PRINCETON
ENCYCLOPEDIA
OF POETRY AND POETICS

PRINCETON ENCYCLOPEDIA OF POETRY AND POETICS

ALEX PREMINGER

EDITOR

FRANK J. WARNKE AND O. B. HARDISON, JR.

ASSOCIATE EDITORS

Enlarged Edition

TO

AUGUSTA FRIEDMAN PREMINGER

Enlarged Edition
First published in the United States 1975
First published in the United Kingdom 1975
Reprinted 1979

Published by
THE MACMILLAN PRESS LTD
London and Basingstoke
Associated companies in New York
Dublin Melbourne Johannesburg and Madras

SBN 333 18121 2   (hard cover)
SBN 333 18122 0   (paper cover)

Printed in Hong Kong by
Bright Sun Printing Press Co., Ltd

PREFACE

The ENCYCLOPEDIA OF POETRY AND POETICS is the most comprehensive treatment of its field yet attempted. It consists of about 1,000 individual entries ranging from twenty to more than 20,000 words, dealing with the history, theory, technique, and criticism of poetry from earliest times to the present. The entries are designed to be useful to the general reader, the student, and the professional scholar. They are supplemented by substantial bibliographies and generous cross-references.

Articles on individual authors, poems, and allusions have been excluded from the ENCYCLOPEDIA as readily available in other reference works. Otherwise, the policy of the editors has been to avoid arbitrary limitations. The danger of too narrow a definition of "poetry" has been recognized, and the reader will find numerous articles dealing with the area between prose and poetry (e.g., VERSE AND PROSE, PROSE POEM, PROSE RHYTHM, FREE VERSE), and topics equally relevant to prose and poetry (e.g., PLOT, MYTH, SYMBOL, IMAGERY). Of particular interest in view of the renaissance of literary criticism in the twentieth century are the numerous articles dealing with poetic theory, schools of criticism, and critical terms. Current interest in poetics also informs many of the entries dealing with the history and forms of poetry.

The entries in the ENCYCLOPEDIA are arranged in alphabetical order. However, they may be grouped under four general headings: (I) History of Poetry; (II) Techniques of Poetry; (III) Poetics and Criticism; (IV) Poetry and its Relationship to Other Fields of Interest.

(I). The history of poetry is treated in terms of languages, movements, and schools. The reader will find entries on the history of each of the major bodies of world poetry—English, American, French, Indian, Arabic, Japanese, etc.—as well as shorter entries on such minor bodies of poetry as Korean poetry, Yiddish poetry, American Indian poetry, and Eskimo poetry. Movements which cut across linguistic or national boundaries are treated in articles such as RENAISSANCE POETRY, ROMANTICISM, and SYMBOLISM. Shorter articles deal with movements or schools peculiar to one country (e.g., DOLCE STIL NUOVO, PRE-RAPHAELITE BROTHERHOOD, PLÉIADE). In every case the aim has been to provide a coherent summary of the important facts illustrated by frequent citations, together with the critical evaluation necessary to an intelligent understanding of the subject.

(II). Technique is covered in articles on STYLE, POETIC DICTION, IMAGERY, RHYME, and the like. There is a general article on FIGURES

OF SPEECH, as well as articles on specific figures like METAPHOR, SIMILE, and CONCEIT. The more important terms of traditional rhetoric are included along with terms which have become current through the influence of modern criticism. The sound values of poetry are treated in SOUND IN POETRY, and in shorter entries on TONE COLOR, ONOMATOPOEIA, ALLITERATION, ASSONANCE, and the like. The major genres, such as tragedy, epic, and lyric, receive extended treatment in terms of both history and theory. More general forms (e.g., DRAMATIC POETRY, NARRATIVE POETRY) are discussed in separate articles, as are such rarely treated subjects as EROTIC POETRY and ORAL POETRY.

Prosody is treated in a general article as well as in more specific entries on CLASSICAL PROSODY, ENGLISH PROSODY, ROMANCE PROSODY, SLAVIC PROSODY, and CELTIC PROSODY, to name only a few. A general article on METER is supplemented by entries on such conventional "types" as HEXAMETER, HEROIC COUPLET, and ELEGIAC DISTICH. Special care has been taken to provide adequate representation for techniques and prosodic forms common in non-Western poetry, e.g., HAIKU, GHASEL, and SLOKA.

(III). Poetics and criticism receive special emphasis in the ENCY-CLOPEDIA. Poetics is treated most generally in POETICS, CONCEPTIONS OF and POETRY, THEORIES OF. These are supplemented by entries dealing with CLASSICAL POETICS, MEDIEVAL POETICS, NEOCLASSICAL POETICS, MODERN POETICS, etc. In addition, the discussions of major literary movements, schools, and genres deal extensively with theory.

The types, objectives, and problems of criticism are explained in CRITICISM, TYPES OF and CRITICISM, FUNCTION OF. They are explored in greater detail in entries on ANALYSIS, EXPLICATION, EVALUATION, and the like. A great many critical terms are discussed separately; e.g., IMAGINATION, FANCY, CONCRETE UNIVERSAL, INVENTION, DECORUM, IMITATION, OBJECTIVE CORRELATIVE, AMBIGUITY, TENSION.

(IV). The relationship of poetry to other fields of interest is examined in articles such as FINE ARTS AND POETRY, MUSIC AND POETRY, PHILOSOPHY AND POETRY, RELIGION AND POETRY, and SOCIETY AND POETRY.

The guiding policies of the editors of the ENCYCLOPEDIA have been accuracy, utility, interest, and (within necessary space limitations) thoroughness. Our contributors have been selected because of recognized excellence in their fields, and we have intentionally refrained from the attempt to impose a preconceived, uniform point of view on their contributions. Each author has been encouraged to present his material in terms of the approach which he feels to be most appropriate. The result is a variety of points of view, representative of the best modern criticism and scholarship. In the opinion of the editors, anything less would be unfair to both readers and contributors.

PREFACE

Two nonsubstantive types of revision have been made by the editors in preparing the manuscript of the ENCYCLOPEDIA for the printer.

(1) Abbreviations have been used throughout in the interests of brevity and consistency of format. As in several continental reference works, the entry word of an article has been abbreviated to its first letter (or letters) when it recurs in the text of the article. Thus *imagery* is abbreviated in the text of that article by *i.; satire* by *s.;* and so forth. Common abbreviations (*c.* for *century* [*ies*]), *Gr.* for *Greek,* etc.) have been used freely. Finally, authors and works referred to frequently throughout the ENCYCLOPEDIA are abbreviated by one or two key words. Full citations of these bibliographic references will be found in the LIST OF ABBREVIATIONS on Page xvi.

(2) Forms of citations, conventions of capitalization, use of italics (e.g., for titles of poems), and the like have been standardized where possible for the sake of consistency.

The ENCYCLOPEDIA OF POETRY AND POETICS has been a cooperative undertaking. It has been made possible only through the learning, dedication, and effort of the contributors. To them the editors wish to extend sincere and warm thanks. A special word of appreciation is due William Arrowsmith, Palmer Bovie, Alfred G. Engstrom, Alvin Eustis, Jr., Paul Fussell, Jr., the late Robert J. Getty, Ulrich K. Goldsmith, Fabian Gudas, Murray Krieger, David I. Masson and Roy Arthur Swanson; as well as M. H. Abrams, George Arms, John Arthos, Paull F. Baum, Max I. Baym, Jess B. Bessinger, Frank M. Chambers, Dorothy Clotelle Clarke, Procope S. Costas, R. S. Crane, Fred A. Dudley, Charles W. Dunn, John J. Enck, Victor Erlich, Robert O. Evans, Solomon Fishman, Wolfgang Bernhard Fleischmann, Richard H. Fogle, Ralph Freedman, Albert B. Friedman, Norman Friedman, Joseph G. Fucilla, Samuel Hazo, Hanford Henderson, Roger A. Hornsby, W. T. H. Jackson, Charles W. Jones, John R. Krueger, Craig La Drière, R.-F. Lissens, Sverre Lyngstad, Clarence A. Manning, Vladimir Markov, Robert Marsh, Earl Miner, Luis Monguió, G. N. G. Orsini, Laurence Perrine, Allen W. Phillips, Seymour M. Pitcher, F. J. E. Raby, Brewster Rogerson, Aldo Scaglione, H. Stefan Schultz, Christoph E. Schweitzer, V. Setchkarev, A. J. M. Smith, Kiril Taranovski, Kurt Weinberg, Philip Wheelwright, A. S. P. Woodhouse, and Lawrence J. Zillman, whose help went beyond the boundaries of their signed contributions. Several scholars, it should be appreciatively acknowledged, also assumed the responsibility for completing or updating the articles of colleagues who had died while the ENCYCLOPEDIA was still in progress.

We are grateful, too, to the following scholars, critics, and poets who are not among our contributors but who have generously given us their advice, specific suggestions, and criticisms: Alfred Adler,

PREFACE

Brooklyn College; Sverre Arestad, University of Washington; Hayden Clair Bell, University of California (Berkeley) ; Armando Correia Pacheco, Pan American Union; Joseph F. de Simone, Brooklyn College; S. Dinamarca, Brooklyn College; David Djaparidze, Princeton University; David M. Dougherty, University of Oregon; Samuel H. Elbert, University of Hawaii; David C. Fowler, University of Washington; Marcel Françon, Harvard University; Thomas Greene, Yale University; Henry Hatfield, Harvard University; Gilbert Highet, Columbia University; Edwin Honig, Brown University; Langston Hughes; Lawrence Hyman, Brooklyn College; Ivar Ivask, St. Olaf College; S. F. Johnson, Columbia University; Walter Johnson, University of Washington; François Jost, University of Fribourg; Adolf D. Klarmann, University of Pennsylvania; Victor Lange, Princeton University; Wallace Lipton, Brooklyn College; Richard A. Long, Morgan State College; Roy MacNab; Percy Matenko, Brooklyn College; Fritz Mautner, Bryn Mawr College; Davidson Nicol, University College of Sierra Leone; Charles Passage, Brooklyn College; Daniel W. Patterson, University of North Carolina; Omeljan Pritsak; Guenther Rimbach, University of California (Riverside); D. W. Robertson, Jr., Princeton University; Alexander Rodger, Edinburgh University; Louis Schoffman, Brooklyn College; Thomas A. Sebeok, Indiana University; Stavro Skendi, Columbia University; Arnold Stein, University of Washington; Claude Vigée, Brandeis University; Eliseo Vivas, Northwestern University; Robert Vlach, University of Oklahoma; Ernst Waldinger, Skidmore College; Ronald N. Walpole, University of California (Berkeley); Sigfried Wenzel, University of North Carolina; Maria Widnäs, University of Oklahoma; and Mary Yiu, Brooklyn College.

We are very much indebted also to Antoinette Ciolli, Brooklyn College Library, Martin Fine, Nicole Stern, Pamela Williams, Jean-Claude Preminger, Toby Preminger, and Tamara Arney for assisting in the preparation of the manuscript.

It remains to thank the Bollingen Foundation without whose aid this book could not have been completed at this time; Mr. Herbert S. Bailey, Jr., director of the Princeton University Press, for his understanding and support; and Mrs. James Holly Hanford, Princeton University Press editor, for her devoted and inspired help.

Flushing, New York
December 1963

THE EDITORS

-[viii]-

PREFACE TO THE
ENLARGED EDITION

In the first edition of this work the editors committed themselves to an ideal of comprehensiveness, hoping to make the *Encyclopedia of Poetry and Poetics* the most complete and accurate reference source of its kind. Nevertheless, there were inevitable oversights. No separate entries were provided for a number of important movements in poetry (HARLEM RENAISSANCE), major aspects of literature (THEME), and perennial issues (CENSORSHIP). The Supplement of about 75,000 words to this new edition of the *Encyclopedia* attempts to rectify such omissions, and it also includes dozens of other new entries that reflect recent developments in poetry and poetics.

Poetry, like any art, is in a constant process of change, and in the nine years since the publication of this *Encyclopedia* there have been many significant shifts in poetic practice and in the intellectual and social world that surrounds the poet's art. Accordingly, the Appendix includes such entries as ROCK LYRIC and COMPUTER POETRY, as well as an overview of contemporary AMERICAN POETIC SCHOOLS AND TECHNIQUES. Moreover, the increased cultural awareness and articulateness of ethnic minorities and emergent nations has required treatment here of such subjects as recent BLACK POETRY in the United States, PUERTO RICAN POETRY, and AFRICAN POETRY in various languages.

Many articles in the Appendix also call attention to recent developments in poetic criticism. An essay on METACRITICISM critically examines criticism itself. Such entries as STRUCTURALISM, PHENOMENOLOGY, and the GENEVA SCHOOL deal with ideas and movements which have proved themselves during the last decade to be of value in the study of literature. Fresh debate over traditional issues is summarized and analyzed in the treatments of HISTORICISM and INTERPRETATION. And new emphases in disciplines ancillary to literature are accounted for in such articles as PSYCHOLOGY AND POETRY and POLITICS AND POETRY.

The editors have again attempted to avoid construing "poetry and poetics" in either too inclusive or too narrow a fashion. They have not tried to encompass the whole area of imaginative literature: such an effort would have resulted in an unwieldy work of many volumes. Instead, they have restricted the province of the *Princeton Encyclopedia of Poetry and Poetics* to metrical or quasi-metrical composition, hoping to maintain a clear unity of subject matter. On the other hand, the editors have included some topics (e.g., articles on criticism or on general literary techniques) which apply to prose as well as to poetry. Moreover, they have made no effort to rule out occasional references to prose works in the entries. As in the first edition, the editors have adopted the policy of entrusting the articles to authorities recognized in their respective fields, and of allowing these contributors considerable freedom in point of view and development.

The editors owe a special debt of gratitude to the following contributors, past and present, for advice, concrete suggestions, and criticisms: Monroe C. Beardsley, David F. Dorsey, Paul Fussell, Fabian Gudas, Lyndon Harries, Kevin Kerrane, Murray Krieger, Sally N. Lawall, Sverre Lyngstad, Wallace Martin, Earl Miner, and Aldo Scaglione.

We should also like to thank: M. H. Abrams, Joseph G. Beaver, Seymour Chatman, Jonathan Culler, Paul de Man, Alvin Eustis, Bernard Wolfgang Fleischmann, Z. Folejewski, Ralph Freedman, Ulrich K. Goldsmith, John Hollander, Douglas Johnson, Samuel R. Levin, Richard A. Long, Louis Monguió, and Barbara Herrnstein Smith.

Various scholars, whose names do not appear in the List of Contributors, have assisted us by careful reading and helpful criticism of entries. We are grateful to: Barry Beckham (Brown University), Wilfred Cartey (Brooklyn College, City University of New York), Marshall Cohen (Graduate Center, City University of New York), Thomas Conley (University of California, Berkeley), Thomas R. Edwards (Rutgers University), Michael Fahey (University of Delaware), Mary Ann Geissal (Northeastern Illinois University), Albert S. Gérard (University of Liège), Norman N. Holland (State University of New York, Buffalo), Nathan Irvin Huggins (Columbia University), F. R. Jameson (University of California, San Diego), David Kalstone (Rutgers University), Edward Maxwell (Northeastern Illinois University), J. Hillis Miller (Yale University), Gerald Moore (University of Sussex), Gerald M. Moser (Pennsylvania State University), Edgar C. Polomé (University of Texas), Anthony Z. Romano (University of Delaware), Don Weller (University of Hawaii), and Carl Woodring (Columbia University).

Special thanks go again to Mrs. James Holly Hanford, our very able and dedicated Princeton University Press editor.

1974

THE EDITORS

ACKNOWLEDGMENTS

Great care has been taken to trace all the owners of copyright material used in this book. If any have been inadvertently overlooked or omitted, acknowledgment will gladly be made in any future editions.

Thanks are due to the following authors, publishers, and representatives who have so courteously granted permission to use selections from copyrighted publications.

The Africana Publishing Corporation for six lines of "Heavensgate" reprinted from *Labyrinths* by Christopher Okigbo, copyright 1971 by Legal Personal Representatives of Christopher Okigbo, by permission of Africana Publishing Corporation.

The Bernice P. Bishop Museum for a nature poem, "Moolelo o Hawaii," manuscript by S. M. Kamakau, translated by M. W. Beckwith and M. K. Pukui.

William Blackwood & Sons, Ltd., Hugh MacDiarmid, and The Macmillan Co. for six lines of "The Bonnie Broukit Bairn" from *The Collected Poems of Hugh MacDiarmid*, copyright 1948, 1962 by Christopher Murray Grieve.

The Bodley Head, Ltd., for four lines by Fedor Tyutchev, from *Modern Russian Poetry. An Anthology.* Chosen and translated by Babette Deutsch and Avrahm Yarmolinsky.

Cambridge University Press, for twelve lines, from *Literary History of the Arabs* by R. A. Nicholson, 2d ed.

Clarendon Press, Oxford, for the first eight lines of "Cheddar Pinks," from the *Poetical Works of Robert Bridges. Excluding the Eight Dramas.*

Editions Gallimard, for four lines by Paul Valéry from *La Jeune Parque*, copyright 1917 by Editions Gallimard, and three lines by Paul Valéry from *Charmes*, copyright 1922 by Editions Gallimard.

Faber and Faber, Ltd., for first stanza of "September 1, 1939," from *Collected Shorter Poems* by W. H. Auden; for excerpts from

-[xi]-

ACKNOWLEDGMENTS

Poetic Diction: A Study in Meaning by Owen Barfield, new ed. 1952; for three lines of "Ash Wednesday," from *Collected Poems* by T. S. Eliot.

Farrar, Straus and Cudahy, for excerpts from *The Heresy of Courtly Love* by A. J. Denomy.

Grove Press, for "Oread," from *Selected Poems by H. D.*, copyright 1957 by Norman Holmes Pearson.

Harcourt, Brace & World, Inc. for three lines of "Ash Wednesday," from *Collected Poems of T. S. Eliot*, copyright 1936 by Harcourt, Brace & World, Inc.

Harcourt Brace Jovanovich, Inc., for the poem "l(a" by E. E. Cummings. Copyright 1958 by E. E. Cummings. Reprinted from his volume *Complete Poems 1913–1962* by permission of Harcourt Brace Jovanovich, Inc.

Harvard University Press, for excerpts from Aristotle, *The Poetics*; "Longinus," *On the Sublime*; Demetrius, *On Style*, Loeb Classical Library.

Heinemann Educational Books, Ltd., for four lines of "The sounds begin again" from *A Simple Lust* by Dennis Brutus and for six lines of "Heavensgate" from *Labyrinths with Path of Thunder* by Christopher Okigbo. These lines reprinted by permission of the publishers, Heinemann Educational Books Ltd., London.

Hill and Wang, for four lines of "The sounds begin again" from *A Simple Lust* by Dennis Brutus. Reprinted with the permission of Hill and Wang, a division of Farrar, Straus & Giroux, Inc. Copyright 1963, 1968, 1970, 1971, 1973 by Dennis Brutus.

Holt, Rinehart and Winston, Inc., for "The Golf Links Lie So Near the Mill," from *Portraits and Protests* by Sarah N. Cleghorn. All rights reserved. Reprinted by permission of Holt, Rinehart and Winston, Inc.

Houghton Mifflin Co., for four lines of "Ars Poetica," from *Collected Poems, 1917–1952* by Archibald MacLeish, reprinted by permission and arrangement with Houghton Mifflin Co. Copyright 1952 by Archibald MacLeish; for "Lilacs," from *Complete Poetical Works of Amy Lowell*. Copyright 1955 by Houghton Mifflin Co.

The Irish Texts Society, for lines from *Aithdioghluim Dana*, edited by L. McKenna.

ACKNOWLEDGMENTS

Alfred A. Knopf, Inc., for first four lines of "Planting Bamboos" by Po-Chüi, from *Translations from the Chinese*, by Arthur Waley.

Little, Brown & Co., for lines from "If I can stop one heart from breaking," from *The Complete Poems of Emily Dickinson*, edited by Thomas H. Johnson.

The Macmillan Company, for six lines of "The Bonnie Broukit Bairn," from *The Collected Poems of Hugh MacDiarmid*, copyright 1948, 1962 by Christopher Murray Grieve; for lines from *The King of the Great Clock Tower, The Collected Plays of W. B. Yeats*, 1952, 1953; for one line of "After Long Silence," the epigram "On Those that Hated 'The Playboy of the Western World,' 1907," four lines of "Sailing to Byzantium," four lines of "Under Ben Bulben V," eight lines of "Why Should Not Old Men Be Mad?" all from *The Collected Poems of W. B. Yeats*, definitive edition, 1956.

The Mediaeval Academy of America, for excerpts from A. J. Denomy, "Courtly Love and Courtliness," *Speculum*, 28 (1953), 44.

New Directions, for third stanza of "To a Friend," translated by Babette Deutsch, from *Selected Writings* by Boris Pasternak; for fifth stanza of "Apparuit," from *Personae* by Ezra Pound, copyright 1926, 1954 by Ezra Pound; for opening sentence from *Under Milk Wood* by Dylan Thomas, copyright 1954 by New Directions. Reprinted by permission of New Directions.

Oliver & Boyd, Ltd. and the Trustees of the Alexander Carmichael estate, for second stanza of "Lament for Seathan," from *Carmina Gadelica*, compiled and translated by Alexander Carmichael.

Random House, Inc., for first stanza of "September 1, 1939," from *Collected Poetry of W. H. Auden,* copyright 1945 by W. H. Auden. For excerpt from *Ulysses* by James Joyce, copyright 1914, 1918 and renewed 1942, 1946 by Nora Joseph Joyce. Reprinted by permission of Random House, Inc.

Charles Scribner's Sons, for excerpt from an Inca prayer, from *Ancient Civilization of the Andes* by Philip Ainsworth Means, copyright 1931 Charles Scribner's Sons, renewal copyright 1959 Louise Muntoe Means, reprinted with the permission of Charles Scribner's Sons; for four lines of "America For Me," from *Poems* by Henry van Dyke.

Speculum, The Editors, for excerpts from A. J. Denomy, "Courtly Love and Courtliness," *Speculum,* 28 (1953), 44.

ACKNOWLEDGMENTS

Stanford University Press, for the following selections in translation: five lines each by Hitomaro, Okura, Akahito, Narihira, Komachi, Yoshitada, Izumi Shikibu, Anon., Yoshitsune, Saigyō, Shunzei, Teika, Tamehide, ex-Empress Eifuku; ten lines by ex-Emperor Hanazono and three lines by Bashō, from *Japanese Court Poetry*, by Robert H. Brower and Earl Miner, copyright 1961 by the Board of Trustees of the Leland Stanford Junior University.

University of Chicago Press, for lines from *Greek Lyrics*, translated by Richmond Lattimore, copyright 1955 by Richard Lattimore.

Twayne Publishers, Inc., for six lines of "If we must die," from *Selected Poems of Claude McKay.*

University of Wales Press, for lines 668–673 from *Canu Aneirin,* edited by Ifor Williams.

A. P. Watt and Son, Mrs. W. B. Yeats, the Macmillan Co. of Canada Ltd., and Messrs. Macmillan & Co. Ltd., for lines from *The King of the Great Clock Tower, The Collected Plays of W. B. Yeats,* 1952, 1953; for one line of "After Long Silence," the epigram "On Those that Hated 'The Playboy of the Western World,' 1907," four lines of "Sailing to Byzantium," four lines of "Under Ben Bulben V," eight lines of "Why Should Not Old Men Be Mad?" all from *The Collected Poems of W. B. Yeats,* definitive edition, 1956.

CONTENTS

LIST OF ABBREVIATIONS

BIBLIOGRAPHICAL

Abrams   M. H. Abrams, *The Mirror and the Lamp. Romantic Theory and the Critical Tradition*, 1953.

AJP   *American Journal of Philology*

AL   *American Literature*

ASch   *American Scholar*

ASEER   *American Slavic and Eastern European Review*

ASR   *American-Scandinavian Review*

AUC   *Anales de la Universidad de Chile*

Auerbach   E. Auerbach, *Mimesis. The Representation of Reality in Western Literature*, tr. W. R. Trask, 1953.

BA   *Books Abroad*

Baum   P. F. Baum, *The Principles of English Versification*, 1922.

Beare   W. Beare, *Latin Verse and European Song*, 1957.

Behrens   I. Behrens, *Die Lehre von der Einteilung der Dichtkunst* (Beihefte zur Zeitschrift für Romanische Philologie, 92, 1940).

BHR   *Bibliothèque d'humanisme et renaissance*

Bowra   C. M. Bowra, *Greek Lyric Poetry from Alcman to Simonides*, 1936, 2d ed., 1961.

Bray   R. Bray, *La Formation de la doctrine classique en France*, 1927.

Brooks and Warren   C. Brooks and R. P. Warren, *Understanding Poetry*, 2d ed., 1950, 3d ed., 1960.

Brooks, *Tradition*   C. Brooks, *Modern Poetry and the Tradition*, 1939.

BZ   *Byzantinische Zeitschrift* (Leipzig)

Cabeen   *A Critical Bibliography of French Literature*, general ed. D. C. Cabeen, 1–   ; 1947–   (in progress).

Cassell's   *Cassell's Encyclopaedia of World Literature*, ed. S. H. Steinberg, 2 v., 1954.

CBEL   *Cambridge Bibliography of English Literature*

CE   *College English*

Chadwick   H. M. and N. K. Chadwick, *The Growth of Literature*, 3 v., 1932–40.

CHEL   *Cambridge History of English Literature*

CL   *Comparative Literature*

CP   *Classical Philology*

CQ   *Classical Quarterly*

Crane   R. S. Crane, *The Languages of Criticism and the Structure of Poetry*, 1953.

Crane, *Critics*   *Critics and Criticism, Ancient and Modern*, ed. R. S. Crane, 1952.

Crusius   F. Crusius, *Römische Metrik*, 2d ed., 1955.

Curtius   E. Curtius, *European Literature and the Latin Middle Ages*, tr. W. R. Trask, 1953.

CW   *Classical World*

Daiches   D. Daiches, *Critical Approaches to Literature*, 1956.

Dale   A. M. Dale, *The Lyric Metres of Greek Drama*, 1948.

Deutsch   B. Deutsch, *Poetry Handbook*, 1957, 2d ed., 1962.

DVLG   *Deutsche Vierteljahrsschrift für Literaturwissenschaft und Geistesgeschichte*

E&S   *Essays and Studies by Members of the English Association*

EIC   *Essays in Criticism* (Oxford)

EIE   *English Institute Essays*

Eliot, *Essays*   T. S. Eliot, *Selected Essays*, 1932, rev. ed., 1950.

Eliot, *Wood*   T. S. Eliot, *The Sacred Wood: Essays on Poetry and Criticism*, 1920.

Empson   W. Empson, *Seven Types of Ambiguity*, 1930, 2d ed., 1947.

FiR   *Filologia romanza*

FM   *Français moderne*

Frye   N. Frye, *Anatomy of Criticism*, 1957.

FS   *French Studies*

Gayley and Kurtz   C. M. Gayley and B. P. Kurtz, *Methods and Materials of Literary Criticism: Lyric, Epic and Allied Forms of Poetry*, 1920.

Gilbert and Kuhn   K. Gilbert and H. Kuhn, *A History of Esthetics*, 1939, 2d ed., 1953.

Hamer   E. Hamer, *The Metres of English Poetry*, 1930.

Hardie   W. R. Hardie, *Res metrica*, 1920.

HR   *Hispanic Review*

HSCL   *Harvard Studies in Comparative Literature*

HSCP   *Harvard Studies in Classical Philology*

HSS   *Harvard Slavic Studies*

JAAC   *Journal of Aesthetics and Art Criticism*

JAF   *Journal of American Folklore*

Jeanroy   A. Jeanroy, *La Poésie lyrique des troubadours*, 2 v., 1934.

ABBREVIATIONS

Jeanroy, *Origines* A. Jeanroy, *Les Origines de la poésie lyrique en France au moyen âge*, 3d ed., 1925.

JEGP *Journal of English and Germanic Philology*

JHI *Journal of the History of Ideas*

JNH *Journal of Negro History*

JWCI *Journal of the Warburg and Courtauld Institute*

Kastner L. E. Kastner, *A History of French Versification*, 1903.

Ker W. P. Ker, *Form and Style in Poetry*, 1928.

Kolář A. Kolář, *De re metrica poetarum Graecorum et Romanorum*, Prague, 1947.

Koster W. J. W. Koster, *Traité de métrique grecque suivi d'un précis de métrique latine*, 2d ed., Leyden, 1953.

KR *Kenyon Review*

Krieger M. Krieger, *The New Apologists for Poetry*, 1956.

Langer S. K. Langer, *Philosophy in a New Key*, 1948.

Lausberg H. Lausberg, *Handbuch der literarischen Rhetorik*, 2 v., 1960.

Lehmann A. G. Lehmann, *The Symbolist Aesthetic in France, 1885–95*, 1950..

Lewis C. S. Lewis, *The Allegory of Love*, 1936.

LonM London Magazine

Martino P. Martino, *Parnasse et symbolisme, 1850–1900*, 1925, 4th ed., 1935.

MdF Mercure de France

MLF *Modern Language Forum*

MLJ *Modern Language Journal*

MLN *Modern Language Notes*

MLQ *Modern Language Quarterly*

MLR *Modern Language Review*

Morris-Jones J. Morris-Jones, Cerdd Dafod, 1925.

MP *Modern Philology*

N&Q *Notes and Queries*

Navarro T. Navarro, *Métrica española: Reseña histórica y descriptiva*, 1956.

NED *New English Dictionary*

Neophil Neophilologus (Groningen)

Nicoll A. Nicoll, *A History of English Drama, 1660–1900*, 6 v., 1952–59.

Norden E. Norden, *Die antike Kunstprosa*, 5th ed., 2 v., 1958.

OED *Oxford English Dictionary*

OSP *Oxford Slavonic Papers*

Parry T. Parry, *A History of Welsh Literature*, tr. H. I. Bell, 1955.

Patterson W. F. Patterson, *Three Centuries of French Poetic Theory*, 3 v., 1935.

PMLA *Publications of the Modern Language Association of America*

PQ *Philological Quarterly*

PR *Partisan Review*

QQ *Queen's Quarterly*

QR *Quarterly Review*

Raymond M. Raymond, *De Baudelaire au surréalisme*, 1933, 2d ed., 1940.

Reallexikon *Reallexikon der deutschen Literaturgeschichte*, ed. P. Merker and W. Stammler, 4 v., 1925–31; 2d ed., ed. W. Kohlschmidt and W. Mohr, 1958– (in progress).

Ren Renascence

RES *Review of English Studies*

RF *Romanische Forschungen*

RFE *Revista de filología española*

RHL *Revue d'histoire littéraire de la France*

Richards, *Practical* I. A. Richards, *Practical Criticism*, 1929.

Richards, *Principles* I. A. Richards, *Principles of Literary Criticism*, 1925.

RLC *Revue de littérature comparée*

RLR *Revue des langues romanes* (Montpellier)

Rom Romania

RPh Roman Philology

Saintsbury G. Saintsbury, *History of Criticism and Literary Taste in Europe*, 3 v., 1900–04.

Saintsbury, *Prosody* G. Saintsbury, *A History of English Prosody*, 3 v., 1906–10.

SAQ *South Atlantic Quarterly*

SAWW *Sitzungsberichte der [österreichischen] Akademie der Wissenschaften in Wien. Phil.-hist. Klasse*

SB *Studies in Bibliography: Papers of the Bibliographical Society of the University of Virginia*

Schipper J. M. Schipper, *Englische Metrik*, 3 v., 1881–1888 (abridged and tr. as *A History of English Versification*, 1910).

Schmid and Stählin W. Schmid and O. Stählin, *Geschichte der griechischen Literatur*, 2 v., 1929–48.

Science and Literature International Federation for Modern Languages and Literatures. *Literature and Science. Proceedings of the Triennial Congress held at Oxford 1954*, 1956.

SD *Studi danteschi*

SEER *Slavonic and East European Review* [title changed to: *Slavic Review*]

SFI *Studi di filologia italiana*

Shipley *Dictionary of World Literature*, ed. J. T. Shipley, 1943, rev. ed., 1953.

ShS Shakespeare Survey

Smyth H. W. Smyth, *Greek Melic Poets*, 1906.

SOED *Shorter Oxford English Dictionary*

SP *Studies in Philology*

SQ *Shakespeare Quarterly*

SR *Sewanee Review*

SRen Studies in the Renaissance

Sutton W. Sutton, *Modern American Criticism*, 1963.

SWR *Southwest Review*

Sym Symposium

TLS *[London] Times Literary Supplement*

TPAPA *Transactions and Proceedings of the American Philological Association*

ABBREVIATIONS

LIST OF ABBREVIATIONS
GENERAL

Am. American
anthol. anthology
assoc. association
b. born
bibliog. bibliography
c. century; centuries
ca. about
cf. *confer*, compare
ch. chapter
cl. classical; classicism
crit. critical; criticism
d. died
dict. dictionary
diss. dissertation
ed. editor; edited (by); edition
e.g. *exempli gratia*, for example
Eng. English
enl. enlarged
et al. *et alii*, and others
ff. following
fl. *floruit*, flourished
fr., frag. fragment
Fr. French
Gesch. *Geschichte*
Gr. Greek
hist. history, *histoire*
i.e. *id est*, that is
introd. introduction
Ir. Irish
It. Italian

jour. journal
L. Latin
lit. literature (s); literary
LL Late Latin
loc. cit. *loco citato*, in the place cited
ME Middle English
ms(s) manuscript(s)
OE Old English
OF Old French
ON Old Norse
p., pp. page; pages
pr. printed
prep. preparation
proc. proceedings
Prov. Provençal
publ. published
q.v. *quod vide*, which see
qq.v. *quae vide*, both which, or all which, see
Ren. Renaissance
repr. reprint; reprinted
rev. revised
Rus. Russian
s. *siècle*
sc. *scilicet*, to wit
Sp. Spanish
supp. supplement; supplementary
t. tome
tr. translated by; translation (s)

* An asterisk at the end of a word or phrase indicates that an entry on this subject will be found in the Supplement.

THE CONTRIBUTORS

Kenneth M. Abbott, Professor of Classical Languages, Ohio State University

M. H. Abrams, Frederic T. Whiton Professor of English, Cornell University

Fernando Alegría, Professor of Spanish and Portuguese, Stanford University

Robert P. apRoberts, Professor of English, San Fernando Valley State College

Arthur J. Arberry, late Sir Thomas Adams's Professor of Arabic, University of Cambridge

George Arms, Professor of English, University of New Mexico

William Arrowsmith, University Professor, Boston University

John Arthos, Hereward T. Price University Professor of English, University of Michigan

Stuart Atkins, Professor of German, University of California (Santa Barbara)

Arra Avakian, National Association for Armenian Studies and Research

María Teresa Babin, Professor of Spanish, Graduate Center, City University of New York

James Baird, Professor of English, Connecticut College

Anna E. Balakian, Professor of Romance Languages and Comparative Literature, New York University

Linton Lomas Barrett, late Professor of Romance Languages, Washington and Lee University

Paull F. Baum, late James B. Duke Professor of English, Duke University

Glen W. Baxter, Lecturer in East Asian Languages and Civilizations, Harvard University, and Associate Director of the Harvard-Yenching Institute

Max I. Baym, Professor Emeritus of the Humanities, Polytechnic Institute of Brooklyn

Monroe C. Beardsley, Professor of Philosophy, Temple University

William Beare, late Professor of Latin and onetime Pro-Vice Chancellor, University of Bristol

Joseph C. Beaver, Professor of Linguistics, Northeastern Illinois University

Richard Beck, University Professor Emeritus of Scandinavian Languages and Literatures, University of North Dakota

Robert Beloof, Professor of Rhetoric, University of California (Berkeley)

Allen R. Benham, late Professor of English, University of Washington

Aldo S. Bernardo, Professor of Romance Languages and Chairman of the Division of Humanities, State University of New York (Binghamton)

Jess B. Bessinger, Jr., Professor of English, New York University

John L. Bishop, Lecturer in East Asian Languages and Civilizations, Harvard University

Harold Bloom, Professor of English, Yale University

Morton W. Bloomfield, Arthur Kingsley Porter Professor of English, Harvard University

Arna Bontemps, late poet and writer

Smith Palmer Bovie, Professor of Classics, Rutgers University

Thomas O. Brandt, late Professor of German and Chairman of the Department of German and Russian, Colorado College

David Bromwich, Scholar of the House in American Literature, Pierson College, Yale University

Cleanth Brooks, Gray Professor of Rhetoric, Yale University

Huntington Brown, Professor Emeritus of English, University of Minnesota

Merle E. Brown, Professor of English, University of Iowa

James Camp, Associate Professor of English, Newark College of Engineering

Leonard Casper, Professor of English, Boston College

Frank M. Chambers, Professor of French, University of Arizona

Kun Chang, Professor of Oriental Languages, University of California (Berkeley)

Seymour Chatman, Professor of Rhetoric, University of California (Berkeley)

Arthur Melville Clark, Reader Emeritus in English Literature, University of Edinburgh

Dorothy Clotelle Clarke, Professor of Spanish, University of California (Berkeley)

Stanley K. Coffman, Professor and Chairman of the Department of English, Bowling Green State University

W. E. Collin, former Professor of Romance Languages, University of Western Ontario

Padraic Colum, late poet and author

J. E. Congleton, Professor Emeritus of English, Findlay College

Mercer Cook, Professor Emeritus of Romance Languages, Howard University

Procope S. Costas, Professor of Classics, Brooklyn College, City University of New York

CONTRIBUTORS

Hardin Craig, late Professor of English, Stanford University, University of North Carolina, and University of Missouri

R. S. Crane, late Distinguished Service Professor of English, University of Chicago

John A. Crow, Professor of Spanish, University of California (Los Angeles)

István Csicsery-Rónay, Hungarian writer and critic

Jonathan D. Culler, Fellow and Director of Studies in Modern Languages, Selwyn College, University of Cambridge

A. Grove Day, Professor Emeritus of English, University of Hawaii

Paul de Man, Professor of Comparative and French Literature, Yale University

Endre De Spur, formerly, The Gypsy Lore Society

Vinton A. Dearing, Professor of English, University of California (Los Angeles)

R. J. Dorius, Professor of English, San Francisco State College

David F. Dorsey, Associate Professor of English and Afro-American Studies, Atlanta University

Fred A. Dudley, Professor Emeritus of English, Washington State University

Charles W. Dunn, Margaret Brooks Robinson Professor of Celtic Languages and Literatures and Chairman of the Department, Harvard University

Robert M. Durling, Professor of English, University of California (Santa Cruz)

John M. Echols, Professor of Linguistics and Asian Studies, Cornell University

Brian R. Elliott, Reader in Australian Literature, University of Adelaide

Robert C. Elliott, Professor of English Literature, University of California (San Diego)

Gerald F. Else, Professor of Classical Studies and Director of The Center for Coördination of Ancient and Modern Studies, University of Michigan

John J. Enck, late Professor of English, University of Wisconsin

Alfred Garwin Engstrom, Alumni Distinguished Professor of French, University of North Carolina (Chapel Hill)

Victor Erlich, Bensinger Professor of Russian Literature, Yale University

Alvin A. Eustis, Professor of French, University of California (Berkeley)

Robert O. Evans, Professor of English, University of Kentucky

Robert P. Falk, Professor of English, University of California (Los Angeles)

Leon Feraru, late Professor and Chairman of the Department of Modern Languages, Long Island University

Palamandadige Eberg Edwin Fernando, Professor of Sinhalese, University of Ceylon

Solomon Fishman, former Professor of English, University of California (Davis)

Wolfgang Bernard Fleischmann, Professor of Comparative Literature and Dean of the School of Humanities, Montclair State College

Richard Harter Fogle, University Distinguished Professor of English, University of North Carolina (Chapel Hill)

Stephen F. Fogle, late Professor of English, Adelphi Suffolk College

Zbigniew Folejewski, Professor of Slavonic Studies and Chairman, Comparative Literature, University of British Columbia

Tatiana Fotitch, Professor Emeritus of Romance Languages and Literatures, Catholic University of America

Wallace Fowlie, James B. Duke Professor of French Literature, Duke University

Jean Franco, Professor of Spanish and Comparative Literature, Stanford University

John Fraser, Professor of English, Dalhousie University

Ralph Freedman, Professor of Comparative Literature, Princeton University

Bernard J. Fridsma, Professor Emeritus of Germanic Languages, Calvin College

Albert B. Friedman, Professor of English, Claremont Graduate School

Norman Friedman, Professor of English, Queens College, City University of New York

Northrop Frye, University Professor, Massey College, University of Toronto

Joseph G. Fucilla, Professor Emeritus of Romance Languages, Northwestern University

Paul Fussell, Professor of English, Rutgers University

Naomi Garrett, Professor of Romance Languages, West Virginia State College

Carolyn F. Gerald, Associate Professor of Black Literature, Atlanta University

Robert J. Getty, late Paddison Professor of Classics, University of North Carolina (Chapel Hill)

Pierre Gilbert, Professor of the History of Art, Université Libre de Bruxelles

G. Giovannini, Professor of English, Catholic University of America

John F. Goins, Professor of Anthropology, University of California (Riverside)

Ulrich K. Goldsmith, Professor of German and Comparative Literature, University of Colorado

Lewis H. Gordon, Professor of Italian and French, Brown University

Bernard Groom, former Professor of English, McMaster University

Fabian Gudas, Professor of English, Louisiana State University

CONTRIBUTORS

Hans G. Güterbock, Tiffany and Margaret Blake Distinguished Service Professor of Hittitology, University of Chicago

Theodore Johannes Haarhoff, Emeritus Professor of Classics, University of the Witwatersrand, Johannesburg

Vernon Hall, Jr., Professor of Comparative Literature, University of Wisconsin (Madison)

Talat S. Halman, Lecturer in Turkish, Princeton University

O. B. Hardison, Jr., Director, The Folger Shakespeare Library

Jacques Hardré, Kenan Professor of French and Chairman of the Department of Romance Languages, University of North Carolina (Chapel Hill)

William E. Harkins, Professor of Slavic Languages, Columbia University

Lyndon Harries, Professor of African Languages and Literature, University of Wisconsin (Madison)

Sylvia C. Harris, Lecturer in German, Birkbeck College, University of London

Samuel Hazo, Professor of Literature, Duquesne University

George T. Hemphill, Professor of English, University of Connecticut

Hanford M. Henderson, formerly, American Academy, Rome

Marvin T. Herrick, late Professor of English, University of Illinois

Daniel G. Hoffman, Professor of English, University of Pennsylvania

John Hollander, Professor of English, Hunter College, City University of New York

C. Hugh Holman, Kenan Professor of English, University of North Carolina (Chapel Hill)

Urban T. Holmes, Jr., Kenan Professor of Romance Languages, University of North Carolina (Chapel Hill)

Roger A. Hornsby, Professor and Chairman of the Department of Classics, University of Iowa

Leo Hughes, Professor of English, University of Texas

Gloria T. Hull, Assistant Professor of English, University of Delaware

W.T.H. Jackson, Professor of German and History, Columbia University

Vera Javarek, former Lecturer in Serbo-Croatian Language and Literature, University of London

Douglas Johnson, Assistant Professor of Black Literature, Federal City College

James William Johnson, Professor of English, University of Rochester

Charles W. Jones, Professor of English, University of California (Berkeley)

Michael K. Joseph, Professor in English, Auckland University, N. Z.

Sholom J. Kahn, Assistant Professor of English, Hebrew University, Jerusalem

John D. Kendall, formerly, School of Library Science, University of Minnesota

Hugh Kenner, Professor of English Literature, Johns Hopkins University

Kevin Kerrane, Associate Professor of English, University of Delaware

Thomas A. Kirby, Professor and Head of the Department of English, Louisiana State University

Charles A. Knudson, Professor of French, University of Illinois

June Q. Koch, Assistant Professor of English, Bryn Mawr College

Miriam Koshland-Joel, writer and translator

Manfred Kridl, late Adam Mickiewicz Professor of Polish Studies, Columbia University

Murray Krieger, University Professor of English, University of California (Irvine)

John R. Krueger, Professor of Uralic and Altaic Studies, Indiana University

James Craig La Drière, Professor of Comparative Literature, Harvard University

Stephen A. Larrabee, author and critic

Sally N. Lawall, Professor and Chairman of the Department of Comparative Literature, University of Massachusetts

Laurence D. Lerner, Professor of English, University of Sussex, England

Samuel R. Levin, Professor of English, Graduate Center, City University of New York

John L. Lievsay, James B. Duke Professor of English, Duke University

Herbert Lindenberger, Avalon Professor of Humanities in Comparative Literature and English and Chairman, Department of Comparative Literature, Stanford University

René Felix Lissens, Professor of Dutch Literature and European Literatures, Universitaire Faculteiten, St.-Ignatius, Antwerp

D. Myrddin Lloyd, Keeper of Printed Books, National Library of Scotland

Edgar Lohner, Professor and Chairman of the Department of German, Stanford University

Richard A. Long, Professor of English and Director, Center for African and African-American Studies, Atlanta University

Albert B. Lord, Arthur Kingsley Porter Professor of Slavic and Comparative Literature, Harvard University

Katharine Luomala, Professor of Anthropology, University of Hawaii

Sverre Lyngstad, Professor of English, Newark College of Engineering

Frederick P. W. McDowell, Professor of English, University of Iowa

John MacInnes, Lecturer in Scottish Studies, University of Edinburgh

Clarence A. Manning, former Associate Professor of Slavic Languages, Columbia University

CONTRIBUTORS

Vladimir Markov, Professor of Slavic Languages, University of California (Los Angeles)

Robert Marsh, Professor of English, University of Chicago

Wallace Martin, Professor of English, University of Toledo

David I. Masson, Librarian in Charge of Brotherton Collection, University of Leeds Library

William Kleesman Matthews, late Professor of Russian Language and Literature and Head of the Department of Language and Literature at the School of Slavonic and East European Studies, University of London

Rigo Mignani, Professor of Romance Languages, State University of New York (Binghamton)

Louis T. Milic, Professor of English, Cleveland State University

Elizabeth Maxfield Miller, former Instructor in French, Concord Academy

Earl Miner, Professor of English, Princeton University

Luis Monguió, Professor of Spanish, University of California (Berkeley)

Stephen L. Mooney, late Professor of English, University of Tennessee

Bayard Quincy Morgan, late Professor of German, Stanford University

Wesley Morris, Associate Professor of English, Rice University

John M. Munro, Professor of English, American University of Beirut

Robert D. Murray, Jr., Associate Professor of Classics, Princeton University

George Nakashidse, former Lecturer in Georgian History and Literature, Columbia University

Lowry Nelson, Jr., Professor of Comparative Literature, Yale University

William Van O'Connor, late Professor and Chairman of the Department of English, University of California (Davis)

John B. Olli, Professor Emeritus of Germanic and Slavic Languages, City College, City University of New York

Ants Oras, Professor of English, University of Florida

G.N.G. Orsini, Professor and Chairman of the Department of Comparative Literature, University of Wisconsin (Madison)

Kostas Ostrauskas, Lithuanian dramatist, literary historian, and musicologist

Lucy B. Palache, editorial research assistant

Douglass S. Parker, Professor of Classics, University of Texas

Richard A. Parker, Wilbour Professor of Egyptology, Brown University

John P. Pauls, Professor of Russian Language and Literature, University of Cincinnati

Hla Pe, Professor of Burmese, School of Oriental and African Studies, University of London

Laurence Perrine, Professor of English, Southern Methodist University

Robert H. Pfeiffer, late Hancock Professor of Hebrew and Other Oriental Languages, Harvard University

Allen W. Phillips, Professor of Spanish, University of Texas

Seymour M. Pitcher, Professor of English and Comparative Literature, State University of New York (Binghamton)

Alex Preminger, Associate Professor, Brooklyn College Library, City University of New York

Frederick James Edward Raby, late Fellow of the British Academy. Honorary Fellow, Jesus College, University of Cambridge

V. Raghavan, Professor Emeritus and former Head of the Department of Sanskrit, University of Madras

Paul Ramsey, Alumni Distinguished Service Professor of English, University of Tennessee (Chattanooga)

Joseph Remenyi, late Professor of Comparative Literature, Western Reserve University

Elias L. Rivers, Professor of Spanish and Chairman of the Department of Romance Languages, Johns Hopkins University

James K. Robinson, Professor and Head of the Department of English, University of Cincinnati

Brewster Rogerson, Professor of English, Kansas State University

George Brandon Saul, Professor of English, University of Connecticut

Aldo Scaglione, W. R. Kenan Professor of Romance Languages and Comparative Literature, University of North Carolina (Chapel Hill)

Bernard N. Schilling, Trevor Professor of English and Comparative Literature, University of Rochester

H. Stefan Schultz, Professor of German, University of Chicago

Alexander H. Schutz, late Professor of Romance Languages, Ohio State University

Christoph E. Schweitzer, Professor and Chairman of the Department of Germanic Languages and Literatures, University of North Carolina (Chapel Hill)

A. Lytton Sells, Professor Emeritus of French and Italian, Indiana University

R. B. Serjeant, Sir Thomas Adams's Professor of Modern Arabic, University of Cambridge

Vsevoled Setchkarev, Curt Hugo Reisinger Professor of Slavic Languages and Literatures, Harvard University

Lawrence A. Sharpe, Associate Professor of Spanish and Portuguese, University of North Carolina (Chapel Hill)

Albert Thompson Shaw, former Director of Music and Art Master, The Royal Grammar School, Worcester, England

CONTRIBUTORS

Eisig Silberschlag, Professor of Literature and Dean, Hebrew Teachers College, Brookline

Isidore Silver, Rosa May Distinguished Professor in the Humanities, Washington University

John I. Simon, drama and film critic

A. Neil Skinner, Professor of African Languages and Literature, University of Wisconsin (Madison)

A.J.M. Smith, Professor Emeritus of English, Michigan State University

Barbara Herrnstein Smith, Professor of Literature, Bennington College

Robert W. Stallman, Professor of English, University of Connecticut

Edward Stankiewicz, Professor of Slavic Languages and Linguistics, Yale University

Martin Steinmann, Jr., Professor of English, University of Minnesota

Stephen Stepanchev, Professor of English, Queens College, City University of New York

Roy Arthur Swanson, Professor of Classics and Comparative Literature and Chairman of the Department of Comparative Literature, University of Wisconsin (Milwaukee)

Kiril Taranovski, Professor of Slavic Languages and Literatures, Harvard University

William Thalbitzer, late Professor of Eskimo Language and Culture, University of Copenhagen

John Thompson, Professor of English, State University of New York (Stony Brook)

Robert D. Thornton, Professor of English and Chairman of the Department of English and World Literature, State University of New York (New Paltz)

Ernst S. Trümpler, Instructor, Kantonsschule Schaffhausen, Switzerland

C. A. Trypanis, former Bywater and Sotheby Professor of Byzantine and Modern Greek Languages and Literatures, University of Oxford

Louis Untermeyer, poet, anthologist, and editor

Gustave Vanwelkenhuyzen, Académie Royale de langue et de Littérature Françaises, Brussels

V. H. Viglielmo, Professor of Japanese, University of Hawaii

Frank J. Warnke, Professor of English and Chairman, Comparative Literature, University of Washington

Weber-Perret, Swiss author, journalist, and educator

Kurt Weinberg, Professor of Foreign Languages and Comparative Literature, University of Rochester

Uriel Weinreich, late Professor of Yiddish Language, Literature, and Culture on the Atran Chair, and Chairman of the Department of Linguistics, Columbia University

Ulrich Weisstein, Professor of German and Comparative Literature, Indiana University

Henry W. Wells, Curator Emeritus, Brander Matthews Dramatic Museum, Columbia University. Former Professor of English, Columbia University

George Whalley, Professor and Head of the Department of English, Queen's University

Philip Wheelwright, late Professor of Philosophy, University of California (Riverside)

Harold Whitehall, Professor Emeritus of English and Linguistics, Indiana University

William Willeford, Associate Professor of English and Comparative Literature, University of Washington

William Carlos Williams, late poet and author

Sir Richard Olaf Winstedt, former Reader in Malay, University of London

A.S.P. Woodhouse, late Professor of English, University of Toronto

Mabel P. Worthington, Professor of English, Temple University

Stephen Wright, formerly, Haile Selassie I University, Addis Ababa

Paul M. Zall, Professor of English, California State University

Henri de Ziègler, former President, University of Geneva

Lawrence J. Zillman, Professor of English, University of Washington

PRINCETON

ENCYCLOPEDIA

OF POETRY AND POETICS

ABECEDARIUS. See ACROSTIC.

ABSOLUTISM IN CRITICISM. See CRITICISM, TYPES OF.

ABSTRACT. See CONCRETE AND ABSTRACT.

ABSTRACT POEM. Dame Edith Sitwell describes the poems in her *Façade* as "*abstract* poems [italics hers]—that is, . . . patterns in sound." She apparently understands "abstract" as it is used in connection with, say, painting (many prefer "nonrepresentational" or "non-objective") and/or in the sense in which music is said to be abstract—though all three arts obviously present *concrete* experiences of sound, shape, color, etc. Insofar as Dame Edith's phrase suggests a poetry of pure sound without sense, it is an exaggeration, for her critics agree that the *Façade* poems exemplify the familiar elaboration of Pope: that the *total* sense of a poem is in part a function of its sound.—E. Sitwell, "On My Poetry," *Orpheus*, 2 (1949); *A Celebration for E. S.*, ed. J. Garcia Villa (1948); J. Lindsay, "Introductory Essay" to E. S., *Façade and Other Poems* (1950); Deutsch.   J.D.K.

ABYSSINIAN POETRY. See ETHIOPIAN POETRY.

ACATALECTIC. See TRUNCATION.

ACCENT. The vocal emphasis with which a syllable is spoken relative to the emphasis received by contiguous syllables. Some linguists and prosodists equate a. with stress (q.v.); some maintain that stress is simply one of the constituents of a.; and some hold that the two are quite different things. Disagreement over the nature of a. is traditional in prosodic theorizing. Does an accented syllable have a higher pitch (q.v.) than an unaccented one? Does it have a longer duration (q.v.)? Is it louder? Has it a unique timbre or quality? Or is its emphatic characteristic connected with some sort of mysterious "energy" or "impulsion" which cannot be described in terms of either pitch, length, loudness, or quality? There is little solid agreement about these questions, even though the coarsest sensibility is capable of perceiving that the line

To me the meanest flower that blows can give

consists of alternating "accented" and "unaccented" syllables. Although it is obvious that there are infinite degrees of a. (whatever it is),

prosodists frequently discriminate three degrees for purposes of scansion (q.v.): primary a., secondary a., and weak a.

Accents are also classified by kind: etymological or grammatical ("lexical" or "word") a. is the accentual pattern customary to the word because of derivation or the relationship of prefix and suffix to root; rhetorical or logical ("sense") a. is the variable degree of emphasis given syllables according to their sense in context, e.g.

Have you the money? Have you the móney?

and metrical a. is the abstract pattern of more or less regularly recurring emphases in a line of fairly orthodox verse. Most modern prosodic theorists would hold that metrical a. almost always yields to rhetorical except in rare cases of presumably intentional "wrenched a.," as in some popular ballads:

And I fear, I fear, my dear mastér,
That we will come to harm.
(*Sir Patrick Spens*)

On the other hand, conservative prosodists of the 18th and early 19th c. frequently maintained that rhetorical a. yields to metrical.

A., however defined, is the metrical basis of Germanic accentual and accentual-syllabic prosodies (see METER), in which, most frequently, the rhetorical importance of words or syllables in context provides the pattern of metrical accents. See STRESS, PROSODY.

R. M. Alden, *Eng. Verse* (1903); J. B. Mayor, *A Handbook of Modern Eng. Metre* (1903); T. S. Omond, *Eng. Metrists* (1921); R. Bridges, *Milton's Prosody* (rev. ed., 1921); Baum; L. Abercrombie, *Principles of Eng. Prosody: Part I* (1923); P. Fussell, Jr., *Theory of Prosody in 18th-C. England* (1954).   P.F.

ACCENTUALISM. See METER.

ACCENTUAL-SYLLABIC VERSE. See METER.

ACCORD. Term used by the unanimists J. Romains and G. Chennevière in discussion of a supposedly new verse technique called by J. Hytier the *vers classique-moderne*. While the unanimists often employed conventional rhyme, in the *accords proprement dits* vowel rhyme is sacrificed and replaced by homophony of at least one of the consonants preceding or following the vowel. Like rhyme, the accord may be *poor*, with homophony of only one consonant (*mer/cor; d'été/sept ans*); *sufficient* (*cri/croc; peste/buste*), or *rich* (*ruche/rêche*); and it may be *masculine* (*bonheur/mort*), *feminine* (*sentinelle/nulle*), or *mixed* (*seule/sol*). The unanimists identified also an *a. renversé*, in which the homophonous consonants are in reverse order (*riche/cher*), and even theoretically an *a. renversé imparfait* (*sac/col*). Its champions considered *le vers accordé* superior to Fr. classical verse in richness and complexity of harmonious relations. Grammont disagreed and proclaimed much of their theory sheer illusion. Romains' use of accords in the poems of *La vie unanime* (1908) and *Odes et prières* (1913) may have influenced the "half-rhyme" verse of Wilfred Owen. See also NEAR RHYME.—J. Romains and G. Chennevière, *Petit traité de versification* (1923); J. Hytier, *Les techniques modernes du vers français* (1923); M. Grammont, review of the preceding study in RLR, 62 (1923); D.S.R. Welland, "Half-Rhyme in Wilfred Owen: Its Derivation and Use," RES, n.s. I (1950).   A.G.E.

ACEPHALOUS (Gr. "headless"). Said of a line whose first syllable is, according to the strict pattern, wanting: "Whán that Áprill with his shóures sóote" (Chaucer, *Canterbury Tales*, Gen. Prol. 1). A. verse rarely occurs in ancient hexameters (but see Homer, *Iliad* 23.2), though it is commonly found in Gr. dramatic and lyric verse. Its effect is subtle when skillfully used by a master such as Pindar. Often, however, a unit labeled a. may more properly be given another name, e.g., in Gr. lyric an a. Ionic *a minore* scans the same as a bacchius ⏑−− (q.v.). In Eng. an iambic line with a monosyllabic first foot is said to be a.—Schipper; P. Maas, *Griechische Metrik* (1929); Dale; Koster.   R.O.E.

ACMEISM (Gr. *acme*, "utmost," "a pinnacle of"). A school in modern Rus. poetry. In 1910, A. Akhmatova, S. Gorodetsky, N. Gumilyov, M. Kuzmin, and O. Mandelstam—a group of young Rus. poets gathered about the magazine *Apollon*—set out to chart a new course in Rus. verse writing. The acmeists spurned the esoteric vagueness of symbolism, which then dominated the Rus. literary scene, its vaunted "spirit of music," i.e., the tendency to achieve maximum emotional suggestiveness at the expense of lucidity and sensory vividness. They strove instead for "Apollonian" clarity, for graphic sharpness of outline, and sought to convey the texture of things rather than their inner soul. To the acmeist, the poet was not a seer or a prophet, but a craftsman (hence the name of the principal literary association of the acmeists, the "Guild of Poets"). These tenets found expression in the highly cultivated poetry of Osip Mandelstam (1891–1942?), which

combines classical learning with "modern" compactness of imagery, and in the sparse, intimate verse of Anna Akhmatova (1889–), one of modern Russia's finest lyrical poets. Nikolay Gumilyov (1886–1921), who, as a leading theorist of the school, preached neoclassicism, often tended in his own poetry toward the flamboyantly exotic and romantic. Acmeism produced some distinguished poetry, yet as a literary movement it proved short-lived and a rather inconclusive venture. After 1917, their aloofness from social problems and their relatively conservative aesthetics made the acmeists unpopular with both the official Soviet critics and the bulk of the literary avant-garde.—D. S. Mirsky, *A Hist. of Rus. Lit.* (1949); L. Strakhovsky, *Craftsmen of the Word* (1949); *A Treasury of Rus. Verse*, ed. A. Yarmolinsky (1949).   V.E.

ACROSTIC. The most common a. is a poem in which the initial letters of each line have a meaning when read downward. There are many variations among which the following are the most important: an a. might be a prose composition in which the initial letters of each paragraph make up the word or words in question; the a. might use the middle (mesostich) or the final letter (telestich) of each line; finally, the key letters might be distributed by stanzas and not by lines.

According to some, the a. was first used as a mnemotechnic device to ensure completeness in the oral transmission of sacred texts. In ancient times mystical significance was attributed to a. compositions. In the Old Testament all the recognized acrostics belong to the alphabetical type (abecedarian). Psalm 119 offers the most elaborate example. Here the 22 letters of the Hebrew alphabet in their proper order form the initial letters of every other line of the 22 stanzas of the Psalm. Another example of this type of a. is Chaucer's poem *An A.B.C.* Gr. authors of the Alexandrian time as well as L. authors (e.g., Plautus) put the title of their plays in the a. verses of the arguments (as did Ben Jonson in *The Alchemist*). During the Middle Ages the a. often spelled out the name of the author or of a saint. Later also the name of the patron or the beloved was thus designated. Among the more famous poets to use the name of their beloveds are Boccaccio and Edgar Allan Poe. In the case of *Der Ackermann aus Böhmen* and of *La Celestina* the name "a." is important evidence for the identification of Johannes von Tepl and Fernando de Rojas respectively as their authors.

By extension, the forming of words—new or old—from the initials of other words is also called an a. In the early Christian church the famous symbol of the fish is the result of this type of a. The initials of the following five words spell out the Gr. word for fish, *ichthys: Iēsous-CHristos-THeou-(H)Yios-Sōtēr.* These words in turn mean Jesus-Christ-God's-Son-Saviour. Modern examples include words like AWOL and CARE.—R. Knox, *Book of Acrostics* (1924); R. Marcus, "Alphabetic Acrostics in the Hellenistic and Roman Periods," *Jour. of Near Eastern Studies,* 6 (1947). C.E.S.

ADNOMINATIO. See PUN.

ADONIC (Adoneus, *versus* Adonius). In Gr. and L. poetry this metrical unit was of the same form as the last 2 feet of the dactylic hexameter and took its name from the cry for the god Adonis:

$$\bar{o} \; t\breve{o}n \; \bar{A}d\bar{o}n\breve{i}n. . .$$

(Sappho, fr. 168 Lobel and Page)

Certain Gr. proverbs were in Adonics, e.g.

$$gn\bar{o}th\breve{i} \; se\bar{a}ut\breve{o}n.$$

The fourth and last line of the Sapphic (q.v.) stanza, as usually printed, was an A., although word-enjambement from the third to the fourth line would suggest that the two lines were metrically one, e.g. Horace's

$$l\bar{a}b\breve{i}t\bar{u}r \; r\bar{i}p\breve{a} \; I\bar{o}v\breve{e} \; n\bar{o}n \; pr\bar{o}b\bar{a}nt(e) \; \bar{u}\text{-}x\bar{o}r\breve{i}\breve{u}s$$

$$\bar{a}mn\breve{i}s$$

(*Odes* 1.2.19–20, a rare example in that poet). Seneca employed the A. sometimes in longer runs of "lesser Sapphics." Some poets later used it stichically:

$$n\breve{u}b\breve{i}b\breve{u}s \; \bar{a}tr\bar{i}s$$

$$c\bar{o}nd\breve{i}t\breve{a} \; n\bar{u}ll\bar{u}m$$

$$f\bar{u}nd\breve{e}r\breve{e} \; p\breve{o}ss\bar{u}nt$$

$$s\bar{i}d\breve{e}r\breve{a} \; l\bar{u}m\bar{e}n.$$

Bowra; J. F. García, "La cesura en el verso 11 del carmen XI de Catulo," *Emerita* 9 (1941); Kolář; U. von Wilamowitz-Moellendorff, *Griechische Verskunst* (2d ed., 1958). R.J.G.

ADYNATON. The use of the a. or *impossibilia* is a natural expression of exaggeration which has been in constant use from the primitive days of mankind. In Gr. and L. literature the two most common varieties are the "sooner-than type" bringing out that the impossible will come true sooner than that which is mentioned by a person will take place, and the "impossible count" type referring to the number of sands on the shore, the stars in the sky, pebbles on the beach, waves in the seas, ears of corn in the fields, etc. These varieties do not occur in the literature of the Middle Ages, or,

in any case, are very rare. In contrast, a different brand was cultivated by OF writers known as the *fatrasie,* dealing with impossible or ridiculous accomplishments (cf. the *fatrasies* of Philippe de Beaumanoir and the anonymous *Fatrasies d'Arras*). Prov. writers used an allied form made popular by Petrarch's sonnet: *Pace non trovo e non ho da far guerra.* The Gr. and L. types were, however, abundantly revived by Petrarchists all over Europe, who primarily made use of them either to emphasize the cruelty of their lady loves, or as an affirmation of their eternal love, praise, loyalty, and the like. Since Petrarchism (q.v.) the device has suffered a marked decline in literary circles.— R. H. Coon, "The Reversal of Nature as a Rhetorical Figure," *Indiana Univ. Studies,* 15 (1928); H. V. Canter, "The Figure A. in Gr. and L. Poetry," AJP, 51 (1930); E. Dutoit, *Le Thème de l'adynaton dans la poésie antique* (1936); J. G. Fucilla, *Studies and Notes* (1953); L. C. Porter, *La Fatrasie et le fatras* (1960). J.G.F.

AEOLIC (properly the name of the dialect of Gr. in which were written the poems of Alcaeus and Sappho) is a term applied to a class of meters in which dactyls and trochees are brought closely together, so that choriambs appear conspicuously. Indeed opinions are divided as to whether choriambic is preferable in Aeolic verse to dactylo-trochaic ("falling") and, alternatively, iambo-anapaestic ("rising") scansion. In several forms the first 2 syllables vary in quantity between long and short and are called the "Aeolic base," the subsequent choriamb may be repeated, and the line may end with an iambic metron. The variability of the first 2 syllables (the first 4 in the case of the "polyschematist," q.v.) and the frequent presence of the choriamb have tempted theorists to see parallels with e.g., Vedic verse.— Hardie; Bowra; Dale; D. Page, *Sappho and Alcaeus* (1955); W. Borgeaud, "Analyse de quelques mètres éoliens," *L'Antiquité classique,* 26 (1957). W.B.

AESTHETIC DISTANCE. Aesthetic or physical d. is essentially a psychological rather than a spatial or temporal concept. It is meant to describe the attitude or perspective of a person toward an object when he contemplates it as separated from any personal or practical interest to himself. In the purely aesthetic sense, as formulated by Münsterberg, Puffer, Bullough, and others, "d." is the indispensable prerequisite for a contemplation of the artistic object as object by either the critic or the creator of it.

According to Bullough, who coined the term in 1912, aesthetic or "psychical d." may vary with respect to the individual and to the character of the artistic object being contemplated. A critic of a poem, for example, may fluctuate in his aesthetic attitude between the dangers of "overdistancing" and "underdistancing." If perspective is "overdistanced," the critic will be "too cold and withdrawn" in his appreciation of a poem. If perspective is "underdistanced," the critic's view will tend to become "unduly subjective and practical" (J. L. Jarrett, *The Quest for Beauty*, p. 112). The proper aesthetic d. could be said to lie somewhere between these two extremes, subject in the final analysis to the variables of individual taste and temperament. To illustrate personal variability with regard to "d.," Jarrett has noted that Bullough himself believed that the most desirable d. was consonant with its "utmost decrease" while Ortega y Gasset held that the ideal was possible only with the "utmost increase" of d. between the viewer and the object. Jarrett attributes this divergence to the romantic character of Bullough's taste as opposed to the more classical preferences of Ortega (Jarrett, p. 117).

The artistic object may itself determine the d. required for its appreciation. With respect to literature, for example, David Daiches has written that each "work of literary art, by its diction as well as other devices, provides an implicit set of directions concerning the distance from the object at which the reader must stand if he is to see it for what it is" (*A Study of Literature for Readers and Critics*, p. 63). Daiches' comment implies that every artist must bear the responsibility of incorporating into his work those devices that will help the reader determine the perspective or d. at which the work should be viewed. Milton's *Paradise Lost*, for instance, requires and demands a greater aesthetic d. for its appreciation than Frost's *Stopping by Woods on a Snowy Evening* or Herrick's *Upon Julia's Clothes*. It follows, therefore, that the artist, like the critic, is subject to the discipline of d. Distance for the artist permits him to cultivate a detachment toward his work even while he is creating it in order to consummate it with the proper "antinomy." D. for the critic enables him to keep his perspective free of irrelevant subjective discoloration in order to see in a work all the nuances that constitute the entirety of its meaning.—E. Bullough, "Psychical D. as a Factor in Art and an Aesthetic Principle," *Brit. Jour. of Psychol.*, 5 (1912); H. S. Langfeld, *The Aesthetic Attitude* (1920); D. Daiches, *A Study of Lit. for Readers and Critics* (1948); J. L. Jarrett, *The Quest for Beauty* (1957). P. A. Michelis, "Aesthetic D. and the Charm of Contemporary Art," JAAC, 18 (1959); S. Dawson, "Distancing as an Aesthetic Principle," *Australasian Jour.*

of Philos. 39 (1961) questions Bullough's assumptions. **S.H.**

AESTHETICISM. A term applied to the point of view that art is self-sufficient, need serve no ulterior purpose, and should not be judged by moral, political, or other nonaesthetic standards. Proponents of a. have often displayed self-consciousness in their rebellion against didacticism in art, since they have often been a minority in middle-class communities distrustful of art and artists.

The genesis of this view of art can be traced to the writers and philosophers of the German romantic movement—Kant, Schelling, Goethe, and Schiller—who were all agreed that art must be autonomous. Kant stressed the "pure" and disinterested existence of the work of art; Schiller, the all-importance of form; Goethe, the work of art as an independent organism; and Schelling, the work of art as a unique revelation of the universal in the particular. In England, these ideas, at least in part, were diffused by Coleridge and Carlyle; in America, by Emerson and Poe; in France, by such enthusiasts for German culture as Mme de Stael, Victor Cousin, and his disciple Théophile Jouffroy. Cousin is reported to have made use of the phrase "l'art pour l'art" in his lectures on *Le Vrai, le Beau et le Bien* of 1818 (which were not printed until 1836); other early examples of the perhaps fortuitous use of this phrase can be found in the *Journal Intime* of Benjamin Constant (1804, publ. in 1895) and in discussion by Victor Hugo in 1829. The idea of "art for art" is also implicit in Hugo's Prefaces to *Cromwell* (1827) and *Hernani* (1830).

The first vigorous, self-conscious expression of a. in modern literature, however, is that of Gautier, who humorously but emphatically denied in the Preface to *Mademoiselle de Maupin* (1835) that art could be in any way useful. From Gautier and from Poe, with his view that poetry is "the rhythmical creation of Beauty" (*The Poetic Principle*, 1850), Baudelaire adopted an aesthetic view of experience, and in writing his poetry rejected all considerations save the sovereignty of the artist and the desire to apprehend an ultimate Reality through the process of creation itself. In his concern with the ultimate implications of his materials, however, Baudelaire revealed that his sensibility was partly moral; and despite his devotion to art in its purity, he was also led to protest against "the childish utopianism of the school of art for art's sake in ruling out morals."

Baudelaire's view of experience as "a forest of symbols" to which the poet must give order and his theory of the "correspondences" existing among the objects of sense and "spiritual reality" and among the perceptions of the various senses themselves were incorporated in the Fr. symbolist movement, with Mallarmé and Verlaine as its leaders. The symbolists tried to communicate concentrated feeling through the use of evocative symbols rather than rational statement, and they also tried to refine and purify language to obtain this sort of communication. Following Poe, they held that poetry was to approximate the disembodied emotion to be found in music and that Ideal Beauty was to be sought beyond the visible world, though paradoxically to be evoked in terms of the visible world—or of symbols (in Wagner, the symbolists found a counterpart of what they were trying to do). The symbolists were also conscientious craftsmen interested in the complex and subtle relationships existing between the total poem and its component words and images. In Fr. literature the line is clear from Mallarmé to Rimbaud, who emphasized "the derangement of all the senses" to achieve new poetic effects and a complete freedom of the mind; to Valéry, who organized his poetry about the vivid image in an effort to achieve a "pure poetry," intellectually as well as emotionally defined; to Apollonaire, who, in his free subjectivism, anticipated the surrealists; and to Breton and Éluard, surrealists who exploited the subconscious in their poetry, often in an hallucinatory ambience.

A. in England was the product of native and Fr. influence both. The sometimes exaggerated individualism and subjectivity of romanticism encouraged the Eng. aesthetic movement of the 1880's. The preponderantly aesthetic values of Keats and Ruskin's enthusiastic worship of beauty were appropriated by the Pre-Raphaelites (see PRE-RAPHAELITE BROTHERHOOD) and made for a decorative art and literature instead of an ethically inspired one. In this decade and later the influence of Walter Pater was great. In the Conclusion to The Renaissance (1873), Eng. a. received almost an official sanction. Pater urged the sensitive individual "to burn always with this hard gem-like flame" and to find the most precious moments of his life in the pursuit of his sensations raised to the pitch of "poetic passion, the desire of beauty, the love of art for art's sake." Pater dominated the poets of the 1890's—Wilde, Dowson, Lionel Johnson, Symons, and the early Yeats. George Moore, Arthur Symons, and Edmund Gosse made the work of the new Fr. writers and painters available to the Englishmen of the 1890's (though Swinburne had previously discovered Baudelaire); somewhat later James Huneker performed a similar service in America. The Eng. poets of the 1890's

were influenced more by the diabolism of Baudelaire and by the insistence of Verlaine that the poet depict nuances of mood and strive for a state of music in verse than by the uncompromising artistry evinced by the work of Mallarmé.

The two British and Am. pioneers of modern verse, Eliot and Pound, were introduced to the work of the Fr. symbolists by Symon's The Symbolist Movement in Literature (1899) and incorporated into the Anglo-Saxon tradition what was most vital in the a. of Fr. poetry, the concept of the impersonal and objective existence of the poem. In America the work of MacLeish, Aiken, Cummings, Marianne Moore, Stevens, Hart Crane, Ransom, and Tate owes much to the symbolists' dedication to, and delight in, the exercise of the poet's craft and to their refusal to be inhibited by moral convention. In England, the followers of Eliot (Auden, Day Lewis, Spender, MacNeice) have absorbed the all-important concept of the autonomy of art, despite their earlier sociological orientation. Modernists like Roy Campbell and Robert Graves write a tightly knit "symbolistic" poetry; and other poets like Edith Sitwell, Dylan Thomas, Lawrence Durrell, David Gascoyne, and George Barker have been influenced by the surrealist descendants of the symbolists. In Germany the earlier verse of Stefan George and Rainer Maria Rilke reveals the influence of Fr. a. In general, all these modern proponents of a., except for some of the surrealists, have tended to regard poetry more as a public and social activity than did Mallarmé and his immediate contemporaries. Yet for all the authors mentioned in this article, the most valid aspect of a.—a realization that the Beautiful has independent importance and that the poet must be technically scrupulous in his work—was the prime motivating factor in their lives as artists.

See books by and about writers mentioned in article. Consult also H. Jackson, The Eighteen Nineties (1913); Martino; J. Farmer, Le Mouvement esthétique et "décadent" en Angleterre (1931); L. Rosenblatt, L'Idée de l'art pour l'art dans la litt. anglaise . . . (1931); Wilson; B. I. Evans, Eng. Poetry in the Later 19th C. (1933); M. Praz, The Romantic Agony (1933); Gilbert and Kuhn; C. M. Bowra, The Heritage of Symbolism (1943); W. Gaunt, The Aesthetic Adventure (1945); G. Matoré, La Preface de 'Mlle de Maupin' (1946); G. Michaud, Le Message poétique du symbolisme (3 v., 1947); T. S. Eliot, From Poe to Valéry (1948); G. Hough, The Last Romantics (1949); W. Fowlie, Age of Surrealism (1950); Lehman; Raymond; T. S. Eliot, "Arnold and Pater," Selected Essays (1950); R. Z. Temple, The Critic's Alchemy (1953); J. Wilcox, "The Beginnings of L'Art pour L'Art," JAAC, 11 (1953); J. Chiari, *Symbolism from Poe to Mallarmé* (1956); H. N. Fairchild, *Religious Trends in Eng. Poetry*, IV-V (1957-62); Wimsatt and Brooks; L. Eckhoff, *The Aesthetic Movement in Eng. Lit.* (1959); E. Starkie, *From Gautier to Eliot* (1959). F.P.W.MCD.

AFFECTIVE FALLACY. The a.f., as defined by W. K. Wimsatt, Jr., and Monroe C. Beardsley, is the critical error of evaluating a work of art in terms of its effects or "its results in the mind of its audience" (*The Verbal Icon*, p. xi). Although significant affective theories of criticism can be traced from Plato through Longinus to I. A. Richards, the fallacy of affective criticism arises from a propensity to confuse the poem with its effect. Wimsatt and Beardsley claim that this propensity of some affective critics often forces much of their criticism—based as it is on the individual critic's response rather than on more formalistic criteria—into the byways of "impressionism and relativism" (*ibid.*, p. 21). David Daiches has questioned this position by claiming that some form of legitimate affectiveness is necessary if the qualified reader is to avoid the "ontological fallacy of believing that a work of art fulfils its purpose and achieves its value simply by *being*" (*Literary Essays*, p. 173). He has suggested that a real relationship does exist between poetic effect and poetic value, and that affectivism can be saved from impressionistic and relativistic fallacies if the reader traces the "actual or potential effect" of the work upon himself to the internal structure of the work which has caused such an effect. Daiches has thus suggested the relevance of "emotional effect as a guide to value" (M. C. Beardsley, *Aesthetics*, p. 491). However, separation of effect and value, i.e., evaluation based upon what a poem *does*, immediately relegates the poem itself "'as an object of specifically critical judgment" (*The Verbal Icon*, p. 21) to a position of subordinate consideration. Such is the outcome and nature of the a.f.—a concern with effect to the subordination or disregard of the effect's source and means of creation. Wimsatt; D. Daiches, *Lit. Essays* (1956); M. C. Beardsley, *Aesthetics: Problems in the Philosophy of Crit.* (1958). S.H.

AFFLATUS (L. *afflo*, "to blow into or on"). In reference to poetry it is a synonym for inspiration (q.v.). It is usually qualified by the adjective "divine." Cicero (*De Oratore* 2.46) says that no man can be a poet "who is not on fire with passion and without a certain touch (*afflatus*) of frenzy." In ·*De Natura Deorum* 2.66: "'No one . . . was ever great without a certain divine afflatus." A.R.B.

AFRICAN NEGRO POETRY. See NEGRO POETRY. AFRICAN.

AFRIKAANS POETRY. See SOUTH AFRICAN POETRY.

AIR. (a) A song, especially a form of strophic song (Eng. "ayre," Fr. *air de cour*, It. *balletto*) in which the upper (melody) line is carried by solo voice or instrument. Because of this arrangement there is greater emphasis on the words, or poetic text, than in such compositions as madrigal or choric song. "A." in the above sense flourished during the 16th c., particularly in the hands of the Eng. lutenist composers like Dowland and Campion. (b) In a strictly musical sense, "a." is used in 17th- and 18th-c. France to refer to dancelike instrumental pieces. (c) In a somewhat recondite sense by Eng. musical writers of the 17th c., "ayre" comes to mean the mode, or key, of a particular musical sequence; thus frequently mentioned are the "aires which the Antiquity termed *Modi*" (Thomas Morley, *A Plaine and Easie Introduction to Practicall Musicke*, p. 147). This usage is supported by that of Charles Butler, Thomas Mace, and other theorists. This sense of the word seems to be the one used by Milton in "Lap me in soft Lydian airs" (*L'Allegro* 1.136).—*The Eng. School of Lutenist Song Writers*, ed. E. H. Fellowes (16 v., 1920–32; 2d ser., 16 v., 1925–27); P. Warlock, *The Eng. Ayre* (1926). J.H.

ALBA (Prov.), *aube, aubade* (Fr.), *Tagelied* (Ger.). A dawn song, ordinarily expressing the regret of two lovers that day has come so soon to separate them. It has no fixed metrical form, but each stanza usually ends with the word *alba*. The earliest examples in Prov. and in Fr. date from the end of the 12th c. The a. probably grew out of the medieval watchman's cry, announcing from his tower the passing of the night hours and the return of day. And in one a. it is a watchman who speaks, a friend of the lover's, who has been standing guard. Others are little dialogues between lover and beloved, with occasional comments from the author. In Eng. poetry, examples can be found in Chaucer's *Troilus and Criseyde* and the *Reeve's Tale*.—A. Jeanroy, *Origines . . .* and *La Poésie . . .* ; R. E. Kaske, "An Aube in the Reeve's Tale," ELH, 26 (1959) and "January's Aube," MLN, 75 (1960). See also TAGELIED. F.M.C.

ALBANIAN POETRY. The Albanians, numerically one of the smallest peoples in Europe, are also one of the most divided. Their struggle to secure their national independence, a unified language, and a modern literature has been complicated and difficult. Their speech has two distinct dialects, Geg (in the north) and Tosk (in the south), and the people are divided into three religious faiths—Roman Catholic, Orthodox, and Mohammedan. Under Ottoman rule, which lasted for more than four centuries, the task of unification was especially difficult, for the Turkish government, while employing many educated Moslem Albanians in high posts, still frowned upon the publication of books in the Alb. language, many of which had to appear abroad in Rumania, Bulgaria, and Egypt.

Alb. folk songs are composed in lines of 7 and particularly 8 syllables, chiefly trochaic. One of the most beautiful cycles of the north, the Mujo-Halil cycle, is in 10-syllable lines. They deal with the exploits of Alb. and sometimes of Slavic heroes, the latter modified to accord with Alb. environment. Yet there are several songs which bear witness to a general Balkan opposition to all invaders from abroad, whether Christian or Mohammedan. Very rare are songs in Albania proper which tell of the national hero George Castriotis, or Skanderbeg, who was reared at the Sultan's palace but died for the Christian cause in Lesh (Alessio) in 1468. However, in the large Alb. colonies in southeastern Italy there exists a whole Skanderbeg cycle. It pictures the violent struggles of feudal and Christian Albania under the leadership of the national hero to preserve her independence against the Turks. The spirit which inspired the songs around Skanderbeg has remained creative until very recent times.

The oldest known example of Alb. poetry is in the dialect of the Italo-Albanians (Tosk) and is by Father Llukë Matranga (1598), from the Alb. settlements in Sicily. In general, Alb. verse has its true birth in the 19th c., largely as a result of the interest in folk poetry which was associated with romanticism. Girolamo de Rada, an Italian of Alb. parentage, collected folk verse and later used some of their materials for his own poetry. Another significant Italo-Alb. poet was Zef Skiro (Schirò). Subsequently the brothers Sami Bey and Naïm Frashëri gave a great impetus to native Alb. culture, Naïm being the apostle-poet of Alb. nationalism. His nephew Midhat Frashëri (Lumo Skendo, 1880–1949), while not a poet himself, published in Sofia a number of important Alb. exile works, among them those of Aleksander Drenova (Asdren). Another important poet, Anton Çako (Çajupi) published most of his lyrics in Egypt.

After Albania recovered its independence in 1919, the poets shifted the center of their activities to their homeland. The focal point of the literary revival was in the Catholic North, and the outstanding poet was Father Gjergj Fishta (1871–1940), whose poetic creativeness had begun to be appreciated as early as the turn of the century. He was the author of lyric, satiric, and dramatic verse as well as of the epic Lahuta e Malcis (The Lute of the Mountains). He has been called Albania's "national poet." Other important figures included Vinçenc Prennushi, Ndre Mjeda, Ernest Koliqi, and Etehem Haxhiademi. F. S. Noli, a bishop in the Alb. Orthodox Church, is known not for his original poems but for his verse translations of such literary masterpieces as Shakespeare's works and Omar Khayyám's Ruba'iyat. Of the younger poets of this time who wrote in Tosk, Lasgush Poradeci aroused the most excitement. With truly new. poetic accents he combined the influences of Goethe, Eminescu, and the Fr. symbolists. A poet who became popular because he created in the spirit of folk poetry and sang of a period on the wane was Ali Asllani.

In the 1930's Albania, despite the pressure of its neighbors, was drawn rapidly into the Western world, and even the Mohammedans tended to study in the West rather than in the traditional center of Istanbul. The country was replacing the tribal organization with national, and in Tirana and other cities groups of literary men were in close contact with Western literary movements. The invasion of Mussolini checked these tendencies and broke up the unity of the Alb. intellectual class, which became involved in the international complications. The Fascists were succeeded by the Communists, and the latter silenced or destroyed most of the older writers who did not find refuge abroad. In the meantime only one sensitive poetic voice emerged, Migjeni. The younger writers, such as Aleks Caci, Mark Ndoja, and Veli Islami have followed the dominant Soviet themes with such Alb. coloring as the authorities allow, but their work is far inferior to that of the older generation, which followed its own inclinations and models.

In Albania so far no poet has arisen who has been able to make his appeal to the whole of this much-torn country, and Alb. literature is still best represented by its epic songs from the past. Little information comes out of the country today, and that little is not particularly hopeful.

ANTHOLOGIES AND COLLECTIONS: Kângë popullorë gegënishte (Geg Folk Songs), comp. V. Prennushi (1911); Anthollogjia Shqipetare, ed. K. Floqi (1923; coll. of epic and lyric verse); T. Mitko, Bleta Shqypëtare (The Alb. Bee), ed. Gj. Pekmezi (1924); Poesia popolare albanese, ed. E. Koliqi (1957).

HISTORY AND CRITICISM: P. F. Cordignano, La poesia epica di confine nella Albania del Nord (1943); G. Petrotta, Svolgimento storico della cultura e della letteratura albanese (1950); S. Skendi, "The South Slavic Decasyllable in Alb. Oral Epic Poetry," [Slavic] Word,

9 (1953) and *Alb. and South Slavic Oral Epic Poetry* (1954); S. E. Mann, *Alb. Lit.* (1955); A. Logoreci, "Dialogue of Modern Alb. Writing," BA, 30 (1956); *Albania*, ed. S. Skendi (1957; ch. on "Lit. and the Arts"). C.A.M.

ALCAIC. Generally a 4-line stanza of Aeolic (q.v.) type, named after the Gr. poet Alkaios (Alcaeus, late 7th and early 6th c. B.C.). The scheme is:

$$\smile \underline{\smile} \smile \smile \underline{\smile} \smile \smile \underline{\smile} \smile \underline{\smile} \ \text{(twice)} \ ||$$
$$\underline{\smile} \smile \smile \underline{\smile} \smile \underline{\smile} \smile \underline{\smile} \ ||$$
$$\smile \smile \smile \smile \underline{\smile} \smile \underline{\smile}$$

Lines 1 and 2 are Greater (or hendecasyllabic) Alcaics; line 3 is a 9-syllable A.; line 4 is a Lesser (or decasyllabic) A. This is the strophe used most frequently—37 times—by the Roman poet Horace (65–8 B.C.). It was adapted in It. by Gabriello Chiabrera (1552–1638), Paolo Rolli (1687–1765), and Giovanni Fantoni (1755–1807). Like Chiabrera, Renaissance metricians in England and France attempted recreation of the A. among other classical meters. In 18th-c. Germany F. G. Klopstock composed 17 A. odes. Hölderlin, von Platen, and others contributed to the tradition of the meter. Tennyson ("O mighty-mouth'd inventor of harmonies, . . ."), A. H. Clough, and Swinburne composed Eng. A. verses. Recent examples of translations from Gr. and L. into Eng. Alcaics are to be found in, e.g., Richmond Lattimore's version of Alcaeus'

Asunnetēmmi tōn anemōn stasin
(*Greek Lyrics*, 1955, p. 27)

and J. B. Leishman's, H. R. Henze's, J. Michie's translations of Horace (1956, 1961, 1963).— For bibliog., see CLASSICAL METERS IN MODERN LANGUAGES. Also, C. H. Moore, *Horace* (1902); H. G. Atkins, *A Hist. of German Versification* (1923); O. Francabandera, *Contribuzioni alla storia dell' alcaica* (1928); G. Highet, *The Cl. Tradition* (1949); Koster; J.P.M. Blackett, "A Note on the A. Stanza," *Greece and Rome*, 2 (1956). R.A.S.

ALCMANIC VERSE. A dactylic tetrameter catalectic *in syllabam* ($\underline{\smile} \smile \smile \underline{\smile} \smile \smile \underline{\smile} \smile \smile \underline{\overline{\wedge}}$), named after the lyric poet Alcman (7th c. B.C.). It is found in the Gr. drama and occasionally in L. dramatic poetry in dactyloepitrite periods or in periods of pure dactyls. The A. strophe is a combination of the A. verse with a dactylic hexameter. It occurs twice in Horace.—Bowra; Koster. P.S.C.

ALEXANDRIANISM. The literary works and critical principles of Hellenistic writers (ca. 325–ca. 30 B.C., the "Golden Age" of A. being ca. 280–ca. 240 B.C.). Chief poetical forms were elegy (e.g., Callimachus, Philetas), epigrams (Callimachus, Asclepiades, Poseidippos, and others), lyric (for instance, the hymns of Callimachus), epic (Apollonius Rhodius' *Argonautica*, Rhianus' *The Messenian Women*, Callimachus' *Hekale*, Philetas' *Hermes*), pastoral (for example, Theocritus' *Idylls*), and didactic (e.g., Aratus' *Phaenomena* and the astronomical works of Eratosthenes). The earlier Alexandrians (Callimachus, Philetas, *et al.*) instituted an experimental and learned fashion of writing. Their followers, the later Alexandrians (e.g., Euphorion, Antipater of Sidon, Archias of Antioch, Philodemos, Parthenios of Nicaea) favored experimental composition in narrative elegy, epigrams, hymns, iambi, *paignia*, the epyllion (or short epic), catalogue poems, and didactic poems, and introduced A. to Roman audiences and artists. The Alexandrians selected their source materials from the more specialized and less known forms of earlier poetry (e.g., the Cyclic poems, Hesiod, the Homeric hymns, and the lyrics of Stesichorus and Pindar). Their reaction against the traditional and popular forms is exemplified by Callimachus' outspoken preference of the epyllion over the epic; his pupil, Apollonius Rhodius, differed with him in this matter and thereupon produced the *Argonautica* in an approximation to the traditional epic manner. Alexandrian drama included Herodas of Cos's *Mimiambi*, which combined archaic form and contemporary content, and the works of the "Tragic Pleiad." Lycophron, one of the Pleiad, is credited with having written the most obscure and recondite poem of his time (of any time, we might say, excluding that of Eliot and Joyce), the *Alexandra* (or *Cassandra*), a dramatic monologue in 1,474 lines, studded with perplexing allusions and periphrases, neologisms, and (over 500) *hapax legomena* ("said only once"). The major movements in Alexandrian criticism were (1) the change from philosophical to scholastic estimates of literature and (2) establishing canons of earlier authors.

Under the Ptolemies a vast number of manuscripts were collected and stored in the Brucheum and Serapeum libraries at Alexandria. The Alexandrian scholars authenticated the works and Callimachus published an initial catalogue (*Tables of Outstanding Writers and their Works*) comprising about 120 books classified according to drama, poetry, legislation, history, oratory, rhetoric, and miscellaneous. Authors preserved in substantial quantity were published in formal editions (*ecdoseis*) accompanied by annotations (*hypomnēmata*). Canons of such authors were drawn up by Aristophanes of Byzantium and Aristarchus; these lists were based on the quantity rather than the quality of extant works: for example, "five" tragedians and "nine" lyric poets represent the authors whose works survived in complete texts and remained current. Unlike their contemporaries, the scholars of Pergamum, who directed their criticism and scholarship toward prose, the principal interest of the Alexandrian scholars was in poetry. They attempted, for example, to determine the original texts of edited authors, especially Homer—evidence of the caliber of their work on Homer is available in the Venetian scholia of the 10th c.—; they introduced the use of critical symbols (e.g., the obelus, asterisk, dipla); seeking to clarify matters of accentuation, they invented accent signs; they also sought to clarify metric.

The Alexandrian influence on L. literature is particularly noticeable in Catullus (poems: 63, *Attis;* 64, *Peleus and Thetis;* 66, *The Lock of Berenice;* and 68. Poems 64 and 68 are epyllionic; 66 is virtually a translation of a poem by Callimachus). Callimachus appears also to have influenced Gallus, Propertius, and Ovid in elegiac composition. Epyllionic composition in general characterized the works of the Neoterici (the Catullan school, including Calvus, Cinna, and Cornificius). It is, moreover, the style and form of the pseudo-Virgilian *Culex* and *Ciris,* Virgil's *Georgics,* and Ovid's *Metamorphoses.* Virgil's *Eclogues* (or *Bucolics*) extend the tradition of Theocritus' *Idylls.* The element of eroticism is fairly standard in Alexandrian lyric and epigram and is sustained in L. elegy.

It is clearly possible to draw an analogy between Alexandrian and modern poetry and criticism. Joyce, Yeats, Pound, and Eliot—to name only the most obvious figures—show an Alexandrian interest in myth, linguistic experiments, eroticism, forgotten areas of history and literature, etc. Likewise, the extensive development of criticism which has occurred since the 1920's might be (in fact, has been) called "Alexandrian."

A. Couat, *La Poésie alexandrine sous les trois premiers Ptolémées* (1882; Eng. tr., J. Loeb, 1931); F. Susemihl, *Gesch. der griechischen Lit. in der Alexandrinerzeit* (1891–92); G. Knaack, "Alexandrinische Lit.," in Pauly-Wissowa, *Realencyclopädie der classischen Alterumswissenschaft* 1.i (1893–); J. E. Sandys, *A Hist. of Cl. Scholarship,* I (3d ed., 1921); J. D. Denniston, *Gr. Lit. Crit.* (1924); P.-E. Legrand, *La Poésie alexandrine* (1924); U. von Wilamowitz-Moellendorff, *Hellenistische Dichtung in der Zeit des Kallimachos* (1924); W. R. Roberts, *Gr. Rhetoric and Lit. Crit.* (1928); A. Körte, *Die hellenistische Dichtung* (1925; Eng. tr., J. Hammer and M. Hadas, 1929); M. M. Crump, *The Epyllion from Theocritus to Ovid* (1931); J. W. H. Atkins, *Lit. Crit. in Antiquity* (1934); W. Van O'Connor, "This Alexandrian Crit.," *A Sch.,* 14 (1945); Curtius, ch. 14; F. C. Sell, "The Fusion of Languages: Modern A.," *Minnesota Rev.,* 4 (1963). R.A.S.

ALEXANDRINE. In Fr. prosody, a line of 12 syllables. The a. has been, since the 16th c., the standard meter of Fr. poetry, in which it has had an importance comparable to that of the quantitative hexameter in L. poetry or blank verse in Eng. poetry; it has been used especially in dramatic and narrative forms. The earliest Fr. alexandrines occur in *Le Pèlerinage de Charlemagne à Jérusalem,* a *chanson de geste* (q.v.) of the early 12th c., which abandons the traditional decasyllabic verse of Fr. epic style for the longer line. However, the a. probably takes its name from a slightly later poem, the *Roman d'Alexandre* (late 12th c.) of Lambert le Tort, a romance based on the legendary exploits of Alexander the Great. Having fallen into disuse in the later medieval period, the meter was revived in the 16th c. by J. A. de Baïf and was widely used by Ronsard and other members of the *Pléiade* (q.v.). After being perfected by the great dramatists of the 17th c., especially Racine, it became the dominant meter of all serious Fr. poetry. A certain regularity, characteristic of even the earlier a. verse, was intensified by the theory and practice of the 17th-c. poets, who developed strict rules for the use of the meter. In particular, the position of the caesura after the sixth syllable tended to become standard:

Je le vis, je rougis, || je pâlis à sa vue . . .
(Racine, *Phèdre*)

After the days of Corneille, Molière, and Racine, each of whom was able to impress the meter with his own personality, the a. tended to become excessively mechanical, until the advent of the Fr. romantics revolutionized it by an extensive use of enjambement (q.v.) and a freer practice of the so-called *alexandrin ternaire,* with its two pauses:

J'ai disloqué | ce grand niais | d'alexandrin . . .
(Hugo)

The evolution is complete with Verlaine who, by his musical fluidity, deemphasizing of rhyme, and offhand treatment of mute *e,* brings the a. to the brink of free verse. Since symbolism, the a. has oscillated, depending upon the poet, between Malherbian rigidity and symbolist evanescence.

The a. has had great importance in the poetry of several other languages, notably Dutch, in which it was the most widely used meter from the early 17th c. until around 1880. It is a common meter in 17th-c. German poetry—widely used in the school of Opitz because of the sanction lent it by *Pléiade* practice, imaginatively exploited by Andreas Gryphius because of its formal appropriateness to his antithesis-filled style. The a. is also

-[11]-

the basis from which developed the *cuaderna via* (q.v.), the important 14-syllable Sp. meter, as well as the It. meter analogous to it. The Eng. a. differs from the Fr. in being actually longer. Composed of iambic feet, it contains 6 stress accents rather than the fluid 4 accents (occasionally 3) of the Fr. poets. Spenser uses the length of the Eng. a. to good advantage in *The Faerie Queene:* the a. which concludes a Spenserian stanza (q.v.) contrasts with the 8-pentameter lines which precede it and enables the poet to achieve both emphasis and stanzaic continuity. Several Eng. works—Drayton's *Polyolbion*, Browning's *Fifine at the Fair*, Bridges' *Testament of Beauty*—are written entirely in alexandrines, but in general the Eng. a. has proved too unwieldy for continuous use in a long work.—H. P. Thieme, *The Technique of the Fr. A.* (1898); V. Horak, *Le vers a. en français* (1911); G. Lote, *L'alexandrin d'après la phonétique expérimentale* (3 v., 1911–12); A. Rochette, *L'alexandrin chez Victor Hugo* (1911); J. B. Ratermanis, "L'inversion et la structure de l'alexandrin," FS, 6 (1952); M. Burger, *Recherches sur la structure et l'origine des vers romans* (1957).   F.J.W.; A.P.

ALLEGORY (Gr. *allos*, "other," and *agoreuein*, "to speak") is a term denoting a technique of literature which in turn gives rise to a method of criticism. As a technique of literature, a. is a technique of fiction-writing, for there must be some kind of narrative basis for allegory. We have a. when the events of a narrative obviously and continuously refer to another simultaneous structure of events or ideas, whether historical events, moral or philosophical ideas, or natural phenomena. The myth and the fable are forms closely related to, or frequently used for, a., and the works usually called allegories are genres of fiction: epic (Dante's *Divina Commedia*), romance (Spenser's *Faerie Queene*), prose fiction (Bunyan's *Pilgrim's Progress*) or drama (*Everyman*). It is continuity that distinguishes a. from ambiguity or simple allusion. Fiction-writing has two aspects: (1) a progression of incidents which are imitations of actions, and (2) elements of meaning or thought which represent a poetic use of ideas. Hence there are two main types of a.: historical or political a., referring to characters or events beyond those purportedly described in the fiction; and moral, philosophical, religious, or scientific allegories, referring to an additional set of ideas. If the allegorical reference is continuous throughout the narrative, the fiction "is" an a. If it is intermittent, if a. is picked up and dropped again at pleasure, as in many works of Ariosto, Goethe, Ibsen, and Hawthorne, we say only that the fiction shows allegorical tendencies. A. is thus not the name

of a form or a genre, but of a structural principle in fiction.

A. may be simple or complex. In simple a. the fiction is wholly subordinate to the abstract "moral," hence it often impresses the literary critic as naive. An example is the fable, which is directed primarily at the set of ideas expressed in its moral. Simple historical allegories (simple at least as regards their literary structure) occur in some of the later prophecies of the Bible, such as the a. of the four kingdoms in Daniel. More complex historical and political allegories tend to develop a strongly ironic tone, resulting from the fact that the allegorist is pretending to talk about one series of incidents when he is actually talking about another. Hence there is a close connection between historical or political a. and satire, a connection marked in Spenser's *Mother Hubberd's Tale* (*Prosopopoeia*), which uses a beast-fable to satirize a contemporary political situation; in Dryden's *Absalom and Achitophel*, which uses an Old Testament story for the same purpose; in Swift's *Tale of a Tub*, and elsewhere.

Moral allegories are apt to be deeply serious in tone. In these the fiction is supposed to provide entertainment and the a. instruction. The basic technique of moral a. is personification, where a character represents an abstract idea. The simpler the a., the more urgently the reader's attention is directed to the allegorical meaning. Hence simple or naive moral a. belongs primarily to educational literature: to the fables and moralities of the schoolroom, the parables and exempla of the pulpit, the murals and statuary which illustrate familiar ideas in official buildings. Often the allegorist is too interested in his additional meaning to care whether his fiction is consistent or not as a fiction. Bunyan, even Spenser, occasionally drop into naive a. In the First Book of *The Faerie Queene*, the Redcross Knight is being taught by Faith, Hope, and Charity, and Hope urges him to take hold of her anchor, the traditional emblem of hope. It is possible to think of Hope as a female teacher lugging this anchor into the lecture room to make her point—such emblems are still brought into classrooms—but it is simpler to think that the literal narrative is being naively distorted by the allegorical interest.

Allegorical interpretation, as a method of criticism, begins with the fact that a. is a structural element in narrative: it has to be there, and is not added by critical interpretation alone. In fact, all commentary, or the relating of the events of a narrative to conceptual terminology, is in one sense allegorical interpretation. To say that *Hamlet* is a tragedy of indecision is to start setting up beside *Hamlet* the kind of moral counterpart to its events that an a. has as a part of its structure. Whole libraries of criticism may be written on the fictions of *Hamlet* or *Macbeth*, bringing out aspects of their meaning that would not occur to other readers, and all such commentary might be said, by a ready extension of the term, to allegorize the plays. But this does not, as is sometimes said, turn the plays into allegories. A glance at *Hamlet* is enough to show that it is not structurally an a. to begin with. If it were, the range of commentary would be greatly limited, because the presence of a. prescribes the direction in which commentary must go. As *Hamlet* is not an a., it has an implicit relation only to other sets of events or ideas, and hence can carry an infinite amount of commentary. Strictly defined, allegorical interpretation is the specific form of commentary that deals with fictions which are structurally allegories. This leaves considerable latitude still, for there are many fictions, notably ancient myths, where the presence or absence of a. is disputable. In this situation the critic must content himself with offering his allegorical interpretation as one of many possible ones, or—the more traditional method—he may assume that the poet has, deliberately or unconsciously, concealed allegorical meanings in his fiction. The history of allegorical interpretation is essentially the history of typical forms of commentary applied to fictions where a. is present, or is assumed to be so.

Of these, one of the earliest and most important is the rationalization of myth, especially classical myth. The stories about the gods in Homer and Hesiod were felt by many early Gr. philosophers to be not serious enough for religion: as Plutarch urged much later, gods who behave foolishly are no gods. A system of interpreting the gods as personifications either of moral principles or of physical or natural forces grew up, known at first not as a. but as *hyponoia*. The practice is ridiculed by Plato in the *Republic* and elsewhere, but it increased with the rise of the more ethical and speculative cults, notably Stoicism. Judaism had similar difficulties, and the extensive commentaries of Philo on the Pentateuch are the most ambitious of the earliest Jewish efforts to demonstrate that philosophical and moral truths are concealed in the Old Testament stories.

With Christianity a special problem arose, that of typology, of which a. formed a part. To some extent the Old Testament had to be read allegorically by the Christian, according to the principle later enunciated by St. Augustine: "In the Old Testament the New Testament is concealed; in the New Testament the Old Testament is revealed." Certain Messianic passages in the Old Testament were held to refer specifically to Jesus; the Jewish law was abolished as a ceremony but fulfilled as a type of the spiritual life. St. Paul in Galatians, commenting on the story of Abraham, Sarah, and Hagar, explicitly says that the story is an a., though it later became more exact to say that such stories had or contained allegorical meanings. Hence a doctrine of multiple meanings in Scripture was elaborated which could be applied to religious literature as well. Dante has given us the best-known formulation of the medieval scheme in his Tenth Epistle, to Can Grande (also at the beginning of the second part of the *Convito*), partly in explanation of his own practice. We begin with the "literal" meaning, which simply tells us what happened; this narrative illustrates certain principles which we can see to be true (*quid credas*, as a popular tag had it), and this is the a. proper. At the same time the narrative illustrates the proper course of action (*quid agas*); this is its moral meaning, and is particularly the meaning aimed at in the *exemplum* or moral fable used in sermons and elsewhere, and which is also employed a good deal by Dante, especially in the *Purgatorio*. Finally there is its anagogic or universal meaning, its place within the total scheme of Christian economy, the Creation, Redemption and Judgment of the world. These last two meanings may also be called allegorical in an extended use of the term.

The allegorization of classical myth continued throughout the Middle Ages, though the emphasis shifted to L. literature, through the popularity of allegorical commentaries on Virgil and Ovid which remained in vogue for well over a millennium. The use of a. for educational purposes, largely popularized by Martianus Capella's *Marriage of Mercury and Philosophy* (early 5th c.), is still going strong in England in Stephen Hawes's *Passtyme of Pleasure* (ca. 1510). In secular literature, the most popular form of a. was the allegory of Courtly Love, which employed an elaborate system of parallels to religion, its God being Eros or Cupid, its Mother Venus, its great lovers saints and martyrs, and so on. A. also of course pervaded the plastic arts, and the emblem books which became popular in the 16th c. are an example of the literary absorption of pictorial iconology.

The original motivation for allegorical systems of commentary had been the defense of the sobriety and profundity of religious myths which appeared, on the face of it, to ascribe capriciousness or indecency to the gods. Hence attacks on Homeric theology by Plato, or on early Christianity by anti-Christian apologists, normally included a rejection, usually with some ridicule, of all such face-saving interpretations. With the rise both of Protestantism and of post-Tridentine Catholicism, the same problem entered literary criticism. Puritans attacked classical mythology as puerile fable, and scoffed at all efforts to allegorize it. In Elizabethan England Gosson's *School of Abuse* was one of the most articulate of such attacks, and was replied to by Sir Philip Sidney and by Thomas Lodge. Lodge concerned himself more particularly with the question of a.: "Why may not Juno resemble the air?" he protested; "must men write that you may know their meaning?" Tasso in Italy also defended his *Jerusalem Delivered* along allegorical lines. The conception of major poetry as concealing enormous reserves of knowledge through an allegorical technique was widely accepted in the Renaissance: the preface to Chapman's translation of Homer expresses it eloquently, and other men of letters discovered their own philosophical interests in classical mythology, as Francis Bacon did in his *Wisdom of the Ancients*.

Gradually the Aristotelian conception of poetry became the main basis for the defense, as well as for much of the practice, of imaginative literature. In the *Poetics*, which influenced criticism increasingly from about 1540 on, poetry is conceived as an imitation of nature which expresses the general and the typical rather than the specific and particular, and which consequently is not to be judged by canons of truth or falsehood. This is obviously far more flexible a principle than the assumption of concealed allegorical meanings, and the latter interpretations fell out of favor. In the romantic period a renewed interest in myth, where the myth became subjective and psychological, a part of the poet's own creative processes, developed a new conception of a., expressed in Goethe, Friederich Schlegel, and Coleridge (notably in the *Statesman's Manual*). In this conception a. is thought of as essentially the translating of a nonpoetic structure, usually of abstract ideas, into poetic imagery, and is thereby contrasted with symbolism, which is thought of as starting with the poetic image, and attaching concepts to it. This contrast then becomes the basis of a value-judgment, symbolism being good and a bad. The distinction is uncritical, because it identifies all a. with naive a., but it became very popular, and helped to rationalize the growing prejudice against a. which still exists. The good allegorists, such as Dante and Spenser, were explained away by other means: readers were taught to think of a. as tedious or pedantic, or were encouraged to read Spenser or Bunyan for the story and let the a. go. Such criticism reflects the romantic conception of a direct firsthand encounter with experience as the key to great literature, in contrast to the secondhand approach to it through books.

Nevertheless, the allegorical tradition survived fitfully. In criticism, it is found notably in Ruskin, whose *Queen of the Air,* a treatise on classical mythology, practically defines a myth as an allegorical story, and classifies the canonical allegories into the moral and the cosmological. In poetry, more or less straightforward a. is found in the second part of Goethe's *Faust;* in Shelley's *Prometheus Unbound;* in Keats's *Endymion;* in Ibsen's *Peer Gynt.*

The new romantic conception of symbolism is illustrated by such fictions as *Moby Dick, The Scarlet Letter, The Golden Bowl, To the Lighthouse,* and others, where there is a central symbol, usually named in the title, with a great variety of suggestive implications, but which lacks the continuity necessary for genuine a. Hawthorne is frequently allegorical in his technique—some of his stories, such as *The Bosom Serpent,* might almost be called naive allegories—but the 19th and 20th c. are notable for fictions which carry a great deal of conceptual weight, such as *War and Peace,* or are mythopoeic, such as *The Plumed Serpent,* and yet are not strictly allegorical. The use of an archetypal model for a fiction, as Joyce uses the Odyssey in *Ulysses* and Faulkner the Passion in *A Fable,* is closer to traditional allegorical techniques. Continuous a., as we have it in Anatole France's *Penguin Island,* usually favors the historical type, with its natural affinity for satire; but the recent vogue of Franz Kafka indicates that even serious moral a. still makes a powerful appeal.

Since 1900 two new forms of allegorical interpretation have crowded out nearly all the older ones. Dreams have been from ancient times recognized as close to a., but it was only after the appearance of Freud's *Interpretation of Dreams* that there developed in criticism a technique of reading works of literature as psychological allegories, revealing the latent sexual drives and conflicts either of their authors or of their readers. There is now an extensive bibliography of such allegorical criticism in literature, most of it either Freudian or Jungian in reference. About the same time Frazer's *Golden Bough* began a school of criticism which approaches literature much as Christian typology related the New Testament to the Old. Works of literature, especially of ancient literature, are regarded as myths which contain and at the same time reveal the significance of earlier rituals and ceremonies. This form of allegorical interpretation, like the other, assumes the unconscious rather than the deliberate concealment of the allegorical allusion.

There is no comprehensive work on the subject: an immense amount of scholarly research has been done on classical and medieval a., much of it in areas remote from literature; critical treatments of modern literature usually deal with mythopoeia rather than a. The following studies are helpful: Lewis; R. P. Hinks, *Myth and A. in Ancient Art* (1939); J. Seznec, *The Survival of the Pagan Gods*, tr. B. Sessions (1953); E. D. Leyburn, *Satiric A.: Mirror of Man* (1956); H. Berger, Jr., *The Allegorical Temper* (1957); E. Honig, *Dark Conceit: the Making of A.* (1959); M. P. Parker, *The A. of the Faerie Queene* (1960); A. C. Hamilton, *The Structure of A. in "The Faerie Queene"* (1961); P. E. McLane, *Spenser's Shepheardes Calender: a Study in Elizabethan A.* (1961); A. Fletcher, *A.: the Theory of a Symbolic Mode* (1964). N.FR.

ALLITERATION. Any repetition of the same sound(s) or syllable in two or more words of a line (or line group), which produces a noticeable artistic effect (see also SOUND IN POETRY and ACCORD). A. may occur involuntarily or by choice. It can produce emphasis and euphony (or cacophony!) comparable to the striking effects of end rhyme. The most common type of a. is that of initial sounds (hence the term "initial rhyme" or "head rhyme"), especially of consonants or consonant groups; a. of initial vowels is less frequent since they do not have the same acoustic impact as consonants. In Germanic alliterative meter (q.v.) or "Stabreim" any vowel can alliterate with any other, probably because the preceding glottal stop constitutes the repetition. A. may, however, include with notable effect the repetition of consonants, vowels, or consonant-vowel combinations in medial or even final position ("That *brave* vibration . . ,"—Robert Herrick). This applies especially in languages which, like Fr., lack stress accent ("J'ai couru les deux mers que sépare Corinthe"—Racine). On the other hand, in languages with stress accent, a. is not confined to stressed syllables, but may extend to the unstressed (called "submerged" or "thesis" a., e.g.: "Suppos'd as forfeit to a confin'd doom"—Shakespeare). Different alliterating sounds can be interwoven to produce intricate patterns extending through the whole or sections of a poem. A. on the one sound or sound combination may be followed by, alternate with, or include another alliterative sequence (*parallel* or *crossed* a.)

Other varieties of a.: the grammatical figure or *polytopon*, Fr. *l'annomination* (diverse forms of the same syllable in successive words not necessarily etymologically related: "vi vitam"—Ennius); *homoeoteleuton* (identity of word endings: "au travers . . . divers"—Mallarmé; really a form of identical rhyme); *suspended* a. (reversal of the alliterating consonant and the succeeding vowel: "Herds of fallow *deer* were *feeding*"—Longfellow. All these varieties are combinations of a. with assonance (q.v.). So-called eye a. consists in identical spelling only: "Have wrought and worshipped" (Swinburne) or "Careless of censure" (Pope). It is doubtful whether such false a. is ever consciously intended by a poet.

In all literatures where a. is practiced, it is subject to changing literary fashions and tastes, but, generally speaking, it is more prominent in the poetry of languages with stress accent (especially where the accent regularly falls on the first syllable, as in Finnish, Esthonian, and Czech) and in verse which is meant to be spoken rather than sung or chanted. Thus in the medieval Germanic idioms (ON, Old High German, Old Saxon, ME), in Finnish (*Kalevala* epic), and in early (7th-c.) Ir., a. served as the chief structural principle and was governed by rigid rules [see ALLITERATIVE METER], whereas in languages with tone systems or quantitative structures it is either completely absent (as in Chinese poetry, which is based on syllable count and tone patterns), or used rarely and only for very special emphasis (as in Sanskrit, e.g., Kalidasa, *Kumarasambhava* 1.18, and in Japanese where an 8th-c. tanka and a 17th-c. kyoka furnish notable but rare examples). In the modern Germanic languages, even after its substitution by end rhyme as a structural principle, a. is still more prevalent than in the chiefly syllable-counting Romance tongues.

Ancient Gr. poetry, based on a quantitative metric, uses a. rarely and only for special onomatopoetic effects. In Roman poetry a. is found throughout, beginning with the Saturnian *carmina* (Latin possesses stress accent, and the quantitative metric was taken over from the Greeks). The Romans used the Gr. term *paromoeon*, while *alliteratio* does not occur until the end of the 15th c. Ennius made ample use of the device and went to absurd extremes. While Cicero disdained it, Lucretius delighted in a. Among the "new" poets, Catullus had a marked preference for alliterative ornament in some parts of his work and practiced abstinence in others. Virgil employed a. with great subtlety as a conveyor of emotions. In late Imperial times and through the Middle Ages a. became a cherished mannerism.

All the troubadour poets of Old Prov. practiced a. (*replicatio*), aiming with great skill at achieving parallelisms between sound and meaning. They favored a. especially at the beginning and at the end of a poem. In the modern Romance literatures, It. poets use a. sparingly, the Sp. more frequently, though with discretion (a manneristic flowering occurred in the 16th and 17th c.). The Fr. used a. very sparingly until the romanticists, symbolists, and moderns sought to endow the Fr. poetic medium with a new musicality. In Baudelaire's *Fleurs du mal* the use of a. often coincides with the division of an alexandrine into anapaests. Mallarmé and Valéry achieve highly sophisticated alliterative effects.

Ir. (Gaelic) is among the most richly alliterative poetic media of world literature. Through the centuries, Ir. verse has preserved an unbroken tradition of decorative a. even though its metric has long since been based on rhyme and syllable count, whereas Welsh poetry uses, even today, the complex, versatile "cynghanedd" (q.v.), an ancient artistic device, involving a. and having a metric function.

In Eng. versification, likewise, a. continued as an ornamental device after its eclipse as a structural principle. In the 16th c., under the influence of rhetoric, which encouraged "the figure of like letter" (also called "parimion" or "letter-tagging"), some poets used it to excess. Shakespeare burlesques alliterative practices in *Love's Labour's Lost*, but where he chooses, he can use it with superb mastery (e.g. Sonnets 18, 29, 30, 128). During the 17th and 18th c., a. lost its importance somewhat. While it was used as an occasional ornament by some poets, such as Dryden, Richard Crashaw, Oliver Goldsmith, it was largely avoided by others, such as Milton. Pope could skillfully avoid the device through long sections of a poem and then suddenly use it with great effect, as at the end of the *Essay on Criticism*. With the romantic poets a new vogue set in. Effects were achieved which aimed to enhance the musicality of the language rather than to produce rhetorical emphasis. The Victorians, Pre-Raphaelites, and moderns continued the practice with further refinement and subtlety. Swinburne parodied his own alliterative abundance in *Nephilidia*. Gerard Manley Hopkins' use of a. (see CYNGHANEDD) is the most willfully original and strikingly bold (see, for example, *The Wreck of the Deutschland*).

The development of a. in Am. poetry runs parallel with the British vogue. Walt Whitman uses it amply, Melville frequently and effectively. T. S. Eliot tends to use repetition of identical words and whole phrases rather than a. proper. Carl Sandburg, Marianne Moore, H. D. like a.; W. H. Auden's *Voices in the Desert* in *The Flight into Egypt* imitates alliterative verse. Wallace Stevens, schooled by the musicality of the Fr. symbolists, does not depend on a. for his sound harmonies, but he can use it most effectively.

In modern German, aside from the sporadic and ineffectual attempts at resuscitating medieval "Stabreim" (W. Jordan, R. Wagner), a. is common as an occasional ornament. In Goethe it is less numerous than in Schiller and the romantic poets, but he uses it frequently enough to permit the conclusion that he did so deliberately, especially to express high emotional tension (e.g., in *Marienbader Elegie*). After the influence of Baudelaire and the symbolists had quickened the renewal of German poetry, a. became a far more consciously used, almost indispensable, euphonic device ("Hiersein ist herrlich"—Rilke; "Ich bin freund and führer dir und ferge"—Stefan George).

R. L. Taylor, *A. in Italian* (1900); K. Florenz, *Gesch. der japanischen Lit.* (2d ed., 1909); Schipper; M. Scholz, "Die A. in der altprovenzalischen Lyrik," ZRP, 37 (1913) and 38 (1914); A. Heusler, "Stabreim," *Reallexikon*, ed. J. Hoops, IV (1919); E. Sikes, *Roman Poetry* (1923); E. Rickert, *New Methods for the Study of Lit.* (1927); H. Schneider, "Stabreimvers," *Sachwörterbuch der Deutschkunde*, II (1930); E. Wölfflin, "Zur A.," *Ausgewählte Schriften* (1933); M. Grammont, *Le Vers français* (4th ed., 1937); R. E. Deutsch, *The Patterns of Sound in Lucretius* (1939); M. Dillon, *Early Ir. Lit.* (1943); U. K. Goldsmith, "Words out of a Hat? A. and Assonance in Shakespeare's Sonnets," JEGP, 49 (1950); N. I. Herescu, *La Poésie latine: étude des structures phoniques* (1960); W. Kayser, *Gesch. des deutschen Verses* (1960).
U.K.G.

ALLITERATIVE METER. A prominent feature of Old Germanic prosody (q.v.) is initial rhyme, used not for mere ornamentation but structurally, to link and emphasize important words within prescribed metrical units. The beginnings of the alliterative tradition are unknown, though one may guess that alliteration was partly a mnemonic aid to primitive oral recitation. Whatever its origins in Germanic antiquity, alliteration is part of a complex prosodic system, and indeed of the fabric of the Germanic languages themselves. The fondness for alliterative formulas is still noticeable in a language like Eng., which uses them easily and habitually in and out of poetry: "might and main," "time and tide," "to have and to hold."

The a. m. of the oldest poetry of Germany, Scandinavia, and England is superimposed upon the speech rhythms of these languages, with their constituent long and short syllabic quantities, in such a way as to increase the rhythmic emphasis of regular numbers of syllables in a given unit of verse, leaving different numbers of subordinatively stressed and unstressed syllables around them. The following lines from the Old Saxon *Heliand* (2242-2247), despite their varying syllabic totals, are metrically identical in that each typographical line (the arrangement of which on the page is a modern editorial convention) contains 4 heavily stressed syllables and several more lightly stressed or unstressed syllables in different patterns. Marks of vowel quantity are omitted from this and subsequent examples, and no attempt is made to indicate secondary accents.

<blockquote>

Thuo bigan thes wédares cráft,
úst úp stigan,   úthiun wáhsan;
súang gisúerc an gimang;   thie séu warð an hrúoru,
wan wínd endi wáter;   wéros sórogodun,
thiu méri warð so múodag,   ni wanda thero mánno nigén
léngron líbes.

</blockquote>

Then the power of the storm, the tempest, became greater; waves grew larger; darkness fell; the sea was stirred up; wind and water contended; the sea raged so that men despaired, nor did one of them expect to live longer.

The long line, it should be noted, is divided into 2 metrically independent verses by a pause, and the verse pairs are linked by the alliteration of 1 or 2 stressed syllables in the first verse with the first stressed syllable of the second verse. Different types of verses will be formed from five possible arrangements of long and short, stressed and unstressed syllables, according to a complex system conventionally described by Eduard Sievers (see bibliog. below). As for the alliteration itself, each consonantal sound rhymes (usually) only with another occurrence of the same sound, but any vowel or diphthong may rhyme either with itself or with another vowel or diphthong. The basic structure of this meter, it must be emphasized, is not stanzaic or even linear: each of the verses in a verse pair is a metrical unit; a sentence may begin or end in the middle of a line, and the verses may be strung together in long verse paragraphs which bring out a characteristic parallelism of thought and diction, like the sequence which concludes the OE *Battle of Brunanburh:*

<blockquote>

            Ne wearð wæl máre
on ðys íglánde   æfre gýta
fólces gefýlled   befóran ðýssum
swéordes écgum   ðæs ðe us sécgað béc,
éalde úðwitan,   sibþan éastan híder
Éngle and Séaxe   úpp becómon
ofer bráde brímu,   Brýtene sóhton,
wlánce wígsmiðas   Wéalas ofercómon,
éorlas árhwate   éard begéaton.

</blockquote>

Never yet in this island was a greater slaughter of an army by the sword's edge, as books tell us, ancient scholars, since the Angles and Saxons came hither from the east over the broad waters, sought out Britain, proud fighters defeated the Welsh, warriors keen for glory won a homeland.

Alliteration, then, is a device which associates phrases or individual verses within the verse pairs, but the series of lines which constitutes the poem may be loosely or compactly joined, depending on the syntax and style of the whole work.

In England the comparatively severe, remarkably regular alliterative poetry of the OE period gave way to a less systematic ME verse which tolerated much more freedom in the alliteration itself, and in the treatment of stressed and unstressed syllables: compare the resemblances to and the departures from the OE norm in the 14th-c. *Piers Plowman:*

<blockquote>

I seigh a tóure on a tóft   trielich ymáked,
A dépe dále binéthe,   a dóngeon there-ínne
With dépe dýches and dérke   and drédful of síght.
A fáire félde fúl of fólke   fónde I there bytwéne,
Of álle máner of mén,   the méne and the ríche,
Wórchyng and wándryng   as the wórlde ísketh.

</blockquote>

I saw a tower on a raised place, excellently built, a deep valley beneath, a dungeon therein with deep dark ditches, dreadful to look upon. In between I discovered a beautiful plain full of people of all kinds, the common and the rich, working and wandering as the world requires.

Sometimes, as in the 14th-c. *Pearl* or *Sir Gawain and the Green Knight,* intricate patterns of rhyme and elaborate stanzaic forms are combined with a freely treated alliterative line. But with the end of the Middle Ages and the assimilation of Fr. and classical syllabic meters into Eng. poetry, the systematic a. m. disappeared for centuries, and only in modern times have Eng. and Am. poets returned to it as a potentially fresh and vital form. It is a hard meter to use well, or even to use at all, if its rhythmic characteristics are more or less faithfully observed; and the retention or rediscovery of its primitive quantitative rules is more difficult still, but not impossible, as shown by C. S. Lewis in the study mentioned below. Poems by Ezra Pound (*The Seafarer*), C. Day Lewis (*As One Who Wanders into Old Workings*), and Richard Eberhart (*Brotherhood of Men*) could be cited as notable experiments in a contemporary alliterative revival. W. H. Auden's *The Age of Anxiety* (1947) is a major work in which many varieties of the Old Germanic a. m. are displayed with great skill. On the Ir. a. m. see below.

E. Sievers, *Altgermanische Metrik* (1893); Saintsbury, *Prosody,* I; J. P. Oakden and E. R. Innes, *Alliterative Poetry in ME: A Survey of the Traditions* (1935); C. S. Lewis, "The A. M.," in *Rehabilitations* (1939); G. Murphy, *Early Ir. Metrics* (1961); A. J. Bliss, *An Introd. to OE*

Metre (1962); M. Borroff, *Sir Gawain and the Green Knight* (1962). J.B.B.

ALLOEOSTROPHA. A term used by Milton in the Preface to *Samson Agonistes* to describe verse composed in stanzas (or strophes) of irregular length and construction. Opposed to the strict and predictable strophic organization of the formal ode (q.v.). P.F.

ALLUSION. Tacit reference to another literary work, to another art, to history, to contemporary figures, or the like. A. may be used merely to display knowledge, as in many Alexandrian and medieval poems; to appeal to a reader or audience sharing some experience or knowledge with the writer; or to enrich a literary work by merging the echoed material with the new poetic context. A. differs from mere source-borrowing, because it requires the reader's familiarity with the original for full understanding and appreciation; and from mere reference, because it is tacit and fused with the context in which it appears. The technique of a. assumes: (1) an established literary tradition as a source of value; (2) an audience sharing the tradition with the poet; (3) an echo of sufficiently familiar yet distinctive and meaningful elements; and (4) a fusion of the echo with elements in the new context. It has analogues in biblical and religious writings, the novel, and elsewhere, and usually requires a close poet-audience relationship, a social emphasis in literature, a community of knowledge, and a prizing of literary tradition.

TYPES. *Topical a.*, normally reference to recent events, is common up to the romantic movement, less frequent thereafter except in humorous poetry or ephemeral *vers de société*. *Personal a.*, reference to facts concerning the poet himself, must be to facts widely known, easily grasped, or made familiar, and varies from Shakespeare and Donne's plays on their own names, to Virgil's lamenting his misfortunes in the *Eclogues*, to Dante's account of his love for an idealized Beatrice; but it should be distinguished from the romantic use of personal experience for subject matter, e.g. Coleridge's discussion of his failing poetic powers in *Dejection: An Ode. Metaphorical a.* is more complex in function and richer in interest and meaning. Found chiefly in periods setting value on tradition (e.g., Augustan Rome, China from early times, 11–14th-c., Japan, 17–18th– and 20-c. Europe), this technique uses the echoed element as a vehicle for the poetic tenor that it acquires in the new context (e.g., Dryden's allusion to *Aeneid* 5 and 6 in his poem to Oldham expresses through metaphor the relation between himself and Oldham and also between Roman and Eng. cultural values). Frequent in the older Chinese and Japanese poetry, such a. can also be found in Goethe (to religious services in *Faust*), in Foscolo (to Homer in *Dei sepolcri*), in Baudelaire (to the *Aeneid* in *Le Cygne*), and broadcast in the major works of Eliot and Pound. *Imitative a.* is either specific (Dr. Johnson to Juvenal, *Satire 3*, in *London*), generic (Dryden to epic in *Absalom and Achitophel*), parodic (Philips to Milton in *The Splendid Shilling*) or, commonly, synthetic (Pope's *Rape of the Lock*—at once specific to Milton and others, generic to epic, and parodic). *Structural a.* gives form to a new work by suggesting the structure of an older work; in this it resembles imitative a., but it is identifiably different when the a. is to other genres or arts (e.g., the *Odyssey* is alluded to structurally by Joyce's *Ulysses*, and music is alluded to by Eliot in *Four Quartets*). And in spite of Lessing's strictures, many poets from the 17th c. to the present have alluded structurally to nontemporal graphic and plastic arts (e.g., Auden to Breughel's *Icarus* in his poem *Musée des Beaux Arts*).

No comprehensive study of a. exists, but the following touch upon representative aspects of the subjects. H. J. Rose, *The Eclogues of Virgil* (1942); H. F. Brooks, "The 'Imitation' in English Poetry . . . Before the Age of Pope," RES, 25 (1949); M. Mack, " 'Wit and Poetry and Pope': Some Observations on His Imagery," *Pope and His Contemporaries* (1949); J. R. Hightower, *Topics in Chinese Lit.* (1950); S. P. Bovie, "Classical Allusions," CW, 52 (1958); R. A. Brower, *Alexander Pope: The Poetry of A.* (1959); R. H. Brower and E. Miner, *Japanese Court Poetry* (1961). E.M.

AMBIGUITY. Term introduced by William Empson, who devoted a book, *Seven Types of Ambiguity* (1930), to an examination of its critical applicability and usefulness. A more reasonable term probably is one employed by Philip Wheelwright, *plurisignation*. Most readers of poetry, Empson felt, reduced the meaning of a given word to a single denotation. For example, he found that Shakespeare editors differed strongly about the meaning of a word like *rooky* (*Macbeth*). Learned reasons were given why a single meaning, and no other meaning, was *the* correct one. Empson inferred that if collectively the editors saw multiple meanings in *rooky*, then Elizabethan audiences must also have seen multiple meanings, and that Shakespeare himself must have seen them "since he was no less sensitive to words than they." In explaining his method, Empson confesses an indebtedness to the analysis of a Shakespeare sonnet by Robert Graves in *A Survey of Modernist Poetry* (1938). (The method was also employed by

Graves in *Poetic Unreason* [1925]). And both Graves and Empson had been anticipated by Frederick C. Prescott in *The Poetic Mind* (1922). Prescott used Freudian terminology, "displacement," "condensation," etc., but his analyses bring out the same sort of thing that Empson does. For example, Prescott analyzes two lines from a speech of Hotspur's against Henry IV: "We must have bloody noses and crack'd crowns/ And pass them current too. God's me, my horse."— "Here the 'crack'd crowns' are first cracked coins, secondly broken heads, and thirdly royal crowns upset. Note too that the third meaning is at once farthest from the literal, the most latent, perhaps the most unconscious (in Hotspur's mind), and the most far-reaching (involving the whole dramatic action)."

Many readers have felt that Empson's insistence on *seven* types of a. is unnecessary and mistaken. William York Tindall, who finds Empson's readings "exemplary," finds the division into seven types "pretentious." There seems little doubt, however, that Empson has helped to teach at least one generation of poetry readers to find more complicated meanings in poetry than they had hitherto been prepared to find. Again, in Mr. Ransom's words, "The ordinary critic cannot read them (Empson's analyses) and be the same critic again. . . ." Mr. Empson summarizes this method in these words: "We call it ambiguous . . . when we recognize that there could be a puzzle as to what the author meant, in that alternate views might be taken without sheer misreading. . . . An ambiguity, in ordinary speech, means something very pronounced, and as a rule witty or deceitful. I propose to use the word in an extended sense, and shall think relevant to my subject any verbal nuance, however slight, which gives room for alternative reactions to the same piece of language."

Empson says, to take an instance, that a concentration of meanings is a characteristic of Augustan poetry: "This way of suggesting grasp of mind, ingenuity, and control over things, this use of a word with several extended meanings so as to contract several sentences into one, is the fundamental device of the Augustan style. The word is usually a verb precisely because the process is conceived as an activity, as a work of the digesting and controlling mind." An example is seen in Pope's *Of the Characters of Women*: "One certain portrait (I grant) may be seen, / Which Heav'n has varnish'd out, and made a queen." The passage refers to Catherine Hyde, wife of the third Duke of Queensbury. There is a little cluster of meanings relevant to the verb "varnish": Heaven, or chance, has dressed her as a duchess, covered her in glistening robes, in the same way varnish gives a glow to the portrait; she is a duchess in name rather than in spirit, and the verb is appropriate in the sense that Pope, as he says, is sketching and finishing portraits. The pun on "queen" is obvious. The virtue in Empson's method is that it helps to enlarge one's sense of what a poem says. A weakness in the method, which Empson himself does not always avoid, is that it invites overly complicated, ingenious, and finally irrelevant readings.

J. D. Hubert (*L'Esthétique des "Fleurs du Mal." Essai sur l'ambiguité poétique, 1953*) applies a similar approach to the poetry of Baudelaire. The categories of a. perceived by Hubert differ from Empson's and thereby not only suggest the unlimited wealth of plurisignation in Baudelaire's work but also indicate the usefulness of the concept as detached from Empson's specific scheme.

As a poetic device, a. also occurs, of course, in other literatures—ancient and modern—e.g., W. B. Stanford (*Ambiguity in Gr. Literature. Studies in Theory and Practice*, 1939) traces a. in Gr. poetry from Homer to Euripides.

J. C. Ransom, "Mr. Empson's Muddles," *The Southern Review*, 4 (1938); C. Brooks, "Empson's Crit.," *Accent Anthol.* (1946); W. Y. Tindall, *Forces in Modern Brit. Lit.* (1947); E. Olson, "William Empson, Contemporary Crit., and Poetic Diction," in Crane, *Critics*; P. Wheelwright, *The Burning Fountain* (1954) and *Metaphor and Reality* (1962); Wimsatt and Brooks. w.v.o'c.

AMERICAN INDIAN POETRY. North America. The poems of the North Am. Indians cannot be fully understood unless the reader has some comprehension of their origins and the human needs and desires that brought them into being. This native poetry grew out of the use of the song as a part of tribal life, and few examples can be found which did not originally serve as the words to a religious or secular chant, ritual, or incantation. Song among the Indians was seldom used merely for entertainment or for voicing the soul-cry of the lyrical individualist. As one Indian said, "If a man is to do something more than human, he must have more than human power." Song was a way to tap this good superhuman force, and was used to obtain success in almost every act of Indian life.

The Indians made poems, then, for many reasons: to praise their gods and ask their help in life; to speak to the gods through dramatic performances at seasonal celebrations or initiations or other rites; to work magical cures or enlist supernatural aid in hunting, plant-growing, or horsebreeding; to hymn the praises of the gods; to chronicle tribal history; to explain the origins of the world; to teach right conduct; to mourn the dead; to arouse warlike feelings; to compel love; to awaken laughter; to ridicule a rival or bewitch an enemy; to praise famous men; to communicate the poet's private experience; to mark the beauties of nature; to boast of one's personal greatness; to record a vision scene; to characterize the actors in a folk tale; to quiet children; to lighten the burden of work; to brighten up tribal games; and, sometimes, to express simple joy and a spirit of fun.

The large majority of translated songs were made for essentially religious or magical purposes. Here is one of the 161 songs from the Navaho "Mountain Chant," translated by Dr. Washington Matthews:

> The voice that beautifies the land!
> The voice above,
> The voice of the thunder.
> Within the dark cloud
> Again and again it sounds,
> The voice that beautifies the land.
>
> The voice that beautifies the land!
> The voice below:
> The voice of the grasshopper.
> Among the plants
> Again and again it sounds,
> The voice that beautifies the land!

Even what seem at first to be poems descriptive of the beauties of nature are often found to be connected in the Indian mind with religion and worship. Many of the short chants of the Midé, the grand medicine society of the Chippewas, reveal a poetic awareness of surroundings. Here is a fresh impression of June days:

> As my eyes search the prairie
> I feel the summer in the spring.

Vision songs are widely found. These are often personal charms composed after fasting, or else spring from cult ceremonies, such as the trance-inspired songs of the revivalist Ghost Dance Religion. This example "summarized the whole hope of the Ghost Dance—the return of the buffalo and the departed dead, the message being brought to the people by the sacred birds, the eagle and the crow."

> The whole world is coming.
> A nation is coming, a nation is coming.
> The Eagle has brought the message to the tribe.
> The father says so, the father says so.
> Over the whole earth they are coming,
> The buffalo are coming, the buffalo are coming.
> The Crow has brought the message to the tribe.
> The father says so, the father says so.

On the secular side, a few pieces of satirical verse can be found, such as the boasting contests of the Northwest Coast. Cradle songs and lullabies are often delightful, and a few songs from games are of poetic value.

The Aztecs, who conducted schools for poets and singers, produced several first-rate lyricists, in particular the reflective royal poet Nezahualcoyotl, but elsewhere the pure lyric is a rare type. Neither is the romantic love song a common form, and with the exception of love-charms to arouse affection by magical means, most such songs are late and reflect the white man's idea of what an "Indian love call" should be.

Among the Indians there is a notable lack of rhythmic work songs comparable to our sea shanties or Negro labor songs. The most surprising lack, however, is in narrative verse. The Indian customarily told his tales and legends in prose, and reserved the poetic style and rhythm for nonprosaic purposes. No examples were found that could correspond to the European epic, ballad, or verse romance. However, the historical chronicle in rude mnemonic lines is fairly well represented by the "Walam Olum" of the Lenape tribe.

Indian songs vary in length from a few words to extended ceremonials that might run on for days at a time. Thus, a song in honor of a Chippewa brave consisted of only two words—one meaning "warrior" and the other the name of the hero. The people were supposed to know his valiant deeds and it was not necessary to mention even one of them. In contrast to this two-word poem, the "Night Chant" of the Navahos contains a sequence of no less than 324 different songs which made up one long ritual poem recited over a succession of days and nights.

Every Indian was a potential poet. Songs were the most important instruments of the medicine man; but any member of the tribe could by means of dreams and visions find a personal song to help in time of need. Many ceremonies encouraged the invention of such songs, which related experiences either real or else seen in visions. The names of the makers of most of the poems surviving among the Indians are unknown. The religious songs, in particular, are always anonymous, for they were presumed to have been inspired by supernatural beings. The lyrics of Nezahualcoyotl and the war songs of Sitting Bull were, however, known to be individual compositions.

The many excellent translations of Indian poetry to be found scattered through dozens of works of the past century are charming contributions to Am. literature. The best literary translations of Indian verse have been made by professional ethnologists who have united with their linguistic learning a talent for poetic rendition. Effective translation is made difficult chiefly because, when a song, chant, or recitative is taken out of its ceremonial setting, the meaning is not always clear to the modern reader. Therefore, explanation is often needed to give the reader an idea of the background from which the poem has come. Translation of meaning is further complicated by the frequent use of symbolism, figurative language, secret or archaic language, and allusions to Indian myths and other parts of the background which the native hearer was supposed to know and take for granted.

Stylistic qualities—such as rhythm, pattern, imagery, contrast, monotony, variation, poetic diction, parallelism, personification, euphony, and onomatopoeia—are found in Indian poetry, but these cannot always be literally translated. Although Indian verse lacks metrical accent and is not composed in iambics or dactyls, there is usually a measured rhythmic pattern for each type of Indian song; vocables are sometimes added to fill out the measure, and accents are misplaced to conform to some melodic scheme. One who listens for hours to the chants and wails of an Indian ceremonial will easily perceive a rhythm of a marked sort —one closely associated with the drum-beat— and this rhythm may often be quite elaborate.

The meaning of an Indian poem is often obscured in Eng. not only because of stylistic problems, but also because Indian verse frequently is intentionally cryptic or ambiguous. To say that we cannot enjoy such a poem in exactly the same frame of mind as that in which it was first heard by Indians, however, is not to say that the poem cannot be enjoyed today in a good Eng. version—particularly if the translator adds some commentary on its origin and background.

H. Hale, *Iroquois Book of Rites* (1883); D. G. Brinton, *The Lénapé and Their Legends* (1885), *Ancient Nahuatl Poetry* (1887) and *Rig Veda Americanus: Sacred Songs of the Ancient Mexicans* (1890); W. Matthews, "The Mountain Chant, a Navaho Ceremony," Bureau of Am. Ethnology, *5th Annual Report* (1887); J. Mooney, "The Sacred Formulas of the Cherokees," BAE, *7th A.R.* (1891) and "The Ghost-Dance Religion," BAE, *14th A.R.* (pt. 2, 1896); A. C. Fletcher, *Story and Song from North America* (1900), and "The Hako: a Pawnee Ceremony," BAE, *22d A.R.* (pt. 2, 1904); N. Curtis (Burlin), *The Indians' Book* (1907, 1923); F. Russell, "The Pima Indians," BAE, *26th A.R.* (1908); F. Densmore, *Chippewa Music*, BAE, *Bull. 45* (1910), *The Am. Indians and Their Music* (1926) and "Songs of the Indians," *Am. Mercury*, 7 (1926); N. Barnes, *Am. Indian Verse, Characteristics of Style* (1921); E. L. Walton and T. T. Waterman, "Am. Indian Poetry," *Am. Anthropologist*, 27 (1925); R. Bunzel, "Zuñi Ritual Poetry," BAE, *47th A.R.* (1932); H. J. Spinden, *Songs of the Tewa*

(1933); R. M. Underhill, *Singing for Power* (1938); F. La Flesche, *War Ceremony and Peace Ceremony of the Osage Indians*, BAE, *Bull. 101* (1939); A. G. Day, *The Sky Clears: Poetry of the Am. Indians* (1951; contains bibliog. and 200 poems in Eng. from 40 tribes), and "The Indian as Poet," *Am. Indian*, 6 (1952); I. Nicholson, *Firefly in the Night: A Study of Ancient Mexican Poetry and Symbolism* (1959).—RECORDINGS: Original Indian songs collected by Miss F. Densmore from at least a dozen Am. tribes are available at the Music Div., Library of Congress.　　　A.G.D.

SOUTH AMERICA. The indigenous poetic literature of the South Am. Indians is of two fundamental kinds: the *poetry of song*, rhythmically repetitive in form and content, often the burden or accompaniment of music, dance, and ritual, turning on various but common themes, which is found universally among the nonliterate native peoples of the continent; and the *poetry of extraordinary speech and thought*, reflective and lyrical, that was achieved at least twice in South America, by the Incas of Peru, and by the Araucanians of Chile and Argentina. This is an oral literature, not originally written down, of which only a few fragments have been preserved from the past, in 16th- and 17th-c. chronicles, and of which only meager examples have been transcribed in the present from the lore of contemporary Indian cultures.

Song covers a wide range of functions, themes, and formal elaborations. At one extreme are series of meaningless syllables in which there are rhythm and regularity but no sense, rude songs that are generally believed to have the power to control supernatural forces; and simple chants of a similar character, with words, such as the two-word verse—*peitolo yavali* (run into the valley)—which the *Lule*, a Chaco tribe, monotonously repeated through a whole night. At the other extreme are complex song recitals of people like the *Tupinamba* (Brazil), which were led by a man singing couplets, with answers in refrain from the whole community, and which were epic in content if not in form. The use of song in connection with magic and religion is primary everywhere in South America, and it is especially marked among tribes of simpler culture in the Circum-Caribbean area and the Pacific lowland. But the poetry of song is not always directed to supernatural purposes alone, and it is not always dependent for effect upon the simple, monotonous rhythms that are usually associated with magic and ritual. Cadenced work songs of native invention are reported for the *Catío*. Festive singing of secular songs with various themes—planting and harvesting, hunting, fishing, animals and birds—is a common form of entertainment. Among the *Oto-*

mac (Venezuela), the whole village is said to assemble every night of the year in three concentric circles, with a leader in the center, to sing and dance together. And purely recreational song that approaches the level of genuine poetry, insofar as words and rhythm become more than the mere burden of melody, attains peculiar importance in a number of Tropical Forest tribes. The singing of such songs, both communally and individually, is the most popular pastime of the *Tenetehara, Tapirapé,* and *Carajá* Indians of Brazil. Improvisation occurs; simile is a highly developed element of style, although evidently not rhyme; and creative excellence is recognized, as among the *Tupinamba,* where, it is said, an outstanding composer might enjoy such prestige that an enemy tribe, taking him prisoner, would release him unharmed.

At a quite different level of achievement, the Araucanians produced a distinctive poetic literature, which, although still rooted in song, began to realize somewhat the inherent rhythms of language itself and to employ them consciously for the more forceful expression of thoughts and feelings. These Indians, socially aggressive and individualistic, placed a peculiarly high value upon eloquence as an art, and oratory was a skill not only esteemed but consciously cultivated and taught. There were "poets," individuals (*ngenpin*) whose sole occupation was the composition of songs for public ceremonial gatherings. Strict metrical forms were not known, nor was rhyme; but poetic style emerged from the rich use of metaphor, simile, and repetitive phrasing. Araucanian songs, whose verses can stand alone as poems, were being composed in the old style as late as the 19th c. and have been the inspiration, indeed, for some modern Chilean poetry. Common themes of Araucanian poetry were romantic love, erotism and sex, war memories, insults and quarrels, satires, death, and events of daily life, like robbery and drunken parties.

Inca poetry was, however, unquestionably the most remarkable literary achievement of the aboriginal New World, and, in its present forms and language, modified through time but still clearly indigenous, it constitutes today one of the genuinely important, living heritages of the native Am. past. Examples of pre-Spanish Inca literature are few, but they are sufficient to suggest the underlying character of the poetry. Expressive of the deepest human sentiment, of moving religious thought and aspiration, sometimes humorous, melancholy, impassioned, noble, and austere, it was a true reflection of a great Andean civilization and of the Indian mind and spirit that created it.

Rowe and others have rightly stressed the unusual, poetical qualities of *Quechua,* the language of the ancient Incas (it is still spoken today by some five million Andean Indians, mainly in Peru and Bolivia), which, by uniformly accenting the penult of words, has a natural rhythm and, through free use of affixes, permits expression of the finest shades of meaning and emotion. In this subtle language were composed the prayers and hymns, long narrative poems (no complete example is known), poetic dramas, and songs that comprised the body of Inca literature. Recited, performed, and sung before large public gatherings, learned and repeated generation after generation, they were not only the repository of mythology, legend, and history, for a people who lacked writing, but a continuing affirmation as well of the Indian's personal relation to man and nature. Here, for example, is an excerpt from an Inca prayer (Means, p. 437):

The Sun—the Moon;
the Day—the Night;
Summer—Winter;
not in vain,
in orderly succession,
do they march
to their destined place,
to their goal.
They arrive
wherever
Thy royal staff
Thou bearest.
Oh! Harken to me,
listen to me,
let it not befall
that I grow weary
and die.

Most Inca poetry was lyric love song, plaintive in spirit and rich in allusions to nature. It is still the commonest poetic form among present-day Quechua Indians; indeed, most popular verse in Peru and Bolivia, whether composed in Sp. or Quechua, bears the stamp of the old Inca style and theme. Beyond this, passages of considerable poetic value occur in modern Quechua dance-dramas, performed by the highland Indians on certain Roman Catholic religious holidays. The death of the Inca Atahuallpa is a favorite subject. Such passages conserve both the spirit and language of a genuinely great and remarkably persistent poetic tradition.

GENERAL: *Handbook of South Am. Indians,* ed. J. Steward (6 v., 1946–49; comprehensive surveys of all tribes, including their lit., with excellent bibliog.).

ARAUCANIAN: T. Guevara Silva, *Historia de la civilización de Araucanía* (1898), *Folklore araucano* (1911); Félix José de Augusta, *Lec-*

turas araucanas (1910).—INCA and QUECHUA: E. Middendorf, *Dramatische und lyrische Dichtungen der Keshua-Sprache* (1891); P. A. Means, *Ancient Civilizations of the Andes* (1931); R. Rojas, *Himnos Quichuas* (1937); J. María Arguedas, *Canto Kechwa* (1938), *Canciones y Cuentos del Pueblo Quechua* (1949); J. Basadre, *Literatura Inca* (1938); J. M. B. Farfan, "Poesía folklórica Quechua." Instituto de Antropología, Tucumán, *Revista*, 2 (1942) and *Colección de Textos Quechuas del Peru* (1952); J. Rowe, "Inca Culture at the Time of the Sp. Conquest," *Handbook of South Am. Indians*, II (1946; best crit. summary, references to early sources); J. Lara, *La Poesía Quechua* (1947; anthol. and crit. analysis); J. Lira and J.M.B. Farran, "Himnos Quechuas Católicos Cuzqueños," *Folklore Americano*, 3 (1955); R. Stephan, *The Singing Mountaineers* (1957; contemp. verse in good Eng. tr.). J.F.G.

AMERICAN NEGRO POETRY. See NEGRO POETRY. AMERICAN.

AMERICAN POETICS. See MODERN POETICS.

AMERICAN POETRY.† While no definitive history of Am. poetry has been written, within existing histories of Am. literature poetry has probably received its fair proportion of regard. Though R. H. Pearce's recent *Continuity of Am. Poetry* most nearly qualifies as a history, he calls his book an "inside narrative" and hopes "some day for a proper literary history, in which we shall be able to comprehend our poetry in its totality." Various extended essays (e.g., H. W. Wells) and introductions (e.g., F. O. Matthiessen) have appeared; studies of particular aspects (e.g., G. W. Allen) have been made; critical biographies of poets have been written; and histories of particular periods, especially the 20th c. (e.g., H. Gregory and M. Zaturenska) are available. Yet compared to the knowledge of other national poetries, that of our own is fragmentary; and perhaps this situation has justification, since such pioneer explorations as those of 17th-c. New England verse (by H. S. Jantz), of southern poets (by J. B. Hubbell), and of the 1890's (by C. T. Kindilien) reveal forgotten poems of interest, but not of greatness. This essay makes no pretense to explore, and depends heavily on works like those cited; in a consciously sketchy fashion it will follow the traditional framework of centuries and of groups within those centuries. If it can advance claims to novelty, these may lie in its implied sense that more sympathetic reading of poets before 1912 will be fruitful, that the revision of poetical reputations is a continuing and healthy process, that even though major groupings and norms may be basically established, they may just as

well be radically revised or significantly modified.

THE 17TH C. For both the 17th and 18th c., the three geographical areas of New England, the middle colonies, and the South reflect significant cultural groupings and such poetical concentrations as existed. Of the writers of the middle colonies there is none now worth recording. The South, with its earlier settlement, can also make its earlier claim to a poet of rank. George Sandys (1578–1644), as colonial treasurer in Jamestown from 1621 to 1625, "bred [his translation of Ovid] in the Newworld, of the rudenesse whereof it cannot but participate," yet he was rewarded by Dryden's praise as "the ingenious and learned Sandys, the best versifier of the former age." Besides the work of Sandys, who was British in reputation and accomplishment, one fine poem emerged—the epitaph on Nathaniel Bacon by John Cotton of Queen's Creek in 1676, which in its compressed colloquialism and homely imagery reminds us of the presence of Vaughan and Herbert in southern colonial libraries. John Donne's not receiving the appointment in the Virginia colony that he may have sought in 1610 raises the interesting speculation of the foremost metaphysical becoming an Am. poet. Other than these matters, the rest is pretty much silence.

In New England, though publication was infrequent, silence hardly characterized the period. The work of Anne Bradstreet (ca. 1612–1672), first published in England in 1650, has long been known; that of Edward Taylor (ca. 1642–1729), was first discovered only in 1937. Perhaps John Saffin, Benjamin Tompson, and Richard Steere come closest to these two, though preferences among the many candidates for a resurrected immortality differ. In tradition, sensibility, and provinciality all are close to their two better known contemporaries. Of these, Bradstreet is less metaphysical or baroque (the choice of terms is in dispute) than Taylor. While qualifying voices have sought to diminish the first enthusiasm for Taylor, the force of his exploration of baroque sensibility in terms of New England religion and common life moves most readers:

Make me, O Lord, thy Spinning Wheele compleat;
Thy Holy Worde my Distaff make for mee.

Certainly Bradstreet and Taylor represent the potential of Am. Puritan poetry better than Wigglesworth's *Day of Doom* (1662) and the *Bay Psalm Book* (1640), for whatever the drawbacks of the Puritan aesthetic, it prized a harmony that was deepened as well as narrowed by its theological concern.

It may well be argued (as has T. M. Pearce,

† In Supplement, see also AMERICAN POETIC SCHOOLS AND TECHNIQUES (CONTEMPORARY).

AL, 14 [1942], 277–84) that literary historians and anthologists have regrettably neglected an important tradition by ignoring Am. Indian poetry (q.v.). Certainly in the 20th c. the interest in it of creative writers has outweighed their interest in poetry of the colonial period; and in a somewhat similar fashion the Negro spirituals and secular songs of the 19th c. have provided sources of inspiration in Am. Negro poetry (see NEGRO POETRY. AM.) of the last sixty years.

THE 18TH C. Though the late baroque writers of New England extend past 1700, by that date they had already begun to show a knowledge of Dryden and the neoclassical movement, as in the work of Cotton Mather. In New England Mather Byles best represents the Am. Augustans. As the century progressed, Am. libraries contained not only the work of Dryden, but of Butler, Swift, Pope, Thomson, Gray, and Goldsmith. By 1770 around Hartford and New Haven there was a flowering in the work of the Connecticut Wits—principally John Trumbull, Timothy Dwight, and Joel Barlow. The Wits were satirical (*The Progress of Dulness*, 1773), didactic (*Greenfield Hill*, 1794), and epic (*The Vision of Columbus*, 1787). They had their conservative Federalism and (though not without exception) their New Haven theology, but can be more usefully seen as early nationalists with the secular ideals of the Enlightenment. Their anthology, *American Poems*, 1783, underscored this national tendency, for it included poems of Freneau of the middle colonies, who was concerned with political revolution and enlightened deism. As a poet Freneau fused Miltonic, neoclassical, and preromantic idioms into an authentic Am. manner. In language and attitudes his "burly expression," as H. W. Wells calls it, still rewards readers who are willing to allow for frequent shortcomings.

Freneau's close connection with Thomas Jefferson and with the Virginia democratic tradition might suggest more poetic activity in the South than we find. In the early 18th c. verse had been widely practiced. Principally under the encouragement of William Parks of the Virginia *Gazette* and of the Timothy family of the South Carolina *Gazette* there was a sense of group interplay that promised more than it yielded. In spite of Ebenezer Cooke's *The Sot-Weed Factor* (1708), William Dawson's *Poems on Several Occasions* (1736), and the work of Richard Lewis and Joseph Brown Ladd, no accomplishment emerged of a group like the Connecticut Wits, of such Philadelphians as Thomas Godfrey and Nathaniel Evans, or of a poet like Freneau.

THE 19TH C. In the post-Revolutionary period in the South we find poets (the best known are Edward Coote Pinckney and Rich-

ard Henry Wilde) who fulfill some of the promise of their by now fairly well composted soil. Yet, as with poets of the same generation in the North (Richard Henry Dana, Sr., Fitz-Greene Halleck, and James Gates Percival, for example), their quality appears petty when set against Bryant or such immediate successors as Poe and the New England worthies.

What were the advantages of the second generation of post-Revolutionary poets over the first? Apart from the sheer good luck of being in the right place at the right time, all of them were literary conservatives, writing within a tradition that absorbed Wordsworth rather cautiously into an essentially neoclassical mood and that neglected Byron and Moore. Lacking the ability to be originals, they had the good sense not to follow the latest fashion; except for Poe and Emerson, they were plodders, yet as plodders contributed a solid body of poetry that has possibly more merit than we are willing to recognize.

Of almost the same age as Dana and Halleck, Bryant published *Thanatopsis* in 1817, followed it with *Poems* in 1821, and by mid-century had come to be regarded as the literary pioneer of the new poetry of his time. Perhaps it is fair to say, as long as saying it does not accuse, that he rewrote *Thanatopsis* many times. With as penetrating a sense of nature as Wordsworth's, he retained a neoclassical vocabulary and stateliness. In no direction did he push very hard: yet his metaphors, his sense of dramatic occasion, even his irony thoroughly suffuse his verses at their best.

Though with individual variations and younger than Bryant by at least a dozen years, the poets that we group with him have much in common. Like him they utilize tradition rather than seek for a new one. Whittier, the least sophisticated, is also the least conscious of the British poets of his own time; and he draws from Burns and other preromantics in his forms and moods. When consciously exploring the paths of Am. history or putting his verse to use in the antislavery movement, he is not at all literary; but at moments when his greatness and his limitations can consort, as in *Snowbound*, *The Pennsylvania Pilgrim*, or *Telling the Bees*, one finds an unpretentious but fully self-sustaining poetry. At the extreme in education from Whittier is Lowell, alert to the younger British romantics and to his own Am. contemporaries. The weakest of the five in the bulk of his poetry, perhaps because he was the least traditional, he had the best potential. This potential—the flexible, digressive, witty verse essay—he unfortunately never quite accepted as his metier; within this genre *The Biglow Papers* and *A Fable for Critics* are recognized for topical reasons; but a rather sizable body of other work in this manner exists (e.g., *Fitz Adam's Story*), and when the now unfashionable odes are read in this light, they cease to become the "factitious rhetoric" that they have been accused of being.

Longfellow and Holmes also ought to be read with a far greater sense of their whimsicality or wit than is common today. Longfellow achieves a poised delicacy of image and sound that entitles him to a high place as a minor poet; his controlled geniality informs a good many of his verses and helps to explain why his didacticism, though misread by the man in the street, could in his time be appreciated by a cultivated audience; and to all readers he gave a cosmopolitan awareness of European literature from Dante to the German romantics. With Holmes, the humor is more open than with Longfellow and in many of his occasional verses becomes too evident. Yet his serious poetry—today pretty much repudiated—also has effectiveness in a tradition of wit. The greater part of this wit is of the 18th c., yet metaphysical techniques are present, for this group of poets did not neglect the school of Donne to the extent that post-1912 critics think. Indeed, looked at as writers accepting the 18th-c. poetic and at least mindful of the 17th c., sympathetic with the romantics but somewhat dubious of their excesses, these five poets exhibit a total quality that places them closer to the 20th-c. movements than we have thought.

In spite of this argument, they admittedly lack the interest for us of Emerson, Poe, Melville, and Whitman. The reasons for the vitality of these four differ from poet to poet, yet all have in common metrical experimentation, an intense sense of symbol, and an emotional or intellectual urgency to drive deep into individual experiences. Though few would agree with Robert Frost in calling *Uriel* "the greatest western poem yet," the judgment has its core of truth. While Emerson was the least professionally devoted of the four, in a mostly casual fashion he brought poetical rhythms close to speech and saw as the stuff of poetry not only common life but the philosophical explorations that he practiced in his essays— "Bread, kingdom, stars, and sky that holds them all." Also as a transcendentalist Emerson not only exhibited this polarity but expressed the infinitude of man, thus furnishing Whitman with his gospel and Poe and Melville with texts for both exegesis and denunciation.

Against the tendency toward colloquialism in Emerson, Poe's experimentation drives toward a highly artificial rhythm and phrasing: a musicality that is at times as bouncing as that of his coexperimenter Chivers and an allusiveness that with its "dark tarn of Auber" and "woodlands of Weir" is either meaningless or so recondite that it has taken scholars a century to identify. Yet this "jingle man" practiced poetry as an experience and even a form of knowledge, and by his Gothic scenery and dead beauties presents an image of life that with all its vulgarity makes him, in the words of Allen Tate, our "dejected cousin"— "if the trappings of Poe's nightmare strike us as tawdry, we had better look to our own." Though we may question the judgment of Baudelaire, Mallarmé, and Valéry in making him the precursor of Fr. symbolism, the historical fact (whatever the reasons or qualifications) assures us that they did. Nor should we neglect the judgment of W. C. Williams on the essential Americanism of Poe: "His greatness is in that he turned his back and faced inland, to originality, with the identical gesture of a Boone."

Of the same age as Lowell, Melville and Whitman spoke late as poets, the first only after his novels, the second after an extended period of journalism. Certainly Melville is the lesser of the two as a poet, for his work has its value more in being that of a great novelist than in having a poetical greatness of itself. Perhaps first recognized by Thorp in 1938, the poetry of Melville has shown an abiding attraction to such critics as Matthiessen, R. P. Warren, and Arvin. Much like Emerson's in its colloquialism, it cultivates roughness more fully. The "dualities and dubieties" of the themes of Melville's major novels fill it, and within its sharpened scope there is a precision that the novels lack.

With an even greater symbolic vision than Melville and with a colloquialism that surpasses any of his contemporaries, the poetry of Walt Whitman has stood so long for literary revolt that we are a little tired of it. Certain qualities may also cause the restrained enthusiasm that was present even in the celebration of the 1955 centennial of *Leaves of Grass*: an oratorical mannerism, a fluidity of symbol that approaches the soggy, a readiness to dismiss human limitations. Yet with all these qualifications, it is hard to shoulder Whitman aside from his claim to the greatest body of poetry in 19th-c. America.

> Failing to fetch me at first keep encouraged,
> Missing me one place search another,
> I stop somewhere waiting for you.

Whatever wayward freedoms he gave to himself as wordmaker, as teacher, or as philosopher, he broke with tradition more thoroughly than Emerson, Poe, and Melville, who with less force (though with more taste) sought the same things. And while the direct line of descent from Whitman has not been an illustrious one in spite of his regard for himself as the progenitor of poets, it is hard to imagine 20th-c. poetry without this barbaric yawper.

Other experimenters in the latter part of the 19th c. shared our own hesitancies about Whitman for literary reasons, though openly they condemned him on sexual grounds: Emily Dickinson's "disgraceful" and Sidney Lanier's "immeasurably shocked." Of the two poets named, Lanier had in common with Whitman (as he occasionally recognized) his thorough wedding of poetry with music, his freely metered verse, his overtures to modern science, his belief in the prophetic role of the poet, and his somewhat superficial transcendentalism. But in spite of such a brilliant tour de force as *The Symphony* and the solid accomplishment of *The Marshes of Glynn*, Lanier cannot survive in his total work as a fully accomplished poet. As with his two Southern poetical masters, Timrod and Hayne, time and place and health were unpropitious; though aware of the drawbacks of romantic attitudes and rhythms, all three duplicated them with intensity rather than questioned them. Lanier, with his faintly metaphysical strain, questioned most; and if he had not sought to restrain his "disposition to push [his] metaphors too far," more of his promise might have been realized.

Between 1858 and 1865, before Lanier had begun his career and while Whitman was preparing his third and fourth editions and Melville was meditating *Battle-Pieces*, Emily Dickinson wrote the greater part of her poetry. Her work is not so far from literary sources and the thought of publication as early critics believed. Nevertheless there is an isolation that still startles in view of the greatness of her accomplishment. Of her Am. predecessors she would appear most dependent on Emerson in her colloquialism and her metrical freedom; but more than Emerson she went back to a Puritan view of man and nature, although she was far from orthodox; and she sensed the fullness of experience that the poem as symbol might allow.

> How frugal is the Chariot
> That bears the Human soul.

Yet as she drew back from a transcendental view of man, she also drew back from full indulgence in symbolism: in their intensity her images are of the metaphysical rather than of the Fr. school. Hesitating at the orthodoxies of the Connecticut valley, she retained the view of limited man confronting sovereign godhead, and from the intensities of that confrontation came a poetry that since its publication in 1890 has constantly meant more to its readers. The extent of her influence has little weight in the 20th c. beside the Fr. symbolists, the metaphysical revival, or Whitmanian self-confidence; rather in Am. literary history her value is that of asserting the greatness that was always possible within provincial confines.

By 1890 what Whitman, Lanier, and Dickinson had understood in their various ways, and what Emerson, Poe, and Melville had anticipated, became still more apparent. The Am. schoolroom poets were close to the end of their careers or were no more; the great Victorians were dying off. The emptiness of the efforts of such late comers as Stedman, Aldrich, and Sill was widely felt if not openly spoken. Yet no poet appeared (except Robinson) who approached the success of Dickinson or Whitman. From either Dickinson or from her cultural situation stemmed several disciples. Stephen Crane confronted a sovereign universe instead of a sovereign god, breaking farther than she from traditional prosody, seeking the sharp but less functioning image. John Tabb attempted a synthesis of his Catholicism and his ante-bellum Southern attitudes. Lizette Woodworth Reese, without the theological strength of Dickinson, provided a counterpart in feminine sensitivity and unpretentiousness. More popular certainly were the pretentious poets, Bliss Carman and Richard Hovey, who took something from Whitman, something from Fr. bohemianism and symbolism, and a great deal from Kipling. Finally, George Santayana, William Vaughan Moody, George Cabot Lodge, and Trumbull Stickney made up an academic group centering at Harvard. The latter three were close to Santayana in displaying, as he stated it himself, verses that "mental and thin as their textures may be, represent a true inspiration." All present a poetry that, while traditional, moves toward modern poetry more certainly than that of either the Dickinson or the Kipling group. Less abstract than the older Santayana, Moody revived an old-fashioned Miltonism, yet at his best did this in order to treat such topical problems as Am. imperialism. Lodge is often merely Tennysonian. More effectively than either, Stickney catches an Am. idiom, elegiac rather than outspoken, but still authentic. For all four, Lodge, whose biography by Henry Adams focuses as shrewdly on the poetical crisis as the *Education* had on the cultural crisis, stated the problem: "The whole core of the struggle, for ourselves and for art, is to emerge from the envelope of thoughts and words and deeds which are not our own, but the laws and conventions and traditions formed of a kind of composite of other men's ideas and emotions and prejudices." Stickney succeeded best, and perhaps his early death in 1904 kept him from greater accomplishment. For again excepting Robinson it was not until the second decade of the 20th c. that Am. poets recovered from the earlier century's failures and triumphs.

AMERICAN POETRY

THE 20TH C. "I suppose," John Crowe Ransom remarked (KR, 13 [1951], 445) of Eng. poetry since 1900, "no other period has been so copious for three hundred years, i.e., since 1600–1650." Even such a claim seems modest, and one might well set only the Am. side of Eng. poetry against the first half of the 17th c. without a sense of its inferior quality.

Both the quantity and diversity of poetry since 1912 make the establishment of norms and groupings difficult. If the attempt is made through decades, the tendency to produce merely a chronicle is hard to overcome; and if one tries to delineate schools, particularly in America the actualities deny the comfort of such an approach. In *Poetry* alone, founded in 1912 by Harriet Monroe and still the most influential magazine of poetry, the range has been consciously broad since the first several volumes, which printed everyone from Lindsay and Sandburg to Pound and Eliot. Perhaps at present one can, then, do no better than roughly group the poets into a first and second generation (with the dividing line for birth about 1907). With the first generation, allegiances are more clearly felt; with the second generation a kind of eclecticism seems to signal individual variations within a general mood rather than groupings. Of the poets of the first generation (from Robinson, 1869–1935, to R. P. Warren, 1905–) the three major allegiances that emerge are those to a renewed tradition, to a self-conscious Americanism that partakes strongly of Whitman, and to Fr. symbolism modified by the Eng. metaphysicals. In each of these is a mixed lot, in the last two are many poets who divide their allegiance, and in the third a dual allegiance is posited in the category itself.

Of Robinson and Frost, who are here presented as renewing the tradition, the first had well preceded the *annus mirabilis* of 1912. The closeness of Robinson and the Harvard academics both physically and spiritually might easily place him with them, were it not that he achieved what they only attempted and that he lived out a full poetical career. Frost too had his Harvard association, which his later association with the British Georgians did not obliterate; in both subject and manner he has much in common with Robinson. The earlier Frost, like the earlier Robinson, looked at the hard and sometimes sordid side of New England farm and village. Though both kept to a traditional prosody, they shared with the moderns an ear for a new poetic speech, a revulsion from standard poetical gestures, a searching for images that would render the poem. If some critics have depreciated Frost (perhaps mostly for his living into the present and for his refusal to participate in fashionable movements), the place of both Frost and

Robinson in modern Am. poetry has remained secure in spite of their lack of concern for the virtuosities of Valéry or of Donne. Edna St. Vincent Millay, a poet twenty years their junior, also had an essential allegiance to a renewed tradition, but her romantic bohemianism has not shown the power to sustain her reputation. A more academic traditionalist than either Robinson, whom he admires, or Frost, whom he has labeled a "spiritual drifter," Yvor Winters has published poetry that displays modern sensibility at its fullest without further involvement in modern manners or beliefs.

Robinson's later use of Arthurian romance and Frost's increasing pastoralism allow us to forget the close association of both poets with the realistic tradition in fiction. Along with the open relationships of the first poet's apostrophes to Zola and Crabbe or the second poet's materials in *The Death of the Hired Man* and *The Hill Wife*, in all their work we can see a pragmatic testing of ideals through concrete situations. Thus Robinson writes in *The Man Against the Sky* that we may

of our transience here make offering
To an orient Word that will not be erased,

and Frost (more casually) observes, "One could do worse than be a swinger of birches."

Even the implication that truth appears only in the situation—a view not remote from a fundamental tenet of symbolism—is found to some degree in those whose allegiance is to Whitman, who had formed a bridge between Am. romanticism and realism of the earlier century. But Sandburg, Lindsay, and Jeffers follow Whitman in their realism rather than the pragmatic novelists. They present actuality and comment on it, or when they do not comment allow it less to speak for itself than for a democratic (or with Jeffers an antidemocratic) idealism. Again like Whitman, all incline toward an oratorical rather than poetic rhythm, and all would seem to mirror themselves as popular bards, not so much renewing a tradition as offering a superficially exciting escape from it. At their best they achieve an immediacy of communication more to be admired than deplored; and the younger poets may find a sustenance in these disciples of Whitman that could help them break from the grip of symbolistic and metaphysical restraints of the older generation.

Some of them have for many years found that sustenance in the work of William Carlos Williams, who essentially may belong to the Whitman group quite as much as to that of the symbolists. From an early association with such poets as Pound, Marianne Moore, and Hilda Doolittle, Williams has kept a concern for genuine speech, concise image, and probing of the human condition. Yet his essays mark him as one of the few poets of stature who have given Whitman unqualified fealty, and though he lacks the transcendental fulsomeness of the Brooklyn poet, his *Patterson* belongs more with *Song of Myself* than the *Cantos*. The work of Hart Crane may also be allied to that of Whitman in its search for emblems of the modern and in its very liberation. Still, Crane's poetry also carries despairing overtones that come not only from the symbolist enmity of the poet and society but from an existential awareness within the poet himself.

Whatever their primary allegiance, Williams and Crane point clearly to the fact that the undiluted tradition of Whitman would not fully serve. Rather it was from the Fr. symbolists (and by way of them from Poe) and from such British interpreters as Arthur Symons that the major impact on modern Am. poetry came. In its unqualified form the symbolist influence may be felt most strongly in Stevens, Pound, and Cummings. With a commingling of the British metaphysicals, we find it in Eliot, Moore, and Ransom. Also with the last three might be allied MacLeish, Gregory, Tate, Merrill Moore, and R. P. Warren, but these five are perhaps most influenced by their older Am. contemporaries. Even with Stevens, Pound, Cummings, Eliot, Marianne Moore, and Ransom, the influence upon each other—after the first stimulus from non-Am. sources—must certainly be kept in mind.

The nature of the symbolistic and metaphysical strains introduced into modern Am. poetry is manifold. Both aspects have in common cosmopolitanism that offered liberation from the 19th-c. Eng. tradition. Both have the sense of the integrity of poetry, whether as a kind of knowledge in itself or as a knowledge fully compatible with other truth. Both reveal an uneasiness about the condition of man. Both assert a kind of exploration in prosody and word and image that marks an impatience with traditional poetics. At the same time they differ as much as the 19th from the 17th c. Symbolism (q.v.) is of modern Europe, is exclusive of logical discourse, urges itself as the only solution of the human problem, looks toward dadaism and surrealism in its denial of past literary values. The metaphysical (q.v.) belongs to a religious age, exults in scholastic logic, asserts a kinship with theology, challenges the literary tradition without discarding it. Possibly in the clash of the disparate elements modern British and Am. poets have found the completely satisfactory literary situation: in Eliot, who polarizes the two sets of values most adeptly, we have our greatest poet.

Though the symbolic-metaphysical impact would seem in perspective to have been decisive, modern poetry first became known as a new departure not through it but through the movement of imagism (q.v.). Related to symbolism, it was also inspired by Chinese, Japanese, and Prov. poetry. As it became popular, especially under the leadership of Amy Lowell and the manifesto of 1915, it quickly hardened into a naive simplicity. If it provided only a basis for poetry and not a fully articulated poetry in itself, it still demonstrated the pervasive necessity of experiment. Imagism also touched firmly upon some of the work of Eliot, Stevens, Moore, and Williams, while it gave major impetus to H. D., J. G. Fletcher, and Amy Lowell.

After his earlier alliance with imagism, Pound moved into symbolism with the Mauberley period and with his *Cantos*. This work, still being written, is certainly his poetic monument, a work of magnificence but also an artifact for examination by technicians. Its fragmentation and perverse social program exemplify one blind alley that symbolism may take. But the poetry of Wallace Stevens, beginning with *Harmonium* and enriched by every later publication until by the end of his career some critics placed him above Eliot, appears the perfection of symbolist technique and morality —an apotheosis of the literary imagination produced by elegance and infinite tact. With a sharpness and open humor lacking in Stevens, but without his elegance, Cummings also has created an enduring poetry. Enjambed, disjointed, and distorted words give to his work an immediate feeling of avant-gardism that Stevens' lacks; but the essentially simple lyric quality does not suffer from these devices and profited from them when a poetic jolting was needed. Though to future readers they may be an obstacle, they will always be a charming one.

Eliot, Marianne Moore, and Ransom, as already noted, drew upon the metaphysical tradition as well as upon the symbolistic, Eliot most fully absorbing Fr. symbolism and Ransom least. Certainly Eliot, who has written poems in the Fr. language, is close to his sources; and we hardly need his testimony of the effect upon him of Arthur Symons' book in 1908 to assure ourselves of his alliance with Laforgue, Rimbaud, and Corbière: The apparent illogic of sequence and the shimmering of the surface over a depth of effect are there:

And I must borrow every changing shape
To find expression. . . .

Symbolism and imagism had also come to Eliot through Pound, whose *Cantos* Eliot has singled out as the only long poem by a contemporary that he could read with enjoyment and admiration. But in Eng. poetry Pound took most from Browning and the group of the nineties, as Eliot said, while in both critical writing and poetry Eliot shows a growing awareness of the school of Donne. Quite probably Eliot had already read Donne as an undergraduate in Cambridge, where Charles Eliot Norton, who in 1895 edited the poet on the basis of Lowell's earlier work, continued prominent after his retirement. *The Waste Land* is "For Ezra Pound"—and not inconsiderably by him; but it implies (negatively) a philosophical base in Christian orthodoxy that, though not unlike Baudelaire's, has little in common with Arthur Symons' but much in common with Donne's. Yet this comment does not suggest simply a return to an older view. In the poem's free use of anthropologists a new psychological frame of reference is provided that had greater moment for later poets than the religious frame of reference that led to *Ash Wednesday* and *The Four Quartets*. In these later poems one feels more and more a metaphysical concern for the image as "objective correlative" (q.v.) and less a concern for the image as a self-sufficient experience. Eliot has never written "about" poetry but about life:

> . . . the light is still
> At the still point of the turning world.

Yet it would be false to regard Eliot's work as merely a coalescence of two aspects of modern poetry, for his greatness lies not in this but in a total effect that makes uniquely his own the newer sense of poetry as a form of knowledge, the traditional sense of poetry as a special kind of knowledge, and the need for a poet to create a new language and rhythm.

By Ransom's own definition of "Major Poet" (as producing "deliverances . . . of vital human importance . . . consistently in some volume . . . freshly rather than repetitiously") both he and Marianne Moore would seem to qualify as minor. Yet both are always memorable, as the former's

> . . . the body bears the head
> (So hardly one they terribly are two)

and the latter's "imaginary gardens with real toads in them." With Moore there is a fuller use of psychological nuance and a more conscious experimentalism than in Ransom, but both share a tightness of structure, an architectural sense of function, and a liveliness of wit. Each has a following, especially the former, whose pervasive influence among the poets of the next generation has almost established a "school of Marianne Moore." But of the five poets mentioned whose source of inspiration belongs to other earlier modern poets (MacLeish, Gregory, Tate, Merrill Moore, and Warren), the latter three are of the Fugi-

tive (q.v.) group and have kept a meaningful association with their former teacher Ransom.

Like him their work has been metaphysical in flavor, and they variously demonstrate what he has indicated as the distinctive characteristics of the poetry of the century: the relaxation of meters, satiric and even "hateful" poetry, extreme condensation and syntactical displacement. But all three have been drawn much more to depth psychology than Ransom, partaking possibly of the anthropological interests of Eliot as well as of the clinical findings of Jung and Freud. In Merrill Moore relaxation of meter, with his remarkable experimentation in the sonnet, is a hallmark: though his poetry is often satiric, the satire is that of the tolerant psychiatrist rather than of the moralist, while his many thousands of sonnets show no more condensation in each than in the number of the whole. Both Tate and Warren, along with their psychological concern, have shown a Christian awareness, the former traditionally Catholic and the latter neo-orthodox. Tate has demonstrated a condensation and syntactical displacement that is much more pronounced than Ransom's; but Warren, as a book-club novelist, has not exhibited a compulsion toward obscurity.

The work of MacLeish and Gregory has also avoided extreme condensation and syntactical displacement. Though MacLeish began his poetical career as much under the symbolistic influence as any modern poet, he turned rapidly toward public speech, for which he has been both condemned and praised. Along with him, Horace Gregory has exhibited a much more marked use of social material and commentary in poetry: and both have been liberals rather than conservatives, humanists rather than supernaturalists. Though in this respect they may be regarded as continuing the tradition of Whitman, their technique does not recall Whitman. As the last of the first generation to be named (but not the last that should be named in any roll call of significant poets) they finally demonstrate the constant crisscrossing of the groupings that have been used. Writing on "Vers Libre and Avant-Garde," Louise Bogan closes her chapter with a consideration of Stevens, Marianne Moore, and Williams as three distinguished experimentalists. In this essay each has been placed in a separate category; but their closeness of personal and literary association also warrants our thinking of them as having a unity of influence, of mood, and of style.

This kind of unity is even more marked in the second generation of modern Am. poets, who largely lack major allegiances that could form even fluid groupings among them. Less difficult is the distinguishing of them from the poets of the first generation, however, though obviously poets born a half-dozen years on either side of the year used as a dividing line (1907—the birthdate of Auden) might well be claimed to be either the poetic fathers or the sons. The principal difference between the two groups is that the second grew up reading Frost, Stevens, and Eliot, or their British contemporaries; they were the heirs of revolt and victory. And as with all heirs of emancipation and property, their systems and substances proved both a sustaining comfort and an embarrassing restriction. Shocks in subject matter or in medium were no longer as easily attained; linguistic and psychological awareness remained rewarding, but lacked novelty. Further, the second generation was working along with the first, for if we take 1885 as a composite date of birth for the first generation, by 1962 it had reached only its seventy-seventh birthday. (By 1912, in contrast, Lowell, Whitman, and Melville would have been ninety-three if they had not died in the early 1890's.) Lacking retirement rules and sustained by geriatric medicines, the first generation has continued in competition with its poetic offspring.

The use of Auden's birthdate as the line of division affords not only a convenience but a recognition of his impact on Am. poetry in the last twenty years. First generally known in this country in the middle 1930's (and later becoming a citizen of the United States in an almost even compensation for Eliot's becoming a British subject), Auden has had a direct effect upon some of the poets of the second generation, and for many others represents the kind of shift in sensibility that has taken place. His casual mastery of modern poetic idiom marks him as the child of his more pioneering but less gracious poetic forebears. This mastery he shares with poets of today; and he has also shared with many of them a thorough grounding in psychological and anthropological explorations, but with a commitment to theological or secular existentialism. He has shared too the renewed impact of a first generation poet, Yeats, and his elegy on Yeats not only deserves its high repute as poetry but documents the new freedom, questioning, indebtedness, and emotional strength.

> In the prison of his days
> Teach the free man how to praise.

With the acceptance of the unique pervasiveness of Eliot ("this dictatorship," as Peter Viereck has called it, of "an ambiguous mixture of snobbism and real excellence"), and with the recognition of a particular attraction by the younger poets for such diverse figures as Hopkins, Lorca, and Rilke, still two other individuals as controlling to a great extent the present poetic destinies may be put forward. One is John Crowe Ransom, whose influence as poet, critic, and editor has hardly been equalled. His presence in the work of such poets as Richard Eberhart—self-contained, traditional, with recognized affinities to Frost—and Theodore Roethke—turbulent, self-conscious, with something of the prophetic quality of Dylan Thomas—suggests the extent of his penetration. The second is Marianne Moore, whose tremendously impressive minor poetry has been valued since its first appearance in 1921, but for whom a real clamor of enthusiasm was delayed until the middle 1950's when even the Ford Motor Company sought her advice (though it did not take it, *New Yorker*, April 13, 1957) on the naming of a new automobile. Among many, two distinguished poets who show her authority—more truly than the Edsel would have under another name—are Elizabeth Bishop and Richard Wilbur. The former stays closer to Moore; but both have brought into our poetry a sustained joyousness of wit—elegant, controlled, a little too mature, but probably lasting. To be contrasted with them are Randall Jarrell and Howard Nemerov, both much more varied and exploratory, deeply indebted to Auden, yet to Auden as a starting point and not as a complete journey. Like Auden they not only accept and probe their progenitors but make a demanding peace with their modern culture.

But these connections with Auden and Moore do not invalidate Ciardi's statement about his contemporaries in his introduction to *Mid-Century Poets:* "These poets are not imagists, nor vorticists, nor classicists, nor existentialists. . . . It is never, then, a poetry of movements or manifestoes." Except for the Beat Poets (q.v.), who have mostly published since 1950, we have been treated to no movements, and as yet it is hard to discern more than tentative accomplishments in this large grouping. Perhaps the best, those at some time associated with Black Mountain College, are also closest to their other academic contemporaries. If so, we must still accept the rest of Ciardi's characterization: "It is more nearly a blend of the classical and the metaphysical, a poetry of individual appraisal, tentative, self-questioning, introspective, socially involved, and always reserving for itself the right to meet experience in its humanistic environment. . . . It is therefore a poetry of great variety, and of some difficulty, but a poetry capable of offering great rewards."

To attempt to select the poets now writing who offer the greatest rewards would be unfair both to those omitted and those named. Instead, we may glance at five poems by poets of the second generation which have recently examined earlier poets of the Am. tradition and which are a happy augury for a continuity that was justly interrupted in 1912 but that never was completely shattered and that now calls for mending. The first, *For T.S.E. Only*, by Hyam Plutzik, upbraids Eliot for his strain of anti-Semitism and for its associated pride, but in a context of the common brotherhood of sinfulness—

> Thomas, Thomas,
> Come, let us pray together for our exile.

Edwin Honig's *Walt Whitman*, placed in juxtaposition with Swinburne's Victorian panegyric and Lorca's surrealistic tribute, sharpens our sense of the fine surface and penetrating depth of which contemporary poetry is capable, while at the same time it exhibits the independence of the 20th-c. Am. poet in his appraisal of a powerful but one-sided poetic tradition. In Winfield T. Scott's *Mr. Whittier* —"It is so much easier to forget than to have been Mr. Whittier"—we find secure recognition of unfashionable virtues by a poet who admires Stevens but loves Thomas Hardy, "warts and all," and who perhaps has most notably displayed in his poetry a consistent wish to simplify the modern poetic manner without losing all of its complexity. Robert Lowell's *Mr. Edwards and the Spider* looks still farther into the Am. past at a poet of the pulpit; it epitomizes the struggle between Lowell's desperate Catholicism and his Calvinistic origins in an intense and gnarled poetic that contrasts with the urbanity of the general poetic of the day. With *Homage to Mistress Bradstreet*, John Berryman has offered to many readers a masterpiece of modern poetry, difficult but not obscure, allusive but not precious, forceful but lyrical. Even though Berryman's concern is with the woman and not the poet, he brings us full circle, suggesting with poetic ·image a historical meaning in the Am. experience of poetry that this essay has labored discursively to outline.

BIBLIOGRAPHIES: Brown University Library, *A Catalogue of the Harris Collection of Am. Poetry* (1886); O. Wegelin, *Early Am. Poetry* (1930); U. S. Library of Congress, *Sixty Am. Poets*, ed. A. Tate (1945, rev. ed. 1954); *Lit. Hist. of the United States*, ed. R. E. Spiller *et al.*, III (1948) and *Bibliog. Supplement*, ed. R. M. Ludwig (1959); current bibliog. in AL and PMLA.

ANTHOLOGIES: *Specimens of Am. Poetry*, ed. S. Kettell (1829); *The Poets and Poetry of America*, ed. R. W. Griswold (1842); *An Am. Anthol.*, ed. E. C. Stedman (1900); *The Poets of Transcendentalism*, ed. G. W. Cooke (1903); *Modern Am. Poets*, ed. C. Aiken (1922); *Major Am. Poets*, ed. H. H. Clark (1936); *Southern Poets*, ed. E. W. Parks (1936); *Minor Knicker-*

bockers, ed. K. B. Taft (1947); *A Little Treasury of Am. Poetry*, ed. O. Williams (1948); *The Poetry of the Negro*, ed. L. Hughes and A. Bontemps (1949); *Mid-Century Am. Poets*, ed. J. Ciardi (1950); *Oxford Book of Am. Verse*, ed. F. O. Matthiessen (1950); *Modern Am. Poetry*, ed. L. Untermeyer (mid-century ed., 1950; new and enl. ed. 1962); *Criterion Book of Modern Am. Verse*, ed. W. H. Auden (1956); *Fifteen Modern Am. Poets*, ed. G. P. Elliott (1956); *New Poets of England and America*, ed. D. Hall *et al.* (1958); *Modern Verse in Eng.*, ed. D. Cecil and A.·Tate (1958); *The Conscious Voice: an Anthol. of Am. Poetry*, ed. A. D. Van Nostrand and C. H. Watts (1959); *The New Am. Poetry 1945–1960*, ed. D. M. Allen (1960).

HISTORY AND CRITICISM: E. C. Stedman, *Poets of America* (1885); W. B. Otis, *Am. Verse 1625–1807* (1909); A. H. Strong, *Am. Poets and Their Theology* (1916); A. Kreymborg, *Our Singing Strength* (1929); G. W. Allen, *Am. Prosody* (1935); L. Howard, *The Connecticut Wits* (1943); H. W. Wells, *The Am. Way of Poetry* (1943); H. S. Jantz, *The First Century of New England Verse* (1944); H. Gregory and M. Zaturenska, *A Hist. of Am. Poetry 1900–1940* (1946); Y. Winters, *In Defense of Reason* (1947); F. W. Conner, *Cosmic Optimism* (1949); J. G. Southworth, *Some Modern Am. Poets* (1950); H. H. Waggoner, *The Heel of Elohim* (1950); L. Bogan, *Achievement in Am. Poetry 1900–1950* (1951); S. K. Coffman, Jr., *Imagism* (1951); S. T. Williams, *Beginnings of Am. Poetry* (1951); B. Deutsch, *Poetry in Our Time* (1952); A. N. Wilder, *Modern Poetry and the Christian Tradition* (1952); G. Arms, *The Fields Were Green* (1953); J. B. Hubbell, *The South in Am. Lit. 1607–1900* (1954); J. .G. Southworth, *More Modern Am. Poets* (1954); C. S. Lenhart, *Musical Influences on Am. Poetry* (1956); C. T. Kindilien, *Am. Poetry in the Eighteen Nineties* (1957); J. M. Bradbury, *The Fugitives: a Crit. Account* (1958); L. Cowan, *The Fugitive Group* (1959); M. L. Rosenthal, *The Modern Poets* (1960); R. H. Pearce, *The Continuity of Am. Poetry* (1961); *Aspects of Am. Poetry*, ed. R. M. Ludwig (1962); G. Cambon, *Recent Am. Poetry* (1962) and *The Inclusive Flame: Studies in Am. Poetry* (1963).

G.A.

AMOEBEAN VERSES (Gr. "responsive verses"). Verses, couplets or stanzas, found chiefly in pastoral poetry (Theocritus, Virgil) and spoken alternately by two speakers. The second character is expected not only to match the theme introduced by the first speaker but also to improve upon it in any way possible. —Koster.

P.S.C.

AMPHIBRACH (Gr. "short at both ends"). A classical metrical foot consisting of a long syllable preceded and followed by a short one:

$$\smile\smile\;; \;habere$$

Rarely used in classical poetry either as an independent unit or in a continuous series. In Eng.

$$\overset{x}{}\;\overset{\prime}{}\;\overset{x}{}\;: \;arrangement$$

the amphibrachic cadence is common in stress-groups.—Koster.

P.S.C.

AMPHIMACER. See CRETIC.

AMPLIFICATION. The enlarging of a statement, dilating an argument, and sometimes diminishing one. (*Meiosis*, q.v., was often used when there was diminution.) A very comprehensive figure, a. is often more than a figure. Cicero (*De Oratore* 3.26) said that the "highest distinction of eloquence consists in amplification by means of ornament, which can be used to make one's speech not only increase the importance of a subject and raise it to a higher level, but also to diminish and disparage it." Quintilian (*Institutiones Oratoriae* 8.4.3) spoke of four principal means of a.: augmentation (*incrementum*), comparison, reasoning, and accumulation (*congeries*). Aristotle, in the *Poetics* (19), mentioned "maximizing and minimizing" as important elements of Thought (i.e., rhetoric) in the drama. In the *Rhetoric* (2.26.1) he remarked that a. and depreciation are "enthymemes which serve to show how a thing is great or small." Aristotle, Cicero, and Quintilian clearly regarded a. as something larger than a figure. So did some of the Renaissance rhetoricians. Melanchthon, for example, in his *Elementorum Rhetorices* (1533, p. 76), said, "The universal design of eloquence consists of three things: first in grammatical speech, next in figures, third in amplifications." Nevertheless, *amplificatio* was also considered a figure. A good example of building up a simple idea into a powerful effect was cited by Quintilian (8.4.4.) from Cicero: "It is a sin to bind a Roman citizen, a crime to scourge him, little short of the most unnatural murder to put him to death; what then shall I call his crucifixion?" Cicero's amplifications, and there are many in his orations, were widely imitated in both prose and verse.

A., which is best suited to the grand or elevated style, is specially prominent in epic and tragic poetry. Among many examples in Shakespeare, one of Othello's speeches is a good one. Othello has just realized that Desdemona is innocent: "Whip me, ye devils, / From the possession of this' heavenly sight! / Blow me about in winds! Roast me in sul-

phur! / Wash me in steep-down gulfs of liquid fire! / O Desdemona! Desdemona! dead!" 5.2. 276–80). More common in dialogue or monologue, a. may yet be very effective in narrative or descriptive passages, as in *Paradise Lost* 2.618–22: "Through many a dark and dreary vale / They passed, and many a region dolorous, / O'er many a frozen, many a fiery Alp, / Rocks, caves, lakes, fens, bogs, dens, and shades of death- / A universe of death."—W. G. Crane, *Wit and Rhetoric in the Renaissance* (1937); Lausberg.

M.T.H.

ANACLASIS (Gr. "bending back"). Interchange of a long and a short syllable in Gr. verse either within a foot or metron or between the end of one foot or metron and the beginning of the next. Thus:

$$\smile\overset{2}{\smile}\smile\smile\;\text{may become}\;\overset{2}{\smile}\smile\smile\smile$$

and

$$\smile\smile\underline{\overset{1}{}/\overset{2}{}}\smile\smile\smile\;\text{may be replaced by}\smile\smile\smile\overset{2}{}/\overset{1}{}\smile\smile\smile$$

W. J. W. Koster, "Over anaclasis en rhythmische metabole in de grieksche verskunst," *Handelingen van het 19.Vlaamse Filologen-congres* (1951).

R.J.G.

ANACOLUTHON (Gr. "wanting sequence"). Primarily a term of grammar designating a change of construction in a sentence that leaves its beginning uncompleted, ordinarily seen as a fault, as betraying a lazy or confused mind. Some rhetoricians, however, have recognized that it is sometimes a quite natural and perspicuous mode of expression in spoken discourse (G. W. Hervey cites *Matthew* 7:9, which runs, in the Authorized Version, "Or what man is there of you, whom if his son ask bread, will he give him a stone?" [*Christian Rhetoric*, 1873, p. 583]). Another authority observes that "Shakespeare sometimes showed depth of feeling in his characters" by this means, as at 4.3.34–36 of *Henry V*, where the King says: "Rather proclaim it, Westmoreland, through my host, / That he which hath no stomach to this fight, / Let him depart" (H. L. Yelland and others, *A Handbook of Literary Terms*, 1950, p. 5). Lausberg finds the commonest form of a. to be the so-called absolute nominative (like that in the lines just quoted from Shakespeare). The particular a. of the absence of the complementary member of a pair of correlative expressions has been known by the term *particula pendens*, where we have to do with correlative particles (like "either . . . or," or "both . . . and"), otherwise by the term *anapodoton* or *anantapodoton* (Gr. "wanting the apodosis," as of a conditional sentence). Thus C. T. Ernesti, *Lexicon technologiae Graecorum rhetoricae*, 1795, cites the authority of a nameless scholiast on a locus in Thucidydes 3.3, which translated runs: "If the attempt succeeds," the understood but unexpressed apodosis being, "it will be well"; so also Lausberg and others. J. Marouzeau, however, distinguishes *anapodoton* from *anantapodoton*, making the former a term for an a. in which after an interruption, an antecedent expression is restated in a changed form ("si vous vous recusez,—et vous en avez le droit,—si c'est là votre attitude, j'agirai en consequence." [*Lexique de la terminologie linguistique*, 1933]). See EPANALEPSIS.   H.B.

ANACREONTIC. Named after Anacreon of Teos (6th c. B.C.), the regular Anacreontic (⌣⌣‒⌣‒⌣‒‒) was the alteration of the lesser Ionic (q.v.) dimeter (⌣⌣‒‒/⌣⌣‒‒) by anaclasis (q.v.), whereby the final long syllable of the first foot was interchanged with the first short of the second. That the A. was an Ionic measure is supported by such passages as Euripides, *Cyclops* 495–502; 503–510; 511–518, where a sequence of Anacreontics is varied by lesser Ionics. Another view is that the A. was originally an iambic dimeter catalectic with the initial foot an anapaest (Sappho, fr. 102 Lobel and Page, combines pure iambic dimeters catalectic with Anacreontics), and iambic dimeters were indeed employed by both Anacreon and the authors of the later *Anacreontea* (composed in imitation of Anacreon between 200 B.C. and 500 A.D.). Whatever their origin, Anacreontics were used in L. apparently by Laevius (1st c. B.C.) and by Seneca, Petronius, Claudian, Martianus Capella, and Boethius. Hadrian's famous reply to Florus,

ĕgŏ nōlŏ Flōrŭs ĕssĕ,

is a notable and particularly good example of the meter, which can be paralleled in Longfellow's *Hiawatha*, e.g., "For a while to muse and ponder / On a half-effaced inscription."— Kolár; Dale; Koster; Crusius.   R.J.G.

The *Anacreontea* or *Anacreontics* comprise about 60 short lyrical poems on wine, love and song—graceful and charming but rather shallow pieces. Edited for the first time by Stephanus (Henri Estienne) in 1554, they had a 'considerable influence on Renaissance and later European poets, e.g., in 16th-c. France, on Ronsard and Rémy Belleau and, in 16th-, 18th-, and 19th-c. Italy, on Tasso, Parini, Monti, Foscolo, and Leopardi who translated and imitated many of these poems. Anacreontic imitation was even more in vogue in 18th-c. Germany among the so-called *Anakreontiker* (Gleim, Uz, Götz, and their forerunner Hagedorn). In England, Abraham Cowley seems to have first used the term in his *Anacreontiques* (1656), but the probably best known verse translation is *Odes of Anacreon* (1800) by the Ir. poet Thomas Moore, dubbed by Byron

"Anacreon Moore."—Schmid and Ständlin, I.; E. Merker, "Anakreontik," *Reallexikon*, 2d ed., I.   P.S.C.

ANACRUSIS (Gr. "the striking up of a tune"). One or more initial syllables which are not part of a regular metrical scheme. This term, for which the adjective "procephalous" would be a more descriptive and better attested alternative, was adopted by Bentley in principle and Hermann in fact, as well as by their successors in the 19th c. through analogy with modern music, i.e., when a note or notes occur before the first actual bar of the melody. Classical scholars have largely abandoned the view that a. could be assumed to alter rising (e.g., iambic) to falling (e.g., trochaic) rhythms, or vice versa. For an example in Gr. poetry see LOGAOEDIC. An example in modern stress verse occurs in Blake's *The Tyger:*

When the stars threw down their spears

And watered heaven with their tears

where classical metricians would not now normally regard the first syllable of the second line as justifying a return to the falling rhythm of the first.—Dale; N. A. Bonavia-Hunt, *Horace the Minstrel* (1954). For a. in OE verse see J. C. Pope, *The Rhythm of Beowulf* (1942).   R.J.G.

ANADIPLOSIS, also *epanadiplosis* (Gr. "doubling"). Twice used by the Gr. rhetorician Demetrius (1st c. A.D.?), once in the general sense of word repetition, e.g., "There were huge serpents in the Caucasus, both huge and many" (*On Style* 66); once where he calls it a "schema," quoting from Sappho to illustrate the "force" and "grace" imparted to her poetry by word repetitions. Observe that the repetitions in this example occur both with and without intervening words (W. Rhys Roberts' tr. in the Loeb Classics ed. is faithful to the original on this point: " 'Maidenhood, Maidenhood, whither away, / Forsaking me?' And her Maidenhood makes reply to her in the same figure: 'Not again unto thee shall I come for aye, / Not again unto thee!' " (140). Synonyms of a. in this general sense of word repetition for emphasis have included *palillogy* (Johannes Susenbrotus, *Epitome troporum ac schematum*, 1541, ed. 1621, p. 45); *epizeuxis* (Herodian, grammarian of the 2d c. A.D., in C. Walz, *Rhetores Graeci*, 9 v. 1832–36, v. 8, p. 603); *conduplicatio* (*Ad Herennium*, 1st c. B.C., 4.28); and still others. In view of this plethora of other terms for the general sense, it would seem well, if the term "a." is to be used at all henceforth, to apply it, as most of the postclassical authorities do, only to the word repetition that serves to link two units of discourse such as consecutive stanzas or sentences (Susenbrotus, p. 45; George Puttenham, *The Arte of Eng. Poesie*, 1589, 1936 ed., p. 200; Henry Peacham, *The Garden of Eloquence*, 1593, p. 46). Such is the link between the final line of the 44th and opening line of the 45th stanza of *The Faerie Queene* 1.2: "Then turning to his Lady, dead with feare her found. / Her seeming dead he found with feigned feare."

Various other kinds of repetition have been distinguished, among others: *antanaclasis* or *traductio* (the witty repetition of a word in a changed sense, Quintilian, 1st c. A.D., *Institutes of Oratory* 9.3.68–73); *epanalepsis* (q.v.); *ploce* (the "weaving" of several repetitions of one or more words through a passage of some length, Quintilian 9.3.40–44); *anaphora* (q.v.); *epiphora* or *epistrophe* (the ending of a series of units of discourse with the same word or words, Peacham, p. 42; Abraham Fraunce, *The Arcadian Rhetorique*, 1588, Dᵛ); *symploce* or *complexio* (*anaphora* and *epiphora* combined, Alexander, Gr. rhetorician of the 2d c. A.D., *Peri schematōn* 2, in Walz, v. 8, pp. 464–65; *Ad Herennium* 4.13); and *climax* (q.v.). H.B.

ANALOGY. See SYMBOL.

ANALYSIS. The resolution or breaking up, at least partially, of anything complex into its various elements; the opposite of *synthesis*. Its necessity is twofold: the experience of a poem, and any discourse about it, both take place in time; unable to read or say "everything at once," we proceed from the parts to the whole.

HISTORY. In Plato and Aristotle we find two basic types of a.: (1) Plato's method, generally, is to analyze an idea *dialectically*, i.e., by examining in a dialogue various definitions of it or aspects of the problem it presents; (2) in an Aristotelian treatise, there may also be a dialectic of ideas, but Aristotle's characteristic method is to *generalize* on the basis of examples (e.g., in the *Poetics*, tragedy, with some comparisons of comedy and epic) expounding the first principles of a subject in the form of definitions and sketching its broad outlines by a classification into genus and species of its various parts or aspects. This contrast between a dramatic-poetic-intuitive method and an empirical-scientific-expository one persists throughout the history of the criticism of poetry. The Platonic and Aristotelian traditions mingled in the Middle Ages (Abelard, Aquinas, Scotus), with that of Aristotle on the whole dominating. Of central importance was the fact that the methods of instruction practiced by the church were based on the inculcation of dogmas, systematically analyzed and formulated, and on the careful study and pre-

cise interpretation of texts. Dante's analyses of his own poems in *Vita Nuova* show the resulting habit of mind being applied on an elementary level; and the allegorical theory of interpretation, derived from Philo of Alexandria (the four levels of meaning distinguished by Aquinas, and by Dante in his letter to Can Grande della Scala), is an application "in depth" of the method of analysis developed by many generations of commentators on the Bible, Homer, and other classics.

In the Eng. tradition, it was Bacon (*Novum Organum*, 1620) who first clearly called for a new "form of induction (i.e., science) which shall analyze experience and take it to pieces," contrasting the conclusions to be extracted thus "out of the very bowels of nature" with those derived "merely out of the depths of the mind." Thus began the empirical-sensationalistic Eng. tradition developed by Hobbes, Locke, and others, with profound consequences for poetry and poetic theory (C. D. Thorpe, *The Aesthetic Theory of Thomas Hobbes*, 1940). The "esprit géométrique" represented by Descartes and Spinoza, also, was a pervasive influence on neoclassical literature, art, and criticism, which can be felt in the poetry of argument and ideas, in the increasingly rational approach to imagery and metaphor, and in other ways. In the arts, its impact is perhaps more obvious: the music of Bach, the architectural designs of Sir Christopher Wren. A key document in this development is W. Hogarth's *The Analysis of Beauty* (1752; ed. J. Burke [1955]), which attempts to relate all visual beauty to a single element (the "line of beauty").

It was in Germany that the problem of taste and judgment was given its classic formulation by Kant in his *Critique of Judgment* (1790). Here the distinction between analytic and synthetic judgments is thoroughly developed. Kant went beyond "synthetic judgments," into "a dialectic of the *Critique* of taste (not of taste itself) in respect of its *principles*." Hegel developed further the dialectical method, as a kind of synthesis of a.-and-synthesis, by means of which he hoped to transcend both; nevertheless, in much post-Hegelian philosophy and aesthetics, the a.-synthesis opposition remains of central importance.

Among the attempts to counter the analytic tendency which have had important consequences for literature and poetics, special mention may be made of Bergson's theories of time as *durée* and of "intuition"; Croce's conception of *Aesthetic as Science of Expression* (1902) or "spiritual activity"; and Whitehead's "organicist" theories of "synthetic prehension."

APPLICATION TO POETRY. In less theoretical terms, we may say that a. (and synthesis) are fundamental activities of the mind that are present in all critical discourse. Among the specific applications of a. to poetry have been:

1) *A. of Language.* As one way of defining grammar, this became, with the publication of Morell's *Analysis of Sentences Explained* (1852), a powerful pedagogic tool in England and the States, which may have influenced habits of reading poetry. More profound, probably, was the general tendency of Eng. to pass from its "synthetic," inflected Indo-European roots to "analytic" language patterns—which, by making the meanings of words dependent on their positions in a sentence or line of poetry, help determine their ambiguities or "plurisignation" (see, for example, W. Empson, *Seven Types of Ambiguity*, 1930; *The Structure of Complex Words*, 1951).

Structural linguistics has begun recently to make its contributions to the a. of poetry (F. L. Utley, "Structural Linguistics and the Literary Critic," JAAC, March 1960; and see the typical countercriticisms of this tendency by Wimsatt and Beardsley, "The Concept of Meter: An Exercise in Abstraction," PMLA, Dec. 1959. The semiotic tradition (Cassirer, Morris, Langer) has been developed by E. G. Ballard toward a conception of the aesthetic object as "a self-significant natural symbol which is intrinsically valued" (*Art and Analysis*, 1957). And another related tendency, at its most ambitious and systematic in K. Burke (see section 6, below), is the return to rhetorical a. (e.g., J. J. Mahoney, "An Analysis of *Winesburg, Ohio*," JAAC, Dec. 1956, concerned with "voice and address" and "tone").

2) *A. of an Idea.* This is a logical process, characteristic of philosophy, which may enter into poetics by way of: (a) definitions (as when Aristotle says that "Metaphor consists in giving the thing a name that belongs to something else; the transference being either from genus to species, or from species to genus, or from species to species, or on grounds of analogy"); (b) critical discussions of such concepts as "nature," "imitation," "romanticism" (or "analysis"!); and (c) historical studies of the changes in meaning undergone by words such as the foregoing (see Empson, *op. cit.*; A. O. Lovejoy, *Essays in the History of Ideas*, 1948; Leo Spitzer, *Essays in Historical Semantics*, 1948; and the *Journal of the History of Ideas*).

3) *A. of a Structure of Ideas.* Often overlapping with no. 2, this may be restricted to individual literary works, as in the writing of briefs, summaries, conspectuses, or synopses (Wilkins, 1668: "A Scheme or Analysis . . . of things belonging to this design"), especially of such elements as their "arguments" or plots; or may be extended to entire systems of ideas —in relation to an individual poet (J. F. Danby,

Shakespeare's Doctrine of Nature, 1949), to a limited age or movement (neoclassicism, imagism), or to an elaborate historical development (A. O. Lovejoy, *The Great Chain of Being*, 1936).

4) *A. of a Text.* This may overlap with no. 3, but is really associated with the writing of critical commentaries (E. Huit, 1664: "The whole Prophecie of Daniel Explained by a Paraphrase, Analysis and Briefe Comment") and various other forms of interpretation (cf. John Wisdom, *Interpretation and Analysis*, 1931; see also articles on EXPLICATION and on TEXTUAL CRITICISM). The problems encountered in the explication of poetry, for example, may be related, theoretically and practically, to those involved in the interpretation of other "works of art" as well (M. C. Beardsley, *Aesthetics*, 1958, ch. 2: "The Categories of Critical Analysis" and Ch. 3: "The Literary Work"), for which D. F. Tovey's *Essays in Musical Analysis* (1935) may be taken as one model. (See also C. L. Stevenson, "On the 'Analysis' of a Work of Art," *Philos. Rev.*, Jan. 1958.)

5) *A. of Causes.* This is necessary for all writers of biography or literary history. Conceptions of causation vary: the Aristotelian a. is the most elaborate; the modern-empirical one has been influenced by developments in the various sciences. Thus, Taine formulated his deterministic a. in terms of race, environment, and time; a Marxist critic will relate a certain style of poetry to the economic and social conditions of the age which produced it; and so forth.

6) *A. Involving Psychology.* Whether in terms of Freudian "psychoanalysis" or an earlier "faculty" psychology, this is required for discussions: (a) of imagination and creative processes and aesthetic experiences (D. H. Parker, *The Analysis of Art*, 1926; D. W. Prall, *Aesthetic Analysis*, 1936; K. Burke, "Freud—and the Analysis of Poetry," *The Philosophy of Literary Form*, 1941; *Art and Psychoanalysis*, ed. W. Phillips, 1957); (b) of poets as individuals, especially in biographies; and (c) of characters or situations in poems.

7) *A. of Types.* Besides psychological types (see no. 6), this has resulted, by a kind of analogy to biological and other types or species, in considerations of literary genres (I. Ehrenpreis, *The 'Types Approach' to Literature*, 1945; S. J. Kahn, "Problems of Analysis and Criticism," in *Science and Aesthetic Judgment*, 1953).

SYNTHESIS AND CATEGORIES OF ANALYSIS. To the extent that a. is systematic, it implies a corresponding impulse toward synthesis, whether revealed by the analyst's choice of elements or categories, or made explicit in terms of some all-embracing philosophy or world-view. Thus, each of the emphases included in our historical sketch can be shown to have had, and to have, natural consequences for poetic theory and the actual practice of criticism; whether out of this variety a total synthesis or organon of analytic methods can emerge is a problem only the future can solve. S. C. Pepper, in *The Basis of Criticism in the Arts* (1945), for example, sketches four alternative syntheses (mechanistic, contextualistic, organistic, and formistic), though he prefers the contextualistic categories for his own "analysis of the aesthetic work of art" (*op. cit.,* "Supplementary Essay"). Thus, the character of the synthesis determines the nature of the a. to which it corresponds.

Though this aspect of our subject is well-nigh inexhaustible, it may help to provide a few illustrations. The Aristotelian analyst will approach the poem in terms of logical divisions of the "concrete whole" into its parts: objects, means, and manner of imitation; plot, character, thought, diction; and material, efficient, formal, and final causes. The Platonist may use similar distinctions, but will tend to subordinate all other elements, through a dialectic of ideas, to the all-embracing Idea of the Good; as the medieval or modern scholastic will, to the nature of God and His creation. The neoclassicist, to put a long story very briefly, will try to harmonize the foregoing categories with the requirements of Cartesian or Newtonian science. The romantic, emphasizing either the individual or the social or the transcendental aspect of experience, will utilize psychological categories (expression, or suppression, of emotion), or invoke humanitarian values, or pinpoint mystical experiences or symbols; and Coleridge's central distinction between "fancy" and "imagination" corresponds roughly to that between a. (in psychology, Lockean and Hartleian "associationism") and synthesis (his "esemplastic" power and the modern "Gestalt"). The naturalist will apply the methods and metaphors of evolutionary science (chiefly biology) in an attempt to achieve objectivity (Taine and Brunetière, in certain respects; L. A. Sherman, *Analytics of Literature,* 1893). The modern pragmatist or instrumentalist will be concerned chiefly with the relations of means to ends in the poem, giving a new formulation to a principle as old as Aristotle's *Poetics* and *Rhetoric;* one form of this tendency in our century is the concern with poetry as a form of communication, the complications of which have led to the young science of semantics, with its elaborate a. of meanings and motives (C. K. Ogden and I. A. Richards, *The Meaning of Meaning,* 1923). In I. A. Richards, to mention one of the most interesting and influential of those who have attempted a new synthesis, we generally find a complex mixture of romantic, pragmatist, and behaviorist psychological tendencies (see "Analysis," pt. 3 of *Practical Criticism,* 1929; also *Principles of Literary Criticism,* 1925; *Coleridge on Imagination,* 1934; *Interpretation in Teaching,* 1938; *How to Read a Page,* 1943).

Sometimes, as in Kenneth Burke ("Lexicon Rhetoricae," in *Counter-Statement,* 1931; *A Grammar of Motives,* 1945; *A Rhetoric of Motives,* 1952), we encounter an ambitious attempt to embrace all these elements, and more, in some sort of dialectical unity. Less ambitious, but more coherent, syntheses are found in P. Goodman, *The Structure of Literature* (1954), which, using a version of the Aristotelian categories, distinguishes "formal, genetic, and final modes of analysis" and applies a method of "inductive formal analysis" to dramatic and novelistic plots, and to lyrical poems; R. S. Crane, *The Languages of Criticism and the Structure of Poetry* (1953) in which various theories of criticism are discussed in the light of Aristotelian principles; and D. A. Stauffer, *The Nature of Poetry* (1946), in which an organic metaphor unites the various analytical chapters.

ULTIMATE ISSUES AND CONCLUSIONS. Behind the problems of synthesis lurk the profounder, often implicit, questions of epistemology and metaphysics—of what we know and of the nature of being. R. Wellek and A. Warren (*Theory of Literature,* 1949) have posed the problem of the "mode of existence" of a poem as follows: "What is the 'real' poem; where should we look for it; how does it exist?" They have based their formulation of the problem of literary study on a distinction between "extrinsic" and "intrinsic" approaches, strongly favoring the latter. Wellek's discussion of "The Analysis of the Literary Work of Art" (Ch. 12) provides a convenient review of our problem—but one subject to the limitation stated in the preceding paragraphs, in that its attempt at a constructive statement of the elements "intrinsic" to the study of literature is based on E. Husserl's "Phenomenology" ("which stresses the careful description of phenomena in all domains of experience without regard to the traditional epistemological questions": *American College Dictionary*), as applied by Roman Ingarden (*Das literarische Kunstwerk,* 1931). This method of a. distinguishes strata of sound, of units of meaning, of "world" (objects represented), and of "metaphysical qualities" (the sublime, the tragic, the terrible, the holy). The present writer, using another metaphysical framework, prefers the more neutral terminology of "external" and "internal" relations (used also by W. Shumaker, *Elements of Critical Theory,* 1952); the "external" relations would include all those elements discussed by Wellek and Warren in their chapters on

-[36]-

biography, psychology, sociology, ideas, and the other arts. All these can be, and should be, embraced by a conception of experience as the interactions of an organism with its environment (S. J. Kahn, "What Does a Critic Analyze?" *Phil. and Phenomenological Res.*, Dec. 1952); and, further, that such an "organic" a. can go beyond a naive "biologism" or "psychologism" or "sociologism" and incorporate the profoundest wisdom of the poets and modern science, if it returns to the full complexity of Aristotle's a. of causation ("Towards an Organic Criticism," JAAC, Sept. 1956).

However such ultimate issues may be settled, we should conclude with the modest caution that a.—however necessary, and even delightful, it may be as an exercise of reason—should never, where poetry is concerned, become an exclusive end in itself. Since poetry, in its nature, is something to be experienced aesthetically and enjoyed and valued, as well as studied and understood, the best style of poetic a. will naturally be one which best leads to the full realization of *all* these ends. Indeed, there are occasions in the reading of poetry, as in life, when a. is unnecessary, or does more harm than good. As T. S. Eliot put it in his lecture on *The Frontiers of Criticism* (1956): since the function of literary criticism is to "promote the understanding and enjoyment of literature . . . we do not fully understand a poem unless we enjoy it." And if, as he quizzically concluded, the literary criticism of the last thirty years "in both England and America . . . may even come to seem, in retrospect, too brilliant," the reason may lie in its overemphasis on a.   s.J.K.

ANALYZED RHYME may be broadly defined as the simultaneous, or interlocked, usage of two or more types of rhyme. Perhaps it is most commonly seen in a combination of assonantal rhyme and consonantal rhyme, as in run, hunt, fin, splint, but it can involve other combinations such as the consonantal and true rhymes in clear, where, tear, air.—S. L. Mooney, "New Devices in Sound Repetition," *Word Study*, 24 (1949); Deutsch.   R.BE.

ANANTAPODOTON. See ANACOLUTHON.

ANAPAEST, anapest (Gr. "beaten back," i.e., either a "reversed" dactyl or a verse begun with a "beat" of the foot). A metrical unit, in quantitative verse, of 2 short syllables followed by 1 long one:

$$\smile\smile-; \; dei\bar{t}as$$

Originally a warlike march rhythm, it was widely used, in combinations and pure, in Gr. melic and dramatic verse, particularly by comic choruses:

$$\bar{e}x \; h\bar{o}u \; g\bar{e} \; ch\bar{o}roisin \; \breve{e}phesteken \; tr\bar{y}gikois \; h\bar{o}$$
$$didaskalos \; hemon$$

(Aristophanes, *Acharnians* 628; anapaestic tetrameter catalectic, i.e., $7\frac{1}{2}$ anapaests, with normal substitution of spondee for a. in the first foot.) It was adopted by the Romans primarily in drama (Plautus, Seneca). The term has been adopted into Eng. for the accentual foot of 2 unstressed syllables followed by 1 stressed one:

$$(\text{x x } \prime; \text{ interrupt})$$

Used mainly in popular verse until the beginning of the 18th c., it was subsequently employed for serious poetry by Cowper, Scott, Byron, Browning, Morris, and especially Swinburne, who used it in lines of every possible length. While the a. is characteristically the foot of hurried motion and excitement:

"The Assyrian came down like a wolf on the
fold"
(Byron, *The Destruction of Sennacherib*)

it can also be slow-moving and effective in conveying mourning or sadness, as, for instance, in Matthew Arnold's *Rugby Chapel*. Pure anapaests are comparatively rare in Eng. and tend to jig unless carefully varied with other feet.—A. Raabe, *De metrorum anapaesticorum apud poetas Graecos usu . . .* (1912); J. W. White, *The Verse of Gr. Comedy* (1912); Baum; Hamer; Crusius.   D.S.P.

ANAPHORA (Gr. "a carrying up or back"); also *epanaphora*. The Gr. rhetoricians Demetrius (1st c. A.D.? [*On Style* 268]) and Longinus later (*On the Sublime* 20.1–2) apply the term *epanaphora* to the repetition of the same word or words at the beginning of several successive sentences or sentence members, and Demetrius (*loc. cit.*) and virtually all postclassical authorities treat a. as its exact synonym. Examples abound in argumentative oratory and sermons and in poetry. Longinus sees in this, as he does in many another figure, an imitation of the thought or action that the words express: " 'By his manner, his looks, his voice, when he strikes you with insult, when he strikes you like an enemy, when he strikes you with his knuckles, when he strikes you like a slave.' Here the orator [says Longinus] does just the same as the aggressor, he belabors the minds of the jury and assaults them again and again." It is, of course, a favorite pattern of Shakespeare's, e.g., for eulogy, as in John of Gaunt's lines on England: "This royal throne of kings, this sceptred isle, / This earth of majesty, this seat of Mars, / This other Eden . . . (*Richard II*, 2.1.40–42), and for expressions of nostalgia, like Richard's lines in the same play: "With mine own tears I wash away my balm, / With mine own hands I give away my crown, / With mine own tongue deny my sacred state [etc.] (4.1.207ff.).

A different meaning, ignored by the later rhetoricians of Europe and best regarded as obsolete, was assigned to a. by the Gr. rhetorician of the 2d c. A.D., Hermogenes (*Peri deinotētos*, ch. 28), namely, the citation of testimony for support (*asphaleia*), as distinguished from *bebaiōsis*, i.e., confirmation thereof for proof ("*pistis*"), e.g., Herodotus: "So say the Corinthians" (*anaphora*), "and the Lesbians concur" (*bebaiōsis*). See C. Walz, *Rhetores Graeci*, 9 v., 1832–36, v. 3, p. 433.　　　　H.B.

ANAPODOTON. See ANACOLUTHON.

ANASTROPHE (Gr. "a turning upside down"). A dislocation of the normal (that is, prose) word order, restricted by Quintilian (1st c. A.D.) to the inversion (L. *inversio* or *reversio*) of only two words, for example, *mecum* for *cum me*, *quibus de rebus* for *de quibus rebus* (*Institutes of Oratory* 8.6.65). Quintilian defines a nearly related term, *hyperbaton* (Gr. "a stepping over," L. *verbi transgressio*) as primarily the separation of two words that normally belong together, by the interposing of an alien sentence element, which thus has to be "stepped over" ("as . . . 'in duas divisam esse partes'; for 'in duas partes divisam esse' was the natural order, but would be harsh and inelegant"). Longinus applies the term *hyperbaton* to an inversion of ideas rather than words, i.e., an inversion of what would seem the expected or logical order of the elements of an argument, in a very interesting passage in which he cites "the speech of Dionysius, the Phocaean, in Herodotus," pointing out what extra force a surprising order imparts to ideas that thus seem "wrung from" the speaker rather than "premeditated" (*On the Sublime*, ch. 22). It is a commonplace that because of the almost unlimited freedom of word order normal in L. and Gr.—at least literary L. and Gr., prose as well as verse—one can hardly identify any inversions in these languages (Quintilian is near to pedantry on the subject), whereas inversions of the much stricter order normal in the modern languages are conspicuous. L. prose would easily tolerate the form of Horace's question, "ridentem dicere verum / Quid vetat?" (*Satires* 1.1.24–25), whereas Milton's word-for-word rendering of it, "Laughing to teach the truth / What hinders?" is distinctly "poetical." Inversions are naturally

most exploited in poetry, whether merely to meet the exigencies of meter or rhyme (as in many a line by "regular" poets of the school of Pope) or for effects of melody or emphasis, or as one among other means by which a poet may impart to his work something of the spirit and prestige of ancient models (e.g., in *Paradise Lost*), or, again, as has sometimes been thought, out of a perverse eccentricity (the more cryptic poems of Browning have not escaped this charge).　　　　H.B.

ANCIENTS AND MODERNS, QUARREL OF. See BATTLE OF THE ANCIENTS AND MODERNS.

ANGLO-SAXON PROSODY. See OLD GERMANIC PROSODY; ENGLISH PROSODY.

ANTANACLASIS. See PUN; ANADIPLOSIS.

ANTHOLOGY. Etymologically a "bouquet"; from Gr. *anthos* (flower) and *legein* (to gather, pick up); originally a collection of poetic epigrams, generally composed in elegiac distichs and referent to specific poets or subjects. Compilations were made as early as the 4th c. B.C. About 90 B.C. Meleager of Gadara collected a *Garland* of short epigrams in various meters, but chiefly elegiac, and on various subjects; some fifty poets from Archilochus (7th c. B.C.) to himself were represented. About A.D. 40 Philippus of Thessalonica collected a *Garland* of exclusively elegiac epigrams by poets since Meleager. Approximately a century later Straton of Sardis put together some hundred epigrams on a single subject, homosexual love. About A.D. 570 the Byzantine anthologist Agathias collected a *Circle* of epigrams in various meters; he included selections, arranged by subject, from both *Garlands* as well as a large selection of contemporary epigrams.

Constantinus Cephalas, a Byzantine Greek who lived during the reign of Constantine VII (912–59), compiled an a. in which he combined and rearranged the collections of Meleager, Philippus, Straton and Agathias. In all, it included 15 divisions: Christian epigrams, descriptions of statuary, temple inscriptions, prefaces (by Meleager, Philippus, and Agathias), erotic poems, dedicatory poems, epitaphs (including Simonides' famous lines on the Spartan dead at Thermopylae), epigrams by St. Gregory of Nazianzus, epideictic epigrams, moral epigrams, social and satirical epigrams, Straton's collection, epigrams in special meters, riddles, and miscellaneous epigrams. The A., or Gr. A., as it is called, was edited, revised, and expurgated in 1301 by the monk Maximus Planudes. His edition was the only available Gr. a. until 1606, when the great Fr. scholar Claude Saumaise (Salmasius) discovered a single manuscript of Cephalas in the Elector Palatine's library at Heidelberg; hereafter it came to be known as the *Palatine A.*; it supplanted the *Planudean A.* but retained a Planudean appendix as a 16th division. The first edition of the *Palatine A.* was published in 13 vols. (1794–1814) by Friedrich Jacobs.

The influence of the *Gr. A.* in the modern world dates from Janus Lascaris' Florentine edition of Planudes in 1494. Translations of the epigrams into L. and later into the vernacular languages multiplied consistently until about 1800, when the enthusiasm for the unpointed Gr. epigram was succeeded by that for the pointed epigram as perfected by the Latin Martial (1st c. A.D.). Renewed interest in the *Gr. A.* is apparent today in current translations, e.g., Kenneth Rexroth's, of selections from it. Other anthologies include the 5th c. Stobaeus' Gr. *Eclogae* (*Selections*) and *Anthologion*, the *Anthologia Latina* (ed. Riese, Bücheler and Lommatzsch, 1894–1926, including otherwise uncollected L. verse and a 6th-c. compilation which contained the *Pervigilium Veneris*), medieval *florilegia*, the *Carmina Cantabrigiensia* (11th c.) and *Carmina Burana* (13th c.), and Erasmus' *Adagia* early 16th c.).

The earliest anthologies in Eng. include: *Tottel's Miscellany* (orig., *Songes and Sonettes, written by the ryght honorable Lorde Henry Haward late Earle of Surrey, and other*, 1557); Clement Robinson's *Very Pleasaunt Sonettes and Storyes in Myter* (1566; surviving *only as A Handefull of Pleasant Delites*, 1584); *The Paradyse of Daynty Devises* (1576); *A Gorgious Gallery of Gallant Inventions* (1578); *The Phoenix Nest* (1593); *Englands Helicon* (1600, 1614); *Davison's Poetical Rapsody* (1602).

Other significant European anthologies are: Jan Gruter's *Delitiae* (It., Fr., Belgian, and German poems in Latin; 1608–1614); J. W. Zincgref's *Anhang unterschiedlicher aussgesuchter Gedichten* (1624); Thomas Percy's *Reliques of Ancient Eng. Poetry* (1765; an a. of early ballads which proved to be considerably influential); Oliver Goldsmith's *The Beauties of Eng. Poetry* (1767); Thomas Campbell's *Specimens of the British Poets* (1891); Palgrave's *Golden Treasury of Eng. Songs and Lyrics* (1861; *the* a. of lyric poetry in Victorian England); *Le Parnasse contemporain* (1866, 1871–76); Sir Arthur Quiller-Couch's *Oxford Book of Eng. Verse* (1900, 1939).

The popularity of anthologies in the 20th c. is so great as to preclude even a representative listing of titles in Eng. Mention should be made, however, of *The New Poetry* (1917) by Harriet Monroe and Alice C. Henderson because of its influence on modern poets, and of such anthologists as Robert Bridges, Louis Untermeyer, Conrad Aiken, Oscar Williams, Selden Rodman, James Reeves, William Cole, and of the collaborators Cleanth Brooks and Robert Penn Warren, whose *Understanding Poetry* (1938, 1950, 1960) is a pedagogical a.

F. Lachère, *Bibliographie des receuils collectifs de poésies publiés de 1597 à 1700* (1901); A. Wifstrand, *Studien zur griechischen Anthologie* (1926); J. Hutton, *The Gr. A. in Italy to the Year 1800* (1935) and *The Gr. A. in France and in the Writers of the Netherlands to the Year 1800* (1946); A.S.F. Gow, *The Gr. A.: Sources and Ascriptions* (1958). L.U.; R.A.S.

ANTIBACCHIUS. See PALIMBACCHIUS.

ANTICLIMAX. First recorded, it seems, by Dr. Johnson in a quotation from Addison, Dr. Johnson's definition being "a sentence in which the last part expresses something lower than the first" (*Dictionary*, 1755). It is commonly extended to include this kind of descent in longer or shorter units of discourse than the sentence, but usually refers only to the concluding part or nadir (1) to designate an ineptly expressed idea meant to be superlatively grandiose or pathetic (in this sense synonymous with *bathos* 1., q.v.), or (2) to designate a deliberately ironical letdown of this kind, as in various absurd similes in Henry Fielding's burlesque of Elizabethan and Restoration tragedy, such as: "King [Arthur, to his queen, Dollalolla] . . . Whence flow those Tears fast down thy blubber'd Cheeks, / Like a swoln Gutter, gushing through the Streets?" (*The Tragedy of Tragedies*, 1731, 1.2.6–7), or Lord Grizzle's impassioned address to the Princess Huncamunca: "Oh! Huncamunca, Huncamunca, Oh! / Thy pouting Breasts, like Kettle-Drums of Brass, / Beat everlasting loud Alarms of Joy / . . ." (2.5.1–3). H.B.

ANTIMETABOLE. See CHIASMUS.

ANTISPAST (Gr. "drawn in the contrary direction"). A metrical foot consisting of 4 syllables, 2 long flanked by 2 short (⌣－－⌣), or iambus and trochee. It is not certain if this foot existed in classical poetry as an independent unit.—P. Shorey, "Choriambic Dimeter and the Rehabilitation of the A.," TAPA, 38 (1907); Koster. P.S.C.

ANTISTROPHE (Gr. "counterturning"). Originally in Gr. choral dance and poetry the second of a pair of movements or "stanzas" in an ode. It corresponds exactly in meter to the preceding strophe. In rhetoric the term means the repetition of words in reversed order, e.g., "The master of the servant and the servant of the master." It also describes the repetition of a word or phrase at the end of successive clauses. See STROPHE; EPODE. R.A.H.

ANTITHESIS, *antitheton* (Gr. "opposition"; L. *contentio*). A contrasting of ideas made sharp by the use of words of opposite or conspicuously different meaning in contiguous clauses or phrases, a form of expression recommended as satisfying by Aristotle "because contraries are easily understood and even more so when placed side by side, and also because a. resembles a syllogism, for it is by putting opposing conclusions side by side that you refute one of them" (*Rhetoric* 3.9.8). Some later authorities likewise stress the clarity and force that an a. may impart to any idea (e.g., the anonymous *Rhetorica ad Herennium*, 1st c. B.C., 4.15.21; Johannes Susenbrotus, 1541, on *contentio*, ed. of 1621, p. 63); but the *Rhetorica ad Herennium* sees in it also a means of embellishing a discourse, and this is the idea mainly emphasized by the moderns (e.g. Henry Peacham, "it graceth and bewtifieth the Oration," *The Garden of Eloquence*, 1593, p. 161; John Smith calls it "a Rhetoricall Exornation," *The Mysterie of Rhetorique Unvailed*, 1657, pp. 172–73).

The a. that draws a broad, simple contrast of idea is the pattern of many a verse in the biblical Book of Proverbs, e.g., "It is better to dwell in the wilderness, than with a contentious and angry woman" (21.19; Smith quotes a number of examples, p. 175), and such antitheses are fairly frequent in Anglo-Saxon poetry, often pivoting on the adversative "nālaes," e.g., "Waraþ hine wraeclāst, nālaes wunden gold" (His lot is the path of exile, by no means twisted gold—*The Wanderer*, 32).

A. was cultivated more or less by the classical poets, and while these poets sometimes contrive a strict balance of form or a complex opposition of idea, e.g., "Non fumum ex fulgore, sed ex fumo dare lucem / Cogitat" (He aims to fetch not smoke from a flash, but light from smoke, Horace, *Ars Poetica* 142–43), this kind of ingenuity is still more characteristic of the Eng. and Fr. poets of the Age of Reason, e.g., "Je veux et ne veux pas, je m'emporte et je n'ose" (I would and would not, I am on fire yet dare not—Pierre Corneille, *Cinna*, 1640, 1.2.122); "Thus wicked but in will, of means bereft, / He left not faction, but of that was left" (Dryden, *Absalom and Achitophel*, 1681, ll. 567–68); "It is the slaver kills, and not the bite" (Pope, *Epistle to Dr. Arbuthnot*, 1735, l. 106). The convenience of the closed couplet, which had early emerged as the preferred verse form of the Restoration and Queen Anne poets, for balanced expressions probably goes some way toward explaining why these poets were minded to exploit a. as they did, sometimes to the point where it amounts to a major element of their style. They found it, in any case, an ideal resource for the display of their satirical wit.

The antitheses quoted above are among the many forms of expression that exhibit two or more "figures of speech," and may be labeled with one term or another according to the particular feature to be distinguished. Thus the second line of the quotation from Dryden exhibits *chiasmus, epanalepsis* (qq.v.), and *isocolon* (equality of length in the cola of a period; see COLON).

In contemporary writing the use of a. is chiefly in humorous verse.—P. Beyer, "Antithese," *Reallexikon*, I; Sister Miriam Joseph, *Shakespeare and the Arts of Language* (1947); Lausberg.   S.F.F.; H.B.

ANTODE (Gr. "opposite song"). In the parabasis (q.v.) of Gr. Old Comedy the lyric odes sung by half the chorus in answer to an earlier ode sung by the other half chorus. Composed in lyric meters which correspond metrically to the ode, it contained an invocation to the gods or muse to assist the chorus. See EPIRRHEMA.—F. M. Cornford, *Origin of Attic Comedy* (1914); Koster.   R.A.H.

ANTONOMASIA (Gr. "naming instead"). A figure of speech, in which an epithet or appellative, or the name of an office or dignity, is substituted for a proper name (e.g., "The Bard" for Shakespeare), or in which a proper name is used symbolically for a class or type: "Some village Hampden that with dauntless breast / The little tyrant of his fields withstood; / Some mute, inglorious Milton here may rest, / Some Cromwell guiltless of his country's blood (Gray, *Elegy Written in a Country Churchyard*). Quintilian (*Institutes of Oratory* 8.6.29) states that a., which is very common in poetry but less so in oratory, may be accomplished in two ways, by substitution of epithets such as "Pelides" (that is, son of Peleus for Achilles), and by substituting the striking characteristics of an individual for his name: "Divum pater atque hominum rex" (Father of gods and king of men) Virgil, *Aeneid* 1.65. To this he adds a third type wherein acts may indicate the individual; however, this type, which does not correspond to his twofold division, may well be a spurious emendation. Puttenham, in his *Arte of Eng. Poesie*, distinguishes carefully between epitheton ("fierce Achilles," "wise Nestor") and a. in which the particular individual is not named but referred to by a "type name," e.g., a "Machiavelli" for a crafty schemer.—Lausberg.   R.O.E.

APHAERESIS (Gr. "a taking away"). Omission of an initial, unstressed syllable, specifically an initial vowel, e.g., mid for amid, as in "Mid the squander'd colour" (R. Bridges, *Cheddar Pinks*). In Gr. poetry the suppression of an initial short "e" following a word ending in a long vowel or diphthong, as in *mē 'gō* for *mē egō*.   R.A.H.

APOCOPATED RHYME (from Gr. *apocope*, q.v.) occurs where the final accented syllables of two words are in true rhyme, but where one word is masculine, one feminine in accentuation, e.g., find, blinder; pal, callow. Though the device may be found most predominantly in modern poets, others (Burns and Spenser, for instance) have used varieties of it.—E. Guest, *History of Eng. Rhythm* (new ed., 1882); S. L. Mooney, "New Devices in Sound Repetition," *Word Study*, 24 (1949); Deutsch. R.BE.

APOCOPE (Gr. "a cutting off"). Omission of one or more letters from the end of a word, e.g., "t'other" for "the other." In Gr. poetry the suppression of a short vowel before a consonant. This may occur within a compound word (*kábbale* for *katéballe*) or when two words are separate (*kap pedion* for *kata pedion*).   R.A.H.

APOLLONIAN-DIONYSIAN. Antinomy first devised by Friederich Nietzsche in *The Birth of Tragedy* (1872). Nietzsche uses Apollo as a symbol for the poet's dream of form: The Apollonian impulse urges the poet to create an understandable and beautiful world. It further guides him to a cognition of symmetry, giving him the power to create an apparently real world within tragedy. By contrast, the Thracian god Dionysus is used by Nietzsche to characterize the poet's sense of music. Music, in this definition, is an expression of that basic awareness of blind irrationality, pain, and suffering in the world which gives rise to the Dionysian dance of orgiastic worship.

Both Apollonian and Dionysian impulses are seen as absolute, nonrational powers which work *through* the poet and are hence independent of his personal feelings or of his audience's understanding. The tragedy of Aeschylus represents the interaction of Apollonian and Dionysian forces at its best. When Socratic skepticism taught the Gr. world to differentiate between appearance and reality, and Euripides consciously separated the "stage world" from the "real world," Gr. tragedy died. Rationalism, with its distinction between "subjective" and "objective" views, undermined both Apollonian and Dionysian impulses. These are, however, perennial forces which, Nietzsche maintains, can re-create true tragedy if properly brought to the surface. In *The Birth of Tragedy*, Nietzsche sees Wagnerian opera as a valid Apollonian-Dionysian interaction—a view which he later abandoned.

The Apollonian-Dionysian antinomy is based, in philosophical conception, upon Schopenhauer's *The World as Will and Idea* (1819).

Further, the intellectual *milieu* of the late 19th c. abounded in the assumption of literary antinomies which, like Nietzsche's, attempt to distinguish instinctive from formal literary creation. The distinction between classicism and romanticism (qq.v.) and Schiller's antinomy of the naive and sentimental (q.v.) are perhaps the most important among these. For these reasons, the influence of the Apollonian-Dionysian antinomy on later poetics must be assessed with caution and only such writers named as adapters of it who explicitly followed Nietzsche's approach. Foremost among these was Stefan George, whose followers (George-*Kreis*) considered his poetry an execution of "what Nietzsche only thought out." Thomas Mann consciously endorsed the Nietzschean view of music as a Dionysian manifestation and made use of the concept in composing the novels *Tristan, Death in Venice,* and *Doktor Faustus.* It was the Dionysian part of the antinomy, also, which enticed the Fr. poetess Comtesse de Noailles to place epithets from *The Birth of Tragedy* over some of her verse. D. H. Lawrence, finally, showed strong interest in the antinomy, though its influence upon his work remains to be assessed.—C. G. Jung, *Psychological Types* (1923); A.H.J. Knight, "Dionysus" in *Some Aspects of the Life and Work of Nietzsche* (1933); O. Kein, *Das Apollinische und Dionysische bei Nietzsche und Schelling* (1935); O. Manthey-Zorn, *Dionysus* (1956); M. Krieger, *The Tragic Vision* (1960). W.B.F.

APOSIOPESIS (Gr. "a becoming silent"). A conscious anacoluthon (q.v.), that is, a speaker's abrupt halt midway in a sentence, accountable to his being either too excited to give further articulation to his thought (so Quintilian, 1st c. A.D., *Institutes of Oratory* 9.2.54) or thinking to impress his addressee the more with this kind of vague hint of an idea too awesome to be put into words (so Demetrius, 1st c. A.D., *On Style* 2.103. These different motives are not always distinguishable in given examples, e.g., Neptune's threat of punishment to the winds: "Iam caelum terramque meo sine numine, venti, / Miscere et tantas audetis tollere moles? / Quos ego—Sed motos praestat componere fluctus" (How dare ye, ye winds, to mingle the heavens and the earth and raise such a tumult without my leave? You I will—but first I must quiet the waves [*Aeneid* 1.133–35, one of Quintilian's illustrations]); or King Lear's threat of vengeance on his wicked daughters: "I will have revenges on you both / That all the world shall—I will do such things—" (2.4.282–83). According to the Gr. rhetorician Alexander of the 2d c. A.D., a. is always followed by the speaker's explanation that he is passing over in silence matters either already known to the addressee or too sordid to be mentioned (*Peri schematōn*, C. Walz, *Rhetores Graeci*, 9 v., 1832–36, v. 8, p. 450); and Quintilian remarks that it is sometimes used as a merely transitional device, where the speaker wishes to introduce a digression or announce an impromptu change in the planned conduct of his argument, such as the circumstances of the moment might suggest (9.2.55–57).

A. should not be confused with *paraleipsis* (Gr. "a passing over," L. *praeteritio, occultatio*), a term for the trick by which a speaker emphasizes an idea by pretending to say nothing of it even while giving it full expression (the difference is explained by Gregory of Corinth of the 12th c., in his commentary on Hermogenes' *Peri deinotētos*, ch. 7 in Walz, v. 7, pp. 1166–67).　　　　　　　　　　　　　　H.B.

APOSTROPHE (Gr. "to turn away"). A figure of speech which consists in addressing a dead or absent person, an animal, a thing, or an abstract quality or idea as if it were alive, present, and capable of understanding, e.g., "Quid non mortalia pectora cogis, / auri sacra fames!" (Virgil, *Aeneid* 3.56); "Ahi, serva Italia, di dolore ostello" (Dante, *Purgatorio* 6.76); "O judgment! thou art fled to brutish beasts" (Shakespeare, *Julius Caesar* 3.2.10); "Milton! thou should'st be living at this hour" (Wordsworth, *London, 1802*); "Ring out, wild bells" (Tennyson, *In Memoriam* 106). The term originally referred to any abrupt "turning away" from the normal audience to address a different or more specific audience, whether present (e.g., one person out of the assemblage) or absent. In narrative verse the poet "turns away" from the generality of listeners or readers to address a specific reader, a character in the narrative, or some other person, thing, or idea. The use of a. gives life and immediacy to language, but is also subject to abuse and open to parody.　　　　　　　　　　　　　　L.P.

ARABIC POETRY. In the rich intricacy of his language the Arab experiences an intellectual and aesthetic pleasure unique perhaps in the world. To him Ar. is the greatest of the arts and its noblest expression is in poetry. Nor is this an art become the thing of a small coterie of the élite, divorced from the life of the common man; it remains a part of every day, to express the emotions, to commemorate an occasion, or to lampoon the latest twist of current politics.

PRE- AND EARLY ISLAMIC VERSE. The earliest known verse is attributed to the time of the War of al-Basūs (ca. A.D. 500), but at no time can an evolutionary stage of ancient Arabian poetry be discovered, for in form, meter, and theme, it is already fully developed at the period from which these first lines have survived.

It has been proposed that the earliest meters are the rajaz:

$$\overline{\text{mus}}\text{-}\overline{\text{taf}}\text{-}\breve{\text{ʿi}}\text{-}\overline{\text{lun}} \: / \: \overline{\text{mus}}\text{-}\overline{\text{taf}}\text{-}\breve{\text{ʿi}}\text{-}\overline{\text{lun}} \: / \: \overline{\text{mus}}\text{-}\overline{\text{taf}}\text{-}\breve{\text{ʿi}}\text{-}\overline{\text{lun}}$$

and its derivative, the basīṭ:

$$\overline{\text{mus}}\text{-}\overline{\text{taf}}\text{-}\breve{\text{ʿi}}\text{-}\overline{\text{lun}} \: / \: \overline{\text{fa}}\text{-}\breve{\text{ʿi}}\text{-}\overline{\text{lun}} \: / \: \overline{\text{mus}}\text{-}\overline{\text{taf}}\text{-}\breve{\text{ʿi}}\text{-}\overline{\text{lun}} \: /$$
$$\overline{\text{fa}}\text{-}\breve{\text{ʿi}}\text{-}\overline{\text{lun}}$$

both of which are much used for verse sung to tunes accompanying actions. The complete verse (*bait*) is composed of a couplet, often rhyming, formed of one of the many patterns (*bis*) of which the two above are examples. Older rajaz and basīṭ poems, however, are often so composed that each half *bait* has the common rhyme of the whole poem, as if complete in itself. The qaṣīdah or ode, however, has the form aabaca, etc. (i.e., the 2 hemistichs of the opening line rhyme; this rhyme is repeated at the end of every line), but in early verse there is an occasional tendency for an internal rhyme *a*, perhaps an archaic survival. Rhyming is a natural grace easily achieved.

Authorities name 16 meters but each has many variations, the metrical systems being based on schemes of long and short syllables. A consonant with a short vowel constitutes a short syllable. A long syllable may be (a) a consonant with a long vowel, (b) a consonant followed by a short vowel and a consonant. Even colloquial Ar. meters today are based on patterns of long and short syllables, notwithstanding the fact that colloquials are nearly devoid of classical Ar. inflections and have numerous contracted speech forms which figure occasionally in ancient Ar. as poetic licenses.

Extant ancient Arabian verse is that of the tribes and chivalry, for artisan and peasant poetry has survived only in rare quotations (e.g., A. Guillaume, *Life of Muhammad* [1955] pp. 228–29). Composed in Bedouin language, it sings of honor, revenge, the tribal preoccupations of war, the fantastic generosity of desert cavaliers like Ḥātim al-Ṭāʾī, encounters with lovely Bedouin girls when the rains have started the desert pastures into life, the boasting (*fakhr*) of one's nobility and doughty deeds with satire of the foe, and descriptions of animals and beasts and hunting. The qaṣīdah has a strict theme sequence, commencing by recalling the girl whose beauty keeps the poet from sleep and the ever shifting movements which inevitably tore her from him. The poet turns to describe his noble beast upon which he flees all too poignant memories—and so to the true subject of his poem. These lines introduce the *Muʿallaqah* of the greatest ancient poet Imraʾ al-Qais, known as the "Errant King." (The word *muʿallaqah* seems to mean a bead from a necklace, to which the Arabs are fond of

-[42]-

comparing the verses of a poem as if they were beads strung together on a cord).

Fa-Tūḍiḥa fa-ʾl-Miqrāti lam yaᶜfu rasmu-hā
Li-mā nasajat-hā min janūb-in wa-shamʾali
Tarā baᶜara ʾl-arʾāmi fī ᶜaraṣāti-hā
Wa-qīᶜāni-hā kaʾanna-hū ḥabbu fulfulī

See the white doe droppings strewn by the wind on them, black on her floor forsaken, fine grain of peppercorn. Here it was I watched her, lading her load-camels, stood by these thorn-trees weeping tears as of colocynth. Here my twin friends waited, called to me camel-borne: Man! not of grief thou diest. Take thy pain patiently (W. S. and A. Blunt, *The Seven Golden Odes of Pagan Arabia* [1903]).

Only by considering how poetry is composed in Ar. can the evolution of the qaṣīdah be reconstructed. In its simplest form, verse is composed extempore, sung to some traditional tune, in one *bait* at a time; it is then taken up by the company, sung to rhythmical movement and hand clapping. Until the poet warms to his work he casts about among the many traditional themes in his conscious and subconscious memory—which doubtless explains the qaṣīdah sequence and the recurrent clichés of both classical and colloquial versification, for in Arabia mere originality for its own sake is not sought. When visited by Inspiration—which the Arabs conceive as supernatural, a species of demon—the poet now turns to the theme he wishes to treat. Preoccupied with the qaṣīdah form, critics have regarded poems on individual themes as pieces (*qiṭᶜah*) developed from the original qaṣīdah, but it is more logical to suppose that the qaṣīdah developed from a medley of single themes, such as the *ghazal, fakhr*, etc.

That ancient verse is couched in a poetic diction relatively unaffected by dialect can be deduced from classical writers and is confirmed by the study of colloquial verse in contemporary Arabia or Ar.-speaking countries. Colloquial Arabian verse today, when treating of heroic or amatory themes, is generally free of the more markedly dialectical forms. In the Koran itself the poetic diction of such passages as those concerned with the "Signs" of God may be contrasted with sections concerned with ordinances and regulations delivered in language which an impartial observer can only pronounce as ordinary and commonplace as the colloquial speech we know today.

Certain critics (D. S. Margoliouth, "The Origins of Ar. Poetry," *Jour. Royal Asiatic Soc.* [1925]) have suggested that ancient poetry, if not mostly spurious, has been much tampered with by philologists, and this view at one time even won some acceptance with the Egyptian critic Ṭāhā Ḥusain (*Fiʾl-Adab al-Jāhilī* [Cairo] 1926. Insofar as their views apply to some limited political categories of verse where an interested motive is easily discernible (many in fact already commented upon by ancient writers), there is a case for rejection. Where the bulk of ancient verse is concerned the evidence for authenticity, apart from minor accidents of time, is overwhelming. It would seem that even in the first century of Islam some tribal *dīwāns* or collections had already been assembled (I. Goldziher, "Dîwâns of the Arabic Tribes," *Jour. Royal Asiatic Soc.* [1897], pp. 325–34), but poetry was usually preserved by professional reciters (*rāwī*), probably families of professional poetasters like the Bā ᶜAṭwah of Ḥaḍramawt today. It is evidence of the soundness of oral tradition that I collected poems from a Bā ᶜAṭwah poet—only to discover that Count v. Landberg had already published some of them. The variants were of a trifling nature, the interval between collectors about fifty years, but the poems were not new then.

UMAIYAD VERSE. For a century and a half of Islam, tribal poetry flourished more or less unchanged. This was the age of that fine exponent of the *ghazal* ᶜUmar ibn Abī Rabīᶜah, but the great personalities of the age are al-Farazdaq and his two rivals, al-Jarīr and the Christian al-Akhṭal with whom for many years he engaged in a contest of lampoon and counterlampoon. Jarīr's panegyric composed on the Umaiyad Caliph became a model imitated by later ages—followed, for instance, by al-Buḥturī (*infra*). The Umaiyad aristocracy were deeply imbued with Bedouinism, retiring whenever possible to the Syrian desert fringes in pursuit of the chase. Poetry at the court continued to be composed in an Arabian milieu. To the dynasty and to its enemies it was in fact an important form of propaganda. This period saw the rise of propagandist poetry for the house of ᶜAli, the prophet's cousin who had married his daughter Fāṭimah. Of this poetry al-Kumait was an early exponent. This period may also have seen the beginnings of the popular verse cycles like the ᶜAntar romance, though the latter is ascribed to the ᶜAbbāsid period.

POETRY DURING THE ᶜABBĀSID PERIOD. With the shift of the capital from Damascus to Baghdad after the ᶜAbbāsids had supplanted the Umaiyads the atmosphere changed. Influences of Hellenism and of Persia came into play, but the most significant new factor for poetry was the change in patronage from a Bedouin court to that of the great bureaucratic officials of the Caliphate and settled urban life. ᶜAbbāsid poetry can hardly be said to be less "Arabic" than Umaiyad, but the Baghdadi poet of mixed ancestry felt toward Bedouin verse sentiments rather similar to those of an "intellectual" for a sporting squire. The new school of smart sophisticated verse current at the Baghdad court is typified in the famous Abū Nuwās who with refined simplicity boasts his debauchery—his winesongs are superb—or lechery, be it with town women or boys. He parodies the Bedouin qaṣīdah:

Let the south-wind moisten with rain the desolate scene
And Time efface what once was so fresh and green!
Make the camel-rider free of a desert space
Where high-bred camels trot with unwearied pace;
Where only mimosas and thistles flourish and where,
For hunting, wolves and hyenas are nowise rare!
Amongst the Bedouins seek not enjoyment out;
What do they enjoy? They live in hunger and drought.
Let them drink their bowls of milk and leave them alone,
To whom life's finer pleasures are all unknown.
(tr. R. A. Nicholson, *Literary History*, p. 286)

Apparently in sober contrast stands the verse of Abu ʾl-ʿAtāhiyah, a low-born client Arab of Kūfah. Failing to win the love of the Caliph's slave-girl ʿUtbah, he assumed the ascetic's robe and abandoned the poetry of love for reflections on religion, man's mortality, and predestination—a poet of pessimism; but a recent critic attributes this change of mood to the constant frustrations besetting a man of low birth in Baghdad:

Men vaunt their noble blood, but I behold
No lineage that can vie with righteous deeds.
(R. A. Nicholson, *op. cit.*, p. 302)

He too turned to simple language from which to shape the stuff of poetry, venturing to introduce new metrical modes, and excelling in the *urjūzah*, couplets in rajaz meter. Persian antipathy to Arab domination finds expression in the verses of the blind Bashshār ibn Burd and his kind, but following the way of Arab poets in all ages he won patronage by the laudatory ode and satirized those who neglected him. Even in the early ʿAbbāsid period there are allusions to popular songs (mawwāl) composed in Ar. not strictly classical and consisting of four verses only.

CRITICS AND ANTHOLOGISTS. Antiquarian interest prompted the collection of ancient verse, the most famous anthologies being the *Muʿallaqāt* of Ḥammād al-Rāwiyah (8th c.), the more varied and extensive *Mufaḍḍalīyat* of al-Ḍabbī (8th c.), the *Ḥamāsah* of Abū Tammām arranged according to motives like hardihood, dirges, manners, love satire, etc. The monumental *Book of Songs* of Abu ʾl-Faraj al-Iṣfahānī (d. 967) contains ancient and modern Arab poems set to music with musicological annotations and a mass of biographical anecdote (Cf. Blachère, *Histoire de la littérature arabe* [1952], pp. 139–52, for a well-documented discussion of this branch of literature). The link between Ar. verse and music is highly significant at all periods.

Early Muslim critics had formulated the principle that verse had attained matchless perfection before Islam, but the critic first to declare that ancient and modern verse should be judged by an aesthetic canon was Ibn Qutaibah (9th c.) contemporary with whom flourished the royal poet Ibn al-Muʿtazz—himself author of a treatise on poetics, *Kitāb al-Badīʿ*. With the critic al-Āmidī, the term *badīʿ* seems to mean the lavish employment of figures of speech in the new style of which he regards Abū Tammām as the epitome. Abū Tammām was unspontaneous, fond of far-fetched metaphors, differing from older poets, inclined to *takalluf* (deliberate composition; later this means affectation) and *ṣanʿah* (consciously creating poetry; later it came to mean artificiality, as opposed to al-Buḥturī who is *maṭbūʿ* (a naturally spontaneous poet). It is the style of Abū Tammām which dominates Ar. poetry up to the 20th c.

The ʿAbbāsid poet who has won the greatest appreciation in the Arab world is al-Mutanabbī, court poet to the Ḥamdānids of Aleppo (10th c.), "panegyriste vénale de Saif al-Dawlah, de Kāfūr, et d'Ibn al-Amid," as Blachère styles him (R. Blachère, Abou t-Ṭaiyib al-Motanabbî [Paris, 1953], p. 319), who has found scant favor with Western critics. The testimony of writers like Abu ʾl-ʿAlaʾ al-Maʿarrī, though conscious of defects in al-Mutanabbī, and modern poets like Shawqī and Ḥāfiẓ Ibrāhīm is, however, incontrovertible evidence of the esteem in which he is held. Though reputedly a townsman, he spent much time with the Bedouin, and it has been suggested that his poetry shows a mingling—even a conflict—of Bedouin ideals and values with those of the sedentary Arabs of the towns and villages.

Western taste, however, appraises highly the Syrian Abu ʾl-ʿAlaʾ born in 973 at Maʿarrah south of Aleppo (R. A. Nicholson, *Studies in Islamic Poetry* [1921], pp. 43–289, is the most accessible study of Abu ʾl-ʿAlaʾ, but many Ar. books have been written on him in recent years). The favor of the West and the Syro-Lebanese writers of North America has enormously enhanced his reputation in Arab literary circles. A visit to Baghdad in his middle thirties turned him from the career of professional poetaster to the practice of asceticism and his later verse displays a boldness of thought coupled with a destructive philosophy which overshadows his high morality. Blachère suggests that the subversive writings of the Ikhwān al-Ṣafāʾ and Ismaʿīlīs had created the atmosphere in which Abu ʾl-ʿAlāʾ could write in such cynical vein without fear of ill consequences, but while this may be, it is a fact that one encounters similar sentiments among quite unlettered persons in Arab countries. Abu ʾl-ʿAlāʾ wrote:

Prophets arose and vanished: Moses, Jesus,
Muḥammad last, who brought the prayers
    five—
And 'tis told there comes another Faith
Than this—and men still perishing away
Between a morrow and a yesterday.

His most curious writing, however, is the *Risālat al-Ghufrān,* in which he pictures a visit to heaven and hell to converse with the poets of olden times. It has been compared with Dante's *Inferno.*

ṢŪFISTIC, RELIGIOUS, AND OTHER VERSE. The Ṣūfis, or Mystics, apply the erotic imagery and symbolism of the *ghazal* to the description of the ecstasy of divine love, so that, says Nicholson (*Studies in Islamic Mysticism* [1921], pp. 163–64), "unless we have some clue to the writer's intention, it may not be possible to know whether his beloved is human or divine —indeed the question whether he himself always knows is one which students of Oriental mysticism cannot regard as impertinent." The Sp. Ibn al-ʿArabī and his contemporary Ibn al-Fāriḍ (d. 1235) are outstanding in this genre which flourishes persistently to this day. Typical of religious verse is al-Būṣīrī's *Burdah,* a panegyric of the Prophet. Mnemonic doggerel composed by the professions from lawyer to sailor, literary tricks, conceits, and artifices abound in all periods.

SPANSH ARABIC VERSE. In close cultural contact with the East, Ar. Spain at first saw verse develop along traditional lines, and the arrival of the singer Ziryāb from Baghdad in Spain in 821 is an important event in the history of Sp. verse. However, with the rise of the Berber Almoravids versification in classical Ar. declined, and the newer forms of *muwashshaḥah* and *zajal* closely associated with music, and in a colloquial Ar. came into general vogue. These forms are held to have originated in the 9th c., and there can be little doubt that this type of Hispano-Ar. poetry strongly influenced troubadour verse in Acquitania and even It. poetry. García Gómez, "Don Nuevas Jarŷas Romances," *Al-Andalus,* 19 (1954), pp. 369–91, has published examples of *kharjahs* or refrains, in a curious mixture of Ar. and Romance, not unlike the mixed Ar. and Hindustani of the poet Yaḥyā ʿUmar in R. B. Serjeant, *Prose and Poetry from Hadramawt* (1951), p. 90. The very word *troubadour* has been connected with the Ar. root *ṭariba,* from which is derived *muṭrib* (singer). The anthologies of Maqqarī and Ibn Bassām are widely known collections of Sp. material. A charming example of sophisticated Sp. lyrical verse in elegant 18th-c. Eng. is quoted by W. A. Clouston (*Arabian Poetry for English Readers* [1881], p. 143): "Verses addressed by Waladata, daughter of Mohammed Almostakfi Billah Khalif of Spain to some young men who had pretended a passion for her and her companions."

When you told us our glances, soft, timid, and
    mild,
Could occasion such wounds in the heart,
Can ye wonder that yours, so ungovern'd and
    wild,
Some wounds to our cheeks should impart?
The wounds on our cheeks, are but transient,
    I own,
With a blush they appear and decay;
But those of the heart, fickle youth, ye have
    shewn
To be even more transient than they.

THE DARK AGE. The Mongol Conquest of Baghdad (1258) closes an era. Though Mameluke poetry is known, the critics are hardly aware of the prolific activity of the 14th-19th c.; what is known appears severely conventionalized. Ar. ceased to be the language of the court and rulers after the extensive Turkish conquests, so patronage doubtless dwindled. It appears that aesthetic impulse was, to an increasing extent, satisfied by verse in one of the numerous Ar. vernaculars while classical composition became a sterile literary exercise. Men of letters often composed in near-classical Ar. known variously as Ḥumainī, Nabaṭī, or, in North Africa, as Malḥūn. In less conventional fields we find the versified shadow play, and the *Qaṣīd Abī Shādūf,* a satirical poem in "vulgar" Ar. on the fellahin of Lower Egypt. Peasants and tribesmen, as ever, composed verse necessary to their social occasions, though little was preserved until Europeans begun to collect it for scientific purposes, but their work has not influenced Arab letters.

THE RENAISSANCE. The 19th-c. impact of Western culture set up a process of ferment, though each country is affected in different degree even within itself. As modern literary movements are diffused over much of the world in journals and newspapers it is difficult to form a coherent picture of them, and older genres survive unaffected by new fashions. Particularly affected by the West are the Lebanese through contact with France and the Syro-Lebanese of the Americas—where al-Rābitah al-Qalamīyah (The Pen Club) was founded to infuse a new creative spirit into Ar. literature. Egypt's first great new poet is al-Bārūdī who studied ʿAbbāsid poets to revive classicism in Ar. verse. More celebrated is Ahmad Shawqī (1868–1932), called "The Prince of Poets." Of mixed racial origins, he is today regarded as the poet of the wealthy aristocracy. His contact with Fr. poetry while he was a student in Paris altered his whole outlook. Though a neoclassicist, his verse has an outstandingly lyric quality which has spread it far and wide, especially through the singers Umm Kulthūm and ʿAbd al-Wahhāb. From 1920 on he identified himself closely with Egypt, and some of his plays have a Pharaonic theme of a type still not unfashionable. Also outstanding is Hāfiz Ibrāhīm (d. 1932) following classical techniques.

Syrian by birth, the journalist Khalīl Mutrān experimented with rajaz and muwashshah. Meter and rhyme, he maintained, should be subservient to the theme. A poem should be considered as a whole, and the *mot juste* carefully selected. In the younger ʿAqqād and Abū Shādī, both acquainted with the West through the medium of Eng., he found response. To Abū Shādī and a modernist group in fact belongs the credit of founding a verse magazine *Apollo* (1932) which, if short-lived, had profound influence. Both Lebanon and Egypt were affected by the symbolist movement of France (studied by Antun Ghattas Karam, *al-Ramzīyah* [Beirut, 1949]), which has as its prominent Ar. exponent Bishr Fāris. Space permits no discussion of the latest trends in Egypt, and only the briefest reference to the many Syrian poets such as Khalīl Mardam Bey, or Sulaimān al-Bustānī, translator of the *Iliad* (1904), to the poets of the New World: Asʿad Rustum, Ilyā Abū Mādī, Jabrān Khalīl Jabrān; the great poets of Iraq's long political emergence al-Zahāwī and al-Rusāfī, and her younger poets and those of other Arab countries experimenting in free verse, without rhythm or meter, influenced by existentialist and other current philosophies. The origins of free verse (*al-shiʿr al-ḥurr*) with no rhyme or fixed meter can be traced back to the Apollo school of poetry; its exponents include Bayātī (Iraq), Nāzik al-Malāʾikah (Iraq), Yūsuf al-Khāl (Lebanon), Salāh ʿAbd al-Sabbūr (Egypt). Free verse is to be distinguished from blank verse (*al-shiʿr al-mursal*) of which ʿAbd al-Rahmān Shukrī (Egypt) is reckoned the first exponent. Though North African Arab poets are little known beyond their borders, the Tunisian Mahmūd al-Masʿadī has made a notable impression with his verse play *al-Sudd* the approach of which is much influenced by Jean

Paul Sartre's works. Nor can colloquial verse be neglected, for it flourishes in all Arab countries, and it too stems from an ancient tradition. Egyptian zajals and mawwāls are heard on the radio, and every country has famous colloquial poets. The Sudan, for instance, has its poets of the Mahdist era, such as Hārdallūh; Baghdad, the humorist al-Karkhī; South Arabia, its Yahyā ʿUmar; while a host of colloquial poets exist in North Africa little known elsewhere; the Persian Gulf and Saʿūdī Arabia have their own favorites. Egypt has begun to collect her colloquial verse in a new journal, *Folklore* (Cairo, 1959–).

The nature movement and nationalist, social, spiritual, and technical trends distinguished by recent authors in modern literary Ar. are mainly of occidental inspiration, for literati look to the West for novelty. Classical Ar. is securely and rightly enthroned in modern Ar., but the heritage of colloquial vocabulary and vigorous idiom could give it rich stimulus. When a new Ar. has been forged from these elements, we may perhaps look to a new era, but the present is an age of experiment.

The following selective bibliography is confined mainly to books in European languages, Eng. where possible. Since the appearance of Brockelmann's last *Supplement* many critical studies, in Ar., of ancient and modern poets have been published. J. D. Pearson's *Index Islamicus* and *Supplement* may be consulted for articles and reviews in Western periodicals; material in Arabic is far from so well served, but J. A. Dagher's two bio-bibliographies (listed below) are helpful.

GENERAL: *Encyclopaedia of Islam* (4 v. and suppl., 1913–38; 2d ed. 1954– ; Eng., Fr., and German ed.; subject-entries, *muwashshah*, *shiʿr*, etc.); J. D. Pearson, *Index Islamicus 1906–1955* (1958; pp. 710–711, 734–743, 746–749 *passim*), and *Supplement 1959–60* (1962; *passim*).

ANTHOLOGIES: *Specimens of Arabian Poetry*, ed. and tr. J. D. Carlyle (1796; elegant 18th c. renderings, perhaps not always accurate); *Arabian Poetry for Eng. Readers*, ed. W. A. Clouston (1881); *Anthol. of World Poetry*, ed. M. van Doren (1929; see pp. 61–95 for Ar. verse); *Ancient Arabian Poetry*, ed. C. J. Lyall (1930); *Modern Ar. Poetry*, ed. and tr. A. J. Arberry (1950; 19th- and 20th-c. verse from most Arab countries); *Moorish Poetry*, tr. A. J. Arberry (1953; tr. of Ibn Saʿīd's "Pennants"); *Al-Shiʿr al-ʿArabī fī l-Mahjar*, ed. Ihsān ʿAbbās and Muhammad Yūsuf Najm (Beirut, 1957; Ar. poets in America).

HISTORY AND CRITICISM: C. Brockelmann, *Gesch. der arabischen Lit.* (2 v., 2d ed., Leyden, 1943–49; 3 suppl. v., 1937–42; immense standard bibliog. of Ar. but difficult to consult for the nonexpert); R. A. Nicholson, *Lit. Hist.*

of the Arabs (2d ed., 1930; standard work); A. R. Nykl, *Hispano-Ar. Poetry and Its Relations with the old Prov. Troubadours* (1946; comprehensive, with full bibliog. in text); L. Veccia Vaglieri, "Notizie bio-bibliografiche su autori arabi moderni," *Annali dell' Instituto universitario orientale de Napoli*, I (1940); J. A. Dagher, *Maṣādir al-Dirāsat al-Adabīyah* (Ṣaidā; I, 1950, in progress); *Leaders in Ar. Moderń Lit.* (Beirut; I, 1956, in progress); H. A. R. Gibb, *Ar. Lit.* (2d rev. ed., 1963).

POETICS: Ibn Qoteiba, *Kitāb al-Shiʿr wa-ʾl-Shuʿarāʾ* (*Introduction au livre de la poésie et des poètes*, tr., introd., and commentary by M. Gaudefroy-Demombynes [1947]); A. Kh. Kinany, *The Development of the Gazal in Ar. Lit.* (Damascus, 1951); ʿAbdullāh al-Ṭaiyib al-Majdhūb, *Al-Murshid ilā Fahm Ashʿār al-ʿArab* (Cairo, 1955; important modern work of crit. of ancient Ar. verse); Amjad Trabulsi, *La Critique poétique des Arabes* (Damascus, 1956); W. Hoenerbach, *Die vulgärarabische . Poetik al-Kitāb al-ʿĀṭil al-Ḥālī wal-Muraḥḥaṣ al-Gālī des Ṣafīyaddīn Ḥillī* (Wiesbaden, 1956; development of postclassical verse forms). R.B.S.

ARAUCANIAN POETRY. See AMERICAN INDIAN POETRY. SOUTH AMERICA.

ARCADIAN ACADEMY (*Accademia dell' Arcadia*). An It. poetic association, organized in Rome in October 1690, by a group of poets and litterateurs who had frequented the Roman salon of Christina, former Queen of Sweden. The principal aim of the group was "to exterminate bad taste and see to it that it shall not rise again." In the early years of the association, the members devoted much energy to a systematic attack on marinism (q.v.), a poetic style which offended their sensibilities by its nonclassical tendencies toward the sensual and the sensational.

The dominant mode of Arcadian poetry was pastoral, and at their meetings the members often appeared in shepherd costume. Despite the sincerity of the Arcadians, and despite the real need for a movement toward simplicity in the poetry of the time, they produced little verse of true merit. Pietro Metastasio (1698–1782) was the only poet of distinction to emerge from the environs of Arcadia. He composed in all forms—lyric, pastoral, idyll, and the rest—but he is especially remembered for his opera libretti. Among the many minor poets of the Arcadia, Vincenzo da Filicaia (1642–1707) and Paolo Rolli (1687–1765) deserve special mention, Filicaia for a sonnet freely rendered in two stanzas of Byron's *Childe Harold's Pilgrimage,* and Rolli for his translation (1735) of *Paradise Lost* and for his defense of Milton and Tasso against their depreciation by Voltaire.

The Academy extended its influence through the establishment of "colonies" in various It. cities. Carlo Goldoni adorned the Arcadian academy of Pisa in the 1740's, shortly before producing his brilliant *Putta Onorata* and *Vedova Scaltra*. Leo XIII's (Gioacchino Pecci, 1810–1903) most interesting secular poem was an ode, lauding such poets as Metastasio, Parini, and Alfieri, and contributed to celebrate in 1890 the 200th anniversary of Arcadia.

The last volume of poems issued by the Academy appeared in 1780, but the organization itself remained in existence, being renamed, in 1925, the *Accademia Letteraria Italiana.*—C. Calcaterra, "Arcadia," *Dizionario Letterario Bompiani*, I (1947); K. Clark, *Landscape into Art* (1949); Wilkins; Van Wyck Brooks, *The Dream of Arcadia* (1958); A. Piromalli, *L'Arcadia* (1963). H.M.H.

ARCHAISM, as a feature of literary style, is especially associated with poetry and was originally connected with meter. It sometimes happened that the older form of a word had, by its different number of syllables, an advantage in a metrical context over its modern equivalent. Readers of Eng. poetry are familiar with such archaism, the best known instance being the option to treat such words as *loved, wished,* etc., as dissyllabic, according to the older practice. Archaic forms of some other words have been preserved for use in verse, e.g., the dissyllabic *marish* as an alternative to "marsh," and the monosyllabic *marge* in place of "margin." In certain languages, too, a select "poetic" body of words has been built up by tradition, since old expressions sometimes carry with them certain associations lost to the contemporary language. In Eng. the richest single source of such language is the King James Version of the Bible. A. has been a feature of much Eng. poetry since the time of Spenser's *Faerie Queene* in which old words are often used for the sake of their association with the chivalry and romances of the past. Milton, the most influential successor of Spenser, also drew on old language, though more sparingly. Since Spenser's time, archaisms such as *morn* for "morning" and *adown* for "down" have been so common in certain types of poetry that it is uncertain whether they have any association with the past or are simply a metrical convenience. Archaic language has sometimes been affected on a large scale, e.g., by the 18th-c. "Spenserians," by Coleridge, William Morris. Nor have archaic words ceased to be used today. In spite of the objection to a. expressed by some modern critics, it is certain that an old word is *le mot juste* in innumerable poetic contexts.—See T. Quayle, *Poetic Diction* (1924); B. R. McElderry Jr., "A. and Innovation in

ARCHETYPE

Spenser's Poetic Diction," PMLA, 47 (1932); O. Barfield, *Poetic Diction* (2d ed., 1952). B.G.

ARCHETYPE. Generally speaking, an a. is an original pattern from which copies are made or an idea of a class of things representing the most essentially characteristic elements shared by the members of that class. It is, in other words, a highly abstract category almost completely removed from the accidental varieties of elements contained in any particular species belonging to it. Thus, for example, the "Platonic" idea of a table would comprise a flat horizontal surface propped by vertical supports, and this is the a. of all tables everywhere when considered apart from their peculiar differences of size, height, material, shape, finish, and so on.

So, in poetry, an a. may be any idea, character, action, object, institution, event, or setting containing essential characteristics which are primitive, general, and universal rather than sophisticated, unique, and particular. This generality and universality may refer merely to similarities among various literary or subliterary works, as when scholars discover variants or analogues in time and place of certain types of legends and folk tales, or it may refer more broadly to similarities found outside of literary works, as when critics seek comparisons to things found in a poem among myths, dreams, and rituals. In the case of *Hamlet*, for example, one could either construct an a. of the revenge play on the basis of similarities found between Shakespeare's play and other revenge plays, or fashion an a. of the Oedipal situation on the basis of the similarities found between Shakespeare's play, myths, legends, folk tales, and anthropological and psychological literature. The former method tends to be more direct, as when one studies a series of hero stories and tabulates the characteristics which they share in common, while the latter method tends to be more tenuous, as when one tries to construct hypotheses to interpret the meaning of such recurrences in terms of the racial unconscious, the ritual origins of poetry, the diffusions of culture, or whatever. Needless to say, these methods may overlap.

Either way, when one speaks of archetypes in poetry one usually refers to basic, general, or universal patterns (cf. IMAGERY) of one sort or another: birth, coming of age, love, guilt, redemption, and death are archetypal subjects; the conflict between reason and imagination, free will and destiny, appearance and reality, the individual and society, and so on, are archetypal themes; the tension between parents and children, the rivalry among brothers, the problems of incestuous desire, the search for the father, the ambivalence of the male-female relationship, the young man from the country arriving for the first time in the city, and so on, are archetypal situations; the braggart, the buffoon, the hero, the devil, the rebel, the wanderer, the siren, the enchantress, the maid, the witch, and so on, are archetypal characters; and certain animals, birds, and natural phenomena and settings are archetypal images. Any of these elements in a poem, either alone or in some combination, when treated in such a way as to bring forth its general and universal attributes, forms an archetypal pattern or patterns.

Historically, the archetypal approach seems to have derived around the turn of the century from two sources: (1) the Cambridge school of comparative anthropology issuing from Sir J. G. Frazer (*The Golden Bough* [1890–1915]), and including, loosely speaking, Gilbert Murray, Jane E. Harrison, Jessie L. Weston, S. H. Hooke, Lord Raglan, E. M. Butler, and Theodor H. Gaster; and (2) the psychology of C. G. Jung (*Psychology of the Unconscious: A Study of the Transformations and Symbolisms of the Libido* [1916]) and, to a lesser extent, that of Sigmund Freud (see, for example, "Symbolism in Dreams" [1915–17], *A General Introduction to Psychoanalysis* [1920]), and including the further work in the psychology of ritual and myth of Theodor Reik, Otto Rank, Erich Fromm, and so on. The combination of comparative anthropology with depth psychology (in conjunction with certain ideas of Cassirer regarding the origins of language) has resulted in the following series of hypothetical arguments for the interpretation of literature: since dreams, myths, and rituals are basically disguised, indirect, and nonutilitarian ways of fulfilling universal emotional needs and resolving universal human problems, and since a symbol is a disguised, indirect, and nonutilitarian way of saying or doing one thing while intending another, therefore dreams, myths, and rituals are symbolic; if dreams, myths, and rituals are symbolic ways of fulfilling universal emotional needs and resolving universal human problems, and if an a. derives from what dreams, myths, and rituals share in common, then an a. is a universal symbol; and if an a. is a universal symbol, and if a given pattern in a poem is archetypal, then it too is a universal symbol (cf. MYTH).

Thus, according to Jung, "The primordial image or archetype is a figure, whether it be a daemon, man, or process, that repeats itself in the course of history wherever creative phantasy is freely manifested. Essentially, therefore, it is a mythological figure. If we subject these images to a closer examination, we discover them to be the formulated resultants of countless typical experiences of our ancestors. They are, as it were, the psychic residue of numberless experiences of the same type." A poet using archetypes, he continues, speaks in a voice stronger than his own: "he raises the idea he is trying to express above the occasional and the transitory into the sphere of the ever-existing. He transmutes personal destiny into the destiny of mankind. . . . That is the secret of effective art" (*Contributions*). Such contemporary critics as Knight, Bodkin, Bachelard, Chase, Campbell, Frye, and Auden have worked out, each in his own way, the implications of these assumptions, or similar ones, for the study of Shakespeare, Blake, Yeats, Wordsworth, Poe, Coleridge, Milton, and so on. So Bodkin can claim, "I shall use the term 'archetypal pattern' to refer to that within us which, in Gilbert Murray's phrase, leaps in response to the effective presentation in poetry of an ancient theme. The hypothesis to be examined is that in poetry . . . we may identify themes having a particular form or pattern which persists amid variation from age to age, and which corresponds to a pattern or configuration of emotional tendencies in the minds of those who are stirred by the theme" (*Archetypal Patterns in Poetry*). And so Frye can say, "By archetype I mean an element in a work of literature, whether a character, an image, a narrative formula, or an idea, which can be assimilated into a larger unifying category" ("Blake's Treatment of the Archetype").

An approach which looks in poetry for echoes and reenactments of ancient and ubiquitous patterns—for (in the words of Thomas Mann) a "mythical identification, as survival, as a treading in footprints already made"—finds general types implicit in the specific elements of a given poem, and then interprets those types as symbols of human desires, conflicts, and problems. It thus emerges as a kind of symbolic approach (cf. SYMBOL). One may trace the image of "The Descent into Hell," for example, from early myth and ritual, to Homer, Virgil, Medieval Romance, Dante, and up to Hart Crane's subway section of *The Bridge* and to T. S. Eliot's *The Hollow Men*, and then interpret it as an a. symbolizing the encounter with one's own repressed guilt. It will be observed further that such mythical identification need not depend upon the explicit and conscious presence in a work of actual names, places, and events from mythology—the procedure rests rather upon finding more or less unconscious similarities and resemblances.

An archetypal symbology may be reconstructed, then, based upon the parallels which exist between the cycles of human life and those of the external world, and the patterns which these parallels have caused to appear in myth, ritual, dream, and poetry: "In the solar cycle of the day," says Frye, "the seasonal cycles of the year, and the organic cycle of human life, there is a single pattern of significance, out of which myth constructs a central narrative around a figure who is partly the sun, partly vegetative fertility and partly a god or archetypal human being" ("The Archetypes of Literature").

On the other hand, many critics (see Block and Douglas, for example) have questioned the soundness of the theory and/or of the practice of the archetypal approach. In the first place, many poems contain symbols which are primarily personal, and to interpret them archetypally is to overread them, if not to misread them altogether. Secondly, even if a poem does contain universal symbols, they may not symbolize those kinds of depth-meanings which archetypal critics are looking for. Thirdly, this approach, in emphasizing the universal and general, tends to be reductive in its view of particular and unique works of art; it is an approach which simplifies a complex thing, and while it is capable of yielding exciting and valuable results, it tends to blur the essential distinctions, as Jung, for example, frequently does (although he is against the genetic fallacy in theory), between good poems and bad ones. Finally, anthropological and psychological specialists, especially of the American pragmatic school (A. Irving Hallowell and Margaret Mead, for example), have been issuing repeated warnings that no two cultures are actually alike and that therefore it is dangerous if not false to seek parallels between European rituals and those of Africa, India, and the South Sea Islands.

Thus, while comparative and archetypal studies of poetry have an obvious value in helping the reader to see and perhaps interpret symbolically real and important resemblances among many different works, it is essential to recognize that such studies often rest upon assumptions and hypotheses whose validity and utility need continual reexamination.

C. G. Jung, "On the Relation of Analytical Psychology to Poetic Art" (1922), *Contributions to Analytical Psychology,* tr. H. G. and C. F. Baynes (1928); C. G. Jung, "The Problem of Types in Poetry," *Psychological Types,* tr. H. G. Baynes (1923); G. W. Knight, *The Christian Renaissance* (1933); M. Bodkin, *Archetypal Patterns in Poetry* (1934); T. Mann, "Freud and the Future," *Freud, Goethe, Wagner,* tr. H. T. Lowe-Porter (1939); E. Cassirer, *Language and Myth,* tr. S. K. Langer (1946); G. Bachelard, *La Terre et les Rêveries du Repos* (1948); R. Chase, *Quest for Myth* (1949); J. Campbell, *The Hero with a Thousand Faces* (1949); N. Frye, "Levels of Meaning in Lit.," KR, 12 (1950) and "Blake's Treatment of the A.," *EIE 1950* (1951); W. H. Auden, *The En-*

ARCHILOCHIAN

ARCHILOCHIAN

chafed Flood (1950); N. Frye, "The Archetypes of Lit.," KR, 13 (1951) and *Anatomy of Crit.* (1957); H. M. Block, "Cultural Anthropology and Contemp. Lit. Crit.," JAAC, 11 (1952); W. W. Douglas, "The Meanings of 'Myth' in Modern Crit.," MP, 50 (1953); *Lit. Symbolism*, ed. M. Beebe (1960); *Myth and Mythmaking*, ed. H. A. Murray (1960); *Symbolism in Religion and Lit.*, ed. R. May (1960); B. Seward, *The Symbolic Rose* (1960); P. Wheelwright, *Metaphor and Reality* (1962); *Myth and Symbol*, ed. B. Slote (1963).　　　N.FRIE.

ARCHILOCHIAN. Archilochus of Paros (8th or 7th c. B.C.) was said to have been the inventor of *metra episyntheta* (lines or couplets in which different meters or metrical cola were combined). The following Archilochian systems of couplets were used by Horace in his *Odes* and *Epodes:* (1) dactylic hexameter and dactylic tripody catalectic *in syllabam* (*hemiepes* [q.v.]), as in *Odes* 4.7; (2) dactylic hexameter and iambelegus, as in *Epode* 13; (3) iambic trimeter and elegiambus, as in *Epode* 11; (4) *versus Archilochius* and iambic trimeter catalectic, as in *Odes* 1.4. The *versus Archilochius* was a dactylic tetrameter (the fourth foot of which, in Horace but not in Gr. verse, was consistently a dactyl and not a spondee) together with an ithyphallic, e.g.

solvitur acris hiems grata vice | veris et Favoni
(*Odes* 1.4.1)

Kolář; B. Snell, *Griechische Metrik* (2d ed., 1957).　　　R.J.G.

AREOPAGUS. The names applied by some literary historians to a conjectural literary group or club active in London in the 1580's. Douglas Bush, among others, has rejected all references to the A. as "stubborn myths" (CL, 7 [1955], 284), and it is certain that no firm evidence for its existence has ever been presented. Still it is true that a group of Elizabethan poets and critics—Sidney, Spenser, Gabriel Harvey, Sir Edward Dyer—were interested in reforming Eng. verse in the direction of classical quantitative prosody, and their common interests may conceivably have led them to organize into a group analogous to the Fr. *Pléiade* (q.v.). Formally organized or not, the common pursuit of the classical meters was short-lived. The autocratic Harvey retained his belief that rhyme and accentual verse were barbarisms, but the great poets, Sidney and Spenser, went on to develop Eng. verse on It., Fr., and native models, stabilizing the principles of rhyme and accent in *The Faerie Queene* and *Astrophel and Stella*.　　　L.B.P.

ARGENTINE POETRY. See SPANISH AMERICAN POETRY.

ARGUMENT has several senses in literary criticism. Loosely used, it can mean "plot." This meaning is sanctioned by classical usage (e.g., Terence: *argumentum fabulae,* the plot of the story) and is common during the Renaissance. It can also refer to the individual debates and logical reasoning which an author must often use in narrative or dramatic poetry (e.g., Portia's defense of Antonio in *The Merchant of Venice,* or the debate of the fallen angels in *Paradise Lost*). But the commonest modern meaning, and the most important, is that of the logical structure of a poem: the framework which would be common both to the poem and to a paraphrase of it. Must a poem have an argument, in this sense? Has its a. much—or anything—to do with its value? Renaissance poetry was written in a tradition which linked poetry with logic, spoke about the "cause" of a poem, and considered details (the images of a lyric, the scenes of a play) in relation to their logical function. In contrast to this is the symbolist view, which sees the value of poetry as lying in those elements which it does not share with prose: the logical (or narrative) structure of a poem can be dispensed with, and this seems to be done in such poems as Mallarmé's *L'Après-midi d'un Faune* or Valéry's *La Jeune Parque* (though not in all Valéry). No logical thread links the images of these poems. Wallace Stevens, T. S. Eliot, Hart Crane, are all at least partly in this tradition.

A rather different antilogical tradition runs from Rimbaud to the surrealists and much of Dylan Thomas: here the brute juxtaposition of imagery is the result not of a careful act of poetic construction, but a direct expression of the unconscious. A modified symbolist theory is found in the criticism (perhaps not in the poetry) of John Crowe Ransom, who values the a., but insists that it exists for the sake of the poem, not the reverse: texture is more important, poetically, than structure. An attempt has been made, notably by Eliot, to see in the metaphysical poets an anticipation of this modern alogical poetry. This is hotly contested by Rosamund Tuve, who bases her a. on Elizabethan critical documents, which she treats with rather more respect than is common. She sees the finding of images as an application of the Aristotelian predicaments, and points out that a great deal which seems "alogical" may be an example of the figure catachresis, the desperate metaphor. This comment of course can be applied to modern as well as metaphysical poetry.

There seem to be three possible conclusions: that a. is unnecessary; that it is important mainly as a sop to the reader, to enable true poetic response to take place; that it is sometimes (always?) part of a poem's true value. It

-[50]-

would not be possible to claim that it was the whole of this value without maintaining that the paraphrase was worth as much as the poem. The first view is the symbolist theory. The second is implicit in some romantic criticism ("word-magic"), and is likely to be held, more or less articulately, by modern admirers of romantic poetry (e.g., Housman). The perfect illustration of it would be a poem like *Kubla Khan*. The third is the traditional view, and in modified form is still common among critics, and almost universal among readers.— P. Valéry, "Avant-propos à la Connaissance de la Déesse," *Variété*, I (1924), "Au Sujet du Cimetière Marin," *Variété*, II (1929), "Questions de Poésie," *Variété*, III (1936); T. S. Eliot, "The Metaphysical Poets," *Selected Essays* (1932); A. E. Housman, *The Name and Nature of Poetry* (1935); J. C. Ransom, *The World's Body* (1938) and "The Bases of Crit.," SR, 52 (1944); Tuve; D. Davie, *Articulate Energy* (1955; discusses symbolist theory, and pleads for "authentic" syntax). L.D.L.

ARMENIAN POETRY. On tablelands south of the Black Sea and the Caucasus Mountains lies ancient Armenia. Its people are the blend of the indigenous stock and the Eastern-migrating Indo-Europeans nine centuries before Christ. Its legendary origin, 1,000 years earlier, identifies patriarch Haïc, great-grandson of Noah, whence the name, in Arm., Haïastan, and the people, Haï. It lies as a frontier between the Moslem East and the Christian West, an important factor in the development of its history and culture. Almost from the beginning a battleground of foreign nations, the territory and the frontiers of historical Armenia have varied greatly throughout the centuries, and what is known today as Armenia—one of the Soviet republics—is only a small part of the ancient country. Under the political domination of many powers, from the Persians in the 6th c. B.C. to the yoke of the Turks and Russians in the 19th and 20th c., Armenia has nevertheless preserved its cultural integrity to this day.

Arm. poetry in its earliest form, the ballad, reflects the dual influence, displaying Eastern iridescence and brilliance with Western restraint and symmetry. Unfortunately, most of the ancient, pre-Christian poetry, which included also hymns and epics, was destroyed when Christianity was adopted in Armenia in A.D. 301. Only some fragments of epics, legends, and songs have survived—collected by Movses of Chorene, 5th-c. Arm. historian, and preserved in his *History of Armenia*. One of the fragments describes, in free verse, the birth of Vahagn, Arm. god of war:

Yercner yercin yev yercir
Yercner yev tzirani tzov
Yercn i tzovoun ouner zcarmric yeghegnicn
. . . .

Heaven and earth were in labor,
The purple sea also labored.
The sea in labor bore a red reed.
From the reed rose smoke,
From the reed rose flame,
And from the flame a young lad sprang.
He had hair of fire,
His beard was of flame,
And his eyes were as the rays of the sun.

The 9th-c. epic of David of Sassoun is lost, but the 19th-c. poet Thoumanian immortalized the hero's struggle against the Arab invader.

The 4th-c. adoption of Christianity presaged the 5th-c. creation of the alphabet of 36 letters by St. Mesrob, introducing a Golden Age of literature with the translation of the Bible and the compositions of the *sharacans* (rows of gems), which are chants and hymns. Written in free or metrical verse, the *sharacans* are the unique property of the Arm. church and the main material in song and chant of its services, with themes of creed, history, the Bible, the life of Christ, the saints, etc. While most *sharacans* were composed in the 5th and 7th c., they continued to be written until the 15th c. Of the score of important later *sharacan* writers the poetess Sahakaduk (8th c.) and Nerses Clayetsi (12th c.) stand out in the poetical quality of their work. Lyric poetry continued to predominate through the following centuries. The 7th c. saw the mystic poetry of Catholicos Comitas (d. 628) and Stephanos Siunetsi. In the 10th c. the great mystic poet St. Grigor Narecatsi (951–1009), called the Pindar of Armenia, wrote his odes, elegies and panegyrics.

The so-called Silver Age of literature (12th-13th c.) witnessed a revival of learning and a new surge of poetical creation. Nerses Clayetsi (1100–1173), mentioned for his *sharacans*, wrote also elegies and narrative poems and left a voluminous body of verse. Other outstanding poets were three ecclesiastics: Constantine Erzincatsi (b. about 1250), Hovhannes Erzincatsi, and Khachatour Cecharetsi (d. about 1330), who wrote under the pen name of Fric. The work of Constantine Erzincatsi and Fric shows Arabic and Persian influences in its sensual mysticism. (Another earlier instance of Arabic influence was the introduction of rhyme in Arm. verse.) With the beginning of the Silver Age a new spirit entered Arm. poetry, and poets once again wrote about nature, valor, love, and beauty—themes which had, since the 5th c., been shunted in favor of hymns and other religious poems. This new spirit can be seen in the poetry of Constantine Erzincatsi and, later, that of Hovhannes Tulkourantsi (1450–1525) and Nahapet Kouchac (16th c.). It is also evident in the popular poetry of the minstrels (*ashough*), which enjoyed great favor. The best known of these was Sayat-Nova (1712–95), whose love songs are famous.

About the middle of the 19th c. a new literary language came into being. Writers and poets began to abandon classical Arm. (except for religious works) and wrote their stories and poems in modern Arm., which differs considerably in grammar but less so in vocabulary from the ancient language. With the division of the country into Rus. and Turkish Armenia two dialects developed: the Western in Turkish Armenia, Anatolia, Constantinople, and Europe, and the Eastern in Rus. Armenia. In both dialects the poets continued to sing of the sadness of the people, their love of homeland, their longing for national freedom. Coming into contact with the European literary tradition, the Arm. poets of the 19th and 20th c. have been influenced in the West by Fr. and It. writers and in the East by German and Rus. schools. Of those writing in the Western dialect, the short-lived Petros Dourian (1851–72) should be mentioned and his brother, the Patriarch Egishé (1860–1930), a master of the language. Among more recent poets Vahan Thekeian (1877–1945) is outstanding, especially by European standards. Two fine lyricists are Daniel Varouzhan (1884–1915) and Atom Yarjanian (Siamantho; d. 1915). Of those writing in the eastern dialect, Khachatour Abovian (1804–48) will be remembered as the founder of modern Arm. literature. Raphael Patcanian and Hovhannes Hovhannesian were leading lyric poets and Hovhannes Thoumanian (1869–1922) the best epic poet. In the Arm. Soviet Republic (since 1920) Avetik Isahakian (1875–1957) must be considered the most important Arm. poet and his great poem *Abou Lala Mahari* perhaps his most significant work. Of the younger generation Gegham Sarian and Gourgen Mahari deserve special mention. There is no dearth of talented poets, but they are subjected to the dictates of socialist realism. A more integral part of the Arm. cultural heritage is the emigré poetry of the first third of the 20th c., a continuation of the Western Arm. literature, which once flourished in Turkish Armenia whence thousands of Armenians fled following the massacres in 1915 and earlier. Especially in three large centers: France (Arshak Tchobanian), the Middle East (M. Ishkan and Andranic Dzaroukian), and the United States (Lootfi Minas) the poetic spirit of Armenia lives on.

COLLECTIONS AND ANTHOLOGIES: *Tonal (Tzaynigh) Sharacan* (Arm. ed., Jerusalem, 1914); *rder of the Services of the Arm. Church* (Arm. ed., Jerusalem, 1915); *Les Trouvères arméniens*, ed. and tr. A. Tchobanian (2d ed., 1906); *Arm. Legends and Poems*, ed., Z. C. Boyajian (1916, repr. 1959); *Arm. Poems Rendered into Eng. Verse*, ed. A. S. Blackwell (1917); *Anthologie des poètes arméniens*, ed. A. Navarian (1928).

HISTORY AND CRITICISM: M. Matindjiane, "Etude sur la poésie populaire arménienne" (Paris, 1907; diss.); Z. C. Boyajian, "Arm. and Eng. Poetry: Some Parallels," *Contemporary Rev.*, 119 (1922); E. Arch. Dourian, *The Hist. of Arm. Lit.* (Arm. ed., Jerusalem, 1933); A. Zaminian, *The Hist. of the Early Lit. of Armenia* (Arm. ed., Beirut, 1941); *The Hist. of Arm. Lit., Part I. From the Beginning to 1700*, ed. Mekhitharist (Arm. ed., Venice, 1944); R. Grousset, *Hist. de l'Arménie des origines à 1071* (1947); V. Brussov, "The Poetry of Armenia," tr. A. S. Avakian, *The Arm. Rev.*, I (1948); M. V. Janashian, *Hist of Arm. Modern Lit.* (Venice, 1953); K. Mekhitarian, "Quarter Century of Arm. Lit. Abroad," BA, 30 (1956).

See also: H. Thorossian, *Hist. de la littérature arménienne . . .* (1951); S. Soghomonian, *A Few Questions on Modern Poetry* (Arm. ed., Erevan, 1960). A.A.

ARSIS AND THESIS (Gr. "lifting up" and "setting down"). Corresponding to the "rise" and "fall" of the foot in the march or dance, these terms meant respectively the upward and downward beat in keeping time to the enunciation of Gr. verse. Thus the long syllable, on which the beat naturally fell, of a simple metrical foot like the dactyl ($-\smile\smile$), anapaest ($\smile\smile-$), trochee ($-\smile$), or iambus ($\smile-$) in meters based on them was regarded as the t. and the remainder of the foot as the a. In the later Roman period a. for a time referred to the first part of a foot and t. to the second, but the grammarians came to think of the raising and lowering of the voice rather than the upward and downward beat, so that the original application of a. and t. among the Greeks was reversed and a. denoted the basically long syllable and t. the rest of the foot. The authority of Richard Bentley (1662–1742) and Gottfried Hermann (1772–1848) has made this meaning of the two words usual, but not universal, in modern works on Gr. and L. meter.—J. Caesar, *Disputatio de verborum "arsis" et "thesis" apud scriptores artis metricae latinos . . . significatione* (1885); E. H. Sturtevant, "The Ictus of Cl. Verse," AJP, 44 (1923); Hardie; Dale; Koster; Crusius; Bearc. R.J.G.

ART FOR ART'S SAKE. See AESTHETICISM; POETRY, THEORIES OF (OBJECTIVE THEORIES).

ARTE MAYOR. As a general Sp. metric term a.m. may mean any line of 9 or more syllables.

However, a.m. almost always refers to a line of a certain pattern or to the strophe composed of such lines. The late medieval poets borrowed the a.m. directly from the Galician-Portuguese of the 13th and 14th c. The form reached the peak of its development in 15th-c. Sp. poetry and gave way to the Italianate hendecasyllable in the 16th, since which time it has occupied only a minor position in Sp. poetry. Juan de Mena (1411–56) is considered its greatest master. A recitative measure, it was the vehicle for most poetry of weighty or serious subject matter of the 15th c. Unlike most learned Sp. verse, the a.m. was not restricted by syllable count, but depended largely on rhythmic beat. The basic pattern was a 12-beat verse divided into 2 hemistichs of 6 beats each and having triple rhythm, thus:

The primary (´) and secondary (˝) stress beats (the latter occasionally lacking) of each hemistich are supplied by accented syllables; the unstressed beats between these two are supplied by 2 obligatory unaccented syllables; the remaining unstressed beats may each be supplied by 1 or 2 unaccented syllables or a rest beat. The pattern was not always strictly followed. The a.m. was normally arranged in groups of 8 lines to form a stanza called *copla de a.m.*, rhyming abbaacca, less often ababbccb or abbaacac. Although the original a.m. enjoyed great rhythmic and syllabic freedom, the line in later centuries became primarily a 12-syllable or a 6-plus-6-syllable verse with marked amphibrachic rhythm.—R. Foulché-Delbosc, "Etude sur le *Laberinto* de Juan de Mena," *Revue Hispanique*, 9 (1902); J. Saavedra Molina, *El verso de a.m.* (1946); P. Le Gentil, *La Poésie lyrique espagnole et portugaise à la fin du moyen âge. 2ᵉ partie. Les formes* (1953); Navarro; D. C. Clarke, *Morphology of 15th C. Castilian Verse* (1964). D.C.C.

ARTE MENOR. Sp. octosyllabic, sometimes shorter, verse. The term is used in contrast to *arte mayor* and is generally applied to the verse characteristic of the *copla de arte menor*, a late medieval stanza having the rhyme scheme of any *copla de arte mayor* or variation thereof (see ARTE MAYOR). Both line and strophe were probably borrowed from the 13th- and 14th-c. Galician-Portuguese.—D. C. Clarke, "*Redondilla* and *copla de a.m.*," HR, 9 (1941); Navarro. D.C.C.

ARZAMAS. A Rus. literary discussion circle which met between 1815 and 1818. Its members, partisans of the elegant, Westernized style of Nikolai Karamzin, included the poets Zhukovski, Batyushkov, Vyazemski, and, most important, Alexander Pushkin. The chief business of the group was the reading of parodies of the conservative Slavonicized style of their opponents, the followers of Admiral Shishkov. The circle was significant for the role it played in fostering the "golden age" of Rus. poetry, which came in the 1820's.—E. A. Sidorov, "Literaturnoe obshchestvo 'Arzamas,'" *Zhurnal Ministerstva Narodnogo Prosveshcheniya*, 6–7 (1901). W.E.H.

ASCENDING RHYTHM (rising rhythm). The rhythm of lines written predominantly in iambic or anapestic feet. The most frequent kind of rhythm in Eng. poetry, a.r. is so called because the reader or hearer is presumed to feel, in each foot (q.v.), an "ascent" from a relatively unstressed syllable to a relatively stressed one. The term is of dubious usefulness, and it may lead to confusion and pedantry unless one remembers that it has no metaphoric or symbolic value whatever: a.r. does not, in itself, transmit a feeling of aspiration, elevation, levity, or cheer. Consider:

The stricken warrior sank to earth.

See DESCENDING RHYTHM.—H. L. Creek, "Rising and Falling Rhythm in Eng. Verse," PMLA, 35 (1920); G. R. Stewart, *The Technique of Eng. Verse* (1930). P.F.

ASCLEPIAD. A meter named after the poet Asclepiades of Samos (ca. 290 B.C.). Whereas the glyconic (q.v.) had 1 choriamb, i.e. the central foot of $\_\_|\smile\smile\smile|\_\_$, the lesser a. had 2 and the greater a. 3. Diaeresis usually occurred between the choriambs, e.g.

Maece|nas ătăvīs||edīte re|gībus
(Horace, *Odes* 1.1.1.)

tū nē|quaesīeris,||scīre nĕfas,||quēm mīhī,

quēm|tĭbī
(ibid. 1.11.1)

The a. was used long before the time of the poet who gave it his name, not only in monodic and choral lyric but also in tragedy. It is very common in Horace who employs five types of asclepiadean strophes.—H. Sądej, "De versu Asclepiadeo minore apud Romanos obvio," *Eos*, 45 (1951); Koster; L. Rotsch, "Zur Form der drei Horaz-Oden im Asclepiadeus maior (1.11; 1.18; 4.10)," *Gymnasium*, 64 (1957); A. R. Bellinger, "The Lesser Asclepiadean Line of Horace," YCS, 15 (1957). R.J.G.

ASSAMESE POETRY. See INDIAN POETRY.

ASSONANCE, sometimes called "vocalic rhyme," denotes vowel identity in the tonic

ASSONANCE

syllables, sometimes supported by the same device in the succeeding unstressed syllables, of words whose consonants differ or, if partly the same, avoid creating rhyme (grave / fate; votive / notice; glory / holy) and which (1) echo each other in the same line or in different portions of a poem, or which (2) appear at the end of successive or alternating lines.

The first type (internal a.) is used exclusively for stylistic effect and often occurs in combination with alliteration and consonance (qq.v.) producing elaborate sound textures (see also SOUND IN POETRY and TONE COLOR). To be noticeable, at least the first two assonances in a sequence must be in close proximity, or in the first and last words of a line. Internal a. is characteristic of poetry in any language. Thomas Gray: "Along the heath and near his favorite tree"; George Herbert: "Onely take this gentle rose." Thomas Hardy's *The Voice* has an assonantal pattern on "u," woven through the whole poem. Baudelaire: "Le gouffre a toujours soif; la clepsydre se vide." Goethe has many subtle internal assonances; for rhyme pair assonances echoing the internal ones see his *An die Entfernte*. Rilke is especially fond of assonances on *a* and *ei* (e.g., *Duineser Elegien* 2. 41–42; 10. 1–5, 73). For an interwoven pattern of alliteration and a. see Shakespeare's Sonnet 12; cf. also Marianne Moore's *Spenser's Ireland*.

The second type represents a device for linking lines or line parts. It is not used by poets of the Eng. language as a deliberate device, except very occasionally (e.g., Marianne Moore: ". . . swiftness / . . . crevices" in *The Fish*). Sometimes an a. has to make up for the lack of a pure rhyme (e.g., the only two certain examples of impure rhyme in Shakespeare's Sonnets: "open / broken," 61.1–3, and "remember'd / tender'd," 120.9–11). In popular verse and folk song ("And pray who gave you that jolly red nose? / Cinnamon, Ginger, Nutmeg, and Cloves") a. appears as the result of "carelessness or blunted ear" (Edmund Gosse). In classical L. Virgil, Cicero, and especially Catullus made subtle use of a. as an alternative to rhyme while in ancient Gr. poetry vocalic rhyme echoes were used effectively within lines (e.g. *Iliad* 1.406). In late Vulgar L. and early romance poetry final a. is part of the verse structure and links contiguous lines of indefinite number. The Sp. romances have up to 50 or 60 lines of *rimas asonantes* with the same a., which never becomes tedious because of the rich vocality of the language. (Note the endless variety of words with *i-a* or *i-o* in the last two syllables). Both the tonic penultimate and the ultimate are in a. Successful use of a. in modern Sp. poetry includes a. on either the ultimate or the penultimate alone (Már-

mol, Bécquer) and mere vocalic analogies, as *e/i* and *o/u* (Martinez de la Rosa). In Rubén Darío's *Sinfonía en gris mayor* lines 2 and 4 of all 8 stanzas are in a. Semivowels *i(y)* and *w(u)* preceding a vowel do not destroy the a. (e.g., "universo / . . . ingenuo" or "Fulgencio / . . . esto"). A. is also used in the Sp. drama (Calderón, Antonio Hurtado, etc.).

The early OF *chansons de geste* have a. in place of rhyme. The assonant line groups are called *laisses* or *tirades* and vary greatly in number; in the *Chanson de Roland* the average *laisse* has 14 lines. A. takes place only between final syllables of the same category (i.e., masculine or feminine). In modern Fr. poetry Charles Guérin's attempt to reintroduce a. in place of rhyme in *Le sang des crépuscules* (1895) has found no imitators.

In Ir. poetry, rhyme includes an elaborate system of assonances (called "amus"), since *g-b-d*, *c-p-t*, or *ch-ph-th* are allowed to "rhyme."

Middle High German poetry uses a. often (but nowhere exclusively) instead of, or intermingled with, rhyme (e.g., in the *Graf Rudolf* fragments 15 per cent of the rhymes are thus "impure"). The German *Volkslied* uses a. occasionally, when at a loss for a rhyme. The attempts of the German romantic poets to reintroduce a. in place of rhyme into German poetry in their translations from the Sp. (the brothers Schlegel) and in their own romances and dramas (Tieck, Arnim, Heine) are *tours de force* rather than genuine artistic successes, since New High German, with its prevalence of the *shva*-sound in final syllables, cannot produce sufficiently strong word echoes without the aid of consonance. Modern poets occasionally use a. with great effect, e.g., Stefan George in *Verschollen des traumes* . . . where identical rhyme is regularly interlaced with a. and in *Der Widerchrist* where assonances tellingly deviate "by a hair's breadth" from full rhyme, just as do the works of the Antichrist from Christ's.

A. W. Schlegel, *Briefe an Tieck*, ed. K. v. Holtei, III (1864), 275ff.; F. Brunetière, "A.," *La Grande encyclopédie* (1886); J. Minor, *Neuhochdeutsche Metrik* (2d ed., 1902); M. Méndez y Bejarano, *La ciencia del verso* (1908); W. Masing, *Sprachliche Musik in Goethes Lyrik* (1910); E. Gosse, "A.," *Ency. Britannica* (11th ed., 1911); A. Fischli, *Über Klangmittel im Versinnern* (1920); P. Habermann, "Assonanz," *Reallexikon*, I; E. Rickert, *New Methods for the Study of Lit.* (1927); L. P. Thomas, *Le Vers moderne* (1943); N. I. Heresu, *La Poésie latine: Étude des structures phoniques* (1960); W. Kayser, *Gesch. des deutschen Verses* (1960); C. C. Smith, "La musicalidad del Polifemo," RFE, 44 (1961).   U.K.G.

ASSYRO-BABYLONIAN POETRY. Babyl. literature flourished in the 2d millennium, and Assyrian from 1500 to 600 B.C.; the Neo-Babyl. period (625–538 B.C.) did not produce significant poetry. Written in cuneiform characters of Sumerian origin, on clay tablets, the poetic texts of Babylonia and Assyria hardly differed at all from each other, although the two spoken dialects differed almost as much as the vernaculars of London and New York. The language is East Semitic.

The meter of Semitic verses is identical to the Sumerian: usually the two halves of a verse have 4 stress accents each; for instance the Creation Poem (*enuma elîš*) begins as follows:

enuma elis la nabu samamu

saplis ammatum suma la zakrat . . . .

When on high the heavens had not been named,
Below the earth's surface had not been called by name . . .

The 2 hemistichs, as here, are usually in parallelism, as is also the case in Sumerian and ancient Near Eastern poetry in general. New in Babyl.-Assyr. poetry of later periods is the use of acrostics, not alphabetic acrostics as in the Hebrew Bible (Psalms 25, 34, 37, 119; Proverbs 31:10–31; Lamentations 1–4, etc.) but forming names and sentences, as "For Janneus A. and his wife." Other acrostics have the word "Nabu" (the god Nebo), or the sentence, "I am Ashurbanipal who invoked thee: grant me life, O Marduk, and I will pay thee thy homage." One poet even repeats the same syllable of the acrostic at the beginning and end of the 4 verses in each stanza, producing a sort of rhyme.

The hymns and prayers used in the Babyl.-Assyr. worship are slightly revised versions from the Sumerian; their diction is so conventional that with hardly a change they could be used for another deity. We have hymns in honor of Anu, Enlil (some of which were later addressed to Marduk in Babylonia and to Ashshur in Assyria), Ninurta, Nabu (we have an antiphonal prayer of Ashurbanipal, with replies of Nabu), the fire gods (Gibil, Nusku, and Gira), and the goddess Ishtar; numerous hymns are addressed to the moon god Sin, the sun god Shamash, and the dying vegetation god Tammuz (Adonis).

Some of the mythological epics were used liturgically in the worship, notably the *Creation Epic* (*enuma elîš*) sung in Babylon to honor Marduk on the fourth day of the New Year festival (4 Nisan, about March 24). It begins with a genealogy of the gods and continues with the attack of the monsters of chaos against the gods, Marduk's victory over Tiamat (the primeval mother who led the monsters), the making of heaven and earth out of the two halves of her body, Marduk's organization of the world and his exaltation among the gods. In the extant Babyl. edition of this poem, Marduk usurps the original place of Enlil. The poem of *Ishtar's Descent to the Nether World*, presumably to bring back to earth her lover Tammuz, was apparently sung during the Tammuz festival. The *Gilgamesh Epic* is the best known and most admirable Babylonian poem. As in the poem about Adapa (who missed partaking of the food of immortality through Ea's wrong guess of Anu's intentions) and the one about Etana (who flew to heaven on the back of an eagle, but failed to obtain the herb of procreation), the theme of the *Gilgamesh Epic* is man's vain search for immortality.

Gilgamesh, whither rovest thou?
The life thou seekest thou shalt not find.
When the gods created mankind,
Death for mankind they set aside,
Life in their own hands retaining.
Thou, Gilgamesh, let full be thy belly,
Make thou merry by day and by night.
(Tablet 10, tr. E. A. Speiser)

The story of the deluge is told in the 11th tablet, but was not part of the Sumerian original of the *Gilgamesh Epic*.

In addition to proverbs and counsels for life, which are also known in Sumerian, Assyr.-Babyl. poetry included the following genres unknown in surviving Sumerian texts: work songs, love poetry (a catalogue of erotic poems, listing the first lines, is known), and pessimistic and skeptical poems.

The best Eng. tr. of Assyro-Babyl. poems will be found in *Ancient Near Eastern Texts Relating to the Old Testament*, ed. J. B. Pritchard (1950; these tr. are repr. in an inexpensive ed. by I. Mendelsohn, *Religions of the Ancient Near East*, 1955). See also A. Heidel, *The Babyl. Genesis: The Story of Creation* (1942), *The Gilgamesh Epic and Old Testament Parallels* (2d ed., 1949).—Tr. in other languages: *Altorientalische Texte zum Alten Testament*, ed. H. Gressmann (2d ed., 1926); G. Contenau, *Le déluge babylonien, suivi de: Ishtar aux enfers, la Tour de Babel* (1941); G. Furlani, *Poemetti mitologici babilonesi e assiri* (1955).—Among the best literary histories are books by B. Meissner (see bibliog. *of* SUMERIAN POETRY for these and other pertinent volumes) and O. Weber, *Die Literatur der Babylonier und Assyrer* (1907). See also *Sumerische und ak-*

kadische Hymnen und Gebete, tr. A. Falkenstein and W. von Soden (1953; important introd.); *Gilgameš et sa légende*, ed. P. Garelli (1960); W. G. Lambert, *Babyl. Wisdom Lit.* (1960).　R.H.P.

ASTEISMUS. See PUN.

ASTROPHIC, *astropha.* Composition in verses without responsion or balancing metrical structure.　K.M.A.

ASYNARTETE (Gr. "disconnected"). A classical verse composed of independent cola (see COLON), loosely or not at all connected with each other metrically. The diaeresis between cola was at first strictly observed, but later poets (e.g., Cratinus) often neglected it. The creator of this type of verse was Archilochus (7th c. B.C.), and the cola he used in his asynartetes were dactylic, trochaic, and iambic. The comic poets made frequent use of these asynartetes.—Kolář; Koster; B. Snell, *Griechische Metrik* (3d ed., 1962).　P.S.C.

ASYNDETON (Gr. "unconnected"). A rhetorical device consisting of the omission of conjunctions, articles, and sometimes even pronouns. A., which enables the poet to achieve effects of extraordinary speed and economy, occurs with special felicity in an inflected language such as L.; Horace and Statius were fond of the device, and their example was followed by many of the medieval L. poets. Medieval German poets (e.g., Walther von der Vogelweide, Wolfram von Eschenbach) also made much use of a. The figure was especially favored by baroque poets in Germany (Andreas Gryphius), Spain, and France.

In Eng. literature a., which Puttenham, in his *Arte of Eng. Poesie,* called "loose language," has occurred particularly in modern poetry—in the work of the imagists, for example, with their cult of brevity, and in W. H. Auden with his fondness for the pithy and loaded phrase. But in the Latinist Milton as well one can find numerous examples: "The first sort by their own suggestion fell, / Self-tempted, self-depraved; man falls, deceived / By the other first: man therefore shall find grace, / The other none." (*Paradise Lost* 3.129-132). See also POLYSYNDETON.—H. Pliester, *Die Worthäufung im Barock* (1930); Curtius; Lausberg.

ATONIC (Gr. "without tone, or stress"). Used in Gr. grammar of words which have no accent (pitch) of their own and are usually attached to another word which precedes or follows. Used in general of the unaccented syllables of a word. In accentual prosody the unstressed syllables of a word or foot.　R.O.E.

AUBADE, *aube.* See ALBA.

AUDITION COLORÉE. An aspect of synaesthesia (q.v.) in which sounds are perceived or described in terms of colors. Coleridge observes in the *Biographia Literaria* that "the poet must . . . understand and command what Bacon called the *vestigia communia* of the senses, the latency of all in each, and more especially . . . the excitement of vision by sound and the exponents of sound." The phenomenon of a.c. is common in literature, where its most famous example is probably Rimbaud's sonnet *Voyelles* (Vowels), beginning: "A noir, E blanc, I rouge, U vert, O bleu, voyelles. . . ." Such terms as *golden voice, coloratura soprano, chromatic scale, Klangfarbe* (German "sound-color," *timbre*) show the assimilation of a.c. into language. A vivid example occurs in Edward Thomas's *Cock-Crow:*

> Out of the night, two cocks together crow,
> Cleaving the darkness with a silver blow.

J. Millet, *A.c.* (1892); E. Noulet, *Le premier visage de Rimbaud* (1953).　A.G.E.

AUREATE LANGUAGE, aureation. A type of poetic diction important in 15th-c. Eng. and Scottish poetry of official praise. It is also an important characteristic of the style of the contemporaneous *rhétoriqueurs* (q.v.) in France. A.l. is based on copious vernacular coinages from Latin ("Haile, sterne superne! Haile, in eterne,"); in its role as an "ornament" to style it illuminates one aspect of late medieval poetics. Although a.l. has generally been ridiculed by literary historians, it was the means by which Scotsman Dunbar, one of the finest of 15th-c. poets, earned his bread. One must also remember that many terms which do not strike us as aureate because they have since been absorbed into our language were indeed exotic coinages in their day. Much of Chaucer's diction may so have struck his contemporaries. Poets other than Dunbar whose work is distinguished by aureation include Lydgate and Hawes in England and King James I and Henryson in Scotland.—J. C. Mendenhall, *Aureate Terms* (1919); C. S. Lewis, *Eng. Hist. in the 16th C.* (1954).

AUSTRALIAN POETRY. Though in touch with trends elsewhere Aus. poetry has evolved along its own lines. It had a rougher origin than Am. or Canadian poetry. In the 19th c. some literary poetry was written, but until recent times almost all Aus. verse was related primarily, not to literature, but to soil and origin.

The difficulty of asserting a native image in

a new country is illustrated by the persistence in early Aus. poetry of points of view inherited, not locally formed. Robert Southey's *Botany Bay Eclogues* (1794) caricature the landscape (which he never saw) in a fatuous pastoralism, a key from which later local poets found it hard to depart. Poets represented New South Wales (settled 1788 as a penal station) as a savage outpost, grim, romantic only by terror and remoteness. (Cf. Goldsmith's view of Georgia in *The Deserted Village*.) Relief was sought in facetiousness, as in the tag ascribed (as a joke) to the gentleman-pickpocket George Barrington:

True patriots all, for, be it understood,
They left their country for their country's good.

Although Australia soon ceased to be a penal colony, adjustment was slow. The European sensibility recoiled from a landscape of unfamiliar forms: "Here nature is reversed," wrote one early observer. Poetry was called upon to bridge an almost complete gap in cultural continuity. Many conventions and clichés were shattered by the change of environment (e.g., strange native animals and flowers; bright but raucous parrots; kookaburras which appeared to laugh at the newcomer; no nightingales; no violets, primroses, etc.). Charles Tompson (1806–83), the first native-born poet, expressed an affectionate but thin elegiac regard for the landscape. In Charles Harpur (1813–68) the true colonial imagination first appeared but was compromised by ineffectual literary imitation (couplet verse in styles from Collins to Wordsworth). His best was seen in a lyric, *Midsummer Noon in the Australian Forest*, and an epic fragment, *The Creek of the Four Graves*, describing a clash between settlers and Aborigines. The most popular colonial poet was Adam Lindsay Gordon (1833–70, came to Australia at the age of 20), known for his energetic meters and homespun tags, which were much appreciated as contributions to colonial morale. His verses as a rule described outdoor life, often associated with horses and riding, and characterized by an Eng. Public-School background, scraps of L. or Gr., and a plangent nostalgic tone. At his worst trite, at his best he really captured the spirit of Aus. life and landscape. His Aus. poems, especially those of a balladlike character, were universally known and repeated in their day, but later he was much criticized for some lines in which he appeared to belittle Australia as a land "where bright blossoms are scentless, / And songless bright birds." He must nevertheless be given credit for certain perceptions and insights, of a quite fleeting but invaluable kind, which endowed the ordinary Aus. landscape

with an archetypal clarity beyond anything as yet seen in any of the arts:

In the Spring, when the wattle-gold trembles
    'Twixt shadow and shine,
When each dew-laden air draught resembles
    A long draught of wine;
When the sky-line's blue burnished resistance
Makes deeper the dreamiest distance. . . .

This quality of essential vision was Gordon's best achievement; he bequeathed it to the painter Streeton.

Immediately following Gordon, Henry Kendall (1839–82, native born) added lyrical refinement to colonial diction. Monotonous but sensitive, his verse flows with musical fluency. Influenced by Poe, Swinburne, Shelley, his mellifluousness is sometimes excessive. His best poem, *Bell Birds* ("By channels of coolness the echoes are calling, / And down the dim gorges I hear the creek calling"), effectively corrects the stock inherited convention that the bush is unmusical.

At its inception (1880), the Sydney *Bulletin*, then a radical and widely circulated weekly, set deliberately about fostering a local literature in prose and verse. Two traditions quickly defined themselves: (1) a campfire style, displayed in what in Australia is called ballad verse, and in anecdotal narrative in prose: and (2) a genteel verse style, refined and "educated" (often naively), of journalistic or drawing-room provenance. A number of women contributed sentimental and picturesque lyrics, often with a decidedly nationalistic bias (e.g., Louise Mack: "Land I love! I will find your meaning. . . . You shall reveal the soul of your song!" etc., etc.) The best of these were men, journalists, and three of them Ir.: Victor Daley, D. M. Wright, Roderic Quinn (the last Aus. born but of Ir. parents). From these, later poets learned some of the needed disciplines of lyric verse. In the campfire style, energy counted for more than subtlety but over a very broad canvas a lively descriptive impressionism was achieved, related to Gordon but freer:

Beneath a sky of deepest blue, where never
    cloud abides,
A speck upon the waste of plain, the lonely
    mailman rides. . . .
    (A. B. Paterson, *The Travelling Post-Office*)

The best of the bush balladists were Henry Lawson and A. B. ("Banjo") Paterson. Others worth naming were John Farrell, Will Ogilvie, Edward Dyson, E. J. Brady, Barcroft Boake; but there were a great many more. Their verses circulated widely in the *Bulletin* and were learned and repeated throughout the country. The bush ballad remains a fundamental Aus. popular idiom. C. J. Dennis' *The Sentimental Bloke* (1915), a wartime city pastoral with vivid local color, preserved the visible outline but not the spirit of the true bush ballad. There have been sophisticated modern treatments of it (e.g., Douglas Stewart, *Glencoe*, 1947), but in its original form its heyday is past. Poems like John Manifold's elegy for John Learmonth and Judith Wright's *Bullooky* (both in the *Penguin Book of Aus. Verse*) reflect its influence significantly. It remains undoubtedly the strongest native strain in contemporary Aus. poetry, and almost certainly accounts for the manifest reluctance of the poets to subscribe to an unreservedly intellectual poetical convention. Underneath every free image or concept there is sustained a hard, earthy skepticism; this seems to be the indwelling Aus. secret, and if it limits the intellectual range, at least it humanizes the effect.

Throughout the colonial period the poets continued obsessed with environment and description; but about 1890–1900 new impulses developed, culminating in three strong poets, Bernard O'Dowd (1866–1953), Christopher Brennan (1870–1932) and William Baylebridge (1883–1942). O'Dowd and Baylebridge were prophets of a new age, political idealists though of contrasting creeds, for whom poetry was an instrument rather than an end in itself. O'Dowd corresponded with Whitman; both were students of Nietzsche. Neither was so attractive a poet as was the sombre Brennan. Brennan represents probably the most brilliant poetic talent yet seen in Australia, the first fully developed literary and critical skill. A symbolist and follower of Mallarmé, a student of European ideas, he was intellectually stranded and alone in Australia, and his poetry suffered in consequence; it was often obscure, sometimes brutal, but never weak. His qualities are only now being recognized; in his own day, except for a limited circle, he was virtually unknown.

In the 20th c., lyrical poetry moves from the exuberant nationalism of Dorothea Mackellar ("I love a sunburnt country, / A land of sweeping plains," etc.—*My Country*, 1914) to a much more objective and critically tempered point of view (e.g., James McAuley's *Envoi*, "The people are hard-eyed, kindly, with nothing inside them, / The men are independent but you could not call them free"). Significant steps were taken by a group early associated with the painter Norman Lindsay (b. 1879) and the poet Hugh McCrae (1876–1958), both of whom boldly advocated a nonlocal subject matter. This amounted to echoing the aesthetic movement in England, with stress upon a Nietzschean or "Dionysian" formula of art and recourse to classical, mythological, or medieval

themes. In McCrae there was wit and delicacy, though too much intellectual dissipation. Stronger work came from the younger poets who followed, first in the publication *Vision* (1923) and afterward independently. Chief of these were Kenneth Slessor (b. 1901), whose elegy *Five Bells* is one of the finest modern Aus. poems, and Robert D. FitzGerald (b. 1902), whose *Essay on Memory* won a sesquicentenary prize in 1938. Two poets whose work appeared about the same time were Shaw Neilson (1872–1942), a sensitive lyrist, and Mary (Dame Mary) Gilmore (1865–1962), who in her nineties could still produce an occasional lyric reminiscent of the wit and precision of her best days. Two wars had an influence on Aus. poetry, but the second had the profounder effect. It first revived, then broke the nationalistic obsession. Jindyworobákism, set up about 1935 by Rex Ingamells (1913–55), was a movement which endeavored to protect the image of Australia against cultural intrusions from abroad (including England), and took as its center the culture of the Aborigine, at once embraced as a valid symbolism by a large number of young followers. Not all of the movement decayed when later developments followed; for example, many still make use of the picturesque *altjira* or "dream time" concept fundamental to all Aus. native mythologies. Between the pre- and postwar moods of youth came the Angry Penguins, an undergraduate group whose brief rebellion was exploded by a widely publicized hoax. Two young soldier-poets (James McAuley and Harold Stewart, in collaboration) sent the editor of the magazine *Angry Penguins* (1944) a sequence of nonsense-poems, *The Darkening Ecliptic*, the work of a circumstantially documented but quite nonexistent poet, "Ern Malley." It was accepted by the editor, Max Harris—himself a poet—and extravagantly praised. The result was the prophylactic collapse of showy but empty forms of "modernism" among the younger Aus. poets, and a new beginning to the art.

Contemporary Aus. verse is lyrical, commentative, satirical, and descriptive. It remains reflective in pattern, and is doggedly traditional by its lights. It has not denied its colonial origins but has developed from them; all the movements mentioned have been assimilated constructively, and it owes little, comparatively, to fashion abroad. Outstanding poets are A. D. Hope, James McAuley, Douglas Stewart, Judith Wright, David Campbell, Rosemary Dobson, Geoffrey Dutton, Vincent Buckley, Ray Mathew. All these are represented in the excellent but necessarily limited *Penguin Book of Aus. Verse*, which also has a good short introduction and brief notes on each of the poets.

ANTHOLOGIES: *A Century of Aus. Verse*, ed.

AUSTRIAN POETRY

D. Sladen (1888; of historical interest mainly); *An Anthol. of Aus. Verse*, ed. G. Mackaness (2d ed., 1952); *Modern Aus. Poetry*, ed. H. M. Green (2d ed., 1952); *Aus. Bush Ballads* (1955) and *Old Bush Songs and Rhymes of Colonial Times* (1957), both ed. D. Stewart and N. Keesing; *A Book of Aus. Verse* (1956) and *New Land, New Language* (1957), both ed. J. Wright; *The Penguin Book of Aus. Verse*, ed. J. Thompson, K. Slessor and R. G. Howarth (1958).

HISTORY AND CRITICISM: T. I. Moore, *Six Aus. Poets: McCrae, Neilson, O'Dowd, Baylebridge, Brennan, FitzGerald* (1942); E. M. Miller, *Aus. Lit. A Bibliog. to 1938, Extended to 1950*, ed. F. T. Macartney (1956); C. Hadgraft, *Aus. Lit.* (1960); H. M. Green, *A Hist. of Aus. Lit.* (2 v., 1962); J. P. Matthews, *Tradition in Exile: A Comparative Study of Social Influence on the Development of Aus. and Canadian Poetry in the 19th C.* (1962); A. D. Hope, *Aus. Lit. 1950–1962* (1964).   B.R.E.

AUSTRIAN POETRY. Though Austr. poetry is lingually an intrinsic part of German lyrics, there is sufficient justification to deal with it separately, particularly since a peculiar multi-ethnic background, history, religion, and nature have drawn its characteristic features. When speaking of Austr. poetry one ought to bear in mind the realms of the Babenbergs and of the Hapsburgs which at various times extended from Switzerland over Hungary and Poland to Russia, and from Silesia and Bohemia to Croatia and Lombardy, as well as the influences from Spain through the imperial court and from Italy through the *commedia dell'arte* and music. Such growth, rarely brought about by wars, frequently by dynastic marriages, has molded Celtic, Roman, German, Slavic, and Magyar elements into a highly diversified and individualistic populace that increasingly cherished a *vita contemplativa* as opposed to a *vita activa*. Its attracting center was Vienna.

Austria in the 12th and 13th c. abounded in a multitude of *Minnesänger* after the stern religious vein exemplified in Frau Ava (d. 1127) and in the *memento mori* of Heinrich von Melk (12th c.) had run its course. Der Kürenberger (ca. 1150–1200) cultivated verses which combined folk song and minnesong in a knightly manner; Dietmar von Aist (d. ca. 1170) composed his verses in praise of love (*Taglieder*); the Alsacian Reinmar von Hagenau (ca. 1160–1205) had come to Vienna to enchant the court of the Babenbergs with his artful, amorous, though elegiac poems. It was he whom Walther von der Vogelweide (b. ca. 1170 in Austria, d. ca. 1230) recognized as his teacher and master, and it was Vienna where Walther, according to his own testi-

mony, had learned "singen und sagen." His poems—with unaffected love, nature, religion, politics, and sagacity as main topics—signal the height of lyric poetry until Goethe, some 600 years later. They reveal a happy meeting of mind and senses, of color and form, music and rhythm, reflection and feeling; they express joy in living and truthfulness, but also sadness at the transitoriness of life. They do so in a manner which renders them timeless and great. This reliance upon eye and ear, the prevalence of the concrete over the abstract and of the mind over the intellect is noticeable also in minor poets of his period to the end of the Middle Ages, e.g., in Reinmar von Zweter and Neidhart von Reuental (both first half of the 13th c.), Der Tannhäuser (ca. 1230–70), Ulrich von Lichtenstein (ca. 1200–1276), Der von Suoneck (ca. 1250), Hugo von Montfort (1357–1423), Oswald von Wolkenstein (1377–1445) and up to our own time.

After the decline of the Middle High German period we listen in vain for a great lyrical voice in Austria (except folk songs) until the romantic period. Whereas Protestant church song, schools, and the homes of Protestant clergymen made the German language a vessel of poetic expression, Catholic Austria—with Latin the language of the church, as well as of the schools conducted predominantly by Jesuits who considered it the worthiest form of expression, and with no ministerial home as a center of learning and scholarship—can offer nothing comparable to the great German baroque poets A. Gryphius, P. Gerhardt, Fleming, Dach, Angelus Silesius, Logau (with the limited exception perhaps of Katharina Regina von Greiffenberg, 1633–94). Even at the time of M. Claudius, Klopstock, Goethe, Schiller, and Hölderlin, poetic art in Austria remained uninspiring, adhering to metric form but lacking in true rhythm—the versifications of Michael Denis (1729–1800), J. B. Alxinger (1755–97), A. Blumauer (1755–98), Karoline Pichler (1769–1843), L. Pyrker (1772–1847), J. C. v. Zedlitz (1790–1862) notwithstanding. Only Marianne von Willemer (b. 1784 in Linz, d. 1860 in Frankfurt o/M.) rose to poetic heights with Goethe in *West-Östlicher Diwan*, but she hardly can be called an Austr. poetess in the proper sense.

The second flowering of Austr. poetry did not occur until the advent of F. Grillparzer (1791–1872, Vienna) and particularly of Nikolaus Lenau (b. 1802 near Temesvar, Hungary, d. 1850, Vienna). Deep melancholy and pessimism, *Weltschmerz*, loneliness, and restlessness pervade Lenau's poetry, during the Metternich period when political stagnation was unsuccessfully challenged by Anastasius Grün (b. 1806, Laibach, d. 1876).

Resignation, a bitter-sweet attitude towards

life, psychological insight, a recognition of the relativity of values, but also a quiet joy in small things—echoes of the Biedermeier (q.v.) period, which was given to introspection and averse to confrontations with materialistic life —characterized Austr. poetry to the end of the 19th c. These traits are expressed in the lyrics of the Viennese E. v. Feuchtersleben (1806–49) and F. v. Saar (1833–1906), the Tyrolian H. v. Gilm (1812–64), and the Moravian M. v. Ebner-Eschenbach (1830–1916). Austr. poetry at that elegant and tender time does not reflect the labor and aftermath of the industrial revolution, and the veins of poetic realism and naturalism are apparent only in her dialect poets (F. Stelzhamer, 1802–74, P. Rosegger, 1843–1918, etc.). Austria then had no poets comparable to G. Keller, C. F. Meyer, Theodor Storm, D. v. Liliencron, F. Freiligrath, Arno Holz, R. Dehmel.

Around 1900, however, there was a lyrical burgeoning in Austria as at the time of Walther. As if latent dispositions had come to the fore and the array of half-tones and a molded heritage had gained sound, music, color, and form, *Lebensweisheit* revealed itself in its ripest lyrical fruit. This spring blossomed in the Indian summer and autumn of a dying era. The sweetness of life, its fragrance and wisdom were gathered once more in irretrievably fading hours while time seemed to allow itself to stand still to behold the gathering riches. With extraordinary sensitivity, sovereignty of rhythmical suggestiveness, uncanny insight, and vocal splendor, R. M. Rilke (b. 1875, Prag, d. 1926) and H. v. Hofmannsthal (b. 1874, Vienna, d. 1929) set music and images into words. Their art, impressionistic yet thoughtful, has no equal in Germany. An exceptional faculty of surrender and understanding of human nature (which for the Austr., as Hofmannsthal said, was a trait extending to the point of loss of character), a melancholy recognition of the futility of human doing and striving, had made the *vita contemplativa* an art in itself. Even a "chronicle" like Rilke's *Die Weise von Liebe und Tod* (1906) is a purely lyrical work. Content and form had become indistinguishable from each other. But beauty and splendor were felt to be, as Rilke put it, only "the beginning of the terrible." "We always play, he who knows it is wise," Hofmannsthal said, and Rilke who by inner necessity had made loneliness and suffering into self-recognition cast his heart into the *Duineser Elegien* and the *Sonnette an Orpheus* (1923), in which human isolation is no longer softened by the warmth of the senses. While R. Schaukal (b. 1874, Moravia, d. 1942), S. Zweig (b. 1881, Vienna, d. 1942, Brazil), K. Kraus (b. 1874, Bohemia, d. 1936), and M. Mell (b. 1882, Marburg) tried to pre-

serve the heritage of the Occident in the purity of poetic creation, it broke quietly but frighteningly asunder in the verses of G. Trakl (b. 1887, Salzburg, d. 1914), to whom beauty had disintegrated into wintry hues and reality had become a decaying concept which he beheld from the threshold of expressionism (q.v.).

It is significant though not surprising that expressionism as a passionate, explosive, truth-seeking, activistic movement brought forth only one Austr. lyric poet of stature, F. Werfel (b. 1890, Prague, d. 1945, Calif.). True, there are certain expressionistic features noticeable in other Austr. poets, e.g., F. T. Csokor (b. 1885, Vienna), A. Wildgans (b. 1881, Vienna, d. 1932), Th. Kramer (b. 1897, near Vienna, d. 1958), but, in general, Austrians who suspect any manifesto or tempestuous confession and prefer compromise over unconditional demands were no partners to this literary movement. Instead, Austr. poetry of the 1920's and 1930's revealed itself with new imagery, melodic rhythm, and sensitivity in its pursuit of adherence to form and in its endeavor to explore man's relationship to himself, to God, and to nature. Vienna in particular, a most humane metropolis, had a cultural climate which blended urbaneness and landscape happily into each other. This union offering perspectives into the past towards Biedermeier, romanticism, and baroque is apparent in the works of the older generation like Th. Däubler (b. 1876, Triest, d. 1934), R. Beer-Hofmann (b. 1866, Vienna, d. 1945, N.Y.), F. K. Ginzkey (b. 1871, Pola), F. Braun (b. 1885, Vienna), but continues to the present also. Rustic elements, objectively and functionally shaped in woodcut manner—as in the work of R. Billinger (b. 1893, Upper Austria), G. Zernatto (b. 1903, Carinthia, d. 1943, N.Y.)—as well as Catholic accents—as in Paula v. Preradović (b. 1887, Vienna, d. 1951)—lend profile to the wealth of lyrical creation. One of the great, unfortunately almost forgotten, is Hans Leifhelm (1891–1947), Austr. by choice, whose nature poems remain almost unexcelled.

Other voices signaling rather the continuation of a long tradition than the beginning of a new one are those of E. Mitterer (b. 1906), A. Lernet-Holenia (b. 1897), E. Schönwiese (b. 1905), E. Waldinger (b. 1896), and J. Weinheber (b. 1892, Vienna, d. 1945). Weinheber in particular reveals in his poetry an Austr. tendency of thinking with the heart and feeling with the mind, a deep mistrust, pessimism, even despair to be borne only by constraining it into form, by resignation, or by humor. Unhappiness, suffering, an inability to accept the conditions of life (prevalent also in Grillparzer, Raimund, Lenau, A. Stifter) pervade his verses that reach from the heroic to rustic strokes, from delicate softness to humor written in Viennese dialect.

After the end of the Second World War the new Austr. generation, inclined as ever to evolution, not revolution, played the chords of old in different keys, advancing an unbroken tradition. In contrast to Germany (disregarding in this connection P. Celan, b. 1920 in what used to be Austr. Bukovina) no neo-expressionistic or surrealistic experimentation of consequence can be discerned. Most of the younger poets adhere to a melancholy and subjective interpretation of life or assimilate thought and emotion to patterns designed in an exclamatory manner, softly and more quietly echoing German postwar tendencies. Worthy of attention and perhaps characteristic of Austria (rather a motherland than a fatherland) is the poetry of women who indeed have contributed most to the lyrical image of Austria after 1945, above all two Carinthians—Ingeborg Bachmann (b. 1926) whose sibylline, quiet rhythm casts the issue of life, love, and death into arresting images with new light and breath in newly revealed words, and Christine Lavant (b. 1915) in whom strength and mourning, apocalyptic visions and whispered tenderness fuse into mythical expression.

ANTHOLOGIES: *Museum aus den deutschen Dichtungen österreichischer Lyriker und Epiker der frühesten bis zur neuesten Zeit*, ed. S. H. Mosenthal (1854); *Deutsche Lyrik aus Österreich seit Grillparzer*, ed. C. Hoffman (1912); *Lyrik aus Deutschösterreich—Vom Mittelalter bis zur Gegenwart*, ed. S. Hock (1919); *Die Botschaft*, ed. E. A. Reinhardt (1920); *Anthologie österr. Lyrik*, ed. E. Rieger (1931); *Die Gruppe*, ed. F. Sacher (1932, 1935); *Österr. Lyrik der Gegenwart*, ed. R. Brasch and R. Schäfer (1934); *Der ewige Kreis*, ed. O. Brandt (1935); *Vom Expressionismus zur neuen Klassik. Deutsche Lyrik aus Österreich*, ed. J. Pfandler (1936); *Um Zeitliches und Ewiges, ein Querschnitt durch Österreichs kämpferische Lyrik*, ed. R. and A. Mühlher (1947); *Österr. Lyrik aus neun Jh.*, ed. W. Stratowa; *Unsterbliches Lied, Hausbuch österr. Lyrik*, ed. F. Sacher (1948); *Das Herz ist deine Heimat*, ed. R. Felmayer (1956); *Österr. Lyrik nach 1945*, ed. E. Schönwiese, 1960.

HISTORY AND CRITICISM: J. W. Nagl, J. Zeidler, E. Castle, *Deutschösterr. Literaturgeschichte* (4 v., 1899–1937); F. Sacher, *Die neue Lyrik in Österreich* (1932); A. v. Schmidt, *Einführung in die Gesch. der deutschen Dichtung in Österreich* (2d ed., 1947); E. Waldinger, "Die österr. Lyrik zwischen 1918 u. 1938," *Erbe und Zukunft*, 3 (1947); J. Nadler, *Literaturgesch. Österreichs* (2d ed., 1951); A. Schmidt, *Dichtung und Dichter Österreichs im 19. und 20. Jh.* (1964). T.O.B.

AUTO SACRAMENTAL. An allegorical play in one act that deals with the mystery of the Eucharist, usually performed on a float or an especially constructed platform, in the public square, on the feast of Corpus Christi, in Spain. The characters of the *autos* are allegorical and represent abstract concepts like virtues, vices, the World, Sin, Everyman, Hope, Faith, Free Will, etc.

During the Middle Ages the word *auto* was used for any dramatic piece, religious as well as profane. Toward the beginning of the 16th c., however, the word came to be applied exclusively to religious plays and eventually to those religious plays that treated the miracle of transubstantiation so that around the middle of the same century the *autos* already show all the features that are part of the *autos sacramentales*. The *autos* are written in verse and contain a variety of metrical forms. Very often some of the best poetry of the age is found in the *autos*.

Although most of the leading playwrights of the Sp. Golden Age, like Lope de Vega, Tirso de Molina, etc., wrote *autos sacramentales*, the unsurpassed writer of *autos* is considered to be Pedro Calderón de la Barca (1600–81). The date of his death coincides with the beginning of the rapid decline of the genre.— *Calderón: Three Plays*, ed. G. T. Northup (1926); A. Parker, *The Allegorical Drama of Calderón* (1943); B. W. Wardropper, "The Search for a Dramatic Formula for the Autos Sacramentales," PMLA, 65 (1950) and *Introducción al teatro religioso del siglo de oro* (1953); E. Frutos Cortés, *La filosofía de Calderón en sus autos sacramentales* (1952); A. Valbuena Prat, *Historia del teatro español* (1956); J. L. Flecniakoska, *La formation de l'"auto" religieux en Espagne avant Calderón* (1961). R.MI.

AUTOTELIC (Gr. *autos*, "self," and *telos*, "end,"—i.e., a work of art or poem having an end-purpose in itself). See POETRY, THEORIES OF (OBJECTIVE THEORIES).

AWDL. The most highly regarded form of Welsh bardic composition. The "chair" of the National Eisteddfod of Wales is awarded for an *awdl*. The word, originally a variant of *odl* (rhyme) came to mean, successively, the stave bearing the rhyme, a run of monorhyming lines, a complete poem in monorhyme, a poem entirely in certain specified a. meters and, since the 15th c., a poem of some length in *cynghanedd* (q.v.) and in one or more of the "24 strict *metres*" including at least some portions not in *cywydd* or *englyn* (qq.v.). Many of the best Welsh poems of the last two centuries, as in the medieval period, are *awdlau*. Among a. meters are (a) *rhupynt*, a 12-syllable line of 3 sections, each of 4 syllables, the first section rhyming with the second, and a consonantal correspondence woven around the main stresses of the second and third sections, and the twelfth syllable bearing the main rhyme: "Iawn o'i berchi i bawb erchi o bob

B

BACCHIUS (also called *bacchiacus* or *bacchiac*). A unit of verse composed of 1 short syllable followed by 2 long ones, $\smile$ _ _ . The name supposedly derives from the use of the unit in ancient Gr. religious songs to the god Bacchus. Although comparatively rare in Gr. lyric verse, it appears frequently in L. poetry, especially in the plays of Plautus, e.g.,

$$nam \; v\bar{o}x \; m\bar{e} \mid pr\breve{e}c\bar{a}nt \; (um \; h)\bar{u}c \mid f\breve{o}r\bar{a}s$$

$$\overline{ex}|c\bar{\imath}t\bar{a}v\bar{\imath}t$$
(*Rudens* 260f.)

where, as sometimes happens, the first syllable is a *longa irrationalis*. In L. verse the unit occurs usually in tetrameters, though sometimes it will be combined with spondees and iambs for a line of verse. The Romans felt it to be especially suitable for a serious and solemn style. Eng. poetry is said to admit the unit in such words as "aboveboard" where the second and third syllables receive about the same amount of stress. But the term is really appropriate to ancient quantitative poetry.— W. M. Lindsay, *Early L. Verse* (1922); P. Maas, *Griechische Metrik* (1929); Dale; G. E. Duckworth, *The Nature of Roman Comedy* (1952); Crusius.   R.A.H.

BALADA. A Prov. dance song, of no fixed form, but with a refrain, which was often repeated several times in a stanza. The b. is hardly to be distinguished from the *dansa* by any objective criterion.—F. Diez, *Die Poesie der Troubadours* (2d ed. by K. Bartsch, 1883).   F.M.C.

BALLAD. The "folk," "popular," or "traditional" b. is a short narrative song preserved and transmitted orally among illiterate or semiliterate people. Story-songs of this kind have been collected in all European countries, and though each national balladry has its distinctive characteristics, certain constants hold for all bona fide specimens: (1) Ballads focus on a single crucial episode or situation. The ballad begins usually at a point where the action is decisively directed toward its catas-

eirchiad"; (b) *long rhupynt* (16 syllables and 4 sections); (c) *cyhydedd naw ban,* a 9-syllable line; and (d) *hir a thoddaid* (long and blending)—a special pattern of 10-syllable lines with its own rhyme scheme and accentuation.— Morris-Jones; Parry.   D.M.L.

trophe. Events leading up to this crucial and conclusive episode are told in a hurried, summary fashion. Little attention is given to describing settings; indeed, circumstantial detail of every sort is conspicuously absent. (2) Ballads are dramatic. We are not told about things happening: we are shown them happening. Every artistic resource of the genre is pointed toward giving an intensity and immediacy to the action and toward heightening the emotional impact of the climax. Protagonists are allowed to speak for themselves, which means, of course, that dialogue bulks large in ballads. At strategic moments, dialogue erupts into the narrative. Such speeches are sparingly tagged; we must frequently deduce the speaker from what is being said. (3) Ballads are impersonal. The narrator seldom allows his own subjective attitude toward the events to intrude. Comments on motives are broad, general, detached. There may be an "I" in a ballad, but the singer does not forget that he is the deputy of the public voice and is not speaking from private judgment. Bias there is in ballads, of course, but it is the bias of a party, community, or nation, not an individual's particularistic point of view. Stylistically the ballad is a species apart. This is because the b., like folk song in general but unlike all the literary genres, is an oral phenomenon, and, as a consequence, preserves traces of the archaic modes of preliterature. The story is the key thing in a b., all other artistic possibilities are subordinated to it. The language is plain and formulaic. A small stock of epithets and adjectives serves for all the ballads in a given language. There are few arresting figures of speech and no self-conscious straining after novel turns of phrase. And because the emphasis is on a single line of action precipitously developed, there is not time in a b. for careful delineation of character or for extensive research into psychological motivation. The heavy amount of repetition and parallelism one finds in the ballads may appear to be merely decorative rhetoric, but it is not so. Repetition in heightened passages was brilliantly explained by Coleridge as the singers' effort to discharge emotion that could not be exhausted in one saying. Much repetition is mnemonic: in a story being recited or sung, crucial facts must be firmly planted in the memory since the hearer cannot turn back a page to refresh himself about a fact that slipped by in a moment of inattention. (Incremental repetition, a rhetorical device in Eng. and Scottish popular ballads for achieving suspense, is discussed separately.)

Between the balladries of Western and Eastern Europe there are marked differences. Except for certain Rumanian ballads, rhyme and assonance are unusual in Slavic territories and in the Balkans, including Greece. The Ukrainian *dumy*, which assonate, are another exception. Finnish ballads employ alliteration as a binding principle. In Western countries, rhyme or assonance is general. All ballads are essentially narrative poems with a greater or lesser infusion of lyrical elements, and the strength of the lyrical quality is another discriminant in the classification of balladries. As a general rule, strophic (stanzaic) ballads tend to be more lyrical than nonstrophic. Rhyme, assonance, refrains, and short meters further suggest lyricism, as do singability and dance animation. Least lyrical are the *viser* of Denmark, lengthy, heroic ballads, which upset the criteria just established in employing rhyme and assonance and being stanzaic; the Serbian men's songs on historical and martial topics, written in a heavy pentameter line; the Sp. *romances* (q.v.), which seem, like the *viser,* to have been cut down from epic lays, and which, though held together by assonance, are not strophic. Lithuania, Poland, France, Italy, and Scotland possess the most lyrical story-songs. As to metrical schemes, British and Scandinavian ballads use a couplet of 4 stresses to the line or the common meter quatrain; an octosyllabic line is the staple of Sp., Bulgarian, Rumanian, and much German b. poetry; France and allied b. territory (Catalonia, Northern Italy, Portugal) take as standard a verse of 12 or 16 syllables broken into 2 equal members which rhyme or assonate with one another; the scansion of the Rus. *byliny* (q.v.) is free and highly irregular —the musical phrasing governing the organization of the verse.

The charms of British balladry were first brought to the attention of the lettered and learned world in the 18th c. During the period 1790–1830 many important recordings from tradition were made. F. J. Child, a professor at Harvard, made the definitive thesaurus of British popular ballads (1882–98), printing 305 ballads, some in as many as 25 versions. In this century, about 125 of Child's ballads have been recovered in the United States and Canada from the descendants of 18th-c. immigrants from the British Isles. *Judas,* the oldest b. in

Child's collection, was recorded in a manuscript of about 1300. It deals with the betrayal of Christ. There are a few other religious ballads, mostly concerned with the miracles of the Virgin, but these are far outnumbered by the pieces dealing with the pagan supernatural, like *Tam Lin, The Wife of Usher's Well, Lady Isabel and the Elf-Knight,* etc. In America the supernatural elements in these ballads has been deleted or rationalized. The commonest b. theme is tragic love of a sensational and violent turn (*Earl Brand, Barbara Allen, Childe Maurice*). Incest and other domestic crimes are surprisingly common. The troubles on the Border in the 15th and 16th c. inspired a precious body of sanguine heroic ballads (*Johnny Armstrong, Hobie Noble, Edom o'Gordon*), many of which are partly historical. Most other historical ballads are the work of minstrels and transparently urge the causes of the minstrels' noble patrons. Propaganda seems also to inform the Robin Hood ballads, which exalt the virtues of the yeoman class.

The origin of the British popular ballads has been hotly argued among b. scholars. A school known as individualists (John Meier, Louise Pound) assert that all ballads are the work of individual poets and are "popular" merely in having been taken up by the folk. Communalists (F. B. Gummere, W. M. Hart, G. L. Kittredge) insist that the prototypical b. was concocted in assemblies of the folk in the exultations of choral dance. Current opinion concedes that the traits of "balladness" may be explained by the communal theory, but holds that all extant ballads are the work of individuals originally. As the individualists failed to understand, however, the work of an individual poet does not become a b. until it is accepted by the folk and remodeled by the b. conventions in the course of its tour in tradition.

Native Am. ballads, influenced partly by the British traditional ballads but mainly by the broadsides, exist alongside the imported ballads. The oldest perhaps is *Springfield Mountain,* the story of a Yankee farmboy fatally bitten by a snake, which may be pre-Revolutionary. Better known are outlaw songs like *Jesse James* and *Sam Bass,* the lumberjack classic *The Jam on Gerry's Rock,* the cowboys' *The Streets of Laredo* and the popular favorites *Casey Jones, John Henry* and *Frankie and Albert* (*Frankie and Johnny*). The last three pieces are sometimes classed as Negro ballads, but they are demonstrably the results of collaboration between the races.

Ballads have had an enormous influence on Eng. and German poetry, though Entwhistle exaggerates when he writes that "the debt of [romantic] literature to the ballad has been comparable to that of the Renaissance to the

Greek and Latin classics." The early 18th-c. imitations, Thomas Tickell's *Lucy and Colin,* for example, patterned themselves on broadsides and dealt mainly with village tragedies. Wordsworth and Hardy pursued a similar vein in much of their b.-colored poetry. Percy, the editor of the famous *Reliques* (1765), sentimentalized and prettified the b. style in *The Hermit of Warkworth,* but some of his completions of genuine fragments were reasonably faithful. His reconstruction of *Sir Cauline* lent many touches to Coleridge's *Christabel.* Scott's poetic career began with a translation of Bürger's *Lenore,* a German b. imitation, and he concocted several counterfeit ballads in early years, but he eventually came to feel that ballad impersonality and the stylization of b. language were contrary to the aesthetic of composed poetry. In the b.-like poems of Coleridge, Keats, Rossetti, Meredith, and Swinburne, we see the popular b. style being crossed with borrowings from medieval romances and from minstrel poetry to yield poems of richer texture, more circumstantial and more contrivedly dramatic than are the ballads. *La Belle Dame Sans Merci* and *The Ancient Mariner,* perhaps the finest of the so-called imitations, could never pass for the genuine article though greater poems than any b. Yeats's ballads (*Moll Magee, Father Gilligan,* etc.) are ballads only in stanza structure and simplicity; they do not employ stock language or the rhetoric peculiar to traditional song.

Herder's encouragement of folk song collecting resulted in Arnim and Brentano's *Des Knaben Wunderhorn* (1805–8), a collection which exerted an almost tyrannical influence over the German lyric all through the 19th c. Many of the best shorter poems of Heine, Mörike, Chamisso, Eichendorff, Uhland, and Liliencron purposely resemble *Volkslieder.* The narrative element in these poems is usually so completely overwhelmed by the lyrical that they would hardly be considered ballads by Eng. standards. See also FOLK SONG.

Child's collection cited above amalgamates the British collections to 1898. *The Traditional Tunes of the Child Ballads* have been edited by B. H. Bronson. The first v. appeared in 1958; the second in 1962; two others are projected. T. P. Coffin, *The British Traditional B. in America* (1950) documents the survival of Child's ballads. For Eng. collections to 1952, the most important of which are edited by C. J. Sharp, see M. Dean-Smith, *A Guide to Eng. Folk Song Collections* (1954). The most valuable post-Child Scottish collection is G. Grieg's *Last Leaves of Traditional Ballads* (1925). The European field is surveyed in W. J. Entwistle, *European Balladry* (1939), which lists the major European collections, among

them A. Durán, *Romancero general* (1849–51), S. Grundtvig and A. Olrik, *Danmarks Gamle Folkeviser* (1853–1920), L. Erk and F. Böhme, *Deutscher Liederhort* (3 v., 1893–94), R. Trautmann, *Die Volksdichtung der Grossrussen* (1935). Of the numerous Am. collections, almost all restricted to particular geographical areas, the best edited are P. Barry and others, *British Ballads from Maine* (1929) and H. M. Belden, *Ballads and Songs . . . Missouri* (1940; 1955). A sampling of ballads from the entire Eng.-speaking world is set out in A. B. Friedman, *The Viking Book of Folk-Ballads* (1956). J. and A. Lomax, *Am. Ballads and Folk Songs* (1934), restrict themselves to this side of the Atlantic.

Especially valuable critical works are R. Menéndez Pidal, *Poesía popular y poesía tradicional* (1922), G. H. Gerould, *The B. of Tradition* (1932), W. Kayser, *Gesch. der deutschen Ballade* (1936), L. K. Goetz, *Volkslied und Volksleben der Kroaten und Serben* (1936–37), M. J. C. Hodgart, *The Ballads* (1950). To be used with caution are F. B. Gummere, *The Popular B.* (1907) and L. Pound, *Poetic Origins and the B.* (1921). The relations of the ballads to official poetry 1100–1960 are explored by A. B. Friedman in *The B. Revival* (1961), which supersedes the works of S. B. Hustvedt. D. K. Wilgus, *Anglo-Am. Folksong Scholarship since 1898* (1959), surveys modern b. criticism and collecting techniques.　A.B.F.

BALLAD METER, or common meter (The C.M. of the hymnals is roughly the same as ballad meter, except that the beat is more regular because of the deliberate style of singing and the first and third lines usually rhyme). In the characteristic ballad stanza the first and third lines are iambic tetrameter, the second and fourth lines iambic trimeter. Only the second and fourth lines rhyme. A typical quatrain:

> The ladies cracked their fingers white,
> The maidens tore their hair,
> All for the sake of their true loves,
> For them they ne'er saw mair.

It has been conjectured that this stanza is actually a couplet composed of two 7-foot lines, the 7-foot line deriving from the septenary (q.v.) of medieval church poetry. The conjecture is borne out to some extent by the musical phrasing of many ballad tunes, for many phrases round themselves over the 7 feet of two lines, ignoring the 4/3/4/3 arrangement of the text. There are so many exceptions to this musical pattern, however, that the conventional practice of printing the ballad stanza as 4 lines is still justified. The stanza is easily managed and is noted for its buoyancy and tunefulness. Folk singers and minstrels as well as the learned poets who have adopted the stanza vary the accentuation of the shorter lines, weighting the line by spondees and lightening it with extra unaccented syllables. An example of the latter effect is Herrick's famous stanza: "Gather ye rosebuds while ye may, / Old Time is still aflying; / And this same flower that smiles today, / Tomorrow will be dying." Although the 4-line ballad stanza accounts for the form of most folk ballads, some of the more important traditional pieces are sung in tetrameter couplets, usually with an irrelevant refrain weaving among the story lines. F. J. Child, G. L. Kittredge, and other ballad scholars considered the tetrameter couplet the older ballad stanza.—See, for a brief discussion, G. H. Gerould, *The Ballad of Tradition* (1932), 124–30. Fuller is J. W. Hendren, *A Study of Ballad Rhythm* (1936).　　　　　　　　　A.B.F.

BALLADE. The most important of the so-called OF forms and the dominant verse form of Fr. poetry in the 14th and 15th c. The most common type of b. is made up of three 8-line stanzas rhyming ababbcbC and a 4-line *envoi* (q.v.) rhyming bcbC. As the capital letters indicate, the last line of the first stanza serves as the refrain, being repeated as the last line of each stanza and also of the *envoi*. In the tightness of its rhyme scheme and in its use of the refrain, the b. is one of the most exacting of verse forms. Some variants of the standard b. utilize 10- or (less often) 12-line stanzas and 5- or 6-line *envois* in place of the more common 8- and 4-line arrangements. The *envoi*, which frequently begins with the address "Prince" (a derivation from the medieval literary compositions at which the judge was so addressed), forms the climactic summation of the poem.

Although the b. may have developed from some Prov. form, it was standardized in Fr. by such 14th-c. poets as Guillaume de Machaut, Eustache Deschamps, and, less so, Jean Froissart. It was carried to perfection in the 15th c. by Christine de Pisan, Charles d'Orléans, and, most of all, François Villon, who made the b. the vehicle for the greatest of early Fr. poetry. Such works as his *B. des pendus* (B. of the Hanged) and his *B. des dames du temps jadis* (B. of Ladies of Times Gone By) achieved an unequaled intensity in their use of refrain and *envoi*. The b. continued in favor until the time of Marot in the early 16th c., but the poets of the *Pléiade*, as well as their neoclassical successors in the 17th c., had little use for the form and regarded it as a barbaric survival. Both Molière and Boileau made contemptuous allusions to the b.

The b. of the great Fr. period was imitated in England by Chaucer and Gower, but it never established itself firmly in that country. In the later 19th c. a group of Eng. poets, including Austin Dobson, Andrew Lang, and W. E. Henley, revived the form with enthusiasm, inspired perhaps by the example of Théodore de Banville in France. But the later b., with the possible exception of a few of Swinburne's, has not even aimed at the grandeur and scope of Villon; it has been essentially a delicate and artificial exercise for light or polite versifiers.

The double b. is composed of six 8-line stanzas or six 10-line stanzas. The refrain is included but the *envoi* is optional.—Kastner; P. Champion, *Hist. poétique du XVᵉ s.* (2 v., 1923); J. Fox, *The Poetry of Villon* (1962).

BARD. A poet among the ancient Celtic peoples, whose function it was to celebrate the heroes, victories, or laws of the nation. By extension, in modern usage, any poet, though the term has often been applied to specific poets, notably Shakespeare and Milton.

The term (Welsh, *bardd;* Ir., *bard*) is used by the later L. writers, Lucan, for example, to describe the poets of Gaul and Britain. The bards, who constituted an entire separate social class with hereditary privileges, became extinct in Gaul at a relatively early date, but their existence in Ireland and Scotland until the 18th c. and in Wales, in some respects, until the present day supplies many details as to their organization.

The 10th-c. Welsh code of *Hywel Dda,* with its division of the bardic class into three categories, the *pencerdd* (chief of song), the *bardd teulu* (household bard), and the *cerddor* (minstrel), suggests the earlier Ir. distinction of *druid, filid,* and *baird.* These groups ultimately fell together under the classification *bard* as their separate functions merged.

The Welsh festivals or contests of poetry, known as *Eisteddfodau* (sing. *Eisteddfod,* q.v.) continued until the reign of Elizabeth I and were revived in 1822, since which date they have been regularly held. In modern Welsh usage, a bard is a poet who has participated in an Eisteddfod.

The art of the bards was essentially social in function, related to the life, traditions, and ideals of the community. Hence, it is in actuality far removed from the personal, lyric emotionalism connected with the term by the 18th-c. Eng. poets, such as Gray and Beattie, who revived it.—E. C. Quiggin, *Prolegomena to the Study of the Later Ir. Bards 1200–1500* (1914); H. I. Bell, *The Development of Welsh Poetry* (1936); G. Murphy, "Bards and Filidh," *Eigse,* 2 (1940); J. J. Parry, "The Court Poets of the Welsh Princes," PMLA, 67 (1952).　　　　F.J.W.; A.P.

BARDOLATRY. Literally, "worship of poets." The word was coined by George Bernard Shaw in the preface to *Three Plays for Puritans* (1901). Shaw used the term satirically to describe the adulation of Shakespeare which he felt was having a stifling effect on Eng. drama. —For a different point of view, see R. B. Heilman, "Bardolatry," *Yale Rev.*, 50 (1961).

A.R.B.

BAROQUE describes the style that prevailed in European literature between, roughly, 1580 and 1680; from the *Gerusalemme Liberata* to the last *autos* of Calderón. For those who view Western literature as a whole, and whose concern is to find a period term for the literary style between the decline of the Renaissance and the rise of the Enlightenment, no other word is as convenient. Indeed, no other could now be imposed. B. is by no means universally accepted as the sole designation for the period; considerable opposition to its use comes from partisans of separate national literatures. Since the term is embattled, and perhaps always will be, it is necessary to deal with its etymological origin and with the history of its application to the arts and to literature. Once a settlement of these questions is generally accepted, it will then be possible to liberate the term from its wayward origins, to lay the ghost of its past, and proceed to investigate the traits of the period style which it designates.

HISTORY OF THE WORD. The usual derivation of "b." from *barroco* (Portuguese: "irregular pearl") and eventually *verruca* (L.: "declivity," "wart") will have to be abandoned. Not only is the linguistic evidence untenable, but also there is practically no textual support. Instead, a good case can be made out for deriving the word from the mnemonic hexameters constructed in the 13th c. by William of Shyreswood as a code version of Aristotle's categories of syllogisms. The early history of the word can be traced by putting together citations from writers like St. Bernardine, Vives, Erasmus, Montaigne, Ferrari, Soldani, Saint-Simon, and others. In all these instances the word *baroco* was singled out as representing the absurd or grotesque pedantry of late medieval logic-chopping.

HISTORY OF THE CONCEPT. Until the later 19th c., "b." was used mostly as a fancy synonym for "absurd" or "grotesque." On occasion one finds it used in the older way: Baudelaire, for example, addressing the city of Paris, speaks of "Tes petits orateurs, aux enflures baroques, / Prêchant l'amour" ("Projet d'épilogue pour la seconde éd. des *Fleurs du Mal*"). The art historians J. Burckhardt (1855) and H. Wölfflin (1888) began the rehabilitation of the term, the first giving it historical limits and the second freeing it of

pejorative associations. It was quickly accepted in art history as a necessary term to designate the period after the High Renaissance; in fact, in the early part of the century, the succession of period styles was made more precise by the definition of an intermediate style between High Renaissance and b., to which the name "mannerism" was given. As far as literature is concerned, the first application of the concept b. was made in 1888 by Wölfflin, who, in his *Renaissance und Barock*, sketched a stylistic contrast between Ariosto (Renaissance) and Tasso (b.), based on the opening stanzas of *Orlando Furioso* and *Gerusalemme Liberata*. He further suggested that the same sort of contrast exists between Boiardo's *Orlando Innamorato* and Berni's *rifacimento* of it. From Boiardo to Tasso he traces a continuous trend away from clear visual imagination toward mood and atmosphere ("weniger Anschauung, mehr Stimmung"). Though literary historians were long in responding, it is from Wölfflin's contrast that we can date the beginnings of interest in b. as a literary concept.

Because of its enormous success, the concept of b. in art history has continued to exert strong influence on its literary counterpart. In 1922 Theophil Spoerri wrote a thorough study, *Renaissance und Barock bei Ariost und Tasso*, which attempted to fill Wölfflin's prescription. By this time Wölfflin had also published his *Kunstgeschichtliche Grundbegriffe* (May 1915; Eng. tr. *Principles of Art History* [1932]), which set forth categories (such as closed *versus* open form, linear *versus* painterly) for distinguishing between Renaissance and b. styles in art. Some have been tempted to apply the categories almost directly to literature, while others have emulated them at a distance. An instance of the former would be D. H. Roaten and F. Sánchez y Escribano, *Wölfflin's Principles in Sp. Drama: 1500–1700* (1952); and of the latter, I. Buffum, *Agrippa d'Aubigné's Les Tragiques: A Study of the B. Style in Poetry* (1951). Buffum takes his point of departure from Wölfflin, as well as purely literary devices such as asyndeton, verbal echo, and oxymoron, and arrives at general characteristics like forcefulness, theatricality, and mutability. With his *Four Stages of Renaissance Style* (1955), W. Sypher increases the indebtedness to Wölfflin. He undertakes to include both literature and art in a set of general stylistic categories drawn from Wölfflin and others. By means of them he attempts to distinguish his four styles: Renaissance (e.g., Spenser); mannerism (*Hamlet, Lear*); b. (*Othello, Paradise Lost*); late-b. (Dryden, Racine).

In varying degrees the debtors to Wölfflin show their awareness of the great difficulties in transferring art categories of style to literature. But in the end the difficulties remain unsolved. More independent attempts to define b. style in literature, based solely on literary aesthetics, have yielded results. Among the first was Fritz Strich, who in 1916 proposed that the use of the rhetorical figure asyndeton (*Worthäufung*) was the most characteristic element of b. style, at least in German poetry. In 1929 H. Hatzfeld, in his analysis of the religious lyric in France, went beyond rhetorical or syntactical devices and derived what he found to be characteristic motifs or themes, such as veiled antithesis (*Schleierantithese*) and solitude (*tout-seul-Formel*). Later, in his book *Literature Through Art: A New Approach to Fr. Literature* (1952), Hatzfeld undertook to establish other motifs common to literature and art of the b.: renunciation, resignation, boundlessness, to name a few.

STATUS OF B. IN IMPORTANT NATIONAL LITERATURES. (*1*) *Germany:* The rapid success of the term among German art historians and the early work of Strich, Viëtor, and others, led to a general acceptance among literary scholars. It is now taken for granted that b. is the proper name for the period embracing, for instance, Grimmelshausen, Gryphius, and Angelus Silesius. (*2*) *Spain:* The old term *siglo de oro* still competes; but the fact that the "century" lasted for considerably more than a hundred years, as well as the renewed interest in the Sp. Renaissance, has opened the way for the use of b. Central figures like Cervantes, Lope de Vega, and Quevedo have been analyzed as b. writers. Góngora, whose rehabilitation began in 1927, is now considered the extreme of b. style. A certain amount of confusion results from the continued use of the term *barroquismo,* which has pejorative and nontemporal connotations. (*3*) *France:* Interest in b. among Fr. critics has arisen mostly since the war. Partly this has come about as a result of revaluating the traditional concept of *classicisme* and the *grand siècle,* and partly from a reconsideration of the poets, such as Saint-Amant and Théophile de Viau, inaccurately called *précieux.* The essays and radical anthologies of Thierry Maulnier and the work of M. Raymond have been influential. So far, apart from the early work of German critics, the most ambitious book has been J. Rousset's *La Litt. de l'Age B. en France: Circé et le paon* (1953). (*4*) *Italy:* Here the b. was a relative decline. In poetry the important figures are few after Tasso, Marino, Tassoni, and Redi. Most scholarship on Marino and his followers has been concerned with mechanical detail, biography, or influence on Fr., German and Eng. poets of the time. *Marinismo* is generally deplored as a disease, and B. Croce finds *barocco* almost synonymous with bad taste.

More recently, however, there has been an upsurge of interest, and no fewer than three congresses on b. have been held since 1954, the latest (*Manierismo, Barocco, Rococò*) in 1962. In general, the term "b." seems to be accepted as the designation for the whole age. (*5*) *England:* Eng. critics have proved the most reluctant to adopt the concept of b. A main source of opposition is the happy coincidence between literary movements and the reigns of kings. The two episodes of the Renaissance in England roughly correspond to the reigns of Henry VIII and Elizabeth, and what elsewhere would be called b. corresponds in its origins to the reign of James I. In Eng. literature we find a special difficulty: the belated flowering of the Renaissance comes so close upon the beginning of the b. that the two styles for a time coexist. Nevertheless, a start has been made in distinguishing the styles, with Morris Croll's early analysis of b. prose style pointing the way.

B. STYLE IN POETRY. Among the least promising ways of approaching the question are to view b. as an eternal phenomenon, recurrent in all ages, or to limit it to the Counter-Reformation, or to depend wholly on the criteria of art history. Far preferable are independent formulations that begin with single works of literature and generalize on the basis of their purely literary traits. Among these we may consider rhetorical figures such as metaphor, the element of time, the dramatic situation of the poem, and the implied world view.

A common way of describing b. poetic style is to say that it abounds in conceits (*concetti, conceptos*), that is, puns or unusual similes. As examples, there is Donne's image of the compass and Marino's statement that if he cannot enjoy sleep he will at least enjoy the image of death (which is, of course, sleep). But it can be urged that such expressions represent habits of thought known in the Middle Ages and Renaissance: e.g., the pen as plowing furrows on the page or Petrarch's "I burn and am as ice." Some critics have tried to show that Eng. metaphysical poetry is characterized by extended metaphors running through the poem, but they have been effectively countered by L. Unger in *Donne's Poetry and Modern Criticism* (1950). It may be suggested that the quality of wit makes the difference; but that remains to be shown.

If a poem is looked upon as a communication in time, then time itself becomes an important element of structure. It can be shown that Renaissance poetry is generally simple in its use of tense and time reference, whereas b. poetry exhibits not only explicit awareness of the nature and passage of time but also a tendency to manipulate time and exploit its paradoxes.

The dramatic situation of a poem can be defined as the interaction between the speaker, the audience, and the reader. In Renaissance poetry, generally speaking, an attitude is expressed and then elaborated. In b. poetry, to state the contrast starkly, a tentative attitude is expressed and then, through interaction of the several dramatis personae, it is gradually modified until in the end a new attitude is achieved.

A final possible criterion is the so-called world-view of b. poetry. B. poetry often attempts to cover the enormous range between religious sentiments and libertinage, beauty and ugliness, egocentricity and impersonality, temporality and eternity. It is not surprising that such issues should arise in b. poetry: whatever their antiquity, they were presented with new immediacy by thinkers like Montaigne, Descartes, and Hobbes. We may look to Montaigne for a touchstone: "Je ne peins pas l'être; je peins le passage." Commonly words like disequilibrium and disillusionment (desengaño) are used of the period. If they are adopted, it may be considered that they express transitory resolutions of the problem of opposites.

It must be emphasized that a theory of b. poetic style ought to strike a balance between the general and the particular; that it ought to be able to account for the major works of the time in such a way as to distinguish their style significantly from what preceded and what succeeded them.

F. Strich, "Der lyrische Stil des 17. Jh.," Abhandlungen zur deutschen Literaturgesch. Festschrift für Franz Muncker (1916); H. Hatzfeld, Don Quixote als Wortkunstwerk (1927) and "Der Barockstil der religiösen klassischen Lyrik in Frankreich," Literaturwissenschaftliches Jahrbuch der Görresgesellschaft, 4 (1929); K. Viëtor, Probleme der dt. Barocklit. (1928); B. Croce, Storia della età barocca in Italia (1929); M. W. Croll, "The B. Style in Prose," Studies in Eng. Philology . . . in Honor of F. Klaeber, ed. K. Malone and M. B. Ruud (1929); W. P. Friederich, Spiritualismus und Sensualismus in der englischen Barocklyrik (1932); R. Wellek, "The Concept of B. in Lit. Scholarship," JAAC, 5 (1946); M. Mincoff, "B. Lit. in England," Annuaire de l'Université de Sofia, Faculté Historico-Phil., 43 (1947); C. Calcaterra, "Il Problema del Barocco," Problemi ed orientamenti critici di lingua e di lett. ital., ed. A. Momigliano (1949); Revue des sciences humaines (numéro spécial), fasc. 55–66 (1949), containing articles by the institutors of B. in France, M. Raymond, R. Lebègue, etc.; O. de Mourgues, Metaphysical, B. and Précieux Poetry (1953); L. Nelson, "Góngora and Milton: Toward a Definition of the B.," CL, 6 (1954) and B. Lyric Poetry (1961); F. Strich, "Die Übertragung des Barockbegriffes von der bildenden Kunst auf die Dichtung," Die Kunstformen des Barockzeitalters, ed. R. Stamm (1956); I. Buffum, Studies in the B. from Montaigne to Rotrou (1957); A. Cioranescu, El barroco (1957); M. Praz, The Flaming Heart (1958); H. Hatzfeld, "Use and Misuse of 'B.' as a Critical Term in Lit. Hist.," Univ. of Toronto Quarterly, 31 (1962). See also J. Rousset, "La Définition du terme 'B.,' " Intern. Comparative Lit. Assoc. Proc. of the Third Congress (1962); R. Daniells, Milton, Mannerism and B. (1963); R. Wellek, Concepts of Crit., ed. S. G. Nichols, Jr. (1963; see "Postscript 1962" to b.).   L.N.

BAROQUE POETICS. It could hardly be claimed that the baroque age was original and productive in elaborating a theory of poetry. Actually, it inherited, modified, and passed on to the age of neoclassicism the formulations of the Renaissance: Castelvetro, Scaliger, Minturno, and others (see RENAISSANCE POETICS) had placed Aristotle in the center of importance where he went almost unchallenged until the stirrings of the romantic revolution. B. poetics, therefore, derived its theory ultimately from the precepts of Aristotle, with a varying admixture of Horatian loci and rhetorical dicta: poetry is both useful and pleasing, the poet must possess the faculty of invention, poetry is related to the real world in that it is an imitation of nature, art is in some way distinct from nature and yet it cannot transgress the norms nature imposes, the poet should be good as well as eloquent. Only in matters of emphasis can a few theoreticians be called original.

Apart from exposition of theory, treatises of the time often had ulterior motives: to reaffirm the worth and dignity of poetry, to provide a didactic guide or handbook to poetic practice, and to make a case for poetry in the vernacular. Such purposes had also been served by Renaissance "defenses" and "arts of poetry"; in fact, there seems little new in most of the many b. treatises of the kind. Martin Opitz' Buch von der deutschen Poeterey (1624), for example, is heavily indebted to Ronsard and Heinsius, among others. Likewise, Ben Jonson's Timber, or Discoveries (first published in 1641) is almost wholly derivative from classical and Renaissance sources. For the most part their fame as critics is due to their chronological originality within the hypothetically closed system of a national literature. On the other hand, Jonson's opinions as recorded in his Conversations (1619) with Drummond of Hawthornden are refreshingly pungent and personal. Though they are hardly argued criticism, they surpass in interest, because of their sharp and imperious phrasing, the many "roll calls" (to use Spingarn's term) from Cervantes' *Viaje del Parnaso* (1614) to Boileau's historical sketch of poetry in his *Art poétique* (1674).

As the 17th c. progressed there was a trend, parallel with the growing influence of Fr. critics, toward stricter and stricter interpretation of neoclassical doctrine. At the same time, several relatively new concepts were given some prominence; relatively new, because in one form or another they could be found anticipated in the Renaissance. In general, they had to do with the "ineffable" in art, the phenomena which escaped traditional analysis. First of all, the notion of taste (*gusto, goût*) became a means of explaining bewildering differences of opinion among readers and unargued judgments of critics. Its consequences for later criticism are much greater than its prominence in the b. Second, the notion of "wit" or "genius" (*ingegno, ingenio, génie* or *esprit*) accounted for the inventive faculty (corresponding to "fancy" or the later "imagination"). The obvious problem presented itself: could a poet without "wit" but possessed of skill write satisfactory poetry; and could a poet with "wit" but without skill do the same? One must keep in mind, while following the word "wit" through its many convolutions, that its meanings, ranging from "ingeniousness" to "imagination," ultimately depend upon the L. substratum *ingenium* and its customary contrast with *iudicium* or "judgment." A third important concept evolved during the age was the *je ne sais quoi* (in the later phrase of Pope, the "grace beyond the reach of art"). It is a vague recognition that the "rules" (q.v.) did not account for everything. Later in the century it may be seen to be related to the new interest in the "sublime" which brought about the resuscitation of Longinus. Again, its substratum is the Latin *nescio quid;* but it is important to observe that the common locution has become almost a technical term. In most instances, however, these relatively new concepts did not receive thorough exposition and analysis until the age of neoclassicism proper.

It is true that there were conservative and liberal interpretations of the rules. There were, in the major European literatures, proponents of the strictest observance (e.g., La Mesnardière, el Pinciano) whose appeal to authority was as dogmatic as it was inadequate. On the other hand, there were independent interpreters of the ancients whose "liberalism" has sometimes been given exaggerated importance. Nothing will make up for the obvious lack of original theory in the age, especially at a time when new modes of lyric poetry and the drama, not to mention the novel, were being created. In England, for instance, Shakespeare, Milton, and Donne had varying receptions at the hands of different critics, but none, despite often recognized excellence, was properly explicated or accounted for by contemporary criticism. The less revolutionary Corneille caused a split in orthodoxy; and even Racine was attacked. Lope de Vega felt himself within the bounds of a liberal classicism, and yet his practice in writing the seemingly hybrid form of the Sp. *comedia* was censured by the strict. In general, it may be said that the critics, as so often happens, were unprepared for novelty: their ready-made theory gave them the hardihood to reject anything for which they could not cite precedent; mere mechanical conformity often received their highest praise.

It is a custom to view Fr. literature at times as a long sequence of controversies or "quarrels." Certainly there is one whose importance cannot be denied and whose international consequences are part of the aesthetics of the age: the quarrel of the ancients and the moderns. The problem of "imitation" (in many of the possible meanings of that unfortunate translation of *mimesis*) led illogically to the problem of how and with what fidelity to "imitate" the ancients, which in turn led illogically to the question of whether the ancients were superior to the moderns. Though the most interesting consequences of that quarrel belong to the succeeding age, it must be recognized that the dispute was already implicit in the tenets of Renaissance neoclassicism, and that it was the newly expounded notion of "progress" that brought it into prominence.

In the larger context of aesthetics and philosophical systems one may find plausible reasons for the absence of an original poetics and for the prevailing poetic practice of the time. Generally speaking, the rationalist cast of thought in Bacon and Descartes required a separation between reason and imagination, thought and feeling. Hence a theoretical "distrust of the imagination" and a "dissociation of sensibility" (q.v.). But Descartes's neglect of aesthetics and Bacon's perfunctory consideration of poetry had no immediate effect on poetics. Whether the anti-Aristotelian reformer, Petrus Ramus, whose works on dialectic (1555, 1556) long remained textbooks, actually influenced poetic practice by making the elements of poetry a part of logic rather than rhetoric, remains a difficult, perhaps wrongly posed, problem. There is a danger in mistaking mere reshufflings of terms and categories for real innovation, just as there is a danger in assuming that poets wrote their poetry according to prescription. Nevertheless, it is obvious that b. poetry is characterized by intricacy and ingeniousness and that the most original poetics of the time were influenced by rhetoric and dialectic, whether the classical-medieval tradition or the newer systems.

Before surveying the major countries, it is appropriate to recall what was in the common heritage, common above all because most of it was in L. Horace was of course immediately available; Aristotle's *Poetics* was in L. and commented and presented by, for instance, Castelvetro; Vida and Scaliger, too, were in the learned language. They also had in common the rhetorical tradition which, unlike the tradition of poetics, had gone unbroken from antiquity through the Middle Ages. In fact, before Aristotle became ascendant in the middle of the 16th c., the poetics were heavily dependent on rhetorical theory. That dependence continued, and can be clearly seen in, for example, Puttenham, Gracián, and Tesauro.

Within Fr. literature of the 17th c. it would be possible to make an elaborate and microscopic analysis of the fortune of various parts of the neoclassical canon, from Malherbe to Boileau. There would, predictably, be the liberals and the conservatives, but the basic theory would appear quite static. If one were to conceive of neoclassicism in the most rigid fashion, it would then be easy to cull eccentric opinions and label them anticlassical (or, as Spingarn does, "romantic"); but the whole question would have been formulated falsely. As for the relation between poetry and theory, it may be said that only as poets began to conform to the "rules" did a rapprochement come about. B. poetic theory was certainly powerless to deal with D'Aubigné or even Théophile de Viau. Its precepts, however, could be made to fit more conservative poets, such as Malherbe and Voiture. Even the doctrines of *préciosité* (q.v.) are more an evidence of neoclassical purism than a defense of novel poetic practice. The triumph of current theory, in a sense its proof after the fact, were the great tragedies of Racine.

In England, aside from occasional comments by Jonson or Milton or other poets (Carew's, in his *Elegy upon the Death of Doctor Donne*, are the most perceptive), perhaps the greatest interest is to be found in b. poetics is the question of epic poetry. It is presented most fully in the exchange between William Davenant and Thomas Hobbes in regard to the former's epic *Gondibert* (1650). Davenant makes the conventional remarks about the epic, and argues that it is proper for him to write on a Christian subject, especially for the purpose of "instruction." True, he allows for effects beyond the rules ("shadowings, happy strokes, secret graces"), but we have seen that b. neoclassicism quickly granted such "libertics." A great deal of the treatise is directed toward demonstrating the moral efficacy of poetry; in fact, he comes close to the *reductio ad absurdum* of neoclassical criticism, the sugar-coated pill theory of poetry. Hobbes's answer is hardly more than a perfunctory agreement. One turns in vain to Cowley's "Preface to *Poems*" (1668) for some sketch of a poetics of the "Metaphysicals"; unfortunately, the few hints of theory are quite traditional. Nor do Henry Peacham's chapter on poetry in *The Compleat Gentleman* (1622) or Henry Reynold's *Mythomystes* (1633?) arouse more than antiquarian interest.

In Italy there is some rapprochement between contemporary practice and theory. From letters and poetic passages of Marino (see MARINISM) one can derive a few traits of a primitive theory of poetry. Its purpose is hardly to instruct at all: it tries to please, to play upon the senses, to be an end in itself. The goal of the good poet is to astonish or dazzle his readers by the brilliance and opulence of his descriptions and turns of phrase. The only important treatise is Emanuele Tesauro's *Cannochiale aristotelico* (1654), which is more a handbook of rhetoric than a poetics. It can be seen as representing the old rhetorical tradition; yet its emphasis on wit and the conceit is relatively novel. Of similar interest is Matteo Pellegrini's *Delle acutezze* (1639).

In Spain the situation is generally as elsewhere: liberals and conservatives manipulate the same counters. There is some novelty and interest in Gracián's treatise *Agudeza y Arte de Ingenio* (1642, 1648), which can be set in the same tradition as Tesauro's. Essentially, it is an elaborate and not always consistent classification of kinds of wit (*ingenio*). With great patience and perseverance it attempts to categorize and exemplify the "ingenious" effects achieved by poets ever since antiquity, with special pride of place for such contemporaries as the Argensolas and Góngora. In the main, however, its theory is traditional: there is a sort of poetic substance on which the poet attaches his "ornament" and the "ornament" is a local achievement which is almost seen as independent of the total poem. Gracián's work is mostly a commented anthology of "ingenious" poems and passages.

It could not be gainsaid that there are points of particular interest in b. poetics, such as the development of some important concepts (taste, wit, the *je ne sais quoi*) and a new compenetration of poetics and rhetoric (e.g., Tesauro and Gracián, and the somewhat exaggerated influence of Ramus). But we must conclude that it was unsuccessful in elaborating an original theory of poetry, that it fails to account for the poetic practice of the age, and that its main importance is to transmit the canons of neoclassical criticism from the Renaissance to the full flowering and achievement of the age of neoclassicism.

SOME ADDITIONAL PRIMARY WORKS: P. de

Deimier, *L'Académie de l'art poétique* (1610);
J. Chapelain, Preface to Marino's *L'Adone*
(1623); P. de la Mesnardière, *Poétique* (1639).
—G. Chapman, Prefaces to his *Homer* (1610–
16?); B. Jonson, "To the memory of my beloved the author, Mr. William Shakespeare"
(1623); W. Alexander, *Anacrisis* (1634?).—G.
Galilei, *Considerazioni al Tasso* and *Postille
all'Ariosto* (ca. 1600); T. Boccalini, *Ragguagli
di Parnaso* (1613); A. Tassoni, *Pensieri diversi*
(1620).—L. A. de Carvallo, *El cisne de Apolo*
(1602); L. Carrillo de Sotomayor, *Libro de la
erudición poética* (1611); C. Suárez de Figueroa, *El pasajero* (1617); J. de Jáuregui, *Discurso poético* (1623).

GENERAL WORKS: M. Menéndez y Pelayo,
Historia de las ideas estéticas en España (9 v.,
unfinished, 1883–91); J. E. Spingarn, *A Hist.
of Lit. Crit. in the Renaissance* (1899) and
Crit. Essays of the 17th C. (3 v., 1909); B.
Croce, *Estetica* (1902; best Eng. ed. 1922) and
"I trattatisti italiani del Concettismo e Bal-
tasar Gracián," *Problemi di estetica* (1909); H.
Gillot, *La Querelle des anciens et des modernes
en France* (1914); Bray; G. Marzot, *L'Ingegno
e il genio del seicento* (1944); H. T. Sweden-
berg, *The Theory of the Epic in England,
1650–1800* (1944); Tuve; E.B.O. Borgerhoff, *The
Freedom of Fr. Classicism* (1950); A. Vilanova,
"Preceptistas de los siglos XVI y XVII," *His-
toria general de las literaturas hispánicas*, ed.
G. Díaz-Plaja, III (1953); M. Raymond, *B. et
Renaissance poétique* (1955); W. S. Howell,
Logic and Rhetoric in England, 1500–1700
(1956); A. J. Smith, "An Examination of Some
Claims for Ramism," RES, n.s., 7 (1956); E.
Haase, "Zur Bedeutung von 'Je ne sais quoi'
im 17. Jh.," *Zeitschrift für französische Sprache
und Lit.*, 67 (1956); Wimsatt and Brooks; S. L.
Bethell, "The Nature of Metaphysical Wit,"
Discussions of John Donne, ed. F. Kermode
(1962).   L.N.

BARZELLETTA. It. verse form originally
characterized by an accumulation of unconnected, bizarre, and sometimes senseless subject matter and by haphazard meter and
rhyme. By the early 14th c. its epigrammatic
qualities were utilized to make the composition a vehicle for moral instruction. By the
end of the 14th c. it had assumed truly artistic
proportions. Notwithstanding its moral, political, or satirical intent, the b. often remained
on the level of the rigmarole full of proverbs
or witty didacticisms in 7-syllable couplets
or unrhymed pentameters, heptameters, or
hendecasyllables with internal rhyme. In the
15th and 16th c. it was known as the *frottola-
barzelletta*, really a sort of *ballata*, and was
much in vogue with courtly poets who used
it to sing of their loves or whims in simple
meters. The octosyllabic carnival songs of

Lorenzo de' Medici afford the most famous examples of these.—V. Pernicone, "Storia e
svolgimento della metrica," in *Problemi ed
orientamenti critici di lingua e di letteratura
italiana*, ed. A. Momigliano, 2 (1948); Wilkins.
                                                    A.S.B.

BATHOS (Gr. "profundity" or "height," according to the point of view, cf. L. *altitudo*).
1. Though Longinus made b. a synonym of
hypsos (the sublime) in *On the Sublime* 2.1),
Pope, who can hardly be supposed ignorant
of Longinus' meaning, took a new departure
and made it an antonym in his parody of
Longinus' treatise, *Peri Bathous: or, Martinus
Scriblerus His Treatise of the Art of Sinking
in Poetry*, 1728. The commonest meaning of
the word ever since has been that of Pope,
namely, an unintentionally ludicrous because
ill-managed attempt at elevated expression, in
the 18th c. most often an expression of pathos
in its wide Aristotelian sense of passion (i.e.,
any of the passions or emotions), later, of
pathos in its more modern, narrower sense of
the sad or pitiable. These meanings are obviously accountable in no small measure to the
accidental similarity of the two Gr. words,
pathos and *bathos*. Pope illustrates with "Ye
Gods! annihilate both Space and Time, / And
make two Lovers happy" (ed. E. L. Steeves,
1952, p. 52); Elizabeth Barrett Browning ardently recalls "Our Euripides, the human— /
With his droppings of warm tears" (*Wine of
Cyprus* 89–90); and Tennyson misfires with
"He suddenly dropt dead of heart-disease"
(*Sea Dreams* 64). A veritable feast of b. is to
be enjoyed in "an anthology of bad verse"
entitled *The Stuffed Owl*, selected and arranged by D. B. Wyndham Lewis and C. Lee
(1930).

2. The use of the word for a deliberately
contrived effect of pathos *manqué* or any kind
of deliberate anticlimax, in the way of irony,
gay or serious, is also current, though less
common, and is perhaps best avoided. See
ANTICLIMAX 2.   H.B.

BATTLE OF THE ANCIENTS AND MOD-
ERNS. The name given to two more or less
specific literary "battles," one in France and
a somewhat related one in England, in the
last part of the 17th and the earliest part of
the 18th c.

The backgrounds are found, first, in the
growth in prominence of France and England,
especially France, economically and culturally,
and the consequent increase of nationalistic
pride; and, secondly, in the growth of the scientific spirit and the idea of Progress. A century before the battle proper, the relative value
of Fr. as against L. for literary purposes had
been argued and explored, most significantly

in du Bellay's famous *Défense et Illustration* (1549). The rise of the Fr. Academy in the first half of the 17th c., and especially the argument over Corneille's *Cid* in the 1630's indicated how deeply some important Fr. minds were committed to the rules derived from ancient poetry and the Aristotelian tradition. Veneration for Homer reached a height in *Discours . . . Moïse et d'Homère* in 1604 and in du Souhait's *Préface* to his translation in 1620. And Descartes' *Discours de la Méthode* in 1636, with its contempt for the past and its wholehearted faith in rational method, was one of the most important books in the development of the modern spirit. Then the several serious, unsuccessful attempts at Christian epics by Saint-Amand, de Scudéry, and Chapelain also helped to prepare the ground.

The battle can be said to have begun with Desmarets de Saint Sorlin's comments on heroic poetry and the Christian Marvellous in the *Préface* to his poem *Marie-Magdeleine*, 1669. In it and *Traité pour Juger des Poètes Grecs, Latins, et Français* (1670), he speaks for modern, Christian poetry as against the pagan, improbable, immoral, and inelegant epics of Homer and Virgil. In 1676, the year of his death, he formally gave over the defense of the cause to Charles Perrault.

In 1678, Perrault, in his introduction to an edition of *Jerusalem Delivered*, praised Tasso over the ancients. In 1682, Pierre Bayle's *Pensées Divers sur la Comète*, a devastatingly brilliant attack on traditional modes of thinking, came out, and the next year Fontenelle, a *précieux* popularizer of the ideas of Bayle, published his *Dialogue des Morts*, where he defends the moderns. In 1687 Perrault's *Le Siècle de Louis le Grand*, an extravagant piece of flattery of the modern century, was answered by La Fontaine's *l'Epître à Huet*, a graceful defense of the ancients, and also attacked by Boileau, Dacier, and Longepierre. Perrault and Fontenelle replied to these attacks in the following year. In 1693 Boileau wrote *Pensées sur Longin* and Perrault wrote a response. By 1694, through the offices of Arnault, the quarrel was pretty well ended, and Boileau set the capstone by a conciliatory letter to Perrault in 1700. A bit over a decade later, there was a flareup of the battle concerning Homer, but it did not last long.

In England the quarrel arose in the 1690's when Wotton and Bentley pointed out some manifest inadequacies in Sir William Temple's classical scholarship (he had praised ancient over modern learning). This is important in that it involved the beginnings of genuine historical scholarship in England and in that, more important from a literary standpoint, it led to Swift's defense of Temple, *The Battle of the Books*.

The quarrel has its paradoxes: its chief historical importance is that it was closely related to a greater quarrel, that between the positivistic and the Christian spirits. Nonetheless, the moderns began by defending the Christian Marvellous, and Pierre Bayle, the greatest of the moderns, contemned the idea of Progress. Perhaps the moral is that the fight and some bigger, later ones need not have occurred. Pascal, in *Fragment d'un Traité sur le Vide*, 1646–51, had explained clearly that the sciences are progressive and cumulative, in a sense "perfectible," in a way that philosophy, theology, and the arts are not.—H. Gillot, *La Querelle des Anciens et des Modernes en France* (1914); R. F. Jones, *Ancients and Moderns* (1936). L. Wencelius, "La Querelle des Anciens et des Modernes et l'Humanisme," *Bulletin de la Société d'Etude du XVIIᵉ s.*, 9–10 (1951).   P.R.

BEAST EPIC. A long tale using animals for characters and told in a quasi-epic manner. The L. fable collection of Phaedrus (1st c. A.D.), based upon what is called Aesop, inspired numerous fables and fable collections in Western Europe, and some of these, simplifying the actions of men under beast forms, were well suited to satire. In the *Fredegarius* (7th c.) there is the story of the deer who had no heart (because the fox had already eaten it). In Lorraine in the 10th c. there were two poetic tales in L.: the *Ecbasis cuiusdam captivi* (leonine hexameters) and the *De Gallo et Vulpe* (iambic dimeter). The second of these is the first appearance of the Chanticleer theme. Around 1152 there was a movement to oppose a continuation of the Second Crusade and Nivard of Flanders composed to this purpose, his *Ysengrimus* (elegiac couplets). This has twelve episodes, all satirical.

The term "beast epic" is properly applied to the *Roman de Renart*. Pierre de Saint-Cloud composed the earliest branch of this (no. 2) in 1173. In this the first episode is the tale of Chanticleer. Gradually the creatures were portrayed as knights on chargers, and their dens were sometimes called castles. Faint mockery of epic themes grew as the Branches continued. In the late 12th c. Heinrich der Glîchezâre adopted some of these tales in his *Reinhart Fuchs*. The finest version, *Van den Vos Reinaerde*, developed in Flanders in the early 13th c. Goethe's *Reineke Fuchs* goes back ultimately to this. Chaucer retold the Chanticleer theme in his Nun's Priest's Tale making use of the Fr., and possibly of the Glîchezâre versions. In these later adaptations there is less epic satire, and more of the animal fable.—H. Büttner, *Studien zu dem Roman de Renart and dem Reinhart Fuchs* (2 v., 1891); L. Sudre, *Les Sources du Roman de Renart*

(1893); L. Foulet, *Le Roman de Renard* (1914); A. Graf, *Die Grundlagen des Reineke Fuchs* (1920); M. de Meyer, *Les Contes populaires de la Flandre* (1921); R. Bossuat, *Le Roman de Renard* (1957); H. R. Jauss, *Untersuchungen zur mittelalterlichen Tierdichtung* (1959).

U.T.H.

BEAT. Regularly reccurring metrical emphasis in accentual poetic lines. The term is often used instead of "stress" (q.v.) by prosodists who are pressing the analogies between verse and music and who are thinking of the metrical foot (q.v.) as an almost exact parallel with the musical bar. The expression "a 5-beat line" emphasizes the "ideal" or "normal" accentual pattern and suggests that the number of syllables may vary as long as the five structural beats are present. See METER.

P.F.

BEAT POETS. The term is applied to a loosely knit group of Am. lyric poets identified more by period of productivity (1955–60), by common outlets (*Evergreen Review, Pocket Poets Series, Beatitudes*), and by a sharing of social attitudes (apolitical, anti-intellectual, romantic nihilism—"beat" meaning variously "beaten down," "beaten up," and "beatific") than by stylistic, thematic, or formal unity of expression. Membership in the group known as beat is or was held by such widely diversified poets as the neo-Whitmanesque Allen Ginsberg (b. 1926), the "spontaneous" automatic writer Jack Kerouac (b. 1922), the pure romantic symbolist Gregory Corso (b. 1930), and the careful dadaist-surrealist (qq.v.) craftsman Lawrence Ferlinghetti (b. 1919). The vague poetic antecedents of beat creation thus include the whole tradition of Am., British, and Fr. romanticism (q.v.), ranging from realistic outbursts of protest in the style of Am. proletarian Marxist poetry of the 1930's through visions of cerebral-emotional ecstasy à la Rimbaud to experiments in language and form tangential to the work of E. E. Cummings. Kenneth Rexroth initially served the movement as a kind of mentor, as did Henry Miller; after their disillusionment with its aims and membership, Paul Goodman and Norman Mailer assumed roles of "adult" sponsors for the b. movement. If b. poetry has any common denominator apart from the proclivity of its authors to make it recitable to the accompaniment of jazz, this would consist in its exaltation of ecstatic, visionary states of emotion and apperception. For that reason, its more religious votaries tend to subscribe to forms of mystical adoration including Roman Catholic (Brother Antoninus, O.P., b. 1912), Jewish (Allen Ginsberg), and Buddhistic (Gary Snyder, b. 1930) modes; more secularly minded b. poets, on the other hand, place explicit

faith in the visionary powers of drugs (Gregory Corso, Michael Rumaker, b. 1932). The work of the b. poets has been widely translated and diffused in Europe, notably in Germany and in the Scandinavian countries. It came to be recognized more fully as an important form of Am. literary expression in the Berlin, Paris, or Copenhagen of 1961 than in its native centers of San Francisco and New York.—*Evergreen Review*, 1, no. 2 (1957) and later issues; W. B. Fleischmann, "Those 'Beat' Writers," *America*, 161 (Sept. 26, 1959); L. Lipton, *The Holy Barbarians* (1959); *The Beats*, ed. S. Krim (1960); *The New Am. Poetry, 1945–1960*, ed. D. M. Allen (1960).

W.B.F.

BEGINNING RHYME. See RHYME.

BELGIAN POETRY (in French. For FLEMISH POETRY see that article). It was about the year 1880 that Belgium awakened to poetry. Romanticism, of course, had already hatched a few talents, but with more sincerity or ambition than real success. To the writers of *La Jeune Belgique* must be granted the merit of having begotten the literary and poetical works which were still wanted, after half a century of independence, by a prosperous nation. Albert Giraud, Ivan Gilkin, and a few others remained true to the motto "l'art pour l'art" of the Fr. Parnassians. In 1887, about ten years after the publication in Paris of the last volume of *Le Parnasse contemporain français*, the poems of eighteen Belg. authors were assembled in *Le Parnasse de la Jeune Belgique*. But already three or four of them were searching other paths. A new way was shown by Georges Rodenbach whose delicate and nostalgic inspiration could not accord his mezzotinto with the austere objectivity of the Parnassian school. Emile Verhaeren, for his part, broke off with Albert Giraud who was the declared enemy of the so-called vers libre. Thus the unity of the group became loose.

About the same time, poets of France and Belgium were regrouping elsewhere. In 1886, the Moréas manifesto and the first issue of *Le Symboliste* came out in Paris. In Liège, Albert Mockel founded *La Wallonie*, which, after an unsteady start, became soon one of the most important spokesmen of the new tendency, with contributions by Charles Van Lerberghe, Max Elskamp, Grégoire Le Roy, Maurice Maeterlinck. André Fontainas introduced there Stuart Merrill and Pierre Quillard, the fellow mates of the lycée Condorcet. In 1887, the Mockel review opened its columns to the set of *Les Ecrits pour l'art* which had ceased their publication in Paris and whose manager, René Ghil, with Emile Verhaeren already known in the Fr. literary world, joined the Belg. group. Moréas, Verlaine, Vielé-Griffin,

-[73]-

André Gide, Henri de Régnier, and Paul Valéry, these two last at their start, sent contributions to the Belg. review, and a binding fellowship mingled ages and nationalities. The bonds were not broken between the prewar poets and the postwar poets like Georges Marlow, Thomas Braun, Jean de Bosschère, Franz Hellens, Pierre Nothomb, Lucien Christophe, Noël Ruet, and others who, after 1918, continued the works of the elders.

Emile Verhaeren, after his tragic death in 1916, stood in all minds with higher honor than any one else, dead or alive, of his generation. His impetuous verse, with fiery rhythm, abode in all memories. He was unforgettable, the visionary of *Les Villes tentaculaires*, the powerful conjurer of the people and sites of *Toute la Flandre*, the marveled songster of *Les Heures*, the social prophet and apostle of human brotherhood, who finds his expression in many other books.

After 1918, the young poets, although they did homage to their predecessors, were seduced by the symbolist renewal which was starting in France. These tendencies found their assertion in *La Lanterne sourde* of Paul Vanderborght (1921) and in *Le Disque vert* which Franz Hellens published at the same time. Both of them arranged meetings of poets of France and Belgium in order to fix the common line of their literary intentions. Ten years later, in 1931, Pierre-Louis Flouquet founded in Brussels *Le Journal des Poètes,* which brought together the newcomers. After the second war, the same paper resumed its mission to defend genuine poetry.

It is difficult to single out, today more than ever, an autonomous poetical current in Belgium, although both the Flemish mood and the Walloon have had an influence on the Fr.-writing authors. It has been admitted that the rally of the Belg. symbolist poets took place on the Walloon territory, but was held by a majority of Flemish-born authors. It seems that the mystery of inner life and the manifestations of subconscious feelings which are the main topics of symbolism are linked with the mystical aspirations expressed by the brilliant school of painting of old Flanders. The innate liking for images, the keen observation of reality inherited from their ancestors, may have disposed these poets toward a symbolic form of expression.

Surrealism did not find as many adepts amidst those who came later. Its fantasy, its hermeticism, its incoherence may have shocked their good sense and their stern and minutely ordained realism. In return, the Walloon, imbued with Latinity and more open to all literary currents, has hailed without umbrage, if not always without surprise, the curious, unexpected and many times successful achievements of surrealism, following the excesses of dadaism. The new generation of Walloon poets has given several clever interpreters to the surrealist movement. To Charles Plisnier, Robert Vivier, Marcel Thiry, Edmond Vandercammen, Robert Goffin, Maurice Carême, Armand Bernier, Roger Bodart and their congeners, Flanders opposes but a very few Fr.-speaking poets, namely Franz Hellens, Marie Gevers, Camille Melloy, Robert Guiette.

If it has happened that Belg. writers have led the way for the Fr. ones—Franz Hellens and Jean de Bosschère were amidst the forerunners of surrealism—how much greater has been the influence of the Fr. poets. Yet the Belg. contribution to the vast Fr. literary production of today is at least as important and original as in the past.

ANTHOLOGIES: *Contemporary Belg. Poetry*, ed. and tr. J. Bithell (1911); *Poètes belges d'esprit nouveau*, ed. P. Vanderborght (1924); *Petite Anthologie des poètes belges d'expression française*, ed. O. Meurice (1932); *Florilège de la nouvelle poésie fr. en Belgique*, ed. G. Norge (1934); *Pages choisies des écrivains français de Belgique*, ed. L. Demeur et G. Vanwelkenhuyzen (1936); *Anthol. de la décade, 1930–40* (1942) and *Anthol. de la deuxième décade, 1940–50* (1951); *Poètes fr. de Belgique. De Verhaeren au surréalisme*, ed. R. Guiette (1948); *Lyra Belgica*, tr. C. and F. Stillman (2 v., 1950–51; in Eng.); *Jeune Poésie fr. de Belgique*, ed. G. Varin (1954).

HISTORY AND CRITICISM: Fr. Nautet, *Hist. des lettres belges d'expression fr.* (2 v., 1892–93); H. Liebrecht and G. Rency, *Hist. illustrée de la litt. belge de langue fr.* (1926); F. Castillo Najera, *Un Siglo de poesia belga* (1931; includes anthol.); G. Charlier, *Les Lettres fr. de Belgique* (1938); G. Deutrepont, *Hist. illustrée de la litt. fr. en Belgique* (1939); G. Charlier and J. Hanse, *Hist. illustrée des lettres fr. de Belgique* (1958). G.V.

BELIEF, PROBLEM OF. As it has recently been formulated, the question of beliefs in poetry primarily concerns the relation of the reader to the poem. It asks how, as readers, we respond to those statements that can be extracted from the literary work as the poet's version of "truth" and, aside from whether we agree or disagree with them, in what ways they enhance or inhibit our aesthetic response to the work as a whole. It is a question that has come increasingly to the fore as positivistic criteria for truth have achieved more exclusive dominance in the philosophical arena.

Of course, from Plato on, writers on poetics have explored the relation of the truths supposedly being expounded in a literary work to the truth of actual reality as maintained by the reader. And since, throughout much of the history of poetics, the presentation of truth has been held to be a major function of poetry (see MEANING, PROBLEM OF), this relation has been seen to be crucial in our valuing of the poem. Aside from the skeptical Plato, few earlier writers questioned the poet's inherent capacity *qua* poet to write truth. The dedication of the poet's talent was generally not so distinguished from that of the philosopher's or the scientist's as to require the setting of any precise "problem of belief" in the way we are now accustomed to finding it set. The reader's or the audience's belief could be taxed only by the patently unbelievable: by the fantastic or, for the more literal-minded, by the obvious delusions—the counterfeiting—of theatrical presentation. Indeed, through much of the 18th c. most of the talk about belief was confined to dramatic poetry. The argument of Samuel Johnson (*Preface to Shakespeare*, 1765) in which, using other terms, he distinguishes stage illusion from delusion—an argument taken up, with certain important changes in emphasis, by Samuel Taylor Coleridge (*Biographia Literaria*, 1817)—comes immediately to mind.

As, with the help of Coleridge and other defenders of poetry on the one hand and antipoetic positivistic thinkers on the other, the opposition of poetry to science was so urgently posed in the 19th c., what we now call the problem of belief was forced to be raised by both sides. For as the one saw the poet as superciliously transcending "mere" scientific truth, so the other arrogantly denied him access to its sacred precincts. In either case something had to be substituted for the poet's previously maintained responsibility to tell us that which, being true, we ought to believe, whether this something be raised to the ultimate mystical truths of the transcendental philosopher or relegated to the emotional satisfactions permitted by the coldblooded devotee of scientism. Since the increasingly scientific temper of the 19th c. was likely to translate the former of these into a kind of wish-fulfillment—of emotional origin itself—it was the latter which found expression as the "problem of belief," "belief" here taking on a meaning utterly separated from that of "truth."

Of course, an additional incentive toward the setting of this problem was found in the difficulty, frequently mentioned but never resolved and rarely specifically confronted, which asked how—if poems were to present statements of truth—we were to handle two or more excellent poems which rested on world-views that were mutually exclusive; or, more personally, how we were to accommodate poems whose world-views were uncongenial to our own.

In several places in his writings, but especially in the opening paragraphs of "The Study of Poetry" (1880), Matthew Arnold puts the problem most cogently. This formulation is very likely not original with him (for example, M. H. Abrams in *The Mirror and the Lamp*—see bibliography—cites earlier and more philosophically sophisticated statements of this position by John Stuart Mill and Alexander Smith of Banff, and, of course, though in a less clear way, by Coleridge himself); but in his influence generally, and specifically on I. A. Richards in our own day, Arnold can claim an especially significant place. In his poetry and prose alike Arnold frequently pines for the lost Christian medieval unity which, addressed primarily to human needs, proved so emotionally satisfying. Unfortunately, as he sees it, this unity had the advantage of being everything but right. And confronted by the truths of modern science, man has no choice but to abandon "the shadows and dreams and false shows of knowledge." But the truth which man gets in exchange for his religion—by the very virtue of being the cold, natural truth rather than the warm, human myth, of being adapted to the facts of nature rather than to the demands of human psychology—has none of the soothing power of the older, blessed falsehoods. Yet as reasoning creatures we dare not let this new truth go, although as feeling creatures we cannot do with it alone.

What is needed, then, is something which will do religion's job while not, like religion, depending upon a falsification of facts to get the job done. But, as we see also in his debates with T. H. Huxley (for example, "Literature and Science," 1882), Arnold appears implicitly to concede to the positivists that science's is the only way of putting the facts that does not falsify them; and this is the cold, humanly unsatisfying way. If poetry, then, is to take religion's place while avoiding its fatal errors, it would seem to be required to serve as a kind of objectless religion which can give us the emotional satisfaction without demanding the commitment. Thus, despite other discussions of his—like those which speak of "poetic truth"—which reveal more than anything else his ambivalence and inconsistencies, Arnold seems to set the terms more systematically employed by I. A. Richards (see PSEUDO-STATEMENT) to dissociate the seeming statements of poetry from any claims to literal truth.

What poetry says it says only provisionally in order to inculcate sufficient make-believe belief to produce the emotional effect which our psychological needs have a right to demand of the poetic occasion. Consequently the poet need fear no clash between the seeming beliefs in his poem and either the truths of science, the seeming beliefs presented in other poems, or the beliefs of his readers. In the realm of myth all can accommodate and be accommodated. And all this becomes precisely the formulation of Richards who, in his discussion of poetry as "emotive" in contrast to "referential" discourse (*Principles of Literary Criticism*, 1924), in his invention of the term "pseudo-statement," and in the very title of the chapter in which he employs this term ("Poetry and Beliefs," *Science and Poetry*, 1926), explicitly sets this forward as a major problem in contemporary literary criticism.

T. S. Eliot's approach to poetics would seem to be diametrically opposed to that of the early Richards. His religious orthodoxy leads to an absolutism that would deny the positivistic psychologizing of Richards. Yet surprisingly we find his ideas about beliefs in poetry close in many ways to Richards'. According to Eliot, the poet borrows his beliefs from his environment and in the poem deals with how it feels for one to hold them. He need neither create his beliefs nor defend them since his concern is not with the beliefs themselves—his mere raw materials—but with their "emotional equivalents," although, as dictated by the "objective correlative" (q.v.) he can convey only the "objective equivalents" of these emotions. Thus the quality of the beliefs is essentially irrelevant to the quality of the poem.

Eliot does realistically acknowledge that beliefs must be fairly "mature" if, though we should not agree with them, they are not to get in the way of our reading of the poem. We must credit them with being respectable enough for a reasonably adult and intelligent man to hold so that we can forget about them and focus on what counts—the objectification of the emotions he feels as a holder of these beliefs. But, as Eliot claims is the case when we read Shelley, if the beliefs are puerile they obtrude upon us and block our attempt to read the poetry sympathetically as poetry.

Thus Eliot too separates the poem and its beliefs from any kind of "truth." The function of the beliefs is the rather negative one of staying out of the way so that the poetry can carry out its emotive assignment. Further, his dichotomy between the beliefs in the poem and the "poetry" in the poem, like the older form-content dichotomy which it resembles, prevents the more organic and contextual treatment of poems which our most influential recent critics have called for. Critics like Allen Tate and Cleanth Brooks, for example, must treat this problem differently from Eliot. They would see the poetic weakness of a Shelley as arising not so much from the puerility of his beliefs as from his failure to hold them in the formal context of his poem. As a result they present themselves out of context as ideas; they leap forth as ideas and plead to be judged

as true or false much as we would judge a scientific or philosophic idea. If they were held in the context, they would never so present themselves and could not fairly be so judged. Of course, it can be argued, if a Shelley were to hold his beliefs in the poem's context in the manner suggested, he would perforce have to give them depth and complexity so that they would no longer betray the puerility with which Eliot charged them.

There is, however, more than a verbal difference between the two charges. While Eliot's objection is aimed at the content side of a form-content dichotomy, the other objection is aimed at a weakness in the unified context which should combine these two elements organically. Our agreement with Eliot's objection would depend upon whether or not we thought the poet's beliefs to be puerile; this is hardly a literary problem and surely not one that can be resolved by reference to the objective features of the work. Our agreement with the other objection would depend on how similar our analysis of the poem would be to that of those making the charge. This is a literary problem which can be solved only by a constant appeal to the objective features of the work. We should have simply to decide, although in practice it is rarely simple, whether or not the poem was functioning as a fully self-contained aesthetic object; to decide, in other words, whether the statements in the poem were functioning merely referentially or whether they were functioning purely cross-referentially, contextually. Thus this matter of beliefs is still a major source of difficulty even in the objective and perhaps somewhat neoclassical form of practical criticism as it is performed today.

I. A. Richards, "Poetry and Beliefs," *Science and Poetry* (1926); T. S. Eliot, "Dante," *Selected Essays 1917–1932* (1932) and *The Use of Poetry and the Use of Crit.* (1933); C. Brooks, "The Problem of Belief and the Problem of Cognition," *The Well Wrought Urn* (1947); A. Tate, "Three Types of Poetry," *On the Limits of Poetry* (1948); M. H. Abrams, "Science and Poetry in Romantic Crit.," *The Mirror and the Lamp* (1953); E. Vivas, "Lit. and Knowledge," *Creation and Discovery* (1955); *Lit. and Belief*, ed. M. H. Abrams (1958; EIE, 1957); K. Smidt, *Poetry and Belief in the Work of T. S. Eliot* (2d ed., 1961); N. Frye, *The Well-Tempered Critic* (1963).   M.KRIE.

BENGALI POETRY. See INDIAN POETRY.

BERGERETTE. See VIRELAI.

BESTIARY. A didactic genre, popular in the Middle Ages, in which moral or religious significance is attached to the real or reputed characteristics of animals, many of them legendary. Written in prose or verse, the medieval bestiaries go back ultimately to a lost Gr. work named *Physiologus* (The Naturalist), which was probably written in Alexandria in the 2d c. It was widely imitated and translated, and versions exist in Arabic, Armenian, Ethiopian, ON, and Old Syriac.

Often referred to as a manual for "unnatural natural history," the b. is important both as a source of symbolic types for later medieval art and as an example of the medieval habit of allegory. Some of the fabulous material of the bestiaries was utilized by such later writers and poets as John Lyly (*Euphues*), Milton, and Dryden.

Most bestiaries date from the 12th–14th c., and examples can be found in various European languages. Although bestiaries are usually Christian in their symbolic application, the *Bestiaire d'amour* (ca. 1250) of Richard de Fournival is a secular love allegory. The earliest surviving example in Fr. is Philippe de Thaon's *Bestiaire* (ca. 1125), written in 6-syllable couplets. Other Fr. bestiaries include *Le Bestiaire divin* (about 1210) by Guillaume le Clerc and the *Bestiaire* (end of 12th or beginning of 13th c.) by Gervaise. Interestingly, this genre was revived by G. Apollinaire with his *Bestiaire* in 1919. The poems on the *Panther* and the *Whale* in the Anglo-Saxon Exeter Book, together with a fragment on the *Partridge,* constitute the earliest Eng. b. A more complete example is the illustrated ME *Bestiary* of the 13th c. Partly rhymed and partly alliterative, it is based on the L. *Physiologus* of Theobaldus (an 11th-c. It. abbot) and other sources.—Fr. Lauchert, *Gesch. des Physiologus* (1889); M. Wellman, "Der Physiologus," *Philologus,* supp. 21 (1930); F. Sbordone, *Ricerche sulle fonti e sulla composizione del Physiologus greco* (1936); G. Cronin, Jr., "The B. and the Mediaeval Mind—Some Complexities," MLQ, 2 (1941); J. Calvet and M. Cruppi, *Le Bestiaire de la littérature française* (1954) and *Le Bestiaire de l'antiquité classique* (1955); F. McCulloch, *Mediaeval L. and Fr. Bestiaries* (rev. ed., 1962). A.P.

BIEDERMEIER. The term was first formulated by Ludwig Eichrodt (1827–1892) in analogy to F. Th. Vischer's bourgeois figure "Shartenmaier." Eichrodt and his circle parodied this bourgeois type and published, from 1885 on, *Die Gedichte des schwäbischen Schulmeisters Gottlieb Biedermaier und seines Freundes Horatius Treuherz* in the *Münchner Fliegenden Blättern.* These naive, rhymed verses were collected later in *Biedermaiers Liederlust* (1869), a book responsible for popu-

larizing the type B. as a philistine caught in a narrowly idyllic conception of the world. These parodies were especially directed at the literary efforts of Samuel Friedrich Sauter.

B. came into prominence as a stylistic and historical term, especially regarding painting, through the 1906 centenary exhibition in Berlin. As the name for a period of German literature, B. was introduced by J. Wiegand, P. Kluckhohn, W. Bietak, G. Weydt, etc. The term was supposed to encompass those writers and poets between romanticism and realism (e.g., Raimund, Nestroy, Niebergall, Grillparzer, Droste-Hülshoff, Mörike, Stifter) who could not be ascribed to the movement *Junges Deutschland.*

The characteristics of B., as defined by the above literary historians, especially P. Kluckhohn, were the degrading of the ideals of the classical and romantic movements to the limited, conservative sphere of a bourgeois idyll, characterized by such terms as "resignation," "love of details," "the glorification of a secure and simple middle-class life." Because of this limited attitude B. exhausted itself in minor literary productions: genre scenes, idylls, brief verse tales etc. The term "B." is, however, insufficient to describe and define adequately the works of major poets such as Stifter, Droste-Hülshoff, Mörike, Grillparzer. As so many other designations of literary periods (e.g., "baroque," "realism," "expressionism," etc.), the term "B." is to be treated with caution. It has never been satisfactorily defined and is beset with ambiguity and vagueness. There is an unbridgeable gulf between the term itself and its application to a literary work of art. Neither the artistic value nor the poetic uniqueness of the major writers of the period can be fully explained by this term. B. is, therefore, only a convenient term for an indistinct period of German literary history.— M. von Boehn, *B.-Deutschland 1815–1847* (1911, 2d ed., 1922); H. Beyer, "Lit. B. in Deutschland," *Reallexikon,* I; P. Kluckhohn, "Die Fortwirkung der dt. Romantik in der Kultur des 19. und 20. Jh.," *Zeitschrift für dt. Bildung* (1928), "B. als lit. Epochenbezeichnung," and "Zur B.-Diskussion," DVLG, 13 (1935) and 14 (1936), respectively; W. Bietak, *Das Lebensgefühl des B. in der österr. Dichtung* (1931); G. Weydt, "Lit. B.," DVLG, 9 (1931); A. von Grolman, " 'B.'-Forschung," *Dichtung und Volkstum* (1935); R. Haller, "Goethe und die Welt des B.," DVLG, 14 (1936); A. Holske, "Stifter und die B. Crisis," *Studies in Honor of John A. Walz* (1941); G. Weydt, "B. und junges Deutschland," DVLG, 25 (1951); B. Emrich, "B.," *Reallexikon,* 2d ed., I. F.L.

BIOGRAPHICAL CRITICISM. See CRITICISM, TYPES OF.

BLANK VERSE. Unrhymed iambic pentameter lines. Neither originally nor exclusively Eng., b.v. is nevertheless the distinctive poetic form of our language; it is the medium of nearly all verse drama and of much narrative and reflective verse. B.v. was introduced with the first substantial body of poetry written in Standard Modern Eng.: Surrey's b.v. translations from the *Aeneid*, written ca. 1540, were printed by Tottel in 1557. In Tottel's *Miscellany*, also 1557, the work of Wyatt, Surrey, and others (including two short b.v. poems by Grimald) introduced the iambic line and decisively marked the course that poetry in the modern Eng. tongue would take.

Some verse forms, like the triolet, the ballad measure, the limerick, seem to carry in themselves a suggestion of meaning or tone regardless of the language set to them; others, like the sonnet or the heroic couplet, have acquired a strong traditional manner from their exemplary employment during one literary period or by one great master. B.v. has no inherent tone. Except for free verse, it is the form closest to the form of our speech. Its stresses alternate as our Eng. speech stresses tend to do, and its measure of 5 strong stresses marked by the juncture of the line end, a measure readily apprehended without counting, both simulates and accommodates the way we make phrases and clauses as we speak. This is perhaps the reason no one poet, not even Shakespeare or Milton, has stamped b.v. forever with the mark of his own style as Pope did the heroic couplet. The freedom of the form is also a challenge; lacking the extrinsic mark of rhyme, poets must prove themselves in b.v. by their powers of conception and by their deployment of the sound-patterns of the language in interaction with the ideal pattern of the metrical form. The shifts of dominance in this interaction constitute the metrical history of b.v.

Surrey evidently sought a close relation between the order of stresses in his phrases and the ideal metrical pattern. Probably borrowing the idea of b.v. from the unrhymed hendecasyllabic *versi sciolti*, q.v. ("freed" verse) of Molza's It. translations from the *Aeneid* (Venice, 1539), and being encouraged perhaps by the dislike of the Eng. classicists Cheke and Ascham for "rude beggarly rhyming," as well as by the tradition of ME unrhymed alliterative verse, he worked closely with the Scots Vergil of Gavin Douglas, which was in couplets (ca. 1515, publ. 1553). He manipulated Douglas' phrases to fit them smoothly into an iambic line.

Clam vp againe in the greit hors maw
(Douglas)

Clambe vp again vnto the hugie horse
(Surrey)

Yet Surrey's lines are not monotonously iambic, his pauses are varied, and as Padelford (Surrey, *Poems* 1928) calculated, run-on lines make up one-fourth of his b.v. Early Elizabethan b.v. shows, in minor works by Turberville, Sackville, Barnaby Rich, Greene, and others, a movement toward strict metrical regularity, culminating in Gascoigne's *The Steele Glas* (1576). Here the stress-pattern is unvaried, run-on lines are rare, and a pause occurs always at the fourth syllable, indicated by punctuation if not by the phrase.

But holla: here, I see a wondrous sight,
I see a swarme, of Saints within my glasse
783–784)

Marlowe's *Tamburlaine* (1587), while not the first Eng. b.v. play (Sackville and Norton, *Gordobuc*, 1562; Gascoigne and Kinwelmarshe, *Jocasta*, 1566), inaugurates the great Elizabethan drama. In metrics, Marlowe exercised originality and freedom in stress and phrasing within the line, but composed his lines as individual units, often balanced in two vivid epithets (H. Baker, *Induction to Tragedy*, 1939); he did not join his lines in longer rhythms.

See see where Christs blood streames in the
firmament,
One drop would saue my soule, halfe a drop,
ah my Christ.
(*Faustus*, 1593; 1463–1464)

Many Elizabethan plays contain passages like this which resist the conventions of scansion. One line here has 11, the other 12 syllables; it would not seem profitable to try to rationalize the stresses. Marked as it is above, the scansion may suit some. Yet the excess of syllables alone might indicate that the lines are meant to strain the metrical pattern to the breaking point. Dramatic verse (like satire) never held to the strict metric developed by other Elizabethan verse, although it was based on the same convention. A line such as

Friends, Romans, countrymen, lend me your
ears,

spoken as marked here, strains at the convention, yet it does not actually violate it. The metrical system provides that while words of more than one syllable must retain their proper sound, monosyllables may be considered either strong or weak-stressed in a line of verse, regardless of their degree of stress in normal speech. The metrical feet have reference only to syllables; they have nothing to do with the divisions into words or phrases of the sounds of speech. This line would be *scanned,* but surely never spoken, thus:

× × / | × / | × / | × / |
Friends Romans countrymen lend me your ears.

Shakespeare, beginning with this convention, kept a relation to it throughout his career; yet it is plain that he often wrote lines which were willing, if temporary, departures. The increasing freedom with the line of Shakespeare and the later Elizabethan and Jacobean dramatists, Fletcher, Middleton, Webster, Massinger, Ford, was only one mark, and perhaps not a necessary one, of the progress made in b.v. The movement of rhythm through a series of lines, and the accommodation of every range of subject, idea, and feeling to the pentameter line gave this verse a flexibility unequalled, so it is sometimes said, in any language. It could shift from excited eloquence to prosaic statement; in fact, Eliot has said that the achievement of b.v. at this time was the evolution from the "intractably poetic" medium of Marlowe to one which could "carry the burdens and exhibit the subtleties of prose" (*Poetry in the 18th C.,* 1930).

Milton, it would appear, worked in *Paradise Lost* (1667) to restore to b.v. both a more poetic tone and a strong conventional relation to the iambic line. To accomplish this, he deliberately distorted the normal syntax and sound-patterns of Eng. speech. He retained the privilege of drastic metrical variation, though by some views he had entirely other principles (F. T. Prince, *The It. Element in Milton's Verse,* 1954). His chief metrical achievement is usually said to be the construction of masterful rhythmic periods and "verse paragraphs," or as he put it in his preface to *PL,* where he maintains that b.v. is the noblest medium for verse, lines with "the sense variously drawn out from one verse to another." In *Paradise Regained* (1671) Milton employed a line generally freer than that of *PL,* and in *Samson Agonistes* (1671) a highly individual form including short lines and rhymes.

During the times of Dryden and Pope, b.v. was practiced by minor imitators of Milton, while the heroic couplet dominated the drama and longer poems. Dryden argued against b.v. (*Essay of Dramatic Poesy,* 1668), although he used it in some later plays, following *All for Love* (1671). When the vigor of b.v. was revived, notably by Thomson in *The Seasons* (1726), some Miltonic mannerisms of diction were retained, and although phrases and sentences were arranged freely to run over the line end, which they seldom did in the 18th-c.

couplet, b.v. in this period did not attain the easy colloquial mode of Dryden and Pope's couplets. Later in the century, Young's *Night Thoughts* (1742) and Cowper's *The Task* (1785) are distinguished by a certain departure from the conventionally "poetic" diction of the time; metrically they are composed largely in the style of the "single-moulded" line, as Saintsbury called it, and they maintain regularity in stress and syllable.

Nearly every great poet of the 19th c. employed b.v. for his longer poems; some, like Tennyson, wrote lyrics in it (*Tears, idle tears,* 1847). The limits and flexibility of the form were established, and while each poet used it in a manner suitable to his own poetic voice, no basic metrical innovations were made. Wordsworth's *Prelude* (1805–50), Keats's *Hyperion* (1820), Browning's *The Ring and the Book* (1868), demonstrate much the same qualities in phrasing and stress-groupings that mark their poetry in other forms.

In contrast with the experimental meters favored by many 20th-c. poets, b.v. for the first time appears as a conservative force. Thus the b.v. in Eliot's *The Waste Land* (1922) appears ordered and traditional in its context, as do Stevens' b.v. poems among his free-verse works. Poets who have maintained the older forms, like Frost and Auden, use b.v. in idioms little different from those of their rhymed poems. Verse drama and longer poems are rare today; b.v. is not a favorite with contemporary poets.

S. Johnson, "Milton," *Lives* (1781); R. Bridges, *Milton's Prosody* (1894); J. A. Symonds, *B.V.* (1895); R. M. Alden, *Eng. Verse* (1903); Saintsbury, *Prosody;* F. G. Hubbard, "A Type of B.V. Line Found in the Earlier Elizabethan Drama," PMLA, 32 (1917); T. Brooke, "Marlowe's Versification and Style," SP, 19 (1922); M. Robertson, "The Evolution of Eng. B.V.," *Criterion,* 2 (1924); H. Baker, "Some B.V. Written by Thomas Norton Before *Gorboduc,*" MLN, 48 (1933); T. S. Eliot, *Elizabethan Essays* (1934); G. K. Smart, "Eng. Non-Dramatic B.V. in the 16th C.," *Anglia,* 61 (1937); C. S. Lewis, "The 15th-C. Heroic Line," E&S, 24 (1938); H. Baker, *Introduction to Tragedy* (1939); A. Swallow, "The Pentameter Line in Skelton and Wyatt," MP, 48 (1950); G. L. Trager and H. L. Smith, Jr., *An Outline of Eng. Structure* (1951); F. T. Prince, *The It. Element in Milton's Verse* (1954); J. Thompson, *The Founding of Eng. Metre* (1961). J.T.

IN OTHER LANGUAGES. B.v. (*versi sciolti,* q.v.) originated in Italy. Its derivation is disputed between those who consider the It. *endecasillabo,* in rhymed form used as early as 1135, an offshoot of the Fr. rhymed decasyllable (later called *vers commun*), and those who trace both these metrical lines to a common double source: L. dactylic tetrameter catalectic and Horatian sapphic. B.v. came into being in response to the need of It. tragedians for a metrical form that would match as closely as possible the iambic trimeter of Gr. tragedy. By adopting unrhymed hendecasyllables, or *versi sciolti*, for his tragedy *Sofonisba* (1515; publ. 1524), Trissino—incidentally, not the first to use b.v.—made this meter the standard one for It. drama. Though b.v. was brought from Italy to Spain in the early 16th c. by Boscán and Garcilaso, *verso suelto* never became assimilated to the Sp. metrical tradition; and the attempts to accommodate *vers blanc* in France were likewise unsuccessful.

Outside of Italy b.v. celebrated its greatest continental triumph in Germany, which received it from England. Notable is a translation of Milton's *PL* as early as 1682. For original creation b.v. was first used much later, namely by Wieland in his *Erzählungen* (1752) and in the tragedy *Lady Johanna Gray* (1758). But it was Lessing's *Nathan der Weise* (1779) which established b.v. as the standard metrical form of German drama, subsequently to be used by such poets as Goethe (in *Iphigenie* and *Tasso*), Schiller, Kleist, Grillparzer, Hebbel, Hauptmann, and others. Broad differences in metrical usage exist from the start, between, say, the predominantly end-stopped lines of Goethe and the typically run-on pattern of Lessing's verse. These divergent practices imply two different theoretical conceptions of b.v.: in the first, the line has preserved its metrical integrity; in the second, it has been replaced by the verse paragraph. Grillparzer is the most conservative in his usage, and his b.v. has a lyrical quality; the verse of Kleist, who most consistently disregards the line as metrical unit, is carried forward by a powerful dramatic impulsion. Schiller's position is an intermediate one. Beginning in *Don Carlos* (1787) with a b.v. much like Lessing's, he adopted from *Wallenstein* (1800) on a more conservative form. Besides Wieland, Liliencron wrote b.v. narrative, and Schiller, Heine, Storm, and George used b.v. in the lyric.

The Scandinavian countries received b.v. from three sources, Italy, England, and Germany, with Germany providing the chief models in the dramatic verse of Goethe and Schiller. With *Balders Død* (1773) Johannes Ewald introduced hendecasyllabic b.v. in Denmark, evidently of It. extraction. Preferring the 10-syllable line with masculine endings, Oehlenschläger created a medium capable of a wider range of dramatic effects; his treatment of b.v. in his numerous historical tragedies is very much like that of the later Schiller. Oehlenschläger's followers in the drama, Ingemann and Hauch, naturally adhered closely to the verse form of their master; more individual is the b.v. used later by Paludan-Müller (in his dramatic poems on mythological subjects) and by Rørdam. In Swedish poetry b.v. was introduced with Kellgren's narrative fragment *Sigvarth och Hilma* (1788), in the It. form acquired from Ewald. Excellent Eng. b.v. appeared as early as 1796 in a few scenes of a projected historical play by the Finn Franzén; but not until 1862 did Wecksell, another Finn, produce the only significant b.v. drama in Swedish, *Daniel Hjort*. Unlike the situation in Denmark and Norway, where b.v. appears infrequently in narrative, didactic, satirical, and reflective poetry, in Sweden b.v. has a long and still living tradition in these genres, with contributions by such poets as Tegnér, Stagnelius, Sjöberg, Malmberg, Edfelt, and Ekelöf. The form of Swedish b.v. is generally conservative, not unlike that of Goethe. Norwegian poets started using b.v. about the same time, but the first significant works in this form are several farces and dramas (beginning in 1827) by Wergeland. Wergeland's metrical usage, modeled on Shakespeare's, is exceedingly free. Neither Andreas Munch's imitations of Oehlenschläger (beginning in 1837) nor Ibsen's *Catilina* (1850) displays a distinctive form of b.v. The rhymed verse intermittently used in *Catilina* is by far superior to the b.v.; this may partly explain Ibsen's subsequent preference for such a form. Bjørnson, on the other hand, composed excellent b.v. in his saga dramas, in a free form which points to Shakespeare and Schiller as the chief models.

In Russia b.v. appeared with Zhukovsky's translation of Schiller's *Die Jungfrau von Orleans* (1817–21). It was subsequently used by Pushkin in *Boris Godunov* (1825; publ. 1831) and his "Little Tragedies," and by Mey, Ostrovsky, and A. K. Tolstoy in their historical dramas. Tolstoy's *Czar Fyodor Ioannovich* (1868) has been a popular success up to recent years. B.v. also appears in narrative and reflective poetry. In Russia, as elsewhere, b.v. varies within a certain range, from the conservative line-structured form with constant caesura of *Boris Godunov* to the more loosely articulated verse of "little tragedies" like *Mozart and Salieri* and *The Covetous Knight*. In Poland, the hendecasyllabic b.v. of It. origin used by Kochanowski in his tragedy *Odprawa posłów greckich* (The Dismissal of the Gr. Envoys, 1578) failed to inaugurate a tradition. Rhymed verse became standard for Polish drama, and neither J. Korzeniowski's many b.v. plays (beginning in 1820) nor his persistent theoretical advocacy of the medium greatly modified the situation. Of individual works in b.v. may be mentioned *Lilla Weneda* (1840), one of Slowacki's best tragedies, Norwid's comedy *Miłość czysta u kąpieli morskich* (Chaste

Love at the Bathing Beach), and J. Kraszewski's epic trilogy *Anafielas* (1840).

In conclusion, it may be noted that, although b.v. in all these countries, except Italy and Poland, is designated as a 5-stress iambic meter, its lines rarely have 5 full stresses. According to K. Taranovski's computation, in *Boris Godunov* only 22.5 per cent of the lines have 5 stresses, 53.5 per cent have 4, and 24 per cent have 3. This distribution also holds roughly for b.v. in the other literatures here treated.

F. Zarncke, *Über den fünffüssigen Jambus mit besonderer Rücksicht auf seine Behandlung durch Lessing, Schiller, und Goethe* (1865); A. Sauer, *Über den fünffüssigen Jambus vor Lessings "Nathan"* (1878); L. Hettich, *Der fünffüssige Jambus in den Dramen Goethes* (1913); H. G. Atkins, *A Hist. of German Versification* (1923); O. Sylwan, *Den svenska versen från 1600-talets början* (3 v., 1925–34) and *Svensk verskonst från Wivallius till Karlfeldt* (1934); A. Heusler, *Deutsche Versgesch.* (v. 3, 1929); K. Taranovski, *Ruski dvodelni ritmovi* I-II (1953); B. O. Unbegaun, *Russian Versification* (1956; with bibliog.); *Poetyka* III: *Wersyfikacja*, v. 3: *Sylabizm*, ed. M. R. Mayenowa (1956; with bibliog.); P. Habermann, "Blankvers," *Reallexikon*, 2d ed., I; W. Kayser, *Gesch. des deutschen Verses* (1960); L. J. Parker, "Wielands *Lady Johanna Gray:* Das erste deutsche Blankversdrama," GQ, 34 (1961). s.L.

BLASON. According to Thomas Sebillet, *Art poétique françoys* (ed. F. Gaiffe, 1932, p. 169–70), the b. is a poetic genre devoted to the praise or blame of almost anything. V. L. Saulnier (see bibliog.) regards Sebillet's definition as too narrow and speaks of two types of b.: the *b. satirique* and the *b. médaillon*. The purpose of the former is sufficiently indicated in the name; that of the latter is to describe briefly a single object. The genre had its origin in 1536 with Clément Marot's *Blason du beau tétin*. Sebillet is inclined to think, incorrectly, that the b. represented an effort to do in poetry what heraldic art did with armorial bearings. In reality, the satiric b. is a distant descendant of the L. satire, while the descriptive b. traces its beginnings to the Gr. epigram. The good b., says Sebillet, will be brief, of 8- or 10-syllable verses, and will have a sharp [i.e., epigrammatic] conclusion. Most *blasons*, like the one by Marot that initiated the genre, celebrated some part of the female body, and by 1550 it was possible to gather many of them into an anthology entitled *Blasons du corps feminin*.—J. Vianey, *Le Pétrarquisme en France au XVIe s.* (1909); R. E. Pike, "The *blasons* in Fr. Lit. of the 16th C.," RR, 27 (1936); V. L. Saulnier, *Maurice*

Scève (2 v., 1948–49); H. Weber, *La Création poétique au XVIe s.* (2 v., 1956). I.S.

BLUES. As folk songs the b. differs strikingly from Negro spirituals (q.v.). Where spirituals are choral and communal, the b. are solo and individual. Where the spirituals sing of heaven, the b. are earthy. The spirituals are fervently hopeful, the b. cry of hopelessness and despair. Originally, the spirituals were sung unaccompanied. The b. always called for instrumental backing. And while the spiirtual has no set verse pattern, the b. song is based on a 3-line lyric: "Sometimes I feel like nothin', somethin' th'owed away / Sometimes I feel like nothin', somethin' th'owed away / Then I get my guitar and play the blues all day." Created by the down-and-out, giving voice to feelings and experiences hard to endure, these brief, agonizing, sometimes impromptu expressions appear to be derived from an earlier form known as "hollers." They did not become known as "b." until introduced into Am. "popular music," through the compositions of W. C. Handy and others. Several Negro poets, notably Langston Hughes and Waring Cuney, have used the verse pattern of the b. for poems intended mainly for reading.—H. W. Odum and G. B. Johnson, *The Negro and His Songs* (1925); C. S. Johnson, "Jazz Poetry and B.," *Carolina Magazine*, 58 (1926); J. W. Work, *Am. Negro Songs* (1940); W. C. Handy, *Father of the B.*, ed. A. Bontemps (1942); *A Treasury of the B.*, ed. W. C. Handy and A. Niles (1949); P. Oliver, *B. Fell this Morning* (1960). A.B.

BOB AND WHEEL. A bob is the refrain of a song or, as first used by E. Guest (*A History of Eng. Rhythms*, 1838), a short line, often only 2 syllables, at the end of a stanza, a device frequently employed in ME romances. A wheel is a set of short lines used at the end of a stanza. Sometimes the first line is very short and is then called a bob and the whole is referred to as a "bob wheel" or "bob and wheel." For example, the unrhymed alliterative stanzas of *Gawain and the Green Knight* each end with a bob of 2 syllables followed by a wheel consisting of quatrains, either in ballad form (8686) or in sixes, rhymed alternately (abab); the bob is rhymed with the second and fourth lines.—Saintsbury, *Prosody*, I. R.P.APR.

BOUTS-RIMÉS. Words rhyming in accordance with a given rhyme scheme, ordinarily that of the sonnet, and used as the basis of a versemaking game. The object of the game, which originated in the *précieux* circles of early 17th-c. Paris, was to write a poem which would utilize the given words as end rhymes yet achieve an effect of naturalness and ease. Accordingly the list of words was made as bizarre and incongruous as possible. The diversion became highly fashionable and remained so, in both France and England, until the 19th c. Such important poets as Corneille and Boileau tried their skill at b.-r., and an amusing sally is attributed to Fontenelle, who, on being given the words *fontanges, collier, oranges, soulier* by a beautiful woman, improvised the following lines: "Que vous montrez d'appas depuis vos deux *fontanges* / Jusqu'à votre *collier!* / Mais que vous en cachez depuis vos deux *oranges* / Jusqu'à votre *soulier.*"

BRACHYCATALECTIC. See TRUNCATION.

BRAZILIAN POETRY. Brazil's three races, Portuguese, Indian, and Negro, severally and in various combinations, account for many factors in the development and the character of her poetry, including its "periods." But more than the racial subject matter and attitudes and, as literature matured, the themes of ever increasing emphasis on reality, what gives unity to Braz. literature is the persistence of the national spirit, once awakened.

After the Jesuits' didactic and religious poems in the 16th c. and the mediocre *vers d'occasion* of the early 17th, the first strong personality in Braz. poetry emerged. Gregório de Matos (1633–96) was the first to depict in verse the defects of colonial society. He reflects not only preoccupation with the landscape, as in his lyrics, which are good but not outstanding, but also concern with the human scene in his satiric poems, his best work. And with the emergence of Man, added to Nature, poets acquired a national consciousness and a desire to be independent of Portugal. During the mid-18th c. gold rush in Minas Gerais were born those who were to form the *mineira* (from "Minas") school. Educated in Portugal, some becoming members of literary "academies" proliferating at the time, these youths wrote poetry in the academic-Arcadian fashion and, once back at home, conspired in the ill-timed, ill-fated *Inconfidência Mineira,* the earliest attempt at revolt. Their artistic leader, Tomás Antônio Gonzaga (1744–1810), is regarded as one of Brazil's greatest lyric poets, as the author of the most popular love poems in the language, *Marília de Dirceu* (1792; the pastoral names stand for "Gonzaga's Maria"). These poems are purely lyrical, all grace and beauty in their exaltation of carnal and spiritual love in balanced proportion. Two other names complete the trio of the great *mineiro* lyric poets, Cláudio Manuel da Costa (1729–89) and Alvarenga Peixoto (1744–93).

Still other *mineiros* wrote the best epics in Brazil. The more original and sensitive, a major precursor of romantic Indianism, is *O Uraguai* (1764), by Basílio da Gama; it recounts the war waged by Portugal with Spain's aid against the Indians of the Mission Towns who rebelled at transfer from Jesuit to Portuguese rule. More truly Braz. in subject, of greater art and culture but less original and less imbued with poetic genius, is *Caramurú,* by Santa Rita Durão; it is the story of Diogo Álvares, the shipwrecked sailor who discovered Bahia and became chieftain among the Indians there under the name of Caramurú (moray). In these poems nature varies from the bucolic, pantheistic nature of Arcady to the majestic indigenous nature as seen through baroque, gongoristic eyes: nature stylized, not as it really is.

The *mineiros,* influenced by theories absorbed from Rousseau and other Encyclopedists, have been called "proto-romantics." But it is only later, with political independence, that romanticism first asserts itself, firmly based, after its early steps, upon the idealized aborigine. The movement, however blurred the lines, falls into four phases:

1. Initiation (1836–40), with lyricism and religious inspiration its major characteristics. Gonçalves de Magalhães (1811–82) is its main representative, although perhaps his importance is more historical than lyrical: his *Essay on the History of Literature in Brazil* (1836) is the equivalent of a romantic manifesto, though the adjective does not figure in it. To theory he added example with *Suspiros Poéticos e Saudades* (Poetic Sighs and Yearnings), finding enthusiastic reception and disciples in Brazil, despite a lack of genuine romanticism and of poetic talent in his work.

2. Indianism (1840–50), with Gonçalves Dias (1823–64) its major exponent. He dominates all romantic poetry through his sense of sobriety and harmony. All is balanced: love and religion, feeling for nature, patriotism, sympathy for the Indian. He, better than most, infused life into the Indian theme. But one of his most famous poems is "Canção do Exílio" (Song of Exile), a delicate, poignant expression of *saudade* (yearning) for Brazil.

3. Phase of individualism, subjectivism, pessimism (1850–60). Least Braz. of all, these poets cultivated the worst habits and practices of the European decadents, and most died young. Principal names: Álvares de Azevedo (1831–52), Junqueira Freire (1832–55), Casimiro de Abreu (1839–60). The last-named is the simplest, most ingenuous of Braz. poets, therefore the favorite of the common folk. Junqueira Freire's poems reflect deeper and more intense suffering than any other Romantic's verse.

4. *Condoreira* (from the condor, bird symbolic of grandeur of flight) school of social poetry (1860–ca. 1880), linked with abolitionism and the Paraguayan War (1865–70). Now

the movement bound itself more closely to Braz. reality while still remaining romantic and lyrical. The great "condor" poet, Castro Alves (1847–71), developed a social conscience, turning away from native Indianism to nativist antislavery themes, so felicitously expressing general contemporary sentiment that he became the most popular poet in Brazil. His verses exude the physical and spiritual anguish of the Negro slave, as they also do the desire of the most progressive elements in Brazil for the abolition of the Empire as well as of slavery. His *Os Escravos* (The Slaves) contains the two poems in which he reaches supreme heignts of inspiration: *Vozes de África* (Voices of Africa) implores justice of God, and *Navio Negreiro* (Slave Ship) evokes the sufferings endured by the black cargo therein. They are impressive despite the defects of grandiloquence inherent in *condoreira* poetry.

Fagundes Varela (1841–75) comes between phases 3 and 4, chronologically, but in his verse all the main trends of Romanticism are found blended.

Sated with such magniloquent flights of language and with the wild subjectivism of the ultra-romantics, poets welcomed Parnassianism as a kind of panacea. Although essentially identical with the Fr. original, the movement shows some tropical modification in Brazil. Alberto de Oliveira (1857–1937), most rigidly Parnassian of the major trio, even so reflects better than the other two the lure of Braz. nature. Raimundo Correia (1859–1911) is more subtle, musical, pessimistic, of graver and more intense emotion. Olavo Bilac (1865–1918) shows a more facile sensibility, an evident virtuosity (Ronald de Carvalho calls him "pan-sensual"), and a fluent, brilliant grace of language. His *Panóplias* (Panoplies, first of three parts of his first edition of poems), contains a profession of faith in his Fr. masters. Parnassianism having entered the country, symbolism inevitably followed, but found fewer disciples, among whom Cruz e Sousa (1863–98) is the major poet in reaction to the narrow materialism of the Naturalists, the chill polish of the Parnassians. Symbolism was short-lived, although its effects proved lasting, as Andrade Murici has shown. The mystic poet par excellence of Braz. symbolism is Alphonsus de Guimaraens (1870–1921), who found inspiration in the themes of his Catholic faith.

The turn of the century saw a complex of influences in Braz. literature: skepticism, the cynicism of an Oscar Wilde, the defeatist satire of an Eça de Queiroz, the "barbaric" meters of a Carducci or a d'Annunzio, the ironic agnosticism of an Anatole France. Poetry was no coherent genre, had no common aim. Constructive action came only in 1922, when a group of young poets of São Paulo and Rio de Janeiro organized a "Modern Art Week" in São Paulo, consisting of a series of concerts, lectures, and exposition of the plastic arts, the whole inaugurated with an address by the celebrated novelist Graça Aranha, who lent his support to the new movement. So began Braz. modernism, not to be confused with other "modernisms."

These poets, at first destructive (first phase, 1922–30) in order to be constructive later, broke with the past, stripped away Parnassian eloquence and symbolist mistiness, cast off logic together with the syntax and vocabulary of Portugal, ignored meter and rhyme in favor of absolutely free verse, extended the scope of poetry to include the most prosaic details of life, and took on a markedly national tone, interpreting their country's past and present and stressing the Negro elements in its formation. Among the pioneers of modernism the principal name is Mário de Andrade's (1893–1945), who in 1922 published his *Paulicéia Desvairada* (Hallucinated City), a volume of modern poems that became the bible of modernism, as its author came to be called the "Pope of the new creed," a role thrust upon him. Not only a poet, he was a master of modernism in music and the visual arts as well as in aesthetics and criticism. Some of the first generation, like Menotti del Picchia (1892–) and Guilherme de Almeida (1890–), were converts from earlier movements; some, like Ronald de Carvalho (1893–1935), Sérgio Buarque de Holanda (1902–), and, greatest of these, Manuel Bandeira (1886–), became literary historians and critics also. Bandeira, called "the Saint John the Baptist of the new poetry" for certain elements in his work prior to 1922, is an independent spirit even though he shared in the establishment of modernism. He warns that the poet must first look to genuine inspiration, and only then to technique. His language is simple, but his concepts are not. His importance lies, besides in his verse, in his rare ability to interpret Braz. poetry and other letters to the public. The world of his poetry is the commonplace daily world, apparently nonpoetic yet transmuted by his genius to lyricism.

The first generation São Paulo poets were the most radical, their liveliest leader Oswald de Andrade (1890–1954; no relation to Mário). The cult of nationalism and regionalism permeated the group, united for a time in the magazine *Klaxon* (a typically grotesque name). The ebullient Oswald de Andrade advocated what he termed "primitivism," something very like the *exotisme* of France. A restless soul, he later formed the group that published the magazine *Antropofagia* (Cannibalism), a name inspired by Montaigne's famous essay. Opposing such Fr. influence, and indeed all alien "isms,"

BRAZILIAN POETRY

Menotti del Picchia, Cassiano Ricardo (1895–) who reached the fullness of his powers only much later, Plínio Salgado (1901–) and others founded the *verde-amarelo* (green-yellow) group, nationalistic on an Amerindian basis; their magazine was *Anta* (Tapir), which they said was an animal that symbolized the barbaric original power of the land.

Modernist groups in Rio were less eager to shock the bourgeoisie, and tended to be more conservative in general. A representative example would be the group that published *Festa* (Holiday), to which many modernists contributed. The highest feminine poetic genius of Brazil, Cecília Meireles (1901–), was a member. Their manifesto included four points: *velocidade* (velocity of expression, not physical speed), *totalidade* (total view of reality in all its aspects), *brasilidade* (Braz. nationality and reality), and *universalidade* (universality).

The next generation of modernists is nationwide in distribution, but in general their verse possesses similar characteristics, philosophical and religious—or, more accurately, socio-political and religio-mystical. Carlos Drummond de Andrade (1902–) represents the socio-political trend. A master of irony, his *Brejo das Almas* (Fen of Souls, 1934) was one of the most important books of the decade. Lately this great poet has lost some of his earlier illusions about politics (e.g., belief in socialism or communism as the ideal society), but none of his reverence for poetry. Murilo Mendes (1902–), Augusto Frederico Schmidt (1906–), and Cecília Meireles are the finest examples of the religious-mystical current. Mendes has written surrealistic poetry, metaphysical in tone; Schmidt (poet-wealthy industrialist-politician!) has combined Biblical inspiration and Whitmanesque rhythms; Cecília Meireles has turned to nature and Brazil's heroic past, as well as to medieval Europe, for her materials. Vinicius de Morais (1913–) and Jorge de Lima (1895–1953) must be mentioned. Despite his youth relative to the first generation, Morais's poetic evolution has brought him closer to those older poets, although his first two books show a sustained gravity of tone in their universal themes of religion and death. Jorge de Lima, he who wished to "restore poetry in Christ" and who wrote the mystical *A Tunica Inconsútil* (The Seamless Robe, 1938), compellingly presents the Negro theme in *Poemas Negros* (1946). His work is profoundly Christian and wholly Braz., grave in tone, deliberate in rhythm, expressed in long lines. His later works, e.g., *Livro de Sonetos* (Book of Sonnets) and *Invenção de Orfeu* (Invention of Orpheus), remain constant in feeling if they lack the proselyting force of his earlier poems. Contemporary with the oldest generation, Jorge de Lima showed himself

highly versatile as he underwent successive spiritual experiences ending with a phase of symbolic verse of personal anguish; indeed, he is really contemporary with all Modernist generations.

The poets who have appeared since 1942 can be categorized only arbitrarily. Some call themselves the "Generation of 1945," although all came on the scene either before or after that year. Amoroso Lima (pseud. Tristão de Ataíde) calls this period *Neomodernismo*, saying that Modernism died in 1945. Lêdo Ivo (1924–), Domingos Carvalho de Silva (1915–), João Cabral de Melo Neto (1920–), and Geir Campos (1924–) are the principal names among these younger poets who have in common an intellectualist attitude and perhaps a touch of Swiss Concretism ("A poem is a *graphic* thing!"), a strangeness of poetic images, and other traits of previous generations, all reduced to what amounts to a system, but characterized by restraint.

Meanwhile, the older poets still living continue their creative work, although most have evolved beyond their early phases, e.g., Cassiano Ricardo, who reached his peak only after the original modernism had declined, turning into a great psychological poet who seeks his material in modern science. Generally there is now a sense of discipline (though complex), with no return to traditional forms but with a policy of aesthetic expression in the construction and the final polishing of the poem.

ANTHOLOGIES: F. A. de Varnhagen, *Florilégio da Poesia Brasileira* (Anth. of Braz. Poetry; v. I & II, Lisbon, 1850; v. III, Madrid, 1863; v. I is a historical sketch of Braz. letters, a genuinely pioneer work of great probity); *A Nova Lit. Bras.: Crítica e Antologia* (The New Braz. Lit.: Crit. and Anthol.; 1936; a collection of modernist poetry with crit. and biographical notes), and *Panorama do Movimento Simbolista Bras.* (3 v., 1951–52; anthol. of Braz. symbolist verse with biogr. & bibliogr. notes), both ed. J. C. de A. Murici; *Antol. dos Poetas Bras. da Fase Romântica* (2 ed., 1940), *Antol. dos Poetas Bras. da Fase Parnassiana* (2 ed., 1940), and *Apresentação da Poesia Bras.*, seguida de uma *Antol. de Versos* (2 ed., 1954; an excellent introd., with crit. essay, to Braz. poetry), all ed. M. Bandeira; *Modern Braz. Poetry* (1962; with extremely brief but informed intr., followed by tr. of poems by twelve modernists), ed. and tr. John Nist.

HISTORY AND CRITICISM (besides above items): S. Romero, *História da Lit. Bras.* (1888; 5 ed., enl., 5 v., 1953–54; sociological attitude causes bias, but basic and standard, although should be reevaluated in light of subsequent criticism); J. V. D. de Matos, *Hist. da Lit. Bras.* (1916; 3 ed., 1954; coldly objective in considering work of art as such, with scant attention to artist as man or to society in which he moves; still basic and standard); R. de Carvalho, *Pequena Hist. da Lit. Bras.* (1919; 7 ed., 1944; valuable for crit. opinions; his attitude a synthesis of Romero's and Matos'); I. Goldberg, *Studies in Braz. Lit.* (1922; a pioneer work in Eng., treating representative figures from viewpoint similar to that of Matos); A. Grieco, *Evolução da Poesia Bras.* (1932); A. A. Lima, *Estudos* (6 v., 1927–33; series of crit. essays on many subjects, including poetry), *Contribuição à Hist. do Modernismo: I. O Pre-Modernismo* (1939), and *Poesia Bras. Contemporânea* (1942); S. Putnam, *Marvelous Journey* (1948; a comprehensive, very readable, introd. in Eng. to four centuries of Braz. writing); *A Lit. no Brasil* (Lit. in Braz.; 3 v. in 5 tomos, 1955–59; a collaboration by many critics in the most ambitious attempt yet at a lit. hist. of Braz. on aesthetic principles), gen. ed. A. Coutinho; M. Bandeira, *Brief Hist. of Braz. Lit.* (1958; tr., introd., and notes by R. E. Dimmick; despite its brevity and the author's modesty about his own role as poet, extremely valuable for the insight of an active participant in and interpreter of Braz. poetry; this ed. incorporates many of the author's notes for revision of the orig. ed., and many helpful data by the tr.). L.L.B.

BRETON POETRY. The language of Lower Brittany (*Breiz Izel*) belongs, like Welsh and Cornish, to the Brythonic or "P"-Celtic group, and is derived from the speech of settlers from southwest Britain who left their homeland from the 5th to the 7th c. when the Saxons were encroaching from the east. The earliest Bret. poetry to survive dates from the 14th c. and consists of a few scraps of verse, discovered in 1913, as doodlings on a copy of a medieval L. text. Though fewer than 20 lines in all they are the residue of a body of popular verse, now almost entirely lost, in an indigenous metrical system related to that of Cornish and early Welsh but with its own characteristics. The main feature is the occurrence in each line of a form of internal rhyme very similar to the Welsh *cynghanedd lusg* (q.v.), although not necessarily with penultimate stress:

An heguen am louenas

An hegarat an lacat glas.
(Her smile gladdened me, the blue-eyed love.)

There is evidence, from Marie de France and others, that medieval Bret. poets sang of heroes and romance, but nothing, except the above-mentioned fragments, has survived of all that was written before the 15th c., and most of the poetry until the 19th c. is of mediocre literary merit, consisting mainly of works of religious edification. Fr. had become the language of the learned and the well-to-do, and this had arrested the development of a cultivated literary norm. Four main dialects have emerged: those of León, Tréguier, Cornouailles, and Vannes, but a literary language common to all four is hard to establish. Stemming from the work of the grammarian, Le Gonidec (1775–1838), there appeared a school of purists bent on ousting as many as possible of the Fr. words in common use, and coining others from Celtic roots. The tendency among 19th-c. poets to follow this lead has reached its extremity in the Gwalarn school of 20th-c. writers. Nevertheless, works of religious edification have continued to appear in the much decried *Brezonec belec* (Priest Bret.).

Most of the verse from the 15th to the beginning of the 19th c. consists of long plays of no great literary merit intended for the untutored peasantry. The native prosody of penultimate rhyme survives to the 17th c. when it is superseded by the Fr. manner of syllable counting and final rhyme, although regularity of stress is not always ignored. The themes of most of the plays are drawn from the Bible and the lives of saints. A few of the most popular plays, such as the *Pevar Mab Emon* (Les Quatre Fils Aymon), are based on themes drawn from chivalry, and there are a few farces. The influence of Fr. models on all these types is evident. Apart from these plays there is very little else in verse until the 18th c. is almost ended, except a few long and dreary religious poems such as the *Mellezour an Maru* (The Mirror of Death, 1519), metrical devout meditations, the Creed in verse, a metrical Book of Hours and a collection of carols (1650).

New stirrings begin with the two mock-epic poems of Al Lae (close of the 18th c.), but the real impetus came with the rise of 19th-c. romanticism. Auguste Brizeux published his *Kanaouennou* (Songs) in 1837. La Fontaine's *Fables* had appeared in Bret. the previous year. The great event was the publication in 1839 of Villemarqué's *Barzaz Breiz* (Poetry of Brittany). Much of the contents is spurious, and the claims of high antiquity are not valid, but the style is vigorous, and the effect was profound. A romantic vision of the Bret. past was created, which stirred the imagination of many, and it led to new literary enthusiasm. Luzel was impelled to collect the genuine Bret. folk poetry, of which there were two main kinds: the *gwerziou*, usually dramatic, in form, direct and simple in style, and concerned with local events, legends, beliefs, and folklore, and the *soniou*, consisting of more lyrical verse, including love songs and satires. Prosper Proux recounted his escapades with rough humor in his native Cornouailles dialect in 1839, but by 1866 he had acquired a more "literary" expression though not without loss of vigor. The Vannetais dialect shared early in the new literary activity, and was used in a volume of Georgics in 1849. A tone of conscious literary creation prevailed throughout the second half of the 19th c. This was set by a group of poets, the *Breuriez Breiz*, who derived their impulse from the purism of Le Gonidec and the romantic nationalism of Villemarqué. Luzel, and the others, many of whom lived uprooted from the Bret. countryside, expressed in a somewhat artificial diction their love of the simple life, of the homeland, and of the inheritance which was no longer secure. This tradition was maintained and reinvigorated in the 90's by the rich lyricism of Taldir, and the more artistic Erwan Barthou. The outstanding poet of the present century has been J. P. Calloc'h, killed in action in 1917, whose posthumously published volume of verse in the Vannetais dialect reveals a poet of very sensitive religious and patriotic feeling.

The 20th c., up to 1944, saw the vigorous growth of Bret. literary periodicals. Poets and other writers formed groups around each journal. Vannetais writers found expression in *Dihunamb*. The Gwalarn group, however, was by far the most enterprising and talented, widest in culture and most creative. Under the leadership of Roparz Hémon they pushed the synthetic and purifying tendencies of the Le Gonidec-Vallée tradition to extreme lengths, thus establishing a literary norm far removed from spoken Bret. New metrical experiments, including vers libre were encouraged, while at the same time the Gwalarn poets experimented with the native metrical system after its long disuse. Their journal, however, did not survive the "Libération." Breton poetry of fine quality continues, nevertheless, to appear, and there are signs of renewed vigor, particularly among the "Al Liamm" group.

ANTHOLOGIES: *Barzaz Breiz*, comp. H. de la Villemarqué (1839); *Gwerziou Breiz-Izel*, comp. F. M. Luzel (2v., 1868–74); *Soniou Breiz-Izel*, comp. F. M. Luzel and A. le Braz (2 v., 1890); *Chrestomathie bretonne*, comp. J. M. Loth (1890); *Les Bardes et poètes nationaux de la Bretagne Armoricaine* (1919) and *La Chanson des siècles bretons*, both comp. C. le Mercier d'Erm; *Barzhaz: kant barzhoneg berr, 1350–1953*, ed. P. Denez (1953). GENERAL SURVEYS, with bibliog.: A le Braz, *Le Théâtre celtique* (1904); P. le Goff, *Petite Hist. littéraire du dialecte bret. de Vannes* (1924); M. Guieyesse, *La Langue bretonne* (1936); R. Hémon, *La Langue bretonne et ses combats* (1947); F. Gourvil, *Langue et littérature bretonnes* (1952); *Istor Lennegezh*

Vrezhonek an Amzer-Vreman, ed. Abeozen, i.e. Y. F. M.. Eliès (1957).   D.M.L.

BREVE. See PROSODIC NOTATION.

BROADSIDE BALLAD. A song printed on a single sheet and hawked about the streets of British towns and at country fairs during the period 1500–1920. The broadsheet was usually decorated with a crude woodcut and advised that the song be sung "To the tune of . . ."—here specifying a tune in the common repertory. Musical notation was seldom given. Although mainly doggerel verse, especially the topical songs, literary poetry was also occasionally vended on broadsheets. In the course of time, the sheets shrunk from five-column folio size to single-column slips. Many broadside ballads were remade by rural tradition into folk song; reciprocally, folk songs were sometimes printed as broadsides. The three of four decades after the Civil War were the heyday of broadside balladry in America; its last stronghold was in Negro communities before World War I.—*The Common Muse*, ed. V. de Sola Pinto and A. E. Rodway (1957); L. Shepard, *The Broadside Ballad* (1962). A.B.F.

BROKEN RHYME refers to the division of a word (not the rhyme) at the end of a line in order to produce a rhyme: for*getful*/*debt* (Pope); *tu*-tor/*U*-niversity (George Canning). Poets from Shakespeare to Ogden Nash have used b.r. for comic or satiric effects; yet Hopkins has taken it as a resource for serious poetry, e.g., in *The Windhover* and *To what serves Mortal Beauty?* J. Schipper (*A History of Eng. Versification*, 1910) cites another type of b.r., which, however, is usually referred to as mosaic rhyme (q.v.).

BUCOLIC. The term is ordinarily used as a synonym of pastoral. Virgil's ten pastoral poems, to which he refers as "pastorem carmen" in the fourth georgic and to which the term "eclogue" is now generally applied, were called "bucolics" by the grammarians. During the Renaissance and 17th c. there was a tendency to reserve the term "b." for Virgil's eclogues and for the imitations of them. The critics argued that in primitive times wealthy men—princes, even—were the keepers of cattle, not the keepers of sheep or of goats. Since pastorals in the Virgilian tradition portray people of culture and refinement, they insisted that it would be more accurate to use the term "b." when referring to poems of this type. In modern Eng. the term has a slightly humorous connotation, though it is too vague to be recorded except in a few dictionaries. See ECLOGUE, PASTORAL.   J.E.C.

BUCOLIC DIAERESIS. See DIAERESIS.

BULGARIAN POETRY. Bulg. literature is old, but Bulg. poetry is relatively young. This paradox can be easily explained by the fact that, although Bulgaria was the original home of the Church Slavonic language, which was spread among all the orthodox Slavs, the Bulg. clergy was predominantly Gr. for many centuries, and their control of the church and the economy forced the Bulgarians into a backward state, while the Turkish political occupation almost completed the ruin of the country.

The early folk poems are of many types. They deal with all the aspects of peasant life and its hardships. Many of them are epic narratives similar to those of the Serbs and dealing with the same heroes, such as Marko the King (Marko Kral) of Prilep. As compared with the Serb epics, they seem to contain more original history and less idealization.

For some centuries in Bulgaria, there was no poetry in the modern sense of the word. Its place was taken by Gr. songs, sometimes with Bulg. phrases inserted in alternate lines. Truly Bulg. poetry was not written until the emergence of modern Bulgaria, usually dated by the *History* of Father Paisi in the latter part of the 18th c.

The earliest writers produced by this revival worked with the object of arousing their people against the Turks. Many of them, such as Dobri Chintulov (1822–86), Georgi Stoykov Rakovski (1821–65), and Lyuben Karavelov (1837–79), had lived in Russia, chiefly in and around Odessa, and thus had come to know Rus. literature, especially the works of the revolutionists of the day. Yet their works are less influenced by abstract ideas than by the needs of the Bulg. people. Perhaps the first author to pass beyond purely political poetry was Petko Rachev Slaveykov (1827–95). A teacher as well as an active patriot, he wrote to replace the popular Gr. songs and produced many lyrics of high quality.

Of this early group the outstanding poet was Khristo Botev (1848–76). A typical revolutionist, he died with a small band of men who tried to cross the Danube into Bulgaria to start an uprising. His poetry is so full of dynamic beauty, together with passion against the oppressors of his people, that his position is secure among the Bulg. people, no matter what the regime.

After the liberation of the country, a somewhat similar position was held by Ivan Vazov (1850–1921). Vazov was the first to introduce a knowledge of world literature into Bulgaria; he handled all forms of writing—poetry, prose, drama—and dealt with all phases of Bulg.

life, from the earliest coming of the Bulgars to his own day. Unlike the storm-tossed Botev, he led a quiet and literary existence and achieved his fame by hard and continued work. He is undoubtedly the foremost Bulg. author of his day.

The next generation was represented by Pencho Slaveykov (1866–1912), Peyu Yavorov (1877–1914), and Petko Yu. Todorov (1879–1916). Definitely poets in the Western sense, these men were self-conscious artists, and their work reflects contemporary movements in the West. They formed, as it were, a reaction against the Rus. tradition and devoted themselves to Western ideas, whether taken from Germany or from Ibsen, although they did not isolate themselves from Bulg. reality.

Symbolism was the next movement to appear in Bulg. poetry. Introduced by Todor Trayanov (1882–), a poet of considerable importance, the movement found further exponents in Dimcho Debelyanov (1887–1916), who was killed in World War I and left only some fifty poems, which are, however, recognized as masterpieces, and in Nikolay Liliyev (1886–).

The defeat of Bulgaria in the Second Balkan War and World War I, and the political and social unrest which followed, changed the spirit of the literature. Less optimistic, the newer generation sought to resolve its problems by mysticism, particularly a revival of Bogomilism, a medieval Bulg. religious movement. It expressed its nationalism in a glorification of the past which developed into a definite historical school. At the same time, there were many independent authors of various types, such as Elisaveta Bagryana (1894–) and Angel Karaliychev (1902–). During these years the more radical poets and those connected with the Peasant Party, such as Geo Melev (1895–1925) and D. Polanov (1899–1953), dropped into the background.

At the conclusion of World War II, the Communists seized control in Bulgaria and forced literature into the mold of socialist realism by silencing or imprisoning all authors who would not accept this doctrine. They reexamined the writers of the past, enthusiastically accepting Botev and overstressing certain aspects of his genius. They have been more hesitant in regard to Vazov. At first they condemned him, but he was so popular that they now tend to praise some of his earlier works, while criticizing or ignoring later ones that do not fit their purposes.

In general terms, the dean of Bulg. authors is now Lyudmil Stoyanov (b. 1888), long accepted as a competent writer with some orientation to the Left, who—after the rise of Fascism—swung definitely into the Communist camp. There are also such men as Anton.

Rastsvetnikov, who began to write before World War II, and Krum Kyulyakov (b. 1893). Still, far too much work has been published like *Partisan Songs* of V. Georgiev (1947), which scarcely goes beyond the setting in verse of the ordinary political clichés.

During the early postwar years when Communism was taking root, literature was heavily controlled. The principles of the Soviet writer Zhdanov were carefully inculcated and followed. Younger authors, such as Khristo Radevski, Mladen Isayev, and others, stoutly pledged their devotion to the Party, and knew no limits to their adulation. This mood was easier to induce because of the pro-Russianism of the population, especially after the events of 1876–77.

With the downfall of the cult of personality as practiced by Chervenkov, signs of revolt appeared, and after the Twentieth Congress of the Party, there were even demands that more freedom be given to the writers, although they were opposed by some of the more ardent. Even Stoyanov pleaded for the recognition of objective truth in literature, but the liberal movement was soon defeated, especially after Khrushchev in 1957 declared that the Party had to maintain control over literature. Since that time Bulg. poetry seems to have acquiesced in its Communist role. It has none of the independence and variety that formerly marked the differing schools of Bulg. writers and found vent in long and earnest discussions.

The contrast between a strong tendency to follow the Rus. spirit and a deep peasant individualism creates the present impasse in Bulg., and it is still too early to see how it is to be solved and what form Bulg. poetry will take.

ANTHOLOGIES: *Poètes bulgares*, ed. G. A. Dzivgov (1927); *Antologia della poesia bulgara contemporanea*, ed. E. Damiani (1950); *Bolgarskiye Poety* (1952); *Canti popolari bulgari*, tr. L. Salvini (1958).

HISTORY AND CRITICISM: D. Shishmanov, *A Survey of Bulg. Lit.*, tr. C. A. Manning (1932); B. Penev, *Istoriia na novata bulgarska literatura* (4 v., 1930–36); N. Donchev, *Influences étrangères dans la litt. bulgare* (1934) and *Esquisse d'un tableau de la nouvelle litt. bulgare* (1935); A. Cronia, *Saggi di litt. bulgara antica* (1936); G. Hateau, *Litt. bulgare* (1937) and *Panorama de la litt. bulgare contemporaine* (1937); C. A. Manning, "Communism and Bulg. Lit.," *Am. Bulg. Review*, 5 (1956); C. A. Manning and R. S. Smal-Stocki, *Hist. of Modern Bulg. Lit.* (1960). C.A.M.

BURDEN, burthen. (a) The refrain or chorus of a song: "Foote it featly heere and there, and sweete Sprights beare the burthen. *Burthen dispersedly*. Harke, harke, bowgh, wawgh"

(Shakespeare, *Tempest* 1.2.380). (b) The chief theme, the leading sentiment, of a song or poem: "The burden or leading idea of every couplet was the same" (L. Hunt, *Men, Women & Books* 1.11.199).—R. L. Greene, *The Early Eng. Carols* (1935). R.O.E.

BURLESQUE. No good purpose can be served by a too rigid insistence upon nomenclature in a discussion of parody, burlesque, or travesty in literature. All three employ the device of incongruous imitation and deflationary treatment of serious themes for satiric purposes. There is some general agreement among authorities that parody (q.v.) is the more exclusively literary and critical method, fixing the attention closely on an individual style or poem, while b. is freer to strike at social or literary eccentricity by employing such established verse conventions as the love-romance, the pastoral, the courtly tradition, or the Homeric manner. More important than such distinctions perhaps is what they have in common. George Kitchin states that parody and b., in modern times, have both represented "the reaction of custom to attempted change" and of established social forces and literary forms to subversive excess. They have increasingly become voices of conservatism. Four main types or genres have become identified with the history of poetic b.: Scarronesque poetry (from Paul Scarron's Fr. *Virgile travestie*, 1648–52); Hudibrastic poetry (from Butler's burlesque poem *Hudibras*, 1663–64); dramatic b. like Gay's *Beggar's Opera*, 1728, a burlesque of It. opera sometimes described as an early forerunner of the operettas of Gilbert and Sullivan; and the straight mock-heroic as practiced by Dryden and Pope. B. poetry has had a long foreground in classic comedy (Aristophanes), in medieval church history and ritual where it usually served as a weapon against hierarchy, in Chaucer who used satire against the medieval romance and mock-heroic technique in "The Nun's Priest's Tale," in the Renaissance when anti-Petrarchans debunked the love and pastoral conventions, and in the 17th c., when metaphysical verse was often burlesqued. About 1650, however, b. began to be used as a conscious critical term derived from the Fr. anticlassical burlesque of Scarron and Boileau (*Le Lutrin*, 1674) in which the primary device was the substitution in a heroic composition of bourgeois for aristocratic manners. Scarron had many Eng. imitators, but it remained for Butler to evolve an original Eng. form of the b. in which jogging couplets and quick turns of mood and line are combined with a central theme parallel to *Don Quixote*, in a broad attack on Puritanism, pedantry, romance, religious bigotry, and superstition. In the 18th c. the accent shifted from Scar-

ron and Butler to mock-heroic verse in couplets. Leaving aside prose burlesques of Defoe,
Swift, and Fielding (and Irving in America),
the historian must mention Dryden's burlesque
animal fable used for polemical purposes (*The
Hind and the Panther*), Pope's vengeful satires
in the *Dunciad* vein, and the dramatic b. of
which Buckingham's *The Rehearsal* was the
archetype. These and other belittling treatments of Augustan modes fall within the class
of the older satirical imitations where types
and general styles, social and religious practices, or literary rivals are the targets. Modern
critical parody of specific poems or poets
emerged as a later form leaving b. mainly as
a form of popular stage entertainment or a
looser form of parody often in prose. Parody
and b. existed side by side in the early *Punch*
which, under Douglas Jerrold's editorship,
was dedicated to liberal social causes. *Punch*
later grew conservative becoming an organ of
well-bred mid-Victorian complacency.

In modern times b. has most commonly been
found on the stage, ridiculing the drama or the
fashions of the day. Fielding's and Gay's satiric
plays (*The Thumb, The Beggar's Opera*) are
early examples. Gay's work anticipates the extremely popular 19th-c. form of musical entertainment exemplified in the work of W. S.
Gilbert, G. A. Sala, and F. C. Burnand. In
Germany stage b. was a popular way of de-
flating the romantic vogue of *Sturm und
Drang* (q.v.) and the classical tragedy or Wagnerian opera. The names of Platen, Heine, and
Johann Nestroy are usually mentioned in accounts of German literary humor. Weber and
Fields turned the stage b. into a musical
vaudeville successful on the Broadway stage
around 1900, and since that time the tendency
of b. has been more and more toward light,
ribald stage effects or comic operas and away
from the critical purpose of literary parody.—
K. F. Flögel, *Geschichten des Burlesken* (1794);
G. Kitchin, *A Survey of B. and Parody in Eng.*
(1931); A. H. West, *L'Influence française dans
la poésie burlesque en Angleterre entre 1660–
1700* (1931); R. P. Bond, *Eng. B. Poetry, 1700–
1750* (1932); E. A. Richards, *Hudibras in the
B. Tradition* (1937); V. C. Clinton-Baddeley,
*The B. Tradition in the Eng. Theatre after
1660* (1952); F. Bar, *Le Genre b. en France au
17e s.: Etude de style* (1960).   R.P.F.

BURMESE POETRY. Many Burm. poems have
been discovered in stone inscriptions of dates
from 1310 A.D. onward. The passages describing the glory and achievements of kings and
princes, and the noble lineage of queens and
princesses are usually in verse, as are also
prayers for the donor and his friends and
curses on those who damaged his benefaction.

These stone poems were clearly designed to
be permanent records.

Side by side with these there existed another
kind of poetry, less formal and more emotional
in character. This was scratched with stylus
on palm-leaves, and the best known of the
older specimens is dated 1455 A.D. From the
15th to the last quarter of the 19th c. under
the patronage of Buddhist monarchs, poems of
varied lengths and on varied subjects were
composed by monks (Shin Thi-la-wun-tha, Shin
Ra-hta-tha-ra), courtiers (Na-wa-de the First
and Nat-shin-naung), or royal ladies (Mi Hpyu
and the Hlaing Princess). Their poems were
not addressed to posterity but to royal patrons
or beloved ones.

There are altogether more than fifty different kinds of poems and songs, among which
the most important are: (1) *E-gyin*, historical
ballads, some of which were sung as cradle
songs while others informed young princes or
princesses of the achievements of their ancestors. (2) *Maw-gun*, panegyric odes, perhaps the
oldest type of poem. Their subjects range from
the arrival at the Court of a white elephant
to the campaign in and conquest of Siam, and
from the completion of a canal to an essay on
cosmography. (3) *Pyo*, metrical versions of
Buddhist and non-Buddhist stories, in narrative or expository form, transferred to a Burm.
setting and made more vivid by small imaginative details, and homilies in verse. (4) *Lin-ga*
(Pali *alankāra*, ornamentation) a variety of
pyo but generally shorter; often used as a
generic term for all kinds of verse. (5) *Ya-du*
(Sanskrit *ritú*, season) the shortest type, usually
of 3 or fewer stanzas, deal generally with romantic subjects such as emotions called forth
by the changing seasons, the mood of longing
and memories of loved ones.

The forms in which Burm. poetry is cast
are of uncertain origin. Writers on Burm.
prosody have attempted to force these poems
into a Procrustean bed of Sanskrit and Pali
pattern. But their distinguishing feature (the
climbing rhyme schemes) appears to be peculiar to Burma and the 4-syllable lines with
an end or break marked by lines of usually 7
syllables, is in harmony with the rhythm of
the spoken language. The foundation of the
verse is the *than-jat* chorus, e.g.: "tabe: ya. lou.
tamu: hlu / dou. shan: taun-dhu / tu-nain you:
la:" // (We, Shan Taungthus, earn one anna
and give away two. Could anyone rival us?)
From this followed the *than-bauk*, a 3-line epigram "min: pari. ye / ngatin.de / na: we male-
shā" // (Poor Nga Tin Dè did not understand
the king's trick!) The rhyme schemes are
rigid. As a rule each line has 4 syllables and
the stanza contains, as in the *than-bauk*, climbing rhymes in groups of three. In other forms
of verse the rhyme scheme is looser. The lines

may consist of 3, 4, 5, or more syllables. A rhyme may be confined to 2 lines. These forms, however, may be regarded as variations of the main scheme of Burm. *pyo* prosody, rather than as an essentially different type of verse.

The last eighty years have seen the advent of the printing press, the cessation of royal patronage in 1885, the introduction of Eng. education, the founding of the University of Rangoon in 1920, and the creation of the Union of Burma in 1948. During this eventful period Burm. poetry underwent significant changes. In the 1930's an influential literary movement called *Khitsan* ("Experiment for a new age") was formed, which stressed simplicity, directness, and purity of language. Commoners have assumed the role of poets and have to cater to a larger public with a catholic taste. Short poems have replaced the traditional long epics. But Burm. poetry still retains its distinctive character.

IN ENGLISH: *Jour. of the Burma Research Soc.*, Rangoon (1910–), esp.: (a) Ba Han, "Seindakyawthu, Man and Poet," v. 8; (b) Po Byu and B. H., "Shin Uttamagyaw and his Tawla, a Nature Poem," v. 7–10; (c) U Ba Thein, "A Dictionary of Burm. Authors," tr. G. H. Luce and Maung Ba Kya, v. 10; (d) G. H. Luce, "Prayers and Curses," v. 26; *Bulletin of the School of Oriental and African Studies* (London), v. 12 and esp. v. 13 (article on *Maw-gun*); *Minthuwun* (a selection of Min-thuwun's poems and prose with Eng. tr. by G. H. Luce, 1961); Maung Htin Aung, *Burm. Drama* (1937); Hla Pe, *Konmara Pya Zat* (pt. 1, introd. and tr., contains various rhyme schemes and forms of Burm. prosody, 1952); U On Pe, "Modern Burm. Lit.: Its Background in the Independence Movement," *Atlantic Monthly*, 201 (Feb. 1958); Hla Pe, *Burm. Proverbs* (1962).

IN BURMESE: *Anth. of Burm. Lit.*, ed. U. Kyaw Dun (4 v., 1926–31); U Tin, *Kabyaban-dhathara Kyan* (1929; Burm. prosody); Saya Lun, *Kabyatharahta Thingyo* (1931; Burm. prosody); Pe Maung Tin, *Hist. of Burm. Lit.* (1947); Zawgyi and Min Thu Wun, *Sa-pe Loka* (1st ser., 1948; "On Life and Letters"; anthol. of verse with comments); E. Maung, *Kabya Pan Gon* (1950; "A Garland of Burm. Poems"). See also Ba Thaung, *Sa-hso-daw-mya Athok-pat-ti* (1962; "Biog. of Burm. Authors"). H.P.

BURNS STANZA, or Burns meter (also called "Scottish stanza," "Habbie stanza," and the "6-line stave"). A 6-line stanza rhyming aaabab, lines 1, 2, 3, and 5 being tetrameter and lines 4 and 6 dimeter. It takes its name from the use made of it by Burns in *To a Louse, Holy Willie's Prayer*, and in many of his other vernacular poems. The stanza, however, may be

found in Prov. poems of the 11th c., and it occurs commonly in Eng. romances and miracle plays of the Middle Ages. Despite its intricacy, the form is highly effective, especially in the hands of a master like Burns. Following the crescendo of the initial tercet, the short lines lend themselves to effects of irony and epigram:

Ye ugly, creepin, blastit wonner,
Detested, shunn'd by saunt an' sinner,
How daur ye set your fit upon her,
   Sae fine a lady!
Gae somewhere else, and seek your dinner
   On some poor body.

                (*To a Louse*, stanza 2)

The meter was also used by Wordsworth in his *At the Grave of Burns*.—A. H. MacLaine, "New Light on the Genesis of the Burns Stanza," N&Q, 198 (1953).

BYELORUSSIAN POETRY reflects the sad fate of its people. Being Eastern Slavs living in the vicinity of Polotsk, Smolensk, Minsk, Homel, and Grodno, the Byelorussians received Christianity and learning from Ukranian Kiev, the center of ancient Rus'. In the 1st half of the 13th c., the Tartars destroyed Kievan Rus' and the B-r. lands were merged with Lithuania, which as a less civilized country adopted B-r. as its official language (actually there was a fusion of B-r., Ukr. and Church Slavic, and the writings are claimed by all Eastern Slavs). After the Union of Lithuania with Poland in 1569, almost all of the B-r. upper class became Polonized and embraced Catholicism, while the peasantry remained Orthodox and preserved the B-r. language and rich folk songs, some of which date from pre-Christian times. The earliest monuments of written literature (in Church Slavic with B-r. influence) are the *Lithuanian Annals* (1380–1446), the *Annals of Avraamka* (1495), Dr. F. Skaryna's (1490–?) Bible translation (in Prague, 1517), and *Poems* by A. Rymsha (16th c.). The Polish Jesuits used B-r. (influenced by Polish) for their rhymed "Intermedia" in the "school dramas" (16th c.). Simon Polotsky (1629–80), the court poet of Tsar Alexis of Moscow, wrote in Rus.: *Rhythmologion, Flowery Plesaunce* (1678) and *Rhymed Psalter*. His baroque style was quite elaborate, but there was little true feeling in his verse.

In 1795 Russia acquired all B-r. territory. Soon after, modern B-r. poetry began with V. Rovinski's travesty of the *Aeneid* after the similar Ukrainian version of Kotlyarevsky (1798) and the anonymous comic epos, *Taras on Parnassus*, ridiculing serfdom. Some liberal landowners contributed to the national awakening. The didactic poet Y. Chachot (1797–1847) and the poet-dramatist V. Dunin-Martsinkevich (1807–84) created romantic types of benevolent landlords, who saw their peasants as human beings (poems: *Hapon*, 1854, *Evening Party*, 1855, *Harvest Festival at Shawrovo*, 1857). I. Nosovich in 1874 collected and published *B-r. Songs*, a collection of folklore and poems on the life of the peasants.

But it was a peasant's son, Maciej Burachok (F. Bahushevich, 1840–1900) who with his *B-r. Flute* (Krakow, 1891) and *B-r. Bow* (Posen, 1894) created realistic, truly national poetry, extolling the human dignity of his countrymen and calling upon them to struggle for a better, freer life. His works, banned in the Rus. Empire, only with difficulty reached his homeland. Similar work was done by Yanka Luchyna (1851–97) and the ardent revolutionist "Ciotka" (the Aunt) Aloyza Pashkevich (1876–1916).

After the Revolution of 1905, the ban on B-r. writing imposed in 1863 was relaxed, and in 1906 the first B-r. literary periodical *Nasha Niva* (Our Field) began to appear in Vilna and marked the real New Renaissance in B-r. literature; all of the younger poets contributed. As a result of their work and the patriotism of the people, an independent B-r. National Republic was proclaimed on February 25, 1918. It was overrun by the Bolsheviks and replaced by the BSSR on January 1, 1919. However, this was partitioned in 1921 by Poland and Soviet Russia, whose armies "united" it again on September 17, 1939. All these turbulent events and wars were deeply reflected in B-r. literature.

Among the new poets was the highly talented Maksim Bahdanovich (1891–1917), a symbolist with strong realistic leanings. In his collection *Wreath* (1912) he treated universal problems and also the simple beauty of Byelorussia and the richness and charm of its nature and stressed the coming of a newer, brighter day.

From the *Niva* group emerged the greatest B-r. poet and spiritual leader, Yanka Kupala (I. Lutsevich, 1882–1942). In his lyric and social poems, *The Flute* (1908), *Eternal Song* (1910), *The Dream on the Mound* (1910), he defended the human dignity of the peasants and their desire "to be called people," and he and Kolas (see below) even won the encouragement of M. Gorky. Kupala's next poems, *Along the Road of Life* (1913), *Legacy, On the Nemen River, The Destroyed Nest* (1919), are his most mature works. He continued to dwell on social problems, urged his people to struggle for an independent Byelorussia, and wrote indignantly after the Bolshevik occupation on August 28, 1919, about "Byelorussia in shackles," an act which caused angry retorts by Communist critics. In 1922, Kupala wrote a highly artistic comedy, *Natives*, and the poem *Facing the Future*. His last free poem was *My Village,*

You are Disappearing, 1929 (about forced collectivization).

In 1929–30 the Bolsheviks began to liquidate "B-r. Nat. Democrats." Kupala was arrested (1930) and attempted suicide in his cell. His life was saved and as the critics said: "The attention [terror] of the Party helped Kupala and Kolas to become active builders of the new, national in form but socialist in content, culture and literature." In his new role he glorified the Party and Soviet reality in various poems, *On the River Aresa* (1933), *Barysaw* (1934), *The Song on Construction* (1936), *To Decorated Byelorussia* (1937). Only in *The Song of Taras* (1939) on the Ukrainian poet Shevchenko and in such short poems as *Lavonikha, Turochka, Alesya* and *Flax*, written in folk song style, did he show his former poetical talent. During the invasion of Hitler in 1941, he composed highly patriotic poems such as *To the B-r. Partisans, The People Arose, Again We Will be Free*, and he showed Soviet fanaticism in *The Dictatorship of Labor* which will "Destroy the palaces, the gangsterism of the dollar" and "build life as in a fairy tale for all ages and generations." However, in Kupala's collected works edited by the Soviets, all his B-r. patriotic poems are excluded.

Yakub Kolas (K. Mitskevich, 1882–1956), the second greatest B-r. poet, showed in his first lyrics, *Songs of Sorrow* (1910), great talent and profound sensitivity to social injustice. In *To Work* (1917) he appealed to God for his people's independence and condemned the Soviet regime in *Native Pictures* (1921) and *Repercussion* (1922). His best works are the *New Land* (1923) on the peasant life in the 19th c. and *Simon the Musician* (1925), depicting a poor village artist who lives to please the people. Some have seen the poem as an allegory with Simon as a renascent B-r. poet, awakening the conscience of his people; his sweetheart Hanna as Byelorussia; the evil Mr. Daminik as an occupying power.

But by 1926 Kolas had embraced communism and expressed his new faith in such works as *Our Days* (1937) and *Under Stalin's Sun* (1940). During World War II, he wrote poems on the partisans such as *Trial in the Forest* (1943) and *Retribution* (1945), and on hardships in Poland, e.g., *The Fisherman's Hut* (1947). In addition he wrote novels, dramas, and articles, and has been considered along with Kupala the real creator of modern B-r. literature.

The pressure applied after 1930 broke the spirit of all the free writers, and if it failed to do so, authors by the hundreds disappeared forever, though a few reappeared after the death of Stalin. It did not spare even earlier Communist authors, such as Tsishka Hartny (Zm. Zhylunovich). Stalinization reached its peak in the submissive, collective poem, *Letter of the B-r. People to the Great Stalin* (1936). Later poets like Zmitrok Byadula (S. Plawnik, 1886–1941) son of the Jewish ghetto, who had been a free spirit and praised an independent Byelorussia, suffered; while M. Lyn'kow, K. Chorny, R. Trus, P. Browka, A. Zvonak, P. Hlebka and K. Krapiva wrote on the duly legalized Soviet themes in terms of Socialist realism.

In 1939 after the liberation of Western Byelorussia, new poets born under Polish rule appeared, such as M. Mashara, P. Pyastrak (Z'vyastun) and the talented Maksim Tank (E. Skurko, b. 1912) who wrote *Naroch* (1937), *Yanuk Syaliba* (1943) and a collection *So They Know* (1947) on Soviet heroism.

In the Zhdanov period (1946) a new campaign was launched against "cosmopolitanism" and in 1951 against "B-r. nationalism." Literature was not affected by the Russian "thaw" (1954–56), but there were enough deviations to arouse Party anger and cause "confessions of errors" by authors during the Twenty-Third Congress (1959). Only Communist didacticism, the cult of Lenin, and the Party are regarded as fit subjects for poets, as is shown by M. Kalachynski's *Harvest Festival at Kalasowka* (1956) which treats the Party Congress as a source of joy in every home, or P. Browka's *Always with Lenin* (1956), *Voice of Mother* (1960), P. Panchenko's *Patriotic Song* (1957), and A. Makayanka's *Lyavonikha in Orbit* (1960). Among the new poets U. Karatkevich and Y. Los' are worthy of mention, but, under the vigilance of the Party, B-r. literature is kept at a provincial "national" level and does not rise to the height of the early achievements of Kupala, Kolas, and their group.

The B-r. Diaspora continues its modest literary tradition; for instance, in Canada there exists a poetical group, *Bayavaya Ŭskalos'*, publishing a journal by the same name, wherein short poems appear by A. Zmahar, P. Sirata, A. Ivers, M. Khvedarovich, and others.

ANTHOLOGIES: *Xrestamatyja belaruskae literatury*, ed. M. Harecki (1921); *Xrestam. novaj b-r. lit.*, ed. I. Dvarcanin (1927); V. Zub, *Mastackae slova* (1956); *Bayavaya Ŭskalos'*, nos. 6 and 7 (Toronto, 1962).

HISTORY AND CRITICISM: E. F. Karskij, *Belorusy*, III (1922) and *Gesch. der weissrussischen Volksdichtung und Lit.* (1926); M. M. Pjotuxovič, *Narysy historyi b-r. lit.* (1928); L. Blende and A. Kuxar, "Mataryjaly da narysow pa historyi b-r. lit.," *Maladnjak*, no. 5 (Minsk, 1931); S. Stankievich, "Kupala in Fact and Fiction," *B-r. Review*, no. 3 (Munich, 1956); *B-r. soveckaja lit.*, ed. V. Barysenka and M. Lyn'kow (AN BSSR, 1958); A. Adamovich, "Forty Years of B-r. Lit. in the BSSR," *B-r. Review*, no. 7 (1959); *Pis'menniki Soveckaj*

Belarusi (1959; biographical directory). See also other articles on B-r. poetry in *B-r. Review*, nos. 1– (1954–); L. I. Zalesskaja, *Poezija Sovetskoj Belorussii* (1960); S. I. Vasilënok, *Fol'klor i literatura Belorussii* (1961). J.P.P.

BYLINA (also called *starina*). A Rus. oral epic, couched in blank verse, with occasional grammatical rhymes, which celebrates in a highly formalized style the exploits of a folk-hero (*bogatyr'*). Typically the action of a b. is set in Kievan Russia of the 10th–12th c. and revolves around an outstanding member of the ruler's retinue and his superhuman deeds of valor. Prince Vladimir, the King Arthur of the Rus. epic tradition, usually appears here as a secondary character. The apotheosis of the hero is bolstered by grandiose similes and extravagant hyperboles. The "ancient history" quality of the b. is reflected in the lavish use of morphological and lexical archaisms. While most of the b. plots seem to have originated in Southwestern Russia, in the Pre-Mongol era, in modern times they were preserved chiefly in the outlying provinces of the Far North, e.g., along the coast of the Arctic Ocean and around Lake Onega. It was there that, in the 18th and 19th c., these epics were heard and recorded by collectors of Rus. folklore such as K. Danilov, Rybnikov, Gilferding. Today the art of narrating *byliny* is well-nigh extinct.—M. Speransky, *Byliny* (2 v., 1916–19); A. Skaftymov, *Poetika i genezis bylin* (1924); N. K. Chadwick, *Rus. Heroic Poetry* (1932); Yu. Sokolov, *Rus. Folklore* (1950). V.E.

BYZANTINE POETRY. The majority of Byz. literary works labor under the classical Gr. linguistic and literary traditions, which smothered much of their originality. Only in religious poetry did Byz. literature break fresh ground and approach greatness, and only from the 13th c. onward did it use a language approximating that spoken by contemporary Greeks.

The first three centuries of the Eastern Roman Empire were a period of transition from pagan Roman and Hellenistic to a Christian Byz. culture. This is reflected in the poetry of the time. Christian fervor appears side by side with an orgiastic love of life; hymns are composed in a Christian and pagan spirit, and grandiose *ekphraseis* (descriptions of works of art) celebrate Christian and pagan masterpieces. Of these the description of the Church of Sancta Sophia by Paul the Silentiary (fl. 563) is undoubtedly the most significant, extolling the twin grandeur of church and state, around which Byz. life was to revolve.

I. RELIGIOUS POETRY. Originally Byz. religious poetry used a number of classical Gr. meters, the hexameter, elegiac, iambic, anacreontic, and anapaestic, as can be seen from the writings of Methodius, Synesius, and Gregory of Nazianzus (4th–5th c.). But very soon the new rhythmic meters prevailed, whose effect relied on the number of syllables and the place of the accents within a line. These, together with the admiration for the martyrs and devotion to the mysteries of the new religion, gave Byz. religious poetry a power and freshness which remained unequaled in subsequent medieval Gr. writings.

The rhythmic Byz. hymns fall into three periods; the first (4th–5th c.) characterized by short hymns, the *Troparia*; the second (6th–7th c.) by long and elaborate metrical sermons, the *Kontakia*; and the third (7th–9th c.) by a form of hymn-cycle called *Kanon*. The second is the great period of Gr. hymnography. In its early part lived Romanus (6th c.) the most celebrated Byz. religious poet. Some eighty-five of his works have been preserved, all metrical sermons for various feasts of the Orthodox Church. They were accompanied by music, which is now lost, and were apparently rendered in a kind of recitative resembling oratorios. Romanus, being a conscientious Christian, treated his subjects exactly as the church ordained. Occasionally, however, he gives rein to his fancy, and at such times becomes grandiloquent in the style of epideictic oratory. His language on the whole is pure; he is rich in metaphor and imagery, and often interweaves in his narrative whole passages from Holy Scripture. His main fault is an oriental love of size, unpalatable to the modern reader. Andrew, Bishop of Crete (ca. 660–740) initiates the third period of Byz. religious poetry with his *Major Kanon,* a composition of huge size, in which elaboration of form results in a decline of power and feeling. The two most important representatives of this period are St. John Damascene (7th–8th c.) and his foster brother Kosmas of Maiouma. As a hymnographer, St. John Damascene was greatly renowned. He returned to the use of quantitative verse, even endeavoring to combine it with modern meters.

The storm of the iconoclastic controversy, which broke out in the lifetime of St. John Damascene, brought in its wake a reaction which resulted in a new florescence of hymnography. Works (mostly anonymous) of writers of this period finally found their way into the liturgy of the Eastern Church, and replaced the older hymns and metrical sermons of the days of Romanos. Of the posticonoclast poets Symeon the Mystic (949–1022) certainly ranks highest. In Byz. poetry he is the most important figure after Romanos, although his fervent mystical poems tend to be formless and often obscure. Moreover, he is the first person known to have used the 15-syllable verse (*politikos stichos;* see VERSUS POLITICUS) in personal poetry, the verse which in later years was to become supreme in the Gr. world.

Byz. religious poetry was to accomplish a great historical mission. It not only kept alive Gr. national and Christian feeling in the face of numerous barbarian invasions, but also scattered to East, West, and North the seeds that later blossomed into the literatures and cultures of other peoples—the Russians, the Southern Slavs, the Rumanians, the Syrians, the Copts, and the Armenians.

II. EPIC POETRY. The historical court epics of the late Hellenistic era survived in the early Byz. centuries. If we are to judge by their scanty remains, they had limited artistic merit. The greatest representative of the historical epic, or rather the epic encomium, and one of the most distinguished Byz. poets was George Pisides (7th c.). Some of his most important verse is in praise of his patron emperor Heraclius, whose victory over the Persians he celebrated. In the hands of Pisides new Byz. meters begin to take shape, and in particular the Byz. 12-syllable iambic verse, which was to become the principal meter of subsequent "highbrow" medieval Gr. poetry. But the most important Byz. epic cycle apparently originated in the provinces of the East in the course of the 10th c. It centered round the heroic figure of Digenes (who symbolized the ideal of medieval Gr. manhood) and spread from the deserts of Syria to the Rus. steppes, and even reached the remote Gr. colonies of Southern Italy. Of this we possess today only a small number of isolated folk songs (the *Akritic Ballads*), some of great power and beauty, and half a dozen versions, ranging from the 12th to the 17th c., of a long poem now lost, the so-called *Epic of Basil Digenes Akritas*. They all differ in language and style and even in the sequence of the narrative. In this epic we find Gr. and Hellenistic motifs blended with Eastern elements, as well as a number of baffling historical facts anything but contemporary.

III. LYRIC POETRY. The epigram in the Hellenistic sense of the term (the short occasional poem) was the type of lyric poetry most cultivated in Byzantium. At first it followed the late Hellenistic patterns, as the works of Agathias (6th c.), Paul the Silentiary, and others show. But from the 7th c. the new religious spirit permeates it and is expressed in the predilection of churches, monastic life, and holy relics as subjects. Theodore Studites (759–826) is the most important representative in this trend. Cassia, often and unjustly called the Sappho of Byzantium, followed him in the 9th c. But the heyday of the Byz. epigram is the 10th and the 11th c. For it was then that John Geometres (Kyriotes), Christophoros of Mitylene, and John Mavropous flourished.

They reverted to the older Hellenistic influences, and their verse displays both feeling and refined wit. The only other type of Byz. "highbrow" lyrical poetry worth mentioning is the *Lament*. This often takes the form of an address to the poet's soul, or of a dirge or complaint, full of the ascetic spirit of the time. It was influenced by the long and insipid autobiographical poetry of Gregory of Nazianzus, yet many important Byz. poets, like George Pisides or Christophoros of Mitylene, indulged in it, and it continued in the form of "a moral admonition" or "the prayer of a sinner" till the end of the Byz. era.

Medieval erudite poetry, permeated as it was by the ascetic spirit, did not draw on profane love for inspiration, one of the greatest sources of lyricism of all centuries. Such Byz. love poetry as has survived is written in a more or less demotic tongue, and is to be found in the love letters (the *Pittakia*) of the verse romances (see below, section 4), or in certain modern Gr. folk songs whose origins can be traced back to the Middle Ages.

IV. VERSE ROMANCES. After the fall of Constantinople to the Fourth Crusade (1204), Frankish chivalrous poetry was translated into Gr. and, influenced by this, a new type of Gr. chivalrous poetry arose. It used a more supple and lively language, and broke away from the sterile tradition of the highbrow Byz. verse romances of Niketas Eugenianos (12th c.) and Theodoros Prodromos (12th c.), which blindly followed the patterns of the late Helenistic romances of Heliodorus and Achilles Tatius. Such are *Callimachos and Chrysorrhoe, Belthandros and Chrysantza, Imperios and Margarona,* and *Florios and Platsiaflora,* all the works of unknown poets. The essence of these tales is boundless romanticism. Arduous love and the amazing fortitude of their heroes color the narrative. Yet in the hands of the Byz. poets the Western were blended with Eastern elements, so that an oriental atmosphere of magic suffuses certain episodes of these poems, lending them a charm and a character of their own. Closely connected to these are two long biographical verse romances, *The Poem of Alexander the Great* and *The Story of the Famous Belissarios.* The first follows the pseudo-Callisthenes life of Alexander, the second has as its subject the deeds of Belissarios the famous general of the Emperor Justinian. To this group one should perhaps add the *Achilleis,* which treats of the life and deeds of the Homeric Achilles, presenting him, however, as a medieval Western knight.

V. SATIRICAL VERSE. In the 12th c. certain satirical didactic poems appeared, permeated by a mordant Byz. humor, not always refined. These are generally grouped under the title of *Prodromic Poems,* and are traditionally attributed to the beggar and scholar Theodoros Prodromos. Their chief interest lies in the picture of the social and monastic life they give, and in the type of language they use, in which spoken (demotic) forms abound.

VI. DIDACTIC POETRY AND DRAMA. If we exclude the epigram, perhaps no other poetic form was so assiduously and continuously practiced in Byzantium as didactic poetry. But these endless prose-in-verse creations on birds, fish, stones, vegetables, etc. are certainly not poetry in the real sense of the word, and it is very doubtful if their authors ever sought an original artistic effect. Information was all they wished to convey. Moreover, drama proper remained unknown in Byzantium. Such literature as exists in dramatic form (of which the 11th-c. cento *Christus Patiens* is the most important example) was always meant to be read and not acted. The dramatic instinct of the Greeks revealed itself in the long dialogues of the *Kontakia* and in the Acclamations to the Emperors, and found ample nourishment in the pageantry of the palace ceremonies and the liturgies of the Gr. Orthodox Church.

ANTHOLOGIES: *Anthologia Graeca Carminum Christianorum,* ed. W. Christ and M. Paranikas (1872); *Byzantinische Dichtung,* ed. G. Soyter (1930); *Poeti Byzantini,* ed. R. Cantarella (2 v., 1948); *Medieval and Modern Gr. Poetry,* ed. C. A. Trypanis (1951; bibliog. on all important Byz. poets in the notes); *Sancti Romani Melodi Cantica,* ed. P. Maas and C. A. Trypanis (1963).

HISTORY AND CRITICISM: K. Krumbacher, *Gesch. der byzantinischen Lit.* (2d ed., 1897; still the standard work on the subject); W. Schmid and O. Stählin, *Gesch. der griechischen Lit.* (1929–48); F. Dölger, *Die byzantinische Dichtung in der Reinsprache* (1948); F. H. Marshall, "Byz. Lit.," in N. H. Baynes and H. St. L. B. Moss, *Byzantium* (1948); N. B. Tomadakis, *Eisagoge eis ten Byzantinen Philologian* (1952). On the *Kontakion* see esp. P. Maas, "Das K.," *Byzantinische Zeitschrift,* 19 (1910). C.A.T.

C

C.M. Abbreviation for common measure or meter. Hymn stanza. See BALLAD METER.

CACCIA. An It. verse form believed by some to have evolved from the madrigal (q.v.), though this is generally disputed since the form was known in late 13th-c. France. Its lines are mostly short, telling as they do of exciting outdoor activity. Like the madrigal, it has a final refrain, but its core consists of an undetermined series of uneven verses with or without rhyme or in assonance. Its name probably derives from the fact that in its early stages its contents dealt chiefly with the hunt. It is also maintained that the name could derive from its musical form which had 2 or more voices repeating, at a distance of 3 or more beats, the same melody and words, thus giving the impression of a "hunt" between the voices. The c. flourished in the 14th and 15th c., especially at the hands of Franco Sacchetti.—V. Pernicone, "Storia e svolgimento della metrica," in *Problemi ed orientamenti critici di lingua e di lett. ital.*, ed. A. Momigliano, II (1948); Wilkins. **A.S.B.**

CACOPHONY. The quality of being harsh-sounding or dissonant; the opposite of euphony (q.v.). Though poets ordinarily avoid c., they may use it deliberately to reinforce meaning. In the following example, the first and third lines may be considered appropriately euphonious, the second appropriately cacophonous:

How charming is divine philosophy!
Not harsh and crabbed as dull fools suppose,
But musical as is Apollo's lute.
(Milton, *Comus*)
L.P.

CADENCE. (1) the expressive melodic pattern (interrogatory, hortatory, etc.) preceding a pause or at the end of a sentence; (2) the rhythm of accentual phrasal units; (3) a term used to describe the rhythmical flow of accentual free verse, Biblical poetry, and "poetic prose." The term when used in this last sense implies a looser concept of poetic rhythm than that assumed by adherents of orthodox graphic scansion (q.v.). The imagists and the vers librists of the early 20th c. frequently exhorted poets to abandon composition by the traditional foot system and to compose instead in loose cadences; as Ezra Pound told his contemporaries, "Compose in the sequence of the musical phrase, not in sequence of a metro-

nome." Again, Pound warns, "Don't chop your stuff into separate *iambs*. Don't make each line stop dead at the end, and then begin every next line with a heave. Let the beginning of the next line catch the rise of the rhythm wave. . . ." (*Make It New*, 1934). W. C. Williams is another modern who has supported composition in loose cadences over composition in more conventional British prosodies. Williams begins with the proposition that the Am. idiom is unique and that it thus requires a unique rhythmical garment, not one imported without alteration from the very different tonalities of the British language. "We must break down," he writes, "the line, the sentence, to get at the unit of the *measure* in order to build again." Williams suggests that much modern Am. poetry is empty, tired, and unreal because poets have maintained a misplaced allegiance to the traditional accentual-syllabic British line in ascending rhythm (q.v.). The "stasis" of much modern poetry, he believes, can be broken if Am. poets will examine their own natural idiom and deduce from it cadences to form the basis for a genuinely native prosody. As he writes, "We have had a choice: either to stay within the rules of English prosody, an area formed and limited by the English character and marked by tremendous masterwork, or to break out, as Whitman did, more or less unequipped to do more. Either to return to rules, more or less arbitrary in their delimitations, or to go ahead; to invent other forms by using a new measure" ("An Approach to the Poem," *EIE*, 1947 [1948]). This "new measure consonant with our day," Williams makes clear, must be a cadence midway in formality between the regularity of traditional British prosody and the whimsical rhythmical anarchy of totally unmetered free verse. The repeated phrasal rhythms of Gertrude Stein's work seem to exemplify the concept of "c." as employed by Pound and Williams. Whitman is clearly one of the important progenitors of the "c." concept. **P.F.**

CAESURA (cesura). A rhetorical and extrametrical pause or phrasal break within the poetic line. If the pause occurs near the beginning of the line, it is called initial c.; if near the middle of the line, medial; if near the end, terminal. A c. is masculine if it follows an accented syllable, feminine if it follows an unaccented syllable. Feminine caesuras are of two types: lyric if the syllable before the pause is the normal weak element in the foot (q.v., and see SCANSION), epic if an extra weak syllable occurs at the pause. The c., which is frequently marked by punctuation, corresponds to a breath-pause between musical phrases, and its constant intersection with the more or less constant metrical scheme of the poem provides a form of expressive counterpoint. A line may have no c., and it may have more than one. It may also have one or more briefer or less conspicuous caesuras called (by conventional prosodists) secondary pauses or (by "linguistic" or "acoustic" prosodists) junctures.

In Gr. and L. metrics, the term "caesura" designates a word end within a foot (opposed to diaeresis, coincidence of word and foot ending); the "main c." in a line is usually found within the third or fourth foot. In classical metrics, c. is an important technical element of composition but is wholly metrical and should not be confused with pause in modern prosodies. In prosodic analysis of classical verse, terms such as "penthemimeral" or "semiquinarian" (i.e., after the fifth half-foot) are employed to designate caesura position. For example, c. occurring after the first long syllable of the second foot, that is, after the third half-foot, is called trihemimeral or semiternarian; c. after the seventh half-foot is called hephthemimeral or semiseptenarian, and so on.

The c. is generally used with great regularity in much classical, romance, and OE verse. It is only with the development of the iambic pentameter line that varied and expressive c. placement (as in Chaucer) becomes, in Eng., a subtle prosodic device. Whereas in OE verse the medial c. had been rather mechanically used to separate each line into 2 isochronous hemistichs and to emphasize the regularity of the structure, in modern Eng. the c. is often used as a device of variety, a device whose purpose it is to help mitigate metrical rigors by shifting from position to position in various lines. In formal verse, whether classical, Romance, or OE, the medial position of the c. is frequently predictable; in verse of greater flexibility and informality, the position of the pauses cannot be anticipated.

In the syllabic Fr. alexandrine (q.v.) the predictable medial c. occurs with great regularity:

Trois fois cinquante jours   le général naufrage
Dégasta l'univers;   en fin d'un tel ragage
L'immortel s'émouvant,   n'eût pas sonné si tôt
La retraite des eaux   que soudain flot sur flot
Elles gaignent au pied;   tous les fleuves s'abaissant.
Le mer rentre en prison;   les montagnes renaissent.
(Du Bartas, *La Première Semaine*)

It is also extremely regular in accentual, alliterative OE poetry:

Hige sceal þe heardra,   heorte þe cenre,
Mod sceal þe mare,   þe ure maegen lytlaþ.
(*The Battle of Maldon*)

In early Eng. blank verse:

O knights, O Squires, O gentle blouds yborne,
You were not borne,   al onely for your selves:
Your countrie claymes,   some part of al your paines.
There should you live,   and therein should you toyle.
(Gascoigne, *The Steel Glass*)

And in much Eng. Augustan poetry:

Careless of censure,   nor too fond of fame;
Still pleased to praise,   nor yet afraid to blame;
Alike averse to flatter,   or offend;
Not free from faults, nor yet too vain to mend.
(Pope, *Essay on Criticism*)

In later blank verse, on the other hand, and particularly in that of Milton, the placement of the c. is extremely flexible:

Thus with the Year
Seasons return, but not to me returns
Day, or the sweet approach of Ev'n or Morn.

And Bush with frizl'd hair implicit: last
Rose as in dance the stately Trees.
(*Paradise Lost*)

Its flexibility is also notable in much modern iambic-pentameter verse:

An aged man is but a paltry thing,
A tattered coat upon a stick, unless
Soul clap its hands and sing, and louder sing
For every tatter in its mortal dress . . .
(Yeats, *Sailing to Byzantium*)

From these examples, one can see clearly that, in general, the c. is used in two basic and quite antithetical ways: (1) as a device for emphasizing formality of poetic construction and distance from colloquial utterance; and (2) as a device for investing fairly strict meters with something of the movement of informal speech. If the c. occurs regularly in the medial position, one is dealing with a different kind of verse from that in which caesura placement is more varied and unpredictable. The surprisingly unvaried medial caesuras in Frost's *Out, Out,* for example, suggest that Frost is seeking to raise a domestic rural tragedy to the level of formal art; while, on the other hand, the unexpectedly varied caesuras in Eliot's *Journey of the Magi* suggest that Eliot, proceeding in the opposite direction, is interested in giving a colloquial cast to speech which might otherwise seem excessively chill, distant, and artificial.

C. M. Lewis, *The Foreign Sources of Eng. Versification* (1898); Saintsbury, *Prosody;* A. L. F. Snell, *Pause: A Study of its Nature and its Rhythmical Function in Verse* (1918); G. R. Stewart, *The Technique of Eng. Verse* (1930); S. E. Sprott, *Milton's Art of Prosody* (1953). P.F.

CANADIAN POETRY. IN ENGLISH. The earliest Eng. Can. poetry was produced by the United Empire Loyalists who emigrated to the Maritime provinces after the success of the American Revolution. The poets of this loyalist tradition were disappointed Tories like Jonathan Odell (1737–1818) and Joseph Stansbury (1740–1809), whose best work consisted of convivial songs and lively political satires, or Puritan evangelists like Henry Alline (1748–84), who wrote hymns and pious ejaculations. The first poet to attempt the inescapable theme of the challenge of the new land to the hardy European settler was a grandnephew and namesake of the famous 18th-c. poet Oliver Goldsmith. The Can. Goldsmith (1781–1861) was born in Nova Scotia and lived there the greater part of his life. In 1825 he published an ambitious descriptive poem in heroic couplets, *The Rising Village,* the sketch of the development of an eventually happy and prosperous community of Loyalist settlers in the Acadian wilderness. The work is a rather pedestrian essay in neoclassic sentimentalism, but it is redeemed by some vivid touches of realism. Joseph Howe (1804–73), editor, political philosopher, and statesman as well as poet, produced in *Acadia* a descriptive and reflective narrative in the same tradition. It is notable for a vivid and painful description of an Indian massacre. The earliest poets in Lower Canada (Quebec and Montreal) were romantic sentimentalists of the school of Byron and Tom Moore. Among these, Adam Kidd (1802–31) enjoyed a popular success with *The Huron Chief and Other Poems* (1830).

No poet of more than spasmodic ability appeared until the 19th c. had reached the halfway mark. The hard task of subduing the wilderness and the achievement of a sense of national unity rising from the War of 1812, the rebellions of 1837, and the growing threat of Am. annexation occupied the energies of the British North Am. colonists, and it was not until the late 1850's and 1860's that a national ideal began to take shape in reality and find expression in poetry. Then in the old-fashioned, high-spirited verses of Alexander McLachlan (1818–96), some of the lyrics of Charles Sangster (1822–93), and the western descriptive pieces of Charles Mair (1838–1927)

Can. poetry began little by little to individualize itself. The most original poet of the pre-Confederation period, however, was Charles Heavysege (1816–76), whose mammoth closet drama *Saul* (1857, 1859, 1869) soars from the almost ridiculous to the near sublime. Showing a greater, if unfulfilled, promise than any of these was George Frederick Cameron (1854–85), whose accurately titled *Lyrics on Freedom, Love and Death* was published posthumously in 1887. Isabella Valancy Crawford (1850–87) in a narrative poem of the western settlement, *Malcolm's Katie* (1884), wrote some descriptions of the northern forest that have not been excelled for vigor and imagination.

What has been called the "Golden Age" of Can. poetry began with the publication by Charles G. D. Roberts (1860–1944) of *Orion and Other Poems* (1880). This was the first of a long series of carefully wrought volumes in which ambitious patriotic odes, nature poems, love lyrics, and transcendental rhapsodies combined native and cosmopolitan elements. A competent craftsman, Roberts' inspiration has been most genuine in his simpler, more homely descriptions and his often classical nature poems. Roberts' early books were followed by those of a remarkable group of friends or contemporaries who all applied a classical distinction of form to descriptions of nature in Canada and to themes of love or philosophical or ethical speculation. The most widely known of the group was Roberts' cousin, Bliss Carman (1861–1929), a mellifluous lyric poet who hymned the beauties of nature, the vicissitudes of love, and the joys of the open road. Among the best of his books were *Low Tide on Grand Pré* (1893), *The Pipes of Pan* (5 vols., 1902–5), and three series of *Songs from Vagabondia* written in collaboration with the Am. poet Richard Hovey (1894, 1896, 1901). Carman's later poetry and his transcendental prose essays are a somewhat vague and diffuse echo of his early work.

Not as widely known as these two New Brunswick poets but equally accomplished as craftsmen were three Ontario poets whose finest work, like theirs, was produced in the 1890's and the early years of the new century. These were Archibald Lampman (1861–99), Duncan Campbell Scott (1862–1947), and Wilfred Campbell (1858–1919). Lampman is generally regarded as the finest of all Can. poets, though his mastery is limited to the vivid and sensitive interpretation of nature. The poems in *Among the Millet* (1888), *Lyrics of Earth* (1893), and *Alcyone* (1901) show his fine painter's eye for details of landscape and are distinguished by an impressionistic radiance and a genuine power. His magnificent sonnet "Winter Evening" (admired by R. L. Stevenson) is characteristic of his best quality. Its close is as fine as any 19th-c. sonnet in Eng.:

. . . soon from height to height
With silence and the sharp unpitying stars,
Stern creeping frosts, and winds that touch like
    steel,
Out of the depth beyond the eastern bars,
Glittering and still shall come the awful night.

Like Lampman, Duncan Campbell Scott spent the greater part of his life as a civil servant in Ottawa. A scholarly poet and a conscientious craftsman, he has a wider range of human interest and a deep knowledge of Indian life and legend that made him successful in ballads and dramatic lyrics. Wilfred Campbell began as a poet of the wild lake country of northern Ontario and achieved his best work in his earliest volume *Lake Lyrics* (1889). Campbell's later work consists of grandiose odes on patriotic and imperialistic themes and Tennysonian closet dramas and is of comparatively little interest. Other poets of this generation were William Henry Drummond (1854–1907), famous for his tender and humorous dialect poems of Fr. Can. farm life, the Indian poetess Pauline Johnson (1862–1913), and the Anglican poet Canon Frederick George Scott, the beloved padre of World War I. The influence of Carman, Roberts, and Lampman had a somewhat overpowering effect on their successors for two generations, and a period of diluted romanticism followed in which European movements such as Pre-Raphaelitism and the Celtic Twilight made themselves felt in the work of such graceful lyricists as Marjorie Pickthall (1883–1922), Francis Sherman (1871–1926), and Audrey Alexandra Brown (b. 1904). The best poets of this period were Theodore Goodridge Roberts (1877–1953), a younger brother of Sir Charles, Tom MacInnes (1867–1955), a West Coast poet whose *Rhymes of a Rounder* (1913) are unique for their high spirits and for the skill with which MacInnes has breathed life into the ballade, villanelle, and rondeau and made them vehicles for the expression of a genial and intelligent bohemianism. Whether Robert W. Service can be regarded as a Can. poet or merely a visiting Englishman, his rollicking vaudeville verses have been read with delight by thousands who never read poetry.

The modern movement in Can. poetry began in the 1920's with a simplification of diction and a broadening of themes. Romanticism began to be modified by realism on the one hand and by the introduction of a metaphysical complexity on the other. Thus Can. poetry followed the same path that can be discerned in Fr., Eng., and Am. poetry in the 20th c. E. J. Pratt (1883–1964) produced a series of forceful narrative poems that include *The Cachalot* (1925), *The Roosevelt and the Antinoe* (1930), *The Titantic* (1935), *Brébeuf and His Brethren* (1940), his masterpiece, *Dunkirk* (1941), and *Towards the Last Spike* (1952), a story of the building of the first Can. transcontinental railway. Pratt created boldly and on a large scale and has achieved a greater measure of popular success as well as critical acclaim than any of his contemporaries in Canada, though the West Coast poet Earle Birney (b. 1904) has shown a comparable energy and virtuosity in the tragic narrative of mountain-climbing, *David* (1942) and the satirical dramatic poem *Damnation of Vancouver* (1952). A native tradition of social realism and proletarian sympathy appears in the work of the western poets Dorothy Livesay (b. 1909) and Anne Marriott (b. 1913) and in the Ontario farm poems of Raymond Knister (1900–1932). With these should be mentioned W. W. E. Ross (b. 1894), whose *Laconics* (1930) is a fine example of imagism devoted to purely Can. themes. The impact of the modern cities of Montreal and Toronto upon the sensitive and disillusioned generations can be noted in the poetry of Louis Dudek (b. 1918), Raymond Souster (b. 1921), and most remarkable of all Irving Layton (b. 1912).

The cosmopolitan tradition of symbolist and metaphysical verse developed in Canada in the late 1920's and 1930's with the work of the Montreal Group, F. R. Scott (b. 1899), A. J. M. Smith (b. 1902), and the magnificent Jewish poet A. M. Klein (b. 1909). These published their early poems in a significant anthology *New Provinces* (1936) in which they were joined by E. J. Pratt, Leo Kennedy (b. 1907), and the Toronto poet Robert Finch (b. 1900). During the 1940's and 1950's these and a number of younger poets, Patrick Anderson and Miss P. K. Page in the war years and more recently Douglas Le Pan, John Glassco, Miriam Waddington, Anne Wilkinson, James Reaney, Jay Macpherson, and Daryl Hine, have developed a modern school of metaphysical or neoromantic poetry in various individual ways that reveal a sensibility and expression unmistakably, if indefinably, Can. At the beginning of the 1960's the poetry of Margaret Avison might be singled out. Collected in *Winter Sun* (1960), it was given the Governor General's award in that year. More original, if more complex and difficult, her poetry is at least as rewarding as the work of any other modern Can. poet.

ANTHOLOGIES: *Selections from Can. Poets*, ed. E. H. Dewart (1864); *Songs of the Great Dominion*, ed. W. D. Lighthall (1889); *Can. Poets*, ed. J. W. Garvin (1926); *The Book of Can. Poetry*, ed. A. J. M. Smith (1943, 3d ed. rev. and enl., 1957); *Other Canadians*, ed. J.

Sutherland (1947); *Can. Poems, 1850–1952,* ed. L. Dudek and I. Layton (2d ed., 1952); *20th C. Can. Poetry,* ed. E. Birney (1953); *Can. Poetry in Eng.,* ed. B. Carman, L. Pierce, and V. B. Rhodenizer (1954); *Can. Anthol.,* ed. C. F. Klinck and R. E. Watters (1955); *The Penguin Book of Can. Verse,* ed. R. Gustafson (1959); *The Oxford Book of Can. Verse* (Eng. and Fr.), ed. A. J. M. Smith (1960); *Poetry 62* (Eng. and Fr.), ed. E. Mandel and J.-G. Pilon (1961).

HISTORY AND CRITICISM: R. P. Baker, *A Hist. of Eng.-Can. Lit. to the Confederation* (1920); A. M. MacMechan, *Head-Waters of Can. Lit.* (1924); L. Stevenson, *Appraisals of Can. Lit.* (1926); L. Pierce, *An Outline of Can. Lit.* (1927); V. B. Rhodenizer, *A Handbook of Can. Lit.* (1930); W. E. Collin, *The White Savannahs* (1936); E. K. Brown, *On Can. Poetry* (rev. ed., 1944); *Leading Can. Poets,* ed. W. P. Percival (1948); D. Pacey, *Ten Can. Poets* (1958) and *Creative Writing in Canada* (2d ed., 1961).   A.J.M.S.

IN FRENCH. The earliest Fr.-Can. poets Joseph Quesnel and Michel Bibaud, were men of the 18th c.: satirists. Under the influence of Rousseau and Lahontan they used the notion of the virtuous Indian to ridicule the pretended virtue of the Fr. residents. What they neglected to do in their satires, that is to note the grandeur of the landscape and celebrate the heroes of the race, the men of the "patriotic" school of 1860 did to their heart's content. Their imaginations were fired by their "national" historian; François-Xavier Garneau, and they found their epic voices in the poetry of Victor Hugo. Much of this fanfare has died away. Of Octave Crémazie all that is left is a song of an old Can. soldier. Louis Fréchette's aim, like that of his idol Hugo, was to dramatize the upward march of a race. His poetry, like his master's, suffers from excessive fervor, overemphasis, the abuse of antithesis and repetition. The next generation of poets, in founding the "Ecole littéraire" (1895), destroyed the formulas of romanticism; they turned their backs on Can. history, refused to worship their ancestors, and sought a purely aesthetic ideal. Parnassians at heart, they introduced into Fr.-Can. literature a sense of formal and exotic beauty which they found in far-away places: France, Italy, Greece, Persia. The poet whose work has endured is Emile Nelligan (1879–1941), a symbolist. Pieces like *Le vaisseau d'or,* in which he pictured his soul as a ship laden with treasures, sailing unknown seas, "shipwrecked in the abyss of Dream," and *Le romance du vin,* in which he made mockery of the philistines by pretending that a poet's life was merry and bright, still shine gemlike in the Can. anthology.

Farther down the river another group made its appearance about this time (1902) in whose work the two patriotic strands, awareness of the grandeur of Can. nature and the cult of ancestors, blended together in what Mgr. Camille Roy, the critic of the day, called literary "nationalism." Because they were concerned with racial survival, religion, language, traditions, people and their work, these poets are often referred to as the "terroir" school. Blanche Lamontagne, the most prolific of the group, is inspired by the folk songs and religious traditions of her native Gaspésie. It is often a question of a peasant at work and folk songs enter the poetry to mark the rhythm of consecrated labor, as in the picture of her grandmother, "la belle et robuste fermière," whom she sees sitting at the window of the old house, spinning. The vogue of this art extended over the first third of the 20th c.

The last twenty years have produced richer and more significant poetry, but more austere, more difficult. Experience has been more complex. Saint-Denys Garneau, François Hertel, and Robert Charbonneau made their debut in 1934, in the pages of a review they launched, *La Relève.* Charbonneau wrote little poetry; he was a novelist, editor, polemist. To him life in Quebec lacked grandeur. He expressed disgust with the prevailing conformist spirit. He tried to open wider the windows of Fr. Canada to take in the great Rus. and Am. writers. It was the appalling conformist spirit that drove Hertel to seek freedom abroad. An ex-Jesuit, he seems to have lost his faith. Even in Paris he is a tormented soul, suffering from fissure, and his imagination, whether it creates verse or prose, expresses itself ironically in the form of brilliant paradoxes. Whereas Hertel writes endlessly, Saint-Denys Garneau (1912–43) wrote very little: a small collection of poems with a metaphysical title, *Regards et jeux dans l'espace* (1937), an odd essay and a *Journal.* Then he died. To him poetry was a child's game because it was a way of building his life with pure motives, unbiased judgments, with charity. When he talked of "bones" he expressed his will to strip language to its essential truth. Garneau was the first to venture away from traditional verse forms, to destroy the tyranny of the alexandrian line. The way for the free rhythms of Edmond Labelle's poetry in *La quête de l'existence* (1944) was prepared by Garneau. Something of Garneau's spirit is found in the poetry of Anne Hébert, his cousin. It expresses a nostalgia for a childhood paradise and at the same time, by means of symbols such as room, drawer, cupboard, courtyard, tomb, it translates an experience of psychic oppression. Alain Grandbois, the most important of the older poets today, expresses his inner life through the symbol "voyage." By this token he recognizes his literary ancestors: Baudelaire and Rimbaud. Grandbois has traveled through Europe, Egypt, and China, and the poems in *Les îles de la nuit* (1947) re-create the nightmares that torment the poet's soul during a voyage over a dark ocean. The lights of islands that appear are points where, in his journey through the unconscious regions of his soul, the poet touches the mystery of life.

A new critical attitude toward the Church and the part it has traditionally played in politics and education and toward Can. federation is found in the poetry of the young rebels who are coming to dominate Fr.-Can. letters. Among the most brilliant of the new men, cosmopolitan or nationalistic, are Pierre Trottier, Gilles Henault, Roland Giguère, J.-G. Pilon, Eloi de Grandmont, Sylvain Garneau, Gilles Vigneault, and the fine woman poet Michèle Lalonde.

ANTHOLOGIES: *Anthologie des poètes canadiens*, comp. J. Fournier and O. Asselin (3d ed., 1933); *L'Ame de la poésie canadienne française*, ed. L. Rièse (1955); *Anthologie de la poésie can.-fr.*, ed. G. Sylvestre (4th ed., 1963). See also CAN. ENG.

HISTORY AND CRITICISM: I. F. Fraser, *Bibliog. of Fr.-Can. Poetry* (1935) and *The Spirit of Fr. Canada* (1939); A. Dandurand, *La Poésie can.-fr.* (1933); J. M. Turnbull, *Essential Traits of Fr.-Can. Poetry* (1938); B. Brunet, *Hist. de la littérature can.-fr.* (1946); J. Paul-Crouzet, *Poésie au Canada* (1946); C. Roy, *Hist. de la litt. can.* (14th ed., 1950); A. Viatte, *Hist. littéraire de l'Amérique fr. des origines à 1950* (1954), G. Tougas, *Hist. de la litt. can.-fr.* (1960).   W.E.C.

CANCIÓN. The term is now loosely applied to any Sp. poem consisting of strophes in Italianate lines (11 and 7 syllables) and in which the poet invents a first strophe and then models all following strophes of the poem exactly after it. *Canciones* of a few lines are often called *liras, canciones aliradas, canciones clásicas,* and *odas.* Many variations have been developed since the Italinate *c.* (cf. CANZONE) was introduced by Boscán and Garcilaso near the middle of the 16th c. The *c. petrarquista* (also called *c. a la italiana, c. extensa,* and *estancias*) is generally considered the purest form of the Italianate type.

In the 15th and early 16th c., before the use of the Italianate form, an entirely different type of *c.*—an octosyllabic form of *cantiga* (cf. DECIR)—was widely employed. Although some variety in pattern was allowed in the early period, by the end of the 15th c. the form was usually restricted to either a quatrain (abab or abba) followed by a *copla de arte menor* (8 lines only) whose last 4 rhymes are identical with those of the initial quatrain though the order of the rhymes may be changed, or a *quintilla* (2 rhymes only, no set order) followed by a *copla real* or a *copla de arte menor* of 9 or 10 lines, whose last 5 rhymes are identical with and follow the same sequence as those of the initial *quintilla.* Variation in the first type, then, may occur only in the order of rhymes, and in the second type, in the length of the second strophe. F. Vendrell de Millás (ed. *El Cancionero de Palacio,* 1945, pp. 95–100) lists other variations. This *c.* may be distinguished from the closely related *villancico* (q.v.), according to P. Le Gentil (*La Poésie lyrique espagnole et portugaise à la fin du moyen âge,* II [1953] 263ff.), by its longer refrain (4 or 5 lines having *redondilla, serventesio,* or *quintilla* rhyme); its *vuelta,* which parallels exactly the initial theme; its shorter length, which rarely exceeds one stanza; and its courtly nature and love theme. See Le Gentil, *loc. cit.,* for examples.   D.C.C.

CANCIONEIROS (Portuguese, "songbooks"). See CANTIGA; GALICIAN POETRY; PORTUGUESE POETRY. CANCIONERO (Sp., "songbook"). See SP. POETRY.

CANTAR. Throughout Sp. literature the term has been used loosely to mean words for a song. In the 15th c. it was probably the equivalent of *cantiga.* In modern times it has come to mean specifically an octosyllabic quatrain having assonance (occasionally consonance) in the even-numbered lines and, preferably, unrhymed oxytones in the odd-numbered: "Algún día me verás / cuando no tenga remedio; / me verás y te veré, / pero no nos hablaremos." The composition, also called *copla,* is usually contained in one strophe. The *seguidilla gitana* (see SEGUIDILLA) is sometimes called c. The c. is sometimes defined as an octosyllabic 5-line poem of one strophe assonating ababa. The *c. de soledad,* also known as *soledad, soleá, terceto,* and *triada gallega,* is an octosyllabic c. reduced to 3 lines. The first and third lines rhyme in either assonance. or consonance and the second is left unrhymed. The form is of popular origin. Dance songs, such as the *jota* and the *malagueña,* are also termed "c." The *c. de gesta,* also called simply c., is an epic poem, usually of the medieval period. The lines vary in length, but are long and divided into 2 hemistichs each. The poem is divided into *laisses* of unequal length. Each *laisse* is monorhymed in assonance. The anonymous *C. de Mio Cid* (c. 1140) is the best known example.—N. Alonso Cortés, *Elementos de preceptiva literaria* (6th ed., 1919); S. G. Morley, "Recent Theories about the Meter of the 'Cid,'" PMLA, 48 (1933); Navarro.   D.C.C.

CANZONE

CANTE JONDO. Andalusian phrase for *cante hondo* (deep song), also called *cante flamenco*. It is the typical folk song (and poetry) of Southern Spain characterized musically by plaintive tremulos and accompanied by the guitar. Assonance is generally used instead of rhyme, and the main themes are love, loss of love, death. The c.j. bears a strong kinship with the music of North Africa, Arabia, and other regions of the Near East. It also resembles the Hebrew lament. The gypsies of Andalusia are particularly noted as c.j. performers. Some musicologists believe that the Moors introduced this style of song into Spain, others that it antedated the Moorish conquest and underwent only slight modification through contact with this extraneous culture. The c.j. is an integral part of Andalusian gypsy dancing, and has inspired many of the finest compositions of Sp. music. During the years between World Wars I and II it became a focal point of poetic creation among the younger writers in Spain, particularly García Lorca. This poet and the composer Manuel de Falla together organized a Fiesta of the *Cante Jondo* in the year 1927, and thus gave further impetus to a tremendous revival of interest in this type of poetry and music all over the Hispanic world. —G. Chase, *The Music of Spain* (2d ed., 1959).　J.A.C.

CANTICUM. In the Roman drama the part of the play that was declaimed or sung to musical accompaniment, as opposed to the *diverbium* (q.v.) or spoken dialogue. The *cantica* of Plautus are very numerous, constituting approximately two-thirds of each play while those of Terence are very few. They are chiefly monodies or duets sung or declaimed by an actor or by actors in a great variety of meters. The *cantica* of Seneca are choral songs written in meters which derive primarily from the metrical system of Horace.—F. Leo, *Die Plautinische Cantica und die hellenistische Lyrik* (1897); G. E. Duckworth, *The Nature of Roman Comedy* (1952); W. Beare, *The Roman Stage* (2d ed., 1955).　P.S.C.

CANTIGA. Term applied to variety of literary and folk songs in the Iberian Peninsula, but commonly referring to around 2,000 Galician-Portuguese lyrics written between the late 12th and 14th c. and contained principally in three great *cancioneiros* of the 14th and 15th c. The four main categories are, according to subject, *cantigas de amigo* (sung by woman to or about her lover), *cantigas de amor* (addressed by a man to his lady), *cantigas de escarnio* (or *de mal dizer*, songs of vilification, sometimes obscene) and religious songs (dealing usually with miracles of the Virgin as in Alfonso X's *Cantigas de Santa Maria*). Prov.

inspiration is quite apparent in *pastorelas* (shepherd songs), *albas* (dawn songs), *bailadas* (dance), etc., but indigenous influences are found especially in the *cantigas de amigo*. The best of these are characterized by *saudade* (melancholy longing), simple haunting rhythms, parallelism in structure, idea, and rhyme, as well as refrains, and restricted vocabulary with systematic synonymy.

TEXTS OF CANCIONEIROS: *Il canzoniere portoghese della Biblioteca Vaticana*, ed. E. Monaci (1875); *Cancioneiro da Ajuda*, ed. C. Michaëlis de Vasconcellos (2 v., 1904) and diplomatic ed. by H. H. Carter (1941); *Cancioneiro da Biblioteca Nacional, antigo Colocci-Brancuti*, ed. E. Pacheco Machado and J. Pedro Machado (7v., 1949–60); *Cantigas de Santa Maria*, ed. Marqués de Valmar (1889) and in course of publication ed. by W. Mettmann (1959).

ANTHOLOGIES: *Cantigas d'amigo dos trovadores galego-portugueses*, ed. J. J. Nunes (3 v., 1926–28); *Cantigas d'amor dos trovadores galego-portugueses*, ed. J. J. Nunes (1932); *Escolma da poesia galega*, v. I, ed. X. M. Álvarez Blázquez (1952); *An Anth. of Medieval Lyrics*, ed. A. Flores (1962; tr).

HISTORY AND CRITICISM: A. F. G. Bell *et al.*, *Da poesia medieval portuguesa* (2d ed., 1947); M. Rodrigues Lapa, *Lições de literatura portuguesa. Época medieval* (4th ed. rev., 1956). On the *cantiga* in Castilian poetry, consult P. Le Gentil, *La Poésie lyrique espagnole et portugaise à la fin du moyen âge. 2. Les formes* (1953).　L.A.S.

CANTO. A subdivision of an epic or narrative poem, that divides and orders the content, like the chapter in a novel. The end of each c., in long epic poems, gave the singer an opportunity to rest for a while or perhaps to defer the rest of the recitation to the following day. The subdivision into cantos may apply to poems of all stanzaic patterns. Although the subdivision into smaller units is found in long epic poems of all times and literatures, the It. word *canto* to indicate such a subdivision was adopted mainly by the Romance and Eng. literatures. It appears in the works of Dante, Ariosto, Tasso, Ercilla, Voltaire, Pope, Byron, etc.　R.MI.

CANZONE. Due to the intimate link between poetry and music the term *canzone* (from *cantio*) has come to be applied to quite a number of verse forms with differing metrical patterns. Among the better known types are the *c. epico-lirica* whose center of diffusion was originally the Gallo-It. dialect area. It belongs to the Celtic substratum and is akin to compositions of the same genre in France and Catalonia. More indigenous to the It.

soil is the *c. a ballo* or *ballata* and other popular compositions such as the *frottola, barzelletta,* the *canto carnascialesco* and the *laude sacra.* At various times these types have been used by the *poeti d'arte,* but the type exclusively employed for refined artistic expression is the so-called *c. petrarchesca.* It is obscure in origin but bears strong traces of Prov. influence. The *strambotto, ballata* and minnesong are also said to have conditioned its architectonic structure. It takes its beginning among the poets of the Sicilian school (q.v.) is employed extensively by Guittone d'Arezzo and his followers and by the poets of the *dolce stil nuovo* (q.v.), but acquires fixed patterns and perfection in Petrarch's *Canzoniere,* hence the qualifying adjective *petrarchesca.* Its greatest vogue in Italy occurred, as one might expect, during the Petrarchistic period. It lasted until the death of Torquato Tasso. While in Eng. the Petrarchistic type of c. was employed by William Drummond of Hawthornden and in German by A. W. von Schlegel and other German romantic poets, Spain and Portugal were really the only countries outside of Italy where it was used to a considerable extent. In this type of poem the division for each of its stanzas is tripartite, consisting of two like parts, *piedi,* and one unlike part, *sirima* or *cauda.* There is usually a single *commiato* at the close of the poem in the form of a valediction to the c. Stanzaic length is indeterminate, varying from a maximum of 20 to a minimum of 7 verses. The lines are normally hendecasyllabic with some admixture of heptameters and pentameters. After Tasso, under the strong influence of the Fr. *Pléiade,* this type was supplanted by new forms labeled *canzoni*—the Pindaric and Anacreontic odes. Chiabrera played a leading rôle in their diffusion. He also revived the *canzonetta* originally employed by the poets of the Sicilian School. This became the favorite type used by Metastasio and the Arcadian school. Toward the close of the 17th c. Alessandro Guidi acclimated the *c. libera* which reached its highest development at the hands of Leopardi.— P. E. Guarnerio, *Manuale di versificazione italiana* (1893); F. Flamini, *Notizia storica dei versi e metri italiani* (1919); R. Murari, *Ritmica e metrica razionale ital.* (1927); E. Segura Covarsí, *La canción petrarquista en la lírica española del Siglo de Oro* (1949); E. H. Wilkins, "The C. and the Minnesong," *The Invention of the Sonnet and Other Studies in It. Lit.* (1959). J.G.F.

CAPITOLO. It. verse form originating either in imitation or parody of Dante's terza rima (q.v.) of which it has all the characteristics. Its name probably derives from the name given by Petrarch to the chief divisions of his *Trionfi.* Up to the 15th c. its subject matter was primarily political or didactic, but by the end of that century it was also widely used to sing of love. Beginning with the 16th c. its use spread to humorous and satirical subjects. Since Ariosto the c. has remained the chief verse form for It. classical satire. A.S.B.

CARMEN. The L. word usually meant "song" or "lyric"; e.g., Catullus' *Carmina* or Horace's *Odes.* On occasion it had a broader meaning of "poetry" including epic, drama, and lampoon. Its broadest usage covered prophecies, oracular responses, incantations, triumphant hymns, epitaphs, charms, and even legal formulas in prose. The word seems to connote divine inspiration, the song of the poet as the agent of a god or muse; e.g., Horace's usage in the *Odes.* The word in modern languages suggests a conscious archaism intending to impart a serious quality to a work of poetry. R.A.H.

CAROL, a light-hearted song of religious joy. The pre-Elizabethan c. was a lyric of definite verse form and reflected stylistically its close connection with the dance, but since the 16th c., the word has come to mean any festive religious song, whatever the metrical or stanzaic form, sung to a tune which in pace and melody follows secular musical traditions rather than those of hymnody. In America the c. is now almost invariably associated with Christmas; this is less true of England, where Easter carols are also widely sung. The Fr. *noël* (from L. *natalis*), a joyous song of the Nativity, is the counterpart of the Christmas c.; it has been an established song type since the 15th c. An earlier Fr. form, the *carole,* was a dance-song similar in structure and movement to the early Eng. c. and probably its ancestor.

The surviving medieval carols are composed of uniform stanzas interspersed with a refrain, usually a rhymed couplet, which seems to have been sung—or read—also at the beginning of the c. A tetrameter triplet (3 rhyming lines of 4 stresses each) makes up the base of the c. stanza. The stanza is completed by a tag line shorter than the triplet lines and normally rhyming with the refrain. The following example is from a 15th.-c. carol of moral advice; it has been slightly modernized:

Man, beware, beware, beware,
And keep thee that thou have no care.

Thy tongue is made of flesh and blood;
Evil to speak it is not good;
By Christ, that died upon the rood,
    So give us grace our tongues to spare.

Commonly the stanza rhymes abab; it may also be extended to 5, 6 or 8 lines and bound together by a variety of rhyme schemes. Refrains, too, are sometimes extended by 1 or 2 lines. Perhaps the most notable single variation from the norm is having the tag line of the stanza identical with a refrain line. This tendency to integrate stanza and refrain frequently sets in when a dance-song ceases to be danced.

In the round dances at which carols were originally performed, the stanza was probably sung by the leader of the dance; the refrain was sung by the chorus as they executed an accompanying dance figure. Modern children's games like "Now We Go 'Round the Mulberry Bush" and "A Tisket, A Tasket" represent corrupt descendants of the medieval round dances —then, of course, an adult pastime. From the violent denunciations of caroling that fulminated from medieval clerics, it is clear that caroling, even though the songs, in most cases, dealt reverently with Christian matter, was regarded as a wicked pagan survival. And, in fact, many of the older specimens are highly erotic and suggest pagan fertility rites. Doubtless the reason why caroling flourished strongest at Christmas and Easter was that these Christian festivals coincided with and supplanted the pre-Christian winter and spring fertility revels. Of some 500 medieval carols extant in manuscript, about 200 deal directly or indirectly with Advent and the Nativity. Easter, the New Year, and Epiphany were less frequently celebrated with caroling. Abundant political, moral, and satirical carols are met with, and there are besides many amorous pieces, some of which are frank to the point of lewdness.

Carols were popular in both courtly circles and among the folk, but most of those that have been preserved show learned influences, such as uncorrupted L. tags, and the various manuscript versions of the same c. do not exhibit the variation that one would expect if carols had been orally transmitted and re-created in the manner of folk song.

With the Reformation the medieval c. began to die out. The decline was mainly due to the more sober fashion of celebrating Christmas and other religious holidays that came to prevail. The formal c. was thus gradually replaced by festive songs learned from broadsides, chapbooks, and devotional songbooks. Some carols of this new kind, like *The Seven Joys of Mary, I Saw Three Ships, God Rest You Merry, Gentlemen* and *The Virgin Unspotted,* are regularly described as "traditional," a term which means only that such pieces were long popular and are anonymous, not necessarily that they are folk songs.

The carols which supplanted the medieval carols were themselves beginning to wither in popularity when musical antiquaries like Gilbert Davies (*Some Ancient Christmas Carols,* 1822) and William Sandys (*Christmas Carols, Ancient and Modern,* 1833) collected and revived them. J. M. Neale and Thomas Helmore in 1852 introduced the practice, since followed in most British and Am. c. books, of plundering Fr., Basque, Dutch, Sp., It., German and Scandinavian collections for tunes to which Eng. words could successfully be adapted. Since 1870 the rural counties of England have been scoured for folk carols and the collectors' discoveries have been impressive. By being made available to school children in excellent arrangements by Cecil J. Sharp, Vaughan Williams, and other folk-music experts, the folk carols have been artificially revitalized among educated people. Folk carols are comparatively rare in America; the only ones widely reported in this century, *The Seven Joys of Mary, Jesus Born in Bethlehem* and *The Twelve Days of Christmas,* are all Eng. imports.

R. L. Greene, *The Early Eng. Carols* (1935) is the definitive collection of medieval carols. Greene furnishes a lengthy crit. introd. His theory of the popular character of the extant carols (also held by E. K. Chambers and W. W. Greg) has been contested by R. H. Robbins in "Middle Eng. Carols as Processional Hymns," SP, 56 (1959), who applies to the Eng. carols current Fr. theories that the *caroles* were composed for ecclesiastical festivals. Carols of the later kind are collected in *The Oxford Book of Carols* (1928 and later ed.). E. Routley, *The Eng. C.* (1959) is a running commentary on the Oxford coll. but includes much information on the reputation of the carols and their modern liturgical use. Sir. R. R. Terry's coll., *Two Hundred Folk Carols* (1933), is notable for preserving the Roman Catholic features of the Continental carols he prints. Folk c. collections of the greatest importance are A. E. Gillington, *Old Christmas Carols of the Southern Counties* (1910), C. J. Sharp, *Eng. Folk-Carols* (1911) and R. Vaughan Williams, *Eight Traditional Carols* (1919). For Am. folk carols, see the *F. C. Brown Coll. of North Carolina Folklore,* II (1952), 199–212, where abundant references to other sources are given. A.B.F.

CARPE DIEM (L. "seize [enjoy] the day"). A motif in poetry which usually advises the enjoyment of present pleasures. The *locus classicus* of the phrase occurs in Horace, *Odes* 1.11, though the fullest treatment of the theme by that poet appears in *Odes* 3.29. The motif, which is found in Gr. poetry (Aeschylus, *Persians* 840–42; Anacreon 4.11.7–10) as well as in L. poetry, arises from the realization of the brevity of life and the finality of death. Hence the injunction to enjoy this life. Such enjoyment ranges in L. poetry from the refined pleasures of the mind and spirit (Horace, *Odes* 3.29) to purely sensual and momentary delights (Catullus, *Carmina* 5). Even at the height of the single, joyous experience the motif encourages objectivity and detachment, implying full awareness of the sadness of the human situation. To this basically epicurean thought Ausonius added the rose motif wherein the brevity of life becomes symbolized by the brevity of the rose (*De rosis nascentibus* 35–36). In subsequent goliardic verse as well as Fr. and Eng. poetry the rose and its brevity further symbolized the loss of virginity (*Roman de la rose*). The 15th c. poets used the c.d. theme and the rose to rail against fruitless chastity (Lorenzo de' Medici, *Corinto* 28–31). In this same tradition were the Eng. Cavalier poets such as Herrick ("Gather Ye Rosebuds").

But in Christian writing and poetry the c.d. theme has been used as a persuasion to goodness (J. Taylor, *Holy Dying*, p. 31). Herbert used the motif to emphasize not only the transitoriness of this life but the eternity of the Christian life, especially after death. So also did Spenser in the *Faerie Queene*. The motif in one aspect or another is found in Carew, Thomas, Marvel, Milton, and Blake. It is found also in Persian poetry (Omar Khayyám) and ancient Egyptian poetry (*The Song of the Harper*).—J. A. Symonds, *Essays Speculative and Suggestive* (1893); F. Bruser, "Comus and the Rose Song," SP, 44 (1947); Frye. R.A.H.

CATACHRESIS (Gr. "misuse"). The misapplication of a word, especially in a strained or mixed metaphor or in an implied metaphor. It need not be a ridiculous misapplication as in bad poetry, but may be a deliberate wresting of a term from its normal and proper significance. Sometimes it is deliberately humorous. Quintilian called it a necessary misuse (*abusio*) of words and cited Virgil's *Aeneid* 2.15–16: "equum divina Palladis arte / aedificant" (They build a horse by Pallas' divine art). Since *aedificant* literally means "they build a house," it is a catachresis when applied to a horse. Puttenham, in his *Arte of Eng. Poesie*, called c. a figure of "plain abuse, as he that bade his man go into his library and fetch him his bow and arrows." Two celebrated examples of this figure are found in Shakespeare and Milton: "To take arms against a sea of troubles" (*Hamlet* 3.1.59) and "Blind mouths! that scarce themselves know how to hold a sheep-hook" (*Lycidas* 119–120). A very effective c. is Shakespeare's " 'Tis deepest winter in Lord Timon's purse" (*Timon* 3.4.15), which suggests comparison with some of the strained metaphors or implied metaphors in more modern poetry, e.g., "The sun roars at the prayer's end" (Dylan Thomas, *Vision and Prayer*, last line).—Lausberg. M.T.H.

CATALAN POETRY. It has been the peculiar fate of the poetry of the Catalans that during a number of centuries it was written by them mainly in languages that were not their own: Prov. in the Middle Ages, Castilian during the age of Sp. ascendancy. It is only since romanticism that a poetry in their own vernacular has continuously flourished in Catalonia and the Cat.-speaking Valencia and Balearics.

In the Middle Ages, the geographic, linguistic, and political propinquity of Catalonia and Provence, and the European prestige of Prov. poetry, caused the Catalans to write theirs in the literary language of Provence, borrowing also the patterns—courtly love, satire, moralization—and the poetics of the troubadours. Most Cat. poets held to this practice from the 12th c. to the 15th. Guillem de Berguedà (1140–ca. 1200) and Cerverí de Girona (fl. 1250–80) are among the best of the early Cat. troubadours and Jaume March (1335–1410?) and Pere March (1338?–1413) among the late ones.

Relics have been found, however, of a poetry written in Catalonia in the same centuries, not in literary Prov., but in Cat.: a popular, religious poetry (mainly Marian, and usually addressed to the Virgin of Montserrat), of a type still common in Cat. literature. Ramon Llull (1232?–1316) wrote more formal poetry in Cat., reaching lyric heights in his *Desconhort* and the *Cant de Ramon*. His greatest lyric is the *Llibre d'Amic e Amat*, a prose poem somewhat under the influence of the Arab mystics and celebrating the ascension of Man's soul toward God through the ways of Love.

In the 14th and 15th c. there appeared in Catalonia a narrative poetry, usually written in octosyllabic couplets. One might include in this type the *Spill* or *Llibre de les dones* by Jaume Roig (d. 1478), a book on the wiles and vices of women, written in 4-syllable couplets.

The close political ties of the Crown of Aragon with Sicily, Naples, and Italy in general, soon added to the Prov. influence the influence of the It. *dolce stil nuovo* (q.v.). A slight Petrarchan tinge has been noticed in the verse of Jordi de Sant Jordi (ca. 1400–1424), although he was still very much a writer in the Prov. tradition. The language of his poetry was quite close to the Cat. of his own time, as we know it from prose literature. Completely Cat. already is the language of the poetry of Ausiàs March (1397–1459), who is the heir to both troubadour and It. lyricism. Within these traditions, March reveals a profound psychological insight that can transform apparently medieval or Italianate topics into expressions of universal human emotions. His work is usually divided into songs of love, songs of death, moral songs and a spiritual song, in all of which—as he himself said—

there is no fiction, but rather truth, trouble, and solitude. To complete a trilogy of great Cat. poets of the 15th c. mention should be made of Joan Roïç de Corella (ca. 1430–ca. 1490), a poet first of sensual love, then of pure love and finally of divine love. He was a writer of great visual and imagistic power, and also the first to introduce into Cat. poetics the It. hendecasyllable.

Just as it seemed that Cat. poetry had established itself in the work of Ausiàs March and Roïç de Corella and the constellation of minor poets that surrounded and followed them, a decadence set in which brought about the almost complete disappearance of Cat. poetry. In fact, from the beginning of the 16th c. to the beginning of the 19th, most Cat. poets abandoned Catalan to write in Castilian, and although the Cat, language remained the tongue of the people of Catalonia, it was used in poetry only by minor writers. The poetry in Cat. that remained truly alive during the period was the ballad and the popular religious song, both transmitted orally by a people more attached to their tradition than were at that time the literate upper classes.

In the 19th c., with the spread of the romantic ideals of individualism and nationalism, a revival or rebirth—la Renaixença—of Cat. literature took place. Romanticism naturally tended to foster a return to the native tongue as the means of expressing the sentiments of the men of a Cat. nation that was finding again its ancient pride and soul. The ode to La Pàtria (1833) by Bonaventura Carles Aribau (1798–1862) has often been cited as the symbolic beginning of this rebirth. Then the work of a number of poet-scholars like Joaquim Rubió i Ors (1818–99) and Manuel Milà i Fontanals (1818–84) gave it momentum, leadership, and organization. The revival in 1859 of the annual "Jocs Florals" (poetry contests) inspired a number of writers consistently to exercise their faculties in the vernacular. This stimulated floods of patriotic, religious, dramatic, and lyric verse, not always of the best; but the instrument was finally ready and all previous efforts were crowned with the work of Jacint Verdaguer (1845–1902), a peasant priest.

After Verdaguer, no Cat. has had to apologize for the literary use of his native tongue. Verdaguer's poetry ranges from the epic of L'Atlantida (1877) and of Canigó (1886), to religious poetry, to nature poetry, to the most subjective and intimate lyricism; his meters range from the short lively quadrisyllable through the traditional and popular ballad meter to the solemn alexandrine, his strophic combinations are varied and always appropriate as he had a keen ear for harmony both formal and internal.

After Verdaguer, modern Cat. poetry, having come of age, shed its Romantico-Renaixença character. Joan Maragall (1860–1911) brought to it a new sense of freedom by using free verse as well as the traditional forms. Maragall's poetry expresses his enjoyment of beauty, his love of life, of nature, of strength, work and creation: what is now called the "Maragallian optimism." Perhaps his best loved books are Pirenenques, Vistes al mar, and Cants. He was the poet whose "measure was human" and could say:

Si el món ja és tan formós, Senyor, si es mira
amb la pau vostra a dintre de l'ull nostre,
què més ens podeu dâ en una altra vida?

If the world is already so beautiful, Lord,
when one looks at it with your Peace within
     one's eye,
what more can You give us in another life?

While Maragall observed or broke the classical rules, the Balearic poets of Cat. language, Miquel Costa i Llobera (1854–1922), the author of Horacianes (1906), and Joan Alcover (1854–1926), the author of Cap al tard (1909) and Poemes biblics (1918), reasserted the love of measure and of wisdom, the classical Mediterranean inheritance of Cat. culture.

The following generation of poets was heir to both the classicism of Costa i Llobera and Alcover and the vitalism of Maragall. For instance, there is Josep Carner (1884) who added grace, lightness, and style to Cat. poetry; Guerau de Liost (pen name of Jaume Bofill i Mates, 1878–1933) with his intellectualism; Josep Maria López-Picó (1886–1959) with his Catholic vision of the world; Josep Maria de Sagarra (1894–1961) with his popularism; Carles Riba (1893–1959), a professor of Gr. by trade, with his "pure poetry."

The post-Spanish Civil War (1936–39) generation of Cat. poets, at home and in exile, continues to write poetry although the political restrictions imposed by the Franco régime on publication in Cat. on the Peninsula have somewhat isolated the poets from their public. Salvador Espriu (1913) is perhaps the best known of the poets living in Catalonia; Agustí Bartra (1910) perhaps the best known of those writing abroad. They carry on the flame of living Cat. expression.

BIBLIOGRAPHIES: J. Massó i Torrents, "Bibliografia dels antics poetes catalans," Anuari de l'Institut d'Estudis Catalans, 1913–14, and Repertori de l'antiga literatura catalana, I, La Poesia (1932); A. Elías de Molins, Diccionario biográfico y bibliográfico de escritores y artistas catalanes del siglo XIX (1889–95).

ANTHOLOGIES: Anthol. of Cat. Lyric Poetry, ed. J. Triadú and J. Gili (1953); and the collection of Cat. classics of Biblioteca Catalana of M. Aguiló (Barcelona).

HISTORY AND CRITICISM: L. Nicolau D'Olwer, *Resum de literatura catalana* (1927); M. de Riquer, *Resumen de lit. catalana* (1947); J. Ruiz i Calonja, *Història de la lit. catalana* (1954); G. Díaz Plaja, *De lit. catalana* (1956); J. Fuster, *La poesia catalana* (2 v., 1956). L.M.

CATALEXIS, catalectic. See TRUNCATION.

CATALOGUE VERSE. A term to describe lists of persons, places, things, or ideas which have a common denominator such as heroism, beauty, death, etc. The device, which may be of any length, is of ancient origin and found in almost all literatures of the world. But the purpose of such verse has changed in the course of the history of literature. One of its original functions was educative. In Polynesian and Abyssinian literature lists of islands and places seem primarily used to inform by supplying geographic information. Rhymed lists of rules of conduct frequently were used to inculcate moral training in the young. Such, too, may be the chief purpose of the genealogical lists found in all ancient literatures and especially in the Bible (Genesis 10). In lists of this sort there is often an encroachment of antiquarian information on the original purpose. But frequently c.v. has a more artistic intention, such as indicating the vastness of a war, a battle, or the power of a prince or king. This is the primary purpose of the catalogue of heroes in epic literature, for example the heroes of the Trojan war found in *Iliad* 2, the Argonauts in Apollonius Rhodius' *Argonautica* 1, the heroes in *Aeneid* 7, and the list of fallen angels in Milton's *Paradise Lost* 2. Closely allied with this notion is the treatment of God's power as found in the canticle, "Benedicite omnia opera Domini" (*Book of Common Prayer*).

The device often appears in secular medieval poetry to enumerate many things such as beautiful women. This seems to follow from ancient example such as Ovid's catalogue of trees in *Metamorphoses*. A similar use appears in modern song writing, for example, Cole Porter's "They couldn't compare with you." Often it has been used for the sake of play or whimsey or because the poet enjoyed the sound of particular kinds of words, e.g., the list of jewels in Wolfram von Eschenbach's *Parzifal*, and Cole Porter's "You're the tops."

In 19th- and 20-c. European poetry a different aspect of c.v. has appeared. Whitman, for example, by employing long lists of things demonstrates the essential unity of the universe, which to him is evident through the individual's awareness of his connection with all aspects of the world (cf. *Crossing Brook-*

lyn Ferry). Modern poets such as Rilke and George as well as Auden and Werfel have in varying degrees followed Whitman in this use. Indeed, in some poems the use of catalogues supplies the meaning of the entire poem rather than illuminates a particular aspect of it as in ancient poetry.—T. W. Allen, "The Homeric C.," *Jour. of Hellenic Studies*, 30 (1910); Chadwick; D. W. Schumann, "Enumerative Style and its Significance in Whitman, Rilke, Werfel," MLQ, 3 (1942) and "Observations on Enumerative Style in Modern German Poetry," PMLA, 59 (1944); L. Spitzer, "La enumeración caótica en la poesía moderna," Instituto de Filologia (Buenos Aires), *Colleción de estudios estilísticos*, anejo 1 (1945); S. K. Coffman, "Crossing Brooklyn Ferry: a Note on the C. Technique of Whitman's Poetry," MP, 51 (1954); H. E. Wedeck, "The C. in Late and Medieval L. Poetry," *Medievalia et Humanistica*, 13 (1960). R.A.H.

CATHARSIS. The use of the word c. ("purgation") in connection with the theory of literature, originates in Aristotle's celebrated definition of tragedy in the sixth chapter of the *Poetics*. Unfortunately, Aristotle merely uses the term without defining it (though he may have defined it in a putative second book of the *Poetics*); and the question of what he actually meant is a *cause célèbre* in the history of literary criticism. Insofar as there is no agreement yet, and none in sight, all definitions, including this one, must be regarded as interpretations only.

The essential function of tragedy, according to Aristotle's definition, is a representation (*mimesis*—q.v.) of an action that is serious, complete, and of an appropriate magnitude; and when such representation is effectively carried out it will succeed "in arousing pity and fear in such a way as to accomplish a purgation (c) of such emotions." The definition was doubtless framed as an answer to Plato's charge that poetic drama encourages anarchy in the soul by feeding and watering the passions instead of starving them. Aristotle held, on the contrary, that anarchy in the soul is most effectively prevented not by starving and repressing the emotions but by giving them expression in a wisely regulated manner. Tragedy he regarded as a chief instrument of such wise regulation, for it works in a twofold way, first exciting the emotions of pity and fear and then allaying them, thereby effecting an emotional cure.

Aristotle's somewhat technical understanding of c. acquires its overtones of meaning from a double linguistic heritage, in part medical and in part religious. On the one hand the idea of c. finds early expression in the writings of the Hippocratic School of Medicine, where

CATHARSIS

it refers to the discharge of whatever excess of bodily elements has produced a state of sickness, and the consequent return of the body to that state of right proportion which is health. There is, in Hippocratic language, a preparatory process of slow "digestion" (*pepsis*), produced by the body's heat, wherein the bodily elements are recombined and fused in such a way that waste products are generated, ready for discharge at the proper time; and when this discharge, or c., has taken place, the result is a new balance or proportion of bodily elements, which is health. Analogously, Aristotle considers that in its "natural" condition the human psyche is well-balanced and serene, but that it falls readily away from this natural state into intemperance; and that the action of a well-made tragedy strikes pity and fear into the beholder in such a way that these emotions become "digested" (as in the Hippocratic description of returning health), with the result that a new proportion and blend of the emotions is produced, and the residue of superfluous emotional impulses is "catharated." The religious meaning of c., on the other hand, finds a diversity of expressions in the dialogues of Plato, and therefore must have entered into the conversations and teachings which surrounded Aristotle during the intellectually formative period of his young manhood. In the *Phaedo*, for instance, Plato declares that c. consists "in separating, so far as possible, the soul from the body, and in teaching the soul the habit of collecting and bringing itself together from all parts of the body, and in living, so far as it can, both now and hereafter, alone by itself, freed from the body as from fetters."

When Aristotle's definition is reconsidered in the light of these two trends of thought, the medical and the religious, an important corollary stands forth. Since the new blending which is attained in the catharic process is psychic, not merely physical, it involves a new emotional perspective, and even, arising from that, a new intellectual vision. A wisdom is distilled from tragic suffering: man is *pathei mathos*, "taught by suffering," as the chorus in the *Agamemnon* sings. The tragic c. and the ensuing emotional calm have produced in the spectator a new insight into what the plot of the drama most essentially represents, what its action—which is to say, its meaning in motion —essentially is. Such insight is what justifies Aristotle's assertion (ch. 9) that "poetry is something more philosophical and more highly serious than history, for poetry tends to express universals, history particulars."

Subsequent critics, on the whole, have been more inclined to accept than to reject the doctrine of c., although their acceptance has usually involved some degree of reinterpretation.

In the It. Renaissance Aristotle's definition was revived by such writers as Minturo (*The Art of Poetry*, 1563) and Castelvetro (*Poetica d'Aristotele volgarizzata e eposto*, 1570), although in the former the emphasis is shifted to the "delight and profit" which result to the spectator from his cathartic experience. In France a century later both Corneille and Racine accept the principle of c. in the fairly plain moral sense of regarding the spectator as purified by the tragedy and thus as deterred from performing such evil acts as he has been witnessing. Corneille, in addition, assumes that either pity or fear might operate separately.

In Germany, Lessing in his influential *Laokoön* (1766) opposed the latter view of Corneille, insisting that the special effect of tragedy must come from the union of the two emotions, from which there emerges the cosmically oriented emotion of *awe*, as the spectator recognizes through the tragedy the sword of destiny that is suspended above us all. Lessing also emphasizes (*Hamburger Dramaturgie*, 1768) the applicability of Aristotle's ethical standard of "due measure" to the principle of c.; for tragedy, if it is to transform our pity and fear into virtue, "must be capable of purifying us from both extremes"—from "too little" by its emotional contagion, and from "too much" by the restraint which its formal pattern imposes. Schiller in his essay "On Tragic Art" (1792) reaffirms the importance of measure, and in "On the Sublime" (1801) he draws two corollaries: that the most perfect tragedy is one which produces its cathartic effect not by its subject matter but by its tragic form; and that it has aesthetic worth only so far as it is "sublime"—i.e., as by representing the indifference of the universe to moral ends it produces in the soul of the spectator an "inoculation against unavoidable fate." Goethe, in his *Nachlass zu Aristoteles Poetik* (1827), sees the main importance of the purgatorial, or cathartic situation, not in reference to the spectator, whose condition is incidental and variable, but in the reconciliation and expiation of the characters in the play. Among later German writers on aesthetics we may note Schopenhauer (*The World as Will and Representation*, 1819), who equates the cathartic principle of tragedy with an idealized and universal experience of fellow-suffering wholly disproportionate to moral deserts; and Nietzsche (*The Birth of Tragedy*, 1872), who interprets the matter through the complementary symbols of Dionysus and Apollo, the unresisting plunge into whatever sufferings and joys life may offer and the calm vision that results from this self-surrender.

Of Eng.-speaking writers, Milton in the Preface to *Samson Agonistes* (1671)· interprets Aristotle to mean that tragic c. operates on

the homeopathic principle, and he draws an analogy from medicine, wherein "things of melancholic hue and quality are used against melancholy, sour against sour, salt to remove salt humours." Wordsworth, shifting the reference from dramatic to lyric poetry, offers a humanitarian interpretation: that readers are to be "humbled and humanized," and to be purged of the prejudices and blindnesses arising from false sophistication and snobbery, "in order that they may be purified and exalted" (Nowell C. Smith, ed., *Wordsworth's Literary Criticism*, 1905). In our own day I. A. Richards (*Principles of Literary Criticism*, 1925) interprets the cathartic process as a reconciliation and reëquilibration of "Pity, the impulse to approach, and Terror, the impulse to retreat," along with various other groups of discordant impulses, and he affirms the importance of tragedy on the ground that "there is no other way in which such impulses, once awakened, can be set at rest without suppression." Among other contemporaries we might mention Elisabeth Schneider (*Aesthetic Motive*, 1939), who has argued that just because the pity and terror are painfully and utterly irreconcilable in real life, the one always driving the other out, we receive the greatest pleasure from their stylized union in art. So here again, at the end as at the beginning of our survey, we are reminded that c. is not a simple elimination, but always operates hand in hand with a process of stylization and an aesthetic creation of significant form.

Aristotle, *Poetics*, or *The Art of Poetry*, tr. Bywater (1909; Fyfe's commentary on a reissue of this translation in 1940 is helpful), Cooper (1913), Butcher (1917), Fyfe (1927), Epps (1942), Wheelwright (1951). See also Else (1957) for a good comprehensive study but controversial theory.—I. A. Richards, *Principles*, chs. 7, 15, 32; M. T. Herrick, *The Poetics of Aristotle in England* (1930); J. C. Ransom, "The Cathartic Principle," *The World's Body* (1938); E. Schneider, *Aesthetic Motive* (1939); *European Theories of Drama*, ed. B. H. Clark (rev. ed., 1947); F. Fergusson, *The Idea of a Theatre* (1949); F. L. Lucas, *Lit. and Psychology* (1951) and *Tragedy; Serious Drama in Relation to Aristotle's Poetics* (rev. ed., 1957); Wellek; R. Kuhns, *The House, the City and the Judge* (1962; ch. 5).   P.W.

CAUDA, coda (L. "tail"). The short line, or tail, which in a stanza of longer lines usually rhymes with another, similar, short line, thus serving to divide the stanza into parts. When the caudae rhyme, the stanza is known as a tail-rhyme stanza, characteristic of Romance languages. The use of caudae was especially popular in medieval metrical romances (e.g., *Aethelston, Horn Childe*). A school of tail-rhyming romance writers is supposed to have flourished in East Anglia in the 14th c. See TAIL-RHYME.   R.O.E.

CAUDATE SONNET. A form of the sonnet in which the normal (usually It.) pattern of 14 lines is supplemented by one or more codas or "tails." Usually the coda is introduced by a half-line, followed by a couplet in pentameters, and this in turn may be followed by additional "tails" in similar line-lengths. The c.s., established by Francesco Berni (1497–1536), has usually been employed for satirical themes, as in Milton's *On the New Forcers of Conscience Under the Long Parliament*, the coda of which, following the 14th line, is as follows:

> That so the Parliament
> May with their wholesome and preventive shears
> Clip your phylacteries, though baulk your ears,
>   And succour our just fears,
> When they shall read this clearly in your charge,—
> New *Presbyter* is but old *Priest* writ large.

J. S. Smart, *The Sonnets of Milton* (1921; p. 127).   L.J.Z.

CAVALIER LYRIC. The term is used to describe not only the work of the Cavalier poets or lyrists but also any poem which, like Browning's *Cavalier Tunes*, is written to illustrate their attitudes and evoke the spirit of their time.

CAVALIER POETS, Cavalier lyrists. A group of Eng. poets in the time of Charles I (1625–49), characterized by the lightness, grace, and polish of their verse and by the wit and gallantry of their attitudes. Since there was no formal group of "C. poets," as such, recognized in the 17th c., it is impossible to determine with precision what poets should be included in the category. Certainly Richard Lovelace and Sir John Suckling, who in their lives as much as in their poems gave an origin to the term, should be included. Other poets who resemble them in both attitude and style are Herrick, Carew, Waller, Randolph, and Godolphin. Love was the favorite theme of the C. lyrists, and their treatments of the subject ranged from the conventional Petrarchism of Lovelace to the cynicism of Suckling and the pagan sensuality of Carew. Poems of courtly compliment, *jeux d'esprit,* and expressions of loyalty to the king are also typical of the Cavaliers.

The greatest influence on the style of the C. lyrists was that of Ben Jonson; indeed, most of them considered themselves "Sons of Ben." Their lyrics usually employ the shorter rhyth-

CELTIC PROSODY

mic line, the more precise diction, the tighter logical structure with which Jonson had signified his departure from his more expansive Elizabethan predecessors. And, like Jonson, the Cavaliers abandoned the sonnet almost entirely. However, Jonson's influence is often modified by that of Donne, particularly in the work of Carew and Suckling. Perhaps the best known of the poems of the C. lyrists are Suckling's *Why so pale and wan, fond lover?*, Lovelace's *To Althea, from Prison* and *To Lucasta, on Going to the Wars*, Herrick's *Delight in Disorder*, and Carew's *Ask me no more where Jove bestows*.—G. Walton, "The C. Poets," *From Donne to Marvell*, ed. B. Ford (1956); R. Skelton, *C. Poets* (1960; Writers and Their Work no. 117).

CELTIC PROSODY. No direct information is available about the nature of the poetry composed by the Celts on the continent of Europe before they settled in the separate areas in which they now live. From Caesar we know that in the 1st c. B.C. students learned verses by memory in the druidic schools of Celt. Gaul, but no actual examples of poetry have survived among the remains of the Gaulish language.

Of the Celt. Poetry composed in Welsh, Cornish, and Breton, and in the Gaelic of Ireland, Man, and Scotland, the earliest remains are Ir. and Welsh. These date back only to about the 7th c. A.D., by which time both the Ir. and the Welsh had begun to use rhyme, familiar to them through the Latin hymns of the church, as their central prosodic device.

Some archaic Ir. texts preserve sporadic examples of an ancient verse form which was presumably the dominant type from prehistoric times down to at least the 6th c. It is derived from the same Indo-European system which can be traced in the gnomic and epic poetry composed in Vedic Sanskrit, Gr., and Slavic. A typical line consists of a free initial colon, a separating break, and a final colon with fixed cadence:

Mo chride crúaid | crechtnaigther.
(Grievously my heart is wounded.)

In the Ir. poetry belonging to this tradition, lines were regulated to certain syllabic counts. Alliteration provided optional decoration but was not, as in later Celt. poetry (and in Germanic), requisite as a patterning device.

The mainstream of Celtic poetry, however, springs from the time that the Celtic peoples heard rhyming L. hymns such as that composed in the 5th c. by Sedulius, which though nominally composed in quantitative iambic dimeter, foreshadowed the stressed, rhyming verse later

to become common in European vernacular poetry:

A solis ortus cardine   a
Ad usque terrae limitem   b
Christum canamus principem   b
Natum Maria virgine.   a

From the quarter of the rising of the sun
to the boundary of the earth
let us sing Christ the Prince
born of the Virgin Mary.

The new prosodic systems inspired by rhyme are in many cases so intricate that their indebtedness to L. is far from obvious, but the relationship is undeniable and is substantiated by the sudden emergence of, for instance, an Ir. stanza which like Sedulius' consists of 4 rhyming lines, each exactly 8 syllables in length.

An early example of the impact of rhyme upon the Welsh is afforded by Aneirin's *Gododdin*, the original of which may reach back to about A.D. 600. In the following stanza the old and the new meet together, for each line is linked to the next by a final rhyme (*-ant*), while the traditional Celt. device of alliteration is retained as an optional decoration (*k* in line 1, *g* in 2, *h* in 3, *l* in 4, *g* in 5):

Kywyrein ketwyr, kyuaruuant,
y gyt en vn vryt yt gyrchassant.
Byrr eu hoedyl, hir eu hoet ar eu carant.
Seith gymeint o Loegrwys a ladassant.
O gyvryssed gwraged gwyth a wnaethant,
llawer mam ae deigyr ar y hamrant.
(*Canu Aneirin*, ed. Ifor Williams [Cardiff, 1938], 668–673.)

As one the warriors arose, foregathered, together attacked with single purpose. Short were their lives, long the lament of their kinsmen for them. Seven times their number of English they slew. Through strife they left women widows, many a mother with tears on her eyelids.

Even in a poem as early as the *Gododdin*, there are other, more intricate stanzaic forms; but these are a mere tentative preliminary to the later developments of Welsh *cynghanedd*, q.v. (harmony), in which rhyme becomes an integral part of an extraordinary network of sound effects. At this subsequent stage, a disciple of the 14th-c. poet Dafydd ap Gwilym writes couplets such as the following:

Dyrcha ael fain, d'orchwyl fu
Dristau gŵr dros dy garu.
(Caradar, *Welsh Made Easy*, III. 92. See *Gwaith Dafydd ap Gwilym*, ed. T. Parry [Cardiff, 1952], p. clxxxvi.)

Raise your fine eyebrows! Your achievement has been to make a man sad for love of you.

Here he not only satisfies the requirements of *cywydd*, q.v. (coupled lines), that each line contain 7 syllables and that each couplet contain an end rhyme between a final unstressed syllable and a final stressed syllable (fu: garu). He has also arranged the *cynghanedd* within the line so that a sequence of as many as 5 or even 6 consonants in the first half of the line recurs in the second half of the line: *d--r--ch--l--f: (n) d--r--ch--l--f; d--r--s--t--g--r: d--r--s--d(t)--g--r*. And, at the same time, he has followed the rule that the corresponding vowels should be dissimilar (*dris-: dros*, etc.). And, throughout the remainder of the poem, he has alternated at will four different kinds of *cynghanedd*, each with its own stringent requirements.

In the Gaelic poetry common to Ireland, Man, and Scotland, rhyme was early developed into an equally intricate prosodic system known as bardic verse. Its chief characteristics are the limitation of each line to a fixed number of syllables (often 7 or 8) and the use of what may be called generic rhyme—that is, any member of a particular genus of phonetically similar consonants may rhyme either with itself or with any other member of that genus, provided that the preceding vowels are identical. These six rhyming groups are as follows:

1.	*c*	*t*	*p*			
2.	*ch*	*th*	*ph*,	*f*		
3.	*g*	*d*	*b*			
4.	*gh*	*dh*	*bh*,	*mh*	*l*	*n* *r*
5.				*m*	*ll*	*ng,nn rr*
6.	*s*					

· The source of the syllabic measure, as in Welsh, is obviously the Latin hymn. The development of generic rhyme is less clear. An analogous system appears in early Welsh, involving four consonantal sets—*g:d:b, dd:l:r, ʒ:f:w*, and certain nasal clusters. This may have been borrowed from Irish, for bards of the two nationalities visited one another; or both systems may have been suggested by the tentative rhymes in early L. hymns. (In Sedulius' stanza quoted above, [*lim*]*item* makes full "Ir. rhyme" in its last two syllables with [*princ*]*ipem*, and [*ca*]*rdine* with [*vi*]*rgine*.)

A typical example of Ir. syllabic prosody is the following stanza composed by an anonymous medieval bard, who is describing an ornate goblet owned by a king of Connaught:

Eoin bas n-dearg 's a n-druim r' a thaoibh,　1
mar do chuim an ceard go côir　2
lucht 'gar chasmhail cleasa ceoil—　3
eoin 's a sleasa d' asnaibh ôir.　4

(McKenna, *Aithdioghluim Dána*, no. 9)

Birds red of claw stand backed against its borders, just as the artist deftly shaped them as figures seeming really to sing—birds whose sides are ribbed with gold.

This particular meter, known as *rannaigheacht mhôr* (the Great Versification), requires a stanza of 4 lines which must each contain 7 syllables and end in a stressed monosyllable.

The last words in lines 2 and 4 must show generic rhyme with one another (*ôir:ôir*). The last words in 1 and 3 must consonate but not assonate with these (the consonants *bh* in *aoibh* and *l* in *eoil* both show generic rhyme with the *r* in *ôir*, while the vowels *aoi* and *eoi* are identical with the *ôi* in 2 and 4 only in length).

All the stressed words in 2 other than the final rhyming word show generic rhyme with stressed words in 1—(*ch*)*uim:(dr*)*uim*, (*c*)*eard:-(d*)*earg*. All the stressed words in 4 other than the final rhyming word must show generic rhyme with stressed words in 3—*eoin:(c)eoil, (sl*)*easa:(cl*)*easa, asnaibh:(ch*)*asmhail*. (In a disyllable such as the last, both syllables must rhyme,—*s:s, n:mh, bh:l*.)

Every line must have at least one alliteration between adjacent stressed words, and in the last line this alliteration must be between the last two stressed words—*dearg, druim; chuim, ceard, côir; chasmhail, cleasa, ceoil; asnaibh, ôir* (a consonant alliterates either with itself or with its corresponding form produced by initial grammatical mutation, and a vowel alliterates with itself or any other).

The professional bard was allowed to use measures less cramping than the 7-syllable line. A stanza from a 16th-c. religious poem will illustrate the greater scope available. The meter is *droighneach*, whose lines average from 9 to 13 syllables. In the following quatrain the lines number respectively 11, 15 (exceptionally), 11, and 13 syllables.

Tairm na nêal, foghar na n-uile ainmhidhe,　1
foghar ainglidhe na n-êan, foghar duille gach
　　dhionnmhuighe,—　2
ag soin moladh na n-dûileadh dâ
　　n-daghruire—　3
bûireadh an doimh dhamhghoire, foghar na
　　fhiodhbhuidhe.　4
(*Aithdioghluim Dána*, no. 76.)

The crash of clouds, the sound of all animals, the angelic sound of birds, the sound of leaves on every hillside, the belling of the stag among the deerherd, the sound of the forest—through these comes the praise of the elements to their kind King.

Such amplitude as this measure permits does not, however, exempt it from the stringencies of bardic law. To conform to the pattern of *droighneach* each line must end in a trisyllable. The finals in 2 and 4 must make generic rhyme—*(dh)ionnmhuighe: (fh)iodhbhuidhe* (*nn* may rhyme with *dh* in a consonant cluster). The finals in 1 and 3 must consonate and must not assonate with the finals in 2 and 4. All the stressed words in 2 except the last must make generic rhyme with words in 1—*(f)oghar* (twice): *(f)oghar, ainglidhe:ainmhidhe, ēan:(n)ēal, (d)uille:uile* (a permissible rhyme). And, similarly, 4 must rhyme with 3—*(b)ūireadh:(d)ūileadh, (d)oimh:-(s)oin, (dh)amhghoire:(d)aghruire, (f)oghar: (m)oladh*. In 2 and 4 at least the last two stressed words must alliterate—*duille, dhionnmhuighe; foghar, fhiodhbhuidhe*. In 1 and 3 at least two of the last three stressed words must alliterate —*uile, ainmhidhe; duileadh, daghruire.*

Since long measures like *droighneach* occur less frequently than the compact 7 or 8-syllable measures such as *rannaigheacht mhōr*, it seems apparent that most bards preferred to work under the more severe limitations of their miniaturist's art. Like the decorators of the *Book of Kells*, they found their satisfaction in challenging their ingenuity to fill each minute space in the most colorful, varied, and exhaustive manner possible.

Medieval Gaelic and Welsh verse was produced by professional poets who were schooled in their art for years. The earliest vernacular manuals of prosody known in Western Europe are the Ir., dating back to the end of the 8th c. (See Thurneysen, in *Göttingen Abhandlungen*, 14, no. 2, 78–89.) It is not surprising, therefore, that the prosodic complexities which the bards evolved have never been matched. Within the realm of European poetry, Norse skaldic verse (see OLD NORSE POETRY) alone approaches Celt. in intricacy, and the reason for its similarity probably lies in the fact that Norse poets attempted to emulate the traveling Ir. bards.

Aesthetic judgment of such poetry is consequently very difficult for those unused to its requirements. In their use of Eng. near-rhyme both Hopkins and Owen have imitated the resources of Celt. generic rhyme, but they have not really accustomed the modern reader to it, for they use such rhyme merely as an optional decoration, not as an unavoidable necessity, and they do not submit to any systematic rules. (For them *rob* would make an equally good rhyme with either *rod* or *rot*; for the Ir. bard only *rod* would be acceptable.) Mere metrical virtuosity will not make an otherwise poor poem remarkable; but a good poem written in the strict Celt. measures derives much of its force from the subtleties of its workmanship.

With the decline of the bardic orders in the Celt. countries, new and simpler meters emerged. In part these are the products of amateur versification, in part they may represent the dignification of popular and perhaps ancient song-meters hitherto unrecorded, and in part they certainly represent the adaptation of alien measures. When the secret of generic rhyme was lost, the most appealing device seems to have been assonance. Thus, in one of the songs of Geoffrey Keating (17th c.), which is typical of the new Ir. stressed verse known as *abhrān*, not only do the final stressed syllables assonate (as in the OF *laisse*), but all the others assonate in order, each of the first stressed syllables with one another, and each of the second, and the third, and the fourth:

$$\overset{}{\breve{O}m}\ \overset{1}{sge\breve{o}l}\ \overset{}{\breve{a}r}\ \overset{2}{ard\text{-}mh\bar{a}gh}\ \overset{}{F\bar{a}il}\ \overset{3}{n\breve{i}}\ \overset{4}{ch\breve{o}dl\bar{a}im}$$
$$\overset{5}{\breve{o}idhch\breve{e}},$$

$$'\text{S}\ \overset{}{d\breve{o}}\ \overset{1}{bhre\breve{o}dh}\ \overset{}{g\breve{o}}\ \overset{2}{br\bar{a}th}\ \overset{}{m\breve{e}}\ \overset{3}{d\bar{a}la}\ \overset{}{\breve{a}}\ \overset{4}{p\breve{o}buil}\ \overset{5}{d\bar{i}lis}.$$

$$\overset{}{G\breve{i}dh}\ \overset{1}{r\breve{o}\text{-}fh\bar{a}da}\ \overset{}{at\bar{a}id}\ \overset{2}{'n\breve{a}}\ \overset{}{bhf\bar{a}l}\ \overset{3}{r\breve{e}}\ \overset{}{br\breve{o}sc\breve{a}r}\ \overset{4}{b\breve{i}odh\text{-}}$$
$$\text{bh}\breve{a}dh,$$

$$\overset{}{F\bar{a}}\ \overset{1}{dh\breve{e}oidh}\ \overset{}{g\breve{u}r}\ \overset{2}{fh\bar{a}s}\ \overset{}{\breve{a}}\ \overset{3}{l\bar{a}n}\ \overset{}{d\breve{o}'n}\ \overset{4}{ch\breve{o}g\bar{a}l}\ \overset{5}{tr\breve{i}otha}.$$

(*Dánta . . . Sheathrúin Céitinn*, ed. E. C. mac Giolla Eáin [Dublin, 1900], no. 3; see Hyde, *Irish Poetry*, p. 128.)

Because of what I've heard about Fail's noble plain [Ireland] I cannot sleep at night, and it has crushed me utterly to think of her noble people. Though in the rampart they have stood too long facing a hostile rabble, enough of these tares at last have spread among them.

The assonance thus runs

$$\bar{o}\text{-}\text{-}\bar{a}\text{-}\text{-}\bar{a}\text{-}\text{-}o\text{-}\text{-}\bar{i}$$

through each line.

Since Keating's time some Gaelic poets have become satisfied to use only a single final assonance. In Wales, though *cynghanedd* is still practiced, many song writers have adopted the patterns familiar to rhymed, stressed Eng. poetry even in such nationalistic songs as the original Welsh version of *Men of Harlech.*

Wele goelcerth wen yn fflamio,	a
A thafodau tân yn bloeddio	a
Ar i'r dewrion ddod i daro	a
Unwaith eto'n un.	b
(Caradar, 3.68)	

Lo, the beacon brightly flaming, and tongues of fire shouting to the brave ones to go once again to strike together.

Only in its alliteration (which is not fully reproduced in the familiar Eng. version of this song) does its prosody retain any peculiarly Celt. flavor. But the most notable mark of the

Europeanizing of Celt. prosody lies in the fact that several of today's outstanding Celt. poets have written their best work in vers libre devoid of any of their traditional devices. See also BRETON POETRY, CORNISH POETRY, IRISH POETRY, SCOTTISH GAELIC POETRY, WELSH POETRY.

IRISH: R. Thurneysen, "Entwicklung der irischen Metrik," *Revue celtique*, 6 (1884; on L. origin of Ir. rhyme), and "Mittelirische Verslehren," in *Irische Texte*, ed. W. Stokes and E. Windisch, III, pt. 1 (1891; cf. Königl. Gesellschaft der Wissenschaft zu Göttingen, Philol.-hist. Klasse, *Abhandlungen*, 14, no. 2, 78–89) (prosodic manuals 8th-11th c.); D. Hyde, *Ir. Poetry* (1902; partly outdated, but imitations in Eng. verse tr. are suggestive); K. Meyer, *A Primer of Ir. Metrics* (1909; still valuable but inadequate—see *Ériu*, 8 (1916), and "Ueber die älteste irische Dichtung," Königl. Preussische Akad. der Wissenschaften, Philos.-hist. Classe, *Abhandlungen*, Jahrg. 1913, nos. 6, 10 (early unrhymed and rhymed poetry 7th–8th c.); O. Bergin, "The Principles of Alliteration," *Ériu*, 9 (1921–23); *Tadhg Dall Ó Huiginn*, ed. and tr. E. Knott (Ir. Texts Soc., 22–23, 1922–26; good introd. to bardic verse); E. Knott, *An Introd. to Ir. Syllabic Poetry* (1928, 2d ed, 1957; thorough and reliable), and *Ir. Classical Poetry* (1957); *Aithdioghluim Dána*, ed. and tr. L. McKenna (Ir. Texts Soc., 37, 40, 1939–40; wide variety of bardic meters, succinctly classified); G. Murphy, *Early Ir. Metrics* (1961); C. Watkins, "Indo-European Metrics and Archaic Ir. Verse," *Celtica*, 6 (1963; important discovery).

SCOTTISH GAELIC: W. J. Watson, *Bardachd Ghaidhlig* (2d ed., 1932; important; though, for bardic rhyme, insufficient).

WELSH: J. Loth, *La métrique galloise* (2 v., 1900–1902; on all W. meters, including comparison with Cornish, Breton, and Ir.); J. Morris-Jones, *Cerdd Dafod* [Poetic Art] (1925; in W., indexed by G. Bowen, *Mynegai i Cerdd Dafod*, 1947); A.S.D. Smith (Caradar), *W. Made Easy*, III (n.d.; very helpful introd.); T. Parry, *A Hist. of W. Lit.*, tr. H. I. Bell (1955; appendices to several chapters discuss meters).　　　C.W.D.

CENTO (L. "patchwork"). A poetic composition made up of passages selected from the work of some great poet of the past. Homer largely served this purpose in Gr. literature from the adaptations by Trygaeus of various lines in the *Iliad* and *Odyssey* (Aristophanes, *Peace* 1090–94) to the *Homerokentrones* of the Byzantine period. Similarly Virgil was the most popular source for centos in later Roman times. The oldest of those extant is the tragedy *Medea* by Hosidius Geta (2d c. A.D.), while the *C. nuptialis* of Ausonius and the *C. Vergilianus* of Proba (4th c. A.D.) are among others drawn

from his work. Renaissance and later works of this kind included the It. *Petrarca spirituale* (1536) and the Eng. *Cicero princeps* (1608), which was a treatise, compiled from Cicero, on government. In the modern era may be mentioned a Shakespearean c. which appeared in *English* (Nov. 1919) and humorous centos which are occasionally published in popular literary reviews.—J. O. Delepierre, *Tableau de la littérature du centon chez les anciens et chez les modernes* (2 v. 1874–75); R. Lamacchia, "Dall'arte allusiva al centone," *Atene e Roma* n.s. 3 (1958).　　　R.J.G.

CENTROID. See PROSODY.

CHAIN RHYME. A rhyming device, akin in structure to *rime riche* (q.v.), which takes up the last syllable of a line and repeats it as the first syllable of the line immediately following. It must be noted that the repeated syllable, though having the same sound as its predecessor, must carry a different meaning: "Dieu gard ma Maistresse et re*gente* / *Gente* de corps et de façon. / *Son* cueur tient le mien en sa *tente* / *Tant* et plus d'un ardant frisson" (Marot). Occasional brief examples of chain r. may be found in Eng., as in Hopkins: "O there's none . . . / Be beginning to despair, to despair, / Despair, despair, despair. / *Spare!* / There is one . . ."—M. Grammont, *Le Vers français* (2d ed., 1913); J. Suberville, *Hist. et théorie de la versification fr.* (new ed., 1956).　　　S.L.M.

CHANSO (*canso, chanson*). A love song, the literary genre *par excellence* among the Old Prov. poets. Its distinguishing characteristics are precisely the two great contributions of the troubadours to all subsequent European literature—a new conception of love involving the exaltation of the lady, and a constant striving for perfection and originality of form. It is impossible to draw a sharp line between the ch. and the older *vers* (q.v.); but by the time the name ch. came into common use (toward the end of the 12th c.), the ideals of courtly love (q.v.) had become generally accepted and the technique of composition more polished, so that the ch. is apt to be more artistic, but also more conventional and artificial, than the *vers*. The typical ch. has 5 or 6 stanzas, of identical structure, plus an *envoi*, or *tornada* (q.v.). Far from following any set metrical pattern, every ch. was expected to have a stanzaic structure and a tune that were completely original. This proved too high a hurdle for many poets, but the metrical diversity of the extant *chansos* is still very impressive. Unfortunately, the same can hardly be said for their contents, which simply ring the changes on a few well-worn themes and situations. The poet's lady love is almost never named, and she is described in such vague generalities that an identification is ordinarily out of the question. The proper names used in a ch. (commonly in the *tornada*) are for the most part those of friends or patrons to whom the poem is dedicated.—Jeanroy, II.   F.M.C.

CHANSONS DE GESTE is the term by which the OF epic poems relating the deeds of Charlemagne and his barons, or other feudal lords of the Carolingian era, were known in their time, principally the 12th and 13th c. "Geste" has, aside from the original sense of "deeds," additional senses of "history" and "historical document," and by further extension it comes to mean "family, lineage." Upward of eighty of the poems survive, in whole or in part, in existing mss., some of them in several redactions. They celebrate heroic actions, historical or pseudo-historical, and the chivalric ideals of a Christian, monarchical, and feudal France. Critics have not succeeded in reaching firm conclusions as to whether the ideological preoccupations are primarily those of Carolingian times or of the period of the Crusades and 12th-c. France. The history is at best considerably overlaid with legend, and many of the epics are largely or wholly fictitious, reworking the themes made popular by the earlier poems. This is particularly true where the taste for the romantic and the fantastic nurtured by the romances imitated from Gr. and L. antiquity, the Arthurian romances, and folklore was carried over into the invention of plots for the epics: this hybrid type is best illustrated by poems like *Huon de Bordeaux, Renaud de Montauban*, and *Le Chevalier au Cygne*.

CYCLES. Several more or less well-defined groups of these poems may be distinguished. The most cohesive of these (24 poems) is the cycle of Guillaume d'Orange, to be identified with the historical Count Guillaume de Toulouse, contemporary of Charlemagne, and in which are recounted his deeds and those of his six brothers, his nephews, particularly Vivien and Bertrand, his father Aymeri de Narbonne, and others of his line. The principal poems of this cycle are *Le Couronnement de Louis, Le Charroi de Nîmes, La Prise d'Orange, Le Couvenant Vivien, La Chanson de Guillaume, Aliscans, Le Moniage Guillaume*, and *Aymeri de Narbonne*.

The so-called cycle of Charlemagne is less extensive and less unified. To it are assigned the poems treating of Charlemagne's wars (*La Chanson de Roland, Aspremont, Les Saxons*) or of his youth (*Mainet*) or of earlier royal heroes such as *Floövant*, son of Clovis. One of these is the partly comic *Pèlerinage de Charlemagne*, which includes the description of a highly fanciful visit to the court of the Emperor of Constantinople.

The third main group has as its common element the theme of a feudal lord's revolt, usually provoked by an act of injustice, against his *seigneur*, who is in several cases Charlemagne, as in *Girart de Roussillon* (the only *chanson de geste* surviving in a dialect of the *langue d'oc*), *La Chevalerie Ogier de Danemarche, Renaud de Montauban*, known also as *Les Quatre fils Aymon*, and *Huon de Bordeaux*. In the oldest poem of this group, the 11th-c. *Gormont et Isembart*, surviving only in a fragment, the renegade Isembart fights against his lord King Louis III. *Raoul de Cambrai* relates the sombre violence of feudal warfare following a forcible dispossession. The unforgiving bitterness of struggle between two great families is the subject of a minor cycle, *Les Lorrains*, of which the principal poems are *Garin le Lorrain* and *Hervis de Metz*.

LA CHANSON DE ROLAND. *La Chanson de Roland* is the masterpiece of the genre and the earliest surviving example, composed most likely in the second half of the 11th c. in continental France and preserved in an Anglo-Norman manuscript of the mid-12th c. (Oxford version). Later versions lengthen the poem and insert additional episodes. The historical event on which the poem is based is the annihilation of Charlemagne's rear guard under Count Roland while recrossing the Pyrenees after an expedition against Saragossa in 778. In the poem the attackers are referred to as Saracens, whereas they were in all probability Basques, and a succession of councils is related, leading to the decision to leave Spain. A traitor Ganelon is introduced, as Roland's stepfather, who urges the Saracens to attack the rear guard in revenge for Roland's having designated him for the perilous embassy to the enemy camp. The disaster is assured when Roland overconfidently refuses to call back Charlemagne by sounding his horn when attacked, in spite of the urgings of his companion Oliver. After the defeat at Roncevaux, the poem ends with another battle in which Charlemagne is victorious, and with the trial and execution of Ganelon.

The *Chanson de Roland* is remarkable for the ideals it exalts—unstinting devotion to God and to feudal lord, and to the fatherland, "douce France,"—for its vigorous and incisive portrayals of great characters, closely knit structure, elevation of tone, and firm, concise language.

FORM, VERSIFICATION, STYLE. The usual line is of 10 syllables, with caesura after the fourth, not counting a possible unstressed syllable with schwa-vowel after the accented tenth syllable or after the accented fourth. Among the earlier epics the 8-syllable or the 12-syllable line may be used (*Gormont et Isembart, Pèlerinage de Charlemagne*). The strophic form is that of the *laisse*, a variable number of lines bound together by the same assonance in the earlier poems, by rhyme in later ones. In the *Chanson de Roland* the *laisses* average 14 lines in length; in later poems they tend to be much longer. In length, the *c.d.g.* range from about a thousand lines (*Pèlerinage de Charlemagne*) to 10,000 lines and over; the *Chanson de Roland* has 4,000 in the Oxford version. As their name would indicate, the *c.d.g.* were sung, and the notation of some music has been preserved.

In coherence of composition, the epics vary greatly, from well-knit poems like the *Chanson de Roland* or the *Pèlerinage de Charlemagne* to rambling and even self-contradictory successions of episodes. The style is vigorous and stamped with the mark of talent in the best poems, but diffuse and filled with *clichés* ("epic formulas") in the poorer ones. The use of *clichés* has been used by some scholars as an argument for the theory that the epics were improvised orally by the performing *jongleur*.

ORIGINS. The debate over the origins and the prehistory of the *c.d.g.* has been, for three-quarters of a century, the outstanding controversy in Fr. medieval literary history. In the 19th c. it was customary to consider the surviving *chansons* as deriving ultimately from poems inspired by contemporary historical events, constantly altered and expanded in the course of oral transmission through two, three, or even four centuries. At the beginning of the 20th c., J. Bédier denied the continuity of transmission and argued to reduce the historic content of the poems to a few data discovered by jongleur-poets in sanctuaries along the pilgrimage routes in the 11th and 12th c. Bédier's "individualism," as it has been called, has increasingly been subject to massive attack by numerous scholars who have revived the older view and buttressed it with new "traditionalist" arguments. It is principally around the *Chanson de Roland* that controversy wages, according to the degree of originality the critic is willing to ascribe to the author of the Oxford version. Traditionalists see him as a mere arranger of a poem with a long prehistory of collective elaboration, an intermediate group see his sources in medieval L. hagiography or epic, while "individualists" minimize his debt to hypothetical predecessors and credit him with the largest possible measure of creativeness.

DIFFUSION. The *c.d.g.* early became popular outside their own domain of northern France and Norman England, being translated notably into Middle High German and Old-Norse-Icelandic. In Italy they were made accessible in an Italianized Fr. before serving as the inspiration for wholly It. poems. They were known in Spain, where, however, national epic heroes were preferred. In France, the 15th and 16th c. knew the epic legends through prose adaptations, before these in turn were forgotten through two and a half centuries of classicism.

In spite of its age and the obsolescence of many of the views expressed, the best general reference is still L. Gautier's *Epopées françaises*, to be consulted in the 2d ed., 4 v., 1878–92, supplemented by his *Bibliographie des c.d.g.*, 1897. J. Bédier's celebrated *Légendes épiques*, 4 v., 1908–13, repr. 1914–21 and 1926–29, is not a general history of the *genre*, but a series of studies which constitute a sweeping criticism of the theory of historical continuity. M. de Riquer's *C.d.g. françaises* (1957), the 2d ed. and tr. of a work originally publ. in Sp., is a very good recent general study, treating at length the most important poems. P. Le Gentil's concise *Chanson de Roland* (1955) is the best and most recent introduction to the study of this poem. Questions of text and prehistory are extensively examined in J. Horrent, *La Chanson de Roland dans les littératures française et espagnole au moyen âge* (1951) and M. Delbouille, *Sur la genèse de la Chanson de Roland* (1954). A compendious *état présent* is furnished by A. Junker, "Stand der Forschung zum Rolandslied," *Germanisch-Romanische Monatsschrift*, 1956.

The arguments for oral transmission with free improvisation of the *c.d.g.* are given by J. Rychner in *La C.d.g.: essai sur l'art épique des jongleurs* (1955), and more briefly in an article in *La Table Ronde* (Dec. 1958). Rychner's views are subjected to close scrutiny and criticism in a study by M. Delbouille, "Les C.d.g. et le livre," in Liège. Université. Faculté de philosophie et lettres. *La Technique littéraire des c.d.g. Actes du Colloque de Liège*, Sept. 1957. (1959). *Les Origines des c.d.g.* by I. Siciliano (1951), the 2d, rev. ed. of the original in It., is a brilliant critique of origin-theories. R. Menéndez Pidal's *La Chanson de Roland et la tradition épique des Francs* (1960), a 2d, rev. ed. of a work first publ. in Sp., is a substantial defense of the neotraditionalist view of Roland origins.

In 1955 the Société Rencesvals was founded at Pamplona for the study of the Romance epic. Communications delivered at meetings of the society have been publ. in *Coloquios de Roncesvalles* (Saragossa, 1956), v. 3 of *Cahiers de civilisation médiévale*, and v. 21 of *Cultura Neolatina*. The society publ. an occasional *Bulletin bibliographique* (1958, 1960, 1963–).

Ample bibliographical treatment will be found in *A Crit. Bibliog. of Fr. Lit.* (D. C. Cabeen, general ed.), I, *The Mediaeval Period*, ed. by U. T. Holmes, Jr., 2d ed., 1952, and more fully in R. Bossuat, *Manuel bibliogra-*

phique de la littérature française du moyen âge (1951) and its two supplements (1955, 1961). C.A.K.

CHANSON DE TOILE. See FRENCH POETRY.

CHANT (OF *chanter*, L. *cantare*, "to sing"). (1) Any song or melody: the "Chant of tuneful birds," *Paradise Regained* 2. 290. (2) Sometimes the actual melody to which the Psalms, Canticles, etc. are sung. (3) Or the Psalm or Canticle itself. (4). A poem intended to be chanted rather than sung or read, as especially those of W. B. Yeats 'or Vachel Lindsay:

Booth led boldly with his big bass drum . . .
(*General William Booth Enters Into Heaven*)

Chants are most commonly found in liturgical services. The Anglican chants, which have doubtless influenced secular poetry intended to be recited in a similar fashion, derive from the Gregorian, the plain song or *cantus firmus* used in Roman ritual and named for Pope Gregory.

When a poem is set to music, the rhythm is controlled by the music, but when it is chanted the musical elements are subordinated to the verbal. Chanting gives verse a "hieratic quality, removing it from the language of common speech, and it thereby increases the exhilaration of poetry, bringing it nearer to the sphere of the heroic . . ." (N. Frye, "Introd.: Lexis and Melos," *Sound and Poetry*, 1957). R.O.E.

CHANT ROYAL. One of the most complex and difficult of the OF verse forms. Related to the ballade (q.v.), the c.r. in its most common form (as described in the 14th c. by Eustache Deschamps) consists of 5 stanzas of 11 lines each, rhyming ababccddedE, followed by an *envoi* (q.v.), rhyming ddedE. It is further distinguished by the use of a refrain—as indicated by the capital letters—at the end of each stanza, including the last line of the *envoi*, and by the fact that, except in the *envoi*, no rhyme words may be used twice. Thus, 60 lines must be rhymed on 5 rhyme sounds, a formidable technical task. Perhaps the technical challenge of c.r. explains the regal element in its name, but it is more likely that it is called "royal" because of its address to the "prince" presiding over a *puy*, or poetic contest. In addition to Deschamps, who composed numerous *chants royaux*, Charles d'Orléans, Jean Marot, and, especially, his son Clément excelled in the use of the form.

Ironically, this most solemn and grandiose of the Fr. forms has had the fate, in the 19th and 20th c., of being employed almost solely as *vers de société* by such light poets as Richard Le Gallienne and Don Marquis.—Kastner; Patterson.

CHANTE-FABLE. A romance of adventure composed, as the name implies, of alternating assonantal verse and prose, the former intended to be sung, the latter to be spoken. Bossuat refers to *Aucassin et Nicolette* (ca. 1200) as the sole witness to a genre that must have had a certain vogue. The rhythmic and musical structure of the verse portions seems to resemble that of the *chansons de geste* (q.v.). The alternation of prose and verse has sometimes been thought to be an imitation of an Arabian technique. *Aucassin* is characterized by the delicate treatment of detail that reminds one of the work of medieval miniaturists, exquisite charm, combined with simplicity and even naïveté in the expression of sentiment, and an every-day realism entirely divorced from crudity.—*Aucassin et Nicolette, chante-fable du XIIIᵉ s.*, ed. M. Roques (1925; 2d ed., 1936; see the crit. biblog., introd. and the note *additionnelle* at the end of the 1936 ed.); R. Bossuat, *Le Moyen âge* (1931); Cabeen, I, nos. 2127–35. I.S.

CHARM. An incantation or spell; a song, verse, phrase, or word sung or spoken to invite or control supernatural power. Charms may ward off evil, expel diseases, destroy enemies, summon spirits, endow objects with supernatural power, attract good luck, win success in love. One of the earliest recorded forms of written literature, charms accompany the magical rites of almost all preliterate peoples. They are universally known in the literatures of all the Indo-European cultures. Their chief influences upon the poetry of literary tradition have been to provide a formulaic structure, traditional content, and incantatory diction for poetry of invocation. These elements have been used in widely varying contexts. E.g., Shakespeare uses charms in the witches' cauldron scene, *Macbeth* 4.1.1–38, to invoke the spirit of evil; in *Lear* 3.4.44f., Edgar invokes snatches of charms against "the foul fiend." Thomas Campion's lyric, *Thrice toss these oaken ashes in the air*, adapted from Ovid's *Metamorphoses*, submits magic to the greater power of his mistress. Modern instances of charms as invectives are James Stephens's *Righteous Anger* and Robert Graves's *Traveller's Curse After Misdirection*. —F. Grendon, "The Anglo-Saxon Charms," JAF, 22 (1909); Chadwick. D.H.

CHASTUSHKA. A short Rus. folk song, often humorous and epigrammatic; at times vulgar. In content it reflects the attitudes of its cultivators, particularly youth, toward current social reality. Rhymed, the c. is usually of four lines, and shows relative rhythmic regularity. Two and six-line forms are also found. The c. has been known since the middle of the 19th c. and has had a steady growth in popularity.—

D. K. Zelenin, "Das heutige russische Schnader-hüpfel," zsp, i (1915); Y. M. Sokolov, "Folk Rhymes," *Rus. Folklore* (1950). w.e.h.

CHIASMUS (Gr. "a placing crosswise," from the name of the Gr. letter X, "chi"; L. *decus-satio,* from the symbol X for ten, "decem"). According to the Gr. rhetorician Hermogenes (2d c. A.D.), the pattern of a sentence consisting of two main clauses, each modified by a subordinate clause, in which sentence each of the subordinate clauses could apply to each of the main clauses, so that the order of these four members could be altered in several ways without change in the meaning of the whole (*Peri heureseōn,* i.e., *On Invention* 4.3, in C. Walz, *Rhetores Graeci,* 9 v., 1832–36, v. 3, p. 157), e.g. "Pardon me, God, I knew not what I did! / And pardon, father, for I knew not thee!" (*Henry VI,* part 3, 2.5.69–70). C. has been more recently defined as the criss-cross placing of sentence members that correspond in either syntax or meaning, with or without word repetition (*Oxford Dictionary;* Lausberg), e.g., "With comely haveour and count'nance sage" (*The Faerie Queene* 3.12.3.8).

The similar figure *antimetabole* (Gr. "transposition," apparently first recorded in Quintilian), though Quintilian defines it merely as a figure of words "repeated with variations in case or tense," is illustrated by him with examples in which two words of the early part of a sentence are later repeated in reverse order, e.g., "Non ut edam vivo, sed ut vivam edo" (*Institutes of Oratory,* 1st c. A.D., 9.3.85); and it is primarily this symmetrical pattern of word repetition (abba) that the term *antimetabole* is most often made to designate by later authorities, e.g., John Hoskins, *Directions for Speech and Style,* ca. 1599 (ed. of 1935, p. 14), John Smith, *The Mysterie of Rhetorique Unvailed,* 1657, and others, most of whose illustrations are from prose. A clear example from Eng. poetry can be seen in the final line of Shakespeare's 154th Sonnet: "Love's fire heats water, water cools not love."

It would seem convenient to use the term "c." for the criss-cross order and correspondence in meaning or syntax of two pairs of words, whether or not involving word repetition, and restrict *antimetabole* to the narrower meaning of a pair of words repeated (usually with some morphological change) in reverse order. h.b.

"CHICAGO CRITICS, THE." Originally the authors of *Critics and Criticism: Ancient and Modern* (1952), so called because of their association with the University of Chicago; the label has since been extended to some of their pupils and to others who have acknowledged indebtedness to them. The present account can touch only on those broad features of their approach to criticism which distinguish them most clearly, as a group, from other contemporary critical schools. These may be summed up under two heads: first, what they have called their "pluralism" and, second, what has been called by others their "Neo-Aristotelianism," the two terms referring respectively to their concern, as theorists and historians of criticism, with investigating the logical grounds of variation among critical positions and to their interest, as students of literature, in exploring the possibilities of one particular approach, which has seemed to them too much neglected, to the analysis and evaluation of literary works.

(1) The most explicit statements of their "pluralism" are contained in McKeon's "The Philosophic Bases of Art and Criticism," Olson's "An Outline of Poetic Theory," and Crane's *The Languages of Criticism and the Structure of Poetry;* the same view also underlies the various studies by these and other writers of figures and episodes in the history of criticism. The basis of the view is the recognition that what any critic says on a literary subject, general or particular, is determined only in part by his direct experience with literary works; it is conditioned no less importantly by the tacit assumptions concerning the nature of literature and the most appropriate method of studying it which he brings to his immediate task: he will say different things about a given poem, for example, or at least mean different things, according as he conceives of poetry as a species of artistic making or as a mental faculty or as a special kind of knowledge, and his results will likewise differ widely according as his reasoning about it rests primarily on literal definitions and distinctions within his subject matter or primarily on analogies between it and other things; and so on through a good many other possible variations in principle and method.

The Chicago writers have thought it likely that much, though by no means all, of the notorious diversity in doctrine and interpretation observable in the criticism of all ages can be accounted for in these terms; and they have taken this possibility as a working hypothesis in their writings on critics and critical movements from Plato and Aristotle to the present day. In these they have sought to judge the achievements of critics, not by any universal criterion of what literature or poetry "truly" is or of what criticism "ought" to be, but by the relative standard of what they have given us, within the limits of their widely variant principles and methods, in the way of verifiable and usable solutions to the different problems they set out to solve. They have gone on the assumption, in short, that though some modes of criticism are more restricted in scope than others, there are and have been many valid critical approaches to literature, each of which exhibits the literary object in a different light and each of which has its characteristic powers and limitations, so that the only rational ground for adhering to one of them rather than to any of the others is its superior capacity to give us the special kind of understanding and evaluation of literature we want to get, at least for the time being.

(2) The so-called Neo-Aristotelianism of the Chicago group represents a choice of this pragmatic sort. The special interest in the *Poetics* which appears in their earlier writings and explains the currency of this label had its origin in their concern, as teachers of literature, with developing a kind of practical criticism of literary texts that would emphasize the specifically artistic principles and reasons governing their construction, as distinct from their verbal meanings, their historical and biographical backgrounds, or their general qualitative characteristics, and that would attach more importance to the principles peculiar to different kinds of texts and to individual texts within a given kind than to those common to literature in general. The questions to be asked of any text in this sort of criticism would concern primarily the problems of organization, presentation, and expression imposed on its writer by the particular end he was trying to achieve in composing it, the nature of the means he employed in solving them, and the reasons governing his choice of these means rather than others; they would be questions, in short, the correct answers to which, since they pertain to a unique work of human art, can never be predicted in advance or deduced from any *a priori* critical theory, but have to be arrived at by considering which one among various conceivable answers best accounts for what is in the text. But if general presuppositions about what any given literary work must be can only serve to impede the critic's inquiry into what its writer was actually attempting to do and why, he is almost certain, on the other hand, to become more accurate and discriminating in his judgments the more he knows of what it might be—of the range of possible things that writers may do in different kinds of works and of their reasons for doing them, insofar as these can be induced from their productions past and present.

The appeal of Aristotle to the Chicago group lay in the fact that he, more than any other critic they knew, had conceived of literary theory in this *a posteriori* and differential way and had not only formulated some of its necessary distinctions and principles in his brief discussions of ancient tragedy and epic but

pointed the way to further inquiries of the same general sort concerning possibilities in these and other literary arts still unrealized at the time he wrote. They have attempted to pursue some of these, and with increasing independence of the letter of the *Poetics*, in their writings on the lyric, the drama, and the novel.

R. S. Crane, W. R. Keast, R. McKeon, N. Maclean, E. Olson, B. Weinberg, *Critics and Criticism: Ancient and Modern* (1952); abridged ed. with new introd. and list of other related writings by the same authors to 1957 (1957). Later publications in the same tradition: W. J. Hipple, Jr., *The Beautiful, the Sublime, and the Picturesque in 18th-C. Brit. Aesthetic Theory* (1957); R. Marsh, "The 'Fallacy' of Universal Intention," MP, 55 (1958); W. C. Booth, *The Rhetoric of Fiction* (1961); N. Friedman and C. A. McLaughlin, *Poetry: An Introd. to Its Form and Art* (1961); E. Olson, *Tragedy and the Theory of Drama* (1961); B. Weinberg, *A Hist. of Lit. Crit. in the It. Renaissance* (1961); A. M. Wright, *The Am. Short Story in the Twenties* (1961). Critical discussions: W. K. Wimsatt, Jr., "The Chicago Critics," *The Verbal Icon* (1954); J. Holloway, "The New and the Newer Critics," EIC, 5 (1955), repr. *The Charted Vision* (1960); Krieger; H. P. Teesing, "The Chicago School," *Orbis Litterarum*, Supp. 2 (1958) ; Sutton. R.S.C.

CHILEAN POETRY. See SPANISH AMERICAN POETRY.

CHINESE POETRY. Nowhere has poetry been more widely or continuously esteemed and practiced than in China. From ancient times it was sung and chanted in the fields and in the halls of kings and princes; long transmitted by memory, it began to be preserved among the earliest records. It has been composed by emperors and concubines, generals and conscripts, governors and prostitutes. It has been written in solitary studies and on the walls of inns and brothels, at farewell meetings of friends or chance encounters by the wayside. Like poetry elsewhere, it has been sometimes a spontaneous expression of genuine feeling, sometimes a product of pure artifice—contrived for a polite occasion, a contest, or even the imperial examinations for public office. Until very recently the writing of verse was an accomplishment expected of any educated Chin., and although many have been remembered chiefly for their poems, only two or three who failed at everything else could be said to have been professional poets. A person could not, in fact, be called a poet in Chin., in the general sense, because there is no Chin. word for poetry—only different words for different kinds of verse.

However, in modern times one of these

words is often used to connote poetry in general. The *shih,* because of its ancient origin, great prestige, and almost unbroken practice over the centuries, may be called the standard class of Chin. verse, subsuming many of its varied forms and styles. The word *shih* first appears as the name for the folk and courtier songs, hymns, and ceremonial libretti which comprise China's earliest recorded poetry, brought together before the time of Confucius (5th c. B.C.) in what came to be known as the *Shih Ching* (Classic of Songs). There is a tradition, not now much credited, that Confucius himself made the collection; he may have revised it. It is certain that he set great store by the *Songs,* both words and music. They were all sung or chanted; in China, as elsewhere, music and poetry were closely related in origin and development.

The main characteristics of Chin. verse are already present in the *Songs:* its strong rhythms, its abundant use of rhyme, its basic expressive devices, its succinctness.

The monosyllabic word, represented by a single graph, is the basic rhythmic unit of Chin. poetry. Length of line therefore sets the meter, so that one speaks of 4-word-line (4-beat) poems, 7-word-line poems, etc. The early ritual chants mix long and short lines, but among the folk songs the uniform 4-word-line poem is predominant. The usual rhyme scheme is ABCB; initial and internal rhyme also appear, as does alliteration. Words are often doubled, usually with onomatopoetic or similar effects—the sound of nets thrown in the water, of fish flapping their tails, the glistening of leaves, the whirling of wind. The first words in the collection are *gwan-gwan,* the cry of the osprey. As in folk poetry the world over, phrases or lines are often repeated from stanza to stanza:

I go out the East Gate—
There are girls like clouds.
Though [many] as clouds,
None absorbs my thoughts.
White robe, grey kerchief,
She delights my heart.

I go out the Gate Tower—
There are girls like reeds.
Though [many] as reeds,
None detains my thoughts.
White robe and madder,
She can delight me.

This simple kind of repetition and variation, a natural and easy unifying device, forcruns a whole complex of structural and verbal parallelisms elaborated in Chin. poetry, as well as in some types of prose, many centuries later.

Despite repetition of components, the *Songs* are remarkably terse, as is Chin. poetry in general—partly because of the nature of the language, and partly because of a preference for suggestion rather than exposition. The *Songs* are by no means reticent, and abound in direct declaration of emotion. Directness, however, does not mean complete statement; Chin. directness may seem like ellipsis to the Western reader. In the poem given above it is not said that "I know a girl who wears a white robe and grey kerchief." The two articles of clothing stand for the girl, and the line stands alone with its syntactical relation to the next line indeterminate (an example not lost on modern poets acknowledging Chin. influence). Comparisons are seldom grammatically indicated with "like" or "as if." Philosophical observation, likewise, is seldom stated, and is sometimes rendered obliquely, as when the imagery of nature is used in contrast to man's plight rather than as a sympathetic reflection of it—the brightness of flowers, the permanence of hills providing a poetic counterpoint to man's sorrow and evanescence.

The themes of the *Songs* are those of an ordered, by no means primitive society: the joys and sorrows of love and marriage, of agricultural labor and feudal service, of food and drink or their lack. Poems by educated courtiers deal with pleasures and trials of court life, praising or blaming the kings and lords. Although the courtier poems are full of stereotypes as compared to the folk songs, many clichés are common to both and are repeated in verse of later centuries. The whole body of Chin. poetry is replete with direct and indirect allusions to the *Songs,* allusions with multiple levels of association derived in part from a moral-allegorical interpretation of the classic text (compare The Song of Solomon) which was standard from the Han dynasty (206 B.C.–A.D. 221) until recent times. Modern scholarship has performed a signal service to literature and anthropology by restoring the *Songs* minus the accretions of intervening ages; but Chin. poetry of these intervening ages owes perhaps more, in allusive subtlety and complexity, to the traditional interpretations than it owes to the *Songs* themselves.

The *Songs* reflect life in the North; China's next known poetry, preserved in the *Ch'u Tz'u* (Elegies of Ch'u) originated in the more luxuriant Yangtze basin, in the Warring Kingdoms period after Confucius. This collection includes the *Nine Songs,* a group of erotic incantations by shamans summoning various deities. Essentially dance libretti, they are rhapsodic in structure and content, richly sensuous in imagery. They were believed to have been set down by Ch'ü Yüan, a loyal minister who drowned himself after scheming courtiers estranged the King of Ch'u from him. Other verse compositions attributed to or associated with him appear in the *Elegies*, notably a long personal lament called *Li Sao* (usually rendered Falling into Trouble). It describes a journey to the gates of heaven and back in vain search of a suitable mate and a prince worthy of Ch'ü Yüan's services. The two goals, curiously confused in the extant text, have been taken as one by commentators (the treatment of love poetry in terms of political allegory being a convention of Confucian critics, often adopted by poets themselves). In addition to its unprecedented length and personal emphasis, the *Li Sao* differs from the classic *Songs* in being independent of music and in employing a new metric. It is mostly in 7-word lines of coupletlike structure: two 3-word groups separated by the extra character *hsi* which effects a central caesura. This *hsi* seems to be equivalent to the indrawn sigh which Chin. to this day sound at the end of a line of verse when intoning it. The *Li Sao* and its companion pieces established a new genre, the *sao* (elegy).

Similar in metric but usually less personal in content was the *fu* (rhymeprose). This generally had a short narrative or expository introduction in prose, and the main body (descriptive or persuasive or both) used rhyme at will, here and there shifting to a different meter. Probably the first Chin. form of "pure" literature, the rhymeprose became the favorite rhythmic vehicle of Han writers. However, tradition dates some of the most remarkable examples considerably earlier and attributes them to Sung Yü, supposedly a nephew of Ch'ü Yüan himself: e.g., the *Kao-t'ang Fu*, a fantastic description of the wonders of Mount Kao-t'ang. Such exuberant exercises in word-magic suggest that the *fu* also harks back to shamanistic incantations. But composition in rhymeprose became progressively regularized, and the "parallel style" (verbal and syntactical balance of lines within couplets or larger groups) became an inseparable element of it. The regularized form was practiced with frequent distinction through the Six Dynasties (221–589), reaching its highest development in the *Lament for the South* by Yü Hsin, a historical and personal poem on the fall of the Liang dynasty. Other outstanding *fu* include Hsi K'ang's *On the Lute*, Lu Chi's *On Literature* (an analysis of the creative process), and Chiang Yen's *On Separation*.

Meantime other verse genres arose. The history of Chin. poetry consistently shows a pattern of overlapping development: as an established genre became rigidly prescriptive in form and imitative in content and diction, poets tended to discover and exploit the novelty of some popular oral type of poetry or song-words. The supplanted genre seldom became obsolete but continued to be used,

generally with a deliberate effect of archaism, occasionally rejuvenated in the hands of some poet of genius. By the end of the Han a new lyric form had emerged, inspired by popular songs and borrowing from them many of its themes.

Chin. music had changed greatly since ancient times, affected by foreign importations during the expansion of the Han empire. Distant military expeditions, foreign trade, and growing cosmopolitanism also gave a wider range of themes to popular song-words, which along with the music were collected and recorded by the imperial Music Bureau (*yüeh-fu*) and are therefore known as *yüeh-fu* poems. (The term is also applied to later popular songs and to countless literary imitations of the genre.) These balladlike lyrics usually present through monologue or dialogue a dramatic situation such as that of the abandoned wife or concubine, the princess sent as bride to a barbarian tribal chief, the abused orphan, the soldier at the front or in captivity.

Early *yüeh-fu* are characterized by mixed meters, but 5-word lines are frequent, and probably from these arose the new 5-word-line *shih*, the dominant verse form for centuries to come. Length and number of stanzas varied, but the individual line became regularized with a caesura after the second word, avoidance of enjambement, use of the couplet as a structural unit, and rhyming of alternate lines. Use of the 5-word-line *shih* by the literati became prominent around the Chien-an period (196–220), which lends its name to a renaissance of lyric poetry at the end of the Han era. This renaissance centered at the court of the Ts'ao family (founders of the succeeding Wei kingdom), and the prince Ts'ao Chih invested the new form with his personal emotions. A sense of transience and insecurity, for himself and for the age, colors his poems.

The period of the Three Kingdoms (including Wei) and the Six Dynasties spanned three centuries of political, social, and cultural disintegration and reformation, during which alien invaders and the foreign missionary religion of Buddhism were gradually assimilated. Many literati, deeply disturbed by the collapse of the imperial structure and its Confucian orthodoxy, retreated into Taoist or Buddhist seclusion, individualistic eccentricity, or the solace of wine—attitudes traditionally typified by a group of poets known as the Seven Sages of the Bamboo Grove. T'ao Ch'ien (T'ao Yüan-ming) shares the conflicts of the period but rises above his contemporaries in stature as a complex personality and an individual stylist. Flight from public office to a life of poverty as a farmer epitomizes his personal tragedy of divided allegiance between Confucian duty and Taoist freedom from social convention; his poetry expresses a mixture of desperation and delight, often with an undercurrent of guilt. Wine, of which he writes often, represents not so much an easy solution as a resigned acceptance of the tangible pleasures in a universe apparently unconcerned with man's questionings and desires (e.g., the poem *Substance, Shadow, and Spirit*). Yet of all Chin. poets he has perhaps the strongest affinity for the world of nature, drawing from it simple symbols (chrysanthemum, pine, homing bird) which acquire special significance in the context of his entire work. He wrote *fu* and some archaistic 4-word-line poems, but is best known for those in pentameter. They show an unstudied parallelism in thought and syntax. Hsieh Ling-yün and Pao Chao, more typical poets of the period and more deliberate in technique, further developed the craft of the 5-word-line poem.

Increasing speculation on the nature and function of literature was beginning to amplify the rudimentary critical theory inherited from Han times. Orthodox tradition regarded the ancient classics as the basis of all literature, and thus viewed the *Classic of Songs* as the fountainhead of poetry and the touchstone for its evaluation. Evaluation was by and large ethical; the standard Han preface to the *Classic of Songs* (*Shih Ching*), defining *shih* as the emotional expression of purposeful thought, stressed the didactic function of poetry allegedly laid down by Confucius.

The concept of poetry as an art was foreshadowed in a fragmentary *Essay on Literature* by Ts'ao P'ei, who became emperor of the succeeding Wei dynasty (220–264). Later in the 3d c., Lu Chi's *Rhymeprose on Literature* gave "expression of feeling" as the motive for any writing beyond the utilitarian; his analysis of the creative process was that of an artist, both in purpose and in effect. He was not, however, seeking to assail the classical tradition, but to revitalize and enrich it. The tradition was brilliantly restated in the most systematic critical work produced in the Liang dynasty (502–556), under which Chin. literary theory reached its height. This was Liu Hsieh's *Wenhsin Tiao-lung* (the title defies translation), which classified all forms of writing in 21 categories, derived from one or another of the Classics: from the *Shih Ching* came the elegy (*sao*), songs (*shih*), the later folk songs (*yüeh-fu*), the rhymeprose (*fu*), praise odes (*sung*), and hymns (*tsan*). He gave examples of each and appraised them on the basis of their suitability to their purpose. Liu's work was by no means merely an elaborate bit of scholasticism; its second half dealt earnestly with the individual creative faculty and process, and astutely with problems of style, technique, and balance of form and content.

Liu Hsieh's patron, the Liang prince Hsiao T'ung, compiled in the *Wen Hsüan* (Anthology of Literature) a large collection of short writings up to his time which is our chief source for Six Dynasties poetry, and upon which later writers drew heavily for both diction and allusion. While ostensibly supporting the didactic tradition in his preface, Hsiao T'ung admitted pleasure as a guiding principle in his selection. Hsiao Kang, his brother and later Emperor, took an extreme position in defining poetry as a medium for free self-expression, and dissociating it from the ethics of canonical literature. His views were implemented in an anthology about love and beautiful women compiled at his order (*Yü-t'ai Hsin-yung* or New Lyrics from Jade Terraces). The contents were mostly by recent poets whose erotic preoccupation, preciosity of diction, and decorative artifice characterized the "palace style," which long continued in fashion. As a narrow preserve of aristocrats at beleaguered regional courts, the "palace style" eventually was pushed aside in the new social synthesis of the T'ang Dynasty (618–907).

The T'ang was another period of imperial expansion, foreign intercourse, and successful assimilation of new ideas and cultural innovations. In these three centuries new verse genres were developed and some old ones revitalized. The 5-word-line poem shared favor with a corresponding form based on a 7-word line with much the same prosodic features, the caesura coming after the fourth word. By the end of the 7th c. both forms had become regularized in such a way as to crystallize the prosodic tendencies of earlier poets. A prominent factor in the new *lü-shih* ("regulated poems") was the requirement of tonal contrast between the two lines of each couplet. Tone (relative pitch) as a phonemic element in each monosyllable undoubtedly had existed in ancient Chin., with a definite if unrecognized function in poetry; but the Chin. seem to have been unconscious of this linguistic peculiarity until zeal to translate the Buddhist scriptures brought them into contact with Sanskrit, which lacked it. In the 5th c. Shen Yo distinguished four tones, which were later grouped in two categories: "level" (constant in pitch) and "deflected" (changing in pitch). On the basis of general tendencies in poetry, Shen Yo formulated a set of euphonic prescriptions which, amplified by the practice of the 6th- and 7th-c. poets, resulted in the "regulated poem."

The great T'ang poets of the 8th and 9th c., in writing their *lü-shih*, conformed to a length of 8 or 12 lines (later 8 became standard), to the use of rhymes only in level tones and at the ends of alternate lines, to syntactical parallelism in certain couplets, and (less strictly) to rules of tonal contrast in all couplets. A poet who chose to work outside these limitations, as all did on occasion, was writing *ku-shih* ("old-style poems"). Some suggestion of the difficulty imposed by verbal parallelism and tonal contrast can be conveyed by a word-for-word translation (followed by a free one) of a *lü-shih* by Wang Wei, accompanied by its tonal pattern. Level tones are indicated by O, deflected tones by X, optional tones by an asterisk, and rhyme-words by an added R:

Late	years	only	love	peace
*	o	o	x	x
x	x	x	o	o-R
Myriad	affairs	not	involve	mind

Self	examine	no	long-term	plan
*	x	o	o	x
*	o	x	x	o-R
Only	know	return	old	woods

Pine	*wind*	*blow*	*loosen*	*girdle*
*	o	o	x	x
o	x	o	o	o-R
Mountain	*moon*	*shine*	*play*	*lute*

Your	question	failure	success	principle
*	x	o	o	x
*	o	x	x	o-R
Fishers'	song	enter	estuary	deep

In later life I only care for peace;
Affairs of state are none of my concern.
I know I have no plan to save the world,
Only my old retreat here in this wood.
My girdle loosened to the cool pine wind,
I play the lute beneath the mountain moon.
You ask the laws of failure and success?
The fishermen are singing in the cove . . .

Besides tonal contrast, note the strict verbal correspondencies of the couplet in italics. Classical allusions expand the meaning of lines 2, 3, and 7; line 8 suggests the typical *non-sequitur* answers of Zen Buddhists to abstruse questions. Such compact verse requires the most exacting economy; each word must contribute its full share of meaning, often on more than one plane. An even briefer form, the *chüeh-chü* ("stop-short"), limited to a single quatrain of five- or 7-word lines, nearly always leaves in suspension several levels of suggestion. The T'ang *chüeh-chü* was often set to music, and may in fact have originated as a song-form upon which the exigencies of tonal contrast were later imposed.

The master poets of the age were Li Po and his friend Tu Fu. They lived in the reign of one of history's most fabled patrons of the arts, Emperor Hsüan-tsung, and through the rebellion which not only ended it but shattered the T'ang empire almost beyond repair. Yet Li Po continued writing much the same sort of poetry as before. He inevitably commands Western attention as being closest to the romantic prototype of poets, self-centered, vola-

tile, incapable of practicality. Impatient of restraint, he usually favored the less stringently controlled verse forms. Into these he put more intensity of feeling and boldness of imagination than profundity of thought, and he was more successful with personal than with social or historical themes. Some of his most celebrated pieces depict fanciful flights into a kind of Taoist fairyland, or at least into the wilder realms of nature. Tu Fu, in many respects his antithesis, was an introspective, disciplined, and responsible personality. A diligent minor official, he felt a personal involvement in the imperial disaster, which indeed brought bitter hardship to him and his family. The humility and sense of empathy pervading his poems have made him for the Chin. a spokesman for the universal suffering of mankind and for its power to endure and hope. A meticulous craftsman, he was a master of the regulated poem, to which he contributed great density of texture and a wealth of learned, though not pedantic, allusion.

Wang Wei, equally noted as painter and poet, retired to a Buddhist monastery after a busy if somewhat equivocal official career. His lyrics reflect his religious bent and his love of rural seclusion. His pastoral experience seems more aesthetic and less grounded in realities than that of T'ao Ch'ien, whom he greatly admired.

Po Chü-i, one of the most translatable of Chin. poets, strove for transparency of idea and simplicity of diction. His work was exceedingly popular, some of it becoming standard repertory among singing-girls, but he was disappointed at the neglect of an experimental group of "new *yüeh-fu*" by which he hoped to call the attention of the throne to social abuses. Much more difficult are the poems of Han Yü, chiefly known in the West as a model prose writer. He championed a return to the simplicity characteristic of Chin. prose before it accumulated a set of elaborate rules for almost verselike regularity. As a poet he accepted and excelled in the regulated forms, but carrying into poetry his dislike of pretty verbiage, he made use of unhackneyed vocabulary and did not hesitate to experiment with harsh combinations when he wanted a harsh effect. His verse thus abounds in the kind of "unpoetic" juxtapositions esteemed in modern poetry. Yet here is a major poet who, despite a complete German translation, is almost totally unrepresented in Eng.

Much of the work of these and most other Chin. poets was written as occasional verse, exchanges with friends or celebrations of social events, and it often suffers from the inconsequentiality or obscurity of such origins. On the other hand its relation to daily experience contributed spontaneity, concreteness, and not infrequently the stimulus for flashes of insight transcending time and circumstance.

Toward the end of the T'ang (907) a previously subliterary genre, the *tz'u* ([song-]words), began to enjoy artistic status. The term referred to songs heard in the brothels and teahouses, following melodies quite different from the old *yüeh-fu* pieces. Further infiltration of music from northern and central Asia, even from India, had again remolded Chin. musical modes. The symmetrical verses of T'ang poets had often been sung to this now domesticated music, but they did not fit its rhythms and melodic contours unless the singers stretched some words and slighted others, or improvised a few here and there. With the political decline of the T'ang, the quality of formal verse (a literary accomplishment required for the state examinations) declined too; young men found it more diverting to write song-words about love and pretty girls, with the uneven lines and varied patterns of rhyme and tone which they heard in the pleasure quarters, such as the following by Yen Hsüan:

Autumn rain,
Autumn rain,
No noon, no night,
Drip, drip, pour, pour.
Lamp gone out, pallet cold, brooding loneliness.
Pretty wench,
So very sad!
West wind rustles faintly in the bamboo by the window,
Stops and begins again;
On painted cheeks two teardrops gleam like jewels.
How many times he promised, "When the wild geese come . . ."
He let the date go by—
The geese returned, he didn't.

First poet to write a great many of these songs was Wen T'ing-yün, whose rich ornamentation of erotic verse-pictures is yet so impressionistic as to be today obscure as often as not. More personal were the bittersweet songs of Li Yü (Li Hou-chu), reminders of the felicities he enjoyed as ruler of the ephemeral Southern T'ang state and lost as prisoner of the conquering Sung emperor. During the Sung Dynasty (960–1280) the *tz'u* took in a much wider variety of subjects and often, especially with Hsin Ch'i-chi, diction from everyday speech. Much of the best Sung verse was written to the hundreds of different *tz'u* patterns. Eventually the tunes were forgotten and only literary models remained, to be carefully followed in form and prosody.

Sung poets also revitalized the rhymeprose, making of it a reflective thing of less rhyme

and more prose; the "prose *fu*" of Ou-yang Hsiu (e.g., one on "The Sound of Autumn") are noteworthy. The most popular Sung poet, Su Tung-p'o, reworked as a *tz'u* one of his two famous *fu* about visits to the Red Cliff. He was also a major *shih* writer, achieving a unified style (informed with wit and good spirits) even while borrowing heavily from the phrases of earlier poets. On the whole, Sung poetry is less imaginative and more philosophical than that of the T'ang period. The tendency of Sung poets to form schools and prescribe methods of composition is exemplified by Huang T'ing-chien, who left a clearly enunciated set of poetic principles, one of which called for constant use of erudite allusion. (Adherence to this method by less gifted men calls to mind Arthur Waley's dictum that classical allusion, always the bane of Chin. poetry, finally destroyed it altogether.)

As poetic creativity among the literati declined and even the *tz'u* became an antiquarian pastime, once again a popular song-form carried the fresher currents of the time. The music of the *ch'ü* came both from South China and from the northern regions controlled by the Tartars of the Chin Dynasty (1115–1234). Similar to *tz'u* in the irregularity of their rhythms, the *ch'ü* allowed greater prosodic freedom in the rhyming of level with deflected tones and in the insertion of any number of extra "patter" words or asides independent of the basic pattern. Linguistically these songs, apparently performed in street entertainments for all to hear, show a greater use of vernacular vocabulary and grammar; the range of subject matter includes social and humorous themes. The device of grouping together tunes in the same mode produced "song chains" with a narrative frame, a device which made the *ch'ü* the prosodic basis of the lyric drama of the Yüan period (1280–1368). Very few of these songs, not to mention the dramas of which they are the artistic core, have been translated.

No further popular genres rose to the literary surface to mold new verse forms. For historical reasons the Ming and Ch'ing (1644–1912) were periods of cultural conservatism. As critics, poets wrote a great deal of reanalysis and reevaluation of their great heritage with the aim of re-creating it in their own work; but, partly from the sheer length and weight of the tradition, in practice they concentrated more on their models than on the creative inspiration they sought to derive from them. The most esteemed models were the major T'ang poets; an 18th-c. lyricist, Huang Chin-jen, perhaps came nearest to recapturing the authentic T'ang manner. Yüan Mei of the same century was almost unique in his "natural inspiration" theory emphasizing the poet's individual endowment; his comparatively transparent and lively verses are conventionally regarded as somewhat frivolous. A stupendous body of verse was produced in these centuries, much of it still read and esteemed, but only in exceptional instances ranked with the poetry of earlier periods.

Although exceptions may be found to any generalization about Chin. poetry, in its totality it shows certain salient differences from that of the Occident. Thematically, it is little concerned with some of the major subjects of Western verse—idealized love, heroic adventure, religious devotion. Feminine charms are often described with delicate and sometimes with heavy eroticism, but consuming passions are reserved for fiction. Unfulfilled love is conventionally presented from the standpoint of the abandoned wife or concubine, though the number of such poems known to be actually by women is comparatively small. Writing in their own person, men prefer the theme of separation and reunion of friends. The epic is unknown, and long narrative poems of any kind are rare. Even the *yüeh-fu* poem usually differs from the European ballad in describing a dramatic situation rather than narrating a sequence of events, and seldom involves ghosts, animals with human attributes, or supernatural intervention. The relatively small place of the supernatural in Chin. poetry is perhaps explained by an absorption with this world, not the next, which on the whole has characterized the Chin. ethos. Religions have colored, but rarely if ever dominated, the poet's view of this world. Chin. poetry often has mystical overtones and Taoist, Buddhist, or other religious referents, but religious verse as such is a very minor category.

Stylistically, Chin. poetry displays a marked restraint in the use of simile, metaphor, symbol, and (almost wholly absent) personification, those figures of speech so common in Western poetry. Complexity is supplied by diction which accumulates through tradition an ever-increasing range of ideological and emotional implication. On the whole, Chin. poets achieve their effects by reticence not rhetoric; draw their images from nature more often than from mythology or religion; imply their emotions instead of anatomizing them; and integrate what they have to say with existing poetic forms and conventions, rather than attempting to create new media to fit individual needs.

The unique nature of the Chin. written language poses unusual problems for the translator of poetry. Amateur sinologists have produced interesting but far-fetched results by a pseudo-semantic method based on a fundamental misconception of the function of the Chin. graphs, supposing that the various pictorial and metapictorial elements of a single character create a word. Generally speaking the opposite is true: a word with a certain sound has a certain meaning, or complex of meanings, and a graph is devised to represent that word. Often the graph contains no more than a vague hint at the general meaning and perhaps a mnemonic device for the approximate sound—the latter frequently being taken by self-taught foreigners as contributing to the meaning. Even when such a phonetic element is absent, it is risky to translate separately the component significs of a single character. The Chin. graph for "autumn" is composed of a sign for "grain" and one for "fire"—but it is no less presumptuous to render it as "season of grain and fire" than it would be for a Chin. to reverse the process and translate Keats's "season of mists and mellow fruitfulness" merely as "autumn."

The feature of Chin. poetry which has had the most influence on modern Western poets is its use of concentrated images instead of diffuse description or exposition. Curiously enough, the imagist movement was the first strong Western influence on Chin. poetry, when in the literary revolution that followed the political one, traditional verse forms were abandoned along with the restricted literary language. Next came the personal and social rhapsody characterized by a recent critic as "Whitmanism." With the imposition of a new (Communist) orthodoxy in continental China, poetic as well as other literary principles and practices became governed by political ideology. Modern Chin. poetry has little connection with that of previous ages and belongs to a separate study, one which cannot yet be undertaken with the hope of any conclusions of lasting validity.

ANTHOLOGIES: *The Temple* (1925), *The Book of Songs* (1937), *Chin. Poems* (1948), and *The Nine Songs* (1955), all tr. A. Waley; *The Jade Mountain*, tr. W. Bynner and Kiang Kang-hu (1931); *Chin. Lyrics*, tr. Ch'u Ta-kao (1937; *tz'u* poetry); *Selections from the Three Hundred Poems of the T'ang Dynasty* (1940), *A Further Selection . . .* (1944), both tr. S. Jenyns; *The White Pony* (1947), *Contemporary Chin. Poetry* (1947), both tr. R. Payne; *Anthologie raisonnée de la litt. chinoise*, tr. G. Margouliès (1948); *La Poésie chinoise*, tr. P. Guillermaz (Paris, 1957); *Ch'u Tz'u, The Songs of the South*, tr. D. Hawkes (1959); *The Penguin Book of Chin. Verse*, ed. A. R. Davis (1962); *20th C. Chin. Poetry: An Anthol.*, ed. and tr. Kai-Yu Hsu (1963).

HISTORY AND CRITICISM: A. Waley, "Notes on Chin. Prosody," *Jour. of the Royal Asiatic Soc.* (1918); Kiang Kang-hu, "Various Poetic Regulations and Forms," *The Jade Mountain*, xxviii-xxxv; C. D. Le Gros Clark, *The Prose-Poetry of Su Tung-p'o* (1935); J. Ingalls, "Chin. for Poets," *Saturday Review* (Mar. 20, 1948); A.

Fang, "Rhymeprose on Literature," *Harvard Jour. of Asiatic Studies*, 14 (1951), "From Imagism to Whitmanism in Recent Chin. Poetry," *Indiana Univ. Conference on Oriental-Western Literary Relations* (1955); G. Margouliès, *Hist. de la litt. chinoise—Poésie* (1951); J. R. Hightower, *Topics in Chin. Lit.* (rev. ed., 1953; with crit. bibliog.), "The *Fu* of T'ao Ch'ien," *Harvard Jour. of As. St.*, 17 (1954), "The Wen Hsüan and Genre Theory," *Harvard Jour. of As. St.*, 20 (1957); G. W. Baxter, "Metrical Origins of the *Tz'u*," *Harvard Jour. of As. St.*, 16 (1953); J. L. Bishop, "Prosodic Elements in T'ang Poetry," *Indiana Conference;* Yi-tsi Mei, "Tradition and Experiment in Modern Chin. Lit.," *Indiana Conference;* Liu Hsieh, *The Literary Mind and the Carving of Dragons*, tr. V. Yu-chung Shih (1959); Ch'ên Shou-Yi, *Chin. Lit.: A Historical Introd.* (1961); J. J. Y. Liu, *The Art of Chinese Poetry* (1962); B. Watson, *Early Chin. Lit.* (1962).

J.L.B.; G.W.B.

CHŌKA. See JAPANESE POETRY.

CHOLIAMBUS (Gr. "lame iambic") or *scazon* (Gr. "limping"). Hipponax of Ephesus (ca. 540 B.C.) employed this meter in his invectives. Its "limping" effect was suggested by the substitution of a spondee (or trochee) for the obligatory iambus in the 6th foot of the normal iambic trimeter. When the 5th foot was also a spondee, the verse was called ischiorrhogic ("with broken hips") and was ascribed to Ananius (also 6th c. B.C.). The c. was used in the Alexandrian period by Herodas for his *mimiambi* and by Callimachus. In L. poetry Catullus and his successors apparently imitated Callimachus in keeping the 5th foot a pure iambus, while they admitted few resolutions in the first 4 feet. An example is:

Mĭsēr | Cătŭl|lē, dē|sĭnās | ĭnēp|tīrē
(Catullus 8.1).

Hardie; Kolář; Koster.

R.J.G.

CHOREE. See TROCHEE.

CHORIAMB (Gr. "consisting of a choree [i.e., a trochee] and an iamb"). A metrical unit of the structure − ∪ ∪ −, frequently found in Gr. dramatic choruses and lyric verse and used often by Sappho, Alcaeus and, in L. poetry, by Horace. It is found mostly in combination with other units, e.g., in glyconics and asclepiads (qq.v.) but is sometimes pure as

deīnā mĕn oūn, | dĕīnā tărāss | eī sŏphŏs oī |

ŏnothĕtās
(Sophocles, *Oedipus Tyrannus* 484)

Some assign it a far greater role in the rationalization of Gr. lyric, either considering it (with Wilamowitz) the basic element in a widespread "choriambic dimeter" whose first foot can evidently be almost anything, or (with Dale) holding it and its resolutions to be one of the two basic "building blocks" of any lyric. In an accentual form, the c. has been used in modern languages, e.g., in German (Goethe's *Pandora*, written in choriambic dimeters) and in Eng. Its occurrence in Eng. verse is fairly rare, but undoubted, varying from single lines such as Marvell's

Lilĭes withoūt, | rŏses withīn

(*The Nymph and her Fawn*) to Swinburne's protracted use in his *Choriambics.*—U. v. Wilamowitz-Moellendorff, *Griechische Verskunst* (1921; 2d ed., 1958); E. W. Scripture, "The Choriambus in Eng. Verse," PMLA, 43 (1928); Hamer; A. M. Dale, "The Metrical Units of Gr. Lyric Verse," CQ, 44 (1950) and CQ, n.s.1 (1951); Koster; E. Martin, *Essai sur les rhythmes de la chanson grecque antique* (1953).

D.S.P.

CHORUS (Gr. *choreuein*, "to dance"). Presumably, Gr. tragedy somehow arose from, or in conjunction with, the lyric and religious performances of a ch. of masked and singing dancers. But despite the crucial bond between tragedy and its characteristic ch. (no extant 5th-c. tragedy lacks a fully developed ch.), our information is lamentably scanty. The following facts, however, deserve mention. (1) The tragic ch., rectangular in formation and often military in movement, is *not* to be confused with the "cyclical" ch. of dithyramb. (2) The early number of the ch. is said (on flimsy evidence and by an improbable analogy with the dithyrambic ch.) to have been 50; Aeschylus (cf. *Agamemnon* 1347–1371) used 12 and Sophocles is said to have raised the number to 15. (3) Choral odes (including *kommoi*) were *sung* by all or part of the ch., while the lines of the *coryphaeus* (or chorus leader) were *spoken*. (4) The expenses of training the ch. were assigned by the state to a wealthy man (called the *choregus*), and the "giving of a chorus" by the archon constituted the poet's official admission to the tragic contest.

Both tragedy and ch. appear to have been religious in origin. However, whereas tragedy and comedy in the later 5th c. became secularized as they lost touch with their ritual origins, the ch. remained the conservative soul of the play, the articulate spokesman for traditional religion and society, clinging stubbornly to the forms and wisdom and even the style of the worshipping group from which it arose. This conservative element is visible not only in the elaborately figured archaic lyrics with their "poetic" syntax and heavy load of Doricisms in sharp contrast to the more colloquial dialogue, but in the traditionalism of its moral beliefs, its conventional theodicy, and its commitment to proverbial social wisdom. And so the normal mode of choral utterance is a characteristic group speech, of great power but often limited precision, rising from sheer banality to the apocalyptic gnomic richness of the Aeschylean ch. Dramatists might adapt the ch. to their practical needs by making it serve such simple functions as spectacle, widening emotional range etc., but they seem to have found it difficult to alter this communal and traditionalizing role of the ch. There is, however, little tension between the nature of the ch. and the dramatist's needs until the time of Euripides. But as Olympian religion declined and the old social order went under in the convulsions of the late 5th c., the ch. lost the context that gave it life as a convention, and in post-Euripidean tragedy appears to have been degraded to ornament. According to Aristotle, it was in the 4th c. that the practice arose of writing choral odes that had little or nothing to do with the play.

Conservatism was strengthened by function. For the ch. attends the action as a dependent society in miniature, giving the public resonance of individual action. Thus the ch. exults, fears, wonders, mourns, and attempts, out of its store of traditional moralities, to cope with an action whose meaning is both difficult and unfamiliar. By so doing, the ch. generalizes the meaning of the action and at the same time the action revives and refreshes the choral wisdom. But almost never is the chorus' judgment of events authoritative; if it is an intruded voice, it is normally the voice of tradition, not the dramatist. In Aeschylus perhaps the ch. is least fallible, but in both Aeschylus and Sophocles the ch. tends to lag behind the meaning implicit in the action; that lag is the secret of the chorus' *dramatic* power and the means whereby the tension between the tragic hero and his society is made clear. Euripides, less easy with tradition and hence self-conscious, tends to rely on his ch. more for poetic intensity than dramatic tension (though in no Gr. play is the ch. so fully and ironically exploited against tradition as in the *Bacchae*).

The power of the choral convention explains why the ch. has been so constantly revived in subsequent literature—in the undramatic virtuoso choruses of Seneca; in Milton's *Samson Agonistes*, formally and dramatically the most perfect Gr. choruses in Eng.; in the quasi-Euripidean ch. of Fr. tragedy; in the cosmic choruses of Shelley and Goethe, and finally in the remarkable ch. of Eliot's *Murder in the Cathedral*, to mention but one of the many modern attempts to resuscitate the choral convention. But with almost all of these revivals, no matter how remarkable the mastery, the choral convention has failed somehow to flourish, or flourished only as a literary and archaic device, deprived of the context and ground that in the Gr. theatre gave it a natural rightness. Only Eliot, by placing his ch. within the context of a religious society in the dramatic act of worship, has overcome the difficulties, but the limits imposed by such a context must prove unacceptable to a living and secular theatre.—A. E. Haigh, *The Tragic Drama of the Greeks* (1896); R. C. Flickinger, *The Gr. Theater and Its Drama* (1916); A. W. Pickard-Cambridge, *Dithyramb, Tragedy and Comedy* (1927) and *The Dramatic Festivals of Athens* (1953); T.B.L. Webster, *Gr. Theater Production* (1956); M. Bieber, *The Hist. of the Gr. and Roman Theater* (2d ed., rev. 1961). w.a.

CHRISTABEL METER. The meter of Coleridge's *Christabel* (free, 4-stress couplets, generally iambic or anapestic, but with frequent substitution). In his preface to the poem Coleridge made three claims: 1. that the meter is based not on a count of syllables, but on a count of accents ("in each line the accents will be found to be only four"); 2. that this is a new principle; 3. that the length of line varies with the passion. As various critics have said, the principle was not new. Coleridge assumed that previous poets had measured their lines by counting syllables (as in Fr. and It. verse), but this is not quite true, for from the earliest times *native* Eng. verse had been accentual, as in the long line of *Beowulf*. With Chaucer there seems to have been a blend of the two systems, accentual and syllabic.

What makes *Christabel* meter different is that in a few places Coleridge went the whole way and reduced the line to 4 syllables only —monosyllabic feet, as in the much-cited *Break, break, break* of Tennyson. As to the success of the handling of the accentual meter in *Christabel*, Bridges' charge seems unanswerable that Coleridge never shook off the tradition of conventional metric stress, as opposed to word or sense stress. Thus, in important respects *Christabel* does not provide a good example of accentual prosody. One might also question the appropriateness of the particular usage of the meter in *Christabel* in relation to its theme and tone. Nevertheless, there is little doubt that the meter was an important milestone on the road to some of the most important accentual experiments and successes of succeeding times.—Saintsbury, *Prosody*; R. Bridges, *Milton's Prosody* (1921); A. R. Morris, *The Orchestration of the Metrical Line* (1923); A.L.F. Snell, "The Meter of Christabel," in

The Fred Newton Scott Anniversary Papers (1929). **R.BE.**

CHRONICLE PLAY. See HISTORY PLAY.

CH'Ü. See CHINESE POETRY.

CINQUAIN. (a) A form of 5-line stanza of varying meter and rhyme scheme; probably of medieval origin. According to Georges Lote, it was used by the author of *Vie de Saint Alexis* and later reemployed by Guernes de Pont-Sainte-Maxence, "et cette fois en alexandrins." The term eventually became generalized to include almost any 5-line stanza: "One of Sher Kan's boon-companions . . . reciting the following cinquains" (J. Payne, *1001 Nights* 2.205). (b) The precise 5-line stanza invented by Adelaide Crapsey for her volume of *Verse*, employing lines of, respectively, 2, 4, 6, 8, and 2 syllables. This stanza is supposed to bear a resemblance to the Japanese *haiku* (q.v.), a form dating from feudal times employing three lines of 5, 7, and 5 syllables, but the resemblance is superficial.—G. Lote, *Hist. du vers français*, II (1951); J. D. Hart, *The Oxford Companion to Am. Lit.* (3d ed., 1956). **R.O.E.**

CLASSICAL METERS IN MODERN LANGUAGES. The ancient Gr. poet marked his arsis and thesis (q.v.) by variance in voice pitch. The "pitch accent" reflected syllable quantity: a syllable was "long" if its vowel was long or diphthongized or if its vowel was short and followed by two consonants (including, in the case of a final syllable, the initial consonant of a following word); a syllable was "short" if its vowel was short and followed by a single consonant sound (see CLASSICAL PROSODY). Vowel quantity can be illustrated by the word *"ibidem"*: the first *i* is short, the second long (by classical standards); in pronunciation the two sounds would correspond respectively to the first and second *i* of "intrigue." (Similarly using the macron (−) to indicate length and the micron (˘) to indicate brevity:

m̄achine, f̄ather, m̆et, m̄eet; ŏbey, m̄ole, p̆ut, cl̄ue.

The Gr. quantitative pitch accent was succeeded by the L. quantitative stress accent, in tune with L. speech and early L. verse patterns, e.g., the Saturnian (q.v.); this succession partially anticipated the full (nonquantitative) stress accent of medieval L. and modern European poetry.

The stress accent of modern languages, including Fr., makes it practically impossible, except by sheer artifice, to divide syllables into "longs" and "shorts." Modern versification depends upon syllable-counting (syllabic verse: flexible in Eng. and German, rigid in Polish and Fr.) and the occurrence of naturally stressed syllables (accentual verse). In Eng. and German the stressed syllables usually alternate with unstressed syllables; in Fr. they occur at the verse's caesura and end. It is safe to say that no modern language approximation to quantitative verse has been completely successful. The most that can be said for Robert Bridges' experiments with Eng. syllable quantities, in testing the theories of his friend W. J. Stone, is that quantity and stress coincide rather frequently. But "quantity" in Eng. is considerably erratic. Except for accent stress, the sounds *e* and *ie* in "believe" are quantitatively equal. But in a *scazon* verse Bridges scans the word as

be͞lie̅ve,

quantitatively invalid, but in keeping with modern stress. Modern language accent stress frequently determines vowel "quantity." In L. and Gr. the reverse is true. Some modern language syllables, when recorded on the kymograph, prove to be six times as "long" as others. Consonant clusters in the modern languages, with the exception of, e.g., It. and Sp., neither regularly render actual syllable quantity (except as in "below" and "bellow") nor regularly determine accent.

Generally, a modern approximation of a cl. meter involves the substitution of stress for quantity. Longfellow's

This is the forest primeval. The murmuring

pines and the hemlocks

would scan, according to quantitative principles alone, something like this: ˘−˘˘−−−− ˘−˘−−˘−. A dactyl, then, in the cl. situation, consists of a long syllable followed by 2 short syllables (−˘˘); in the modern situation it consists of a stressed syllable followed by 2 unstressed syllables (´ x x).

The earliest recorded attempt at quantitative "versing" in Fr. is the elegiac couplet written by Estienne Jodelle in 1558:

Phebus, Amour, Cypris, veut sauver, nourrir et orner

Ton vers cuer et chef, d'ombre, de flamme, de fleurs.

As in all such modern attempts it is not quantity as such, but coincidence of accent with "quantity" that marks the scheme. In or about 1567 Antoine de Baïf attempted to classify syllables as "longs" and "shorts" in effecting various "quantitative" strophes, such as the sapphic. His effort forced him to adopt phonetic spelling.

In 1555 Conrad Gessner, a German Swiss, produced a *Mithridates* in spondaic hexameters. Phrases like

$$\text{alle díe / eere}$$

show how questionable his "quantity" is. But his accent coincidence is quite regular. Dean W. R. Inge quotes Goethe's "pentameter" line,

$$\text{Rothstrúmpf ímmer gehásst und Víoletstrúmpf}$$
$$\text{dazu}$$

and rightly asks "If the vowel of *strumpf* is not long by position [i.e., followed by more than one consonant] what vowel can be?"

The Renaissance *literati*, in exalting, discovering, and reexamining literary products of the cl. world, were seriously concerned with the reproduction of cl. quantitative meters. Successful reproduction was limited, however, to the L. language itself, e.g., Petrarca's unfinished and unpublished *Africa* and the *Davidiad* of Marco Marulo (1450–1524) in 14 books. The vernacular languages did not and could not sustain quantitative distinctions. In Spain Estéban de Villegas produced sapphics and hexameters by substituting stress for quantity. Gabriello Chiabrera similarly attempted cl. meters, including the sapphic, in It. In France Ronsard and the Pléiade imitated Horace and translated his quantitative L. odes into stress-accentual Fr. verse. The Renaissance spirit of classicism is reintroduced into It. by the 19th-c. poet, Giosuè Carducci, whose *Odi barbari* (init. 1887) include cl. meters in stress-accentual modern It.

Rus. poetry does not originate before the post-Renaissance period (ca. 1650). There have not been many attempts made in Rus. to reproduce cl. quantitative meters. The "learned" meters include binary iambics and trochaics and ternary dactylics, amphibrachics ($\smile\acute{}\smile$) and anapaestics. Rus. verse disallows feet of more than 3 syllables (e.g., the proceleusmatic, $\smile\smile\smile\smile$).

Likewise stress-accentual is the meter in the modern Gr. "sequel" to the *Odyssey* by Nikos Kazantzakis. His verse measure comprises 17 syllables and 8 stresses. Traditionally, the modern Gr. verse measure comprises 15 syllables and 7 stresses. Kazantzakis achieved a closer approximation to the Homeric hexameters (5 dactyls and a spondee = 17 syllables) in the matter of syllabism but did not minimize the force of stress.

Early attempts to introduce quantitative verse into Eng. were mediocre at best. (See Thomas Watson's hexameter version of the first two lines of the *Odyssey*, noted by Roger Ascham in *The Scholemaster*, 1570.) In the discussion between Edmund Spenser and Gabriel Harvey the great problem began to appear: Should "length" be determined by cl. rules or by ear? Poetically, a high point of Eng. experiment in cl. meters was reached in the examples (especially "Rose-cheeked Laura") offered by Thomas Campion to illustrate his modified cl. system based on stress-equivalents to cl. feet (1602).

In the middle of the 17th c. John Milton "rendred almost word for word without Rhyme according to the Latin Measure [third asclepiadic strophe], as near as the Language will permit" an Eng. version of Horace's Ode 1.5:

$$\textit{Quis múlta grácilis te púer in rosa}$$

His first line, "What slender youth bedew'd with liquid odours," is not "according to the Latin Measure" of the poem, since it is more nearly an accentual approximation of the choliambic line. Possibly "without Rhyme . . . Measure" means simply "without rhyme as in Latin poetry"; but Horace's ode presents skillfully wrought internal rhyme. Milton's impatience with quantitative "versing" is expressed in his sonnet to Mr. H. Lawes. Of the many experiments in Eng. during the 19th c. none fully reproduced its cl. exemplar. Tennyson, intensely concerned with syllable quantity, concluded that the Eng. hexameter was "only fit for comic subjects." He comments accordingly in one of his humorous elegiac distichs:

$$\text{These láme hexámeters the stróng-wing'd}$$
$$\text{músic of Hómer!}$$
$$\text{No—but a most burlesque barbarous experi-}$$
$$\text{ment.}$$

The proper accents of "hexameters" and "experiment" have been sacrificed in the interest of "quantity." A. H. Clough used a stress-accentual hexameter for light effect:

$$\text{Tea and cóffee were there; a júg of wáter for}$$
$$\text{Héwson. . . .}$$

Swinburne's stress-accentual choliambics, sapphics, hendecasyllabics, and elegiacs show no concession to quantity. Both Tennyson and George Meredith imitated Catullus' galliambic. Tennyson's version is the more rigidly "quantitative": e.g.,

$$\text{Mad and máddening all that heard her in her}$$

fierce volubility.

His quantitative alcaic ode to Milton, e.g.

Whose Tītăn ăngēls, Gābrĭĕl, Ābdĭĕl . . .

Rīngs tŏ thĕ roar ŏf ăn angĕl ōnset

is perhaps as close to perfection as any Eng. poet has come in this endeavor. The 20th c. has seen no Tennysonian concern for quantitative cl.-verse equivalents. But accentual cl.-verse equivalents are still, indeed perennially, attempted, primarily in translation, e.g., J. B. Leishman's Horace, Helen R. Henze's *The Odes of Horace* (1961), and Rolfe Humphries' Ovid (*The Art of Love*, 1957).

STUDIES OF CLASSICAL METRICS: W. Christ, *Metrik der Griechen und Römer* (1874); J.H.H. Schmidt, *Introd. to the Rhythmic and Metric of the Cl. Languages*, tr. J. W. White (1883); Hardie; Dale; W. Rupprecht, *Einführung in die griechische Metrik* (3d ed., 1950); Kolář; Crusius; U. v. Wilamowitz-Moellendorff, *Griechische Verskunst* (2d ed., 1958); G. Thomson, *Gr. Lyric Metre* (2d ed., 1961).—MODERN LANGUAGES: Kastner; Schipper; W. R. Inge, "Cl. Metres in Eng. Poetry," Royal Soc. of Lit. of the United Kingdom, *Transactions*, 3d ser., 2 (1922); R. C. Trevelyan, "Cl. and Eng. Verse-Structure," E&S, 16 (1930); J. Körner, *Einführung in die Poetik* (1949); G. L. Hendrickson, "Elizabethan Quantitative Hexameters," PQ, 28 (1949); V. Turri, U. Renda, P. Operti, *Dizionario storico della letteratura italiana* (3d ed., 1951–52); R. Graves, "Harp, Anvil, Oar," *The Crowning Privilege* (1955); B. O. Unbegaun, *Rus. Versification* (1956); Beare; J. B. Leishman, *Translating Horace* (1958); J. Thompson, *The Founding of Eng. Metre* (1961); W. Bennett, *German Verse in Cl. Metres* (1963).   R.A.S.

CLASSICAL POETICS. 1. DEFINITION. Cl. poetics can be defined in either of two ways: (1) as the aggregate of opinions and doctrines which were put forward concerning poetry during cl. antiquity, i.e., roughly, between 750 B.C. and A.D. 200, or (2) as that more or less coherent body of critical doctrine which is represented for us chiefly by the *Poetics* of Aristotle and the so-called *Ars Poetica* of Horace and which gave rise, during the Renaissance, to the poetic creed called "classicism" (q.v.). We shall take the term here in the first and broader of the two senses, but with particular attention to the origin and development of classicism.

2. PRE-PLATONIC POETICS AND CRITICISM. So far as the Western world is concerned, the very concept of poetics, in fact of literary criticism in general, is a Gr. invention. Although it is a commonplace that criticism follows rather

than precedes the making of literature, in the case of the Greeks the striking thing is not how late the critical impulse was in making its appearance, but how early. Criticism followed close on the heels of poetry, and insisted from the beginning on raising fundamental questions and fundamental issues.

Before summarizing this earliest stage of Gr. criticism, we must point to certain tacit presuppositions which it shared with Gr. poetry itself and which underlie the whole later development, namely, that (1) the chief subject of poetry is man, his life—and death—, his actions, his happiness. (The Homeric gods, with their advanced anthropomorphism and their consuming interest in men, confirm rather than belie this principle.) (2) Poetry is a *serious, public concern*, the cornerstone of education and of civic life. (3) It is also a *delightful thing*, endowed with a fascination that borders on enchantment. (4) It is not merely terrestrial and utilitarian, but somehow or other *divine*, being inspired by the gods or the Muses. (5) It is at the same time an *art* (*techne*), a craft or profession, requiring native talent, training, and long practice. (6) The poet, though inspired from on high, is after all not a priest or a prophet but a *secular person*. His work is respected, even revered, but it can be criticized.

Some of these preconceptions can 'be detected in the Homeric poems themselves, especially the *Odyssey*; in any case the poems were later judged by the Greeks in terms of them. Gr. criticism was born and grew to maturity on Homer, assuming implicitly that he was—as indeed he had become—the teacher of his people. The earliest criticisms were not "literary" or aesthetic but moral and philosophical, and the issues they raised were fundamental ones, as to the truth and moral value of poetry. Hesiod (7th c. B.C.; *Theogony* 27–28) and Solon (early 6th c.; frag. 21 Diels) agree that, as the latter puts it, "The bards tell many a lie." Xenophanes (end of the 6th c., beginning of the 5th) objects to the immoral goings-on of Homer's gods and casts ridicule on the whole concept of anthropomorphism; see frags. 11–16 Diels. These are, for us, the opening guns of what Plato (*Republic* 10) calls "the ancient feud between poetry and philosophy." The objectors grant that poetry, especially the epic, is a source of delight and the recognized custodian of truth and moral values, but insist that she is an unworthy custodian. This struggle between poetry and philosophy for the position of teacher to the Gr. people is of fundamental importance for later theory.

One way of saving Homer's gods was to take their quarrels as representing conflicts of natural elements (earth, air, etc.) or of social and political principles. This "allegorical interpretation," which was to have a long history, originally sprang from a scientific motive and went hand in hand with the rise of cosmology and the natural sciences. Appearing as early as the end of the 6th c. (Theagenes of Rhegium), it was adopted by some of the Sophists and later by the Stoics, though rejected by Plato (*Phaedrus*).

The aristocratic Theban poet Pindar (518–ca. 445 B.C.) shows an interesting blend of traditional and personal attitudes toward poetry. For him it is (see particularly his *First Olympian* and *First Pythian*) both a high and exacting craft and a thing inspired. The poet's wisdom (*sophia*) embraces technical proficiency and insight into truth; his mission is to glorify great prowess or achievement ("virtue," *arete*) and guide his fellow men. Pindar was conscious of the dubious morality of some of the older tales. His solution was to "pass by on the other side" and leave them untold.

In the 5th c. poetry was still, as it had always been, the basis of primary education and an official repository of truth. But two potent new forces came into play at Athens which enhanced and at the same time threw doubt upon the honor traditionally paid to it. These were (1) the drama and (2) the Sophists. Tragedy and comedy, with their vividness of presentation and their semiofficial status, tended to bring every citizen into direct contact with literature and make him a potential critic. Moreover the Old Comedy arrogated to itself the right to satirize anything and everything, including poetry. The Sophists were characteristically, in addition to their other activities, grammarians, philologians, and expounders of literature. But they were also, characteristically, rationalists, skeptics, and positivists, and the net effect of their teaching was to break down traditional standards, in literature as in other fields. It has been suggested but not proved that Gorgias was the first promulgator of a poetic theory; in any case he had a shrewd and accurate idea of the *effect*, particularly the emotional effect, of poetry on its hearers.

We can gauge the impact of these new tendencies by the reaction they called forth in Athens' premier comedian and judicial critic, Aristophanes (ca. 445–ca. 385 B.C.). His brilliant gift for literary satire, especially parody, was exercised above all on Euripides and other representatives of modernism (intellectualism, skepticism, preciosity, etc.) in poetry. His unremitting crusade against Euripides (see particularly the *Acharnians* and the *Thesmophoriazusae*) reaches its climax in the *Frogs* (405 B.C.), the most sparkling exhibit of judicial criticism in antiquity. Aeschylus, champion of old-fashioned moral principles and lofty style, finally wins his bout against the challenger

Euripides—logic-chopper, corrupter of morals, and writer of dull prologues—but not before the two combatants have agreed (lines 1009, 1055) that the poet's duty is to instruct and improve his fellow citizens. We may be sure that most Athenians accepted this principle, at least in theory.

3. PLATO (427–347 B.C.). With Plato, a born poet and lover of poetry who renounced it for the higher truth of philosophy, the "ancient feud" reaches a major climax and crisis. There is no room in Plato's thought for literary criticism or theory as a separate intellectual pursuit. Truth is one, and Poetry must appear before that inflexible judge on the same terms as any other human activity. Nevertheless the great issue of the justification of literature haunted Plato all his life, and he grapples with it repeatedly in the dialogues—nowhere, however, in truly complete and systematic form. He tends to view poetry from two quite different, perhaps incommensurate, points of view: as "inspiration" (*enthousiasmos*) and as "imitation" (*mimesis*). Seen inwardly, in its native character as experience, poetry is inspiration or "possession," a form of madness quite beyond the poet's control. The reality of the experience is unquestionable; its source and value remain an enigma. Is it merely irrational, i.e., subrational (*Ion*; cf. the end of the *Meno*), or might there be a suprarational poetic inspiration, winged by Love (Eros), that could attain Truth (*Phaedrus*)? The question is left open. Meanwhile, viewed externally, in its procedures and its product, poetry appears as "imitation" (q.v.), and as such falls under the ban of excommunication (*Republic* 3, 10) or at least under rigid state control (*Laws* 2 and 7). Plato's utterances about poetry have a deep ambivalence which has aroused fascinated interest, but also fierce protest, ever since. Outwardly he seems one with the Puritans and obscurantists who have always wanted to banish or muzzle the poetic impulse; inwardly he is one of those who feel poetry to be, not merely a technical pursuit and not merely a representation of men, or action, or whatever, but a *communication from the soul*: supremely personal, then—and supremely dangerous.

4. ARISTOTLE (384–322 B.C.). Aristotle was no poet. His cooler spirit was devoted to poetry in quite another way: as an objective, uniquely valuable presentation of human life in a particular medium. The *Poetics* is not formally or in method a polemical work, but in effect it constitutes an answer to Plato's doubts and objections and thereby a resolution of the "ancient feud." Here, conducted in a dispassionate, scientific spirit, is an inquiry into the nature of poetry which restores it to an honorable—not a supreme—place in the scheme of things. The heart of Aristotle's achievement

is a new theory of *poetic structure,* based on a new concept of "imitation" not as a copying of ordinary reality but as a generalized or idealized rendering of character and action (ch. 9). In proportion as poetry attains this goal it approaches the condition of drama, and the drama, as the most perfectly objective presentation of action, is the supreme poetic genre (ch. 4, 26). In Aristotle's eyes, that which constitutes poetry is not the writing of verses but the building of a poetic "structure of events." This structure is the plot (*mythos*) of the poem; it therefore is by far the most important part of the poet's task (ch. 6, 9). The other constituent elements of the poem, or rather of the art of making a poem (*poiesis,* "making"), viz. (1) character portrayal (*ethos*), (2) "thought" (*dianoia*), i.e., the presentation of ideas or arguments by the characters, (3) poetic language or expression (*lexis*), (4) song composition (*melopoiia*), and (5) costuming (*opsis*), stand in decreasing order of importance (ch. 6); none can vie with plot. The making of plots is essentially a creative activity. But poetic creativity is not, for Aristotle, a subjective efflorescence. It goes to the bodying forth of reality, the essential truth about human beings and their actions, not the invention of fantasies or private worlds.

A poetic structure should be *beautiful.* This requires (a) unity (the famous "unity of action"; see UNITY), (b) symmetry of the parts with each other and with the whole, and (c) proper length, such that the poem can make a sizable aesthetic impression but not so great as to blur or dissipate it. The crux of the matter is the unity of action, and the corollary —duly emphasized by Aristotle himself—is that the events which constitute the action must succeed each other according to the law of necessity or probability. This is what he means by the famous statement (ch. 9) that poetry treats of "universals" while history deals with particulars.

A tragedy ought to be not only serious and beautiful, but tragic as well (whether this requirement also applies to the epic is a question to which the *Poetics* gives no clear answer). Plato had said (*Republic,* 10) that poetry threatens the moral equilibrium in states and individuals alike by "feeding" the appetitive and emotional side of human nature, especially its tendencies to pity and fear. Aristotle implicitly sets aside this verdict. But he also calls for something to be done to or with or through pity and fear which he designates by the obscure term "catharsis" (q.v.). All that can be said with confidence is that the tragic catharsis somehow represents a defense and acceptance of the emotional side of the drama, against Plato. If pity and fear are desirable effects of tragedy, certain kinds of plot are better fitted

to arouse them than others. All tragic actions involve a change or passage from one pole of human fortune—"happiness" or "unhappiness" —to the other (ch. 7, end). In a simple plot the change is direct, unilinear; in a complex plot it is brought about by a sudden and unexpected reversal (*peripety*), or a recognition (*anagnorismos*), or both (ch. 11). Aristotle demands that the hero who undergoes the tragic vicissitude be a good man, but not a perfect one. The change to unhappiness, which is the tragic change *par excellence,* should not be caused by wickedness but by some *hamartia* (ch. 13). Here, as in the case of "catharsis," battles of interpretation have raged (does *hamartia* mean "moral flaw" or simply "error"?), without conclusive result. Aristotle further prescribes (ch. 15) that the tragic characters be "appropriate," i.e., true to type; "like," i.e., true to life or human nature in general; and self-consistent.

Aristotle regarded the linguistic side of the poet's activity as needful in order to please and impress the public, but ultimately less important than plot construction and character-drawing. The first virtue of poetic diction, as of language in general, is to be *clear* (ch. 22). But it should also not be "low": that is, it should maintain a certain elevation above the level of ordinary life, through the use of archaic, foreign, or unfamiliar words, ornamental epithets, and figures, especially metaphor. For further remarks on style, including poetic style, see Book 3 of the *Rhetoric.*

The discussion of the epic (ch. 23–25) forms a kind of appendix to Aristotle's analysis of tragedy. Its outstanding feature is that he measures the epic by the drama and insists that it should follow the model of the latter as far as it possibly can. The logical, though paradoxical, result is that Homer figures as the supreme poet not so much *qua* epic poet as *qua* dramatist. The epic should have a central action, like tragedy, but may "dilute" it generously with episodes. It also has a special license to deal in marvels and the supernatural. In these, and indeed in all respects, Homer is the perfect exemplar.

Aristotle's main discussion of comedy is lost (it was contained in a second book), but enough remains to show that he disliked the formlessness and satiric bent of the Old Comedy and approved the trend of his own time (represented subsequently by the New Comedy and its imitators at Rome, Plautus and Terence) toward regular plots and the humorous portrayal of generalized character types rather than the pillorying of individuals.

The *Poetics* is a work of paramount importance, not only historically, as the fountainhead of "classicism," but in its own right. But from neither point of view is it a complete treatise on poetry. Aside from the loss of the main discussion of comedy, it deals only sparsely and obliquely with the epic and all but ignores lyric, not to mention other genres which were not cultivated in Aristotle's day. Moreover it is very uncertain whether the *Poetics* was directly known to anybody in antiquity after Aristotle's death, though many of his ideas were transmitted by his pupils. In any case the fully developed doctrine of classicism embraces a number of interests and attitudes which are not Aristotelian, and which still remain to be accounted for.

5. HELLENISTIC POETICS (3d–1st c. B.C.). Both poetry and poetic criticism were carried on in a new environment in the Hellenistic age. The center of gravity in literature, as in other fields, shifted from old Greece, with its civic traditions, to Alexandria, Pergamum, and other royal courts. Alexandria in particular, with its Library and "Museum"—originally sprung from the Lyceum—was a hive of *literary scholarship* (philology, grammar, editing of texts, *Literaturgeschichte*), with which criticism now came in close contact. Indeed we owe the terms "critic" and "criticism" to the Hellenistic grammarians, who regarded the judgment of poems, *krisis poiematon,* as the climax and capstone of their art. The typical critic is now a scholar who dabbles in poetry and poetic theory. Unfortunately, of the lively critical squabbles of the time we have only *disjecta membra* such as Callimachus' disparagements of long poems: "I loathe the cyclic poem" and "Big book, big nuisance" (it may be only a coincidence that he was the compiler of the catalogue of the Alexandrian Library, in 120 volumes), or Eratosthenes' dictum that "poetry is for delight."

We can, however, make out that two ideas of basic importance for the development of classicism were, if not invented, at least given canonical form in the Hellenistic period: (a) the concept of a "classic" (the word is Roman but the idea Gr.), and (b) the concept of genre. A belief which had been implicit in the *Poetics* was now proclaimed explicitly, that the great age of poetry lay in the past (7th through 5th c.) and that it contained all the models of poetic excellence. This backward-looking view was enshrined in official lists (*kanones*): the Nine Lyric Poets, the Three Tragedians, etc. Further, each poetic "kind" was thought of as an entity more or less to itself, with its special laws of subject matter, arrangement, and style, and its particular supreme model, Homer for epic, Sappho or Alcaeus for love poetry, Archilochus for "iambic" poetry, and so on. These ideas needed only to be reinforced by the rhetorically inspired idea of imitation (see below, section 7) to become the full-fledged doctrine of classicism. Since the genres were defined primarily by their versification and style, a further result was a tendency toward absorption in style at the expense of other interests.

The philosophical schools participated unevenly in the critical development. The Stoics officially approved of poetry, especially the Homeric epic, but tended to judge it by moral and utilitarian standards and therefore indulged rather freely in the allegorizing of Homer. Orthodox Epicureanism frowned on poetry as "unnatural" and a bait for the passions, but Philodemus, an Epicurean (1st c. B.C.) and himself a poet, put forward a theory that recognized multiple forms and aims of poetry and granted wide autonomy to the poet. Philodemus lived at Rome and Naples for many years and had influence on Horace and other Roman poets. From polemical remarks of his we can further reconstruct a Peripatetic doctrine, put forward by one Neoptolemus of Parium in the 3rd c., which has been shown to underlie Horace's *Ars Poetica.* In it the subject was treated under the triple heading of *poiesis,* the poetic process of composition, *poiema,* the poem, and *poietes,* the poet. Actually *poiesis* had to do chiefly with the selection or invention and the arrangement of subject matter (*hypothesis* or *pragmata; res*) and *poiema* chiefly with style (*lexis; elocutio*).

Others, for example the Platonizing Stoic Posidonius (1st c. B.C.), accepted at least parts of this scheme, and it provided a handy framework for discussion of three cardinal issues that were much agitated in the Hellenistic period: (a) which is more important, subject matter or expression? (b) which is the purpose or function of poetry, instruction or delight? and (c) which is more essential for the poet, native genius (*physis; igenium*) or art (*techne; ars*)? In these formulations we see the cl. poetics taking on the physiognomy which it was to keep down through the Renaissance. The answers were various. We have already quoted Eratosthenes' dictum that the end of poetry is delight; others, especially among the Stoics, argued the claims of (moral) instruction; while the Peripatetic view called for both (Horace: "omne tulit punctum qui miscuit utile dulci"). Similarly with the debate over subject matter and style. It would seem, however, that a considerable amount of tacit agreement underlay the dispute, namely that poetry is a way of discoursing about "things," and that these things, whether matters of historical or scientific fact (*historia; fama*), myth (*mythos; fabula*), or pure invention (*plasma; res ficta*), were all equally admissible (hence, e.g., didactic poetry, which Aristotle had excluded from the realm of poetry altogether) and had essentially the status of facts, i.e., were to be judged by reference to the ordinary laws of reality.

Nowhere do we find a reaffirmation of Aristotle's principle that the objects of poetry are universals.

6. HORACE (65–8 B.C.). We have devoted what may seem a disproportionate amount of space to the Hellenistic period because, although most of its critical production is lost, it played an even more important role than Plato or Aristotle in the rise of classicism and exerted a decisive influence upon Roman and therefore upon Renaissance thinking about poetry. The most significant transmitter of this influence is Horace. To be sure, neither Horace nor his literary milieu was Gr. He was a thorough Italian, blessed with a consuming interest in people, a sharp eye for their foibles—and his ówn—, and sturdy independence of judgment. He came to literary criticism by an indirect road, through satire, and to the end his treatment of it remained occasional and essentially unsystematic. Criticism of his own Satires led him (Satires 1.4 and 10) to a spirited defense of the genre and of his right to pursue it in his own way. He admits that satire is not quite true poetry, because it lacks inspiration and sublimity of style (1.4.43: "mens divinior atque os magna sonaturum"); but it performs a useful and honorable social function by exposing vice and folly. Attacked for depreciating his predecessor Lucilius, Horace insists (1.10) on appropriateness of style and above all on elegance and polish, attained by hard work. Again and again (Satires 2.1.12ff.; Epistles 2.1.208, 250ff.; cf. Odes 1.6; 4.2) he resists the importunities of well-meaning friends, urging him to write epic or drama: it is essential that the poet choose and stick to the genre or genres for which he is best fitted.

These themes recur in the three major critical letters in verse which constitute the second Book of the Epistles, but against a broader background. The Epistle to Augustus (2.1) surveys the current literary scene, derides the blind worship of the poetry of the past (the Roman past), and deplores the vulgarity of popular taste. The essay, with its blend of urbanity and seriousness, reveals especially well two important aspects of Horace's classicism: (1) He felt deeply that Rome deserved and was capable of a great literature, to set alongside that of cl. Greece; but (2) he was convinced that the result could be achieved only by hard work and the emulation of that same cl. Gr. literature. Thus classicism was in Horace's eyes a progressive and patriotic creed, the means to a specifically Roman achievement. The paradox has significant parallels in the Renaissance, in both Italy and France.

The Epistle to Florus (2.2) returns to one of Horace's favorite themes, the haste and sleaziness of much of the current scribbling of poetry ("scribimus indocti doctique poemata passim"). But it is in the Epistle to the Pisos (2.3), the so-called Ars Poetica, that he gives fullest expression to his view of poetry. Based though it is on the Hellenistic poetics mentioned above (section 5), it carefully maintains the easy, discursive air appropriate to its genre: it is after all a verse epistle, not a formal treatise. Still, the tone is a shade more systematic and apodictic than usual. Poiesis (see above, section 5) is dealt with summarily in the first 45 lines, with a plea for poetic unity. The rest of the first section, down to line 294, really treats of Horace's main interest: style and matters connected therewith—originality and appropriateness (decorum—46–98); emotional appeal (99–113); faithfulness either to poetic tradition or to general type in character portrayal (114–178). As he progresses it becomes clear that Horace, following the Peripatetic doctrine (not the state of affairs at Rome in his own day), is assuming the drama, and particularly tragedy, to be the major poetic genre. Hence we find a number of detailed prescriptions for the dramatist (179ff.: no deed of violence on stage; five acts, no more and no less; three actors; choral odes germane to the plot; etc.), a thumbnail history of the drama, interrupted by a long passage on the satyr-play, and finally (280ff.), the adjuration— really the most important of all in Horace's codex—to polish, polish, polish ("the labor of the file") rather than publish, publish, publish. The last section of the poem (295–476), is devoted to the poet: his training (309–332), with emphasis on moral philosophy (Socratic dialogues); his purpose, which may be either to profit or to please or, best of all, to do both (333–346); his faults, venial and otherwise (347–390); his need for both ability and training, and for unsparing criticism (419–452). The end-piece (453–476), is an uproarious sketch, in Horace's best satirical vein, of the mad poet.

Our summary may suggest how many of the leading ideas of classicism are enshrined in the Ars Poetica. What no summary, and no translation, can convey is the brilliance of the poem as a poem: not in its structure but in its texture, its striking figures, and memorable phrases. "Purpureus pannus" (purple patch, q.v.); "brevis esse laboro, obscurus fio"; "in medias res" (q.v.); "bonus dormitat Homerus," and dozens of others have passed into the common stock. To the It. critics of the Renaissance, Latinists and stylists all, it was a breviary. They might admire Aristotle; Horace was in their bones. And they learned more from him than rules. He encouraged them in the proud belief that poetry is an honorable and exacting craft, fit to offer serious counsel and occupy a high place in a nation's culture.

7. RHETORICAL CRITICISM, GREEK AND ROMAN. The establishment of rhetoric as the prevail-

ing mode of higher education, especially at Rome in the 1st c. B.C. (in Greece proper it goes back to the 4th c.), had major effects on both poetry and poetics. Poetry itself began to show rhetorical tendencies; and, more important for our purpose, literary criticism now tended to become the professional property of the rhetoricians. (Horace is the lone exception among extant critics from this period.) In the rhetorical schools poets were read, and to an increasing extent imitated, on the same basis as prose writers. This practice helped to foster the extension of two influential concepts from the rhetorical sphere to the poetic: (1) "imitation," in the sense of imitation of authors (see IMITATION), and (2) the analysis of style into three (occasionally four) kinds or levels, high, middle, and low or plain (see SUBLIME). It also tended to dislodge poetry from its old preeminence, in favor of a more catholic and eclectic view of all "literature" (grammata; litterae), prose and verse alike, as belonging to a liberal education.

The extant critical works which represent this trend all belong—not by accident—to the 1st c. B.C. and A.D. We can mention them here only briefly, without distinction between Greeks and Romans (in any case rhetorical study and theory in that period were essentially international). The treatises of "Demetrius" On Style (1st c. B.C.?) and of Dionysius of Halicarnassus On Literary Composition (actually on the placing of words; perhaps around 10 B.C.), though technical and rhetorical in nature, deal with prose and poetry impartially. Poets like Sappho, Pindar, Sophocles, Euripides, and above all Homer, are cited and analyzed, particularly by Dionysius, in illuminating detail. Cicero is a conservative but intelligent and informed critic of poetry, ancient and modern, a not contemptible poet himself, and a firm believer (see particularly the speech For Archias and the De Oratore) in the necessity of a liberal, i.e., a literary, education for the orator and man of affairs. Tacitus's Dialogue on Orators (date uncertain; perhaps a youthful work) canvasses the reasons for the decline of oratory and of literature in general, and presents poetry as a garden of refreshment and delight, a retreat from the hurly-burly of everyday life. Quintilian, Imperial Professor of Rhetoric, incorporated into Book 10 of his major work, the Institutio Oratoria (The Training of the Orator; after A.D. 88) a complete thumbnail sketch and appraisal of all the important Gr. and L. authors, poets and prose writers, from the point of view of their uses in education and as exemplars of style.

"Longinus" (see SUBLIME) stands apart, a "sport" among the rhetoricians. In his lexicon, Homer and Archilochus, Pindar and Sophocles figure equally with Plato and Demosthenes—

Homer, in fact, above the rest—as models of greatness of spirit. It is he who gives us the best definition of a classic, as a work that has pleased men of all ages, tastes, and situations throughout the centuries. "Longinus'" enthusiasm for great literature is perennially infectious. But with his indifference to poetic structure, and to genre and the rules of genre, he really stands outside the tradition of classicism as it was formulated in antiquity.

8. SURVIVAL AND INFLUENCE. Ancient criticism was never, at any stage of its history, a continuing, stable enterprise. Its survival into the modern world was even more precarious. From cl. Greece, only Aristophanes, Plato, and Aristotle outlasted antiquity. Plato, though preserved complete, was not completely known or studied in the West until the Renaissance, and then seen mainly through Neoplatonic spectacles. The Poetics survived only as a torso (see above) and apparently by accident, through its inclusion in a miscellany of rhetorical works by "Demetrius," Dionysius, and others. A medieval L. translation by William of Moerbeke (1278) has come to light in the last twenty years; otherwise the treatise was available to the Middle Ages and the early Renaissance only in a L. translation of an Arabic paraphrase by Averroes. Horace and the Roman rhetoricians were never lost, though considerable parts of Cicero and Quintilian were not recovered until the Renaissance.

Poetic theory could not flourish as such in the Middle Ages, being assigned normally, like rhetoric, to a humble place in the trivium, as a part of grammar or logic. Petrarch and his followers, the humanists of the early Renaissance, began the process of recovery of the ancient heritage, but only gradually and, as it were, backward. The literary ideal of the Quattrocento was the Poeta Orator, and its critical attitudes were mainly Horatian, rhetorical, and based on L. literature. To the early It. humanists, whose consuming passions were L. style (in prose and verse) and personal glory, Horace, Cicero, and Quintilian spoke a familiar language that the Greeks could not rival. Plato, however, was drawn to some extent into the battle over the defense of poetry, which gained new point from the reawakened enthusiasm for pagan literature. In this struggle it was natural that he should appear now on the side of the attackers, e.g., Savonarola (in the De Divisione ac Utilitate Omnium Scientiarum, ca. 1492), now on that of the defense: in the latter case either for the idea of inspiration or for the notion—actually Neoplatonic in origin—that the artist creates according to a true "Idea."

Systematic theorizing about the art of poetry as such, its nature, effects, and species, appears only in the 16th c., in the train of the rediscovery and gradual dissemination of the *Poetics* (L. tr. by Giorgio Valla, 1498; *editio princeps* of the Gr. text, *Aldus*, 1508; L. tr. by Paccius [Pazzi], 1536, It. by Segni, 1549; commentaries by Robortelli, 1548, Madius [Maggi], 1550, Victorius [Vettori], 1560, Castelvetro, 1570, and many others). The first treatises on poetics, by Vida (1527), and Daniello (1536), were still essentially L. and Horatian. It was Minturno's *De Poeta* (1559) and Scaliger's *Poetices Libri Septem* (1561), together with Castelvetro's commentary, that established Aristotle's dictatorship over literature; but even these works are only very imperfectly and halfheartedly Aristotelian.

In spite of the rage for "Longinus" in the 18th c., and sporadic phenomena like Shelley's literary Platonism in the 19th, the prestige and influence of cl. poetics have waned steadily since Lessing's dethronement of the "French" —actually the It.—rules (*Hamburgische Dramaturgie*, 1767–69). The last twenty years, however, have witnessed a revival of critical allegiance to Aristotle, on the part of the so-called Chicago school (see CHICAGO CRITICS) and others (see IMITATION). The interest of this newest phase of Aristotle's influence is that he is now being viewed and interpreted directly, instead of through the distorting prism of Horace and the cl. tradition as a whole.

PRIMARY WORKS. (1) PLATO: *Ion; Phaedrus; Republic* 10. For these dialogues as well as the remarks on poetry scattered through other dialogues see the standard tr. of B. Jowett (5 v., 1892); *Phaedrus, Ion*, etc., tr. L. Cooper (1938); *Republic*, tr. F. M. Cornford (1941). (2) ARISTOTLE: *Poetics:* See L. Cooper and A. Gudeman, *A Bibliog. of the Poetics of A.* (1928), with supp. by M. T. Herrick, AJP, 52 (1931); G. F. Else, "A Survey of Work on A.'s Poetics," CW, 48 (1954–55). *Eds. with Gr. text and comment.:* A. Rostagni (1927, 2d ed. 1945; best ed., excellent It. introd. and notes); A. Gudeman (1934; radical text, fullest comment [German], but judgments erratic). *Text, tr., and comment.:* I. Bywater (1909; text outdated, but only complete comment. in Eng.; tr. often repr.); S. H. Butcher, *A.'s Theory of Poetry and Fine Art* (4th ed. 1911, repr. 1951; good text, standard Eng. tr., essays in lieu of comment.; excellent but sometimes overmodernizes A.); mod. Gr.: S. Menardos (tr.) and I. Sykutris (excellent text, comment., introd.; 1937). *Text and tr.:* S. H. Butcher (4th ed. 1907; as cited above, without essays); French: J. Hardy (1932; "Budé" ed.). *Eng. tr. without text:* L. Cooper (2d ed. 1947; with supplementary illustrations for studs. of mod. lits.); L. J. Potts, *A. on the Art of Fiction* (1953; original, sometimes erratic); G. M. A. Grube (1958). "Amplified versions" of the *Poetics* include L. Cooper, *A. on the Art of Poetry* (1921), *An Aristotelian*

Theory of Comedy (1922). *Rhetoric:* ed. and tr. with comment. by E. M. Cope and J. E. Sandys (3 v., 1877). (3) HORACE: *Ars Poetica:* text and Eng. tr., H. Fairclough (Loeb ed.), 1929. Convenient for comparisons is A. S. Cook, *The Poetical Treatises of Horace, Vida, and Boileau* (1892). (4) RHETORICAL CRITICS: Demetrius, *On Style*, and Dionysius of Halicarnassus, *The Three Lit. Letters* and *On Lit. Composition* (1902, Loeb ed. 1927; 1901; 1910). Cicero, *Pro Archia, Brutus, Orator*, and *De Oratore*, all available in the Loeb series. Tacitus, *Dialogue on Oratory*, tr. W. Peterson (1914; Loeb). Quintilian, *Institutio Oratoria*, tr. H. E. Butler (4 v., 1920–22; Loeb). Longinus: see SUBLIME.

SECONDARY WORKS. (1) GENERAL: Besides the general histories of crit. by Saintsbury (thin and outdated) and Wimsatt and Brooks, see K. Borinski, *Die Antike in Poetik und Kunsttheorie* (2 v., 1914–24); C. S. Baldwin, *Ancient Rhetoric and Poetic* (1924; fresh and vigorous); E. E. Sikes, *The Gr. View of Poetry* (1931; somewhat sketchy); J. F. D'Alton, *Roman Lit. Theory and Crit.* (1931); J. W. H. Atkins, *Lit. Crit. in Antiquity* (2 v., 1934; full but not definitive); J. J. Donohue, *The Theory of Lit. Kinds* (2 v., 1943, 1949); W. C. Greene, "The Gr. Crit. of Poetry," HSCL, 20 (1950; good survey); A. D. Gomme, *The Gr. Attitude to Poetry and Hist.* (1954). (2) PRE-ARISTOTELIAN CRIT.: M. Pohlenz, "Die Anfänge d. gr. Poetik," *Göttinger Nachrichten* (1920); G. Finsler, *Platon und die Aristotelische Poetik* (1900); W. C. Greene, "Plato's View of Poetry," HSCP, 29 (1918). (3) ARISTOTLE: J. Vahlen, "Beiträge zu Aristoteles Poetik," SAWW (1865–67, repr. 1914; fundamental work of interpr.); A. Rostagni, "Aristotele e aristotelismo nella storia dell' estetica antica," *Studi Ital. di Filol. Class.*, n.s., 2 (1922; fullest survey); L. Cooper, *The Poetics of A., Its Meaning and Influence* (1923; brief, lucid); F. L. Lucas, *Tragedy in Relation to A.'s Poetics* (1927); A. P. McMahon, "Seven Questions on Aristotelian Definitions of Tragedy and Comedy," HSCP, 40 (1929); E. Bignami, *La Poetica di Aristotele* (1932); S. H. Butcher, *A.'s Theory of Poetry and Fine Art:* see above under primary works; H. House, *A.'s Poetics* (1956; shrewd, sensible); G. F. Else, *A.'s Poetics: the Argument* (1957); J. Jones, *On Aristotle and Gr. Tragedy* (1962). (4) HORACE: J. F. D'Alton, *Horace and His Age* (1917; ch. 7); G. C. Fiske and M. A. Grant, *Cicero's De Oratore and Horace's Ars Poetica* (1929); O. Immisch, "Horazens Epistel über die Dichtkunst," *Philologus*, Supplementband 24, Heft 3 (1932); C. O. Brink, *Horace on Poetry: Prolegomena to the Lit. Epistles* (1963). G.F.E.

CLASSICAL PROSODY is, with respect to Gr. and L., the science which deals with the nature of syllables, whereas meter is the technique of their arrangement. In its technical sense Gr. *prosōdia* (L. *accentus*) meant primarily accentuation as determined, in Gr. at any rate, by musical pitch; but the scope of the word was subsequently extended, and prosody is now regarded as describing the facts concerning the "quantities" of syllables, i.e., the time taken to pronounce them. Quantity, not stress, was the basis of cl. Gr. and L. metric, with the possible exception of the Saturnian measure in early L. Syllables were regularly either long (_) or short (ᴗ), the latter quantity being the time unit (Gr. *chronos*, L. *mora*), and a long syllable was conventionally regarded as equivalent in time value to two shorts (_ = ᴗᴗ). As variations of this simple "disemic" scheme, syllables with greater or less length than either quantity have been postulated in modern times on the ground that syllabic irrationality was apparently recognized in antiquity, not indeed by metricians, but in rhythmical and musical theory. But while the hypothesis of the existence of such irrational syllables in metric was acceptable to scholars of the 19th c. who tried to explain Gr. lyric meters in the light of their own conjectures about the accompanying music, it has little favor with the modern school which adheres to the "graphic" prosody of the long and short syllables of spoken verse. (See CYCLIC FOOT, DISEMIC and TRISEMIC, and MORA.)

Most Am., British, and German metricians, accustomed as they are to stress accent in their own languages, maintain that the L. accent was similar, and many have held that coincidences or clashes of *ictus* (q.v.) and accent were intentional in certain writers (e.g., Plautus and Virgil). But the existence of a pitch accent is arguable from the testimony of the Romans themselves, and Fr. scholars, with the example of their own language before them, are convinced that such was the nature of the L. accent, at any rate during the literary period. Whichever it was, in cl. and post cl. L. it conformed to the "penultimate law," whereby the accent of a dissyllabic word fell on its first syllable, while a polysyllabic word was accented on its last syllable but one if this was long, and on the syllable before that if the penultimate was short.

A syllable containing a short vowel was normally short if the vowel was followed by a single consonant either in the same word or at the beginning of the next, or by no consonant at all. In L. *qu* was regarded as a single consonant, *h* was ignored metrically as being no more than an aspirate [as in transliterated Gr.], and occasionally, in the republican period, a final *s* preceded by short *i* or *u* was disregarded if the following word began with a consonant, e.g.

mēntĭbŭs[s] căptī.

On the other hand a syllable was long by nature if it contained a long vowel or diphthong, and long by position if its vowel, being short, was followed either by a double consonant (zeta, xi, or psi in Gr. or *x* or *z* in L.), or by two or more consonants. However, since a mute and a liquid consonant in sequence (like *gr, pl, pr,* etc.) could be pronounced together, a syllable containing a short vowel which immediately preceded such a combination in the same word or at the beginning of the next might remain short or be scanned as long in verse (except that of Gr. comedy and early Roman tragedy and comedy where it was not lengthened), e.g.

ăgrestis

If, however, the mute and the liquid belonged to separate words or to separate parts of a compound word, the syllable was long by position, e.g.

incumbīt ripis, ōb-ruit

The varying quantity before a mute and a liquid is sometimes referred to as *syllaba anceps* (syllable with two possibilities), but the term is usually applied to the particular case where the final syllable of a verse was permitted to be either short or long.

Metricians and linguists, with the support of ancient authorities like Dionysius of Halicarnassus (1st c. B.C.), generally maintain that a syllable with a short vowel is long if it is "closed," i.e., ends with a consonant (or consonants) not belonging to the next syllable. This is so with the first (or more) of a group of consonants which, in their respective languages, cannot normally begin a Gr. or L. word, e.g., the syllables of *am|bo, an|trum,* or *sanc|tus* must be divided as shown. A double consonant is divisible between two syllables (e.g., *x = c + s*) and the combination of mute and liquid in the same word may be divided or not as occasion demands. But a single consonant between two vowels is assumed to belong to the syllable containing the second and (as a rule) at the end of a word to be theoretically transferable to the first syllable of the next word in the same verse, if this word has an initial vowel or diphthong, without regard to the intervening punctuation. Thus in the division of feet within the L. hexameter

exsequā|r. hanc etī|am, Mae|cena|s, aspice|

partēm

the final consonants of the first and fourth words belong respectively to the first syllables of the second and fifth feet. But the occasional retention of the final consonant with the word to which it belongs is at least a mechanical explanation of the not infrequent lengthening in hexameters of short syllables in the first place or "rise" of the feet to which they belong, e.g.

ipse ubi tempus erīt omnis in fonte lavabo.

The treatment in syllable division of the final consonant of a word is thus parallel to the functioning of vowel elision and hiatus. Elision occurred in Gr. when a word which began with a vowel or diphthong was preceded by another which ended with a short vowel other than *y* (or, on occasion, with the diphthongs *ai* and *oi*) and the first vowel (or diphthong) disappeared in the second. In L. verse it was usual for a vowel or diphthong (or for a short vowel followed by *m* which presumably nasalized it) to be likewise elided, although some scholars, particularly in continental Europe, prefer to apply the cl. term *synaloepha* (coalescing) to describe what happens to a long vowel or diphthong in elision. In written Gr., but not L., elision is regularly indicated by omitting the elided vowel and inserting an apostrophe, e.g., *legoim' an* for *legoimi an.* Hiatus on the other hand occurred when the final and the initial vowel or diphthong remained separated each in its own syllable, particularly when there was a recognized metrical division or sense-pause between them. A strong sense-pause, however, was not an obstacle to elision, which might take place even when there was simultaneously a change of speaker in drama. An example, first of elision and then of hiatus, is provided by the L. hexameter:

ūt vī|di (elision or *synaloepha* of the final *i*),

ūt perī|ī (hiatus), *ūt|me mălu|s abstuli|t error.*

In Gr. metric, when a short initial vowel was absorbed into a long vowel or diphthong at the end of the preceding word, this occurrence is called *aphaeresis* or *prodelision* and was especially common in dramatic verse. Akin to elision and prodelision are *crasis* (q.v.) and *synizesis* or the combination of two separate vowels within a word into one, e.g.,

deīnde for *deīnde.*

In L. the shortening, without elision or *synaloepha,* of a long before a short vowel in the next word, e.g.

an quī amant,

was, as a prosodic expedient, much rarer than in the Gr. hexameter or elegiac couplet,

where such "correption" of a long vowel or diphthong was convenient for either of the two shorts in the second half of a dactyl ($\_\smile\smile$) and can be illustrated by the shortening of the second element in

agroŭ ep' eschatiēs

and of the third in

andrā moĭ ennepe.

This too was a form of elision, inasmuch as the second of the two temporal units into which the quantity of the long syllable could be resolved ($\_=\smile\smile$) was elided to leave the first in its place. Other apparent anomalies of quantity in Homeric verse are often to be explained by the disappearance from the traditional text of consonants which were once valid in pronunciation, especially the digamma, which had the sound of L. *v* or Eng. *w.*

A knowledge of syllabic quantity is the indispensable introduction to any study of the various metrical forms. It is to be acquired in the first place only by means of a thorough acquaintance with vocalic quantity, which of course has to be learned by students of both languages as an essential of pronunciation. But, when this has been done, the laws of cl. prosody are on the whole straightforward.

E. Kalinka, "Griechisch-römische Metrik und Rhythmik im letzten Vierteljahrhundert," Bursian's *Jahresbericht,* 250 (1935), 290–507; 256 (1937), 1–126; 257 (1937), 1–160; A. M. Dale, "Gr. Metric 1936–1957," *Lustrum* 2 (1957), 5–51; P. W. Harsh, "Early L. Meter and Prosody 1935–1955," *Lustrum* 3 (1958), 215–280. —E. H. Sturtevant, *The Pronunciation of Gr. and L.* (2d ed., 1940); Kolář; P. Chantraine, *Grammaire Homérique: Tome I, Phonétique et Morphologie* (1948); J. D. Denniston and J. F. Mountford, "Metre, Gr." and "Metre, L.," respectively, *The Oxford Cl. Dict.* (1949), pp. 564–570 (with brief but important bibliog.); M. Platnauer, *L. Elegiac Verse* (1951); C. G. Cooper, *An Introduction to the L. Hexameter* (1952; contains a careful account of syllable division); Koster; Crusius; Beare; P. Maas, *Gr. Metre,* tr. H. Lloyd-Jones (1962).   R.J.G.

CLASSICISM. A definition of the term will be attempted here in the form of an analysis of its divergent and often contradictory meanings and of the different ways in which "classic" and "classical," root adjectives of "cl.," are understood. Six different meanings of "classic," "classical," and "cl." may be used as a frame of reference for a general definition. It should be emphasized that these meanings will not include connotations of the term "cl." in reference to arts other than literary (music, painting, architecture, etc.): the object of this analysis is solely to furnish a way of understanding the main contexts of cl. within the development of poetics and of the theory of literature.

A. As "Great" or "First Class." This meaning stems from the oldest application of the term to literary matters. Aulus Gellius, a grammarian of the 2d c. A.D., cites (*Noctes Atticae* 9.8) Cornelius Fronto as distinguishing a *scriptor classicus* from a *scriptor proletarius*, a "classical" from a "proletarian" writer. The terms *classicus* and *proletarius* were taken from Roman tax law: the first designated a member of the highest income bracket; the second, a wage-earner with an income below the taxable minimum. Fronto's distinction, as cited by Aulus Gellius, was made in reference to the use of genteel language by the *scriptor classicus* and was by that token alone a social distinction which the borrowing of terminology from the tax collectors served to enhance: the *scriptor classicus* writes for the few; the *proletarius*, for the many. This meaning of "classic" and "classical" has survived only indirectly: its original antonym, "proletarian," has become a term in Marxist criticism to designate the opposite of aristocratic or bourgeois literature. In the Soviet presentation of the literary history of Russia, however, predominant poetic styles in the reign of Catherine the Great, termed c. are contrasted with the contemporaneous rise of "popular" elements in letters —in this instance, the old Gellian dichotomy is preserved.

B. As "What Is Read in School." This meaning was first formed in the 6th c. A.D. by Magnus Felix Ennodius who spoke (*Dict.* 9) of a student who attends classes in school as a *classicus*. *Classicus* (*classique, classico*) was sometimes used by Fr. and It. Renaissance critics of the 16th c. to describe works of literature read in school. Since what is used as a school text was usually adjudged excellent, a combination of definition A ("first-rate") and of the present meaning formed a concept of cl. as denoting general excellence or "of value as a model" which will be discussed under the next heading. Modern Fr. and It. meanings of *classicisme* and *classicismo* are still colored, however, by the earlier association of the term with school usage of texts.

C. As a Term Used to Denote "Greatest" or "Standard" Works of Literature or Periods of Eminent Literary Development. This definition, still current in both Germanic and Romance languages, was first developed in the 16th c. Thomas Sebillet's *Art Poëtique Françoys* (1548) speaks of Alain Chartier and Jean de Meung as "bons et classiques poëtes françoys," i.e., as standard or model authors. The *Discorsi Fiorentini* (1581) of Agnolo Segni speak of "Autori classichi e toscani" in the

same sense. The *New Eng. Dictionary* gives instances of the use of "classicall" as synonymous with "canonical" or "worthy of imitation" for the years 1599 (Sir George Sandys) and 1608–11 (Bishop Hall). The German term *klassisch* (*classisch*) to denote standard works of literary excellence did not become current until the second half of the 18th c.

Modern uses of the term "classic" in this sense are the division of the history of letters into "classic ages" (e.g., the Elizabethan Age as the classic age of Eng. literature), ages of highest poetic achievement rather than of specific literary forms, and the naming of collections which include works of recognized merit, though of no common literary form, as "classics." Thus the *Harvard Classics* include the *Arabian Nights* and Charles Darwin's *Voyage of the "Beagle"* as well as the *Odyssey* and the *Aeneid*. *Les Classiques Français du Moyen Age* contain over 80 outstanding literary products of the Middle Ages in France which, for the most part, have no connection with that form of Fr. literature called cl. Sainte-Beuve, Babbitt, and others have attempted to give formal definitions of what a classic, understood as a work of general excellence, should be. T. S. Eliot's answer to *What is a Classic?* (1944) is that such a work must be the product of a mature civilization reflected in a mature mind and must show a "common style" which fully exploits the possibilities of the language in which the work is composed. Further, a classic should comprehensively represent the spirit of the nationality it belongs to and have some claim to universal meaning, to dealing with questions of general philosophical import.

D. As Specifically Gr. and Roman—Cl.—As the Imitation of Ancient Gr., and Roman Authors. As the writers of Gr. and Roman antiquity became increasingy standardized both as models for imitation and as school-texts, a fused meaning of definitions A, B, and C ("first-rate," "school-text," "standard work") became current in the 17th c.: Cl. was made synonymous with the imitation of Gr. and Roman authors who, in turn, captured the appelation "classics" as a collective term for their works. At present this meaning still stands. In the 20th c., critics use it, however, to designate two different practices: sometimes cl. denotes the imitation of Gr. and L. themes in the modern literatures (as in G. Highet, *The Classical Tradition*, 1949); at other times, cl. is taken to mean the imitation of Gr. and Roman literary forms in composing works on any theme. It is thus necessary to divide the discussion of this definition into one of *thematic* and one of *formal* imitation.

D. 1. *As the thematic imitation of Gr. and Roman models.* Under this heading, much of

Roman literature constituted cl. in that Gr. letters furnished its themes. Seneca's imitation of Aeschylus, Sophocles, and Euripides; and Virgil's emulation of Homeric themes would be cases in point. In modern literature, thematic imitation of Graeco-Roman models began with the Fr. and German courtly romances of the 12 c. (Benoît de Saint Maure's *Le Roman de Troie*, Heinrich von Veldeke's *Eneit*). These inaugurated a tradition, continuous to the present, of recasting Gr. and Roman stories into the language of the day and country. To a great degree, this meaning of cl. was to merge with the emulation of Gr. and Roman poetic forms (See D. 2., below). In the late 19th and early 20th c., however, many works have used Graeco-Roman myth and legend as an apt commentary on perennial human problems, though their authors paid no heed to the literary forms in which their stories had been cast in Gr. and Roman literature. In the field of lyric poetry, Stéphane Mallarmé's *L'Après Midi d'un Faune* (1876), Carl Spitteler's *Der Olympische Fruehling* (1900–10), and T. S. Eliot's *The Waste Land* (1922) could be cited as notable examples of this trend. The modern novel shows this aspect of cl. in James Joyce's *Ulysses* (1922), André Gide's *Thésée* (1946), and Elisabeth Langgaesser's *Die maerkische Argonautenfahrt* (1950). Notable examples in drama are O'Neill's *Mourning Becomes Electra*, Sartre's *Les Mouches*. In the 20th c., anthropology, psychiatry, and psychology have also added to renewed interest in the thematic imitation of Graeco-Roman models. Sir J. G. Frazer (1854–1941), in *The Golden Bough*, showed Gr. and Roman myth to be linked to the agricultural and sexual myths of primitive peoples and hence to be of far more general import to the understanding of the human imagination than had been supposed before. Sigmund Freud (1856–1939), looking at Gr. myth from his psychoanalytic point of view, found it to illustrate striking parallels to certain unconscious drives manifested in the symbolic pattern of dreams. Some of the neurotic situations in the Freudian system received Gr. mythological names (Oedipus complex, Electra complex). Finally, the work of C. G. Jung (1875–1961) has shown myth to be an aspiration of the "collective unconscious," i.e., a wish-fulfillment of desires perennially present in man. Frazer's anthropology, Freud's psychoanalysis, and Jung's research in psychology have all contributed heavily to the present resurgence of interest in Graeco-Roman myth and legend which is reflected in 20th-c. literature.

D. 2. *Cl. as the Formal Imitation of Gr. and Roman models.* Cl. in this sense concerns the attempt to construct, from Gr. and L. sources, a poetics for vernacular literature. The imitation of modern "classical" poetics in the crea-

tion of vernacular literature is also subsumed here. Two works of antiquity, one Gr., the other Roman, may be used as keys to an understanding of formal cl.: Aristotle's *Poetics* and Horace's *Art of Poetry*. During the It. revival of Graeco-Roman letters in the 15th and 16th c., the *Poetics* of Aristotle achieved attention which was to earn its rules a complete tyranny over the development of European drama from 1560 to 1780. The ideas of poetry as imitation (to be interpreted in 17th-c. France "as a mode of imitation of nature, with Aristotelian regularity understood as nature"), the exaltation of tragedy and epic as "highest" forms of poetry, and, above all, the idea of unity of action in tragedy (to be extended, by later critics, to unities of place and time) were the main tenets of the neo-Aristotelian poetics. These were disseminated by 16th-c. It. commentators on Aristotle's *Poetics* like Fr. Robortelli (1548), B. Segni (1549), V. Maggi (1550), P. Vettori (1560), L. Castelvetro (1570), and A. Piccolomini (1575). Julius Caesar Scaliger's *Poetica* (1561) and Giorgio Trissino's work of the same name (1563) used Aristotle's theory as a basis for practical criticism. Coincidental with the rise of neo-Aristotelian poetics was a revival of interest in the drama of Seneca. Thus Senecan tragedies of the 16th c. like Trissino's *Sofonisba* (1515), Jodelle's *Cléopâtre captive* (1553), and Sackville and Norton's *Gorboduc* (1561) combined with concurrent interest in Aristotle's *Poetics* to create a background for European "classical" drama of the 17th and 18th c.

If Aristotle's ideas influenced the development of a theory of "imitation" and effected the regularization of the drama, it was Horace's *Art of Poetry* which inspired that idea of *propriety* (*decorum*) in composing poetry central to imitative cl.: the use of the right form for a suitable subject (only an epic may accommodate giants), of language to suit the dramatic character's social and native background, and of action to match the nature of the character (Medea, a mother, cannot slaughter her children on stage). In addition, Horace stressed the importance of polished craftsmanship, of long labor to achieve a consciously balanced work of art, a doctrine much stressed in the poetics of this aspect of cl. Important works which spread the Horatian doctrine in 16th-c. Italy were Vida's *De Arte Poetica* (ca. 1520), Robortello's paraphrase of Horace in an appendix to his edition of Aristotle's *Poetics*, important for the coupling of the two critical theories in one volume, and Minturno's *De Arte Poetica* (1563). In France, Joachim du Bellay's *Défense et illustration de la langue française* (1549) and Pierre de Ronsard's *Abrégé de l'art poétique français* (1565) were poetics Horatian-Aristotelian in spirit with an almost immediate effect on the development of styles and forms in Fr. verse and drama. Even though the Horatian-Aristotelian doctrine found critical exposition in Sir Philip Sidney's *Apologie for Poetry* (1595) and Martin Opitz's *Buch von der deutschen Poeterei* (1624), its canon was to dominate 17th-c. literature only in France. In the 18th c., when the emulation of Graeco-Roman form was central to critical doctrines in England, Germany, and elsewhere, the expositions of Fr. 17th-c. critics, rather than the Ancients themselves, were looked to for guidance. For this reason, c. as a mode of imitation of form is often identified totally with Fr. emulation of Graeco-Roman doctrines and forms, notably with the canon of Nicolas Boileau-Despréaux' *Art Poétique* (1674).

Boileau's defense of Horatian proportion and Aristotelian "regular tragedy" is supported by the philosophical framework of Cartesian rationalism: reason should be the poet's guide in selecting what he desires to imitate from nature; outstanding Gr. and Roman works are even safer to imitate than nature itself since the perennial character of what they have described assures the rationality and universality of their themes. Indeed they were, in a sense, nature. As Alexander Pope's *Essay on Criticism* (1711), a guide for critics based on Boileau's poetics, was to say of Virgil's imitation of Homer: "Perhaps he seem'd above the Critic's law / And but from Nature's fountains scorn'd to draw: / But when t' examine ev'ry part he came, / Nature and Homer were, he found, the same" (132–135). Of Gr. and Roman *genres* to be imitated, Boileau stressed the epic, tragedy, comedy, ode, eclogue, elegy, satire, and fable. He did not reject, however, forms of poetic expression inaugurated or developed mainly in the vernacular tradition—the novel, the sonnet, or the ballad—but demanded that these forms also follow the same regularity of proportion and observe the same proprieties as genres imitated from the ancients. The doctrine of formal imitation of Graeco-Roman letters thus gained ascendancy over all directions of poetic activity in France. It was supported, in this respect, by a series of outstanding works which anticipated, paralleled, or reflected theories codified in the *Art Poétique:* the most important of these were the tragedies of Pierre Corneille (1606–84), Jean Racine (1639–99), and Voltaire (1694–1778), the comedies of Molière (1622–73), the fables of Jean de La Fontaine (1621–95), and Boileau's (1636–1711) own satires. In England, Boileau's critical precepts were expounded by John Dryden (1631–1700), Thomas Rymer (1641–1713), and Alexander Pope (1688–1744) and were best reflected in the literary productions of the first and last named, in tragedies like Thomas Otway's *Titus and Berenice*

(1677) and Joseph Addison's *Cato* (1713), and in the satirical style of Jonathan Swift (1667–1745). While Daniel Georg Morhof's *Unterricht von der deutschen Sprache und Poesie* (1682) already upheld Corneille and Molière as dramatic models for the German theatre and Boileau's verse was imitated, during his lifetime, by Friedrich von Canitz (1654–99), the Fr. canon of formal classical imitation was introduced to Germany by Johann Christoph Gottsched (1700–1766). His *Versuch einer kritischen Dichtkunst* (1730) was a paraphrase of Boileau's *Art Poétique;* Gottsched's almost single-handed theatrical reforms placed the German stage under a Fr. neo-Aristotelian spell for a dozen years. Yet Gottsched had few followers: the only German poets of some merit to follow Fr. critical doctrine were Gottsched himself, the fabulist Friedrich von Hagedorn (1708–54), and the dramatic poet Johann Elias Schlegel (1718–49). Later in the 18th c., German literature was to develop another aspect of formal cl., to be discussed below.

In France, England, and Germany, the critical vocabulary of Boileau and his followers became part of the philosophical polemic between partisans of the "ancients" who saw Greece and Rome as storehouses of perennial wisdom and the "moderns" who saw current progress in the arts. Works like Swift's *Battle of the Books* (1704) on the "ancient" or Charles Perrault's *Parallèles des Anciens et des Modernes* (1688) on the "modern" side which drew readers from beyond literary circles perhaps intensified the importance which neoclassical critical theory (as opposed to poetic practice) seems to have had in these countries. In Spain and Italy, where the "quarrel of the ancients and moderns" was not fought in the 18th c., the followers of Boileau were of a more academic character and had, besides, less influence upon the poets. In Italy, Gian Vincenzo Gravina's *Della tragedia* (1708) and Saverio Bettinelli's *Lettere Virgiliane* (1757) expressed a Fr. neoclassical canon which was to be eminently realized only during the last quarter of the 18th c. when Vittorio Alfieri (1749–1803) created some 19 tragedies in the style of Corneille and Racine. The learned *Poética* (1737) of Ignacio Luzan, based on Horace and Boileau, fell short of animating outstanding literary productions in Spain. In one measure or the other, however, Fr. neoclassical doctrine became known and imitated in the 18th-c. literature of almost every European country—Sweden, Denmark, Holland, Russia, Poland, and Hungary all had their "classical" periods under Fr. influence. Thus the term cl., in the critical sense, refers, in most European literary histories, to the imitation of Gr. and Latin models by Boileau's rules, or to the emulation of Fr. works "classical" by virtue of their Horatian-Aristotelian character.

The main exception to this rule is German literary historiography, where cl. (*Klassik*) carries a meaning distinct from the appelation of Fr. neocl., German cl. (*Klassizismus, Klassik*) consciously rejects both Fr. neoclassical poetics and Roman works of art as models for emulation in favor of a direct imitation of Gr. forms. German concentration of interest upon Greece was animated, during the latter half of the 18th c., by the work of Johann Joachim Winckelmann (1717–68) who saw Gr. graphic and plastic forms as models of human perfection. His conception of all Gr. art as the emanation of a harmonious soul was challenged by Gotthold Ephraim Lessing (1729–81) whose *Laokoon* (1766) points to the realism of Gr. literature manifested in its portrayal of both beautiful and ugly elements in human nature. Winckelmann's and Lessing's controversy, far from being destructive of a German understanding of Greece, helped to redefine it: Gr. letters were now seen as both preeminent aesthetically and human in their emotional appeal: Lessing's *Hamburgische Dramaturgie* (1767–69) sought to reinterpret Aristotle's *Poetics* as placing emphasis upon the purgation of pity and fear in the spectator to tragedy, rather than on the formal unities inherent in the play. In so doing, Lessing rejected the tragedies of Corneille and Racine insofar as these claimed to be true imitations of Aeschylean and Sophoclean tragedy. Among German writers, Johann Wolfgang von Goethe (1749–1832), Friedrich Schiller (1759–1805), and Friedrich Hoelderlin (1770–1843) most eminently imitated Gr. forms in some parts of their work. The most noteworthy aspect of their emulation of Gr. forms is that they used these in the portrayal of non-Gr. themes or for the expression of personal feelings. Outstanding examples are Goethe's epic *Herrmann and Dorothea* (1797), Schiller's tragedy *Wilhelm Tell* (1804), and the Pindaric hymns of Hoelderlin (1801ff.). Friedrich Nietzsche's (1844–1900) preoccupation with the Apollonian-Dionysian (q.v.) components of Gr. tragedy as well as the use of elegy and hymn in the poetry of Stefan George (1868–1933) and Rainer Maria Rilke (1875–1926) can be seen as aspects of a German cult of Gr. form which extends from Winckelmann through Goethe and Hoelderlin to the 20th c.

E. As the Antithesis of Romanticism. The antinomy cl. vs. romanticism (q.v.) was first coined by Friedrich von Schlegel (1772–1829) who saw cl. as an attempt to express infinite ideas and emotions in finite form (*Das Athenaeum*, 1798). Schlegel envisaged a finite (classical) poetics coexisting with his own idea

of romanticism—a progressive universal poetry in the making of which the poet was law unto himself. Mme de Staël (1766–1817), whose *De l'Allemagne* (1813) first brought the antinomy to the attention of Fr. and Eng. critics, drastically rejected cl. as a sterile form of literary creation: a mechanical imitation, by means of predetermined rules, of Graeco-Roman models statically conceived. Whereas Schlegel saw his idea of romanticism as antithetical to Goethe's *Klassik* and with implicit reference to Schiller's antinomy of the naive and sentimental (q.v.) poet. Mme de Staël attacked in cl. the poetics of Boileau and of his followers. Her polemic rejected the Fr. tradition of classical imitation not only on aesthetic but on political grounds. Accordingly, *De l'Allemagne* engendered 19th-c. views of cl. vs. romanticism as meaning "conservative" vs. "revolutionary" as well as "bound by sterile rules" vs. "originally creative." Goethe (in a conversation with Eckermann, 1820) originated yet another view of this antinomy by equating cl. with health and romanticism with sickness. This idea has remained current in the 20th c. (cf. M. Praz, *The Romantic Agony*, 1933). Generally, however, 20th-c. critics have come to see the contrast between cl. and romanticism as an emphasis on poetic form and conscious craftsmanship opposed to a poetics of personal emotion and logically incommensurable inspiration. It is in this sense that T. S. Eliot (*The Sacred Wood*, 1920) rejected romanticism in letters in favor of cl.

F. As a Period Designation in Literary History. The confusion engendered by the many meanings which "classic," "classical," and cl. have carried throughout the last 1700 years is reflected in the designation of "classical" movements and epochs by 20th-c. historians of literature. Since those authors whose works have fallen under the heading of cl. in literature, as discussed in definitions D. 1 and 2, above, seldom referred to their own creations as "classical," the aesthetic and historical grounds for establishing national or general classicisms in literature have had to be reconstructed from hindsight. In this respect, historians of Fr. literature have had the easiest task since the polemics of Fr. romanticism clearly defined what its contrary, cl., was and the canon of Boileau's precursors and followers created a clear-cut vocabulary for purposes of grouping and analysis: In the histories of Fr. literature (and in works on general and comparative literature from a Fr. point of view) the period 1660–1700 is noted as the high point of Fr. cl.; the influence of its critical theory and works upon the literatures of 18th-c. Europe constitutes an international age of cl. German literary historians tend to see the Fr. classical canon as a neocl. (with the pejorative connotation of mannerism and second-rate literary production) and include the period of adherence to Boileau's standards in the development of German letters (ca. 1725-45) within the neoclassical category. By contrast, the period 1787-1800, when Goethe's and Schiller's emulation of Gr. form reached its high point, is taken to be the epoch of true German cl. Since there is no clear-cut distinction on aesthetic grounds between that *Klassik* and the romantic period which begins at an overlapping point in time, historians of German literature and some comparative literature scholars have tended to borrow from art history plastic concepts which would distinguish the restrained style of what is considered classical from the "open" forms of romanticism and the irregularities of baroque (q.v.) literature. Further, the notion of "classic" as "model" (definition C) tends to enter German notions of cl.—since Goethe, Schiller, and Hoelderlin represent the best of German literature, their age is therefore *classical*. Historians of Eng. literature are beset by a central problem when questions relating to a definition of Eng. cl. arise: Emulation and imitation of Graeco-Roman motifs and forms runs through Eng. letters from 1550 to the present and was perhaps more intensive among the "romantic" and "Victorian" poets of the 19th c. than among the avowed followers of Boileau in the late 17th and 18th c. Historians of Eng. letters have, especially of late, chosen to speak of classical "contexts" and "aspects" related to individual works or groups of writers—a definition of cl. in Eng. literature, based on these phenomena, is yet to be formed. Historians of other European literatures have generally restricted themselves to employing the term cl. to epochs in which their national literature imitated the Fr. 17th-c. doctrine of formal classical imitation. Scholars of comparative, general, or world literature have either analyzed European cl. as a Fr. or Gallic phenomenon or have attempted the difficult task of seeing the poetics of such diverse writers as Boileau, Goethe, and T. S. Eliot as aspects of one historical trend. The question can be asked, legitimately, whether the term cl. continues to be useful or instructive as a description of periods of literary history. Its many and at times contradictory meanings should certainly lead scholars to apply it with great caution.

A. Spingarn, *A Hist. of Lit. Crit. in the Renaissance* (1908); G. Murray, *The Cl: Tradition in Poetry* (1927); F. Strich, *Deutsche Klassik und Romantik* (1928); Wellek and Warren; H. Peyre, *Le Classicisme français* (1942) and "Classicisme" in *Hist. des litt. occidentales*, ed. R. Queneau (1956); P. Van Tieghem, *Hist. littéraire de l'Europe et de l'Amérique de la*

Ren. à nos jours (1946); Curtius; T. E. Hulme, "Romanticism and Cl.," in *Modern Lit. Crit.*, ed. R. B. West (1952); W. Rehm, *Griechentum und Goethezeit* (1952); A. Heussler, *Klassik und Klassizismus in der deutschen Lit.* (1952); W. P. Friederich, *Outline of Comparative Lit.* (1954); H. Levin, *Contexts of Crit.* (1957); G. Luck, "Scriptor Classicus," CL, 10 (1958); R. Wellek, "The Concept of Cl. and Classic in Lit. Scholarship," in Intern. Comparative Lit. Assoc., *Proc. of the 4th Congress* (1965). W.B.F.

CLAUSULA. See PROSE RHYTHM.

CLERIHEW. A form of comic poetry invented by Edmund C. (for Clerihew) Bentley (1875–1956). A c. consists of two couplets of unequal length often with complex or somewhat ridiculous rhymes and presents a potted biography of a famous personage or historical character. The humor consists in concentrating on the trivial, the fantastic, or the ridiculous and presenting it with dead-pan solemnity as the characteristic, the significant, or the essential. Actually it celebrates the triumph of the *nonsequitur* and indirectly satirizes academic pedantry as well as amateur inconsequence in biographical research. Bentley wrote his first c. as a schoolboy of sixteen.

> Sir Humphrey Davy
> Detested gravy.
> He lived in the odium
> Of having discovered sodium.

Famous as the author of the "perfect" detective novel *Trent's Last Case*, Bentley is honored by a coterie of enthusiastic connoisseurs for three collections of capsule biographies: *Biography for Beginners* (1905), *More Biography* (1929), and *Baseless Biography* (1939). In the "Introductory Remarks" to an omnibus volume, *Clerihews Complete*, the author states and illustrates the nature of his work:

> The Art of Biography
> Is different from Geography.
> Geography is about Maps,
> But Biography is about Chaps.

It is clear that this art form, which is not unrelated to the limerick (q.v.), is very British and quite Old School Tie, but it has nevertheless attracted many practitioners in America as well as England, among them being W. H. Auden, Clifton Fadiman, Ellen Evans, Diana Menuhin, and others.—C. Fadiman, "Cleriheulogy" in *Any Number Can Play* (1957).
A.J.M.S.

CLICHÉ. A phrase or figure which from overuse, like a dulled knife, has lost its cutting edge; a trite expression. Clichés in verse result when the poet's inspiration arises from other poems rather than from a fresh response to experience. Examples of poetic clichés are: fettered soul, eagle-eyed, break of day, rolling wave, purling brook, whispering breeze, ruby lips, pearly teeth, white as snow. Good poets sometimes use clichés intentionally for ironical purposes.—E. Partridge, *A Dictionary of Clichés* (1947); L. D. Lerner, "Clichés and Commonplace," EIC, 6 (1956) presents a different view. See also T. Y. Booth, "The Cliché: A Working Bibliog.," *Bulletin of Bibliog. and Magazine Notes*, 23 (1960).   L.P.

CLIMAX (Gr. "ladder"). (1). As a term of rhetoric, according to the anonymous *Ad Herennium* 25, and Quintilian (*Institutes of Oratory* 9.3.54–57), both of the 1st c. A.D., and the Gr. rhetorician Demetrius (*On Style* 270, 1st c. A.D.?), c. is the pattern of a series of sentences or other units of discourse linked chainwise, a meaning of the term now mostly abandoned for fear of confusion with sense 2 below. The opening word or words of each unit after the first repeats a word or words, usually the final ones, of the preceding unit, sometimes with a morphological change. The purpose is commonly to build up a crescendo of force or excitement, e.g., "I will grind your bones to dust / and with your blood and it I'll make a paste, / And of the paste a coffin I will rear / And make two pasties of your shameful heads, / And bid that strumpet, your unhallow'd dam, / Like to the earth swallow her own increase" (Shakespeare, *Titus Andronicus* 5.2.187–92). A c. is known as a *sorites* when the linked elements are truncated syllogisms in a chain of argument, the conclusion of each before the last becoming the premiss of the next (see, e.g., Richard Whately, *Elements of Logic* 2.4.7). (2). The meaning currently designated by c. is the point of supreme interest or intensity of any graded series of events or ideas, most commonly the crisis or turning point of a story or play, e.g., the fall of Adam in *Paradise Lost* or the murder of the king in *Macbeth*.   H.B.

CLOAK AND SWORD. See COMEDIA DE CAPA Y ESPADA.

CLOSET DRAMA is designed for reading in the study (closet) or to small groups rather than for performance on the public stage. Classifying a specific play as c.d. can be difficult since it is not always clear what the dramatist intended. In some cases he may well have hoped for theatrical production but have been rejected by a theatre catering to a nonreceptive audience. The classic example, Seneca, wrote at a time when the Roman stage was monopolized by mimes and tumblers. It seems

clear that such Senecan plays as *Hercules Furens, Phaedra,* and *Thyestes,* all highly rhetorical pieces, were designed for oral reading at most, though centuries later, in the Elizabethan period, they were to exert a strong influence on such important dramatists as Marlowe and Kyd. In the period of great dramatic activity in England from 1580 to 1642 at least a few c.d. appeared. These seem to have been written in academic or provincial isolation from a theatre restricted almost entirely to the London populace. Milton also wrote for the closet. His *Samson Agonistes* might have suited the Athenian stage; it was clearly not intended for the Restoration one.

The period most productive of c.d., the 19th c., affords the clearest example of divergence of dramatist and audience. Shelley, Keats, Landor wrote a highly poetic though perhaps inadequately dramaturgic form of tragedy usually based on Gr. or Elizabethan models. Shelley's *Prometheus Unbound* and *Cenci*— this last piece was produced generations later by the poet's admirers—are excellent examples of the type. In France the plays of Alfred de Musset, though several were eventually performed, belong in the class of c.d. In the 20th c. much "poetic" drama would appear to fit the definition of c.d., in its ultimate fate if not because of the authors' intentions. The plays of Yeats, Eliot, and Fry, for example, are better known in the "closet" than on the stage though they were clearly intended for the theatre. Only a few minor figures, such as Lawrence Binyon or W. W. Gibson, wrote plays for the reader alone.—F. E. Schelling, *Elizabethan Drama 1588–1642* (1910); H. A. Smith, *Main Currents of Modern Fr. Drama* (1925); T. S. Eliot, "Seneca," *Selected Essays* (1932, 1950); P. W. Harsh, *A Handbook of Classical Drama* (1944); Nicoll.   L.H.

COBLA. This is the usual word for "stanza" in Old Prov. It is also used, either alone or in the expression *c. esparsa* (isolated stanza), to designate a poem consisting in its entirety of a single stanza. These *coblas* are fairly common from the end of the 12th c. on. In theme they are usually like miniature *sirventes* (q.v.), and in their concision they represent the troubadours' closest approach to the epigram. It often happened that a *cobla* would inspire an answering *cobla,* and this might well follow the metrical structure of the first, in which case the resultant combination resembles a short *tenso* (see under TENZONE).—Jeanroy, II.   F.M.C.

COCKNEY SCHOOL OF POETRY. A derisive name applied (*Blackwood's Magazine*, Oct. 1817) to a group of writers, including Keats, Shelley, Leigh Hunt, and Hazlitt, who were

Londoners by birth or adoption. Hunt, and Keats as his protégé, were the chief targets of the anonymous attack (long but, as it appears, mistakenly attributed to J. G. Lockhart), which was motivated at least as much by the reviewer's opposition to the radical social and political views of the group as by his disagreement with the artistic principles which he believed they shared, a motivation which is underlined by his references to the humble origins of Keats and Hunt. The term was also used by John Wilson Croker in the course of his notorious attack on Keats' *Endymion* (QR, Sept. 1818).

COLOMBIAN POETRY. See SPANISH AMERICAN POETRY.

COLON (Gr. "limb"). A colon may be composed of a number of feet or metra or else may be a single sequence which cannot be thus analyzed. As a metrical phrase it should not exceed 16, 18, or 25 morae in, respectively, isomeric, diplasic, and hemiolic genres (where the constituent feet can be classified as divisible into parts in the respective proportions of 1:1, 1:2, and 2:3 morae). In Gr. lyric verse cola may be combined into a *periodos* or subordinate period, but colometry (i.e., their identification within a passage) is not always easy to decide. —Kolář; Dale; Koster.   R.J.C.

COMEDIA DE CAPA Y ESPADA. A play of intrigue, very popular during the Sp. Golden Age, that elaborates upon the life of the lower aristocracy or of the upper middle class and takes its name from the cloak (*capa*) and sword (*espada*) that were part of the street costume of these classes. The plot is usually centered on the obstacles which chance or society create to the marriage of one or two couples, and the obstacles are overcome at the end. A comic level is provided by a parallel situation that arises among servants and also ends happily in marriage. The plot is often complicated by disguises, mistaken identities, and misunderstandings. Although the origin of the *comedia* . . . may be seen in the *Comedia Ymenea* (1517) by Torres Naharro, the great masters of this dramatic form are Lope de Vega (1562–1635) and Pedro Calderón de la Barca (1600–81). The *comedia* . . . , like all other plays of the Sp. Golden Age, is in verse. Lope de Vega in his *Arte nuevo de hacer comedias* (1609) gives advice (which he did not always heed himself) on the type of verse to be used for each dramatic situation: *décimas* (q.v.) for sad scenes, *romance* (q.v.) for narration, *redondillas* (q.v.) for love scenes, and sonnets and tercets for grave and serious matters.—R. Schevill, *The Dramatic Art of Lope de Vega* (1918); M. Menéndez y Pelayo, *Estudios sobre el teatro de Lope de Vega* (7 v., 1919–27); A. Valbuena-Prat, *Calderón* (1941).   R.MI.

COMEDY. Homer's Odysseus affords us in some respects the first of the ancient prototypes for c. His characteristics are in many ways the opposite of those we associate with protagonists in tragedy. Clever, flexible, resourceful, when confronted with a serious challenge or obstacle, Odysseus applies his wits to good effect or nimbly gets out of the way. He is never at a loss; he can extricate himself from the tightest scrapes, and his shrewdness renders him, like many clever gentlemen among his successors, the object of some suspicion. Indeed, the Eng. word most frequently used to describe him is "wily," suggesting perhaps the faintly or clearly disreputable qualities often associated with many of the greatest figures of c. Nevertheless, the amiability and energy of Odysseus, and of later figures with his temperament more properly called "comic," are attractive to other characters and to listeners and readers alike. Comic characters of this type always seem to be freer than we are, partly able to ignore or transcend ordinary relationships between people and events. The predicaments in which they find themselves seem to be, if anything, tests of their quickwittedness, and not necessarily, as in tragedy, means for exhibiting their characters. The problems they face are usually worked out on the level of action rather than of abstract thought. Their minds are strictly empirical. They believe in what they can touch, see, and understand, and in preserving—not too pompously—their sense of dignity and, above all, their lives. The varieties of comic character, however, may be even greater than those of tragic. Characters of a kind very different from these sketched here—those who are startled, baffled, or defeated by everything, who mistake the nature of everything they see, who respond to the world in exaggerated, uncontrolled, inflexible, or irrational ways, or who are as predictable as simple animals or machines—are equally interesting comic types, in a tradition at least as old as Aristophanes. We often laugh at the comic eccentric (odd in mind or body), the butt, gull, zany, pantaloon, braggart, and clown because they seem to cut a more ridiculous figure than we. But we may also laugh with or at the rogue, trickster, wit, or the court fool of earlier drama because they outsmart or outmaneuver the world that we find so troublesome. We may suspend judgment about their morality because of our delight in their freedom.

From Aristotle's few extant remarks on the nature of c. to the writings of Freud and Bergson and beyond, valuable insights have illuminated the subject from very diverse points of view. Theories of comedy discriminate with difficulty between work of art and the feelings of audience or reader, antic clown and laughing observer, object and subject. Two of the principal "stimulus" theories—one pointing out our satisfaction in feelings of superiority and the other our perceptions of contrast in c. or sense of sudden disappointment—attempt to bring object and subject into a relationship with one another. The theory of superiority, developed by Hobbes, Bergson, Meredith and others, emphasizes our delight in seeing ourselves less unfortunate than some human beings; that of contrast, developed by Aristotle, Kant, Schopenhauer, and others, emphasizes our delight in any form of incongruity, any difference between our ideas of things and things themselves: what ought to be as opposed to what actually is. The former, now the principal theory, often emphasized our feelings of derision or need to degrade. The two are often combined, and neither perhaps fully accounts for the laughter of the holiday spirit. A fusion of sympathy and laughter is possibly the most pervasive kind in c., in which there is a union between mocker and mocked, and in which art holds the mirror, however exaggerated, up to our own natures. Other, but related theories of c. often stress an element of triumph or liberty, and they take many specialized forms, emphasizing humor as aggression or as playfulness, the liberation of energy, the removal of inhibitions, or a return to childhood. Laughter can be construed as the sudden relief from tension, fear, or danger, the overcoming of tragedy, or as a failure of vital energy, the freezing of life in a stereotype or automatism. A comedy can involve our "thoughtful" laughter at the spectacle of the tensions between the sexes in society, or the simpler laughter associated with motor activity, or its suddenly being arrested. Much c. is conservative. It justifies, defends, or elevates us in relation to the oddity, the alien, the scapegoat. It enables us to surmount our doubts about those who are different by laughing them out of existence. But the implications of c. can also of course be profoundly revolutionary.

An author therefore seems to write c. for a wide variety of reasons—because he finds the entire spectacle of human life, or a small part of it, amusing or absurd, because he wishes to satirize, mock, scorn, or ridicule this spectacle, because he wishes to correct or reform it, because he feels that it cannot be corrected, because he wishes to caricature, parody, or burlesque it, to grace, embellish, or even to destroy it. And as listeners or readers we laugh when we perceive that the relationship of anyone to himself, to society and its conventions, to nature or natural law is very different

from our own, or from what we pretend is true for ourselves. We laugh when established roles or patterns are altered, and someone behaves like a god, animal, an inanimate object, or like someone very different from himself. We may laugh "at" a comic character, in detachment or scorn, or we may feel somehow allied with him, and laugh "with" him, recognizing common human failings. Or we may even feel inferior to or uneasy about him, laughing in embarrassment or a kind of fear. Like most forms of the drama, c. is in part an art of juxtaposition—the tall and short, fat and thin, clever and dull, formal and informal, brave and cowardly, idealist and realist frequently occur together: Falstaff and Justice Shallow, Don Quixote and Sancho Panza, and so on.

If c. is related to our perceptions of incongruity, it follows that a congruity of meanings must be securely established first, before such perception can be possible. Patterns in society or in art must be generally acknowledged before varying or breaking them proves to be amusing. Thus most societies seem to develop clearly recognized traditions and conventions before their great artists turn to c. Both c. and tragedy present individuals in the context of groups, of society, or of human life generally. The individual's variation from the norm of thought or behavior is the source for much of the dramatic tension in both genres. But in c., unlike tragedy, this variation is without serious or fatal consequences; hence, in part, the feeling of exhilaration and release we derive from much c., Hobbes's "sudden glory." We are delighted to see persons acting stupidly, oddly, or recklessly with relative impunity, or to see the exceptional so freed from the "laws" governing everyday life that it elicits neither our disapproval nor our strong sympathy.

By and large, c. is a more secular and earthbound form than tragedy. It concentrates upon the local, established, familiar, upon problemsolving, the probable rather than, as in tragedy, upon mystery or wonder. It usually emphasizes the middle range—neither pity nor terror, neither the sublime nor the extremely grotesque. The well-known commonplace—that c. is the expression of the man who thinks and tragedy of the man who feels—possesses this grain of truth: strong feeling is inimical to the experience of much c., the object of its mockery rather than the effect it seeks to induce. The norm in c. frequently lies in the group, in society, or in a social arbiter of some kind, and it is often suggested through the author's point of view or tone. Indeed, the arbiter is often clearly the author himself. The exceptional behavior of heroes, which in tragedy may be admirable or appalling, is laughable in c. In the latter the central virtues are not the ability to endure, courage, or heroic magnanimity, but the ability to adjust, common sense, and humility, or a clear-eyed sense of one's relationship to others. Inflexibility, obsession, vanity, or pride—all frequently allied with tragic grandeur—and hypocrisy or folly have always been the targets of c.

Relationships between plot, character, and action are usually very different in c. from what they are in tragedy. Events in c. frequently do not follow one another with the same sense of inevitability as they do in tragedy, and they do not seem to grow out of or in turn to shape character to the same degree. Indeed, as we have seen, it is the apparent dislocation of events in a series, the disruption of laws of cause and effect or other kinds of logical relationships, that gives the audience in c. its sense of freedom from everyday patterns. Plot or story is often of the essence in this genre. The comic writer tends to choose a rapidly moving plot or dialogue, affording him a diversity of surprises within an over-all unity. C. frequently gives the impression of exploring horizontally rather than vertically: it often suggests meaning in depth by a manipulation of elements on the surface. The writer of c. also tends to choose or to invent individuals with a dominant trait or traits—physical, mental, emotional, or moral—anything in appearance, character, behavior, or all three which will serve as an index to essential human nature. Much of the apparent ease with which comic situations can be manipulated derives from this necessity in c. for heightening and exaggerating. Thus style is of the utmost importance. This is not to imply, of course, that c. need be in any way superficial, in choice or treatment of subject matter or in effect. Indeed, the evocation of an entire world through revelation of a part is the goal of every art.

The imprecise terms we employ for the major types of c.—c. of humors or of character, of intrigue, of manners, of ideas; high c., sentimental, romantic, realistic, social, or fantastic c.; satire, farce, and so on—are scarcely adequate for distinguishing between the varieties of c. that may occur even within a single great play. And there are many comic forms and styles. Most c. falls somewhere in the range between "high" or "pure" c. (presenting a world of uniform tone in which virtually no one is exempt from comic treatment) and mixed forms, such as romantic c., problem c., or tragicomedy. The poetic language of c. is as various as the range of man's comic attitudes, forms, and purposes—from the rich exuberance of Aristophanes, Plautus, or Lope to the more formal manner of Restoration c. Clearly the poetry of an author who wishes to comment significantly upon life will be composed as carefully as that in tragedy. A rela-

tively small part of the world's humorous, witty, or satiric writing in verse occurs in dramatic form, and the following brief survey will be concerned only with major dramatists of the West.

Though it has since Aristotle frequently been considered an inferior form, c. can be the vehicle for insights as profound as those of tragedy. On the highest level, furthermore, it is as rare as tragedy, perhaps even rarer. Much of the great poetic c. of the Western world appears approximately in the same periods as its great tragedy—in the 5th and 4th c. B.C. in Greece and in Europe in the 16th and 17th c. Greek c. was from the beginning associated with the worship of Dionysos, with the *komos* or revel, and emphasized a chorus, often fantastically garbed as animals. As it developed, its emphasis shifted from a concern with gods, to heroes, to mortal men. At the head of c. stands Aristophanes (448?–?380 B.C.), whose plays show great variety, verbal brilliance, and daring, and who wished to reconcile man to the world he inhabits and yet to save Athens from impending doom. He is the master of an art in which poetry, dance, and drama form a unity, and which combines vigorous mockery or satire of contemporary customs and living persons—social, political, and literary—with a series of fantastic plots and characters. Few writers of c. have ever profited as has Aristophanes from so much freedom, and Middle C., which began to emphasize escape from trouble through fantasy, produced no successors whose work has survived. It is the New C. of Menander (343?–?291 B.C.) which has exercised the greatest influence over later writers. In this c., in which the first fairly complete play, the *Dyskolos*, has recently been discovered, the emphasis is social rather than political, the chorus is less important, and young love is the theme. Frequently a slave or parasite enables a young man to win his girl, over opposition, and the slave is then given his freedom. This is a c. of manners, employing domestic situations and frequently mythological themes. Menander's plots, his stock types of character, and his comic attitudes are adapted or taken over in detail by the only other writers of verse c. in the ancient world of whom we have adequate record, the Romans Plautus (254?–184 B.C.) and Terence (190–159 B.C.). Here too, the theme is the difficulties confronting young love, and many of the stock types of character are the opponents of the lovers—the wealthy rival, the slave merchant, and the old parents. The lively figures and situations in the c. of these poets serve in turn as patterns for much of the subsequent c. in Europe written up through the Renaissance and beyond. Apart from a few academic exercises, very little dramatic c. is produced in the Middle Ages, though the medieval farce and interlude are frequently lively forms. The word "c." comes to be applied to any narrative or poem with a happy ending, as in Dante's *Divine Comedy*. With the Renaissance, the word is restored to the theatre, and a distinction of Aristotle's remains generally applicable: tragedy attempts to depict persons who are "better" than we are; c., those who are "worse."

The burst of great c. in the Renaissance is richly indebted to the perennial c. of the folk and of traveling entertainers, as Gr. c. is to the Megarean farce and Roman to the *mimus*. But the rediscovery of and renewed interest in the classics are paramount in giving the new men of the theater a sense for drama as a literary form, with act and scene divisions and a highly organized structure. In Spain the prolific and versatile Lope de Vega (1562–1635) and the graver Calderón (1600–1681) and other gifted writers produce a brilliant variety of verse comedies, both romantic and realistic, chiefly on the usual Sp. themes of love and its intrigues and honor and its defense. Their plays, few of them what we would call "pure" comedies, employ many different styles and meters and soon furnish the dramatists of northern Europe with countless clever plots and with vivid types of character. The precept and example of Italy prove to be equally exciting for northern playwrights. Though few It. comedies achieve the stature of those in other countries, the It. store of folk and literary tales and the professional and popular theater developed in the 16th and 17th c., the *commedia dell' arte*, are enormously influential. The *commedia* is a c. of improvisation, in which a few stock types of character—Harlequin, Columbine, Pantaloon, the Doctor, Punch, and the braggart captain—invent dialogue and action according to a few basic types of plot, often derived from antiquity. Its fullest flowering can be seen in the later It. comedies of Goldoni (1707–93) and the Fr. c. of Marivaux (1688–1763).

From the verse c. of Shakespeare (1564–1616) and Ben Jonson (1573–1637) to the prose c. of Bernard Shaw (1856–1950), the Eng. theater is distinguished by a remarkable number of comic writers. The romantic c. of Shakespeare and some of his contemporaries and the c. of humors (of types or idiosyncrasies) of Jonson suggest from the outset two dominant directions which later comic writers will take: a c. which revolves about love and marriage and which frequently employs nature and its rhythms as central to both dramatic structure and theme, and a more "classical" c. which satirizes hypocrisy, eccentricity, manners, and morals, and which is predominantly urban. In the development of later comedies of intrigue

and manners, many writers adopt elements from both of these forms. As in *Volpone* and *The Alchemist*, few of Jonson's characters, following ancient example, are exempt from comic treatment. These plays exhibit a uniform tone and great vitality, and are built around a central image or theme. Shakespeare's comedies usually exhibit a central character, frequently a woman, who partly directs, tests, illumines, and transforms those around her. The particular balance between the wit and humor of Shakespeare's verse and the earnestness of his preoccupation with the mystery of the seasons, with birth and death, loss and restoration, sickness and healing, is rare in the history of c. The poetic elements of this c. are very similar, however, to those of many of Shakespeare's Eng. contemporaries: an alternation between rhymed verse, blank verse, and even prose, many songs, and an experimenting with all kinds of comic tone—from the merry "Roman" farce of *The Comedy of Errors*, through the witty lyricism of *As You Like It* and the bitter probing of the problem c., *Troilus and Cressida*, to the serenity of the last romances (*The Tempest*).

The great age for nondramatic comic verse in England (if we exclude a few great figures like Chaucer) extends from about the first quarter of the 17th c. to about the middle of the 18th. Much of the comic verse of this period is witty, ironic, or satiric, and it is often characterized by rather strict forms, direct (or disguised) reference to persons still alive, and a subtle and precise adjustment of the tone and texture of a poem to the character of the person or occasion for which it is written. Poets as different as Marvell, Dryden, and Pope, writing in or near an age of great comic drama, command many of the resources of dramatic dialogue. A similar mastery of tone and style is achieved by the writers of Restoration stage c. Congreve and his fellows write a series of glittering comedies of manners, but the language of dramatic c. is now chiefly prose. Similarly, after the Restoration, most of the greatest writers of c. turn toward nondramatic poetry (Pope or Byron) or, in ever greater numbers, toward prose (Swift, Fielding, Sterne, Jane Austen, Dickens, and so on). The only comic dramatists (whose works are still performed today) of the 18th (Goldsmith and Sheridan) and later 19th c. (Wilde) also write almost wholly in prose. In the 20th c., Yeats, Synge, Eliot and others have written comic dramas in poetry, or something like poetry, with varying degrees of success.

The greatest writer of c. in France, Molière (1622–73), is also, like Aristophanes or Shakespeare, one of his country's greatest poets. In both prose and verse, he writes a c. of situation, of intrigue, of manners, and of character (almost of humors), in a variety of modes that range from farce, which he revived, through *comédie-ballet* to something near tragedy. Inheriting the "masks" of It., Sp., and early Fr. c., he turned them into fascinating characters. His plays do not primarily concern love or the exploring or refining of attitudes toward it, as in Shakespeare. They revolve, as in *Tartuffe, Le Misanthrope,* and *Les Femmes Savantes,* around basic human frailties or obsessions, like exaggerated purity, avarice, hypocrisy, snobbery, or pride. Though written in part for an aristocratic audience, Molière's twenty-two c. are universal, based as they are upon native Fr. tradition (folk play, farce, and *sottie*), classical example, and the *commedia dell' arte*. Many of his verse lines, like Shakespeare's in Eng., have sunk deeply into the fiber of the language. Molière's great contemporary, Corneille, also writes c., similar to the Sp. c. of intrigue (*Le Menteur*). Comic styles in Fr. throughout the 18th and 19th c. vary greatly—c. of manners, and moralizing, sentimental, romantic, and realistic c. But even the most interesting of the later writers—Marivaux, Beaumarchais, de Musset, and so on—in France as in other countries, write primarily in prose. Since c. now takes many lesser forms —farce, tearful c. and operetta—the marvelous balance of elements in the c. of Molière and other writers of his century is weakened. This is not to imply, of course, that writers of the later 19th and the 20th c. in all countries have ceased to entertain, characterize, or satirize the world. Ibsen (writing partly in verse) in Norway, Chekhov in Russia, Shaw in England, Pirandello in Italy, Giraudoux and Anouilh in France, Brecht (partly in verse) in Germany, and many more recent writers (such as Beckett and Ionesco) have written prose c. of ideas, of social conditions, of manners, of fantasy, and many other forms which will probably rank with the comic writing of the last hundred years in the short story or the novel. And during the last 200 years, in an allied form of theatre, a series of composers with a genius for c., from Mozart through Rossini, Verdi, and beyond, have produced a number of brilliant comic operas.

G. Meredith, *An Essay on C. and the Uses of the Comic Spirit* (1877); H. L. Bergson, *Laughter* (1912); F. M. Cornford, *The Origin of Attic C.* (1914); S. Freud, *Wit and its Relation to the Unconscious* (1916); W. Smith, *The Nature of C.* (1930); G. Norwood, *Gr. C.* (1931); K. M. Lea, *It. Popular C.* (2 v., 1934); J. Feibleman, *In Praise of C.* (1939); H.T.E. Perry, *Masters of Dramatic C. and their Social Themes* (1939); E. E. Stoll, *Shakespeare and Other Masters* (1940); P. A. Chapman, *The Spirit of Molière* (1940); M. Turnell, *The Cl. Moment* (1947); L. J. Potts, *C.* (1948); A.

Koestler, *Insight and Outlook* (1949); D. H. Monro, *Argument of Laughter* (1951); G. E. Duckworth, *The Nature of Roman C.* (1952); L. Kronenberger, *The Thread of Laughter* (1952); A. Rapp, *The Origins of Wit and Humor* (1952); *Eng. Stage C.*, ed. W. K. Wimsatt, Jr. (1954); H.D.F. Kitto, *Form and Meaning in Drama* (1956); W. Sypher, *C.* (1956); Frye; P. A. Arnott, *An Introduction to the Gr. Theatre* (1959); C. L. Barber, *Shakespeare's Festive C.* (1959); M. T. Herrick, *It. C. in the Renaissance* (1960); M. C. Swabey, *Comic Laughter* (1961); A. Nicoll, *The World of Harlequin* (1963).   R.J.D.

COMEDY OF HUMORS. The comedy of humors was an outgrowth of the Renaissance stress on decorum in life which required a well-balanced personality unmarked by any grave eccentricities. The concept of humors was derived from a traditional theory of physiology in which the state of health—and by extension the state of mind, of character—depended upon a balance among the four elemental fluids: black and yellow bile, blood, and phlegm. Though perhaps first applied to drama by Chapman, the notion, by then largely analogical or figurative, was seized and fully developed into a theory of comedy by Ben Jonson, whose bent toward a satiric and normative drama is clearly shown in his first play, *Everyman in His Humour* (1598). In this and subsequent plays, such as *The Silent Woman* (1609) or *The Alchemist* (1610) Jonson parades before his audience a variety of eccentrics, each marked by some particular bias of character, some folly or meanness—short, however, of crime—which prevents his being satisfactorily human. Hence Jonson's humors comedy is closely related both to comedy of character, since he deals with peculiarity of character as a root of action, and to comedy of manners, since he goes to contemporary society for his norm. Though he had ardent followers in later generations—Shadwell, even Congreve, in the drama, Smollett and Dickens in the novel—this type of comedy is usually associated in literary history with Jonson and his times. Obviously Jonson used the term *humor* in a far more restricted sense than we do today when it can mean a great many things.—F. E. Schelling, *Elizabethan Drama 1558-1642* (1910); Ben Jonson, *Works*, ed. C. H. Herford and P. and E. Simpson (11 v., 1925-54); P. V. Kreider, *Elizabethan Comic Character Conventions as Revealed in the Comedies of George Chapman* (1935); H. L. Snuggs, "The Comic Humours: a New Interpretation," PMLA, 62 (1947); Nicoll; J. J. Enck, *Jonson and the Comic Truth* (1957).   L.H.

COMMON RHYTHM. See RUNNING RHYTHM.

COMPARATIVE CRITICISM. See CRITICISM, TYPES OF.

COMPENSATION. One of several devices used to schematize a basically irregular foot or line (see METRICAL VARIATIONS). A pause (see REST) is sometimes said to substitute (or compensate) for a missing part of a foot or a whole foot. This is one of two main varieties of c. The other kind occurs when an extra syllable in one foot may be said to compensate for a missing syllable in another, or when a missing metrical unit in one line may be compensated for by an extra unit in an adjacent line.—Baum; Deutsch. R.BE.

COMPLAINT. A plaintive poem, plaint. (1) Often the c. of a lover to or about an unresponsive mistress (cf. *Greek Anthology*, Villon, Surrey's *A Complaint by Night of the Lover Not Beloved*); (2) a plaint in which the poet seeks relief from his unhappy state (Chaucer's *A Complaint unto Pity*); (3) a plaint about the sorrows of the world or the poet's affairs (Spenser's *Complaints*); (4) less frequently a c. in a lighter vein about some trivial subject (Chaucer's *The Complaint of Chaucer to his Purse*). Usually the poem is in the form of a monologue in which the poet explains the cause of his sorrow and pleads for a remedy. Ponsonby, the printer, claims Spenser's complaints are more serious than usual, that the book is composed of "all complaints and meditations of the worlds vanitie, verie graue and profitable." Dr. Johnson disliked the form, saying that Cowley's ode, *The Complaint*, "seems to have excited more contempt than pity." Sometimes a mournful c. is indistinguishable from a lament (q.v.).—J. Peter, *C. and Satire in Early Eng. Lit.* (1956). R.O.E.

COMPLEXIO. See ANADIPLOSIS.

COMPOSITE VERSES. Verses composed of feet of different kinds, e.g., dactylo-trochaic. See also *episyntheton*. K.M.A.

CONCEIT. An intricate or far-fetched metaphor, which functions through arousing feelings of surprise, shock, or amusement; in earlier usage, the imagination or fancy (qq.v.) in general. The term is derived from the It. *concetto* (concept), and all types of conceit share an origin which is specifically intellectual rather than sensuous. The poet compares elements which seem to have little or nothing in common, or juxtaposes images which establish a marked discord in mood. One may distinguish two types of c.: (1) the Petrarchan, in which physical qualities or experiences are metaphorically described in terms of very different physical objects; it often verges on hyperbole (q.v.):

Quando a gli ardenti rai neve divegno
When I turn to snow before your burning rays. . .
(Petrarch, *Canzone* 8)

(2) the "metaphysical," in which the spiritual qualities or functions of the described entity are presented by means of a vehicle which shares no physical features with the entity:

As lines, so loves, oblique may well
Themselves in every angle greet;
But ours, so truly parallel,
Though infinite, can never meet.
(Marvell, *The Definition of Love*)

The Petrarchan type, valid for its originator and the more gifted of his followers because of the rich psychological content it often implies, degenerated ultimately into the fanciful and decorative figures of marinism (q.v.), but it was widely employed by the Elizabethan sonneteers and by Tasso. The metaphysical type, so-called from its use by the metaphysical poets (see METAPHYSICAL POETRY), was characteristic not only of Donne and his followers in 17th-c. England and their contemporaries on the Continent, but also of the Fr. symbolists in the latter 19th c. It has been widely used by contemporary poets.

The metaphysical c. is usually intended in critical discussions of the c. Within this type of c. one may perceive two general forms: (1) the extended, in which the initial analogy is subjected to a detailed and ingenious development, as in Donne's famous figure from *A Valediction: Forbidding Mourning*:

If they be two, they are two so
As stiff twin compasses are two;
Thy soul, the fixed foot, makes no show
To move, but doth, if th' other do . . .

(2) the condensed, in which the ingenious analogy or discordant contrast is expressed with a telling brevity, as at the opening of T. S. Eliot's *The Love-Song of J. Alfred Prufrock*:

When the evening is spread out against the sky
Like a patient etherised upon a table.

The lines of Eliot will serve to typify two important aspects of the c.: its subtle use of controlled connotation to enrich the meaning of the poem, with the associated dependence on the imaginative sensitivity of the reader, and its consistent evocation of paradox (q.v.).

The faculty of wit (q.v.), the capacity for finding likenesses between the apparently unlike, is central to the c., and the presence of this faculty largely determines the success of a given c. For the emotion evoked by a good c.

is not simply surprise, or, in Dr. Johnson's terms, wonder at the perversity which created the c., but rather a surprised recognition of the ultimate validity of the relationship presented in the c., which thus serves not as an ornament but as an instrument of vision.

R. M. Alden, "The Lyrical C. of the Elizabethans," SP, 14 (1917) and "The Lyrical Conceits of the Metaphysical Poets," SP, 17 (1920); K. M. Lea, "Conceits," MLR, 20 (1925); E. Holmes, *Aspects of Elizabethan Imagery* (1929); G. Williamson, *The Donne Tradition* (1930); C. Brooks, "A Note on Symbol and C.," *Am. Review*, 3 (1934); M. Praz, *Studies in 17th-C. Imagery*, I (1939); G. R. Potter, "Protest against the Term C.," PQ. 20 (1941); Tuve; T. E. May, "Gracián's Idea of the 'Concepto,'" HR, 18 (1950); J. A. Mazzeo, "A Critique of Some Modern Theories of Metaphysical Poetry," MP, 50 (1952); D. L. Guss, "Donne's C. and Petrarchan Wit," PMLA, 78 (1963).   F.J.W.; A.P.

CONCEPTISM. See CULTISM.

CONCRETE AND ABSTRACT. In poetics concreteness has usually been valued and abstractness decried. Sidney in *The Defense of Poesie* (1583) exalted poetry above philosophy because of poetry's greater concreteness. Later neoclassical doctrine shifted to a distinction between generality and particularity, and in keeping with the neoclassical interpretation of nature preferred generality. Sir Joshua Reynold's conception of the ideal is literally an abstraction of chosen qualities, and Dr. Johnson praised Shakespeare for the generality of his characterizations. The preference for concreteness reappears with romanticism, in Wordsworth's and Coleridge's attacks upon stock poetic diction and abstract personifications and in Shelley's reinforcement of Sidney in his *Defence of Poetry* with a new theory of metaphor and an enlarged conception of poetry's function ("We want the power to imagine that which we know"). Keats's "Axioms in philosophy are not axioms until they are proved upon our pulses" is his characteristic phrasing of the general romantic distrust of the "understanding," or abstract reason.

In the 20th c. the distinction between the concrete and the abstract has been turned against the romantics, chiefly because modern poets and critics have suspected the romantics of smuggling in scientific and philosophic statement disguised as poetry. Ezra Pound (in his early days), T. E. Hulme, and the imagists tried before 1920 to formulate a wholly concrete poetry of things uncontaminated by idea and statement. The imagists oversimplified the problem, but their position was refined and strengthened by T. S. Eliot, whose famous "objective correlative" (q.v.) is a blow for con-

creteness, by John Crowe Ransom, who found in *The World's Body* that "the rich, contingent materiality of things" is poetry's proper matter, by I. A. Richards and, after him, Cleanth Brooks and others, who condemned "exclusive poetry" and the poetry of statement in favor of inclusiveness and the poetry of metaphor and indirection. During the 20th c. the distinction has been no longer, as it was in Sidney, between the abstractness of philosophy and the concreteness of poetry, but between the abstraction which science uses as its weapon and the disinterested concreteness and wholeness of poetic contemplation.—O. Barfield, *Poetic Diction* (1928); J. C. Ransom, *The World's Body* (1938); C. Brooks, *The Well Wrought Urn* (1947); R. H. Fogle, *The Imagery of Keats and Shelley* (1949; ch. 5); Wimsatt.   R.H.F.

CONCRETE UNIVERSAL, the term and in part the concept, has come to literary criticism from idealist philosophy. Hegel proposed his theory of the c.u. as a solution to the ancient philosophical problem concerning the nature and reality of universals. Later idealists regarded this theory as revolutionizing the study of logic and metaphysics and, like Hegel, drew out its implications for ethics, politics, and aesthetics. In the works of these philosophers the c.u. (or organic universal) is opposed to the abstract universals, or general ideas, of science and Aristotelian logic. Abstract universals, whether they be concepts of attributes ("blue," "round") or of syntheses of attributes ("dog," "man"), are only mental creations and, as such, have no "real" existence. Philosophy must go beyond the abstract universals of science and be oriented to the study of the "individual," the "true" or "concrete" universal. The criteria for determining whether or not an object is a c.u. are diversity of parts, interrelatedness of parts, completeness, unity, independence, and self-maintenance. In terms of these criteria, the only true c.u. is the "Absolute" or "World Whole"; but the phrase is also used in a secondary sense to denote microcosms within this macrocosm. A human being, a work of art, or an integrated society would be examples of such "finite" concrete universals.

J. C. Ransom has long been an opponent of holistic theories in aesthetics and literary criticism. In the 1930's and 1940's he repeatedly attacked the idealist notion of the c.u. and the more recent versions of holistic theory expressed in the terminology of "organic whole," "functional unity," "fusion," or "funding." In Ransom's opinion, to call a poem a c.u. is either to state a "gaudy paradox" or to class it with the products of applied science ("Art Needs a Little Separating," p. 121). Ransom's model for the c.u. is a complex machine in which each part has significance and justification only as it works with the other parts to achieve the purpose for which the machine was designed. A natural object is not a c.u. in this sense; it always exhibits characteristics which are "irrelevant" in terms of human conceptions of order and purpose. Poetry (and literature generally) arises from the human desire to contemplate, love, and enjoy the confused multitudinous particularity of nature for its own sake. Hence holistic structure in poetry, which would necessarily impose a "rational order" on the objects imitated, would prevent the satisfaction of this desire. An analysis of a good poem will indeed show the presence of a "logical structure" or "argument" that provides a skeletal organization for the poem and may be interesting or valuable in itself; but it will also show the presence of irrelevant "local details" which reflect the particularity of nature and which cannot be fitted into or assimilated by the logical structure. Should analysis show that the local details in a poem are being used only to support, illustrate, or express the argument, the poem may justly be called a c.u., but it then becomes a species of what Ransom has called "Platonic poetry"—discourse "which is really science but masquerades as poetry by affecting a concern for physical objects" (*The World's Body*, pp. 121–22).

The holistic connotation of "c.u.," which made Ransom view the term with suspicion, has made it an attractive term for other modern critics who argue that a work of literature should be regarded as an organic unity from which nothing can be subtracted and to which nothing can be added without detriment to the whole. W. K. Wimsatt, Jr., in his article "The Structure of the 'Concrete Universal' in Literature" (1947), formally proposed "c.u." as a key term for a holistic poetics which would be "objective and absolute" (p. 279). He classifies as a c.u. any natural or artificial object which exhibits "organized heterogeneity" of a complexity sufficiently great to make it seem "in the highest degree individual" (*ibid.*, pp. 270–72). In poetics he recommends that the term be used to denote not only the poem as a whole but also any of its distinguishable parts, such as characters or metaphors, which may be considered as small wholes within the larger whole. Perhaps the chief reason for Wimsatt's preference for "c.u." is that it provides him with a pair of polar terms which suggest the structure of the organic unity of the poem. He regards a work of literature as discourse which expresses a "meaning," "value," "idea," "concept," or "abstraction" (the universal) by means of the specific details (the concrete) which constitute the matter of the poem. Thus the meaning is the form or

unifying principle; and the poem is an organic unity if the characters, actions, metrical devices, words, and metaphors combine to body forth this universal. Furthermore, the concrete is the only possible means for expressing the universal, which (in a good poem) is so subtle and individual that ordinary language cannot provide a substantive class name for it. For example, the unique feeling of surprise which receives its formulation in Keats's *On First Looking into Chapman's Homer* can be conveyed only by the sequence of the particular metaphors which appear in the poem.

Wimsatt accepts this theory of the structure of the c.u. in literature because it can be used successfully for the analysis and evaluation of poetry and because the history of literary and aesthetic criticism shows that critics have been preoccupied with an opposition in which one extreme is called "universal," "general," or "abstract," and the other "particular," "individual," or "concrete." Critics have used this opposition to define poetry, to determine its subject matter and structure, and to generate principles for evaluation. It has been incorporated in critical dicta like the following: poetry "tends to express the universal, history the particular" (Aristotle); the poet "coupleth the general notion with the particular example" (Sidney); "The business of a poet is to examine, not the individual, but the species" (Johnson); the object of poetry is "truth, not individual and local, but general, and operative" (Wordsworth); Shakespeare had "the universal, which is potentially in each particular, opened out to him" (Coleridge); "All sensuous and concrete ideas, even abstract thought-sequences as embodied in a whole of individual and typical import, can be the material of this [penetrative] imagination, and therefore it enters into and is operative in all recognition and production of the beautiful" (Bosanquet). The recurrence of this opposition suggests that the concepts of "concrete" and "universal" must both appear in any acceptable theory of the nature and structure of poetry. Wimsatt says that modern criticism, especially that of Empson, Brooks, Blackmur, and Tate, has finally formulated correctly the doctrine which had been adumbrated in earlier critical writings.

Ransom took the occasion of the republication of Wimsatt's article in *The Verbal Icon* for a fresh restatement of his poetics and his arguments against "Hegelianism." In the past he had made frequent attempts to distinguish the different elements or components which are found in poetry and to state their relationship. He had spoken of "contingents" and "constants"; "thing" and "idea"; "local texture" and "logical structure"; "particularity" and "universality." Regardless of how he had named the components, he had always looked upon a poem as an "aggregate" in which several different interests are loosely combined. He is now willing to accept "c.u." as a term designating the components if a "Kantian," rather than "Hegelian," relationship between them is allowed (that is, if the term can be used in a nonholistic sense).

The preceding discussion suggests that in modern criticism "c.u." is an ambiguous term naming a variety of concepts. It functions as both a descriptive and an evaluative term, carrying the recommendation that of the objects which have in the past been denoted by the term "poetry" only those which also fall into the genus "c.u." are to be considered "true" poems or "good" poems. "C.u." should be useful to critics who wish to defend one of the following positions (or some combination of these): (1) that a poem or other literary work should (or should not) be an organic whole; (2) that a poem should be both a concrete object and a universal object; (3) that the elements found in poems may be exhaustively classified into those which are concrete and those which are universal and that a certain proportion or relationship should be maintained between these two sets of elements; or (4) that poetry is a peculiar use of language that "fuses" the concrete and the universal, or "reveals" the universal "hidden" in the concrete, or expresses a universal theme, meaning, or archetype (by way of the concrete of allegory, example, symbol, or metaphor) which could not receive as precise or as effective a statement in any other way. Because of the notorious vagueness and ambiguity of "concrete" and "universal" (Wimsatt and Brooks list nine different meanings for "universal" in their *Literary Criticism: A Short History*, pp. 331–33), varying concepts of the c.u. can also be developed within any one of these four broad positions. Some objection may be raised to the substitution of "c.u." (in its holistic sense) for "unity in variety" or "organic whole." In spite of Ransom, holism dominates modern literary theory and aesthetics and will presumably continue to do so. However, some holistic critics may argue that "c.u." begs the question with respect to the structure of the organic unity which is (or ought to be) present in literary works.

J. Royce, *The Spirit of Modern Philosophy* (1892; especially pp. 222–27, 492–506); B. Bosanquet, *The Principle of Individuality and Value* (1912); F. H. Bradley, *The Principles of Logic* (2d ed., 1922); J. C. Ransom, *The World's Body* (1938), "Crit. as Pure Speculation," *The Intent of the Critic*, ed. D. A. Stauffer (1941), "Art Needs a Little Separating," KR, 6 (1944), "Art Worries the Naturalists," KR, 7 (1945), and "The C.U.," KR, 16 (1954), 17 (1955); W. K.

Wimsatt, Jr., "The Structure of the 'C.U.' in Lit.," PMLA, 62 (1947) and *The Verbal Icon* (1954); Wheelwright; Wimsatt and Brooks. F.G.

CONDUPLICATIO. See ANADIPLOSIS.

CONNECTICUT WITS. See AMERICAN POETRY.

CONNOTATION AND DENOTATION. Contemporary critics who have concerned themselves with the "multi-dimensionalism" of language and who advocate that poets should exploit the full resources of language have found the terms "c." and "d." useful to mark distinctions among these resources. These terms are usually applied only to words, and d. almost always signifies the intension and/or extension of a word; however, c. names a variety of concepts.

C. has been used to designate any or all of the responses which a word in a particular context disposes a reader to make other than his recognition of its denotative meaning. Thus c. may be (1) any sensory or emotional response; (2) any cognitive response which is a consequence of suggestion, association, or inference, or of the look, spelling, or sound of a word, or of some device such as Empsonian ambiguity or the symbolic use of a word. Most critics, however, prefer to call such responses the result of the "extralogical" dispositions of words, and use c. as a name for *one* of these dispositions.

M. C. Beardsley (in his *Aesthetics*, pp. 125–126; see also pp. 116–124, 149–151) has proposed the following terminology: the "signification" of a term is the sum total of its "conceptual" or "cognitive" meaning; the "denotation" is the referent it points to; the "designation" is the set of characteristics that the referent must have to be correctly denoted by that term; and the "connotation" is the "secondary" or "accompanying" meaning. (Empson's "Implication" is another name for such secondary meaning.) Connotative meanings are also characteristics of the referent: "What a word connotes . . . are the characteristics that it does not designate but that belong, or are widely thought or said to belong, to many of the things it denotes" (*ibid.*, p. 125. "Characteristic" is interpreted broadly and includes the effects, uses, etc. of the referent. Beardsley should have added that sometimes some of the most important connotations are characteristics that a speech-community thinks a referent *ought* to have). Beardsley says that the connotations of a term are just as "objective" as its designation, and are to be distinguished from "personal associations" which have little value for the explication of poetry. In literature the connotations of a word are "liberated," especially by the power of metaphor, and the explication of metaphor consists in listing the connotations of the "modifier" that may appropriately be attributed to the "subject."

The value of c. depends on the value of the effects the poet can produce by its use. C. has been praised as one of the means by which poetic language achieves depth, density, thickness, richness, and condensation. Enthusiastic critics have said that the meanings of great poems are infinite and hence inexhaustible. But tastes differ; and although some latent or hidden meaning is present (or can be discovered) in all poetry, even the humblest (see Beardsley's interpretation of *Little Jack Horner, ibid.*, p. 405), the recommendations of critics and the practice of poets show no uniformity with respect to the amount of c. and other implicit meaning that is desirable in an imaginative work (see Bateson and Tillyard). Certainly, "The more connotation, the better!" must not be irresponsibly urged; and, as has often been pointed out (see Sparrow, Tate, and Winters), neglect of d. in favor of c. leads to obscurity and incoherence or, at best, to a very limited range of poetic effects.

L. Abercrombie, *The Theory of Poetry* (1926); G. H. W. Rylands, *Words and Poetry* (1928); W. Empson, *Seven Types of Ambiguity* (1930, rev. ed. 1947), and *The Structure of Complex Words* (1951); F. W. Bateson, *Eng. Poetry and the Eng. Language* (1934); J. Sparrow, *Sense and Poetry* (1934); E. M. W. Tillyard, *Poetry Direct and Oblique* (1934); A. Tate, "Tension in Poetry," *Reason in Madness* (1935); Y. Winters, "Preliminary Problems," "John Crowe Ransom," *The Anatomy of Nonsense* (1943); C. Brooks, *The Well Wrought Urn* (1947); R. B. Heilman, "Preliminaries: Crit. Method," *This Great Stage* (1948); M. C. Beardsley, *Aesthetics* (1958); I. C. Hungerland, *Poetic Discourse* (1958).　　　　F.G.

CONSONANCE. Aside from the broader meaning of a pleasing combination of sounds or ideas, it is (1) the counterpart of assonance (q.v.) and refers to partial or total identity of consonants in words or syllables whose *main* vowels differ (e.g., *pressed-past, shadow-meadow*). For c. restricted to sounds following the main vowel, see NEAR RHYME. As a deliberate device to replace rhyme, rich (i.e., total) c. has been used in a number of poems by Wilfred Owen, e.g., "Has your soul sipped / Of the sweetness of all sweets? / Has it well supped / But yet hungers and sweats?" Such poems as his *Strange Meeting* are virtually entirely constructed with this type of impure rhyme, intended no doubt to convey the discordant anguish of war and death. (2) In Ir. poetry there is c. ("uaithne") between words when the corresponding vowels are of the same quantity, the corresponding consonants or consonant groups of the same class, and the final consonants of the same class *and* quality.—E. Rickert, *New Methods for the Study of Lit.* (1927); W. Owen, *The Poems of W. Owen*, ed. E. Blunden (1931); E. Knott, *Ir. Syllabic Poetry 1200–1600* (2d ed., 1957).　　U.K.G.; S.L.M.

CONSTRUCTIVISTS. A group of young Soviet poets founded in 1924, including Ilya Selvinski, Vera Inber, and, as the group's theoretician, K. L. Zelinski. The c. declared that a poem should be a "construction," in which all images and devices should be directed toward the subject. Thus, a poem about war might employ a marching rhythm. This rigid aesthetic was never followed very literally, and the movement itself broke up around 1930.—"Konstruktivizm," *Literaturnaya entsiklopediya*, v (1931).　　W.E.H.

CONTE DÉVOT. A pious tale, in prose or verse, in the 13th and 14th c. It is distinct from the saint's life and from the moral tale. The most famous one is the *Tombeor Nostre Dame*, or *Jongleur de Notre Dame*, where a minstrel, whose only talent is dancing, performs before the image of Our Lady, to her approval. Such tales were undoubtedly inspired by the big collections known as the *Vita Patrum* and the *Miracles Nostre Dame*. Most of these contes are miracle tales, but not all. There is the *Conte del'hermite et del jongleour*. A holy hermit is told by an angel that his companion in heaven will be a minstrel. The hermit is disgusted and goes to the town marketplace. There he talks with a poor minstrel and hears his life story. Knowing that the poor man is better than he the hermit repents, and eventually the two are admitted to heaven together.—O. Schultz-Gora, *Zwei altfranzösische Dichtungen* (4th ed., 1919); E. Lommatzsch, *Del Tumbeor Nostre Dame* (1920).　　U.T.H.

CONTESTS, POETIC. See POETIC CONTESTS.

CONTRACTIONS. See POETIC CONTRACTIONS.

CONVENTION. By "c." is meant (1) "rule that, by implicit agreement between a writer and some of his readers (or of his audience) allows him certain freedoms in, and imposes certain restrictions upon, his treatment of style, structure, and theme and enables these readers to interpret his work correctly" or (2) "product of the observance of such a rule." The number of readers who are parties to the agreement (that is, who have knowledge of the c.) may be very small indeed; else a writer could never create a new c. (for example, free verse or sprung rhythm), revive an old (alliterative verse, in the 14th c. and, by Auden, in the 20th), or abandon an old (the heroic couplet). Readers who are not parties to the agreement (that is, who are ignorant of—or, at least, out of sympathy with—the c.) must to some extent misinterpret a work that exemplifies it; and, when the number of such readers becomes large, writers may abandon the c. —though, of course, works that exemplify it remain to be interpreted (or misinterpreted). The conventions of the pastoral elegy are instances of abandoned conventions; and Dr. Johnson is an instance of a reader who misinterprets a work (*Lycidas*) because he is ignorant of or out of sympathy with these conventions. Conventions both liberate and restrict the writer because they usually go in sets, because, therefore, a writer's decision to use a certain c. obliges him either to use certain others or to risk misleading his reader, and because the freedom given him by the set as a whole or by some of its parts may well be restricted by other parts. The conventions of the epic, for example, allow a writer to achieve the sublime but compel him to forgo the conversational idiom of the metaphysical lyric (and thus, of course, to risk, as Milton does, the censure of those modern critics who take the conventions of that lyric to be *the* conventions of all poetry). Some examples of conventions of style are the rhyme scheme of the sonnet and the diction of the ballad; of structure, beginning an epic *in medias res* and representing the subject of a pastoral elegy as a shepherd; and, of theme, the attitudes toward love in the Cavalier lyric and toward death in the Elizabethan lyric.

To break with conventions (or "rules") is sometimes thought a merit, sometimes a defect; but, merit or defect, such a break is never abandonment of all conventions but replacement of an old set with a new. Wordsworth condemns 18th-c. poetry for using poetic diction (Preface to the 2d edition of the *Lyrical Ballads*); F. R. Leavis condemns Georgian poetry for adhering to "nineteenth-century conventions of 'the poetical'" (*New Bearings*, p. 14). But—though conventions come and go and though we may regret the passing of the old or welcome the advent of the new—literature, new or old, cannot escape conventions.

Insistence upon the necessity of knowing what the conventions of a given work are (as in the criticism of E. E. Stoll) does not entail, as some theorists wrongly hold (for example, Wellek and Warren, *Theory of Literature*, pp. 32–33), either judgment of the work by the extent to which it conforms to the conventions of its genre or the "intentional fallacy" (or, if it entails the latter, then insistence upon the necessity of knowing the Elizabethan sense of, say, "passing"—as in "passing fair"—also entails that "fallacy"). The concept of genre nowadays is in some disrepute (or, more exactly, sets of conventions are looser than they used to be); but now as always a c. in Sense 1 is a rule of interpretation; and, to understand a given work, a reader must understand its conventions—not only its linguistic ones, but its more specifically literary ones of style, structure, and theme.

R. S. Crane proposes that the sense of "c." be restricted in such a way that "'convention' denotes any characteristic of the matter or technique of a poem the reason for the presence of which in the poem cannot be inferred from the necessities of the form envisaged but must be sought in the historical circumstances of its composition . . ." (*The Languages of Criticism*, p. 198, n. 62). In other words, those conventions that all works in a certain genre must, by definition, share are not (in Crane's sense) conventions. Thus he would not count an unhappy ending as a c. of tragedy but does count the chorus in Gr. tragedy as such. But he acknowledges that his proposed sense does not conform to modern usage of "c."—S. Johnson, *Lives of the Eng. Poets* (1779–81); W. Wordsworth, Preface to the *Lyrical Ballads* (2d ed., 1800); J. L. Lowes, *C. and Revolt in Poetry* (1922); E. E. Stoll, *Poets and Playwrights* (1930); F. R. Leavis, *New Bearings in Eng. Poetry* (1932); M. C. Bradbrook, *Themes and Conventions of Elizabethan Tragedy* (1935); Wellek and Warren; Crane. M.S.

CONVERSATION PIECES. The c. piece or poem is relaxed and informal, but serious. Like Horace's epistles and satires, from which it probably springs, it is a genre intermediate between poetry and prose—*propriora sermoni*, which in Coleridge's case Charles Lamb translated as "properer for a sermon." Not uncommon in the latter part of the 18th c., the c. poem is peculiarly a favorite with Wordsworth and Coleridge, doubtless because of its unique combination of unpretentiousness and depth, attributes given it by Cowper. Wordsworth's *Expostulation and Reply* and *The Tables Turned* are c. poems, though blank verse is the genre's most appropriate medium; the Lines *Composed a Few Miles Above Tintern Abbey* might be thought of as a c. piece which got out of hand and burst its bounds. Coleridge's *Dejection: an Ode* is another such, but as a Pindaric ode it does not quite correspond to the type. Coleridge, however, is the great practitioner of the c. piece in *The Eolian Harp, This Limetree Bower My Prison, The Nightingale, To William Wordsworth,* and a number of other poems. We have nothing quite like this genre today, but W. H. Auden and perhaps Theodore Roethke might be mentioned as poets who have written in its spirit. G. M. Harper, "Coleridge's C. Poems," QR, 244 (1925); D. G. James, *The Romantic Comedy*

(1948); R. H. Fogle, "Coleridge's C. Poems," TSE, 5 (1955). R.H.F.

COPLA. Since the Sp. term "c." often means simply stanza, it is necessary to specify the type, such as *c. de arte mayor* (see ARTE MAYOR) or *c. de arte menor* (see ARTE MENOR). The *c. de pie quebrado,* developed during the 14th and 15th c., is any variation of the *c. de arte menor* in which one or more lines have been reduced to half-length (4 syllables or their equivalent) and/or half-lines have been added. The most famous, though not the most common, has the rhyme scheme ABcABcDEfDEf and is often called *c.* (or *estrofa*) *de Jorge Manrique,* or *c. manriqueña* after the author of the famous *Coplas por la muerte de su padre.* The *c. real* (also called *décima, décima falsa, estancia real,* or *quintilla doble*) is an important 15th-c. variation of the *c. de arte menor.* It is a 10-line octosyllabic strophe, the equivalent of two *quintillas,* the two usually having different rhyme schemes. The *c. real* was widely used in the 16th c., but in the 17th gradually gave way in popularity to one of its late 16th-c. variations, the *espinela.* See also CANTAR.—F. Rodríguez Marín, *El alma de Andalucía en sus mejores coplas amorasas* (1929); D. C. Clarke, "The *c. real*" and "The 15th C. *c. de pie quebrado,*" HR, 10 (1942); Navarro. D.C.C.

COQ-À-L'Âne. Name derived from an OF proverbial expression, "C'est bien sauté du cocq a l'asne," which was, and still is, used to describe an incoherent manner of speaking or writing. The content of the genre is the satiric treatment of the vices, faults, and foibles of individuals, social groups, and even institutions. Clément Marot, who created the form in 1530, was the author of four *coq-à-l'âne,* all of them in the form of (generally) octosyllabic verse epistles of varying length.—J. du Bellay, *Deffense et Illustration de la Langue Françoyse,* ed. H. Chamard (1904), pp. 218–21; C. E. Kinch, *La Poésie Satirique de Clément Marot* (1940); article by H. Chamard in *Dictionnaire des Lettres Françaises: Le Seizième Siècle* (1951). I.S.

CORNISH POETRY. The Corn. language, now extinct, belonged to the Brythonic or 'P'-Celtic group, but had closer affinities with Breton than with Welsh. It died out in the 18th c. Apart from one long narrative poem and five plays, all on religious topics, the literary remains are meager in the extreme. Although Cornwall must have supplied to medieval romance a good deal of the "Matter of Britain" in the extant Corn. literature, this rich vein is left unexploited. The earliest verse to survive is a fragment of 41 lines on a charter dated 1340, but the poem may have been copied on it

some sixty years later and seems to be part of a lost play. The speaker is offering a lady in marriage and giving her advice based on Corn. folklore. The rhyme scheme is aabccb, with lines varying from 4 to 9 syllables. *Pascon agan Arluth* (The Passion of our Lord) is a narrative poem, consisting of 259 stanzas of 8 lines, each line of 7 syllables, trochaic, and the lines rhyme alternately. The earliest manuscript is mid-15th c. The theme is the fasting and temptation of Christ, followed by the story of Holy Week, based on Biblical and apocryphal sources.

The main interest of Corn. poetry lies in the plays. They were composed by men of learning but for a popular audience, and were performed in open-air theatres, the "plenys-angwary," spaces enclosed by circular banks of earth, now known as "rounds," some of which can still be seen, e.g., at St. Just and Perranzabuloe. Three of the plays, called the *Ordinalia,* form a sequence. These are the *Origo Mundi* (2,846 lines), based on Old Testament history and some incongruent legendary material, the *Passio Domini* (3,242 lines) recounting the life and death of Christ, and the *Resurrectio Domini* (2,646 lines) which has a greater accretion of legend including lives of saints and the death of Pilate. Rhythm is basically trochaic, but stress regularity is not meticulously observed. Rhymes are often stricter to the eye than to the ear, a sure sign of "learned" or "literary" composition. Full lines of 8 or 7 syllables can rhyme alternately, shorter lines or half-lines of 4 syllables can do likewise, and lines of varying or equal length within the same sequence or "stanza" can conform to aabccb or aabaab rhyme schemes. More intricate patterns also occur, but otherwise such metrical features as alliteration and internal rhyme are random and not woven into a strict pattern like Welsh *cynghanedd* (q.v.).

Beunans Meriasek (The Life of St. Meriasek, 4,568 lines), was discovered by Dr. Whitley Stokes in a manuscript written in 1504. This play has linguistic forms which indicate a later period than the *Ordinalia,* but metrically it is similar. Local references associate it with the cult of Meriasek at Camborne, a 7th-c. saint whose legendary life, told with anachronisms involving the appearance of Pope Sylvester and the Emperor Constantine, forms the topic of the play. The latest, at least in its extant form, of the Corn. plays is *Gwreans an Bys* (The Creation of the World, 2,548 lines). The earliest MS bears a colophon in the hand of William Jordan, of Helston, and is dated 1611. The play borrows much from *Origo Mundi,* but has features of its own. Lucifer and his demons revert to Eng. except when they are on their good behavior—then they speak Corn. The most noticeable metrical innovation is a more frequent disregard of syllable-counting. In all the plays there are passages of touching poignancy, and considerable literary merit, but the quality is not sustained.

The few remaining scraps of late Corn. verse (mostly 17th c.) indicate a falling away, foreshadowed in *Gwreans an Bys*, from the more strictly syllabic verse patterns of medieval Corn. It may be asked whether this was merely a phase of the decay of the language, or an increased awareness of stress as a metrical principle. The remains, however, are too scanty for one to judge with assurance. A few enthusiasts in our own day have learned Corn., and poems in this long neglected Celtic tongue have been written and published of recent years.—H. Jenner, *Handbook of the Corn. Language* (1904; general survey, with bibliog.). See also the following editions and translations: E. Norris, *The Ancient Corn. Drama* (1859); W. Stokes, "Pascon agan Arluth," TPS (1860–61), "Gwreans an Bys," TPS (1863) and "Beunans Meriasek," TPS (1872). D.M.L.

CORONACH. A funeral lament or dirge, originating in Ireland and in the Scottish Highlands. The term, which in Gaelic means "wailing together," owes its currency in Eng. literary history to Sir Walter Scott, who refers to the custom in his novels and introduces into his *Lady of the Lake* (3.16) a c. of his own composition, beginning: "He is gone on the mountain. / He is lost to the forest, / Like a summer-dried fountain, / When our need was the sorest . . ." According to Scott's presentation, the c. was usually sung by women.

CORRELATIVE VERSE takes its name from the literary device of correlation which consists in a linear relationship of two or more members (first correlative plurality), matched by at least another one (second correlative plurality) whose members are symmetrically related to the members of the first plurality. A Gr. epigram from the *Anthologia Graeca* (3.241) gives a very clear idea of this type of poetry in one of its simplest forms: "You [wine, are] boldness, youth, strength, wealth, country [1st plurality] / to the shy, the old, the weak, the poor, the foreigner." [2d plurality]. Examples of correlation are found in Gr. poetry starting with the 3d c. B.C. and in L. poetry starting with the 1st c. A.D. Medieval L. poets were very fond of this device, and early Romance poetry, especially Prov., made use of it too.

A special type of correlative poetry, the disseminative-recapitulative type, used by Petrarch, spread, together with Petrarchism (q.v.), in Italy, France, Spain, and England during the Renaissance and the baroque period. An example of the disseminative-recapitulative type is the following first quatrain of a sonnet by the Elizabethan poet Thomas Watson: "Here end my *sorrow*, no here my sorrow springeth / Here end my *woe*, no here begins my wailing: / Here cease my *griefe*, no here my griefe deepe wringeth, / Sorrow, woe, griefe, nor ought else is auailing" with the recapitulation in the last line.

Correlative poetry has been found in Sanskrit, Persian, and Arabic literatures and—even though its relationship to the Western tradition has not been studied yet—it seems to offer to the scholar a valid tool to investigate the propagation of literary material within and without the Western tradition.—Curtius; D. Alonso and C. Bousoño, *Seis calas en la expresión literaria española* (1951); D. Alonso, "Antecedentes griegos y latinos de la poesía correlativa moderna" in *Estudios dedicados a Menéndez Pidal*, IV (1953); J. G. Fucilla, "A Rhetorical Pattern in Renaissance and Baroque Poetry," SRen, 3 (1956); D. Alonso, "Poesía correlativa inglesa en los siglos XVI y XVII," *Filología moderna*, 2 (1961). R.MI.

COUNTERPOINT (syncopation). A rhythmical effect achieved through metrical variations. C. results from the establishment of a relatively stable metrical structure (e.g., iambic pentameter) and then the occasional departure from this structure so as to create a sense of two metrical patterns, the old and the new, continuing at once. C. is impossible except in moderately regular metrical compositions, for any variation must have something fixed to vary from. In general, at least two contiguous feet must be varied or reversed from the initial metrical pattern if a counterpointed rhythm is to be felt. In the following line by G. M. Hopkins,

> The world is charged with the grandeur
> of God,

the third and the fourth foot constitute a counterpointed section, for they interrupt and "reverse" the ascending rhythm (q.v.) of the earlier part of the line. See METRICAL VARIATIONS.—"Author's Preface," *Poems of Gerard Manley Hopkins*, ed. R. Bridges and W. H. Gardner (3d ed., 1948). P.F.

COUPLET. Two lines of verse, usually rhymed. Ever since the advent of rhymed verse, the c. has counted as one of the principal units of versification in the Western literatures, whether as a stanzaic form in extended composition, as a subordinate element in other stanzaic forms, or as an independent poem of an epigrammatic nature. The c. composed of two lines of iambic pentameter—the so-called heroic couplet (q.v.)—is the most important c. form in Eng. poetry. As perfected by Dryden and Pope, the heroic c. is "closed"—syntax and thought are fitted neatly into the envelope of rhyme and meter—and in this form it dominates the poetry of the neoclassical period: "Know then thyself, presume not God to scan; / The proper study of Mankind is Man" (Pope, *Essay on Man*). Although the heroic c. is generally associated with its 18th-c. masters, one should recognize that it is a form of great antiquity, used by Chaucer in *The Legend of Good Women* and most of *The Canterbury Tales*, by Marlowe, Chapman, and other Elizabethans, and by Donne, whose free use of enjambement achieves effects utterly different from those of Pope and Dryden.

The iambic tetrameter or octosyllabic c. (see OCTOSYLLABIC VERSE) has a distinguished history in Eng. verse as the form of Milton's *L'Allegro* and *Il Penseroso*, Marvell's *To his Coy Mistress*, and Coleridge's *Christabel* (see CHRISTABEL METER). The 4-beat couplets of Samuel Butler's *Hudibras* really constitute a separate type, known as Hudibrastic couplets. Not all Eng. couplets utilize regular line length. Poets as diverse as George Herbert and Robert Browning have developed verse forms in which the couplet rhyming of irregular lines occurs: ". . . With their triumphs and their glories and the rest. / Love is best!" (Browning, *Love Among the Ruins*.).

The c. of rhyming alexandrines is the dominant form of Fr. narrative and dramatic poetry (see ALEXANDRINE). In the hands of the classical masters—Corneille, Molière, Racine, La Fontaine—the alexandrine c. is end-stopped and relatively self-contained, but a freer use of enjambement is found among the romantics. Under Fr. influence, the alexandrine c. became the dominant metrical form of German and Dutch narrative and dramatic verse in the 17th and 18th c. After being neglected during this period, a more indigenous German c. form, the tetrameter c. called *Knittelvers* (q.v.), was revived by Goethe and Schiller.

Although the c. ranks as one of the major forms for extended poetic composition, its function as a constituent of more complex stanzaic forms is scarcely less important. The principal stanzaic forms created by the later Middle Ages and the Renaissance—ottava rima and rhyme royal (qq.v.)—both conclude with a c., which may be used for purposes of formal conclusion, summation, or epigrammatic comment. The pithy qualities inherent in c. structure are evident not only in these stanzas but also in the independent epigrammatic c., and in the Shakespearean sonnet (see SONNET), which concludes with a c.

As a unit of dramatic verse the c. occurs in the classical Fr. drama, the older German and Dutch drama, and the "heroic plays" of Restoration England. It also fills an important function in Elizabethan-Jacobean drama as a variation from the standard blank verse; its principal use is at the conclusion of a scene or at a peak of dramatic action. The relative frequency of couplet variation is an important means of determining the chronology of Shakespeare's plays, as he tended, with increasing maturity, to abandon the device.

In Fr., the term *couplet* is sometimes used with the meaning of stanza, as in the *couplet carré* (square couplet), a stanza composed of 8 lines of octosyllabic verse. See also DISTICH.

F.J.W.; A.P.

COURTLY LOVE (Fr. *amour courtois*, It. *amore cortese*. Prov. *domnei*, German *Frauendienst*) is a group of conventions widely observed in the amatory poetry and romance writing of Western Europe during the Middle Ages and continued in much of the literature of the Renaissance both on the Continent and in England. In the general sense in which the term is usually employed, c.l. is primarily a literary phenomenon; though there is little doubt about the actual existence of courts of love as a form of social diversion, they did not exist as formal judicial assemblies.

During the earlier Middle Ages the status of woman was vastly different from that which obtains today. There was no concern about passionate love between male and female as a normal feeling. Such love was frowned upon by the theologians, even to the extent of being considered improper between husband and wife. Woman was the perennial Eve, and man regarded her primarily as the potential mother of his children, hardly as a companion enjoying equal status, and certainly never as a lady commanding abject devotion. In the early 12th c. a markedly changed view of man's relationship to woman developed in southern France in the poetry of the troubadours (q.v.), a concept which is perhaps most clearly reflected in the lyrics of a poet who wrote during the last half of the century, Bernart de Ventadorn. It is this treatment of love which has come to be known as c.l., though the term itself was unknown in medieval times; it is derived from a phrase *amour courtois*, coined by Gaston Paris in 1883 to describe the new concept.

C.l. is a noble passion; the courtly lover idealizes his beloved; she, his sovereign lady, occupies an exalted position over him; his feelings for her ennoble him and make him more worthy; her beauty of body and soul makes him long for union with her, not for passion's sake but as a means of achieving the ultimate in moral excellence. It is a striking paradox that love as presented by most of the troubadours is adulterous and illicit and, at the same time, ennobling and conducive to virtue. "C.l. is a species of that movement inherent in the soul of man towards a desired object. It is this object, the final object, which specifies love and differentiates one from the other. When the object of love is the pleasure of sense, then love is sensual and carnal; directed towards the spiritual, it is mystic, towards a person of the opposite sex, sexual, towards God, divine. C.l. is a type of sensual love and what distinguishes it from other forms of sexual love, from mere passion, from so-called platonic love, from married love is its purpose or motive, its formal object, namely, the lover's progress and growth in natural goodness, merit, and worth" (A. J. Denomy, *Speculum*, 28:44).

The product of an essentially aristocratic and chivalric society, c.l. is essentially Ovidian in much of its machinery, but it also owes much to the feudalism under which it flourished (the lover as vassal, for instance) and the Christianity of the day, especially the cult of the Virgin (e.g., the exaltation of the beloved). The troubadour concept of love spread to Italy, where it attained its ultimate refinement in the poetry of the *dolce stil nuovo*, q.v. (e.g., Guinicelli, Cavalcanti) and especially in the *Vita Nuova;* to northern France, where it provided the essentials for the love poetry of the trouvères (q.v.) and became an important element in the romances (cf. especially Chrétien de Troyes' *Le Chevalier de la Charrette*, the most polished early treatment of the Lancelot and Guinevere story); to Germany, where it enriched the poetry of the Minnesingers (q.v.); to England, where it found its fullest early use in Chaucer, particularly his *Troilus and Criseyde*. Through the poetry of Petrarch especially (but not exclusively) c.l. came to the Eng. poets of the 16th c. (notably the sonneteers and Spenser) as well as to the Fr. poets of the *Pléiade*, q.v. (e.g., Ronsard, Du Bellay). Thus any attempt to frame a single brief statement adequately describing the concept as reflected in so many literatures and literary forms spread over so many centuries is basically impossible. Much of the confusion concerning c.l. stems from the assumption that there was a single generalized type which all authors, writing in different genres at various times in several languages, celebrated or at least drew upon. The nonsensual, idealized love of the troubadours, the *fin amors* of the *canzon*, is hardly the same as the adulterous love of Tristan and Isolde or of Lancelot and Guinevere, nor is married love totally excluded (e.g., *Parzifal* and Chrétien's *Yvain*). "The novelty of C.L. lies in three basic elements: first, in the ennobling force of human love; second, in the elevation of the beloved to a place of superiority above the lover; third, in the conception of love as ever un-satiated, ever increasing desire. Of course, the troubadour lyrics were embellished with other conceits, formulae and situations: the nature introduction, the personification of love as a god with absolute power over his army of lovers, the idea of love as a sickness with all its familiar exterior manifestations, the ceaseless fears of the lover at losing his beloved, at not being worthy of her, at displeasing her, the position of inferiority of the lover and the feeling of timidity to which the feeling gives rise, the capriciousness, haughtiness and disdain of the beloved, the need of secrecy, stealth and furtiveness in the intrigue, the danger of tale-bearers, and so on. These notions and conceits have their parallels and analogues in classical literature, in medieval Latin and Arabic love literature. They are not peculiar to C.L., but are, rather, universally human and belong to the general fund of love literature. It is, on the contrary, the three basic elements of the conception of love as desire, the ennobling force of love, and the cult of the beloved that make C.L. to be C.L. and which set it apart from all other conceptions of love. They provide, as it were, the skeleton framework, the mechanics or thought pattern of C.L.: the surge of the lover to rise in worth and in virtue towards the beloved through the force and energy of desire" (A. J. Denomy, *The Heresy of C.L.*, pp. 20–21).

For general purposes, the codification attempted by Andreas Capellanus in the late 12th c., the *De Amore*, is still helpful as a point of reference; its alternate title, *De Arte Honeste Amandi*, which is found in some mss., is more aptly descriptive, for the idea of love as an art is basic to the notion of c.l. The fact that Andreas obviously wrote with tongue in cheek and that he is often contradictory does not reduce the value of his treatise for the modern reader.

T. P. Cross and W. A. Nitze, *Lancelot and Guenevere: A Study on the Origins of C.L.* (1930); C. S. Lewis, *The Allegory of Love* (1936); A. Capellanus, *The Art of C.L.*, tr. J. J. Parry (1941); A. J. Denomy, "An Inquiry into the Origins of C.L.," *Mediaeval Studies*, 6 (1944); A. J. Denomy, *The Heresy of C.L.* (1947); T. Silverstein, "Andreas, Plato, and the Arabs: Remarks on Some Recent Accounts of C.L.," MP, 47 (1949); A. J. Denomy, "C.L. and Courtliness," *Speculum*, 28 (1953); H. J. Weigand, *Three Chapters on C.L. in Arthurian France and Germany* (1956); D. de Rougemont, *Love in the Western World*, tr. M. Belgion (rev. ed., 1957); W. T. H. Jackson, "The *De Amore* of Andreas Capellanus and the Practice of Love at Court," RR, 49 (1958); M. Valency, *In Praise of Love* (1958); J. F. Benton, "The Court of Champagne as a Lit. Center," *Speculum*, 36 (1961); G. de Lorris and J. de Meun,

The Romance of the Rose, tr. H. W. Robbins (1962); D. W. Robertson, Jr., "Some Medieval Doctrines of Love," *A Preface to Chaucer* (1962).   T.A.K.

COURTLY MAKERS. A group of court poets who, during the reign of Henry VIII, introduced the characteristic forms of Renaissance poetry into England from Italy and France, and thereby laid the foundations for the great poetic achievement of their Elizabethan successors. One of their number, Sir Thomas Wyatt (1503?–1542), wrote the first Eng. sonnets, and another, Henry Howard, Earl of Surrey (1517?–1547), is credited with the first Eng. blank verse. Most of the work of the c.m. does not have major artistic importance. Some of the best of it was compiled from manuscript collections and published as *Tottel's Miscellany* in 1557. The work had a great influence on the Elizabethans.

The term *maker*, as a literal translation of the Gr. *poiein* from which *poet* is derived, was in common use in 15th- and 16th-c. England and Scotland.—J. Stevens, *Music and Poetry in the Early Tudor Court* (1961); R. Southall, *The Courtly Maker* (1964).

CRASIS (Gr. "mixing," "blending"). The fusion in Gr. of a vowel or diphthong (usually in a monosyllable like the forms of the definite article, the conjunction *kai*, and the exclamation of address *o*, but sometimes at the end of a dissyllable like *mentoi*) with another which follows, e.g., *haner* for *ho aner*, *kago* for *kai ego*, *onax* for *o anax*, and *mentan* for *mentoi an*.—Koster; A. Sidgwick and F. D. Morice, *An Introd. to Gr. Verse Composition* (new impression, 1955).   R.J.G.

CREATIONISM. One of the many postwar poetic *isms* that endeavored to annul past literary tendencies and establish a new aesthetic creed. Vicente Huidobro, a Chilean, propounded the central ideas of c. in Buenos Aires in 1916, and the Fr. poet Reverdy initiated the movement in France. Huidobro's visit to Spain in 1918 made the new creed known there, where it was received with intense but brief and limited enthusiasm. Ultraism (q.v.), however, carried on many of its tendencies. Juan Larrea and Gerardo Diego are the two Sp. poets whose works most reflect the ideas of c.

"To create a poem as Nature creates a tree," is the core of c. according to Huidobro. In daring, oftentimes strained metaphors, he and his followers tried to create a new pure poetry which broke abruptly with the past, and which brought a sense of Godification to the written word. Huidobro wrote:

Why do you sing the rose, O, poets?
Make it flower in the poem.

Only for you
Live all things under the Sun.
The poet is a small God.

G. de Torre, *Las literaturas europeas de vanguardia* (1925); R. Cansinos-Asséns, *La nueva literatura*, III (1927); A. de Undurraga, "Teoría del creacionismo," Vicente Huidobro, *Poesía y prosa. Antología* (1957); *Antología de la poesía española e hispanoamericana*, ed. F. de Onís (1961).   J.A.C.

CRETIC or amphimacer (Gr. "long at both ends"). The cretic foot ($-\smile-$) and verse form are thought to have originated with a Cretan poet called Thaletas (7th c. B.C.) and to have been at first a meter for the hyporchema (q.v.). As is obvious from resolution of either long syllable, the c. is really a form of the paeon (q.v.) and cretic-paeonic measures, though rarely employed in the choruses of Gr. tragedy, are not infrequent in comedy. Cretics occur in early Roman drama and are common in the *clausulae* of Cicero (see PROSE RHYTHM). An example in the former is the song of Phaedromus in Plautus, *Curculio* 147–154:

$$\bar{pes}\breve{su}li,\ heu\bar{s}\mid \bar{pes}\breve{su}li,\mid \bar{vos}\ s\breve{a}lu\mid \bar{to}\ l\breve{u}b\bar{e}ns,$$

$$\bar{vos}\ \breve{a}mo,\mid \bar{vos}\ v\breve{o}lo,\mid \bar{vos}\ p\breve{e}to\ \bar{at}\mid que\ \bar{obsecro}$$

the meaning and meter of which G. E. Duckworth thus reproduces: "Bolts and bars, bolts and bars, gladly I greetings bring, / Hear my love, hear my prayer, you I beg and entreat." Imitations of cretics are not common in Eng., but lines composed of single feet are found in Tennyson's *The Oak*. Coleridge imitated and described the c. thus: "First and last being long, middle short, Amphimacer / Strikes his thundering hoofs like a proud high-bred Racer."—E. W. Scripture, "The Choriambus in Eng. Verse," PMLA, 43 (1928); Dale; G. E. Duckworth, *The Nature of Roman Comedy* (1952); Koster; Beare.   R.J.G.

CRISIS. See PLOT.

CRITICISM. FUNCTIONS.† This article differs from the longer article on types of criticism (q.v.) in being less thorough and more theoretical: it divides criticism according to its possible purposes, a division which cuts across that into schools. There are four (some would say five) functions of c.: technical, social, practical, theoretical. Judicial is a doubtful fifth. There are also a number of related purposes which are not strictly critical.

By technical c. is here meant a guide to the actual practice of writing. There is no recognized term for this, and we might equally well call it "workshop," "didactic" or "pragmatic" c., or even "creative" c. (though this last might

† In Supplement, see also METACRITICISM.

cause confusion with the kind of c. associated with Carlyle and Lamb, in which a foiled creative impulse uses the critical essay as a pretext for its own expression). Such technical c. was common in Elizabethan times: George Gascoigne's *Certayne Notes of Instruction concerning the Making of Verse or Ryme in Eng.* announces its purpose in its title, and Puttenham's *Arte of Eng. Poesie* tells us that its chief purpose is "the learning of Ladies . . . or idle Courtiers . . . to make now and then ditties of pleasure." No serious critic would undertake this task today. Our respect for the individuality of the work of art is so great that we no longer believe that any issues of real concern to the practicing poet can be discussed in general terms: rules and common problems (from the metrical details of Gascoigne up to the theory of the unities) may have an approximate validity or relevance, but they must always in the last resort be considered in relation to the aims of the particular work. If there can be technical c., it must be specific, as in the creative writing class.

Of more importance is the indirectly technical. A great deal of c. which takes the form of comment on existing texts has as one of its aims the improvement of literature as yet unwritten. Thus Donald Davie says of his *Purity of Diction in Eng. Verse* (which is about the attitude of Augustan and romantic poets to their language) "It is to the would-be poet of today that I should like to address myself." The leading examples of this sort of practitioner-critic are Ezra Pound and T. S. Eliot. Eliot has observed that the reader for whom Pound wrote his early c. was primarily "the young poet whose style was still unformed." This concern with the future of poetry is found not only in the prose of Pound, but also in much of his verse: in *Hugh Selwyn Mauberley*, or in his monstrous translation of *The Seafarer*, defensible only as a stylistic hint to the young poet. In the same essay, Eliot observes of himself "the best of my *literary* criticism . . . is a by-product of my private poetry workshop." This would not necessarily make it technical, since we are concerned with function, and not with origins; but it is also the case that in drawing attention to the resemblances between the Fr. symbolists and the 17th-c. metaphysicals Eliot's aim was not only to promote understanding of these poets, but also to open a vein that would be fruitful in modern Eng. poetry. So that although his reading of the metaphysical poets can be challenged (as it has been by Rosemond Tuve and others), the use to which this reading (or misreading) has been put, by Eliot himself and by others, is an achievement that cannot be undone.

It is important that poetry should matter, and should be felt to matter, in the community; and as well as its more specific tasks, c. has what we may call a social, or journalistic, function: the building up of the prestige of literature. This can be done at many levels. At the lowest, it does not matter what is said, as long as books are talked about: the function of the book page in a daily or weekly paper is not merely (perhaps not mainly) to assess the books actually reviewed, but to contribute to the ceaseless discussion of literature. At a rather higher level, this social function consists in the arousing of enthusiasm: the work of such writers as Robert Lynd, Desmond McCarthy, Philip Toynbee, as well as popular academics like Sir Arthur Quiller-Couch, falls here. To read them is to meet a (usually attractive) personality describing with obvious sincerity his love of literature. The dangers of such writing are clear: explicit enthusiasm easily becomes strident (as often in Swinburne), the display of the critic's personality easily becomes exhibitionist, the *rapport* with a wide public is too easily attained by philistinism; but insofar as it sets people reading, and talking about what they read, it is wholly admirable. Once this sort of c. becomes more serious, it will take on one of the other critical functions. The review, if it has something to say about its book, becomes practical c.; remarks on the importance and value of literature, if they become systematic, turn into apologetics, which is a branch of theoretical c. We now turn to these two, which are by far the most important critical functions.

Practical c. is not very old. Few if any commentaries on individual works before the 18th c. are either thorough or illuminating. Such things begin, perhaps, with Addison's *Spectator* essays on *Paradise Lost,* and some of the close attention paid to Shakespeare by such writers as William Richardson and Maurice Morgann; but the real father of practical c. is Coleridge. In him we can for the first time see the qualities of the best of the "New Critics": intense brooding on a work to grasp its essential quality, and illustrating this by careful and subtle reference to details. The editors of *Scrutiny* or the *Kenyon Review* would readily have accepted Coleridge's discussions of Wordsworth or *Venus and Adonis* (from *Biographia Literaria*) or some of his Shakespeare lectures, whereas one fancies they might boggle over Addison's papers on Milton. Not even Coleridge, however, is a fully formed, modern specimen of the practical critic, and most of the leading names in 19th-c. criticism (Bagehot, Pater, Arnold) leave us dissatisfied with their particular comments, or else conceding that their aims were slightly different from ours. Matthew Arnold's idea of "touchstones," for example, looks at first like the sort of comparison of actual passages that is so popular today, but in fact it is only pioneer work—it has none of the careful choice of comparable passages, the juxtaposition of like with almost like, that the good modern critic will insist on. One of Arnold's successors in the Chair of Poetry at Oxford, A. C. Bradley, though his critical approach is no nearer to modern tastes, was far more conscientious about getting down to detail; and his *Shakespearean Tragedy*, though based on assumptions about the nature of drama almost universally rejected now, conducts its argument with a thoroughness and particularity congenial to the rejecters, and eminently worth attacking.

By practical c. is meant the close study of particular works; and if it has a beginning, it was on the day in the 1920's when I. A. Richards started giving unsigned poems to his students at Cambridge for their comments and appraisal. The result was horrifying. Magazine poetasters were extravagantly praised, Donne, Hopkins, and Christina Rossetti firmly damned; every felicity was ridiculed, and every absurdity praised, by large minorities and even majorities. Richards described the experiment in *Practical Criticism*, and added a discussion of the main problems of c. This book and its sequel (*Interpretation in Teaching*) are among the main sources of what has become standard lecture-room practice in America and (to a lesser extent) in England: close reading, or *explication de texte* (for it had always been standard practice in France). Outside the universities, a similar direction was being given to c. by the work of a number of poets: Robert Graves, T. S. Eliot, William Empson. Eliot's *The Sacred Wood* has become the most influential critical work of the century; it mingled a habit of wild and radical generalization with great shrewdness in commenting on actual quotations. Graves and Riding's *Survey of Modernist Poetry* discussed Shakespeare as well as Hopkins and E. E. Cummings: it was a main influence behind the vastly more subtle and daring work of William Empson. Empson carried the search for hidden meanings in great poetry further than ever before, and began a growing and often fantastic hunt for puns, ambiguities, and multiple ironies. Empson's fundamental position is that all great poetry is complex: "Whenever a receiver of poetry is seriously moved by an apparently simple line, what are moving in him are the traces of a great part of his past experience and of the structure of his past judgements." If this is so, there is clearly a great deal for the practical critic to say. Other influences in this movement are F. R. Leavis, Cleanth Brooks, R. P. Blackmur, John Crowe Ransom, and L. C. Knights. Leavis has always maintained that the critic should deny himself the

luxury of any general remarks that cannot be clearly related to particular texts: his own best practice has always conformed to this, and the precept is embodied in the title as well as the contents of *Scrutiny*, the periodical run by him and his collaborators for twenty-one years. Brooks is the great popularizer of the movement, not only in his own critical works, but in the college textbooks written with Robert Penn Warren. A typical product of such c. is the collection of essays by various hands, each on a single poem or book: such as *Determinations*, edited by Leavis, or *Interpretations*, edited by John Wain.

Practical c. is a method as well as an aim. As a method, it consists in basing closely on actual texts whatever one is doing; as an aim, it is pedagogic, and its goal is the full appreciation of the work discussed. Once a reader has appreciated the poem, the commentary (as far as he is concerned) ceases to matter, just as technical c. ceases to matter to a poet once he has written the poem it was intended to stimulate in him. This aim, of course, assumes that there is such a thing as the right reading of a poem, toward which the reader is being led, and objections to practical c. as an aim have mainly been based on denial of this.

The extreme objection is that since taste is subjective, each man's reading is valid only for himself: if two readers disagree about the meaning or value of a poem, each of them, so far as he himself is concerned, is right. F. L. Lucas is an extreme exponent of this position. This view is more often stated than believed. Taken literally, it would make literary discussion futile; there would not even be any point in rereading in order to sharpen and improve one's reactions, since if there is no external standard there can be no improvement. The theoretical answer to this objection is contained in Charles Morris' doctrine of intersubjectivity; and in practice even the strongest relativists pay more attention to the interpretations of some readers than of others, and speak of particular commentaries in such normative terms as shrewd, eccentric, sensitive, or imperceptive.

A less radical but more serious objection is that a work of art is a growing thing, and changes with succeeding generations. When a new work of art is created, says T. S. Eliot, "something . . . happens simultaneously to all the works of art which preceded it." This view received its best theoretical statement in the discussion by Wellek and Warren of the mode of existence of a literary work (*Theory of Literature*, ch. 12); and it is perfectly exemplified in the impact of Eliot's own poetry. It leads naturally to a historical relativism: to the belief (as stated for example by C. Day Lewis) that "every classical poem worth trans-

CRITICISM

lating should be translated afresh every fifty years," and to the observation that every generation reads the masterpieces of the past in its own way.

It is not enough to reply that there may nonetheless be a right reading for one's own time. Epochs overlap, and what seems an eccentric reading may be the first signs of a new movement, or the last fizzle of the old; and the chronological division between generations easily extends itself to include a division between different communities or different viewpoints (such as Catholic, liberal humanist, and Marxist in our time), and even perhaps between different personality types. This line of argument need not lead us back into complete relativism: it means that instead of one right reading we must postulate an area of readings, shading through the doubtful and the eccentric to the absurd, through the tendentious to those incompatible with our own point of view, and perhaps through the old-fashioned to the outmoded. How much variety is allowed among "legitimate" readings will depend largely on the work itself. A lyric by Campion, Landor, or Housman will very nearly have one right reading, which will not even change much with time; while at the other extreme the number of defensible readings of *King Lear* (and even more of *Hamlet*) is clearly very large. In the case of *Lear* this is due to the range and richness of experience embodied in it; in the case of *Hamlet*, to that, and also to certain ambiguities in the nature of the work.

This discussion has assumed that the practical critic influences not only our interpretation but also our judgment of a poem, thus rejecting the view that interpretative and judicial are two separate critical functions. For it is at least arguable that a really thorough interpretation of a poem must be evaluative: as we consider the exact meaning and associations of each phrase, its relation to the whole, the effect of the poem's rhythm and formal qualities, we are either assuming that these effects are achieved, or else drawing attention (implicitly at least) to inadequacies. As for purely judicial c., it is hard to see what this can consist in (apart from a dogmatic assertion that a poem is good or bad) unless it is substantiated by a discussion of the success of actual details. Judicial c. may be a by-product or a conclusion of practical c.: it cannot exist without it.

How far can practical c. go? When two readers disagree about a work, can they be reconciled by one persuading the other that he has misread it? Or must we assume that they are reading the same poem, but reacting differently because they look for different things in poetry? C. S. Lewis, disagreeing with

Leavis about the style of *Paradise Lost,* says "he sees and hates the very thing that I see and love." If this is a typical literary disagreement, there is very little for practical c. to do; but if readers with similar general positions differ in their ability to see exactly what is happening in a poem, then the practical critic has a task: to enlighten those readers who lack his sensibility, or his experience, or his special knowledge, or even his opportunity to devote a great deal of time to puzzling over a work.

Finally, theoretical c. This is a consideration of what literature is: it is a descriptive study insofar as "imaginative" or "creative" writing is being distinguished from science, propaganda, entertainment, or memoirs, and a normative study insofar as genuine literature is being distinguished from inferior. Whereas the practical critic asks "What is this poem saying?" and "Is it good?," the theoretical critic asks, "What constitutes poetic merit?" Apart from the cases in which such an issue arises out of specific disagreements, theoretical c. is c. in its own right: its existence assumes that when we have read and reacted to a poem, it is natural and proper to ask, disinterestedly, what exactly we have done. The first great work of theoretical c. is Aristotle's *Poetics*; and Longinus' *On the Sublime* is probably theoretical in intent. Defenses of poetry, which have been common since ancient times, naturally tend toward systematic apologetics, and so raise the question of the nature of literature and the literary experience.

This question has always been, and must be, the central concern of c. The answers depend of course on the general social or ethical attitudes of the critic, or even on a polemical literary purpose: theories of literature depend far more on a concern for its future (and so shade into the indirectly technical) or for its contemporary influence, than upon a detached reflection on its past. For a full treatment of this problem, see POETRY, THEORIES OF; here we can only indicate some of the main positions.

Cognitive theories assert that literature conveys knowledge, or states truths. This is a commonplace of Renaissance and neoclassic c.: the fictions of the poet are a means toward the formulating of some general truth—particular truth is the province of the historian, universal of the poet. This view is used by the Augustans to justify a poetic style that refuses to number the streaks on the tulip; the romantics, though rejecting the style, often retain the theory, Wordsworth for example applauding Aristotle and saying that the object of poetry is "truth, not individual and local, but general, and operative." Poetic knowledge is not the same as ordinary knowledge, and the difference is usually stated in terms of a contrast between imaginative or emotional knowledge, and mere intellectual acquiescence. This contrast is found in Shelley's *Defence of Poetry,* and implied in Keats's famous reference to "proving on the pulses." If literature is purely cognitive, it is difficult to see how, in principle, it differs from science, and the cognitive view has traditionally been combined with the affective view that it arouses emotion. In symbolist theory, and in much of the poetry associated with it, we can see the first systematic attempt to reject the cognitive completely: to Valéry and (especially) Mallarmé, as largely to Eliot, poetry should reject the prose functions of narrative, exposition, and argument, confining itself to the building of a nonrepresentational universe like that of music. Parallel to this movement, though distinct from it, is the transfer of interest from conscious to unconscious mental processes, and the claim that poetry should talk the language of dreams, not that of ratiocination. Rimbaud, Lautréamont and Lewis Carroll are immediate ancestors of this movement, and its theory is formulated in surrealism. Even more far-reaching than the contrasting views over the cognitive nature of literature, is the contrast between didactic views, which emphasize the effects of the literary experience, and aesthetic views, which emphasize the experience itself. The traditional view is didactic. The Horatian commonplace (*dulce et utile*) combines didactic and affective views, and is cited almost universally until the 18th c.: its naiveté (to modern eyes) consists in its assumption that these two purposes are independent and unaffected by each other. Only if you believe that literature affects the attitudes (and ultimately the conduct) of its readers can you claim for it a useful social function, so that all apologists must take a didactic view, whether naively like most of the Elizabethans, or in a more sophisticated form like that of I. A. Richards. The weaknesses of didactic theories are these. First, their corollary that literature is replaceable: could not something else produce the improvement in morals or the finer organization of attitudes that results from the appreciation of poetry—a change of environment, a course in psychoanalysis, or a drug? This corollary it shares with purely cognitive theories, and while we ought perhaps to be prepared to contemplate a social order in which the arts will have no part to play, the thought arouses violent and natural hostility in the breasts of the literary. Second, didactic views often seem remote from the actual appreciation of poetry: hence the attractiveness of the critic whose theories spring from an intense awareness of what it is like to be moved by a poem, even if this leads to a total lack of interest in its consequences. Such awareness lies behind T. S. Eliot's insistence that "poetry is not a substitute for philosophy or theology or

religion," Keats's objections to didacticism, or Dewey's belief that a philosopher's capacity to build a theory of aesthetics (based on an awareness of what a work of art is actually like) is a test of the capacity of his system to grasp the nature of experience itself. These three very different thinkers are all concerned that talk about poetry should not distort its nature. Finally, the didactically minded critic is greatly tempted to judge a poem by extrinsic and (strictly speaking) irrelevant standards. Dr. Johnson, for example, condemned Pope's *Elegy to the Memory of an Unfortunate Lady* for the sympathy it showed for a disobedient daughter. Since there is nothing in the poem to attach it to such a situation, Johnson can be accused of passing off his disapproval of Pope's personal action in entering the quarrel as if it was a disapproval of the poem. To draw the borderline between such external points, and what is part of the poem's effect, and therefore the concern of a legitimate didactic theory, is often very delicate; c. of such modern writers as Pound and Lawrence has been much concerned with this problem.

Perhaps the first demand we make on theoretical c. today is that it should not go back on the achievements of the "close reading" movement; and the best meaning that can be given to the overworked phrase "New Criticism" is that it is c. which, whatever its aim (practical, theoretical, didactic, even noncritical) tries to preserve and use these achievements. It is even possible for the theoretical critic to begin, like the practical, from an *explication de texte;* whether he does this or not may depend largely on whether he was trained as a philosopher or a man of letters. Almost all the work of William Empson is closely related to actual poems: but he often takes for granted the appreciation of what he is discussing, and concerns himself with the general literary or semantic issue which it raises. At the other extreme, we have works like *The Principles of Art,* by R. G. Collingwood, or *Art as Experience* by John Dewey, or the *Principles of Literary Criticism* of Richards: here the contrast in title with *Practical Criticism* points clearly the distinction in function. Somewhere between these extremes come writers such as W. K. Wimsatt (*The Verbal Icon*) or John Crowe Ransom (*The World's Body*). Each of the major figures in the history of Eng. c. has dealt with theoretical problems; most prominently, perhaps, S. T. Coleridge (e.g., *Biographia Literaria,* chs. 12–14).

If we interpret "c." strictly, as a concern for literature *as literature* rather than as evidence for some other study, then these are its only functions. There are other disciplines which use the same subject matter, but they do not center, as c. must, on the response of the modern reader, but may provide the means for c.: such are textual studies, bibliography, and other forms of "scholarship" (in the narrow meaning of this term); or they may set themselves other aims. Mainly, there are two such aims, historical and psychological. The literary historian concerns himself with what past generations have thought poetry to be, or have found in a particular poem, and refuses to start from the critic's basic assumption, that the poem has something to say to him, here and now. The psychological student of literature studies the relation of a poem to its origins in the poet's personality, but without necessarily altering its meaning for us. The historian certainly, and perhaps the biographer and the psychologist also, can provide certain necessary aids to the critic: in the case of a poem written several centuries ago, the literary historian may need to tell us what some of its words meant then before we are in a position to react fully to its poetic quality. Literary history, biography, and the study of the creative process, however, insofar as they are studies pursued in their own right, strive to be impersonal, rather than, as c. must be, committed.   L.D.L.

For bibliog., see below.

TYPES. The various patterns of critical interests that are commonly regarded as types have achieved their status not because they fit together into any preconceived system, but simply because they recur constantly and independently in the actual study of literature. A few represent theoretical cross sections of c.; for example, the evaluation of works and authors is sometimes distinguished from analytical description on one side and literary theory on the other and considered as a type—judicial c. Others arise out of philosophical issues that extend into and beyond literature, e.g., absolutist and relativist c. Such theoretical distinctions cut across another range of types, those which correspond to the different fields of knowledge or opinion upon which critics often draw in interpreting their literary experience. Most of the generally recognized types belong to this last category.

No critic can deal with literary phenomena without relating them either implicitly or explicitly to some framework of facts or ideas, and his choice of a framework may have a determining influence upon the kinds of results he can achieve. He may choose to limit his context to specifically literary facts and ideas, as the formal critic does when he treats the individual poem as a self-contained universe and the poet strictly as a maker of poems. On the other hand, he may find that for him the central avenue into literature lies through history or anthropology or psychoanalysis or some other related discipline, so that the most mean-

ingful way for him to take hold of his literary experience is to place it in the perspective of that second field. Out of this procedure come the several types of c. that are known as sociological, psychological, and so on.

Such labels obviously do not tell the whole story when they are applied to individual critics. Though it is convenient to speak of the historical critic or the psychological critic as though he were a distinct order of being with a fixed quota of interests and a standard set of methods, no individual critic is quite so pure a specimen. In practice, he may habitually move back and forth from one context to another, becoming formal analyst, historian, and ethical or social commentator by turns. But like everyone else, he is subject to academic shorthand, and if his predominating interests seem to lie in some one of these directions, he will hardly escape being classified accordingly.

The one critical context that is automatically available to every reader, if he chooses to exploit it, is himself. No one, from the casual reader who "knows what he likes" to the most subtly trained of observers, can detach himself altogether from his own temperament and personal history, and from the judgments that spring out of them. But critics differ widely in their willingness to depend upon openly personal estimates. Some regard it as the first duty of c. to establish checks and balances against the subjectivity of individual taste; others, notably the critics who are classified as impressionists, deliberately depend upon personal estimates and, without arguing the point, take the private sensibility as the only meaningful context for critical discussion.

Though impressionistic c. may draw at will upon history and other disciplines for all sorts of incidental information, it owes its name to the habit of concentrating on the direct insights and "impressions" of an individual reader. Typically, the impressionistic critic gives his account of a poem by singling out the most vivid of the sensations and attitudes it evokes in him and exploring them as he pleases, sometimes within the framework of the poet's other writings, but more often within a free range of his own literary and personal experience. He assumes, with Walter Pater, that "in aesthetic criticism the first step towards seeing one's object as it really is, is to know one's own impression as it really is, to discriminate it, to realise it distinctly" (Preface, Studies in the History of the Renaissance). He seldom attempts to reinforce his impressions by any appeal to literary theory, or to round out methodical descriptions of the poems and poets he discusses. Conscious impressionism is likely to rely heavily on good stage management, as the critic, well aware that it is his own sympathetic imagination that is on view, dramatizes his individual impressions one by one. In effect, he may create a second work of art interpreting the first. It is thus no accident that such critics often have a reputation of their own as personal essayists—witness Hazlitt and Lamb, Anatole France and Virginia Woolf. As critics they have a difficult balance to keep, to avoid toppling off into sheer autobiography on one side and a random feasting upon sensations on the other; less skillful writers, by losing that balance, have brought the method itself into disrepute, until nowadays it is usually mentioned only to be dismissed as *mere* impressionism. But such c. at its best is not the shallow and fragmentary thing that some of its detractors seem to imply; it has a personal coherence of its own, and often an atmospheric suggestiveness that enables a reader to see something new for himself, so that it has its uses as a kind of c. by contagion.

Nevertheless, when c. aspires to offer something beyond what Anatole France asked of it —the adventures of the soul among masterpieces—it is obliged to find more "objective" methods. Virtually all the other types of c. supply some context that is more accessible than that of the impressionist's mental world, some method that is more regular and sharable than his purely intuitive one. Each aims at results that can be observed and described in some consistent way and referred to definite principles. Of all the types, those that adopt the most exclusively literary context for their observation of poetry are the different branches of *technical* (i.e., *formal* and *stylistic*) c. As their background they take no field of interests outside literature, but simply the collective experience of poetic structure and style. For the purist these types constitute what is meant by "literary" c. in the strict sense. Technical critics have generally gone about their work in one of three different but complementary ways: by relating the individual poem to a *genre* or kind of poetry, by taking it as a formal entity complete in itself, or by studying it as a phenomenon of style.

Genre-c. is essentially a means of classifying poems by their formal properties, and thus of setting up fairly definite expectations as to the elements they will contain and the kind of effect they will produce. During the two centuries or so from Vida's time to Dr. Johnson's, it was a basic procedure in c. A critic like Addison (see his *Spectator* papers on *Paradise Lost*) accepts the independent validity of certain "kinds" of poems mostly inherited from ancient literature, and his first question in taking up a new work is likely to be, "What kind of poem is it?" If it purports to be an epic, for example, it will presumably have certain parts that belong to the form by definition—

not merely certain sections and conventional devices, but generalized elements of the sort that Aristotle had found in tragedy (plot, character, diction, and the rest), all of them adjusted to one another in such a way as to create a recognizable literary pattern. If some of these ingredients are missing, or their balance is altered, the structure and effect will be altered correspondingly; the poem may differ from epic in one set of ways and be a heroic romance, in another and be a mock-epic, in another and be merely a miscalculation. In any case, the critic cannot apply the relevant standards until he knows what kind of object it is. But once he has classified it, he can move on to observe (as Addison did with Milton) how the poet uses the essential resources of the form, adapting each of the "parts" to his chosen subject and bringing them all into unity.

The prescriptive authority of the *genre*-system fell apart during the 18th c.; and though critics did not abandon its basic vocabulary, and some of the most important of them (e.g., Goethe and Schiller) concerned themselves with reinterpreting its principles, *genre*-analysis as a means of concrete literary description was largely handed over to the historian rather than pursued and extended by the critic. As a result, though it established itself in literary historiography, little was left of it in the mainstream of c. beyond certain traditional distinctions among types of poetry —epic, lyric, dramatic, and so on. Today, in a climate more favorable to a close structural analysis of poetry, the purely descriptive side of *genre*-theory is once more in common use. It cannot be said to have regained a place as an independent type of c., let alone the ruling type, but it is an indispensable fixture in historical c., and critics of all persuasions draw upon it for a standard glossary of forms, from the tragedy down to the limerick. The forms are no longer regarded as autonomous, but that they have an identity at all is an indication of the perseverance of *genre*-theory.

A second way in which the technical critic may operate is to take the individual poem itself as his context, conceiving of it as a unique entity, the product of a unique combination of elements. He may find the idea of *genre* incidentally useful, but he is less interested in charting class-relations among poems than in seizing on the specific means of integration in any given one. In his view the form of a poem, like the life of an organism, is a property of the individual, not of a class; and the aim of c. should be to observe how every detail in the poem shares in the determination of this individual form. One of the most publicized of critical developments in this century has been the rise of a painstaking technical analysis of poetry from this point of view, accepting the notion of "organic form" as a basic metaphor, and redefining form so as to make it immediately correlative with "meaning."

Since the materials out of which form or meaning is realized are *words,* modern analytical critics have concerned themselves intensively with the various ways in which words act and react upon one another in a poem, and their study of a text is characteristically devoted to a close *explication* (q.v.) of the interconnected verbal patterns that make it up—their literal sense, their figurative and symbolic suggestions, the images they produce, their rhythmical texture, and so on. Among the critics prominently associated with this technique are I. A. Richards (whose theoretical work on meaning in poetry was a strong initial stimulus), William Empson, and Cleanth Brooks and Robert Penn Warren (whose *Understanding Poetry* brought the method into uncounted Am. classrooms). Such analysis at its strictest, being unconcerned with any hierarchy of values outside the poem, confines itself to judging internal relations, and thus at most to distinguishing good poems from bad; it does not readily lend itself to ranking one good poem above or below another (except on grounds of comparative intricacy) or explaining how one poem is great and another simply good. In practice, of course, the method is often yoked to some independent set of standards, moral or social—as in the work of F. R. Leavis—by which the critic relates the poem to a wider area of experience.

Much of the technical equipment of both *genre*-c. and modern formal explication is shared with or reinforced by *rhetorical* analysis. Yet the stock image of a "rhetorical critic" is that of a man who goes through a text marking splendid examples of *zeugma* and *hysteron proteron* without much concern for the totality of the meaning. Traditional rhetoricians often have gone through a text marking figures, but not because the total meaning did not matter; each figure was a tactical move creating a certain localized effect in a larger design. The classical authorities on rhetoric from Aristotle to Quintilian handed down an elaborate roster of such figures of thought and language, from tropes and personifications to devices of syntax and meter, each representing a different artifice by which an orator could give a special force or color to what he was saying at any point. Originally a kind of applied psychology for the public speaker, the whole loose system of figures proved easy to transport into the analysis of prose and verse in general, and even in classical times it was not restricted to oratory. In medieval and Renaissance education it held an important place; and though it began to be elbowed off

the stage as early as the 17th c., the study of the figures continued to have practical consequences in poetic technique for another hundred years and more. Nowadays it is so far fallen that a man who knows the difference between *syllepsis* and *chiasmus* has presumably just looked them up; yet remnants of the old system are still everywhere in the standard language of literary description (e.g., metaphor, antithesis, onomatopoeia), and various other figures have been absorbed into new contexts by modern rhetorical theorists such as I. A. Richards and Kenneth Burke.

More important than the figures, however, is a general conception that underlies them—the conception of *style.* For the classical rhetorician, a discourse consisted not only of certain things that were said and a certain order in which they were placed, but of a certain manner of expression—a high or middle or low "style" that suited the purpose of the discourse and the dignity of the subject. It was with this conception that traditional rhetoric supported the theory of *genres,* for it was universally held that the difference between the elevated forms like tragedy and epic and the lower ones like comedy and elegy inhered in their manner no less than their matter, and much of the discussion of *genres* hinged upon this decorum of style. But style has proved to be an endlessly expansible concept. Almost any quality that can be attributed to literature can be regarded from some point of view as a stylistic quality, with the result that the c. of style, far from remaining the property of the rhetorician, has come to belong equally to the impressionist who may waive all technical analysis and the historian who may often take such analysis largely for granted. Critics have used it not only for describing the texture of language in a poem (rough or smooth, plain or flamboyant, and so on) and for generalizing upon modes of literary experience (sublime, pathetic), but for defining the special manner of an individual poet (Virgilian, Petrarchan, Byronic), or the expression of national character (Gallic, Germanic), or even the "spirit" of whole eras in the arts (Hellenistic, Baroque). Stylistic discussion may therefore seem at times to be carried on at a considerable remove from the observation of specific poems.

Two independent techniques for keeping such discussion rooted in concrete detail require to be noticed here: *metrical analysis* and *stylistics.* Though metrical theory has been in an embattled condition for centuries, faced with an extremely complicated body of linguistic and rhythmical problems, critics have fortunately been able to make themselves understood with a variety of pragmatic systems for pointing out the metrical movement of a poem and for characterizing an author's metrical habits. Even a rough and ready prosody is sensitive enough to find distinctive idioms not only in verse with a strongly marked manner, such as Milton's or Hopkins', but in the work of poets far less unusual in their metrical behavior. Such rhythmical idioms have often been taken as keys to a poet's style, and related significantly to his rhetorical technique, his place in a particular tradition, and his individual temperament. Whereas metrical analysis is a traditional tool for the exploration of style, stylistics (q.v.) is comparatively new and highly specialized. Professedly a branch of linguistic science, it aims primarily at characterizing the total system of expressive conventions that make up a given language at a given time; some students of the field, however, extend it into the analysis of individual and period styles, taking the view that any style is a distinctive selection from the total system that is available, and that it should therefore be possible to describe it in concrete and objective terms.

Literary study is often held to be at its most objective when it concerns itself with enterprises of this kind—with collecting and authenticating various kinds of "facts," and not with evaluating works and authors. It has long been a custom to distinguish such fact-finding operations from c. by describing them rather loosely (not to say disparagingly) as *scholarship*. The exact relations between scholarship and c. have been argued and reargued at length, often with a practical turn toward the problem of training critical scholars and scholarly critics (see, for example, Foerster *et al.*, *Literary Scholarship*; Wellek and Warren, *Theory of Literature*, chs. 6 and 20; Daiches, *Critical Approaches to Literature*, ch. 6). For some writers, auxiliary studies such as paleography and bibliography, the establishment of texts, linguistic and literary history are preliminary to c., in the sense that their results have to be in before the work of interpretation and evaluation can properly begin. For others, these disciplines cannot come into play at all without involving a constant exercise of literary judgment, so that they are at least implicitly forms of c. in their own right. The issue is complicated by the fact that the various branches of scholarship depend upon literary judgment in differing degrees and for different reasons.

Textual c., for example, certainly does not profess to say how good a poem is, nor to give any interpretative account of it; instead, it provides the indispensable Exhibit A, an accurate text. It aims at reproducing exactly what the author wrote, with all doubtful readings and corruptions cleared away as far as possible and all the evidence duly recorded. Editors have been known at times to take a

high hand with their materials, putting their literary judgment ahead of documentary evidence; Pope's edition of Shakespeare and Bentley's of *Paradise Lost* are notorious instances of an editor's freely emending a text on the basis that his author surely could not have intended a given passage as it stood, or that if he did, he was writing much below his usual manner and deserved to be protected from himself. But such instances chill a modern editor's blood. Since the middle of the 19th c., editors have generally outlawed any kind of personal interference with the text, and have followed a strict and often highly ingenious editorial logic that tries to take into account all ascertainable facts about the history and transmission of the text—the origin, date, and comparative reliability of each separate manuscript or printing, and all the possible sources of error or confusion at every stage from the time the work left its author's hands. It is in the highest attainable degree an objective weighing of the evidence. Inescapably, however, the evidence will sometimes be artistic evidence. To the extent that there is a recurrent necessity of judging which of two readings equally attested in the sources is more probable in the context—or simply of deciding whether a given reading is a corruption, a misprint, or a characteristic license of the author's style—there is still a last appeal to literary acumen in the editing of texts. To that very limited extent, the editor serves in advance as a critic of the poem.

When he goes on to annotate his text, providing the information that a reader will need to understand the language, to follow the allusions to persons and places and ideas, and to set the work in its historical matrix, he draws more fully and obviously upon his literary judgment. Though he may be chiefly concerned with detailing the facts that seem to be relevant, it is for him to decide what the grounds of relevance are. Time after time he must decide whether a given passage does or does not invoke a certain precedent, whether it does or does not presuppose some special knowledge or some pattern of associations, and so on. To the extent that he must explicate the poem in advance, his scholarly findings rest upon his critical sense and literary experience. At the same time, he generally thinks of it as his fundamental job not to evaluate, but to explain.

When c. interests itself systematically in some range of explanatory materials outside the poem, its center of gravity naturally shifts from the poem alone to the relation between the poem and its setting. Several of the types of c. (historical, biographical, sociological, psychological) have distinctive ways of defining that relation and of investigating the background of a poem—which is to say, they have their own criteria of relevance in c., and their own scholarship to depend upon. Though most of them have more than one point of entry into c., their approach to a poem is commonly genetic: they seek to explain how it came into being, and what influences were at work to give it exactly the qualities that it has. Characteristically, they try to suggest what is in the poem by showing what lies behind it. And since for them the poem is one element in a partly nonliterary situation, and thus may be regarded not only as a product of the situation but as an expression of it in turn, these types of c. are quite ready to treat the poem itself as documentary evidence. They may use the background to illuminate the poem, or the poem to illuminate the background. Modern formal critics have often objected to this procedure on the grounds that there is no necessary connection between an idea or experience inside a poem and that "same" idea or experience outside it; but the procedure is nonetheless standard in what Wellek and Warren have called the "extrinsic" approaches to the study of literature.

The *historical* critic may agree with the formal analyst that a poem should be accepted on its own terms, but he may well take issue with him as to what those terms actually are. For him the poem is essentially a historical phenomenon, arising out of conditions of thought and experience that may differ in countless ways from modern conditions, and that therefore require to be studied if the poem is to yield up its full meaning. He attempts to set the poem once again in its original context in time, reconstructing the circumstances of its composition and public reception, pointing out its connection with the artistic and intellectual assumptions of its age, and thus restoring as fully as he can the aspect it would have worn for a contemporary reader. He may tend to identify the poem with its original meaning, and insist that it is accessible only to a thoroughly instructed reader; this extreme position, in terms of which a critic could not hope to discuss the *Aeneid* intelligently without committing himself to think and feel as an Augustan Roman would (and in L.), is often to be found in historical c. Or he may take the less stringent view that any poem will offer the reader more in proportion as he learns to see the sense it makes historically, and thus that the study of many sorts of detail—the conventions of courtly love, the psychology of humors, the political difficulties of Charles II, or the influence of Frazer's *Golden Bough*—may help to clarify and enrich a given poem here and now. Though he is well aware that a modern cannot turn himself into an ancient by an act of will, nor even arm himself at all points with the appropriate knowledge,

the historical critic nonetheless regards the past of the poem as implicit in its present, and devotes himself to learning as much of it as he can.

As historian, however, he has a broader terrain to cover than the background of any single poem. His work is to generalize from all such backgrounds an account of the literary past. Notable historians of literature such as Friedrich Schlegel, Taine, De Sanctis, and Courthope have differed greatly in scope and method and individual sympathies, but have had in common a conception of their task not as the reporting of a gigantic congeries of mere events and names and dates, but as the finding of meaningful patterns and correlations, the sorting out of the facts that have consequences from those that seem to have none. Their work is critical from the beginning, in the sense that at every stage they must make the basic distinctions between what is and what is not literature, between authors who do not count and those who do. But there is an important reservation to be made about the range of critical judgment in such histories, apart from the fact that they may occasionally impose patterns from outside fields upon the data of literature. To the historian's eye, certain works and authors may stand out above their surroundings because they bring some new development into play, or because they represent with unusual clarity some element in the life of their time. For him, such works and authors have a greater "significance" than others, and he naturally gives them a special prominence. He may go further and assert that they are good in themselves, or great, and it is within his prerogative as a critic to do so; but in doing so he makes a leap beyond what history can tell him. Historical evidence by itself may reveal the instrumental value of poems and poets—their representativeness or their influence in producing historical consequences—but not their intrinsic value. It is the failure to distinguish between these two things, the tendency to assume that what is "significant" is by that very fact good, that opens the gates to enormous amounts of antiquarian research into third-rate literature, thus widening the gap between scholar and critic to the disadvantage of both.

Beyond literary history lie the realms of cultural and ideological history in which literature is only one of many sources of evidence. The cultural historian may or may not expect to find uniformities among all the productive activities of a given age, but he regards them all as expressions of the age as well as "institutions" with a continuity of their own. The particular kind of cultural history known as *Geistesgeschichte* does look for uniformities within any given age, its premise being that every age is informed by a certain *Zeitgeist,* a distinctive spirit that underlies its ways of thought and action and reveals itself in all contemporary institutions. The historian of this *Zeitgeist* takes his lead from the formal philosophy as well as the sciences, arts, and social conventions of an era, and may be interested in literature only as testimony to the ideological pattern of the time—or possibly, as in the extreme case of Spengler's *Decline of the West,* to the value of his own theory of civilization.

Another province of intellectual history, more explicitly philosophical and less concerned with the "spirit" of individual ages, is the study called by its founder Prof. A. O. Lovejoy the "history of ideas," which aims at tracing specific motifs in philosophical thought from their origin to their dissolution, showing how their implications fan out not only into the systems of particular philosophers but into many different cultural phenomena over long periods of time. For such history, literature provides a major source of illustrative detail. (See the opening chapter of Lovejoy, *The Great Chain of Being,* for the classic statement of the method.) The use of such disciplines as these for the practicing critic lies partly in their constant association of literature with the other forms of creative expression, but even more immediately in the fact that they may alert him to the intellectual assumptions in a poet's work —to meaning that is below the surface, implied rather than expressed, but nonetheless central to the coherence of the whole.

Another related province with its own principles of organization is that of the sociologist. *Sociological* c. begins with the axiom that literature is an expression of society: that social forces inescapably form and condition the poet and his work and his audience, and that what he creates is therefore to be studied as a social phenomenon. Though the status of literature as a product and a reflection of society interested many earlier thinkers from DuBos to Madame de Staël, the introduction of a full-fledged sociological c. is usually credited to the Fr. historian Hippolyte Taine, who set out to interpret the course of a whole national literature in strictly scientific terms (*History of Eng. Literature,* 1863–67), and who proposed for that purpose the celebrated formula "the race, the *milieu,* the moment." These three factors, the second being the totality of social conditions and attitudes existing at a given time, were taken as the essential determinants of literary history. As if by chemical action, they combined to make a certain author inevitable at a certain time and to govern the character of his work. Later sociologists of literature have abandoned virtually all of Taine's majestic generalizations

beyond the handy concept of the writer's *milieu;* but there has often remained in the background a faith in the possibility that literature and the other arts conform ultimately to general laws of society—or at the very least that their development can be explained in large part by the analysis of environmental causes. The sociologist thus may go considerably beyond the issues that are central to c., since he is concerned with all the aspects of literature as a social institution that can be examined statistically, or reported in factual terms. According to his lights, he may concentrate upon the environment of the poet as a private man or as a professional writer, the image of society that emerges from his writings and the social attitudes implicit in them, the causes and consequences of shifts in public taste, or the mutual relations between social ideologies and artistic movements. (See Duncan's *Language and Literature in Society* for an extensive bibliography in each of these fields.) Most of the practical c. of poetry along such lines has been devoted to the influence of a given poet's *milieu* upon his work (e.g., F. W. Bateson's *Eng. Poetry: A Critical Introduction,* and many essays of Edmund Wilson), or to the social origins of various forms and conventions and movements (e.g., Herbert Read's *Phases of Eng. Poetry,* much of the scholarship in folklore, or almost any attempt at defining the concept of "modernity" in literature). These interests shade off naturally into psychological biography on one side and anthropology on the other.

Such c. is not always primarily descriptive and interpretative. A critic who regards a poem as the reflection of certain social or ideological forces is likely to have his own views as to the health or malignancy of those forces, and he may therefore assert himself for or against them, in effect holding the writer responsible for promoting some end outside his work, and even requiring him to be an advocate for the critic's own views. Thus, Tolstoi would require a writer to put himself directly into the service of the Christian brotherhood of man; Vernon Parrington would find better things to say of a writer who professed Jeffersonian principles than of one who did not; Julien Benda would make it a condition of praise that a writer should detach himself from popular ideologies and function as a reproving force against them—in itself a requirement no less limiting than the others. Of the kinds of c. that make specific ideological demands upon the artist, the most prevalent in this century has been *Marxist* c. Marxism is first a philosophy of history and second a program of political action; it is only derivatively a theory of c., and from the beginning it has had the disadvantage that the founders of its doctrine, Marx and Engels, provided little in the way of a ground plan for relating their economic determinism to questions of aesthetic value. One prominent Marxist frankly pointed out that the virtue of Marxist theory lay not in evaluating works of art but in explaining the basic social and economic influences that operated to produce them; but this was Trotsky (*Literature and Revolution*, tr. 1925), and Trotsky did not carry the day. The more common approach of the Marxist critic has been to take on both tasks, and to view a given work not only as a reflection of the class interests and aspirations of its author, but as a valuable or a hurtful contribution to the understanding of the true goals of society. In its crudely militant form, Marxism asks of the writer that he should use his art as a weapon, exposing the falsities of bourgeois culture, and becoming a propagandist for the destined society in which all men will be happy and free because they will have lost their economic chains; the writer who does not subserve these ends is unacceptable and even dangerous, since his art may encourage the formation of erroneous "group psychologies" (Nikolai Bukharin: see bibliog.). Such starkly utilitarian principles, taking a work of art almost exclusively as a political document, can often lead to bizarre results—as when one critic sees *The Tempest* as Shakespeare's study of the political basis of colonial expansion, and Caliban as the only genuine lover of freedom in the play. It is clear that if such judgments were all that Marxist c. had to offer, it would not have made a perceptible impact outside its ideological circle. But at one remove from the stresses of polemical warfare, it has seemed to many critics to provide a useful added dimension in the study of literary history, through its insistent focus upon the influence of class structure and the distribution of wealth and social power from age to age. Critics who hold no brief for a rigid economic determinism have sometimes derived much of their equipment for inspecting the economic background of literary tendencies from the Marxists. Thus a highly diversified group of writers have made constant or occasional use of Marxist theory in discussing poetry—Christopher Caudwell, Kenneth Burke, William Empson, and D. S. Savage, among others. Perhaps the most influential of European Marxist critics at present is the Hungarian Gyorgy Lukács, much of whose work is as yet unavailable in Eng.

In the types of "genetic" c. so far mentioned, the individual poet himself may sometimes seem to vanish behind a thicket of influences and forces and tendencies; but there is one type of historical c., the *biographical*, in which he obviously holds the center of the stage. The motto of the biographical critic might well be Sainte-Beuve's remark in his *Nouveaux lundis* ("Chateaubriand"), "I can enjoy the work itself, but I find it hard to judge in isolation from the man who wrote it." The assumption is that the life and personality of the author, down to the last apparently trifling detail, may provide an essential key to the understanding and thus the appraisal of his poetry. Much literary biography, of course, has been written without any such regard to its critical relevance. The lives of authors may be interesting quite independently of their possible bearing upon the works, and many a student has been interested in both without supposing that there is any inevitable correspondence between them. For example, Boswell's *Life* does not undertake to "explain" the works of Johnson by tracing them to their origins in his personal experience, nor does it rest any case for their value upon the personality behind them; it aims simply (if that is the right word) at delivering to posterity a just image of a great man who is also a great author. Similarly, Johnson's own *Lives of the Poets* make a fairly plain distinction between the biographical enterprise, which has its own humane interest, and the critical one; the specifically critical part of each "life" is usually a separate section, a formal review of the man's works, after the portrait has been duly accomplished. Such biography is very different, as David Daiches says (*Critical Approaches to Literature*, p. 250) from the kind "which draws from the psychology of the author clues for the interpretation and appreciation of what he has written"—or from the kind that reverses the process, drawing upon what he has written for clues to his life and personality. Biography of these latter sorts is largely an outgrowth of romantic literary psychology, with its stress upon individual creativity and its absorbed contemplation of the Poet. Carlyle furnishes a good example; his studies of such men as Schiller, Burns, and Shakespeare are heroic portraits, in which the literary works figure chiefly as elements in that "greatest work of every man, the Life he has led." Sainte-Beuve himself, little as he has in common otherwise with Carlyle, takes the personality of the author as his principal object, immersing himself in historical and personal detail, and bringing the works and the life together in a single impression. His *Causeries du lundi* form a celebrated casebook of such c. If such a critic has an occupational hazard, it is the temptation to use the life and works interchangeably to illuminate each other, deducing the personality from the poetry and then judging the poetry in the light of the personality. The tendency is outstandingly obvious in the attempts of Georg Brandes and later critics to read Shakespeare's plays and sonnets biographically; but it is implicit in much other biography—in works written under the influence of Stefan George's concept of "inner form," for instance, and in such a study as Tillyard's *Milton*, which holds that the real subject of a poem is the state of the author's mind at the time of composition. But in all biographical c., from the casual reminiscences of a Frank Harris to the comprehensive life-and-times scholarship of a David Masson, there is the fundamental conviction that though the events of a writer's life may be only behind the work, his personality is in it and of it, and an evaluation which ignores his presence there is doomed to miss the mark. The critic who declared that the author of the *Iliad* could not have written the *Odyssey* because no one man could have two such different attitudes toward dogs was not writing authentic biography, perhaps, but he was illustrating very clearly the fact that the movement from the work to the man and back again is an all but involuntary impulse in c.

In recent years, biographical c. has drawn a new if somewhat reckless vitality from important developments in psychological theory, especially those that are popularly lumped together under the name of psychoanalysis. Though the various branches of *psychological* c.† are by no means exclusively genetic or biographical in their approach to poetry, the most influential ones (leaving aside the work of I. A. Richards) have been those that center upon the personality of the poet or that seem to offer some clue to the mysteries of the creative process. The idea of the poet as the half-unwitting instrument of irrational or at least obscure forces has a history reaching back to Plato's *Ion;* it is implied in every invocation to the Muse, and in every reference to the *furor poeticus*, the divine fire of inspiration. Though modern critics are not fond of such terms, they have made unparalleled efforts to analyze the creative activity itself, or at least to see how far it can be analyzed. The most famous detailed study of an individual poet in action, J. L. Lowes' *Road to Xanadu*, attempts to track the synthesizing imagination of Coleridge through the vast mazes of his reading, showing the raw materials he had to work with and the transformations that they underwent, if not the way in which the transforming was done. Another approach, represented in such a book as *Poets at Work* (ed. C. D. Abbott, 1948), has been to examine the stages through which a poem has passed during composition, as far as they are apparent in the author's drafts and worksheets; here the emphasis is often more formal than psychological, concentrating on the deliberate changes that the author made in his text, and leaving a margin

for that unexplained something at the beginning that, as Stephen Spender says in *The Making of a Poem*, is simply "given." The mysterious force is still there. But many critics, taking their cue from Sigmund Freud and his followers, have looked for that force in the promptings of the poet's "unconscious," and have turned therefore to one or another of the several versions of psychoanalytic theory as at least a partial answer to the riddle of personal creativity.

Even apart from the differences between early Freud and late, and between the contending systems of his successors, the relation of psychoanalytic theory to c. is too complex and unsettled to be summarized in brief. But in rough terms the basic connection arises from the concept that an individual personality is constituted in part by needs and cravings which the mind in its conscious activity rejects or represses, and that these powerful drives, constantly seeking an outlet, thrust their way to the surface in disguised forms, expressing themselves not openly but symbolically—in dreams, for example, and in works of art. A poem may thus be read as a symbolic expression of the author's unconscious fantasies and desires, and as such it offers a conjectural means of access to the hidden depths of his personality. Not all the prominent psychoanalytical critics have focused on the inner life of the poet; Charles Baudouin's study of Verhaeren, for instance, devotes itself at some length to psychoanalytic factors in the reader's response to poetry (*Psychoanalysis and Aesthetics*, tr. 1924). But most such investigations are irresistibly drawn at last into the subliminal storehouse of the author's mind. Ernest Jones' *Hamlet and Oedipus*, probably the best-known Freudian study of a literary subject, is first of all an attempt to explain Hamlet's irresolution as the result of an Oedipus complex; but the quest is not finished until it develops that Hamlet's latent conflict is "an echo of a similar one in Shakespeare himself"—a biographical finding that is somewhat diluted by the further comment, "as to a greater or less extent it is in all men." Freud's own view that the early sexual history of the individual is of prime importance in the determination of his latent drives has met with much opposition, but it has been enormously influential. The roster of poets whose salient qualities have been traced to Oedipus complexes, castration fears, repressed homosexuality, infantile menstruation traumas, and other felicities is truly impressive. But since it is a major tenet of Freudian doctrine that such phenomena are universally distributed among mankind, the apparently high incidence of them among poets would seem to mean nothing more than that the supposed evidence in their cases, being in

† In Supplement, see also PSYCHOLOGY AND POETRY.

print, is relatively easy to collect. Neither Freud's influence nor the relevance of his findings to literature can be said to rest on such studies. But whatever may be thought of them, there is a further range for the qualified critic in the interpretation of works that are directly indebted to Freudian or other psychoanalytic ideas. Hardly any writer for the last forty years or more can have been wholly untouched by Freud's vision of man and the controversies it has provoked (see the titles by Trilling and Hoffman in the bibliography), and a critic can do much for the reader by elucidating the effects of that influence in actual poems and plays and novels.

In some of Freud's work (e.g., *Totem and Taboo*) and much more extensively in the work of Carl Jung, the search for recurrent patterns of symbolism has gone beyond the practical limits of individual experience, into the realm of a more general cultural heritage. It was Jung who formulated the search as an investigation of the "collective unconscious," the primitive layer of the individual psyche that serves as a reservoir of racial memory. Many critics who accept little else in Jung's psychology have found this concept a fruitful one in accounting for the steady reappearance and powerful impact of certain stories and "motifs" in the literature of different ages. His emphasis on primordial images or "archetypes" (q.v.) has gone along with independent research in several fields—anthropology, comparative religion, classical archaeology, iconology in the graphic arts, and the study of symbolism in language—to focus attention upon the ritualistic and mythical elements in literature (see MYTH); and out of this potent combination of sources has sprung a whole school of critical mythography that is at present one of the most vigorous influences in c. The taproot of this interest is as much anthropological as psychological, and if any single book has been fundamental to it, it is not one of Jung's, but Sir James Frazer's *Golden Bough*. The breadth of implication in such studies may be seen in a work like Suzanne Langer's *Philosophy in a New Key;* from the standpoint of literary c. the most elaborate theoretical essay in the field to date is Northrop Frye's *Anatomy of C.* Of critical works directly indebted to Jung himself, the most instructive is still Maud Bodkin's *Archetypal Patterns in Poetry* (1934).

Apart from the psychoanalytic movement there are at least two branches of current psychology that are directly concerned with literary questions, and neither of these is primarily genetic. One is the experimentalist school, from Fechner to Birkhoff and beyond, which has attempted to get at the bases of aesthetic judgment by a variety of statistical techniques—aptitude and preference tests, projective devices such as the Thematic Apperception Test, and physiological studies of aesthetic responses. The other is the "Gestalt" school, which has centered upon the process of perception, working out the implications of its theory that aesthetic and other insights are characterized by the apprehension of complex wholes as wholes, rather than by a merely additive recognition of parts and their relations. A brief summary of the accomplishments of both schools in studying the arts may be found in the essay by Douglas N. Morgan listed below. Most students of literature have found the experimentalist approach largely unpromising; and though Gestalt psychology has produced interesting results in the analysis of perceptual patterns in the visual arts, it has so far been unable to transfer its methods into literary analysis with any degree of success. See, however, Rudolf Arnheim's "Psychological Notes on the Poetical Process," in *Poets at Work*, which once more turns back to the poet himself.

Of the important contribution of I. A. Richards, with his theory of aesthetic experience as the harmonious integration of impulses, little can be said here. It has already been mentioned that his stress upon the interplay of various properties of language in a poem helped to launch the modern development of close verbal analysis. It may be added that in his early stand against the idea that poetry has a cognitive or knowledge-giving validity (see PSEUDO-STATEMENT), he brought on a renewal of an age-old dispute in c. as to the relation between art and "truth"—or in his terms, poetry and science. Though many of Richards' views have altered since he published *The Foundations of Aesthetics* (with C. K. Ogden and James Woods) in 1921, his first positivistic spelling-out of the function of poetry has remained one of the most productive irritants in modern literary theory. On his views and their influence, see John Crowe Ransom's *The New C.* (1941), Murray Krieger's *The New Apologists for Poetry* (1956), and chs. 27–28 of Wimsatt and Brooks.

In contrast to the types of c. so far discussed, the type known loosely as *comparative* c. draws such unity as it has from its method rather than from any one distinctive body of knowledge or theory. The method is that of directly comparing one work with another, one artist with another, one artistic movement with another. Since such comparison may be made from any of the points of view already mentioned—since it may be formal and stylistic, or historical, or sociological, and so on—this kind of c. cuts obliquely across the other types, and might reasonably be taken as a subdivision of each of them. But it does have a sphere of its own, in that the name "comparative" properly refers to c. that jumps the boundary lines between national literatures, comparing (say) Shakespeare with Racine or Lope de Vega, or between the different arts, comparing Milton with Poussin, Shakespeare's *Othello* with Verdi's, or the formal balance of Augustan verse with that of Palladian architecture. A great deal of such c. has been incidental rather than systematic, aimed at isolating particular qualities of style, particular themes and motifs, or special analogies among the arts. But there is nonetheless a natural tendency in such c. to lead on into historical generalizations that attempt to catch the *Zeitgeist* in action, or into aesthetic theory. An interest in the theoretical and practical connections among the arts has figured in c. since the day of Leonardo da Vinci's *Paragone,* sometimes as a major issue, producing scores of essays on the "parallels" of poetry with painting or music or some other art, along with some noted works that stand out against the trend and insist on the folly of confusing the arts—e.g., Lessing's *Laokoön* and the *New Laokoön* of Irving Babbitt. (See Wimsatt and Brooks, ch. 13.) Modern aesthetics itself may be said to have sprung out of 18th-c. comparative c. on the theoretical level.

When any of the foregoing types of c. advances a judgment as to the value of a poem or the artistic rank of an author, it becomes to that extent *judicial* c. In one sense, as has already been suggested, c. is bound to involve implicit value-judgments even in its earliest stages; merely to recognize a literary phenomenon is to place it in some way, at least tentatively, and thus to have an attitude toward it. The attitude may turn out to need revision, but it is normative from the first. But c. becomes fully and explicitly judicial when it measures out praise and blame to a poem or a poet in accordance with some generalized *standard* of excellence. Although standards of value may seem to differ so widely in practice that there is little hope of finding common denominators among them, they do fall into various categories, and each type of c. has its own appropriate range of them. One broad distinction may be made between aesthetic and ideological standards. The critic for whom a poem is something to be contemplated in and for itself will make judgments of value that are primarily aesthetic, keyed to the inner economy of the piece and the uniqueness of its psychological effect; see the discussion of modern technical analysis above. Such a critic may go on to apply other standards, but formal and (immediate) psychological values are his home ground. On the other hand, the critic for whom a poem is interesting chiefly as a commentary on experience will judge it primarily by the ideological standards—political, social, ethical, religious—that seem to him to matter most in judging experience as a whole. In an extreme instance, as in Marxist c., or any c. based single-mindedly on social or religious commitments, the ideological implications of a poem may mean everything, and the fact that it is a poem little or nothing. But the great bulk of ideological c. is not so doctrinaire as to demand that a poem support the critic's own views or devote its powers to a practical cause. The central position of such c. is simply that literature draws much of its value out of a serious and complex relevance to the rest of experience, and that in evaluating a poem one needs to consider what that relevance is, how far it goes, and what light there may be in it.

From the beginning, the most pervasive of ideological standards in the critical tradition have been *ethical* standards. The profound moral influence that poetry is capable of exerting has been an active issue in c. since Plato banished from his ideal republic all poetry except hymns to the gods and praises of famous men. For much subsequent c. the problem of the relation between moral and aesthetic standards was posed in Horace's finely ambiguous formula that the end of poetry is "aut prodesse aut delectare," to instruct or to delight—or both. The grounds on which Renaissance critics defended poetry from philistines and philosophers were ethical: poetry incited men to virtue through representing the beauty of noble actions. And this was no mere tactical maneuver. It was an axiom in older *genre*-theory that each of the major forms had its own contribution to make toward the inculcation of valuable ideas about human conduct; Rapin and LeBossu, not to mention Virgil and Spenser, regarded the epic as potentially a lesson in ethical and even political wisdom. Between the two extremes of outright didacticism and "art for art's sake" there has traditionally been a wide range of argument; to disagree with Tolstoi is by no means to agree with Oscar Wilde.

Few would deny the proposition that literature exhibits human character and action in situations that have serious moral meaning, and thus that it is in part, in Matthew Arnold's phrase, a criticism of life. It is when the critic assumes that the prime function of a poem is to deal in a morally positive way with experience, to punish vice and reward virtue, or to provide improving images of goodness—in short, when he judges the poem as a right or wrong reaction to life—that ethical c. becomes overbearing and runs into opposition. For even if art were definable simply as the representation of life, it is not the same thing as the life it represents, and the standards by which it is to be judged must take account of the difference as well as the likeness. This is basically the distinction that underlies the much-quoted observation of T. S. Eliot in *Religion and Literature:* "The 'greatness' of literature cannot be determined solely by literary standards; though we must remember that whether it is literature or not can be determined only by literary standards." It is characteristic of ethical c.—as of ideological judgment in general—that it does attempt to grapple with the problems of truth and greatness in literature, the very problems that aesthetic or "literary" standards alone seem least able to solve.

Critics have often applied their judicial standards without looking into the philosophical status of the values they entail. But there is a long-standing theoretical dispute about the very nature of values and the way in which they get into experience, and critics customarily take part in it, even if only inadvertently and by implication. They are likely to feel a strong temperamental assurance either that the values they discover in poems are aspects of a permanent and unalterable reality, or that those values, while firm and vivid enough in present experience, are dependent upon all sorts of temporary conditions, and thus may change as the conditions change. The first attitude is that of the so-called absolutist, the second that of the relativist. The *absolutist* position is that there is one universal order of things, and thus one ultimate hierarchy of values, lying behind the variety of appearances, and that the diversity of standards on every side is simply an indication of the difference in the power of individuals (and even of whole eras) to see through to the truth. This is generally an unpopular view today, to judge by the number of critics who congratulate themselves and others on being relativists. But there are several possible meanings of the word *relativism;* the two most common forms of relativist doctrine in c., though they agree in accepting a psychological rather than an ontological definition of value, do not necessarily agree either in their implications or in their critical methods. These two chief forms are personal and historical relativism. The first holds that all valuation is subjective, that values therefore may differ from one man to another, that no man's perceptions in this kind are to be regarded as definitive, and that, in fact, *de gustibus non est disputandum.* A thoroughgoing impressionist might be expected to take this stand, though there is nothing to keep him from believing instead that his own values are indelibly graven in the nature of things. The extreme subjectivity of personal relativism is missing from the other form, historical relativism, which stresses the influence of social and educational conditioning

upon the individual. The historical relativist holds that values change as times and manners change, that what is significant and satisfying to one age or nation may seem the very reverse to another, and that in judging the work of any poet the critic must take into account the standards of the age in which he lived. For a lively exposition of this point of view, see Frederick A. Pottle's *The Idiom of Poetry* (2d ed., 1947).

One final type of c. calls for comment, though there is a reasonable doubt that it does or can exist. Whether there is such a thing as *scientific* c. depends mainly upon definition. The various operations that have been described occasionally as scientific c.—sociological, psychological, and anthropological studies of different sorts, but also linguistic commentary, textual editing, attribution, the dating of manuscripts, and even biography—are not distinguished by any uniformity of criteria as to what constitutes a science. Most writers who refer to such studies as scientific mean presumably that they exhibit a high respect for empirical fact and strive for the utmost clarity and consistency in describing their data. If this is science, then there is no doubt that c. should bend its efforts toward becoming altogether a science, as critics sometimes propose. But it may be observed that a study is scientific only as far as its materials and their relations prove to be subject to empirical verification, so that the laws of their behavior can be inferred and prediction can be based on them. Whatever may be said of phonemes, watermarks, and rates of respiration, values are not amenable to such treatment. They are not "public" data; they can be reported and discussed but not "verified," as that term is understood by the scientist. Until there is an empirical science of value (as opposed to a mere statistical technique for finding out how many people prefer Keats to Wordsworth), there can be no science of c. in any but a superficial sense. In the meantime, for those who regard "science" as an honorific name, it will have to continue to apply to the various factual disciplines that inform and support but cannot in themselves complete the act of c.   B.R.

J. Guyau, *L'art au point de vue sociologique* (1889); M. Dessoir, *Aesthetik und allgemeine Kunstwissenschaft* (1906); Eliot, *Wood;* Richards, *Principles* (1924); and *Practical C.* (1929); C. S. Lewis and E. M. W. Tillyard, *The Personal Heresy in C.* (1934); E. Pound, *Guide to Kulchur* (1938); C. Brooks, *Modern Poetry and the Tradition* (1939); Gilbert and Kuhn; T. M. Greene, *The Arts and the Art of C.* (1940); F. A. Pottle, *The Idiom of Poetry* (1941; enlarged ed. 1946); N. Foerster *et al., Literary Scholarship* (1941); Langer; H. J. Muller, *Sci-*

ence and C. (1943); F. J. Hoffman, *Freudianism and the Literary Mind* (1945); S. Pepper, *The Basis of C. in the Arts* (1945); H. Levin, "Lit. as an Institution," *Accent*, 6 (1946); C. Brooks, *The Well Wrought Urn* (1947); *The Importance of Scrutiny*, ed. E. Bentley (1948); S. E. Hyman, *The Armed Vision* (1948); Wellek and Warren; H. Dingle, *Science and Literary C.* (1949); D. N. Morgan, "Psychology and Art Today: A Summary and Critique," JAAC, 10 (1950); L. Trilling, *The Liberal Imagination* (1950); *The Creative Process*, ed. B. Ghiselin (1952); Abrams; H. D. Duncan, *Language and Lit. in Society* (1953; bibliog. 143–214); Wimsatt; V. Erlich, *Rus. Formalism* (1955; see esp. ch. 6, "Marxism versus Formalism"); Daiches; Wimsatt and Brooks; Frye; F. Kermode, *The Romantic Image* (1957); Y. Winters, *The Function of C.* (1957); F. Bowers, *Textual and Lit. C.* (1959); H. Gardner, *The Business of C.* (1959); L. D. Lerner, *The Truest Poetry* (1960); S. E. Hyman, *Poetry and C.* (1961); R. E. Lane, *The Liberties of Wit . . .* (1961); C. S. Lewis, *An Experiment in C.* (1961); N. Frye, *The Well-Tempered Critic* (1963); R. Wellek, *Concepts of C.*, ed. S. G. Nichols (1963); Sutton; *Explication as C.*, ed. W. K. Wimsatt (1963).

B.R.; L.D.L.

CROWN OF SONNETS. Traditionally a sequence of 7 It. sonnets so interwoven as to form a "crown" of panegyric for the one to whom they are addressed. The interweaving is accomplished by using the last line of each of the first 6 sonnets as the first line of the succeeding sonnet, with the last line of the seventh being a repetition of the opening line of the first. A further restriction prohibits the repetition of any given rhyme sound once it is used in the crown. Employed first in Italy early in the development of the sonnet as a form, the c.o.s. is probably best known in John Donne's *Holy Sonnets*, where it stands as a prologue to the sequence proper, the 7 sonnets being titled as follows: *La Corona, Annunciation, Nativitie, Temple, Crucifying, Resurrection,* and *Ascension;* with the opening and closing line of the series being "Deigne at my hands this crown of prayer and praise." L.J.Z.

CUADERNA VÍA. A Sp. meter (also called *alejandrino, mester de clerecía, nueva maestría*) in which syllable-count verse was used for the first time in Castilian, though the line soon deteriorated or was modified to one of somewhat more flexible length. It was introduced, probably under Fr. influence, in the first part of the 13th c. or earlier by the clergy (hence the name *mester de clerecía* in contrast to the *mester de juglaría,* or minstrel's meter or craft, typical of the popular epic and other narrative poetry). This meter, particularly in the work

of its earliest known exponent, Gonzalo de Berceo (late 12th to mid-13th c.), is noted for its rigidity of form: lines were made up of carefully counted syllables; each line consisted of 2 hemistichs of 7 syllables each; the lines were grouped into stanzas of 4 monorhymed lines each, the rhymes being in consonance. According to Fitz-Gerald, hiatus was obligatory, though contraction, apocope, aphaeresis, dialysis, synizesis, and sometimes syncope were permitted. An example of the c.v. from the work of Berceo is the following:

Yo Maestro Gonzalvo de Berceo nomnado,
iendo en romeria, caeci en un prado,
verde e bien sencido, de flores bien poblado;
logar cobdiciaduero pora homne cansado.

The best known works written largely in c.v. are Juan Ruiz's *Libro de buen amor* and López de Ayala's *Rimado de Palacio,* both of the 14th. c. The c.v., which was employed for most of the serious poetry written in the 13th and 14th c., was completely supplanted in the 15th by the *arte mayor* (q.v.).—J. D. Fitz-Gerald, *Versification of the C.V. as Found in Berceo's Vida de Santo Domingo de Silos* (1905); J. Saavedra Molina, "El verso de clerecía," *Boletín de Filología,* 6 (1950–51); Navarro. D.C.C.

CUBAN POETRY. See SPANISH AMERICAN POETRY.

CUBISM is the name that in mockery Henri Matisse gave in 1908 to the new school of art in Paris which under the leadership of Picasso and Braque was trying to represent modernism. A common denominator for art and poetry, at the dawn of the 20th c., was recognized by a number of poets, most gifted among them Guillaume Apollinaire and Pierre Reverdy. The cubists veered away from the reproduction or imitation of the dimensions and perspectives of nature. While retaining concrete forms and living entities as subject matter, they appeared to reduce them to simplified or stylized geometric patterns. But Apollinaire, better than the art critics, understood that the dehumanization and the distortion of reality, which resulted from a new concept of beauty, were in effect investing geometry with a fourth dimension. His book, *The Cubist Painters,* explained the united effort of the poet and the painter to renew nature's appearances and to convey the inner sense rather than the outer forms of reality, thereby stretching the limits of human imagination. For poets of that prewar epoch, c. became the bridge from traditional techniques toward a more subtle and flexible comprehension of the subject-object relationship in the arts.—G. Lemaître, *From C. to Surrealism in Fr. Lit.* (1941); W. Sypher, *Rococo to C. in Art and Lit.* (1960).   A.E.B.

CUBO-FUTURISM. A school in Rus. poetry, which originated on the eve of World War I. The first c.-f. miscellany, *Sadok sudei* (A Trap for the Judges) appeared in 1910. At first they called themselves "budetlyane" (Rus. neologism for "men of the future"). Only as late as 1913 did they begin to call themselves futurists. In their manifestos (1912–14) D. Burlyuk, V. Khlebnikov, A. Kruchonykh, and V. Mayakovsky called for a complete overhauling of poetic language, for doing away with any and all literary conventions—from the "sentimental" themes of love and romance to the "obsolete" rules of grammar. The iconoclastic arrogance of this credo is clearly reminiscent of the leader of It. futurism (q.v.), F. I. Marinetti. Yet in their tendency toward "creative deformation" of reality, and toward free, untrammeled verbal play, the Rus. futurists were more akin to the cubists (hence the term "c.-f.") and to the Fr. dadaists. Not unlike the latter, the cubo-futurists espoused the gospel of pure euphony; they favored the sound, or more broadly the sensory texture of the word, at the expense of its semantic aspect. This revolt against meaning found its expression in the slogan of "trans-sense language" (*zaumny yazyk*) and in Kruchonykh's and Kamensky's attempts to write verse composed solely of arbitrary combinations of sounds.

More rewarding than the crude experiments with nonsense syllables was the path-breaking poetry of Velimir Khlebnikov (1885–1922). His poem, *Incantation by Laughter*, based entirely on an ingenious play with derivatives, is perhaps the most characteristically "futurist" Rus. poem. Khlebnikov was deemed too difficult by the general public, but for many young poets his linguistic discoveries were a major source of inspiration. If Khlebnikov was the most original figure in Rus. futurism, its most popular exponent was Vladimir Mayakovsky (1894–1930), who combined poetic craftsmanship with boisterous coarseness and a genuine lyrical talent with a blatant propagandistic zeal. In the first years of the Revolution, Mayakovsky and some of his futurist confrères sought hegemony in Soviet letters, but their Bohemian antics were viewed with increasing disfavor. By the mid-1920's the Rus. futurist movement had run its course.—A. Kaun, *Soviet Poets and Poetry* (1943); C. M. Bowra, *The Creative Experiment* (1949); D. S. Mirsky, *A Hist. of Rus. Lit.* (1949); R. Poggioli, *The Poets of Russia* (1960); *An Anthol. of Rus. Verse*, ed. A. Yarmolinski (1962); V. Markov, *The Longer Poems of Velimir Khlebnikov* (1962).   V.E.

CUECA CHILENA. A South Am. popular dance song, also called *chilenita, zamacueca, zamacueca peruana*. It is an 8-line *seguidilla* (q.v.) in which the basic quatrain is separated from the *estribillo* (refrain) by the insertion of a line that is a repetition of the fourth line plus the word *sí*.—F. Hanssen, "La seguidilla," AUC, 125 (1909).   D.C.C.

CULTERANISM. See CULTISM.

CULTISM, which may be considered synonymous with gongorism and culteranism, is best understood in relation to conceptism. Traditionally, in Sp. literary history, cultism describes a poetic style in which learned words, Hispanized from L. and Gr., are prominent. Conceptism, on the other hand, is a style in poetry or prose characterized by ingenious or "precious" ideas. In other words, according to this view, cultism concerns poetic vocabulary and conceptism concerns the expression of thought in literature. But even in theory this is too simple: it is impossible absolutely to divorce thought from expression. In practice, cultism and conceptism are often found intermingled. If they are kept provisionally separate in the interest of analysis, cultism may be found best exemplified in Luis de Góngora y Argote (1561–1627) and his followers, and conceptism best exemplified in Francisco de Quevedo y Villegas (1580–1645) and Baltasar Gracián (1601–58).

While it is true that Góngora often drew on L. in fashioning neologisms, it must be recognized that L. has always been the reservoir of Sp. and also that many new creations did become permanently naturalized. Contemporary testimony in the form of satire (e.g., Quevedo's "La Culta Latiniparla") is misleading in that it suggests that Góngora and his school wilfully displaced good Sp. words with Latinisms and various preciosities. More characteristic of Góngora is his strange use of common words: e.g., *peinar* ("to comb") in the sense of "to plow" or "to pass through" (as in "peinar el viento"). The effect is that of a striking and original metaphor, and, in general, of a new linguistic system built right into the old. In the new language common objects or qualities take on a multiple existence: grain becomes gold and wool becomes snow; white may be snow or crystal or ivory. In syntax, Góngora tends to compress by following as closely as Sp. inflection allows the freedom of L.; hyperbaton, dislocated word-order, is the result. For instance, "De este, pues, formidable de la tierra / bostezo, el melancólico vacío / a Polifemo, horror de aquella sierra, / bárbara choza es, albergue umbrío / y redil espacioso . . ." (Describing a cave: "For the melancholy void of this formidable yawn of the earth is for Polyphemus, terror of that range, rude hut, shady lodging, and roomy sheepfold").

The major literary contest in the Sp. baroque age was carried on by Góngora and Quevedo, supported on either side by lesser partisans. If Quevedo refrained from using Latinate words and bending Sp. words to his own esoteric uses, nevertheless he made capital of word play, drawing on slang (*germanía*), double meaning, and etymology. He is also fond of syntactical contrast, paradox, and oxymoron. It can be seen, therefore, that Góngora and Quevedo had several things in common: a use of language (whether in "word" or "thought") which broke with usual Renaissance practice in its expanded and "indecorous" vocabulary, its compressed and "difficult" expression, its thorough exploitation of multiple meaning. Quevedo's criticism of Góngora may be reduced, without much loss, to his disapproval of Latinizing Sp. Indeed, cultism may be restricted to describing this aspect of gongorine style. The true affinities of the two poets are best seen under the light of general baroque (q.v.) poetic style. Their close relation was, in effect, recognized by the chief theorist of the time, Baltasar Gracián, in his highly specialized anthology and commentary, the *Agudeza y Arte de Ingenio* (1648; earlier version, *El Arte de Ingenio*, 1642). Gracián himself is a master of baroque artifice, and his work, while emulating the older rhetoric, is in part an original analysis of poetic taste and practice of the time. In it, Góngora and Quevedo, as well as the whole range of ancient and modern poetry, serve side by side as examples of wit and ingeniousness and art.—B. Croce, "I trattatisti italiani del concettismo e Baltasar Gracián," *Problemi di estetica* (1905); L. P. Thomas, *Le Lyrisme et la préciosité cultistes en Espagne* (1909); D. Alonso, *Evolución de la sintaxis de Góngora* (1928), *La lengua poética de Góngora* (1935, 3d corr. ed., 1961) and *Poesía española* (2d ed., 1952); E. Mérimée and S. G. Morley, *A Hist. of Sp. Lit.* (1930); W. Pabst, "Góngoras Schöpfung in seinen Gedichten *Polifemo* und *Soledades*," *Revue Hispanique*, 80 (1930); T. E. May, "Gracián's Idea of the 'Concepto,'" HR, 18 (1950); F. García Lorca, "La imagen poética en don Luis de Góngora," *Obras completas* (1954); D. Alonso, *Góngora y el Polifemo*, II (1961). L.N.

CURSUS. See PROSE RHYTHM.

CYCLIC FOOT. The "cyclic dactyl," which is rejected by almost all modern metricians, was a faulty assumption by J. A. Apel in 1806 from a passage in Dionysius of Halicarnassus (1st c. B.C.) that the component syllables of dactyls in lyric verse might on occasion have

their morae or time-units in the proportion of 1½: ½: 1 (indicated by ‿⌣=‿⌣) instead of the normal ratio 2: 1: 1 (indicated by ‿⌣⌣). In other words such dactyls (and anapaests) were assumed to be in triple instead of common time (diplasic instead of isomeric). See CLASSICAL PROSODY.—J. W. White, *The Verse of Gr. Comedy* (1912); Hardie; Kolář; Koster. R.J.G.

CYNGHANEDD. A scheme of sound correspondences peculiar to Welch poetry, involving accentuation, alliteration and internal rhyme. Described by Gerard Manley Hopkins as "chimes," he admitted that they were a main influence on his own formal experiments. In Welsh it was well developed by the 14th c., although not finally codified until the Caerwys Eisteddfod (Bardic Assembly) of 1524. It was, and still is, a main feature of strict-meter poetry, but it has often been practiced, with varying degrees of strictness, in the free-meters, and in our own day even in vers libre.

Cynghanedd is of three kinds: consonantal; *sain*, involving both rhyme and alliteration; and *lusg* (dragging), a form of internal rhyme, which was practiced also in Breton.

Consonantal c. is of three kinds: crossing, leaping, and interlinked crossing. In all examples of the "crossing" type, the alliteration forms a pattern in relation to 2 stressed vowels—the last before the caesura and the last in the line. There are three kinds of "crossing": stressed, unstressed, and "uneven-falling." In the first type, for example, the 2 stressed vowels above-mentioned are not followed by unstressed vowels within the same half-lines. In this type, all consonants within the half-lines which precede the final stressed vowels must be repeated in the same order, e.g.

Yr ydwyf í / ar dy fedd (r d f́ / r d f́).

In the unstressed and "uneven-falling" types, the sound relations, though similar to the above, are more complex. In the "leaping" types, the correspondences are as for the "crossing" types, except that, after the caesura, the repetitions are preceded by one or more unrepeated consonants, and where the "crossing" is interlinked, the repetitions begin before the caesura. In *c. sain* the line is in 3 sections, each with a main stress, the first section rhyming with the second, and the second related to the third as in consonantal c. In *c. lusg*, each line must end with a penultimate stress, the unstressed final syllable bearing the main rhyme, and the preceding stressed syllable rhyming with one of the earlier syllables in the same line, which may be stressed or post-stressed.

The rules of c. are stated above only in broad outline. Much of the skill and delight

CZECH POETRY

of c. poetry is in the variation of types in successive lines, and in the contrasting of vowel sounds alongside the repetition of consonants. It is an art form capable of a very rich, melodious, highly wrought and subtle effect, extensively exploited by Welsh poets.— Morris-Jones; Parry. D.M.L.

CYWYDD. A group of Welsh meters, including the *cywydd deuair hirion*, popularized by Dafydd ap Gwilym (14th c.). The 14th to the early 16th c. are known as the Cywydd Period because during this time it became the normal Welsh meter. It was revived in the 18th c. by Goronwy Owen and Ieuan Fardd and is still popular. The earliest known examples are without *cynghanedd* (q.v.). Dafydd, however, embellished most of his lines with *cynghanedd*, and in the 15th c. this became obligatory in every line. The *c.* is closely similar to Ir. *debhidhe*. It is composed in rhyming couplets (aa, bb, cc, etc.), each line having 7 syllables, with the accentuation of the rhyming endings uneven, that is, with the stress penultimate in the one and final in the other. Unlike the rule for *debhidhe*, either type of ending may precede the other.—Morris-Jones; Parry. D.M.L.

CZECH POETRY. The earliest known example of verse in the Cz. vernacular is a hymn dating from the late 12th or early 13th c., addressed to the patron saint of Bohemia, Václav ("Good King Wenceslaus"). The 14th c. saw a great flowering of Cz. poetry, epic and lyric. Outstanding are an epic about Alexander of Macedon, and the numerous verse legends of lives of New Testament figures and saints, in particular a *Life* of St. Catherine of Alexandria noted for the brilliance of its imagery. These works all had medieval L. prototypes, but were often original in details. The lyric also came to Bohemia, especially from France and Italy; worthy of note is a Cz. variant of the Prov. *aubade*. An indigenous satiric poetry also flourished in the 14th c.: perhaps the most original example is a burlesque disputation, *Podkoní a žák*. (The Groom and the Student), in which each antagonist maintains that his life is the better. The form of most of Cz. 14th-c. verse was an 8-syllable trochaic line with couplet rhymes, though chronicle and lyric verse showed variations.

The Hussite period of the early 15th c. severely curtailed poetic expression, though it did produce interesting polemic poetry. Humanism brought new forms of L. verse, but poetic expression in the vernacular lagged behind, though the Cz. humanists made their native prose one of the most expressive of the written languages of Europe. The Counter-Reformation, which followed the loss of Cz. independence in 1620, saw the cultivation of

a contemplative religious poetry of hymns and prayers, remarkable for their brilliant, flowery imagery and plays upon words, if at times too sentimental and overburdened with diminutives of endearment.

The end of the 17th and the 18th c. witnessed the virtual death of national literature; not till the latter half of the 18th c. were systematic attempts begun to revive Cz. as a literary language. This movement was nationalistic and patriotic; opposing the Jesuit Baroque heritage, it reached back further to the Cz. Protestant humanist tradition of the 16th and early 17th c. The result was that written Cz. as revived was somewhat archaic, and has remained so until today. But this tie with an ancient literary tradition has given modern Cz. a decided advantage over many other Central and East European literary languages.

Classical influences were strong in the early 19th c., and a period of vacillation between quantitative and qualitative (accentual) systems of verse ensued. Eventually qualitative verse triumphed (Cz. has a weak stress fixed on the first syllable), but length of syllables undoubtedly plays an important prosodic role in Cz. verse.

Didactic, biblical, laudatory and idyllic verse predominated at the end of the 18th c. in the work of such poets as A. J. Puchmajer (1769–1820). The beginning of the 19th c. brought preromanticism and a poetry dedicated to the national patriotic cause. The kinship of Czechs and other Slavic peoples was stressed. The Slovak poet Ján Kollár (1793–1852), who wrote in Cz., produced a collection of sonnets, *Slávy dcera* (The Daughter of Sláva, 1824 and 1832), a grandiose and sometimes moving attempt to construct a Slavic mythology and to foretell a happier future for the Slavic peoples. F. L. Čelakovský (1799–1852) utilized the inspiration of Slavic folk songs in his *Ohlasy* ("Echoes") of Rus. and Cz. folk songs (1829 and 1839, respectively).

Romanticism came full-fledged with K. H. Mácha (1810–36), probably, in spite of his early death, the greatest Cz. poet. His solitary masterpiece, the narrative poem *Máj* (May 1836), is Byronic in subject, but is remarkable for the saturated intensity of the imagery, which portrays the poet's favorite romantic antitheses of age and youth, love and death. May is the time of youth and love:

Byl pozdní večer—první máj—
večerní máj—byl lásky čas.
Hrdliččin zval ku lásce hlas,
kde borový zaváněl háj.

It was late evening, the first of May—
Evening May—it was the time of love.

-[177]-

The voice of the turtle-dove summoned to
love
Where the pine grove wafted its scent.

These opening lines are the best known in all
Cz. poetry. But this time of childlike innocence
is fleeting:

Daleko zanesl věk onen časů vztek,
dalekot' jeho sen. . . .
to jestit' zemřelých krásný dětinský čas.

The fury of the times bore that season far
away,
Far off his dream. . . .
The fair childhood age of the dead.

Mácha introduced iambic verse to Cz.: before
him modern Cz. verse had been exclusively
trochaic (even Kollár's sonnets were in trochees); occasional iambic lines were considered
as trochaic with anacrusis. This was because
Cz. has fixed stress on the first syllable, so that
lines normally open with a stress. Mácha varied
the treatment of the first foot of the line and,
emphasizing the iambic character of the other
feet, thus shaped a true iambic verse. More
conservative was K. J. Erben (1811–70), who
created the Cz. romantic ballad, inspired by
the popular ballad of folk poetry.

The failure of the Revolution of 1848
brought an end to the movement for independence and to the first wave of romanticism.
Not till the 1860's did a strong new romantic
movement emerge. The national cause was
once again dominant, but now found a more
practical expression through the creation of
popular institutions, including a national theater. Writers were concerned with social problems: democracy, the emancipation of women,
the correction of economic injustice, as well as
with the longing for national independence.
The leading poet of this period was Jan
Neruda (1834–91), who strove to develop national consciousness, at times indulging in
sharp ironic criticism of his too contented
people. During the 1870's and 1880's the nationalist tendency continued to dominate, notably in the work of Svatopluk Čech (1846–
1908), a follower of the Pan-Slavic poet Kollár.
Cech's style, often bombastic, at times attained
real rhetorical power. In his lyrics he dealt
with the political misfortunes of his people
and, like Neruda, was capable of sarcasm at
the expense of national self-satisfaction.

The technical side of Cz. verse had suffered
during this era, but the 1870's saw it rise to a
new brilliance with the work of the Parnassian
poet Jaroslav Vrchlický (pseudonym of Emil
Frída, 1853–1912). A superb technician,
Vrchlický introduced many new forms as well
as poetic themes from abroad; in this he and
his followers opposed the more nationally
minded poets who were his contemporaries.

Vrchlický even rejected the traditionally canonized use of folk motifs and forms in Cz. higher
poetry. He wrote voluminously, and translated
from most contemporary European tongues as
well as from the classical languages; his total
production exceeds one hundred volumes, and
includes much narrative and dramatic as well
as lyric verse. A follower of Victor Hugo's
evolutionary optimism, he was more limited
in ideas than in form. Tending towards aestheticism and the cult of classical antiquity, he
failed, however, to turn the current of Cz.
poetry permanently in either direction.

Vrchlický was followed by J. S. Machar
(1864–1942), who sought to create a great poetic
panorama of world history; like Nietzsche, he
believed that history follows a spiral movement, alternately rising and falling. Greater
as poets were the Cz. symbolists, influenced by
Fr. and Belgian symbolism. The most important of these was Otokar Březina (pseudonym of V. I. Jebavý, 1868–1929), who wrote
rhapsodic verse celebrating the mystic union
of all men and of man and cosmos. Themes of
decadence appear in the work of such poets as
Jiří Karásek ze Lvovic (1871–1951) and Karel
Hlaváček (1874–98). Viktor Dyk (1877–1931)
wrote sarcastic epigrams on superficial Cz.
patriotism, as well as giving a poetic portrait
of the contemporary "lost generation" of the
fin-de-siècle. The Cz. symbolists, particularly
Březina and Antonín Sova (1864–1928), did
much to strengthen the musical aspect of Cz.
verse as well as to cultivate an impressionistic
imagery.

The achievement of national independence
in 1918 was followed by a period of intense
creativity. The early 1920's brought a wave of
so-called proletarian poetry, expressing a warm
if naive sympathy for the Soviet experiment.
The leading poet of this trend was Jiří Wolker
(1900–1924). The late 1920's saw a sudden and
violent shift to "poetism," a school of "pure
poetry" which had its roots in dadaism, futurism (qq.v.) and vitalism. The poetists sought
to create a poetry of joy of living, of urban
life and technology, a poetry inspired by peripheral arts such as the film, circus, and
musical revue. Leading "poetists" were Vítěz-
slav Nezval (1900–58) and Jaroslav Seifert
(1901–   ).

The early 1930's saw the sudden collapse of
poetism as a movement: Nezval went over to
surrealism, while Seifert turned to a more personal poetry of sensual imagery. The period
also saw the cultivation of a spiritual and
meditative poetry in the work of Josef Hora
(1891–1945) and such Catholic poets as Jaroslav
Durych (1886–1962) and Jan Zahradníček
(1905–60). Probably the greatest poet of this
period is František Halas (1901–49), a complex
writer obsessed by themes of death, old age,

and decay. Most of these poets (except the Catholics) were leftists in politics, but their poetry remained individualist.

World War II and the subsequent Communist coup virtually destroyed the older poetic tradition. Durych was silenced, as was Seifert until 1955, while Zahradníček was long imprisoned. In the spring of 1956 demands for greater freedom began to be heard, and Seifert and František Hrubín (1910–) sharply criticized the restrictions imposed on literature. But it is still too soon to determine whether any significant relaxation will be effected.

Cz. poetry has almost always been the dominant form of expression in Cz. literature, and prose has lagged far behind. The poetic culture attained a particularly high level under symbolism and again in the 1920's and 1930's. This occurred in spite of the frequent predominance of nationalist and didactic trends, and of the relative weakness of aestheticist, Parnassian, or classicist tendencies in modern Cz. literature. The native folk lyric has had a strong influence in many periods, as has the folk epos of other Slavic peoples: Russians and Serbs. During the 19th c. the leading foreign influences were those of Shakespeare, Milton, Goethe, Schiller, Byron, Pushkin, Mickiewicz, Béranger, Heine and Hugo, with the Fr. symbolists, Whitman, and Verhaeren important at the very end of the century. The 20th c. has seen extreme variety of foreign influence.

The lyric has had a stronger tradition than the epic; perhaps the lack of a native folk epos is to blame here. But the ballad, a mixed epic-lyric form influenced by the Cz. folk ballad, has been important. Dramatic poetry is on the whole weak, though there are many plays in verse. In the 20th c. the predominance of the lyric has been absolute, as in European poetry generally.

In prosodic form binary meters are virtually exclusive, since the language has a tendency to accent on every odd syllable. Mixed trochaic-dactylic forms based on classical or native folk models are common, however, particularly under romanticism.

ANTHOLOGIES: *Česká poesie XIX. věku*, I-III, "Máj" (1897–98); *Česká lyra* (1911) and *Ceská epika* (1912), both ed. F. S. Procházka; *Modern Cz. Poetry*, ed. P. Selver (1920); *Anthologie de la poésie tchèque*, ed. H. Jelínek (1930); *Zpěv českého obrozeni, 1750–1866*, ed. M. Očadlík (1940; poetry of the Cz. Revival); *Lyrika českého obrození*, ed. V. Jirát (1940); *Modern Cz. Poetry*, ed. E. Osers and J. K. Montgomery (1945); *Česká poesie*, Československý spisovatel (1951); *Nová česká poesie*, Československý spisovatel (1955); *A Book of Cz. Verse*, ed. A. French (1958); *The Linden Tree*, ed. M. Otruba and Z. Pešat (1963).

HISTORY AND CRITICISM: J. Jakubec and A. Novák, *Gesch. der tschechischen Lit.* (1907); P. Selver, *Otokar Březina* (1921; in Eng.); J. Král, *O prosodii české*, I (1923); F. Chudoba, *A Short Survey of Cz. Lit.* (1924); R. Jakobson, *Základy českého verše* (1926; opposes Král's book); H. Jelínek, *Hist. de la litt. tchèque* (3 v., 1930–1935); J. and A. Novák, *Přehledné dějiny literatury české* (1936–39; most thorough survey; abridged and supplemented as *Stručné dějiny lit. české*, 1946); F. X. Šalda, *Studie literárně historické a kritické* (1937) and *Kritické glosy k nové poesii české* (1939; poetry of the 1920's and 1930's); J. Mukařovský, *Kapitoly z české poetiky* (3 v., 1948); B. Meriggi, *Storia della letteratura ceca e slovacca* (1958); J. Hrabák, *Studie o českém verši* (1959; studies of Cz. verse). W.E.H.

CZECH PROSODY. See SLAVIC PROSODY.

D

DACTYL (Gr. "finger"). A metrical unit, in quantitative verse, consisting of a long syllable followed by two short ones:

$$- \smile \smile;\ f\bar{\imath}lius$$

In accentual verse, an accented syllable followed by two unaccented ones:

$$\acute{/}\ x\ x;\ \text{tenderly}$$

Widely used in classical poetry, especially in the hexameter and the elegiac distich (qq.v.), where it may be replaced by a spondee ($--$).

Also, in lyric verse, pure or in combination with other forms, such as the epitrite (one short and three long syllables, in any order; see DACTYLO-EPITRITE). Except in imitations of the classical hexameter, the use of the d. as a basis for Eng. verse is infrequent till the 19th c., when Browning, Scott, Swinburne, and others employed it, and is still rarely done well, its prolonged use tending to override the normal word-accent and result in a grotesque jigging. But this very grotesqueness is sometimes what is wanted in modern . verse.— Hardie; Hamer; Koster; U. v. Wilamowitz-

Moellendorff, *Griechische Verskunst* (2d ed., 1958). D.S.P.

DACTYLO-EPITRITE. This Gr. lyric meter of Pindar, Bacchylides, and the drama is a compound of dactyls, spondees, and epitrites. The dactyls generally form cola of the type ‒∪∪‒∪∪‒ (dactylic tripody catalectic *in syllabam* or *hemiepes*) and ‒∪∪‒∪∪‒‒, and the epitrites are normally of the form ‒∪‒‒ rather than ‒‒∪‒. The name "dactylo-epitrite" as a compound word is not ancient but was given currency by the 19th-c. metricians A. Rossbach and R. Westphal. See EPITRITE.—Hardie; Kolář; Dale; U. von Wilamowitz-Moellendorff, *Griechische Verskunst* (2d ed., 1958). R.J.G.

DADAISM. In Zurich in 1916, a Roumanian, Tristan Tzara, an Alsatian, Hans Arp, and two Germans, Hugo Ball and Richard Huelsenbeck, chose a word to represent their need for total freedom. The word was "Dada," independent of specific connotations, signifying everything and nothing at the same time, primitive but all-encompassing. In 1919 Dada moved to Paris, where its international character became even more pronounced. Dadaism proved a potent nucleus for the poetically ardent, socially rebellious Fr. youths, including André Breton, Philippe Soupault, Paul Eluard, Louis Aragon, Georges Ribemont-Dessaignes and others, who were seeking to shape a new "cenacle." The Dadaists received encouragement and assistance from the slightly older and equally unconventional cubists. The basic word in the vocabulary of the Dadaists became "nothing." Dissatisfied with reason, morality, and religion, which they believed to have led the world into a senseless war, they undertook to sweep clean all the ideals and rules prevalent among the successful poets and artists of their time. Their performances consisted of public demonstrations verging on exhibitionism; "collage" in art and poetry, consisting of the juxtaposition of unrelated objects or words picked out at random and linked into an illogical unit; and poems and manifestoes which appeared in their official journal, *Dada*, and other periodicals. They waged war against cliché imagery, and standard syntax, and they invested the metaphor with elements of absurdity and irony. In 1921 they considered Dada to have outlived its usefulness and thereupon buried it, making way for surrealism (q.v.), which the Paris contingent proceeded to endow with a more solid and more positive *ars poetica*, conceived in the spirit of Dada. Elsewhere, particularly in Germany and America, under the initiative of Hülsenbeck and Arthur Cravan respectively, and with the cooperation of many artists, dadaism has survived as a trademark. However,

its most permanent effects are deemed to have been felt by the poetry of France.—*The Dada Painters and Poets, an Anthol.*, ed. R. Motherwell (1953); *Dada, Monograph of a Movement*, ed. W. Verkauf (2d ed., 1961); R. Hülsenbeck, *En avant Dada. Eine Gesch. des Dadaismus* (1920). A.E.B.

DAINA. See LITHUANIAN POETRY; LATVIAN POETRY.

DANISH POETRY. Rune (q.v.) inscriptions indicate that the ancient Danes were familiar with the verse form of Norse heroic poetry; however, no Dan. heroic poetry has been preserved in the original form. When Saxo Grammaticus (fl. 1200) recorded the oral poetic traditions, he used L. prose and hexameter, and furthermore the material is adulterated with non-Dan. elements. The reconstructed poems reflect the ethos of a ruling aristocracy: the main themes are war, love, and loyalty. *Bjarkamál*, whose heroes also appear in the Anglo-Saxon poems *Widsith* and *Beowulf*, is a powerful war song in dialogue form; the lay of Ingjald (ca. 950) is the monologue of an old warrior who castigates the ruling king's cowardice in failing to avenge his father's murder. The prevailing genre was the *kviða* (lay), a short heroic narrative in which one simple action, involving a limited number of characters, is rushed to a violently dramatic climax. The most common stanza used, *fornyrðislag* (q.v.), consists of 8 lines—each with 2 heavy beats—rhyming alliteratively in pairs.

In the Middle Ages (1100–1500) Dan. poetry assimilated the spirit and form of European courtly poetry. The folk ballad, which is the chief poetic monument of the age, reached Denmark from France in the early 12th c. But the Dan. ballad, with its rapid dramatic narrative, has also preserved essential elements of the old native poetry; and like the latter, it mirrors the life of the nobility. The most important single poem of the age is *Den danske Rimkrønike* (The Dan. Rhymed Chronicle, ca. 1478), written most likely by Brother Niels of Sorø. In the 16th c., poetry in the vernacular was still medieval in spirit and form; the folk ballad and the rhymed chronicle dictated the styles, notably subject to a growing German influence. In the drama, which was late in developing, the first significant contributions were those of Hieronymus Justesen Ranch (1537–1607), particularly the masterly farce *Karrig Nidding* (The Miserly Miscreant), the best Dan. play before Holberg. The form is the *knittelvers* (q.v.) rhymed couplet, interspersed with lyrical measures.

In the 17th c., when the Renaissance reached Denmark, the poets endeavored to create a national Dan. poetry on classical models. Foremost was Anders Arrebo (1587–1637), whose *Hexaëmeron* (ca. 1622; pr. 1661), based on Du Bartas' *La Semaine,* was composed partly in twice-rhymed hexameter, partly in alexandrines. The style, with its classical-mythological imagery, is ineluctably artificial, achieving transparency only in rare passages of nature description. Most eminent of the grammarians who were simultaneously developing a theory of Dan. metrics was Hans Mikkelsen Ravn (1610–63), who in *Ex Rhythmologia Danica epitome brevissima* (1649), following Opitz, Ronsard, and Bembo, analyzed and illustrated a variety of metrical forms, mostly classical. This theoretical work provided the necessary technical instruments for the two greatest poets of the century, Bording and Kingo.

Anders Bording (1619–77) is best known as a versatile singer of wine, women, and song. But he also wrote delightful nature lyrics, although the classicizing tendency occasionally proved baneful, as in his *Phaetonvise* (Phaeton Ballad). In his hand the novel metrical forms became subtle vehicles of poetic expression. Thomas Kingo (1634–1703), however, was the first poet great enough fully to exploit the new-found metrical variety. He is remembered primarily for his *Aandelige Syngekor I, II* (Spiritual Choirs, i, ii, 1674, 1678). Kingo's hymns, largely inspired by the Hebrew prophets, are unmistakably baroque in style, a characterization borne out by their thematic counterpoints and sensuous imagery. Metaphors are often forced and images revolting, especially in poems on the Passion and on death. He is most successful where the baroque does not predominate, as in his morning and evening hymns. Here a devout fervor has achieved a sublimely simple and forceful expression.

Whereas in the 17th c. the dominant foreign influence in Dan. poetry was German, in the 18th c. Fr. neoclassicism as formulated by Boileau provided the models. This change was due mainly to the activity of the Norwegian Ludvig Holberg, important both in Dan. and Norwegian literature. Although known chiefly as the creator of bourgeois prose comedy, in his verse mock-epic *Peder Paars* (1719–20), Holberg achieved notable distinction. Influenced by Boileau's *Le Lutrin* and Cervantes' *Don Quijote,* the satire of the poem was both literary and social. In the battle between the ancients and the moderns Holberg sided with the latter, employing Homer, Virgil, and their heroic lines as vehicles of commonplace emotion. Simultaneously, he attacked the pedantry and narrow-mindedness of the official dignitaries and the superstition of the commoner. The poem marks Holberg as the first great spokesman of the middle classes in Dan. literature.

Lyric poetry was in the first half of the 18th c. represented by Ambrosius Stub and Hans Adolf Brorson. Stub (1705–58) practiced a wide variety of genres, from the religious lyric to the drinking song. His form, influenced by the It. operatic aria, is concise as well as graceful; his style, in its delicate picturesqueness, has some features of the rococo. As Holberg expressed the rationalism of the age, Brorson expressed religious pietism, which especially during the reign of Christian VI (1730–46) was a strong cultural force in Denmark. In the second half of the century the rationalistic and the sentimental currents in Dan. literature assumed new and more programmatic forms. The inheritance from Fr. neoclassicism and Eng. empiricism was taken up by the Norwegian authors then settled in Copenhagen, who in 1772 organized *Det norske Selskab,* q.v. (The Norwegian Society); the claims of feeling and imagination were upheld by *Det danske Litteraturselskab* (The Dan. Literary Society), organized in 1774, with Johannes Ewald as honorary member. Decisive for the development of Ewald (1743–81), the preromantic poet of Denmark, was the German poet Klopstock, who with his Nordic dramas had adumbrated a Germanic renaissance. Klopstock introduced Ewald to Saxo Grammaticus; simultaneously Ewald read Macpherson's *Ossian* and Shakespeare. His first important poetic drama, *Balders Død* (The Death of Balder, 1773), is a mixture of Fr. classical and Klopstockian Nordic tragedy, composed in blank verse with feminine endings, a form Ewald was the first to use in Dan. His most mature play is *Fiskerne* (The Fishermen, 1780), which was revolutionary by its treatment in the grand style of the life of the common man. The only noteworthy poet of the last twenty years of the century was Jens Baggesen (1764–1826), a mercurial spirit who alternated between 18th- and 19th-c. sensibility in accordance with the tenor of his personal experience.

Guldhornene (The Golden Horns, 1802) by Adam Oehlenschläger (1779–1850), the greatest poet of Denmark, precipitated the romantic movement. Oehlenschläger's genius was awakened—and his poem inspired—by the Norwegian Henrik Steffens, who in 1802 expounded the aesthetic theories of Schelling and the two Schlegels in Copenhagen. The poem condemns the rationalist and glorifies the born genius, alone capable of interpreting nature and history and of joining past and present. The form, an adaptation of Old Icelandic *fornyrðislag,* objectifies this historical consciousness, which enabled Oehlenschläger to create a Nordic as well as a nationally Dan. poetry. Oehlenschläger's works embrace epic, lyric, and drama. Noteworthy are his romances—based on native ballads, but composed in forms like ottava and terza rima—and the Shakespeare-inspired *Sanct Hansaften-Spil* (Midsummer Night Play, 1803), a lyrical comedy in *knittelvers* which ironically satirizes the contemporary view of poetry. The chief vehicle of Oehlenschläger's romantic philosophy is *Aladdin* (1805), a fairy-tale drama in blank verse with a Shakespearean richness of contrasting moods ranging from the sublime to the quotidian. After 1806, Oehlenschläger's subjectivism became tempered by his admiration for Goethe's and Schiller's objective poetry. Swayed by the German-national Heidelberg romanticism, he recast his universalist art into a national mold. *Nordiske Digte* (Northern Poems), published in 1807, contained *Baldur hin Gode* (Balder the Good), *Thors Rejse* (Thor's Journey), and his best drama, *Hakon Jarl*, a blank verse tragedy modeled on Schiller's *Wallenstein*. Although the principal value of these works was cultural, in that they restored, in artistic form, the heritage of Scandinavian myth, even their purely aesthetic merits are high, in some respects surpassing those of their German predecessors. National in inspiration was also the work of another romantic of stature, N.F.S. Grundtvig (1783–1872), who, less poet than cultural leader, nevertheless created an enduring monument in his hymns. In their imagery, impregnated with Dan. landscape and Nordic mythology, these hymns represent a deeply original poetic achievement, in its power comparable to that of Kingo.

About 1830 the older naive form of romanticism was superseded by *romantisme*, at the same time more socially aware, more contemplative, and formally more sophisticated. Johan Ludvig Heiberg (1791–1860), its chief representative, is noted for his romantic plays, which by their charming alternation between actuality and the dream world—as between prose and poetry—dissipated the public's desire for Oehlenschläger's tragedies. Although social satire abounded, as in *Syvsoverdag* (Seven Sleepers' Day, 1840), it was only with the delightful apocalyptic comedy *En Sjæl efter Døden* (A Soul after Death, 1841) that satire of bourgeois inanity became Heiberg's primary purpose. The soul, used to the "fat, phlegmatic life on earth," adjusts painlessly to hell, the realm of the immediate, where no idea ever enters.

As early as the 1820's Steen Steensen Blicher (1782–1848) and Poul M. Møller (1794–1838) had written poems of realistic inspiration. Blicher's best work, *Æ Bindstouw* (The Knitting-room, 1842), which is a collection of stories with interspersed poems and ballads, marks not only the beginning of Dan. regional poetry, but also the first modern use of dialect. With Frederik Paludan-Müller (1809–76), second only to Oehlenschläger among Dan. poets, appeared critical realism, in his case the outcome of a rigorous ethical philosophy. The early lyric-narrative poem *Dandserinden* (The Dancing Girl, 1833) still exuded aestheticism; inspired by Byron's *Don Juan*, it features the ottava rima and a style alternating between pathos and ironical satire. After writing three successive mythological dramas, the poet reassumed the Byronic manner and form in his principal work, the three-volume epic *Adam Homo* (1841–48), in order to present a satirical picture of contemporary Dan. culture. Like Heiberg in *En Sjæl efter Døden* he found it stripped of idealism and dominated by the insidious spirit of compromise.

Realism and satire notwithstanding, the same period brought forth, in the poetry of Ludvig Bødtcher, Emil Aarestrup, and Christian Winther, the fairest flowers of romanticism, now largely aesthetic in inspiration. These poets express the subtly Epicurean side of the Dan. temperament, Bødtcher (1793–1874) and Aarestrup (1806–56) through their love lyrics, in a minor and major key respectively. The poetry of Winther (1796–1876), one of Denmark's finest lyrists, is more complex. His themes, nature and love, are usually intimately combined, as in *Træsnit* (Woodcuts, 1828), ten romances giving genre pictures from the village. His greatest achievement, besides the poignant love poetry in *Til Een* (To Someone, 1843, 1849), is the romance *Hjortens Flugt* (The Flight of the Deer, 1855). The verse form used in this series of medieval idylls is a freely modified Nibelungen stanza (q.v.); the idiom is colloquial and slightly archaizing.

Winther's lyricism, which excels in the idyll, typifies Dan. lyric poetry in general in that the latter is seldom pure, but usually combines lyric and narrative elements. This feature may derive from the particular deficiencies and excellences of the Dan. language. Compared to Swedish and Norwegian, Dan. evinces but slight sonority, modulation, and melody; and the glottal stop causes a measured, if not staccato, rhythm. These qualities make Dan. only moderately effective as a medium for conveying high passion, whether erotic or cosmic, an area in which Swedish is supremely expressive. Also, they indicate a lack of the rhythmical impetus required for great dramatic poetry, the demands of which Norwegian more readily fulfills. Generally, the strength of Dan. lies in delicate and intimate lyricism and in descriptive poetry. With its subdued music and unemphatic but varied rhythm it is also an effective vehicle for reflective and satirical poetry, a significant tradition in Dan. literature from Holberg to the present. To illustrate the qualities of Dan., which like the other Scandinavian languages lends itself with about equal felicity to each of the four metrical movements, here is a stanza from Winther's poem *Hvile* (Repose, 1858), in dactylic-trochaic rhythm:

Solen er slukket, dagen forstummer,
skyerne staa ved himlens rand.
Stjernerne smile; drømme og slummer
favne i stilhed hav og land.

The sun is extinguished, day's voices
drowned,
The clouds hover at heaven's end.
The stars are smiling; in stillness wound
Dreamy slumbers clasp sea and land.

A new age was marshaled in by the critic Georg Brandes, who demanded a literature that "subjected problems to debate." He could hardly fail to affect the work of three contemporary poets, Jens Peter Jacobsen (1847–85), Holger Drachmann (1846–1908), and Karl Gjellerup (1857–1919). By way of Edgar Allan Poe, Jacobsen found his form in the capriciously winding monologues he called "arabesques," free-verse poems whose violent coloring and veiled music suggest a subconscious origin. Drachmann was in *Digte* (Poems) of 1872 a revolutionary Brandesian, most characteristically so in *English Socialists*. Later he turned from radicalism both in politics and love, and a neoromantic attitude marks the plays which, like *Der var engang* (Once Upon a Time, 1885), dramatize themes from medieval fairy tales. But in the verse drama *Vølund Smed* (Wayland Smith, 1894), influenced by Shakespeare and Wagner, he appeared again as a passionate eroticist. In his best collection, *Sange ved Havet* (Songs by the Sea, 1877), Drachmann evoked with deep empathy the changing moods of the sea, where he perceived an image of his own protean spirit. As a lyric poet Drachmann is undoubtedly Denmark's greatest; at its best his style is distinctively individual. By varying line length and loosening rhythm, he created a most flexible form, preserved from flux through structural rhyme.

In the 1890's naturalism retreated before a neoromantic movement. Its program was formulated in *Taarnet* (The Tower, 1893–94), a monthly published jointly by Johannes Jørgensen (1866–1956), Viggo Stuckenberg (1863–1905), and Sophus Claussen (1865–1931). With *Stemninger* (Moods, 1892) Jørgensen, the editor, had introduced the dreams and visions of Fr. symbolism into Dan. literature. His later poetry, mostly reflective, is marked by his conversion, in 1896, to Roman Catholicism. The lyrics of Stuckenberg, usually love poems pale in color and melancholy in tone, universalize intimately personal experience. The quality of Claussen's verse, which is highly original, was largely determined by his doctrinal adherence to symbolism, not only as an aesthetic theory, but as a metaphysic. This is evident in his erotic poetry, where beneath the surface theme an ontological pattern is discernible, a tension of irreducible opposites. Dualism also permeates the splendid hexameter poem *Atomernes Oprør* (Revolt of the Atoms, 1925), in which Claussen foresaw the Atomic Age. Two other neoromantics were Helge Rode (1870–1937) and Ludvig Holstein (1864–1943). Rode's lyricism is notable for its ethereal quality. In this, as also in its deep concern with death, his best work, *Ariel* (1914), is reminiscent of Shelley's poetry. The best of Holstein's simple lyrics, quite unaffected by symbolism, flow from his steady vision of man's oneness with nature.

Dan. poetry of the 20th c. has precipitated various currents and styles, determined partly by international vogues, partly by socio-political events. The prewar period broke with the soul-searching symbolist lyricism of the 1890's; this was the decade of Jutland regional poetry, dominated by Jeppe Aakjær (1866–1930) and Johannes V. Jensen (1873–1950). Aakjær, a disciple of Blicher and Robert Burns, was also the poet of the fourth estate, whose sensibility he articulated in vigorous, eminently singable verse. Ultimately, however, he embraced the entire people, its past as well as its present. Jensen's expansion was cultural and racial: Inspired by the doctrine of evolution, he created a strange myth about the progressive "Jute-Anglo-American" race, whose mentality he saw epitomized in Columbus, the explorer. Accordingly, the main themes of his poetry are vitality and longing, alternating with the *Weltschmerz* that ineluctably accompanies the fulfillment of desire and dream. Jensen's diction, which in its incongruous mixture of brutally suggestive realism and florid sensuousness seeks to render living reality in all its changeableness, has been vastly influential in modern Dan. poetry, as has his free verse influenced by Jacobsen and Whitman. Traditional in form, the voluminous and varied production of Valdemar Rørdam (1872–1946) is comparable in its manly vigor and musical resonance to the poetry of Drachmann.

During and after World War I, Dan. poetry experienced a veritable renewal, which continued throughout the 1920's. Inspired by Jensen and by expressionism in painting and in German poetry, Emil Bønnelycke (1893–1953) and Tom Kristensen (b. 1893) developed a revolutionary aesthetic designed to create new forms of beauty as well as new social forms. Kristensen's *Fribytterdrømme* (Freebooter's Dreams, 1920), which projected the restless spirit of the Jazz Age, conveys the brutal explosions of instinct in a style intoxicated with color and sound. In singular contrast stands the work of Otto Gelsted (b. 1888), whose *Reklameskibet* (The Show Boat, 1922) recalls *The Waste Land* of T. S. Eliot. An admirer of

Jensen, Gelsted maintained the radical-humanistic tradition in Dan. poetry between the Wars. Informed with humanism is also the poetry of Nis Petersen (1897-1943) and Paul La Cour (1902-56), who dominated the scene in the 1930's. Petersen displayed, especially in *Brændende Europa* (Europe Aflame, 1933), a gloomy concern for Western culture. La Cour, whose sensibility was formed by Claussen and modern Fr. poets, especially Paul Eluard, was able to combine the quest for the secret sources of personal renewal with a view of poetry which emphasized its profoundly cultural value. Two significant individualists were Per Lange (b. 1901), whose lapidary verse shows a supreme artistry, and Jens August Schade (b. 1903), an earthy philosophical humorist of surrealist affinities.

Under the pressure of war and foreign occupation the 1940's instilled new vigor and urgency into Dan. poetry. Inspirational was the work of Gustaf Munch-Petersen (1912-38), a modernist rebel who, through his death in Spain fighting against Franco, became the prototype of the "engaged" writer. Another originative poet was Morten Nielsen (1922-44), who in a hard, weighty, and unfinished form expressed a deep reverence for life and freedom. Closely related to these two figures are Halfdan Rasmussen (b. 1915) and Erik Knudsen (b. 1922). The second main group of young Dan. poets, whose original forum was the periodical *Heretica* (1948-53), is religiously oriented. Inspired by the example of T. S. Eliot, Ole Sarvig (b. 1921) and Ole Wivel (b. 1921) embody in their poetry, by way of an essentially Christian symbolism, the pattern of rebirth after catastrophe and wasteland. Stylistically, however, Sarvig's closest affinities are with abstract painting, Wivel's with Rilke. Rilke-inspired is also Thorkild Bjørnvig (b. 1918), perhaps the most significant of the new poets. Finally, one may mention Jørgen Nash (b. 1920), a gay heir of Munch-Petersen; Tove Ditlevsen (b. 1918), the best living poetess; Ove Abildgaard (b. 1916), a baroque antiromantic; Frank Jæger (b. 1926), a droll successor to Schade; and Robert Corydon (b. 1924), whose objective nature poetry is distinguished by stylized imagery. Although in the 1950's prose again predominated, these and the preceding contemporary poets justify optimism in regard to the immediate future of poetry in Denmark.

ANTHOLOGIES: *A Book of Dan. Verse*, tr. S. F. Damon & R. S. Hillyer (1922); *The Oxford Book of Scandinavian Verse*, ed. E. W. Gosse and W. A. Craigie (1925); *A Book of Dan. Ballads*, sel. Axel Olrik, tr. E. M. Smith-Dampier (1939); *A Second Book of Dan. Verse*, tr. C. W. Stork (1947); *Ung dansk Lyrik*, ed. N. K. Johansen (1949); *20th C. Scandinavian Poetry*, ed. M. Allwood (1950); *Modern Dan.*

Poems, ed. K. K. Mogensen (2d ed., 1951); *Danske lyriske Digte,* ed. M. Brøndsted and M. Paludan (1954); *Ti danske Poeter,* ed. E. Knudsen (1956; a selection of recent lyricism); *Den danske Lyrik 1800-1870,* ed. F.J.B. Jansen (2v., 1961).

HISTORY AND CRITICISM: G. Brandes, *Danske Digtere* (1877); E. W. Gosse, *Northern Studies* (1890) and *Two Visits to Denmark* (1911); J. Jørgensen, *Gesch. der dänischen Lit.* (1908); A. Olrik, *The Heroic Legends of Denmark,* tr. L. M. Hollander (1919); C. Rimestad, *Fra Stuckenberg til Seedorf* (2 v., 1922-23); H. G. Topsøe-Jensen, *Scandinavian Lit. from Brandes to Our Own Day,* tr. I. Anderson (1929); C. S. Petersen and V. Andersen, *Illustreret dansk Litteraturh.* (4 v., 1924-34; standard lit. hist.); H. Kjærgaard, *Die dänische Lit. der neuesten Zeit* (1934); F.J.B. Jansen, *Danmarks Digtekunst* (3 v., 1944-58; a fine hist. of Dan. poetry); S. Norrild, *Dansk Litt. fra Saxo til Kaj Munk* (2 v., 1949; an informative survey); E. Bredsdorff *et al., An Introd. to Scandinavian Lit.* (1951; useful short survey); P. M. Mitchell, *A Bibliog. Guide to Dan. Lit.* (1951); M. Paludan, *Ti unge Lyrikere* (1951); J. Claudi, *Contemporary Dan. Authors,* tr. J. Andersen and A. Rush (1952); F.J.B. Jansen, "Romantisme Européen et Romantisme Scandinave," *L'Âge d'Or* (1953); O. Wivel, *Poesi og eksistens* (1953); S. M. Kristensen, *Dansk Litt. 1918-52* (1956); P. M. Mitchell, *A Hist. of Dan. Lit.* (1958; best survey in Eng.); G. C. Schoolfield, "The Recent Scandinavian Lyric," BA, 36 (1962).   S.L.

DEAD METAPHOR. A metaphor which has been used so often in common parlance that its force as a figure of speech is no longer felt and which, therefore, is used as a literal expression. Max Müller found, upon investigating etymologically the history of languages, that a very large proportion of words in current use which are taken literally today were once metaphors. Most words describing the operations of the mind, for example, derive ultimately from descriptions of physical processes—such as "conceive," which goes back to the L. *concipere,* "to take." Or again, the word "metaphor" itself goes back to the Gr. *metapherein,* "to carry over." Müller termed this sort of figure "radical" (i.e., understood in terms of roots or origins), and it has also been called "fossil" or "faded" or "petrified" metaphor. Owen Barfield has suggested that it is the special duty of the poet, in his effort to achieve vividness, to use such expressions in a poem so as to revive their lost metaphorical powers. So, too, the critic, in his search for avenues of interpretation, may trace apparently literal words in a poem back to their source so as to uncover relevant meanings.—M. Müller, *Lectures on the Science of Language* (2d ser.,

1864); G. Buck, *The Metaphor* (1899); G. Stern, *Meaning and Change of Meaning* (1931); O. Barfield, *Poetic Diction* (2d ed., 1952).

N.FRIE.

DÉBAT. See POETIC CONTESTS.

DECADENCE. A term used ostensibly in reference to periods or works whose qualities are held to mark a "falling away" (L.: *de-cadere*) from previously recognized conditions or standards of excellence. The term is often applied in relation to the Alexandrian (or Hellenistic) period in Gr. letters (ca. 300–ca. 30 B.C.) and to the period in L. literature after the death of Augustus (14 A.D.). In modern poetry d. has been identified most persistently in works related to the Fr. symbolist-decadent movement of the late 19th c., whose influence in the British Isles encouraged native tendencies already nurtured by the ideas of Walter Pater, the poetry of Rossetti and Swinburne, and the general ambience of the Pre-Raphaelite Movement. Symbolist influence was widespread also among the poets of *fin-de-siècle* Europe outside France. It did not significantly affect the poetry of the United States until the 20th c., although Poe was himself a progenitor of important ideas and practices of the Fr. symbolists.

In a limited sense, d. may be seen exemplified in the tastes and habits of such fictional characters as Petrus Borel's Passereau l'Ecolier, Poe's Roderick Usher, Huysmans' Des Esseintes, Wilde's Dorian Gray and Lord Henry Wotton, and Villiers de l'Isle-Adam's Axël d'Auersperg; in passages like those on the language of decaying civilizations by Baudelaire (in the note to his poem *Franciscae meae laudes*) and by Gautier (in his essay on "Charles Baudelaire" [1868], probably the most memorable passage ever written on d.); in the apostrophe of Mallarmé's Hérodiade to her mirror; in Verlaine's verses beginning "Je suis l'Empire à la fin de la décadence. . . ."; in Wilde's *Salomé* and Dowson's famous poem to Cynara; in the affectations of Count Robert de Montesquiou-Fezensac and the remarkable production in 1891 of P. N. Roinard's *Cantique des cantiques* in the perfumed atmosphere of Paul Fort's Théâtre d'Art. D. in this sense was in great part a mannerism of the sort prevalent in the England of the "Yellow Nineties," with its brilliant and superficial *fin-de-siècle* aesthetic pose that played perhaps a more significant rôle than is generally recognized in opposition to the crushing force of modern materialism. But the word *decadence* has come to be used by hostile critics in a larger sense than this.

A basic characteristic of d. has been a failure to recognize objective or timeless values that transcend and give form and direction to individual experience and effort. In these terms the decadent poet is seen living in a state of Heraclitic or Bergsonian flux, with his values confined within narrowly egocentric limits and unlikely to satisfy his desires. Here the poet tends to be concerned not with "the fruit of experience" but with "experience itself" and with private sensations; and his poems are likely to reveal a number of the following "decadent" characteristics: search for novelty with attendant artificiality and interest in the unnatural; excessive self-analysis; feverish hedonism, with poetic interest in corruption and morbidity; abulia, neurosis, and exaggerated erotic sensibility; aestheticism, with stress on "Art for Art's Sake" in the evocation of exquisite sensations and emotions; scorn of contemporary society and mores; restless curiosity, perversity, or eccentricity in subject matter; overemphasis on form, with resultant loss of balance between form and content—or interest in jewel-like ornamentation, resulting at times in disintegration of artistic unity; bookishness; erudite or exotic vocabulary; frequent employment of synaesthesia (q.v.) or *transpositions d'art;* complex and difficult syntax; attempt to make poetry primarily a means of enchantment, with emphasis on its musical and irrational elements; experiments in the use of new rhythms, rich in evocative and sensuous effects, alien to those of tradition and often departing from the mathematical principles of control in established prosody; anti-intellectualism and stress of the subconscious; abandonment of punctuation, and use of typography for visual and psychological effects; substitution of coherence in mood for coherence and synthesis in thought; "postromantic" irony in the manner of Corbière, Laforgue, and the early Eliot; obscurity, arising from remote, private, or complicated imagery or from a predominantly connotative and evocative use of language, with obvious reluctance to *"name* an object" ("Le suggérer, voilà le rêve."); an overall aura of something lost—a nostalgic, semi-mysticism without clear direction or spiritual commitment, but with frequent reference to exotic religions and ritual, or to such mysterious substitutes as Tarot cards, magic, alchemy, Rosicrucianism, Theosophy, the Kabbala, Satanism, and the like.

Dr. Emile Laurent (1897) even thought he could identify certain characteristics of a *physiognomie décadente:* a lack of forehead; prognathous features; oddly shaped heads ("plagiocéphales, oxycéphales, acrocéphales"); deformed noses; glabrous, asymmetrical faces; wide ears; enormous cheek bones, etc., etc. All this was a continuation of the thesis of Max Nordau's *Entartung* (Degeneration) [1892–93], which found that the Fr. symbolists "had in common all the signs of degeneracy and imbecility." G. B. Shaw's "The Sanity of Art"

DECASTICH

(1895) was an effective reply to this sort of nonsense.

In a discussion of important modern and contemporary poets, the term *decadence* can hardly on the whole be applied and interpreted to suggest decline in literary quality from an immediately preceding period. The decline seems to be rather in the values in terms of which earlier poetry had been made. Unusual distinction is evident in many modern poets who have been identified as showing "decadent" tendencies (e.g., Whitman, Baudelaire, Verlaine, Mallarmé, Rimbaud, Valéry, Rilke, Yeats, Hart Crane, Eliot, Pound, to mention only a few). Even hostile critics recognize that poets "decadent" in this sense have furnished much of the most memorable poetry of the modern world.

C. Baudelaire, note to *Franciscae meae laudes* in 1st ed. of *Les Fleurs du Mal* (1857); T. Gautier, "Charles Baudelaire" (1868); J.-K. Huysmans, *A rebours* (1884; esp. chs. 3, 12, 14); M. Nordau, *Entartung* (Degeneration) (1892–93); A. Symons, "The Decadent Movement in Lit.," *Harper's Magazine*, 87 (1893); G. B. Shaw, "The Sanity of Art" (1895); E. Laurent, *La Poésie décadente devant la science psychiatrique* (1897); A. Cassagne, *La Théorie de l'art pour l'art en France* (1906); I. Babbitt, *The New Laoköon* (1910) and *Rousseau and Romanticism* (1919); H. Jackson, *The Eighteen Nineties* (1913); E. von Sydow, *Die Kultur der Dekadenz* (1921); J. W. Duff, *A Lit. Hist. of Rome in the Silver Age from Tiberius to Hadrian* (1927; 2d ed., 1960); G. L. Van Roosbroeck, *The Legend of the Decadents* (1927); A. J. Farmer, *Le Mouvement esthétique et décadent en Angleterre* (1873–1900) [1931]; M. Praz, *The Romantic Agony* (1933; 2d ed., 1951); Y. Winters, *Primitivism and D.* (1937); H. W. Rosenhaupt, *Der deutsche Dichter um die Jahrhundertwende und seine Abgelöstheit von der Gesellschaft* (1939); O. Cargill, "The Decadents," *Intellectual America* (1941); C. M. Bowra, *The Heritage of Symbolism* (1943) and *The Creative Experiment* (1949); W. Gaunt, *The Aesthetic Adventure* (1945); C. E. M. Joad, *D.: A Philosophical Inquiry* (1948); J. M. Smith, "Concepts of D. in 19th-C. Fr. Lit.," sp, 50 (1953); O. Ragusa, "Fr. Symbolism in Italy," RR, 46 (1955); A. E. Carter, *The Idea of D. in Fr. Lit., 1830–1900* (1958); G. R. Ridge, *The Hero in Fr. Decadent Lit.* (1961). A.G.E.

DECASTICH. A poem composed of 10 lines. See also DIZAIN, a Fr. stanza or poem of 10 lines, and DÉCIMA, the 10-line stanza of classical Sp. poetry.

DECASYLLABLE. Line of 10 syllables. Appeared in Fr. verse about the middle of the 11th c. in *La Vie de St. Alexis* and *Le Boèce* (later in *La Chanson de Roland*) as a line of 10 syllables with a pause (*coupe*) after the fourth and 2 fixed accents on the fourth and tenth syllables (M. Burger, *Recherches sur la structure et l'origine des vers romans*, 1957, p. 20). In It. the *endecasillabo* appeared early in the 12th c.: "Li mile cento trenta cenqe nato, fo questo tenplo a san Gogio donato . . ." (*Iscrizione Ferrarese,* / 1135 [*Testi volgari italiani*, ed. A. Monteverdi]) and was used by Dante, Petrarch, and Boccaccio. Chaucer may have discovered the line through their work if he had not already become acquainted with it in Machault, Deschamps, Granson, etc. His influence helped to associate the d. with the 5-stress line, and thus to provide (whether one is syllable- or stress-counting) a line which becomes fundamental to the sonnet, the Spenserian and many other stanza forms, the heroic couplet, and blank verse. The real number of syllables in a d. varies in accordance with fashions in pronunciation and with conventions of prosodic practice: thus the Fr. line frequently has 11 syllables because of the addition of a feminine ending; it may have 12 if a further syllable is added at an epic caesura. The It. d. always has at least 11 because a feminine ending is required. In Eng. feminine endings are also employed, but the d. may have as few as 9 syllables when an initial syllable is omitted, resulting in an acephalous line. Frequently what appear to be extrametrical syllables are suppressed by one form of elision or another: "When such / was heard / declar'd / the Almightie's will" (Milton, *Paradise Lost* 7.181).—B. Ten Brink, *Chaucer's Sprache und Verskunst* (1885); M. Kaluza, *A Short Hist. of Eng. Versification* (1911); P.-E. Guarnerio, *Manuale di versificazione italiana* (1913); R. Bridges, *Milton's Prosody* (1921). R.O.E.

DÉCIMA. Sp. stanza form used loosely to denote any 10-line stanza, but now usually used as the equivalent of *espinela* (q.v.), occasionally of *copla real*. The first *décimas* approximating the final form were the 14th- and 15th-c. 10-line variations of the *copla de arte menor*, though 10-line stanzas may be found earlier. The *d. italiana*, probably first used in the 18th c., is an octosyllabic strophe rhyming ababc:dedec, the c rhymes being oxytones and the colon denoting a pause. Other meters, particularly the hendecasyllable with heptasyllable, may be used and the rhyme scheme and position of the pause may vary, or lines may be unrhymed provided that the two oxytones rhyme and be found one at the end of the strophe and the other at the pause. This strophe is directly related to the *octava italiana*.—Navarro. D.C.C.

DECORUM

DECIR. Most of the Castilian court poetry of the pre-Renaissance period (late 14th through early 16th c.) may be divided, according to Le Gentil, into two principal categories: the free-strophe composition intended to be read or recited and the poem of fixed form intended to be sung, generally termed *decir* (or *dezir*) and *cantiga* respectively. Both forms were borrowed from the Galician-Portuguese, but show Fr. influence. The d. usually is narrative, satiric, didactic, or allegorical and sometimes attains considerable length. The *copla de arte mayor* (see ARTE MAYOR), rarely used for the *cantiga* type of poem, was considered the appropriate meter for d., though the *copla de arte menor* (see ARTE MENOR) was also employed. The strophes of a given poem have the same pattern, but are otherwise metrically independent of each other. The best known examples of the d. are *Decir a las siete virtudes* heretofore generally attributed to Imperial, and Juan de Mena's *Laberinto de Fortuna*, both of the 15th c.—P. Le Gentil, *La Poésie lyrique espagnole et portugaise à la fin du moyen âge. 2e partie. Les formes* (1953); Navarro. D.C.C.

DECORUM in poetry is propriety, a careful attention to what is proper and becoming in action, character, and style. In a good poem, action should fit situation and character, thought and feeling should fit character, expression should so fit subject matter that weighty matters are treated with dignity and trifling matters with humbleness.

Cicero, in the *Orator* (21), defined the term in its general application to real life, oratory, and poetry. Horace illustrated its specific application to poetry, at least to epic and dramatic poetry. Cicero remarked that *decorum* was the L. equivalent of the Gr. *prepon*, which pointed straight to Aristotle's discussion of propriety of style in the *Rhetoric* (3.7.1–2 and 3.7.6). Aristotle also used *prepon* in ch. 17 of the *Poetics*, wherein he recommended that the tragic poet visualize every scene he composes so that he will devise what is appropriate and avoid incongruities. In an earlier chapter, 15, Aristotle used *harmotton* to define appropriateness of dramatic character, and this term was virtually synonymous with *prepon*. There is no evidence that the Romans knew the *Poetics*, but when the Renaissance rediscovered the treatise Aristotle joined Cicero and Horace as leading arbiters of poetic d. In 1536, Paccius translated *prepon* as *decorum* and *harmotton* as *conveniens;* the terms were interchangeable, but d. became the favorite.

Although Horace never actually used the word *decorum* in his *Ars poetica,* his chief doctrine was literary propriety. The favorite passage for his modern disciples was lines 89–127, wherein Horace argued that each style should keep its proper place since a speaker's words should never be discordant with his station; it makes a great difference whether a god or a hero or a slave is speaking, an old man or a youth, a great lady or a nurse, a merchant or a plowman, an Assyrian or a Greek. Moreover, comic themes are distinct from tragic, and the two should never, or very rarely, be mingled. Throughout the Renaissance and long afterward this doctrine of d. was paramount in the theory of poetry and highly influential in its practice. Milton, in his *Tractate of Education,* spoke of the crowning study of poetry as "that sublime art which in Aristotle's *Poetics,* in Horace, and the It. commentaries of Castelvetro, Tasso, Mazzoni, and others, teaches what the laws are of a true epic poem, what of a dramatic, what of a lyric, what *decorum* is, which is the grand masterpiece to observe." As interpreted by the critics and commentators, d. called for distinct poetic genres, consistent characters, and the careful observance of the classical hierarchy of styles (grand, moderate, plain). Neoclassical d. came to emphasize literary propriety in the sense of elegance and correct taste, a propriety that avoided the vulgar as well as the unconventional.

Even while this neoclassical theory of d. was forming, however, it was being challenged by some poets. As Croce has said in his *Aesthetic,* art is intuitive, the rules of criticism concepts, and intuitive poets are always upsetting the rules. Medieval poets had more often than not either ignored or modified classical d., and many Renaissance poets, influenced by the Bible and Christian literature as well as by the medieval anarchy of forms, flouted fixed genres, conventionalized characters, the hierarchy of styles, and studied elegance of expression. "Right" tragedies and comedies, "true" epic poems and odes were written, but along with these neoclassical productions there also flourished tragical comedies, comical tragedies, tragicomedies, histories, romances, simple narrative poems and lyrics. To name just one example among several notable rebels, the actor-playwright Angelo Beolco (b. 1502), better known as Ruzzante from his favorite role, understood classical d. which fostered "literary" poetry, but argued for a different kind of artistic propriety, namely, simple nature. The characters in his peasant eclogues and farces spoke in their native dialects, using the most naive and sometimes the coarsest expressions.

Ruzzante of Padua was a naturalist, and soon turned from verse to prose as even more appropriate for his representations of pure nature. Naturalism in poetry, however, has always distrusted the conventional and traditional d. Wordsworth's revolt against "false refinement" and "poetic diction" was in large part the revolt of the naturalist against an artificial d. As he explained in his Preface to the *Lyrical Ballads*, he had chosen incidents and situations from "humble and rustic" life, and had related these in a "selection of language really used by men." Although Coleridge, in his *Biographia Literaria*, showed that the very act of "selection" plus the use of meter removed this poetry from rusticity, Wordsworth was demonstrating the truth of Croce's assertion that the intuitive artist is always upsetting the rules. For Wordsworth, not rules but the author's own feelings were his "stay and support."

It should be said, however, that although the neoclassical d. that long governed both critics and poets has fallen into disrepute, the original Ciceronian-Aristotelian concept of d. is still valid. No sensible poet or critic can quibble very much with the admonition that it is unseemly to use high-sounding expressions when speaking of the gutter and equally unseemly to use mean expressions when speaking of the majesty of Rome.—R. K. Hack, *The Doctrine of Lit. Forms* (HSCP, 1916); G. C. Fiske, *Cicero's De Oratore and Horace's Ars Poetica* (1929); J. W. H. Atkins, *Lit. Crit. in Antiquity* (1934); M. T. Herrick, *The Fusion of Horatian and Aristotelian Lit. Crit.* (1946); Wimsatt and Brooks; Weinberg.　M.T.H.

DEFECTIVE FOOT. In a conventional metrical line, a foot which lacks one or more unstressed syllables. In this example,

This is the forest primeval,

the last foot is defective: the normal pattern calls for a final dactyl, but the clause ends with a trochee instead. The term "defective" is unfortunate, for a foot lacking one or more syllables can be considered "faulty" only by those who are gratified by absolute metrical monotony. See TRUNCATION; METRICAL VARIATIONS.　P.F.

DENOTATION. See CONNOTATION AND DENOTATION.

DÉNOUEMENT. See PLOT.

DESCENDING RHYTHM (falling rhythm). The rhythm of lines written predominantly in trochaic or dactylic feet. D.r. is so called because the reader or hearer is presumed to feel, in each foot, a "descent" from a relatively stressed syllable to a relatively unstressed one. The traditional jest that the firm name Batten, Barton, Durstine, and Osborn sounds "like a trunk falling downstairs" will suggest something of the nature of d.r. The term is useful

only if one remembers that it has really no metaphoric or symbolic connotation: d.r. does not, in itself, transmit a feeling of depression, gloom, or physical descent. See ASCENDING RHYTHM.　P.F.

DESCORT. A Prov. song whose distinguishing feature is its irregularity. Instead of having all its stanzas alike, as in the ordinary *chanso* (q.v.), the d. theoretically has them all different. These stanzas are often quite long and the individual verses quite short. In one poem called a *descort*, the stanzas are similar in structure, but all are in different languages, to furnish the "discord" which the genre demands.—I. Frank, *Répertoire métrique de la poésie des troubadours*, I (1953).　F.M.C.

DIAERESIS. The pronunciation of two successive vowels as separate sounds and not as a single vowel or diphthong, e.g., Chloë, coöperate. In classical prosody d. denotes the coincidence of a word-ending with the end of a metrical foot or unit, e.g.

spārsīs | hāstīs | lōngīs | cāmpūs | splēndĕt ||

ēt | hōrrēt
(Ennius, *Scipio* 6)

A dactylic hexameter such as this, in which d. after every foot precludes caesura, is an example of the hyporrhythmic (i.e., deficient) verse. D. after a fourth-foot dactyl is called "bucolic d." by virtue of its frequency in pastoral or bucolic poetry. D. is often confused with caesura (q.v.), which in Gr. and L. poetry strictly means the ending of a word within a foot. D. can be used for a deliberate effect as in the example from Ennius, and in certain verse forms such as the elegiac distich. In the classical hexameter, however, it was generally avoided as being disruptive to a line of verse. The coincidence, within a line, of a sense-pause with a d. is called a diaeresis-pause. D. can occur in the verse of modern languages, e.g.,

Had cást | him oút | from Heáv'n, | with

all | his Hóst
(Milton, *Paradise Lost* 1.37)

The pause after "Heav'n" might be termed diaeresis-pause, but in Eng. versification it is permissible to label it a caesura.—Hardie; Schipper; H. Drexler, "Hexameterstudien," *Aevum*, 25 (1951).　R.A.H.

DIALECT IN POETRY. The social values of literature determine that most writing will at the time of its composition be regarded as standard speech. But dialectal peculiarities are, nevertheless, of great significance. Many of the most important poems in any literature are in the dialects of the provinces or in an idiom deliberately given the patina of the antique. Mastery of several dialects is essential to the thorough appreciation of any literature.

Since dialects are more generally distinguished by divergence from the standard language phonetically than semantically, much of the stylistic significance of d. poetry derives from the ear. It is, accordingly, a favorite device of poetry for the stage or for recitation. In Aristophanes' comedies, for example, Spartan and Athenian characters speak the idiom of their respective regions. Such shadings as a rule much embarrass translators, but B. R. Rogers, in his celebrated translation of *Lysistrata,* by placing a Scottish d. in the mouths of the Spartans achieved a memorable linguistic *tour de force.* Obsolete linguistic forms are occasionally used for poems with subject matter suggesting a past age. A defensible instance occurs in Adriaan Barnouw's rendering of Chaucer's *Canterbury Tales* into a Dutch having a number of archaisms. Edmund Spenser affected an archaistic style, as, to a still greater degree, did Thomas Chatterton.

The theory of d. commonly presumes that local characteristics are best revealed in local speech. So a Southerner is most expressive of his native characteristics when speaking in his native idiom. Shakespeare, in *Henry V.,* offers a picture of a united people by sketching soldiers of the Eng. army from various sections of Great Britain, representing different temperaments, each using a different idiom. It has been of special importance for popular poetry that as class distinctions in the modern world have increased, d. has acquired new values, as conspicuously seen in London at the close of the 19th c. In another context, much of the vitality of Ir. poetic drama since 1900 reflects the playwrights' knowledge of d.

In classical poetry, d. is often used to distinguish foreigners or countryfolk from citizens, and a similar distinction remains notable in It. verse throughout the Renaissance. In England an artful use of d. with a dramatic sensibility occurs in Chaucer's *Canterbury Tales,* especially the *Friar's Tale.* Much of the finest medieval Eng. verse, including the work of the "Pearl poet," was in the native dialects, ranging from Devonshire to Lancashire and Kent. Scottish poetry has been most retentive of the Eng. d. forms, as seen from Henryson and Dunbar to Robert Burns and Edwin Muir. It is typical that Burns commanded a greater artistic skill when using his mother tongue, that of Ayrshire, than when writing in the standard idiom of literary London. In modern times Tennyson exploited d. in his *Northern Farmer —Old Style.* Some of Thomas Hardy's best poems use Dorset speech. James Russell

Lowell's *Bigelow Papers* are a comic reflection of New England rural speech, and Rudyard Kipling's *Barrack Room Ballads* are in cockney and with a dash of slang. (Slang consists of dialectal usages in the lowest levels of society. Outstanding poetry devoted in subject matter to the poorer classes has flourished in Europe, from Pushkin to Bertolt Brecht). In America the largest part of d. poetry appears in the unselfconscious art of ballad singers, especially Negroes, but Robert Frost has written much poetry echoing New England d. Because of the preponderant importance of the voice in d. poetry, the phonographic recordings of the British Dialect Society and the Library of Congress, and the readings by Dylan Thomas and Robert Frost surpass whatever can be provided by critical or scholarly commentary.

H.W.W.

DIALOGUE. There are two major meanings to the term. In its more general sense it signifies an exchange of words between any number of imaginary speakers, in fiction, drama or poetry. So we may speak of d. in a novel. In its more limited sense it denotes a literary usage largely or entirely based on speaking parts without intention of theatrical presentation. The word has an identical meaning in referring to verse or prose, although used more often for the latter. It is best employed to signify a general method of composition, not a particular genre. Nevertheless, based on the use of verse d. several traditional forms have been established, such as the satirical poem after the Horatian manner, in which an exchange of words between two speakers often occurs. In such instances it is correct to speak of a "d. poem" as well as to say that the poem uses d. The term has been most frequently employed in the case of poetry where two speakers are present, but this numerical limitation is inessential. Poems having only a minor portion of their lines in direct discourse are seldom included under the term, although works may be so described where a moderate amount of the lines remains outside direct speech, especially if the leading voice addresses an imaginary audience and speaks in the first person. A series of monologues, as in Robert Browning's *The Ring and the Book,* does not constitute d.

Although not essential to drama, since there are brilliant specimens of the dramatic monologue, or address to one or more silent figures, d. lies at the basis of the theatre, and the writing of successful d. constitutes a large part of the dramatist's task. In the limited sense of the word, d. is a literary device containing a germ of the theatre that remains only in its initial stage, a change of scene, for example, being generally avoided. The most celebrated prose dialogues, those by Plato, are said to have been founded on dramatic works, the mimes, in the 5th c. B.C., by the Sicilian poets, Sophron and Epicharmus. D. verse in some instances remains purely literary; in others, its direct speech has encouraged either recitation, where the words are spoken, as in an argument, or musical forms, such as the duet or the oratorio, where the words are sung. D. has often been used in conjunction with the antiphonal forms of music, as appears in religious chants, hymns, and litanies. But the word is not used where a refrain introduces a voice unheard elsewhere in the poem. D. signifies an exchange of words, not a monologue punctuated by interruptions nor a poem in which an interlocutor merely starts the main speaker on his way. It is much at home in love lyrics, where the lovers address each other.

During the Classical Age, verse d. flourished in the pastoral, the satire, and the philosophical poem. In the Middle Ages it appeared with much frequency as "debates" and "flytings" (scolding matches). A favorite subject was the debate between the Soul and the Body. The philosophical dichotomies of the times encouraged this form, a good example of which in Middle Eng. is *The Owl and the Nightingale*. D. in the more general sense abounds in medieval allegories and romances to such a degree that doubt occasionally arises whether a manuscript presents a poem for reading or one intended for the stage. This condition is common in the Orient. D. is often employed in the popular ballad; it is also found in satirical poetry (for example, in that of Robert Burns, who, though writing in the last quarter of the 18th c., wrote in close touch with medieval tradition).

The philosophical verse d. enjoyed much popularity in the Renaissance, as seen in the poetry of Samuel Daniel, author of the much-admired dialogue, *Ulysses and the Siren*. Songs with questions and answers are also common, as may be observed in lyrics from Shakespeare and Sir Philip Sidney to Robert Herrick. Andrew Marvell found use for the form, as in *A Dialogue Between the Resolved Soul and Created Pleasure*. Direct speech is freely used in the poetry of the 18th c., as in Alexander Pope's *Satires*. Although subjectivity in the romantic period conferred a relative advantage on the monologue, the d. was not forgotten. Examples of Eng. d. poems of this period are found in the work of Walter Savage Landor, although the greater number of his dialogues are in prose. It found much favor with German and Scandinavian writers of romantic song and ballad.

D. poems have often been dialect poems, as in the Dorset eclogues by William Barnes. Verse dialogues are notable in Robert Frost's

North of Boston and other volumes by this poet where the influence of the classical eclogue is still perceptible. As example of d. in more recent verse may be cited William Butler Yeats's *Dialogue of Self and Soul*. The radio provides a new field for verse-d. Although Dylan Thomas's *Under Milk Wood* has been called a play, with equal propriety it may be called a d. The device assists nondramatic poetry in obtaining dramatic tension and vigor and in objectifying its subject. It must be recognized as one of the major resources of the poet's art.—A. H. Hawkins, *D.* (1909); E. Merrill, *The D. in Eng. Lit.* (1911); H. Thielmann, *Stil und Technik des Dialogs im neueren Drama* (1937); R. Wildbolz, *Der philosophische D. als literarisches Kunstwerk* (1952); J. Andrieu, *Le D. antique, structure et présentation* (1954).   H.W.W.

DIBRACH. See PYRRHIC.

DICHOREE. See DITROCHEE.

DICHRONOUS (Gr. "of 2 times or quantities," "common"). Term applied to the Gr. vowels alpha, iota, and upsilon, each of which may be either short or long. In some words a syllable containing a dichronous vowel is likewise variable, e.g.,

$$\bar{A}res \; \breve{A}res$$

at the beginning of a Homeric hexameter.—Koster.   R.J.G.

DICTION, POETIC. See POETIC DICTION.

DIDACTIC POETRY is poetry which is primarily intended to instruct. Most commonly, the label is used for poetry which teaches a moral. It can also refer to poetry which conveys factual information, like astronomy, mathematics, or rhetoric; or systematic philosophy. Aesthetically it seems to be the first stage in the evolution of literary forms: the earliest literature we possess, Eastern, Hebrew, Greek, is in verse and uses meter as a mnemonic device to make the hearer remember and thereby learn what is being said. The seed of all literature is the proverb, the gnomic line, the memorizable rhyme ("Thirty days hath September"), and from such seeds d. poetry evolved in antiquity as it was to do again in northern Europe in the early centuries of the Christian era. The truest d. poetry, in accordance with Horace's *utile et dulce*, both explains and provides subjective experience of that which is explained, e.g., Virgil's *Georgics* (cf. L. Richardson, *Poetical Theory in Republican Rome*, 1944).

As a genre, d. verse is difficult to define and

somewhat foreign to the usual poetic taste. Aristotle explicitly excluded it from the branches of poetry when he said "Homer should be called a poet, while Empedocles should be called a natural philosopher rather than a poet" (*Poetics*, 1). In A.D. 9 Ovid disparaged "technical" poems as trivial (*Tristia* 2. 471–492), and 17 centuries later when d. poetry was about to become fashionable in Eng. literature Thomas Hobbes challenged it anew. "The subject of a poem is the manners of men, not natural causes," Hobbes wrote, and denied poets the right to use "terms from any science, as well mechanicall as liberal" (*Answer to Davenant's Preface to Gondibert*, 1650). Nevertheless, d. verse entered early into the stream of Western literature and has periodically risen to eminence, in antiquity, in the Middle Ages and Renaissance, in Eng. literature of the 17th and 18th c., serving poets from the earliest times down to the present (cf. V. Sackville West, *The Land*, 1926) as a valid means of artistic expression.

1. IN ANTIQUITY. Formal d. poetry begins with Hesiod, who wrote at the end of the 8th c. B.C., and whose principal works, the *Theogony* and the *Works and Days*, represent two related types of d. composition. They have in common the "didactic" purpose, which means that they are written to instruct the reader (or listener), to pass on knowledge; but it is apparent from Hesiod's example that the poet can "teach" in two different ways and make use of two different kinds of subject matter. As in the *Theogony*, he can convey myths, or a knowledge of the gods (his emphasis is along genealogical lines), inform man of the nature of the gods, or of the nature of things (i.e., the cosmos), inform man of his spiritual obligations and cultural ancestry, tell him significant stories about his past. Or, as in the *Works and Days*, he can convey useful information about work techniques (in this case, how to farm) and describe the rules and laws governing a specific technical method. In general, all d. poetry falls into one or the other of these two categories: it instructs the reader either along general lines, objectively, telling him *what* he ought to know about his world and its structure, or along specific lines, telling him *how* to do different kinds of things.

In theory, Gr. literature distinguishes between d. as a branch of *epē*, or lengthy verse written in hexameters, and *melē*, the lyric modes, and although d. poetry did eventually assume elegiac and iambic meters, the immediate followers of Hesiod continued to employ the hexameter framework. D. poems, now lost, were written which apparently were modeled on Hesiod and therefore came to be known as works of the school of Hesiod. Then, in the 6th and 5th c. B.C. appeared the writings of

philosophers and moralists, e.g., Xenophanes (fl. 535), Parmenides (ca. 450), Empedocles (fl. 444–41). From the fragments now left it seems definite that d. poetry was well established as an instructive literary genre, its purpose being to advance speculative knowledge of the cosmos. At this point d. poetry disappeared from the scene of Gr. literature, to emerge several centuries later, during the Alexandrian Age. What then came back was the manual type of "applied" poetry descended from the *Works and Days*. Such Alexandrian writers as Aratus and Nicander of Colophon represent the new cosmopolitan vogue for technical, erudite verse packed with information. In Gr. literature d. poetry continued to serve this purpose as a minor form until the 4th c. A.D.

Roman literature made impressive use of the d. genre. Even the early writers Ennius and Accius probably experimented with the form, and in the 1st c. B.C. d. poetry soared to great heights. Translations of Empedocles existed; Cicero in his youth made an adaptation of Aratus' *Phaenomena,* and work of this sort inevitably paved the way for the two notable masterpieces, Lucretius' *De Rerum Natura* and Virgil's *Georgics*. The former, a lengthy expository poem concerned with science, ethics, and the philosophy of materialism, and the latter, a beautifully proportioned work of some 2,188 lines on the subject of "how to farm," both satisfy to a singular degree the requirements of the two types of d. poetry that originated seven centuries earlier. In quite different vein, Horace's *Art of Poetry* (ca. 13 B.C.) and Ovid's *Art of Love, Art of Makeup and Remedy of Love* (ca. 1 B.C.) are related to the d. genre. Horace's "instructions" are more aesthetic than methodological; his verse letter is a critical masterpiece that sharpens the reader's powers of literary observation and elevates his taste. In the course of the poem Horace formulated an aesthetic ideal that corresponds closely to the ideal of d. poetry: "omne tulit punctum qui miscuit utile duci / lectorem delectando pariterque monendo" (The man who mingles the useful with the sweet carries the day by charming his reader and at the same time instructing him, *Epistles*, ("Art of Poetry," 2.3. 343–44). Ovid's witty pointers for getting on "in the field of sex and society" are little more than a travesty of the d. ideal, although this *reductio ad infandum* of methodology may be one of the poet's greatest strokes of irony. However, the various purposes of Roman d. poetry may be compared and evaluated, four major poets in the golden age turned their attention to the didactic medium. Minor works ensued, chief among them Manilius' five-book poem on astrology.

In summary, d. poetry offered writers of antiquity certain real possibilities, and underlying the whole theory is perhaps the larger relationship of science and religion to human affairs. How was civilized man to absorb and codify his knowledge of the nature of things? How was he to apply the knowledge? D. poetry helped make it possible for men to remember what they ought to know or ought to do. Speculative knowledge having been made more widely available, the later d. literature became narrowly technical and dwindled into insignificance. Other literary forms could satisfy the general need for instruction more satisfactorily than the d. genre—moral instruction would readily find outlet in the major literary forms, while technical information would flourish in prose treatises, or simply in directions for the use of tools.

2. IN THE MIDDLE AGES AND RENAISSANCE. Medieval literature was, in one sense, entirely d., for it stressed moral content in accordance with Christian doctrine and always sought to inform and enlighten the reader. From Martianus Capella's *On the Marriage of Mercury and Philology* (primarily, a work in the form of Menippean Satire) on through Spenser's *Faerie Queene* an unending succession of allegorical poems conveyed various kinds of doctrine. The most outstanding example is perhaps *Le Roman de la Rose*. In addition, medieval literature abounded in rhymed chronicles, metrical *specula*, or encyclopedias, and offered many examples of metrical and later dramatic versions of saints' lives, miracle stories, popularized excerpts from church doctrine, and collections of aphorisms. Chaucer epitomized the dominant tendency when his narrator concluded the *Nun's Priest's Tale* by saying:

For seint Paul seith that al that writen is,
To oure doctrine it is ywrite, ywis;
Taketh the fruyt, and lat the chaf be stille.

This seems to suggest that all knowledge and all understanding should accord with Christian truth (for if that is *the* truth, how can anything contradict it?), and represents the widespread medieval attitude. But spiced though it was with information and misinformation, and seasoned with moral flavors, medieval literature could nevertheless assume an aesthetic quality distinct from knowledge *per se*, as it did in such works as *The Divine Comedy* or the medieval romances, or the poetry of Chaucer.

It remained for the Renaissance to give another impetus to the composition of d. poetry based on Gr. and L. models. The movement began in Italy before the 16th c. and continued well on into the 18th c. in England. It. Renaissance theory led the way by affirming the ancient ideal of conveying information in artistic form, one writer for instance claiming that

Virgil was a better teacher than Cato or Varro *because* he wrote poetry (Fracastoro, *Naugerius sive De Poetica dialogus*, 1555). From the mid-16th c. on, d. poetry found favor among Eng. writers (T. Tusser, *Hundreth Pointes of Good Husbandry*, 1557) and became so popular indeed that by the mid-18th c. d. poetry virtually dominated the field of lyric composition.

3. IN THE 18TH C. AND AFTER. A variety of works in a variety of meters satisfied the 18th-c. Englishman's demand for a descriptive nature poetry that was realistic, methodological, informative, and beautiful by analogy with the landscape painting of the period. The 18th-c. "georgic," epitomized in James Thomson's staggeringly successful *Seasons* (1726) manifested considerable changes from the classical models. It emphasized heterogeneous information rather than detailed instructions; it exalted landscape over work processes; it invited the reader to feast on the native beauties of rural life, not to wring a living from the recalcitrant soil.

Thomson's *Seasons* was translated into Fr. for the first time in 1759; later on in the century the widely admired poet Jacques de Lille (1758–1813) was chiefly instrumental in bringing the *genre descriptif* into considerable vogue, with his translation of Virgil's *Georgics* and his original d. poem *Les Jardins*. In German literature "d. poetry" is generally taken to refer only to medieval examples of moralizing verse, e.g., *Bescheidenheit* by "Freidank" (1215–16) or *Der Renner* (ca. 1300) by Hugo von Trimberg; or to refer to such Reformation satires as *Narrenschiff* by Sebastian Brant (1494) or *Narrenbeschwörung* (1512) and *Gauchmatt* (1514) by Thomas Murner. In Sp. literature d. poetry makes its appearance in the Golden Age briefly and incidentally in the form again of moralizing treatises or discussions of aesthetics, by such authors as Francisco Pacheco, Lope de Vega, and Cervantes, the works in question being of distinctly minor importance.

In It. literature few traces of d. poetry may be detected except for imitations of Virgil's *Georgics*. Poems of a generally diffused moral intent, e.g., the satires of Parini, cannot be placed within the tradition of d. poetry without extending the category beyond its reasonable bounds. Pope's "Essays," for instance, or Boileau's *L'Art Poétique* belong to the category of argumentative moral verse rather than to that of d. poetry proper with its emphasis on technical content. The line between d. purpose and moral content is real, for while the d. authors occasionally step over it, they always return ultimately to their own area of knowledge and instruction, in the interests of which the whole poem has been originally conceived. Satire in general offers another instance of the point of departure at which in formation and instruction leave off and fiction and moral implication assume the main function in the literary design. A· moral poet or a satirist expects the reader to be somewhat the better for having read his work; the d. poet expects him to be better informed.

By the end of the century (e.g., Cowper's *Task*, 1785) the Eng. fashion of "georgic" poetry was on the decline, and this style of writing has never reappeared in our literature on any comparable scale. In the late 18th and early 19th c. more "georgics" were composed, but the genre was virtually obsolete. Nevertheless, in view of the fact that it did assume so phenomenal a place in the aesthetic experience of neoclassical England (continental examples being negligible), we may conclude this survey by evaluating the theory and purposes animating the poetry in its final phase. The Eng. poems are subjective, rambling, effusively appreciative of nature. But if ancient writers tended to separate knowledge of nature from knowledge about utilizing her resources and to write either one or the other kind of d. poem, the most popular 18th-c. writers managed to combine both elements again and to incorporate them in single works. Their mission was neither so explicit nor so limited as the mission of the classical d. poets. Inquiring studiously into the facts, the later writers were concerned with teaching the reader to visualize, to understand, and even to rejoice in nature.

Throughout its history, d. poetry has coincided with scientific awareness. The early writers after Hesiod produced poems virtually coterminous with the first great advances in Ionian speculative science. Again, d. poems coincided with the rising scientific interest of the Alexandrian Age. Lucretius and Virgil were Romans, i.e., members of a society with a strong affinity for technological progress. The "new science" of the Renaissance found its counterpart to some degree in the d. poems of Italy and their early Eng. descendants. The Newtonian world of the Enlightenment in England accorded the warmest hospitality of all to a great number and great variety of d. poems. The somewhat elusive genre, d. poetry, has perhaps not always conveyed "the impassioned expression which is in the countenance of all Science," but it has quite frequently displayed the glow of understanding that steals over the face of inquisitive man.

There is no comprehensive book on the subject of d. poetry. The best guides to the subject are: (1) for the classical period, the articles in the *Oxford Cl. Dict.* under "D. Poetry," and separate scholarly editions of the works of the major authors. (2) For the Eng. tradition, Dwight L. Durling, *Georgic Tradition in Eng. Poetry*, 1935. This thoroughgoing study contains an invaluable discussion of the whole subject and includes a comprehensive bibliog. See also G. Pellegrini, *La poesia didascalica inglese nel settecento italiano* (1958).   s.p.b.

DIIAMB. A syzygy consisting of 2 iambs (˘–˘–) and known also as iambic monometer. It is occasionally found in combination with or as part of other cola.—Kolář; Koster. p.s.c.

DIMETER (Gr. "of 2 measures"). A line consisting of 2 metra or measures. In classical iambic, trochaic, and anapaestic verse the metron is a dipody (pair of feet). Thus the trochaic dimeter

$$\text{blastāneī kāi} \mid \text{sykophāntei}$$
(Aristophanes, *Birds* 1479)

contains 4 feet. But, as used by Eng. prosodists, "-meter" is synonymous with foot. The Eng. dimeter (a 2-stress line), therefore, consists of 2 feet, the trimeter of 3 feet, etc.   p.s.c.

DIMINISHING METAPHOR. A type of metaphor which utilizes a deliberate discrepancy of connotation between tenor and vehicle (q.v.). It is thus a type of conceit (q.v.), but its special quality lies in its use of a pejorative vehicle in reference to a tenor of value or desirability. One of the most extreme examples of d.m. occurs in Donne's *First Anniversary*, in which the surpassing and divine virtue of Elizabeth Drury, the subject of the obsequies, is described in these terms.:

But as some Serpent's poyson hurteth not,
Except it be from the live Serpent shot,
So doth her vertue need her here, to fit
That unto us; shee working more than it.

The function of d.m. seems thus to lie in its forcing on the reader an intellectual rather than a sensuous reaction. It is, understandably, a figure especially favored in metaphysical poetry (q.v.) and in the work of many modern poets.   f.j.w.

DINGGEDICHT. A type of poetry concerned with the description of objects from within rather than from the point of view of the observer. Early examples are to be found in the poetry of Eduard Mörike (*Auf eine Lampe*) and C. F. Meyer (*Der römische Brunnen*). As a form, the D. is fully developed in R. M. Rilke's *Neue Gedichte* (1907). These are parodied by Christian Morgenstern in certain of his *Galgenlieder*. Based on Goethe's ("Die Schöne bleibt sich selber selig"—Beauty rests content with itself) and Mörike's ("Was aber schön ist, selig scheint es in ihm selbst" —But that which is beautiful seems [or shines] content with itself) concept of beauty, the D.— a name first given to the genre by K. Oppert—

deifies the object by stressing its self-sufficiency and its imperviousness to change. The object, to which a pure state of being is attributed, is said to be "separated from chance and time" (Rilke). The theory underlying the D. is implicitly stated in Rilke's essays on Rodin, where *Skulptur* and *Ding* are treated as synonyms. This explains the close relationship between the D. and the art of sculpture. Although, strictly speaking, the term D. refers only to German poetry of the 19th and early 20th c., certain parallels can be drawn between it and the art of the *Parnassiens* in France (with its emphasis on sculptural hardness) and that of the imagists in England and America (with its craving for spatialization).— K. Oppert, "Das D.," DVLG, 4 (1926); W. Rehm, "Wirklichkeitsdemut und Dingmystik," *Logos*, 19 (1930); E. Feise, "Rilkes Weg zu den Dingen," *Monatshefte*, 28 (1936); H. Kunisch, *Rainer Maria Rilke und die Dinge* (1946); F. Martini, "D." in *Reallexikon*, 2d ed., I. U.W.

DIPODIC VERSE. Verse constructed rythmically so that, in scansion, pairs of feet must be considered together. That is, the metrical unit is less the individual foot than a dipody (2 related but slightly dissimilar feet, one of which normally has a stronger stress than the other). Crude dipodic verse, of the sort encountered in children's rhymes, nursery songs, and popular ballads, provides simple examples:

$$\text{Taffy was a} \mid \text{Welshman,}$$
$$\text{Taffy was a} \mid \text{thief.}$$

Here the first 4 syllables in each line constitute similar dipodies: to scan as if each line began with a trochee and a pyrrhic would be to underemphasize the force of the "secondary accent" on the word "was"; to scan as two trochees would be to overemphasize the stress on "was." More complex dipodic arrangements are to be found in a poem like Masefield's *Cargoes*.—G. R. Stewart, *Modern Metrical Techniques as Illustrated by Ballad Meter, 1700–1920* (1922) and "The Meter of the Popular Ballad," PMLA, 40 (1925); L. Woody, "Masefield's Use of Dipodic Meter," PQ, 10 (1931). P.F.

DIPODY (Gr. "combination of 2 feet"). In classical prosody, a group of 2 metrical feet constituting a single measure. A ditrochee.

DIRGE. The name derives from the beginning of the antiphon in L. of the Office of the Dead ("Dirige, Domine . . ." adapted from Psalms 5.9). As a literary genre it comes from the Gr. *epicedium* (q.v.), the song sung over the dead, and the threnody (q.v.), sung in memory of the dead, both of which were found in the

L. *nenia*. Although in ancient literature it was sometimes influenced by the *consolatio* and closely connected with the elegy, its chief aim was to lament the dead, not console survivors. The meter in L. was the hexameter or the elegiac distich. The subject matter included lamentation and eulogy, often with consolatory reflections, apostrophes, invocations, etc. Not only may human beings be mourned but animals as well (cf. Catullus 3.). Simonides, Pindar, and the Alexandrian poets used the genre in Gr. In L., Calvus and Catullus first used it and Propertius brought it to its greatest perfection (4.11). The medieval writers combined the L. form with the church's lamentation for the dead, employing in the process Christian themes. In Eng., such poems as Henry King's *Exequy* on his young wife or George Meredith's *Dirge in the Woods* are examples of dirges.—G. Herrlinger, *Totenklage um Tiere in der antiken Dichtung* (1930); E. Reimer, *Die rituelle Totenklage der Griechen* (1938). R.A.H.

DISEMIC (Gr. "of 2 time-units"). Term applied to the regular principle of Gr. and L. prosody whereby a long syllable was regarded as equivalent to 2 shorts (the short syllable being the time-unit or mora). See CLASSICAL PROSODY, MORA, and TRISEMIC. R.J.G.

DISINTERESTEDNESS IN CRITICISM. "D." is a key word in "The Function of Criticism at the Present Time," first delivered by Matthew Arnold as an Oxford lecture in 1864 and published as the opening essay of *Essays in Criticism* (1865). In the first paragraph of the essay, Arnold quotes his own definition of the function of criticism, first enunciated at Oxford in "On Translating Homer, Lecture II" of 1860. Criticism is "the endeavour, in all branches of knowledge, theology, philosophy, history, art, science, to see the object as in itself it really is." That is, criticism is properly a broadly cultural rather than merely belletristic activity, objective rather than partisan or given to practical ends.

Such activity depends on an attitude toward the objects of criticism which Arnold calls "d.," a free play of mind or consciousness. Obstructed by the practical character of the modern Englishman and the conservatism of the age, criticism in the 1860's, Arnold says, must take d. as the rule for its course. It must keep aloof from practical considerations and partisan causes, must come to know "the best that is known and thought in the world and by in its turn making this known, to create a current of true and fresh ideas" out of which can come a new creative epoch of literature. D. is thus an antidote to the predominantly provincial, self-interested criticism of his time. Arnold's disinterested critic is to allow his mind to play freely with the best ideas in the world.

Arnold recommended, and sometimes exhibited, a disinterested disposition, a detached stance. He also often adopted a disinterested manner as a rhetorical strategy. As early as his 1849 sonnet, *To a Friend,* he praised Sophocles, "Who saw life steadily, and saw it whole." Several of the subjects in *Essays in Criticism* were chosen as examples of the disinterested disposition: Maurice de Guérin, Joubert, Marcus Aurelius display unified aims, generous elevation of feeling, predominance of spirit over everything else. Arnold used d. as a strategy by professing concern for his subject matter not as material for the world of facts but for the world of ideas, by disavowing fixed principles, and by assuming an attitude of great intellectual flexibility, of modesty to the point of self-depreciation. However, though he argued the cause of d. with eloquence, Arnold himself had a disposition not basically disinterested, and, as he moved from literary to social criticism, even his strategy ceased to be disinterested.

Important modern critics, from Eliot on, have expressed sympathy for Arnold's principle of criticism as a disinterested endeavor, though some of them have adopted a highly interested point of view in their practical criticism.

H. W. Garrod, *Poetry and the Crit. of Life* (1931); E. K. Brown, *Matthew Arnold: A Study in Conflict* (1948); G. Tillotson, "Matthew Arnold: The Critic and the Advocate," *Crit. and the 19th C.* (1951); D. G. James, *Matthew Arnold and the Decline of Eng. Romanticism* (1961).   J.K.R.

DISPONDEE. A combination of 2 spondees into a single measure (– – – –). It is seldom found as an independent foot and never occurs in a connected series.—Koster.   P.S.C.

DISSOCIATION OF SENSIBILITY. The terms "d.o.s." and "unification of sensibility" were introduced into the discussion of Eng. literary history by T. S. Eliot in an essay entitled "The Metaphysical Poets" (1921). Some students believe, however, that, insofar as they relate to "metaphysical" poetry (q.v.), concepts similar to Eliot's (in which there has been discovered the influence of Rémy de Gourmont or, alternatively, of F. H. Bradley) considerably antedate Eliot's formulations.

In his essay, Eliot sets out to discover what, if anything, justifies us (and Dr. Johnson) in considering the "metaphysical" poets a "school" or (aberrant) "movement" in the history of Eng. poetry; he concludes that there is no such justification. He therefore adopts the hypothesis that, rather than an aberration, they are "the direct and normal development

of the precedent age. . . ." Furthermore, he sets out (by implication) to counter the view which he supposes to underlie Johnson's adverse criticism of the metaphysicals: the view that in poetry, thought, as manifested in learning and wit, is incompatible with feeling. To compass this end, Eliot offers the theory of unified and dissociated sensibilities. The early 17th-c. poets, he suggests, were learned men in the tradition of Dante and the *stilnovisti* (see DOLCE STIL NUOVO) and equipped like them with a "mechanism of sensibility" (or unified sensibility) which has subsequently and unfortunately disappeared. Through this "mechanism" they were capable of a "direct sensuous apprehension of thought" such that; for them, thought and feeling were "fused." After Donne and Herbert of Cherbury, however, "a dissociation of sensibility set in, from which we have never recovered." The results of the d., aggravated by the peculiar excellences of Milton and Dryden, were a refinement of language together with a progressive crudeness of feeling, and later a sentimental revolt "against the ratiocinative" in the 18th c. Since then poets have "thought and felt by fits, unbalanced."

Although Eliot has recorded his astonishment at the success of the theory, and although he soon began to make statements about Donne which are diametrically opposed to those in "The Metaphysical Poets," the theory gained widespread acceptance during the 25 years after it was enunciated; more recently, it has been subjected to considerable criticism on logical, psychological, and historical grounds. It is accepted and elaborated with particular reference to Donne and the "metaphysicals" by Williamson (1930) and with reference to 17th-c. intellectual history in general by Willey (1934). Reflexes of the theory are to be found in the poetics of such critics as Cleanth Brooks, Ransom, and Tate. Knights (1946) follows Eliot and Willey, but finds evidences of the d. already in the style of Bacon, Donne's older contemporary. O'Connor (1948) accepts the main outlines of Eliot's theory as elaborated by Williamson and Willey as the basis of his study of 20th-c. poetics and poetry. Maxwell (1952) accepts the concepts of unified sensibility and "felt thought," but finds that they are conditions aimed at by Donne (and not perfectly achieved even by Dante) rather than conditions inherent in a culture and thus necessarily imposed upon its representatives.

On the other hand, since at least 1939 doubts have been expressed as to the validity of the theory and of its elaborations. The mild skepticism of Spencer and Van Doren (1939) and of Dobrée (1946) gives place to the thoroughgoing criticism of Unger, who (1950, 1956) tests and finds wanting many of the assertions about "metaphysical" poetry by Williamson, Ransom, Brooks, and Tate from Eliot. Bateson (1951, 1952) finds Eliot guilty of equivocation in his use of the term "sensibility" and traces both term and equivocation to the "ram-shackle" psychological theory of Gourmont. Leishman (1951) finds that the fusion of thought and feeling, the hallmark of the undissociated sensibility, is evident in few of Donne's poems and that Eliot's theory is more intelligble as a program for a poet in the 20th c. than as an account of poetry in the 17th. Kermode (1957) finds the theory un-satisfactory as historical explanation and con-siders it merely an attempt to rationalize the position of the poet in a scientific world.

The fullest accounts of the theory and of its elaborations are to be found in the critiques of Unger, Leishman, and Kermode, the fullest applications in Williamson and Willey.—[T. S. Eliot], "The Metaphysical Poets," TLS, Oct. 20, 1921 (repr. in *Selected Essays* [1932]); G. Williamson, *The Donne Trad.* (1930); B. Willey, *The 17th C. Background* (1934); T. Spencer and M. van Doren, *Studies in Metaphys. Poetry* (1939); L. C. Knights, *Explorations* (1946); B. Dobrée, "The Claims of Sensibility," *Humanitas* (Manchester), 1 (1946); W. V. O'Con-nor, *Sense and Sensibility in Modern Poetry* (1948); L. Unger, *Donne's Poetry and Modern Crit.* (1950) and *The Man in the Name* (1956); F. W. Bateson, "Contributions to a Diction. of Crit. Terms II. D.o.S.," EIC, 1 (1951) and "D.o.S.," EIC, 2 (1952); J. B. Leishman, *The Monarch of Wit: an Analytical and Comparative Study of the Poetry of John Donne* (1951); D.E.S. Maxwell, *The Poetry of T. S. Eliot* (1952); H. W. Smith, " 'The D.o.S.,' " *Scrutiny*, 18 (1952); E. Thompson, "D.o.S.," EIC, 2 (1952); F. Kermode, *Romantic Image* (1957). See also F. M. Kuna, "T. S. Eliot's D.o.S. and the Critics of Metaphysical Poetry," EIC, 13 (1963).

J.D.K.

DISSONANCE. The quality of being harsh or inharmonious in rhythm or sound; akin to cacophony (q.v.). Insofar as the terms may be distinguished, cacophony is what is harsh-sounding in itself, d. is that which is discordant or inharmonious with what surrounds it. By extension the term may refer to poetic ele-ments other than sound that are discordant with their immediate context. Donne and Browning have made notable use of d.—J. B. Douds, "Donne's Technique of D.," PMLA, 52 (1937).

L.P.

DISTICH. A couple of metrical lines, usually rhymed and expressing a complete idea (see COUPLET). In classical poetry the most common d. is the elegiac (q.v.), consisting of a dactylic

hexameter followed by a dactylic "pentameter." It was very often used by writers of epigrams and is common in modern Gr. poetry.—Koster; G. Soyter, "Das volkstümliche Distichon bei den Neugriechen," *Laographia*, 8 (1925). P.S.C.

DIT (many other terms are used as synonyms: *conte, lai, traitie, essemple*). This is primarily an exemplum, a poem which has some instruc-tional value, without necessarily supporting a moral. There is the *dit d'Aristote* which has something to say about the wiles of women; there is the *dit des rues de Paris* which lists all 310 of the streets as they were at the close of the 13th c. Since the middle of the 13th c. the term began to be used particularly for a long poem of contemporary observation and reflection. It could be a treatise on how to be-have: *le dit d'Urbain le Courtois;* it might be concerned with religion and morals; it could be satire; it could be personal musing; it could even be an historical account. Guillaume de Machaut made use of the term for narratives that described his love adventures, allegorical and real. The *Voir Dit,* or "True Story," had to do with his relations with Peronelle d'Ar-mentières. The inspiration for the *dit* comes from the L. exemplum and treatise of the 12th c. At first the form was the 8-syllable rhymed couplet; but soon, with Jean Bodel and Gautier de Coincy, 4-line monorhymed stanzas in alex-andrines came into vogue.—*Hist. littéraire de France,* XXIII (1895). U.T.H.

DITHYRAMB. Gr. choric hymn, accompanied by mimic gestures, describing the adventures of Dionysus, the god of fertility and procrea-tion. The etymology of the term is not very certain. Many consider it of Thracian or Phrygian origin. It was probably introduced into Greece early in the 7th c. and became very popular among the Dorians. In its earliest form it was led off by the leader of a band of revelers, a group of dancers, probably dressed as satyrs and dancing around a burning altar. Arion of Corinth (ca. 600 B.C.) gave it its regu-lar form and raised it to the rank of artistic poetry. Shortly before 500 B.C. it was intro-duced into Athens by Lasus of Hermione and was soon recognized as one of the competitive subjects at the various Athenian festivals. For more than a generation after its introduction into Athens the d. attracted the most famous poets of the day and reached its highest point of development in the hands of Pindar and Simonides. By this time, however, it had ceased to concern itself exclusively with the adven-tures of Dionysus and begun to choose its sub-jects from all periods of Gr. mythology. Furthermore, even as early as before the mid-dle of the 5th c. the d. had begun to undergo changes which affected seriously its original

DOLCE STIL NUOVO

character. These changes consisted primarily in the abandonment of the antistrophic arrangement of the verses introduced by the Dorians, greater metrical freedom, the preponderance of the music over the words, the introduction of solo songs, and the use of bombastic and affected language. The results of these changes are illustrated in the lyric passages of the poet Timotheus (fl. 400 B.C.). In the 4th c. and subsequently, the d. continued to lose steadily in importance, even in Athens. But we know that it was performed there as late as the imperial period.

In modern literature pure dithyrambs have been very rare. In Eng. poetry the d. probably finds its best expression in Dryden's *Alexander's Feast* (1697). The adjective "dithyrambic" is often used to describe both an enthusiastic and elevated and a wildly vehement and passionate composition.—Smyth; A. W. Pickard-Cambridge, *D., Tragedy and Comedy* (1927); Schmid and Stählin, I; G. A. Privitera, *Appunti intorno agli studi sul ditirambo* (1957).   P.S.C.

DITROCHEE, *dichoree.* Two trochees or chorees viewed as a unit (-◡-◡). It is also known as trochaic monometer and is found in combination with other cola and is used occasionally as a *clausula* (see PROSE RHYTHM).—Koster.   P.S.C.

DITTIE, ditty, dictie, etc. (a) a composition intended to be sung, a lay; now any short, simple song—sometimes disparaging in tone; or, more generally, any composition in verse, particularly a ballad (Kipling, *Departmental Ditties & Barrack-Room Ballads*). (b) Sometimes the words of a song as separate from the music; i.e., the theme or burden. (c) The verb, meaning to sing a dittie, or (rarely) to adapt the words to music, is now obsolete.   R.O.E.

DIVERBIUM. The spoken dialogue in the Roman drama to be distinguished from the *cantica* (see CANTICUM), the sung or declaimed part. It was written, as a rule, in iambic senarii. In some manuscripts of Plautus the d. is indicated by DV and the *canticum* by C.—Hardie; W. M. Lindsay, *Early L. Verse* (1922); W. Beare, *The Roman Stage* (2d ed., 1955).   P.S.C.

DIZAIN. A Fr. poem of 10 octosyllabic or decasyllabic lines which, with Clément Marot, Hugues Salel and Mellin de Saint-Gelais, had the rhyme scheme ababbccdcd. On the same scheme Maurice Scève wrote the 449 related *dizains* of his *Délie* (1544). When the d. stood alone as a separate composition, it tended to have the characteristics commonly associated with the epigram (q.v.), and Thomas Sebillet

in his *Art poétique françoys* of 1548 (ed. F. Gaiffe, 1932, p. 110), defines the d. as "l'épigramme aujourd'hui estimé premier." Three or five *dizains*, each group with an *envoi*, could be brought together to form a *ballade* or a *chant royal* (qq.v.), respectively. As employed later by the *Pléiade*, the d. has the rhyme scheme ababccdeed, is less often found as a separate poem, and may be composed of verses of different length.—P. Martinon, *Les Strophes* (1912); H. Chamard, *Hist. de la Pléiade*, IV (1941).   I.S.

DOCHMIAC or dochmius (Gr. "slanted"). A metrical foot of 3 long and 2 short syllables occurring most commonly in the form ◡--◡-. Very often each long syllable is resolved into 2 short ones, and the first and fourth syllables may be long. Dochmiacs are almost exclusively used in Gr. tragedy, chiefly in passages expressing intense emotion, agitation, or grief, and are frequently found in combination with iambs, anapaests, and cretics. As for Roman drama, the existence of dochmiacs in Plautus is disputed. In the *hypodochmius* or anaclastic dochmius, the first two elements are inverted.—J. F. A. Seidler, *De versibus dochmiacis tragicorum graecorum* (1811); Dale; Koster.   P.S.C.

DOGGEREL (origin unknown). Rough, poorly constructed verse, characterized by strong, monotonous rhyme and rhythm, cheap sentiment, triviality, and lack of dignity. Chaucer referred to his burlesque *Tale of Sir Thopas* as *rym doggerel*, and Dr. Johnson stigmatized the vice in the following parody:

> As with my hat upon my head
> I walk'd along the Strand,
> I there did meet another man
> With his hat in his hand.
> (G. Steevens, *Anecdotes of Johnson*
> [Miscellanies] p. 315.)

Northrop Frye (in *The Anatomy of Criticism,* 1957) has characterized d. as the result of an unfinished creative process, in which a "prose initiative" has never assumed the associative qualities of true poetry, revealing its failure in a desperate attempt to resolve technical difficulties through any means which suggest themselves. There are, however, some works of real poetic value in which doggerel-like features are deliberately used for comic or satiric effect. John Skelton, Samuel Butler, and Jonathan Swift are all masters of artistic d., and much German *Knittelvers* (q.v.) also achieves a brilliant parodistic effect.   L.B.P.

DOLCE STIL NUOVO. The style of It. lyric poetry written in the second half of the 13th c.; marked by sincerity of feeling and musicality of verse. The term was first used by Dante, "Purgatory," 24.57, where it is spoken by the poet Bonagiunta Orbicciani of Lucca. Dante's term has considerable validity. The "sweetness" of his style is attained, analysts have discovered, through his careful selection of words of pleasurable sound and their ordering. The "newness" scholars have long disputed. Most probably Dante refers to the poet's creative variations on traditional poetic themes. As we shall see presently, Dante's content is not without some new accent and variation. The literary background from which the *stil nuovo* emerged included the tradition of 200 years of Prov. troubadour poetry. This tradition was still vital in Italy at the time of Dante's birth. From Prov. poetry the *stilnovisti* learned the conventions of courtly love with its religious overtones, its idealization of women, its emphasis on gentility (*gentilezza*), and its faith that love is an ennobling influence on the lover. From Prov. poetry the *stilnovisti* also learned how to use intricate poetic forms like the *trobar clus*, a lesson which is important for the development of such native forms as the *canzone* and the sonnet. A second influence important for the *stil nuovo* is the Franciscan revival, which stressed sincerity, simplicity and a feeling for the unity of man with nature. Finally, philosophy had an important influence on the s.n. From Guido Guinizelli to Guido Cavalcanti and even Petrarch all of the important *stilnovisti* had contact with the University of Bologna where Thomistic theology and medicine were taught, both of which were allied to the great 13th c. revival of Aristotelianism. Avicenna on medicine and Averroes on Aristotle were not without their influence too. The result of these influences was to deepen the analysis of love found in the poetry of the s.n. In fact, it has been suggested (e.g., Karl Vossler) that the philosophical and often metaphysical bent of the poetry of the s.n. is its most distinctive characteristic. Another important influence is that of the Sicilian school (q.v.) of poets which flourished in the 13th c. and whose most prominent figure is the Notary Jacopo da Lentini.

The first of the triad of poets who composed important doctrinal *canzoni* is the jurisconsultant Guido Guinizelli. His contribution was imitated by Dante, the third member, in the first *canzone* of the *Vita Nuova*. Guinizelli repeats the trobador commonplaces, but seems to expand on the basis of platonic doctrine. The eyes (as in Plato's *Republic* Book 4) are the most beautiful part of the body—the windows of the soul. The *saluto* ranks second (in accordance with Aristotle's teaching of the "smile"). Love and the noble heart are one and the same. Love cannot exist anywhere save in a noble heart, and a noble heart cannot exist without love. This nobility is of the spirit, not of heredity through blood. It derives from one's own virtue. In Guido's conception, the beloved activates the lover's inborn disposition toward good and is instrumental in raising the lover's soul to the Highest Good, making for communion with the Absolute and the Eternal. Guinizelli's method is scholastic—a mode that developed to its perfection contemporaneously with Aristotelianism. His manner is distinguished by use of scientific observation of natural phenomena in images and similes to objectify the internal sensations of love. Cavalcanti, Dante's "first friend," is the second member of the triad. He devoted the best of his two *canzoni* to his Christian, neoAristotelian understanding of love. He deals with Love's origins and nature and may possibly show some overtones of Averroes' notions. Cavalcanti is concerned with profoundly intimate reveries upon womanly beauty. He is haunted by the phantom of Love and Spectre of Death amid the agitation and anguish of his state.

Dante brought the literary trend to a climax in the first *canzone* of the *Vita Nuova*. His earliest poetry is in the s.n., but that *canzone* (composed about 1289) and the several subsequent sonnets in the *Vita Nuova* (compiled probably in 1292, two years after Beatrice's death) show his adoption of Guinizelli's view of love, although he rejects Cavalcanti's views. The later poems of the *Vita Nuova* begin a series of paeans of "praise." They contain elements of the platonic outlook, particularly the seeing of the beloved as an angel-lady. The death of the lady in the case of Dante's Beatrice (as well as of Petrarch's Laura) is a supreme milestone in the pilgrim's progress in love. Having died, she becomes an angelic form, who through the light of the eyes and radiance of the smile, leads the lover as true guide, symbol of virtue, to God in His Goodness, to the ideal of perfection. In Dante's *Convivio* (1308), we learn (2.15.10; 2.16; 3.12.2-3; and 4.2) that he reserved a special manner of sweetness of expression for rhymes of love and that his conception of *amore* included the eager pursuit of knowledge. In his L. *De Vulgari Eloquentia*, written in about the same period (2.8, 12), Dante further elaborates his ideas as to style (the tragic being the highest); as to language (the illustrious vulgar being the sweetest); as to form (*the canzone, sonetto, ballata* being the noblest); and as to meter (hendecasyllabic being the most excellent). In the same work he names Cavalcanti, Lapo Gianni, himself, and Cino da Pistoia, whom (we do not understand why) he favors especially for his subtlety and sweetness, as partakers in the "sweet new style." Dante's remarks have led some critics to feel that there was a more or less self-conscious "school" of the *dolce s.n.* More likely it was a group of friends with more or less common poetic interests. Critics have added to the supposed group Gianni Alfani, Dino Frescobaldi, Guido Orlandi, and even Guido Novello da Polenta, Dante's host in days of exile.

Petrarch throughout his several reworkings of his *Canzoniere* shows much influence of the *dolce s.n.* However as Nesca Robb aptly points out, he was not altogether successful in his attempt to subjugate his "very mortal passion" to the Dantean ideal. His awareness of this dilemma is expressed in the crescendo and diminuendo, the ebb and flow throughout the carefully contrived *Canzoniere*. Later followers of the *stilnovisti* include Matteo Frescobaldi, Franceschino degli Albizzi, Sennuccio del Bene, Boccaccio (the last two, poetic correspondents of Petrarch), Cino Rinuccini, and Giovanni Gherardi da Prato. Through the influence of Petrarch, the conventions of the s.n. were spread throughout Europe and profoundly affected the development of lyric poetry in France, Spain, England, and elsewhere. Lorenzo de' Medici, the reviver of Petrarchism for the It. *Quattrocento,* consciously imitated the s.n. He also appreciated the minor *stilnovisti,* as is evidenced by the letter to Frederico of Aragon accompanying the anthology of early It. poetry he compiled for him (see A. Lipari, *The Dolce S.N. According to Lorenzo de' Medici* [Yale Romanic Studies, XII], 1936). Later, Michelangelo, Pietre Bembo, and Torquato Tasso showed the influence of the s.n., as did Ugo Foscolo in the 19th c. An It. refugee in England, Dante G. Rossetti, reintroduced Eng. Victorians to the s.n. through both translations and original compositions. The continuing significance of the s.n. is apparent in the critical discussions of the school by Ezra Pound and (more recently) Francis Ferguson, Edward Stambler, and John Anthony Mazzeo.

K. Vossler, *Die Göttliche Komödie* (1906; tr. *Mediaeval Culture,* 1929; surveys the philos. background of the poetic development); A. Figurelli, *Il Dolce S.N.* (1933; surveys historically attitudes toward poetically inspiring love, see review by M. Casella, SD, 18 [1934]); J. E. Shaw, "Guido Guinizelli, Cavalcanti, Dante," and "The Dolce S.N.," *Guido Cavalcanti's Theory of Love, The Canzone d'Amore and other Related Problems* (1949; penetrating analysis); U. Bosco, "Il 'Nuovo Stile' della Poesia Dugentesca," *Medievo e Rinascimento, Studi in onore di B. Nardi,* ed. C. Antoni (2 v., 1955; sensitive and discerning); A. Del Monte, "Dolce S.N.," *FiR,* 3 (1956); J. A. Mazzeo, "The Analogy of Creation in Dante," *Speculum,* 32 (1957) and *Structure and Thought in the Paradiso* (1958); L. Russo, "Lo Stilnovo," *Storia della lett. ital.* (3 v., 1957; magnificent survey);

G. Favati, *Guido Cavalcanti Rime* (1957; culmination of a polemic on text and interpretation); *Poeti del Duecento,* ed. G. Contini (2 v., 1960); G. Petrocchi, *Il Dolce S.N.* (1960). L.H.G.

DOUBLE, DUPLE METER. (a) Any meter in which the feet are composed of 2 syllables; i.e., iambic or trochaic, exemplified by most Eng. verse. (b) But in classical poetry the double measure, or dipody, was usually thought to contain 2 feet; thus the Gr. iamb, a dipodic measure, contained 4 syllables, the first either long or short, the second long, the third short, the fourth long, though in comedy considerable freedom of construction was allowed. (c) The term "duple meter" is sometimes used to describe dipodic verse (q.v.) in Eng. R.O.E.

DRAMATIC IRONY. See IRONY.

DRAMATIC MONOLOGUE. See MONOLOGUE.

DRAMATIC POETRY. The limits of genres, upon whose conventions most creativity and surely all criticism in the arts depend, keep shifting from one generation to the next. On the other hand, were the boundaries of poetic categories, such as lyric, narrative, and dramatic, wholly fixed, writing would long since have grown mechanical. The 20th c. has prized the dr. highly, thus its emphasis on *show* rather than *tell* and its addiction to formulae such as, "never apologize, never explain," for authors. Poets, particularly, have taken to dramatization: they speak through interior monologues or assume masks; they liberate minor objects and elevate them as striking symbols; they indulge in contrasts between great and small, or private and public, or ancient and contemporary, or elegant and tawdry —in short, they strive for a heightening, not by connected discourse, but by ellipses. A major advocate for this manner, T. S. Eliot, observed that the past directs the present, which then may modify former orders. Consequently, by the standards of this century works have been resurrected from neglect or undergone revaluation. One criterion for excellence rests on how objective, and therefore dr., poets now sound. It follows that Dante, creating a self and expressing it through concrete figures, enjoyed a revival, and that Milton's reputation resting on vague images and didacticism declined. Donne, with two personalities of sinner and prelate, rose in popularity among readers who appreciated his nervous juxtapositions and vivid contrasts. Baudelaire's creating from a dandy's sensibilities an anxiety and vocabulary more witty and analytic than Tennyson had risked placed the Fr. master of postromantic despair far beyond his Eng. counterpart. Examples might extend for paragraphs. The result of this tendency complicates a definition of dr. poetry: older lines have blurred so that much more poetry now sounds dr., and the word has partly lost its descriptive nature and nearly changed into a standard for evaluation.

The traditional groupings of lyric, narrative, and dr., nevertheless, help delimit basic boundaries. Whether any man ever composed as a man rather than self-conscious poet probably no one can affirm. Certain poems do look almost anonymous, perhaps sincerely naive, as though the author expressed only his direct perception and, in some cases, his audience. With such compositions, however dramatized their images, the lyric attributes stay predominant. The narrative poem (including the epic) tells a story so that the writer speaks in his own person while setting the scene or giving exposition, but he puts on varied personalities and adopts different voices as the episodes require. In the dr., finally, the bare narrative fades away, and a group of characters embodied by actors remains. These distinctions have no fixed historical developments, and some works may partake of all three: Shakespeare's sonnets offer an instance. By itself the sonnet generally belongs to lyric poetry. Taken together the separate parts interact and produce a narrative which tells a kind of story. To the extent that the individual sonnets constitute a unified whole for which the author appends no direct commentary, it may look dr. The frequently explicated sequence lacks the precise lines which dr. poetry needs. One can compare Shakespeare's with other lyric poems and his *Troilus and Cressida*, for all its idiosyncrasies, with other plays, but one can scarcely cite any other dr. composition, however loosely that term is applied, quite like the sonnets. When a word which should describe a genre extends to embrace almost unique titles, it has lost its primary function.

Putting aside the subtleties of aesthetic and subjective prejudices, one might then agree upon the approximate range for dr. poetry. Its origins provide clues for the abiding attributes. In the Western world drama had two origins, one in Gr. festivals and, after nearly disappearing, another in the medieval church. A very early example from the Christian era belongs to the enactment of the Easter story called, after the angel's inquiry, the *Quem Quaeritis* Trope. Drama poses a question whose answer must unfold in human terms and not as abstract theology or a single emotion. For another dimension: the development of plays in Gr. culture depended upon adding to the traditional chorus in Dionysiac festivals a speaker, called the *hypocrites* or answerer. The questioner receives his reply from someone who need not reveal all he knows. Taken together these two (or more) constitute the cast or

dramatis personae. In its origins *persona* seems associated with the term for mask; those who ask and respond assume a distinct personality and project their special traits through what they say. Finally, drama derives from *dran*, to do or act, so that the development does not occur simply as a dialogue but as a recognizable imitation of a happening. Why these speeches initially appear in poetry causes no uncertainty for the moment; it existed before plays themselves as part of the rites. Prose, although it soon enters in passages or takes over entirely, may represent a decline, just as pieces which deviate too far from the stage may grow overly speculative.

One paradox in evaluating any play depends upon its need for production; until having seen a performance one can scarcely possess a very accurate grasp of it, but, afterwards, that single interpretation may unduly influence one's judgments. This condition marks all drama, but, especially, the poetic will partake of the cast's inflections. A more vexing question hinges upon whether a prose translation of a play in verse distorts it seriously, whether, for example, Yeats's prose rendering of *Oedipus Tyrannus* gets closer to or further from Sophocles than Gilbert Murray's stanzas do. Similar problems hinge upon performances; does a dedicated troupe of students declaiming *The Birds* in the original before a non-Gr. audience commit a greater violence on Aristophanes than a professional company acting *Lysistrata* in translation? Here, again, to emphasize dr. qualities and the primacy of the theatre itself at least helps. At present, the Comédie Française in Paris, the Piccolo Teatro in Milan, the Old Vic of London, and the Burgtheater of Vienna among others keep on their active repertoire Molière, Goldoni, Shakespeare, and Schiller respectively in productions which, with varying degrees, exhibit tradition and experiment. Drama, to a greater extent than most other arts, relies on continued revaluations; every mounting entails another approach and in instances will stress novel aspects. At the same time, since printing, plays also remain available on the page, and, no matter how drenched in atmosphere with scrims, lighting, music, and stylization, dr. poetry needs, self-evidently, its language and not just the shifting tricks which directors, rather than authors themselves, may stumble upon through private predilections.

The kind of verse congenial to the stage varies a good deal from country to country and a bit less from time to time, as does the strictness of its uses. Generally the complete script rather than impressive parts sets the prevalent tone. Some examples might help define these conditions. When Lear realizes that Cordelia is dead, he says, in a moment of tragic recognition, "Thou'lt come no more, / Never, never, never, never, never!" The celebrated line, which out of context hardly looks striking, depends for its effects upon many circumstances: the suffering king whom it describes, his change from irascibility at the opening and rage on the heath, pity for Cordelia, and tragic awe. By itself it is not necessarily poetry, but the dr. rhythm undeniably reaches one of its heights here. In contrast, at the end of *Ghosts,* as Oswald declines into imbecility, he mutters, "Mother, give me the sun. . . . The sun, the sun," and Mrs. Alving wonders whether she can ever bring herself to poison him. Whatever pathos the scene may arouse, the line, scannable in translation, does not partake of poetry because the play throughout relies upon prose and a more pragmatic level—hence the irony of the title—than verse allows. At another extreme, to close *The Rake's Progress* a quartet sings a warning, "For idle hands / And hearts and minds / The Devil finds / A work to do, / A work, dear Sir, fair Madam, / For you and you." This passage indisputably belongs to verse and also the stage. About its merits opinions may differ, depending perhaps upon how clearly the echo from the end of *Don Giovanni* comes through. Opera, however, does not count as dramatic poetry because it fits more suitably into another genre where music has taken over as the medium and replaced a sustained repetition in the movement of language. For their effectiveness many operas rely upon the simplicity of the words. Finally, when Samson laments his condition, "O dark, dark, dark amid the blaze of noon / Irrecoverably dark, total eclipse / Without all hope of day," the poetry projects a special fervor but does not move rightly on the stage. At least, from a few experimental productions *Samson Agonistes* has not held its own and so fits more suitably with closet drama, dialogue designed only for the printed page. To turn back, finally, to Aristotle for a confirmation of such points—and he, of course, knew only plays in verse and closely associated with festivals—drama must contain plot, character, diction, thought, spectacle, and song. Although Aristotle, like most academicians since, did not rate spectacle highly, to ignore it raises too many extraneous questions.

Dr. poetry seldom exists in its pure state, just as, perhaps, *Oedipus Tyrannus* alone quite fits Aristotle's definition of tragedy. Granted imprecise limits, where it leaves off and turns into something else, basic essentials for its unique attributes do emerge. In addition to the general qualities which distinguish all poetry, metrical language, especially when recited on a stage, sustains the tableaux at a more intense level, whether for grandeur or satire, than prose can. Moreover, every production must establish some kind of rhythm, and, here again, if the voice as well as the body furthers the tempo, the performance gains commensurately. Prose has its own cadences, many brilliantly orchestrated, as in Congreve's comedies, and actors may, indeed, sometimes prefer it because it encourages their own mannerisms to cover a wider range. Over the years poetry has held its own for reasons which no one has yet fully explained; were no mystery connected with it, probably it would long since have vanished. One cause for its continuity may hark back to its origins: the theater retains aspects of participation by a group in an established ceremony. For this reason, among others, poetry has seldom attained prominence in motion pictures or television, which direct their products to frankly commercial ends. To mention individual titles as illustrations will probably pin down the range which poetry can encompass more effectively than added speculation here will. Before a chronological survey, one representative title—not necessarily the greatest within the conventional divisions of comedy and tragedy—will establish bases for noting later deviations.

A neoclassical play, obeying the rules promulgated in 17th-c. France, *Phèdre,* observes nearly impeccable proportions. Racine's language, in the expected couplets, establishes a tragic, elevated tone so that, with its deliberate aloofness, it creates its speakers as both individuals and types. Inside such confines it can, exploiting restricted variations, display much subtlety for both euphony of phrase and nuance. It investigates a persistent problem, that of passionate love, here a woman's for her stepson, but the *dénouement* cannot, by definition, dispel the mystery beyond clarifying the particular circumstances. By restricting himself to his notoriously small vocabulary, Racine manages a full exploration of his complex theme. The concepts must refer to psychological complications, and the fewer purely external interferences, the better: character is fate. Inevitability unfolds with unswerving logic. As Phèdre describes her suffering to the confidante, with a minimum of gestures reinforcing the words and in a functional *mise en scène,* the mind operates upon but fails to quell the emotions, which, expressed through the analytic alexandrines, gather to themselves intensity and amplitude. For an indicative comparison, Robert Lowell's Eng. rendering, with gratuitous figures and intensifying words added, sinks into rant and does not commensurately rise to terror. As with architecture, so with poetry in the theatre: less is more. In Fr. the deliberate artificiality of the verse prevents the frenzy from spilling over into mere bombast. *Phèdre* stays a nearly unique example, even for the Fr. theatre and Racine, and, like most models, the very lack of singularity may restrict it as less engrossing than others with slightly distorted proportions. To place *Phèdre* at a figurative center will indicate different types of diction in plays on similar themes, not by implication better or worse.

When the emotions no longer quite contain themselves in such simplicity of language, and when the characters fall victim to forces disproportionate to their strength and situations, the effect tends toward melodrama, for instance Dryden's heroic play *Aureng-Zebe*. To sustain mounting tensions the story may swell with improbabilities or collapse in an anticlimax. If a musical accompaniment serves to hold the whole together and make acceptable simplified exaggerations which the poetry by itself can no longer contain, the result grows entirely operatic, Verdi's *Don Carlos* based on Schiller's romantic play. Toward an opposite direction, when Phèdre herself serves as not merely a woman but directly embodies a myth, the situation may call for more than she can say in her own person, particularly if an awareness of her as an archetype emerges for an audience to whom she reveals, partially, a religious mystery. The play may then need a chorus for commentary with ceremonial songs and dances, the difference between Racine's *Phèdre* and Euripides' *Hippolytus*. If, too, as in the Gr. tragedy, the obsessive emotions loom as almost supernatural and Artemis and Aphrodite actually occupy the stage, then the verse may incorporate incantation, verging on the goal of all rituals, which bring knowledge of earth from heaven. If one thinks of these two movements as upward and downward, then toward the left, should Phèdre lose her status as a queen, a woman elevated, and become an unhappy wife, the verse may seek more idiomatic turns, paradoxically often away from directness, the effect in Lope de Vega's *Punishment without Revenge*. Eventually it may terminate with a domestic tragedy in prose, such as *Desire Under the Elms*, set forth through O'Neill's typically choked dialogue. Opposite from this point, to the right, when the characters begin uttering words meant primarily to evoke patterns nearly independent of the tableaux, then the effect approaches closet drama or, ultimately, ballet, where the voice separates from individuals and the poet gives up dramatization through words, such as Cocteau's ballet based on *Phèdre*. These directions are not absolutes, and intricate variations may arise through joining them, but, generally, diction must shape and control the episodes; when it no longer does, then a genre freed from the conventions strictly governing a play in verse has evolved.

If tragedy depicts the analysis of a continuing enigma, comedy explodes false mystification through people who should shun pretensions. The language, consequently, revels in weird extravagances. *Volpone*, for example, like *Phèdre* belongs to the neoclassical pattern of the 17th c. It shows three men bringing presents in order to be named the sole heir of a man who pretends to be dying. Because the characters deceive themselves, their vocabulary has lost touch with reality. Vain ambitions, which they project through their speeches, puff all of them. Commensurately with this bent, their baseless wishes swell as disproportionate and ridiculous. Only Jonson's firmly reined blank verse prevents parts from disintegrating into rant. Whereas tragedy must veil an uncontainable fate, comedy must expose people who deceive themselves. In tone comic diction ranges from satire to benignity, from Aristophanes to Molière. Comedy also expands in four approximate directions. That acceptable examples of tragedies on similar topics come to mind at once, whereas nearly every memorable comedy in verse looks nearly unique, suggests that the ridiculous must examine contemporary failings, which seldom endure. When it reverts to an affirmed joy, that man with all his limits will ultimately triumph, it partakes of its origins in celebrating fertility or harvests, and all may dissolve in songs, feasts, games, and wedding ceremonies.

Comparable with tragedy's approach to opera, comedy may quite yield to spectacle so that in the 17th c. the masque (q.v.), where décor buried the poetry, may supersede it and, in the 20th, musical comedy, where prose ties together a spate of lyrics. Again, parallel with tragedy, if the scene grows domestic and the language idiomatic, then what passes for comedy in popular usage has evolved. Finally, just as tragedy veers toward slighting language, comedy may abandon thought and revert to a clown's pantomime, where a touching tragic admixture occurs in the very inarticulate quality of its performers' lacking eloquence. Although circus and farce do not enjoy very high reputations at the present time (nor, until recently, has the musical comedy as evolved in the United States, nor, except to academic studies, have whatever spring rites may survive), these forms, if they overcome clichés, need not be judged by their natures minor; they simply have left off being instances of dr. poetry.

Such a schematic outline does violence to the wayward growth of the drama itself, and a loosely chronological order will help modify the generalizations. The Gr. theatre, to which nearly all western developments owe some debt, arose out of rituals, for tragedy those devoted to Dionysus. The large amphitheatres still remaining attest to its popularity, and authors received official prizes for their works. Drama itself started when a speaker exchanged dialogue with the chorus which sang in a rhythmic movement. Consequently, the poetry attendant upon all religious ceremonies accompanied secular plays from the outset, as did dancing or, at least, formal movement. The very nature of this diction required stylization, and the staging itself corresponded, with the actors garbed for tragedy in high masks. The short lines exchanged between speakers, stichomythia, kept to a rigorous pattern. Varied meters served, particularly for the chorus with its standard turns divided into strophe, antistrophe, and epode, but dialogue stayed chiefly in alexandrines. Plays by three writers of tragedy remain, although in each case far from the total number which they composed. Their styles differ, but all elude translation; recently the challenge has intrigued a number of poets in England and the United States, and their versions remove the seeming falsifications perpetrated by preceding centuries. The problem, of course, plagues all dr. poetry. By its nature it incorporates deliberate artificiality, and, yet, if it sounds only stiffly contrived, it fails to catch living accents. As a result, any translation must adhere to limits acceptable by literary and idiomatic standards for less than a century. Moreover, the Gr. dramatists worked in traditional materials so that their audiences could often respond with a directness to nuances not understandable later. Aeschylus, the earliest, while observing an austerity in plots and actions, can rise to solemnity and exuberance poetically. Sophocles indulged in a more personal vocabulary which favored the ironic implications of words as well as action. The characters' discovering the full implications of their sentences and deeds only with the unfolding of the story constitutes his theatrical effectiveness. With Euripides the tone sounds decidedly more mixed. His tragic figures, the women, especially, reveal psychological suffering in images more tortured than his predecessors'. The action, likewise, draws mixed responses; the puzzling *Alcestis* still causes controversy.

Where and how Gr. comedy originated remains more debatable. Aristophanes has left the first surviving examples, although he clearly drew upon antecedents. Indicatively the oral and physical extravagances which adhere to comedy occur in all his plays, as men search vainly to realize their desires and endure indignities, such as ascending to heaven on a beetle. Somehow, in spite of their bewilderment by an unpredictable world, they ultimately triumph. The language features sharply biting exchanges, and the plots revel in exaggerations unavailable to the stage since. The basically personal bias, using more meters than tragedy, represents old comedy. The need for this mode

to depict mainly contemporary foibles restricts it more persistently to an idiom of an obvious verisimilitude than tragedy must observe. As part of this nature, Gr. comedy apparently moved through a middle phase, which stays conjectural, and a late phase called new comedy, with which the works of Menander have become virtually synonymous; the recently discovered *Dyskolos* is the only reasonably complete play extant by which Menander's talents can be judged. Although prized above Aristophanes by some critics, Menander's poetry represents a descent toward mere speech. He specializes in the stereotypes who form so conspicuous a part of comedy and who, themselves unchanging, always mouth the fashionable clichés so that plays featuring them age quickly. Plautus and Terence, the Roman dramatists who copied Menander, fill their plots with similar intrigues and cross purposes. While differences set off these two writers, they treat the same topics: clever slaves, lost children, braggarts, and wayward sons. These complications may copy life, particularly Gr. and Roman life, but for language they necessitate a looseness which no versification can entirely rescue and require those embarrassing notes in which editors translate foreign idioms into the outmoded slang of their own youth. As a whole, such works probably give the social historian more pleasure than the playgoer. Seneca, the author of L. tragedies, barely exceeding closet drama, retains an ambiguous reputation. His tortured syntax and melodramatic twists perhaps deserve mention more for their later influence than achievements on their own; in the 17th c. the Roman dramatists exerted a heavier influence than the Gr.

With the medieval period, almost all drama of any sort disappeared, as far as records can prove, until it sprang again mainly from the churches. For a second time European theatre took direction from a religious ceremony. Although some critics make the development one toward secularization, or an intrusion of realistic material, such a theory denies art special attributes and reduces it to mirroring events rather than reinterpreting persistent impulses in human terms. For whatever causes, during the 17th c. both tragedy and comedy reached their most impressive achievements since the classical era. Among the conflicting factors credited—such as a popular and/or aristocratic audience, the appearance of gifted authors and/or actors, a culmination from earlier developments, and simply the historical moment—a large measure indisputably depends upon making and perfecting a native idiom for stage poetry in each country. Without merely copying classical patterns, the stage took over its measures and fitted them to the vernacular so that they display both directness and grace.

DRAMATIC POETRY

No single tendency will define all of them, but everywhere the crossing between the native and the classical accounts for the vigor. The proportions vary, with the Fr. theater almost determinedly neoclassical and the Eng. more mixed.

For England, *Gorboduc* in the mid 16th c., whatever its limits, hit upon blank verse, which continues almost the basis in Eng. dr. poetry. Until Marlowe's *Tamburlaine,* with his modulation of the line into a more pliant instrument, stage verse stayed awkwardly stiff. His swelling syllables reinforce a conqueror's vision and emphasize man's despair in containing human wishes. In spite of its seeming freedom, Elizabethan poetry obeyed, while expanding, the formal rules for grammar, rhetoric, and logic formulated by Renaissance rhetoricians, who founded their trivium upon classical models. Nevertheless, later, under less skilled hands, drama may disintegrate into mere melodrama or sensational effects of speech and action, a danger perhaps inherent from the outset in Kyd's *Spanish Tragedy* with its Senecan touches. To count Shakespeare the heir of these earlier writers emphasizes once again how greatly any artistic creation must exceed the source upon which it draws. Indeed, to the astounding degree that Shakespeare excels any other dramatist, at least in the qualities now prized, counting him the measure for excellence may limit one's appreciation of other, not necessarily less interesting, playwrights. In language, as any other theatrical trait, he ranges as he chooses and breaks rules with impunity. This very assurance leads lesser authors to fiascoes, as, for example, the succession of dull plays based vaguely upon *Hamlet* sufficiently proves. His poetic resources can range in tragedy from passages of formal balance to quite simple, idiomatic speeches without disrupting a deeply sustained tone. Because his career traces a consistent development, no single title can wholly exemplify his technique, although the movement in diction strives toward greater freedom with meters and a simplified vocabulary. In the great tragedies, through the metaphors, the exploration of thought and emotions ranges so widely that it almost exceeds containable limits. The presence of running patterns in imagery, which comments upon the story, contributes further to this richness. Passages in prose handle effects from realism to humor which verse by itself probably could not sustain.

In comedy he likewise displays assurance from the tavern scenes with Falstaff to the happy endings for lovers. Shakespeare excels in comedy which relies upon romance, but infrequently, except in early works, does he undertake the grotesque extremes in which Jonson specialized. Jonsonian comedy, as in *Volpone,*

already discussed, loses contact with actuality while the vocabulary further distorts the speakers' swollen dreams. Few other writers commanded Jonson's assurance, and comedy, even in the Jacobean period, stressed such pyrotechnics less and relied more upon a kind of realism and prose. Tragedy, while partly leaning toward domestic commonplaces after Shakespeare, became generally more extreme with an emphasis upon nearly pathological states. The verse, unable always to contain these effects, therefore verged upon pathos and grew sentimental except in Webster and, unevenly, Ford. The hiatus in theatrical production for nearly twenty years cleared the way for a different style with the Restoration. Comedy moved almost uniformly into prose and explored the foibles of fashionable society. Tragedy, influenced to a degree by the Fr. theatre, abandoned blank verse briefly and copied the foreign couplets. The narrow limits of this mode, and its requiring a simplified diction, could not hold the scene very long. Moreover, by featuring unexpected reversals in plots and reducing psychology to the claims of love and honor, debated at length, the action lay stilted and frozen. Nevertheless, the impetus from which much of this derives, the Fr. theatre, yields far richer effects.

In France a group of dramatists devotedly serving restrictions more severe than those which Aristotle promulgated produced tragedies distinguished by lines nearly as clear-cut as the Elizabethan and Jacobean are diversified. With Corneille, not wholly happy in the conventions which he obeyed, the theme of love and honor, more congenial to Fr. than Eng. psychology, took readily to couplets, which heightened the antitheses. The style culminates with Racine, although a criticism sometimes directed at his plays holds that the analyses of emotion grow too rarefied and overly refined. In comedy, on the other hand, Molière often serves as a paragon with his graceful emphasis on common sense, on types who violate social standards, on a genial wit, and on easily conversational movement in his verse. He may in instances skirt dangerously close to prosaic moralizing, but by its nature comedy inevitably runs this risk. How closely dramatists succeed in various modes may attend upon native patterns of language. For example, the Sp. theatre of Lope de Vega and Calderón, nearly contemporary with the Fr. and Eng., like the Elizabethan may mix emotions and employ varying styles. The *comedia de capa y espada* (q.v.) drew upon such mixed tendencies with a wider range of versification than contemporary plays elsewhere in Europe employed. After the general flowering of drama throughout Europe during the 17th c., the one following witnessed a decline into wholly stilted plays on classical themes or sentimental domestic pieces. In both cases the diction almost disintegrated into artificiality or cloying affectation.

With the approach of the 19th c., the triumphant romanticism which swept through every country brought along a reemphasis upon the theatre based chiefly on the new enthusiasm for Shakespeare, particularly in England and Germany. An anomalous aspect of the romantic temperament often trapped it between the lyric, the desire to express fresh, spontaneous feelings, and the dr., the compulsion to impose novel and generally self-conscious poses. Consequently, nearly every romantic poet sought—or expressed the wish—to write a play and failed in the effort. In plots, despite an earnestness, their plays often touch bathos, and the verse emphasizes more twists of speculation than the stage can contain while action itself languishes for long stretches. In England nearly every major poet of the century set his hand to plays, all of which, to 20th-c. tastes, look unstageworthy. With scarcely more memorable results, the Fr. poets, likewise, assaulted the theatre. Despite minor rebellions in style, exciting at the time, Hugo's plays, like most romantic drama, sound operatic, and, significantly, some, such as Hernani, have furnished the material for libretti. In Germany, as well, the romantic era encouraged a similar development, but philosophizing nearly predominates over psychology, as in Schiller and Goethe. These two directions, toward a lyric expression and toward a versified metaphysic, pulled in opposite directions and, for the period, reached a symbolic culmination with the interminable mythologies of Wagner's operas and Mallarmé's fragmentary prose-poem Igitur, admittedly closet drama. By and large the romantics did not admire intentional comedy, which disintegrated with popular playwrights into mere farce, and the serious theatre itself yielded to problem plays, well made in utilitarian prose.

In the 20th c., despite many attempts at revitalization, these two extremes survive to hamper dr. poetry: efforts to project a lyric slightness or to express transcendant generalizations. In Eng. Yeats favored enigmatic material influenced by what he made of the Japanese Nō (q.v.) plays. Hugo von Hofmannsthal in Germany experimented with a similar mode before, largely, turning to the books for Richard Strauss' operas. With both authors purely dr. poetry fell into abeyance. On the other hand, modifying Elizabethan approaches, T. S. Eliot through his own theatrical development almost repeated the historical growth of the drama, starting with a religious pageant, The Rock, its choruses using irregular meters, and subsequently working through plays which in-

corporate themes from Gr. tragedies in modern settings. His language has, similarly, modified blank verse and shuns any self-conscious artificiality. Christopher Fry, with The Lady's not for Burning, sporadically achieved the exuberance of an essentially comic verse. An instance of how tragedy demands tighter diction occurs in his The Dark Is Light Enough, which tries for greater pathos and fails to encompass the theme convincingly. Unfortunately, a promising departure for plays in verse, one based on the idioms of jazz, has not come into its own apart from musical comedies, where undistinguished prose holds together the songs and dances. The most interesting experiments along such lines, the collaborations between W. H. Auden and Christopher Isherwood, suffer from an excessive indulgence in wit. The two titles of an incomplete work in this vein by T. S. Eliot, originally published as "Wanna Go Home, Baby?" but changed to "Fragment of an Agon," exemplify the difficulties which this manner imposes. The colloquial sounds only trite, no matter how serious the puns, and the formal a bit too stiff and ironic for its subject. Furthermore, with the disappearance of the authentic sources for this speech, even as expressed in vaudeville and the music hall, the future will have no place from which to draw the raw materials.

Indeed, at present the entire concept of poetry in the theatre relies less and less upon language and increasingly on the special contributions from stagecraft. Here, again, the 20th-c. tendency to exploit the unique materials of the arts as expressive in themselves perhaps has had an influence. Thus, painting no longer favors a subject, music has abandoned programmatic notes, and sculpture concentrates upon mass and space. The emotions associated with the arts have, as a result, shifted. In many ways the short story provides the sudden insight once reserved for lyric poetry. On the other hand, the novel since James has taken to dramatizing subjects, and the major novelists in this century have annexed what remains of the epic, if not precisely the heroic. What the theatre can best trade upon remains problematic. If the term dr., as applied to poetry, now connotes praise, for the theatre itself it sounds almost pejorative, synonymous with commercial or, nearly, anti-poetic. Works belonging to the "Theatre of the Absurd" with their destructive tendencies drawn from early Dada and later existentialism have sought to destroy conventional language along with other middle-class clichés. Whatever originality such plays exhibit, their dialogue—or, frequently soliloquies even when involving two or more speakers—relies on prose whether sinewy as Beckett's or explosive as Genet's. The efforts of others to sustain a poetry sound puerile and not, unfortunately, by design. Dryden started "An Essay of Dramatic Poesy," "It was that memorable day, in the first summer of the late war," but removed his debaters from the conflict so they could discuss their points leisurely. At the moment, caught between the claims of disinterested art and engagement, the theatre has not yet hit upon any effective substitute for poetry. No one has recently succeeded in bringing forth any enduring verse for the stage, either. See also COMEDY AND TRAGEDY.

GENERAL: critical prefaces and essays of Aristotle, Sidney, Jonson, Lope de Vega, Corneille, Molière, Racine, Dryden, Johnson, Lessing, Schiller, Goethe, Coleridge, and Hugo; A. Nicoll, *Theory of Drama* (1923); G. Baty and R. Chavance, *Vie de l'art théâtral des origines à nos jours* (1932); E. A. Drew, *Discovering Drama* (1937); Wellek and Warren; M. E. Prior, *The Language of Tragedy* (1947); *Understanding Drama*, ed. C. Brooks and R. B. Heilman (1948); J. L. Barrault, *Reflections on the Theatre* (1951); S. H. Butcher, *Aristotle's Theory of Poetry and Fine Art* (4th ed., rev., 1951); M. McCarthy, *Sights and Spectacles* (1956); Frye; A. Artaud, *The Theater and Its Double* (1958).

SPECIALIZED STUDIES: N. Díaz de Escovar and F. de P. Lasso de la Vega, *Historia del teatro español* (2 v., 1924); W. B. Yeats, *Essays* (1924); H. C. Lancaster, *A Hist. of Fr. Dramatic Lit.* (1929-1942); E. E. Stoll, *Poets and Playwrights* (1930); C. V. Deane, *Dramatic Theory and the Rhymed Heroic Play* (1931); J. S. Kennard, *The It. Theatre* (2 v., 1932); T. S. Eliot, *Elizabethan Essays* (1943), *Poetry and Drama* (1951); H. Granville-Barker, *On Poetry in Drama* (1937); M. Bieber, *The Hist. of the Gr. and Roman Theater* (1939; 2d ed., 1961); U. Ellis-Fermor, *Frontiers of Drama* (1945); A. Nicoll, *The Development of the Theatre* (3d ed., rev., 1946); R. Peacock, *Poet in the Theatre* (1946); F. Fergusson, *Idea of a Theater* (1953); R. Langbaum, *The Poetry of Experience* (1957); R. Lattimore, *The Poetry of Gr. Tragedy* (1958); D. Donoghue, *The Third Voice: Modern British and Am. Verse Drama* (1959). J.J.E.

DRAME (*romantique*). A dramatic form of the 19th c. often written in prose. As concerned with Fr. poetry, the term is used in the sense discussed by Victor Hugo in his *Préface de Cromwell* (1827). The d. breaks from the "cage of the unities," keeping only unity of action, is impregnated with local color, avoids classical *récits* and seeks to offer a great amount of action on the stage. It keeps verse as a barrier against the commonplace and is faithful to rhyme, "that slave-queen" (Boileau had called rhyme only "a slave"); but its verse is freer than that of classicism, with enjambement

(q.v.) encouraged and displacement of the caesural pause. On occasion it develops a notable lyricism. Among characteristic weaknesses of the genre (exemplified in such plays as Hugo's *Hernani* [1830], *Le roi s'amuse* [1832], and *Ruy Blas* [1838]) are its melodramatic plots, exaggerated emotionality, and superficial characterization. It has been said with some justice that the d.r. of this sort differs from melodrama primarily in that it is in verse, is more literary, and ends unhappily. In the last quarter of the century such authors as Henri de Bornier, François Coppée, and Jean Richepin wrote plays in verse that mark a brief return to the d.r. The last great success in the genre is *Cyrano de Bergerac* (Dec. 1897) by Edmond Rostand.—E. Sée, *Le Théâtre français contemporain* (1928). A.G.E.

DRÁPA. An elaborate skaldic poem consisting of a number of stanzas in the same metrical pattern (often *dróttkvætt*, q.v.), with a refrain of 2 or more half-lines at regular intervals. Shorter court poems, without a refrain, were known as *flokkr*, and were regarded as inferior eulogistic offerings. With its resonant rhythmical effect the d. lent itself particularly well to impressive recitation in the presence of the king (or other chieftain) and his court. To this day Icelandic poets resort to the time-honored and sonorous d. form when they wish to write a eulogy of especially high order. A notable example from recent years is Einar Benediktsson's *Drápa* composed in honor of King Christian X of Iceland and Denmark and publicly recited in his presence during his visit to Iceland in 1921.—*The Skalds*, tr. and ed. L. M. Hollander (1945). R.B.

DREAM-ALLEGORY is one variety of the vision literature popular in the Middle Ages. The allegory may vary widely in purpose and extent and is often fused with other, frequently more interesting, elements. The framework, however, shows little variety. Springtime commonly provides the season. The poet finds himself in a pleasant wood or garden; falls asleep to the music of birds and brook; dreams; and in the dream beholds either real people performing symbolic actions or, more commonly, certain abstractions personified and going through a set of motions which to the conscious mind will have other significance. The type apparently received a major impulse from Macrobius' commentary upon the *Somnium Scipionis* in Cicero's imperfectly preserved *Republic*. Probably its best known representative, vastly influential, was the *Roman de la Rose*. In Eng., the type is best represented by Langland's *Piers Plowman;* and, among many others, both the anonymous *The Pearl* and Chaucer's *Parlement of Foules* have been considered dream-allegories.—E. Langlois, *Origines et sources du Roman de la Rose* (1891); W. H. Schofield, "The Nature and Fabric of *The Pearl*," PMLA, 19 (1904); E. Rickert, "A New Interpretation of *The Parlement* . . . ," MP, 18 (1920); C. S. Lewis, *The Allegory of Love* (1938); A. A. T. Macrobius, *Commentary on the Dream of Scipio*, tr. W. H. Stahl (1952); G. de Lorris and J. de Meun, *The Romance of the Rose*, tr. H. W. Robbins, ed. C. W. Dunn (1962). J.L.L.

DRÓTTKVÆTT (*dróttkvæðr háttr*). The elaborate and most common measure of skaldic poetry. Each stanza consists of 8 lines of 6 syllables, 3 of which are accented and 3 unaccented, with each line regularly ending in a trochee. Every 2 lines are bound together by alliteration, which must fall on the first stressed syllable of the second line, with 2 alliterations in the first line as well. This measure is also characterized by internal rhyme, full rhyme in the even lines, half rhyme (assonance) in the odd lines. Besides the extravagant use of kennings (q.v.), and other specific poetic vocabulary, the arrangement of words and the sentence structure are highly intricate. The following lines will illustrate the basic metrical rules generally observed:

Brunnu beggja kinna

björt ljos a mik drosar.

The d. measure, in all its main features, is already found in the remaining stanzas of *Ragnarsdrápa* by Bragi the Old (first half of 9th c.), who may even have devised this verse form. It has survived in Icelandic poetry down to the present day.—*The Skalds*, tr. and ed. L. M. Hollander (1945). R.B.

DUMY. See UKRAINIAN POETRY.

DURATION. The length of time phonetic phenomena (particularly syllables) continue. One of the four characteristics of a spoken sound, the others being pitch (q.v.), loudness, and quality. Since poetry is constructed of spoken sounds, duration of syllables, as well as of feet, lines, and stanzas, is an important consideration in analyzing the phonetic construction of a poem. The shortness of many of the important vowels in Pope's line

Not so, when swift Camilla scours the plain
(*Essay on Criticism* 2.372)

contributes to the effect of rapidity and delicacy which the line conveys. Some prosodists have attempted to explain accent (q.v.) in terms of d. P.F.

DUTCH POETRY. (Flemish poetry from the beginnings until 1600 is treated concurrently with D. poetry; for an account of FLEMISH POETRY from 1600 to the present, see the separate article on that subject.)

The earliest monuments of D. poetry are the works of Hendrik van Veldeke, a Fleming who lived during the latter part of the 12th c. The absence of any older vernacular literature may be attributed to the dominance of L. in both courtly and ecclesiastical circles, a dominance which is a recurrent complicating factor in the literary history of the Netherlands. Van Veldeke wrote a versified life of St. Servatius and a courtly romance epic, *Eneïde*, which shows a marked influence of Fr. courtly literature, as do his lyrics. The first great development of D. poetry occurred in the 13th c., reaching a climax in the religious verse of the Flemish nun and mystic Hadewych (fl. 1240). A creation of a very different sort is the beast-epic *Van den Vos Reinaerde* (Reynard the Fox), one of the finest of the genre, which may probably also be assigned to the early 13th c. It is an irreverent treatment of society, written with wit and charm, from a decidedly non-aristocratic point of view.

These works, the most important of the early period, typify the three main currents of medieval D. poetry—the courtly, the religious, and the bourgeois—related at once to different classes of society and to different ways of looking at experience. All three types of vision were to be of continuing importance in the intellectual and artistic history of Holland, and they were ultimately to give rise to a significant dichotomy which shaped that history. For D. poetry, in its later manifestations, was to tend toward extremes of bourgeois practicality and conformity and of individualistic aestheticism and revolt. The religious impulse itself was to find a double expression—in socially oriented didacticism and in unfettered mysticism.

Courtly, religious, and bourgeois elements were combined in the work of another Fleming, Jacob van Maerlant (ca. 1235–ca. 1288), who has sometimes been called "the father of D. poetry," a title he merits for productivity if for no other reason. In his early period he wrote courtly romances on the standard subjects of the aristocratic tradition—the quest for the Grail, the siege of Troy, and the legendary adventures of Alexander. Later, in his *Rijmbibel*, he treated religious themes, and in his compendious works of erudition—the *Spieghel Historiael* (Mirror of History) and *Der Naturen Bloeme* (Flowers of Nature)—he catered to the growing bourgeois taste for enlightenment and edification. Van Maerlant's importance is more cultural than artistic.

After the 14th c., a period of relatively little

poetic activity in the Low Countries, a new poetic period began. It manifested itself first in the *rederijkerskamers*, "Chambers of Rhetoric," (see REDERIJKERS), bourgeois poetic associations organized in Flanders and, later, in Holland. The *rederijkers* were interested primarily in the theater, and they carried the traditions of the morality play into the period of the Renaissance. *Elckerlyc* (ca. 1490), which was probably the source of the Eng. *Everyman,* was the most notable product of *rederijker* art. The members of the Chambers of Rhetoric also interested themselves in problems of language and metrics, and, though it is easy to be amused by their pedantry and their addiction to complex rules, one should not underestimate their role in laying a foundation for the great literary works of the 17th c. The practice of the *rederijkers,* for example, firmly established the rimed alexandrine couplet as the major vehicle for dramatic and heroic verse in D., and it was to remain the most important form for the next three centuries.

The influence of the It. Renaissance entered D. poetry in the early 16th c. in the work of the Flemings van der Noot and van Mander and the Hollanders van Hout and Coornhert. A kind of fusion of *rederijker* tradition and Renaissance influence is evident in the poetry of the later *rederijkers* Visscher and Spieghel, both residents of Amsterdam, which began to assume a position of cultural dominance after the fall of Antwerp in 1585. The 17th c., the greatest period in D. literature, was characterized by an emphasis on the drama and the lyric, and in both these forms one finds a typical mixture of native tradition with themes and techniques borrowed from the It. Renaissance. Pieter Corneliszoon Hooft (1581–1647) was the true founder of the poetic drama in Holland. Though he was a staunch Calvinist, his imagination was fired by the spirit of the southern Renaissance, which he experienced on a youthful trip to Italy. His plays, though written in the rimed alexandrines of his predecessors, follow the standard Renaissance models. *Granida* is a pastoral drama in the fashion of Guarini and Tasso, *Gerard van Velsen* is a Senecan tragedy, and *Warenar,* his best-known work, is based on the *Aulularia* of Plautus. Hooft's brilliant younger contemporary Gerbrand Adriaenszoon Bredero (1585–1618) worked more closely with the native tradition and was inspired primarily by his instinctive realism and his observing eye. *De Spaansche Brabander* (The Spanish Brabanter) is an excellent romantic comedy, but Bredero's distinctive art reaches its peak in his great *kluchten,* or farces, chief of which are *De Klucht van de Koe* (The Farce of the Cow) and *Der Klucht van de Molenaer* (The Farce

of the Miller). In these works the standard alexandrine couplet is treated with freedom and virtuosity; the strictness of the form never seems to conflict with the raucous quality of the action or the detailed realism of the observation.

Joost van den Vondel (1587–1679), the greatest of D. poets, is also the greatest D. dramatist. Master of a poetic style which suggests Milton in its sublimity, Vondel was at the same time more clearly the heir of the writers of the morality plays than were Hooft and Bredero. For his dramatic art is always ultimately ethical and devotional in its impulse, and these qualities are noticeable both in the early *Palamedes,* a political allegory attacking the strict Calvinists, and in the towering works of his maturity—*Lucifer* (1654), *Jephta* (1659), and *Adam in Ballingschap* (Adam in Banishment, 1663). The dramas of the early and middle years are of many different types. *Gijsbrecht van Aemstel,* one of his finest works, is an historical and patriotic drama, which, through its sympathetic presentation of Catholic ritual (a symptom of Vondel's approaching conversion to that faith), aroused the ire of the more intransigent Amsterdam Protestants. *Maagden* (The Maidens), a work of the same period, is a dramatized saint's legend, and *De Leeuwendalers* is an idyllic pastoral drama. But Vondel's mature dramatic powers expressed themselves in a long series of remarkable biblical dramas in which the spirit of the old morality plays is given Sophoclean form and articulation. Particularly noteworthy are *Lucifer,* probably his masterpiece, and *Jephta.* The expansiveness and sublimity of *Lucifer,* in both conception and imagery, contrast with the restrained inevitability of *Jephta,* and the contrast suggests the range of the poet's powers. Most of Vondel's plays are written basically in alexandrine couplets. *Jephta,* however, utilizes a five-beat couplet which Vondel handles with equal skill. A noteworthy feature of all his dramas is the use of choruses, which are written in a variety of free and strikingly lyrical forms. The choruses of *Gijsbrecht van Aemstel* and *Lucifer* are among his finest achievements. Vondel's nondramatic production is immense —elegies, epithalamia, poems of description— expressed in a wide variety of forms, many of them utilizing internal rime endings and a skillful repetition of the diminutive endings in which the D. language abounds. One should also mention his political poems, his satires, his occasional pieces, and his epic, *Johannes de Boetgezandt* (John the Baptist).

Vondel's fellow-Amsterdammers, Hooft and Bredero, are also noted for their lyric poetry, and in their lyrics we find an illuminating formal contrast. Hooft, the Italianate aristocrat, is a master of metrical variety. He is

particularly fond of the contrapuntal interplay of rime and line length, as exhibited in
the following passage:

Amaryl, de deken sacht
   Van de nacht,
Met sijn blaewe wolken buijen,
Maeckt de starren sluimerblint
   En de wint
Soeckt de maen in slaep te suijen.

Amaryl, the cover light
   Of the night,
With its bluish clouds aheap,
Makes the stars all slumber-blind,
   And the wind
Seeks to lull the moon asleep.
                    (tr. F. J. Warnke)

Noteworthy also is his tendency to substitute
anapestic movement for the dominant D.
iambics. Bredero, on the other hand, adheres
more closely to the metrics of the folk song,
and at his best he achieves the deceptive simplicity of that form.

In their imagery, the three great Amster-
dammers show a common love for the pictorial
and the detailed, a kind of imaginative observation of the visible world which allies
them to the great D. painters and which serves
to define one of the continuing characteristics
of D. poetic tradition. If Vondel has a special
kinship to a painter, it is to Rubens, in the
lushly Baroque magnificence of his conceptions. Bredero, in contrast, has more affinity
with the realistic genre painters, with Jan
Steen and Frans Hals.

The great poetry of the D. Renaissance was
not confined to the Amsterdam circle. To the
west, in the vicinity of The Hague, two other
poets of note were active—Jacob Cats and Con-
stantijn Huygens. Cats is the bourgeois poet
par excellence. His didactic verse, devoted to
the ethics of practicality, codified homely advice on subjects ranging from home economics
to sexual intercourse. He became the most
widely quoted of D. poets, but his reputation
has undergone an inevitable decline. His friend
Huygens is a poet of a very different sort. An
admirer of John Donne and of Rembrandt,
he is one of the "metaphysical poets" of Holland. But his love for the conceit is noticeable primarily in his epigrams and in his
translations of Donne's *Songs and Sonets*. His
long descriptive pieces, *Batava-Tempe* and
Hofwijck, have more in common with the poetry of Sir John Denham than with that of
Donne. Jan Starter, a follower of Bredero, and
the religious poets Revius, Camphuyzen, Stal-
paert, and Dullaert should also be mentioned.
The last great poet of the Golden Century was
Jan Luyken, whose religious verse is among the
finest written in Holland.

Toward the end of the 17th c., a decline in
the quality of D. poetry initiated a period of
relative barrenness which was to last for two
centuries. The lyric tradition of Vondel declined in the hands of his last disciple,
Antonides van de Goes, and the drama, already
decadent in the sensation-seeking work of
Jan Vos, was given its death-blow by the
derivative neoclassicism preached by *Nil Volentibus Arduum* (q.v.), an Amsterdam poetic society which flourished between 1669 and 1681.
D. poetry of the 18th c. is characterized by a
consistent but futile striving to escape the
double bondage of an imported neoclassicism
and a moribund poetic diction. Hubert
Corneliszoon Poot, a lyric poet from a peasant
background, spoiled his gift for natural observation by imitating the mythological machinery of Hooft. Other poets of the period
attempted to revivify their country's poetry by
introducing ideas and models from England
and Germany. But H. van Alphen, who was
influenced by Lessing, Klopstock, and Riedel,
was a better critic than poet, and Rhijnvis
Feith, who at a later date imitated the graveyard poetry of Young and Blair in *Het Graf*
(The Grave), was less talented than his models,
and even more lugubrious.

The greatest poetic figure of Holland between 1700 and 1880 was Willem Bilderdijk
(1756–1831), and he is, today as in his own
time, a controversial figure. The paradox of
his nature, at once rationalistic and romantic,
Calvinistic and passionate, did not prevent him
from being one of the most prolific of D. poets,
though it did, in all probability, lead to
internal conflicts which prevented him from
ever achieving the coherent artistic expression which the poetry of his country needed.
His production embraced lyrics, dramas, didactic pieces, long narrative poems (*Elias, Urzijn
en Valentijn*), an unfinished epic entitled *De
Ondergang der Eerste Wereld* (The Fall of the
First World), and a series of ballads, imitated
from Eng. and Scottish sources, which are
among his best works.

But the deficiencies of Bilderdijk's art are
manifest in the work of his disciples, Da
Costa and Tollens, who are remembered as
perhaps the most reputable poets of the most
sterile age of Holland's poetry, the early 19th c.
I. Da Costa's ponderous didacticism has not
worn well, and H. Tollens' *De Overwintering
op Nova Zembla* (The Winter on Nova
Zembla), once praised as a high point in D.
descriptive poetry, is now felt to be a futile
set-piece composed of superficial rhetoric and
facile sentimentality. The triumph of bourgeois sensibility was complete in the Holland
of the post-Napoleonic period, and that sensibility no longer seemed to possess the moral
courage of Bilderdijk, the eloquence of Vondel,

or even the stalwart common sense of Jacob Cats. In such an atmosphere, the romanticism which dominated European letters could find no roots, and the two D. poets of the period who may be classified as "romantics"—van Lennep and Beets—are only the palest reflections of their respective models, Scott and Byron.

As the 19th c. progressed, bolder spirits in D. artistic and intellectual circles grew indignant at the low state to which their country's poetry had fallen. With his friend, the critic Coenrad Busken Huet, E. G. Potgieter founded *De Gids* (The Guide), a review dedicated to the revival of literary and intellectual vitality. As a poet, Potgieter was handicapped by a temperament which was too self-conscious and critical, a style which was too ponderously learned and allusive. But his example simplified the work of his great successors.

The decade of the 1880's was one of the most significant in the history of D. literature. For at that time a group of gifted, iconoclastic, and energetic young poets set to work to revive their country's poetry and to place it once more on the level of general European poetry. The great names of the *Beweging van Tachtig* (Movement of the Eighties) (see TACHTIGERS) are Willem Kloos (1859–1938), Frederick van Eeden (1860–1932), Albert Verwey (1865–1937), and Herman Gorter (1864–1927). The first three founded *De Nieuwe Gids* (The New Guide), a review which, in its very name, aimed at following newer paths than even the more progressive elements of the immediate past. The work of the *tachtigers* was not entirely without forerunners. D. poetry in the 1870's had received tremendous impetus from the publication of the sonnet sequence *Mathilde* by the precocious and gifted Jacques Perk (1859–1881), who had reintroduced into D. poetry that important form which had been neglected since the days of Hooft. Perk's mastery of the sonnet form was only one manifestation of his metrical virtuosity. His *Iris* displays a flexibility of meter which had been sorely lacking in the poetry of the 18th and 19th c.:

Ik ben geboren uit zonne-gloren
En een zucht van de ziedende zee,
Die omhoog is gestegen, op wieken van regen,
Gezwollen van wanhoop en wee . . .

I was born of the streams of the morning's
　　beams
And a sigh of the surging sea,
Ascending again on wings of the rain,
Swollen with tears and dismay.
　　　　　　　　　　(tr. F. J. Warnke)

The meter is immediately recognizable as that of Shelley's *The Cloud,* on which *Iris* is based, and the young poet's allegiance to the Eng. romantics was also prophetic of the direction to be given D. verse by Kloos and Gorter. Kloos was important both as poet and critic. The sonnets contained in his *Verzen* of 1894 and 1895 are among the finest in the language, and his motto, "De aller-individueelste expressie van de aller-individueelste emotie" (The most individual expression of the most individual emotion), summed up the estheticism, realism, and individualism which were the artistic goals of his group. Gorter's *Mei* (1889) is one of the most ambitious European poems of the century. Of novel-length, it is a narrative poem with epic overtones and passages of lyric beauty. It is clearly suggestive of Keats' *Endymion*, both in its mythopoeic power and in its metrical features—loosely enjambed pentameter couplets varied with lyric passages in more irregular meter. But it is essentially an original poem, in the course of which Nordic mythology becomes fused with meticulous observation of nature in its cyclic changes.

The group centering around *De Nieuwe Gids* had, in their exaltation of individualism and in their advocacy of passion and realism in both imagery and emotion, revived two of the constant elements of D. culture—respect for the individual and delight in accurate visual representation. Their doctrine of "art for art's sake," however, left out of account a third element of D. tradition—concern for the community, for the collective whole—which had given their nation's culture its distinctive bourgeois quality and which was expressing itself, politically and economically, in the great achievements of late 19th-c. D. liberalism. So it was on the issues of individualism and art for art's sake that the *Nieuwe Gids* group dissolved around 1890. Kloos, the intransigent individualist, remained loyal to his original ideals, but his influence steadily waned. Verwey, after a period of silence, produced in his *Aarde* (Earth) (1896) the product of his contemplation, a kind of poetry devoted more to the inner life than to the external realities which had consumed his interest in the days of *tachtig*. Van Eeden, novelist, poet, and dramatist, the most versatile member of the group, began the long spiritual pilgrimage which was to lead him through Utopian socialism to the Roman Catholic Church, a pilgrimage which he documented in his lengthy *Het Lied van Schijn en Wezen* (The Song of Appearance and Reality), a philosophical poem in skillful terza rima, which stands with his dramatic poem *De Broeders* (The Brothers) among the most important works of the tachtigers. Gorter, after the publication of *Mei*, devoted himself to the cause of the proletariat. His communism found expression in *Klein Heldendicht* (Little Epic) (1906), an unsuccessful attempt to write traditional heroic verse with a symbolic worker as hero. But Gorter's proletarianism was essentially an intellectual effort; basically he remained a bourgeois liberal whose individualism expressed itself in such experimental work as his *Sensitieve Verzen*. Eng. romanticism remained the strongest influence on the *Beweging van Tachtig*, but it was modified by Fr. and German influences, notably that of Stefan George on Verwey, who was his close friend.

In a short time the poets of *tachtig* had done their work, and on the foundation laid by them the poets of the 20th c. continued to build. Verwey had perhaps the greatest influence on the younger generation, through his important journal, *De Beweging* (The Movement) (founded 1905). But before passing to the more recent poets of Holland, one must consider the work of three important poets who stand between the generation of the 1880's and that of the first World War—J. H. Leopold (1865–1925), Henriette Roland-Holst (1869–1952), and Pieter Corneliszoon Boutens (1870–1943). Leopold, considered by many to be Holland's greatest lyric poet since Vondel, was influenced to some degree by the aestheticist and individualist doctrines of the tachtigers, but finely organized lyrics such as his famous *O Nachten van Gedragene Extase* (O Nights of Ecstasy's Duress) show the influence of his classical training. Boutens resembles Leopold both in his classicism and in his introspectiveness, but his Platonic inner vision is modified by a passionate sensitivity to external nature; he ranks with Gorter as modern Holland's supreme poet of nature, and none of his contemporaries has so well rendered the distinctive beauty of that flat, misty, and infinitely various land. Henriette van Roland Holst displayed in her work a movement from nature poetry to poetry of social protest, and in her proletarianism she has links both to Gorter and to the popular socialist poet Adama van Scheltema.

D. poetry of the 20th c. has partaken of the variety characteristic of modern poetry as a whole, and has shown an increasing tendency to share in international artistic and intellectual movements. Rilke, George, Verlaine, and Yeats have been important influences on such followers of Verwey as Martinus Nijhoff and Adriaan Roland Holst, and China has influenced the poetry of J. J. Slauerhoff as India influenced that of his older contemporary J. A. Der Mouw. A vigorous expressionist movement under the leadership of the gifted Hendrik Marsman (1899–1940) dominated the poetry of the 1920's, but called forth a reaction in the more socially oriented work of the group centering around the periodical *Forum*,

the most important members of which were the critic Menno Ter Braak and the poet and novelist Simon Vestdijk, perhaps the most influential writer in contemporary Holland. More recently, D. poetry has received important impetus from the "moderate surrealists" Gerrit Achterberg and Ed. Hoornik, and the Catholic Bertus Aafjes. The current generation of D. poets, including such names as Lucebert, Gerrit Kouwenaar, and Remco Campert, shows energy and promise.

Despite a healthy diversity in both style and outlook, D. poetry of the 20th c. has developed organically from the romantic revival of the 1880's. It has, while ratifying its membership in the international world of art and thought, consistently adhered to those preoccupations which are the historical heritage of the D.—the honest and vivid representation of observed reality and the untiring exploration of the delicate relationship which exists between the individual and the community.

ANTHOLOGIES: *Zeven Eeuwen*, ed. K. H. de Raaf and J. J. Griss (4 v., 1932; a crit. anthol.); *Coming After*, ed. A. J. Barnouw (1948); *Spiegel van de Nederlandse Poëzie door alle Eeuwen*, ed. V. E. van Vriesland (3 v., 1953–55); *Een Inleiding tot Vondel*, ed. A. Verwey (n.d.; a generous sel. of Vondel's works, with crit. comments).

HISTORY AND CRITICISM: E. Gosse, *Studies in the Lit. of Northern Europe* (1879); H. J. C. Grierson, *The First Half of the 17th C.* (1906; excellent chapters on D. poetry of that period); G. Kalff, *Studiën over Nederlandsche Dichters der 17de Eeuw* (1915); H. Robbers, *De Nederl. Litt. na 1880* (1922); A. J. Barnouw, *Vondel* (1925; a biog. in Eng.); H. J. C. Grierson, *Two D. Poets* (1936; studies of Hooft and Boutens); J. A. Russell, *D. Poetry and Eng.* (1939); G. Knuvelder, *Handboek tot de Geschiedenis der Nederl. Letterkunde* (4 v., 2d ed., 1957); Th. Weevers, *Poetry of the Netherlands in its European Context* (1960); F. Baur *et al.*, *Geschiedenis van de Letterkunde der Nederlanden* (7 v. to date, 1939– ; this ambitious work will be, when completed, the definitive hist. of D. lit.); P. Brachin, *La Littérature néerlandaise* (1963). F.J.W.

DYFALU. A poetic technique in Welsh poetry which reaches its highest excellence in the work of Dafydd ap Gwilym (14th c.), but which long remained current practice, and after its degeneration was ridiculed by Ellis Wynne in his *Visions of the Sleeping Bard* (1703). The term also means to guess and has affinities with the riddle poem. D., at its best, is an animated play of fancy, whereby the object on which the poet's mind dwells—it may be the stars, or mist, or a bird, a girl's yellow hair, or her white arms—is rapidly compared in a concatenation of metaphors of strong visual imagery, with other objects in nature. The stars are the sparks of a conflagration lit by the saints, berries belonging to the frozen moon, the reflection of hail on the sun's bright floor. This onrush of metaphors is well suited by its exuberance to convey Dafydd ap Gwilym's exciting vision of the ever renewed miracle of creation. Other poets, such as Dafydd Nanmor, in the 15th c., employ the same device with fine effect, but later it became mechanical and stereotyped.—Parry.　　　　　D.M.L.

E

ECHO. Any recurrence of the same sound or combination of sounds at intervals near enough to be perceptible to the ear. Thus, alliteration, assonance, consonance, near-rhyme, rhyme, repetend, and refrain (qq.v.) all constitute kinds of echo. Used either internally or terminally, such repetitions are a means of "orchestrating" verse, may be used both for their musical appeal and as a means of structuring verse by linking words or lines related in meaning. Poe's line "The viol, the violet, and the vine" shows an obvious compact use of echoes, as does Bridges' "In secret sensuous innocence."—A. Oras, "Surrey's Technique of Phonetic Echoes: A Method and Its Background," JEGP, 50 (1951).　　　　　L.P.

ECHO VERSE. A line (or, usually, a poem of such lines) of which the final syllables are repeated, as by an echo, so as to provide a reply or a comment, often a punning one. E.g., "Qu'est-ça du monde la chose la plus infame? Femme!" (G. du Pont, 1539); "Echo! What shall I do to my Nymph when I go to behold her? Hold her!" (Barnabe Barnes, 1593). Echo verse goes back to the *Gr. Anthology*, the earliest known example being by Gauradas. It flourished in Western Europe in Fr., It., and Eng. verse of the 16th and 17th c. Found most often as a device of pastoral poetry or drama, it has unrequited love as its commonest subject, but has also been used for religious poetry, political satire, and society verse. Well-known examples are George Herbert's *Heaven* and Swift's *A Gentle Echo on Woman.*—E. Colby, *The Echo-Device in Lit.* (1920).　　　　　L.P.

ECLOGUE. A short, conventional poem, usually a pastoral, in the form of a dialogue or soliloquy. Ordinarily it is without appreciable characterization or action; the setting, described either by the poet or by one of the characters, is objective; and the highly finished verse is smooth and melodious. Originally the word, derived from *eklegein* (to choose), meant "a choice poem." The spelling *aeglogue* (or *eglog*), popularized by Dante, was based on the false etymology which derived the word from *aix* (goat) and *logos* (speech) and was construed to signify, as "E. K." argued, "Goteheards tales." The term was first applied to Virgil's bucolic poems, and from this association became the designation of a formal pastoral poem following the traditional technique derived from the idylls of Theocritus. Though there are precedents in both classical and Renaissance literature of city and piscatory eclogues, most eclogues are pastorals. The term, however, signifies nothing more than structure. The Renaissance was the heyday of the eclogue. Negligible as a genre in the Middle Ages, it was revived by Dante, Petrarch, and Boccaccio and came to full flower under the culture of the humanists of the 15th and 16th c. Widely studied and of dominating influence (as evidenced by Shakespeare's well-known comment, "Ah, good old mantuan! . . . who understandeth thee not, loves thee not") were the eclogues of Baptista Mantuanus Spagnuoli. Still considered the best modern examples of the genre are those by Garcilaso de la Vega and Edmund Spenser. Pope's eclogues, though called *Pastorals*, epitomize the neoclassic eclogue and rococo art. In the 18th c. new matter was poured into the mold and a variety of eclogues—town, exotic, political, war, school, culinary, Quaker—was produced. The most celebrated of the nonpastoral eclogues is Swift's *A Town Eclogue. 1710. Scene, The Royal Exchange.* See PASTORAL, GEORGIC.—M. H. Shackford, "A Definition of the Pastoral Idyll," PMLA, 19 (1904); W. W. Greg, *Pastoral Poetry and Pastoral Drama* (1906); W. P. Mustard, "Introduction" to *The Piscatory Eclogues of Jacopo Sannazaro* (1914), and "Notes on *The Shepheardes Calendar*," MLN, 35 (1920); R. F. Jones, "E. Types in Eng. Poetry of the 18th C.," JEGP, 34 (1925); M. K. Bragg, *The Formal E. in 18th C. England* (1926); D. Lessig, *Ursprung und Entwicklung der spanischen Ekloge . . .* (1962).　　　　　J.E.C.

EGO-FUTURISM. An ephemeral movement in early 20th-c. Rus. poetry. The term was coined by, and is mostly used with reference to, Igor

EGYPTIAN POETRY

Severyanin (1887-1942), whose tuneful, gaudy and blatantly egotistical verses enjoyed a brief vogue on the eve of World War I. Outside of its name, a distinct proclivity for neologism and a shrill rejection of the literary tradition, e.-f. had little in common with the more creative variety of Rus. futurist poetry, as represented by V. Khlebnikov and the early Mayakovsky. See CUBO-FUTURISM.—D. S. Mirsky, *A Hist. of Rus. Lit.* (1949); *An Anthol. of Rus. Verse,* ed. A. Yarmolinsky (1962).   V.E.

EGYPTIAN POETRY. The prosody of ancient Eg. is not fully known to us. Since the writing does not take note of vowels, we are not able to judge the relations between long and short measures. But the facility with which one word can replace another of a different number of syllables suggests that Eg. prosody was based on a succession of fairly free rhythmic accents rather than on a system of quantities.

The scribes who copied the poems have at times separated verses by a red point. Most frequently, the form does not permit distinguishing poetry from prose. So we waver. For example, should the moral works known as *Wisdom Texts* be considered prose because of their plain tone and the rarity of images or rather as very simple poetry, whose rhythm attracted attention and made it easier to remember?

In the Old Kingdom, besides the *Wisdom Texts,* the largest collection is that from the pyramids. But these inscriptions—which comprise narrations, incantations, invocations intended to promote the passage of the soul of the king in the other world—have, despite certain poetic resonances, more interest to the student of religion than to the student of poetry.

One of the first works of true poetry, which admirably represents the noblest kind, is a sort of *ode* from the period of trouble which followed the Old Kingdom, inserted in *The Dialogue of the Despairing Man with his Soul.* Because of the violence of his time, the unhappy man wishes to die in order to find justice in the beyond: "Death is before me today / Like health for the invalid / Like going out after an illness. / Death is before me today / Like the odor of myrrh, / Like sitting under the sail on a windy day . . . / Death is before me today / Like the desire of a man to see his home again / After numberless years of captivity." The poetry is characterized here by an abundance of images, and the human profundity of emotion. The regularity of the refrain and the parallelism of ideas produce patterned stanzas. Official poetry has always preferred this lyricism of fixed composition, whose fault, when the sentiment weakens, is to fall into formalism.

At the beginning of the Middle Kingdom, about 2000 B.C., a celebrated writer, Khety, composed—besides *The Instructions of King Amenemhet I to his Son,* intended to reinforce the renascent order—a spirited arraignment of the different professions, in order to proclaim as unrivaled that of scribe. He also composed a *Hymn to the Nile* in which inspiration causes the poet to abandon the formal framework of the traditional hymn. In this hymn, rich and poor, great and small fraternize in the joy of seeing the Nile, at the expected moment, fertilize Egypt with its inundation. To the end of the Middle Kingdom belongs the *Song of the Harper,* which celebrated, for a King Intef, the pleasure of living contrasted to the prospective annihilation of death. This is an anticipation of Horace's *carpe diem* theme.

In the New Kingdom, some poems reiterate in free stanzas the invitation to rejoice in life, but blend with it the hope that simple and pure joys are only an initial stage of the happiness reserved for the just in the other world. A second harpist, in the Theban tomb of Neferhotep, at the middle of the 14th c. B.C., replies to the first by a *Song of Trust in Death,* where all those who are loved and who love repose in peace in a mysterious union.

But one must not think that death was the most popular subject of Eg. poetry. The victories of the Pharaoh and the relief that he brings to the country menaced or struck by invasions, are brilliantly celebrated in several epic pieces, of which the best known is the recital of *The Battle of Qadesh.* In this poem Ramses II, before the Syrian town of Qadesh, unperturbed in the middle of the attacking wave of Asiatics, single-handedly saves the situation, thanks to his youthful courage and his unshakable confidence in his father, the great god Amon.

In the first half of the 14th c. B.C. another king, Amenophis IV, who had become the impassioned advocate of a monotheistic reform of the Eg. religion, addressed to his sole god, visible in this world under the aspect of the sun, personal hymns which are splendid effusions of the heart and spirit before the divinity who is glimpsed in nature:

"All who fly and flap (their) wings / Live again at your rising. / Ships emulously go up and down the river, / Every way is open because you appear; / The river fish jump before your face, / Your rays go to the heart of the sea. /

"You develop the germ in women / And of the seed make men, / Supporting the son at the breast of his mother / And soothing him so that he does not cry. . . . / The chick in the egg speaks while in the shell, / For you give it breath inside in order to make it live."

The hymns which have such a broad religious scope and which sacrifice mythological allusions and theological ideas to a spirituality strictly poetic are much influenced by profane poetry, which is above all a poetry of love.

The New Kingdom has left us a whole series of compilations of love poems. Small pieces are grouped together so as probably to constitute entire programs of entertainment (we would say "soirées"), designed to refresh the attention of the audience sometimes by the diversity of tone and sometimes, conversely, by the linking together of the poems into a kind of small novel or psychological dialogue. The form, apparently, is that of free verse in a composition itself often free. It is a *poetry of feeling*, grave or vivacious, humorous or tender, in which the impulses of the heart matter more than those of the senses. It is alive with appreciation of nature. Often the scene is a garden. The charm of the flowers and the birds envelops the charm of the maidens. Anxious lovers seek to console themselves before a beautiful landscape. Often these lovers are in quite humble circumstances. In a small house, the young man, in the midst of his own, watches for the passing-by of his sweetheart, who delights in awaiting his look: "I passed near his house; / I found the door open, / My friend remained beside his mother, / All his brothers and sisters with him. / They are taken with sympathy for him, / All those who pass on the way. . . . / He looked at me when I passed. . . ."
The indications of place are seen to be exact and graphic, but fleeting, the ebb and flow of impressions counting infinitely more than external facts.

It is probably by this poetry, young and fresh under the sun, that Egypt touches us the most. In antiquity the Hebrews drew inspiration from it in the Song of Songs, less restrained and more passionate; and perhaps Theocritus in his dialogues, composed in part in Egypt, has enlarged the model of the alternating songs of Sicily after the example of the Eg. poems of love when he awakens our sympathy for modest and ingenuous lovers endowed with the most delicate sensibilities.

G. Maspero, "Les chants d'amour du papyrus de Turin et du papyrus Harris 500," *Etudes égyptiennes*, I (1886) and *Causeries d'Egypte* (1907); W. M. Müller, *Die Liebespoesie der alten Ägypter* (1889); *Ägyptische Sonnenlieder*, ed. and tr. A. Scharff (1922); *Anthol. of Ancient Eg. Poems*, ed. S. Elissa Sharpley (1923); H. Ranke and H. Gressmann, *Altorientalische Texte zum alten Testament* (1926); A. Erman, *The Lit. of the Ancient Egyptians*, tr. A. M. Blackman (1927); A. Moret, "Chants d'amour de la vieille Egypte," *Revue de Paris* (Feb. 1, 1930); A. H. Gardiner, *The Library of A. Chester Beatty* (1931); T. E. Peet, *A Comparative Study of the Literatures of Egypt, Palestine and Mesopotamia* (1931); A. and J. Baillet, "La chanson chez les Egyptiens," *Mélanges Maspero*, I, Orient ancien 1934; P. Gilbert, *La poésie égyptienne* (1943, 2d ed., 1949); M. Lichtheim, "The Songs of the Harpers," *Jour. of Near Eastern Studies*, 4 (1945); M. Murray, *Eg. Religious Poetry* (1949); *Altägyptische Liebeslieder*, ed. and tr. S. Schott (1950); A. Hermann, "Zur ägyptischen Lit.," "Zur ägyptischen Stilistik," both in *Orientalische Literatur Zeitung*, 50 (1955) and *Altägyptische Liebesdichtung* (1959); B. de Rachewiltz, *Liriche amorose degli antichi Egiziani* (1955); I. Donadoni, *Storia della letteratura egiziana antica* (1957); G. Nolli, *Canti d'amore dell' antico Egitto* (1959). P.G. (tr. R.A.P.)

EISTEDDFOD (bardic session or assembly). A main feature of Welsh literary activity which can be traced back with certainty to the 15th c. and perhaps to the bardic festival held by Lord Rhys in 1176 at Cardigan. The early e. was an assembly of the guild or order of bards, convened under the aegis of a distinguished patron, and in the 16th c. even under royal commission. The chief function was to regulate the affairs of the profession, such as the establishment of metrical rules, and the issue of licenses to those who had completed the prescribed stages of their apprenticeship. Awards were also granted for outstanding achievements in poetry and music. The most important of these *eisteddfodau* were Carmarthen (ca. 1450), and Caerwys (1523 and 1568). Decay then set in, and the institution degenerated to the tavern *eisteddfodau* of the 18th c. These were meetings of poetasters, announced in almanacks, and mere scenes of disputations in very indifferent verse. After a period of decline, the e. were revived during the 19th c. Today the National E. of Wales is a cultural festival of wide range and influence which provides for poetry, prose, drama, massed choirs and other vocal and instrumental music. It has given much needed patronage and publicity to poetry and has enabled several important literary critics to impose standards and to mold literary taste. D.M.L.

ELEGIAC DISTICH. The Gr. *elegeion* (a word of uncertain derivation which first occurs in Critias frag. 4.31 Diehl) was a distich or couplet which was composed of a heroic or dactylic hexameter followed by a pentameter (q.v.). As is shown by Ovid's address to *flebilis Elegeia* (*Amores* 3.9.3), the word was connected in antiquity with the later meaning of *elegos* ("song of mourning" as in Euripides and Apollonius Rhodius 2.782), but its use for epitaphs and laments is probably not quite so ancient as its beginnings in the 8th or 7th c. B.C. with flute songs (Archilochus, Callinus, Mimnermus), war songs (Tyrtaeus), and dedications. It was used for many purposes in the classical age of Greece and, notably but by no means exclusively, for love poems in the Alexandrian, Roman, and Byzantine periods. In L. the Augustan elegiac poets (Tibullus, Propertius, and Ovid) tended to make the sense coincide with the couplet, whereas in Gr. poetry and Catullus it was often continuous for two or more distichs. Among the refinements which in time became regular in the Roman elegists and particularly in Ovid was the restriction of the final word in the pentameter to a dissyllable.

The classic description and imitation of the elegiac distich in the accentual verse of a modern language is Schiller's couplet:

Im Hexameter steigt des Springquells flüssige Säule,
Im Pentameter drauf fällt sie melodisch herab,

which Coleridge thus reproduced:

In the hexameter rises the fountain's silvery column,
In the pentameter aye falling in melody back.

The form has been imitated in Eng. by Spenser, Sidney, Clough, Kingsley, and Swinburne and, in German, by Klopstock and Goethe in addition to Schiller. (See also CLASSICAL METERS IN MODERN LANGUAGES).—Hardie; Hamer; D. L. Page, "The Elegiacs in Euripides' Andromache," Gr. Poetry and Life (1936); C. M. Bowra, Early Gr. Elegists (1938, repr. 1960); M. Platnauer, L. Elegiac Verse (1951); Koster; M. L. Clarke, "The Hexameter in Gr. Elegiacs," CR, n.s. 5 (1955); D. A. West, "The Metre of Catullus' Elegiacs," CQ, n.s. 7 (1957). R.J.G.

ELEGIAC STANZA (also known as elegiac quatrain, heroic quatrain, Hammond's meter). The iambic pentameter quatrain, rhymed abab, has apparently acquired the name of elegiac stanza through its use by Thomas Gray for Elegy Written in a Country Churchyard (1751). It is identical in form with the quatrain used in Shakespearean sonnets, where its use has no elegiac connotations, and it was frequently employed without elegiac feeling or intention by other poets, e.g., Dryden in his Annus Mirabilis. However, according to W. J. Bate (The Stylistic Development of Keats, 1945), the pentameter quatrain was "almost invariably employed for the writing of elegiac verse" from about the middle of the 18th c. until almost a century later, beginning with James Hammond's Love Elegies (1743). But even Gray's use of the form in his great poem failed to establish a quatrain tradition, both Shelley's Adonais and Arnold's Thyrsis being written in more complex stanzas. S.F.F.

ELEGIAMB(US). In Gr. and L. metric a dactylic (generally hemiepes, q.v.) followed by an iambic colon, e.g., Horace, Epodes 11.2:

$$scr\bar{\imath}b\bar{e}r\breve{e} \mid v\bar{e}rs\breve{\imath}c\breve{u}|l\bar{o}s \mid\mid \breve{a}m\bar{o}|r\breve{e} \ p\breve{e}r|c\bar{u}ss\bar{u}m \mid gr\breve{a}v\bar{\imath}$$

(hemiepes and iambic dimeter acatalectic) . See ARCHILOCHIAN and IAMBELEGUS. R.J.G.

ELEGY (from Gr. elegeia, "lament"). A lyric, usually formal in tone and diction, suggested either by the death of an actual person or by the poet's contemplation of the tragic aspects of life. In either case, the emotion, originally expressed as a lament, finds consolation in the contemplation of some permanent principle. Any discussion of the origin of the e. is complicated by a shifting of definitions. The term in Gr. literature referred both to a specific verse form (couplets consisting of a hexameter followed by a pentameter line) and to the emotions frequently conveyed by that verse form. Originally, any poem in this distich form (with the exception of the epigram) was known as an e., whether it concerned the dead, was a war song, a political satire, or dealt with love. The pastoral laments, such as those of Theocritus, which seem in subject matter to be prototypes of the modern elegy, were classed by the Greeks as idylls. The distich form of e. was employed by the Alexandrian Greeks chiefly for erotic and suggestive verse. The Latin e. itself was initially distinguished from other literary genres by the distich meter, the tone of complaint, and the theme of love, as in Gallus, Propertius, Tibullus, and their successors. In Ovid the distich and the tone of complaint are already extended to other subjects as in Tristia and Ex Ponto, although love remains his dominant theme.

In early 16th-c. Italy, when other experiments in the imitation of classic meters were being made, the content and subject matter of the e. were taken over into terza rima by such writers as Bernardo Tasso and Ariosto, whose Rime and Satire received the label of elegies only after his death. The elegiac strain of extended lyrics expressing melancholy and tender sentiments was represented in the baroque period by Filicaia and continued into 19th-c. It. letters by Leopardi and Carducci. In modern times there have even been metrical experiments with the classic distich by D'Annunzio.

In Spain, the e. began as imitations of It. models, as in Garcilaso de la Vega's First

Eclogue (ca. 1535) on the death of his lady, in the tradition of the pastoral e. and in some of his other poems modeled upon the work of Bernardo Tasso. Lope de Vega (1562-1635) used octaves and other stanzaic measures in imitation of Tasso for his elegiac verse. In the present century, the prevailing tone of Juan Ramón Jiménez in his *Arias Tristes* and *Elegías* is melancholy and elegiac. The work of Federico García Lorca, in *Elegía a Doña Juana La Loca* and *Llanto por Ignacio Sánchez Mejías* shows a more direct obsession with the presentiments of death.

In France, the first attempt at copying the e. form from the ancients was by imitating the classic distich in alexandrine couplets, alternating masculine and feminine rhymes, later by alternating decasyllabic with octosyllabic lines, an experiment of Jean Doublet in his *Élégies,* 1559. Ronsard, in his *Élégies, Mascarades, et Bergeries,* 1565, abandoned the attempt to reproduce the classical meter and returned to the subject matter of the classical elegists. This treatment of the e. was also adopted by Louise Labé and Malherbe. In *l'Art Poétique,* Boileau insists on themes either of love or death for the e., and the genre comes to deal in the 18th c. with the tender and the melancholy rather than with deep grief. The climax of this tendency was reached with André Chenier, at the end of the century:

Mais la tendre élégie et sa grace touchante
M'ont séduit; l'élégie à la voix gémissante,
Aux ris mêlés de pleurs, aux longs cheveux
　　épars,
Belle, levant au ciel ses humides regards.

After Lamartine's *Méditations,* 1820, the elegiac tendency in Fr. literature becomes confused with others, and whole poems in the genre appear only sporadically.

In Germany, the subject matter of the e. has been so little restricted that Sir Edmund Gosse could say that the e. as a poem of lamentation does not exist in Germany. There had been a number of attempts during the Renaissance to write elegies in L., but it remained for Opitz, in the early 17th c., to write elegies in the vernacular. His equivalent for the classic meter was alexandrines in couplets, with alternating masculine and feminine rhymes. Klopstock, with greater metrical freedom, turned to sentimental subjects, general sadness, the troubles of love, as well as the memorializing of actual death. The influence of the "graveyard school" of Eng. poets as well as of Young, Goldsmith, Gray, Ossian, and others was also felt heavily in Germany. The *Römische Elegien* of Goethe, although imitative of the L. elegiac meter, should probably be classed as idylls, his chief elegy being *Metamorphosen der*

Pflanzen. Schiller, in his essay, "On Primitive and Sentimental Poetry," distinguishes the elegiac from the satiric and idyllic, by saying that the elegiac longs for the ideal, while the satiric rails against the present situation and the idyllic represents the ideal as actually existent. His notion of the elegiac is illustrated in his own *Die Götter Griechenlands, Die Sehnsucht,* and *Der Pilgrim.* Hölderlin's elegies also deal with the impossibility of attaining an ideal and the longing for the golden days of youth. Mörike and Geibel produced the only German elegies of note in the remainder of the 19th c. The ten *Duino Elegies* (1912-1922) of Rainer Maria Rilke constitute an important renewal of the genre in modern literature and have been widely influential outside of Germany as well as within.

In England, there were a few Renaissance attempts, as, for example, by Sidney, Spenser, and Harvey, to imitate the quantitative verse of the classical distich, but these, like other attempts to write quantitatively in an accentual language, failed. The term *elegie* was used in the 16th and early 17th c. for poems with a variety of content, including Petrarchan love poetry as well as laments, but the connection between death and e. was made more clear with the use of "funeral elegy" in the title of one section of Donne's *An Anatomy of the World* (1611). Milton's pastoral e., *Lycidas,* (1637) helped to establish the e., a lament for the dead, as a separate genre in Eng. Eng. literature has not lacked meditative and reflective verse, but a distinction has grown up between this as "elegiac" and the e. proper, although the boundary is by no means sharp. For examples of the former, see Gray's *Elegy Written in a Country Churchyard* (1750), Young's *Night Thoughts,* Samuel Johnson's *Vanity of Human Wishes,* and Whitman's *When Lilacs Last in the Dooryard Bloomed.* In the e. tradition belong such poems as Pope's *Elegy on the Death of an Unfortunate Lady* and Tennyson's *In Memoriam* (1850). A notable example of the modern e., this one employing three very different metrical patterns, is W. H. Auden's *In Memory of W. B. Yeats.* The pastoral (q.v.) elegy, notably illustrated in Eng. by *Adonais* (1821), Shelley's poem on the death of Keats, and *Thyrsis* (1867), Arnold's monody on the death of Clough, derives from a different tradition, being thought of as a subdivision of the idyll or eclogue. In classical literature, the *Lament for Bion* (traditionally attributed to Moschus but probably by an unknown disciple of Bion) and Virgil's Fifth *Eclogue,* as well as the First Idyll of Theocritus and the Tenth Eclogue of Virgil, both of which combine the themes of love and death, were the chief models.

M. Lloyd, *Elegies, Ancient and Modern*

(1903) ; J. H. Hanford, "The Pastoral E. and Milton's Lycidas," PMLA, 25 (1910); Gayley and Kurtz; H. Hatzfeld, *Die französische Renaissancelyrik* (1924); J. W. Draper, *The Funeral E. and the Rise of Romanticism* (1929); F. W. Weitzmann, "Notes on the Elizabethan *Elegie*," PMLA, 50 (1935); C. M. Bowra, *Early Gr. Elegists* (1938); F. Beissner, *Gesch. der deutschen Elegie* (1941, 2d ed., 1961); G. Luck, *The Latin Love E.* (1960) .   S.F.F.

ELISION (L. "striking out") a general (metrical) term for the omission or blurring of a final unstressed vowel (vowel sound) followed by a vowel or mute consonant; cf. Fr. *l'épée*, *l'heure*. The Gr. equivalents *ecthlipsis* and *synaloepha* (q.v.) nowadays tend to have specialized meanings. In Gr., elision—which is variable in prose but more regular in poetry —is indicated by an apostrophe (') to mark the disappearance of the elided vowel (generally short alpha, epsilon, and omikron as well as the diphthong *ai* occasionally in Homer and in comedy); but, when e. occurs in Gr. compound words, the apostrophe is not used. In L. a final vowel or a vowel followed by *m* at the end of a word was not omitted from the written language, but as a rule it was ignored metrically when the next word in the same measure began with a vowel, diphthong, or the aspirate *h*. In Eng. syllable-counting measures, e. is a kind of fiction, two syllables being reckoned as one to make the line conform to the metrical scheme. Or, as S. E. Sprott (*Milton's Art of Prosody*, 1953, p. 63) has it: e. is the "process by which two syllables are reduced to the prosodical value of one." In accentual meters it gives the appearance or illusion of smoothness. A similar phenomenon, not properly to be called e., occurs in such forms as "we'll" for "we will." Cf. HIATUS, the opposite or avoidance of e. See also POETIC CONTRACTIONS; CLASSICAL PROSODY; ROMANCE PROSODY.   R.J.G.; P.F.B.

ELLIPSE (Gr. "leaving out," "defect"; L. *detractio*). A figure wherein a word, or several words, usually of little importance to the logical expression of thought but ordinarily called for by the construction, are omitted. Quintilian (*Institutes of Oratory* 9.3.58) exemplifies with Caelius' denunciation of Antony: " 'stupere gaudio Graecus,' the Greek began to be astonished with joy, for 'coepit,' began, is readily understood." The device may be used for a number of psychological reasons, including, according to Quintilian, considerations of modesty: "Novimus et qui te, transversa tuentibus, hircis, / et quo, sed faciles Nymphae risere, sacello" (You—while the goats looked goatish —we know who, / And in what chapel—but the kind nymphs laughed) Virgil, *Eclogues*

3.8. Gr. rhetoricians permitted omission of substantives, pronouns, objects, finite verbs, main clauses, and (rarely) subordinate clauses; modern poets allow omission of almost any member so long as the meaning remains clear. Quintilian distinguishes e. from aposiopesis (q.v.) on the ground that in the latter it is uncertain what is suppressed. "Where wigs [strive] with wigs, [where] with sword-knots sword-knots strive" (Pope, *The Rape of the Lock* 1.101). In their eagerness not to be diffuse, 20th-c. poets (especially Pound, Eliot, Auden, William Carlos Williams, etc.) are particularly attracted to the device.   R.O.E.

EMBLEM. A didactic device consisting, normally, of three parts: a "word" (*mot* or *motto*), a woodcut or engraving symbolically expressing the "word," and a brief verse *explicatio* or application of the idea expressed in the combination. The e. exhibits varied and close affinities with proverb, fable, and epigram. Emblems were introduced into European literature by the *Emblematum liber* (1531) of Andrea Alciati, and for two centuries thereafter enjoyed an enormous vogue. The first Eng. e. book was Geoffrey Whitney's *Choice of Emblemes* (1586), the most notable probably the *Emblemes* (1635) of Francis Quarles. In recent times the form receives amusing illustration in R. L. Stevenson's *Moral Emblems*. As the form developed it became customary to present the *motto* in one language, the *explicatio* in a different language; and many bilingual or multilingual e. books served incidentally as language manuals. Originally erudite productions, e. books became increasingly instruments of popular education, especially in Jesuit hands during the 17th c. Above all, they were a gold-mine of imagery for poets, Spenser, Shakespeare, Donne, Quarles, and Crashaw being notably thus indebted.—H. Green, *Andrea Alciati and His Books of Emblems* (1872); M. Praz, *Studies in 17th-C. Imagery* (2 v., 1939–47); E. James, "The Imagery of Francis Quarles' *E.*," UTSE (1943); R. J. Clements, "Cult of the Poet in Renaissance E. Lit.," PMLA, 59 (1944), "Condemnation of the Poetic Profession in Ren. E. Lit.," SP, 43 (1946), "Ars emblematica," *Romanistisches Jahrbuch*, 8 (1957) and *Picta Poesis: Lit. and Humanistic Theory in Ren. E. Books* (1960); J. Lederer, "John Donne and the Emblematic Practice," RES, 22 (1946); R. Freeman, *Eng E. Books* (1948).   J.L.L.

EMOTION. A poem involves two people, writer and reader; and a discussion of the place of e. in poetic theory can be divided accordingly. The division is chronological as well as logical: until the end of the 18th c., emphasis fell on the reader's e.; since the romantics, it has shifted to the poet's.

A good poem moves the reader: this has been a critical truism (perhaps even *the* critical truism) since literary criticism as we know it began, and hardly anyone disputes it, even today. The e. may be aroused for purely aesthetic purposes—for "delight"—or else as an indirect means of inciting to virtue. This latter is the Horatian view that poetry is both *dulce et utile*—that it "teaches delightfully"—and it is by far the more common in the Renaissance: it can be illustrated from almost any 16th-c. poet who discusses his craft: "O what an honor is it, to restraine / The lust of lawlesse youth with good advice . . . / Soone as thou gynst to sette thy notes in frame, / O, how the rurall routes to thee doe cleave! / Seemeth thou dost their soule of sence bereave . . ." (Spenser, *The Shepheardes Calender*).

Is the emotional effect normative—i.e., can we say that a good poem arouses strong emotions, and a bad poem doesn't? Aristotle probably thought not: he admits in the *Poetics* that terror and pity can be aroused by the spectacle (this is not of course an inferior poem, but an inferior element of poetry; but we can surely extend the argument by analogy), though it is preferable to raise them by the words, and he does not indicate that the less preferable method arouses a weaker or even a different e. The usual answer, however, was yes. When Sidney confesses "I never heard the olde song of *Percy* and *Duglas,* that I found not my heart mooved more then with a Trumpet," he clearly assumes that this is a testimony to the poem's excellence. This normative view was carried much further in the 18th c., when it was claimed explicitly and at length (notably by Diderot) that the good poet must be judged by his power to arouse our emotions. Thus Pope: "Let me for once presume t' instruct the times, / To know the Poet from the Man of rhymes: / 'Tis he, who gives my breast a thousand pains, / Can make me feel each Passion that he feigns; / Inrage, compose, with more than magic Art, / With Pity, and with Terror, tear my heart" (*To Augustus*). This is an aspect of neoclassic doctrine that passed unchanged and naturally into romanticism.

One common objection to using one's emotional reaction as a touchstone is that it is too completely subjective: a poem has many readers, and they cannot compare their private emotions. The theoretical reply to this is contained in the doctrine of intersubjectivity (as formulated, for example, by Charles Morris): the use of language as a means of comparing purely private experiences. Nonetheless, the objection is useful if taken as a warning to the practical critic to talk about the words of the poem, rather than the e. it arouses in him:

for the latter will result either in vagueness, as in most impressionistic or rhapsodic criticism, or in such physiological descriptions as Housman's account of his skin bristling, or Emily Dickinson's "If I feel physically as if the top of my head were taken off, I know that is poetry."

A poem, then, arouses in the reader an emotional response which is intersubjective: what is this e. like? The first question here is whether there is such a thing as a purely aesthetic e. The experience of reading, say, a satire of Pope is not the same as being angry; but critics are divided on whether the difference can profitably be described by postulating a specific poetry-reading or aesthetic emotion, which has no more to do with anger than with any other feeling.

The Horatian (*dulce et utile*) tradition would tend to answer yes. The e. of reading poetry was usually called, quite simply, pleasure; but it was clearly thought of as a special kind of pleasure, and there was some discussion in the 18th c. of its exact nature (e.g. by Hume in his essay on tragedy). Modern critics who believe in this emotion include Clive Bell ("The starting point for all systems of aesthetics must be the personal experience of a particular emotion . . . All sensitive people agree that there is a peculiar emotion provoked by works of art") and T. E. Hulme ("You could define art as a passionate desire for accuracy, and the essentially aesthetic emotion as the excitement which is generated by direct communication"). One can also mention Freud, who believed that there was a "purely formal, that is, aesthetic pleasure" offered by poetry, and who also (not surprisingly) believed it was unimportant: an "increment," a "bribe," to release a greater pleasure arising from deeper sources in the mind. Freud held exactly the opposite view to Hume (and Wordsworth) on this point: for him, the aesthetic pleasure, or fore-pleasure, is a trigger that releases a discharge of e. that provides the true enjoyment of literature; whereas for Hume the aesthetic pleasure "softens," for Wordsworth it "tempers" the passions.

Up till the 18th c., the two main views of the reader's e. were the Horatian (that it was a pleasure) and the Aristotelian (that it was a catharsis). There was a potential contradiction between these two, as we see by remarking that the catharsis-view would tend, implicitly, to deny the aesthetic e.: it was real pity and real terror that were to be felt. In modern times, it is denied by those anxious to repudiate an ivory tower or esoteric view of literature: by Marxists; by I. A. Richards (who says curtly that "psychology has no place for such an entity"); and, in effect, by John Dewey who, though he uses the term "aesthetic motion," insists that it is "not cut off by a chasm from other and natural emotional experiences," and complains that those who believe in "an emotion that is aboriginally aesthetic . . . relegate fine art to a realm separated by a gulf from everyday experiences."

In talking of the reader's e., one must mention those critics who deny that e. has any place at all in his reaction. This denial can come from mainly theoretical motives, as in the case of Eliseo Vivas, who wishes to substitute "attention" as the key concept; or as part of a specific literary program, as in the case of T. S. Eliot. Eliot (who, however, is not always consistent) suggested that the emotions provoked by a work of art "are, when valid, perhaps not to be called emotions at all." This can be linked with his doctrine of impersonality (he tends to think of an e. as something personal, even self-regarding), and his emphasis on the physical ("the cerebral cortex, the nervous system, and the digestive tracts") that sometimes leads him to prefer the term "feeling." Thomas Mann has also expressed the view that "art is a cold sphere." The "calm" or "cold" that these writers find in the poetic response might by others be considered a kind of e., but there is a real cleavage here. What no one (presumably) denies is that even if the poem kills the e., it must deal with a situation that would have aroused e. in the first place.

Critics who try to describe the reader's e. are likely to apply to it some of the favorite modern conceptions for assessing a poem: especially particularity and complexity. It is generally agreed today that any good poem has an element of the specific and the individual: can we say that it arouses a particular, and even a unique e.? There are of course only a limited number of emotions, perhaps a dozen in common recognition; nonetheless, Collingwood maintains that beyond classifying "the anger which I feel here and now" as anger, one must add that "it is a peculiar anger, not quite like any anger that I ever felt before;" and to become fully conscious of it (which in his view is the first step towards its poetic expression) means "becoming conscious of it . . . as this quite peculiar anger." Dewey too (whose views on art and e. are often very like Collingwood's) maintained "save nominally, there is no such thing as *the* emotion of fear, hate, love. The unique, unduplicated character of experienced events and situations impregnates the emotion that is evoked." And the individuality of the work of art, he believes, comes from its faithfulness to this individual e. Eliot has also, on occasion, linked the precision of good poetry to the definiteness of its e.

As for complexity, I. A. Richards has frequently maintained that a response to poetry is highly complex, and reading a poem a matter of emotional accommodation and adjustment. He prefers however to direct attention away from e., and to speak of attitudes ("imaginal and incipient activities or tendencies to action") which poetry organizes in the reader "for freedom and fullness of life." This organization is the function of emotive language, sharply distinguished by Richards from referential language, which makes statements. William Empson, whose view of language is similar and influenced by Richards, goes even further in not wishing to discuss the emotions aroused by words: "Normally they are dependent on a Sense which is believed to deserve them," and the way to discuss the emotional impact of a poem is to analyze the structure of sense and implication in its key words.

Most of the remaining problems are best discussed under the heading of the poet's e. (Naturally, insofar as a poem is a successful act of communication, this division is artificial.) The first point to note, when considering the e. of the poet, is that it must be a descriptive and not a normative inquiry. A poem in itself can never offer conclusive evidence that the poet did not feel a certain e., nor (except on certain rather naive theories) that he did; this external, biographical fact can only be established separately, and has no critical relevance. Ruskin tried to classify forms of poetry as worse than others according to whether the poet was insincere or—worse still—deliberately, in hardness of heart, weaving intricate metaphors "with chill and studied fancy." Here we have left literary criticism for moralizing. As a reaction against this sort of thing, some modern writers on aesthetics (notably Beardsley and Osborne) have tried to make logical mincemeat of the very concept of artistic expression. It is much easier for them to do this when they are considering it as a normative concept than when treating it as part of literary psychology.

And as part of such a descriptive inquiry, there is a great deal to say about the poet's e. First of all, does he need to feel any? The view that he does not—that Shakespeare's sonnets, say, are literary exercises—repels most readers; but it is a view that seems to be supported by the pronouncements of some poets, very conscious of the hard work involved in composition. The Horatian-Renaissance critical tradition, with its manuals of instruction and its advice on decorum, has little to say on the poet's feelings, and a great deal on his craft. Even the famous line in the *Ars Poetica*, "si vis me flere, dolendum est primum ipsi tibi" (if you wish to make me weep, you must first feel grief yourself) is addressed to characters in a play, and refers simply to the need for good writing or good acting. It might be thought that the Platonic doctrine of inspiration ran counter to this tradition, but as expressed by Plato (and, generally, by everyone else) this has nothing to do with the poet's emotions: inspiration comes to him from without, and enables him, with the Muse's help, to solve problems in his craft that would be beyond his unaided wit; but they remain problems of craft. The doctrine that art is the expression of e. is one we owe to the romantic movement; earlier statements of it are very hard to find.

It is obviously a true doctrine, though there is room for great controversy within it. There is, first, the question whether the e. expressed in a poem is the same as that originally expressed by the poet. Most of the difficulties here vanish if we reject too naive a view of the temporal priority of this original e. What a poem expresses is clearly not the e. of the poet *before* he began writing it, but it may be his original e. insofar as the writing of the poem helped him to discover, even to feel it: "Expression is the clarification of turbid emotion," says Dewey. Samuel Alexander, however, prefers to postulate two emotions, the material passion ("the passions appropriate to the subject") and the formal passion (the "passion proper to the artist" which guides him "more surely than conscious ideas . . . unifying his choice of words . . . into an expressive whole"). This formal passion is clearly the equivalent for the poet of the aesthetic e. of the reader; Alexander suggests that the material passion need not be present, citing the example of dramatic poetry: "It is not necessary to suppose that Meredith or Shakespeare actually felt the emotions of his characters, but only that he understood them." It might however be truer to say that the material passion is not the e. of Macbeth himself, but Shakespeare's e. about the *Macbeth*-situation, which is contained, probably implicitly, in the play, and which Shakespeare presumably felt as well as understood. Unless we say this, Alexander's view can be turned into a craft-theory.

The central difficulty in any view of art as the expression of e. is to find a way of indicating that the poet, though in the grip of an e., is also in control of it: that he is possessed by his e., but also possesses it. A critic's way of resolving this paradox may often show the heart of his doctrine. A typical Victorian answer is that of Ruskin, for whom the second order poet is in the grip of his feelings (or chooses to write as if he was), whereas the first order poet has command over himself, and can look round calmly. When it comes to applying this distinction to poems, Ruskin shows a naïveté that is almost ludicrous: the great poet's "control of emotion" consists mainly in

avoiding metaphor and factually untrue statements, even in preferring similes to metaphors. A glance at such a view makes it clear how greatly criticism has deepened its powers in the last century.

For it is not merely a question of the difference between first and second order poets, but between the control of e. necessary for its expression, and the inability to express oneself at all. Croce views expression as either aesthetic or naturalistic: "there is . . . an abyss . . . between the appearance, the cries and contortions of some one grieving at the loss of a dear one and the words or song with which the same individual portrays his suffering at another time." Dewey makes a distinction between giving way to, and expressing, an impulse: raging is not the same as expressing rage; and he links it with his more general theory that the arresting of the physiologically normal outlet of an impulse is the necessary precondition of its transformation into a higher level of experience. Perhaps the most valuable formulation of the difference is that of Collingwood, who distinguishes between expressing and betraying an e., linking this with his view of art as an enlarging and clarifying of consciousness.

These are philosophical formulations; to the poet and practical critic, what matters is the application of the distinction to the actual language of poetry. The classic instance of failure to draw this distinction is Johnson's attack on *Lycidas* on the grounds that "where there is leisure for fiction, there is little grief." The naturalistic discharge of grief may have no such leisure, but its expression has. This element of control in expression was no doubt one of the things Coleridge wished to indicate by attributing to imagination "a more than usual state of emotion, with more than usual order"; and that Eliot was thinking of when he described poetry as "an escape from emotion." Eliot's objections to *Hamlet* spring from a feeling that loose e., inadequately expressed, is betrayed in the play, though he shows some uncertainty whether the emotion is Shakespeare's, or also Hamlet's.

Wordsworth's account of poetry as originating in "the spontaneous overflow of powerful feelings" looks like a discharge-theory, but he goes on to add that as well as having "more than usual organic sensibility" the poet must be someone who has "thought long and deeply." Wordsworth was in fact usually aware (though he is inconsistent) that the e. as expressed is not the same as that originally felt: in his account of e. recollected in tranquillity, he remarks that the recollected e., that which issues in the poem, is "kindred" to the original one.

Of all modern theorists, the one who perhaps comes closest to a view of art as the mere discharge of e. is Freud. He happens to be talking of the reader's e., but his view (already mentioned) seems relevant here. He recognizes no element of control in the "release of tension" provided by literature, and sometimes indicates a view of art that equates it with indulgence in wish-fulfillment. (At other times he holds what amounts to a cognitive view.) Jung, though his interpretation is different, holds the same view of what the poetic e. is like, and describes it with the same metaphors: "the moment when the mythological situation appears is . . . as though forces were unloosed of the existence of which we had never even dreamed; . . . we feel suddenly aware of an extraordinary release."

There can be no doubt that this distinction between expressing and betraying is invaluable in the actual criticism of literature. Collingwood applies it, briefly but brilliantly, to *Tess of the D'Urbervilles* and to Beethoven; it provides the best terminology for sorting good from bad in writers like Shelley, Carlyle and Lawrence. Where Henry James censured the bad parts of *Daniel Deronda* as cold and intellectual, F. R. Leavis, in more modern terminology, can show that they are really too emotional.

How does e. work in the creative process? If writing a poem is like driving a car, the e. can be thought of as the destination or as the gasoline: the subject of literary creation, or the force that renders it possible. Eliot holds the first view: "What every poet starts from is his own emotions," he says, in contrasting Shakespeare with Dante, and suggests that Dante expresses not belief but certain emotions of believing. Alexander on the other hand holds the second view: "The artist aims to express the subject which occupies his mind in the means which he uses. His purpose may be dictated by passion but is still a passionate *purpose*." The resolution of this dispute (which may be partly terminological) lies outside literary theory; but the dangers and implications of each view are worth noting. If you believe that a poet's emotions are the subject of his poem, you are likely to emphasize, even overemphasize, the typicality of poems dealing explicitly with emotions, such as Shakespeare's sonnets, Coleridge's *Dejection*, and even perhaps (in the case of many romantic critics) lyric poetry in general. If on the other hand you regard emotion as merely the fuel, literature may become assimilated to philosophy.

However clearly we may perceive that the question of the poet's emotion is not normative, and therefore, strictly speaking, not relevant to criticism, there is no doubt that it will continue to be used, not only in literary psychology, but also by critics. For it is a useful short cut, a formulation that fits admirably into our habits of thinking. We persist in remembering that every poem had an author, who, as Eliot remarks in a similar context, meant what he said. To consider what drove him to write as he did may be the most convenient way of perceiving and evaluating what are really elements in our own reaction.

Plato, *Ion* (early 4th c. B.C.); Aristotle, *Poetics* (4th c. B.C.); Horace, *Ars Poetica* (ca. 12 B.C.); Sidney, *Apology for Poetry* (1595; typical Renaissance document); Boileau, *L'Art Poétique* (1674; typical neoclassic document); Diderot, *Le Paradoxe du Comédien* (written 1770–78, publ. 1830); Wordsworth, *Preface to Lyrical Ballads* (1800); Coleridge, *Biographia Literaria* (1817); Ruskin, "The Pathetic Fallacy," in *Modern Painters*, iii, 4 (1856); Croce, *Aesthetic*, tr. D. Ainslie (1909); T. S. Eliot, "The Perfect Critic," in *The Sacred Wood* (1920), "Tradition and the Individual Talent," "Shakespeare and the Stoicism of Seneca," "Dante," in *Selected Essays* (1932); I. A. Richards, *Principles of Lit. Crit.* (1924), *Practical Crit.* (1929); S. Freud, "The Relation of the Poet to Day-Dreaming," tr. G. Duff, in *Collected Papers*, IV (1925); C. G. Jung, "On the Relation of Analytical· Psychology to Poetic Art," in *Contributions to Analytical Psychology*, tr. H. G. and C. F. Baynes (1928); W. Empson, *Seven Types of Ambiguity* (1930), *The Structure of Complex Words* (1951); S. Alexander, *Beauty and Other Forms of Value* (1933); J. Dewey, *Art as Experience* (1934); E. Vivas, "A Definition of the Aesthetic Experience," *Jour. of Philos.*, 34 (1937); R. G. Collingwood, *Principles of Art* (1938); H. Osborne, *Aesthetics and Crit.* (1955; ch. 7 attacks the expression theory); Wimsatt. See also H. Osborne, "The Quality of Feeling in Art," *Brit. Jour. of Aesthetics*, 3 (1963).

L.D.L.

EMPATHY AND SYMPATHY. E. is the projection of ourselves into, or the identification of ourselves with objects either animate or inanimate. S. is a fellow-feeling with the ideas and emotions of other human beings, or with animals to whom we attribute human ideas and emotions. E. (*Einfühlung*) has been boldly conceived as the agent of our knowledge of nature, and in regard to poetics as the source of personification, or as the basis for all metaphor that endows the natural world with human life, thought, and feeling. In this aspect it is identical with what modern critics have termed the mythical view, and as such it is the essential attitude of poetry and art.

E. has, however, a more limited sense as a species of metaphor which conveys the meaning of an object by evoking a powerful physical response to it. In its projection into or identification with the object (the metaphysical crux of romantic nature poetry) it is distinguishable from s. by its element of sensation and its more intimate union with its object—s. runs parallel, while e. unites. S. may be intellectual only, or it may combine thought and feeling, and it need not deal with physical things, which along with the sensations evoked by them are indispensable to e. The importance of s. to poetics lies in its relation to extra-poetic issues. The sympathetic imagination, for example, makes possible organized social action by awakening us to the kinship of all things in unity. The Ancient Mariner's crime is a failure of s. toward a creature that has, significantly, already been associated to humanity: "As if it had been a Christian soul, / We hailed it in God's name." In his *To a Young Ass* Coleridge laid himself open to ridicule by sympathetically regarding the likenesses and defying the differences between himself and an underprivileged donkey: "Innocent foal! thou poor despis'd forlorn! / I hail thee *Brother*—spite of the fool's scorn! / And fain would take thee with me, in the Dell / Where high-soul'd Pantisocracy shall dwell!"

Empathic identification depends upon motor-imagery, allied with tactile and muscular impressions, with sensations of tension and release. E. is, then, relatively physical and instinctive, while s. is relatively intellectual and self-conscious. Keats's lines: "Crag jutting forth to crag, and rocks that seem'd / Ever as if *just rising from a sleep, / Forehead to forehead held* their monstrous horns . . ." aptly illustrate the empathic interpretation of objects by physical suggestion. E. is valuable to the critic as an instrument for focusing and organizing his perception of certain powerful poetic effects. It is especially helpful to romantic criticism, which tries to reconcile the poem, the reader, and the poet in a single critical act, since in this process both the reader's and the poet's emphathic response to the object can be regarded as relevant.—H. Lotze, *Microcosmus*, tr. E. Hamilton and E. E. Constance Jones (1886); V. Lee, *The Beautiful* (1913); H. S. Langfeld, *The Aesthetic Attitude* (1920); L. P. de Vries, *The Nature of Poetic Lit.* (1930); J. T. Shipley, *The Quest for Lit.* (1931); C. D. Thorpe, "E.," in Shipley, *Dict.*; W. J. Bate, *From Cl. to Romantic* (1946; chap. 5); N. F. Ford, "Keats, E., and 'The Poetical Character,'" SP, 45 (1948); R. H. Fogle, *The Imagery of Keats and Shelley* (1949; chap. 4); M. H. Abrams, "E. and S.," *A Glossary of Lit. Terms* (1957).   R.H.F.

ENCOMIUM. A Gr. choral song in celebration not of a god but of a hero, sung at the *komos*, the jubilant or reveling procession which celebrated the victor in the games. While Simonides and Pindar wrote encomia, Aristotle says that both the e. and the myth are parts of all early poetry. In later times the term acquired the meaning of any laudatory composition in verse or prose but it applied more often to a rhetorical exercise in prose, exalting the virtues of some legendary figure or praising the extraordinary deeds of a human being. Aristotle considers it a subdivision of declamatory oratory (*Rhetoric* 1358 b 18ff.). The best examples of this type of e. in the classical period were written by Isocrates. It became very popular in the time of the New Sophistic and was widely imitated by Roman, Byzantine, and modern writers. Occasionally, however, the contents of this type of e. degenerated into the silliest and most trivial and extravagant of subjects. Erasmus' *Praise of Folly* is perhaps the best known example of the rhetorical kind of e. in modern literature. In the Hellenistic period many encomia were composed in the epic style. Theocritus wrote one in honor of Ptolemy Philadelphus (Idyll 17). In later times this type of composition was imitated by several Roman poets.—G. Fraustadt, *Encomiorum in litteris graecis usque ad Romanam aetatem historia* (1909); A. S. Pease, "Things Without Honor," CP, 21 (1926); H. K. Miller, "The Paradoxical E. with special Ref. to its Vogue in England, 1600–1800," MP, 53 (1956).   P.S.C.

ENDECHA. The Sp. e. is a dirge or lament, usually written in 5-, 6-, or 7-syllable verse having assonance in the even-numbered lines, though any simple rhyme scheme in consonance and any type of verse may be used, since the name refers primarily to subject matter. The strophe employed in the *e. real*, however, introduced in the 16th c., is usually limited to 4 lines, generally 3 heptasyllables plus 1 hendecasyllable, the second and fourth lines assonating and the others left unrhymed. The position of the hendecasyllables may vary, or the strophe may alternate hendecasyllables with heptasyllables. Alternating rhyme (*serventesio*) in consonance may be used. The short-line forms, according to Le Gentil, are found as early as the 15th c., although the typical assonance of the learned poetry is a development of the 16th. The e. is sometimes called *romancillo*. A famous example is Lope de Vega's *Pobre barquilla mía*.—P. Le Gentil, *La Poésie lyrique espagnole et portugaise à la fin du moyen âge. 2e partie. Les formes* (1953); Navarro.   D.C.C.

ENDING. See LINE ENDINGS.

END RHYME. See RHYME.

END-STOPPED. A term applied to poetic lines in which both meaning and meter undergo a pause at the end of the line. End-stopped lines, like closed couplets (q.v.), are characteristic of the heroic couplets of Eng. 18th-c. poetry: "Hope springs eternal in the human breast; / Man never is, but always to be, blest" (Pope) and of the alexandrine verse of the Fr. neoclassicists. The term "end-stopped" is opposed to *run-on*, or *enjambé* (see ENJAMBEMENT), terms which are used to describe the free and uninterrupted carryover of the grammatical structure from one line to the other, as in most Eng. blank verse and most romantic poetry. The relative occurrence of end-stopped lines has been used as a means of determining the chronology of Shakespeare's plays and of other works.

ENGLISH POETICS. See MEDIEVAL, RENAISSANCE, BAROQUE, NEOCLASSICAL, MODERN POETICS.

ENGLISH POETRY. The early literature of England falls into two divisions: Old Eng. literature, the beginning to 1066; Middle Eng. literature, 1066 to 1500. The body of poetry we possess from the OE period is only a fragment of the poetry, oral or written, which existed in Anglo-Saxon times and it has survived the hazards of over a thousand years in four manuscripts: Cotton Vitellius AXV, the Exeter Book, the Vercelli MS, and the Junius MS. Despite the ravages of the centuries, we possess in OE poetry a vernacular literature by far the oldest in Western Europe.

The Germanic tribes who invaded Britain in the middle of the 5th c. after the evacuation of the Romans were an illiterate people who possessed, in common with all the Germanic peoples, a body of oral literature celebrating the legendary exploits of the heroic age of migrations. Within three centuries after landing in Britain, the Anglo-Saxons had achieved in the northern kingdom of Northumbria a degree of culture unsurpassed in Western Europe. Here, in the last half of the 7th c. and in the 8th c. the bulk of OE poetry was produced. The chief agent effecting this change was Christianity, for with conversion came literacy. But though Christianity provided the means and the stimulus for producing written literature and the theme for a good deal of OE poetry, it did not preclude the production of some poetry dealing with material from heroic times and reflecting both heroic ideals and pagan attitudes toward life.

OE poetry, then, has two major divisions: poetry in the Germanic heroic tradition and poetry dealing with Christian stories and themes. The heroic poem most suggestive of the rich knowledge the Anglo-Saxons had of continental history and legend is the *Widsith,* a mnemonic catalogue of the great figures of Germanic heroic poetry. Another poem containing allusions to such heroes is *Deor,* a poem unique in OE in its division into six short strophes of irregular length each followed by a refrain. The *Waldere,* of which only two very short fragments survive, is a telling, possibly on an epic scale, of the legend of Walter of Aquitaine. An older type of Germanic heroic poetry, the heroic lay, is represented by *The Fight at Finnsburh* (or the *Finnsburh Fragment*). It is one of only two surviving lays which represent the poetry of the migration period, the other being the Old Saxon *Hildebrandslied.*

The culmination of heroic poetry in OE and, indeed, the greatest Anglo-Saxon literary product is the *Beowulf.* The poem is an account of the fabulous adventures of Beowulf, a hero possessed of superhuman qualities, in overcoming two trolls and, at the cost of his life, a fire-breathing dragon. *Beowulf* is a folk epic not unworthy of comparison with the *Iliad* and the *Odyssey.* The epic effect is achieved by three means. First, the verse form (Germanic alliterative meter [q.v.]) has a powerful, skillfully varied rhythm and a strong melody which are particularly effective for the heroic subject matter of the poem. Second, the fabulous adventures are placed in an historical setting enriched by detailed allusions to 6th-c. costumes, customs, political institutions, and so forth. Third, the principal characters, particularly Beowulf, exemplify the high ideals of conduct of the Germanic *comitatus:* generosity in the king and undying loyalty in the retainer. The consensus of scholarly opinion is that the poem was composed in Northumbria between 675 and 750. Recent criticism views the poem as the work of one author and finds in the details and digressions a unity which shows an impressive artistic control of material.

Though *Beowulf* is the high-water mark of the heroic tradition in England, two late pieces testify that the tradition remained strong throughout the Anglo-Saxon period. The *Battle of Brunanburh* is a short panegyric which appears in the *Anglo-Saxon Chronicle* for the year 937. A magnificent expression of the heroic spirit is the *Battle of Maldon* (after 991). The words of an aged retainer as he rallies his comrades for a fight to the death after their lord has been cut down are still a moving expression of courage:

Hige sceal þē heardra, heorte þē cēnre,
mōd sceal þē mare, þē ūre maegen lytlað.

The spirit must be hardier, the heart bolder,
courage must be greater, the more our might
    lessens.

Although there is a marked cleavage between the themes of heroic poetry and those of Christian poetry, the two have much in common. *Beowulf* has a strong Christian element, and the heroic spirit informs the retelling of biblical and holy stories. The relationship between Christ and his apostles might be that between a chief and his followers. The Hebrew patriarchs of the Old Testament and the saints of medieval legend are made into Germanic heroes and their exploits are described as though they were warriors. Even the processes of nature are thought of in terms of heroic struggle—"rime and frost, hoary warriors, fettered the land of heroes."

According to Bede, the first religious poet was Caedmon, a lay worker in the monastery of Whitby in Northumbria, upon whom the gift of song was miraculously bestowed. The only work which can be definitely ascribed to him is the short hymn which Bede records as having been divinely inspired. Bede tells us, however, that after having received his divine gift, Caedmon turned many biblical stories into poetry. Chiefly on the basis of Bede's account, the poems of the Junius MS—*Genesis, Exodus, Daniel, Christ and Satan*—were for a long time attributed to Caedmon and are still referred to as the Caedmonian poems though they were composed by different authors at different times.

The only other OE poet beside Caedmon whose name we know is Cynewulf. His name in runic letters is worked into the text of four poems—*Christ II, Juliana, Elene,* and the *Fates of the Apostles*—so that the reader may pray for him. Aside from a few autobiographical details in the signature passages, we know nothing about him. The poems of Cynewulf are more personal and lyrical than the Caedmonian poems and more artfully conscious and learned in the tradition of medieval rhetoric. In subject matter they consist of poetic versions of the L. prose lives of two saints, Juliana and Helena, of a L. prose homily of Gregory the Great on the Ascension, and a short recounting of the work and manner of death of the twelve apostles. But these poems are not mere translations; everywhere they are informed with the poetic spirit. This is particularly true of passages which treat of battle or the sea; the description of Helena's voyage is one of the finest sea pieces in OE poetry. The first 1,664 lines of the Exeter Book have been given the title *Christ*. These lines divide into three sections, which modern scholars number I, II, and III because each has a different subject matter. *Christ II* contains the runic signature of Cynewulf and, from a conservative point of view, is the only section which can be ascribed to Cynewulf. While *Christ I* and *Christ III* cannot be definitely attributed to Cynewulf, they can be assigned to a group of poems which are often referred to as Cynewulfian because in theme, style, and diction they resemble the signed poems. Among these

are the *Dream of the Rood*, a lyric dream vision in which the Cross tells its story; *Guthlac A* and *B*, two different versions of a L. legend of St. Guthlac of Croyland; the *Phoenix*, a Christian allegory based on a L. poem and a fine piece of religious verse; and the *Andreas*, an account of the legendary exploits of St. Andrew with interesting parallels in style to the *Beowulf*.

Leaving aside some fragmentary and minor religious poems and such subliterary products as the *Charms* and the *Gnomes*, we can complete our brief survey of OE poetry by speaking of the *Riddles* and the lyrics or elegies. The seventy odd riddles contained in the Exeter Book cover a wide range of subjects from Old English daily life. Many are very ingenious, some are of high poetic merit, and some are wittily lewd. Also included in the Exeter Book are a group of five short lyrics which because of their mood are generally called elegies. Two of these are outstanding. The *Wanderer* is a superb expression of the grief felt by one who has lost his lord and companions and who broods on the transience of things. The *Seafarer*, which contains fine descriptions of the hardships and fascination of the sailor's life, is probably best interpreted as a Christian allegory of the renunciation of worldly pleasures and the endurance of the hardships of pilgrimage in order to win eternal life.

Practically all OE verse is composed in the Germanic alliterative meter (q.v.), which the Anglo-Saxons brought from the continent. It was intended for oral delivery and was recited to the accompaniment of the harp. The principal stylistic traits of OE poetry are the extensive use of compound words, its heaping up of words in apposition, and the use of the kenning (q.v.).

The OE poetry which we possess is practically all written in West Saxon but most of it was composed in Northumbrian. Northumbrian culture was brought to an end in the 9th c. by the Danish invasions and its poetic products which have survived were transported to Wessex where they were copied by West Saxon scribes.

With the Norman Conquest the tradition of OE literature comes to an end. OE alliterative verse with its 4-beat line continued in use throughout the ME period (1066–1500) and was the form of some outstanding poems. But the spirit, the themes, and the dominant verse forms derived chiefly from France. From 1066 to the last half of the 14th c., Eng. poets were apprentices learning to handle new verse forms and new types of poetry, and they did not become masters until the appearance of Chaucer and Gower. Nearly all poetry in this early period consists of translations and adaptations of foreign works, chiefly Fr., to provide the middle and lower classes with the entertainment and information which their social and intellectual superiors enjoyed in Fr. and L. While alliterative verse continued to be used, end rhyme became practically universal. The commonest verse forms were the octosyllabic couplet from the Fr., the fourteener from medieval L., and, after Chaucer, the iambic pentameter couplet. But in the romances and particularly in the lyrics, many stanzaic forms, some of great complexity, were used.

New literary forms emerged in great multiplicity. There is a large body of religious poetry: moral didactic pieces such as the early *Poema Morale* (ca. 1170), *exempla* such as those contained in *Handlyng Synne* by Robert Mannyng of Brunne (begun 1303), many saints' lives, miracles of the Virgin, of which the best collection is the *Vernon*, lyrics and carols. Secular works cover a wide range: debates such as *The Owl and the Nightingale* (ca. 1225); *fabliaux* such as *Dame Siriz* (ca. 1275); chronicles such as the *Cursor Mundi* (ca. 1260); tales such as those in *The Seven Sages of Rome* (13th c.); a multitude of songs and lyrics, some of very high quality; Breton *lais*, short poems of romantic adventure often involving the fairy world, such as *Sir Launfal* (14th c.); and, two types which deserve more detailed comment—the *ballad* and the *romance* (qq.v.).

There are references to ballads from the 13th c. on, but the great age of the ballad was the 15th c. The ballad of this period was usually in a 4-line stanza rhyming abcb, the *a* and *c* lines in iambic tetrameter, and the *b* lines in iambic trimeter. Often a refrain was added and dramatic tension was increased by incremental repetition. The form was well adapted to musical accompaniment. Excluding variants, about 300 genuine Eng. and Scottish ballads survive. In subject they cover a wide range: domestic tragedy (*Edward*), border feud (*The Battle of Otterburn*), betrayed love (*Lord Randal*), outlaw life (*Johnny Armstrong*), riddles (*Riddles Wisely Expounded*), the supernatural (*The Wife of Usher's Well*), the fairy world (*Thomas Rymer*), and humor (*The Farmer's Curst Wife*). There is one outstanding ballad cycle, the Robin Hood sequence. During the preromantic period (ca. 1750–1800), there was a widespread revival of interest in ballads, and many were transcribed for the first time. The most notable early collection of ballads was that of Bishop Percy, *Reliques of Ancient English Poetry* (1765); the greatest that of F. J. Child, *Eng. and Scottish Popular Ballads* (1892–98).

The romances are conveniently classified by their subjects or "matters." The Matter of England consists of romances such as *King Horn*, the earliest Eng. romance (ca. 1225), and *Havelok the Dane* (ca. 1275) which celebrate the exploits of Eng. heroes. The Matter of France, which dealt with Charlemagne and the Twelve Peers, did not produce any romance of distinction in Eng., the best being *The Taill of Rauf Coilyear* (ca. 1475). The Matter of Rome includes the legends of Alexander and Troy, and in Eng. these legends are closer to metrical chronicles than romances.

Of all ME romances the most popular were those concerned with the Matter of Britain, the stories of Arthur and the Knights of the Round Table. About 1155 the Anglo-Norman poet Wace wrote the *Roman de Brut*, a poetic paraphrase of Geoffrey of Monmouth's *Historia Regum Britanniae*. This work was translated by Layamon into a ME form of the earlier alliterative verse in his *Brut* (ca. 1200). The best handling of the full story of Arthur is the alliterative *Morte Arthur* (ca. 1375). Lancelot is the hero of only two Eng. romances, but one of these, the stanzaic *Le Morte Arthur* (ca. 1400), is a fine telling of the story of the Maid of Ascolot, the discovery of the love of Lancelot and Guinevere, and the destruction of Arthur and his court. The favorite Arthurian hero for the Eng. is Gawain, who is the subject of more metrical romances than any other knight of the Round Table and who, in nearly all, is portrayed as the exemplar of chivalry. The best of these romances are *Yvain and Gawain* (ca. 1325), *The Weddynge of Sir Gawain and Dame Ragnell* (15th c.), *Golagrus and Gawain* (ca. 1400), and, finest of all Eng. metrical romances, *Sir Gawain and the Green Knight*. This last romance is one of four poems contained in a single manuscript generally ascribed to an unknown writer who is referred to as "the Pearl poet" after the title of one of his poems, *The Pearl*. The poems are all written in the West Midland dialect and were composed between 1360 and 1400. All are in alliterative verse: *The Green Knight* employs stanzas of irregular length, each stanza ending with 5 short rhymed lines; *The Pearl* employs a 12-line rhymed stanza with heavy, but irregular, alliteration; *Patience* and *Purity* are in long alliterative lines. *The Pearl*, an elegy in dream vision form on the death of a little girl, and *The Green Knight* are among the finest poems in ME.

Belonging to the same period as the Pearl poet are John Gower and the author of *Piers Plowman*. Gower is notable for competence and prolixity. His one long poem in Eng., the *Confessio Amantis* (1390), runs to 33,000 lines of proficiently handled octosyllabic couplets. The poem is a collection of stories illustrating the Seven Deadly Sins as applied to love. Poetry much more vigorous than Gower's is shown in *The Vision Concerning Piers Plowman*, a poem in three versions—A (ca. 1362–63), B (ca. 1376–77), C (ca. 1392–93 or 1398–99). It is the longest and most complex of a group of poems criticizing the social conditions of the period and is a series of dream visions which depict allegorically the state of society and the falling away from Christian ideals. The poem has much that is rude and formless, but impassioned reforming zeal animates the vivid picture of contemporary society.

The finest flower of ME poetry is the work of Geoffrey Chaucer (ca. 1343–1400). His early works—*The Book of the Duchess* (1369) and some short poems—are strongly marked by the influence of Fr. courtly poetry. Although not lacking in originality, they do not reach the level of his later pieces. Traditionally, the deepening of Chaucer's art has been attributed in part to the influence of the great It. authors, Dante, Petrarch, and Boccaccio. *The House of Fame* shows some influence of Dante and *The Parliament of Fowls* some of Boccaccio. *Troilus and Criseyde* (ca. 1382–1385), Chaucer's greatest complete work, is a retelling of Boccaccio's *Il Filostrato* which sees in Boccaccio's story of an unhappy love affair an illustration of the view of life given in Boethius' *Consolation of Philosophy*, a work Chaucer translated into prose. Apparently after a false start at a frame-story in the unfinished *Legend of Good Women* (the *Prologue* is one of Chaucer's most charming pieces), Chaucer hit upon the device of a pilgrimage to provide the framework of a series of tales and so produced the most celebrated of all his works, *The Canterbury Tales.* Some of the stories are slight or dull but most are brilliant. The range is great—courtly romance in the *Knight's Tale*, fabliaux such as the *Miller's* and the *Reeve's* tales, a miracle of the Virgin in the *Prioress's Tale*, folk tales in the *Man of Law's* and the *Clerk's* tales, a beast fable in the *Nun's Priest's Tale*, a Breton lai in the *Franklin's Tale*, a burlesque metrical romance in *Sir Thopas*, medieval "tragedies" in the *Monk's Tale*, an exemplum in the *Pardoner's Tale*. But the brilliance of the tales themselves is only part of the artistic merit of the work. There are two points of striking originality about the *Canterbury Tales.* First, the frame is not a mere mechanical or introductory device for a series of stories (as it is is the *Legend of Good Women*); links between the stories provide the sense of a continuing journey and of the presence of the pilgrims. Second, the tales are related to the characters of the tellers and to their reactions to other pilgrims or to problems in which other pilgrims are interested. The result is that sense of verisimilitude which has charmed readers from Chaucer's day to the present. He was also an innovator in verse form. His two chief innovations are rhyme royal (q.v.) and the iambic pentameter couplet.

Except for ballads, the 15th c. was a barren one in England. After Chaucer there was no poet worth naming in a survey as brief as this. The only poetry worthy of the name was written in Scotland by a group of poets who, though influenced by Chaucer, did not, as his Eng. followers did, slavishly imitate him. Though writing before the 15th c. John Barbour should be mentioned. His *Bruce* (ca. 1370), though not great poetry, is great in its reflection of the Scottish spirit. An offspring of the *Bruce* is the popular epic, Blind Harry's *Wallace* (ca. 1460). James I of Scotland wrote one poem, *The Kingis Quair* (ca. 1423), which is memorable because its conventional love allegory is informed by the spirit of the true love which inspired it. Robert Henryson (ca. 1430–ca. 1506) wrote some delightful animal fables and a short but effective sequel to Chaucer's *Troilus, The Testament of Cresseid.* The finest of the so-called Scottish Chaucerians (q.v.), though much of his work comes after 1500, may be mentioned here. William Dunbar (ca. 1465–ca. 1530) shows the least influence of Chaucer and the greatest vigor and originality. His works are those of a highly skilled, thoroughly professional poet who delights in high style, elaborate metaphor, and that coinage from L. which has given to the Scottish school the appellation *aureate* (q.v.).

Poetry, then, in the ME period reaches its culmination in the period of Chaucer. Except in Scotland, it did not again reach such a high level until the Renaissance.

BIBLIOGRAPHIES: CBEL; A. H. Heusinkveld and E. J. Bashe, *A Bibliog. Guide to OE* (1931); W. L. Renwick and H. Orton, *The Beginnings of Eng. Lit. to Skelton* (1953).—J. E. Wells, *A Manual of the Writings in ME, 1050–1400,* with 9 supp. (1916–51); E. P. Hammond, *Eng. Verse between Chaucer and Surrey* (1920); L. L. Tucker and A. R. Benham, *A Bibliog. of 15th C. Lit.* (1928); C. Brown and R. H. Robbins, *Index of ME Verse* (1943).—W. Geddie, *A Bibliog. of Middle Scot Poets* (1912). See also the bibliog. in the lit. histories by E. K. Chambers and H. S. Bennett, below.

TEXTS: Consult the publications of the Early Eng. Text Society, the Scottish Text Society, and the Chaucer Society. The standard ed. of the corpus of OE poetry is the *Anglo-Saxon Poetic Records,* ed. G. P. Krapp and E.V.K. Dobbie (6 v., 1931–53). For ed. of specific poems, see the bibliog. in these vols. and those cited above. The most comprehensive 1-v. tr. of OE poetry into prose is that by R. K. Gordon, *Anglo-Saxon Poetry* (rev. ed., 1954); a convenient anthol. of translations into verse is that of C. W. Kennedy, *An Anthol. of OE Poetry* (1960). The best ed. in Eng. of *Beowulf* are those by Fr. Klaeber (3d ed. with 1st and 2d supp., 1950) and by A. J. Wyatt and R. W. Chambers (1921). The best introduction to the poem for the beginning student is W. K. Lawrence, *Beowulf and Epic Tradition* (1930); for the advanced student, R. W. Chambers, *Beowulf: An Introd. . . .* (3d ed., 1959). A. G. Broduer's *The Art of Beowulf* (1959) is the best discussion of the artistic unity of the poem. The best ed. of Chaucer is that of F. N. Robinson (2d ed., 1956).

HISTORY AND CRITICISM: C. W. Kennedy, *The Earliest Eng. Poetry* (1943; best study of OE poetry in Eng.); J. C. Pope, *The Rhythm of Beowulf* (1942) and A. J. Bliss, *The Metre of Beowulf* (1958) are studies of OE prosody.—CHEL I and II; W. H. Schofield, *Eng. Lit. from the Norman Conquest to Chaucer* (1906); Saintsbury, *Prosody*, I (1906; the best work in Eng. on ME metrics); E. K. Chambers, *Eng. Lit. at the Close of the Middle Ages* (1945); H. S. Bennett, *Chaucer and the 15th C.* (1947); A. C. Baugh *et al.*, *A Lit. Hist. of England* (1948); G. Kane, *ME Lit.* (1951); R. M. Wilson, *Early ME Lit.* (1951).—*Scottish Poetry: A Crit. Survey*, ed. J. Kinsley (1955).   R.P.APR.

SINCE 1500. Eng. poetry has generally dominated its accompanying poetics and criticism. It is empirical in its use of ideas and rules, and free of logical extremism. Fed by other literatures and cultures, like the Fr. and It., it has always possessed the creative power to absorb and transform them. In Eng. poetry after 1500 there are two periods of full expansion: the Elizabethan flowering, and the romantic movement. The metaphysical 17th c. is a gallant withdrawal to the conservative neoclassicism of the Augustans, who consolidated new positions at the rear. The second half of the 18th c. witnesses an irregular and straggling advance, which nevertheless culminates at the border of a new frontier in Eng. romanticism. The age of Victoria is a long and gradual breaking-up, which reaches with the Georgian poets into the 20th c., until the moderns reorganize and intervene with Yeats and Eliot. Those contemporary critics who have been able to descry a tradition in Eng. poetry have ordinarily found it in the metaphysicals of the early 17th c. The central tradition, however, cannot be located in any one period or group. It lies as it were in poetic creation itself, and it has been most evident at those times when the poets have believed that they had something to say, without too many obstacles in their road. Eng. poetry has always tried to assert the primacy of the spirit. It has best succeeded when it has been neither too defeatist nor too defiant.

THE RENAISSANCE. Tudor and Elizabethan poetry is at once conventional and spontaneous. In its vast body of lyrics individuals are little distinguishable, but all are remarkable for vigor and ease. Themes, imagery, and metrics owe something to native tradition, and in the late 16th c. something to the Fr. *Pléiade,* but most of all to It. Petrarch's sonnets especially, with their Renaissance version of courtly love, affected Eng. poetry. The pastoralism of Elizabethan lyrics is also primarily It. and conventional. In the Arcadianism of a typical anthology, *England's Helicon* (1600), the lover and his beloved are stock figures and Nature is Arcadia in eternal spring, but the verse is nevertheless charming and fresh.

John Skelton (1464?-1529) is a medieval, not a Renaissance figure. *The Bouge of Court* (1498 or 1499) is in the tradition of the dream allegory of Jean de Meung and many others, and his massive *Magnificence* (1515-16) is a morality play. Skelton is most esteemed today for the "Skeltonics" of *Philip Sparrow, The Tunning of Elinor Rumming, Colin Clout,* and *Why Come Ye Not to Court,* his most individual and characteristic poems. *The Garland of Laurel* (1523), in praise of the Countess of Surrey and other ladies, is like *The Bouge of Court* a dream allegory. Skeltonics (q.v.) are irregular and jagged short lines, with rhyme their only fixed principle. The number and positions of the stresses vary. Skeltonics owe something to medieval L. verse, but they are more irregular than their models. Skelton's decided interest for some modern poets probably lies, in fact, in his daring in wrenching earlier forms to the very limits of the formal.

Sir Thomas Wyatt (1503?-42) is the first Eng. poet of the Renaissance. The first considerable collection of his poems was published, with those of Henry Howard, Earl of Surrey (1517?-47) and others, in *Songs and Sonnets,* usually known as *Tottel's Miscellany* (1557). Wyatt's lyrics, chiefly in native modes, are now highly thought of, but he is remembered historically as the introducer into Eng. of the sonnet, the classical epigram, and the semiclassical satire, as well as the stanza forms of ottava rima and terza rima. Surrey gave to the sonnet its distinctive Eng. movement and rhyme pattern (ababcdcdefefgg), as opposed to the typical abbaabbacdecde of the It. sonnet. Surrey's most important innovation, however, was blank verse, which he invented in a partial translation of Virgil's *Aeneid* as an Eng. equivalent of Virgil's dactylic hexameters. His propagation of the rocking-horse "poulter's measure," widely used in 16th-c. drama and narrative verse, has occasioned less gratitude.

The great body of fine Elizabethan lyrics is preserved in such collections as *A Hundreth Sundrie Flowres* (1573), *The Paradise of Dainty Devices* (1576), *A Gorgeous Gallery of Gallant Inventions* (1578), and *A Handful of Pleasant Delytes* (1584?). The titles are publisher's come-ons, but not unfaithful to the contents. The harmonious relation of words and music in the Elizabethan song is exemplified in the work of poet-composers like Thomas Campion. Many of the finest songs came from drama and prose romance, such as the songs of Shakespeare's plays: "My true love hath my heart and I have his," from Sidney's *Arcadia*; and "Love in my bosom like a bee," from Thomas Lodge's *Rosalind*. The sonnet rose to new refinement in the sonnet-sequences of the 1590's. The vogue of these is usually attributed to Sir Philip Sidney's *Astrophel and Stella* (1591), which also marks the coming-of-age of Elizabethan prosody. Samuel Daniel, Lodge, Edmund Spenser, Michael Drayton, and particularly Shakespeare contributed to the sonnet, with other lesser poets. The next great practitioner, Milton, transferred his allegiance to a modified It. form, which Wordsworth also was later to use.

The main themes of Elizabethan lyricism are on the one hand pastoral love, on the other this world's illusion—also from the pastoral ideal of permanence and serenity. They are further developed in the Ovidian narrative and the long reflective poem. The reflective or philosophical poem came from the middle ages, through the medium of Sackville's *Induction* (1563) to the popular *Mirror for Magistrates*. Between 1590 and 1610 Sir John Davies, George Chapman, Samuel Daniel, and Fulke Greville, Lord Brooke, wrote largely of large issues, in such poems as Davies' *Orchestra* (1596) and *Nosce Teipsum* (1599), Daniel's *Musophilus* (1599), Chapman's *Tears of Peace* (1609), and Greville's *Treatie of Humane Learning*. These were didactic, as was the Elizabethan theory of poetry, but they were spacious and vital. The Ovidian narrative poem (Ovid's *Metamorphoses* had been translated into Eng. in 1567) is represented by Marlowe's *Hero and Leander* (1593?) and Shakespeare's *Venus and Adonis* (1593) and *The Rape of Lucrece* (1594). Glowingly pictorial, they illustrate the Renaissance version of Horace's *ut pictura poesis* doctrine that painting is silent poetry and poetry a speaking picture. Michael Drayton's *Endymion and Phoebe* (1595) anticipates Keats's *Endymion* in using sensuous love as a metaphor of spiritual exaltation. Chapman also uses sense-experience for allegory in Ovid's *Banquet of Sense*.

The Renaissance greatly respected the classical epic, although it did not always distinguish its qualities clearly. Chapman translated Homer's *Iliad* (1598–1611) into vigorous "fourteeners": "He took much ruth to see the Greeks by Troy sustain such ill, / And mightily incenst with Jove stooped straight from that steep hill . . ." and added in 1614 a translation of the *Odyssey*. Tasso and Ariosto were accepted as epic poets; Edward Fairfax's translation (1600) of Tasso's *Gerusalemme Liberata* and Sir John Harington's translation of Ario-

sto's *Orlando Furioso* (1591) were tributes to the heroic, although Harington's Orlando is not an epic hero.

Edmund Spenser (1552–99) writes his version of epic, undifferentiated from other narrative forms, in *The Fairie Queene* (1590). *The Fairie Queene* from its Arthurian antecedents is related to medieval romance; it looks back to Dante's famous letter to Can Grande in its multiple allegory; and it draws from the mixed narrative of Ariosto, which had set the It. critics at each other's throats. In the variety and scope of his achievement Spenser is the epitome of his time. He is successful in many of its characteristic forms: at the sonnet-sequence in *Amoretti*, and at the pastoral in the half-Eng., half-Virgilian *Shepherd's Calendar* (1579). In *Prothalamion* and *Epithalamion* Spenser fused the classical wedding ode, the Theocritan elegy, and the It. *canzone*, bequeathing an instrument to Milton for *Lycidas*. Spenser's influence upon Eng. poetry has been enormous from his own days until the 20th c. Dryden, Milton, Thomson, Collins, Gray, Wordsworth, Byron, Keats, Shelley, Tennyson, and Arnold were all in varying degrees his followers. Spenser's "grand style," heightened with archaisms and mythological allusions, led eventually through Milton to the artificial poetic diction which Wordsworth castigated in the 1800 Preface to the *Lyrical Ballads*.

Elizabethan and Jacobean poetic drama has a long medieval tradition behind it of miracle and morality plays, and also a classical background from the comedies of Plautus and Terence and Seneca's rhetorical tragedies. Nicholas Udall wrote a Plautine comedy with Eng. local color (*Ralph Roister Doister*, ca. 1553), about the same time as *Gammer Gurton's Needle*, a more Eng. comedy, was being performed at Cambridge. In 1562 Sackville and Norton produced *Gorboduc*, the first Eng. tragedy. *Gorboduc* is Senecan, declamatory, and vicariously and indiscriminately bloody (its murders are announced by messenger), but it is important as a tragedy in blank verse. Tragedy had to wait upon Marlowe and Kyd for real significance. Meanwhile the playwrights wrote in alexandrines, or fourteeners, or the combination of these called poulter's measure. Preston's sprawling and bombastic *Cambyses* (ca. 1569) is an instance of the popular drama that Sidney scorned in his *Defence of Poesy* (1581), and that Falstaff and Ancient Pistol were to burlesque. Christopher Marlowe (1564–93) brought Elizabethan tragedy to maturity with *Tamburlaine*, *Edward II*, *Doctor Faustus*, and *The Jew of Malta*. He contributed a new command of blank verse ("Marlowe's mighty line"), a new insight into dramatic character, and a troubled but expansive humanism. Thomas Kyd (1557?–1595?) supplied in *The Spanish Tragedy* an unprecedented skill in plot.

William Shakespeare (1564–1616) is of course too large for the perspective of this essay, and the variety of his achievement makes it impossible to characterize. Shakespeare has been anomalous to the neoclassics, romantic to the romantics, and metaphysical to the moderns. He was capable of excelling in classical L. comedy (*Comedy of Errors*) and in the courtly comedy of manners and affectation (*Love's Labour's Lost*), as well as in the mixed romantic comedy of *Midsummer Night's Dream, As You Like It, Much Ado About Nothing,* and *Twelfth Night.* His history plays, *Julius Caesar, Antony and Cleopatra, King John, Richard II* and *Richard III, Henry IV I and II, Henry V,* and the *Henry VI* plays stem organically from the development of the 16th-c. stage, but so far transcend their origins as to constitute a new dramatic genre. The enigmatic "problem plays," *Measure for Measure, All's Well That Ends Well,* and *Troilus and Cressida* also rise above the ground that nourished them. Of the tragedies, *Romeo and Juliet, Hamlet, King Lear, Macbeth, Othello,* and *Coriolanus,* it is useless to speak here. They correspond with but go beyond our general characterization of Elizabethan drama, while *The Winter's Tale* and *The Tempest* defy classification. Perhaps the one form unattempted by Shakespeare is the classical "regular" tragedy, to which category *Othello* most closely approaches.

From our point of view Shakespeare and Shakespearean blank verse dominate the Elizabethan and the Jacobean stage, and the subsequent history of poetic drama. In actual fact the Eng. Renaissance theatre had dozens of gifted poets writing for it, at the only time in Eng. stage history when the poetic and the popular play have been identical. The roll of dramatists is too long to do more than mention names, and we cannot here, like the players in *Hamlet,* enumerate dramatic genres. Before 1600 came John Lyly (1554?–1606) with Euphuistic prose comedies, Robert Greene's (1558–1592) *Friar Bacon and Friar Bungay,* and George Peele's *Arraignment of Paris.* Ben Jonson (1573?–1637) moved toward another and a neoclassical age in his comedies of the "humours" and his learned tragedies, *Sejanus* and *Catiline.* Dryden was to praise Shakespeare eloquently in his *Essay of Dramatic Poesy* (1667–68), but he chose Jonson's *Silent Woman* to analyze as a model of dramatic structure. Francis Beaumont (1584–1616) and John Fletcher (1579–1625) point also toward the Restoration, lowering tragedy to pathos, and Aristotle's "terror" of tragic effect to "admiration." The roster of playwrights is long—Thomas Heywood (1575?–1641), George Chapman (1559–

1634) with his tragedies from recent Fr. history, John Marston (1575–1634), of whom it has been unkindly said that "the first part of his *Antonio and Mellida* was the worst tragedy in Eng. till the second part appeared," Thomas Middleton (1570?–1627), Philip Massinger (1583–1640), John Ford (1583–1640?), and James Shirley (1596–1666). John Webster (1580?–1625?), who "was much possessed by death," is inheritor of Shakespeare's tragedy in *The White Devil* and *The Duchess of Malfi,* but his poetry and subtle thought stand apart from his shapeless plots. Cyril Tourneur (1575?–1626) brings the Senecan tradition to a turbulent end in *The Revenger's Tragedy.*

The Elizabethan and Jacobean drama are expansive and energetic. They are spacious and profuse in metaphor and imagery, fluid, swift, and various in movement, by classical standards loose in structure, and extravagant in event. In energy and variety they are predominantly "romantic," and in their romanticism they are for good or ill the norms of the poetic drama in Eng.

To return to nondramatic poetry, the influence of Spenser continued in the 17th c. in George Wither, William Browne, Giles and Phineas Fletcher, and Michael Drayton. Of these Drayton is most notable, for his sonnets, his narrative *Endymion and Phoebe,* his patriotic odes, his pastoral *The Muses' Elysium,* and his massive *Poly-Olbion,* an historico-patriotic-geographic poem *sui generis.* The main lines of the 17th c. up to the Restoration, however, followed Ben‿Jonson and John Donne. It is convenient to label Jonson and his "sons of Ben" neoclassical, and to call Donne and his group metaphysical. Herrick and the cavalier poets, Carew, Lovelace, and Suckling are thus Jonsonian and classical, with Donne, Herbert, Crashaw, Vaughan, Marvell, Cowley, and Cleveland in the metaphysical line. The classification, however, must be cautiously used. Jonson sometimes wrote like Donne and Donne like Jonson, Carew is both metaphysical and classical in his famous "Ask me no more where Jove bestows," as is Marvell in *To His Coy Mistress,* and the Horatian Herrick is capable of metaphysical wit in "Julia's Clothes" and elsewhere. They were all poets of the 17th c., with the same Elizabethan heritage to profit from and to react against. In the main they wrote short lyrics; the long Spenserian narrative and the didactic poem of reflection had gone out of fashion. Under the hand of Jonson, who developed the heroic couplet and the classical epigram, the lyric ceased to sing and became a talking poem, elaborated and refined in technique, with less exuberance and more apparent art than its 16th-c. counterpart. The transition from singing to talking is even more evident in Donne, who perfected the logical, argumentative structure already available in the Elizabethan sonnet.

Metaphysical poetry was first labeled in mockery by the conservative Drummond of Hawthornden, who disliked its "scholastic quiddities." Dryden employed the term unfavorably in describing Donne's love poetry, and Dr. Johnson made it stick in his life of Cowley (1779), still the *locus classicus* of discussion. The adjective is apt in connoting both cosmic largeness of view and subtle logical distinction. Metaphysical poetry reacts against the expansive affirmations, the optimistic humanism, and the conventionality of the Elizabethans, much as modern poetry has reacted against the 19th-c. romantics. Its world derives from the hierarchical world of the 16th c., but instead of accepting the orderly layers of being and meaning which harmonize so well with the methods of Spenserian multiple allegory, metaphysical poetry drives these layers violently together. It takes special delight in unifying, *discordia concors*, widely disparate elements. John Donne (1572–1631) wrote of sacred and profane love, the hope of heaven and the fear of hell, and frequently all these themes in the same poem or even in the same metaphor. Donne wrote songs, sonnets, satires, and meditations, but one thinks of him first as the author of dramatic lyrics like *The Canonization*, which fuses sex with saintliness, or *A Valediction: Forbidding Mourning*, with its famous conceit of the compass. By his mingled levity and seriousness, his ironic egocentricity, his rhetoric of shock and outrage, his subtle ambiguities, and his mastery of dramatic development of theme, Donne has profoundly affected 20th- as well as 17th-c. poetry. His use of counterpoint, in opposition in metrical and rhetorical stress, has had marked consequences in later versification.

George Herbert (1593–1633) is a quieter poet. His poetry is a record of religious experience, dramatized by conflict of the individual with the divine will. Herbert is fond of the "emblem" (q.v.) fashion of allegorical interpretation, to the point of giving some poems an emblematic physical shape. Richard Crashaw (1612–13–49) in his *Steps to the Temple* (1646) and other work is the most flamboyant and "baroque" of the metaphysical poets, his conceits more Sp. and It. than Eng. Henry Vaughan (1622–95) in the two parts of his *Silex Scintillans* (1650 and 1655) is a Christian neoplatonist whose almost pantheistic view of nature distinguishes him from the other metaphysicals in imagery and in thought. Bishop Henry King is remembered for his wonderful *Exequy*. Thomas Traherne (1637?–1674) was unpublished till the 19th c. Traherne like Vaughan was a mystic, who saw God immedi-

ately in nature. John Cleveland, once a great name, has been little read since the 18th c., and Abraham Cowley (1618–67) has now a merely historical interest from his elaborate "Pindaric" odes and his epic the *Davideis*. Cowley alone among the metaphysical poets welcomed the rise of science, which had already dismayed Donne in the new astronomy—

And new philosophy puts all in doubt;
The element of fire is quite put out—

and which was to have depressing effects upon the poetry of the future. A better poet than Cowley, the Horatian classicist Robert Herrick (1591–1674), is primarily a follower of Ben Jonson, but he is perhaps most enjoyed now for a latent metaphysical strain of tough-minded wit. Herrick's *Corinna's Maying* is like *Lycidas* in its harmonious fusion of pagan with native elements, though in Herrick's poem there is little of the Christian. Andrew Marvell's (1621–78) *To his Coy Mistress*, *The Garden*, and the *Horatian Ode upon Cromwell's Return from Ireland* today seem flawless. Less scholastic and more classical than Donne, Marvell at his best suits all tastes.

John Milton (1608–74) is traditionally second to Shakespeare among the Eng. poets, though powerful 20th-c. iconoclasts, especially T. S. Eliot and F. R. Leavis, have tried to overthrow him. Milton is the last and belated product of the earlier Renaissance, and the fulfillment of its dearest aspirations. He excelled in all but comedy and satire; a comedy by Milton is inconceivable, and his satire is all-out vituperation. Until the Restoration, satire did not prosper in the 17th c. Donne and Marvell tried it, but their satirical impulses were given better expression in the irony of their complex lyrics. Milton began his career with an Italianate baroque ode, *On the Morning of Christ's Nativity*, proceeded to better Ben Jonson in the urbane and charming pastoralism of the twin *L'Allegro* and *Il Penseroso*, and again in the masque of Comus; and brought the pastoral elegy to its consummation in *Lycidas*. In its exquisite mastery of its convention *Lycidas* is a wonderful tour-de-force, but recent critics have been most interested in its mythical pattern of death and rebirth. Milton's fine sonnets, chiefly Italianate, transmit the sonnet-form to the 18th and 19th c. *Paradise Lost* is the only successful epic in Eng. literature, and *Samson Agonistes* the only successful attempt at classical tragedy. As with Shakespeare in the drama, Milton's blank verse and his poetic diction, in the tradition of Spenser, so mastered later poetry that no poet could avoid them. Their power prevailed from Dryden to Robert Bridges.

THE AUGUSTANS. The tone of poetry from

the Restoration of Charles II to about 1750 was lowered by exhaustion from the religious ardors and domestic broils of the interregnum. There was a general distrust of "enthusiasm," which was associated with Puritanism, non-conformity, and extremism of all kinds. Further, the rise of physical science, with the prestige behind it of Bacon, Hobbes, and the Royal Society, tended to deprive poetry of its ground. The Royal Society's drive for denotative accuracy of language struck at the validity of poetic imagery and figure. The poets lost confidence in their calling; they retreated, and tried to consolidate and stabilize their new position. The age paradoxically combined humility with self-confidence. The Augustans, as the name indicates, thought their time comparable in refinement to the days of Virgil and Horace. They did not, however, suppose themselves to rival their forebears in genius; not merely the ancients but even their Eng. predecessors had stolen their best thoughts. Dryden looks back with awe to "the giants before the flood," and Pope pays tribute in the mock-heroic *Rape of the Lock* to an achievement beyond his reach. Retreating before science, poetry sought both refuge and reconciliation, on the one hand in the traditional authority of the great classics, on the other by limiting its subject matter to ethics, the manners of men in society, and the norm of human nature as attainable by reason—topics outside the interests of the physical sciences. Poetry tended, then, toward limitation and uniformity, and its ideals were "correctness," decorum, and consistency. The chief virtues of Augustan poetry are balance, restraint, control, and unillusioned realism, as in the sinewy verses of Swift, the arguments and satires of Dryden, and the ethical epistles of Pope. This poetry is an artifact, an object not large but consummately wrought.

The Augustans used many verse forms, but their characteristic measure is the heroic couplet, as in this famous passage from Sir John Denham's *Cooper's Hill*, which was held a model for the closed couplet structure in its "correctness" and its coherence of metrical with rhetorical accent: "O could I flow like thee, and make thy stream / My great example, as it is my theme! / Though deep yet clear; though gentle yet not dull; / Strong without rage, without o'erflowing full." The balanced parallels and antitheses of the heroic couplet embody the contradictions of the Augustan mind: its love of consistency and reason but also its perception of something ungraspable and beyond reason, whose presence the antithesis admits in paradox, but against which it is a weapon in mockery. The heroic couplet persists beyond the great Augustans in Dr. Johnson's Juvenalian *London* (1738) and *The*

Vanity of Human Wishes (1749), and in Oliver Goldsmith's *The Traveller* (1764) and *The Deserted Village* (1770). It continues into the early 19th c. as a vehicle for ethical reflection and satire. Byron used it effectively in *Eng. Bards and Scotch Reviewers* (1809), but it no longer expressed a real way of thought.

The chief genres of Augustan poetry are the satire and the reflective or argumentative poem. The mock-heroic narrative is a subtype and vehicle of satire, which after Samuel Butler's tetrameter *Hudibras* (1663) came fully of age in Dryden's *Absalom and Achitophel* (1681) and *Mac Flecknoe* (1681–82). The poem of reflection was often purely argumentative or reflective, as in Dryden's *Religio Laici* (1682) and *The Hind and the Panther* (1687), or Pope's *Essay on Criticism* (1711), which enunciated the central critical dictum of the era in

True wit is nature to advantage dress'd,
What oft was thought, but ne'er so well
                                        expressed.

There are also poems, however, which mingle reflection with natural and topographical description, such as Denham's *Cooper's Hill* (1642–55), Pope's *Windsor Forest* (1713), Thomson's *Seasons* (1726–30), Goldsmith's *Traveller* and *Deserted Village*, and William Cowper's *The Task* (1785). The mock-heroic narrative takes on its own individuality in Pope's *Rape of the Lock* (1711, 1714) and *Dunciad* (1728).

The Augustans also practiced the Pindaric ode, an elaborate form at the opposite pole from the heroic couplet. Dryden's ode to Mrs. Anne Killigrew (1685) and *Alexander's Feast* (1697) are brassy but impressive set-pieces. The form persisted, and was employed again by Thomas Gray (1716–71) and William Collins (1721–59). Gray's *The Progress of Poesy* is Augustan, but *The Bard*, like his later *The Fatal Sisters* and *The Descent of Odin* reflects the growing interest of the second half of the 18th c. in primitive and bardic poetry. Collins' *Pity, Fear, Simplicity, The Poetical Character, Evening, The Passions*, and *Popular Superstitions of the Highlands* show a new delicacy of feeling. To go beyond the 18th c., Coleridge's *Dejection: an Ode* (1802) and Wordsworth's *Ode on Intimations of Immortality* (1806) transformed the Pindaric into an instrument of individual emotion and philosophic speculation, and Tennyson revived its original public and formal function with amazing success in his official *Ode on the Death of the Duke of Wellington*.

To return to the Augustans, John Dryden (1631–1700), the most versatile and probably the most considerable poet of his era, excelled in all the characteristic genres, and was also critic, playwright, and translator. In 1672 he produced the best of the Heroic Plays in couplets, *The Conquest of Granada,* and did still better in *All For Love* (1678), a blank-verse imitation of Shakespeare's *Antony and Cleopatra.* Dryden's version is enormously lower in intelligence and vitality than Shake-peare's, but *All For Love* is nonetheless a thoroughly satisfying "regular" play, which challenges Otway's *Venice Preserved* for the title of the finest poetic tragedy of its time. In his later days Dryden translated L. and Gr. classics, notably the *Eclogues,* the *Georgics,* and especially the *Aeneid* of Virgil, and in his *Fables* (1700) imitated poems and tales from Chaucer and Boccaccio with great success and later consequences in Wordsworth and in Keats's *Lamia.* In connection with Dryden it is well for us to remember that Augustan neo-classicism, though it was largely imported from France, was much less doctrinaire and more flexible and tolerant than Fr. neoclas-sicism. The better Eng. poets and critics could never be induced to disavow Shakespeare, the irregular play, and in general their heritage of great native poetry. Dryden appreciated Chaucer and Spenser, and was influenced by Donne; Pope translated Homer, but he also edited Shakespeare with considerable insight; and the formidable Dr. Johnson himself ad-ministered the *coup-de-grace* to the neo-classic "three unities."

Throughout his entire career Alexander Pope (1688–1744) progressed steadily toward a limited and uniform perfection. With con-summate self-knowledge, or "judgment" as his age would have said, he settled and fixed upon his forte. After some casual philandering with feeling and imagination in poems like *Pastorals* (1709), *Windsor Forest* (1713), and *The Elegy to the Memory of an Unfortunate Lady* (1717), he turned decisively to satire and to didactic essays and epistles in the manner of Horace, the favorite poet of the Augustans. He would have it his praise, as he wrote in his *Epistle to Dr. Arbuthnot,* "That not in fancy's maze he wandered long, / But stooped to truth, and moralized his song." Pope wrote the finest neoclassical poem in Eng. in *The Rape of the Lock.* His translations of Homer's *Iliad* (1715–20) and of part of the *Odyssey* (1725–26) were influential as late as the 19th c., but they bore the reproach of corrupting taste by their vicious "poetic diction."

THE ROMANTICS. Eng. romanticism has been traced in a bewildering variety of tendencies and poets. Some critics have even found a foretaste of it in the *Windsor Forest* and the *Elegy to . . . An Unfortunate Lady* of the arch-Augustan Pope. As the "Return to Na-ture" it has been perceived in James Thom-son's *Seasons,* Lady Winchilsea's *Nocturnal*

Reverie (1714), and John Dyer's *Grongar Hill* (1726). As the "Awakening of Feeling" it is prepared for by Rousseau and the sentimental-ists, and is connected with the bitter-sweet melancholy of Gray's *Elegy Written in a Coun-try Churchyard* (1750), Edward Young's *Night Thoughts* (1742), and Robert Blair's *Grave* (1743). A revival of interest in the Middle Ages, and in native folk poetry and culture as against the prevailing classicism and internationalism of the Augustans, appears in the poetry and criticism of Joseph and Thomas Warton, and in Bishop Percy's ballad collection, the *Reliques of Ancient Eng. Poetry* (1765). The Wartons revived appreciation of Spenser, and Joseph Warton wrote a poem significantly en-titled *The Enthusiast,* or *The Lover of Nature.* Burns made literature of the Scottish scene and song.

Eng. romanticism has also been variously identified with humanitarianism, democracy, and the doctrine of the perfectibility of man, and organicism in reaction against the New-tonian mechanical universe of science. It should not be confined to any single notion, however, without due caution. Like Eng. neo-classicism, Eng. romanticism is relatively loose, nontheoretical, and tolerant of self-contradic-tions. Unlike the German romantics, who established a definite critical program, the Eng. generally wrote the poetry first and de-cided afterward what it signified. Coleridge's account of the purposes of the *Lyrical Ballads,* which is the nearest to a definite romantic credo, was written long after the poetic facts that occasioned it. The poets were not con-scious of forming a romantic school. Neverthe-less, romanticism is an intelligible and a useful concept if we take care to make it broad enough. The sense of infinite potentiality, the organic view of the mind and nature, the re-spect for imagination and poetic truth, the shift from poetry as imitation to poetry as creation, are different aspects of the same object. The main current of romanticism runs in Blake, Wordsworth, Coleridge, Shelley, and Keats, but Scott, Burns, and Byron are also romantics.

The romantic period brought about no abso-lute changes in versification and poetic genres. The traditional genres remained, although less rigidly distinguished from each other than they had been under the Augustans. The poets returned to the study of Chaucer and the great Elizabethans, and to Milton, whom they now saw in a new light. They reacted against the Augustans but nevertheless made use of them; for romanticism is not a rejection of reason but a resynthesis of reason and feeling, of the head and the heart. Compared to the Augustans they were daring and various in their versification, but they were seldom really radical. The reflective poem was continued, generally in blank verse, by Wordsworth and Coleridge, the sonnet was again practiced, especially by Wordsworth and Keats, the metrical romance was widely current and popular, Byron and Landor wrote classical epigrams, the Elizabethan song was reborn in Blake and Shelley, and the epic was attempted unsuccessfully by Southey in *Madoc* and *Thalaba* and inconclusively by Keats in his splendid, unfinished *Hyperion* (1818). Satire existed, but notably only in Byron's *Vision of Judgment* (1822) and *Don Juan* (1819–24). The Augustan interest in manners had generally lapsed, and it was not a satiric time. Perhaps epic was no longer possible, and *Don Juan* and Wordsworth's *Prelude* were in their different ways the 19th c. equivalents of epic. The elaborate pastoral elegy, neglected by the Augustans and condemned by Dr. Johnson, reappeared in Shelley's *Adonais*.

In the latter half of the 18th c. two forgers of literary antiquities achieved poetry in their forgeries: James Macpherson (1736–96), and the pathetic Thomas Chatterton (1752–70), whom later poets set up as the type of poetic genius. These men were more or less isolated from their society, as was Christopher Smart (1722–71), who wrote his astonishing *Song to David* in a madhouse. The theory has recently been advanced with some earnestness that in the state of literary culture of the late 18th c. insanity was the best equipment for a poet, and Smart, William Cowper, and William Blake have been proposed as instances of proof. Blake (1757–1827) was certainly not mad, but so unprecedented were his personality and art that many of his contemporaries found madness the simplest explanation for them. Blake is today accepted as both a great poet and a great painter, and his radical doctrine of poetic imagination is thoroughly congenial to the modern critic. In *Songs of Innocence* and *Songs of Experience* Blake is an unsurpassed lyricist, but the poetic status of his gigantic *Prophetic Books* is still in doubt. There is no doubt about their intellectual energy, but it is not clear that their content is fittingly clothed in form. It is possible, however, that their very magnitude obscures their artistic outlines.

William Wordsworth (1770–1850) and Samuel Taylor Coleridge (1772–1834) are the fullest and most characteristic exponents of Eng. romantic poetry. Unlike Blake, who on behalf of imagination denied external reality, Wordsworth and Coleridge believed in the essential unity of the mind and nature. Their joint *Lyrical Ballads* (1798) introduced a new kind of poetry, and in his 1800 Preface Wordsworth challenged neoclassicism with a daring attack upon poetic diction, demanding for poetry "a language really spoken by men." Both Wordsworth and Coleridge, however, were well acquainted with the Augustans and their immediate successors, and Wordsworth in particular had many points of kinship with them.

Wordsworth is too prolific for satisfactory summary. In the posthumous *Prelude* (1850), an autobiography of his poetic development, he turned the action of the epic inward. *The Prelude* was to introduce a trilogy, *The Recluse,* which would have spanned the whole relationship of man to nature and society. The existing *Recluse* is only an introductory fragment. In *The Prelude* and *The Excursion* (1814) Wordsworth remade the 18th-c. reflective-topographical poem, transforming nature by his shaping imagination. Coleridge's greatest poetic achievements are *The Ancient Mariner, Dejection: an Ode,* and the unfinished *Kubla Khan* and *Christabel.* He was also happy, however, in the "conversation poem," a relaxed and intimate meditation in blank verse, which owed much to the 18th c. and something to the epistles of Horace. Of this group of poems *Frost at Midnight* is the most perfect and *This Limetree Bower My Prison* the richest. Lord Byron (1788–1824), arrogant, passionate, and wayward, was Augustan in theory although seldom in practice. Byron, once thought of as the crown and epitome of romanticism, has in the 20th c. sunk lower than his deserts because of his comparative lack of verbal distinction. Since his forte is quasi-oratorical amplification, he is at his best in bulk. Byron was a hasty and voluminous writer who succeeded too easily and too soon, but his poetry steadily improved throughout his short and crowded career. Aside from Burns he is the only romantic with wit, and with that anticlimactic self-mockery which has been labeled "romantic irony." Chiefly with the aid of the It. tradition of Pulci and Ariosto, he developed the loose narrative romance from the early *Childe Harold* to his highest achievement in *Don Juan.*

Percy Bysshe Shelley (1792–1822) combined the pastoral tradition of Petrarch, Spenser, and the Sicilian Greeks with his own social idealism and Platonic thought. In *Adonais* and his lyrical drama *Prometheus Unbound* he revitalized myth for contemporary purposes. With Byron and Keats he is a romantic Hellenist. Shelley is a virtuoso of metrics and of language who during most of the 19th c. was considered like Spenser before him the ideal poet's poet, but his passionate idealism has repelled the metaphysical critics of our own time. Shelley, like Blake, conceived of the poet as prophet and law-giver; John Keats (1795–1821) thought of him primarily as an artist, though not in the limited Augustan sense of craftsman. Of all the romantics Keats, at least in his early poetry, attacked the Augustans most forthrightly, and in *Endymion* (1817) he followed Leigh Hunt's lead in giving narrative speed and variety to the heroic couplet. Later, however, he went to school to Dryden for the couplets of *Lamia* (1819). Like Shelley Keats revitalized Gr. myth, most fully in the unfinished epic *Hyperion* (1818–19), which makes use of the entire theogony of the ancients. With Shelley and Wordsworth he mastered Miltonic blank verse, and of all the romantics drew most extensively upon the Elizabethans. Keats aspired to Shakespearean dramatic objectivity, but he returned in *The Fall of Hyperion* to Spenserian allegory, which he might in time have significantly refashioned. In his six "great odes" Keats developed a new stanza form out of the sonnet and the Spenserian stanza.

Robert Burns (1759–96) is romantic in his democratic sympathies, his attachment to folk tradition, and his gift of imaginative realism, of discerning the unusual within the usual circumstances of ordinary life. Burns inherited a long and not unlearned Scottish tradition, and as his stanza forms often show, something of Fr. as well. Burns's songs are matchless, and his narrative *Tam O'Shanter* a comic masterpiece. His impressive *The Jolly Beggars* is an adaptation of the ballad-opera like Gay's famous work. Sir Walter Scott (1771–1832) shared Burns's devotion to Scottish songs and ballads in his *Minstrelsy of the Scottish Border* (1802–3). Scott's metrical romances of Scottish history, such as *The Lay of the Last Minstrel*, *Marmion*, and *The Lady of the Lake*, are superficial but graceful and stirring. Robert Southey, once a great name, is now read only by scholars, and not even scholars are generally conversant with Campbell and Samuel Rogers. In 1819 Byron challenged the position of the "Lakers," Wordsworth, Coleridge, and Southey, with "Scott, Rogers, Campbell, Moore, and Crabbe will try / 'Gainst you the question with posterity." Byron was speaking for orthodox and popular taste, but he was mistaken in betting against Wordsworth and Coleridge. Crabbe's genuine virtues lack glamour, and Moore's Oriental *Lalla Rookh* has gone the way of Southey. Leigh Hunt and John Clare must be neglected here, as also Walter Savage Landor, a considerable but not an influential poet.

Since Dryden there has been little vital relationship between Eng. poetry and the stage. The 18th c. admired Congreve's *Mourning Bride* (1697) and Addison's *Cato*, and among the romantics Coleridge's *Remorse* and Byron's revivals of Restoration heroics enjoyed some success. Shelley's *The Cenci* (1820) is the finest Eng poetic drama of the 19th c., but because of its monstrous theme it has never been tested in genuinely public performances. Blake and Keats left fragments of Shakespearean blank-verse plays, and the young Wordsworth made a serious attempt in *The Borderers*. Among the Victorians Tennyson, Browning, and Swinburne all wrote ambitious plays, but they were essentially untheatrical, despite the efforts of Irving for Tennyson and Macready for Browning.

THE VICTORIANS. The Victorian period should be thought of as running from the 1830's to the eve of World War I, a boundary comparable to the civil wars of the 17th c. The number of competent poets whose work falls within these limits is too great to permit even summary justice in dealing with them. Tennyson stands at one end of the era, and Hardy, who lived till 1928, at the other. Victorian poetry is a continuation of romantic poetry in its feeling for nature, its idealism, its subjectivity, and its variety. Romanticism, however, got there first, and preempted broad territories which the Victorians could only divide and cultivate. The romantics were able, in Coleridge's words, "to bring the whole soul of man into activity" as the Victorians could not: among them the romantic synthesis of heart and head broke down. The new findings of science deprived the Victorians of the romantic creed of nature; Tennyson, Browning, Arnold, Hardy, Housman, and others possess the romantic sensibility without the romantic belief. There was a difference, too, in the poet's relation to his audience. The great mid-Victorians, whatever their private peculiarities, were more central to their society and closer to a general audience than the romantics were, and like the Victorian novelists they incurred special responsibilities and were bound by special conventions by their relation to their audience. The last third of the 19th c. reacted to earlier pieties in the neopaganism of Swinburne, of Edward Fitzgerald's *Rubaiyat of Omar Khayyam*, and later on of A. E. Housman; in the Pre-Raphaelites Rossetti and Morris; and in the art-for-art's sake impressionism of the poets of the 1890's, indicated by the shift in taste from Ruskin's art theories to Whistler's. Despite much fine poetry, the result is a derivative and decorative romanticism which brought down upon itself the antiromanticism of the 20th c.

Like the romantics, the Victorians worked in many genres and metrical forms. The long narrative or metrical romance is less prominent than it had been, though far from being completely neglected. Browning's dramatic lyrics and monologues are highly characteristic of his age, as well as being significant for the future. His massive *Ring and the Book* (1868–69) foreshadows modern prose-fictional experiments in pure point of view. Hardy's dramatically ironic lyrics also owe something to Browning. Tennyson took up the dramatic monologue effectively in *Ulysses*, and more elaborately in the psychological "monodrama" *Maud* (1855). Tennyson frequently employed what might be called the lyrical monologue, where a dominant theme is projected through a single character in feeling and pictorial description: *Oenone* and *Tithonus* are outstanding examples of the type. Lyrical drama, in the manner of Shelley's *Hellas* and *Prometheus Unbound*, is represented among the Victorians in Arnold's *Empedocles upon Etna* (1852) and Swinburne's *Atalanta in Calydon* (1865), the latter of which led to Sir Gilbert Murray's later translations of Greek tragedy. Hardy's tremendous panorama of the Napoleonic Wars, *The Dynasts* (1903–8), is of the same general pattern.

The literary ballad of the romantics is refined and attenuated by Rossetti and by William Morris, who added the atmosphere of Keats's *La Belle Dame sans Merci* to the ballad-refrain and produced musically nostalgic poems like Morris's "Two red roses against the moon"—parodied by C. S. Calverley in "The auld wife sat by the ivied door—/ Butter and eggs and a pound of cheese." Keats's influence, transmitted through Tennyson, was the chief direct contribution of the romantics to Victorianism. His modulations of Miltonic blank verse are evident in the heightened narrative, too densely pictorial and static for epic, of Tennyson's *Idylls of the King*. Pastoral, a little declined from Wordsworth's *Michael*, continues in Tennyson's *Enoch Arden* (1864), and in Arnold's more classical *Scholar Gipsy* (1853) and George Meredith's intoxicating *Love in the Valley* (1851, 1878). The sonnet tradition, lapsed after Wordsworth, revived in sonnet-sequences like Rossetti's *House of Life* (1848–81) and Meredith's *Modern Love* (1862). Matthew Arnold, with his respect for the classics, tried his hand at epic in the marmoreal *Sohrab and Rustum* (1853), and at the pastoral elegy in *Thyrsis* (1863). Tennyson's freer adaptation of the pastoral tradition in *In Memoriam* (1850) produced a more vital and representative poem, more central to its age.

The Victorians, who valued humor more than wit, were not notable satirists. They were more inclined to exercise their combative impulses in plain personal vituperation. Browning's *Caliban upon Setebos* and *Mr. Sludge the Medium*, however, demonstrate a genuine flair for satire, quite un-Augustan in its intricacy and its fondness for the grotesque and particular. Nonsense-verse and parody, not of course previously unknown, appeared as distinct genres in Edward Lear, Lewis Carroll (Charles Lutwidge Dodgson), C. S. Calverley, and W. S. Gilbert. The earlier didactic-reflective poem became a form of *vers-de-societé* in Tennyson's *Princess* (1847) and Arthur Hugh Clough's *The Bothie of Tober-na-Vuolich* (1848); and a rhapsodic oration in Swinburne.

The Victorian giants are Alfred, Lord Tennyson (1809–92), Robert Browning (1812–89), Matthew Arnold (1822–88), and Thomas Hardy (1840–1928). Of these Tennyson, though now least influential of the four, is doubtless greatest, in technique, sensibility, and concentrated moral power. Browning's force and originality would be more evident if he had written less. Arnold, with his wide range and keen intelligence, is not, like Tennyson, totally committed to his craft; if judged by the highest standards his poetry is tentative and experimental. Hardy is closest to us in spirit, with his tragic irony, his colloquial and technical vocabulary and his metrical harshness and indecorum, but he is Victorian in his old-fashioned scientific materialism on the one hand and on the other a now-vanished traditional *virtus* and ancestral piety. Gerard Manley Hopkins (1844–89), who was substantially unpublished till 1918, by his "inscape" and "sprung rhythm" (qq.v.) has influenced much modern poetry. Some critics have placed him in the highest company.

In our own century the Georgian poets included in Sir Edward Marsh's anthologies (1911–22) belong on the whole to the Victorian rather than the modern tradition. Two of them, however, Walter de la Mare (1873–1956) and Robert Graves (1895–) have won major reputations, and D. H. Lawrence must be mentioned. John Masefield's (1878–) merits are perhaps obscured by popularity and official honors, while poets like J. E. Flecker (d. 1915), J. C. Squire, and John Drinkwater for the present have little to say to us. Among the war poets Wilfred Owen is most important. In addition to his intrinsic worth, which goes beyond the humanitarian indignation that gave him impetus, his metrical experiments look toward the future. Rupert Brooke, Edward Thomas, and Isaac Rosenberg were killed like Owen in the war, and Siegfried Sassoon's best verse dated from the war years.

THE MODERNS. Modern poets have been oppressed both by science and society, and have felt a more than usual sense of crisis. The effects of two world wars, the breakdown of cultural tradition, loss of religious faith, the rise of media of mass-communication, and the declining importance of the individual have all conspired to drive the poets into self-conscious isolation. The language of modern poetry is difficult, obscure, and "pure"; the poets have sought to avoid the terms in which our society expresses itself, distrusting them as stereotypes of mass emotions. Rejecting also the poetic diction and rhetoric of the past, they have been forced to invent their own vocabulary, and, in the fragmentation of our culture, their own philosophy and myths as well.

In reaction on the one hand against the denotative language of science and on the other against the debased currency of popular feeling and decadent romanticism, most modern poets have rejected direct statement for indirection, and logical development of ideas for either a "metaphysical" exploration of the logic of metaphor or a "symbolist" development of the multiple associations of words. Both techniques are often to be found in the same modern poem. The result is ambiguity, complexity, and irony, dramatically organized in a structure of opposing tensions which it is the business of the poem to resolve. Modern poetry has had to cope with new doctrines and systems—Marxism, depth psychology, comparative anthropology, neo-Thomism—and has fought to assimilate their internal relationships to systems of poetic structure, and their contents to myths. Myth has assumed overwhelming importance, as a poetic truth independent of the privative truths of science.

The traditional genres still exist in modern poetry, but for the most part they have undergone radical changes. The dramatic lyric has become the norm of poetry, and the longer narrative and reflective poems have largely disappeared. True narrative now seems impossible, since the poet no longer finds significance in external action, but the reflective poem appears in a new guise in Eliot's *Waste Land* and *Four Quartets*. W. H. Auden and others have at times made use of the verse-epistle. In its habitual mingling of levity and seriousness, modern poetry continually verges upon satire and *vers-de-société*, both generally mordant. Eliot has practiced both, and his poetry of the inhuman modern city is descended not only from Baudelaire but from the informal mock-heroics of Swift. His famous comparison in *Prufrock* of the evening sky to "a patient etherized upon a table" resembles Swift's epic simile in *A Description of a City Shower* in spirit if not in form:

Meanwhile the South, rising with dabbled
    wings,
A sable cloud athwart the welkin flings,
That swilled more liquor than it could contain,
And, like a drunkard, gives it up again.

W. B. Yeats and W. H. Auden have written satire, and Auden's *In Memory of W. B. Yeats* is a carefully modern pastoral elegy.

Modern poetry began with imagism, a movement more notable for its manifestoes than its accomplishments. It aimed at distinctness and precision in imagery and an organic unity obtained by the use of free verse, in reaction to late-romantic haziness and conventionally regular meters. Pure imagism is difficult to adhere to, and few poets did. T. E. Hulme's scanty but provocative work exercised a disproportionately large influence, and D. H. Lawrence's (1885–1930) verse was partly imagist. In 1917 Eliot's *Love Song of J. Alfred Prufrock* struck a new note, and his criticism, his startling and cryptic *The Waste Land* (1920), along with the publication of Sir Herbert Grierson's anthology of *Metaphysical Lyrics and Poems of the Seventeenth Century* (1921) ushered in a fully modern poetry, an antiromantic blend of the post-Versailles temperament, the metaphysical poets, and the Fr. symbolists, seasoned with a dash of Freud, Dante, and *The Golden Bough*. The chief poets of the 1930's were prevailingly post-Eliot, though Auden, C. Day Lewis, Louis MacNeice, and Stephen Spender were all more directly concerned than was Eliot with the contemporary scene and social problems. These were not only postwar but post-Depression poets. W. B. Yeats was active almost up to his death in 1939, but his influence is much less clearly marked than Eliot's.

Dylan Thomas (1914–54) was assisted in establishing his own utterance by the Celtic tradition of verbal splendor, by the poetry of Hopkins, and by Hart Crane's kaleidoscopic associational imagery. The publication of his collected poems shortly after his death was treated as a major literary event. George Barker (1913–) is like Thomas in intensity and violence. Modern poetry escapes the classifying eye as it nears the present, but Sir Herbert Read has fostered the neoromanticism of Henry Treece and others, perhaps closer to surrealism than to traditional romanticism.

The poetic drama has stayed alive, perhaps even gained a little. Early in the century Lascelles Abercrombie and Gordon Bottomley experimented both with diction and staging. Like them, Yeats turned from the photographic realism of the 19th c., until in his latter plays the drama became ritual, symbol, and dance. Eliot has tended in the other direction, from his earlier *Family Reunion* and *Murder in the Cathedral* to *The Cocktail Party* and *The Confidential Clerk*. He has striven to achieve colloquial dialogue without falling into prose, whereas Christopher Fry has frankly sought Elizabethan color and music in his efforts to restore the nobleness of life.

William Butler Yeats (1865–1939), Thomas Stearns Eliot (1888–), and Wystan Hugh Auden (1907–) are the chief figures of modern Eng. poetry. Some critics would admit Thomas to their company. Yeats is perhaps the greatest of these, Eliot the most influential, and Auden the most widely representative of modern ideas. Yeats, a fine Pre-Raphaelite and then a great modern poet, was able to move without a break from an older tradition, and without losing his singing voice in the process. He is distinctively modern in his absolute rejection of science in favor of myth; like Blake he is a radical of the imagination. Like the romantics, however, he maintains the gospel of the heart, and keeps up a connection with folk ballad and song. His transformation from Pre-Raphaelite to modern was most apparent in *The Tower* (1928).

An account of T. S. Eliot is an account of modern poetry itself, so marked is his originality, and so powerful his prestige. The prevalence of organization by mythical motif, ironical juxtaposition, and metrical cacophony are all due to his practice of them. Eliot's early theme of the hollow men gradually gave way to meditations upon the hope of Grace, but the manner of his faith is itself an indictment of our ordinary world. Exquisitely austere, his poetry gives the effect of a dramatic struggle for an impossible annunciation.

In W. H. Auden contemporary thought is most comprehensively if not most intensely presented. Dazzlingly versatile and agile, Auden has ranged from the *canzone* to the popular song, from OE accentual verse to Byronic ottava rima. He reclothes old pieties and values in modern, sometimes modish terms, as when in *Petition* God is requested to function as a power-and-light company, or as in *September 3, 1939* romantic sympathy is indistinguishable from antiromantic Marxism. It grows increasingly unnatural to make absolute distinctions between Eng. and American poetry. It may be that the two will become one in the poetry of Auden, now for some years an American citizen.

ANTHOLOGIES: *A Select Collection of Old Plays*, ed. R. Dodsley (12 v., 1744, 1780, 1825; 16th- and 17th-c. poetic drama); *The Works of the Eng. Poets, from Chaucer to Cowper*, ed. A. Chalmers (1810; a famous coll., containing Johnson's *Lives*); *The Eng. Poets*, ed. T. H. Ward (5 v., 1880, 1918; from Chaucer to Rupert Brooke, with a famous introd. by Arnold); *The Oxford Book of Eng. Verse, 1250–1900*, ed. A. T. Quiller-Couch (1900); *Georgian Poetry*, ed. E. Marsh (6 v., 1912–22); *Metaphysical Lyrics and Poems of the 17th C.*, ed. H. J. C. Grierson (1921; an epoch-making anthol.); *Circumference*, ed. G. Taggart (1929; a broad interpretation and selection of metaphysical poetry); *Understanding Poetry*, ed. C. Brooks and R. P. Warren (1938, 1950, 1960; the most influential modern textbook anthol.); *Poets of the Eng. Language*, ed. W. H. Auden and N. H. Pearson (5 v., 1950; an excellent sel. of poetry from Langland to Yeats); *Six Centuries of Great Poetry*, ed. R. P. Warren and A. Erskine (1955; concise, well-chosen, and inexpensive); *New Poets of England and America*, ed. D. Hall *et al.* (1958); *Modern Verse in Eng.*, ed. D. Cecil and A. Tate (1958); *Modern British Poetry*, ed. L. Untermeyer (new and enl. ed., 1962); *The Oxford Book of 19th-C. Eng. Verse*, chosen by J. Hayward (1964).

HISTORY AND CRITICISM: T. Warton, *Hist. of Eng. Poetry* (1774–81; 4 v., 1871; the first comprehensive study); S. Johnson, *Lives of the Eng. Poets*, ed. G. B. Hill (3 v., 1905; the classic practical crit. of the Augustans, and in the life of Cowley the definition of metaphysical poetry); C. Lamb, *Specimens of Eng. Dramatic Poets* (1808) in *The Works of Charles and Mary Lamb*, ed. E. V. Lucas, IV (1904); S. T. Coleridge, *Biographia Literaria* (1817, ed. J. Shawcross, 2 v., 1907; see esp. chs. 14, 15, 16); W. Hazlitt, "Lectures on the Eng. Poets" (1818; *The Complete Works*, ed. P. P. Howe, V, 1932); "Lectures on the Dramatic Lit. of the Age of Elizabeth" (1820; *Complete Works*, VI; the romantic viewpoint); W. J. Courthope, *A Hist. of Eng. Poetry* (6 v., 1895–1910; the most extensive general hist., ending with the romantic movement); J. M. Berdan, *Early Tudor Poetry, 1485–1547* (1920); R. D. Havens, *The Influence of Milton on Eng. Poetry* (1922); G. Hughes, *Imagism and the Imagists* (1931; the authoritative treatment); Wilson (an objective examination of symbolist influence upon modern poetry); D. Bush, *Mythology and the Renaissance Tradition in Eng. Poetry* (1932); *Mythology and the Romantic Trad. in Eng. Poetry* (1937); *Science and Eng. Poetry* (1950); *Eng. Poetry* (1952; an excellent brief survey from Chaucer to the 1950's); J. C. Ransom, *The World's Body* (1938; exposition of metaphysical poetics); C. Brooks, *Modern Poetry and the Trad.* (1939); *The Well Wrought Urn* (1947; Eng. poetry and the metaphysical trad.); D. Daiches, *Poetry and the Modern World* (1940); B. I. Evans, *Trad. and Romanticism* (1940; reconciliations of classic and romantic tendencies in Eng. poetry); G. N. Shuster, *The Eng. Ode from Milton to Keats* (1940); F. A. Pottle, *The Idiom of Poetry* (1941; periods of poetry treated as shifts of sensibility); R. P. Warren, "Pure and Impure Poetry," KR, 5 (1943); J. Miles, *The Continuity of Poetic Language: Studies in Eng. Poetry from the 1540's to the 1940's* (1951; close studies of the vocabulary of periods); D. Stauffer, *The Nature of Poetry* (1946; argues against a rigid "tradition" of Eng. poetry); H. J. C. Grierson and J. C. Smith, *A Critical Hist. of Eng. Poetry* (1947; a good 1-v. hist.); Tuve (emphasizes contemp. rhetorical and philos. bases); A. Warren, *Rage for Order* (1948; techniques of various periods); T. S. Eliot, *Selected Essays* (new ed., 1950; influential discussions of the Elizabethans, the Jacobeans, the metaphysicals, and the general trad. of Eng. poetry); C. S. Lewis, *Eng. Lit. in* the 16th C. Excluding Drama (1954); A. Alvarez, *Stewards of Excellence. Studies in Modern Eng. and Am. Poetry* (1958); D. Daiches, *Crit. Hist. of Eng. Lit.* (2 v., 1960); J. Press, *Rule and Energy: Trends in British Poetry Since the 2d World War* (1963). R.H.F.

ENGLISH PROSODY. It is more accurate to speak of Eng. prosodies than of Eng. prosody, for, historically considered, the phenomena of Eng. versification are too manifold and complex to be explained according to a single metrical system, although some scholars and critics have expended whole careers in unhappy attempts to show that all Eng. verse of whatever period manifests one prosodic principle. Only the following three feeble generalizations would seem to hold true for all Eng. verse: (1) Because Eng. is a more markedly accentual language than the Romance tongues, stress has generally played a more notable part in the structure of Eng. verse than it has in many continental poetries; (2) the Eng. language, when metered by whatever system (see METER), appears to flow most pleasingly and naturally in ascending rhythms (q.v.); and (3) most Eng. poetry seems naturally to seek a line-length neither short nor long: the most "natural" line-length in Eng. would appear to be one of 4 or 5 isochronous units, as in the O. Eng. 4-stress accentual line or the Shakespearean "iambic pentameter" (it is well to remember that about three-fourths of all Eng. poetry is in blank verse). Other than sharing these few common characteristics, the poetries of various periods manifest very few prosodic similarities, and their unique characteristics are best seen if we isolate them philologically.

OLD ENGLISH (ca. 500–ca. 1100). The powerful accents of the OE language supply a natural basis for a heavily accentual prosody (see METER) in which sense rhythm, at every point, provides the meter. The standard OE line consists of 4 strongly stressed syllables arranged, together with any number of unstressed syllables, in 2 hemistichs (or half lines) of 2 stresses each. Stressed syllables frequently alliterate, and stichic rather than strophic structure prevails. The 2 hemistichs are separated by an invariable medial caesura (q.v.). "Rests" and the occasional omission of stressed syllables (especially in the second hemistich) provide a sort of syncopation or counterpoint (q.v.) which keeps the prosodic structure varied and expressive (see Pope, *The Rhythm of Beowulf*). The following example from *Beowulf* (lines 4–7) shows the "normal" line structure (second line) and the possibilities of variation through rest and omission of stress (third and fourth lines):

Oft Scýld Scéfing   sceaþena þréatum,

mónegum mǽgþum   méodsetla oftéah,

égsode eorlas   syþþan ǽrest wearþ

féasceaft funden   he þaes frofre gebad . . .

Pope has conjectured that, in recitation, the "normal" position of stresses was signaled by a chord on a harp; this constant "beat" would provide a sort of metrical underpinning against which rhythmical variations dictated by rhetorical emphasis would be strikingly noticeable. Despite its apparent simplicity, OE prosody is an instrument of extremely subtle expressiveness: its variations from the "ideal" meter and its returns to it give the rhythm a constantly shifting surface of great sophistication. (See also ENG. POETRY; OLD GERMANIC PROSODY.)

MIDDLE ENGLISH (ca. 1100–ca. 1500): After the Norman Conquest, the rapid changes in the language (loss of inflection, Romance incursions into what had been primarily a Germanic vocabulary, the multiplication of dialects) quickly complicated the principles of Eng. prosody. Although it persisted for a time in the new language, the OE accentual line, with its varying number of unaccented syllables, is gradually abandoned in favor of a line in which syllabic numeration becomes, for the first time, one of the structural criteria. One can observe the phenomenon of the 2 hemistichs of the OE line transforming themselves into the alternating 4- and 3-stress lines of the ballad meter (q.v.). Strophic construction makes inroads on stichic, and elaborate "tail-rhyme" stanzas begin to appear. The strongly Germanic accentual quality of the language begins to weaken slightly, and instead of a prosody of powerful and emphatic pressures at equal times we find a prosody more conscious of the qualitative similarities between stressed and unstressed syllables. The linguistic complexities of the period created a situation in which many unique prosodies are actually to be found simultaneously. We find (1) a continuation of OE prosody adapted (often by the addition of assonance and rhyme) to an increasingly uninflected language; (2) accentual-syllabic rhyming verse in lines of 4 stresses, gradually lengthening to become the heroic couplet (q.v.) of Chaucer and Lydgate; (3) accentual verse in hexameter line-lengths with a strong pseudo-classical air; and (4) a sort of "sprung rhythm" (q.v.), especially in songs and other lyrical pieces set to music. Out of all this complication, and with the relative stabilization of language and dialects, the decasyllabic, 5-stress line of Chaucer gradually emerged, and this line provides the basis for Renaissance developments.

MODERN ENGLISH (ca. 1500–); *16th and 17th C.:* Three circumstances are of great importance in Renaissance prosody: (1) The Eng. language attained a period of relative stability; (2) the widespread admiration of the classics of antiquity served to focus attention on the apparently unsystematic and occasionally rather coarse quality of earlier Eng. metric; and (3) rhetorical and metrical criticism, in the manner of the ancients, began to be written and to be read. These circumstances gave impetus to that stream of systematic and academic prosodic speculation and dogmatizing which has continued without break to our own times.

The Renaissance admiration for Gr. meters impelled one school to attempt to import into Eng. practice Gr. quantitative theory, and theorists, dilettantes, and poets like Cheke, Ascham, Sidney, Dyer, Drant, Spenser, Greene, Campion, Harvey, and Stanihurst labored, with varying degrees of seriousness and success, to imitate the classical heroic hexameter or the Gr. lyric measures. Since the poet was obliged, however, to remember constantly the predetermined "quantities" of the syllables he was using, composition was a laborious, academic-theoretical business, and little work of any natural virtue resulted (see METER).

Along with this impulse to "refine" Eng. poetry by making it mimic Gr. rhythms went the development of the Chaucerian accentual-syllabic pentameter line as a vehicle for dramatic expression. Both Marlowe and Shakespeare use it with consummate mastery, calmly inventing new tonalities when they have exhausted the old, and even the lesser dramatists of the period reveal, through their instinctive feeling of comfort within it, that this is going to be, for whatever reason, The Eng. Line. In lyric verse, the song writers, often obliged to fit words to preexisting airs, produce free accentual lines which foreshadow the sprung rhythm (q.v.) of Hopkins, and lyric practitioners like Donne, Crashaw, Herbert, and Marvell make of the iambic tetrameter or pentameter line a vehicle for wit, shock, and ecstasy by shifting or adding stresses boldly.

And yet, in the midst of all this freedom and inventiveness, signs of an impulse toward greater regulation and predictability are apparent: Daniel's *Defense of Rhyme* (?1603) is a conservative document which anticipates the practice of Denham and Waller, and 20th-c. students (Bridges, Sprott) have shown that Milton, in *Paradise Lost,* despite the expressive variation or omission of stresses, was adhering consciously to a fixed decasyllabic limitation. The end of the Renaissance thus sees a movement away from the metrical spontaneity of the Elizabethans; prosody, both in theory and practice, is now moving toward an ideal of strict syllabic limitation and relative predictability of stress placement.

18th C.: Post-Restoration prosody reveals strong Fr. syllabic influence: the number of syllables instead of the number of stresses becomes the essential criterion of the poetic line. Theorists like Edward Bysshe, Richard Bentley, and Henry Pemberton are to be found advocating rigid regularity in the heroic line, and poets like Richard Glover are to be seen composing strictly "ideal" (i.e., regular) accentual-syllabic verse. This lust for regularity and "smoothness" is clearly one expression of the orderly and rationalistic impulses of the age.

Soon after 1740, however, a reaction to metrical rigidity manifests itself in the prosodic writing of Samuel Say, John Mason, and Joshua Steele. These theorists point out that monotony results from iambic lines long continued without trisyllabic substitution, and that the shifting or omission of stresses is an expressive tool which the poet who wishes to tap all resources of poetry cannot do without. The writings of this "preromantic" school advocate a return to "sense rhythms" after the predominance of "metrical rhythms" earlier in the century, and the positions of this school issue from an early "romantic" aesthetic of impulse, spontaneity, and surprise rather than from an Augustan aesthetic of stability, reason, and quietude. By opposing the poetic contractions (q.v.) required by a syllabic prosody, the late 18th-c. theorists sought to create an "expandable" line which could swell or diminish expressively according to the rhetorical pressure within it.

Unlike the sparse prosodic speculation of the Renaissance, that of the 18th c. is copious; it is also relatively systematic, and, under the influence of Locke, remarkably "psychological." Throughout the period, the practice of the poets substantially corroborates the findings of the prosodists: although such masters as Pope and Johnson shift stresses freely and instinctively, even they never violate the strict syllabic limitation, and the lines of most of the lesser manufacturers of the heroic couplet will be found to be strikingly regular in the disposition of stressed and unstressed syllables.

19th C.: The major phenomenon in 19th c. Eng. prosody is a rejection of strict accentual-syllabism and a reaching toward accentualism. Coleridge, in *Christabel,* publicly practiced for a wide audience the principles of trisyllabic substitution advocated a half-century earlier by Say, Mason, and Steele. As a result of this new accentualism, the Eng. pentameter line tends to lose its formal, Augustan oratorical tone and to take on a tone of almost colloquial intimacy (*The Prelude, Fra Lippo Lippi*). In prosodic writing, accentualism soon expressed

ENGLISH PROSODY

itself in musical theories and scansions (Lanier), and the rise to fashion of Germanic philology, which helped remind prosodists that Eng. was solidly a Germanic tongue, fanned the accentual fires. The development of "free" or "cadenced" (qq.v.) verse in the middle of the century was generally an expression of impatience with the metrical constraints of the previous century. Triple rhythms, in music as well as in poetry, are attempted more and more in "serious" works (Longfellow, Poe). But despite these new departures, many prominent poets (Tennyson, Arnold) continue to exercise themselves in what is fundamentally the line of the Augustans, with its syllabic limitation and conservative placement of stresses. W. J. Stone, with his *On the Use of Classical Metres in English* (1898), attempted to interest the more academic spirits in quantitative prosody once more, but the decay of classical learning and enthusiasm deterred all but Robert Bridges from experimenting seriously with quantitative prosody. Gerard Manley Hopkins was moved to revive the medieval and Renaissance technique of overstressing called "sprung rhythm" (q.v.), and it is notable that this technique can be thought of only in a strongly accentual prosodic climate.

The numerous 19th-c. divagations from accentual-syllabic prosody and the general air of quest and experimentation during the period suggest widespread dissatisfaction with the sound of conventional Eng. verse, and this dissatisfaction may have some philological cause. For example, the gradual separation of the Am. from the British language may have had something to do with the new metrical tonalities which the 19th c. sometimes frenetically sought; so may the gradual replacement of classical by modern language studies in schools and universities. Whatever the causes of the dissatisfaction, it is clearly an expression of the age's lust for reform and its commitment to the idea of progress.

20th C.: Most of the prosodic mutations of interest in the 20th c. have been associated with the United States. During the twenties and thirties, the work of Pound and Williams tightened the freely cadenced line of Whitman and made of it a witty instrument in the short poem. Eliot's poetic dramas have used subtle accentual lines with great skill, and Auden has written accentual, accentual-syllabic, and syllabic poems with equal facility. But even after such bold experiments as the "spatial cadences" of E. E. Cummings, the incremental variation of Stein, and the cadenced syllabism of Marianne Moore, 20th-c. poetry still continues the 19th century's quest for new prosodies to express an alarmingly changed social, political, and intellectual order.

The failure of many of the experiments of the twenties and thirties to arrive at any very profoundly expressive mode of metric has impelled many post-World War II poets to return to stable lyric measures: Wilbur, Shapiro, Lowell, and others have had happy results with traditional accentual-syllabic lines, and a return to conservatism in metrical structure seems apparent in the pages of little magazines and literary reviews. How closely this return to conservatism in prosody is connected with the similar movement in contemporary politics and intellectual life it would be hazardous to say. It will be obvious, however, to those who have seen in history the intimate alliance between metrics and the general intellectual and emotional tendencies of an age, that no prosodic phenomenon is devoid of wider meaning if only we can learn to read it correctly.

The area of prosodic investigation has been entered in our own time by the so-called acoustic or linguistic prosodists, who, with elaborate machinery (for example, the kymograph and the oscillograph), are trying to discover what actually goes on in the oral delivery of verse. Although this characteristically technological 20th-c. approach to problems which have traditionally been investigated prescriptively or subjectively has yet to demonstrate its full usefulness to metrical study, it has undeniably laid the groundwork for much valuable future study. The very fact that even the machine has finally been called to the assistance of the prosodist helps indicate the continuing pressing interest in the elusive and mysterious prosodies which emerge from Eng. poetry.†

Saintsbury, *Prosody*; T. S. Omond, *Eng. Metrists* (1921); R. Bridges, *Milton's Prosody* (rev. ed., 1921); L. Abercrombie, *Eng. Prosody* (1923); G. R. Stewart, *The Technique of Eng. Verse* (1930); G. W. Allen, *Am. Prosody* (1934); E. Olson, *General Prosody* (1938); J. C. Ransom, *The New Crit.* (1941), pp. 254–69, 297–330; J. C. Pope, *The Rhythm of Beowulf* (1942); M. M. Holloway, *Prosodic Theory of Hopkins* (1947); K. Shapiro, *A Bibliog. of Modern Prosody* (1948); G. L. Hendrickson, "Elizabethan Quantitative Hexameters," PQ, 28 (1949); G. L. Trager and H. L. Smith, Jr., *An Outline of Eng. Structure* (1951); P. F. Baum, "Eng. Versification," in Shipley; S. E. Sprott, *Milton's Art of Prosody* (1953); P. Fussell, Jr., *Theory of Prosody in 18th-C. England* (1954); "Eng. Verse and What It Sounds Like," KR, 18 (1956; articles by J. C. Ransom and others); R. Beum, "Syllabic Verse in Eng.," *Prairie Schooner*, 31 (1957); E. L. Epstein and T. Hawkes, *Linguistics and Eng. Prosody* (1959); J. Thompson, *The Founding of Eng. Metre* (1961). P.F.

† In Supplement, see also AMERICAN POETIC SCHOOLS AND TECHNIQUES (CONTEMPORARY); PROJECTIVE VERSE.

ENGLYN. A group of Welsh meters. The *englyn unodl union* (direct monorhyme e.), which first appeared in the 12th c., has become the most popular of all the "strict" meters. This kind of e. has 30 syllables, the "shaft" having 16, and the "wings" 14. In the classical period there is always a pause after the 5th syllable. The main rhyme first occurs on the 7th, 8th or 9th, and then on the 16th, 23rd, and 30th. The *gair cyrch* ("reaching-out word," cf. Gerard Manley Hopkins's "outriders") which extends from the 1st main rhyme to the 10th syllable need only be related to what follows by means of light alliteration, whereas strict *cynghanedd* (q.v.) has been observed in all other parts since the 15th c. Uneven end stress, as in *cywydd*, is the rule in the "wings" since the 13th c.—Morris-Jones; Parry.   D.M.L.

ENJAMBEMENT or enjambment. The completion, in the following poetic line, of a clause or other grammatical unit begun in the preceding line; the employment of "run-on" lines which carry the sense of a statement from one line to another without rhetorical pause at the end of the line:

> . . . Yet I know her for
> A spleeny Lutheran . . .
> (Shakespeare. *Henry VIII*, 3.2)

The term is also applied to the carrying over of meaning from one couplet or stanza to the next.

E., a device widely used by the Elizabethans and by Milton, fell into disrepute in 18th-c. poetry but was revived by the romantic poets, who saw in it a symbol of liberation from neoclassical rules. Keats's *Endymion* supplies some extreme examples of e.

The technique of e. has been a subject of controversy in Fr. poetry. Rarely found in OF poetry, e. was widely used in the 15th and especially 16th c. (Ronsard and the *Pléiade*). In the 17th c. it was frowned on by Malherbe and, later, by Boileau. These neoclassical authorities, however, allowed its use in certain circumstances—in decasyllabic poetry and in the less "noble" genres such as comedy and fable. Occasionally, e. occurs even in tragedy (e.g., Racine, *Britannicus*). Since André Chénier, e. has been accepted in all genres. The device was exploited to the full by Victor Hugo, whose famous e. at the beginning of *Hernani* ("Serait-ce déjà lui? C'est bien à l'escalier // Dérobé. . . .") had all the force of a manifesto. E. is a freely used technique of modern poetry.—M. Grammont, *Petit traité de versification française* (5e éd. revue, 1924).

ENOPLIUS (Gr. "in arms," "martial"). In Gr. lyric, verse of the scheme

$$\smile\smile - \smile\smile - \smile\smile - -$$

The catalectic form of the e. is the *prosodiacus* (see PROSODION).—Dale.   K.M.A.

ENSALADA. A Sp. poem consisting of lines and strophes of varying lengths and rhyme schemes, generally depending on the music to which the poem is sung. According to P. Henríquez Ureña (*La versificación irregular en la poesía castellana*, 2d ed., 1933), the earliest known e. is one by Fray Ambrosio Montesinos (d. ca. 1512) found in Barbieri's *Cancionero musical de los siglos XV y XVI* (no. 438). The e. apparently was never very popular.—Navarro.   D.C.C.

ENSENHAMEN. A didactic poem in Old Prov., ordinarily composed in a nonlyric meter, such as rhymed couplets, and designed to give advice or instruction to an individual or a class of persons. Some of these poems are like little books of etiquette. Others are addressed to the jongleurs (q.v.) who sang the poets' compositions, telling them the things they should know and how they should perform their task. The knowledge expected is doubtless exaggerated, but the poems have a certain interest for what they reveal about contemporary taste in literature and other matters.—J. Anglade, *Hist. sommaire de la litt. méridionale* (1921).   F.M.C.

ENVELOPE. The e. pattern is a special case of repetition (q.v.) A line or stanza will recur in the same or nearly the same form so as to enclose other material. A line or significant phrase may thus enclose a stanza or a whole poem; a complete stanza may be repeated to enclose a poem or a section of a larger poem. The effect of the e. pattern is to emphasize the unity of the enclosed portion, to indicate that elaborations or parallels of statement have not departed from the original focus. Also the repeated words carry an added richness and meaning from the intervening lines, sometimes acquiring an almost incantatory force. The e. pattern is distinguished from the refrain (q.v.) in that the repetitions here affect the enclosed material rather than the material preceding each occurrence. The single-line e., as it applies to a stanza, may be seen in both stanzas of James Joyce's *I Would in That Sweet Bosom Be*, as it applies to an entire poem, in the *Eighth Psalm* or Whitman's *Joy, Shipmate, Joy*. A stanza used as an e. for an entire poem may be seen in Blake's *The Tyger* and in Keats's *The Mermaid Tavern*.—R. B. Lewis,

Creative Poetry (1931); G. W. Allen, *Am. Prosody* (1935).   s.f.f.

ENVOI, envoy. (Prov. *tornada*; G. *Geleit*). A short concluding stanza found in certain Fr. poetic forms, such as the *ballade* and the *chant royal*. In the *ballade* it normally consists of 4 lines, in the *chant royal* of either 5 or 7, thus repeating the metrical pattern of the half-stanza which precedes it, as well as the rhyme scheme of that half-stanza. The e. also repeats the refrain which runs through the poem (e.g., Villon's "Mais ou sont les neiges d'antan?"). In its typical use of some form of address, such as "Prince," the e. shows a trace of its original function, which was to serve as a kind of post-script dedicating the poem to a patron or other important person. However, its true function during the great period of the OF forms was to serve as a pithy summing-up of the poem. For this reason the Prov. troubadours called their envoys *tornadas* (returns). Among the Eng. poets, Scott, Southey, and Swinburne employed envoys. Chaucer wrote a number of *ballades* (e.g., *Lenvoy de Chaucer a Scogan*), in which he departs from the customary form by closing with an e. which is equal in length to a regular stanza of the poem, usually his favorite rhyme royal (q.v.).

EPANADIPLOSIS. See ANADIPLOSIS.

EPANALEPSIS (Gr. "a taking up again"). 1. Anciently most often defined as the repetition of a word or words after an intervening word or words, whether (a) for emphasis (Rutilius Lupus, ?1st c. B.C., *De figuris sententiarum et elocutionis* 1.11, cited C. T. Ernesti, *Lexicon technologiae Graecorum rhetoricae,* 1795), e.g., ". . . Hell at last / Yawning received them whole, and on them closed, / Hell their fit habitation . . ." (Milton, *Paradise Lost* 6.874–76); or (b) for mere clarity, as to resume a construction after a lengthy parenthesis (Demetrius, 1st c. A.D.?, *On Style* 196), e.g. "Say first, for heaven hides nothing from thy view, / Nor the deep tract of hell, say first what cause / Moved our grand parents . . ." (*Paradise Lost* 1.27–29). 2. By modern authorities, most often and most usefully defined as the ending of a sentence with its own opening word or words; so Abraham Fraunce, *The Arcadian Rhetorike,* 1588 (D3ʳ) who quotes for illustration, "Multa super Priamo rogitans, super Hectore multa" (*Aeneid* 1.750), and "They love indeed who quake to say they love" (Sir Philip Sidney, *Astrophel and Stella,* sonnet 54); so also Henry Peacham, *The Garden of Eloquence,* 1593, p. 46; and others. Various types have been distinguished in Walt Whitman; more than 40 per cent of the lines of the final version of *Leaves of Grass* employ

e. of one sort or another. Sometimes the device enters into the texture of an entire passage (or poem) affecting a high percentage of the words. (A. N. Wiley, "Reiterative Devices in *Leaves of Grass*," AL, 1 [1929]).   R.O.E.; H.B.

EPANAPHORA. See ANAPHORA.

EPIC. HISTORY. See NARRATIVE POETRY.

EPIC. THEORY. Already in the Heroic Age of Greece the e. bard and his disciples and imitators were marked as men possessing peculiar qualities of memory and vision. In fact the purveyors and refurbishers of popular tradition concerning gods and heroes, they were credited with being able, by special inspiration, to transcend the limitations of sense (some are said to have been blind), and to rescue the past from oblivion, restoring it to life and moving their hearers to pity and fear. The early philosophers, e.g., Heraclitus, Empedocles, and even Democritus, agree that there is something more than natural about such faculties as respects their origin, their working, and its effect upon men.

There was no speculation on the proper nature of e. until its usefulness had been questioned. Socrates, though he steadily testified to the exemplary value of the old poems and offered no other explanation of Homer's felicitous expression and greatness of mind than divine prompting, began to find fault with the poets as thinkers and historians. He noted in them error in fact and warned against their more general ignorance. In the *Republic* Plato, his pupil, began an attack particularly on e. and drama. Tragedy and comedy Plato disapproved because they imitate and cause us to imitate—that is, they bring to life before us all kinds of men and women, encouraging us to identify ourselves with them indiscriminately. He allowed e. partial merit as a mixed kind, imitative but also narrative. He seems to have thought that as narrative it was more safely and clearly discernible as opinionative and interpretative; its audience was less likely to be taken in. Plato, however, decried the effect of the Homeric poems on the young; they reported scandal of the gods and suggested weakness in the heroes. At the end of his career, in the more tolerant vein of the *Laws,* he argued that his elder citizenry would find more pleasure in e. than in other forms of literature, perhaps because its leisurely pace and patent artifice would appeal more to them than the intensities and realism of tragedy.

Aristotle in the *Poetics* replied to Plato's strictures against imitative poetry. He claimed for e. and tragedy a convincingness beyond ordinary probability and verisimilitude and a moral purposefulness in the pleasure they could create; both imitate men as they are and as they ought to be; both are concerned with actions consequent upon good moral choices, but also with errors and frailties, with happiness and unhappiness; both characteristically present outstanding and noble people, for such are famous for their deeds and for their suffering. The actions treated have clearly defined beginnings and ends with middle parts amplified by appropriate episodes; more of the latter may feasibly be used in e. In e. simultaneous happenings may be consecutively developed. Although its imaginative length is unlimited, in reading or in recitation e. may conveniently approximate a dramatic trilogy; too often it is unduly prolonged and hence "diluted" in effect. Tragedy and e. normally center in one man, but it is a mistake to show the whole life from beginning to end; instead, an important segment should be chosen for emphasis. The movement may be either simple and straightforward, or (preferably) complicated by recognition scenes and reversals of direction. Stress may be on character or on suffering. E. more effectively stimulates amazement as a response; improbabilities may more plausibly be introduced in it since it is less obligated than tragedy to sustain the illusion of actuality. Finally, e., unlike tragedy, uses throughout a single meter (dactylic hexameter), which is suited to narrative for its dignity and to figurative language for its flexibility. Aristotle's remarks on e. show no recognition of it, in contrast with tragedy, as being peculiarly interpretative of life, nor does he conceive it to be the vehicle of propaganda for general ideas.

Fuller recognition of the achievement and potentialities of e. was not possible until a poet able to challenge the Homeric epics demonstrated his powers. Virgil's *Aeneid* is a creative imitation of the *Iliad* and the *Odyssey*, but its differences from its predecessors are as important as its similarities. It is deliberately conceived, as they had not been, to give meaning to the destiny of a people, asserting the implications of their history and recognizing the significance of contemporary events in relation to the past. Although Virgil left no theoretical writings, his purposes, which are common to his age, are voiced by other writers. Horace, for example, sensed Rome's civilizing role, understood her traditions as Virgil did; he repeatedly testifies also to his regard for Homer and the Greeks, believing their precedent in literature ought to be imitated. Distant echoes have been found in Horace's *Ars Poetica* (13 B.C.?) of Aristotle's admonitions on probability and on consistency in characterization. He adds little to e. (and dramatic) theory beyond the observation that action should begin in the midst of things (*in medias res*), an opinion which may echo distantly Aristotle's rejection of the tedious biographical poem. Many of these ideas appear in Cicero (*De Oratore*, 55 B.C.) and Quintilian (*Institutio Oratoria*, A.D. 93). The former, sketching the ideal character of oratory, no doubt encouraged reflection on the nature of the literary genres. The latter, comparing Virgil with Homer, scarcely acknowledged his countryman's inferiority, applauding his deliberate workmanship and preferring his steady excellence to the purple passages of the *Iliad* and the *Odyssey*.

In the 1st c. A.D. Lucan's *Pharsalia* broke with tradition by taking events of recent and actual history as its subject and dispensing with supernatural "machinery"—the manifest intervention of gods and goddesses in human affairs. Objection to this new direction was voiced by Petronius in a well-known definition of epic's proper content, as follows: "Things actually done are not to be put into verses, for historians treat them far better; instead, through enigmas, interventions of gods, and a fictional intertwining of purposes (*fabulosum sententiarum tormentum*), the free spirit is to rush; so there is evidenced rather the vaticination of a raging mind than the testimony of scrupulous statement by witnesses" (*Satyricon* 118). Lucan had no immediate followers, whereas a series of poets—Silius Italicus, Valerius Flaccus, and Statius—imitated Virgilian style and episode. In the 4th c., commentators like Servius Honoratus and Macrobius glorified Virgil.

In the Middle Ages occasional restatements of earlier opinions occur. Isidore of Seville (*Etymologiae*, 6th c.) defines heroic verse as being so named "because in it the affairs and deeds of brave men are narrated (for heroes are spoken of as men practically· supernatural and worthy of Heaven on account of their wisdom and bravery); and this meter precedes others in status." In unconscious defiance of Aristotle, Suidas (10th c.) confuses e. with history on the ground that in the manner of history it narrates in verse the life of a man who deserves the name of hero. Classifications of the kinds of literature sometimes allow for e. as a mixed form combining drama and narrative (so Diomedes, Isidore, and Bede), but in the 12th c. Vincent of Beauvais and John of Garland know nothing of e. as a genre. The continuing veneration of Virgil as sage and poet, though sometimes degenerating into superstition, culminates in Dante's idealization of his character in the *Divine Comedy* (begun in 1307).

In the It. Renaissance, Vida celebrates Virgil rapturously in his *Ars Poetica* (1527). Though the subject of this work is heroic verse (*carmen heroicum*), it is not really theoretical; Vida's practical advice to poets largely derives from Horace and Quintilian. His *Christiad* (1535), in the breadth of its conception, is profoundly imitative of Virgil. Theoretical discussion of the e. did not begin until the rediscovery of Aristotle's *Poetics*. In the 13th c. Roger Bacon had warned that the Romans were unoriginal thinkers and had noted the desirability of study of their Gr. sources, including for literary theory the *Poetics*. There was no wide knowledge of the work until the Gr. text was printed (1508) and translations into L. (1498, 1536) and It. (1549) had appeared. Trissino's *Poetica* (1528–63), citing important passages from Aristotle as criteria, began a discussion of the achievement of It. literature to date. His *Italia Liberata* (1547) is modeled on Homer and written in It. in blank verse (*versi sciolti*).

There followed an intense controversy, engaging the suddenly numerous critics, over the success of such epic-like poems as those of Boiardo and Ariosto and the medieval *chansons* and romances from which they in part derived. Of this Aristotle was the acknowledged arbiter, though his preference of tragedy over e. was disregarded. A few representative names can be introduced here. Giraldi Cinthio (*Discorsi intorno al comporre de i Romanzi*, 1554) attempted to justify medieval and recent as well as ancient practice by distinguishing three heroic forms: e. (as defined by Aristotle), romance (many invented actions of many men), and biographical poem (the whole history of one man). Minturno (*L'Arte Poetica*, 1564) argued that all heroic poetry, in contrast with tragedy, should move men to the admiration of extraordinary virtue. He advocated that the subject matter of the romances, including their Christian marvels and machinery, should now become the materials of a regular classical e. He is responsible for the notion that the action of e. should be limited to one year; others stipulated one month or the length of a summer's military campaign. Castelvetro (*Poetica d'Aristotele vulgarizzata et sposta*, 1576) broke with Aristotle in maintaining that e. may handle the various acts of a single person or many people, and even the action of a whole race. It is imaginative history. According to Torquato Tasso (*Discorsi del Poema Epico*, 1594) e. should concern itself with heroic acts of Christian knighthood performed in the medieval past. He would leave to tragedy the pity of human frailty and the disasters of fortune; it is also made responsible for the punishment of the wicked. As for the structure of e., he calls for unity in diversity; an e. may contain as much material (but only as much) as a man can retain in memory while reading.

Although in France by the middle of the 16th c. the writers of the *Pléiade* were calling for a national e. on a patriotic theme and in the vernacular, there was little contribution to the theoretical discussion of that subject for a hundred years. Then appeared the pronouncements of Mambrun (*de Poemate Epico*, 1652), Scudéry (Preface to *Alaric*, 1674), Rapin (*Réflexions sur la Poétique*, 1674), Boileau (*Art Poétique*, 1674), Le Bossu (*Traité du poème épique*, 1675), and the rest, inspired by the high-flown idealism of the age and aimed at the codification of rules. The consensus of their views was that e. is the most lofty undertaking of the human imagination; it demands in the poet both inspiration and deliberation. It must be based on a moral proposition (*fable*) to be illustrated allegorically in a unified action and didactically inculcated. Its delineation of character presents man in his perfection as understood in Christian conceptions of valor and virtue. And these qualities must be rewarded in the end, preferably by happiness. Decorum, i.e., truth to type in characterization and suitability in all things, is to be faithfully preserved. Nothing may violate verisimilitude or probability, although the marvelous shall be introduced to create awe and reverence. The whole is to constitute a pleasing imitation of Nature in her dignity and truth. It has been ironically observed that during the period (1650–70) when these principles were being most emphatically enunciated, the Fr. produced forty epics, all of them failures. Neoclassicism, however infeasible for poets, thus reached its theoretical apex.

Certain difficulties were discovered by the Fr. themselves. For example, Boileau could not stomach the use of Christian machinery and argued that pagan divinities and demons have an appropriateness for poetry which renders them inoffensive. And Le Bossu, faithful to Aristotle, argued that defects might be present even in virtuous heroes, his reason being that something is to be learned from the bad as well as from the good.

Fr. neoclassicism was imported into England with the Restoration, its dogmas on the e. being purveyed by such writers as Davenant (Preface to *Gondibert*, 1650), Hobbes (*Answer to Davenant's Preface*, 1650, and Preface to *A Translation of Homer*, 1675), Cowley, (Preface to *Poems*, 1656, and Preface to *The Cutter of Coleman Street*, 1663), Dryden (*An Apology for Heroic Poetry*, 1677), and Mulgrave (*Essay upon Poetry*, 1682). Most of the Eng. critics add something of their own. Davenant proposes that e. should approximate drama as closely as possible, even to the point of being divided into five books (acts) and several cantos (scenes). Cowley rejects "mad stories" of ancient gods and medieval knights in favor of biblical subjects. The reflections of Milton on e. themes and form show that he was generally more influenced by It. than by Fr. thought. He

EPIC

suggested a distinction between diffuse and brief e. (*Reason of Church Government*, 1642). Dryden defends the heroic play as resembling e. in loftiness of conception and nobility of characterization. On the e. Dryden mainly repeats Le Bossu, the chief authority of the time, but he diverges in advocating absolute perfection in the hero; he acknowledges, to be sure, that the public virtues of rulers and heroes are more appropriate than the private virtues of piety. For epic machinery he proposes that poets use "Guardian Angels." Dryden is perhaps the first to argue that e. should strive for that *sublimity* of expression which "Longinus" had found in Homer. Addison in his *Spectator* essays (1711–12) discovers this quality in Milton.

The 18th c. in England sees a general assault on the authority of Fr. neoclassicism, and the "rules" (q.v.) are subjected to a more analytical criticism. The attack on Le Bossu is led by Pope himself in his burlesque *Art of Sinking* (1727–28). Reverberations are heard in such writers as Joseph Warton (*Essay on the Genius and Writings of Pope*, 1756), Murphy (*Gray's-Inn Journal*, no. 92, 1756), Gibbon (*Critical Observations on the Aeneid*, 1770), Hayley (*Essay on Epic Poetry*, 1782)—but most impressively in Kames (*Elements of Criticism*, 1762) and Johnson (*Life of Milton*, 1779). Kames, indeed, questions whether the forms of poetry can be distinguished on a theoretical basis. In the main, nevertheless, the critics hope merely to broaden and clarify the definition of e. Fielding (Preface to *Joseph Andrews*, 1742) would extend the concept to include all narrative, whether tragic or comic in spirit, verse or prose. Presently the novel is asserted to be the modern e. (Beattie, *Of Fable and Romance*, 1783; Reeve, *Progress of Romance*, 1785; Millar, *On the Epic*, 1818). In support of such opinions, Pye (Commentary on Aristotle's *Poetics*, 1792) argues, on Aristotle's authority, that e. as a term covers both verse and prose. Le Bossu's emphasis upon the didactic purpose of e. is now repeatedly rejected; Johnson finds Milton the only poet who ever took it seriously. His dictionary (1755) definition of e., particularly in what it omits, sums up the semantic change in the meaning of the word: "Narrative; comprising narrations, not acted but rehearsed. It is usually supposed to be heroic, or to contain one great action achieved by a hero." Aikin (*Letters*, 1793) even ridicules the notion that e. exists to stimulate "admiration." At the same time there were changes in the reputation of e. poets. Homer, after Blackwell's *Enquiry into the Life and Writings of Homer* (1736) came to be exalted as an original and primitive genius who knew and needed no rules. Goldsmith (*Art of Poetry on a New Plan*, 1762) objected to all the poets who had tried to imitate him. Pinkerton (*Letters*, 1785) singled out Virgil for blame on that score. Hurd (*Letters on Chivalry and Romance*, 1762) praised the writers of romance, and notably Ariosto and Spenser, for their preference of poetic truth to realism, and for their freedom from restraint in respect to the marvelous. He roundly condemned Davenant and Hobbes for having introduced Fr. theories in England.

Meanwhile in France, although Mme Dacier (Preface to the *Iliad*, 1711) had given her allegiance to Le Bossu, a more severe rationalism, as epitomized by Voltaire (*Essay on Epic Poetry*, 1733, *et passim*) began to urge the relativity of taste among different peoples and in various ages. Definitions are dangerous, Voltaire asserts, because they discourage experimentalism and imagination; it is the nature of genius to attempt new ventures. For him, then, an e. is best defined in a noncommittal way, as "a narration in verse of heroic adventures." He ridicules, as do almost all 18th-c. critics, the idea of using Gr. and Roman mythological personages in modern literature. Judgment now is advocated as a check upon the marvelous, which must be handled with good taste as well as probability. Other critics attack the belief that literature should serve morality rather than pleasure. The imitation of antiquity is deplored. As in England, there is dispute whether Christian machinery is appropriate in e.; this leads to Chateaubriand's rhapsody (*Le génie du christianisme*, 1802) on the poetic qualities of the Christian marvelous.

With the development of romanticism in England, the concept of the e. as a genre falls apart. Not only is the uniqueness of every poetic expression emphasized; the critic is freed from rules and encouraged in impressionism. The nature of poetry intrigues the speculative mind rather than the definition of kinds. From Germany (see particularly Wolf's *Prolegomena ad Homerum*, 1795) come theories about the folk origins of the *Iliad* and the *Odyssey*, and the old views of their supposed author's profound wisdom and deliberate artistry have to be revised. Virgil is now little valued. Milton, for Coleridge (*passim*), seems to typify the modern subjective poet. Dante and Milton are contrasted with the simple and objective bards of primitive times. Long poems come under attack as straining patience; Coleridge (*Biographia Literaria*, 1817) and in America Edgar Allan Poe ("The Poetic Principle," 1845) deny their legitimacy altogether.

At the end of the 18th c., Germany was the chief source of theoretical speculation on the nature of e. Goethe and Schiller collaborated in an essay *Über epische und dramatische Dichtung* (1797). E., they assert, deals with public actions in the past, drama with inner suffering in the present; e. stirs to contemplation, drama requires complete involvement in the experience of the moment. Goethe generally opposes any confusion of these genres, but Schiller was led to the paradoxical conclusion that e. will make past events immediately concrete, whereas drama will make present events universal. For Schiller, violent action, stimulating strong emotional response, is inappropriate to e. And he also breaks with established tradition (from Aristotle onward) in contending that the marvelous is inappropriate to the clarity demanded of e. Jean Paul Richter (*Vorschule der Ästhetik*, 1804) modifies the ideas of Goethe and Schiller, maintaining that, although e. reflects and interprets the past, drama has implications for the future, and lyric centers wholly in the present. Following Wolf, Friedrich Schlegel (*Prosaische Jugendschriften*, 1794–1802) sees the e. as a series of loosely concatenated chance events, beginning and ending *in medias res* (q.v.); this he contrasts with the purposefully unified tragedy of fate and necessity. Schelling (*Philosophie der Kunst*, 1802) constructs a theory of the evolution of genres, the philosophical poem, as exemplified by the *Divine Comedy*, being seen as a stage of development beyond the impersonal e. Hegel (*Vorlesungen*, 1835) argues that drama marks the combination of the e. and the lyric, the objective and the subjective; also he remarks that e. is an expression of nationalism. The ideas of the Germans spread rapidly to England (Coleridge, *passim;* Dallas, *Poetics*, 1852), to France (Mme de Staël, *de l'Allemagne*, 1802; Hugo, Preface to *Cromwell*, 1825) and to Italy (Leopardi, *Discorsi*, 1818; Foscolo, *Petrarcha*, 1823).

The 20th c. has seen sober consideration of the accumulated facts, inspired by historical research and characterized by rigorously analytical procedures. Particularly notable are C. M. Bowra's studies of the contrast between "oral" and "written" e. (*From Vergil to Milton*, 1945; *Heroic Poetry*, 1952). He manifests little interest in theory, but regards e. as "a narrative of some length" which "deals with events which have a certain grandeur and importance and come from a life of action, especially of violent action such as war. It gives a special pleasure because its events and persons enhance our belief in the worth of human achievement and in the dignity and nobility of man." E.M.W. Tillyard (*The English Epic and its Background*, 1954) rejects merely nominal and formal criteria in an attempt to state what many poems and prose writings (even histories) which we call e. in spirit have in common. He remarks, first off, seriousness of tone and excellence in expression. Secondly, he notes scope and inclusiveness: e. gives us the whole truth as its author sees it, and what he says impresses us as normal and sane. Thirdly, his work manifests structural control throughout: inconsistencies and fragmentariness are disqualifications. There is an impression of deliberateness, and there is notable exercise of will in the conduct of the hero or in the poet's own accomplishment. Fourthly, the e. poet speaks for his *own* time, sometimes for a people, sometimes for a whole age; he does not speak for all time. Tillyard also observes that he is not necessarily limited to the use of established myth: he may create his own symbolic materials. A. B. Lord (*The Singer of Tales*, 1960) is concerned with "oral epic song," particularly as it is found in Yugoslavia today. Following the earlier studies of Antoine Meillet and Milman Parry, he establishes the thesis that it is the modern counterpart of the Homeric e., "composed in a manner evolved over many generations by singers of tales who did not know how to write; it consists of the building of metrical lines and half lines by means of formulas and formulaic expressions and of the building of songs by the use of themes." Lord points out that these formulas are not "ossified clichés" but capable of change and productive of other and new formulas.

PRIMARY SOURCES: Plato, *Phaedrus*, etc., tr. L. Cooper (1938); *Lit. Crit.: Plato to Dryden*, ed. A. H. Gilbert (1940); *The Art of Poetry, The Poetical Treatises of Horace, Vida, and Boileau*, ed. A. S. Cook (1926); *Lit. Crit.: Pope to Croce*, ed. G. W. Allen and H. H. Clark (1941); *Idées et doctrines littéraires*, ed. F. Vial and L. Denise (3 v., 1922–28); *Crit. Essays of the 17th C.*, ed. J. E. Spingarn (3 v., 1908–9); *Essays of John Dryden*, ed. W. P. Ker (2 v., 1926); *18th C. Crit. Essays*, ed. S. Elledge (2 v., 1961).

SECONDARY SOURCES: R. C. Williams, "It. Influence on Ronsard's Theory of E.," MLN, 35 (1920); "E. Unity (Vida to Castelvetro)," MP, 18 (1920); "It. Crit. Treatises of the 16th C.," MLN, 35 (1920); "Poetics and E.," RR, 12 (1921); "Some It. Critics of the 16th C.," RR, 12 (1921); "16th C. Critics on Metrical Form of E.," MLN, 36 (1921); and "Two Studies in E. Theory," MP, 22 (1924); C. S. Baldwin, *Ancient Rhetoric and Poetic* (1924); *Medieval Rhetoric and Poetic* (1928); and *Renaissance Lit. Theory and Practice*, ed. D. I. Clark (1939); C. E. Whitmore, "The Validity of Lit. Definitions," PMLA, 39 (1924); J. E. Spingarn, *Hist. of Lit. Crit. in the Renaissance* (1925); L. Abercrombie, *Theory of Poetry* (1926); J.W.H. Atkins, *Lit. Crit. in Antiquity* (2 v., 1934), *Eng. Lit. Crit.: The Medieval Phase* (1943); *The Renaissance* (1947); and *17th and 18th C.* (1951); Behrens; H. T. Swedenberg, *The Theory of the E. in England, 1650–1800* (1944); C. M. Bowra, *From Vergil to Milton* (1945) and *Heroic Poetry* (1952); A. H. Warren, *Eng. Poetic Theory,*

EPIGRAM

1825–65 (1950); D. M. Foerster, "The Crit.
Attack upon the E. in the Eng. Romantic
Movement," PMLA, 69 (1954); "Crit. Approval
of E. Poetry in the Age of Wordsworth," PMLA,
70 (1955) and *The Fortunes of E. Poetry* (1962);
E.M.W. Tillyard, *The Eng. E. and its Back-
ground* (1954); Wellek; A. Warren, "Lit.
Genres," in Wellek and Warren; Wimsatt and
Brooks; A. B. Lord, *The Singer of Tales* (1960);
M. Di Cesare, *Vida's "Christiad" and Vergilian
E.* (1964).   s.m.p.

EPIC CAESURA. See CAESURA.

EPIC SIMILE. See SIMILE.

EPICEDIUM (L. spelling of Gr. "funeral
song"). A song of mourning in praise of the
dead, sung in the presence of the corpse and
distinguished from *threnos,* a dirge, which was
not limited by time or place. The word does
not occur before the Alexandrian period or in
L. before Statius (1st c. A.D.), although the
lamentations over the bodies of Hector and
Achilles in Homer are, properly speaking,
epicedia. It became very popular in the Hellenistic period and was widely imitated in L.
literature. It was accompanied by a solemn
dance with music provided by a flute in the
Lydian mode. Written originally in a variety
of meters it became, after the classical period,
wholly elegiac or hexametral. *Epicedia* included lamentations in verse for pet animals
and birds (e.g., Catullus 3, Ovid, *Amores* 2.6,
Statius, *Silvae* 2.4 and 5).—Smyth; Schmid and
Stählin; G. Herrlinger, *Totenklage um Tiere
in der antiken Dichtung* (1930).   p.s.c.

EPIDEICTIC POETRY. Poetry following the
rules of the epideictic category of oratory.
From Aristotle on, rhetoric was divided into
three parts, deliberative (political debate), judicial (legal argument), and epideictic (or
demonstrative). The e. category was arbitrarily
described as oratory in praise or blame of
something, primarily for the pleasure and edification of the audience. During the classical
decadence poetry became increasingly epideictic. Statius's *Silvae* is one of the finest, and
perhaps the best, L. collections of poems on e.
themes. Common e. types are encomium, epithalamium, epicede, ecphrasis (or *descriptio*),
etc.—in short, the types which are usually
classified today as occasional poetry. The continuity and importance of the e. tradition may
be illustrated by the fact that the rules for
the types given in Scaliger's *Poetices Libri
Septem* (1561) are almost identical with those
given in the 3d c. B.C. by Menander in his
Peri Epideiktikon (On E. Oratory).—T. Burges,
E. Lit. (1902); O. B. Hardison, Jr., *The Enduring Monument* (1962).   o.b.h.

EPIGRAM. A form of writing which makes a
satiric, complimentary, or aphoristic observation with wit, extreme condensation, and,
above all, brevity. As a poetic form, the e.
generally takes the shape of a couplet or
quatrain, but tone, which is usually either
ironic or gnomic, defines it better than does
verse form. An example from Matthew Prior,
one of the best Eng. epigrammatists, displays
the personal, specific quality which distinguishes the e. from the proverb (q.v.) or the
apothegm:

> Sir, I admit your general rule,
> That every poet is a fool:
> But you yourself may serve to show it,
> That every fool is not a poet.

The etymology of the term (Gr. *epigramma,*
"inscription") suggests the features of pithi-
ness and economy of language which have always characterized the form; from an inscription carved on a monument or statue, the
classical Gr. e. developed into a specific literary type, typified by the epigrams contained
in the *Gr. Anthology,* which covered a wide
range of subjects and attitudes.

The e., as cultivated in the earlier Renaissance in both L. and the vernacular languages,
owed more to the coarse, harshly satirical examples of Martial and other Roman writers
than to the more polished products of the
Anthology, but the 17th and 18th c., the greatest periods of epigrammatic writing in England, saw a variety of epigrammatic types,
ranging from the brutal thrusts of Donne to
the delicate compliments of Herrick.

Epigrams have existed not only as independent poems but also as units in the composition of larger works; Pope's *Essay on Criticism*
and *Essay on Man,* for example, are made up
of epigrammatic couplets which are often
quoted as self-contained observations:

> We think our fathers fools, so wise we grow;
> Our wiser sons, no doubt, will think us so.
>   (*Essay on Criticism*)

Although the satiric spirit dominated the
18th-c. e., the 19th c. produced some which,
in their delicacy and gracefulness, recall the
amatory epigrams of the *Gr. Anthology:*

> Stand close around, ye Stygian set,
>   With Dirce in one boat conveyed!
> Or Charon, seeing, may forget
>   That he is old and she a shade.
>   (Landor, *Dirce*)

The e. holds an important place in the
poetic history of France and Germany as well.
In France, where the vernacular e. was initiated
by Marot and St.-Gelais in the early 16th c.,

-[247]-

the satiric and personal e. reached perfection in the hands of Boileau, Voltaire, and Lebrun:

Eglé, belle et poète, a deux petits travers:
Elle fait son visage, et ne fait pas ses vers.
(Lebrun).
Aegle, beauty and poet, has two little crimes;
She makes her own face, and does not make her rhymes.
(tr. Byron).

In Germany, on the other hand, the didactic e., or *Sinngedicht*, has occupied a position of special importance from the time of the *Priameln* (q.v.) of the 13th c. to the time of such masters as Logau, A. G. Kästner, Lessing, Goethe, and Schiller.

The e. is one of the most persistent types of literary expression, as it embodies certain permanent qualities of the human spirit. Such diverse modern epigrammatists as Ezra Pound and Edna St. Vincent Millay in Eng., Christian Morgenstern and Erich Kästner in German, have carried on the tradition, and W. B. Yeats's e. *On Hearing that the Students of our New University Have Joined the Agitation against Immoral Literature* is equal, in bite and precision, to the best of Prior or Voltaire.

COLLECTIONS: *Select Epigrams from the Gr. Anthology*, ed. J. W. Mackail (3d ed., 1911); *The Soul of Wit* (1924) and *Wit's Looking-Glass* (1934; Fr. epigrams tr.), both ed. G. R. Hamilton; *The Hundred Best Epigrams*, ed. E. B. Osborn (1928); *Epigrammata, Gr. Inscriptions in Verse . . .* , ed. P. Friedländer (1948).

HISTORY AND CRITICISM: R. Reitzenstein, *Epigramm und Skolion* (1893); T. K. Whipple, *Martial and the Eng. E. . . .* (1925); P. Nixon, *Martial and the Modern E.* (1927); H. H. Hudson, *The E. in the Eng. Renaissance* (1947); O. Weinreich, *Epigrammstudien* (1948); W. Preisendanz, *Die Spruchform in der Lyrik des alten Goethe und ihre Vorgeschichte seit Opitz* (1952).   F.J.W.; A.P.

EPINICION. A triumphal song, an ode commemorating a victory at one of the four great Gr. national games. It was sung either on the victor's arrival at his native town or during the solemn procession to the temple or at the banquet especially held to celebrate his victory. The ordinary e. consisted of a number of groups of 3 stanzas each (strophe, antistrophe, epode) and contained an account of the victory of the hero, a myth, the most important part of the poem, relating the victor's deed to the glorious past of his family, and the conclusion which returned to the praise of the victor and ended with reflective admonitions or even a prayer. The most eminent representatives of this type of composition are Simonides, Pindar, and Bacchylides. One of the latest *epinicia* on record is that composed by Euripides for Alcibiades on the occasion of the latter's victory in three chariot races at Olympia (420 B.C.).—Smyth; Schmid and Stählin; G. Norwood, *Pindar* (1945).   P.S.C.

EPIPHORA. See ANADIPLOSIS.

EPIPLOCE (Gr. "plaiting together"). Term applied by ancient metricians to alternative possibilities of regarding a metrical sequence. Thus, with redistribution of the syllables between the feet, an iambic or anapaestic series could be regarded as trochaic or dactylic respectively, for example, a trochaic trimeter catalectic ($-\cup-\cup|-\cup-\cup|-\cup-$) might be described as an acephalous iambic trimeter, i.e., an iambic trimeter minus its first syllable ($-\cup|\cup-\cup-|\cup-\cup-$).   R.J.G.

EPIRRHEMA (Gr. "that said afterwards"). In the parabasis (q.v.) of Attic Old Comedy the speech delivered to the audience by the leader of one half of the chorus after an ode had been sung by that half of the chorus. Composed usually in trochaic tetrameters, its content was satire, advice, or exhortation. The structure in the parabasis of an ode sung by half of the chorus, an epirrhema, an antode (q.v.) sung by the other half of the chorus and an antepirrhema is called "epirrhematic syzygy." Such an arrangement of lyrics by the chorus and speech or dialogue by a character is found in Aeschylus' and Sophocles' plays.— F. M. Cornford, *The Origin of Attic Comedy* (1914); G. Norwood, *Gr. Comedy* (1931); Aeschylus, *Agamemnon*, ed. E. Fraenkel, III (1953).   R.A.H.

EPISTLE, verse. A poem addressed to a particular patron or friend, written in a familiar style. Two types of verse epistles exist: the one on moral and philosophical subjects which stems from Horace's *Epistles* and the other on romantic and sentimental subjects which stems from Ovid's *Heroides*. Though the verse e. may be found as early as 146 B.C. with Sp. Mummius' letters from Corinth and some of the satires of Lucullus, Horace perfected the form. Employing the hexameter, he used plain diction, personal details, questions, etc. to lend a familiarity to his theme which was usually some philosophical subject. Ovid used the same style for his *Tristia* and *Ex Ponto*, but developed the sentimental e. in his *Heroides* which are fictional letters from women to their lovers. Throughout the Middle Ages the latter seems to have been the more popular type, for it had an influence on the courtly love (q.v.) poets and subsequently inspired Samuel Daniel to introduce the form into Eng. literature, e.g., *Letter from Octavia to Marcus Antonius*. Such also was the source for Donne's copy of the

Heroides and Pope's *Eloisa to Abelard*. But it was the Horatian e. which had the greater effect on the Renaissance and subsequent poetry. Petrarch, the first humanist to know Horace, wrote his influential *Epistulae Metricae* in L. Subsequently, Ariosto's *Satires* in terza rima employed the form in the vernacular It. In all these epistles Christian sentiment made itself felt. In Spain Garcilaso's *Epístola a Boscán* (1543), and the *Epístola moral a Fabio* in blank verse and terza rima introduced and perfected the form. The Fr. especially cultivated it for its "graceful precision and dignified familiarity." Although others wrote verse epistles, Boileau's twelve (1668–95) in neoclassic couplets are considered the finest examples in Fr. Ben Jonson began the Eng. use of the Horatian form (*Forest*, 1616) and was followed by others, e.g., Vaughan, Dryden, Congreve. But the finest examples in Eng. are Pope's *Moral Essays* and the *Epistle to Dr. Arbuthnot* in heroic couplets. The romantics did not especially use the e., though Shelley, Keats, and Landor on occasion wrote them. Recent examples are W. H. Auden's *New Year Letter* and Louis MacNeice's *Letters from Iceland.*—H. Peter, *Der Brief in der römischen Lit.* (1901); G. Curcio, *Q. Orazio Flacco, studiato in Italia dal secolo xiii al xviii* (1913); E. P. Morris, "The Form of the E. in Horace," YSC, 1931; J. Vianey, *Les Epîtres de Marot* (1935); E. L. Rivers, "The Horatian E. and Its Introd. into Sp. Lit.," HR, 22 (1954); W. Grenzmann, "Briefgedicht," *Reallexikon*, 2d ed., I; J. A. Levine, "The Status of the Verse E. before Pope," SP, 59 (1962).   R.A.H.

EPISTROPHE. See ANADIPLOSIS.

EPISYNTHETON (Gr. "compound" sc. meter). Meter composed of cola (see COLON) of different kinds. Archilochus (7th c. B.C.) is said to have been the first to use *episyntheta*.—Kolář.
                                      K.M.A.

EPITAPH (Gr. "[writing] on a tomb"). A literary production suitable for placing on the grave of someone or something, though this need not actually be done or even intended. The e., which is a shortened form of the elegy (q.v.) and which may vary in tone from panegyrical to ribald, indicates in brief compass the outline of a complete life. It attempts to arrest the passer-by, compelling him to read, to reflect on the life of the one commemorated and, by implication, on his own life. The earliest epitaphs are Egyptian, written on sarcophagi and coffins. They have generally the name, the person's descent, his office, and a prayer to some deity. Gr. and Roman epitaphs are often highly personal, sometimes epigrammatic. They may be written in verse (usually the elegiac distich) or in prose. Their details may include the name of the person, his family, the facts of his life, a prayer to the underworld (especially so in Roman epitaphs) and a warning or imprecation against defilement. Rarely are all these details found in a single e. On those from Greece and Rome are found varying concepts of Fortuna and Fate, literary figures such as the thread of life, the removal from light, the payment of a debt as well as various kinds of consolation and lamentation.

The major collection of classical epitaphs is Book 4 of the *Gr. Anthology*. The epitaphs in this collection are of high poetic quality and cover the whole range of the form from satiric and comic to intensely serious. They have influenced subsequent writers of epitaphs from Roman times (e.g., Martial, Ausonius) through the Renaissance (Pontanus, Erasmus, More, Jonson) and on into the present period (Pound, Yeats). Perhaps the single most famous e. from the *Anthology* is that on the dead at Thermopylae: "Go, tell the Lacedaimonians, passer-by, / That here obedient to their laws we lie."

The Middle Ages used the Latin e. both in prose and verse, often leonine verse. Following the themes and practices laid down by the Greeks and particularly the Romans, the Eng. used the form, developing it to an exceptionally high art in the 15th and 16th c., e.g., William Browne on the Dowager Countess of Pembroke, or Milton on Shakespeare. Both Dr. Johnson and William Wordsworth wrote essays on the e. as an art form.

The e. has not always been used to commemorate the dead. It has been put to satirical use against an enemy who is alive, and it has been aimed even at an institution, e.g., Piron's e. on his rejection by the Fr. Academy. As a literary form without a specific occasion it has continued in use into the 20th c., e.g., O. St. J. Gogarty, *Per iter tenebricosum*, W. Stevens, *Death of a Soldier.*—S. Tessington, *Epitaphs* (1857); H. W. Wells, *New Poets from Old* (1940); R. Lattimore, *Themes in Gr. and L. Epitaphs* (1942); *Epigrammata*, ed. P. Friedländer (1948); Frye; R. W. Ketton-Cremer, "Lapidary Verse," *Proceedings of the British Academy*, 45 (1959).
                                      R.A.H.

EPITHALAMIUM (Gr. "at the bridal chamber"). Any song or poem sung outside the bridal chamber on the wedding night; perhaps the intention behind such a song is the encouragement of fertility. Sappho is apparently the first to use it as a distinct literary form, though such a song does appear in Homer's *Iliad* and in Hesiod's *Shield of Herakles*. Brief nuptial songs appear in Aristophanes' *Peace* and *Birds*, but Theocritus is the most significant Gr. poet to have used the form (Eclogue 18 on the marriage of Helen and Menelaus). Among L. writers who used it were Ovid, Statius, and Claudian, but the most important for literary history was Catullus (*Carmina* 61, 62, 64). Medieval literature has devotional poems entitled *Epithalamia*, but these have no connection with the classical genre. The Renaissance revived the form and used it to great advantage: Tasso and Marino in Italy; in France Ronsard, Belleau, Du Bellay; in England Spenser, Sidney, Donne, Jonson, Herrick, Crashaw, Marvell, Dryden. Perhaps the greatest Eng. e. is Spenser's on his own wedding.

The form of the poem as established by the Renaissance poets includes the following conventions: the context is of course a wedding; the characters are the husband and wife who, when not fictional, are upper class, and the poet who is the public celebrator of the couple's private experience; the events of the entire wedding day form the basis of the organization of the poem; and classical allusions and *topoi* are included.—R. H. Chase, *Eng. Epithalamies* (1896); A. L. Wheeler, *Catullus and the Traditions of Ancient Poetry* (1934); A. Gaertner, *Die englische Epithalamienlit. im 17. Jh. und ihre Vorbilder* (1936); T. M. Greene, "Spenser and the Epithalamic Convention, CL, 9 (1957); A. K. Hieatt, *Short Time's Endless Monument* (1960).   R.A.H.

EPITHET. See POETIC DICTION.

EPITRITE (Gr. "one-third as much again," "one and one-third"). A foot containing 1 short and 3 long syllables, so described because the ratio of 2 longs to a long and a short is, in time-units or morae, 4: 3. The position of the short syllable determines the description of the epitrite as first, second, third, or fourth (respectively ⏑‒‒‒, ‒⏑‒‒, ‒‒⏑‒, ‒‒‒⏑). The first and fourth, however, were avoided by the Gr. poets as unrhythmical. See DACTYLOEPITRITE.   R.J.G.

EPIZEUXIS. See ANADIPLOSIS.

EPODE (Gr. "sung after"). In the lyric odes of, for example, Pindar, Bacchylides, and the Gr. dramatists, the epode completed an epodic triad by following the strophe and antistrophe (qq.v.), from which it differed in metrical form. In this sense, the Gr. word *epodos* could be feminine in gender, whereas when masculine it also denoted the shorter verse of a couplet, notably an iambic dimeter following an iambic trimeter. (The alternating lines of poems composed in such couplets might, however, be in different meters; for example, a dactylic hexameter might be followed by an

iambic dimeter or an iambic trimeter by a dactylic *hemiepes*.) Archilochus seems to have been the founder of this kind of composition which was used for invective and satire. Horace claims to have introduced the form into L. poetry in his "Iambi," which subsequent grammarians called epodes.—Hardie; Koster; B. Kirn, *Zur literarischen Stellung von Horazens Jambenbuch* (1935); E. Fraenkel, *Horace* (1957).   R.J.G.

EPYLLION (Gr. "little epos," "versicle," "scrap of poetry"). Such was the classical meaning of a word which, in the sense of "little epic," is apparently an invention of the 19th c. to describe a short narrative poem in dactylic hexameters. This so-called genre embraced mythological subjects which often contained a love interest. It was characterized by elaborate and vivid description, learned allusion, lengthy digression, and an interest in psychology. It was especially cultivated in the Alexandrian period (e.g., by Callimachus and Theocritus), and such compositions were widely imitated and served as models in the late Republican and early Augustan periods of L. literature. Catullus, for example, in his 64th poem which dealt with the wedding of Peleus and Thetis and included a digression about the abandoned Ariadne on Naxos. The Byzantine period had its "epyllia" which were longer than these narrative poems of Alexandrian and Roman times and were in effect brief epics. The counterparts of the shorter narrative poems of classical times were in the Middle Ages and afterwards the troubadour songs, the Russian *byliny*, the Scandinavian sagas, the modern Gr. *kleftic* songs. Shakespeare's "Lucrece" and Tennyson's *Oenone* are perhaps the best examples of epyllia in Eng. poetry.—J. Heumann, *De Epyllio Alexandrino* (1904); M. M. Crump, *The E. from Theocritus to Ovid* (1931); L. Richardson, Jr., *Poetical Theory in Republican Rome* (1944); J. F. Reilly, "Origins of the Word 'E.,' " CJ, 49 (1953–54); V. d'Agostino, "Considerazioni sull' epillio . . . ," *Rivista di studi classici*, 4 (1956); W. Allen, Jr., "The E.," TAPA, 71 (1940) and "The Non-Existent Classical E.," SP, 55 (1958).   R.J.G.

EROTIC POETRY. Poetry which deals with the sexual in more or less explicit detail. *Erotic poetry* is distinct on the one hand from *love poetry* which avoids specifically sexual details (such as Petrarch's *Canzoniere*) and on the other from mere *pornographic* (Gr. *pornē*, "harlot," and *graphē*, "writing") or obscene *verse*, which does not meet the aesthetic criteria understood in this article to be implied by the term *poetry*. In e. poetry the sexual is by some process of ordering (intellectual, emotional, stylistic—preferably all three) made to subserve an aesthetic effect, to submit to the artistic stylization of experience in the poem. However, although the imposition of stylistic and imaginative unity upon subject matter in poetry is analogous to moral integrity and self-control in practical matters, to demand control in poetry is not to require the poet to adhere to our own particular moral standards. Even thoroughly amoral works such as Ovid's *Ars amatoria* and Marlowe's *Hero and Leander* can have high aesthetic merit when the firm control of structure and style "diffuses a tone and spirit of unity" (Coleridge).

The erotic is not a *genre* but rather a recurrent *theme* of poetry, which may be treated in many genres. We shall be concerned with works a principal subject of which is sexual love, and only with the most important of those. The greatest e. literature of the East is that of India. Secular e. poetry appears early in the history of classical Sanskrit literature. Most important are perhaps Kalidasa's luxuriant *Meghaduta* (5th c.; tr. G. H. Rooke, 1936); Bharitrari's graceful century of quatrains, *Sringasataka*, the first of three centuries which lead from sexual love to worldly wisdom and finally to renunciation (7th or 8th c.; tr. J. W. Kennedy, 1914); and Bilhan's impressive *Pancaçika* (11th c.; tr. E. P. Mathers in *Eastern Love Songs*, 1953). Since perhaps the 4th c. A.D., Hinduism has recognized a passive or female principle (*Sakti*) in the universe, and the mythological sexual relations of the gods have traditionally been understood to represent the interaction of spirit (male) and matter (female). E. episodes in the ancient epics were early given mystical interpretation, especially the *Prem Sagar*, "The Ocean of Love," the tenth book of the *Bhagavatapurana* (before A.D. 900), which has formed the basic scripture of the Vaishnava cults. Vaishnava worship singles out for special attention the loves of Krishna (one of the ten incarnations of Vishnu) and Radha; perhaps the most significant of the richly ornamented, highly traditionalistic Indian e. poetry has been written in connection with this cult. Jayadeva's lyrical drama *Gita Govinda* (12th c.; tr. G. Keyt, 1947) and Vidyapathi's *Bangiya Padabali* (15th c.; tr. A. Coomaraswamy, 1915) refer simultaneously to divine love and highly sensual earthly love.

Secular e. poetry, both heterosexual and homosexual, is much more common among the Arabs than is religious e. poetry. The pre-Islamic Arab poets set a standard of grace and restrained intensity which dominated Arabic poetry for centuries. There are two principal collections of their poems: the *Hamasa*, made by Abu Temmam in the 10th c. (selections in C. Lyall, *Translations of Ancient Arabian Poetry*, 1885; German tr. by Friedrich Rückert, 1846), and the *Muallakat* (the seven "golden

odes," tr. in A. J. Arberry, *The Seven Odes*, 1957). These fairly extended "odes" (*kasidas*) of Imru-alqais and others regularly begin with nostalgic love episodes and proceed to the praises of chieftains or to set descriptions of desert life. Perhaps the most characteristic form of Islamic e. poetry is the *ghazal*, a short lyric, notably practiced by the cynical court poet of the Abassids, Abu Nuwàs (756–810); by the authors of the *Thousand and One Nights* (before 990); by the Persian Hafiz (ca. 1320–1389; tr. John Payne, 2 v., 1901); and by such graceful Moorish poets as Ibn Hazm, the author of an important treatise on love (*The Dove's Neck Ring*, tr. A. J. Arberry, 1953), and Ibn Zaidun and Al-Mutamid (1003–71 and 1040–95 respectively; selections tr. in A. R. Nykl, *Hispano-Arabic Poetry and its Relations with the Old Prov. Troubadours*, 1946 and in A. J. Arberry, *Moorish Poetry*, 1953). Although Islamic e. poetry is usually secular, the Prophet promised sexual joys in heaven, and the Sufi mystics sometimes used sexual symbolism, for example Ibn Al-Farid (1182–1234; *The Mystical Poems of Ibn Al-Farid*, tr. A. J. Arberry, 1956) and Rumi (1207–73; *Rumi, Poet and Mystic*, tr. R. A. Nicholson, 1950; *The Ruba'iyat of Jalal al-Din Rumi*, tr. A. J. Arberry, 1950). The Persian Jami (d. 1492) wrote a brilliant version of the Talmudic tale of Joseph and Potiphar's wife, *Yusuf and Zalaikha* (incomplete tr. by R. T. H. Griffith, 1881; Fr. tr. by A. Bricteux, 1927), in which the richly e. tale has detailed mystical meaning. In Jami's *Salaman and Absal* (tr. E. FitzGerald, 1856; see A. J. Arberry, *FitzGerald's Salaman and Absal. A Study*, 1957), on the other hand, sexual love is made representative of all that binds the soul to earth. Religious sexual symbolism entered the Western heritage with the biblical Song of Songs, whose imagery bears a clear family resemblance to that of pre-Islamic Arabic poetry and of the remnants of Egyptian e. poetry (S. Schott, *Altägyptische Liebeslieder*, 1950). The Song of Songs is probably secular in origin; the most likely theory identifies it as a collection of wedding songs. It has traditionally been interpreted as an allegory, whether of God's love for Israel or of Christ's love for the church or for the soul.

The Greeks produced lyric e. poetry with their characteristic ease and delicacy, from the intensities of Sappho to the uncomplicated and cheerful libertinage of Anacreon and his followers and the e. epigrams of the *Gr. Anthology* (collected in the 10th c. by Constantinus Cephalus). Aside from mildly e. episodes in Homer and Apollonius of Rhodes, there is little Gr. narrative e. poetry. Musaeus' *Hero and Leander* (4th or 5th c. A.D.) might be mentioned because of its influence on Christopher Marlowe. The few e. Idylls of Theocritus (most notably xxvii) were influential in the late 16th and the 17th c. The Gr. influence on later European e. poetry was, however, relatively slight, and that the most important influence was Roman, and especially Ovidian, is perhaps regrettable. A combination of factors, such as the tradition of the *hetairai*, the dominant classical conception of sexual passion as a form of madness, and the official puritanism of Augustan Rome, made it inevitable that Roman e. poetry should be produced in a spirit of libertinism. While the libertinism of Catullus and Propertius has its deeply serious side, in Ovid's *Amores* and *Ars amatoria* the deliberately outrageous is made a sophisticated amusement, and the epigrams of Martial and his imitators degenerate into obscene and cruel joking. Although the traditional mystical interpretation of the Song of Songs made possible such magnificent mystical poetry as that of St. John of the Cross (1542–91), there is little in Western poetry to compare with the simultaneous validation of earthly and mystical love in Indian and Persian poetry. Until the late 19th c., European e. poetry is, for the most part, wittily libertine or coarsely humorous, or else it descends out of the sphere of poetry into mere pornography.

While much love-making is described with gusto in such romances as *Huon of Bordeaux*, the medieval romance often treats sexual passion as tragic or impure even when, like Gottfried of Strassburg's *Tristan* (13th c.; tr. A. T. Hatto, 1960) and Wolfram von Eschenbach's *Parzifal* (tr. Mustard and Passage, 1961), they are outspoken on sexual matters. The doctrine of *courtly love* (q.v.) often included a final turning away from earthly passion to the love of God (cf. the influential treatise, *De Arte honeste amandi*, by Andreas Capellanus, 1174–86; tr. J. J. Parry, 1914). On his conversion, Peter Abelard destroyed all of his e. poems. Chaucer's *Troilus and Criseyde*, based on Boccaccio's *Filostrato* (tr. N. E. Griffin and A. B. Myrick, 1930), is beyond compare the best Eng. treatment of the theme. Much of the e. poetry of the goliards in the *Carmina Burana* and the so-called *Cambridge Songs* (tr. H. Waddell, *Medieval L. Lyrics*, 5th ed., 1951), overtly rebellious against the prevailing social norms, is unusually fresh and graceful in its lyricism.

The coarsely humorous medieval poetry of sex is best exemplified in the octosyllabic-couplet *fabliaux* (q.v.). These tales of low-life cuckoldings and gullings, which Douglas Bush has described as "broader than they are long," are illuminated by genius in Chaucer's "Miller's Tale" and "Reeve's Tale." Closely related to the *fabliau*, as well as to the Italian *novella*, is the 17th- and 18th-c. stanzaic *conte*, of which the best known writer is La Fontaine (*Nouvelles en vers*, 1665; *Contes et nouvelles*,

1666). Some of the verse collected in such volumes as the famous *Cabinet satyrique* (1618; critical ed., 1924), like the best broadside ballads of this and later periods, is on the level of the best bawdy jokes; most of it, however, is mere obscenity.

The writers of the so-called romantic epic adapted *fabliaux* and *novelle*, Boiardo in his *Orlando innamorato* (1483–95) and Ariosto in his *Orlando furioso* (1516–32); they added another element which was to have a considerable vogue later in the century: e. episodes based on such portions of Ovid's *Metamorphoses* as the myths of Salmacis and of Caenis. The episode of Paridell and Hellenore in Book III of Spenser's *Faerie Queene* (1590) is a particularly good specimen of the type. The myth of Circe was a favorite with the writers of romantic epic: Ariosto, Trissino (*L'Italia liberata dai Goti*, 1547), Tasso (*Gerusalemme liberata*, 1583), and Spenser all used it. The mythological e. poem, related to the ancient epyllion (q.v.) as practiced by Catullus (44), but owing most to the spirit of Ovid, was most notably practiced by Christopher Marlowe (*Hero and Leander*, 1598) and Shakespeare (*Venus and Adonis*, 1593) in England, where the vogue was most intense. In the hands of the It. mannerist G. B. Marino (*L'Adone*, 1624), it became an epic *omnium gatherum* and soon died out, although La Fontaine published an *Adonis* in 1669. A favorite type of e. poetry in the 17th c. was the pastoral, either narrative or lyrical, on whose development Theocritus, Longus, Tasso, Marino, and Ronsard were major influences.

Equally important with the influence of Ovid's *Metamorphoses* in the Renaissance was that of his *Amores* and *Ars amatoria*. Most of the 15th- and 16th-c. humanists wrote e. Latin poetry based on the *Amores* and Catullus. The best of them is beyond question Gioviano Pontano (1426–1503). The e. lyrics of Marino and his followers are also based primarily on Ovid's *Amores* and *Ars*. In France, the vogue of the *Amores* bore fruit in the cult of "l'amour simple"—uncomplicated sensual love, in part a reaction against Platonism—of which the best product is probably Ronsard's *Les amours de Marie* (1555). At some point in his career, Marlowe translated the *Amores*; the best example of the Eng. vogue is Donne's *Songes and Sonnets* and *Elegies* (1633).

Edmund Spenser's *Epithalamion* may well be the greatest e. poem in the literature of the world. Many epithalamia, of course, avoid mention of sexual detail. Those which do not tend to draw either upon folk songs or upon Pontano's adaptation of Ovidian instructions, as do Johannes Secundus (1511–36), Ben Jonson (*Hymenaei*, 1606), and Marino. Spenser united classical (Sappho, Catullus) and oriental (The Song of Songs) elements in a noble celebration of physical love sanctioned and ordered in a Christian and Platonic framework. Milton's Spenserian mode of celebrating married love (*Paradise Lost*, Book 4, 1667) is not the rule in the later 17th c., however. The Ovidian verse of Hoffmanswaldau, Colletet, Rochester, and others and the licentious songs popular on the Restoration stage in England (many are collected in Thomas D'Urfey's *Pills to Purge Melancholy*, 1684–1720) carry to new extremes the characteristic libertine paradox of slyly obscene content in elegant form.

The 18th c. saw the breakdown of these various traditions of e. poetry, as of the Renaissance tradition in general. The Ovidian elegy was revived in a lively and characteristically original manner by Goethe (*Römische Elegien*, 1795), the mythological e. poem by Keats (*Endymion*, 1818), and the comic-erotic epic by Byron (*Don Juan*, 1818–24), but with these and a few other exceptions (such as the songs of Béranger), little significant e. poetry was produced until the advent of the revolutionary Fr. symbolists, of whom an important precursor was Théophile Gautier (*Albertus*, 1833). Baudelaire (*Les fleurs du mal*, 1857), Mallarmé (*Hérodiade*, 1869; *L'après-midi d'un faune*, 1876), and Verlaine (*Parallèlement*, 1889; *Chansons pour elle*, 1891; *Odes en son honneur*, 1893) exploited various kinds of sexual abnormality, corruption, and diabolism and in general opened the way for serious poetic treatment of a wide range of sexual matters. The Victorian era in England saw a revival of interest in e. themes, of which the Pre-Raphaelite movement was a principal agent. Dante Gabriel Rossetti (*Poems*, 1870; *The House of Life* in *Ballads and Sonnets*, 1881) and Algernon Charles Swinburne (*Poems and Ballads*, 1866) evoked considerable controversy (e.g., Robert Buchanan, *The Fleshly School of Poetry*, 1872). In America, portions of Walt Whitman's *Song of Myself*, as well as his *Children of Adam* (first included in the 1860 edition of *Leaves of Grass*), brought a charge of immorality on the book which cost Whitman his position in the Indian Bureau. In the 20th c., e. poetry reflects the influence of Freudian and Jungian theories of the unconscious. Among the most important modern poets who have written serious e. poetry are: in Germany, Rainer Maria Rilke; in Spain, Federigo García Lorca; in France, Paul Valéry and Paul Eluard; in Great Britain, W. B. Yeats and D. H. Lawrence; in the United States, E. E. Cummings and Robinson Jeffers.

The standard lit. histories and bibliog. should be consulted. GENERAL: P. Englisch, *Gesch. der erotischen Lit.* (1927); C. von Bolen, *Erotik des Orients* (1955); F. Saba Sardi, *Sesso e mito. Storia e testi della letteratura erotica* (1960).—INDIA: P. N. Sinha, *The Bhagavata-Purana: a Study* (1901); R. Schmidt, *Beiträge zur indischen Erotik* (2d ed., 1911); A. Coomaraswamy, *The Dance of Siva* (1919); *India Love Poems*, ed. Tambimuttu (1954); W. G. Archer, *The Loves of Krishna in Indian Painting and Poetry* (1957).—ARABIA, PERSIA, MOSLEM SPAIN: *Arabic-Andalusian Casidas*, tr. H. Morland (1949); A. Kh. Kinany, *The Development of Ghazal in Arabic Lit.* (1951); A. J. Arberry, *The Seven Odes: The First Chapter in Arabic Lit.* (1957).—BIBLICAL: *The Song of Songs:* H. H. Rowley, "The Interpretation of the S. of S.," *Jour. of Theological Studies*, 38 (1937); R. Gordis, *The S. of S.* (1954).—EGYPT: W. M. Müller, *Die Liebespoesie der alten Ägypter* (1899).—CLASSICAL: A. L. Wheeler, *Catullus and the Tradition of Cl. Poetry* (1934); L. P. Wilkinson, *Ovid Recalled* (1955). MEDIEVAL: K. Breul, *The Cambridge Songs* (1915); J. Bédier, *Les Fabliaux* (4th ed., 1925); Jeanroy, *Origines*; F. J. E. Raby, *A Hist. of Secular L. Poetry in the Middle Ages* (2d ed., 2 v., 1957).—RENAISSANCE AND LATER: *Eng. Epithalamies*, ed. R. H. Case (1896); D. Bush, *Mythology and the Ren. Tradition in Eng. Poetry* (1932) and *Mythology and the Romantic Trad. in Eng. Poetry* (1937); J. H. Wilson, *The Court Wits of the Restoration* (1948); M. Praz, *The Romantic Agony*, tr. A. Davidson (2d ed., 1951). R.M.D.

ESKIMO POETRY. Esk. humanism, or spiritual culture, strikes many chords. We find no sentimentality, but a great deal of intimacy. There is a sufficiency of longing, with ensuing disappointments, and surprises; exaggerations, grotesque sorcery, and magic conjuring (*qila*) abound; there are even glimpses of sublime pathos—beside indignation and irony—in some arctic poems. According to Knud Rasmussen, Esk. poetry manifests a profuse and lofty imagination, a "fertile, creative fantasy [that] . . . lifts us . . . up . . . to the great spaces." But it can also exude a passionate earthiness, as in the cultic and dramatic games, which often surge with an abandoned eroticism. One can, however, hardly find a wooing ballad or a sentimental-frivolous love song. A national epic does not exist, and war songs are equally lacking.

The Eskimos have everywhere had a broad unwritten literature, including numerous legends and a nucleus of classical poems, mostly anonymous. The poems often consist of roughly uniform couplets which vary the same thought; often the poetic unit is a long, polysynthetic word which corresponds to two shorter words in the next line A kind of rhyme easily arises by two lines varying two verbs having the same grammatical endings, as, for instance, in the hymn of the angakok:

ilēgiakka	I explored them,
kagersēwimakki	these wide fjords.
ajangēleqākka	I was repelled by them.
nawiangēleqākka	I started being afraid of them,
ākitte, annikitte etc.	their small and big boats of skin (kayaks, umiaks)

A poem is poetically called the "breath" of the author (*anertsā* < *anér* "to breathe") or his *taigdliā* (from *tai* "to name, or mention, something"), actually "verbal art-work." The poem is considered the author's property (*pia*) as long as he is alive. Only after his death can it become common property; and the name of the author is forgotten at his death (cf. name-taboo). The great significance of poetry in Esk. culture was indicated by one of Knud Rasmussen's Esk. friends, Apákaq, who explained: ". . . festivity cannot be enjoyed with dance and song alone. The most festive thing of all is joy in beautiful smooth words. . . ." The poets observe the natural rhythms, cadences, and musical accents of the words. Most of the poems are intended to be sung, Esk. style; but petting songs for children and certain fairy tales are recited, in a peculiarly subtle manner. This is neither speech nor song, but an intermediate mode, with a fixed musical diction, crystallized from natural colloquial speech.

A. OCCULT AND INTIMATE POETRY. *Genre I: Magic prayers.* The Esk. magic prayers (*serhrät*) are ancient formulas transmitted clandestinely from the forefathers, thus constituting an occult tradition. They are recited in solitude in a low voice, at a moderate pace, and with regular pauses. Every adult would make sure to learn from an older person a number of such charms, enlarging his collection in response to the needs of new situations until he knew some ten or twenty of them. The young people asked; the old ones offered, confidentially, adding the following advice: "Do not use it too often! Do not wear them out! Be sparing of them!" The charm was supposed to be paid for with a costly gift. Magic prayers operate against attacks of disease, the evil effects of shooting stars, the cunning of a foe, and envy. According to Esk. thinking, every human being has many souls, a little one in each joint, more vital ones in the nape of the neck, the throat, and the diaphragm; by seizing upon these souls, evil men or spirits can cause disease. The victim seeks a cure in an appropriate formula. When death occurs, strict mourning-taboos are observed, especially by women; when the taboo is lifted, the bereaved one charms, murmuring: "Once more I step out upon the thin skin of the ice; I have become as poor now as the new earth, the poor one here, ea, ea!"

Genre II: Intimate poetry. To the intimate genre belongs the mothers' lullaby, e-e-e-a, used as a means of soothing; it consists of the magic refrain, which has been lengthened to an adagio of two see-sawing tones. Besides, every baby receives as a christening gift its own individual petting song (*aqaut*), a short or long poem alluding to the child's name—surname and nickname—or behavior.

B. The following genres are largely public and generally accessible. *Genre III:* The epic-lyrical genre embraces a great quantity of poetry, principally in short poems rarely divided into stanzas; the verse consists of freely flowing, rhythmically composed lines. The genre falls into several subvarieties, with or without melody and refrain. In the kayak-songs, the hunter sings (*ivnger-*) while rowing his kayak so that he is heard on shore. Using the tones of the drum-song, he sings about his catch (to signal the kind of seal caught), about the voyage, the weather and the ice—and about his wife: "She shall receive a coat of the finest fur (crested seal)." More closely connected with ancient tradition are the short poems that occur in certain legends: In *Ariagssuaq* the dead drummer-boy rises, a skeleton, from his grave to sing his approaching opponent to death, using his shoulder blade for a drum. In an East Greenland variant of the legend about the geese—a legend which is of pan-Esk. tradition—the death-song of the drowning raven resounds as he sinks into the sea with a last shriek. This is a dramatic poem, very artistically executed.

Genre IV: The cultic-religious hymns are partly traditional songs attached to old rites (festivals in the *qagssit's*, or communal houses), partly occasional poems composed by fully educated shaman priests *(angákut)* at the performance of their office. For instance, when at seances, with the aid of the sorcerer's drum, they conjure up their assisting spirits and speak with them in the presence of the congregation, the choir cooperating.

Genre V: In the juridical verse lampoons (*piseq*, pl. *pitsit; iver-, soqula-*) two men or women, facing each other in a drumming contest, alternately sing and drum-dance; they sing a dueling-feud in the circle of visitors, which participates as choir and court. The songs are composed and rehearsed in the homes of the duelists before they depart for the place of the meeting; the contents are poetically executed accusations, most often in the form of ironical suggestions woven into long refrains.

Genre VI: The dramatic drum-dance roles are partly cultic, connected with religious festivals, or quite profane games played in the huts during the winter season. Some of them lack the melodic element; they are just recited, rhythmically and expressively—in jest.

C. THE POETRY OF MODERN GREENLAND. Since 1721, when missions from Denmark, Norway, and Germany established themselves on Greenland, the people have become Europeanized and are now strongly mixed. A Christian-ecclesiastical literature was fostered when the natives learned how to read and write. From ca. 1860 on, periodicals and newspapers in the West Greenland language, which is an Esk. dialect, have been ¬published. At Godthåb there is a printing press. Modern authors like Henrik Lund (1875–1948), Pavia, and Jonatan Petersen have composed many fine hymns and secular poems, mostly in Danish romance style, but in the Greenland-Esk. language. Jonatan Petersen wrote a textbook on Greenland metrics. Other natives have composed novels and plays. Apart from a few transitional poems from the last century, the traces of the old-world heathen poetry are quite extinguished; this poetry is only faintly remembered in East Greenland.

TEXTS AND TRANSLATIONS: H. J. Rink, *Eskimoiske Eventyr og Sagn* (2 v., 1866–77); *Tales and Traditions of the Esk.* (1875–77) and (with F. Boas) "Esk. Tales and Songs," JAF, 2 (1889), 7 (1894), 10 (1897); W. Thalbitzer, "Old-fashioned Songs" (pp. 289–317) in *Phonetical Study of the Esk. Language* (Meddelelser om Grønland, 31, 1904), "Texts from East Greenland [Poetry]," *The Ammassalik Esk.*, 2d pt., pp. 184–378, 496–543 (Medd. om Grønland, 40, 1923), *Légendes et chants esquimaux du Groenland* [Leroux] (1929), *Esk.-Liederen van Oost-Groenland* [Mees] (1933), *Inuit Songs and Dances from Greenland* [Munksgaard] (1939); K. J. V. Rasmussen, *Snehyttens Sange* (1930) and *The Eagle's Gift*, tr. I. Hutchison (1932); *Beyond the High Hills: A Book of Esk. Poems*, comp. and tr. K. J. V. Rasmussen (1961).

GENERAL: H. J. Rink, "Eskimoisk Digtekunst," *For Idee og Virkelighed* (1870); F. Boas, "The Central Eskimo," U.S. Bureau of Am. Ethnology. 6th *Ann. Rep.* (1888) and "The Folklore of the Esk.," JAF, 17 (1904); K. J. V. Rasmussen, *The People of the Polar North* (1908) and *Report of the Fifth Thule Expedition 1921–24*, VII-IX (1930–32); W. Thalbitzer, "Poetics. Language and Folklore," *The Ammassalik Eskimo*, 2d pt., pp. 160–80 (Medd. om Grønland, 40, 1923) and "Grønlandsk litteraturhistorie," in *Grønlandsbogen*, ed. Schultz, II (1950, pp. 255ff.); H. C. Glahn, ["On the Poetry of the Greenlanders in the Rev. Glahn's Relations"] *Dagbøger* (Diaries) written in Greenland 1763–68, ed. H. Ostermann in Det grønlandske Selskabs *Skrifter*, 4 (1921); C. W. Schultz-Lorentzen, "Intellectual Culture of the Greenlanders," in *Greenland*, ed. M. Vahl, II (1928);

S. Frederiksen, "Henrik Lund, A National Poet of Greenland," Am. Philos. Soc. *Proceed.*, 96, no. 6 (1952) and *Stylistic Forms in Greenland Esk. Lit.* (Medd. om Grønland, 136, no. 7, 1954).
w.t. (arr. and tr. s.l.)

ESPINELA. An octosyllabic 10-line Sp. stanza form having the rhyme scheme abba:accddc. There is a pause after the fourth line as indicated by the colon. The strophe was supposedly invented by Vicente Espinel (1550–1624) and is named after him. The e. is occasionally augmented by 2 lines rhyming *ed*. Also called *décima* or *décima espinela*. It has been termed "the little sonnet," and justly so, since some of the most beautiful lines in Sp. poetry (e.g., in Calderón's *La vida es sueño*) have taken this form. Since its introduction in the late 16th c., the e. has been widely employed.— D. C. Clarke, "Sobre la e.," RFE, 23 (1936); J. Millé y Giménez, "Sobre la fecha de la invención de la décima o e.," HR, 5 (1937); J. M. de Cossío, "La décima antes de Espinel," RFE, 28 (1944); Navarro. D.C.C.

ESTONIAN POETRY. The Est. language, akin to Finnish, has the word-accent on the first syllable, is highly inflected, and tends toward polysyllabism. Its relatively small number of initial consonants favors alliteration, which, however, is unobtrusive because of the unemphatic articulation. Oral folk poetry, alive in some parts of Estonia until fairly recently, and recorded in hundreds of thousands of items, prefers an octosyllabic meter combining quantitative and accentual principles, as that of the Finnish *Kalevala*. The lines, trochaic when sung, permit initial short syllables of words to be stressed only at the beginning of the verse, e.g.:

$$\text{K\'ohise, k\'ohise, keeli,}$$

$$\text{L\'aja v\'astu, l\'aasi, s\'uuri.}$$

Ring, ring, tongue,
Resound, great forest

The trochaic pattern is not followed when the verses are spoken. Parallelism and periphrastic formulae—not unlike *kenningar* (see KENNING) abound, creating a rich, ornamental style capable of strong lyrical and dramatic effects. Written poetry since the 17th c. almost entirely discarded this form, using instead either syllabo-accentual or purely accentual meters, largely owing to German influence. The numerous polysyllables, with only one clearly audible stress, often count as one long metrical foot; more frequently, however, the slight secondary stresses are exploited metrically, producing iambic or trochaic patterns. Dactylic, amphibrachic, and anapestic patterns are also frequent enough. There is considerable disinclination to use the weakly stressed inflections as rhymes. Near-rhymes, permitting a fuller use of the vocabulary and surprise effects, have become more common since the 1920's.

Foreign—Baltic-German and Rus.—social, economic, and political pressure slowed up the intellectual life of the Estonians until the early 19th c., when poetry, along with other cultural pursuits, began to flower. Stimulated by the romantic conception of a national genius, the leading poets of the Est. national Renaissance drew much of their inspiration from folklore, aided by their study of classical antiquity, Finnish, German, and partly British romantic and preromantic poetry. The first notable poet, the short-lived Kristjan Jaak Peterson (1802–22), wrote inspired Pindarics. F. R. Kreutzwald's epic *Kalevipoeg* (The Kalevid, 1857–61), based on runic folk ballads, whose meter it uses, and of decisive importance as a cultural stimulus, owed much to Lönnrot's Finnish *Kalevala*. The powerful patriotic lyrics of Lydia Koidula (1843–86) with great independence developed the romantic *Lied* genre. Later in the century, political and social changes led to a less public, more intimate and more individually differentiated poetry, most impressively exemplified in the profoundly personal, tragic symbolism of the seemingly simple lyrics of Juhan Liiv (1864–1913). Symbolism in its Western form, intellectually searching, with much emphasis on a highly individual, sophisticated style, characterizes the verse of the Noor-Eesti (Young Estonia) group, above all that of its leader, Gustav Suits (1883–1957), a revolutionary experimentalist and idealist, constantly torn between high flights of emotion and bitter, satirical skepticism. The poignancy, subtlety, formal richness, and exploratory boldness of his verse decisively affected the further course of Est. poetry. The quiet, introspective mysticism of Ernst Enno (1875–1934), the sensitive island landscapes of Villem Grünthal-Ridala (1885–1942), influenced by Carducci, and the archaic ballads of Jaan Lôo (1872–1939) all added new wealth of language, imagery, and versification to a rapidly expanding literature. A discordant but effective note was struck by the gloomy, visionary primitivism of Jaan Oks (1884–1918).

Toward the end of the First World War, shortly before the Est. declaration of independence in 1918, a new group, named after a mythological bird, "Siuru," inaugurated an era of lyrical exuberance and extreme individualism of both form and content. Its leaders, Marie Under (1883–) and Henrik Visnapuu (1889–1951), soon abandoned subjectivism for strenuous thought, more universal themes, and more firmly crystallized form. Marie Under, the greatest master of lyrical intensity, passed through psychological and metaphysical crises culminating in a poetry of extraordinary translucency and human insight. The eclectic but keen picturesque aestheticism of Johannes Semper (1892–), the intimate dialect verse of Artur Adson (1889–) and Hendrik Adamson (1891–1946), the principally Rus.-inspired experiments in melodic instrumentation of Valmar Adams (1899) preceded a temporary trend towards robust, nonphilosophic realism, which dominated the early thirties, but was followed by a strong idealistic reaction. The deeply rooted native tendency toward symbolism, in a new, disciplined form, reasserted itself in the verse of the "Arbujad" (Magicians) group, including Uku Masing (1909–), Bernard Kangro (1910–), and, above all, Heiti Talvik (1904–46) and Betti Alver (1906–), both intellectually among the subtlest, formally among the most brilliant of Est. verse writers. Keenly aware of the great tradition of European poetry and thought, these poets sought "to enclose in slim stanzas the blind rage of the elements" (H. Talvik), imposing the finality of perfect expression on the emotional turbulence of a world heading toward chaos. This is equally apparent in the extreme, explosive, but fully controlled condensation of Talvik and in the more many-sided output of Betti Alver, whose intense inner struggles are expressed with classical poignancy and clarity, her seriousness being tempered by self-irony, and sometimes also by warm humor. Bernard Kangro's sensitive application of legendary and country lore added a special touch to the verse of this group.

Since the Second World War, which led to the Sovietization of Estonia, only the refugees have been able to write freely and to produce real art. Some of them, especially Marie Under, Bernard Kangro in some of his work, and Gustav Suits in his last, extensive volume of verse, have grown in breadth and depth of outlook. New talents—Kalju Lepik, Ivar Grünthal, Harri Asi, Arno Vihalemm, Raimond Kolk, Ilmar Laaban—vigorously voice the experiences of war and exile in a great variety of approaches, ranging from strict traditionalism to surrealism. Aleksis Rannit, though known before, has only recently developed his special style of delicate definition of impressions of art. Irony, rueful resignation, a delight in vivid, grotesque imagery characterize the strong rhythms of Arno Vihalemm. Even greater irony, an aggressive, expansive temperament, and an insatiably probing intellect are prominent in the verse of Ivar Grünthal, whose metrical virtuosity can be dazzling. The dominant tone of Est. poetry—restless intellectual quest—remains strongly pronounced.

ETHIOPIAN POETRY

ANTHOLOGIES: *Estnische Klänge,* ed. A. Kallas (1911); *Almanach estnischer Literatur und Kunst* (1927); *An Anthol. of Modern Est. Poetry,* ed. W. K. Matthews (1953); *Est. Lit. Reader,* ed. A. Oras (1963).

HISTORY AND CRITICISM: W. F. Kirby, *The Hero of Estonia* (2 v., 1895; on *Kalevipoeg*); M. Kampmaa, *Eesti kirjandusloo peajooned* (4 v., 1924–36; hist. of Est. lit.); F. R. Kreutzwald, *Kalevipoeg* (2 v., 1934–36); W. K. Matthews, "The Est. Sonnet," SEER, 25 (1946–47); E. H. Harris, *Lit. in Estonia* (2d enl. ed., 1953); H. Salu, *Eesti vanem kirjandus* (1953); G. Suits, *Eesti kirjanduslugu,* I (1953); A. Oras, "Est. Poetry," *N.Y. Publ. Lib. Bull.,* 61 (1957) and "Storia della letteratura estone," in *Storia delle letterature Baltiche,* ed. G. Devoto (1957, 2d ed. in prep.); For *A.O.: Studies in Est. Poetry and Language,* ed. V. Kõressaar and A. Rannit (1964).   A.O.

ESTRIBILLO. A refrain in Sp. lyrics and ballads which apparently originated in the *zéjel* (q.v.), of Arabic origin. The *zéjel* came through the Galician-Portuguese to the Sp. court lyric in the 14th c., where it developed into the *cantiga,* which in turn produced various types of poems during the pre-Renaissance period. In the early period the e. was the introductory stanza—stating the theme and often called *cabeza* or *texto*—of a poem and was repeated at the end of each stanza of the poem. Later it is sometimes found at the end of each stanza only.—Navarro.   D.C.C.

ETHICAL CRITICISM. See CRITICISM, TYPES OF.

ETHIOPIAN POETRY may be divided into three classes: (1) verses written in Ge'ez (Ethiopic), a language which ceased to be spoken (except in the church) some four or five hundred years ago, though it remained the normal medium for literary expression until the end of the 18th c.; (2) popular verse composed in Amharic (now the official and most widely used language), Tigrinya, Tigré, Harari, or other local vernaculars; and (3) modern secular or semireligious poetry in Amharic.

In all types of Ethiop. poetry the principal formal characteristic is rhyme, which is constituted by consonant plus vowel (not vowel plus consonant): rhyming lines must end in the same combination of consonant and following vowel. When the last word in the line ends with what in ordinary speech is a. consonant, in poetry a vowel (something between short *e* and short *i*) must be sounded after it. Vowels alone do not constitute a rhyme, though sometimes (notably in Tigré verse) a stanza may contain lines ending in, say, *nu, ru,* and *lu,* each occurring four or five times in no par-

ticular order. The general rule is for one full rhyme to persist for several lines, then for another to be started, differing in both consonant and vowel.

In most Ethiop. poetry meaning is more important than sound; the succession of images and metaphors aims at subtle allusion, not at beauty of words and rhythm. Thus in Ge'ez verse, which is almost exclusively religious in character, double meanings are ingeniously devised which often require, for their full understanding, a profound knowledge of the Bible, of sacred legends, and of dogma. A couplet will be admired for its concise allusiveness rather than for its musical sound. Ge'ez poems are normally intended to be sung to some traditional musical mode, which makes it less necessary to provide music in the words themselves.

In Ge'ez poetry there are several fixed types as regards number and length of lines, ranging from epigrammatic couplets through the 9-line *mawaddes* (praise) to long hymns—of which a favorite form is the *malk'e* (likeness) addressed usually to a saint; it consists of some fifty 5-line stanzas, each of which begins *salām* and is a salutation to a different physical or moral attribute of the subject. The earliest hymns are attributed to Yared, who lived in the 6th c., but the surviving poems mostly date from the 15th and succeeding c.; both in form and in content there has been little change of style, and in monastic schools, where the composition of Ge'ez verse continues to be taught, ancient models are faithfully followed. Ge'ez poems are also still written by and for learned ecclesiastics and laymen; their themes are sometimes secular, but they invariably contain allusions to sacred subjects.

Popular verse in Amharic and other vernaculars has for centuries been composed by professional minstrels, mostly at the courts of kings and princes, or at weddings, funerals, and other celebrations; the earliest known are 14th-c. songs in honor of the Emperor. Such verse is "occasional," and only a small proportion has more than a temporary vogue, when it relates to celebrated persons or events, or is exceptionally witty. There are also some love songs and patriotic ditties of recent date. Like Ge'ez poetry, popular verse aims at subtle allusion, through puns and plays on words, rather than at beauty of diction. For example:

Yimallisau inji iraññāu bāwwaqa—
Yammichilau yallam—yās lām ka-zallaqa.

A more or less literal translation is:

He will bring it back, indeed, will the herdsman, in (the way) he knows—
There is none (other) who can—that cow that has strayed.

-[257]-

A simple rustic situation is described in simple language. But it is possible to take *yās lām* not as "that cow" but as *yā-(i)slām*, "those Moslems." The couplet is now transformed: the "herdsman" stands for God; and *zallaqa* is to be taken in a secondary sense of "infiltrate," thus we have a pointed comment upon the infiltration into Christian Ethiopia of Moslems whom only God knows how to send away again.

It is only during the present c., and particularly since the restoration of independence in 1941, that Amharic has begun to be used for more individual poetic expression. Even so, the traditional rhyme system is followed, though with a tendency toward shorter series of rhymes. The usual line is a hexameter with a strong caesura in the middle. Poems are mostly lengthy and didactic, with morality and patriotism the commonest themes. Verse drama displays most variety and originality. The "elevated" style is characteristic of modern Ethiop. verse.

ANTHOLOGIES: *Lieder der Tigrēstämme*, ed. E. Littmann (*Publications of the Princeton Expedition to Abyssinia*, v. 3 [text], 4A, 4B [tr.], 1913); *Matshafa qenē*, ed. Heruy Walda-Sellāsié (1926; 1,100 Ge'ez poems); *Inē-nnā wedājochē*, ed. Heruy Walda-Sellāsié (1935; Ge'ez and Amharic poems); *Yāddis zaman mazmur*, ed. Yilmā Dērēsā (1941; 36 Amharic poems by young writers); *Amāriññā qenē*, ed. Māhtama-Sellāsié Walda-Masqal (1955; over 1,150 short Amharic poems, mostly anonymous); *Malk'a qubā'ē*, ed. Tesfā Gabra-Sellāsié (1955; coll. of Ge'ez hymns called *malk'e*).

HISTORY AND CRITICISM: I. Guidi, *Proverbi, strofe e racconti abissini* (1896; with texts and tr.); M. Chaîne, "La poésie chez les Ethiopiens," *Revue de l'Orient Chrétien*, 3e sér., 2 (1920–21); M. Cohen, "Couplets amhariques du Choa," *Jour. asiatique* (Juillet–Sept. 1924); J. M. Harden, *An Introd. to Ethiopic Christian Lit.* (1926); I. Guidi, *Storia della letteratura etiopica* (1932); W. Leslau, "Chansons Harari," *Rassegna di studi etiopici* (1947); E. Cerulli, *Storia della lett. etiopica* (1956). s.w.

EUPHONY. The quality of having a pleasant and smooth-flowing sound, free from harshness; the opposite of cacophony. E. arises largely from ease of articulation. The vowel sounds, which demand no cessation of breath, are considered more euphonious than the consonants, with the longer vowels being preferred to the shorter. Of the consonant sounds the most euphonious are the liquids and semivowels: *l, m, n, r, y, w.* Poe, considering long *o* the most sonorous vowel and *r* the most reproducible consonant, chose "Nevermore" as refrain word for *The Raven*, a word combining three vowels, four liquids, and a soft *v*. Opinions differ as to the order in which the other consonants follow, but in general those most easily produced are felt to be most pleasing. E. results not only from choice of sounds but from their arrangement. Sounds may be arranged so that they flow easily into each other, or may be placed in difficult combinations, demanding more muscular effort. Meter also will play a role, sometimes clogging a line with heavy accents, sometimes spacing them out more agreeably.

The importance of e. to total poetic effect is a matter of dispute, some finding great pleasure in "linkèd sweetness long drawn out"; others insisting that "mere sound in itself can have no or little aesthetic effect" (Wellek and Warren). Since too much euphoniousness may give the effect of weakness, some poets (e.g., Browning) have reacted against it. In general, however, e. is a desired characteristic, and most poetry is more euphonious than ordinary speech. Nearly all would agree, however, that e. is to be desired chiefly as a means rather than as an end, and that the first test of its desirability is appropriateness. The lines " 'Artillery' and 'armaments' and 'implements of war' / Are phrases too severe to please the gentle Muse" are much more euphonious than those written by Byron in *Don Juan*, but Byron's are much to be preferred as more consonant with their idea: "Bombs, drums, guns, bastions, batteries, bayonets, bullets,— / Hard words, which stick in the soft Muses' gullets." See also SOUND IN POETRY.—G. R. Stewart, *The Technique of Eng. Verse* (1930); A. Spire, *Plaisir poétique et plaisir musculaire* (1949). L.P.

EUPHUISM describes the style and subject matter of John Lyly's two novels *Euphues: the Anatomy of Wit* (1578) and *Euphues and His England* (1580), as well as his comedies. There is every reason to confine the term to the twenty or thirty years of Lyly's vogue in England, and leave the term mannerism (q.v.) to cover all ornate styles.

It was long assumed that Lyly carried to extravagance certain stylistic traits of Humanist Ciceronianism, until M. Croll proposed what he considered more direct origins in rhetorical teachings of the Middle Ages. Whatever the ultimate origins, Lyly was strikingly anticipated by Antonio de Guevara (various of whose works went through twenty-four editions in Eng. before 1578) in the elaborate and persistent use of balance and antithesis both in sound and sense. Aside from style, there are other influences on Lyly, e.g., Renaissance treatises on the education of the courtier or prince. Not only did their conventional themes influence Lyly, but also their advocacy of elegance in manners and speech, and, in general, of the ideals of aristocratic refinement. Hence the significance of the name "Euphues," meaning "well-grown."

All the characters in *Euphues* discourse in the same polished manner, using a wealth of rhetorical devices, such as balance, antithesis, homoeoteleuton, and paranomasia in numerous patterns. Moreover, learned allusions, elaborate comparisons and far-fetched metaphors occur without regard to any canon of verisimilitude. In general, e. is a highly analytical style which ceaselessly dissects, catalogues, compares, and contrasts; it aspires thereby to represent the polite discourse of urbane and elegant persons.

In determining the influence of e. on prose and poetry of the time, we must always consider the question of whether similarities come one from the other or whether they are merely parallel. One clear case of influence is found in the prose and even the verse of Shakespeare's early comedies, notably *The Comedy of Errors, Two Gentlemen of Verona* and *Love's Labour's Lost.* In these plays, and still more obviously in *Henry IV,* part 1 (2.4; direct parody of a passage from *Euphues*), Shakespeare is satirizing affected euphuistic speech, but we must not assume that his satire is meant to be devastating: it was partly from Lyly that he learned to make his own style pointed, elegant, and witty.

While it is possible to trace the influence of e. on the drama, it is difficult to do the same in lyric poetry. Even Lyly's own lyrics hardly show the mark of e.; his one verse play is singularly free of it. In general, it can be said that e. had less of a chance in the lyric, because the exigencies of rhyme and stanza made such immediate demands that the additional formal requirements of e. could not easily be honored.—F. Landmann, *Der Euphuismus, sein Wesen, seine Quelle, seine Geschichte* (1881); C. G. Child, *John Lyly and E.* (1894); A. Feuillerat, *John Lyly* (1910); M. Croll, "Intro." to his and H. Clemons' ed. of *Euphues* (1916); J. A. Barish, "The Prose Style of John Lyly," ELH, 23 (1956) and *Ben Jonson and the Language of Prose Comedy* (1960); G. K. Hunter, *John Lyly* (1962).   L.N.

EVALUATION. The act of ascertaining or judging the value or worth (from L. *valere*, "to be strong," or "worthy") of a poem. Since the word may appear in relation to (1) a general theory of "value" (and, more specifically, aesthetic or poetic value), (2) the designation or analysis of specific "values" found in a poem (e.g., maturity, harmony, texture, irony), (3) the process of "evaluation" (sometimes "valuation"), or (4) the final result of this process—it has, in a sense, become almost synonymous in our day with "criticism" itself,

as seen from a special point of view. Our concern here is to trace the development of that point of view and to discuss its achievements and the problems it presents.

HISTORY OF THE TERM. The critic or theorist who speaks of e. today is referring, *mutatis mutandis,* to the same general areas referred to by earlier critics who spoke of the problem, or the faculty, of taste (q.v.) and who pronounced judgment on poets and poems (see "Judicial criticism," under CRITICISM, TYPES OF). More or less rough equivalents of the modern notion of "value" were implicit in the Platonic Idea of the Good; in the Aristotelian "telos" (end), "entelechy," and final cause; and in the medieval and Renaissance concepts of "virtue." In the early stages of modern criticism, a "neoclassicist" might speak of a poet's "virtues" and "vices" (or "beauties" and "faults"); and, with the development of aesthetics, of Beauty in general (cf. *Philosophies of Beauty,* ed. E. Carritt, 1931).

The modern word was originally used in the sciences (referring especially to mathematical and physical "values"), but first gained more popular currency in economic theory (Adam Smith, in *The Wealth of Nations,* 1776). Thus, originally at least, it implied an attempt at technical precision.

In his three great *Critiques,* Kant attempted to justify the "validity" of the ancient trinity of values (Truth, Good, Beauty), in the face of the denial of their objective existence by the empirical science of his day; and the foundations of "value theory" were subsequently laid by post-Kantian philosophers, chiefly in Germany (R. H. Lotze and A. Ritschl, at Goettingen; C. von Ehrenfels, *System der Werttheorie,* 1897; A. Meinong, *Zur Grundlegung der Allgemeinen Werttheorie,* 1923). Nietzsche's "transvaluation of all values" (*Zur Genealogie der Moral,* 1887) and W. James's "pragmatism" (which considered values in relation to their practical consequences) were less technical explorations of the same problem. Out of an extensive and ever-growing literature in Eng., we may mention: W. M. Urban, *Valuation: Its Nature and Laws,* 1909; R. B. Perry, *General Theory of Value,* 1926; O. Pell, *Value Theory and Criticism,* 1930; J. Dewey, *Theory of Valuation,* 1939. As one practical consequence, these theories have led to new concepts and techniques of testing and grading students in educational situations (including literary composition), concerning which there is an extensive literature (A. Gates *et al., Educational Psychology,* 1942).

AXIOLOGY. We may well begin by asking what has been gained for poetics from the science of "axiology" (a word newly coined from a Gr. root to designate the *general* theory of value)—by speaking of e. rather than "judgment," of poetic "values" rather than "virtues" or "beauties"? In a sense, perhaps, comparatively little: a new fashion in terminology does not necessarily settle ancient issues, and we must beware of merely importing a specious "scientific" quality into discussions of the art of poetry. To cite one fairly typical example: W. Shumaker (*Elements of Critical Theory*, 1952) concludes an elaborate and sensitive exploration of e. with little more than the following (quoted from D. Daiches, *New Literary Values*, 1936): "The ideal criticism begins with a philosophic view of life as a whole, proceeds with the separating out of literary activity from human activity in general and the assessing of their mutual relations, deducing from this a norm of literary value, and concludes by the application of this standard to the individual instance." In such a sensible statement, however one may want to criticize it, certain classical conceptions of criticism may have been made a bit more precise, perhaps, but they hardly seem to have been superseded. The achievement we are attempting to summarize thus consists chiefly of: (1) the restatement and clarification (sometimes complication—whether useful or not, is a matter for debate in each instance) of certain fundamental distinctions and issues; and (2) an attempted reunification of realms which modern philosophy and practice (unlike that of the Greeks) have tended to keep separate.

Axiology seeks to establish a soundly based theory of value in general, and to distinguish the various forms or species of that genus. Theories of value tend naturally to be influenced by more general philosophical positions, particularly those that have to do with the objectivity and subjectivity of phenomena, and some of the issues that cluster around this polarity will be touched on in the section on the locus of aesthetic values. Furthermore, since controversy on fundamental principles is still very much alive, any single theory of value will probably fail to satisfy certain needs and, particularly when stated briefly and without development or qualification, be open to some objections. Nevertheless, we offer the following as a widely accepted definition of "value" useful for our purposes: *A quality of an object or experience which arouses and/or satisfies our interest, appreciation, or desire.* The latter are all psychological terms, and value theories often carry the implication (if not the explicit invocation) of a hedonistic psychology. This general quality may then be subdivided into classes: economic, ethical (including the social and political), aesthetic, logical (as when certain logicians speak of "truth-value"), religious—and perhaps others, which are probably subdivisions of one or another of these.

A primary distinction is that between instrumental and intrinsic (or terminal or immediate) values: e.g., the "exchange value" of gold, as against its color and hardness; the lamp originally created primarily as a means of illumination, as against the same lamp exhibited in an art museum as an object of beauty; and the use of literature for purposes of propaganda, as against the "purely poetic" values of the poem, however these may be defined. Obviously, what originally had instrumental value only, or chiefly, may come to be cherished for their intrinsic values, as "goods in themselves." Most value theorists restrict the latter to the ethical, logical, aesthetic, and religious values (good, truth, beauty, holiness, in early philosophies). These major kinds of intrinsic value, though attempts may sometimes be made to reduce some of them to others, seem to be more or less clearly distinguishable. They are also, however, naturally related to one another, within our experiences (as Dante's *Divine Comedy*, Pope's *Essay on Man*, or any poem for that matter, may be read in terms of any one of these values, or of all four together), and also in the sense that one such value may be "weighed" against another (as a poem may be found to forego aesthetic subtlety of form in order to achieve clarity of statement; or as a reader may choose to overlook the theology of Milton's *Paradise Lost* the better to enjoy its "organ tones").

Most contemporary theories tend to treat values as relative to human situations and to the personal limitations of those who experience them. However, in the past there have often been attempts to relate them to one another in terms of some hierarchy or scale, leading up to Absolute Value, which has been seen as an ultimate Reality (sometimes God), or at least as the ultimate standard by which the others are "weighed." One recent theory sees values as more or less elaborate rationalizations (in the best sense of that much-abused word) of the primitive fact of *choice* or *preference*: "I like Keats" becomes "Keats is a good poet because. . . ."; and, on a higher level of complexity, "I like Keats better than Shelley" becomes "Keats is a better poet than Shelley because. . . ." On the false analogy of economics, where "price" (cf. the value-verb: "to prize") provides a neutral measure, various attempts have been made with limited success, to translate the conditions of these choices into quantitative terms—as with Bentham's "hedonistic calculus" of his utilitarian ethics, and grading scales in commerce and education (but see G. D. Birkhoff's persuasive *Aesthetic Measure*, 1933). As against the methods of comparison and measurement, there is a point of view which stresses the uniqueness of each individual person, experience, work of art, or value situation.

THE LOCUS OF AESTHETIC VALUES. It is sometimes held that poetry is most properly appreciated for its intrinsic (or internal) values, and that so-called nonpoetic elements (philosophic or religious ideas, political propaganda, etc.) are to be excluded from evaluation (Abbé Bremond, *La poésie pure*, 1926)—in opposition to the ancient tradition which held that poetry should teach as well as delight (Horace) and should move to right action (Minturno, Sidney). This scientific attitude—which is as old as Aristotle, though it has been given special emphases by modern critics—usually involves close attention to the internal relations of parts in the poem, to its formal values (hence the label "formalism") considered more or less as ends in themselves: e.g., unity and variety, antithesis and contrast, structure and pattern, and so forth. The classical tradition, however, especially those aspects of it embodied in principles of rhetoric (for example, decorum), would urge us to relate the formal aspects of the poem or oration to the immediate and ultimate ends it is designed to serve and to the motives of the poet or orator, with inevitable consequences for our evaluations. Thus, a work of propaganda, or didactic poetry, may also be great literature—and in such a case it is artificial to separate its formal values from the values of the cause it is designed to serve, or the truths it seeks to teach.

In the total aesthetic situation, we encounter a complex interplay of (1) the poet, (2) the poem, and (3) the reader-critic, the first two involving the process of *expression*, and the poem acting eventually as a vehicle of *communication* between the poet and the reader. Thus, aesthetic values may be viewed in any of three ways, at least, depending on who is involved and where the critic may choose to place his primary emphasis: (1) as expressive of the poet's intention, to the extent that this can be ascertained; (2) in terms of the poem itself, not excluding its various contexts, past and present; or (3) in terms of the immediate experience of the critic as he reads the poem. Since the first alternative tends to lead away from immediate values into second-hand statements, which may or may not be relevant to the poem, or into problems of biographical or historical fact which are scientific and not aesthetic in essence, the last two would seem to bring us closest to the poetic values themselves; and the locus of critical reading would seem to lie in a constant interaction between the qualities of the poem as an aesthetic object and the subjective states of mind of the reader. The full exploration of this question would involve us, ultimately, in metaphysical issues (see ANALYSIS, especially the references

to Pepper and Wellek). What concerns the less philosophical critic more immediately is the problem of the validity of his evaluations: Are these merely subjective, his own private preferences or hallucinations which might result in an attitude of extreme impressionism or relativism? Or are they objective facts, that should be shared by all or most men— resulting in an emphasis on tradition (the "common reader") and attempts at scientific objectivity?

Since both extremes can easily be shown to be wrong in some respects (i.e., to have their limitations), the truth probably lies somewhere between. The most useful formulation is that which locates the values of the poem in the aesthetic experience of the poem, giving that term its fullest possible significance as representing the total "interaction of the organism with its environment"—in this case, of "the live creature" with "the expressive object" or poem, to use Dewey's language in *Art as Experience* (1934). In the aesthetic experience itself there occurs a fusion of the outer and the inner, an organization of energies such that "the object and pleasure are one and undivided in the experience." E. Vivas, a critical follower of Dewey, has stated the case, briefly and well, for what he calls an "objective relativism," according to which "we evince interest in [the work of art] because it actually possesses objective features that are capable of eliciting our [one's] interest" (art. on "Value," *Dictionary of World Literature*, ed. J. Shipley, 1943). Only by some such formulation, we think, can justice be done both to the subjective variety of tastes, and the intimate nature of the aesthetic experience, on the one hand; and to the sense we have that our poetic values are not merely arbitrary, and to the objective social and educative functions of poetry, on the other.

THE PROCESS OF EVALUATION. Though metaphysical issues may, in one fashion or another, ultimately determine our judgments, philosophical training is no sure guarantee of sensibility or taste. For the study of poetry, then, broad generalities may be less useful than an examination of the actual process of e. as it may be observed in our own reading and in the practice of critics.

The first point to be made, perhaps, is the great variation—not incompatible with objectivity—not only of judgments, but also of methods and styles of criticism (" 'Tis with our judgments as our watches, none / Go just alike, yet each believes his own"): some may depend more on intuition and *aperçus*—others, on rules and principles; some may prefer obiter dicta—others, to "damn with faint praise." Also, since criticism is, after all, not a science, but an art, our evaluations (the end-results of the process), especially of poetry, can never be made mathematically exact, but change with time, within an individual's biography and in the development of a literary tradition, even in relation to the very greatest poems and poets. We can only venture a few tentative generalizations, then, about this most subtle and mercurial of processes.

The first set of problems encountered revolves around the element of "immediacy" in our evaluations. On first acquaintance, before the intellect has had much chance to meddle, we like or dislike a poem, or it leaves us indifferent: ". . . The reason why I cannot tell; But this alone I know full well, I do not love thee, Doctor Fell." Or we are gripped, rapt, thrilled, moved: "don't ask me why." The initial e. distinction is therefore: "This poem is worthy of my interest and attention—that one is not." The sources of such preferences may vary considerably: some are the products of training, of the conventions of one's age or circle (social or literary), of mere habit, and even of "irrelevant" prejudices; some may be the results of "chance," as when a poem finds an immediate response in a receptive public, or is "stillborn" because it fails to find readers (perhaps to be discovered by a later generation, as with Emily Dickinson and Gerard Manley Hopkins). At the stage of immediacy, the emphasis may be on partial values ("What a lovely line!" "The perfect word." "How unexpectedly true!"), rather than on a total evaluation: the appeal to the ear, the sense of texture (Edith Sitwell, John Crowe Ransom, R. P. Blackmur), and so forth. In relation to these it is difficult to distinguish instinctive elements of feeling from that high degree of training which may result in a kind of "immediate analysis."

The next set of problems has to do with the rationalization of such immediately sensed values, and this is the part of the process which is most usually called "critical." The two essential processes are those of (1) analysis —with its twin, synthesis; and (2) abstraction. The poem, as an historical entity, both has its unique inner form and is involved in an intricate web of organic relationships with its poet-creator and critic-reader. To put a very complex matter briefly, these various relationships, both those internal to the text and those external to it, may be explored and analyzed more or less thoroughly: some degree at least of such exploratory analysis seems to be necessary for a truly critical e. (see ANALYSIS).

But the relationships between these two elements are not easy to state clearly. Shumaker (op. cit., esp. ch. 8: "Moving from Analysis to Evaluation") considers the problem in some detail (using an article by A. Kaplan, "On the So-Called Crisis in Criticism," JAAC, Sept. 1948), only to come out with the negative conclusion that none of the theoretical explanations is wholly satisfactory: (1) logical consequence (for example: complexity is valuable; this poem has such-and-such complexities; therefore, it is a good poem—the Q.E.D. need not follow); (2) verification (the initial judgment is in the nature of an hypothesis—but the "evidence" for or against it presumably offered by textual analysis is not "scientific," since it assumes to begin with the very values to be verified; and (3) causal (analysis, by helping us to perceive values, *causes* appreciation— but the desired e. need not necessarily follow, as every teacher has had occasion to know!). As Shumaker puts it: "Only value facts have evaluative consequences. Facts-simple (analytic findings) have none." A similar distinction between the processes of description and judgment is made by M. C. Beardsley (*Aesthetics*, 1958).

However, in defiance of such reasonings, the practical (historical and educative) fact remains that the two have gone, and do go, hand in hand. Perhaps all we need keep in mind is the caution to "judge in detail and *judge while analyzing,* instead of making the judgment a pronouncement in the final paragraph" (Wellek and Warren, *Theory of Literature,* ch. 18, our italics; this entire chapter is a penetrating exploration of problems of e., from a formalist point of view. See also W. K. Wimsatt, Jr., "Explication as Criticism," *The Verbal Icon.*

Another problem much debated in recent criticism is that of abstraction. Obviously, any discourse *about* a poem necessarily involves some degree of both analysis and abstraction; what is meant by those who speak of "the heresy of paraphrase" (e.g., Cleanth Brooks, *The Well Wrought Urn,* ch. 11) is that the critic's abstraction should not be taken as an equivalent of, or substitute for, the poem itself. Each poem is indeed, in a trivial sense, unique; but the logical *reductio ad absurdum* of an emphasis on this fact would be that all the critic-evaluator could properly do is quote the entire poem, and let it speak for itself. No abstraction can ever be completely "true"; therefore, we make a distinction between false and true abstractions, and our effort (shared by the philosopher and scientist) is to make our abstractions *as true as possible* (S. J. Kahn, *Science and Aesthetic Judgment,* 1953, ch. 4). The first level of abstraction would be that involved in the initial analysis or paraphrase of the poem; a next would result from comparisons made among the poems by one writer, or among those of a number of writers; and thus we may proceed by stages to the highest level, in theories of poetics and aesthetics. On none of these levels is it possible to avoid making value judgments, and presumably the "truer" the abstraction, the sounder will be the judgment with which it is involved.

No single sketch of the process of e. could cover more than a fraction of the actual cases, since each critic's procedure is properly individual, but that analysis and abstraction must be involved at one stage or another seems indisputable. They are present, if only implicitly, even in the most impressionistic critical sketch.

TOTAL E. AND ITS CRITERIA. The highest stage of abstraction and synthesis is achieved by what T. S. Eliot, in "Tradition and the Individual Talent," called the "ordering" of the values found in, for example, a national literature, or the European tradition, and ultimately in "world literature." This raises the problem of greatness vs. mediocrity, the ranking of poems and poets according to hierarchies or scales of value, and of the criteria or standards by which we make such total evaluations.

The difficulties here encountered may spring from the changes in our feelings (of respect, reverence, or spontaneous affection) toward the great poetry of the past, and the desire to justify new values introduced by modern innovators. However, the fact remains that, despite constant demotions and promotions in the lower echelons, the top-generals of the poetic army seem to remain secure in their eminence down the ages: Homer, Dante, Shakespeare, at least, "have a permanent, though not a 'fixed' position" (Wellek and Warren). It is when we attempt to state philosophically the grounds for such rankings, in terms of specific criteria, that the value differences emerge most clearly.

To cite one example: T. M. Greene, in *The Arts and the Art of Criticism* (1947), invokes four general criteria which he discusses under the headings of "style, perfection, truth, and greatness." At first glance, there may seem to be a conflict between the first two and the last two of these criteria, especially in modern literature: thus, perfection of a limited sort seems most possible to the minor poet or poem ("In small proportions, we just beauty see; And in short measures, life may perfect be"); while the striving toward "truth" and "greatness" (which are extra-aesthetic criteria) may imply the penalty, or at least risk, of disproportion and occasional dullness or bathos (with perhaps two exceptions: Homer and Dante). A similar conflict of values seems to recur in a variety of forms: the beauty-sublimity distinction (Edmund Burke, Kant); the classical vs. the romantic styles of beauty; so-called easy vs. difficult beauty (Bosanquet, *Three Lectures on Aesthetic*, 1915)—though few things are more difficult to achieve than "easy beauty"; and the contrasting values of simplicity and complexity (see C. Lalo, "The Aes-

thetic Analysis of a Work of Art," JAAC, June, 1949).

G. Boas (*A Primer for Critics*, 1937) argues for the principle of "multivalence," a form of the complexity-principle which would account for the recurrent appeal of great works to various individuals and ages (a criterion found in Longinus and Dr. Johnson) by the multiplicity or richness of values they embody. S. C. Pepper (*The Basis of Criticism in the Arts*, 1945) expounds a systematic eclecticism, presenting the critic with four sets of more or less equally valid criteria (mechanistic, formistic, contextualistic, organistic). Cleanth Brooks may represent the dominant values of an influential and gifted group loosely referred to as the "New Critics" in his assumption of such criteria as "functional imagery, irony, and complexity of attitude" (*op. cit.*, appendix I, "Criticism, History, and Critical Relativism"). Greene, however, provides a more liberally conceived analysis of artistic perfection (different from the more limited one suggested above) in terms of Aristotle's doctrine of the mean, as the resolution of three "polar tensions": (1) simplicity and complexity, into organic unity; (2) order and novelty, into expressive originality; and (3) denial of the medium and overinsistence on the medium (in poetry: language), into expressive exploitation of the medium (*op. cit.*, ch. 22). For the issues which have clustered around such concepts as "style," "greatness," and "artistic truth," the reader is referred to Greene's work, or to comparable discussions.

It seems to the present writer that the organic concept, adequately developed and applied can do justice (without relaxing into a lazy eclecticism) to the widest range of criteria and values, including those developed by Greene. In opposition to those critics who, in the name of "pure poetry," would reject criteria drawn from life (ethics, society, science, religion), we are committed to the acceptance of the latter, in one form or another, by our earlier position on "interaction" and on the relevance of both internal and external relationships to poetic analyses: aesthetic values are practically meaningless or empty without the context of other human values to which they give expression or are otherwise related.

CONCLUSIONS: Is it possible to make any large generalizations concerning the traits of an "evaluative" critic, as distinct from the earlier varieties? We think not. Perhaps the "science of value" is too young and unsettled as yet to permit us to do more than discern certain tendencies. To begin with, the extensive theoretical discussions have not been carried to the point where they can provide a substitute for "good taste"; as Wellek and Warren conclude: "A reasoned judgment, in matters of literature, cannot be formulated save on the basis of some *sensibility*, immediate or derivative" (our italics). Central, perhaps, to the "evaluators" has been a desire to create for poetry an autonomous realm, in terms of purely aesthetic principles; but, in actual practice, they have not been able to ignore (though they have often tried to restate) such extra-aesthetic issues as are presented by religious or political "beliefs," or to escape the truth of T. S. Eliot's remark: "The 'greatness' of literature cannot be determined solely by literary standards. . . ." The upshot of our exploration of the implications of axiology for poetry may be little more startling than a restatement of the need for a sense of proportions and a "sense of the whole" (the whole poem and the whole of life) for a proper assessment of values—a clearer, because more explicit, form of Arnold's injunction "to see life steadily and see it whole." If no final definition of "poetic value" has emerged, the complex possibilities may have been more fully explored and spread out to view in this recent literature, than in most earlier theories of criticism. And if no final set of criteria or standards has been provided for the practicing critic to override the age-old differences of schools of taste, value-theory has at least made the process of e. more mature, more aware, and thus more responsible, by clarifying some of the hidden assumptions upon which evaluations may actually be based.

ADDITIONAL BIBLIOGRAPHY. E. AND AESTHETICS: B. Croce, *Aesthetic* (best Eng. ed. 1922) and *The Essence of Aesthetic* (1921), both tr. D. Ainslie; L. A. Reid, *A Study in Aesthetics* (1931); B. C. Heyl, *New Bearings in Esthetics and Art Crit.: A Study in Semantics and E.* (1943); W. Empson, *The Structure of Complex Words* (1951; chs. on value theory); R. McKeon, "The Philos. Bases of Art and Crit.," *Critics and Crit.*, ed. R. S. Crane (1952); *Symbol and Values: An Initial Study*, ed. L. Bryson *et al.* (1954; a symposium); *Proceedings* of the Third International Congress on Aesthetics (Torino, 1957; see under the headings: "Valore, Giudizio, Critica") and the Fourth International Congress on Aesthetics (Athens, 1961; see under the headings: "Aesthetic and Critical Judgment," "Functional Value and Artistic Value"); *Rivista di Estetica,* III (1958); M. C. Beardsley, *Aesthetics* (1958; ch. 10: "Crit. E." and ch. 11: "Aesthetic Value").

THEORY OF VALUE: H. Muensterberg, *Eternal Values* (1909); B. Bosanquet, *The Principle of Individuality and Value* (1912); D. W. Prall, *A Study in the Theory of Value* (1921); W. M. Urban, "Theory of Value," *Ency. Britannica* (14th ed., 1928, 1932); S. Alexander, *Beauty and Other Forms of Value* (1933); J. R. Reid, *A Theory of Value* (1938); C. I. Lewis, *An Analysis of Knowledge and Valuation* (1946); De Witt H. Parker, *The Philosophy of Value* (1957); S. C. Pepper, *The Sources of Value* (1958); W. J. Oates, *Aristotle and the Problem of Value* (1963).   s.j.k.

EXEMPLUM. A short narrative used to illustrate a moral point. The term is applied chiefly to the stories used in medieval sermons, though the illustrative anecdote is still, perhaps, the commonest feature of public speaking. Chaucer's *Pardoner's Tale* furnishes an example; not only the main story but many lesser narratives are used as *exempla* of the Pardoner's text. The most famous source of such stories was the L. prose *Gesta Romanorum* (13th c.), but collections for the use of preachers were also made in poetic form, e.g., *Handlyng Synne* (begun 1303) by Robert Mannyng of Brunne, a treatise on the Seven Deadly Sins with illustrative stories. A secular use is shown in John Gower's poem, *Confessio Amantis* (ca. 1385), where the *exempla* illustrate sins against Venus.—G. R. Owst, *Preaching in Medieval England* (1927) and *Lit. and Pulpit in Medieval England* (1933);. J.-Th. Welter, *L'Exemplum dans la litt. religieuse et didactique du moyen âge* (1927).   R.P.APR.

EXOTICISM. Any persistent incidence in poetry of nostalgia directed toward the distant and the strange for the sake of novelty is a manifestation of e. Poetry in the exotic mode is usually reflective upon objects and settings foreign to the culture of the artist. It may be clearly distinguished from primitivism (q.v.) by its superficial concerns. Primitivism implies a search for ideal states of human society, the artist turning from his own culture in recognition of its inherent evils. E. displays indifference to questions of cultural adequacy; it is marked by sensuous reverie upon the distant and the untried. A condition for its appearance in poetry would seem to be eclecticism in sophisticated taste. In the arts of design the exploration of foreign cultures creates a taste for objects of strange color or unaccustomed voluptuousness, as in, for example, an eclectic architectural style which imports Islamic motifs and superimposes these upon indigenous forms. E. in the arts, and particularly in poetry, often derives from the literature of travel. In poetry of the 19th and 20th c. e. is related to Orientalism in Western art. The interest of Théophile Gautier and his daughter Judith in the arts of China, Japan, and the Near East gave to Fr. poetry of the latter 19th c. a distinctive preoccupation with the imagined qualities of Asian cultures. Judith Gautier's *Livre de Jade* (1867) exerted a particularly strong influence upon a generation of exotic poets, among whom Hérédia, Cros, Bouilhet, and Renaud figure prominently. In Germany a comparable exotic Orientalism appeared some years later in such collections of verse as *Die chinesische Flöte* (1907) by Hans Bethge. The interests of the Fr. school are also reflected in the e. of the Am. imagist poets, particularly John Gould Fletcher and Amy Lowell. Fletcher's "Oriental" *Symphonies*, written during 1914 and 1915, are poetic reveries upon Chinese landscape. His influence is evident in Miss Lowell's "Japanese" poems in *Pictures of the Floating World* and *Fir-Flower Tablets* (1919).

In all critical discussions of e. in poetry a clear distinction should be made between *pure e.* as in the work of the Fr. school and its derivatives, and *exotic elements* as in the work of poets not primarily exotic. The poetry of William Butler Yeats, for example, frequently exhibits exotic motifs (e.g., *Lapis Lazuli*). Yet it is quite apparent that Yeats is concerned with major issues of human existence rather than with exotic excursions of a vagrant fancy.—*Poésies de l'époque des Thang*, tr. D'Hervey-Saint-Denys (1862); H. Bethge, *Die chinesische Flöte* (1907); L. Cranmer-Byng, *A Lute of Jade* (1909); A. Lowell, *Pictures of the Floating World* (1919); W. L. Schwartz, *The Imaginative Interpretation of the Far East in Modern Fr. Lit., 1800–1925* (1927); P. Jourdà, *L'Exotisme dans la litt. fr. depuis Chateaubriand* (1938); J. G. Fletcher, *Selected Poems* (1938); M. D. Camacho, *Judith Gautier* (1939); J. Baird, *Ishmael* (1956).   J.B.

EXPLICATION. Also called formal, structural, or textual analysis, e. examines poetry or any work of literature for a knowledge of each part and for the relation of these parts to the whole. For Eng. poetry it begins in the late 1920's with Laura Riding and Robert Graves's *A Survey of Modernist Poetry* (1928), I. A. Richards' *Practical Criticism* (1929), and William Empson's *Seven Types of Ambiguity* (1930). The relation of these critics to *explication de texte* as practiced in Fr. and British schools seems inescapable, though the educational use seldom went beyond paraphrase. They probably did not know the earlier Rus. formalism (q.v.); and while e. was implicit in Aristotle, had appeared once in Longinus, and occurred in neoclassical critics, Richards and his associates derived mostly from Coleridge's organic concept of poetry. Cleanth Brooks introduced e. into the United States and brought it a widespread following through *Understanding Poetry* (1939), written with Robert Penn Warren. All the New Critics have made e. the basis of their findings, and so have the Chicago Critics (but with some differences in theory). Such periodicals as *Scrutiny* (1932–1953), *Southern Review* (1935–1942), *Kenyon Review* (1939–), and *Essays in Criticism* (1951–) contain many explications; and *The Explicator* (1942–), which has popularized the term, has been devoted solely to them. Though today few critical essays or books fail to use e., the movement has had many detractors—principally in its early years among literary historians and more recently among proponents of a mythic approach to poetry.

Poetry, as seen by e., is characterized by three major qualities. Self-sufficiency, the first of these, affirms the poem as impersonal and autonomous. Biographical considerations are ignored or at most given slight regard, poetry is detached from its historical context, and the poem is judged for itself rather than for its effect upon a reader. In place of intentional, historical, and affective fallacies, the starting place becomes the point of view within the poem and the tone that develops from it. A second major characteristic, that of unity, is traditional. But e. has insisted upon a comprehensive organicism, has studied the relation of structure and materials, has usually urged the importance of theme, and has occupied itself with the contextuality of poetic truth. A final characteristic is complexity, which stands in antithesis to a simplicity of plainness but not to a simplicity of articulated function. Rather, it senses unity through a *discordia concors* that informs all good poetry and not merely that of the metaphysical school. In its zeal e. has at times attempted too much in revealing ironies, ambiguities, and paradoxes, but whether or not they are the central element of poetry as some have held, the pervasiveness of some kind of countersuggestion in the language and symbols of poetry and in their fusion has won recognition. In treating all these qualities various groups and individuals exhibit differences, and none urge the characteristics as absolute, since to make a poem unmitigatedly unique would not allow a reader to comprehend it in any degree.

E. does not claim to be an act of evaluation (q.v.), but rather to serve as the basis of literary criticism and history. As W. K. Wimsatt has shown ("Explication as Criticism"), there are serious problems in adjusting the polarities of part and whole, value and disvalue, and value and neutrality. Though he believes that "the extreme theory of explicative criticism cuts apart understanding and value," he also regards successful e. as rising "from neutrality gradually and convincingly to the point of total judgment." When the organic form has been established in its self-sufficiency and complexity, a judgment upon the relationship quite naturally follows. See also ANALYSIS; MODERN POETICS. 20TH C. FR.

BIBLIOGRAPHIES: R. P. Basler, C. C. Walcutt, M. Greenhut, et al., "A Checklist of E.," *Explicator*, 3—(1945–), June issues; G. Arms and J. M. Kuntz, *Poetry E.: A Checklist* (1950; rev. ed. by Kuntz, 1962).

HISTORY AND CRITICISM: Wellek and Warren, ch. 12; L. Fiedler *et al.*, My "Credo," KR, 12–13 (1950–51); W. K. Wimsatt, Jr., "E. as Crit.," *EIE 1951*, and *The Verbal Icon* (1954); Crane; J. P. Kirby, "'The Last Verse . . . Is Not Sufficiently Explicated'!" *Va. Librarian*, 2 (1956); Daiches, ch. 15; Krieger; Wimsatt and Brooks, "Epilogue"; G. Arms, "Poetry," *Contemporary Lit. Scholarship*, ed. L. Leary (1958). See also *E. as Crit.*, ed. Wimsatt (1963). G.A.

EXPOSITION (of a plot). See PLOT.

EXPRESSION, THEORY OF. Rhetoric has always been concerned with e. or *elocutio*. The perfectly achieved expression of a thought in words was always considered a poetic beauty. The complete adjustment of the words to the thought was seen to be an organic unity already by Cicero (*De Oratore* 3. 5–6). In the Renaissance a theory of poetry as e. emerges in G. Fracastoro's *Naugerius* (1555): "The poet has no other aim than to speak well, absolutely, about anything that suggests itself to him" (Kelso ed., p. 59). In the 17th c. aesthetics developed out of the rhetorical theory of elocution in contrast with the dialectical theory of logic. In the early 18th c. Pope said: ". . . true expression, like the unchanging sun, / Clears, and improves, whate'er it shines upon." (*Essay on Criticism*, 315–16). In the later 18th c. Romantic poetics (e.g., Herder) asserted that true e. is inseparable from thought. In 19th-c. England a theory of emotional e. was developed by several critics. Coleridge stressed the organic unity of thought and e.: e.g., *Biographia Literaria* (1817), ch. 1. In 1833 J. S. Mill argued that poetry is "the expression or uttering forth of feeling" and consequently lyrical poetry was "more eminently and peculiarly poetic than any other." At about the same time John Keble in his lectures (1832–41) developed the theory that poetry is the indirect e. of emotions too strong to be expressed directly. Both the substance of plot and the form of meter were considered by him indirect expressions of emotion. In 1857 George Eliot spoke of the poet as always "true to his own . . . inward vision" or "mental state"; this became "truth to the vision within" in Walter Pater's *Essay on Style* (1888), which contains the most advanced expressionist theory of the age: "all beauty is in the long run only fineness of truth, or what we call expression, the finer accommodation of speech to that vision within." In this aesthetic truth Pater found

the absolute ("that absolute accordance of expression to idea") which he could not find elsewhere. An Eng. philosopher of the idealistic school, R. L. Nettleship, made the organic unity still tighter: "The feeling is not truly felt till it is expressed, and in being expressed it is still felt but in a different way . . . so that it is not strictly correct to call the word the expression of what we meant before we found it" (*Remains*, I, 132). On the continent an expressionist aesthetic was formulated by Eugène Véron in the 1870's: "Art is the manifestation of emotion, obtaining external interpretation now by expressive arrangements of line, form or color, now by a series of gestures, sounds or words governed by particular rhythmical cadence" (tr., p. 89).

But the most comprehensive theory of poetry (and art in general) as e. was worked out by Benedetto Croce. He began in 1893 by turning Hegel's "Beauty is the sensuous manifestation of the Idea" into "Beauty is the expression of a content." In the *Aesthetic* of 1902 he argued that poetic e. is not the direct e. of emotion, but the e. of an intuition. An intuition for Croce is the fully fashioned mental picture of a particular object: a character, a place, an incident, a story. It is through the mental picture, or "image," that the emotion is expressed. The act of e. is defined as an *a priori* synthesis: the emotion does not exist until it is expressed, the image exists only as the e. of the emotion (cf. Nettleship above). Thus *Hamlet* is for Croce the expression of a mood of melancholy and disgust with life, a mood such as no one expressed before and which can be conveyed only by the pattern of words which the poet chose for it. The characters, the situations, the action and the catastrophe are all expressions of different shades and tones of the basic mood and in perfect work of art constitute an indissoluble unity. From the example given it will be clear that the theory considers that all kinds of poetry are basically expressive of emotion, whether they are narrative or dramatic in form, and that all genres are basically one, the lyrical. This provides the foundation for a theory of criticism which offers three objects to the critic: the image, the emotion, and the way the two are fitted together. The function of the critic is to characterize the image, to define the lyrical theme or emotion, and to evaluate their adjustment. In a defective poem there is either excess of emotion over the image (romantic poetry) or a deficiency of emotion, which is replaced by the repetition of images taken from other works (classicism).

According to Croce the modes of e. do not preexist to the act of e., so there is no fixed poetic vocabulary, no set pattern of style or laws of composition or structural principles other than those required by the particular subject of the individual poem, and these are not good for any other poem. However, every act of e. arises upon previous acts of e., and uses them as raw material: every image is a synthesis of previous images, integrated in a new manner to suit the new emotion. The converse of this, which may be called the principle of integration, is the principle of contextuality: single words exist only in context, isolated words are mere abstractions catalogued in dictionaries. The unit of e. is not the word but the sentence, understood not in the grammatical sense but as a complete unit of meaning, whether consisting of a single phrase or of a whole poem. Both these principles are reducible to one organic unity or, as Croce calls it, *a priori* synthesis.

Croce dealt with the theory of poetry most fully in his untranslated book, *La Poesia* (1936). Here he acknowledged that set forms and patterns, while not regulative, are useful to the poet as reminders of previous expressions: the poet should keep them in mind and allow them to operate upon his mind. Some of them will become part of a new e. in a way that is unpredictable in advance. Also, the structure of a long poem or drama is now seen as a device which is sometimes unpoetic but which the poet adopts to bring together different groups of images, and it cannot be eliminated without breaking up the whole poem. On the other hand it must not be evaluated as a form of art, for it is something external to poetry. Instances of such "structural parts" are the expository portions of poems and plays, the chorus in Gr. tragedy, and incidents or characters which are introduced to carry on the action. Indeed, plot is often a mere traditional framework "upon which a poet weaves his own poetry, sometimes covering up and concealing the warp completely, at other times allowing it to remain visible to a greater or smaller extent." Such are the plots of Shakespeare. Poetic e. must also be distinguished from other forms of e. which have practical or expository purposes, such as "oratory" which for Croce is any form of writing which is addressed to the emotions rather than to the imagination. See also POETRY, THEORIES OF (EXPRESSIVE THEORIES).

E. Véron, *Aesthetics*, tr. W. H. Armstrong (1879); R. L. Nettleship, *Philos. Lectures and Remains* (1897); B. Croce, *The Essence of Aesthetic*, tr. D. Ainslie (1921), *Aesthetic as Science of E. and General Linguistics*, tr. D. A. (2d ed., 1922), *Conversazioni critiche*, III (1932), 36-39 (for the rhetorical tradition), *La poesia* (1936); R. G. Collingwood, *The Principles of Art* (1938); C. La Drière, "E.," in Shipley; Abrams; G. N. G. Orsini, *B. Croce as Philosopher of Art and Lit. Critic* (1961).　G.N.G.O.

EXPRESSIONISM. A term coined, probably by L. Vauxcelles, after a series of paintings by Julien-Auguste Hervé exhibited in 1901 under the title *Expressionismes*. In Germany, where it was most frequently used, it was first applied to painting around 1911 and to literature around 1914. Mainly concerned with the forceful representation of emotions, the expressionist painters took recourse to ever more abstract configurations and, on the whole, preferred nonrealistic technique to the use of local color. Edvard Munch and van Gogh (in his final phase) are usually regarded as forerunners of pictorial e. In France, the movement came to the fore with the first exhibition of *Les Fauves* in 1905. In Germany, the *Brücke* group held its first exhibition in 1906, while *Der Blaue Reiter* followed approximately five years later. The chief theorists of e. in art are Wilhelm Worringer (*Abstraktion und Einfühlung*, 1908) and Wassily Kandinsky (*Über das Geistige in der Kunst*, 1912). In literature, Kasimir Edschmid (*Über den Expressionismus in der Literatur und die neue Dichtung*, 1919) became its principal spokesman.

While it is impossible to find a common denominator for all the qualities generally supposed to be typical of literary e., a few critical observations may elucidate the major tendencies of the movement. The expressionistic practice springs from a violent antirealism and is based on the refusal to imitate, repeat, reproduce that which already exists ("Die Welt ist da. Es wäre sinnlos, sie zu wiederholen"—The world is there. It would make no sense to repeat it). Instead, turning toward the soul, the expressionists sought to capture its movements in their prearticulate purity. Hence their urge to abstract from reality, to give "Farbe ohne Bezeichnung, Zeichnung und kein Erklären, im Rhythmus festgesetztes Hauptwort ohne Attribut" (Däubler—Color without name, drawing [or image] without explanation, rhythmically determined noun without attributes). As irrationalists and visionaries, they poured out their emotions ecstatically and with a pathos almost forgotten since the age of the Storm and Stress (see STURM UND DRANG). In the expressionistic plays and poems, expression always precedes, and thus determines, form—rhythm being far more important than harmony. This explains the disjointed syntax, the dynamic use of imagery and the discontinuity of thought and action. Repudiating the aesthetic world view of impressionism (q.v.), the expressionist is preoccupied with man and his fate in a world about to disintegrate. He is a humanist before, a pacifist during and a socialist after the war. He also considers his art to be merely the outward manifestation of a new ethos.

In Germany, as elsewhere, e. is most characteristically represented in poetry and the drama. Under the influence of Strindberg, German expressionist playwrights from Wedekind to Barlach have made significant contributions to world literature. In poetry, the era of e. extends from approximately 1910 to the mid-twenties, when it was supplanted by that of surrealism (q.v.) and of the new realism known as *Neue Sachlichkeit* and exemplified by the poems of Bertolt Brecht's *Hauspostille* (1927). Subdivisions were first introduced by H. E. Jakob in the preface to his anthology *Verse der Lebenden* (1924). Alfred Mombert and Theodor Däubler, whose epic *Nordlicht* appeared in 1910, may be regarded as direct ancestors of the movement. Its early phase is constituted by the poetry of Georg Heym (*Der ewige Tag, Umbra Vitae*), Ernst Stadler, and Georg Trakl. The latter's *Gedichte* (1913) and *Sebastian im Traum* (1914) display a peculiar *Weltschmerz* and are distinguished by a dreamlike quality that is hardly typical of expressionistic poetry as a whole. The main representatives of poetic e. can be divided into groups according to their artistic, metaphysical, and political attitude. Franz Werfel (*Der Weltfreund*) is a deeply religious humanist, J. R. Becher an activist fond of futuristic word cascades, Else Lasker-Schüler a poet dwelling in a decidedly exotic atmosphere. Gottfried Benn (1886–1956), whose *Morgue* offers a poignant example of poetic nihilism, lived to proclaim the beginning of a second phase of e. Perhaps the greatest German poet of his generation, he did not share the ethos of his fellow-expressionists and soon developed an esoteric cult of the word that seems to have its origin in Baudelaire's cult of beauty.

In his magazine *Der Sturm*—together with *Die Aktion* the most influential expressionistic periodical—Herwarth Walden published the work of August Stramm, the most radical of the expressionists. Stramm's poetry reflects an urge toward abstraction which compelled the poet to express himself by means of word formations to which no meaning is assigned in the dictionary. Serious though Stramm may have been in the pursuit of his goal, many of his poems clearly anticipate the anti-art of Dadaism (q.v.). The nature of poetic e. is nowhere better revealed than in the anthology *Menschheitsdämmerung*, which Kurt Pinthus edited in 1920.

Outside of Germany, e., until recently, has been poorly understood and little appreciated. In France, the movement failed to gain any foothold whatsoever, while in Anglo-Saxon literature—with the exception of Wyndham Lewis and the few other practitioners of vorticism (q.v.)—its influence has been restricted to the drama. O'Neill's *Hairy Ape*, Elmer Rice's *Adding Machine,* and Thornton Wilder's *Skin of our Teeth* clearly betray the influence of Strindberg and his German emulators. In the field of poetic drama, the plays Auden and Isherwood wrote for the Group Theatre manifest similar tendencies. Eliot's *Sweeney Agonistes,* where jazz rhythms are effectively used to heighten the irrational element, shows how often these affinities are of a purely formal nature.

In poetry proper, Edith Sitwell's *Façade*—which is the result of pseudo-expressionistic "inquiries into the effect on rhythm and on speech of the use of rhymes, assonances and dissonances"—shows a superficial resemblance to August Stramm's convulsive lyrical outbursts. The imagists, like the expressionists, wanted to grasp the essence of things rather than their outward appearance. The static brilliance of the images they fashioned, however, implies a betrayal of the dynamic principle which lies at the root of e.

A. Soergel, *Dichtung und Dichter der Zeit. Neue Folge: Im Banne des Expressionismus* (1925); F. L. Schneider, *Der expressive Mensch und die Lyrik der Gegenwart* (1927); B. Fehr, "E. in der neuesten englischen Lyrik," in *Brittanica: Max Förster zum 60. Geburtstag* (1929); W. Rose, "E. in German Lit." and "The Spirit of Revolt in G. Lit. from 1914–1930," in *Men, Myths and Movements* (1931); D. W. Schumann, "E. and Post-E. in G. Lyrics," GR, 9 (1934); L. V. Palmer, "The Language of G. E." (diss. Univ. of Illinois, 1938); S. Spender, "Poetry and E.," *New Statesman and Nation*, March 12, 1938; W. Stuyver, *Deutsche expressionistische Dichtung im Lichte der Philosophie der Gegenwart* (1939); R. Samuel and R. H. Thomas, *E. in German Life, Lit. and the Theatre* (1939); E. Sitwell, "On My Poetry," *Orpheus*, 2 (1949); M. Freedman, "T. S. Eliot and Jazz," SAQ, 51 (1952); U. Weisstein, "Gottfried Benn and E.," *The Folio*, 19 (1954); *E.: Gestalten einer Bewegung*, ed. H. Friedmann and O. Mann (1956); M. Hamburger, "1912" and "Georg Trakl" in *Reason and Energy* (1956; the first essay to be read with caution); C. Heselhaus, *Die Lyrik des Expressionismus* (1956); F. Martini, "Expressionismus," *Reallexikon*, 2d ed., I (contains a fine bibliog.); W. H. Sokel, *The Writer in Extremis: E. in 20th-C. G. Lit.* (1959; of limited value to students of poetry); R. Brinkmann, *Expressionismus. Forschungs-Probleme, 1952–60* (1961). U.W.

EYE RHYME. A rhyme which gives to the eye (that is, in spelling) the impression of perfect rhyme but to the ear (that is, in pronunciation) the effect of, at best, an approximation, as in near rhyme (q.v.). In general, eye rhymes represent obsolete or merely regional pronunciations which are inexact in standard modern Eng. or Am. speech. Some prosodists refer to such eye rhymes as *love-prove, flood-brood* as historical rhymes because it is almost certain that these pairs once rhymed perfectly. Note, however, that histori-cal rhymes are not always eye rhymes, e.g., Pope's *tea-away,* words which once echoed each other, "tea" being pronounced "tay" in the early 18th c.—H. C. Wyld, *Studies in Eng. Rhymes from Surrey to Pope* (1923) .   s.l.m.

F

FABLE IN VERSE. F. is supposed to have originated in the primitive allegory which presented animals and plants speaking like human beings. It has been suggested that the multiple stories in the *Panchatantra* are the fountainhead of the European f., but the genre probably arose spontaneously in ancient Greece. Hesiod's poem of the hawk and the nightingale (8th c. B.C.) is the oldest known Gr. f.: after that, Archilochus' fragments on the fox and the eagle. The first repertory of Gr. fables is attributed to Aesop (6th c. B.C.), but our knowledge of them is indirect. They were written down by Demetrius of Phalerum (4th c. B.C.); yet even this text is known only through the edition (14th c.) of Maximus Planudes. The Aesopic fables conveyed moral or satirical lessons in the briefest and driest of verses; there is no reason to suppose that Aesop was anything of a poet.

Phaedrus (1st c. A.D.) imitated Aesop in iambic trimeters, but also invented many new fables, recounted anecdotes of his contemporaries and introduced political allusions. Babrius, who wrote in Gr. (2d c. A.D.) went further. He invented racy epithets and pic-turesque expressions, and enlarged the formula of the genre in the direction of satire and the bucolic. His f. of the fox and the raven is scarcely inferior to La Fontaine's. He was the first of the fabulists who may be reckoned a real poet.

In the 10th c. a prose version was made of Phaedrus and Babrius, under the title of *Romulus.* This was retranslated into elegiac verse and enjoyed a celebrity lasting into the 17th c. The best of the medieval fabulists was Marie de France who, toward A.D. 1200, com-posed 102 fables in octosyllables (some in An-glo-Norman). Although she usually treated Gr. and Roman themes, she was an excellent ob-server of beasts and men, possessed the ironic and whimsical touch of her nation, and gives many glimpses of the feudal society of her times. The age was liberal, and she criticized high and low without favoritism. The *Ysopets* (13th and 14th c.) were Fr. verse translation of older L. apologues.

The *Fables du très ancien Esope Phrygien* (1542) were an adaptation, in which Gilles Corrozet used verses of different length and thus was to show La Fontaine the advantages of this freer form. Meanwhile, the Indian apologues which, deriving from the *Pancha-tantra* (2d c. A.D.?), were adapted in an Arabic edition of the 8th c. A.D. as the *Kalīla wa Dimna,* had been taken up in Italy by Agnolo Firenzuola and Doni. They were later pub-lished in a Fr. translation of 1644 as *Le Livre des Lumières* and attributed to a mythical Pilpay.

Jean de la Fontaine (1621–95) raised the f. to the level of a great poetical genre. In his earlier fables he drew mainly from Aesop and Phaedrus: the Indian apologues supplied some inspiration for the last six books. He united naïveté and culture, the simple wonder of a child with wide reading and exquisite taste. Into traditional themes he breathed poetry, irony, and knowledge of life; he treated them dramatically and also made them a vehicle for lyric poetry and philosophical disquisition. He has been widely and brilliantly translated and ranks as the world's greatest fabulist.

Among La Fontaine's imitators or emulators, mention should be made of Eustache le Noble (1643–1711), John Gay (1685–1732), J.-P.-C. de Florian (1754–94), and Tomás de Iriarte (1750–91). Gay's fables, though racy and vigorous, lack the robust originality of his operas. Florian rehandled the fables of his predecessors, but gave them a political or sentimental turn. In Germany, C. F. Gellert (1715–69) modeled his fables after La Fontaine, but G. E. Lessing (1729–81) considered the simple f. of Aesop the ideal model.

The f. had now begun to play an important part in the development of Rus. literature, by training writers in the realistic manner. Of these the greatest was Ivan Andreyevich Krylov (1769–1844), who made his first translations from La Fontaine in 1805. The twenty-three fables published in 1809 won a success un-precedented in Rus. literary annals. Written mostly between 1810 and 1820 Krylov's fables appeared in nine books, and their popularity was due both to the substance and the style. His attitude was one of sound but prosaic common sense. He satirized the ineptitude and absurdity of officials, but his satire was general and his weapon ridicule. He used the language of the street and the tavern, although in a classical manner and with a mastery of the art of compression.

A. Loiseleur-Deslongchamps, *Essais sur les fables indiennes* . . . (1838) ; W. G. Rutherford, *The Hist. of Gr. F.* (1883); L. Hervieux, *Les Fabulistes latins depuis le siècle d'Auguste jusqu'à la fin du moyen-âge* (5 v., 1883–89); M. Marchianò, *L'Origine della favola greca* . . . (1900); H.-A. Taine, *Essai sur les fables de la Fontaine* (1853); *Krylov's Fables*, tr. B. Pares (1921); M. Stege, *Die Gesch. der deutschen Fabeltheorie* (1929); *La Fontaine's Fables*, tr. E. Marsh (2 v., 1931); C. Filosa, *La favola e la letteratura esopiana in Italia* . . . (1952). A.L.S.

FABLIAU. A short story in verse, usually in octosyllabic couplets, relating a comic or bawdy incident from middle-class life. The fabliaux, which originated in France, flourished there in the 12th and 13th c., but an 8th-c. warning against them, in Egbert's *Poenitentiale*, shows that they must have existed centuries before. *Richeut* (1159) is regarded by some authorities as the oldest surviving f., but other scholars feel that the *Isopet* of Marie de France is, in effect, an earlier example of the genre.

Opinion is sharply divided as to the origin of the f. and its themes: questions under controversy include whether the genre was bourgeois or courtly in origin, and whether or not its themes derive from oriental sources. It seems likely that all classes of society supplied writers of fabliaux, although the anonymous authorship of so many of them makes this difficult to establish. Writers who can be identified include Rutebeuf, Philippe de Beaumanoir, and Jean Bodel.

The typical f. is realistic in setting, coarse in treatment, and ribald in material. Its favorite theme is cuckoldry, usually achieved through the use of guile, and it frequently contains sharp anticlerical satire. Some critics have seen in its cynical attitude toward women a reaction against the deification of woman implicit in the code of courtly love (q.v.), which permeated the *lais* and romances of the time.

In the 14th c. the vogue of the f. spread to Italy and to England, where Chaucer imitated the form in his *Miller's Tale* and *Reeve's Tale*. F. tradition continued in the prose *nouvelle*, but the influence of the older form may be noted, centuries later, in the poetry of La Fontaine in France, C. F. Gellert in Germany, and I. A. Krylov in Russia.—J. Bédier, *Les Fabliaux* (5th ed., 1928); P. Nykrog, *Les Fabli-*

aux (1957); J. Rychner, *Contribution à l'étude des fabliaux* (2 v., 1960).

FALLING ACTION. See PLOT.

FALLING RHYTHM. See DESCENDING RHYTHM.

FANCY is an abbreviation of fantasy (L. *phantasia*, itself a transliteration from the Gr., and later replaced in L. by *imaginatio*). Whether regarded as synonyms or differentiated in meaning, f. and *imagination* are closely related and cannot be explained without cross-reference. The number in parentheses refers to the relevant paragraph in the article on IMAGINATION (q.v.).

In medieval L. the terms are sometimes synonymous (e.g., in Aquinas), sometimes differentiated (e.g., in Albertus Magnus, with imagination the repository of images, and fantasy the active power operating upon them). In It. the term *fantasia* comes to be appropriated by the higher or creative artistic activity and *immaginazione* relegated to a lower (cf. 21). So also in German; *Phantasie* comes to occupy the higher place and *Einbildungskraft*, despite the influence of Kant (14), sinks to a lower: for Jean-Paul *Phantasie* is "the power of making all parts into a whole" while *Einbildungskraft* is merely a "highly coloured memory." In England (with the exceptions noted below) *imagination* and f. were generally treated as synonyms till the beginning of the 19th c. Dryden's assignment of a comprehensive role to imagination while limiting f. to language and the "variation" of a thought (12) allows the context to fix the two meanings, but in assigning the more limited function to f. points the way to future development. By Reynolds imagination is bracketed with genius, f. with taste (10); by Hume the legitimate and indeed necessary exercise of imagination is distinguished from "the loose reveries of fancy" (11); by Duff creative imagination is contrasted with a "sportive fancy" (11), and by Stewart f. (as in Dryden) is restricted to language while imagination creates action, character, and scene (11). Thus the restriction or depression of f. is plainly apparent before Coleridge elaborated his famous distinction.

If, as has been suggested, this distinction owes something to Jean-Paul, it is notable that Coleridge conforms to Eng. usage by naming the more general and also the higher activity *imagination* (Kant's *Einbildungskraft*), and the lower and restricted activity f. (Jean-Paul's *Einbildungskraft* as opposed to his *Phantasie*). For Coleridge (15) f. is a distinct faculty, dependent of course for its materials on the primary imagination, and up up to a point analogous in its operations to the secondary imagination, but limited in its scope,

FARCE

confined to the phenomenal (having no access to the noumenal), with power more or less capriciously to manipulate its materials, but none to modify, reshape, and unify them. "The fancy is indeed no other than a mode of memory emancipated from the order of time and space"; and "equally with the ordinary memory the fancy must receive its materials ready-made from the law of association." These materials are fixed objects (*natura naturata*): f. cannot rise to an imitation of *natura naturans*. That imagination and f. may appear in the same work; that they may sometimes treat, each in its own mode, the same material; that imagination may even require f. "as its complement" since "the higher intellectual powers can only act through a corresponding energy of the lower," Coleridge does not deny. Such concessions, however, should raise no doubt of the reality or importance of the distinction for him. Though they had contributed greatly to each other's thinking, Wordsworth (16) diverged from Coleridge on the f. For Wordsworth f. differs less in the kind than in the degree and value of its operations. "To aggregate and associate, to evoke and combine" belong to both imagination and fancy; and "fancy, as she is an active, is also . . . a creative faculty." But she is content with materials which are susceptible of little if any modification at her touch, and with effects that are transient and of small value. In his own experience (to which Wordsworth referred every theory) f. developed with imagination, as the *Prelude* makes clear; and it was this copresence of the two, said Coleridge, that misled Wordsworth and prevented his accepting the distinction in its entirety.

It is natural that the higher or more comprehensive term (in Eng., *imagination*) should be dwelt upon, and the lower and more restricted (in Eng., *fancy*) be defined always in relation to it. Ruskin (19) will serve as illustration. And in the 20th c. (though with the traditional It. reversal of terms) Croce (21), after assigning to imagination (*fantasia*) a central role in aesthetic experience, dismisses as irrelevant images appearing either in accidental succession or forced combination, and declares this to be the real distinction underlying all efforts to discriminate between imagination (*fantasia*) and f. (*immaginazione*). A.S.P.W.

For bibliography see IMAGINATION.

FARCE. If, following the suggestion of *Rambler* no. 125, we confine ourselves to purpose and ignore the more accidental feature of means, we should have no difficulty in arriving at an acceptable definition of f. Its object is to provoke the spectator to laughter, not the reflective kind which comedy is intended to elicit but the uncomplicated response of sim-

ple enjoyment. Its means are often shared by other comic forms, such as burlesque (q.v.), thus giving rise to frequent confusion among them. Once purpose is established these means are not hard to visualize. F. exploits the surprise of sudden appearance or disclosure, the mechanism suggested by many physical actions, repetition, gross exaggeration of character, and so on. Since it does not share with higher comedy the responsibility of commentary on social conduct it may pursue its laughter into a world of fantasy where the unpredictable, even the impossible, is commonplace.

The origins of f. are doubtless hidden somewhere beyond the beginning of recorded literary history since the propensity to horseplay seems as natural to man as the trait of laughter, which is alleged to separate him from the other animals. The presence of f. in Aristophanes and the Roman comic writers and its popularity in the mimes and Atellanan pieces of the Romans suggest an early origin. Something of the crude horseplay common to f. and such kindred forms as burlesque, mime, and satyr play may be observed in surviving vase paintings and statues. The first plays of record to bear the name were Fr., for the name was devised in France from the L. *farcire,* to stuff. The 15th c. reveals Fr. f. at an early peak as it was developed especially by the "joyous societies" who contrived numerous little pieces from the stuff of folklore and fabliau. Usually rendered in lively octosyllabic couplets, these medieval Fr. farces exploited themes of commercial trickery and sexual infidelity, to show a life both coarse and vibrant in which the conventions, particularly the conventional respect for women and the clergy, were flaunted. Two examples of many possible ones may be cited: *Le meunier et le gentilhomme* (ca. 1550), which treats a folk motif traceable back as far as the 7th c. and appearing on four continents, and *Maître Pierre Pathelin* (ca. 1465), most famous of all. F. never quite regained in France the level of popularity it had reached in the Middle Ages, yet it managed to survive and to enjoy a popular esteem, even in the classical period, when Molière as both actor and playwright helped restore it to theatrical recognition. It managed to survive the competition of *drame bourgeois* in the 18th c. and of *mélodrame* and romantic drama in the 19th though perhaps no name greater than that of Labiche came to its support. Italy, Spain, and Germany meanwhile had their f. writers, though *writer* is slightly misapplied in the case of Italy since the bulk of It. f. was supplied by the improvisations of the widely popular and influential *commedia dell'arte* troupes which flourished from the 16th to the 18th c.

The first Eng. f. writer of note—there are

farce episodes in the earlier mystery plays—
is the 16th-c. John Heywood, a somewhat isolated figure in that he chose to borrow from
and imitate Fr. f. and also developed an independent genre. The common practice, following the triumph of classical models just as
the professional Eng. theatre was beginning,
was to mix farcical episodes in with more
serious matter. In Shakespeare's *Comedy of
Errors,* for example, or *Merry Wives,* in Jonson's *Silent Woman,* even more in such popular anonymous plays as *Mucedorus,* we find f.
scenes mingled with intrigue, romance, and
the satirical portraiture of "humours" comedy.
Only in the droll of the Commonwealth period
was Eng. f. independent of other forms before
the coming of the afterpiece at the beginning
of the 18th c. With the establishment of the
afterpiece and the consequent demand for
short pieces in the Eng. repertory f. came into
its own as a distinct genre. For much of the
next two centuries it thrived vigorously. As
taste declined, f. took its place, with sentimental comedy and melodrama, as one of the
staples of theatrical fare. Of the hundreds of
farces written in this period of its flourishing
few worthy of preservation appeared. Only at
the very end, with Wilde and Pinero, did f.
aspire to be literary, an aspiration usually
fatal to the genre. Though it still has its
place in the popular theatre and always will
have, it no longer enjoys quite the vogue it
did a century ago. Even in the cinema, where
with Chaplin and other producers of short
pieces it had a renewal of life, the more traditional f. with human actors has been displaced
by the animated film.

L. Petit de Julleville, *Hist. du théâtre en
France* (1880–89); K. Holl, *Gesch. des deutschen Lustspiels* (1923); W. S. Jack, *The Early
Entremés in Spain* (1923); K. Lea, *It. Popular
Comedy* (1934); W. Klemm, *Die englische F.
im 19. Jh.* (1946); I. Maxwell, *Fr. F. and John
Heywood* (1946); Nicoll; G. Frank, *The Medieval Fr. Drama* (1954); L. Hughes, *A Century
of Eng. F.* (1956); E. Bentley, "The Psychology
of F.," *New Republic,* 138 (Jan. 6 and 13,
1958); M. Bieber, *A Hist. of the Gr. and Roman Theater* (2d ed., 1961); B. Cannings,
"Toward a Definition of F. as a Lit. Genre,"
MLR, 56 (1961).   L.H.

FATRAS (also called *fatrasie, fratrasie, res-
verie*). An irrational or obscure piece of verse,
which originated in the Middle Ages. It is
generally lively and joyous in style, full of
plays on words, ridiculous associations of ideas,
and deliberate nonsense. E. Langlois defines
two forms of this genre: the *f. possible,* which
offers a coherent text, and the *f. impossible,*
which, like the later *coq-à-l'âne* (q.v.), seems to
make no coherent sense at all. *Qua* genre, how-

ever, it is not the incoherence of content that
constitutes the f., but its very special form:
a strophe of 11 lines, the first and last of
which form a distich placed at the beginning
as the theme of the composition. This is
known as the *f. simple.* The *f. double* is
formed from this by "restating the initial
[distich] in reverse order, and adding a second
strophe of ten lines ending with an eleventh,
a restatement of line one of the [distich]."
L. C. Porter distinguishes between the (13th-c.?)
fratrasie and the f., a later (14th-c.?) development. The former invariably is composed of
a single strophe of 11 lines, and its content
always is irrational. In the f. the opening
distich introduces the next 11 lines, serving
as their first and last line and imparting a
uniform rhythm to the whole poem.—E. Langlois, *Recueil d'Arts de seconde rhétorique*
(1902; p. 192, n. 1); R. Bossuat, *Le Moyen âge*
(1931); Patterson; P. Zumthor, *Hist. litt. de la
France médiévale* (1954); L. C. Porter, *La
Fatrasie et le f.* (1960).   I.S.

FEELING. See EMOTION.

FEIGNING. As far back as Plato, and probably much farther, fiction has been identified
with poetic imitation (q.v.). Plato's *Republic*
condemned the "lies" of poets like Homer
and Hesiod and barred all imitative poetry
from the ideal commonwealth since it was
detrimental to the understanding of truth.
Aristotle, in his *Poetics,* challenged the Platonic doctrine by arguing that imitative poetry is more philosophical and a higher thing
than historical fact, that the poet imitates
what ought to be rather than what is. According to Aristotle, Homer was a poet because he
was an imitator or maker, Empedocles merely
a physicist writing in verse, and Herodotus'
history still history even if it were turned into
verse.

Aristotle apparently regarded poetic imitation as idealized fiction based on probability
rather than on literal truth. Certainly succeeding critics so interpreted poetic imitation.
Horace's *Ars Poetica* praised the learned imitator (*doctus imitator*) as the ideal creative
artist and condemned the servile copyist. (The
leading commentators on Horace maintained
that it is feigning (*fingere*) that distinguishes
the true poet.) Plutarch's essay on *How the
Young Man Should Study Poetry* called poetry
an imitative art which brings pleasure when
its fictions are created in the semblance of
truth—i.e., verisimilitude.

Consequently it became a commonplace
even before the full impact of the revival of
learning in the early 16th c. to equate the Gr.
mimesis with the L. *fictio* or *fabula* or *inventio*
or *verisimilitudo.* The 14th book of Boccaccio's

Genealogy of the Gods (ca. 1360) described poetry as a "fervid and exquisite invention," a fiction which reveals a hidden or allegorical truth. The leading poets and critics of the 16th c., e.g., Torquato Tasso, Giraldi Cinthio, J. C. Scaliger, Castelvetro, Ronsard, Sir Philip Sidney, accepted imitating or feigning as indispensable to the poet. Scaliger went so far in his praise of the creative poet as to call him "almost a second deity," and Sidney echoed him. For Castelvetro, the essence of poetry was invention. Ronsard summed up Renaissance theory as well as any one in his famous *Abrégé de l'art poétique français* (1565): "As the aim of the orator is to persuade, so that of the poet is to imitate, to invent and represent things which are, or which may be, like the truth (*vraisemblables*)."

Very little has been added in later times to these ancient and Renaissance concepts of poetry as feigning. Although terminology may have changed somewhat, and the theory of art as an imitation or representation of nature is not accepted by every one, poetry is still regarded as something above and beyond the communication of literal truth. Croce's "instantaneous imaginative fusion" (*Defence of Poetry*, 1933) suggests the older *fictio* or *inventio*. Wimsatt and Brooks, in their *Literary Criticism* (1957), are more specific; they equate (p. 751) the "art of fiction" with Aristotle's *poiētikē* and acknowledge (p. 686) that although fiction may be sharply differentiated from lyric poetry "the lyric shares with the novel a common fictionality."—See also L. Lerner, "The Truest Poetry Is the Most Feigning," *The Truest Poetry* (1960).　м.т.н.

FÉLIBRIGE. A Fr. literary association, founded near Avignon in 1854, for the purpose of reviving the Prov. language, literature, and culture. Its most important member was Frédéric Mistral, and its membership included Joseph Roumanille, its first leader, and Théodore Aubanel. The accomplishments of the *félibres* included the reform of Prov. spelling and the standardization of the Prov. vocabulary. Perhaps their most lasting achievement consisted in the creation of such works as Mistral's *Miréio* and Aubanel's collection of love poems, *La miougrano entre duberto*, and in the impetus which their example gave to dialect literature in France, not only among their Prov. followers, who included Félix Gras, but also among the speakers of Gascon, Béarnais, and Auvergnat. The official organ of the F. is the *Armana* (Almanach) *prouvençau*, which has existed since 1855.—E. Ripert, *Le F.* (3d ed., 1948); A. Gourdin, *Langue et littérature d'oc* (1949); A. V. Roche, *Prov. Regionalism* (1954); A. del Monte, *Storia della letteratura provenzale moderna* (1958).

FEMININE ENDING. See LINE ENDINGS; for FEMININE RHYME, see RHYME.

FESCENNINE VERSES. A form of L. poetry, of great antiquity, which originated as crude, ribald, or abusive songs sung at harvest and vintage festivals and also at weddings. They were roughly dramatic in structure, having the form of a dialogue between peasants, and were probably composed in the Saturnian (q.v.) meter at first. In antiquity the name "Fescennine" was derived either from *fascinum*, a phallic emblem worn as a charm, or, as is more likely, from the town of Fescennium in Etruria. In the period of the Empire, F. verses were used for personal invective to such an extent that a law was passed against their circulation. Livy (7.2) implies that the F. verses developed into Roman satire and comedy, but the question has been much controverted.— G. E. Duckworth, *The Nature of Roman Comedy* (1952); W. Beare, *The Roman Stage* (2d ed., 1955).　r.j.g.

FIGURES OF SPEECH are traditionally considered to be words and expressions used in ways that are out of the ordinary, serving primarily as ornament and making their appeal through novelty. Although the distinction between f. of speech and f. of thought was standard in ancient rhetoric, there has never been agreement upon the differentiation. Quintilian, elaborating on Ciceronian rhetoric, provides the simplest and perhaps best test: f. of speech may be changed or removed without changing the sense of what contains them, but f. of thought cannot be so changed (*Institutes* 9.1.17). F. of speech are either grammatical or rhetorical (as aphaeresis, antithesis, isocolon, anaphora). F. of thought are words or expressions used in different senses from those which properly belong to them (as metaphor, metonymy, synechdoche, irony), and these are frequently classified as tropes when they approximate metaphors.

Study of the various f. was originally a branch of rhetoric but came to be included in poetics. Longinus considered that the f. of rhetoric were controlled by what was known to be true and thought to be probable, but the use of similar f. in poetry was to be governed by other considerations, and particularly by their effectiveness in achieving elevation and transport. During the Middle Ages and the Renaissance, partly through the continuing influence of Cicero, the distinction of Longinus was lost, and poetry was very generally thought of as versified rhetoric.

Quintilian divided f. of speech into three classes: those formed by the addition of elements (anaphora, polysyndeton, etc.); those formed by subtracting elements (asyndeton, zeugma, etc.); and those formed through the use of comparable or parallel constructions (antithesis, paranomasia, etc.). Bede, following Isidore of Seville, carried over the classification that had originated in ancient rhetoric in which the major classes were of schemes and tropes (see TROPE). Geoffrey of Vinsauf, the leader in the identification of rhetoric and poetics, listed 34 f. of speech (frequently in the Middle Ages called "colors"), 19 f. of thought, and 10 tropes. Innumerable refinements were developed in the Renaissance, and the classifications were multiplied. In the 16th c. Thomas Wilson listed 19 f. of speech, 27 f. of thought, and 13 tropes. Puttenham changed the basis of the initial classification. He devised three classes of f.: those that made their appeal to the ear (of which there were 21), those appealing to the mind (25), and those that appealed to both (62). In this as in other matters Puttenham was breaking away from the confusion of poetics and rhetoric. Ramus's reform of traditional rhetoric involved the idea that style was the whole of rhetoric, and that f. and tropes, which were the substance of style, should be distinguished from invention and arrangement, which Ramus considered parts of Logic.

That f. of speech are ornaments has been a dominant idea in the history of literary criticism. Through many centuries the mastery of f. was considered a sign of virtuosity, and much of the pleasure of reading was thought to depend on the pleasure of discriminating among the devices. Both Longinus and Quintilian argued against the use of f. according to fixed rules, and Thomas Wilson was returning to their position when in his *Art of Rhetoric* (1551) he proposed that they be used according to principles that would justify them in their context, what he called the principles of clearness and fitness and beauty. Puttenham in his *Art of Poetry* (1589) carried this reasoning further: for him poetry took feeling and nature as its guides, decency and decorum were proposed as laws of nature, and f. of speech, formed according to the demands of feeling and decorum, were employed in order to achieve "good grace." Such theories were an improvement on the medieval doctrine of rhetorical colors but continued to stress the ornamental aspect of the f. By the time of Dryden and Pope the doctrine of decorum (q.v.) and the prevailing rationalism caused the f. to be ever more closely bound to content and argument.

In the later 18th c. the development of psychology supported an emphasis on the criticism of particular poems and particular effects, and with Coleridge there was the beginning of a system in which it may be said that all f. aspired to the state of metaphor and indeed to metaphysical reference. The issues raised by this development have continued to be among the most significant ones for literary criticism in the 20th c. The New Critics and the Chicago Critics have been profoundly concerned with f., as with other phases of the relation of rhetoric to poetics. A paradoxical aspect of some of this interest is that f. of speech are often taken to be the quintessence of poetry when in the past they were primarily valued as ornaments to meaning or the substance of style. See also IMAGERY, RHETORIC AND POETICS, and articles on individual f. of speech, e.g., METAPHOR, SIMILE, METONYMY, ASYNDETON.—G. Dzialas, *Rhetorum antiquorum de figuris doctrina* (Breslavia, 1896) ; E. Faral, *Les Arts poétiques du XIIe et du XIIIe s.* (1923); A. K. Coomaraswamy, *F. of Speech or F. of Thought?* (1946); J. W. H. Atkins, *Eng. Lit. Crit.: The Renascence* (1951); Crane; Wimsatt; W. S. Howell, *Logic and Rhetoric in England, 1500–1700* (1956); Lausberg. J.A.

FINE ARTS AND POETRY. No branch of aesthetic criticism has produced a more curious crop than the critical treatises, versified art theory, and biographical and personal chit-chat about the interrelations of poetry and the fine arts. In this article the fine arts will be defined as painting, sculpture, and architecture—for many aestheticians, the *major* arts. Even if opinions vary as to which arts are *fine* or *major,* and why they are so, these three arts long have been called sisters, and the relationship has often been extended to include poetry, an art of immaterial words and sounds. Indeed, Poesy seemed no ordinary sister but a rival of Mnemosyne in sponsoring a brood of arts, fine and unrefined. Now, it appears, poetry is a subdivision of literature, and poets, no longer star attractions, are pleased to find occasional service as attendants in the passages leading to the main theater of the arts.

The notion that the fine arts are similar to poetry in intention, means, possibilities, and achievements flourished under the aesthetic cover-all of Art as imitation (q.v.) or *mimesis.* But what poet ever held his mirror up to nature so effectively as Pygmalion, who. was rewarded by having his handiwork come to life? With artistic activity regarded as imitation, and with artists described as skilled in using "the life-resembling pencil," the arts very easily approached each other, especially in the pseudo-Aristotelian theory of the Renaissance. Before the close of the 17th c., when the most praiseworthy imitation reflected the ability to apprehend and body forth the Neo-platonic ideal and composite beauties superior to the ordinary forms in nature, the arts moved even closer to poetry.

While its supremacy among the arts was challenged and sometimes denied by the painters, most conspicuously. Leonardo da Vinci, poetry generally carried the standard of art; and the poets, a numerous and very vocal group, discovered the merits of their own art in painting and sculpture and, somewhat later, architecture. All the arts appeared fine, liberal, "poetical": *ut poesis artes.* Artists often put on the badge of poetry, and few were those who did not believe, with the poets, that their activities were more "philosophical" than philosophy.

Personally and in groups or "schools," the poets played favorites among the arts, at various times lending encouragement and approval to one or more arts, borrowing a little extra glory from an individual art, or illustrating theories of poetry with principles from the sister-arts.

Majestic, nervous, bold and strong,
Let ANGELO and MILTON vie;
Oppos'd to WALLER'S amorous song,
His art let wanton TITIAN try.
(Anon, *Mount Pleasant,* 1777)

Painting, their first favorite, held that position into the 20th c. Without resorting to statistics, one may hazard the conjecture that poets have written more lines about paintings, painters, and painting than about buildings and statues, architects and sculptors, or architecture and sculpture, even though the latter arts have inspired several of the best poems, for example, works by Hölderlin, Rimbaud, Rilke, George, and others. In Eng., few, if any, poems about painting surpass Keats's *Ode on a Grecian Urn* and Wordsworth's *Inside of King's College Chapel, Cambridge.*

As a mode of epic, history-painting represented for the late Renaissance the highest reach of the pictorial art. Pastoral poets regarded themselves as painters of landscape and were pleased that the artists followed suit as "poets" of color and design or expressive line and contour. Claude Lorrain was celebrated as a painter of Theocritean and Virgilian scenes. According to Reynolds, Michelangelo carried "painting into the regions of poetry" and emulated "that art in its most adventurous flights" by Homer and Shakespeare (*Discourse* 15, 1790). In the 19th c. a band of Eng. poets looked back to the Pre-Raphaelite painters. Until recently there was an abundance, even overabundance, of pictorial poetry—"word-painting" or "painting" in sounds. Many prose-poems came into being as "pictures," and the highest praise went to a novelist's or essayist's picturesque or poetic prose. Poets and critics

vied with one another and with aestheticians in adapting the terminology of painting to poetry. Poets have displayed interest in almost every phase of "modern" painting. Moreover, the painting of the East, especially China and Japan, has for decades attracted poets of the West.

Sculpture followed close upon painting in the esteem of poets, and the assumed simplicity, unity, and grandeur of free-standing figures and monumental works occasionally suggested imagery to poets. Thus, there were 12th-c. Thomas of Britain's description of Tristan's Hall of Images with the almost-living figure of Ysolt; the "counterfeits of nature" and the "life-resembling" colored statues and sepulchral effigies in many Renaissance dramas and poems; the posings of neoclassical and romantic heroines *à la* Venus de' Medici (most famous of all, James Thomson's Musidora in *Seasons,* 1730) and the comparisons of heroes to some Apollo, Bacchus, or marble Faun, the Elgin Theseus, or even the Torso Belvedere; the Praxitelean shapes by Shelley; and numerous "stationings" of Grecian, Egyptian, Gothic, and Druidic figures by 19th-c. poets. Blake, poet and artist, beheld the records of the Cosmic Memory as "the bright sculptures of Los's Halls"—some as linear and relief-like engravings and others as figures in the round, like his Originals of the Greek Statues (*Jerusalem,* I, part 16, 62, and *Descriptive Catalogue, Works* [Keynes], p. 781). Along with mythological, historical, and technical interests in the broken and unbroken marbles of classical antiquity, which "went for much" until recently, the poets envied most of all, very likely, the sculptor's reputed ability to represent or re-create human feeling, passion, emotion, and thought in materials more enduring than words or sounds. Sculpture, they felt, offered significant "moments" made eternal and ever-beautiful—"fair attitudes" in marble (often but not always Parian and white) or "masque-like figures on the dreamy urn."

Poets in many lands found analogies between poetry and the careful carving, clear design, outline, and relief—with or without suggestions of the third dimension—of the sculptors. Some became "carvers of verbal agates," writing their "sculptures" and cutting their "gems" after visiting studios and galleries or looking at illustrated volumes, or with their eyes on gems, intaglios, animated or reposeful busts, high or low reliefs, and storied or well-wrought urns. Even at the peak of the interest in "word-painting," the persistent attractiveness of Alexandrian "metrical carvings" was illustrated, for example, by E. C. Stedman and T. B. Aldrich's *Cameos Selected from the Works of Walter Savage Landor* (1874). Later, Yeats came to admire most of all the gold metalwork, ivories, and mosaics of Byzantine craftsmen in the age of Justinian, even wishing that he might become a work of perfect art which in turn might inspire other finely hammered, enduring artifacts of gold. Keats had wanted to participate in the perfect expression of emotional activity he imagined in the cold pastoral on a Grecian urn; but Yeats would be the work of art itself, with a dual role in the artifice of eternity as object of contemplation and contemplator of Being. Other modern poets have dreamed of producing—or becoming—works of art.

From the early 19th c. onward, poets and theorists often borrowed critical terms from the art of sculpture: statuesque, sculptural, sculpturesque. Individual works and sculptors as well as the technique and principles of the art influenced the Parnassians and, in the early 20th c., the "imagists," the "objectivists," and many poets without classification or program. In America and Europe a number of poets preferred to alter the Horatian comparison of painting and poetry into *Ut sculptura poesis.*

A popular revision, today, might be *Ut architectura poesis;* for the most generally admired artists or "poets" are now the architects—engineers and scientists—who plan and make stadiums, turnpikes, city-plans, skyscrapers, housing and industrial projects, and houses or rooms as "space" for gracious living. In short, architects create works which not only suggest what earlier generations called the sublime and the beautiful but which also serve useful functions. The bridge was an appropriate epical symbol for Hart Crane, however defective his own poetic design and achievement.

Architecture, moreover, surpasses both sculpture and painting in supplying terms which the critic-poet uses without embarrassment. Structure, frame of reference, design, architectonic(s)—in varying degrees connotative of architecture—may be applied to poetic activity and to individual poems. Critical reference may be either to "well-built," "unornamented," "clean," or "economical" poems or to the "organic," "dynamic," or "functional" principles according to which poems are designed and fabricated.

The many critics, artists, and poets, who, from the Renaissance through the 19th c., engaged in discussing the parallels between the fine arts and poetry would be surprised today not only by the multiplicity of artistic interests among poets and critics in their efforts to absorb the specialized knowledge of the arts ("style-concepts" and studies in iconology and iconography) but even more, perhaps, by the relatively humble status of poetry. With the demotion of poetry to a minor classification of literature has come a great advance in the standing of her sisters, especially "the modern art of music" and its "frozen" but now thawed-out relative, architecture. While a visiting critic from the 17th c., for example, might search long before tracking down a poet who turns out "word-paintings," he would find many craftsmen studying the lesser or decorative branches of several arts and occasionally displaying their careful workmanship in "poetic" medallions, cameos, icons, mosaics, metalworks, montages, collages, mobiles, and even immobiles. The visitor might then observe that poetry has all but dropped its dramatic, epic, narrative, and didactic pinions, and that poets strive to be specialists in the technics of a special and exacting artistic medium while the practitioners of less rigorous arts, major and minor, move into the poets' former area of operation.

The critic from the past concludes, perhaps, that poetry survives, even in a zealously guarded preserve of diminished song. A poem may mean much or little, but it is made, first of all, to be itself a work of art: "a poem is a poem is a poem." Who seriously disagrees? Yet what becomes of the general critic's occupation if that is all we need to know?

S. Rocheblave, "L'Art français au XVIIe s. dans ses rapports avec la littérature," *Hist. de la langue et de la litt. fr.,* ed. L. Petit de Julleville, v (1898); K. Borinski, *Die Antike in Poetik und Kunsttheorie* (2 v., 1914-24); L. Binyon, "Eng. Poetry in its Relation to Painting and the Other Arts," *Proc. British Acad.,* 8 (1918); E. Panofsky, "Idea" . . . , *Studien der Bibliothek Warburg,* 5 (1924) and *Studies in Iconology* (1939); Bray; F. P. Chambers, *Cycles of Taste* (1928) and *Hist. of Taste* (1932); F. Maury, *Arts et litt. comparés* (1933); H. Read, "Parallels in Eng. Painting and Poetry," *In Defence of Shelley and Other Essays* (1936); A.H.R. Fairchild, *Shakespeare and the Arts of Design* (1937); S. A. Larrabee, "Crit. Terms from the Art of Sculpture," N&Q, April 3, 1937 and *Eng. Bards and Grecian Marbles* (1943); C. B. Tinker, *Painter and Poet* (1938); T. M. Greene, *The Arts and the Arts of Crit.* (1940); L. Hautecoeur, *Litt. et peinture en France* . . . (1942); E. Souriau, *La Correspondance des arts* (1947); T. Munro, *The Arts and Their Interrelations* (1949); K. Gilbert, *Aesthetic Studies: Architecture and Poetry* (1952); H. A. Hatzfeld, *Lit. through Art* (1952); Wellek and Warren, 2d ed., ch. 11 and bibliog.; J. H. Hagstrum, *The Sister Arts* (1958); W. Sypher, *Rococo to Cubism in Art and Lit.* (1960); R. G. Saisselin, "Ut Pictura Poesis: From Du Bos to Diderot," JAAC, 20 (1961). See also UT PICTURA POESIS.   S.A.L.

FINIDA. In 14th- to early 16th-c. Sp. poetry the f. is the approximate equivalent of the *remate* (q.v.) of the later *canción petrarquista.* Lang says: "Like the Provençal *tornada,* the finida serves as a conclusion to a poem, and with the *tornada* and kindred forms, such as the *envoi,* the *desfecha,* the *estribote* and others, this stanza was originally, in all probability, a sequence to a musical composition. According to the Leys d'Amors, the *tornada* repeats in its rhyme-order the second part of the last stanza in case this has the same number of verses; otherwise it may have one verse more or less than the last half-stanza. In the Portuguese . . . the *finida,* which is regarded as essential to a perfect composition, may have from one to four verses, and must rhyme with the last stanza or, if the poem be a *cantiga de refram,* with the refrain. The practitioners of the *Cancionero de Baena* [ca. 1450] appear to have followed the example of the Provençals and Catalans."—H. R. Lang, "Las formas estróficas y términos métricos del Cancionero de Baena," *Estudios eruditos "in memoriam" de Adolfo Bonilla y San Martín,* I (1927); Navarro.   D.C.C.

FINNISH POETRY. Historically, there are only two periods of Fin. poetry, the old and the new. For centuries the Fin. people remained at the very outskirts of European civilization largely owing to Finland's geography. With the advent of Christianity the isolation was broken; gradually, the new ideas became interwoven with the old nature myths and tribal heroic legends. The outcome of this fusion of the old and the new culture was a wealth of folklore. For many centuries it lived as an oral tradition, originating in the southwest and gradually receding into the less populated southeast, where it was collected by 19th-c. scholars.

More than a million lines of this anonymous poetry have been recorded. It consists of epic and lyric elements. A very good selection of it was published by Elias Lönnrot in 1835 and 1840, under the titles of the *Kalevala* and the *Kanteletar.* The former is an amalgam of ancient nature myths, heroic tales, and assimilated Christian legends, all woven together into an epic form. Its verse has 8 syllables with 4 stresses (Longfellow used this meter in *Hiawatha*). The *Kanteletar* is a collection of lyrics, ballads, and legends, like the *Kalevala* frequently based on historical events. They display an engaging directness and simplicity of manner: a maiden sings while waiting for her lover; a shepherd gives voice to his cares while tending his herd. In these poems nature, as if endowed with a soul, rejoices and mourns with the singer.

In keeping with the principles of the Lutheran Reformation, the Old and New Testaments were translated into Fin. in the 16th and 17th c. Despite this undertaking, the usage of Fin. was for a long time limited to the lower classes. The language of higher social levels was Swedish, which had prestige as the vehicle of the government and the civil administration. But the Swedo-Fin. authors could not found a national literature. Eminent poets like Jacob Frese (1691–1729), Gustaf Filip Creutz (1731–85), and Frans Michael Franzén (1772–1847), though credited with a Fin. sensibility, left their native country for Sweden, and their production was absorbed by the *rikssvenska* (national-Swedish) tradition. When the Swedish period (1155–1809) came to an end in consequence of the Napoleonic wars and Finland became annexed to Russia, the literary situation was fundamentally changed. The separation from Sweden, concurrent with the romantic movement in European literature, turned the eyes of the cultural leaders of Finland to the common people and the Fin. folk culture as the chief potential sources of strength in the struggle to save their country as a national entity.

The literary revival which ensued came about through the joint endeavors of Fin. and Swedo-Fin. writers. The slogan for the national movement was formulated by the pioneer agitator A. I. Arwidsson (1791–1858): "We are not Swedes, we will not become Russians, and so we must be Finns." A major event was the founding in 1831 of the Fin. Literary Society, still in existence. Most far-reaching in their consequences for Fin. poetry were the labors of Lönnrot (1802–84), who by collecting the *Kalevala* and the *Kanteletar* showed the people how rich their poetic heritage really was. It was, however, two Swedish-language poets, Johan Ludvig Runeberg (1804–77) and Zachris Topelius (1818–98), who first assimilated the spirit of this heritage. Runeberg's significance in Fin. poetry is twofold. First, in conformity with the program of National Romanticism, he gave his people a national-literary identity, principally through his heroic cycle *Fänrik Ståls sägner* (The Tales of Ensign Stål, 1848–1860). These poems, which are based on memories of the wars with Russia, articulate a fervent Fin. patriotism. Secondly, through his formal virtuosity Runeberg became the preceptor of the Fin.-language poets. When these poets began to develop the resources of their language in the 1860's, their main ambition was to transpose into Fin. the metrical and stanzaic forms that Runeberg had earlier worked out in Swedish. Topelius is important for his elusive idylls written in mellifluous verse. Beside Runeberg, however, he appears rather pale.

The emergence of art poetry in Fin. occurred between 1860 and 1880; but, with the exception of Aleksis Kivi (1834–72), the poets showed greater formal talent than creative power. Under the pseudonym Oksanen, A. Ahlqvist (1826–89) published *Sparks* (1860–68), the aim of which was to illustrate the use of various verse forms in Fin.; it established him as the lawgiver of Fin. poetry. Two poets who helped in accommodating Runeberg's and Topelius' formal patterns to Fin. were J. H. Erkko (1849–1900) and Kaarlo Kramsus (1855–95). Erkko followed his masters also in spirit, by cultivating the idyll. Kivi, primarily a novelist and dramatist, was in his poetry more original. His poems, written in unrhymed verse of irregular rhythm, express deep and spontaneous feeling.

Toward the end of the century the results of the Fin. revival became evident in poetry. A number of young men educated in Fin. schools and dedicated to the idea of creating a truly native artistic culture appeared on the scene. They called themselves "Young Finland," and their circle embraced men working in all fields of art—the composer Sibelius, for example, was one of the group. Utilizing folklore motifs and following the examples of the best in world literature, three poets, Leino, Manninen, and Koskenniemi, became the agents of the poetic breakthrough. With *Songs of March* (1896) Leino (1878–1926), the most gifted of them, initiated a career notable for its variety and vigor. He was equally distinguished in narrative and lyric forms. Through his acquaintance with Scandinavian poetry and his deep penetration of the ancient Fin. heritage, Leino was able to relieve the close formal dependence on Runeberg and Topelius in Fin. poetry. Interesting is his use of Fin. myth, not in the spirit of National Romanticism, but as a means of articulating personal and universal experience. His verse is melodious, and much of it is transparent, as, for instance, his ballad *Ylermi*, which deals with a superman who violates all conventions.

Ylermi ylpeä isäntä
Ajoi temppelin ovesta,
Lausui kirkon laivan alta:
"Täss'on mies tämän sukuinen,
Kadu ei tehtyä tekoa,
Ei parane palkan eestä."

(Ylermi, the proud knight, dashed into the temple on his mount, and shouted from under the arch: "Here is a man of such kinship that he never regrets his deeds and will not change his ways for any price.") Otto Manninen (1872–1950) displayed in *Stanzas* (1905, 1910) and *Calm of the Stream* (1925) verses of the utmost perfection, distinguished by formal refinement, subtle symbolism, and ethical depth. He made notable translations into Fin. of Homer, Molière, Ibsen, and Runeberg. V. A. Koskenniemi (1885–1962) was Finland's first philosophical poet. Having the closest affinities with the classical and the French traditions, Koskenniemi is noteworthy for the noble sentiment and the pure artistry of his verse. Both he and Manninen show a precision of language unequaled by their predecessors.

In more recent years Fin. poetry has been well represented by gifted young writers participating in all the cultural and intellectual trends of our time. Foremost are a group of poets who in some ways parallel the Swedish-Finnish modernists (q.v.), *Tulenkantajat* (The Torchbearers, 1924–30); in its more extreme forms, their style is characterized by primitivism, surrealism, and free verse. Most talented were Uuno Kailas (1901–33), a tormented poet tempering passionate reflection by Parnassian form, and Katri Vala (1901–44), a dithyrambic counterpart to Edith Södergran. The leaders of the later leftist group *Kiila* (The Wedge), Arvo Turtiainen (b. 1904) and the poetess Elvi Sinervo (b. 1912), wrote much of their poetry before and during the last war in prison. In laconic verse reminiscent of Manninen, Yrjö Jylhä (1903–56) immortalized the events and moods of that war. After 1945, two somewhat older poets who in the 1920's had been close to the Torchbearers, P. Mustapää (pseudonym for Martti Haavio, b. 1899) and, especially, Aaro Hellaakoski (1893–52), reinvigorated the Fin. lyric. A man of great emotional power and wide intellectual range—he was scientist, educator, painter—Hellaakoski forged from his passionate and divided experience poetry characterized by formal harmony, marvelously sensitive rhythm, and symbolic resonance. The young poets coming to maturity in the 1950's, like Lassi Heikkilä (b. 1925), Lassi Nummi (b. 1928), and Paavo Haavikko (b. 1931), assimilated the new style, which avoided both the subjective excesses of extreme modernism and the national pathos characteristic of much traditional lyricism.

Whereas from the 1860's on Fin.-language poetry was thriving, Swedish poetry in Finland languished. The last noteworthy achievement for some time was the still actable verse drama *Daniel Hjort* (1862) by J. J. Wecksell (1838–1907). In the 1880's Karl August Tavaststjerna (1860–98) introduced a more realistic note into lyric poetry, which had become monopolized by the Topelian idyll. When lyricism again began to flow more freely in the 1890's and after, it expressed the moods of pessimism natural to a minority group which foresaw its gradual severance from Fin. national life. The predominant themes were alienation and loneliness, compensated either by recourse to regionalism or exoticism, or by aristocratic idealism and internationalism. The existing situation of permanent entrenchment has tended to give Swedo-Fin. poetry a more severe form than that typical of Swedish poetry. This becomes evident in the work of Michael Lybeck (1864–1925) and Bertel Gripenberg (1878–1947). Best known for his flaming erotic poetry in incantatory verse, Gripenberg in later life adopted the sonnet form. His celebration of Fin. heroism during and after the Fin. Civil War is a proud testament to his aristocratic attitudes. Comparable in stature to Gripenberg is Arvid Mörne (1876–1946), whose early regionalism was followed by an intense poetic battle for the idea of a Swedish nationality in Finland. Other significant poets were Hjalmar Procopé (1868–1927), a philosophical ironist, Emil Zilliacus (1878–1961), a learned classicist, and the younger Jarl Hemmer (1893–1949), an extreme romantic.

With *Dikter* (Poems, 1916) by Edith Södergran (1892–1923) was inaugurated the movement of the Swedish-Finnish modernists (q.v.). This movement, the most original one in 20th-c. Swedish-language poetry, was a poetic response to the sense of crisis and apocalypse which attended the Rus. Revolution and the Fin. Civil War. However, no uniformity of inspiration existed. The poetry of Södergran herself and of Elmer Diktonius (1896–1961) approaches the prophetic mode, but the former's exaltation is cosmic, the latter's social-revolutionary. The inspiration of both Gunnar Björling (1887–1960) and Rabbe Enckell (b. 1903) is aesthetic, but Björling's verse is surrealist, Enckell's classical. And the style of Henry Parland (1908–30) has affinities with the futurism of Mayakovski. What held the group together was their novel and more profoundly social conception of poetry. Of more recent modernists may be mentioned Ralf Parland (b. 1914), Solveig von Schoultz (b. 1907), and Bo Carpelan (b. 1926). The conservative modernism of Enckell has been important to both von Schoultz and Carpelan, an indication of the formal discipline of Swedo-Fin. poets.

The early triumph of modernism in Swedish Finland was due largely to the international orientation and the aesthetic cast of mind fostered by social alienation. Recently, however, even those poets who stay close to their native habitat and to traditional form, the regionalists, have adopted modernistic techniques. One of them, Anders Cleve (b. 1937) applies surrealistic imagery and free form to poetry about his native Helsingfors (Helsinki), which he envisions as a matrix of myths.

ANTHOLOGIES. FIN.: *Voices from Finland*, ed. E. Tompuri (1947); *Lukemisto uudempaa suomalaista kirjallisuutta*, ed. E. A. Saarimaa (1948); *Nuori kiila runoantologia*, ed. E. Sinervo et al. (1948); *Suomen Runotar*, ed. J. V. Lehtonen and E. Cederberg (4th ed., 1951); M. Haavio, *Kirjokansi, suomen kansan ker-*

tomarunoutta (1952); *Tuhanten rantain partahilla*, ed. A. Salmela (1954); *Ny finsk lyrik*, tr. E. Repo and N.-B. Stormbom (1960).—SWEDISH: *Finländsk litt. utom Runeberg*, ed. G. Castrén (1922); *Finlandssvensk lyrik från Edith Södergran till nu*, ed. P. E. Wahlund (1947); *Ur Finlands svenska lyrik*, ed. E. Kihlman and Th. Warburton (2v., 1949); *20th C. Scandinavian Poetry*, ed. M. Allwood (1950); *40 år finlandssvensk lyrik*, ed. S. Carlson (1955).

HISTORY AND CRITICISM. FIN.: D. Comparetti, *Traditional Poetry of the Finns*, tr. I. M. Anderton (1898); J. Bouchot, *La Litt. finnoise* (1914); F. A. Hästesko, *Kalevalan kauneus* (1927); A. Kallio, *Uudempi suomalainen kirjallisuus* (2v., 1928–29); H. Grellmamm, *Finnische Lit.* (1932); J. L. Perret, *Panorama de la litt. contemporaine de Finlande* (1936); R. Beck, "Fin. Lit.," in *Hist. of the Scandinavian Literatures*, ed. T. Blankner (1938); V. Tarkiainen, *Finsk litteraturh.* (1950) and, with E. Kauppinen, *Suomalaisen kirjallisuuden historia* (2d ed., 1961); A. Sakari, *Litt. finlandaise* (1952); E. R. G. Gummerus, *Storia delle letterature della Finlandia* (1957); I. Havu, *Finlands litt., 1900–1950* (1958).—SWEDISH: R. Hedvall, *Finlands svenska litt.* (1917); J. Landquist, *Modern svensk litt. i Finland* (1929); E. N. Tigerstedt, *Det religiösa problemet i modern finlands-svensk litt.* (1939); B. Holmqvist, *Modern finlandssvensk litt.* (1951); Th. Warburton, *Finsk diktning i svensk dräkt: En översikt* (1960); G. C. Schoolfield, "The Recent Scandinavian Lyric," BA, 36 (1962). J.B.O.; S.L.

FLAMENCA. See SEGUIDILLA.

FLEMISH POETRY. (For Flemish poetry prior to 1600 see DUTCH POETRY.) After the division of the Netherlands (fall of Antwerp, 1585), the southern provinces (now known as Flanders, or Flemish Belgium) lost their economic, cultural, and literary predominance. Nevertheless, the movements of the modern period, such as the Reformation and the Renaissance, had taken their first flight in this region. Renaissance poetry of the Netherlands reached its high point in the northern provinces, specifically in the work of P. C. Hooft, but the renewal itself originated in the south. In the circles of the *rederijkers* (q.v.) one finds an interest in humanism, a gradually growing understanding of the spirit of antiquity, and a sensitivity to new moral and aesthetic ideas and to new forms. Transitional figures are Lucas de Heere (1534–84) and Carel van Mander (1548–1606), in whose work one encounters, side by side with conventional *rederijker* poems, new poetic forms, and a new handling of verse itself. De Heere, an admirer of Marot, introduced the sonnet into the poetry of the Netherlands, wrote odes and epigrams, and applied himself to the purification of verse, although his alexandrines still stand close to the twelve-syllable verse of the *rederijkers*. Van Mander wrote sonnets and alexandrines and translated the *Bucolics* and *Georgics* of Virgil into iambic verse (1597). But the spirit as well as the form of poetry was rejuvenated by Jan van der Noot (ca. 1540–1595/1600), nobleman, humanist, and man of letters. Self-satisfied and ambitious, exalting beauty and poetry, an admirer of Petrarch and the *Pléiade* (especially Ronsard), he wrote sonnets in alexandrines after the Fr. manner, odes, and an epic; he practiced by preference the iambic pentameter and the alexandrine, he purified the language—all this not in a narrowly formalistic manner but with the inspiration of a true poet (*Het Theatre*, 1568; *Het Bosken*, 1570(?); *Cort Begrijp der XII Boeken Olympiados*, 1579).

After the definite political separation of the northern and southern Netherlands, the poetic climate was principally determined by the Counter-Reformation. In the first half of the 17th c., however, the Renaissance found further echoes among the *rederijkers* and even, formally, in religious song books. The Renaissance was represented by J. D. Heemssen, J. Ysermans, and the most prominent poet of the time, Justus de Harduyn (1582–1636), whose beautifully formed elegiac poetry is still alive. In his youth he celebrated the beauty and grace of his beloved in a cycle of songs, odes, elegies, and sonnets (*De weerliicke liefden tot Roose-mond*, ed. 1613). Later, as a priest, he wrote sacred love lyrics (*Goddelicke lofsanghen*, 1620)—more internally experienced, less "literary," and in some songs connected with the religious lyrics of the Middle Ages. The triumphant Counter-Reformation made itself felt here, as also in the work of L. Makeblyde, B. van Haeften, Aeg. Hafacker, L. van Mechelen, and in the pious and serene lyrics of D. Bellemans. Under the influence of this powerful religious movement, secular poetry (love songs, epithalamia, drinking songs, amorous or edifying sonnets, odes, pastoral poems) was obliged more and more to yield to poetry of religious inspiration. This type of poetry was, in its most typical forms, moral-didactic and popular. Its most distinguished representative was the wise and humorous Jesuit Adriaan Poirters (1605–74), who created, in *Het masker vande wereldt afgetrocken* (1645) (The World's Mask Removed), the successful genre of the spiritual emblem book: in form, an alternation of prints, long poems, and prose pieces (these latter in turn interspersed with short rhymes and verse narratives); in content, at the same time, narrative, didactic, satirical, and polemic; in spirit, religious and moralistic. In addition to being a popular poet, Poirters was a medi-

tative and ascetic poet who had contact with interior piety as well as with the grandiose accents of the affective, emotional Baroque. Baroque elevation also appears in Michiel de Swaen (1654–1707), who closes the 17th c. His religious contemplative poetry suited the spiritual climate, but was distinguished from the popular-didactic poetasting of Poirters' disciples by its more individual experience and its exalted literary aims. Vondel, Cats, and the Fr. classicists were his models. These influences appear also in his literary treatise, *Nederduytsche digtkonde of rijmkonst* (ca. 1700), which displays a certain independence.

The 18th c. was a period of decadence. Poetry was devoid of personal accents, partly because poets of distinction were lacking, and partly because the now-dominant Fr. classical poetics (Boileau's *Art Poétique*, translated in 1721 and 1754) discouraged individual expression, though it promoted regularity, as may be noted in the recommendations of such theorists as J. P. van Male and J. B. Bouvaert, the latter of whom also defended blank verse. A poetically and spiritually monotonous expanse of moral observations, didactic verses, complimentary and occasional poems, secular and religious verses, fables, translations, and adaptations lies between the alexandrine didactic poem *De gramschap* (Anger, 1725) of Livinus de Meyer (1655–1730) and the *Ode aan de vryheid* (Ode to Freedom, 1790) of P. J. de Borchgrave (1758–1819), in whose predominantly classical poetry various shades of feeling, national pride, and devotion to nature are visible.

These very elements made themselves felt more and more at the beginning of the 19th c., and led to the breakthrough of romanticism, which occasioned the rebirth of Flem. literature. The harmonious Karel Lodewijk Ledeganck (1805–47) and the extraordinarily prolific Prudens van Duyse (1804–59), who practiced all genres and forms, directed poetry away from the classical style; poetry became free and spontaneous in the popular rimes of Th. van Rijswijck (1811–49), and found in J. A. de Laet (1815–91) an interpreter of *Weltschmerz*. Imagination, sentiment, national inspiration, and introspection broadened the range of poetry; verse narratives, legends, ballads, elegiac musings, songs in the manner of the old *volkslied*, and historical tableaux varied the pattern. But the assertion of an individual life was lacking: such an assertion had naturally no chance for existence in the climate of moderate realism which, since the 1850's, had expressed itself in pictures from the life of the people (J. van Beers), songs and airs dealing with the joys and sorrows of domestic life (G. Dodd, Fr. de Cort, G. Antheunis), political and social verses (J. Vuylsteke, J. de

Geyter), cantatas and oratorios (E. Hiel), and epic tableaux (J. de Geyter, L. de Koninck). Strange but not very convincing are the formal-technical experiments undertaken by the so-called "taalvirtuozen" ("language-virtuosos")—J. M. Dautzenberg, Fr. de Cort, and J. van Droogenbroeck—on the model of Platen and Rückert (see GERMAN POETRY), although Dautzenberg achieved some results which, with the simple anecdotal poems of Rosalie and Virginie Loveling (*Gedichten*, 1870), belong to the best work brought forth by this period.

One of the most extraordinary assertions of individuality in the modern lyric is to be met in the poetry of Guido Gezelle (1830–99). A paradox of this work is that it was lived and written by a humble and learned priest. One had to wait for him in order to hear individual emotion sing out completely and sometimes passionately, and at the same time to see a wonder—that this individual life is rooted in the divine world-order, in which man, as well as the stars, the flowers, and the ants, stands in the sign of eternity. Gezelle's emotional life shows an astonishing variety of light and dark variegations. His sensuous empathy and his interpretation of nature are probably without equal in the lyrics of the world. His religious life, perhaps, brought him close to the mystical experience. But he does not speak; he sings: his lyric work is an original and highly perfected phenomenon of language, rhyme, and rhythm—plastic and musical, drawn from his own creative strength and distilled from the treasury of popular, dialectal forms of expression, at the same time refined and spontaneous. He draws from the mysterious well of poetry itself, and he liberates the word. Van Ostaijen in the 1920's and the experimental poets who appeared some fifty years after Gezelle's death recognized in him their great predecessor (*Dichtoefeningen*, 1858; *Kleengedichtjes*, 1860; *Gedichten, gezangen en gebeden*, 1862; *Tijdkrans*, 1893; *Rijmsnoer*, 1897).

Gezelle remained for a long time on the periphery of recognized poetry. The young titan Albrecht Rodenbach (1856–80) wrote, in traditional meters and with neoromantic inspiration, militant songs, epic verses, and reflective poetry which binds one with its deeply human content. Among a group of "intimate" poets, the impressionistic formalist Pol de Mont (1857–1931) fought for "art for art's sake," and Prosper van Langendonck (1862–1920) interpreted the incurable anguish of the *poète maudit* (q.v.). Both, especially the latter, anticipated the *fin de siècle* poetry of Karel van de Woestijne (1878–1929), a Flem. nuance in the individualistic symbolism of the era. He was a hypersensitive and hyperintellectual self-tormenter who explored, in his first life-weary

and listless volumes—*Het vader-huis* (The Paternal House, 1903); *De boom-gaard der vogelen en der vruchten* (The Orchard of Birds and Fruits, 1905); *De gulden schaduw* (The Golden Shadow, 1910)—the furthest reaches of sensuous experience and of spiritual love between man and woman; he clothed his pride and fear in a superabundant baroque garment of sensations, images, symbols, word-garlands, and slow rhythms. In his later, more sober verses—*De modderen man* (The Muddy Man, 1920); *God aan zee* (God at the Sea, 1926); *Het bergmeer* (The Mountain Lake, 1928)—in which human insufficiency rises up once more in a supreme wave of impurity and loathesomeness, a great concern with God and eternity appears, and the poet reaches a state of renunciation and purification. Van de Woestijne is master of the poetic landscape of his day, in which the most striking features are the pithy, plastic verses of O. K. de Laey, the social and political lyrics of R. de Clercq, the "irrequietum" of the symphonies and musings of the visionary Cyriel Verschaeve (1874–1949), the mannered poems of Karel van den Oever (1879–1926), and the minor tone of the amiable stoic Jan van Nijlen (1884–).

In the early years of the 1920's, expressionism broke radically with the aesthetically oriented poetry of impressionism as well as with traditional verse construction in order, under the influence of Verhaeren, Whitman, Tagore, the Fr. *unanimistes,* and, above all, the German expressionists, to proclaim a coming world of goodness and brotherhood—in emotional free verse with spasmodic imagery (P. van Ostaijen, W. Moens, A. Mussche), or in moral anecdotes (M. Gijsen). Paul van Ostaijen (1896–1928), who stood at the beginning of this humanitarian expressionism with his volume *Het sienjaal* (The Signal, 1918), came rapidly under the spell of dadaism (*Bezette stad*, Occupied Town, 1921), Apollinaire, Cocteau, and, especially, Aug. Stramm's experiments with the "concentrated word." In acute essays (*Gebruiksaanwijzing der lyriek*—Directions for the Use of the Lyric) he formulated a theory of pure poetry, based on the isolated word and on association. He had just time enough to give reality to his insights in a few poems, now become classics, in his posthumous volume, *Het eerste boek van Schmoll* (The First Book of Schmoll, 1928).

Van Ostaijen's spiritual adventure is one of the great moments in the modern poetry of the Low Countries. His spiritual relatives V. J. Brunclair and G. Burssens took part in it, and it had a fertilizing effect on M. Gilliams and P. G. Buckinx, who, sounding the depths of pure essence, brought the word back into its syntactic context. Nevertheless, after the early death of Van Ostaijen, the dominant force for a couple of decades remained traditional: post-symbolist in U. van de Voorde and H. Hensen, tart and hoarse in R. Minne, thoughtful in R. Herreman, antipoetically sober in W. Elsschot, vitalistic in R. Verbeeck, B. Decorte and B. Peleman, disenchanted in K. Jonckheere, pithily erotic in L. van Brabant, collectivist in F. Vercnocke and K. Vertommen, the last-mentioned of whom revert to old forms such as the ballad and the epic.

Around 1950 the experimental poets H. Claus, R. van de Kerckhove, A. Bontridder, B. Cami, M. Wauters, E. van Ruysbeek, A. de Roover, and P. de Vree sounded a new note. Their attempts participate in the process of the absolutizing of the word, a process initiated on an international level early in this century and as yet far from completed. Most of these new poets do not "write verses"; they construct poems with words, which are, first of all, magic signs of sound and rhythm, and with images, which, by means of intuitive associations and analogies, interpret emotion directly from the unconscious. The traditional conception of poetry as a statement or an avowal in the inherited language of forms retains, however, a strong attractive power, and is practiced by, among others, A. van Wilderode, H. van Herreweghen, J. de Haes, Reninca, and Chr. d'Haen.

ANTHOLOGIES: Onze dichters, ed. Th. Coopman & V. dela Montagne (1880); Vlaamsche oogst, ed. Ad. Herckenrath (1904); De Vlaamsche jongeren van gisteren en heden, 1910–1927, ed. Aug. van Cauwelaert (1927); Vlaamsche lyriek 1830–1890, ed. M. Gilliams (1937); De Vlaamsche poëzie sinds 1918 (v. 2, Bloemlezing), ed. A. Demedts (2d ed., 1945); Breviarium der Vlaamse lyriek, ed. Marnix Gijsen (4th ed., 1953); Vlaamse dichtkunst van deze tijd, ed. P. de Ryck (2 v., 2d ed., 1954); Waar is de eerste morgen?, ed. J. Walravens (2d ed., 1959).

HISTORY AND CRITICISM: E. Rombauts, "Humanisme en Renaissance in de Zuidelijke Nederlanden" and "De letterkunde der XVIIe eeuw in Zuid-Nederland" in Fr. Baur and others, Geschiedenis van de letterkunde der Nederlanden, III (1945) and v (1952); A. Demedts, De Vlaamsche poëzie sinds 1918 (v. 1, Studie, 2d ed., 1945); M. Rutten, Nederlandse dichtkunst van Kloos tot Claus (1957); R. F. Lissens, De Vlaamse letterkunde van 1780 tot heden (3d ed., 1959); P. de Vree, Throw in (1959).

R.F.L. (tr. F.J.W.)

FLESHLY SCHOOL OF POETRY, THE. First part of the title of an article in the October 1871 issue of Contemporary Review, signed "Thomas Maitland" but actually by Robert Buchanan. Buchanan saw Rossetti, Swinburne, and Morris as poets united by perverse loyal-ties toward one another and against all that was normal and decent. His primary target was Rossetti, whose recently published Poems provided the occasion for the article. His chief objections to the "School" were that they were "fleshly" and that they were aesthetic: "The fleshly gentlemen have bound themselves by solemn league and covenant to extol fleshliness as the distinct and supreme end of poetic and pictorial art; to aver that poetic expression is greater than poetic thought. . . ."

In attacking "fleshliness" Buchanan was exploiting a general mid-Victorian prejudice against exposure of the body in life and art (and also betraying his own prurience). The graver charge, and the one more disturbing to the "School," was that their work was morally irresponsible, for, however much they may have contributed to the "aesthetic movement," none of these poets believed in the autonomy of art or exalted form over content.

Deeply hurt, Rossetti entered a dignified protest in "The Stealthy School of Criticism," Athenaeum, December 16, 1871. Swinburne, delighted at the opportunity to strike another blow in his private war with Buchanan which had begun with the latter's attack on Poems and Ballads (1866), published in 1872 a savage pamphlet entitled Under the Microscope. Virulent exchanges between Swinburne and Buchanan continued for the next four years, ending only with Buchanan's victory over Swinburne's publisher in a libel suit. While the "Fleshly School" controversy may have hastened Rossetti's death, it undoubtedly ensured the failure of Buchanan's literary career. —T. Maitland, "The Fleshly School of Poetry; Mr. D. G. Rossetti," Contemporary Rev., 28 (1871), expanded and publ. under Buchanan's own name in The F.S.o.P. and Other Phenomena of the Day (1872); D. G. Rossetti, "The Stealthy School of Crit.," Athenaeum, Dec. 16, 1871; A. C. Swinburne, "Under the Microscope" (1872); O. Doughty, "The F.S.o.P.: 1871–72," Dante Gabriel Rossetti (1949); J. H. Buckley, "The Fear of Art," The Victorian Temper (1951); J. A. Cassidy, "Robert Buchanan and the Fleshly Controversy," PMLA, 67 (1952); G. G. Storey, "Robert Buchanan's Critical Principles," PMLA, 68 (1953). J.K.R.

FLYTING, fliting. A poetical invective—often a kind of intellectual game—in which two poets assail each other alternately with scurrilous, abusive verse, e.g., The Flyting of Dunbar & Kennedie. The form is especially typical of 16th-c. Scottish poets; despite the excess profanity, flytings have freshness, color, and a rich power, and are not infrequently superior in quality to Eng. poetry of the same period. Probably influenced Skelton.

While the f. tradition is at the heart of

Scottish poetry and extends from William Dunbar (ca. 1460–ca. 1520) to Hugh Mac-Diarmid in the 20th c., cursing matches in verse are found in other literatures as well, e.g., Gr., Arabic, Celtic, It., and, of course, Prov. (see TENZONE).—A. Mure Mackenzie, *A Historical Survey of Scottish Lit. to 1914* (1933); C. S. Lewis, *Eng. Lit. in the 16th C., Excluding Drama* (1954); K. Wittig, *The Scottish Tradition in Lit.* (1958).　　R.O.E.

FOCUS. A photographer so aims and adjusts his camera that there will be one point in his picture to which all other elements are subordinated. This point is the center of interest or focus. In literature, also, f. is the organizational center of the work—that element which organizes and unifies all other elements. In Browning's *My Last Duchess* the f. is the characterization of the Duke. In Tennyson's *Mariana* it is a mood of melancholy and dejection. In Frost's *The Death of the Hired Man* it is the conflict of justice vs. mercy which finds expression in the two definitions of home.
　　　　　　　　　　　　　　　　　L.P.

FOLÍA. A Sp. stanza form, popular 4-line variation of the *seguidilla* (q.v.), probably related to a Portuguese dance-song form and normally expressing a nonsensical or ridiculous thought. The lines may be octosyllabic or shorter; if the lines are not of equal length, the even-numbered are generally the shorter and very often —some think properly so—oxytonic. The origin is undatable, but *folías* dating before 1600 are known. The following example is from Cervantes' *Rinconete y Cortadillo*:

> Por un sevillano
> rufo a lo valón
> tengo socarrado
> todo el corazón.
> 　　　　　　　　D.C.C.

FOLK SONG, a body of song preserved and transmitted by oral tradition. A folk song is the expression not of any individual poet but of the whole singing community, and it is uninfluenced by contemporary literary conventions or sophisticated cultural norms. F.s. embraces work songs, folk lyrics, sea shanties, traditional ballads, religious songs, lullabies, play games, carols and dance songs. Although, taken altogether, f.s. is a distressingly amorphous mass, certain types have distinctive formal characteristics. The European traditional ballad, the narrative department of f.s., is the most important such type and will be separately treated. Here we shall discuss only nonnarrative f.s., song that does not pretend to tell a story.

Primitively, f.s. was poetry, music, and dance all in one, but since the Middle Ages, the bulk of f.s. has ceased to be danced. Some folk songs have even lost their musical dimension; longer pieces, especially, began long ago to be recited instead of sung. But music remains an important part of f.s., though it is music of a simple kind. Harmony occurs rarely in f.s. and is suspect when it does. Polyphonic singing, however, sometimes implicating as many as four voice lines, is highly cultivated by Slavic singers, particularly the Russians. But it is in tonal organization that folk music differs most widely from art music. Some of the finest European folk tunes are based on the modal scales (Aeolian, Mixolydian, Dorian, etc.) of medieval church music rather than on the modern major and minor scales. Unfortunately, the early collectors did not understand the modal system and consequently tortured the tunes into the modern system—with deplorable results. Many of Thomas Moore's *Irish Melodies* are spoiled for just this reason. As to performance, modern concert singers usually accompany themselves; authentically the folk singer seldom does, but sings without instrumental accompaniment or is accompanied by someone else. Choral accompaniment by voice, by a chorus of whistlers or by handclapping and foot-stomping may also figure in a folk performance. In England the most elaborate type of f.s. musically is the round. Here the singers divide themselves into three or four groups, each of which begins the melody at staggered intervals, as in the nursery song *Row, row, row your boat. Sumer is a cumen in,* a round preserved in a 13th-c. manuscript, is considered the oldest extant Eng. f.s.

F.s. flourishes best in the backwaters of civilization, in illiterate communities where class distinctions are vague and where people are racially homogeneous. Illiteracy is the prime condition, for f.s. substitutes for literary expression among people without letters. A song may have been originally composed by an individual, but it does not become f.s. until it is adopted by the folk and re-created communally. Thus f.s. is never self-conscious, since it is a collective creation expressing representative feelings. The style reflects the way the song has come into being and is transmitted. The sophisticated poet's main research is to find the peculiar figure or the unique phrase that will project imaginatively what he sees and feels; the f.s. employs stock figures and formulaic phrases, and the arresting and magically poetic effects achieved in f.s. are the successes of the conventions and not the result of painstaking artistic calculations. Because f.s. is sung, the verses have a melodic fluency about them. Short meters are characteristic. And because folk poetry is carried in memory, the songs are free of unnecessary complication.

For the same reason, various kinds of repetition are employed for mnemonic purposes. Since the songs are the possession of the folk, they naturally reflect the naïveté and directness of those who have created and cherished them.

In the late Middle Ages, folk and literary poetry were less widely estranged than they have been since that period; nevertheless, folk songs were only sporadically recorded in manuscripts. The greater part of the national repositories were contributed by collectors who, beginning in the 1790's, scoured out-of-the-way rural districts for traces of traditional song. These basic field collections were usually published as the f.s. of a given principality (Germany), province (France), shire (Britain) state or region (America) since the sponsors were local antiquarian and folklore societies. The divisions thus established are largely artificial; folk songs do not observe political boundaries. Even the provincial grouping of Fr. songs, by far the least artificial, is not entirely satisfactory. Normandy and Brittany are, to be sure, integral f.s. regions, but a province like Guyenne contains the *pays* of Quercy, Périgord, and Rouerge whose folk songs are interestingly distinct. Still, for convenience, scholars accept the present parochial arrangements, though this concession does not inhibit them from making blanket statements about a whole nation's or language's f.s.

A broad survey of European f.s. reveals that as one moves south the lyrical element tends to dominate the narrative. Danish songs are mainly narrative, and narrative of a peculiarly stiff and heroic kind. Germany is rich in both veins; in France the lyric predominates, as it does even more decisively in Italy. Sicily, a seminal region for It. lyric forms, is exceptional in possessing a great number of historical narratives as well. And the Sp. storysongs, the world-renowned *romances* (q.v.), are of greater aesthetic value than the vastly more numerous *coplas* (q.v.) or the *soleares* and *siguiriyos* of *cante jondo*, q.v. (deep song; Gypsy style). In traversing Europe north to south, one notes also the progressive ascendancy of assonance over rhyme. Slavic collections are remarkable for their greater quantity of nonstanzaic songs and for a generally heavier and longer basic verse. The division of parts of the Slavic repertory into men's songs and women's songs introduces a principle rarely found elsewhere in Europe.

Among the more curious genres of continental f.s. are the following: the *cloer*, the complaint of a Breton seminarian whose lovesickness makes him uncertain of his priestly vocation; the *pastourelle*, q.v. (northern France) in which a shepherdess is accosted by a lecherous gallant; the Bavarian *schnadahüpfl*, an impromptu song of one or two couplets sung traditionally by reapers; the Czech *kaledy*, a conjurer's chant; the Andalusian *saeta*, a fervent religious apostrophe addressed to an image carried in procession; the Sicilian *ciuri* (in Tuscany, *stornelli*, q.v.), short invocations to a loved one symbolized as a flower:

Flower of the palm!
In vain I fly, in vain I search for calm.
My life's gone stale since I have lost your charm; . . .

and the passionate Corsican *voceri*, keening songs at the wake of a person who has suffered a violent death. Impressive among group songs are the Hebridean waulking chants, which are shared by leader and Gaelic chorus as they knead and hand around a length of cloth that is being shrunk.

Scottish folk lyrics deal mainly with courtship and unrequited love (*Waly, Waly*) or, as in *Auld Lang Syne*, with convivial friendship. Some of Robert Burns's most esteemed lyrics— *A Red, Red Rose,* for example—are simply tidied versions of Scottish folk songs of this kind. Cryptic political ditties of Jacobite sympathies once bulked large in the Scotsman's repertory, but they are now forgotten. With the exception of the anti-Papist *Lilliburlero,* the same fate has overtaken the political songs of England. Amorous dalliance and love laments are the chief subjects of Eng. song; interspersed with them are drinking songs and humorous pieces, the latter concerned heavily with the malice and vices of incompatibly married couples. Marriage is the blissful goal of the love songs; love is seldom mentioned in songs about the married. *I Wish I Were Single Again* exists in versions for both sexes. Notable among Eng. love songs is the frequent *chanson d'aventure* opening which finds the narrator walking abroad on a May morning and overhearing the lament of a disappointed lover. In *Where Are You Going, My Pretty Young Maid?* there is a trace of the brutally realistic Fr. *pastourelles*. But only a faint trace, for the song in England has sunk to the children's level.

Importations from Britain make up the core of Am. f.s. *The Butcher Boy* and *The Cuckoo*, both tales of disappointed love, can be traced to transatlantic origins, as can *A Paper of Pins* and most other Am. courting play games. Some Am. lyrics (for example, *Who's Gonna Shoe Your Pretty Little Foot?*) are excerpts from long British ballads. Definitely of native origin are *Rye Whiskey, Old Rosin the Beau,* and a host of other drinking songs and the "interminables" like *Old Joe Clark* and the cowboy favorite *The Old Chisholm Trail,* both of which have grown innumerable additional stanzas.

Marriage remains a butt of jokes in the New World; an equally common motive for humor is exploited in the frontier songs which complain with boisterous exaggeration about the hardship of life in the raw territories. In the spirituals, religious songs written in the rhythms of secular songs rather than in those of hymnody, the folk have expressed their naive faith. There is nothing in America that compares with the chants and festival songs that have grown up in European countries around each of the holy seasons.

The Negro spirituals, though they derive from revival songs sung in white camp-meetings, have taken on a radically different musical and poetic form in Negro throats. How much of this novel rhythmic system goes back to African sources has yet to be determined. The Negro has also a rich songbag of hollers, work songs, and prisoners' laments. Negro jingles in which companionable animals figure are fairly numerous, but this sort of thing is better done in the Negro folk tales. The "blues" (q.v.) is the characteristic Negro love complaint, the depressed cry of an abandoned lover. Hardly Negro at all are such dialectical pieces as *Old Zip Coon* and *The Blue-Tail Fly*. These are rather the products of the blackface minstrels and have only a vague connection with the songs of the plantation Negroes. See BALLAD.

There is no respectable compendium of European f.s. and no single work that surveys the field. Excellent and accessible collections are: F. R. Marin, *Cantos populares españoles* (1882–83); C. Nigra, *Canti populari del Piemonte* (1888); G. Pitré, *Canti populari siciliani* (1891); L. Erk and F. Böhme, *Deutscher Liederhort* (3 v., 1893–94); C. J. Sharp, *Folk Songs of England* (1908–12); P. W. Joyce, *Old Ir. Folk Music* (1909); J. Canteloube, *Anthologie des chants populaires français* (1951). The best Am. collections are: C. J. Sharp, *Eng. Folk Songs from the Southern Appalachians* (1932); V. Randolph, *Ozark Folksongs* (1946–50); a commercial venture, J. and A. Lomax, *Am. Ballads and Folk Songs* (1934) and, recently, A. Lomax, *The Folk Songs of North America in the Eng. Language* (1960). For a critical history of f.s. study, see D. K. Wilgus, *Anglo-Am. Folksong Scholarship since 1898* (1959).

A.B.F.

FOOT. A measurable, patterned unit of poetic rhythm. The concept of the f. has been imported into modern accentual-syllabic prosody (see METER) from classical quantitative practice, and disagreement over the nature (and even the "existence") of the f. has been traditional since the late Renaissance. The Eng. f. is customarily defined by the orthodox as a measure of rhythm consisting of 1 accented (stressed, "long") syllable (or 2, as in the spondee) and 1 or more unaccented (unstressed, "short," "slack") syllables. The poetic line in a more or less regular composition, say the traditional prosodists, consists of a number of feet from 1 to 8; conventionally, the feet are to be roughly of the same kind, although metrical variations (q.v.), produced by the occasional "substitution" of different feet, are permissible so long as these substitutions do not efface for long the repeated pattern of the prevailing f.

In traditional Eng. accentual or accentual-syllabic verse (see ENG. PROSODY), the following feet are the most common:

IAMB (iambus); iambic, × / as in destróy

ANAPEST (anapaest); anapestic × × / intervéne

TROCHEE; trochaic / × tópsy

DACTYL; dactylic / × × mérrily

SPONDEE; spondaic / / ámen

PYRRHIC × × the séa | son of | místs

Iambic and anapestic feet are called ascending (q.v.) or rising feet; trochaic and dactylic, descending (q.v.) or falling. Feet of 2 syllables are called duple feet; feet of 3, triple. Spondaic (except in sprung rhythm, q.v.) and pyrrhic feet are generally "substitute" feet (see METRICAL VARIATIONS). Some prosodists recognize also a monosyllabic f. consisting of 1 stressed syllable. The exemplification of these feet by single words, above, of course distorts their nature: it is important to remember that f. divisions do not necessarily correspond to word divisions, and that the structure of a f. is determined contextually by the nature of the feet which surround it.

The f. bears a close resemblance to the musical bar: both are arbitrary and abstract units of measure which do not necessarily coincide with the phrasal units which they underlie. The major difference between them is that the bar always begins with a "stress."

It is perhaps unfortunate that the terminology of feet is borrowed from classical quantitative prosody, where practice is in general much more regular than in most Eng. verse and where "substitutions" are largely governed by rule rather than by whim or instinct. In addition to those listed above, the following feet are among those used in Gr. and L. poetry (where, of course, duration of syllables rather than stress determines "long" and "short"):

AMPHIBRACH ⌣‒⌣
ANTISPAST ⌣‒‒⌣
BACCHIUS ⌣‒‒
CHORIAMBUS ‒⌣⌣‒

CRETIC (or amphimacer) — ⌣ —
DOCHMIAC ⌣ — — ⌣ —
EPITRITE ⌣ — — — (called 1st, 2d, 3d, or 4th according to position of the short syllable)
IONIC
  a majore — — ⌣ ⌣
  a minore ⌣ ⌣ — —
MOLOSSUS — — —
PAEON — ⌣ ⌣ ⌣ (called 1st, 2d, 3d, or 4th according to the position of the long syllable)
PROCELEUSMATIC ⌣ ⌣ ⌣ ⌣
TRIBRACH ⌣ ⌣ ⌣

See PROSODY, SCANSION, METER, ENG. PROSODY, CLASSICAL PROSODY.

R. Bridges, "On the Use of Gr. Terminology in Eng. Prosody," *Milton's Prosody* (1921); Saintsbury, *Prosody;* Baum; Hamer; Koster.
P.F.

FORM in poetry, simply defined, is the manner in which a poem is composed as distinct from what the poem is about. The latter may be called the subject or the substance of the poem, its subject matter or content as distinct from its form or manner. "Form" being a term with a variety of denotations, some of them closely connected with particular systems of philosophy, poetic f. also admits of several meanings, some so divergent from each other that they are contradictory.

To take first one of the commonest meanings, the f. of a poem may be its meter, poetry being usually composed in verse. Modern alternatives to regular verse such as free verse and patterned prose would also constitute the formal element of the poem in this meaning of the term. Alternatively, the words used in the poem, its language and diction, may be considered the f., as distinct from the thought or subject matter of the poem. By extension, f. may be the style in which the composition is written. Most of these meanings are implied when one speaks of the "cult of form" or formalism in poetry, which is making art consist essentially in the skillful handling of words and phrases, verse and rhyme, style and diction. Formalists believe that the value of a poem depends exclusively on the quality of its f., in that sense. They tend to give poets advice such as Horace's to use unsparingly "the labor of the file," revising and polishing the f. until it is perfect, or the injunction from the Parnassian poet who proclaimed that "form is everything": *"Sculpte, lime, cisèle"* (T. Gautier, preface to *Mlle de Maupin,* and *L'art*). Critics of a different persuasion are apt to object that in this meaning f. "is something superficial, general, diagrammatic. We speak of empty form, mere form, formal politeness; it is opposed to the heart and soul of any-

thing, to what is essential, material, and so forth" (B. Bosanquet, *Three Lectures on Aesthetic,* 1916, p. 15).

W. P. Ker pointed out that "from another point of view, however, which is just as common, it is the scheme or argument that is the form, and the poet's very words are the matter with which it is filled. The form is not that with which you are immediately presented, or that which fills your ears when the poem is recited—it is the abstract original scheme from which the poet began. . . . If it is said that a poem is formless—Wordsworth's *Excursion,* for example—what is meant is generally that the argument is not well planned" (*Form and Style in Poetry,* p. 138). In this sense f. is the structure, tight or loose, supple or flaccid, of the whole composition, "this kind of form being in strictness neither prosaic nor poetical, but just as much the one as the other" (p. 139). This brings us to another widely accepted meaning of f., viz. genre or kind of composition. The epic, the lyric, the drama, with all their subdivisions, are said to be the forms of poetry (see GENRES). This meaning of f. as kind may derive from the ancient philosophical meaning of the term (as with Plato's *eidos*), which has been defined: "that which an object has in common with other objects is its form." Accordingly what a poem has in common with other poems—its presentation as dialogue or narrative or as personal effusion—is its f. or kind. The kind or genre is then conceived to determine the structure of the poem, which is the previous meaning of f.

On the other hand, a philosophical meaning which is practically opposite to the last may be defined as follows: "In a broad sense, whatever in the make-up of an object helps one to perceive it as a whole is its form" (V. M. Ames in V. Ferm, ed., *History of Philosophical Systems,* 1950, p. 555). This makes f. the unifying factor in the poem. In this sense we find it applied also to the novel: "Form represents the final unity of a work of fiction, the successful combining of all parts into an artful whole" (R. B. West and R. Stallman, *The Art of Modern Fiction,* 1949, p. 647). It is therefore much more than the "abstract argument" or "original scheme": it is the actual welding of all parts into a whole, the individual organization of a work so that all its constituents, however defined—words, thoughts, diction, style, or meter—cohere and harmonize. In this sense f. is often called organic f. and sharply distinguished from abstract structure, especially as determined by genre. The external and preconceived structure depending on genre is correspondingly named mechanical or abstract f. in contrast with organic. This famous dichotomy of organic vs. mechanical f. found its classical formulation in A. W. Schlegel's

Lectures on Dramatic Literature (1809–11), where the free and supple f. of Shakespearean tragedy is defended as organic, in contradistinction of the mechanical regularity imposed by the rules and unities of neoclassicism. Thus Schlegel finally solved the problem of the artistic pattern of Shakespeare's plays, which had puzzled critics throughout the 18th c. In Coleridge's felicitous translation Schlegel's formula found its way into Eng. criticism and there fructified and proliferated, until it has now become almost a commonplace, and its original author and application often forgotten. In the 20th c. the organic unity of f. and content was the subject of another classic pronouncement by A. C. Bradley in his famous inaugural lecture of 1901, "Poetry for Poetry's Sake." He formulated a dichotomy of "form and substance" and argued: "If the substance means ideas, images, and the like taken alone, and the form means the measured language taken by itself, this is a possible distinction, but it is a distinction of things not in the poem, and the value lies in neither of them. If substance and form mean anything *in* the poem, then each is involved in the other, and the question in which of them the value lies has no sense. . . . The true critic in speaking of these apart does not really think of them apart; the whole, the poetic experience, of which they are but aspects, is always in his mind; and he is always aiming at a richer, truer, more intense repetition of that experience" (pp. 16–17). Bradley then used the phrase "significant form" for the unified whole (p. 19), a phrase which shortly afterwards became the key term in Clive Bell's theory of art (1913).

This concept of f. as the result of the operation of the plastic and unifying imagination was developed by romantic criticism and aesthetics, although the concept of f. as a dynamic unifying principle is as old as Aristotle. In Book 7 of the *Metaphysics* Aristotle applied to art his ontological concept of f. determining matter, such as the idea of the statue which is the form in the mind of the sculptor and which he then imposes upon some kind of material: the resultant work is thus a synthesis of f. and matter produced by human intelligence, while living beings are a synthesis of f. and matter produced by nature. This f. might therefore be said to be organic by analogy. But unfortunately in the *Poetics* Aristotle was diverted by the Gr. conception of poetry as mimetic (see IMITATION; POETRY, THEORIES OF; and POETICS, CONCEPTIONS OF) from applying this concept of organic f. to poetry. The recognition of the relationship of the quality of Beauty to the inner f. (*éndon eidos*) was Plotinus' constructive contribution to aesthetics. From Kant onward f. assumes an epistemological significance as the active mental factor in the organization of experience from the manifold of sensations. Schiller then made poetic f. a force that controls and transforms blind impulse into the material of art: in that sense (and not in the sense of the superficial formalism mentioned above) he could say that "Art consists in the destruction of matter by form" (*Letters on Aesthetic Education* 22). On the other hand, in Hegel art is defined as the sensuous appearance of the Idea, which makes f. consist of the sensuous element and matter becomes the spiritual element or the Idea, thus showing again the polysemanticism of these terms.

The organic concept of f. and content has as its logical corollary that there is no such thing in art as the same f. with different content: alteration in one produces alteration in the other. Hence the rejection of the common concept of genre or kind as an empty form into which a separate matter is poured, as in a mold or vessel (cf. Schlegel). The ultimate consequence of this argument is the rejection, by Croce and others, of genres and kinds from the domain of criticism, f. being conceived as individual and as unique as matter, or as "the efficient equivalent" of a poem's unity (L. Abercrombie, p. 62).

The concept of Inner F. in German criticism is apparently a variant of organic f. It appears as early as 1776 in young Goethe's criticism of dramatic rules and of the unities (*Jubiläum Ausgabe*, 36.115). It has been traced back to Plotinus through Shaftesbury, and forward into romantic criticism as well as into W. von Humboldt's theory of language, which also makes use of the concept of Inner F. In the present century it has been used by the school of George in biographical studies in which the "Inner F." of a great mind has been investigated.

A. C. Bradley, *Oxford Lectures on Poetry* (1909); B. Croce, *Aesthetic,* tr. D. Ainslie (2d ed., 1922); E. Panofsky, *Idea* (1924); L. Abercrombie, *The Theory of Poetry* (1926); W. P. Ker, *F. and Style in Poetry* (1928); H. Read, *F. in Modern Poetry* (1932) and *The True Voice of Feeling* (1953); R. Schwinger, *Innere F.* (1935); O. Walzel, *Grenzen von Poesie und Unpoesie* (1937); G. McKenzie, *Organic Unity in Coleridge* (1939); H. Cherniss, "The Biographical Fashion in Lit. Crit.," *Univ. of Calif. Publications in Cl. Phil.,* 12 (1943); J. Benziger, "Organic Unity: Leibniz to Coleridge," PMLA, 66 (1951); C. La Drière, "F.," in *Dict. of World Lit.,* ed. J. T. Shipley (rev., 1953); V. M. Hamm, "The Problem of F. in Nature and the Arts," JAAC, 13 (1954); F. Schiller, *The Aesthetic Education of Man,* tr. R. Snell (1954); R. H. Fogle, "Organic F. in Am. Crit., 1840–1870," *Development of Am. Lit. Crit.,* ed. F. Stovall (1955); *Stil und*

Formprobleme in der Literatur, ed. P. Bockman (1959); P. Fussell, Jr., *Poetic Meter and Poetic Form* (1965). G.N.G.O.

FORNYRÐISLAG. An ON (Eddic) verse form consisting of a 4-line stanza, each line divided by a caesura into 2 half-lines, which in turn have 2 accented syllables and 2 (or 3) unaccented ones. The 2 half-lines are linked together by alliteration, which in case of the first-line could fall on one or the other of the stressed syllables, but in the second half-line had to fall on the first stressed syllable. The alliteration of the first half-line was called *stuðlar* (props), the one in the second half-line (*höfuðstafr* (head-stave). The alliteration, in reality an initial rhyme, consists of consonants alliterating with the same consonant, except *sk, sp,* and *st,* which could only alliterate with themselves, and of a vowel alliterating with any other vowel, as well as with j. The opening lines of the famous *Völuspá* (Sibyl's Vision) will serve as an example of the form, illustrating the metrical principles outlined above: "*H*ljóðs bið ek allar *h*elgar kindir / *m*eiri ok *m*inni *m*ögu Heimdallar." The great majority of the Eddic poems are composed in this measure, which Icelandic poets still use on occasion.—*The Poetic Edda,* tr. H. A. Bellows (1923) and tr. L. M. Hollander (1928, rev. ed. 1962). R.B.

FOUR AGES OF POETRY. Essay (1820) of about 5,500 words by Thomas Love Peacock, purporting to demonstrate the irrelevance of poetry in modern culture, and now known chiefly by title as having provoked Shelley's *Defence of Poetry.* In a witty conspectus, Peacock declares that classical Gr. and L. verse passed through ages of (1) iron, or crude primeval vigor, (2) gold, or Homeric mastery, (3) silver, or Virgilian refinement, and (4) brass, or "the second childhood of poetry." Then he forces postclassical poetry into the same cycle for the purpose of ridiculing, as exemplars of the new age of brass, "that egregious confraternity of rhymesters, . . . the Lake Poets." Wordsworth (whom he elsewhere treats with respect) is contemned not only as a silly poet, but because any new poetry is a silly pastime in the modern world, which has for its major concerns politics and philosophy and science, and for its amusement the treasures of classical poetry. The essay begins in clever gaiety and ends in jolly outrageousness; like one of the convivial parsons in his own puckish novels, Peacock pushes his argument into preposterous audacity for the sheer fun of it. Inflated praise of the contemporary giants of practical intellect, at the expense of the "drivellers and mountebanks" who still write poetry, may be taken as an ironical gibe at the idea of prog-

ress; but no serious purpose is evident. The solemn reply by his intimate friend Shelley takes a much higher tone. Richards' *Science and Poetry,* a century later, is a similarly earnest refutation of Peacock on different grounds.—See the essay in Peacock's works, ed. Brett-Smith and Jones (1934), vol. VIII, or ed. R. Garnett (1891), vol. entitled *Calidore and Miscellanea;* Shelley, *Defence of Poetry,* many printings; I. A. Richards, *Science and Poetry* (1926). F.A.D.

FOURTEENER. An Eng. meter of 7 iambic feet. See HEPTAMETER and SEPTENARY.

FREE-METRE POETRY. All metrical forms known to Eng. poetry, however strict, would be included among the "free metres" of Welsh poetry. It is a generic term for all possible metrical forms not included among the "strict-metres" (q.v.) of the Welsh professional bards, i.e., the various kinds of *awdl, cywydd,* and *englyn* (qq.v.), which in their final forms were codified by the poet Dafydd ab Edmwnd in the Carmarthen Eisteddfod (ca. 1450) as the "twenty-four metres." Rapid growth of "free-metre" poetry in Welsh is largely a consequence of the breakdown of the bardic orders and the influx of foreign influences following the social changes of the Tudor period.—Morris-Jones; Parry. D.M.L.

FREE VERSE. A term popularly, but not accurately, used to describe the poems of Walt Whitman and others whose verse is based not on the recurrence of stress accent in a regular, strictly measurable pattern, but rather on the irregular rhythmic cadence of the recurrence, with variations, of significant phrases, image patterns, and the like. F.v. treats the device of rhyme with a similar freedom and irregularity. The following quotation, from Whitman's *Song of Myself,* is fairly typical:

I celebrate myself;
And what I assume you shall assume;
For every atom belonging to me, as good belongs to you

I loaf and invite my soul;
I lean and loaf at my ease, observing a blade of summer grass.

There are two opinions about the form and Whitman's use of it. Some say that his practice is no more than rhythmical prose. Others that it has distinctively "poetic" qualities. Both of these opinions are consistent with the following addition to the definition given above in paragraph one: whenever and however, either by the agency of the eye or ear, a persistent irregularity of the metrical pattern is established in a poem, it can justly be called f.v. The irregularity involves both the eye and the ear. Whether the measure be written down with a view to the appearance of the poem on the printed page or to the sound of the words as spoken or sung is of no consequence so long as the established irregularity is maintained.

Many antecedents have been cited in the attempt to discover the origins of f.v. Gr. and L. "art prose" (cf. Norden, *Die Antike Kunstprosa*) bears obvious resemblances to the modern form, as do the medieval tropes and sequences. Alliterative verse suggests the tendency of the Germanic languages to seek forms other than traditional quantitative or accentual verse. In England, the King James translation of the Psalms and the Song of Songs, based in part on the original Hebrew cadences, provided a powerful and inspiring model for nonmetrical verse, the influence of which is evident in the work of Whitman and most of his successors. Technically, Milton's verse is regular, but its effect in *Lycidas, Paradise Lost,* and *Samson* is that of extreme freedom, a fact evident in Milton's tendency to make the verse paragraph rather than the line his basic unit. And although Fr. neoclassicists prided themselves on their regularity, certain modern theorists (Robert de Souza, Georges Lote) have demonstrated that the Fr. alexandrine is extremely irregular if scansion is based on reading rather than syllable-counting.

The neoclassic movement hindered the tendency evident in the baroque Pindaric ode to move toward f.v. Interest revived, however, as the romantic movement gained momentum. Macpherson's *Ossian Poems* are in rhythmical prose, and Christopher Smart's *Jubilate Agno* is f.v. in the tradition of the King James Psalms. In Germany Klopstock (*Messias*), Goethe (*Prometheus*), and Novalis (*Hymnen an die Nacht*) show a similar tendency. Romantic experimenters in f.v. and related forms include Blake and Arnold (f.v.); Lamb, de Quincey, and Poe (prose tending to poetry); Hölderlin, Heine, and Nietzsche (poetic prose, prose poem); Bertrand, Hugo, Baudelaire (f.v., prose poem). Toward the end of the 19th c. the Fr. symbolists had gone far toward establishing the prestige and flexibility of f.v. on the continent; while Whitman (who had influenced the symbolists through Baudelaire) and Gerard Manley Hopkins, whose "sprung rhythm" (q.v.) is a kind of mid-point between f.v. and tradition, moved toward the form in England and America.

During the 20th c. f.v. has become so common as to have some claim to being the characteristic verse form of the age. Merely listing the significant poets who have used f.v. would be a tedious and futile task, but among typical practitioners may be mentioned Rilke, Apollinaire, St.-John Perse, Eliot, Ezra Pound, and William Carlos Williams. It may be noted that the most important Eng. and Am. f.v. poets of the first half of the century were either involved in or influenced by the imagist program formulated by T. E. Hulme and Ezra Pound between roughly 1905 and 1915.

In all modern literatures f.v. has been defended as more "natural" than regular meter, and it has often, though by no means always, been described as innately "democratic" or even revolutionary. In England and America it has been argued (especially by Pound and Williams) that conventional meters, being based on analogies to Gr. and L. quantitative forms, deform the natural speech pattern. This deformity is most marked in Milton—despite the fact that Milton in some ways anticipated the effects of f.v.—and his techniques, minus his talent, helped to create the artificial diction typical of much 18th- and 19th-c. poetry. On the other hand, the Gr. and L. contour of phrase which Milton and the Elizabethans learned in the schools was capable of effects unprecedented in the colloquial idiom. That, in essence, is still the stumbling block to an easy, not to say natural, poetry in Eng.

A language or practice of speaking or writing which will not conform to rigid prosodic rules is forced to break those rules if it is to be retained in its own character. More accurately, it must adopt a new set of rules which it can obey, find another way of speaking and writing. It is the refusal of Eng. (especially Am. Eng.) to conform to standard prosody which has given rise to "f.v." However, the term can be misleading. Being an art form, verse cannot be "free" in the sense of having *no* limitations or guiding principles.

The crux of the question is measure. In f.v. the measure has been loosened to give more play to vocabulary and syntax—hence, to the mind in its excursions. The bracket of the customary foot has been expanded so that more syllables, words, or phrases can be admitted into its confines. The new unit thus created may be called the "variable foot," a term and a concept already accepted widely as a means of bringing the warring elements of freedom and discipline together. It rejects the standard of the conventionally fixed foot and suggests that measure varies with the idiom by which it is employed and the tonality of the individual poem. Thus, as in speech, the prosodic pattern is evaluated by criteria of effectiveness and expressiveness rather than mechanical syllable counts. The verse of genuine poetry can never be "free," but f.v., interpreted in terms of the variable foot, removes many artificial obstacles between the poet and the fulfillment of the laws of his design. See also VERS LIBRE.

T. S. Eliot, "Reflections on Vers Libre," *New*

Statesman, 8 (1917); A. Lowell, "The Rhythms of F.V.," *Dial*, 64 (1918) and "Walt Whitman and the New Poetry," *Yale Review*, 16 (1927); H. Monroe, *Poets and Their Art* (1926); E. Pound, *Make It New* (1934); G. W. Allen, *Am. Prosody* (1935); A. Closs, *Die freien Rhythmen in der deutschen Lyrik* (1947); Y. Winters, *In Defense of Reason* (1947); C. A. Allen, "Cadenced F.V.," CE, 9 (1948); W. C. Williams, "An Approach to the Poem," *EIE, 1947* (1948); L. Bogan, "Vers Libre and Avant-Garde," *Achievement in Am. Poetry, 1900–1950* (1951); *Discussions of Poetry*, ed. G. Hemphill (1961). w.c.w.

FRENCH POETICS. See MEDIEVAL, RENAISSANCE, BAROQUE, NEOCLASSICAL, MODERN POETICS.

FRENCH POETRY. It has been frequently claimed, e.g., by A. E. Housman in a Cambridge conversation with André Gide (1917), that there is in Fr. poetry no tradition comparable to that of England or Germany or Italy. Housman stated that between Villon and Baudelaire—for 400 years—Fr. poetry was given over to rhymed discourse in which eloquence, wit, vituperation, and pathos were present, but not poetry. Even the romantics with their abundant lyricism have been denied a place among the legitimate poets.

Gide's first answer to this challenge was to acknowledge that perhaps the Fr. as a nation do have a deficiency in lyric sentiment, but that this very deficiency accounts for the elaborate system of Fr. prosody which developed in the course of those 400 years. Strict rules of versification, acting as constraints on the poet's spontaneity, caused poetry to be looked upon in France as a difficult art form, which had been more rigorously perfected there than in other countries. In answer to Housman's second question, "After all, what is poetry?" Gide turned to a definition of Baudelaire's in notes for a preface to the *Fleurs du Mal*. "Rhythm and rhyme," Baudelaire wrote, "answer man's immortal need for monotony, symmetry, and surprise, as opposed to the vanity and danger of inspiration." This theory, whereby poetry is related to music in that its prosody springs from the deepest, most primitive part of nature, illuminates not only the entire history of Fr. poetry, but also Baudelaire's significant revolution in that history with the publication of *Les Fleurs du Mal*.

I. The earliest Fr. *lyric* poems date from the first part of the 12th c. Called *chansons de toile*, they were short poems probably accompanying needle work and tapestry weaving. In Southern France, a rich school of Prov. poetry, that of the troubadours (q.v.), flourished during the 12th c. In the north, the poets who followed them chronologically and adopted many of their forms were known as trouvères (q.v.). The best of these was Rutebeuf, a 13th-c. contemporary of St. Louis. A forerunner of Villon, he spoke directly of himself, his moral and physical sufferings, the falseness of his friends, and his unhappy marriage.

During the 14th c. the forms of the various types of poems became fixed, the most important being the ballade and the rondeau (qq.v.). Guillaume de Machaut, a canon of Rheims, practically founded a school of poetry. Eustache Deschamps, of Champagne, was perhaps the century's most fecund poet; he composed 1,500 ballades in addition to poems in all the other known genres. Alain Chartier is today most famous for his *Belle Dame sans Merci*. Charles d'Orléans is the first Fr. poet a few of whose poems are well known today, his rondeau, for example, which begins:

Le temps a laissé son manteau
De vent, de froidure et de pluye . . .

The weather has left its mantle
Of wind and cold and rain . . .

Great poetry was first created in France by François Villon from the depths of his affliction, poverty, and suffering. In his two *Testaments*, Villon illustrates the principle of Christian metaphysics that man exists by some mystery—he is unable not to exist. For Villon, as for most medieval writers, the world is only an illusion, and the one reality is his own nature. Although Villon himself had no order in his life, his poetic imagination shows that he shared his time's passion for order. This order is the two natures of man, with the supremacy of spiritual nature over temporal nature. Villon was formed not only by the genius of his race, but by the faith of his mother, of his protector, and of his age.

Dame du ciel, régente terrienne,
Emperière des infernaux palus,
Recevez-moi, votre humble chrétienne,
Que comprise soye entre vos éleus.

Lady of heaven, queen of earth,
Empress of the infernal swamps,
Receive me, your humble Christian,
That I may have my place among your elect.

At the dawn of Fr. thought, the poet knew, above all, the night of the world: war, famine, poverty. He sees himself in many of his characters, especially in the role of poverty-stricken culprit. "Le pauvre Villon" betrays coquetry and narcissism. He appears neither heroic nor stoical. He is a poor lover, or, more simply, the poor man surrounded by all the legendary heroes. He is not alone, because he under-

FRENCH POETRY

stands the greatness of the men who lived before him, who live again in him and in his memory, and who will continue living after his death. It is especially this feeling of union with what is above time that makes Villon a poet. All the themes of the 15th c. are in his work: the Virgin, death, fortune, the martyr-lover, "la Dame sans merci," the harlot, the shepherd, the malice of priests, the vanity of this world, the flight of time. And all of these themes find their purest expression in his art.

Formerly considered the wasteland of Fr. lyric poetry, the period of the *grands rhétoriqueurs*, lying roughly between Villon and Clément Marot, is now seen in its true perspective as a time of audacious formal innovations characterized by exuberance of vocabulary, syntax, prosody, and rhetoric. The *rhétoriqueurs*, especially the greatest of them, Jean Lemaire de Belges, were gifted humanists who created a pre-Renaissance of sorts and interpreted the events, customs, and ideals of their time in the light of ancient wisdom. Court poets, they were hardly refined, speaking out vehemently against contemporary abuses and endowing modern Fr. poetry with some of its earliest significant satire.

Long *narrative* epic poems, called *chansons de geste* (q.v.) and dating from the 11th and 12th c., marked the beginnings of Fr. literature. Most scholars today accept, at least in part, Joseph Bédier's thesis (*Les Légendes Épiques*) that these poems originated in churches and monasteries where the monks furnished the half-legendary, half-historical narratives glorifying their sanctuaries. The *chansons de geste* celebrating Charlemagne and the other great feudal lords form cycles of poems of which *La Chanson de Roland* is the acknowledged masterpiece. A single rearguard action is sung of as an epic battle. Historical characters are converted into stylized types: Roland the rash young warrior, Charlemagne the emperor and patriarch, Olivier the wise friend and counselor, Turpin the priest-warrior. Christianity, chivalry, and patriotism are exalted. The other two cycles comparable to the *chansons de geste* deal with Celtic material or antiquity. *Le Roman d'Alexandre* used a 12-syllable line which became the standard Fr. line (the alexandrine, q.v.). The *lais* of Marie de France are short narrative poems by the first Fr. poetess, writing at the end of the 12th c.

The most fertile narrative poet of the 12th c. was Chrétien de Troyes. The principal author of courtly romances in Fr., he drew upon the Arthurian legends of the Round Table in his effort to reconcile the earlier warlike ideals of the *chansons de geste* with the new devotion to woman—whence such characters as

Merlin, Lancelot, and Queen Guenivere. Those poets who continued Chrétien's work added poems on the Grail Legend and the story of Tristan, narrated principally by Béroul and Thomas. To the same courtly tradition may be added a charming "chante-fable," *Aucassin et Nicolette*, half prose and half poetry, alternately recited and sung, and describing the trials inflicted by destiny on two lovers before their final happiness.

The *fabliaux* (q.v.) were short comic narratives characterized by immorality and coarseness. Their humor and irony had been more fully developed in *Le Roman de Renart*, a long satirical poem written in several parts, or "branches," and probably by several poets of the 12th and 13th c. A society of animals stands for human society and presents a caricature of feudal aristocracy, clergy, and literary themes. Renart the fox symbolizes human intelligence using trickery and ruse in order to mock authority. The multiple sources of this work are to be found in fables of antiquity and European folklore.

The outstanding Fr. allegorical work of the Middle Ages is *Le Roman de la Rose*, in two separate parts, the first written by Guillaume de Lorris in the first half of the 13th c. and the second, by Jean de Meung, in the second half of the same century. Guillaume de Lorris' poem is a manual of courtly love. He was familiar with Ovid's *Art of Love* and the allegories used by the *clercs* to describe the phases of love. His work is essentially moralistic in its analysis of sentiments and shadings of sentiment. The longer part of the poem, by Jean de Meung, is composed in a far different style and spirit, the fictional element being a mere pretext for digressions on cosmology, life, religion, and morals. Encyclopedic and pedantic, this philosophical treatise is quite emancipated from theology. Nature is the key to man's rights and virtues; it is the principle of beauty, reason, and the good. This second part of *Le Roman de la Rose* is the genesis of a moral philosophy which was continued in varying degrees in the writings of Rabelais, Montaigne, Molière, and Voltaire.

The first form of *dramatic* poetry in France was the liturgical drama (*drames liturgiques*), closely connected with church ceremonies. Originally acted within the church, the dramas were then performed outside on an improvised stage. Gradually, texts became secularized. *Le Jeu de Saint Nicolas*, by Jean Bodel, at the end of the 12th c., represents the definitive form of religious theatre: a combination of miracle and farce, with many themes and accessory plots. Miracle plays (*miracles*), dealing with the intercession of the Virgin, flourished especially in the 14th c. Morality plays, satires (*soties*), and mystery plays (*mystères*) flourished in the 15th c. These last, of excessive length and demanding several days for performance, constituted a popular treatment of religious history from the Creation to the time of Saint Louis. The more purely secular comic theatre comprised the pastoral play, such as *Le Jeu de Robin et Marion,* and a more complex type, half satiric, half comic, *Le Jeu de la Feuillée,* both by Adam de La Halle (13th c.), as well as farces (15th c.). The masterpiece of the medieval comic theatre dates from the middle of the 15th c., *La Farce de Maître Pathelin.* In character development and plot, it is a full-fledged comedy, a distant ancestor of Molière's art.

II. Clément Marot (1496–1544) was a Renaissance court poet whose gift for satire was stimulated by his contacts with the law students and lawyers of Paris (*La Basoche*), with Marguerite de Navarre, the King's sister, who encouraged him, with the It. court of Ferrara (where he was able to give free expression to his religious and satiric themes), and with the court of Francis I. His satirical tone is varied and subtle rather than vehement. Although he continued medieval forms—the farcical, rambling, and sometimes obscene *coq-à-l'âne,* the *rondeaux* and *ballades*—he also practiced with forms that were to be developed especially in the 17th c.: the *épître,* a long poem written in the form of a letter addressed to someone, and the *épigramme,* a short, concise poem, usually satiric and with a sting in its tail. Marot was probably the first sonnet writer in Fr.

Marguerite de Navarre (1492–1549) was the first important Fr. woman poet. She was not a profound theologian in her religious poetry, *Les Prisons;* but she drew abundantly on Plato and the fundamental doctrines of Christian theology. She participated in all the humanistic activities of the Renaissance, in philosophy, politics, and poetry; however, the sentiment which directed her life was her love of God and her quest and need for the Absolute.

Poetry flourished in Lyons, especially during the reign of Francis I. The one subject of the three elegies and the twenty-four sonnets of Louise Labé (1526–66) is love, carnal love. In the 500 lines comprising her poetic output, she expresses vibrantly the causes and symptoms of her suffering without psychological subtleties. She had obviously read Petrarch, but never plagiarized his text. She is far less complicated than Maurice Scève (1511–64), both in form and sentiment. Scève, too, wrote against a background of very conscious literary and philosophical enthusiasms. Platonism and Petrarchism had been the two current fashions in Lyons ever since their introduction by the Florentines in the 15th c. and by Marguerite

de Navarre and her court in the early 16th c. Plato's influence is even more apparent in Marguerite's religious poetry than in Scève's *Délie.* Platonism, as taught in Italy in the 15th c., especially by Marsilio Ficino, had taken on in France the amplitude of a movement of ideas when, in Paris and in Lyons, Ficino became one of Marguerite's favorites. Scève was probably presented to her when she stopped in Lyons between April and July 1536. The title of Scève's work, *Délie,* is an anagram of the word, "l'idée," but it is also the fictitious name given to the lady whom Scève loved and with whom all the 449 *dizains* (or poems of 10 lines) are concerned. Since each of the *dizains* relates one aspect or moment of the same experience, the work possesses an organic composition. Many of the *dizains* follow the tradition of describing the particular beauties of Délie's countenance and body. But in the far more striking *dizains* where Scève analyzes the impossibility of being loved as he loves, he describes a progressive self-knowledge and self-torment which give the work its profoundest unity. The end of the long sequence of poems apostrophizes death, not as a union with the beloved, but as a liberation from amorous torment. The absence of any religious philosophy gives Scève's psychology a relentless terror and bareness, which is not at all characteristic of the Middle Ages and the Renaissance, but rather annunciatory of the modern period.

The seven poets known as *La Pléiade* represent the most spectacular triumph of Fr. poetry in the Renaissance. Some of their poetry is of a springlike tenderness and hopefulness, despite their awareness of life's uncertainties and the destruction of sentiment and beauty that the passing of time brings. Their art is a union of mythology and nature—a combination of pedantic constructs and simple, heartfelt popular poetry. Rivers, woods, roses, dew, and nymphs are everywhere in their verses, forming the natural setting for the serious themes of happiness, love, and death. Pierre de Ronsard (1524–85), the greatest poet of the *Pléiade,* left a long and varied work. His sonnets, *Les Amours,* have immortalized three women: Cassandre, Marie, Hélène: "Quand vous serez bien vieille, au soir, à la chandelle, / Assise auprès du feu, dévidant et filant, / Direz chantant mes vers, en vous esmerveillant: / Ronsard me célébroit du temps que j'estois belle" (When you are old, in the evening, by candlelight, Seated near the fire, unwinding and spinning, You will say reciting my verses and marvelling at them: Ronsard sang of me when I was beautiful). His *Odes* and *Hymnes* made him the most celebrated poet in Europe. Ronsard demanded for the poet the highest position, that of *vates,* of a glory similar to the hero's. The earlier poets had had a sense of professional honor; Villon had been a conscientious writer, as was Scève, with a sense of higher worldly position. But Ronsard instituted the doctrine of poetic *gloire,* a gift which the poet can bequeath and sell. In 1549, Joachim du Bellay (1525–60), the second most important member of the *Pléiade,* drew up the new poets' program and beliefs in the *Défense et Illustration de la langue française.* Although Du Bellay treated the ancients with almost fanatical respect, his treatise's chief purpose was to prove that the Fr. language was equal in dignity to Gr. and L. He advised a complete break with medieval tradition and the imitation of classical genres: tragedies and comedies, for example, should supplant the *mystères* and *miracles* of the "Gothic" period. Du Bellay was to a certain extent responsible, in *L'Olive* (1549), for the love sonnet which was to have such success in the 16th and 17th c. and, in *Les Antiquités de Rome* and *Les Regrets* (1558–59), for the satiriç sonnet.

Agrippa d'Aubigné (1550–1630) was a prophet-poet as well as a soldier and memorialist. His *Tragiques* are as strongly a satiric work as Hugo's *Châtiments.* They testify to his Calvinist faith and demonstrate a close application of Holy Scripture to the accidents of mortal existence, to the predestined significance of seeming chance happenings. The 7 books composing *Les Tragiques* describe France in a state of civil war. They denounce the Valois princes, the chambers of justice, and the holocausts of the century and reflect all the latter's styles and beliefs: something of Ronsard's sensitive lyricism; a humanistic understanding of man, to a stronger degree; a biblical and apocalyptic interpretation of the day, to an overwhelming degree.

III. The 20th c. has witnessed the rehabilitation of the baroque poets who, from Ronsard's decline to Boileau's rise, enriched Fr. poetry with themes and forms (largely of It. origin) running counter to the then-shaping classical tradition. Jean de Sponde and Aubigné in the 16th c. and Malherbe himself (in a youthful folly, *Les Larmes de Saint-Pierre*), Théophile de Viau, Saint-Amant, and Tristan L'Hermite in the 17th were the chief representatives of a movement that turned one current of Fr. poetry into a contest with the indefinable, strangely mingling religious and profane elements, building up tensions, piling up images, and torturing syntax. By the unfinished ("open") character of their poems, their deliberate striving for obscure, bizarre effects, and their stretching of one image over several stanzas or an entire poem, these solitary geniuses differed from the 17th-c. *précieux* poets, who wrote polished verse filled with discreet allusions, witty epigrams, and short metaphors for a well-defined, aristocratic audience.

The influence of François de Malherbe (1555–1628) dominated poetic matters in the first half of the 17th c. His work as grammarian, poet, and critic helped to define the precepts of a Fr. art which was to be called "classical" and which occupies the central place in the history of Fr. culture. In a celebrated passage of his *Art Poétique,* Boileau was later to hail the advent of Malherbe's authority in all things poetical: "Enfin Malherbe vint . . ." (At last Malherbe appeared). He was the first craftsman in the history of Fr. poetry who discussed analytically, even pontifically, the rules of his craft. He denounced erudition in poetry and the unrestrained outburst of lyricism. He purified the Fr. language by narrowing its range and making it capable of enunciating truths rather than personal passions. Ronsard and the other *Pléiade* poets had insisted on loftiness of theme and diction. Malherbe was the first to claim ordinary speech for poetry.

The tendencies toward bombast (*emphase*) and preciosity which had developed during the 16th and early 17th c., largely because of It. and Sp. models, were opposed by Boileau (1636–1711), whose authority was strong under the reign of Louis XIV. He was a bourgeois of Paris, like Molière and Voltaire, and thus interrupted the central tradition of Fr. literature, which before his day had been largely aristocratic. Boileau, Molière, and Pascal, in their critical attitudes, represented a strong reaction against the spirit and the *précieux* poetry of the *salons* and *ruelles.* Boileau attacked the pedantry of Chapelain and the Fr. imitation of It. models. He was backed by La Fontaine, Racine, and Molière, and eventually won over to his side the public and the King himself. Imitation of nature is the highest rule for Boileau: "Que la nature donc soit notre étude unique." (Let nature be our one study.) But this imitation must be carried on rationally, and only insofar as nature conforms to itself, only insofar as it is universal. Hence, the law of the three unities is applicable in tragedy because it is natural and reasonable. Preciosity, which in poetry emphasized overrefined sentiment and periphrastic ornamental language, should be condemned because it is unnatural to obscure willfully one's thought by language. An artist as well as a bourgeois, Boileau was also a craftsman and a painstaking theorist.

The critic Faguet claimed that a century of Fr. poetry came to a close with Jean de La Fontaine (1621–95). Eclectic in the choice of his masters (he owed allegiance to Villon, Marot, and Voiture, as well as to Boccaccio and Rabelais), he converted his imitations into an art that is very much his own. His care for technical perfection he owes as theory to Malherbe, but the works themselves, *Adonis,* for example, and *Psyché,* long narrative poems, and his *Contes,* are triumphs in poetic grace, melody, and sentiment. La Fontaine recreated the genre of the fable, writing what he himself called "the one hundred act comedy whose stage set is the universe." Scenes, characterizations, dialogues are all struck off with remarkable clarity and concentration. Each fable is a dramatization. The moral value of his teaching has been often questioned, but the poems themselves appear as original creations, thanks to La Fontaine's psychological penetration and his subtle, varied use of free verse. The final lines of *Les Deux Pigeons* illustrate this art of nuance and sentiment: "Amants, heureux amants, voulez-vous voyager? / Que ce soit aux rives prochaines. / Soyez-vous l'un à l'autre un monde toujours beau, / Toujours divers, toujours nouveau" (Lovers, happy lovers, do you want to travel? Do not go very far. Be for each other a world always beautiful, always different, always new).

Pierre Corneille (1606–84) was the first poet to apply with any lasting success the principle of the three unities to Fr. tragedy. He was a major pioneer in classical art. His poetry is vigorous but tends toward the bombastic. His language seems today somewhat archaic and oratorical, but he did master the alexandrine verse. His poetic style has clarity and precision and a strong sense of rhythm. The poetry of his best tragedies, *Le Cid, Horace, Cinna, Polyeucte,* is a poetry of action and an intellectual language describing the feelings and dilemmas of the characters.

Jean Racine (1639–99) holds a high place among the religious poets of France. His choruses from *Athalie* and *Esther,* as well as his four *Cantiques Spirituels,* testify to a remarkable lyric perfection. The achievement of Racine as dramatist is due in part to his theory of tragic action and to his penetration as psychologist, but in part also to his poetic gifts, the elegance of his expression, and the magic of his style. Racine's particular triumph is in the fusion of meaning and music, of tragic sentiment and the pure sound of his alexandrine line. The prestige of poetic language is fully present in such totally simple, yet meaningful, lines as

Retournez, retournez à la fille d'Hélène
(*Andromaque*)
La fille de Minos et de Pasiphaé
(*Phèdre*)
Que le jour recommence et que le jour finisse,
Sans que jamais Titus puisse voir Bérénice.
(*Bérénice*)

Racine was trained in the school of the *précieux;* and there are elements of preciosity

throughout his tragedies. But on the whole he rejected superfluous ornaments and excluded unusual words from his vocabulary. When the occasion calls for it, Racine can write lines as vibrantly eloquent as Corneille's. Fr. poetry was not to know again such human poignancy and such artistic simplicity and dramatic meaning until the publication of Baudelaire's poetry in the 19th c.

Several of the major comedies of Molière (1622–73) were written in verse: *L'Ecole des Femmes, Le Tartuffe, Le Misanthrope, Amphitryon, Les Femmes Savantes,* etc. As Racine did in the case of tragedy, Molière, in his treatment of comedy, fused language with situation and poetry with characterization. Molière's language is at all times vigorous, varied, and colorful. He knew the language of the people, the bourgeoisie, and the *précieux.* In the high comedies, composed in alexandrines, one has the impression of listening to conversation, and at the same time, to something more substantial, thanks to the skillful sentence organization, the lilt of the rhythm, and the resounding rhymes. Molière's style is purely theatrical—the dramatic suitability of the poetic expression was his guiding rule.

IV. The richest periods for lyric poetry in France were, first, the 16th c., when a renaissance of spring abundance had favored the delicate, witty songs of Marot, the sadder, more metaphysical verse of Labé and Scève, and the full maturity of the *Pléiade* poets; and, secondly, the 19th c., with its three so-called schools of poetry: romantic, parnassian, and symbolist, which are but three aspects of a single development in modern art and sensitivity and which continued in the major poets of the 20th c.

In the two intervening centuries, lyric poetry had been subdued or lost in other forms of writing. During the 17th c., the lyric genius was always subordinated to the dramatic genius. The drama of Racine's poetry had been prepared by almost 200 years of lyric poetry, from Villon at the end of the Hundred Years' War to the advent of Louis XIV. The effusiveness and facility of lyric verse, which are its constant dangers, had been chastened and channelled in the tragedies of *Andromaque* and *Phèdre,* as, in the 19th c., the expansiveness of romantic verse would be chastised by the strict form of the Parnassians and by the severe experience of the symbol in Mallarmé's poetry. During the 18th c., the poetic genius was taken over by the philosophers, and the exploration of self gave way to the explorations of society and of the universe. In the wake of many versifiers, André Chénier (1762–94) appeared at the end of the 18th c. as its one legitimate poet. Before his execution by the guillotine, he wrote his prison poems, *Les Iambes,* a work which in satiric force and vituperation takes its place beside d'Aubigné's *Tragiques* and Victor Hugo's *Châtiments.*

The form of poetic tragedy perfected by Racine declined rapidly. In the 18th c., it became a conventional, weak genre. Voltaire alone showed some competence in his imitation of Racine. The style of *Zaïre,* for example, has a classical clarity but is lacking in strong characterization. Voltaire tried all forms of poetry. His epic *La Henriade* celebrates the religious wars and the advent of Henri IV. His philosophical poems, epistles, and satires were more successful, yet they are lacking in any real sensitivity. His short poems, *pièces de circonstance,* are perhaps his best in their elegance and wit.

The major poetic work of the 18th c. was, paradoxically, written in prose. Its author, Jean-Jacques Rousseau, was certainly concerned with ideas, but he felt them as a poet might, and he succeeded in transmitting them to the romantic poets of the 19th c. Passages from all Rousseau's writings, but especially his last book, *Rêveries d'un Promeneur Solitaire,* fixed the characteristics of the romantic temperament and gave the first fevers to a malady which was to deepen during the next hundred years. Jean-Jacques preached that man's oneness with nature was a state to be recaptured. The first stage of the new lyricism was one of "rêverie"; and it was largely narcissistic. With Chateaubriand's *René* (in poetic prose) at the turn of the century and during the first decade of romantic poetry (1820–30), Rousseauistic rêverie underwent an important modification. Nature continued to be the fountain of Narcissus for the romantic hero, but the traits he saw reflected in it were no longer peaceful. His dissatisfaction, vague nostalgia, tearfulness, and even sorrow had changed the visage of the self-seeking and self-reflected hero.

Lamartine (1790–1869) in his *Méditations Poétiques* of 1820, expressed this new sensibility in his constant wanderings through all the sites of nature and in his efforts to capture moments of the past when he had experienced happiness. For Lamartine, the resurrection of his memory was that of happiness and even ecstasy; his belief in the future, although indistinct, was formed in hope and optimism. It was only the terrible present for which he felt no genius. The state of disillusionment reached its most bitter expression in the verse of Alfred de Vigny (1797–1863). To the disappointment which Lamartine felt in the flux of time, Vigny added an attack on the infidelity of woman and nature herself and on the religions of the world as beneficent lies. The early romantic disillusionment thus culminated with him in undisguised pessimism. He was an uneven poet, but a forceful thinker. To his innate pessimism, Vigny opposed stoicism and a philosophy founded on work and intellection. Coldness and aloofness characterized his attitude, as well as a nobility of thought akin to that of the ancients. Although Vigny did not believe in the ultimate salvation of mankind, he did believe in the greatness of effort, the majesty of human suffering, and the achievements of philosophers and scientists: "J'aime la majesté des souffrances humaines" (I love the majesty of human suffering). The impertinence and facility of Alfred de Musset's (1810–57) early poems changed after tragic experience with George Sand. The "enfant terrible" of the early romantics became in his *Nuits* "un enfant du siècle," the type of the suffering poet and the victim of what has been called *pélicanisme* in accordance with the poet's own interpretation of the pelican symbol in *La Nuit de Mai.*

The position of Victor Hugo (1802–85) in the development of 19th-c. poetry is extraordinarily important. He played a preponderant part in the gradually increasing violence of the romantic malady by the very vigor of his character and his verse. His first volumes (*Odes et Ballades* and *Les Orientales*) were roughly contemporary with the first of Lamartine and Vigny, and his last volumes (*La Légende des Siècles* and *La Fin de Satan*) came at the time of Baudelaire and Mallarmé. During this long career, which encompassed the other more significantly brief careers of Nerval, Baudelaire, Lautréamont, Rimbaud, and Mallarmé, Hugo's philosophy or, more explicitly, his cosmology developed into a form of pantheism which is the source of his best poetry. After being a mirror for narcissistic Rousseau, a site for the anguished wanderings of Chateaubriand and Lamartine, and a distant, unconsoling splendor for Vigny, nature was sometimes raised by Victor Hugo to a level of religious significance: "J'étais seul près des flots, par une nuit d'étoiles. / Pas un nuage aux cieux, sur les mers pas de voiles; / Mes yeux plongeaient plus loin que le monde réel" (I was alone near the waves, during a starry night. Not a cloud in the heaven, on the sea no sail. My eyes saw farther than the real world). External nature, of which man is but one element, was for him a multiform manifestation of occult forces and divinity. A peculiar interpretation of the Old Testament and the Kabbala led Hugo to believe that the animation of nature, when it should be realized, would in turn animate man and solve his problems. Some of Hugo's dramas were written in verse: *Hernani, Ruy Blas, Les Burgraves,* etc. Their value is more in their lyricism than in their dramatic or psychological conceptions. There are many bravura passages, love dialogues, and meditations in which the dramatist is essentially a poet. (At the end of the century, in 1897, *Cyrano de Bergerac* by Edmond Rostand would represent a return to the early romantic drama. It had in its poetry many of the elements of Hugo's plays: heroism, grace, bombast, wit. The play had a tremendous success at a time when the naturalistic theatre was flourishing.)

Théophile Gautier (1811–72) defined in his poem *L'Art* some of the principal tenets of the parnassian school which grew up in opposition to the excessive subjectivity of romantic poetry. Art, he claims, finds its justification in its own intrinsic beauty and not in its relevance to morality or philosophy. Art alone has eternity, and especially that kind of art whose form is difficult to achieve. This doctrine of "art for art's sake" was believed in by Hérédia and Leconte de Lisle. Traces of the same convictions are visible in the poems of Baudelaire and Mallarmé.

Hugo's pantheism had represented a moment in the history of man's hope and religious illumination. The prose and poetry of Charles Baudelaire (1821–67) holds out the hope of magic in nature. Baudelaire was the greatest poet of the second half of the 19th c., in the sense that *Les Fleurs du Mal* (1857) was the richest source of creativeness, being both an achievement in art and a criticism for art. (Similarly, Rimbaud was to be the greatest poet for the first forty years of the 20th c., in the sense that *Les Illuminations* and *Une Saison en Enfer* are the two guiding psychological documents for the period and contain rhythms and images which have been preserved in some of the new European and Am. art.) Baudelaire's significance lies not solely in his conception of nature as the source of sensations and the key to the world of the spirit. It lies even more preeminently in his despair over inertia and acedia, in his despair over his lack of despair which prevented him from willing not to sin. Hope in nature, in the whole created universe as the reflection of some half-experienced sense of unity or Divine Love on the one hand, and on the other, the incapacity to feel deeply enough the infractions against the laws of man and God in order to cease perpetrating the infractions, are the two aspects of Baudelaire's art, which he calls the *idéal* and the *spleen*. This new definition of man's basic dualism and struggle with the forces of good and evil springs from the sensitivity of the 19th-c. artist. Baudelairian "idéal" was yet another expression of romantic exoticism and Hugo's hope in nature. It was the need to go to the most distant, and therefore the most purifying, parts of the world, to scenes different from the familiar, where the heart of man could be itself unashamedly in all of its fathomless innocence. Likewise, Baudelairian "spleen" was still another expression of romantic introspection and Vigny's pessimism: "Pluviôse, irrité contre la ville entière, / De son urne à grands flots verse un froid ténébreux / Aux pâles habitants du voisin cimetière / Et la mortalité sur les faubourgs brumeux" (November, angry with the whole city, from its urn pours out a dark cold over the pale inhabitants of the nearby cemetery and mortality over the foggy suburbs). Spleen was the poet's incapacity to move out from himself, to disengage his spirit from the center of his dilemma, from the center of his body which had been enslaved. It was the poet's velleity and ennui which, even if they are absences and negations, may grow to uncontrollable proportions. "Idéal" in Baudelaire is often translated by the image of a sea-voyage, by *L'Invitation au Voyage;* and "spleen" is often translated by the image of a closed room or cell, by a closed brain or a closed body. "Idéal" is the desire to move and to be free. "Spleen" is the horror of being unable to move and of being caught in bondage.

The poems of Arthur Rimbaud (1854–91) are the first representations of his life (*Poètes de Sept Ans* and *Mémoire*) and his first visions (*Bateau Ivre*). His prose work, *Une Saison en Enfer*, is fairly devoid of visions. It is almost a retractation, an effort to understand his past and his revolt against Christianity. It is his confession of failure. The prose poems, *Les Illuminations*, are best understood as coming after *Une Saison* in a new movement of hope and almost mystical belief in himself as poet and visionary. In the earlier works, the poet had learned his language of *voyant* and something concerning the failure of living as an artist. *Les Illuminations* have behind them an experience comparable to the mystic's initiation to failure. Rimbaud's example will remain that of the poet opposing his civilization, his historical moment, and yet at the same time revealing its instability and quaking torment. He is both against his age and of it. By refusing to take time to live, he lived a century in a few years, throughout its minute phases, rushing toward the only thing that mattered to him: the absolute, the certainty of truth. He came closest to finding this absolute in his poet's vision. That was "the place and the formula" he talked of and was impatient to find, the spiritual hunt that did not end with the prey seized. Rimbaud's is the drama of modern man, by reason of its particular frenzy and precipitation; but it is also the human drama of all time, the drama of the quest for what has been lost, the unsatisfied temporal existence burning for total satisfaction and total certitude.

As early as Gérard de Nerval (1808–55), who incorporated the speculations of the 18th-c. *illuminés*, poetry had tried to be the means of intuitive communication between man and the powers beyond him. Nerval was the first to point out those regions of extreme temptation and extreme peril which have filled the vision of the major poets who have come after him.

Stéphane Mallarmé's (1842–98) lesson is the extraordinary penetration of his gaze at objects in the world and the attentive precision with which he created a world of forms and pure relationships between forms. The object in a Mallarmé poem is endowed with a force of radiation that is latent and explosive. The irises, for example, in *Prose pour des Esseintes*, have reached a "purity" from which every facile meaning has been eliminated. This purity is their power to provoke the multiple responses of the most exacting readers, those who insist that an image appear in its own beauty, isolated from the rest of the world and independent of all keys and obvious explanations. Mallarmé's celebrated sonnet on the swan caught in the ice of a lake illustrates this power of a metaphor to establish a subtle relationship between two seemingly opposed objects in the world: a swan and a poet. The relationship is not stated in logical, specific terms, but is implied or suggested or evoked by the metaphor.

Le vierge, le vivace et le bel aujourd'hui
Va-t-il nous déchirer avec un coup d'aile ivre
Ce lac dur oublié que hante sous le givre
Le transparent glacier des vols qui n'ont pas fui!

Will the virginal, strong and handsome today
Tear for us with a drunken flap of his wing
This hard forgotten lake which the transparent glacier
Of flights unflown haunts under the frost!

For the role of magus and prophet for the poet, so histrionically played by Victor Hugo, was thus substituted the role of magician, incarnated not solely by Rimbaud (whose *Lettre du Voyant* of 1871 seems to be its principal manifesto), but also by Nerval and Baudelaire who preceded him, by his contemporary Mallarmé, and by his leading disciples, the 20th-c. surrealists, 30 years after his death. This concept of the poet as magician dominates most of the poetic transformations and achievements of the last century. The poet, in his subtle relationship with the mystic, rids himself of the traits of the Hugoesque prophet, as well as the vain ivory-tower attitude of a Vigny. Emphasis on the poet as a sorcerer in search of the unknown and the surreal part of his own being has also caused him to give up the poetry of love, especially the facile love poetry of a Musset.

Jules Laforgue (1860–87) has been gradually assuming a place of real importance in the history of symbolism. The first constituted group of symbolist poets were active during 1880–85. The word "decadent" has been associated with them. As opposed to the symbolists, the decadents allowed in their verse the direct transcription of emotion and phenomena. There is nothing in the later Laforgue of the grand style of romantic poetry. He is concerned with depicting the shifts and variations of feelings in scenes of the modern city. The dominant mood Laforgue expresses is one of emotional starvation and emotional inhibition. The parody of his own sensibility becomes, in Laforgue's *Moralités Légendaires*, the parody of some of the great myths of humanity. He recapitulates the stories of the masters: Shakespeare's Hamlet, Wagner's Lohengrin, Mallarmé's Pan, Flaubert's Salomé, and alters them in order to infuse new meanings. No such thing as a pure hero exists for this poet. He sees the so-called heroes as ordinary creatures and gives them the psychological characteristics of his Pierrots—nervousness, anxiety—and an ephemeral existence.

The first edition of Tristan Corbière's one book, *Les Amours Jaunes*, appeared in 1873, which was the year of Rimbaud's *Une Saison en Enfer* and Verlaine's *Romances sans Paroles*. No attention whatever was paid to these three books at that time. Corbière died two years later, at the age of thirty. Not until 1883, in Verlaine's series of essays on *Les Poètes Maudits*, was Corbière presented to the Paris public as a poet of importance. This first label of *poète maudit* (q.v.) has remained associated with his name. He refused to write poetry in accordance with traditional forms. He even refused to be a traditional bohemian. "An ocean bohemian," Laforgue once called him, since most of his life was spent in Brittany, in the towns of Morlaix and Roscoff, and since the themes of his personal suffering are mingled with the dominant theme of the sea. In many ways, Corbière was the spiritual descendent of Villon, especially in his self-disparagement. He looked upon himself as a failure, both as a man and as a poet, and he looked upon his life as a marriage with disaster. There are strong reminiscences of Baudelaire in *Les Amours Jaunes* and Baudelairian traits in Corbière's impenetrability. There are *concetti* and antitheses almost in Góngora's style and rhythmical innovations and patterns which Verlaine will develop. Corbière's control of his art is less strong than Baudelaire's or Rimbaud's; his revolt against order and convention is less metaphysical than Rimbaud's.

Mallarmé and Rimbaud are the greatest poets of the symbolist period, although, paradoxically, neither one is purely representative of the symbolist creed. To a far lesser degree, the example of Paul Verlaine (1844–96) counted also in the symbolist period. His was the poetry of the heart and pure sentiment, a tradition maintained, for example, by Francis Jammes (1868–1938), who belongs to the first generation of the 20th-c. poets. Even more isolated from the central evolution of Fr. poetry stands Charles Péguy (1873–1914), celebrated for his deeply religious poetry on Notre-Dame de Chartres and for his *Mystère de la Charité de Jeanne d'Arc* (1910).

V. Paul Valéry (1871–1945) had listened in his early twenties to Mallarmé's conversations on poetry. In his celebrated definition of symbolism, Valéry states that the new poetry is simply trying to recapture from music what belongs to it. But in the practice of so-called symbolist poetry, he revived, and adhered to, all the classical rules of prosody. If the music of language is to be rediscovered and recreated, a long process of "research" is necessary into the sounds of syllables, the meanings of words, and word phrases and their combinations. The symbol in poetry establishes a relationship between things and ourselves. It is a kind of bond uniting man with the universe. Valéry appropriates some of the oldest symbols (or myths) of the world, e.g. Narcissus and the Fates, which are the titles of two of his greatest poems. Most of the poems in *Charmes* derive their title from the leading symbol: *L'Abeille* (bee), *Palme, Au Platane* (planetree), *La Ceinture* (sash). Valéry is a singer of knowledge, of subterranean knowledge, where thought may be studied at its birth, in the intermediary stage between the subconscious and the conscious. His poems are metaphysical debates, as in the poems on Narcissus, where a veritable self-inquisition takes place: "Un grand calme m'écoute, où j'écoute l'espoir . . . / Jusque dans les secrets de la fontaine éteinte. / Jusque dans les secrets que je crains de savoir . . ." (A great calm heeds me in which I listen to hope. In the secrets of the extinguished fountain. In the secrets which I fear learning—[Extrait de *Charmes* de Paul Valéry. © Editions Gallimard 1922]). At the beginning of *La Jeune Parque*, we learn that some kind of metaphysical catastrophe has taken place; the poem develops the consequences of this catastrophe. Valéry's fame has been built upon fragments: poems, aphorisms, dialogues, brief essays. He is the supreme example of a writer indifferent to his public, detached from any need to please his public. The dialogue which he instituted with himself and with the few great writers he turned to appears with the passage of time increas-

ingly dramatic. *Eupalinos* as well as *Mon Faust* are comparable to the form of the Socratic dialogue in which the resources and agility of man's conscience are explored.

Rimbaud's importance, especially the spiritual significance of his work, was first revealed by a poet who has recently died, Paul Claudel (1868–1955). Deep within a work which seems to be composed largely of revolt and blasphemy, Claudel discovered traces of a religious drama which spoke directly to him and to which he owed his return to Catholicism. The reading of Rimbaud and the religious experience he underwent at the age of eighteen changed the world for Claudel. These were revelations whereby he saw the world as the work of God and worthy of the poet's paean of praise. This was the genesis of his great theme of Joy, the one reality for Claudel, the one requirement for the making of an artistic work. By temperament, Claudel belongs to the race of revolutionaries and conquerors, poets like d'Aubigné and Rimbaud; but he is also like Mallarmé in his will to define poetry in its essence. From Mallarmé, Claudel learned especially about the metaphor, which is the essential element in his poetics. A metaphor is a relationship between two subjects; it may even be a relationship between God and the world. The poet's role is to apprehend the metaphors which exist in the world. This means naming each object and restoring it to its rightful place in a new ordering of the universe, in a new lexicon of the world. By naming an object, the poet gives it its meaning, as God had originally done in creating the world—by naming it. The total word, or the total poem, is, therefore, the universe. Each poet bears in himself a picture of the universe, a subjective maze of images which have relationships with one another. Mallarmé had followed an instinctive quest in naming various objects and seeking to understand their metaphorical meaning; Claudel goes farther in willing this quest as if it were a religious obligation. Symbolism, under the guidance of Mallarmé, had been a spiritual way of understanding and celebrating the universe; in the art of Paul Claudel, it became a more frankly religious way of discovering, in the midst of endless variety, a secret unity. In his *Art Poétique* (1903), Claudel states that the metaphor is the logic of the new poetry, comparable to the syllogism of the older logic. Things in the world are not only objects to be known; they are means by which man is being constantly reborn. Claudel's plays are the most important poetic dramas in 20th-c. Fr. literature. They are concerned with human passion (*Partage de Midi*) and religious themes (*L'Annonce faite à Marie*). Despite the difficult style and the highly metaphorical language, these plays reveal in production a grandeur and solemnity not found in the art of any other Fr. playwright.

It was quite appropriate that Guillaume Apollinaire (1880–1918), coming after the highly self-conscious symbolist school, would, in rebellion against such artifice, seek to return to the most primitive sources of lyricism. But by his lesson of freedom, gratuitousness, and individual morality, Apollinaire prolongs the lessons of Rimbaud and Mallarmé; like them, he considers poetic activity as a secret means of knowledge—self-knowledge and world knowledge. The miracle of his poetry is the number of word surprises it contains and the abrupt appearances and disappearances of emotions and images. In his verses the great myths crowd close upon purely personal inventions. He calls upon his immediate knowledge of cities and ports, of unscrupulous *voyous* and popular songs, but speaks in the tone of a prophet and discoverer. The contrast between Apollinaire's extraordinary erudition, nourished on pornography, magic, popular literature, and encyclopedias, and his total simplicity as a song writer explains the profound irony pervading most of his poetry. Apollinaire's appearance, at the beginning of the 20th c., coincided with many new aesthetic preoccupations to which he brought his own inventiveness and speculative inquiry. His work. joined that of the poet Max Jacob and the painters Picasso, Braque, Derain, Matisse in a series of artistic fantasies that have gone far in shaping modern sensibility. A farcical, festive air presided over many of the modes of art of that time, which were given the names of cubism, fauvism, Negro art, cosmopolitanism, or erotology. Apollinaire himself was responsible for the term "surrealism." He literally became a prophet in his support of aesthetic innovations which were to become the accepted forms of the future.

Surrealism, thanks to the examples furnished by Rimbaud and Apollinaire, was to recognize that the real domain of the poet is just outside what is called the world of reason. Apollinaire had taught that the poetic act is the creative act in its fullest purity. Whatever the poet names possesses an ineffable quality; his function is precisely to explain *that*, to study what refuses to be cast into explicit language. In this way, poetry is able to restore to language something of its primitive origins and mystery. Poetry like Apollinaire's does not try to fathom the supernatural or the miraculous, but simply to state the incomprehensibleness of the ordinary and the commonplace. Every human expression Apollinaire saw became sphinxlike for him, and every word he overheard resembled a sibyl's utterance. His language has a baptismal gravity.

Nascent language, it would seem to be, rediscovering its virginity, as the poet, performing his earliest role of demiurge, calls the world to be born again by naming it.

The surrealist poets, Breton, the early Aragon, Eluard, Tzara, and Soupault prolonged the tradition of the 19th-c. *voyant*. In the wake of Baudelaire, Rimbaud, and Mallarmé, poetry continued to be for them the effort to find a lost language. The image or the metaphor is the result of a certain kind of alchemy. In symbolism, the alchemy had tried to go beyond the elaborate consciousness of symbolism to the very source of poetic imagination, to the sleep in which the myths of man are preserved. Breton (1896–) and Eluard (1895–1952), especially, have discovered (or rediscovered) the pure love of woman and sung of this love as ecstatically and vibrantly as any Ronsard. Their very intoxication with liberty seems to find an outlet in their love of woman, in their joy over their love. The human spirit's secrets were revealed to the surrealists, one after the other, in spontaneous and involuntary fashion. Their concept of woman seems to spring from the deepest part of their subconscious and to rise up to their consciousness with a primitive, almost sacred insistence. The surrealists have contributed to a rehabilitation in literature of the role of woman as the bodily and spiritual partner of man. Love is the immediate. (Eluard has entitled one of his volumes *La Vie Immédiate*.) The mystery of passion is a dialectic in which man makes an extraordinary request, but one which is clearly articulated in the most serious part of the surrealist program. In asking for the experience of passion, he asks for the resolution, or the dissolving, of the antinomy between the subject and the object, between love and death, between man and woman.

The generation of poets writing in France at the turn of the mid-century is more dramatically allied with action, with the war and the Resistance, than the earlier poets of the century. Sartre defined the new literature as being "engaged" (*la littérature engagée*), and the term applies to the poetry of this generation so directly concerned with actual circumstances and events. The lesson taught by Mallarmé that there is no such thing as immediate poetry is, however, to such a degree the central legacy of modern poetry that the younger poets pass instinctively from the immediate toward the eternal myths which are just beyond the events, the first reactions, and the first sentiments.

The greatness of Jouve (1887–) brilliantly illustrates this use of the immediate event in poetry. René Char (1906–) is one of the best poets of the south. He was a maquis captain in Provence at the end of the war and has written movingly in his poetry of his war experience. Existentialism, as a literary movement, has not developed any poets, with the possible exception of Francis Ponge, on whose work Sartre himself has written a long essay. Although Ponge was born in 1899, his first important publication was in 1942, *Le Parti Pris des Choses*, a poetic work of great rigor and objectivity, and one completely lacking in any subjective lyricism.

In private life Saint-John Perse is Alexis St. Léger Léger, born in the Fr. West Indies in 1887 and, until 1940, a Fr. diplomat and Secretary-General of Foreign Affairs. He has taken his place beside the four or five major poets of modern France: Baudelaire, Mallarmé, Rimbaud, Valéry, Claudel. Like them, his work defies any facile nomenclature of romantic or classical. Perse and the other poets whose tradition he continues represent extremes in their role of demiurge and in their traits of passivity to the cosmic forces. They are extraordinary technicians drawing upon all the known resources of their art, upon the most modern beliefs in ancient poetic wisdom, and upon the most ancient tenets still visible in symbolism and surrealism. Saint-John Perse's *Vents* (first published in 1946), as well as Rimbaud's *Illuminations* and, to some extent, Baudelaire's *Fleurs du Mal*, are among those modern works of poetry reflecting the complex degree of sensibility which man reached in the 19th c. and continues to maintain in the 20th. The meaning of the winds which blow over the face of the earth and disturb all perishable things is the subject matter of his poem. The opening words speak of the winds in quest, of oracles and maxims, and of the narrator who seeks for his poem the favor of a god. Poetry, in such a work as *Vents*, reaffirms its power and its destiny to draw upon all forms of knowledge: psychoanalysis, history, phenomenology, autobiography. It is perhaps the one art of synthesis able to show at moments of intense illumination the once-complete form of our shattered world. The long work *Amers* (Seamarks) of 1957 is about the sea, about man submitting to the sea and forming with the sea an alliance. During the course of the poem the sea becomes a part of the inner life of the poet. Just as navigators take a steeple or a cliff on the mainland as a seamark (*amer*) in their navigation, so the reader of *Amers* learns to take the marine cosmos, which is the personal universe of the poet, as a guide to the understanding of man and his work. *Chronique*, a magnificent, but shorter, poem to the glory of humanity, is the fitting summation of the poet's evolution and was chiefly responsible for his being awarded the Nobel Prize in 1960.

ANTHOLOGIES: *Poètes d'aujourd'hui*, ed.

A. van Bever et P. Léautaud (3 v., 1929); *Petite Anthologie poétique du surréalisme*, ed. G. Hugnet (1934); *Introd. à la poésie française*, ed. T. Maulnier (1939); *Anthol. de la poésie religieuse fr.*, ed. D. Aury (1943); *Anthol. de la poésie fr. moderne*, ed. V. Bastos (1945); *Anthol. de la poésie fr.*, ed. A. Gide (1945); *Anthol. de la poésie fr. depuis le surréalisme*, ed. M. Béalu (1952); *An Anthol. of Mod. Fr. Poetry*, ed. C. A. Hackett (1952); *The Poetry of France*, ed. A. M. Boase (1952); *Panorama critique de Rimbaud au surréalisme*, ed. G.-E. Clancier (1953); *Panorama critique des nouveaux poètes fr.*, ed. J. Rousselot (1953); *Poètes du 16e s.*, ed. A.-M. Schmidt (1953) ; *Fr. Poetry of the Renaissance*, ed. B. Weinberg (1954); *Anthol. de la poésie fr.*, ed. M. Arland (nouv. éd., 1956); *Mid-Century Fr. Poets*, ed. W. Fowlie (1956); *The Oxford Book of Fr. Verse. XIIIth C.-XXth C.*, chosen by St. John Lucas (2d ed., ed. P. Mansell Jones, 1957); *The Harrap Anthol. of Fr. Poetry*, ed. J. Chiari (1959); *Séquences. Anthologie permanente de poésie française contemporaine*, sous la direction littéraire de J. Nielloux, I (1959–); *Anthol. de la poésie baroque fr.*, ed. J. Rousset (2 v., 1961); *Three Centuries of Fr. Verse, 1511–1819*, ed. A. J. Steele (rev. ed., 1961); *Penguin Book of Fr. Verse* (4 v., 1958–61); *An Anthol. of Fr. Poetry from Nerval to Valéry in Eng. Tr., with Fr. Originals*, ed. A. Flores (new, rev. ed., 1962).

HISTORY AND CRITICISM: C. A. Sainte-Beuve, *Tableau de la poésie fr. au 16e s.* (2d ed., 1838); G. Paris, *La Poésie du moyen âge* (2 v., 1885–95); F. Brunetière, *L'Evolution de la poésie lyrique au 19e s.* (1894); H. Guy, *Hist. de la poésie fr. au 16e s.* (v. I, *L'Ecole des rhétoriqueurs*, 1910); Jeanroy, *Origines*; E. Faguet, *Hist. de la poésie fr. de la renaissance au romantisme* (1929–30); R. Lalou, *Vers une alchimie lyrique* (1927); Raymond; A. Beguin, *L'Ame romantique et le rêve* (1946); R. Lebègue, *La Poésie fr. de 1560 à 1630* (2 v., 1951); H. Peyre, *Connaissance de Baudelaire* (1951); J. Chiari, *Contemp. Fr. Poetry* (1952); W. Fowlie, *Mallarmé* (1953); J. Rousset, *La Littérature de l'âge baroque en France* (1953); R. Winegarten, *Fr. Lyric Poetry in the Age of Malherbe* (1954); G. Brereton, *An Introd. to the Fr. Poets* (1956); M. Gilman, *The Idea of Poetry in France* (1958); A. M. Schmidt, "Littérature de la Renaissance," *Hist. des littératures*, ed. R. Queneau, III (1958); J. Frappier. *Poésie lyrique en France au 17e et 18e s.* (1960); A. Bosquet, *Verbe et vertige* (1961). W.F.

FRENCH PROSODY. See ROMANCE PROSODY.

FRENZY. See POETIC MADNESS; INSPIRATION.

FRISIAN POETRY. Fris., the nearest continental relative of Eng., was once the speech of an independent and extensive maritime nation along the North Sea coast, but is today the language of a minority people living partly in the Netherlands and partly in Germany. It exists in three forms: East and North Fris., spoken in Germany; and West Fris., spoken in the Netherlands. Only West Fris., which now has legal status both in the schools and in the public life of Netherlands Friesland, has developed into a full-fledged literary language and *Kultursprache*.

As in the case of other Germanic peoples, literature among the Frisians began with the songs of bards celebrating the great deeds of kings and heroes. Of those early alliterative epics, none has come down to us. What has come down is a valuable body of Fris. law, and that in a form justly described as "more original and distinctive than that of any other Germanic people." This legal literature, the earliest of which dates from the 11th c., is reminiscent of the lost epics, for it not only employs such literary devices as alliteration and parallelism, but often it is also genuinely poetic in thought and feeling.

When about the year 1500 Friesland came under foreign control, Fris. lost its position as a language of law and public life. The loss of freedom ushered in a period of national passivity, and Fris. literature sank to a deplorably low level. No great poetic figure appeared on the scene until Gysbert Japicx (1603–66), an eminent Renaissance poet, who with his *Rymlerije* (Poetry), published posthumously in 1668, reestablished Fris. as a literary and cultural language. The book is divided into three parts: love lyrics, dialogues, and poetic versions of the Psalms. Japicx' love verse and dialogues are written with spontaneity and charm; his Psalms, composed later in life, testify to genuine religious emotion, but suffer somewhat from the heaviness of their baroque style.

The 18th c. saw the rise of many followers and imitators of Gysbert Japicx, as for instance Jan Althuysen (1715–63) and Dirk Lenige (1722–98). However, no outstanding poetic figure came to the fore. In the 19th c., Eeltsje Halbertsma dominated the scene. Much of his work is folk poetry inspired by German romanticism. Another outstanding figure at this time was Harmen Sytstra (1817–62), a romanticist inspired by his country's heroic past. In him there is something of a national prophet and seer. His work embodies patriotic, social, and satirical elements; it is characterized by a manly and epic quality, and reveals a desire to restore the old Germanic verse forms. The latter half of the 19th c. produced many folk poets, the most popular of whom

were Waling Dykstra (1821–1914) and Tsjibbe Gearts van der Meulen (1824–1906). Their work is, on the whole, uninspired, rationalistic, and didactic. Piter Jelles Troelstra (1860–1930), with themes centering on love, nature, and the fatherland, ushered in a second romantic period.

The 20th c. began to bring a new spirit to Fris. poetry. It was perhaps first evident from the simple and pensive verse of J. B. Schepers, but even more clearly from the work of Simke Kloosterman (1876–1938), whose poetic art is both individualistic and aristocratic. In *De wylde Fûgel* (The Wild Bird, 1932) she gives intense and passionate utterance to the longings and disillusionments of love. Rixt, the pen name of Hendrika A. van Dorssen (b. 1887) also writes verse characterized by emotional intensity. A first-rate poet at the beginning of the century was Obe Postma (1868–1963). His quiet verse is simple and unrhetorical, with no display of craftsmanship. However, it has vigor, penetration, and philosophic insight. Much of it is poetry of reminiscence; still more of it is a paean to life and the good earth. Postma was the first to use free verse in Fris. and to use it well.

The new spirit at the beginning of the century came to full expression in the Young Fris. movement, launched in 1915 and led by the young and daring nationalist Douwe Kalma (1896–1953). The movement ushered in a national resurgence and a literary renaissance. Kalma, himself a talented poet and critic, sharply denounced the mediocrity and provincialism into which Fris. letters had fallen during the 19th c. With him and his movement Friesland began to have an independent voice in European culture. Kalma's genius probably appears at its freshest in his classic *Kening Aldgillis* (King Aldgillis, 1920), an epic drama in verse. The play was later republished in abridged form in his important *Keningen fan Fryslân* (Kings of Friesland, 2 v., 1949 and 1951), a series of historical plays, in blank verse, featuring the Fris. kings and depicting the struggle between heathendom and Christianity. Kalma's lyric poetry, collected in *Dage* (Dawn, 1927) and *Sangen* (Songs, 1936) displays great technical skill and beauty of form, but its content is often unsubstantial and nebulous. His work—as well as that of his school—suffers somewhat from aestheticism and a poetic jargon leaning heavily on newly coined words and archaisms.

Among the poets of merit who had their start in the Young Fris. school are R. P. Sybesma, an excellent sonneteer; D. H. Kiestra, a poet of the soil with a vigorous talent; and J. H. Brouwer, a more conventional figure. For decades the most popular and widely read poet was Fedde Schurer (b. 1898), a versatile artist with preference for national and religious themes. His early poems show the influence of Young Fris. aestheticism; those written after 1946 are more direct, unadorned, and modern. His *Simson* (Samson, 1945), a biblical drama in verse, gained him the Gysbert Japicx Literature Prize. In 1946 he helped launch *De Tsjerne* (The Churn), a literary periodical with which most of the important names in contemporary Fris. letters are associated.

Around 1935 some of the younger poets showed signs of breaking away from the Young Fris. movement, both in spirit and in poetic diction. This was true of J. D. de Jong and Ype Poortinga but especially so of Douwe A. Tamminga (b. 1909). The latter in his *Brandaris* (Lighthouse, 1938) created his own poetic idiom, based largely on the language of the people, which he transfigured and sublimated into pure art.

Since the Second World War, poetry in Friesland has been less in the romantic and classical tradition. Much of it breathes the spirit of postwar disillusionment and cultural pessimism. Garmant N. Visser in his *Jolm* (Flotsam, 1948) gives expression to loneliness, bitterness, and emotional despair. Anne Wadman in his *Op koart Front* (On Short Front, 1946) and *Fan Tsien Wâllen* (From Ten Shores, 1946) presents poetry that is proud and independent in spirit. Though original and arresting, it is largely negative in tone, revealing youthful contempt for tradition, convention, shallowness, and sham. Sjoerd Spanninga's poetry, rich in imagery and figures of speech, is exotic and almost oriental in spirit. The verse of Martin Sikkema, Freark Dam, and Klaes Dykstra is more traditional in theme, but nonetheless of definite merit. Reimer van Tuinen has proved an impressive writer of expressionistic free verse. Among the younger poets, perhaps two deserve separate mention. They are Jan Wybenga, who in 1953 made his debut with *Amoeben* (Amoebae), a volume in a very modern, experimentalist vein (though without the usual traces of pessimism); and Tsjits Peanstra, a poetess whose more traditional collection *Underweis* (On the Way, 1955) shows both dedication and promise. Of the youngest avant-garde, now publishing in the journal *Quatrebras*, little can as yet be said. In 1961 this group of experimentalists brought out a small anthology, called *op fjouwer winen* (On Four Winds). Its verse, obscure and esoteric at times, registers a complete break with the past. Of the work represented, perhaps that of Durk van der Ploeg, Jelle de Jong, and Tjitte Piebenga (who has published two meritorious collections of his own) stands the best chance of survival.

ANTHOLOGIES: *Bloemlezing uit Oud-, Middel-* *en Nieuwfriesche Geschriften,* ed. F. Buitenrust Hettema (1887); *It Sjongende Fryslân* (1917; poetry since the 17th c.); *De nije Moarn* (1922; an anthol. of Young Fris. verse); *De Fryske Skriftekennisse fen 1897–1925* (2 v., 1928–31) and *De Fryske Skriftekennisse fen 1876–1897* (1939), all ed. D. Kalma; *Fiif en tweintich Fryske Dichters,* ed. F. Schurer (1942); *Frieslands Dichters,* ed. A. Wadman (1949; an excellent anthol. of poetry since 1880, with a valuable introd. and tr. in Dutch); *op fjouwer winen,* ed. A. R. Oostra *et al.* (1961; anthol. of young experimentalists).

HISTORY AND CRITICISM: C. Borchling, *Poesie und Humor im friesischen Recht* (1908); T. Siebs, "Gesch. der fries. Lit." in Paul's *Grundriss der germanischen Philologie* (1909); D. Kalma, *Gysbert Japiks* (1939); J. Piebenga, *Koarte Skiednis fen de Fryske Skriftekennisse* (1939, 2d ed., 1957; a valuable hist.); A. Wadman, *Kritysk Konfoai* (1951; important essays on contemp. poetry); E. H. Harris, *Lit. in Friesland* (1956; fairly good survey, with tr. *in situ,* in Eng.). B.J.F.

FROTTOLA. See BARZELLETTA.

FU. See CHINESE POETRY.

FUGITIVES, THE. A group of Southern poets and critics who met as teachers and students at Vanderbilt University, and published *The Fugitive* magazine (19 issues, from April 1922, to December 1925). Among the original members of the group were Allen Tate, John Crowe Ransom, and Donald Davidson. They were joined in 1923 by Robert Penn Warren. The Fugitives were Southern Agrarians, who stood for the South, traditionalism, and regionalism, and correspondingly in aesthetics for concreteness and particularity. They opposed the industrial big-city civilization of the North, with its liberal humanitarianism, its doctrine of progress, and its glorification of science. Allen Tate, the movement's most powerful proponent, significantly linked economic and social behavior to aesthetics and poetry. The effect of their repudiation of scientific abstractions and their preferences for concrete particularity can be interestingly traced in the poetics of John Crowe Ransom.—*The Fugitive,* ed. Walter Clyde Curry, Donald Davidson, Merrill Moore, J. C. Ransom, and others (1922–25); *Fugitives, an Anthol. of Verse* (1928); *I'll Take My Stand, the South and the Agrarian Tradition by Twelve Southerners* (1930; Ransom, Tate, *et al.*); J. M. Bradbury, *The Fugitives: A Crit. Account* (1958); D. Davidson, "The Thankless Muse and Her Fugitive Poets," SR, 66 (1958); L. S. Cowan, *The Fugitive Group: A Lit. Hist.* (1959). R.H.F.

FUROR POETICUS ("poetic madness"). The phrase, which is not classical, is perhaps a translation of the Gr. *mania* or *enthousiasmos*, which were both used for poetic inspiration. In Ficino's translation of Plato (1482) the *Ion* is given the subtitle, *De Furore Poetico*, and thereafter the term is common in L. and vernacular critical works. See POETIC MADNESS and INSPIRATION.　　　　　　　　　　　A.R.B.

FURY (L. *furia*, "rage" or "madness"). See FUROR POETICUS.

FUTURISM. The first futurist manifesto appeared in 1909, in the *Figaro*, written by the It. F. T. Marinetti who remained, until his death in 1944, the staunchest and, after the twenties, the lone member of the movement he had created. Between 1909 and 1930 the movement launched dozens of manifestoes intended to reform all the arts and most human activities, spreading from Italy to other European countries, like France, Germany,' and Russia, where it enjoyed a limited success and often merged with other artistic movements of the time like cubism and dadaism.

As the name proclaims, f. was intended as a violent rebellion against the whole tradition of the 19th c., in all aspects of life, and as an attempt to express, through the arts, the dynamic life of the 20th c. In literature the main targets of f. were the lingering sentimental traces of romanticism together with the complicated psychology of the symbolists. It appealed to the pure instinct, to the elementary passions of violence, strife, and irresponsibility. Hence it encouraged a poetry of speed, movement, color, change, achieved through verbal formulas geometrically conceived and free from any reminiscence of traditional poetry. In style, it encouraged the use of free verse and of free association of words together with the suppression of capital letters, adjectives, adverbs, punctuation, and the conjugated forms of the verb (the infinitive was the only accepted form). The typographical composition of the page was also quite elaborate: not only did futurists use different characters to signify the distinct weight of each word in the sentence, but they also added mathematical signs to indicate the various connections of the parts to the whole.

Although f. was best known in the figurative arts and in architecture, some futurist poets achieved a momentary fame, in Italy, in 1925, when an anthology of their poems, *I nuovi poeti futuristi*, was published. It contained poems by Marinetti, Carli, Settimelli, Govoni, Buzzi, etc., some of whom had also achieved a certain literary fame outside the movement. For Papini, Soffici, and Prezzolini, who had manifested an active interest in the movement at the time of *Lacerba* and *La Voce,* f. was only a short-lived experiment. A great number of artists, in all fields, who were not already settled in their ways in the first decade of this century went through the futurist experience and ended by finding their own personal way of expression. Some of the futurist experiments are reflected in the poetry of G. Apollinaire (1880–1918), Gerardo Diego, Antonio Espina, etc. In Russia the best known poet to have experimented in this direction was V. Mayakovsky (1894–1930).

F. proved to be a very profitable stimulus in the elimination of the less vital parts of literary tradition, even though its more ostentatious efforts to break with the past seem quite senseless—as, for example, the long poem by Marinetti entitled *Zang-tumb-tuuum*, or the collection of short poems by Soffici called *Bif§z+18*. If one disregards the products and the extravagant proposals of the various futurist manifestoes and considers instead the movement as a challenge offered to the young artist to revise his values, one cannot fail to understand why f. is more than a literary curiosity. See CUBO-FUTURISM; EGO-FUTURISM.

F. Flora, *Dal romanticismo al futurismo* (1925); A. Bobbio, *Le riviste fiorentine del principio del secolo, 1903–1916* (1936); E. Falqui, *Il futurismo e il novecentismo* (1953); *Piccola antologia di poeti futuristi*, ed. V. Scheinwiller (1958); R. T. Clough, *F.: The Story of a Modern Art Movement* (1961); S. Pacifici, *A Guide to Contemp. It. Lit.: From F. to Neorealism* (1962).　　　　　　　　　　R.MI.

FYRTIOTALISTERNA ("The Poets of the Forties"). A group of Swedish modernist poets of the 1940's whose work is characterized by ideological pessimism and complexity of form. The movement precipitated by the group—at its height between 1944 and 1947 when its main literary organ, *40-tal* (The Forties), came out—was novel chiefly by its breadth. The number of talented new poets was remarkably high. The leaders were Erik Lindegren (b. 1910) and Karl Vennberg (b. 1910); of the disciples one may mention Sven Alfons (b. 1918), Stig Sjödin (b. 1917), and Ragnar Thoursie (b. 1919). Intellectually, the movement was a response to the ideological crisis brought about by the positivist Uppsala philosophy of Axel Hägerström; socially and culturally, it was conditioned by the catastrophe of World War II. These factors are evident particularly in the work of Vennberg, whose collection *Halmfackla* (Straw Torch, 1944) was diagnosed by Lindegren as a "vanmaktens katharsis" (catharsis of impotence). Vennberg's poetry has been greatly influenced by Franz Kafka; it is existentialist in the sense that it is a means of confirming *Angst*. Both because of his lack of a passionate sensuality and his analytic-objective method, Vennberg could more easily become the leader of the younger poets than Lindegren, whose work, like that of Stephen Spender, is centered on imaged feeling.

Technically, the poetry of the forties utilizes all the devices of free association, condensed imagery, ambiguity, literary allusion, and abstraction made available by psychoanalysis and the practice of poets like T. S. Eliot, Dylan Thomas, the Fr. surrealists, and preceding Swedish modernists. In many of the f. the semantic dimension of poetry is less significant than the poetic syntax, which is *sui generis* and cannot be rendered in terms of prose. The internal tensions of image, feeling, and idea create a self-subsistent structure; this structure demands to be experienced by the total personality rather than to be merely understood by the rational mind. From this point of view, the movement of the forties appears a parallel to 19th-c. Phosphorism, which claimed for the imagination an independent function, equal to that of reason. Reaffirming the autonomy of the creative imagination, the achievement of f. can be considered one of the most courageous and intelligent protests against a nonhuman universe and a dehumanized science and society.—*40-talslyrik,* ed. B. Holmqvist (1951); *Svensk 40-talslyrik* (1951) ; O. Sjöstrand, "Fire svenske lyrikere," *Vinduet,* 9 (1955).   s.l.

G

GAI SABER (*gaia sciensa*). The art of composing love songs. These terms are most often used in connection with the Academy established at Toulouse in the 14th c. to instill a semblance of life into the dying Prov. lyric.—Jeanroy, I.
F.M.C.

GAITA GALLEGA. A 2-hemistich verse having marked ternary movement and a variable number of syllables, usually averaging about 10 or 11. It is primarily a Galician-Portuguese meter used in Sp. popular, rarely learned, verse. It is thought to be related to the *muiñeira,* a song to be accompanied by the bagpipe. P. Henríquez Ureña (*Versificación irregular en la poesía castellana,* 2d ed., p. 239) says: "It seems hardly necessary to note that this meter, in spite of its relationship with the 15th-c. *arte mayor,* cannot be confused with it, because, even in the most regular forms, it employs the anapestic decasyllable; moreover, the latter becomes characteristic of the new regular form."   D.C.C.

GALICIAN (OR GALLEGAN) POETRY. Spreading from the pilgrimage center of Santiago de Compostela throughout Galicia and northern Portugal, Gal.-Portuguese *cantigas* (q.v.) were among the earliest lyric poetry in the Iberian peninsula and imposed their linguistic form as a sort of *koiné* or common dialect on troubadours from non-Gal. speaking regions of Spain. Most of the secular *cantigas* are preserved in the *Cancioneiro* (song book) *da Ajuda* (mid-14th c.), *Cancioneiro da Vaticanq* (end of 15th c.), and the more extensive *Cancioneiro Colocci-Brancuti* (now *Cancioneiro da Biblioteca Nacional de Lisboa,* 16th c.). King Alfonso X is responsible for the religious *Cantigas de Santa Maria* (13th c). Some Galicians from the period of greatest brilliance, 1200–1350, are Martin Codax, Afonso Eanes de Cotón, Bernal de Bonaval, Joan (Garcia) de Guilhade, Joan Airas, Pai Gomes Charinho, Airas Nunes, Pero Garcia, and Pedro Amigo de Sevilla, plus poets from Portugal and other regions of the peninsula. The Gal.-Port. school, though employing the types of the Prov. troubadours, is most distinguished by the supposedly native *cantiga de amigo.* Possessing a metrical and verbal parallelism, these songs portray the melancholy nostalgia (*saudade* or *soidade*) of a simple maiden's lament for her absent lover. Realism in description of lowly occupations, a meeting with the lover, the mother's attitude, and the very language employed lend to this form a poignancy uncommon in Provenzalesque songs.

After the death of Port. King Diniz (1325) the old lyric declines and after 1400 Castilian begins to replace Gal. in Peninsular poetry. The bilingual *Cancionero de Baena* (1445) still contains a few Gal. poems by Macías "o Namorado" (fl. 1360–90), el Arcediano de Toro (fl. 1379–90), and Alfonso Alvarez de Villasandino (1340?–1428). Perhaps the rhymed chronicle *Poema de Alfonso Onceno* (Poem of Alfonso XI) was originally Gal., but from this time until the end of the 18th c. little other than oral literature was produced in the vernacular dialects. Diego A. Cernadas de Castro (1698–1777), "el Cura de Fruime," captures the lyrical nature and rustic language of his parishioners in bilingual occasional verse and together with Manuel Freire Castrillón (1751–

1820) represents an incipient literary "galeguidade" (Galicianism).

Romanticism inspired greater interest in and consciousness of the past of Galicia, its ancient literature, folklore and sociological characteristics. Antolín Faraldo (1823–53) defended the autonomy of Galicia and with Aurelio Aguirre (1833–58), the "Galician Espronceda," communicated youthful enthusiasm for literary regionalism. Although Nicomedes Pastor Díaz (1811–63) wrote little in Gal., he characterized the gentler, nostalgic romanticism of the "Celtic" northwest. José García Mosquera (1810–68) is remembered for his Horatian A vida do campo (Country Life), and Francisco Añón y Paz (1812–78), "el Patriarca," for patriotic odes and humorous poems. Alberto Camino (1821–61) with his sentimental, folkloristic and elegiac compositions is an important precursor of the Renacimento (renaissance) which produced the triumvirate, Rosalía de Castro, Pondal, and Curros Enríquez. This renaissance was heralded by the "Juegos Florales" (Floral Games) held in La Coruña in 1861, the winning poems of which were published in the Álbum de Caridad (1862). In the following year Rosalía de Castro published her Cantares gallegos (Gal. Songs) and in 1880 Follas novas (New Leaves). Like most compatriots, she also wrote in Castilian, but it is in Gal. that her own melancholy life, saudade for home, sympathy for the suffering of her people, sincerity and simplicity have created such genuine "folk" songs as:

> Doces galeguiños aires
> quitadoriños de penas,
> encantadores das augas,
> amantes das arboredas,
> músicas das verdes canas
> do millo das nosas veigas,
> alegres compañeiriños,
> run-run de todal-as festas;
> leváime nas vosas alas
> com' unha folliña seca.

Sweet Galician breezes,
dear banishers of sorrow,
charmers of the waters,
lovers of the groves,
music of the green stalks
of maize in our meadows,
gay little companions,
chattering away at every festival,
carry me on your wings
like a dry little leaf.

Eduardo Pondal y Abente (1835–1917) in Queixumes dos pinos (Complaints of the Pines) reveals himself as a pagan Celtic bard. The early anticlerical poems of Manuel Curros Enríquez (1851–1908) forced him to emigrate to Cuba where he shared in the morriña

("saudade") of his fellow emigrants. His Aires da miña terra (Airs of My Land, 1880) contains poetic legends, songs, and scenes from folk life. Valentín Lamas Carvajal (1849–1906) sang especially of the life of the peasantry with elegiac overtones in Espiñas, follas e frores (Thorns, Leaves and Flowers, 1875), Saudades gallegas (Longing for Galicia, 1880), and A musa das aldeas (Village Muse, 1890). Other poets active in the second half of the 19th c. are: José Pérez Ballesteros (1833–1918), most important for his 3-volume collection Cancionero popular gallego (1885–86); the humorous Enrique Labarta Pose (1863–1925); Manuel Leiras Pulpeiro (1854–1912) with his folkloristic Cantares gallegos (1911); and Manuel Lugrís Freire (1863–1940), author of Soidades (Longing, 1894).

Among contemporary poets there are broader horizons. The language, still with many characteristics of a folk speech, has become a more sophisticated instrument. Troubadour traditions, saudade, and Galicianism are still present, but many foreign poetic movements have contributed new nuances. The foremost poets of the early 20th c. are Antonio Noriega Varela (1869–1947), Ramón Cabanillas Enríquez (1876–1959), Victoriano Taibo García (b. 1885), and Gonzalo López Abente (b. 1878). Noriega is close to the previous generation in his rural, folkloristic themes, but Cabanillas reflects Sp. (-American) modernismo (q.v.) in a varied and abundant production. Taibo with great richness of vocabulary, borrowed from various dialects, is perhaps the best craftsman. The most original poet of the vanguard was Manuel Antonio (Pérez Sánchez, 1900–1928) who collaborated in the iconoclastic manifesto "Mais Alá" (Beyond, 1922) and wrote a small volume of sea poetry De catro a catro or Follas sin data dun diario de abordo (Leaves without Date from a Ship's Diary, 1928). Luis Amado Carballo (1901–27), without abandoning Gal. forms and themes, created a modern sensual pantheistic verse full of original images. Fermín Bouza Brey (b. 1901) has imitated the style of the medieval cancioneiros, and Alvaro Cunqueiro (b. 1911) likewise has much from the troubadours but is very personal. Lack of opportunities for systematic instruction in the Gal. language, for publication, and even for wide critical attention has not prevented the appearance of many active and promising young poets. Even an outsider like García Lorca was so impressed with the language and its possibilities that he published Seis poemas gallegos (Six Gal. Poems, 1935).

ANTHOLOGIES: Cancionero popular gallego, ed. J. Pérez Ballesteros (2 v., 1942; first publ. in 1886); Escolma de poesía galega (v. I, Escola medieval galego-portuguesa, 1952; v. II, A poesía dos séculos XIV a XIX, 1959, both ed.

X. M. Alvarez Blázquez; v. III, *O século XIX*, 1957; v. IV, *Os contemporáneos*, 1955, both ed. F. Fernández del Riego. Contain biogr. and critical notes.) See also CANTIGA.

HISTORY AND CRITICISM: A. Couceiro Freijomil, *Diccionario bio-bibliográfico de escritores* (3 v., 1951–54; includes Galicians writing in Sp.); F. Fernández del Riego, *Historia de la literatura gallega* (1951); B. Varela Jacomé, *Historia de la lit. gallega* (1951); R. González Alegre, *Poesía gallega contemporánea* (1954); R. Carballo Calero, *Sete poetas* (1955; appr. same ground covered in Castilian in *Aportaciones a la lit. gallega contemporánea*, 1955); J. L. Varela, *Poesía y restauración cultural de Galicia en el siglo XIX* (1958).   L.A.S.

GALLIAMB(US). This meter was associated in antiquity with the worship of Cybele, the Magna Mater or great mother-goddess. It derived its name from her priests, the Galli, and was adopted by Callimachus and his contemporaries in the Alexandrian period. In L. its most celebrated occurrence is in the Attis poem of Catullus (no. 63). Technically described as ionic tetrameter catalectic (4 ionic feet with suppression of the final syllable), it had diaeresis regularly after the second foot and was used by Catullus with anaclasis, resolutions (particularly of the penultimate long syllable in the theoretical scheme of pure minor ionics as the components of this meter: ◡◡−−|◡◡−−‖◡◡−−|◡◡−), and contractions. Catullus' poem is full of such variations and verse 54 is unique in beginning with 2 pure minor ionics:

ĕt ĕar(um) ōmnĭ(a) ădīrem‖furĭbundă lătĭbŭlā

Verse 1 is more typical with anaclasis (q.v.) in its first and resolution (q.v.) in its second half:

sŭpĕr āltă vĕctŭs Āttīs‖cĕlĕrī rătĕ mărĭā

J. P. Postgate, *Prosodia Latina* (1923); Kolář; Koster; Crusius.   R.J.G.

GAUCHO POETRY. Taken literally, G. poetry is the name for poetic compositions, anonymous or otherwise, which deal with the life and adventures of the Argentinean cowboy. It would be a mistake to apply the same denomination to all popular poetry produced in Sp. America.

Popular poetry, which had its origin in the Sp. *Romancero*, flourished at the end of the 18th c. and reached its peak by the middle of the 19th c. In Uruguay and Argentina, learned writers invaded the field of folk poetry and produced a number of compositions imitating the style of early *Payadores*, or singers of popular poetry. The first of these poets, in chronological order, was the Uruguayan Bartolomé

Hidalgo (1788–1822), whose famous dialogues expressed the sentiments of the G. in regard to the war of independence against Spain. He was followed by the Argentine Hilario Ascasubi (1807–1875), who played an active role in the struggle against the dictatorship of Rosas and who published a number of G. ballads dealing with the siege of Montevideo (*Paulino Lucero o los gauchos del Río de la Plata, cantando y combatiendo contra los tiranos de las repúblicas Argentina y Oriental del Uruguay, 1839–1851*). *Santos Vega, o los mellizos de la Flor* (1851, 1872), his greatest achievement in this type of poetry, tells the story of two brothers, one of whom becomes an outlaw. The main value of the poem resides in its accurate and colorful description of country and city life in Argentina at the middle of the 19th c. Estanislao del Campo (1834–1880) followed the example of these writers and employed pure G. dialect in his *Fausto* (1866), a parody of Gounod's opera.

The greatest of the G. poems is *Martín Fierro* (1872, 1879) by the Argentine José Hernández (1834–86). A well-educated man and a writer deeply conscious of his social mission, Hernández set out to prove the moral fortitude of the G. and his right to gain a respectable position in the life of his country. Dealing with the problem of civilization and barbarism in the Am. continent he criticized the defenders of "civilization" for their irresponsibility in ruthlessly destroying the traditions of native populations, especially in the case of the nomad Gauchos. He praised the stoicism of the Sp.-Am. peasants, and with true romantic spirit he envisioned the birth of a new way of life from their epic fight in the midst of a wild continent. Encouraged by the success of his poem Hernández wrote a second part (1879) in which he told of Martín Fierro's return from the Indian country where he had sought refuge from persecution by the city authorities. The tone of this continuation is no longer rebellious but moderately didactic. Hernández' poem owes its immense popularity in Sp. America to its virile exaltation of freedom and courage, to its forceful display of nationalism, popular wisdom, and pride in the virtues of people who hold fast to the tradition of their fatherland. The critics of yesterday and today are unanimous in considering *Martín Fierro* the highest expression of popular poetry in Sp. America.

At the present time G. poetry is going through a period of stagnation. The same may be said about popular poetry in general throughout Sp. America. Scholars and students of the subject are busy organizing and editing the production of past years.

ANTHOLOGIES: *The G. Martín Fierro*, tr. W. Owen (1935); *Poetas gauchescos: Hidalgo,*

Ascasubi, del Campo, ed. E. Tiscornia (1940);
La poesia gauchesca en lengua culta [por] R.
Obligado (1943); *Poesia gauchesca*, ed. J. L.
Borges and A. Bioy Casares (2 v., 1955).

HISTORY AND CRITICISM: M. W. Nichols, *The
G.: Cattle Hunter, Cavalryman, Ideal of Ro-
mance* (1942); A. Torres-Rioseco, *The Epic
of Latin Am. Lit.* (1946); E. Larocque Tinker,
G. Lit. of Argentina and Uruguay (1961).
F.A.

GENIUS. See INSPIRATION.

GENRES. The theory of g. in Western poetics
originates from a distinction made by Plato
between two possible modes of reproducing an
object, thing, or person: (1) by description
(i.e., by portraying it by means of words) or
(2) by mimicry (i.e., by imitating it). Since poetry according to the mimetic theory (see
IMITATION; POETRY, THEORIES OF and POETICS,
CONCEPTIONS OF) was conceived as such a reproduction of external objects, these two modes
became the main divisions of poetry: dramatic
poetry or the theatre was direct imitation or
mimicry of persons, and narrative poetry or
the epic was the portrayal or description of
human actions. And as this crude division obviously left out too much, a third division was
inserted between the two others (*Republic*
3.392 d): the so-called mixed mode, in which
narrative alternates with dialogue, as is usually
the case of epic poetry which is rarely pure,
unadulterated narrative. But no new principle
of classification was thereby introduced, so
no room was left for the genre of self-expression or the lyric, in which the poet expresses
directly his own thoughts and feelings. Such
a subjective point of view was outside the
purely extrinsic and objective scheme used
for the nonce by Plato, and taken up later
by Aristotle in the *Poetics*, ch. 3, where it becomes the foundation of his main classification
of poetic g. No express recognition of the
lyric genre is to be found there, much less
in his statement that in the second of these
g. the poet "speaks in his own person": that
is merely Aristotle's way of saying that the
narrative is the poet's own discourse and not
a speech by a fictitious character of drama.
So the traditional triple division of poetic g.
or kinds into the epic, the drama, and the
lyric, far from being a "natural" division first
discovered by the Gr. genius, is, it appears, not
to be found in the creative age that preceded
Aristotle or in Aristotle himself. It was rather
the result of a long and tedious process of
compilation and adjustment, through the repetition with slight variations of certain traditional lists of poetic g., which did not reach
the modern formula of the three divisions
until the 16th c.

During the great Attic age we do not find
a simple, clear-cut division, but a wide variety
of terms for specific g.: the epic or recited poetry, the drama or acted poetry, the latter subdivided in tragedy and comedy; then iambic
or satirical poetry (so called because written
in iambic meter), and elegiac poetry also written in a distinctive meter, the elegiac couplet,
with its offshoots, the epitaph and the epigram (all classed together because composed
in the same meter). Then there was melic
poetry (as it was called later), or poetry sung
usually by a chorus to the accompaniment of
a flute or of a stringed instrument. Melic poetry comes closest to our concept of the lyric,
but still it excluded what we would consider
the essentially lyrical genre of the elegy, and
the epigram which was to develop into the
beautiful lyrics of the later *Gr. Anthology*.
In addition, there was the hymn, the dirge or
threnos, and the dithyramb, the latter a composition in honor of the god Dionysus which
could be anything from a hymn to a short
narrative or a miniature play. Songs of triumph or of celebration, chorally recited, were
paeans, encomia, epinikia, and epithalamia.
There was certainly plenty of material in Gr.
poetry to make up a concept of lyrical poetry,
but the Greeks of the Attic age apparently
never took that step and contented themselves
with classifying these g. by such criteria as
metrical form. Aristotle in the *Poetics* does not
even attempt to enumerate all these g., but
concentrates on tragedy, comedy, and the epic,
with occasional passing references to some
others.

After Aristotle, it was Alexandrian scholarship that undertook the first comprehensive
stock-taking of Gr. poetry and began the
process of grouping, grading, and classifying
poems. Lists or "canons" of the best writers
in each kind were made, which led to a
sharper awareness of g. The first extant grammarian to mention the lyric as a genre was
Dionysius Thrax of the 2d c. B.C., in a list
which comprises, in all, the following: "Tragedy, Comedy, Elegy, Epos, Lyric, and Threnos,"
lyric meaning for him and other Greeks "primarily what the name implies—poetry sung to
the accompaniment of the lyre" (Smyth). In
Alexandrian literature other g. were added to
the list, the idyll and the pastoral, not to
speak of prose fiction. But the classification
which prevailed and which was repeated afterwards for centuries was a mere return to the
Platonic modes, found in the grammarian
Diomedes of the 4th c. A.D.: the *genus activum,
enarrativum*, and *mixtum*.

Gradually the exact meaning of the terms
was forgotten, and the closing of the theatres
in the Middle Ages obliterated all notion of
drama and dramatic performance. "In Byzan-

tine writing, *drama* means the novel; in the West, it means a philosophical dialogue" (Behrens, p. 38). By the time of Dante the notion of the theatre was lost: for him, the *Aeneid* was a tragedy and his own poem was a comedy. The latter is comic because it is a tale that ends with happiness (in Paradise) and because it is composed in the "middle" style, the other two styles being the "noble" and the "humble": the noble being reserved for "tragedy" or the epic, and the humble for "elegy"—a complete confusion of ancient classifications. Of course, the Middle Ages had g. of their own, but no Aristotle to attempt a classification of them. The It. Renaissance achieved a more exact notion of ancient literature, revived the theatre in its classical form, and rediscovered the *Poetics*, which had actually been translated in the 13th c. but completely neglected by medieval writers. The fresh resort to the original text of the *Poetics* early in the 16th c. came as a revelation to critics and produced a host of commentaries and adaptations, and eventually of criticism and rebuttal. The theory of g. was taken as the foundation of the critical system, and elaborate codes of rules were built up, supposedly out of Aristotle, for the epic and the drama. This led to critical controversies about great medieval poems like Dante's which could not be fitted into the classical schemes or the newly fashioned rules, and about Renaissance poems modeled upon the medieval romances, like Ariosto's and Spenser's (see RENAISSANCE POETICS). It was also impossible to ignore the lyric any longer as a major genre, since Petrarch's love poems had set a standard of poetry for the whole age. At first the Aristotelian critics tried to fit the lyric into the mimetic scheme by arguing that the lyrical poet was also an "imitator"—he "imitated himself." This rather clumsy device was rejected by the more rigorous theorists, some of whom inclined to exclude the lyric from poetry altogether, since it could not be made to fit into the scheme. But there was no lack of critics who came to the defense of the lyric, and in 1559 we find it listed by Minturno as one of the three great g. of poetry. But he still described the third genre, which he called "melic," as "imitating actions" and "now narrating and now introducing some other speaker," falling back into the traditional two modes of Plato. The lyric genre really did not come into its own until the romantic movement.

Even in the Renaissance some of the more independent thinkers rejected the classification of poetry by g., and Bruno roundly declared that "there are as many genres of poetry as there are poets." The greatest damage the g. system and its correlative rules was oduced by the flourishing of irregular drama,

such as the Elizabethan or Sp. theatre, composed outside such rules as those of the three unities, and which finally discredited both the rules and the genre system. Other controversies arose in the 17th and 18th c. about minor g. such as the pastoral and the burlesque or mock-epic. The romantic movement inspired a revolt against (first of all) rigid barriers between g., such as comedy and tragedy. Some romantic critics then favored the mingling or interpenetration of all g. into a single, comprehensive poetic form; others argued in favor of new g., such as the historical novel or historical drama or the *Märchen*. Others extolled the lyric, defining it as the essence and animating spirit of all poetry (Herder). Finally some envisaged the abolition of all definitions and classifications by genre, as F. Schlegel in his *Dialogue on Poetry* (1800) and in his essay on Goethe (1828). His brother August William hit upon the idea of fitting the three g., now fixed in the triad of lyric, epic, and drama, into the dialectical trinity of "Thesis, Antithesis and Synthesis: the Epic is objective, the Lyric is subjective, and the Drama is the interpenetration of both" (*Lectures* of 1801–2).

This neat parallel became very popular, and is still the foundation of many current classifications. It can be imagined to what a riot of dialectic it led in Hegel's Aesthetic, which should have been a warning, but acted instead as an incentive to the metaphysical aestheticians of the 19th c., each with his own system of the arts and of the g. Evolutionary thinking, claiming to be as scientific as Darwin, took over bodily the classification by g., as it did many other traditional ideas, and built up evolutions of g., a process culminating in the work of Brunetière. This led to viewing the masterpieces of literature as the result of something like "natural selection," proceeding by the gradual accretion of plots, devices, and conventions. G. were also found convenient devices for grouping large numbers of works in the histories of literature, and as such are still in current usage. Attempts are continually being made to invest these traditional formulas with some critical substance, and to achieve a final definition, e.g., of the "tragic spirit" or the "essence of comedy." But the field is littered with the ruins of past definitions which have convinced no one save their author, and the advance of modern writing is so vast and multifarious that all classifications crumble in front of it. The most radical rejection of g. in modern times was made by Croce, who considered them mere abstractions, useful in the construction of classifications for practical convenience, but of no value as aesthetic categories.

F. Brunetière, *L'Evolution des g.* (1892);

Saintsbury, II (1900); H. W. Smyth, *Gr. Melic Poets* (1900); R. K. Hack, "The Doctrine of Lit. Forms," HSCP, 27 (1916; against the genre theory); B. Croce, *Aesthetic*, tr. D. Ainslie (2d ed., 1922, pp. 87-93, 436-49), "Per una Poetica moderna," *Vossler Festschrift* (1922); *La Poesia* (1936, pp. 177-83, 333-36), *Poeti e scrittori del pieno e del tardo rinascimento*, II (1945), 109-18; N. H. Pearson, "Lit. Forms and Types; or, a Defense of Polonius," *EIE 1940* (1941; for the genre theory); J. J. Donohue, *The Theory of Lit. Kinds* (2 v., 1943-49); Behrens (best historical account of the development of genre classification in Western lit.); I. Ehrenpreis, *The "Types Approach" to Lit.* (1945; gives an objective account of discussions pro and con the theory); M. Fubini, *Critica e poesia* (1956); Fry (reaffirms g.).   G.N.G.O.

GEORGIAN POETRY. The people of Georgia had their own independent state from before the Christian era, although they suffered much from the Iranians and later from the Arabs and Turks. At times they were compelled to acknowledge the suzerainty of one or other of their neighbors, but in the early part of the 19th c. they were annexed by the Rus. Empire and despite frequent revolts they were unable to secure their independence until the Rus. Revolution in 1917. The independent Georg. Republic was short lived, for in 1921 it was seized by the Communists, forced into the Soviet Union, and Communist rule was ruthlessly enforced.

The Georgians have had a written literature with their own alphabet since the time of the Illuminatrix of Georgia, St. Nino, about A.D. 325. There are traces of even earlier folk poems, dating from the pagan period, but none of these have been preserved unless their remains are buried in later works. As the earliest literature was dominated by the church, secular poetry was slow in developing, and, when it did, it bore marked traces of Arab and Iranian influence.

The Golden Age of Georg. literature was from the reign of David II (the Builder) through the great Queen Thamar to the Mongol invasion, a period from 1089 to 1234. The most brilliant era was during the reign of Queen Thamar, when the court in Tiflis counted many distinguished poets, among them Chakhukhadze, secretary of Queen Thamar, whom he glorified in a series of odes. The outstanding poet of this period was Shot'ha Rust'haveli (1172-1216). Like the other poets of his day he was attached to the court and is said to have been in love with Thamar. His great poem was *The Man in the Panther's Skin* (*Vephkhis Tqaosani*), the national saga of Georgia. The theme is the friendship between Tariel and Avt'handil and

the success of the two men in winning their beloveds, Nestan-Daredjan, and Thinat'hin. Although the former is called King of India and the latter King of Arabia, they are very obviously Georgians and show all the characteristic features of the traditional Georg. chivalry. The poem consists of 1,576 quatrains of 16 syllables each with tonic accent and 8 trochaic feet divided by a caesura. The style is heavily allusive, and many passages are very difficult to decipher. There is a marked religious tolerance in the poem, far greater than we would expect in a country that was constantly embattled against enemies of an alien faith. Despite Byzantine and Neoplatonic ideas, the poem, with its praise of friendship and womanhood, and its generally cheerful outlook on life, is typical of the Georg. character in all stages of its history.

The following centuries of national decline produced far less important poetical works, but the poetic art revived with King T'heimuraz (1588-1663) and heralded in the so-called Silver Age. Several of the Kings were poets themselves—for example, T'heimuraz and Archil III (1647-1712), who wrote the *Archiliani*, a verse encyclopedia of Georg. life in more than 12,000 verses. David Guramishvili (1705-86) also composed a verse history of Georgia as well as odes and other lyric poems, many in the Persian style. The reign of King Heraclius II continued the same tendencies with signs of a reaction against the Iranian style and a tendency to return to native Christian models; but other poets continued to follow the Iranian style of verse, as in the work of Bessarion Gabashvili (1749-90).

Throughout the 18th c., Georgia had sought for Christian help to protect it against Turkish and Iranian pressure and had drifted into a sort of dependence upon Russia. In 1800 Tsar Paul ordered the annexation of Georgia to the Russian Empire, and this was carried out by Alexander I, who seized the Georg. throne for himself. His successors continued the policy, and by 1864 all the Georg. dynasties in the different semi-independent provinces had been deposed and the whole of Georgia had been forcibly reorganized on the Russian pattern. This influenced the literature. The poets of the nobility who were accepted in their rank by the Russians speedily modeled their works on Russian poetry, but this was the period when Russian poetry itself was heavily under Fr. influence and so there arose a new Georg. poetry based on Russo-Fr. models and avoiding the old national patterns and themes. The first writer of this group was Alexander Chavchavadze (1786-1864), called the Anacreon of the Caucasus, because of his lyric poems imitating the Anacreontic odes of Derzhavin. The mood soon changed with the romantic movement in Rus. literature, and Nicholas Baratashvili (1815–45) and Gregory Orbeliani (1800–83) reflect the newer school of the lyrics of Pushkin and Lermontov, both of whom were strongly influenced by Byron. George Eristhavi (1811–64) pushed much further this adaptation of Georg. poetry and extended it by translating the poetic dramas of Racine, Schiller, Pushkin, and Mickiewicz. He was the leading author in the popular (not the classical) language of his day. Realism was not long in coming to Georgia and, again following the Rus. pattern, Ilya Chavchavadze (1837–1907) turned away from the romantic school which sang of the Georg. knightly figures and adopted a naturalistic and realistic type of writing which sought its heroes in the common people. His contemporary and friend Akaki Tsereteli (1840–1915) excelled in lyric, dramatic, and epic poetry. In his main work, the epic *Thornike Eristavi*, he evoked the grandeur of Georgia's past. Another important 19th c. poet Vazha Pshavela (1861–1915) revived the heroic epos of the Georgian mountaineers. His poems depict realistically their lives, customs, and characters.

In the 1880's a newer radical poetry began to develop. The Young Georgia movement was formed, which clustered around Michael Gurgenidze's literary review, *Imedi* (Hope), founded in 1881 to oppose the *Iveria* of Ilya Chavchavadze. Here belonged Gregory Volski, Dominika Mdivani, Gregory Abashidze, and others, most of whom had a pessimistic philosophy. In the 1890's Marxist doctrines penetrated Georg. literature, and there was a small but active group of writers trying to express Marxist philosophy.

The Western influence received a new impetus with the arrival of symbolism on the Georg. literary scene. The 1909 issue of the Georg. revue *Phaskundji* (Griffin) printed *The Raven* by Edgar Allan Poe. Soon other poems in the same vein followed. But it was not until the appearance of the magazine *Tsispheri q'antsebi* (Blue Horns, 1916) that the Georg. literary society became aware for the first time of the existence of a whole group of young and dynamic poets who publicly professed themselves admirers and followers of the Fr. symbolists Baudelaire, Mallarmé, Verlaine, and Rimbaud. The most remarkable members of this group were: P. Iashvili, T. Tabidse, K. Nadiradse, V. Gaprindashvili, Sh. Apchaidse, C. Tsirekidse and, for a short time only, G. Tabidse. The well-known writer, critic, philosopher and poet G. Robakidse became the recognized leader of this boastful but extremely talented group.

In 1917 the Rus. Revolution and soon thereafter the establishment of the free Georg. Republic created favorable conditions for the development of Georg. poetry and literature. But the overthrow of the independent Georgia by Soviet Russia in 1921 changed the fate of the country and its writers. At first most poets persisted in their opposition to the Soviet regime, but when in 1934 the writers of all Soviet republics were compelled to join the Union of Soviet Writers and ordered to make communism *the* subject matter of literature, the poets of Georgia had the choice of either joining the regime or perishing. The great majority joined.

Yet the true voice of poetry has not been stilled in Georgia. Aside from works cast in the mold of socialist realism, historical poems, nature and love poems are still being written. The older and well-known poets such as Grishashvili, Shanshiashvili, G. Tabidse, Leonidse, Chichinadse, P. Iashvili have not lost the mastery of their craft, and the younger generation (Mashashvili, Gomiashvili, K. Kaladse, I. and G. Abashidse, and many others) show remarkable poetic vigor, imagination, and technical skill.

Shot'ha Rust'haveli, *The Man in the Panther's Skin*, tr. M. S. Wardrop (1912); *Visramiani* (The Story of the Loves of Vis and Ramin, a Romance of Ancient Persia), tr. from the Georg. version by O. Wardrop (1914); Ch. Beridze, "Georg. Poetry," *Asiatic Review* (1930–31); R. P. Blake, "Georg. Secular Lit.: Epic, Romance and Lyric (1100–1800)," *Harvard Studies and Notes on Phil. and Lit.*, 15 (1933); J. Karst, *Litt. géorgienne chrétienne* (1934); A. Shanidze, *Dzveli kartuli ena da literaturea* (9th ed., 1947); D. Djaparidze, "Litt. géorgienne," *Hist. des littératures*, ed. R. Queneau, II (1956); K. Kekelidze, *Kartuli literaturis istoria* (new ed., 1961). C.A.M.; G.N.

GEORGIANISM. A poetic movement of the early 20th c. in England, named by its founders for the reigning monarch (George V) and to suggest "that we are the beginning of another 'Georgian period' which may take rank in due time with several great poetic ages of the past." Thus Edward Marsh prefaced *Georgian Poetry, 1911–1912* (1912), the first of five anthologies in which the work of poets associated with that movement was presented. Marsh himself edited these offerings, having been affected by the enthusiasm of Rupert Brooke in 1910 for the then-neglected younger poets. Important members of the Georgian group included Lascelles Abercrombie, Brooke, W. H. Davies, John Drinkwater, James Elroy Flecker, W. W. Gibson, Ralph Hodgson, Harold Munro, J. C. Squire, and W. J. Turner; others were occasionally published in *Georgian Poetry* but not directly associated with the Georgians, as, for instance, Robert Graves, D. H. Lawrence and James Stephens. Although members of the movement varied widely in talent and in style, "Georgian" poetry—the idiom common to their generation—was typically bucolic in mood, presenting delicate emotion in meters and forms for the most part traditional. Their poetry is often Wordsworthian but lacks the intensity of vision which transmuted Wordsworth's descriptions of nature into great art. Consequently, they are often accused of sentimental pastoralism or "week-end ruralism."

That Marsh intended no revolutionary manifesto may be inferred from the dedications of two of his anthologies to such respected elders as Robert Bridges and Hardy. His success in gaining public favor for the Georgians was so great that, as Frank Swinnerton observes in *The Georgian Literary Scene, 1910–1935* (1950), "inclusion in his book gave a writer cachet," and those who were left out attacked Marsh for "trying to establish a canon." When, in the preface to his final anthology, *Georgian Poetry, 1920–1922* (1922), Marsh rejoined, "Much admired modern work seems to me, in its lack of inspiration and its disregard of form, like gravy imitating lava," the opponents of Georgianism could regard the movement as conservative. A rival publication devoted to modernism was *Wheels*, established by Edith, Osbert, and Sacheverell Sitwell.

The Georgian maintenance of traditional romantic realism was hardly touched by the upheavals of the First World War and failed to reflect contemporary sensibility. In consequence the influence of this movement rapidly waned in the early 1920's. D.H.

GEORGIC. A didactic poem primarily intended to give directions concerning some skill, art, or science. In his "Essay on the Georgic" (1697), which is the most important discussion of the genre, Addison specifically distinguished this kind of poetry from the pastoral and crystallized the definition of the g. by pointing out that this "class of Poetry . . . consists in giving plain and direct instructions." The central theme of the g. is the glorification of labor and praise of simple country life. Though this didactic intention is primary, the g. is often filled with descriptions of the phenomena of nature and likely to contain digressions concerning myths, lore, philosophical reflections, etc., which are somehow suggested by the subject matter. The g. begins as early as Hesiod's *Works and Days* (ca. 750 B.C.) and was used by many of the great ancients—Lucretius, Ovid, Oppian, Nemesianus, Columella. Some of the better known poems in the tradition are Tusser's *Five Hundreth Points of Good Husbandry* (1573), Poliziano's *Rusticus* (1483), Vida's *De Bombyce* (1527), Alamanni's *La Coltivazione* (1546), Rapin's *Horti* (1665), Jammes's

Géorgiques chrétiennes (1912). The finest specimens of the type are the *Georgics* of Virgil. Virgil's purpose is to pay tribute to Augustus for the new security he brought to the empire and to inspire the farmers to take up afresh the industry of the fields long wasted and neglected. Virgil's *Georgics* cast a long shadow over the poetry of the late 17th and 18th c. Dryden called the *Georgics* "the best poem of the best poet." James Thomson, because of his *Seasons*, was known as the "English Virgil," and William Cowper's *Task* resembles the g. in inspiration and execution. Thomson's far-reaching influence was strongly felt, even on the Continent. Though the term "g." does not appear in the title, scores of poems were written which imitate Virgil's georgics in form and content—poems on the art of hunting, fishing, dancing, laughing, preserving health, raising hops, shearing sheep, etc. Sometimes the serious imitation can hardly be separated from the burlesque, as in Gay's *Trivia; or the Art of Walking the Streets of London* (1716). Because Virgil was addressing his emperor and was intent on glorifying rural occupations, he raised the style of his *Georgics*. Attempting to elevate a lowly subject by elegant circumlocutions led many of his 18th-c. imitators to grotesqueries of style which are easy to ridicule.—M. L. Lilly, *The G.* (1919); D. L. Durling, *G. Tradition in Eng. Poetry* (1935). J.E.C.

GERMAN POETICS. See MEDIEVAL, RENAISSANCE (BIBLIOG.), BAROQUE, NEOCLASSICAL, MODERN POETICS.

GERMAN POETRY. In speaking of G. poetry it should be borne in mind that it was not until the second half of the 8th c. A.D., with the Christianization of Germany and the scribal activities carried on within the monasteries of the Carolingian Renaissance that G. poetry began to develop its individual character. Although the Old High G. dialects were beginning to break away from the other West Germanic dialects in the latter half of the 6th c., throughout the entire Heroic Age (the time of the Migration of Peoples, ca. A.D. 350–600) and up into the second half of the 8th c., Old High G. poetry still formed part of the oral tradition of pagan Germanic poetry, sharing both thought-content, verse forms, and spiritual attitude with that of other Germanic peoples such as the Anglo-Saxons and Scandinavians. The main poetic genres were the *Heldenlied* (heroic lay), the pagan religious poem, the *Preislied* (encomiastic poem) and the *Zauberspruch* (magic charm). The traditional alliterative verse form of Germanic poetry underwent no revolutionary change in Germany until the introduction of end rhyme and the longer alliterative line (8 main stresses) by the Alsatian monk, Otfrid of Weissenburg, in his *Evangelienharmonie* (Gospel Harmony) completed A.D. 863–71, a verse form which was also adopted in the *Ludwigslied* (Lay of Ludwig, A.D. 881–82).

The earliest Germanic verse is mentioned in very general terms by some L. historians, e.g., Tacitus in his *Germania* (A.D. 98), but no conclusions can be drawn about its nature from their remarks. The extant remains are all relatively late. The Anglo-Saxon *Beowulf*, composed about A.D. 750 (MS ca. A.D. 1000) probably exhibits the sustained narrative form at its best, but there is some influence of Christianity and perhaps even of classical verse. Some parts of the *Elder* or *Poetic Edda*, composed during the 9th, 10th, and 11th c. (MS 13th c.) and the Old High G. *Hildebrandslied* (Lay of Hildebrand) composed ca. A.D. 770–90 (MS around A.D. 800) represent the heroic lay. The lays are terse almost to the point of obscurity sometimes, but vigorous in portraying action and character. The longer heroic epics, such as *Beowulf*, although discursive, have a sense of structure and the vigor of the shorter poems. Germanic narrative poetry was written in alliterative verse (*Stabreim*) whose determining features are: 4 main stresses in each line; at least 2 initial sounds alliterating in syllables which bear the stress and an indefinite number of unstressed syllables. Even in its mutated and imperfect state, the *Hildebrandslied* affords a sufficiently clear idea of what the earlier heroic lay was like. Crisp and concise in style, the poem begins without preamble and proceeds with a minimum of commentary, developing the dramatic, increasingly tense situation in the dialog of the father and the son, who refuses to realize that he is about to fight to the death with his own father.

The alliterative verse form was employed exclusively in narrative poetry, and indeed it is not until the 12th c. that we have written evidence of lyric verse in G. in the so-called *Tegernseerbriefe* (Tegernsee letters) written by a young nun to her teacher, a cleric:

> I am thine, thou art mine,
> Take this as a certain sign.
> Imprisoned thou art
> Within my heart
> And lost forever is the key:
> So thou must abide in me.

This charming love lyric is in several respects typical of the G. spirit as it finds expression in lyrical (i.e., personal) poetry. Unforced, natural speech, simple and straightforward thought, and a marked irregularity of form are characteristics of G. folk song—and a considerable portion of G. lyric poetry—down to

the present day. Lyrics are also found among the song collections composed by wandering scholars and clergy in the 12th and 13th c. such as the famous *Carmina Burana,* the main themes of which are wine, woman, and song. These lyrics are sometimes in L., sometimes in G., and sometimes a mixture of both. The love lyrics often contain simple descriptions of nature as a setting.

Within this tradition of the simple love song are the later 12th c. poets of the Danubian region such as the Kürenberger and Dietmar von Aist, although they are not uninfluenced by the lyrics of the troubadours at the courts of Provence. This native type of early G. love song is usually known as a *trutliet* as opposed to the more courtly love lyric or *minneliet.*

The latter part of the 12th c. produced in Germany, especially in the Rhineland and the south-west, a sudden flowering of the courtly love lyric (the period known as *Minnesangsfrühling,* see MINNESINGERS) which cannot be wholly accounted for by Fr. influence, although there is no doubt that Heinrich von Veldeke, Friedrich von Husen, Reinmar von Hagenau, and Heinrich von Morungen, the chief exponents of this art, were strongly influenced by Prov. models in their choice of poetic forms, style, and vocabulary in addition to basic themes. These themes were derived from the literary fiction of *minnedienst* (love homage) paid by the poet to the noble, and usually married, lady of his choice, to whom he addresses his poems and whose husband is his patron and benefactor. The most versatile and the most prolific of the minnesingers was Walther von der Vogelweide (ca. 1170–ca. 1230), a pupil of Reinmar von Hagenau at the Viennese court. Walther had the courage and power to break through the conventional rules of the day and to sing of love as poets have always sung of it, with simplicity and directness. His most successful poem in this vein has become a classic in Germany. The poem is reminiscent, in its setting, of the pastoral poems of the wandering scholars, although the mood is quite different, for the experience is retold in the more sensitive words of the girl:

> Under the spreading
> Linden in heather,
> Where for our love a bed we found,
> You may see us bedding
> Fair together
> Crushed flowers and grass upon the ground.
> By the forest, in a vale,
> Tandarady
> Sweetly sang the nightingale.

Hand in hand with the development of the courtly love lyric in Germany goes that of the courtly epic of chivalry embodying a highly idealized conception of knighthood, which included the feudal virtues of loyalty, constancy, and generosity in relations between liege-lord and vassal, God and Man, knight and lady, and a number of other virtues, all of which should be in perfect balance and proportion. Some of the qualifications for knighthood were hereditary ones such as noble birth and riches, fair appearance etc., whereas others were to be acquired through knightly training. The precourtly epics of chivalry such as the *Rolandslied* (ca. 1170, a version of the Fr. *Chanson de Roland*) are based on the conception of the Christian knight, and the ennobling influence of courtly love is completely absent. This influence, however, is emphasized in the courtly epics such as those of Hartmann von Aue, *Erec* (ca. 1180–85) and *Iwein* (ca. 1200)—both of these based on epics by Chrétien de Troyes —*Tristan und Isolde* (ca. 1210) by Gottfried von Strassburg, and *Parzival* (ca. 1200–1210) by Wolfram von Eschenbach, who employs the story of Parzival's search for the Holy Grail in order to show the highest possible form of knighthood, which combines the attainment of worldly and spiritual happiness. The subject matter of the courtly epics of chivalry written during the so-called classical period of Middle High G. literature (ca. 1180–1250) is taken from the Celtic tales of King Arthur and the Knights of the Round Table through the intermediary of Fr. sources, and the verse form is that of the rhymed couplet.

Especially popular at the courts of southeastern Germany and Austria was the heroic epic, a continuation of the heroic lay, in which the subject matter is derived from Germanic traditions which arose around the figures and events of the Heroic Age and in which the ancient virtues of courage and loyalty to one's blood relations are all-important. Since these epics were composed by anonymous wandering court poets for the delectation of a courtly audience, ancient heroic virtues are combined with Christian courtly ones, familiar to us from the courtly epics of chivalry, and the milieu is courtly-Christian, not heathen-Germanic. Yet the spirit of the *Nibelungenlied* (Lay of the Nibelungs, ca. 1200–1204) and the ethics of most of its protagonists belong to an earlier age when dark fate ruled over a world of deceit, murder, hatred, revenge, heroic courage, victory, and defeat. Conflicting loyalties produce the tragic and highly dramatic situation where Kriemhild kills her brothers in order to avenge the murder of her husband Siegfried. The heroic epics, unlike the courtly epics of chivalry, were written in 4-line strophes, rhyming aa bb, the so-called *Nibelungenstrophe* (q.v.).

The term *Minnesang* included in its widest sense all artistic *lyrical* poetry of the Middle High G. period, but there also existed at this time a body of poets whose poems were concerned mainly with didactic, religious or political themes, the so-called *Spruchdichter*. It was out of these uncourtly, speculative, partly pious, poems that that phenomenon developed, the *Meistergesang*. The *Meistersinger* (q.v.) are treated in a special article, and we will merely touch upon the most notable of them, the master cobbler Hans Sachs (1494–1576). A native of Nuremberg, he composed more than 6,000 works, using in most of them the *Knittelvers* (q.v.) which is now commonly traced back to him. A man of real talent and some originality, he achieved more than passing success in two forms: the *Schwank*, a comic narrative in verse, and the *Fastnachtspiel* (Shrovetide play), a farce, written and performed as entertainment for the day or days immediately preceding Lent. In these two types, which resemble each other in both substance and form, Sachs displayed a delightful awareness of the foibles and frailties of the common people. His figure lives today primarily through Richard Wagner's *Meistersinger von Nürnberg* (1868).

Much of Hans Sachs's energy was devoted to the cause of the Protestant Reformation, inaugurated by Martin Luther (1517), and most of the poetry of the Reformation period and the period immediately following it was of a polemical, usually satirical, nature, either pro- or anti-Reformation. One of the most important and effective poets of this period, who wrote in the cause of the Reformation, was the humanist knight Ulrich von Hutten (1488–1523).

Although it is true to say that the lyric on the whole reached a low ebb in the 16th c., in the field of the *religious* lyric this would not be true. In introducing congregational singing into the church service and through his own fine hymns, Luther gave the religious lyric enormous prestige. And while the 16th c. brought forth no great G. lyricist, it did experience, in common with the preceding 15th c., a rich flowering of the folk song, which had enjoyed a wider transmission since the invention of printing (mid-15th c.).

In 1624, six years after the outbreak of the Thirty Years' War, the Silesian Martin Opitz, recognizing the need for a revival of the art of writing poetry in Germany, brought out his manual of poetics *Das Buch von der Deutschen Poeterey*. G. poetry at this time was inferior to that of other countries such as England and France, and although Germany had some promising poets such as Paul Fleming (1609–40), they were not writing in G. but in L. The principal precepts laid down by Opitz were the return to ancient classical (Gr.) literature as model and inspiration, the insistence on using natural word accent as the foundation for poetic rhythm, and the emulation of the Fr. alexandrine (q.v.) verse in place of the native G. *Knittelvers,* which had degenerated so far as to forfeit all the good qualities which had once made it so popular and were later to restore it to favor. Opitz' work has often been unfavorably criticized as providing rigid and mechanical rules for composing poetry, culled from foreign models such as Ronsard in France, but actually Opitz took care to stress the fact that he did not believe that a poet could write to order if he followed the instructions carefully, but that he must first find inspiration. Opitz also laid emphasis on the role played by the imagination in the creative process of writing poetry.

In view of the prevailing religious and political conditions during the first part of the baroque era in Germany, which corresponded roughly to the period of the Thirty Years' War, it is not surprising that the lyric of that time was pervaded by the following themes: a feeling that life was full of uncertainties and governed by fickle Fortune, an inconsistent and definitely hostile force, an ever-present awareness of the transitory nature of all earthly things and of the imminence of death, a conviction that nothing *is* as it *seems* (the interplay of "Sein" and "Schein"), and a preoccupation with the concept of Time.

In the G. lyric of the 17th c. great attention was paid to form and style, and in this sense the G. lyric enjoyed an artistic renaissance. The term "baroque" was borrowed from the field of architecture where the buildings of the new style which began in Spain and Italy as an artistic expression of the Counter-Reformation contrasted strongly with the symmetry of Renaissance architecture. Above all, the poetry of the 17th c. should appeal to the senses, although sensuous effects are somewhat less marked in the more contemplative poets such as Paul Fleming or Simon Dach. The baroque lyric therefore abounds in visual and sound effects, and much use is made of startling contrasts. In order to build up the tension and sense of eternal motion, which one feels in a baroque church, word is piled upon word or phrase upon phrase until the potentialities of the language are strained almost to the breaking point. All the elements of style just mentioned are to be discovered in the lyrics of Hofmann von Hofmannswaldau (1617–79), the supreme exponent of stylistic virtuosity, who wrote with extreme elegance and surprising facility.

Among the outstanding poets of the baroque era were the two admirers of Opitz, Paul Fleming (1609–40) and Simon Dach (1605–59), whose optimism derived from their unshakable religious faith and, in the case of Fleming, the conviction that man can become master of his fate if he first learns to master himself. No one at the time treated the themes of vanity, death, and destruction in more powerful language than Andreas Gryphius (1616–64), the most outstanding poet and one of the few effective dramatists of the period. His *Sonnets* (1639) and his *Odes* (1643) show a deeply religious mind of strong imagination. In startling contrast to the heartfelt poetry of these three men were the delightful but playful efforts of the Nuremberg circle led by Georg Philipp Harsdörffer, Johann Klaj, and Sigmund von Birken. Their poems reflected an idyllic world of nymphs and shepherds, with no deep problems and are characterized by the decorative element of their graceful style, reminiscent of the light and airy rococo, a further development of the baroque in the plastic arts. Two of the most gifted and popular poets were the rivals Johann Rist (1607–67) who produced sincere and simple hymns, yet at the same time some of the most ornate pastoral songs, and Philipp von Zesen (1619–89), a talented and versatile lyric poet and an enterprising pioneer in his attempts to improve the status of G. as a literary language, a fit vehicle for poetic thought. We have already mentioned the lyrics of Hofmann von Hofmannswaldau, who exploits every stylistic device of his predecessors, and it only remains to point to the fine body of hymns which were produced during this chaotic period by both Roman Catholics and Protestants. The hymns reflect the same basic preoccupations which supplied the themes for the contemporary secular lyric and often show a high degree of formal and stylistic artistry. Among the Catholics we should certainly mention the Jesuit Friedrich von Spee (1591–1635) and the convert Angelus Silesius (i.e., Johann Scheffler, 1624–77), author of *Der cherubinische Wandersmann* (1657). Foremost of the Protestants was Paul Gerhardt (1607–76) considered by many to be the greatest of the G. hymn writers. Many of these hymns have survived up to the 20th c., and the poetic quality of the hymns composed in the 17th c. has not been equalled since.

In a more didactic vein were the poems of the Silesian Friedrich von Logau (1604–55), whose *Sinngedichte* (1654) make him perhaps the greatest epigrammatist of all G. literature. Logau made it his business to criticize the foreign customs and the morals of contemporary society, and in this he was joined by Hans Michael Moscherosch (1601–19) and the preacher Abraham a Sancta Clara (1644–1709).

At the beginning of the 18th c., we find G. poetry at a very low ebb. The Hamburg citizen B. H. Brockes (1680–1747), however, freed poetry from the inflated style of Góngora and

Marino and, impressed by Pope's *Pastorals* and *Windsor Forest,* published in 1721 the first part of *Irdisches Vergnügen in Gott* (Earthly Delight in God) which went through seven editions in the next twenty-three years. A much stronger talent, in his virtues as well as in his vices, was Johann Christian Günther (1695–1723). A lyricist of power and imagination, he has been considered by many a forerunner of the young Goethe. The so-called Anacreontic poets, especially Friedrich von Hagedorn (1708–54), gave to poetic language the ease and gracefulness needed after a long preponderance of didactic verse.

Just as Opitz felt called upon to do something (theoretically as well as practically) about the parlous state of G. poetry, and just as the Schlegels were to set forth the theoretical bases of the romantic school before there was, officially speaking, any writing called romantic (whereas elsewhere in Europe it was afterthought which identified the new style of writing as "romantic"), so the new and necessary revival of G. poetry in the 18th c. was consciously planned and announced in advance by a truly dedicated poet, F.G. Klopstock (1724–1803), the first modern G. not only to make his living as a poet, but also to exalt the position of the poet as the religious and national educator and prophet of his people. Klopstock's name and fame are bound up with two poetic fields which are not sharply distinguished in his case: the epic and the lyric. His portentous epic, *Der Messias* (The Messiah, 1748–73), did three important things for G. poetry: (1) for the first time since the Middle Ages, Germans were held spellbound by a poetic narrative of high seriousness and inspiring character; (2) the sincere religious feeling of the age was brought into active play as by no document other than the Bible; (3) with keen ear and true poetic instinct, Klopstock adapted for his poem the dactylic hexameters of the Homeric poems, thus paving the way for later masterly uses of that verse by Goethe and others. The dactylic hexameter is alive in Germany to this day. (See, for example, Gerhart Hauptmann's *Till Eulenspiegel,* 1927, and R.A. Schröder's translations of the *Odyssey,* 1910, and *Iliad,* 1943.) To us today, *Der Messias* is nearly unreadable, the presuppositions for its appreciation having disappeared with the age of its creation. It lacks outward action, but samples, especially from the earlier of its 20 cantos, still convey to us the uniquely moving quality of its language. Its eminence as a major literary document remains, and the development of G. poetry is unthinkable without it, just as it is unthinkable without Klopstock's lyrical poetry. It was he who, rejecting rhyme as a superficial decoration, focused attention on the poetic idea and introduced "free rhythms" into modern G. and, indeed, into European poetry. Klopstock was not a "Lieder" poet. Intellectual tension, an elevated tone, and the intent to praise characterize his "Oden" and "Hymnen," which are written either in Gr. forms (alcaic, asclepiadean, sapphic, or in Klopstock's own variations of these) or in free rhythms which in turn were developed from Pindar's odes and which were later to be refined to supreme mastery by Goethe and Hölderlin. Klopstock also was among the first to sound a distinctly patriotic note, seeking to replace Gr. mythology by imaginative rather than historically accurate versions of Germanic myths. The impression made by Klopstock on his own age was probably greater than that of any other G. poet before or possibly even since his time.

ANTHOLOGIES: *Deutsche Barocklyrik* (1945) and *Dt. Lyrik des Mittelalters* (1955), both ed. M. Wehrli; *Dt. Liederdichter des 13. Jahrhunderts,* ed. C. v. Kraus and H. Kuhn (2 v., 1952–58); *Althochdeutsches Lesebuch,* ed. W. Braune (13th ed. by K. Helm, 1958); *Des Minnesangs Frühling,* ed. K. Lachmann (32d ed. by C. v. Kraus, 1959). See also anthol. at end of article.

HISTORY AND CRITICISM. GENERAL: G. Ehrismann, *Gesch. der deutschen Literatur bis zum Ausgang des Mittelalters* (2d ed., 4 v., 1932–35); A. Heusler, *Die altgermanische Dichtung* (1943); P. Hankamer, *Dt. Gegenreformation und deutsches Barock* (2d ed., 1947); J. K. Bostock, *A Handbook on Old High G. Lit.* (1955); R. Newald, *Die dt. Lit. vom Späthumanismus zur Empfindsamkeit, 1570–1750* (2d ed., 1957); H. de Boor and R. Newald, *Gesch. der deutschen Lit.* (4th ed., 1960–); P. Wapnewski, *Die dt. Lit. des Mittelalters* (1960); H.J.T. Hettner, *Gesch. der deutschen Lit. im 18. Jh.* (2 v., repr. 1961); M. O'C. Walshe, *Medieval G. Lit.: A Survey* (1962).—SPECIAL: A. Heusler, *Dt. Versgesch.* (3 v., 1925–29); A. Moret, *Le Lyrisme baroque en Allemagne* (1936) and *Les Débuts du lyrisme en Allemagne* (1951); M. Ittenbach, *Der frühe dt. Minnesang* (1939); M. Thorp, *The Study of the Nibelungenlied from 1755 to 1937* (1940); see also more recent studies, e.g., by F. Panzer, W. J. Schröder; M. F. Richey, *Essays on the medieval G. Love Lyric* (1943); H. Schneider, *Heldendichtung, Geistlichendichtung und Ritterdichtung* (2d ed., 1943); H. Kuhn, *Minnesangs Wende* (1952); H. Kolb, *Der Begriff der Minne und das Entstehen der höfischen Lyrik* (1958); S. Beyschlag, *Die Metrik der mittelhochdeutschen Blütezeit in Grundzügen* (3d enl. ed., 1959); W. Kayser, *Gesch. des deutschen Verses* (1960); O. Paul and I. Glier, *Dt. Metrik* (4th ed., 1961); H. Schneider and W. Mohr, "Höfisches Epos," *Reallexikon,* 2d ed., I.

S.C.H.; B.Q.M.

GERMAN POETRY

The history of G. poetry, in contrast to that of Eng. or Fr. poetry, shows neither an unbroken continuity nor a sustained level of quality. The fact that the great period of G. epic and lyric poetry in the 12th and early 13th c. was forgotten for more than half a millennium would appear to be a phenomenon restricted to G.-speaking nations. There were, to be sure, impoverished periods in France and England, too, but G. poetry seems to be sharply characterized by solitary literary peaks rising from qualitative lowlands.

Modern G. poetry did not find its voice until the age of Johann Wolfgang Goethe (1749–1832). Yet Goethe seems to have made up for the long delay; he spoke not only for his own time, but for much of the past and the future as well. His poetry, although unmistakably stamped by his own personality, runs the whole course from Anacreontic rococo to the mystic symbolism of old age. It employs all imaginable forms and genres: the song, the hymn, the ode, the rhapsody as well as the sonnet, the elegy, the epic and the philosophical poem. His artistic personality seems, like Proteus, to have changed: the Leipzig songs show 18th c. conventional sentiments and sentimentality, the Strassburg lyrics bring new motifs and a fresh language (e.g., *Willkommen und Abschied*—Welcome and Departure); to the Weimar period belongs the adagio mood of the two "Night Songs" and the "Moon Song" (*Wanderers Nachtlied I & II; An den Mond*). Twenty *Römische Elegien* (Roman Elegies) in distichs and forty-three *Venetianische Epigramme* (Venetian Epigrams) in the critical vein of Martial are among the fruits of Goethe's Italian journey, 1786–88. A happy fusion of the concreteness of the ancients and the fluid mood of the moderns marks the two elegies *Alexis und Dora* (1796) and *Euphrosyne* (1798), the latter perhaps the most perfect threnody in G. poetry. *Der Erlkönig* (The Erlking), famous above all through Schubert's musical setting, belongs to Goethe's early ballads (1782); the most accomplished ballad form was achieved in 1797 with *Die Braut von Korinth* and *Der Gott und die Bajadere*. The first dramatizes by the use of the vampire motif the clash between the pagan and the Christian faiths, "The God and the Bayadere" treats of sin and redemption in striking variations of 8-line trochees and 3-line dactyls. In the same year, 1797, the hexametric epic *Hermann und Dorothea* was published, "born of nature and carefully nurtured through art," as Goethe's friend Schiller put it. Goethe there transformed the everyday life of solid burghers from the ordinary and limited sphere to a grandiose and moving picture of the world against the sombre background of the Fr. Revolution, a time at which it seemed "as

though the form of the world were to dissolve into chaos and night" ("Alles regt sich, als wollte die Welt die gestaltete, rückwärts / Lösen in Chaos und Nacht sich auf und neu sich gestalten"). The feeling of being exposed to threats from the daemonic forces of life were answered by Goethe in a cycle of seventeen sonnets in 1807–08. The very restriction imposed by this form seemed the natural antidote to the topic of passionate love. As early as 1800 Goethe had announced his belief in an attitude of restraint and renunciation: the sonnet *Natur und Kunst* (Nature and Art) closes almost triumphantly with the words "Und das Gesetz nur kann uns Freiheit geben" (. . . only law can give us freedom). In 1814–15, Goethe added a new province to his poetic kingdom in *West-Oestlicher Divan* (West-Easterly Divan). Stimulated by F. von Hammer-Purgstall's translation of Hafis' *Divan*, Goethe went on a spiritual "hegira" similar to his own flight to Rome in 1786–88, this time to taste the air of the patriarchs in the "pure East." In twelve books of unequal length he ranges over the themes of poetry, love, wine, anger, contemplation, parables, and the ultimate union of the individual with divine love. The tone of these poems comprises the whole scale from the casual and even flippant to the most serious and to the deepest wisdom of old age: West and East intermingle, the waters of Euphrates and of the Main are united, Tamerlane may be Napoleon and Hatem is another name for Goethe himself. Playful irony and veiled wisdom, secret symbolism and sharp consciousness are expressed in frequently brief, easy-flowing, 4-line strophes. There seems to be no slackening of poetic strength until the very end of Goethe's life. At the age of seventy-five, he wrote the so-called *Marienbader Elegie*, later enlarged to *Trilogie der Leidenschaft* (Trilogy of Passion). To his eightieth year belongs *Vermächtnis* (Testament), in many ways the sum of Goethe's insights into the world of nature and of man, of history and moral conduct, and last not least into the "work of love" created by the poet. In Goethe's poetry the G. language became the idiom of world literature. The variety of his metrical forms equals his range of thematic content, especially if we add to the lyrics proper such dramatic pieces as *Iphigenie auf Tauris* (1787) or *Torquato Tasso* (1790) which many critics regard as dramatic failures precisely because of their lyrical excellence; or if we take note of the many occasional masques, or of *Pandora* (1806–8) with its "long-tailed trimeters"; or if we recall the wealth of rhythmic innovations in the second part of *Faust*. Goethe's own dictum that all his poems were "part of a great confession" has too frequently been used to stress the personal experience behind the poem. The same Goethe, however, said that poetry at its best was quite "external," i.e., pure form. Actually, Goethe would have held that poetry, like nature, had "neither kernel nor shell," but was both at once. G. literature, at any rate, possessed, at Goethe's death, a body of poetry which could nourish many generations, regardless of their "classic" or "romantic" inclinations.

Older and younger contemporaries of Goethe added their distinctive voices. Goethe's youth coincided with the literary movement called *Sturm und Drang*, q.v. (Storm and Stress) and with the general enthusiasm for "original genius." The hatred of the despotism of absolute princes and the love of freedom were primarily expressed through dramas, but two poets ought to be mentioned who at least chronologically belong to the period of revolutionary ferment. Both use the popular tone in keeping with the prevalent theories of "folk poetry." Gottfried August Bürger (1747–94) is famous for his ballads, especially *Lenore* (1773), but was also skilled in the sonnet *An das Herz* (To my Heart, 1792). Christian Friedrich Schubart (1739–91), for ten years imprisoned by the Duke of Württemberg, left unpretentious and lovely lyrics such as *Schwäbisches Bauernlied* (A Suabian Farmer's Song, 1786) as well as the heart-rending *Kaplied* (Song of the Cape of Good Hope, 1787) for those of his fellow-men the Duke had sold as soldiers to the East-India Company. Friedrich Schiller (1759–1805) had in his youth also paid tribute to the Storm and Stress motive of "In tyrannos" through tragedies such as *Die Räuber* (The Robbers, 1781) or *Kabale und Liebe* (Intrigue and Love, 1784). His classical dramas and his incisive aesthetic writings belong to the years of his close friendship with Goethe (1794–1805). Schiller is a master of the quotable line; his rhetorical power achieves its best effect in the philosophical and didactic genre (*Das Ideal und das Leben*—Ideal and Life, 1795), in the comprehensive view of human civilization (*Der Spaziergang*—The Ramble, 1795, in distichs) and in many ballads written in 1797. The antithesis of reality and ideality, the recognition that whatever wants to live on in song must first perish in life are among Schiller's cardinal tenets (cf. *Nenie*—Dirge). The Suabian Friedrich Hölderlin (1770–1843) followed in his early rhymed hymns to human ideals in the footsteps of his countryman Schiller. He found his own incomparable tone after 1796 in Alcaic and Asclepiadean measures, in the long hexametric elegies and in the free rhythms of *Der Rhein, Der Einzige* (The Only One), or *Patmos. Der Archipelagus* (The Aegean Sea, 1800) resurrects in 296 hexameters Ancient Greece and the Olympian gods, in order to give to the Germans, living in the darkness of Hades with-

out an intimation of divine things, their Elis and their Olympia, a common spirit above their barbarous and sterile labors. Renewal and return not only of the gods, the last of whom is Christ, "Hercules' brother," but of all the forces of nature is Hölderlin's theme. The G. image of Greece, as it developed from Lessing through Winckelmann, Goethe and Schiller, achieved in Hölderlin's innate Hellenism its consummation; he understood something of "the language of the gods, change and becoming" ("die Göttersprache, das Wechseln und das Werden"). When insanity silenced him in 1806, his fate was fulfilled as he once had predicted: Apollo struck him as he had struck Achilles, Hölderlin's favorite among all heroes. His own time had neither ears nor eyes for the powerful beauty of the language or the great art of composition, nor did it understand the true prophetic tone or acknowledge the office of poets: "to stand with bared head in God's storms, to seize with their own hands the Father's bolt of lightning and to hand to the people the heavenly gift garbed in song" (*Wie wenn am Feiertage*—As on the Lord's day, 1800).

The so-called First G. Romantic School was strong in critical theory, but counted only one original creative poet among its members: Friedrich von Hardenberg (1772–1801), better known under his pseudonym of *Novalis*. His *Hymnen an die Nacht* (Hymns to Night, 1797) praise death as the true life and night as true being and deepest love. The fifth of the six hymns invents that modern mythology for which Friedrich Schlegel among others had been clamoring: the worlds of the pagan gods, of Christ and of the wisdom of India, fused into a vision of mankind in which the romantic aims of individuality and universality achieve a measure of realization. Some of Novalis' *Geistliche Lieder* (Spiritual Songs, ca. 1799) have become part of Protestant hymnals, e.g., *Wenn alle untreu werden*—If all to thee are faithless).

Of the "Younger Romantic School," Clemens Maria Brentano (1778–1842) and his brother-in-law, Achim von Arnim (1781–1831), are best known for their edition of *Des Knaben Wunderhorn* (The Boy's Magic Horn, 3 v., 1806–8), a collection of G. folk songs and art lyrics from the late Middle Ages to the present, a "German Percy" of considerable influence on subsequent G. lyric poetry. Brentano himself was one of the most musical of G. poets, playing with facile skill on the instrument of language. What A. F. Bernhardi, Ludwig Tieck's brother-in-law, had proclaimed in his *Sprachlehre* (1803) as "the idea of producing music through vowels" became actuality in the triple and quintuple rhymes of Brentano's *Nachklänge Beethovenscher Musik* (Echoes of Beethoven's

Music). Brentano's most ambitious and abortive effort were twenty *Romanzen vom Rosenkranz* (Romances of the Rosary) in which he imitated and varied the Sp. *versos redondillos;* the fourth Romance uses in 113 four-line stanzas throughout an *a-o* assonance. Brentano's Catholicism cries often from the depth of misery (*Frühlingsschrei eines Knechtes aus der Tiefe*—Lamentation de profundis of a servant in spring time); the strong faith of Josef von Eichendorff (1788–1857), in contrast, bridges the chasm between his native woods and mountains of Silesia and his true homeland in heaven. Night as the time that binds anew what the day has separated, longing for peace after worldly battles, but also a feeling for the daemonic and uncanny characterize Eichendorff's melodious lyrics.

A catalogue of poets born in the 1780's would contain among other names those of Adalbert von Chamisso (1781–1838) and Ludwig Uhland (1787–1862); although some of their ballads and lyrics became and still are very popular, they cannot rank with the truly great European poets of the 19th c.

Heinrich Heine (1797–1856) continues by many to be considered the foremost representative of G. lyric poetry. Actually, most of the poems in his *Buch der Lieder* (1827) merely echo the 4-line stanza of the folk song and treat of sweetly sentimental moods. The "unfrocked romantic" brought the romantic topic of the identity of Love and Death to the level easily grasped by the rising middle class. By adding exotic touches like lotus flowers dreaming of the moon and by immediate identification in the manner of "Du bist wie eine Blume" (Thou art like a flower), Heine gave his readers in the rising industrial age a golden glimmer of poesy in a life that grew increasingly prosaic and drab. His cycle *Die Nordsee* (The North Sea) added the poetry of the sea to the familiar woods and dales and domesticated the Olympian gods in the same way in which Daumier's lithographs reduced them to the bourgeois sphere of nightcaps and flannel drawers.

Heine's contemporary, Annette von Droste-Hülshoff (1797–1848), is the most original G. woman poet. The lowliest life in nature—insects and grasses, toads and polecats, titmice and foxes—moves through her poems. This is partly a sign of the new realism, but also of the romantic union with the blood of the earth. Her cyclical treatment of the church year (*Das geistliche Jahr*) is less an affirmation of her Catholic faith than the anguished probing of a modern soul "who loves God more than it does believe in Him." The poetry of Eduard Mörike (1804–75) is frequently relegated to the "Biedermeier" (q.v.), that peaceful world between 1820 and 1845 of harmless joys

and not without a touch of Philistinism. Yet some of his poems equal those of Goethe in intensity. *An einem Wintermorgen vor Sonnenaufgang* (On a Winter's Morning before Sunrise), *An eine Aeolsharfe* (To an Aeolian Harp), *Gesang zu zweien in der Nacht* (Duet at Night) convey the energies of the elements as they press upward into the pure harmony of the airs. Wind and meadow, the darkness of night and the inner light of the soul, the "whirring" music of the stars and the gently passionate lament over a lost friend are woven into the firm texture of 5- or 6-foot iambs, of hexameters, or of intoxicating rhymes. And there is that rare reverence in the face of beauty: "Trägst du der Schönheit Götterstille nicht / So beuge dich! denn hier ist kein Entweichen" (If you cannot bear the godlike stillness of beauty, bow down! For here is no escape).

Heirs to a great tradition of thought and formal mastery have a hard time when aspiring to greatness without being of the highest rank. August Graf von Platen (1796–1835) mastered in his *Gaselen* (1821–23) the oriental form of the ever recurring identical rhyme, while his *Sonette aus Venedig* (1825) secured for him the first place among the G. writers of sonnets. Best known is his poem *Tristan* ("Wer die Schönheit angeschaut mit Augen, / ist dem Tode schon anheim gegeben"—Whoever has looked at beauty is already doomed to die) partly on account of Thomas Mann's appreciative essay on Platen (1930) and the story *Tod in Venedig* (Death in Venice, 1913). Friedrich Rückert's (1788–1866) prolific output contains some good poems such as *Du bist die Ruh* (Thou art rest) set to music by Franz Schubert, and many inferior ones such as the *Kindertotenlieder* (1834) which furnished the text for Gustav Mahler's composition. There are many other poets whose names are as good as forgotten while their words are still being sung. One of them is Wilhelm Müller (1794–1827) whose *Müllerlieder* and *Winterreise* (1818) supplied the words for the most celebrated songs of Schubert. Friedrich Hebbel (1813–63) often allowed reflection to intrude upon the pure presentation of mood and atmosphere; yet some of his poems are unalloyed "symbolism" long before the term had been invented, e.g. "Sie sehn sich nicht wieder . . ." (They will not meet again). The recognized initiator of the symbolist manner in G. poetry is the Swiss Conrad Ferdinand Meyer (1825–98). A Stygian mood is evoked in his many references to the "nightly boat" (*Spätboot, Abendboot*); a hidden past frequently permeates the living present with regret; the symbol of the mirror, already used by Droste-Hülshoff, expresses self doubt. Meyer filed his poems with the utmost care and the greatest economy of language and published his *Gedichte* for the first time only at the age of sixty-five. At the same time, the romantic tradition of expressing feeling with immediacy was carried on by Theodor Storm (1817–88) whose lyrics had on Thomas Mann the immediate effect of "contracting his throat and seizing him with the inexorably sweet and sad feeling of life" (cf. Mann's essay on Storm in *Leiden und Grösse der Meister*—Sufferings and Greatness of the Masters, 1930).

By the last decade of the 19th c., G. poetry had again become provincial. Some literary historians claim that Detlev von Liliencron's (1844–1909) poetry of the "plein air" brought a fresh breeze into the stale atmosphere. However, there seem to be only three lyrical poets whose work transcends the national sphere during the last decade of the 19th c. and in the years before and after the First World War: Stefan George, Hugo von Hofmannsthal, Rainer Maria Rilke. George's (1868–1933) congenial translations from Baudelaire, Verlaine, Mallarmé, Swinburne, Rossetti, Verwey and others established the connection with European movements, such as the Fr. symbolists, the Eng. Pre-Raphaelites, or the Dutch *De Nieuwe Gids* (The New Guide). The founding of the *Blätter für die Kunst* (1892) and his own poetic production engendered a new attitude toward art. George wrote nothing but poetry with the exception of one slender volume of highly stylized prose. His earlier cycles breathe the air of the *fin de siècle* and its predilection for the choice and the rare, e.g., *Algabal* (1892). *Der Teppich des Lebens* (The Tapestry of Life, 1901) brings the return from the friendly West to the simple and strict lines of his native Rhenish lands. *Der Siebente Ring* (The Seventh Ring, 1907) announces the coming of the new god, while *Der Stern des Bundes* (The Star of the Covenant), published just before the outbreak of the First World War, established in the manner of the old *Spruchdichtung* (q.v.) the firmly centered realm of the spirit. George's beginnings appear on the surface to be pure *l'art pour l'art;* in his later works the prophet and warner speaks with authority words of praise and blame.

The Viennese Hofmannsthal (1874–1929), today best remembered as the librettist for many of Richard Strauss's finest operas (*Elektra*, 1903–08; *Der Rosenkavalier*, 1910; *Ariadne auf Naxos*, 1910–16), wrote poems and lyrical plays of matchless beauty while quite young. The Austrian critic Hermann Bahr characterized his poetry as early as 1892 as an example of modern symbolism. But Hofmannsthal was aware of the dangers of the purely aesthetic life, for instance in his verse play *Der Tor und der Tod* (The Fool and Death, 1893) or in a series of sophisticated reviews of the works of Walter Pater, D'Annunzio, and Oscar Wilde.

He abandoned the lyric at the end of his twenties for the sake of the drama and thus tried to resolve the conflict between what he called the "aesthetic" and the "social" spheres. The melodiousness of a seemingly effortless mastery of language frequently veils a soft melancholy: the poet "cannot wipe from his eyes the lassitudes of long forgotten nations nor keep from his terrified soul the silent fall of distant stars." Hofmannsthal's office was not revolutionary innovation but rather the living preservation of a European tradition from the Greeks (*Idylle*, 1893), the Renaissance (*Der Tod des Tizian*, 1892), the Middle Ages (*Jedermann*, Everyman, 1911) or the Sp. theatre of Calderón (*Das Salzburger Grosse Welttheater*, 1922).

Rilke (1875–1926), born in Prague, developed as a poet of truly international stature rather late in his life. His early poetry (*Buch der Bilder*—Book of Images, 1902; *Das Stundenbuch*—Book of Hours, 1905) is precious and sentimental, but shows a great facility for internal and end rhymes. Rilke knew of "the old curse of poets" who use language for the description of their hurts instead of "transforming themselves into hard words as the stone-mason of a cathedral obstinately translates himself into the equanimity of the stone." (*Requiem für Wolf Graf von Kalckreuth*, 1908). He achieved objective distance and strictness with his *Neue Gedichte* (New Poems, 1907–8) and crowned his oeuvre after almost ten years of "unproductivity" with the ten *Duineser Elegien* (Duino Elegies, 1912–22) and two books of *Die Sonette an Orpheus* (Sonnets to Orpheus, 1922). Cardinal problems for Rilke were "destructive time," death, and God. His ripe poetry attempted to overcome all three and to transform them into an indestructible inner world (*Weltinnenraum*, "a whole inner world as if an angel, comprehending all space, were blind and looking into himself"). This process of metamorphosis meant a violent struggle against the customary distinctions between here and beyond, present and past, creature and creator. Death is for Rilke only the "sore side" of life, the poet does not stand opposite God but looks with the gods in the same direction. There sometime rises from terrible doubt ("Who if I cried would hear me from the orders of angels?") a joyous affirmation of the Here and Now, and Orpheus is Rilke's symbol for the ultimate union of disparate things in song. But there is no certainty for the permanence of victory in the finally established *Gestalt*, as Rilke clearly indicated in *Imaginärer Lebenslauf* (An Imaginary Life, 1923): after the speaker's apparent achievement of freedom in "space, ease and coldness" God rushes forth from his ambush.

Concurrently with these three poets the generation born in the mid-1880's into comparative prosperity and peace was to profess a spirit of revolt against their fathers. The movement became later known as expressionism (q.v.). Titles of periodicals founded around 1910 are indicative of the activist tendency: *Die Aktion, Der Sturm* (The Tempest), *Revolution, Die Flut* (The Flood). Many of these poets, for instance Franz Werfel (1890–1945), Ernst Stadler (1883–1914), Ludwig Rubiner (1882–1920), were published in Kurt Wolff's series *Der jüngste Tag,* a title meaning both "Doomsday" and "The Newest Day." Destruction of the old, a last judgment, and the proclamation of the new brotherhood of Man were themes which found expression both in the old form of carefully rhymed stanzas and in ecstatic cries that disregarded the conventional syntax. By the mid-1920's the movement had run its course in G. A lone survivor was Gottfried Benn (1886–1956), a physician whose first collection *Morgue* (1912) shocked the public by its imagery of putrescence and cancerous flesh. Benn accepted the fact that his poetry was cerebrospinal and yet begged to be "de-brained" (*enthirnt*). He was a nihilist singing of the late and lost "I," the rotten soul, the "moi haïssable"; yet in 1931 he wrote the words for Paul Hindemith's oratorio "Das Unaufhörliche" (Eternal Continuity) in which beyond all change and ruin ageless man will become part of creation. All but forgotten during the twelve years of Hitler's thousand-year Reich, Benn achieved fame once more after 1948. He seemed to speak for the young and disillusioned generation in poems such as *Verlorenes Ich* (Lost I, 1943) which took its title from a passage in Spengler's *Decline of the West* (1918–22) and neatly expressed the reduction of nature and man to mere "functions," "relations," and "processes." What remains for Benn in the dark void enveloping us is perhaps, cometlike, "A word, a phrase: from cyphers rise / Life recognized, a sudden sense" (*Ein Wort*—A Word, 1941). The dramatist Bertolt Brecht (1898–1956) never found even such fleeting sense in life. Criticism of bourgeois society and of its liking for the "soulful cheese" of the bourgeois theatre was the principal theme of his lyrics, which are scattered throughout his plays like street songs from Hogarth's time. Brecht is a moralist and rightly claimed that the Bible was the model for his language. His only collection of lyrics is appropriately entitled *Hauspostille* (Homilies for Home Use, 1927) and divided into "Lessons." Some critics have called it "the devil's prayer book" because they failed to see the compassion of the author for the downtrodden "who have always lived in hell." But not all poets spoke of despair; a "classical" tradition in the Goethean vein was carried on by such respect-

able writers as Hans Carossa (1878–1956) and Rudolf Alexander Schröder (1878–1962), while the "romantic" tone lived on in the poetry of Ricarda Huch (1864–1948) and Hermann Hesse (1877–1962), to name only a few. Serious poetry in the lighter vein is rare in G. literature. Although Christian Morgenstern (1871–1914) valued his melancholic, mystical poetry more, he became famous through his grotesque, fantastic, and humorous *Galgenlieder* (Gallows' Songs, 1905), to which later were added the collections *Palmström* (1910), *Palma Kunkel* (1916) and *Der Gingganz* (1919). Morgenstern's playing with language might best be likened to Edward Lear and Lewis Carroll.

The most interesting phenomenon in recent G. poetry is the changed role which nature plays in poetic imagery. Industrialization and urbanization at first, and afterward the destruction of this very civilization, made an idyllic or pastoral view of nature an impossibility. Lilies and violets yielded to wolf's bane and cow-parsnip, the evil side of nature ranks with the beneficial. This is not Keats's "poetry of earth" nor is it analogous to G. pastoral poets of the 16th, 17th, or 18th c., as some critics have claimed. There is no gentle melancholy, but a sharp awareness of the inextricable fusion of suffering and joy: "the thorn and the flesh belong together." Oskar Loerke (1884–1941) thus called his poetry at one point "a bunch of flowers plucked at the Acheron." His poem *Schöpfung* (Creation) from the collection *Der längste Tag* (The Longest Day, 1926) describes in two stanzas the disintegration of nature and man, the merely nominal character of earth and seed rather than the awakening of the germ by the spirit. Loerke's friend Wilhelm Lehmann (1882–) joins the world of nature with that of mythology, the saga, and the fairy tale. While his poetry sometimes runs the danger of a facile mannerism it presents at its best (*Der Grüne Gott*—The Green God, 1942; *Entzückter Staub*—Delighted Dust, 1946) such convincing combinations as those of Oberon's golden harness and ripe oats or Daphne's young breasts and quinces. Lehmann's language and rhythm are less harsh than Loerke's so that even the deadly terror of 1944 or 1947 contains some "nourishing magic of song." Elisabeth Langgässer's (1899–1950) cyclical poems, with the exception of her first volume *Der Wendekreis des Lammes* (Tropic of the Lamb, 1925), condense the experience contained in her long novels. The experience might perhaps best be described as the transformation of nature gods and daemons of the Western Classical heritage into Christian-Paulinian energies and powers. Readers of *Tierkreisgedichte* (Poems of the Zodiac, 1935) may be reminded of esoteric allegories as practiced in 16th- and

GERMAN PROSODY

17th-c. art; yet these poems are actually filled with the reality of earth and sky, plant and animal, birth and death; equally real, however, are the names of Virgo and Libra or Persephone and Ceres. Langgässer's method can well be seen in her tripartite poem *Daphne an der Sonnenwende* (Daphne at the Summer Solstice, 1948) in which the author herself believed that she had successfully "drawn the Christian cosmos into the world of nature of classical antiquity." It would be impossible, even if space were to allow it, to characterize the G. poets born in the 20th c. The impact of the Second World War struck different age groups differently. Those who had consciously experienced the First World War could often speak as warners or comforters. Those born during the second decade of the century reported on their experience, as for instance Hans Egon Holthusen (1913–) in *Tabula Rasa* (Clean Slate) or Karl Krolow (1915–) in *Lied, um sein Vaterland zu vergessen* (A song to forget one's country). Many of the youngest generation never returned from the war or remained anonymous. A look at an anthology such as *De Profundis* (1946) will show that Rilke's poetry exerted the strongest influence in imagery and in linguistic patterns. Critics who describe contemporary poetry and its variety of expression variously as "electicism," "surrealism," or "littérature engagée" are probably equally right according to the poems they have in mind. In thematic content we find acknowledgment of guilt, atonement, prayerful requests for the return of a whole world, realization of the loss of all guide posts. The poet exists at constantly shifting border lines, he moves from threshold to threshold and ends in silence. A widely used technical principle is that of montage, the putting together of anything at hand so that the poem becomes "a molecular model built of vowels, a church window made up of nouns, a spider web formed from memories, a prism made up of utopias, a starry configuration made from omissions." An obvious danger of such procedure is the likelihood of empty play instead of the precision of verbal mathematics. It would seem that the work of Ingeborg Bachmann (1926–) and Paul Celan (1920–) has enduring qualities. Bachmann's collection *Die gestundete Zeit* (Reprieve, 1953) symbolizes in its title the human situation, while Celan's latest book of poems *Sprachgitter* (Verbal Lattices, 1959) indicates an openness through which anything may enter as well as escape.

ANTHOLOGIES. GERMAN: numerous anthol. by F. Avenarius, R. Borchardt, A. Closs and T. P. Williams, T. Echtermeyer-B. v. Wiese, C. v. Faber du Faur and K. Wolff, H. G. Fiedler, B. v. Heiseler, L. Reiners, W. Vesper. *Das Jahrhundert Goethes*, ed. St. George and K. Wolfskehl (2d ed., 1910); *Menschheitsdämmerung*, ed. K. Pinthus (1920; poetic expressionism); *De Profundis*, ed. G. Groll (1946; poems of the 12 years of Nazi control); *Deutsche Gedichte der Gegenwart*, ed. G. Abt (1954); *Ergriffenes Dasein: deutsche Lyrik 1900–1950*, ed. H. E. Holthusen and F. Kemp (1955); *Transit*, ed. W. Höllerer (1956); *Junge Lyrik 1960*, ed. H. Bender (1960); *A Book of Modern G. Lyric Verse, 1890–1955*, ed. W. Rose (1960). ENGLISH: consult B. Q. Morgan, *A Crit. Bibliog. of G. Lit. in Eng. Tr., 1481–1935* (2d enl. ed., 1938) nos. C 109, C 44, C 373, C 41, C 17, C 244, C 372, C 311, C 28, C 531, C 423, C 95, C 129, and the unnumbered suppl. *20th-C. G. Verse*, tr. H. Salinger (1952); *An Anthol. of G. Poetry from Hölderlin to Rilke*, ed. A. Flores (1960); *The G. Lyric of the Baroque*, tr. G. C. Schoolfield (1961); *Modern G. Poetry, 1910–1960: An Anthol. with Verse Tr.*, ed. M. Hamburger and C. Middleton (1962).

HISTORY AND CRITICISM. GENERAL: J. Lees, *The G. Lyric* (1914); P. Witkop, *Die deutschen Lyriker von Luther bis Nietzsche* (2 v., 3d ed., 1925); E. Ermatinger, *Die deutsche Lyrik seit Herder* (2d ed., 1925); N. MacLeod, *G. Lyric Poetry* (1930); J. Klein, *Gesch. der deutschen Lyrik* (1957); A. Closs, *The Genius of the G. Lyric* (2d ed., 1962).—PROSODY: A. Heusler, *Deutsche Versgeschichte* (3 v., 1925–29); W. Kayser, *Gesch. des deutschen Verses* (1960). GENRES: K. Viëtor, *Gesch. der deutschen Ode* (1923); G. Müller, *Gesch. des deutschen Liedes* (1925); W. Kayser, *Gesch. der deutschen Ballade* (1936); P. Böckmann, *Formgesch. der deutschen Dichtung* (only v. I, from the Middle Ages to Storm and Stress, 1949); W. Mönch, *Das Sonett* (1955); F. Beissner, *Gesch. der deutschen Elegie* (2d ed., 1961).—INTERPRETATIONS: S. S. Prawer, *G. Lyric Poetry* (1952); *Wege zum Gedicht*, ed. R. Hirschenauer and A. Weber (1956); *Die deutsche Lyrik, Form und Geschichte*, ed. B. v. Wiese (2 v., 1957); W. Killy, *Wandlungen des lyrischen Bildes* (2d ed., 1958); C. Heselhaus, *Deutsche Lyrik der Moderne, von Nietzsche bis Yvan Goll* (1961, includes crit. interpretation).   H.S.S.

GERMAN PROSODY. The Germanic type of verse (see OLD GERMANIC PROSODY) was succeeded by meters which used end rhyme, imitated from Church Latin but which still retained the basic 4-stress, 2 full beat form. The number of unstressed syllables was at first indeterminate, but during the 12th c. the line for all narrative verse gradually approached a standard pattern, although complete standardization was never attained. The lines had either 4 main stresses, the last of which fell on the last syllable of the line (*voll*) or 3 main stresses with a secondary stress on the last syllable

(*klingend*). According to Heusler's theory—
still widely accepted, but attacked by Kayser,
Glier, and others—there are always 2 full beats
of musical time, even though a quarter or
even half beat may be represented by a pause.
The *Nibelungenstrophe* (q.v.) thus would be
basically a 2-beat, 4-stress form, but it combines 2 such lines into a long line and the
last stress in each such long line is actually
represented by a syllable only at the end of
the strophe. Elsewhere it is represented by a
pause. Earlier critics and some modern prosodists think that we may be certain only
that the lines in the romances had 3 or 4
beats and that in the *Nibelungenlied* all half
lines except the last had 3. Lyric verse forms
were probably borrowed directly from the
Romance languages and are closely bound up
with music. By the end of the 12th c., in imitation of Romance songs with syllable-counting
lines, regular alternation of stressed and unstressed syllables as well as regular dactylic
rhythms (the so-called MHG dactyls) became accepted patterns. The length of the lines could
vary according to the music, but the best
poets observe meshing of the lines within each
strophe to produce a specific number of beats
of musical time for the strophe as a whole.
The *Meistergesang* observed only the number
of syllables and ignored coincidence of word
accent with verse stress.   W.T.H.J.

In the 16th c. the dominant form in narrative and drama was the *Knittelvers* (q.v.),
which derived from the rhymed couplet of
medieval narrative and which, like the lyric
Meistergesang, in its so-called strict form noted
only the number of syllables and took no account of the coincidence of word accent with
metrical stress (a "free" form of the *Knittelvers*,
followed by some poets, allowed for an unlimited number of unstressed syllables). The
reform in versification effected by Martin Opitz
in the early 17th c. restored natural accentuation to G. verse and established a strict alternation of stressed and unstressed syllables. For
more than a century after Opitz the dominant
line in serious verse was the rhymed *Alex-
andriner*, a 12-syllable iambic line modeled
superficially after the Fr. alexandrine (q.v.),
but quite different in effect because of the
strongly accentual quality of the G. language.
Certain metrical conventions which have
persisted in G. verse for the last two centuries
were initiated in the mid-18th c. by F. G.
Klopstock, who succeeded in adapting several
Gr. and Roman meters to G. and in developing the so-called free rhythms. Searching for
a suitable metrical form into which to cast
his epic *Der Messias*, Klopstock hit upon the
idea, then regarded as revolutionary, of utilizing the unrhymed classical dactylic hexameter.

For his odes he adapted the stanzaic forms of
Sappho, Alcaeus, and Asclepiades. In each instance this adaptation took place through the
substitution of stressed and unstressed syllables
for the classical long and short syllables. Klopstock's free rhythms, employed in odes such as
Die Frühlingsfeier, are essentially what we
today mean by free verse; like his classical
odes, they dispense with rhyme, yet they do
not attempt to follow a consistent metrical
or stanzaic scheme. Many major works in G.
poetry derive ultimately from Klopstock's
metrical forms, e.g., the classical meters of
Goethe's *Römische Elegien* and *Hermann und
Dorothea* and Hölderlin's odes and elegies;
the free rhythms of Goethe's *Prometheus*,
Hölderlin's late hymns, Heine's *Nordsee* and
Rilke's *Duineser Elegien*.

The example of Lessing's *Nathan der Weise*
(1779) established unrhymed iambic pentameter, modeled after Eng. blank verse, as the
prevailing line of G. verse drama, but certain
notable exceptions can be singled out, above
all, Goethe's *Faust*, which revives the "free"
form of *Knittelvers* and also employs most of
the other metrical forms to be found in G.
poetry. As a result of Herder's efforts to arouse
interest in the national past around 1770, and
through the influence, much later, of Arnim
and Brentano's collection of folk songs, *Des
Knaben Wunderhorn* (1806-8), G. poets came
increasingly to imitate the tone, language, and
metrical forms (especially quatrains with 3-
and 4-stress lines) of G. folk poetry. Besides
this folk strain, which characterizes many of
Goethe's early lyrics, as well as the major work
of such later poets as Brentano, Eichendorff
and Heine, G. poetry during the age of Goethe
assimilated an amazing number of foreign
forms, among them the It. ottava rima and
terza rima, Sp. assonantal forms, and the Persian *ghazel* (though certain importations, e.g.,
the It. madrigal and sonnet, were revivals
of forms prevalent in the 17th c.). During the
remainder of the 19th c., G. poets built upon
and refined the metrical forms and traditions
which they had inherited, but during the
naturalist and expressionist periods and again
since 1945, G. verse has displayed intense experimentation in free verse (e.g., A. Holz,
E. Stadler, B. Brecht), influenced by foreign
free-verse movements as well as by native traditions.

During the last two centuries—the period in
which G. has achieved the stature of a major
world literature—G. verse has probably been
characterized by a greater degree of metrical
theorizing and conscious metrical experimentation, plus a more systematic adaptation of
foreign and earlier native forms, than have
the other literatures of Western Europe during this same period. It is significant that the

work of individual poets often displays major achievement within quite divergent metrical traditions—classical meters, free verse, and folk song in Goethe and Mörike, complex rhymed forms and free verse in Rilke. Moreover, one could describe the whole history of G. prosody as a continual veering between two central traditions—an "art" tradition based on strict syllable-counting ("strict" *Knittelvers*, classical meters, the various stanzas borrowed from the romance literatures) and a "native" tradition which does not regulate the number of unstressed syllables per line ("free" *Knittelvers*, free verse, the folk song and its romantic imitations).

Just as G. poets have tended to show a high degree of interest in prosodic matters, so G. literary scholarship has been particularly rich in systematic attempts to describe the history and nature of G. prosody. Among the most notable of these are H. Paul's *Deutsche Metrik* (1905), F. Saran's *Dt. Verslehre* (1907) and A. Heusler's *Dt. Versgeschichte* (3 v., 1925–29). Recent, more popular discussions of G. prosody include W. Kayser's *Kleine dt. Versschule* (1946) and *Gesch. des deutschen Verses* (1960) and O. Paul and I. Glier's *Dt. Metrik* (4th ed., 1961). H.L.;B.Q.M.

GESELLSCHAFTSLIED. (As opposed to the folk song) a song for several voices, written, composed, and performed by and for, educated society, primarily in the baroque and rococo periods in Germany. It originated toward the end of the 16th c. The first, musical, impetus for the G. came with the adoption of It. song forms: the courtly, nonstrophic madrigal, the strophic Neapolitan *villanella* (street song), and the *canzone* (qq.v.). The pleasures and sorrows of love and convivial joys, such as drinking and dancing, are preferred subject matters.

There is a close affinity between the G. and the lyrical poem proper. Hence the high-flowering period of lyrical poetry (1620–1680; Simon Dach, Martin Opitz, G. R. Weckherlin) had an ennobling effect upon the G. Many of the composers wrote their own texts (H. L. Hassler, Adam Krieger). From 1680–1740 the G. was overshadowed by the artistic aria, although the production of *Gesellschaftslieder* did not stop. The second great vogue of the G. occurred between 1740 and 1780. Both the idea of "humanity" and the renewed interest in the folk song caused the artist to write in a more popular vein (J. A. Hiller, J. A. P. Schulz, J. André; J. F. Reichardt was the first to set Goethe's poems to music).

Due to the renewed interest of Herder and the romanticists in folk literature, the G. had to yield its place to the revived folk song after the turn of the 18th c., while compositions of high poetry (*Kunstlieder*) became monodic, required the art of the trained singer, and were reserved for the concert stage.

Hoffmann v. Fallersleben, *Gesellschaftslieder des 16. und 17. Jhs.* (1860); A. Reissmann, *Das deutsche Lied in seiner historischen Entwicklung* (1861); F. W. v. Ditfurth, *Dt. Volks-und Gesellschaftslieder des 17. und 18. Jhs.* (1872); M. Friedlaender, *Das dt. Lied im 18. Jh.* (2 v., 2d ed., 1908); R. Velten, *Das ältere dt. G. unter dem Einfluss der italienischen Musik* (1914); G. Müller, *Gesch. des deutschen Liedes vom Barock zur Gegenwart* (1925); H. Cysarz, *Deutsches Barock in der Lyrik* (1936); M. Platel, *Vom Volkslied zum G.* (1939); C. v. Faber du Faur, *German Baroque Lit.: A Catalogue of the Coll. in the Yale Univ. Library* (1958); W. Flemming, "G.," *Reallexikon*, 2d ed., I; W. Kayser, *Gesch. des deutschen Verses* (1960). U.K.G.

GHASEL (*ghazal*). Name given to a lyric in eastern literature, especially Arabic, Persian, Turkish, Urdu, and Pashto, from the 8th c. onward. Such a poem, whose theme is generally love and wine, often mystically understood, varies in length from 5 to 12 couplets all upon the same rhyme. The poet signs his name in the final couplet. Hundreds of poets have used this form, most famous among them the Persians Saʿdī (d. 1291) and Ḥāfiẓ (d. 1389). The g. was introduced to Western poetry by the romanticists mainly Fr. Schlegel, Rückert, and von Platen (*Ghaselen*, 1821) in Germany, and was made more widely known by Goethe, who in his *West-östlicher Divan* (1819) deliberately imitated Persian models. See also ARAB POETRY, PERSIAN POETRY.—J. H. S. V. Garcin de Tassy, *Hist. de la litt. hindouie et hindoustanie* (2 v., 1839–47); E. J. W. Gibb, *Hist. of Ottoman Poetry* (6 v., 1900–1909); E. G. Browne, *Lit. Hist. of Persia* (4 v., 1928). A.J.A

GLOSA. A Sp. metric form, also called *mote* or *retruécano*, closely related to the *cantiga*, introduced in the late 14th or early 15th c. by the court poets. In strict form it is a poem consisting of a line or a short stanza, called *cabeza* (also *mote, letra,* or *texto*), stating the theme of the poem, and followed by 1 stanza for each line of the *cabeza*, explaining or glossing that line and incorporating it into this explanatory stanza, often at the end as a refrain. Strophes may be of any length and rhyme scheme. Loosely, the g. is any poem expanding on the theme presented in the opening stanza and usually repeating one or more lines of that stanza. A famous late 16th-c. g. is one by Vicente Espinel beginning "Mil veces voy a hablar / a mi zagala."—H. Janner, "La g. española. Estudio histórico de su métrica y de sus temas," RFE, 27 (1943); Navarro. D.C.C.

GLYCONIC. Named after a poet Glycon whose date and place are unknown, this verse form was familiar in Gr. and L. lyric poetry. As used by the poets of the personal Gr. lyric and their Roman imitators, it was normally octosyllabic

$$(\smile\smile|-\smile\smile-|\smile\smile),$$

but choral lyric and drama admitted longer variants of this scheme with resolutions of the long syllables into 2 shorts. With one exception (*Odes* 1.15.36), Horace began his glyconics with 2 long syllables. The catalectic form

$$(\smile\smile|-\smile\smile-|\smile)$$

of the glyconic was called the pherecratean after the Gr. comic poet Pherecrates (fl. ca. 430–410 B.C.).—Bowra; Kolář; Koster; B. Snell, *Griechische Metrik* (2d. ed., 1957). R.J.G.

GNOMIC POETRY. Term applied to poetry which consists largely of gnomes or which has a strong gnomic content. A gnome is "a short pithy statement of a general truth; a proverb, maxim, aphorism, or apothegm" (OED). An example is provided by the first recorded Germanic gnome, given by Tacitus: "Women must weep and men remember." The name "gnomic" was first applied to a group of Gr. poets who flourished in the 6th c. B.C., Theognis, Solon, Phocylides, Simonides of Anorgos, and others. But ancient Egyptian literature, Chinese literature (the *Shih* and the *Shǔ* with pieces going back before the 2d millennium B.C.), and the Sanskrit *Hitopadésa* testify to the long-standing and widespread popularity of the gnome. The most familiar collection of gnomic utterance is the Book of Proverbs. Old Ir. provides an example in *The Instructions of King Cormac MacAirt* and ON a particularly interesting one in the *Hávamál*. The popularity of gnomes among the Germanic peoples is also shown by the two collections in OE, the *Cotton* and the *Exeter* gnomes. The term "gnomic" has, however, been extended beyond mere collections of gnomes to apply to any poetry which deals in sententious fashion with questions of ethics. Ancient literature abounds in gnomic passages, e.g., the Gr. tragedies, particularly the choruses, or many passages in the *Beowulf*. Gnomic poetry has been cultivated in more modern times, in England by Francis Quarles (*Emblems*, 1633) and in France by Gui de Pibras whose *Quatrains* (1574) were a direct imitation of the gnomic poets and enjoyed a great success. —B. C. Williams, *Gnomic Poetry in Anglo-Saxon* (1914); The *Hávámal*, ed. and tr. D.E.M. Clarke (1923); K. Jackson, *Early Welsh Gnomic Poems* (1935); R. MacGregor Dawson, "The Structure of OE Gnomic Poems," JEGP, 61 (1962). R.P.APR.

GOLIARDIC VERSE. A type of medieval poetry, traditionally attributed to the goliards, wandering "scholar-poets" who flourished especially in 12th- and 13th-c. England, France, and Germany. The origin of the term "goliards" is still not clear. There are references to their belonging to the "household of Golias," whose name, in turn, appears in the rubric of about twenty manuscripts. Yet, according to Hanford, Rozhdestvenskaĩa (Dobïash), Raby, and other scholars, there was no Golias; nor was there an *ordo vagorum*, an order or guild of goliards. It seems that the name was used as a term of reproach, perhaps by analogy with Goliath of Gath—the symbol of lawlessness—or by derivation from the L. *gula* (glutton)—the sin of gluttony—and was attached to poets who attacked the Papal curia and their ecclesiastical superiors.

That wandering clerks existed, Helen Waddell (*The Wandering Scholars*, 1927) has shown, but they were not organized, nor does it seem very likely that they had the thorough knowledge of classical and medieval L. poetry, the familiarity with vernacular poetry (learned and popular), and—last but not least—the technical skill to write the so-called goliardic verse. The real authors of some of these poems are known. They were accomplished and even famous poets, such as Hugh Primas, the Archpoet, and Walter of Châtillon.

Whatever its origin, "goliardic" verse constitutes one of the most vigorous poetic expressions of medieval Europe. Although the so-called goliards wrote a few authentic religious lyrics, their characteristic productions are (1) satiric, directed almost always against the church and the Pope and (2) profane, devoted to the pleasures of the bed and the tavern in a spirit of reckless hedonism. Their underlying theme is the Horatian *carpe diem* (q.v.). The most notable collection of L. lyrics which contains some "goliardic" poems is the *Carmina Burana*, published by Joseph Andrews Schmeller in Germany in 1847 and, in part, translated by John Addington Symonds in *Wine, Women and Song* in 1884.

The term "goliardic measure" refers to a stanza form much favored by these poets—a stanza of four monorhymed lines of 13 syllables each, sometimes ending with a hexameter, called an *auctoritas*, quoted from some classical source.

The only complete text of the *Carmina Burana* is still the one published by Schmeller, 4th ed., 1907. The best ed. is the one by A. Hilka and O. Schumann, but only v. I, pts. 1 and 2 and v. II, pt. 1 were published in 1931–41. J. M. Manly, "Familia Goliae," MP, 5

GRAVEYARD POETRY

(1907–8); J. H. Hanford, "The Progenitors of Golias," *Speculum*, 1 (1926); B. I. Jarcho, "Die Vorläufer des Golias," *Speculum*, 3 (1928); O. Rozhdestvenskaiâ (Dobïash), *Les Poésies des goliards* (1931; includes some texts and a list of mss.); *The Goliard Poets*, ed. G. F. Whicher (1949; texts and Eng. verse tr.); *Hymnen und Vagantenlieder*, comp. and tr. K. Langosch (1954; contains texts of Hugh Primas and the Archpoet); F. J. E. Raby, *Hist. of Secular L. Poetry in the Middle Ages*, II (1957); *The Penguin Book of L. Verse*, comp. F. Brittain (1962; texts and tr.). A.P.

GONGORISM. See CULTISM.

GÖTTINGER DICHTERBUND, Göttinger *Hain, Hainbund*. An association of young German poets, students at the University of Göttingen. It was active from 1772, the year of its founding, until about 1776. Inspired by the dynamic subjective art of Klopstock and by a revived interest in the folk song, the poets of the *Hain* wrote fresh lyrics on the themes of nature, friendship, and patriotism. Their organ was the *Musenalmanach*. The members of the *Hain* included Ludwig Hölty (the most talented member of the group), Voss, the two cousins Miller, and the two brothers von Stolberg. The *Hainbund* had similar aims as the Strasburg *Sturm und Drang* (q.v.) movement in its protest against the enslavement of feeling and imagination by the rigid rationality of the enlightenment.—H. Grantzow, *Gesch. des G. und des Vossischen Musenalmanachs* (1909); R. Bäsken, *Die Dichter des G. Hains und die Bürgerlichkeit* (1937); G. Fricke, "G. Hain und G. Ballade," *Studien und Interpretationen* (1956); W. Kohlschmidt, "G. Hain," *Reallexikon*, 2d ed., I.

GRAMMAR AND POETRY. See LINGUISTICS AND POETICS.

GRAND STYLE. A phrase made famous by Matthew Arnold in his Oxford lectures *On Translating Homer* (publ. 1861) and *On Translating Homer: Last Words* (publ. 1862) but used by him as early as the Preface to *Poems*, 1853. Though, as he says in *Last Words*, "The grand style is the last matter in the world for verbal definition to deal with adequately," he gives examples from Homer, Pindar, Virgil, Dante, and Milton, and says it arises in poetry "when a noble nature, poetically gifted, treats with simplicity or with severity a serious subject." In the "grand style simple," of which Homer is the best model, "a noble nature and a poetical gift unite to utter a thing with the most limpid plainness and clearness." In the "grand style severe," of which Milton is perhaps the best model, a thing is said "with a

kind of intense compression, or in an allusive, brief, almost haughty way, as if the poet's mind were charged with so many and such grave matters, that he would not deign to treat any one of them explicitly." The "severe" may seem grandest when we attend most to the noble nature of the author, the "simple" when we attend most to the poetical gift. Arnold prefers the "simple" because it is more magical, more disinterested. Unlike the "severe" it is not intellectual, and so does not encourage imitation by a poet in whom the poetical gift is either lacking or inferior.

The concept of the Grand Style affected Arnold's practice both as poet and critic. In his long poems, *Sohrab and Rustum* (1853) and *Balder Dead* (1855), he aimed, not altogether successfully, at the g.s., and in his essay, "The Study of Poetry" (1880), he declared that all his touchstone (q.v.) poets had the g.s. Since nine of the eleven touchstone passages in the essay are from poems of epic length, Arnold gives the impression that by the g.s. he means the epic style. Though Arnold made the term famous, he did not invent the concept. It had seriously engaged the attention of such predecessors as Longinus, Reynolds, and Ruskin. In many respects the g.s. is the "sublime" (q.v.) of Longinus, who gave as two sources of the sublime noble diction and elevated composition, and who saw in Homer the supreme example of sublimity. Sir Joshua Reynolds, after Burke the Englishman, most influenced by Longinus, discussed the g.s. in relation to "History-Painting" in the *Idler*, nos. 79 and 82, and in *Discourses* 3, 4, 5, and 15. Ruskin, in *Modern Painters*, v. III (1856), took the Longinian position that the distinction between "Great" and "Mean" art was primarily a matter of nobility in the creator. See also STYLE.—A. J. Boyd, *Arnold and the G.S.* (1934); L. Trilling, *Matthew Arnold* (1939); A. H. Warren, Jr., "John Ruskin," *Eng. Poetic Theory: 1825–1865* (1950); Abrams, ch. 6. J.K.R.

GRAVEYARD POETRY. A type of meditative poetry, having as its major themes the melancholy fact of mortality and the hope of a future life, g.p. is so called from its favorite setting. Fundamenally a preromantic phenomenon, it arose in 18th-c. England, largely as a reaction against Augustan fastidiousness and avoidance of enthusiasm. Although there are some earlier examples of g.p. (e.g., Andreas Gryphius, *Kirch-hof Gedancken*, in mid-17th-c. Germany), Thomas Parnell's *Night-Piece on Death* (1721) is the first full-blown flower of the school, which reached its mature growth in Edward Young's *Night-Thoughts* (1742) and Robert Blair's *The Grave* (1743).

Sometimes religious in its attitudes, g.p. is

-[325]-

more significant as a new aesthetic movement. In the latter half of the 18th c. it became a general European phenomenon. Examples of Continental graveyard verse are: GERMAN: von Creutz, *Die Gräber;* von Cronegk, *Einsamkeiten.*—DUTCH: Rhijnvis Feith, *Het Graf.*—SWEDISH: Oxenstierna, *Natten;* Bellman, *Aftonkväde;* Lidner, *Yttersta domen;* Kellgren, *Förtvivlan.* ITALIAN: Pindemonte, *dei Sepolcri.* Ugo Foscolo's answer to Pindemonte, *I Sepolcri,* is perhaps too great a poem to be wholly typical of the fashion, and the same may be said for Thomas Gray's famous *Elegy Written in a Country Churchyard* (1751).— A. L. Reed, *The Background of Gray's Elegy. A Study in the Taste for Melancholy Poetry, 1700–51* (1924); P. Van Tieghem, *Le Préromantisme* (3 v., 1924–47); J. W. Draper, *The Funeral Elegy and the Rise of Eng. Romanticism* (1929); E. M. Sickels, *The Gloomy Egoist* (1932); C. A. D. Fehrman, *Kyrkogårdsromantik* (1954). F.J.W.; A.P.

GREEK POETICS. See CLASSICAL POETICS.

GREEK POETRY. CLASSICAL. Poetry was uniquely important in ancient Greece, as a means not only of expression, but also of communication, commemoration, and instruction. As early as the 9th c. B.C., the bard was thought to possess keener than normal insights into the nature of man and gods; in later centuries, the poet of ability was regarded as the peer of the philosopher and statesman. In part, this unusual recognition of the value of poetry may be ascribed to the tendency, so marked in the Gr. tradition, to identify beauty, moral good, and truth; in part, to the Greek's inherited consciousness of the power, rhythms, and patterns of speech.

The history of Gr. poetry before the Hellenistic period falls into three major phases, each characterized by the predominance of a single poetic genre: the age of epic, in the 9th and 8th c.; lyric poetry, in the 7th and 6th; drama, in the 5th c. To a considerable extent, these phases accurately reflect the nature of their social contexts: the epic, as expressive of the values of an aristocratic, feudal society; the lyric, of a changing world in which traditional values were questioned and individualism thereby encouraged; the drama, of the solidarity of the city-state, its democratic values (in Athens), and the conflict of ideas engendered by the development of the new, open society.

The earliest extant Gr. poems are the Ionian epics of Homer, probably composed, but not set in writing, in the 8th c. Based on a long tradition of orally created and transmitted heroic poetry, the *Iliad* and *Odyssey* are artistically unified works which exhibit a highly developed stylistic virtuosity and remarkable poetic sensitivity. The verse, the standard meter of ancient epic, is the dactylic hexameter. The epics were composed for recitation, as court entertainment, by rhapsodes of singularly retentive memory. In consequence, the technique of composition is basically oral, and marked by frequently recurring formulae, especially at the end of the hexameters. Such stock motifs are, nonetheless, seldom embarrassing, for they are usually skillfully integrated into the texture of the verse.

Although they were composed for recitation before an aristocratic audience, and embody many of the values of a feudal society, the epics evidence a deep understanding of the comic and tragic dimensions of the human dilemma. Doubtless it was for this reason that the Homeric poems were considered throughout the history of ancient Greece as the richest source of moral and religious instruction. Homer's contribution to the tradition and development of Gr. poetry cannot be overestimated. While there were many heroic epics, which survive only in fragments, written in imitation of his works, apparently none of them equalled his artistry. Hesiod's didactic epics (probably of the 8th c.) have been preserved. They are directed to the peasant of Boeotia rather than the Ionian aristocrat, being concerned with the morality and beliefs of the small farmer toughly confronting a life of ceaseless labor and few rewards. While they cannot be compared to Homer's works in scope or genius, they often display much poetic power.

Lyric poetry as currently defined, and as a literary genre, was apparently a creation of the 7th c., although its roots may be traced to a much earlier period (there is good evidence for its existence as a folk form in pre-Homeric Greece). It should be noted, however, that the term "lyric" normally meant, to the ancient Gr., "sung to the lyre," and that poetry composed for accompaniment by other instruments or designed for unaccompanied recitation was regarded as belonging to other genres. Further, lyric poetry proper was distinguished into two categories; choral lyric, intended for delivery by a chorus of up to fifty voices, and monodic lyric, composed for recitation by one singer. Monodic lyric poetry flourished in the Aeolian islands, especially at Lesbos, the center of an old but rapidly changing civilization, torn by economic unrest and by dissonance between newly emerging political ideals and traditional oligarchic principles. It is primarily a poetry of personal feeling, with a range of subject matter extending from political diatribe to conviviality, friendship, and love. The most famous, and probably the most talented, of the Aeolian poets were Alcaeus, a skilled and versatile writer, and Sappho, whose craftsmanship is sometimes equaled by other Gr. poets, but whose simple charm and emotional intensity are seldom rivaled. Each composed in a wide variety of meters, all marked by a consistent avoidance of groups of three short syllables (a unique feature of Aeolic poetry), and typically cast in stanzaic form, as in these first lines of Sappho's *Ode to Aphrodite*

poikilothron' athanat' Aphrodita,
pai Dios doloploke, lissomai se,
mē m' asaisi mēd' oniaisi damna,
potnia, thymon.

Splendid throned, immortal, O Aphrodite,
child of Zeus and weaver of charms, I beg you
not with grief and anguishing pains to crush
my spirit, O goddess

Although pitifully little Aeolic verse survives, enough is extant to assure us of the excellence of these two poets, and they must be regarded as the greatest of the monodic lyricists. The work of Anacreon of Teos, also a 6th c. poet, is in many ways similar to that of the Aeolian school, although he was an Ionian. His poetry, while finely wrought, is less ambitious than that of Alcaeus and Sappho.

Choral lyric poetry was in large measure a creation of the Dorian Greeks. It became an art form first at Sparta, where it was associated with the name of Terpander of Lesbos; he is a shadowy figure to us today. More is known of the Spartan Alcman (7th c.), especially through a long and lovely fragment of a maiden-song. Nonetheless, it is impossible to form now a reliable estimate of the merit of choral poetry before the 5th c., because of the scantiness of the literary evidence.

With Pindar (5th c.), however, we are on firm ground. A Boeotian aristocrat who inherited the then long tradition of Dorian poetry, he is deservedly the most famous of the choral poets whose works are extant. From his vast production only the *epinicia*, odes in honor of the victors at athletic festivals, have been preserved in better than fragmentary condition. Pindar's genius enables him to surmount the strictures imposed on him by the occasional nature of the epinician ode; his poems, although elaborately formal, evince a striking intensity of emotional content. Pindar, perhaps more than any other Gr. poet, seems to think perceptually rather than conceptually, to move from idea to idea by suggestion of image or mythic association rather than with the design of logic. In consequence, the odes are characterized by a dazzling sequence of images and mythological reference. This aspect of his work is illustrated in brief by the following passage, which concludes the third *Nemean Ode*. Here he addresses once more the victorious Aristocleides, winner in the *pancration*:

> Farewell, my friend. I send you this,
> honey mixed with white milk,
> wreathed with the foam of stirring,
> a poet's draught with breath of Aeolian flutes,

> late though it come. The eagle is swift among
>   birds.
> From afar he hovers and swoops, suddenly, and
>   takes the bloody game with his claws.
> The chattering daws range at humble height.
> On you, by grace of Clio of the fair throne,
>   and for your victor's temper,
> From Nemea, and Epidaurus, also from Me-
>   gara, the light has flashed.

The meters of the epinicia, and indeed, of all choral poetry, are highly complex and varied; Pindar writes in dactylo-epitritic, logaoedic, and paeonic. With a single exception, no two of the forty-five odes are metrically identical, a fact that may serve further to underline this poet's restless artistic individualism.

In much choral lyric, including the Pindaric epinician, a triadic structure is common, in contrast to the predominantly stanzaic form of monodic lyric. Two rhythmically identical series, the "strophe" and "antistrophe," are followed by an "epode," which is based on a different but related metrical pattern. A poem may contain any number of these triads, all of which are metrically alike. Like the occasions served by choral poetry, the subject matter was extremely diversified, ranging, for example, from the epinician to the hymn, the dirge, the maiden-song, and the dithyramb. In short, the choral poet is the voice of the community, expressing the attitudes of his fellow citizens toward events or achievements of moment; but in Pindar's case, at least, this public responsibility in no degree violates the poet's artistic integrity or binds his individuality. Of choral poets other than Pindar, Simonides and Bacchylides (both of the 5th c.) deserve mention. Lamentably little of the former's work in this genre is extant, and the latter's works, although they display much narrative grace, lack the imaginative fire of the Pindaric ode.

In addition to the lyric proper, two other related genres, elegiac and iambic poetry, achieved popularity in Greece. Elegiac poetry originated as a song accompanied by the flute. Its meter, the elegiac couplet, is a modification of the dactylic hexameter, and felt to be lighter than that epic verse form. The first verse is the normal hexameter, while the second member of the couplet is a dactylic pseudo-pentameter in the following form:

$$-\smallsmile\smallsmile|-\smallsmile\smallsmile|-||-\smallsmile\smallsmile|-\smallsmile\smallsmile|-.$$

Elegy was not primarily the vehicle of the lament, but was used for a number of purposes, including military exhortation, historical description, expression of love, and pronouncement of personal opinion on almost any kind of subject. Perhaps the most skilled of the elegiac poets was Mimnermus of Colophon (7th c.). Much of his work focused, it is said, on historical and geographical subject matter. He is better known to us, through the extant fragments, as a writer preoccupied with the despair of youth's fading, and the deeper horror of the ugliness of old age and the finality of death. Even from the little verse that has survived, we can sense his mastery of the illuminating symbol and the incisive image. Still more impressive is the degree to which he controls the flow of elegiac rhythms to support and inform ideas and attitudes. Tyrtaeus (7th c.) and Solon (fl. ca. 600) do not rise to Mimnermus' height, since they appear to lack the sophistication of his technique. They are, however, poets of stature: the former as the voice *par excellence* of Spartan military exhortation; the latter as the reflective and sensible spokesman of Athenian rationality and judicial wisdom. The Megarian Theognis (6th c.), an articulate aristocrat embittered by a society which was uprooting the values to which his class was committed, is a remarkably uneven poet, usually at his best (because most original) when his despair is fullest. An accretion of numerous elegies by other writers, but ascribed to Theognis, has come to us in our manuscripts; many of these can be distinguished from the genuine poems on stylistic or historical grounds, and are of similarly disparate merit.

The remaining major genre, iambic poetry, was principally reserved for the expression of satire and invective, and also for the fable. Simpler and less musical than the lyric or elegiac, it more closely approximated the rhythms of ordinary speech. Archilochus of Paros (7th c.) became and remained the undisputed master of this genre. His inventive, humorous, and often devastatingly vitriolic poems reveal a genius of the first order; they display an engagement not only with personal attack, but (especially in his elegiacs) with deep reflection and introspection. Semonides of Amorgos (7th or 6th c.) is a clever, but lesser, poet, while the Villonesque Hipponax of Ephesus (6th c.) is a precise craftsman within the narrow restraints he accepts with his subject matter. Viewed as a group, and with the exception of Archilochus, the iambic writers must be regarded among the minor poets of ancient Greece.

With the stabilization of the Gr. world in the later 6th and 5th c., the poetry of personal expression was eclipsed by the rise of the drama, especially tragedy. The seeds of tragedy are probably traceable to ritual observances, primarily choral in form, in honor of Dionysus. The decisive steps in the transformation from choral ritual to drama were said to have been taken by Thespis, who added an actor, and Aeschylus, who made true dramatic conflict possible by the addition of a second. At the risk of some oversimplification, the following common characteristics may be observed in the works of the three great tragedians of the 5th c., Aeschylus, Sophocles, and Euripides: a preoccupation with the problems of the city-state, man's relations to it, and to the gods; the use of themes from myths related by Homer and the other epic poets, rather than the creation of "original" plots; an elevated but by no means wholly artificial diction; and finally, an astoundingly dexterous use of imagery to support and illuminate dramatic movement.

The poetic form of the classic tragic drama owes much to the earlier traditions of the various genres. The meter of the dialogue is iambic, and that of the choral odes is as varied and complex as the meter of the earlier and contemporary choral lyrics. The triadic structure of the choral ode is often retained and put to effective dramatic use; indeed, it is singularly appropriate for drama, since the amoebic strophe and antistrophe can serve to set forth a miniature aesthetic parallel of the larger dramatic antagonisms, and the epode, or refrain, to suggest the tragic solution or synthesis.

The history of 5th-c. tragedy is a story of diversity within unity. Aeschylus, the true father of tragic drama, is not thereby, as some would have it, an "archaic" poet, but the master of his preferred dramatic techniques. Concerned as he was with the continuous evolution of God, man, and city-state out of the conflicts and sufferings of the historical cosmic process, he saw the tragic trilogy as the natural, comprehensive vehicle for his humanistic, monotheistic views. The grandeur of his characters and the somber, elemental atmosphere of the plays contribute integrally to the tragic power of his themes, as do the magniloquent diction and the extraordinary metaphors (the wheels of the war chariot "shriek fear"; Helen of Troy is "a thought of windless calm, a delicate jewel of wealth, the soft arrow of the eyes"). The seven tragedies which survive are the product of insight and conscious artistry, not of the tentative experiments of an inventive primitive.

The universe of Sophocles, unlike that of Aeschylus, is static; for this reason, he abandoned the trilogic form and focused the intense light of single dramas on crucial moments in the lives of heroic, epic figures. His is a mysterious cosmos, for these men seem to meet their doom less for what they have done than for what they are; yet there emerges the mystical conviction that their sufferings have transmuted evil into good for their fellows. The style of Sophocles, in his seven extant plays, is simpler and less elegant than his predecessor's, but no less subtle. The power of his key dramatic device, tragic irony, will be attested by anyone who has witnessed a performance of his masterpiece, *Oedipus Tyrannus*.

Euripidean tragedy is less easy to characterize. We possess nineteen of his plays, and he was a notable experimenter and innovator; we owe to him, for example, the invention of melodrama, and probably, in the *Alcestis*, true tragicomedy. The common judgment that much of his writing is "realistic" and prosaic is in large part insubstantial. It is true that his diction, settings, and circumstances of plot may often be drawn from the Athens of his day, but not in reportorial style; "realistic" detail seems to be introduced for the purpose of juxtaposing the shabbiness of contemporary life and the heroic motif, thereby criticizing, rather than reporting, the inversion he felt had taken place in Athenian values. There is much of the reformer, a little of Shaw, in Euripides. At the same time, one finds in most of the plays a lyricism of high order.

As Euripides compared the grandeur of the heroic tradition with the pettiness of his modern world, so his younger contemporary, Aristophanes, juxtaposed the beautiful and the grotesque, in his eleven extravagant, uninhibited comedies. Full of hearty earthiness and brilliant satire on the life of Athens, his plays epitomized the "Old Comedy," a genre which soon deserted the stage forever; the clouded political scene of later centuries could not tolerate the freedom of expression which Aristophanes adorned, but did not conceal, with his melodic fantasies.

Toward the close of the 5th c., Gr. poetry experienced the beginnings of a transformation which was to affect it radically. With the rise of science and philosophy, the faith of the Greeks in the value of poetry as a vehicle of truth began to decline, a trend underlined a little later by Plato's attacks on the poets as mere technicians who possess no real knowledge. The result of the new eagerness for conceptual knowledge was, for many writers, a turning away from the ambiguity of poetry to the clarity and precision of historical and philosophical prose. The artist who continued to choose verse as a medium of expression was faced, then, with a double dilemma: poetry could no longer be regarded as the best possible means of communication of significant ideas, and further, he seldom felt that he could seriously challenge the excellence of the older writers of epic, lyric, and dramatic poetry, forms which appeared to have run the full

course of their development. Consequently, the Hellenistic period is notable for the emergence of poets who emphasized elegance of style and beauty and novelty of technique, sometimes at the expense of clarity and earnest communication. No longer did the poet feel that he was the voice of the community (which itself had begun to dissolve as a result of movements toward political and philosophical cosmopolitanism), or that he was bound by strict and important moral obligations to his society; instead, he tended, in his search for new and unexplored modes of expression, to limit his audience to a coterie of artists and intellectuals. Only the New Comedy remained a fully "public" form, and the one major genre through which the poet spoke to the society at large. But even the renowned Menander (342–291 B.C.), with his polite, rather prosy treatment of conventionally romantic plots, is not deeply concerned with enlarging the experience of his audience. More typical of Hellenistic attitudes is the "manifesto" of the Alexandrian Callimachus:

> I hate the epic poem,
> nor do I like the public highway.
> I abhor the wandering lover,
> I will not drink from the common spring,
> and despise everything popular.

Despite, however, the Hellenistic inclination to restrict the range and popular appeal of poetry, many of the experiments of the age— varyingly realistic, romantic, and baroque— bore valuable fruit. Especially remarkable was the school which developed at the new city of Alexandria, and, under the patronage of the Ptolemies, confirmed and defined the poetic trends already being shaped by changing tastes. The literary consequences of the foundation of the Museum and Library were those to be expected of any nationally sponsored academy; the many poets attracted to the Egyptian city gained a professional security they had not known at the cost of at least a portion of the freedom of expression which was their normal prerogative. Nonetheless, the Ptolemaic patronage assisted the talents of the three greatest Hellenistic poets, Callimachus, Apollonius, and Theocritus. The first of these was a precise formalist who composed in several genres, including the *Hymns* (artificial, in that they are court poems without religious content), and the *Aitia*, an etiological work which occasionally sparkles, but impresses mostly with its scholarly aridity. He is at his best (at least to modern taste) in the epigram. This traditional form, which is based on the elegiac couplet, and traces its origins to functional dedicatory and sepulchral inscriptions of the 7th c., received a rare polish from the terseness and wit of the Callimachean technique. Apollonius, against the tenor of the times, attempted to revitalize the epic in his *Argonautica;* although he is consciously indebted to Homer, the result is not heroic, but psychological and romantic, and foreshadowed the development of the ancient prose novel. Theocritus is probably the finest of these three poets. His *Idylls* (a term of uncertain meaning, but without bucolic reference), written primarily in hexameters, reflect a singular versatility of talent, with equal mastery of the highly musical and romantic pastoral, escapist but never totally divorced from reality, and the realistic mime which gently satirizes the life of his age. Theocritus is a crucial figure in the development of pastoral poetry, for his catalytic skills fused an energetic folk art with the rich inheritance of Gr. literature to create bucolic verse which, for its sureness of touch, its fluidity, and its crisp pictoriality, many feel is unequaled in the tradition of the genre.

With these three major writers of the 3d c. B.C., the great age of Gr. poetry came to an end. Only the collection of epigrams known as the *Greek Anthology* testifies to the continuance of some creativity. This amazing compilation, gathered in the 10th c. A.D., has given us about 4,000 poems, mostly in elegiacs, attributed to poets from the 7th c. B.C. to the high Byzantine era. Much of the later work included is tedious and imitative, but the *Anthology* is adorned by the rich love poetry of Meleager (fl. 100 B.C.) and the verses of a number of minor poets worthy of the older tradition. But by and large, the stage was vacated in favor of the L. writers who, through a synthesis of the Gr. heritage and the creative energy furnished by an expanding civilization, infused a new vitality into Western poetry.

It is not easy to summarize the major qualities of a poetic tradition as diversified and rich as that of the ancient Greeks. There are, however, certain recurrent characteristics, observable in varying measure in Gr. writing of every period: simplicity and directness (virtually bareness, by the standards of Eng. poetry) but with subtlety of suggestion, a tendency to understatement, avoidance of sentimentality, close and careful organization, architectonic balance of composition, and musicality. The last three of these qualities can be illustrated readily by reference to the odes of Sappho, the choral odes of tragedy, or the works of almost any important Gr. poet. The first three are fully demonstrated in the epigram written, in the 5th c., by the famous Simonides, when he was called on to compose an epitaph for the tomb of the 300 Spartans, under Leonidas, who died at Thermopylae and by their death preserved the armies defending Gr. freedom. The epitaph contains no resounding words of praise, no lengthy expression of grief. It states simply, but with reverberating connotations,

O xein', angellein Lakedaimoniois, hoti tēde keimetha tois keinōn rhēmasi peithomenoi.

Stranger, tell the men of Lacedaemon that here we lie, and obeyed their commands.

GR. TEXT: *Anthologia Lyrica Graeca,* ed. E. Diehl (6 fasc., Leipzig, 1925), rev. *alii* (3d ed.), fasc. 1 (1954), 3 (1952), 4–6 in prep. *Theognis,* ed. D. Young (1961) supplants fasc. 2.; *Poetarum Lesbiorum Fragmenta,* ed. E. Lobel and D. Page (1955); *Poetae Melici Graeci,* ed. D. Page (1962). ANTHOLOGIES IN TR.: *Lyra Graeca,* ed. and tr. J. Edmonds (2d ed., 3 v., 1928; also contains Gr. text and a valuable historical survey); *Elegy and Iambus,* ed. and tr. J. Edmonds (2 v., 1931; also contains Gr. text); *Oxford Book of Gr. Verse in Tr.,* ed. T. Higham and C. M. Bowra (1938); *Gr. Poetry for Everyman,* ed. and tr. F. Lucas (1951); *Gr. Lyrics,* ed. and tr. R. Lattimore (2d ed., 1960; brief, but the finest tr.). METRICS: G. Thomson, *Gr. Lyric Metre* (1929, rev. ed., 1961); Dale; P. Maas, *Gr. Metre* (1962). HISTORY AND CRITICISM: A. and M. Croiset, *Histoire de la litt. grecque* (5 v., 1909–28; old, but critically dependable); J. Symonds, *Studies of the Gr. Poets* (3d ed., 1920); J. Mackail, *Lectures on Gr. Poetry* (2d ed., 1926); A. Koerte, *Hellenistic Poetry* (1929); Schmid and Stählin (esp. useful bibliog.); A. Couat, *La Poésie alexandrine . . .* (1882; Eng. tr. J. Loeb with suppl. ch. by E. Cahen, 1931); C. M. Bowra, *Gr. Lyric Poetry from Alcman to Simonides* (1938, 2d ed., 1961; controversial but perceptive) and *Early Gr. Elegists* (1938); G. Norwood, *Pindar* (1945; a thorough treatment of Pindaric technique); D. Page, *Sappho and Alcaeus* (1955; close analysis of the poems); R. Lattimore, *The Poetry of Gr. Tragedy* (1958). R.D.M.

MEDIEVAL GREEK POETRY. See BYZANTINE POETRY.

MODERN. After the fall of Constantinople to the Turks in 1453, and until the Gr. War of Independence (1821–28), poetry flourished mainly in the Frankish-occupied Gr. lands. The island of Crete was the most important center. In the 16th and first half of the 17th c. it gave birth to a poetry that, though depending on It. models, has a force and character of its own. The masterpiece of Cretan literature is the *Erotokritos,* an epico-lyric poem of 10,052 rhyming 15-syllable political verses, composed by Vitzentzos Kornaros. The story—the chivalrous love of Erotokritos for Aretousa, and their union after long and arduous adventures—follows the Frankish romance *Paris et Vienne,* which the author of the Cretan epic probably knew through an It. translation. But at the same time the influence of Ariosto, and also of the Cretan folk song, is evident. Western influence is also felt in the Cretan drama, the most important examples of which are *The Sacrifice of Abraham* by an anonymous poet, and the tragedy *Erophile* by George Chortatzes. Comedy and the pastoral were also written there, and had the fall of Crete to the Turks in 1669 not put an end to the cultural life of the island, modern Gr. literature might well have followed a different course.

In the remainder of the Gr. world, then under Turkish rule, the only noteworthy poetry composed were the folk songs. Their heyday was the 18th c., and many love songs, songs of travel, lullabies, and dirges are of a remarkable beauty and freshness, superior to any poetry in Gr. since the close of the 9th c. In the 18th c. we also meet with the first influence of Fr. literature upon Gr. writing with the so-called *Phanariots* (the educated Greeks who had clustered round the Oecumenical Patriarch in Constantinople), an influence which also largely determined the writings of Athanasios Christopoulos and John Velaras, the two most important precursors of the poetry which followed the liberation of Greece.

The liberation, finally achieved in 1828 after a long and bitter struggle, made the capital of the country the center of all intellectual life. It was there that the Romantic School of Athens flourished, whose founder and leading spirit was Alexander Soutsos (1803–63). He was a fervent admirer of Victor Hugo and Byron, but his exuberant romantic and patriotic writings did not capture the spirit of their models. As a satirist, however, he is terse and vigorous. The influence he exercised upon Gr. poetry was for many years great, though not always beneficial. The other main representatives of the Romantic School of Athens, Panagiotis Soutsos, Alexander Rizos Rangavis, George Zalokostas, Theodore Orphanidis, Elias Tantalidis, and John Karasoutsas were all slaves of an exaggerated romanticism. On the whole, they use a stilted and archaic form of Gr. (the *katharevousa*), and are painstakingly patriotic. Achilles Paraschos (1838–95) is the leading figure in the last period of the school. Alfred de Musset, Victor Hugo, and Byron were his idols, but the rhetorical profuseness and mock-heroic patriotism of his verses kept him far below their level, though a spark of real poetry appears here and there. His contemporaries George Paraschos, Angelos Vlachos, Alexander Vyzantios, Demetrios Paparrhegopoulos, Spyridon Vasiliadis, and George Vizyenos were all overshadowed by his reputation, in spite of the greater sincerity and more delicate technique of many of their writings. The Romantic School of Athens with its rhetorical profuseness, hackneyed patriotism, and stilted purist Gr. was superseded by the New School of Athens, which resulted from a fresh assessment of Gr. national values and the linguistic movement to introduce the spoken tongue (the *Demotiki*) into literature. The latter turned the attention of the nation to the School of the Ionian Islands, by which that form of language had already been successfully used. The founder and greatest representative of the School was Dionysios Solomos (1798–1857). Like other members of the Ionian aristocracy of his day, he was bilingual, and, having received his education in Italy, wrote his first poems in It. He soon, however, developed a preference for Gr. His early works in Gr. were short lyrics, but the War of Independence stirred him to more ambitious projects. As the years passed his philosophic approach to art and life deepened, and expressed itself in verses of unique delicacy and balance, unsurpassed to this day in modern Gr. He is a figure outstanding in the whole of European literature, because he finally succeeded in combining harmoniously the classical and the romantic spirit. From the *Hymn to Liberty* (the first stanzas of which became the Gr. national anthem) to the *Free Besieged*, which sing of the heroic resistance and sally of Missolonghi, we can trace the agony and artistic achievement of a highly spiritual nature. Unfortunately most of his mature work is known only from fragments. The instability of Solomos' disposition seems to have prevented him from finishing many of his major works. In the struggle that continued from Byzantine days between the *Katharevousa* and the *Demotiki* as the language of literature, Solomos marks a turning point. For by choosing the latter he pointed the way which all subsequent Gr. poetry worthy of the name was to follow. Moreover, he introduced a number of Western metrical forms (the sestina, the ottava, the terza rima) into Gr., which freed Gr. poetry from the monotony of the 15-syllable verse which had formerly characterized it. Of the other poets of the Ionian School (George Tertsetis, Julios Typaldos, Gerasimos Marcoras, Lorentzos Mavilis, Andreas Calvos, and Aristotle Valaoritis, the most important are Calvos (1792–1869) and Valaoritis (1824–39). Calvos drew his inspiration from the Gr. classics, and indulged in an austere and moralizing poetry which exercised no notable influence on subsequent literature. Valaoritis, though overromantic and grandiloquent, was greatly admired, and is the link between the Ionian School, the "Demotic Movement," and the New School of Athens.

About 1880, a young group of poets, influenced by the violent criticism of E. Rhoides and by the feeling that Gr. poetry by employing the *kat harevouse* and its excessive romanticism was heading for sterility, formed the New School of Athens. They aspired to become the Gr. *Parnassiens*, masters of a restrained and objective art. Once again the influence of Fr. literature was making itself felt. The central figure of the new school was Kostis Palamas (1859–1943), a man of talent and wide reading. In his many and important works were blended the ancient and modern Gr. traditions, as well as the social and spiritual convulsions of the late 19th and early 20th c. *The Dodecalogue of the Gipsy* is perhaps his central achievement. Its hero the Gypsy musician, a symbol of freedom and art, gradually deepens into the patriot, the Greek, and finally the "Hellene"— citizen and teacher of the world. Together with this powerful epico-lyrical work, *The King's Flute*, a historical epic, and *Life Immovable*, the most important of his lyrical collections, have established his reputation not only in Gr. letters, but throughout Europe. The influence of Palamas on contemporary poets such as George Drosinis, John Polemis, and George Stratigis was profound, and was felt in more ways than one by most of his successors. John Gryparis, in his mastery of language, Constantine Hatzopoulos, in his excellent sense of rhythm, Miltiadis Malakasis and Lambros Porfyras in their sad and playful charm, and Costas Crystallis in his virile idyllic tone betray in more than one way their debt to the leader of the school. It is the poets of this generation who also introduced symbolism and free verse into Gr. poetry, which greatly enriched and enlivened it in the 20th c.

After Palamas the most important figure in Gr. poetry is undoubtedly Angelos Sikelianos (1884–1952). His powerful verse has its roots in the New School of Athens, but his thought followed a different and obscurer course. Gr. nature and history are seen in the light of a Dionysiac mysticism. This together with a rich, incisive diction that brings landscape, the human form, and abstract thought in clear-cut relief before the eyes, has produced some of the most striking lyrical poetry written in the 20th c. in the West. His tragedies, however, are theatrically imperfect. The one significant Gr. poet who remained untouched by the influence of Palamas and the New School of Athens is Constantine Kavafis (1868–1933). An Alexandrian both by birth and spiritual inclination, his main theme is the tragic glory of Hellenistic Greece and its decadence. But in his work historical memories and personal experiences are inextricably blended. In no other Gr. poet is the tragedy of life expressed more sensually, nor sensuality more tragically. Nikos Kazantzakis (1885–1957), well known as a novelist,

is the author of a formidable 33,333-line poem called the *Odyssey* (translated into Eng. verse by Kimon Friar, 1958). Its hero, a modern Odysseus, wandering in the world of thought, is haunted by the idea of nihilism. The size and style of the work are overpowering, and there are many passages of great beauty. Of the many poets living and writing in Greece today at least two should be mentioned in a short survey of this nature. George Seferis (b. 1900), who was awarded the 1963 Nobel Prize for Literature, is a genuine symbolist who records in true poetic and lyrical manner the fate of modern man; and finally Elytis (b. 1912) writes verse full of the light and color of the Aegean islands.

The fact that in the last hundred years much greater poetry has been written in Gr. than in the fourteen centuries which preceded them, and that in the last fifty Gr. poetry by giving up its political or purely national aspirations has achieved universal validity and a European significance, augurs well for the future. It should be remembered that poetry written in Gr. has the longest and perhaps the noblest uninterrupted tradition in the Western world.

ANTHOLOGIES: *Anthologia 1708–1933*, ed. E. N. Apostolidis (n.d.); *Poetry of Modern Greece*, tr. F. McFerson (1884); *Songs of Modern Greece*, tr. G. F. Abbott (1900); *Anthologie Populaire de la Grèce Moderne*, tr. H. Pernot (1910); *Modern Gr. Poems*, tr. T. Stephanidis-G. Katsimbalis (1926); *Anthol. des Poètes Néo-Grecs, 1886–1929*, tr. J. Michel (1930); *Eklogae apo ta tragoudia tou Hellenikou Laou*, ed. N. Politis, 3d ed., 1932); *Medieval and Modern Gr. Poetry*, ed. C. A. Trypanis (1951; includes extensive bibliog. on all important modern Gr. poets); *Six Poets of Modern Greece*, tr. E. Keeley and Ph. Sherrard (1961).

HISTORY AND CRITICISM: D. C. Hesseling, *Hist. de la Litt. Grecque Moderne* (1924); E. Voutieridis, *Syntomi Historia tis Neohellenikis Logotechnias* (1933); J. Panagiotopoulos, *Ta Prosopa kai ta keimena* (5 v., 1942–48); S. Baud-Bovy, *Poésie de la Grèce Moderne* (1946); A. Kambanis, *Historia tis Neas Hellenikis Logotechnias* (1948); C. M. Bowra, *The Creative Experiment* (1949); C. Demaras, *Historia tis Neohellenikis Logotechnias* (1955); Ph. Sherrard, *The Marble Threshing Floor* (1956); B. Knös, *L'Histoire de la Litt. Néogrecque . . .* (1962). C.A.T.

GREEK PROSODY. See CLASSICAL PROSODY.

GUJARATI POETRY. See INDIAN POETRY.

GYPSY POETRY (folk tales, folk poetry, folk songs). Romany is the spoken language of the Gypsies (originally, a neo-Indic dialect of the Northwestern area, based on Sanskrit and Prakrit, including additions from several Asiatic [no Arabic] and many European languages). Though noticeably fading away, it is still a living idiom in its many—in Europe at least 16—dialects. Attempts to trace its development to a literary language have failed up to now.

Fortunetelling is still a flourishing branch of family business with the majority of Gypsies. (The It. popular art of the 17th c. pleasantly immortalized it in the rhymes and tunes of the "Zingaresca" stanzas). The G. is a gifted narrator, talkative, with a retentive memory, a lively temperament, and a fertile imagination. An echo of the rich, impressive faith of his Indian ancestors binds him to his amulets, charms, dreams, omens, and mysterious forces, making the G. communities—whatever religion they may follow nominally—live in the state of animism. The repertoire of G. story tellers appears to conform naturally enough to that of the land of their sojourn. In essentials the Indo-European stockpot is common to all genuine folk tales. The recital of a G. tale is a most dramatic action in which the form of the oral transmission—with its definite openings, links, and tags as stereotyped as the familiar Eng. "once upon a time"—is regarded seriously.

G. folk poetry shows a primitive degree of natural development, with simple (mostly parallel) rhymes without any strophical construction. The not too numerous samples contained in the collections (by H. Wlislocky, A. Hermann, A. Colocci, J. Sampson and a few others) vigorously echo the sound reaction of the G. soul to all that may appeal to the primitive masses of nature-loving European peoples:

Phen ta mange čaje,
Kames man voj ni či?
Kamau tut, kamau tut,
Si nastig bristav tut

Tell me, my Sweetheart,
Do you love me or don't you?
I love you, I love you,
I cannot forget you.
(Collected by I. Csenki)

Their lyric vaguely mirrors some characteristics and the primitive verse-making technique of the surrounding folk poetry, showing naive sincerity in expression. The predominant themes remain nature and love with overtones ranging from manly and parental tenderness down to the merciless cruelty of the revengeful lover and more or less coarse love. Besides the primary devices of repetition and parallelism, metaphor, simile, and alliteration are not unknown in G. poetry. The few samples of epic verses in Romany (kalo) language hardly qualify as folk ballads, though the suggestive imagery in the descriptive tale reaches, at times, real dramatic depth. The kind of music-

hall or highway poetry, mostly a creation of inspired aficionados of the rather romanticized figure of the 18th-19th c. G., thickened into a sui generis "gypsified literature" in a few European countries. It culminated, perhaps, in the performances of the suburban type of the flamenco caste in Andalusia, successors of a mixture of western and oriental minstrel tradition.

The genuine folk poetry of the G. has so far not been sufficiently studied for conclusions about its relationship to the field of genuine G. music, another topic over which the mystic fog of romantic conception is still hovering in most countries of the world. As it is, the world possesses comparatively little information about the genuine music of the Gypsies. The bulk of instrumental or vocal music, known and propagated as Hungarian, Russian, Rumanian, or Spanish G. music (from the tune material of the Hungarian Rhapsodies by F. Liszt down to the tunes sung by the Rus. choirs, and the flamenco music of Spain), is not G. music in the folkloristic sense of the term. F. Liszt's much discussed Des Bohémiens et de leur musique en Hongrie (1859) bears the leonine part of responsibility for the still persisting erroneous belief that the said art music (its melodic material and the instrumental style of its performance) is genuinely G. A remarkable stock of folk songs of the nonmusician Gypsies, collected recently by Hungarian folklorists in continuation of the fundamental work by B. Bartok and Z. Kodály on the Magyar peasant song, seems to support the possibility of some comprehensive conclusions as a result of extended further research in this direction among the Gypsies all over the world.

ANTHOLOGIES: Volksdichtungen der siebenbürgischen und südungarischen Zigeuner, ed. and tr. H. Wlislocky (1890); "Ciganyok" [Gypsies], Pallas Lexikon, ed. and tr. A. Hermann and H. Wlislocky (1893); G. Folk Tales, ed. and tr. F. H. Groome (1899); The Wind of the Heath, ed. and tr. J. Sampson (1930); A Book of G. Folk Tales, ed. and tr. E. D. Yates (1948); Bazsarozsa, 99 G. Folk Songs, ed. I. Csenki and M. Paszti (1955).

HISTORY AND CRITICISM: G. F. Black, A G. Bibliog. (1914); Leeds Univ. Romany Catalogue (D. U. McGrigor Phillips Collection, 1962); Jour. of the G. Lore Society, 1-3 (1888–92); n.s. 1-9 (1907–1915/16); ser. 3, 1- ; 1922- ; A. Hermann, Ethnologische Mitteilungen aus Ungarn (1892–1907); all are indispensable sources for studies of G. lore.—H. M. Grellmann, Die Zigeuner (1787); G. Borrow, The Zincali (2 v., 1841); F. Miklosich, Über die Mundarten und Wanderung der Zigeuner Europas (1872–77); A. F. Pott, Die Zigeuner in Europa und Asien (1884); A. Colocci, Gli Zingari (1888); A. Thesleff, "Report on the G.

problem," JGLS, n.s. 5 (1911–12); I. Brown, *Deep Song* (1929); C. J. P. Serboianu, *Les Tsiganes* (1930); E. Pittard, *Les Tsiganes ou Bohemiens* (1932); M. Block, *Zigeuner* (1938); I. Csenki, "Collecting Folk Songs among the Gypsies of Hungary," *Koddly Album* (1943);

B. Bartok, "G. Music or Hungarian Music," *Musical Quarterly*, 33 (1947); E. De Spur "Liszt's and Brahms' so-called G. Music," JGLS, ser. 3, 28 (1949) and "Myth and Truth about G. Music," *Almanaque da Gazeta Hungara* (1957 and 1958; on the G. folk song).   E.DE S.

H

HAIKU (also called *haikai* or *hokku*). This Japanese lyric form of 17 syllables in lines of 5, 7, 5 syllables emerged in the 16th c., flourished from the 17th-19th c., and has adherents today. Each h. must state or imply a season or New Year's Month and, except for modern innovations, is almost wholly restricted to natural images, whose symbolic force is based upon literary tradition and a cultural mingling of Buddhism, Taoism, and native animism.

H. became widely known in the West about the turn of the century. Its elliptical nature, its dependence on traditional associations for images, and the fact that Western poets interested in it knew no Japanese combined to produce results which often had little to do with h. Since Japanese prosody is syllabic, and since metrical and rhymed translations of such a short poetic form produce jingles, many early translators rendered h. into free forms or prose, leading some imitators to find h. an argument for vers libre in poetry on almost every subject and indispensable in imitations of haiku. Inspired by exoticism, the vogue for imitations of h. began in France ca. 1905. Marcel Revon's important *Anthologie de la Littérature Japonaise* (1910) demonstrated the real syllabic prosody and natural subject matter of h. and fostered a great popularity for imitations. The *Nouvelle Revue Française* published "haiku" by a dozen poets of note in 1920 and held something of a haiku competition in 1924, receiving a thousand entries. Interest waned about 1925, but h. had taken Orientalism from exoticism to serious imitation. Writers agreed that haiku's most important lessons were condensation, definite imagery, and freedom from didactic comment.

H. attracted the interest of the Anglo-Am. poets associated with T. E. Hulme and in the imagist movement about 1910 (and independently at Harvard University about 1912), an interest at first mirroring Fr. ideas, but soon assuming a life of its own. As in France, h. appealed first to exotic tastes but seemed increasingly relevant to experimental interests, vers libre, and imagery; but in England and the United States these concerns were carried farther and had greater effect upon poetic theory and practice. The most notable among the theorists were F. S. Flint, Ezra Pound, Amy Lowell, and John Gould Fletcher. On the model of h., Pound devised a "form of superposition," or use of a vivid image in combination with a more discursive or less vivid passage. This technique, begun with *In a Station of the Metro*, marks many shorter poems and, in somewhat altered form, is employed in *Mauberly* and the *Cantos*. The technique was widely imitated (occasionally to the point of parody), and can be found in the work of Flint, Aldington, Amy Lowell, Fletcher, and of such of the non-imagists as Frost, Aiken, Stevens, Yeats, MacLeish, and many others. Pound gave the technique a new form when, in the *Cantos*, he used Sino-Japanese characters rather than conventional images in super-pository fashion.

Many attempts have been made to imitate h. in Eng., Fr., German, Sp., It., and perhaps other European languages, but usually with exotic motives and almost always with trivial results. H. is too reduced a form and grows too complexly out of its cultural background to be adaptable as a whole into Western languages. Efforts by Amy Lowell and numerous translators to adapt h. prosody as a Western poetic or stanzaic form have been uniformly unsuccessful. The most haiku-like poems are those which, in addition to being written by poets, adapt the techniques for other purposes—e.g., Pound's *Liu Ch'e* (Japanese in technique, Chinese in materials) and Stevens' *Thirteen Ways of Looking at a Blackbird*. These show that h. has encouraged a style in which imagery, especially natural imagery, is the crucial vehicle of meaning; and in which imagistic techniques give order to poems, passages, and sequences. A few poets (e.g., Pound and Fletcher) have derived philosophies of poetry from h., and others (e.g., Edmund Blunden, William Plomer, and Sherard Vines) have used h. images or subjects in forms otherwise unrelated to Japan. See also JAPANESE POETRY.

Extensive bibliographies of primary materials can be found in the following studies. W. L. Schwartz, *The Imaginative Interpretation of the Far East in Modern Fr. Lit., 1800–1925* (1927); G. Hughes, *Imagism and the Imagists* (1931); S. F. Damon, *Amy Lowell* (1935); E. V. Gatenby, "The Influence of Japan on Eng. Lang. and Lit.," Japan Society (London), *Trans. and Proceed.*, 34 (1936–37); S. K. Coffman, *Imagism* (1951); D. Keene, *Japanese Lit.* (1953); E. Miner, *The Japanese Tradition in British and Am. Lit.* (1958). E.M.

HAINBUND, GÖTTINGER HAIN. See GÖTTINGER DICHTERBUND.

HAITIAN POETRY. Poetic expression in Haiti was born of the patriotism accompanying the attainment of independence in 1804. The struggle with France had produced heroes of epic proportions—Toussaint, Dessalines, Christophe, Pétion—perennial sources of inspiration for the aspiring poet. Moreover, to weld the heterogeneous groups of former slaves into a nation, civic-minded intellectuals often resorted to poetic exhortation, exultation, and encomium. One of the first to recognize the effectiveness of this expedient was Antoine Dupré (?–1816), whose *Hymne à la liberté* rallied the new citizens to the defense of their country's freedom. Perhaps the finest example of this genre is the tribute *A Henry Christophe* by Luc Grimard (1886–1954).

France furnished models for the poetry as she had for all institutions of her former colony. With the indignities of slavery still fresh in their minds, Haitians could not view their ties with Africa objectively; the stigma of color prodded them to prove that black men could emulate Lamartine, Hugo, and Musset. Thus, Hait. verse became and, for the most part, remained throughout the 19th c. an imitation of Fr. romanticism. Oswald Durand (1840–1906) was one of the few who took notice of the special charm of his native land; he even pioneered by writing in Creole the poignant lyric *Choucoune*, which still stands as one of the landmarks of Hait. verse.

Early in the second quarter of the present century incidental forces kindled a revolt among Hait. youths, turning them to introspection and exploration of native life and society. Their country was suffering an embarrassing foreign intervention and military occupation brought on by corrupt and inept politicians. Dissatisfied with their elders and resentful of the invader, young writers sought escape within themselves and their traditions —places inaccessible to the ideas of the foreigners. In 1925 Emile Roumer (1903–) startled his Fr. and Hait. readers with the publication in Paris of his *Poèmes d'Haïti et de France*. He then returned home to become the leader of a group of young intellectuals determined to give their country a literature representative of its people. As a vehicle for their works and theories, they founded the *Revue indigène*. Impetus for the movement came from the ethnological studies of Dr. Price Mars which were later published as *Ainsi parla l'oncle* (1928). These essays stressed the importance of recognizing the lower classes and of finding in their abundant folklore and traditions the material needed to revitalize the arts in Haiti. Further encouragement stemmed from the works of Negro poets in the U.S.A. and from the renewed Fr. interest in African art. As a result, although agreeing that their poetry should be indigenous, these young intellectuals differed as to the nature and degree of this quality, for native inspiration meant unity of ideals, not similarity of method.

Accordingly, their verse, which covers the whole range of expression, reveals atavistic memories and treats sympathetically the beliefs and superstitions of the masses. It bemoans the unhappy lot of the peasants, pleading for improvement in their social and economic life. It seeks to approximate the verse of other peoples with similar backgrounds. Frequently it exemplifies a *négritude* closely related to that of the brilliant Senegalese poet, Léopold Sédar Senghor, or of the gifted Martinican, Aimé Césaire. Much of it is protest poetry, condemning injustice, oppression, and exploitation. In *Vous*, Carl Brouard (1902–) attests the importance of the hitherto neglected peasants:

Vous êtes les piliers de l'édifice;
ôtez-vous
et tout s'écroule, châteaux de cartes.

You are the pillars of the structure;
stand aside
and everything will crumble, like castles of
cards.

Modern Hait. verse shows a strong influence of contemporary Fr. techniques, modified by original devices. Native Creole words, expressions, and constructions are fused with Fr. to express Hait. realities and concepts. Rich and colorful metaphors are selected from the tropical scene. Rhyme is often replaced by the rhythm of the Haitian's emotional life. While most of the poets prefer liberated meter to emphasize their break with the past, Jean F. Brierre (1909–) sometimes retains the rhymed alexandrine to voice his new thoughts as in his *Me revoici Harlem*, which manifests solidarity with U.S. Negroes: "Quand tu saignes, Harlem, s'empourpre mon mouchoir" (When you bleed, Harlem, my handkerchief turns crimson).

With the Revolution of 1946 Hait. poetry

has tended to become more utilitarian. Characterized by rebellion and protest, it suggests action. Many of the younger writers believe that their art must be functional in order to exist. However, poets like Léon Laleau (1892–), Philippe Thoby-Marcelin (1904–), Félix Morisseau-Leroy (1912–), Roussan Camille (1915–60), and René Belance (1915–) represent the more desirable tendency of combining social purpose with a careful consideration of art. In the final analysis, Hait. poetry is still in the process of finding its way. Its progress is often handicapped by political and economic conditions; publication is difficult and expensive, for illiteracy and poverty restrict the potential market. Literary magazines are ephemeral and increasingly rare; current exceptions are *Conjonction* and *Optique*. Roumer and Brouard no longer write poetry; death has silenced Jacques Roumain and Luc Grimard. On the other hand, poets remain numerous. One has only to view the incredibly beautiful Hait. landscape to understand the irresistible urge to write verse. From servile imitation of the Fr., this poetry has succeeded in rooting itself firmly in the native soil; it promises to become a reflection of the collective conscience.

ANTHOLOGIES: *Anthologie d'un siècle de poésie hait.* (1817–1925), ed. L. Morpeau (1926); *Panorama de la poésie hait.*, ed. C. Saint-Louis and M. Lubin (1950); *Poésies haitiennes*, ed. M. Lubin (1956).

HISTORY AND CRITICISM: J. Blanchet, *Le Destin de la jeune littérature* (1939); M. Cook, "Trends in Recent Hait. Lit., JNH, 32 (1947); J. Antoine, "Lit.—From Toussaint Louverture to Jacques Roumain," *An Introd. to Haiti*, ed. M. Cook (1951); *Pages de la littérature hait.*, ed. P. Pompilus (1951); W. J. Smith, "Land of Poets," *Américas*, 5 (Nov. 1953); N. Garrett, *The Renaissance of Hait. Poetry* (diss., Col. Univ., 1954, Paris, 1963); A. Viatte, *Histoire littéraire de l'Amérique française* (1954); W. Fowlie, "The Poets on Haiti's Map," *Portfolio*, 1 (1959).   N.G.; M.C.

HALF RHYME. See NEAR RHYME.

HEAD RHYME. See ALLITERATION.

HEADLESS LINE. See ACEPHALOUS.

HEBRAISM-HELLENISM. Antinomy devised by Matthew Arnold in chapter 4 of *Culture and Anarchy* (1869). Hebraism denotes that facet of man's nature which demands strict obedience to a moral code; it is best exemplified by Old Testament Judaism. In Arnold's view, moreover, other spiritual movements in Western civilization, notably Pauline Christianity, medieval asceticism, and the Puritan

Reformation show Hebraic "strictness of conscience." Hellenism is, by contrast, that combination of intellectual curiosity and *joie de vivre* of which classical Gr. civilization offers the best example. The European Renaissance is seen as a second Hellenic movement in which artistic productivity is combined with a strong expression of the urge "to see things as they are." Hebraism and Hellenism are, in essence, not contradictory since "the desire, native in man, for reason and the will of God, the feeling after the universal order" is their common goal. Yet a purely Hebraic civilization is doomed to fall by stagnation within its rigid code; a purely Hellenic one, by its valuation of intellect over morality and law. Arnold sees Hebraism and Hellenism as civilizing strains which should be combined judiciously to bring out the best forces in any Western culture. In terms of 19th-c. England, he feels that its essentially Hebraic Puritanism, inherited from the Reformation, should receive an admixture of Hellenic desire for truth and aesthetic "spontaneity of consciousness."

In relation to poetics, the Hebraic-Hellenic antinomy offers a division of world literature into two major categories: Judaeo-Christian documents, and works belonging to classical antiquity and to the Renaissance Arnold's drawing together of Gr. and Renaissance sensibilities had a strong influence on the Hellenism of Walter Pater. It is easy, however, to overestimate the standing of Arnold's Hebraic-Hellenic antinomy in the intellectual perspective of the 19th c. Its basic distinction between Judaeo-Christian asceticism (Hebraism) and a Hellenism generally defined as a love of realities had been drawn by Henrich Heine in an essay "Ueber Ludwig Boerne" as early as 1840. In addition, Ernest Renan foreshadowed Arnold's historical development of Hebraic-Hellenic strains in *Les Origines du Christianisme* (1863) and later expanded this idea in a preface to his *Hist. des peuples d'Israël* (1887–93).—T. S. Eliot, "Arnold and Pater" in *Selected Essays* (1932); L. Trilling, *Matthew Arnold* (2d ed., 1949); F. Faverty, *Matthew Arnold, The Ethnologist* (1951); W. Robbins, *The Ethical Idealism of Matthew Arnold* (1959).   W.B.F.

HEBREW POETRY. I. BIBLICAL PERIOD. The poetic vein in Heb. literature runs rich and deep. Not only war and victory are celebrated in early biblical documents like The Song of Deborah and The Song of Moses but work and dance—these mother-forms of human activity —are accompanied by rhythmic verses (Numbers 21:17–18; Exodus 15:21). In unabated productivity of more than three millennia Heb. lit. shows a preponderance of poetic output. The ethical ideas which constitute its chief contribution to the humanization of the West made their abiding impact because they were couched in poetic language.

Some of the most ancient books of the Hebrews must have been pure poetry if the few fragments from *The Book of Yashar* (Joshua 10:12–13; 2 Samuel 1:18–27 and possibly 1 Kings 8:12–13) and the single quotation from the uncertain *Book of the Wars of Yahweh* (Numeri 21:14–15) which are preserved in the Bible are any indication. The Bible—not a book but a literary miscellany of a thousand years—is largely poetry in form. In content it is a tripartite history of an ancient people: the Pentateuch is the great epic of the nation's commencement, the Former Prophets continue the story to the first experience of political annihilation while the so-called Latter Prophets dramatize the high moments of inner and outer struggles, the Hagiographa which are lyric and philosophic in inspiration reiterate to a certain extent the nation's story and continue it beyond the period of Babylonian activity. But even the prose of the great histories in the Pentateuch, in Joshua and in Judges, in the two books of Samuel, Kings and Chronicles, in the memoirs of Ezra and Nehemiah, has a poetic rhythm. And Esther and Ruth, predecessors of the short story in modern literature, approximate poetry in their cadenced sentences.

Classical and Semitic scholars love to compare the relative merits of Gr. and Heb. poetry. Of greater importance is the fact that an epic tradition of the Mediterranean East, antedating the earliest histories of the Gr. and Heb. peoples, feeds the Homeric and biblical books. The musical variety of Gr. meters has no parallel in Heb. poetry. An infinite amount of ingenuity and labor, from the Church Fathers to the biblical scholars of our own time, has failed to establish in the Bible dactylic hexameter—the great metric scheme of the Gr. epic—or the iambic pentameter, the great metric scheme of Gr. tragedy. Scholarly emendations of the Bible for the sake of a nonexistent metrical scheme have ended in a *cul de sac*. Only rudimentary meter exists in Heb. poetry just as rudimentary symmetry, of which the caesura is perhaps a remnant, graces Gr. poetry.

Instead of symmetry of feet which is the basic principle of Western poetry, the Egyptians and the Canaanites, including the Hebrews, developed in their poetry a symmetry of units. Though it was noticed by medieval Jewish commentators of the Bible, it was given its scientific name—*parallelismus membrorum*—more than 200 years ago by Robert Lowth, the celebrated scholar and Anglican bishop. Parallelism exhibits essentially three types: sameness, antithesis, and complement. The verse

from Psalms 102:7 is a good example of sameness: "I am like a pelican of the wilderness; / I have become like an owl of the ruins." The desolate despair of the poet, symbolized by the loneliness of the pelican, is accentuated by another denizen of the ruins, the owl. And the symmetry of ideas and imagery is strengthened by repetition. In the original Heb. perfect symmetry is achieved by three words in each unit or line: "Damiti li-Ḳeat Midbar / Hayiti ke-Kos Ḥorobot." The internal rhyme "Damiti-Hayiti" in this beautiful verse is sheer accident: Heb. poetry knew no rhyme until the early development of liturgy in the Synagogue.

There is no better example of antithesis than this pithy epigram in Ecclesiastes 3:4:

> A time to weep,
> And a time to laugh.

It is based on the eternal contrast of two common feelings and is part of a series of opposites which has delighted lovers of poetry for more than twenty-five centuries. In the original Heb. two words in each unit suffice to express the thought:

> ᶜEt li-Bekot
> we-ᶜEt li-Sehok.

The verse from Proverbs 19:21 is a good example of complementary units: "A man may have many plans in his mind; / But the counsel of the Lord—that will stand." This idea, as is well known, has been incorporated in the Eng. proverb "Man proposes but God disposes." It was given its rhyming form by Thomas à Kempis in his *Imitatio Christi:* "Nam homo proponit, sed Deus disponit." In the original Heb. four words in each unit serve to express the simple thought: "Rabot Maḥshabot be-Leb Ish / wa-ᶜAẓat Adonai Hi-Taḳum."

These examples indicate that the Heb. poet strove for symmetric perfection of form and content. And he achieved it in Psalms, in Proverbs and in Job, in the Song of Songs, in Lamentations, in Ecclesiastes, and even in some prosaic segments of the Old Testament. The most powerful poetic effects, however, were created by the Heb. prophets. They escaped monotony—an ever-present danger in the use of frugal form—by the powerful impact of their emotions. And they wrote or spoke inspired poetry—half-oracular and half-conscious—which contained timeless insight and wisdom.

Up to the beginning of this century Bible critics of Germany who set the tone for Bible critics all over the world delighted to denude biblical poetry of all originality. As the important archeological and epigraphic discoveries from former territories of the Arab and

Egyptian, the Sumerian and Akkadian, Syrian, Hurrian, and Hittite peoples inundated the field of biblical criticism, scholars discovered that similarities to biblical poetry often bore the relationship of rough poetic material to the finished poem. The high antiquity of Heb. poetry and the unparalleled accuracy of biblical texts was securely established by the archeological finds of Ras Shamra in northern Syria —ancient Ugarit—where hundreds of clay tablets and clay fragments in alphabetic cuneiform characters from the 14th c. B.C. were excavated by C. F. A. Schaeffer. The dean of American archeologists, William Foxwell Albright, could justly claim that "the flood of light now being shed on biblical Hebrew poetry of all periods by Ugaritic literature guarantees the relative antiquity of its composition as well as the astonishing accuracy of its transmission." Prayers and rites, laws and myths abound in these texts. The protagonists in some fragmentary poems resemble well-known entities in the Bible: *El*, the supreme God in the Ugartic mythology, is the generic name for God in the Bible; *Ashirat*, his consort, is the well-known Astarte; *Baal*, the god of rain and fertility and the virgin *Anath*, the war-goddess, are mentioned in the Bible; *Yam*, the god of the sea and *Mot*, the god of death, have lost their divine character in biblical Heb. and have come to denote "sea" and "death" respectively. An exquisite refinement of expression has been achieved in the Bible though numerous vocables and images and proverbs of Canaanite provenance found their way into the ancient lit. of Israel. By 586 B.C. [587?] when the Chaldeans conquered Judaea, the Hebrews attained a greatness in the domain of poetry which was not equaled anywhere in that remote period of history. The intelligent absorption and transformation of neighboring cultures was and still is the singular peculiarity of Heb. genius.

Heb. poetry is intinately linked with prophecy which has no parallel among Eastern or Western peoples. In spite of superficial resemblances to ecstatic practices in the ancient East, it is a unique phenomenon. According to Maimonides, the great medieval sage, "It is the greatest perfection man can attain." According to the acute critic of prophecy, Sigmund Mowinckel, prophets—"the *Nebiim* . . . were filled by divine power to raving point." Generations of scholars, Jewish sages and Church Fathers, philosophers and poets tried their intuitive and reasoning powers on the solution of the sphinxlike riddle of prophecy. But it has eluded their intellectual and spiritual grasp. At best it can be described and evaluated in subjective terms. Intensity of experience and intensity of expression are its dominant characteristics. But the great poetry of a Shakespeare and a Goethe may also boast such distinction. What makes prophets unique poets is a belief and a claim that their words are inspired by an all-seeing, all-knowing Power which transcends human wisdom: God. From that point of view prophets are poets of faith. The misnomer "prophet" which has the meaning "one who foretells" in Gr. and in the languages of the West, contributed to the misunderstanding of his function. For the Heb. equivalent of the term, *nabi*, probably means "one who is called." But whatever the nature of that divine power or ecstatic experience of the prophets, be it supranormal or a heightened form of psychic tension, the timelessness of their utterance and the universalism of their message has been noted by their admirers and detractors. Yet they never lost sight of Israel, which they wished to elevate by sheer moral power above all its neighbors. Chauvinism and universalism were intertwined in their utterance.

Prophets were also builders of ideal dreamlands in verse, and they served as examples and prototypes to Sir Thomas More and Samuel Butler, Sebastian Mercier and Restif de la Bretonne, Bellamy and Orwell. They did not use the word "utopia" which in Gr. means "nowhere" and which More chose as the title for his book, but they said "the end of days." It should be borne in mind, however, that ancient Israel, like its near neighbors in the Fertile Crescent and the more distant neighbors in Greece had also a dim recollection of a Golden Age in the beginning of days. Most of the prophets experienced the tension of their country's imminent doom. At least two of them—Jeremiah and Ezekiel—lived during the destruction of Jerusalem and the annihilation of the Jewish state, and only a few of them witnessed the rebirth of their puny country under adverse conditions. Since they opposed the surrounding cultures and their ethical *laissez-faire* with all the great eloquence at their command, they were driven to advance the Jews to the status of a chosen people. This idea, maligned through the ages and rejected by Jewish Reform and Reconstructionism in our own times, had nothing in common with the supercilious attitude of the Greeks to other nations. It was elevated by duty to humanity and service to mankind. In spite of the great diversity of prophetic writing, the idea of service and duty gives them their unity. This idea is no stranger to the philosophic lit. of the Greeks but it reached only highly cultured individuals. The prophets, who were poets and who couched their simple ideas in images and visions, had an abiding influence on their people and, through them, on the entire world. They may be said to have shaped a nation in their image—perhaps the only example of a people transformed by the magic touch of poetry.

Like the prophetic books, the collection of 150 Psalms is an anthology *sui generis*. The lyrics of a Sappho or an Archilochus cannot be compared with them. Some of the Orphic hymns, some Babylonian odes reach to their inspiration. But the Psalms are unique in their God-intoxicated expression. Nature or humanity do not exist as independent factors in the universe; they are the manifestations of a transcendental power.

When I see your heavens, the work of your
  fingers,
The moon and the stars, which you have
  formed;
What is man, that you remember him?
  And the son of man, that you should care
  for him?
(Psalms 8:4–5)

Another feature of the Psalms is the blurred boundary between the individual and the nation. These merge so often that "I" in the Psalms is often an individual or a group or both. The reason for this peculiarity is, according to the theories of the greatest commentators of the Psalms in this century, Hermann Gunkel and Sigmund Mowinckel, that psalm poetry is mainly cultic poetry or liturgy which is associated with the worship in the Temple.

If the Psalms may be described as a collection of hymnal lyrics, addressed to God, then the Song of Songs is a collection of love lyrics addressed to a human being and the Book of Lamentations is a sheaf of elegiac lyrics on the ravaged city of Jerusalem. The influence of the Song of Songs loomed large in the history of world lit. The European love lyric has rarely equaled its naïveté and immediacy of expression. In Heb. lit. it was regarded with special reverence after the revered Rabbi Akiba interpreted it as an allegory of love between God and Israel and declared that "all the books in Scripture are holy but the Song of Songs is the holy of holies" (Mishnah, *Yadayim* 3:5).

When in more sophisticated ages the Hebrews aspired to philosophic expression, they also used poetry. The authors of Job and Ecclesiastes are poets first and philosophers last. Though the former stresses patience in suffering and the latter examines the vanity of all endeavor, both are poets of pessimism. Whether the author of Ecclesiastes was a resident of Phoenicia, employing Phoenician orthography and locutions—as Father M. J. Dahood argues in a recent study—or whether he wrote in Aramaic—as H. L. Ginsberg, one of the outstanding biblical scholars of our time

—maintains, we must content ourselves with the extant Heb. text which, in spite of occasional corruptions, is one of the great classics of ancient literature. But the difficulties of exegesis have been such that Heinrich Heine described the book as "the quintessence of scepticism" and Franz Delitzsch, the celebrated German scholar, regarded it as "the quintessence of piety."

Like the author of Ecclesiastes, the author of Job may have been a foreigner or borrowed a foreign, possibly Edomite, tale for his book. But he transformed it into the dramatic query of the ages: why do the wicked prosper? Why do the righteous fail? Whether he meant to offer a solution is open to doubt. The finale, the dialogue between God and Job, is a climax of frustration. The inscrutable ways of Providence can neither be challenged nor changed by man:

Scatter abroad the rage of your wrath;
And look upon everyone that is proud and
  abase him.
Look upon everyone who is proud and bring
  him low;
And crush the wicked where they stand.
Bury them in the dust likewise:
Bind up their faces in the hidden place.
Then I indeed will praise you,
That your own right hand can deliver you.

I know that you can do all things;
And no plan is too difficult for you . . .
Therefore I retract and repent,
In dust and ashes.
(Job 40:11–14; 42:2, 6)

II. The Postbiblical Period is an intermediary period in Heb. poetry which lasted roughly from the final edition of the Bible in the 2d c. B.C. to the emergence of liturgical poets known as *Paytanim* in the 6th or 7th c. A.D. The bulk of Heb. lit. which succeeded the Bible may be regarded as a vast commentary on the Bible—a poetic, homiletic, mystic, or philosophic interpretation of that classic which was never surpassed. Through the L. translation, the so-called Vulgate version, the Bible also exerted a paramount influence on the Christian Middle Ages, and through vernacular translations, on the Renaissance and the post-Renaissance period. In the original text it never ceased to inspire a scholarly and intellectual élite in the West. And it shaped the character and destiny of the people which authored its contents.

Postbiblical lit. is dominated by the theme of Wisdom which has developed from simple proverbs offering sage advice on a worldly plane to elaborate tracts offering religious and moral norms of perfection. This love of wisdom which colors Job and Ecclesiastes, Proverbs and even the Psalms, amounts to an apotheosis in post-biblical lit. Didactic poetry, anemic and intellectual, largely supplants lyric poetry. The books which immediately follow the Bible and eventually become the extra-biblical canon of Apocrypha and Pseudepigrapha, teach rather than inspire. A favorite theme is good and evil and a favorite purpose is theodicy: God is right. This is true of Ecclesiasticus or The Wisdom of Ben Sira, The Wisdom of Solomon and The Psalms of Solomon which are merely exercises in "learned psalmography." But a great deal of theoretical and practical wisdom is often incorporated in these books.

The hoard of manuscripts known as the Dead Sea Scrolls has brought interesting additions to Heb. poetry from the philological and semantic point of view. From the literary point of view there is little of value in them in spite of the claims which were made for such pale imitations of the Psalms as the Hymns of Thanksgiving. It must be borne in mind, however, that sound appraisal of the Dead Sea Scrolls will be only possible when they are all unrolled and published in accessible form.

In the immediate postbiblical period poetry copied biblical prototypes. Even its mystical and apocalyptic aspect had its origin in the biblical Daniel. But the language of the Jews, Heb., slowly gave way to Aramaic. In the hellenistic age powerful centers of Jewish culture developed outside Palestine. In Alexandria where Jews spoke Gr., Philo created a new philosophy which, according to the monumental researches of Professor Harry Austryn Wolfson, shaped the course of philosophy for 1,500 years. The less-known Ezekiel of Alexandria wrote his play Exagogē (Exodus) in conformity with classical Gr. tragedies. In Palestine itself various cities were totally Hellenized. As the Jews spread all over the mediterranean countries and later penetrated into the heart of Europe, they developed their lit. in numerous languages and created immense and fascinating difficulties for the literary historian. For no lit. in the world was to exhibit such striking cross-pollinations as that of the Jews. Yet Heb. remained the preferential language. Even in the three centuries—the 11th, 12th and 13th—which are regarded as the Golden Age of Sp. Jewry poets wrote chiefly in Heb. Philosophers who were also poets, Halevi and Gabirol for instance, exhibited a strange dichotomy: they composed their philosophic works in Arabic and their poems in Heb.

III. MEDIEVAL PERIOD. Just as the Hellenic conquest of the Orient was to impress the peoples of the civilized world for a thousand years, so the Arabic conquests after the death of Mohammed created a new civilization in the Orient and in some European countries, notably in Spain, in Provence, and in parts of Italy. Together with the Jews, the Arabs ushered in the Eastern Renaissance in the beginning of the Middle Ages. It antedated the It. Renaissance by several centuries and it exhibited a similar breadth of intellectual interests. Its great men were predecessors of the uomo universale and cultivated poetry and philosophy, history and geography, natural science and law. Kinship in language and race was responsible for close cultural ties between Arabs and Jews. While Gr. models were sparsely used in Heb. poetry during the Hellenistic period, Arab models were slavishly imitated during the Arab period in Jewish history. New poetical techniques were borrowed to such an extent that Halevi rebelled against the imposition of alien shackles and complained that "Jews long for a prosody in imitation of other peoples, in order to force the Hebrew language into their metres." Parallelism was abandoned in favor of metrical systems which were difficult to master and difficult to adapt to Heb. prosody. Since Arabs delighted in convivial and even lax poetry, Jews also contented themselves with euphonious verses on wine and women, war and friendship, love and landscape. Thematic redundancy characterized their poetic effusions. Yet sea poetry, a rarity in Heb. lit., made its debut in the Middle Ages. Humorous verse, an even greater rarity, found an accomplished master in Abraham ibn Ezra, probable prototype of Robert Browning's "Rabbi Ben Ezra" and in Yehudah al-Harizi, the Heb. version of a wandering troubadour. By the 12th c., the poetaster superseded the poet, the art of versification smothered genuine inspiration. Even such impossible subjects as grammar, chess, and natural science were used as grist for the poetic mill.

Only one domain of poetry was safe from cumbersome or frivolous incursions: liturgy. Galut and Geulah, diaspora and redemption, were the magic themes which invigorated Heb. poetry. The humiliation of persecution which was characteristic of the Jewish Middle Ages, the promise of future happiness which was associated with redemption—these were the sources of spiritual strength in medieval Heb. poetry. It was in liturgical poetry that greatness has been achieved by Samuel the Prince and Solomon ibn Gabirol, Yehudah Halevi, and Moses ibn Ezra. Recent and improved editions of their works validated their fame in past centuries and won them new acclaim in our own time. In the case of Samuel the Prince a hoard of poems, forgotten for centuries, revealed a unique master of the abstruse and the obscure. The proud sorrows of Solomon ibn Gabirol, the musical charm of Yehudah Halevi, the penitential strength of Moses ibn Ezra deserve to be better known by lovers of poetry throughout the civilized world.

It is common knowledge that the Semitic genius penetrated and transformed the West in the Middle Ages. Even It., Fr., and German Jewry did not escape the influence of Arabic exemplars. But they favored, in imitation of Fr. *chansons de geste*, epic poetry where legend and history mixed in happy innocence. Instead of jousts and tourneys they described the splendor and the awe of ancient ritual in the Temple. They also cultivated the sonnet and used it as a vehicle for roisterous badinage and high-spirited lechery not unworthy of a Boccaccio. An Immanuel of Rome shocked the sensibilities of Jews to such an extent that the authoritative code of religious practice, the *Shulḥan ʿAruk*, prohibits the reading of "profane talk and erotic discourse such as the *Book of Immanuel*." It is not without interest that the church legislated against poets because of their alleged preoccupation with pornography. And had it not been for the nobleman who welcomed them to his castle and the commoner who encouraged them, they would have met with a worse fate than they actually had to contend with. Like their Christian brethren, Heb. poets in the Middle Ages depended on the patron. But the rich who had often vulgar tastes were not as generous as the poets expected them to be. Even when they were as cultured as Ḥasdai ibn Shaprut, they subjected their charges to humiliation. The poets who had a sense of humor laughed away their misery or took to the road and changed patronage with inordinate frequency.

IV. MODERN PERIOD. The banishment of Jews from Spain in 1492 was a cultural loss to the Iberian peninsula and a boon to its neighboring countries. The dispersal of Jewish poets and scholars brought a refinement of arts and sciences to their new homelands in Italy, North Africa, and Turkey. Like the classical poets and scholars who were compelled to leave their homes after the destruction of the Byzantine Empire in 1453, they had a considerable share in the development of the Renaissance. During the 455 years, between the expulsion of the Jews from Spain in 1492 and the establishment of the State of Israel in 1947, Heb. lit. shifted its centers of activity to the far reaches of Eastern Europe, America, and Palestine. But only in the domain of legal lit. did Eastern Europe of the 16th and 17th c. equal the achievements of the Golden Age of Spain. In poetry there was a noticeable decline.

Modern Heb. lit. does not begin, as standard textbooks indicate, with Moses Ḥayyim Luzzatto or Moses Mendelssohn. No such *terminus a quo* can possibly be accepted for a multitude of writings which appear not in one country but in numerous lands. Modern Heb. lit. has its beginnings in various countries at different times: in Italy in the 16th, in Holland in the 17th, in Germany in the 18th, in Poland and in Russia in the 19th c. A convenient starting point for modern Heb. lit. is 1492: the date of the Jewish exile from Spain.

The revival of poetic drama—another indication of modernity in Heb. letters—was the great achievement of It. and Dutch Jewry. First there was imitation and adaptation of such trusted models as the *Tragicomedia de Calisto y Melibea* (*The Celestina*) which probably was written by the convert Fernando de Rojas. Later original plays appeared in increasing profusion. But the synagogue, unlike the church, had an ancient aversion to the theatre, which was a semireligious, idolatrous institution in Hellenistic times when the Jews became aware of its existence. Yet popular plays thrived in spite of religious frowns. Amateurish companies produced dramatizations of the story of Esther and Joseph. Leone de Sommi Portaleone is the author of a prose comedy on marriage—the first original play in Hebrew—and a handbook on theatrical art in It. Moses Zacuto of Sp. ancestry, Dutch birth, and It. sojourn, wrote two dramatic poems which resemble Christian morality plays. But they were written for libraries and readers rather than for the stage.

Moses Ḥayyim Luzzatto marks the culmination of a vast dramatic literature. His plays, reminiscent of Tasso and Guarini, have exercised a decisive influence on subsequent poets. And his style, modeled on the classical lines of the Bible, dominated the Heb. language for 150 years. In the hands of epigones it was to degenerate into a patchwork of biblical phrases and verses. Though Luzzatto's use of allegory was a retarding factor and his characterization verged on the naive, his fresh delight in the pastoral aspects of nature and his quest for mystic illumination are still potent forces in modern Heb. poetry. It was because of his influence that the idyll became the preferred vehicle of Heb. poets. Not only was the first original Heb. novel *Ahabat Ẓion* (The Love of Zion) by Abraham Mapu idyllic in tone and semipoetic in rhythm, but the poems of the Lebensohns, father and son, and some epics of J. L. Gordon vaunted rural bliss, while Tschernichowsky and Shimoni, reaching for the source, adapted the hexametric molds of Theocritus to the Heb. idyll. Luzzatto's quest for mystical illumination and the religious fervor of Hasidism inspired a vast literary activity and left a mark on contemporary poets —on Shalom and Melzer, Lamdan and Gruenberg.

The so-called Heb. Renaissance of the 19th

and 20th c.—a misnomer like the Celtic Renaissance—was imbued with nationalist aspirations which included the cult and cultivation of the Heb. language. As in 10th-c. Spain so in the first two decades of 20th-c. Russia and Poland, Galicia and Bessarabia, a fusion of Hebraic and non-Hebraic elements of culture among the outstanding representatives of Heb. lit. resulted in significant poetry. But history never repeats itself. In Spain Heb. poets had absorbed Heb. learning when it was in fullest bloom, and the sciences when they had a veritable rebirth in all their wide ramifications. In Eastern Europe where Heb. poets, with few exceptions, were obsessed with provincial interests, the fusion of Hebraic and non-Hebraic elements of culture occurred at lower tension. Bialik, the most popular representative of the Heb. Renaissance, had only a meager knowledge of contemporary trends in world poetry. In his ardent search for his own roots in childhood and for national roots in the childhood of Jewry, in his assiduous recreation of this twin motif, he is both the most personal and the most national of poets. Like his biblical predecessors he knew how to blend individual and communal traits. Translations in Eng. do not reflect the sweetness and the grandeur of his poetry. Many have attempted but few succeeded in mirroring his felicitous imagery which seems traditional but is, in reality, a bold departure from tradition. Like prophets and psalmists he castigated and comforted. But he also imposed an unprecedented lyricism on a people which, steeped in the study of impersonal legalism, eagerly accepted the subjective relief.

It was, perhaps, the misfortune of Tschernichowsky to have been a contemporary of Bialik. In another age he would have created a school: his knowledge and mastery of classical and postclassical meters and forms gave him an advantage over all his contemporaries. Epic in inspiration, he discovered for Heb. poetry the mythical past of Judaism—the worship of Tammuz, the Semitic Adonis, and Astarte, the Semitic Venus. What Yeats did for Ir. poetry in revivifying the Ir. myth, Tschernichowsky accomplished for Heb. poetry in recreating the Semitic pantheon. Another contemporary poet, Zalman Shneur, wove an interesting poetic tapestry out of ancient Heb. myths and legends. Together these three poets may be regarded as the progenitors of contemporary Heb. poetry in Israel and America—a phase which began with the aftermath of the First World War.

For more than a hundred years Heb. lit. had been concentrated in Eastern Europe. After the Rus. Revolution in 1917 a small center emerged in America, a few splinter centers thrived for a number of years in Poland and in Germany, and a larger center in Palestine, which had played a subsidiary role in Heb. lit. for the past thousand years, assumed increasing importance. The Am. center conquered new ground for modern Heb. poetry. The fate of the indigenous Indian and the imported Negro had a special fascination for Heb. poets in America. And the life of the Am. Jew was richly reflected in narrative poetry. The heavy orientation toward Israel was merely the perpetuation of an anomaly which had its roots in the political annihilation of Judea in the 1st c. A.D.

It was after the First World War, then, that the old home of Heb. poetry became its new home again. The reclamation of the land by the pioneer, the Ḥaluz, and the desperate difficulties which attended the process—these were voiced in Isaac Lamdan's cycle of poems *Massadah* which had no rival in popularity in the 1920's and 1930's. Characteristically, after the Second World War, another book with a symbolic name, *Reḥobot ha-Nahar* by Uri Zevi Gruenberg became the important poetic document of Israel. This biblical place name, mentioned in Genesis 36:37 and 1 Chronicles 1:48 in connection with the princes of Edom—a symbol of Christianity in medieval Heb. lit.— is an indictment of the civilized world which permitted the slaughter of millions of Jews. Different in its Whitmanesque technique from *Massadah*, the book shares its deep pessimism.

The older and the younger poets of Israel—Fichmann, Shimoni, and Cohen, Shalom, Alterman, and Shalev, Guri, ʿAmiḥai, and Zak—have rediscovered the Palestinian landscape and reintroduced the living variety of animate and inanimate life into their works. Some of them brought back the indigenous inhabitant, the Arab and the Oriental Jew, after a millennial absence. The Ingathering of Exiles—a cornerstone of political policy in the young State of Israel—had become poetic policy, unconscious and unpremeditated, years before the establishment of the State of Israel. Not a few of the able younger poets were women who had been barred for centuries from the high roads of learning and literary expression and who had few opportunities to voice their luckless lot in verse.

The War of Independence, succeeding the establishment of the Jewish State, led to a certain vulgarization of the Heb. language in prose and poetry. Young soldiers and veterans, indigenous and immigrant, affected spoken Heb. with picturesque oddities and slang elements from Arabic, German, Yiddish, Polish, Rus., and Eng. But they also composed war poetry which had a fresh intensity and immediacy of experience. Together with earlier poets, especially the nimble master of the language, Abraham Shlonsky and his numerous followers, the soldier-poets gave a new elasticity to the Heb. language. Some of them have joined the extreme Canaanites who reject the entire period of Jewish dispersion as an inconsequential incident in Jewish history. All of them succeeded in modernizing the Heb. language and in widening its powers of expression.

SOURCEBOOKS AND ANTHOLOGIES IN ENG. TRANSLATIONS: *The Bible: An Am. Tr.*, ed. J. M. Powis Smith (1935; modern version of the O.T.; quotations in the article, with slight modifications, from this Am. tr.); *Ancient Near Eastern Texts Relating to the O.T.*, ed. J. B. Pritchard (1950; largest coll. of text-tr. relating to the O.T.); *Apocrypha and Pseudepigrapha of the O.T.*, ed. R. H. Charles (2 v., 1913; standard Eng. ed.); *An Anthol. of Medieval Heb. Lit.*, ed. A. E. Millgram (1961); *A Treasury of Jewish Poetry*, ed. N. and M. Ausubel (1957); *Post-Biblical Heb. Lit.*, ed. B. Halper (2 v., 1921; sel. of medieval texts and tr.); *A Golden Treasury of Jew. Lit.*, ed. L. W. Schwarz (1946; from the 12th c. B.C. until the present); *Titans of Heb. Verse*, ed. H. H. Fein (1936); *Israel Argosy*, ed. I. Halevy-Levin (7 v., 1952–60; contemp. Heb. prose and poetry in tr.).

HISTORY AND CRITICISM: R. H. Pfeiffer, *Introd. to the O.T.* (1941; an appraisal of biblical lit. in the light of the present state of higher crit.); *The O.T. and Modern Study*, ed. H. H. Rowley (1951; excellent survey and crit. appreciation by 12 leading scholars); S. C. Yoder, *Poetry of the O.T.* (1948; useful introd. and repres. coll. of biblical poetry); C. C. Torrey, *The Apocryphal Lit.* (1945; concise handbook of Jew. postcanonical lit.); N. Slouschz, *The Renascence of Heb. Lit.* (1909); J. Klausner, *A Short Hist. of Modern Heb. Lit.* (1932); S. Halkin, *Modern Heb. Lit.* (1950; record of historical and social forces which have motivated Heb. Lit. in modern times); M. Ribalow, *The Flowering of Modern Heb. Lit.* (1959); S. Spiegel, *Hebrew Reborn* (1930); E. Silberschlag, "Heb. Lit. in America: Record and Interpretation," *Jew. Quarterly Rev.*, 45 (1955) and *Heb. Lit.: An Evaluation* (1959); M. Wallenrod, *The Lit. of Modern Israel* (1956); M. Waxman, *A Hist. of Jew. Lit.* (5 v., 1960).

SOME WELL-KNOWN ANTHOLOGIES IN HEB.: *Be-Ron Yaḥad*, ed. A. M. Habermann (1945; ancient and modern liturgy); *Mibḥar ha-Shirah ha-ʿIbrit be-Italia* (1934; Heb. poetry in Italy) and *Ha-Shirah ha-ʿIbrit bi-Sefarad u-bi-Provence* (2 v., 1954–56; in Spain and Provence), both ed. J. Schirmann; *Mibḥar ha-Shirah ha-ʿIbrit ha-Ḥadashah*, ed. A. Barash (1938; modern); *Anthologiyah Shel ha-Shirah ha-ʿIbrit ba-America*, ed. M. Ribalow (1938); *Ha-ʿAnaf ha-Gaduʿa*, ed. A. Kariv ([new ed.?] 1954); *Sifrutenu ha-Yafah*, ed. H. Toren (3 v., 1953–

54; contemp. Heb. lit.); *Shiratenu*, ed. J. Lichtenbaum (2 v., 1962; modern).

SOME WELL-KNOWN HISTORICAL AND CRITICAL STUDIES IN HEB.: Y. Ḳeshet, *Shirat ha-Miḳra* (1954; on the poetry of the Bible); A. Ben-Or (Orinovsky), *Toldot ha-Shirah ha-ʿIbrit bi-Ymei ha-Benayim* (2 v., 1934; hist. of medieval Heb. poetry); I. Zinberg, *Toldot Sifrut Yisrael* (6 v., 1955–60; Heb. lit. from A.D. 500 to the 1850's); F. Lachover, *Toldot ha-Sifrut ha-ʿIbrit ha-Ḥadashah* (4 v., 1936–48; modern); J. Klausner, *Historiyah Shel-ha-Sifrut ha-ʿIbrit ha-Ḥadashah* (6 v., 1930–50; modern); A. Ben-Or, *Toldot ha-Sifrut ha-ʿIbrit be-Dorenu* (2 v. [v. I: Poetry], 1954–55; contemp.); D. Miron, *Arbaʿ Panim be-Sifrut ha-ʿIbrit Bat Yamenu* (1962; contemp.).   E.S.

HELLENISTIC POETICS. See CLASSICAL POETICS.

HEMIEPES (Gr. "half-hexameter"). A dactylic trimeter catalectic ending in a long syllable ($-\cup\cup-\cup\cup-$) corresponding to the earlier part of a dactylic hexameter before the penthemimeral caesura. It occurs frequently and in various combinations with other cola in Gr. lyric verse. The second line of Horace's

$$\bar{D}\bar{\imath}f\!f\bar{u}ger\breve{e}\ n\bar{\imath}v\breve{e}s,\ r\breve{e}d\bar{e}unt\ \bar{\imath}am\ gr\breve{a}m\bar{\imath}n\breve{a}\ c\bar{a}mp\bar{\imath}s$$

$$\breve{a}rb\breve{o}r\bar{\imath}b\bar{u}squ\breve{e}\ c\bar{o}m\breve{a}e$$
(Odes 4.7.1–2)

is an example of h. following a dactylic hexameter.—Dale; U. von Wilamowitz-Moellendorff, *Griechische Verskunst* (2d ed., 1958).
                                                        R.J.G.

HEMISTICH (Gr. "half line"). A half line of verse divided at the caesura. It usually forms an independent colon. The device is used in drama where at least two characters exchange half lines of dialogue to create an effect of sharp argument. Such a series of half lines is called *hemistichomythia*. In other types of poetry a hemistich may create an effect of great emotional or physical disturbance, e.g., Virgil's isolated half lines in the *Aeneid* (1.534; 2.233). In Germanic verse the h. is the primary metrical structural unit as is shown in the poetry of OE, Old High German, Old Saxon, and ON. Often in modern poetry any metrically incomplete line is called a hemistich. W. H. Auden's *Always in Trouble* uses this device.—J. L. Hancock, *Studies in Stichomythia* (1917); J. C. Pope, *The Rhythm of Beowulf* (1942).   R.A.H.

HENDECASYLLABIC (Gr. "11-syllable"), also called *Phalaecean*, after the Gr. poet Phalaikos (4th c. B.C.?). The scheme is $\cup\cup$ (or $\cup-$; $-\cup$;

--) ‿‿‿‿‿‿‿‿‿. It is used by Sophocles (*Philoctetes* 136, 151), Aristophanes (*Ecclesiazusae* 942ff.). The Alexandrian poets employed it as the meter for complete poems, e.g., Theokritos (*Epode* 20), Phalaikos (*Anthologia Palatina* 13.6). Catullus (84–54 B.C.?) perfected it in L., e.g.,

Ādest (e, h) ēndĕcăsўllăbī, quŏt ēstīs

Forty of his 113 extant poems are in h. verses, ranging in function from love lyricism to invective. The It. h. line is used in sonnets, terza rima, and ottava rima by e.g., Dante and Petrarca; unrhymed lines (*endecasillabi sciolti*) after the L. are prominent in the tragic and epic poetry of Giangiorgio Trissino (1478–1550), in the poetry of Gabriello Chiabrera (1552–1638), and in that of Guiseppe Parini (1729–99), Ugo Foscolo 1778–1827), Giacomo Leopardi (1798–1837), and Alessandro Manzoni (1785–1873). The Marquis de Santillana (Juan de Mena) adapted the h. to the Sp. sonnet form in 1444. In general, the development of the h. in Spain followed the same pattern as that in Italy. In Germany Heinse and Goethe imitated the It. h. Modern-language hendecasyllabics are "syllabic" rather than "accentual" (see CLASSICAL METERS IN MODERN LANGUAGES); Tennyson, however, attempted the classical-accentual equivalent, e.g.

Āll cŏmpōsĕd īn ă mētĕr ōf Cătūllŭs,

as did Swinburne. W. S. Landor wrote L. hendecasyllabics. For a recent (1957) rendering of this meter, see F. O. Copley's translation of Catullus' 28th poem (*Catullus, The Complete Poetry*).—For bibliog., see CLASSICAL METERS. . . . Also, W. Thomas, *Le Décasyllabe roman et sa fortune en Europe* (*Travaux et mémoires de l'Univ. de Lille*, n.s., I, fasc. 4, 1904); M. Serretta, *Endecasillabi crescenti . . .* (1938); E. Pound, *Lit. Essays* (1954).   R.A.S.

HENDIADYS (Gr. "one through two"). The use of two substantives or sometimes a substantive and attributive genetive or adjective, connected by a conjunction to express a single, complex idea: "chrono kai poliorkia" (by length of time and siege; i.e., "by a long siege" —Demosthenes 19.123); "we drink from cups and gold" (Virgil, *Georgics* 2.192); "nice and warm" (in place of "nicely warm"—Fowler, *Modern Eng. Usage*). Sometimes h. is confused with simple parallelism, in which the substantives are equivalent: "might and main." Some grammarians argue the term is merely descriptive; others claim no such figure exists. E. A. Hahn contends the term "h." is a misnomer when applied to Virgil; that is, when Virgil chose to write as if he had two ideas,

"he really did have two." Hence a phrase, "membris et mole valens," really contains two intentionally distinct ideas, "membris valens" and "mole valens," though it is usually translated simply "strong limbs." H. is found at all periods, usually for purposes of increased emphasis:

The heaviness and guilt within my bosom
Takes off my manhood.
(Shakespeare, *Cymbeline* 5.2.1–2)

E. A. Hahn, "H.: Is there Such a Thing?" cw, 15 (1921–22).   R.O.E.

HEPHTHEMIMERAL. See CAESURA.

HEPTAMETER. A line of 7 feet, metrically identical with the septenary (q.v.) and the fourteener. The meter exists in classical Gr. and L. prosody (chiefly in comic verse in the latter), and has great importance in Eng. prosody. It flourished in the narrative poetry of the Elizabethans, who coined for it the term *fourteener*, but later appearances of the heptameter line, printed as such, are infrequent. Wordsworth's *The Norman Boy*, E. B. Browning's *Cowper's Grave*, and Whittier's *Massachusetts to Virginia* are instances of post-Elizabethan h. On the whole, however, it has proved unsuitable for the long and elevated verse narrative because of its tendency toward monotony, but Chapman's translation of the *Iliad*, and Coleridge's *Rime of the Ancient Mariner* are notable exceptions. When divided into two parts, the h. becomes the familiar ballad meter (q.v.) or common measure (C.M. of the hymnbooks) of alternating 4- and 3-stress lines.—G. Stewart, *The Technique of Eng. Verse* (1930); J. Thompson, *The Founding of Eng. Metre* (1961).   A.P.

HEPTASTICH. A group or stanza of 7 lines.

HEPTASYLLABIC. A line or colon of 7 syllables.

HERESY OF PARAPHRASE. This term (or, occasionally, "periphrastic heresy") was introduced and its concept discussed, by Cleanth Brooks, in *The Well Wrought Urn* (1947), pp. 176–238. It means "the erroneous opinion that a poem is paraphrasable." If "paraphrase" means "say the same thing in other words," then a poem cannot, Brooks holds, be paraphrased. For it has a dramatic, not a logical structure; or, as he sometimes says, it is a structure of attitudes or (following R. P. Blackmur) of "gestures." It is not a statement, but (following Kenneth Burke) a symbolic action; and (following W. M. Urban) its form is inseparable from its content. It may contain statements among its elements; but they are not its essence, have no primacy over other elements, but are organically related to them. Though they can be paraphrased, the paraphrase "is not the real core of meaning which constitutes the essence of the poem" (p. 180); and they are to be judged not by their truth, but by their dramatic propriety. In other words, Brooks (following I. A. Richards) distinguishes between scientific discourse, which can be paraphrased, and poetic, which cannot. But unlike Richards he believes that, though what a poem says is otherwise ineffable, it does say something—that poetry is not emotive, or emotive alone, but cognitive. Poetry is didactic; it contains wisdom. But it does not state its wisdom; it enacts it. And "A poem . . . is to be judged, not by the truth or falsity as such, of the idea [the wisdom] which it incorporates, but rather by its character as drama—by its coherence, sensitivity, depth, richness, and toughmindedness" (p. 229).

In the communion of the faithful, Brooks counts (in addition to Blackmur, Burke, Urban, and Richards) René Wellek and Susanne K. Langer; among the heretics, Yvor Winters, Donald A. Stauffer, Herbert J. Muller, Frederick A. Pottle, and John Crowe Ransom. For a more recent use of the term, and a comprehensive discussion of the issues that are the context of the term, see M. Krieger, *The New Apologists for Poetry* (1956).   M.S.

HERMETICISM. Derived from Hermes Trismegistus, reputed author of several works on symbolism and the occult. The term refers generally to poetry using occult symbolism (see PLATONISM AND POETRY), and in particular to a phase or "school" of early and mid-20th-c. poetry having a direct line of descent from the poetry and theories of Novalis and Poe as modified in the works of such Fr. symbolists as Baudelaire, Mallarmé, Rimbaud, and Valéry. Notwithstanding the international flavor of the term, which is often associated with the works of such seemingly divergent writers as Verhaeren, Jammes, Maeterlinck, Claudel, Apollinaire, Gide, Proust, Ibsen, Hauptmann, Strindberg, and Yeats, its denotation of a specific phase of recent poetry has peculiarly It. roots. It was first fully defined in 1936 by Francesco Flora in his study *La poesia ermetica* which traces its primary sources to Baudelaire, Mallarmé, and especially Valéry, and singles out Giuseppe Ungaretti as the chief It. exponent.

The generally recognized It. pioneer of such poetry was Arturo Onofri (1885–1928) who had been strongly influenced by the theosophy of Rudolf Steiner as well as by the works and theories of the Fr. decadents and their concept of "pure poetry." Following the clash between advanced guard ideas and reactionary tendencies that took place in It. literary and artistic circles in the second decade of this century Onofri emerged as the foremost exponent of a "new" poetic which has been alluded to as "a sort of literary asceticism" or "aesthetic mysticism." It was in part an attempt to arrive at "naked poetry" by concentrating all the lyrical potential in the individual word deprived of its decorative or logical elements. The new emphasis was to be on the musical suggestiveness and alliterative powers of the word rather than on its meaning. Similarly what was to matter most in the poem as a whole was the magical interplay between sound and silences, between moments of "illumination" and moments of "white blankness," rather than the balanced structure of verses and stanzas. Poetry was to be a sort of "intellectualized music" in which narrative and logical elements played no part. The poet's inspiration might encompass an instant (atomism) or longer periods of sustained intuition. This attempt to "render sensible the world of the supersensible" led quite naturally to the use of highly subjective language, experiences and complex devices (analogy), whence the sense of obscurity usually associated with the movement. The term "hermetic poetry" thus moved beyond Flora's definition of a poetry on the borderline of music (Hermes) to a poetry implying conscious obscurity and enigma. In time, however, the movement acquired a more sober perspective as a result of a return to such classical poets as Leopardi and Petrarch, and of the influence of such foreign poets as García Lorca, Paul Éluard, and T. S. Eliot. The outstanding poets of this latter phase have been Giuseppe Ungaretti (in his later works), Eugenio Montale, and Salvatore Quasimodo.—A. Onofri, *Il nuovo Rinascimento e l'arte dell' Io* (1925); A. Gargiulo, *Letteratura italiana del novecento* (1940); V. Rossi, *Storia della lett. it.* (1946); E. Williamson, "Contemp. It. Poetry," *Poetry*, 79 (1951–52); O. Ragusa, "Fr. Symbolism in Italy," RR, 46 (1955); V. Orsini, *Ermetismo* (1956).   A.S.B.

HEROIC COUPLET (also riding rhyme, rhymed decasyllables, rhymed 5-beat lines, etc.). Iambic pentameter lines rhymed in pairs; one of the most important meters of Eng. syllabic verse; origin unknown. The Eng. form is often thought to have developed with Chaucer under influence from the Old Fr. decasyllable rhymed in couplets: e.g., "A toy, Henry, dous amis, me complain, / Pour ce que ne cueur ne mont ne plein . . ." (Machault, *Complainte écrite après la bataille de Poitiers et avant le seige de Reims par les Anglais*, 1356–58). Chaucer's *Compleynte to Pitee* was probably written before his It. journey, 1372–73; hence Fr. influence seems prior to It. However, ten Brink has shown that Chaucer's heroic verse, of which there are some 16,000 lines, differs from the Fr. in almost all respects in which the It. does, and Skeat and Lewis have also expressed some reservations about Fr. influence.

Moreover, it now seems Eng. syllabic verse developed naturally from a disintegration of the old alliterative meters (J. P. Oakden, *Alliterative Poetry in Middle Eng.*, 1930), with doubtless some encouragement from Fr. forms. Accordingly couplets may have arisen as the natural result of a strong native tradition. In any case, couplet rhymes, showing little if any continental influence, appear very early in verses of uneven length: "Castelas he let wyrcean. / And earme men swithe swencean. / / Se cyng waes swa swithe stearc, / And benam of his undertheoddan manig marc . . ." (*Rime of King William* in *Anglo-Saxon Chronicle*). For development of an octosyllabic couplet, such verses would need only slight regularization, and the decasyllabic couplet would seem to be a natural extension. Moreover, as Saintsbury points out, sporadic heroic couplets occur fairly frequently in pre-Chaucerian poetry, concealed in stanzas. But credit for development of the form as a medium for sustained expression belongs to Chaucer.

Although Neo-Chaucerians of the 15th c. did not abandon the h.c. (e.g. Henryson, *Orpheus and Eurydice*), they showed distinct preference for stanzaic verse. In the 16th c. there was a steady increase in its use for occasional, reflective, critical, complimentary, and topical verse, the form reaching a high state of development by 1557 (Nicholas Grimald in *Tottel's Miscellany*). Some scholars distinguish between two distinct varieties of h.c., though the differences may be essentially chronological. The first is the Chaucerian type used by Marlowe and Spenser, the latter making it a suitable medium for satire (*Mother Hubberd's Tale*). The other has come to be known as the classical variety, of which Jonson is the most important source: "To draw no envy, Shakespeare, on thy name, / Am I thus ample to thy book and fame . . ." (*To the memory of my beloved the author, Mr. William Shakespeare, and what he hath left us*). Both types exhibited medial pause, balance, antithesis, crisp diction, parallel construction, contrasted clauses, inversions, etc., but the classical type is supposed to have differed somewhat from the Chaucerian in that thought tended to become more, and narrative less important. Sandys, Hall, Drayton, Fletcher, Beaumont, Fairfax, Donne, Waller, Denham, Oldham all made extensive use of the form before Dryden brought it to near perfection.

In the great dramatic verse of the Elizabethan period the h.c. is used sporadically. It is employed sparingly in Shakespeare, in pastoral drama (e.g. Peele's *Arraignment of Paris*), and it often appears as a device for metrical variation, a commonplace means of terminating blank-verse speeches, and, less frequently, as a link between speeches. D'Avenant and Etheredge made use of the form after the Restoration, and Dryden made it the principal medium for dramatic verse (*Tyrannick Love, Aureng-Zebe,* etc.). The critical controversy over rhyme during this period concerns mainly the use of the h.c. as opposed to blank verse, for tragedy: Dryden allows Lisideius to argue, in the *Essay of Dramatic Poesy*, that he prefers rhyme to the Eng. "way of writing in tragedies . . . in blank verse." To Dryden also belongs credit for making the h.c. the principal nondramatic, neoclassical meter; he became a master of the epigrammatic quality now especially associated with the period: "During his office, treason was no crime; / The sons of Belial had a glorious time . . ." (*Absalom and Achitophel,* 597–98). Pope brought this quality to an even higher state of perfection, paying special attention to the use of anticlimax: "Here thou great Anna! Whom three realms obey, / Dost sometimes counsel take—and sometimes tea. . . ." (*Rape of the Lock* 3.7–8). Johnson, Goldsmith, Crabbe, Cowper, Byron, Hunt, Keats, Shelley, Browning, Swinburne, and Morris all made notable use of the h.c., though the form began to decline in prominence early in the romantic period.

Many variations of the h.c. are possible, particularly as the caesura is shifted; indeed, excepting the rhyme requirement, the form is nearly as flexible as blank verse (e.g. Browning's *My Last Duchess*). The simplest, formal separation into types is into (1) closed couplets, those in which a semi- or full stop is employed at the end of the second rhyme, and (2) open couplets, in which the thought continues from the second rhyme into the following line. Similar couplets occur in most European languages, excepting Sp. which makes little use of the decasyllable, but the term h.c. is usually reserved for the Eng. meter.

C. M. Lewis, *The Foreign Sources of Modern Eng. Versification* (1898); F. E. Schelling, "Ben Jonson and the Cl. School," PMLA, 13 (1898); B. ten Brink, *The Lang. and Metre of Chaucer* (1901); R. M. Alden, *Eng. Verse* (1903); Saintsbury, *Prosody*; J. S. P. Tatlock, "The Origin of the Closed C. in Eng.," *The Nation*, 98 (April 9, 1914), 390; E. C. Knowlton, "The Origin of the Closed C. in Eng.," *The Nation*, 99 (July 30, 1914), 134; R. C. Wallerstein, "The Development of the Rhetoric and Metre of the H.C., esp. in 1625–1645," PMLA, 50 (1935); W. C. Brown, *The Triumph of Form* (1948).   R.O.E.

HEROIC PLAY. Modern critics have applied the term "h.p." to a Restoration fashion in tragedy. It was an exploitation of the epic mode of heightened admiration of heroism. It gave up blank verse for the rhymed couplet, which was suited to declamation on the stage. Its rhetoric was extravagant, and its concept of tragedy erroneous. We have Dryden's word for it that it was based on the work of Sir William Davenant, whose *The Siege of Rhodes* (1656) and *The Cruelty of the Spaniards in Peru* (1658) were much admired. With Davenant came magnificence in staging and the presence of an operatic element. Sir Robert Howard's *The Indian Queen* and its sequel by Dryden, *The Indian Emperor*, set the fashion, and Dryden's *Conquest of Granada* is perhaps the finest example. Two things perhaps served to bring this "highfalutin" drama down to earth. One was the famous burlesque, *The Rehearsal*, by the Duke of Buckingham and his collaborators, and the other was the superior tragic genius of Thomas Otway.—B. J. Pendlebury, *Dryden's H. Plays* (1923); A. Nicoll, *A Hist. of Restoration Drama, 1660–1700* (1928); C. V. Deane, *Dramatic Theory and the H.P.* (1931); *A. Hist. of Eng. Lit.*, ed. H. Craig (1950); T. J. Fujimura, "The Appeal of Dryden's H. Plays," PMLA, 75 (1960).　　　H.C.

HEROIC POETRY. See EPIC; NARRATIVE POETRY. **HEROIC METER** or line. The meter characteristic of heroic poetry, e.g., the dactylic hexameter in Gr. and L.; the iambic pentameter (5-stress line, unrhymed as in blank verse or rhymed in pairs as in the heroic couplet) in Eng.; the alexandrine in Fr.; and the hendecasyllable in It. **HEROIC QUATRAIN** or stanza. The iambic pentameter quatrain, rhymed abab. **HEROIC SIMILE.** See SIMILE.

HEXAMETER (6-measure), refers to the classical 6-foot catalectic dactylic line whose scheme is

$$\overline{1} \; \overline{2} \; \overline{3} \; \overline{4} \; \overline{5} \; \overline{6}$$

Foot 5 may be a spondee, in which case the line is called "spondaic." The last syllable in the line may be long or short and is called *syllaba anceps*. The caesura, or major pause, may occur *within* foot 3 (penthemimeral, i.e., after 5 half-feet), 4 (hephthemimeral), or 2 (trihemimeral); a line may have as many as 2 minor pauses. Diaeresis (coincidence of word and foot endings), e.g.

kūmătă lĕipĕi

is fairly common in foot 5. Homer tends to avoid it in foot 4 (bucolic diaeresis, q.v.) and more particularly in a foot-4 spondee or foot-3 dactyl. The L. h. is in general less flexible than

the Gr.; it avoids the foot-3 "feminine" caesura (−⌣‖⌣), which is frequent in Homer. Coincidence of metrical and word accents is common in Lucretius, avoided in Virgil. The use of a foot-5 spondee became a feature of Alexandrian verse and was imitated by the Romans, often as a mere fashionable trick, e.g., Cicero's parody (*Atticus* 7.2.1):

flauit ab Epiro lenissimus Onchesmites.

The h. in antiquity is used in lyric, gnomic, elegiac, philosophical, and satirical poetry but is primarily the meter of epic, e.g., *Iliad, Odyssey, Aeneid, Pharsalia*. It is also the meter of the "epyllion," an epic-style short poem (ca. 300–500 lines), e.g., *Ciris*, Catullus 64. It is to classical poetry what the alexandrine is to Fr., the iambic pentameter to Eng. poetry. During the early Middle Ages (4th-6th c.) Christian epics were produced in dactylic h. by, e.g., Juvencus, Sedulius, Arator, and Avitus. The quantitative L. h. continued to be used during the Middle Ages (e.g., John of Salisbury's *Entheticus*), despite the growing preponderance of syllabic, stress-accentual (see CLASSICAL METERS IN MODERN LANGUAGES), and rhymed verses (including especially the leonine), and during the Renaissance, despite the new vernacular-language verse forms.

In the *certame coronario* of 1441, L. B. Alberti and Leonardo Dati introduced experimental *esametri italiani*. In the next century Claudio Tolomei, followed by other poets, experimented with the re-creation of quantitative h. verse.

Richard Burgi, studying early Slavic literature, suggests on the basis of his observations that this literature "produced the first verse rendering of Homer in a non-classical language." Early in the 16th c. Maksim the Gr. made the first attempt in Rus. at a quantitative prosody based on an artificial and arbitrary classification of long and short vowels (*Maksimovskaja prosodija*). According to Burgi the year 1704 "marks the first appearance in print of the standard accentual prosody of classical Russian verse"—a pair of rhymed hexameters in syllabic verse. Accentual hexameters were revived in Russia toward the end of the 18th c. The translation of the *Iliad* into Rus. h. by N. Gnedič is considered one of the great achievements of Rus. literature; it was greatly admired by Pushkin, who himself wrote much h. verse. V. Brjusov, one of the Rus. symbolists, translated the *Aeneid* and I. Račinskij, a philologist, all of Lucretius in hexameters.

When Andreas Arvidi's *Det Svenska Poeteri*, the first Swedish *Ars Poetica*, was published in 1651, the *knittelvers* (doggerel) was being displaced in ballads and chronicles by both the h. and the alexandrine. George Stiernhielm's monumental *Hercules* (1658) was composed in hexameters. Other important h. poems in Swedish include Thomas Thorild's *Passionerna* (1781) and Johan Ludvig Runeberg's *Julkvällen* (1841). Eventually the alexandrine displaced the h. in Swedish poetry.

Notable hexameters in German literature include F. G. Klopstock's *Der Messias* (1748–73), J. H. Voss's *Homer* and *Luise*, and Goethe's *Reineke Fuchs* and *Hermann und Dorothea* (a "pastoral epic"—1798).

The h. is, at best, merely incidental to the traditions of Fr. and Sp. poetry (see CLASSICAL METERS . . .). Nicaragua's Rubén Darío (1867–1916) composed his *Salutación del optimisto* in h. verses varying between 13 and 18 syllables, with most verses consisting of heptasyllabic and decasyllabic hemistichs; the verses are marked by many dactylic clausulae, common in Gr. lyric poetry but alien to epic.

Eng. poets since the 16th c. have been perennially ambitious in hexametrical endeavors, both accentual and syllabic, but particularly so in the 19th c. (see CLASSICAL METERS . . .). One of the earliest (16th c.) examples is Thomas Watson's "All travellers do gladly report great praise of Ulysses, / For that he knew many men's manners and saw many cities"—less wretched, perhaps, than Sidney's hexameters, e.g.

Ōpprest with ruinōus conceits by the help of
  an outcry

Spenser had seen the root of the problem (viz., stress-accent vs. quantitative accent) when he suggested that we retain normal accents for speech but quantitative accents in prosody. This was the problem faced by Southey, Kingsley, Coleridge, Longfellow, Clough, Tennyson, and Swinburne. Robert Bridges' syllabic hexameter is trying, e.g. for

Ibant obscuri sola sub nocte per umbram

he has

They wer' amid the shadows by night in loneliness obscure.

C. Day Lewis' translation of the *Aeneid* (1956) is a stress-accentual h. version with lines varying from 12 (alexandrine) to 17 (full Latin-h.) syllables.

Of Scandinavian languages Danish and Swedish are particularly apt for h. verse. In the former, Sophus Claussen's poem *Atomernes Oprør* (1925) is noteworthy; in the latter, Georg Stiernhielm's epic *Hercules* (publ. 1658) and, in the 19th c., Esaias Tegnér's *Fritiof'tager arv* . . . stand out. H. poetry became also somewhat popular in Icelandic literature during the 19th c., according to S. Einarsson, who

notes that Steingrímur Torsteinsson's mock-heroic *Redd-Hanne-sarríma* (first ed. in 1925) marked the initial use of the h. for a reasonably long narrative poem. Torsteinsson was followed by his contemporaries, Benedikt Gröndal and Matthias Jochumsson, who wrote shorter mock-heroic h. poems.

For bibliography, see CLASSICAL METERS IN MODERN LANGUAGES. Also, R. Bridges, *Ibant Obscuri* (1916); H. G. Atkins, *A Hist. of German Versification* (1923); A. Izzo, "L'esametro neo-classico italiano," R. Accad. . . . dei Lincei. *Rendiconti*, 7 (1932), fasc. 6; J. S. Molina, *Los hexámetros castellanos y en particular los de Rubén Darío* (1935); G. L. Hendrickson, "Elizabethan Quantitative Hexameters," PQ, 28 (1949); G. Highet, *The Cl. Tradition* (1949); C. G. Cooper, *An Introd. to the L. H.* (1952); S. Einarsson, "H. in Icelandic Lit.," MLN, 68 (1953); Koster; R. Burgi, *A Hist. of the Rus. H.* (1954); Navarro; A. Gustafson, *A Hist. of Swedish Lit.* (1961).   R.A.S.

HEXASTICH. See SEXAIN.

HIATUS. (a) A gap which destroys the completeness of a sentence or verse: "A Dunce-Monk, being [about] to make his epitaph . . . left the Verse thus gaping, *Hic sunt in fossa Bedae—ossa,* till he had consulted with his Pillow to fill up the *Hiatus*" (Fuller, *The Church—History of Britain,* II, iii). (b) Grammar and prosody: a break between two vowels coming together without an intervening consonant in successive words or syllables to prevent vowel clash, where neither aphaeresis, crasis, nor elision (qq.v.) is operative. In Eng. the indefinite article may be altered by addition of a nasal to prevent hiatus: *an action.* Elision to avoid h. is permissible (R. Bridges, *Milton's Prosody,* 1921). In the classical languages (see CLASSICAL PROSODY) h. is common in Gr. epic poetry, rarer in L. In languages in which number of syllables is an important aspect of verse, like Fr., an understanding of h. is essential both for scansion and for writing verse. In Fr. h. was generally permissible until (at least) the 14th c.; there is no elision to prevent h. in *Saint Alexis* (about 1040), but in Froissart (ca. 1337–ca. 1410) there are 132 cases of elision against 5 of h. (G. Lote, *Hist. du vers français,* III, 87). The two phenomena may be observed, with the same words in *Chanson de Roland:* "Jo i ferrai de Durendal m'espee" (v. 1462)—h.; "Jo i puis aler, mais n'i avrai guarant" (v. 329)—elision. In Sp., It., and Portuguese, h. is usually eliminated by contraction.   R.O.E.

HINDI POETRY. See INDIAN POETRY.

HISTORY AND POETRY. These two disciplines are usually distinguished in terms of poetry as fiction and hist. as fact. This distinction governs the crucial ch. 9 of the *Poetics* (see below), where Aristotle sees poetry tending toward fiction as its proper form: poetry refers to a possible and hist. to an actual order of things. In the scholia on Dionysius Thrax (ed. Hilgard, p. 449) hist. is contrasted with the fictitious but possible and the strange or impossible. This pattern of differentiation, the basis of differentiation among literary forms in Roman antiquity (Cicero, *De inventione* [*rhetorica*] 1.19.27, Quintilian 2.4.2.), was preserved by L. grammarians (ed. Halm, pp. 202, 486, 552) and in standard reference works of the Middle Ages (Isidore's *Etymologiae* 1.44, Vincent of Beauvais' *Speculum doctrinale* 3.127). To Dante poetry is simply "fictio rethorica" (*De vulgari eloquentia* 2.4), and the sense of poetry as a structure of new things—utterly new, "inauditas inventiones," says Boccaccio, *Genealogia deorum gentilium* 14.7—is assimilated into Renaissance poetics (Sidney, *Apology*; Bacon, *Advancement* 2.4; Jonson, "What Is a Poet?" in *Timber*) and becomes a foundation of the modern conception of poets as "Creators, such as raise admirable Frames and Fabricks out of nothing" (W. Temple, *Of Poetry*; cf. Macrobius, *Saturnalia* 5.1–2). Truth was expected under the cover of fiction: Dante defines the *Comedy* as a treatise in moral philosophy (Epistle to Can Grande 9, 16); Sidney classifies the poet as "the right popular philosopher." But in medieval as in later criticism it is the fictional mode of treatment (*fictivus*) which produces the poetry, the fictional sometimes remaining the only distinguishing element, "the forme and Soule of any Poeticall worke" (Jonson).

The contrast between hist. as fact and poetry as a discipline transcending fact, a contrast based on the *Poetics* 9, survived into the 19th c. (Wordsworth, 1800 Preface; Newman, *Poetry*). But it has been largely replaced by the contrast between science and poetry (I. A. Richards, *Science and Poetry*, ch. 6; cf. Coleridge, *Biographia Literaria*, ch. 14). In both types of contrast since the romantic period, and in recent definitions of poetry as pseudo-statement (Richards) or mythopoeic (H. Read, *Collected Essays*, p. 102), some traditional sense of poetry as fiction remains. But the term fiction has been increasingly applied to prose narrative, and in popular usage today fiction is synonymous with the novel, and poetry with some kind of knowledge beyond the reach of prose and in some special way involving a truthful rendering of emotion in a biographic or dramatic lyric—a sense anticipated by Wordsworth: "Poetry is passion: it is the history or science of feelings" (Note to *The Thorn*).

The association of poetry with hist. has been as persistent as the dissociation and occurs early and late in criticism. Ezra Pound's definition of his *Cantos*, "An epic is a poem including history" (*Literary Essays*, ed. Eliot, p. 86), is a rephrasing of an old conception that poetry is a record of useful and memorable things (Cicero, *Pro Archia* 10; Strabo 1.2), and has "something of the Historical in its Nature, and never shines more, than when it alludes to Characters and Things of past Times" (Welsted, *Epistles*, 1724, p. xlvi). To Manzoni (*Lettre à M. Chauvet*) fiction is minimal and unessential: "tous les grands monumens de la poésie ont pour base des événemens donnés par l'histoire," the poet's function being to see data from the inside and give esthetic form to motives and emotions that hist. omits or reduces to an abstraction. Sometimes the fictional is radically undervalued: "an Irish peasant with a little whisky in his head will imagine and invent more than would furnish forth a modern poem" (Byron, *Letters*, ed. Prothero, v, 554), or opposed as falsehood to a positivistic sense of truth: "Who sayes that fictions onely and false hair Become a verse? Is there in truth no beautie?" (G. Herbert, *Jordan*). This serious conception of poetry as a representation of "cose veramente avvenute" (Muratori, *Opere*, 1769, ix, pt. 1, 78), which modern criticism developed against "the vulgar conceit of men, that Lying is Essential to good Poetry" (Cowley's Preface, *Poems*, 1656), is a refinement of an ancient conception of the poet as historian found in Lactantius (*Divinae institutiones* 1.11; repeated in Isidore's *Etymologiae* 8.7.10 and Vincent of Beauvais's *Speculum doctrinale* 3. 110). To invent everything, says Lactantius, "id est ineptum esse, et mendacem potius quam poetam." The conception of poetry as historical by nature and deriving value from historical reality (Puttenham, *Arte of Eng. Poesie* 1.19, ranks it next to divine) is the corollary of a theory of poetic origins inherited from antiquity and summarized by Wordsworth: "The earliest poets of all nations generally wrote from passion excited by real events" (*Appendix*). Evanthius (ed. Kaibel, pp. 63–64) remarks that primitive poetry was historical, and Aristotle suggests as much in outlining the development of dramatic forms (*Poetics* 9.4–6). Early Christian apologists utilized the theory: poetic myths about the gods are distortions of human hist. (Lactantius, *Divinae institutiones* 1.15; Augustine, *De civitate Dei* 18.14), or corrupt versions of Old Testament hist. (Tertullian, *Apologeticus* 47.12–14; cf. Raleigh, *Hist. of the World* 1.6; T. Gale, *Court of Gentiles*, 1669, pt. 1, 275–398). The euhemeristic explanation was fully detailed by Vico in *Della discoverta del vero Omero*. He relies on Lactantius, and on the passage in Strabo 1.2.6 describing poetic discourse as anterior to prose, but develops his theory of the historical origins of poetry on two romantic assumptions: that the poetic process is by nature particularistic, distinct from the metaphysical; and that primitive man was naturally truthful, incapable of inventing, since he was controlled by a sensuous imagination and lacked the power of reflection. So Vico concludes that poetic myths at their birth were "narrazioni vere e severe" which later underwent many changes and descended to Homer in corrupt and incredible forms (*Opere*, ed. Nicolini, pp. 739–45, 749).

The association of poetry with hist. is sometimes complicated by the conception of poetry as philosophy in its origin and function—a conception which was already ancient in the time of Strabo (1.2.3), remembered in the Middle Ages ("Poetas philosophorum cunas esse, celebre est," John of Salisbury, *Metalogicon* 1.22), and a commonplace in modern criticism where it is often thought to have the support of the *Poetics* 9.3 (see below). Modern poetic theory has developed confusedly along two main lines marked out in antiquity—one toward conceiving the poem as a structure of particulars historical or invented (e.g., Vico; cf. Plato, Republic 10, who discredits poetry as phantasmal imitation of appearances), and the other toward the poem as a structure of true universals ("La Poesia non è altro che una prima filosofia," Giraldi Cinthio, in *Lettere*, ed. Poracchi, 1565; cf. Maximus Tyrius, *Dissertationes* 4, Teubner ed.). Attempts to reconcile the two directions—notably in Agnolo Segni (see Bibliog. below), Sidney, Butcher on the *Poetics* (4th ed., pp. 191–92)—have issued in the conception of poetry as an organization of concrete universals. To Sidney it is a perfect organization ethically informed, mediating between the particularistic and the abstract which in Plato stand in absolute opposition: hist. and philosophy, says Sidney, "do both halt," for one lacks a general principle of conduct and the other the example; but poetry "coupleth the general notion with the particular example" and so performs its ethical function perfectly. An important source of poetry conceived as a concrete universal is the celebrated passage in the *Poetics* 9.3: "poetry is something more philosophic and of graver import than history, since its statements are of the nature rather of universals, whereas those of history are singulars" (Bywater's tr.). This passage has often been read as an equation of poetry and philosophy, the poet sharing in "the philosopher's quest for ultimate truth"(Atkins, *Literary Criticism in Antiquity*, 1.80; cf. Butcher, pp. 164, 168, 184); or misread in favor of the preeminence of poetry as knowledge: "Aristotle, I have been told, has said, that Poetry is the most philosophic of all writ-

ing" (Wordsworth, 1800 Preface). But it is very doubtful that Aristotle means to say universals should be philosophically valid to satisfy the requisite of poetic art, which is giving a pleasure peculiar to it. His theory runs in a contrary direction, made clear at 24.18–19, 25.4–8, 26–31, that poetry is not restricted to true statements. From ch. 25 emerges the large proposition, empirically derived from the successful practice of poets, that what may enter poetry is not only the ideal (what ought to be) and the actual (and therefore the probable or possible), but also the impossible, the false, and matters of mere opinion. The passage at 9.3 is perhaps to be understood in terms of the general sense of the *Poetics* that poetry is essentially fiction: the philosophical bent of poetry—and the passage clearly indicates no more than this—is inside a fictional structure which derives no special value from it.

Gr. tragic poets had traditionally exploited material accepted as historical, and at 9.4–8 Aristotle raises the question of the relative value of fiction and hist. only to dismiss it: there are wholly fictitious tragedies, "e.g. Agathon's *Antheus*, in which both incidents and names are of the poet's invention; and it is no less delightful on that account." The definition of tragedy as hist. was current in Hellenistic times (perhaps it was current in Aristotle's time, see Tragedy and Hist., Bibliog. below), and as found in ancient grammarians (ed. Hilgard, p. 307; ed. Kaibel, pp. 17, 58, 66, 67, 72) the definition involves a stated or implied contrast with comedy: tragedy is a hist. of disasters which happened to heroic figures of a remote past, comedy is a fiction about private persons in everyday life. This distinction was preserved during the Middle Ages (Isidore, *Etymologiae* 8.7.6; Vincent of Beauvais, *Speculum doctrinale* 3.110) with, however, only a shadowy sense of its dramatic import, Dante, e.g., applying it to kinds of narrative (Epistle to Can Grande 10; but see Mussato below). It. Renaissance criticism inherited this distinction, sometimes expanding it to include the epic as hist., and made it an important issue in discussions of verisimilitude, catharsis, and ethical function (see Historical Realism, Bibliog. below). The question of the relative merit of fiction and hist. in serious poetry aroused a bitter controversy (Giraldi Cinthio, Castelvetro, Tasso, Piccolomini) the echoes of which are still heard in Lessing (*Hamburgische Dramaturgie*) and as late as Manzoni's essay (see above).

The controversy is reflected in Sidney: "and do they not know that a Tragedy is tied to the laws of Poesy, and not of History?" During the Eng. Renaissance the ethical and political value of hist. informs popular literature (*Mirror for Magistrates*, 1559), the drama (over 150 plays are based on Eng. hist.; Schelling, *Eng. Chronicle Play*), and apologies for the stage (Lodge, Nash, T. Heywood). The definition of tragedy as hist. was familiar enough to force Prynne into a particular attack on "reall tragicall Histories" (*Histrio-Mastix*, 1633, pp. 789, 940–41). But Eng. criticism generally followed Bacon (*Advancement* 2.4.2): poetry should correct hist., which is little else than a sorry record of man's injustices, and followed Dryden (Pref., *Troilus and Cressida*): the tragic plot need not be historical, but only probable, "*probable* being that which succeeds, or happens, oftner than it misses." The doctrine that poetry is generically fiction, and that epic or tragedy is no exception to it, did not seriously affect practice. Even Giraldi, who followed Aristotle and wrote the wholly fictitious *Orbecche* after the example of Agathon's *Antheus*, turned to hist. and legendary hist. in his other tragedies. Jonson summarizes the doctrine: "Poets never credit gain'd / By writing truths, but things, like truth, well feigned" (2nd Prol., *Silent Woman*); yet for his tragic plots he sought the authority of hist. Hist., in fact, is the source of the conception of the earliest regular and secular tragedies in the vernacular: Trissino's *Sofonisba* (ca. 1513) drawn from Livy, Jodelle's *Cléopâtre* (ca. 1552) from Plutarch, Ferreira's *Inez de Castro* (ca. 1558) from Portuguese chronicles, Sackville and Norton's *Gorboduc* (1562) from Geoffrey of Monmouth. But the conception runs back to Dante's contemporary Mussato, whose *Eccerinis* based on the career of the ferocious tyrant Ezzelino III, is the first indication of tragedy in the classical sense of hist. in dramatic structure (cf. Mussato's *Epistola* 1, and Dazzi's comments, *Giornale storico della letteratura italiana*, 1921). From Mussato to Eliot's *Murder in the Cathedral* there is a continuous tradition of secular hist. in drama serving ethical, political, social, or nationalistic ends. Hist. furnished material for a large body of narrative poetry— classical epic, romantic epic, chanson de geste, ballad—from Homer to Pound's *Cantos*. The epic in practice is often associated with authentic hist. as its primary base—a practice honored by Dante who places Lucan among the great poets of antiquity (*Inferno* 4.88–89), and an association which may have influenced Milton to abandon an Arthuriad when he found the historical authenticity of Arthur in question (Brinkley, *Arthurian Legend*, ch. 4). The practice in treatment of hist. varies; but in general poets have "altered and transposed and invented incidents" to suit purpose and design (MacLeish, Note to *Conquistador*). The most significant innovation in treatment and material is in Pound's *Cantos*, which introduce economic and monetary hist. in poetry after the example of Dante and exploit the subject

for educative ends, even to the extent of including precise bibliographical information: "mentions distributive justice, Dante does, in Convivio / Four, eleven" (Canto 93).

In every age poetry has gravitated toward hist., and historiography toward poetic fiction, as in a type of Hellenistic hist. imitating tragedy (a type castigated by Polybius, Plutarch, Lucian; see Hist. and Tragedy, Bibliog. below), medieval rhyming chronicles, and modern histories that read like fictions (e.g., C. Bowen's *John Adams*). The historian Duris, censored by Plutarch, defines this type in Aristotelian terms of mimesis and pleasure (Jacoby, *Fragmente der Griechischen Historiker*, pt. 2A, 138), though Aristotle nowhere suggests poetic norms for historiography. The question implicit in Duris, whether hist. is an art or a science, has often been discussed since the romantic period (see Poetry of Hist., Bibliog. below; Bury, G. M. Trevelyan, Croce) and sometimes resolved by conceiving hist. as meditating between art and science (T. M. Greene, *Yale Review*, 1944). In Aristotelian terms the question is not momentous: Aristotle's distinction, art is concerned with making and science with knowing by principle and system (*Ethics* 6.3–4) suggests that the discipline of hist. is under science, and that problems of historiography are only incidentally problems of art and essentially problems of cognition. It is extravagant to claim that hist. as science "cannot ever exist" because of difficulties in determining principles of causation and the like (Trevelyan, *Clio, a Muse*, 1931, p. 143). The difficulties, which are after all comparable to those in other sciences, merely indicate more subtle instruments for the systematic cognition of "dead documents," so called by the Crocean school.

Trevelyan (*Clio*, pp. 155–56) advises the literary scholar to soak himself in social and political hist. The wealth of historical poetry in every age, the relevance of topical information to the study of satire, the pervasive sense of hist. in modern poetry (e.g., Eliot's *Waste Land*) make the advice generally sound. The historical method (Morize, *Problems and Methods in Literary Hist.*, 1922) has been attacked for raking up data irrelevant to literary value (see issues debated in Crane, "Hist. and Poetry," EJ, 1933; Cunningham, "Ancient Quarrel between Hist. and Poetry," *Poetry*, Sept. 1949; PMLA, Dec. and Feb., 1951; Bush *et al.*, KR, 1950–1). But the method itself has obvious uses, among them "to divest ourselves of the limitations of our own age" (Eliot, *On Poetry and Poets*, p. 130), and needs no justification: it is a natural act of the understanding; and to justify it as an act of the evaluating intelligence (literary hist. has been renamed *historical criticism*) is to confuse its function, which is explanatory and preliminary to evaluation. In practice the historical method (which includes *explication de texte* closely connected with the New Criticism) is largely this, with evaluation merely implied or summary. See CRITICISM, TYPES OF; and La Drière, Bibliog. below.

B. Fioretti, *Proginnasmi poetici*, v (1639), 10–60; W. Cloetta, *Beiträge zur Literaturgesch. des Mittelalters und der Renaissance* (1890–92); A. Benoist, "Théories dramatiques avant les discours de Corneille," *Annales de la Faculté des Lettres de Bordeaux* (1891), pp. 334–41; P. Scheller, *De hellenistica historiae conscribendae arte* (1911); A. Belloni, *Il poema epico* (1912), ch. 5, 6; R. C. Williams, "Purpose of Poetry," RR, 12 (1921) and "Two Studies in Epic Poetry," MP, 22 (1924); R. Bray, *Tragédie cornélienne* (1927), 34–55; A. P. McMahon, "Seven Questions on Aristotelian Definitions of Tragedy and Comedy," HSCP, 40 (1929); B. L. Ullman, "Hist. and Tragedy," *Proc. of the Am. Philol. Assoc.*, 73 (1942); G. Giovannini, "Tragedy and Hist. in Ancient Crit.," PQ, 22 (1943), "Agnolo Segni and a Renaissance Definition of Poetry," MLQ, 6 (1945) and "Historical Realism and the Tragic Emotions in Ren. Crit.," PQ, 32 (1953); H. T. Swedenberg, *Theory of the Epic in England* (1944); E. Neff, *Poetry of Hist.* (1947), ch. 7, 8; J. V. Cunningham, *Woe and Wonder* (1951), ch. 3; C. M. Bowra, *Heroic Poetry* (1952), ch. 14; A. W. Gomme, *Gr. Attitude to Poetry and Hist.* (1954); J. C. La Drière, *Directions in Contemp. Crit.* (1955), 84–85, n.67; F. W. Walbank, "Hist. and Tragedy," *Historia*, 9 (1960); H. S. Hughes, *Hist. as Art and Science* (1964). G.G.

HISTORY PLAY. Any play based heavily on history may be termed "h.p." Since the distinction between myth, legend, and formal history is relatively late, Gr. tragedy and Christian mystery and miracle plays (qq.v.) could be called h.p. Usually, however, the term is applied to plays based on secular history and following it rather closely. *The Persians* by Aeschylus is the first h.p. in the formal sense and the only example of the genre surviving from Gr. drama. Roman critics had a formal term (*fabula praetexta*) for drama on historical subjects, but only one example, the *Octavia*, attributed to Seneca, has survived.

Renaissance dramatists frequently drew on both ancient and modern history, and several critics (e.g., Lodovico Castelvetro) argued that tragedy should always be based on historical events, if only to make the stage action more convincing. The achievements of Eng. dramatists in the form are so preeminent that frequently the terms h.p. and chronicle play are used to refer simply to Eng. works of the late 16th and early 17th c. H.p. is somewhat more inclusive than chronicle play, the latter term being usually reserved for plays based on

Holinshed's *Chronicles of England, Scotland, and Ireland* (1577–87). The earliest Eng. plays on historical subjects are loose, didactic, tinged with morality-play influences, and range from Eng. history (Bale's *King John*), through legend (Sackville and Norton, *Gorboduc*), to ancient and oriental history (the anonymous *The Wars of Cyrus*, Preston's *Cambises*, Marlowe's *Tamburlaine*). A high level of excellence is reached in Marlowe's *Edward II* and maintained in such 17th-c. plays as Fletcher's *Bonduca* and Ford's *Perkin Warbeck*. The greatest h.p. are those by Shakespeare, which form a cycle beginning with *Richard II* and extending through *Henry VIII*.

H.p., usually on Roman subjects, continued to be written in Italy, France, and England throughout the 18th c., but the only writer to achieve genuine greatness in the form was Schiller (*Wallenstein* trilogy; *Maria Stuart*), and with Schiller we have already entered the romantic period. During the 19th and early 20th c. Dumas, Hugo, Pushkin, and Strindberg produced significant h.p. More recently, Claudel, T. S. Eliot, Maxwell Anderson, Robert Sherwood, and Arthur Miller have dramatized historical materials. If cinema is considered a form of drama, a plethora of examples of h.p. may be adduced to demonstrate that the public is just as eager today for dramatic re-creations of historical events as it was during the age of Shakespeare, and no more critical.

F. E. Schelling, *The Eng. Chronicle Play* (1902); *Marlowe's Edward II*, ed. W. D. Briggs (1914; see long introd.); W. Farnham, *The Medieval Heritage of Elizabethan Tragedy* (1936); E.M.W. Tillyard, *Shakespeare's H.P.* (1946); L. B. Campbell, *Shakespeare's "Histories"* (1947); A. Nicoll, *World Drama* (1950); I. Ribner, *The Eng. H.P. in the Age of Shakespeare* (1957); T. F. Driver, *The Sense of Hist. in Gr. and Shakespearean Drama* (1960); M. M. Reese, *The Cease of Majesty: A Study of Shakespeare's H.P.* (1962).

HITTITE POETRY. The Hittites, who lived in Turkey in the second millennium B.C. and spoke an Indo-European language, have left a few poetical texts in the royal archives of their capital, Hattusa, modern Boghazkoy, 100 miles east of Ankara. The texts are written in cuneiform, a system of writing that the Hittites borrowed from Babylonia. It uses word signs and syllables; this causes the following difficulties for the reading of poetic texts: (1) clusters of two or more consonants at the beginning and end, and of three or more consonants in the interior of a word had to be broken up by the addition of mute vowels; (2) the Hittite reading of some word signs is still unknown (such words will be rendered by their Eng. equivalent in capitals).

HOMOEOTELEUTON

The Indo-European Hittites superseded an earlier population who spoke an unrelated language, called Hattic by scholars and for the most part undeciphered. Among the Hattic texts used by the Hittites in the cult of the gods of the land, there are some that are written in stanzas of 3 to 5 verses which are separated by horizontal rules. In contrast to these Hattic poems, Hittite poetical texts are not written in separate verses but rather consecutively, like prose. The oldest example is a short song, contained in an historical text of the Old Kingdom (ca. 1700–1600 B.C.) and introduced by the words "Then he sings." Among texts of the New Kingdom (ca. 1400–1200 B.C.), some hymns and epics seem to be written in verse, e.g., a hymn to Istanu, the Sun God, which begins: "Istanui iskha-mi / handants hannesnas iskhas" (Oh Istanu, my lord! / Just lord of judgment).

From the epic literature of the New Kingdom we quote passages of The Song of Ullikummi. The first stanza of 4 verses, which was a prooemium of the type known from Homer, is mutilated; its last line reads: "dapiyas siunas attan Kumarbin iskhamihhi" (Of Kumarbi, father of all gods, I shall sing). The story itself begins in the fourth stanza:

11 man-tsa Kumarbis hattatar istantsani piran
   das
   nas-kan kiskhiyats sara hudak arais
   kessarats STAFF-an das
   padas-sas-ma-tsa SHOES liliwandus huwan-
   dus sarkwit

15 nas-kan Urkisats happirats arha iyannis
   nas ikunta luli-kan anda ar(a)s

11 When Kumarbi wisdom into (his) mind had
   taken,
   from (his) chair he promptly rose,
   into (his) hand a staff he took,
   upon his feet as shoes the swift winds he
   put;

15 from (his) town Urkis he set out,
   and to a cool(?) pond(?) he came.

Although both the lines and the stanzas have different length, and although it is impossible to establish a meter, it is clear from the term "song" used in the original title of the epic as well as from the structure of the text that we are dealing with some sort of bound language. Occasional rhyme occurs (das in 11 and 13, perhaps aras in 16, if the a was pronounced; arais in 12 and iyannis in 15), but it is not systematically used throughout the text. The same is true of parallelism of the type known from the Bible: it is used occasionally, but is not an essential feature. Other devices of the epic style, like standing epithets,

repetition of standard lines and of whole passages, are common.

H. Th. Bossert, "Gedicht und Reim im vorgriechischen Mittelmeergebiet," Geistige Arbeit, 5 (1938), no. 18, 7–10 (poetic texts in Hittite and other Mediterranean languages, with special emphasis on rhyme) and "Zur Entstehung des Reimes," Jahrbuch für Kleinasiatische Forschung, 2 (1951–53), 233f. (see also Mitteilungen des Instituts für Orientforschung, 2 [Berlin Academy, 1954], 97f.).— TEXTS discussed here and by Bossert: H. G. Güterbock, Keilschrifturkunden aus Boghazköi, 28 (1935) nos. 10–49 (cuneiform Hattic text; p. iv on stanzas); B. Hrozný, Archiv Orientálni, 1 (1929) 297 (Old Kingdom song); E. Tenner, "Zwei hethitische Sonnenlieder," Kleinasiatische Forschungen, 1 (1930), 387–92 (text and tr. of Sun hymns, analyzed by Bossert, loc. cit.); H. G. Güterbock, Jour. of the Am. Oriental Society, 78 (1958), 239 (text and tr. of Sun hymn quoted here) and "The Song of Ullikummi," Jour. of Cuneiform Studies, 5 (1951), 135–61, 6 (1952), 8–42 (text and tr., metrically arranged, of the epic; pp. 141–44 on form).— See also I. McNeill, "The Metre of the Hittite Epic," Anatolian Studies, 13 (1963), 237–42.— GENERAL: O. R. Gurney, The Hittites (2d ed., 1954). H.G.G.

HOKKU. See HAIKU; JAPANESE POETRY.

HOMOEOMERAL (Gr. "having like parts"). In prosody the term means portions which are metrically the same, e.g., strophe and antistrophe (qq.v.), or the repetition of the same stanzaic form.—Kolář. R.A.H.

HOMOEOTELEUTON (Gr. "similarity of endings"). This stylistic term, which first occurs in Aristotle, Rhetoric 3.9.9, is particularly apt with respect to inflected languages like Gr. and L. in that it describes similar case-endings in proximity, whether in prose or verse, e.g., in Naevius' Saturnian: "bicorpores Gigantes || magnique Atlantes." When h. of more than one syllable occurs at the end of two or more lines in succession, it becomes rhyme, e.g., Cicero can end three consecutive hexameters with monebant, ferebant, and iubebant. Rhyme, because of the heavier case-endings of L., is more common in that language than in Gr. It is generally agreed that h. and rhyme in quantitative meters were intentional, whether the effect was similar or not to that achieved by their use in the accentual verse of later L. and of modern languages. See also RHYME, HISTORY OF.—J. Marouzeau, Traité de stylistique latine (2d ed., 1946); J. Cousin, Bibliographie de la langue latine, 1880–1948 (1951); N. I. Herescu, La poésie latine (1960). R.J.G.

-[353]-

HORATIAN ODE. See ODE.

HOVERING ACCENT. A term suggestive of the effect of slowness and rhetorical weight produced by the spondaic foot (q.v.) or by a quasi-spondaic foot consisting of 1 primary stressed syllable and 1 secondary stressed syllable. In the iambic pentameter line

Unfriend|ly lamp | light hid | under | its shade, |
(Yeats, *After Long Silence* 3)

the third foot may be described as consisting of a hovering accent.—Brooks and Warren. P.F.

HRYNHENT. A variety of skaldic meter consisting of an 8-line stanza, and otherwise similar to *dróttkvætt* (q.v.), except that each line was lengthened by the addition of trochee. Used in some notable court poems from the 11th to the 13th c., h. is the verse form of the much admired sacred poem *Lilja* of the 14th c., from which it became known as *Liljulag,* and has down to the present day been employed by Icelandic poets for poems specially elevated in theme and form.—*The Skalds,* tr. and ed. L. M. Hollander (1945). R.B.

HUDIBRASTIC VERSE. The distinctive octosyllabic verse, rhyme use, characteristic satirical tone, and frequently impious imagery—widely imitated but never equalled—employed by Samuel Butler (1612–80) in his *Hudibras.* The meter would appear joggingly monotonous were the reader not kept constantly engrossed in the wide-ranging, conversational, sparkling wit; and constantly alert for the unexpected rhymes, many of them feminine, which, as an anonymous writer has remarked, "seem to chuckle and sneer of themselves." Butler speaks, for example, of "Dame Religion,"

Whose honesty they all durst swear for,
Tho' not a man of them knew wherefore;

of a time when

The oyster women picked their fish up
And trudged away to cry No Bishop;

and of Hudibras:

He knew the seat of Paradise,
Could tell in what degree it lies; . . .
What Adam dreamt of, when his bride
Came from the closet in his side; . . .
If either of them had a navel;
Who first made music malleable;
Whether the Serpent, at the Fall,
Had cloven feet, or none at all:
All this, without a gloss or comment,
He could unriddle in a moment. . . .
(Canto 1, Part 1)

Saintsbury, *Prosody*; I. Jack, "Low Satire: Hudibras," *Augustan Satire, 1660–1750* (1952); C. L. Kulisheck, "Swift's Octosyllabics and the Hudibrastic Tradition," JEGP, 53 (1954). L.J.Z.

HUITAIN. A form of the 8-line strophe with 8-syllable or 10-syllable lines, written on 3 rhymes with one of these appearing 4 times, and with the same rhyme for the fourth and fifth lines. The order is commonly ababbcbc, sometimes abbaacac. The h. may be a complete poem in 8 lines or it may be employed as the structural unit for longer poems. In the 15th c., François Villon wrote his *Lais* and the body of *Le grand testament* and most of its ballades in *huitains*. The form was popular in France in the first half of the 16th c. (e.g., with Marot), and it was sometimes employed in 18th-c. epigrams. In his *Petit traité de poésie française* Banville regrets the abandonment of the h. by modern Fr. poets and calls it (with the *dizain*) "perhaps the most perfect thing our lyric art has produced."—Kastner; M. Grammont, *Petit traité de versification fr.* (5e éd. revue, 1924). A.G.E.

HUMANISM, NEW. See NEO-HUMANISM.

HUNGARIAN POETRY. The Hung. word for poet, *költő,* was popularized in the 18th c., and the word for poetry, *költészet,* was coined in the fourth decade of the 19th c. In the Middle Ages and for a long time afterward the poet was called *regős, dalos, énekes, igric, hegedős, kobzos;* some of these terms having Hung. roots and others being of It., Slav, or Turkish origin. The heroic legends of the Huns and Magyars were, of course, in the Hung. language, as were romances, ceremonial verses, pastorals, warrior songs, chronicles, fairy and comic tales, parables and fables. Learned works, however, were written in Latin. Little of this poetic heritage survived (and what has is of rather dubious authenticity, although for about three centuries it was handed down orally from one generation to another. It is reasonable to assume that much crude poetry and perhaps many lovely songs and short and lengthy epic poems were lost. Converted to Christianity, the kings and feudal lords, assisted by the clergy, condemned them as undesirable pagan relics. The splendid Transylvanian-Hung. (*Székely*) ballads—products of later centuries—and folk songs, striking examples of an animated imagination endowed with a sense of the concrete, confirm the supposition that early Hung. poetry must have had similar qualities.

In the Middle Ages and in the Renaissance and baroque periods much Hung. poetry was written in L.: it was primarily devotional poetry, in some instances not without literary merit. The Hung. Latin poet, János Csezmiczei, known as Janus Pannonius, expressed the spirit of the Renaissance. The translation of the Book of Psalms into Hung. by Albert Szenczi Molnár was an important contribution to the devotional poetry of the Hung. Protestants.

The first important poet who wrote in Hung. was Bálint Balassa, a 16th-c. warrior. He lived a tempestuous life; his destiny as a man and as a lyric poet was bound up with that of his nation. Next to Balassa, Count Miklós Zrinyi, the 17th-c. epic poet must be mentioned. In the 18th c., when Hungary seemed on the verge of national death, poets—drawing strength from the historical past and from the beauty, pliability, and force of their native tongue—implanted confidence into the people. The craftsmanship and versifying resourcefulness of Mihály Csokonai Vitéz, the late 18th-c. poet, were such that even today his works, in which auditory and visual images mingle with pathos and humor, offer definite pleasure to the discerning reader.

Toward the end of the 18th c. and in the first half of the 19th c. an extraordinary revival of creative and critical intelligence characterized Hungary. Influenced by Gr., L., German, Fr., and Eng. poets and writers and by the mental climate of the Age of Reason, Hung. men of letters examined old texts, concentrated on the development of their agglutinative language, contemplated the intricacies of grammar and style, and devoted much time to a discussion of prosody in which Ferenc Kazinczy and Ferenc Kölcsey excelled. The metrical structure of traditional Hung. poetry, based on the rhythm of the language, was discussed, as was the question of how to apply the quantitative versification of the Greeks and Romans or the stress-accent of Western European poets to Hung. poetry. Romantic themes began to appear, and stylistic realism—the use of normal speech in poetry—was gradually accepted by some. The odes of Dániel Berzsenyi, the figurative language of Mihály Vörösmarty, the epic imagination of János Arany, the lyrical spontaneity of Sándor Petőfi, the elegiac tone of Mihály Tompa, the successful application of ancient and new meters and stanzaic forms, the variation of themes, the fresh treatment of folk subjects and individual experiences, the relationship of poetry to folklore, not only enriched national literature, but also created substantial contacts with world literature.

Mihály Vörösmarty (1800–55) voiced in his poetry the lofty ideas of Széchenyi's great Reform Era, while some of his works reveal the eternal search of romanticism for happiness. In his apocalyptic visions of the fate of his nation and mankind, born from the defeat of the War of Independence, he reached artistic heights which are still unsurpassed in Hung. poetry.

Sándor Petőfi (1823–49) started his meteoric career by revolutionizing poetry through the adaptation of the popular style. His poems, celebrating love and liberty, are of a great immediacy and freshness. The following short poem contains the credo of his art and his life—sacrificed later in a battle of the War of Independence.

Szabadság, szerelem!
E kettő kell nekem,
Szerelmemért föláldozom
Az életet.
Szabadságért föláldozom
Szerelmemet.

Freedom, love!
These two I need.
For my love I sacrifice
Life.
For freedom I sacrifice
My love.

János Arany (1817–82), though born a peasant, became the most erudite man of his generation. His poetry was firmly anchored in the deepest strata of his people's instincts—yet, he is considered the most classical of all Hung. poets.

In the second half of the 19th c. János Vajda, Gyula Reviczky, Jenő Komjáthy, and József Kiss, albeit conscious of their national obligations, turned to a kind of "cosmopolitan" philosophy. While industrially and commercially the country progressed and there was an extension of human rights, poets, like many of their confrères in Western Europe, felt alien to the growing materialism of their age. There were poets who received their impetus from national pride or anxiety: e.g., Pál Gyulai, József Lévay, Kálmán Thaly, Andor Kozma, Gyula Vargha. They believed that the true purpose of Hung. poetry was to give expression to their nation's instinct for self-preservation. Most of these poets used simple metrical forms, especially when they were motivated by warm, uncomplicated personal feelings about love, nature, God, family life, homestead. They conventionalized Hung. poetry and were still popular in the early 20th c. "Pure" poetry was unknown; however, in the first and second decades of the 20th c. poets appeared on the Hung. Parnassus, such as Endre Ady, Mihály Babits, Dezső Kosztolányi, and Árpád Tóth, whose sense of verbal music and color and at times unorthodox psychology fitted into the exquisite pattern and metaphorical uniqueness of the Parnassians and symbolists.

Endre Ady (1877–1919) is the most important Hung. poet of the 20th c. In a titanic rebellion against God, cosmic order, and human morality, he professed, as Anti-Christ, a new salvation for mankind—only to fall, after realizing the limitations of human existence, into the most profound humility, in which he sought and discovered the God of the Bible and expressed a glowing but anxious love for his perishing people. Under such pressure, the Hung. language melted and was cast by his art into a new and marvelous mold. His *œuvre*, consisting of almost 1,000 poems, is considered by many the Hungarian *Divina Commedia*.

Between the two World Wars formalistic devices in conflict with sophisticated or primitive impulses indicated confusion in taste and confusion concerning the function of poetry. The avant-garde movements, symptomatic of Western European poetry, had their exponents in Hungary. Among the poets, Gyula Juhász and Attila József harmonized respect for form with ethnic attachments and social conscience. There is creative authenticity, resolved and unresolved tension of varying degrees, in the works of Lajos Áprily, József Erdélyi, Gyula Illyés, Lajos Kassák, László Mécs, Miklós Radnóti, István Sinka, Lőrinc Szabó, Sándor Weöres, and others. Some are traditionalists, others *vers-libristes;* some emulators of centuries-old folk songs and soldier songs, others expressionistic or surrealistic experimenters; some regionalists, others religiously, intellectually, morally, aesthetically, ironically, or hedonistically disposed, or revolutionary in ideas but—paradoxically—sometimes conservative or classical in technique. The most characteristic poet of this era is Lőrinc Szabó.

During and after World War II, the pressure of the rapidly succeeding periods of Nazi influence, the democratic era, Stalinism, the thaw, and the 1956 revolution stimulated a new flowering of Hung. poetry. In these two decades the poets completed the process of synthesis between the rich Eastern heritage of the people (hitherto submerged) and Western traditions—a synthesis initiated by Endre Ady and (in music) by Béla Bartók. Great poems were created out of the poets' protest against the inhumanities of both Nazism and Communism. Though the new regime made serious efforts to educate a new generation of poets in its own image, after Stalin's death the disillusioned Communist poets (László Benjámin, Zoltán Zelk, Lajos Kónya, Péter Kuczka) joined the heretofore silenced non-Communist poets in preparing, intellectually, for the revolution. The high point of these feverish years was marked by Gyula Illyés' visionary poems which also constitute a revolutionary breakthrough in form, compared with his earlier sober and repressed style.

In recent years, in an atmosphere of both relative freedom and hopelessness (the consequences of a first victorious, then crushed national uprising), most poets—among them Weöres, the visionary of cosmic scale; Illyés, now very mature and melancholy; the Catholic and pessimistic János Pilinszky; and Ferenc Juhász, the greatest young talent—continue to publish their works. In exile, many poets keep alive the spirit of freedom and humanity (László Cs. Szabó, Victor Határ, János Csokits, Alajos Kannás, Áron Kibédi Varga, etc.). The year 1962 saw the first full-scale appearance of Hung. poetry as a part of world literature: a 500-page anthology in Fr. translated by the best Fr. poets.

ANTHOLOGIES: *Magyar népköltési gyüjtemény*, ed. L. Arany and P. Gyulai (1872–82); *Magyar Poetry* (1899) and *Modern Magyar Lyrics* (1926), both ed. W. N. Loew; *Neue ungarische Lyrik in Nachdichtungen*, tr. H. Horvát (1918); *Anthologie de la poésie hongroise*, ed. I. Goll (1927); *The Magyar Muse* (1933) and *A Little Treasury of Hung. Verse* (1947), both ed. W. Kirkconnell; *Modern Magyar Lyrics*, ed. B. Balogh (1934); *Magyar versek könyve*, ed. J. Horváth (2d ed., 1942); *Négy nemzedék: élő magyar költők*, ed. I. Sőtér (1948); S. Petőfi, *Sixty Poems*, ed. E. B. Pierce and E. Delmar (1948); *Hét évszázad magyar versei*, ed. T. Klaniczay (1951); *Magyar versek Aranytól napjainkig*, ed. L. Cs. Szabó (1953); *Magyar versek, 1953–1956*, ed. N. Baudy (1958?); *Anthol. de la poésie hongroise du XIIᵉ s. à nos jours*, ed. L. Gara (1962).

HISTORY AND CRITICISM: F. Toldy, *A magyar költészet története* (1854); L. Négyesy, *A magyar verselmélet kritikai története* (1888) and *A mértékes magyar verselés története* (1892); F. Riedl, *Poétika* (1889) and *A Hist. of Hung. Lit.* (1906); J. Pintér, *Magyar irodalomtörténet* (8 v., 1930–42); A. Szerb, *Magyar irodalom története* (1935); A. Eckhardt and L. Molnos, *André Ady, poète hongrois et européen* (1947); J. Horváth, *A magyar vers* (1948) and *Rendszeres magyar verstan* (1951); J. Reményi, *Sándor Petőfi, Hung. Poet* (1953). L. Bóka and P. Pándi, *A magyar irodalom története 1849–ig* (1957); T. Klaniczay and others, *Hist. of Hung. Lit.* (Eng. ed., 1964); J. Reményi, *Hung. Writers and Lit.*, ed. A. J. Molnár (1964). J.R.; I.C.-R.

HYMN. In its broadest sense a hymn is an ode composed in honor of gods and sung or recited in religious festivals or other celebrations of a public character. In the ancient world hymns were an important feature of such ceremonies, and many specimens of the lyric ode—certainly musical in origin—have been preserved in Gr. literature, though the Romans (with the notable exception of Horace) wrote little for public performance.

In defining the content of the h. it must be observed that in classical antiquity the word might also be used to signify a song composed in honor of a hero or other famous man. In the Christian church the Fathers accepted St. Augustine's definition which may be stated as "Praise of God in Song." By a later (11th c.) definition praise was extended to His saints. Despite the rise of vernacular verse after the 12th c. only Latin hymns were used in public worship, and the emphasis, in accord with Ambrosian tradition, was doctrinal. However, before Luther paraliturgical vernacular verses had been worked into services in some churches.

Hellenic hymns in general consist of a group of metrically related lines of varying length cast in the form of strophe and antistrophe. The so-called Homeric hymns are in hexameter verse as were also most of the hymns of Callimachus (ca. 305–ca. 240 B.C.) and the celebrated Stoic h. to Zeus composed by Cleanthes of Assos (331–232 B.C.). The theurgic hymns of the mythical Orpheus, in hexameter verse, chanted by initiates in the "mysteries" have been assigned to a period ca. 580 B.C. but may perhaps be products of the Alexandrian school in the early years of the Christian era.

The metrical pattern of the ancient Egyptian hymns to Ra and Amen and of the later New Kingdom hymns of Akhenaten is obscured by our ignorance of Egyptian phonetics, but a form of parallelism can be discerned, e.g., in the structure of a coronation ode of the XX Dynasty, 1168 B.C. Meanwhile, in India (ca. 1200 B.C.), the great collections of hymns of which the Rig Veda is the oldest were being written in archaic Sanskrit. More than 2,000 years later the Indian mystic Kabir (A.D. 1440–1518) used his gifts to compose songs in the old Hindi and Punjabi languages.

Parallelism, both "synonymous" and "antithetic" is a distinguishing feature of the Ugaritic poetry which the Hebrews encountered in Canaan. They adopted and developed the Ugaritic manner in their own poetry, and with them the h. first reached perfection as a devotional medium. In the psalter—a compilation from Davidic and Levitical sources—parallelism of the two halves of a couplet or line is most commonly combined with a balanced accentual pattern (3:3). The halting rhythm (3:2) called in the Hebrew *qināh* (employed to produce an emotional effect) is an exception to the general rule. The "Psalms of David" continued to be employed in the worship of the primitive Christian church. They retained their unique position until prejudice against the use of nonscriptural matter weakened and the way was opened—first in the Eastern church—for new compositions. 4th c. Gr. hymns made use of the hexameter and pentameter as well as Anacreontic, Ionic, iambic, and other lyrical measures. All these fell into disuse before compositions of a later date. Of the few primitive Gr. hymns which have survived the best known is probably *Phōs hilaron hagias doxēs* from the 3d c. or earlier.

Scriptural texts appointed to be said or sung at a very early date include the Angelic song at the nativity *Gloria in excelsis* and the three Gospel canticles: *Magnificat,* the song of the Blessed Virgin Mary; *Nunc dimittis,* the song of Simeon; and *Benedictus,* the song of Zacharias. The *Tersanctus* (the L. title of the triumphal h. in adoration of the Trinity which is found in all the early liturgies of the Eastern and Western churches) is probably the most ancient and universal of all Christian hymns of praise.

L. hymns were introduced into Western Christendom by St. Hilary of Poitiers as a means of combating the Arian heresy in the 4th c. He was closely followed by St. Ambrose of Milan. Up to the 6th c. the iambic dimeter employed by Ambrose was most favored. It may here be observed that many short Eng. religious lyrics have been made from centos of long L. poems, e.g., *Jerusalem the golden* and *The World is very evil* from Bernard of Morlas' *De contemptu mundi.* L. hymns continued to be written throughout the Middle Ages. The masterly h. *O quanta qualia* (dactylic) comes from *Hymnus Paraclitensis,* which Abelard (1079–1142) wrote for Heloïse; but at the time of the Renaissance many of the old rugged and objective hymns were drastically revised to suit Humanist conceptions of classical Latinity.

In the 16th c. the twin influences of the Renaissance and the Reformation gave an impetus to the emergence of the vernacular in hymns and metrical versions of the psalms. Luther and his collaborators zealously extended congregational singing in vernacular, translating and adapting L. hymns as well as composing new hymns in the tradition of medieval fairs and camps. In the 16th c. German tunes retained a considerable degree of accentual freedom and the poet who wrote verses for singing was at liberty to follow a free rhythm. Paul Gerhardt (1607–76), author of the great Passion h. *O Haupt voll Blut und Wunden,* wrote exquisite lyrics of deep, tender feeling. The hymns of Franck (1618–77) and Scheffler (1624–77) and some of the works of the later Pietists are also meritorious.

But in Germany as in England and elsewhere post-Reformation religious lyrics which are first-rate as poetry are not common. Poetry in the h. is rare largely because few writers have succeeded in composing objective (not personal or metaphysical) verses capable of being sung by mixed congregations; moreover, because the h. is the ordinary man's theology and its stanzas must be married to tunes which can easily be memorized, rhythmic simplicity is essential.

Modern Eng. hymnody derives from the Metrical Version of the Psalms known as the "Old Version" of Sternhold and Hopkins which, in its turn, reflected the ideas of the Genevan reformers as expressed in the Fr. version of Marot and Beza. Neither the "Old" nor the "New" version has any poetic merit; we may dismiss them from consideration. It is remarkable that despite the glory of Elizabethan literature no indigenous congregational hymnody appeared before the 18th c. The literary poems of George Herbert (1593-1633) were not written for public performance. Many of them, like *Let all the world in every corner sing* (10.4. 6.6. 6.6. 10.4), are in peculiar meters. The work of his contemporary George Wither (1588-1667), few of whose many religious songs are in common use, illustrates the practice of composing verses to suit existing ballad tunes. Donne (1573-1631), the great poet of the metaphysical school, was not a h. writer. His intensely personal *Wilt thou forgive that sin*, which has found its way into a modern book, is not suitable for public singing.

Isaac Watts (1674-1748) was the creator of the modern Eng. h. in which singleness of theme is combined with brevity and songfulness. *O God, our help in ages past*, in C.M., with much use of metaphor and simile, is perhaps the greatest h. in the language, while *When I survey the wondrous Cross* may be the most moving. After Watts we enter upon the great age of evangelical hymnody—a century of divine songs. Cowper (1731-1800), one of the few great poets to write hymns, collaborated with Newton (1725-1807); his brilliant lyric *Sometimes a light surprises* is an illustration of the truth that good hymns begin well.

Charles Wesley (1707-88) is the greatest writer in the devotional sphere. His hymns are characterized by great fertility of metric invention. *Wrestling Jacob*, a lyric drama in 14 stanzas, is his finest poem and one at least of his hymns for children, *Gentle Jesus, Meek and Mild*, has something of the precision and penetrating power of Blake's winged thought.

During the 19th c. there was a great outpouring of religious verse on both sides of the Atlantic. The great bulk of it was weak and unsatisfactory, but in England Heber (1783-1826) "inaugurated the literary hymn aiming not merely at the expression of religious feeling but also at deliberately controlling that expression by the canons of the poetic art." (C. S. Phillips). Am. writers who enriched Eng. hymnals as well as their own include John Greenleaf Whittier (1807-92), Oliver Wendell Holmes (1809-94), Ray Palmer (1808-89), and Samuel Johnson (1822-82).

In the 20th c. many poor hymns which had found favor in the past were courageously dropped from new and revised hymnals. Authors tended to write "hymns" of a subjective and nonscriptural character with a special stress on the idea of "social service." A poem, however, if it is rightly to be interpolated into the Office must be in accord with the linguistic tone of scripture and liturgy. Secular poems with a human interest may fall short of this ideal, but where they are yoked to tunes suitable for congregational singing they may be suitable for use in public gatherings of an undenominational character.

SOURCES: *Sequentiae ex Missalibus*, ed. J. M. Neale (1852); *Anthologia Graeca Carminum Christianorum*, ed. H. A. Daniel (5 v., 1855-6); *Analecta Hymnica Medii Aevi*, ed. G. M. Dreves, C. Blume and H. M. Bannister (55 v., 1886-1922); *Piae Cantiones*, 1582, ed. G. R. Woodward (with pref., 1910).—COLLECTIONS: *Hymns from the Yattendon Hymnal*, ed. R. Bridges and H. Ellis Wooldridge (1899); *Songs of Syon*, ed. G. R. Woodward (1910); *The Four-part Chorals of J. S. Bach* (German text with Eng. tr.), ed. C. S. Terry (1929); *Hymn Book of the Protestant Episcopal Church of America* (1940).

GENERAL: *Hymns A. and M.* (with introd. by W. H. Frere, hist. ed., 1909); *A Dictionary of Hymnology*, ed. J. Julian (1925); J. M. Gibbon, *Melody and the Lyric* (1930); *Homeric Hymns*, ed. T. W. Allen et al. (2d ed., 1936); M. Britt, *Hymns of the Breviary and Missal* (rev. ed., 1936); C. S. Phillips, *Hymnody Past and Present* (1937); H. W. Foote, *Three Centuries of Am. Hymnody* (1940); B. L. Manning, *The Hymns of Wesley and Watts* (1942); T. H. Robinson, *Poetry and the Poets of the Old Testament* (1947); F. J. E. Raby, *A Hist. of Christian L. Poetry* (2d ed., 1953) and *The Poetry of the Eucharist* (1957); A. T. Shaw "Hymns and Anthems," *Cassell's*; E. Routley, *The Music of Christian Hymnody* (1957); L. F. Benson, *The Eng. H.* (1962). A.T.S.

HYPALLAGE (Gr. "exchange"). A change in the relation of words whereby a word, instead of agreeing with the word it logically qualifies, is made to agree grammatically with another word; h. is usually confined to poetry: "neikos andron xunaimon" (kindred strife of men *for* strife of kindred men; Sophocles, *Antigone* 794). Quintilian (*Institutes of Oratory* 8.6.23) does not distinguish clearly from metonymy (q.v.): "Cererem corruptam undis" (Ceres by water spoiled; Virgil, *Aeneid* 1.177). Characteristic of Virgil, Spenser, Shakespeare, Milton. Shakespeare not only depends heavily on the device but also uses it with a flavor of parody: "I see a voice. Now will I to the chink, / To spy and I can hear my Thisby's face" (*Mid-*

summer Night's Dream 5.1.189–90). Cf. Sister Miriam Joseph, *Shakespeare's Use of the Arts of Language* (1947). Lausberg, discussing "die metonymischen Epitheta," distinguishes syntactical and other varieties.   R.O.E.

HYPERBATON. See ANASTROPHE.

HYPERBOLE. (Gr. "overshooting," "excess"). A figure or trope, common to all literatures, consisting of bold exaggeration, apparently first noted by Isocrates and Aristotle. Quintilian says, "an elegant straining of the truth, and may be employed indifferently for exaggeration or attenuation" (*Institutes of Oratory* 8.6.67): "Geminique minantur / In caelum scopuli" (Twin rocks that threaten heaven—Virgil, *Aeneid* 1.162).

Not all the waters in the rude rough sea
Can wash the balm from an annointed King.
                    (Shakespeare, *Richard II* 3.2.54)

Any extravagant statement used to express strong emotion, not intended to be understood literally. According to Puttenham, the figure is also used to "advance or . . . abase the reputation of any thing or person" (*The Arte of Eng. Poesie*, 1589). P. called it "over-reacher" or "loud liar" equating it with L. *dementiens*.

Grammarians and rhetoricians sometimes consider h. to be among the second order of figures of speech, along with amplification, examples, images, etc. Use of h. in Elizabethan drama, particularly Jonson, with special reference to the development of comic irony, is discussed by A. H. Sackton, *Rhetoric as a Dramatic Language in Ben Jonson* (1948). See also: R. Sherry, *Treatise of the Figures of Grammer and Rhetorick* (1555); H. Peacham, *The Garden of Eloquence Conteyning the Figures of Grammer and Rhetorick* (1577, enlarged 1593); W. S. Howells, *Logic and Rhetoric in England, 1500–1700* (1956); Lausberg.   R.O.E.

HYPERCATALECTIC. See TRUNCATION.

HYPERMETRIC (Gr. "beyond the measure"). In prosody a line which has an extra syllable or syllables at the end, or a syllable which is not expected in the regular metrical pattern, e.g., a hypercatalectic line (see TRUNCATION). In classical poetry a verse in which the vowel at the end of one line elides with the vowel beginning the following line: "sors exitura et nos in aeternum / exsilium impositura cumbae" (Horace, *Odes* 2.3.27–28). In Old Germanic poetry a verse expanded by means of an additional initial foot, or, according to the rhythmic theory, by means of doubling the time given to it.—E. Sievers, *Altgermanische Metrik* (1893); Hardie; J. C. Pope, *The Rhythm of Beowulf* (1942); Koster.   R.A.H.

HYPHAERESIS (Gr. "a taking away from beneath"). In Gr. the disappearance of short "e" before a vowel, e.g., *nossós* for *neossós*. Generally, the term is used to indicate the omission of a letter from the body of a word as in "o'er" for "over."   R.A.H.

HYPORCHEMA (Gr. "song accompanied by dancing"). This Gr. choral song accompanied by dancers who did not sing was supposed to have been invented by Thaletas of Gortyn in Crete (ca. 7th c. B.C.), but Athenaeus found its origins in Homer. It was, however, characterized by its use of Cretic measures. As a hymn in honor of Apollo, the h. was akin to the paean (q.v.) as it was later to the dithyramb (q.v.) in praise of Dionysus. Pindar, for example, wrote both hyporchemata and paeans. In tragedy the term was applied by Eucleides, an authority cited by Tzetzes, to lyric passages where the chorus was evidently dancing. Consequently some modern scholars have unnecessarily imagined it as a kind of lively stasimon (q.v.), e.g. in several passages of Sophocles where jubilation of the chorus at the arrival of glad tidings is followed by the catastrophe of the play.—Smyth; Schmid and Stählin; Koster; A. W. Pickard-Cambridge, *The Dramatic Festivals of Athens* (1953).   R.J.G.

HYPORRHYTHMIC. See DIAERESIS.

HYSTERON PROTERON (Gr. "later earlier"). A figure in which the natural order of time in which events occur is reversed, usually because the later event is considered more important than the former: "trophe kai genesis" (in Shakespeare's phrase, "for I was bred and born"; Xenophon, *Memorabilia* 3.5.10); also found in Virgil: "Moriamur et in media arma ruamus" (Let us die and rush into battle; *Aeneid* 2.353). According to Puttenham, "We call it in English proverbe, the cart before the horse, the Greeks call it *Histeron proteron*, we name it the preposterous . . ." (*The Arte of Eng. Poesie*). "How wild a Hysteron Proteron's this, which Nature crosses, / And far above the top the bottom tosses" (Joseph Beaumont, *Psyche* 1.85). But in poetry especially the device may be highly effective without seeming preposterous.—S. E. Bassett, "Hysteron proteron Homerikos," *Harvard Studies in Cl. Philology*, 31 (1920); Lausberg.   R.O.E.

I

IAMB (Gr. *iambos*, a word of unknown etymology but certainly very ancient). A metrical unit, in quantitative verse, of a short syllable followed by a long:

⏑–; *ămāns*

The iambic rhythm was thought in antiquity to be nearest to ordinary speech; it was in its 6-foot form (see TRIMETER; L. *senarius*) the standard meter for dialogue in drama and for invective. A clear distinction was made between the strong iambic ryhthm and the lighter, more unstable trochaic rhythm (–⏑). Catullus gains a special effect in two poems by using pure iambs, unvaried by spondees. Hipponax invented the *scazon* (q.v.), the "limping" iambic. For the longer iambic lines, see SEPTENARIUS (15-syllabler) and OCTONARIUS (16-syllabler). The iambic dimeter (*quaternarius*, 8-syllabler) sometimes occurs in Plautus; in Horace it sometimes alternates with the trimeter; it is found in a few inscriptions. It came into its glory in the 4th c. A.D., when Ambrose adopted it for his hymns:

aetērnĕ rērum condĭtor

Hardy; Dale; Beare.   W.B.
   The term has been adopted into Eng. for the accentual foot of an unstressed followed by a stressed syllable:

×́́ ́; impose

This alternation, no doubt because it fits the natural patterns of Eng. words and phrases, has become overwhelmingly the commonest type in all Eng. verse. Its use is complemented by secondary accent:

personification

and is varied by occasional substitution of the trochee:

Milton! thou shouldst be living at this hour

or anapest:

Pure as the naked heavens, majestic, free

By these and similar devices the iambic movement is spared monotony and made capable of almost every kind of metrical effect.—Baum.

IAMBELEGUS. In Gr. and L. metric an iambic followed by a dactylic colon (the latter being generally *hemiepes* [q.v.]), as in Horace, *Epodes* 13.2:

nĭvēs|quĕ dē|dūcūnt | Iŏvĕm; || nŭnc mărē |
nūnc sĭlŭ|āē

(iambic dimeter acatalectic and *hemiepes*). See ARCHILOCHIAN and ELEGIAMB(US).   R.J.G.

IAMBES (LES). Fr. satiric poems of variable length in *rimes croisées* (abab, cdcd, etc.), in which a 12-syllable verse alternates throughout with one of 8 syllables. The term *iambe*, whose satiric sense is rooted in a very ancient tradition deriving from the notoriously bitter and supposedly lethal iambics of the Gr. poet Archilochus (8th or 7th c. B.C.), came into Fr. as a generic term with the posthumously published *Iambes* of André Chénier (1762–94) and *Les iambes* (1830–31) of Auguste Barbier. Violent contrasts in rhythm from line to line make the Fr. iambe a remarkably appropriate medium for satire: "Nul ne resterait donc . . . / Pour cracher sur leurs noms, pour chanter leur supplice? / Allons, étouffe tes clameurs; / Souffre, ô coeur gros de haine, affamé de justice. / Toi, Vertu, pleure si je meurs." (A. Chénier, *Iambes* 9).—M. Grammont, *Le vers français* (1913) and *Petit traité de versification française* (5e éd. revue, 1924); A. Chénier, *Oeuvres complètes* (1940).   A.G.E.

IBYCEAN. See LOGAOEDIC.

ICELANDIC POETRY. (For Icel. poetry prior to 1400 see OLD NORSE POETRY.) The basic fact in the history of Icel. literature is its unbroken continuity. Every age produced some writers of note; the ancient literature never lost its hold on the people, but remained a source of strength and inspiration. The vitality of the native poetic tradition is strikingly illustrated in *Háttalykill* (Key to Meters), a cycle of 90 love songs in as many meters, by Loftur Guttormsson (d. 1432), a prominent chieftain and the greatest Icel. poet of the day. With this remarkable work he proved himself a worthy heir of Snorri Sturluson, the author of the *Prose Edda*.
   The most important poet of the first half of the 16th c. was the great patriot Jón Arason (1484–1550), the last Catholic bishop of Iceland, equally renowed for his sacred and secular poetry. A cultural leader of truly heroic mold,

and deeply rooted in the national literary tradition, he brought to Iceland the first printing press about 1530. The leading Icel. poet of the Reformation, on the other hand, was the Reverend Einar Sigurðsson (1539–1626); many of whose poems reflect the spirit and style of the ballads and other folk poetry. Two poets of the 17th c., in whose works the national tradition is a prominent feature, tower above their contemporaries. The Reverend Hallgrimur Petursson (1614–74), whose inspired *Passiusálmar* (Passion Hymns) have appeared in more than fifty editions, was one of the great Lutheran hymn writers of all time, and has profoundly influenced the life of the Icel. people. He also wrote secular poetry of great merit, although, in that respect, he was more than equaled by his fellow-clergyman, the Reverend Stefan Olafsson (1620–1688), noted in particular for his realistic, often satirical, portrayal of everyday life, and a master of fluent and varied form.

A notable literary and cultural figure of the 18th c. was Eggert Ólafsson (1726–68), who wrote edifying and inspirational poems in the spirit of the Enlightenment, but is of much greater importance as a fervent patriot, the leader of a nationalistic movement of far-reaching influence. The outstanding poet of the century, however, was the Reverend Jón Þorláksson (1744–1819). His extensive original production, noteworthy as it is many ways, is overshadowed by his translations, especially those of Milton's *Paradise Lost* and of Klopstock's *Messias*. With them he became the great pioneer in the realm of Icel. translations and a trail-breaker for the poets of the next generation. Effectively and often brilliantly rendered into the elevated *fornyrðislag* (q.v.) measure of Eddic fame, his translations eloquently attest the vigor and continuity of the Icel. poetical tradition.

That observation applies, in varying degrees, to the Icel. poets of the 19th c., whose works are strongly national in spirit, while they were at the same time stimulated by foreign influences, notably the romantic movement. During the latter part of the period realism and neoromanticism were also influential. The pioneer romanticist in Iceland was Bjarni Thorarensen (1786–1841), whose best poems, frequently Eddic in spirit and form, are characterized by vigor, penetration and rich imagery. In the works of his younger contemporary, Jónas Hallgrímsson (1807–45), the romantic love of beauty and of homeland find an exquisite and delicate expression. While he employed Eddic and skaldic meters with great skill, he also enriched Icel. literature with foreign verse forms such as the sonnet, the terza rima, the strophe, and others. He has deeply influenced later Icel. poets.

During the second half of the century, a large number of uncommonly gifted poets carried on, more or less, the tradition of Thorarensen and Hallgrímsson. These successors of the great masters included Grímur Thomsen (1820–96), Benedikt Gröndal (1826–1907), Steingrímur Thorsteinsson (1831–1913), and Matthías Jochumsson (1835–1920), generally regarded the greatest Icel. poet of the day, whose versatile genius is revealed in inspiring historical and memorial poems, as well as in equally noble hymns, including the Icel. national anthem.

The native poetical traditions run particularly strong in the works of the gifted unschooled poets of the period: Hjálmar Jónsson (Bólu-Hjálmar, 1796–1875), Sigurður Breiðfjörð (1798–1846), and Páll Ólafsson (1827–1905). While the two first-named, and Breiðfjörð in particular, carried on with great success the tradition of the *rímur*-poetry, all three were masters of the time-honored Icel. quatrain (*ferskeytla*).

Among leading poets who were influenced by realism are Þorsteinn Erlingsson (1858–1914), Hannes Hafstein (1861–1922), and Guðmundur Friðjónsson (1869–1944). In their works nationalism is also prominent. The same is true of the greatest poets of that generation, Stephan G. Stephansson (1853–1927) and Einar Benediktsson (1864–1940). Despite many dissimilarities, these two poets share unusual creative genius, robust intellectual qualities, and a superb mastery of their native tongue. Other poets of note, whose works belong primarily to the 20th c., are: Jón Þorkelsson (1859–1924), Sigurjón Friðjónsson (1867–1950), Þorsteinn Gíslason (1867–1938), Guðmundur Guðmundsson (1874–1919), Sigurður Jónsson (1878–1949), and Sigurður Sigurðsson (1879–1939).

Icel. poetry since the turn of the century reflects various tendencies, ranging from realism through neoromanticism to outright leftist revolutionary views. Generally speaking, however, the national note continues very strong, expressing itself in an interest in various phases of the native culture. Side by side with the traditional verse forms, new meters have been introduced, including free verse and other modern forms of poetic expression. The traditional verse forms, characterized by alliteration, are, however, still dominant.

Space permits only the mere mention of the most important of the large array of 20th-c. poets: Hulda (Unnur Benediktsdóttir 1881–1946), Örn Arnarson (Magnús Stefánsson, 1884–1942), Jakob Thorarensen (b. 1886), Stefán Sigurðsson (1887–1933), Jakob J. Smári (b. 1889), Davíð Stefánsson (b. 1895), Jón Magnússon (1896–1944), Sigurður Einarsson (b. 1898), Jóhannes Jónsson (Jóhannes úr Kötlum, b. 1899, Jón Helgason (b. 1899), Tómas Guðmundsson (b. 1901), Guðmundur Böðvarsson (b. 1904), Snorri Hjartarson (1906), and Steinn Steinarr (Aðalsteinn Kristmundsson (1908–58), not to mention a number of gifted and very promising younger writers. There is also a large group of gifted Icel.-Am. poets, mostly of the older generation. Stephan G. Stephansson is the most important of these.

ANTHOLOGIES: *Ny-Islandsk Lyrik* (1901) and *Udvalgte islandske Digte fra det nittende aarhundrede* (1919), both tr. O. Hansen; *The Oxford Book of Scandinavian Verse*, ed. W. A. Craigie (1926); *Icel. Lyrics* (1930; 2d ed., 1956) and *Icel. Poems and Stories* (1943), both ed. R. Beck; *The North Am. Book of Icel. Verse* (1930) and *Canadian Overtones* (1935), both tr. W. Kirkconnell; "Iceland," ed. S. Einarsson in *20th C. Scandinavian Poetry*, general ed. M. S. Allwood (1950); P. Bjarnason, *Odes and Echoes* (1954); *Northern Lights*, tr. J. Johnson (1959).

HISTORY AND CRITICISM: K. Küchler, *Gesch. der isländischen Dichtung der Neuzeit* (2 v., 1896–1902); J. C. Poestion, *Isl. Dichter der Neuzeit* (1897) and *Eislandsblüten* (1904); H. Hermannsson, *Icel. Authors of Today* (1913); *The Passion-Hymns of Iceland*, tr. C. V. Pilcher (1913); S. Nordal, *Udsigt over Islands litt. i det 19. og. 20. aarhundrede* (1927); R. Beck, "Icel. Lit.," *Ency. of Lit.*, ed. J. T. Shipley (2 v., 1946) and *Hist. of Icel. Poets, 1800–1940* (1950); G. Finnbogason, "Lit.," *Iceland*, ed. T. Thorsteinsson (1946); K. E. Andrésson, *Íslenzkar nútimabókmenntir 1918–48* (1949); B. M. Gíslason, *Islands litt. efter Sagatiden* (1949); S. Einarsson, *A Hist. of Icel. Lit.* (1957). R.B.

ICTUS (L. "beat"). Roman writers like Horace and Quintilian used this word to describe the movement of the foot or the hand in keeping time with the rhythm of a verse. Audible i. is more than dubious in Gr. verse where the accent was one of pitch, not stress, in the classical period and later. In L. the occurrence of i. has been generally assumed in modern times by those who also believe that words were pronounced with stress; but a recent writer (W. Beare, see bibliog.) thinks that such an assumption "may be due merely to our craving to impose on quantitative verse a rhythm which we can recognize." Whatever its nature was, this rhythmical i. is regarded as falling on the long syllable (i.e., the arsis [q.v.] in the currently accepted sense of that word) of a basic foot like the iambus ($\smile \acute{}$) or anapaest ($\smile \smile \acute{}$) in rising, or the trochee ($\acute{} \smile$) or dactyl ($\acute{} \smile \smile$) in falling measures; but, with resolution (q.v.), the i. is marked on the first of the two short syllables which replace the long. Thus Terence begins a senarius (q.v.) in rising rhythm with

$$h\bar{\imath}nc\ \acute{\bar{\imath}l}|la\bar{e}\ l\acute{a}cr\breve{\imath}|ma\bar{e}$$

and Horace a hexameter (q.v.) in falling rhythm with

$$h\bar{\imath}nc\ \acute{\bar{\imath}l}|la\bar{e}\ l\acute{a}cr\breve{\imath}|ma\bar{e}$$

See ARSIS AND THESIS and CLASSICAL PROSODY.— W. Beare, *L. Verse and European Song* (1957); P. W. Harsh, "Ictus and Accent," *Lustrum*, 3 (1958); A. Labhardt, "Le Problème de l'I.," *Euphrosyne*, 2 (1959); O. Seel and E. Pöhlmann, "Quantität und Wortakzent im horazischen Sapphiker. Ein Beitrag zum Iktus-Problem," *Philologus*, 103 (1959); H. Drexler, "Quantität und Wortakzent," *Maia* n.s., 12 (1960); R. G. Tanner, "The Arval Hymn and Early L. Verse," CQ n.s., 11 (1961). R.J.G.

IDYL(L). A short poem or prose composition which deals charmingly with rustic life; ordinarily it describes a picturesque rural scene of gentle beauty and innocent tranquillity and narrates a story of some simple sort of happiness. There are no requirements of form, such as are prescribed in the stricter types (limerick, sestina, and sonnet) or even in the looser types (ode and ballad). The earliest commentators used the term to designate a great variety of short poems of domestic life in which description of beautiful rural scenery was an essential element. But, because the scholiasts used the term in connection with the poems of Theocritus, Bion, and Moschus, it has often been considered a synonym for pastoral (q.v.); and Theocritus' ten pastoral poems, no doubt because of their superiority, became the prototype of the i. In the 16th and 17th c., especially in France, there was frequent insistence that pastorals in dialogue be called *eclogues;* those in narrative, *idylls.* Dictionary definitions from Edward Philip's *New World of Words*, 1678, to the *New Eng. Dictionary*, 1888–1929, have emphasized two restrictions; first, that the term derives from *eidyllion*, meaning "little picture" (which was construed to mean "framed picture"); second, the term is used to designate poems of rustic life, such as that in the pastoral poems of Theocritus. Critics and scholars also have tried to confine the subject matter of the i. within those limits. In 1555 Vauquelin de la Fresnaye, comparing the terms i. and pastoral, declared that the name "of idyl seemed to me to be more closely related to my purposes, especially as it signifies and represents only diverse small images resembling those engraved on stone or on chalcedony to serve sometimes as a seal." And as late as 1904 Martha Hale Shackford was contending that the i. is "a picture of life as the human spirit wishes it to be, a presentation of the chosen moments of earthly content." Two biblical selections are customarily referred to as idylls—Ruth and The Song of Songs. Among the major writers in Eng. literature, however, there is scarcely a poem to meet these specifications, unless such poems as Marlowe's pastoral *The Passionate Shepherd to His Love* or Burns's realistic narrative *The Cotter's Saturday Night* are included. Poems bearing this designation may be found in the works of minor poets, such as Salomon Gessner's *Idyls* or Anna Nicholas' *Idyl of the Wabash*. And among many major poems frequently there are episodes which may justly be called "idyllic," like the Nausicaa episode in the *Odyssey*, the Palemon and Lavinia episode in Thomson's *Seasons*, and the Juan and Haidée episode in Byron's *Don Juan*. Typical prose idylls are illustrated by Barrie's *Auld Licht Idyls*. It must be pointed out, however, that writers have often ignored the prescriptions. A notable instance occurred even as early as the 17th c. in Marc-Antoine de Gérard, sieur de Saint-Amant's *Moyse sauvé*, 1653, an "idylle héroïque" of 6,000 lines. In more recent times such use, or abuse, of this term has been made by Victor de Laprade, *Idylles héroïques*, 1858, and Tennyson, *Idylls of the King*, 1859. Perhaps Tennyson thought the use of the term was appropriate for his poem; each i. contains an incident in the matter of Arthur and his Knights which is separate (or framed) but at the same time is connected with the central theme; the contents treat the Christian virtues in an ideal manner and in a remote setting. Such freedom led to a wide imitation of the term by poets. For instance, there is little in the matter of Robert Browning's *Dramatic Idylls*, 1879, 1880, which deal for the most part with psychological crises, to place them in the tradition. Obviously, then, the i. cannot be called, either because of form or of content, a definite poetic type. Actually, after such uses of the term as those cited above, it would be rather difficult to say what might not be called an i. The signification of *idyllic*, however, has been more constant. Usually it is applied only to writings which present picturesque rural scenery and a life of innocence and tranquillity.—M. H. Shackford, "A Definition of the Pastoral I.," PMLA, 19 (1904); R. G. Moulton, "The Song of Songs," *Modern Reader's Bible* (1926); P. van Tieghem, "Les Idylles de Gessner et le rêve pastoral," *Le Préromantisme*, II (1930). J.E.C.

IMAGERY. An image is the reproduction in the mind of a sensation produced by a physical perception. Thus, if a man's eye perceives a certain color, he will register an image of that color in his mind—"image," because the subjective sensation he experiences will be an ostensible copy or replica of the objective color itself. The mind may also produce images when not reflecting direct physical perceptions, as in the attempt to remember something once perceived but no longer present, or in the undirected drifting of the mind over experience, or in the combinations wrought out of perception by the imagination, or in the hallucinations of dreams and fever, and so on.

More specifically in literary usage, *imagery* refers to images produced in the mind by language, whose words and statements may refer either to experiences which could produce physical perceptions were the reader actually to have those experiences, or to the sense-impressions themselves. When Archibald MacLeish says, in *Ars Poetica*, that a poem should be "Dumb / As old medallions to the thumb," he not only *means* that the language of poetry should make important use of i., he also *exemplifies* what he means by expressing it in terms of i.: a poem, he implies, should make its impact upon the imagination rather than upon the intellect, much as a person feels an old coin with his fingers (a physical perception). When, however, he says "A poem should not mean / But be," his meaning is the same but his language is not, for this statement is abstract rather than concrete and imagery-bearing, dealing as it does with an idea or concept rather than a perception or sensation. This combination of meaning and imagery may indicate the confusion which can result when "i." is applied to literary study, for it is used variously to refer to the meaning of a statement involving images, to the images themselves, or to the combination of meaning and images. Thus Miss Downey says, "The image must not be conceived as a material copy or thing but merely as the content of a thought in which attention is centred on sensory quality of some sort." Or Miss Spurgeon says, "I use the term 'image' here as the only available word to cover every kind of simile, as well as every kind of what is really compressed simile—metaphor." Or C. Day Lewis says, "It is a picture made out of words." Or Fogle refers to it as "the sensuous element in poetry."

For the purposes of the present discussion, the various definitions of imagery can be reduced essentially to three: (1) "mental i.," (2) i. as "figures of speech," and (3) i. and image patterns as the embodiment of "symbolic vision" or of "nondiscursive truth." Interest in the first is focused on what happens in the reader's mind (effect), while in the second and third it is focused on the imagery-bearing language itself and its significations (cause). None of these categories, of course, is entirely separate from any of the others, but such a breakdown is helpful in making a beginning.

IMAGERY

The first definition emphasizes the relation of the statement on the page to the sensation it produces in the mind, and involves two parallel problems: first, to describe objectively and analytically the sensory capacities of the poet's mind; and second, to test, and perhaps improve, the reader's capacity to appreciate i. in poetry. The method is statistical; that is to say, the analyst reads a given poem and then reports numerically and by categories the different images the poem is capable of stimulating, or he asks a subject to read the poem and report similarly on *his* (the subject's) reactions. Interest in this field was apparently first provoked by the early experiments in the psychology of perception of Sir Francis Galton ("Statistics of Mental Imagery," *Mind*, 5 [1880], 301–18), who discovered that people differ in their image-making habits and capacities ("How much of this morning's breakfast-table can you recall to mind and describe now?" the questionnaires ran). While one person may reveal a predominating tendency to visualize his reading, memories, and ruminations (as indeed many people do), another may favor the mind's "ear," another the mind's "nose," or yet another may have no i. at all.

While this first definition makes no distinction between literal and figurative i.—sometimes centering on the one, sometimes the other, and sometimes both—the second concentrates on the nature of the relationship between a subject and an analogue, i.e., on metaphor. Although it is the analogue which is, strictly speaking, the image, the term is often used to refer to the entire subject-analogue relationship. Beginning with the work of Max Müller, whose "Lectures on the Science of Language" were delivered at the Royal Institution in 1861–64 (and were subsequently published under that title in two series), the nature of metaphor—hitherto almost categorized out of existence by the traditional rhetoricians—became once again an open question. Why does the poet liken his lady to a rose (*how,* and *in what ways,* are further questions to be discussed in due course)? Müller's answer, although its assumptions have been questioned, is still influential today: man, as he develops his conceptions of immaterial things, must perforce express them in terms of material things because his language lags behind his needs—the literal mode becomes ineffective, inexact, or incomplete. That is to say, figurative i. often makes for greater precision of expression; thus language, as it seeks exactitude, grows through metaphor.

Finally, the third definition is concerned basically with the function of image patterns, whether literal or figurative or both, as symbols by virtue of psychological association (cf. SYMBOL). The problems here are to ascertain how the poet's choice of i. reveals not merely the sensory capacities of his mind but also his interests, tastes, temperament, values, and vision; to determine the function of recurring images in the poem in which they occur as tone-setters, structural devices, and symbols; and to examine the relations between the poet's over-all image patterns and those of myths and rituals (cf. ARCHETYPE). Once again the method is statistical. It involves tabulating not merely the kinds of mental i. to be found in the work of any given poet but also the areas of subject matter from which they derive. Although Caroline Spurgeon's ideas were anticipated by Walter Whiter (*A Specimen of a Commentary* [1794]) and William Spaulding (*A Letter on Shakespeare's Authorship of "The Two Noble Kinsmen"* [1876]), her work in 1935 on Shakespeare's i. was largely responsible for stimulating contemporary interest (both favorable and unfavorable) in this field.

Mental i., figurative i., and symbolic i. It may be now asked what is involved in each definition, how each is related to the others, and what the values of each are. Psychologists have identified a number of different kinds of mental images: visual (sight, which can be further subdivided for brightness, clarity, color, and motion), auditory (hearing), olfactory (smell), gustatory (taste), tactile (touch, which can be further subdivided for heat, cold, and texture), organic (awareness of heartbeat, pulse, breathing, and digestion), and kinesthetic (awareness of muscle tension and movement). Obviously these categories, although perhaps somewhat overelaborate for the purposes of literary criticism, are preliminary to the other approaches to i., for they define the very nature of the materials. And several valuable results have emerged from the application of these distinctions to literature (e.g., Downey). In the first place, the concept of mental i. has encouraged catholicity of taste, for once it has been realized that not all poets have the same sorts of sensory capacities, it is easier to appreciate different kinds of poetry. Much of Browning's i., for example, is tactile, and those who habitually visualize are unjust in laying the charge of obscurity at his door (see J. K. Bonnell, PMLA, 37 [1922], 574–98). Or again, the frequently voiced complaint that Shelley's poetry is less "concrete" than Keats's suffers from a basic misconception of the nature of i., for Shelley's poetry contains just as much i. as Keats's, although it is of a somewhat different kind (see Fogle [Bibliography]). In the second place, the concept of mental i. provides a valuable index to the type of imagination with which any given poet is gifted. To know that Keats's poetry is characterized by a predominance of tactile and organic i., for example, or that Shelley's is characterized by a predominance of the i., of motion, is valuable knowledge and provides important descriptive terms with which to define the achievement of each poet. Thirdly, the concept of mental i. is pedagogically useful, for a teacher or a critic may encourage better reading habits by stressing these aspects of poetry. Thus, because the reader is encouraged to make specific images in his mind as he reads, aesthetic appreciation can be improved in a very literal sense.

But the disadvantages of the mental i. approach almost outweigh its advantages. To begin with, it repeatedly runs into an insoluble methodological problem: if poets differ in their imagery-making capacities, so do readers, and therefore the attempt to characterize the imagination of any given poet is inextricably bound up with the imagination of the critic who analyzes it. An image which appears obviously tactile to one reader, for example, may seem clearly visual to another. Secondly, it tends to over-emphasize the role which mental i. plays in the understanding and appreciation of poetry, and an excessive concern of this nature can actually impede pleasure and comprehension—for poetry also operates through meaning, feeling, and sentiment (see G. H. Betts, *The Distribution and Functions of Mental Imagery* [1909]).

In the third place, and most important, in focusing upon the sensory qualities of images themselves, it diverts attention from the *function* of these images in the poetic context. It is crucial, for example, to distinguish between literal and figurative i., and to decide in the case of the latter just how the analogue should be taken. The functioning of T. S. Eliot's famous simile of the "patient etherized upon a table" (analogue, or figurative image) need depend very little upon the question of whether or not either Eliot or the reader has reproduced in his mind the various sensations which this image is potentially capable of stimulating—the sickly sweet smell of the anaesthetic, the feeling of numbness, the buzzing in the ears, the sense of lying prone, the white and silver gleam of the operating room, and so on. This sort of deliberate exploitation may or may not assist the reader in grasping the use of this image in the poem, but to *understand* that this image is one of half-life, half-death, of suspended animation which is the symbol of spiritual debility, and which is therefore highly appropriate not only to the setting of twilight (half-light, half-dark) but also, in terms of revealing Prufrock's state of mind, to the conceptual problem of death-in-life in the speaker's world around which the poem is built, need not of necessity require any such effort. One can therefore best discuss the functioning of a poem's i. without becoming overly involved in the question of the sensations in the reader's or the poet's mind.

And that is where the study of i. as a device of poetic language turned its attention, in the course of time; for i., whatever its sensory qualities may be, may function either literally, figuratively, symbolically, or in some combination. Thus, an investigation of figurative i. involves such problems as that of rhetorical types, that of the kinds of relationships which may obtain between subject and analogue, that of the nature of symbolic expression, and that of the use of figures in poetry, which the study of mental i. either confused or ignored.

Traditional rhetoricians developed elaborate systems of classification for figures of speech, but they were rarely as guilty of mere mechanical pigeon-holing as many modern critics have claimed. The common types distinguished now, however, have been reduced to about six: synecdoche, metonymy, simile, metaphor, personification, allegory, and—a related but different device—symbol. Each of these figures is a device of language by means of which one thing is said (analogue) while something else is meant (subject), and either the analogue, or the subject, or both, may involve i. Although merely identifying and analyzing types of figures is no guarantee of understanding their function in a particular poem, identification and analysis do involve issues which are germane to that end. Classification rests upon the kinds of relationships which may obtain between what is said and what is meant. Thus, in synecdoche and metonymy the relationship between thing said and thing meant is based largely upon some sort of contiguity regarding class and species, cause and effect, and so on, while in the remaining figures, on the other hand, the relationship is based largely upon similarity in difference. It was because of this that Aristotle could say of the power of making metaphors, that "it is the one thing that cannot be learnt from others; and it is also a sign of genius, since a good metaphor implies an intuitive perception of the similarity in dissimilars" (*Poetics*, 1459a 5–7).

The placing, then, of two different kinds of things in significant ratio is the central characteristic of these figures. Subject and analogue (or "tenor" and "vehicle" [q.v.] as I. A. Richards and other modern critics after him have come to designate them) may be related with respect to physical resemblance—as when Homer compares the charge of a warrior in battle to that of a lion on the sheepfold—in which case the study of mental i. provides useful distinctions. But many figures relate two different things in other ways: a lady's blush, her delicate skin, or her fragrance may find physical analogues in the color, texture, or odor of a rose, but her freshness, and beauty are qualities suggestively evoked by the rose rather than images tangibly displayed by it—what Burns's speaker is saying, after all, is that his lady is to him as June is to the world, in the sense of bringing joy. Or, as indicated above, a twilight sky and a patient etherized upon a table are related mainly in terms of attitude, emotion, and idea: sky is to light as patient is to life, in the sense of being half and half (there is also involved here, it may be supposed, a physical relationship between the patient's proneness and the clouds resting horizontally on the horizon during twilight). Furthermore, the two things related may each be images, or each may be feelings or concepts, or the subject may be an image and the analogue a feeling or concept, or the subject may be a feeling or concept and the analogue an image. Some critics have even claimed that the subject or tenor of a figure is in reality the relationship itself, and that therefore the analogy or vehicle includes the two things related. Thus, although the term "i." is commonly used to refer to all figures of speech, further distinctions are obviously necessary.

The kinds of things related and the nature and function of their relationship provide grounds upon which these distinctions may be made. It was once common to claim that proper practice precluded mixing one's analogues in any one figure (see Jennings), while critics today argue that no such rule is universally valid, especially in poetry (see Brooks). Or it was once considered good form to teach students to visualize all figures, but it has been repeatedly pointed out that not only are most metaphors constructed on other bases than mental i. but also that much mental i. is other than visual—in fact, persistent visualizing will break down the relationship entirely between subject and analogue in many figures (see Richards). Again, much attention has recently been focused upon that kind of figure in which the difference between subject and analogue is especially great, and which, since it is believed that such a figure was used mainly by Donne, Herbert, Marvell, Vaughan, Traherne, and so on, has been termed the "metaphysical image" (see Wells, Rugoff, Tuve) —although Miss Holmes has argued that it was derived from Elizabethan drama. Or again, much has been made of the function of the "central" or "unifying image" in a poem, according to which the poet develops a sustained analogy, which serves as the core of his poem.

When these distinctions serve as the basis for various speculations regarding the nature and development of poetic language, or the quality of the poetic imagination, "i." be-

comes one of the key terms of criticism. The New Critics (see NEW CRITICISM) generally hold that metaphor is not a rhetorical device but rather a mode of apprehension, a means of perceiving and expressing moral truths radically different from that of prose or scientific statement. If Max Müller thought that primitive man *compared* abstract ideas to concrete things because his conceptions outran his vocabulary, modern cirtics believe that the primitive *identified* the two in a rich and imaginative fashion (Buck and Barfield anticipated this view.) Thus "spirit," meaning "breath," was not borrowed as a concrete term to express the abstract concept of "soul," but rather "soul" was identified with "breath." Prescientific man (and that includes everyone up to around 1700), therefore, was supposed to be gifted with a "unified sensibility," and poets today are engaged in a mighty struggle to rectify the "dissociation of sensibility" created by science in the imaginations of men.

From these notions, a value-system has been constructed according to which a good poet "reconciles" abstract and concrete, thought and feeling, reason and imagination, and a bad poet, like the scientist, separates them. Thus the good poet aims at wholeness of experience by means of the poetic imagination or "mythic consciousness," whereby he sees facts in terms of values, and continually invents fresh metaphors (myths in little) and symbols (expanded metaphors). Richards, speaking of the artistic use of metaphor, claims "It is the supreme agent by which disparate and hitherto unconnected things are brought together in poetry for the sake of the effect upon attitude and impulse which spring from their collocation and from the combinations which the mind then establishes between them. . . . Metaphor is a semi-surreptitious method by which a greater variety of elements can be wrought into the fabric of the experience . . . what is needed for the wholeness of an experience is not always naturally present, and metaphor supplies an excuse by which what is needed may be smuggled in" (*Principles*). Modern critics accordingly prefer metaphor to simile, symbol to personification, and myth to allegory on the grounds of their superior unifying powers; and they prefer a poet who never explains but always implies what he means through i. (compare Archibald MacLeish's rather self-contradictory poem, *Ars Poetica*, cited above, for a well-known instance of this idea).

Modern criticism, then, has developed what it views as a radically "functional" theory of i. on the assumption that figures are the differentiae of poetic language and poetic language is the differentia of the poetic art. Its favorable terms are "rich," "complex," "concrete," "ambiguous," "ironic," "symbolic," "mythic," "sensuous," "unified," "wholeness," and so on, while its pejoratives are "sentimental," "prosaic," "didactic," "dissociated," and so on. This assumption, derived largely from Richards's reconstruction of Coleridge's theory of the imagination and from Eliot's reinterpretation of the Metaphysical Poets, has been placed against what the New Critics (J. C. Ransom, Cleanth Brooks, Allen Tate, R. P. Blackmur, W. K. Wimsatt, Jr., and so on) take to be the "decorative fallacy" of the traditional rhetoricians (who were supposed to have claimed that figures are pleasant but unnecessary adornments to plain sense) and the "heresy" of modern positivist semantics (which is supposed to claim that logic and the experimental method are the only avenues to truth and that poetry is either a harmless pastime or an actual waste of effort). Although certain other critics have questioned their emphases as well as their assumptions (see Tuve, Fogle, Muir, and *Critics and Criticism*, ed.. R. S. Crane [1952]), the New Critics have defined an important if limited problem and their views have achieved a wide currency.

The study of figurative i. anticipates and overlaps the subsequently developed study of symbolic i. Here the essential question is how the patterns of i.—whether literal, figurative, or both—in a work reveal things about the author and/or his poem. The basic assumption is that repetition and recurrences (usually of images, but also on occasion of word patterns in general) are in themselves significant. Hence the method involves an amateur application (and, sometimes, distortion) of some elementary statistical principles. These patterns may either be within the work itself, or among literary works and myths in general (see ARCHETYPE), or both.

Assuming for the moment that repetitions are indeed significant, the nature of the significance must next be examined. What, exactly, will counting image clusters tell the critic? There are at least five distinguishable answers; they are, in increasing levels of complexity: (1) texts of doubtful authorship can be authenticated (see Smith); (2) inferences can be made about the poet's experiences, tastes, temperament, and so on (see Spurgeon, Banks); (3) the causes of tone, atmosphere, and mood in a poem or play can be analyzed and defined (Spurgeon); (4) some of the ways in which the structure of conflict in a play is supported can be examined (see Burke, *Philosophy of Literary Form* [1941], etc.); and (5) symbols can be traced out, either in terms of how image patterns relate to the author or of how they relate to archetypes, or some combination (Frye, Knight, Heilman).

The first two approaches relate to problems extrinsic to the work itself, although they seek internal evidence. The procedure involves counting all the images in a given work or in all the works of a given poet (and here the various problems of what an image is, what kind it is, and whether it is literal or figurative, must be resolved anew by each critic doing the counting) and then classifying them according to the areas of experience from which they derive: Nature—Animate and Inanimate, Daily Life, Learning, Commerce, and so on. Since these categories and their proportions represent aspects of the poet's imagination and perception, two inferences can be made on the basis of the resultant charts and figures: first, that these patterns are caused by the poet's personal experiences with life and that, therefore, they give a clue to the poet's personality and background; and second, that since they are unique, they offer a means of determining the authorship of doubtful works. Perhaps the second inference is sounder than the first, although both rest upon dubious assumptions, for frequently images appear in a work not because of the poet's personality or experience but rather because of literary and artistic conventions (see Hornstein, Hankins).

The third and fourth approaches relate to problems intrinsic to the artistic organization of the work itself. "One cannot long discuss imagery," says Burke, "without sliding into symbolism. The poet's images are organized with relation to one another by reason of their symbolic kinships. We shift from the image of an object to its symbolism as soon as we consider it, not in itself alone, but as a function in in a texture of relationships" (*Attitudes toward History* [1937], v. 2, pp. 154–55). Certain plays of Shakespeare, it was discovered, are saturated with one kind or another of similar images or "clusters" (usually figurative)—the i. of light and dark in *Romeo and Juliet*, for example, or of animals in *King Lear*, or of disease in *Hamlet*, and so on—and it was reasoned that these recurrences, although barely perceptible except upon close examination, are continually at work conditioning the reader's responses as he follows the action of a play. Thus F. C. Kolbe, a pioneer—along with Whiter and Spaulding—of cluster criticism, claimed in 1930: "My thesis is that Shakespeare secures the unity of each of his greater plays, not only by the plot, by linkage of characters, by the sweep of Nemesis, by the use of irony, and by appropriateness of style, but by deliberate repetition throughout the play of at least one set of words or ideas in harmony with the plot. It is like the effect of the dominant note in a melody" (*Shakespeare's Way*). Modern critics have added that clusters may form dramatic discords as well as harmonies.

From this argument it was a small step to

classify images according to their relationship to the dramatic conflicts in the work. There are basically two sorts of clusters: the recurrence of the same image at intervals throughout the work, or the recurrence of different images together at intervals throughout the work. If the same image recurs in different contexts, then it (theoretically) serves to link those contexts in significant ways, and if different images recur together several times, then the mention of any one will serve to call the others to mind. Thus Brooks, in discussing the implications of Spurgeon's discovery of clothes-imagery and the i. of the babe in *Macbeth*, argues: "Perhaps her interest in classifying and cataloguing the imagery of the plays has obscured for her some of the larger and more important relationships." He continues: "I do not know whether 'blanket' and 'pall' qualify as garment metaphors in Miss Spurgeon's classification: yet one is the clothing of sleep, and the other, the clothing of death—they are the appropriate garments of night; and they carry on an important aspect of the general clothes imagery." What he makes of his classification as opposed to Spurgeon's is as follows: "The clothed daggers and the naked babe—mechanism and life—instrument and end—death and birth—that which should be left bare and clean and that which should be clothed and warmed—these are facets of two of the great symbols which run throughout the play. . . . And between them—the naked babe, essential humanity, humanity stripped down to the naked thing itself, and yet as various as the future—and the various garbs which humanity assumes, the robes of honor, the hypocrite's disguise, the inhuman 'manliness' with which Macbeth endeavors to cover up his essential humanity—between them they furnish Shakespeare with his most subtle and ironically telling instruments" (*Well Wrought Urn*).

The next and fifth step was to reason once again from inside to outside the work, but this time ostensibly for the sake of returning to it with greater insight. According to Burke, a poem is a dramatic revelation in disguised and symbolic form of the poet's emotional tensions and conflicts, and if, therefore, some idea of these tensions and conflicts in his personal life can be formed, the reader will then be alerted to their symbolic appearance in his works. Thus Burke can make equations among Coleridge's image clusters by comparing the poet's letters with *The Ancient Mariner*, and can conclude that the albatross symbolizes Coleridge's guilt regarding his addiction to opium, and this, he reasons, illuminates the "motivational structure" of that particular poem.

It is not difficult, on the other hand, to equate image clusters in a particular work with larger patterns found in other works and myths instead of with the poet's personal life (a dream is the "myth" of the individual, a myth is the "dream" of the race), as does Northrop Frye, and even Burke himself, for the "action" of which a poem is "symbolic" frequently resembles larger ritualistic patterns such as purgation, scape-goating, killing the king, initiation, and so on, although expressed on a personal level and in personal terms. R. P. Warren sees in the *Ancient Mariner* a symbol of the artist-archetype, symbolized in the Mariner, torn between the conflicting and ambiguous claims of reason, symbolized by the sun, and the imagination, symbolized by the moon: thus the crime is a crime against the imagination, and the imagination revenges itself but at the same time heals the Mariner; the wandering is also a blessing and curse, for the Mariner is the *poète maudit* (q.v.) as well as the "prophet of universal charity" (see Elder Olson's review of Warren's interpretation in *Critics and Criticism*, pp. 138–144). Thus, in large and general terms, the artist is seen as the hero and his art as a sacrificial ritual, and he is seen as dying to his life in order to be reborn in his art as the redeemer (see Otto Rank, "Myth and Metaphor," *Art and Artist*, tr. C. F. Atkinson [1932], pp. 207–31). One may find implicit images of descent, guilt, purification, and ascent running throughout a poem whose literal action may be of quite a different nature. Image clusters are seen, then, as forming a "spatial pattern" or even a "subplot" calling for special attention in itself.

The difficulties with the fourth and fifth approaches are: first, that the concern centers rather exclusively on problems of moral vision, on the assumption that the really important thing about poetry is its way of viewing life and experience, a "mode of apprehension"; second, that, as a result, almost any poem or play is read as an allegorical struggle between Good and Evil, Reason and Imagination, Guilt and Redemption, or any other favored pair of opposites, and this is excessively reductive; third, that many such inferences as those discussed above are made on the basis of insufficient evidence and faulty or incomplete hypotheses (a statistician could point out, for example, that *some* recurrences are accidental, and a logician could point out, for example, that a favored hypothesis, in order to be valid, must be tested against other alternatives); fourth, that the *literal* action of a poem or play, when viewed as an artistic construct, tends to be inordinately deemphasized or even ignored altogether; and fifth, that these approaches tend to be so loosely oriented and vaguely defined as to allow anything and everything in a work to be seen in terms of anything and everything else.

The importance, however, of these approaches to i. in a work is that they did indeed refocus critical concern on the work itself, and its parts and devices, at a time when attention was wandering down the bypaths of literature rather than the main highway. Nor does the dubious validity of some of the theorizing necessarily cancel out the worth of all the practical results it fostered.

It may now be asked, what i. does in a poem. Although many good poems contain little or no imagery, i. has come to be regarded as a special poetic device. Neither its presence nor the use of one kind of i. or another, however, makes a good poem; the poet needs more than a unified sensibility in order to compose poems —he needs, in addition, certain constructive powers. That is to say, i., if used, must be part of a larger whole and cannot in and of itself constitute a whole. Far from being itself a unifying form, it must be unified along with all the other elements of a poem (such as rhyme and meter, stylistic, rhetorical, and grammatical schemes, patterns of sequence and order, the devices of point of view, the methods of amplification and condensation, the methods of selection and omission, aspects of thought and character and action, and so on). I., then, is either material or technique—what is being represented or how—rather than form.

It may be, in the first place, the speaker's subject, what he is talking about, whether present before him or recalled to mind afterwards. Included here are, roughly speaking, people, places, objects, actions, and events. In Arnold's *Dover Beach,* for example, the speaker and his lady are physically located by the English Channel, and the speaker describes the view—the full tide, the fair moon, the light gleaming on the French coast, the cliffs of England, the tranquil bay, the sweet night air, the beach, and the grating roar of the waves on the pebbles. Furthermore, we may infer that he is looking out of the window of some sort of seaside dwelling and talking to his lady, whom he asks to join him there. All of this comprises literal i. of subject matter.

Since economy is a fundamental artistic principle, it may be said that usually literal i. is converted into a pseudo-subject, becoming the symbol of something else as a result of the speaker's reflective and meditative activity. Mere scenery, that is, is rarely enough in itself, except in descriptive poems, to justify its presence in a poem. Thus Arnold converts the scene into a symbol as follows: as it begins to signify sadness to the speaker, it reminds him of Sophocles listening long ago by the Aegean and reflecting similarly. Although the literal sea before him at Dover Beach is now at full tide, the "Sea of Faith" now seems to him to be ebbing. Thus the problem which is troubling the speaker (the discord he senses between an apparently meaningful world and an actually meaningless one) finds its image in the contrast between what he sees—the calm sea, the full tide, the fair moon, the bright gleam of lights, the tranquil bay, the sweet night air—and what he hears—the partially submerged and ominous sound of

the grating roar
Of pebbles which the waves suck back, and fling,
At their return, up the high strand,
Begin, and cease, and then again begin,
With tremulous cadence slow, and bring
The eternal note of sadness in.

It will be noted that the language of this passage is set in contrast to that used above: grating roar, suck back and fling, tremulous, slow, and sadness, as opposed to calm, full, fair, glimmering, vast, tranquil, and sweet. Still talking in terms of the pseudo-subject in the second paragraph, the speaker contrasts what Sophocles heard and thought to what he hears and thinks: the great dramatist, long ago and in another place, heard this same "grating roar" and it brought to his mind "the turbid ebb and flow / Of human misery," while the modern Eng. speaker finds "also in the sound a thought, / Hearing it by this distant northern sea." Taken in context, since the meaning is not wholly explicit, this may imply that Sophocles found *some* meaning, however tragic, in the coming and going of the waves, while Arnold's speaker, focusing now not on the rapid motion of the waves but rather upon the slow ebb and flow of the tide (a shift in i. of which some critics have complained), sees only the absence of any meaning whatever. To the ancient Greeks, that is, the world made sense in moral terms (e.g., the catharsis or sense of justice produced by the tragedies of Sophocles), while to the modern European the world is devoid of value. Thus, although the physical tide is full, the moral tide is ebbing, and he can

only hear
Its melancholy, long, withdrawing roar,
Retreating to the breath
Of the night-wind down the vast edges drear
And naked shingles of the world.

At the end, therefore, since the faith of humanity at large is gone, he can appeal to his lady to reaffirm at least their own faith in one another, "for the world, which seems / To lie before us like a land of dreams" (a reference back to the opening description), is really joyless, confused, and without love. Thus does Arnold's sea-imagery function at once as subject and symbol.

IMAGINATION

Thirdly and lastly, images may function as analogies brought into the poem from outside the world of the speaker, apart from his literal subject, to function in a purely figurative fashion. In *Dover Beach,* in addition to the i. already discussed, there are several figures of speech: the "Sea of Faith" once "Lay like the folds of a bright girdle furled," the world seems "To lie before us like a land of dreams," "And we are here as on a darkling plain etc." The girdle, land of dreams, and darkling plain (battlefield), that is, do not derive from the speaker's literal subject at all.

It may be asked, finally, what the poet gains by the use of such devices. I., especially of the figurative or symbolic sort, may, in the first place, serve as a device for explaining, clarifying, and making vivid what the speaker is talking about. Arnold was not content with merely locating his speaker geographically, but had him register his awareness of the precise physical details of the scene before him so that the reader would not only know but feel what he (the speaker) is responding to. Secondly, and correspondingly, the terms in which he is making that response serve to reveal implicitly the mood of tempered sadness in which we find the speaker. Thirdly, and consequently, since this scene serves to call up to the speaker's consciousness—and thereby becomes the vehicle of—a problem which has long been troubling him, it stimulates and externalizes further his mental activity. Fourthly, the poet's handling of i., through his selection of detail and choice of comparisons, serves to dispose the reader either favorably or unfavorably toward various elements in the poetic situation. That faith, therefore, the loss of which the speaker mourns, is made to seem worthy of his lament not only because the reader knows in general what the speaker is talking about but also and more particularly because he compares it to a bright girdle, thereby arousing in the reader's mind the connotations of a thing of value and ornament, pleasant, precious, and useful. I. may serve, fifthly, as a way of arousing and guiding the reader's expectations. Thus, since he places "sea" as the second word of his poem, Arnold prepares the reader for the speaker's symbolic lament: "The Sea of Faith / was once, too, at the full."

I., then, may derive from the speaker's subject, if that happens to involve a person, place, object, action, or event; from a symbolic combination of subject and meaning, if his thought happens to find its expressive vehicle in his physical experience; or from exterior analogies, if he happens to use figures of speech. It may be interpreted in terms of whether it functions to vivify the subject, reveal the speaker's mood, externalize the speaker's thought, direct the reader's attitudes, or guide his expectations.

Although these categories are merely suggestive, an interpretation of i. in a given poem would do well to examine it, at least to begin with, strictly in relation to the particular context and in terms of such distinctions.

F. I. Carpenter, *Metaphor and Simile in the Minor Elizabethan Drama* (1895); G. Buck, *The Metaphor: A Study in the Psychology of Rhetoric* (1899); J. G. Jennings, *An Essay on Metaphor in Poetry* (1915); H. W. Wells, *Poetic I.* (1924); Richards, *Principles;* S. J. Brown, *The World of I.* (1927); O. Barfield, *Poetic Diction* (1928); J. E. Downey, *Creative Imagination* (1929); E. Holmes, *Aspects of Elizabethan I.* (1929); C.F.E. Spurgeon, *Shakespeare's I. and What it Tells us* (1935); I. A. Richards, *The Philosophy of Rhetoric* (1936); U. Ellis-Fermor, *Some Recent Research in Shakespeare's I.* (1937); I. A. Richards, *Interpretation in Teaching* (1938); M. A. Rugoff, *Donne's I.* (1939); C. Brooks, "Metaphor and the Tradition," *Modern Poetry and the Trad.* (1939); M. B. Smith, *Marlowe's I. and the Marlowe Canon* (1940); L. H. Hornstein, "Analysis of I.: A Critique of Literary Method," PMLA, 57 (1942); E. A. Armstrong, *Shakespeare's Imagination* (1946); C. D. Lewis, *The Poetic Image* (1947); C. Brooks, "The Naked Babe and the Cloak of Manliness," *The Well Wrought Urn* (1947); Tuve; R. B. Heilman, *This Great Stage: Image and Structure in "King Lear"* (1948); R. H. Fogle, *The I. of Keats and Shelley* (1949); Wellek and Warren, ch. 15; D. A. Stauffer, *Shakespeare's World of Images* (1949); T. H. Banks, *Milton's I.* (1950); W. H. Clemen, *The Development of Shakespeare's I.* (1951); K. Muir, "Fifty Years of Shakespearean Crit.: 1900–1950," ShS, 4 (1951); F. Marsh, *Wordsworth's I.* (1952); J. E. Hankins, *Shakespeare's Derived I.* (1953); Frye; F. Kermode, *Romantic Image* (1957); C. Brooke-Rose, *A Grammar of Metaphor* (1959); D. C. Allen, *Image and Meaning: Metaphoric Traditions in Renaissance Poetry* (1960); J. W. Beach, *Obsessive Images: Symbolism in the Poetry of the 1930's and 1940's* (1960); R. Frazer, "The Origin of the Term Image," ELH, 27 (1960); *Metaphor and Symbol,* ed. L. C. Knights and B. Cottle (1960); H. Musurillo, *Symbol and Myth in Ancient Poetry* (1961); P. Wheelwright, *Metaphor and Reality* (1962). N.FRIE.

IMAGINATION is derived from L. *imaginatio,* which was a late substitute for *phantasia* (a simple transliteration of the Gr. from which fancy is derived. The two terms, with their derivatives, long appeared as synonyms designating the image-receiving or image-forming faculty or process. From philosophy they were borrowed by criticism, and in both contexts were subject to different evaluations by different schools. Their history, though far from a simple linear development, falls into fairly clearly marked divisions.

I. CLASSICAL AND MEDIEVAL. (1) The history starts with the elementary recognition, first, of a mental image accompanying sense perception (and viewed by the materialist as real and an impress made by the object, by the idealist as mere appearance, by the dualist with depreciation as dependent on matter and the senses), and, secondly, of images occurring in the absence of any object, and in various combinations, which might be depreciated as fictitious, suspected as proceeding from the passions, valued as divinely inspired, or simply examined as psychological phenomena.

(2) All these attitudes find some reflection in Plato, who further recognizes a connection of art and poetry with i. Initially, he regards the image as illusory, yielding no knowledge of reality (since of the "idea" one can form no image) but confined to appearance and opinion, and a prey to every prompting from the irrational soul; hence in part the limitations of artist and poet. Thus Plato inaugurates a long tradition of distrust, which was little mitigated by his own important second thoughts, namely, that "images answering to true opinions are true," that to form images from "ideas" was indeed possible to the god, that an image of pure beauty (subsuming the ideas of truth and goodness) while it could not be produced by any activity of the soul, might be passively received from above, or even "remembered" from the soul's earlier state, a process in which earthly images of beauty might be instrumental, and, finally, that provision was perhaps made (in close proximity to the irrational soul) for a reflection, in the form of images; of ideas entertained by the rational soul. But the gap between "ideas" and "images" was never securely closed. At most the soul could passively receive an image reflecting an idea: it could not actively produce such an image. In the Platonic tradition the distrust of phantasy is emphatic; not until it is dissipated can Platonism make its full contribution to the theory of i. (see below 12, 13, 15, 18).

(3) Aristotle's interest, in the De Anima, was psychological and free from prejudice. Set in motion by sense perception, phantasy forms images of objects and their relations; and from such images reproduced, reason abstracts its ideas. Thus, in the process of deriving knowledge from experience, images are the intermediaries between sense and thought; and in the act of choice images have an equally essential role. Aristotle's failure, however, to invoke his theory of the reproductive image in expounding, in the Poetics, his view of art as an "imitation of nature" at once realistic and philosophical, was to impede the recognition

of the imagination's role in poetry (see below 7).

(4) Distrust of phantasy is dominant in the Stoics (despite some inheritance from the De Anima). Neoplatonism, as represented by Plotinus, is more ambivalent. His emanationist theory permitted him to distinguish a higher and a lower phantasy: the lower dependent on sense and a function of the irrational soul, the higher reflective of ideas because a function of the rational soul, but with the lower capable of being brought into harmony with the higher because it is indeed its shadow. Further, as soul was an emanation of mind, nature was an emanation of soul, inferior to it because lacking, among other powers, that of phantasy and, consequently, all perception of its own activity, namely, the imposition of forms upon matter (the last and lowest of the emanations). Here was a philosophy with large, if undeveloped, possibilities for poetic theory: for the imaginative reflection of the ideal, and even for something like Coleridge's conception of "poesy or art" (see 15).

(5) Though, in discussing the art of poetry, Horace had ignored i. and thus impeded its recognition (cf. 7), Quintilian, with illustrations from Virgil, recognizes that by visiones (or phantasies) absent things seem present, whence the orator can feel and, by his eloquence, arouse emotion; and Longinus, with illustrations from Euripides, recognizes i. as a source of sublimity when "moved by enthusiasm and passion you seem to see the things whereof you speak and place them before the eyes of your hearers." Here as later (cf. 10, 18) i. and passion unite to characterize poetry and eloquence. A further development is adumbrated in Philostratus, when imitation is declared to be inferior to phantasy, since it can represent only what has been seen, but phantasy what has never been seen, fashioning it according to the analogy of the real.

(6) While Christian asceticism, with biblical phrases about vain i., no doubt fortified existing prejudices, St. Augustine distinguished the reproductive from the simple sensory image, reserving to the former the term phantasia or imaginatio. He recognized its role when, in reading history, or in writing and reading fables, we see in our mind's eye persons and scenes; he further noticed the interdependence of the reproductive image and the will in the hypothetical representations formed by addition, subtraction, or combination of attributes. But for him i. remained inferior to intellect: to the former prophetic vision might be vouchsafed, but its interpretation only to the latter. In the "faculty psychology" of the Schoolmen, where this order is maintained, i., like the other faculties, is given its location and its distinctive function, namely, with or

as the *sensus communis*, to produce from sense data the images of objects and their relations, and (sometimes under the designation of *phantasia*) to reproduce and combine images at will. Of the truth of images reason must judge, and from them it abstracts ideas, which memory in turn retains. This is the basic scheme, of which there were many variants. Dante's interest centered on ascent from the image of earthly beauty to intellectual or heavenly love, and on the image divinely bestowed or inspired; but his practice as poet outran his theory: where, in the *Divine Comedy*, he finally declares that i. fails, he is actually making his most effective use of the symbolic image, and in his account of the poem's fourfold meaning he does not refer to i. at all.

II. RENAISSANCE TO ROMANTICS. (7) In Pico della Mirandola's *On Imagination*, the early Renaissance combined a renewed reference to classical sources with much from medieval tradition. Those critics who, in the 16th c., commenced to formulate the principles of neoclassicism, built upon Aristotle and Horace and largely ignored imagination in favor of the imitation of nature; and even when Scaliger and Sidney acclaimed the poet as a "creator," they still clung to the doctrine of imitation. Puttenham's summary of current theories which ascribe poetry to creation, imitation, natural endowment, divine inspiration, etc., remarks (under the first of these) that the poet may indeed be likened to the Creator "who without any travail to his Divine Imagination made all the world of nought," but also bears testimony to long-established prejudice in his defense of i. as, in its healthful state, no wise irregular but very orderly, productive of "beautiful visions," and so helpful to invention that "without it no man could devise any new or rare thing." But it is not till Bacon that i. really begins to claim a central role in poetry—and then with an attendant limitation, for poetry ceases to be knowledge and becomes fiction and play. "History," he writes, "is referred to memory; poesy to imagination; philosophy to reason." With "the primary materials of knowledge" the "mind . . . exercises itself and sometimes sports. For as all knowledge is the exercise and work of the mind, so poesy may be regarded as its sport." For "being not tied to the laws of matter," as are memory and reason, i. "may at pleasure join that which nature hath severed and sever that which nature hath joined" and give thereby "some shadow of satisfaction to the mind of man" by representing "a more ample greatness, a more exact goodness, and a more absolute variety than can be found in the nature of things."

(8) For immediate acceptance this view ran too completely counter to the neoclassical conception of poetry as an imitation of nature. In England, however, neoclassicism early sought its philosophical basis in empiricism, and while it regarded poetry as an imitation of empirical reality (a severely limiting criterion, as seen in Hobbes) and yielded i. only a secondary role, a philosophy which grounded all knowledge in sense experience had less reason to distrust i. than had rationalism in its Cartesian or any other form, and psychological interest prompted a study of its operation. Hobbes sums up his view of poetry in the dictum: "Time and education beget experience; experience begets memory; memory begets judgment and fancy; judgment begets the strength and structure, and fancy begets the ornaments, of a poem." But this did not close the subject. I. or fancy, drawing all its data from sensation, was in its "simple" form, he averred, merely the memory of sensory images; but it had also the power of "compounding" them to form new images. Further, images presented themselves in "trains," the result of undirected association, or (more significantly) of a directing desire or design, in which case i. (cooperating with judgment) became the indispensable instrument of invention in "whatsoever distinguisheth the civility of Europe from the barbarity of the American savages." In critical theory Addison, in effect, grafts Hobbes's psychology of the i. upon Bacon's theory of poetry.

(9) For Addison all the data of i. are supplied by the sense of sight. Its primary process is to form visual images of objects in their presence. Its secondary is to reproduce their "ideas" (i.e. images) "when the objects are not actually before the eye, but are called up into our memories or formed into agreeable visions of things that are either absent or fictitious." Here indeed are two processes: simple reproduction of images, and "altering and compounding those images . . . into all the varieties of picture and vision. . . . ; for by this faculty a man in a dungeon is capable of entertaining himself with scenes and landskips more beautiful than any that can be found in the whole compass of nature." And "because the imagination can fancy to itself things more great, strange or beautiful than the eye ever saw, and is still sensible of some defect in what it has seen, . . . it is the part of a poet to humour the imagination . . . by mending and perfecting nature where he describes a reality, and by adding greater beauties than are put together in nature where he describes a fiction." In "the fairy way of writing" the poet quite loses sight of nature and "out of his own invention" represents "ghosts, fairies, witches, and the like imaginary persons" (which Hobbes had specifically rejected as contradict-

ing nature). In a word, i. "has something in it like creation: it bestows a kind of existence."

(10) To the influence of Addison's *Spectator* papers much of the emphasis on i. in 18th-c. criticism may be traced. "In the fairyland of fancy," wrote Edward Young, "genius may wander wild; there it has a creative power and may reign arbitrarily over its own empire of chimeras." Reynolds, abandoning "ideal form" for "appeal to the imagination" as his criterion in art, declares that its aim "is to supply the natural imperfection of things" and "to gratify the mind by realizing . . . what never existed but in imagination." Unlike the majority of his predecessors, he makes some distinction between i. and fancy in the assertion: "Raphael had more taste and fancy, Michelangelo more genius and imagination." Such theorists as Lord Kames and Alison anticipate the romantics in their emphasis on emotion and its dependence upon i.

(11) Meanwhile Hume, having deposed reason, in effect replaced it by i., which he was careful to distinguish from "the loose reveries of the fancy." Adam Smith made sympathy, the groundwork of the moral sentiments, depend on i. Alexander Gerard, attempting an empirical account of genius, describes it as fertility in associating ideas, and attributes this in turn to an active i., as also does William Duff, in whom merge the cults of i., of genius, and of the primitive: the mark of genius is "an inventive and plastic imagination" which "sketches out a creation of its own," and is something quite different from the mere "quickness and readiness" of "a sportive fancy"; and genius, thus conceived, flourishes best in primitive societies. Blackwell, Wood, Blair, and other primitivists expatiate on the metaphorical character of primitive poetry; and while not all attribute this mainly to i., all would agree with Vico (in Italy) that "imagination is more robust in proportion as reasoning power is weak." Vico's importance lies less in his theory of i. ("imagination is nothing but extended or compounded memory") than in the results which he attributed to it in ancient poetry and myth, thereby anticipating modern anthropological criticism. To Herder and the Germans it chiefly fell to take up and develop Eng. ideas of primitive poetry and the i. of the folk. More central are the interests of Dougald Stewart, who ascribes imagery wholly to "fancy," the power that "supplies the poet with metaphorical language," while i. (freed from its close association with the image) is the power "that creates the complex scenes he describes and the fictitious characters he delineates," as illustrated in Milton's Eden, Harrington's Oceana, and Shakespeare's Falstaff or Hamlet. This is perhaps the final development and utmost reach of the tradition that stops short of making for i. the transcendental claims put forward by the romantics.

(12) Of such claims there were, however, some intermittent premonitions. After basing his early aesthetic on Hobbes, but unlike Hobbes attempting some distinction between i. and fancy (*imagination* connoting the general power whose first activity is "invention or finding of the thought," while its second activity is "fancy or variation . . . of that thought"), Dryden became restive under its limitations and (with liberal quotation from Bellori) advanced the theory that i. could reach to images of the essential ideas of things, which images were the models for painter and poet when they would represent "nature wrought up to a nobler pitch." There are hints of a similar doctrine in William Collins and the eclectic Reynolds; but it could make little headway against the prevailing empiricism. Nor must it be forgotten that the tradition opposed to empiricism, and represented by Shaftesbury, set its own limits on i. Shaftesbury's famous pronouncement on the true poet as "a second maker, a just Prometheus under Jove" speaks in terms of the imitation of nature, not of i., which indeed it disparages in accordance with his oft-repeated Stoic prejudice. In It. criticism attention was being given to the i. with somewhat different results, and notably by Muratori in his defense of the It. poets against the strictures of Fr. neoclassicists. In order to please, poetry must present what appears to be true and beautiful, marvelous but verisimilar. Herein intellect and i. must cooperate and good taste control. If intellect alone works upon the images, the result is philosophical knowledge; if i. alone, dream and delusion. "Simple" or "natural" images appear immediately true to both. Others may appear immediately true to i., but only mediately to the intellect: such are those images, described as "artificial" or "fantastic," which are applied metaphorically under the stress of emotion. Both kinds are approved by Muratori and copiously illustrated from the poets. In German criticism Eng. ideas on poetry and i. were sometimes grafted on the different philosophical stock of Leibniz, as by Bodmer and Baumgarten. But it is to Kant and his followers in Germany and to the romantic poets in England that we must look for the final exalting of i.

III. THE ROMANTICS. (13) Blake takes an extreme line. Ultimate reality is spiritual, and the i. is the organ of its perception: "Imagination is spiritual sensation." It is the "first principle" of knowledge, "and all others are derivative." It perceives—almost one might say, confers—form and value: "Nature has no outline, but Imagination has: / Nature has no tune, but Imagination has. / Nature has no supernatural and dissolves: Imagination is Eternity." In his reaction against empiricism and the theories of art based thereon, Blake condemns all those "who pretend to Poetry that they may destroy Imagination by imitation of Nature's Images drawn from Remembrance." Nothing but i. can resolve the antinomy of material object and spiritual reality, nothing, that is, but the power to look upon the object and see the reality: "to the eyes of the man of Imagination, Nature is Imagination itself." Creative i. issues not in fiction but in the highest truth. Without benefit of German metaphysics, "English Blake" reverses the assumptions of the empirical tradition.

(14) Meanwhile, in the *Critique of Pure Reason*, Kant had emphasized the role of i. (*Einbildungskraft*) in the formation of knowledge, describing it as "an active faculty for synthesis," which unites and unifies the manifold data of sense perception. Without it, no subjective knowledge would be possible, and no ordered knowledge of an objective world. It is "a necessary ingredient of perception itself" and the indispensable mediator between "mere sensibility and understanding"; and, in order to account for these empirical results, Kant has further to infer "a transcendental synthesis of imagination." Nor is this all. In the *Critique of Judgment* he treats i. in another context, which places it in a different relation to understanding and brings into relief free (as opposed to determined) activity. In aesthetic judgment, "we do not refer the representation . . . to the object by means of understanding, with a view to cognition, but by means of imagination (acting perhaps in conjunction with understanding) we refer the representation to the subject and its feeling of pleasure or displeasure." There i. is free: not simply "reproductive" under "the laws of association," but "productive and exerting an activity of its own"; and even when it is restricted by the form of the object of sense represented, and "does not enjoy free play as it does in poetry," the representation is still judged in relation to such a form "as the imagination, if left to itself, would freely project in . . . general conformity to the law of the understanding." In a word, in cognition i. is at the service of understanding; in aesthetic judgment, "understanding is at the service of imagination" in its free activity. Kant's antinomy of the necessary and the free becomes in Schelling that of the real (nature, the finite and determined) and the ideal (mind, the infinite and free) subsisting within the absolute, and the function of art is to mediate between them, to build the infinite into the finite, through the active and intermediary power of "intelligence," which no doubt subsumes i.: "Intelligence is productive in two ways . . . , unconsciously in the per-

ception of the universe, consciously [and, he adds, with freedom] in the creation of an ideal world."

(15) In Coleridge there are elements from both Kant and Schelling. I., he defines as the intermediate faculty which joins the predominantly passive and predominantly active elements in thinking, but as applied to poetry it connotes "a superior degree of the faculty joined to a superior voluntary control over it." And in a more famous passage he writes: "The primary imagination I hold to be the living power and prime agent of all human perception, and as a repetition in the finite mind of the eternal act of creation in the infinite I AM. The secondary imagination I consider as an echo of the former, co-existing with the conscious will, yet still as identical with the primary in the kind of its agency, and differing only in degree and in the mode of its operation. It dissolves . . . in order to recreate or . . . to idealize and to unify." It is thus sharply differentiated from fancy, which is a mere "mode of memory emancipated from the order of time and space" but receiving "all its materials ready made from the law of association." Coleridge is critic as well as philosopher, and one of his concerns is to validate, against empiricism, the productions of the "secondary" i., the creative i. of poet or artist, by identifying it in kind with the "primary" i., the finite counterpart of God's creative act, and thereby to give philosophic ground and content to the traditional idea of the poet as creator. Unlike fancy and understanding, which are confined to the level of the phenomenal, of *natura naturata*, reason and creative i., aspiring to the noumenal, approximate to each other, so that i. becomes (in Wordsworth's phrase) "reason in her most exalted mood." Deliberately Coleridge seeks to unite creative i. with the imitation of nature, properly understood. For "poesy or art" does not "copy" *natura naturata* but "imitates" *natura naturans;* and thus to imitate nature is in effect to interpret it in and by "symbols," "living educts of the imagination, of that reconciling and mediatory power which, incorporating the reason in images of the sense, and organizing (as it were) the flux of the senses by the permanence and self-encircling energies of the reason, gives birth to a system of symbols, harmonious in themselves and consubstantial with the truths of which they are the conductors."

(16) *Imagination,* says Wordsworth, "has been forced to extend its services far beyond the point to which philosophy would have confined them: "the word . . . has been overstrained . . . to meet the demands of the faculty which is perhaps the noblest of our nature." His own criterion is not philosophic but experiential; and he rejects a complete

differentiation of i. and fancy, listing them together as *one* of the qualities requisite for the poet—deceived (Coleridge thinks) by their co-presence in his own poetry. They differ indeed, but mainly in respect of value: "Fancy is given to quicken and to beguile the temporal part of our nature, imagination to incite and to support the eternal." He was early conscious of creative activity in perception itself—"creative sensibility" as he was to call it. This is the beginning of the long evolution traced in the *Prelude,* and the end, a recognition of i. as the organ equally of truth, of beauty and of spiritual love: "This spiritual love acts not, nor can exist / Without imagination, which in truth / Is but another name for absolute power / And clearest insight, amplitude of mind, / And reason in her most exalted mood."

(17) Though still concerned with the image, Coleridge and Wordsworth extend the sway of i. to "thoughts and sentiments," "characters" and "actions": Wordsworth distinguishes the "human and dramatic" i. of Shakespeare from the "enthusiastic and meditative" of the Bible, Milton, and (he adds) Spenser; and Coleridge between the i. of Shakespeare, by which he goes forth and identifies himself with his subject, and Milton's, by which he brings everything to a center in his own experience. But above all i. manifests itself in the unity of the whole: it draws (says Wordsworth, quoting Lamb) "all things to one" and makes them "take one colour and serve to one effect"; it reveals itself, says Coleridge, "in the balance or reconcilement of opposite or discordant qualities; of sameness with difference, of the general with the concrete . . . , the individual with the representative, . . . the sense of novelty and freshness with old and familiar objects, [and] a more than usual state of emotion with a more than usual order. . . ."

(18) Others are more eclectic: Hazlitt, who emphasizes the dependence of poetry on emotion, and of emotion on i.; Keats, whose insights include stress on the poet's imaginative sympathy (these with no distinction of i. and fancy), and (with some attempt at distinction) Leigh Hunt, who notes that i. can dispense with the sensory image and wishes for a new term. Shelley attributes to i. all creative activity in life as well as art, sets it in opposition to reason, and claims for it alone that access to the realm of ideas which Plato had seemed to deny to it; he further assigns to i. a central role in ethics, as it begets and diffuses sympathy, a conception which looks back to Adam Smith and on to John Galsworthy. Though "more Platonic than Plato," Joubert, in the name of i., opposed the master on poetry: by i., "active and creative" and the very "eye of the soul," the poet "purifies and empties the forms

of matter and shows us the universe as it is in the mind of God. . . . His portrayal is not a copy of a copy, but an impression of the archetype." "In their quest of beauty poets come on more truth than philosophers in their quest of truth."

(19) Ruskin distinguishes three modes in which i. operates: the "penetrative" (whereby the artist, reacting to the inner "verity" of his subject, can present it directly, without resort to metaphor or symbol), the "associative" (the instinctive process, contrasted with conscious "composition," whereby he harmonizes every detail so that it may contribute to the effect of the whole), and the "contemplative" (whereby the artist, in treating a subject that transcends nature and the concrete image directly employed, resorts to an analogical or figurative use of image to convey its meaning and suggest the attendant emotion). None of these modes does he regard as "creative," however. For art to create is to depart from truth and produce fiction, and this is the lower activity of three modes of fancy corresponding to the three modes of i. But, despite his characteristic schematism, Ruskin really cares little for terminology, so long as he can assert that great art embodies truth intuitively apprehended and beyond the reach of reasoning. The criticism of reason usually entails a distinction of its discursive and intuitive operations; but Arnold chooses rather to contrast reason and the senses with i. and the heart (i.e., feeling) and, finding neither satisfactory, seeks his ideal in what he calls "imaginative reason" as exemplified in the greatest poetry. In general, however, the Victorians contributed little to the theory of i., using the term so vaguely that G. H. Lewes complained: "there are few words more abused."

IV. THE TWENTIETH C. (20) In popular criticism the word *imagination* and its derivatives are still encountered, if less frequently. Their meaning is sufficiently vague, connoting most often perhaps sustained fantasy as opposed to realistic writing; but it is largely devoid of the transcendental overtones inherited from the romantics. One could expect no less from the widespread and varied reaction against romanticism in general and transcendentalism in particular. An example of this reaction was seen in Am. humanism, though Irving Babbitt conceded the importance of i., and a distinction between the "ethical" (or classic) i. and the "idyllic" (or romantic) is pivotal in his doctrine. More unequivocally hostile to i. as such was the whole naturalistic movement in thought and letters (which the humanists also opposed). In and beyond its ill-defined boundaries transcendentalism is of course out of fashion. If, for example, Coleridge is to be accepted by I. A. Richards, he must first be divested of his metaphysics. The psychology and aesthetics of the romantics have been in part repudiated, in part developed. Whatever their metaphysical affinities, the romantics had assumed that essentially art was the expression of emotion, with emotion and i. indissolubly linked therein. Here contemporary opinion sharply divides, with one school of critics denying or markedly qualifying the dependence of art on emotion, while others (whose interests are more psychological than purely aesthetic) retain it. Again, if we hear relatively little about i., we hear a great deal about the image. The dominance of the image is a principle, and its investigation a method, common to groups holding divergent views on the nature of poetry: the Freudians who regard poetry as wish-fulfillment and analogous to dreams; cultural anthropologists who see it as reducible to archetypal myths and patterns, and those critics who regard the poem as a self-contained entity without significant external relations, whose meaning and effect reside in a pattern of interdependent images. This concentration has restored attention to the image-forming process, often at the expense of those wider powers manifested in description, characterization, narration, and structure, which with increasing emphasis previous criticism had ascribed to i.; but it has borne fruit in a closer study of the image as symbol. Such study looks back in part to Coleridge, and it is significant that Richards should find Coleridge on the i. of absorbing psychological interest. The Freudian association of i. with dream is as old as Plato, and the view of poetry as wish-fulfillment is fundamentally Baconian. Cultural anthropologists, though immediately responsive to Frazer and Jung, are the distant descendants of Vico and Blackwell. And Croce and Collingwood, among exponents of the aesthetic as an area and mode of knowledge, and the role of i. therein, are evidently continuing the explorations of Kant.

(21) In Croce's doctrine of art as intuition (where intuition demands expression and expression is art), i., as productive of the unifying image, is in its turn identified with intuition, so that the doctrine might as well be phrased, art as i. The central role here accorded to i. (fantasia) implies a sharp distinction from the mere recalling of images in accidental succession or arranging them in constrained or capricious combinations.

(22) R. G. Collingwood, in expounding a not dissimilar theory, treats i. in greater detail. I. is neither mere sensibility, which is passive and below the level of consciousness, nor intellect, whose activity issues in thought, in the formation and ordering of concepts: it is an activity of mind which coexists with full consciousness, and it is the intermediary between the other two. It furnishes "the basis for a theory of aesthetic experience"; and it fills an essential "place in the general structure of experience" since it provides the means whereby "the activity of thought makes contact with the merely psychic life of feeling." It is creative because it is an activity of mind and produces something, namely, the work of art. Its product is not, however, mere make-believe, but a form of knowledge and, within its own terms of reference, true. For it is not only creation, but expression, and what it expresses is real feeling, raised in the process to the level of consciousness. Nor is this all. If the psychic life is nothing but feeling, thought, the activity of intellect, also carries its "emotional charges," and to these likewise i. can give expression in its own proper medium, which is art. Nowhere, perhaps, in contemporary aesthetics are so many of the past findings on the i. critically examined and, if they survive the test, built into a coherent theory of art.

REFERENCES AND BIBLIOGRAPHY BY NUMBERED PARAGRAPHS (1–6) M. W. Bundy, Theory of I. in Classical and Mediaeval Thought (1927); (2) Plato, Republic 10 (595–608), Phaedrus (245, 247, 250–51), Philebus (38–40), Timaeus (70–71); (3) Aristotle, De Anima 3.3–8 (427–31); (4) Plotinus, Enneads, as in Bundy ch. 6; (5) Quintilian, Institutio Oratoria 6.2.29–32, 10.7.15; Longinus, On the Sublime 35; Philostratus, Life of Apollonius 6.19; (6) St. Augustine, Epistles 6,7; Bundy ch. 9; (7–12) L. P. Smith, "Four Romantic Words," Words and Idioms (1925); J. W. Bray, Hist. of Eng. Crit. Terms (1898); A. S. P. Woodhouse, "Collins and the Creative I.," Studies in Eng., ed. M. W. Wallace (1931), "Romanticism and the Hist. of Ideas," Eng. Studies Today, ed. C. L. Wrenn and G. Bullough (1951); G. Williamson, "Restoration Revolt against Enthusiasm," SP, 30 (1933); R. S. Crane, "Eng. Neoclassical Crit.," Critics and Crit. (1952); D. Bond, " 'Distrust of I.' in Eng. Neoclassicism," PQ, 14 (1935), "Neoclassical Psychology of the I.," ELH, 4 (1937); W. J. Bate, "Sympathetic I. in 18th C. Eng. Crit.," ELH, 12 (1945); W. J. Bate and J. Bullitt, "Distinctions between Fancy and I.," MLN, 60 (1945); (7) Puttenham, Arte of Eng. Poesie; Bacon, Advancement of Learning, Descriptio Globi Intellectualis, De Augmentis Scientiarum 2.1.13, 5.1; Bundy, " 'Invention' and 'I.' in the Renaissance," JEGP, 29 (1930), "Bacon's True Opinion of Poetry," SP, 27 (1930); (8) Hobbes, Answer to Davenant, Leviathan 1.2–3,8; C. D. Thorpe, Aesthetic of Thomas Hobbes (1940); (9) Addison, Spectator, nos. 411–21; C. D. Thorpe, "Addison's Theory of the I.," Papers of the Michigan Acad. of Science etc., 21 (1935); (10) Young, Conjectures on Original Composition; Reynolds, Discourses, Notes to Mason's tr. of Du Fresnoy; J. Warton, Essay on Pope, Ode to Fancy; H. Home, Lord Kames, Elements of

Crit.; Alison, *Essays on Taste;* (11) Hume, *Treatise of Human Nature;* Adam Smith, *Theory of the Moral Sentiments;* Gerard, *Essay on Genius;* Duff, *Essay on Original Genius;* Blackwell, *Enquiry concerning Homer;* Blair, *Lectures on Rhetoric;* Vico, *Scienza Nuova* (tr. T. C. Bergin, M. H. Fisch, 1948); D. Stewart, *Philos. of the Mind* 1.3, 5, 8; (12) Dryden, Preface to *Annus Mirabilis, Parallel of Poetry and Painting;* Collins, *Ode on the Poetical Character;* Shaftesbury (3d Earl), "Advice to an Author" (in his *Characteristics*); Muratori, *Della Perfetta Poesia Italiana;* J. G. Robertson, *Studies in the Genesis of Romantic Theory* (1923; ch. 3). (13–18) Wellek; Woodhouse, "Romanticism and the Hist. of Ideas" (above); Abrams; (13) Blake, Letter to Trussler, Aug. 23, 1799, *Milton, Ghost of Abel, Marginalia to Wordsworth, Vision of the Last Judgment* (in *Descriptive Catalogue*); (14) Kant, *Critique of Pure Reason* (tr. N. K. Smith), *Critique of Aesthetic Judgment* (tr. J. C. Meredith); E. L. Fackenheim, "Schelling's Philos. of the Lit. Arts," *Philos. Quart.,* 4 (1954); (15–17) Coleridge, *Biographia Literaria* (ed. J. W. Shawcross), *Poesy or Art, Lay Sermon, Table Talk;* Wordsworth, Preface to *Poems* (1815), *Prelude* (esp. Bk. 14); (18) Hazlitt, "Poetry in General" (*Lectures on Eng. Poets*); Hunt, *What is Poetry?;* Shelley, *Defence of Poetry;* Joubert, *Pensées;* (19) Ruskin, *Modern Painters* 3.1.15.2–3; 3.2.1–4 (and see Index); Arnold, "Pagan and Mediaeval Religious Sentiment" (*Essay in Crit.,* 1st ser.); G. H. Lewes, *Principles of Success in Lit.,* ch. 3; (20) I. Babbitt, *Rousseau and Romanticism* (1919); I. A. Richards, *Principles of Lit. Crit.* (1924) and *Coleridge on Imagination* (1934); (21) Croce, *Aesthetic* (tr. D. Ainslie, 1922); (22) R. G. Collingwood, *Principles of Art* (1938).   A.S.P.W.

IMAGISM refers to a concept of poetry associated with a school or movement that flourished between 1912 and 1917. Neither the theory nor the school, however, is clear enough in outline to justify confident, satisfactory definition, and i. can only be discussed after this concession has been made.

In 1912 appear Ezra Pound's first recorded references to it and, in the appendix to *Ripostes,* his somewhat archly allusive comment that established its associations with T. E. Hulme. The next year he and F. S. Flint further publicized the school through articles in *Poetry: A Magazine of Verse,* and in 1914 Pound brought out *Des Imagistes: An Anthology.* By this time, however, his interest had declined, and Amy Lowell displaced him as leader of the group. Under her leadership anthologies called *Some Imagist Poets* were published for the three years 1915–17, but by 1917 she felt that the movement had run its

effective course. Her first two anthologies contained prefaces which, along with the *Poetry* articles, constitute the most deliberate statements of imagist theory and which stand therefore as its manifestoes.

The poems of the anthologies are at least a partial illustration of those principles that can be isolated from the manifestoes. Though they may appear to have merely casual relation to Pound's definition of the Image, they place their values in clarity, exactness or concreteness of detail, if only through their preoccupation with the objective world; in economy of language and brevity of treatment; in an organic basis for the selection of rhythmic patterns. Poems and manifestoes, together with isolated opinions expressed in print by poets who contributed to one or another of the anthologies, come to a definition of i. that might be stated in this way: a belief in the short poem, structured by the single image or metaphor and a rhythm of cadences, presenting for direct apprehension by the reader an object or scene from the external world, and refusing to implicate the poem's effect in extended abstract meaning. Thus H. D.'s *Oread:*

Whirl up, sea—
Whirl your pointed pines,
Splash your great pines
On our rocks,
Hurl your green over us,
Cover us with your pools of fir.

Working from this basis, but realizing that individual poems, except for a few like *Oread,* or Pound's *In a Station of the Metro,* or some of the imitations of Japanese forms, seldom satisfy all of these requirements, it is possible to see i. as an experiment toward the rejuvenation of the language of poetry, a reaction against the flabby, abstract language and structure into which poetry of the 19th c. had degenerated. As such it has parallels with, for example, the romantic reaction a century earlier against the poetic diction of degenerate neoclassicism, and its concentration on the object and the realistic bias which accompanies this recall similar strictures in Wordsworth's *Preface* to the *Lyrical Ballads.*

In its concern with technique and its restriction of meaning, however, it belongs with more nearly contemporary developments which reflect poetry's attempt to redefine its values in resistance to the pressures of science. It is a stage in the growth of a formalist aesthetic beginning with Poe, finding expression in the reticent commentary of Mallarmé, and culminating in the "new criticism." Pound's insistence upon recharging the word and the general agreement upon the immediacy of effect that arises from close association of word and object are in part a program for improving the craft of writing. Taken with the rejection of "message" as an integral part of the poem, however, they lead in the direction of an emphasis upon writing as an art distinct in its medium and justified by it.

It is in the theory of T. E. Hulme that the movement seems most modern. Here the poem is a moment of discovery or awareness, created by effective metaphor which provides the sharp, intuitive insight that is the essence of life. The quality of this insight, marked by irony, the imagists were scarcely aware of; but through Hulme and its own allusions to the image, the movement drew attention to a metaphorical or analogical basis for structure, as well as to a concept of form that was the basis for the symbolism of Mallarmé and the poetics of Eliot, Richards, Ransom, and others. Since imagist form is reducible to style or technique and since i., in its concern with surfaces, light and color, has links with impressionism, it is not wholly to be associated with formalism. At the same time, this is the gist of Pound's theory. The general trend of the movement toward encouraging formal experimentation, especially with image and metaphor, is probably more significant than the occasional instances of its direct influence on the work of poets like Eliot, Crane, and Stevens. For Russian i. see RUSSIAN POETRY.

E. Pound, *Ripostes* (1912), "A Few Don'ts by an Imagiste," *Poetry*, 1 (1913), "Affirmations," *The New Age*, 16 (1915), "This Hulme Business," *The Townsman*, 2 (1939), *The Letters of Ezra Pound*, ed. D. D. Paige (1950); F. S. Flint, "Imagisme," *Poetry*, 1 (1913) and "The History of I.," *The Egoist*, 2 (1915); R. Aldington, "Modern Poetry and the Imagists," *The Egoist*, 1 (1914); T. E. Hulme, *Speculations*, ed. H. Read (1924), *Notes on Language and Style*, ed. H. Read (1930), *Further Speculations*, ed. S. Hynes (1955); R. Taupin, *L'Influence du symbolisme français sur la poésie am.* (1929); M. Roberts, *T. E. Hulme* (1938); S. K. Coffman, I. (1951); H. Kenner, *The Poetry of Ezra Pound* (1951); W. C. Pratt, *The Imagist Poem* (1963). s.k.c.

IMITATION. Until very recently, when it was restored to the critical vocabulary by Francis Fergusson, Kenneth Burke, and members of the "Chicago school" (see also Auerbach's *Mimesis*), "i." had been out of favor as a literary term since the 18th c. Its eclipse began with the critical stirrings that led the way to romanticism, when "i." was more and more felt to be out of keeping with the new spirit of spontaneity and self-expression. Its revival today is associated with other manifestations of a reaction against romanticism, a tendency to adopt a more objective view of the poet's relation to his subject.

"I." the Latin *imitatio*, is a translation of Gr. *mimesis*. The original connotation of the latter seems to have been dramatic or quasi-dramatic (see MIMESIS). Whether any theory of poetry as i. was developed before Plato is uncertain. Gorgias's notion of tragedy as a "beneficent deception" (*apate*) perhaps anticipated it in part; and Democritus certainly held that the arts in general arose out of imitation of nature: singing, for example, from imitation of the birds. But the first place where we can actually grasp *mimesis* as a critical term is Plato's *Republic*, Books 3 and 10. In Book 3, however, the context is political and pedagogical rather than merely literary. Plato's concern there is with the education of his élite corps of Guards, and he judges poetry strictly by that criterion. "I." is identified almost exclusively with the dramatic mode: i.e., with the direct impersonation of literary characters. This involves an identification of oneself with others which is perilous for the young; it may lead them away from their best selves to an indiscriminate i. of low and unworthy persons. Hence poetry, but especially the drama, must be banished from the professional education of the ideal ruler. In Book 10 Plato renews his attack on a broader front. I. is now identified as the method of *all* poetry, and of the visual arts as well. The poet, like the painter, is incapable of doing more than counterfeit the external appearance of things; Truth, the realm of Ideas, is inaccessible to him. In this second discussion (perhaps written later) Plato's attention has shifted from the method of i. to its object, and i.—i.e., art—is condemned not merely for its moral effects but because it cannot break through the surface of Appearance to the reality it ought to reproduce, the Ideas.

This crushing verdict upon "i." does not result, as we might expect, in banishing the term from Plato's world of discourse; on the contrary, it permeates his thinking more and more in the later dialogues. In the *Sophist* (236) he hints at the possibility of a "true i.," which would reproduce the real nature and proportions of its object. Indeed Plato came to think of the whole complex relation of Becoming to Being, Particular to Idea, as a kind of i. Thus the *Timaeus* (27ff.) presents the universe itself as a work of art, an "image" of the world of Ideas made by a divine craftsman. From this it is only a step to conceiving visual art, and then poetry, as a sensuous embodiment of the ideal. The Neoplatonists (see Plotinus, *Enneads* 5.8, and cf. Cicero, *Orator* 2.8–9) took this step, but Plato himself did not. The condemnation of poetry in the *Republic* was never explicitly revised or withdrawn (it is substantially repeated in the *Laws*, Books 2 and 7), and the developments just mentioned remain hints (highly fruitful ones for later thought) rather than a new positive doctrine of poetic i.

Aristotle accepts i. (*Poetics*, ch. 4) as a fundamental human instinct—an *intellectual* instinct —of which poetry is one manifestation, along with music, painting, and sculpture. His real innovation, however, and the cornerstone of his new theory of poetry (see CLASSICAL POETICS), is a redefinition of *mimesis* to mean not a counterfeiting of sensible reality but a presentation of "universals." By "universals" he means (ch. 9) not metaphysical entities like the Platonic Ideas, but simply the permanent, characteristic modes of human thought, feeling, and action. It goes without saying, or at least Aristotle does not bother to say, that knowledge of such universals is not restricted to the philosopher. The poet can represent them, and his readers can grasp them, without benefit of metaphysical training. Poetic i. is of *action* rather than simply of men, i.e., characters. Tragedy (and, with certain reservations, the epic) is an i. of a single, complete, and serious action involving the happiness of an important human being. More specifically, the i. is lodged in the *plot* (*mythos*) of the poem; and by "plot" Aristotle means not merely a sequence but a *structure* of events, so firmly welded together as to form an organic whole. It follows that the poet's most important duty is to shape his plot. He cannot find it already given; whether he starts from mythical tradition, history, or his own invention, he is a poet only so far as he is a builder (*poietes*, "maker") of plots. Thus "i." comes very close to meaning "creation." But the poet's creation is not of some "second nature" existing only in his fancy; it is a valid representation of the actions of men according to the laws of probability or necessity.

Aristotle's concept of i. was subtle and complex. His chief successors in criticism were men of another stamp, more literary than philosophical in their view of poetry. So far as i. remained a key term in the Hellenistic age (actually we do not hear a great deal about it), it seems to have been conceived as meaning the portrayal of standardized human *types:* the hot-headed man, the braggart soldier, the wild Thracian, etc. Aristotle's "probability" (*to eikos, verisimile*), and the even more characteristic concept of "appropriateness" (*to prepon, decorum*), are now tailored to the measure of particular social standards and conventions more than to any permanent principles of human nature. At the same time Aristotle's insistence on action gives way to more relaxed and eclectic views: the object of i. may be character, thought, or even natural phenomena. Anything can be imitated, in accordance with the laws of the *genre* one has chosen,

and the object, whether fable, fact, or fiction, is tacitly assumed to have more or less the same status as a natural object (see CLASSICAL POETICS).

Alongside the Aristotelian concept of i., thus denatured, another of very different provenience—and still easier to understand—took on increasing importance in the Hellenistic and Roman periods. This was the relatively simple idea of imitating the established "classics" (the word is Roman, the concept Gr.), the great models of achievement in each *genre*. Its origin was rhetorical (see CLASSICAL POETICS), but it ended by spreading impartially over prose and poetry. The treatise of Dionysius of Halicarnassus *On Imitation* is lost except for fragments, but we can get some idea of the theme from the second chapter of Book 10 of Quintilian's *Institutio Oratoria*. From these two authors, and more particularly from "Longinus" (see SUBLIME), we can see that the doctrine had its higher side. I. of the great writers of the past need not and should not be merely a copying of devices of arrangement and style, but a passionate emulation of their spirit. Dryden (in the *Essay of Dramatic Poesy*) puts it very well: "Those great men whom we propose to ourselves as patterns of our imitation, serve us as a torch, which is lifted up before us, to illumine our passage and often elevate our thoughts as high as the conception we have of our author's genius." Here i. is united with its apparent opposite, inspiration. Nevertheless, both in antiquity and in the Renaissance, i. in the sense of emulation of models meant chiefly stylistic i., and thus helped to fortify the prevalent understanding of poetry as an art of words.

The Renaissance inherited at least three major concepts of i. from antiquity: (1) the Platonic: a copying of sensuous reality, (2) the Aristotelian: a representation of the universal patterns of human behavior, and of an action embodying these, and (3) the Hellenistic and rhetorical: i. of canonized literary models. But each of these was further complicated by a deviation or variant interpretation: (1) the Platonic by the Neoplatonic suggestion that the artist can create according to a true Idea, (2) the Aristotelian by the vulgarization of Aristotle's "universals" into particular social types belonging to a particular place or time, and (3) the rhetorical by its rather adventitious association with "enthusiasm" and the *furor poeticus* (a good example is Vida's *Ars Poetica* 2.422–444). That this mixed inheritance did not lead to complete critical chaos was due partly to the chronological accident that the *Poetics* did not become known in Italy until well after 1500 (see CLASSICAL POETICS, sec. 8), partly to the incorrigible syncretism of the humanists, which refused to give up any part of the ancient tradition but insisted on blending it into a new amalgam, and partly to the plain fact that the chief literary creed and inspiration of the It. Renaissance was rhetorical. Humanism was an imitative movement in its very root and essence: the i. of classical, particularly classical Latin, literature was its life-blood. Thus the burning question in the 15th c., and well into the 16th, was not What is imitation? or Should we imitate? but Whom (i.e., which classical author or authors) should we imitate? The fiercest battle was waged over prose style, i.e., over the question whether Cicero should be the sole and all-sufficient model for L. prose or others such as Sallust, Livy, Seneca, Tacitus might be admitted also. Lorenzo Valla spoke to this issue in a spirit of enlightened Ciceronianism, in his *De Elegantiis Linguae Latinae* (between 1435 and 1444) and about seventy years later (1512) we find Gianfranco Pico della Mirandola, nephew of the more famous Count Giovanni, and the learned Pietro Bembo (later secretary to Leo X, and Cardinal) debating it once more, with references to a previous controversy between Cortesius and Politian (cf. the latter's *Epistles*). Pico takes the eclectic side, Bembo the Ciceronian, as Politian and Cortesius had done before them. The Ciceronian squabble was more or less ended by Erasmus's *Ciceronianus* (1528). Alongside it ran a similar but less acrimonious dispute over poetic i., centering around Virgil and ending in his canonization by Vida (1527) and Scaliger (1561) as the supreme poet and perfect model.

Meanwhile an issue of more theoretical, or at least of more general, interest was presented by the perennial need for a *defense of poetry* against doctrinal and moral objections from the side of the Church. In this struggle it was only natural that Plato's indictment of poetry as mere i. should be pressed into service by the attackers, e.g., by Savonarola in his *De Divisione ac Utilitate Omnium Scientiarum* (1492), while on the other side "Platonic"—actually Neoplatonic—ideas of poetry as a showing forth of Truth and Beauty made their appearance on the other side. The younger Pico (see above) invoked such ideas in his plea for a broad view of "i."

A genuine theoretical interest in the concept of poetic i. as such could not arise, however, until Aristotle's *Poetics* had come to light again and begun to be studied: that is, until after the first quarter or third of the 16th c. Vida's *Art of Poetry* (1527) is still innocent of this new trend. It preaches the i. of "nature" (2.455: *nil conarier artem, Naturam nisi ut assimulet propiusque sequatur*), but for no other real purpose than to inculcate the i. of the ancient poets, above all Virgil, who fol-

lowed her to the best advantage (*hanc unam vates sibi proposuere magistram*). Daniello (*Poetica*, 1536) knows Aristotle's definition of tragedy as i., but hardly knows what to make of it, since he draws only a faltering distinction between poetry and history. Robortelli, in his commentary on the *Poetics* (1548), allows the poet to invent things that transcend nature. Fracastoro (*Naugerius, sive de Poeta Dialogus*, 1555) pieces out Aristotle's concept of i. with the Platonic idea of beauty, identifying the latter with the universal. Scaliger (1561) recommended the i. of Virgil because Virgil had created a "second nature" more beautiful than the first; and Boileau gave the problem its definitive formulation for neoclassical theory: the surest way to imitate nature is to imitate the classics. But the real difficulty and challenge of Aristotle's idea of i. had not been grasped, much less solved. The later Renaissance was as unable as the earlier to make an effective distinction between poetry and history on the one hand, and between poetry and rhetoric on the other, because it could not seize and define any true "universal" as the object of poetic i., except in vague Platonic (Neoplatonic) terms, and so fell back into regarding poetry as essentially a special way of discoursing about "things." As for the treatises *De Imitatione* penned by humanists north of the Alps in the 16th c.—Camerarius (1560), Sturmius (1574), Ascham's discussion of the subject in the *Scholemaster* (1570)—they belong almost entirely to the history of L. pedagogy, not to criticism.

Although i. was implicitly accepted down through the 18th c. as the goal and method of the fine arts in general, including poetry and painting, it began to slip into disrepute after 1770, being felt more and more to imply a derogation of the artist's integrity. Edward Young sneered at "the meddling ape, Imitation," and Coleridge opined that "To admire on principle, is the only way to imitate without loss of originality." The revival of "i." in our own day (see first paragraph above) has very little to do with either the classical or the neoclassical tradition; it goes straight to Aristotle, not through intermediaries, and views i. above all as a structural concept, the principle of organization of poetic wholes.

S. H. Butcher, *Aristotle's Theory of Poetry and Fine Art*, ch. 2 (4th ed., 1911; suggestive, but overmodernizes A.); U. Galli, "La mimèsi artistica secondo Aristotele," *Studi Ital. di Filol. Class.*, n.s., 4 (1926), comprehensive, covers Plato also; J. Tate, " 'I.' in Plato's *Republic*," CQ, 22 (1928) and "Plato and 'I.,' " CQ, 26 (1932); R. McKeon, "Lit. Crit. and the Concept of I. in Antiquity," MP, 34 (1936), enlightening survey, and "I. and Poetry," in *Thought, Action and Passion* (1954); W. J. Verdenius, *Mimesis:*

Plato's Doctrine of Artistic I. and its Meaning for Us (1949; prudent, well documented); F. Fergusson, *The Idea of a Theater* (1949), esp. ch. 1 and Appendix; K. Burke, "A 'Dramatistic' View of 'I.,'" *Accent*, 12 (1952); Auerbach; H. Koller, *Die Mimesis in der Antike* (1954; ambitious but unreliaƀle); G. F. Else, *Aristotle's Poetics: the Argument* (1957) and "'I.' in the 5th C.," cp, 53 (1958). See also ORIGINALITY.   G.F.E.

IMPRESSIONISM. The term i. is commonly said to have been derived from Claude Monet's painting *Impression: Soleil Levant* first exhibited in Paris in 1874. Monet, Sisley, and Pissarro (the chief representatives of the impressionistic school of painting) sought to capture the fleeting impression of the moment by means of pure spectral colors, which they applied to the canvas in small, irregular brush strokes. When viewed from the proper distance, these dabs were to merge in the observer's eye. Scorning the use of local color, the impressionists wanted to record the light as it is reflected from objects through the air surrounding them. In their paintings, all outlines are blurred and all formal values slighted. But around 1885 a new interest in form was already aroused under the impact of Seurat's pictorial divisionism (pointillism). In the impressionistic tone ' poems of Claude Debussy, emphasis is laid on the tone color and the overlapping of melodic fragments (vibration) rather than on rhythmical progression.

It is no easy task to define i. in literature, let alone in poetry. Hermann Bahr spoke of it as subjective naturalism and defined it by saying that, in it, the naturalistic *états de choses* have been replaced by the corresponding *états d'âme*. In prose literature, the works of the brothers Goncourt are generally regarded as impressionistic. The impressionist poets, like their fellow painters, desired to capture the fleeting impression at the very moment in which sensations are transformed into feelings. On the whole, their art is strictly nonintellectual and—if carried to the extreme—defies all rational explanation. It scorns logical progression and relies on the unpredictable movement which is effected by mental associations. Here, too, outlines are blurred, forms dissolved and images stillborn. Instead of naming the thing he is concerned with, the impressionist describes the effect which it produces. As the observer disappears, the organs of sense perception are confused (synaesthesia), and the poet turns into a medium through whose nervous system sensations and indistinct feelings communicate (Mallarmé's "céder l'initiative au verbe"). Impressionistic poetry aspires in general to the condition of music, but never attains it, since words are in themselves

symbols and have rarely direct access to the world of our senses. A poem composed of words that have an established meaning simply cannot be regarded as an abstract symphony of moods, since to regard it as such would mean to negate the very properties by which language is distinguished from other modes of expression.

Perhaps there is no better way of defining the limits of poetic i. than to study its relation to other types of poetry which are sometimes mentioned in connection with it. As for its affinity to symbolism (q.v.), one can only agree with Ruth Moser that "en littérature, le symbolisme et l'impressionisme se servent, en partie, des mêmes formes d'expression." The main difference would seem to lie in the impressionists' negative attitude toward the symbol. The symbol, after all, carries with it the suggestion of meaning; and there is nothing the impressionist dreads more than an epistemological interpretation of the sense data he has assembled. In that sense, Verlaine's *Art Poétique* may be called a manifesto of poetic i., whereas the poetry of Baudelaire, Mallarmé, and Valéry is more concerned with the intellectual. A similar discrepancy exists between poetic i. and imagism (q.v.); for while the impressionist denies the existence of clearly circumscribed forms, the imagist aims at producing poetry that is "hard and clear, never blurred or indefinite." And whereas the impressionist joyfully immerses himself in the stream of life and consciousness, the imagist, lifting the fleeting impression out of the flux, transforms it into an "emotional and intellectual complex" (Pound). However, since poetic theory is one thing and poetic practice another, we can discover much that is impressionistic in the poetry of the imagists Amy Lowell and John Gould Fletcher. Although the impressionist creed is opposed to the cult of form indulged in by Stefan George and his circle, the early volumes of George's *Blätter für die Kunst* contain many a statement that conforms with the tenets of genuine *Eindruckskunst*. And along with Hofmannsthal's *Vorfrühling*, George's *Komm' in den totgesagten Park und schau* offers the best example of i. in German poetry.

While there is little use in speaking of an impressionistic school of poetry in Fr. or Anglo-Am. literature, German literary historians are unanimous in designating Detlev von Liliencron (1844–1909) as the leader of a school which also includes Richard Dehmel (the naturalistic aspect of his poetry excepted), Max Dauthendey, Gustav Falke, and a number of minor poets. Many of these German impressionists, however, rely all too heavily on the use of onomatopoeia and of slang or dialect. Theirs seems to be a poetry in which the

IMPRESSIONISTIC CRITICISM

naturalistic technique of imitation has been most radically exploited. In spite of the typographical idiosyncrasies which are embedded in them (notably the consistent use of the so-called *Mittelachse*), the poems contained in the original version of Arno Holz's *Phantasus* come much closer to fulfilling the conditions we have set up for a truly impressionistic poetry.

H. Bahr, *Die Überwindung des Naturalismus* (1891); R. Hamann, *Der Impressionismus in Leben und Kunst* (1907); L. Thon, *Die Sprache des deutschen I.* (1928); A. Burkhard, "The Language of Detlev von Liliencron's Lyrics and Ballads," JEGP, 30 (1931); Ch. Bally *et al.*, *El Impressionismo en el Lenguaje* (1936); D. W. Schumann, "Detlev von Liliencron," *Monatshefte*, 36 (1944); R. Moser, *L'Impressionisme français* (1951); B. J. Gibbs, "I. as a Literary Movement," MLJ, 36 (1952); H. Sommerhalder, *Zum Begriff des literarischen Impressionismus* (1961). U.W.

IMPRESSIONISTIC CRITICISM. See CRITICISM, TYPES OF.

IN MEDIAS RES (L. "into the middle of things"). A common way of opening an epic, a drama, or a work of fiction. The author chooses as his beginning some crucial situation in the middle of a series of related events which will begin a chain of incidents and at the same time be the result of preceding ones. Thus he may work forward and backward in time to narrate his story or action. The effect is to arouse the reader's suspense and interest. In his advice to the young poet, Horace in the *Ars Poetica* 148–150 gives perhaps the *locus classicus* of this point: "semper ad eventum festinat et in medias res / non secus ac notas auditorem rapit, et quae / desperat tractata nitescere posse relinquit" (Always he [the poet] hastens to the outcome and plunges his hearer into the midst of events as though they were familiar, and what he despairs of treating effectively he abandons). R.A.H.

IN MEMORIAM STANZA. So called from its use in Tennyson's *In Memoriam*. A stanza of 4 lines of iambic tetrameter, rhyming abba:

I hold it true, whate'er befall;
 I feel it when I sorrow most;
 'Tis better to have loved and lost
Than never to have loved at all.
(*In Memoriam*, 27)

Although Tennyson believed he had invented the stanza, it may be found in earlier poetry, notably in that of Ben Jonson (*If Beauty be the Mark of Praise*), Lord Herbert of Cherbury (*Ode upon a Question Moved, whether Love Should Continue for ever*). It is true however, that Tennyson exploited the inherent formal capacities of the stanza with a greater mastery than did his predecessors. In particular, he utilized its suitability for successive, mutually independent philosophical observations, each enclosed within its "envelope" of stanzaic pattern; and its possibilities for special emphasis through the rhyme of first and fourth lines. Later uses of the stanza are rare. An interesting example is Oscar Wilde's *The Sphinx*, in which the stanza is printed as 2 lines.—H. Corson, *Primer of Eng. Verse* (1892); E. P. Morton, "The Stanza of I. M.," MLN, 21 (1906) and "Poems in the Stanza of I. M.," MLN, 24 (1909); Baum; Hamer.

INCA POETRY. See AMERICAN INDIAN POETRY. SOUTH AMERICA.

INCANTATION (L. "to consecrate with charms or spells"). The use of a formula of words, spoken or chanted, to produce magical effect or charm; more generally, use of magical ceremonies, sorcery, enchantment: "With nigromaunce he wolde assaile To make his incantacion" (Gower, *Confessio Amantis* 3.45). Also, the magical spell, usually a poem, itself: "Double, double, toil and trouble . . ." (Shakespeare, *Macbeth*). Sometimes the term refers to any verses intended to be sung or chanted. Incantation is common in primitive literatures, e.g., Am. Indian, Eskimo, Negro poetry. See also SOUND IN POETRY. R.O.E.

INCREMENTAL REPETITION. A phrase coined by F. B. Gummere to describe a rhetorical device peculiar to Eng. and Scottish folk ballads. In i.r. a line or stanza is repeated several times with some small but material substitution at the same crucial spot. A sequence of such repetition accounts for the entire structure of some few ballads, among them *Lord Randal* and *Edward*. More usually, however, i.r. spans a passage of only 3 or 4 stanzas, and it is frequently confined to the lines of a single quatrain, as in the following stanza from *Sir Hugh; or, The Jew's Daughter:*

Then out and came the thick, thick blood,
 Then out and came the thin;
Then out and came the bonny heart's blood,
 Where all the life lay in.

Suspense is the principal effect achieved by this device, for with each iteration and its substituted element, tension mounts until the climactic substitution, which resolves the pattern, is reached. Gummere interpreted i.r. as another proof of the choric origins of traditional balladry; he argued that it was a certain test of what was and was not a ballad. More recent ballad theorists, like Louise

–[382]–

Pound and G. H. Gerould, hold that i.r. is generally rhetorical not structural and that it is not a determining characteristic of the orally transmitted traditional ballad.—I.r. is elaborately illustrated throughout F. B. Gummere, *The Popular Ballad* (1904, 1907), esp. pp. 117-24. For pugnacious crit. of Gummere, see L. Pound, *Poetic Origins and the Ballad* (1921), pp. 121-35. G. H. Gerould, *The Ballad of Tradition* (1932), pp. 105-10, arbitrates the dispute. A.B.F.

INDIAN POETICS. The Vedic Seers, being self-conscious poets, made observations on their art: they spoke of Speech being refined in their intellects, as flour in a sieve, being imparted beauty and fitted into measured lines, even as chiseled pieces of wood into a chariot. The Muse they said chose to yield herself to the elect, even as a wife to her husband. It was in a state of afflatus, a magnification of personality, that they uttered their hymns with which they established rapport with the Gods they adored. The Vedic Seer-poet was called *Rishi* and *Kavi*, "Seer" and "Maker," which as the 10th-c. Kashmirian critic Tota explained, emphasized that poetry depended both on vision and expression. The hymn was also called *Rasa*, "essence or most delectable thing," and the Upanishad said that what was well done and perfect was indeed the most delectable thing (*Rasa*). Here can be seen the concept of *Rasa* which later became the core of Ind. aesthetics.

In the epics there is mention of literary qualities like sweetness, beauty, richness of thought, and the power to make the past live through the graphic narrative. The Rāmāyana has a story of its origin in which the epic states that it was emotion (*Rasa*), pathos in its case, that became poetry.

The earliest and fullest surviving treatise on theory is Bharata's *Nātya Śāstra* which deals with dramaturgy in all its aspects and includes topics of poetics, language, meter, figures of speech, literary flaws, stylistic qualities, and above all, the emotions (*Rasas*) without which, Bharta said, nothing stirred in a drama. The story of a play was minutely analyzed and five elements, stages, and junctures were established for the gradual unfolding of the plot. Similarly, character-types were also studied and ten types of drama were described; but all these were to subserve the main purpose of evoking emotional response. Of emotions, eight or nine were emphasized: Love, Heroism, Pathos, Laughter, and so on. Each *Rasa* developed from a basic mood which inhered in all human hearts as a permanent instinct and was fed by a number of minor feelings—longing, despondency, envy, etc.—common to more than one mood. When the hero and heroine or the hero and his adversary presented the effects of their emotions, the corresponding emotion in the spectator's heart was stimulated in a pleasurable manner. Bharata stated that the best spectator was one who could enter into the play and feel glad when the character is joyous and sad when he is sorrow-stricken. Bharata defined drama as Imitaton, or as his commentator Abhjnavagupta explained, as Representation, of men and women in different actions and states of feeling.

Poetics developed out of the theories of Bharata, but the early rhetoricians held that the emotions primarily pertained to drama, and in poetry which was narrative, they could be brought out only indirectly through description. Bhāmaha and Dandin (ca. 700 A.D.), as also Vāmana (ca. 800), defined poetry as Word and Sense in unison and endowed with beauty: this beauty was the result of the choice of proper words and constructions, avoidance of literary flaws, addition of stylistic qualities and figures of sound and sense and emotions. The emotions too, they said, went to embellish only the expression in poetry, and hence these ancient critics who emphasized "Form" could be styled "Expressionists."

But in the beginning of the 9th c. A.D. the idea began to gain ground that emotions were the center of appeal in poems also, and soon there appeared in Kashmir the foremost Ind. aesthete Ānandavardhana (9th c.) who unified criticism by taking drama and poetry together and applied to all forms of literary expression —play, poem, lyric, and stray verse—the same principles of analysis and evaluation. Taking his stand on emotion, which he reemphasized as the soul of poetry, he directed his main inquiry to the intriguing question of how this emotion was conveyed by the text of the poem and realized by the reader or spectator. Obviously the express mention of an emotion could not evoke an emotional response. Emotional experience could not be part of the direct meaning of words and sentences, nor of their secondary significance. Between the text and the emotions, the only possible relation is suggestion, manifestation, or revelation—*Dhvani, Vyanjanā, Prakāśa*. Suggestion is a unique process and could be employed even in realms where the primary or secondary capacities of words were enough to convey an idea. Even figures could be rendered more attractive by suggestion; in fact, suggestion added a new dimension to speech, and reinforced the power of the limited medium of language. It was by the symbolism of suggestion that even the message of a whole work was conveyed by the poet. Ānandavardhana thus emphasized content or emotion as against formal features, style, figures, etc.—all of which he put in a subordinate place. The formal features were to be evaluated as good or bad, not by themselves, but in relation to the emotion which they were to suggest, and this relative value of expression called *Auchitya* (adaptation or appropriateness) was developed by Kshemendra (11th c.) as a life-giving complement to the principle of emotional suggestiveness.

There was still the moot question: How could the emotion of one, the actor and character, be relished by another, the spectator; for in life, one's emotion produces diverse and disparate reactions among the onlookers. Another eminent Kashmirian critic of the 10th-c., Nāyaka, offered the solution that in poetry the artistic medium generalized or universalized or abstracted the emotion from its contextual references, and this enabled the emotion as such, not as the emotion of a particular person and situation, to touch the corresponding emotion in the spectator's heart. Nāyaka did not accept Suggestion as all-in-all in poetry, though he accepted it as one of the many resources at the command of the poetic genius. He and his younger contemporary Kuntaka emphasized the unique *way* (*kavi-vyāpāra*) of the poet's genius as the basic principle in poetry. Comparing poetic expression with law and scripture on one hand, and story and news on the other, Nāyaka said that in the former the letter mattered; in the latter, the substance alone mattered; in poetry the *way* a thing was said or conveyed was all-in-all.

Abhinavagupta, the outstanding Kashmirian philosopher and critic (ca. A.D. 1000), accepted Nāyaka's theory of universalization (*sādhāranī-karana*) of emotion and pointed out that aesthetic experience was a unique category, unlike any of the known epistemological processes—sense-perception, inference, remembrance, etc. It manifested itself on the presentation of the artistic stimulus which conditioned its duration; it was a cycle which started with the poet and the poem and completed itself in the heart of the connoisseur who had become, by constant literary activity, attuned to the poet and was hence called *Sa-hridaya*, "one of the same heart." Aesthetic enjoyment is not a joy in any mundane sense, for it is a repose of the heart. It is the equilibrium, the peace and poise of the soul, which is constantly disturbed by worldly preoccupations and which the artistic experience restores for the nonce. Adopting more clearly the view of Self according to Sankara's philosophy, Jagannātha (17th c.) clarified this theory of aesthetic bliss as the manifestation of the inner light and bliss of the Self when the encrustations obscuring it are broken down by the impact of art. He accordingly defined poetry as expression in a verbal medium whose contemplation results in a supramundane bliss-

fulness. This has been the prevailing mode of criticism ever since; but in the 11th c. A.D. the royal polymath, King Bhoja of Dhar, propounded an out-of-the-way theory that the inner sublimated Ego or Self-consciousness or Self-love of men is *Rasa* or Emotion par excellence and that it is not only the basis of all other namable emotions, but lies at the root of all creative art and higher cultural activity.

The poetic theories of Sanskrit, the figures, styles, and *Rasa* served as poetic theory for all the Ind. literatures. *Rasa*, like *Dharma*, is one of the key-words of Ind. culture, characterizing its aesthetic side. Modern writers of India have used the terms of Eng. criticism, but the more authentic voices like Tagore reemphasized the traditional approach, expressing emphatically their Vedantic orientation, viz., that aesthetic joy is a foretaste of spiritual realization and that all art is thus a spiritual aid (*sādhana*). At the same time, it may be noted that echoes of the Ind. theories of Suggestion and *Rasa* are evident in the writings of Western critics like Abercrombie, Richards and Eliot.

R. Tagore, *Creative Unity* (1925), *Sadhana* (1926), and *Personality* (1926); V. Raghavan, *The Number of Rasas* (1940), *Studies on Some Concepts of the Alankara Sastra* (1942), *Bhoja's Srngara Prakasa* (full ed., 1963); "Sanskrit and Prākṛit Metres," and "Sanskrit Drama and Performance," *Jour.* of the Madras Univ. (Section A., Humanities), 23 (1952–53) and 29 (1957–58); P. J. Chaudhury, "Ind. Poetics," JAAC, 19 (1961); S. K. De, *Sanskrit Poetics as a Study of Aesthetic* (1963). v.R.

INDIAN POETRY. SANSKRIT. Ind. poetry represents a continuous and copious literary activity which, in its time-space sweep, comprehends 4,000 years and about a score of cultivated languages of two major linguistic groups, the Indo-Aryan and the Indo-Dravidian. For 3,000 years, it was predominantly Sanskrit literature, with a subsidiary contribution in the earlier popular forms of Sanskrit, viz., Pāli, Prākrit, and Apabhramśa. The last 1,000 years witnessed the growth of the modern Ind. languages and literatures. A popular devotional and religious literature was the first form for which these regional languages were employed, and along with that adaptations and translations of Sanskrit originals were also produced in them. For higher philosophical and technical literature, the spoken languages looked to Sanskrit which continued to set the norms. To this day, the underlying unity of Ind. literatures is what the common heritage of Sanskrit gives them.

Sanskrit poetry begins with the very first stratum of that language, the *Rigveda*, a collection of poetic hymns sung by sages in praise of deities worshipped by them. The Vedic poet employed meter with skill, added sound effects and end rhymes and gave brilliant descriptions of his deities, many of whom were personifications of natural phenomena, the Sun, the Dawn, the Wind, etc. The Rigvedic poet reveled in figures of comparison and could give graphic natural descriptions and had a gift for bodying forth abstract speculations in sublime words.

The Veda was thus the foundation of Ind. poetry, not merely of Ind. religion and philosophy. The meters of classical Sanskrit were a direct development from the Vedic. In the Vedas, there are also hymns praising patrons and heroic kings, and dialogues, myths, and legends, and in the later portions there are examples of narrative literature. All these supplied the themes for the later literature, the heroic lays sung by bards from which the next important phase of epic poetry, couched in a more popular language, developed. The following description of dawn from the *Rigveda* will illustrate vedic style:

adhi pesāmsi vapate nrtūrivā-

pornute vaksha usreva barjaham /

jyotir visvasmai bhuvanāya krnvatī

gāvo na vrajam vyushā ā vartamah //

Beauteous forms doth She put on like a danseuse;
Her bosom she maketh bare, like unto the milch-cow its udder;
Extending light to the entire universe,
Like unto cows coming to their pen (doth she come back to the East).
Thus hath Dawn dispelled darkness.
(*Rigveda* 1.92.4)

The two great epics of India are the *Rāmāyana* of Vālmīki and the *Mahābhārata* of Vyāsa, which have been, as it were, the two eyes of the nation; with their characters, they have molded the ideals of the whole nation and in their sway over the peoples and the religious movements they gave birth to, they outgrew their pure literary character. The *Rāmāyana* in 24,000 couplets and the *Mahābhārata* in a million couplets, are both composed in the heroic measures *śloka* (*anushtubh*) and *upajāti*. The former shows greater unity of authorship while the latter incorporated into the framework of its main story many ancient lays and edifying dialogues and discourses on ethics or philosophy. Vālmiki, like the Vedic poets, delighted in similes, and among human emotions, he depicted not only the great love of Rāma and Sītā and the poignant suffering undergone by the latter, but also portrayed as leading motifs such emotions as friendship, brotherly love, and, above all, the love of the father for the son. In his hero Rāma, Vālmīki presented an embodiment of truth and righteousness, who could, for the sake of these principles, sacrifice even his dearest. The *Rāmāyana* has been called the first of poems, *Ādi-kāvya*, and truly did Vālmīki lay down the path for the later classical poets, in formal features, in the development of the theme, in the portrayal of character and the delineation of emotion.

Vyāsa depicted in his hero Yudhishthira the same ideal of righteousness; his *Mahābhārata* is the story of the feud and fratricidal war of the cousins Kauravas and Pandavas, through which Vyāsa sought to emphasize the vanity of earthly possessions and the futility of wars on their behalf. Some of the old stories imbedded in this great epic, e.g., of Nala and Damayanti, are superb for their simplicity, grace and pathos; of the many great dialogues and discourses here, that between Lord Krishna and Arjuna on the eve of the battle, the *Bhagavad Gītā*, has today been translated into every language of the world.

The passage from the natural epic to the shorter artificial epic poem is obscured by the loss of the creations of the early classical poets. The two epics supplied the themes and on them poets wrote the major poetic type called the *Mahā-kāvya* extending from 8 to 20 cantos, and the major dramatic type, the *Nāṭaka* in 5 to 10 acts. Side by side with the two epics, the great storehouse of popular stories, fables, and romances, the *Brihatkathā* (Great Story), served as a source for plays and romances. In poetry, there developed the minor variety of short poem, "centuries of verses" on specific descriptive and reflective themes, the prose romance, storybooks, lyrics, gnomic and didactic writings, historical poems, and a genre called *Champū* in which prose and verse were mixed. In drama, there were besides the heroic *Nāṭaka*, the social *Prakarana*, and the graft-type *Nāṭikā*, derived from the above two. There were also nine other varieties of which two were more systematically developed, the farce and the monologue of amour; allegorical and philosophical plays, irregular dramatic compositions, and musical ones done with song and dance were also developed, the last-mentioned category deriving inspiration and material from local folk forms also.

Sanskrit poetry and drama set as its aim the presentation and evocation of emotion or *Rasa* and subordinated character and plot to it. A large variety of striking meters were employed by the poets. Sanskrit language has a rich sonorous music in it and the Sanskrit poet was a past master in making sound echo the sense. In natural descriptions, he was a capable miniature painter. With his Vedantic background he saw the one life pulsating in man, animal, tree, and creeper, and consequently, the integration of man and Nature formed a lining, as it were, to his poetry. In drama, the Sanskrit poet was moved primarily by the ideal of presenting *Rasa*. The most obvious feature of the Sanskrit drama is its bilingualism, which is part of its realistic features, as also its mixture of prose and verse. Unity of time or place was not insisted upon, but unity of emotional impression was zealously safeguarded. In the main scenes, the dramatist concentrated on the dignified, sweet, and emotional aspects of the story and left the rest to be communicated in the interludes. While tragic complication, opposition, and suspense were duly introduced, tragedy as understood in the Gr. or Western sense was not countenanced, for the Ind. attitude did not accept the eventual triumph of evil and held that the play should show virtue as finally victorious. The plays opened with an informative and suggestive prelude which Goethe borrowed in his *Faust*.

Exemplifying the above characteristics, there was vast output of classical Sanskrit poems and plays roughly from about 500 B.C. Many of the early specimens are lost and we have more survivals of early drama than of early poetry. In the 3d c. B.C. the Mauryan minister Subandhu wrote a rather out-of-the-way play, emboxing act within act and combining a romance of King Udayana with a court intrigue. After Subandhu, probably, came Bhāsa who wrote many plays marked by simplicity, without allowing their action to be smothered by poetry. The period between 2d c. B.C. and the 4th c. A.D. is one of unsettled literary chronology, but it was the period when the three foremost Sanskrit poets and dramatists flourished, Kālidāsa, Aśvaghosha, and Śūdraka. Aśvaghosha was a Buddhistic poet who pioneered in harnessing poetry and drama for the service of his new faith; he wrote two poems and a drama on the Buddha.

Kālidāsa was indeed the finest flower of Ind. culture; he was a supreme aesthete who, at the same time, reflected in his works the well-rounded picture of the Ind. attitude and ideals in life, viz., the balanced pursuit of virtue, gain, enjoyment and, above all, the spiritual emancipation for which he prayed as he laid down his pen at the close of his masterpiece, the *Śākuntala*. In depicting love, in which he was the unrivaled master, he employed the idea of separation and suffering and introduced the child also, both as means of purifying and stabilizing love into a lasting spiritual union. It is Kālidāsa's harmonizing of the here and the hereafter that made Goethe speak of the union of heaven and earth, of flower and fruit, in the *Śākuntala*. His style is marked by grace, economy, and suggestiveness. Like the Vedic poets and Valmiki, he is celebrated for his similes. Kālidāsa wrote four poems and three plays. In an early effort of his, the *Ritusamhāra* (Cycle of Seasons), he sang of the six seasons of the year as a descriptive poem and a love lyric. In a second short poem, the *Meghadūta* (Cloud Messenger), a separated lover sends a love message to his far-off beloved through a floating cloud. This lyric is the best tribute to Kālidāsa's originality, inventive skill, and richness of imagination, and the spell which it cast resulted in numberless imitations. The *Raghuvamśa* (The Line of Raghu), on the kings of the Solar dynasty (among whom is God incarnated as Rama), is his longest poem. It is in 19 cantos and reflects all the sides of the poet's mind.

In a shorter poem of 8 cantos, the *Kumārasambhava* (Birth of the (War-Lord) Kumāra), the poet depicts the Father and Mother of the Universe, Siva and Devi, yearning in penance for each other, and thereby gives expression in a unique way to his ideal of sublime love. The poet wrote three plays also: The *Mālavikāgnimitra* (Mālavikā and Agnimitra) is a romance in the harem of King Agnimitra of the Sunga dynasty, full of plot interest and attractive motifs of dance, painting, etc. In his second play, the *Vikramorvaśiya* (Urvasi attained by valor), the poet shows the influence of Nature on a love-lorn heart. Here as well as in his last testament, the dramatic masterpiece *Śākuntala*, the poet introduces separation to chasten love and the child to fasten the tie of love into an inseparable unity. After Kalidasa, all dramas, *Nātikās* or *Nātakas*, follow the *Mālavikāgnimitra* or the *Śākuntala*.

If the *Śākuntala* is the outstanding specimen of an idealistic play, the *Mricchakatika* (Little Clay cart) of Śūdraka is the foremost Ind. achievement in the field of social play. The social play called *Prakarana* holds up the mirror, as it were, to life and features characters drawn from the common classes; it assigns greater place to suffering and tragic developments. Śūdraka brings out the possibilities of this type to the utmost in his production, the most stage-worthy of ancient Ind. plays and most interesting to a modern audience because of the variety of its interest, story, characterization, and humor.

Kālidāsa was followed by two important poets who produced the artificial epic with success: Bhāravi, author of the *Kirātārjunīya* (Siva as a Hunter and Arjuna), and Magha, author of the *Śiśupālavadha* (killing of Sisupāla); both poets had undoubted poetic gifts, and have left some exquisite passages on love and life and descriptions of Nature; but with them started the tendency to overload the poem with longer and longer descriptive digressions, the introduction of learned ideas and the display of the skill of the poet in composing difficult verses involving pictorial designs. Even gifted writers allowed themselves to be smothered under these learned and recondite displays; they began packing two themes in one poem by sustained *double entendre*, and composing poems illustrative of rules of grammar or different continued sound effects or pictorial designs.

While such undesirable developments were taking place in the form of the artificial epic, there were some healthy departures in its theme. The historical poem dealt with a contemporary king or line of kings. The outstanding example of this is the *River of Kings* (*Rāja-tarangini*), valuable for the history of Kashmir. Historical poems arose on almost all the local dynasties from about the 11th c. A.D., but these generally had romantic and poetic effusions which reduced their historical value.

Classical Sanskrit prose literature is dominated by Subandhu and two outstanding masters, Bāna (7th c. A.D.) and Dandin (ca. A.D. 700). The earlier specimens are lost. Bāna wrote a romantic story in prose called *Kādambari* in which two pairs of lovers pass through more than one birth and gain each other, and the *Harshacharita* in which he told the stories of himself and his royal patron, King Harshavardhana of Kanauj. Encyclopaedic in his knowledge, Bāna is also a master of the sheer music of words which makes his prose an endless delight to the sensitive Ind. reader. Dandin, who was equally encyclopaedic in his knowledge, adopted a style of simplicity and grace; his *Story of the Ten Princes* (*Daśakumāra-charita*) is realistic and holds up the mirror to life, particularly of the underworld.

When prose and verse had been fully exploited, poets evolved the new form called *Champū*, mixing prose and verse, in which they dealt with the traditional themes. A theme innovation was wrought in this type by an 18th-c. South Ind. poet who presented in his *Viśvagunādarśa* (Mirror of the Characteristics of the Universe), the pros and cons of everything through two reviewers of the world, an admirer and an unsparing critic.

The new lines of development were now mostly in the shorter poem and reflective writing, collections of stray observations or minor poems on a single topic, lyrics, didactic writings, etc. The most celebrated collection of this type is that of the three centuries of verses on proper conduct, love, and dispassion by Bhartrihari, reputed to be a royal writer and philosopher; many centuries of verses on these three topics arose later, for example, "on proper conduct," the 120 verses ascribed to Sundarapandya is an excellent collection on wisdom; "on love," the century of Amaruka is easily the best in the whole field of Sanskrit. Lyrical poetry in Sanskrit has two gems, the

Cloud Messenger (*Meghadūta*) of Kālidāsa already mentioned, and the dramatic poem called *Gitagovinda* (Song of Lord Govinda) on the love of Krishna and Rādhā, composed by Jayadeva (ca. A.D. 1200), which like the former is originally conceived and endlessly imitated; also the same musico-dramatic poem served as a religious inspiration to Vaishnavites and as a model for music and dance-drama compositions and traditions in all parts of India. Lyric poetry comprises also a vast amount of prayers, praises, and psalms by poets, religious teachers, and philosophers. Among the many collections of verses of reflective, didactic, and moral value to which the compact expression possible in Sanskrit lent itself admirably, the *Anyāpadeśa* is a class giving criticisms of life and reflections on men and their virtues or vices through praise or blame of animals, birds, etc.; two effective performances in this category are the "centuries" of the Kashmirian Bhallata (9th c. A.D.) and the South Ind. Nīlakantha Dīkshita (17th c. A.D.); the latter had indeed a flair for satire and wit and gave other minor poems of direct criticism of professional quacks, cheats, pests, parasites, poetasters, etc. (the *Kalividambana* and the *Sabhāranjana*); but before Nīlakantha, the Kashmirian polymath Kshemendra (11th c.) had pioneered in the line of satires with many a minor poem of his.

One of the most significant branches of Sanskrit literature which had gained for India world-wide celebrity in ancient times is animal-fable literature, *Panchatantra* (The Five Expedients) and *Hitopadeśa* (The Salutary Advice) (prose and verse), to which all the animal fables of the world can ultimately be traced. In the category of stories, a number of works were produced but the most important of these is the old store-house of stories, the *Brihatkathā*, originally written in the Paisachi dialect, but now available in three later Sanskrit versions.

The field of drama had some distinguished names to succeed to Kālidāsa and Śudraka. King Harshavardhana of Kanauj (7th c.) wrote three plays of which *Nāgānanda* (The Joy of the Serpents) is on the unique theme of the hero sacrificing his life to save the serpents from annihilation. In the same age, South India could also boast of a royal dramatist in Mahendravarma Pallava of Kānchī who produced two brilliant farces, in one of which he made use of the yogic feat of entering another's body to make a courtesan talk *Sāmkhya* philosophy and an ascetic coquette with his pupil. Bhavabhūti (ca. A.D. 700) attempted both the social and the heroic, but his success lay in the latter, where he was acclaimed as a master of pathos for his play on the *Later life of Rama* and the abandonment of Sitā; Bhavabhūti's expression reveled in profusion, and like Bāna, he was master of the music of Sanskrit. Viśākhadatta, member of a royal house (8th c. A.D.), produced two masterly creations in political drama: the *Mudrārākshasa* (Rakshasa secured through the Signet Ring) on the Mauryan emperor Chandra-gupta and his famous minister Kautilya-Chānakya, the author of the great treatise on polity, the *Artha Śāstra*; and the *Devī-Chandragupta* (The Queen and Chandragupta) on the inside story of the greatest ancient Ind. monarch Chandragupta II Vikramaditya of the Gupta dynasty. Among the smaller plays, the monologue of amour, like the farce, afforded scope for satire and humor; four early specimens of this class, published under the title *Chatur-bhānī* (the Four Bhanas), and numerous good specimens produced in the South in the 18th-19th c. are known. Among the lost dramatic masterpieces is a precious social play *Pushpadūshitaka* in which the playwright depicts the suffering of a virtuous housewife, the purity of whose character had been, on circumstantial grounds, impugned. New ground was cut in drama when the logician-poet of Kashmir (9th c.) produced his play on the different schools of philosophy disputing among themselves. Already Asvaghosha had produced centuries previously a Buddhistic play with allegorical characters. Krishna Miśra (11th c.) was the author who perfected the allegorical play for the *advaita* school of philosophy and this type was later imitated by poet-protagonists of different schools of philosophy and religion, and even of the science of medicine and the planets.

In the different categories described above, a voluminous output of poems and plays and shorter literary pieces continued to appear down the centuries. The countless poets included over thirty women poets. The Muslim period even saw some translations from Persian and some cultivation of Sanskrit and literary creation in it by Muslims. With the advent of the British and the contact with Western literature, Sanskrit began to adopt some Western trends: minor poems, easy straightforward prose, both narrative and expository, short stories, novels, plays, biographies, satires, and similar new forms. The Ind. Independence movement inspired many minor poems, as also longer poems and prose works on the political leaders, Gandhi, Tilak etc. Sanskrit which is one of the languages enumerated in the Constitution of Free India continues today to be used for poetic and dramatic creations and the present writer himself recently received a title for a long Sanskrit poem of his on the life of a celebrated musician-saint of South India.

PRĀKRITS. Of the early Prākrits or popular forms of Sanskrit, the dialect called Mahārāshtri in the Dekkan was cultivated for poetry and the earliest literature in this is an anthology, the *Gāthā-Saptaśatī*, 700 love lyrics and stray descriptive verses put together by King Hāla Sātavāhana of the 2d or 3d c. A.D. Two other similar collections are the *Vajjālagga* and *Gāthākośa*. These Prākrit verses are examples of sweet diction, fine feeling and exquisite cameos of rural life, and on the subject of love, formed the sources on which later lyricists drew. On the romance of King Hāla himself, there is a beautiful story-poem in Prākrit verses called *Līlāvatī*. In Prākrit medium, replicas of the Sanskrit artificial epics were also produced, the best example of which is Pravarasena's *Setubandha* (The Building of the Causeway). In drama where Prākrit was always used, a type wholly in Prākrit called the *Sattaka* was developed later. The Jains produced some voluminous and valuable religious works in Prākrits, e.g., *Kuvalayamālā* (8th c.).

In Apabhramśa, which was the next popular linguistic development, works on the model of the Sanskrit and Prākrit poems grew and Jains especially contributed much to this literature. Out of the Apabhramśa, the modern Indo-Aryan vernaculars of the North started growing from the 11th c. A.D. onward: Marathi in the South, Kashmiri, Panjabi, Rajasthani, Sindhi and Gujarati in the North and West, different Hindi dialects in the middle, and Assamese, Bengali, Bihari and Oriya in the East. The cultivated languages of the South, Tamil, Telugu, Kannada and Malayalam belong to the Dravidian family and have an old literature, particularly Tamil.

The literary efforts in all these languages took the form of translations and adaptations of Sanskrit or original productions on themes from Sanskrit; the literature of these is thus an extension of Sanskrit. There is none among these languages which does not have its own *Rāmāyana* and *Mahābhārata* or works based on them; in fact, some of the vernacular *Rāmāyanas* command as great a devotion as the Sanskrit original, e.g., the *Rāmāyana* of Kambar in Tamil and of Tulasidās in Hindi (Avadhi). The literature in all these languages underwent a uniform revolution on the impact of Western contact: first new forms of poetry and plays on Western models arose in all the literatures. Blank verse, sonnets and short lyrical poems were introduced. Then new ideas of social reform influenced writings; social plays, humorous skits and satires arose. With the rise of nationalism and the freedom struggle, patriotism became an inspiration and there was a rediscovery of the past and the country's soul; the egalitarian political ideologies sweeping the West swayed India also, and among younger writers a new kind of progressive writing before whose iconoclasm traditional patterns and old ideals have been crumbling has been manifesting itself. This is,

INDIAN POETRY

however, a recent trend and it is too early to assess all this seething contemporary literary activity or to predict whether an authentic and characteristic Ind. harmony will emerge from it. Of forms, the short story has become extremely popular; the novel comes next. In poetry and drama, the former has fared better, though great poetry cannot be said to be plentiful. Drama which faced a paralysis before the cinema, is being nursed now by the radio and academies and may recover.

MODERN INDO-ARYAN

MARATHI. Marathi literature begins with the religious and philosophic writings of saints and adherents of different sects and cults. The leading saint-poets of Mahārāshtra whose influence is somewhat pan-Indian, are Jnāneshvar (1271–96), Nāmdēv (1270–1350), Ēkanāth (16th c.), Tukhārām (1608–49) and Rāmdās (1608–81). Among poets of this class were many drawn from the lowest strata of the society. These authors brought the Sanskrit classics, chiefly *Bhāgavata* and *Gītā* to the Marathi masses. Mukteshvar, grandson of Ēkanāth, rendered the *Mahābhārata*. The political victories of the Marathas in the 17th and 18th c. gave rise to the heroic ballads called *Powadā*. Side by side with these developed the love lyric called *Lāvanī*. In the modern age, Mahārāshtra had been, like Bengal, in the forefront of several socio-political and literary movements. The modern Marathi stage had a rapid growth from the last quarter of the 19th c. After a period of musical vernacular adaptations of Sanskrit plays, Shakespeare was studied and plays on contemporary social themes were produced. Minor poems, lyrics, rural poetry, children's poetry, all arose in due course and mention may be made here of Keshavasut, N. W. Tilak, Vinayak, R. G. Gadkari, Balkavi, Muralidhar Gupte and, among the more recent, Y. D. Pendharkar (Yeshwant), S. K. Kanetkar (Gireesh), M. T. Patwardhan (Madhav-Julian), A. R. Deshpande (Anil) and V. V. Shirwadkar (Kusumagraj).

GUJARATI. The Jain monk and Sanskrit polymath Hemachandra Sūri (1089–1173) is the founder of modern Gujarati. Among the early authors in this tongue are the Vaishnavite saints, mystics, and preachers among whom are the Princess Mira (1403–70) and Narasimha Mehta (1415–81) whose songs are sung all over India; others of this type are Akho, the goldsmith (1615–75), Premanand (1636–1734) and Dayaram (1767–1852). The modern period was ushered in by the scholars and poets Dalpatram (1820–98) and Narmadasankar (1833–86). Among Parsis who contributed to the growth of modern Gujarati poetry are B. M. Malabari and A. F. Khabardar. Nanalal, poet laureate of Gujarat, has been a prolific poet, and equally

prolific has been, despite his political and organizational preoccupations, K. M. Munshi (born 1892), the author of many dramas. The modern Gujarati stage has developed forms like dramatic dialogues styled *Nātya Rūpak* and ballets or *Nritya Rūpak* in songs with prose links. Among other poets and playwrights are to be noted Sursinghji, chief of Lathi State, B. K. Thakore, R. V. Desai, Umashankar Joshi, Sundaram, Sundarji Betai, Batubhai Umarwadia, Yashwant Pandya, Pranjivan Pathak, Gulabdas Broker, Jayanti Dalal, and Chunilal Madia. Gujarat which gave to India Gandhi and some of his ablest lieutenants has perhaps been most successful in modern Gujarat prose, criticism, biography, journalism, etc.

PANJABI. Panjabi literature comes into prominence with the rise of the Sikh religion in the latter part of the 15th c. The most important and basic Panjabi literature is the collection of the religious and didactic teachings in the form of songs which the founder of Sikhism, Nanak, and his successors sang and which have been collected in the *Adi-Granth* (*The First Book*) and its supplements. The Muslims of the Panjab developed their own sectarian literature in Panjabi and the Sufis made significant contribution to Panjabi poetry. A popular ballad poetry also existed. Real modern Panjabi literature started growing only with the present century and the study of Panjabi in schools and colleges. Among modern poets are Vir Singh and Puran Singh, and of playwrights are to be noted I. C. Nanda, Gurbaksh Singh, and Kirpa Sagar. Younger writers today include some leftists.

KASHMIRI. The earliest phase of the rather meagre literature of Kashmiri is represented by the verses of the Saivite lady-mystic Lalla Devi. Lalla Devi was followed by Noor-ud-Din, a didactic poet. Then came the age of love-lyrics, some of which were mystic and some contributed by women like the famous peasant girl who became a Queen, Haba Khatoon (16th c.), and Arnimal (18th c.) of sad fate. Kashmiri has its quota of poetic renderings or versions of the old Sanskrit epics and myths done in the 19th c., e.g., the Rāmāyana of Prakasa Ram, the Sivalagan, the Sudāmacharita, etc., of Paramanand. The blend of Persian culture in Kashmiri brought Persian themes, meters, and forms, as also some Muslim writers of Kashmiri. Dance-songs and folk forms were also taken up for fresh literary developments. New life was infused into Kashmiri writing only very recently, and about the beginning of the present century new types of modern Kashmiri writings arose. The new political, social, and economic movements gave a fresh direction to authors: Ghulam Ahmed Mahjur is a pioneer in this line; Zinda Kaul is a lyricist; Nadim, Roshan, Rahi and Premi are contemporary poets who have stood for Kashmiri against outside political aggression or interference. The effort in drama has been meager.

HINDI. Hindi or Khariboli, the federal language of India to be, is a recent development, its precursors being a number of dialects: Rajasthani, in which there was bardic poetry; Brajabhasha, the medium of expression for Krishna-devotion; Avadhi, the language of Rāma-devotion; and Bhojpuri, in which the Hindu-Muslim eclectic preacher Kabir (1399–1518) sang his numerous songs. The fervent devotional movements centering round Rāma and Krishna produced in the 16th c. the foremost poets and singers: Tulasidas, author of the *Rāmāyana* which has usurped the place of the Sanskrit original in the whole of the Hindi-speaking area and Sūrdās of Agra (1483–1563), the blind singer on Krishna. Bihārilāl (1603–63) wrote 700 couplets (*Satsai*) of fine poetry on Rādhā-Krishna love. Malik Muhammad Jayasi (ca. 1540) composed the masterpiece of a historical poem in his *Padumāvat*. The Mughal period saw the rise of Muslim writers in Hindi, some of whom were devoted to Hindu deities, e.g., Abdul Rahim Khankhana, Raskhan, Kabir Mubarak, and Usman. New trends began to show with the beginning of the 19th c., and the pioneering stage is dominated by the prolific and versatile Bhāratendu Hariśchandra (1850–83), author of 175 works, including 18 plays and 1,500 lyrics. The new Hindi writing was successively under the influence of the movements *Chāyā-vāda* (or romanticism), *Prayoga-vāda* (or experimentalism), and *Pragati-vāda* (or progressivism and leftism). There is also a school of writers of rural poetry. Jayasankar Prasad (1889–1937), Sumitranandan Pant (b. 1901), "Nirala" Suryakant Tripathi (1896–1961) and Mahadevi Varma (b. 1907) have been reflective and mystically inclined. Maithilisaran Gupta (b. 1886), Makhanlal Chaturvedi (b. 1889), Siyaramasaran Gupta (1895–1963), and Subhadra Kumari Chauhan (1904–48) have been ardent nationalistic poets. The writings of Tara Pande, Ramesvari Devi, and Hridayesa have a pessimistic tone. Harivamsa Rai (b. 1907) and Girijakumar Mathur have been in the romantic camp and Balakrishna Rao is noted for his sonnets. Others among the old and the young who must be mentioned are: Mahavir Prasad Dvivedi (1868–1938), Balakrishna Sharma Navin (1897–1960), "Dinkar" Ramdhari Sinha (b. 1908), "Suman" Sivamangal Singh (b. 1916), a progressivist, Narendra Sarma (b. 1916), and Bhagavati Charan Varma (b. 1903). In drama, Bhāratendu was followed by Lakshminarayan Misra (b. 1903), Ram Kumar Varma (b. 1905), Upendranath Ashk (b. 1910–), Uday Sankar Bhatta, and others, and these have produced all types of plays,

romantic productions, historical pieces, social plays, satires, farces, etc.

URDU. Urdu language and literature, like Muslim architecture, is one of the cultural products of Indo-Islamic contact on the soil of India. If the increase of the Persian element produced Hindustani, further Persianization and use of Arabic script gave rise to Urdu. It is used both in the North and the Dekkan. Urdu is mostly poetical in its literary output. The greater of the early Urdu poets of the Dekkani and the Northern Muslim courts are Nusrati, Shamsuddin Waliullah, Qadi Mahmud Bahri, Mirza Janijanan Mazhar, Mir Taqi Mir, Mir Dard, Ghulam Hamdani Mushafi, Wali Muhammad Nazir, Haidar Ali Atish, Imam Baksh Nasikh, Anis and Salamat. The 1857 upheaval ushered in the modern phase of Urdu; Azad and Hali were the pioneers in this new movement; its greatest figures were Ghalib and Iqbal. There are several leading contemporary Urdu poets, e.g., Hasrat Mohani, Fani, Ashgar, Jigar; there are other Urdu poets who show Hindi influences and reflect fully the composite Indo-Islamic culture. The political and ideological revolutions have had their effect on Urdu also, which has its own group of iconoclastic writers. In drama, curiously, it was the Urdu *Indra Sabha* and the Urdu playwrights employed by the Parsi Theatrical Co. that led to an all-India theatre-enthusiasm; but modern Urdu has expressed itself very meagrely in the drama.

MAITHILI. Very close to Bengali is Maithili, still struggling for public and scholarly recognition of its separateness. The most famous name among the early makers of Maithili is Vidyāpati whose devotional love lyrics spread far and wide. There was a Maithili song-drama which mixed Maithili and Sanskrit, the best known specimen of which is the *Pārijātaharana* (The Taking of the Pārijāta Tree from Heaven) of Umāpati. In the 19th c. the versatile Chanda Jha produced the Maithili version of the Rāmāyana; the major and minor poem-types of Sanskrit were imitated in Maithili by several poets. Among modern writers of verse, the most noteworthy is Sitarama Jha. Of younger ones, Ishanatha Jha is a poet and playwright and Jivanatha Jha, Kashikanta Misra and several others are contributing to modern Maithili poetry. In drama, Jivana Jha broke new ground by eschewing Sanskrit bilingualism and by taking to social themes. The humorous one-act play is very popular.

BENGALI. Bengal led modern India in several fields and its greatest writer in modern times, Rabindranath Tagore, was an inspiration for all India. The most prominent among the early Bengali productions are the devotional lyrics of Chandidas (14th–15th c. A.D.). In epic, Krittivas gave the *Rāmāyana* in Ben-

INDIAN POETRY

gali (A.D. 1420), Maladhar Basu (1473–80) and Raghunātha (16th c.) the *Bhāgavata,* and Kavindra, Srikara Nandi (ca. 1500) and Kasirama (17th c.) the *Mahābhārata*. In the devotional field the appearance of Chaitanyadev (1483–1534) created new inspiration, both within Bengal and without. The Muslim contact gave a noteworthy group of Muslim writers who also rendered Hindi and Persian works into Bengali. The modern post-Eng. phase of Bengali starts with Michael Madhusudan Datta and Bankim Chandra Chatterji, the latter the creator of the immortal song on Mother India *Vande Mātaram,* which inspired the country in the freedoɪn struggle. Among the earlier modern Bengali poets are Rangalal Banerji (1827–87), Viharilal Chakravartti (1835–94), and Navin Chandra Sen (1847–1909). The earlier dramatists are Dinabandhu Mitra (1830–73), Rajkrishna Roy (1852–95), Amritalal Bose (1853–1929), and the greatest and most prolific of them all: Girish Chandra Ghosh (1844–1911), author of about 90 plays. The next age of Bengali literature is dominated by the greatest, most versatile and prolific of modern writers, poet Rabindranath Tagore (1861–1941), whose securing of the Nobel Prize for literature (1913) brought modern Ind. literature to the notice of the world. Tagore has left his mark on new India as one of the architects of cultural renaissance, and his song on Mother India *Janagana* is today the official National Anthem. Besides Tagore, there have been in his period a number of important poets and playwrights: Devendranath Sen, Akshaya Kumar Baral, Rajani Kanta Sen, Mrs. Kamini Ray, Satyendranath Datta, Dvijendralal Ray (best known among these), Kshirod Chandra Vidyavinod (author of about 50 plays), and Atul Prasad Sen (lyricist). Nazrul Islam, Jibanananda Das, Premendra Mitra, and Buddhadev Bose are three progressive writers.

ASSAMESE. Creative work opens in Assamese at the end of the 13th c. with the artificial epic poems on the Sanskrit model and on the mythological themes by Hema Sarasvati, Harihar, and Kaviratna, followed by translations of the *Rāmāyana* and the *Mahābhārata* by Mādhava Kandali (11th c.) and Rāma Sarasvati, and the *Bhāgavata* and *Gītā* by Bhattadeva. Fresh impetus to devotional literature centering round Krishna was given by the Vaishnava movement among the masses in the 15th–16th c. and the greatest saint of this school, Śankaradev, and his pupils produced, besides translations and original poems, songs called *Borgīts* and devotional dance-drama compositions called *Ankiya Nats*. The pioneering Eng.-educated modernist in Assamese literature was Hemchandra Barua (1835–96), a scholar and playwright. Lakshmīnath Bezbarua (1868–1938) is the foremost figure among mod-

ern Assamese poets and dramatists. Chandrakumar Agarwalla is a lyricist; Kamalakanta Bhattacharya, a fervent nationalist; Hiteswar Barbarua, historically inclined; Raghunath Ghoudhuri, a Nature-poet; the lady Nalinibala Devi, mystical; and Sarat Chandra Goswani (1886–1944), a realist. Hem ·Barua is a progressive. Gunabhiram Barua, Padmanath Gohain Barua, Chandradhar Barua, Nakul Chandra Bhuyan, Prasannalal Choudhury, Daibachandra Talukdar, Chandrakanta Pukan, and Surendranath Saikia may also be mentioned.

ORIYA. The Oriya *Mahābhārata* was produced by Sarala Das (14th c.), the Oriya *Rāmāyana* by Balarama Das and the Oriya *Bhāgavata* by Jagannath Das. Oriya versions of other Sanskrit mythological works followed. Sanskrit devotional adaptations went on till i700. Upendra Bhanja was the most accomplished composer of difficult and highly artificial types of verses. The next phase was a series of devotional and religious works chiefly on Krishna-worship. In the Bṛitish period, Ramashankar Roy and Radhanath pioneered in blank verse. Fakirmohan Senapati (1843–1918) was both prolific and versatile; Gopabandhu Das combined literary work with constructive activity. In drama fresh interest was infused into traditional dance-drama, and original plays were produced by Ramashankar Roy, Kamapala Misra, Vikaricharan Patnaik, Govinda Surdeo, Asvini Kumar Ghosh, and Kalicharan Patnaik. There was also a group of writers who took inspiration from Tagore of the neighboring Bengal which has always exerted literary and cultural influence on Orissa. Orissa too is having its quota of Freudian and Marxian writings today.

INDO-DRAVIDIAN

TAMIL. Of the Indo-Dravidian languages, Tamil possesses the oldest literature. As in the case of Sanskrit, the earliest literature in Tamil has been collected and preserved in anthologies. The Sangam works, the oldest corpus of Tamil poetry, whose date comes up to about A.D. 300, reveals over 500 poets, some of whom are women, e.g., Avvaiyār, the great moralist. The corpus comprises 8 anthologies, 10 idylls, and 18 didactic works bearing medical metaphorical names. The early anthologies and works of this corpus contain verses and short and long poems on love and war, glimpses of rural and social life and customs, moral maxims, proverbs, praises of the Tamil kings, Pallavas, Cholas, Pandyas, and Cheras, and their exploits and liberality, devotion to different deities, description of cities and ports and Tamil trade, which had overseas connections from early times. Special mention must be made of two works in the didactic collection, the *Tirukkural* of Tiruvalluvar and

INDIAN POETRY

the *Four Hundred Quatrains* called *Nāladiyār*. The former is a marvel of brevity and a tabloid of wisdom. It deals with virtue, spirituality, material welfare, and love and has been widely translated. Tamil language received elements from Munda and Sanskrit. The Sanskrit epics *Rāmayana* and *Mahābhārata* had begun to appear in Tamil even in the earliest period. Like Sanskrit, Tamil also has five major *kāvyas* or artificial epics of which the best in the *Lay of the Anklet* (Chilappatikāram), the sad story of the chaste wife Kannaki who was later deified. As in Kannada, in Tamil too, the Jains made copious contributions. The next stage of Tamil is the reaction against Buddhism and Jainism which had spread in the South. In the 6th, 7th, and 8th c., a line of saints and devotees of Siva and Vishnu, *Nāyanārs* and *Ālvārs*, arose who, with their soul-stirring songs set to music, made Tamil country the springboard of Hindu revival. The sweet and appealing quality of Tamil is best enjoyed in Tamil hymnology. In the great days of the Imperial Cholas (10th to 13th c.), there were important poets in Tamil, Kambar, Jayankondār, Ottakkūttar, and Puhalēndi, but the greatest of all these is Kambar (12th c.), author of the Tamil *Rāmayana*, expounded and listened to with as much devotion as the Sanskrit original of Vālmīki. Modern Tamil starts with the arrival of European missionaries two of whom, De Nobili and Fr. Beschi, naturalized themselves as native teachers and wrote Tamil works and poems. New trends started in Tamil too with the establishment of modern universities and contact with Eng. literature. It was not till the Freedom Movement, however, that the Tamils got their great modern poet, Subrahmanya Bharati, author of India's finest patriotic poetry. Bharati is the only genuine and considerable poet of modern Tamil, but in his wake there have been talented followers: S. D. S. Yogi, Surabhi, Desiga Vinayakam Pillai, and Namakkal Ramalingam Pillai. The chief characteristics of modern Tamil are its simplicity of diction, patriotic feeling and zeal for social equality. As elsewhere these trends have led Tamil into leftism. Tamil has a good heritage of music, dance and dance-drama. The devotional song-poems of Gopalakrishna Bharati, couched in popular Tamil, are the most outstanding of this class in modern times. Tamil drama started with the *Manonmaniyam* of Sundaram Pillai and the efforts of Suryanarayana Sastri. P. Sambandha Mudaliar, the doyen of the amateur stage, has written countless plays, translations from Sanskrit and Eng., and also original ones. Tamil genius is effective in the satirical social drama; and the Tamil stage now can boast of a number of enjoyable social hits.

TELUGU. Telugu poetry on a large scale starts with Nannayya (11th c.). He, Tikkana (13th c.) and Yerrapragada (14th c.), produced the Telugu *Mahābhārata*. Several poets did the *Rāmayana* into Telugu. Potana's Telugu *Bhāgavata* (15th c.) rises to the heights of the Sanskrit original. Other Sanskrit philosophical classics and mythological works were also rendered into Telugu. Saivism inspired Somanatha, who produced two substantial and erudite poems. Nonreligious Sanskrit works also attracted the attention of the Telugu poets: the prose romance of Dandin, the *Ten Princes*, was adapted by Katana, and the most accomplished of Telugu poets Śrīnātha produced his masterly poem, the Telugu *Naishadhīya Charita* (*Story of the king of Nishadha*, Nala) and his patriotic poem on the heroes of Palnad. The Vijayanagar empire (14th to 17th c.) greatly stimulated the Sanskrit and Telugu renaissance, and the great king of this line, Krishnadevaraya, had eight poets as the eight pillars of his court. As in Malayalam, so in Telugu, this age developed the type called *Prabandha*, mixing prose and verse on the Sanskrit *Champu* model, and dealt with all kinds of stories in this medium. The Sanskrit *Sataka* or century of verses on themes like love, devotion, ethics, etc., was developed on a large scale in Telugu. The Sanskrit saturation of Telugu diction can be compared only with that of Malayalam. Telugu has also been the favorite medium of South Indian music and dance, the best of which was developed more in the heart of the Tamil country, Tanjore.

K. Veeresalingam Pantulu inaugurated modern Telugu poetry, drama, prose, etc. Vedam Venkataraya Sastri was a similar all-round genius of prodigious accomplishment. On themes of social reform, modern plays were produced by Ch. Lakshminarasimhan, G. Appa Rao, and Bellary Krishnamacharlu. Inspired by Eng. minor poems and the renaissance in Bengali, a new movement of *Bhāva-kavitva* or lyric was started, and B. Appa Rao, A. Bapu Raju, Tirupati Venkata Kavulu, R. Subba Rao, D. V. Krishna Sastri, V. Satyanarayana and D. Rami Reddi took part. The motif and song-medium of simple rustic folk were employed by some of these writers with great success. Among contemporary playwrights are Justice P. V. Rajamannar and Narla Venkatesvara Rao. As in other regions, in Telugu also there has been a swinging of the pendulum to right and left; if realists have rebelled, a school of neo-classicists has also arisen in Telugu and has done well indeed.

KANNADA. Jains pioneered in making Kannada literature in its earliest stages. Kannada versions and adaptations of the Sanskrit epics, mythological literature and classical works started; the *Champu* or *Prabandha* form, mixing prose and verse, was favored here also. Pampa, Ponna, and Ranna of the 10th c. brought the *Mahābhārata* and the *Rāmāyana* into Kannada. The immortal Sanskrit prose-romance *Kādambarī* was done into Kannada by Nāgavarman at the end of the same century. There was then a swing toward simplicity, native meters, and a fresh approach to the masses, partly inspired by the Vira Saiva movement. Along with it, the Vaishnava movement of the Haridāsas approached the masses through music and song in homely language. The patronage of the Vijayanagar kingdom introduced a fresh classicism and return to Sanskrit sources, especially by Kumāra Vyāsa and Kumāra Vālmīki. In drama, the traditional dance-drama called *Yakshagāna* achieved its greatest successes in the 18th and 19th c. Modern Kannada literature has been made by the trinity, B. M. Srikanthayya, D. V. Gundappa, and Masti Venkatesa Ayyangar, whose works enriched poetry, drama, story, etc. Other poets at the present day are Govinda Pai, Bendre, K. V. Puttappa, V. Sitaramiah, P. T. N. Rajaratnam, Mugali, Madhura Chenna, K. Narasimhaswami, Adiga, Sridhara, Vinayaka, etc., who have tried every modern form of poetry. The new drama, especially with social themes, developed in the hands of Huylgol, Kerur, T. P. Kailasam, Adya, and Gokak.

MALAYALAM. Evidence of Malayalam as distinct from Tamil appears in the 9th c. A.D., but the influence of Tamil continued up to the 14th c., in works like the *Rāmacharitam* and the *Mahābhāratam songs*. Soon the influence of the highly learned Namputiri Brahmans Sanskritized the language and its literary forms. Malayalam is the most highly Sanskritized Ind. language and has a regular genre of its literature called *Manipravala*, an euphonically and rhetorically perfected Sanskrit-Malayalam bilingual form. The outstanding Malayalam poet is Tunchattu Ezhuttacchan (15th c.) who gave in Malayalam measures called *Kilippāttu* (Parrot's song), versions of the Sanskrit epics *Mahābhārata* and the *Adhyātma-Rāmāyana*. Kerala, the land of this literature, is famous today for its national art of dance-drama called *Kathakali* for which a corpus of song-plays on mythological stories was produced from the 17th c. onward. A second popular dance-drama form called *Ottan-Tullal* was introduced by *Kunchan Nampyar* (18th c.) who made this a humorous and satirical medium of public criticism and moral edification. With the impact of Eng. education, Malayalam also entered on its modern phase and can today boast of a literary renaissance of all-round richness including classical authors (e.g. Ulloor Paramesvara Aiyar), romantic and lyrical authors (e.g. Kumaran Asan, Vallathol, G. Sankara Kurup,

Changampuzha Krishna Pillai, Vailoppali Sridhara Menon, Pala Narayanan Nair), progressive writers and dramatists (E. V. Krishna Pillai, C. J. Thomas, M. Govindan).

INDO-ANGLIAN. Among the non-Eng. speaking countries, India is unique for its cultivation of the King's or Queen's Eng. with industry and care. Like Sanskrit in the past, Eng. has been in the last century and a half the common medium of communication for all India, and a medium of expression of all aspirations. Though the political slavery of India prevented Ind. Eng. from attaining any distinct recognition, some Indian speakers like V. S. Srinivasa Sastri and writers like Sarojini Naidu and Nehru have drawn the admiration and praise of Englishmen for the correctness and charm of their Eng. Eng. has developed in India in journalism, essay, exposition, short story, and the novel; but the output in poetry has also been considerable. The more successful among the early Ind. writers of Eng. verse came from Bengal: Michael Madhusudan Dutt (d. 1875), the lady Toru Dutt (1856–77) (*A Sheaf Gleaned in French Fields, Ancient Ballads and Legends of Hindustan*), Romesh Chunder Dutt (*Lays of Ancient India*, 1894; *Mahabharata* and *Ramayana* in verse, 1898, 1900), Sarojini Naidu who produced some volumes of exquisite poetry (*The Golden Threshold*, 1905; *The Bird of Time*, 1912; *The Broken Wing*, 1917); and last but not least the mystic Aurobindo Ghose whose collected poems and narratives—lyrical, dramatic, mystic, metaphysical—run to 700 pages. Among non-Bengalis, while there have been writers of creative Eng. in all parts of India, the South Indians specialized, so to speak, in Eng. Two outstanding examples of South Ind. Eng. poets are G. K. Chettur and Manjeri S. Isvaran, the latter, author of several volumes of poetry. In drama mention should be made of the plays of Harindranath Chattopadhyaya and the Madras lawyer and judge, V. V. Srinivasa Ayyangar (*Dramatic Divertisements*).

ANTHOLOGIES AND TRANSLATIONS: *The Ind. Heritage*, ed. V. Raghavan (1956; an anthol. of Sanskrit Lit. Translations and narrative versions. Includes Vedas, Upanishads, the two epics, the Gita and the Bhagavata Pura.ıa); *Select Specimens of the Theatre of the Hindus*, tr. H. H. Wilson (3d ed., 1871); *Sakuntala and Other Writings of Kalidasa*, tr. A. W. Ryder (1912); *The Little Clay Cart (Mricchakatika), a Hindu Drama Attributed to King Shudraka*, tr. A. W. Ryder (1905); *Rajatarangini of Kalhana: The Saga of the Kings of Kashmir*, tr. R. S. Pandit (1935); *The Kadambari of Bana*, tr. C. M. Ridding (1896); *The Ten Princes: Dandin's Dasakumaracarita*, tr. A. W. Ryder (1927); *The Satakas or Wise Sayings of Bhartrihari*, tr. J. M. Kennedy (1913); *Indian*

Poetry, Containing "The Indian Song of Songs" from the Sanskrit Gita-Govinda of Jayadeva, tr. E. Arnold (6th ed., 1891); Hitopadesa, the Book of Wholesome Counsel, a Translation, F. Johnson and L. D. Barnett (1928).—Psalms of the Maratha Saints, tr. N. Macnicol (1919); Mirabai—Songs, Tr. from the Original Hindi, R. C. Tandon (1934); The Adi-Granth or the Holy Scriptures of the Sikhs, tr. E. Trumpp (1877); The Words of Lalla the Prophetess, tr. R. C. Temple (1929); Kashmiri Lyrics, J. L. Kaul (1946); Prthvīrāj-rāsau of Chand Bardai, ed. and tr. J. Beames and A. F. R. Hoernle (2 pts., 1873–86); One Hundred Songs of Kabir, tr. R. Tagore (1926); The Holy Lake of the Acts of Rama; Eng. tr. of Tulasidas's Rama-charitamanasa, W. D. P. Hill (1952); Mathura, tr. F. S. Growse (tr. of poems of worshippers of Krishna); The Padumavati of Malik Muhammad Jayasi, ed. and tr. G. A. Grierson and M. S. Dvivedi (1896–1911); The Quatrains of Hali, ed. and tr. G. E. Ward (in prose) and C. S. Stute (in verse) (1932); Vidyapati: Bangiya Padavali. Songs of the Love of Radha and Krishna, tr. A. K. Coomaraswamy and A. Sen (1915); R. Tagore, Collected Poems and Plays (1937); Selections from Oriya Lit., ed. B. C. Majumdar (3 v.); Ten Tamil Idylls (Pattupp-pāttu), tr. J. V. Chelliah (1947); The Śilap-padikāram or the Lay of the Anklet, tr. V. R. R. Dikshitar (1939); Two Thousand Years of Tamil Lit., J. M. Somasundaram Pillai (1959); The Sacred Kural or the Tamil Veda of Tiruvalluvar, tr. H. A. Popley (1931); Kamba Rāmāyanam, V. V. S. Aiyar (1950); The Verses of Vemana, tr. C. P. Brown (1829); Modern Ind. Poetry, ed. G. Goodwin (1927); An Anthol. of Indo-Anglian Verse, ed. A. R. Chida (1935).

HISTORY AND CRITICISM: A. A. Macdonell, India's Past (1927); A. B. Keith, The Sanskrit Drama (1924) and A Hist. of Sanskrit Lit. (1928); M. Winternitz, A Hist. of Ind. Lit., I (Calcutta, 1927); Aurobindo Ghose, Kalidasa (1st ser., 1929; 2d ser., 1954); V. Raghavan, The Social Play in Sanskrit (1952) and Love in the Poems and Plays of Kalidasa (1954); G. A. Grierson, The Modern Vernacular Lit. of Hindustan (1889); S. K. Chatterji, Indo-Aryan and Hindi (1942); Sahitya Akademi, New Delhi, Contemporary Ind. Lit. (1957); K. M. Munshi, Gujarat and its Lit. (1935); Mohan Singh, A Hist. of Panjabi Lit., 1100–1932 (n.d.); Indar Nath Madan, Modern Hindi Lit. (1939); Ram Babu Saxena, A Hist. of Urdu Lit. (1927); J. K. Misra, A Hist. of Maithili Lit. (2 v., 1949—1950); D. C. Sen, Hist. of Bengali Lang. and Lit. (1911); B. K. Barua, Assamese Lit. (1941); P. T. Srinivasa Lyengar, Hist. of the Tamils to 600 A.D. (1929; hist.-cum-anthol.); S. C. Chitty, Tamil Plutarch (new ed., 1946; biographies); S. Vaiyapuri Pillai, Hist. of Tamil Lang. and

Lit. (1956); P. Chenchiah and Raja M. Bhujanga Rao Bahadur, A Hist. of Telugu Lit. (1928); E. P. Rice, A Hist. of Kanarese Lit. (1918); K. Godavarma, A Short Survey of Malayalam Lit. (1945); K. R. Srinivasa Iyengar, The Ind. Contribution to Eng. Lit. (1945; hist.-cum-anthol.).　　　　V.R.

INDIAN PROSODY. Ind. poetry is remarkable for the large variety and beauty of its meters. Its earliest form, the Veda, is called simply "the measured utterance" (Chandas). Mystic values were often attached to meters. Vedic poetry employs fifteen meters, seven of these being popular and three most frequent. They show flexibility of form and richness of design. The Vedic line was neither completely fluid nor completely fixed, the concluding syllables always being more defined, in terms of an iambic or trochaic cadence. The 8-, 11-, and 12-syllable lines composed the most common meters, and out of these grew in well-defined syllabic instants, long and short, the most popular epic and classical meters, Anushtubh and Upajāti. As the meters passed from the Vedic to the epic and from the epic to the classic, the character of each syllable progressively hardened and the bulk of classical meters are scanned by schemes of long and short in the constituent syllables, with marked caesura recognized in some. Less frequent are meters in which the 4 feet are not equal; there is also a class of meter measured merely by total quantity of morae (mātrā) per foot, and this is more commonly used in drama, lyric, and Prākṛit poetry. Mostly the meters bear charming feminine and lyrical names, due probably to their use in early drama, song, and lyric poetry; there are some in which the rhythm has sharp rise and fall, showing their greater musical character. About 850 meters are defined in a corpus of literature on prosody comprising about 150 treatises. A good many of these were developed by the mixture of typical cadence patterns comparable to Gr. cola. Poetic practice shows that about a score of these meters were frequently handled, and from the same poetic practice we could deduce certain broad principles underlying the use of meters for specific purposes, themes, and emotions.

Indians read different meters in different recitative styles. Prākṛit prosody was based mostly on the total quantity of each foot, each short syllable being one mātrā and the long one being two; Prākṛit prosody employed alliteration and rhyme, but Sanskrit only rarely and under the influence of Prākṛit. Prākṛit meters were also more distinctly musical. The metrics of the Dravidian literatures is based on a different and more complicated scheme of scanning but during the long course of co-existence and mutual contacts, there has been give and take of metrical patterns and practices on both sides, Sanskrit and the Dravidian. Like the Prākrit meters, the Dravidian also employ features of alliteration, are dependent more on the *mātrās* or morae and tend to be, at least in the later measures, more definitely rhythmical than Sanskrit.—B. Brown, *Sanskrit Prosody* (1869); E. W. Hopkins, *The Great Epic* (1900; ch. 5); E. V. Arnold, *Vedic Metre* (1905); Rajagopala Rao, *Comparative Prosody of the Dravidian Languages* (n.d.); A. C. Chettiar, *Advanced Studies in Tamil Poetry* (1943); H. N. Randle, "Sanskrit and Gr. Metres," *Jour. of Oriental Research* (Madras), 17 (1947); H. D. Velankar, *Jayadāman* (1949; four prosody texts); V. Raghavan, "Sanskrit and Prākrit Metres," *Jour.* of the Madras Univ. (Section A., Humanities), 23 (1952–53).   v.r.

INDONESIAN POETRY, as distinguished from Malay poetry, which has been largely common to both Indonesia and Malaya, is defined here as the poetry written in the Indon. language or Malay of Indonesia now called *Bahasa Indonesia.* The period of modern Indon. literature begins with 1917 and since most of the modern poets have received a Western education it is not surprising that the *pantun* and *sjair* of older Malay literature (see MALAY POETRY) have been replaced by Western verse forms.

One of the first of the modern Indon. poets was Mohammad Yamin (1903–62), who introduced the sonnet form into Indon. poetry. His earliest poems deal with his homeland, at that time Sumatra, and appeared in 1922. Entitled *Tanah Air* (My Fatherland), they reveal a strong sentimental and lyrical tone. Yamin was greatly influenced by Rabindranath Tagore, who visited Indonesia in 1927 and one of whose works Yamin translated as early as 1928. A contemporary of Yamin is Rustam Effendi (1903–), author of the volume of lyrical poems *Pertjikan Permenungan* (A Sprinkling of Meditations), which appeared in 1926. In 1927 Sanusi Pané (1905–) published his *Puspa Mega* (Flowers of the Clouds) and in 1936 appeared *Tebaran Mega* (Scattered Clouds), a volume of moving poems by Sutan Takdir Alisjahbana (1908–), which was published just after the death of his first wife and dedicated to her. Prominent among the members of the *Pudjangga Baru* (New Writer) circle were Takdir Alisjahbana, Sanusi Pané, and Amir Hamzah (1911–46), son of a ruling family in North Sumatra, who is generally regarded as the outstanding poet of this pre-World War II group. Extremely sensitive, steeped in the older classical Malay language and literature, his reputation as a poet has steadily increased in Indonesia, though, for one with little knowledge and background in this field, his language is often difficult to understand. He was not a prolific writer, his best known collection of poems being *Njanji Sunji* (Songs of Loneliness), which shows the strong influence of the East as does Sanusi Pané in contrast to Takdir Alisjahbana who is more Western-oriented. Amir Hamzah also translated a number of poems from Eastern literatures and published these in 1939 under the title *Setanggi Timur* (Incense of the East).

During the Japanese Occupation (1942–45) literary activity was rather circumscribed and a strong censorship prevailed. It was, however, during this period that many of the prominent poets of the present day first began writing. Foremost among these was Chairil Anwar (1922–49), who is generally regarded as the leader of the so-called Generation of '45, a group which played a leading role during the Revolution (1945–50). Its poetry is characterized by a strong sense of realism with short, pungent, direct phrases and sentences and with emphasis upon content rather than upon form in distinct contrast to the prewar poets who composed largely in the romantic vein, using polite phrasing in long and often involved sentences. The latter group came under the influence of the Dutch Generation of '80 (Tachtigers, q.v.), especially the writings of Perk and Willem Kloos. Chairil Anwar's poems have been posthumously collected in several volumes, notably *Deru Tjampur Debu* (Melee of Noise and Dust), and *Kerikil tadjam dan Jang Terampas dan jang putus* (Sharp Gravel and Plundered and Broken). His influence upon his contemporaries as well as upon those of the next generation has been inestimable.

Among other poets of the Generation of '45 should be mentioned Rivai Apin, Asrul Sani, and Sitor Situmorang. In the meantime a new generation ('50) has appeared on the scene and some of its representatives, W. S. Rendra, Kirdjomuljo, and Nugroho Notosutanto, show considerable promise. Though writing almost exclusively in Dutch the Javanese poet Noto Soeroto (1898–1951) published a number of volumes of poetry which had considerable influence on such poets as Yamin. One of his best known collections is called *Melatiknoppen* (Jasmine Blossoms) and appeared in 1915.

ANTHOLOGIES AND TRANSLATIONS: *Poeisi Baroe,* ed. S. T. Alisjahbana (1946); *Kesusasteraan Indonesia dimasa Djepang,* ed. H. B. Jassin (1948); *The Flaming Earth,* ed. A. Ali (1949); *Gema Tanah Air: Prosa dan Puisi,* ed. H. B. Jassin (3d ed., 1954); *Indon. Writing in Tr.,* ed. J. M. Echols (1956); *Anthol. of Modern Indon. Poetry,* ed. B. Raffel (1964).

HISTORY AND CRITICISM: A. Pané, *Kort overzicht van de moderne Indonesische literatuur* (1949); J. S. Holmes, "Angkatan Muda, a

Checklist of Writings in Western Lang. Tr.," *Indonesië,* 5 (1951–52) and "A Quarter Century of Indon. Lit.," BA, 29 (1955); H. Subandrio, "La poésie indonésienne," *France-Asie,* 6 (1952); W. A. Braasem, *Moderne Indonesische literatuur* (1954); R. B. Slametmuljana, *Poëzie in Indonesia* (1954); A. Teeuw, *Pokok dan tokoh dalam kesusasteraan Indonesia baru* (3d ed., 2 v., 1955; best general survey) and "Iets over de jongste indonesische letterkunde: het werk van Sitor Situmorang," *Bijdragen tot de taal-, land- en volkenkunde,* 112 (1956); S. T. Alisjahbana, "Le développement de la langue et de la litt. indonésiennes," *Cahiers d'histoire mondiale,* 2 (1955); H. B. Jassin, *Chairil Anwar, pelopor Angkatan 45* (2d ed., 1959) and *Kesusastraan Indonesia modern dalam kritik dan esei* (2 v., 1962).   J.M.E.

INITIAL RHYME. See ALLITERATION.

INITIATING ACTION. See PLOT.

INSCAPE AND INSTRESS. Inscape in the aesthetic of Gerard Manley Hopkins, who coined the term, refers to the principle of physical distinctiveness in a natural or artistic object. Rooted in the Scotist concept of *haecceitas* or "thisness," inscape is whatever uniquely differentiates a thing from whatever was, is, or shall be. Hopkins himself somewhat inadequately defined the term in a letter to Robert Bridges as "design" or "pattern." (*The Letters of G. M. H. to Robert Bridges,* ed. C. C. Abbott, 1935, p. 66). In his critical study of Hopkins, W. A. M. Peters gives a more elaborate definition of inscape as "the outward reflection of the inner nature of a thing, or a sensible copy or representation of its individual essence." (*G. M. H.: A Critical Study Toward the Understanding of His Poetry,* 1948, p. 2). W. H. Gardner states simply that inscape is "the name for that 'individually-distinctive' form (made up of various sense-data) which constitutes the rich and revealing 'one-ness' of the natural object." (*Poems and Prose of G. M. H.,* 1953, p. xx).

Inscape and instress are closely related terms —inscape, the principle of individuation, and instress, the force which sustains and emanates from inscape. In the words of Gardner, instress is essentially the "sensation of inscape," the impulse "which acts on the senses and, through them, actualizes the inscape in the mind of the beholder" (*op. cit.,* p. xxi). Peters notes that instress is the force that "holds the inscape together" as well as "the power that ever actualizes the inscape" (pp. 14–15). For Hopkins, instress is the energy by which "all things are upheld" (*Note-books and Papers of G. M. H.,* ed. H. House, 1937, p. 98).—J. Pick,

G. M. H.: Poet and Priest (1942); *G. M. H.,* ed. J. C. Ransom and C. Brooks (1945); W. H. Gardner, *G. M. H.: A Study of Poetic Idiosyncrasy in Relation to Poetic Tradition* (2 v., 1948–49); *Immortal Diamond: Studies in G. M. H.,* ed. N. Weyand (1949); A. Heuser, *The Shaping Spirit of G. M. H.* (1959).   S.H.

INSPIRATION is the urge that sets a poet to work and the devotion that keeps him at it. There have been two theories of the origins of this urge and devotion. The first, more widespread in space and time than the second, is that i. comes from outside the poet; the second, that it comes from within him. The data on which this first concept is based come from literature and anthropology; the data for the second, from psychology.

In a passage from *On the Orator* (2.46.194) Cicero comments: ". . . I have often heard that—as they say Democritus and Plato have left on record—no man can be a good poet who is not on fire with passion and inspired by something like frenzy." And Plato (*Laws* 719c) alludes to the same view. He often refers to it, sometimes at length (e.g., *Symposium* 197A; *Phaedrus* 244–45). One brief dialogue, the *Ion,* is wholly devoted to a discussion of i. There Plato suggests, borrowing from Democritus, that just as iron filings become magnetized through the power of the magnet, so the poet is inspired through divine power, and that that power is conveyed by him to those who recite poetry—the professional rhapsodists—and, in turn, to their audiences. (See R. C. Lodge, *Plato's Theory of Art,* 1953).

Cicero discussed i. in his *On Divination* (1.18.37), *On the Nature of the Gods* (2.66: "No man was ever great without divine inspiration"), *On the Orator,* and *The Tusculan Disputations* (1.26). In modern Eng. translations of these passages (e.g., in the Loeb Library) the word *inspiration* is used but the words so translated are in Cicero *afflatus, instinctus,* or *concitatio: inspiratio* does not appear until the late Latin period.

Some recent discussions of Aristotle on this point (see A. H. Gilbert, *Literary Criticism, Plato to Dryden,* 1940, pp. 117, 118) conclude that Aristotle rejected i. as the source of the poet's power. (But see Aristotle, *Rhetoric* 3.7). So did Castelvetro in 1570, Dryden in 1679, and William Morris in the 19th c.

Testimony to i. from the poet's point of view occurs as early as *Odyssey* 22.347–48, where the bard, Phemius, says, ". . . the god has put into my heart all manner of lays, and methinks I sing to thee as a god. . . ." Homer, Hesiod, and Pindar invoke divine i. and so does Theocritus, but with the latter perhaps the invocation is just a literary convention. Virgil's address to the muse is well-known, and Ovid also has references to i. (*Ars Amatoria* 3.549; *Fasti* 6.5).

Longinus opens another aspect of the subject. He thinks of i. from the consumer's point of view. When a poem brilliantly imitates the work of another, we think its author inspired (13, 32). Likewise, when we read or hear a poem that is far beyond our experience, we again think it inspired (15).

When Christianity became the official religion of the Roman Empire, a Judaeo-Christian strain was added to the Graeco-Roman tradition that poetic i. came from outside the poet. For the Hebrew contribution consider Joel 2:28–30 and Ezekiel 2:1–10. The Church Fathers—Jerome in particular—often referred to David as the perfect poet-prophet, inspired by God.

From the 8th c. through the first quarter of the 19th we have many testimonies to a belief in the idea that poetic i. comes from outside the poet. Consider the following literary references: Bede (*Ecclesiastical History of the Eng. Nation* 4. 24; account of Caedmon); Dante, *Purgatorio* 1. 1–20; Boccaccio, *Genealogy of the Gods* (tr. Osgood), 14, 15.39, 15.99, etc.; J. C. Scaliger, *Poetics* (tr. Padelford), 1. 2; Sidney, *Defence of Poetry* (ed. Cook), pp. 8, 43; Francis Bacon, *Advancement of Learning* (World's Classics edition), p. 90; and Ben Jonson, *Discoveries* (ed. Schelling), pp. 74–76. The most significant, and probably the most serious, expression of the idea of i. in Eng. poetry of the 17th c. is found in Milton's invocations in Books 1, 3, 7, and 9 of *Paradise Lost*. Milton's Muse is not a tired literary convention carried over from classical poetry but a source of enlightenment comparable to the Protestant "inner light" and equated with the spirit from whom Moses received the Ten Commandments.

In the 18th c. i. was suspected of being "enthusiastic," as were the sermons of the more radical Protestant preachers. To classicists, who believed that the artist should rely primarily on conscious craftsmanship, this was undesirable (e.g., Shaftesbury's *Letter on Enthusiasm*); but to preromantics i. remained important: e.g., Edward Young's *Conjectures on Original Composition* (ed. Edith Morley), p. 30; William Blake's letter to Thomas Butts of April 25, 1802; Wordsworth's conclusion to *The Recluse;* Coleridge's account of the origin of *Kubla Khan* (see E. Schneider, *Coleridge, Opium, and Kubla Khan*, 1953, ch. 2); Poe's *Poetic Principle;* Emerson's *The Poet*.

So much for the first theory, the traditional one, that the poet's i. comes from outside himself, usually from the gods or God. Now for the second theory, that i. comes from within the poet. Of this there are two varieties, the first of which, the theory of genius, will serve as a transition between the two main theories

of i. The idea of genius, characteristically, was held by the romantic writers (ca. 1760–1840), who were severely taken to task for this view by Irving Babbitt in his essays *On Genius* and *On Being Original.*

Genius is a L. word, probably considered by the Roman as the equivalent of the Gr. *daimon* (demon). Socrates regarded himself as directed by his *daimon*. We still have in common parlance the phrases "good genius" and "evil genius." When Christianity became the official religion of the Roman Empire *daimon* came to be thought of primarily as diabolical. In late L., however, *genius* came to be used as the equivalent of *ingenium* and its operation was transferred from the outer to the inner world of the poet. *Genius* appears in the Eng. language as early as the 16th c. It came to mean *native talent*. By romanticists, however, a distinction was made between *genius* and *talent;* the former being something more significant than talent. (See S. T. Coleridge, *Biographia Literaria*, chs. 2, 15). Between 1751 and 1774, twelve publications treat the concept *genius*. The most important and influential of these was Edward Young's *Conjectures on Original Composition* (1759) in which one finds most of the romantic ideas which Irving Babbitt attributes to Rousseau and his influence. (See especially E. Morley's edition of Young's essay, 1918, p. 13). William Hazlitt published two essays on *Genius and Common Sense* (in *Table Talk*) and one on *Whether Genius Is Conscious of Its Power?* (in *The Plain Speaker*). See also Charles Lamb, *The Sanity of True Genius* (in *Essays of Elia*).

The second variety of the modern notion that the poet's i. comes from inside himself is due to the labors of psychologists who from about 1840 on were trying to make their field a true science. These researches are found in systematic treatises on descriptive or experimental psychology, in accounts of abnormal or subliminal psychology, and in volumes like Th. Ribot, *Essay on the Creative Imagination* (1906) or R. M. Ogden, *Psychology of Art* (1938). They give us many data on, but fail to solve the mystery of, the poetic temperament. The most coherent body of literary theory that has emerged from these researches is that named *surrealism* (q.v.) which draws on Marxian interpretations of Hegel as well as on psychological studies such as those of Freud and Jung. The surrealists believe that i. arises from the poet's observations of his own suppressed desires, but they also stress an objective factor—the observation of conflicts in society and the economic and political conditions from which the poet rebels. Thus the surrealists have reverted to the position of Blake in his *Marriage of Heaven and Hell* and (in fact) of Heraclitus (fl. 504 B.C.). Herbert

Read, who describes surrealism as "the resurgence of romanticism" in the essay listed in the Bibliography (below), says that with the aid of Marx and Freud the surrealists have arrived at a scientific basis for creative activity in terms of its own dynamics.

But even in the midst of this, Croce can still refer to the theory of external i.: "The person of the poet is an Aeolian harp which the wind of the universe causes to vibrate." The problem of the poetic mind is still a mystery. See also IMAGINATION, INVENTION, WIT.

G. E. Woodberry, *The I. of Poetry* (1910; Lowell Lectures); F. C. Prescott, *The Poetic Mind* (1922); R. M. Ogden, *The Psychology of Art* (1938); Gilbert and Kuhn (see index); A. H. Gilbert, *Lit. Crit. from Plato to Dryden* (1940; see index); N. K. Chadwick, *Poetry and Prophecy* (1942); J.W.H. Atkins, *Eng. Lit. Crit., Medieval Phase* (1943); R. Harding, *An Anatomy of I.* (3d ed., 1948; a "case book," somewhat similar to Ghiselin's *The Creative Process*); H. Read, "Surrealism and the Romantic Principle," *Crit.*, ed. M. Schorer, J. Miles, G. McKenzie (1948); H.J.C. Grierson, *Crit. and Creation* (1949); W. Fowlie, *Age of Surrealism* (1950); B. Ghiselin, *The Creative Process* (1952; a "case book," testimonies from mathematicians, musicians, novelists, painters, philosophers, poets, psychologists. Dryden and Mozart earliest); Abrams; C. M. Bowra, *I. and Poetry* (1955; see opening article). A.R.B.

INSTRESS. See INSCAPE AND INSTRESS.

INTENSITY is a fundamentally romantic criterion of poetic value, which, however, goes back to Longinus, *On the Sublime*. Longinus' use of ecstasy as the criterion of excellence anticipated the romantic reliance upon sensibility and taste. M. H. Abrams remarks that "the opinion of some nineteenth century critics that only the intense and necessarily brief fragment is quintessential poetry had its origin in Longinus' emphasis on the transport that results from the lightening revelation, the shattering image, or the stunning burst of passion." This tendency to isolate a pure poetry, and to locate it in individual figures and scattered passages, is to be found in Shelley, De Quincey, Lamb, and Hunt, more prominently in Keats, and most significantly in .Hazlitt, where as a doctrine of "gusto" it leads to Pater and impressionistic criticism. Poe carried the tendency to its logical extreme in his requirement that poems be short: "It is needless to demonstrate that a poem is such, only inasmuch as it intensely excites, by elevating, the soul; and all intense excitements are, through a psychal necessity, brief."

This emphasis upon the sudden single flash does not, however, represent the whole of Longinus' meaning, nor perhaps the most important consequences of his treatise for the romantics. Intensity is also a power of mind which interfuses its quality throughout the entire fabric of a poem. In his discussion of Sappho's ode Longinus makes i. the reconciler of opposites, with an effect objectively evident in the artistic unity of the whole. "Extremes meet"—the lover freezes and burns, is joyous and wretched simultaneously, and Sappho is able to render these contradictions acceptable. So in Keats i., like imagination, is a power, exemplified poetically in the *Ode to a Nightingale*, the *Ode on Melancholy*, and the *Ode on a Grecian Urn*, which "brings the whole soul of man into activity." It is not merely passion, but insight as well. "The excellence of every art is its intensity, capable of making all disagreeables evaporate, from their being in close relationship with Beauty and Truth. Examine 'King Lear,' and you will find this exemplified throughout" (Keats, *Letters*).

Equally important, in Longinus i. is the ultimate justification for the rhetorical and the poetic figures, the element which gives life to his elaborate analysis of figures. This with the Eng. romantics: Wordsworth, Coleridge, and Shelley find in i. of feeling the origin and justification for poetic language and metaphor, the quality which distinguishes poetry from poetic diction.—T. R. Henn, *Longinus and Eng. Crit.* (1934); Abrams. R.H.F.

INTENTIONAL FALLACY. See INTENTIONS, PROBLEM OF.

INTENTIONS, problem of. The chief end of criticism is to elucidate the literary work or the relation of the reader or of the author to the literary work. All critical discourse can be classified under one or more parts of this three-part relationship: author to literary work to reader. The critic at his best recaptures what the author created, *or* either more or less than what the author achieved in creating from conscious or unconscious intentions. Original i. and achieved i. are not the same thing, and in most instances there is probably a considerable discrepancy. "One would think it a matter of mere common sense, that in order to criticise justly you must put yourself, for the time being, as nearly as possible at the author's point of sight; form a sympathetic estimate of what he is striving to do, and then you can tell how nearly he attains his purpose" (Harriet Beecher Stowe). What the author was striving to do is "intentional," whereas what he achieved within the work is "actual." As distinguished from (1) original i., (2) the actual i. is the effect which the work aims to evoke, the organizing principle informing the whole, or the meaning which the work manifests or suggests. We may know what the author was striving to do because he has set down what he intended in public prefaces (Henry James) or in letters (Hart Crane). We know also what the author was striving to achieve by evidence of the work itself; he has achieved what he was striving for insofar as he has achieved a work of art. The problem of i. arises from the fact that the author's declared i. as to his design or meaning are one thing, and his achieved i.— the actual intention or meaning framed within the work itself—quite another thing, even when the one and the other happen to agree or coincide.

Also, ingenious interpretations or apparently far-fetched readings give rise to the question of i. Every freshman, confronted with what his teacher finds in the text or reads into it, asks the question: "How do you know that's what Shakespeare intended?" "The view that the genuine poem is to be found in the i. of the author is widespread even though it is not always explicitly stated. It justifies much historical research and is at the bottom of many arguments in favor of specific interpretations. However, for most works of art we have no evidence to reconstruct the i. of the author except the finished work itself. . . . 'Intentions' of the author are always *a posteriori* ratiocinations, commentaries which certainly must be taken into account but also must be criticized in the light of the finished work of art" (René Wellek). Assuming that the work warrants certain interpretations, how do we know that the author "intended" them?

"What did the author set out to do? Was his plan reasonable and sensible, and how far did he succeed in carrying it out?" (Goethe). What Matthew Arnold set out to do in *The Last Word* we know by evidence of the poem alone. Also, we know by the poem itself—on evidence of its contradiction in the intended effect or meaning—that his plan was not reasonable and consequently he could not succeed in carrying the poem through to a successful conclusion, for the ending of *The Last Word* contradicts the beginning in mood and theme. Furthermore, every work of art undergoes from age to age various interpretations, taking on new significances or shedding former ones— "colours which the artist neither foresaw nor intended." Writers frequently "compass more than they intend." "It can hardly be denied," writes a reviewer in the London *Times Literary Supplement* (Dec. 10, 1954), "that the excellence of any work of art must depend on the degree in which the artist has achieved what he intended—or, in Croce's language, has succeeded in expressing his own impressions." True—insofar as "what he intended" is taken to mean what resides within the text rather than outside it. Nothing the author asserts

about his i. can possibly establish the status of his work as work of art, for obviously what tests it as such is finally the work itself.

When the critic relies upon the author's declared intention, either the author's work or the critic's interpretation of it is deficient. Once the work is produced, it possesses objective status—it exists independently of the author and of his declared intention. It contains, insofar as it is a work of art, the reason why it is thus and not otherwise. The difference between art and its germinal event is absolute. The best artist constructs his work in such a way as to admit of no interpretation but the single intended one; its single i. being a single effect, one over-all meaning, one composite theme. All parts of the work of art are, ideally, relevant or functional to the whole. Irrelevant to the objective status of the work *as* art are criteria which dissolve the work back into the historical or psychological or creative process from which it came. "The function of the objective critic is by approximate description of poems, or multiple restatements of their meaning, to aid other readers to come to an intuitive and full realization of poems themselves" (W. K. Wimsatt, Jr.). The critic answers the question: What is the work's organizing principle? Analysis discovers what is intended by each part, all parts having relationship one to the other (the Jamesian canon). All analyses are open to criticism, all judgments are corrigible. The critical reader is the ideal reader.

While it may be supposed that the ideal reader is the author himself inasmuch as he presumably knows what he intended, such is not generally the case. Some German poets, replying to a questionnaire sent out by an ingenious psychologist at Munich, are reported to have become indignant at the imputation that they knew what they were doing. Hart Crane, on the contrary, knew precisely what he was doing, as evidenced by his letter on *At Melville's Tomb* (reprinted in *The Critic's Notebook*, 1950). Authors in the main tend toward concealment of their secret intention (if they have one) and write facetiously about it— Mark Twain, for example. In public pronouncements they play down or belittle the conception of themselves as the conscious craftsman. They obfuscate what their books are really all about by issuing bogus trade-secrets. They deny that their work has any artistic scheme or significance. A notable exception is Henry James in his Prefaces (collected in *The Art of the Novel*, 1934). "Never trust the artist. Trust the tale. The proper function of a critic is to save the tale from the artist who created it" (D. H. Lawrence).

Even when the critic's interpretation coincides with the author's declared intention, such a case of author's approval does not preclude interpretations by other critics; no one interpretation is the authorized one. If it were otherwise, then to grant validity to this correlation between the critic's interpretation and the author's declared intention presupposes that his declared i. is identical with his achieved one; but how can we ascertain this identity of i.? For, according to this conception, a work possesses not objective, intrinsic, or resident values; but only subjective, extrinsic, or nonresident ones. And the criteria for judgment would then be located in external, rather than internal, evidence. Again, the critic is using the work of art as a means for the reconstruction of the author's original intention, and the critic's practice is being judged not by other critical readers but by the author himself, as if the author were the only one who can properly measure the success of his critic's interpretation.

These assumptions are not valid and the questions based upon them are misleading. Even our most conscious craftsmen do not know fully what they intended during the process of creation. As T. S. Eliot remarks, a great deal more goes to the making of poetry than the conscious purpose of the poet; but apart from this consideration, not every artist creates consciously. Though Poe was a conscious craftsman and analyzed *The Raven* as a consciously constructed work, nevertheless his "Philosophy of Composition" remains a fabrication subsequent to the creative process or event. (Cf. W. E. Leonard's "The Poetic Process from the Inside," *Bookman*, Aug. 1932.) Where the artist reconstructs his blueprint of his creative process or original intention, as Poe and Stephen Spender have done, this avowed and externably ascertainable intention constitutes extrinsic evidence which, critically considered, is irrelevant or supererogatory. The work itself takes unconditional precedence, in establishing its status as work of art, over any externally ascertainable data which the author or commentator supplies about its genesis. The author's supposed or avowed i. must not be permitted to intrude or modify our interpretation of his achieved intention. The avowed intention of the author and/or the private history of his work provide clues to the critic for interpreting the work, but not the ultimate grounds for evaluating it. For the i. of a work resides within the work: "No judgment of intention has relevancy unless corroborated by the work itself, in which case it is supererogatory. It is therefore circular and misleading to speak of judging the work with respect to its success in carrying out the author's intention" (Wimsatt).

As for the critic's reconstructing from the work the author's germinal state of mind at the moment of creation (Tillyard to the contrary), the only concrete and full revelation of his state of mind is the work which has issued from it (Wellek and Wimsatt). The creative process "is a process of discovery which objectifies itself as a making," wherefore the artist does not know his actual intention until he achieves it (R. P. Warren). The only thing the artist can know to be what he meant to say is what he said *in the work* (Croce). Often his only "intention" may be simply to make a work of art. And once he has created a work the author becomes simply another reader of his work and, as such, is liable to misinterpret it (Wellek). Consequently, all questions about the author's own attitudes to his utterances within the work of art are critically irrelevant (C. S. Lewis).

M. C. Beardsley and W. K. Wimsatt, Jr., "Intention," in Shipley and "The Intentional Fallacy," SR, 54 (1946); R. W. Stallman, "The Crit. Reader" and "A Note on I.," CE, 9 (April 1948) and 10 (Oct. 1948); *The Critic's Notebook*, ed. R. W. Stallman (1950; ch. 8). For items not listed in *Critic's Notebook*, see E. Vivas, "The Objective Basis of Crit.," WR, 12 (1948); L. Fiedler, "Archetype and Signature: A Study of the Relationship between Biography and Poetry," SR, 60 (1952); L. Thompson, *Melville's Quarrel with God* (1952); R. Stewart, "New Critic and Old Scholar," CE, 15 (1953); R. W. Stallman, "The Scholar's Net: Lit. Sources," CE, 17 (Oct. 1955); cf. F. W. Bateson in CE, 17 (Dec. 1955), 131–35 and R. W. Stallman, *ibid.*, 180; Wellek and Warren; T. M. Gang, "Intention," EIC, 7 (1957).　　　R.W.S.

INTERLUDE (L. *inter* "between," *ludium* "play") is an ancient term denoting a brief entertainment (dramatic, acrobatic, mimetic or musical), introduced as a sort of break or recess between the courses of a feast or the acts of a play. In the Renaissance drama of Italy, the term used for short pieces inserted between long acts was *intermedii*. In France comic or satiric pieces of a similar type were known as *entremets* and in Spain as *entremés*. The latter became a distinct dramatic genre. In England the term "i." seems to have been applied, first by J. Payne Collier, to the plays of the transitional period between the medieval religious drama—mysteries, miracles, and moralities—and the professional drama that appeared after theaters were built and companies of actors organized, roughly from about 1500 to 1576. It is still a vague term, since the context of the concept is very mixed. It is used to designate not only early forms of romantic drama (Henry Medwall's *Fulgens and Lucrece*, 1497) but farce (John Heywood's *The Pardoner and the Friar* and *The Four PP*), morality plays (*Mundus et Infans* and Medwall's *Nature*), late mystery plays (*Godly Queen Hester* and John Bale's *Kyng Johan*), imitations of L. comedy and tragedy (Udall's *Ralph Roister Doister* and Preston's *Cambises*) and various dramatic survivals and new inventions. There is thus no clear line to be drawn between the i. and the earlier drama, nor, indeed, between the i. and the Elizabethan drama proper.—A. W. Ward, *A Hist. of Eng. Dramatic Lit. to the Death of Queen Anne* (3 v., rev. ed., 1875); C. F. Tucker Brooke, *The Tudor Drama* (1912); F. S. Boas, *University Drama in the Tudor Age* (1914) and *An Introd. to Tudor Drama* (1933); E. K. Chambers, *The Elizabethan Stage* (4 v., 1923); A. W. Reed, *Early Tudor Drama* (1926); A. P. Rossiter, *Eng. Drama* (1950).   H.C.

INTERNAL RHYME. See RHYME; LEONINE RHYME.

INVENTION. Ancient theories of social rhetoric commonly listed five "parts" of oratory: invention, disposition (or arrangement), elocution (or expression or style), memory, and delivery. The first three of these concepts have been widely employed also in the discussion of poetry to distinguish not only the tasks and abilities or faculties involved in writing poems but also the elements of poems themselves. In the typical statement of classical rhetoric, i. (*heuresis; inventio*, "discovery" [cf. also *ennoeō; excogitare*, "to think of"]) refers to the nature and source of *what* is said rather than to *how* it is said; it is, for example, "the excogitation of true or plausible things which render one's cause probable" (*Rhetorica ad Herennium* 1.2.3; cf. Aristotle, *Rhetoric* 2.26.1403^{a}34–^{b}1; Cicero, *De inventione* 1.7.9). Likewise, in poetics—although the concept has sometimes been used in such a way as to indicate the production of form or structure (e.g., in Aristotle's *Poetics*, Ch. 14), or of language or style (e.g., in J. du Bellay's *Deffense et illustration de la langue françoyse* 1.8 [1549] and the passages on Homer's "expression" in Pope's Preface to the *Iliad* [1715]), or of poetry in general (e.g., in Boccaccio's *De genealogia deorum* 14.7 [ca. 1365]), or of specific poetic kinds (e.g., in J. C. Scaliger's *Poetices libri septem* 1.1 [1561]), or of a particular whole work of art (e.g., in A. Gerard's *Essay on Genius* 1.3 [1774])—"i." has reference most often to finding, or otherwise producing, the subject matter or "content" of poems. The special meanings given to the term within this general usage, however, have been numerous. Sometimes, for example, i. is contrasted with "imitation" (of prior models), thus signifying originality and independence in the production of subject matter (see Horace, *Ars poetica* 119–20; Quintilian, *Institutio oratoria* 10.2.12; John-son, *Rambler*, no. 121 [1751]; E. Young, *Conjectures on Original Composition* [1759]); sometimes it is contrasted with "judgment" and thus refers to the native power of producing poetic substance as opposed to the control of that power by reason or convention (see Pope, *Essay on Criticism* 1.114 [1711]; Preface to the *Iliad*); sometimes it refers to the production of things "fanciful" or incredible (see Johnson, *Rambler*, no. 4 [1750]); sometimes it means the production of "fiction" as opposed to historical truth (see the discussion of comedy in L. Castelvetro's *Poetica d' Aristotele* [1571]); sometimes it indicates the artful combination of historical truth and imaginative falsehood (see G. de Scudéry's preface to M. de Scudéry's *Ibrahim* [1641]).

Basic differences in the conception of poetic i. are in large part functions of more general differences in poetic theory, particularly regarding what is necessary, practicable, or desirable in poetic subject matter, and why. Some of the principal theoretic variations may be suggested here. (See also IMAGINATION; IMITATION; EXPRESSION; INSPIRATION.)

In one large group of theories, in which essentially rhetorical principles and doctrines are predominant but are combined in various ways with ideas found originally in the "mimetic" poetic theories of Plato, Aristotle, and Democritus, poetic i. of the proper sort is a matter primarily of the proper imitation of nature (in one or another of several senses), since, it is argued, the desired effects of poetry are possible only through positive images or likenesses of real or natural things (see, e.g., Plutarch, *Moralia* 17–18; Thomas Aquinas, *In libros Posteriorum analyticorum expositio* I, Lectio 1; P. de Ronsard, *Abrégé de l'art poétique françois* [1565]; Dryden, *Parallel betwixt Poetry and Painting* [1695]; Johnson, Preface to *Shakespeare* [1765]). "Imitation of nature," however, has been a very inclusive concept, and in some theories in this tradition poetic i. legitimately embraces the powers of "imagining" things and of producing visionary, supernatural, and "marvelous" subjects; but the justification of these products usually remains the achievement of the proper effects of poetry, or those of a particular poetic kind, in an audience for which such things have, through education and tradition, become "natural" (see, e.g., G. Giraldi Cinthio, *Discorso al comporre dei romanzi* [1549]; Dryden's essay on "heroic plays" prefixed to *The Conquest of Granada* [1672]; A. G. Baumgarten, *Meditationes philosophicae de nonnullis ad poema pertinentibus*, 43–59, 109–14 [1735]).

With this group should be mentioned also certain other theories strongly influenced by the tradition of ancient rhetoric (e.g., those of Demetrius, Horace, Dionysius of Halicarnas-

INVERSION

sus, Longinus, Dante, and Pope) in which earlier Greek conceptions of poetic mimesis are somewhat less important and the poet (or other writer) is said to produce his subject matter more by drawing from his own natural and acquired fund of imagery, thought, feeling, or argument and by artfully imitating or emulating prior literary models than by copying from reality or nature. (Cf. R. McKeon, "The Concept of Imitation in Antiquity," in *Critics and Criticism,* ed. R. S. Crane [1952].)

There have been, on the other hand, a number of theories (including those of some of the Stoics and Neoplatonists, and, more recently, of "romantics" like Shaftesbury, Akenside, Herder, and Coleridge) in which rhetorical principles are less central and true poetic i. is conceived as the production of subject matter which in a radical dialectical sense transcends "ordinary" human images or ideas of nature and the natural, because the poet can best be justified not as one who satisfies a particular human audience but rather, e.g., as one who rivals or reflects a higher, "creative" being. Sir Philip Sidney's statement is characteristic: "Only the poet [of all human artists] . . . lifted up with the vigor of his own invention, doth grow in effect into another nature, in making things either better than nature bringeth forth, or, quite anew, forms such as never were in nature. . . . Neither let it be deemed too saucy a comparison to balance the highest point of man's wit with the efficacy of nature; but rather give right honor to the heavenly maker of that maker, who, having made man to his own likeness, set him beyond and over all the works of that second nature; which in nothing he showeth so much as in poetry, when with the force of a divine breath he bringeth things forth far surpassing her doings" (*Defense of Poesie* [1583; 1595]). In some theories in this general tradition (e.g., in those of Shelley and Emerson) the emphasis is on the poet's special inspired or intuitive "vision" of ultimate reality, since poetry must be justified by its provision of a better kind of "cognition" than that obtainable from ordinary human discourse. In others (e.g., those of A. W. Schlegel and Wordsworth) the emphasis is on the poet's power of supremely great or original thought and feeling, since poetry should be defended not as primarily depictive, plastic, or imagistic, but rather as a superior kind of "expression." Later dialectical theories have tended particularly to stress the need for a combination or coalescence of two or more transcendent powers, as in W. K. Wimsatt's conception of poetry as a "tensional union of making with seeing and saying" (*Literary Criticism: A Short History* [1957], pp. 752–55; cf. B. Croce, *Estetica* [1901]; J. Maritain, *Creative Intuition in Art and Poetry* [1953]; P. Wheel-

wright, *The Burning Fountain* [1954]; E. Vivas, *Creation and Discovery* [1955]).

It has sometimes been said that, while the original meaning of "i." involved primarily the idea of "finding" subject matter (even by imitating or borrowing from other writers), the term later came generally to suggest, through association with the concept of imagination, not so much finding as "creating." This observation has some validity, but it should not be allowed to obscure the fact that there never was a time in the history of European criticism when poetic i. was not conceived by someone in terms of the poet's creative or imaginative ability to transform given or discovered materials (for better or worse) or to produce entirely fictional or fantastic ("invented") subjects. And perhaps the most significant development in the recent history of the concept has been a general shift of emphasis, beginning in the 18th c. (see Pope's Preface to *Shakespeare* [1725]), away from the principle that the poet produces his subject matter (and his form and style) by habits or deliberate acts of learned artistry, including the imitation of prior works as well as the imitation of nature, to the converse principle that poetic substance (or at least the better poetic substance) is generated in the poet's soul, either in organic processes or in mechanical operations, by God or nature. (On the varieties of "organic" and "mechanical" theories of i. in 18th- and 19th-c. criticism, see M. H. Abrams, *The Mirror and the Lamp* [1953], pp. 156–225.)

C. S. Baldwin, *Ancient Rhetoric and Poetic* (1924) and *Medieval Rhetoric and Poetic* (1928); M. W. Bundy, " 'Invention' and 'Imagination' in the Renaissance," JEGP, 29 (1930); *The Great Critics,* ed. J. H. Smith and E. W. Parks (3d. ed., 1951; *index*); R. McKeon, "Imitation and Poetry," in *Thought, Action, and Passion* (1953); W. S. Howell, *Logic and Rhetoric in England, 1500–1700* (1956); Weinberg.   R.M.

INVERSION. (a) Rhetoric: turning an opponent's argument against him; (b) Grammar: reversal of normal word order, for the sake of meter ("Thus ceased she: and the mountain shepherds came" [Shelley]), rhyme scheme, or emphasis ("Down comes the winter rain—" [Hardy]). I. is often frowned upon as a device for securing emphasis, though it is frequently used. (c) Prosody: commonly the turning about of a foot by substituting stressed for unstressed, unstressed for stressed syllables, e.g., using a trochee for an iamb in iambic verse:

Catcht by|Conta|gion, like|in pun|ishment
(Milton, *Paradise Lost* 10.544).

In traditional Eng. verse inversion of stress is

a common device for securing variation, occurring most frequently in the initial foot and often immediately after the caesura, only very rarely in the final foot. Efforts by prosodists to limit the term to its meaning in the sense of reversed word order seem unrealistic.   R.O.E.

INVOCATION. A request for assistance addressed by the poet to a muse, patron spirit, or deity. The i. is standard in classical lyric and narrative poetry, and particularly in the epic. It usually comes at the beginning of a poem but invocations can be used for emphasis at critical moments in a narrative to introduce subsections of a work as, for example, books of an epic. Serious invocations are found at the beginning of the *Iliad*, the *Odyssey*, and the *Aeneid*. Invocations to God, Christ, or the Holy Ghost are common in early Christian poems (e.g., Sedulius, *Carmen Paschale;* Aldhelm, *De Virginitate*). Renaissance poems continue to use invocations, sometimes pagan and sometimes Christian (e.g., *Gerusalemme Liberata* and *Paradise Lost*). Mock-heroic poetry naturally produced mock invocations (e.g., Pope's *Rape of the Lock*; Byron's *The Vision of Judgment*). With the decline of classical influence the i. has ceased to be an important poetic convention but is still occasionally used as, for instance, in Hart Crane's *The Bridge* and St.-John Perse's *Amers*.   A.R.B.

IONIC. The origin of this verse form was associated with the Ionians of Asia Minor who appear to have used it in the orgiastic worship of Dionysus and Cybele (cf. the galliambic). The greater I. foot (*ionicus a maiore*) was composed of 2 long followed by 2 short syllables ($--\smile\smile$), whereas in the lesser I. (*ionicus a minore*) the 2 short preceded the 2 long syllables ($\smile\smile--$). Ionics were employed by some of the Gr. lyric poets (especially Anacreon) and by the tragedians, particularly Euripides, whether in monometers, dimeters, trimeters, or tetrameters (including galliambics). Horace, *Odes* 3.12, furnishes a good instance of lesser Ionics in a longish sequence:

miserārum̄ est|neque amorī|dāre ludūm|neque

dūlcī, etc.,

where the frequency of diaeresis may be noted. The use of regular *ionici a maiore* seems to have originated in the Hellenistic period, and in Latin an example is provided by Varro, *Satirae Menippeae* 489. An instance in Eng. poetry of lesser I. trimeter is Browning's "In the midnight, in the silence of the sleep-time." —J. W. White, *The Verse of Gr. Comedy* (1912); Hardie; Hamer; Dale; B. Gentili, "Gli ionici a maiore nella poesia greca," *Maia,* 2

(1949); Koster; P. Habermann, "Antike Versmasse," *Reallexikon,* 2d ed., I.   R.J.G.

IRANIAN POETRY. See PERSIAN POETRY.

IRISH LITERARY RENAISSANCE, Irish Literary Revival, Irish Renaissance. The Ir. Lit. Ren.—which flowered during the half-century beginning about 1885, and which had minor sister movements in Celtic Britain—constitutes the most striking general literary phenomenon of its period and represents a major segment of the clearest post-Victorian phase of the romantic movement. But though it has strands reaching into other segments of that movement (particularly symbolism), it is not parochial in appeal, despite a certain self-containment referable to its spiritually well-defined racial quality. And as the expression of a people in whom the lyric and romantic impulses had blossomed before Continental Europe was out of the dark ages, it found its most intense expression in verse, in dream-wound plays, and in short prose fiction. It was not technically inventive, unless in portions of James Joyce and sporadic efforts to imitate the technical effects of early Ir. verse such as those of F. R. Higgins; a conservative tradition as old as the *filid*—the ancient scholar-poets—operated generally to limit technical aspiration to the perfection or modulation of established forms (some of whose characteristics, from internal rhyme to assonance, may have been Celtic inventions). Its real glory —and power—lies in its fusing of delicacy with extravagance, of the tender with the heroic: it is constantly a revelation of restrainedly savage vitality and spiritual sensitivity. Its ethical background is largely Protestant or nonorthodox; its significant statement is in Eng. But in the end one leaves it in the conviction that it is a logical reiteration of that wild beauty smoldering in the hero-tales and romances, the intricately fashioned lyrics, of centuries gone— this despite touches of overlush romanticism and the fact that ancestral tradition was often a harder and more "realistic" thing.

Initially, this Ren. was sparked primarily by the desire of W. B. Yeats and his literary friends to create "a national literature that made Ireland beautiful in the memory," by the antiquarian and political impulses of Sir Charles Gavan Duffy (in 1842 one of the founders of the *Nation*) and his kind, and by the linguistic and historical enthusiasm of Dr. Douglas Hyde and his sympathizers. Behind the activities of these men, of course, lay the spadework of numerous historians, translators, and miscellaneous intellectuals; among the journals hospitable to their work may be mentioned especially the *Dublin University Review, Sinn Féin* (a 1906 transformation of *The United Irishman*), and Æ's *Irish Homestead*.

Indubitably the finest poet of the movement
—and quite clearly one of the finest lyrists
the world has yet seen—was W. B. Yeats (1865–
1939), behind whose early work stand most
clearly Blake, Morris, Shelley, and Whitman,
with Donne a subsequent exemplar. But there
is also a tremendous amount of excellent stuff
in the verse of Æ (G. W. Russell), James
Stephens, Dr. Oliver St. John Gogarty, Padraic
Colum, F. R. Higgins, and many others. Unfortunately, limitations of space do not permit
a proper estimate of this mass of work; much
less of the remarkable body of drama and
prose fiction accompanying it. Suffice it to say
in conclusion that the Ren. brought not only
recreation of heroic Ir. story (as in Yeats's
Wanderings of Oisin) and "reincarnations" of
verse originally in Ir. (as in some of Stephens'),
but also mystical and transcendental lyricism
linked with Emerson and the East (as in Æ),
a remarkable development of the reined-in line
of Keats, Poe, and Morris (especially in Yeats),
a revival of balladry, an extension of the
"metaphysical" element, an infusion of the
personal lyric with dramatic surcharge more
powerful than ever before evident in Eng.
(again, most strikingly in Yeats), and a notable evocation of natural accent and speech
rhythms.

There is no definitive account of the movement in all its aspects. The following books
will be found *generally* useful: G. Moore, *Hail
and Farewell* (3 v., 1911–14); F. L. Bickley,
J. M. Synge and the Ir. Dramatic Movement
(1912); M. Bourgeois, *John Millington Synge
and the Ir. Theatre* (1913); C. Weygandt, *Ir.
Plays and Playwrights* (1913); E. A. Boyd, *Ireland's Lit. Ren.* (1916, rev. 1922); L. R. Morris,
The Celtic Dawn (1917); A. E. Malone, *The
Ir. Drama, 1896–1928* (1929); S. L. Gwynn, *Ir.
Lit. and Drama* . . . (1936); W. B. Yeats, *Auto-
biography* (1939); U. M. Ellis-Fermor, *The Ir.
Dramatic Movement* (1939); R. Farren, *The
Course of Ir. Verse in Eng.* (1947).   G.B.S.

IRISH POETRY. EARLY PERIOD. Early Ir. poetry is inevitably of special interest to the
prosodist. This is not to deny the existence of
scattered pieces of naive charm or occasionally
moving content: it is merely to emphasize the
constricting concern with early-established,
early-codified, and highly conservative lyric
techniques. Epic—like formal drama—is nonextant, its nearest approximations being confined to certain adventure stories like *Immram
Snédgusa ocus Maic Riagla* (Voyage of Snédgus
and Mac Riagla: ?10th c.), a tale of monkish
pilgrimage, and—perhaps—some of the verse
interpolations in the *uirscéal*, or "romance,"
into which the Ir. preferred to channel their
heroic stories. So one may for brief comment
concentrate on the lyric tradition, which

reaches back to two or three gnomic pieces
fancifully attributed to Amergin, reputedly
one of the invading "Sons of Milesius" in pre-
Christian times.

Actually, much of the earliest Ir. verse appears to have emanated from the southern
half of the island: verse largely rhetorical and
genealogical in character, accentually controlled in some degree, loose in syllabic line-
structure, and marked by protracted alliterations. (Northern poetry was technically somewhat more regular and less alliterative: one
may cite, with Flower, the *Voyage of Bran*.)
This early material (6th c. and later) was
eventually supplanted by verse based on syllable-counting, complicated patterns favoring
short-lined quatrains conceptually self-contained, and consonantal rhyme governed by
arbitrary grouping of the consonants (e.g.,
words ending in *ll* could rhyme only with those
ending in *m, nn, ng,* and *rr*). Behind this intricate verse lie 8th-c. L. influences; in it are
to be found many anonymous monkish quatrains, often preserved in tracts or on manu-
script-borders. The first clearly isolated poet,
the Connachtman Fland mac Lonáin, emerges
in the 9th c., to which also belongs the anonymous lyric in which a wandering Leinster
scholar compares himself to his cat, *Pangur
Bán*—the lyric named by Flower as the first
manuscript example "of the personal poetry of
the Irish."

That early lyricism seems in general most
moving in its nature pieces and elegies; for it
has few love poems, and its numerous eulogies
—like its historical pieces—have small interest
for the general reader. Between the 7th and
17th c. appeared also much religious verse,
seldom poetically consequential; its better
authors, known and unknown, include the
13th c. Donnchadh Mór Ó Dálaigh.

Early Ir. verse was, of course, a special concern of the fabulously privileged *fili*, a man
highly trained in law and history as well as
poetry, whose terrifying satires, with their supposedly magical effectiveness, helped ensure
popular respect; and of the humbler *bard*.
(And one may note that the Ir. distinguished
between "poetry" and "bardcraft.") But the
filid eventually lost status, perhaps during the
Scandinavian invasions; the *baird* emerged
after the Anglo-Norman invasion as in many
cases retainers of wealthy and influential families—and composers of quantities of tiresome
encomiastic verse.

In the Anglo-Norman aristocracy, artificial
Fr. lyrical conventions found a channel permitting fusion with Ir. practices, though the
preserved evidence is largely of the 16th and
17th c. Certainly, however, this tradition explains such work as that of the 14th-c. "Gerald
the Rhymer," Earl of Desmond, to mention

only one polished practitioner. To these initial modern centuries, incidentally, belong some very earthy lyrics out of anonymous clerical tradition—lyrics underscoring the realism and irony which, sentimental assumptions to the contrary, give Ir. poetry its real character.

With the dispersal of the aristocracy in the 17th c., and consequent loss of patronage, the "Bardic Schools"—organizations which had originated among the *filid*, and which had imposed rigorous metrical training upon their neophytes—began to break up (cf. here the verse of David O'Bruadair), and a loosening of the strict metrical system (whose rules the bards had codified) followed. Vowel-rhyme, stress-government, and long lines began to appear; but structure still remained far from simple, not least in respect to internal assonance.

Much postmedieval Ir. verse, which includes a good many "vision" poems, can interest few except the dedicated. Thus, e.g., the entire 17th c. seems to offer little more exciting than the tiresome *Contention of the Bards*, though—like its successor—it produced many ballads exploiting the matter of the great Fenian storycycle, as well as patriotic pieces poetically negligible. And perhaps the only approximations of major work in the 18th c. prior to Brian Merriman's effort are Michael Comyn's *Laoi Oisin i dTír na nÓg* (Lay of Oisin in the Land of the Young), a work underlying Yeats's *Wanderings of Oisin*, and *Torolbh Mac Stairn*, an adventure story suggestive in flavor of the latemedieval.   G.B.S.

LATER IR. POETRY, GAELIC AND ENG. As practiced by professionals, significant Ir. poetry in the vernacular came to an abrupt end about 1780 with Brian Merriman's *Cúirt An Mheadhán Oidhche* (The Midnight Court). What followed for over a century were the semiliterate productions of rural poetasters given to satiric, patriotic, and religious versifying. Their technique, based on Ir. forms, passed eventually into street-songs made in Eng. With the 20th c. there developed a linguistic enthusiasm which provoked some interesting, though not widely known, work. That nothing of consequence should have succeeded Merriman's poem is surprising, for *The Midnight Court*, a thousand lines in length, shows no decadence: it is exuberant, and while keeping to the machinery of the traditional *aisling* and using the elaborate pattern of bardic poetry, it has a new outlook; nostalgia is changed to extravagance and earthiness. Nevertheless, Ir. poetry from Goldsmith on (*The Traveller* is dated 1765; *The Deserted Village*, 1770) becomes mainly poetry in Eng.

Signs of such a development had, indeed, become apparent during the century preceding Goldsmith's, though much of the evidence could be called literature only by courtesy. Examples can be culled from the work of such figures as Sir John Denham (1615–69), the Virgilian who wrote *Cooper's Hill* (1643) and who was actually named "one of the fathers of English poetry" by Samuel Johnson; Thomas Duffet (fl. ca. 1676); Dryden's collaborator Nahum Tate (1652–1715); the nimble-witted Mrs. Mary Monk (?1677–1715); *et al.* But it remained for Goldsmith to prove himself the first Anglo-Ir. poet of any stature.

Eventually Ir. poetry began to attain intermittent racial distinctiveness through translations of native folk song or through the writing of verse in Eng. for the old harp music. An instance would be *The Outlaw of Loch Lene*, a translation (1798) by Jeremiah Joseph Callanan which reproduces the unemphatic rhythm and assonantal effects of the Ir.: "Oh, many a day I made good ale in the glen, / That came not from stream nor from malt, like the brewing of men. / My bed was the ground, my roof the greenwood above, / And all the wealth that I sought, one fair kind glance from my love." Afterward Thomas Moore (1780–1852), following the pattern of the old music, achieved a like unemphatic rhythm—something different from the usual Eng. metric with its stress on particular words: "At the mid hour of night, when stars are weeping, I fly / To the lone vale we loved when life shone warm in thine eye, / And I think that, if spirits can steal from the region of air / To revisit past scenes of delight, thou wilt come to me there, / And tell me our love is remember'd even in the sky!" Moore was spiritually responsive to traditional Ir. material, though imperfectly aware of it. At his best in *Ir. Melodies*, of which ten numbers—the verses set to traditional music—appeared between 1807 and 1834, he shows less depth than facility in the songs. *The Harp That Once through Tara's Halls*, however, remains a superb specimen.

Moore's pathetic younger contemporary, James —self-baptized "Clarence"—Mangan (1803–49) made the only other pronounced verse contribution to the romantic movement then surging in Eng. literature. Quite rightly, the *Concise Cambridge History of Eng. Literature* has credited Mangan with having anticipated Poe "in his use of a repeated and varied refrain." His distinctive poems are based on translations of Ir. originals; examples would be *The Lament for the Princes of Tir-Owen and Tir-Connail, Dark Rosaleen, Kathleen-ni-Houlihan*, and O'Hussey's *Ode to the Maguire*. These versions are closer to the originals than Mangan usually gets credit for being. In *Ode to the Maguire* the verse is like the storm that spends its fury on the chieftain addressed; it rises and falls, pauses and lashes out. *The Lament for the Princes of Tir-Owen and Tir-*

Connail has magnificent structure. The structure of *Dark Rosaleen* is weak, but the piece has a fervor and a flashing imagery that make it one of the world's greatest patriotic poems. *Dark Rosaleen* is an address to Ireland under the "secret" aristocratic name; *Kathleen-ni-Houlihan* is an address under the "secret" peasant name, and in it Mangan achieves a charmingly varied rhythm.

With Sir Samuel Ferguson (1810–86) came the first significant attempts to exploit legendary Ir. saga in verse. *Lays of the Western Gael* (1864), *Congal*—an attempt at epic (1872), and the other matter leading to the collected *Poems* of 1880 testify to soundness of intention, at least, though a genuine poetic gift is harder to find here than metrical talent abetted by antiquarian scholarship. Yet one can understand the enthusiasm of the young Yeats in referring to Ferguson as "the one man of his time who wrote heroic poetry," even while one prefers the translated folk-songs—*Cashel of Munster, Dear Dark Head*, etc.—to the original matter.

Like Ferguson, more to be praised in the intention than in the achievement, is Aubrey de Vere (1814–1902), who in *The Foray of Queen Maeve* . . . (1882) and elsewhere reflected his own explorations of Ir. saga and romance. And with him might perhaps be mentioned William Allingham (1824–89), a fellow of the British Pre-Raphaelites whose *The Fairies*, at least, seems safely corralled by the anthologists.

Much patriotic verse, poetically of little consequence, had, it should be added, begun to be printed after the "Young Ireland" group got its own periodical—*The Nation*—in 1842. But conditions in Ireland during these years were hardly conducive to the development of a literary culture. In 1846 the dreadful famine struck; in 1848 the abortive rising under William Smith O'Brien led to deportation and voluntary exile for some promising literary figures; in 1867, scarcely two years after the birth of William Butler Yeats, came the unsuccessful Fenian rising.

In Yeats (1865–1939), of course, the first indubitably great Ir. poet arrived. It is his *Wanderings of Oisin* (1889—preceding by five years George Russell's *Homeward: Songs by the Way*) that really ushers in the "Irish Literary Renaissance" (q.v.). Herein Yeats takes up where the bardic poets left off, so to say, for his story of the younger hero of the Finn saga in the Land of the Young is rooted in Comyn's *Lay of Oisin*.

Through his long life, by example and discourse, Yeats was to lead the poets of his country away from what was facile and rhetorical. A personal passion, a deliberate style, a language that was living speech were the constituents he stood for. He discounted the nationalist propaganda which previous poets thought it was their duty to offer and which, even when not explicit, made their verse rhetorical. The discipline he insisted on is bound to have an enduring effect on Ir. poetry:

> Irish poets, learn your trade,
> Sing whatever is well made,
> Scorn the sort now growing up
> All out of shape from toe to top.

And as creator of a national theatre he gave a new faculty to the poets, whose rhythms and accents sometimes recalled those of Dr. Douglas Hyde's translations. Meanwhile such collections as O'Grady's *Silva Gadelica* (1892) and Sigerson's *Bards of the Gael and Gall* (1897) had helped to consolidate interest in traditional Ir. lyricism, as well as to intensify concern with that of the many poets of the Renaissance stimulated by Yeats's example. P.C.; G.B.S.

ANTHOLOGIES AND OTHER MATTER IN TR.: *The Love Songs of Connacht* (1893) and *The Religious Songs of Connacht* (8 v., 1906), both ed. and tr. D. Hyde; *The Voyage of Bran*, ed. and tr. K. Meyer (2 v., 1895–97; with an essay by A. Nutt); *Duanaire Finn, the Book of the Lays of Finn*, ed. and tr. E. MacNeill (1908); *Selections from Ancient Ir. Poetry*, ed. and tr. K. Meyer (1911); *An Anthol. of Ir. Verse*, ed. P. Colum (1922; enl. 1947); *Bards of the Gael and Gall*, ed. and tr. G. Sigerson (3d ed., 1925); K. A. Jackson, *Studies in Early Celtic Nature Poetry* (1935) and *A Celtic Miscellany* (1951); *The Silver Branch*, tr. S. O'Faoláin (1938); *The Fountain of Magic* (1939) and *Kings, Lords, & Commons* (1959), both tr. F. O'Connor; *1000 Years of Ir. Poetry*, ed. K. Hoagland (1947); *Ir. Poets of the 19th C.*, ed. G. Taylor (1951); *Early Ir. Lyrics*, ed. G. Murphy (1956); *Oxford Book of Ir. Verse*, ed. D. MacDonagh and E. S. L. Robinson (1958).

HISTORY AND CRITICISM: D. J. O'Donoghue, *The Poets of Irel.* (1893, 1911); D. Hyde, *A Lit. Hist. of Irel.* (1899); E. Hull, *A Text-book of Ir. Lit.* (2 v., 1906–8); R. I. Best, *A Bibliog. of Ir. Philol. and of Printed Ir. Lit.* (1913) and *A Bibliog . . . of Ir. Philol. and of Manuscript Lit . . . 1913–41* (1942); E. Quiggin, *Prolegomena to the Study of the Later Ir. Bards 1200–1500* (1914); D. Corkery, *The Hidden Irel.* (1925); E. Knott, *Ir. Syllabic Poetry* (1928, 2d ed., 1957); St. J. D. Seymour, *Anglo-Ir. Lit., 1200–1582* (1929); J. Vendryes, *La Poésie de cour en Irlande et en Galles* (1932); R. Flower, *The Ir. Tradition* (1947); M. Dillon, *Early Ir. Lit.* (1948); G. B. Saul, *The Shadow of the Three Queens* (1953); R. K. Alspach, *Ir. Poetry from the Eng. Invasion to 1798* (rev. ed., 1958).

See also *Six Ir. Poets*, ed. R. Skelton (1962); *New Poets of Ireland*, ed. D. Carroll (1963); A. and B. Rees, *Celtic Heritage* (1961). G.B.S.

IRONY

IRISH PROSODY. See CELTIC PROSODY.

IRISH RHYME. See ODL; CELTIC PROSODY.

IRONY. (Gr. *eironeia*, originally, "dissimulation," especially through understatement). The *eiron* of Gr. comedy was the underdog, weak but clever, who regularly triumphed over the stupid and boastful *alazon*. The later usage of the term shows the influence of its origin. In Plato's *Dialogues*, for example, Socrates acts the part of an *eiron*. His questions seem naive, often pointless, and even foolish; in the end, however, it is Socrates' antagonist whose case is demolished. Hence the term *Socratic irony*.

Classical rhetoricians distinguished several varieties of i. In i. proper, the speaker is conscious of double meaning and the victim unconscious; in sarcasm both parties understand the double meaning. Other forms include meiosis and litotes (understatement); hyperbole (overstatement); antiphrasis (contrast); asteism and charientism (forms of the joke); chleuasm (mockery); mycterism (the sneer); mimesis (imitation, especially for the sake of ridicule). Depending on their use, pun, paradox, conscious naïveté, parody, etc. can all be ironic. Renaissance critics inherited the whole cumbersome schema of figures worked out by classical rhetoricians. They added little to the critical understanding of i. during the 16th and 17th c. On the other hand, baroque poets and dramatists exploited i. more fully and more consciously than their predecessors. They bequeathed a generally ironic point of view to the writers of the 18th c. In Voltaire and Addison i. is frequently a device for avoiding commitment—perhaps a reflection of skepticism and rationalism. In Swift, one of the great ironists, it is the masque of a *saeva indignatio* directed against the complacency of the age.

To the German romantics (Schlegel, Tieck, Solger) i. was a means of expressing the paradoxical nature of reality. Since it expressed two meanings simultaneously it could suggest the polarities (e.g., absolute vs. relative; subjective vs. objective; mental categories vs. *Ding an sich*) which post-Kantian philosophy found everywhere in experience. *Romantic i.* is a special form of irony described by Tieck and practiced most notably by Jean-Paul Richter and Heinrich Heine: the writer creates an illusion, especially of beauty, and suddenly destroys it by a change of tone, a personal comment, or a violently contradictory sentiment.

Modern discussions have tended to emphasize two main categories of i.: simulation (verbal i) and dramatic i.

Verbal i. is a form of speech in which one meaning is stated and a different, usually antithetical, meaning is intended. In understatement the expressed meaning is mild, and the intended meaning intense; as, for example, Mercutio's comment on his death-wound, "No, 'tis not so deep as a well, nor so wide as a church door; but 'tis enough, 'twill serve." In overstatement, a device especially common in Am. folk humor, the reverse is true. Often a statement becomes ironic because of its context. When one looks out of his window at a rain storm and remarks to a friend, "Wonderful day, isn't it?" the statement can only be understood in an ironic sense. When Hamlet rejects the idea of suicide with the remark, "Thus conscience does make cowards of us all," his remark is unconsciously ironic because *conscience* is a sacramental word associated with moral goodness, whereas *coward* has pejorative connotations. The same kind of i. is illustrated in Comus' speech of seduction, where a true principle (natural fertility) is used to prove an untrue doctrine (libertinism). Often, i. can arise from explicit or implicit contradiction, as when Marvell begins his proposition to his coy mistress with the remark that time is short, and ends with the observation that love can make time pass more quickly ("Thus, though we cannot make our sun / Stand still, yet we will make him run.") Finally, foreshadowing is often ironic. Hamlet's speech on the fall of the sparrow has one meaning in its immediate context and a somewhat different one when considered in connection with Hamlet's own "fall" at the end of the scene.

Naïveté is a special form of i. half way between verbal and dramatic i. Basically, it is a pose of innocence or simplicity. Socrates used it; it appears frequently in the literature stemming from St. Paul's remark that the wisdom of God is the folly of this world, and the wisdom of this world is the folly of God. The tradition of ironic naïveté can be traced in *The Praise of Folly*, Shakespeare's fools and clowns, *Gulliver's Travels*, Blake's *Songs of Innocence*, Dickens' *Barnaby Rudge*, Dostoevski's *Idiot*, and Faulkner's *Sound and the Fury*. An extremely rudimentary example of this form of i. is the stanza,

The golf links lie so near the mill
    That almost every day
The laboring children can look out
    And see the men at play.
        (Sarah N. Cleghorn)

Dramatic i. is a plot device according to which (a) the spectators know more than the protagonist; (b) the character reacts in a way contrary to that which is appropriate or wise; (c) characters or situations are compared or contrasted for ironic effects, such as parody; (d) there is a marked contrast between what the character understands about his acts and what the play demonstrates about them.

Tragedy is especially rich in all forms of dramatic i. The necessity for a sudden reversal or catastrophe in the fortunes of the hero (Aristotle's *peripety*, which, he said, is found in all true tragedy) means that the fourth form of i. (form d) is almost inevitable. *Oedipus Rex* piles i. on i. For example, form (a) is present because of the fact that the audience becomes increasingly conscious as the play progresses that Oedipus is rushing blindly to his doom. Form (b) is present because of Oedipus' insistence on pursuing his investigation to its bitter climax (and the fact that his basic motivation is a desire for justice and public welfare is a further i.—his fall is in part caused by his nobility). Form (c) is illustrated in the parallel between blind Tiresias (who can "see" morally) and the figure of Oedipus when he, too, has gained "vision" after blinding himself. Form (d) is, of course, present in the contrast between what Oedipus hopes to accomplish and what he finally does accomplish.

Among later ironists, Chaucer, Montaigne, Shakespeare, Voltaire, Swift, Fielding, Flaubert, Henry James, and Thomas Hardy are especially noteworthy, although this list can only suggest the richness and variety of dramatic i. Shakespeare's plays, because of their multiplicity of characters and fluid act and scene structure abound in dramatic i. of form (c); and often several characters are placed in analogous situations, so that their reactions ironically contrast with each other (e.g., the lovers in *As You Like It*). The 19th-c. determinists often emphasize "i. of fate," by which is meant the contrast between the individual's conscious aspirations and what fate (or biology or society or psychology or the "immanent will") eventually makes of him. *Cosmic i.* is the contrast between man's feverish efforts and the indifferent universe, as in Hardy's *The Dynasts*.

A variety of reasons can be given for the presence of i. in literature. J. H. Robinson, for example, says that man is a child and a savage, the victim of conflicting desires. Man may talk like a sentimental idealist and act like a brute. "Human thought and conduct, can only," he says, "be treated 'broadly and truly in a mood of tolerant irony." Certain literary critics in the 20th c., including I. A. Richards, Cleanth Brooks, and Robert Penn Warren, have insisted that the truly good poem or work of fiction employs a method of i., in the sense that a writer is aware that his proposition or belief may be relative to opposed propositions and beliefs and, being aware, he expresses a temper of mind and employs a language that is necessarily ironic. Kenneth Burke has said that i. is especially common in 20th-c. literature, and the reason, as he has it, is that we live with "relativistic

sciences," like psychology and anthropology, which have tended to undermine once stable values. Whether Burke is correct or not, it remains true that the ironic attitude is common in modern literature. Possibly it is a safe generalization to say that periods in which religious and social opinions are relatively homogeneous will feel less need for the skeptical and ironic mind, but even in such periods i. functions as an agent of qualification and refinement.

J. A. K. Thomson, *I., an Historical Introd.* (1926); G. G. Sedgwick, *Of I., Especially in the Drama* (1935); C. Brooks, *Modern Poetry and the Tradition* (1939); D. Worcester, *The Art of Satire* (1940); W. Van O'Connor, *Sense and Sensibility in Modern Poetry* (1948); Wellek; Wimsatt and Brooks; G. Dempster, *Dramatic I. in Chaucer* (1959); R. B. Sharpe, *I. in the Drama* (1959); I. Strohschneider-Kohrs, *Die romantische Ironie in Theorie und Gestaltung* (1960); N. D. Knox, *The Word "I." and its Context, 1500–1755* (1961). w.v.o'c.

ISOCHRONISM. The equality of successive temporal units. In prosody, the assumption that meter (q.v.) consists of a succession of equal-time units (feet, lines, stanzas), said to be isochronous. I. is a term frequently employed by accentual and temporal prosodists (as distinguished from syllabic or accentual-syllabic prosodists) and by those theorists who describe the phonetic phenomena of verse in musical terms. Many maintain that Eng. is a naturally isochronous language, characterized by "a tendency to squeeze units into relatively equal time spans, marked by stress pulses" (S. Chatman, "Robert Frost's 'Mowing': An Inquiry into Prosodic Structure," KR, 18 [1956], 421–38). Those committed to i. as a prosodic assumption (these theorists are sometimes called "stress-timers") hold that a dissyllabic and a trisyllabic foot occupy equal intervals of time. See PROSODY.   P.F.

ITALIAN POETICS. See MEDIEVAL, RENAISSANCE, BAROQUE, NEOCLASSICAL, MODERN POETICS.

ITALIAN POETRY. 1200–1400 THE SEED. It. poetry is rooted in spiritual song. The first noble composition in an It. dialect was a deeply felt, though brief, song of thanksgiving and praise to God. Written by St. Francis of Assisi early in the 13th c., it is usually referred to as the *Laudes Creaturarum* (Praises of God's Creatures). Starting with the word *Altissimu*, and ending with the word *humilitate*, the poem is a sustained outpouring of gratitude to God by all of creation for its existence, beauty and goodness. Despite a rather complex versification and rhyme the form as a whole is marked by a primitive simplicity.

The earliest forceful poet in It. poetry was Jacopone da Todi (ca. 1230-1306). His collection of 100 *laude* reveals a highly ascetic and penitent spirit seeking self-annihilation in God through sacred song. His almost morbid descriptions of rotting flesh and the horrors of death achieve poetic proportions when used as analogies to the sinful soul. It is, however, in those poems intended to provide an antidote for this negativism that Jacopone is at his best. Here he points the way to possible redemption in the contemplation of the Incarnation and Passion through the eyes of the Virgin. Only through complete absorption in God can true Love be achieved—the loftiest of all possible goals:

Amore; amore che sì m'hai ferito,
altro che amore non posso gridare;
amore, amore, teco so' unito,
altro non posso che te abbracciare;

Love, oh love, you have wounded me so
that no other word can I cry out;
Love, oh love, so united am I with you
that only you can I embrace . . .

At about the same time that Umbria was producing this spiritual poetry, Sicily was being hostess to the brilliant court of Frederick II. Having become an international cultural center, this court gave a new direction to It. poetry. From the Emperor on down, everyone seemed to dabble in poetry—especially the type of courtly love poetry imported from Provence. In reworking the manifold aspects of this theme, this first group of It. poets established metrical forms that set the pattern for two of the principal It. lyric forms, the *canzone* and the sonnet. The best known members of this "Frederician Circle" were Jacopo da Lentino, Pier della Vigna, Giacomino Pugliese, and Rinaldo d'Aquino. (See SICILIAN SCHOOL.)

With the collapse of Frederick's court in the middle of the 13th c., It. poetry underwent its next significant changes in Tuscany. Here it first experienced a period of abstruse contents and complex form at the hands of staunchly individualistic writers. The most typical representative of this period as well as the first prolific It. poet was Guittone d'Arezzo (d. 1294) whose poetry, on a great variety of themes, was highly intellectual.

By the third quarter of the 14th c. what may be called a new movement in poetry had spread from the University center of Bologna to Florence. Because of a fortunate phrase used by Dante, this movement has since been referred to as the *dolce stil nuovo*, q.v. ("sweet new style"). Its essence consisted in a formal Christian spiritualization of courtly love. The Beloved actually becomes an Angel of God. The poet whom Dante called the "father" of the school was Guido Guiñizelli (ca. 1240-1276). It was his *canzone* starting *Al cor gentil repara sempre Amore* . . . that set the pattern for the new direction. The last stanza in Rossetti's translation typifies the new approach:

My lady, God shall ask, "What dared'st thou?"
    (When my soul stands with all her acts review'd);
"Thou passed'st Heaven, into My sight, as now,
    To make Me of vain love similitude.
    To Me doth praise belong,
    And to the Queen of all the realm of grace
    Who endeth fraud and wrong."
Then may I plead: "As though from Thee he came,
    Love wore an angel's face:
Lord, if I loved her, count it not my shame."

As this approach to love gained more adherents, the philosophical-mystical elements were supplanted by technical and intellectualistic ones.

Another important member of the movement was Guido Cavalcanti (ca. 1255-1300). His principal contribution consisted in a detailed "psychological" analysis of love as a passion, using "spirits" and "little spirits" to represent various states of mind. This led to a highly involved theory of love which found expression in the dense and lengthy *canzone* beginning *Donna mi prega*. . . . It is not here, however, that Cavalcanti excels as a poet. It is rather in those sonnets, ballads and *canzoni* in which he sings of his own love experiences, and in which he reveals an anguished restlessness and passion.

It remained for Dante Alighieri (1265-1321) to gather together the various threads seen thus far. Many and varied were the poems that Dante had composed prior to the *Divine Comedy*, and everywhere is the influence of his predecessors evident—particularly in his earliest ones. In Dante's hands, however, the theme of *fino amor* undergoes a significant change: from worldly and self-centered it now becomes religious and selfless. It too is inspired by a beloved, but this time she bears the name *Beatrice*, a name that assumes a progressively deeper significance as Dante's artistry matures. Already in his earliest noteworthy poem Dante had her partake of the miraculous:

For as she goes by
Into foul hearts a deathly chill is driven
By love, that makes ill thought to perish there;
While any that endure to gaze on her
    Must either be made noble, or else die. . . .
Also this virtue owns she, by God's Will:
Who speaks with her can never come to ill. . . .

Humbleness, and the hope that hopeth well,
　By speech of hers into the mind are brought,
And who beholds is blessed oftenwhiles.
　　　　　　　　　　　　　(Rossetti)

Her presence not only purifies and ennobles, but can even result in actual salvation. By 1293 Dante gathered 31 of his poems on Beatrice, connected them with prose commentaries and called the work the *Vita Nova* or "New Life." The booklet's importance lies in its being a prefiguration of the *Divine Comedy.* Dante's apparent concern for artistic effect in his use of a highly mystical and Christian symbolism makes of the book an exalted effort to define the nature of Beatrice and the love she inspires in terms that are highly poetic and Christian at the same time. By the end of the *Vita Nova* Beatrice stands in relation to Dante as Christ stands in relation to humanity. The entire drama nevertheless remains within the framework of an intensely lyrical story of young and devoted love. Most of the other poems written by Dante in his youth but not included in the *Vita Nova* bear the imprint of experimentation in technique rather than true lyrical inspiration. Three of these, three long *canzoni,* Dante incorporated into his highly learned and unfinished *Convivio* or "Banquet," through which he desired to share his fund of knowledge with other men. The *canzoni* were to serve as courses while elaborate commentaries were to be the bread. The moral and social direction that the commentaries give to the poems deprive them of whatever freshness they might have originally possessed.

Dante's true greatness as a poet rests, of course, on his *Divine Comedy.* In it Dante succeeds in giving a vision of life based on the highest ideals and aspirations of Christianity. By making us see the universe through the eyes of God whose presence is reflected everywhere in the poem, Dante achieves a sublimity which has since been unrivaled. Everywhere in the poem one encounters the hand of the Triune God: the terza rima, the 3 *cantiche,* the 33 *canti* in each *cantica,* the 9 divisions of each realm, the very year in which the story unfurls (1300), etc. Everywhere in the poem must one be prepared to see beneath the surface of the image presented to the mind's eye, for to understand God's language calls for maximum concentration. Thus, just as Dante himself, the protagonist, stands for something more than Dante, the same holds true of the hundreds of other characters and events found in the work. But what gives the work exceptional poetic breadth is the drama of love that unfurls from beginning to end, for in showing mankind the way to salvation Dante has recourse to his love for Beatrice who in her death has become the handmaiden of God and the

Revealer of the Truth. The *Comedy* is a veritable paean of Love.

Other poets of the time associated with the "Sweet New Style" were Lapo Gianni, Gianni Alfani, Dino Frescobaldi and Cino da Pistoia (ca. 1265–1337).

With Francesco Petrarca (1304–74) It. poetry reaches its loftiest lyrism. Few poets before Petrarch had sung of human love with longer strain or deeper penetration. No poet has, indeed, exerted a more lasting influence on love poetry throughout the world. Unlike Dante, Petrarch refused to let metaphysical preoccupations interfere seriously with his view of life. He was essentially a moralist whose knowledge of antiquity, unparalleled in his own day, had convinced him that in the ethical area there was no conflict between his three favorite thinkers, Cicero, Seneca, and St. Augustine. It is no wonder, therefore, that his chief poetic symbol, the name of his beloved, should possess an ambiguity not present in Dante. Laura, the ancient laurel or the Christian palm, possesses, as poetic imagery, an internal tension which at the hands of Petrarch attains lofty lyric heights.

Of the more than 400 It. poems written by Petrarch, 366 form his *Canzoniere* on which his reputation rests. Most of the poems are sonnets, but there are many *canzoni,* ballads, and madrigals. The collection as a whole is basically a diary or story of Petrarch's love for Laura, proceeding from the life to the death, and then to the transfiguration of the beloved. The work is divided into two parts; the first comprising 263 poems written during Laura's life, the remaining after her death. There are a number of poems on other themes, but the basic theme is the perennial one of unrequited love, with the one actor a poet of exceptional sensibility, refinement and culture. Thus each love poem is a highly polished song revealing a new psychological facet of the drama. While there are many traces of the influence of his Prov. and It. predecessors in Petrarch's lyrics, his Laura is a far cry from the beloved sung by the poets of the "Sweet New Style." The general tone of the collection is neither religious, nor Platonic, nor sensual; it oscillates between these three poles. Just as it is usually the absent rather than the present Laura that is the more suggestive, in the same way those love poems written after her death surpass the others in vividness as the poetry becomes pure reminiscence. Other distinctive features of the *Canzoniere* are: a new stress on nature description as background for the love motif; an almost haunting sense of the passage of time and the vanity of all things; an intense awareness of the conflict between spiritual and temporal values; a strong interest in public affairs and in the welfare of friends. The opening and closing poems of the collection are recantations for having succumbed to a sinful passion. The very last word of the final poem is *Peace* which throughout remains the longed-for but unachieved goal.

Technically, Petrarch achieved new levels of perfection in the *canzone* and the sonnet. His keen sense of euphony, proportion and linguistic exactness gives to his verse an impeccable artistic polish. On the other hand, to use the words of a critic: "Petrarch's very sensitiveness to verbal sounds, to variations in mood, and to imagined similarities betrays him, at times, into plays on words, into over-heightened contrasts, and into strained metaphors that are unworthy of his finer verse—but were appropriated all too readily by his imitators." It was this negative quality of Petrarchan verse that was later to form the substance of "Petrarchism" (q.v.). The other It. work of Petrarch that deserves mention is the *Trionfi* (Triumphs) which qualify as lofty poetry in their grandeur of conception and in certain isolated portions.

Though possessing neither great depth nor originality, the approximately 125 surviving lyrics of Giovanni Boccaccio (1313–75) possess considerable merit. In them, sonnets, *ballate* and *canzoni*, the characteristics of the "Sweet New Style" as modified by Dante and Petrarch receive an imprint of secular sprightliness reminiscent of the spirit of the *Decameron*. The beloved is now named *Fiammetta*, "Little Flame," and the background the social scene of Naples. Boccaccio's reputation as a poet rests, however, on a series of longer poems that either became milestones in the evolution of It. poetic genres or had a significant influence on foreign poets, especially Chaucer. These include the *Caccia di Diana*, the first It. hunting poem; the *Filostrato*, the first It. romance using ottava rima and written by a nonminstrel; the *Teseida*, the first epic by a Tuscan writer; and the *Ninfale fiesolano*, the first It. idyll. Except for the first of these, all of the poems are written in ottava rima, which subsequently became the standard form for It. narrative poetry. Unless the poems are read as Christian or moral allegories, their true value resides primarily in their technical achievements.

Among the many minor lyrists of the mid-14th c., the two outstanding ones were Franco Sacchetti (1330–1400) for the variety of his verse, and Fazio degli Uberti (ca. 1305–1368) for the deeply personal nature of his love poetry.

1400–1600. THE FLOWERING. The moral decadence accompanying the political and social crises of the Christian world during the 14th c. led to a religious revival in the first decade of 1400. As a result the *lauda* came once again

into its own, receiving further amplification in the direction of the religious drama. Among the writers of such pieces, the outstanding were Feo Belcari (1410–84) and Giovanni Dominici (1356–1419). Popular poetry also enjoyed a great vogue at this time. Such poems of this period are usually referred to as *giustinianee*, after Leonardo Giustinian (1388–1446) whose *strambotti* and *canzonette* captured the folk spirit so perfectly that many of them have become part of the folk repertory.

By mid-century vernacular poetry had become so sterile that a contest was organized in 1441 by the famous humanist, Leon Battista Alberti. Known as the *certame coronario*, "the contest for the crown," it offered a laurel crown of silver to the poet submitting the best poem in It. Not only was there no winner, but the only significant results of the contest were the first attempts to use Latin meters in It. verse.

By the third quarter of the century, a revival set in. The man primarily responsible for the revival was Lorenzo de' Medici (1449–92) in whom was found the rare admixture of the intellectual and practical ruler. He was quick to see the political advantages of encouraging a culture that combined classical elements with the popular tradition. His princely freedom enabled him to write lyrics whose merit and variety made him the most representative poet of the new era. The variety of Lorenzo's verse is reflected not only in the number of different metrical forms he used (*canzoni, sestine, ballate, canti carnascialeschi, laude, capitoli, terza rima, ottava rima*), but also in the spirit of the poetry, constantly fluctuating between a sensual licentiousness, an intellectual mysticism that often seems sincerely religious, and a sensitivity to the psychological complexities of love, often recalling the *stilnovisti* or Petrarch but with stronger Platonic overtones. Lorenzo's chief poetic works are his *Rime* and his *Commento sopra alcuni de' suoi sonetti*. The former consists of sonnets done mostly after the Petrarchan manner; the latter of about 40 sonnets connected with a prose commentary after the manner of the *Vita nuova*. His *canzoni* and *sestine* attest to his versatility; while his two rhapsodies, the *Selve d'amore* (Improvisations on Love), envelop the love theme with classical-idyllic imagery so typical of later Renaissance verse. Having made the pre-Lenten celebration of Carnival more spectacular than ever before, Lorenzo also achieved notoriety as writer of the songs sung by participants. Known as *ballate* or *canti carnascialeschi*, many are licentious and even obscene. In fact, the spirit of Lorenzo's age is often summarized with the concluding verses of one such song which every It. schoolboy memorizes at an early age:

Quant 'è bella giovinezza,
che si fugge tuttavia!
Chi vuol esser lieto, sia:
di doman non c'è certezza.

How beautiful is youth,
which is in constant flight!
Let whosoever wishes be joyful:
there is no certainty of tomorrow.

Notwithstanding their intellectual bent, Lorenzo's nine religious *laude* reflect the spirit of Lent as convincingly as his carnival songs the spirit of Carnival.

The outstanding poet of Lorenzo's circle was Angelo Ambrogini, or Poliziano, as he called himself (1454–94), whose intensely humanistic training made him excel as a writer of odes and epigrams in L. and Gr. Of the various moods reflected in Poliziano's It. lyrics, the most successful one, poetically, was the carefree gaiety of youth against the background of beautiful landscape. Many of his numerous *rispetti* reflect this mood, but it is in his dance songs, and above all in his *Stanze per la giostra* (Stanzas for the Tournament) that it achieves superb lyrical expression. The enchantment of the music and polish of Poliziano's verse often conceals a vein of melancholy deriving from the often cited "sense of limit" that characterized much Renaissance poetry. His *Stanze per la giostra* are as typical of It. Renaissance lyric poetry as Botticelli's work is of early Renaissance painting. The poem was originally intended to celebrate a tournament won by Giuliano, Lorenzo's brother. Giuliano's untimely death, however, caused Poliziano to leave the poem unfinished at a point where the tournament was about to start. Since the 125 octaves of the first book as well as the 46 of the second had been devoted to a highly lyric depiction of the transfiguration of a youth as he enters adolescence and suddenly falls under the magic spell of Beauty and Love, the poem becomes a sublime expression of what one critic calls "the very dream of life." By symbolizing the essence of youth in the adventurous and carefree spirit of the dedicated hunter, and the transfiguration to adolescence in the sudden trapping of the unsuspecting hunter who one day chases a deer to a clearing in which sits a girl of captivating beauty, Poliziano hits upon poetic imagery of superb effectiveness. By then objectifying the power of love and beauty and its relation to youth in an elaborate and vivid description of the Realm of Venus, the poet intensifies still further the poetic effectiveness of the imagery. Stopping where it does, the poem remains a portrayal of youth and love still in potential, unfulfilled and vibrant, thereby leaving the reader with a sense of dream and myth.

The vigorous humanism that gave Florence undisputed supremacy in practically all fields by the end of the 15th c., received a temporary setback in the very last years as a result of the short-lived religious revival led by Savonarola. Meanwhile the Aragonese court of Naples was also sponsoring a group of distinguished poets and artists. One was Benedetto Gareth, better known as Il Cariteo (1450–1514), whose poetry, full of exaggerated Petrarchism and conceits, established him as a true pioneer of *secentismo*. Another was Jacopo Sannazzaro (1456–1530) who also wrote Petrarchan sonnets and *canzoni*. The idyllic qualities of his piscatorial eclogues in Latin and of his renowned pastoral novel, the *Arcadia*, also inform his It. lyrics. His verse furthermore gives evidence of a linguistic polish resembling the forthcoming purism of Bembo's circle.

Elsewhere in Italy, conventional vernacular verse of this period limited itself pretty much to a rather servile Petrarchism. Among the names most often cited as writers of such verse in the latter half of the 15th c. are those of Serafino Aquilano, Antonio Tebaldi, better known as Tebaldeo, and Matteo Maria Boiardo (1434–94) whose collection of lyrics, the best of the century together with those of Lorenzo and Poliziano, is usually overlooked because of his more renowned *Orlando Innamorato*.

Following the eclipse of the carnival song in Florence at the close of the century, popular poetry elsewhere in Italy continued to show signs of life with the *frottola* and the *barzelletta* (q.v.). At the same time, while lyric poetry was becoming mired in the quicksand of an artificial and uninspired Petrarchism, another form of popular poetry, the narrative poem, was coming into its own. Carolingian legends had from very early times taken root in the repertories of It. *cantastorie* or minstrels. As these evolved throughout the peninsula, not only were new characters and situations introduced, together with other distinctively It. traits (such as use of the ottava rima, the divisions into two feuding families, etc.), but a new spirit, sometimes verging on irrespect for and mockery of the traditional Paladins and Charlemagne, became typical. It was at the Court of Lorenzo, in the third quarter of the 15th c., that Carolingian matter became for the first time grist for the pen of a court poet. At the request of Lorenzo's mother, Luigi Pulci (1432–84) undertook to write an epic in the popular style with a view to rehabilitating Charlemagne's reputation. In the first version of Pulci's work, the *Morgante*, this goal was not achieved. Pulci seemed rather to find delight in lingering on the doings of the famed giant, Morgante, of oral tradition, and of the semi-giant, Margutte, an original creation and the first fully developed picaresque figure in European literature. The droll, Rabelaisian spirit given to the work by the antics of these two, received further stress in a later version bearing the title of *Morgante Maggiore*.

At about the same time, the highly aristocratic court of Ferrara, under the house of Este, was finding special pleasure in the sentimental refinement of Arthurian romances. These also had long been popular in Italy, having been imported from France in the latter half of the 13th c. In Tuscany minstrels had adopted many of the stories either as prose romances or as plots for their *cantari*. But Tuscan audiences found greater delight in the stirring Carolingian tales. For the almost medieval court of Ferrara, on the other hand, composed of knightly gentlemen and cultured ladies, the Arthurian legends had special appeal. It is not surprising therefore that at this time one of its poets, Boiardo, should have undertaken a serious work dealing with Arthurian matter. In fact, by successfully fusing Arthurian matter with the Carolingian tradition in a single poem, Boiardo initiated a new epic cycle. The work, entitled *Orlando Innamorato*, still retains the Roland of Carolingian fame as its hero, but he now exemplifies Arthurian romantic love rather than Carolingian prowess. Throughout the poem, written in ottava rima, there is a skillful interweaving of plots and subplots as the poet takes his audience to distant lands of enchantment. The poem was never completed because of the poet's untimely death.

The new epic cycle instituted by Boiardo had such appeal for the Court of Ferrara that by 1506 another poet, Ludovico Ariosto (1474–1533), undertook to complete Boiardo's poem. In taking up Boiardo's story where it had left off, Ariosto cures Roland of his skirt-chasing vice by leading him through a series of events culminating in a violent insanity which leaves him only after divine intervention. Roland thus becomes once again the champion of yore as he leads Charlemagne's forces to ultimate victory. Some distinctive features of the poem include: an unparalleled perfecting of the ottava rima as well as of the technique of keeping several plots going simultaneously; a highly effective irony resulting from the periodic intrusion of the poet reminding the listener or reader that the story is fictitious; a sane and robust humor that prevails even in the most serious episodes; the complete rehabilitation of Charlemagne; numerous episodes open to allegorical interpretation; and a pervasive sense of classical beauty.

Throughout the turbulent years of the 16th c. Petrarchism reigned supreme in It. lyric poetry. By the first quarter of the century,

it had actually become a literary canon or doctrine largely through the efforts of Pietro Bembo (1470–1547), an active courtier who eventually became literary dictator of his age. Much of the Petrarchan verse in the first half of the century, however, escaped the stigma of cold imitation, first because of the influence of the Neoplatonic movement of the time; and secondly because of a sense of formal elegance and good taste that dominated the versification. At the head of the better followers of the Petrarchan manner at this time must be placed Bembo himself, whose sonnets, *canzoni*, and *ballate* reflect an elegance that contrasts sharply with the distorted Petrarchism of a Cariteo or a Tebaldeo. Yet, even his poetry contains a virtuosity of diction that attests to the refined tastes of a literary admirer of Petrarch rather than to the effects of personal inspiration. There were also a number of women who wrote personal *Canzonieri*. Among these, the most capable were Vittoria Colonna, Gaspara Stampa and Veronica Gambara.

Notwithstanding the temptation of confusing poet and artist, the evaluation of the lyrics of Michelangelo (1475–1564) as among the best of the 16th c. is certainly justifiable. His about 200 completed poems as well as many of the uncompleted ones contain many echoes of the "Sweet New Style," of Dante, of Petrarch, of Savonarola and of the Neoplatonism of Ficino.

Despite the general disagreement among critics regarding the relative merits of the lyrics of Torquato Tasso (1544–95), recent criticism has tended to reevaluate his poetry on the basis of its modern traits. Of his nearly 2,000 lyrics, a good number suffer from a formal Petrarchism or from an intellectualistic vein. The great majority of the poems are inspired by ladies in whose understanding and beauty Tasso sought consolation. The inspiration found expression in traditional lyric forms, but the better ones, especially among the madrigals, possess a musical and rhythmic beauty and a wealth of imagery that often seem to anticipate 19th c. Fr. symbolism. This was the same Tasso who wrote the *Gerusalemme Liberata* (completed in 1575), Italy's foremost "heroic poem." Just as in the high Renaissance Boiardo and Ariosto had turned to Carolingian-Arthurian matter to write a narrative poem that would appeal to the highly secular Court of Ferrara; so a half century later, in the same Court, but in the midst of the Counter-Reformation, Tasso turns to the first Crusade in his attempt to write a truly Christian epic. Like the *Furioso*, Tasso's poem uses the Christian-Saracen conflict as its theme; concentrates on knightly prowess; makes wide use of love as a motivating drive; abounds in episodes of feminine valor and of fantastic adventures; and has frequent recourse to enchantments and divine intervention. However, while Ariosto had sung of "ladies, knights, arms, loves, courtesies and bold adventures," Tasso now sings "the pious arms and the Captain who liberated the great sepulchre of Christ."

There is little doubt that in the storming and capture of Jerusalem Tasso saw a theme open to spiritual interpretation. In fact, he himself wrote a highly medieval allegorization of the poem. His lyrical nature, however, had made him succeed much more with those episodes depicting the varying emotions of the several lovers than with those intended to portray the love affairs as sinful temptations that obstruct man's road to salvation. When he later tried to correct this by eliminating a number of such episodes and adding others, the result, entitled *Gerusalemme conquistata*, was but a cold echo of the *Liberata*. Rather than the vigor, irony and good humor of the *Furioso*, the dominant qualities of the *Liberata* are a sweetness touched with melancholy, and a sustained dignity. Tasso's was one of the last great voices that had helped Italy maintain a cultural predominance over the rest of Europe for three centuries. The three great themes of its poetry since 1200 had been love, religion, and patriotism. It was in a sense unfortunate that all three themes found sublime expression in the early stages of the rise of the vernacular, for as a result the imitation of Dante, Petrarch and Boccaccio became the rule, rather than personal inspiration. This, of course, could only lead to stagnation.

1600–1760. THE DROUGHT. The stagnation of It. poetry in the 17th c. was actually due to a variety of causes. Not only did political and religious factors tend to stifle inspiration, but the fact that poetry had already undergone its period of glory while other arts, especially music and architecture, were about to reach new levels of vitality, now relegated poetry to the role of handmaiden rather than mistress. It was indeed these two arts that now gave poetry still another direction, for musicality together with elaborate and extended figures of speech and constructions became the most desired qualities of versification. The metaphor tending toward shocking conceits and witticisms became the order of the day. Figures such as "the young leaf that weaves the shade together with the sun" enjoyed high favor. As for the contents, no matter was too trivial. In retrospect, however, these general tendencies of *secentismo*, as the movement was called (from Seicento-17:h c.), and as is the case with all decadent tendencies, contained within them a seed for future growth. This was a new consciousness of the intrinsic value of the written and spoken word which is capable of arousing images, impressions and sensations that constitute the essence of life. Naturally, a great deal of exaggeration resulted from the application of this new discovery, but it is not difficult to see latent within it an attitude suggestive of modern theories of aesthetics.

These new tendencies were pushed to their extremes by Giambattista Marino (1569–1625) whose name is often used to designate the movement (*marinismo*, q.v.). Poetry for Marino was but a means to personal glory, and had as its chief object the arousing of surprise and marvel. Whence the exaggerated rhetorical devices that abound everywhere in his poetry. His principal work is the long, lascivious poem *Adone*, published in Paris in 1623. Intended originally as an account of the simple love story of Venus and Adonis, the poem took about 20 years to complete and in its 20 cantos in ottava rima covers an abundance of heterogeneous material abounding in far-fetched and sometimes bizarre situations and figures of speech. His three other collections of lyrics were the *Lira*, the *Galleria*, and the *Sampogna*. In each work the lyrical and suggestive power of the word seems to be Marino's basic concern. Admirers of Marino's manner were not only numerous, but in many cases ranged far beyond the master's extremes. The excesses of the extremists were such as to produce a poem comparing Mary Magdalen's hair to a river, her eyes to suns, and, consequently, her weeping over Christ to bathing His body with suns and drying it with rivers!

There was also a less radical side to *secentismo*. Among those who were almost untouched by the excesses of *marinismo* and who felt instead the pull of classical versification, the outstanding one was Gabriello Chiabrera (1552–1638). Of his massive production, his pindaric *canzoni* and especially his anacreontic *canzonette* are the only ones possessing some poetic virtues. A deep religious faith inspired the most powerful poetic voice of the It. 17th c., that of the dominican Tommaso Campanella (1568–1639). Despite a life fraught with persecutions, Campanella was the author of a prodigious number of works in both prose and poetry, in L. and It. His lyrics develop primarily the three themes of the greatness of God, the ignorance and evil of man, and the praises of God's creatures.

Between 1690 and 1760 a concerted drive was made against the excesses of 17th c. poetry. An actual Academy was organized in 1690 with the specific purpose of eliminating bad taste from It. poetry by returning to classical standards. Since the new goal was to be a pastoral simplicity, the name given to the Academy was "Arcadia." In its condemnation of *marinismo* and promotion of classic taste, the movement performed a noble literary service, but poetry now became but a form of rhythmic and musical virtuosity. For this reason it found its best expression in the arias and other lyrical moments of the *libretti* of Pietro Metastasio (1698–1782) and in his separate *canzonette* and sonnets.

1760–1860. THE NEW ROOTS. The political vicissitudes of Northern Italy during the early and middle portions of the 18th c. generated a social consciousness which began to find its way into poetry toward the third quarter of the century. Its first clear voice was that of Giuseppe Parini (1729–99) who in 1763 began publication of Italy's most famous satire, a long poem in blank verse entitled *Il Giorno*. The poem depicts the typical day of an It. *giovin signore*, or gallant, of the times as seen through the eyes of his preceptor. The work is divided into four parts, Morning, Noon, Evening, and Night. The distinctive quality of the poem is a persistent irony arising from the deadly serious tone with which the poet treats the triviality and pettiness of the gallant's activities. The pervasive elegance of the verse, with its mixture of classical and baroque imagery, adds considerably to the irony. In exposing the absurdity, the injustice and the cruelty of the reigning aristocracy, the poem is a lofty expression of deep indignation. Parini's moral, civic and pedagogical convictions form the basis of 19 odes which, in their lyrical treatment of subject matter (civic, pedagogic) that had hitherto been considered outside the province of poetry, represent a reaction against Arcadia and the opening of new horizons for subsequent It. poetry.

The poet who, next to Petrarch and Michelangelo, gave the strongest personal imprint to the It. sonnet was Vittorio Alfieri (1749–1803), known primarily as Italy's foremost tragedian. Inspired essentially by an overpowering sense of liberty, Alfieri's sonnets are spontaneous outcries of an intensely proud and strong-willed soul rebelling against any form of undue restriction. This, together with a highly personal style, causes even his love lyrics, of obvious Petrarchan inspiration, to assume distinctive qualities. The principal themes of Alfieri's poetry are love, glory, liberty, art and death; while its predominant tone is tragic and melancholic and seems to have its roots in the perennial dissatisfaction and restlessness that typified the poet's own life and prompted some critics to characterize him as "protoromantic."

The most distinctive quality of It. poetry since 1200 had been its literary and learned character. It was largely bookish and scholarly in its conscious attempt to reflect a high degree of culture. In fact, few were the better poets who were not also noteworthy men of letters. The neoclassical tastes of the third quarter of the It. 18th c., together with the new advances of the Enlightenment, made it a propitious time for this quality of It. poetry to emerge full force. With Vincenzo Monti (1754–1828) we have the lettered poet *par excellence*. Everywhere in his poetry can be heard echoes either of Antiquity or of Dante or of the Renaissance or of the recent Ossianic fad. (*Basvilliana, Il Bardo della selva nera, Promoteo*)

The infiltration of northern romanticism into Italy never succeeded in entirely supplanting the essentially classical traits of It. poetry. The poems of Ugo Foscolo (1778–1827) represent the almost perfect fusion of the spirit of romanticism with the classical sense of harmony and beauty. Foscolo's early poetry reflects a variety of influence, ranging from Petrarch, the Arcadia, and Parini, to Ossian, Rousseau and Young. Though mediocre for the most part, it reveals a constant improvement in technique—especially in the composition of the ode, a form in which Foscolo seemed to be most at home. His romantic side emerges full force in his twelve sonnets, many of obvious Petrarchan inspiration, which are usually listed among the best of the 19th c. Foscolo's best known work is *Dei sepolcri* (On Sepulchers), a long poem in blank verse, in which the classical and the romantic are in almost perfect harmony. The basic inspiration is the strong personal reaction of the poet to a Fr. decree stating that all tombstones in Milan were thenceforth to be of identical size and form. In arguing against the decree, the poem becomes the answer of the heart to what appears to be inexorable reason. Despite the dialectic, the poem proceeds by lyrical flights as the poet adduces the history of civilization, the cult of the dead in various epochs, and great men of the past and present. The second half of the poem, however, is a hymn to immortality in which can be felt a tragic sense of illusion as the poet becomes aware of the fact that even the grave is a temporary expedient in the unending flux of life. For many, Foscolo's masterpiece is an unfinished elaborate poem entitled *Le grazie* in which the poet attempts to depict the function and mission of the Graces as initiators of wisdom and beauty.

Just as Parini, Alfieri and Monti had been the chief poetic voices of the It. *Rinnovamento*, the "Renewal" of It. thought and letters; so Foscolo, Manzoni and Leopardi are the first three great poets of the *Risorgimento*, the great political "Resurgence" of Italy extending from Napoleon's death to the establishment of the It. Kingdom in 1870. Of these, Alessandro Manzoni (1785–1873) was not only most directly involved in the political events of the period but was among the chief It. theoreticians of romanticism. Though his fame rests upon his novel *I Promessi Sposi,* he wrote many lyrics attesting to his greatness as a poet. The single event of his life that had the deepest influence on his poetry was his conversion to Catholicism in 1810. Prior to this time he had written much poetry in the conventional neoclassic manner, some of which (*In morte di C. Imbonati, Qual su le Cinzie cime, Urania* and *Adda*) contained promise of potential blossoming. Following his conversion, his poetry constantly reflected a highly Christian philosophy. Between 1812 and 1822 he wrote five *Inni sacri* intended as lyrical glorifications of the principal feast days of the Church: the Resurrection, the Name of Mary, Christmas, the Crucifixion, and Pentecost. Each hymn consists of 12 or more stanzas, but the metrical structure varies. The tone is solemn and dignified, after the classical manner, but the spirited fluency with which Manzoni gives human significance to divine rites reveals a distinctive modernity. Manzoni's lyrism also takes wing in his two historical tragedies, *Il Conte di Carmagnola* and *Adelchi,* written in the years 1816–22. Tragedies only in outward form, they are rather lyric resolutions of tragic situations. This might also be said of his famous ode, *Il cinque maggio,* on the rise and fall of Napoleon's star.

With Giacomo Leopardi (1798–1837) we come to the poet who, alongside Petrarch, represents the highest point of development of It. lyric poetry. It is to Leopardi that 20th-c. It. poets have turned as master. Yet, despite its modernity, Leopardi's poetry affords an outstanding example of how the literary and learned nature of It. poetry can be made to reinforce its lyric power. In relation to the poetry of Manzoni, Leopardi's is, as it were, the other side of the same coin. While Manzoni's seeks to resolve the perennial grief and despair of mankind in the utter abandonment and faith in God and in the Hope of a better world to come; Leopardi's is basically the recognition of the illusory nature of this solution and the acceptance of the nonexistence of any solution. Life, for Leopardi, is but a Great Betrayal by nature, and man's greatness consists in his awareness of this fact.

Leopardi's lyrics, usually collected under the title of *Canti,* fall into four distinct periods. In the pre-*Canti* period (1810–18) we see the youthful poet, eager for knowledge and fame, revealing such traits as the admiration for unsuccessful valor and civic pride (*La morte di Ettore, La morte di Saulle*); a deeply idyllic temperament (*La Campagna, La Mietitura*); as well as a bent for light verse verging on satire (*Alla sorella, La Dimenticanza*). This was also a period of intensive study and meditation which bore fruit in the second period (1818–1823). During these years Leopardi wrote five great patriotic *canzoni* on the vicissitudes of Italy and on her state of vile subjection (*All'Italia, Sopra il monumento di Dante, Nelle nozze della sorella Paolina*). It is also at this time that the illusory nature of human values begins to emerge as a recurrent theme. Thus, in the *canzone, Bruto minore,* Leopardi has Brutus proclaim virtue utter folly as he is about to take his life: "Foolish virtue, misty caves and fields of restless larvae are your schools, and repentance is your reward to your followers." Only the Patriarchs knew happiness, for they lived in the age of myth when harmony prevailed between man and nature (*Alla primavera, Inno ai Patriarchi*). One of Leopardi's loftiest lyrical moments is his short idyll, *L'Infinito,* in which the poet finds a temporary solution to the problem of human misery in a self-annihilation in the infinity of space and time. In almost all these poems there is a constant clash between the serenity of nature and the state of the poet. The second period ends with a ray of hope as the poet seeks solace in human love; but even his lady turns out to be but an illusory ideal. (*Alla sua donna*).

The third period (1824–28) was likewise one of deep meditation. This found expression in several prose works of a philosophic or philological nature, and, ultimately, poetic sublimation in the poems of the fourth period (1828–37). Rays of light also dot the works of this period. In *Il Risorgimento* the poet expresses a strong will to live, even if life is grief, and a willingness to succumb to some of the illusions besetting mankind. In *A Silvia* the dreams of youth emerge as symbols of Hope. But these themes are quickly supplanted by the conviction that pleasure is but the cessation of pain (*Quiete dopo la tempesta*) or that it is nothing more than an anticipation (*Il sabato del villaggio*). The tragic sense of human unhappiness emerges again in the famous *Canto notturno di un pastore errante dell'Asia* in which an oriental shepherd gives voice to his bewilderment as he observes the relentless working of Nature. The ecstasy of love and delusion is sung in a series of poems that includes *Il pensiero dominante* and *A se stesso,* of which the latter again echoes a bitter outcry for self annihilation. *La Ginestra,* Leopardi's last and most significant poem, is a panoramic synthesis of his entire outlook on life. The lowly broom plant on the slopes of Vesuvius serves as a symbol of the tenacity with which life and beauty continue to survive despite the enmity of nature. Man must accept his destiny heroically without recourse to forces other than those residing within himself, for these are the bonds of human brother-hood.

The greatness of Leopardi's poetry lies in the fact that it takes the very essence of the thought and feeling of a highly learned and extremely sensitive poet and converts it into notes of sublime song. Every line, every word gives evidence of an extraordinary acuteness for tonality and rhythm. As a result, its musicality seems to produce what has been called "a catharsis of grief."

Romanticism assumed distinctive character-istics in Italy, and for a variety of reasons pro-duced only minor poets. One of the chief rea-sons was that It. energy was at that time being channeled in the direction of national unity. As a result, most of the poetry was inspired by patriotic zeal or by a spirited longing for free-dom and independence. One of the earliest and strongest exponents of romanticism in Italy was Giovanni Berchet (1783-1851). In 1816, in a pamphlet entitled *Lettera semiseria di Grisos-tomo*, he defended the position that poetry should be addressed, not to the intellectuals nor to the ignorant, but to those classes in-between; that it should deal with matters of national or contemporary interest; and that it should be a direct expression of feeling. As a poet, he tried hard to achieve these goals, but with little success. Among the satirists of the period, Giuseppe Giusti (1809-50) was the most brilliant. Typically composed of brief stanzas and short lines, his satires are founded on a great love of Italy. They satirize such evils as bureaucracy, pacifism, false patriots, mechanized education and demagoguery.

The new romantic emphasis on popular themes resulted in a widespread use of dialect in verse. In fact, two of Italy's greatest dialect poets wrote at this time. The first was Carlo Porta (1775-1821) who used the dialect of Milan in writing a number of humorous pieces relating to the contemporary scene. The other was Giuseppe Belli (1791-1863) whose two thousand sonnets represent the epic of the common people of Rome.

A poet whose reputation suffered consider-ably because of an erratic personality was Niccolò Tommaseo (1802-74) known also for his novels and philological studies. Religion, Grief, Nature, and the Cosmos are the chief themes of his poetry. Perhaps the most typi-cally romantic It. poet of the mid-19th c. was Giovanni Prati (1815-84). His prolific output brought him much popularity in his day, es-pecially his long Byronic poem on contempo-rary Venetian life, *Edmenegarda*. His best work appears in the two collections *Psiche* and *Iside*, especially in the latter in which he analyzes the manifold aspects of Nature in an atmos-phere of dream and myth. One of the more powerful poets of mid-century was Giacomo

Zanella (1820-88), a priest and professor whose staunch faith inspired many poems on the re-lationship of religion and science. His salute to scientific progress is tempered by the strong sense of Man's original stain. All the inven-tions of science, he sings in one poem, "do not decrease the grief which, eternal companion to the weak Adam, flows through the furrows of earth."

Around mid-century a group of Roman poets, known as the "Roman School," or-ganized a resistance movement against the in-roads of Fr. and Eng. romanticism and called for the reinstatement of puristic classical stand-ards. In reaction there arose in Milan a group of poet-artists, styled the *scapigliati* ("the di-sheveled ones"), who advocated daring novel-ties in all the arts. Influenced strongly by such continental poets as Baudelaire, De Nerval, Verlaine, Rimbaud, and Mürger, their rallying principle was the affinity of the arts. In ac-tuality they represent but a link between *secentismo* and the forthcoming "isms" that form the intermittent chain of decadentism in It. art and letters. Three of the stricter ad-herents of the group were Emilio Praga (1839-75), Arrigo Boito (1842-1918), and Giovanni Camerana (1845-1905).

1860-1960. THE NEW HARVEST. A reaction to the excesses of romanticism and of the *scapi-gliati* was inevitable. It was led polemically and in practice by Italy's outstanding poet of the third quarter of the century, Giosuè Carducci (1835-1907). His "reform" was basically a re-turn to the noble and learned tradition of It. poetry and a revolt against the sentimentality and morbidity of nordic romanticism. Reared in rough country by a rude and liberal father, and strongly influenced by a highly humanistic education, Carducci developed a robust char-acter typical also of his writings. At twenty-one he founded a literary society of "Pedant Friends" whose object was the defense of clas-sical and pagan values. His anticlerical con-victions never left him, though they were, along with others, somewhat tempered in later life. At the age of twenty-five he became Pro-fessor of It. Literature at Bologna; and in 1906 he won the Nobel Prize for literature. In his first collection, *Juvenilia*, we see the young poet feeling his way as he imitates great classi-cal and It. poets. In the *Levia gravia* (Light and Serious Verse), the poet, in his early thirties, becomes aware of the stark reality that impedes his ideals. In 1863 his true character bursts forth in his *Inno a Satana* (Hymn to Satan), exalting the forces of nature and Rea-son and denouncing the repressions of tradi-tional religion. This was followed by a collec-tion of *Giambi ed epodi* (Iambics and Epodes) representing the loftiest political poetry of the 19th c. With the *Rime nuove* Carducci reached his poetic maturity. The old spirit of rebellion is still present, but with stricter control. All of Carducci's world finds echo for the first time in this collection: his youthful aspirations, past memories, nature, and significant moments of Italian history. Among the more famous poems are: *Traversando la maremma toscana* (On Crossing the Tuscan Maremma), *Il bove* (The Ox); *San Martino; Pianto antico; Primavere elleniche; Davanti San Guido; Faida di comune* (Communal Feud); and *ça ira* (the battle cry of the Fr. Revolution). In his *Odi barbare* (Barbarian Odes) Carducci imitates the cadences and patterns of Latin strophes in an attempt to give to what he considered classic moods an expression far removed from the simple Romantic forms. The *Rime e ritmi* continue the same strains, with the Alps as background and the poet, standing on the mount of centuries, looking deeply into the past to prophesy the future. Generally speaking, the chief characteristics of Carducci's poetry are an intense hatred for moral decadence, a confidence in Man, Nature, and Art, a worship of the classical past, an intense conviction that the seeds of greatness still lie in Italy, and a constant concern for form.

There followed in the wake of Carducci a rather widespread movement in the direction of what has been called "professorial poetry." This had as themes not only nature and personal feelings but historical and civic ones as well. Its solemn and dignified tone as well as its obvious pedagogical intent attested to learned authors rather than to poets in close communion with nature.

A typical characteristic of European poetry in the last quarter of the 19th c. was a constant wavering between the exaltation of scientific progress and a state of bitterness or dis illusion toward the sciences. This was also true in Italy. A poet who gave voice to both attitudes was Mario Rapisardi (1844–1912), professor and translator of Lucretius, Horace, Catullus, and Shelley. In four of his poems, *Palingensi, Lucifero, Giobbe, and Atlantide*, he attempted a sweeping historical panorama of his age, including such areas as the new social ideals, the assault of Science on Dogma, and the overpowering sense of Mystery and Grief. The same general tendencies may be observed in the poetry of Arturo Graf (1848–1913), likewise a professor of literature.

The anxieties and turmoil occasioned by the sweeping social changes at the turn of the century were sung with depth and feeling by a poetess, Ada Negri (1870–1945). Work and maternity, used as symbols of punishment for the transgression of Adam and Eve, constitute her chief themes. Despite the softer accents of many of her lyrics, Ada Negri remains essentially a rebellious, strong and impetuous soul

in her resentment over the working and living conditions of the lower classes. *Fatalità, Tempeste, Maternità* are the titles of her earlier works.

An almost perfect fusion of the traditional erudition of It. poetry and the spiritual disorientation of the turn of the century occurred in the poetry of Gabriele d'Annunzio (1863–1938). A child prodigy, he became a versatile writer as well as a daring patriot and adventurer. His prodigious poetic output and incredible linguistic facility has been variously adjudged a continuation of the sensual and erotic poetry stemming from the Ovidian tradition, the work of a dilettante in sensations, or effusions of an orator. While all these judgements contain some truth, the formidable influence exerted by d'Annunzio on It. poetry cannot be minimized. His earliest verses, *Primo vere* (In Early Spring), already contain the germs of the later d'Annunzio: an heroic accent, a love of fatherland, a taste for the morbid, a voluptuous delight for beautiful and musical words set in classical rhythms, and a special predilection for transfiguring the physical aspects of Nature into song. The influence of Carducci, obvious in this first collection, largely disappears in the second, *Canto novo*, despite the continued presence of classical elements. Here the prevailing tone is a "cosmic exuberance" that prompted one critic to refer to the collection as, "an explosion of colors, of lights and of Wagnerian sonorities." With his *Intermezzo di rime* d'Annunzio achieves a stylistic mastery of the sonnet and the ottava, and, at the same time, abandons himself to the excesses of decadentism. In the collections, *Isotteo* and *La chimera* we see d'Annunzio's relentless experimentation with form. The first is an elaborate redoing of 14th and 15th c. Tuscan lyrical forms, while the second contains elaborations of the sensual motifs of the *Intermezzo* in a variety of forms, including a Japanese *outa*.

The 25 *Elegie romane* are basically a love song with Renaissance and 17th c. Rome as background. In the *Poema paradisiaco*, on the other hand, the poet's romanticism bursts forth as he celebrates the simple family life following a life of utter dissipation. The poem might be said to represent a spiritual convalescence, and offers many indications of the influence of Verlaine and Maeterlinck. With the *Laus vitae* we come to another phase in the spiritual evolution of d'Annunzio: the celebration of heroic morality, or the heroism of the Nietzschean Superman. The new hero is a reborn pagan Ulysses, superior to Christ Himself. In this hymn to life, which often reaches dionysian proportions, d'Annunzio used an original form: stanzas of 21 verses with verse lengths varying from 5 to 9 syllables. *Alcyone* marks the peak of d'Annunzio's artistry, symbolized in the image of Summer whose celebration constitutes the main theme of the collection. The poem is a fulfilment of the poet's conviction that Man's ultimate destiny is an harmonious identification with Nature, and in it he portrays his spirit as being abandoned "to the voracious melodies of the winds." All of nature consequently becomes musical sensation. The *Alcyone* has been called one of the greatest poems of the last two centuries.

Despite the widespread influence of d'Annunzio, the most accomplished poet of the turn of the century was Giovanni Pascoli (1855–1912) who has been called "poet of the neutral zone of our spirit . . . of the indefinite and the occult . . . the most original of the It. 20th c. . . . because nurtured by a more profound classical culture which became *humanitas. . . .*" His youth, spent amidst the simplicities of rural life, plus a series of domestic tragedies and hardships left deep impressions on the poet's sensibility. Successor of Carducci at Bologna and renowned classical scholar, Pascoli spent his last years teaching and writing poetry. The title of his first collection, *Myricae* (Tamarisks) already attests to a new sort of inspiration. Of Virgilian derivation, the title refers to the idyllic-descriptive nature of the short poems that constitute its bulk. They deal mostly with the manifold aspects of country life, none of which were too small or too insignificant for the poet's keen sensibility. This can be seen in such titles as, *Trees and Flowers, The Hedge, The River, The Nest*. The greater part of these earlier lyrics gives the impression of having been written by a young boy who, in his musings, discovers that in order to recall pleasant things, they must first come to an end or die . . . that beauty exists only because of death. In keeping with this child-like perspective, the verses are brief and rapid, with onomatopeia a recurring device and with a conscious predilection for minute distinctions of form, sound and action. Two subsequent collections, *Canti di Castelvecchio* and *Poemetti*, renew and extend the themes and moods of the *Myricae*, though there now prevails an elegiac-meditative tone. The sense of the mystery of life and death becomes stronger as the poet's vision begins to range beyond the simple rural life and he feels the full anguish of mankind surrounded by the mystery of its destiny. Pascoli is at his greatest when, in an almost childlike stupor, he attempts to penetrate the essence of the simple and the little. As he does so, his marvel increases upon discovering that in each small life there is a new universe surrounded by mystery. By translating this experience into images and sounds betraying the bewildered heart of the young child, Pascoli succeeds in creating a fusion of myth and reality. In addition, he uncovered new stamping grounds for It. poetry, grounds whose location in the neutral, greyish zones of consciousness was to be typical of the poetry later called *crepuscular*.

The term "crepuscular poetry" was first used by G. Borgese to refer to "the voice of a great poetry which is passing away," meaning by this the poetry written after Carducci, Pascoli and d'Annunzio. The expression, however, has since acquired ideological connotations. It also refers to the poetry of the period having all or some of the following characteristics: the poet's propensity for solitude, a subdued tone akin to Christian humility, a predilection for viewing Nature at dusk, a philosophical intuition of life symbolized by the daily passage of light into shadow, a preference for simple themes dealing with domestic and rural life with all its goodness and serenity, a "poetry like prose," and a heavy sense of weariness.

Of all the crepuscular poets, Guido Gozzano (1883–1916) continues to be the most popular. His fanatic determination to escape the influence of d'Annunzio led to an ironical tone that in turn smacks of the superman, while the women he sings attest to a sensuality and a worldliness akin to d'Annunzio's. Another crepuscular poet was Corrado Govoni (1884–) who came closest to Pascoli in the vastness of his production on rural life.

The antitraditionalism of the apparently defunct *scapigliati* erupted anew in the manifesto of the so-called school of futurism (q.v.). In an attempt to oppose something new to the poetry of Carducci, d'Annunzio, and Pascoli, the manifesto proclaimed complete anarchy not only in versification but in the use of words and in inspiration. Blank verse was the new king, and the electric motor was the symbol for the new dynamic spirit that was to invest poetry. In some manifestations it had much in common with Fr. surrealism and dadaism. But being a polemical rather than a strictly poetic movement, Futurism produced no noteworthy poetry.

It might be mentioned parenthetically that dialect poetry also prospered at this time, primarily at the hands of the Neapolitan, Salvatore di Giacomo (1860–1934) and the two Romans, Cesare Pascarella (1858–1940) and Carlo Salustri (1873–1950) better known as Trilussa.

The one poet who from the early twenties has held a place apart in the development of contemporary It. poetry and yet is today considered one of the top three, is Umberto Saba (1883–1957). In 1928 he integrated his several collections into a single one entitled *Il canzoniere*, intending thereby to establish a link with the past masters, Petrarch and Leopardi. His essential inspiration is a detailed analysis of the "convolutions of his mind." This autobiographical direction resulted in a prosaic tone that often interfered with the quality of his earlier verses, and even in his later ones creates the misconception that they are of an extreme simplicity. The style also contributes to this effect, interspersing clearly traditional expressions with dialectical ones and even with the obscurities of the decadents. It is, however, in the originality of his conception rather than in his technique that his merit emerges. The theme of the poet's life as a prototype of poetry, in that it was but a constant panting after the resolution of discords, is a recurring one. The conflict between the poet's desire to verbalize his love of life in its external aspects and the compelling necessity of turning inward to examine his actual status produces disturbing tensions and discords leading to an oddly appealing lyrical unease.

Saba's isolated position receives relief when we consider that the other two of the top three contemporary It. poets, Giuseppe Ungaretti (b. 1888) and Eugenio Montale (b. 1896) spawned a movement known as *hermeticism* (q.v.), which emerged in Italy following the clash between supporters of advance guard ideas and reactionaries. The conflict imperceptibly led to what has been called "the progressive erosion of the narrative and logical elements" in poetry, which in turn led to a poetry based on the compelling need to project internal movements immediately and photographically at their moment of inception, the so-called "flash of inspiration" or "pure poetry" that could encompass an instant (atomism) or longer periods of sustained inspiration. This new poetry also entailed widespread use of highly personalized language, experiences and complex devices (analogy) which, when used to excess, often produced eccentric and bizarre poetry. One of the first singers of the new poetry was Dino Campana (1885–1932) whose *Canti orfici* (1914) and eccentric personality (strongly resembling Rimbaud) had a strange appeal to younger writers. His constant striving after a poetry which would establish a direct contact with another "reality" by being shorn of all intellectual categories led to a poetry whose merits are still being debated.

Ungaretti's figure still looms the largest among the exponents of hermeticism. His earlier collections center around his experiences as a soldier, and often contain extremely brief pieces whose full effect was intended to be conveyed as much by the silences and the blankness surrounding them as by the words. The extreme example is a poem entitled *Una colomba* (A Dove), consisting of a single verse:

D'altri diluvì una colomba ascolto.

I listen to a dove of other floods

At other times the technique attempts to prolong a single instant eternally, as in *Godimento*:

. . . . Stanotte
avrò
un rimorso
come un latrato
perso
in un
deserto.

Tonight I shall have a remorse
like a howling lost in a desert.

Most of Ungaretti's earlier poems were collected in a single collection under the title *Vita d'un uomo* (1947). He published another collection, *La terra promessa*, in 1950 in which the tendency to make technique a primary preoccupation gives way to more classic inspiration.

The third member of the triumvirate is Eugenio Montale. His early and strong interest in T. S. Eliot had a direct bearing on the direction of his poetry. As one critic pointed out, ". . . . better than any other Italian Montale has realized the objective correlative [q.v.], and his complete identification of sentiment with things seems to have been a particular difficulty for It. critics, who are fond of pointing out the 'scabrosity' and 'rockiness' of Montale's poetry." His earlier poetry does linger on well-defined concrete images which are used as a rocky enclosure for a terribly arid life vainly seeking relief in a metaphysic which is itself in turn engulfed in the "scabrosity." This is especially true in his collection significantly entitled *Ossi di seppia* (Sepia Bones, 1925) in which the poet's cosmos is essentially a prison. In this earlier poetry, Montale's inspiration, unlike Eliot's, seems to proceed from an external object to the correlated feeling. As the poet moves to his later collections, *Le occasioni* (1939) and *Finisterre* (1943), there is a progressively greater turning inward and humanization: "the psychological element takes control and the new work becomes a labyrinth of presences in a kind of timeless time where there are memories of the future and previsions of the past."

If post-World War II poetic merit can be based on the winning of one of the better poetry prizes offered annually in Italy, the following poets deserve mention: Sergio Solmi, *Fine di stagione* (1933), *Poesie* (1950); Camillo Sbarbaro, *Trucioli* (1949); Libero de Libero, *Banchetto* (1949); and especially Alfonso Gatto whose *Nuove Poesie* (1950) and *La forza degli occhi* (1954) have been called "from the standpoint of technique, the most exciting volumes to appear in these last years." On the other hand, two of the best known poets in Italy today are Salvatore Quasimodo, and Leonardo Sinisgalli. Both these poets exemplify hermetic poetry in its most recent stage.

Although the best It. poetry written since the close of the Second War has been by hermetic writers, their production shows signs of a progressively closer bond with the past. In 1949, precisely 30 years after the *Ronda* had advocated a neoclassicism with Leopardi as model, eight poets published a manifesto advocating a new "lyric realism." In 1919 the leader of the movement had been Vincenzo Cardarelli (1887–1959) whose poetry, *Poesie* (1936), put into practice what its author had preached. In 1949 the writer of the manifesto was Aldo Capasso (b. 1909), also a poet of considerable merit, (*Il passo del cigno,* 1930). The manifesto was essentially a revolt against the linguistic acrobatics, the arbitrary symbolism and the irrationality of hermetic poetry. It takes a firm stand against the creation of "'another reality' opposed to daily reality, a magic freed from feeling and logical coherence." However, it is also against "that narrow traditionalism . . . which, today, after the second world war, wishes to take up again the classicism of Carducci or the romanticism of Hugo or even the more recent formulae of Moréas and Hérédia." It seems, rather, to seek a middle road: "Instead of rebelling against logical coherence . . . the task of poets is to give men coherent, fully comprehensible expressions of normal humanity, and at the same time to incorporate in the words the imponderables which the language of pure logic does not recognize." Though this had already been more or less realized in the poetry of Saba and the later Quasimodo, it remains true that just as the first half of the century opened with a revolt against d'Annunzio, the second half has opened with a revolt against Ungaretti. It is interesting to note that the 1959 Nobel Prize for literature was awarded to Salvatore Quasimodo who attributed the award to his conviction that "poetry is not a game." The progression from the relatively early collection *Ed è subito sera* (1942) through four others, and then to *La terra impareggiabile* (1958) attests to the seriousness of this conviction.

ANTHOLOGIES: *An Anth. of It. Poems, 13th to 19th C.,* tr. Lorna de' Lucchi (1922 and later); *Rimatori del dolce stil nuovo,* ed. L. Di Benedetto (1925; representative of the movement); *I classici italiani,* ed. L. Russo (1940); *Poeti lirici moderni e contemporanei,* ed. G. de Robertis (1945); E. M. Fusco, *Antologia della lirica contemporanea, dal Carducci al 1940* (1947; annotated and with fine introd.); H. H. Blanchard, *Prose and Poetry of the Continental Renaissance in Tr.* (1949); G. Spagnoletti, *Antologia della poesia italiana* (1909–1959) (1959; standard); *The Oxford Book of It. Verse* (2d ed., 1952); *Lirica del Novecento,* ed. L. Anceschi and S. Antonielli (1953; standard); *The Promised Land, and Other Poems,* ed. S. Pacifici (1957); *The Penguin Book of It. Verse,* ed. G. Kay (1958); *Canzoniere italiano: Antologia della poesia popolare,* ed. P. P. Pasolini (1961); *Contemp. It. Poetry, an Anthol.,* ed. C. L. Golino (1962).

HISTORY AND CRITICISM: A. R. Gaspary, *The Hist. of Early It. Lit. to the Death of Dante,* tr. H. Oelsner (1901); L. Einstein, *L. Pulci and the Morgante Maggiore* (1902); E. G. Gardner, *The King of Courts Poets* (1906); J. E. Shaw, *Essays on the Vita Nuova* (1929); C. G. Osgood, *Boccaccio on Poetry* (1930); C. R. Miller, *Alfieri* (1936); E. R. Vincent, *The Commemoration of the Dead: a Study of "Dei Sepolcri"* (1936); S. E. Scalia, *Carducci: His Critics and Tr. in England and America, 1881–1932* (1937); C. Calcaterra, *I lirici del Seicento e dell'Arcadia* (1936); C. Calcaterra, *Nella selva del Petrarca* (1942; for motivating and unifying forces in P's works); U. Bosco, *Petrarca* (2d ed., 1961; best on P. as poet); J. F. De Simone, *A. Manzoni: Esthetics and Lit. Crit.* (1946); A. Momigliano, *Manzoni* (1948); V. Branca, *Alfieri e la ricerca dello stile* (1948); B. Croce, *La letteratura italiana del Settecento* (1949); C. S. Singleton, *An Essay on the Vita Nuova* (1949; for stylistic and aesthetic insight) and *Dante Studies 2: Journey to Beatrice* (1959); E. H. Wilkins, *The Making of the Canzoniere and Other Petrarchan Studies* (1950; for philol. insight); U. Cosmo, *A Handbook to Dante Studies,* tr. D. Moore (1950); S. A. Chimenz, *Dante* (n.d.); M. Fusco, *La lirica* (1950; a basic source for the present art.); E. Williamson, "Contemp. It. Poetry," *Poetry,* 72 (1951–52); I. Origo, *Leopardi* (new and enl. ed., 1953); A. Galletti, *Il Novecento* (3d ed., 1954; standard on 1900); A. Belloni, *Il Seicento* (2d ed., 1955; standard study on 1600); A. S. Bernardo, "Petrarch's Attitude toward Dante," PMLA, 70 (1955, p. 488 for basic distinctions between poetry of the two poets); G. Natali, *Il Settecento* (4th rev. ed., 1955; standard on 1700); O. Macrì, *Caratteri e figure della poesia it. contemporanea* (1956); G. Mazzoni, *L'Ottocento* (6th repr. with rev., 1956; standard on 1800); V. Rossi, *Il Quattrocento* (6th repr. rev., 1956; standard on 1400); N. Sapegno, *Il Trecento* (2d ed., 1960; standard on 1300); G. Toffanin, *Il Cinquecento* (6th rev. ed., 1960; standard on 1500); E. Auerbach, *Dante, Poet of the Secular World,* tr. R. Manheim (1961); S. Pacifici, *A Guide to Contemp. It. Lit.: From Futurism to Neorealism* (1962).

See also *The Complete Poems of Michelangelo,* tr. J. Tusiani (1960); *L'antologia dei poeti italiani dell'ultimo secolo,* ed. G. Ravegnani and G. Titta Rosa (1963); *The Triumphs of*

Petrarch, tr. E. H. Wilkins (1962); L. Anceschi, *Le poetiche del Novecento in Italia* (1962). A.S.B.

ITALIAN PROSODY. See ROMANCE PROSODY.

ITHYPHALLIC (from Gr. "erect phallus," "ode and dance performed in festivals of Dionysus"). This short verse with the appearance of 3 trochees (brachycatalectic trochaic dimeter), but usually with a long syllable at the end, could be used as a colon (q.v.) or closing element (clausula) of a long line, e.g., the Archilocheans of Horace's *Odes* 1.4 are composed of dactylic tetrameters and ithyphallics:

$$\bar{sol}\breve{vitu}|r \ \bar{a}cr\breve{is} \ h\breve{i}|\bar{e}mps \ gr\breve{a}|t\bar{a} \ v\breve{ice} \ || \ v\bar{e}r\breve{i}|s \ \bar{et}$$

$$F\bar{a}|v\bar{on\bar{i}}$$

The i. is as old as Archilochus and Sappho but is rare in Gr. choral lyric. Plautus often used it after cretics and sometimes substituted a spondee for the second trochee:

$$r\bar{em} \ acc\breve{i}|p\bar{e} \ hanc \ \bar{ab} \ | \ n\bar{ob\bar{is}}$$
(*Casina* 830)

More rarely he permitted resolution of the penultimate syllable:

$$c\bar{um} \ l\breve{u}|cr\bar{o} \ r\bar{es}|p\breve{i}c\breve{i}\breve{as}$$
(*Pseudolus* 264)

W. M. Lindsay, *Early L. Verse* (1922); Dale; Koster; Crusius. R.J.G.

IVORY TOWER (Fr. *tour d'ivoire*) owes its currency in its commonest sense—as a metaphor for intellectual or artistic isolation—to Sainte-Beuve, who adopted the phrase (biblical in origin; cf. Song of Songs 7:4) in characterizing the "meticulous and delicate" Vigny and comparing him with the "tough partisan," Hugo ("A M. Villemain," *Pensées d'Août*, 1837).

Only one in a series of sculptural or architectural images (e.g., white marble statue, column, obelisk) by which Sainte-Beuve sought to express his judgment of Vigny's character, life, and work, the phrase *tour d'ivoire* apparently symbolized for Sainte-Beuve what he considered to be Vigny's defective sense of reality, his love of illusions, and his subjection to chimeras; his obtusely haughty, aristocratic, detached personality; his view of the position of the poet as an isolated sufferer, and his exaltation of art above practical concerns, which, he believed, would make it their slave; his hostility to politics and to everything not of the pure realm of the spirit, and his consequent lack of commitment to any social value or institution save the sterile and useless one of military honor; and, finally, his pure, delicate, polished, classical, but socially and intellectually uncommitted verse. With its heavy emphasis on Vigny's isolation, Sainte-Beuve's phrase suggests but imperfectly the social implications of Vigny's commitment to "the reality of the ideal" and his view of the poet, even in his isolation, as a messianic spiritual leader.

Although "tower of ivory" may still be used in its biblical-liturgical sense (cf. W. R. Childe, "Turris Eburnea"), *tour d'ivoire* in Fr. and "ivory tower" in Eng. have become idiomatic in the sense derived from Sainte-Beuve. "Ivory tower" is now used as a metaphor for unawareness of, indifference to, or isolation from concerns held to be important by the user, and thus as a means of depreciating intellectual or artistic attitudes or pursuits held to be "unreal" or impractical or irrelevant to those more important concerns. According to Panofsky, it "combines the stigma of egotistical self-isolation (on account of the tower) with that of snobbery (on account of the ivory) and dreamy inefficiency (on account of both)"; to these may be added the stigmata of affectation, of pusillanimity, and, in connection with poetry, of obscurity. The currency of the phrase in these senses is doubtless to be explained chiefly by the urgency and frequency with which, during the 19th and 20th c., men of letters and social theorists have agitated the question adumbrated by such phrases as "the social responsibility of the artist," "art for art's sake," "the alienation of the artist," and "the treason"—or "the flight"—of the intellectuals.—C. A. Sainte-Beuve, "Poètes et Romanciers Modernes de la France. XIX. M. de Vigny," *Revue des Deux Mondes*, 4. sér., 4 (1835), *Pensées d'Août* (1837), "Portraits de Poètes Contemporains. M. de Vigny," *Revue des Deux Mondes*, 2. pér., 50 (1864); H. Levin, "The Ivory Gate," YSS, 13 (1954); E. T. Underwood, "Blueprint for an Ivory Tower: Vigny and Sainte-Beuve," (Ph.D. diss. Univ. of Wisconsin, 1955); E. Panofsky, "In Defense of the Ivory Tower," *Centennial Review of Arts and Science*, 1 (1957). J.D.K.

J

JAPANESE POETRY. In every historical period J. poetry has reflected a knowledge of Chinese or Western poetry, but its origins remain native in a prehistoric past and the autonomous character of its language and prosody. (For reasons of definition, not quality, the following are excluded from this survey: poetry in Chinese by J., folk song, art song, and most dramatic verse.) The agglutinative, highly vocalic character of this apparently discrete language was kept pure for centuries by the exclusion of Chinese loan words, which seemed alien and unassimilable, incapable at first of adaptation to the syllabic prosody of alternating 5's and 7's defined sometime about the 7th c. and still the basis of all prosody apart from vers libre. Initially the language—with its modal and aspectual inflections of verbs and adjectives and its dominantly concrete, imagistic nouns—later, tradition, and elements in the J. sensibility itself have made J. poetry intellectually thin and undidactic, but have given it unusual affective depth. Philosophically dominated by a residual Shinto animism and imbued from early historical times with Buddhism, it tends: to mold its affective wealth into a poetry of states, often in harmonies of different states of awareness and perception; to explore feeling; to use images at once as concrete details and for metaphorical implications (rather than representations); and to excel in tonal rather than thematic complexity. The traditional interest in the circumstances of composition, real or imagined, has led in many periods to small aesthetic distance between poet and materials, but until modern times the social ambience of J. poetry has been so pronounced that almost the whole range of J. poetry seems to be a lyricism emerging from social contexts—leading J. to distinguish between formal poetry (written with great care for a large social audience) and informal (written less carefully for but one or a few readers). Public poetry achieves greatness only in the Early Literary period; thereafter, however elevated or social poetry may become, it is uniformly private.

I. PRIMITIVE PERIOD, TO A.D. CA. 685. Primitive poetry and song survive in about 500 examples embedded and distorted in alien contexts of two chronicles, the *Kojiki* (712) and the *Nihongi* (720), and in some later collections. Contextual interpretations, often odd ones, attribution to fictional authors, and (often) revision by the chroniclers—such factors make accurate assessment of Primitive verse exceedingly difficult. The syllabic prosody and literary forms were apparently unfixed, and the best poems appear to have been revised at a late date. Revision involved the syllabic regularizing of the line, alternation of long and short lines, the introduction of complex forms of parallelism, apparently under Chinese influence, and recasting into such later forms as the *tanka* and *chōka* (see below). The poems are of such types as songs of praise or lament, of clan heroes, of private or social occasions, and of work or play. Early clan structure included guilds of reciters to repeat the history of the clan, and there were also mummers to entertain. Few primitive songs are of intrinsic interest, the usual range of expression and thought being limited; some possess a racy or vivid immediacy and the corpus of early poetry already shows the lasting tendency to relatively short, affective expression.

II. POETRY OF THE COURT, CA. 685–1350. The unification of the country led rapidly to a remarkable efflorescence of native culture, stimulated by an influx of Chinese ideas. Poetry was defined in two major forms: the *tanka* (also *uta, waka*) in 5 lines of 5,7,5,7,7 syllables and *chōka* (also *nagauta*), of alternating 5 and 7-syllable lines (the longest extant *chōka* is of 149 lines) concluding with an extra one of 7 and commonly followed by one or more envoys (*hanka,* also *kaeshiuta*) in the *tanka* form. Other forms, notably the *sedōka* (two tercets of 5,7,7), were experimented with in the Early Literary period but soon fell into desuetude, as also the *chōka* after the Early Literary period. The Court periods produced what may be regarded as the greatest and classical achievement of Japanese poetry. After the early flowering, there is a decline, then successive periods of redefinition of poetic aims and practices, with a growing tendency toward refinement and kinds of neoclassicism. Poetic diction, subjects, ideals of achievement, and prescriptions of practice become more explicitly set, traditionalism vying with freshness and increasing technical complexity.

A. *The Early Literary Period, ca. 685–784.* Gradual and largely obscure as the transition from primitive to Court poetry is, it can be defined in terms of the one great early anthology extant, the *Man'yōshū,* which contains some Primitive verse and whose last datable poem is of 759. The bulk of the some 4,500 poems date from 600–750; they are selected from various collections no longer extant and from the personal collections of the compilers, whose methods of compilation vary in method and critical sophistication. The *Man'yōshū* contains the longest and some of the greatest J. poetry. In particular, Kakinomoto Hitomaro (fl. ca. 680–700), Yamabe Akahito (d. ?736), Yamanoe Okura (?660–?733), Ōtomo Tabito (665–731), and Ōtomo Yakamochi (718–85) display a variety and grandeur that render the *Man'yōshū* special to the J. (Clan names or surnames are here given first in J. fashion, although poets are commonly referred to by given names, styles, or pen-names.) Hitomaro is unquestionably the greatest poet, combining as he does lyricism with narrative forms, public subjects (elegies for princes, imperial excursions, visits to former capitals, and poems on the death of private individuals) with such rhetorical techniques of the period as extremely complex parallelisms and the pillow-word (*makurakotoba*), a prefixed conventional attribute or word, usually in a 5-syllable line, used for amplifying and imagistic purposes. His grand openings, subtly developed and warm ironies, skill with imagery and phrasing, and sustained, complex structures are of an extraordinary richness seldom rivaled. His tone at least can be inferred from an envoy to *On Passing the Ruined Capital of Ōmi.*

> The Cape of Kara
> At Shiga in Sasanami yet remains
>   As it ever was,
> But though it wait throughout the ages,
> The courtiers' pleasure boats will not return.

(Translations of poems from the Court period are by R. H. Brower and E. Miner, *J. Court Poetry*, copyright 1961, Stanford University Press; other translations in this article are by E. Miner, copyright 1961, *Orient/West*.)

Okura's intense feeling and terse style conveyed a more moral vision and at times a didactic vein resembling certain kinds of the poetry of China, where he had studied. His style is seen at its best in an envoy to an elegy on his son.

> Since he is so young,
> He will not know the road to take:
>   I will pay your fee—
> O courier from the realms below,
> Bear him there upon your back!

Akahito's lovely descriptive styles introduced new elements, but his supremacy in *tanka* foretells the decline of the *chōka*. His lyric description has a fresh purity seen in this envoy to a *chōka* on the Yoshino Palace.

> The jet-black night
> Deepens to a hush among the birches

> In the stream's pure bed,
> Where the plovers softly raise their call
> Above the gentle murmur of the stream.

Toward the end of the period the *chōka* was given a final greatness in the subjective, reflective style of Yakamochi. There is also a good deal of poetry in the *Man'yōshū* by anonymous, pseudonymous, and little known authors; and verse from the provinces and poems composed in reality or fiction by such authors as workmen, frontier guardsmen, beggars, and even prostitutes. But the greatest poets are courtiers of middling rank, scholarly inclination, and pronounced individuality of outlook.

B. *The Early Classical Period, 784–1100.* A transitional period in which Chinese poetry flourished unchallenged as serious literature was followed by a reaction and redefinition of J. poetry into highly subjective, witty, high-spirited, and often conceited styles expressed wholly in the *tanka* form. Various Chinese ideals and techniques, as well as a remarkable personality, were integrated into a new poetry early in the period by poets like Ariwara Narihira (825–80), whose subjective and extremely concentrated style achieves something like philosophical weight.

> What now is real?
> This moon, this spring, are altered
>   From their former being—
> While this alone, my mortal body, remains
> As ever changed by love beyond all change.

The poetess Ono no Komachi (fl. ca. 850) wrote of, and with, a strength of passion unknown earlier.

> On such a night as this
> When the lack of moonlight shades your way to me,
>   I wake from sleep my passion blazing,
> My breast a fire raging, exploding flame
> While within me my heart chars.

Their poetry and that of the generation of Ki no Tsurayuki (884–946), Ki no Tomonori (fl. ca. 890), Ōchikōshi Mitsune (fl. ca. 900), Lady Ise (fl. ca. 935), and others was collected in the 1st and most influential of the 21 imperial anthologies, the *Kokinshū* (ca. 905), Tsurayuki's Preface to which is the first major critical document in J. poetry. The generation of Tsurayuki and the next few following generations stabilized poetry by giving it a rationale, setting subjects and diction, creating doctrines of decorum, and defining the anthology as a genre with two main groups of subjects, seasonal and love poems, and several shorter groups. Throughout the period there is a questioning of subjective reality with constant reference to dream experience or comparisons between very different poetic elements. Although the pillow-word continues to be used, the characteristic rhetorical device is the pivot-word (*kakekotoba*), which utilizes a single series of sounds to yield two or more parsings and meanings. The consolidation and critical definition of poetry, the experimentation with mixed genres of poetry and prose, the rise of such socio-literary phenomena as the poetry contest, and the assured tone of literature reflect the fact that court society was now at its zenith. There is a falling off in poetic quality in the late 10th and 11th c., accompanied by an intensification of critical interest and experimentation with new styles. Some poems by Sone no Yoshitada (fl. ca. 985) anticipate, inspite of certain eccentricities, later descriptive poetry—

> The sun sets,
> And the luminous underleaves
>   Low upon the trees
> Are stifled in the shadowing
> Of the frightening summer dark.

But the poetry of Lady Izumi Shikibu (ca. 970–1030) is more normative for the tradition and more recognizably human.

> Lying down alone,
> My thoughts are fixed on you—so deeply
>   That I have forgot again
> The tangles of my long black hair
> In yearning for the hand that stroked it clear.

Poets not so given to experiment or expression of passion were, however, over-cautious. Tsurayuki's definition of poetry into formal styles had been more than successful; signs of lassitude and conventionalism increased.

C. *The Mid-Classical Period, 1100–1241.* The slow decline of the Court in power and wealth continued after the establishment of the first feudal government in the late 12th c. and gradually led to poetic changes: a greater seriousness, a conventionalizing of poetic subjects, borrowings from graver Chinese poets, formalizing of the conditions of poetry, and a neoclassical veneration of the past. Such changes came slowly, crystallizing towards the end of the period in the 8th imperial anthology, the *Shinkokinshū* (1206), 2d in historical importance only to the *Kokinshū*, and most admired by J. today after the *Man'yōshū*. The new styles are largely descriptive, and the natural elements described function symbolically to imply human responses. The dominant tones are those related to loneliness, whether miserable in the now almost uniformly unhappy poems of Courtly love, or sad but comforted with beauty in the numerous superb autumn poems of the period. Nouns, rather than the verbs of the preceding period, fill the poems;

the pillow-word and pivot-word are retained, but the most significant technique is allusive variation (*honkadori*), in which the neoclassicism of the age expresses itself by the allusion to older poems.

> Dimly, dimly,
> In the morning mist that lies
>   Over Akashi Bay,
> My longings follow with the ship
> In vanishing behind the distant isle.
>   (Anon., *Kokinshū*)

> Pillowed above the oars
> And deep in sleep until dawn breaks,
>   I awake to find no ship:
> The one which bears my longing in the dream
> Has borne me in the daylight from this boat.

The Abbot Jien (1155–?1225) has here incorporated the earlier love poem into one dealing with the sadness of travel. Other poems show that the passage of time and cultural change weigh heavily upon the poets.

> The plank-roofed halls
> Of the barrier fort of Fuwa "The Enduring"
>   Are emptied of their men,
> And in the ruin of all that was before,
> Only in the rustle of the autumn wind.
>   (Fujiwara Yoshitsune, 1169–1206)

The descriptive symbolism commonly employs a muted natural scene.

> While denying his heart,
> Even a priest must feel his body know
>   The depths of a sad beauty:
> From a marsh at autumn twilight,
> Snipe that rise to wing away.
>   (Priest Saigyō, 1118–90)

Fujiwara Shunzei (1114–1204) resolved the experimentation of earlier poets and directed the energy of the age by setting forth ideals of tradition in some realms and of creative change in others. Since he aimed at depth, he may incorporate in a single autumn poem descriptive symbolism, allusive variation on two earlier poems, and a strong implicit sense of time.

> As evening falls,
> From along the moors the autumn wind
>   Blows chill into the heart,
> And the quails raise their plaintive cry
> In the deep grass of secluded Fukakusa.

The depths of allusion are not always to be felt by the Western reader unfamiliar with the works alluded to. A poem by the greatest poet of the age, Shunzei's son Teika (1162–1241), alludes both to an earlier poem and to

The Tale of Genji; but its syntactical, metaphorical exchange of subjects and predications produces an atmosphere of beauty intelligible to any reader.

> For her straw-mat bedding
> The Lady of the Bridge of Uji now
> Spreads the moonlight out,
> And in the waiting autumn night
> Still lies there in the darkening wind.

Teika's many styles and his criticism dominate an age richly endowed with both. It had developed slowly but flowered in a host of great poets, including such others as ex-Emperor Go-Toba (1180–1239), Fujiwara Ietaka (1158–1237), Fujiwara Ariie (1155–1216), Princess Shokushi (d. 1201), and Shunzei's Daughter (fl. ca. 1200). Although practiced earlier, the poetry contest between two appointed sides and on set poetic topics now becomes, with the composition of poetic sequences modeled on the imperial collections, a major means of "publishing" formal poetry. Records of the contests, many sequences, private collections, and other sources survive to amplify the canon of the age far beyond the imperial anthology.

D. The Late Classical Period, 1241–1350. The grandchildren of Teika fell out over financial and poetic disputes, the senior line ultimately winning and dooming Court poetry to living death in conventionalism. The junior lines produced but two imperial anthologies, the *Gyokuyōshū* (ca. 1313) and *Fūgashū* (ca. 1345), which show remarkable originality and talent. The originality lay partly in the focus upon the intense moment or the intensely minute, but also in the development of styles of total description (imagery alone) for seasonal poems and of no imagery for love poems. Reizei Tamehide (d. 1372) shows the intensely perceived imagistic moment.

> Even in the flashing
> Of the lightning that does not linger
> Even for a moment,
> The very number of the drops of rain
> Could be counted on the leaves of plants.

So intense is the scrutiny of the moment that there are often surprising changes, as in this image-less poem.

> In my heart,
> Weakened now by your betrayal
> To the point of death,
> Even misery takes on pathetic beauty
> And my bitterness is gone.
> (ex-Empress Eifuku, 1271–1342)

The experimentation of the period and its search for intensity led to the increased use of such rhetorical devices as reversed diction (a kind of hypallage) and synesthesia, and even

to the introduction of novel subject matter, as in the following by ex-Emperor Hanazono (1297–1348).

> No trace remains
> Among all the crumbling hovels
> Of their bamboo fences,
> And only a dog breaks the silence,
> Barking from the hindmost shack.

Another of his poems, a complex allegory on the Bodhisattva Beautiful in the *Lotus Sūtra,* shows even in its imagistic vehicles the new beauty of religious poetry.

> The sun at dusk
> Fades in brightness from the eaves
> Where swallows twitter;
> And among the willows in the garden
> Blows the green breeze of the spring.

The counterpart of such rich detail is the extreme difficulty of the minute distinctions in the generalized language of the love poetry. At its best the age produced an intense new poetry, at its unhappiest mere agitation in the verse of the innovative poets and utter sinking into convention by the conventional. Other major poets of the age are Kyōgoku Tamekane (1254–1332), Lady Jūsammi Chikako (fl. ca. 1300), ex-Emperor Fushimi (1265–1317), Lady Jūsammi Tameko (fl. ca. 1300), ex-Emperor Go-Fushimi (1288–1336), and Saionji Sanekane (1249–1322).

III. THE LATER FEUDAL PERIODS, 1350–1867. The political and economic decline of the Court from the 12th c. led at first to gradual, and later to radical, social change. *De facto* power was exercised by successive feudal regimes, the last and most enduring of which was established in 1603. In response to such changes, in reference to Chinese culture, and especially in cognizance of the Court tradition, the poetry of Feudal times developed its distinctive forms. These rose alongside the earlier forms and styles, which continued to be taught and practiced—often with distinction and well into Modern times—by the hereditary schools of Court poets. Indeed, such Court poetry dominated the Feudal literary scene in volume and in prestige, maintaining an organic connection with the past and influencing the new poetry in both general and particular ways.

A. The Mid-Feudal Period, 1350–1600. The fall of the Court into ceremonial and conventional nullity was slow, and the new genres grew organically out of old forms. Nō (q.v.) owed much of its theatrical debt to forms not respected by the Court, but its aesthetic and the style of its poetic passages grew in major degree from Court poetry. The prosody combines the old syllabic 5's and 7's with the freer rhythms of popular songs; such rhetorical tech-

-[426]-

niques as the pivot-word and allusive variation (on Court poetry and Buddhist texts) are skillfully employed. The cultural continuity was provided in large degree by Zen priests of the so-called Five Temples (*Go-San*), who were patronized by a succession of aesthetically-minded Feudal rulers versed in the cultural traditions of the Court. Zen priests and Late Classical poets had been on close terms, sharing *inter alia* enthusiasm for Sung poetry and criticism. Reflecting monastic rather than Court life, the principal Feudal genres developed are "linked" forms—*renga, haikai*—composed in alteration and according to extremely elaborate rules by a small group of poets. *Renga* has a long pre-Feudal history. In Mid-Classical times it had served Court poets as relaxation after the rigors of composing in the *tanka* form. As such, it tended to frivolity, but its serious consideration by ex-Emperor Go-Toba in particular led to distinctions between serious (*ushin*) and playful (*mushin*) forms. In Late Classical times, Nijō Yoshimoto (1320–88) codified the elaborate rules developed for *renga,* establishing the genre in the form it possessed till modern times. *Renga* grew from the diction, rhetoric, aesthetic, and certain formal aspects of Court poetry. The standard *renga* consisted of 100 stanzas alternating the first (5,7,5) and second (7,7) "halves" of the *tanka* in a fashion like the 100-poem sequences of Court poetry; the stanzas were integrated with the same techniques of association and progression developed originally for private sequences and for the imperial anthologies (see below). Yoshimoto and the first major period of the *renga* built upon the aesthetic and style of the conservative Nijō poets of Late Classical times. The second flowering of *renga* came with the priests Shōtetsu (1381–1459) and Shinkei (1406–75), who returned to Teika's ethereal early style for ideals they termed coolness (*hie*) and slenderness (*yase*). Sōgi (1421–1502) sought new ideals in the liberal Late Classical poetry of the Kyōgoku-Reizei schools. A third peak was reached by poets associated with Satomura Shōwa (?1523–1602). Parallel in development with *renga, haikai* or *haikai renga* grew from the concept of playful (*mushin*) *renga*. Sōgi's major distinction between *haikai* and *renga* was apparently the use of Chinese words in *haikai*. More fundamental distinctions between the two forms were made by Arakida Moritake (1473–1549) and Yamazaki Sōkan (?1465–1553), who disregarded some of *renga's* more elaborate rules and introduced colloquial diction and wit. Sōkan's poetry verged at times upon mere playfulness, but Moritake's possessed a depth and seriousness capable of further development. It must be added that the *renga* is of such formidable complexity that it is the least studied and understood of all J. genres.

B. Late Feudal Period, 1600–1867. Priests, courtiers, and a few cultivated warriors had developed Mid-Feudal poetry, but the stability and prosperity of Feudal society enabled large numbers of the battleless warriors, prosperous farmers, and wealthy townsmen to participate in the development of the characteristic genres of Late Feudal poetry, which grew from the *haikai* of Moritake and others. (*Haikai* was later called *renku,* and the first stanzas, or the *hokku,* of *haikai* were often treated specially. But *haiku* conceived of as discrete poems of 5,7,5 syllables is a concept and form of Modern times.) Through most of late Feudal times, serious poetry is conceived of in terms inherited from the *haikai* of Moritake, as redefined by Matsunaga Teitoku (1570–1653), whose study of *tanka* and *renga* brought a new formal seriousness to *haikai* (though his followers often became over-witty); by Nishiyama Sōin (1604–1682), who introduced a prosodic freedom and less restricted diction; and by Kamijima Onitsura (1660–1738), who sought greater tonal elevation. But Onitsura's contemporary, Matsuo Bashō (1644–94) proved to be the greatest and most influential of Late Feudal poets, gathering about him a wide following. Creator of many styles and a master at the mixed genre of *haikai* and prose, *haibun,* Bashō formed his practice and criticism on neoclassical and religious lines. He studied and often alluded to Court poetry; especially the priest Saigyō, to whose ideal of *sabi,* or loneliness, he gave a patina of his own. The *renga* poets, especially Sōgi, earlier *haikai* poets, and the more restrained, descriptive Chinese poets were especially congenial to his ideals. This background enabled him to endow the simple or even the low with a profundity of associational richness. Yet in his varied styles, the elegant, the humorous, the ironic, and the grand also appear. Modern readers have read him with over-literal biographical sentiment, failing to see that his art has shaped, e.g., the mingled poetry and prose of *Oku no Hosomichi* (The Narrow Road of Oku, ca. 1689) from a diary into fiction. Among his best known poems, the following are typical of different styles.

Kareeda ni
Karasu no tomarikeri
    Aki no kure.

A crow is perched
Upon a leafless withered bough—
    The autumn dusk.

• •

Inazuma ya
Yami no katayuku
Goi no koe.

The lightning flashes!
And slashing through the darkness,
A night-heron's screech.

* *

Tabi ni yande
Yume wa kareno o
Kakemeguru.

Stricken in travel,
And turning over withered moors,
A world of dreams.

Bashō was accompanied by a host of distinguished *haikai* poets, whose successors degenerated steadily. The revival of *haikai* in the 18th c. can be epitomized by Bashō's greatest successor, Yosa (or Taniguchi) Buson (1716–83). Study of *renga* and classical literature, familiarity with Chinese criticism of painting, his own stature as a painter, and reinterpretation of Bashō's ideal of "elegance" led him to a style of somewhat greater objectivity and concrete imagistic beauty, often with a strong pictorial conception.

The sea in springtime,
All the warm day in breathing swells,
In breathing swells.

* *

The moon passes
In splendor through its central heavens
And I through wretched streets.

The strength of *haikai* lay in its depth of tradition and in its assumptions of integration of separate stanzas. Bashō and Buson composed integrated sequences (themselves or in company with others) and a number of *hokku*, opening stanzas. These were regarded as the crucial base for subsequent stanzaic development; and collections of *hokku*, or of separate stanzas intermingled with prose (*haibun*) were common. After Buson *haikai* once more deteriorated, as can be seen both in the famous though largely sentimental poetry of Kobayashi Issa (1763–1827) and in the development of the parodic form of the *hokku* of *haikai*, *senryū*. *Senryū* possess at times an incisive wit bringing the world into proportion and grows from the daily life of feudal Japan. But wordplay is commonly an end in itself, and the best *senryū* of Karai Hachiemon (1718–90; pen name Senryū) and others are in reality *hokku manqué*.

IV. THE MODERN PERIOD, 1868—. To the inherent difficulties of assessing recent times must be added other matters—the sudden proliferation of literature in a nation achieving nearly total literacy in a short period; the tendency of Modern J. writers to group into schools of small groups and short lives; an abundance of skilled poets; and a scarcity of truly great ones.

There are a few new and consistent phenomena: the enormous impact of Western culture, the rise of the professional writer to accepted social status, a romantic prizing of individualism, and the dominance of a many-faceted, peculiarly J. "Realism."

A. The "Enlightenment" and After, 1868–1931. The 15–20 years following the opening of Japan brought in a flood of foreign culture and technology that threatened to overwhelm the indigenous civilization. Writers seemed uncertain whether to make the foreign Japanese or to give native literature a foreign cast, as the New Style poetry (*Shintaishi*, ca. 1882) shows. Molding the traditional syllabic 5's and 7's into single lines, the New Style poets translated Gray, Shelley, and other Eng. poets. The academic exercise retains a historical importance, while the use of such compound lines (1897) by the novelist-poet Shimazaki Tōson (1872–1943) returned to so native a tone and language that there seemed little reason for the new prosody, though his style possessed a moving and influential romanticism. The awaited revolution came with Masaoka Shiki (1867–1902), perhaps the greatest, certainly the most seminal, of Modern poets. Prolonged study of *haikai* led him to radical revisionism: scorn of *haikai* and collections of *hokku*, sifting of Bashō, and praise of Buson. His eloquent criticism led him to adumbrate the ineffable "Objective Realism" that pervades modern J. poetry. Essentially aesthetic in aim, highly imagistic in method, it yet prizes individual "sincerity" and abjures "artifice." Its Western inspiration came, in a historical accident, with the simultaneous introduction to Japan of romanticism, realism, and naturalism —with a host of other postromantic schools following hard after. Shiki's achievement lay in his holding Western thought at arm's length in order to return to what he felt essentially J. qualities. He built on the work of Feudal scholars and lesser predecessors, and his *haiku* styles change as his ideas develop, his best *haiku* showing often the pictorial qualities of Buson.

The ocean freshly green,
Mountain on mountain peaked with snow,
Birds homing to the north.

From ca. 1898 Shiki turned to the reformation of *tanka* poetry. The National Scholars (17th-19th c.) had laid the foundations for his reformation by their study of the great works of the Court, by their veneration of the *Man'yōshū* as the supreme J. poetic achievement, and by their own poetry imitative of certain Man'yō styles. Shiki's revisionism went further, entailing the rejection almost *in toto* of the poetry of the Classical and subsequent periods for its presumed artifice and the elevation of the *Man'yōshū* to a touchstone of objectivity, realism, sincerity, and the truly J. poetic spirit. Such primitivism had the good effect of refreshing study of older poetry, but it led to useless theories and sentimentalism, a quality seen broadcast, but found with a mingled self-consciousness and social concern in the work of Ishikawa Takuboku (1885–1912). Yet one of the most individual voices was that of Yosano Akiko (1878–1942), whose *tanka* more than recall the frank passion of Komachi and Izumi Shikibu.

> Piling on *The Spring Dawn*
> Yet another romance, *The Tales of Ise,*
> Gives too weak a pillow:
> The agitation of our making love
> Yielded in a moment to collapse.

Such wry and historically resonant vividness was rare, however; most of the good poetry, whether *tanka* or *haiku*, tended to fill out or extend with practice the outlines set forth by Shiki's theories. Many experiments with free verse followed upon the discovery of Western symbolism (ca. 1905) and, in spite of prosodic uncertainties, greatly increased the range of J. poetry. Free verse was, however, identified with foreign or unorthodox ideas. Before World War I Takuboku had voiced socialism in this medium, and the avant-garde in Tokyo was often better abreast of events in Paris than German, Eng., or Am. poets.

B. *Wars and Repression, 1931–1945.* Government repression had begun early in the new century, but it was strongly opposed and evaded until the outbreak of the Pacific War closed the country and introduced economic sanctions. J. "Objective Realism" had from the beginning had strong ties with romantic nationalism, and during this period there is much fresh (as well as misdirected) study of the *Man'yōshū*, the poet-scholar Saitō Mokichi (1882–1953) showing in his monumental study of Hitomaro (5 v., 1934–40) and his *tanka* an exceptional dignity and intellect. His roots were in the creative Early Modern years, however, and although younger writers of free verse sought to maintain contact with (and to emulate) such Western movements as symbolism and imagism, repression stiffened as conditions worsened, until the deteriorating economic situation made poetry an unsupportable luxury. It seemed as if only isolated and radically individualistic poets like Miyazawa Kenji (1896–1933) could create original styles—his being rather feverish and uneven poetry that came to public notice only after his death. The old barely survived, and then largely discredited by the young while the only thing new of literary value to emerge was the terrible subject of repression, war, and suffering.

C. *After the Wars, 1945—.* Social and economic collapse after 1945 made conditions worse in some ways than during the war. In the confusion of forms and values, there was an initial rejection of all poetry associated with prewar days when not connected with literary or social liberalism. Some earnest but dull proletarian poetry appeared—reviving Takuboku and a few other writers not associated with the totalitarian regime. Many sought to learn what had happened in the West during the years of repression, and as the country rebuilt itself Fr. movements were once more conveyed by translation and discussion, a modified existentialism and decadence proving popular. T. S. Eliot's intellectual style, if not his ideas, and then the later poetry of Yeats brought a new toughness and a degree of abstraction into the poetry of numerous coteries. Within about 15 years after the end of war, the old *haiku* and *tanka* schools had revived; but the dominant poetry of the time was a more objective, intellectual, and often wholly obscure free verse. Problems of prosody and of rapport with society, of creating native canons for free verse (many poets wrote in Western languages) remained crucial; and as at the beginning of the Modern period or in ca. 1930, poets often felt themselves stranded in the middle of the bridge between J. reality and Western modernity.

Although a review of the Modern period shows an impressive variety of as yet inadequately sifted or assessed poetry, it may be divided into three forms: the *tanka*, strongly influenced by Feudal and Modern interpretations of the *Man'yōshū* and other aspects of Modern taste; the *haiku*, developed in a multitude of traditional and experimental styles; and free verse. If free verse be considered the distinctive Modern achievement, its range and tendencies (beyond those of the writers already mentioned) can be exemplified by some of the best contemporary writers. Hagiwara Sakutarō (1886–1942) seemed to many to image the Modern world in his lyricism, pessimism, and symbolism. In both practice and translation, Horiguchi Daigaku (1892–) has introduced Fr. literature into Japan, just as the poetry, teaching, and translations of Nishiwaki Junzaburō (1894–) has naturalized 20th-c. Eng. poetry. Both Kitagawa Fuyuhiko (1900–) and Takenaka Iku (1904–) are representative and influential poets whose connections with various literary magazines and movements have contributed to the definition and practice of contemporary poetry. The socialism of Kondō Azuma (1904–) typifies a large number of politically activist poets, though few have achieved his moving intensity and depth.

So brief a survey of the centuries of J. poetry omits not only numerous great and good poets but also certain outstanding features of the literature of a nation irresistibly given to verse. (Some say that in the mid-1950's there were 1,000 or more poetry magazines.) Foremost among the omissions is discussion of the survival of old styles and forms. Only two forms and few styles have died—the Court long poem (*chōka*) and the "linked" poetry of Feudal times. The *tanka* in particular has lasted from earliest historical times to the present, always exercising powerful (if sometimes negative) influence on J. poetry and the J. sensibility. In any given period, the styles of several previous periods are usually practiced by descendants of the originators and by other cultivated people. Often there is a decorum of styles—the old, new, descriptive, or passionate being appropriate for this or that occasion.

The two forms lost show how the history of J. poetry exhibits two powerful and contradictory tendencies—to fragmentation and integration. The giving way of *chōka* to the shorter *tanka* led to prose contexts, often relating several *tanka;* while the anthology came to be a distinct form integrated beyond Western conceptions. Beginning with the *Kokinshū*, imperial collections were integrated by temporal progressions in seasonal and love poems. To progression was gradually added close association of successive poems by complex manipulation of imagery, rhetoric, and shifting viewpoint. It is scarcely an exaggeration to say that the approximately 1,980 poems of the *Shinkokinshu* are integrated into a single poem of several parts and almost 10,000 lines. The methods of association and progression were embodied in the poetic sequences of, commonly, 100 poems composed by single poets in Mid- and Late Classical times and led naturally to *renga* and *haikai*. These "linked" forms —with their breakage of the *tanka* into two parts for stanzas and their composition by several authors at one sitting—show the persistent fragmentation; the extremely elaborate rules for composition show the contrary integration. In Modern times, as the *haikai* and *tanka* were set apart or fragmented into such discrete units as *haiku*, poems were often integrated by grouping into variations on a theme; but integration of sustained poetry has been sought chiefly in free verse.

The several kinds of integration were philosophically based upon the Buddhist sense of continuity in flux and the poetic tendency to deal less with conceptualized thought than with states of mind and feeling. But the emphasis upon the social contexts of composition has also assisted integration, both in de-emphasizing the discreteness of single poems (as assumed in the West) and by clustering poets into groups that tended to corporate conceptions of poetry and integrated collections of their poems. The tendency to form houses, dynasties, and coteries of poets is a constant feature of J. Poetry after the Early Classical period; and in Modern no less than in Feudal times, a single leader has usually gathered a group which may last for centuries or splinter at any time into groups with their own momentum. The groups are all but invariably dominated by a strong individual; members commonly owe social allegiance to the leader, but in practice may compose in styles traditional, official for the group, and idiosyncratic.

No problem for the Western critic of J. poetry is less capable of solution than that related to the concept of genres. J. poetry is usually thought of as wholly lyric; if so, then Western assumptions about poetry, the range of lyricism, and concepts of poetry need revision. The J. concept of poetry (its nature, aesthetic distances, and social functions); the fact that almost 800 poems are blended into the great "novel," *Genji Monogatari* (The Tale of Genji, ca. 1010); other mixed genres of poetry and prose; the mingling of casualness and unbelievably intricate rules in the jointly composed "linked" forms—such elements suggest that neither "lyric" nor any other Western generic term really applies to J. poetry.

The human as well as historical dynamism of J. poetry consistently emphasizes the strength of tradition or the survival of the old alongside the new. In any given period or poet's canon the forms and styles of earlier ages are apt to outnumber the productions we may associate with the temper of the age or with individual originality. Since the Early Classical period, there are almost no poets unassociated with groups of like-minded, socially obligated, or personally related (father to son, teacher to disciple) writers. Yet every period has been initiated by poets of strongly individualistic genius and decidedly individual character. The original might latterly become the traditional or the personal the oft imitated, but the great poetry has exemplified in practice as well as theory an originality and integrity with the poet's personality unknown in the West before the romantic movement. Moreover, if the emulators of a Teacher-poet, of Chinese poets, or of Western movements have not infrequently lapsed into numerous small idiosyncrasies or stereotyped imitation, the great original poets have consistently achieved their innovations and break-throughs by creative study of the traditional past. J. poets have, in such manner, over some 15 centuries achieved greatness in writing poems of personal response (conventionalized to the point that men create women speakers in courtly love poetry or that confession and diary become set genres) to audiences of fellow poets;

and in finding creative originality in a tradition that became, over the centuries, various enough to hold as traditional numerous departures from tradition. With much of the poetic past alive or latent in every period, each age has awaited its great strong personalities to bring a new poetry into being. The uncertainties of the latter 20th c. have frequently been seen before, and there is no reason to think that the old ways of resolving them will fail in the future.

BIBLIOGRAPHIES: *Kokubungaku Kenkyū Shomoku Kaidai*, ed. I. Asō (1957, Annotated Bibliog. of J. Lit.); Japan P.E.N. Club, *J. Lit. in European Langs.* (1957?); annual bibliog. issue of *Journal of Asian Studies*.

ANTHOLOGIES AND TRANSLATIONS. *Kokka Taikan*, ed. D. Matsushita and F. Watanabe (2 v., 1903, Great Canon of J. Poetry); *Zoku Kokka Taikan*, ed. D. Matsushita (2 v., 1925-26, Great Canon . . . Cont.); *Kōchū Kokka Taikei* (28 v., 1927-31, Great Compendium of J. Poetry, Collated and Annotated); *An Anthol: of Haiku Ancient and Modern* (1932) and *Masterpieces of J. Poetry Ancient and Modern* (2 v., 1936), both ed. and tr. A. Miyamori; *Anthol. de la poésie japonaise*, comp. G. Bonneau (1935); *The Manyōshū, 1000 Poems* pub. for Nippon Gakujutsu Shinkōkai (1940); *Haiku* (4 v., 1949-52) and *Senryu, J. Satirical Verses* (1950), both ed. and tr. R. H. Blyth; J. Konishi, *Haiku: Hassei Yori Gendai Made* (1952, Haiku: From its Begin. to Modern Times); *Gendai Nihon Shijin Zenshū*, ed. A. Kōno, et al. (16 v., 1951-53, Complete Works of Contemp. J. Poets); *Anthol. of J. Lit.* (1955) and *Modern J. Lit.* (1956), both comp. and ed. D. Keene; *Minase Sangin Hakuin*, ed. and tr. K. Yasuda (1956, renga of 3 Poets at Minase); *An Anthol. of Modern J. Poetry*, ed. and tr. I. Kono and R. Fukuda (1957, free verse); *Nihon Kagaku Taikei*, ed. N. Sasaki (6 v., repr. 1958, Great Compendium of J. Poetic Treatises) and . . . *Bekkan*, ed. N. Kyūsōjin (2 v., 1958, Supplement to . . .); *Nihon Shiikashū*, ed. K. Yamamoto (1959, a comprehensive, 1-v. anthol. of J. poetry); *Nihon Koten Bungaku Taikei*, various editors (1957ff., Great Compendium of J. Classical Lit., a monumental annotated ed., incl. poetry from earliest through Feudal times).

HISTORY AND CRITICISM: *Nihon Bungaku Daijiten*, ed. T. Fujimura (4 v., 1935; 1 v., 1955, Dict. of J. Lit.); S. Hisamatsu, *Nihon Bungaku Hyōronshi* (5 v., 1936-50, Hist. J. Lit. Crit.); Y. Yamada *Renga Gaisetsu* (1937, General Explanation of Renga); G. Bonneau, *Hist. de la litt. j. contemp.* (1940); O. Benl, *Die Entwicklung d. j. Poetik bis z. 16 Jh.* (1951); J. Konishi, *Nihon Bungakushi* (1953, Crit. Hist. J. Lit.); D. Keene, *J. Lit.* (1953); *Nihon Bungakushi*, ed. S. Hisamatsu (6 v., 1955-59, Hist.

J. Lit.); Y. Okazaki, *J. Lit. in the Meiji Era*, tr. V. H. Viglielmo (1955); J. Konishi, "Association and Progression: . . . Integration in . . . J. Court Poetry, A.D. 900-1350," *Harvard Journal of Asiatic Studies*, 21 (1958); R. H. Brower and E. Miner, *J. Court Poetry* (1961).

NEW TITLES: *Penguin Book of J. Verse*, tr. and ed. G. Bownas and A. Thwaite (1964); D. Keene, *Modern J. Poetry* (1964).　　E.M.

JARCHA (written *kharja* in Eng.). See SPANISH POETRY.

JAVANESE POETRY. The influence of Sanskrit literature upon Jav. literature has been very great and, for the most part, this influence has persisted through the centuries. Divided into three periods which are called for convenience's sake Old Jav. (1000-1500), Middle Jav. (1500-1830) and Modern Jav. (1830-), the first two periods exhibit especially significant Indic influence while the third period is characterized by a conservatism based on the forms inherited from the earlier stages of Jav. literature. The early literature in the Jav. language is largely in the form of poetry termed *kakawin* which includes epic, lyrical, erotic, and didactic art forms in Hindu style. The *kakawins* form a distinct and important group among the various literary genres in Old Jav. literature and their number is considerable. During the 19th c. Dutch and Indonesian scholars edited, published, and sometimes translated all or portions of the more significant *kakawins*. Among these are the *Rāmāyana* of the 10th c., *Ardjunawiwāhā* (Ardjuna's Wedding) by Mpu Kanwa in the 11th c., the *Bhomakāwya*, the *Bhāratayuddha* and the historically important *Nāgarakrtāgama* of Prapancha (1365), alleged to be a contemporary account of the Mojopait Empire of East Java. In form, old Jav. poetry, like L. and Gr., was quantitative rather than qualitative.

Alongside the Sanskritized court verse forms found in the *kakawin* there developed during the Middle Jav. period a popular verse form called *kidung*. There were two types, *tengahan* and *matjapat*, the latter type consisting of a number of irregular lines in contrast to the court poetry in which all verses are of equal length. *Tengahan* differs in some technical aspects from *matjapat*. Since there was neither word stress nor quantitative distinctions in Jav. proper, rhythm played no role. Two of the best-known examples of *kidung* verse are the *Sudamala and Kidung Sundāyana*. An example of *matjapat* verse is the following:

The son of regent Andajaningrat
At Pengging
And the son of His Majesty the Sultan
Prince of Panggung by name

Came to obtain knowledge
From Siti Djenar

The Golden Age of Jav. literature flourished from the 11th to the 15th c., and Professor C. C. Berg has compared its products favorably with the best the Middle Ages in Europe has to offer. After the fall of the Mojopait Empire and with the advent of Islam Jav. literature went into a recession. While Arabic verse forms seem to have exercised some influence on Malay literature, there is no evidence for such influence upon Jav. poetry. A new indigenous verse form, a kind of *sloka*, appears at this time; it has 4 lines of 16 syllables but is not based on quantity. Modern Jav. literature is generally conceded to begin after the Java War of 1825–1830, when poetry in the Jav. language underwent a renascence with the appearance at the courts of Central Java of such poets as Mangkunegara IV, Jåsådipurå father and son, and the most famous of them all, Raden Ngabèhi Rånggåwarsitå (ca. 1803–74). Rånggåwarsitå's poetry, which exhibits some Western influence acquired through his close association with several budding Dutch scholars in the field of Jav. studies, is probably best represented by the poem *Tjemporèt* (1856) which treats of the marriage of a prince and princess of olden times. The language used is excessively refined, even the peasants speaking this lofty language among themselves. All situations are described in great detail and, for the modern reader, the narrative moves very slowly. There is very little evidence that Jav. poetry in modern rhythms or even in traditional style is being composed at the present time to any great extent.

ANTHOLOGIES: *Proza en poëzie van Oud-Java*, ed. C. Hooykaas (1933); *Proza en poëzie van Oud- en Nieuw-Java*, ed. T. J. Bezemer (1942).

HISTORY AND CRITICISM: *Wrtta-sañćaya. Oud-javaansch leerdicht over versbouw*, ed. H. Kern (1875); "Literatuur (Javaansche)," *Encyclopaedie van Nederlandsch-Indië*, IV (1918); G. A. J. Hazeu, *Oud en nieuw uit de Javaansche letterkunde* (1921); C. C. Berg, *Kidung Sundáyana (Kidung Sunda C)* (1928) and *Hoofdlijnen der Javaansche litteratuurgeschiedenis* (1929); Th. Pigeaud, "Over de beoefening der Javaansche letterkunde in de laatste 40 jaren," *Djåwå*, 12 (1932); R. M. Ng. Poerbatjaraka and T. Hadidjaja, *Kepustakaan Djawa* (1952; the nearest thing to a general survey of Jav. lit.; no adequate survey exists as yet); R. B. Slametmuljana, *Poëzie in Indonesia* (1954); R. Hardjowirogo, "R. Ng. Ranggawarsita," *Buku kita*, 1 (1955). J.M.E.

JE NE SÇAI (SAIS) QUOI. A prize specimen in the curio-cabinet of critical terms which enjoyed a widespread vogue in the literature

of France in the 17th c. and was used occasionally later as an expression for the indefinable grace that was regarded as "a sine qua non in every phase of life and art" (W. E. Thormann). A critical theory of poetry was only incidentally related to the discussions of the *je ne sçai quoi*. First used in England in 1656 for that "strange" feeling of being ill without apparent reason, the term served, particularly in the early 18th c., as a cover-all for the "superior beauties" or qualities which connoisseurs of poetry could only label as an indescribable, inexpressible, unanalyzable "something"—the *I-know-not-what*. Thus Alexander Pope wrote that the term "was the very support of all ignorant pretenders to delicacy" (*Observations on the Catalogue [of Homer]*). Still, in England as in France the notion behind the expression proved very useful for many persons, including "wise" pretenders to taste like Pope himself. The age of canons and rules was also the age of critical speculation about poetry with nameless graces beyond definition. The *je-ne-sçai-quoi* therefore saw considerable service along with *nescio quo modo* (I know not how), *il poco più* and *il poco meno* (the little more and the little less), and similar expressions of persons of taste. "How do the slight touches of the chisel, the pencil, the pen, the fiddlestick, *et cetera*,—give the true swell, which gives the true pleasure!" (*Tristram Shandy* 2.6)

Before the close of the 18th c. the *je-ne-sais-quoi* disappeared from fashionable theorizing about poetry and the arts but was occasionally used to describe a general "air" of elegance or indefinable grace, as in the original Fr. expression. In "The Je Ne Sçai Quoi. A Song" by William Whitehead, poet laureate, the singer amusingly attributed the indescribable *I-know-not-what* that accounted for his falling in love to "the provoking charm of Caelia altogether." The term reappeared in the light verse of the late 19th c. to characterize the taste, appearance, and manners of the poetical-aesthetic, *je-ne-sais-quoi* young man of *Patience*.—Bray; E. B. O. Borgerhoff, *The Freedom of Fr. Classicism* (1950); E. Kohler, "Je ne sais quoi, ein Kapitel aus der Begriffsgeschichte des Unbegreiflichen," *Romanistisches Jahrbuch*, 6 (1953–54); W. E. Thormann, "Again the 'Je Ne Sais Quoi,'" MLN, 73 (1958). S.A.L.

JINGLE. Any verse which pleases the ear by catchy rhythm and pronounced sound-repetitions, as rhyme or alliteration, usually at the expense of sense. *Eeny meeny miny mo* and *hickory dickory dock* are jingles. Because they are easily memorized and repeated, jingles are often as enduring as the loftiest poetry. Mark Twain in "Punch, Brothers, Punch" (*Tom*

Sawyer Abroad, . . . and Other Stories) humorously describes his "catching" and passing on a contagious newspaper jingle. The term is sometimes depreciatively applied to any poetry which makes pronounced use of sound-effects. Addison (*Spectator* no. 297) criticizes Milton for often affecting "a kind of Jingle in his Words" in *Paradise Lost.—The Oxford Book of Nursery Rhymes*, ed. I. and P. Opie (1951).
L.P.

JOC PARTIT (Prov.), *jeu parti* (Fr.). See PARTIMEN.

JONGLEUR. A wandering musician and entertainer of the Middle Ages, somewhat analogous in function to the Anglo-Saxon scop (q.v.) or to the minstrel, *trouvère*, or troubadour (qq.v.) of a later era. Although the word dates only from the 8th c., jongleurs seem to have existed in France from the 5th c. to the 15th. In the earlier period the name was applied indiscriminately to acrobats, actors, and entertainers in general, as well as to musicians and reciters of verse. From the 10th c. on, however, the term is confined to musicians and reciters of verse, largely because the church favored them.

At one time the terms "j." and "troubadour" seem to have been used interchangeably; later, however, as the gulf between creative and performing artist deepened, the term "j." came to denote an entertainer who presented material not of his own composition. Material drawn from the great *chansons de geste* (q.v.) often formed an important part of the jongleur's repertoire. The jongleurs were of great importance in the transmission of medieval literary forms from one country to another.— E. Faral, *Les Jongleurs en France au moyen âge* (1910); P. Wareman, *Spielmannsdichtung. Versuch einer Begriffsbestimmung* (1951); R. Menéndez Pidal, *Poesía juglaresca y orígenes de las literaturas románicas* (6th rev. and enl. ed., 1957); M. Valency, *In Praise of Love* (1958).
F.J.W.; A.P.

JUDICIAL CRITICISM. See CRITICISM, TYPES OF.

JUGENDSTIL. In 1896 Georg Hirth established the liberal journal, *Die Jugend*, which was for long, together with *Simplicissimus*, *März*, and *Süddeutsche Monatshefte*, one of the leading literary journals published in Munich.

Essays on art and literary criticism were the main features of the first volumes, and cartoons and sketches by important artists of the day (e.g., A. Weisgerber, F. V. Ostini, Mattei *et al.*) were contained in each issue. The journal itself provided the name for the common style which these artists developed: *Jugendstil* is the name of the decorative style that prevailed in Germany from about 1893 to 1910. Gothic art, Japanese colored wood-cuttings and motifs from the Eng. Pre-Raphaelites influenced its development. Its linear and spatial ornamentation often employed garlands, fruit, foliage, birds, etc. in a highly stylized form.

J. is one of the many terms (e.g., "baroque," "Biedermeier," "impressionism," etc.) which was first employed in the history of art and was subsequently applied to literature (cf. the writings of F. Strich and O. Walzel in bibliog.). The term has been clearly defined in the history of art; in its application to literature it remains, as all the other terms, extremely ambiguous. In some literary histories the young Rilke, Hofmannsthal, and George, as well as Beer-Hofmann, Dehmel, M. Dauthendey, and R. v. Schaukal, are regarded as belonging to J., whereas in others they are considered to be "impressionists" or "neoromantics"—each time because of almost the same stylistic features: exploitation of language for its ornamental value, abundant use of both adjectives and adverbs, preference for the flowing effect created by intransitive and reflexive verbs. If "ornament" is in fact the characteristic feature of J., can all literature in which ornament is of the essence (e.g., the literature of the 17th c., Joyce's *Finegans Wake*, etc.) be considered as J.? From an over-all view of European literature in the 19th and 20th c., the development and main featuers of literature cannot be understood by postulating a variety of "isms," but by taking it as a whole and analyzing and perceiving the structural and stylistic elements which such poets and writers as Baudelaire, George, Benn, W. Stevens, Flaubert, James have in common.—O. Walzel, *Wechselseitige Erhellung der Künste* (1917); F. Strich, *Deutsche Klassik und Romantik* (1922); G. K. Schauer, "Neue Literatur zur Jugendstilfrage," *Imprimatur*, N. F. (1956–57); V. Klotz, "J. in der Lyrik," *Akzente*, 4 (1957); W. Lennig, "Der literarische J.," *Deutsche Universitätszeitung*, 13 (1958); E. Klein, *J. in der deutschen Lyrik* (1958); *J.—der Weg ins zwanzigste Jahrhundert*, ed. H. Seling (1959).
E.L.

K

KANNADA POETRY. See INDIAN POETRY.

KASHMIRI POETRY. See INDIAN POETRY.

KATHARSIS. See CATHARSIS.

KENNING (pl. *kenningar*). An implied simile in circumlocution for a noun not named; a feature of the diction used with Old Germanic prosody (q.v.). It ranges in kind from stereotyped descriptive compound epithets varying the plain name of a thing (*dispenser of rings: lord*) to complex metaphorical periphrases, especially in skaldic verse (*sea of Odin's breast: divine mead of inspiration: poem*), and thence beyond legitimate poetic functions, through more and more turgid conceits, into affectation and enigma. In such highly formulaic poetry as the Old Germanic, the kenningar were sometimes, understandably enough, petrified expressions which might not be especially appropriate to a given poetic need; but in the best poetry they were more frequently portmanteau devices whose suggestive associations deserve to be unpacked with care. The most familiar k. encase perceptions of some delicacy or power (*God's beacon: sun; foamy-necked floater: ship under sail; joy of a bird: feather*). Very different values are conveyed by these apparently similar k. for "sea, ocean," all used in *Beowulf: windgeard* "enclosure or home of the winds": the sea, its storms, its difference from other kinds of "yards" on land, its aspect as an area to be traversed by sailing ships; *ganotes bæð* "bath of the gannet": a shoreward salt-water area where the sea-fowl dips, fishes, sports, bathes; *hronrád* "riding place of the whale": not "the whale's road," but the great open ocean where the whale rides massively, impressively.—R. Meissner, *Die K. der Skalden* (1921); H. Van der Merwe Scholtz, *The K. in Anglo-Saxon and ON Poetry* (1927); M. Marquardt, *Die altenglischen K.* (1938); C. Brady, "The Synonyms for 'Sea' in *Beowulf*," in *Studies in Honor of Albert Morey Sturtevant* (1952); D. C. Collins, "The Kenning in Anglo-Saxon Poetry," E&S, 12 (1959).　　J.B.B.

KHARJA. See SPANISH POETRY.

KIND. Term widely used in 17th and 18th c. Eng. for genre or literary type, e.g., epic, tragedy. See GENRES.

KNITTELVERS (also *Knüttelvers, Knüppelvers, Klippelvers*). A derogatory name ("badly knit verse," doggerel) applied by Opitz and other classical poets of the 17th c. to a popular meter of 15th- and 16th-c. German poetry. K. consists of lines of 4 stresses each, rhyming in couplets; in its earlier form (*freier K.*) the meter uses an indeterminate number of unstressed syllables (as in *Christabel* meter, q.v.), but as employed by Hans Sachs and others in the 16th c. the meter (*strenger K.*) contained a regular total of 8 or 9 syllables per line. The reforms of the Opitzian school resulted in the substitution of the French-derived alexandrine (q.v.) for the 4-beat line, but K. was revived in the 18th c. by Gottsched, who restricted it to comic effects, and by Schiller (*Wallensteins Lager*) and most notably by Goethe (*Hans Sachsens poetische Sendung*; the older parts of *Faust* 1.).

> Habe nun, ach! Philosophie,
> Juristerei und Medizin,
> Und leider auch Theologie
> Durchaus studiert, mit heissem Bemühn.
> Da steh ich nun, ich armer Tor!
> Und bin so klug als wie zuvor.
> (Goethe, *Faust* 1.354–59).

Later poets who used the meter include Gerhard Hauptmann.—O. Flohr, *Gesch. des Knittelverses vom 17. Jh. bis zur Jugend Goethes* (1893); A. Heusler, *Deutsche Versgesch.*, III (1929); W. Kayser, *Gesch. des deutschen Verses* (1960).

KNOWLEDGE AND POETRY. See MEANING, PROBLEM OF; POETRY, THEORIES OF (OBJECTIVE THEORIES); CRITICISM, FUNCTION OF (COGNITIVE THEORIES).

KOREAN POETRY should be divided into two broad categories: that composed in a kind of Sinico-Kor. and that composed in the indigenous tongue. The former body of verse will not be treated here, although in quantity, and occasionally in quality, it exceeds that of the latter. Furthermore, prior to the invention of the alphabet, or *han'gŭl*, in 1443, even in pure Kor. verse a special writing system called *idu*, or "official reading," was developed which employed Chinese characters to eke out the sounds, and often even the meaning.

The oldest verse form is doubtless the *tusolga*, which is thought to mean "sounds for appeasing spirits." Most of the poetry of the Ancient, Three Kingdoms, and Unified Silla periods (ca. 1st c. B.C.–A.D. 935) is linked with religious myths or legends. Fourteen *hyangga*, or "native songs," of the only twenty-five extant are preserved in the 13th-c. compilation by the Buddhist monk Ilyŏn, *Samguk Yusa* (Remaining Records of the Three Kingdoms). This verse form employs 4, 8, or 10 lines divided into two stanzas of 8 and 2 lines respectively. The number of syllables in each line can vary from as few as 4 to as many as 15. Several of the poems describe natural scenes, although always in a religious context.

In the Koryŏ Dynasty (935–1392), poetry was divided clearly along class lines. The aristocracy developed the *kyŏnggich'aega*, or the "kyŏnggi-style poem," in which both stanzas ended with the fixed refrain, "kyŏnggi yŏha," or "the scene, how is it?" Educated men and scholars employed this form largely to eulogize natural beauty, and the poems contain little romantic element. The common people, however, had their own verse form, the *changga*, or the "long poem," of 10 or more lines or stanzas, with refrains at the end of each. Most of the *changga* dealt with the theme of love. At the end of the Koryŏ Dynasty a new poetic form, the *sijo*, emerged, putting an end to literary class-division, since it came to be composed by both groups. It became the most significant Kor. poetic genre, occupying much the same position which the *tanka* does in Japan. Indeed it must be considered the foremost contribution of Korea to world literature, since Korea did not achieve any great success in prose.

The word *sijo* means, literally, "melody of the times"; as this implies, it was originally sung or chanted according to fixed tunes and to the accompaniment of musical instruments. These tunes have since been largely lost, and only the words remain. The *sijo* came to consist of 3 lines, each composed of 4 groups of syllables. The first and middle lines each had 3, 4, 3 or 4, and 4 syllables in its four groups, but the last line had a pattern of 3, 5, 4, and 3 syllables. Thus, the first 2 lines had either 14 or 15 syllables in all, and the last line a fixed 15. The *sijo*, as a whole, then, could range from 43 to 45 syllables. Although the major breaks came at the end of the first and middle lines, there were secondary breaks at the end of the first 2 syllable groups in each line. Rhyme is not an important feature, although it is not specifically avoided. Head rhyme, however, is often found. The fixed prosody for the *sijo* did not prevent certain poets from writing poems which have more or less than the usual 43 to 45 syllables.

An example of one of the first and best known *sijo* is the following:

Paeksŏl-i chajajin kot-e
kurŭm-i mŏhŭraera
Pangaon maehwa-nŭn
ŏnŭi kot-e p'iŏnŭngo
Sŏkyang-e hollo sŏsŏ
kal kot molla hanora.

In the valley of deep snows
    the clouds gather;
The long-awaited plum flower—
    In what place does it bloom?
At sunset I stand alone,
    not knowing where to go.

During the Yi Dynasty (1392–1910) the *sijo* was further refined, and leading poets, such as Yi I (1536–84) and Chŏng Ch'ŏl (1536–93), emerged. It treated a broad range of themes, but as in most lyric verse, those of nature and love predominate. Many of the poems show a curious mixture of Confucian and Buddhist thought, attesting Korea's intermediate position between China and Japan.

The *kasa*, or "song words," and the *chapka*, or "miscellaneous songs," were subsidiary verse forms which developed during the long Yi period. The former usually contained 8 syllables in a line, which was further subdivided into two phrases, usually of 4 syllables each; some variation was permissible. There was no limit to the number of lines, and many *kasa* had hundreds of them. The foremost poet in this form was the aforementioned Chŏng Ch'ŏl, whose *Melody of Beauty* is an acknowledged masterpiece. *Chapka* were long narrative poems sung by male professional entertainers.

In the modern period (1910–) many poets have abandoned traditional forms to experiment with the free-verse styles of contemporary Western poetry. Outstanding among such free-verse poets is Kim Ki-rim, who employs a subtle, intellectual style. Other modern poets, however, have maintained the long and great *sijo* tradition.

ANTHOLOGIES: *Ch'ŏnggu Yŏng-ŏn* (modern ed. [1930]) of oldest and largest anthol. of Kor. poetry, comp. by Kim Ch'ŏn-t'aek [1727], containing over 1,000 *sijo* and *kasa* from the late Koryŏ period to the early 18th c.); *Haedong Koyo* (modern ed. [1930]) of work comp. by Kim Su-jang [1763], containing 883 songs, 149 by the compiler, of Koryŏ and Yi poets); *The Orchid Door: Ancient Kor. Poems*, tr. J. S. Grigsby (1935, free-verse tr. with brief introd.); *Hyŏndae Chosŏn Munhak Chŏnjip: Siga-jip*, ed. Pang Ŭng-mo (1938; containing poems and biogr. sketches of 33 contemp. poets); *Chosŏn Minyo-sŏn*, ed. Lim Hwa (1939; containing songs never before recorded); *An Anthol. of Modern Poems in Korea*, ed. Zong In-sob (1948); P. P. Hyun "Seven Modern Kor. Poems, Selected and Tr. with an Introd.," *New World*

Writing (1955); "Tr. from Cl. Kor. Poetry," *Kor. Survey*, 4 (1955), by V. H. Viglielmo; *Songs of Ancient Korea, an Anthol. of Poems in the Sijo Form*, tr. V. H. Viglielmo (forthcoming).

HISTORY AND CRITICISM: Cho Yun-je, *Chosŏn Siga Sagang* (1937; an account of Kor. poetry from ancient times to 1910) and *Chosŏn Siga ŭi Yŏn-gu* (1948; a coll. of essays on *hyangga, sijo, kasa*); Pang Chong-hyŏn, *Ko-sijo Chŏnghae* (Detailed Commentary on Old *Sijo*) (1949); D. S. Suh, "The Kor. Mind as Revealed Through Cl. Poems," *Kor. Survey*, 5 (1956), with tr. poems by V. H. Viglielmo; *Voices of the Dawn: A Selection of Kor. Poetry from the 6th C. to the Present Day*, tr. P. Hyun (1960).

NEW TITLES: *Anthol. of Kor. Poetry*, comp. and tr. P. H. Lee (1964); P. H. Lee, *Kor. Lit.: Topics and Themes* (1964). V.H.V.

KVƍUHÁTTR. An ON alliterative verse form which resembles the *fornyrƍislag* (q.v.), "with the difference that instead of having four syllables in each line, its lines alternate between three syllables and four" (Turville-Petre, *Origins of Icelandic Lit.*, p. 34). The earliest poem in which k. is found is *Ynglingatal* (before 900). In the 10th c. Egill Skallagrímsson used it effectively in his famed poems *Arinbjarnarkviƍa* and *Sonatorrek*, and it was also used by some of his contemporaries and later skalds. The following lines from his first-named poem will serve as an illustration:

> Vask árvakr, bark orƍ saman
> meƍ málþjóns morginverkum

In his equally renowned poem *Höfuƍlausn* Egill introduced end rhyme into Icelandic poetry with a meter called *runhent*, modeled upon an OE verse form.—*The Skalds*, tr. and ed. L. M. Hollander (1945). R.B.

L

L.M. Abbreviation for long measure or meter. Hymn stanza.

LAI (Fr.), lay (Eng.). A short lyrical or narrative poem. (1) The oldest lyric *lais* in OF are by Gautier de Dargies who flourished in the first third of the 13th c. The l. is addressed to an earthly lady, or to the Virgin, but it differs from other poems of this theme by having varying rhymes and syllable counts in its stanzas, without refrain. One of the most interesting by Ernoul le Vieux has no love theme; it is the *Lai de l'ancien et du nouveau testament*. It is not certain that l. and *descort* are the same thing. (2) The oldest narrative *lais*, almost always written in octosyllabic verse, are the *contes* or short romantic tales originated by Marie de France in the third quarter of the 12th c. She had Breton themes for most of these, but a few of them are based on local traditions and folk elements. Later the term "l." became synonymous with *conte*. As for the origin of l., some authorities believe that the word is derived from a Celtic form similar to Old Ir. *loid* (song). (3) The term "Breton lay" was applied in 14th-c. England to poems set in Brittany, written in a spirit similar to that of Marie's, or, often, simply because the poem says so. About a dozen Breton lays are extant in Eng., among them *Sir Orfeo, Sir Launfal, Emare*, and Chaucer's *Franklin's Tale*. Since the 16th c. "lay" has been used for song, and in the early 19th c. the term was sometimes used for a short historical ballad, e.g., Scott's *Lay of the Last Minstrel.—Lais et descorts fr. du XIIIᵉ s.*, ed. A. Jeanroy and others (1901); E. Hoepffner, *Les Lais de Marie de France* (1935) and "The Breton Lais," *Arthurian Lit. in the Middle Ages*, ed. R. S. Loomis (1959). U.T.H.

LAISSE. In the OF epics or *chansons de geste* (q.v.) this is a stanzaic, or paragraph, division of no specified length. The length of each l. depends upon the emphasis which the poet wishes to make. Each of these divisions has its own assonance, or—in later poems—rhyme. Sometimes the content of a l. would be repeated item for item in one or two following *laisses*, with differing assonance or rhyme, of course. Such repetitions are called *laisses similaires*.—A. Monteverdi, "La Laisse epique," Liège. Université. Faculté de philosophie et lettres. *La Technique littéraire des chansons de geste* (1959). U.T.H.

LAKE POETS, L. school, Lakers: Wordsworth, Coleridge, Southey. In the first number of the *Edinburgh Review* (Oct. 1802) Jeffrey began twenty years' abuse of these three as a "new school" which in 1807 he coupled with "the Lakes of Cumberland." A denunciation of Wordsworth in Jan. 1809 is listed under "L.p." in the ten-year index of 1813, but a review of

Feb. 1812 is the first to use the expression in context. The poets are called "Lakers" in Nov. 1814, and thereafter such references are common.

Wordsworth wrote all his long life about his "dear native regions." Coleridge linked his name with Wordsworth's by collaborating in the *Lyrical Ballads* and then by following his friend to the north. Southey in turn followed his brother-in-law Coleridge and outstayed him by thirty years. In 1813 Southey's appointment as Poet Laureate and Wordsworth's as a Distributor of Stamps drew attention to their Lake-district residence and invited Byron's continuing ridicule. Circumstance and coincidence, extending to 1843 when Wordsworth succeeded Southey as Laureate, thus lent support to the fiction of a "school." The "system" ascribed to it was Wordsworth's program of simplicity in diction and subject; Coleridge's collaboration was brief, and Southey's not direct or systematic.—F.A.D.

LAMENT. A nonnarrative type of poetry, arising as part of oral tradition, expressing profound regret, sorrow, or concern for a loss of a person or, sometimes, position. The l. seems to have arisen alongside heroic poetry and exists in almost all languages, including Hebrew, Chinese, Zulu.

> Ye daughters of Israel, weep over Saul, who
>   clothed you in scarlet . . .
>   *David's Lament for Saul and Jonathan,*
>   1017 B.C.(?)

> Thou hast finished, finished the nations,
> Where wilt thou go forth to battle now?
> J. Shooter, *The Kafirs of Natal* (1857).

In *Deor's Lament* (Anglo-Saxon) the scop regrets his change of status, having been displaced in the favor of his patron by a rival. Many poems which rely heavily on the *ubi sunt* (q.v.) theme are, in a general sense, laments. Also the separate tragedies in the *Mirror for Magistrates*, wherein a ghost relates the story of his fall from fortune, were called laments (e.g., Sackville's "Lament" for the Duke of Buckingham), and so were in Scotch and Ir. folk music the airs used on occasions of mourning. Any dirge or mournful type of complaint (qq.v.). The essential characteristic seems to be the sense of personal loss.—Chadwick; C. M. Bowra, *Heroic Poetry* (1952).—R.O.E.

LAMPOON. A personal satire, often scurrilous. The word is said to derive from Fr. *lampons*, "let us drink," associated with the slang term *lamper*, to guzzle, swill down. Lampoons abound particularly in the Restoration and 18th c., as do public professions of abhorrence.

Dryden, a magnificent lampooner, abjures the form as dangerous and unlawful: "We have no moral right on the reputation of other men." The l. is often differentiated from satire (q.v.) on grounds that it is (a) personal, (b) motivated by malice, (c) unjust; thus John Dennis: ". . . Satire . . . can never exist where the censures are not just. In that case the Versifyer, instead of a Satirist, is a Lampooner, and infamous Libeller." While the word dates only from mid-17th c., the thing itself is as old as poetry, and as widespread.—*An Anthol. of Invective and Abuse*, ed. H. Kingsmill (1929); J. Dryden, "A Discourse concerning the Original and Progress of Satire" (1693), *Works*, ed. W. Scott and G. Saintsbury (1882–93), XIII, 82–84; J. Addison, *The Spectator*, no. 23; J. Dennis, *Works*, ed. E. N. Hooker (1939–43), II, 325, 396–97.—R.C.E.

LATIN POETICS. See CLASSICAL POETICS; MEDIEVAL POETICS.

LATIN POETRY, CLASSICAL. L. poetry is commonly censured as derivative. The L. poets wrote in meters originated by Greeks, employed a more or less assimilated Gr. mythology as a poetic vehicle, and confined their efforts, for the most part, to genres already well established when Rome was little more than a barbarous village. Yet, despite this real dependence, there remains nothing less Gr. than the masterpieces of L. poetry, whose imitation of the Gr. was never slavish, and whose tradition was a double one. On one side stood the centuries of developed Gr. literature, a literature of infinite variety and vast achievement, supplying L. poets with models and sanctions, and the more valuable for being foreign without being alien. On the other stood the developing corpus of L. literature, steadily informing the cultural context within which a given poet wrote and lived. Between these two traditions the tension was lively and fruitful for Republican poetry especially; if the earlier poetry can be generally divided between a "Romanizing" school on the one hand and a "Hellenizing" school on the other, for later poets the problem is one of preserving the double loyalty they felt without doing damage to either tradition. This double loyalty, it needs to be said, was not maintained by the simple mechanical act of domesticating Gr. meters and forms or adapting them to a specifically Roman sensibility, but by the far more delicate operation of blending the strengths and virtues of both sensibilities in a common form. This marriage of two traditions was the achievement of Virgil more than any other L. writer; and for Virgil's followers his example looms so large that their problem is less whether they should be Greeks or Romans than whether they shall be Virgilians or something else.

Further governing the finished L. poem were two states of mind almost completely alien to classical Gr. poetry. The first was the L. poet's *consciousness* of his tradition and his place in it. Like the Roman historian, the L. poet was intensely aware of his tradition and normally intensely loyal to it; and at times his humility before his tradition's authority approaches servility. It is this intense traditional loyalty that most nearly explains the small range and variety of L. poetry when measured against Gr. or Eng. poetry. Tradition for the L. poet early acquired an enormous authority, extending to subject, conventions, form, and even rhetorical modes; it was something to be exploited but the exploitation is an exercise in humility and craft, a constant refinement of a more or less dominant mode. Rarely does the L. poet rebel against his tradition, though he may rebel against one of its modes for another. In poetry as in character the virtue of *pietas* (dutiful loyalty) is central, and *continuity* is therefore one of the dominant features of L. poetry: in all essential respects the poetics of Virgil and the poetics of Claudian four centuries later are the same. But for the same reason that L. poetry exhibits a restricted range, it also exhibits much less flagrant sensationalism and striving for originality; yet it would be a mistake to suppose that L. poets were indifferent innovators or that style is somehow impersonal. Nowhere is sensationalism of rhetoric and situation more prevalent than in L. poetry, and especially in post-Virgilian verse; but it needs to be observed that rhetorical innovation is almost always marginal, an elaborate, sometimes frigid, refinement of the dominant rhetoric of the language. Almost never is there revolution at the core or rejection of the cardinal principles of traditional poetics. Combined with consciousness of the tradition, the second dominant characteristic of L. poetry was the passion for *utility* in literature, for its application to some patriotic or instructive end —a passion never really absent, even in the hyperesthetic pieces where the poet emphasizes its existence by his determined avoidance of it. But it is not difficult to see how the poetry that emerged from the juggling of these elements was completely different from any Gr. poetry ever written.

Origins. Traces of wholly indigenous L. literature are almost nonexistent. There were rude farces, in the rough Saturnian stress-meter, before the irruption of Gr. culture into Latium, but we possess no fragments. This meter, however, was employed in the first L. poem of which we have even the barest knowledge—a translation of the *Odyssey* written about the middle 3d c. B.C. by Livius Androni-

cus, a Gr. ex-slave. He handled the jigging, heavily accented iambo-trochaic movement of his verse with little distinction, but he had the incalculable advantage of being first, and his work was used as a school text for more than two centuries. His younger contemporary, Gnaeus Naevius, represents a further stage in the transition. His versified chronicle of the First Punic War was done in the same meter, but he seems to have owed much to Homer, while he also wrote tragedies and comedies on Attic models where he employed Gr. meters, based on syllabic quantity rather than stress. But the towering figure of the early years is Quintus Ennius (239–169 B.C.), in the wreck of whose work we may discern the roots of most subsequent L. poetry. He wrote tragedies, comedies, didactic poems and epigrams, all largely derived from the Greeks, but his most important work was the *Annals,* an epic chronicle recording the history of Rome from the arrival of Aeneas down to Ennius' own times. The fragments of this work—which established the dactylic hexameter as the medium of L. epic—still serve to illustrate the peculiar nature of L. poetry. Based openly on the Homeric poems, and in some sense a continuation of them, it seems to have been influenced by Hellenistic poetic histories, and fused these two sources, separated by centuries in time and outlook, into something distinctly Roman by its dedicated patriotic and instructive bias. Ennius' somewhat older contemporary, Titus Maccius Plautus (250–184 B.C.), set a number of plays of the Gr. New Comedy into L., but his debt to the rough native dramatic tradition is probably quite great, as the rather tired comedy of manners of the late Hellenic and Hellenistic ages suffers a sea-change, becoming excellent, bawdy farce. The twenty-one Plautine comedies which we possess are rude, colloquial and frankly aimed at the pit, but they are funny and vital as well.

Preclassical. The 2d century B.C. saw Rome's first literary-philosophical coteries, a gathering of philhellenes centered around the younger Scipio Africanus for the purpose of the serious study and adaptation of Gr. culture. The two great poets of the century were active members of this Scipionic circle. The first was Terence (Publius Terentius Afer, 195?–159), whose six verse-comedies show a definite reaction from the "excesses" of his predecessors, such as Plautus, back to the pure Menandrean ideal of the Gr. New Comedy. The purity and beauty of Terence's language is a definite landmark; but more important is the implication of his subtlety. In stressing form, expression, and relationships at the expense of strength, character, and humor itself, he clearly turned away from the general public to address the educated classes—a situation that had not oc-

LATIN POETRY

curred in Greece until the beginning of the Hellenistic Age, but a necessary step in this grafting of a sophisticated (Gr.) tradition onto a crude but vital (Roman) one. Henceforth, with few exceptions, L. poetry was by learned poets for a more or less learned audience. The other great name was Gaius Lucilius (180–102 B.C.), commonly called the father of satire, the only genre to whose invention Rome can lay fair claim—though the satirical attitude has a long history in Greece, and Lucilius was directly influenced by the Alexandrian Gr. Callimachus. His work itself, some thirty books of miscellanies, or *saturae*, ranged discursively over human experience, the moralizing appropriate in a poet who was a member of a clique whose orientation was largely Stoic. We possess numerous fragments of his work, but none, unfortunately, of any length. Like Terence, he addressed himself to the man of some culture.

Late Republican. The 1st century B.C. witnessed the rise of rhetoric and the fall of the Roman Republic, both of them events of prime importance for poetry. But the first important poem of which we possess any considerable remnants was the translation by the orator Cicero (106–43) of the *Phaenomena* of Aratus of Soli, an Alexandrian didactic work which combined devout Stoicism with a notably faulty astronomy and meteorology and was destined to be translated twice more in the next 500 years. Cicero was no great poet, but his phraseology (and, by reaction, his Stoicism) had a great influence on the most remarkable poem of the period, the *De Rerum Natura* ("On Nature") of Lucretius (Titus Lucretius Carus, 99?–55?), a delineation, in 6 hexameter books, of the Epicurean natural philosophy. The models were the 5th-c. Gr. philosopher Empedocles, also the author of a poem *On Nature,* and Ennius—but the Ennius of the *Annals,* not of the didactic efforts. The result is certainly the fairest didactic poem ever written. Though a missionary, and passionately convinced that his doctrine was needed to free the Roman mind from superstition and the fear of death, Lucretius confined his psychagogic outbursts to clearly discerned "purple patches," letting reason carry the argument through the rest of the poem. The resultant transitions are often jarring, and the versified physics has repelled casual investigators and particularly those to whom Epicureanism is merely unqualified hedonism or non-Roman quietism; but in spite of this, and in spite of its unfinished state, the *De Rerum Natura* stands alone. It even stands outside the mainstream of poetic development at Rome, which was at this time sharply divided, as the patriotic and utilitarian old guard came under attack from a group which styled themselves the "New Poets." These adopted the standards and forms of Alexandrian criticism and performance, preferring the brief, highly-wrought genres—epyllion, lyric, epigram, elegiac—to full-scale epic and didactic. Chief among this learned circle was Gaius Valerius Catullus (84?–54?), whose range was remarkably wide. He wrote epyllia in the Hellenistic fashion which are remarkable for the variety and beauty of their textures, their care for responsion and juxtaposition, as *The Marriage of Peleus and Thetis,* a marvelous instance of unity in layered diversity. In his intenser, shorter pieces, however, he turned from Gr. practice—though not from Gr. theory—employing the full range of colloquial L., in a wide variety of meters, to greet friends, damn enemies, and celebrate and abuse his mistress. These, and especially the last group, are not the white-hot yawps that romantic criticism has dotingly supposed: Catullus in love is a learned poet still, and to say that he conveys the immediacy of passion more directly than any other L. poet is not to deny the elaborate learned intricacy of even his shortest poems.

Augustan. The Hellenizing New Poets never succeeded in making—if they ever intended—a full break with the didactic-patriotic tradition, and ironically enough, their achievements were incorporated into the superb and subtle didactics of the next age. This is best shown in the work of Rome's greatest poet, Virgil (Publius Vergilius Maro, 70–19 B.C.), His first considerable work was the *Eclogues* or *Bucolics,* a collection of ten pastoral poems which observed the New Poets' architectonic structure, intense attention to the word, and approved Hellenistic sources—in this case the Alexandrian Theocritus. But with this significant difference: Virgil's shepherds are not Gr., but Italian, and the pastorals expound openly and covertly on everything from partisan patriotism to literary politics. The same tendency is heightened in the *Georgics,* a poem modeled on the didactic farming-poem of the Gr. Hesiod, the *Works and Days,* but transcending its agricultural poetics with a magnificent celebration of man in general and It. man in particular. Virgil's *magnum opus,* the *Aeneid,* represents an ostensible return to Homeric epic. But Homer is built upon, not imitated, and the whole poem is devoted, in form and subject alike, to the marriage of the hitherto divided traditions of Gr. and Roman sensibility. The *Aeneid's* achievement is the willful creation of a culture, fusing apparently disparate and warring traditions into the full *mythos* of L. culture, and this synthesis perfectly mirrored and supported in the almost miraculous marriage of form to subject. Poetry and history alike meet in the *Aeneid* and the New Rome which is its subject, and the formulation is so perfect that it came almost to be final as well. Virgil, that is, almost usurps the entire tradition, and his example (and the prestige of his success) was so great that it practically compelled subsequent poetry into its path and rendered it impossible by its exhaustion of the ground. The poem is overtly and proudly patriotic and hymns the New Rome of Augustus Caesar by showing it to be the product of ineluctable fate. This end was not wholly of Virgil's choosing; it had been urged by the ·age's most important literary force, Augustus' desire for poet-propagandists. But to see in Virgil merely an imperial propagandist of immense talent is to ignore the quality of the commitment in the omniscience of hindsight. We know now the despotism which Augustus' principate inaugurated; but the *Aeneid* is the poem of a convinced and partisan genius in which the brightness of the affirmation is undercut, not by insincerity, but by a tragic vision.

Horace (Quintus Horatius Flaccus, 65–8 B.C.) is a clearer example of persuaded commitment than Virgil. His earliest works—the *Epodes*—polished iambic poems based on the Gr. Archilochus—and the *Satires*—much more skillful, polished and kindly developments of Lucilius' form—show occasional praise of Rome in their survey of human foibles. But in his transfer of the lyric forms of Sappho and Alcaeus to L., the *Odes,* Horace became both great poet and persuasive propagandist. These lyrics (written ca. 30–23 under the patronage of Augustus' loyal aide Maecenas) treat, in various meters, in a felicity of language equaled only by Virgil, in exquisitely formal precision, love and wine lightly, life and death deeply, and the Augustan virtues from the approved Stoic point of view. In this Tennysonian approach to what amounted to a laureateship, Horace was completely successful. His later works consist of a Roman centennial ode (written to order in the lyric Sapphic strophe), and a collection of mildly satirical verse epistles in three books, of which the last, the famous *Ars Poetica,* versified the literary doctrines of the 3rd-c. Gr. Neoptolemus of Parium, and formulated for all time the basic Roman literary tenet: the successful poet must mix the useful (*utile*) with the pleasing (*dulce*).

Augustus' patriotic *utile* was not so easily urged in another quarter, however. Though Gr. elegiac poetry is various in theme, Roman elegy, which derived from Catullus, Alexandrian elegy, and Gr. New Comedy, was largely restricted to one theme—love, not in the Horatian sense, but as the most important thing in the world. If Albius Tibullus (54?–19) was ever approached by Augustan officials, he declined, for his spare-dictioned, deceptively simple elegies treat, with flowing structure, only of his mistress, his farm, peace, and oc-

casionally the praise of his patron, Augustus' disenchanted lieutenant Messalla. Sextus Propertius (ca. 50?–after 16), most violent and original of Roman poets in his structure, language, and imagery, fared differently. Though protesting, he was persuaded by Maecenas away from the intense, introspective poems on his mistress which comprise his earliest collection to the odd sort of "official" poetry found in his fourth and last book (publ. in 16)—an adaptation of the learned Callimachean etiological poem as a vehicle for retelling incidents from Roman history. With the last of the great Roman elegists, the recruiting system broke down completely. Ovid (Publius Ovidius Naso, 43 B.C.–A.D. 17?) utilized every bit of his formidable rhetorical training in his poetry, seeking, even at his wittiest, to elicit the underlying human reality by an intense exploitation of the conventional poses of the amatory elegist. Thus, in his love elegies, the *Amores* and *Heroides* (verse letters from famous women of Gr. mythology to their lovers), and even in his double-edged satirical treatments of didacticism and love-practice (*The Art of Love* and *The Remedy of Love*), he develops the unheard-of concept of equality between the partners in a love affair. But erotic poetry stabilizes no moralizing empire, and when Ovid's greatest work, the *Metamorphoses,* ostensibly an epic glorifying Augustan Rome, turned out to be an interweaving (on the thread of "form-changing") of 250-odd stories and epyllia, most of them amatory, which exalted the individual at the expense of temporal and divine authority, Augustus had had enough. Ovid, already compromised by the supposed lasciviousness of the *Ars Amatoria,* became involved in some unsavory affair and was summarily banished to Tomi on the Black Sea—an event which brought to a premature end his *Fasti,* a versified Roman calendar made up of poems resembling Propertius' etiological efforts. His last collections, the *Tristia* (Sorrows) and *Epistulae ex Ponto* (Letters from the Black Sea), return to the elegiac form, protesting or admitting guilt and complaining of his bitter life in his Gothic outpost.

Post-Augustan. The last considerable age of classical L. poetry shows only too clearly the cramping effects of authoritarianism, and the changes made in the social life of poetry by despotism. Rhetoric, already of danger to poetry, became now an end rather than a means. The literary past, both Greek and Roman, assumed enormous authority and became a cramping power, and especially the example of Virgil, whose great success with epic tended to demote all other genres by comparison with the prestige of the grand manner. Characteristically, Silver L. poetry exhibits a spectacle of uprooted rhetoric, flourishing for its own sake or supporting grandiose mythological structures lacking almost any social or political relation with the times; socially, it is the age of the dilettante poet and public recitations, in which genuine talent was suppressed or prevented by politics or poverty. Only in satire does Silver L. verse show vigor and power, and here the greatest part of the vigor derives from the fact that the satirist normally wrote in colloquial, or at least less formidably literary, L. and possessed a real attitude to his age.

The worst of the age's poetry was little more than pious imitation of Virgil, as in the Virgilian pastorals of Calpurnius Siculus (under Nero); the wretched Virgilian epic on the career of Scipio Africanus, the seventeen-book *Punica* of Silius Italicus (late 1st c.); and the competent, scholarly but lifeless Virgilian reworkings of familiar Gr. epic material—the *Thebaid* and unfinished *Achilleid* of Statius and the *Argonautica* of Valerius Flaccus. Others turned to the cultivation of harmless genres. Manilius used inaccurate astrology as a peg for Ovidian wit and rhetoric, though not Ovidian poetry, in his *Astronomica*. Phaedrus versified the fables of Aesop; Statius wrote polished occasional verse in his *Silvae*. In satire, however, there are three notable figures. Martial (d. 104?) raised the L. epigram to its highest level of compression and wit, and his personal satire, epigrammatic though it is, is one of Rome's real contributions to world literature. Persius (Aulus Persius Flaccus, 34–62) left 6 crabbed, priggish, yet powerful Stoic satires, and Juvenal (Decimus Iunius Iuvenalis, fl. ca. 100–130), whose tight and memorably phrased indictments of human pretense and weakness are Rome's greatest, wittiest, and angriest satires, is an appealing, passionate figure in an age of limp rhetorical coterie-literature. Elsewhere the blending of Stoicism and rhetoric which moved satire worked less well. The closet dramas of the younger Seneca tend to work over the subtle motivations of the great Attic tragedians with a lurid rhetorical gloss, and the result is too often impoverished bombast, while the greatest epic of the age, the *Civil War* (sometimes called the *Pharsalia*) of Seneca's nephew Lucan (39–65), in spite of some glorious passages, remains, by forcing rhetoric to obscurity and humanity to a bleak and rigid philosophical scheme, a work of unfulfilled promise. It is, finally, the novelist-satirist Petronius (d. 66) who makes the most positive poetical advance of this last age. In the love lyrics left in the section we possess of his great Menippean satire, the *Satyricon*, and in the L. Anthology, Catullan intensity is combined with the Ovidian ability to dissociate, pointing beyond the subsequent inroads of Christianity and late—though able—archaizers like Claudian to the secular lyrics of the Mid-

dle Ages, and thence to modern poetry. Of subsequent L. poetry, apart from a few poems of Claudian, Ausonius, and the *De Reditu Suo* of Rutilius Namatianus, little of value remains. The lovely delicacy of the *Pervigilium Veneris*, still unsatisfactorily dated, is, so far as classical L. poetry is concerned, a sport, and it is rightly regarded as the first of the great L. lyrics of the Middle Ages.

GENERAL: W. Y. Sellar, *Roman Poets of the Augustan Age* (2 v., 1897); H. E. Butler, *Post-Augustan Poetry* (1909); E. E. Sikes, *Roman Poetry* (1923); T. Frank, *Life and Lit. in the Roman Republic* (1930); J. F. D'Alton, *Roman Lit. Theory and Crit.* (1931); J.W.H. Atkins, *Lit. Crit. in Antiquity*, II (1934); L. Richardson, Jr., *Poetical Theory in Republican Rome* (1944); H. J. Rose, *A Handbook of Lat. Lit.* (2d ed., 1949); J. W. Duff, *A Lit. Hist. of Rome from the Origins to the Close of the Golden Age* (3d ed., 1960) and *A Lit. Hist. of Rome in the Silver Age* (2d ed., 1960), both ed. A. M. Duff; K. Buechner, *Römische Literaturgeschichte* (3d ed., 1962); K. Quinn, *L. Explorations: Crit. Studies in Roman Lit.* (1963).

SPECIALIZED STUDIES: M. M. Crump, *The Epyllion from Theocritus to Ovid* (1931); J. W. Duff, *Roman Satire* (1936); G. E. Duckworth, *The Nature of Roman Comedy* (1952); W. Beare, *The Roman Stage* (2d ed., 1955); F. O. Copley, *Exclusus Amator: A Study in Lat. Love Poetry* (1956); *Critical Essays on Roman Lit.: Elegy and Lyric*, ed. J. P. Sullivan (1962).—E. E. Sikes, *Lucretius, Poet and Philosopher* (1936); A. L. Wheeler, *Catullus and the Traditions of Ancient Poetry* (1934); E. A. Havelock, *The Lyric Genius of Catullus* (1939); K. Quinn, *The Catullan Revolution* (1959); H. J. Rose, *The Eclogues of Vergil* (1942); W.F.J. Knight, *Roman Vergil* (2d ed., 1944); V. Pöschl, *The Art of Vergil*, tr. G. Seligson (1962); L. P. Wilkinson, *Horace and His Lyric Poetry* (1945); E. Fränkel, *Horace* (1957); S. Commager, *The Odes of Horace* (1962); H. F. Fraenkel, *Ovid: A Poet Between Two Worlds* (1945); L. P. Wilkinson, *Ovid Recalled* (1955); *Ovidiana, Récherches sur Ovide*, ed. N. I. Herescu (1958); G. Highet, *Juvenal the Satirist* (1954). W.A.; D.S.P.

MEDIEVAL AND MODERN. The history of med. and Renaissance L. poetry is not the history of an unreal and artificial literary activity but part of the history of a literature which had a living relation to the intellectual, religious, and social conditions of a period covering many centuries.

Med. L. poetry begins as the poetry of the new Christian civilization of the West. Christian L. literature had sprung up in Africa and in Italy to meet the needs of an educated class which now formed a substantial element in the church. The language of the liturgy finally changed from Gr. to L., and, as the use of hymns was brought in from the East, L. hymns appear for the first time, in the compositions of St. Hilary of Poitiers and of St. Ambrose. The future lay with the hymns of Ambrose, whose iambic dimeters and 4-line strophes easily developed into rhythmic verses of 8 syllables, adorned, as time went on, with regular rhymes. So the foundation of all Western L. hymnaries was laid.

We need only mention the strange verses of Commodian (4th c.) and Augustine's *Psalm against the Donatists*. Besides these semipopular compositions there was a large body of more sophisticated poetry, the work of men who had been trained in the old schools of grammar and rhetoric. Prudentius (d. ca. 405) stands apart as the creator of the Christian ode and of the Christian poetical allegory as well as of some compositions in lyric measures in honor of the martyrs. In Gaul, especially in the 5th c., the Christian epic flourished, where, following the example of Juvencus and Sedulius (a Spaniard and an It. respectively), a number of versifiers set forth the story of sacred history and similar themes in Virgilian dress. Paulinus of Nola (d. 431) showed more originality in personal poetry and in his invention of the Christian elegy. To the 6th c. belong Boethius, who seems to represent the close of the old order, and Venantius Fortunatus (d. ca. 604) who in his mystical hymns (*Vexilla regis; Pange, Lingua*) is perhaps the herald of the new.

In a manner that is still somewhat obscure, rhythm and rhyme were beginning a long and wonderful career; for they were destined to guide and transform the vernacular literatures of Western Europe. The mysterious writings of Virgil the Grammarian show that rhyme and rhythm were well known in 6th c. Gaul; and, possibly from Gaul, they were adopted by the Ir., whose fondness for the new forms is evident in the *Bangor Antiphonary*, the *Liber Hymnorum*, and the *Book of Cerne*. Columba's (d. 597) impressive *Altus prosator* struck the imagination of many generations. Bede was well acquainted with the technique of rhythmical verse and the Anglo-Saxons were not slow in experimenting with it. But in England, at Canterbury, Jarrow, and York, the old classical tradition, under It. influences, reasserted itself, and when with Alcuin from York, Theodulf from Spain, and Paul the Deacon and Peter of Pisa from Italy, the so-called Carolingian revival began, in the Frankish kingdom there was a great flowering of verse in classical meters: epic, occasional, and religious. At the same time, especially in Italy, there was a large output of rhythmical poetry, much of it secular in character. To the 10th c. belong the

songs, *O Roma nobilis, O tu qui servas*, and *O admirabile Veneris idolum*.

It was an age of musical development, centering mostly in the monasteries, which were the home of the most important new literary and musical composition, the sequence, which was sung at Mass between the Epistle and the Gospel by alternate choirs. It began as prose, usually with parallel strophes and, if rhythmical at all, with a rather indeterminate rhythm based upon the melody; and it developed in the course of time into an elaborate composition, still with parallel strophes, but in full rhythm with a regular scheme of rhyme. The early development, though not the origins, is associated with Notker of S. Gall (d. 912) and it culminates in the 12th c. with the regular sequences of Adam of S. Victor.

The 11th and 12th c. were a time of immense growth in all directions. A great intellectual movement began whose home was, mainly, the Cathedral schools, especially those of France. A new class of men of letters appears, many of whom were poets who took their craft seriously, corresponded with one another, and, if they imitated ancient models, wrote on matters of current interest in epigrams, poetical epistles, and occasional verses, composing also religious rhythms and hymns. It is necessary only to mention here such names as Fulbert, Hildebert, Marbod, and Baudri. The 2-syllabled feminine rhyme was developed and there was a passion for leonine measures. This experimentation with the application of rhyme to hexameters and pentameters began about the 9th c. with assonance or with rhymes of 1 syllable, until, later, we have rhymes of 2 syllables, and the elaborate scheme of internal and tailed rhymes in Bernard of Cluny's *De contemptu mundi*.

The appearance of satire is the mark of a sophisticated society, Nigel de Longchamps' *Speculum Stultorum*, an ambitious satirical allegory in elegiacs, was much read and was known to Chaucer. By the side of historical poems on contemporary events were long hexameter epics, like the *De bello Troiano* of Joseph of Exeter, and the *Alexandreis* of Walter of Châtillon.

The art of versification was studied, and treatises appeared, such as Geoffrey of Vinsauf's *Poetria nova* (ca. 1210), which exercised a considerable influence on vernacular poetry. The most significant and fruitful development in this period was that of the L. lyric, which is to be associated, not with "wandering scholars," but with the needs of a society becoming more cultivated and refined—with princely and episcopal households, with the Cathedral schools—in short, with circles in which a taste for music, and presumably for the new polyphony, created a demand for songs of every kind: moralistic, satirical, erotic, and, in the extraliturgical sense, religious. The collections of this kind of poetry, ranging from the *Cambridge Songs* to the *Carmina Burana*, are literary and social documents of great importance. The *Cambridge Songs*, collected in the 11th c., are a mixture of profane and religious pieces, gathered perhaps for some Rhineland bishop. They form what is essentially a songbook, and, apart from pieces in early Sequence-form, contain, among other things, some secular love lyrics which are a prelude to the full achievement of the 12th-c. poets. Among the most original poets of that century was Peter Abelard, whose hymns and, especially, his *Planctus*, are worthy of his outstanding genius.

One of the most accomplished masters of rhythmical verse was Hugh of Orleans, known as Primas, a needy poet, living as best he could on the bounty of the great, and ready to be satirical or spiteful at the expense of his benefactors. He had a great facility in the use of rhyme in hexameters as well as in rhythms. Equally accomplished and equally disreputable is the mysterious Archpoet, the author of the famous *Confessio*, in the "goliardic" measure, which begins: "Boiling in my spirit's veins with fierce indignation, / From my bitterness of soul springs self-revelation: / Framed am I of flimsy stuff, fit for levitation, / Like a thin leaf which the wind scatters from its station." (J. A. Symonds). This measure was widely used, mainly for satirical pieces (for the term goliard is to be associated with satire), but it lent itself equally well to the mystical raptures of Archbishop Pecham's *Philomena*. Walter of Châtillon was fond of using it with a classical verse, hexameter or pentameter, to close the stanza. Walter, a great scholar and a canon of Reims, was not merely a satirist; he wrote songs for the Feast of Fools, *pastourelles*, songs of love and springtime, and poetry of a deeply personal character.

Another important poet is Philip the Chancellor of Paris (d. 1236), a famous theologian, known for his disputes with the University and with the Friars. Besides his admirable hymns on Mary Magdalene are numerous pieces, designed to be sung, motets, *conducti*, etc., of a moralistic, satirical, or philosophical character. The greater part of the lyrical verse of this time is anonymous, and is to be found in various collections of which the most famous is the Benediktbeuern Collection (*Carmina Burana*), made, probably in Bavaria, early in the 13th c. (SEE GOLIARDIC VERSE). With this lyrical poetry, we can join the numerous "poetical debates," representing a *genre* which may have a combined classical and popular origin. Of this literary form, the *Conflict of Wine and Water* is a good example. The

authors of all this "lyrical" poetry had been trained in schools where they had learned to compose in classical measures and they were well acquainted with the old L. poets as well as with mythology and the rules of rhetoric.

The vogue of this poetry, as well as of the devotional poetry, associated largely with the Franciscan movement and culminating in the *Stabat Mater*, the *Dies Irae*, and in the religious verse of Thomas Aquinas and of John of Howden continued in the 13th c. and beyond. But the vernacular literatures had now come into their own, and the beginnings of the Renaissance brought a definite turning away from rhyme and rhythm to poetry based on a closer study and understanding of classical L. versification. The result, from the 14th to the 16th and early 17th c., was an immense output of what may be called humanistic poetry, which, in the eyes of contemporaries existed by as good a title as that of the vernacular poets, who were, indeed, profoundly influenced by it; Petrarch centered his hopes of future fame on his L. poems and Dante had considered the use of L. for his *Divine Comedy*.

This new poetry was inspired by a sense of form. which was largely lacking in the medieval versifier, who had little feeling for formal perfection or the evocative power of great poetry. Italy was its first home and its Golden Age was the second half of the 15th c. The themes and forms were varied; the poets took their themes very much from contemporary life and their own experience even if the forms chosen had classical models, such as Virgil's Eclogues and the *Aeneid*, Ovid's *Amores* and *Tristia*, as well as the measures used by the great lyric poets. The output of verse was enormous, and only a few names can be mentioned here: in Italy Politian, Pontano, Marullo, Sannazaro, Mantovano, and Navagero; in France Remacle d'Ardenne, Baïf, Belleau, and Macrin; in Holland Johannes Secundus; in Germany Conrad Celtis. Among the numerous religious poets were the Polish Jesuit Casimir Sarbiewski (d. 1640) and the German Jesuit Jacob Balde (d. 1668). In Tudor England Constable, Skelton, Lily, Leland and Thomas More are conspicuous names. In the 17th c. L. poetry began to be little more than an academic exercise. John Barclay (d. 1621) was indeed widely read, and in France J. B. Santeuil wrote hymns, which, like those of Coffin later, found their way into Fr. hymnaries. And, even after the final triumph of the vernacular, the composition of L. verses has survived until our own day, in schools and universities, as an accomplishment proper to a classical scholar.

MIDDLE AGES. Anthologies: *Analecta Hymnica Medii Aevi*, ed. G. M. Dreves, C. Blume and H. M. Bannister (55 v., 1886–1922; a vast coll. of hymns, sequences); *Early L. Hymns*, ed. A. S.

Walpole (1922); *Med. L. Lyrics*, ed. H. J. Wad-
dell (1929); *Les poésies des Goliards*, ed.
O. Dobiache-Rojdestvensky (1931); J. Lindsay,
Med. L. Poets (1934) and *Song of a Falling
World* (1948); *The Goliard Poets*, ed. and tr.
G. F. Whicher (1949); F. Brittain, *The Med.
L. and Romance Lyric* (2d ed., 1951); *Hymnen
und Vagantenlieder*, comp. and tr. K. Langosch
(1954); *Oxford Book of Med. L. Verse*, ed.
F.J.E. Raby (1959).—*Hist. and Crit.*: M. Manitius, *Gesch. der christlich-lateinischen Poesie bis
zur Mitte des VIII Jhs.* (1891) and *Gesch. der
lat. Lit. des Mittelalters* (3 v., 1911–31; for
reference); M.L.W. Laistner, *Thought and Letters in Western Europe, A.D. 500–900* (1931;
new ed., 1957); F. A. Wright and T. A. Sinclair, *Hist. of Later L. Lit. from the Middle of
the 4th to the End of the 17th C.* (1931); J. de
Ghellinck, *Litt. latine au moyen âge* (2 v., 1939)
and *L'essor de la lit. latine au XII⁰ s.* (2 v.,
1946); M. Helin, *A Hist. of Med. L. Litt.* (1939);
F.J.E. Raby, *Hist. of Christian L. Poetry* (2d
ed., 1953) and *Hist. of Secular L. Poetry in the
M.A.* (2d ed., 2 v., 1957; each work has a full
bibliog. and complete texts or extracts from
many poems); K. Strecker, *Introd. to Med. L.*,
rev. R. B. Palmer (1957).

RENAISSANCE AND LATER: *Anthologies:*
E. Costa, *Antol. della lirica latina in Italia nei
secoli XV e XVI* (1888); M. Herrmann and
S. Szamatoski, *Lateinische Litteraturdenkmäler
des XV und XVI Jhs.* (1891–1912); W. P. Mustard, *Studies in the Ren. Pastoral L. Texts*
(6 v., 1911–28).—*History and Criticism:* G. El-
linger, *Italien und der deutsche Humanismus
in der neulat. Lyrik* (1929) and *Die neulat.
Lyrik Deutschlands in der ersten Hälfte des
XVI Jhs.* (1929); D. Murarasu, *La Poésie neo-
latine et la Ren. des lettres antiques en France,
1500–1549* (1928); L. Bradner, *Musae An-
glicanae. A Hist. of Anglo-L. Poetry 1500–1925*
(1940); P. van Tieghem, *La Litt. lat. de la Ren.*
(1944; the best and most useful general survey).

RECENT TITLES (Middle Ages): *Poesia latina
medievale*, ed. and tr. G. Vecchi (2d ed., 1958);
J. Szövérffy, *Die Annalen der lateinischen
Hymnendichtung: ein Handbuch* (1964).
F.J.E.R.

LATIN PROSODY. See CLASSICAL PROSODY.

LATVIAN POETRY. Folk poetry apparently
preceded the reduction of Latv. to writing,
which took place in the 16th c. under the impact of the Reformation. The earliest references to this anonymous poetry (*tautas dziesmas* or *dainas*) go back to the 17th c., but it
did not become widely known till Herder inserted specimens of it in his *Stimmen der
Völker in Liedern* (1807). K. Barons's standard
edition of the *dainas* did not begin to appear
till 1898 and was completed only after Latvia

had won her independence. Since then several
new collections have been published. Barons's
contained 35,000 originals, without variants,
and now this figure has more than doubled.
The *dainas* are mostly in the form of unrhymed octosyllabic quatrains, e.g.

Smagi pūta sila priedes
Smalka lietus pielijušas:
Gauži raud tie bērnini,
Kam nav tēva māmulinas.

The forest pines sighed heavily,
Besprinkled with fine rain:
Those little children weep bitterly
Who have neither father nor mother.

Here we note a trochaic movement (as Latv.
words are stressed on the first syllable) and a
characteristic parallelism of images. Occasionally the rhythm is checked by resort to monosyllables in the middle of the verse; rhyme may
also appear; and now and then alliteration is
used (as in the first line above). These devices
help to vary the relative rhythmic monotony
of the *dainas*, and stanzaic variation (couplets,
sextets, even paragraphs) contribute to their
flexibility. The themes are mainly individual
experiences, social customs, and mythological
matter. Many of the *dainas* embody an expression of the emotional life of a woman but
there are also men's songs. A considerable
amount of research on the *dainas* was done in
Independent Latvia by such investigators as
P. Šmits, L. Bērziņš, A. Švābe, and K. Strau-
bergs, and this research is being continued by
the last two in exile. These scholars and others
have helped to establish the chronology of the
dainas, which conjecture has pushed back well
beyond the later 12th c., when the Germans
first established themselves in Riga.

Many centuries later the successors of these
Germans gave Latvia its earliest written
literature. Most of the authors who wrote the
language between the early 17th and the early
19th c. were German Lutheran pastors, among
whom the outstanding personalities were
Mancelius, Fürecker, Glück, and the elder
Stender. Christopher Fürecker contributed notably to Latv. hymnology (cf. *Lettische geistliche Lieder und Collecten*, ed. H. Adolphi,
1685), and Gothard Stender (1714–96), a typical
product of the Age of Enlightenment, tried to
wean his flock away from their "silly" songs
(*dainas*) by writing sentimental ditties (*zinges*)
and translating Gellert and Brockes. At the
beginning of the 19th c. other German pastors
(K. G. Elverfeld, J. Lundberg, K. Hugenberger)
wrote Latv. secular verse with equal competence and continued to acquaint their readers
with some of the products of German sentimentalism and romanticism. The native Latv.

poets who followed them wrote their poetry in the spirit and within the bounds which their German predecessors had set.

It was only in the middle of the 19th c. that the Latv. national revival (*atmoda*) took place. Among its leaders were Krišjānis Barons (1835–1923), who confined himself mainly to collecting *dainas*, and Juris Alunāns (1832–64), who followed classical as well as German models in his *Dziesmiņas* (Ditties, 1856) and was the stronger poet of the two. This volume marks the real beginnings of Latv. poetry and illustrates measures and stanzas which have been imitated since then. The heralds of the national revival were followed by its most conspicuous poets, Andrējs Pumpurs (1841–1902), author of the epic *Lāčplēsis* (The Slayer of the Bear, 1888), and Auseklis (M. Krogzems, 1850–79), the "morning star" of the revival and the first significant name in the history of Latv. poetry. Pumpurs had more enthusiasm than talent, but his influence was considerable; for it was he who created the symbolic hero of the Latv. people, whom Rainis (Jānis Pliekšāns, 1865–1929) immortalized later in his verse drama *Uguns un nakts* (Fire and Night, 1907). Rainis represents the next phase in the evolution of Latv. poetry and began and ended his career as a symbolist. He wrote most of his verse dramas while in exile, but added considerably to his creative work after his return to Independent Latvia in 1920. In spite of his dramatic bent, Rainis was essentially a poet who has covered the whole gamut of human experience from passion to contemplation. His contemporaries, Aspazija (Elza Rozenberga), J. Poruks, Anna Brigadere, and K. Skalbe were unique in their idealism and in the outstanding quality of their poetic talent. All of them were already known before the advent of Latv. independence.

Between 1919 and 1940 Latv. poetry was first inspired by these and then gradually developed a national style, which reached a peak in the powerful poetry of Edvarts Virza (Liekna, 1883–1940), the singer of Ulmanis's authoritarian regime. Since Virza's death immediately before the loss of independence, the figure of Aleksandrs Čaks (Čadarainis, 1902–50) has loomed particularly large. Though Čaks accepted the Soviet order, he had been closely connected with poetic developments in the authoritarian period, and so seems to bridge the gap between Independent and Soviet Latvia.

The Soviet annexation has led to the creation of a center of Latv. poetry outside the USSR. While poetry in Latvia since 1945 has been subjected to the dictates of socialist realism, which has encouraged uniformity and mediocrity, the spirit of Independent Latvia still survives in the poetry of the many talented Latv. poets (e.g., A. Eglītis) living in enforced exile.

ANTHOLOGIES: *Les Chansons mythologiques lettonnes*, ed. M. Jonval (1929); *Latvju modernās dzejas antologija*, ed. A. Čaks and P. Ķikuts (1930); *Latvju lirika*, ed. R. Egle (1934); *Dziesmas mīlai; dzejoļu antologija*, ed. J. Dreimanis (1936); *Latv. Poetry*, ed. A. Baumanis (1946); *Latviešu tautas dziesmas*, ed. A. Švābe *et al.* (12 v., 1952–56; includes Barons's ed. and that of the Latv. Archives of Folklore); *Dzīvā dzeja: Latviešu lirika u. liroepika 99 gados: 1856–1955*, ed. A. Johansons (1955); *Lettische Lyrik*, ed. and tr. E. Eckardt-Skalberg (1960; new and enl. ed.); *Dzejas un sejas / Latviešu dzeja svešumā*, ed. T. Zeltiņš *et al.* (1962).

HISTORY AND CRITICISM: V. Plūdonis, *Latviešu rakstniecības vēsture* (3 v., 1908–32); A. Upītis, *Latv. jaunākās raktsn. vēst.* (2 v., 1921); J. Lautenbachs, *Latv. literātūras vēst.* (2 v., 1922–28); T. Zeiferts, *Latv. rakstn. vēst.* (3 v., 1926–34); *Latv. lit. vēst.*, ed. L. Bērziņš (6 v., 1934–47); U. Katzenelenbogen, *The Daina* (1935; also anthol.); W. K. Matthews, *The Tricolour Sun* (1936; also anthol.); E. Blese, *Latv. lit. vēst.* (1947); A. Johansons, "Latv. Lit. in Exile," SEER, 30 (1952); J. Andrups and V. Kalve, *Latv. Lit.* (1954); W. K. Matthews, *A Century of Latv. Poetry* (1957; also anthol.). See also *Storia delle letterature baltiche*, ed. G. Devoto (1957). W.K.M.

LAUDA. It. verse form with religious content having as its origin popular adaptations of church liturgy. The oldest examples, in Latin, date back to the 13th c., the most famous being the *Stabat mater* and the *Dies irae*. The earliest in It. was the *Laudes creaturarum* of St. Francis. The form gained widespread popularity through the confraternity singing of the Flagellants whose movement arose in Umbria in 1260. Their songs, following the general pattern of the *ballata*, were either incitements to the good life, or lyrical-narrative stories of Christ or of the saints. The responsive participation called for by many of the songs invited a development of the form along dramatic lines, with actual dialogue occurring among the various characters. The versification in both the lyrical and dramatic types evolved from the unrefined meter of the *cantilene* to that of the *ballata* and of the octosyllabic *sestina* with alternating rhyme in the quatrain followed by a rhymed distich. By the 15th c. the lyrical *l.* became a regular art form, but practically ceased to be written by the beginning of the next century.—G. Ippoliti, *Dalle sequenze alle laudi* (1914); Wilkins. A.S.B.

LEICH. A medieval German lyric form (similar to the OF *descort*, q.v.), which was widely used between ca. 1200 and 1350. It was designed to be sung to music, and, as its etymology suggests, was probably originally accompanied by dance. The *Leich* is distinguished from the *Liet*, or *Lied*, in that its stanzaic form is irregular and nonrepetitive; accordingly, its musical accompaniment was continuous and nonstrophic. The distinction between *Lied* and *Leich* was consciously made as early as 1022. Although the *Leich* probably derived from the ecclesiastical chant, it came to embrace a variety of themes. In general, three types may be distinguished: the *Tanzleich* or "dance lyric," the *religiöse Leich* or "religious lyric," and the *Minneleich* or "love lyric." After the 14th c. the form survived only in religious verse. Noted medieval composers of *Leiche* include Walther von der Vogelweide, Ulrich von Lichtenstein, Konrad von Würzburg, and Tannhäuser.—F. Wolf, *Über die Lais, Sequenzen und Leiche* (1841); O. Gottschalk, *Der deutsche Minneleich und sein Verhältnis zu Lai und Descort* (1908); G. and E. Hüsing, *Dt. Leiche und Lieder* (1932); H. Kuhn, "Leich," *Reallexikon*, 2d ed., II.; S. Beyschlag, *Die Metrik der mittelhochdeutschen Blütezeit* . . . (3d enl. ed., 1959).

LENGTH. See DURATION.

LEONINE RHYME. Strictly used, the term means a disyllabic rhyme of the last syllable of the second foot and the first syllable of the third foot, with the two syllables of the sixth foot of a Latin hexameter. More commonly it indicates the rhyme of the word preceding the caesura with the final word in both hexameters and pentameters. Although known in classical L. (e.g., Ovid, *Ars Amatoria* 1.59), it was not greatly favored. But around the 12th c. writers began to cultivate it assiduously as, for instance, Bernard of Cluny in his *De Contemptu Mundi* (in couplets). It was used in particular as a mnemonic device and for epitaphs, e.g., "Hac sunt in fossa, Bedae venerabilis ossa." It also appears in the OE *Rhyming Poem*, where it contributed to the decline of the long line of alliterative verse by tending to break the verse into two hemistichs. Some attribute the name to Leoninus, canon of St. Victor's in Paris (12th c.); others to Pope Leo.—Schipper; H. G. Atkins, *A Hist. of German Versification* (1923); J. W. Draper, "The Origin of Rhyme," RLC, 31 (1957); finds l. r. in the *Gāthās* and *Yashts* of the *Avesta*); F. J. E. Raby, *A Hist. of Secular L. Poetry in the Middle Ages* (2d ed., 2 v., 1957). R.A.H.

LETRILLA (diminutive of *letra*, a short gloss). A Sp. poem generally written in short lines, often having a refrain, and usually written on a light or satiric topic. Such poems can be found in Sp. literature as early as the 14th c. at least, but were apparently not given the name *letrilla* until much later. Famous examples are Góngora's *Andeme yo caliente, y ríase la gente* (As long as I am comfortable, let people laugh if they wish) and Quevedo's *Poderoso caballero es don Dinero* (A powerful gentleman is Sir Money).—Navarro. D.C.C.

LETTER IN VERSE. See EPISTLE.

LIGHT VERSE. A name rather loosely given to a wide variety of types or forms of metrical composition, worldly in character and most often witty, humorous, ingenious, or satirical. Among the kinds of poem that fall into this category are *vers de société*, occasional verse, satire, burlesque, the mock heroic, nonsense poetry; such brief forms as the epigram, the comic or ironic epitaph, the limerick, and the clerihew; and all types of tricky and ingenious verse as acrostics, shaped or emblematic poems, alliterative or rhyming *tours de force*, riddles, puns, and other forms of versified trivia. Usually a certain standard of excellence, or at least competence, in the handling of verse forms is assumed in the writer of l.v., and a certain finish or polish is characteristic of this kind of poetry no matter how trivial its subject or frivolous its treatment. Elegance, polish, and refinement of taste can sometimes impart a serious poetic significance to l.v., particularly, for example, in the Petrarchan love poems of the 16th c., the Cavalier lyrics of the 17th. or the satirical heroic couplets of the 18th.

An interesting early attempt to define l.v. was made by Frederick Locker-Lampson in the Preface to his anthology *Lyra Elegantiarum* (London, 1867). This Victorian anthologist limits his consideration to *vers de société* and the elegant classicism of aristocratic poetry mainly in the traditions of Anacreon, Theocritus, or Horace, but his analysis is sound and illuminating as far as it goes. Locker-Lampson begins by distinguishing his collection of l.v. from the many popular collections of "sentimental, heroic, humourous, juvenile, and devotional" poems. He then describes the limits and province of his anthology and in doing so supplies us with an excellent, if necessarily restricted, working definition of l.v. He calls it "another kind of poetry which was more in vogue in the reign of Queen Anne, and, indeed, in Ante-Reform Bill times, than it is at the present day; a kind which, in its more restricted form, has somewhat the same relation to the poetry of lofty imagination and deep feeling, that the Dresden China Shepherds and Shepherdesses of the last century bear to the sculpture of Donatello and Michael Angelo; namely, smoothly written verse, where a boudoir decorum is, or ought always to be, preserved; where sentiment never surges into passion, and where humour never overflows into boisterous merriment." The characteristics of l.v. here distinguished are elegance, decorum, moderation, neatness of expression, perfection of form, and coolness of sentiment and tone. This is the classical respect for the golden mean, an Horatian, or more precisely, an Addisonian ideal, with just an overtone also of Victorian squeamishness. The writers of verse who fit into it most comfortably would be such men as Campion, Herrick, Lovelace, Prior, Goldsmith, Cowper, Oliver Wendell Holmes, W. M. Praed, C. S. Calverley, and Austin Dobson. Many of the Elizabethan miscellanies and song books contain madrigals and other poems that would be considered light either by the standards of Locker-Lampson or of later critics. These can be conveniently sampled in the late 19th-c. collection edited by A. H. Bullen, *Lyrics from the Song-Books of the Elizabethan Age* (London, 1888). The more ribald, but often quite as smoothly turned verse of the 17th c. and the Restoration are represented in two other anthologies edited by Bullen, *Speculum Amantis* (1888) and *Musa Proterva* (1889). The nature of the verses collected by Bullen (or defined by Locker-Lampson) is well described in a prefatory quatrain on the flyleaf of *Musa Proterva*:

Gay, frolic verse for idle hours,
    Light as the form whence Venus sprang;
Strains heard of old in courtly bowers,
    When Nelly danced and Durfey sang.

The Durfey referred to here is Thomas D'Urfey (1653–1723), one of the earliest and best collectors of l.v., his *Wit and Mirth, or Pills to Purge Melancholy* (1719) being an interesting collection of the comic and erotic songs of the Restoration period.

Locker-Lampson's definition limits itself to *vers de société*. The definition is amplified by some nice discriminations: l.v., the critic wrote, "should be short, graceful, refined, and fanciful, not seldom distinguished by chastened sentiment, and often playful. The tone should not be pitched high; it should be terse and idiomatic, and rather in the conversational key; the rhythm should be crisp and sparkling, and the rhyme frequent and never forced, while the entire poem should be marked by tasteful moderation, high finish and completeness. . . . The poem may be tinctured with a well-bred philosophy, it may be whimsically sad, it may be gay and gallant, it may be playfully malicious or tenderly ironical, it may display lively banter, and it may be satirically facetious; it may even, considered merely as a work of art, be pagan in its philosophy or trifling in its tone, but it must never be flat, or ponderous, or commonplace." Most of this is discrimi-

nating and accurate, but the limitations imposed are narrow and, the modern reader may feel, snobbish rather than genuinely aristocratic; and they lead the Victorian anthologist to exclude much that modern anthologists of l.v. (David McCord, Michael Roberts, J. M. Cohen, or W. H. Auden) would wish to include. One poem, for instance, is left out as being too broadly humorous, another as too satirical and savage, others as too pathetic, too serious, too homely, too fragmentary, or too lengthy. Comic poetry, as such, nonsense poetry, and the merely tricky or ingenious are excluded. More important, savage satire and bitter irony, because of their intensity, are outside the pale of l.v. *The Rape of the Lock* is l.v. (indeed, except for its length it might be considered as the ideal exemplar of what l.v. ought to be), but *The Dunciad* is not; the sophisticated urbanity of Prior and Gay is certainly light, but the savage indignation and cool ferocity of Swift is not. Popular folk poetry is excluded as being "low."

Modern criticism has widened (and deepened) the scope of what can be considered l.v. All of the categories excluded by the Victorian anthologist have, under certain circumstances, been considered by 20th-c. anthologists and critics to fall within the scope of l.v. The conditions are that the point of view should be worldly or secular, the finish polished or ingenious, and the attitude objective and superior; but the tone, particularly in satire, may be as intense or coarse as the occasion and purpose demand. Hard-boiled popular poetry and rough invective have been admitted into the canon, and while intellectual brilliance is still demanded of the writer of l.v., his social credentials are not nearly so strictly aristocratic. This wider view of the inclusiveness of l.v., and, indeed, of the "serious" import of kinds of poetry that have usually been thought of as merely casual or frivolous owes something perhaps to Freudian ideas of the significance of the insignificant. As Geoffrey Grigson remarked in the preface to his *New Verse Anthology*, "It is a fact that an epic and a limerick are poems. You cannot suppose a divine or an inspired origin for one against a secular or rational origin for the other. You can only distinguish in them differences of effect and quality." This is what W. H. Auden in the Introduction to the *Oxford Book of Light Verse* set himself to do. Like Grigson, Auden sees no *essential* distinction between the light and serious elements in poetry or between l.v. and serious poetry. The difference—or, more precisely, the source of the difference—lies in the relation between the author and society. "When the things in which the poet is interested, the things which he sees about him, are much the same as those of his audience, and that audience is a fairly general one, he will not be conscious of himself as an unusual person, and his language will be straightforward and close to ordinary speech."

The result is, Auden believes, that the verse of such a poet will be "light." It will fall into one of three categories, which Auden defines as follows: "(1) Poetry written for performance, to be spoken or sung before an audience, e.g. Folk Songs, the poems of Tom Moore. (2) Poetry intended to be read, but having for its subject-matter the everyday social life of its period or the experiences of the poet as an ordinary human being, e.g., the poems of Chaucer, Pope, Byron. (3) Such nonsense poetry as, through its properties and technique, has a general appeal, e.g. Nursery Rhymes, the poems of Edward Lear." Thus Auden seems to equate l.v., or, perhaps, what might better be called "light poetry," with classical poetry (in its more aristocratic aspects) and with popular balladry and folk song (in its more plebeian connections). The conditions postulated in the first two categories above favor the production of unadventurous descriptive verse and simple narrative, of convivial or amorous songs, and Tory satire, any of which may or may not be "light." As a result, the *Oxford Book of Light Verse* is a curious conglomeration of poetry and rhyme, ranging from doggerel street ballads to *The Rape of the Lock* and from medieval carols and Elizabethan madrigals to 19th-c. songs like *She was poor but she was honest*. The only element they have in common is that they are all extremely lively. Their "lightness" is due to the absence of pretentiousness, solemnity, and self-regard; and although the standards of excellence by which each poem must be judged are various, the excellence of each piece *as poetry* is never in doubt for the modern reader. That this should be so is due in part to the impact of the criticism of T. S. Eliot, especially to its emphasis on "unity of sensibility" and its precise analysis of the "wit" of the metaphysical poets. Indeed, the essential characteristic of genuine l.v. has been described by Mr. Eliot in defining the "wit" of Andrew Marvell's *To his Coy Mistress*, as "a tough reasonableness beneath the slight lyric grace" by which the seriousness of the poem is unexpectedly enhanced. "Tough reasonableness"—an absence of squeamishness, hard-headedness, good sense, intelligence, a sense of values, a rational worldliness—these are the qualities of attitude and tone which condition the spirit of l.v.; "slight lyric grace" (*slight* means *unostentatious*), verbal elegance, technical accomplishment, perfect and economical adaptation of means to ends—these are the formal requirements of the art.

L.v. can be regarded as *poetry at play*. Much of it is characterized by ingenuity and displays of technical virtuosity, particularly in the handling of complex meters and polysyllabic rhymes but also in the manipulation of intricate stanza forms and in the exploitation of verbal meanings, as in puns, and of verbal patterns involving tricks with syllables and letters, as in anagrams, palindromes, and *tours de force* of alliteration. Most of these devices have on occasion been used in serious poetry, as in Browning's skillful use of complex and divided rhymes or in some of the conceits of the 17th-c. metaphysical poets, but generally the display of technical and linguistic ingenuity for their own sake or in an unusual degree serves notice that the mind is at play and that what we have before us—if it escapes the abyss of the merely silly—is l.v. Complex and divided rhymes are found often in limericks, a neat example being the one that tells how "a great Congregational preacher" complimented a hen, which immediately laid an egg in his hat, and ends "Thus did the hen reward Beecher." W. S. Gilbert in his *Bab Ballads* and in the Savoy operas is a master of the comic effect of intricate rhymes, while among the moderns, Ogden Nash has added the effect of phonetic spelling to catch the rhyme and distort the word. Leigh Hunt wrote a piece of verse consisting of a series of triplets, the rhymes in each of them being achieved by dropping the initial letter from the word ending the previous line. The most famous and difficult display of ingenuity in alliteration is the poem by Alaric A. Watts that begins

An Austrian army awfully arrayed
Boldly by battery besieged Belgrade

and goes on with undiminished vigor through the whole alphabet. Other successful displays of "apt alliteration's artful aid" are found in parodies of Swinburne—Arthur C. Hilton's *Octopus*, Mortimer Collins' *Salad*, and Swinburne's own *Nephelidia*, and in such a quatrain as this from *The Mikado*:

To sit in solemn silence in a dull dark dock,
In a pestilential prison, with a life-long lock,
Awaiting the sensation of a short sharp shock,
From a cheap and chippy chopper on a big
    black block!

Not only verbal or metrical complexity but demanding stanzaic patterns and formal shapes have proved stimulating to writers of l.v. The strict and sometimes very difficult Fr. or It. forms, such as ballade, double ballade, rondeau, sestina, and the brief, fragile triolet (qq.v.) have all been used with considerable skill by writers of l.v., particularly in the production of *vers de société*. Certain Eng. writers of the 70's, 80's, and 90's of the last century wrote much that has charm and grace in these forms. Among them should be noted C. S. Calverley, W. E. Henley, Andrew Lang, and, most accomplished of all, Austin Dobson. Emblematic verses (verses whose shape on the printed page is imitative of the poem's theme) had been much in vogue among Eng. religious poets in the 16th and 17th c., but in the 20th c. the device came to be used occasionally by experimental poets—Guillaume Apollinaire in *Caligrammes* and E. E. Cummings *passim*—in l.v., that is not the less light because its intention is often serious.

Serious l.v., as it is found in British and Am. poetry in the 20th c., is not, of course, a modern invention nor an Eng. one. It is found at its purest in Horace and at its most intense in Catullus, Ovid, and Propertius. European romanticism proved favorable to one of its most fruitful sources of inspiration—the mixture of egoistic sensibility and ironic self-questioning that can be found in Byron and Heine alike and that came into modern poetry through Fr. poets of the latter half of the 19th c., particularly Théophile Gautier, Tristan Corbière, and Jules Laforgue. The influence of all these on the lighter side of Ezra Pound and T. S. Eliot is clear and unmistakable, while the *Homage to Propertius* and translations of lyrics from *Die Heimkehr* of Heine by Pound transmitted the quality of serious l.v. to later modern poets with inescapable gusto. Serious l.v. flourishes so richly today that one is tempted to see it as the characteristic expression of the modern temper. Among its authors, besides Eliot and Pound, are W. B. Yeats, E. E. Cummings, W. H. Auden, and many lesser figures.

L.v., in the more ordinary sense in which it is understood, as humorous, comic, or ingenious verse, is also very widely and skillfully produced. Among the best of the contemporary writers are Ogden Nash, Richard Armour, Phyllis McGinley, Franklin P. Adams, Morris Bishop, Arthur Guiterman, and David McCord in the United States, and Sir Owen Seaman, A. P. Herbert, and John Betjeman in England. ANTHOLOGIES: (NB: Items marked with an asterisk contain valuable critical material): *Wit and Mirth, or Pills to Purge Melancholy*, ed. T. D'Urfey (1719); *Lyra Elegantiarum, ed. F. Locker-Lampson (1867); *Musa Proterva*, ed. A. H. Bullen (1889); *A Vers de Société Anthol.*, ed. C. Wells (1900); *Poetica Erotica*, ed. T. R. Smith (1921); *A Little Book of Am. Humorous Verse*, ed. T. A. Daly (1926); *An Anthol. of L.V.*, ed. L. Kronenberger (1935); *The Oxford Book of L.V.*, ed. W. H. Auden (1938); *The Faber Book of Comic Verse*, ed. M. Roberts (1942); *The Stag's Hornbook*, ed. J. McClure (2d ed., 1943); *What Cheer*, ed. D. McCord (1945); *The Worldly Muse*, ed.

A. J. M. Smith (1951); *Comic and Curious Verse*, ed. J. M. Cohen (1952); *Verse and Worse*, ed. A. Silcock (1952); *The Silver Treasury of L.V.*, ed. O. Williams (1957); *The Fireside Book of Humorous Poetry*, ed. W. Cole (1959).

GENERAL: L. Untermeyer, *Play in Poetry* (1938); R. Armour, *Writing L.V.* (1947).
A.J.M.S.

LIMERICK. A verse form composed of 5 lines rhyming aabba, of which the first, second, and fifth are trimeter and the third and fourth dimeter. Occasionally it is written in 4 lines, the third line being in tetrameter with invariable internal rhyme. The dominant rhythm is anapestic, and the final line is often a repetition, or varied repetition, of the first, as in the following example by Edward Lear (*Book of Nonsense*, 1846), the unquestioned master of the form:

> There was an Old Man of the Dee,
> Who was sadly annoyed by a Flea;
> When he said, "I will scratch it,"
> They gave him a hatchet,
> Which grieved that Old Man of the Dee.

The l. is unique in that it is the only Eng. stanza form used exclusively for light verse. Always comic, it is often nonsensical and frequently bawdy. Theories concerning its origin range from the belief that it was an old Fr. form brought to the Ir. town of Limerick in 1700 by returning veterans of the Fr. war to the theory that it originated in the nursery rhymes published as *Mother Goose Melodies for Children* (1719). What is certain is that the l. may be found in a volume entitled *The History of Sixteen Wonderful Old Women*, published by J. Harris in 1821, and in *Anecdotes and Adventures of Fifteen Gentlemen*, published by John Marshall about 1822 and possibly written by one R. S. Sharpe. The latter volume is cited by Lear as having given him the idea for his l. Whatever its origin, the l. has a secure, if eccentric, place in the history of Eng. verse. In the wake of Lear such notable authors as Tennyson, Swinburne, Kipling, Stevenson, and W. S. Gilbert attempted the form, and by the beginning of the 20th c. it had become a veritable fashion in England. The etymology of the term "l.," never used by Lear, is unknown.

The chief tendency in the modern l., as exemplified in the practice of the Am. light poet Morris Bishop, has been the development of the final line for purposes of surprise or witty reversal, in place of the simply repeated last line of Lear's day. See also LIGHT VERSE, NONSENSE VERSE, CLERIHEW.—*Dict. of Nursery Rhymes*, ed. I. and P. Opie (1951); C. Fadiman, *Any Number Can Play* (1957).
F.J.W.; A.P.

LINE. A formal structural division of a poem, consisting of one or more feet arranged as a separate rhythmical entity. The line, as Brooks and Warren point out, is a "unit of attention," but it is not necessarily a unit of sense: in fact, poems are rather rare in which individual lines constitute complete sense units. For this reason, line divisions, unless they happen to coincide with sense pauses (whether indicated by punctuation or not), are often as unrelated to the rhetoric of poetic assertions as foot divisions. Lines are commonly classified according to their length in feet:

monometer	a line of 1 foot
dimeter	2 feet
trimeter	3 feet
tetrameter	4 feet
pentameter	5 feet
hexameter	6 feet (see also ALEXANDRINE)
heptameter	7 feet
octameter	8 feet

Because the memory can retain a rhythmical pattern of only a limited duration, heptameters and longer lines tend to receive from reader or hearer an unconscious restructuring: the heptameter commonly breaks into a tetrameter and a trimeter (as in ballad meter, q.v.), the octameter into two tetrameters, and so on. Line divisions frequently function like foot divisions in providing a form of counterpoint (q.v.) to the rhetorical and syntactical design in a poem. Although generalization on this point is traditionally hazardous, it may be suggested that short lines (trimeter and shorter) tend to imply levity of tone, and that the pentameter line (or a line of similar duration, measured by whatever system of scansion) has proved the most flexible in Eng.—Baum; Brooks and Warren.   P.F.

LINE ENDINGS. Divided prosodically into two general types depending upon the position of the final stress in relation to the other syllables near the end of the iambic or anapestic line. A *masculine ending* (generally productive of an effect of some force or weight) has the stress on the final syllable of the line:

x /
Upon the moon I fixed my eye
(Wordsworth, *Strange Fits of Passion* 9)

A *feminine ending* has the last stress on the penultimate (or even the antepenultimate) syllable and most often requires terminal extrametrical syllables:

/ x / x / x x
Whatever ails me, now a-late especially,

/ x x
I can as well be hanged as refrain seeing her
(Middleton, *The Changeling* 2.1)

† In Supplement, see also GENERATIVE METRICS.

Feminine ending is very common in the blank verse of the Elizabethan and Jacobean drama, where it is frequently used to give the verse a suggestion of colloquial informality, lightness, or irregularity. The term *weak ending* is sometimes used to describe masculine ending with a secondary (instead of primary) degree of stress. Marianne Moore's *In Distrust of Merits* is full of weak endings. See TRUNCATION.—P. W. Timberlake, *The Feminine Ending in Eng. Blank Verse* (1931).   P.F.

LINGUISTICS AND POETICS.† The study of a literary work of art, like that of any organized form, requires for its proper conduct a knowledge of the principles according to which such works are constructed and a theory by means of which these principles can be ordered into some rational and consistent whole. Since Aristotle's classic work on the subject, the study of these principles and theories has been designated by the name "poetics." Poetics, so understood, is thus the most general, hence fundamental, discipline of literary criticism in its widest sense. Inasmuch as it is language which lies at the base of literary studies, it is not surprising that scholars and literary theorists of various backgrounds and persuasions have explored the linguistic characteristics of literary works of art in formulating their particular systems of poetics. It would thus be possible in an article on linguistics and poetics to discuss at some length the contributions of Leo Spitzer, Dámaso Alonso, Amado Alonso, and various other scholars and critics. Since, however, this article is concerned primarily with post-Bloomfieldian linguistics, only passing mention can be made of their contributions. (But see MODERN POETICS. 20TH C. FR. AND GERMAN, IT., SP., and the articles on EXPLICATION, STYLISTICS, and RUSSIAN FORMALISM.)

Just as we may say of linguistics that it is the study of language and intend thereby that it is the study of its principles of organization and of explanatory theories, so we may, similarly for reasons of convenience—and also for the purposes of this Encyclopedia, which is limited to poetry—refer to poetics simply as the study of poetry. On these assumptions, it would appear, inasmuch as language is the medium of poetry, that 1. and poetics have (at least in part) a common function. But this conclusion requires some consideration. For, granting that language is the medium of poetry, a poem's status as a linguistic production is nonetheless different from the status of ordinary language productions. The task is thus to ascertain whether any but purely linguistic factors contribute to the different status which a poem enjoys and then, to the extent to which the answer to this question is negative, to determine whether the theories and techniques of 1., designed as they are to deal with ordinary language productions, are adequate to the linguistic analysis of poetry.

Of the various views that have been advanced concerning extralinguistic contributory factors, only one will be specifically considered here, namely, the view which would attribute the poem's different status to special psychological sets or responses on the part of the reader (or hearer). The discussion of this view, however, may be taken as paradigmatic for all other extralinguistic factors which might be adduced to explain this special quality of a poem.

It is not ordinarily in the province of l. to deal with psychological sets or responses. But if the poem induces psychological responses beyond those of ordinary communication, then one may reasonably expect to find some linguistic feature or features in the poem to correlate with these responses. If such responses occur for which no linguistic correlate is to be found in the poem, then they would seem to constitute data for psychologists, not linguists. If it should be asserted that such responses in fact constitute the given data of poetics, then there can be no argument from the side of l.; l. simply has nothing to say about them. Further, a psychological set, or *Einstellung*, would seem to be significant only if the reading of the poem sustains that set, and here again one might expect to find correlating linguistic features in the poem. In this case, too, if no linguistic correlation can be established, l. gives over to some other line of inquiry. The approach suggested here has the virtue that it implicitly establishes a hierarchy of validity for critical judgments. From the point of view of l., those judgments that can be supported by linguistic correlates naturally occupy a higher rank in the hierarchy than do those that cannot.

According primacy to those critical judgments for which support can be found in the language of the poem resembles the practice in certain contemporary critical approaches which maintain that the poem must be judged in terms of itself alone. But this view of the New Criticism embodies a response to a poem not merely in terms of the reader's linguistic capabilities, but also in terms of his critical faculties and sensibilities. Linguistic analysis of poetry does not insist on this added requirement. Insofar as it is feasible, linguistic analysis of poetry is usually content to accept the judgments of literary critics, to whom superiority of response is accorded, on the basis of their experience, sensitivity, and general critical capacity, and then to set out and find linguistic correlates for these judgments. If such attempts are made and fail, then two inferences are possible: either the critical responses are occasioned by extralinguistic factors, or the failure to find linguistic support for them reflects present inadequacies in linguistic theory or techniques. Only in this way, by more and more intensive linguistic analyses attempting to explain various critical responses, can the question be settled of whether a poem's special status is due exclusively to linguistic factors.

Whether a poem's special status is a function of its language alone thus remains to be demonstrated. Some linguists, however, tend to proceed on the assumption that it is. In doing so they are not necessarily making a factual claim to this effect—although some of them do. It is rather that a good many critical statements that are purportedly historical, cultural, or biographical, or, alternatively, mythic, doctrinaire, or aesthetic are held by linguists to be prompted *immediately* by the language in a poem, and it is the language that thus deserves the most immediate systematic study. In the same way a good many value statements may turn out to have linguistic correlates in the poem and, that being the case, it is certainly advisable to describe the latter. Thus, while the question of whether, ultimately, the impact of a poem can be explained entirely in terms of its linguistic composition is obviously one of great theoretical interest, it is clear that a good deal of significant work can be done in the linguistic analysis of poetry without waiting to see whether and how the question will finally be answered.

From the point of view of l., the more substantive question is whether or not the theories and techniques of linguistic analysis are adequate to deal with the purely linguistic aspects of poetry. To provide an answer to this question requires some discussion of the aims and capacities of linguistic analysis. To begin with, linguistic analysis is primarily concerned with language, not with language events. It of course analyzes language events, but it does so only with the view of establishing the system which lies behind these events and makes them possible—the system as such not being available for analysis. One distinguishes in this connection between *langue* and *parole*, or code and message, or grammar and utterance. A poem is (to select one alternant) an utterance (where this subsumes written as well as spoken language productions). But the question immediately arises whether a poem is a manifestation of the same grammar as the grammar manifested by ordinary language utterances. This question has nothing to do with the presence in poetry of such conventional features as rhyme, meter, alliteration, etc., inasmuch as these features accompany a language which is independently distinctive. Since, for reasons of convenience and utility, l. has dealt largely with regular utterances, most linguistic descriptions or theories have resulted in or implied grammars such that poetry would fall outside their scope. This would make it appear that, for descriptive purposes at any rate, poetry is written according to grammatical rules that are different from the grammatical rules governing ordinary language utterances. It would of course be possible to revise grammatical descriptions or theories so as to take account of poetic utterances directly, by increasing the scope of the grammar. But such a course would have two disadvantages. In the first place the grammar would lose a good deal of its generality; in the second place, and more important from the point of view of poetics, this course would preclude the use of the grammar as a standard or norm against which to explain the way in which poetic language is distinctive. As a matter of fact, a good deal of recent work in linguistically oriented poetics has adopted the position, explicitly or implicitly, that poetic language is characterized by deviation from grammatical rules.

Another problem derives from the fact that most work in l. has proceeded on the assumption that the sentence is the highest-level linguistic unit about which grammatical statements can be made. L. Bloomfield's statement (*Language* [1933], p. 170) that ". . . each sentence is an independent linguistic form, not included by virtue of any grammatical construction in any larger linguistic form" has, as one of its corollaries, the fact that linguistic forms larger than the sentence, if they are unified at all, are unified by relations that are different from the relation of grammatical construction. Thus, while relations of some sort certainly bind sentences together into larger units, it is not yet sufficiently clear, from the point of view of linguistic analysis, just what these relations are. The measure for intra-sentence relations is grammaticality, for supra-sentence relations, coherence; and linguistic techniques for dealing with the latter are not yet very highly developed. Moreover, those supra-sentence relations which most immediately come to the linguist's mind—features like anaphora, tense sequence agreement, etc.—have little interest for stylistic analysis, inasmuch as they reflect, in the main, obligatory constraints.

There have been a few attempts to discover and account for supra-sentence relations. Z. Harris, in his "discourse analysis," has suggested techniques for judging sameness and difference of structure in the sentences making up a complete discourse ("Discourse Analysis," *Language*, 28 [1952], 1–30, and "Discourse Analysis: A Sample Text," *ibid.*, 474–94). More recently, M. W. Bloomfield and L. Newmark have adapted generative grammar to the generation of complete discourses (not merely sentences); cf. *A Linguistic Introduction to the History of Eng.* (1963), pp. 240,

260ff. Consistent with these procedures is the definition of style proposed by A. Hill, according to which it ". . . concerns all those relations among linguistic entities which are statable, or may be statable, in terms of wider spans than those which fall within the limits of the sentence" (*Introduction to Linguistic Structures* [1958], pp. 406ff.). Levin's book (1962) is an attempt to describe the structure of poetry along these lines. It must be admitted, however, that in the area of discourse analysis (a poem being a discourse in this sense) l. has not yet gone very far. What is needed is to develop means for analyzing the linguistic devices which contribute to the coherence and unity of multi-sentence units, to ascertain what sort of inter-sentence relations these devices enter into, and then to determine the status and function of these devices in the general linguistic system. For a start in this direction, see M. Halliday, "The Linguistic Study of Literary Texts," *Proceedings of the IXth International Congress of Linguists* (1964).

L. has dealt with poetic language on the levels of phonology, word, and syntax. Phonology is divided by l. into two aspects: segmental and suprasegmental (or prosodic). The former aspect deals with those phones (sounds) that appear in morphemes, words, and longer sequences composed of these units, whereas suprasegmental phonology deals with the dynamic features—stress, pitch, and juncture (pausal and transition phenomena)—that accompany the segmental units in the speech act. In actual language utterances, of course, segmental and suprasegmental features occur simultaneously. A morpheme, word, or longer stretch is accompanied by stress(es), pitch(es), and junctures. For purposes of analysis, however, these co-occurring features must first be separately isolated before their mutual relations and their function with the segmental material can be properly evaluated. In general, the study of segmental phonology in poetry is relevant to the question of sound-texture, and the study of suprasegmental phonology is relevant to the question of meter.

In this discussion sound-texture is understood as the texture imparted to a poem by various patterns and configurations of its segmental phones. The standard forms of such patterns and configurations are of course rhyme and devices like alliteration and assonance. Frequently, however, it is possible to discern less obvious phonological patterns in a poem, patterns which similarly play a constructive role in its organization. An attempt at codifying many such patterns is D. Masson, "Sound-Repetition Terms," *Poetics. Poetyka*, pp. 189–99. Analyses of the latter kind—in which vowels, consonants, diphthongs, and even distinctive features have been shown to pattern in some nonrandom way—have been carried out by Firth, Fónagy, Masson, Oras, and others. Findings of phonic pattern-regularity have a rather obvious bearing on the question of poetry's higher degree of textural density as well as on questions of greater organizational unity. On the assumption that sounds possess phonaesthetic properties, attempts have also been made to correlate such findings with judgments of a poem's tone or affective address. Other studies (J. Lynch, "The Tonality of Lyric Poetry: An Experiment in Method," *Word*, 9 [1953]; D. Hymes, "Phonological Aspects of Style: Some Eng. Sonnets," *Style in Language*, pp. 109–31) have gone further and have attempted to show that in certain sonnets and other short poems the phonic patterns thus found frequently converge in a single "summative" word occupying a strategic place in the poem. This pattern thus represents one mode in which form and meaning may be fused in poetry.

Metrics has been one of the most significant areas of convergence for l. and literary analysis. Concerned as it is with the phonological tissue of poetry—an isolatable and measurable thing—it has long attracted literary scholars who like exactness of statement and linguists who have aesthetic yearnings. At the turn of the present century, a great search was made for precision in metrics by means of what some might consider the ultimate sacrilege, the machine. The development of devices for analyzing speech sounds, like the Marey tambour (sometimes called the kymograph) and later the oscilloscope, led to mechanical displays of verse like those of Scripture and Schramm. Earlier workers (like Warner Brown, Ada Snell, P. Verrier, and Amos Morris) had exploded long-believed fictions like the literal equality of feet and the long-short dichotomy, but Scripture was the first to outline an entire theory of meter on a mechanical basis. Recognizing the phonetic complexity of metrical elements, he discarded the traditional identification of ictus with "stress," substituting the concept of "centroid" instead. The centroid was the sum of features like greater auditory impressiveness, intenser loudness, pitch change, slowed transition, and more precise pronunciation. Scripture's basic unit of description was the line: "a stretch of the verse-stream that coincides with the printed line." He denied the existence of feet, since they could not be found in the phonetic trace. Nor, for that matter, could one discover syllables in a trace—all that exists, he contended, is syllabicity. He developed an elaborate terminology to describe linear kinds, inventing such terms as "nucretic," "nudiambic," "nuclydonic," etc. His entire emphasis was to discover the vast variety of phenomena occurring in recited verse, and he was all too successful in his search. Schramm also presented a visual display or "score" of verse performance, although his terminology was somewhat more conventional ("accent," "stress," etc.). Intonational curves, calibrated to the musical scale, were marked on one staff, and intensity was presented on a cotemporal one. Time was divided by vertical bars at one-second intervals. Unlike Scripture, Schramm continued to use the concept of foot—although he recognized its purely formal mode of existence—as a convenient tool of analysis.

Recent developments in acoustic phonetics (frequency and intensity analyzing machines) have made the mechanical analysis of verse performance much easier and more exact. But, at the same time, the rise of phonemic theory has shown the need to correlate physical data with the *system* that language is today universally recognized to be. Thus—and especially for metrical analysis—not raw phonetics but functional phonology, the system of linguistic sounds that mark semantic differences, must be consulted. The need was recognized as early as 1933 by Jakobson in words which laid the groundwork for modern metrics. Jakobson pointed out that meter could not be studied as a purely phonetic object: "Not the phone, but the phoneme as such is utilized as the cornerstone of verse." Although work had been carried on by European linguists like Mukařovský, Lotz, and de Groot, the first recognition and practical application of this notion to Eng. meter came in the 1950's in work by Whitehall, Hill, Chatman (1956), Epstein and Hawkes, and Smith. Whitehall, alone and in collaboration with Hill, first suggested the utility of structural linguistics to metrics and pointed to the Trager-Smith description of the Eng. stress system as an excellent vehicle for precision in metrical statement (G. L. Trager and H. L. Smith, Jr., *An Outline of Eng. Structure* [1951]). Chatman attempted the first application by analyzing a variety of recitations of a given poem to show how variously meter is actualized in performance. Epstein and Hawkes presented what might be called the orthodox Trager-Smith metrics, elaborating the concept of "relative strength" and providing a somewhat vast inventory of foot-types, although only four basic feet were recognized, spondees and pyrrhics being declared impossible on the contention that one syllable must always be louder than the other. They postulated 6,236 kinds of iambs, 2,376 kinds of trochees, and a vaster number of three-syllabled feet. The most suggestive concept educed by Epstein and Hawkes was that of the foot as the *simplest* recurring unit, on principles of homogeneity and regularity.

Smith reviewed and elaborated upon some of the Epstein-Hawkes procedure. Wells (*Style in Language*, pp. 197–200), coming to the subject from a slightly different angle, applied a technique of "logical construction" to the Trager-Smith system, distinguishing the abstract meter from (1) the orthographic record, (2) a recitation of the poem (a more adequate record), and (3) the phonemic system itself. He also suggested the possibility of considering metrics as a derivational or extractional process based upon operational (not prescriptive) rules, the most important being the "maximization principle": one picks the interpretation which gives the maximally regular meter. Thompson (*Poetics. Poetyka*, pp. 167–75) wrote essentially a historical treatment, showing how the Trager-Smith analysis could help to understand how Eng. meter as we know it today was substantially formed in the 16th c.

A different analysis of Eng. intonation, stress, and related features—that of Bolinger ("A Theory of Pitch Accent," *Word*, 14 [1958]) —formed the basis of the most recent linguistic metrics, by Chatman (1964). Distinguishing on purely rhythmical grounds between *event* and *prominence* features in the metrical construct, he identified the syllable as the linguistic actualizer of the former, but found the latter more complex; metrical prominence could be actualized by one of several features: linguistic stress, or accent, or linguistic zero (no overt performance feature at all). He asserted the need to distinguish between performance (a purely linguistic record), scansion (the reduction of linguistic data to the metrical system in one performance), and metrical analysis (the sum of all reasonable scansions), demonstrating these distinctions by analyzing in acoustic and phonemic depth several recorded performances of Shakespeare's eighteenth sonnet. He developed the concept of simplicity suggested by Epstein and Hawkes, presenting formal guidelines for defining the metrical concepts and procedures in terms of efficiency of metrical design.

These assertions of the utility of l. for metrics have not gone uncontested. A significant critique of linguistic procedure (as well as other procedures) was offered by Wimsatt and Beardsley, who objected chiefly to what they considered an excessive concern for linguistic as opposed to metrical detail in some of the early studies. A defense was made by Pace ("The Two Domains: Meter and Rhythm," PMLA, 74 [1959]), who suggested that not all linguists would agree to the formulations already presented. It is undeniable that there exists nothing so monolithic as *the* linguistic position. Further, it is to be hoped that Wimsatt and Beardsley's very perceptive criticism has been or will be successfully answered in later work. Happily, at least three literary scholars who are not primarily linguists— Thompson, Hollander, and Halpern—have used the linguistic approach without apparent injury to their critical sensibilities.

A matter related to but not to be identified with meter is that of verse performance. Modern techniques of phonological analysis, particularly as they apply to stress, intonation, and related phenomena, have made it possible to discuss problems of oral recitation in increasingly finer detail. One subject of interest has been the analysis of the various components of the ultimate performance—what identifies the reader's concept of the *persona* of the poem (an old man, a neurotic, a duke who has had his wife put to death, etc.) and of the *persona's* attitude (anger, fear, etc.)— particularly as these relate to unavoidable carryovers of the reciter's own speech (his general intonational range, voice quality, etc. [Chatman, 1962]). Another concerns the normative problem of reading: what is the proper interpretation of a line? And how does that interpretation relate to meter? Chatman's argument that meter could be used to assist in interpretation and that performance and meter are cross-revealing (1956, 1957) was criticized by Wimsatt and Beardsley as a confusion between meter and intonation, and his argument that metrical ambiguity is more apparent than real and that performances usually demand resolution was contested by Levin ("Suprasegmentals and the Performance of Poetry," *Quarterly Jour. of Speech*, 48 [1962]), who argued that certain syntactic ambiguities cannot be resolved in performance and that forced oral resolutions may do a serious disservice to poetry's richness.

Relevant to the question of performance is the discussion by Trager ("Paralanguage: A First Approximation," *Studies in L.*, 13 [1958]) of the role played in the speech act by such features as voice set, voice quality, and vocalizations—laughing while speaking, crying, whining, vocal intensity, general pitch height, etc. Such features do not appear to be structured systematically as are other linguistic features, but they obviously do signal relevant information. Investigation of these features has been conducted by linguists in some psychiatric interviews. As is suggested by the description of these features and also by the fact that they are studied in clinical situations, "paralinguistic" features signal information about the speaker, not about the message. For this reason their study is quite peripheral to linguistic analysis. In evaluating the oral performance of poetry, however, one must deal with them, if only to discriminate between what is linguistically relevant and what is not.

Grammatical studies of poetic language may be divided according as the emphasis is on words, and according as it is on grammatical sequences of words. Under the first subdivision fall those studies that are concerned with a poem's diction, and under the second those that are concerned with a poem's syntax. Diction studies may in turn be divided into those that deal with the meanings of words and thus lend themselves to statements of a poem's content or import, and those that deal with words primarily as grammatical entities and leave semantic considerations aside. Because words as grammatical entities are much more susceptible to properly linguistic statements, it is with diction in the latter sense that linguistic analysis of poetry has been chiefly concerned. Assuming that part-of-speech membership is given—either tacitly or by analysis—then the words occurring in poetry lend themselves readily to quantitative analysis, and such analysis can be used as a linguistic correlate for certain judgments about a poet's style or aesthetic orientation. Thus, using the data presented by Josephine Miles in an earlier article ("Eras in Eng. Poetry," PMLA, 70 [1955]), in which she distinguished quantitatively between verbal style and substantival style in several centuries of Eng. poetry, A. Kroeber showed that it is in the work of "reasoning" poets like Jonson, Donne, Coleridge, etc. that verb forms predominate, whereas in the work of sensory or visually imagistic poets like Spenser, Milton, Tennyson, etc. the adjectival forms predominate ("Parts of Speech in Periods of Poetry," PMLA, 73 [1958]). Studies with more highly developed statistical techniques have been conducted by Yule and Herdan. In the work of these men there is a greater concern with the problem of establishing adequate statistical procedures, but here also the statistics are used to determine stylistic indices on the basis of the frequencies with which word-classes are represented in literary works. Herdan in fact is interested in establishing a field of "stylostatistics." Although worth-while results may be expected from statistical analyses, certain methodological difficulties remain to be overcome. Two problems mentioned by Plath ("Mathematical L.," *Trends in European and American L.* [1961], pp. 21–57) are that of deciding on the optimal size and nature of the sample to be used, and that of finding statistical measures which will hold no matter what the sample size, so that results obtained from texts of different lengths may be compared directly. Both Yule and Herdan have suggested techniques for dealing with these difficulties, and no doubt statistical procedures will ultimately be refined to the point where such quantitative studies will yield more important results for stylistic analysis.

In syntax the development by Chomsky of generative grammar (*Syntactic Structures* [1957]) offers considerable promise for the analysis of poetry. The aim of all linguistic analysis, as has been stated, is to arrive at a statement and understanding of the grammatical system of the language. Unlike the descriptive approach, however, which proceeds directly from a corpus of actual linguistic material to a statement of the grammar, the generative approach proceeds from a set of rules for generating sentences, where these rules in fact constitute the grammar. The form which the grammar takes on the descriptive approach is one stressing primarily the different classes of grammatical entities, whereas on the generative approach the emphasis is on the rules. Inasmuch as descriptive grammar assigns elements to classes on the basis of their ability to enter into certain combinations with other grammatical elements, it would appear that the rules could be educed from the statements governing the classification. As a matter of fact, a descriptive grammar will in most cases comprise statements concerning sentence types. Usually, however, these are of rather gross sentence types, and only rarely are all the constraints discovered in the classifying process incorporated into them. When aberrant sentences turn up in an extension of the original corpus, or even in that corpus itself, they are usually listed as reflecting exceptional sentence types. Many sentences occurring in poetry would be treated in this manner. In the main, this procedure seems to work: the extension of the corpus reveals few sentences whose members cannot be fitted into the pre-established categories. For purposes of ordinary language analysis this procedure thus has practical value. Its method of dealing with aberrant sentences renders it fairly uninteresting, however, from the point of view of poetic language. Unusual sentences are either lumped in with regular sentences, in this way obviating the possibility of using the grammar for explicative purposes, or they are simply listed as falling outside the domain of the grammar, in this way characterizing them as unusual.

In generative grammar one starts with rules for sentence generation. Unlike descriptive grammar, in which methodological considerations govern the analysis at every step, generative grammar is not concerned, theoretically, with the question of how the rules are arrived at. In practice, of course, the rules result from many of the same kinds of observations that lead to the establishing of classes in a descriptive grammar. The strict adherence in the latter approach to methodological requirements makes it difficult, however—in some cases impossible—to incorporate certain types of grammatical relationships into the description. By proceeding deductively, generative grammar overcomes this disability. Moreover, there is a check on a generative grammar also; it comes at the output end of the generative process, namely, in the form of the sentences which the particular set of rules logically entails. If the output sentences are all grammatical and all grammatical sentences are generated, then the rules are adequate; if the rules do not meet these requirements, then they are defective. In the course of making such a set of rules adequate, it develops that more and more constraints on co-occurrability must be built into the rules; this to ensure grammatical outputs. Many of these constraints would, as a matter of fact, be considered lexical in nature. A generative grammar is thus very finely articulated. It is this articulation which renders generative grammar a suitable tool for poetic analysis.

The language of poetry is referred to in various ways that attest to its distinctive character. Pre-systematically, one uses such terms as different, novel, arresting, etc. Aristotle noticed this property of poetic language, and much later, in the 1920's, the Prague School aestheticians signalized it, referring to the "foregrounded" or "deautomatized" expressions of poetry. Attempts to explain these effects have usually centered on the notion of deviation from the norm. The problem has been, however, to characterize the norm. In eras governed by normative dicta, there may be in effect certain linguistic conventions binding literary forms, and transgressions of these conventions would constitute deviations. From the linguistic point of view, however, such norms are artificial, grafted upon antecedent and more fundamental, genuinely linguistic norms. Attempts to specify these linguistic norms have taken three main approaches in modern linguistic studies: statistical, information-theoretical, and grammatical.

In statistical studies of diction, counts are made of the incidence of various words, types of words, or parts of speech. This same procedure can naturally be employed in dealing with syntactic units like phrases, clauses, and sentences. Assuming that a body of statistics on such units was gathered from a corpus of ordinary language texts, then the frequencies of syntactic units found in poetry could be matched against these original statistics (which would be taken as constituting the norm) and in this way the distinctive effect of the poetic units would be explained as stemming from their statistical rarity or preponderance. Frequently, moreover, deviations are effected in poetry for which the explanation is to be sought not in respect to an external norm, but in respect to a norm built up within the poem itself. Such a situation arises where a poem builds up a statistical preponderance of certain kinds of syntactic patterns (phrase types, clause types, sentence types, etc.), or, in fact, of any linguistic features, and then deviates from this pattern at some subsequent point in the poem. Dealing with such intra-poem statistics is a rather straightforward process, but the problem of explaining deviation in poetry with respect to statistics on ordinary language frequencies is not so simple, since the difficulties mentioned earlier as attending on statistical sampling are naturally pertinent here too. As a matter of fact, these problems are intensified in the area of syntax. For in poetic analysis a good deal of the interest attaches to *particular* syntactic sequences; one is interested, that is, not merely in the *types* of syntactic construction used in a poem, but to an even greater extent in the actually occurring syntactic sequences. In order to provide a statistical background of any reliability, therefore, the sampling would need to be much more extensive and fine-grained. Statistical work of the required magnitude does not yet seem to have been achieved.

The principles of information theory have recently been discussed as perhaps affording another avenue for explicating deviation in poetic language. Information theory approaches the question of deviation not in terms of frequency of occurrence, as does statistics, but from the point of view of transitional probability. Given an inventory of elements and the permitted sequences of these elements, information theory incorporates a measure for assigning probabilities to the occurrence of each element in the inventory at any given point in a sequence. Based on these calculations some elements may have zero probability of occurring at a certain point in a sequence, others one hundred percent probability (complete predictability), and others a probability somewhere in between these limits. Information theory thus measures the rarity or surprise factor of a given element at a given position. It thus amounts to a formal apparatus for explaining deviation. But the problems of data-sampling arise here too in rather severe form. Information theory is an excellent tool for dealing with the transitional probabilities of small inventories of elements, such as phonemes or letters, but in the field of syntax, where the probabilities would have to be established for millions (actually an infinite number) of combinations, it does not seem to offer more than an interesting theoretical possibility.

In discussing descriptive grammar it was pointed out that deviant sentences could be simply listed as exceptions to the stated rules. This of course amounts to a rather trivial explanation of deviation. The corresponding decision in a generative grammar would be made where the sequence or sentence in question was not an output of the grammar. *Ipso facto* such a sequence would constitute a deviation. But using a generative grammar as a norm does not limit one simply to absolute decisions of this kind. Since a generative grammar consists of a finely articulated set of grammatical rules, one can test the deviant sequence against these rules and in this way determine in just what particular respect the sequence is deviant. Generative grammar thus makes it possible to arrive at decisions on kinds and degrees of deviation.

A generative grammar, at least in most versions, comprises a transformational level. On this level sentences are transformed from one grammatical shape into another; e.g., actives into passives, statements into questions, and sentences into nominalizations. In addition to these transformations, various other and more complex grammatical structures can also be shown to stand in the transform relation to each other. This formalized technique for showing relations between different sequence and sentence forms can be put to use in bringing to light certain regularities that lie, as it were, beneath the linguistic surface of the poem. If the grammatical structures occurring in a poem are similar or identical to any appreciable extent, that is obviously a stylistic fact of some importance. But if such similarities or identities are not discoverable in the actual language of a poem, it need not follow that there is no regularity of syntactic structure to be discovered. For it may turn out that there is indeed a regularity of structure, but it is manifested in the fact that various of the sequences in the poem are related to each other transformationally. Thus, transformational analysis provides an additional linguistic means for confirming judgments of a poem's unity of structure.

E. W. Scripture, *Grundzüge der englischen Verswissenschaft* (1929); R. Jakobson, "Über den Versbau der serbokroatischen Volksepen," *Archives néerlandaises de phonétique expérimentale,* 7–9 (1933); W. Schramm, *Approaches to a Science of Eng. Verse* (1935); G. U. Yule, *The Statistical Study of Lit. Vocabulary* (1944); H. Whitehall, "From L. to Crit.," KR, 13 (1951); S. Chatman, "Robert Frost's 'Mowing': An Inquiry into Prosodic Structure," KR, 18 (1956) and "L., Poetics, and Interpretation: The Phonemic Dimension," *Quarterly Jour. of Speech,* 43 (1957); J. R. Firth, "Modes of Meaning," *Papers in L. 1934–1951* (1957); B. Havránek, "The Functional Differentiation of the Standard Language," *A Prague School Reader on Esthetics, Lit. Structure and Style,* ed. P. Garvin (1958); J. Mukařovský, "Standard Language and Poetic Language," *A Prague School Reader;* H. Whitehall and A. A. Hill, "A Report on the Language-Lit. Seminar," *Readings in Applied Eng. L.,* ed. H. B. Allen (1958); E. L. Epstein and T. Hawkes, *L. and Eng. Prosody* (1959); M. Riffaterre, "Criteria for Style Analysis," *Word,* 15 (1959); H. L. Smith, Jr., "Toward Redefining Eng. Prosody," *Studies in L.,* 14 (1959); W. K. Wimsatt, Jr. and M. Beardsley, "The Concept of Meter: An Exercise in Abstraction," PMLA, 74 (1959); G. Herdan, *Type-Token Mathematics* (1960); R. Jakobson, "L. and Poetics," Conference on Style, Indiana Univ., 1958. *Style in Language,* ed. T. A. Sebeok (1960); M. Riffaterre, "Stylistic Context," *Word,* 16 (1960); S. Saporta, "The Application of L. to the Study of Poetic Language," *Style in Language* (1960); International Conference of Work-in-Progress Devoted to Problems of Poetics. 1st, Warsaw, 1960. *Poetics. Poetyka . . .* (1961; see the various articles dealing with l. and poetics); S. Chatman, "Linguistic Style, Lit. Style and Performance: Some Distinctions," *Georgetown Monograph Series on Language and L.,* 13 (1962); S. R. Levin, *Linguistic Structures in Poetry* (1962); S. Chatman, *A Theory of Meter* (1965).   s.c.; s.r.l.

LIRA. A Sp. stanza form of 4, 5, 6, or, rarely, more Italianate hendecasyllables and heptasyllables, the term denoting loosely any short-strophé *canción* (q.v.) in Italianate verse. The name was first applied to the form aBabB and was taken from the end of the first line of Garcilaso's *A la flor de Gnido.* Garcilaso (1501?–1536) supposedly imitated it from Bernardo Tasso, who is credited with its invention. This form is sometimes designated the *l. garcilasiana* and has come to be known also as *estrofa de Fray Luis de León, l. de Fray Luis de León,* and *quintilla de Luis de León* for being popularized through Fray Luis de León's works and later being replaced in popularity by other forms, particularly the *l. sestina* (aBaBcC, also called *media estancia*).—Navarro.   D.C.C.

LITHUANIAN POETRY. Of the two varieties of Lith. poetry one belongs to folklore and the other to literature proper. The anonymous folk songs (Lith. *dainos,* singular *daina*) antedate personal expression in verse by several centuries, and are mentioned in medieval sources, whereas written literature arose in Lithuania during the Reformation and Counter-Reformation. The *daina* comprises the most numerous and original part of Lith. folklore (about 200,000 folk songs have now been recorded). It is best represented by the purely lyrical love songs. The lyrical nature of poetic expression is very characteristic of *daina* in general, and it is strongly evident even in the war songs and ballads. Other types of *daina* include songs of work, dancing, and games, which are the oldest, various holiday songs and songs of family life, among which the wedding songs and funeral lamentations are of particular interest. Mythological and historical songs are rather rare. The originality of the *daina* lies chiefly in various poetic artifices and their specific usage. The most typical among them are the numerous diminutives, lavishly used in various forms and degrees, the highly developed parallelisms, and a rather intricate symbolism, basically of an erotic nature. The metrical structure of the *daina*, which is often of considerable length, is rather complex and quite frequently defies the familiar prosodic standards. Because the text and melody are integrally connected in the *daina*, the rhythm is of great importance, and, as a result of the free stress in Lith., it is variable and often mixed. The rhyme, however, is not essential. The stanzas have mostly two, three, or four lines, either with or without refrain. Some older songs have no stanzas at all.

The first three *dainos* to appear in print were selected and published, with a German translation, by P. Ruhig (1675–1749) in 1745 and attracted Lessing's attention. Subsequently Herder incorporated eight in his collection of folk songs (1778–79), one of which, originally from Ruhig, was woven by Goethe into his "Singspiel," *Die Fischerin*. As a result of this attention, the collection and publication of the *daina* was undertaken on a large scale in the 19th c. and has continued with increasing scholarship to the present. The earliest collection (1825), was by L. Rhesa (1776–1840), the largest (4 v., 1880–83), by A. Juškevičius (1819–80). Eventually the tradition of folk poetry became a strong factor in the formation of the distinctly national character of Lith. poetry, its influence extending to many contemporary poets.

Written Lith. poetry begins in the 16th c. with versions of canticles and hymns, including those of Martynas Mažvydas (Mosvidius, d. 1563), who also prepared in Königsberg the first printed Lith. book, *Catechismusa prasty szadei* (1547), a translation of the Lutheran catechism, and prefaced it with a rhymed address to his compatriots. Until the end of the 18th c., hardly anything of higher poetic value, with one significant exception, was achieved. The exception was the appearance in Prussian Lithuania of Kristijonas Donelaitis (Donalitius, 1714–80). His major work, *Metai* (The Seasons, 1765–75, published 1818), is a long poem (about 3,000 lines in hexameter) which exhibits in forceful language a keen love

and observation of nature and depicts vividly the life and character of the common people. The poem is comparable to similar work of James Thomson and Ewald von Kleist.

A more active literary movement appeared at the beginning of the 19th c., marked first by pseudo-classicism and sentimentalism and later by the influence of romanticism and a growing interest in Lith. folklore. The latter trend was particularly evident in the poetry of Antanas Strazdas (1763–1833), who was one of the first to merge the folk-song tradition with personal expression. The next peak in the development of Lith. poetry after K. Donelaitis was Antanas Baranauskas (1835–1902), the author of the lengthy, picturesque poem *Anykščiu šilelis* (The Grove of Anykščiai, 1858–59), a veiled lament for Lithuania under the czarist Russian regime. The pre-20th c. development of Lith. poetry was concluded by Maironis (pen name of Jonas Mačiulis, 1862–1932), the creative embodiment of the ideals of the national awakening and a foremost lyric poet (cf. his collection *Pavasario balsai* / Voices of Spring, 1895), whose formal and structural innovations (e.g., the introduction of a new tonal structure instead of the former syllabic versification, and the normalization of the poetic language) had great influence on the growth of the new Lith. poetry.

The beginning of the 20th c. brought changes of great importance. The general relaxation of Rus. political pressure and the ever growing cultural consciousness increased literary production and widened its horizon. The utilitarian aims of poetry were less emphasized and, inspired by literary movements abroad, new approaches to poetry were sought that would fit the Lith. spirit and satisfy purely aesthetic demands. Although evident before World War I, these trends were fulfilled after the war, during the period of independence (1918–40), when Lith. poetry reached high standards of creative art. Symbolism left a strong imprint on the early poetry of this period, best represented by Balys Sruoga (1896–1947), also an outstanding dramatist, Vincas Mykolaitis-Putinas (b. 1893), later a leading novelist as well, and Faustas Kirša (1891–1964). This group can be supplemented by Jurgis Baltrušaitis (1873–1944), who, after achieving distinction among the Rus. symbolists, began to publish verse in his native Lith. around 1930. In the 1920's the more conservative trends were countered by the futurist and, to some extent, by dadaist and surrealist poets who, led by Kazys Binkis (1893–1942), formed the group of *Keturi Vėjai* (Four Winds), which further rejuvenated poetic form and content. Somewhat later, neoromanticism, neosymbolism, aestheticism, and expressionism appeared on the scene, while the group *Trečias Frontas*

(Third Front) advocated poetry of leftist orientation.

These trends were transcended, however, by the individual traits and achievements of the four leading poets of the second generation: Jonas Aistis (b. 1904), a highly intimate poet and a master of subtle and refined expression, Bernardas Brazdžionis (b. 1907), whose poetry, sometimes rhetorical and of prophetic overtones, is a synthesis of national traditions, modern life and religious conceptions, and Antanas Miškinis (b. 1905) and Salomėja Nėris (pen name of S. Bačinskaitė-Bučienė, 1904–45), both of whom have transformed the best qualities of the *daina* into their own personal expression. The transitional features leading to the poetry of the next generation were best reflected in the verse of Vytautas Mačernis (1920–44).

The natural development of Lith. poetry has been disrupted by the annexation of the country by the USSR during World War II. This event is responsible for the· schism that has since divided Lith. poetry. On the one hand, in Lithuania, poetry is dominated by the paralyzing ideology of socialist realism. A few of the older poets, such as Salomėja Nėris, Liudas Gira (1884–1946), and Teofilis Tilvytis (b. 1904), have become eulogists of the Soviet regime, while the others, e.g., V. Mykolaitis-Putinas and A. Miškinis, are laboring less conspicuously. Among the younger ones, more prominent are Eduardas Mieželaitis (b. 1919), Algimantas Baltakis (b. 1930), and Justinas Marcinkevičius (b. 1930). On the other hand, the spirit and tradition of the poetry of Independent Lithuania is continued, with the absorption of contemporary movements in Western poetry, by the poets in exile, especially in the United States. Among them, J. Aistis, B. Brazdžionis, and F. Kirša are pursuing their former creative paths, while Henrikas Radauskas (b. 1910) has developed into a first-rank poet of the modern idiom in classical form. Of the younger emigré poets, who have reached maturity in exile, the leading ones are Kazys Bradūnas (b. 1917), the bard of the native soil, Alfonsas Nyka-Niliūnas (b. 1919), an existentialist of a deeply felt philosophical thought, and Henrikas Nagys (b. 1920), who embraces both emotional expressionism and neoromanticism.

ANTHOLOGIES: *The Daina*, ed. U. Katzenelenbogen (1935); *Aus litauischer Dichtung*, ed. and tr. H. Engert (2d ed., 1938); *Litauischer Liederschrein*, ed. V. Jungfer (2d ed., 1948); *Lietuvių poezijos antologija*, ed. J. Aistis and A. Vaičiulaitis (1951); *Lietuvių liaudies dainos*, ed. J. Čiurlionytė (1955); *Lith. Folksongs in America*, ed. J. Balys (1958); *The Green Oak: Selected Lith. Poetry*, ed. A. Landsbergis and C. Mills (1962).

HISTORY AND CRITICISM: M. Biržiška, *Lietuvių dainų literatūros istorija* (1919); B. Sruoga, "Lith. Folksongs," *Folk-lore* (London), 43 (1932); V. Mykolaitis-Putinas, *Naujoji lietuvių literatūra* (1936); V. Jungfer, *Litauen: Antlitz eines Volkes* (1938); J. Mauclère, *Panorama de la littérature lithuanienne contemporaine* (1938); A. Vaičiulaitis, *Outline Hist. of Lith. Lit.* (1942); J. Balys, "Lith. Folk Song," *Funk and Wagnalls Standard Dict. of Folklore . . . , II* (1950); J. Balys, *Lith. Narrative Folksongs* (1954); *Lietuvių literatūros istorija*, ed. K. Korsakas (1957 ff.); A. Senn, "Storia della letteratura lituana," *Storia delle letterature baltiche*, ed. G. Devoto (1957; 2d ed. in preparation). W.K.M.; K.O.

LITOTES (Gr. "plainness," "simplicity"). A figure, related to meiosis (q.v.), employing deliberate understatement for purposes of intensification, or affirmation by the negative of the contrary, usually used to secure emphasis or irony; however, according to Lausberg, "Die Ironie ist in der Litotes nicht total, sondern nur graduell" (*Handbuch der literarischen Rhetorik* 586). Servius, commenting on Virgil's *Georgics* 2. 125 says, "non tarda, id est, strenuissima: nam litotes figura est" (not slow, that is, most brisk: for the figure is litotes), though in fact it seems to be hyperbole. The figure is used so frequently in *Beowulf*, and other OE poetry, that it has become (with kennings) a distinguishing mark of that literature: "þæt wæs god cyning" (that was a good king), following a passage telling how the king flourished on earth, prospered in honors, brought the neighboring people to obey him and pay him tribute. "Nor are thy lips ungraceful, Sire of Men, / Nor tongue ineloquent" (Milton, *Paradise Lost* 8). Effects vary from the obvious ironies of *Beowulf* to the sophisticated subtleties of Pope; l. is also an effective satiric instrument: "He was nat pale as a forpyned goost. / A fat swan loved he best of any roost" (Chaucer, *The Canterbury Tales*. Gen. Prol. 205–6). As an affirmation by negative of the contrary: "I'll bet you won't" meaning "I'm certain you will."—O. Jespersen, *Negation in Eng. and Other Languages* (1917); A. Hübner, *Die "MHD Ironie" oder die L. im Altdeutschen* (1930); F. Bracher, "Understatement in OE Poetry," PMLA, 52 (1937); L. M. Hollander, "L. in Old Norse," PMLA, 53 (1938); Lausberg. R.O.E.

LJÓÐÁHÁTTR. An Eddic meter, of which the first and third lines of each stanza are similar to the usual line of the *fornyrðislag* (q.v.), while the second and fourth lines are shorter and have no caesura. The short line, which may have 3 or more accented syllables, is an independent unit, which alliterates in itself:

Deyr fé, deyja frændr,

deyr sjálfr it sama.

L. is the metrical form of *Hávamál* and other, especially didactic, Eddic poems.—*The Poetic Edda*, tr. H. A. Bellows (1923) and tr. L. M. Hollander (1928, rev. ed. 1962).   R.B.

LOGAOEDIC (Gr. "prose-poetic"). Term invented by metricians of Roman imperial times as a general description of mixed anapaestic and iambic or dactylic and trochaic cola (ascending and descending rhythm respectively) in Gr. lyric verse. L. anapaestic cola may be composed of 2 or more anapaests followed by an iambic dipody catalectic or, more usually, by a single iambus, and l. dactylic cola of 2 or more dactyls followed by a trochaic dipody (the last syllable being *anceps*), or by a trochaic dipody catalectic. Anacrusis (q.v.) sometimes is postulated in the latter category, e.g., in Pindar's famous description of Athens:

o tai liparai kai iostephanoi kai aoidimoi

To the varieties of l. dactylic cola belong the Ibycean (−⏑⏑|−⏑⏑|−⏑|−|) and Praxillean (−⏑⏑|−⏑⏑|−⏑⏑|−⏑|−≏), and with both anacrusis has been assumed. Some modern metricians abhor the name "logaoedic," e.g., A. M. Dale, CR, 62 (1948), 124, who prefers to speak of "prosodiac-enoplian."—T. D. Goodell, *Chapters on Gr. Metric* (1901); J. W. White, *The Verse of Gr. Comedy* (1912); Kolář; Dale; Koster.   R.J.G.

LONG (syllable). See MORA; CLASSICAL PROSODY.

LONG METER (L.M. of the hymn books). In effect a variant of ballad or common meter, for if the trimeters of that 4343 pattern are lengthened, the 4444 pattern of l.m. results. The foot pattern is sometimes trochaic, but usually iambic as in Burns's

Ye banks and braes o' bonnie Doon,
  How can ye bloom sae fresh and fair?
How can ye chant, ye little birds,
  And I sae weary fu' o' care?

Instead of the abcb rhyme scheme, l.m. is frequently found in abab, and even in aabb, the latter differing from octosyllabic couplets in thought development and by being printed as quatrains on the page. The aabb pattern gives a different "turn" to the ideas and is especially well suited, although not limited, to poems of light compliment.   L.J.Z.

LYRIC. The term used to designate one of the three general categories of poetic literature, the others being narrative and dramatic. Although the differentiating features between these arbitrary classifications are sometimes moot, l. poetry may be said to retain most pronouncedly the elements of poetry which evidence its origins in musical expression—singing, chanting, and recitation to musical accompaniment. Though the drama and epic as well as the l. may have had their genesis in a spontaneously melodic expression which soon adapted itself to a ritualistic need and thus became formalized, music in dramatic and epic poetry was secondary to other elements of the works, being mainly a mimetic or mnemonic device. In the case of l. poetry, however, the musical element is intrinsic to the work intellectually as well as aesthetically: it becomes the focal point for the poet's perceptions as they are given a verbalized form to convey emotional and rational values. The primary importance of the musical element is indicated in many generic terms which various cultures have used to designate nonnarrative and nondramatic poetry: the Eng. "l.," derived from the Gr. *lyra* or musical intrument; the classical Gr. *melic*, or *mele* (air, melody); the Chinese *shih*, or "word song."

To speak of the "musical" qualities of l. poetry is not to say that such poetry is written always to be sung. Neither does the appellation of "musical" indicate that l. poetry possesses such attributes as pitch, harmony, syncopation, counterpoint, and other mechanical characteristics of a tonal, musical line or sequence. To define the quality of lyricism in this way is to limit a l. poem to the manner in which it is presented or to its architectonic aspects. This is largely the approach which classical criticism and its followers have taken in their treatment of l. poetry. On the other hand, an equation of poetic lyricism with the non-architectural or "emotional" qualities of music is even less profitable from the critical point of view, because it leads to such question-begging definitions of the l. as "the essence of poetry," "pure poetry," or, most vaguely, "poetry." To declare that "the characteristic of the l. is that it is the product of the pure poetic energy unassociated with other energies, and that l. and poetry are synonymous terms" (Drinkwater) is as extreme a definition of lyricism as to claim that a passage is lyrical simply because it possesses "the quality of metrical construction or architecture" (Gilbert Murray).

Most of the confusion in the modern (i.e., 1550 to the present) critical use of the term "l." is due to an overextension of the phrase to cover a body of poetic writing that has drastically altered its nature in the centuries of its development. The first critical use of the word *mele* by the Greeks was for the purpose of broadly distinguishing between various nonnarrative and nondramatic types of poetry: the melic poem was intended to be sung to musical accompaniment, as contrasted with the iambic and elegiac poems, which were chanted. The first general use of "l." to characterize a selection of poetic literature encompassing several genres did not come until the Alexandrian period. Then "l." became a generic term for any poem which was composed to be sung, and this was the meaning which it largely retained until the Renaissance. The preoccupation of Aristotle, Horace, Josephus, Jerome, and other pre-Renaissance critics with the metrics of melic or l. poetry was entirely appropriate to the principle upon which the category was established.

But with the Renaissance, poets began suiting their work to a visual rather than an auditory medium; even while such critics as Minturno, Scaliger, Sidney, and Puttenham were formulating their discussions of l. poetry, the l. was becoming something quite different from the classical melic poem. No longer a performing bard, scop, or troubadour, the poet ceased to "compose" his poem for musical presentation but instead "wrote" it for a collection of readers. The l. poem, nominally successor to a well-established poetic method, inherited and employed specific themes, meters, attitudes, images, and myths; but in adapting itself to a new means of presentation, the l. found itself bereft of the very element which had been the foundation of its lyricism—music.

At the time the l. was undergoing this important metamorphosis, critics of the 15th and 16th c. chose either to ignore the genre or to treat it in the same quantitative or metrical fashion as the classicists had done. Until the end of the 17th c., therefore, critics failed to distinguish between the true or melodic l., such as the "songs" of Shakespeare, Campion, and Dryden, and the nonmusical, verbal lyrics of Donne, Marvell, and Waller. Both the straightforward, clear song-poem and the more abstrusely phrased print-poem were called "l.": to refer to the "sweetness of numbers" in Waller or Dryden was the critic's substitute for precision of terms in distinguishing poems intended for musical accompaniment from those not so designed. The neoclassical critical concern in 18th-c. France and England with the tragic and epic genres was sufficiently overwhelming to permit the l. to become somehow lost as a subject for discussion; and when the romantic movement came with its championing of lyrical modes, terminological confusion continued in the equation of "l." with "poetry" by Wordsworth, Goethe, Coleridge, Poe, and other literary theorists. The 19th-c. development of a scientific methodology, with consequent insistence on accuracy of terms and precision of generic distinctions, translated itself in the field of literary criticism into a

concern with the intrinsic and characteristic nature of the l. The definitions by Drinkwater and Murray were the overinclusive and overexclusive criteria which resulted from this concern; and critical attempts to reestablish the melodic or musical substance of l. poetry were a third, and equally unsuccessful, method of dealing with the paradoxical nature of a "musical" poetry which was no longer literally "melodic." Such, in greatly simplified lines, is the background of the verbal ambiguity with which post-Renaissance critics concealed their basic failure to define exactly the nature of the l. genre which distinguishes it from narrative and dramatic poetry and which includes all the disparate types of poem commonly called "lyrical."

Critical attempts to define l. poetry by reference to its secondary (i.e., nonmusical) qualities have perhaps suffered by being descriptive of various historical groupings of lyrics rather than definitive of the category as a whole. Among the most well-known and popularly cited proscriptions regarding the l. are that it must necessarily be brief (Poe); "be one, the parts of which mutually support and explain each other; all in their proportion harmonizing with, and supporting the purpose and known influence of metrical arrangement" (Coleridge); be "the spontaneous overflow of powerful feelings" (Wordsworth); be an intensely subjective and personal expression (Hegel); be an "inverted action of mind upon will" (Schopenhauer); or be "the utterance that is overheard" (Mill).

Though the attributes of brevity, metrical coherence, subjectivity, passion, sensuality, and particularity of image are frequently ascribed to the l. genre, there are schools of poetry obviously l. which are not susceptible to such criteria. Milton's mood poems, L'Allegro and Il Penseroso, as well as the most famous of the Eng. elegies are "brief" in only the most relative sense. Much of the vers libre of the present age contradicts the rule of metrical coherence. Imagist lyrics are hardly "empassioned" in the ordinary sense of the word. The "lucubrations" of the metaphysicals are something less than sensual in the romantic meaning of the term. The problem of subjectivity must always plague the critic of the Elizabethan love l. And, finally, the common artistic admission that the universal can be expressed best, and perhaps solely, through the particular image largely invalidates any distinction between the l. and non-l. on a metaphoric or thematic basis.

The irreducible denominator of all l. poetry must, therefore, be those elements which it shares with the musical forms that produced it. Although l. poetry is not music, it is representational of music in its sound patterns, basing its meter and rhyme on the regular linear measure of the song; or, more remotely, it employs cadence and consonance to approximate the tonal variation of a chant or intonation. Thus the l. retains structural or substantive evidence of its melodic origins, and it is this factor which serves as the categorical principle of poetic lyricism.

Contemporary critics, predicating the musical essence of the l. as its vital characteristic, have come close to formulating an exact, inclusive definition of the genre which eliminates semantic contradictions. "Words build into their poetic meaning by building into sound . . . sound in composition: music" (R. P. Blackmur). "A poet does not compose *in order to* make of language delightful and exciting music; he composes a delightful and exciting music in language *in order to* make what he has to say peculiarly efficacious in our minds" (Lascelles Abercrombie). Lyrical poetry is "the form wherein the artist presents his image in immediate relation to himself" (James Joyce). "Hence in lyrical poetry what is conveyed is not mere emotion, but the imaginative prehension of emotional states . . ." (Herbert Read). It is "an internal mimesis of sound and imagery" (Northrop Frye). Thus, in contemporary critical usage it may be said that "l." is a general, categorical, and nominal term, whereas in the pre-Renaissance sense it was specific, generic, and descriptive. In its modern meaning, a l. is a type of poetry which is mechanically representational of a musical architecture and which is thematically representational of the poet's sensibility as evidenced in a fusion of conception and image. In its older and more confined sense, a l. was simply a poem written to be sung; this meaning is preserved in the modern colloquialism of referring to the words of a song as its "lyrics."

However useful definitions of the l. may be, they cannot indicate the great flexibility of technique and range of subjects which have helped this category to comprise the bulk of poetic literature. There are literally dozens of l. genres, ranging from the ancient *partheneia* to the modern vers libre; and no topic, whether a cicada or a locomotive, has been neglected by the l. poets. Though it is manifestly impossible to say everything about the historical development of the l. in a short summary, certain general facts prove interesting as pieces in an evolving pattern of theories about and treatment of the lyrical mode between various ages, cultures, and individuals. The l. is as old as recorded literature; and its history is that of human experience at its most animated.

It is logical to suppose that the first "lyrical" poems came into being when men discovered the pleasure that arises from combining words in a coherent, meaningful sequence with the almost physical process of uttering rhythmical and tonal sounds to convey feelings. The instinctive human tendency to croon or hum or intone as an expression of emotional mood is evidenced in the child's babbling; and the socialization of this tendency in primitive cultures by the chanting or singing of nonsense syllables to emphasize tribal rites is a well documented phenomenon. At that remote point in time when the syllables ceased to be nonsense and became syntactically and connotatively meaningful, the first l. was composed but in what Cro-Magnon or Neanderthal cave this took place, no one will ever know, though speculations about the folk origins of literature range from those of Herder to Jung to A. B. Lord. The earliest recorded evidence of l. poetry would indicate that such compositions emerged from ritualistic activity accompanying religious ceremonies and were expressive of the mystical experience which the "poet" or speaker was undergoing. The dividing line between the nonsense babblings of the Pythoness at Delphi and the transliteration by the priests into a coherent unit of thought is indicative of the fashion in which many of the early religious lyrics came into existence. Scholars have found evidence to support this theory of the religious derivation of poetry in general and the l. in particular in such literatures as the Sanskrit, Celtic, and Japanese, as well as the Gr.

The most complete written evidence of early l. activity is the Egyptian: the Pyramid Texts (ca. 2600 B.C.) includes specimens of the funeral song (elegy), song of praise to the king (ode), and invocation to the gods (hymn); and tomb inscriptions from the same period include the work songs (*chansons de toile*) of shepherds, fishers, and chairmen. Also among the earliest l. writings of the Old Kingdom are the dialogue, the proverb, and the lament (complaint). Works from the New Kingdom (ca. 1555 B.C.) include the love song, the song of revelry and the epitaph. Although relatively unsophisticated, the Egyptian l. contained in nascent form many of the elements which were to become characteristic of later l. poetry. The poetic lines were probably some form of free rhythm without rigid meter. Alliteration and parallelism were devices frequently used, as was paronomasia or punning. Irony and paradox were present in a primitive form; and these first of all lyrics were already treating such subjects as death, piety, love, loneliness, jealousy, martial prowess, and happiness. Furthermore, the personal tone of the l., though not ubiquitous, was apparent in such poems as those enclosed in *The Dispute with His Soul of One Who Is Tired of Life*.

Remains of such other ancient literatures as

the Babylonian and the Assyrian are too fragmentary to disclose much in the way of advancement over the Egyptian l. poems, which the inhabitants of the Fertile Crescent appear to have imitated in certain obvious ways. The most complete of the ancient bodies of lyric poetry is the Hebrew, which, while owing something to Egyptian and Babylonian sources, nevertheless marked positive improvement in the l. technique. These lyrics, well known to modern readers because of their religious associations and highly important because of their effect on the patristic lyricists of the Middle Ages, are among the most strikingly beautiful ever written. Though textual evidence indicates that some Hebrew l. poetry was written as early as the 10th c. B.C. (notably the *Song of Deborah*), many poems were of a later date; and the earliest Jewish literary criticism dealing with the l. was as late as the time of Christ. Philo Judaeus (ca. 20 B.C.–A.D. 50) indicated the Egyptian origin of some Hebrew lyric techniques by declaring that Moses was taught "the whole theory of rhythm, harmony, and meter" by the Egyptians; and Flavius Josephus (ca. A.D. 37–95), dealing with the famous hymn of Moses in Exodus 15:1–2 ("I will sing unto the Lord, for he hath triumphed gloriously") said that it was written in hexametric verse. The hymns and songs of David, Josephus also wrote, employed various meters, including trimeter and pentameter. Later discussions of Hebrew meters were carried on by Origen, Eusebius, and Jerome; but it is questionable how applicable to Hebrew lyrics the Gr. metric nomenclature was in fact, and it must be conceded that very little is known even yet about the nature of ancient Hebrew l. meters. It is known, however, that the lyrics were accompanied by such instruments as the harp, sackbut, and cymbals; and suggestions of the manner in which hymns, elegies, songs of rejoicing, and songs of triumph were composed and performed may be found in the story of David in I Samuel 16:23 and II Samuel 1:17–27, 6:5, 15–16.

The ancient Jewish poets were proficient in the use of parallelism and alliteration, perfecting these devices and using them in a variety of ways. Parallelism is obvious in such lyrics as Psalm 19 ("The heavens declare the glory of God, and the firmament sheweth his handiwork") and in Proverbs 21:17 ("He that loveth pleasure shall be a poor man: he that loveth wine and oil shall not be rich"); but it is also, more subtly, used as in Jeremiah 6:24 ("Anguish hath taken hold of us, and pain, as of a woman in travail"). The use of tropical devices is highly developed in Hebrew l. poetry, with similes and metaphors predominating; the apostrophe and hyperbole increase the personal tone of the l. far beyond the Egyptian.

Many of the lyrics indeed appear intensely subjective, as Psalm 69 ("Save me, O God; for the waters are come in unto my soul. I sink in deep mire, where there is no standing"); but even these poems reflect what Frye has called "the sense of an external and social discipline." Yet the personal tone remains and is essential to the lyricism of such passages as those in Isaiah 5:1 ("Now will I sing to my well beloved a song of my beloved touching his vineyard"); Psalm 137 ("By the rivers of Babylon, there we sat down, yea, we wept, when we remembered Zion"); and II Samuel 1:19 ("The beauty of Israel is slain upon thy high places: how are the mighty fallen!").

The Hebrew lyricists developed a number of types and subtypes of the l. genre, which are classified by method of performance, source of imagery, or subject matter. These include the psalm (derived from the Gr. *psallein*, "to pull upon a stringed instrument"); the pastoral, which draws heavily upon the agrarian background of Hebrew culture; and the vision or apocalyptic prophecy, which employs the indirection of the trope to imply its perceptions. Other types include the proverb, the epigram, and similar forms of "wisdom" literature; the descriptive love l.; the triumph; various sorts of threnody; panegyrics of different kinds; and even a lyrical dialogue (or "drama") in the Book of Job. Some overlapping of these types is obvious (the triumph was frequently a panegyric on some hero, and the threnody or elegy was often pastoral); but the ambiguity is an historical one and terminological distinctions have yet to be drawn. Viewed as descriptions, the types are helpful in understanding the characteristics of the variations of the l. expression.

Like the Egyptian and Hebrew, the Gr. l. had its origins in religious activity; the first songs were probably composed to suit an occasion of celebration or mourning. Gr. lyrics were chanted, sung, or sung and danced; each of these lyrical methods of presentation is traceable to some form of religious practice. The dithyramb, for example, may have been composed to commemorate the death of some primitive vegetable god or the birth of Dionysus; in any case, it was originally sung to the accompaniment of the flute playing a melody in the Phrygian mode, which the Greeks considered the most emotional. In time, the dithyramb took on a more particular form involving formalized dance steps corresponding to passages in the text: these rhythmical and thematic patterns conceivably were the prototype of the fully developed ode, or song of celebration, with its divisions of strophe and antistrophe as written by Pindar, Sophocles, and others. Similar tracings of the development of other lyrical modes in Greece from the Heroic Age to the Homeric to the Periclean may be made, though it must be remembered that all are largely hypothetical.

The essential element of the Gr. l. was its meter, which was of two kinds: the stichic, that spoken or recited; and what may be termed the melic, that suited for singing or singing and dancing. Stichic meters were well demarcated lines of equal length and repetitive rhythm that can be broken into equivalent feet or metra. Melic meters were composed of phrases of varying length or movement, the cola, which were combined into a unit rhythmically complete or rounded, the *periodos*. Some cola are rhythmically repetitious in themselves and may be broken into dimeter or trimeter; but in the melic poems, it was the *periodos* or stanza that constituted the l. unit. Melic meters were obviously subject to wide adaptation by individual writers, and most of the best known Gr. lyrical meters are named for the poets who developed and customarily used them: the Alcaic, Anacreontic, Pindaric, and so on. The earliest Gr. lyrics were folk in origin, but even in the works of Homer and Hesiod there is evidence of an artistic concern with the lyrical mood and subjects, if not the lyrical form. In the *Iliad,* for instance, there are such embryonic lyrics as Helen's laments, Achilles' speech at the death of Patroklos, and the elegiac statements at Hector's funeral. The hymn was among the first developed of the definably l. genres, being composed in significant numbers before 700 B.C. The Homeric Hymns date from this period and indicate the religious nature of the first lyrics: they are addressed to Artemis, Dionysus, Heracles, Helios, Selena, *et al.,* and the pattern of some became a distinct type of l. hymn (i.e., the "paean" was a hymn to Apollo). The hymns employ devices appropriate to the apostrophe but are not very expansive in their tropes, chiefly using the attributive epithet, as in the hymn to Hera, XII (Evelyn-White trans.): "I sing of golden-throned Hera, whom Rhea bare. Queen of the immortals is she, surpassing all in beauty."

The Homeric epigrams are attributed to this period, also, thereby setting up an archetype for the later iambics: "Thestorides, full many things there are that mortals cannot sound; But there is nothing more unfathomable than the heart of man." The period from 700–500 B.C. saw the rise of elegiac and political verse, written by Solon among others, and the personal lampoon in iambics, by Archilochus, Hipponax, and Simonides of Amorgos. After 660 B.C., melic poetry developed, primarily in two strains: the Aeolian, or personal, lyrics written at Lesbos by Sappho and Alcaeus; and the Dorian, or objective, by Alcman, Arion, Stesichorus, and Ibycus. This group of lyrics

may also be categorized by method of performance as solo or choral, but the dividing line is not sharp, as Gr. scholars have pointed out. Although the ancient distinctions of melic poetry on the basis of metrics may have indicated separate categories, the modern definition of the l. would be hard pressed to differentiate between such poems as those of Ibycus, Sappho, and Alcman: (Lattimore tr.)

Blessed is the man who blithely
winds out all days of his life
without tears. But I must sing the
light of Agido. O see her
like the sun that Agido
summons up to shine upon us.
(Alcman)

Now in this season for me
there is no rest from love.
Out of the hard bright sky,
a Thracian north wind blowing
with searing rages and hurt—dark,
pitiless, sent by Aphrodite—Love
rocks and tosses my heart.
(Ibycus)

Throned in splendor, deathless, O Aphrodite,
child of Zeus, charm-fashioner, I entreat you
not with griefs and bitternesses to break my
spirit, O goddess. . . .
(Sappho)

The 5th c. in Greece produced some of the best of the l. poets: Simonides, Pindar, and Bacchylides; it was then that the l. found such magnificent expression in the choral odes of Sophocles, Aeschylus, and Euripides. Melic poetry became national in tone, with the Dorian mode prevailing; there was an abundance of such l. types as the hymn, paean, dithyramb, processional, dance song, triumph, ode, and dirge. Other popular genres were the *partheneia* (songs sung by virgins to flute accompaniment); *nomos* (ode or war song); *kommos* (a mournful dirge sung in Attic drama by an actor and the chorus alternately); *prosodion* (processional song of solemn thanksgiving); *hyporcheme* (a dance song); *epinicion* (song of victory); *threnos* (a dirge); wedding songs for men; and the *scolion* (a banquet song accompanied by the lyre and supposedly originated by Terpander).

The Gr. critics were less concerned with l., or melic, poetry than with the tragedy and the epic; the few extant comments which they made predicate the musical nature of the genre. Plato's denunciation of all poetry, especially the "representational" tragedy, included the melic, which Plato considered "untrue" or false in its depiction of reality. Stripped of musical coloring and laid bare as ideas, the melic poems revealed the ignorance of the poet, which clothed itself in "rhythm, meter, and harmony." (*The Republic* 10.4) Aristotle, in the *Poetics* (1-4) observed the absence of a generic term which might denote such non-epic and nondramatic kinds of poetry as the works in iambic, elegiac, and similar meters, which imitated "by means of language alone" as contrasted with the melic poems, which used rhythm, tune, and meter "all employed in combination." This statement indicates the existence of poetry, l. in the modern sense, which was not melic in the Gr. sense; but the Alexandrian use of "l." to indicate such disparate types as the dithyramb, iambics, elegies, and sapphics, while a broad attempt to repair the deficiency noted by Aristotle, was inexact and confusing.

Roman critical remarks on the l. would indicate that the term was used in the sense of melic poetry or poetry sung to the tune of the lyre. Horace indicated a belief that l. poetry was less substantial in content than epic poetry, being the *jocosa lyra;* and Quintillian concurred in the view that l. poetry was less weighty than epic though the ode might be worthy of more significant themes. To Horace's mind, the "dainty measures" were suited to "the work of celebrating gods and heroes, the champion boxer, the victorious steed, the fond desire of lovers, and the cup that banishes care"; they included the iambic, trimetric, and elegiac distich. These general criteria for form and content were adopted by most of the commentators following Horace—Ovid, Petronius, Juvenal, Pliny the Younger—so that, in l. theory, the Romans were little advanced beyond the Greeks.

In practice, Roman poets tended to imitate the Alexandrian l. writers, who composed works primarily meant to be read rather than performed. Moses Hadas has pointed out that this practice tended to produce l. poems more enigmatic and allusive than earlier "sung" poems had been; and it may be generally noted that Roman l. poets are more subject to examination as formulators of a "personal" or subjective poetry than the Greeks. The extent to which the lyrics of Sappho and the Aeolian school reflected the true feelings of their authors must be largely postulated; but with the Roman l. poets, sufficient internal detail in the poems plus objective evidence recorded of the poets' lives tempts the critic to speculate on the relationship between the nature of the l. mode and the private feelings of the lyricist. Thus, while they modeled their poems on the hymns of Callimachus, the Idyls of Theocritus, the epigrams of Anacreon, the elegiac laments of Bion and Moschus, and the later Gr. lyrics, Roman poets adapted the l. to produce a more subjective or autobiographical utterance. Conventional and minor Roman lyricists were con-

tent with the school of "fastidious elegance" which kept them copying the Greeks, and which Catullus mocked, but the Roman genius emphasized his particularized experiences: Propertius in his observations, Catullus in his amours, Virgil in his rustic pleasures, Ovid in the sorrows of his exile, Tibullus in his love pangs, Martial and Juvenal in their private asperities, and so on.

The private insight, the subjective focusing of experience is more keenly apparent in Roman lyrics than in other ancient works: in Ovid's *Tristia* 1.8. ("To their sources shall deep rivers flow"); Martial's *Epigrams* 1.8 ("Thou hast a name that bespeaks the season of the budding year, when Attic bees lay waste the brief-lived spring"); Catullus' *To Hortalus* 65 ("Though I am worn out with constant grief and sorrow calls me away"); and Tibullus, *To Delia* 1.2 ("More wine; let the liquor master these unwonted pains"). Coincidentally, there are many more "occasional" lyrics among the Roman poets which celebrate private rather than public festivals, with a greater proportion of such genres as the prothalamium and epithalamium (wedding songs), the *vale* or farewell, the epigram, the satire, and the epistle. Topicality is a notable element in many L. lyrics.

The formalistic approach to meter which typifies the l. writers of the pre-Augustan and Augustan periods of Roman literature began to weaken by the middle of the 1st c. A.D. and a greater flexibility of form resulted. The rigid preoccupation of the Horatian and Virgilian schools with the exact meters dictated by the system of quantitative verse was probably a classical attempt to substitute precision of metrics for the abandoned melodies of the true l. In any case, the lyrics of Petronius, unlike the imitative formal measures of the Statian odes, were experimental in form; and during the 2d c., definite steps were made by writers of L. lyrics toward a nonquantitative or accentual form of verse. In the 3d c., the completely new principle of rhyme could be found in the verse of the patristic lyricist, Commodian; it was then that the principles which were to guide medieval L. verse—rhyme and accent—were established.

As in the case of the Jews and the Greeks, the patristic critics of literature were an Epimethean lot, choosing to discuss forms and practices long established rather than treating contemporary practices. Eusebius and Jerome were concerned with examining Hebrew l. modes in terms of Gr. meters; Origen's comments were similarly analytical of metrics; and the anthologer, Isidore of Seville, discussed Hebrew and Gr. meters in conventional fashion, noted the musical element of l. poetry, but still failed to make any distinctions between the various genres. Patristic l. criticism throws little light on the practice of the times.

The first church lyrics were, not surprisingly, hymns which were patterned on the Hebrew Psalter and the Gr. hymns. The earliest verse hymns were those of St. Hilary, who probably used meter for its mnemonic effectiveness and who employed the meter that was to become a favorite with Prudentius, Fortunatus, and Thomas Aquinas as well as the basis for several of the medieval sequences: the *versus popularis* or trochaic tetrameter catalectic. St. Ambrose developed the use of iambic dimeters grouped in quatrains (the "Ambrosian" stanza); St. Jerome made L. more flexible as the language of poetry; and Augustine wrote a didactic poem which Brittain has said to contain in embryo the three elements of Medieval L. versification: accentual rhythm, isosyllabism, and rhyme. The Rule of St. Benedict, drawn up in the 6th c., required hymns to be sung at all the canonical hours, and this edict spurred on the writing of numerous lyricists. It should be noted that once more lyrics were composed to be sung or chanted; the indissoluble connection between the L. words and meters and the melodic line must not be forgotten. The Sequence depended on the repetition of phrases, both verbal and musical; and the involved meters as well as the simple rhymes of the hymns which Abelard wrote for Heloise and her nuns to sing were due to their avowedly musical nature:

> Christiani, plaudite,
> (Resurrexit Dominus)
> Victo mortis principe
> Christus imperat.
> Victori occurite,
> Qui nos liberat.

The church lyrics of the 12th and 13th c. are among the most perfect produced in the centuries of liturgical literature: the *Stabat Mater* and *Dies Irae* must be included in any list of the world's great lyrics, and there are numerous other examples of accomplished l. art: sequences, *cantiones*, nativities, and hymns of various kinds. The importance of patristic songs cannot be exaggerated in the history of the l.: not only is the body of church lyrics significant in itself, but it presages most of the metric and tropic techniques which are the foundation of the modern l.

Related to the development of patristic l. poetry was the Mozarabic poetry of Spain. Mozarabic writers inherited from the Visigoths the hymns of various Church Fathers—Hilary, Prudentius, Ambrose—transcribed into Gothic characters. Maurico, the compiler of Mozarabic l. in the 10th and 11th c., collected a large number of the hymns and songs written by Mozarabic poets of earlier periods and patterned on the Gothic and L. copies of patristic l. The Mozarabic l. include hymns, psalms, pleas, and such occasional poems as arose from the ordination of bishops, the building of churches, and the births and deaths of nobles. Though in time the Mozarabic l. adapted itself to accommodate characteristic cultural themes and attitudes of its era of Sp. history and came to be written in the vernacular, it remains one of the least known of all bodies of European l. poetry. Doubtless its claim to being the earliest vernacular poetry of the postclassical period in Europe will lead to its fuller investigation and evaluation in the future.

The centuries between A.D. 300 and A.D. 1200 also produced two separate traditions which must be noted in any tracing of l. development. One of these, the Anglo-Saxon, was Western; the other was Eastern. Anglo-Saxon poetry is interesting as an example of a community literature with ancient religious origins. The verse form, composed to be sung and presented by bards or scops, consisted of a heavily accentual rhythm of a 4-beat line with a caesura; thematically, the poetic lines, redolent of Egyptian and Hebrew poetry in their parallelism and alliteration, were developed through the kenning (metaphor). The range of Anglo-Saxon lyrics, subjected to various influences, includes the gnomic verse, the rune, the lament, the complaint, the elegy, and the hymn. In lyric mood and subject matter, *The Wanderer* and *The Seafarer* touch on the highly emotional and personal; *The Phoenix* is an example of descriptive allegory; *The Wife's Lament, Deor,* and *Widsith* represent differing experiences and attitudes; and the Caedmonian hymns display the superimposition of the patristic tradition of hymn-writing on the Anglo-Saxon. The Anglo-Saxon l., long ignored except by such rare commentators as Sir William Temple, has come in for great enthusiasm in recent years because of the efforts of such imitators as G. M. Hopkins, Ezra Pound, and W. H. Auden.

Chinese poetry is almost entirely lyrical: although the earliest lyrics, folk in origin, were composed before the 6th c. B.C., the perfection of the Chinese l. came during the T'ang Dynasty (A.D. 600–900) when such lyricists as Yüan Chieh, Li Po, and Po Chü-i lived. The ancient folk ballads and odes for sundry occasions were replaced in the 4th c. B.C. by the lyrics of Ch'ü Yüan, author of the *Li Sao.* From the first types of "art" l.—the lament, the nostalgic complaint, the pastoral description—the Chinese poem developed into other areas: the political allegory ("The Liberator" by Wu-ti), the marching song ("Song of the Men of Chin-ling" by Hsieh T'iao), the satiric song ("Tchirek Song"), and, finally, the controlled descriptive or mood poems of Li Po. In the 8th c. A.D., Po Chü-i adapted the l. to instructive purposes, writing with the utmost stylistic simplicity in describing scenes which served as the basis for serious reflection.

Unrewarded, my will to serve the State;
At my closed door autumn grasses grow.
What could I do to ease a rustic heart?
I planted bamboos, more than a hundred
  shoots. . . .
                    (tr. Arthur Waley.)

The succinct quality of these Chinese lyrics, as well as their visual effects, has had a decided effect on the imagists of the 19th and 20th c.

Though roughly contemporaneous with Chinese poetry, Japanese l. poetry is a completely separate tradition. The first Japanese l. poetry was reputedly composed by the god Iza-nagi and his descendants, and it is reasonably certain that a few kinds of folk l. were composed in the centuries before Christ: the war song, drinking song, and ballad. It is impossible to date the origins of what are apparently the earliest regular forms of Japanese poetry—the *chōka* (also, *nagauta*); the *tanka*, which was used either autonomously or as envoys to *chōka*; and the *sedōka*. The first extant anthology to include them was the *Man'yōshū* (compiled late 8th c. A.D.), after which the *chōka* and *sedōka* died out as vehicles of great poetry. The tanka, the most popular of Japanese l. forms for centuries, is composed of 31 syllables, and the haiku (or hokku) is composed of 17 syllables; each has alternating lines of 5 and 7 syllables. Though a relative late comer to Japanese poetry, the haiku has been perfected since its inception in the 15th c. by a long line of masters: Sōkan, Moritake, Teitoku, and the great Bashō. Fusing in its brief span references to nature, human emotion, time, mood, infinity, the haiku is perhaps the most concise kind of l. poetry ever devised.

Another oriental l. tradition which should be mentioned is the Persian, ancient in origin but flourishing in the 12th through the 15th c. Persian lyrics, originally religious and objective in nature, became more personal in the works of Omar Khayyam, Saʿdi, and Hafiz: the famous Rubáiyát of Omar being a specimen of the Persian philosophical wit poem. Other highly developed l. types included the *qasida* (hymn), *hajw* (satire), *marthiya* (elegy), *qitʿa* (a fragment characterized by its prosody), *ghazal* (ode), and learned and descriptive poetry. The vogue for oriental literature in 18th and 19th c. England served to reveal Persian l. poetry to Eng. writers and thus to cause the oriental l. to affect directly the western lyric tradition.

In Europe, the 12th and 13th c. saw the growth in popularity of the wandering minstrel: the quasi-ecclesiastical goliards, who wrote secular songs in L.; the trouvères in northern France, and the troubadours in the south; the Minnesinger in Germany. The l. was sung, or sung and danced, widely. The troubadours, composing in the vernacular, produced the *chanso* (song, often of love), *sirventes* (topical songs of satire, eulogy, or personal comment), the *planh* (complaint), *tenso* (debate), *pastorela* (account of a pastoral episode), *alba* or *aubade* (dawn song), and some songs designed for dancing (*balada* and *dansa*). Much has been said about the differences between the *chansons courtois* and *chansons populaire*, the *caroles* and *rondets* for dancing and the chansons designed for singing only, the *chansons de toile* (work songs) and their subspecies in a number of excellent studies. Few areas of l. history have been as thoroughly dealt with as the medieval.

Medieval lyrics remain in abundance and they exert a special charm for the modern reader in their mixture of naïveté and sophistication. They range from the slapstick "macaronic" songs (a jumble of languages) to the simple understatement in "Foweles in the frith," from the obvious but delightful "Sumer is icumen in" to the complex rondeau of Chaucer's "Now welcom somer, with thy sonne softe" and his ballade, "Hyd, Absalon, thy gilte tresses clere." Although this period produced such masters of the written "art" l. as Chaucer, Bertrand de Born, Chrétien de Troyes, Walther von der Vogelweide, Rutebeuf, Pierre Vidal, and Sordello, l. poetry was still a thing of the people, composed to be sung and enjoyed. The melodic element of the l. genre in the medieval period has not been equalled since the dawn of the Renaissance.

This is not to say that after 1400 the l. and music were immediately and completely disassociated; but in time, the divorcement became more apparent with the rise of such primarily melodic forms as the madrigal, glee, catch, and round which subordinated words to the musical line. In spite of the later efforts of writers primarily poets and not composers—Swinburne, Hopkins, Yeats, Vachel Lindsay, and Edith Sitwell—the l. genre since the Renaissance has remained a verbal rather than a musical discipline and the traces of a melodic origin have become largely vestigial. The influence of the Roman metricians on the It. and Fr. lyrical theorists of the Renaissance may have helped to produce the latter day emphasis on meter as a substitute for melody. Or Renaissance lyricists, writing for an aristocratic audience of readers, may simply have unconsciously adapted their forms to a different medium. In any event, the l. suffered a sea change after the 15th c. with the consequences noted above.

Renaissance lyrics, diffused as they are through several countries and centuries, nevertheless share certain general characteristics which are evidence of their common origin in the earlier Prov. lyrics. In Spain, l. poets fused their Mozarabic and Prov. traditions to perfect some older forms (the *cantiga* and possibly the *cossante*) and to develop some new ones (the *bacarola, bailada*, and others). After its inception in the Sicilian court of Frederick II, the *sonetto* rose to full perfection in Dante's *Vita Nuova* and Petrarch's *Sonnets to Laura*. Petrarch's *Canzoniere*, the prototype of It. l. poetry, contained sonnets, sestinas, ballatas, and even a few madrigals. In such Sonnets as nos. 33 ("Gia fiammeggiava l'amorosa stella") and 35 ("Solo e pensoso i piu deserti campi"), Petrarch struck the thematic chords that were to echo in the lyrics of countless imitators in Italy and England in the following centuries. In spite of excellent *canzone* written by Ariosto and others, it is Petrarch whose name remains synonymous with Renaissance It. art lyrical verse. More popular vernacular verse in Italy—the *strambotto* and *rispetto*—was also composed in great numbers.

What Petrarch was to lyric poetry in Italy, Ronsard was to the poetry of Renaissance France. The leader of the *Pléiade*, a stellar group of poets including Joachim Du Bellay, Ronsard published his version of the sonnets to Laura in *Les Amours* in 1552, and a later collection of sonnets, the *Sonnets pour Hélène*, in 1578. In addition to writing sonnets, Ronsard also composed odes, mythological and philosophical *Hymnes*, and elegiac and pastoral poems. Scorning the older forms of the rondeau and rondelle, Ronsard explored the whole range of lyric images and emotions in his sonnet collections. Though the earlier sonnets contained frank Petrarchan notes (e.g. "Cent et cent fois penser un penser mesme"), the later works were perfectly Ronsard's own ("Adieu, cruelle, adieu, je te suis ennuyeux"). The later ages of Fr. literature have traced Fr. lyricism back to Ronsard just as often as they have traced its antithesis back to Malherbe.

In England, the publication of *Tottel's Miscellany* in 1557 marked the beginning of the most lyrical of England's poetic eras. A collection of "songs," sonnets, and other kinds of verse, the *Miscellany* evidenced the musicality of Eng. poets of earlier periods and set up a form of anthology to be imitated by scores of compilations from *The Phoenix Nest* and *England's Helicon* to the eventual *Broadside Ballads* and Bishop Percy's *Reliques*. Wyatt and Surrey were among the first in England

to test the possibilities of the sonnet's thematic and metrical subtleties; and dozens of Eng. sonneteers—Sidney, Daniel, Spenser, Shakespeare *et al.*—published lengthy sonnet sequences, more or less directly patterned on Petrarch's. Certain old forms of the lyric were redeveloped in England, e.g. the prothalamium and epithalamium; and adulation for Horace and other L. lyric poets caused the vogue of the ode to become widespread. The song remained popular, both in its melodic and ballad forms, being written by such experts as Campion, Sidney, Ben Jonson, and Shakespeare.

In general, it may be said of Renaissance l. poetry that it was a succinct example of the philosophy of humanism. The lyric's preoccupation with the subjective self dovetailed neatly with the humanistic interest in the varied forms of human emotion; and the new geographical concerns of the Renaissance supplemented the pastoralism of the traditional l. to produce an imagery that enforced a fusion of the scientific and poetic perspectives. The effect of printing on the lyrical poets has already been touched on; and though the shifting nature of l. poetry was not apparent to those Renaissance critics who discussed that "divine" art—Minturno, Scaliger, Torquato Tasso, Sibilet, Gascoigne, Sidney—its aftermath was important in poetic practice as well as theory.

Although the past 300 years in the history of the l. may be divided into certain chronological "periods" (i.e., the Renaissance, Restoration, Augustan, *Fin de siècle*) or certain distinctive "movements" (metaphysical, neoclassical, romantic, symbolist, expressionist, naturalist, hermeticist, and so forth), these terms reveal little about the true nature of lyrical poetry and practice. Far more accurate is the designation of all l. poetry after 1600 as "modern." The range of this body of lyrics from the most objective or "external" to the most subjective or "internal" may be included in three chief l. types: the Lyric of Vision or Emblem, the Lyric of Thought or Idea, and the Lyric of Emotion or Feeling.

The L. of Vision or Emblem, although it has its antecedents in classic, Anglo-Saxon, and Chinese poetry, is nevertheless fundamentally the product of the Age of Type. It is this sort of lyric that Ezra Pound has discussed as "Ideograms" and Apollinaire has called "calligrammes." This is the most externalized kind of l., utilizing the pictorial element of print to represent the object or concept treated in the context of the poem itself: it is a literal attempt to follow MacLeish's admonition that "a poem should not mean, but be." The optical l. exists, therefore, in itself without need of reference to a private sensibility, whether of poet or reader. The first use of the visual in the modern l. came in the Elizabethan Age with the experiments of Gascoigne and George Puttenham, who wrote critical appraisals of the technique. Renaissance poets printed poems in the shape of circles, spires, and pillars. Later, George Herbert showed wings, altars, and floor patterns in poems on the subject; and the prevalence of pictorial lyrics among Fr. and Eng. poetasters of the 17th and 18th c. drew Dryden's scorn in *Macflecknoe* and Addison's laughter in *The Spectator*. The imagists of the 19th and 20th c., under Chinese influence, revived the practice; the symbolists were influenced by it; and the most recent practitioners of lyrical emblemism include Amy Lowell, H. D., William Carlos Williams, E. E. Cummings, and the French dadaists of the 1920's.

Somewhat more personal but still objective in tone and method is the L. of Thought or Idea, which may be divided into the Expository or Informative and the Didactic or Persuasive (critics like Drinkwater believe "l." and "didactic" to be contradictory terms). This school of lyricists is classically oriented, believing with Horace that poetry must be *utile* as well as *dulce* and consequently emphasizing musicality of form to balance prosaic content. The Expository l. writers include Boileau, Dryden, Cowper, Schiller, and Tennyson in former years; and such modern poets as Rainer Maria Rilke in his early descriptive works, the Sp. "naturalists" (Juan Ramón Jiménez, Jorge Guillén, Rafael Alberti), St. John Perse and T. S. Eliot are formulators of a lyrically expositional verse. The preoccupation of 19th- and 20th-c. poets with "sound" and verse form has produced vers libre, which is an obvious effort to accompany poetic statement with musical techniques just as the rigid heroic couplets of the neoclassical poetry of statement were.

The Didactic or Persuasive L. includes the allegorical, satiric, exhortatory, and vituperative species. L. allegory is apparent in the animal myths of La Fontaine, Herrick's use of Cupid, Mandeville's bees, Heine's Atta Troll, Arnold's merman, Davidson's dancers in the house of death, and Frost's departmental ants. The satiric l. includes, of course, the l. parody, such as Lewis Carroll's burlesques of Wordsworth and Swinburne's mockery of Tennyson; but it also includes directly satiric verse: Donne's verses on women, Mayakovsky's *Bedbug*, Bertolt Brecht's acrid observations on romantic love, Ogden Nash's disillusionment with life in Old Virginia. The exhortatory l. is often patriotic or moralistic as in the Elizabethan panegyrics on England, Burns's call to the Scots, Gabriel D'Annunzio's fervent championing of life and freedom, or Kipling's tributes to Britannia. The vituperative l. aims its darts everywhere: against critics (Pope's *Epistles*); convention (Rimbaud's *Illuminations*); war (Owen and Sassoon); poverty and suffering (Antonio Machado's Del Camino); or against the world in general (Allen Ginsberg's *Howl*). No discussion of the Didactic L. can ignore Ezra Pound's *Cantos*, which combine all of the subtypes—allegory, satire, exhortation, and vituperation—in a unique manner.

The most subjective or "internal" strain of modern l. poetry is the L. of Emotion or Feeling. It is this lyrical type which has become synonymous with "poetry" through the criticism of the romantic school and which is the prototype of the "personal" or "experienced" l. expression. The L. of Emotion comprises three major groups: the sensual l., the "imaginative" l. which intellectualizes emotional states, and the mystical l. The mystical l. is antipodal to the lyric of emblem: these two varieties of "vision" l., one literal and the other metaphorical, mark the extreme limits of objectivity and subjectivity which confine the l. genre.

The sensual l. enjoys an unbroken continuity from the 16th c. to the 20th in the sonnets of Ronsard and the *Pléiade*, the love poetry of the Elizabethans and metaphysicals, the erotica of the restoration and 18th c., the synaesthetic images of Keats and the romantics, the symbolist glorification of the self and its peculiar sensations, the neurotic sensualism of the Yellow Nineties, and the "new" sensualism of the Lost Generation, the Existentialists, and the Beat Generation. Ranging from the *carpe diem* to the *memento mori*, the sensual tradition is sustained in differing forms by Shakespeare, Donne, Collins, Herder, Heine, Baudelaire, Mallarmé, Whitman, D'Annunzio, Millay, and Dylan Thomas.

The "imaginative" or "intellectualized" l. of emotion furnishes a host of examples. The German lyricists provide a large number of these (notably Goethe and Schiller with Rilke, Hauptmann, and Stefan George as more recent examples). The "verbalized feelings" of the Eng. romantics and the Fr. symbolists have their modern counterparts in the lyrics of Apollinaire and Valéry, as well as in the poetry of García Lorca and the It. hermeticists, Ungaretti and Montale. Many of the lyrics of Pushkin and Boris Pasternak fall in this category. Writers of British lyrics of this type are Auden, MacNeice, Empson, and Spender; Americans include Emerson, Emily Dickinson, Frost, Jeffers, MacLeish, Wallace Stevens, and Marianne Moore. Finally, the poetry of mysticism is significant in modern l. history, possibly being an attempt to find some substitute for the Gr. myths which provoked the classic lyrics, or for the Christian mythology which stimulated the medieval l. Foremost among the mystical lyricists are Herbert, Vaughan, Smart, Blake, Hopkins, Baudelaire, Claudel, Yeats, and Rilke.

The abundance of lyrical poetry in the modern period is equaled, if not exceeded by the plethora of critical comments on and theories about that poetry. Mention was made above of the development of lyrical theory from Sidney to Joyce, but this is a meager indication of the vast body of critical writing resulting from the application of scientific methods to literary criticism. Perhaps the most exhaustive studies of the l. are contemporary German ones. Behrens, Rauch, Closs, Ermatinger, von Wiese, and Witkop are among those who have contributed expansive studies of the history of various l. traditions; and the theories of Staiger, Petsch, and Friedrich supplement this historical scholarship. In France, there are a number of academic critics, such as Henri Bonnet and Gaëtan Picon, although there are increasing numbers of writer turned critic who deal with literary theory and practice: Maurice Blanchot, Jean Rousselot, Seghers, Cocteau as well as Sartre and the existentialist critics belong to this group. In Spain, there is Ortega y Gasset. The Eng. tradition of the poet writing about poetry has developed into the backbone of criticism in England and America, where such practicing poets as Eliot, Auden, MacNeice, Empson, Thomas, Ransom, Tate, Warren, Elder Olson, Randall Jarrell, and Karl Shapiro have also doubled as critics of their own and others' work. There are, however, still a number of contemporary critics of the l. who are primarily critics and not creative writers: Cleanth Brooks, Edmund Wilson, I. A. Richards, Ivor Winters, Babette Deutsch, and the rest. So diverse are their theories of the l. that the interested must go to the original works for an accurate understanding of the distinguishing tenets of each critic's beliefs. Perhaps the task of future encyclopedists will be eased by a discriminating time which illuminates the outstanding critical works of the 20th c. while throwing the rest into darkness.

Thus from its primordial form of the song as the embodiment of an emotional reaction, the l. has been expanded, discussed, altered, and developed through the centuries until it has become one of the chief literary instruments which focus and evaluate the human condition. In flexibility, variety, and polish, it is perhaps the most proficient of the poetic genres. In the immediacy and keenness of its expression, it is certainly the most effective. These qualities have caused the 19th and 20th c. to look upon the l. as largely their own

work, but l. poetry has belonged to men of all ages.

GENERAL AND BIBLIOGRAPHICAL WORKS: F. B. Gummere, The Beginnings of Poetry (1901); J. Drinkwater, The L. (1915); Gayley and Kurtz; J. Pfeiffer, Das lyrische Gedicht als aesthetisches Gebilde (1931); M. R. Ridley, "The L.," E&s, 19 (1933); Behrens; G. Benn, Probleme der L. (1954); C. Heselhaus, Die L. des Expressionismus (1956); Frye.

SPECIALIZED STUDIES: J. Erskine, The Elizabethan L. (1903); F. E. Schelling, The Eng. L. (1913); G. B. Gray, The Forms of Hebrew Poetry (1915); E. Ermatinger, Die deutsche L. (1925); P. Witkop, Die deutschen Lyriker (1925); A Erman, The Lit. of the Ancient Egyptians, tr. A. M. Blackman (1927); P. S. Allen and H. M. Jones, The Romanesque L. (1928); H. J. C. Grierson, Lyrical Poetry of the 19th C. (1929); G. Murray, The Cl. Tradition in Poetry (1930); K. Rauch, Der L. eine Bresche (1931); G. Kar, Thoughts on the Mediaeval L. (1933); A. L. Wheeler, Catullus and the Traditions of Ancient Poetry (1934); Bowra; R. Brittain, The Mediaeval Latin and Romance L. to A.D. 1300 (1937); A. Closs, The Genius of the German L. (1938) and Die neuere deutsche L. (1951); M. Kastendieck, England's Musical Poet, Thomas Campion (1938); H. Färber, Die L. in der Kunsttheorie der Antike (1939); R. Petsch, Die lyrische Dichtkunst (1939); G. Errante, Sulla lirica romanza delle origine (1943); E. Staiger, Grundbegriffe der Poetik (2d ed., 1946); E. K. Chambers, Early Eng. Lyrics (1947); Dale; C. M. Ing, Elizabethan Lyrics (1951); J. Wiegand, Abriss der lyrischen Technik (1951); N. Maclean, "From Action to Image: Theories of the L. in the 18th C.," in R. S. Crane, Critics; M. Hadas, Ancilla to Classical Reading (1954); H. Friedrich, Die Struktur der modernen L. (1956); W. Killy, Wandlungen des lyrischen Bildes (1956; 2d enl. ed. 1958); J. L. Kinneavy, A Study of Three Contemporary Theories of L. Poetry (1956); B. von Wiese, Die deutsche L. (1957); C. Heselhaus, Deutsche L. der Moderne. Von Nietzsche bis Ivan Goll (1961); E. Muir, The Estate of Poetry (1962).　　　　J.W.J.

LYRICAL CAESURA. See CAESURA.

LYRISME ROMANTIQUE. An aspect of Fr. lyricism that drew upon the individual poet's private experience and emotions with an immediacy, particularity, and depth unprecedented in the language. Its development has been traced to the Rousseauistic cultivation of the self in profoundly subjective terms, which led to the romantic moralité des passions and in expression lent on occasion so lyric a quality even to prose that the first great poets of

Fr. romanticism have been identified as Rousseau and Chateaubriand. This contact with *le moi profond* introduced a new musicality into Fr. verse, and prepared for a revolution in Fr. poetic imagery and for at least a partial break with the domination of rhetoric in Fr. poetry. It lies also in the background of the irrational stress on the subconscious in symbolist and surrealist lyricism.—A. Monglond, *Le préromantisme français*, II (1930), 355–67; A. Thérive, "La nouvelle théorie du lyrisme," *La revue de Genève*, 4 (1922); H. Read, "The Romantic Revolution," *LonM*, 2 (1955). A.G.E.

M

MACARONIC VERSE incorporates words of the writer's native tongue in another language and subjects them to its grammatical laws, thus achieving a comic effect. The traditional basic language for m.v. is L. Tisi degli Odassi seems to have been the inventor of m.v.; he interspersed L. with It. (*Carmen maccaronicum*, 1488). Teofilo Folengo, however, using the same mixture, lent m.v. its renown through his famous mock-epic *Maccaroneae* (1517–21). Its anonymous Fr. translator (1606) describes Folengo as the "prototype of Rabelais." According to Folengo, the name "m.v." indicates a crude mixture—like that of flour, cheese, and butter in macaroni—and its burlesque appeal. The Fr. m. classic was Antoine de la Sablé. Priests (or Protestants) and literati were the favorite targets of m. satire. The wealth of German m. production (*Nudelverse*) is second only to that of the Italians, but, prior to Folengo's influence, it may have originated independently in Germany, that is, in student circles and with the mere intent to amuse. One of the rare examples of true m.v. in Eng. is the short 17th-c. epic *Polemo-Middinia*, ascribed to W. Drummond, in which L. terminations are skillfully tacked on to the Lowland Scots vernacular.

Loosely speaking, the term "m.v." has also been applied to any verse mingling two or more languages together, as in the OE *Macaronic Poem* (Krapp-Dobbie VI, 69–70), Máel Ísu Úa Brolchán's *Deus Meus* (*Early Ir. Lyrics*, ed. G. Murphy, 1956), the poems by J. Skelton, R. Brathwait's *Barnabae itinerarium* (1638), and, more recently, in the humorous verse of the American J. A. Morgan.

F. W. Genthe, *Gesch. der maccaronischen Poesie* (1829); J. O. Delepierre, *Macaronéa ou mélanges de litt. macaronique des différents peuples de l'Europe* (1852); J. A. Morgan, *M. Poetry* (1872); *Die Floia und andere deutsche maccaronische Gedichte*, ed. C. Blümlein (1900); *Anglo-Saxon Poetic Records*, ed. G. P. Krapp and E. V. Dobbie (6 v., 1931–53); W. O. Wehrle, *The M. Hymn Tradition in Medieval Eng. Lit.* (1933); U. E.

Paoli, *Il latino maccheronico* (1959); B. Ristow, "Maccaronische Dichtung in Deutschland," *Reallexikon*, 2d ed., II. U.K.G.

MACRON. See PROSODIC NOTATION.

MADNESS, POETIC. See POETIC MADNESS.

MADRIGAL. A short monostrophic, polyphonic song form. It originated in northern Italy in the 14th c.; those with texts written by Petrarch are good examples of the early type. Revived in the 16th c., the m. underwent a tremendous vogue which extended as far as England, where it was assiduously cultivated by the Elizabethan poets and composers.

In its metrical form the m. displays considerable variety, particularly in its later manifestations. The m. of the 14th c. was usually composed of 2 or 3 tercets followed by 1 or 2 rhyming couplets, the lines generally being of 7 or 11 syllables. By the time of its 16th-c. revival, however, its metrical form had become so free that Bembo, himself a composer of madrigals, wrote that it is bound by no rule concerning number of lines or arrangement of rhymes. But the last 2 lines almost always rhymed, and madrigals seldom exceeded 12 or 13 lines.

The following song from Shakespeare's *Measure for Measure* is a good example of the type of verse to which the term "m." was applied in the later Renaissance:

Take, O, take those lips away,
    That so sweetly were forsworn,
And those eyes, the break of day,
    Lights that do mislead the morn;
But my kisses bring again, bring again,
Seals of love, but seal'd in vain, seal'd in vain.

The echoing device in the final couplet is a characteristic refinement of the later m. verse.

The content of the earlier madrigals is generally pastoral, and the consistent themes of the form, throughout its history, remained nature and love. Verse of the m. type was written in the 19th c. by Carducci and D'Annunzio in Italy, by Goethe and Platen in Germany. The 20th c. has seen a great revival of m. singing in both England and America.— E. H. Fellowes, *Eng. M. Verse, 1588–1632* (1920), *The Eng. M. Composers* (1921) and *The Eng. M.* (1925); A. Einstein, "It. M. Verse," *Musical Ass., Proc.,* 63 (1937), *The It. M.* (3 v., 1949); B. Pattison, *Music and Poetry in the Eng. Renaissance* (1948).

MAGYAR POETRY. See HUNGARIAN POETRY.

MAITHILI POETRY. See INDIAN POETRY.

MAL MARIÉE. An OF song, often in ballade meter with a 2-line refrain, in which a married woman is overheard lamenting her marriage and calling upon her lover. In some of these the lover then appears and rescues her. A common variant is the lament of the nun who wants her *ami* to take her from the convent. Jeanroy insisted that this is a popular type which has spread from the Franco-Prov. border region; but it could be aristocratic in origin. There is one *malmaridada* by King Denis of Portugal, in imitation.—J. Bédier, "Les fêtes de mai et les commencements de la poésie lyrique au moyen âge," *Revue des deux mondes*, 135 (1896); Jeanroy, *Origines.* U.T.H.

MÁLAHÁTTR. An Eddic measure closely related to *fornyrðislag* (q.v.); each line of the 4-line stanza is divided into 2 half-lines by a caesura, and the half-lines have 2 accented and 3 (or even 4) unaccented syllables. The alliteration is similar to that of *fornyrðislag.* The following lines from *Atlamál en grænlenzku,* the only Eddic poem to employ this measure in its pure form, will serve as an example of its metrical construction:

Horsk vas húsfreyja, hugði at mannviti,

lag heyrði orða hvat á laun mæltu

The Poetic Edda, tr. H. A. Bellows (1923) and tr. L. M. Hollander (1928, rev. ed. 1962). R.B.

MALAY POETRY. Rude rhythmical verse, with stock tags to cover the reciter's flagging memory or inspiration, appears to have been the Malay's first essay in poetry. Known by a Tamil name, the form may have come from southern India. Specimens occur in the *Hikayat Raja-raja Pasai,* written between 1350 and 1500, but the best are found in the shaman's incantation, in Minangkabau songs of origin from Negri Sembilan and in such folk tales as *Awang Sulong, Maᶜlim Deman* and *Sri Rama.* With the *pantun,* they reach the highest level of Mal. poetry. Rhapsodist recitation of this verse left Mal. prose "a legacy

of balance and antithesis, like the antiphons of the Psalms, a device due not only to the need of chanting passages twice over for the ears of an audience liable to inattention but also to the relief afforded to a reciter, whose memory and inventiveness could not be at full stretch all the time."

While rhythmical vers libre must have been the oldest popular form, the earliest court verse recorded is on an Achehnese royal tombstone, dated A.D. 1380, in a pre-Muslim Indian script; this form is in the Sanskrit *upajátiᶜ* measure, which was employed by the Javanese also and may have given rise to the classical Mal. *shaᶜer* with its 4 rhyming lines. Many *shaᶜer* derive from the 15th c. and probably from Malacca where Mal. and Javanese mingled. A typical example, indebted to Java's *Panji* tales, is the *Ken Tambuhan.* But the Mal. *shaᶜer,* in such poems as the *Sĕri Bĕnian* and *Bidasari,* is inspired also by Indian romances of the period transitional between Hinduism and Islam. Later *shaᶜer* contain the folklore of the Muslim Deccan or are adapted, as by Hamzah of Barus at the end of the 16th c., for propagating Islamic mysticism. A good example from 18th c. Perak describes a royal picnic. And the next century saw *shaᶜer* on such various topics as a fire in Singapore, the Russo-Turkish War of 1854, the eruption of Krakatau, and Mal. pearl-fishing in Australia. But the favorite topics have been erotic or didactic and owe a debt to Persian and Arabic models. Today, in Indonesia, the *shaᶜer* form, outworn as the heroic couplet, has been supplanted by a variety of novel meters due to European influence.

By far the best and most interesting Mal. verse form is the *pantun,* which does not occur in literature before the 15th c. It would seem to have been begotten by jingling riddles (with assonance of internal as well as final syllables) upon the Indian *sloka* (q.v.), as it occurs in the *Ramayana* and *Sakuntala.* Like the *sloka* the Mal. quatrain may have all four lines rhyming, but in most the first line rhymes with the third, and the second line rhymes with the fourth. The Chinese ode, too, seems to have influenced the *pantun,* for in both, before coming to the topic of the poem, some natural object or well-known event is mentioned to prepare for what follows:

Asal kapas mĕnjadi bĕnang,
　Asal bĕnang mĕnjadi kain.
Asal lĕpas, jangan di-kĕnang,
　Sudah mĕnjadi orang lain.

From cotton coarse our thread we fashion,
　From the thread our cloth is wove.
No remorse! When sped the passion,
　I'm another, not your love.

In its assonance the *pantun* resembles the Persian *tarsi*, but at its best is "simple, sensuous and passionate." See also INDONESIAN POETRY.

ANTHOLOGIES: *Pantun Mĕlayu*, ed. R. J. Wilkinson and R. O. Winstedt (2d ed., 1955; an anthol. of verses by different poets—anonymous as always till lately); *Kesusasteraan Mĕlayu*, ed. R. Winstedt (6 v., 1958; anthologies of Mal. history, poetry, etc.); *Modern Mal. Verse, 1946–61*, eds. O. Rice and A. Majid (1963).

HISTORY AND CRITICISM: R. O. Winstedt, *The Malays, a Cultural Hist.* (1950) and "A Hist. of Mal. Lit." [rev. ed.], Royal Asiatic Society, Malayan Branch, *Jour.*, 31 (1958); E. Marrison, "A Mal. Poem in Old Sumatran Characters," Roy. As. Soc., Malayan Branch, *Jour.*, 24 (1951); P. G. Brewster, "Metrical, Stanzaic, and Stylistic Resemblances between Malayan and Western Poetry," RLC, 32 (1958). R.O.W.

MALAYALAM POETRY. See INDIAN POETRY.

MANNERISM in literature has the general meaning of affected or excessive use of a peculiar style; recently, in imitation of art history, it has been used to designate a period style between Renaissance and baroque. In tracing the origin of the word, we must go back to Vasari (1511–74), who used the word *maniera* to mean impressive and distinctive quality, and more particularly, the ability to join together single beauties into a beautiful whole. It came to mean affected style in the 17th c., and when it appeared in the form of an "-ism" in the chief European languages around 1800, it meant more or less artistic affectation. In this century a main effort in art history has succeeded in imposing a neutral and chronological meaning on the word. Between Michelangelo and Rubens lies the trajectory of a whole period, within which flourished artists like Tintoretto, Cellini, Breughel, and El Greco.

If m. were applied to a similar period in European literature, it would include authors like Antonio de Guevara (1480?–1545) and John Lyly (1554–1606), and perhaps others such as D'Aubigné and Tasso. In the case of the first two, the difficulty would be in distinguishing their style from similar styles in late antiquity and the Middle Ages; and, in the case of the latter two, it would be in distinguishing their style from baroque. An ambitious scheme, deriving from the art-historical concept of mannerist style, is attempted in *Four Stages of Renaissance Style* (1955) by W. Sypher. In Donne and *Hamlet*, e.g., he finds a kind of instability which, according to the scheme, existed between the two syntheses of Renaissance and baroque. More

demonstration would be needed, especially on a European scale.

In the meantime, the most useful application of m. to letters is in the general, nonhistorical sense of literature which depends heavily on ornament or ingeniousness. Prime examples would be the elaborately balanced or antithetical styles of Guevara and Lyly, the lush ornate style of Marino, the evocative sensual style of D'Annunzio and Valle-Inclán, and numerous artificial styles in poetry since Mallarmé. Among rhetorical devices used in abundance by mannerists are, to follow E. R. Curtius, hyperbaton, periphrasis, *annominatio* (paranomasia), and affected metaphors. Others would of course be found in particular cases. —Curtius; E. B. O. Borgerhoff, "M. and Baroque: A Simple Plea," CL, 5 (1953). See also A. M. Boase, "The Definition of 'M.,'" Intern. Comparative Lit. Assoc. *Proc. of the Third Congress* (1962); R. Daniells, *Milton, M. and Baroque* (1963). L.N.

MARATHI POETRY. See INDIAN POETRY.

MARINISM can usefully be accorded three ranges of meaning: the poetic style of Giambattista Marino (1569–1625); the style of a number of It. poets who may be considered direct disciples; and the general influence Marino had on other poets in Europe in the baroque period. It is often thought vaguely equivalent to preciosity, gongorism, euphuism, etc., usually by way of wholesale condemnation. A more precise view would hold that marinism is a species of baroque (q.v.) poetic style, and therefore a cousin to preciosity and gongorism, but only distantly related to euphuism.

Marino's several collections of lyrics, *La Lira* (1602–14), *La Galleria* (1620) and *La Sampogna* (1620), show the usual baroque gamut of subject matter, from sensuality to religiosity. His knowledge of It. poetry was considerable; one finds especially the influence of Ariosto and Tasso. There is, however, less direct Petrarchan influence than among the so-called *antimarinisti;* instead of ideal, nostalgic, tender love, Marino celebrates actual, languid, sensual love-making. His great reservoir, particularly for his most imposing work *L'Adone* (1623), is the whole of polished or sentimentalized mythology to be found in poets like Ovid and Claudian. The "fable" of this enormous poem (5,123 octaves) is, to cite Marino's own words, "narrow and incapable of incident"; nevertheless, he manages to "lengthen it with digressions and other luxuriances." His means are an unsparing use of catalogues, processions, tableaux, and miscellaneous descriptions. The style is characterized by rambling syntax, correlative clauses, inexorably pursued metaphors; moreover, the language is highly adjectival and sensually suggestive. As in Góngora's poems and Shakespeare's *Venus and Adonis*, frozen metaphors become, so to say, *lingua franca* in the poem: "purple" takes the place of "blood," "ivory" or "snow" of "white," etc.

It must be granted that Marino's poetry has variety within its narrow limits and that it has a mellifluousness remarkable even in It. poetry. There is also merit in the satirical and burlesque poems, especially in the *Murtoleide* (publ. in 1619) which was directed against the poetaster Gaspare Mùrtola. It is there that we find the supposed "poetics" of Marino ("Fischiata XXXIII"): "The poet's goal is wonder (I speak of the excellent and not the clumsy poet): he who does not know how to astonish, let him take up the currycomb!"

During Marino's stay in Paris (1615-23) at the court of Marie de Médicis and Louis XIII, there is no evidence that he frequented the Hôtel de Rambouillet (see PRÉCIOSITÉ); yet one of its habitués Jean Chapelain wrote a "Lettre ou Discours . . . sur le Poëme d'Adonis du Chevalier Marino" in extravagant praise of the poet, which he later modified, saying that the poem was "a bottomless and edgeless sea and that no one but Saint-Amant has been able to survey it completely." In Italy, of course, Marino's influence was pervasive. His best known direct disciple is Claudio Achillini; yet even his opponents, such as Tommaso Stigliani and Gabriello Chiabrera could hardly escape his impress. Elsewhere, in England, his love lyrics had a certain vogue, and were translated or imitated by such poets as William Drummond of Hawthornden, Thomas Carew, Edward Sherburne, and Thomas Stanley. Marino's greatest influence here is on Richard Crashaw, who translated, under the title *Sospetto d'Herode* (1637), the first book of his *Strage degli Innocenti* (publ. in 1632). In Germany Marino's chief debtor was Christian Hofmann von Hofmannswaldau. In Spain the situation was, in a sense, reversed; not only did Góngora occupy any possible place Marino might have taken, but also Marino found himself tempted to borrow from Lope de Vega.

B. Croce, *Lirici marinisti* (1910) and *Storia dell' età barocca in Italia* (1925); L. P. Thomas, *Góngora et le gongorisme considérés dans leurs rapports avec le marinisme* (1911); G. Balsamo-Crivelli, "Introduzione" to his ed. of *L'Adone* (1922); M. Praz, *Seicentismo e marinismo in Inghilterra* (1925); A. Belloni, *Il Seicento* (1929); H. Geibel, *Der Einfluss Marinos auf Christian Hofmann von Hofmannswaldau* (1938); D. Alonso, "Lope de Vega despojado por Marino" and "Adjunta a Lope de Vega despojado por Marino," RFE, 33 (1949); *Marino e i marinisti*, ed. G. G. Ferrero (1954); F. J.

Warnke, "Marino and the Eng. Metaphysicals," *SRen*, 2 (1955); F. Croce, "Nuovi compiti della critica del Marino e del marinismo," *Rassegna della letteratura italiana*, 61 (1957); J. V. Mirollo, *The Poet of the Marvelous: Giambattista Marino* (1963).   L.N.

MARXIST CRITICISM. See CRITICISM, TYPES OF.

MASCULINE ENDING. See LINE ENDINGS; for MASCULINE RHYME, see RHYME.

MASQUE. The m. developed in the Renaissance as an entertainment in which a procession of masqued or otherwise disguised figures represented a highly imaginative action interspersed with speeches and songs. Many native and foreign traditions contributed to its various forms—morris dancing, mummers' pageants, *ludi*, "disguisings," "triumphs," ballets, morality plays, etc. In Italy, where the m. first acquired a distinctive form, the splendor of the spectacle was of the greatest importance to the presentation of the mythological or similarly fantastic subjects that provided the usual themes. Settings were designed by the greatest artists, Brunelleschi and Leonardo among them, according to the most sophisticated and imaginative taste, and machines were invented to incorporate fountains, artificial clouds, and fire in the production. A single setting might include several scenes in which more than one action or dance would be performed, concurrently or in sequence. The court masques of England equalled these in magnificence and taste even when they were being developed towards a more definite dramatic structure.

Circe, a *ballet de cour* produced in Paris in 1581, exerted a great influence on Eng. masques in providing the example of greater dramatic and thematic unity than had previously been usual. Ben Jonson's and Inigo Jones's *The Masque of Blacknesse* in 1605 moved still further toward establishing dramatic unity as a principle governing the structure of masques by fixing a single concentrated scene for the action upon a stage erected at one end of the hall.

Jonson conceived of the m. as primarily the work of a poet. In the preface to *Hymenaei* (1606) he argued that the design and the words of the m. are its soul, the spectacle and mime and dancing its body. He was thus proposing for the m. a fixed principle, Neoplatonic not merely in declaring the "body" of the m. to be the expression of the "soul," but in claiming the invention itself to be the expression of ideal beauty and truth. To Jonson is also due the credit of inventing the antimasque, a briefer m. to accompany the main one, ordinarily preceding it. This would represent grotesque or comic figures to contrast with the mythological or allegorical personages that were the staple of the main m. For both parts Jonson supplied erudite illustrations in marginalia, partly to point to the philosophic and emblematic nature of the very conception of the works.

Jones, Jonson's collaborator from 1605–31, regarded the spectacle as the main thing, and his own work, after the separation from Jonson, continued to give the greatest scope to visual magnificence. The means for such productions was made available from time to time during the reign of Charles I (Shirley's *Triumph of Peace* [1634] was as lavishly produced as anything under Henry VIII), but with the fall of the Stuarts and the destruction of the conditions that had made the court m. possible, the interest in masques was absorbed in various theatrical and operalike productions.

There had been some place for masques on the Elizabethan stage. The informal, improvised kind that seems to have been very popular in actuality is briefly shown in *Romeo and Juliet*. The more elaborate forms are rather fully presented in *Cymbeline, The Winter's Tale* and *The Tempest*. In the Jacobean and Stuart periods the establishment of the proscenium arch advanced a special form of the m. that has been called "the substantive theatre masque." After the Restoration, masques were sometimes assimilated in the new operatic forms, but in independent productions they appear to have been offered as special kinds of opera, as one may think the 18th-c. productions of *Comus* were regarded. Whatever the variations, one might say that a m. always derives its form from the initial conception of royalty assuming the role or joining the company of the allegorized divinities of classical belief and, after the fable and dancing are concluded, reverting to its own splendor. Such a combining of dynasty and fancy and moralizing expresses the highest aspirations of a humanist society, the partnership of power and culture in a sententious and joyful entertainment. In the concluding dance, when the masquers, now unmasqued, take their partners from the audience, there is the culminating recognition of the ease and grace and blessedness of the society the actors and dancers in their true selves govern. The spirit of the m. is the opposite of that of the carnival, being royal and noble and classical.

The anti-m. is the other side of the coin, the comic treatment of the unruly, of the forces and elements royalty subdues. To remain true to the tone of the m., the anti-m. opposes it not in satire, which would be alien to the assurance of the rulers, but in the grotesque, the wicked, useless, and amusing imaginings of the ignoble and unworthy.

The combining of music and dancing with drama and spectacle was directed toward a balance that excluded the tensions of drama, and much of the controversy between Ben Jonson and Inigo Jones relates to the problem of how much the burden of meaning and the presentation of character may be allowed to challenge the primarily choreographical and musical movement. Similarly, the spectacular effects were important as much for their variety and their changes as for their dramatic propriety.

R. Brotanek, *Die englischen Maskenspiele* (1902); A. Solerti, *Musica, Ballo e drammatica alla corte Medicea dal 1600 al 1637* (1905); P. Reyher, *Les Masques anglais* (1909); H. Prunières, *Le Ballet de cour en France avant Benserade et Lully* (1914); L. B. Campbell, *Scenes and Machines on the Eng. Stage During the Renaissance* (1923); *Designs by Inigo Jones for Masques and Plays at Court*, ed. P. Simpson and C. F. Bell (1924); E. Welsford, *The Court M.* (1927); A. Nicoll, *Stuart Masques and the Renaissance Stage* (1938); D. J. Gordon, "Poet and Architect: The Intellectual Setting of the Quarrel between Ben Jonson and Inigo Jones," JWCI, 12 (1949); J. Arthos, *On A Mask Presented at Ludlow-Castle, by John Milton* (1954); E. Haun, "An Inquiry into the Genre of Comus," in *Essays in Honor of Walter Clyde Curry* (1954); *Les Fêtes de la Renaissance*, ed. J. Jacquot (1956).

J.A.

MASTERSINGERS. See MEISTERSINGER.

MATHEMATICAL LINGUISTICS. See LINGUISTICS AND POETICS.

MEANING, PROBLEM OF. In treating the nonaesthetic functions of poetry, we may pose problems about its social or political function, its moral function, its religious function. But logically prior to these problems is the problem which asks about the kind of meaning we find in poetry if, indeed, what we find is anything like what we conventionally call "m." For what we think about the social-political, the moral, or the religious function of poetry depends largely on what we conceive to be the capacity of poetry to make meaningful statements about these spheres of human activity. And to determine this capacity we must know whether poetry can make meaningful statements about anything; and, if it can, in what way it manages to do so.

Of course, in these days of such extensive semantic analysis in philosophy, the very meaning of "m." is continually disputed. And especially worrisome is the use of this word in reference to the peculiar kind of symbols employed in poetic discourse. For purposes of economy we shall simply restrict "m." to its primitive sense which concerns the reference of verbal symbols and their syntactic relations to the outside world of things and their real relations. This limitation will immediately dismiss that perhaps eccentric sense of "m.," in somewhat common usage of late in poetics, which would treat only the aesthetic, intramural coherence among the words of a literary work in accordance with the internal consistency of their closed system of interrelations.

Because of the dominance of "imitationism" in the history of criticism through much of the 18th c., the simple referential view of poetic m. also went without serious challenge. Whether, like Sir Philip Sidney, critics approved or, like Plato, disapproved what poetry was saying, they were in wide agreement about its ability to say it. It is true, however, that in following the doctrine of imitation critics have been of two kinds, those who proclaimed the objective of poetry to be literal imitation or imitation of the particular and the far greater number who proclaimed it to be ideal imitation or imitation of the universal. Both could invoke the backing of Aristotle and even of Plato, whether they wanted poetry to copy life as it really is or to capture life as, freed from the imperfections of individuality, it ideally ought to be. Literary realists or literalists there have always been; but even as sophisticated and influential a recent philosopher as Charles W. Morris— who, as an anti-Platonist denies any relation of art to universals—appears to join the literal imitationists in his contribution to aesthetics of the notion of the "iconic sign."

Those who, like Samuel Johnson, thought purely in terms of an expanded concept of imitation that would deal not with the individual but with the species, have been far more influentially concerned with the nature of poetic m. For once poetry is not considered as a detailed mirror of minute actuality, the truth of its m. must for the imitationist depend on the general statements it makes or illustrates, since the representative type given us in a poem is treated as a sign pointing to a universal, which has an objective reality more certain and significant than that of mere particulars. As Sidney, citing Aristotle, puts it, poetry is superior to both history and philosophy. History describes particulars only; as descriptive it can never give us universal truth or tell us how to act. Philosophy can do both, but its terms are too general for us to apply the universal truth or general precept to the individual case. Poetry surpasses history in that its universal truths tell us how life *ought*

to be and it surpasses philosophy in that it gives us the particular example. In this way Sidney resolves the ever-present problem of poetic theory which asks how poetry can be at once universal and particular. The poem exists primarily for its message or paraphrasable m., with its content irrevocably separated from its form, which—as merely a suitable felicity of language—can act only as embellishment. The felicity is there to help persuade, but it is thus performing a rhetorical rather than a poetic function. In addition to Sidney and Johnson, a greater number of distinguished writers in our critical tradition have maintained at least a qualified version of this view of poetic m. than have held any other: Horace, medieval writers like Dante and Boccaccio, most 16th-c. It. critics, neoclassicists like Dryden, Boileau, Addison, and Pope. Even in our own time, when, as an aftermath to Victorian didacticism, the wide acceptance of organicism has made this an unpopular view, we may detect an affinity to it in the neo-Humanists and even, perhaps, in Yvor Winters as well as in aestheticians like T. M. Greene.

However, as philosophic realism had sanctioned imitationism in poetics, so philosophic idealism often led to the opposite, poetic expressionism. For the idealist, the pure, mental creations of what William Blake termed the poetic genius could become a measure of ultimate reality more trustworthy than the limiting illusions of the external world. And poetry was to reflect the godlike mind rather than what was outside it. So profound a difference had to make itself felt in conceptions of poetic m. Thus there have been other, more romantic critics who have claimed there is more than one kind of m. and who would not lower the dignity of poetry by having it at the service of so inferior a kind of m. as the one here described as propositional. Rather, in seeing a psychological opposition between the reason and the imagination, they have regarded poetry as dedicated to the kind of m. furnished by the unbounded powers of the latter faculty. Since the imagination, as the poetic faculty, is considered the only means of reaching this transcendent m., their claims would make the cognitive function of poetry a unique and irreplaceable one, whereas the more traditional view we have examined sees poetry as involved with the same kind of m. as can be obtained—and probably more immediately, if less persuasively, obtained—from more directly discursive modes of language.

The first hint we get of this intuitionist view, strangely enough, may very well also come from Plato, who in his *Ion* pictures the poet as divinely inspired and even as possessed. He is the man chosen by the gods to intuit the highest truths. This definition of the poet was developed into the first theories of imagination by Dion Chrysostom, Philostratus, and finally by the Neoplatonic Plotinus. But it does not attain its most systematic and influential expression until the conception of imagination becomes a central concern of German idealism and is passed on to segments of British as well as German romanticism. Closer to our own period, Henri Bergson and Benedetto Croce are the principal exponents of this general position.

It is a position that would seem to demand a special metaphysic. If we look, for example, at the influential theory of F.W.J. Schelling, the theory that provided Coleridge with his concept of imagination, we find that he can grant such cognitive powers to the imagination only because he posits a monistic universe whose divine essence or ground lies immanently within every particular object. If the whole is in every part and never exists except in the part—if the ground, in other words, is only immanent and never transcendent—then only by fully apprehending the part can we intuit the indwelling whole. This activity certainly is not to be entrusted to our abstract reasoning power, which can never fully appreciate the particular. Nor need our intuition be subject, like propositional truth, to a rational check since imagination, beyond reason, can hardly be contained by the inferior disciplines which reason provides. The imagination, then, is the faculty which produces art since it captures the particular completely and sees through it to the underlying essence. And the act of imagination—the perception of a particular and seemingly lifeless object, which infuses it, through the power of mind, with the dynamic essence of the universe—is literally an act of cognition, the most crucial act of cognition we can perform. Of course, the relation between the universal and particular given us by Schelling is not at all like that given us by Sidney. Sidney considered poetry, with its use of particulars, as another path to propositional truth—from below, as it were, rather than from above. For Schelling the truth of poetry is the only final truth. The m. of the universe is revealed intuitively, through the vehicle of art, or it is not revealed at all.

But there are those too who have denied that poetry has any important dealings with any kind of m. They have not been interested in relating what is in the literary work to the nonaesthetic world outside—to life, as we usually term it. Rather they have sought to locate the function of poetry solely in its affective relations with its reader. Poetry for them exists not for what it is or for what, in terms of life generally, it means but for what

it can do for us. While the older version of this approach commonly ended in hedonism, the more recent version—perhaps following a different path out of the Aristotelian tradition —usually ends by seeing poetry as therapy. Once poetry is denied the power of illumination that we associate with life-meanings, the only justification that can be claimed for its existence is the pleasure it can provide or the emotions it can affect. As the view that poetry yields propositional m. was seen to concentrate on the content or the teaching aspects of the poem, so this view concentrates on the formal or the pleasing aspects of the poem.

Many have held the view, that, as pleasure-giving, poetry is its own justification. As has been intimated, it has cropped up here and there as a minority version of Aristotelianism. A very few 16th-c. It. critics, notably Castelvetro and Mazzoni, expounded varying forms of this heresy amid the flourishing didactic theories. Only a faint, dissident voice in the Renaissance, this view was comparatively without adherents until the 19th c. But from the time that Gautier enunciated the slogan "l'art pour l'art," the movement grew. With its notion of pleasure restricted to the delicate aesthetic pleasure, it has since dominated the Fr. symbolist and Eng. aesthetic movements. And more recently it has dominated such "formalists" in the plastic arts as Clive Bell and Roger Fry, some Rus. literary formalists, and those who may constitute the only equivalent school in current Am. literary criticism, the Chicago neo-Aristotelians.

In order to assert poetry's affective function, the various proponents of this view, whatever their differences, have denied its cognitive function. Thus the neo-Aristotelian Elder Olson has suggested that it is absurd to think of a poem having a m. since the poem means only itself. Only those who are unmoved by the emotional effect of the poem feel the need to justify it by an irrelevant search after m. Frequently, too, critics who have taken this position have been forced to deny poetry any real importance in the total human economy unless, for the sake of a pure, unburdened art and the rarefied aesthetic emotion it permits, they deny the importance of all man's other and more time-consuming activities. But this is the by-product one would expect of a theory whose increasing popularity in the last hundred years has been largely dependent on the increasing dominance of the intellectual arena by scientific positivism. If knowledge is to be restricted to the sort of thing that allows of proof in the laboratory manner so that even speculative philosophy comes to be considered emotive rather than meaningful, how can poetry, so much less rigorous a mode of discourse, be justified except by abandoning any pretense at m. in order to seize upon its unquestioned capacity to please and to move?

While I. A. Richards (see BELIEF, PROBLEM OF) explicitly renounces any pleasure-theory, in denying m. to poetry and in claiming that poetry operates therapeutically by improving our neurological health, he may seem dangerously close to such a theory. He sees "referential discourse," with its use restricted to science, as giving propositional truth. In order to do so efficiently it must employ signs that are as transparent as possible: the relation of the sign to the thing or concept it represents must be as close to one-to-one as possible. But if this thin discourse is lucid, it is also—compared to less exact and more distorted discourse—cold and unfeeling. Thus there is also a need for an "emotive discourse," although as a positivist Richards cannot allow it a claim to truth. For it is not referential in character; if it were it would lose its warmth, its capacity to appeal to large and complex groups of impulses in readers. Instead of statements, then, poetry, as emotive, contains "pseudo-statements" (see PSEUDO-STATEMENT); it is pure myth. It exists only to affect our total psychology, a function until now and in the foreseeable future beyond the cold powers of laboratory-controlled knowledge. Since emotive discourse does not literally mean anything, since it finally points only to itself, there is no need for clarity. Ambiguity may be allowed, even encouraged, since the denser the discourse the more complexity it has and the more effectively it can perform its neurological task, which Richards defines as the arousal in the reader of as broad an organization of impulses—and of opposed impulses—as possible. The emotive-referential dichotomy, used by Richards to find an important place for poetry in an age of science, has also been commonly used to the detriment of poetry by philosophers of a positivistic bent who are more antihumanistic in intention.

However, some antipositivistic modern critics—for example, Allen Tate, Cleanth Brooks, and in places John Crowe Ransom—transform the elements of Richards' dichotomy in order to restore m. to emotive discourse, although, since the dichotomy is still maintained, it is a very different sort of m. from that yielded by referential discourse. They put in Richards' referential category the abstractions from the world made by science or philosophy for its own purposes. But this is for them hardly the only kind of m. there may be since the abstractions of science or philosophy hardly exhaust all that there is in the world. Indeed either science or philosophy must leave unaccounted for what is to these critics the most significant aspects of the world we experience

—what Ransom calls the particularities in "the world's body"—since these are the aspects which must slip through the inhumane sieve of formulae which either discipline must use to accomplish its limited purposes. These critics see the inadequacy of philosophy as well as of science, of propositional discourse in general, to be caused by the fact that it is and ought to be so purely referential. Because it is thin and its relation to things one-to-one, it cannot help but be generic, abstract. Brooks, for example, claims that, as ideally pure symbols, the terms of science are to be static and unyielding and are thus not to be highly charged and made dense with contextual qualifications and complexities. They obviously cannot be intended to do justice to the dynamics and the fullness of our experiential world. But in poetry the endless verbal complexities produced by qualifications, ambiguities, paradoxes, and ironies keep the alert reader from using the poem crudely, from treating it as a mere sign. The involved data of human experience must be sifted as little as possible, so that as much as can be aesthetically accommodated may come through into the poem.

According to this view, poetry, in a sense less useful because it is literally confounded, has a kind of m. afforded by no other form of discourse. It is different from propositional m., as we have seen; nor is it the intuitional m. suggested for poetry by the romantics discussed earlier. It is not related to any faculty-psychology and it is not to break through to the essential realities of a noumenal world. Rather it is related to the immediate world of our experience. Its difference from referential m., a difference caused by the peculiar and complex nature of the poetic context, is that it deals with a world differently conceived in accordance with a difference of purpose—or indeed a suspension of any precise and systematic purpose. And, as contrasted to referential m., the m. yielded by the poetic context might be termed "presentational m.," a many-faceted reflection of the fullness of experience which has its own rightful place as a possible cognitive function of discourse.

C. K. Ogden and I. A. Richards, *The Meaning of M.* (1923); I. A. Richards, *Science and Poetry* (1926); C. W. Morris, "Esthetics and the Theory of Signs," *Jour. of Unified Science*, 8 (1939); "Science, Art and Technology," KR, 1 (1939); T. M. Greene, *The Arts and the Art of Crit.* (1940); J. C. Ransom, "Wanted: an Ontological Critic," *The New Crit.* (1941); J. Hospers, *M. and Truth in the Arts* (1946); C. Brooks, "The Heresy of Paraphrase" and "The Problem of Belief and the Problem of Cognition," *The Well Wrought Urn* (1947); A. Tate, "Lit. as Knowledge," *On the Limits of Poetry* (1948); E. Olson, "A Symbolic Reading of the Ancient Mariner," in Crane, *Critics*; W. K. Wimsatt, Jr., "The Concrete Universal," *The Verbal Icon* (1954); E. Vivas, "Lit. and Knowledge," *Creation and Discovery* (1955); Krieger; Wheelwright; Frye; M. Krieger, "Recent Crit., Thematics, and the Existential Dilemma," *The Tragic Vision* (1960); R. Foster, *The New Romantics* (1962).   M.KRIE.

MEASURE. A metrical group or period. The m. may consist of the dipody as in classical iambic, trochaic, and anapaestic verse, or of the foot as in Eng. verse. In the so-called musical theories of versification the m. is usually the time sequence consisting of syllables beginning with a main accent and running to the next: "Night's / candles / are burnt / out, and / jocund / day" (*Romeo and Juliet* 3.5.9). In this example the initial word is an example of anacrusis (q.v.); there follow 4 measures of 2 syllables each, of relatively equal time; the final word belongs to the m. ended in the initial syllable of the following line.   R.O.E.

MEDIEVAL POETICS. All art of the Middle Ages is unified by Christianity and therefore begins with Christ and the Apostles. There is as yet no definitive study of med. poetics. This article especially refers to Western Christendom, where L. was the language of criticism, even of vernacular poetry.

The nearly fifteen centuries are divided into three periods of roughly equivalent length: (1) A *patristic period,* in which the foremost minds of the ancient world (*patres,* Fathers) developed a catholic culture out of diverse cultures—Semitic, Persian, Coptic, Hellenic, Italic, Celtic. The unifying element was belief in the Incarnation as revealed in the rhetoric of Christ and the Apostles (*traditio*) and the literature of the Holy Spirit (*sacrae scripturae*). (2) A *scholastic period,* in which that culture was transmitted to all people, largely barbarian and predominantly illiterate, by the regular (monastic) or secular clergy. (3) A *secularizing period,* in which the verbal arts, for half a millennium the special language of that single profession, spread to the nobility, the emergent professions, and the bourgeoisie.

(1) Throughout the pagan Empire, *poet* was primarily defined in four ways: by derivation, as a maker or creator; by assimilation, as a *vates,* who penetrated into very nature; by discrimination, as a fabulist devoted to entertainment (*dilectatio*) as contrasted with the historian devoted to record (*res gestae*); by synecdoche, as a versifier. Since in the creed of the Fathers God alone created, poetry in the first sense was false; "poet" became an opprobrious term for those who created false gods, to the delusion of the people. To the second sense the Fathers were more favorable; the Hebrews had regarded writing as more divine than had the rhetorically inclined Greeks and Romans. The poet did not create; but by the will of God he discovered the Truth, as did prophets. And he cast this living Truth into literary form. God, Himself the Creator, allowed His poem to be seen in fragments or shadows, except in the single instance of the Incarnate Christ, the Logos. Verbalized revelation of that True Poem in the Catholic Scriptures was the measure of all. Since these scriptures were, in the main, not versified, few Christian writers used *poet* in the fourth sense, lest it confuse the central issue; for metrical and other regulated lines they used *versus* and the like. Nevertheless, they intensely studied and practiced metrical and ornamental arts, which were aspects of Truth, discovered by or revealed to man. But perhaps poetry was most widely thought of in the third sense; for most Fathers, including Augustine, regarded the poets as fabulists, valuable only as their fables induced good morality. As such they were to be despoiled (as Moses despoiled the Egyptians) for Christian doctrine.

Adherence to these principles meant that poetics, in the classical or neoclassical sense, would not be composed; for theory could not guide creation, nor could criticism influence it. Nevertheless, the recipient of True Poetry needed to understand it. Consequently nearly all that the Fathers wrote was interpretation of Scripture—that is, exegesis—and may therefore in a general sense be regarded as poetics. Unlike the rhetoricians, the Fathers addressed themselves to readers as individuals; each reader was responsible for the effect of the poetry upon himself.

The center of exegesis was Alexandria, where *grammar,* that is, study of letters, had developed in the last pre-Christian centuries. Secondary centers were the apostolic sees of Antioch and Rome, and Caesarea, which early developed a great Christian library. In the Gr. world, Constantinople (Byzantium) became the heir to this Christian learning. There an active literary life continued until the 15th c. As in all aspects of its culture, Byzantine literary criticism was ultraconservative. Photius (ca. 820–897) and Tzetzes (1110–ca. 1183) are outstanding. But Byzantine criticism had almost no effect upon the West from the 6th to the 14th c.

At Alexandria, Philo the Jew, contemporary with Christ, established allegorical interpretation of Hebrew Scriptures. Clement of Alexandria and his pupil, the amazing Origen, predicating a perfect unity in a corpus of "canonical" works, resolved apparent discrepancies among the literal statements by an allegorical method—not verbal allegory, which is characteristic of poetry in any age, but an allegory of things—an actual relationship as of type and typed between events, expressed by verbal symbols. Only the chosen few (*eruditi, electi, philosophi*) had the power of apprehending the true meaning beneath the integument; the unsophisticated mass must be content with the literal (*carnalia, superficialia, historia*). This distinction of audience was akin to, but not identical with, the classical distinction of liberal and servile. The new form of polysemous interpretation, though intensely popular, especially with the monks, had its detractors in the Antiochene school. Nevertheless, both parties gave themselves wholly to understanding Truth through writing: Gr. Fathers like Athanasius, Eusebius, Basil, the two Gregorys, Theodore of Mopsuestia, John Chrysostom; Latin Fathers like Tertullian, Cyprian, Arnobius, Lactantius, Ambrose, Rufinus, and Vincent of Lerins, but especially Jerome and Augustine.

Jerome, translator of the Scriptures, composed commentaries upon virtually every book of the canon and wrote many tracts upon literary education, methods of translation, inspiration, and literal and figurative meaning. His *Illustrious Men* was a literary history designed to give status to the Christian writers above the pagans; his hagiography encouraged Western Christians to cultivate the arts of "Greek romance"; his *Chronicle* formulated world history for later writers; his textual criticism formed the "Vulgate" of the West; his exegesis detached veneration from verbalism and centered attention on the thing expressed. He established, or confirmed, the lasting principle of Christian and pagan literary correspondence. Augustine, himself a professor of rhetoric before his conversion, especially through his earlier *Master* and *Order* and his later *Christian Doctrine*, stamped with the approval of the most influential Father the concept of seven disciplines as rational steps to True Philosophy. Since these disciplines, as he formulated them, consisted of grammar as the base with rhetoric and dialectic as other verbal arts, and music, geometry, astronomy, and "numbers" as rungs leading from material to pure intelligence, poetry was excluded, except as a kind of servant of grammar. These Latin Fathers played down form while emphasizing image and figure.

(2) In the 5th c. and thereafter to, roughly speaking, the Norman Conquest of England and Italy, the collapsed western empire, overrun by Teutons, Moslems, Hungarians, and Scandinavians, had only the claustral clergy to preserve and disseminate culture. Because their business was teaching at an elementary level, the culture was markedly traditional and scholastic. Though the very foundations of modern poetry were laid and its conventions shaped in this period, there was neither leisure nor inclination for criticism. Following Augustine, four writers whose texts became standard also neglected poetry. Boethius furnished the scholastic basis for philosophy, translating Aristotle's and others' works on rhetoric and logic, but he was executed before he treated poetics, if indeed he ever intended to. Cassiodorus, his successor as Master of Offices under Theodoric, founded a monastic school in southern Italy and wrote a syllabus for it (*Institutiones*). He adhered to the seven disciplines, as did the African Martianus Capella (*De Nuptiis*). Isidore of Seville, whose compendious encyclopaedia (*Etymologiae*) was very popular, treated the seven arts in detail, but relegated poetry to a book (8) in which he treated all forms of heresy and the pagan philosophers, poets, Sibyls, magi, and gods; his notion of poets as pseudo-creators influenced nearly every schoolboy. Bede treated *The Art of Meter*, in which the isosyllabic rhythms were first identified, and *Figures and Tropes*; he emphasized the kinship of pagan and Christian poetry by drawing his examples of classical poetic figures from the sacred scriptures. The masters whom Charlemagne assembled in an abortive renaissance, led by Alcuin from England, Paul the Deacon from Lombardy, and Theodulf from Visigothic Spain, partially revived study of ancient poetry, especially bucolics and epic, but their critical statements are of little importance now. John Scotus, who with Heiric and Remigius of Auxerre introduced the method of scholastic glosses, did begin a revival of Neoplatonism, which smoldered for two centuries before bursting into flame at Chartres. Perhaps the most original work of this scholastic period was the *Book of Sequences* of Notker Balbulus of St. Gall, who prefaced the collection of his own sequences with a description of methods of composition.

(3) During the 11th c. there were increasing signs that the long period of migration, chaos, poverty, and rudimentary teaching was passing. About the year 1000 the feudal nobility, born of the wars, had consolidated their holdings sufficiently to begin to build in stone, and castles and courts heralded a new stability. Wealth and manpower appeared in abundance. By the year 1100, the West had so far regained its balance as to be able to spend in excess upon crusades, schools, a resurgent papal church, and the arts. The time had arrived to disseminate the culture which had for so long remained with the clergy. The cathedral schools, which were the sole agency

of public education beyond the primary training given by parish priests, had existed precariously; York (8th c.), Orleans and Auxerre (9th c.), Reims and Paris (10th c.), had barely kept the Boethian tradition alive. But under Fulbert, a disciple of Gerbert at Reims, the School of Chartres took on new life at the beginning of the 11th c., intensively studying the *auctores*, that is, the major classics, with emphasis upon poetry. Teachers like Bernard and Theodoric instructed novices who became poets of some stature. Simultaneously, Orleans, Reims, and Paris welcomed the younger sons of nobility displaced by primogeniture, who feted poetry despite the strictures of some schoolmen (e.g., Abelard, *Introductio ad Theologiam* 2.2). As court chaplains, archdeacons, and chancellors, they passed along to the nobility and the expanding bourgeoisie the skills formerly limited to the clergy. The 12th and first half of the 13th c. saw the production of many an "Art of Poetry" hastily coined to supply the trade: Marbod of Rennes (*De Ornamentis Verborum*), Alan of Lille (*Anticlaudianus*), Geoffrey of Vinsauf (*Poetria Nova*), Matthew of Vendome (*Ars Versificatoria*), Alexander of Villa Dei (*Doctrinale*), Eberhard of Bethune (*Graecismus*), Everhard the German (*Laborintus*), John of Garland (*Poetria*), and others.

It is hardly to be expected that, in such a period of expansion and reorientation, criticism of lasting merit would appear; but these authors made up in zeal, variety, and naive combinations of commonplaces what may have been lacking in taste. They often misapplied methods which were satisfactory for ecclesiastics: allegory, that is, verbal figures, took on pretensions of scriptural allegory, classical poets were "moralized" to accord with spurious Christian doctrine, and flowers of rhetoric were cultivated for their own sake. Yet the very excesses led to a new romantic idiom, giving Dante and Chaucer a language of color and emotion never known before. Concurrently, the need for *summae* in the emerging universities created a new kind of textbook in which treatment of poetry as an authentic art found place (Vincent of Beauvais; Brunetto Latini). True, Paris in the north, with its emphasis upon dialectical theology, and Bologna in the south, emphasizing law, soon overshadowed other schools, and study of poetry again languished. After the middle of the 13th c., the schools and universities no longer advanced the cause.

But they had done their work. While they preserved ancient poetry and justified its study, they taught the laity not only how to compose but how to sing. They codified both rhythms and meters, and adapted their L. principles to the vernacular tongues. New lyric, narrative, and dramatic verse, originated in the cloisters and developed in the schoolrooms, now emerged as a modern synthesis; hence the concept of poetry was unified throughout the western *Kulturgebiet*, no matter what vernacular was chosen for composition.

Averroes' paraphrase of Aristotle's *Poetics* was translated by Hermannus Alemannus, ca. 1250 (see G. Lacombe, ed., *Aristoteles Latinus* I [1939], 212-3), but seems to have had little significance. A purely western criticism developed among the late troubadours: Raimon Vidal de Besalú (*Las razos de trobar*) and Uc Faidit (*Donatz proensals*); at Toulouse in the 14th c. poetical questions were settled by a kind of judicial procedure, recorded in *Leys d'Amors* (see Hist. litt. de la France, XXXVIII [1949], 139-233). But already northern Italy had begun to cultivate poetic theory with a vigor characteristic of the rising communes. The new art found its greatest critic in Dante, not only in his *Vita Nuova, Convivio,* and letters (especially Epistle 10), but in a monumental though unfinished poetics, *De vulgari eloquentia.*

Dante's intent was to discover the appropriate and inevitable language and form of poetry. It is but one of the glories of his work that he saw the future of poetry in the vernaculars (the "natural" tongues) and not Latin ("grammar"). The diction must be *illustrious* (i.e., exalted), *cardinal* (standard), *courtly* (noble), and *curial* (judicial). Such a special language must be screened from all the separate dialects and be characteristic of none. He examines this diction with the discrimination of the scholar and the taste and perception of the poet. He then proceeds to consider the proper subjects of poetry, which are the *salus, venus,* and *virtus* ("safety, love, virtue"; cf. *De vulgari eloquentia* 2.2.70) of the troubadours in the exalted senses of the *dolce stil nuovo* (q.v.), and their proper forms (the hendecasyllabic line and *canzone* structure are his ideal). Tragic style is elevated, comic is middling, and elegiac is the style of the wretched. The illustrious vernacular should never be used for lowly or vulgar themes. Particularly striking is Dante's conception of the evolution of language and his discrimination of formulated from natural language. Had *De vulgari eloquentia* had the audience which it merited during the Humanist period, we may believe that poetical theory would have been much advanced.

PRIMARY WORKS: As yet, no useful collection of texts; representative of each period is: (1) Basilius Magnus Caesareae, *Sermo de legendis libris gentilium,* ed. J. P. Migne, *Patrologia Graeca,* XXXI, 563-90. (2) Bede, *De arte metrica,* ed. H. Keil, *Grammatici Latini,* VI. (3) Dante, *De vulgari eloquentia,* tr. A. G.

Ferrers Howell, *The L. Works of Dante* (Temple Classics), pp. 1–124.

SECONDARY WORKS: P. Lehmann, "Literaturgesch. im Mittelalter," *Germ.-rom. Monatschrift*, 1912, pp. 569ff. and 617ff.; Saintsbury, v. I (comprehensive and still provocative); Norden (important); E. Faral, *Les arts poétiques du xiie et du xiiie s.* (1924; incl. texts); H. Brinkmann, *Zu Wesen und Form mittelalterlicher Dichtung* (1928); G. Paré, A. Brunet, F. Tremblay, *La Renaissance du XIIe s.: Les écoles et l'enseignement* (1933); H. H. Glunz, *Die Literaturästhetik des europäischen Mittelalters* (1937; uneven); H. Scharschuch, *Gottfried von Strassburg: Stilmittel, Stilästhetik* (1938; stylistics of a poet at the crossroads); Behrens (pp. 33–66 a systematic brief survey of period); É. Lesne, *Les écoles de la fin du VIIIe s. à la fin du XIIe s.* (Hist. de la propriété eccl. en France, v, 1940); E. deBruyne, *Études d'esthétique médiévale* (3 v., 1946); L. Arbusow, *Colores rhetorici* (1948); H. I. Marrou, *St. Augustin et la fin de la culture antique* (2d ed., 1950); E. Dekkers and E. A. Gaar, *Clavis Patrum Latinorum* (1951; *Wegweiser* for Latin Fathers to Bede); Curtius (his exceptional critical monographs listed, p. 600 of his *European Lit. and the Latin M.A.*); R. McKeon, "Rhetoric in the Middle Ages," pp. 260–296, "Poetry and Philosophy in the 12th C.," pp. 297–318, in Crane, *Critics*; H. Roos, *Die Modi Significandi des Martinus de Dacia* (1952; pp. 72–120 an excellent survey of the scholastic period); G. E. von Grunebaum, "The Aesthetic Foundation of Arabic Lit.," *CL*, 4 (1952); J.W.H. Atkins, *Eng. Lit. Crit.: The Med. Phase* (rev. ed., 1952); M. T. Houtsma *et al.*, *The Encyclopedia of Islam* (new ed., 5 v., 1953ff.); R. H. Bolgar, *The Cl. Heritage and its Beneficiaries* (1954); G.W.H. Lampe and K. J. Woollcombe, *Essays on Typology* (1957; esp. pp. 39–75 on theological allegory); E. Auerbach, *Literatursprache und Publikum . . . im MA* (1958); *Crit. Approaches to Med. Lit.*, ed. D. Bethurum (1960). c.w.j.

"MEDIEVAL POETRY" is not yet a definite term. Some critics have worked to discover and describe latent unity in the literature of med. western Europe in studies of genres like hymnography, dramaturgy, and mythology, and of arts of prosody, music, and rhetoric, while some aestheticians and historians like de Bruyne, Curtius, Auerbach, and Bezzola have tried to distinguish an essentially med. poetic vigor. But still others look upon med. poetry as debased classicism or a primitive stage of the several national literatures.

Except for fragments of oral verse caught up in letters, our heritage from the Middle Ages consists of works designed to be read or to be recited in accordance with a script. It is therefore literary poetry. The roots of literary poetry are L. L. Christianity introduced from the Alps to Iceland an alphabet, writing materials, schools and libraries, and an idiom primarily developed for religious expression by a clerical class. It fused elements of Semitic and Hellenic diction, syntax, and figure with the Roman imperial language. This Christianity embraced Celtic, Teutonic, and Scandinavian peoples who had developed indigenous oral poetry; and it was affected, though very lightly, by Byzantium and the Muslim world. In the course of ten centuries Western social systems changed radically as a whole and regionally. Consequently there are marked diversities, first as the exclusive cultures acquired the L. arts, then as vernaculars, now Latinized in various degrees, became literary and spread from clerical to noble and bourgeois classes. Particularly from the 7th to the 12th c. did regional poetry receive its L.-Christian impress, which makes the "western tradition."

I. LATIN POETRY. Especially in the century following the Nicene Council (A.D. 325), brilliant, rhetorically trained Romans devoted themselves to developing and disseminating Christian doctrine and liturgy. They supplied the language of med. poetry, primarily in prose: Ambrose's hymns and addresses, Jerome's translations of Scriptures (the basis of the Vulgate), and Augustine's doctrinal works expressed insensible realities in sensible terms. At the same time, Roman versifiers like Prudentius and Paulinus turned the Hebrew-Christian poetry into traditional L. genres. This patristic writing, the staple of early med. schools and libraries, was popularized in sermons, liturgy, and paraliturgy as a unified body of doctrine, tradition, legend, and myth which was, or might be, poetical.

A. *Prosody and Verse Form*. Med. verse evolved from meters to rhyme and rhythm. The great influx of foreigners, at first from the east and later from the north, affected L. metrical purity as early as the 2d c.; at the end of the 4th c. Augustine stated that his students could no longer distinguish between long and short syllables. Though learned poets continued the composition of meters throughout the Middle Ages, popular poets developed patterns derived in part from *Kunstprosa*, which had taken on "Asian" flourishes including homophony such as alliteration, homeoteleuton, and rhyme. Isosyllabism (as in Augustine's *Psalm Against the Donatists*), which supplanted meters, was not alone decor; it aided memory and helped to preserve the text. Such classical meters as had been isosyllabic (e.g., trochaic septenarius, iambic dimeter) acquired additional popularity as being simultaneously traditional and modern; at the same time, isosyllabic substitutes were developed for popular classical meters like the heroic, elegiac, and sapphic. Emphasis, as in Ambrose's hymns, upon linear units of thought, partly because of choral antiphony, stimulated growth of patterned terminal rhythms, which became stressed in Teutonic regions. However, there is at present only partial agreement about the evolution of stress and tonic accent. By the end of the 7th c., terminal rhyme, or at least homeoteleuton and assonance, was a common verse pattern. As L. increasingly became a scholastically acquired second language, these figures of sound increased. By the 12th c., complex 2- and 3-syllable terminal rhyme was standard.

Strophaic patterns seem to have followed these patterns of rhyme and rhythm. Long lines separated at rhymed caesuras. For example, the dactylic hexameter became *leonine*, that is, with rhyme at caesura and term, or, eventually, even more complex. Then versifiers learned to double or triple the number of lines with the caesural rhyme. The septenarius was another long verse which evolved into a cadenced stanza. Refrains became more common and regular.

Vernacular and L. verse tended to interchange sound patterns, but eventually L. predominated. There are a very few early attempts to compose L. verses in Teutonic stress rhythms. But the L. isosyllabism, rhyme, and patterned terminal accent became the vernacular standard. The octosyllabic developed from the Ambrosian iambic dimeter; the decasyllabic and It. hendecasyllabic (though long thought to be Fr.) probably partly from dactylic tetrameter catalectic and partly from Horatian sapphic. However, once the principles were established, both L. and vernacular versifiers tried every variation. The *sequence*, which began from the 9th c. as musical prose, introduced flexibility. By the middle of the 13th c. composers in L. had ceased to invent, and vernaculars led the development.

B. Characteristics. The clergy preserved selected classics especially adaptable to the schools, but Scriptures, including ancillary apocryphal writings and hagiography, were primary. Before about A.D. 1050, the word "poet" or "maker" was hardly ever used for a contemporary writer or versifier, even if he composed learnedly in meters; for God was the sole Creator. It was applied to classical poets somewhat pejoratively, though Virgil became *Poeta* as Aristotle eventually became *Philosophus. Author* was similarly affected. Versifiers were apt to designate their work as *rhythmi, versus, carmina,* but not *poemata.* Reverence for scriptures, that is, literature, exalted the science of *grammar,* and dislike of pagan eloquence as prideful depressed *rhet-*

oric. Words needed to reveal simultaneously (according to traditional interpretation) the highest exaltation and the most mundane sensibility. The polysemous allegory which developed would have been ambiguous beyond understanding were its interpretation not anchored in a common doctrine. This doctrine had to be carried in the mind, for books were expensive and literacy uncommon; hence mnemonic formulas strongly determined med. aesthetics, including use of *carmina figurata* (see PATTERN POETRY), number symbolism, etymologies, and topics. The classical distinction between the content of poetry and prose disappeared. An author quite customarily wrote the same matter twice, once in prose for meditation and once in verse for recitation. Sometimes, in the model of Martianus and Boethius, he would alternate prose and verse (Sedulius Scotus, *Liber de rectoribus christianis;* cf. Boccaccio, *Ameto*). Contrast and color, more than formal unity, were desired.

Hence genres are difficult to identify. At the early centers of literacy, hymnody, hagiography, and scholastic verse were basic.

1. *Hymnody* was the heart of lyric poetry and scriptural psalms and canticles its muscle. Hymns (q.v.), defined as songs of praise, were admitted to the Office on sufferance after Hilary and Ambrose led the way. Later, sequences developed in the Mass from extension of Hebraic jubilations like the *Alleluia.* Their melodies spread to the market places as paraliturgy. Med. love of parody and inversion grew with adaptation of these religious pieces to profane use.

From the 10th c. liturgical drama developed slowly out of hymnody by expansion of tropes (q.v.) and use of processionals, until extensive representations of scriptural narrative in the form of Passion and Nativity Plays and Cycles ("mysteries," see MYSTERY AND MIRACLE PLAYS) came to be presented by laity as popular entertainment. Concurrently a more secular drama based on legends ("miracles") developed, quite possibly in the schools, since the earliest (Hildesheim) plays are scholastic. Dramatized allegories ("moralities," q.v.) and professional divertissements ("interludes" and "farces," qq.v.) do not appear to have become conventional before the late 14th c.

2. *Hagiography,* which in the late classical period had arisen as *acta martyrum* and *vitae patrum,* was designed for edification; in various proportions it combines semitic narrative, epideictic eloquence, and "Greek romance" in pious tales for conversion, meditation, and instruction in manners. Because in cloisters it was employed for reading in nocturnal office and in refectory as well as for private meditation, demand and supply were high. The oriental tradition of monasticism determined

that oriental narratives and narrative devices should predominate. The romantic narrative tradition is markedly hagiographical: poetized knighthood takes its start from the Pauline arming of the Christian warrior in Ephesians; chivalry from the beast and saint of, for instance, Jerome's *Malchus*; peerage (the Twelve Peers of France) from discipleship; quests (*quaerere*) from oriental seekers, and gestes (*gesta* is hagiographical synonym for *virtutes* and *miracula*) from superhuman accomplishments; love and joy from *amor Dei* and *gaudia Christi*; courtliness from *cohors* (cognate *garden*) which in hagiography combined notions associated with Eden, the pastoral Canticles, the *locus amoenus* ("lovely spot"; cf. Horace, *Ars Poetica* 17; Isidore, *Etymologiae* 14.8.33) and the cloister.

3. *Scholastic verse* was ancillary to the other two, but helped to preserve classical tradition for useful adaptations. The scholars, as the only literates, composed occasional verse: epistles, eclogues, epigrams, panegyrics, processionals, and the like, usually in meter. Secular dráma (e.g., the Nicholas plays) developed from exercises based on Terence, a model of style. Scholastic imitations of Roman epics (Abbo's *Siege of Paris*) doubtless affected narrative verse. Even textbooks were sometimes cast into meter, partially as models. A most fruitful activity was student composition. Walafrid's *Visio Wettini* (9th c.) is a prototype of the *Commedia*. The St. Gall (?) *Waltharius* may be called the first chivalric epic; it phrases a Teutonic tale in the language of Virgil and Prudentius. The *Ecbasis Captivi* (from Toul ?) is a progenitor of beast epics (q.v.), and *Ruodlieb*, from Tegernsee, of the Parzival-type of psychological tale. Scholars provided the often quite imaginative verse chronicles and the *specula* or "mirrors" for leaders of church and state; they ranged from manners and advice to sheer trifles for amusement, in verse or prose.

As the West produced more scholars than the church could absorb, vagrants and wits became increasingly apparent, though they had always existed (see Augustine's *De opere monachorum*). They converted ecclesiastical art to a wider public, composing especially parodies, drinking and love songs, and scurrilities, often called goliardic verse (q.v.). Especially as they located posts in civil life as chaplains or chancellors, they were prime agents in adapting form, imagery, idiom, and melody of L. verse to the emergent vernaculars of the secular classes. The mendicant orders, especially the Franciscans (13th c.), composed some of the most moving lyrics (*Stabat Mater, Dies Irae*) of all time.

Petrarch represents the entire middle age in regarding L. as the language of true poetry;

Dante's exaltation of the *eloquentia vulgaris* as a fit poetical medium is exceptional.

II. VERNACULAR POETRY. *A. Celtic*. The term refers to what seems indigenous that has survived from Ireland, Wales, and Scotland. Caesar's observation (*Bellum gallicum* 6.14) that the Druidic schools kept some for twenty years memorizing verses, for letters were irreligious, is indicative. There are native words for poet (*bard*), musician, and song; but the earliest Welsh codices of poetry, four in number, date from the end of the 12th to the 15th c., the Scotch-Gaelic are later, and the Ir., except for scraps from the pens of Carolingian migrants, have only slightly greater range and number. Scholars try to distinguish in these documents what is indigenous from southern importations, but they often disagree; to compare L. works from the pens of known Celts like Erigena or treatments of Celtic materials by Latinate writers like Geoffrey of Monmouth or Gerald of Wales is infrequently helpful. The Celts seem to have enjoyed lyric, melodic strains, varieties of word play and rhyme, pathos, a sensuous view of external nature, cult of women, a demimonde of fairies and pixies, formulated codes and "prohibitions," and imaginativeness at the expense of coherence. There is reason to believe that the Celtic revivalists have not greatly erred in their instinctive choices of what to accent, though as with their literate and literary med. predecessors, they may have imposed an uncharacteristic form upon tradition.

B. Teutonic. The verse of Goths, Franks, Germans, and Eng. was primarily mytho-historical, but they were also given to charms, riddles (qq.v.), and convivial songs. The few genres seem to have been customarily composed in unmetrical lines of 4 stresses with alliteration. The Teutons lacked the lyricism of the Celts: Tacitus speaks kindly of their heroic songs, but Fortunatus complains of the dull thump of their conviviality. King Theodoric, reared at Constantinople, as king of the Goths and the Romans worked to transmit classical culture to the Teutonic races; he lived on in German poetry as the hero Dietrich.

The earliest vernacular documents are Eng. and do not precede Bede's description (*Historia ecclesiastica . . . 4.22*) of Caedmon, the earliest identifiable poet. According to Bede, he dreamed a hymn to the Maker of Heaven and Earth; thereafter, monastic doctors taught him Scripture, which he converted to verse for their transcription. Early verse was adapted transcription (*Widsith, Beowulf*), transference (*Genesis*), or imitation (*Phoenix*), of great poetic power. After the outburst in the century following Caedmon, OE poetry declined; the later survivals draw nearer L. models. Only after the Norman conquerors and their language and poetry had been absorbed did a ME poetry emerge. Though fecund and, in Chaucer's verse, magnificent, and though provincial versifiers revived and for a time enlivened some elements of native tradition (*Piers Plowman, Pearl, Gawain*), this late med. period depended upon France and, later, Italy.

The early Eng. missionaries on the continent transmitted Caedmon's art, and during the 9th c. German poets followed the methods of their Eng. relatives. The *Hildebrandslied* survives incompletely in a monastic (Fulda) codex as the only transcription of native song; but Otfrid's *Gospel Book*, the *Muspilla,* and the *Heliand* show how Caedmon's tradition was transplanted. Late in the century the *Ludwigslied* followed the trend of L. secular panegyric. Verse gave way to prose until the century after A.D. 1175. That glorious period under the Hohenstaufen emperors is marked by the lyrics of the Minnesinger (q.v.), with Walther von der Vogelweide at the head, the beast epic *Reinhart Fuchs*, the courtly tales of Hartmann von der Aue and Gottfried von Strassburg, the psychological and symbolical *Parzival* of Wolfram von Eschenbach, and the epic *Nibelungenlied*. Almost certainly, noble patronage and the exhilaration of crusade and discovery fertilized this bloom, which quickly withered. The 14th and 15th c., dominated by Meistersinger (q.v.), are crabbed in comparison.

C. Scandinavian. Though it acquired a life of its own, Scandinavian may be regarded as a branch of Teutonic. The lyrics are largely preserved in the Icelandic collections formed in the 13th c. by Snorri Sturluson and his nephews, but also as incorporated in *sagas.* These are a rich and independent form, though in some debt to the Ir. Unversified, designed for recitation with appropriate formal conventions of diction and phraseology, they more resemble poetry than eloquence. Their clear-eyed simplicity and accuracy of observation add force and conviction to heroic tales strongly historical. Composed by the governing class, they were written down after Christianization in the 11th c., apparently without notable change in form. From the 13th c., many poets went to the continent for education, and their works became romanticized. But the borrowing was not reciprocal, and only in the 19th c. when antiquarians revived the poetry did it measurably affect the Western stream.

D. Romance. The earliest (ca. 880) verses in romance vernacular are a paraliturgical exaltation of an early virgin martyr *Eulalie* in unevenly decasyllabic assonanced lines. That same codex contains both a L. *Eulalia* with lines borrowed from Prudentius and also the *Ludwigslied;* this suggests that monks sup-

plied matter and form and Teutons supplied incentive for vernacular composition. A line through *Eulalie* and *Alexis* (11th c.) to the *Chanson de Roland* (12th c.) indicates the secularization of liturgical form in Fr. *épopées,* and Bédier and followers have, somewhat overzealously, described how the content accrued around shrines. The approximately 80 chansons, nearly all in decasyllabic assonanced verses, were recited, chanted, and possibly mimed at fairs, markets, camps. The *Poema del Cid* (12th c.), of similar genre, inaugurates Sp. poetry. Heroic in the 12th c., the chansons declined later to sheer buffoonery.

A parallel form of narrative was the courtly tale, which seems to have been secular edification growing out of scholastic verse, of which *Waltharius* is a prototype. Consolidation of feudality in castles and manors, burgeoning of schools, spread of literacy to the counties, induced poetry for a noble class almost as cloistered as the monks. For manorial festivals, clerks composed recitations in *roman,* commonly in octosyllabic rhymed couplets. The content was described by Bodel, one such *trouvère* (q.v.), as matter of Rome, France, or Britain; that is, tales drawn from scholastic classics about Troy, Alexander, Caesar, or tales of Charlemagne and his peers, or Celtic tales of Arthur and others. Centered in northern France, these romances spread in all directions, to become poetic models for diverse nations. As might be expected, the profanity, secularity, and virtual anarchical exaltation of the individual man on horseback and the *dames* with castellar pallor contrast with the often patriotic and religious fervor of the early chansons, though the genres overlap. Emphasis upon the *tale,* which now attracted an avid audience, resulted in ransacking all sources; the crusades, not only in Palestine but throughout eastern Europe, Byzantium, and Muslim Spain and Africa, were a fertile supply.

The first extant romance lyrics were composed by Duke William IX of Aquitaine (d. 1127), and the 12th c. witnessed an outpouring of lyrics in *langue d'oc.* Comparative peace and isolation in the 11th and 12th c. bred, as it were, a group of wealthy prisoners, and their verse, like prison literature, emphasized forms, enigmas, ambiguities, acuity, and surprise, with restricted content. New stanzaic structure for each song, within the restrictions of rhyme and rhythm, became prerequisite. The subjects were *salus, venus, virtus* ("safety, love, virtue"; cf. Dante, *De vulgari eloquentia* 2.2.70). The fruits of this cultivation ripened elsewhere. As civil war and other Prov. disruptions interfered with the art at home, the poets stimulated others elsewhere, especially the Portuguese, the Eng., the trouvères, the Minnesinger, and the Italians. The It. lyric began at the

Sicilian court of Frederick II, but soon burst out in the north, eventuating in the *dolce stil nuovo* (q.v.) of Guido Guinicelli and then Dante and his contemporaries—a spiritualizing and, in some ways, platonizing of an earthbound tradition. Dante's *Vita Nuova* and his critical *De vulgari eloquentia* demonstrate that vernacular poetry was coming of age. The *Commedia* was indeed in many respects the voice of ten silent centuries; for if there is a middle age, that poem is at once its representation and supreme achievement. Through long vicissitude Italy had lost but never forgotten its Roman heritage; the new bourgeoisie of Tuscany and Lombardy held the pass from the cultivated barbarism of the north to Rome and even India. Dante, with transalpine scholasticism and cisalpine catholicity, bound in one volume the scattered leaves of the med. world. His two great Tuscan successors, Petrarch and Boccaccio, in their quite different ways catching Dante's high conception of the poet's function, returned to earth his exalted vision. Petrarch, primarily a rhetorician, but a priest of poetry, revived antiquity in receiving the laurel; his L. epic *Africa* was archeology, but his *Canzoniere,* replete with feeling and perception, imposed a stamp, not always felicitous, upon modern verse. Boccaccio, father of It. prose but meriting attention as font for Chaucer and many another, composed as his own epitaph, *studium fuit alma poesis* ("My study was nourishing poetry"). Medieval poetry had moved on from the days when *poeta* was an opprobrious word. See also EPIC, LYRIC, MEDIEVAL ROMANCE, etc. and the various national poetry articles.

ANTHOLOGIES: All major collections of med. texts are limited to a single language, nation, or genre. For initial guidance, consult F. Baldensperger and W. P. Friederich, *Bibliog. of Comparative Lit.* (1950); K. Strecker, *Introd. to Med. Latin,* ed. and tr. R. B. Palmer (1957); R. Bossuat, *Manuel bibliographique de la litt. fr. du moyen âge* (1951) and supplements; CBEL; W. Bonser, *An Anglo-Saxon and Celtic Bibliog.* (2 v., 1957); W. Stammler and K. Langosch, *Die deutsche Lit. des Mittelalters: Verfasserlexikon* (5 v., 1931–55). Standard collections containing the bulk of Latin verse: *Patrologiae cursus completus* [ser. Latina], ed. J.. P. Migne (221 v., 1844–64); Monumenta Germaniae historica: *Auctores antiquissimi* (15 v., 1877–1919), *Poetae Latini medii aevi* (5 v., 1881–1939), *Scriptores* (32 v., 1826–1934); *Rerum Britannicarum medii aevi scriptores,* "Rolls Series" (99 titles in 254 v., 1887–96) esp. *The Anglo-Latin Satirical Poets,* ed. T. Wright (2 v., 1872). Convenient anthol. in tr.: *Med. Lit. in Tr.,* ed. C. W. Jones (1950); *Med. Romances,* ed. R. S. and L. H. Loomis (1958); *Lyrics of the MA,* ed. H. Creekmore (1959); *Med. Epics,* tr. W. Alfred *et al.* (1963).

HISTORY AND CRITICISM: *Hist. littéraire de la France* . . . (38 v., 1865–[1949]; reaches beyond Fr. lit.; use indexes); E. K. Chambers, *The Med. Stage* (2 v., 1903); M. Manitius, *Gesch. der lateinischen Lit. des MA* (3 v., 1911–31; standard ref., by authors, through 12th c.); J. Bédier, *Les Légendes épiques* (3d ed., 4 v., 1926–29; standard, though theories discounted); K. Young, *Drama of the Med. Church* (2 v., 1933; with L. texts); Jeanroy; J. de Ghellinck, *Litt. latine au m.a.* (2 v., 1939) and *L'Essor de la litt. lat. au xiie s.* (2d ed., 1955); R. R. Bezzola, *Les Origines et la formation de la litt. courtoise en occident* (3 v., 1944–63); G. Graf, *Gesch. der christl. arabischen Lit.* (5 v., 1944–53); *Oxford Hist. of Eng. Lit.* (v. 1 to appear; v. 2, in 2 pts., 1947); G. Lote, *Le Vers français* (3 v., 1949–55); Curtius (see esp. listing of his monographs, p. 600); Auerbach (pp. 50–231 on med. "realism"), and, *idem., Literatursprache und Publikum in der lat. Spätantike und im MA* (1958); F. J. E. Raby, *Christian L. Poetry* (2d ed., 1953) and *Secular L. Poetry* (2d ed., 2 v., 1957; standard surveys of med. L. lyric); H. A. W. de Boor, *Gesch. der deutschen Lit.,* v. 1, 2, 5 (1955–62); *Le Origini,* ed. A. Viscardi and others (1956); F. Artz, *Mind of the M.A.* (3d ed., 1958; survey and bibliog.); D. Norberg, *Introd. à l'étude de la versification lat. med.* (1958); W. T. H. Jackson, *The Lit. of the MA* (1960; useful bibliog.); O. H. Green, *Spain and the Western Tradition,* I (1963). c.w.j.

MEDIEVAL ROMANCE. The meaning of the term "r." is obscured by the fact that both in medieval and modern times it has been used so loosely. In France, where it originated, it was applied at first to vernacular Fr. (versus L.) literature. Later it came to refer to imaginative works in verse whose subject matter was felt to be fictional or nonhistorical. By the 13th c., however, this distinction was becoming blurred. Any tale of adventure, whatever the origin of its matter, could be a r., and the adventure could be chivalric or merely amorous. Furthermore, r. soon began to be written in prose. Most modern critics distinguish r. from narrative poems treating national themes such as the *Volksepos* in Germany, the *chanson de geste* in France, and the national epic in Spain, even though the treatment of these subjects in the later Middle Ages can hardly be distinguished from that of r. There are several important r. cycles, such as those of Arthur and Alexander, which are associated more by a common background than the presence of a particular character.

The cycles are usually divided by scholars according to their subject matter: (1) "The Matter of Britain" (subdivided into "Arthurian

Matter"—r. derived from Breton lays—and "English Matter," e.g., *King Horn*). (2) "The Matter of Rome" (stories of Alexander, of the Trojan war and its heroes, of Thebes, and of the Orient). (3) "The Matter of France" (titles of Charlemagne and his knights).

In general, r. is distinguished from the older *chanson de geste* (q.v.) and epic forms by its less heroic tone, its greater sophistication, its fondness for the fantastic, its more superficial characterization, (often) looser structure, and unity of action. The sources of r. are legion, and there is controversy over which is primary. According to one influential school (e.g., W. P. Ker), the form is the result of the sentimentalization of the earlier heroic materials which occurred when they were combined with such typically high medieval ideals as chivalry and courtly love (q.v.). Others stress classical sources and/or such late classical r. as *Daphnis and Chloe* by Longus and the *Aethiopica* (3d c. ?) of Heliodorus. Arthurian r. has received particularly full treatment. The theory of Celtic origins has been most vigorously propounded by Roger Sherman Loomis. An opposing school of thought, best represented in America by Urban T. Holmes, Jr., argues with equal vehemence that Chrétien de Troyes must be regarded as the inventor of Arthurian r. Other theories have also been advanced, but an early settlement of the controversy seems unlikely.

Although it is not confined to r., the courtly background is virtually indispensable to them. It is not a realistic background of contemporary courts but an ideal of chivalry, with stress on mercy to an opponent, good manners, and artistic sensitivity as well as the virtues of bravery, loyalty, and preservation of honor. The milieu of r. is tournaments, adventures, and particularly love. The winning of a lady is an essential part of all early r., and it is achieved by "love service," that is by worship, formal courtship, and unremitting attention to her wishes. In its highest form this love ennobles a man and makes him capable of deeds beyond his normal powers. A man truly in love lives a full life, both for his lady and for adventure. Such love may be between man and wife, as it is, after trials, between Erec and Enide, Yvain and Laudine, Parzival and Condwiramurs. It may be adulterous, as between Lancelot and Guinevere and Tristan and Isolde. Married love holds together society, adulterous love destroys it. In both the power of love is predominant over everything else. Later r., although they often paid lip service to the power of love, tended to regard it as merely one more adventure.

Although Arthurian r. are by far the most famous and influential, the earliest extant r.

do not belong to this cycle. They are r. of antiquity, rather misleadingly called the "Matter of Rome." An anonymous *Roman d'Enée* was written about 1150. Virgil's *Aeneid* was its source but its tone is emphatically medieval. The work becomes a love adventure with destructive love (Dido) spurned and true love (Lavinia) finally triumphant. The characters behave like medieval knights. A reworking by the German Heinrich von Veldeke (*Eneide*, ca. 1180) retains these characteristics. The greatest of Troy r., the *Roman de Troie* of Benoit de Ste. Maure (ca. 1165), tells the full story of the Trojan War, based on the L. account by "Dares Phrygius." Again love interests predominate, particularly that of Achilles and Polyxena and—probably Benoit's own invention—of Troilus and Cressida. Here the code of chivalry is applied fully to the warriors of Troy.

Although not originated by him, Arthurian r. is closely associated with Chrétien de Troyes. Chrétien's works are the earliest and greatest of the r. in Fr. Nothing is known of the author except that he was associated with the court of Marie de Champagne. He may have been a cleric. His r. appeared in the order *Erec et Enide*, *Lancelot* or the *Knight of the Cart*, *Yvain*, and *Perceval* or *Li Contes del graal*. *Cligès*, written after *Erec*, is an Eastern r. with Arthurian elements. Common to all these is the acknowledged superiority of Arthur's court as a center of civilized behavior, a high standard of manners, courage, and love of service, of which Gawain is the perfect type and Sir Kay the antitype. The world outside is full of uncouth creatures and is fit only for adventure. *Erec* and *Yvain* handle two facets of the same problem, the maintenance of equilibrium between love and adventure. In both cases married love is fulfillment and true adventure is possible only in the service of love. *Lancelot* shows this love carried to absurdity, for the lover, a brave knight, is made to obey every whim, however foolish, of his lady. Chrétien did not finish the work, and it is hard to deny that it is ironical. *Perceval* was clearly intended to show a knightly service higher than that of Arthur's court, for the foolishly simple Perceval is destined for the service of the Grail, which is definitely a religious symbol however mysterious it may be otherwise. The parallel adventures of the perfect secular knight Gawain again express the theme of the higher destiny. Chrétien did not finish the work but Wolfram von Eschenbach about 1210 used his work and other material as a source for *Parzival*. Here the Grail, a precious stone, becomes the gift of Paradise, the center of a band of religious knights whose king must be above the love-adventure morality of Arthur's courts. Parzival's pilgrimage takes him through innocence, error, pride, despair, and repentance, to humility. It is the way of the Christian man but not of any Christian man, for Parzival is a chosen king, an Arthurian warrior on his father's side, a grail warrior on his mother's. In *Parzival* r. reaches its highest spiritual manifestation while maintaining the essential characteristics of the type—adventure, love, and ideal background of chivalry.

If *Parzival* is the noblest romance, Gottfried von Strassburg's *Tristan and Isolt* (ca. 1210) is the most polished and in some ways the most intellectually satisfying. Gottfried used the fine courtly r. of Thomas of Britain (ca. 1180) as a source but his hero is in fact more a minstrel and artist than a knight. The love episodes are courtly only on the surface, for Gottfried shows that courtly love is empty. His lovers seek a deeper, more spiritual, less attainable love which destroys both them and society.

With few exceptions the history of the r. in the 13th and 14th c. is one of decline. The chief characteristic is loss of form and purpose. The Alexander r., for example, the earliest of which date from ca. 1120, were capable of indefinite expansion by increase of incident; and the prose versions of Arthurian r. become highly involved adventure stories in which characters appear and disappear. New and voluminous r. were written about minor Arthurian knights and on persons hitherto hardly known. Two exceptions stand out. *Sir Gawain and the Green Knight* by an anonymous writer of the Eng. Midlands is a superb study of the moral problem of courage. Gawain undertakes a test of courage which he feels is his duty as the model Arthurian knight. He survives a planned assault on his virtue by a lady in the castle where he is staying. Yet he cannot resist the temptation of accepting a charm against wounds, even though it is dishonorable for him to do so. Sir Thomas Malory's misnamed *Morte d'Arthur* is best known in the form in which Caxton rearranged it. It is a final accounting of the Arthurian cycle, with a strong feeling for the fate which the sin of adultery brought to the ideal world of chivalry.

The traditions of r. lingered on, though often in distorted and even parodied form, to the Renaissance. Ariosto's *Orlando furioso*, the *Teuerdank* of Maximilian I, *Amadis de Gaule* all show the conventions of chivalry, and the humor of *Don Quixote*, as well as its tragedy, depends on a recognition of r. conventions.

COLLECTIONS: *ME Metrical Romances*, ed. W. H. French and C. B. Hale (1930); *Medieval Romances*, ed., R. S. and L. H. Loomis (1957).

HISTORY AND CRITICISM: W. P. Ker, *Epic*

and R. (1897); W. Golther, *Tristan und Isolde in der Dichtung des Mittelalters und der neuen Zeit* (1907); G. Schoepperle, *Tristan and Isolt* (2 v., 1913); M. Wilmotte, *De l'origine du roman en France* (1923); E. K. Chambers, *Arthur of Britain* (1927); R. S. Loomis, *Celtic Myth and Arthurian R.* (1927) and *Arthurian Tradition and Chrétien de Troyes* (1949); C. B. Lewis, *Classical Mythology and Arthurian R.* (1932); R. R. Bezzola, *Les Origines et la formation de la litt. courtoise, 500–1100* (2 v., 1944–60); U. T. Holmes, Jr., *A New Interpretation of Chrétien's Conte del Graal* (1948); E. Neumann, "Der Streit um 'das ritterliche Tugendsystem,'" *Festschrift für Karl Helm* (1951); G. Cary, *The Medieval Alexander* (1956); J. Frappier, *Chrétien de Troyes* (1957); *Arthurian Lit. in the Middle Ages*, ed. R. S. Loomis (1959); L. A. Hibbard, *Medieval R. in England* (rev. ed., 1961); M. J. C. Reid, *The Arthurian Legend: A Comparison of Treatment in Medieval and Modern Lit.* (1961); R. S. Loomis, *The Development of Arthurian R.* (1963) and *The Grail* (1963).   W.T.H.J.

MEIOSIS (Gr. "lessening"). A figure employing ironic understatement, usually to convey the impression that a thing is less in size, or importance, than it really is; generally synonymous with *litotes* (q.v.), though sometimes considered more generic in application. Quintilian discusses m. as an abuse or fault of language which characterizes obscure style rather than one lacking ornament, but he indicates that deliberately employed m. may be called a figure, and promises to discuss it later, though he neglects to do so (*Institutes of Oratory* 8.6.51). Puttenham distinguishes m. more particularly: "If you diminish and abbase a thing by way of spight . . . , such speach is by the figure *Meiosis* or the disabler" (*The Arte of Eng. Poesie*). "Long for me the rick will wait, / And long will wait the fold, / And long will stand the empty plate, / And dinner will be cold" (A. E. Housman, *A Shropshire Lad* 8.21–24). A singularly persuasive literary device which may dominate an entire poem, as Auden's *Musée des Beaux Arts* or *The Unknown Citizen*. M. may also occur with startling simplicity as part of a longer narrative; e.g., Dante's famous "quel giorno più non vi leggemmo avante" (We read no more that day) from the Paolo and Francesca episode (*La Divina Commedia: Inferno 5*), or the concluding lines of Wordsworth's *Michael*. Note also Shakespeare's later tragedies, especially *Lear*, wherein simplicity and understatement often mark the most dramatic moments.   R.O.E.

MEISTERSINGER. German burgher poets of the 14th, 15th, and 16th c. The heirs of the earlier Minnesinger (q.v.), they traced their ancestry traditionally to twelve "Meister," including such figures as Frauenlob, Walther von der Vogelweide, and Wolfram von Eschenbach, but in practice they generally replaced the erotic themes of the earlier poets with religious and didactic material.

The M. were characterized by their organization into guilds and by the rigidly formalistic nature of their productions. Some scholars believe the guilds originated in groups of laymen organized by the church to sing at public occasions. Whatever their origins, the M. had a remarkable fondness for rules and categories. Before becoming a *Meister*, an aspirant was obliged to work his way up through the grades of *Schüler* (pupil), *Schulfreund* (school-friend), *Singer*, and *Dichter* (poet). Even when the highest rank was reached, the *Meister* found his material and technique severely restricted. At the *Schulsingen*, or formal meetings, he could treat only religious subjects; at the *Zechsingen*, or informal meetings, frequently held in taverns, a wider range of material was permissible. In technique, the M. were restricted to certain set *Töne*, or patterns of tune and meter; the metrics were determined by syllabic number and often displayed great intricacy. In fitting words to the *Töne*, the M. followed the *Tabulatur*, an extensive and pedantic code of rules.

Famous M. include Hans Folz (d. ca. 1515), who successfully established the right of the Nuremberg *Meister* to introduce new melodies as well as new metrical patterns, and Hans Sachs, used by Wagner as the hero of his opera, *Die Meistersinger von Nürnberg*, a work which affords in general an accurate picture, though Wagner took liberties in presenting the art of the *Meister* as being subject to public appreciation and approval. He also idealized their performances to some extent. A very considerable body of scholarship (see B. Nagel, *Der Meistersang*, 1962) has maintained that the *Meistergesang* developed from the didactic poems of the so-called *Spruchdichter* of the 13th and 14th c.

The M. flourished for the most part in the Rhineland and in southern Germany; there were some individual *Meister* in the north, but the characteristic guild organization seems not to have existed there.

COLLECTIONS: *Die Meisterlieder der Kolmarer Handschrift*, ed. K. Bartsch (1862); *Die Singweisen der Kolmarer Handschrift*, ed. P. Runge (1896); H. Folz, *Meisterlieder*, ed. A. L. Mayer (1908).—HISTORY AND CRITICISM: A. Taylor and F. H. Ellis, *A Bibliog. of Meistergesang* (1936); C. Mey, *Der Meisterges. in Gesch. und Kunst* (1901); A. Taylor, *Lit. Hist. of Meisterges.* (1937); C. H. Bell, *Georg Hager, a M. of Nürnberg (1552–1634)* (4 v., 1947), *The Meistersingerschule at Memmingen*

and Its "Kurtze Entwerffung" (1952) and "A Glance into the Workshop of *Meisterges.*," PMLA, 68 (1953); B. Nagel, *Der deutsche Meistersang* (1952); E. Geiger, *Der Meisterges. des Hans Sachs* (1956).　　F.J.W.; A.P.

MEIURUS or *myurus* (Gr. "tapering," "mousetailed"). A hexameter verse in which the first syllable of the last foot is short instead of long. The classic example is: "Troes d' errhigesan, hopos idon aiolon ŏphin" (*Iliad* 12.208), translated by Terentianus Maurus as: "attoniti Troes viso serpente pavĭtant," where in both cases the penultimate syllable in the line is naturally short instead of long. M. was recognized by the ancients as a special verse and was used frequently. It is also called *teliambos*.—T. F. Higham, *Gr. Poetry and Life* (1936); Koster; Kolář.　　P.S.C.

MELIC POETRY (Gr. "connected with music," "lyric"). Poetry sung or sung and danced. In the classical period the Greeks applied the name to all forms of lyric poetry in which music played a very important part. However, it did not include elegiac, iambic, and epic poetry because in these genres the musical accompaniment was not particularly significant. M. poetry was chiefly developed by the Aeolians and the Dorians and was written in a great number of meters. Its most brilliant period was between the 7th and the 5th c. B.C. It was divided into two classes, monodic or solo lyric and choral lyric. The monodic lyric was sung by a single voice and expressed the emotions and feelings of one individual. Its stanzas, usually made up of 4–5 lines, were repeated without interruption. Its chief representatives were Sappho, Alcaeus, and Anacreon. The choral lyric expressed the emotions of the group and was sung by a chorus. Its strophes were arranged in triads (strophe, antistrophe, epode) repeated several times. It was chiefly written by Alcman, Stesichorus, Simonides, Pindar, and Bacchylides. The main subdivisions of m. poetry as given by the Alexandrian scholars were: hymns, paeans, dithyrambs, *epinicia, scolia*, epithalamia, and *partheneia*. In Alexandrian and subsequent times this type of poetry is referred to as lyric.—Smyth; Bowra; J. M. Edmonds, *Lyra Graeca* (3 v., 1952).　　P.S.C.

MESODE. In Gr. drama, a portion of a choral ode which occurs between a strophe and its antistrophe. A m. has no antistrophe.　　R.A.H.

MESOSTICH. See ACROSTIC.

MESUR TRI-THRAWIAD. A Welsh meter consisting of dactylic half lines of 6, 6, 6, 5; 6, 6, 6, 3 syllables. It derives its name ("3-

stroke meter") from the 3 stresses only of the last line, which serve to slow down the movement and thus provide a finished effect. Not one of the "24 strict-meters" of Welsh poetry, it became commonly practiced in the 17th c. in popular verse, reached high perfection in the 18th-c. pastoral poetry of the scholarly Edward Richard, and in the 20th c. it has been embellished with full *cynghanedd* (q.v.), and very effectively used, particularly by Cynan in a poem set in the Aegean islands. It is a meter of great smoothness capable of lush effects, but also highly suitable for poetry of a reflective quality.—Morris-Jones; Parry.

D.M.L.

METAPHOR. A condensed verbal relation in which an idea, image, or symbol may, by the presence of one or more other ideas, images, or symbols, be enhanced in vividness, complexity, or breadth of implication.

The nature and definition of metaphorical terms and of the relations between them have both been matter for much speculation and disagreement. It is unlikely therefore that a more specific definition will at first be acceptable. The metaphorical relation has been variously described as comparison, contrast, analogy, similarity, juxtaposition, identity, tension, collision, fusion; and different views have been held regarding the nature, operation, and function of metaphor in poetry. In recent years the view has gathered weight that m. is the radical process in which the internal relationships peculiar to poetry are achieved; some critics maintaining that m. marks off the poetic mode of vision and utterance from the logical or discursive mode; others, usually on anthropological evidence, that all language is m. The traditional view, however, is that m. is a figure of speech, or a family of tropes, involving two (occasionally four) operative terms, and that it is used for adornment, liveliness, elucidation, or agreeable mystification.

The view of m. as tropical may be considered first. For this view Aristotle is taken to be the prime authority, particularly in his statement that "metaphor consists in giving the thing a name that belongs to something else; the transference being either from genus to species, or from species to genus, or from species to species, or on grounds of analogy" (*Poetics* 1457b). Some of these instances of "transference" have been classed by grammarians—not without ingenuity and precision—under such names as synecdoche, metonymy, catachresis, and so on—the terms not coinciding with Aristotle's division. And Aristotle's fourfold classification is found, without significant qualification, at the end of a neo-Aristotelean pronouncement in 1950 (see Crane, *Critics and Criticism*, 1952, pp. 80–82).

Grammarians since Cicero and Quintilian, again on Aristotle's authority (though based upon the *Rhetoric* where the discussion is limited to prose), have insisted upon the harmony or congruity of metaphorical elements, and upon a measure of visual clarity. Hence the traditional condemnation of "mixed metaphor" and the limiting of m. to a descriptive or expository function: so that, for example, George Campbell (*Philosophy of Rhetoric*, 1841) writes: "In metaphor the sole relation is resemblance." Grammarians, noticing some logical incongruity between the elements in m., have also suggested that m. not only transfers and alters meaning but may also pervert it; and this suspicion is preserved in the single definition offered by soED: "Metaphor. The figure of speech in which a name or descriptive term is transferred to some object to which it is *not properly applicable*" (cf NED: ". . . some object different from, but analogous to, that to which it is properly applicable"). Philosophers particularly have indulged the suspicion—at least as old as Locke, though recently much encouraged by Wittgenstein—that m. is an "improper" connection of terms, regarding m. as a decorative but inexact alternative to what honest and forthright consideration would disclose in a literal form, and implying that the use of m. is a mark of carelessness, haste, or intellectual unchastity (cf *Poetics* 1458b 17 which, if read out of context, might seem to support this view).

Traditionally, m. has been represented as a trope of transference in which an unknown or imperfectly known is clarified, defined, described in terms of a known. This is exhibited as an overt or implied predication of the form (*a*) A is [like] B, or (*b*) A is as B—that is, A is [like X] as B [is like Y]. In this scheme a m. is explicated by translating it into a predicative form that will reveal the relation of resemblance. For example: (*a*) 1. "Love is a singing bird" = "Love is like a singing bird" or "Love makes you feel like (or, as though you were listening to) a singing bird"; 2. "the proud nostril-curve of a prow's line" = "a prow's line with the same curve as a proud man's nostril"; 3. "Her head . . . with its anchoring calm" = "Her head that, with its air of calm, makes you feel as secure (? and hopeful) as an anchor would in a ship"; 4. "a Harris-tweed cat" = "a cat that looks (smells, feels) as though it were made of Harris tweed"; (*b*) 5. "My love is . . . begotten by despair upon impossibility" = "My love is conceived as though its father were despair and its mother impossibility"; 6. "Hatred infects the mind" = "Hatred is like an infection in the mind"; 7. "Admiral earth breaks out his colours at the forepeak of the day" = "The earth discloses its colors in the morning with the same abrupt brilliance as the breaking-out of an admiral's colors (ensign) at the forepeak of his flagship."

All these examples happen to be "good" metaphors; the only objection would be to the method of exposition. Certainly there are "low-grade" metaphors, e.g., "Animal life always lives in the red," "He bull-dozed his way through all difficulties"; and the term "pro-saic" m. might be used to mark these off from the "essential" m. that has preoccupied 20th-c. criticism, e.g., "the mill of the mind / Consuming its rag and bone." But such a dis-tinction would turn less upon a definable difference in verbal events than upon the reader's (or writer's) attitude to m. in any particular passage. A m. becomes "dead" when the user forgets or does not know that a metaphorical relation was in the past implied or is still capable of being implied (e.g., "arrive" = late L. *arribare, adripare, ad ripam* [*appelere, venire*] = to call ashore, to come ashore or into harbour). The "prosaic" m. concentrates upon describing, clarifying, de-lineating, comparing—or is seen as doing so—, and is—or is seen as—subject to the limitations of plausibility or of logical harmony. "Essen-tial" m. deals in—or is seen as dealing in—a more complex, instantaneous, and even non-logical relation.

An unprejudiced examination of the exam-ples given above suggests that although analy-sis by resemblance may be suitable for analys-ing resemblance, it is inadequate—even irrele-vant—in most of these cases if we take into account not merely some notion of semantic equivalence but the actual sensation these met-aphors induce. First, the apparently simple metaphors 1 and 4 have at least two or three simultaneous meanings; and this occurs not because of a variety of resemblances but be-cause of a substantial though paradoxical co-incidence of terms: each term preserves its dis-tinctness, yet in the momentary coincidence—or identity (to use a term applied at least as early as 1930 by Bowra)—each term is changed. Second, examples 3 and 6 show that what ap-pears to be a simple two-term relation can be a condensed four-term relation. Third, the function of the transitive verb in analogical m. (A is to X as B is to Y) is very important (with "hatred infects the mind" cf "hatred is [like] an infection in the mind" or "hatred works in the mind as infection works in the body"); to reduce or expand an analogical m. to predica-tive form destroys its vitality. These results may be tentatively consolidated. The radical form of m. is either A is B (a momentary or hypothetical identity being involved), or sim-ply A-B (parataxis, the juxtaposition of two terms, e.g., "sphinx-woman" and 2, 3, 4 above). The analogical m. achieves strength and avoids a simple relation of resemblance by forming itself around a transitive verb (e.g., "bright chanticleer explodes the dawn," "the ship ploughs the waves").

Historically, however, the view of m. as primarily a figure for extending description, comparison, and exposition reflects literary usage rather than critical obtuseness. Rosa-mund Tuve, for example, has pointed to the 16th-c. emphasis, in handbooks and in prac-tice, upon the delight roused by deft and sustained *translatio*, the exploration by meta-phorical means of minute similarities within clearly defined fields of relationship (see *Eliza-bethan and Metaphysical Imagery*, 1947, pp. 121ff., 223–24). Guided by a clear notion of the didactic and explicatory function they wished m. to serve, writers of that period saw no reason to extend or explore the outer reaches of m. And Milton's use of epic simile, as compared with the Homeric use, is a refined development of *translatio* in the direction of multiple logical resemblances (see SIMILE be-low). Although at practically all periods we find instances of m. serving important poetic functions outside the scope of the received grammatical definition, these were evidently not thought important enough to modify the defi-nition. Even the extended range of m. used by, say, Shakespeare, Milton, and Donne happened not to be matched by any extension in analysis or theory. And if Johnson may be regarded as representative of his age, he looked back at least two centuries when he said: "As to meta-phorical expression, that is a great excellence in style, when it is used with propriety, for it gives you two ideas for one."

In fact, Aristotle's doctrine of m., though fragmentary, was far more comprehensive than his successors had reason clearly to recognize. He had also said that "the greatest thing by far is to be a master of metaphor. It is the one thing that cannot be learnt from others; and it is also a sign of genius, since a good metaphor implies an intuitive perception of the simi-larity in dissimilars" (*Poetics* 1458b; cf *Rheto-ric* 1405a); and that "from metaphor we can best get hold of something fresh [new]" (*Rhetoric* 1410b), that "Liveliness [?energy] is specially conveyed by metaphor" (*Rhetoric* 1412a), and that "of the four kinds of Meta-phor the most taking is the proportional [4-term analogical] kind"—e.g., "The sun sheds its rays" (*Rhetoric* 1411a). He had not only implied a sharp distinction between the uses of m. in prose and in poetry, but had also emphasized the energetic character of m. by choosing examples, not in predicative form, but as formed around vigorous verbs. In show-ing the relation between riddle and m. he had in a sense anticipated the doctrine of para-tactic m. But tradition, and many later critics, neglected these niceties.

Although discussion about m. during the last thirty years has been concentrated upon "essential" m., the discourse has often carried within itself relics of the grammarians' empire, unexpunged because unexamined. The grammarians' view of m., however, cannot be dismissed as altogether irrelevant; for the grammarian has a legitimate claim to pronounce upon the form and use of figures as far as these can be manipulated according to rhetorical technique. Nor can the "prosaic" m. be banished from poetry as "not a genuine m."; for the dividing line between "prosaic" and "essential" m. is never in general distinct, and what is a "prosaic" m. in isolation may become an "essential" m. by being put back into its context or by an appropriate adjustment of the reader's attention. Most grammarians and many literary critics have failed to notice that the *matrix* of a m.—the vital context, often considered over a wide range—is an indispensable component of "essential" m. Once precise control of the matrix is lost—and one's memory of the history of a word can be an important part of the matrix—the m. dies.

The publication within less than ten years of Grierson's edition of Donne, Hopkins' poems, Eliot's *Waste Land*, three volumes of Yeats's mature poetry, Pound's paraphrases of Fenollosa, and Joyce's *Ulysses* brought to attention poetic facts and relations that were not to be explained on the traditional view. The New Criticism, which first established itself less as a systematic order of criticism than as a method of explication with a strong pedagogical bias, was quite early overtaken by the clamorous but intermittent inquiry into m. and symbol which has dominated criticism in this century. If there are few modern examinations of m. on any scale of completeness, this is to be explained by a remark of Middleton Murry (1927): "The investigation of metaphor is curiously like the investigation of any of the primary data of consciousness: . . . Metaphor is as ultimate as speech itself, and speech as ultimate as thought. If we try to penetrate them beyond a certain point, we find ourselves questioning the very faculty and instrument with which we are trying to penetrate them" (in *Countries of the Mind*, 2d ser., 1931, p. 1).

Eliot's doctrine of the unity of sensibility in Donne may first have raised the question how widely disparate elements came to be unified in poetry; but it was the deliberate and powerful articulation of symbol and myth (sometimes private symbol and myth) by Yeats, Eliot, Pound, and Joyce that raised some even more awkward questions. Pound's doctrine—which he shared with the Fr. *symbolistes*—that m., like the Chinese ideogram, was a matter of abrupt juxtaposition, carried the question beyond grammatical limits and suggested a direct connection with Aristotle's *mimesis*. Certainly the implied extension of this principle of juxtaposition in Eliot's *Waste Land*, in Joyce's *Ulysses*, and in Pound's *Cantos* showed that large-scale ryhthms could be secured within a whole work by the abrupt juxtaposition of blocks of disparate material and by swift unmodulated shifts of emphasis from one focus to another over a large or small scale. Nevertheless there is danger in allowing the term "metaphor" to become too inclusive. Some anthropological arguments, and even Empson's illuminating analysis of the metaphorical structure of drama, seem to move toward the conclusion that *any* juxtaposition whatsoever is m. The corollary would be that no combination of words is not-metaphorical: and a useful term and a fruitful distinction is thereby destroyed.

The view that the term m. could legitimately be extended was encouraged by the work of Max Müller (1862–65) and by a succession of anthropologists, linguists, and psychologists who have studied the genesis and history of language. These have produced conflicting and even misleading hypotheses, and by customarily neglecting the evidence of developed literature have provided results not always serviceable to literary criticism. But they have helped to confirm the conclusion, drawn with increasing insistence from literary evidence, that in m. we see that "most vital principle of language (and perhaps of all symbolism)" (Susanne K. Langer, *Philosophy in a New Key*, 1953 ed., p. 112; here discussing Philip Wegener), and that "The genesis of language is not to be sought in the prosaic, but in the poetic side of life" (Otto Jesperson, *Language*, 1933). Shelley incidentally had already noticed this in a luminous if isolated passage: "Language is vitally metaphorical; that is, it marks the before unapprehended relations of things and perpetuates their apprehension, until words, which represent them, become, through time, signs for portions or classes of thought instead of pictures of integral thoughts: and then, if no new poets should arise to create afresh the associations which have been thus disorganized, language will be dead to all the nobler purposes of human intercourse" (*Defence of Poetry*).

The link with a rhetorical past was not easily broken. Much effort—both before and since the 1920's—has been spent on contriving terms suitable for describing how m. works: with distinctions between "what was said" and "what was meant," between "literal" and "metaphorical" meaning, between "idea" and "image," "form" and "figure," and so on. But it is dangerous to assume a readily distinguishable external datum of literality, for the literal meaning in each case is determined *within* the context; and the way Richards' terms "tenor" and "vehicle" fluctuated, even in his own hands (1936), arises from his attempt to answer both the question *"how does metaphor work?"* and the much more profitable question "what happens in a metaphor?" Some answers to this second question turned up not through consistent analysis but in more or less isolated *appercus.* T. E. Hulme's dictum that "the great aim [in poetry] is accurate, precise and definite description" (*Speculations*, 1924) obviously needed repudiating. Richards stated in 1925 that m. is "the supreme agent by which disparate and hitherto unconnected things are brought together in poetry for the sake of the effects upon attitude and impulse which spring from their collocation and from the combinations which the mind then establishes between them. There are few metaphors whose effect, if carefully examined, can be traced to the logical relations involved" (*Principles of Literary Criticism*, 1925, p. 240). C. Day Lewis' neat epigram has been influential: "We find poetic truth struck out by the collision rather than the collusion of images" (*The Poetic Image*, 1947, p. 72). Richards' *Philosophy of Rhetoric* (1936), though disappointing, emphasized the "organizing" activity in some kinds of m., pointed out that a word may be simultaneously "literal" and metaphorical, and introduced Coleridge into the discussion—a man who had already made at least a perceptive route-traverse of the country with the eye of a psychologist and linguist as well as of a poet and critic. John Crowe Ransom's introduction, from idealist philosophy, of the term "concrete universal" provided a useful name for an old and abiding paradox of poetry: that poetry evokes its universals not by generalizing or direct description but by an acute concentration upon the concrete particular, discovering directness in obliquity.

Max Black's analysis (Aristotelean Society, 1955) provides a useful summary and stopping place. He wished to assail the philosophical commandment "Thou shalt not commit metaphor" and in looking for a use of m. acceptable in philosophical discourse analysed previous accounts of m. into three "views": *substitution, comparison,* and *interaction.* The first two he dismissed (with qualifications), but found that the third, as represented chiefly by Richards (though again with some qualifications), offered "some important insight into the uses and limitations of metaphor." He starts with Richards' definition: "In the simplest formulation, when we use a metaphor we have two thoughts of different things active together and supported by a single word, or phrase, whose meaning is a resultant of their interaction" (*Philosophy of Rhetoric,* p. 93);

but rejects the word "interaction" in favor of the image of a *filter.* The metaphor-word—the *focus*—calls up a system of "associated commonplaces" which are in turn related .with various aspects of the principal subject: e.g., "Man is a wolf." "The metaphor [in this case] selects, emphasizes, suppresses, and organizes features of the principal subject by implying statements about it that normally apply to the subsidiary subject." Although Black recognizes that the elements of m. are "systems of things" rather than "things," and insists that these metaphors are untranslatable and that the secondary implications of a m. can be extremely intricate, his illustrations—as one would expect of a philosopher—are stated in propositional form. The outcome then is actually a comparison-metaphor, though of a much more highly organized and finely controlled kind than the comparison-metaphor recognized by tradition. Richards had clearly intended to go beyond his point, as some of his uses of the terms "tenor" and "vehicle" show. He wanted to talk about the "total meaning" of m. as arising from the *interaction* of elements. He had quoted Coleridge with approval: "A symbol is characterized by the translucence of the special in the individual . . . It always partakes of the reality which it renders intelligible; and while it enunciates the whole, abides itself as a living part in that unity, of which it is the representative." He seems to have chosen the word *interaction* with care: it allowed him to think of the metaphorical elements as preserving their integrity, and to think of the "total meaning" as the outcome of the impact of elements rather than as a derivative by comparison, fusion, or combination. If he had written his book ten years later he might have said that "interaction" was not like chemical combination but like nuclear fission. Richards' view is not definitive, but it either represents or has stimulated much of the more recent discussion. W. B. Stanford's definition, quoted with approval by W. K. Wimsatt in a review of Martin Foss, includes all the aspects Richards seems to have envisaged: "Metaphor is the process and result of using a term (X) normally signifying an object or concept (A) in such a context that it must refer to another object or concept (B) which is distinct enough in characteristics from A to ensure that in the composite idea formed by the synthesis of the concepts A and B and now symbolized in the word X, the factors A and B retain their conceptual independence even while they merge in the unity symbolized by X" (*Greek Metaphor,* 1936, p. 101).

An important adjunct to these views—and it is contained within the word "process"— was the New Critics' insistence upon tension, paradox, ambiguity, and irony as principles of poetic energy. As a means of reconciling these intimations of dualism, such words as "unification," "identity," and "fusion" have tended to come into use to express the complete metaphorical relation. Yet these images—as far as they are images of oneness—do not satisfactorily describe the sensations, emotional and semantic, induced by even such a simple transposing m. as "He has burnt his boats at both ends"; nor do they give an appropriate indication of what happens in the last two stanzas of *Sweeney among the Nightingales* or in Yeats's *The Second Coming.* It is conceivable that, if energy involves "tension" or bipolarity, m. like poetic experience exhibits an incorrigible dualism—or duplicity; and that although logical analysis can exhibit the vertiginous complexity of some metaphorical dualities, it can neither interpret them satisfactorily nor reduce them to monism except by radical distortion. We may well be able to apprehend metaphorical relations without being able to translate them into logical or any other terms.

Ingenious analyses of m. have been conducted by reducing all m. to the predicative form "A is B" and tracing the nexus of logical relations involved in an *identity* of A and B; identity, not mere similarity, being postulated for the relation. An interesting—and infinite —series of identifications, and identifications of identifications, then emerges. Clearly, if A is B, then A is not not-B; and also, in some sense, B is A, and B is not not-A. But beyond this, A is also not-B and B is not-A; otherwise the statement "A is B" or "B is A" would be tautological ("A is A" and "B is B"). Thereby a complete set of contrary relations is established. This procedure is capable of much more intricate and illuminating results than the repellant algebraic formulation would suggest; but it tends to preclude the controlled consideration of affective metaphorical context, and perhaps only comes into its own in analyzing the relations between symbols, myths, or archetypes. It is certainly a good way of analyzing all the logical implications of a statement of the form "A is B" where identity of A and B is assumed; but it is unlikely to commend itself to those who regard m. as a nonlogical—even antilogical—mode of connection, and therefore as a relation that by definition is *not* expressed in the form "A is B."

In an area so beset with the brambles of conflicting doctrine, some single view must be attempted. As a general definition Stanford's account serves very well. Certain observations and suggestions may be added. (The additional remarks accord—in some ways at least—with Martin Foss's *Symbol and Metaphor in Human Experience,* but are not derived from that study.) (1) M. is not simply a problem of language. Though m. is seen in a highly developed form in poetry, and is the characteristic mode of energetic relation in poetry, it may also prove to be the radical mode in which we correlate all our knowledge and experience. (2) M. is a nonpredicative energy-system, different from and opposite to (or complementary to) the logical mode. The m. is to poetry what the proposition is to logic. (3) When poetic energy is low the m. gravitates toward predication and simile—toward the "prosaic" m. (4) M. can fall into a large number of different grammatical patterns. Grammatical construction does not identify "essential" m., and is only a rough guide even to "prosaic" m. The line of division between "essential" and "prosaic" occurs at about the level of *simile* (q.v.); but some passages in the simile-form achieve a genuine metaphorical relation, and some passages in the metaphor-form are submerged similes. Also the analogical m. can be either "prosaic" or "essential": cf. "The chairman ploughed his way through the agenda" and "The ship ploughs the waves." (5) What Richards calls "interaction" may be called *confrontation.* This would imply, on the analogy of human relationship, juxtaposition (parataxis) *and* interaction—even a desire to communicate, to enter into communion—without either the merging or unification of elements or the destruction of integral individuality. (6) Although the verb "to be" is a primary mark of metaphorical coincidence or identity, the "prosaic" m. is usually (*a*) one in which immediacy of confrontation is destroyed by the verb "to be," "to seem," etc. (even when omitted), the space being bridged by the logical processes of comparison, descriptive emendation, and substitution (e.g., "to barter in the bawdyhouse of fame / their birthright for a misbegotten song": the apparent m. "bawdyhouse of fame" = "fame is a bawdyhouse," and anyway the whole m. is out of control); "When the play ended, they resumed / Reality's topcoat": the apparent m. "Reality's topcoat" = "Reality is a topcoat." Again, "prosaic" m. is often (*b*) one in which the setting does not prepare and control confrontation. (7) Metaphorical process may operate over a very limited or a very wide range. The tendency of metaphorical energy to spread outward and to draw other elements inward may be called *resonance.* (This at the logical level is what tradition meant by "consistency," "congruity.") The resonance of a m. is a function both of the setting (which may be extensive) and of the nature of the elements brought into relation: for example, a m. which relates symbolic and mythical elements tends to be, but is not necessarily, more resonant than a m. which relates only elements which are dominantly visual or conceptual. It would be profitable to see how resonance is affected by various parts of speech (verb, adjective, noun, etc.) and by sound and rhythm. It would also be profitable to find out how there is metaphorical resonance in a phrase like Donne's "a bracelet of bright haire about the bone," and in passages where most of the elements are abstract terms and the syntactical relations apparently discursive (see for example Wordsworth, *Immortality Ode* 140–50, or Preface to *The Excursion* 62–71). (8) "Essential" m. cannot be translated without severe cognitive loss, and is inexhaustible to analysis. The only sure test is the actual relation in the individual instance, and the actual degree and scope of resonance.

The Works of Aristotle, ed. W. D. Ross, XI (*Rhetoric*, tr. W. Rhys Roberts; *Poetics*, tr. I. Bywater) (1924); M. Müller, *Lectures on the Science of Language*, 2 ser. (1862, 1865); H. Paul, *Principles of the Hist. of Language* (1888); A. Biese, *Die Philosophie des Metaphorischen* (1893); P. Wegener, *Untersuchungen über die Grundfragen des Sprachlebens* (1898?); J. G. Jennings, *An Essay on M. in Poetry* (1915); H. Werner, *Die Ursprünge der Metapher* (1919); I. A. Richards, *Principles; Coleridge on Imagination* (1934), *The Philos. of Rhetoric* (1936); J. M. Murry, "M." (1927) in *Countries of the Mind*, 2d ser. (1931); O. Barfield, *Poetic Diction* (1928); H. Konrad, *Etude sur la métaphore* (1939, 2d ed., 1958); H. W. Fowler, *A Dict. of Modern Eng. Usage* (1940; art. "M." and "Simile & M."); Langer; M. Foss, *Symbol and M. in Human Experience* (1949); W. Empson, *The Structure of Complex Words* (1951); H. Kenner, *The Poetry of Ezra Pound* (1951); Crane, *Critics*; G. Whalley, *Poetic Process* (1953); P. Wheelwright, *The Burning Fountain* (1954) and *M. and Reality* (1962); M. Black, "M.," *Proc. of the Aristotelian Society*, n.s., 55 (1955); Frye; C. Brooke-Rose, *A Grammar of M.* (1958); *M. and Symbol*, ed. L. C. Knights and B. Cottle (1960); M. I. Baym, "The Present State of the Study of M.," BA, 35 (1961); C. M. Turbayne, *The Myth of the M.* (1962).   G.W.

METAPHYSICAL POETRY. The poetry written by John Donne, George Herbert, Henry Vaughan, Andrew Marvell, and other 17th-c. Eng. poets, distinguished by ingenuity, intellectuality, and, sometimes, obscurity. By extension, any poetry which displays similar qualities. M.p. of the 17th c. is characterized by a marked dependence on irony and paradox (qq.v.) and by the use of the conceit (q.v.) as well as such figures as catachresis and oxymoron (qq.v.). In its earlier manifestations (e.g. the *Songs and Sonets* of John Donne), Eng. m.p. was further distinguished by revolutionary and highly original attitudes toward

sexual love. Donne rejected not only Petrarchan rhetoric (see PETRARCHISM) but also the pose of abject worship of the mistress which the 16th-c. poets had inherited, via Petrarch, from the troubadours. A new kind of sexual realism, together with an interest in introspective psychological analysis, thus became an element in the metaphysical fashion.

Realism, introspection, and irony remained the dominant features of Eng. m.p., but the greatest of Donne's successors—Herbert, Crashaw, Vaughan—generally chose to embed these qualities in a religious rather than an amorous context. The great body of m.p., including much of Donne's own, is devotional, sometimes mystical. Although some authorities regard the term "m.p." as a misnomer, pointing out that its practitioners are seldom overtly concerned with questions of metaphysics or ontology, others have maintained that the distinctive quality of m.p., the occasion of its technique, is precisely that the subject—love, death, God, human frailty—is presented in the context of some metaphysical problem. Whatever its theme or subject matter, 17th-c. m.p. showed relatively little dependence on sensuous appeal. As the preceding comments on their technique suggest, the m. poets employed primarily a kind of imagery which requires the mediation of the intellect for full comprehension. In this respect m.p. differs from the 17th-c. baroque (q.v.) poetry with which it is often associated. There are, however, a few poets who, like Crashaw, manifest aspects of both fashions. The assumption, made by most earlier critics, that Eng. m.p. derives primarily from attempts to imitate Donne has been successfully challenged by modern scholarship, which has demonstrated not only the notable individuality of such poets as Herbert and Marvell but also the fact that many features we usually associate with the metaphysical style were actually present in much poetry written either shortly before or during the time when Donne wrote his *Songs and Sonets*, by such poets as Southwell, Fulke Greville, and William Alabaster. Furthermore, modern research has drawn our attention to many poets on the European Continent, predecessors or contemporaries of Donne, who wrote poems in a strikingly similar style. Such poets as La Ceppède in France, Huygens in Holland, and Quevedo in Spain seem certainly to deserve the name "metaphysical poets." If there can be said to be a "School of Donne" in England, it consists really of such minor amorous lyrists as Lord Herbert of Cherbury, Carew, and Suckling, not of the great devotional poets.

Poets and critics during the heyday of m.p. had almost no awareness of that kind of poetry as a separate stylistic phenomenon; most theorists of the age continued to describe poetry in terms of traditional Renaissance poetics (see BAROQUE POETICS). However, some It. and Sp. writers did offer the doctrine of "universal analogy" as a basis for conceit and farfetched metaphor in general, and the term "strong lines" was used by Eng. writers to designate the intricate intellectual quality of Donne and many of his contemporaries. The term "m." was first suggested by John Dryden (*Discourse of the Original and Progress of Satire*, 1692), in a reference to Donne: "He affects the metaphysics not only in his satires, but in his amorous verses, where nature only should reign, and perplexes the minds of the fair sex with nice speculations of philosophy." It remained for Dr. Johnson to supply the first analysis of m. imagery as well as to establish the term "metaphysical" permanently in Eng. literary criticism. Johnson described the basis of m. imagery as a kind of *discordia concors*, through which "the most heterogeneous ideas are yoked by violence together," and criticized the school for its lack of naturalness. The rejection implied by both Dryden and Johnson leads to some consideration of the wavering reputation of the m. style. Dominant until the Restoration of 1660 and the associated triumph of neoclassicism, m.p. went into a period of eclipse throughout the 18th and 19th c. Although such poets as Coleridge and Browning admired Donne, he and his successors were generally regarded as frigid and pretentious purveyors of intentional obscurity. A great revival of interest in the m. poets coincided with the development of "modern" poetry in the period of the first World War. T. S. Eliot, for example, saw in those poets, as in the Jacobean dramatists, the quality of "unified sensibility," a capacity for "devouring all kinds of experience" which he contrasted with the singleness of tone of the romantics and Victorians.

Some critics of the 1920's and 1930's, influenced by Eliot, went perhaps too far in stressing the modernity of the m. group, but balance has been achieved in recent years through scholarly studies which have demonstrated the links between m.p. and the phenomena of its own age—such phenomena as scholastic philosophy, Renaissance logic and rhetoric, the new science of the 17th c., and the practice of formal religious meditation. Nevertheless, Eliot has been one of the most provocative writers on m.p. It is to him, largely, that we owe the expansion of the term's denotation from the historical to the generic. Eliot implies three great epochs in which m.p. has flourished: 13th- and 14th-c. Italy, from Guido Guinicelli to Dante; 17th-c. England, in the lyric poetry of Donne and his "school" and in the drama of Shakespeare and his successors; France in the later 19th c., in the poetry of Baudelaire

and his symbolist progeny. The last grouping is susceptible to a further extension: through Eliot, initially a follower of Laforgue and Corbière, and through Yeats, initially influenced by Mallarmé, 20th-c. Eng. and Am. poetry derives a decidedly m. cast which continues to characterize the work of the younger poets at mid-century.

If Eliot's perception is valid, one may be justified in seeking common historical causes for the periodic emergence of the m. fashion. Perhaps our own century, under the disturbing impact of scientific relativity, social fragmentation, and political chaos, stands in an intrinsic kinship both to the 17th c., when, in Donne's phrase, "new philosophy calls all in doubt," and to the 14th c., in which the medieval synthesis began to break up. Certainly the m. style, in its introspective and realistic orientation as in its wide-ranging metaphor and daring rhetoric, aims at creating a precarious unity from the scattered materials of an existence which has grown puzzling and unfocused. The m. poet, whether Donne, Baudelaire, Rilke, or Eliot, is perhaps compelled to "unify his sensibility" because he can find no unity in his world.

S. Johnson, "Life of Cowley," in *Lives of the Eng. Poets* (1781); H.J.C. Grierson, *Metaphysical Lyrics and Poems* (1921); G. Williamson, *The Donne Tradition* (1930); J. Smith, "On M.P.," *Scrutiny*, 2 (1933); J. Bennett, *Four M. Poets* (1934); J. B. Leishman, *The M. Poets* (1934); H. C. White, *The M. Poets* (1936); R. Tuve, *Elizabethan and M. Imagery* (1947); C. Brooks, *The Well Wrought Urn* (1947); T. S. Eliot, "The M. Poets" and "Andrew Marvell" in *Selected Essays* (1950); L. Unger, *Donne's Poetry and Modern Crit.* (1950); M. Nicolson, *The Breaking of the Circle* (1950, rev. ed., 1961); O. de Mourgues, *M., Baroque and Précieux Poetry* (1953); L. L. Martz, *The Poetry of Meditation* (1954); J. E. Duncan, *The Revival of M.P.* (1959); A. Alvarez, *The School of Donne* (1961); L. Nelson, *Baroque Lyric Poetry* (1961); F. J. Warnke, *European M.P.* (1961). See also R. Ellrodt, *L'Inspiration personnelle et l'esprit du temps chez les poètes métaphysiques anglais* (3 v., 1960).

F.J.W.

METER. More or less regular poetic rhythm; the measurable rhythmical patterns manifested in verse; or the "ideal" patterns which poetic rhythms approximate. If "m." is regarded as the ideal rhythmical pattern, then "rhythm" becomes "m." the closer it approaches regularity and predictability. The impulse toward metrical organization seems to be a part of the larger human impulses toward order: m. is what results when the rhythmical movements of colloquial speech are heightened, organized, and regulated so that pattern emerges from the relative phonetic haphazard of ordinary utterance. M. is thus one of the fundamental and most subtle techniques of order available to the poet, like rhyme, line division, stanza form, and over-all structure.

Most theorists agree that poetic m., even when most primitive, produces a pleasant effect, but there is widespread disagreement among critics and scholars over the reason for the universal popularity of metered compositions. According to some theorists (mostly rationalists), m. is pleasant because it focuses attention and refines awareness; according to others (mostly romanticists), on the contrary, it is pleasant because it produces a lulling, drugging, or hypnotic effect. One theory holds that, since the beat in most accentual poetries is slightly faster than the normal heart-beat, the apprehension of poetic m. produces a physically exhilarating effect on hearer or reader: his heart-beat, the theory contends, actually speeds up to "match" the slightly faster poetic rhythm. The pleasure universally resulting from foot-tapping and musical time-beating seems to suggest that the pleasures of m. are definitely physical and that they are as intimately connected with the rhythmic quality of man's total experience as are the similar alternating and recurring phenomena of breathing, walking, and love-making. Perhaps one could untangle some of the disagreements about the pleasures of m. by suggesting that the quality of the apprehender will determine the nature of the pleasure in each case: children and the unsophisticated receive from m. primarily physical pleasure which manifests itself in foot- or finger-tapping, head-nodding, and the like; on the other hand, the more experienced and sensitive reader will probably derive most of his metrical pleasure from the higher level of rhetorical attention which m. enforces ("Meter keeps the mind on the stretch," one critic has observed), or from an intellectual delight in witnessing order and containment brought out of chaos and flux. Medieval theories of m., in fact, frequently assume that the pleasure man takes in m. is an image of the pleasure he takes in the observation of the principle of order in a universe which is itself will and order incarnate.

"M." derives from the Gr. term for "measure," and one way to investigate various meters or metrical systems is to examine what is being measured in each. On this basis, four metrical systems are generally—if not quite adequately —discriminated: the syllabic, the accentual, the accentual-syllabic, and the quantitative.

Syllabic prosody measures only the number of syllables per line: hence the term "numbers," frequently used as a synonym for "versification" by syllabic metrical theorists. In syllabic m. stress or accent is usually only a device of embellishment and not a criterion of the basic metrical "skeleton" of the line. Poetry in the Romance languages and in Japanese is fundamentally syllabic in construction. Some Eng. poetry after the Restoration became markedly syllabic (perhaps as a result of Fr. influence) until about 1740, but since that time syllabism has seldom been revived except as an experimental novelty: Robert Bridges, Dylan Thomas, W. H. Auden, and Marianne Moore are some of the recent poets who have experimented with syllabism. It would probably be agreed that syllabism is not a natural m. in a Germanic language so accentual as Eng., although interesting (if perhaps hypersubtle) effects can result from it (here and below, all examples are of poetry in Eng. for purposes of comparison):

> Mid the squander'd colour
> idling as I lay
> Reading the Odyssey
> in my rock garden
> I espied the cluster'd
> tufts of Cheddar pinks
> Burgeoning with promise
> of their scented bloom . . .

(R. Bridges, *Cheddar Pinks* [6- and 5-syllable lines alternating; stress used as embellishment])

One clear disadvantage of syllabic construction is that the reader, to sense the form of the poem, must halt unnaturally at line endings: the reader naturally measures by stresses, not by number of syllables, and he finds it almost impossible to grasp the metrical shape of the poem without an elaborately unnatural pause at the end of each line.

In accentual m., on the other hand, only the accents are measured; syllables may vary in number, it being assumed that 3 or 4 syllables can be uttered in the same time as 1 or 2. Most Germanic poetries, including OE, are based on accentual meter, as are most Eng. poems in which the number of syllables varies (through trisyllabic substitution, for example) from line to line:

> Why should not old men be mad?
> Some have known a likely lad
> That had a sound fly-fisher's wrist
> Turn to a drunken journalist;
> A girl that knew all Dante once
> Live to bear children to a dunce;
> A Helen of social welfare dream,
> Climb on a wagonette to scream.

(W. B. Yeats, *Why Should not Old Men be Mad?* [4 stresses per line, with number of syllables varying from 7 to 9])

METER

I sit in one of the dives
On Fifty-Second Street
Uncertain and afraid
As the clever hopes expire
Of a low dishonest decade:
Waves of anger and fear
Circulate over the bright
And darkened lands of the earth
Obsessing our private lives.

(W. H. Auden, *September 1, 1939* [3 stresses
per line, with number of syllables varying
from 6 to 8])

Sometimes accentual meters like the two above
are called "loose iambic."

The third metrical system, the accentual-
syllabic, represents really a tightening of the
accentual. Here, both number of accents and
number of syllables are measured (frequently
through the measuring of "feet" [see FOOT] of
stated patterns). Variations in accent placement, addition, or omission are much more
readily "allowed" than variations in number
of syllables per line. The result of this strictness is a metrical container of some rigidity
and inflexibility, but, at the same time, of
great compressive power. Fairly strict accentual-syllabic m. will generally be found used
by conservative practitioners in Eng.: Dryden,
Pope, Swift, and Johnson are examples. One
may conjecture that accentual-syllabic m. has
been fashionable in Eng. primarily during
periods marked by an interest in classical
rhetoric and by a commitment to the maintenance of a sense of order and limitation, for
of all Eng. metrical systems, it is the one most
hostile by nature to impulse, irregularity, and
unrestrained grandiosity:

Creatures of every kind but ours
Well comprehend their natural powers;
While we, whom reason ought to sway,
Mistake our talents every day.

(Swift, *The Beasts' Confession to the Priest*
[octosyllables with 4 stresses; "natural" in line
2 reduced to a dissyllable by syncope])

In a slightly looser form, sometimes tending,
that is, toward accentualism, the accentual-
syllabic system is the basis for the standard
Eng. meters, such as iambic pentameter (blank
verse), or iambic and trochaic tetrameter. The
presence or absence of trisyllabic substitution
often determines whether a given meter is to
be classified as strictly accentual or accentual
syllabic.

In quantitative m., finally, durational rather
than accentual feet are measured, and each
foot consists of a particular pattern of "long"
and "short" syllables. Sanskrit, Gr., and later
Roman poetries are quantitative, and there
have been attempts (particularly during the
Renaissance) to write Eng. verse according to

the principles of duration rather than stress:
"Unhappy verse, the witness of my unhappy
state, / Make thyself flutt'ring wings of thy
fast flying / Thought, and fly forth unto my
love, wheresoever she be: / Whether lying restless in heavy bed, or else / Sitting so cheerless
at the cheerful board, or else / Playing alone
careless on her heavenly virginals" (Spenser,
Iambicum Trimetrum [quantitative imitation
of classical iambic trimeter]). Inspired by the
theorizing of William J. Stone, Robert Bridges,
among others, has performed some interesting
experiments in our own time with quantitative
Eng. verse. It must be said, however, that despite occasional successes with the quantitative
principle in Eng., the language seems to be so
heavily accentual by nature that no other
characteristic can serve adequately as a basis
for m. Bridges has testified to the difficulty of
thinking in quantities instead of accents, and
his experience suggests that a m. customary in
a given language is customary just because it
"measures" the most characteristic quality of
the language.

In poetry, which is the most organic and
"total" mode of verbal expression, m. (like
the other formal elements) serves as one of
the primary correlatives of meaning: since m.
is an indispensable contributor to meaning, it
follows that the m. of a poem, in and by
itself, means something, and even that the m.
maintains a portion, at least, of its meaning
whether symbolic sounds are attached to it or
not. A good illustration of this basic alliance
of m. with meaning (perhaps through association only) is the function of m. in the limerick,
where the short anapestic lines are themselves
expressive of light impudence. The fact that
a "translation" of a limerick into another m.
(say, iambic tetrameter) seriously impairs the
comic tone which is a part of the total expression indicates the large burden of meaning which m. alone carries. In the same way,
most sensitive Eng. poets have discovered that
triple meters (anapestic, dactylic) tend to have
something vaguely comic, light, or superficial
about them (some, like Longfellow in *Evan-
geline*, apparently have made the discovery too
late), and they tend to eschew such meters in
favor of duple rhythms for the treatment of
more or less serious subjects. Taking a somewhat more complex illustration than a limerick, we can see the relationship of m. to meaning in Shakespeare's 129th sonnet:

Th'expense of spirit in a waste of shame
Is lust in action; and till action, lust
Is perjur'd, murd'rous, bloody, full of blame,
Savage, extreme, rude, cruel, not to trust;

Here the metrical disorder and violence of the
4th line is intimately allied with the violence
and extremity of the statement, and indeed

-[498]-

both creates and is created by that violence. One has only to imagine the same statement expressed in a regular anapestic m. to perceive how m. and meaning are indissolubly married here. In a good poem, thus, limerick or sonnet, rhythmical pattern (together with expressive variations from it) is a constituent and a source of significance; it is never a mere embellishment, appliquéd from the outside onto what would otherwise be "prose" utterance; it issues from the pressure of feeling and reasoning at every point in the poem (see METRICAL VARIATIONS).

In addition to serving as a major technique for the reinforcement of meaning, m. performs more general functions in a poem. It often establishes a sort of "distance" between both poet and subject and reader and subject by interposing a film of unaccustomed rhythmical ritual between observer and experience. It can thus help to control emotion and inhibit cliché responses in both poet and reader. This ritual "frame" in which m. encloses what is often perfectly everyday experience resembles the frame or artificial border of a painting. It reminds the apprehender unremittingly that he is not experiencing the real object of the "imitation" (in the Aristotelian sense) but is experiencing instead that object transmuted into symbolic form. M., as a device of artificiality and unnaturalness, is thus a primary technique of artifice in poetry, just as similar conventions (the palpably artificial stone flesh of statues, for example) are primary techniques of artifice in the other arts. M. also tends to suggest (since ordinary people don't speak in meter) the vatic rôle of the poet, just as it tends to invest with a mysterious air of permanence and authority the words which are cut to its pattern. The strange power of m. to burnish the commonplace has even tempted some thinkers to regard metrical patterns as Platonic forms, themselves inherently and permanently beautiful, which the poet perceives unconsciously and towards which he constantly impels his own utterance.

If one regards absolutely regular m. (as some Platonists do) as the "ideal," then one becomes extraordinarily sensitive to those points in the poem where the "sense" pattern of the language rhythm lies at some distance from the normal or "base" abstract rhythm of the presumed metrical scheme. Prosodists and critics who have studied closely this frequent distance between a poem's "ideal" and "real" m. have developed a theory of prosodic "tension": these theorists maintain that one of the sources of metrical power and pleasure is just this tension between perfect and imperfect metrical patterns. To these theorists, the perpetual tension between "metrical" and real rhythms constitutes the sort of "play" or "suspension" (or even the Coleridgean reconciliation of opposites) which is the secret source of illumination and delight in all art.

A complete discussion of the nature of m. would require not only a consideration of the function of poetic m. in general, but also some investigation of the unique functions of m. in different kinds of poetry. Except for its most obvious offices, it is apparent that m. does not do the same things in lyric that it does in poetic drama; nor does it do the same things in narrative poetry that it does in satiric. Its function is mnemonic in "Thirty days hath September" and in the metered genealogies of epic; musical and hypnotic in *Kubla Khan*; and oratorical and analytically pedagogic in the *Essay on Man*. See PROSODY; ENG. PROSODY; LINGUISTICS AND POETICS.†

T. S. Omond, *Eng. Metrists* (1921); E. A. Sonnenschein, *What is Rhythm?* (1925); P. Barkas, *A Critique of Modern Eng. Prosody* (1934); Y. Winters, "The Influence of M. on Poetic Convention," *Primitivism and Decadence* (1937); J. C. Ransom, *The New Crit.* (1941), pp. 254–69, 297–330; D. A. Stauffer, *The Nature of Poetry* (1946); K. Shapiro, *A Bibliog. of Modern Prosody* (1948); Wellek and Warren; A. Stein, "A Note on M.," KR, 18 (1956); J. C. Ransom, "The Strange Music of Eng. Verse," KR, 18 (1956).　　　P.F.

METONYMY (Gr. "change of name," "misnomer." L. *denominatio*). A figure, related to *synecdoche* (q.v.), in which one word is substituted for another with which it stands in close relationship: in common language such substitutions as *hippos* (literally horse) in place of *to hippikon* (meaning cavalry); *o katharma* (literally "that which is thrown away in cleansing" for "you scum"). Quintilian (*Institutes of Oratory* 8.6.23–27) does not distinguish clearly from *hypallage* (q.v.), but he does classify m. into various kinds: e.g., the name of the inventor or possessor, for the invention or possession; the container for that which is contained; to which may be added modifier for modified, symbol for thing symbolized, etc.: "Pallida mors aequo pulsat pede pauperum tabernas" (Pale death with equal foot knocks at the poor man's door—Horace, *Odes* 1.4.13). Common to all poetry, m. is well exemplified in Shakespeare: m. of the efficient cause—"As Ovid be an outcast quite abjur'd" (*The Taming of the Shrew* 1.1.33); m. of the material cause—"he tilts / With piercing steel at bold Mercutio's breast" (*Romeo and Juliet* 3.1.163); m. where effect is substituted for cause —"I have made my way through more impediments / Than twenty times your stop" (*Othello* 5.2.263). The major effect is to communicate through abstract, intangible terms the concrete

† In Supplement, see also GENERATIVE METRICS.

or tangible; according to Kenneth Burke, abstract and spiritual words are metonymic in origin ("Four Master Tropes" in *A Grammar of Motives*, 1945, pp. 503f). There is some reason to believe that m., with metaphor, is more intimately related to the processes whereby experience becomes language and thought than study of it as a figure would suggest; Wellek and Warren write, "Recently some bolder conceptions of m. . . . have been suggested, even the notion that m. and metaphor may be the characterizing structures of two poetic types—poetry of association by contiguity, and poetry of association by comparison, joining in a plurality of worlds, mixing in the striking phrase of Bühler [*Sprachtheorie*, 1934], a 'cocktail of spheres' ". (*Theory of Lit.*, 2d ed., 1956, pp. 184–85).—A. Fraunce, *The Arcadian Rhetorike* (1588; ed. E. Seaton 1950); Lausberg.

R.O.E.

METRICAL ROMANCE. See MEDIEVAL ROMANCE.

METRICAL VARIATIONS. A term covering the techniques of departing from metrical regularity for the purposes of either sheer variety or rhetorical reinforcement. Strictly speaking, m.v. are possible only in verse composed with a more or less regular base rhythm; they do not exist as such in cadenced or free verse.

"Substitution" (according to conventional graphic scansion) is the most frequent technique of metrical variation. Here, once a basic metrical pattern has been established, the rhythm may be varied by the introduction of a "substitute" foot to replace one or more of the normal ones. In the following example,

An aged man is but a paltry thing,
A tattered coat upon a stick, unless
Soul clap its hands and sing, and louder sing
For every tatter in its mortal dress, . . .
(Yeats, *Sailing to Byzantium*)

each line uses a substitution for one of the "expected" iambic feet: line 1 has a pyrrhic in the third position; line 2 a pyrrhic in the third; line 3 a trochaic (or spondaic) substitution in the first position; and line 4 a pyrrhic in the third. These substitutions serve both to alleviate the metrical monotony of the long-continued iambic pentameter and to allow the metrical structure to "give" and shape itself according to the rhetorical pressures of the statement. In the following lines by Matthew Arnold,

Listen! you hear the grating roar
Of pebbles which the waves draw back, and
fling,
At their return, up the high strand,

Begin, and cease, and then again begin, . . .
(*Dover Beach*)

one can see substitutions used with even stronger intentions of sense reinforcement. Against an iambic background, the initial trochaic substitution in line 1 constitutes an unexpected reversal of the metrical movement which emphasizes a shift in the address; in line 2, the spondaic substitution in the fourth position suggests the slowness of the sea wave as it coils back upon itself, gathering force to shoot itself up the beach; in line 3, the pyrrhic substitution in the 1st position suggests the speed with which the wave "flings" itself up the sand; and in line 4, the return to iambic regularity, after these suggestive variations, transmits a feeling of the infinite, monotonous continuance of the wave's process. In Eng. verse, the most common substitution is the replacement of the initial iamb by a trochee, as in the first line of the Arnold example. This initial trochaic substitution is usually found even in the most metrically regular poems, for the unvaried iambic foot becomes insupportably tedious after very many repetitions. In fact, a failure to employ m.v. is one of the stigmata of the bad poet. In the following example: "I know that Europe's wonderful, yet something seems to lack: / The Past is too much with her, and the people looking back. / But the glory of the Present is to make the Future free— / We love our land for what she is and what she is to be" (Henry Van Dyke, *America for Me*) the absence of an instinct for meaningful m.v. goes hand in hand with the complacent ignorance of the ideas and the fatuity of the rhetoric.

In addition to the device of dissyllabic substitution, lines can also be varied by the addition or subtraction of unaccented syllables, which is frequently accomplished by either trisyllabic or monosyllabic substitution. Trisyllabic substitution is regarded by conservative metrists as a "bolder" form of substitution than dissyllabic, for, in duple measures, trisyllabic substitution increases the syllabic length of the line.

As the examples above help illustrate, the fundamental principles of metrical variation are these: (1) a succession of stressed syllables without the expected intervening unstressed syllables tends to transmit an effect of slowness, weight, or difficulty; (2) a succession of unstressed syllables without the expected intervening stressed syllables tends to suggest an effect of rapidity, lightness, or ease; and (3) an unanticipated reversal in the rhythm (as in the first line of the Arnold passage, above) suggests a new direction of thought, a new tone of voice, or a change in poetic address.

The fact that m.v. such as these can be

illustrated by scansion and analyzed dispassionately should not cause the reader to believe that, from the point of view of the poet (at least the good poet), they are anything but instinctual. Many poets whose work can be analyzed metrically according to the foot system would be astonished to be told that they have indulged in "substitution": the genuine poet composes according to the rhythms which his utterance supplies, and, although these rhythms frequently turn out to consist of "normal" and "substitute" feet, they do not necessarily begin that way. See METER, PROSODY, SCANSION, COUNTERPOINT, FOOT.—Saintsbury, *Prosody*; Baum; Brooks and Warren; L. Perrine, *Sound and Sense* (1956). P.F.

METRICUS, *metrici* (Gr. *metrikos*, *metrikoi*, student(s) of metrics). The *metrici* represented a school of ancient metrical theorists who held that only long and short syllables need be considered in analysis, and that the long syllable was always twice the length of the short, variations being too slight to be of consequence. In opposition to this group were the *rhythmici*, who maintained that long syllables differ greatly from one another in quantity, and that even short syllables may differ in some degree, thus demanding much more complicated methods of analysis. At present the speculations of both schools hold only historical interest.—T. D. Goodell, *Chapters on Gr. Metric* (1901); U. von Wilamowitz-Moellendorff, *Griechische Verskunst* (2d ed., 1958). K.M.A.

METRON. In Gr. and L. verse the unit of measurement. In dactylic (–∪∪), cretic (–∪–), and bacchiac (∪––) verse the unit is a single foot (e.g., the dactylic hexameter contains 6 feet) and the scansion is according to the foot (*kata poda*). On the other hand, in other dissyllabic and trisyllabic feet, e.g., iambic (∪–), trochaic (–∪), and anapaestic (∪∪–), which do not contain more than 4 morae, the unit is 2 feet, i.e., a dipody or syzygy, and the scansion is according to the metron (*kata metron*). Thus the iambic dimeter, trimeter, or tetrameter is a verse of 4, 6, or 8 feet.

The importance and value of the distinction may be observed in the L. iambic trimeter as contrasted with the iambic senarius. In the former the inner thesis (of feet 2,4,6) must be "pure" (the even-numbered feet must not be spondees). Here the dipody is the unit of composition. Where, as in the senarius, and in fact most L. verse (not Gr.), no distinction between the inner and outer thesis or arsis (q.v.) is observed by the poet, the dipody is merely traditional and the true m. is the foot.—Koster. K.M.A.

MEXICAN POETRY. See SPANISH AMERICAN POETRY.

MIME (Gr. "imitation"). A dramatic form in which players rely mainly on gestures to tell a story. Found in ancient Greece and Rome the m. probably arose from the natural impulse to imitate persons or scenes from daily life. As a literary genre, however, it developed in Sicily and southern Italy where Sophron of Syracuse (5th c. B.C.) wrote in colloquial prose realistic scenes which border on the gross. Subsequently Herodas (3d c. B.C.) used metrics in his *mimiambi* which in turn influenced the Alexandrian poetry of Theocritus and the L. poets Plautus, Terence (dramatists), Horace (*Epodes, Satires*), and the Roman m. writers, Decimus Laberius and Publilius Syrus (1st c. B.C.), whose works except for fragments are not extant. The genre is basically comic but differs from comedy in that it need not have a plot, emphasizing instead the portrayal of character. Ribaldry and burlesque were its chief ingredients and hence its source of great popularity. The Christian church waged war on the m. and its actors so that finally in the 5th c. A.D. all who took part in it were under ban of excommunication. As a genre it again became popular in 16th-c. Italy in the *commedia dell' arte* whence it spread to France and England. In 19th-c. France *L'Enfant Prodigue*, a three-act m. play, culminates the history of the genre. In the contemporary world the m. again is popular but as a part of dramatic technique. Today it relies exclusively on gesture, avoiding entirely the use of words.—H. Reich, *Der Mimus* (1903); O. Crusius, *Die Mimiamben des Herondas* (1926); A. Körte, *Hellenistic Poetry* (1929); A. Nicoll, *Masks, Mimes and Miracles* (1931); W. Beare, *The Roman Stage* (2d ed., 1955). R.A.H.

MIMESIS. A Gr. term, customarily translated "imitation," but with a different and somewhat broader range of meaning than the Eng. word. Ultimately derived from *mimos*, which in the historical period denoted the "mime" or an actor therein, *mimesis* seems to have meant originally the mimicking of a person or creature through dance, facial expression, and/or speech and song. But the object so "imitated" might be a god, a mythical hero, or a fabulous creature, e.g., the Minotaur; in other words, m. could refer to an idea or a type as well as to an actual individual. For the extension of m. to literature in general and its establishment as a central concept in literary theory by Plato and Aristotle, see IMITATION; POETRY, THEORIES OF (MIMETIC THEORIES). G.F.E.

MINNESINGERS, authors of *Minnesang* (the first body of poetry in German to rank as part of world literature), which in its widest sense includes all artistic lyrical poetry of the Middle High German period and was composed to be sung or recited (not read) for the entertainment of courtly society. In the narrow sense it is a specific kind of love poetry, the aim and reward of the man's spiritual devotion to woman (*hohe minne*) being "that your worth be enhanced and you gain a joyous elation therefrom" (Albrecht von Jahnsdorf).

It flourished first in the Rhine regions, then chiefly at the courts of Austria and Southern Germany for a 200-year period, which may be subdivided into (1). *Minnesangs Frühling* (Spring of minne song), middle to end of 12th c. (e.g., Der Kürenberger, Heinrich von Veldeke, Dietmar von Aist, Meinloh von Sevelingen); (2). the great flowering, end of 12th to beginning of 13th c. (hardly more than 20 years, e.g., Hartmann von Aue, Albr. von Johansdorf, Heinrich von Morungen, Reinmar von Hagenau, Walther von der Vogelweide); (3). late *Minnesang*, beginning of 13th to beginning of 14th c. (e.g., Ulrich von Lichtenstein, Neithart von Reuenthal), generally considered a period of decline. The early poets came from the higher nobility, later ones also from the lower (professional or semiprofessional minstrels, or *Spielleute,* under the patronage of great nobles).

Love (*minne*) is the chief theme, although there is much formal treatment of nature and reference to contemporary history: the crusades, the poet's relationship to his princely employer, the state of the Empire (Walther!). Love had in earlier eras been condemned by the church as lust (*luxuria*). Since, however, *Minnesang* is court poetry, the relationship between man and woman assumes certain noble characteristics of the lord-vassal relationship. The *man* is vassal to his *frouwe* and he wishes to receive a reward (*lón*) for his service (*dienest*). As the aim of German court society at the time of the Staufen dynasty was the perfect man, who achieved self-discipline and balance (*máze*) by constant training (*zuht*), the value of the *minne* relationship shifted from the attainment of possession to the arduous but ennobling way which might lead to it. The woman, by this process, became so idealized that the goal became in fact unattainable, and the whole relationship fictitious. Only thus can one understand the apparent paradox of the poet's praise of the virtue of a married noble lady (often the wife of the minnesinger's own lord) whom he implores to relax her standards in his particular case. *Minnesang*, in the work of its greatest representatives, is an elevation of womanhood. In its quasi-religious praise of the Eternal-Feminine, this poetry re-

flects elements of the worship of the Virgin Mary. In the hands of the lesser practitioners, especially in the late period, *Minnesang* became a social game or empty conventionality to the point of caricature. There is, however, a more realistic strain; even the great singers around 1200 and certainly the late M. would write of sensual love, attainable from women of the lower classes (*niedere minne*). This poetry bears the marks of personal experience and expresses personal feelings.

Minnesang has strong affinities with the love poetry of the Fr. troubadours, but elements of older G. secular love poetry can also be discerned. It is often less gallant and more spontaneous than its Fr. counterpart. A relationship may, moreover, exist between *minne* song and medieval secular love poetry in L. (*Vagantenpoesie*). Lastly, the Arabic sung strophic love lyrics, placing woman in an exalted position, practiced at the Arabic princely courts of Spain, and antedating the troubadour poetry, must be considered in any attempt at historio-genetic explanation.

Form (1). The principal form used by the M. is the *lied* i.e., the strophic poem (the strophe represents both the poetic and the musical unit, as with the troubadours), a frequent variety (from Walther on) being the *Tagelied* (q.v.). While metric structure and rhyme patterns were, at first, indebted to prov. models, variations and innovations were developed from ca. 1180 on. (2). There is also the nonstrophic *leich* (q.v.) with varying length and number of lines, and set to continuous music. (3). For the short (originally 1 stanza) poem, which since Walther may deal with political and religious themes, Simrock and Wackernagel (1833) misleadingly introduced the term *Spruch*. It is really the same as a short *lied*; for it is not spoken, but also sung, and must not be confused with the didactic *Spruch* (q.v.) proper.

COLLECTIONS: *Minnesinger,* ed. v. d. Hagen (4 v., 1838, new printing 1923); *Die Schweizer Minnesänger,* ed. K. Bartsch (1886); *Der Minnesang des 12. bis 14. Jhs.,* ed. F. Pfaff (2 v., 1891–1895); *Deutsche Liederdichter des 12. bis 14. Jhs.,* ed. K. Bartsch and W. Golther (8th ed., 1928); *Herbst des Minnesangs,* ed. H. Naumann (1936); *Trouvères et minnesänger,* ed. I. Frank (I, texts, 1952) and J. M. Müller-Blattau (II, music, 1956); *Die Lieder Neidharts,* ed. E. Wiessner (1955); *Deutsche Lyrik des Mittelalters,* ed. M. Wehrli (1955); *Dt. Liederdichter des 13. Jhs.,* ed. C. v. Kraus and H. Kuhn (2 v., 1952–58); *Die Gedichte Walthers v. d. Vogelweide,* ed. C. v. Kraus (12th ed., 1959); *Des Minnesangs Frühling,* ed. K. Lachmann (32d ed. by C. v. Kraus, 1959).
HISTORY AND CRITICISM: A. Lüderitz, *Die Liebestheorie der Provençalen bei den Min-*

nesingern der Stauferzeit (1904); W. Wilmanns, *Walther v. d. Vogelweide*, ed. V. Michels (4th ed., 1916–24); K. Burdach, "Über den Ursprung des mittelalterlichen Minnesangs," *Berliner Sitzungsberichte* (1918); G. Müller, "Studien zum Formproblem des Minnesangs," DVLG, 1 (1923); L. Ecker, *Arabischer, provenzalischer und deutscher Minnesang* (1934); C. v. Kraus, *Walther v. d. Vogelweide* (1935) and *Des Minnesangs Frühling: Untersuchungen* (1939); M. Ittenbach, *Der frühe dt. Minnesang* (1939); M. F. Richey, *Essays on the Mediaeval German Love Lyric* (1943); T. Frings, *Minnesänger und Troubadours* (1949); A. Moret, *Les Débuts du lyrisme en Allemagne* (1951); F. Maurer, *Die politischen Lieder W's v. d. Vogelweide* (1954); H. Kolb, *Der Begriff der Minne und das Entstehen der höfischen Lyrik* (1958); B. Kippenberg, *Der Rhythmus im Minnesang* (1962). U.K.G.

MINSTREL. A professional entertainer of the Middle Ages, successor to the earlier scop (q.v.), gleeman, or jongleur (q.v.). Minstrels flourished particularly in the 13th and 14th c.; their activity decreased in the 15th c., and with the invention of printing their function in society ceased to be meaningful.

As in the case of the jongleur, it is difficult to determine with certainty the nature and role of the medieval m. Some were attached to a court or a noble household; others wandered from town to town; some even performed in the public streets. The social position of the m. presents a similar problem. Sometimes the term is applied to the troubadours and *trouvères* (qq.v.), true poets and often men of education and social standing; on other occasions it denotes the wandering acrobats and buffoons. Some scholars have suggested that the more sophisticated entertainers rose out of their class as a result of their talents.

In any case, the literary productions of the minstrels are clearly distinguished in pace and tone from those of the two other main categories of medieval writers—the clerical and the aristocratic. For the most part, the minstrels retold the familiar stories of tradition, as derived from a variety of sources ranging from the *chansons de geste* (q.v.) and the Germanic legends to the later romances and folk ballads. Independent love lyrics are also attributed to minstrel authors. The romantic writers of the late 18th and early 19th c., influenced by a belief in the virtues of "primitive" poetry, endowed the minstrels with the colorful and picturesque aura which surrounds them, even today, in the popular mind.—E. Faral, *Les Jongleurs en France au moyen âge* (1910); H. Naumann, "Spielmannsdichtung," *Reallexikon*, III; P. Wareman, *Spielmannsdichtung. Versuch einer Begriffsbestimmung* (1951);

R. Menéndez Pidal, *Poesía juglaresca y orígenes de las literaturas románicas* (6th rev. and enl. ed., 1957). A.P.

MIRACLE PLAYS. See MYSTERY AND MIRACLE PLAYS.

MOCK EPIC, MOCK HEROIC. Terms used in a broad sense to describe a satiric method in poetry and prose and, more specifically, a distinct verse form which seeks a derisive effect by combining formal and elevated language with a trivial subject. The mock-heroic poem *per se* consciously imitates the epic style, follows a classical structure and heroic action for deflationary purposes, and employs some of the standard paraphernalia of the epic—i.e., invocations, dedications, celestial interventions, epic similes, canto-divisions, and battles.

The Homeric *Batrachomyomachia* (Battle of the Frogs and Mice) served as a model for many an 18th-c. battle in mock-epic strain. The 1717 version of this work by Thomas Parnell belongs with many such neoclassic, burlesque battles of pygmies or cranes or rats or hoops or books or sexes. Chaucer had employed the mock-heroic style in *Nun's Priest's Tale*, but Boileau's *Le Lutrin* is commonly mentioned as the most influential modern poem magnifying a trivial subject on an ambitious scale. Dryden's *MacFlecknoe* and Pope's *Rape of the Lock* and *Dunciad* are classic examples of Eng. mock-heroic poetry aiming their shafts at literary pretence and social folly. Mock odes, mock elegiacs (Gray's ode *On the Death of a Favourite Cat . . .*), and mock eclogues abound in Eng. verse, but the mock heroic held supremacy among them until it blended with later burlesque and satiric modes.—R. P. Bond, *Eng. Burlesque Poetry, 1700–1750* (1932); K. Schmidt, *Vorstudien zu einer Gesch. des komischen Epos* (1953). R.P.F.

MODERN POETICS. I. 1750–1900. Modern poetics is distinguished by a gradual dislocation of traditional standards based on the neoclassical interpretation of Aristotle's *Poetics* and on the models of classical antiquity. These changes, and reactions against them, which have become most pronounced since the mid-18th c., may be clarified by an arbitrary division of the period into four phases: *empiricism, transcendentalism, realism, idealism,* and *the revival of classicism,* and *symbolism.*

1. *The Empiricist Phase:* In the *empiricist phase* of the later 18th c., under the impact of philosophers like Locke and Hume, a critical reorientation tended to replace external authority by the individual mind. Subjectivity and historal relativism in matters of taste and a degree of license in poetic forms

and levels of style were the result of this development. But in stressing the individual self, this position also provided fertile ground for conceptions of the self as a principle of inspiration, in a Neoplatonic and Longinian sense, which had been implicit in neoclassical poetics. By suggesting that in inspiration a poet intuitively fathoms universal forms and truths, this principle reconciled a subjective view of creation with an insistence on classical rules.

In *France,* this reorientation is reflected in the work of the pre-Revolutionary generation of critics like Voltaire and Diderot. François-Marie Voltaire (1694–1778) combined a subjective theory of taste with a practical belief in the touchstones of critical judgment, harmony and decorum. Thus, Voltaire combined the famous dictum of "each to his own taste" with a belief in "good" taste that favored lucid, metrically sound verse and strict adherence to dramatic rules. He could praise Shakespeare's genius and yet condemn his rude violations of classical conventions. Differences between Homer, Tasso, and Milton are accounted for by a distinction between *conventional* beauties (locally determined) and *essential* beauties (based on universal reason). Denis Diderot (1713–84) worked more narrowly within the tradition of empiricism. Borrowing from the Lockean sensationalism of the Comte de Condillac (1715–80), Diderot developed a theory of signs according to which poetic language pictures the sounds and shapes of external nature and registers human emotions as they are experienced by the mind. Consequently, Diderot preferred descriptive and narrative poetry and employed it in the service of his particular moral didacticism. Later, his attention shifted from the poet and reader to "real" beauty, an eternal form beyond human perception, embedded in nature and copied by the work of art. Among other Fr. critics of the age, various accommodations between an empirical and a Neoplatonic position are found from the rationalism of the Comte de Buffon (1707–88) to the increasingly radical sentimentalism of Jean-Jacques Rousseau (1712–78) and Sébastien Mercier (1740–1814).

In *England,* a similar dual position is suggested by the continuing impact on 18th c. poetics of the Neoplatonic tradition of the Earl of Shaftesbury on the one hand and by Lockean and Humean doctrines of imagination and taste on the other. The concept of "original composition" of Edward Young (1683–1765) suggests that genius works through a supernatural power which enables the poet to penetrate to eternal forms despite the fact that each man is born an original. Underlying such theories is not only a Neoplatonic metaphysic but also a belief in the universality

of taste and the generality of human, moral, and external nature held by critics like Sir Joshua Reynolds (1723–92) and Dr. Samuel Johnson (1709–84). Dr. Johnson's criticism favored the universal, disparaged the grotesque in construction and style, minimized the poet's individual imagination, and stressed the need for rationally valid rules of good taste and sound moral judgment superimposed upon an enlightened historical relativism. At the same time, Eng. and Scottish critics like Henry Home, Lord Kames (1696–1782), Richard Hurd (1720–1808), James Beattie (1735–1803), or Hugh Blair (1718–1800) developed the implications of Lockean psychology—based on the apprehension and association of ideas and their signs (words) by the individual mind—for emotion, imagination, and taste in poetry. But while these critics contributed much to the refinement of poetic theory, they were also compelled to reconcile their views with the need for common standards of agreement in Dr. Johnson's sense.

In addition to Neoplatonism, these standards were to some extent provided by the "common sense" school of philosophy, exemplified by Thomas Reid (1710–96), which insisted that the mind intuitively apprehends matters of fact "as they are," knowledge of which is founded in men's common consciousnesses. In thinkers like Adam Ferguson (1723–1816) and Dugald Stewart (1753–1828), this view led to a definition of "imagination" as an innate, universally human power of abstraction and ordering which acts upon assemblages of sensible materials supplied by the lower "fancy." Thus, each of these theories is forced to deal with the problem of reconciling individual experience and emotion with an objective aesthetic. Edmund Burke (1729–97) offered a solution with his distinction between rationally accessible *beauty* and the *sublime* apprehended only as the result of grotesque and individual imagination. Paralleling this development is a growing belief in primitivism and an interest in history. The "discovery" of James Macpherson's "Ossian" and the vogue of folk poetry, as demonstrated by the activities of Thomas Percy (1729–1811), were explained on the grounds that primitive language and poetry are "purer" than civilized poetry because they are more immediately expressive of emotions. The view of poetry as an historical phenomenon, associated with the work of Joseph Warton (1722–1800) and his brother Thomas Warton (1728–90), is the result of an historical relativism in poetry impelled by the empirical point of view. On the whole, such criticism and poetry exhibit, ultimately, that very rejection of universality which Dr. Johnson had deplored. This tendency is revealed in the interest in bizarre subject matter, narrative verse reflecting individual experiences, and the decline of poetic drama during the second half of the 18th c.

Moreover, in England, as elsewhere in Europe, this development tended to weaken the Horatian notion, which had dominated Western poetics since the Renaissance, that a poem must teach as well as delight. What had been self-evident to Sir Philip Sydney and Alexander Pope required a Neoplatonic rationale or Dr. Johnson's stern defense in terms of the psychological and common sense doctrines of his time. As poetry became more and more associated with individual inspiration and expression, moral purposes requiring universal truths became more and more the insights or visions apprehended by individual poets. Didacticism continued in a different order of mystical apprehension in Blake, Wordsworth, or Shelley.

In *Germany*, the central conflict of 18th c. poetics was focused in the opposition of Gotthold Ephraim Lessing (1729–81) and Johann Gottfried von Herder (1744–1803). In his essay "Laokoon oder über die Grenzen der Malerei und Poesie" (1766), Lessing developed a theory of signs according to which the *co-existent* signs of the pictorial arts (denoting extension and form) and the *successive* signs of poetry (denoting action in time), must not encroach upon one another. Hence, despite some later modifications, Lessing was led to reject descriptive and to neglect lyrical poetry and to extol the epic and drama in which action predominates. Herder, on the other hand, stressed meaning and *organic form* which bind literary signs together through energy linking subject and object, space and time, in imaginative apprehension. Herder's concept of organic form, which in Italy was independently developed by Giambattista Vico (1668–1744), was applied to the evolution of history, language, and poetry, and led to an adulation of Homer, "Ossian," and Shakespeare as poets of nature. Herder expressed the protest against a prevailing prosaic rationalism by the generation of the *Storm and Stress* which also included the young Schiller, Goethe, and Wieland. These developments, however, were modified towards the end of the century. Friedrich Schiller (1759–1805) distinguished between ancient *naive* poetry, which was essentially poetry of nature, and modern *sentimental* poetry, which was poetry of art, the former being identified with intuitive emotion, the latter with intellectual reasoning. Schiller's famous theory of art as play, moreover, placed poetry in an art-world of illusion in which the opposites of sense and intellect, subject and object, nature and art are resolved in an apprehension of eternal verities conceived in the spirit of Shaftesbury

and Kant. At the turn of the 19th c., both Schiller and Johann Wolfgang von Goethe (1749–1832) had reconciled their conception of poetry of nature and organic form with an essentially Neoplatonic view of an ideal unity of language and form inspired by the models of antiquity. The history of German poetics in the 18th c. shows a fluctuating development, ranging from a rigid neoclassicism and didacticism early in the century to the emotionalism and the belief in genius, primitivism, and organic unity held by Herder and the *Storm and Stress* movement, to the temporary reconciliation of both in the "classicism" of the mature Goethe and Schiller.

In *Italy* the second part of the century saw the triumph of sensationalism over the rationalism of Descartes and the intellectualism of Leibniz, which had dominated the earlier half of the century. The ideas of the German philosopher were reflected in the poetics of L. A. Muratori, G. Gravina, and A. Conti. Their basically classicistic attitudes were superseded by the sensationalist speculations of Pietro Verri, Cesare Beccaria, Saverio Bettinelli, and Giuseppe Parini, who centered their attention on the hedonistic aspect of art and attempted various ways to reconcile it with more traditional didactic views as well as with the new emphasis on the role of individual "genius," personal "taste," and free "imagination." The outstanding critic of the later 18th c. was Giuseppe Baretti (1719–89), who criticized Voltaire's strictures of Shakespeare, rejected most of Fr. neo-classicism and philosophy, and extolled the critical ideas of Dr. Johnson. His notions of the rational naturalness of expression ("direct construction") were later refuted by Melchiorre Cesarotti, (1730–1808) the translator of "Ossian." In *Spain*, one of the foremost neoclassical works of criticism in the 18th c. was Ignacio de Luzán's *Poética ó reglas de la poesia en general y de sus principales especies* (1737).

2. The Transcendentalist Phase: As Kantian metaphysics sought to oppose an apparent trend towards skepticism in 18th c. empiricism and sentimentalism, so the poetics developed from the Kantian *Critiques* sought to restore "objectivity" to criticism. In his first two critiques, *Die Kritik der reinen Vernunft* (1781–87) and *Die Kritik der praktischen Vernunft* (1788), Immanuel Kant (1724–1804) distinguished three realms of knowledge, that of sensibility or sensual apprehension, of understanding or rational knowledge of the world of appearances (*Verstand*), and that of truly "real" things-in-themselves, the world of transcendental Reason (*Vernunft*) which cannot be known empirically or rationally but which is accessible through adherence to the universal moral law. In his *Kritik der Urteilskraft*

(1789–93) Kant defined the beautiful as "free," that is, as bound neither by the rules of the understanding nor by those of the moral duty. By this he meant that beauty is a *disinterested* emotion; the beautiful object manifests "purposiveness without a purpose"; its objective harmony serves only aesthetic enjoyment as an end in itself. At the same time, disinterested pleasure (beauty) and awe (sublimity) allow us to entertain *visions* of the transcendental world of Reason, but, since they exist autonomously, they cannot give us any *knowledge* of things-in-themselves which exist in the realm of Reason. Kant's successors, however, like Johann Gottlieb Fichte (1762–1814) and Friedrich Schelling (1775–1854), developed from this position an aesthetic which viewed the beautiful as yielding actual knowledge of the world of Reason; it becomes a cognitively accessible symbol of the transcendental ideal. Indeed, Schelling's *Die Philosophie der Kunst* (1802–3, publ. 1859) defined art as the presentation of the absolute or transcendental ideal in the sensible particular.

In *Germany,* this transcendentalist position was self-consciously applied to poetics in romantic criticism. Although Friedrich Schlegel (1772–1829) vacillates in his definitions of "romantic," a transcendentalist point of view is usually implied. The "romantic" mode is the essential characteristic of all poetry, an ideal distinguishing poetry from non-poetry, art from non-art, and thus approximating transcendental definitions of beauty. The term "romantic," however, is also used to distinguish between ancient and modern poetry as Schiller had distinguished between "naive" and "sentimental." In this formulation, "romantic" denotes the opposite of classical beauty which distiguishes Christian poetry since the Middle Ages sharply from the ideal poetry of Gr. antiquity. "Romantic" thus designates the unordered and complex, all that is connoted by the task of representing the infinite in finite perception. In consequence, Friedrich Schlegel's notion of *irony* assumes significance in transcendental terms. A discrepancy is created between the poem as finite artifact and the infinite ideal which it mirrors in *transcendental poetry.* Irony points up this discrepancy and thus exhibits aesthetically the union (in opposition) of the personal creation and the impersonal ideal which it mirrors.

Other romantic writers like Ludwig Tieck (1773–1853) or Ernst Theodor Amadeus Hoffmann (1776–1822) included in this notion of irony devices like the deliberate breaking of an aesthetic illusion to show the continuous interrelation of finite, subjective perception and infinite, impersonal art. The elaborate *Vorschule der Aesthetik* (1804) by Jean Paul Richter (1763–1825) includes a view of *humor* as a bridge from the finite world of sense experience to the infinite world of the ideal. August Wilhelm Schlegel (1767–1845) also utilized the transcendental definition of poetry. He echoed his brother's distinction between pure limited classical form and limitless romantic form which, in turn, is based on a definition of poetry as organic and on a transcendentalist conception of modern poetry as reflecting the infinite. A. W. Schlegel defined poetic imagination as a universal, undiversified power through which all art is created, but he defended differentiation of genres and rigorous metrics by suggesting that poetry is not the image but the *symbol* of the infinite. In this way, he could stress the organic conception of character (in Herder's sense) rather than the mechanical conception of fate as the driving power of dramatic form and defend Shakespeare against the invocation of Aristotelian rules. The distinction between "classical" and "romantic" was obliterated on transcendental grounds by Adam Müller (1779–1828) who defined poetry as the creation of life in which all oppositions (including that of classical and romantic) are joined.

A further outgrowth of the transcendentalist point of view in poetics is a new conception of the poet and hero. Friedrich von Hardenberg (Novalis) (1772–1801) developed a "magical idealism" through which the poet unites himself with the world of experience in the synthesizing apprehension of the ideal world reflected in transcendental poetry. The poet or hero whose perceptions and dreams become the material of poetry functions as the intermediary between finite nature and infinite art. Allegory and myth were the most likely means whereby the aesthetic synthesis could be accomplished. Novalis worked out a theory of the poet as a "supreme mimic" who incorporates within himself alien points of view and who thus becomes the poet's aesthetic self ironically representing both the finite self from which he is derived and the infinite which he symbolizes. The "classical" enthusiasm, in verse and prose, and the philosophical deliberations of Friedrich Hölderlin (1770–1842) represent one slightly atypical manifestation of this trend; Freiherr Josef von Eichendorff's nature poetry and symbolic fiction is another.

Among other German romantic writers, these views found more radical expression in three interrelated forms: (1) the supersedure of prescribed genres and forms by undifferentiating imagination and genius as advocated by Heinrich von Kleist (1777–1811), Achim von Arnim (1781–1831), and others; (2) the definition of poetry as an ideal language mirrored in our language of sense and a concomittant elevation of music (and hence of the lyric) as the crucial criterion of poetry, suggested especially by Bettina von Arnim (Brentano) (1785–1859); (3) the transformation of Herder's emphasis on myth as the basis of poetry into a self-conscious return to national folk myth and, in consequence, a gradual destruction of the previous cosmopolitan character of the romantic movement. This development was signaled early in the century by the collection of folk poetry *Des Knaben Wunderhorn* (1808) by Achim von Arnim and Clemens Brentano (1778–1842). Later, it was manifested in the linguistic studies, translations, and collections of Germanic myths by Jakob Grimm (1785–1863) and his brother Wilhelm Grimm (1786–1859). This shift in interest was explained by a distinction between *natural poetry,* expressing a national consciousness in its totality, and *art poetry,* reflecting artificially this expression of a national soul. This distinction was a radical and nationalistic echo not only of Herder's definitions of poetry but also of the Schlegels' transcendentalist derivations from Schiller's concept of naive and sentimental poetry.

The tendency of the later romantic movement to abandon aestheticism in favor of an increasing emphasis upon emotionalist and didactic interpretations was expressed by Friedrich Hegel (1770–1831). For Hegel's philosophy suggests a shift in transcendentalist doctrines of poetry from concern with the object mirroring the ideal to the ideal itself. Although for Hegel art is both *concrete* and *universal,* its development must lead away from its most concrete manifestations to higher universal forms in which art *qua* art ultimately disappears. Viewing poetry in three stages, symbolical or primitive allegories, classical or concrete and well-formed poetry, and romantic poetry, Hegel defined the last as the final stage in the development of poetic forms, as the overflowing of the absolute spirit. Although poetry is the highest form, approximating the ideal most closely through its simultaneous interaction of content and form in abstract and intellectual signs, it must also be superseded, for the approximation to spiritual reality (in a philosophical sense) is the ultimate end. The emphasis, therefore, remained on the spirit rather than on the form of art, and on its manifestation in a constantly evolving historical and dialectical process towards the ideal. The reformulation of Kant and Schelling by Arthur Schopenhauer (1788–1860), according to which poetry led to the necessary destruction of the transcendental Will through disinterested contemplation, was opposed to this trend, but Schopenhauer was less significant to his contemporaries than to succeeding generations. As a whole, from the 1830's on, transcendentalism

survived chiefly as an extra-literary framework within which poetry was judged. The revolt of the *Jung-Deutschland* group, which included, among others, Heinrich Heine (1797–1856) against the literary dictatorship of Goethe and the aestheticism of the Schlegels tended to abandon more and more the symbolic implications of a transcendentalist poetics but almost unconsciously retained its nonaesthetic, ideological emphasis as suggested, in part, by the Hegelian formulation. As a result, philosophical idealism, subjectivism, and political purposes became the standards guiding critical discussion.

In *England,* the first impulse toward a transcendentalist position was not so much concerned with first principles as with new conceptions of nature and of the function of poetic language. Although the relationship of the poet to his world and his art was equally explored, the more empirical spirit which pervaded British thought during the closing decades of the 18th c. focused attention primarily on the world of experience and on the language through which it was to be communicated. The *Preface to the Lyrical Ballads* (1798–1800) by William Wordsworth (1770–1850) and Samuel Taylor Coleridge (1772–1834) (as substantiated by the poems themselves) sought to demonstrate this change and thus became the first document of romantic principles in England. Nature was not a universal principle but the particularized, sensibly accessible external world. Similarly, human nature was not defined by a universal principle but by the particular psychology of "simple" men who lived close to nature. Poetic language, against the opposition of critics like Francis Jeffrey (1773–1850), was to express the language of these people ("common speech") truthfully as well as to reflect suitably images of external nature. At the same time, as their various writings suggest, Wordsworth's and Coleridge's views of aesthetic perception were colored by empirical doctrines of psychology available to them in David Hartley's Lockean treatise *Observations on Man* (1749): The 18th c. disjunction between poetic perception, viewed in empiricist terms, and poetic imagination, defined in the inspirationalist terms of Shaftesbury and Neo-Platonism, entered into the distinction between *fancy* and *imagination* which was redefined in romantic poetics. For Wordsworth, *fancy* denoted aesthetic perception and association, whereas *imagination,* the intuitive fathoming of eternal forms, became an understanding of an all-pervading divine spirit within nature of which the poet was a part and which was hence no longer directly related to neo-classical definitions of form. Poetry as the "overflow of powerful feelings . . . recollected in tranquility" became the means whereby the poet established his identity with nature.

S. T. Coleridge recognized the kinship of the distinction between fancy and imagination with the aesthetic theories of Kant, Schiller, and Schelling. Identifying "fancy" with Kantian understanding (*Verstand*) and "imagination" with reason (*Vernunft*), Coleridge defined primary imagination as "a repetition in the finite mind of the eternal act of creation in the infinite I Am," and secondary imagination as the power of expressing this insight formally. In making these distinctions Coleridge echoed the 18th c. Eng. tradition associated with Shaftesbury, but from his German readings he understood that in the 19th c. this is also a transcendentalist formulation: the poet fuses himself and the world of objects into a transcendental reality of the spirit, exhibited in the poem as the result of the unifying or "esemplastic" power of the imagination. This point of view influenced Coleridge's discussions of meter and language in his criticisms of Wordsworth and his critical judgments of Shakespeare (whatever his debt to A. W. Schlegel may have been). Meter establishes aesthetic distance through its tension with the natural rhythm of language and thus unifies and objectifies the passions. Coleridge's view of the totality of the work of art, mirroring the totality of life, which he applied to his Shakespeare criticism, reflects the transcendentalist notion according to which the poem as a total and organized unit mirrors the unity of life as a whole.

Among other Eng. critics of the age, essayists like William Hazlitt (1778–1830) and Charles Lamb (1775–1834) emphasized the evocative and metaphoric nature of poetry and criticism in their general views and in their criticisms of Shakespeare and other poets. More central to the current of transcendentalist poetics was the thought of Thomas de Quincey (1785–1859) who favored Kant's philosophy and Jean Paul's views of the relationship of poetry and dream. De Quincey's distinction between *literature of knowledge* (impermanent assemblages of facts) and *literature of power* (lasting works of creative imagination) reflects Coleridge's distinction of fancy and imagination in terms of the Kantian dualism. Linking up this view with the notion that superior awareness resides in dream (often stimulated by drugs), De Quincey conceived of the self, in its heightened imaginative act, as the instrument of the reason and thus opened the way to the kind of transcendentalist poetics we find later in Poe, Baudelaire, Rimbaud, and the symbolist movement.

The distinction between the passive conception of self as experiencer and the active conception of self as attaining to superior truths in inspiration is applied to conceptions of the self as hero in the poetry of Lord George Gordon Byron (1788–1824) and Percy Bysshe Shelley (1792–1822). The passive self is dramatized into the suffering as well as perceiving hero, the active self into that of the poet-hero as the conqueror of opposing external forces. At the same time, Shelley's *Defence of Poetry* (1821, publ. 1840), directed against Thomas Love Peacock's *Four Ages of Poetry* (1820), explores the relation of the poet to his craft and to the external world. Shelley defines imagination as a heightened experience, an inexpressible state of mind in which the mind is a bright coal fading in the actual process of creation. But he also views the poet as an active knower, an "unacknowledged legislator" of the world, who, while he expresses emotions, also copies eternal ideas through his language, and, beyond language, through symbols. Although John Keats (1795–1821) also identified truth and beauty, his concept of "negative capability" sought to exclude from the poet's search for truth a deliberate striving for perfect knowledge (which was to be left to the philosopher). For Keats, truth reveals itself in the act of feeling and creation through the genius of poetry rather than through the poet's self-conscious quest. Among later Eng. critics, Thomas Carlyle (1795–1881) did much to stimulate interest in German romanticism in England through translations and studies. The transcendentalist emphasis upon the self led in Carlyle's thought to an extension of the concept of the active hero into the supreme knower and creator with whom the poet was identified, as his work was identified with the echo of the divine ideal. In the *United States*, various derivations of transcendentalism from German and Eng. sources supplied defining characteristics to the mid-century flowering of romanticism in New England. Ralph Waldo Emerson (1803–82) sought a fusion of 18th-c. Eng. Neoplatonism and 19th-c. German transcendentalism. In his view, the soul rises to a comprehension of the universal order, to a realm of the spirit symbolized in external nature, which can be shared by the poet himself.

In *France*, the generation of François-René Chateaubriand (1768–1848), which was contemporaneous with Wordsworth, Coleridge and the older romantics in Germany, reflected views more easily associated with 18th-c. subjective empiricism and inspirationalism, coupled with neoclassical standards than with romantic formulations. With the appearance of *De l'Allemagne* (1813) by Mme de Staël (Germaine Necker) (1766–1817) German ideas in philosophy and literature were introduced into Fr. letters, but Mme de Staël's interpretation of these ideas emphasized the subjectivism of German romantic theories and ignored their objective formulations. Alphonse de Lamartine (1790–1869) pointed the way to an increasingly subjective, lyrical view of the nature of poetry which was reinforced by his growing affinity with Byron and other romantic writers. In addition to its concern with the relaxation of dramatic rules, the issue in Fr. romanticism was lyricism. Poets like Alfred de Vigny (1797–1863) and Victor Hugo (1802–85) aimed at the liberalization of verse forms and of distinctions between genres and levels of style in favor of poetic inspiration. Victor Hugo viewed art as a totality, a complete reflection of beauty founded in myth, and thus believed in the identity of form and content and in the reconciling power of the imagination. Essentially, Hugo's romanticism implied, in various degrees, rebellion against authority, whether in drama, poetry, criticism, or politics, and a view of the poet as the towering exile whose vision is perpetually misunderstood. Among other romantic poets in France, Gérard de Nerval (1808–50) is noteworthy not only for his translation of *Faust* (1830) but also for his fusion of imagination, image, and dream which contributed to the transformation of romantic into symbolist poetics.

In *Italy*, the romantic position in the debate with classical authority had been foreshadowed by Vittorio Alfieri (1749–1803), who conceived the role of the poet as that of an inspired upholder of freedom and fighter against tyrants. The more mature romanticism was represented, among others, by Ugo Foscolo (1778–1827), Alessandro Manzoni (1785–1873), and Giacomo Leopardi (1798–1837). Their views of the nature of poetry and the poet, of imagination and prescribed form, reenact Fr. and German debates of the 18th and 19th c. Most influential during the second half of the century was the scholar and critic Francesco de Sanctis (1817–83). In his critical essays and lectures, as well as in his *Storia della letteratura italiana* (1870–71), De Sanctis held transcendentalist views of poetics in their Hegelian formulation; yet, more rigorously than Hegel, he taught strict adherence to aesthetic form which rises to the poet's mind simultaneously with the idea which it seeks to express. In *Spain*, the attempts to define the nature of folk poetry by Manuel Milá y Fontanals (1818–84) and the views of the role of metrics in verse romance advanced by Angel de Saavedra, Duke of Rivas (1791–1865) are of special interest. The reciprocal effect on Sp. poetics of the German romantic enthusiasm for Sp. medieval and Renaissance masterpieces, the influence of Fr. and It. poetics, and the mid-century vogue of German metaphysics (based on the derivative theories of Friedrich Krause [1781–1832])

channelled poetics in Spain in a romantic direction. In *Russia*, a neoclassic attitude towards poetry early in the century was gradually displaced by a new spirit in the 1820s when Byron became a vogue. Alexander Pushkin (1799–1837) and Michael Lermontov (1814–41) are perhaps the foremost representatives of this spirit. On the whole, Fr. and German ideas contributed to the formulation of romantic poetics in Russia which, as elsewhere in Europe, were interwoven with political issues.

3. *Realism, Idealism, and the Revival of Classicism:* Transcendentalism was a philosophical expression of the poet's new relationship with himself as experiencer and actor and with the world of nature as a sensibly accessible univese of experience. An important force in the growing rejection of romanticism emerged in the empiricist and scientific *positivism* of Auguste Comte (1798–1857). Positivism brought with it the suggestion that poetry is necessitated by its external conditions and can be explained by them. This attitude is enhanced by the writings of social reformers like Claude-Henri Saint-Simon (1760–1825) and Pierre-Joseph Proudhon (1809–65), who focused on the social origin of poetry, as well as by theorists like the painter Gustave Courbet (1819–77), who believed that any imposition of convention upon a rigorously executed reproduction of the external world had to be dismissed as an objectionable "aristocratic pose." Both these formulations required *realism*, i.e., the depiction of the world "as it is," in vision and technique. At the same time, realism also became an important *aesthetic* reaction against romantic idealism. This position is evident in the antiromantic posture of the *Parnassian School* of Théodore de Banville (1823–91), Théophile Gautier (1811–72), and others, who sought to represent concrete objects and to manipulate them in language and verse forms following neoclassical conventions. But unlike the realism advocated by Courbet, the realism of this school served purely aesthetic purposes which anticipate the art-for-art's sake movements later in the century. In the *Eng.* language, on the other hand, the use and advocacy of realistic techniques in the poetry and poetics of Alfred Tennyson (1809–92), Robert Browning (1812–89), or Walt Whitman (1819–92) was combined with an idealistic and often even mystical world view, a combination still betraying the lasting influence of Wordsworth. Similarly Wordsworthian, John Stuart Mill (1806–73) extended the identification of poetry with feeling by applying to it an associationist psychology without the aesthetic limitations drawn by Wordsworth's theories of memory and imagination. If Courbet's realism tended to dismiss poetry altogether by condemning

all conventions, and if the Parnassian poets dissolved poetry into pure rhetoric, Mill's position allowed poetry to evaporate into pure feeling, a view which is epitomized in the contemporary positivism advocated in the early work of I. A. Richards.

The conception of realism which subjects poetry to its determining influences is evident in the historical theories of Ernest Renan (1823–92) and Hippolyte Taine (1828–93). Taine's slogan "race, milieu, moment" states that the moment and conditions of creation are sufficient to reveal the nature of poetry. In *England*, this point of view was reinforced by the rise of *Darwinism* as reflected in the writings of Thomas Henry Huxley (1825–95) and Herbert Spencer (1820–1903). Darwinist theories of evolution, in turn, affected continental poetics, as shown, for example, in the literary theory of Ferdinand Brunetière (1849–1906), according to which each literary genre is defined by its evolution and the manners which determine its changes during its progress through time. In *Russia*, the view of poetry as an expression of society was advocated by the Saint-Simonian Socialist Alexander Herzen (1812–70), Vissarion Belinsky (1811–48), and N. A. Dobrolyubov (1836–61). Belinsky, famous for his sociological criticism based on Feuerbach's materialistic interpretation of Hegel, identified poetry with society. Leo Tolstoy (1829–1910), from a very different ideological position, viewed poetry as a vehicle for the expression of emotions, for the communication of accurate perceptions of external reality, and for the implementation of desirable social and religious ends. The notion of literature as a social phenomenon serving the criticism of society, the *naturalism* of Émile Zola, most immediately affected prose fiction and the drama, but as a critical theory it also became profoundly significant to poetry.

The extension of romanticism into an increasingly *idealistic* conception of poetry is distinct from, though interrelated with, the positivistic point of view and the practice of realism. In the *United States*, Emerson had applied Coleridge's definition of the imagination to the notion of a universal spirit, which, through manifestation in the world of sense, unites the poet with the spiritual and moral order of which he is a part. Walt Whitman celebrated the poet as seer who found the universal truths embedded in the physical universe. Poetic language must express this impulse of identity with the universe, a view which accounts for Whitman's free verse as well as for his realistic techniques. Whitman's pantheism, by focusing on the immanence of the spirit in physical and human nature, reconciled his idealism with a sociological view of poetry as a mirror of democratic society. In *Germany*, post-Hegelian transcendentalism influenced both early Marxist and idealistic views of poetry. Realistic technique affected the extension of romantic nature poetry into the late 19th c., but at the same time essentially idealistic theories of symbolism and tragedy emerged under the aegis of Schopenhauer, in his reformulation of Kant, whose influence rose markedly during the second half of the century. The view propounded by Richard Wagner (1813–83) that *music* is the *pure,* aesthetic component of all artistic language and that all forms of art are fused into a music of ideas caught in the complex of aesthetic symbols profoundly influenced symbolist poetics in France.

Although he was deeply opposed to Hegelianism, Friedrich Nietzsche (1844–1900) incorporated in his view of tragedy the unity and opposition of formal and antiformal elements. Contrasting classical *Apollonian* order with the *Dionysian* annihilation of the limits of existence, Nietzsche viewed the former as the common characteristic of beauty and the latter as the true essence of tragedy. (See APOLLONIAN-DIONYSIAN). In the great Gr. tragedies both these elements are juxtaposed and intermingled, defining and opposing one another in mutual interaction. In this way, the poet of true tragedy can reenact man's fundamental impulses, founded in myth, through symbolic characters and events and provide a regeneration of these impulses through which alone man can satisfy his striving for existence. Similarly, the aesthetic speculations of Fyodor Dostoyevsky (1821–81) and the theological treatises of Søren Kierkegaard (1813–55) furthered the concept of the poet as attempting to annihilate the paradoxes of existence within a framework whose oppositions and reconciliations recall a Hegelian world view despite their profound rejection of the Hegelian system.

Post-Hegelian transcendentalism also directed historical, ideological, and philological approaches to poetry. Despite overt rejections of Hegel during some phases of the later 19th c., Hegel's identification of poetry with history, which obliterated the distinctions between genres and rendered poetic rules obsolete, resulted in a displacement of critical by historical criteria which had been prepared for by the historical and philological preoccupations of the Brothers Grimm. In a philosophical historian like Wilhelm Dilthey (1833–1911), the historical idea was fused with a psychological and cultural view of the relationship of poetry to man and society. As a result, Dilthey advocated an historical approach in which poetry was judged not by its inherent properties but by its manner of shaping and being shaped by its historical evolution and by its manner of mirroring the ideas and attitudes appropriate to its particular position in time. In this form, German *Geistesgeschichte,* which viewed the poem in terms of the spirit of the era which produced it (including its language, philosophy, science, painting, music, etc.) and in terms of the poet himself as the exemplar of this spirit, has determined much of the most important German criticism to this day. At the same time, the Hegelian conceptions of poetry did not necessarily displace tradition and poetic rules.

The criticism of Charles Augustin Sainte-Beuve (1804–69) was both impressionistic and traditionalist, his method historical and analytic. In Sainte-Beuve's view, poetry is an expression of the poet's personality, a manifestation of the poet's intuition and of the social and historical context which shaped him. But at the same time Sainte-Beuve derived his critical standards from within the Fr. classical tradition. This dual position was fortified by thories of critics like Ferdinand Brunetière and literary historians like Gustave Lanson (1857–1934). A similar outlook, however, was sharpened in the criticism of Matthew Arnold (1822–88) into a well-defined classical position. Arnold combined his historical idealism (based on Coleridge, Shelley, and Goethe) with a classical point of view. On the one hand he viewed poetry as part of a movement of ideas and the poet as the intuitive critic of ideas. On the other hand, he insisted on the *permanence* of literary values both in his reaction against Carlyle and German romanticism and in his debate with scientific naturalism. This position is evident in Arnold's belief in the "touchstones" of great art and in his confidence in the models of the ancients. Taking issue with the scientific exclusion of poetry from actual knowledge, he claimed for poetry an all-inclusiveness traditionally reserved for philosophy and a moral efficacy traditionally associated with religion.

The vogue of Hegelianism, and its variants, in late 19th-c. philosophy produced many theories important to 20th- rather than 19th-c. poetics—notably Bernard Bosanquet's theory of catharsis, Henri Bergson's analysis of intuition and time, Benedetto Croce's analysis of art as expression and intuition and his Hegelian dissolution of genres into the flow of history. Manifesting themselves in realistic and idealistic positions, transcendentalism and positivism ushered in the major critical theories which have dominated 20th-c. poetics: the sociological and psychological theories of Marxist, Freudian, and behavioristic poetics, the impressionism and biographical approaches of George Saintsbury and Edmund Gosse, the emphasis on the history of ideas so important

to critical discussion in Germany, France, and, recently, the United States. The stress upon tradition and classicism, moreover, aided in the development of modern formalist theories, which logically emerged from the *symbolist* implications of transcendentalism.

4. *The Symbolist Phase:* Symbolism, as a rebellion against both the traditionalism of Sainte-Beuve and the naturalism of Taine and Zola, originated in an aesthetic interpretation of transcendentalist poetics which was greatly affected by the ideas of Edgar Allan Poe (1809–49). Despite his rejection of Emerson, Poe's remarks about the nature of poetry and beauty are by no means unrelated to the transcendentalist tradition, but rather develop a symbolic concept of poetry, which returns to the early romantic conception of the ideal attained to in poetry as essentially aesthetic. Poe thought of the poet as the reflector of "supernal" beauty, an ideal reached by the marshalling of all the senses not to mirror objects of experience but to transform them symbolically. Beauty, moreover, is also *feeling;* poetry, distilled from the discursive functions of its language, is *music* which, through its dispositions of sound, organizes the essences of all experiences into art. So defined, pure poetry represents an end in itself, unalloyed by considerations of moral, social, and other didactic purposes.

In *France,* Charles Baudelaire (1821–67), under the influence of Poe, Gautier, Swedenborg, Wagner, and others, viewed the poet as translating his experiences into symbols of a transcendental reality through a fusion of all the senses. These symbols are concrete, preferably artificial forms which obtain an existence of their own as images from a realm beyond sense. Uniting his craft with the crafts of other arts, such as music and painting, the poet thus strives to capture the infinite within the finite limits of his poem. The result has been lyrical poetry in which, despite important modifications in metrics, the personal experience is translated into an aesthetic experience chiefly through imagery reflecting artificial objects and often through an allegorical or stylized depiction of external, human, and moral nature. Arthur Rimbaud (1854–91) extended Baudelaire's notion of the poet's function in a more radical direction. He enacted the role of the poet as seer who, in a heightened state of awareness often stimulated by intoxication and drugs, accumulates within himself all possible experiences, especially those arising from unconscious dream. Through an intense disordering of all the senses, the poet becomes "another" by recreating his conscious and unconscious perceptions in detached forms, manipulated neither by laws of psychology nor by logical or dramatic sequence but by aesthetic dispositions of color, imagery, and sound.

The symbolist point of view was developed further by Paul Verlaine (1844–96) and by the practice of poets like Tristan Corbière (1845–75). It was crystallized in the Symbolist Manifesto of 1886 in a pointed exchange between Anatole France (1844–1922), the exponent of rationalism and classicism, and Jean Moréas (1856–1910). Poets responsible for the symbolist program in France and Belgium (Gustave Kahn, Francis Viélé-Griffin, Stuart Merrill, Maurice Maeterlinck, Emile Verhaeren, and others) were intensely concerned with dissolving the *logic* of Fr. poetry. They seized upon *music* as the most striking method whereby logical sequence could be "liquefied." Denying, with Verlaine, poetic language its communicative function, symbolists viewed the language of poetry as a veil preventing rather than enhancing intelligible communication. At the same time, paradox, as developed from the concept of romantic irony, was used not in a logical function but precisely in an illogical fashion—to destroy logic through unexpected contradiction. But the poet's duty was also to transcend the world of sense by absorbing its inherent contradictions. The dreams of his subconscious, reflections of a higher order, became concrete, though detached symbols, which, in their illogical connections and sound and image patterns, manifested that higher reality. The symbolist position, therefore, entailed an extreme subjectivism, a concern with the darkest aspects of the subconscious (which led to a label of "decadent"); paradoxically, however, it was also characterized by an extreme aesthetic detachment and by a preference for the artificial. The greatest exponent of symbolism was Stéphane Mallarmé (1842–98) who furthered the dissolution of logical verse into music and illogical paradox and resolved the apparent contradiction between the subjective origin of a poem and its objective detachment through form by counselling total annihilation of the "life" emotion which inspired the poem. The more rigidly the poetic symbol excludes the world of natural reality and the initial emotion the more closely it approximates the ideal of art.

In *England*, the art-for-art's-sake movement represented a fusion of native Platonism (developed from Coleridge and Shelley), a resurgence of Hegelianism, and Fr. symbolism and "decadence." John Ruskin (1819–1900), William Morris (1834–96), and others returned to "imagination" as the source of poetic genius and as a means whereby a transcendent realm could be reached in which ethical truth and aesthetic form were one. Walter Pater (1839–94) carried Ruskin's Platonic aestheticism further by identifying the aesthetic function of poetry with the production of pleasure valuable for its own sake. The "Pre-Raphaelite" circle of Dante Gabriel Rossetti (1828–82), his sister Christina Rossetti (1830–94), and others, was a movement originally concerned with painting, insisting that conventions imposed since Raphael had obscured the eye for the object "as it is." Advocating the minute, photographic representation of objects rather than the use of objects as concretized symbols of inner states, the Pre-Raphaelites approached more a Parnassian than a symbolist aestheticism. Algernon Charles Swinburne (1837–1909) was one of the first important Eng. poets and critics to acknowledge the significance of Fr. poetry and to identify himself publicly with the art-for-art's-sake implications of Parnassian and symbolist aestheticism. In his essay on Blake (1868), he proclaimed the didactic heresy (*l'hérésie de l'enseignement*) and asserted a rigorous classical position of *pure* art. His dandyism was a Baudelairean rejection, as he understood it, of the bourgeois optimism of his time; his criticism a deliberate attempt to use the standards of Gautier, Baudelaire, and Mallarmé in the analysis and writing of Eng. poetry. Oscar Wilde (1856–1900) similarly acknowledged Fr. poetry as an important model for Eng. aestheticism. He celebrated art as the model of nature, and beauty as a symbol of ultimate truth "because it expresses nothing." George Moore (1857–1933) knew intimately, through reading and personal acquaintance, many of the important symbolist writers and introduced their notion of purity into the antididactic movement of the last decades of the century. Finally, Arthur Symons' (1865–1945) devoted summary of *The Symbolist Movement in Literature* (1899) attests to the decisive mark which Fr. aestheticism and symbolism left on *fin de siècle* poetics in England.

Aestheticism in poetry pervaded most of Europe during the closing decades of the 19th c. In *Russia*, a formalist movement under the aegis of Fr. symbolism is associated with the names of Konstantin Balmont (1867–1943), Valery Bryusov (1873–1924), Vyacheslav Ivanov (1866–1949), Andrey Bely (1880–1934) (pseud. for Boris N. Bugayev), and Alexander Blok (1880–1921). In conjunction with academic criticism and scholarship, it gave rise to an important formalist school of criticism, poetics, and linguistics during the first three decades of this century. In *Spanish* literature, the Nicaraguan Rubén Darío (1867–1916) was a foremost exponent of the movement of *modernismo,* which drew heavily upon Fr. Parnassian and symbolist sources. Juan Ramón Jiménez (1881–1958) struggled towards a "pure poetry," ranging from an early dependence on Fr. symbolism to an increasing simplicity of

MODERN POETICS

style. Federico García Lorca represents the culmination of a modern development of poetry and poetics in Spain, both in the scope and in the quality of his achievement. In *Italy*, Gabriele D'Annunzio (1863–1938) stands out as a representative of a poetic theory which emphasized aesthetic form while celebrating subjective and unconscious inspiration. In *Germany*, the aestheticism of the school surrounding Stefan George (1868–1933), primarily influenced by Fr. symbolists, Nietzsche, and the Eng. Pre-Raphaelites, introduced a notion of poetry as prophecy and a highly formal and precious language which was not meant to serve immediate didactic ends but which, aristocratically divorced from life, was meant to transmit a visionary incantation of higher truths. Apart from the George circle, and often in opposition to it, Rainer Maria Rilke (1875–1926) developed a musical and pictorial approach to poetry which was reinforced by the models of Baudelaire and Verlaine. Rilke's theory of *Dinge* defined the phenomena experienced by the poet as concretized abstractions, which, obtaining a life of their own, are caught by the poet and reconstituted in art—a further refinement of symbolist method. At the turn of the 20th c., the symbolist position was extended by the rationalistic mysticism of Paul Valéry. Moreover, 20th-c. "classicism," as formulated by T. E. Hulme, Ezra Pound, T. S. Eliot, and others, while rejecting the transcendentalist rationale of symbolism, nonetheless retained its analysis of the manner in which emotion in life is reformulated as emotion in art.

To avoid duplication, only a few items from the latter 18th c. are included in this biblog. For further references to this period, see NEO-CLASSICAL POETICS.

PRIMARY WORKS: M. Arnold, *Essays in Crit.*, 1st ser. (1833), 2d ser. (1888); T. Carlyle, *Critical and Miscellaneous Essays* (5 v., 1839); S. T. Coleridge, *Lectures on Shakespeare*, 1st ser. (1808), 2d ser. (1811–12), *Biographia Literaria* (1817); R. W. Emerson, *Essays*, 1st ser. (1841), 2d ser. (1844); W. Hazlitt, *Lectures on the Eng. Poets* (1818); S. Johnson, *Prefaces to the Plays of Shakespeare* (1765), *The Lives of the Eng. Poets* (1779–81); W. Pater, *The Renaissance. Studies in Art and Poetry* (1910); E. A. Poe, "The Philosophy of Composition" (1846), "The Poetic Principle" (1850); W. Wordsworth, "Essay Supplementary . . ." (1815).—W. Dilthey, *Das Erlebnis und die Dichtung* (1906); F. von Hardenberg (Novalis), *Fragmente und Studien, 1798–9, Novalis Schriften*, ed. Kluckhohn (4 v., 1929; 2 and 3); H. Heine, *Die romantische Schule* (1833); J. G. Herder, *Über die neuere deutsche Lit.* (1767), *Briefe zur Beförderung der Humanität* (1793–97); F. Nietzsche, *Die Geburt der Tragödie* (1871); Fr. Schiller, *Über*

naive und sentimentalische Dichtung (1795), *Briefe über die aesthetische Erziehung des Menschen* (1795); A. W. Schlegel, *Gesch. der deutschen Sprache und Poesie* (1818–19, ed. J. Körner, 1913); Fr. Schlegel, *Gespräch über die Poesie* (1800), *Gesch. der alten und neuen Lit.* (1812); L. Tieck, *Kritische Schriften* (4 v., 1848–52). C. Baudelaire, "Edgar Poe, sa vie et ses oeuvres" (1856), "Notes Nouvelles sur Edgar Poe" (1857), *L'Art romantique* (1868); M. H. Beyle (Stendhal), *Racine et Shakespeare* (1823); H. Bergson, *Le Rire* (2d ed., 1901); F. Brunetière, *L'Évolution des genres dans l'hist. de la litt.* (1890); F.-R. de Chateaubriand, *Essai sur la litt. anglaise* (1836); D. Diderot, *Paradoxe sur le comédien* (1778, publ. 1830); T. Gautier, *Hist. du romantisme* (1874); V. Hugo, "Préface de *Cromwell*" (1827), *William Shakespeare* (1864); S. Mallarmé, *Divagations* (6th ed., 1922); A. Rimbaud, "Letters to Charles Izambard and Paul Demeny" (1870) in *Lettres de la vie littéraire d'Arthur Rimbaud*, ed. J.-M. Carré (1931); C.-A. Sainte-Beuve, *Portraits littéraires* (3 v., 1862–64); H. Taine, *De l'idéal dans l'art* (1867), *Introd. à l'hist. de la litt. anglaise*, ed. I. Babbitt (1898).—*Discussioni e polemiche sul romanticismo (1816–26)*, ed. E. Bellorini (2 v., 1943); G. Baretti, *A Dissertation upon It. Poetry* (1753), *Discours sur Shakespeare* (1777); G. Carducci, *Discorsi letterari e storici* (1868–88); F. De Sanctis, *Teoria e storia della lett.*, ed. B. Croce (2 v., 1926); U. Foscolo, *Essays on Petrarch* (1823); G. Leopardi, *Zibaldone di pensieri* (1817–32); A. Manzoni, Preface to *Il Conte di Carmagnola* (1820); E. Visconti, *Idea elementaria sulla poesia romantica* (1818; in *Discussioni . . .*, I).—M. Menéndez y Pelayo, *Estudios de crítica literaria* (5 ser., 1884–1908) and *Historia de las ideas estéticas en España* (9 v., new ed., 1890–1912); M. Milá y Fontanals, *Observaciones sobre la poesía popular* (1853) and *Principios de lit. general* (1874); F. de Paula Martínez de la Rosa, *Poética* (1827); A. de Saavedra, Duque de Rivas, Preface to *Romances históricos* (1841).—V. Belinsky, *Lit. Reveries* (1834), *Thoughts and Notes on Rus. Lit.* (1846), *Selected Philosophical Works* (Moscow, 1948, tr. anon.; contains both the above items); A. Bely, *Symbolism* (1910)*; A. Blok, "On the Present State of Symbolism" (1910)*; V. Bryusov, *Rus. Symbolists* (1894)*; A. Potebnya, *Lectures on Lit. Theory* (1894)*; A. Pushkin, *Preface to Boris Godunov* (1827); L. Tolstoy, *What is Art?* (5th ed., tr. A. Maude, 1899). * These titles are translated from the Rus. The books and essays in question are not yet available in Eng.

SECONDARY WORKS. Consult: Abrams; A. Béguin, *L'Âme romantique et le rêve* (1939); C. M. Bowra, *The Heritage of Symbolism* (1943); *The Romantic Imagination* (1949);

–[513]–

P. Van Tieghem, *L'Ère romantique* (1948); Wellek; Wimsatt and Brooks.—W. J. Bate, *From Classic to Romantic* (1946); F. O. Matthiessen, *Am. Renaissance* (1941); R. Z. Temple, *The Critic's Alchemy* (1953); B. Willey, *19th C. Studies, Coleridge to Matthew Arnold* (1949); R. Wellek, *Immanuel Kant in England, 1793–1838* (1931).—R. Benz, *Die deutsche Romantik* (3d ed., 1956); E. Cassirer, *Idee und Gestalt. Goethe, Schiller, Hölderlin, Kleist* (1921); H. A. Korff, *Geist der Goethezeit.* (4 v., 1923–53); O. Walzel, *Die deutsche Lit. von Goethes Tod bis zur Gegenwart* (5th ed., 1929), *Grenzen von Poesie und Nichtpoesie* (1937).—A. Cassagne, *La Théorie de l'art pour l'art chez les romantiques et les premiers réalistes* (1906); K. Cornell, *The Symbolist Movement* (1951); T. S. Eliot, *From Poe to Valéry* (1948); E. Fiser, *Le Symbole littéraire* (1941); Lehmann; Martino; Raymond; M. A. Souriau, *Histoire du romantisme en France* (2 v., 1927); B. Weinberg, *Fr. Realism. The Critical Reaction, 1830–70* (1937).—G. Borgese, *Storia della critica romantica in Italia* (2d ed., 1920); G. Citanna, *Il Romanticismo e la poesia ital. dal Parini al Carducci* (1949); B. Croce, *Aesthetic,* tr. D. Ainslie (2d part, 2d ed., 1922), *Poesie e non poesia* (1923), *La Lett. ital.* (4 v., (1956–61; III); M. Fubini, *Romanticismo ital.* (1953); G. Getto, *Storia delle storie letterarie* (2d ed., 1946).—I. L. McClelland, *The Origins of the Romantic Movement in Spain* (1937); E. A. Peers, *A Hist. of the Romantic Movement in Spain* (2 v., 1940).—H. Bowman, *Vissarion Belinsky, 1811–48* (1954); V. Erlich, *Russian Formalism* (1955); *L'estetica e la poetica in Russia,* ed. E. Lo Gatto (1947; anthol. of essays by Russian poets and critics); O. A. Maslenikov, *The Frenzied Poets: The Russian Symbolists* (1952); D. S. Mirsky, *A Hist. of Russian Lit.* (1949).   R.F.

II. 20TH-C. AMERICAN AND BRITISH. Under the influence of developments in other disciplines, especially philosophy and psychology, the theorizing about poetry that has gone on in this century has been multifarious. Since a good deal of it has been by critics, to classify the various approaches would be to duplicate too much what is done in *Criticism, Types of* (q.v.); and to attempt to deal with every figure who has at one time or another enjoyed some kind of prestige is clearly unfeasible. (But see the secondary works listed in the bibliography below.) Accordingly, most of the attention in this brief article will be directed to writers who have both contributed something new to poetic theory and have had, or seem likely to have, a marked effect on the writing, criticism, and teaching of poetry; and the subject will be treated mainly chronologically, with a view

to exhibiting a distinctively 20th-c. pattern of development.

Most of the writers involved (a considerable number of whom have themselves been poets) have tended to concentrate on some or all of four closely related topics—the processes of poetic creation, the poetic medium, the process of reading a poem, and the cognitive status of poetry. The influence most widespread among them has been Coleridge's, especially his concept of the organic unity of a poem (see ORGANISM), and most of them have been concerned to redefine and defend poetry's autonomy. The pattern of development referred to above is as follows. Owing in part, no doubt, to the continuing influence of the *symboliste* movement (see SYMBOLISM), the first phase of "modernist" theorizing involved a revulsion from the then common notion that poetry is primarily interesting for its autobiographical revelations or for the profundity of its thought; a major effect of this revulsion was the theoretical banishment from poetry of much that has generally been thought to give it seriousness (and the ruling out, by implication, of the kind of sensitively and complexly philosophical approach employed by a critic like George Santayana); and the need of subsequent writers has been to find ways of reasserting the seriousness of poetry without falling into oversimplifications or sacrificing the best modern insights.

The notion that poetry should be restricted to being mimetic in the simpler of Aristotle's senses of the term—namely, concerned with representing physical phenomena—was first reasserted in this century by T. E. Hulme (between 1909, approximately, and 1917) and by Ernest Fenollosa in *The Chinese Written Character as a Medium for Poetry* (written before 1908, in Ezra Pound's hands by 1913, and first published by him in 1920). Influenced by their studies of, respectively, Bergson and ideographic literature, both writers argued that reality was, in effect, a kind of flux, unseizable by means of "abstract" language and traditional logic. And, especially when taken in conjunction with the ideas of Remy de Gourmont (and, to some extent, of W. B. Yeats) and publicized by Ezra Pound, the prescriptions for poets that they set up on this metaphysical basis have had a very marked effect on modern poetry and poetics.

This influence was particularly prepotent during the formative decade between 1910 and 1920. Hulme's insistence on concreteness of presentation (which Fenollosa also advocated) and on sharpness of visualization, and his belief that emotion could best be conveyed by describing natural objects, were taken up for a time by Pound and the Imagists and almost certainly contributed to the formulation and

MODERN POETICS

acceptance of T. S. Eliot's notion of the "objective correlative" (q.v.). Influential, similarly, was Hulme's demand that poetry be dry, witty and anti-sentimental in tone, as was his support of the Free Verse movement. But perhaps most potent of all was the insistence of both Hulme and Fenollosa that ordinary daily language was imprecise and shop-worn, that poets should endeavor to revivify the language of their times, and that the essential strength of poetry lay in figurative language, especially metaphors; and the notion (held, to some extent, by Yeats too) that poetic language should be, in effect, an intensified and enriched form of contemporary speech was taken up influentially by Eliot and subsequently considerably developed and refined by F. R. Leavis.

But while most of these notions have become common currency, a number of objections to some of them have been raised at various times, and some of the most important ones can appropriately be mentioned here. First, (influenced by Irving Babbitt) Yvor Winters has argued that poetry is not mimetic at all but meditative—a poet's experience *plus* his understanding of it. Second, in *The Problem of Style* (1922) J. Middleton Murry, in addition to denying the primacy of visualization in poetry (as Leavis has done too), argued that a poet need by no means always employ metaphors or concrete particulars as symbols of his emotions, but that under certain conditions even ideas could be adequate symbols. Third, Murray Krieger, adopting a somewhat Crocean position, has recently argued that despite Hulme's emphasis on using words freshly, his emphasis on the presentation of things already apprehended tended seriously to undervalue the role of language in literary creation. And, lastly, the basic antithesis between "concretions" and "abstractions" has been challenged by T. C. Pollock and Donald Davie, who have argued that both are alike abstractions from an individual's total apprehension of a situation.

If Hulme, Fenollosa and Pound were much concerned with prescribing for others, T. S. Eliot was apparently considerably concerned in his most influential criticism (that between about 1917 and 1925) with indirectly defining and defending the kind of poetry that he himself wished to write; and the terms in which he did so were largely those of the psychology of poetic creation (a topic, incidentally, which has considerably interested such other writers as Robert Graves, Maud Bodkin, and Kenneth Burke). To extract a systematic poetics from this criticism is difficult, for Eliot's terminology is sometimes unclear and it is often difficult to determine whether he is speaking analytically or impressionistically, and whether of all poets, of some poets, or only of himself. But

the main outline of his position appears to be roughly as follows. Essentially, a poet's task during creation is to give expression to some extremely complex state of mind that has been forming itself unconsciously out of his stored experiences and is now beginning to agitate him obscurely. If he is successful, the resultant poem will be, in a sense, impersonal (for it is not the direct emotional response of the poet to some particular situation in his own life); and it should not be valued for its ideas as such but for its demonstration of what it feels like to the poet to have them. But this does not mean that intelligence has no role in poetry. On the contrary, the more intelligent a poet is, the broader his education, and the more he belongs to a coherent cultural tradition, the better; for the greater then will be the variety of experiences and ideas that, given a suitably flexible sensibility, he will be able to absorb emotionally so that they can become, poetentially, fit material for poetry. And what he should attempt to achieve in his poetry (and, presumably, in his consciousness too) is the kind of reconcilement of opposites, the ability to mingle seriousness and levity, and the mature poised tone (coming, in part, from a critical awareness of the limitations of the experiences involved) that Eliot saw as especially characterizing some of the metaphysical poets—notably Marvell.

Much careful criticism of Eliot's position has been offered by such writers as John Crowe Ransom, Eliseo Vivas, Murray Krieger, René Wellek, Leonard Unger, Marshal Van Deusen, and, most notably, Yvor Winters. The most serious point that has been made against it is, perhaps, that Eliot has attempted to draw too absolute a distinction between a man's poetic activities and his other activities. For ideas do not seem in fact to be the essentially public, static, and impersonal things that Eliot apparently supposed them to be, and some kind of emotional modification of a person's being, as Van Deusen has argued, is always involved in the having of them. And by dwelling so heavily upon the importance of a poet's objectifying his consciousness, rather than upon his endeavoring to understand it and modify his attitudes accordingly, Eliot would seem, in effect, to be denying to a poet the opportunity to work out in his poetry the kinds of moral or religious concerns that seem to play crucial roles in normal human consciousness. Manifestly Eliot himself, in his later poetry, has not been handicapped in this way; and in some of his later criticism, principally "Dante" (1929) and "Poetry and Propaganda" (1930), he has concerned himself more fully with the problem of belief (q.v.) and poetry. But his discussions still do not indicate clearly how moral activity can go on in the writing and reading of poetry, and seem reducible to little more than the formula that some poets give sensuous life to abstract ideas, their own or other people's; that the extent to which they believe in them can vary considerably from poet to poet; that, other things being equal, it is reasonable to prefer the poetry whose ideas seem to one the truest; but that even when the ideas seem untrue one can still reasonably enjoy successful poetry for the enlargement of awareness that it promotes.

Debatable though some of Eliot's conclusions may be, he has the distinction of having raised and confronted, in a seminal way, most of the major problems in modern poetics. And it seems reasonable to suppose that the challenge of this comprehensiveness considerably helped to stimulate the almost equal comprehensiveness of I. A. Richards. But whereas Eliot wrote primarily as a poet, Richards approached poetry as a psychologist and semanticist concerned to view poetic language under the aegis of language as· a whole and refusing to regard poetic creativity as essentially different from other kinds (as A. E. Housman and Herbert Read, for instance, believed it to be). In his extremely influential *Principles of Literary Criticism* (1924) and *Practical Criticism* (1929) he founded his system of poetic value on the concept of psychological-physiological "impulses"—largely those of the reader. In a person's daily life, he argued, the greater part of the impulses towards action that are aroused are suppressed in the interests of self-consistency. In the reading of poetry, however, a far greater number than usual can be aroused and so harmonized (by way of the "reconciliation of opposites" that Coleridge described) that no suppression is necessary. And the effect on the reader is a sense of intensified and freshly-ordered life.

Much criticism has been levelled at this theory, especially by such writers as Eliot, Ransom, D. G. James, and Krieger. The weaknesses most often criticized in it are that there is no scientific way of giving any precise account of the 'impulses' in any particular situation, that the theory is too general and relativistic to be of much help to the practicing critic, and that by ignoring the question of poetic form Richards does not seem adequately to differentiate poetry from other forms of art. However, at least two corollaries of Richards' approach have had a very considerable influence on subsequent criticism. By insisting that the 'meaning' of a poem is not something objective and absolutely definable but is created afresh, and somewhat differently in every case, by each reader, Richards did much to encourage William Empson's concern, especially in *Seven Types of Ambiguity* (1930), with multiple meanings in poetry—a concern

aroused, in part, by Laura Riding and Robert Graves's *A Survey of Modernist Poetry* (1927) and to some extent anticipated also in F. C. Prescott's *The Poetic Mind* (1922). And Richards' argument that by its inclusiveness a poem could be invulnerable to irony was later extended further by Cleanth Brooks, who argued that irony and paradox were in fact characteristics of virtually all good poetry. Influential, too, have been Richards' discussions of such more practical matters as figurative language (especially metaphor), rhythm, the components of poetic meaning (sense, feeling, tone, intention), and the ways in which poetry can be misread.

That discussions of poetics tended increasingly to focus upon the question of the differences between poetry and non-poetry and of the cognitive value of the former was also largely Richards' doing. In *Science and Poetry* (1926) he resolutely adopted the positivist position that knowledge comes, in language, only by way of publicly verifiable statements; and since many poetic utterances are clearly not of this nature they must therefore, he argued, be simply expressions of emotion. (The notion that poetry is nonreferential has also been arrived at, by a circuitous route, by Vivas and Krieger.) Such a position, obviously, makes poetry a far less intellectually respectable activity than science; and it must be said that the first major challenges to Richards (with the possible exception of Owen Barfield's *Poetic Diction*, 1928) did not do much to improve matters. Returning to near Hulme's position, Max Eastman, in *The Literary Mind* (1931), and John Crowe Ransom (especially between 1930 and 1938) objected independently of each other that actually science is concerned not with pure knowledge but with understanding relationships for the sake of their usefulness, whereas poetry results from a heightened and disinterested consciousness of things in their concrete particularity—for Ransom a consciousness informed by love—and a desire to render them in words. But when Ransom started to deal with poetry more concretely and historically than Hulme had done, a further serious difficulty of this mimetic position began to emerge.

That poetry simply describing natural scenes and objects could be very pleasant had been demonstrated by many Imagist poems and by the poems in George Moore's *Pure Poetry: An Anthology* (1924); but its range, Ransom pointed out, was very narrow. Yet to prefer, as Ransom did, the metaphysical poetry of the 17th c. necessitated a confrontation of the fact that the latter contained a good many complex, serious, and sometimes decidedly abstract ideas and was concerned with considerably more than natural objects. This difficulty

Ransom tried to resolve by treating the intellectual elements in this poetry as predominantly only delighted perceptions of unexpected resemblances, as manifested in the Metaphysicals' extensive use of figurative language. But, as Richards pointed out in *The Philosophy of Rhetoric* (1936), a figure comprises both a vehicle *and* a tenor (q.v.); and when finally in *The New Criticism* (1941) Ransom himself came to argue that most poems do in fact contain a paraphraseable argument, this only brought out more acutely a point that Allen Tate had drawn attention to indirectly by his argument (apropos of "tension" in poetry) that many good poems are highly denotative as well as highly connotative. Either, that is to say, poems must be considered simply prose statements made less coherent (though pleasanter) by meter and other irrelevancies; or else if one believes that poetry, as Tate argued elsewhere, can provide a very important kind of knowledge of the world that is obtainable by no other means, then it is well to have sound theoretical grounds for this belief.

Two approaches seem to have been especially fruitful in confirming the essential seriousness and meaningfulness of poetry. The first, a fresh approach to the whole problem of referentiality, was, paradoxically, initiated by Richards. In *Coleridge on Imagination* (1934) he accepted the Kantian theory that each person creates his own reality out of the undifferentiated stimuli he receives, and that even the things in the realm of practical everyday experience are mental constructions. Therefore, Richards argued, the constructions that a poet makes by combining those things are not, generically, any less real than the constructions that a scientist makes by abstracting from them—a position that was adopted, too, by D. G. James in *Scepticism and Poetry* (1937). But it was Philip Wheelwright who, in *The Burning Fountain* (1954), most powerfully reasserted the claims of poetry to be knowledge. Emotional assent, he argued, is an essential element in the whole concept of truth, and emotion can have, positively, a semantic role. "Some degree of judgement," he insisted, "is implicit in all experience, emotive as well as sensory, and this implicit judgement tends to make some claim about the nature of things." And he accordingly grouped together poetry, symbolism, myth, and religion as the areas in which the emotional response can be at its most intense and a knowledge of the world be obtained that can be obtained in no other way. (Large-scale synthesizing expeditions into these regions have also been undertaken by Susanne K. Langer in *Feeling and Form*, 1953, and Northrop Frye in *Anatomy of Criticism*, 1957.)

Since then, Isabel C. Hungerland has attacked the fallacy of "regarding scientific discourse as the paradigm of language in general" and argued persuasively, in *Poetic Discourse* (1958), that "all the modes of meaning, features, and functions of everyday language are found in poetry."

The second approach has been the attempt to show how ideas and moral values can exist in a poem without its being merely didactic. The traditional notion that poetry provides imitations not so much of objects as of human (and morally evaluable) actions and thoughts —i.e., that it is mimetic in the second and more important of Aristotle's senses of that term—has been reaffirmed most explicitly in this century by the Chicago "Neo-Aristotelians," especially R. S. Crane, from about 1935 onward. (See CHICAGO CRITICS.) A number of other writers (including Cleanth Brooks, R. P. Blackmur, and especially Kenneth Burke with his theory of symbolic action, q.v.) have discarded the concept of mimesis altogether and taken the stand that essentially a poem is *itself* an action, the poet's own struggle to work out problems, insights, valuations. (See also NEW CRITICISM.) And it is the latter approach, perhaps, that logically permits the completest kind of moral evaluating of a poem. Two writers in particular have demonstrated how such evaluating can effectively be carried on. Since about 1929 Yvor Winters has governed his own criticism by the theory that a successful poem is the culmination of a writer's effort to understand experiences rationally and respond justly to them emotionally—the poem being a final act of perception in which emotion and understanding are simultaneously realized, with the use of verse permitting a more finely controlled emotional response than is possible in prose. (A synthesis of important elements in Winters' position and Wheelwright's has been effected by Van Deusen; Donald Davie has investigated the kind of control attainable through syntax.) And the poetic criticism of F. R. Leavis since 1932, with its concern with the extent and equality of of "felt life" in a poem and degree of maturity in the poem's tone, and its alertness to ways in which the psyche can be enriched or impoverished in its dealings with language, has been perhaps the finest demonstration in our time of the complexity and subtlety of the process of adjustment that can go on in the relating of a poet's experiences and values (as manifested in his poems) to one's own.

By way of conclusion, this much, perhaps, can be ventured. 20th-c. Am. and Brit. writers on poetics have undoubtedly shed more light on their subject than any previous group in British or Am. criticism. But if future writers are to benefit fully from their labors it can surely only be by giving up the attempt to separate poetry rigidly from other forms of discourse and by recognizing that there must be room in poetry, theoretically as well as practically, for all of man's deepest concerns—if, that is, any kind of support is to be given to I. A. Richards' splendid and traditional claim that "poetry is the completest mode of utterance."

PRIMARY WORKS: T. E. Hulme, *Speculations*, ed. H. Read (1924), and *Further Speculations*, ed. S. Hynes (1955); W. B. Yeats, *Essays* (1924); T. S. Eliot, *The Use of Poetry and the Use of Crit.* (1933), *Selected Essays, 1917–1932* (rev. ed., 1950) and *On Poetry and Poets* (1957); M. Bodkin, *Archetypal Patterns in Poetry* (1934; a predominantly Jungian approach); F. R. Leavis, *Revaluation* (1936), " 'Thought' and Emotional Quality," *Scrutiny*, 13 (1945), and *The Common Pursuit* (1952); C. Caudwell, *Illusion and Reality* (1937; the most ambitious of the Marxist studies of poetry); J. C. Ransom, *The World's Body* (1938); C. Brooks, *Modern Poetry and the Tradition* (1939), *The Well Wrought Urn* (1947), and, with R. P. Warren, *Understanding Poetry* (1938); K. Burke, *The Philos. of Lit. Form* (1941); T. C. Pollock, *The Nature of Lit.* (1942); R. P. Warren, "Pure and Impure Poetry," KR 5 (1943); Y. Winters, *In Defense of Reason* (1947; coll. of three earlier books) and *The Function of Crit.* (1957); *The Importance of Scrutiny*, ed. E. Bentley (1948); *Critiques and Essays in Crit., 1920–1948*, ed. R. W. Stallman (1948; extensive coll.; valuable bibliog.); R. Graves, *The Common Asphodel* (1949); Wellek and Warren; E. Pound, *The Letters of Ezra Pound, 1907–1941*, ed. D. D. Paige (1950), and *Lit. Essays*, ed. T. S. Eliot (1954; comprehensive coll. of Pound's crit. since 1913); *Lit. Opinion in America*, ed. M. D. Zabel (rev. ed., 1951; extensive coll. of 20th-c. crit.; valuable bibliog. appendices); *Critics and Crit.*, ed. R. S. Crane (1952; essays by the "Chicago Critics"); W. K. Wimsatt, *The Verbal Icon* (1954); D. Davie, *Articulate Energy* (1955); A. Tate, *The Man of Letters in the Modern World* (1955); G. Santayana, *Essays in Lit. Crit.*, ed. I. Singer (1956); F. Kermode, *Romantic Image* (1957; analysis of Symbolist assumptions in 20th-c. theory); L. M. Van Deusen, "In Defense of Yvor Winters," *Thought*, 32 (1957). See also E. Vivas, *Creation and Discovery* (1955) and *The Artistic Transaction and Essays on Theory of Lit.*

SECONDARY WORKS: S. E. Hyman, *The Armed Vision* (1948; still the most comprehensive study of 20th-c. crit., by an admirer of Kenneth Burke); S. Coffman, *Imagism* (1951); W. V. O'Connor, *An Age of Crit.: 1900–1950* (1952); W. K. Wimsatt and C. Brooks, *Lit. Crit.; a Short History* (1957); R. J. Foster, *The New*

Romantics; a Reappraisal of the New Crit. (1962). See also M. Krieger, *The New Apologists for Poetry* (1956) and "After the New Crit.," *Massachusetts Rev.*, 4 (1962); Sutton.   J.F.

FRENCH AND GERMAN. Continental poetics remain remarkably autonomous and isolated within their national traditions. A few major figures extend their influence beyond the national borders and there are instances of fruitful cooperation between writers from different nationalities. But on the whole there is less contact between, for instance, Fr., G. and It. poetical theorists than there is between the actual poets of these countries.

In France, up to a recent date, literary theory was overshadowed by the techniques of "explication de texte," a discipline which is not primarily concerned with poetics. It aims at the correct reading of literary texts and is pedagogical rather than critical in purpose. To the extent that it contains an implicit theory of poetry, this theory is positivistic. From Taine, it inherits a considerable interest in the extrinsic forces that act upon literature: social, intellectual, and political history play a large part in the works of the most eminent representative, Gustave Lanson. Its methods are highly analytical and characterized by the virtues of precision and caution inherited from the natural sciences. Because of the particular structure of Fr. literary history, with its high period in the classical 17th and 18th c., the method was primarily devised to deal with authors of that period, hence the emphasis on rhetoric. Orthodox explication is much less at home with 19th-c. romantic and especially symbolist literature, avowedly antirhetorical in purpose. The gap between live poetry, which continued to develop in the wake of symbolism, and the methods taught in the schools kept widening and a reaction was bound to occur.

One should mention Bergson and Valéry among the main initiators of this reaction, because both translated the heritage of symbolism into poetic theory. In Valéry's case, this continues the tradition of a poetry which, ever since Baudelaire and Mallarmé, had been acutely aware of the problems created by its own existence, and had often expressed itself on matters of a theoretical nature. Valéry's main contribution may well have been his help in reawakening interest in theoretical poetics as such, by the numerous and widely read essays in which he advocates a direct study of poetic creation, independently of historical and critical considerations. His efforts culminated in the establishment of a chair in Poetics at the Collège de France, where Valéry himself, from 1937 to 1945, delivered a series of lectures which, unfortunately, have not been recorded. The actual content of his theory has been less influential, possibly because it did not mark such a sharp departure from the premises of the natural sciences. It was primarily the self-reflective, hyper-conscious aspect of symbolism (especially in Mallarmé) that interested Valéry; his thought aims at a rational description of the poetic act, often using his own creative experience as a starting-point towards "reducing poetry to a scientific operation of feeling" (Jean Hytier). Devoid, as Valéry deliberately was, of Mallarmé's dedication to the poetic work as an absolute expression of the human spirit, his theories lead to valid insights but remain, on the whole, the isolated display of his own intellectual idiosyncrasies. Nevertheless, his writings on poetics contain suggestions of great value on the relationship between the workings of the poetic and the rational mind, such as his critique of naive conceptions of "inspiration" and his emphasis on the deliberate, calculated aspects of poetic composition.

Although he was not primarily concerned with poetics and did not write systematically on the subject, Bergson exercised a profound influence on Fr. poetic theory. His constant emphasis on the presence, in human consciousness, of subjective elements pertaining to memory, imagination, intuition, next to—though sharply separated from—elements that possess objective reality, amounts in fact to a poetization of human experience. The entire area of man's contact with the outside world (perception, sensation, etc.) becomes similar to the experience found in works of art and literature. The poetic image, for instance, becomes a close verbal approximation to what perception and sensation are actually like, much closer, at any rate, than the purely intellectual representation of reality found in the scientific concept. Poetics thus becomes a vital source for theoretical psychology, rather than a minor part of it. It has been shown (among others by Fiser) that Bergson's conception is a close equivalent, in philosophical language, of the kind of imagery used by symbolist writers, from Baudelaire to Proust. The unity of a symbolist work always resides in the inner coherence between its images, a coherence similar, in Proust's words, "to the single relationship which, in the world of science, is called the law of cause and effect. . . ." Bergson's work is concerned with this same process as the unifying theme of human consciousness.

Later thinkers such as Jean Wahl or Gaston Bachelard are not to be considered Bergson's disciples in the usual sense of the term, but their independent speculations pursue a direction which Bergson had initiated. By his writings on poetry, by the considerable place he allots to poetics in the field of metaphysics and by his influence as a teacher, Jean Wahl has contributed to a renewal which by now has reached down into the field of practical literary criticism. By means of poetry, as Wahl puts it in a very Bergsonian formula, man will again be able "to communicate substantially with what is substantial in things"; genuine metaphysical thought can also achieve this, but poetry and thought are so closely related as to be almost one and the same thing. A similar insight, more systematically developed, appears in the series of studies which Gaston Bachelard, a philosopher of science, has devoted to what he calls "material imagination." He shows the imagination as acting in a manner which differs from rational cognition by being a direct, unmediated apprehension of matter, a "dreaming about" matter rather than an act of knowledge (one notices the similarity with Bergson's critique of the scientific "symbol" as the sole mode of cognition). In a series of four books, Bachelard attempts a typology of the poetic imagination, cataloguing images according to their dominant material element (fire, water, earth, air). The resulting method does not cover the entirety of the literary work: it describes only the imagery and, it could be argued, only a certain kind of imagery; when used without the inner sympathy with the poet's imagination which Bachelard constantly demands, it could easily become mechanical. The impact of these studies on current Fr. literary criticism is considerable. They allow for a return to the poetic experience as an experience of *concrete* reality, a return which is implicit in Bergson's philosophy.

Although often critical of Bergson, Jean-Paul Sartre is close to him in his contributions on poetic theory. His study of the imagination insists upon the radical distinction between perception and imagination, a thesis which figures prominently in Bergson's early *Matière et mémoire* (1900). The method of existential psychoanalysis which he advocates in *l'Être et le néant* (1943) involves an interpenetration between matter and consciousness which, despite important differences of emphasis, remains Bergsonian; its similarity to Bachelard's theory of material imagination would suffice to indicate this. Sartre's own literary criticism contains examples of such analyses, but in younger critics it is often difficult to separate Sartre's influence from that of Bachelard. In later writings, such as the essay *What is Literature?* (1949), Sartre has abandoned the pursuit of theoretical poetics which was at least potentially present in his earlier work. By drawing a sharp distinction between literary prose and poetry, he reintroduces interpersonal, ethical considerations in his evaluation of literature and, for the time being at least, puts aside problems of theoretical poetics.

Bachelard and Sartre's poetics are attempts at a phenomenology of the poetic conscious-ness. They differ from each other by the original situation which is taken as a starting-point: in Bachelard it is man's relationship to the texture and the spatial dimensions of matter, in Sartre it is the existential situation. Another writer who belongs in the same group, Georges Poulet, starts from the poet's sense of temporality, and shows how the structure of the style expresses his specific experience of time; aside from its philosophical implications, the interest of this approach stems from its concern with style and from the possible link it suggests between phenomenological analysis and stylistics. The manner, however, in which Poulet establishes this link remains prob-lematic and in need of a theoretical founda-tion.

Such a foundation can only be discovered in an exhaustive study of the poetic act; Fr. lit-erary theory has more and more felt the need for an ontology of the poetic as preliminary to a study on such a highly integrated level as that of style. The writer who has perhaps gone furthest in the formulation of such an ontology is Maurice Blanchot. If Valéry and Bergson can be considered as the theorizers of symbolism, Blanchot appears in a somewhat similar relationship to the surrealist move-ment. Already in the oblique and subtle essays of Jean Paulhan and in the tormented medita-tions of Georges Bataille, some of the surreal-ist themes had continued to find expression. Blanchot shows how the works of poets gravi-tate around the ontological question, how they try and fail always again to define human existence by means of poetic language. His writings are unsystematic and highly subjec-tive, but if the necessity for a fundamental questioning of the poetic act is granted, it is bound to begin as a tentative, difficult explo-ration, and not as a self-assured doctrine.

Practical applications of these and related theories to criticism and history have multi-plied in later years. As could be expected, they are centered in the area of the 19th' c., and they have modified the traditional picture of Fr. literary history as dominated by 17th-c. classicism. The success of historical studies founded on a symbolist poetics, such as Albert Béguin's book on romanticism (*L'Âme ro-mantique et le rêve,* 1937) or Marcel Ray-mond's study of symbolism (*De Baudelaire au surréalisme,* rev. ed., 1952) illustrates this trend. The study of the 16th and 17th c. has also been influenced by the new trends, and the new emphasis on 16th-c. baroque can undoubtedly be traced back to the same shift in orientation. Among typical examples of books which make use of phenomenological poetics, one should mention Jean Pierre Rich-ard's essays in the 19th-c. novel and symbolist poetry (*Littérature et sensation*) with an im-portant preface by G. Poulet, 1955, *Poésie et profondeur,* 1956) as well as his recent study of Mallarmé (*L'univers imaginaire de Mal-larmé,* 1962) which give a clear picture of the possibilities and the limits of the method. Roland Barthes's *Le Degré zéro de l'écriture,* 1956) is noteworthy because it suggests con-nections between phenomenological analysis and the structure, history and sociology of style. The very brief essay merely indicates the problem, but if further studies could help to bring these various disciplines closer to-gether, Fr. poetics would move on to a stage where synthesis becomes possible.

While Fr. *explication de textes* derived its methods primarily from the natural sciences, German literary studies of the same era seem to have been especially eager to emulate the social sciences, as they were practiced in Ger-many at the turn of the century. Various forms of organic historicism appear as the dominant characteristic of several works. Sometimes, as in H. A. Korff's *Geist der Goethezeit* (5 v., 1925–57), the concept of history is triadic and Hegelian; in others, such as Walzel or Richter, it is derived from the visual arts—in this case Wölfflin's theories of vision and of "open" and "closed" form. Others still search for historical continuity in specific literary traditions and *topoi* (Curtius), in recurrent themes and atti-tudes (Unger, Rehm), in archetypal patterns (Kerenyi), in philosophical or aesthetic atti-tudes (Cassirer, Auerbach). In all these in-stances, the problem is essentially one of his-torical continuity: a certain theory of history is shown to bring order and coherence in the apparently erratic development of literature. Some of the authors mentioned have pro-duced works of lasting value which often go far in revealing the inner workings of the poetic mind. But since they all start from the literary work as an unquestionable empirical fact, they do not claim to be writing on poetics, in either sense of the term. It is partly in re-action against the considerable authority of much philological and historical literary sci-ence that a new concern with poetics de-veloped, not unlike that in France, although the issue is much less clearly defined.

As one significant example of such reactions, the disciples of the poet Stefan George set themselves up as deliberate opponents of the prevalent methods of literary study. Although George claimed that "from him, no road led to science," most of his later followers taught in universities. Since several among them were men of considerable learning, they exercised a great deal of influence. Their approach was antiphilological in the extreme (no footnotes, sources or bibliographies), but their merit lies rather in their respect for the autonomy of the poetic mind than in their attacks on traditional methods. The writer on literature must come as close as possible to the creative experience itself, helped in this by admiration and love for his subject rather than by scruples of accuracy and objectivity. There is great emphasis, also, on the messianic role of the poet as an almost superhuman figure, to be dealt with in a language closer to that of myth or religion than that of science. That such an approach is not always incompatible with true learning is clear from Gundolf's books on Shakespeare and Goethe. Only a few of George's disciples are still alive, and a vigorous reaction has, in turn, set in against the arbitrary elements in their works. This reaction, however, should not blind one to their contribution. It was certainly necessary, around 1910, to bring G. philology into closer contact with live poetry; George's disciples renewed the established image of Goethe, they were instrumental in the discovery of Hölderlin and contributed to the emphasis on the neo-Hellenic tradition which runs as a continuous strand through G. literature, from Winckelmann to the present. But if the George Circle was militantly aware of the need for poetic autonomy, the contribution of its members to poetics remains diffuse, mostly because their insistence on the messianic element tends to overshadow the formal element of poetry altogether. In their master, George himself, the tangible expression of the transcendental value of poetry was to be found in the perfection of the form; it was by the act of extreme formal discipline, a kind of askesis of the form, that the poet earned the right to statements of prophetic weight. If this formal discipline is taken away, the entire messianic attitude becomes dangerously arbitrary. Significantly, it is after he had left the George Circle that one of the most gifted among its members, Max Kommerell, wrote studies on the drama, on Faust and on Hölderlin that show real insight in poetic motivation and its relation to formal structure.

More recently, another challenge has been offered to G. philology, emanating this time from a philosopher, Martin Heidegger. In 1937, Heidegger began the publication of commentaries on the poetry of Hölderlin and in subsequent works, he has given an increased importance to the poetic as a prominent part of his philosophy, with occasional excursions in the practical field of exegesis. Heidegger's conception of the poetic is part of his attempt to reach beyond what he considers the limits of the Western metaphysical tradition. Because of their greater proximity to language, poets reflect the fundamental tensions of human existence more faithfully than even the great-est among the metaphysicians. And the purest of them all, the poet who, according to Heidegger, has been able to name the very essence of poetry, Hölderlin, offers therefore an insight into Being which is without antecedent in the history of human thought. Whoever is able, with the assistance of the commentary, to listen to Hölderlin, will stand in the presence of the poetic itself and discover that it is the unmediated language of Being. For Heidegger, the poet's language has eschatological power and is to be interpreted, not by means of a critical analysis which assumes a common frame of reference, but as a kind of revelation which, at best, we can hope to perceive but never to grasp critically, as one can grasp a concept. The methodological consequences of this attitude go against the very foundation of philological science. The implication is that traditional philological methods, based on the assumedly objective status of the work, are themselves imprisoned within Western rationalism, and therefore unable to gain true poetic insight. This inability extends to the era where the authority of philology reigns undisputed, that of the correct establishment of texts—and Heidegger has participated, directly and indirectly, in the controversies that surround the critical edition of Hölderlin's complete works. He has often been accused of stretching and distorting texts to make them conform to his own views; these controversial readings, however, are always consistent with his own philosophical assumptions and they can only be discarded or criticized within the context of this philosophy.

If Heidegger's commentaries are an extreme example of a poetics founded on "creation," G. scholars have also made important contributions to the poetics of style. Stylistic research (*Stilforschung*) is probably the most international among the trends we have mentioned. It originated out of an encounter between G. philology and the philosophy of the It. aesthetician Croce. One would expect Croce's main influence to be in the field of history of literature, since this is the area with which his massive philosophical work is primarily concerned; the orientation of his numerous It. disciples has generally been in this direction. But it seems now as if his impact is perhaps most strongly felt in stylistic studies, although he was himself somewhat reticent towards *Stilforschung*. The close friendship between Croce and the G. philologist Karl Vossler, leader of the Munich school of stylistic criticism to which Leo Spitzer also belongs, is an important personal factor in this influence. Croce and Vossler's intellectual kinship has for its common root the revolt against the scientific positivism of the 19th c., which it criticized in the name of Hegelian idealism;

the revealing title of Vossler's first work is *Positivismus und Idealismus in der Sprachwissenschaft* (1904). Vossler's later work is mainly a study of the dominant stylistic traits of literary language, as a key, not only to the personality of an author but even, as in his book on France (*Frankreichs Kultur und Sprache*, 1929), to the spirit of a nation. Leo Spitzer, using more intricate and more refined techniques, pursues a similar aim: he selects a distinctive feature of the style to penetrate into the work and reach the distinctive quality of a poetic personality: the study of one crucial passage in *Phèdre*, for instance, allows for a general interpretation of Racine. Such attempts may seem purely technical, but they are in fact a practical application of the monistic assumptions that dominate Croce's poetics. The writers of the Munich school derived from Croce the precept that, since poetic style is not to be separated from poetic experience and personality, it is legitimate to reach an exhaustive interpretation on the basis of the aspect of the work that is most readily and objectively available, namely the style. This kind of stylistic analysis differs sharply from positivistic stylistics in that it assumes the work to be an autonomous aesthetic unit. It restored to the systematic study of poetry values of taste and sensitivity, without falling back on impressionistic subjectivism, and it refined the tools of analysis and interpretation to a considerable extent. Vossler enjoyed a high reputation in Spain and thus established a link between G., It., and Sp. literary studies; Dámaso Alonso's book on Góngora was perhaps the most accomplished work to come out of this school.

Partly in reaction against the psychological aspects of Vossler's method, a new trend in stylistic study has recently originated in Zürich around Emil Staiger and the review *Trivium* (now no longer published). Staiger's techniques are still those of stylistic analysis, based on close reading, study of syntactical, rhythmical, and metaphorical structure, but his ultimate purpose is to reveal the metapersonal attitude of the poet toward the fundamental categories of existence, especially temporality. One is reminded of similar trends in France; Staiger, however, is backed by the highly developed methods of stylistic research established by his G. predecessors. His most theoretical work, *Grundbegriffe der Poetik* (1946), is based on the classical distinction between the three genres, lyrical, epic, and dramatic. It is especially noteworthy for its description of the lyrical as the fundamental poetic genre, the ideal from which all poetry springs forth and to which it tends to return. In this assertion, Staiger makes explicit a preference which is found in most of the tendencies that have been mentioned. Because it draws on a variety of

doctrines, Staiger's school offers a balanced method of descriptive poetics. It is avowedly better suited to deal with the details of relatively brief lyrical poems, rather than with larger dramatic units. This reveals once more what has been apparent throughout this survey: the recent trends in Fr. and G. poetics (and in European poetics in general) are the theoretical expression of the poetics implicitly contained in the 19th-c. romantic and symbolist poetry.†

A. FRANCE. 1. G. Lanson, "Quelques mots sur l'explication de textes" in *Methodes de l'histoire littéraire* (1925), R. Vigneron, *L'explication de textes* . . . (1928).—2. P. Valéry, "Introduction à la méthode de Léonard de Vinci," "Avant-propos à la connaissance de la déesse" in *Variété* I, "Léonard et les philosophes," "Questions de poésie" in *Variété* III, "Discours sur l'esthétique" in *Variété* IV, "Poésie et pensée abstraite," "Première leçon du cours de poétique," "L'enseignement de la poétique au Collège de France" in *Variété* V; *Cahiers*, 29 v. to date (1957–); M. Bémol, *Paul Valéry* (1949), J. Hytier, *La poétique de Valéry* (1953).—3. H. Bergson, *Essai sur les données immédiates de la conscience* (4th ed., 1904), *Le rire* (1908); V. Jankélévitch, *Bergson* (1931), E. Fiser, *Le symbole littéraire* (1941).— 4. J. Wahl, *Traité de metaphysique* (1953), *Poésie, pensée, perception* (1948); G. Bachelard, *Lautréamont* (1939), *La psychanalyse du feu* (1940), *L'eau et les rêves* (1942), *L'air et les songes* (1943), *La terre et les rêveries du repos* (1948), *La poétique de l'espace* (1957); J. P. Sartre, *L'imaginaire* (1940), *Situations* (3 v., 1947–49); G. Poulet, *Études sur le temps humain* (Edinburgh, 1949), *La distance intérieure* (1952; v. 2); J. Paulhan, *Les fleurs de Tarbes ou la terreur dans les lettres* (1945); M. Blanchot, *Faux pas* (1943), *La part du feu* (1949), *L'espace littéraire* (1955); M. Merleau-Ponty, "Le langage indirect et les voix du silence," *Signes* (1960); J. Starobinski, *J. J. Rousseau: la transparence et l'obstacle* (1958), *L'oeil vivant* (1961).

B. GERMANY AND RELATED SUBJECTS. 5. O. Walzel, *Gehalt und Gestalt im Kunstwerk des Dichters* (1923); R. Unger, *Aufsätze zur Prinzipienlehre der Literaturgeschichte* (2 v., 1923), *Herder, Novalis, Kleist: Studien über die Entwicklung des Todesproblems* (1923); E. Cassirer, *Die Philosophie der symbolischen Formen* (1924); H. Pongs, *Das Wortkunstwerk* (1926); W. Rehm, *Der Todesgedanke in der deutschen Dichtung* (1928); Auerbach; Curtius; F. Strich, *Deutsche Klassik und Romantik* (4th ed., 1949); M. Wehrli, *Allgemeine Literaturwissenschaft* (1951); K. Kerenyi, *Geistiger Weg Europas* (1955).—6. F. Gundolf, *Shakespeare und der deutsche Geist* (1911); *Goethe* (1916), *George* (1920); M. Kommerell, *Der Dichter als*

† In Supplement, see also GENEVA SCHOOL; PHENOMENOLOGY; STRUCTURALISM.

Führer in der deutschen Klassik (1928), *Geist und Buchstabe der Dichtung* (1944); H. Rössner, *George Kreis und Literaturwissenschaft* (1938).—7. M. Heidegger, *Erläuterungen zu Hölderlins Dichtung* (1950), "Der Ursprung des Kunstwerkes," "Wozu Dichter . . ." in *Holzwege* (1950), ". . . dichterisch wohnet der Mensch," in *Vorträge und Aufsätze* (1954); E. Buddeberg, "Heidegger und die Dichtung," DVLG, 26 (1952); B. Alleman, *Hölderlin und Heidegger* (rev. ed. 1957).—8. *Carteggio Croce-Vossler 1899–1949* (1951); L. Spitzer, *Stilstudien* (2 v., 1928), *Romanische Stil und Literaturstudien* (1931), *Essays in Stylistics* (1948); E. Staiger, *Die Zeit als Einbildungskraft des Dichters* (1939), *Die Kunst der Interpretation* (1955).

See also: A.4. G. Poulet, *La métamorphose du cercle* (1961), *L'espace proustien* (1963); J. Rousset, *Forme et signification* (1962). B.7. H. G. Gadamer, *Wahrheit und Methode* (1960); R. Ingarden, *Das literarische Kunstwerk* (2d ed., 1960).

Concerning the relationship between Marxism and poetic theory, see the Hungarian G. Lukács' effort at a comprehensive aesthetic, *Die Eigenart des Ästhetischen* (2 v., sec. 1 of his *Ästhetik*, 1963). P. DE M.

ITALIAN. Poetic theory in 20th-c. Italy has been dominated by the overwhelming personality of Benedetto Croce (1866–1952), whose *Estetica* appeared in 1902. In polemical reaction to late 19th-c. positivism, and in the tradition of G. Vico and F. De Sanctis, Croce, an idealist philosopher of the Hegelian school, held that art is the first of the four forms of spiritual activity (art seeking the beautiful, philosophy the true, ethics the good, economy the useful), and can be defined as expression of intuition, whereas philosophy consists of logical thinking. Art materializes through several media and in different degrees, but is ultimately one, and poetry (or lyric) is only the name of its pure form in the literary medium, whether in verse or not. It is not the technique of a particular medium which gives origin to art, but, vice versa, the naive, free imagination ("fantasia") creates its own medium and technique; hence, language is expression, originally poetic, and the particular use of the language (= style) cannot be separated from the individual and singular experience or intuition it expresses. Image is the poetic nucleus of the work of art, the concrete manifestation of the intuition, and the word is the sensorial sign of the image. A collective language is originally made of images. The distinction between poetry and nonpoetry (or plain "literature") is basic in Croce's thought and in his method of literary criticism, and it was brought to a focus in his definitive book of theory, *La Poesia* (1936, untranslated).

Croce's position was challenged by Giovanni Gentile (1875–1944), a "pure idealist" and the authoritative founder of *attualismo*. Gentile objected to Croce's emphasis on distinctions, and countered it with his emphasis on the basic unity of spiritual life. For him the poet, the logician, and the critic are essentially one in that the faculties which preside over their respective activities can be distinguished only from the outside, in techniques and methods, not from the inside—the inner "taste" that guides them all. Ultimately they all are pure modes of existence of the spirit, "pure acts."

Gentile has had a very limited influence on practical criticism, a more noticeable one on cultural historiography (for instance in the field of the Renaissance); Croce's impact in Italy has been all-pervasive both on theory and practice. The metaphysical foundations of his system have by now been challenged from several quarters, but the basic methodological aspect of his aesthetics has left very deep roots in all segments of It. culture: I refer to his disqualification, in the field of art, of "raw" sentiment (the source-material of art, not the actual content), of intellectualism (ideas are not found in art *qua* art), of moralism and utilitarianism (the rapport between the work of art and prevailing ethical standards or its practical functionality for its society is an extrinsic question, irrelevant to aesthetic judgment). In the last decades an articulate reaction to Croce has loomed ever larger, even though he is such a giant as to have overshadowed all other It. theorists. Nevertheless, all modern critical currents have been actively represented in Italy, from G. Pascoli's postromantic doctrine of the poet as a perennial child (the "fanciullino"), or G. D'Annunzio's decadent view of poetry as the verbal triumph of the "superman," to A. Tilgher's concept of art as *amor vitae* and representation of the impossible, E. Paci's and N. Abbagnano's existentialism, and G. Rensi's relativistic scepticism.

Formally speaking, radical Crocian attitudes seem consistent with the productive movement toward "pure" poetry known as Hermeticism, which during the Fascist years attracted most of the best talents by assuring an escape from trivial and undignified *engagement* through the initiation into a sophisticated expression as subjective, suggestive, and symbolic in its language as it was universal in its matter. But outside and against Crocian orientations (normally emphasizing the exclusive "ontological" approach to the intrinsic, aesthetic qualities of the work of art), one can see fully developed three main theoretical currents which correspond closely to their respective applications in literary criticism: (1) the emancipation of stylistic study, principally in the wake of Leo Spitzer (B. Terracini) but also on quite independent tracks (G. de Robertis, G. Devoto, M. Fubini, G. Contini), in a more or less close cooperation with modern philology and linguistic theory; (2) the stressing of the rapports between the work of art and the circumstances in which it found its natural genesis, from the psyche of the author and the vicissitudes of his life to the broader, social and political setting of his work (the most extreme example of this trend, but far from being the most productive, is the Marxist: cf. A. Gramsci, A. Banfi, C. Luporini); (3) the elaboration of the formal categories (implicitly regarded by Croce as nominalistic illusions or intellectualistic, pseudo-metaphysical intrusions), exemplified at best by the renewed interest in the Baroque (L. Anceschi). All this is in addition to the more common, though not more trivial, study of the works as part of a cultural, and specifically literary, tradition. See also FUTURISM, HERMETICISM, EXPRESSION, THEORY OF.

PRIMARY WORKS: B. Croce, 'La filosofia dello spirito': 1. *Estetica come scienza dell'espressione e linguistica generale* (1902), 2. *Logica* (1905), 3. *Filosofia della pratica* (1909), 4. *Teoria e storia della storiografia* (1917), all tr. D. Ainslie respectively in 1922², 1917, 1913, 1921, *Breviario di estetica* (1912), *Nuovi saggi di estetica* (1920), *The Essence of Aesthetic*, tr. Ainslie (1921), *La poesia di Dante* (1921), tr. Ainslie (1922), *Poesia e non poesia* (1923), *European Lit. in the 19th C.*, tr. Ainslie (1924), *Filosofia, poesia, storia* (1951); G. Gentile, *La filosofia dell'arte* (1931); A. Tilgher, *Estetica* (1931), *Studi di poetica* (1934); G. Della Volpe, *Fondamenti di una filosofia dell'espressione* (1936); G. Calogero, *Estetica, semantica, istorica* (1947); U. Spirito, *La vita come arte* (1948); A. Gramsci, *Letteratura e vita nazionale* (1950); A. Gargiulo, *Scritti d'estetica* (1952); L. Pareyson, *Estetica. Teoria della formatività* (1954); L. Stefanini, *Trattato di estetica* (1955).

SECONDARY WORKS: S. Caramella, *Storia del pensiero estetico e del gusto letterario in Italia* (1924), G. Bertoni, *Lingua e poesia. Saggi di critica letteraria* (1937); M. Apollonio, *Ermetismo* (1945); A. Ruschioni, *Sommario di storia dell'estetica letteraria* (1952); L. Russo, *La critica letteraria contemporanea* (3 v., new ed. 1953); M. Petrucciani, *La poetica dell'ermetismo italiano* (1955), *Poesia pura e poesia esistenziale* (1957); O. Macrí, *Caratteri e figure della poesia italiana contemporanea* (1958); A. Frattini and M. Camilucci, *La giovane poesia italiana e straniera. Aspetti e problemi* (1959); G. N. G. Orsini, *B. Croce, Philosopher of Art and Literary Critic* (1961); and for a detailed survey of the whole discipline, *Mo-*

menti e problemi di storia dell'estetica, pt. 4 (Marzorati ser., 1961).   A.S.

SPANISH. The 20th-c. renaissance in Sp. letters is in large part due to the excellence of its lyric poets. Despite their marked individuality, they all seem to share one general theoretic aim: to adopt a new aesthetic in which contemporary European trends are harmoniously blended with the most valuable of their own poetic tradition. Such an attitude implies, of course, a blending of revolution and continuity, reassessment of the literary past and tacit acceptance of foreign artistic influences.

The first revolutionary impulse to revitalize languid Sp. poetry at the turn of the century was the cosmopolitan *modernism* introduced into peninsular literature mainly by the Nicaraguan poet Rubén Darío. The influence of *modernism* was brief but decisive. However, major poets such as Antonio Machado and Juan Ramón Jiménez, despite their admiration for Darío himself, soon rejected its brilliant superficialities; Unamuno never could embrace its art-for-art's-sake doctrines; but still others (Villaespesa) were not ever able to break away from its exotic and facile charm.

Partly as a result of world crisis and partly as a Sp. counterpart of the various European isms, in 1919 an aggressive avant-garde movement known as *ultraism* appeared in violent opposition to an outmoded *modernism*. *Ultraism* produced little or no poetry of value, and its exponents disbanded as a militant group in 1922. However, its theories of the rehabilitation of the poem and the suppression of all extraneous material not strictly lyric were highly beneficial. The ultraists advocated the absolute supremacy of image and metaphor. Their poems were often merely a stringing together of ingenious and overwrought metaphors. Sentimentalism was rejected and narrative anecdote eliminated. As in all postwar movements—and *ultraism* aspired to be a synthesis of all avant-garde tendencies—the poets recognized the limitations of logic and reacted strongly against such an interpretation of reality. Furthermore, *ultraism* recommended a stripped down syntax, certain new typographical arrangements, and the inclusion in poetry of objects typifying modern civilization. Although it is impossible to clearly establish priorities, at about the same time the Chilean poet Huidobro brought with him to Madrid, via Paris, still another ism, that of *creationism*. As the name implies, *creationism* affirmed an attitude of independence with relation to reality and nature. In order to *create* new realities in poetry, Huidobro sought to *create* rather than represent the object. What is really significant in all this avant-garde ferment is that now Spain was undergoing a similar artistic upheaval *simultaneously* with that of other European nations.

Such unrest and experimentation were fruitful as a preliminary for the emergence of a really important literary generation, that of 1927. Because of the complex nature of the various artistic doctrines which converge and intermingle in the individual work of these writers of 1927, we shall be content to point out here only a few general trends. Above all, these poets wished to create a poetry which was essentially pure and genuinely lyric. In this connection, the poetic theories of Jiménez were particularly influential in the decade 1920–1930. This influence was twofold: the example of his person and also of his work. He encouraged the younger writers and opened to them the pages of his own exclusive poetry reviews. At this time too his own poetry became more synthetic, lucid, and concentrated. As Juan Ramón evolved toward greater formal liberty, he also sought to rid his verse of all decorative elements which he considered impurities. A more intellectual concept of poetry had now replaced the sensuous, impressionistic, and vaguely romantic verse of former years. His complete dedication to literature, his constant striving for perfection in art, and his personal austerity became an ideal for the young poets. As early as 1916 he had written: "¡Inteligencia, dame / el nombre exacto de las cosas! / . . . Que mi palabra sea / la cosa misma, / creada por mi alma nuevamente." This dictum was accepted by the new generation of poets. To this general poetic orientation should be added the more intellectual and philosophical influence of Ortega y Gasset who rejected all frivolity in his thinking and writing. The intensified use of metaphor was a typical quality of these poets, and this is not surprising since many of them fell momentarily under the spell of Góngora, whose tercentenary was enthusiastically celebrated in 1927. This interest in the 17th-c. poet gave rise to a direction known as *neogongorism,* readily visible in some of the verse of this generation. Moreover, several Andalusian poets, the early Lorca and Alberti, for example, cultivated a neopopular style in which popular motifs were highly stylized and cast in traditional forms such as the ballad. Still another new poetic influence can be traced to Fr. surrealism, but it is difficult to clearly determine any *direct* contact of the Sp. poets with the initiators of the movement in France. The Sp. writers, among them Lorca, Alberti and Aleixandre, accepted certain new liberties afforded them and benefited from some expressive techniques of surrealism. However, Sp. surrealism is not orthodox, and the poets did not embrace the more irrational aspects of André Breton's theories of automatic writing,

nor did they accept the dogmatic laws he advocated. Of this generation Guillén and Salinas did not write surrealist poetry. They both tended toward a more intellectualized and disciplined style. Juan Larrea was perhaps the most surrealistic of the Sp. poets.

Poetic tradition was naturally disrupted in Spain following the Civil War. The poets of today, however, tend toward an expression which is more social, more "realistic" and committed than that of previous generations. They wish to be heard and understood. Their language is less metaphorical, more direct and conversational in tone. Free verse is the norm, and the purely aesthetic is to some degree sacrificed to other ends.

As an important correlative to 20th-c. Sp. poetics themselves, final mention should be made of two critics, Dámaso Alonso and Amado Alonso, who have made outstanding contributions to stylistics. Of the former, his *Poesía española. Ensayo de métodos y límites estilísticos* (1952) is of particular significance. The remarkable studies of Amado Alonso in the interpretation of literary texts are too numerous to quote, but in the posthumous and miscellaneous volume *Materia y forma en poesía* (1955) are included ample definitions of his theories and their application. Moreover, each has trained a number of very distinguished disciples who are publishing important studies in this field of criticism. For additional bibliographical information the pertinent sections of Helmut A. Hatzfeld, *A Crit. Bibliog. of the New Stylistics* (1953) and (with Y. Le Hir) *Essai de bibliographie critique de stylistique française et romane (1955–1960)* (1961) are useful.

J. Ortega y Gasset, *La deshumanización del arte . . .* (1925; Eng. tr. by H. Weyl, 1948); G. de Torre, *Literaturas europeas de vanguardia* (1925) and *La aventura y el orden* (1948); *Antología de la poesía española e hispanoamericana,* ed. F. de Onís (1934, 1961); A. Machado, *Juan de Mairena* (2 v., 1942); J. López Morillas, "Antonio Machado's Temporal Interpretation of Poetry," JAAC, 6 (1947); P. Salinas, *Literatura española. Siglo XX* (1949); G. Díaz-Plaja, *Modernismo frente a noventa y ocho* (1951); D. Alonso, *Poetas españoles contemporáneos* (1952); Navarro; L. Cernuda, *Estudios sobre poesía española contemporánea* (1957); L. F. Vivanco, *Introducción a la poesía española contemporánea* (1957); J. R. Jiménez, *Pájinas escojidas* (Prosa), ed. R. Gullón (1958); A. W. Phillips, "Sobre la poética de García Lorca," *Revista Hispánica Moderna* 24 (1958); P. Salinas, *Ensayos de literatura hispánica* (1958; pp. 290–395); *Poesía española,* ed. G. Diego (1959); J. L. Cano, *Poesía española del siglo XX* (1960); J. M. Castellet, *Veinte años de poesía española, 1939–*

1959 (1960); G. de Torre, "Contemp. Sp. Poetry," *Texas Quarterly*, 4 (1961); C. Zardoya, *Poesía española contemporánea. Estudios temáticos y estilísticos* (1961). See also bibliog. to CREATIONISM, MODERNISM, NEOGONGORISM, and ULTRAISM.   A.W.P.

SLAVIC. Rus. poetics in the first two decades were largely determined by the symbolist school. The study of versification, widely neglected in the second half of the 19th c., became the main point of interest. Whereas the leader of the symbolists, Valery Bryusov, tried to systematize and popularize the poetics of the Fr. symbolists and to adapt them to the special requirements of the Rus. language, the symbolist poet and prose writer Andrey Bely developed original theories in Rus. versification combined with a rather mystic philosophy trying to explain the phenomenon of creative artistic intuition. The most important point in his verse theories is the clear realization of the moment of pyrrhics in Rus. verse. He maintained that it should be possible to characterize single poets by the distribution of pyrrhics in their poems. From graphs based on tables of pyrrhic frequency he obtained geometrical figures which varied with every poet and thus represented the starting point of their characterization. The sound pattern of each poem was closely examined; in fact, sound became sometimes more important than contents (e.g. in poets like Balmont and Blok). Very soon sound became a kind of a symbol out of which a rather vague ideology was not difficult to develop. The theoretical discussion of poetics as seen by the symbolists received valuable contributions in the articles of the outstanding poet Innokenty Annensky (e.g. in his essay "Balmont—lirik" in *Kniga otrazheniy* I, pp. 169-213). He developed the idea of a general "lyrical ego," which explains why everyone has the same subconscious emotional reaction to the given form of poem.

The poetical school which followed the symbolists, the acmeists, preserved the stress on form, but denied its symbolic meaning. In their general attitude to poetry they adopted to a certain degree the views of the Fr. *Parnassiens*, but of course the polemical tendency against the Rus. symbolists and the excellent knowledge of their poetry colored their theoretical writings. Very important are the essays of Osip Mandelstam and Nikolay Gumilyov, published for the most part in the review *Apollón*. In explaining their discrepancies with the symbolists they gave many valuable contributions to the theoretical understanding of Rus. verse.

The occasionally exaggerated demands of the Rus. futurists, who followed the acmeists, culminated in the work of Velimir Khlebnikov who inaugurated a kind of mysticism and mythology of words: he tried to reduce Rus. vocabulary to a number of ideologically valued roots which when varied and ramified by means of prefixes, infixes, and suffixes, helped him to form a kind of poetic language which did not follow logical but "translogical" (*zaumny*) associations. Basic ideas were originally expressed in basic sounds; poetry should help to restore this correspondence of sound and meaning which has been destroyed by common speech. A rebirth of language as such was expected from the new poetry.

The structuralists (a better word than the usual "formalists") continued to stress the poetic "word as such" and the detailed analysis of the poetic text. Important are Osip Brik's articles about sound repetitions in poems (e.g. "Zvukovye povtory," *Poetika*, 1919), Roman Jakobson's analysis of Khlebnikov's poetry (*Noveyshaya russkaya poeziya*, 1921) and the very valuable book by Boris Eichenbaum *Melodika stikha* (1921). The distinction Eichenbaum makes between the songlike and the rhetoric diction in poetry proved to be a consequential step in Rus. poetics. The structuralists described poetic language as a special device to make us feel the word in its double quality: as a label designating a certain object and as a sound and sense pattern having a weight and an essence of its own. The result of the interest in the structure of poetic works were several excellent and conclusive theoretical works giving a complete system of Rus. versification: Yury Tynyanov tried to establish the specific quality of the poetic speech in *Problema stikhotvornogo yazyka* (1924); Boris Tomashevsky gave a comprehensive presentation of Rus. metrics (*Russkoe stikhoslozhenie*, 1923); and Viktor Zhirmunsky discussed exhaustively the composition of lyric poems and the different aspects of rhyme (*Kompozitsiya liricheskikh stikhotvoreniy*, 1921 and *Rifma, ee istoriya i teoriya*, 1923). Soviet poetics did not add anything new to the discussion of technical questions; but there are some valuable works about the language of individual poets strongly influenced by the structuralists, e.g. Viktor Vinogradov's impressive *Yazyk Pushkina* (1935). "Formalism" is not accepted officially in Soviet Russia.

In other Slavic countries, the main influence was that of Fr. symbolist poetics during the first two decades of the 20th c. Afterwards structuralism took firm hold only in Czechoslovakia. One of its principal champions in Russia, Roman Jakobson, went to Prague in 1920 and applied the structuralist methods to Czech verse, comparing it in part with Rus. verse (*O chéshskom stikhé preimúshchstvenno v sopostavlénii s rússkim*, 1923). The works of Jan Mukařovský, especially his study of the poetry of K. H. Mácha, present one of the best analyses in Slavic poetics. In Poland structuralism was accepted and applied to Polish verse by Manfred Kridl and Franciszek Siedlecki. But on the whole the strictly historical approach still prevails. This has resulted in some excellent works about the development of Polish verse, as e.g., Maria Dłuska's *Studia z historii i teorii wersyfikacji* (1948–50) or the encyclopaedia of poetics edited by Maria Renata Mayenowa (*Poetyka, Zarys encyklopedyczny*, 1956–57). In Yugoslavia the special qualities of the Serbian, the Croatian and the Slovenian languages, above all the musical accent, account for the long disputes between the "syllabists" and the "tonists" in the beginning of this century (and earlier). These were not very productive. A consistent poetics of the South Slavic languages began to develop when Roman Jakobson (using the Serbian popular songs), Kiril Taranovski (using the popular as well as the literary poetic language) and A. Isátchenko (on the basis of the Slovenian language) began to apply the methods of the Rus. "formalists" and the linguistic school of Prague. They clearly showed that all prosodic elements play an important part in shaping this specific verse: the stress, the musical pitch and the length and number of syllables. See also RUSSIAN FORMALISM.

A. Bely, *Simvolizm* (1910) and *Lug Zelony* (1910); V. Bryusov, *Kratky kurs nauki o stikhe* (1919; a brief introd. to versification) and *Osnovy stikhovedeniya* (1924; the basic concepts of versific.); B. Eichenbaum, *Lermontov* (1924; an exemplary application of poetic theories); R. Jakobson, *Základy českeho verše* (1926; basic concepts of Czech verse); V. Khlebnikov, *Sobranie proizvedeniy* (1928–33); F. Siedlecki, "Sprawy wersyfikacji polskiej," *Wiadomości Literackie* (1934; basic concepts of Polish verse); K. W. Zawodziński, *Zarys wersyfikacji polskiej I* (1936; same); M. Kridl, *Wstęp do badań nad dzielem literackiem* (Z zagadnień poetyki I) (1936; a crit. survey of lit. theories); J. Mukařovský, *Kapitoly z české poetiky* (3 v., 1941; an application of structuralist theories and a discussion of basic concepts of poetics); K. Taranovski, *Ruski dvodelni ritmovi* (1953; an exhaustive discussion of the Rus. 2-foot meters) and *Principi srpsko-hrvatske versifikacije* (1954); R. Wellek, "Modern Czech Crit. and Lit. Scholarship," *Harvard Slavic Studies*, 2 (1954); B. O. Unbegaun, *Rus. Versification* (1956). v.s.

MODERNISMO. The movement in Hispanic letters which began in the 1880's in Sp. America, blending Sp., Fr., and other foreign influences in the creation of a new poetic diction. The area's relative stability during the last quarter of the 19th c. made possible this first widespread literary movement of the Southern countries, and marked their cultural maturity. Literature, previously composed in great haste and for a political purpose, now became an art form. Old poetic forms such as the *romance* octosyllable, the hendecasyllable, tetrasyllable, the alexandrine, monorhyme, and the classic Greco-Latin hexameter were revived and polished. New meters of 10, 11, 12, 15, or more syllables, and new metric combinations, were widely used and gave a new fluidity to poetic expression. The result was a complete renovation of metrical resources. Spritely metaphors, elegant musicality, linguistic impressionism, and synesthesia (q.v.) were also characteristic of the modernist style. The clichés of romanticism were zealously avoided by the new writers, and exotic gallicisms were deliberately and judiciously employed to bring zest and flavor both to poetry and to prose. Syntax was simplified, difficult inversions avoided, and language, though overly ornate in many early modernist writings, was gradually made more crystalline and more harmonious.

M. blended romanticism, Fr. symbolism and Parnassianism in its strong Sp. Am. crucible. The Orient, classic and Nordic mythology, Sp. literature of the pre-Golden and Golden Ages, and the United States were also sources of inspiration, as were the traditions of the Am. peoples and the Am. earth. The skillful fusion of all these resources resulted in a cosmopolitan perspective, a new concinnity of language, and a new poetic diction which were the main contributions of m. to Western literature.

The initiators of m. were Gutiérrez Nájera of Mexico, José Asunción Silva of Colombia, Julián del Casal and José Martí of Cuba. Martí was a unique figure whose life, speeches, and writings exemplified both fine literature and political action. The most famous modernist was Rubén Darío of Nicaragua, whose influence carried the new movement to Spain. Among the other modernists were José Enrique Rodó of Uruguay, Amado Nervo and Enrique González Martínez of Mexico, José Santos Chocano of Peru, Leopoldo Lugones of Argentina, and the Machado brothers of Spain. Hispanic literature entered the gates of m. with Rubén Darío and left them in the poetry of Juan Ramón Jiménez of Spain—so writes one of the best historians of the movement, Federico de Onís.

Despite their lack of a keen social sense, the modernist writers established a feeling of spiritual and cultural kinship among themselves and among their nations. On the other hand, m. erected a beautiful literary façade behind which lay an economic and a political shambles. The subsequent literature of the Mexican Revolution and other more recent writings destroyed the façade and exposed the shambles.

ANTHOLOGIES: *An Anthol. of the Modernista Movement in Sp. America*, ed. A. Coester (1924); *Antologia de la poesia española e hispanoamericana*, ed. F. de Onís (1934, 1961; contains excellent crit. essays); *Poetas modernistas hispanoamericanos*, ed. C. García Prada (1956); *Swan, Cygnets and Owl*, tr. M. E. Johnson (1956); *Antologia critica del modernismo hispanoamericano*, ed. R. Silva Castro (1963).

HISTORY AND CRITICISM: I. Goldberg, *Studies in Sp. Am. Lit.* (1920); P. Henríquez-Ureña, *La versificación irregular en la poesia castellana* (1920) and *Lit. Currents in Hispanic America* (1945); J. R. Jiménez, "El modernismo poético en España e Hispanoamérica," *Revista de América* (April 1946); G. Díaz-Plaja, *Modernismo frente a noventa y ocho* (1951); M. Henríquez-Ureña, *Breve historia del modernismo* (1954, 2d ed., 1962; best general survey); R. A. Arrieta, *Introducción al modernismo literario* (1956); Navarro.   J.A.C.

MODULATION. See METRICAL VARIATIONS.

MOLOSSUS. In classical prosody, a metrical foot consisting of 3 long syllables ($-\,-\,-$). It is found very rarely as an independent foot and never in a connected series. Sometimes it replaces an Ionic (q.v.) *a minore* by the contraction of the first 2 short syllables, and less often an Ionic *a maiore* or a choriamb (q.v.).
—Dale; Koster; Crusius.   P.S.C.

MONGOLIAN POETRY. The chief source of early Mo. poetry is an imperial chronicle of Genghis Khan's house, the *Secret History of the Mongols* (A.D. 1240), which contains many rough-hewn alliterated verses of irregular length, and of no set pattern of repetition for the initial alliterating syllables. Some later historical chronicles of the 17th c., as the *Erdeni-yin Tobči* (Jewelled Summary), contain sophisticated and polished quatrains of even length and fixed form, particularly at points of direct discourse in the narrative.

The bulk of native literary expression is in the form of *üliger's*, orally transmitted epic stories in verse, which may reach 20,000 verses in length, and are recited from memory by bards. They relate the adventures of real or legendary heroes and villains, as Genghis Khan, Erintsen Mergen, Gesser Khan, and Janggar. These heroes struggle against the many-headed *manggus*, who is defeated in the end. The internal structure of these poems is quite stylized and may be diagrammed as a series of rounds between the hero and his adversary.

Mo. verse is alliterative (although rhyme is found in a few instances, such as the Sino-Mo. inscription of 1362). This alliteration chiefly occurs on the initial syllable (the entire syllable, and not just the first phoneme), but internal alliteration is also found. In epic poetry, alliteration is in couplets or is irregular, and in lyric poetry (here used in the strict sense of the word, "composed for the lyre," hence, in stanzas), it is in quatrains. The best-styled verse has 7 to 8 syllables with 3 or 4 internal stresses, but this is only a general guide to its construction. One may also encounter in texts the so-called graphic alliteration, by which some letters of identical shape in the Mongolian script (as *t/d, o/u*) may alliterate (cf. Eng. "eye-rhyme").

The characteristic feature of form is parallelism, the same idea reiterated in slightly different words in the succeeding verses. This usage is very similar to the Hebraic parallelism made familiar by the Old Testament Psalms. The chief theme of Mo. poetry has been the great epic legends, with their elaborate descriptions of heroic deeds, royal palaces and maidenly beauty. There are also shorter poems with love themes, nature themes, and religious themes.

One of the finest poems in Mo. is the *Lament of Toghon Temür*, six well-polished stanzas uttered by that ruler when he was driven from Khubilai's palace and the throne of China in 1368. In bemoaning the loss of that residence, he draws on an accretion of Mo. legends which were likewise used by Marco Polo in his description. This account was later taken by Purchas for his travel book, whence it filtered through Coleridge's subconscious to emerge as *Kubla Khan*.

As a general sample of Mo. verse, the following stanzas may be cited. The free translation accompanying employs both initial alliteration as well as end rhyme to convey the poetical nature of the original, although rhyme is not present there. The parallelism between the stanzas will be evident.

> *dobo děre urgasan*
> *dolōn zuilīn tsetseg bī;*
> *dolōn zuilīn tanarta*
> *domgīn dū ailadxan bi.*

> *namag děre urgasan*
> *naiman zuilīn tsetseg bī;*
> *naiman zuilīn tanarta*
> *nadmīn dū ailadxan bi.*

Sitting in their hillside bowers (are)
Seven sorts of hillside flowers;
Seven sorts of stories, too,
Soon I'll say in song to you.

Garlands of the gloomy swamp,
Grow eight flowers in their pomp;
Games and gladness, eight kinds too,
Give I gladly now to you.

N. Poppe, *Khalkha-mongol'skii geroičeskii èpos* (The Heroic Epic of the Khalkha Mongols, 1937), *Mongolische Volksdichtung* (1955) and "Der Parallelismus in der epischen Dichtung der Mongolen," *Ural-Altaische Jahrbücher*, 30 (1958); K. Grønbech, "Specimens of Mo. Poetry," *The Music of the Mongols* (1943); P. Pelliot, *Hist. secrète des Mongols* (1949); Damdinsüren, *Monggol uran jokiyal-un degeji jagun bilig orusibai* (One Hundred Extracts from Mo. Lit., 1959); J. R. Krueger, "Poetical Passages in the *Erdeni-yin Tobči*, a Mo. Chronicle of the Year 1662 by Sagang Sečen," *Central Asiatic Studies*, 7 (1961).　　J.KRU.

MONK'S TALE STANZA. A stanza composed of 8 lines of iambic pentameter, rhyming ababbcbc, used by Chaucer in *An A.B.C.*, *The Monk's Tale* (in *The Canterbury Tales*), and a few other short poems. The stanza is, in all certainty, one of the Fr. ballade stanzas. It is, however, not used with distinction in *The Monk's Tale*, which suffers from excessive end-stopping and rhythmic monotony. The stanza had some popularity in the 15th c., but its major importance is as a possible inspiration of the Spenserian stanza (q.v.), which is achieved by the simple addition of an alexandrine line which duplicates the final rhyme of the stanza.

MONODY. Originally in Gr. lyric poetry an ode sung by a single voice, e.g., by one of the characters in a tragedy. It came to be associated with the lamentation of a single mourner, and hence became a dirge (q.v.) or a funeral song. In metrical form the strophes are repeated without variation. In Eng. poetry, Milton referred to his *Lycidas* as a m., as the epigraph of the poem indicates. Matthew Arnold applied the term to his elegy on A. H. Clough: *Thyrsis, A. M.*　　R.A.H.

MONOLOGUE. The word "m." is used in several distinct senses all of which have in common the conception of one person speaking alone, who may or may not have an audience. The meaning of the term for poetry is elucidated by its use entirely apart from any art form, where it means simply "the prolonged speech of an individual." In colloquial usage the word often has a prejudicial sense, as a "m." that prevents freedom of conversation. In its more general literary sense it signifies any prolonged utterance, in direct speech. There may, for example, be monologues within novels, plays, or poems. It is even correct to describe a work of great length as a m. if it is couched in a framework of direct address. But the speaker should preferably be the principal character. Meditations may in this sense also be called monologues. The common use stresses speech as well as the individual speaking; words uttered constitute a purer form of m. than those merely thought or written. The epistle is not a m., since it is imagined as read, not spoken.

Despite its limitation to a single speaker, the m. naturally assumes a dramatic character. For vocalization itself craves an object—one or many persons to constitute an audience. Thus the audience as well as the speaker becomes a part of the total area of imagination. In Chekhov's play, *Tobacco*, the speaker addresses the theatre audience believing it to be a jury sitting in judgment on the morality of his actions. This unusual play becomes a m. on two accounts: because the dramatist imagines his speaker and because the speaker imagines his audience. The m. requires not only a single speaker but an advanced degree of impersonation.

The soliloquy of theatrical tradition becomes a form of m. when sufficiently prolonged. The word applies equally to the soliloquy that is an interior debate, as Hamlet's speech, "To be or not to be," or Falstaff's direct address on honor, delivered downstage to the audience. The m. may be either heard or overheard. Many of the outstanding passages of dramatic poetry are in this form. The overheard m., or the speaker's talking to himself, is a favorite vehicle for self-expression and subjective utterance. Passages of this nature introduce many plays, as Marlowe's *Doctor Faustus*, Goethe's *Faust*, and Byron's *Manfred*. Not only in its theatrical form but in nondramatic poetry it becomes a favorite device of the romantic poets. But the origins of m. are too ancient to be sketched in more than conjecture. As the germ of drama, it may well precede even the dialogue. A lament may be regarded as a tragic form of m.; a clownish harangue, a comic form. In biblical literature the poetic m., usually embedded in larger forms, is brought to a high degree of perfection. Specimens are *The Song of Deborah*, *The Song of Hannah*, and Jeremiah's lament over Jerusalem. From biblical poetry comes also the soliloquy of the personified city. A variety of m. is the prayer, where the devotee addresses the deity who hears but deigns no reply.

Although the m. as a distinct literary form is inconspicuous in early Gr. poetry, the art is brought to refined development within the drama, epic, and ode. Long speeches in highly cultivated rhetoric appear in most of the longer literary forms. On the stage the convention of a colloquy between a single actor and the chorus considerably reduces the tendency to monologue, but impressive achievements of this nature are nevertheless found, as in Aeschylus' *Prometheus Bound*. M. was prominent in miming, though dialogue enjoyed greater popularity. Admirable examples are found among the idyls, especially those of Theocritus. The classical shepherd is by tradition fond of declamation; pathos discourages question or conversation. Notable instances of m. are found among the poems of Ovid and Propertius.

The subjectivity prevalent in Germanic literature favored m. Some of the finest Anglo-Saxon poems, as *The Wanderer, The Seafarer,* and *The Wife's Lament,* afford good examples. Christian devotional literature abounds in such verse, as in poems where the Virgin addresses the Cross, or where, similarly, the Soul addresses the Body. An advance toward the dramatic appears in poetry of the later Middle Ages and early Renaissance, where the formula of "the complaint," or "the address," appears. This becomes happily conspicuous among the Scotch Chaucerians, notably Dunbar, Henryson, and Lyndsay, as well as in the work of John Skelton. Imitations of the Horatian or Ovidian epistle aid the rise of the more dramatic forms of address. This development extends throughout the 16th c., from Wyatt through *The Mirror for Magistrates,* and the work of George Gascoigne to the more refined art of Raleigh and Drayton. It offers an important contribution to the perfection of Elizabethan dramatic verse. M. appears in all periods of Eng. literature, though in some more abundantly than in others. Robert Burns made important contributions to the form partly through his familiarity with the Scottish tradition. Sidney Smith's *Imaginary Addresses* represent an admirable development in humorous verse.

In instances where the speaker is strictly identified with the poet, as in much romantic verse, the absence of impersonation vitiates the achievement of m. in the more usual sense of the word. The highest form of m. is dramatic and is best illustrated by the dramatic monologues of Robert Browning. His works in this kind show two contrasting influences: those in stanzaic forms, which are in the majority, betray inspiration from the popular ballad that often employs a single imaginary speaker; those in couplets or in blank verse derive most clearly from the stage; they may be described as drama in miniature. Browning's dramatic monologues may also be regarded as closet dramas where only one person speaks. Such pieces as *My Last Duchess* may be imagined as scenes with a crowded stage and only one speaker. So powerful are Browning's dramatic monologues that his discoveries in the genre surpass those in the realm of the poetic style.

Some of the most important verse in Eng. since Browning plays variations upon his development of the m. Many of Thomas Hardy's,

Rudyard Kipling's, and Ezra Pound's works follow Browning's use closely; T. S. Eliot's *The Love Song of J. Alfred Prufrock* is a m. addressed *in vacuo;* several of E. A. Robinson's finest poems, as *Toussaint L'Ouverture,* are addressed to imaginary hearers. An interesting variation is seen in Robinson's *Rembrandt to Rembrandt,* his own favorite among his poems, where one phase of the painter's soul is imagined as conversing with another in his mirror. Conrad Aiken, Edgar Lee Masters, and Robert Frost have contributed further variations.

The m. becomes an especially enlivening form for poetry in any literature tending to neglect the vital relations of poetry to the spoken voice. With Browning as a pathfinder, it has assumed great value for Eng. verse of the 20th c., as this drastically divorces itself from the comparatively bookish diction of Tennyson and Swinburne. But it may safely be concluded that much of the world's finest poetry has in all ages been in the m. form.— I. B. Sessions, "The Dramatic M.," PMLA, 62 (1947); B. W. Fuson, *Browning and his Eng. Predecessors in the Dramatic M.* (1948); R. Langbaum, *The Poetry of Experience* (1957).
H.W.W.

MONOMETER. A line consisting of one meter, either a dipody or foot. In classical iambic, trochaic, and anapaestic verse the metron is a dipody (pair of feet). As used by Eng. prosodists, "-meter" is synonymous with foot. The Eng. monometer (a 1-stress line), therefore, consists of 1 foot. Probably the most famous examples in Eng. poetry are by Herrick, *The Bridegroom; Upon his Departure Hence:*

> Thus I
> Passe by
> And die:
> As one, . . .

R.O.E.

MONORHYME refers to a passage in a poem, to a strophe, or to an entire poem in which all lines have the same end rhyme. It is often used capriciously as an artificial device for producing satirical or comical effects, or even as a mnemotechnical aid. Aside from this it occurs in various languages as a component part of certain meters and is, in this instance, purely conventional. It is fairly frequent in the Romance and Slavic languages where it may be applied with greater ease as in German or in Eng. It occurs in medieval L. poetry; thus, in the poems of Commodian, in a psalm by St. Augustine consisting of 288 lines all ending in -e or -ae (tirade rhyme), in the sequences of Notker (echoing the -a of the Alleluja), in the *Carmen Mutinense*, and in the poems of Gottschalk. It has also been used by the goliards in strophes of four 13-syllable lines (*Vagantenstrophe*). In Old Fr. m. appears in *laisses* of varying length in the medieval *Alexander Romances* while, later, it is restricted to quatrains and tercets which, in turn, were imitated in Spain (the *cuaderna via* as practiced by Berceo and the *tercetos* of Pedro de Veragüe's *Doctrina cristiana*). In modern Fr. it has been employed by Voltaire, Lefranc de Pompignan, and Théophile Gautier. German examples of m. (*gehäufter Reim*) are rare and so are Eng. In Arabic poetry m. is the rule, and there exists a mystical poem of 700 lines with the same end rhyme. In Welsh poetry, likewise, m. is functional. It appears in the *awdl* (ode) and is sometimes used to link a chain of *englynion* (*gosteg o englynion*). T.F.

MONOSTICH. (a) A single line of verse; (b) a poem one line long (cf. *Anthologia Palatina*, 11. 312). MONOSTROPHIC. (a) A poem one strophe or stanza long; (b) a poem in which all the strophes or stanzas have the same metrical form.

MORA (L. "delay" but *mora temporis* "space of time." The Gr. equivalent is *chronos*, literally "time.") Term used to denote the duration of a short syllable, which was the time-unit of Gr. and L. quantitative verse. The normal or "disemic" principle of classical metric was to regard a long syllable as equivalent to 2 morae, while rhythmical theory distinguished "trisemes," "tetrasemes," and "pentasemes" (conventionally indicated in modern times by ⌞ or ⌟, ⊔, and ⊔⊔) for syllables of the length of 3, 4, and 5 morae respectively. See CLASSICAL PROSODY, DISEMIC, and TRISEMIC. R.J.G.

MORAL CRITICISM. See CRITICISM, TYPES OF.

MORALITY PLAYS. The m.p. is a dramatized allegory. This is a useful definition, since it enables us to discriminate between the morality proper and the multitude of other plays, both medieval and modern, that introduce allegory and allegorical characters. Allegory was common to medieval literature of all kinds. In the m.p. emphasis was placed on those allegorical figments that expressed the fate of man on earth. Life was compared to a journey: we have the motif of the pilgrimage of the life of man; to an enterprise ending in death: we have the *Dance of Death;* to a battle between the forces of evil: we have the *psychomachia*—the warfare between the seven deadly sins, assisted by various vices,

and the four cardinal and the three theological virtues.

The most important idea, the one that lies back of the earliest m.p., is man's achievement of salvation. Man, conceived in sin, is obliged by his corrupted nature to plunge into sin. In order to be saved, he must repent, believe, and submit himself to divine mercy. These facts determine the essence of the m.p. as a dramatic genre. Man in the generalized form of Mankind, Everyman, *Homo*, or *Humanum Genus* behaves positively and objectively, suddenly and immediately without inward struggle. Temptation beckons him and he becomes a sinner. Later Conscience, Conviction of Sin or Repentance comes to him, and again, since abstractions cannot feel, he follows these agents without hesitation.

There was an extensive development of the m.p. in France and to a lesser degree in Germany, Spain, and elsewhere, but, so far as one can see, the perfectly generalized career of man on earth appears first in England and forms the salient characteristic of Eng. moral plays.

The crisis in the full-scope moralities is the unexpected arrival of Death, and the Dance of Death epitomizes this aspect of morality. It had impersonation and dialogue and needed only event, or the experience of an individual, to make it a complete m.p. Two Eng. plays border on the Dance of Death: *The Pride of Life*, from an imperfect Dublin manuscript and going back probably to the end of the 14th c., and *Everyman*, printed by Pynson in 1509, but so primitive and pure in its conception as to suggest great age. The former actually has no provision for salvation. One manuscript contains three full-scope moralities all belonging to the 15th c.: *The Castle of Perseverance*, dated by W. K. Smart about 1405 and the most elaborate and learned of all early moralities, *Mankind*, a play badly degenerated and vulgarized by ignorant rural players and possibly written early in the 15th c., and *Mind, Will and Understanding*, a later play probably from London and dramatizing quite generally the faculties of the human mind. Other early plays of this same complete generality are *Nature* (ca. 1530) by Henry Medwall, *The Nature of the Four Elements* (ca. 1519), *Hyckescorner* (pr. ca. 1512), and *Mundus et Infans* (pr. 1522). There are others of this kind, and the mode of complete generality was never lost, but in practice the way to find new subjects was specialization—childhood instead of the whole of human life, man in particular situations and subjected to special temptations, trades, professions, and social classes instead of man in general.

What happened may be described as a flood of m.p. of every conceivable sort, a flood that continued until the 17th c. We may mention *Gentleness and Nobility* by John Rastell, *Magnificence* by John Skeleton, *All for Money* by T. Lupton, *Lusty Juventus* by R. Wever, *The Interlude of Youth* (anonymous), *The Longer Thou Livest, the More Fool Thou Art* by W. Wager, *The Tide Tarriest No Man* by George Wapull, and *The Conflict of Conscience* by Nathaniel Woodes. Among the Elizabethan m.p. are Robert Wilson's *The Three Lords and Three Ladies of London*, the excellent anonymous play *A Knack to Know a Knave*, Marlowe's *Dr. Faustus*, Dekker's *Old Fortunatus*, and Jonson's *The Staple of News*. The titles will suggest the range but not the numbers. These plays are successes, but, in point of fact, the m.p. underwent great degeneration in its later life. Allegory was introduced everywhere, as also the Devil and the Vice, not because these things were needed, but because the popular audiences of the time demanded them.

Stylistically m.p. are uncertain and poor. *The Pride of Life* is in simple quatrains, *Everyman* in couplets of long lines suggestive of tumbling measure, *Mankind* has worse lines of the same sort with varied and ill-defined stanzas. *The Castle of Perseverance* is syllabic in form and better set up, with elaborate and well-constructed stanzas. *Wisdom* again is badly mixed, but seems to prefer the Chester rhyme-scheme. All these are medieval. The latter m.p. reflect the mixture of new forms with old that characterizes dramatic style during the first three-quarters of the 16th c.

L. Petit de Julleville, *Répertoire du Théâtre comique* (1886); W. R. Mackenzie, *The Eng. Moralities* (1904); C. F. Tucker Brooke, *The Tudor Drama* (1912); W. K. Smart, *Some Eng. and L. Sources and Parallels for the Morality of Wisdom* (1912) and articles in learned journals; H. Craig, *Eng. Religious Drama of the Middle Ages* (1955); D. M. Bevington, *From Mankind to Marlowe* (1962). H.C.

MOSAIC RHYME has at least one rhyme-fellow made out of more than one word, as in the following from Whittier's *Barclay of Ury*: *master / passed her, save us / Gustavus, pray thee / slay thee, greet me / meet me.* A fair proportion of feminine rhymes are of this kind. Browning who was partial to the device has 16 out of a possible 37 in *A Grammarian's Funeral*, including such unconventional ones as: *fabric / dab brick, far gain / bargain, all meant / installment, failure / pale lure, soon hit / unit, loosened / dew send.* A.M.C.

MOTE. A Sp. poem consisting of a single line or 2 lines, rarely more, containing a complete thought. Usually, but not always, this thought is glossed in verse, the whole composition then being called either *mote* or *glosa*, occasionally *villancico* or *letra*. One m. may be glossed by several poets or by the same poet in several versions. The m. was particularly popular in the 15th c.—Navarro. D.C.C.

MOZARABIC LYRICS. See SPANISH POETRY.

MULTIPLE OR POLYSYLLABIC RHYME. Also known as triple rhyme and, rarely, quadruple rhyme. Correspondence of more than 2 syllables in rhyming position (*nascitur / pascitur*) is a feature of medieval L. and other Romance verse, but it never established itself strongly, except for special effects, in less heavily polysyllabic languages like Eng. Sidney mentions *sdrucciola* (triple rhyme) in the *Defence of Poesie*, and has virtuoso examples of it in the *Arcadia*, but it is chiefly used for comic effects, as by Byron in *Don Juan* and by Gilbert in his ballads. G.T.H.

MÜNCHENER DICHTERKREIS. A circle of German poets (E. Geibel, P. Heyse, H. Lingg, M. Greif, W. Herz, F. Bodenstedt, Graf von Schack *et al.*) writing during the middle of the 19th c., who were invited by Maximilian II, King of Bavaria, to take residence at his court in Munich. In imitation of the Duke of Weimar, Maximilian wanted to enable these poets to devote all their time to literary activities.

This group first came together, under the guidance of E. Geibel, in the literary club "Das Krokodil," founded in 1856 by P. Heyse after the model of the Berlin club "Der Tunnel über die Spree." In 1862 Geibel edited the *Münchner Dichterbuch*, which was to be authoritative in matters of artistic taste. The poetic genres represented here were mainly "Lied," ballads, sententious lyric poetry, and verse tales. Geibel instructed his associates in ways to achieve a superficial flawlessness of diction, stanza form, and rhyme scheme. He was opposed to irregular and unusual sentence structure and hyperbolical metaphors. Geibel confused strict precision in language with aesthetic beauty. Important motifs in the works of the M.D. are complaints against the transience of all life, loneliness, and isolation; predominant are the atmosphere of autumn and the longing for peace and rest. All of these poets were epigones. After the death of Maximilian (1864) the circle lost its impetus. In 1882 Heyse made an attempt to revive the circle when he published *Das neue Münchner Dichterbuch*, a collection artistically even more fragile than the first. It was published at a time when new literary movements were emerging, and had nothing in common with the new aesthetic principles of works published in the same year: Ibsen's *Enemy of the People,* Nietzsche's *Fröhliche Wissenschaft,* and the Hart brothers' *Kritische Waffengänge.* In 1883 "Das Krokodil" had its last meeting.—F. Burwick, "Die Kunsttheorie des M.D." (diss. Greifswald, 1932); W. Sieber, "Der M.D. und die Romantik" (diss. Bern, 1937); L. Ferrari, "Paul Heyse und die literarischen Strömungen seiner Zeit" (diss. Bonn, 1939); E. Petzel and W. Kohlschmidt, "M.D.," *Reallexikon,* 2d ed., II; F. Martini, *Deutsche Literatur im bürgerlischen Realismus 1848–1898* (1962).   E.L.

MUSE. One of the nine Gr. goddesses who preside over poetry, song, and the arts, traditionally invoked by poets to grant them inspiration. ("Sing, Goddess, the wrath of Achilles, Peleus' son . . ." Homer, *Iliad* 1.1). At first indefinite in number, the M., daughters of Zeus and Mnemosyne (goddess of memory), were first celebrated in Thrace near Mt. Olympus and Pieria. Hence that peak was regarded as their home and the Pierian Spring as the fountain of learning. Probably before Homer's time their worship had spread southward to Helicon and thence to Delphi; it eventually became a common feature of Gr. religious culture. By the 3d c. B.C. the festival of the Heliconian Muses at Thespai was patronized by Athens and the important guild of artists of Dionysus; here all the poetic and musical talent of Greece was consecrated. Elsewhere, observance of the M. became attached to the worship of Apollo.

The attribution of particular arts to each M. is a late development, and there is some duplication of influence. The M. are: Calliope (epic or heroic poetry); Clio (history, lyreplaying); Erato (love poetry, hymns, lyre-playing, pantomime); Euterpe (tragedy, flute-playing, lyric poetry); Melpomene (tragedy, lyreplaying); Polymnia or Polyhymnia (hymns, pantomime, religious dancing); Terpsichore (choral dancing and singing, flute-playing); Thalia (comedy); and Urania (astronomy, i.e., cosmological poetry).

With the recovery of classical writings in the later Middle Ages the tradition of invoking the Muse or Muses was revived. In Dante (where Beatrice herself fulfills the Muse's role), there are references to the Muses of antiquity (*Inferno* 2.7f.; 32.10f.; *Paradiso* 2.8; 18.82f.). Milton invokes the pagan M. but transforms her into a specifically Christian inspiring power: "Descend from Heaven, Urania, by that name / If rightly thou art called . . . / . . . for thou / Nor of the Muses nine, nor on the top / Of old Olympus dwell'st, but heavenly-born . . . / Thou with Eternal Wisdom didst converse." (*Paradise Lost* 7.1ff.).

For other Renaissance poets, however, the M. of antiquity could be accepted without relinquishing their pagan attributes. Thus Spenser commences *The Faerie Queene:* "Me, all too meane, the sacred Muse areeds / To blazen broad amongst her learned throng; / Fierce warres and faithfull loues shall moralize my song." (1.7–9). The unnamed "sacred Muse" is either Clio (history) or Calliope (epic). The Petrarchan love poets, too, invoked their inspiring spirit: "Fool said my muse to me, look in thy heart and write" (Sidney, *Astrophel and Stella,* 1.14). The beloved herself sometimes assumed the role of M. The tradition continues into modern times of invoking or referring to the Muse or Muses for inspiratory power (cf. Thomas Gray, *The Progress of Poesy*). For a provocative discussion to poetic homage to the M. from ancient to modern times see Robert Graves, *The White Goddess* (3d ed., 1958).—L. R. Farnell, *The Cults of the Gr. States,* V (1909); G. Murray, *The Cl. Tradition in Poetry* (1927); G. Highet, *The Cl. Trad.* (1949).   D.H.

MUSIC AND POETRY undoubtedly arose in common historical sources of primitive prayer, working chants and the like, and notwithstanding the diverse development of literature and music as human institutions, the histories of both have remained in many ways mutually contingent. It has been frequently observed that more or less primitive oral traditions make no conceptual differentiation between narrative or lyric texts and the melodies and/or accompaniments to which they are sung. Even the sophisticated aesthetic speculations of classical antiquity, however, blended together in the notion of *mousike* those activities which we should today distinguish as music, poetry, and dance. And while we know that throughout classic times textless, instrumental music continued to develop its own conventions, it was only rational music, given meaning by the text sung to its melody, that could serve as a subject fit for philosophical speculation. A powerful additional bond between text and melody in actual practice was effected by the fact that a common over-all rhythm governed both of them. (A modern reader might see this most clearly in the testimony of the musical notation of the ancient world, which consisted of pitch indication alone, the durations and stressed groupings of notes being generally determined by the prosody of the text. As long as the meter of poetry retained its significance in what we should call today a musical sense, the monistic character of *mousike* remained unthreatened. But as soon as poetic conventions of a purely schematic type could allow literary conceptions of poetry to replace more fundamentally phonic ones, a fracturing of the united notion of *mousike* could occur. What was properly the *meter*, the governing principle of poetic construction, became something independent of sound alone; and where the quantitative prosody of Gr. was forced onto the unyielding sound structure of L., for example, word stress had generally to be ignored in the metrical scheme, which latter tended more and more to become a purely graphematic arrangement.

It was by no means the case, however, that with the decline of the classic world, poetry and music as we would distinguish them proceeded to develop as separate and independent arts. It must be remembered that the growth of instrumental music was a long and gradual one, that it was not until late in the 16th c. that instrumental and vocal music became independent practices to any degree at all. It was only after instrumental compositions grew beyond their prior status of being merely *versions* of either vocal settings or of dances, that pure instrumental sounds could serve as the pure type of music in the abstract, as we know it today. And it was only with the development, during the Renaissance and after, of forms of lyric poetry completely divorced from either the intention or effect of *song*, that any concept of "the music of poetry" might emerge. Such a notion, describing the operation of the nontonal but merely linguistic sounds of poetry, thus relates those sounds to the tones of modern, abstract music. Both, it is generally felt, move to affect a listener in some subrational fashion, just as both are in some way involved with the communication of feeling rather than of knowledge.

In general, a number of phases might be distinguished in the relationship between music and poetry in the Occident. In the first of these periods, the two are completely identified, as in pre-Attic epochs, in Germanic languages up to about the 9th c., and in pre-literary folk traditions up through modern times. Here poet and composer are the same person, and they practice one craft, even after (as in fact actually occurred) the poet ceases to be the sole performer as well. It will be noted that, at such a stage, the one human occupation which might involve the production of melodies without texts would be dancing. But social rituals invariably operated to unite most occasions for dancing and singing.

A second stage could be said to emerge during the Attic period of antiquity, during which both music and poetry began to flourish individually. Scientific and philosophic interest in the nature of pure sound, on the one hand, and *literary* (i.e., linguistic and mythical)· criticism of poetic style, on the other, urged a gradual conceptual differentiation between the two disciplines. And it might be guessed that the attacks on textless music (for being irrational) of Plato, Aristotle, Aris-

toxenus and others were certainly directed at actual instrumental musical practices. Most important of all, however, in the incipient bifurcation of *léxis* and *mélos*, was the gradual development, during the classic period, of purely literary conventions, and the replacement, by *readers*, of *audiences* in the stricter sense. This whole second stage in the development of music and poetry was marked by unequal growth in the two, however; and it seems to have been the former that, surging ahead, forced the cleavage between them.

But it was for many centuries that music in the West followed in the footsteps of its sister art, unable quite to develop independently. With the fall of the Roman world, both music and poetry were to be found primarily in the liturgy of the church, and in the earliest vernacular narratives. The latter represent, of course, the earliest unified musico-poetic stage. Scop, minstrel and bard were all poet-musicians whose muses might be concretely identified both in their musical instruments and in their "word-hoards," their linguistic stocks in trade. But the subsequent development of both music and verse fell under the guidance of the church, which at once could control access to the practices of antiquity, and could itself establish and preserve linguistic and musical conventions. After the codification of the musical liturgy by Gregory I at the end of the 6th c., we may distinguish a third phase of musico-poetic history. Here it is that the development of music eventually permits it to compete with poetry for independence; it is during the period from 900–1400 in particular that theoretical and practical problems of music alone give gradual rise to a craft and a concern quite distinct from that of the writer. It is meaningful, throughout the Middle Ages, to speak of the task of the composer as that of setting a pre-existent text to music. To this extent, word and tone are still inextricably involved, but musical and poetic invention have become separated as matters of technique.

It is in the troping of "original" fragments of music into the codified plain-chant of the liturgy that the earliest instances of such musical invention may be observed. It must be remembered, however, that the additional musical material always accompanied some newly composed bit of Latin, inserted between words of the canonical text. While it is in these *tropes* and *sequences* that early examples of actual composition may be identified, it is only with the beginnings of polyphony in the 10th c. or thereabouts, and the subsequent development of the typical intricacies of Western music both within the church and outside of it, that purely musical exigencies began to cause composers to neglect, and even to subvert, formal and structural elements of the text. By the beginning of the 13th c., the establishment of polyphonic music in the uses of the church was complete, and was accompanied by the utilization of adjunct instruments, and by the first appearance of identifiable composers who signed their compositions. During the period from 1100 to 1450, however, it is primarily in the domain of the secular lyric that anything of the earlier phases of unification may be observed. The L. *conductus*, the troubadour *canzo* and *vers*, the Northern *chanson*, *rondeau*, *virelai* and *ballade*, the *bar* and *leich* of the Minnesinger, were all musico-poetic forms, and their authors were also their composers. It is significant that the music here was in most cases monodic (i.e., it consisted of a single melodic line), and also that the occasional instrumental preludes (only possibly were there rudimentary accompaniments) that preceded the singing of a troubadour or trouvère song were invariably performed by a jongleur servant of the poet himself. But this period of unified activity was accompanied by such diverse institutions as the spread of the early polyphonic motet, which often had as many texts as there were musical parts: a sacred L. text in the *tenor*, and a Fr. hymn and a bawdy drinking song in the upper voices frequently occurred together. It was into the polyphonic tradition, ultimately, that the monodic, courtly secular lyric was absorbed, and perhaps the last truly great poet-composer of this epoch was Guillaume de Machaut (1300–77), who flourished during the musical era of the "ars nova." It was during this period that the technical concerns and advances of composers and theorists grew to involve the text less and less, and moved music more and more towards autonomy.

In the Renaissance, finally, a kind of historical irony emerges with the observable development of an ideological concern for the reunification of music and poetry, coexistent with the spread and refinement of just those elements of musical practice which best operated to prevent that reunification from permanently taking hold. The 16th c. saw the rise of instrumental music in its own right, the beginnings of virtuoso performance, and the institutionalization of concern with harmony in the modern sense, for example. But it also produced the neoclassic aesthetic of such groups as the *Camerata* in Florence and the *Pléiade* (q.v.) in France, both openly committed to an ideal identification of text and melody, based on the practices of antiquity as they understood them. Corresponding to the attempts of many writers and critics to establish classical scansion as the governing prosodic principles for the poetry of their respective modern languages, there arose in the later 16th c. a concerted interest in the

purification of music, in restoring the importance of the text, and in reclaiming for vocal music, at any rate, a truly expressive function that had been lost early in the development of "modern" polyphony. This sort of argument led, within Jean-Antoine Baïf's circle in France, to experiments in the so-called *musique mesurée,* or vocal settings designed to point up a quantitative scansion for their Fr. texts. The It. circle who met at the house of the Count Bardi, however, produced a lasting influence on the music of the following centuries in the invention of *recitative.*

With the beginning of the baroque era, we may distinguish another phase of musico-poetic relations in which the two arts are adjudged to have a complementary relationship to each other: music might be said to have stood to poetry as feeling to knowledge, or, as Hobbes put it, "as Fancy to Judgement." It was this sort of distinction that prevailed throughout the 17th and earlier 18th c., during which period the status of both music and poetry as utterly independent practices remained unchanged. The growth of opera, of course, provided an area in which the two might be mutually effective. But the general trend of baroque music was toward a kind of technical standardization, treating the human voice as an instrument, etc. and the achievements of poetry remained in an intellectual domain.

Most 18th-c. aestheticians would have wanted to distinguish between the instruction and embellishment whose purposes were respectively served by the cognitive and ornamental elements in poetry alone. Alexander Pope could insist in *An Essay on Criticism* (1709) that, in any poem, "The sound must seem an Echo to the sense"; but this same author could, a few lines earlier, condemn all those who "to Church repair, / Not for the doctrine, but the music there." In general, a neoclassic aesthetic that could so sharply distinguish between "music" and "sense" could not help but trivialize the importance and power of the first with respect to that of the second. And similarly but conversely, a romanticism that sought to reject what it considered the artificialities of the preceding century and a half could almost not help but celebrate music and feeling at some expense of language and thought. What might have been an attempt to blur a previous epoch's distinctions only managed to cut their lines more deeply.

Since the 18th c., both opera and "art-song" have flourished as legitimate genres, but by and large, the relationship between music and poetry (as a branch of literature) has remained very much the same. It has been observed that the romantic era, with its prescriptions of emotional experience for poetry, actually main-

MUWASHSHAH

tained the conceptual dualism of the previous epoch while trying in practice to destroy it. Even as "pure" instrumental music became more literary and "programmatic," poetry sought to develop, in its texture, a music of its own. For literature, generally, music has continued to invoke the Irrational, just as musicians have, on the whole, turned to literary underpinnings (in titles, covert myths and programs, epigraphs, etc.—aside from actual sung texts) for a basis of emotional content.

De la musique avant toute chose,
Et pour cela préfère l'Impair
Plus vague et plus soluble dans l'air . . .

Paul Verlaine's aesthetic manifesto, in urging a commitment to the priority of sound over sense, is enjoining a more general rejection of knowledge for the sake of feeling. And this peculiar notion of sound, the "music of poetry" continues to represent today the significant characteristic of music in its relation to literature: namely, that the power of music to affect a hearer remains a model for the potential effectiveness of poetry, if only because the workings of the former seem to be so much more mysterious than those of the latter. See LYRIC, SONG.

S. Lanier, *The Science of Eng. Verse* (1880); J. B. Beck, *Die Melodien der Troubadours* (1908); P. Aubry, *Trouvères et Troubadours* (1909); R. Noble, *Shakespeare's Use of Song* (1923); J. M. Gibbon, *Melody and the Lyric* (1930); T. S. Eliot, *The Music of Poetry* (1942); G. Reese, *Music in the Middle Ages* (1940) and *Music in the Renaissance* (1954); C. Sachs, *The Rise of Music in the Ancient World* (1943) and *The Commonwealth of Art* (1946); B. Pattison, *Music and Poetry of the Eng. Ren.* (1948); *Source Readings in Music Hist.*, ed. O. Strunk (1950); W. Mellers, *Music and Society* (2d ed., 1950); J. S. Manifold, *The Music in Eng. Drama* (1955); A. Einstein, *Essays on Music* (1956); B. Nettl, *Music in Primitive Culture* (1956); J. Hollander, "The Music of Poetry," JAAC, 15 (1956) and *The Untuning of the Sky: Ideas of Music in Eng. Poetry, 1500–1700* (1961); *Sound and Poetry*, ed. N. Frye (1957); J. Stevens, *Music and Poetry in the Early Tudor Court* (1961); F. W. Sternfeld, *Music in Shakespearean Tragedy* (1963).　　J.H.

MUWASHSHAH (*muwashshahah*). See ARABIC POETRY (Spanish-Arabic section).

MYSTERY AND MIRACLE PLAYS. In American and continental usage the term *mystery* refers to plays based on the Bible, in particular those parts of the Scripture that tell the story of man's Creation, Fall and Redemption, and *miracle* refers to plays that treat the lives and martyrdoms of saints. The former, which are the earlier, appeared as additions to the services of the liturgical year. Each period of the year had its own special readings, called *lectiones,* and a good deal of the Scripture read was dramatized, bit by bit, from the 9th to the 16th c. Mystery p. did not grow from one stem in one place, but were varied both in location and degree of development, in spite of occasional imitation and borrowing. In some locales the early or middle forms remained almost unchanged for centuries; in others extensive dramas in the vernacular were built up.

Mysteries began in what are called tropes, which were additions to the regular services, and began to appear during a musical and artistic renaissance in the 9th c. It happened that one of these tropes, the *Quem quaeritis* trope representing the visit of the Three Marys to the sepulchre of Christ, contained the three fundamental elements of drama, namely, impersonation, dialogue, and event. The fact that these elements were present in the *Quem quaeritis* trope caused it to grow by incremental additions into a complete drama of the Resurrection. The main additions were the visit of the disciples Peter and John to the tomb, the appearance of Jesus to Mary Magdalen in the Garden, the Journey of Cleophas and Luke to Emmaus, followed by the Incredulity of Thomas, and two secular elements, the Ointment Seller and Pilate's Setting of the Watch. This growth occupied about two centuries, and during that time the dramatizing habit had so asserted itself within the liturgy that little L. plays, so-called dramatic offices, had made their appearance at Christmastide in the form of Nativity plays, including ultimately the Messianic prophets (*Ordo prophetarum*), the Shepherds (*Pastores*), the Magi, which introduced Herod, the villain of the piece, the Flight into Egypt, the Slaughter of the Innocents, and the Death of Herod. It is also possible that the so-called eschatological plays, Antichrist and Judgment Day, which had originated in Advent, were in some places united with the Christmas–Epiphany cycle. In addition to these there were many plays on special subjects originating at special festivals. Some of these were no doubt absorbed in larger units, although some of them, such as the Conversion of St. Paul and the play of the Wise and the Foolish Virgins, led independent existences throughout the period. The story of the Passion seems to have been dramatized toward the end of the 12th c. as an appropriate introduction to the already highly developed play of the Resurrection, and, when it did appear, its dramatic interest was so great that it assumed a central position. Indeed, the common popular name for mystery

-[536]-

p. on the continent of Europe became Passion plays (q.v.).

The Latin drama of the church was fairly complete in its treatment of religious themes by the year 1200. The records are almost nil, but we know from the results what happened in the 13th c. Most of the plays were translated into modern languages, and they left the church and appeared in the churchyard or in the street. They seem moreover to be no longer in the hands of the clergy but in those of the laity, probably in the care of ecclesiastical and (later) secular guilds. However, the transitional period is obscure.

The establishment of the feast of Corpus Christi in the early 14th c. was an event of great importance to the mystery p. The directions for the celebration of the feast called for a procession, and each ecclesiastical district was allowed to decide what the features of the procession should be. At some place, we do not know where, a brilliant idea was evolved. The mystery p. were already in the hands of the people, and the Easter and Christmas plays were highly developed. The idea was not only to transfer the plays to the new feast of Corpus Christi sixty days after Easter, when the weather would be good, but to arrange them chronologically. The result was a processional drama that extended from the Creation to Doomsday. This great play did not appear everywhere. Examples are preserved from Germany, Spain, the Low Countries, and England, particularly the north and east of England. An alternative common in France, Germany, and parts of England was continued separation of the Christmas and Easter groups, the latter of which grew to great proportions. The result was the great German Passion plays of Frankfurt, Alsfeld, Heidelberg, Eger, Innsbruck, and Künzelsau; the Fr. plays of Arras, Troyes, and Valenciennes; the great redactions by Jean Michel and Arnoul Greban and many others; and numerous cycles in Provence, Italy, and elsewhere.

The plays of London and the south of England were in the continental form, but they are all lost except one great, but possibly not representative, cycle in the ancient Cornish language. What we have are rather ample remains of the Corpus Christi plays and numerous records of lost plays of that kind. We have the great and almost complete cycle from York and that from Wakefield (Towneley), originally identical with the York cycle. There are also the Chester plays, preserved in five late manuscripts, the simplest of all the cycles, and a cycle called mistakenly *Ludus Coventriae,* now frequently designated as the Hegge plays. This cycle is complete, theologically very learned, and possibly is a Corpus Christi play from Lincoln. Besides these, there are several single plays and fragments of lost cycles.

The records of the Corpus Christi play have been so abundantly preserved that there is an idea abroad that all mystery p. were composed and acted after the Corpus Christi model, but, in point of fact, the variety was very great. Not only were there many independent single plays, like the Conversion of St. Paul or the Play of St. Mary Magdalen; but the whole body of plays from London, the south of England, and no doubt elsewhere were passion plays like those prevailing on the continent. Such plays were acted on fixed stages with conventional treatment of time and space, whereas the Corpus Christi plays were played as single scenes on pageant wagons drawn in chronological order to fixed places or "stations" about the cities where a Corpus Christi play was maintained. The decay and abandonment of the mystery p. came about gradually through the influence of Protestantism and the change of public manners and tastes brought on by the Renaissance. The end in England was in the later 16th c., but they lived on in a few places on the continent, such as Oberammergau, until modern times.

The earliest Eng. mystery p. were in rhymed couplets and quatrains and in *rime couée* ($aa^4b^3aaa^4b^3$), which were the forms current in L. and Fr. poetry of the 11th and 12th c. They were well suited to simple scriptural themes. Mainly out of these elements Middle Eng. poetry built stanzas of considerable variety and complexity, and the mysteries were often revised in these forms. The Chester plays, however, were written in a ballad stanza to which they usually adhered through many redactions.

MIRACLE PLAYS. In Am. and Continental usage the term "miracle p." is applied to medieval dramas that treat of the lives and martyrdoms of saints and of their intercessory functions. In Great Britain this term is sometimes applied to both saints' plays and those derived from the Bible. The difference in origin between the two kinds is negligible; both grew out of an expansion of the church services beginning in the 9th c. The lives and deeds of the saints were precisely as sacred and important as were those of patriarchs, prophets, and disciples. There was, however, a significant dramatic difference between miracle and mystery plays. The subjects of the latter were dictated and largely controlled by the services of the liturgical year, but the former had much greater range of plot and situation and greater freedom of choice, so that, as pointed out by Manly, miracle plays must have had important influences in the creation of the secular plays of the Tudors. Only four L. miracle p. are preserved. All deal with St. Nicholas and are clearly derived from the liturgy of his feast (Dec. 6). They are usually dated in the 11th or 12th c. St. Nicholas was the patron saint of boys in school, and the play must have been widely distributed. We know that there must have been other L. saints' plays at an early date. There was such a play of St. Catherine performed at Dunstable at the end of the 11th or the beginning of the 12th c., and William Fitzstephen (fl. 1170–86) in his life of Thomas Becket declares that in his times plays dealing with the miracles of holy saints and confessors were regularly enacted in London. There are other evidences, but England and other Protestant countries have so swept away texts and records that one has to make a beginning in France.

There are two purely vernacular miracle p. that seem to have special significance: *Le Jeu de Saint Nicolas* by Jean Bodel of Arras, which develops in spirited fashion the theme of one of the L. plays on St. Nicholas, and *Le Miracle de Théophile* by Rutebeuf, which belongs to the 13th c. It details a miracle of salvation by the Blessed Virgin Mary and, so far as we know, may be the first *miracle de Nôtre Dame.* The fashion at any rate took hold in France, and the great 14th-c. manuscript (Bibl. Nat. 218 and 219) contains no less than forty *Miracles de Nostre Dame par personages,* highly developed and drawn from a wide area of subjects. There are many other miracles of Notre Dame, and the 14th and 15th c. filled France with miracle p., which appeared, too, in other countries—Germany, Spain, England, Scotland, Holland, and elsewhere, but not nearly so plentifully as in France.

The Reform in England did an almost complete job of destruction. Records show lost miracle p. on many subjects: St. Catherine at Coventry, St. Nicholas at Trinity College, Cambridge, and at Aberdeen, St. Andrew in Scotland and at Braintree in Essex, St. Christiana at Bethersden in Kent, St. Clotilda at Windsor, St. Margaret and St. Lucy in Southwark, St. Thomas Becket at King's Lynn, and many others. In point of fact only one complete miracle p. has been preserved, the so-called *Croxton Play of the Sacrament,* a rather crude and nontypical example. There were so many Croxtons in the Midlands that one does not know which of them was the home of our only miracle p. in Eng. There is also preserved the role of the principal actor in another miracle p. It bears the name of the leading actor and is called *Dux Moraud.*

There is, however, a play *The Life of St. Meriasek* in the ancient Cornish language which enables one to form an idea of the common run of popular miracle p. It is a long play in two parts probably acted, like the *Origo Mundi,* in a circular earthen amphitheatre. St. Meriasek was venerated in Britanny, Cornwall, and Wales, where the Cymric

dialect of Celtic was the language. He was the son of the Duke of Britanny, carefully reared and given every opportunity, including a brilliant marriage, but he renounced the world for the service of God. He performed his first miracle; then sailed for Cornwall, where he tamed a wolf and built his hermitage, both by miraculous means. His great miracle, however, was the routing of robbers and pagans. The second part is located in Rome, where he performed other miracles and became a bishop. Both parts end with an invitation to the audience to drink and dance.

The remains of Eng. miracle p. are so meager as to afford little material for the determination of poetic form and style. That many of them were exciting dramas there can be no doubt. If one may judge from Fr. miracle p., one would say that the early forms were probably in simple measures and that, as time went on, the plays were written in more and more elaborate stanzas.

L. Petit de Julleville, *Les Mystères* (2 v., 1886); W. Creizenach, *Gesch. des neueren Dramas* (esp. I, 1893); E. K. Chambers, *The Mediaeval Stage* (2 v., 1903); G. R. Coffman, *A New Theory Concerning the Origin of the Miracle Play* (1911) and articles in learned jour.; J. M. Manly, "Miracle P. in Mediaeval England," Royal Soc. of Lit., *Trans.,* ser. 3, 7 (1927); K. Young, *The Drama of the Medieval Church* (2 v., 1933); H. C. Gardiner, *Mysteries' End* (1946); A. P. Rossiter, *Eng. Drama from Early Times to the Elizabethans* (1950); H. Craig, *Eng. Religious Drama of the MA* (1955); E. Prosser, *Drama and Religion in the Eng. Mystery Plays* (1961); A. Williams, *The Drama of Medieval England* (1961). H.C.

MYTH† may be defined as a story or a complex of story elements taken as expressing, and therefore as implicitly symbolizing, certain deep-lying aspects of human and transhuman existence. This definition is framed in such a way as to avoid two contrary and one-sided views of the matter. The one, represented by Cassirer, treats myth as primarily a kind of perspective, and in this vein Cassirer speaks of "transposing the Kantian principle"—that all knowledge involves, at the instant of its reception, a synthesizing activity of the mind —"into the key of myth." Evidently m. here becomes synonymous with the mythopoeic mode of consciousness; it is simply a basic way of envisaging experience, and carries no necessary connotation of storytelling. At the opposite extreme stands the view that m. is *merely* story. In its popular form this gives rise to the colloquial use of the term "m." to mean a tale that is not according to the facts, and the adjective "mythical" as a synonym

† In Supplement, see also MYTH CRITICISM.

MYTH

for "false." A more reflective development of
the same general attitude finds expression in
Chase's view that "myth is literature and must
be considered as an aesthetic creation of the
human imagination"; in other words, that the
earliest mythologizers were individual poets—
which is to say "makers," or storytellers—constructing out of their especially active imaginations tall tales characterized by a peculiar complication "of brilliant excitement, of the ter-
rific play of the forces natural and human,"
and eventuating in some deeply desired and
socially sharable feeling of reconciliation
among those forces. As distinguished from
Cassirer's position our proposed definition includes the idea of narrative as an essential
part of the meaning of m.; but as distinguished
from Chase's position it insists that the original sources of such storytelling lie somehow
below or beyond the conscious inventions of
individual poets, and that the stories themselves thus serve as partly unconscious vehicles
for meanings that have something to do with
the inner nature of the universe and of human life.

The partial validity of each of the views
mentioned, as well as the variable relationships
between m. and poetry, become more evident
when we distinguish between the two main
senses of m.—as mythopoeia and as mythology.
Friedrich Max Müller (*The Science of Religion*, II, 1864) has proposed that the adjective
"mythic" be employed for the first meaning,
where no clear-cut ideas of true and false have
yet emerged, and "mythical" for the second,
where some degree of deliberate fable-making
is implied.

Giambattista Vico (*La Scienza nuova*, 1725)
was the first important writer to emphasize
that primitive thought is essentially poetic, in
that the endowment of inanimate objects with
life, will, and emotion is at once the natural
tendency of primitive man and the most sublime task of poetry—a point of view carried
on with various modifications by Herder
(1744–1803) and by Shelley (*A Defence of Poetry*, 1821). The word "mythopoeia" has come
into vogue as designating the human outlook
and forms of expression most characteristic of
that early stage of culture when language is
still largely ritualistic and prelogical in character. Each of these two aspects of the character of primitive language has a decisive
bearing upon the formation of both m. and
poetry. The relation of ritual to the rhythmic
and eventually the metric element in poetry
needs no demonstration. The ritualistic basis
of m. has been emphasized by a number of
anthropologists and classical scholars during
the last few decades, notably in such works
as: Jane Harrison, *Themis* (1912), Francis M.
Cornford, *The Origins of Attic Comedy* (1914),

A. B. Cook, *Zeus* (1914), S. H. Hooke, ed.,
Myth and Ritual (1933), Lord Raglan, *The
Hero* (1937), and Theodore H. Gaster, *Thespis*
(1950). Harrison cites an ancient Gr. definition
of m. as "ta legomena epi tois dromenois" (the
things that are spoken in ritual acts). The
reason why ritual tends to engender m. becomes more evident when we consider that
genuine ritual is celebrative and therefore
participative. Seasonal ritual (as Gaster has
shown with respect to the ancient Near East)
expresses something of the worshippers' joyful sense of the coming of spring, or of the
summer solstice, or of the gathering of grain,
and at such times the worshippers feel themselves to be participating in the great rhythmic
movement of nature. Dance and song are the
natural expressions of such participation, and
the words of the song tend to describe or to
address or to enact the personified forces that
are being celebrated. From description to
address it is an easy step in a culture which
does not sharply distinguish between person
and thing nor between adjective and noun.
When the ancient Canaanites described a
storm, "Baal opens a rift in the clouds and
gives forth his holy voice," they probably got
as close to a naturalistic description as their
language would allow them to go; the metaphors that make the description possible are
such that Baal is envisaged not as an abstraction but as a superhuman operator, to be
addressed and to be ritually enacted. Where a
set of linguistic habits is such that virtually
no distinction is made between the literal and
the figurative there is likely to be just as little
distinction between the descriptive and the
fanciful. Such psychic and linguistic amalgams
are one of the most important factors in the
genesis and early growth of m.

The role of metaphor in primitive language
is a second factor joining poetry and m. Our
reference here must be to primary, or radical
metaphor. Metaphor in the familiar sense of
"the transference of a name from the thing
which it properly denotes to some other
thing" (Aristotle, *Poetics*) is rhetorical, not
primary, for it is possible only where certain
terms with fixed meanings are already available as starting-points; it is, therefore, more
characteristic of the post-mythological and
sophisticated than of the primitive phase of
m. There is a prior semantic activity which
operates, perhaps preconsciously, by fusing
certain raw elements of experience—qualities,
relationships, capabilities, emotional colorings,
and whatever else—into a unity of reference
which some symbol is taken to represent. Thus
in Vedic Sanskrit the word *agni* meant fire
in its various culturally important aspects:
fire as lord of the sacred hearth, fire as "the
spoon-mouthed one" which receives the obla-

tion of sanctified butter from a spoon or ladle, fire as the messenger which crackles and leaps as it bears this offering to the gods on high, fire as the dispeller of darkness and hence of evil, fire which punishes evil-doers by its burning heat, fire as the generative urge in the loins of animals, and Lord Agni as a member of the Vedic pantheon. The hymns addressed to Agni in the *Rig-Veda* are thus able to designate the god with a connotative fullness appropriate to poetry, while they also stir up mythic inquiries by suggesting relations between some of these traits and others. Again, in the ceremony of the Night Chant practiced by the Navajo Indians the giant corn plant growing at the Red Rock House and the giant squash vine growing at the Blue Water House are employed as symbols of the masculine and feminine principles respectively, as symbols of food and therefore of plenty, as magically efficacious healing devices, and hence (through the idea of regeneration implicit in each of these aspects) as symbols of man's aspiration to spiritual rebirth. Such symbols have on the one hand a richness of reference, not overexplicit, that makes them suitable materials for poetry; while on the other hand the jostling of different and sometimes incongruous meanings may stimulate the invention of mythic tales to comment upon and partly explain how those meanings are related.

In recent years, particularly through the researches of Dr. Carl G. Jung at his school, a promising line of inquiry has been developed into the collective psychology underlying primary myth-formation. Jung postulates a "collective unconscious" which consists of "primordial images" or "archetypes"—i.e., transindividual ideas with a strong feeling-tone and with a tendency to find expression in characteristic imagistic forms. The Divine Father, the Earth Mother, the World Tree, the satyr or centaur or other man–animal monster, the descent into Hell, the Purgatorial stair, the washing away of sin, the castle of attainment, the culture-hero such as Prometheus bringing fire or other basic gift to mankind, the treacherous betrayal of the hero, the sacrificial death of the god, the god in disguise or the prince under enchantment—these and many other archetypal ideas serve as persistently recurrent themes in human thought. Since they have furnished story elements to the literature of widely different cultures, Jung and Kerenyi have employed Herder's word *mythologem* to designate this aspect of them. Jung holds that they are buried deep in man's psyche, below the suppressed or inchoate memories belonging to the individual, and that the libido has recourse to them "when it becomes freed from the personal-infantile form of transference."

The epic poet's invocation of the Muse would represent, in one aspect, the poet's desire to free himself from the "personal-infantile" type of thinking through being borne along by the more deeply expressive power of archetypal thought patterns.

The emergence of a definite mythology, recognized as such, represents on the whole a later and more sophisticated stage of human thought, when the primitive mythopoeic way of envisioning the world has been largely replaced by definite conceptions and a greater reliance upon reasoning, with the result that the older mythic stories have become materials to be embellished, recontextualized, and often reinterpreted by the poet's conscious art. The *Iliad* and the *Odyssey* represent two early phases of the development of mythological out of mythopoeic thought. While they contain many traces of an earlier mythopoeic attitude and of a ritual stylization (which the practice of minstrelsy in Homer's time doubtless did much to preserve), yet the voice and genius of an individual poet are unmistakably present, selecting and regrouping and articulating the older stories according to a freshly conceived design. Aeschylus' *Oresteia*, Virgil's *Aeneid*, Dante's *Commedia*, Shakespeare's *A Midsummer Night's Dream* and *The Tempest*, and Milton's *Paradise Lost*, represent in different perspectives the zenith of literary exploitation of mythology. The mythic ideas of the emergence of divinely sanctioned Gr. law out of tribal vendetta, of the destined founding of Rome, of the faery life of the Eng. countryside, of Neoplatonic hierarchies, and of Christian eschatology are here deliberately reconceived and reformulated through the imaginatively constructed medium of the poem. Yet some degree of positive belief is still operative in each of these works, giving spiritual force to the presentation and integrating without too much apparent artifice the diverse particulars. As the attitude towards mythology becomes more overtly sophisticated—e.g., in Ovid's *Metamorphoses*, Goethe's *Faust*, and Eliot's *The Waste Land*—the problem of finding a stable unifying philosophy by which to interpret a given subject matter becomes of increasing concern to the poet (cf. PHILOSOPHY AND POETRY).

The spiritual problems of the poet in contemporary society arise in part out of the lack of myths which can be felt warmly, envisaged in concrete and contemporary imagery, and shared with a wide body of responsive readers. Consequently, since the time of Herder there has been a gradually increasing insistence upon the need of what Friedrich Schlegel (*Gespräch über die Poesie*, 1800) calls "the mother-soil of myth." Unlike Herder, who urged the revival of Teutonic mythology as a rich mine of folk imagination available to German poets, Schlegel looked toward a new and more comprehensive mythology which would combine and blend folk elements with the idealistic philosophy of Fichte and Schelling, the pantheism of Spinoza, and the sacred writings of ancient India, thus achieving a "hieroglyphical expression" of nature conceived as a system of correspondences and symbols. However, Herder was careful to warn (what every good poet knows) that the m. must be related to the poem organically, not by way of a conscious effort to plug a gap. In other words, m. in poetry is not to be conceived merely as a narrative structure, but should enter into the very life-blood of the poem—that is, into its very mode of envisaging and formulating its materials. Accordingly, Friar and Brinnin declare that "the use of metaphysical and symbolist devices has grown out of the modern poet's search for a mythology which might offer him some concrete body for metaphor and metaphysic." Thus in St.-John Perse's *Anabasis* the mythic sense of race, of rootage in the soil, of space as the area in which man moves and settles, of matter as the quarry of his building stones, of time as the cycle of seasons shot through with a firm line of communal action in the erection of cities, all conduces to an archetypal image, concretely and movingly envisaged, of the human caravan as massively operative in man's collective prehistory. Rilke's reenvisagement of the Christian mythos ("Every angel is ringed with terror"), Yeats's gradual construction of a highly individual but nonetheless powerfully expressive mythology out of the marriage of Ir. folklore with gnostic theosophy, and Eliot's synthesis of anthropology, Christian mysticism, and Gr. and Hindu metaphysics are further outstanding examples of the poetic revitalization of m. and the fresh exploration of the philosophical and religious possibilities of

mythic experience through the medium of poetry in our time.

G. Vico, *The New Science* (1725; Eng. tr. 1948); T. S. Eliot, "Ulysses, Order, and M.," *The Dial*, Nov. 1923; E. Cassirer, *The Philosophy of Symbolic Forms*, II, "Mythical Thought" (1923–29; Eng. tr. 1955) and *Language and M.* (Eng. tr. 1946); F. C. Prescott, *Poetry and M.* (1927); St.-J. Perse, *Anabasis* (Eng. tr. by T. S. Eliot, 1930); H. Rosenberg, "M. and Poem," *The Symposium*, 2 (April 1931); D. Bush, *Mythology and the Renaissance Tradition in Eng. Poetry* (1932) and *Mythology and the Romantic Trad. in Eng. Poetry* (1937); M. Bodkin, *Archetypal Patterns in Poetry* (1934) and *Studies of Type-Images in Poetry, Religion, and Philosophy* (1951); Langer, ch. 7; M. Schorer, *William Blake* (1946; esp. ch. 2); P. Ure, *Towards a Mythology: Studies in the Poetry of W. B. Yeats* (1946); J. Campbell, *The Hero with a Thousand Faces* (1949); R. Chase, *Quest for M.* (1949); E. Drew, *T. S. Eliot: The Design of his Poetry* (1949); T. H. Gaster, *Thespis: Ritual, M. and Drama in the Ancient Near East* (1950); K. Friar and M. Brinnin, "M. and Metaphysics," pp. 421–443 of *Modern Poetry*, ed. by the same (1951); A. W. Watts, *M. and Ritual in Christianity* (1954); H. Weisinger, *Tragedy and the Paradox of the Fortunate Fall* (1954); Wheelwright, chs. 7–10; *M.: A Symposium*, ed. T. A. Sebeok (1955; separate issue of JAF, v. 68, no. 270); Frye; K. Burke, "Myth, Poetry and Philosophy," JAF, 73 (1960); *Myth and Mythmaking*, ed. H. A. Murray (1960); *M. and Symbol*, ed. B. Slote (1963). See also J. Campbell, *The Masks of God* (1959–68); M. Eliade, *The Sacred and the Profane* (1959) and *M. and Reality* (1963); R. Y. Hathorne, *Tragedy, M. and Mystery* (1962).

P.W.

MYTHOPOEIA. See MYTH.

N

NAGAUTA. See JAPANESE POETRY.

NAIVE–SENTIMENTAL. Poetic antinomy devised by Friedrich Schiller in an essay "Ueber naive und sentimentalische Dichtung" (1795–96), primarily designed to define the poet's relationship to nature. Schiller divides all poets into two classes: The naive poets (Homer, Shakespeare, Goethe) who strive, as best they may, to project nature as they embody it, and the sentimental poets (Schiller himself and

most poets associated with classicism, q.v.) who have lost contact with nature and attempt to portray it as a sought-for ideal. The naive poets create by instinct since they must only express themselves to express nature—they are realists since they embody and produce reality. Sentimental poets, on the other hand, create formally since they strive to reproduce that ideal of nature which lies beyond them—they are hence idealists. Since nature is particularized in the form of the naive poet, the conception of nature which he can express is limited: he cannot transcend himself. The poetic possibilities of the sentimental poet are, by contrast, infinite since he continues to seek nature which he does not experience—but in that last condition lies his limitation. An overcoming of the boundaries with which the naive and sentimental poetic visions are beset is most nearly accomplished by the poetic genius. For, though he may be, by virtue of his emotions and beliefs, a sentimental poet, he is naive by virtue of his genius. He is best able to create that full vision of nature which only a simultaneous possession of naive instinct and sentimental control of form could procure.

It was Schiller's vision of the poetic genius and his definition of the "naive" which became, more than his justification of the sentimental poet, a leading concept in 19th c. thought. The poetics of German romanticism (q.v.) some aspects of Eng. romantic criticism (notably Coleridge's *Lectures on Poesy and Art*), Nietzsche's Apollonian-Dionysian antinomy (q.v.), Thomas Mann's thinking on the creative process, and German literary historiography to the present day are all, to a measure, indebted to this concept.—U. Gaede, *Schillers Abhandlung ueber naive und sentimentalische Dichtung* (1899); H. Meng, *Schillers Abhandlung ueber naive und sentimentalische Dichtung* (1936); F. Schiller, *Ueber n.u.s.D.*, ed. W. F. Maitland (1951).　　w.b.f.

NARRATIVE POETRY. A n. poem is one that tells a story. The two basic types are epic and ballad. Although metrical romance is often considered as a third basic type, it is probably rightly to be thought of as a kind of epic, because it shares important recurrent themes with epic and presents them in the same narrative manner. Both epic and ballad have a long history as oral literature before they are recorded and literary forms of each emerge. The history of their literary forms is a matter of record; the origin of oral epic and of ballad is undoubtedly to be sought in the prehistoric past.

Story telling in verse form is sometimes thought to have its beginning in the chanting of myth relating to ritual. Vestiges of this earlier mythic connection of n. poetry can be seen in: (a) the very fact that the story is told in verse, not in prose; for the rhythms of verse are associated with "magic" effectiveness (not, as is often stated, because verse is easier to remember than prose!); (b) the pervasiveness of alliterative and assonantal techniques in epic, which are also associated with incantation; (c) the structure of the commonest stories, which coincides with the structure of myths; (d) the association of the singing of epic with religious festivals; and (e) the tradition that the bard is a seer.

In answer to the question of why a story should be told in verse, and in *sung* verse, at that (since both epic and ballad were originally sung or chanted), it is often said that the verse serves a purely mnemonic purpose; the story in verse is easier to remember than that in prose. Actually there is little or no basis for this conclusion. Studies of oral poetry that have appeared in this century and research still in progress show clearly that oral n. poetry is not memorized textually, that, indeed, its style has evolved to make a kind of "improvisation" rather than memorization possible. Moreover, the oral transmission of the tale indicates that prose can be handed on with as great ease as poetry and with almost as great, perhaps even greater, fidelity. It seems more likely that the story sung in verse had a magical purpose and was in some way connected with ritual. Such an origin would explain the pervasiveness of repetitions of sounds (alliteration and assonance) in n. as well as in all other kinds of oral poetry; for such phonetic characteristics are essential to the effectiveness of incantations. This technique later loses its overt magical function, but is preserved first as a device to aid in composition, and later as a convention.

The teller, singer, or poet would have been a kind of magician, a mediator between the other world and this world, a specially marked individual, inspired by the "muses." The listeners would be participants in the rite, sharing both individually and as a group in the benefits to be gained from the ritual myth. Such an origin would also then explain the position of the "bard" in society. It would, moreover, make reasonable the persistence of certain story patterns and details as well as provide a residual or vestigial meaning for them in later epic and ballad.

It seems probable that epic and ballad are both cognate in ritual, rather than, as has been often thought, that the one originated from the other. The ballad would represent the joining of the narrative with the dance; whereas the epic would be the joining of the narrative with incantation. In the drama one would see the survival of the three elements of ritual still in conjunction, namely, n. myth, music in its two aspects of chant and dance, and pantomime, the acting out of the myth either directly or in symbols.

There was perhaps a differentiation in performance between original epic and ballad. Epic would have been performed by an individual as priest or magician; ballad would have been performed by a dancing and singing group of devotees with a choral leader who sang the burden of the tale, while the dancing chorus came in with a refrain. Whether the myth became attached first to the incantation or first to the dance song may be a moot point, but it would seem that we should think of the myth, or n., as being joined to two already existent forms, that is, incantation and dance song, rather than of short forms becoming long or long forms being split into shorter ones.

The commonest form for epic poetry is stichic, nonstanzaic sequence of verses. N. poetry, like all poetry, was originally sung or at the very least chanted in a kind of recitative. It was usually accompanied by a musical instrument, the function of which was to maintain the rhythm of the line and of composition, although in the earliest period it may well be conjectured that the musical accompaniment was also associated with magic. There were, nevertheless, elements sometimes present that led in the direction of stanzaic form. One of these was the tendency to join lines in couplets, a natural result of syntactic parallelism on the one hand and of antiphonal singing, where it existed, on the other. The melodic patterns reflect this tendency as well, because in such couplets the real cadence comes only at the end of the second line. Since the parallelism is not only syntactic but often phonological as well, the linking of lines may go beyond the couplet. In those languages in which morphology and syntax conspire to make a series of lines ending in rhyme, there develops a convention of maintaining this rhyme as long as the singer is able. Albanian epic tradition follows this pattern. It is entirely possible that this practice is the cause of the *laisses* of the *chansons de geste* with their assonantal verse endings.

Yet it may be doubted that this tendency ever led to the development of a true stanza. The origin of the stanzaic form of the ballad must, I think, be sought elsewhere. Stanzaic form presupposes a more complex musical structure with a final melodic cadence coming after three or four lines of verse. Moreover, it may very well, as the derivation of the word "ballad" itself implies [OF *ballade,* a dancing song], have been associated with the dance. On the whole this form is less suited to extended n. than is the nonstanzaic. It is closer to the pantomime of ritual and to the choral ode of drama.

Once the myth is incorporated into epic and ballad, there is great possibility for exchange of subject matter from one to the other, and also, in most languages, even for exchange of some of the formulas, provided the metrics allow. Epic and ballad are then from the beginning two aspects of the same n. ritual impulse.

Probably the most significant shift in the history of n. poetry, second only to the creation of the myth itself and its joining to song, took place when the mythic and overtly magical content was transformed into stories of human beings told for no ostensible magic purpose, but to honor or remember great men. We might explain this by saying that the god of the myth becomes a divine king and the king then loses his divinity and becomes a human hero. The framework or structure of the myth remains but its meaning is reinterpreted on a human level. Conflicts with supernatural beings by supernatural beings become conflicts with supernatural beings by human heroes, and then the opponents of the heroes become the tribal and later the national enemy. This is not to argue that the hero is a "faded god," but that the hero has taken the place of the god in the story and the story has been modified to suit him, and he, in turn, acquires some of the characteristics of his predecessor. Epic is not *born* in a heroic age but rather in such an age it is clothed in a new garment.

It may be supposed that when divine kings, demigods, and finally mortal heroes replaced the gods of the myth, the stories too took on the aspect of human events unrolling in the real world. The secularization of epic leads to that branch known as heroic poetry. The story is told for its own sake and becomes a vehicle for moral and ethical teaching by example. The perseverance of the hero, his defense of his own prestige, his fighting for a cause, in short all those ideals that we commonly group under the concept "heroic" become of primary importance. Here stand the epic of Gilgamesh, the *Iliad,* the *Odyssey, Roland, Beowulf,* and so on. The fantastic element in these epics serves to emphasize the superior qualities of the hero.

There is a possibility that the change just outlined, from ritual myth to history with real heroes as *dramatis personae,* is aided by a concurrent development of n. poetry from a related yet distinctly different source. Myths of origins would be related to ritual myths but their purpose would be the gaining of power by incantation over the thing or person whose origin is told. No ritual drama is involved; the ritual is restricted to the incantation itself. The best examples of these myths of origins are to be found in Finnish epic lore. In order to gain control over an iron axe which has caused a wound, one chants the myth of the origin of iron. The singer of the myth is a magician. When the thing to be controlled is the spirit of a dead man, potentially a hostile force, his origin and deeds and perhaps also his death and vengeance may be sung. Epic has a close connection with the cult of the dead and with another poetic form, the lament (q.v.).

If the emphasis on the hero who has taken the place of the god in mythic material leads in a warlike society to what we call heroic epic, the stressing of the element of fantastic adventure and of the "love interest" leads to what is later termed "romance." These romantic and supernatural elements become the focus of the story and the tale is merely a series of strange adventures told for their own sake as entertainment. Some of the later *chansons de geste*, as *Huon de Bordeaux*, and the Gr. metrical romances, fall into this category. Both heroic elements and romance are found in the oral epic of the Yugoslavs, for example, not as separate genres sung by different singers to different audiences, but in the repertories of all singers for all audiences.

There seem to have been four main periods when oral n. poetry was recorded: (1) ca. 2000 B.C. in Sumer, Egypt, and generally in the Middle and Near East; (2) ca. 1000–400 B.C. in Babylon, Greece, and Palestine; (3) the Middle Ages in Europe; and (4) modern times, beginning about 1750 and coming down to the present day. The best known monuments of n. poetry from the earliest period are the Creation Epic and the Epic of Gilgamesh, preserved most fully in Akkadian texts, but known also from Sumer where they were probably original. The second period of the recording of oral texts yielded the Homeric poems, Hesiod, and the Cyclic epics in Gr. and parts of the Old Testament in Hebrew. In the case of the first period we are not sure whether the texts belong to oral or written literature (although very probably the former); it is just possible that written poetry developed this early. On the other hand, we know that an authentic written tradition of n. poetry eventually emerged in Gr., following the model of the recorded oral material, but no longer part of a living oral poetry.

Our earliest truly written n. texts of any length are the n. odes of Pindar. His choral odes from the early 5th c. B.C. are n. in that they recount a myth or myths associated with the athletic victory they celebrate. Pindar's Fourth Pythian tells the story of Jason and the Argonauts and is our earliest full form of that tale. With Pindar should also be mentioned Stesichorus, Simonides of Ceos, and Bacchylides. Our earliest written epic, the *Argonautica* of Apollonius of Rhodes, had to await the scholarly interests of the Alexandrian period. Apollonius' poem in four books totals 5,834 lines in an age that preferred shorter poems. In fact, he quarreled bitterly with his older contemporary, Callimachus, who is reported to have said that a long book is a great evil. Callimachus (b. ca. 330 B.C.) wrote

short epics, *epyllia*, which form a separate division of n. poetry. Two of his epyllia have echoes in Roman times; *Hecale*, which tells how Hecale entertains Theseus on his way to kill the bull of Marathon, is like the story told by Ovid of Philemon and Baucis; and *The Lock of Berenice*, which we know from Catullus' version of it (the original is lost). Callimachus also wrote a work in elegiac meter in four books entitled *Aetia*, a series of narratives concerning the origin of customs and of legends, in form not unlike Ovid's *Metamorphoses*. Theocritus, too, a younger contemporary of Callimachus, wrote epyllia, such as *Helen, Hylas, The Infant Heracles,* and *The Dioscuri.* The epyllion, with its tendency to satire and mock heroic, will continue to cross our path in later centuries.

The written literary tradition thus established in Greece continued through Roman and medieval times to our own day, now and then meeting with a native vernacular oral tradition. Eventually it cast all these into the background, triumphing over and assimilating unto itself local or tribal subjects. Thus, while there was probably a native Italic oral tradition of n. poetry in the Saturnian verse, into which Livius Andronicus translated the *Odyssey* in the 3d c. B.C. and in which Naevius wrote his *Bellum Punicum*, the first L. epic, none of these oral poems seems to have been written down or to have survived. For Ennius, the next epic writer in line after Naevius, in his *Annales* borrows the hexameter from the Greeks, and henceforth the "matter of Rome" is native merchandise carried in foreign bottoms.

Rome has bequeathed to us the first historical epic in Naevius' *Bellum Punicum* and Ennius' *Annales.* Virgil's *Aeneid*, though dealing with early Roman legend and based on the Homeric model, is filled with historical overtones and in Book 6 presents us with a brief panorama of Roman history.

Ovid's *Metamorphoses* in hexameters goes back to the same structural frame as Callimachus' *Aetia*, relating one after another, a series of tales of transformations, something like a strong of epyllia. Virgil's *Aeneid* and Ovid's *Metamorphoses* were the most lasting and influential of the n. poems of the Augustan period in Rome. The Empire boasted of Lucan (*Bellum Civile*), Statius (*Thebais* and *Achilleis*), Valerius Flaccus (*Argonautica*), and Silius Italicus (*Punica*). Claudian's *De Raptu Proserpinae* comes after some break in time (late 4th c.) and marks the close of classical L. epic. Lucan's fierce poem distorts history for partisan purposes and disdains the divine machinery of previous epic. In the Silver Age, epic preferences were divided. But the tradition ends with a return to myth in Claudian's poem.

NARRATIVE POETRY

Several centuries elapse before we find Greek epic poetry again in Quintus Smyrnaeus' *Posthomerica* (ca. A.D. 400), Nonnus' *Dionysiaca* (ca. A.D. 420), Tryphiodorus' *Taking of Troy* (ca. 470), Colluthus' *Rape of Helen* (ca. 490), and an anonymous *Argonautica* in a collection called *Orphica* (ca. 400). In the middle of the 6th c. Musaeus wrote the last of classical Greek n. poems, *Hero and Leander*. As striking as the long period of time, from the 3d c. B.C. to the 5th c. of our era, during which epic poetry seems to have been written in Gr. is that the poems which we have or know about are concerned with the ancient pagan myths and legends. Unlike Roman n. poetry, that of ancient Greece never turned to history for its subjects.

THE MIDDLE AGES. L. n. poetry did not die out after the classical period. The tradition of Virgil and Ovid was transformed to some extent by Christianity, or, perhaps better, accepted Christianity. The Gospel story was told in L. hexameters in Juvencus' *Evangeliorum Libri* (ca. 330) some sixty-five years before the poem of Claudian (ca. 395). Juvencus' poem contained more than 3,000 lines. In the first half of the 5th c. Sedulius wrote a *Paschal Poem* in five books. Both these poems of the Christian story became well known in the Middle Ages. At the end of the 5th c. Dracontius treated the Creation in his poem *In Praise of God;* and in the 6th c. Arator wrote a poem on Acts. Thus in these centuries at the dawn of the Middle Ages a Christian n. poetry came into being in the literary tradition of Virgil and in dactylic hexameters (or in other cases in elegiac couplets). These were significant moments; for the new mythology of Christianity was replacing paganism in paganism's literary forms.

We are not surprised to find hagiographic works in verse as well as in prose, although prose antedates verse in this genre. Early in the 8th c. Bede wrote lives of St. Cuthbert in both prose and verse, and the following century saw a number of such lives. Milo of St. Amand (ca. 810–71) wrote a versified life of St. Amandus in 2,000 lines, and Heiric of Auxerre did a life of St. Germanus in 3,400 lines.

Historical poems in L. verse also appeared in the Carolingian period. The Saxon Poet's verse annals of Charlemagne reach nearly 3,000 hexameters and elegiac couplets, and the monk Abbo of St. Germain wrote two books of L. epic (ca. 900) on the Norman attack on Paris in 885–86. Ermoldus Nigellus had celebrated the deeds of Louis the Pious (ca. 826) in something like 2,500 lines of elegiac couplets.

The saints' lives may be regarded as continuations of the tradition of songs about the gods as well as songs about heroes. At about this same time, in the early Middle Ages, there began to appear another vastly important branch of n. poetry, romance; and it is to be noted that, like the saint's life and chronicles or annals, the romance can be either in verse or in prose, or in both. Prose romance seems to antedate versified romance in our manuscripts. The Pseudo-Callisthenes Gr. original of the Alexander Romance seems to belong to the 2d c. of our era, and was translated into L. by Julius Valerius in the 3d c., but the verse tales are much later. The earliest apparently to be found in L. belongs to the 13th c. (1236, *Alexandreis* by Quilichinus of Spoleto) and the earliest vernacular poem in the West is a fragmentary Prov. octosyllabic text attributed to Albéric of Besançon of the late 11th c. The L. prose of Dictys Cretensis goes back to the 4th c. and that of Dares perhaps to around 500. But the first L. poem to come to our notice is in the 12th c. (Simon Chèvre d'Or's poem in leonine elegiacs in the middle of the century, and Joseph of Exeter's *De Bello Trojano* in 1187–88)—the same century in which there appeared Joannes Tzetzes' Gr. hexameter poem *Iliaca*, and also the first poem in the vernacular, the famous 30,000 line *Roman de Troie* of Benoit de Sainte-More (ca. 1184).

If we turn to a consideration of n. poetry in Byzantium, or in the Gr. East, we find a somewhat similar situation. Nonnus, who had written the *Dionysiaca* in ca. 420, had also produced a Paraphrase of the Gospel of St. John in dactylic hexameters. Saints' lives, however, in the East seem to be almost entirely in prose. The verse autobiography of Gregory Nazianzus (ca. 329–ca. 89) appears to be *sui generis*, in his own day at least. Historical poems in Gr. are found beginning in the 7th c. with George Pisida, who wrote a description of the campaigns of the Emperor Heraclius against the Persians, another on further exploits of the emperor, and still another on the attack of the Avars on Constantinople in 626. There are but a few scattered poems from then until the 12th c., when the verse chronicle of Constantine Manasses was written and another Constantine, Stilbes, composed two poems on two fires in Constantinople in 1197 and 1198!

In the field of romance we do not encounter metrical tales until the 12th c. when we find fragments of the *Loves of Aristander and Callithea* by the chronicler Constantine Manasses. Early in the same century Prodromus wrote a long poem on *Rhodanphe and Dosicles*. In the 13th c. the famous and anonymous *Belthandros and Chrysantza* appears.

Allegory as a literary form (not merely the rhetorical trope) seems to have appeared comparatively early in n. poetry. Examples of personification are, of course, to be found in Ovid and Virgil and other L. poets, but probably the first full dress allegory is the *Psychomachia* of Prudentius (A.D. 348–ca. 410), which depicts a battle of the virtues and vices. Thus allegory entered the service of morality and religion. Not only was the mythic battle of prehistory, refined by the heroic and by the historic, easily adaptable, as we have seen, but also the other basic mythic material, that of the journey, could easily be suited to Christian concepts, as had already been done in saints' lives and in apocryphal tales. The supreme example of religious allegory, Dante's *Divine Comedy*, is structurally a journey into the other world and a return after the gaining of knowledge. The cult of courtly love (q.v.), a kind of secular religion, led allegory captive and produced the "allegories of love" of which the *Roman de la Rose*, begun about 1230 by Guillaume de Lorris and completed about 1270 by Jean de Meun, is the best known instance.

Oral epic for the first time since the 8th c. B.C. began again to be written down, now in the vernaculars of the West as well as in Middle Gr. Only one poem in the latter can probably be classed as oral, the *Digenis Akritas*. The hero belongs to the 8th or 9th c. (or possibly the 10th), but the earliest Gr. manuscript is probably of the 14th c. Grégoire refers the formation of the epic to the 10th c. and the Rus. version of it to the 12th. In Old Sp. the *Cid* is said to have been composed about 1140 about a hero, Don Rodrigo Díaz, who died in 1099. Our unique manuscript of the poem is actually dated 1307. The thirty odd separate poems in the ON collection entitled the *Elder Edda* are thought to have been written down in the 12th c.; they are mythological and heroic in character. The Anglo-Saxon *Beowulf* has been assigned to the middle of the 8th c., but its only manuscript dates from about the year 1000. There are somewhere around a hundred *chansons de geste*. The earliest is the famed *Chanson de Roland*, referring to the battle of Roncesvalles in 778, and earliest preserved is the Oxford manuscript of about 1170. The oldest German poem is a fragment of the *Lay of Hildebrand* in Old High-German of ca. 800. Surely the best known of the Middle High German epics is the *Nibelungenlied*, which seems to belong to the early part of the 13th c.

The question as to whether these vernacular poems are oral or written is still being debated. In those cases where there are a number of varying manuscripts over a period of time there is a possibility that some are oral and some written. At any rate it seems very probable that written versions, imitating the oral

vernacular songs, appear at least as early as the 14th c. and probably earlier. In German and in OF the appearance of rhyme and the rewriting of some of the stories in rhymed rather than alliterative or assonantal verse seems to indicate a new formal tradition, generally associated with writing, coming into existence.

Contemporary with the vernacular epics and the whole group they represent is another body of n. poems in the vernacular on religious subjects. Thus, in Anglo-Saxon there are poems on Genesis, Exodus, Daniel, Christ, and Andreas, all of which are assigned dates close to that of *Beowulf*. Some of these poems are ascribed to Caedmon, others to Cynewulf, others are of unknown authorship. In Old High German there is a *Liber Evangeliorum* (Book of the Gospels) by Otfrid of Weissenburg in the 9th c., and about 830, the *Heliand* recounts the life of Christ. In other words both religious and secular "epic" are written in vernacular (one might also say "oral") style during this period. Somewhat earlier, it will be remembered, L. was the language (except for Gr. in the East) used for the metrical religious narratives including saints' lives. When history appears in verse in the West it is in L., the language of learning.

In the case of the medieval romances, it may be that some are oral and some written, although it is generally assumed, perhaps correctly, that they are written. Besides the material on Troy and Alexander, that on Arthur and his knights is the most widespread (see MEDIEVAL ROMANCE).

In the 14th c., at the end of the Middle Ages, there appear in England, contemporary or slightly later than Dante in Italy, other n. poems that are neither epic nor romance. One of them, *The Vision of Piers Plowman*, is allegory, and is written in three versions in alliterative verse. Part of it was long attributed to William Langland (ca. 1332–ca. 1400). It is a kind of frame story, in the conceit of a dream. The author says that he went walking and sat down and fell asleep beside a brook, and then he dreamed a succession of things, including the Vision of the Field of Folk, Holy Church, and Lady Meed, and the Vision of the Seven Deadly Sins. Another Eng. poet to grace the 14th c. n. scene is, of course, Geoffrey Chaucer (ca. 1343–1400), whose *Canterbury Tales* is perhaps the most famous frame n. in Eng. literature. Here allegory bows to realism as the first person convention does to the proper third person of n.

Elsewhere than in England in the 14th c. n. poetry was also practiced. In Italy this is the century not only of Dante, but also of Petrarch and Boccaccio. We may think of Petrarch chiefly as a writer of sonnets, but he fancied himself also as an epic poet; his *Africa*, on the theme of Scipio Africanus and Roman history, is in L., it will be noted, not It. Boccaccio is known best for prose n. in the frame tradition, in his *Decameron*, but his metrical romance *Filostrato*, on the story of Troilus and Criseida, drew from the Trojan romance and influenced Chaucer in his n. of *Troilus and Criseyde*. He also wrote *Teseida* (the story of Arcita and Palemone) in ottava rima. Metrical romance was also being cultivated in Gr., as evidenced by *Callimachus and Chrysorrhoë*, which probably belongs to the 14th c.

THE RENAISSANCE. The great Renaissance tradition of epic poetry begins with Matteo Maria Boiardo (1441–94) and continues with Ludovico Ariosto (1474–1533) in Italy. Boiardo is famous for his *Orlando Innamorato*, an unfinished epic, or perhaps more properly romance, with Roland, the hero of the OF *chanson*, as its principal figure. Ariosto's even more famous *Orlando Furioso* picked up the same theme and completed Boiardo's story. The hero in both these poems is in name only the hero of the older epic; he is in them rather the hero of romance. The older kind of epic might well have died in Italy had it not been for an even greater poet of the following century, that of the "high Renaissance," namely Torquato Tasso (1544–95), who combined the more classical idea of the heroic epic, as it was known in those days from ancient models, with the romance. The result was his *Gerusalemme Liberata* (Jerusalem Delivered). For the heroic part of this epic, as distinguished from its romantic part, Tasso turned to the history of the first crusade, to the fairly distant past, therefore; on the other hand the two chief 16th-c. epics of the Iberian peninsula, *La Araucana*, by Alonso de Ercilla y Zúñiga (1533–94) in Spain, and *Os Lusiadas* by Luis de Camoëns (1524–80) in Portugal treated more recent history. The former deals with the conquest of South America (the Araucanians being a tribe of South American Indians in central Chile) by the Spaniards, and the latter with the voyaging to India by Vasco da Gama in 1497–99. One might say that for the first time since Virgil's day one had again a really national epic. 16th-c. France was not much given to epic, although mention should be made of Pierre de Ronsard's (1524–85) *La Franciade*, unfinished but published in 1572. The theme was obviously national here too, and the return to the decasyllables of early medieval times was an archaism not in keeping with a new age. All three of these epics, in France, Spain, and Portugal, were historical, national, and classical, looking backward to Virgil and to classical mythology, and not, as Tasso, toward romance. There was in France another epic poet in the 16th c., a Huguenot,

Guillaume de Salluste du Bartas (1544–90), who turned, or returned, to one of the most ancient of subjects for epic, namely to the creation of the world. In 1578 he published *La Sepmaine*, a poem very popular in its day not only in France but also in England. With his *Judith* (1573) he was employing a theme well liked in Renaissance painting.

With Du Bartas, indeed, we are carried in two directions; one is toward England and ultimately to Milton, the other is toward Dalmatia and to the figure of Marko Marulić (1450–1524) of Split, the "father" of Croatian literature. He was not a Protestant, but he also wrote a *Judita* in his native Croatian, in 1501, which went into three editions during his lifetime (1521, 1522, 1523). Like Du Bartas, Marulić did not approve of the pagan themes and settings, and his L. epic *Davidijada* returns to biblical stories rather than to classical antiquity. It is worthy of note that n. poetry was flourishing also in Dalmatia during the 16th c. under the influence of the It. Renaissance. On the island of Hvar the poet Petar Hektorović wrote a n. poem telling of a fishing expedition, *Ribanje i ribarsko prigovaranje* (1555), partly in imitation of It. models of "fishing pastorals" (fishermen and nymphs instead of shepherds and nymphs), but completely realistic, *sans* nymphs. It included, however, the singing of folk songs, some of them n. ballads. A friend of Hektorović's in Dubrovnik, Mavro Vetranić (1482–1576) wrote an unfinished philosophical-allegorical epic entitled *The Pilgrim*, picturing man as a traveler through the three conditions of sin, repentance, and perfection. Petar Zoranić (1508–?1569) of Zadar on the Dalmatian coast wrote a pastoral romance in verse and prose entitled *Planine*, "The Mountains" (1536, published 1569) in which a shepherd named Zoran goes to the mountains to find herbs to cure him of lovesickness. Among other adventures he encounters a mountain spirit named Croatia, who complains of the lack of interest in the Croatian tongue. This national theme appears again in the later work of two other poets of Zadar, Brno Krnarutić (1520–72) and Juraj Baraković (1548–1628). Krnarutić's fame comes from his epic on a contemporary theme, *The Capture of the City of Sziget*, which fell to the Turks in 1566 after a heroic defense by Nikola Zrinski. And Juraj Baraković published in 1614 his *Vila Slovinska*, devoted to the past and contemporary history of Zadar. It is in the early 17th c. that Dalmatia produces her Tasso, in the person of Ivan Gundulić (1588–1638) of Dubrovnik, whose unfinished epic *Osman* follows Tasso's theory of the combining of the classical heroic with the romantic, with this difference, however, that Gundulić chose a theme from contemporary

Balkan history, in the spirit of Christendom's crusade against the Turks with the Polish prince as its heroic champion.

Although the pastoral (q.v.) romance has its roots deep in the past with the idylls of Theocritus and Bion and their descendants (for example, in the *Eclogues* of Virgil) and although one can find examples in the 15th c. such as Boccaccio's *Ameto,* in prose and verse, it is common to date pastoral romance from the publication of J. Sannazaro's *Arcadia* in 1504, also a work combining verse and prose. The pastoral romance is distinguished by the fact that its protagonists are shepherds, its background and scenery are the countryside where shepherds and shepherdesses tend their flocks, and its adventures are in keeping with its protagonists in love. All is ideal and paradisiacal. The limitations of such a form are obvious and its possibilities were exhausted in England actually by the end of the 17th c. The pastoral impulse went elsewhere, into pastoral drama, lyric, and even into the novel.

Eng. n. poetry other than pastoral of the 15th and 16th c. follows patterns well established on the continent. The prolific John Lydgate's *The Fall of Princes* (36,000 lines), for example, is a translation of Boccaccio's *De Casibus Virorum Illustrium,* and his *Troy Book* (1412) was a translation of Guido. Hawes' *Pastime of Pleasure* (1509) was an allegory, a pilgrimage of the soul of the active man. In the same century Spenser's *Faerie Queene* indulged in the allegory of courtly love; and we have at least two historical narratives in Edward Hall's *Chronicle* and Samuel Daniel's (1562–1619) *Civil Wars* (1595). With Michael Drayton it is abundantly clear that we are in a period when forms shorter than the older epic and romance have become attractive. Once again we see appearing what we might call the Ovidian collection of epyllia, that is, Drayton's *England's Heroical Epistles* (1597).

And at the fairs and in the streets of London and throughout the cities of the British Isles appeared in ever greater numbers the cheap broadsides with their n. ballads. In 1520 *Robin Hood* was being sold at Oxford in broadsides. Our oldest copy of *Chevy Chase* is in a manuscript of ca. 1559. The earliest collection of broadsides comes from the first two decades of the 17th c., and the Percy Folio Manuscript of ballads and broadsides is dated about 1650. But it is to the 18th c. that one must turn for the real history of ballad collecting and publishing.

THE 17TH AND 18TH C. TO ROMANTICISM. It has already been seen that the activity in n. poetry in the 16th c. was ebullient, and it welled over into the next. The world was changing, however, in the 17th c., and as the century wore on n. poetry, with certain notable exceptions, gave place to occasional poems and especially to satire. This state of things lasted actually until after the middle of the 18th c., when romanticism brought n. poetry as such back into favor. In Italy and Germany this intermediate period was especially barren. France presents us with some interesting exceptions. We find Nicolas Boileau's *Le Lutrin* (lectern) a mock epic, written in 1673–83; some of the *Fables* of La Fontaine (1621–95) are n. poetry; but more important, two works, one in the 17th c., Fénélon's "prose poem" *Télémaque* (1699), which tells the tale of Odysseus' son in search of his father and his adventures, and the other in the 18th, Voltaire's *Henriade* (1728), a national epic on the religious wars. Actually both these works, one from ancient story and the other from recent history, are used by their authors as platforms from which to expound their educational, social, or political views. In parts they tend to be tracts, or to be mere rhetoric. It almost seems that epic, and, as we shall soon see, the short n. forms, move easily in the direction of satire. The story is amusing, or biting, or formally perfect; it has lost its lure as a story for entertainment.

At the close of the 16th c. in England we might note two links with the past. Christopher Marlowe (1564–93) wrote a poem on *Hero and Leander* (1593), completed and published by George Chapman in 1598. By it we are reminded of Musaeus' epyllion that marked the end of the ancient Gr. epic tradition. And Abraham Cowley (1618–67) wrote a *Davideis* (1656) which remained unfinished, a biblical epic in Virgilian style. This was a different task from the *Davidijada* of Marko Marulić mentioned above, which was a more or less direct paraphrase of the biblical story.

But the picture in the 17th c. is dominated by John Milton and his *Paradise Lost* (1667). Milton went back to the wellsprings of epic for his subject, to religious myth, to the creation, to the war of the gods. He thought to fashion a new hero in Adam, and thus misjudged the tradition of the heroic. Yet his magnificent poem stands as perhaps the last great epic in Western literature. There are examples of the genre later, but they are either *tours de force* or weak in their concept of the hero, as in the Victorian epic.

When the other great poets of these centuries, whose chief fields were either drama or satire, turned to n., it was to translation rather than to original creation, yet their translations became classics. Such are the renderings by John Dryden of Ovid, Virgil, Chaucer, and Boccaccio; that of the Homeric poems by Alexander Pope (1688–1744) and by William Cowper (1731–1800). The best of all translations of Homer, however, in this early period was that of George Chapman (1559–1634).

NARRATIVE POETRY

ROMANTICISM. A new interest in n. poetry began to grow from about the middle of the 18th c., no longer a neoclassical movement (which seemed pretty well exhausted), but a movement in the direction of the songs of the common people. This was, of course, in keeping with the times. The opening gun of this new interest in n. might be said to be the publication in 1765 by Thomas Percy of his *Reliques of Ancient Eng. Poetry*. In this the term "Ballad" was limited to those songs which described action, and the term "Song" was used for thóse which expressed a sentiment. Actually the publication of Percy's book was preceded by a few years by the "hoaxes" of James Macpherson (1736–96), *Fragments of Ancient Poetry collected in the Highlands of Scotland* (1760), *Fingal, an Ancient Epic Poem in Six Books, together with Several Other Poems composed by Ossian, the Son of Fingal, translated from the Gaelic Language* (1761), *Temora* (1763) and *The Works of Ossian* (1765).

From the point of view of n. poetry and aside from the question of the value of their content, these two books or groups of books exerted influence in three important directions. First, they encouraged through the work of men like Johann Gottfried von Herder (1744–1803) and the brothers Grimm, Jakob and Wilhelm, the collecting and studying of folk ballads and folk epic song throughout Europe. Secondly, they led to the unearthing, publication, and scholarly investigation of medieval manuscripts of epic which were revived during the 19th c. Thirdly, they inspired written ballads in a literary tradition. To these three influences it might be added that they played no small role in the beginning of the romantic movement in general with its theories about the origins, transmission, and composition of poetry, with its new view of the world and of the past, and the revival of some of the themes of epic from antiquity retold in the romantic spirit.

Of the first of these something has been said in the article on oral poetry. Of the second there has been some treatment both in that article and in this. It is of the third that we must speak further here.

Burns and Scott would seem to be the best examples of the impact of the ballad on written n. poetry. They both knew the popular form from an early age. Robert Burns (1759–96) is more given to lyric, but in such poems as *Tam o'Shanter* he exhibited his skill with the ballad spirit. N. was more serious a matter for Sir Walter Scott (1771–1834), whose *Minstrelsy of the Scottish Border* (1802–03), a collection of the ballads of Scotland, prepared him well for his own *The Lay of the Last Minstrel, Marmion,* and *The Lady of the Lake.*

Scott's instinct for story, a true n. instinct, expressed itself more genuinely perhaps in his novels, the real successors of epic. Scott is a more veritable follower of the n. genius in Western literature than many another, for the story interests him above all.

And this is the fate of n. poetry after 1750. William Wordsworth (1770–1850) turns to the common folk and tells stories of local events, as in *Goody Blake and Harry Gill,* but it is a self-conscious attempt. *Michael* is more sentimental than the popular ballads, although it has something of their spirit in that the kind of change that comes over Luke in the evil cities of men is not untypical. In *Laodamia* Wordsworth is consciously telling a tale from the past, a tale that touches the heart of epic mythic origins, and one that he retells with perfection. It is not his fault but that of the moment of intellectual history that the perfection of the poet in his craft is more significant than the story of *Laodamia*. We might, I suppose, call *The Prelude* n., but the first person in ballad is pure convention, and to concentrate upon it as the real subject of the tale is contrary to the objectivity of traditional story poetry. True, there are famous examples in epic where a character, as, for example, Odysseus in the *Odyssey*, tells a long tale in the first person, but Odysseus is not Homer. In Samuel Taylor Coleridge (1772–1834), whose *The Rime of the Ancient Mariner* is surely one of the best known n. poems of this period, together with his unfinished, and somewhat less known *Christabel,* we find an artistic sense of and feeling for the ballad situation and an uncanny ability effectively to present weird tales. The ballad manner and the traditional phrasing are lacking, of course, and the intensity of the poet lends an air of its own. The style here, too, and the poet are what count rather than the story.

And what should we say of George Gordon, Lord Byron (1788–1824) and n. poetry? He is closest to story telling in his oriental tales, in *The Giaour,* for example. Here is story telling for its own pleasure. *Beppo* is good n. but also an excellent illustration of the use of n. for satire. The Romans were past masters of this genre. In *Don Juan* the story is but a vehicle for all the views of the poet. And *Childe Harold's Pilgrimage,* while ironically enough it takes us back to the tale of a journey, so basic to n. myth, is only veiled autobiography. Perhaps it is truly n. only in its digressions. John Keats (1795–1821) is objective enough to be a master of n., and some might say that his perfection of style serves the n. rather than that the n. serves the style. This certainly seems true for *The Eve of Saint Agnes* and for *Lamia.* Whether he could have sustained this balance

-[549]-

to complete the longer epic is doubtful perhaps, to judge from the fate of *Hyperion*.

FROM THE VICTORIAN AGE TO THE PRESENT. N. poetry comes more into its own in the Victorian Age, when writers had greater interest in the story and less in form. It should be sufficient to name the more famous poets and their equally famous works. Alfred, Lord Tennyson's (1809–92) *Idylls of the King* takes us back to the romances of chivalry, and, indeed, it is a revival of old subjects that faces us. Thomas Babington, Lord Macaulay (1800–59) in his *Lays of Ancient Rome* went even further back than Tennyson, to early Roman times. Matthew Arnold (1822–88) follows fashion in his interest in oriental tales, and his *Sohrab and Rustum* drew from ancient Persian history and epic, which lies a bit uneasy in its 19th-c. sentimental cradle. And, finally, William Morris (1834–96) reminds one of Scott in the earlier part of the century; he too had a real instinct for n. and a sense of story telling of the past, as can be seen from his saga translations, for example. His *Jason* is probably our last telling of the tale of the Argonauts. *The Earthly Paradise* not only returns us to Gr. myth in some of its tales and emphasizes as well the mythic tales of the Scandinavians, but also takes us back to the frame story. And the story for the frame is an ancient mythic one of wanderings. We have thus returned to the beginning of our account. The date was 1866–70, nearly a hundred years ago.

There has been some n. since then, of course, but our own age has felt that the genius of poetry was lyric, or fashionably dramatic. It has scorned n. poetry in general and sought its stories for entertainment, instruction, or artistic edification in the novel. When poetry is thought of as form and ecstasy, then n. poetry is an anomaly. Rudyard Kipling's (1865–1936) ballads took the fancy of a generation, John Masefield (b. 1878) had a real talent for n., and many will remember his *The Everlasting Mercy* (1911) and *The Widow in the Bye Street* (1912). Stephen Vincent Benet's (1898–1943) *John Brown's Body* (1928) is an interesting almost-epic experiment in n.

Ten years later (1938) in Greece and in Gr. there was published the n. poem that ends our own tale, *The Odyssey, a Modern Sequel*, by Nikos Kazantzakis; the translation into Eng. of this poem, which narrates the further wanderings and adventures of Odysseus, appeared in 1958.

W. P. Ker, *Epic and Romance* (2d ed., 1908) and *Form and Style in Poetry* (1928); G. H. Gerould, *The Ballad of Tradition* (1932); Chadwick; Lewis; W. J. Entwistle, *European Balladry* (1939); D. Bush, *Eng. Lit. in the Earlier 17th C., 1600–1660* (1945; 2d ed., 1962); E. K. Chambers, *Eng. Lit. at the Close of the*

Middle Ages (1945; especially chap. 3, "Popular N. Poetry and the Ballad"); C. M. Bowra, *From Virgil to Milton* (1948) and *Heroic Poetry* (1952); E.M.W. Tillyard, *The Eng. Epic and Its Background* (1954); R. Poggioli, "The Oaten Flute," *Harvard Library Bulletin*, 11 (1957); K. Kroeber, *Romantic N. Art* (1961).

A.B.L.

For further consideration of the epic in the various literatures, see the articles on ASSYRO-BABYLONIAN POETRY, ENG., FINNISH, GR., INDIAN, L., OLD NORSE, etc. Consult also EPIC THEORY, ORAL POETRY, CHANSONS DE GESTE, and refer to such bibliographic titles as: E. W. Hopkins, *The Great Epic of India* (1901; the *Mahābhārata;* also some discussion of the *Rāmāyana*); L. Abercrombie, *The Epic* (1914); R. Heinze, *Virgils epische Technik* (3d ed., 1915); H. V. Routh, *God, Man, and Epic Poetry* (2 v., 1927); W. W. Lawrence, *Beowulf and Epic Tradition* (1928); J. M. Parry, *L'Epithète traditionelle dans Homère* (1928) and "Traditional Metaphor in Homer," CP, 28 (1933); C. M. Bowra, *Tradition and Design in the Iliad* (1930); R. Menéndez Pidal, *Historia y epopeya* (1934) and *La epopeya castellana a través de la literatura española* (1945); C. S. Lewis, *A Preface to Paradise Lost* (1942); E. Mudrak, *Die nordische Heldensage* (1943); D. Knight, *Pope and the Heroic Tradition* (1951); U. Leo, *Torquato Tasso* (1951); Auerbach; Curtius; G. R. Levy, *The Sword from the Rock* (1953); A. Heusler, *Nibelungensage und Nibelungenlied* (5th ed., 1955); C. Whitman, *Homer and the Homeric Tradition* (1958); R. W. Chambers, *Beowulf: An Introd.* (3d ed., 1959); A. B. Lord, *The Singer of Tales* (1961); G. S. Kirk, *The Songs of Homer* (1962); T. M. Greene, *The Descent from Heaven: A Study in Epic Continuity* (1963).

NATURALISM. In applying this much-maligned term to poetry, we must beware of following Georg Brandes (*Naturalism in 19th C. Eng. Literature*) and Stopford Brooks (*Naturalism in Eng. Poetry*), who use it much in the same sense in which we use the word "romanticism." Unlike realism, which is the artistic expression of an attitude toward reality common to numerous individuals in many different ages, n. is the aesthetic correlate of a philosophical doctrine that has its place in 19th-c. history. It is a movement, and not merely a way of looking at things. Based on a stringent disbelief in teleological explanations, philosophical n. considers natural causes to be responsible for all movements of mind and matter (determinism). In art, this materialistic attitude finds its most poignant expression in the works of Émile Zola, whose *Le Roman Experimental* (1880)—which is based on Claude Bernard's *Introduction à l'Étude* *de la Médecine Expérimentale* of 1865—forms the keystone of naturalistic aesthetics. In this treatise, Zola urges the writer to imitate the scientist by observing reality (the *how*) without inquiring into its ultimate causes (the *why*). He charges him with establishing an inner and outer milieu, into which the characters, whose behavior he wants to observe, are to be placed. Underlying this experimental method, we recognize a humanitarian desire to change the existing social conditions; hence the close relation between n. and socialism.

Ample space being required for the environmental experiment, the naturalists preferred the dramatic and novelistic genres to that of lyric poetry. Nevertheless, Émile Zola attempted to formulate a naturalistic theory of poetry when he reviewed the Fr. poetry of his own century in an essay entitled "Les Poètes Contemporains" (1878). In François Coppée and Sully Prudhomme he thought to have discovered the forerunners of a school of poetry capable of creating that *langue nouvelle* which was to be the true expression of the scientific age. No such development took place, however, since none of Zola's contemporaries dared to cast aside all poetic conventions, as the master had demanded.

It was only in its application to German literature of the 1880's that the term "n." was used to designate a specific school of poetry. In his preface to the anthology *Dichtercharaktere* (1884), Karl Henckell defined the new poetry as "a characteristically embodied image of all the suffering, longing, striving and struggling of our time." Only gradually, German naturalistic poetry succeeded in ridding itself of the humanitarian and nationalistic pathos which marks its early stages. This emancipation was completed by Arno Holz who, apart from Richard Dehmel, is the only genuine poet among the German naturalists. In *Die Kunst, ihr Wesen und ihre Gesetze* (1890), he argued that the greater a work of art the greater its tendency "wieder Natur zu sein" (to turn back into nature). In order to facilitate this process of retransformation, Holz introduced the *Sekundenstil* (a photographically minute reproduction of each phase in a given development). While the *Sekundenstil* technique remains more or less restricted to prose, poetry was to achieve a similar purpose by a voluntary renunciation of such formal devices (rhyme, stanzaic pattern, set meter) as stand in the way of an accurate transcription of reality. In advocating a form that was to be the direct expression of subject matter, Holz developed what he called a consistent naturalism in poetry. Formally described in *Revolution der Lyrik* (1899), the new style was put to the test in *Phantasus,* a collection of verse which contains Holz's maturest poetry. In its

preoccupation with mood, however, *Phantasus* clearly foreshadows the end of n., a development which Hermann Bahr had foreseen as early as 1891. And already at the turn of the century, the predominant style was to be that of impressionism (q.v.).—N. M. Thompson, "Arno Holz and the Origins of the New Poetry," *Washington Univ. Studies,* 8 (1920); F. Doucet, *L'Esthétique de Zola et son application à la critique* (1923); H. Röhl, *Der deutsche Naturalismus* (1927); R. Leppla, "Naturalismus" in *Reallexikon,* II; R. König, *Die naturalistische Aesthetik* (1931); K. Turley, *Arno Holz* (1935); M. Cowley, "Not Men— A Natural History of Am. N.," KR, 9 (1941); deals mostly with fiction); R. Hamann and J. Hermand, *Naturalismus* (1959); *Literarische Manifeste des Naturalismus 1880–1892,* ed. E. Rupprecht (1962). u.w.

NATURE. To deal with n. in poetry is, in some sense, to deal with nearly the whole task of poetry. For poetry is, to paraphrase John Dryden, the "image of nature." All theories of poetry have made some allowance for both terms ("image"—a thing in itself, a construct; "nature"—what the poem imitates or speaks about), however much a given theory may stress some peculiar aspect of the many interconnections. Hence, n., both as subject and as involved in poetic theory, is central in poetry.

It is symptomatic of our times, semanticism being in some measure a product of the Cartesian division and romantic doubts about n., that "nature" is so often thought of by modern writers as primarily an ambiguous *word.* But the situation is not quite so desperate as might appear from the articles of Lovejoy and Wilson ("Nature as Aesthetic Norm," *Essays in the History of Ideas,* 1948; and "Some Meanings of 'Nature' in Renaissance Literary Theory," JHI, 2 (1941), respectively). For the galaxy of meanings there adduced do have a center-reality, manifested in this way or that—and the crucial differences in meaning are more ontological than semantic.

Man has puzzled much about his relation to n. throughout the history of thought. People have felt that man is in, but not of, n.; or of, but not quite in, n.; or, in any case, that he is a very special part of n. (astronomically speaking, man is the astronomer). And from the earlier semireligious, semimaterialistic speculations about the n. of things, literature and men's views about n. have been mutually though not exclusively causative, and considerably complicated.

NATURE IN POETRY. In Homer, n., though mythic and under the sway of supernatural beings, is a large, solid, brilliantly lighted world of objects, and every episode is presented in detail, forcibly, with precision

(Erich Auerbach, *Mimesis*, pp. 1-20). Life and n. are accepted, and presented, in their own right. In the Old Testament, n. is rigorously subordinated to God, and details are given, never for their own sake, but for the sake of religious truth. They may be simple exterior parts of the story briefly, sometimes naively, put forward (the bear and the children, the direct account of events in Kings and Chronicles, important because Jewish history is uniquely sealed by God), or they may have supernaturally illumined potency (the burning bush, the deep where the fish takes Jonah), or may be poetically magnificent responses to God and created beauty (the Psalms, the Song of Solomon). In Job, a n. apparently indifferent to man's moral purposes is explored with agonizing brilliance, the resolution remaining in the inscrutable will of the Deity.

In Gr. thought and literature, n. becomes many things: god-haunted, a goddess herself, a demiurge, a Heraclitean flux, an unreal world of appearances, an unceasing and godless play of atoms. She usually, however, keeps a more substantial independence (even when conceived as unreal) than in Jewish ontology, because the Jews, unlike the Greeks, think of n. as created. God is supreme reality and fact. Heraclitus, whose philosophical fragments are great poetry, sees the world as change, and transformation, and flux (though he apparently also accepts a divine order behind the flux), and the idea of n. as flux has influenced poets from the Ovid of the *Metamorphoses* through Gerard Manley Hopkins and T. S. Eliot in the *Four Quartets*. In Sophocles' *Oedipus*, as in other plays and poems, man and n. are joint heirs of weal and of woe; the plague, caused by Oedipus' wicked deeds, falls on land and people alike: n. is subject to the (partially unknowable) moral order.

Parmenides and Plato, in their different ways, found the world to be delusive (how much their conclusions come from the technical arguments regarding motion and concepts respectively, and how much from religious insight must remain an open question). Platonic scholars and literary critics still disagree whether Plato finally rejects poetry and poets, but it is clear enough that he does reject most poetry from the ideal kingdom, as appertaining to the lesser world. But the idea of n. as appearances, with its subsidiary idea of the ladder of reality, is among the most telling ideas in history, in poetry and criticism as in religion and ethics. It comes through Plotinus and the Neoplatonists and Christian theology, and is a Renaissance commonplace, however powerful the contrary impulse to accept, explore, and control a thoroughly real natural world. It informs Sidney's great sonnet, "Leave me, O love, that reachest but to dust,"

and Spenser's four Hymns, and reappears, in moods and with differences, in Wordsworth's *Peele Castle* ("the light that never was on sea or land") and Shelley's *Hymn to Intellectual Beauty*, however far some of these manifestations may be from Plato or Socrates or Parmenides.

But n. is not only the world-view which a poet assumes or wrestles with: it was, and is, place—the rocks, streams, hills that men can admire, live among, or fancifully rearrange. In the pastorals of Theocritus and Virgil, a gentle, special world is selected *from* n. to serve as a counterpoise of spirit for man's hectic life in courts and cities and to serve the perpetually recurring theme of (and need for) innocence and freshness. But the genre is no simple one, and it grows: it includes elegy, disguised autobiography, battles of wit, half-mocking or tender praises of love; it can deepen to allegory, drama, passion, and prophecy. A somewhat parallel and, later, overlapping tradition is found in the shepherds' plays of the Middle Ages. The tradition is rediscovered in the Renaissance and developed by such writers as Politian, Mantuan, Sannazaro, the *Pléiade*, Tasso, Guarini, and Spenser. It takes various forms: (1) the pastoral novel of Sidney, Honoré d'Urfé, and others; (2) the pastoral play or masque (Fletcher and Jonson, as well as the Shakespeare of *As You Like It* and scenes from *The Winter's Tale* and *The Tempest*); (3) the more common pastoral eclogues. The tradition culminates, but does not end, in *Lycidas*. In pastoral, n. is refined, humanized, decorated, elaborated, simplified, yet this recreated n. can have, as in Virgil and Milton, a deeply natural and quickening power of its own. "Pathetic fallacy" and "decoration" alike are far too crude to describe the dense reality and interplay between man, n., and God in *Lycidas*.

The *Georgics* of Virgil (which are founded largely on the poems of Hesiod) show n. in a special view. In one sense a technical manual of agriculture, they nonetheless show forth a deeply humanized n., impregnated by civilization, by man's rational and earnest cultivation, that in turn gives to man rootedness and stability and pious accord with the past. In the *Aeneid*, n. keeps the qualities of the *Georgics*, but deepened, made more dignified and pious, stately. The epic simile presumes man's separation from the natural world, the orderliness of n., and dignifies man and natural world alike.

N. can be for the Greeks and Romans a goddess, and remains so for centuries, at least in literature. Even Lucretius, whose materialism is stubborn and basic, hymns Venus, the creative power of n., in verse that becomes religious in quality, and achieves a poetic naturalism whose closest modern parallel is perhaps some of the philosophic prose of George Santayana. "Natura" (or "Physis") as a generative and intervening goddess, appears in poetry from Ovid's *Metamorphoses*, through Claudian and the Orphic hymns of the 3d and 4th c., down through such medieval writers as Bernard Silvestris of Tours (*De universate mundi*, 1145–53) and Alan of Lille (*De planctu naturae*, and *Anticlaudianus de Antirufino*, 1182 or 1183). In the process of partially Christianizing the pagan goddess, there derives a new poetic genre, the philosophical-theological epic, in which the Christian view of the world provides the end and frame for the story, but various pagan or semipagan deities and demigods are the actors. This tradition worked against obstacles, in part because of the multiple Christian attitudes toward n.: n. is created, hence good; n. is fallen, hence evil, especially so as involved in sensuality (here Manichean and Platonic pressures are felt). As innocent or as redeemed, n. can be lovely and holy. In the Middle Ages (and of course the Middle Ages are not entirely Christian), various Christian attitudes to n. appear, especially in the complex tradition of courtly love (C. S. Lewis, *The Allegory of Love*; Denis de Rougemont, *Love in the Western World*; M. C. D'Arcy, *The Mind and Heart of Love*). In the two parts of the 14th-c. *Romance of the Rose* there are two "natures," both quite medieval, incorrigibly different. In the first part, by Guillaume de Lorris, n. is gardenlike and delicate of bloom; in Jean de Meun's second part n. means rank and sprawling sensuality.

The n. in the literature of the semi-Christian and courtly world of the Middle Ages is different in kind and emphasis from the n. found in poems of the semi-Christian and courtly world of Old Eng. In the latter, the most successful natural descriptions, in poems like *Beowulf*, *The Wanderer*, and *The Seafarer*, are of the bleak and great and spare: the bitter sea of exile, the fens and fastnesses where demons walk, a great and lonely funeral pyre. But in the medieval *Sir Gawain and the Green Knight*, n. is magnificent, various, and brilliantly colored, even when expressive of grim fears; and in the *Pearl*, as in many medieval carols and lyrics, the loveliness of the landscape is dipped in supernatural hues. N. is selective, holy. Chaucer is a master of natural description, n. in many moods and features: symbolically black rocks, the delicacy of Love's gardens (a delicacy parallelled in Fr. n. poets: Deschamps, Machaut, Froissart), the natural and vigorous earth the pilgrims travel over, the invented and phantasmagoric landscape (or airscape) of *The House of Fame*, and the world of many spheres rising toward God (the *Knight's Tale*; *Troilus and Criseyde*). He learned much, borrowed much, and trans-

formed much from Dante, who, though his greatest poem is almost entirely set in supernature, has perhaps the most exact eye for physical detail of any poet. Light in the *Paradiso* becomes the most eloquent of all literary symbols (for mind is there illumined by the supernatural); yet he uses similes with a businesslike attention to the point of the resemblance that presumes the genuine importance of the intellect in its own capacity and the Thomistic reliance on the senses, the plainly visible.

The great poets of the Eng. Renaissance—Shakespeare, Spenser, Milton—share some fruitful, if tangled, assumptions about n.: that n. is created, hierarchical, symbolic, full of personal-social-physical-theological correspondences, struck with sin, powerfully threatened, and these assumptions appear whether they write of real or imaginary or metaphysical fields (Agincourt or the Bower of Acrasia or the Garden of Eden). One of their great motifs is the overthrow of n., physical n. being stubbornly involved in the moral world; and the supreme correspondences of man and nature are expressed in *King Lear*.

The medieval tradition of meditation on the features of the world (as image of God's glory, or symbols of temporal vanity, or to express the coinherence of the church and the mystical life) is kept alive in the devotional poetry of Southwell, Donne, Herbert, Vaughan, Crashaw and (in fragments such as the beginning of *Religio Laici*) in Dryden. In general, Dryden keeps the theory of a symbolical and hierarchical world, but relaxes the practice, except in moments and in the semi-Miltonic *Absalom and Achitophel*. For Pope, the more traditional view has faded. N. exists to serve philosophical argument, for primitivistic sentimentalizing, for faint pastoral or fainter Christian pastoral, but he speaks with power and pungently naturalistic detail when he deals with bugs, worms, toads, chicks in satiric attack or when he sees, in the bitterness and magnitude of the *Dunciad's* close, the wreck of a former world. In Voltaire, n. exists almost exclusively for argument (even Candide's garden to be cultivated is as much an example as an exception), to "prove" the existence of the deistic God by its noble and orderly design or to "disprove" Christian providence by its cataclysmic and meaningless evils.

Shaftesburian and Rousseauistic optimistic benevolism and antirational associationism (n. conceived as innately good and sponsoring social as well as sentimental feeling) rules much of the 18th and to some degree the 19th c., even though Miltonic diction for describing a well imagined literary nature has its influence too, and the long standing epideictic tradition (poetry as praise of God through praise of the natural creation) shows attractively in Thomson's *The Seasons,* magnificently in Smart's *A Song for David,* and deistically and thinly in Addison's *Hymn.* Gray and Collins and Blake achieve some unique and beautiful effects of natural description.

The theory of "general nature," as expressed by Rapin and Boileau and vividly by Johnson when he advises against numbering the streaks of the tulip, is never completely obeyed by its proponents, but Blake contemns the idea ("To Generalize is to be an Idiot"—itself a generalization!) and seeks knowledge inhering in and through particular images of the poetic vision, achieving thereby some very profound and some densely obscure images. Wordsworth has some excellent passages of particular description, but his landscapes are more apt to be generalized, important for their effect on the soul or their correlate philosophical and religious meaning. His poetic theory insists more on the general than the particular. In Goethe, n. shows range, but not a return to the Renaissance. Whether serving as a mirror for the sorrows of a young poet, or as the ground for man's reclamation in the second part of *Faust,* it is essentially passive and, by romantic projection and by engineering, bears man's stamp.

Wordsworth and Coleridge, however much they differ in specific poetic ideas, are very seriously puzzled about n. Earlier poets widely believed in, or simply assumed, spiritual power in or behind n.; they frequently gave n. human qualities without embarrassment (they had rhetorical terms, prosopopoeia or personification, for such devices). Coleridge, Wordsworth, Shelley, Keats were at once more passionate and more uncertain about physical n. The term "pathetic *fallacy*" is, significantly, a 19th-c. invention. The question of projection vs. perception was perhaps the most agonizing that these poets dealt with, and they strongly feared the negative conclusion (that men merely read meaning into a deterministic and meaningless world). All of them have, like the Victorians after them, their moments of great doubt. They also have their great moments of vision. Wordsworth perhaps came off best in the struggle, largely by strength of character and a certain instinctive distrust of philosophical speculation. In the latter part of the century, the problem was intensified by the Darwinian concept of n. as blindly evolving, "red in tooth and claw."

In the Fr. poetry of the 19th c., this reduced view of n. appears in at least three different ways: the praise of n. as admirably alien from man; the re-creation of a "Parnassian" n. from refined natural elements; the belated, personal, and desperate attempt of the symbolists to achieve medieval views of analogy by a desperate leap of the "angelical imagination" (a phrase Tate uses in speaking of Poe, the hero of the symbolists). The first and second ways combine beautifully in such a poem as de Lisle's *Les Eléphants,* the second and third ways magnificently in the poems of Baudelaire with their queer mixture of romantic charlatanism and a revived and deadly sense of sin (inherited in some part from the meditative and powerful Jansenism of Racine). And in passages of such poems as De Vigny's *La Maison du Berger* or *La Mort du Loup* (as in Tennyson's *In Memoriam*), there is a rediscovery of the meditative tradition, only drawing strength and profundity from doubt rather than faith, "questioning all with inquietude" (as De Vigny says in another context).

The typical n. of 20th-c. poetry is that of Eliot's *The Waste Land* and Crane's *The Bridge,* where the natural—and human—world is conceived of as shattered, fragmentary, painful. Eliot's poem attempts to express this confusion: Crane's does express the confusion in the very failure of his attempt to unify American experience (but achieves much coherence within the partially broken frame). Stevens broods freshly the projection-perception puzzle, with faint hope, ironic irresolution, loud and deliberately literary creations of an elegant or amusing n., or with the starkest vision of a world devoid of meaning except for the motion of naked particularity. In Valéry, n. is presented with an almost pitiless brilliance of detail and a highly subtle ambivalence of feeling and belief. Auden handles natural imagery imitatively (i.e., of the n. of OE poetry) or with journalistic aplomb or so as to express the *oddness* of particularity. Less commonly and more seriously, he offers redemptive glimpses of supernature through n. or celebrates n. lyrically. Yeats in a curious way bridges the chasm: his natural imagery is magical, hieroglyphic, wavers; or it is solid and Ir.: it can serve for savage espousal of the harshest naturalism or for images that beget images of supernature. R. P. Warren is bold with the pathetic fallacy and attains a genuine nightmarish intensity at times, at rare times a beauty of light and color, but he seems to feel the fallacy as fallacy and commits it stridently. In much minor poetry, n. is interior, contrivedly Freudian, uglily symptomatic, or academically tentative. In some of the best free verse (for instance, in much of H. D.'s and W. C. Williams'), the very line shape expresses the fragmentation of n., but seen with a fresh, loving, and particular eye. Some poets, such as St.-John Perse and Dylan Thomas in some moods attempt in the Whitman tradition to make n. paradise by dithyrambic lyricism, and by harmonizing conscious and unconscious meanings of natural symbols. Allen Tate in

Ode to the Confederate Dead presents in great bitterness an alien and deadly n. which undoes man's best hopes and visions. In his later poem *The Swimmers* (actually one section of a long uncompleted poem) he approaches older views of n. (and the work of such modern, traditional poets as Edwin Muir and Robert Bridges). N. in that poem serves him for symbols of moral and psychological depth, but is also the place where the action occurs and has the wholeness and resonance of places of boyhood remembered and, though distinct from man, is, like man, under the aegis, the brooding presence of the moral law. Two younger distinguished poets, Robert Lowell and Anne Sexton, present n. brilliantly, almost solipsistically, yet focusing moral and religious as well as personal problems.

NATURE IN CRITICISM. Critical theory, from Plato on, has almost always centered in ideas of n. Platonic theories of the world and the "image" have influenced criticism as well as poetry, despite Plato's (at least partial) rejection of poetry as an imitation of the world of appearances and as baneful in moral influence. Modern "Platonic" theories (those of the Abbé Bremond, Wallace Fowlie, to some degree those of Maritain) conceive of art as imitating or somehow partaking of, at least by analogy, the transcendent world, a privilege reserved in Plato for the trained and morally good philosopher. The doctrine in *Ion* of the poet as inspired seems to be ironic, but it has extended a major influence, not ironic.

The central theory of criticism has been, however, the Aristotelian, whose primary concept is poetry as the imitation of n. In this theory n. enters into both terms, since the imitation is not only of n. (man's n. primarily), but is natural (according to nature), since it is natural for men to delight in imitation and to respond with moral sympathy to the joys and terrors of men not too unlike themselves. As developed by the rhetoricians Cicero and Quintilian, who insist on the propriety of the three styles, high, middle, and low, to various subject matter, and reinterpreted by Renaissance critics (who yoke, with some violence, Horace's *Art of Poetry* to Aristotle's *Poetics*), the theory has been *the* Western critical tradition, and its major concepts—imitation and propriety—though rejected in most modern theory, are still unavoidably *used* in most criticism.

In this theory, "n." means the subject of imitation; the foundation of accords between emotion, idea, and subject; and the poet's inborn talent ("n." as opposed to "art," "art" meaning the cultivation of one's powers by judgment and practice). The consistency and intelligibility of n. is the ground for the "rules." The theory of the rules is often mis-understood, however sensibly they were or were not applied. Dryden puts the case clearly: there is only one primary rule, as certain as reason itself—that good poetry should be in accordance with n., both as an imitation (that is, poems should have verisimilitude) and as something made (poems should be in accord with the moral and aesthetic law and permanent human n.—else they cannot long please). All other rules are secondary and uncertain, and therefore judgment, tradition, mediation, and good sense are permanent essentials of criticism, which is not an exact science.

In the last two centuries, the ideals of imitation and propriety have been widely replaced by the Coleridgean ideals of imagination and organic form (which Coleridge derived from such Germans as Herder and Schelling). In this view, poetry is like n. rather than an image of it or proper to it. Poems and physical n. are, according to Coleridge, created by different but analogous acts of human imagination. But the newer theory sometimes conceals the old. The notion of literature as a proper imitation of nature is a hardy plant, and critics nowadays (sometimes in the teeth of their theories) let us know what poetry does or should represent: the organic biological essence of life (Susanne Langer); the harmonizing of emotions (the earlier I. A. Richards); God by analogy and intuition (Wallace Fowlie); the poet's soul (many); the mobile flow of free personality (Herbert Read); Jungian archetypes (Elizabeth Drew); the "tough" ambiguous uncertainty of life (Cleanth Brooks); the particulars in which reside all truth (W. C. Williams and Ezra Pound). In some versions of the notion of organic form (e.g., Herbert Read's), organic form is the chief good because it better fits (is more *proper* to) the idea of natural evolution than are older theories. Or it is sometimes argued, in flamboyant self-contradiction, that a dynamic, nonmimetic theory is proper to the modern notion of a purposeless n., since value must come from within the human mind rather than from n. Croce's theory of expression is based, explicitly, on the idea of a coherent and permanent human n., and the looser forms of expressionism tacitly or explicitly assume that poetry should imitate, be like, the chaotic and meaningless flux that is reality (n.).

C. V. Deane, *Aspects of 18th C. N. Poetry* (1935); L. Welch, *Imagination and Human N.* (1935); J. W. Beach, *The Concept of N. in 19th-C Poetry* (1936); M. J. Adler, *Art and Prudence* (1937); H. McCarron, S.J., *Realization: a Philos. of Poetry* (1937); K. E. Gilbert and H. Kuhn, *A Hist. of Aesthetics* (1939); T. Spencer, *Shakespeare and the N. of Man* (1942)

H. Trowbridge, "The Place of Rules in Dryden's Criticism," MP, 44 (1946); W. V. O'Connor, "N. and the Anti-Poetic in Modern Poetry," JAAC, 5 (1946); H. Read, *Form in Modern Poetry* (1948); N. MacLean, "From Action to Image," in Crane, *Critics;* Curtius; L. L. Martz, *The Poetry of Meditation* (1954); Wellek; R. Tuve, *Images and Themes in Five Poems by Milton* (1957); R. Langbaum, "The New N. Poetry," *A Sch.*, 28 (1959); C. S. Lewis, *Studies in Words* (1960); P. Van Tieghem, *Le Sentiment de la n. dans le préromantisme européen* (1960); D. B. Wilson, *Ronsard, Poet of Nature* (1961); P. Ramsey, *The Lively and the Just* (1962).　　　　　　　P.R.

NAVAHO POETRY. See AMERICAN INDIAN POETRY. NORTH AMERICA.

NEAR RHYME. The repetition in accented syllables of the final consonant-sound without correspondence of the preceding vowel- or consonant-sounds, and either with or without "feminine" unaccented syllables following (which should be largely identical). E.g., *grope-cup, maze-coze, drunkard-conquered.* It is a special case of CONSONANCE (q.v.), and is called by such various names as slant rhyme, half rhyme (also applied to rich consonance), oblique rhyme, para-rhyme. An old device in Icelandic, Ir., and Welsh verse, n.r. appears to have been deliberately used in Eng. first by Vaughan, who was influenced by Welsh practice. Both internally and at line ends such inexact echoes can be found occasionally in all poetry, especially in ballad, folk, and popular song. Swift rhymed "justice" with "hostess," Emily Dickinson "port" with "chart," Osbert Sitwell "war" with "armchair" (which last have *no* true echo in Standard British Eng.). But no major poet in Eng. had used n.r. consistently until Hopkins and Yeats. Hopkins knew George P. March's work in Icelandic and himself studied the Welsh. Yeats, although not a student of Ir., knew of Ir. metrics through Kuno Meyer and others. Once considered an oddity in the work of such poets as Emerson and Emily Dickinson, n.r. is now accepted and used by nearly all 20th-c. poets, not to supplant perfect rhyme but to supplement it, so as to provide a greater range and freedom for the poet. The Am. poet Trumbull Stickney uses n.r. systematically intertwined with regular rhyme in *Mnemosyne.* For examples of n.r. in modern poetry, see Hopkins, Yeats, Ransom, Eliot, Owen, Tate, Wylie, and Auden.—G. P. March, *Lectures on the Eng. Language* (1859; anticipates modern borrowing and experimentation); K. Meyer, *A Primer of Ir. Metrics* (1909); E. Rickert, *New Methods for the Study of Lit.* (1927); T. W. Herbert, "Near-Rimes

and Paraphones," SR, 14 (1937); G. Symes, "A Note on Rhyme," *Eng.*, 7 (1949).
　　　　　　　　　　　　　　　　S.L.M.; U.K.G.

NEGRO POETRY. AFRICAN.† Traditional Afr. Negro poetry cannot be labeled as poetry in the strict sense of the term, and therefore is often called rhythmic prose. This terminology originates in the fact that the people of Africa themselves designated poetry as "chant," much as the Greek and Romans called a poem an "ode," or "carmen" or "cantus." Because of recent studies of the languages of Senegal, of the Bantu, Peulh, Dahomey, and Ruanda, it is now known that the chants and dances at religious, social, and domestic ceremonies were actually poems. The following Bayeke chant is a typical example:

> Nabula kusekula
> Mulume walala ni nzala
> Mabulanda, mayo
> Mulume walala ni nzalae!
>
> I have not milled (the maize)
> My husband went to sleep hungry
> Yes, this is very sad, O mother
> My husband criticized me,
> My husband went to bed hungry!

Afr. authors have asserted that "a poem is any work of art" (Léopold Sédar-Senghor) or a poem is "words pleasing to the heart and ear" (a Peulh proverb). However, the content of Afr. traditional poetry was originally quite clearly defined, comprising the unwritten history of clans, families, and tribes, and expressing conquests, defeats in battles, the praise of ancestors and chiefs, the description of social and family life, religious beliefs, and the explanation of the phenomena of nature. Other common types were occupational songs to accompany canoe-paddling, milling of rice, marching, nursing of children; also funeral songs, marriage or death songs, chants of witch doctors or soothsayers, and the like. Traditionally the poet composes his verses *ex tempore*, at times varying the conventional materials with topical references. Many chants, however, were memorized and carried from generation to generation for centuries.

Imagery and rhythm are the two basic characteristics of Afr. traditional poetry. Few abstract poems exist, for the Afr. Negro poet stresses the concrete aspect of life. In contrast to Indo-European languages, where a logical syntax is used, the Afr. Negro uses an intuitive syntax. The principle of both traditional and contemporary Afr. Negro poetry is essentially rhythm combined with the word; this is eventually combined with music and the dance. The poetic line is normally quan-

† In Supplement, see also AFRICAN POETRY: VERNACULAR, ENG., FR., PORT.

titative—an alternation of short and long syllables with accentual emphasis on specific syllables. In the regular traditional poem each verse has the same number of accents, while in contemporary poetry this is no longer the case.

It is impossible in the present brief survey to treat even the most outstanding examples of traditional Afr. poetry. One must bear in mind that there is not one Afr. literature but many: Yoruba, Malinke, Zulu, Bantu, to mention but a few. South of the Sahara, more than 600 languages are spoken, not including dialects and secret languages which raise the number to about 3,000. We know that each Court had its poet; the profession of the poet was taken over by the son from the father; each tribe had its "griot" (professional poet); chants or poems were numbered chronologically; about 200 dynastic traditional poetic chants are recorded. For adequate discussion of the material, the reader is referred to the bibliography.

Turning to contemporary Afr. Negro poetry, we see a tragic conflict between tradition and progress in the attempt to create a specifically Afr. poetic style. Many Afr. poets live abroad, and those who have adopted the language of their new homeland are no longer truly "African" because they have tried to find a synthesis between Africa and Europe. Their poems, written in Fr. or Eng., have lost much of their Afr. character. On the other hand, the native Afr. poet cannot find a large audience for his work, for if he writes in his own Afr. language, he is understood by a small circle of readers only. Destroyed tradition cannot be revived, and the Afr. Negro poet has yet to establish a specific Afr. style and language in which he can create an authentically "African" poetry.

Many contemporary Afr. poets emphasize political themes. Among them are David Diop (Senegal, 1927–), Bernard Dadié (Ivory Coast, 1923–), J. R. Jolobe (Indwe, S. A., 1902–), Dennis C. Osadebay (Nigeria, 1911–), Theko Bereng (Basuto, 1900–). Their poems express protest against colonialism and the disregard of tradition. There are relatively few lyrical poets in the manner of Léopold Sédar-Senghor (Senegal, 1906–) who is undoubtedly the most lyrical of the contemporary Afr. poets as his Chants pour Naett and Chants d'Ombre show. Aimé Césaire (born in Martinique, 1913; now living in Paris) is considered an Afr. poet with a knowledge of the Fr. language almost unsurpassed even by Fr. poets. His style shows surrealistic elements borrowing from traditional Afr. chants, ancestral myths, magic and ancient rites. In his poems Soleil Cou Coupé, Batouque and many others, he combines surrealism with a kind of esoteric and intel-

lectual word game, developing in many of his poems into a revolutionary message. Another lyrical poet is Efua Sutherland.

A number of literary reviews have appeared in the past years. The most important ones are: La voix du Congolais (Elisabethville), Jeune Afrique (Elisabethville), La revue du monde noir (Paris), Présence Africaine (Paris and Dakar), Makerere (Uganda), University Herald (Nigeria), African Drum (Johannesburg), Black Orpheus (Nigeria), Odu (Nigeria). Africa South (Johannesburg and London), West African Review (London) and African Affairs (London) contain occasional literary essays and poems.

Afr. Negro poetry has undergone many transformations: colonization, expatriation, the consequences of being uprooted, a metamorphosis of spiritual and intellectual concepts following the meeting of Africa with the West. There is no doubt that a truly Afr. Negro poetry in at least some of the Afr. countries will emerge when the many errors and insecurities of style are overcome.

ANTHOLOGIES: Anthologie aus der Suaheli Lit., ed. C. G. Büttner (1894); Les Chants et les contes des Ba-rongas, ed. H. A. Junod (1897); Myths and Legends of the Bantu, ed. A. Werner (1933); Anthol. nègre, ed. B. Cendrars (1947); Les plus beaux écrits de l'Union Française et du Maghreb (1947) and Anthol. de la nouvelle poésie nègre et Malgache (1948), both ed. L. Sédar-Senghor; Poètes d'expression fr. 1900–1945, ed. L. G. Damas (1947); Chansons d'ébène en langue d'ivoire (n.d.) and Poètes et conteurs noirs (1948), both ed. O. de Bouveignes; Le Monde noir, ed. T. Monod (1950); Anth. of W. Afr. Verse, ed. O. Bassir (1957); Voices of Ghana, ed. H. Swanzy (1958); Yoruba Poetry, ed. and tr. B. Gbadamosi and U. Beier (1959); Afr. Voices, ed. P. Rutherford (1960); An Afr. Treasury, ed. L. Hughes (1960); Schwarzer Orpheus, ed. J. Jahn (4th ed., 1960). See also Antologia da poesia negra de expressão portuguesa, ed. M. Andrade (1962); Modern Poetry from Africa, ed. G. Moore and U. Beier (1963); Poems from Black Africa, ed. L. Hughes (1963).

HISTORY AND CRITICISM: H. Grégoire, De la lit. des nègres (1808); P. Cultur, Histoire du Sénégal du XVe s. à 1870 (1910); C. Meinhof, Die Dichtung der Afrikaner (1911); J. Roscoe, The Baganda (1911); E. Hurel, La Poésie chez les primitifs (1922); R. S. Rattray, Religion and Art in Ashanti (1927); Chadwick; M. J. Herskovits, Dahomey (1935); W. D. Hambly, Source Book for Afr. Anthropology (1937); H. Baumann and D. Westermann, Les Peuples et les civilisations de l'Afrique (1948); L. Homburger, The Negro-Afr. Languages (1949); L. Frobenius, Kulturgeschichte Afrikas (1954); J. Jahn, Muntu: An Outline of Neo-Afr. Culture, tr. M. Grene (1961); L. Harries, Swahili

Poetry (1962); B. W. Andrzejewski and I. M. Lewis, *Somali Poetry* (1964). M.KO.-J.

AMERICAN (U.S.).† A sudden burst of poetic expression in Harlem in the 1920's produced "more confident self-expression" by Negro Americans, according to one observer, than the centuries that preceded.

The poets of the Harlem Renaissance were born nearly 200 years after the first Am. Negro poet, Lucy Terry, the slave girl whose semi-literate *Bars Fight* is a verse account of an Indian raid on old Deerfield in 1746. The second important Am. Negro poet is Phillis Wheatley, who was born in Senegal, West Africa, sold into slavery in early childhood and brought to Boston in 1761. *A Poem by Phillis, a Negro girl in Boston, on the death of the Reverend George Whitefield*, published when she was just seventeen, heralded the beginning of a unique writing career, culminating in *Poems Religious and Moral*, published in 1773 in England, where she had gone for her health. Lucy Terry and Phillis Wheatley, along with such other Am. Negroes as Jupiter Hammon and George Moses Horton, belong to a tradition of writers in bondage which goes back to Aesop and Terence.

Marked changes in the pattern of slavery in the United States followed the Revolutionary War. Laws were passed in the slave states making it a crime to teach a slave to read and write. Formal poetry by Negroes, it needs scarcely be said, suffered. Except for such writings in Fr. by free men of color in Louisiana as were collected in the anthology *Les Cenelles* (1845), and a few scattered lyrics by Horton and Frances E. W. Harper elsewhere, the richest self-expression by Negroes in the 19th c. was not written. It consisted of spirituals, seculars, narrative poems, proverbs, and aphorisms, animal tales and the like.

About 120 years after Phillis Wheatley, Paul Laurence Dunbar greeted the 20th c. with several volumes of lyrics, including such representative poems as *Dawn, Little Brown Baby, When Malindy Sings*, and *Compensation*, together with scores of others which, more than half a century later, have a host of admirers to whom they remain fresh and poignant. His *Collected Poems* (1913), have never been out of print. A strong sense of melody and rhythm was a feature of Dunbar's poetry, as it has been of nearly all the Negro poets of the United States. Dunbar's delightful country folk, his broad, often humorous, dialect failed to create a tradition, however. Later Negro poets have held that the effective use of dialect in poetry is limited to humor and pathos. Accordingly, most of them have abandoned it. The colloquial speech used now and then by poets like Langston Hughes and Sterling A. Brown is something else.

A contemporary of Dunbar's was James Weldon Johnson, but Johnson's *God's Trombones*, a collection of folk sermons in verse and his most important poetic achievement, was not completed until late in his career. Meanwhile William Stanley Braithwaite, best known for his series of annual *Anthologies of Magazine Verse* (1913 to 1929), published two volumes of his own lyrics (1904 and 1908), neither of them recognizable in any way as "Negro poetry." Selected editions of Johnson's and Braithwaite's poems were published in 1930 and 1948 respectively. Angelina W. Grimke, Anne Spencer, Georgia Douglas Johnson and Jessie Redmond Fauset are women whose poems appeared here and there before the Harlem poets arrived. Miss Grimke's *The Black Finger*, Miss Spencer's *Letter to My Sister*, Miss Johnson's *The Heart of a Woman*, and Miss Fauset's *Enigma* are typical. Fenton Johnson, their contemporary, is remembered best for free-verse vignettes like *The Banjo Player, Aunt Jane Allen*, and *The Scarlet Woman*. Three small volumes of his poetry came out between 1914 and 1916.

With the arrival of Claude McKay in the United States Negro poetry welcomed its strongest voice since Dunbar. Born in Jamaica, B.W.I., McKay published his first book, *Songs of Jamaica*, at the age of nineteen. *Constab Ballads*, also written in West Indian dialect, followed about a year later, and presently the young McKay migrated to the United States to attend Tuskegee Institute and, later, Kansas State University as a student of Agriculture. Two years of this was enough for him. He moved on to New York and began contributing verse to American magazines. McKay went to Europe in 1919 and published in London his slight but appealing collection *Spring in New Hampshire* (1920). On returning to America he became associated with Max Eastman in the editing of the *Liberator*. *Harlem Shadows*, the book by which he became widely known to poetry lovers, and which touched off much subsequent literary activity in Harlem, came out in 1922. *The Tropics in New York* and the famous sonnet *If We Must Die* represent McKay's range as well as his special quality. Attention was drawn to the universality of the latter poem when Winston Churchill quoted it as the conclusion to his speech before the joint Houses of Congress prior to the entrance of the United States into World War II:

If we must die, O let us nobly die,
So that our precious blood may not be shed
In vain; then even the monsters we defy
Shall be constrained to honor us though dead!

• • • • • • • •

† In Supplement, see also BLACK POETRY, RECENT (U.S.); HARLEM RENAISSANCE.

Like men we'll face the murderous, cowardly
pack,
Pressed to the wall, dying, but fighting back!

The poems of Langston Hughes, meanwhile,
had been attracting attention in the *Crisis*,
a magazine which had since 1911 welcomed
contributions by Negro poets. Hughes quickly
identified himself as a distinctive new voice.
His *The Negro Speaks of Rivers* appeared soon
after his graduation from high school in 1920
and was reprinted far and wide. The first
collection of his poems was *The Weary Blues*
(1926), but no less than half a dozen volumes
have followed, all of them marked by an ease
of expression and a naturalness of feeling that
make them seem effortless. Hughes's art can be
likened to that of Jelly Roll Morton and the
creators of jazz. His sources are street music.
His language is Harlemese. In his way he is
an Am. original.

Countee Cullen, another of the poets who
helped to create the mood of the 1920's in
Negro poetry, was quite different. Educated
in New York City, he adopted the standard
models, from John Keats to Edna St. Vincent
Millay. But the ideas that went into Cullen's
sonnets and quatrains were something new in
Am. poetry. His long poem *Color,* for example,
which gave its title to his first book (published in 1925 while Cullen was still an undergraduate at New York University), is the poet's
treatment of the problem of race prejudice as
he saw and experienced it. His *Heritage* shows
him seeking a nostalgic link with the Africa of
his dark forebears. His *Incident* tells how the
color problem startled an impressionable child.
All these are included in *On These I Stand*
(1947). Jean Toomer's small output belongs to
this same period. His *Cane* (1924), like Sterling Brown's *Southern Road* a decade later,
highlighted significant folk values.

Four Negro poets have received critical attention since the Harlem period. Margaret
Walker won the Yale University Younger Poets
award in 1942 with her volume *For My People*,
the title poem of which has become a favorite
of Negro speakers and readers. Her *Molly
Means* has become popular with verse choirs.
Gwendolyn Brooks's first book was *A Street in
Bronzeville* (1945). Her *Annie Allen*, which
followed in 1949, was awarded the Pulitzer
Prize for poetry, the first time this honor had
been given to any Negro writer. She has since
published fiction as well as poetry for children.
Owen Dodson's *Powerful Long Ladder* (1946),
gets its idiom more from the New Poetry of
our time than from Negro folk sources, and
probably for this reason is less known among
Negro readers than his sensitive novel *Boy at
the Window* (1951). The two books of Melvin
B. Tolson's poetry also represent two attitudes
toward his material. *Rendezvous with America*
(1944), shows the influence of Langston Hughes
and Negro folk sources. His *Libretto for the
Republic of Liberia* (1953), while treating a
Negro theme, is an exercise in poetics better
understood by New Critics than by readers
accustomed to traditional forms, folk or otherwise. Nevertheless it won him honors from the
government of Liberia. A collection of Robert
E. Hayden's poems appeared in England in
1962 under the title *Ballad of Remembrance*.
Other young poets whose reputations at that
time rested mainly on appearances in anthologies and periodicals included Moses Carl
Holman, Gloria Oden, and LeRoi Jones.

ANTHOLOGIES: *Carolling Dusk,* ed. C. Cullen
(1927); *The Book of Am. Negro Poetry*, ed.
J. W. Johnson (2d ed., 1931); *Negro Poets and
Their Poems*, ed. R. T. Kerlin (1935); *Golden
Slippers*, ed. A. Bontemps (1941); *The Negro
Caravan*, ed. S. A. Brown (1941); *The Poetry
of the Negro, 1746–1949* (1949) and *The Book
of Negro Folklore* (1958), both ed. L. Hughes
and A. Bontemps; *Am. Negro Poetry*, ed.
A. Bontemps (1963); *New Negro Poets, U.S.A.*,
ed. L. Hughes (1964).

HISTORY AND CRITICISM: B. G. Brawley, *The
Negro in Lit. and Art in the U.S.* (1918), *Early
Negro Am. Writers* (1935) and *The Negro
Genius* (1937); V. Loggins, *The Negro Author*
(1931); S. A. Brown, *Negro Poetry and Drama*
(1937; essential introductory statement; some
attention to origins and folk sources); J. S.
Redding, *To Make a Poet Black* (1939; a closer
look at the work of representative Negro
poets); J. Wagner, *Les poètes nègres des Etats-
Unis: Le sentiment racial et religieux dans la
poésie de P. L. Dunbar à L. Hughes* (1963).
A.B.

NEOCLASSICAL POETICS. From about 1650
to about 1800, development of interest and
activity in "poetics"—in discussion, within
the general province of criticism, of the nature
and value specifically of poets and poetry—
was rapid and widespread. It was not, however,
the development of a single, harmonious system of principles and doctrines. Sometimes,
for example, theories were developed around
questions primarily of "art" (as by Boileau,
Rapin, Le Bossu, Dryden, Gottsched, and
Lessing), while sometimes "nature" was of
primary importance (as for Johnson, Edward
Young, Rousseau, and Herder); sometimes,
again, questions of the ends or effects of poetry
were primary (as for Boileau, Rapin, Dryden,
Addison, and Johnson)—and this was the orientation most characteristic of the period—
while sometimes heavy emphasis was placed
on the powers and habits of poets (as by
Bouhours, Joseph Warton, and Young). Moreover, within each of these broad and overlap-

-[559]-

ping divisions, and others like them, the specific doctrines and methods of reasoning were various. It is possible, nevertheless, to describe in very general terms (1) some of the different kinds of discussion and inquiry characteristic of the period and (2) some of the principal shifts and developments in dominant interest, emphasis, and orientation.

1. In the sense of discussions designed specifically to state the nature, problems, and excellence of poetry, neocl. poetics took two principal forms: "technical" and "qualitative"; the distinction between them turns on the special kind of question and poetic phenomenon with which each was primarily concerned. The "technical" poetics—deriving its problems and terms mainly from Horace and Aristotle (but largely in interpretations which blurred their radical differences) and from Renaissance and 17th-c. critics who combined "Horatian" and "Aristotelian" doctrines with elements especially from Cicero, Quintilian, and certain Neoplatonists—is found, to list a few characteristic examples, in works like Dryden's *Essay of Dramatic Poesy* (1668) and Preface to *Troilus and Cressida* (1679), Fielding's Preface to *Joseph Andrews* (1742), Boileau's *L'Art poétique* (1674), Rapin's *Réflexions sur la poétique d'Aristote* (1674), Voltaire's Preface (and accompanying letters) to the 1730 edition of his *Oedipe*, Ignacio Luzán's *Poética* (1737), Gottsched's *Versuch einer kritischen Dichtkunst* (1730), Lessing's *Hamburgische Dramaturgie* (1767-69), Gravina's *Ragion poetica* (1708), and his *Della tragedia* (1715), Metastasio's *Estratto dell'arte poetica d'Aristotile* (1782), and numerous others. Its principal task was to answer questions of artistry and poetic construction, viewed largely in terms of the ends and means appropriate to the different species of writing; and it did this mainly by a process of deducing "rules" and "beauties" from considerations of the "art" of poetry, the powers and practices of poets, and the needs and demands of audiences.

The "qualitative" poetics—deriving from the tradition represented by Demetrius, Dionysius of Halicarnassus, Quintilian, Cicero, and especially "Longinus"—is found in such works as Dryden's "Preface to the Fables" (1700), Pope's "Preface to the Iliad" (1715), many of Johnson's *Rambler* papers on poetic topics (1750-52), parts of Voltaire's "Discours sur la tragédie" (1731), Bodmer's *Critische Abhandlung von dem Wunderbaren in der Poesie* (1740), J. E. Schlegel's *Vergleichung Shakespears und Andreas Gryphs* (1741), and Pietro Calepio's *Paragone della poesia tragica d'Italia con quella di Francia* (1732). It sought its principles, characteristically, in the demands and responses of the audience and the practices and powers of the poet; its task, however, was to answer questions not of specific form and technique but rather of the qualities and values which characterize poetry in general or distinguish one writer or work from another, either ignoring questions of species and established styles or subordinating them to broader considerations of matter and manner, thought, mind, expression, and the like.

With the major developments in and between these two principal modes of poetics—and often, in given discussions, inseparable from them—arose also two special kinds of inquiry in general criticism and aesthetics. On the one hand, historians and critics began increasingly to examine the special rhetorical circumstances, environmental causes, and historical setting of an author's production—his gifts, education, life, audience, geographic location, climate, nationality, language, and the spirit or condition of his age—thus providing, in general, a variety of explanations and justifications of the peculiar forms and qualities of the works of poets in different social conditions, ages, and nations. This kind of discussion is found in such early works as François Ogier's Preface to Schélandre's *Tyr et Sidon* (1628), parts (e.g., 2.1) of D'Aubignac's *Pratique du théâtre* (1657), Saint-Évremond's *De la tragédie ancienne et moderne* (1672)—and many other contributions to the ancients-moderns controversy—Temple's essays "Upon Poetry" and "Upon Ancient and Modern Learning" (1690), Dryden's "Origin and Progress of Satire" (1693), and passages (e.g., 1.118-23; 2.394-407) of Pope's *Essay on Criticism* (1711); more fully developed in such later works as Voltaire's *Essay upon Epic Poetry* (1727), Thomas Blackwell's *Enquiry into the Life and Writings of Homer* (1735), Johnson's "Preface to Shakespeare" (1765) and parts of his *Lives of the Poets* (1779-81), Thomas Warton's *History of English Poetry* (1774-81), Herder's "Briefwechsel über Ossian und die lieder alter Völker" and his essay on "Shakespeare" (1773), Gravina's *Ragion poetica* (in part), F. X. Quadrio's *Della storia della ragione d'ogni poesia* (1739-52), Vico's *Principii d'una scienza nuova* (1744); and in general in the various apologies for "runic," "oriental" (especially the Hebrew), "primitive," and "gothic" poets and poetry, as in the works of Lowth, Hurd, Blair, Hamann, Herder, and Melchiorre Cesarotti.

On the other hand, philosophers and critics began increasingly to explore the bases of all the arts, in "scientific" and "philosophical" analyses of human nature, the mind, works of art, and the properties of the world. This kind of discussion is exemplified by Dryden's "Parallel betwixt Poetry and Painting" (1695), Shaftesbury's *The Moralists* (1709), Addison's *Spectator* papers on "the pleasures of the imagination" (1712), Bouhours's *La manière de bien penser dans les ouvrages de l'esprit* (1687), Du Bos's *Réflexions critiques sur la poésie et sur la peinture* (1719), Batteux's *Beaux arts réduits à un même principe* (1746), Arteaga's *Investigaciones filosóficas sobre la Belleza Ideal* (1789), Muratori's *Riflessioni sopra il buon gusto nelle scienze e nelle arti* (1708), Giuseppe Spalletti's *Saggio sopra la bellezza* (1765), Baumgarten's *Aesthetica* (1750–58), Lessing's *Laokoon* (1766), among many others.

In spite of the different objects, purposes, and methods represented in these various discussions, more or less common use was made of a body of critical concepts and distinctions which, in a general way, may be described as "neocl." There were, in the first place, those familiar general analytical and descriptive devices having reference to the various species or types of composition and their rules and principles of subject matter, structure, and style: terms and distinctions such as tragedy, comedy, epic, satire, ode, epigram, epistle, pastoral; matter and manner, argument and design, thought and expression; invention, arrangement or disposition, and expression; thought and passion, fable, manners, and sentiments; the elevated, the middle, and the low styles. In the second place, there were those still more general concepts and oppositions of concepts having reference not to specific kinds or elements of poems but to the bases, circumstances, causes, subjects, ends, effects, and qualities of literature as a whole: nature and art, pleasure and instruction, invention and judgment, imagination and reason, originality and the imitation of models, the imitation of nature and fanciful invention, general nature and particular nature, men of taste and the common reader, simplicity and refinement, the just and the lively, truth and novelty, the regular and the irregular, the sublime and the beautiful, the picturesque, the ridiculous, and many others. These are not, of course, examples of doctrine or, in any simple sense, of "neocl. tastes" in poetry, but rather of a highly amorphous body of "commonplaces" in terms of which doctrines were stated or tastes defined. Nevertheless, not only do they differ, as a whole, from those especially characteristic of earlier and later periods, but also they derive mainly from a common critical tradition which had its origins in the rhetoric of Alexandrian Greece and the Rome of Horace, Cicero, and Quintilian; and in these common conceptual materials a general continuity in poetic theory and criticism did exist throughout the neocl. period (See R. S. Crane, in UTQ (22 [1953], 376–91).

2. It was, however, a continuity of terms and distinctions, not a static unity of principles or doctrines, and one of the important developments in the poetic theories of the period involved a basic shift of emphasis in first principles from one side to the other of the most general and inclusive conceptual opposition in ancient criticism—from "art" to "nature." In many cases, this shift began with an inclination—often motivated by nationalism or religion—to defend poems and poets that presumably did not meet the "artistic" standards set by the admired Gr. and Roman critics and models, according to common 17th-c. and earlier interpretations of those critics and models. The significance of this inclination was in part its stimulation of fresh inquiries into poets' environmental conditions, especially into differences among audiences, as well as into general audience psychology and the ends and means of poetry. Those familiar controversies, for example, regarding "marvelous" and "probable" subject matters, or "true" and "false" wit, or the propriety or possibility of portraying Christian martyrs and the subject of love in tragedy, or the three unities, or the use of rhyme in tragedy and epic, turned upon freshly stated questions of what a given audience or society would or would not accept, of the real substance and structure of the nature imitated (or in general the subject matter expressed) in different kinds of poems, and of what, after all, poetry is supposed to accomplish. Such inquiries were accompanied and followed by those familiar qualitative reappraisals and rediscoveries of the works of poets (e.g., Shakespeare, Homer, "Ossian") who revealed more "imagination" than "reason" or "learning," more "liveliness" than "justness," more "invention" than imitation of proper models. Out of this general process of reexamining established rules and criteria arose, among other things, the compelling question—going quite beyond the issue of a poet's relative "rationality," "correctness," or "judgment"—of the necessity or reliability, for actually achieving the ends of poetry, of any rules based merely on the practices of past poets. As a result, critics tended more and more to look for the true laws and ideals of poetry (in its various forms and qualities) in laws and ideals of nature instead of in the established precepts and models of the art. From the beginning, of course, the importance of "nature," in one or another of its senses, was never disputed, but for writers like Rapin, Le Bossu, Dryden, Gildon, Dennis, Luzán, Gottsched, G. M. Crescimbeni, and Gravina the major concern was the rules and standards of the art, especially as based on what the great poets had done and on the principles and doctrines of great critics who had based their systems on the practices of the poets, whereas for later writers like Diderot, Rouseau, Johnson, Young, Burke, Kames, Reynolds,

Baretti, Beccaria, Hamann, and Herder, the major concern was some ideal or universal kind or aspect of nature—human, "external," or divine—to which "rules" could be subordinated or in terms of which "art" itself could be defined. Commonly, the example of models of the past which clearly reflected the prior example of nature continued to be maintained as relevant to poetic theory; but explaining the "beauties" and effects of great works in relation primarily to their "natural causes" had become increasingly popular early in the 18th c. (e.g., with Addison, Du Bos, and Fontenelle), and after the middle of the century some writers—e.g., Burke, on the *Sublime and Beautiful* (1757), Lord Kames, in his *Elements of Criticism* (1762), and Beccaria, in his *Ricerche intorno alla natura dello stile* (1770)—sought to reject the guidance not only of established rules of the art but also of all past models ("natural" or "artificial," primitive or refined, ancient or modern, "oriental" or "Hellenic," "vulgar" or "classical"), in favor of direct investigation of natural phenomena; by the close of the century the attempt to establish the true principles of poetic subject matter, structure, and style in "nature" was a very popular activity.

A second development in the period, occurring for the most part concomitantly with this shift of emphasis from art to nature, entailed increasing concern with questions of the powers and habits of the poet as means to the ends, or cause of the effects, of poetry. From the beginning the poet had been required to possess both genius or imagination and judgment or learning (both "nature" and "art"). Moreover, nearly all the great critics of antiquity had made allowance for the spontaneous, for divine inspiration, or for the natural, untutored "original," and by the last quarter of the 17th c. some critics—e.g., Bouhours, in his *Entretiens d'Ariste et d'Eugène* (1671) and Temple, in his essay "Upon Poetry"—had begun to refurbish these old principles. Even without invocation of such a concept as the "je ne sais quoi" (q.v.), the desire to explain or defend the obvious differences in the poetry of different ages and nations led to inquiry into the effects of climate, terrain, political organization, and accidents of history on the mind and practice of the poet, or into the inherent differences of poetic mentality and habits of different races, nations, and languages, especially at different stages of development, or into different *bona fide* kinds and uses of genius that could be looked at as potentially common to all races, ages, and societies. It all amounted to a significant increase in attention given to questions of the poet's mind and conduct; whereas in the earlier years the poet himself had been subordinated, in a

general way, to considerations of the "art" of poetry and the audience, at the close of the 18th c. most poetic theorists did not hesitate to give a central position to the man who produces the poems. It remained, however, the position largely of writer of poetry—of responsibility for certain subject matters, arrangements, styles, and qualities of composition—and to most neocl. critics poetry was significant primarily for its effects upon an audience, not (in any independent sense) for its "sources" in the poetic mind.

Audiences differ, however, and a third important development involved a change in dominant principles of audience appeal; it was scarcely an even and complete alteration of values, but in general by the middle of the 18th c., poetic theorists were willing to reject not only specific preestablished rules of poetry but also the common conceptions of the "proper" audience in terms of which they had frequently been justified. In the earlier years, the dominant concern tended to be either with the accidental but legitimate demands and needs of various kinds of spectators and readers existing in a given society (as for Corneille or Sir Robert Howard) or with the demands of a special man of taste, virtue, or judgment (as for Chapelain, Racine, Voltaire, Dryden, Dennis, Addison, Muratori, Forner); in the later years, it tended to be with the requirements of "general humanity" (as for Johnson) or with the automatic responses of an essential or "natural" human being (as for Burke, Reid, Dugald Stewart, Beccaria, Rousseau). The first basis for such a development lay in the special character of many of the "historical" and comparative inquiries which appeared early in the period. In order, for example, to explain adequately the different subjects and styles of different societies and ages, it was frequently thought to be necessary not only to recognize an author's "rhetorical circumstances." (gifts, education, and special audience demands) but also to assume, at least tacitly, the existence of either a basic humanity, in both the poet and his readers, upon which differences of climate and terrain or social structure could act as differentiating causes (as for Bouhours and Fontenelle), or an ideal of humanity or society from or toward which different societies moved (as for Vico), or some combination of these (as for Shaftesbury); and such inquiries were frequently deliberate attempts to defend works which seemed to violate rules and criteria held to be established in part through analysis of different kinds of readers or through the demands of the "most judicious." Moreover, with the publication of Boileau's translation of Longinus in 1674 and his *Réflexions* on the treatise in 1693, attention was directed to a critical document, however poorly understood, in which, in relation to to the art of sublimity, special differences of audiences are not emphasized. This influence, in turn, was supplemented especially by the increasing amount of theorizing concerning the universal principles of aesthetic response, and by the end of the 18th c. a sort of general "universalizing" of the audience, though in a variety of senses, had taken place.

The growing popularity of Longinus is related to another development, of greater significance for the whole of European criticism: a general shift in dominant interest away from genres and established techniques to general qualities of art and nature—in short, a shift from technical to qualitative poetics. There was no need, in Longinus' analysis of the art of sublimity, for distinctions of poetic genres or special forms of discourse; the quality of sublimity was sought in all forms, and in both prose and verse. However, since early neocl. writers (e.g., Boileau, Dryden, Dennis) tended to work the Longinian terms and doctrines into systems in which distinctions of genre were still important, it is doubtful whether the new popularity of Longinus could alone have brought about the growing vogue of qualitative poetics, and this development, too, was stimulated both by the increasing practice of comparing the poets and poetry of different ages and nations and by the many "philosophical" inquiries concerning the universal bases of the arts. In any case, by the last quarter of the 18th c., concern with poetic genres and types of composition had given way, with few important exceptions (notably in Lessing), to a dominant interest in general qualities or in formal distinctions (e.g., tragedy and epic) translated into qualitative distinctions (e.g., the pathetic or the heroic), by means of which poets and poems could be described and evaluated, comparatively and individually. Thus whereas in the early years (as by Boileau and Dennis, among others) poetic faculties and types of learning, for example, were sometimes systematically adjusted to different species of poems, in the later years (as by Young, Bodmer and Breitinger, and Muratori) such adjustments were made, if at all, to very general qualities of subject matter, mind, and manner. Similarly, whereas in the early years (as by Rapin and Dryden) audiences were sometimes differentiated in part on the basis of their demand for different species or styles, in the later years (as by Beaumarchais, Hume, Goldsmith) they were differentiated, if at all, on the basis of their demand for or response to general qualities of subject matter and expression.

Finally, in most of the earlier examples of qualitative poetics—notably in Boileau, Dryden, and Muratori—the emphasis tended to be on qualities (e.g., wit and judgment, regularity and irregularity) referring to the matter and manner of works conceived at least in part as the products of art (and often related to models of the past upon which "specific" rules had been based), whereas in the later examples—notably in Johnson, Herder, and Pagano—the qualities (e.g., the sublime and the beautiful, "truth" and novelty) tended to be drawn consciously and more directly from some view of nature, as related to the mind of the poet, the properties of the universe, or the response of the audience. No radically new terminology was necessary for this development, of course, since the issues of "art" and "nature" had always been present in both technical and qualitative poetics, in the works, for example, of both Horace and Longinus, and since the qualitative terms, whatever their original significance, received their special meanings from the immediate "natural" or "artificial" frameworks in which they were employed.

Nor was any major revolution necessary against the characteristic neocl. orientation toward the demands, needs, and responses of the audience. Nevertheless, when the emphasis came to be placed on the natural responses or needs of a "universal" human being instead of the demands of specially differentiated kinds of readers, it was relatively easy for the poet also to be viewed "universally" in terms of natural response and conduct, and with the general increase of interest in the mind of the poet and the rise of a mode of qualitative poetics whose values and ideals often had reference especially to poetic mentality, transition was easy to the period we call "romantic," in which "poetry" (as a superior quality of thought and expression) could be distinguished from "poems," and in which the main controlling reference in poetics was no longer the audience but the psychology and moral nature of the poet.

SOME ADDITIONAL PRIMARY WORKS: J. Dryden, *Essay of Heroic Plays* (1672); T. Hobbes, "Preface to Homer's Odysses" (1675); T. Rymer, *A Short View of Tragedy* (1693); Dryden, Dedication of the *Aeneis* (1697); J. Dennis, *Grounds of Crit. in Poetry* (1704); A. A. Cooper (Third Earl of Shaftesbury), *Soliloquy; or Advice to an Author* (1710); J. Trapp, *Praelectiones poeticae* (1711–15); C. Gildon, *Complete Art of Poetry* (1718); J. Spence, *Essay on Mr. Pope's Odyssey* (1726–27); R. Lowth, *De sacra poesi Hebraeorum praelectiones* (1753); T. Warton, *Observations on the Fairy Queen* (1754, 62); J. Warton, *Essay on the Genius and Writings of Pope* (1756, 82); O. Goldsmith, *Present State of Polite Learning in Europe* (1759); E. Young, *Conjectures on Original Composition* (1759); R. Hurd, *Letters on Chiv-*

alry and Romance (1762); H. Blair, Crit. Dissertation on the Poems of Ossian (1763); Hurd, "The Idea of Universal Poetry" (1765); R. Wood, Essay on the Original Genius and Writings of Homer (1769); J. Reynolds, Discourses (1769–90); P. Stockdale, Inquiry into the Nature and Genuine Laws of Poetry (1778); Blair. Lectures on Rhetoric and Belles Lettres (1783).—P. Corneille, Discours and Examens (1660); J.-B. Poquelin (Molière), Préface de Tartuffe (1664); J. Racine, Préfaces (1664–91); C. M. Saint-Denis (Saint-Évremond), Sur les caractères des tragédies (1672); R. le Bossu, Traité du poème épique (1675); Saint-Évremond, Sur les poèmes des anciens (1685); B. B. de Fontenelle, Digression sur les anciens et les modernes (1688); C. Perrault, Parallèles des anciens et des modernes (1688–97); J.-B. Bossuet, Maximes et réflexions sur la comédie (1694); F. M. Arouet (Voltaire), Vie de Molière (1739); "Dissertation sur la tragédie ancienne et moderne" (in Sémiramis; 1748); G.-L. Leclerc (Comte de Buffon), Discours sur le style (1753); D. Diderot, Discours sur la poesie dramatique (1758); J.-J. Rousseau, Lettre à D'Alembert sur les spectacles (1758); Voltaire, Commentaires sur Corneille (1764).—B. J. Feijóo, Teatro crítico universal (1724–41); A. de Montiano y Luyando, Discursos sobres las tragedias españolas (1750–53); N. F. de Moratín, Desengaños al teatro español (1762); F. Nieto de Molina, Los críticos de Madrid, en defensa de las comedias antiquas y en contra de las modernas (1768); A. de Capmany, Filosofia de la elocuencia (1777); V. de los Ríos, Análisis del Quijote (1780); J. P. Forner, El asno erudito (1782); T. de Iriarte, Fábulas literarias (1782); Forner, Oración apologética por la España y su mérito literario (1786); M. J. Quintana, Las reglas del drama (1791); S. Barbero, Principios de retórica y poética (1805).— G. M. Crescimbeni, Della volgar poesia (1700); L. A. Muratori, Della perfetta poesia italiana (1706); G. C. Becelli, Della novella poesia, cioè del vero genere e particolari bellezze della poesia ital. (1732); S. Bettinelli, Lettere Virgiliane (1757); G. Gozzi, Giudizio degli antichi poeti sopra le moderne censure di Dante (1758); M. Cesarotti, Ragionamento sopra il diletto della tragedia (1762); G. Baretti, La frusta letteraria (1763–65); M. Zanotti, Dell'arte poetica (1768); G. Tiraboschi, Storia della lett. ital. (1772–82); G. Parini, Sui principi di belle lettere (1773–75); C. Goldoni, Memoirs (1783–87); M. Pagano, Sull'origine e natura della poesia (1783); V. Alfieri, Del principe e delle lettere (1788).—J. J. Bodmer and J. J. Breitinger, Von dem Einfluss und Gebrauche der Einbildungskraft (1727); J. C. Gottsched, Ausführliche Redekunst (1736); Breitinger, Critische Abhandlung von der Natur, den Absichten und dem Gebrauche der Gleichnisse

(1740); Critische Dichtkunst (1740); Bodmer, Critische Betrachtung über die poetischen Gemälde der Dichter (1741); Critische Briefe (1746); J. G. Hamann, Kreuzzüge des Philologen (1762); H. W.-von Gerstenberg, Briefe über Merkwürdigkeiten der Lit. (1766–67); J. G. Sulzer, Allgemeine Theorie der schönen Künste (1771–74); J. G. Herder, Vom Geist der Ebräischen Poesie (1783).

SECONDARY WORKS: J. G. Robertson, Studies in the Genesis of Romantic Theory in the 18th C. (1923) ; Crane, Critics; Wellek, I.; J. W. Draper, 18th C. Eng. Aesthetics: A Bibliog. (1931); S. H. Monk, The Sublime (1935); CBEL, II; R. Wellek, The Rise of Eng. Lit. Hist. (1941); J. W. H. Atkins, Eng. Lit. Crit.: 17th and 18th C. (1951); A. Bosker, Lit. Crit. in the Age of Johnson (2d ed., Groningen, 1953); R. S. Crane, "Eng. Neo-Classical Crit.," in Shipley and "On Writing the Hist. of Eng. Crit., 1650–1800," UTQ, 22 (1953).—Bray; G. Lanson, Manuel bibliographique de la litt. fr. moderne, XVIe au XIXe s. (new ed., 1921); A Crit. Bibliog. of Fr. Lit., ed. D. C. Cabeen (IV, 1951).—F. Fernández y González, Historia de la crítica literaria en España . . . (5 v., 1867); M. Menéndez y Pelayo, Hist. de las ideas esteticas en España (2d ed., 9 v., unfinished, 1890–1912); J. Hurtado and A. González-Palencia, Hist. de la lit. española (6th ed., 1949).—B. Croce, Estetica (1902, Eng. tr. D. Ainslie [1921]); H. Quigley, Italy and the Rise of a New School of Crit. in the 18th C. (1923); Storia letteraria d'Italia (13 v., 1929–35; Il Seicento by A. Belloni [1929]; Il Settecento by G. Natali [3d ed., 2 v., 1950]); M. Fubini, Dal Muratori al Baretti (1946); "Arcadia e illuminismo," Questioni e correnti di storia letteraria (v. III of Problemi ed orientamenti critici di lingua e di lett. ital., ed. A. Momigliano [1949]).— E. Grucker, Hist. des doctrines litt. et esthétiques en Allemagne (1883); K. Borinski, Die Antike in Poetik und Kunsttheorie . . . (2 v., 1914–23); Annalen der deutschen Lit., ed. H. O. Burger (1952); O. Olzien, Bibliog. zur deutschen Lit. (1953; 1955; suppls. to the Burger, Annalen). R.M.

NEOCLASSICISM. See CLASSICISM.

NEOGONGORISM. Hispanic ultraism (q.v.) led the young writers of Spain and Sp. America toward a new gongorism in which the attempt to create striking metaphors was intrinsic. García Lorca, Jorge Guillén, Gerardo Diego and Rafael Alberti of Spain all loudly espoused the poetic genius of Góngora in speech and writing. The revival of interest in the classic Góngora, blended with 20th c. literary tendencies, and fused onto the rock of popular language and tradition, provided the keynotes of Hispanic poetry of the post-war era. Lorca, quoting Góngora, pointed out that the only thing which could give a kind of immortality to a poem was "a chain of images."—*Antología poética en honor de Góngora, desde Lope de Vega a Rubén Darío*, ed. G. Diego (1927).　　　　　　　　　　J.A.C.

NEO-HUMANISM. A movement in Am. criticism which had greatest impact in the years 1915–33. Neo-h. had no direct relationship to Renaissance humanism or to other expressions of humanism in letters and philosophy, except to emphasize human dignity, moral strenuousness, and exercise of the will and reason. Primarily, neo-h. defended conservative ethical, political, and aesthetic standards against 19th-c. romantics, liberals, and empiricists and their 20th-c. counterparts. Irving Babbitt (1865–1933) in *Literature and the Am. College* (1908) formulated its program which remained essentially unchanged; and Paul Elmer More (1864–1937) was his associate.

Despite their emphasis upon reason, the neo-humanists felt that ultimately intuition was the source of philosophical truth. Certain permanent, distinctively "human" qualities, they said, could be ascertained by looking within; they thus took over the neoclassic concept of ethical and aesthetic universals. They not only repudiated all formal philosophies based upon nature, like those of Dewey, James, and Bergson, but the romantic nature-worship of 19th-c. poets like Wordsworth, Coleridge, Emerson, Goethe, Byron, Meredith, and Whitman. They also condemned a negative approach to nature like that of Thomas Hardy. To ethical emphasis in these and other writers, the neo-humanists were, however, sympathetic; and they tended to judge literature by ethical rather than by aesthetic criteria. Drawing heavily on Christian moral tradition while opposing Christian dogma and formal theology, the neo-humanists pictured man in a continuing, dualistic struggle between lower and higher impulses, between expansive natural desires and the "inner check" or "will to refrain." At the end of his life, Paul Elmer More came to feel that the absolute nature of the values he had embraced required the additional sanction of revealed religion.

The neo-humanists owed much to Matthew Arnold. They distrusted his liberal bias in politics and religion, and they sometimes thought he was too subjective in his judgments; but on the whole they regarded him as their chief 19th-c. precursor. His condemnation of the romantics, his ethical view of literature, his conviction that the "best self" (compare More's "inner check") must prevail over the "ordinary self," his view of man as discontinuous with nature, and his belief in an intellectual aristocracy (a "saving remnant")—all ally him with the neo-humanists.

In literature, the neo-humanists were hostile to the concept of original genius, particularly in the work of Rousseau and of 19th-c. writers. In his best book, *Rousseau and Romanticism* (1919), Babbitt flayed Rousseau and the romantic poets for their primitivism, optimism, and uncontrolled emotionalism. As classicists, the neo-humanists stressed the rational rather than the emotional in art and life; perfection of form rather than experimentalism; serenity, order and repose rather than manifestations of undisciplined creative energy. In emphasizing the need for selection of detail, they were hostile to realism in poetry and fiction. In *The Genteel Tradition at Bay* (1931) George Santayana judged neo-h. to be a survival from the genteel tradition in Am. culture; in the aversion of neo-humanists to literary realism, in their squeamishness about sexual experience, in their emphasis upon the identity of the good, the true and the beautiful, and in their moralism they perhaps deserved Santayana's criticism. The neo-humanists, however, repudiated genteel ideality and optimism. In Babbitt's *Democracy and Leadership* (1924) and More's *Aristocracy and Justice* (1915), anti-democratic, antihumanitarian, and anti-individualistic tendencies of the movement are evident.

From the beginning of World War I until about 1924, Stuart P. Sherman (1881–1926) was chief spokesman for neo-h. After his defection to modernism in 1924 as first editor of *New York Herald Tribune "Books"* and his accidental death in 1926, the chief popular and academic publicist for the movement was Norman Foerster (1887–) in *American Criticism* (1928), *Toward Standards* (1930), and the anthology he edited, *Humanism and America* (1930). The attack upon the neo-humanists was represented in another anthology edited by C. Hartley Grattan, *The Critique of Humanism* (1930). With the publication of these anthologies and with Babbitt's death in 1933, the movement had spent its force. The principal issues in "the great critical debate" between neo-humanists and their liberal and radical opponents in the 1920's and early 1930's were the extent of the artist's freedom to create without restriction, the relationship between the absolute and the relative, and the relevance of philosophic naturalism to the spiritual life.

For lasting significance in criticism and aesthetics, the neo-humanists were too negative, too concerned with the ethical, too inflexible in applying their formulas, and too unsympathetic to modern literature. In insisting upon standards for literary judgment when criticism had become largely impressionistic, in challenging the frequently deterministic implications of modern naturalism, and in emphasizing—like Pound and Eliot later—the philosophical inadequacies of romanticism, they had an important and beneficial influence. More's critical instincts were sounder than Babbitt's, and at his best he achieved Arnold's fusion of discriminating sensibility with moral insight. In the *Shelburne Essays*—the chief contribution to literature by the neo-humanists—More exposed incisively the ideological weaknesses, in particular, of the Eng. Victorian and romantic poets. From the neo-humanists, Eliot in part developed his conservative and classical bias, though he repudiated their aesthetic insensitivity and their rejection of formal Christianity. Either directly or through Eliot, other critics and poets like the Southern Agrarians (Ransom, Tate, Warren, Donald Davidson) and Yvor Winters were influenced to adopt conservative moral, aesthetic and religious standards.

See books by and about writers mentioned. Also the following: L. J. A. Mercier, *Le Mouvement humaniste aux Etats-Unis* (1928), *The Challenge of Humanism* (1933); *I'll Take My Stand, the South and the Agrarian Trad. by Twelve Southerners* (Ransom, Tate *et al;* 1930); T. S. Eliot, "The Humanism of Irving Babbitt," and "Second Thoughts on Humanism," *Selected Essays* (1932, 1950); L. Lewisohn, *Expression in America* (1932); *Lit. Opinion in America*, ed. M. D. Zabel (1937, 2d ed., 1951); R. Shafer, *Paul Elmer More and Am. Crit.* (1938); E. Wilson, *The Triple Thinkers* (1938); R. P. Blackmur, "Humanism and the Symbolic Imagination," *Southern Review*, 7 (1941); A. Kazin, *On Native Grounds* (1942); J. P. Pritchard, *Return to the Fountains* (1942) and *Crit. in America* (1956); Y. Winters, *In Defense of Reason* (1947); R. E. Spiller, "The Battle of the Books," *A Lit. Hist. of the U.S.*, ed. R. E. Spiller *et al.,* II (1949); W. V. O'Connor, *An Age of Crit., 1900–1950* (1952); *The Development of Am. Lit. Crit.*, ed. F. Stovall (1954), pp. 159–98; *The Achievement of Am. Crit.*, ed. C. A. Brown (1954); F. J. Hoffman, *The Twenties* (1955); J. H. Raleigh, *Matthew Arnold and Am. Culture* (1957); A. Warren, "The 'New Humanism' Twenty Years After," *Modern Age* (1959); A. H. Dakin, *Paul Elmer More* (1960); Sutton.   F.P.W.MCD.

NEOPLATONISM. See PLATONISM AND POETRY.

NEOTERICI (L. "the new ones"). The name given by Cicero to the coterie of "new poets" of his age who took their inspiration and models from the Gr. Alexandrians. Catullus is the most famous, but others whose work survives in fragments are Calvus, Cinna, Cornificius, Furius Bibaculus, and Ticidas. Diomedes

and Terentianus Maurus, grammarians, cite another group of n. who flourished during the reign of Hadrian. Their verse was characterized by tricks of meter, scansion, and syntax with variety and cleverness at a premium.— A. Baehrens, *Fragmenta Poetarum Romanorum* (1886); C. L. Neudling, *A Prosopography to Catullus* (1957); K. Quinn, *The Catullan Revolution* (1959).   R.A.H.

NEO-THOMISM AND POETRY. For the neo-Thomist, poetry is essentially the artistic realization of a unique form of knowledge. St. Thomas Aquinas conceded this vestigially when he wrote that poetic knowledge or "poetica scientia" cannot be seized by but must beguile the reason by certain similitudes ("quibusdem similitudinibus"). Because of the paucity of allusion to poetry in St. Thomas' writings, it has remained the lot of such contemporary Thomists as Maurice de Wulf, Thomas Gilby, John Duffy, Eric Gill, E. I. Watkin and, particularly, Jacques Maritain to formulate more fully the meaning of poetry in the Scholastic tradition.

Maritain, for example, has written that poetry originates, according to a recent paraphrase, in a moment of "subjective communion with objective reality" (W. K. Wimsatt, Jr., and C. Brooks, *Literary Criticism, A Short History*, 1957, p. 753). Maritain explains that such a communion brings into existence in the poet a true and existential knowledge of the object he is contemplating. This "poetic knowledge" is intuitive rather than discursive, experiential and connatural rather than conceptual, originating in "intuitions of sense." Gilby has noted that poetic knowledge is actually capable of being acquired *only* when "intelligence" is "united with sense" (*Poetic Experience*, 1933, p. 17). In brief, the germinative power of poetry is inherent in poetic knowledge. As Maritain has written, poetic knowledge is "the intrinsic moment from which creation emanates" (*The Range of Reason*, 1952, p. 18). Such knowledge, by nature inexpressible in concepts or judgments, demands, in the case of a true poet, to "take form in a poem."

To make possible the conversion of poetic knowledge into the completed poem, Maritain claims that the poet must be actuated by an inspiration, "a creative impulse transcending the limits of reason and employing as it elevates every rational energy of art" (*Art and Scholasticism*, 1927, p. 54). Inspiration in turn actuates the all-important creative intuition, "the incitation to create," which immediately begins to reshape the sense-intuitions constituting poetic knowledge into the first, primitive forms of the yet-to-be-perfected poem. The process of art, which is the process of making or productive action (*factibile*), originates when the creative intuition starts to operate, when the creative idea of the poet catalyzes and transfigures poetic knowledge into new and artistically beautiful forms. What results in the finished poem, therefore, is both a simultaneous and integrated revelation of objective reality (intuitively apprehended and artistically re-created) together with something of the creative subjectivity of the poet himself. The poem thus becomes both "an obscure grasping of the real" as well as "an obscure grasping of the soul of the poet" (Maritain, *The Situation of Poetry*, 1955, p. 84).

True poetry, according to Maritain, is thus characterized by a spirit of "transfigurative realism," which is opposed to representationalism and naturalism on the one hand and nonrepresentationalism and suprematism on the other. Maurice de Wulf notes that it springs from a need "to interpret and dominate reality" (*Art and Beauty*, 1950, p. 30). Such transfigurative realism implies that there is a fusion in the poem of the poet's subjectivity together with the reality whose existence he has intuitively shared, known and re-created. Since the poet's knowledge of reality is inextricably involved with himself, his poetry becomes a vision of himself in things, as it were. In this regard, Duffy has stated that the poet's contemplation of a poem is one of "complete penetration" even "while the poem is being created" (*A Philosophy of Poetry Based on Thomistic Principles*, 1945, p. 217). Similarly, E. I. Watkin has written that "the artist's personality largely determines what significant forms he shall see in nature and shall display, and under what aspect he shall see and display them" (*A Philosophy of Form*, 1935, p. 350).

The signally important term in the Thomistic theory of poetry as Maritain has interpreted it is the creative intuition, which is the indispensable link between the acquisition of poetic knowledge and the actual exercise of the virtue of art in the making of a poem. Creative intuition makes poetic expression possible by releasing and shaping poetic knowledge for artistic ends. It locates the source of poetry in the intellect's intuitive activity and determines, by its presence or absence in a poem, whether a poem is genuine or pastiche. Although poetic knowledge and inspiration are important to the poetic process, it is the creative intuition "to which the entire work to be engendered in beauty, in its perfect singularity as a kind of unique cosmos, is appendent" (*Creative Intuition in Art and Poetry*, 1953, pp. 59–60). By identifying the creative intuition as "the first ontological root of the artistic activity," Maritain is able to give a final definition of poetry as a "divination of

the spiritual in the things of sense, which will also express itself in the things of sense" (*Art and Scholasticism*, p. 75).—J. Maritain, *Art and Poetry* (1945), *Art and Faith* (with J. Cocteau, 1948); R. W. Rauch, "Esthetic of Maritain," *Thought*, 6 (1931); Gilbert and Kuhn; E. Gill, *Autobiography* (1941); G. A. McCauliff, "Intuition in Christian Lit.," *Ren.*, 3 (1951); S. J. Hazo, "An Analysis of the Aesthetic of J. Maritain" (unpubl. diss., Univ. of Pgh., 1957) ; F. J. Kovach, *Die Ästhetik des Thomas von Aquin* (1961). s.h.

NEW CRITICISM. The n.c. is perhaps not susceptible of a formal definition, for "new" in this context is not much more than a vague pointer. When John Crowe Ransom published *The New Criticism* in 1941 he apparently meant no more than to designate the criticism then current. (Either he was not aware of, or not concerned with, the fact that Joel E. Spingarn had already preempted the term in a different connection—in an address delivered at Columbia University in 1910.) The critics with whom Ransom was primarily concerned were I. A. Richards, William Empson, T. S. Eliot, and Yvor Winters. But Ransom's book was a sustained, though respectful, attack upon these four figures; and the critic that he desired to see, an "ontological critic," was conspicuous by his absence from the modern scene. The book closed with an invitation for him to appear. Ransom showed himself fully aware of the sharp differences in assumptions and method that separated the modern critics whom he discussed, and he did not insist upon such traits as they held in common. Yet with the publication of his book, "the n.c." as the name of a species gained immediate currency, and has been used constantly, if not very responsibly, ever since.

There are doubtless reasons for this phenomenon. The increased critical activity in our time has brought about the need for a term that would characterize a kind of literary interest which, though difficult to define, seems to many people clearly to exist. Certain polemicists have seized upon the term with joy, content with allowing it to mean no more than "that criticism that I don't like." On the other hand, critics like Allen Tate, R. P. Blackmur, Kenneth Burke—not to mention those discussed in *The New Criticism*—have resisted acceptance of the term and would have great difficulty in recognizing themselves as the members of a guild.

One aspect of the n.c. which is often seized upon as central is the "close reading" of poetry, and certainly a concern for nuances of words and shades of meaning has characterized much of modern criticism. But "close reading" as such is a superficial trait. The Fr. *explica-*

tion de texte involves close reading but few would call it "n.c." Much will depend upon what one intends to do with a text and upon what he regards as an adequate reading of it. The application of semantics to literary study, a development which owes most to men like I. A. Richards and William Empson, has indeed been very important. Yet the early Richards' affective bias and Empson's inveterate psychologizing about both writer and reader run quite counter to the antiexpressionistic tendencies of a T. S. Eliot, for example, or to the insistence on a *cognitive* criticism by other "new critics."

Other foci of interest have to be taken into account. An important one has been a concern with a specifically *literary* criticism as distinguished from a study of sources or of social backgrounds or of the history of ideas or of the political and social effects of literature. The n.c. has tended to explore the structure of the work rather than the mind and personality of the artist or the reactions of his various readers. No one is forgetting (though the critics in question have frequently been accused of forgetting) that literary works are written by human beings, and may exert all sorts of effects upon the human beings who read them. But the "new critics" have characteristically attempted to deal with the literary object itself rather than with its origins and effects—to give a formal rather than a genetic or affective account of literature.

In this connection one may recall that a number of years ago I. A. Richards argued that we needed a spell of purer criticism before we returned to the problems of the interrelation of man's various activities. The "new critics" may be said to have undertaken seriously this purification of literary criticism though surely at the risk of being blamed for having cut literature off from life. The related charge that the n.c. represents a revival of the doctrine of art for art's sake runs into complications when one notices how many of this group have a definite religious position. (Perhaps because they do, they have found it the easier to reject Matthew Arnold's attempt to have poetry assume the duties of religion. They have attempted to distinguish art from religion and morality rather than to make art a substitute for religion and morality.)

Another aspect of the n.c. is to be seen in its resolute attempt to set up an organic theory of literature. One of the few things which these critics do have in common is a profound distrust of the old dualism of form and content, and a real sense of the failure of an ornamentalist rhetoric to do justice to the interpenetration of the form and matter achieved in a really well-written work. These critics, then, have attempted to take the full context into account and to see each individual word of a work, not only as contributing to the context, but as deriving its exact meaning from its place in the context. Hence the development of terms like irony, plurisignation, ambiguity, etc., to indicate the richness and complication of meanings developed in a poetic context.

The concern of the new critics with the structure of a work including the intricacies of structure has led to a number of attacks upon this criticism as being too narrowly concerned with the verbal medium. This was the gist of the attack by the University of Chicago critics some years ago in their volume *Critics and Criticism;* and also, more moderately, of Francis Fergusson in his *The Idea of a Theater* (1949). Such critics, remembering their Aristotle, would find the soul of a work in its "plot" or "action," and not in the words which they regard as merely the means for exhibiting that action. But this conception of the "verbal medium" seems to deny the organic theory of art—at least as it is interpreted by the "new critics." The kind of distinction proposed seems to reintroduce the old dualism, this time between a nonlinguistic meaning and words as mere husks of meaning. The new critics would refuse to admit any divorce of words from action in any such sense. For they are interested in words as nodes of meaning, and literary form is for them the very organization of meaning.

Here follows a very brief selected bibliog. The works are of varying merit. Some are cited because they represent typical responses to the n.c.: J. C. Ransom, *The N.C.* (1941); S. Hyman, *The Armed Vision* (1948); A. Tate, *On the Limits of Poetry* (1948); W. Elton, *A Glossary of the N.C.* (rev. ed., 1949); *Critiques and Essays in Crit., 1920–1948,* ed. R. W. Stallman (1949; extensive bibliog.); D. Daiches, *Crit. Approaches to Lit.* (1956); Krieger; J. P. Pritchard, *Crit. in America* (1956); Wellek and Warren, 2d ed.; Wimsatt and Brooks; R. Foster, *The New Romantics, a Reappraisal of the N.C.* (1962). C.B.

NEW HUMANISM. See NEO-HUMANISM.

NEW NORSE. A Norwegian language norm constructed by Ivar Aasen (1813–96) from the less adulterated rustic dialects in order to give his country a language directly descended from ON and to provide the rural population, constrained by Dano-Norwegian, with a natural medium of literary expression. In a modest way Aasen proved the poetic viability of his *landsmaal* (now called *nynorsk*—New Norse). Formally notable is *Haraldshaugen* (The Mound of King Harold), in which he achieved

a masterly recreation, with addition of end rhyme, of the ON alliterative measure *fornyrðislag* (q.v.). Of later poets who helped to create the national N.N. poetry envisaged by Aasen may be mentioned Aasmund Vinje, Arne Garborg, and Olav Aukrust, who demonstrated the remarkable power and rich melody of the new medium. In present-day Norway, N.N. enjoys the same official status as the *bokmål*, a misnomer ("literary language") for Dano-Norwegian.—H. Bourgeois, "Une Langue nouvelle: La 'Landsmaal' norvégienne," *Revue de linguistique et de philologie comparée*, 43 (1910); I. Lillehei, "*Landsmaal* and the Language Movement in Norway," JEGP, 13 (1914); O. J. Falnes, *National Romanticism in Norway* (1933).
S.L.

NEW ZEALAND POETRY. New Zealand's small and recent literature shows greater diversity and development in poetry than in any other form. Although it is essentially true that this poetry did not begin to mature till after World War I, it began to exist over a century ago. The early settlers were often cultured men, and some wrote verse, like Alfred Domett's Maori epic *Ranolf and Amohia* (1872), which imitates the more popular romantic and Victorian poets.

A tradition of vernacular rhyming survived in local laureates like John Barr of Craigilee; but the country inherited little that was validly traditional. "Serious" verse, such as that of the journalist and politician Thomas Bracken, was fluent and undistinguished; and the real sense of historic events—exploration, settlement, Maori wars, gold rushes—remained unexpressed. Even when the colonists wrote best, on the country's impressive landscapes, the work was often false-colored by nostalgia for their Eng. "Home."

The 1890's brought modest prosperity, and second-generation settlers became conscious of themselves as a people. William Pember Reeves, Parliamentarian and reformer, spoke in easy and popular verse for the idea of N.Z. as "social laboratory"; the work of Jessie Mackay and Blanche Baughan showed a stronger and more genuine talent. But, on the whole, the anxious desire for a distinctive national literature did not begin to be realized for another generation.

Early 20th-c. writers shared the mediocrity of contemporary Eng. poets who were often their models; but, like certain of the Eng. "Georgians," some achieved significant poetry without radical innovations of manner—Arnold Wall, Alan Mulgan, J. C. Beaglehole, and, even more, Ursula Bethell and Eileen Duggan, Walter D'Arcy Creswell and R. A. K. Mason. Ursula Bethell described the Canterbury scene with virtuosity and an intense contemplative affection. Eileen Duggan has evolved independently the concrete and energetic idiom of her later poems. Creswell and Mason both strike out attitudes toward their country: Creswell's, more highly mannered, expresses the ambivalent emotion of a kind of exasperated love affair; Mason's is that of a Roman stoic, looking on the brevity of life and the fall of empires.

Although many of the poems collected in *Kowhai Gold* (1930) were still feeble, changes had begun in the 1920's. It is only roughly true to think that the achievements of modern N.Z. poetry began in the 1930's, and to connect them with the depression, political ferment, social anger, and the conscious experience of a growing community finding its place in a disturbed world. N.Z. poets came abreast of European writers—not only the younger Eng. poets (Auden, MacNeice, etc.) with whom they seemed to have most in common, but older masters like Eliot, Pound, or Rilke. It was, however, a transformation rather than a revolution. The whole process can be seen in the work of the versatile "Robin Hyde" (Iris Wilkinson), which develops from late romantic aestheticism to a contemporary idiom; another kind of example is the accomplished traditional verse of J. R. Hervey and Basil Dowling.

The mature work of older poets overlapped with that of younger men, particularly A. R. D. Fairburn, Allen Curnow, Denis Glover, and Charles Brasch. In expression they can be both tough and sensitive, romantic and ironic, as can be seen in a long sequence like Fairburn's *Dominion* or a short lyric like Brasch's *A View of Rangitoto*. They have a developed awareness of their own country as well as of the general human situation, most clearly voiced by Curnow, who sees his country's history as a continuing reality in time:

> All in that strange sea-dimension
> Where Time and Island cross.

At the end of this period it could be seen that N.Z. poetry was coming of age: this is marked by the appearance in 1940 of McCormick's study and M. H. Holcroft's essays (see bibliography), and a few years later, of Curnow's anthology and the first issues of Brasch's periodical, *Landfall*.

These expressed, among other things, a myth of N.Z. as an island place, distinct in space and time, enigmatic, even hostile, in which the writer could see reflected his own situation, and in discovering which he discovered himself. A body of symbols reflecting this understanding—island, ocean, beach, mountain, "bush"—has arisen naturally and become common to nearly all N.Z. writers, e.g., Ursula

Bethell's *The Long Harbour*, Creswell's *Lyttleton Harbour*, Curnow's *At Dead Low Water*, Fairburn's *Letter to a Friend in the Wilderness*. The type-figure of the solitary, the unattached man (Mason's swagman, or Glover's Harry or Arawata Bill) links this mental landscape with some significant N.Z. fiction.

Among the most recent poets, there has been a conscious and sometimes factitious reaction against this "myth of insularity." In practice this means that certain writers have widened their range of reference to include more of the urban scene and to accept the influence, e.g., of Baudelaire, Hart Crane, Robert Lowell, or Dylan Thomas. A similar indication is the growing tendency toward the longer poem or sequence, as in Alistair Campbell's *Elegy*, Keith Sinclair's *Ballad of Half-Moon Bay*, or Pat Wilson's *Staying at Ballisodare*. Yet this newer work often represents an extension, rather than an extinction, of the island-myth and what it signifies, as can be seen also in the poetry of Kendrick Smithyman, Mary Stanley, Ruth Dallas, and others whose work is represented in Louis Johnson's annual anthology. Most of all it appears with varied range and tone in James K. Baxter, who combines the attitudes of the *poète maudit* (q.v.) and the bard.

Despite its limited public, N.Z. poetry has been quite liberally published in recent years; and few poets are exempt from the danger of sometimes publishing below themselves. Opportunities for extended criticism are few, and it seems that N.Z. poetry has reached the stage where criticism—and self-criticism—is what it most needs. The writers of the last thirty years have at least produced a body of work upon which such criticism can properly operate.

ANTHOLOGIES: *N.Z. Verse*, ed. W. F. Alexander and A. E. Currie (1906), rev. but without preface as *A Treasury of N.Z. Verse* (1926); *Kowhai Gold*, ed. Q. Pope (1930); *Lyric Poems of N.Z., 1928–42*, ed. C. A. Marris (n.d.); *A Book of N.Z. Verse, 1923–45*, ed. A. Curnow (1945; rev. ed. 1950; an important anthol. with preface); *N.Z. Poetry Yearbook*, ed. L. Johnson (1951–); *An Anthol. of N.Z. Verse*, ed. R. M. Chapman and J. Bennett (1956; comprehensive and up-to-date); *Penguin Book of N.Z. Verse*, ed. A. Curnow (1959).

HISTORY AND CRITICISM: E. H. McCormick, *Letters and Art in N.Z.* (1940); M. H. Holcroft, *The Deepening Stream* (1940), *The Waiting Hills* (1943), *Encircling Seas* (1946, collected as *Discovered Isles*, 1951); J. C. Reid, *Creative Writing in N.Z.* (1946, two brief but informative chapters on poetry); J. K. Baxter, *Recent Trends in N.Z. Poetry* (1951) and *The Fire and the Anvil* (1955); E. H. McCormick, *N.Z. Lit., a Survey* (1959; "based on *Letters and Art in N.Z.*"). M.K.J.

NIBELUNGEN STANZA, *Nibelungenstrophe, Kürenbergstrophe*. The most important stanza of Middle High German epic poetry, it is named from its use in the *Nibelungenlied*, although its earliest recorded use is by Der von Kürenberg (fl. 1150–70). It is composed of 2 pairs of lines (*Langzeilen*). For a long time Heusler's somewhat conjectural analysis of the N. stanza was accepted as authentic: A line consists of 2 hemistichs (*Kurzzeilen*), of which the first usually contains 4 stresses, the third and fourth stresses occurring in the same word (*klingende Kadenz*), while in the second hemistich the fourth stress is replaced by a metrical pause (*stumpfe Kadenz*) except for the last hemistich of the stanza which has 4 stressed syllables. Thus, ending with a full cadence, the stanza has the character of a distinct formal unit. Its basic scheme is as follows:

$$\overset{\prime}{-} - \overset{\prime}{-} - \overset{\prime}{-} - \overset{\prime\prime}{\wedge}\,\|\,\overset{\prime}{-} - \overset{\prime}{-} - \overset{\prime}{-} - \overset{\prime}{\underline{\wedge}}$$
$$\overset{\prime}{-} - \overset{\prime}{-} - \overset{\prime}{-} - \overset{\prime\prime}{\wedge}\,\|\,\overset{\prime}{-} - \overset{\prime}{-} - \overset{\prime}{-} - \overset{\prime}{\underline{\wedge}}$$
$$\overset{\prime}{-} - \overset{\prime}{-} - \overset{\prime}{-} - \overset{\prime\prime}{\wedge}\,\|\,\overset{\prime}{-} - \overset{\prime}{-} - \overset{\prime}{-} - \overset{\prime}{\underline{\wedge}}$$
$$\overset{\prime}{-} - \overset{\prime}{-} - \overset{\prime}{-} - \overset{\prime\prime}{\wedge}\,\|\,\overset{\prime}{-} - \overset{\prime}{-} - \overset{\prime}{-} - \overset{\prime}{-}$$

The rhyme scheme for hemistichs 2, 4, 6, 8 is aabb; caesural rhyme occurs occasionally. Modern prosodists (Thomas, Glier) confine themselves to a purely and cautiously descriptive formula according to which hemistichs 1 to 7 contain three stresses each, the eighth 4, and 1, 3, 5, 7 as a rule have feminine and 2, 4, 6, 8 show masculine endings. The use of the N. stanza has continued over the centuries in many variants, e.g., among the *Meistersinger* (q.v.) as "Hönweis," in the church hymn (P. Gerard, *O Haupt voll Blut und Wunden*), and in the modern worldly *Lied*, especially among the romanticists (L. Uhland, *Des Sängers Fluch*), even in the drama (Z. Werner, *Die Söhne des Thals*, (1803).—A. Heusler, *Deutsche Versgesch.* (3 v., 1925–29) and *Nibelungensage und Nibelungenlied* (4th ed., 1944); P. Habermann, "N. Strophe," *Reallexikon*, II; F. Panzer, *Das Nibelungenlied* (1955); U. Pretzel and H. Thomas, "Dt. Verskunst, mit einem Beitrag über altdt. Strophik von H. Thomas," *Dt. Philologie im Aufriss*, ed. W. Stammler, III (1957); O. Paul and I. Glier, *Dt. Metrik* (4th ed., 1961). U.K.G.

NICARAGUAN POETRY. See SPANISH AMERICAN POETRY.

NIL VOLENTIBUS ARDUUM (Nothing is Difficult to the Willing). A society of Dutch poets, founded at Amsterdam in 1669 by Lodewijk Meyer, Andries Pels, and others. The major concern of the society was the establishment of Fr. neoclassical artistic principles in Dutch dramatic poetry. The members of the

N.V.A. interpreted these principles so strictly that they condemned not only the decadent and sensational drama of Jan Vos and Blasius but also the earlier classical drama of Hooft and Vondel, since regarded as one of the high points of Dutch poetry. Like its earlier counterpart, Samuel Coster's *Duytsche Academie*, N.V.A. also exerted its influence by giving courses in grammar and philosophy. The writings of its members include Andries Pels' *Horatius' Dichtkunst op onze tijden en zeden gepast* (Horace's Art of Poetry revised to fit our times and customs, 1677). In 1681, after the death of Meyer and Pels, the society began to decline in influence.—A. J. Kronenberg, *Het kunstgenootschap N.V.A.* (1875); J. Bauwens, *La Tragédie française et le théâtre hollandais au XVIIᵉ s.* (1921).   F.J.W.

NŌ. This relatively short Japanese dramatic form, employing poetry, prose, patterned movement, dance, and music, was perfected in the 14th c. Adapting with some variations, the traditional syllabic fives and sevens, the poetry is highly allusive and elevated. Such elevated richness, the religious subjects, and the slow tempo of most nō create a drama akin to the Gr., which it further resembles in its use of traditional materials, masks, male performers, and a chorus (that takes no part in the action).

Nō has broadly and rapidly influenced Western drama, nondramatic poetry, and literary criticism since Ezra Pound first received (1914), studied, revised, and published (1916) Ernest Fenollosa's notes and rude translations. Pound felt that nō showed how to write a long Vorticist (i.e., imagist) poem, since he saw in it a technique by which crucial images unified whole plays or passages. He utilized both allusions to nō and this technique of "Unity of Image" in the *Cantos* by employing certain recurring, archetypical images—e.g., light, the literary journey, and the heavenly visitor to earth—to unify his poem. Often these images take on an additional oriental dimension, since the heavenly visitor to earth may be the central character of the nō *Hagoromo* as well as Diana; or it may be the Sino-Japanese character for "brightness" combined with other imagery of light.

Pound had discussed his interests with Yeats, who became so absorbed that he completely reshaped his later dramaturgy in the image of nō. On this Japanese model, he fashioned an "aristocratic form" employing a bare stage, masks, dance, a few rhythmic instruments, a chorus not part of the action, and other characteristics of nō. Some of his "Noh plays," as he called them, have elements borrowed from specific nō: e.g., the blue cloth centrally onstage in *At the Hawk's Well* is modeled on the brocade cloak of *Aoi no Ue*; and *Words*

Upon the Window-Pane and *The Dreaming of the Bones* borrow the *Nishikigi* motif of unmarried ghostly lovers from a distant past. Yeats seems to have come upon the idea of a unifying-image technique in nō independently of Pound, using it to give coherence to such plays as *The Only Jealousy of Emer, Calvary,* and *A Full Moon in March,* through dramatic focus on an object onstage (Cuchulain's body, Christ hanging on the cross) or an imagistic pattern (of moon and cat's eyes). The importance of nō to Yeats can be measured by his use of it to form a new poetic drama, by his use of images and techniques related to it in his nondramatic poems, and by his statement that the Japanese dramatists were more like modern Western man than either Shakespeare or Corneille.

Yeats's enthusiasms, the Fenollosa-Pound adaptations, Arthur Waley's translations and commentaries, and the monumental studies of Noel Peri, *Cinq Nô* (1929) and *Le Nô* (1944) have influenced many other playwrights, especially those concerned with the poetic or semiprivate theatre. Yeats induced his friend T. Sturge Moore to write "Noh plays," and such others as Gordon Bottomley and Laurence Binyon soon followed. In Germany, Berthold Brecht conceived his two didactic plays, *Der Jasager* and *Der Neinsager,* in the light of Waley's translation of *Tanikō;* and in France, Paul Claudel, who had seen nō performed in Japan, borrowed techniques for his marionette plays. Similarly, Thornton Wilder modeled the bare-stage technique of *Our Town* in part upon nō and has adapted the *waki* (deuteragonist) and the chorus of nō into a *raisonneur* for many plays. Such other, lesser known writers as S. Foster Damon and Paul Goodman have written plays modeled on nō, and Stark Young's *Flower in Drama* uses earlier ideas about nō as antinaturalistic dramatic criteria. If haiku (q.v.) has influenced more Western poets than any Japanese or other non-European form in this century, the nō may be credited with having produced a larger amount of first-rate literature, especially in Eng., through its influence upon dramatists and poets. See also JAPANESE POETRY.—W. B. Yeats, Introd. to *Certain Noble Plays of Japan* (1916); A. Nicoll, *World Drama* (1949); D. Keene, *Japanese Lit.* (1953); E. Miner, *The Japanese Tradition in British and Am. Lit.* (1958).   E.M.

NONSENSE VERSE is, quite simply, a type of verse which does not make sense. Although seemingly obvious, the point is worth making because to most people, including the compilers of many so-called nonsense anthologies, any verse which relates an absurd or improbable story, or makes extensive use of exaggenerated parody, far-fetched rhymes and neologisms, is nonsense. Yet, a great deal of this kind of verse depends for its effect not on the reader's willingness to accept it as n. but on a recognition of the writer's ingenuity. This is especially true of many so-called n. limericks, whose appeal lies not so much in their subject matter as in the dexterity of the writer in finding suitable rhymes for the most improbable words. Such a limerick as this cannot rightly be called n.:

> There was a sculptor named Phidias
> Whose statues were perfectly hideous;
> He made Aphrodite
> Without any nightie
> And shocked the ultra-fastidious.

Similarly, parody cannot be called n., because its appeal lies in the writer's ingenuity, in his ability to suggest by means of distorted exaggeration the writer he is parodying. For all its absurdity, a poem such as Cuthbert Bede's *In Immemoriam* is not really n.:

> We seek to know, and knowing seek;
> We seek, we know, and every sense
> Is trembling with the great intense,
> And vibrating to what we speak.
>
> We ask too much, we seek too oft;
> We know enough and should no more;
> And yet we skim through Fancy's lore
> And look to earth and not aloft.

Perhaps closer to n. are those verses which invert the natural order of things, but it is doubtful whether they are really pure n. The very consistency of the inversion suggests that behind the poem lies a rational intellect displaying its skill in a systematic reversal of the expected. The following anonymous poem is typical:

> 'Tis midnight and the setting sun
> Is slowly rising in the west.
> The rapid rivers slowly run.
> The frog is on his downy nest.
> The pensive goat and sportive cow
> Hilarious, leap from bough to bough.

This is not really a n. world: it is simply an inversion of the normal one, and our appreciation is the result of recognizing the deviations from the familiar. Similarly, a poem such as Thackeray's *The Sorrows of Werther*, included in Carolyn Wells's nonsense anthology, is not pure n. either, because here again the effect depends on our recognition of how normal people behave and noting the way Werther and Charlotte contradict the expected:

> Werther had a love for Charlotte
> Such as words could never utter;

> Would you know how first he met her?
> She was cutting bread and butter.
>
> Charlotte was a married lady,
> And a moral man was Werther,
> And for all the wealth of Indies
> Would do nothing for to hurt her.
>
> So he sigh'd and pined and ogled
> And his passion boil'd and bubbled,
> Till he blew his silly brains out
> And was no more by it troubled.
>
> Charlotte having seen his body
> Borne before her on a shutter,
> Like a well-conducted person
> Went on cutting bread and butter.

None of these verses can properly be called n., because appreciation depends not on a willingness to accept the irrational laws of topsy-turvydom so much as a recognition of the writer's ingenuity or clear-headed common sense. Pure n. is entirely dependent on the rejection of what most people consider logical or even normal and an acceptance of the conventions of a completely different universe.

This fact is convincingly demonstrated in the limericks of Edward Lear. In his verses the Old Men and Old Women persist in a behavior so palpably absurd that it outrages the sensibilities of all those proper and sensible people whom Lear refers to quite simply as "They." Such is the case concerning the

> . . . Old Man in a Garden
> Who always begged everyone's pardon,
> When *they* asked him, What for?
> He replied, "You're a bore!
> And I trust you'll get out of my garden."

In this instance "They" were apparently sent about their business, but quite frequently "They" make life extremely unpleasant for the eccentrics. The Old Man of Montrose, "who walked on the tips of his toes," was told that his behavior was not at all "pleasant" and that he was "a stupid Old Man of Montrose"; and "They" even went to the extreme of "smashing" the Man of Whitehaven, whose only sin was to dance with a raven. N. simply cannot exist in the world of common sense and the Old Person of Basing who

> . . . purchased a steed
> Which he rode at full speed
> And escaped from the people of Basing

did indeed show "a presence of mind that was amazing," for he realized that freedom for pure n. could only be obtained in a place where the conventions of common sense were completely disregarded.

The world of pure n. is an autonomous

world, a world which operates according to its own laws and into which sane people can never really penetrate. It is true that we can make some sense out of Lewis Carroll's "Jabberwocky," but it is doubtful whether we could manage without Humpty Dumpty's gloss in chapter 5 of *Through the Looking Glass.* Consider the opening four lines for example:

'Twas brillig and the slithy toves
Did gyre and gimble in the wabe;
And mimsy were the borogroves
And the mome raths outgrabe.

It may be that we do not need to be told that "slithy" is a "portmanteau" word derived from "lithe" and "slimy," or that "gyre" means "to go round and round like a gyroscope," but certainly, without Humpty Dumpty telling us that "toves" are "something like badgers . . . something like lizards . . . something like corkscrews," or that a "rath" is "a sort of green pig," we would be at a loss to account for their appearance. Although by exercising our ingenuity we can make some sense of Carroll's coinages and even arrive at an approximate · meaning of the poem, we cannot go further. The Jabberwocky world remains a rather forbidding place where strange creatures move and behave in an incomprehensible way, and even though the Jabberwock is slain in a most appalling manner we remain quite unmoved by his death, because he bears so little resemblance to anything which is even remotely familiar.

It is one of the characteristics of pure n. that the most violent things can happen without evoking in us the slightest compassion or sympathy, as in this limerick of Lear's, for example:

There was an Old Man who screamed out
Whenever they knocked him about
So they took off his boots, and fed him on
        fruits
And continued to knock him about.

The idea of an old man being subjected to such barbarous treatment is discomforting, no matter how flippantly it is expressed. Yet, in this limerick there is not the faintest assault on our sensibilities. However, if for the third line we substitute, "So they averted their eyes and stifled his cries," the result, although not profoundly moving, at least causes us some emotional unease. The reason for the change of effect lies in the substitution of a logical statement for a blatantly illogical one, which focuses the reader's attention on certain elements natural to such a situation—the inability of the knockers about to look at the old man and the necessity they feel for stifling his cries —rather than to the irrelevant taking off of

the Old Man's boots and the feeding him fruits.

It is not simply that our sympathy is diverted by the illogical behavior of Lear's knockers-about; we are drawn even further from emotional participation by the writer's choice of two objects, "boots" and "fruits," which carry no emotional significance at all. These two words are, in Coleridgean terms, "fixities and definites" and the poem as a whole is evidently the product of the Fancy. "The Fancy," wrote Coleridge, ". . . has no other counters to play with, but fixities and definites. The Fancy is indeed no other than a mode of Memory emancipated from the order of time and space; while it is blended with and modified by that empirical phenomenon of the will, which we express by the word CHOICE. But equally with the ordinary memory the Fancy must receive all its material ready made from the law of association." Change "association" to "dissociation" and this is a remarkably just description of the process behind the making of a poem of pure n. All pure n. adopts a similar technique, for it is only by concentrating our attention on "fixed" and "definite" irrelevancies that we can exclude the emotions and so avoid the reader's sympathetic involvement with the events in the poem.

This theory is confirmed by the emphasis on precision and regularity in n. verse. We are reminded in *The Walrus and the Carpenter,* for example, that it would take "Seven maids with seven mops," sweeping for "half a year" to clear away the sand from the beach where the oysters dwell, and the Old Person whose habits "induced him to feed upon rabbits" actually ate eighteen before he turned green. The meticulous regularity of the rhythms of n. verse is another way in which we are reminded of the "fixed" and "definite" nature of the n. world, and of course the fact that so many writers of n. have felt it necessary to support their writing with precise line-drawings so as to indicate the character and appearance of their creations, is still another way by which these writers direct our attention to definite things and keep our imagination and sympathy from intruding.

In some n. verse, however, we see beyond the "fixities and definites" to an emotional reality which transcends the n. Such poems owe more to Coleridge's Imagination than Fancy. Coleridge maintained that the ideal poet ". . . diffuses a tone and spirit of unity, that blends, and (as it were) *fuses* each into each, by that synthetic and magical power, to which we have exclusively appropriated the name of imagination. This power, first put in action by the will and understanding, and retained under their irremissive, though gentle and unnoticed control (*laxis effertur habenis*) reveals itself in the balance or reconcilement of opposite or discordant qualities . . . and while it blends and harmonises the natural and the artificial, still subordinates art to nature, the manner to the matter; and our admiration of the poet to our sympathy with the poetry."

This definition of what Coleridge considers as the highest kind of poetical activity, also describes quite accurately such a poem as Lear's *The Dong with the Luminous Nose*. Here, in contrast to, say, Lewis Carroll's *The Walrus and the Carpenter*, Lear does indeed "blend" the "natural and the artificial," for he subordinates his ingenuity to the sympathetic portrayal of the "natural" behavior of the forsaken Dong, and while we admire the poet's technical virtuosity we also feel "sympathy" for this unfortunate creature, jilted by his Jumbly girl and ever in search of her.

The essential difference between *The Dong with the Luminous Nose* and *The Walrus and the Carpenter* is that behind Lear's poem we can sense the personality of the poet. Lear was himself a pathetically ugly, restless wanderer who traveled extensively, evidently seeking some kind of repose, and although Carroll, too, was a timid, unhappy man, he did not subconsciously dramatize his predicament as Lear seems to have done. In Carroll's n. world, particularly in the "Alice" stories, the emotions are rigorously excluded and the particulars are presented with an unequivocal precision. On the other hand, Lear, in the "Dong" poem, presents a world of evocative vagueness, similar to that of the Gothic imagination:

When awful darkness and silence reign
Over the great Gromboolian plain,
Through the long, long wintry nights;—
When the angry breakers roar
As they beat on the rocky shore;—
When storm-clouds brood on the towering
  heights
Of the hills of the Chankly Bore:—
Then, through the vast and gloomy dark,
There moves what seems a fiery spark,
A lonely spark with silvery rays
Piercing the coal-black night,—
A meteor strange and bright:—
Hither and thither the vision strays,
A single lurid light.

The Dong with the Luminous Nose does, in fact, evoke a natural, sympathetic response, which makes one hesitate to call it n.

Possibly, Lear's poem has as much right to be called surrealist as n. Certainly, the line between n. verse and surrealism (q.v.) is often difficult to distinguish. Influenced by Freudian theories of the unconscious, by the ideal of free association, by Jungian concepts of the archetypal, or perhaps just out of boredom with existing poetic modes, many artists in the 20th c. have produced poetry very similar to n. Such poetry, however, is based on a serious theory of poetic communication. As Sir Herbert Read remarked in an essay occasioned by the London Surrealist Exhibition of 1936, "surrealism is . . . the romantic principle in art" and takes its form and substance from the individual unconscious of the creator; therefore such a poem as the following, which many people might regard as n., has an emotional quality suggesting the workings of the Coleridgean imagination:

du dubon dubonnet
the snake laughs brightly
rumble rumble rumble
in the infinite womb of dreams
i in my isolation
asking the way

Here, the opening line recalls the signs that flash past in the Paris *metro*, and once we recognize this, most of the other details of the poem fall into place. The actual meaning of the poem may still be obscure, but at least the reader is able to discern the controlling image which holds the poem together. It should be noted, however, that in so far as surrealism is a formal program for the exploitation of the unconscious—an idea emphasized by surrealism's chief theoretician, André Breton, in his *First Surrealist Manifesto* (1924) —it differs from n., which is opposed to all programs.

N. then, occupies the narrow ground between wit and humor on the one hand, and surrealism on the other. Although at first sight it has the appearance of being a fairly prolific genre, there is surprisingly little true n. verse. Pure n. is completely negative in its effect. The poet must avoid the temptation to turn an amusing phrase or relate a recognizably humorous anecdote, and he must be equally cautious of allowing his imagination to intrude. It is essentially a poetry of escape, a conscious refusal to communicate anything which could be considered positive, a form which demands unceasing control and a disposition more cerebral than emotional. Hence, it is not surprising that the two most successful n. writers in Eng. were not poets at all, but men engaged in work which demanded precision and exactness—Lear, a professional illustrator of scientific books of natural history, and Carroll, a professor of mathematics.

G. K. Chesterton, *The Defendant* (1902); *A N. Anthol.*, ed. C. Wells (1903); E. Cammaerts, *The Poetry of N.* (1925); L. Reed, *The Complete Limerick Book* (1925); A. L. Huxley, *Essays New and Old* (1927); C. L. Dodgson, *The Complete Works of Lewis Carroll*, illustrated by J. Tenniel (1936); *Surrealism*, ed. H. Read (1936); E. Partridge, *Here, There and Everywhere* (1950); E. Lear, *The Complete N. of Edward Lear*, ed. and introd. H. Jackson (1951); E. Sewell, *The Field of N.* (1952); G. Orwell, *Shooting an Elephant* (1954).

See also the discussion of the German Christian Morgenstern as an intermediate figure between Carroll and Lear and the surrealists in L. W. Forster, *Poetry of Significant N.* (1962).

J.M.M.

NORSE PROSODY. See OLD GERMANIC PROSODY.

NORSKE SELSKAB, DET (The Norwegian Society). A social-literary club (1772-1812) of Norwegian students, teachers, and writers resident in Copenhagen. It carried on the inheritance from Fr. neoclassicism and Eng. empiricism and opposed Klopstockianism and its Danish adherents. Some poets associated with it were Johan Nordahl Brun (1745-1816), Claus Frimann (1746-1829), Thomas Rosing de Stockfleth (1743-1808), Johan Herman Wessel (1742-85), and Jens Zetlitz (1761-1821). The poetic endeavors of the members comprised most neoclassical genres, from heroic drama and fables in verse to elegy and epigram. Worthy of note as Norway's first national-historical play is Brun's *Einar Tambeskielver* (1772). By the emphasis it placed on the use of Norwegian subject matter in poetry and on a national manner of treatment, the society laid the foundations for the literary renascence that came with Henrik Wergeland. —F. Bull, *Fra Holberg til Nordal Brun* (1916); A. H. Winsnes, *Det norske Selskab, 1772-1812* (1924).

S.L.

NORWEGIAN POETRY. At the height of the Middle Ages (ca. 1250), when the tradition of ON poetry (q.v.) had ceased to inspire any major literary activity, the vogue of versified Fr. romances and troubadour poetry overshadowed any individual creations in the vernacular. The chief original poetic monuments of the age are the folk ballads, which employed a new, nonalliterative style derived from troubadour verse. In spirit and form they are close to the Eng. and Scotch ballads, with their hero worship and dramatic narrative. A ballad of a special kind is *Draumkvæde* (The Dream Ballad), a superb example of visionary poetry unique in Scandinavian literature. The poem, whose narrator-dreamer visits the "other world" and attends a Last Judgment reminiscent of Ragnarok, is notable for its perfect synthesis of the pagan and Christian traditions.

The first known poet of significance to Norway was the Dane Anders Arrebo (See DANISH POETRY), who was for a time bishop of Trond-

heim; the epic narrative of his *Hexaëmeron* is interspersed with passages describing Northern Norway. Petter Dass (1647-1707), the first Norw. poet of stature, continued Arrebo's topographical poetry in *Nordlands Trompet* (The Trumpet of Nordland, ca. 1700; pr. 1739) in a meter and style strictly his own. His religious poetry embraces versifications of Biblical stories as well as paraphrases of Luther's Catechism. The verse of Dass is in feeling and tone close to folk poetry.

With Ludvig Holberg (See DANISH POETRY) a Norw. writer attained European dimensions. Holberg (1684-1750), who spent most of his mature years in Denmark and wrote his comedies and satires largely about Danish conditions, is significant for Norw. literature mainly because of his brilliant example. Still Danish subjects, his countrymen drew faith in their creative talent from this example and, besides, derived from it an enduring conception of poetry as criticism of life. The first ambition of Norw. poets, however, was misdirected; the poetic tragedy in neoclassical Fr. style which they endeavored to create in the 1770's was not a success. The only memorable result was the delightful tragic parody *Kierlighed uden Strømper* (Love Without Stockings, 1772) by Johan Herman Wessel (1742-85), a successor to Holberg whose elegant ironical satire, embodied in graceful alexandrines, put an end to the imitation of It. opera and Fr. tragedy. Wessel also wrote some excellent comic narratives, like *Smeden og Bageren* (The Blacksmith and the Baker), in which conversational passages in free rhythm vary with epigrammatic couplets. The second principal genre practiced by the poets of this period—most of whom, like Wessel, belonged to *Det norske Selskab*, q.v. (The Norw. Society)—was the descriptive poem, composed in an individual and national spirit. Claus Frimann (1746-1829) evoked in simple, fresh language the life of peasant and fisherman. *Hornelen,* a descriptive poem by his brother Peder Harboe Frimann (1759-1839), deviated from earlier nature poetry both in its subject, a stark wild mountain, and in its unconventional style. Edvard Storm (1749-94) wrote some truly original nature lyrics in dialect, *Dølevisor* (Dalesmen's Songs), which express to perfection the spirit of the Norw. seasons.

Whereas in Denmark and Sweden romanticism had already produced a great poetry by the first and second decade of the 19th c. respectively, Norway experienced a similar awakening only in the 1830's and 1840's. The manner of this awakening was determined by the persisting cultural dominance of Denmark, despite the political independence which Norway had gained in 1814. The 1830's precipitated a "culture feud," the issue of which was whether to follow the ideas of the Danish romantics or to disregard the "400 years of darkness" and create a literature on purely native grounds. Also involved was the question of what formal principles should guide the new poetry. Henrik Arnold Wergeland (1808–45), leader of the Patriots, was a man of supreme gifts and inexhaustible energies; his activities ranged from those of political editor, orator, and popular educator to those of satirical farceur, heaven-storming dramatist, and sublime lyrist. A born genius to whom poetry meant rapture and accordingly tended to create its own free design, he contrasted diametrically with the leader of the Intelligentsia Party, Johan Sebastian Welhaven (1807–73), a poet of quiet reflection who, following the Danish poet-critic J. L. Heiberg, emphasized the necessity of a chiseled form. The traditions established by these two men have thenceforth coexisted in Norw. poetry, although by 1900 they tended to interweave.

Wergeland defies classification. In some ways he fulfilled the era of Enlightenment ushered in by Holberg; but he was also Norway's first great romantic poet. His philosophical rationalism, suffused with a mystical pantheism similar to Shelley's, was expressed in *Skabelsen, Mennesket og Messias* (Creation, Man, and Messiah, 1830), an enormous lyrical drama which he himself called an "epic of humanity." Its publication caused an attack by Welhaven, who criticized the poem for its inflated imagery and lack of form. Subsequently, Welhaven wrote *Norges Dæmring* (The Dawn of Norway, 1834), a series of sonnets in epigrammatic style exposing not only Wergeland's artistic deficiencies, but also the uncritical cultural nationalism of the Patriots. Wergeland's achievement as a narrative and lyric poet, however, is impressive. His best narratives are *Jøden* (The Jew, 1842), *Jødinden* (The Jewess, 1844), and *Den engelske Lods* (The Eng. Pilot, 1844). A poem *sui generis* is *Jan van Huysums Blomsterstykke* (Jan van Huysum's Flowerpiece, 1840), a sensitively imaginative interpretation of a work of art in story form. Among shorter lyrics, *Til min Gyldenlak* (To My Wallflower) and *Til Foraaret* (To Spring) are supreme.

Only in the 1840's did Norw. literature develop a romanticism of the kind initiated in Denmark by Oehlenschläger. This romanticism defined itself largely by a diligent search for the values hidden in the folk culture. An important step in this search was the recording of the native ballads, a work begun by Jørgen Moe (1813–82) and continued by M. B. Landstad (1802–80), whose collection *Norske Folkeviser* (Norw. Folk Ballads, 1853) exerted a broad influence on poetry. The New Norse (q.v.) movement, originated by Ivar Aasen (1813–96) as a means of giving the rural population its own literary medium, was another manifestation of National Romanticism. Of the more important poets, Welhaven was in his later phase a National Romantic: his poetry of personal reminiscence was broadened to embrace the entire country and its historical past, which he celebrated in the tone of ballad or romance. In his nature poems he introduced fairies and trolls to suggest an authentic native atmosphere.

National Romanticism reached its climax with Ibsen and Bjørnson, beside Wergeland the greatest Norw. poets of the 19th c. Together with them may be mentioned the New Norse writer Aasmund Vinje (1818–70), unique both as poet and critic. The two decades from 1850 to 1870 were a transition period in which realism and romanticism coexisted, a fact clearly exemplified by Vinje, a Norw. Heine whose double vision shuttled him back and forth between sublime pathos and sardonic irony. To his romantic output belongs the first authentic lyricism of the Norw. mountains, at the same time intimate and magnificently grand. Henrik Ibsen (1828–1906) carried on the Welhaven tradition in Norw. literature, both in his National-Romantic and in his satirical poetry. But despite influences, among which Heine was another, everything Ibsen wrote is impregnated with an individual style. His concentrated, even laconic, lyric verse is singularly powerful, conveying its meaning, often symbolic, with a minimum of imagery. Ibsen's chief poetic contribution to National Romanticism was the drama *Gildet paa Solhaug* (The Feast at Solhaug, 1856), a historical idyll metrically and stylistically influenced by the ballad. With *Kjærlighedens Komedie* (The Comedy of Love, 1862), which from a Kierkegaardian point of view satirized bourgeois materialism, a realistic period began. The poetry, in skipping iambic pentameters with varying rhyme, abounds in caricature and paradox. *Brand* (1866), more somber in mood, is an impressive dramatic statement of Ibsen's central theme, the "contradiction between aspiration and ability, between will and possibility." In this play, as in *Peer Gynt* (1867), the satirist in Ibsen became fused with the National Romantic. For at the same time as they scathingly satirized the Norw. national character, they cast a romantic glamor over the Norw. landscape—with its lakes and rivers, its fabled fjords and mountain peaks. In *Peer Gynt*, moreover, Ibsen succeeded in portraying dramatic symbols which have universal as well as national significance. The major theme—the fanciful, self-indulgent man ultimately saved, if saved at all, through a noble woman's love—recalls both the *Divine Comedy* and *Faust*, a fact which suggests the scope and depth of Ibsen's vision. Formally, also, *Peer Gynt* is superior to *Brand*.

Whereas in *Brand* iambic *knittelvers* (q.v.) determines the movement throughout, in *Peer Gynt* the predominantly trochaic rhythm alternates with anapaestic parts where a more conversational effect was desired. Ibsen amply demonstrated in his plays, especially in *Peer Gynt*, the effectiveness of the Norw. language as a poetic-dramatic medium, capable of infinite variations of rhythm and melody. As such a medium, Norw. seems to possess greater expressiveness than either Danish, whose verbal music is subdued and rhythm unemphatic, or Swedish, whose rich sonority and surging rhythm may prevent dramatic transparency.

Whereas Ibsen focused his attention on the individual and at times represented attitudes which approach *l'art pour l'art* and anarchism, Bjørnstjerne Bjørnson (1832–1910), who considered himself literary heir to Wergeland, was concerned with the individual's duty toward society and the world. His saga dramas, *Halte-Hulda* (Lame Hulda, 1858), *Kong Sverre* (1861), and *Sigurd Slembe* (1862), were deliberately undertaken in order to give his country a national gallery of dramatic heroes to match those of other European countries, an ambition which accorded with the National-Romantic program. Dramatically, these plays were not successful; their chief merits are historical verisimilitude and a saga tone. It was as narrative and lyric poet that Bjørnson excelled. *Arnljot Gelline* (1870), his greatest narrative poem, is a cycle of 15 romances in various measures in the style of Oehlenschläger's *Helge*, Tegnér's *Frithiofs saga*, and Runeberg's *Kung Fjalar*. The imagery is profusely rich, the diction colloquial and varied; and the meter, mostly trochaic and dactylic, is skillfully attuned to the changing moods. As a lyric poet Bjørnson bears comparison with the best European masters. Notable is the influence of classical sculpture, the effects of which are clearly perceptible, for example, in *Olav Trygvason* and *Bergljot* (in *Digte og Sange*, 1870); within a few dramatically tense scenes these poems present an entire tragic action. Worthy of special mention is *Salme II*, a magnificent hymn to ever resurgent life which both intellectually and technically marks the highpoint of his lyricism.

When, after the prosaic 1870's and 1880's, poetry again appeared, it sounded a more personal note, often produced by an intimate fusion of individualism and nature mysticism; and the poets moved as much in the realm of fantasy as in actuality. Fr. symbolism—largely as mediated by Swedish and Danish neoromantic poetry—Nietzsche, and the painting of Edvard Munch were the principal sources of inspiration. The most important exponents of *fin de siècle* moods were Vilhelm Krag (1871–1933) and Sigbjørn Obstfelder (1866–1900), the former expressing a rather conventional melancholy, the latter celebrating the wondrous mystery of life in a highly original form characterized by repetitions, abrupt transitions, pauses, and incompleteness. A contrasting temperament was that of Nils Collett Vogt (1864–1937), a radical child of the 1880's who, however, attained poetic maturity only with the collection *Fra vaar til høst* (From Spring to Fall) published in 1894. Here, in the spirit of Swinburne, he sang dithyrambs in praise of an individualistic classical paganism. In his later work Vogt followed the Wergeland-Bjørnson tradition, both formally and intellectually. Also New Norse poetry had a revival in the 1890's, through the work of Arne Garborg (1851–1924) and Per Sivle (1857–1904). Although best known as a naturalistic novelist, Garborg gave in *Haugtussa* (The Hill Innocent) and *I Helheim* (In Hel's Home) a unique expression to the contemporary need for a religious conception of life. Both poems evoke uncannily the dark forces in man and nature. Neoromantic in inspiration is also the poetry of Knut Hamsun (1859–1952) and Hans E. Kinck (1865–1926), both best known as novelists. *Det vilde Kor* (The Wild Chorus, 1904) showed Hamsun as a supreme lyrist, ranging in tone from the personal mood of mystical recollection in *Skjærgaardsø* to the national chords of his anniversary salute to Bjørnson (*Bjørnson paa hans 70-Aars Fødselsdag*). Kinck's dramatic poem *Driftekaren* (The Drover, 1908) in unmusical but richly textured verse explores the division the poet discerned in the Norw. folk psyche, torn between conventional rationalism and imaginative vision.

About 1910 a lyric breakthrough came about in Norway, largely due to Hermann Wildenvey (b. 1886) and Olaf Bull (1883–1933). Inspired by Hamsun's *Det vilde Kor*, Wildenvey brought a new spirit as well as a new rhythm and style into poetry. A fresh paganism animates his seductive erotic lyrics in *Nyinger* (Bonfires, 1907); pantheism pervades his regional nature poetry. His verse is identified by the anapaestic, "billowy" line, which lends itself to conversational, but highly melodious, effects. His diction, compounded of elements from Bible and folk song as well as from jargon and slang, is arresting and brilliantly original. Undoubtedly the greatest Norw. lyrist in this century, Bull was Wildenvey's opposite both in temperament and formal talent. Symbolist in conception, his work is profoundly personal, centered on the tensions of inner experience. Usually starting with a minimum of observation, the poems are given substance by a powerful visionary imagination and provided with philosophical perspective by a mind schooled in Bergson and in modern science.

Especially notable, both for its intellectual scope and its imaginative transmutation of scientific abstractions, is the grandiose cosmic fantasy *Ignis Ardens* (1929), an artistic synthesis of the evolution of life on a Bergsonian basis.

New Norse poetry found worthy exponents in Olav Aukrust (1883–1929) and Tore Ørjasæter (b. 1886), in whose works religious and philosophical problems are treated in a national spirit and in a form deriving from the Edda and the ballad. Aukrust masterfully demonstrated the technical possibilities of NN, especially for the expression of elemental passion and grotesque humor. In these areas the power of NN, with its wide range of vowels and diphthongs and its strong rhythm, comes close to that of Swedish. The few lines below from Aukrust's principal work *Himmelvarden* (The Cairn Against the Sky, 1916) will suggest the kind of expressiveness the language possesses:

Grøne havmerri skumblaut ris,
frauden voggar
og velt um lenderne,—
kvart eit andlit vert bleikt som is,
og stormflod-fjelli stig inn på strenderne.
Skume dagen vert svart som natti,
og eldingregn gjenom myrkret susar. . . .

Look at the sea horse, green-soaked, rise!
The surf rocks
And breaks about its flanks,—
Every face becomes pale as ice,
And the storm-ridden flood mounts on the
    banks.
Dusky day turns black as night,
And lightning rain whizzes through the
    dark. . . .

In the 1920's, a rich period in Norw. literature, two intellectual currents clashed—a liberal conservatism of Christian inspiration and a radical socialism allied with psychoanalysis. The above NN poets represented the former; a leading radical was Arnulf Øverland (b. 1889), whose great powers, evidenced in *Brød og vin* (Bread and Wine, 1919), were called forth by World War I. Much of his poetry is inspired by a religious devotion to the ideal of socialism, interpreted humanistically, often in biblical symbols. Øverland's suppressed fire, truncated poetic form, and monumental use of simple unadorned words mark him as the latest great Norw. poet in the Welhaven-Ibsen tradition. The best work of Nordahl Grieg (1902–43) and Gunnar Reiss-Andersen (b. 1896) belongs to the 1930's and later. In his ceaseless activity reminiscent of Wergeland, Grieg wrote chiefly socially oriented patriotic poetry, in a style of impassioned magniloquence. His greatest success was *Krigsdikter* (War Poems, 1945), where his

rhetorical pathos was poetically justified. Reiss-Andersen, whose sheer formal talent has no equal in Norw. poetry, combines sensitivity to the everyday idyll with a broad social awareness. Remarkable for its imaginative scope, rhythmical virtuosity, and colorful imagery is *Norsk freske* (Norw. Frieze), written in Swedish exile during the German occupation. Two other poets, Emil Boyson (b. 1899) and Rolf Jacobsen (b. 1907), were significant as forerunners of poetic modernism in Norway. Jacobsen created an objective poetry, characterized by free verse and technical imagery, through which he rendered the life of the modern city.

Of the poets who came to maturity in the 1940's, Inger Hagerup (b. 1905) has produced condensed love lyrics reminiscent of Øverland; André Bjerke (b. 1918) composes highly finished verse of elegant sensuousness; and Claes Gill (b. 1910) writes reflective poetry in the surrealist manner. Notable is a group of vers librists strongly influenced by modern Am. and Eng. poetry. Of these, Per Arneberg (b. 1901), whose work shows a deep affinity with Whitman's lyricism, has rendered *Song of Myself* into Norw.; Paal Brekke (b. 1923), the most self-consciously modernistic poet, has translated *The Waste Land* by T. S. Eliot. NN poetry, fairly represented by the enraptured and musical verse of Tormod Skagestad (b. 1920), remained strongly imbued with National Romanticism. The 1950's witnessed a debate between the traditionalists—headed by Arnulf Øverland, the uncrowned poet laureate —and the modernists. The latter looked either, like Erling Christie (b. 1928), to T. S. Eliot or, like Carl Keilhau (1919–57), to Rilke and modern Danish poets. Of great significance to the movement has been Tarjei Vesaas' adherence to modernism in his lyric production, which has maintained a steady flow from 1946 on; in adopting this style, Vesaas (b. 1897), who is the leading writer of fiction in NN, has shown that a tenacious traditionalism is not necessarily part of the NN poetic idiom. Other modernists are Astrid Hjertenæs Andersen (b. 1915), Harald Sverdrup (b. 1923), and Gunvor Hofmo (b. 1921); of the youngest generation of poets, Per Bronken and Stein Mehren show unusual promise. The great number, besides, of excellent traditional poets will guarantee the future continuance of the two Norw. poetic traditions, those of Wergeland and Welhaven. Also, undoubtedly, satire will continue to hold an important place, as will national and religious pathos, all elements which have been present in Norw. poetry from its very beginning.

WORKS AND ANTHOLOGIES: B. Bjørnson, *Arnljot Gelline*, tr. W. W. Payne (1917; annotated); H. Ibsen, *Peer Gynt*, tr. W. and C.

Archer (1923); *The Oxford Book of Scandinavian Verse*, ed. E. W. Gosse and W. A. Craigie (1925); *Anthol. of Norw. Lyrics*, tr. C. W. Stork (1942); *Eagle Wings: Poetry by Bjørnson, Ibsen and Wergeland*, tr. A. G. Dehly (1943); *Norsk litt. gjennom 1000 år*, ed. E. and V. Skard (3 v., 1948); *Modern Norw. Poems*, tr. I. Allwood (1949); *Norsk lyrikk gjennom tusen år*, ed. C. Kent (2d ed., by E. Kielland, 2 v., 1950; a compreh. anthol.); *20th C. Scandinavian Poetry*, ed. M. Allwood (1950); P. Dass, *The Trumpet of Nordland*, tr. T. Jorgenson (1954); *Den unge lyrikken 1939–1954*, ed. P. Brekke (1956).

HISTORY AND CRITICISM: E. W. Gosse, *Northern Studies* (1890); P. H. Wicksteed, *Four Lectures on Ibsen* (1892); I. Grøndal and O. Raknes, *Chapters in Norw. Lit.* (1923); K. Elster, "Three Lyric Poets of Norway," ASR, 13 (1925); H. G. Topsøe-Jensen, *Scandinavian Lit. from Brandes to Our Own Day*, tr. I. Anderson (1929); F. Bull, "Bjørnsons lyrikk," *Streiftog i norsk litt.* (1931); T. Jorgenson, *Hist. of Norw. Lit.* (1933); K. Elster, *Illustrert norsk litteraturh.* (2d ed., 2 v., 1934–35; an illuminating crit. hist.); F. Bull, *Henrik Ibsens Peer Gynt* (1947); H. Schneider, *Gesch. der norwegischen und isländischen Lit.* (1948); E. Bredsdorff et al., *An Introd. to Scandinavian Lit.* (1951; a useful short survey); J. Lescoffier, *Hist. de la litt. norvégienne* (1952); F. Bull et al., *Norsk litteraturh.* (6 v., 1924–55; standard lit. hist.); H. Beyer, *A Hist. of Norw. Lit.*, ed. and tr. E. Haugen (1956; best survey in Eng.); G. C. Schoolfield, "The Recent Scandinavian Lyric," BA, 36 (1962). s.L.

NOVAS RIMADAS (in the plural, even for a single composition). A Prov. nonlyric poem, ordinarily written in octosyllabic rhymed couplets. Both narrative and didactic poems are so named, though the original meaning of the word was surely "tale," like the modern Fr. *nouvelle* and other words of similar derivation.—J. Anglade, *Hist. sommaire de la litt. méridionale* (1921). F.M.C.

NUMBER(S). (a) The prosodical meters of both classic and modern poetry; hence, (b) poems, lines, strophes, etc. As originally applied to quantitatively scanned poetry, the notion of "numbers" involved the idea of metrical *proportion*, and was thus linked to the proportions of musical harmonies (and, in the Middle Ages, of musical rhythm). In the Renaissance, "numbers" simply means poetry in general, although the extension to music and musical compositions may also be invoked, as in "In full harmonic number joined . . ." (Milton, *Paradise Lost* 4. 687); the most general sense of musico-mathematical proportion is preserved in such commonplace references to

Plato as one affirming that he held that "the mynd was made of certaine harmonie and musicall nombers" (E. K., *Gloss to Spenser's Shepheardes Calender* "October" 27). Ing argues for an Elizabethan distinction between "number," or mere syllable-count, and "numbers," used in its traditional sense for quantitative prosody.—St. Augustine, *De Musica; Elizabethan Crit. Essays*, ed. G. G. Smith (1904); C. M. Ing, *Elizabethan Lyrics* (1951). J.H.

NURSERY RHYMES. A nursery rhyme may be defined as a rhyme or verse preserved in the world of children. Examples are:

Humpty Dumpty sat on a wall,
Humpty Dumpty had a great fall—
All the King's horses and all the King's men
Couldn't put Humpty Dumpty together again.

Rain, rain, go away,
Come again another day.

The origins of the r. are manifold, but except for lullabies and those verses which accompany infant games ("This little piggy") very few originated in the nursery. Material from adult life was introduced to children either for reason or by accident, often simply because of its memorability; that material which proved popular with the children survived, and with surprisingly little alteration, despite the fact that some of it disappeared from print for two centuries at a time.

Peter Opie estimates that at least one-fourth, and probably one-half, of the r. known to Eng.-speaking children today are more than 200 years old. It is impossible to be precise about the age of most of the verses. "White bird featherless" appears in L. in the 10th c.; "Two legs sat upon three legs" in Bede, "Thirty days hath September" in Fr. in the 13th c., "Matthew, Mark, Luke, and John" in German in the 15th c.; but it is likely that these r. existed many, perhaps hundreds, of years before they were set down. References in Gr., Roman, and Oriental literatures would indicate that children's games and verses analogous to ours were known in these cultures, and some scholars believe that some "classic" r. (e.g., "Buck, buck," "Humpty Dumpty") are thousands of years old. The theory would be supported by the prevalence of a number of the r. or their analogues throughout Europe. One cannot of course ignore the likelihood that many were carried from country to country by armies, travelers, missionaries, and, in latter days, translators; many Eng. r. have been translated into Hindustani, Malayan, Russian, etc. But the possibility exists that some of the lore came down in an unbroken line from the ancient world.

It is possible to trace the sources (or define

-[579]-

the types) of many of the later r.—those of the last 300 years. Some of these sources are: (1) *Songs*. These include ballads and folk songs ("One misty moisty morning"); drinking songs ("I've got sixpence"); war songs ("The King of France went up the hill"); songs from plays ("There was a jolly miller"—but probably this song existed before it was incorporated in *Love in a Village*); romantic lyrics ("Where are you going, my pretty maid?"); popular songs of recent date ("Where, o where has my little dog gone?"); lullabies proper ("Rockabye, baby"). (2) *Street cries* ("Hot Cross Buns"). (3) *Riddles* ("Little Nancy Etticoat"). (4) *Proverbs* ("Needles and Pins"). (5) *Custom and ritual* ("London Bridge"). (6) *Religious and anti-religious matter* ("Matthew, Mark, Luke, and John," "Good morning, Father Francis"). (7) *R. about historical personages* ("Lucy Locket," Robin Hood rhymes). (8) *Poems by recent authors* ("Twinkle, twinkle, little star," by Jane Taylor). (9) *Words accompanying games* ("Here we go round the mulberry bush"). (10) *Counting out r.*, many of which seem to have derived from old Celtic numbers preserved among primitive people in England and still used for counting sheep, fish, stitches in knitting, etc. ("Eena, meena, mina moe," "One-ery, two-ery," and originally "Hickory Dickory Dock"). The above classifications are rough and do not account for all the r.; they will serve, however, to show from what a variety of sources the lore of the nursery is culled.

The first published collection of nursery songs was *Tommy Thumb's Pretty Song Book* (1744); there is a single extant copy of the second of its two volumes, containing about 40 songs, in the British Museum. In ca. 1765 appeared *Mother Goose's Melody, or Sonnets for the Cradle*; in 1784 came *Gammer Gurton's Garland*. In America, in 1719, appeared *Songs for the Nursery, or Mother Goose's Melodies for Children*; no copies are extant. There is a story that the printer named the book after his mother-in-law, née Elizabeth Goose. The r. are usually called "Mother Goose R." in America, but the origin of "Mother Goose" seems to be Fr. The term "Nursery R." was not used in England until the 19th c.; before that they were "Tommy Thumb's songs." During the past century and a half hundreds of collections of the r. have been issued.

The first scholar to concern himself with the material was James Orchard Halliwell, whose collection of 300 r., most of them still popular today, was published by the Percy So-

ciety in 1842. His work has been superseded by that of Iona and Peter Opie, whose *Oxford Dictionary of Nursery R.* contains 550 entries, with many variants, important notes, and a valuable introduction.

During the 20th c., scholars and other interested persons have proffered various theories concerning the r. One of these, the *historical* theory, tries to identify the "real personages" of the verses: e.g., Old King Cole is a British king of the 3d c.—or the father of St. Helena —or the father of Finn McCool; Georgie Porgie is George I—or the Duke of Buckingham; the Queen the pussy-cat went to see is Elizabeth I. Although some of these "identifications" must be described as wild surmise, there is evidence for the historicity of a number of the characters: Elise Marley was a famous alewife, Lucy Locket and Kitty Fisher courtesans of the time of Charles I, and Jack Horner probably a steward of the Abbot of Glastonbury, whose "plum" was a deed to valuable property still in the Horner family.

Henry Bett believes that the r. (as well as many children's tales and games) reflect nature myths ("Jack and Jill" is about the tides), custom ("London Bridge" echoes the old rite of human sacrifice necessary to appease the water over which a bridge was built), and history ("John Ball"). James Joyce owned a copy of Dr. Bett's book and apparently found much to agree with in it. Joyce's *Finnegans Wake* contains a multitude of references to about 70 rhymes; the author uses them to reinforce his concept of ever recurrent motifs in human existence; he sees the r. as embodying myths which express the experiences of the human race. In this use of the r. Joyce illustrates what may be called the *psychoanalytic* theory, a theory recently put forth (not specifically about nursery r., but about folk material in general) by Joseph Campbell, in *The Hero with a Thousand Faces*.

J. O. Halliwell, *The Nursery R. of England* (1842); H. C. Bolton, *The Counting Out R. of Children* (1888); L. Eckenstein, *Comparative Studies in Nursery R.* (1906); H. Bett, *Nursery R. and Tales* (1924); D. E. Marvin, *Historic Child R.* (1930); V. Sackville-West, *Nursery R.* (1947); I. and P. Opie, *The Oxford Dict. of Nursery R.* (rev. ed., 1952; best general survey) and *The Oxford Nursery R. Book* (1955); P. Opie, "Nursery R.," in Cassell's; M. P. Worthington, "Nursery R. in Joyce's *Finnegans Wake*," JAF, 70 (1957); P. H. Evans, *Rimbles* (1961).　　　　　　　　　　M.P.W.

O

OBJECTIVE CORRELATIVE. T. S. Eliot introduced the term "o.c." into modern literary criticism in the essay "Hamlet and His Problems" (1919; *The Sacred Wood*, 1920). *Hamlet* is an "artistic failure," according to Eliot, chiefly because its central character "is dominated by an emotion which is inexpressible, because it is in *excess* of the facts as they appear." "The only way of expressing emotion in the form of art is by finding an 'objective correlative' in other words, a set of objects, a situation, a chain of events which shall be the formula of that *particular* emotion; such that when the external facts, which must terminate in sensory experience, are given, the emotion is immediately evoked." Shakespeare has failed to provide Hamlet with any such o.c.

Since Eliot introduced the term, it has doubtless been more often discussed than used; it may well be one of those "notorious phrases which," he said in 1956, speaking of his own literary criticism, "have had a truly embarrassing success in the world." In any case, Eliot's argument bristles with difficulties (due to loose writing given an air of precision by such mathematical expressions as "formula" and "equivalent" [Unger]). Let us agree, with Eliot, that disgust is a part of Hamlet's state of mind. To what, then, does the term "o.c." apply? To Hamlet's gross language in 3.4 and elsewhere, which in a simple sense "expresses" that disgust? Or, as Eliot oddly implies, to Gertrude and her misdeeds (the inadequate "equivalent" for Hamlet's disgust)? Eliot appears to confound the expression of an emotion with the occasion of that emotion. Again, who is being thought of as "expressing" emotion, Hamlet, or Shakespeare, or both? Or again, how can we say that an emotion is *inexpressible* merely because it is excessive in relation to its occasion (if it is)? Finally, what is the relation between "expression," "communication," and "evocation" as Eliot understands them? One concludes that Eliot here uses the term "expression" in a special sense, according to which a state of mind which is inadequately accounted for is inadequately expressed; it fails to engage fully the audience's sympathies, and has therefore not been successfully turned into "the form of art."

The concept of the o.c. has been traced variously to Washington Allston (Wellek), Santayana (McElderry), Pound (Praz), and Poe (Winters). Allston (*Lectures on Art*, 1850) uses the phrase itself in a discussion, in terms reminiscent of Emerson, of the relation between the mind and the external world: "the mind . . . needs . . . , as the condition of its manifestation, its objective correlative"—the external world, objects in which bear a "predetermined" relationship to ideas "preexisting" in the mind and cooperate in the realization of the mind's potentiality for "pleasurable emotion." Here Allston is speaking of the mind in general, but later, in discussing the distinctive qualities of the artist, he defines one of them, originality, as "the power of presenting to another the *precise* images or emotions as they existed in himself." The implication of Allston's remarks is that one, at least, of the functions of art is the expression and communication of emotion. Santayana (*Poetry and Religion*, 1900) takes a similar position, but adds to the notion of expression that of evocation: "The poet's art is to a great extent the art of intensifying emotions by assembling the scattered objects that naturally arouse them." By uniting "disparate things having a common overtone of feeling," the poet evokes that feeling. He seeks or invents "correlative objects" for the expression of feeling, though, according to Santayana, "expression" is a misleading term, implying as it does that something already experienced and/or otherwise known is "expressed," while the fact is that the very act of expression itself may so modify the feeling expressed as in effect to constitute the invention of a totally new feeling. Praz believes that "Pound's idea of poetry . . . [*The Spirit of Romance*, 1910] as of 'a sort of inspired mathematics, which gives us equations, not for abstract figures, triangles, spheres, and the like, but equations for the human emotions,' may be said to be the starting point of Eliot's theory of the 'objective correlative.'" Winters agrees with Praz's estimate of the importance of Pound's influence, but asserts that "this particular theory is at least as old as Poe and is more likely older, and Poe states it much more nearly in Eliot's terms." He then quotes the passage, from the essay on Hawthorne, in which Poe sets forth the doctrine of the single "preconceived effect."

Overlooking possible difficulties in the theory of literature apparently implied by the o.c., Matthiessen finds its importance in its apparent insistence on definiteness and particularity of language and situation; and indeed its original use by Eliot and its subsequent vogue are doubtless related to the passion for the concrete and definite exemplified by Imagism and are part of the 20th-c. reaction against Shelleyan and late Victorian vaguenesses. Matthiessen refers to the passage in which the concept is enunciated as "a *locus classicus* of criticism" and finds in it "the exact clue to the triumph of *Samson Agonistes*," in which, presumably, Milton has successfully "expressed" his own emotions "in the form of art" by depersonalizing and objectifying them in the story of Samson, their perfect o.c.

Other critics, however, have found the concept more or less unsatisfactory. In some doubt as to the meaning of the phrase, Wellek is content to keep it "as a convenient word for the symbolic structure of a work of art," but only, it would appear, at the expense of the notion that the o.c. is a deliberately sought device for the expression and evocation of a state of mind. Winters concludes that "the idea of the objective correlative is this: that the poet starts with an emotion and after casting about finds objective data which he believes can be used to embody it; nothing more." As a rationalist, Winters objects to the concept on the ground that it implies the priority and primacy of emotion in literary composition. Vivas, who infers that the concept was "devised to explain how the poem expresses the poet's emotion," believes that it assumes a "dubious psychology" and an untenable literary theory; that Eliot implies that poems are composed exclusively of objectifications of emotions and feelings; and finally that it is hardly possible that any given concrete object or set of circumstances will express for the poet and arouse in the reader precisely the same "*particular* emotion."

T. S. Eliot, "Hamlet and His Problems" (1919), in *The Sacred Wood* (1920); F. O. Matthiessen, *The Achievement of T. S. Eliot* (1935, 1947); M. Praz, "T. S. Eliot and Dante," *The Southern Rev.*, 2 (1937); J. T. Shipley, "O.C.," *Dict. of World Lit.* (1943); Y. Winters, *The Anatomy of Nonsense* (1943); E. Vivas, "The O.C. of T. S. Eliot," *The Am. Bookman*, 1 (1944); *The Critic's Notebook*, ed. R. W. Stallman (1950); R. Wellek, "The Crit. of T. S. Eliot," *SR*, 64 (1956); B. R. McElderry, Jr., "Santayana and Eliot's 'O.C.'," *Boston Univ. Studies in Eng.*, 3 (1957).　　J.D.K.

OBJECTIVISM. A term used to describe a mode of writing, particularly the writing of verse. It recognizes the poem, apart from its meaning, to be an object to be dealt with as such. O. looks at the poem with a special eye to its structural aspect, how it has been constructed. The term originated in 1931 with a small group of poets calling themselves "The Objectivists," who used it to signalize their work: George Oppen, Louis Zukofsky, Charles Reznikoff, Lorine Niedecker and W. C. Williams. Individually they published several books and together, in 1932, *An "Objectivists" Anthology*. The movement, never widely accepted, was early abandoned. It arose as an aftermath of imagism (q.v.), which the Objectivists felt was not specific enough, and applied to any image that might be conceived. O. concerned itself with an image more particularized yet broadened in its significance. The mind rather than the unsupported eye entered the picture.　　w.c.w.

OBJECTIVITY. See SUBJECTIVITY AND OBJECTIVITY.

OBLIQUE RHYME. See NEAR RHYME.

OBSCURITY. Almost invariably the critics and historians of modern poetry have observed that it is as a body of poetry more obscure than the poetry of earlier periods—and have then proceeded to give reasons for this phenomenon. At least two critics, F. W. Dupee and John Crowe Ransom, see o. as largely a matter of deliberate intention. Dupee says that neoclassical poetry, for example, exhibits "a peculiarly brilliant and aggressive clarity," that this is a "stylistic feature of the school of Pope," and that modern poetry, on the other hand, is aggressively obscure and difficult. No single poet is to be held responsible for this; o. and difficulty are characteristics of "a general style." Dupee adds that this style is the poets' way of implying a negative judgment on the complexities of modern life, on the relatively inaccessible sciences, on the multiple beliefs we are asked to discriminate among, on the separation of art from everyday life, and so on. The poets' private myths, allusiveness, and ambiguity are their way of saying nay to a world they do not approve of. Ransom's theory is somewhat similar to this. He holds that in our post-Renaissance era knowledge has become more and more narrow and intensified, especially in the realms of science and applied science. In the process, poetry has lost a good deal of its power and prestige. "The poets," Ransom says, "are in the spirit of their time. On the one hand, they have been pushed out of their old attachments, whereby they used to make themselves useful to public causes, by the specialists who did not want the respective causes to be branded with amateurism. On the other hand, they were moved by a universal tendency into their own appropriate kind of specialization, which can be, as they have been at pains to show, as formidable as any other." Ransom's point, of course, is that modern poets have played down poetry-as-communication or as message and concentrated on exploiting poetry as medium.

Both of the above theories participate in the conception of the poet as alienated from his society, a conception that has given rise to many articles and books. Delmore Schwartz and William York Tindall have made interesting contributions to this literature. Schwartz says that as early as the 17th c. there was "a break between intellect and sensibility [what is commonly called the "dissociation of sensibility"]; the intellect finds unreasonable what the sensibility and the imagination cannot help but accept." There was a general suspicion of language used for emotional and imaginative purposes—for myths. Science and applied science made tremendous strides, thereby greatly increasing the industrialization of society. An unfortunate consequence of this, Schwartz says, is that there was little or no room left for the cultivated man. Poetry as a part of culture became more and more autonomous, and therefore more and more self-regarding and specialized, the poets writing for themselves or for small coteries. Tindall sees the exile of the poet as a break with the middle class. "Accustomed to expressing feelings and ideas shared with their literate audience, poets slowly realized their disinclination or inability to express feelings so much coarser than their own. About the middle of the century Baudelaire looked out of his window and was filled with the 'immense nausea of billboards.' The rest follows from this." The poets tend to write not about public matters but about themselves, and to write for others equally sensitive. Randall Jarrell has described the way in which many modern poets regard their medium as: "very interesting language, a great emphasis on connotation, texture; extreme intensity, forced emotion—violence; a good deal of obscurity; emphasis on sensation, perceptual nuances; emphasis on details, on the part rather than on the whole; experimental or novel qualities of some sort; a tendency toward external formlessness and internal disorganization—these are justified, generally, as the disorganization required to express a disorganized age, or alternatively, as new-discovered and more complex types of organization; and extremely personal style—*refine your singularities;* lack of restraint —all tendencies are forced to their limits; there is a good deal of emphasis on the unconscious, dream-structure, the thoroughly subjective." This statement is probably most appropriate as a description of the more willful modern poets. Yet if it is taken as a slightly exaggerated statement it can stand as a description of the way the medium of poetry has been employed by modern poets.

There is undoubtedly a good deal of truth in these various theories, but perhaps all of them put a little too much emphasis on the poet's choosing to write obscurely, and not enough emphasis on the factors in modern culture that make at least a certain degree of o. inevitable. R. P. Blackmur says this about poetry in ages prior to the 20th c.: "The artist's task was principally to express the continuity of his culture and the turbulence that underlay it. That is perhaps why we find the history of criticism so much concerned with matters of decorum: that is to say, with conformity, elegance, rhetoric, or metrics: matters not now commonly found or considered in our reviews." Of the major imaginative works of our own time, he says this: "Those who seem to be the chief writers of our time have found their subjects in attempting to dramatize at once both the culture and the turbulence it was meant to control, and in doing so they have had poetically to create—as it happens, to re-create—the terms, the very symbolic substance, of the culture as they went along." One may illustrate Blackmur's comment by references to the cultural "history" that Yeats wrote as background for his poetry, the myths that Eliot used in order to dramatize his vision of a modern waste-land, or the theory of aesthetics that Stevens worked out both in the writing and in the justifying of his poetry. (The same sort of thing could be said about Joyce or Mann.) As Blackmur puts it, the modern poets must create or re-create their very symbolic structures. Perhaps one should qualify this, by saying that the remarks pertain especially to "major" poets, to those who create coherent and self-defined mythic visions. These poets have felt and suffered from what Marc Friedlander calls a loss of the "common store" —"the loss of a frame of traditional values in which the artist and his audience move easily and with confidence." We no longer have the classical myths which were understood by poets and audiences down into the Victorian world, and even our Christian myths (the Bible, legends of saints, etc.) are available only to certain groups. Nor can it be assumed that any two "educated" men know the same facts or believe in the same values. "The elimination of obscurity in our literature waits upon the reconstitution of the audience of which the poet may feel a part, upon the creation of a common store of reference, familiarity with which would be shared by all who might properly be called *educated*."

J. C. Ransom, "Poets Without Laurels," *The World's Body* (1938); R. Jarrell, Preface to "The Rage for the Lost Penny," *Five Young Am. Poets* (1940); D. Schwartz, "The Isolation of Modern Poetry," KR, 3 (1941); W. Y. Tindall, "Exiles: Rimbaud to Joyce," *Am. Scholar*, 14 (1945); F. W. Dupee, "Difficulty as Style," *ibid.;* M. Friedlander, "Poetry and the Common Store," *ibid.;* W. Van O'Connor, "Forms of O.," *Sense and Sensibility in Modern Poetry* (1948);

A. Tate, "Understanding Modern Poetry," *On the Limits of Poetry* (1948); R. P. Blackmur, "A Burden for Critics," *Lectures in Crit.* (1949); J. Press, *The Chequer'd Shade: Reflections on O. in Poetry* (1958; systematic and comprehensive). w.v.o'c.

OCCASIONAL VERSE. Any poem, light or serious, good or bad, written for a special occasion and with a special purpose, as, for example, the memorial pieces in honor of Edward King, among which *Lycidas* was one; the birthday odes expected of a poet laureate; tributes to a poet placed at the beginning of his volume particularly in the 16th and 17th c.; epithalamia, such as those by Spenser and Donne; funeral elegies, respectful or ironic; sonnets or odes memorializing some state occasion or historic event; or the prologues and epilogues to 17th- and 18th-c. plays. O.v. is public poetry and has a practical social function to perform.

Certain modern poets, e.g., W. B. Yeats, Ezra Pound, William Carlos Williams, have written a good deal of o.v. Some modern occasional poems are Hardy's *On an Invitation to the United States,* Yeats's *Easter, 1916,* and Auden's *September 1, 1939.* A characteristic brief example is Yeats's epigram *On Those that Hated 'The Playboy of the Western World,' 1907:*

> Once, when midnight smote the air,
> Eunuchs ran through Hell and met
> On every crowded street to stare
> Upon great Juan riding by:
> Even like these to rail and sweat
> Staring upon his sinewy thigh.
>
> A.J.M.S.

OCTAMETER. A line of 8 measures or feet, rare in classical poetry (see OCTONARIUS); rarer still in Eng., though Poe claimed some lines of *The Raven* were in o. acatalectic. The most noteworthy, if not the only true, example in Eng. is found in Swinburne's *March,* from *Poems and Ballads.* OCTASTICH. A group or stanza of 8 lines; also an huitain (q.v.), a poem of 8 lines.

OCTAVE, octet. A group of 8 lines, either a stanza (ottava rima, *Monk's Tale* stanza, qq.v.) or part of a stanza, as the first 8 lines of a sonnet (usually rhyming abbaabba) are called the octave, or octet. "I Have finished the First Canto, a long one, of about 180 octaves," Byron, *Letter to Murray.* R.O.E.

OCTONARIUS (L. "of 8 each"). The Roman equivalent of the Gr. acatalectic tetrameter. Whereas the latter was divided into four complete pairs of feet or dipodies, the iambic, trochaic, and anapaestic octonarius of early Roman drama were each regarded as composed of 8 complete feet.—W. M. Lindsay, *Early L. Verse* (1922); Crusius. R.J.G.

OCTOSÍLABO. See OCTOSYLLABIC VERSE.

OCTOSYLLABIC VERSE. Tetrameter verse in iambs or trochees, with variants limited to prevent "tumbling verse." It forms the structural line of several stanzas (long meter, *In Memoriam* stanza, etc.) but is more commonly associated with couplets. Byron's reference to "the fatal facility of the octo-syllabic meter" recognizes the danger of sing-song monotony, a danger offset, however, by the feeling of rapid movement inherent in the pattern which makes it an excellent medium for narrative verse. In the hands of a skilled craftsman monotony is not difficult to avoid, as is evident in Milton's *Il Penseroso:*

> Come, pensive Nun, devout and pure,
> Sober, steadfast, and demure,
> All in a robe of darkest grain,
> Flowing with majestic train,
> And sable stole of cypress lawn
> Over thy decent shoulders drawn.
> Come; but keep thy wonted state,
> With even step, and musing gait . . .

The o. couplet derived from late medieval Fr. poetry (with a fusion of L. verse elements) in the chronicles, romances, and legends of the 12th c. (Wace, *Roman de Brut*); the romance of manners, *lais,* and *dits* in the 13th c. strengthened its position. In the course of time its association with verse essentially frivolous or gay marked its use in France, and even as late as the 18th c. Le Sage, Peron, and Voltaire employed it thus for popular appeal. The form (normally in varied rhyme schemes rather than couplets) reached Spain in the 14th c. (Ruiz, *Libro de Buen Amor*) from the Prov. troubadours by way of Galician-Portuguese sources, and strengthened a native tendency toward it in earlier Sp. poetry. By the 15th c. it was firmly established through collections of courtly lyrics (e.g., *Cancionero de Baena*), and since that time has come to be "the national meter par excellence."

In England the influence of Fr. o. verse in the 12th and 13th c. (through Anglo-Norman poets like Gaimar, Wace, Benoit) led to refinement on the common accentual 4-stress Anglo-Saxon structure for narratives, with evidence of growing syllabic regularity as the couplet developed through a flexible use in Chaucer (*The Boke of the Duchesse,* etc.), monotonous regularity in Gower (*Confessio Amantis*), and so to miracle and morality plays and a lessening Elizabethan use. The vehicle next of shorter poems, descriptive or philosophical, by Jonson, Milton, Dyer, Parnell, Gay, Swift, Collins, and others, its most notable 17th-c. narrative use was in the widely imitated *Hudibras* of Samuel Butler (1612–80), the individuality of whose jogging satiric verse with its ingenious rhymes has distinguished it as "Hudibrastic verse" (q.v.). Serious or whimsical narrative was again written in the form as Burns, Wordsworth, and Coleridge, but especially Byron, Scott, and later, Morris, brought the couplet to its height in the 19th c. Other more varied patterns have tended to overshadow if not to replace the o. couplet in modern poetry, although an occasional distinctive use will be found, as in Edna St. Vincent Millay's popular *Renascence*.—Saintsbury, *Prosody;* Schipper; Hamer; E. N. S. Thompson, "The O. Couplet," PQ, 18 (1939); D. C. Clarke, "The Sp. Octosyllable," HR, 10 (1942); J. Saavedra Molina, *El octosílabo castellano* (1945); M. D. Legge, *Anglo-Norman Lit. and Its Background* (1964).   L.J.Z.

ODE (Gr. *aeidein* "to sing," "to chant"). In modern usage the name for the most formal, ceremonious, and complexly organized form of lyric poetry, usually of considerable length. It is frequently the vehicle for public utterance on state occasions, as, for example, a ruler's birthday, accession, funeral, the unveiling or dedication of some imposing memorial or public work. The o. as it has evolved in contemporary literatures generally shows a dual inheritance from classic sources, combining the reflective or philosophic character of the Horatian o. with the occasional character of the Pindaric o. (e.g., Tennyson's *Ode on the Death of the Duke of Wellington*). Frequently elaborate and complex stanzas are used, based ultimately upon either the triadic structure of the Pindaric o. or upon imitations of or developments from it, combining great variety in length of line with ingenious rhyme schemes. The serious tone of the o. not only calls for the use of a heightened diction and enrichment by poetic device, but thus lays it open, more readily than any other lyric form, to burlesque. A third form of the modern o., the Anacreontic, is descended from the 16th-c. discovery of a group of some sixty poems, all credited to Anacreon, although the Gr. originals now appear to span a full thousand years. In general the lines are short and, in comparison with the Pindaric o., the forms simple, with the subjects being love or drinking, as in the 18th-c. song "To Anacreon in Heaven," whose tune has been appropriated for "The Star-Spangled Banner."

In Gr. literature, the odes of Pindar (522–442 B.C.) were designed for choric song and dance. The words, the sole surviving element of the total Pindaric experience, reflect the demands of the other two arts. A strophe, a complex metrical structure whose length and pattern of irregular lines varies from ode to ode, reflects a dance pattern, which is then repeated exactly in an antistrophe, the pattern being closed by an epode, or third section, of differing length and structure. Length of the o. itself (surviving examples range from fragments to nearly 300 lines) is achieved through exact metrical repetition of the original triadic pattern. These odes, written for performance in a Dionysiac theatre or perhaps in the Agora to celebrate athletic victories, frequently appear incoherent through the brilliance of imagery, abrupt shifts in subject matter, and apparent disorder of form within the individual sections. Modern criticism has answered such objections, which date from the time of Pindar himself and range through Gr. and L. to modern times, by discerning dominating images, emotional relationships between subjects, and complex metrical organization. The tone of the odes is emotional, exalted, intense, and the subject matter whatever divine myths can be adduced to the occasion being celebrated. In L. literature, the characteristic o. is associated with Horace (65–8 B.C.), who derived his forms not from Pindar but from less elaborate Gr. lyrics, through Alcaeus and Sappho. The Horatian o. is stanzaic and regular, based upon a limited number of metrical variations (Alcaics, Sapphics, etc.). It is personal rather than public, general rather than occasional, tranquil rather than intense, contemplative rather than brilliant, and intended for the reader in his library rather than for the spectator in the theatre.

Throughout Europe the history of the o. commences with the rediscovery of the classic forms. The humanistic o. of the 15th and earlier 16th c. shows the adaptation of old meters to new subjects by Fifelfo, in both Gr. and L., and by Campano, Pontano, and Flaminio in neo-Latin. The example of the humanistic o. and the publication in 1513 of the Aldine edition of Pindar were the strongest influences upon the vernacular o. In Italy, tentative Pindaric experiments were made by Trissino, Alamanni, and Minturno, without establishing the o. as a new genre. More successful were the attempts in France by members of the *Pléiade*, where, after minor trials of the new form by others, Pierre de Ronsard in 1550 published *The First Four Books of the Odes* with stylistic imitations of Horace, Anacreon, and (in the first book) Pindar. Influenced by Ronsard, Bernardo Tasso and Gabriele Chiabrera later in the century succeeded in popularizing the form in Italy, where it has been used successfully by, among others, Manzoni, Leopardi (in his *Odicanzone*), Carducci (*Odi barbare*, 1877), and

D'Annunzio (*Odi navale*, 1892). In France, the example of Ronsard was widely followed, notably by Boileau in the 17th c., and by Voltaire and others in formal, occasional verse in the 18th. The romantic period lent a more personal note to both form and subject matter, notably in the work of Lamartine, Musset, and Victor Hugo. Later, highly personal treatments of the genre may be found in Verlaine's *Odes en son honneur*, 1893, and Valéry's *Odes*, 1920.

The o. became characteristically German only with the work of G. R. Weckherlin (*Oden und Gesänge*, 1618–19), who, as court poet at Stuttgart, attempted to purify and refashion German letters according to foreign models. In the middle of the next century Klopstock modified the classic models by use of free rhythms, grand abstract subjects, and a heavy influence from the Lutheran psalms. Later Goethe and Schiller returned to classical models and feeling, as in Schiller's *Ode to Joy*, used in the final movement of Beethoven's Ninth Symphony. At the turn of the century Hölderlin in his complex, mystical, unrhymed odes united classic themes with the characteristic resources of the German language. Since Hölderlin, few noteworthy odes have been written in German, with the possible exception of those of Rudolph Alexander Schröder (*Deutsche Oden*, 1912).

The few attempts at domesticating the o. in 16th c. England were largely unsuccessful, although there is probably some influence of the classical o. upon Spenser's *Prothalamion* and *Epithalamion*. In 1629 appeared the first great imitation of Pindar in Eng., Ben Jonson's *Ode on the Death of Sir H. Morison*, with the strophe, antistrophe, and epode of the classical model indicated by the Eng. terms "turn," "counter-turn," and "stand." In the same year began the composition of Milton's great o., *On the Morning of Christ's Nativity*, in regular stanzaic form. The genre, however, attained great popularity in Eng. only with the publication of Abraham Cowley's *Pindarique Odes* in 1656, in which he attempted, like Ronsard and Weckherlin before him, to make available to his own language the spirit and tone of Pindar rather than to furnish an exact transcription of his manner. With Dryden begin the great formal odes of the 18th c.: *Alexander's Feast, Ode to the Memory of Mrs. Anne Killigrew*, and, marking the reunion of formal verse and music, the *Song for St. Cecilia's Day* (1687). For the 18th c. the o. was the perfect means of expressing the sublime, whether approached through the allegorical, the descriptive, or through terror, as in Gray's *The Bard*. In the mid-18th c., the odes of Collins and Gray used less elaborate devices and more romantic themes. The true romantic o. in Eng. literature begins with Coleridge's

Dejection: An Ode (1802) and Wordsworth's *Ode on Intimations of Immortality* (written 1802–4, publ. 1815). Wordsworth's *Ode,* with its varied line lengths, complex rhyme scheme, and stanzas of varying length and pattern, has been called the greatest Eng. Pindaric o.:

> The rainbow comes and goes,
> And lovely is the rose;
> The moon doth with delight
> Look round her when the heavens are bare;
> Waters on a starry night
> Are beautiful and fair;
> The sunshine is a glorious birth;
> But yet I know, where'er I go,
> That there hath past away a glory from the earth.

Of the other major romantic poets, Shelley wrote the *Ode to the West Wind*, and Keats wrote the *Ode on a Grecian Urn, Ode to a Nightingale*, and *Ode to Autumn*, probably the most brilliant group of odes in the language. Since the romantic period, with the exception of a few brilliant, isolated examples, such as Tennyson's *Ode on the Death of the Duke of Wellington*, the formal Pindaric o. has been neither a popular nor a really successful genre in Eng. Among modern poets, the personal o. in the Horatian manner has been revived with some success, notably by Allen Tate (*Ode to the Confederate Dead*) and W. H. Auden (*In Memory of W. B. Yeats, To Limestone*).

G. Carducci, "Dello svolgimento dell'ode in Italia," *Opere*, xvi (1905); R. Shafer, *The Eng. O. to 1660* (1918); K. Viëtor, *Gesch. der deutschen O.* (1923) ; A. W. Pickard-Cambridge, *Dithyramb, Tragedy and Comedy* (1927); F. Neri, "O.," *Enciclopedia italiana*; Bowra; G. N. Shuster, *The Eng. O. from Milton to Keats* (1940); G. Highet, *The Cl. Tradition* (1949); *Annalen der deutschen Literatur*, ed. H. O. Burger (1952); N. Maclean, "From Action to Image: Theories of the Lyric in the 18th C.," in Crane, *Critics*; C. Maddison, *Apollo and the Nine: A Hist. of the O.* (1960); N. E. Collinge, *The Structure of Horace's Odes* (1961); G. Thomson, *Gr. Lyric Metre* (rev. ed., 1961); S. Commager, *The Odes of Horace: A Crit. Study* (1962). s.f.f.

ODL (rhyme). Both end rhyme and internal rhyme are features of Welsh poetry from the beginning (6th c.), and *cynghanedd* (q.v.) involves internal rhyming. Repetition of final unstressed vowels together with the consonants which follow them is adequate in Welsh verse (father/sister), for all vowels are distinct, stress accent is not very strong, and the rhyming of final syllables was established before the shift of accent from final to penultimate syllables. Rhyming of stressed with unstressed syllables (stick/ecclesiastic) is common in Welsh, and in some meters (*englyn* and *cywydd*) is obligatory. There are two kinds of partial rhyme in Welsh: (a) "Ir." rhyme, as in Gaelic, where only the vowels correspond, and the consonants following them need only to belong to the same phonetic group; (b) *proest*, where the consonants following the vowel correspond exactly, and the vowels (or diphthongs) are only of the same length (an, in, on). Nostalgia, or a sense of loss or incompleteness can be very effectively conveyed thus. Wilfred Owen made much use of *proest* in Eng.—Morris-Jones; Parry. D.M.L.

OLD GERMANIC PROSODY. The Teutonic peoples of the early Middle Ages had a remarkably homogeneous prosodic system, specimens of which have survived in runic inscriptions and poetic manuscripts. The majority of these are in the Old English (OE) and Old Norse (ON) languages, but enough survives also of the Old Saxon (OS) and Old High German (OHG) poetic documents to allow some generalizations about a large corpus of poetry.

No matter what its theme or place of origin, and in spite of the comparatively late time at which most of it was copied into written form, Old Germanic (OGc.) poetry is highly formulaic and formalistic, so that its techniques are comparable from century to century and from one linguistic area to another. The material versified is of many kinds: legal texts, mnemonic lists of rulers and peoples, heroic epics and religious narratives, reflective or elegiac lyrics, sober collections of maxims, encomiastic pieces, and others besides, including a variety of satirical and erotic verses.

The most important key to the governing style of OGc. poetic composition is the fact that the poetry was so largely an oral phenomenon prior to the introduction of Christianity and the Latin alphabet into the Gc. area. That is, oral composition upon traditional themes helped create and perpetuate a leisurely, formulaic, periphrastic, and repetitious style, with considerable freedom in syntax, and an elaborate poetic diction in which the kenning (q.v.) is a conspicuous feature. This flow of verse (spoken, chanted, or sung) is rhythmically organized into a series of short, metrically independent phrases or verses. The verses contain 2 stressed syllables which are long in quantity, and differing numbers of syllables in addition which are relatively unstressed and may be long or short in quantity. A "resolved stress" sometimes occurs when two short syllables, only the first of which is accented, replace a single long accented syllable. The quantitative and accentual unit thus formed will resemble one of five metrical

"types"—patterns of long and short, stressed and unstressed syllables—analytically described by Eduard Sievers (see below) as common to all OGc. verse; a detailed examination of these basic patterns would be beyond the scope of this survey. Finally, this independent basic verse or metrical unit is linked to another by the rhyming of initial sounds in some, not all, of the stressed syllables, and the verse-pairs so created are centrally divided by a pause. In modern editions of the poetry these verse-pairs are printed as a single typographical line. The alliteration within the verse-pairs is systematic, not occasional or ornamental. As a rule, each initial consonantal sound rhymes with itself only; any vowel or diphthong rhymes with itself or with any other vowel or diphthong. Thus an alliterative meter (q.v.), ordering and emphasizing what would be the normal spoken accents of successive phrases, is the conservative foundation upon which most OGc. poetry is built. Side by side with this complex poetic form there may well have existed similar but less exacting popular meters which are now lost beyond hope of recovery. But the written records, faulty as they often are, display a poetic tradition which is at best superb, perhaps especially in the epic recitative of long narrative poems, where with vigorous stresses and sonorous vowel music the linked verses flow, wheel, and clash by turns, moving with a magisterial deliberation proper to the art of the court singer, or, to give him his Anglo-Saxon name, the scop (q.v.). This is an oral poetry not merely in the circumstances of its origins, but also in the sense that it must be heard aloud if justice is to be done to its essential nature.

A passage from the OE *Beowulf* (205–16) will demonstrate the structure and illustrate some of the stylistic features just described. In this and the following examples, marks of vowel quantity are ignored and secondary stresses are also left unmarked.

> Hǽfde se góda   Géata léoda
> cémpan gecórone   þára þe he cénoste
> fíndan míhte;   fíftyna súm
> súndwudu sóhte,   sécg wísade,
> lágucræftig món   lándgemýrcu.
> Fýrst fórð gewat;   flóta wæs on ýðum,
> bát under béorge.   Béornas géarwe
> on stéfn stígon,—   stréamas wúndon,
> súnd wið sánde;   sécgas bǽron
> on béarm nácan   béorhte frǽtwe,
> gúðsearo géatolic;   gúman út scufon,
> wéras on wílsið   wúdu búndenne.

The hero had chosen fighters from the men of the Geats, the boldest he could find; he and fourteen others went to the sea-wood [i.e., ship]; the man skilled in the craft of the sea showed the way to the shore. The time came that the vessel was in the waves at the foot of the cliff. Ready warriors climbed aboard; currents eddied, sea against sand; men brought bright treasure and splendid war-gear into the ship's bosom; mariners pushed off the trim craft on the journey they eagerly sought.

The same basic metrical structure and stylistic manner are evident in the OS *Heliand* (2005-2012):

> Wérod blíðode,
> wárun thar an lúston líudi atsámne,
> gúmon gládmodie. Géngun ámbahtman,
> skénkeon mid scálun, drogun skírianne wín
> mid órcun endi mid álofatun; was thar érlo dróm
> fágar an fléttea.

The troop was in good spirits; people there were happy together; men were cheerful. Servants went around with pitchers; they poured clear wine with cups and vessels; there was a splendid revelry of heroes in the hall.

An equally pronounced repetitive and periphrastic style will be noted in the OHG *Hildebrandlied* (63-68):

> Do léttun se ǽrist ásckim scrítan,
> scárpen scúrim, dat in dem scíltim stónt.
> Do stópun tosámane, stáimbort chlúbun,
> héuwun hármlicco húitte scílti,
> únti im iro líntun lúttilo wúrtun,
> giwígan miti wábnum.

Then first they let fly spears, sharp weapons, so that they stuck in the shields. Then they strode together, split the bucklers, hacked grimly at the bright linden shields until they were cut to bits, destroyed by weapons.

ON verse bears a strong family resemblance to other Gc. national poetry, especially in the narrative stanza known as *fornyrðislag* (old lore meter); but in this example, chosen from the *Darraðarljóð*, it will be noted that the stanzaic form itself (one of several common in ON verse) contrasts with the stichic or nonstanzaic poetry of other Gc. traditions:

> Víndum, víndum véf dárraðar,
> þars vé váða vígra mánna;
> látum éigi líf hans fárask;
> éigu válkyrjur váls um kósti.

We weave, we weave the web of the spear, while the brave warrior's standard advances; we shall not let him lose his life; only the valkyries may decide who shall be slain.

The ON stanza, concentrating as it does upon one verse paragraph at a time, lends itself to a less relaxed and flexible style, and easily achieves a greater intensity than will be found, for instance, in OE epic verse. During the 9th c. and afterward in Norway and Iceland, this concentration, accompanied by an elaboration of kenningar, developed into the extraordinary complexity and artifice of the skaldic stanzas, as in the court measure or *dróttkvætt* (q.v.).

It remains to be said that some technical aspects of OGc. prosody are still disputed even after many decades of study. At present little is known about the partnership of the verse with the vocal and instrumental music which must have been associated with it in early times. Contradictory theories about the exact scansion of the verse itself—for example, the arrangement of strong and subordinate stresses, the scansion of certain expanded verses, and the use of pauses or rests within the verse-pairs—continue to be advanced, and cannot be discussed in a short space; a few important and suggestive works are listed below. However, the student who has made a beginning at the languages themselves will find that he can read the verse with pleasure if he is careful to observe and reproduce aloud whenever he can the rhetorical intention of the poet-singer, who based his art upon the natural (that is, the logical and grammatical) patterns of stress in Gc. speech rhythms.

E. Sievers, *Altgermanische Metrik* (1893) and *Zur Rhythmik des germanischen Alliterationsverses* (anastatic reprint, N.Y., 1909); A. Heusler, *Die altgermanische Dichtung* (1923); J. C. Pope, *The Rhythm of Beowulf* (1942); M. Daunt, "OE Verse and Speech Rhythm," Philological Soc., *Transactions*, 1946 (1947); P. F. Baum, "The Meter of the *Beowulf*," MP, 46 (1948-9); F. P. Magoun, Jr., "Oral-Formulaic Character of Anglo-Saxon Narrative Poetry," *Speculum*, 28 (1953); W. P. Lehmann, *The Development of Gc. Verse Forms* (1956); J. C. Pope, *OE Versification* (mimeographed ed., Yale Univ., 1957); A. J. Bliss, *The Metre of Beowulf* (1958) and *An Introd. to OE Metre* (1962). J.B.B.

OLD NORSE POETRY. The term "Old Norse" (ON) is here used in its broad sense of "Old Scandinavian" (*norrænn*), with particular reference to Norway and Iceland.

The creative poetic genius of the early Scandinavians, more specifically of the Norwegians and the Icelanders, found a lasting expression in two main branches of poetry: The Eddic Poems and the Skaldic or Court Poetry, both of which are rooted deep in the cultural soil of ancient Scandinavia and embody age-old Germanic traditions as well. The bulk of the Eddic Poems, 29 out of the 34 usually included in the *Elder* or *Poetic Edda*, are preserved in the precious 13th c. Icelandic manuscript *Codex Regius (Konungsbók)* in the

Royal Library at Copenhagen. All that we know for certain about its history is that it came into the possession of the learned humanist and antiquarian, Bishop Brynjólfur Sveinsson of Skálholt, in 1643. He ascribed the collection to Sæmundur Sigfússon the Learned (1056–1133), and gave it the title of *Sæmundar Edda,* although the designation *Elder* or *Poetic Edda* later gained currency. It should be added that there is no reason to believe that Sæmundur the Learned, whatever else he may have written, had any connection with this priceless manuscript. The title *Edda* was, however, correctly applied to Snorri Sturluson's famed handbook for poets, briefly considered below. Various theories have been advanced concerning the meaning of the word "Edda," the most plausible of which is the explanation, originally suggested by Eiríkr Magnússon, that it means "The Book of Oddi," linking it to the long-time intellectual and cultural center by that name in southern Iceland.

The Eddic Poems have, as already indicated, their roots deep in ancient Germanic and Scandinavian soil. Their authors and compiler are unknown to us, although some ingenious conjectures have been made concerning the authorship of several of these poems. Their date of composition is also a matter of conjecture among specialists in the field. On the basis of the available evidence, they appear, generally speaking, to have been composed between 800 and 1100, while most of them were probably put into writing between 1150 and 1250. Limitation of space excludes extended discussion of the much-debated question of the home of the Eddic Poems. Iceland, Norway, and the Western Islands all have had their advocates, and the specialists still continue to disagree on the point. Professor Jón Helgason of the University of Copenhagen has succinctly summed up the whole matter: "Clear and definite answers to the age and home of each individual poem are not available and will not be forthcoming. The only absolutely certain fact is that the poems have come down to us in Icelandic manuscripts, the most important of which are from the 13th century. The burden of proof rests on the one who wishes to seek their origin in remote ancient times or distant regions" ("Norges og Islands digtning," *Nordisk Kultur VIII B,* 1952, p. 69).

The 34 poems included in the *Poetic Edda* cover a wide range in terms of subject matter, mood, and style. They encompass such diverse productions as the majestic *Völuspá* (The Sibyl's Vision), with its "magnificent panorama of the course of the world"; the gnomic *Hávamál* (The Sayings of the High One) graphically expressing the practical wisdom of the Norse race; *Þrymskviða* (The Lay of Thrym), a rollicking ballad, describing in a

striking fashion Thor's recovery of his missing hammer; and a memorable cycle of heroic poems containing a Northern version of the Nibelung story. As befits the elevated theme of many of the Eddic Poems they are composed in a simple but dignified meter. In common with other early Germanic poetry, the meter is based on alliteration. The three principal verse forms are *fornyrðislag* (Old Meter), *ljóðaháttr* (Song Measure), and *málaháttr* (Speech Measure), all of which are explained more fully in individual entries. The significance and general character of the Eddic Poems are excellently summarized by Professor Lee M. Hollander in the opening words of the introduction to his translation of *The Poetic Edda* (1928, p. VII): "What the Vedas are for India, and the Homeric poems for the Greek world, that the Edda signifies for the Teutonic race: it is a repository, in poetic form, of the mythology and much of their heroic lore, bodying forth the ethical views and the cultural life of the North during Heathen times."

The Skaldic or Court Poetry flourished simultaneously with the Eddic Poems from the 10th to the 13th c., but they differ fundamentally from the *Edda* in subject matter and metrical form. In contrast to the Eddic Poems, with their relative variety of themes, the Skaldic Poems, of which a very large number has been preserved, consist primarily of praise of kings and other chieftains by poets (skalds), attached to their courts. Again, in contrast to the simple meters of the Eddic Poems, the Skaldic Poetry is characterized by an intricate, alliterated verse form, the most common being *dróttkvætt* (*dróttkvæðr háttr*) [q.v.] as well as by a specific poetic diction abounding in metaphorical descriptive terms (kennings). The more elaborate of these Skaldic Poems are known as *drápa* (q.v.). Despite the pictorial quality and the sonorous effect of these poems, generally they have much greater historical than artistic value.

The names of a great many of the court poets, as well as their life stories in varying detail, are known to us. The earliest of them were Norwegian, of whom the following are the most important: Bragi Boddason the Old, of the first half of the 9th c., whose *Ragnarsdrápa* is the pioneer poem in that genre; Þjóðólf of Hvin and Þorbjörn Hornklofi, both of whom were members of the court of King Harold Fairhair (ca. 860–933); and Eyvindr Finnsson skáldaspillir (ca. 910–ca. 990), the leading Norwegian court poet who has immortalized King Haakon the Good in his famous *Hákonarmál.*

From the 10th c. and on, the Icelanders monopolized and elaborated the art of Skaldic Poetry. Prominent among such Icelandic poets were: Kormákr Ögmundarson (ca. 935–ca. 970), the foremost love poet among the Icelandic skalds; Hallfreðr Óttarson (970–1007), attached to the court of King Olaf Tryggvason and the first Icel. court poet to deal with Christian themes; and Sighvatr Þórðarson, the court poet and devoted friend of King Olaf Haraldsson (Saint Olaf). The greatest of these Icel. skalds, however, was Egill Skallagrímsson (900–983), whose rugged viking character, robust intellect, and poetic genius are memorably revealed in his *Sonatorrek* (Sons' Lament), an impressive elegy commemorating his two sons. The *kviðuháttr* (q.v.) verse form harmonizes well with the tragic theme.

The Skaldic Poetry, in all its aspects, is brilliantly interpreted and illuminated in the *Prose* or *Younger Edda* by Snorri Sturluson (1178–1241), indeed a remarkable *ars poetica* of its kind.

When the Court Poetry, for various reasons, went out of general favor at the close of the 13th c., Icel. poets began writing poems on religious subjects in elevated Eddic meters or more frequently in Skaldic verse forms. The most noteworthy among the earlier poems of this type was *Sólarljóð* (Lay of the Sun), by an unknown author, from about 1200. A vision poem, composed in the resonant *ljóðaháttr*, it is highly didactic in theme, but marked by uncommon descriptive power and imaginative quality. Akin in theme and spirit, and occupying a prominent place in ON literature of the period, is the Norwegian vision poem, *Draumkvædet* (The Dream Vision), originally composed around the year 1200, but handed down in oral form until the 19th c. The most outstanding literary production of the 14th c. was the sacred poem *Lilja* (The Lily), by the Icel. monk Eysteinn Ásgrímsson (d. 1361). Written in the sonorous *hrynhenda* form (q.v.), it is an eloquent and masterfully constructed interpretation of medieval religious teachings.

Dance-songs of foreign origin were common in Iceland during the 12th and 13th c., but are now largely lost. They gradually developed into a new kind of poetry, the *rímur* (q.v.), which arose in the 14th c. and enjoyed great popularity into the 19th c., and even to this day have their admirers. Generally speaking, the cultural and linguistic importance of the *rímur* is, however, much greater than their literary significance.

ANTHOLOGIES: *Den norsk-islandske Skjaldedigtning*, ed. F. Jónsson (4 v., 1912–15); *Anglo-Saxon and Norse Poems*, ed. and tr. N. Kershaw (1922); *Rímur fyrir 1600*, ed. B. K. Þórólfsson (1934); *O.N. Poems* (1936) and *The Skalds* (1945), both tr. L. M. Hollander; *Eddic Lays*, ed. F. T. Wood (1940); *A Pageant of Old Scandinavia*, ed. H. G. Leach (1946); *Icel. Christian Classics*, tr. C. V. Pilcher (1950);

Sýnisbók íslenzkra rímna, ed. W. A. Craigie (3 v., 1953; specimens of Icel. *rímur*).

HISTORY AND CRITICISM: E. Mogk, *Gesch. der norwegisch-isländischen Lit.* (2d ed., 1904); W. P. Ker, *Epic and Romance* (1908); F. Jónsson, *Den oldnorske og oldislandske Litteraturs Historie* (2d ed., 3 v., 1920–24); R. Meissner, *Die Kenningar der Skalden* (1921); *The Hávamál*, ed. and tr. D. E. Martin Clarke (1923); F. Paasche, *Norsk Litteratur-historie*, I (1924); E. Noreen, *Den Norsk-Isländske Poesien* (1926); *The Poetic Edda*, tr. H. A. Bellows (1923) and tr. L. M. Hollander (1928, rev. ed., 1962); *The Prose Edda*, tr. A. G. Brodeur (1929); B. Nerman, *The Poetic Edda in the Light of Archaeology* (1931); H. Hermannsson, *Old Icel. Lit.* (1933); B. S. Phillpotts, *Edda and Saga* (1931); J. Helgason, *Norrön Litteraturhistorie* (1934); M. Schlauch, *Romance in Iceland* (1934); W. A. Craigie, *The Art of Poetry in Iceland* (1937); R. Beck, "Icel. Lit.," *Ency. of Lit.*, ed. J. T. Shipley (2 v., 1946); E. Ól. Sveinsson, *The Age of the Sturlungs*, tr. J. S. Hannesson (1953); G. Turville-Petre, *Origins of Icel. Lit.* (1953); S. Einarsson, *A Hist. of Icel. Lit.* (1957); E. Ól. Sveinsson, *Íslenzkar Bókmenntir í Fornöld* (1962).   R.B.

OMAR KHAYYÁM QUATRAIN (or *Rubáiyát* stanza; from Persian *rubāʿī*, quatrain). A stanza of 4 decasyllabic lines rhyming aaba (rarely aaaa). The name comes from Edward FitzGerald's *Rubáiyát of Omar Khayyám*, which is a loose adaptation of the Persian original (see PERSIAN POETRY), employing the same rhyme scheme but lacking the subtle rhythm: "I sometimes think that never blows so red / The Rose as where some buried Caesar bled; / That every Hyacinth the Garden wears / Dropt in its Lap from some once lovely Head." By leaving the third line blank FitzGerald avoids much of the monotony of the quatrain stanza. Swinburne's imitation, in *Laus Veneris*, links third lines in pairs. FitzGerald usually employs enjambment in the initial couplet, and his stanzas frequently have a sententious effect.   R.O.E.

ONOMATOPOEIA. Strictly, o. refers to the formation or use of words which imitate sounds, such as *hiss, snap, buzz, clash, murmur*. Broadly, the term refers to combinations of words in which any correspondence is felt between sound and sense, whether of sound, of motion, or of mood. In Tennyson's

The moan of doves in immemorial elms
And murmuring of innumerable bees,

only *moan* and *murmuring* are strictly onomatopoetic, but their reinforcement by the repeated m's, n's, and r's of *immemorial, innumerable*, and *elms* makes the whole passage onomatopoetic in the broader sense.

Whether sounds of themselves can suggest meaning has been much disputed. Riding and Graves in *A Survey of Modernist Poetry* (1928) point out that the suggestiveness of Tennyson's lines is lost if their sounds are reproduced in a line of different meaning: "More ordure never will renew our midden's pure manure." Experimental evidence, however, indicates that sounds do have limited capacity for suggesting meaning; e.g. agreement will be almost universal as to which of the nonsense words *taketa* or *naluma* should go with a curved diagram and which with an angular one (W. Kohler, *Gestalt Psychology*, 1947). Undoubtedly this capacity has been often exaggerated and many purely fanciful correspondences discovered. Pope's dictum that "the sound must seem an echo to the sense" seems a reasonable view, since an echo comes after rather than before the event it accompanies. Most readers would agree that Tennyson's lines are more appropriate to their meaning than the following revision:

The moan of doves in stately ancient oaks
And quiet murmuring of countless bees.

The importance of o. to poetry has also been much disputed, some considering it the crowning technical achievement of the poet, others decrying it as a technical bauble quite removed from the essential nature of poetry. The historical record indicates that great poetry has existed without it, but that great poets in all languages have sought it. In Virgil's "Quadrupedante putrem sonitu quatit ungula campum" has been heard the gallop of a horse, and in Ennius's "At tuba terribili sonitu taratantara dixit" the sound of a trumpet. See also SOUND IN POETRY.—G. R. Stewart, *The Technique of Eng. Verse* (1930); L. P. Wilkinson, "O. and the Sceptics," CQ, 36 (1942); N. C. Stageberg and W. L. Anderson, *Poetry as Experience* (1952); C. R. Woodring, "O. and Other Sounds in Poetry," CE, 14 (1953). L.P.

ORAL POETRY is poetry composed *in* oral performance by people who cannot read or write. It is synonymous with traditional and folk poetry, the latter term being an unfortunate product of German romanticism, and begetter by translation of "popular." This definition *excludes* verse composed *for* oral presentation, as well as verse that is pure improvisation outside of traditional patterns. All o. poetry is sung or, at the very least, chanted, and can be divided into three general classifications: ritual, lyric, and narrative. The origins of o. poetry are those of poetry itself. As literacy spreads throughout the world at a now rapid pace, o. poetry seems destined in time to disappear.

The two main types of o. narrative poetry, in fact of all narrative poetry (q.v.) both o. and written, are epic and ballad. The former is stichic, the same metric line being repeated for the entire song; whereas the latter, the ballad, is stanzaic. This seems to be the most reliable distinction between the two forms. All other points of difference between them probably stem from the different manners in which they are performed. The epic tends to longer songs because of the rapidity of telling; whereas the ballad tends to be shorter since the stanza is usually a slower method of narration and an audience runs quickly out of patience.

The nonnarrative types of o. poetry include (a) the incantation or charm, (b) the love song, (c) the lament, (d) the wedding ritual songs, and (e) other ritual songs for special festivals. Indeed all these types, including the love song, are ritual in origin and in ultimate purpose.

The most distinctive characteristic of o. poetry is its fluidity of text. While this is best seen in long epic songs, where the length renders impossible exact memorization from frequent repetition, it is discernible also with shorter poems. In them, however, the text becomes more stable in the hands of a single singer in direct proportion to the number of times that it is sung. Such stability is the result of habit and does not arise from any idea that there is a single unalterable text. In the case of magic incantations (and they would belong in the category of o. poetry if they were in verse), the exact reproduction of a text would seem sometimes to be necessary to make the magic effective; but our evidence here should be reviewed with care, because it may be that only certain alliterations or assonances rather than certain words and phrases must be repeated. When illiterate people inform us that a text must be repeated exactly word for word, we know from a comparison of performances that they mean essential characteristic for essential characteristic; for their concept of a word is different from ours.

Fluidity of text, or, to put it in reverse, the absence of a single fixed text, arises from the technique of o. composition, which the poet learns over many years, no matter which genre of verse is in question. It is a technique of improvisation by means of "formulas," phrases which say what the poet wants and needs to say, fitted to the varying metrical conditions of his tradition. These "stereotyped" phrases have often been thought of as the building blocks from which the poets construct their lines. Actually, they are probably not so stereotyped as was at first thought. For one thing, the "formulas" pervade the poetry; every line and every part of a line in o. poetry is "formulaic."

It is not a question of merely a comparatively few noun-epithet combinations or frequently used metrical units for introducing speeches; everything in the style is in the category of formula. The most often used phrases, the ones that a singer or poet hears most frequently when he is learning and therefore learns first, establish the patterns for the poetry, its characteristic syntactic, rhythmic, metric, and acoustic molds and configurations. In time the individual practitioner of the art can form new phrases, create formulas, by analogy with the old as needed. When he actually has become proficient in thinking in the traditional patterns, including the traditional phrases and everything else like them, he is a full-fledged singer of o. poetry. He composes naturally in the forms of his tradition, unconsciously, and often at very rapid speed.

Even as the formulas and their basic patterns make composing of lines possible in fast performance, so the associative use of parallelism in sound, syntax, and rhythm aids the o. poet in moving from one line to another. A line suggests what is to follow it. At times the complexity of structural interconnections between verses in o. style is so great that it seems that man could have attained it only with the aid of writing. Such a conclusion has an almost ironic flavor; for the truth probably is that these intricate architectonics of expression were developed first in o. verse, thus establishing from very archaic times the techniques which man with writing inherited and then believed himself to have "invented" with the stylus, the quill, and the pen.

O. poetry is of *necessity* paratactic. Its style has been called an "adding" style, because the majority of its lines *could* terminate in a period, insofar as their syntax is concerned; instead, however, another idea is "added" to what precedes, and so on for line after line. A comparatively small percentage of necessary run-on lines is, therefore, another distinctive and symptomatic feature of o. style.

What has been said above is applicable to all o. verse, albeit in varying degrees, whether it be ritual, lyric, or narrative. Meaning is conveyed by the sounds, rhythms, and figurative patterns of the words as well as by their conventional denotation and their connotation. The purpose of ritual is fulfilled, its magic is made effective, by these meanings. The same can be said for lyric verse. But o. narrative poetry, be it ballad or epic, has a story to tell, and the fact that the tale is being told in o. traditional verse imparts to its form certain necessary characteristics and may even be said to have some bearing on the kind of story chosen to be thus related.

Because there is no fixed text, o. narrative is not, *cannot* be, memorized, and is in constant flux, both in regard to its text and in respect to its story. Although there are many repeated incidents, scenes, and stock descriptions, these remain themselves ever flexible, susceptible to expansion or contraction; a journey may be related briefly or with copious details, the description of armor may occupy one line or a hundred, and still be termed the same "theme," as such repeated incidents and descriptions are called. Each theme has a minimum core, not in terms of lines or parts of lines, but in terms of essential ideas. Its outward form is ever changing; its essence remains. The theme is multiform, and has existence only in its multiforms. Habit and frequent use may set its form in the practice of a single singer to some degree of stability, but no given form is sacrosanct. Themes are useful, even as the "formulas," in any song in which the incident or description may belong. The journey framework may be employed in any number of stories; the assembly of men or of gods is common to many tales in song. In learning a song the singer needs only to remember the proper names of people and places and the sequence of events; he has no necessity to memorize, even were there a fixed text available, because he has the building blocks and the techniques for rapid-fire composition.

The configuration of themes that form a song in o. tradition is similar to the single theme in its fluidity. Like the themes that make it up, the song may be long or short according to the desires of the singer at the moment of performance. It may be ornamented to a greater or less degree. It, too, has multiforms. They are usually called variants, or versions. Probably the term "multiform" is better, more accurate, because both "variant" and "version" carry greater implication of an "original" that has undergone some kind of change resulting in the text before us. These terms arose from the belief that a well-defined and well-made original, a fixed text, became changed and "corrupted" through the faults of o. transmission and that lapses of memory and imperfections of memory gave opportunity for addition of new material or substitution of new incidents. Such "oral transmission" surely has taken place, in later stages of ballad tradition especially, and in a tradition after the initial recording period when fixed texts, or for example, broadside ballads, were available to be memorized, well or badly, and "corrupted." But this is not pure o. transmission, particularly in the epic forms. Pure o. transmission involves not memorization but recomposition; it does not consider any text, i.e., any performance, as an "original" or in any way fixed. It results in a retelling, not in a reproduction. Each performance, or multiform, has its own validity and is unique, whether it be a "good" or a "bad" performance of the song.

In o. poetry one can, and must, distinguish three meanings of the word "song," especially in the narrative forms, but also in ritual and lyric as well. The first is that of any performance; for, as we have just said, each performance is unique and valid in its own right. The second might be called that of the specific subject matter; e.g., the song of the capture of Bagdad by Sultan Selim. Combining the first and the second meanings, one can say with accuracy that there will be as many texts of the specific song as there are performances, whether they are recorded or not. This distinction between songs is not in the subtle sense of, let us say, interpretations of a play (with fixed text) by different actors, or by the same group of actors on different evenings. The divergencies are greater. The third meaning of "song" could be called the "generic." The story of the capture of Bagdad (the specific song) falls into the configuration of a number of stories dealing with the capture of cities, just as the *Odyssey*, for example, falls into the general category of songs recounting the return of the hero after long absence from home. The texts of this "song" would be very numerous, of course, and would reach back into the depths of human history.

The generic song is of considerable importance in o. poetic tradition. It is not merely a convenient method of classification. It represents rather the significant core of ideas in a song that survive reinterpretation and specific application to "history," a core held together by tensions from the past that give a meaning to the song not apparent on its surface, no matter how lowly or local any given performance may be. Because of this core one might say that each song in o. tradition has its "original" within it and even reflects the origin of the very genre to which it belongs.

In o. poetry the question of authorship is as complicated as the apparently simple problem of what constitutes a "song." Yet it is clear, to use the first of the three meanings of song, given above, that the performer, the folk singer, if you will, is the "author" of his particular performance. The performer is composer as well. One has, therefore, multiple authors, even as one has multiple texts, of any specific or generic song. But of any given text, there is but one author, its performer-composer. This is a different concept of multiple authorship from that historically employed in Homeric and other epic criticism since Wolf. This concept, furthermore, does not agree with the "communal" authorship put forth by scholars of the romantic period.

The date of any o. poem is, therefore, the date of the performance, or composition; that of the specific song would be the date on which some singer for the first time adapted existing themes and configurations to other specific people and events, that is to say, it would be the date of the first performance. The latter is ordinarily out of our grasp. The date of the generic song is lost in prehistory. And what has been said of date and authorship of an o. song can also be said about the date and authorship of any theme in the narrative poetry, and perhaps even of any formula or group of formulas. Each of these units has a life of its own as well as a life in any given song or context, and each has then a history of its own in addition to its history in the song. The author of any multiform of a theme (or of a formula) is the performer whom we see and hear, and its date is the date of our seeing and hearing. The analogy with language is especially cogent. Any phrase we use in ordinary speech is ours, but it has a history of its own outside of, but including, our own usage. The analogy is close because the language of o. poetry, formulaic though it be, is in fact an organic language, an organism of man's imaginative life.

The study of o. poetry as such is still very young and scholars are only now beginning to explore some of its problems. O. poetry long played an integral role in the life of human beings and social communities; its practice provided that spiritual activity necessary to man's existence; its bonds with everyday life were manifold and close. Its outlines and even a few of its deeper qualities are now becoming clear, as we can sift them from the crude ore of the transitional periods in which they were first recorded. As we come to know how o. poetry is composed and transmitted, we see new modes for its evaluation. And these modes lead us back to the symbols and meanings of poetry itself.

M. Parry, *L'Epithète traditionelle dans Homère* (1928), *Les Formules et la métrique d'Homère* (1928) and "Studies in the Epic Technique of O. Verse Making, I: Homer and Homeric Style, II. The Homeric Language as the Language of an O. Poetry," HSCP, 41 (1930), 43 (1932); Chadwick; A. B. Lord, "Composition by Theme in Homer and South-slavic Epos," TPAPA, 82 (1951), "Homer's Originality: O. Dictated Texts," TPAPA, 84 (1953) and *The Singer of Tales* (1960); Wellek and Warren; C. M. Bowra, *Heroic Poetry* (1952); G. S. Kirk, *The Songs of Homer* (1962). A.B.L.

ORGANISM. Critics as diverse as Aristotle, Longinus, Emerson, Henry James, Croce, Dewey, and Brooks have analogized artistic works to living things. However, the analogy has been most fully exploited by the German romantic critics and Coleridge, who were trying to formulate a "nonmechanistic" aesthetics and psychology of the creative process. The poem, they said, begins as a "seed" or "germ" in the creative imagination of the poet; its growth, primarily an unconscious process, consists in assimilating to itself foreign and diverse materials; its development and final form are self-determined; the result is an artistic work which in essence is like a living thing in that multiplicity and unity, the particular and the universal, content and form have coalesced and fused.

In contemporary criticism "organic," though widely used, has all but lost its metaphoric significance. The term is claimed by or attributed to critical systems which hold that the chief concern of criticism should be with the unity of the literary work. This stand is based on the conviction that artistic objects are complex integrated wholes which secure their aesthetic effects primarily as a consequence of their being such wholes. Thus it follows that the parts of an artistic whole have qualities, meanings, or effects which they would not have separately and that the most important excellence that can be attributed to any of the parts is to show that it is a necessary element of that whole. If all the distinguishable parts of a whole are essential and in the proper order and if the whole lacks no part necessary for its completeness, then the parts are "organically related" and the whole has "organic unity."

Despite disagreements over what is "true organicism," organicists are united in their opposition to form-content dualisms, to "ornamental" metaphor or any other separation of style and meaning, to any "mechanical" or "external" unity imposed by genre requirements or "rules," and to any criticism which treats the parts of a literary work as discrete elements and judges the value of these parts by separate aesthetic criteria. See also FORM.

C. Brooks, "The Poem as O.," *Eng. Institute Annual* (1941) and "Implications of an Organic Theory of Poetry," *Lit. and Belief (EIE, 1958)*; S. C. Pepper, *The Basis of Crit. in the Arts* (1945); M. Weitz, *Philos. of the Arts* (1950); Abrams; W. K. Wimsatt, Jr., "Explication as Crit.," *The Verbal Icon* (1954); R. H. Fogle, "Organic Form in Am. Crit., 1840–1870," *The Development of Am. Lit. Crit.*, ed. F. Stovall (1955); H. Osborne, *Aesthetics and Crit.* (1955); E. Vivas, "What Is a Poem?" *Creation and Discovery* (1955); Krieger; R. H. Fogle, *The Idea of Coleridge's Crit.* (1962). F.G.

ORIGINALITY. In poetics, o. names a relational property indicating some degree of difference in matter or form that a new poem exhibits when it is compared with the total body of existing literature. Thus o. is opposed to the conventional and traditional; to plagiarism and imitation; to the hackneyed and the stereotyped. In a trivial sense, all poems are originals in that the peculiar combination of words that constitutes a particular poem did not exist before the poem was written. More importantly, o. has been attributed to a poem if it reflects novelty in diction, imagery, stanza form, or technical and structural devices; if it modifies an existing genre or establishes a new genre; if it treats of some facet of human life that had escaped literary treatment; if it describes something which could not be characterized as belonging to human life (Shakespeare's fairy lore); if it offers a new interpretation of human activity and destiny derived from philosophy, psychology, or some other science (compare Homer's treatment of Odysseus with that of Dante, Tennyson, and Joyce).

O. usually appears in systems of poetics as an aesthetic norm. Theorists from the beginning of criticism have disagreed as to whether o. is desirable and, if it is, to what extent it is desirable and in what aspects of a poem it should be reflected. Extreme positions have been defended. Coomaraswamy, speaking for a tradition that in Western poetics goes back to Plato, severely condemns the contemporary search for individuality and novelty: Eternal Truth does not change; the artist's function is to communicate Eternal Truth; any novelty in his work is therefore a defect. On the other hand, Edward Young, reacting to neoclassic recommendations to imitate the ancients, says, "We read *Imitation* with somewhat of his languor, who listens to a twice-told tale: Our spirits rouze at an *Original;* that is a perfect stranger, and all throng to learn what news from a foreign land. . . . All eminence, and distinction, lies out of the beaten road" (*Conjectures on Original Composition*, 1759). And in some versions of modern expressionist poetics o. is highly prized on the grounds that a poem should reflect a poet's unique personality or state of mind or his individual vision of reality. Most frequently, however, theorists have tried to recognize the claims of both tradition and individual talent, the original and the familiar, though not all theorists have given the same importance to both. Thus Coleridge recommends the reconciliation in a poem of "the sense of novelty and freshness, with old and familiar objects"; he says that his and Wordsworth's intention in *Lyrical Ballads* was to unite "the power of exciting the sympathy of the reader by a faithful adherence to the truth of nature, and the power of giving the interest of novelty by the modifying colors of imagination" (*Biographia Literaria*, ch. 14). Like Irving Babbitt, T. S. Eliot has attacked the modern tendency to recommend "the aggrandisement and exploitation of *personality*" in literature: "What is disastrous is that the writer should deliberately give rein to his 'individuality,' that he should even cultivate his differences from others; and that his readers should cherish the author of genius, not in spite of his deviations from the inherited wisdom of the race, but because of them." Eliot argues that a poet, under most circumstances, is successful only when writing within a tradition and that therefore his search for originality should be confined to producing "finer variations within a form." Thus the basic problem in evaluating a new poem is this: "Has this poet something to say, a little different from what anyone has said before, and has he found, not only a different way of saying it, but *the* different way of saying it which expresses the difference in what he is saying?" Finally, some systems of poetics reject o. as an aesthetic norm. Beardsley points out that since a poem can be original and good or original and bad, o. cannot be a valid standard, at least within the system of objective aesthetics that he is advocating. O. is a reason for admiring the poet and not his work.

I. Babbitt, "On Being Original," *Lit. and the Am. College* (1908) and "On Being Creative," *On Being Creative and Other Essays* (1932); J. L. Lowes, *Convention and Revolt in Poetry* (1919); L. P. Smith, *Words and Idioms* (1925); T. S. Eliot, *After Strange Gods* (1934) and *On Poetry and Poets* (1957), esp. "Johnson as Critic and Poet"; E. L. Mann, "The Problem of O. in Eng. Lit. Crit., 1750–1800," PQ, 18 (1939); A. K. Coomaraswamy, *Why Exhibit Works of Art?* (1943); M. C. Nahm, *Aesthetic Experience and Its Presuppositions* (1946) and *The Artist as Creator* (1956); M. C. Beardsley, *Aesthetics* (1958). A.R.B.; F.G.

ORIYA POETRY. See INDIAN POETRY.

OTTAVA RIMA. A stanza of 8 iambic lines, rhyming abababcc. Its origin is obscure, being variously attributed to development from the ballade or the *canzone* (qq.v.) or to imitation of the Sicilian *strambotto* (q.v.). However, it was in use in the religious verse of late 13th-c. Italy, and it was given definitive artistic form by Boccaccio in his *Teseida* (1340–42) and his *Filostrato* (1339–40). Becoming almost immediately the dominant form of It. narrative verse, it was developed by Poliziano, Pulci, and Boiardo in the 15th c. and reached its apotheosis in the *Orlando Furioso* (1516) of Ludovico Ariosto, whose genius exploited its potentialities for richness, complexity, and variety of effect. Later in the same century, Tasso showed his mastery of the form. The poets of Renaissance Spain and Portugal followed It. example in adopting the form for narrative purposes.

Notable epics in o.r. are Ercilla's *La Araucana* in Sp. and Camões' *Os Lusíadas* in Portuguese.

Although the form was occasionally used by the Eng. Renaissance poets (e.g., Wyatt, Spenser, and Drayton), it was not until the romantic period that the form found a true Eng. master in Byron, whose translation of a portion of Pulci's *Morgante Maggiore* seems to have made him aware of the stanza's possibilities. He employed the stanza in *Beppo, The Vision of Judgment*, and, with greatest success, in *Don Juan*. Keats and Shelley also wrote poems in o.r.

The work of the great masters of the stanza —Ariosto and Byron—suggests that o.r. is most suited to work of a varied nature, blending serious, comic, and satiric attitudes and mingling narrative and discursive modes. Byron, referring to the work of Pulci, calls it "the half-serious rhyme" (*Don Juan* 4.6). Its accumulation of rhyme, reaching a precarious crescendo with the third repetition, prepares the reader for the neat summation, the acute observation, or the epigrammatic twist which comes with the final couplet:

And Julia's voice was lost, except in sighs,
Until too late for useful conversation;
The tears were gushing from her gentle eyes,
I wish, indeed, they had not had occasion;
But who, alas, can love, and then be wise?
Not that remorse did not oppose temptation:
A little still she strove, and much repented,
And whispering "I will ne'er consent"—consented.

(Byron, *Don Juan* 1.117)

Furthermore, the stanza is long enough to earry the thread of narrative but not so long that it becomes unmanageable.—Schipper; Hamer; V. Pernicone, "Storia e svolgimento della metrica," in *Problemi ed orientamenti critici di lingua e di letteratura italiana*, ed. A. Momigliano, II (1948); Wilkins; G. M. Ridenour, *The Style of Don Juan* (1960). F.J.W.; A.P.

OXYMORON (Gr. "pointedly foolish"). A figure of speech which combines two seemingly contradictory elements. It is a form of condensed paradox (q.v.): "O heavy lightness! serious vanity! / Mis-shapen chaos of well-seeming forms! / Feather of lead, bright smoke, cold fire, sick health!" (Shakespeare, *Romeo and Juliet* 1.1). Although o. has been a recurrent device in poetry from the time of Horace ("concordia discors rerum"—the jarring harmony of things—*Epistulae* 1.12.19) to the time of Dylan Thomas, it is, *par excellence*, the rhetorical expression of the baroque era. Such poets as Marino in Italy, Góngora in Spain, Crashaw in England made it a primary vehicle of the 17th c. sensibility:

Welcome, all wonders in one sight!
Eternity shut in a span,
Summer in winter, day in night,
Heaven in earth, and God in man!

As the above quotation indicates, o. is particularly effective in evoking religious mysteries or other meanings which the poet feels to be beyond the reach of human sense. Its popularity in the late Renaissance owes something to the heightened religious concerns of that period and something to the revival of the habit of analogical thinking.

O., which reveals a compulsion to fuse all experience into a unity, should be carefully distinguished from antithesis (q.v.), which tends

P

PAEAN (Gr. *paian*). The earliest mention of a p. is in *Iliad* 1.473, where, after the plague which Apollo had sent upon them, the Achaeans sought to propitiate the god with song. Apollo in his capacity as god of healing came to be invoked as *Paian* ("healer"), whence choral songs in his honor or in that of his sister Artemis were called "paeans." The p. as a literary form was employed by Pindar and others in the classical period of ancient Greece. As time went on, it might also be addressed to a successful general like Lysander or T. Quinctius Flamininus. The p. should be distinguished from the paeon (q.v.) which, however, has the same derivation.—A. Fairbanks, *A Study of the Gr. P.* (1900); Smyth; G. Norwood, *Pindar* (1945). R.J.G.

PAEON. A metrical unit consisting of 1 long and 3 short syllables: first p., $-\smile\smile\smile$; second p., $\smile-\smile\smile$; third, $\smile\smile-\smile$; fourth, $\smile\smile\smile-$. The first and the fourth p. are, in effect, cretics ($-\smile-$) by resolution of their last and first syllables respectively. The second and the third p., however, exist only in ancient metrical theory, and the fourth is quite rare. Paeonic verse, especially the first p., is found in Gr. poetry and more frequently in comedy than in tragedy. Cretics and paeons may occur in combination (cf. Aristophanes, *Acharnians* 210ff.). In Eng. poetry all four types have been used in combination with other kinds of feet. While the first and fourth p. are rare, the second and especially the third are not uncommon in modern accentual verse:

The appealing | of the Passion | is tenderer |

to divide and categorize elements of experience. Significantly, the latter figure, with its basis in rationality, dominates the poetry of the 18th c., a period which regarded the figures of the baroque poets as examples of "bad taste" or "false wit." But o. is not exclusively suited to religious poetry. Against Milton's use of the figure in *Paradise Lost* to evoke the unimaginable glories of God we may place the lines from Shakespeare quoted earlier, the stock Petrarchan figures for love's contradictions, and many passages in which Keats expresses the paradoxes of man's sensuous experience. See also CATACHRESIS, SYNAESTHESIA.—Lausberg; E. Mc Cann, "O. in Sp. Mystics and Eng. Metaphysical Writers," CL, 13 (1961). F.J.W.; A.P.

in prayer apart"
(G. M. Hopkins, *The Wreck of the Deutschland*).

J. W. White, *The Verse of Gr. Comedy* (1912); Dale; Hamer; B. Ghiselin, "Paeonic Measures in Eng. Verse," MLN, 57 (1942). D.S.P.

PAINTING AND POETRY. See FINE ARTS AND POETRY.

PALILLOGY. See ANADIPLOSIS.

PALIMBACCHIUS. Also known as the antibacchius. A metrical unit in Gr. lyric poetry composed of 2 long syllables and 1 short one: $--\smile$. It is the reverse (Gr. *palin* "back") of a bacchius (q.v.).—Dale; Koster. R.A.H.

PALINDROME (Gr. "running back again"). A word, sentence or verse which reads alike backward or forward. Its reputed inventor was Sotades, a lascivious poet of the 3d c. B.C., from whose name the palindromes are often referred to as Sotadics. There are no examples from the classical Gr. period. The best known p. in Gr. is "nipson anomemata me monan opsin" (wash my transgressions, not only my face), attributed to Gregory of Nazianzus and often inscribed on fonts in monasteries or churches. A familiar one is also the Latin "Roma tibi subito motibus ibit amor." The following line by Camden illustrates a more refined type of p. in which each word reads alike backward or forward: "Odo tenet mulum, madidam mappam tenet Anna, Anna tenet mappam madidam, mulum tenet Odo." Palindromes were popular in Byzantine times. We possess a number of them written by the emperor Leo the Wise (10th c.). In 1802 Ambrose Pamperis published, in Vienna, a pamphlet containing 416 palindromic verses recounting some of the campaigns of Catherine the Great. Among the best known examples in Eng. are perhaps the following: "Madam, I'm Adam" and "Able was I ere I saw Elba," a saying attributed to Napoleon. Also called *carcinoi, versus anacyclici, versus echoici.*—K. Preisendanz, "Palindrom," A. Pauly, G. Wissowa, and W. Kroll, *Real-Encyclopädie der classischen Altertumswissenschaft*, XVIII, 2 (1949).   P.S.C.

PALINODE. Originally a term applied to a lyric by Stesichorus in which he recanted his earlier attack upon Helen as the baneful cause of the Trojan War. Hence, any poem or song of retraction. The p. as a theme, or a conceit, in literature has been common in love poetry since Ovid's *Remedia Amoris*, supposedly written to retract his *Ars Amatoria*. It appears in medieval literature in *The Romance of the Rose* and in the courtly love poetry. Chaucer uses it as a device throughout his poems and as the reason for his *Legend of Good Women*, written to retract the effect of *Troilus and Criseyde.*—Lewis.   R.A.H.

PALINODIC. Originally in Gr. lyric poetry an arrangement of two metrically corresponding members (e.g., strophe and antistrophe) interrupted by another pair of similarly corresponding members. Thus the "stanzas" are arranged in the pattern abba, with *ab* the "ode" and *ba* the "palinode"; e.g., *a* is strophe, *a*, antistrophe, *b* and *b* the second strophe and antistrophe. The term is now used of any such arrangement in any poetry and may also be applied to single lines in such a pattern.— U. von Wilamowitz-Moellendorff, *Sappho und Simonides* (1913).   R.A.H.

PANEGYRIC. A speech or poem in praise of an individual, institution or group. Originally p. was a rhetorical type belonging to the epideictic category of oratory. Its rules are given in the rhetorical works of Menander and Hermogenes and famous examples include the *Panegyricus* of Isocrates, the p. of Pliny the Younger on Trajan, and the eleven other *XII Panegyrici Antici* (4th c.). Much primitive poetry is p. in nature, consisting of the praises of heroes, armies, victories, states, etc. Pindar's odes have been loosely described as panegyrics. After the 3d c. B.C., p. was accepted as a formal poetic type and its rules were given in handbooks of poetry. It became popular during the decadence of classical poetry and like other such forms persisted until the Renaissance. Scaliger gives its rules in his *Poetices Libri Septem* (1561).

P. is almost indistinguishable from encomium, but according to Scaliger it tends to deal with present men and deeds, while encomium deals with the past. Among significant examples of p. poems are Sidonius' poems on the Emperors Avitus, Majorian, and Anthemius; Claudian's on Honorius and on the consulship of Probinus and Olybrius; the p. on the death of Celsus by Paulinus of Nola; Aldhelm's *de Laudibus Virginum;* and innumerable poems in praise of Mary, the cross, the martyrs, etc. In the Renaissance the tradition continued unabated with perhaps more emphasis on the praise of secular figures and institutions. One notable feature of p. is its tendency to develop toward epic, which it heavily influenced in the Renaissance.— T. Burges, *Epideictic Lit.* (1902); Chadwick.   O.B.H.

PANJABI POETRY. See INDIAN POETRY.

PANTOUM. A poem of indeterminable length, composed of quatrains in which the second and fourth lines of each stanza serve as the first and third lines of the next, the process continuing through the last stanza. In this quatrain the first line of the poem also reappears as the last and, in some Eng. pantoums, the third line of the poem as the second. Thus, the p. begins and ends with the same line. Another distinct feature is that different themes must be developed concurrently in the p., one in the first 2 lines and the other in the last 2 lines of each quatrain, the 2 pairs of lines being connected only by their sound.

A distinct Malayan verse form (*pantun,* see MALAY POETRY), the p. was introduced into Western poetry by the Fr. orientalist Ernest Fouinet and was established by the practice of Victor Hugo in his Notes to *Les Orientales.* In Fr. the form was effectively used by Théodore de Banville, Louisa Siefert, Leconte de Lisle, and, with considerable variations, by Charles Baudelaire; in Eng. by Austin Dobson, Brander Matthews, and others. Despite its oriental origin and its relatively late Western adoption, the p. is often listed with the much older Fr. forms, such as rondeau, triolet, ballade, and villanelle (qq.v.).—Kastner; M. Grammont, *Petit traité de versification française* (7th ed., 1930); P. G. Brewster, "Metrical, Stanzaic, and Stylistic Resemblances between Malayan and Western Poetry," RLC, 32 (1958; finds European analogues of the p. in the German *Schnaderhüpfel,* the Russian *chastushka,* the Sp. *copla,* the Latvian and Lithuanian *daina*).   A.P.

PARABASIS (Gr. "coming forward"). A choral performance, composed mainly in anapaestic tetrameters, in Old Gr. Comedy. During an intermission in the action the chorus, alone in the orchestra and out of character, came forward without their masks to face the audience and delivered, in song or recitative, views which the author felt strongly on various matters, such as politics, religion, etc. The parts of a complete p. were said to be introductory song (*kommation*), parabasis (properly so called), *makron* or *pnigos* (to be recited at one breath), strophe or ode (*melos*), epirrhema, antode or antistrophe, and antiepirrhema. Not all parts occur in every p.—J. W. White, *The Verse of Gr. Comedy* (1912) ; F. M. Cornford, *The Origin of Gr. Comedy* (1914); G. Norwood, *Gr. Comedy* (1931); Schmid and Stählin. R.A.H.

PARADOX. A statement which seems untrue but proves valid upon close inspection. E.g.: "The longest way round is the shortest way home;" or, "When my love swears that she is made of truth / I do believe her, though I know she lies" (Shakespeare, Sonnet 138). P. was recognized by ancient rhetoricians (Menander, Hermogenes, Cicero, Quintilian, etc.) as one of the standard figures. It was popular during the decadent period of Graeco-Roman literature in such forms as paradoxical encomium, *controversiae,* and *suasoriae.* During the Middle Ages paradoxical arguments were used to train students in rhetoric and for humor or irony in literature, as in the arguments against chastity in the *Romance of the Rose.* The most famous Renaissance example of sustained p. is *The Praise of Folly* by Erasmus; but because of the paradoxical nature of Christian values, p. abounds in both popular and esoteric literature of the later Middle Ages and Renaissance. In literature of the Renaissance, p. is handled with moderation and is merely one of several popular figures. However, during the baroque period, p. became a central poetic figure. It is particularly important in the prose and poetry of Donne. One of his earliest works is the prose collection *Paradoxes and Problems;* and the techniques of paradoxical argument developed in this collection are evident throughout his *Songs and Sonnets* and his sermons. Fondness for p. is evident in poetry of the later 17th c. and the 18th c. However, as in Dryden and Pope, it tends to be verbal p., reflected in the use of balance and antithesis in the heroic couplet, rather than paradoxical argument. Hazlitt called neoclassic poetry "the poetry of paradox" and contrasted it with what he felt was the far richer "poetry of imagination" written by the Elizabethans.

Both Friederich Schlegel and Thomas De Quincey argued that p. is a vital element in poetry, reflecting the paradoxical nature of the world which poetry imitates. DeQuincey wrote in the *Autobiography,* ". . . to speak in the mere simplicity of truth, so mysterious is human nature, and so little read by him who runs, that almost every weighty aspect of truth upon that theme will be found at first sight to be startling, or sometimes paradoxical. And so little need is there for chasing or courting paradox, that, on the contrary, he who is faithful to his own experiences will find all his efforts little enough to keep down the paradoxical air besieging much of what he *knows* to be the truth. No man needs to *search* for paradox in this world of ours. Let him simply confine himself to the truth, and he will find paradox growing everywhere under his hands as rank as weeds."

As a widely employed critical term, p. is peculiar to 20th-c. criticism. The rediscovery of Donne and Marvell undoubtedly played a part in its usage, as well as our general awareness of the need for the ironic mind. It is in Cleanth Brooks' *The Well Wrought Urn* that p. is most closely examined. Brooks says, in "The Language of Paradox," that p. is a form of indirection, and indirection is a general characteristic of poetic language and structure. Brooks brings a good deal of evidence to bear in support of his thesis, showing examples of p. in a poet like Wordsworth, whom one might expect to be a poet of simple, direct statement. An issue that he touches on but probably does not develop sufficiently is the difference between *verbal paradoxes* and *paradoxical situations.* Because he does not sufficiently stress this distinction, Brooks is sometimes accused of reducing poetry to "screaming paradoxes." Obviously, as his analysis of Wordsworth's *Composed upon Westminster Bridge* shows, Brooks does not insist merely on witty paradoxes. He is more concerned, and rightly so, to show that many interesting and good poems are written from insights that dramatically enlarge or in some way startlingly modify our commonplace conceptions and understandings, and these we call paradoxical. A good poet might, for example, take Eliot's p., "Liberty is a different sort of pain from prison," and make it into a full poem. Whether he kept Eliot's own verbal p. or chose to render the idea either by a series of examples or of simple direct statements would be of little significance. His poem would remain paradoxical.—Brooks and Warren; C. Brooks, "The Language of P.," *The Well Wrought Urn* (1947); R. Crane, "The Critical Monism of Cleanth Brooks," *Critics and Crit.* (1952); D. Daiches, "Poetry and P.," *Crit. Approaches to Lit.* (1956); H. K. Miller, "The Paradoxical Encomium . . . ," MP, 53 (1956). W.V.O'C.

PARALEIPSIS. See APOSIOPESIS.

PARALLELISM (Gr. "side by side"). In poetry a state of correspondence between one phrase, line, or verse with another. P. seems to be the basic aesthetic principle of poetic utterance. According to B. R. Lewis, *Creative Poetry* (1931), primitive man, "if strongly aroused, and if his emotion was sustained, . . . must have repeated . . . the same sequence of sounds. . . ." Such repetitions as "Nyah eh wa, Nyah eh wa," of the Am. Indian, "Ha-ah, Ha-ah," of the New Zealander, "Wa-la-wa, Wa-la-wa," of the *Beowulf* poet, are parallel refrains of the most elemental, lyrical nature. Tense emotion, such as joy, grief, anger, longing, seems naturally to give rise to parallel utterance, and, doubtless, p. was the basic element of primitive poetry before such refinements as meter and rhyme were invented.

P. of clauses is the central principle of biblical verse, a fact not fully understood by the translators of the Authorized Version. The principle was rediscovered by Bishop Robert Lowth who called it *parallelisimus memborum* and noted several distinct varieties; in fact many structural types have been described, including especially those based on sameness, antithesis, and complement. But in the Bible there seems not only to have been structural and rhythmic p. but also p. on an interpretive level. Thus the significance of a figure may be understood by the envelope or stanzaic pattern formed by the relations of the members. Accordingly the Lord's Prayer might be printed:

> Our Father which art in heaven:
> Hallowed be thy name,
> Thy Kingdom come,
> Thy will be done,
> In earth as it is in heaven.

Therein all the parallel clauses are connected with both the opening and closing, and the meaning becomes: "Hallowed be thy name in earth as it is in heaven; Thy kingdom come in earth as it is in heaven, etc.," thereby considerably enriching the interpretive value. This principle has been of some importance to modern biblical commentary.

Doubtless p. occurs in all languages in which there is poetry dealing with feelings of a religious or exalted nature or where strong emotion is expressed. But the poet who has certainly made the most use of this device in Eng. is Walt Whitman. G. W. Allen divides Whitman's devices into four main types: (*1*) *Synonymous p.*, where the second line enforces the first by repeating the thought: "I too am not a bit tamed. I too am untranslatable. / I sound my barbaric yawp over the roofs of the world" (*Song of Myself*, Sec. 52). (There may or may not be repetition of the actual words). (*2*) *Antithetical p.*, where the second line denies or contrasts the first. (*3*) *Synthetic or*

cumulative p, where the second line, or several consecutive lines, supplements or completes the first. (*4*) *Climactic p.*, or "ascending rhythm," where each successive line adds to its predecessor, usually taking words from it and completing it. However, as C. M. Lewis, *The Foreign Sources of Modern Eng. Versification* (1898) claims, there is "no modern poetry of any great importance in which this principle is the only determinant of form."—Bishop R. Lowth, *Isaiah, a New Tr., with a Preliminary Dissertation* (1778); C. A. Smith, *Repetition and P. in Eng. Verse* (1894); R. G. Moulton, *The Lit. Study of the Bible* (1895); G. W. Allen, *Am. Prosody* (1935). R.O.E.

PARAPHRASE, HERESY OF. See HERESY OF PARAPHRASE.

PARARHYME. See NEAR RHYME.

PARNASSIANS. The "Parnassiens" were the group, or groups, of Fr. poets who were born about 1840 or 1850 and gravitated around Leconte de Lisle. They treated a number of nonpersonal themes taken from history, science, philosophy, nature, or contemporary life; but some were mainly lyrists. They respected and often followed their elders; used traditional verse forms; and regarded the cult of poetry as a religion. *Le premier Parnasse contemporain* (1866) was followed by other *recueils* in 1871 and 1876; but the works of individual "Parnassiens" covered the period from 1865 to the end of the century and represented the norm of Fr. poetry between the romantic era and the symbolists. Among recent critics, Souriau regards Leconte de Lisle as the "chef-d'orchestre" of the "école parnassienne"; in his view, the only true P. were this poet and his disciples Dierx and Heredia. But Ibrovac, Martino and Peyre have brought out the complexity of "Le Parnasse" and shown that the poets composing it did not for the most part echo Leconte de Lisle. A. Schaffer has developed these views and explained the great variety of attitudes and genres that existed.

The movement was initiated by Catulle Mendès and L.-X. de Ricard in the early 1860's and the P. first met in Lemerre's bookshop and in the salon of the Marquise de Ricard; later they foregathered in the salon of Mme Leconte de Lisle, whose formidable husband was regarded as an oracle. Of the fifty or more poets called Parnassian only a few can be mentioned here. Among the more independent, Albert Glatigny (1839–73) was a wit and virtuoso who took his cue from Banville. Sully-Prudhomme (1839–1907) explored the secrets of the inner life in verses as poignant as Heine's but without Heine's bitterness. He wrote philosophic poems, using a delicate imagery drawn from the natural sciences. François Coppée (1842–1908) described the life and problems of humble folk and, like Sully-Prudhomme, was sensitive to the writer's moral responsibilities. The followers of Leconte de Lisle respected traditional morals, but worshipped "Art." Gautier as well as Banville remained a potent influence. Léon Dierx (1838–1912) wrote tragic poems on historical themes and struck a note of despair. Jean Lahor (1840–1909) exhaled his melancholy in Buddhistic verses. J.-M. de Heredia (1842–1905) drew inspiration from the Gr. myths, from the epigrams of the Gr. *Anthology* and from the L. poets. He was something of a scholar and palaeographer, but above all a finished artist. Most of his *Trophées* (1895) are sonnets, and he is the outstanding sonneteer of modern France. Anatole France (1844–1924) was more independent. Although a versatile neo-Hellenist, he was also, in his *Poèmes dorés,* an exquisite nature poet. Jules Lemaître (1853–1914), the critic and literary historian, was also a delightful *conteur* and poet.

Though some of them underwent the influence of Ménard, the P. were not primarily Hellenists, nor were they as a whole impassive or impersonal. If they had anything in common, it was a love of precision, a devotion to formal beauty and the cult of rhyme; beyond that, in Henri Peyre's words, "un romantisme assagi et mitigé."

C. Mendès, *La légende du Parnasse contemporain* (1884); R. Canat, *Une forme du mal du siècle. Du sentiment de la solitude morale chez les romantiques et les Parnassiens* (1904) and *La Renaissance de la Grèce antique* (1911); M. Ibrovac, *J. M. de Heredia: sa vie, son oeuvre* (1923); T. Martel, *Le Parnasse* (1923); Martino; F. Desonay, *Le rêve hellénique chez les poètes parnassiens* (1928); E. Estève, *Le Parnasse* (1929); A. Therive, *Le Parnasse* (1929); A. Schaffer, *Parnassus in France* (1930) and *The Genres of Parnassian Poetry* (1944); M. Souriau, *Hist. du Parnasse* (1930); H.-M. Peyre, *Louis Ménard (1822–1901)* (1932) and *Bibliog. critique de l'hellénisme en France de 1843 à 1870* (1932); F. Vincent, *Les Parnassiens* (1933); M. G. Rudler, *Parnassiens, symbolistes et décadents* (1938); Z. Rosenberg, *La persistance du subjectivisme chez les poètes parnassiens* (1939); A. Lytton Sells, "Heredia's Hellenism," MLR, 37 (1942); V. Errante, *Parnassiani e simbolisti francesi* (1953). A.L.S.

PARNASSUS. An 8,000 foot mountain in Phocis in Greece. On its slopes were the Castalian Spring (sacred to the Muses) and the Oracle of Delphi. It had two peaks, one sacred to Apollo and one to Dionysus. It was the traditional haunt of the Muses, q.v. (cf. Pro-

pertius 3.13.54; Persius, Prologue to the *Satires;* Chaucer, Prologue to *Franklin's Tale,* etc.). References to P. abound in postclassical literature. Usually it stands by synecdoche for poetic achievement. In the 17th c. a genre of satirical criticism arose which may be called "Parnassus-literature" (e.g., *Ragguagli di Parnaso,* 1612; *The Pilgrimage to Parnassus* and *The Returne from Parnassus,* ca. 1600). See also PARNASSIANS. A.R.B.

PARODOS (Gr. "the way past"). The odes sung by the chorus in an ancient Gr. drama upon entering the orchestra for the first time. The word also means either of the two passageways between the spectators and the scene-building into the orchestra in an ancient Gr. theatre.— A. Pickard-Cambridge, *The Dramatic Festivals of Athens* (1953); M. Bieber, *A Hist. of the Gr. and Roman Theater* (2d ed., 1961). R.A.H.

PARODY (Gr. *parōdia*). DEFINITIONS. P. is as old as poetry itself. One fundamental distinction can be made between comic p., which is close to burlesque (q.v.), and literary or critical p., which follows more closely a given author's style or a particular work of art. In the broader sense p. and literary burlesque originated in classic drama where they expressed a basic impulse for emotional counterpoint to tragic themes. From Aristophanes to Shakespeare and into our time the comic interlude, with its ludicrous parallel of the main plot, has functioned as a parody—to provide a breather or the catharsis of laughter. It is, therefore, somewhat beside the point to regard all p. with suspicion or distrust. For, although a parasitic art and written at times with malice, p. is as fundamental to literature as is laughter to health.

Critical p. has been defined as the exaggerated imitation of a work of art. Like caricature it is based on distortion, bringing into bolder relief the salient features of a writer's style or habit of mind. It belongs to the genus *satire* (q.v.) and thus performs the double-edged task of reform and ridicule. Eccentricity, sentimentalism, pedantry, dullness, pompousness, and self-importance are among its major targets, and at its best it is a critical instrument of telling force because it approaches the subject from within rather than from without, and thus avoids the reproach of poets and creative writers that a critic is simply a disappointed artist. P. usually makes its point by employing a serious style to express an incongruous subject, thus disturbing the balance of form and matter. It keeps attention focused on the poem imitated with, in most cases, a deflationary intent.

The best p. surpasses mere imitation. It stands on its own feet, containing enough independent humor to be funny beyond aping of the original. The following brief example of modern p. will illustrate its insistence upon common sense and reality against what Mark Twain termed "girly-girly romance." Bret Harte's sequel to Whittier's sentimental ballad *Maud Muller* details the long connubial years of Mrs. Judge Jenkins and closes with a deft p. of the final familiar couplet by showing us the other half of the coin:

> If of all words of tongue or pen
> The saddest are 'It might have been,'
>
> Sadder are these, we daily see,
> 'It is, but hadn't ought to be!'

There are as many different motives for p. as there are parodists. Sometimes, especially in the 18th-c. coffee houses, it was personal spite. More often the parodist employed the style of his original to poke fun at current follies or vices. He might have a social axe to grind or he might wish to expose a certain literary school or mannerism which had hardened into conventionality. Thus Cervantes dealt a classic blow to the fiction of knight-errantry and Fielding punctured the Richardsonian novel of sentiment in *Joseph Andrews*. A familiar example of the double-edged p. in verse is Lewis Carroll's *Hiawatha's Photographing* in which the rhythms of Longfellow are employed to poke fun at the then novel practise of the family photograph. J. C. Squire aped Gray's *Elegy* and at the same time aimed his p. at the Spoon River series of Masters; and E. B. White in *A Classic Waits for Me* has written a fine take-off on the Classics Club selection of best sellers in the rolling lines of Whitman.

HISTORY. P. was originally "a song sung beside," i.e., a comic imitation of a serious poem. The imitation may be of the actual words or of the manner; the comic effect may be achieved by applying high-flown language or meter to trivial themes or by some other form of incongruity or caricature. The instinct to burlesque any lofty or pompous performance is deep in our nature; but with us p. proper is a form of literary criticism which consists in heightening the characteristics of the thing imitated. Aristotle (*Poetics* 1448ª12) attributes the origin of p. as an art to Hegemon of Thasos, because he used epic style to represent men not as superior to what they are in ordinary life but as inferior. Hegemon was, we are told, a comic poet of the 5th c. who was the first to introduce parodies into the theatre (Athenaeus 15.699a); he was reciting his p. of the *Battle of the Giants* in the theatre when the news arrived of the disaster in Sicily. Athenaeus elsewhere quotes Polemo as saying that p. was invented by the iambic poet Hipponax (6th c. B.C.), who had himself been the victim of

caricature at the hands of the sculptors and painters; we have a few lines of his mock-heroic epic on the adventures of a glutton. Athenaeus also refers to Epicharmus and two poets of the Old Comedy, Cratinus and Hermippus. Much earlier than these was the pseudo-Homeric *Margites*, known to Archilochus (Bergk, *Poetae Lyrici Graeci*, Archilochus fr. 117), which set forth in hexameters (with intermingled iambics) the story of a fool. We still have the *Battle of the Frogs and Mice*, which parodies Homer. Athenaeus has preserved a long passage by Matron setting forth in epic style an account of an Athenian banquet. The supreme parodist in antiquity was Aristophanes, who may be thought to have reached his highest level in the *Frogs*, where he parodies the styles of Aeschylus and Euripides. But almost every page of Aristophanes contains a touch of p. In later comedy this element dwindles. Plato imitates the styles of several prose writers with amusing effect; in the *Symposium* (194e–197e) he puts into Agathon's mouth a speech in the manner of Gorgias. Lucian has a good many touches of p. or burlesque, for example in Dialogue 20, the *Judgment of Paris*, where the comic effect is achieved by making the divine characters talk in the language of ordinary life.

Roman humor had a strong element of satire; the phlyax pots and the performances which they presumably illustrate must have appealed to the Romans. In L. comedy we find occasional burlesque of the tragic manner, e.g., in the prologues to the *Amphitryon* and the *Rudens*, the mad scene in the *Menaechmi*, and Pardalisca's mock-tragic outburst (*Casina* 621ff.)—passages which, whatever the original may have been, owe their effect to the language and the meter. A more delicate irony is shown in Syrus' mocking reply to the sententious words of Demea (*Adelphoe* 420ff.). Lucilius imitates the style of the Roman tragic poets, for example Pacuvius' unusual words and awkward compounds. The fourth poem of Catullus is closely parodied in *Catalepton* 10. Persius ridicules by imitation the styles of Pacuvius and other poets. Petronius (*Satyricon* 119–24) gives us a long hexameter poem on the Civil War, parts of which may be meant as a caricature of Lucan.

In its later days the Roman mime parodied the rites of the Christian church. During the later Middle Ages parodies of liturgy, well-known hymns, and even the Bible were popular. Renaissance authors, when not embroiled in the polemics of the Reformation, preferred to parody the classics or such "gothic" phenomena as romance and scholasticism—e.g., Boiardo's *Morgante Maggiore*, Cervantes' *Don Quixote* (p. of romance); Giambattista Gelli's *Circe*, Tassoni's *La Secchia Rapita*, Scarron's

Virgile Travesti (p. of the classics); Erasmus' *Praise of Folly*, Rabelais' *Gargantua and Pantagruel* (p. of scholasticism). Of these authors Rabelais is the most universal, the richest, and the most difficult to classify.

P. became institutionalized during the 17th c. The existence of academies and distinct literary movements, particularly in Italy, France, and England, encouraged debates in which p. was used as a weapon of satire. Boccalini's *Ragguagli di Parnasso* (1612) was the origin of a whole *genre* employing p. as a device for criticizing contemporary authors.

Eng. p. had its beginnings in ecclesiastical litany and the Mass. It was employed in the Miracle Plays where a scene of common life (the Mak episode in *The Second Shepherd's Play*) provided comic relief. Chaucer's *The Rime of Sir Thopas* parodied the grandiose style of medieval romances. Shakespeare burlesqued his own romantic love plots with *rustic amours*, and John Marston, in turn, wrote a rough, humorous travesty of *Venus and Adonis*. In 1705 John Phillips (*The Splendid Shilling*) used the solemn blank verse of Milton to celebrate ludicrous incidents. One of the best-known 17th c. parodies was the Duke of Buckingham's *The Rehearsal* (1671) which leveled its shafts mainly at Dryden's *The Conquest of Granada* and at the grand manner of heroic drama. In the next century, Sheridan's *The Critic* took a similar target. Exceptions to the general rule that p. rarely outlives the literature parodied, *The Rehearsal* and *The Critic* have been revived in the 20th c.

The Golden Age of p. in Eng. poetry paralleled the rise of romantic and transcendental attitudes, perfect targets for the literary head-shrinkers. Canning, Ellis, and John Hookham Frere produced a series of parodies in the *Anti-Jacobin Journal* (1790–1810). Here the Southey-Wordsworth brand of Fr. revolutionary sympathy for knife-grinders and tattered beggars provided good anti-Jacobin sport. Byron's *Vision of Judgment* and Shelley's *Peter Bell* likewise parodied Southey, Wordsworth, and "elemental" poetry. James Hogg in 1816 took off most of the Eng. romantics, and in 1812 James and Horace Smith published *Rejected Addresses*, a landmark in Eng. p., in which the styles of Scott, Wordsworth, Byron, Coleridge, Dr. Johnson, and others were skillfully but not uproariously parodied. In the later 19th c. names and titles continue to multiply. Tennyson, Browning, Longfellow, Poe, Swinburne, and Whitman become the chief targets for such parody artists as J. K. Stephen, C. S. Calverly, J. C. Squire, Lewis Carroll (*Father William* after Southey's *The Old Man's Comforts*), Swinburne (*The Higher Pantheism in a Nutshell* à la Tennyson and *Nephelidia*, a self-parody), Andrew Lang, and Max Beer-

bohm. In America the names of Phoebe Cary, Bret Harte, Mark Twain, Bayard Taylor, H. C. Bunner, and J. K. Bangs were most prominent before 1900. In the present century *The New Yorker* has carried on the tradition established by *Punch* and *Vanity Fair*. During the 1920's p. found a highly congenial atmosphere when such talented writers as Corey Ford, Louis Untermeyer, Frank Sullivan, Donald Ogden Stewart, Wolcott Gibbs, James Thurber, Benchley, Hoffenstein, and E. B. White persisted in seeing the funny side of the hard-boiled generation in prose and verse. With a history of twenty-five centuries behind it, p., it seems, is here to stay. Like all literature it has had its ups and downs, but at its best it is more than a parasitic art. It has attracted men and women of major stature and at times has shown the capacity to outlive the serious work which has inspired it. See also BURLESQUE.

COLLECTIONS: *Parodies of the Works of Eng. and Am. Authors*, ed. W. Hamilton (6 v., 1884–89); *A P. Anth.*, ed. C. Wells (1904); *A Book of Parodies*, ed. A. Symons (1908); *A Century of P. and Imitation*, ed. W. Jerrold and R. M. Leonard (1913); *Am. Lit. in P.*, ed. R. P. Falk (1957); *Parodies, an Anthol.*, ed. D. MacDonald (1960).

HISTORY AND CRITICISM: A. T. Murray, *On P. and Paratragoedia in Aristophanes* (1891); A. S. Martin, *On P.* (1896); C. Stone, *P.* (1915); P. Lehmann, *Die Parodie im Mittelalter* (2 v., 1922); E. Gosse, "Burlesque," *Selected Essays, First Series* (1928); G. Kitchin, *A Survey of Burlesque and P. in Eng.* (1931); A. H. West, *L'Influence française dans la poésie burlesque en Angleterre entre 1660–1700* (1931); R. P. Bond, *Eng. Burlesque Poetry, 1700–1750* (1932); G. Highet, *Anatomy of Satire* (1962; chap. on p.).　　　　　　　　　R.P.F.; W.B.

PAROEMIAC (Gr. "proverbial"). An anapaestic dimeter catalectic commonly used in proverbial and popular expressions, with metrical form

$$\smile\smile-\mid\smile\smile-\mid\smile\smile-\mid\underline{\smile}$$

It is often employed as a clausula (see PROSE RHYTHM) in anapaestic systems.—Koster; L. Parker, "The Incidence of Word-End in Anapaestic Paroemiacs and Its Application to Textual Questions," *CQ*, n.s. 8 (1958); U. von Wilamowitz-Moellendorff, *Griechische Verskunst* (2d ed., 1958).　　　　　　　P.S.C.

PARONOMASIA. See PUN.

PARTICULA PENDENS. See ANACOLUTHON.

PARTIMEN (also called *joc partit*, Fr. *jeu parti*). A specialized variety of *tenso* (see under TENZONE) in which one poet proposes two hypothetical situations (e.g., whether it is better to love a lady who does not love you, or to be loved by a lady whom you do not love). The second poet chooses and defends one of these alternatives, while the first poet upholds the other. After each has had his say in the same number of stanzas (usually three), all identical in structure, they commonly refer the debate to one or more arbiters for settlement. There are also *partimens* involving three poets and three choices, but these are far less frequent. It seems certain that these *partimens* really represent the cooperative work of two or more poets; but in view of the difficulties involved it is unlikely that they were actually improvised, as they purport to be. Sometimes it is even clear from the poem itself that the poets were writing back and forth over a considerable distance.—L. Selbach, *Das Streitgedicht in der altprovenzalischen Lyrik* (1886); Jeanroy, II.   F.M.C.

PASSION PLAY. The play of the Resurrection was elaborately developed in the Middle Ages before the events of the Crucifixion were dramatized. Two brief L. plays from Benediktbeuern, Upper Bavaria, in the *Carmina Burana* manuscript (13th c.) indicate that the plays of the Passion proper were invented as prologues to the Resurrection. Once on the stage such plays, because of their greater interest, quickly became more popular than the Resurrection from which they had originated, so that in time the combined dramas came to be called P. plays. In some places P. plays became parts of the Corpus Christi cycle, but in larger areas on the continent of Europe and the south of England they remained separate from the plays of the Nativity and became enormously popular. Most of them came to an end in the 16th and 17th c., but a few of them in remote places in Germany, Austria, and Switzerland lived on until later dates. The well-known Oberammergau P. play has continued to be acted, usually at ten-year intervals, for hundreds of years. The play has, however, been recast on the lines of classical drama. P. plays seem to have been brought to America by the Spaniards and to have survived in degenerate forms in Sp. America.—W. Creizenach, *Gesch. des neueren Dramas* (3 v., 1893–1903); J. E. Wackernell, *Altdeutsche Passionsspiele aus Tirol* (1897); E. K. Chambers, *The Mediaeval Stage* (2 v., 1903); G. Frank, *The Medieval Fr. Drama* (1954).   H.C.

PASTORAL. HISTORY. The p. imitates rural life, usually the life of an imaginary Golden Age, in which the loves of shepherds and shepherdesses play a prominent part. To insist on a realistic (or even a recognizably "natural") presentation of actual shepherd life would ex-

clude the greater part of the compositions that are called p. Only when poetry ceases to imitate ordinary rural life does it become distinctly p. It must be admitted, however, that the term has been and still is used to designate any treatment of rural life, as for instance Louis Untermeyer's speaking of Robert Frost as a "pastoral" poet or John F. Lynen writing on his "P. art." Perhaps most critics agree with Edmund Gosse that the "pastoral is cold, unnatural, artificial, and the humblest reviewer is free to cast a stone at its dishonored grave." But there must be some unique value in a genre that lasted 2,000 years. This long-lived popularity, it seems, derives from the fact that the shepherd—a simple swain, with whom everyone may easily identify himself—deals with a universal subject—something fundamentally true about everyone. Thus the complex is reduced to the simple; the universal is expressed in the concrete.

For all practical purposes the p. begins with Theocritus' *Idyls*, in the 3d c. B.C. Though the canon of his work is unsettled, enough of the poems in the collection made by Artemidorus are certainly his to justify the claim that Theocritus is the father of p. poetry. No. 11, for example, in which Polyphemus is depicted as being in love with Galatea and finding solace in song, becomes the prototype of the love lament; no. 1, in which Thyrsis sings of Daphnis' death, sets the pattern and, to no small degree, the matter for the p. elegy; no. 5 and no. 7 introduce the singing match conducted according to the rules of amoebaean poetry. And no. 7, in the appearance of contemporary poets under feigned names, contains the germ of the allegorical p. Theocritus wrote his pastorals while he was at Ptolemy's court of Alexandria, but he remembered the actual herdsmen of his boyhood and the beautiful countryside of Sicily; so he, like the p. poets who followed him, was a city man longing for the country. But perhaps no other p. poet has ever been able to strike such a happy medium between the real and the ideal.

Virgil's *Eclogues* refine and methodize Theocritus' idyls. Expressing the sentiment inspired by the beauty of external nature in her tranquil moods and the kindred charm inspired by ideal human relationships (love in particular) in verse notable for its exquisite diction and flowing rhythm, they consolidate and popularize the conventions of p. poetry. During the Middle Ages, the p. was chiefly confined to the *pastourelle* (q.v.), a native type of dialogue poem, and to a few realistic scenes in the religious plays. The vast body of the modern p.—elegy, drama, romance, p. poetry in general—is a direct outgrowth of Renaissance humanism.

The p. elegy, patterned after such classical

models as the *Lament for Adonis*, credited to Bion, the *Lament for Bion*, traditionally ascribed to Moschus but most probably by a disciple of Bion, and Theocritus' first idyl, became conventional in the Renaissance. The traditional machinery with variations was the invocation, statement of grief, inquiry into the causes of death, sympathy and weeping of nature, procession of mourners, lament, climax, change of mood, consolation. Marot and Spenser contributed Renaissance specimens, and numerous other p. poets, including Pope, Ambrose Philips, and Gay, tried their hand at the genre. Milton's *Lycidas* and Shelley's *Adonais* conform rather closely to the classic conventions, and vestiges of them can be seen even as late as Arnold's *Thyrsis*.

The p. drama was latent in the idyls and eclogues, for the brief dialogue was easily expandable. Even as early as Boccaccio's *Ninfale Fiesolano* the dramatic intensity of the eclogue was considerably heightened. With the addition of the crossed love plot and secret personal history, the p. drama emerged and grew in popularity as the medieval mystery plays lost ground. Poliziano's *Favola di Orfeo* (1472), is perhaps more correctly classified as an opera, but p. elements are prominent. Agostino de' Beccari's *Il Sacrificio* (1554), the first fully-developed p. drama, led to the heyday of the p. drama in Italy during the last quarter of the 16th c. Tasso's *Aminta* (1573), an allegory presenting the court of Ferrara, is no doubt the greatest of the kind and has exerted the most far-reaching influence on the tradition. Second only to it is Guarini's *Il Pastor Fido* (1583), the first important tragicomedy. In France, the most famous drama is Racan's *Les Bergeries* (1625), founded on d'Urfé's *Astrée*. It was followed by countless *bergeries*, which, after the mode of *Astrée*, were so filled with *galant* shepherds and beautiful nymphs that the type wore itself out with its own artificiality. England's first noteworthy p. dramas—Lyly's *Gallathea* and Peele's *Arraignment of Paris*—were both published in 1584, and the most excellent—Fletcher's *Faithful Shepherdess* (imitating Tasso's *Aminta*)—in 1610. Because of the constant pressure of Eng. empiricism and the austerity of the Puritan taste, the p. drama in England never reached the extravagant artificiality that it attained on the Continent. The last p. drama in England was the belated *Gentle Shepherd* by Allan Ramsay in 1725. Written in Lowland Scotch, picturing particular Scottish scenes, and using "real" shepherds, it was highly praised by the early romantic poets and critics.

The p. romance usually takes the form of a long prose narrative, interspersed with lyrics, built on a complicated plot, and peopled with characters bearing p. names. Anticipated by Boccaccio's *Ameto* (1342), a mixed composition of graceful prose and tuneful verse, the genre is usually dated from Sannazaro's *Arcadia* (1504), a remarkable composition, written in musical prose and filled with characters who live in innocent voluptuousness. Popular imitations are Montemayor's *Diana* (1559?), in Portugal, and Cervantes' *Galatea* (1585), in Spain. In France the indigenous *pastourelle* held back the p. romance; but Rémy Belleau's *Bergerie* (1572), established the type and in d'Urfé's *Astrée* the baroque p. romance found its most consummate example, as nymphs bedizened in pearls and satin cavort with chivalric shepherds. The most celebrated Eng. p. romance is Sir Philip Sidney's *Arcadia* (1590). Its lofty sentiment, sweet rhythm, ornate rhetoric, elaborate description and high-flown oratory, display one aspect of the Italianate style of Elizabethan courtly literature. In spite of the riddle of its plot, in which the strange turns of fortune and love make all the virtuous happy, it is still good reading as a romance of love and adventure. The literary influence of the *Arcadia* was pervasive: Greene and Lodge, for example, imitated it; Shakespeare drew from it for the character of Gloucester in *King Lear*; on the scaffold Charles I recited an adaptation of a Pamela's prayer; in translation the *Arcadia* contributed to the elaborate plots of the Fr. romances; and traces of it may perhaps be seen even in Richardson and Scott. The sustained elaboration of its structure marks another step in the development which distinguished the novel from the short story and the picaresque tale. Robert Greene's *Menaphon* (1589; reprinted as *Greene's Arcadia* in 1590), conventional and imitative, adds little to the genre except some delightful lyrics. Thomas Lodge's *Rosalynde* (1590), in the style of Lyly's *Euphues* but diversified with sonnets and eclogues, was dramatized with little alteration by Shakespeare in *As You Like It*.

Early in the 14th c. the p. eclogue was profoundly influenced by the new learning, when Dante, Petrarch, and Boccaccio wrote L. eclogues after the mode of Virgil. They continued the allegory of their master, extended its political and religious scope, and introduced the personal lament. About the turn of the 15th c. Baptista Spagnuoli Mantuanus exploited the satirical possibilities of the p. by using rustic characters to ridicule the court, the church, and the women of his day. Late in the century Marino (1569–1625) developed a style paralleling gongorism and euphuism. His *Adone* (1623), filled with affected word-play and outrageous conceits, represents a baroque aberration of the genre comparable to the contemporaneous *Astrée*. The *Pléiade* transplanted the classical eclogue into France, and Marot and Ronsard and many imitators produced conventional eclogues. In England, aside from the inferior works of Barclay and Googe, p. poetry may be dated from Spenser's *Shepheardes Calender* (1579). Though Spenser follows the conventions of the classical eclogue, he aims at simplicity and naturalness by making use of rustic characters speaking country language. During the last quarter of the 16th c., England continued to produce much p. poetry in imitation of Spenser. According to modern taste and judgment, those of most merit are Michael Drayton's *Shepherds Garland* (1593), and William Browne's *Britannia's Pastorals* (1613–16). In his *Piscatory Eclogues* (1633), Phineas Fletcher imitated Sannazaro, who may have taken his cue from Theocritus' fisherman's idyl, no. 21.

The swan song of the p. was sung by the Eng. poets of the 18th c. Revived by Pope and Philips, whose rival pastorals appeared in Tonson's *Miscellany* in 1709, the p. attracted a surprising amount of interest. Pope, inspired by Virgil's *Eclogues*, produced one of the showpieces of rococo art—a part of "Summer" being so tuneful that Handel set it to music. Philips, under the rising influence of Eng. empiricism, tried to write pastorals that came closer to the realities of Eng. rural life. The followers of neither poet wrote any p. worthy of mention, and the genre soon died of its own inanition. So artificial and effete had it become that Gay's *Shepherd's Week*, in broad burlesque, was sometimes read as a p. in the true Theocritean style. The outstanding example of the romantic p. is Salomon Gessner's *Daphnis* (1754), *Idyllen* (1756), and *Der Tod Abels* (1758); and Wordsworth's *Michael*, reflecting the empirical element of Eng. romanticism, well marks the end of serious attempts in the genre.

E. Gosse, "An Essay on Eng. P. Poetry," *Complete Works in Verse and Prose of Edmund Spenser* (1882); M. H. Shackford, "A Definition of the P. Idyll," PMLA, 19 (1904); J. Marsan, *La Pastorale dramatique en France* . . . (1905); E. K. Chambers, *Eng. Pastorals* (1906); W. W. Greg, *P. Poetry and P. Drama* (1906); J. Marks, *Eng. P. Drama* . . . (1908); J. H. Hanford, "The P. Elegy and Milton's *Lycidas*," PMLA, 25 (1910); H. M. Hall, *Idylls of Fishermen* (1912); H. A. Rennert, *Sp. P. Romances* (1912); J. P. W. Crawford, *Sp. P. Drama* (1915); H. E. Mantz, "Non-dramatic P. in Europe in the 18th C.," PMLA, 31 (1916); J. W. MacKail, "Allan Ramsay and the Romantic Revival," E&S, 10 (1924); M.ˉK. Bragg, *The Formal Eclogue in 18th C. England* (1926); P. van Tieghem, "Les Idylles de Gessner et le rêve p.," *Le Préromantisme*, II (1930); W. P. Jones, *The Pastourelle* (1931); W. Empson, *Some Versions of P.* (1938); T. P. Harrison,

The P. Elegy (1939); M. I. Gerhardt, *La Pastorale* (1950); J. Duchemin, *La Houlette et la lyre: Recherche sur les origines pastorales de la poésie* (1960–); J. F. Lynen, *The P. Art of Robert Frost* (1960).

THEORY: Sustained criticism of the p. begins with the essays of the Renaissance humanists, the most important being Vida's *Ars Poetica* (1527), Sebillet's *Art Poétique françoys* (1548), Scaliger's *Poetices* . . . (1561), and "E.K.'s" epistle and preface in 1579. The interest of these critics in the p. sprang from their desire to enrich the vernacular by imitating the "ancients" in this genre and to exploit its allegorical potentialities.

But mere imitation of Theocritus and Virgil did not long suffice, as the debate over Guarini's tragicomedy *Il Pastor Fido* illustrates. In his *Discorso* (1587), Jason Denores attacked this play because, he argued, it is a bastard genre, unauthorized by Aristotle. In *Il Verato* (1588), and *Il Verato Secondo* (1593), Guarini secured the new form against his adversary, thereby widening the scope of the genre. D'Urfé, in "L'Autheur à la Bergere Astrée" (1610), further extended the bounds of the p. when he turned critic to defend his baroque romance. Though Marini never expressed his critical ideas, his aberration of the genre in his extravagant p. idyl *Adone* (1623), made him the main target of the neoclassic attack.

In 1659 René Rapin argued that p. poets should return to the ancient models, and to his *Eclogae sacrae* he prefixed "Dissertatio de carmine pastorali." Reaching the apogee of authoritarianism in p. theory, he declares that he "will gather" all his theory from "*Theocritus* and *Virgil*, those . . . great and judicious Authors, whose very doing is Authority enough," and concludes "that *Pastoral* belongs properly to the Golden Age."

The most significant rebuttal to Rapin's theory is Fontenelle's "Discours sur la nature de l'eglogue" (1688). Whereas Rapin looked for his fundamental criterion in the objective authority of the ancients, Fontenelle, like his master Descartes, sought a subjective standard in and expected illumination from "the natural light of Reason." Fontenelle's method is deductive. He starts with a basic assumption, the self-evident clarity of which he thinks no one will question: "All men would be happy, and that too at an easy rate." From this premise he deduces the proposition that p. poetry, if it is to make men happy, must present "a concurrence of the two strongest passions, laziness and love."

This quarrel between the ancients and the moderns was transferred directly to England; Rapin was translated by Thomas Creech in 1684, and Fontenelle was "Englished by Mr. Motteux" in 1695. The clash between the objective authority of the classics and the subjective standards of reason divided the critics into two schools of opinion, which are best denominated as neoclassic and rationalistic. The immediate source of the basic ideas of the Eng. neoclassic p. critics, the chief of whom are Walsh, Pope, Gay, Gildon, and Newbery, is Rapin's "Treatise." Pope, in practice as well as in theory, epitomizes the neoclassic ideal, explicitly admitting that his "notions concerning" the p. "were derived from . . . *Theocritus* and *Virgil* (the only undisputed authors of P.)."

The immediate source of the basic ideas of the Eng. rationalistic critics, the chief of whom are Addison, Tickell, Purney, Johnson, and *Mirror* no. 79, is Fontenelle's "Discours." But the Eng. followers of Fontenelle insist that the p. conform to experience as well as to reason. Though Dr. Johnson's *Rambler* essays on the p. in general observe both rationalistic and empirical premises, his "true definition" of a p. poem, in which he asserts that a p. is nothing more than a poem in which "any action or passion is represented by its effects on a country life," is basically empirical.

Romantic p. theory evolved from rationalistic theory. As the critics became more certain of their empirical grounds, they showed more freedom to disregard the form and the content of the traditional p.; to look on nature with heightened emotion; to endow primitive life with benevolence and dignity; and to place a greater value on sentiment and feeling. For example, in *An Essay on the Genius and Writings of Pope* (1756), Joseph Warton, by arguing that Theocritus was primarily a realistic poet and that the Golden Age depicted in his poetry may be equated to 18th-c. rural life, substitutes cultural primitivism for the chronological primitivism of the Golden-Age p. In "Discours Préliminaire" to *Les Saisons*, Jean-François de Saint-Lambert disregards the distinction between the p. and descriptive poetry and speaks with enthusiasm concerning the beauty of fields, rivers, and woods and of the felicity of rural life as he knew it in his childhood. In *Lectures on Belles Lettres*, 1783, Hugh Blair singles out Salomon Gessner's *Idyllen* as the poems in which his "idea . . . for the improvement of Pastoral Poetry are fully realized." Blair's essay, along with Wordsworth's *Michael* (which exemplifies much of Blair's theory), ends serious consideration of the p. After that poem and Blair's essay, the genre belongs to the academicians.

N. Drake, "On P. Poetry," *Lit. Hours* (1798); W. W. Greg, *P. Poetry and P. Drama* (1906); E. C. Knowlton, "The Novelty of Wordsworth's *Michael* as a P.," PMLA, 25 (1920); M. K. Bragg, *The Formal E. in 18th C. England* (1926); E. Wasserman, "Introd." to Thomas Purney's

A Full Enquiry into the True Nature of P. (1948); J. E. Congleton, *Theories of P. Poetry in England: 1684–1798* (1952); R. Poggioli, "The Oaten Flute," *Harvard Lib. Bull.*, 2 (1957). J.E.C.

PASTOURELLE (Prov., *pastorela*). A short narrative poem of the Middle Ages which relates the encounter of a knight (who tells the story) and a shepherdess. The form was not fixed; only this conventional situation defines the genre. In the typical p., the knight, while riding along one morning, spies a pretty shepherdess beside the road. He proceeds at once to make advances to her, advances backed up by small gifts or greater promises. In some poems the shepherdess yields with pleasure after very little persuasion. In others, the knight takes by force the favors she tries to deny. In still others, she cleverly outwits him by one stratagem or another, or she is rescued by friendly shepherds, and the knight rides away humiliated or even beaten.

The p. was most popular and had its most typical development in OF in the 13th c. Prov. literature offers relatively few examples (though one of these, by Marcabru, is the earliest extant p. in any vernacular literature), and those few depart widely from the standard pattern. In German, Neidhardt von Reuenthal and his successors developed accessory and subsequent details (the mother's attitude, later developments, scenes of rustic revelry, etc.). The genre has been traced back with some show of probability to certain Latin poems slightly older than the vernacular pastourelles; but the characters in these poems are not a knight and a shepherdess, as they always are in the true p. Whatever its ultimate origin, the p. is the aristocratic product of a superficially polished age, which could find humor in the plight of a silly peasant girl seduced by a man of high rank, as well as in the far less probable discomfiture of the knight outwitted by a peasant girl cleverer than he. It is interesting to note that the delightful little play *Robin et Marion* is nothing more than an expanded p. of this second type.—E. Piguet, *L'Evolution de la p. du XIIe s. à nos jours* (1927); J. W. Powell, *The P.* (1931); Jeanroy, II; W.T.H. Jackson, *"The Medieval P. as a Satirical Genre,"* PQ, 31 (1952). F.M.C.

PATHETIC FALLACY. A phrase coined by John Ruskin and discussed in "Of the Pathetic Fallacy," ch. 12 in *Modern Painters*, III (1856). It describes the tendency of poets and painters to credit nature with the feelings of human beings. This fallacy is caused by "an excited state of the feelings, making us, for the time, more or less irrational." It is the "error . . . which the mind admits when affected strongly by emotion," a "falseness in all our impressions of external things." To illustrate his definition Ruskin quotes from Kingsley's *The Sands of Dee*

They rowed her in across the rolling foam—
The cruel, crawling foam

and says, "The foam is not cruel, neither does it crawl. The state of mind which attributes to it these characters of a living creature is one in which the reason is unhinged by grief."

The highest (creative) order of poets (Homer, Dante, Shakespeare) seldom admit this falseness. It is the second (reflective or perceptive) order (Wordsworth, Coleridge, Keats, Tennyson) who "much delight in it." Ruskin puts his two orders of poets in perspective when he includes them in his four "ranks of being," using the reaction of Wordsworth's Peter Bell to the primrose as a touchstone. The nonpoet is "the man who perceives rightly because he does not feel, and to whom the primrose is very accurately the primrose because he does not love it." The second-rank poet is "the man who perceives wrongly, because he feels, and to whom the primrose is anything else than a primrose." The first-rank poet is "the man who perceives rightly in spite of his feelings, and to whom the primrose is for ever nothing else than itself—a little flower, apprehended in the very plain and leafy fact of it." The inspired poet is a strong man who nevertheless is submitted to influences stronger than himself and who sees inaccurately because what he sees is inconceivably above him. Ruskin thus finds the pathetic fallacy in second-rank poets and in inspired poets. In the former the fallacy is to be condemned as a sign of morbid feeling or inaccurate perception. Inspired poets, on the other hand, quite validly resort to the fallacy, for they are ever aware of the fact qut of which strong feeling comes. Ruskin's attack on what he considers to be a morbidity of mind in modern painters and poets, the overpowering of intellect by narrow feelings, follows naturally from his moral theory of art, in terms of which the fallacy of this group is to distort truth, to "miss the plain and leafy fact."

Ruskin coined the phrase, the "p.f.," to attack the secular sentimentalism of his contemporaries. It existed, of course, long before Ruskin named it as a traditional figure of speech, a species of personification going back as far as Homer. But the late 18th c. saw its extensive use. There are numerous figures in Gray, Collins, Cowper, Burns, Blake, Wordsworth, Shelley, and Keats which attribute to natural objects human feelings and powers. Mountains mourn, winds sigh, fields smile. Wordsworth justified such expressions by asserting that "objects . . . derive their influ-

ence not from properties inherent in them . . . , but from such as are bestowed upon them by the minds of those who are conversant with or affected by these objects."

The morbid use of the p.f., which Ruskin denounced in theory, Tennyson refined and diminished in poetic practice. Not the large natural forms but individual objects with their peculiar characteristics came to be celebrated for their overtones of human emotion. Knowing more about science than any Eng. poet before or since (except possibly William Empson), and being near-sighted to boot, he took a close look at natural objects. His verse from 1842, as Josephine Miles has shown, reveals a markedly less frequent resort to the fallacy than theretofore. Rather than stress the great likeness between man and nature in terms of sympathies of feeling, he heralded a new emphasis on qualitative comparison between objects in terms of sense perception. The old order, then, had already begun to yield to the new when Ruskin named and denounced the morbid use of the fallacy. After Ruskin, and perhaps because of him, use of the fallacy declined markedly. The Pre-Raphaelites, in paint and language, tried to set down what was really there. Hopkins followed them in his concern with "the plain and leafy fact" of the primrose, though, of course, his inscapes are of a vital nature. Among 20th-c. poets use of the p.f. has continued to decline, although Dylan Thomas used it with brilliant effectiveness.

J. Ruskin, "Of the P.F.," *Modern Painters*, III (1856); J. Miles, *P.F. in the 19th C.* (1942); A. H. Warren, Jr., "John Ruskin," *Eng. Poetic Theory: 1825–1865* (1950); B. Morris, "Ruskin on the P.F., or On How a Moral Theory of Art May Fail," J.ᴬᴄ, 14 (1955); J. D. Thomas, "Poetic Truth and P.F.," *Texas Studies in Lit. and Language*, 3 (1961).   J.K.R.

PATHOS (Gr. "suffering," "passion"). That quality which evokes feelings of tenderness, pity, and sorrow in the reader or beholder. See SENTIMENTALITY.

PATTERN POETRY.† Verse in which the disposition of the lines is such as to represent some physical object or to suggest motion, place, or feeling in accord with the idea expressed in the words. The pattern poem, or "shaped" poem, first appears in Western-world literature in the works of certain Gr. bucolic poets, notably in a few poems of Simias of Rhodes (ca. 300 B.C.), later much imitated. It is unlikely that the form is a Gr. invention; its origin has been thought to be Eastern. The true oriental p. poem (Persian or Turkish) blends several visual arts and bears more relation to acrostics, calligraphy, and illumination than to poetry proper. Among the shapes com-

† In Supplement, see also CALLIGRAMME; CONCRETE POETRY.

monly represented in such poems have been axes, eggs, spears, altars, wings, columns, pyramids, diamonds, and other geometric figures. The chief agent in transmitting p. poetry from antiquity to modern times was the Planudean version of the *Gr. Anthology*. An extravagant instance of figure-poems is the *Musarum libri* (1628) of Baldassare Bonifacio, whose whole volume is devoted to the type. The first Eng. p. poems belong to the 16th c. (Stephen Hawes, 1509; Richard Willes, 1573; George Puttenham, 1589), though the best known is doubtless the *Easter Wings* of George Herbert. Modern practitioners of the form, or of related graphic devices, include Guillaume Apollinaire, Dylan Thomas, and E. E. Cummings.—G. Puttenham, *The Arte of Eng. Poesie*, ed. G. Willcock and A. Walker (1936; Bk. 2); M. Church, "The First Eng. P. Poems," PMLA, 61 (1946); Wellek and Warren; A. L. Korn, "Puttenham and the Oriental P.-Poem," CL, 6 (1954). J.L.L.

PAYADA. Argentine term referring to extemporaneous poetic contest of questions and answers among the Gauchos. Made famous in many gauchesque poems, particularly in part II of *Martin Fierro* by José Hernández, in which there is a long p. between the protagonist and a Negro. Many of the questions and answers are of a philosophic and lyrical nature, such as: "What is the song of the earth?" "What is the song of the sky?" In the p. contest the Gaucho who is unable to answer, or who answers in an inferior fashion, loses. The p. is also called *contrapunto*. The champion Gaucho singers are highly regarded in Argentine legend and poetry. Santos Vega was one of the best known of these legendary Gaucho troubadours. J.A.C.

PEGASUS. In mythology, a winged horse born from the blood of Medusa and favored by the Muses (q.v.). He assisted the Gr. hero Bellerophon in slaying the Chimaera, but threw him when he attempted to fly to heaven. He was not associated with poetry beyond the fact that his hoofprint produced Hippocrene, the fountain of the Muses, on Mount Helicon. In postclassical times, however, he is frequently referred to as a symbol of the poetic imagination, either soaring to the heavens of invention or in need of the restraining bit. (Cf. Hesiod, *Theogonia* 280ff., 325ff.; Pausanias 2.3.5, 2.31.9, 9.31.3; Boileau, *Art Poétique* 1.6.) A.R.B.

PENTAMETER (Gr. "of 5 measures or feet") should mean a line of 5 measures. The term was actually applied in antiquity to a dactylo-spondaic line consisting of two equal parts $(2\frac{1}{2} + 2\frac{1}{2}$ feet):

In thĕ Pĕn|tămētĕr | āye || fāllĭng ĭn | mĕlŏdў |

b̄ack
(Coleridge)

The first 2 feet may be either dactyls or spondees; then comes a long syllable; the second half consist of 2 dactyls, followed by a long syllable. The division between the two halves is marked by a break between words; there must not be hiatus, elision, or *syllaba anceps* (short allowed to stand for long) at this position. The p. is normally the second part of the elegiac distich (q.v.), the first part of which is a hexameter. The classical p. should not be confused with the so-called Eng. p. (5-stress line), which is usually iambic and generally regular. See BLANK VERSE; HEROIC COUPLET.—Hardie; K. Rupprecht, *Einführung in die griechische Metrik* (1950); U. von Wilamowitz-Moellendorff, *Griechische Verskunst* (2d ed., 1958). W.B.

PENTAPODY (Gr. "5 feet"). A group or line of 5 feet. The most common pentapodies in Gr. poetry are the dactylic, iambic, and trochaic.—Koster.

PENTARSIC (Gr. "of 5 rises"). Having 5 metrical beats. See ARSIS AND THESIS. R.J.G.

PENTASTICH. A group, stanza or poem of 5 lines of verse. See also QUINTET, and CINQUAIN, a special form of a 5-line stanza.

PENTHEMIMER (Gr. "of 5 halves"). In Gr. and L. verse a metrical unit consisting of $2\frac{1}{2}$ feet. When these feet are dactylic, the unit is also called *hemiepes* (q.v.). Correspondingly, the caesura which occurs in the dactylic hexameter and iambic trimeter after the first syllable of the third foot is called penthemimeral.—Koster. P.S.C.

PERFECT, TRUE, OR FULL RHYME. The correspondence in accented syllables of the vowel-sound and the following consonant(s) but not of the consonant(s) before the vowel. It is single, duple, or triple: *Keats-beets, Shelley-jelly, Tennyson-venison* (J. C. Ransom's "Survey of Literature"). P.r. is the equivalent of Fr. *rime suffisante* (cf. *rime très riche, vaillant-travaillant*, in which the preceding vowel and consonant are also identical; *rime riche, éclaire-crépusculaire*, in which the preceding consonant is also identical; and *rime pauvre, ami-fini, mont-ton*, where the vowel stands alone or is followed by different unpronounced consonants; if the latter are pronounced, rhyme has weakened to assonance [q.v.]). The designation "perfect" points to the acceptance of varieties of rhyme not perfect, which may have been taken from Ir., Welsh, Icelandic, and other sources into Eng. to make up for the relative scarcity of perfect rhymes in the language, as contrasted with the abundance of such rhymes in other languages; the main varieties are consonance and near rhyme (qq.v.). P.r. has not, however, been displaced by these new devices, which remain still supplemental and not central. s.l.m.

PERIPHRASIS as a round-about way of naming something makes its meaning apparent by approximating a whole or partial definition. Quintilian distinguished two kinds, the euphemistic (as in the phrase "the Lord of Hosts" to signify God) and the descriptive (as in the phrase "the wandering stars" to signify planets. *Institutes* 7.6.59). The distinction is the fundamental one. Of the first kind are also those which are meant to weaken the thought of evil (the *absit omen* motif, as in the phrase "passing away" to signify death); the descriptive kind includes most of those which approximate the two-word definition in the combination of a specific with a general term ("the finny tribe" to signify fish). While widely used in biblical and Homeric literature, the development of p. as a truly important feature of poetic style begins with Lucretius and Virgil, and through their influence it became an important feature of epic and descriptive poetry throughout the Middle Ages and into the Renaissance. Its use in the earlier period, however, was possibly supported by the use of kenning (q.v.) in Germanic poetry. The practice of the *Pléiade* in the 16th c. gave periphrases a new vogue throughout Europe and led directly to the establishment in the late 17th and 18th c. of a whole battery of phrases many of which conformed to the growing interest in scientific definition (as in the phrase "liquid ambient" to signify water). Since the 18th c., the form has lost much of its prestige, and more often than not survives in inflated uses for purposes of humor, as it does in Dickens. In the history of rhetoric p. is most generally characterized as a trope, and its function has been best analyzed by Longinus who shows how it serves the elevation of thought, and how by unfitting use it becomes gross and turgid (28–29).—E. Krantz, *Essai sur l'esthétique de Descartes* (1882); J. Arthos, *The Language of Natural Description in 18th C. Poetry* (1949). j.a.

PERSIAN POETRY. Though poetry was certainly written and sung in Persia long before that country was invaded and converted to Islam by the Arabs during the 7th c. A.D., the term "Pers. poetry" is customarily used to indicate the practice of the poetic art since the Muslim conquest. It is in this sense that the term is interpreted in this essay. It must also be remarked by way of commentary that poetry has been written in postconquest Pers. not only in Persia itself, but also in Turkey, Afghanistan, India, and now Pakistan and some Central Asian republics of the Soviet Union.

It took two to three centuries for Pers., an Indo-Aryan language, to shed most of its ancient inflections and to assimilate those Semitic elements of Arabic origin which enriched its vocabulary and modified its rhetoric. A considerable quantity of fragments from the verse of this transitional period has survived. However, the first major poet of Pers. literature, incidentally the greatest of his kind, was Firdausī (d. ca. 1020), author of the epic *Shāh-nāma*. This immense work in some 60,000 couplets rehearses the legendary history of the ancient kings of Persia, and was based upon material that goes back to the pre-Muslim period. It is a true masterpiece, for the great breadth of its canvas is matched by brilliant portraiture of individual incidents, of which the best known recounts the tragic story of Sohrab and Rustum, a theme familiar to readers of Eng. poetry through its treatment by Matthew Arnold. All Pers. meters, with a single exception, were derived from Arabic prosody and are quantitative; the meter of the *Shāh-nāma* is *mutaqārib*.

$$\smile\!-\!-\,|\,\smile\!-\!-\,|\,\smile\!-\!-\,|\,\smile\!-$$
$$\smile\!-\!-\,|\,\smile\!-\!-\,|\,\smile\!-\!-\,|\,\smile\!-$$

chu nuh māh: bigzasht: bar dukht-i shāh
yakī kūdak āmad chu tābanda māh
chu khandān shud ū chihra shādāb: kard
urā nām: Tahmīna Suhrāb: kard

When nine slow-circling months had roll'd
  away,
Sweet-smiling pleasure hailed the brightening
  day.
A wonderous boy Tuhmeena's tears supprest,
And lull'd the sorrows of her heart to rest;
To him, predestined to be great and brave,
The name Soohrab his tender mother gave.
   (tr. J. Atkinson)

The rhyming couplet (*mathnavī*) had been used in Arabic poetry, but was not very popular with a people who greatly preferred to write in monorhyme. The epic, though attempted by a few Arab poets, proved alien to the literary genius of the Arabs. The Persians made these two distinctive contributions to poetic form—the perfecting of the rhyming couplet, and its exploitation in extensive compositions.

None since Firdausī has successfully composed a long and discursive epic on the scale of the *Shāh-nāma*, though he has had not a few imitators. Epics of lesser magnitude and with more restricted range have been written by many authors, some of great brilliance. Firdausī himself is doubtfully credited with one such idyll on the theme of Joseph and

Potiphar's wife; several later writers attempted the same subject, but the most admired treatment is that of Jāmī (d. 1492). The best esteemed of the idyllists is Niẓāmī (d. ca. 1203) who composed five minor epics, the longest being upon the legend of Alexander the Great; he also retold the Arab desert romance of Majnūn and Lailā, while ancient Persia provided him with the heroic themes of two other poems. His writings, like Firdausī's Shāh-nāma, inspired Pers. artists to paint their finest miniatures. Jāmī composed in all seven idylls, interpreting as mystical allegories such familiar stories as the tragic love of Salāmān and Absāl. His nephew Hātifī (d. 1521) wrote an epic on the conquests of Tamerlane, and his idyll Lailā u Majnūn also enjoys a certain popularity.

The romantic idyll, like the epic, was composed in rhyming couplets, but the poet had a variety of meters from which to choose, though only one meter might be used in a given poem. Didactic verse also followed the epic form, and indeed sometimes reached truly epic proportions, notably in the mystic Mathnavī of Jalāl al-Dīn Rūmī (d. 1273). This famous poem, venerated almost equally with the Koran, describes in a wealth of anecdote the soul's quest after union with God; it runs to about 25,000 couplets and is composed in the ramal metre.

bishnav az nai chūn ḥikāyat mīkunad
az judāyīhā shikāyat mīkunad
kaz nayistān tā marā bibrīda and
az nafīram mard u zan nālīda and

Hear, how yon read in sadly pleasing tales
Departed bliss and present woe bewails!
'With me, from native banks untimely torn,
Love-warbling youths and soft-ey'd virgins
mourn.'
(tr. Sir William Jones)

Rūmī's chief predecessors in applying the epic form to mystical purposes were Sanā'ī (fl. 1150) who wrote among other things a remarkable Pilgrim's Progress, and Farīd al-Dīn ʿAṭṭār (d. ca. 1230), a voluminous author whose most celebrated idyll is the Bird-Parliament translated in epitome by Edward FitzGerald. A more commonplace and popular note was struck by Saʿdī (d. 1292) in his Būstān, which makes a pair with his prose and verse miscellany the Gulistān; both books are admired for their practical wisdom enshrined in simple yet elegant language. The tradition was continued in modern times by Sir Muḥammad Iqbāl (d. 1938) of Lahore, whose Secrets of the Self and Mysteries of Selflessness express attractively their author's religiopolitical philosophy; he also composed many graceful lyrics which proclaim his indebtedness to Rūmī.

The formal ode (qaṣīda), copied from its Arabic model, has been popular throughout Pers. literary history chiefly as an instrument for courting the favour or appeasing the displeasure of kings and princes. Poets have also employed this form to canvass religious, mystical or ethical ideals, to describe the beauties of nature or to commemorate an interesting event, to congratulate a patron or a friend upon some good fortune or to condole with him in a bereavement. The ode may extend to as many as 100 couplets or more, all having the same rhyme; it is thus taken as a chance to display craftsmanship and virtuosity, qualities which appeal greatly to the primary audience but largely vanish in translation. Hyperboles, rhetorical embellishments, and verbal conceits are the accepted stock-in-trade of the skilful ode-maker. The meters employed vary considerably, and there is a preference for the long and swinging line; the following are the commoner patterns:

Ramal	‿‿‿ | ‿‿‿ | ‿‿‿ | ‿‿‿
Hazaj	‿‿‿‿ | ‿‿‿‿ | ‿‿‿‿ | ‿‿‿‿
Mujtass	‿‿‿‿ | ‿‿‿‿ | ‿‿‿‿ | ‿‿‿‿
Muẓāriʿ	‿‿‿‿ | ‿‿‿‿ | ‿‿‿‿ | ‿‿‿‿

The court poets who have won greatest fame by their odes include Rūdagī (d. 940), Farrukhī (d. 1038), Anvarī (d. ca. 1190) and Khāqānī (d. 1200). Nāṣir-i Khusrau (d. 1061) is esteemed for his religious and moralizing odes, while Sanā'ī, ʿAṭṭār and Rūmī used the form in their mystical poetry. In modern times the best known ode writers include Qāʾānī (d. 1854), Adīb-i Pīshāvarī (d. 1931), Parvīn (d. 1941), and Bahār (d. 1951); the convention is now found appropriate to political and social broadsides. Parvīn revived charmingly the old moralizing themes made famous by Saʿdī; Bahār's most splendid poem is a formal panegyric composed in honor of Firdausī at his millenary.

The lyric (ghazal) looks at first sight to be simply a short ode, its length averaging between 5 and 15 couplets, all monorhymed. The same range of meters is employed, though the line is often apt to be somewhat briefer. As an art form it appears to have evolved out of the so-called nasīb (erotic prelude) with which the old Arab poets began their odes; its central theme is love, to which wine-drinking is an almost inevitable accompaniment. The beloved may be either male or female; sometimes the person intended is the royal patron; by the mystical poets he is identified with God, and wine is taken as a symbol for ecstatic emotion. The acknowledged master of the lyric is Ḥāfiẓ (d. 1391), to whom some 500 ghazals are attributed; the following is a brief specimen.

When my Beloved the cup in hand taketh
The market of lovely ones slack demand taketh.
I, like a fish, in the ocean am fallen,
Till me with the hook yonder Friend to land
　taketh.
Every one saith, who her tipsy eye seeth,
"Where is a shrieve, that this fair firebrand
　taketh?"
Lo, at her feet in lament am I fallen,
Till the Beloved me by the hand taketh.
Happy his heart who, like Hafiz, a goblet
Of wine of the Prime Fore-eternal's brand
　taketh.

(tr. J. Payne)

The foregoing version ingeniously imitates
both the rhythm and the rhyming scheme of
the original. Other famous lyrical poets are
Sanāʾī, Rūmī, ʿIrāqī (d. 1289), Saʿdī, Amīr
Khusrau (d. 1325) and Jāmī. Many are writing
lyrics at the present day, some under the influence of European literature; it is worth mentioning that the Soviet poet Lāhūtī took Stalin
for his Beloved. Khānlarī reflects Wordsworth
and Tennyson; the genius of Valéry and the
imagists has fired the imagination of such
writers as Gulchīn, Shahriyār, and Tavallalī.

It appears that the only original contribution made by the Persians to poetic form and
prosody consists in the quatrain (rubāʿī); and
it is just therefore that this should happen to
be the form best known to the general public,
thanks to the great and continuing popularity
of its adaptation by an Eng. translator. Edward FitzGerald's Rubáiyát (1st ed., 1859)
gives a true picture of the rhyme pattern
(AABA, occasionally AAAA) of the Pers. original, though not of its subtle rhythm. Tradition makes out that the invention of the
quatrain meter was quite accidental—the glee-
ful shout of a child at play, overheard and
adopted by a passing poet. Most Pers. poets
have composed quatrains, which have generally
retained the authentic flavor of spontaneity,
succinctness, and wit; the rubāʿī is essentially
an occasional poem, and the impression of
continuous composition conveyed by FitzGerald's paraphrase is wholly misleading. The
most illustrious practitioner of this literary
form was ʿUmar Khaiyām (d. 1132), who may
have composed as many as 750 quatrains. The
following quotations illustrate the pattern of
the rubāʿī, and the venial infidelity of Fitz-
Gerald to his Pers. model.

---∪∣∪--∪∣∪--∣≃∪-

khurshīd: kamand-i ṣubḥ: bar bām afgand
kaikhusrav-i rūz: muhra dar jām afgand
mai khur ki nidā-yi ʿishq: hangām-i saḥar
āvāza-yi ishrabū dar aiyām afgand

Wake! For the Sun, who scatter'd into flight
The Stars before him from the Field of Night,

Drives Night along with them from
　Heav'n, and strikes
The Sultan's Turret with a Shaft of Light.

(tr. E. FitzGerald)

The sun has cast the noose of morn
　Athwart the roof-top of the world;
　The emperor of day has hurled
His bead, our goblet to adorn.

Drink wine: for at the first dawn's rays
　The proclamation of desire
　Rang through the universe entire,
And bade men drink through all the days.

(tr. A. J. Arberry)

The quatrain is today felt to be the ideal form
in which to compose a political squib.

This brief review of Pers. poetic forms is
not complete without a mention of certain
rarer varieties. The quatrain has a pair in the
dū-baitī, a folk convention having the same
rhyming pattern but a different and simpler
meter. The only poet who has given semiclassical shape to this rustic doggerel is the
wild mystic Bābā Ṭāhir (fl. 11th c.). The qiṭʿa
is a brief occasional poem in monorhyme; its
most accomplished exponent was Ibn Yamīn
(d. 1344). The tarjīʿ-band is a device for linking together a succession of lyriclike stanzas,
a couplet in the form of a refrain being interposed between each component. The spirit of
emulation which encourages the Pers. poet to
pay tribute to by seeking to outrival the work
of his predecessors has engendered the mu-
khammas and musaddas; a given lyric is expanded by inserting four or five lines between
each line of the original.

Out of obscure and humble beginnings, the
Pers. poetic genius suddenly broke into full
flower in Firdausī's masterpiece. Other poetic
forms—the ode, the lyric, the quatrain, the
idyll, didactic verse—quickly matured thereafter, and a classical tradition was firmly established by the end of the 12th c. Toward the
year 1500 this transition reached its climax, to
be succeeded by a slow decline; though Pers.
poetry enjoyed a long Indian summer under
the Moghul empire. Royal and princely patronage had throughout these centuries encouraged the poet to give of his best, and so
much of Pers. poetry is courtly in theme and
tone; yet the portrayal of mystical ideas liberated the individual writer from too strict bondage to earthly rulers and gave him scope to
express his personal experiences and his relationship with the Divine Beloved. It is only
in this century that the poets of Persia have
discovered anew the creative impulse of a
most gifted people. The rise of democratic
institutions, and intellectual and cultural contacts with Western countries, have set up a
new ferment in the Pers. mind, the full effects
of which are yet to be seen.

PERSONIFICATION

ANTHOLOGIES: *Flowers from Pers. Poetry*, ed.
N. H. Dole and B. M. Walker (2 v., 1901); *A
Pers. Anthol.*, ed. E. G. Browne (1927); Badī'al-
Zamān Bishrūya, *Sukhan u Sukhanvarān* [Po-
etry and Poets] (1929); *Poets and Poetry of
Modern Persia*, ed. M. Ishaque (2 v., 1933);
H. Pizhmān, *Bihtarīn ash'ār* [Best Poems]
(1934); *Immortal Rose* (1948; anthol. of tr.
lyrics) and *Pers. Poems* (1954; comprehensive
anthol. of tr.), both ed. A. J. Arberry.
HISTORY AND CRITICISM: E. G. Browne, *The
Press and Poetry of Modern Persia* (1914) and
A Lit. Hist. of Persia (4 v., 2d ed., 1928; a
splendid and complete survey); A. V. Williams
Jackson, *Early Pers. Poetry* (1920); R. Levy,
Pers. Lit. (1923; introd. manual); Rizā-zāda
Shafaq, *Tarīkh-i adabīyāt-i Irān* [Lit. Hist. of
Persia] (1942); A. J. Arberry, *Cl. Pers. Lit.*
(1958); G. M. Wickens, "Poetry in Modern
Persia," *Univ. of Toronto Quarterly*, 29 (1960).
A.J.A.

PERSONIFICATION, as a manner of speech
endowing things or abstractions with life, has
been a feature of European poetry since
Homer. Psychologically and rhetorically it
may be described as "a means of taking hold
of things which appear startlingly uncontrollable and independent" (T. B. L. Webster). But
the famous personifications of Strength and
Force in *Prometheus Bound* parallel and challenge the figures of gods in myths, and according to a theory now current, supported
by Cassirer, Cornford, and others, personifications replace mythical figures when rational
attitudes supersede the primitive imagination.
This theory had an ancient presentation in
the Stoic doctrine that abstractions in the
form of personifications express demonic force.
In the early Christian and medieval ages
the history of p. is closely associated with the
rise of allegory (as in the *Psychomachia* of
Prudentius, *The Romance of the Rose*, and
Piers Plowman). It was almost equally important in the mingled development of mythological and romantic poetry in the Renaissance
(Poliziano, Spenser). Here, too, as in Ariosto's
descriptions of war and in Spenser's *Muta-
bilitie Cantos*, the personifications aspire to
the power and automatism of mythical figures.
Such is the central personification of Spenser's
Hymn to Love:

For Love is lord of truth and loyalty.

In the 18th c. personifications lost much of
their emotional and quasi-mythical power to
the degree that poetry subscribed to the vague
anthropomorphism of deistic philosophy, but
their vogue increased even as they themselves
became, as in much nature poetry, barely more
than abstractions. The development of sym-

bolist poetry in the 19th c. largely smothered
the use of p. as a figure in which the rational
element is the determining character. But this
kind has returned again to fashion in Auden
(*At the Grave of Henry James*), while the
more nearly mythological forms have been
employed by Dylan Thomas (*The force that
through the green fuse drives the flower*).

H. Usener, *Götternamen* (1896); J. Tambor-
nino, *De antiquorum daemonismo* (1909);
R. Hinks, *Myth and Allegory in Ancient Art*
(1939); B. H. Bronson, "P. Reconsidered," ELH,
14 (1947); E. R. Wasserman, "The Inherent
Values of 18th-C. P.," PMLA, 65 (1950); T.B.L.
Webster, "P. as a Mode of Gr. Thought," JWCI,
17 (1954); C. F. Chapin, *P. in 18th-C. Eng. Poetry* (1955); N. Maclean, "P. but not Poetry,"
ELH, 23 (1956); Lausberg. J.A.

PERUVIAN POETRY. See SPANISH AMERICAN
POETRY.

PETRARCHISM. In the broadest sense of the
word P. is the direct or indirect imitation of
Petrarch's L. or It. writings whether in prose
or in verse. However, it is in connection with
his It. poetry that the term has most commonly been employed, alluding almost exclusively to derivations from the *Canzoniere*
or Song-book and compositions by others using
Petrarch's collection for imitative purposes.
This type of poetic borrowing started during
Petrarch's lifetime in the 14th c., reached considerable proportions in the last half of the
15th c. and became the predominant mode of
poetic expression in the 16th not only in Italy
but throughout Western Europe as well. Most
of the lyric poets of the last mentioned period,
and they were legion, wrote under the influence of P. In Italy they include such first-rate
artists as Ariosto, Della Casa, Michelangelo,
Gaspara Stampa, Vittoria Colonna, Tansillo
and Torquato Tasso; in France, Maurice Scève,
Louise Labé, Ronsard and his fellow-poets in
the *Pléiade*, and Desportes; in Spain, Garcilaso
de la Vega, Cetina, the Argensola brothers,
Herrera, Lope de Vega, Quevedo, and Góngora;
in Portugal, Sá da Miranda, Camoëns, Bernardes, and Antonio Ferreira, in England,
Wyatt and Surrey, Shakespeare, and most of
the Elizabethans. The authority of Cardinal
Pietro Bembo, amounting to a literary dictatorship, exercised through his *Asolani* (1505),
which set up the Petrarchan and Neoplatonic
doctrines of love as the great archetypes to be
followed, and through his *Prose sulla Volgar
Lingua* (1525) which proclaimed Petrarch's
It. poems as the unique linguistic models for
composition in verse, did much to firmly establish the tradition. Reacting against the excesses of *Quattrocentism*, Bembo was instru-

mental in the restoration of good taste in poetry. He performed the function of systematizing P. Other contributing factors were the diffusion of printing and the vogue of the vernacular as the common medium for love-poetry. It goes without saying that these external stimuli would soon have lost their rousing power were it not for the fact that the *Canzoniere* is a great poetic masterpiece—the subjective expression of a deep emotional and spiritual conflict, intensely and variously voiced, and in a language that stylistically approaches perfection. Petrarch was aware that he was attempting something new. He refers to *le mie rime nove* in the sonnet, *L'arbor gentil* . . . His followers, especially in the 16th c., appreciated this originality and correctly assessed the superlative lyric value inherent in the poems. Those among them who were true poets were able to use the collection as a model and still rise to lyric heights with a minimum of violence to their artistic personalties. On the other hand, numerous others, constituting the majority, indulged in imitation merely because it was a literary fad. They were primarily enticed by the rhetorical elements lurking here and there in Petrarch's verse, and by dint of constant repetition reduced many of its genuinely poetic features to conventional commonplaceness. Some of the most stereotyped features that characterize this type of P. are the description of the physical beauty of one's lady-love—she is apt to have golden hair, ebony brows, rose lips, teeth or fingers of pearl, forehead or hands of ivory, neck of alabaster; her eyes are stars or suns, etc. Morally she is chaste, angelic, and has a miraculous power over men and nature. These two types of beauty lead to contrasting effects: milady's physical beauty, giving rise to hope, and her moral beauty, to despair. Countless poems are addressed to her eyes, hands, and hair. Invocations to night, sleep, wild nature, rivers, the breeze, and jealousy abound. This literary mannerism soon became an object of ridicule and the term "Petrarchistic" acquired a derisive connotation because of it, undeservedly casting a pall of opprobrium upon the movement as a whole. Actually, P. represents one of the most revolutionary advances in the history of modern poetry.

E. H. Wilkins, "An Introductory Petrarch Bibliog.," PQ, 27 (1948) and "A Gen. Survey of Renaissance P.," CL, 2 (1950); C. Calcaterra, "Il Petrarca e il Petrarchismo," in *Questioni e correnti di storia letteraria* (1949); L. Baldacci, *Il Petrarchismo italiano nel Cinquecento* (1957); J. G. Fucilla, *Estudios sobre el petrarquismo en España* (1960); B. T. Sozzi, *Petrarca* (1963).　　　　　　　　　J.G.F.

PHALAECEAN. See HENDECASYLLABIC.

PHERECRATEAN. Named after the comic poet Pherecrates (5th c. B.C.), this classical meter was the catalectic form of the glyconic (q.v.). Apart from *syllaba anceps* (q.v.) in the final syllable, it permitted resolutions only in the quantities of the base (i.e., the first 2 syllables). The P. occurs, usually with one or more glyconics, chiefly in Anacreon, the choruses of Gr. tragedy, and Horace (in whom the base was regularly spondaic). An example is Horace's

$$\text{gra\bar{t}o,} \mid \text{P\bar{y}rrh\breve{a}, s\breve{u}b \ \bar{a}n}\mid\text{tr\bar{o}}$$
(*Odes* 1.5.3.).

Bowra; Dale; Koster; Crusius.　　P.S.C.

PHILIPPINE POETRY. Although Sp. "cross and crown" colonial policy in the 16th c. required destruction of pre-Christian writings, a strong oral tradition has kept alive even until today Indonesian-Malayan origins of Filipino culture. Riddles and rituals in verse, for the planting-harvest cycles; *kumintang*, war songs; *kundiman*, plaintive love lyrics; *talindao*, boat songs; poetic debates and epics—all these have survived in relatively pure form, ironically because colonial administrations withheld the fruits of the Sp. Renaissance from the governed classes. Consequently, sources of a nativist resurgence have always been present.

The necessity of preserving vernacular literature orally has made both primitive and even modern poetry inseparable from song and the drama. One of the most popular forms of self-entertainment during fiestas in rural *barrios* is *balagtasan*, a kind of spontaneous debating in verse, to test wit rather than reason. To the same heritage belong the *duplo* and *karagatan*, dramatic debates employed to fulfill social requirements at a wake, to relieve the living during the interval between religious ceremonies. Often the rhyming begins with a fanciful criminal accusation, which the innocent must disprove. Losers forfeit objects which can be reclaimed only after a *loa*, a declamation such as this from the Visayas:

Nag tanum ako limon
putus brillante ang dahon;
ang tauo nga makapasilong
luas gid sa Kamatayon.

I planted a lemon tree,
Its leaves all diamonds;
Anyman in its shelter
Will find immortality.

Two days are required to recite the epics of the Ifugaos, heirs to the ancient mountain rice terraces: the *Hudhud* relates the creation of the world and tribal progenitors; the *Alim*, like the Indian *Ramayana*, describes collective life among the gods. The Moro epics (*daran-gan*)—*Bantugan, Bidasari,* and others—require a week for declamation, but are valued for absence of Western intrusions. The Ilocano *Lam-ang* is generally considered a lesser epic because its present form betrays the influence of 17th-c. Christian fathers.

Even when alien themes or forms were borrowed, however, some native element persisted, making the composite unique. Church litanies have suggested a special kind of two-part verse, with *talindao* (leader) and *pabinian* (chorus); dramatic reading of the Bible has led to development of several *Pasions* in verse, to be wailed for days during the Eastertide, to improvised melodies. In the same manner of development, the dance of armed Moros in 1750, during celebration of Ali Mundi's conversion, Mohammedan leader, inspired imitations called *moro-moro* plays, melodramatic extravaganzas representing colorful conflicts between Muslims and Christians, religious differences often serving only as temporary obstacle to a mixed love pact. Although Christian triumph is made inevitable, a high degree of invention often has kept poetic expression of tournament and courtship lively. Similarly, the Filipino *awit* (chivalric-heroic romance) and *corrido* (legendary or religious tale) are exaggerated adaptations of Sp. material, and exhibit, respectively, the indigenous preference for 12- and 8-syllable lines. The scene of the most distinguished *corrido, Florante at Laura,* was situated in Albania to enable its author, Francisco Balagtas (1788–1862), to describe Phil. conditions without fear of censorship. Consequently it is remembered for the felicity of its Tagalog (the principal vernacular) rather than for its substance.

Despite over three centuries of Sp. rule, imposed national distinctions prevented writing of verse in Sp. until the late 1800's. Pedro Paterno's *Sampaguitas y Poesias Varias* (1880), first collection by a Filipino-Sp. poet, had to be published in Europe. Characteristically, poems in Sp. were serenades and lyrics, written for entertainment of friends, or for the accumulation of prestige required by a forensic career. More permanent are the prophetic, patriotic verses of Jose Rizal (whose *Ultima Adios* composed the day before his execution in 1896, ironically helped provoke an armed revolt which he had worked to prevent) and of his contemporaries whose writings, published in Madrid to change colonial policy at the summit, later were smuggled into the Philippines. The most striking example of early 20th-c. crossroads culture is Jose Palma's *Filipinas:* written in Sp. (after the mode of Rizal) under Am. rule, eventually it became the Phil. national anthem.

With the introduction of widespread educa-

tion, Eng. served to help unify an archipelagic nation otherwise divided among nine major dialects. By the 1930's, Quezon as first President of the Commonwealth ordered organization of a national language institute based on Tagalog. Meanwhile, however, just before the outbreak of war he awarded national prizes for literature in the three major languages. One of the prize poems, Zulueta da Costa's *Like the Molave,* is in the declamatory tradition of Whitman, badly imitated—the pseudo-epic style so attractive to chauvinistic writers substituting enthusiasm for art. The craft of imagery and personal idiom had to wait for Jose Garcia Villa, an expatriate in America, for realization. Villa's theme of estrangement from God and country, pending recognition of equality, has found radiant expression in *Have Come, Am Here* (1943) and *Volume Two* (1949), the latter containing Villa's unique "comma poems." Meditative weight is provided each word through indiscriminately regular recurrence of commas, functioning as "holds" rather than as punctuation. Unfortunately, poor imitations of Villa have been a source of "unpoetics" second only to misunderstood Whitman. More recent poets in Eng., often trained and published in the United States, have achieved coalescence of native traditions (dramatic tableau, employment of cryptic and colorful language), New Critical formalism (to shear off excesses of sentimentality and wordiness), and personal vision. Especially important is Edith Tiempo's apocalyptic verse, and Bienvenido Santos' commemoration of lost dignity redeemed through long-suffering. Reanimation of the narrative line, in modern form, is already apparent in the verse dramas of Alejandrino Hufana, who is also coeditor of *Signatures,* first poetry magazine in Eng., founded in 1955. Even if Tagalog succeeds in becoming the language of literature as well as of elementary communication, Am. emphasis on the dramatic and concrete has at least hastened the decline of the romantic abstract and essays-in-rhyme in Phil. poetry.

ANTHOLOGIES: Diwang Kayumanggi, ed. J. C. Laya (4 v., 1947–48; Tagalog prose and poetry); *Heart of the Island,* ed. M. Viray (1947); *Phil. Cross Section,* ed. M. Ramos and F. B. Valeros (1950); *Phil. Harvest,* ed. M. Ramos (1953); *Phil. Writing,* ed. T. D. Agcaoili (1953); *Six Filipino Poets,* ed. L. Casper (1955); *Kathâ I: an Anthol. of Phil. Writing in Eng.,* ed. J. C. Tuvera (1955).

HISTORY AND CRITICISM: T. del Castillo y Tuazon, *A Brief Hist. of Phil. Lit.* (1937); *The Lit. of the Filipinos,* ed. J. V. and C. T. Panganiban (1954); L. Casper, "Filipino Poet: Erect and Audible," *Phil. Studies,* 4 (1956), "Reconnaissance in Manila," *Antioch Review,* 17 (1957) and *The Wayward Horizon: Essays on Modern Phil. Lit.* (1961).   L.C.

PHILOSOPHY AND POETRY. A poem may be philosophical in either of two main senses. It may serve as a vehicle of some philosophical teaching which is essentially independent of the poem itself and could therefore be paraphrased in a set of logically developed statements without loss or distortion of meaning: e.g., Lucretius' *De Rerum Natura*, Pope's *Essay on Man*, and Bridges' *A Testament of Beauty*. Or on the other hand, and by a more deeply characteristic procedure, it may employ its full linguistic, rhythmic, and associational resources to open up new insights into values, relationships, and significant possibilities, such as could not be adequately restated, except with gross distortion, outside the particular poem that has succeeded in expressing them. Shakespeare's *King Lear*, Keats's *Ode to a Grecian Urn*, and Eliot's *Four Quartets* may be taken to illustrate this second type.

Even in those cases where an explicit philos. serves as the main subject matter of the poem, it is never quite identical with the whole of the integral philos. that is being poetically expressed. A poem whose meaningful utterances were confined strictly to general propositions in their abstract character would be little more than a didactic tract, and any concrete details which it might employ would function as allegory rather than as poetic symbolism (see SEMANTICS AND POETRY). Where a poem succeeds in conveying an explicit philos. and in being good poetry at the same time, this combination is mainly a result of its employing language in such a way as to generate implicit insights, adumbrated by poetic rather than logical means, so as to deepen and enliven the explicit teachings that furnish the scenario of the poem. Thus in *De Rerum Natura* the otherwise dry doctrine of universal atomism is watered by fresh insights that find expression in such memorable images as "the flaming ramparts of the universe" (*flammantia moenia mundi*) and the "compacts of love" (*foedera Veneris*) that draw and bind the atoms together. Such imagery is not merely decorative, but constitutive. The word *foedus*, with its plural *foedera*, carries a political connotation and suggests, perhaps subconsciously, that the atoms are drawn together by a kind of Roman agreement, instead of being hooked up mechanically as Democritus had supposed. Thus the poet's awe in the presence of cosmic majesty and his tranquil remembrance of the sweet unions sanctified by the goddess of love are real contributions to the total philos. which *De Rerum Natura* expresses. Accordingly the very opening line of the poem—"Aeneadum genetrix hominum divomque voluptas" (O mother of the race of Aeneas, who stirrest desire in men and gods)—may be taken as an announcement of the philosophical themes to follow, for it succeeds with remarkable economy in doing three things at once: it sets a Roman tone for the poem by its opening word; it invokes Venus, the symbol of archetypal womanhood in its dual aspect of desirable femininity and bounteous motherhood; and it acknowledges Venus' cosmic power, through arousing love, of producing and sustaining life.

The foregoing distinction between explicit and implicit philos. finds a counterpart in the distinction put forward by T. S. Eliot, in his essay on Dante, between intellectual lucidity and poetic lucidity, and correspondingly between "belief attitudes" or "philosophical beliefs" on the one hand and "poetic assent" on the other. Even in Dante's *Divine Comedy*, where the philosophical beliefs are logically and overtly the same as those of Thomas Aquinas, Eliot points out that the belief attitude of a man reading the *Summa Theologica* must be different from that of the same man adequately responding to the *Commedia*. For the *Commedia*, unlike the *Summa*, is constructed according to a "logic of sensibility" representing "a complete scale of the depth and height of human emotion." Correspondingly, Eliot argues, Dante's poetic assent, which is to say his total belief attitude, is inseparable from the elaboration of images which are "not merely antiquated rhetorical devices, but serious and practical means of making the spiritual visible."

The view that a poem may express truths by virtue of its peculiar poetic character and may thus claim to be inherently philosophical, was first overtly enunciated by Aristotle in his famous remark that "poetry is more philosophical than history, for poetry deals with universals, history with particulars." No doubt Aristotle was moved to this declaration by the Platonists' denunciation of poetry, as recorded in the 10th book of Plato's *Republic*. According to this Platonic view the outer world is half unreal, a mere shadow of the ever enduring Forms, or universal meanings and ideals, that find imperfect expression in it; and the arts are declared to be still further removed from the white light of reality, since they irresponsibly pick out elements of the natural world to represent them through their respective media—words and rhythms, or painted and figured surfaces—and thus what they produce is merely "a copy of a copy." Aristotle, on the other hand, regards the world of nature as holding within itself the potentialities of all things, and as striving, with variable success, to realize them; hence "Art partly imitates nature and partly carries to completion what nature has left incomplete," he declares in his *Physics*. But the carrying to completion of nature's partly realized tendencies is what establishes art as a philosophical operation;

for artistic creation, since it is conceived as imitating, must therefore in turn symbolize creative nature at work. Later versions of the Aristotelian principle have held that the universals which poetry expresses are such as to constitute *natura naturans* as distinguished from *natura naturata;* the world's soul rather than the world's body; concrete rather than abstract universals; the creative impulse rather than the finished product.

The Aristotelian idea of poetry as at once reflecting and developing the activity of creative nature is notably carried forward by Goethe (1746–1832). Somewhat like Kant in his relatively late *Critique of Judgment* but independently of him, Goethe holds that evidences of immanent purpose can be found alike in the growth and evolution of natural organisms and in the humanly creative activities that constitute art. The role of mind is not to impose its laws upon an alien world of sense-data (as Kant had taught in his earlier work, *The Critique of Pure Reason*); its true role is "thinking in objects" (*gegenständliches Denken*), which involves the discovery of harmonies and analogies between the creative processes of nature and of art, and thus comes to grasp "Ideals," or archetypes, which are present in both of them. However, the Goethean archetype is not, like the Platonic *eidos*, something sharply distinguishable from the particulars that embody it; rather it exists only "in and through" particulars, and thus can be known only to one whose eyes and ears and heart are responsively open to the sensuously living world. Among these sensuous particulars that flow through one's "living experience" (*Erlebnis*, as distinguished from "conventional experience," *Erfahrung*) the rôle of mind is to discover "eminent instances," each of which is "a living-moment disclosure of the Inscrutable"—a disclosure which would never have been made were it not for just this individual manifestation. Poetry has therefore, by its very nature, something of the character of revelation: not because it proclaims universal truths as such, but because "by grasping the particular in its living character it implicitly apprehends the universal along with it."

The essentially philosophical nature of poetry is reaffirmed, on a variety of grounds, by a number of German and Eng. writers representing the romantic movement. The earlier German romantics—particularly the two Schlegels, Novalis, and Schelling—tend to confuse the issue by broadening the idea of poetry to such a degree as to include, in Friedrich Schlegel's words, that "unformed and unconscious poetry which stirs in planets, shines in light, . . . and glows in the loving bosoms of women" (*Gespräch über die Poesis*, 1800). His brother, August Wilhelm, frames this view

with a more definite logic: arguing that as all things in nature are interrelated, so each thing in some way signifies everything else and thus mirrors the whole; and that whereas commonplace awareness is a disturbing medium that obscures the vision of the whole, the imagination (*die Fantasie*) breaks through this medium and plunges us into the real universe, where nothing is either static or in isolation, but everything participates in everything else in a state of continual metamorphosis. Both Novalis (1772–1801) and Schelling (1775–1854) are in general agreement, describing nature's power to fuse and create as *love*, which Novalis identifies with "the highest natural poetry" and which Schelling describes as "the spirit of nature that speaks to us only through symbols."

Two later German philosophers, Schopenhauer and Nietzsche, have made notable contributions to the topic. Schopenhauer (1788–1860) holds that nature operates primarily not by love but by will, and that the various grades of will in nature, from inorganic matter up through the plant and animal species to man, are distinguished by the Ideas (in something like Plato's sense) which represent the working of will, or desire, at a given level. Art, including of course poetry, he defines as the kind of knowledge concerned with the Ideas, and declares that "its only aim is the communication of knowledge." The highest art and the highest philos. are therefore one, since they both aim at that painless state in which "the wheel of Ixion stands still" and "we are for the moment set free from the miserable striving of the will." In Nietzsche (1844–1900) the will becomes more vigorously characterized as "the will to power," but this conception is broadened to include such diverse manifestations as the violence of the thunderstorm, the tropisms of a sprouting plant, the babe emerging from the womb, the battle-lust of marching Prussian regiments, the creative sensitivity of the artist, and the asceticism of the saint. In the artist the will to power assumes the complementary aspects of Dionysian creative frenzy (*Rausch*) and Apollonian love of form with its attendant illusion of universality; together they produce the aristocratic passion of "self-overcoming," in which philosophical wisdom and artistic creation are combined. Philos. and poetry are fundamentally one, because "wisdom is a woman" and can only be wooed by one who is "careless, mocking, forceful." Hazardous flashes of poetic insight, not demonstrative arguments, are the way to truth.

In England during the romantic period the identification of poetry and philosophy was a familiar theme, as illustrated in Shelley's declarations that poets are "philosophers of the very loftiest power" and that poetry is "the center and circumference of all knowledge." Coleridge adds the qualification that the poet is implicitly, not explicitly a philosopher. Both he and Wordsworth, moreover, base their view of the implicitly philosophical nature of poetry upon a theory of the imagination, derived in part from Kant. Now Kant's word for imagination is not *Fantasie* but *Einbildungskraft*, connoting by its etymology a power (*Kraft*) of making (*bilden*). Analogously Wordsworth characterizes imagination as "the faculty by which the poet conceives and produces—that is images [verb] —individual forms in which are embodied universal ideas or abstractions." Coleridge takes the further step of distinguishing between the Primary Imagination, the "living power and prime agent of all human perception" (virtually equivalent to Kant's "transcendental unity of apperception") and the Secondary Imagination, a combination and reflection of the Primary, guided by artistic aim and control. All imagination, both primary (metaphysical) and secondary (artistic), is "a repetition in the finite mind of the eternal act of creation in the infinite I AM"; and thus there is a firm continuity between a genuine poet's philosophical insights and his poetic creations.

In the past few decades one result of the reaction against romanticism has been a frequent disposition to deny any important connection between poetry and philos. Archibald MacLeish's aphorism, "A poem should not mean / But be," expresses the preference felt by many a poet, especially in a period of philosophical disorientation, to be judged as a maker rather than as a seer. I. A. Richards has provided a semantic groundwork for the divorce between poetry and philos., stressing the role of poetic utterances "as means to the manipulation and expression of feelings and attitudes" (*Practical Criticism*, 1929) and therefore as "pseudo-statements" (q.v.) to which judgments of true or false in the philosophical sense are irrelevant. However, more recent studies of the semantics of poetry, including some of Richards' own, have tended to recognize the inseparability of being and meaning, or of sentiment and idea, and accordingly to attempt a more adequate understanding of the role of meaning and belief in poetry. For an elaboration of this aspect of the subject see SEMANTICS AND POETRY.

Plato, *Phaedrus* (the best tr. is by Lane Cooper, 1938); Aristotle, *Poetics*, or *The Art of Poetry*, tr. by Bywater (1909), Cooper (1913), Butcher (1917), and others; S. T. Coleridge, *Biographia Literaria* (1817; esp. ch. 14); A. Schopenhauer, *The World as Will and Representation* (1818; pt. 3); P. B. Shelley, *A Defence of Poetry* (1821); F. Nietzsche, *The Birth of Tragedy* (1872); G. Santayana, *Three Philosophical Poets* (1910); T. S. Eliot, *Dante*

(1930); J. M. Murry, "The Metaphysics of Poetry," in *Countries of the Mind* (2d ser., 1931); G. Boas, *Philos. and Poetry* (1932); D. G. James, *Scepticism and Poetry* (1937); W. M. Urban, *Language and Reality* (1939); K. Burke, *Philos. of Lit. Form* (1941); E. M. W. Tillyard, *The Elizabethan World Picture* (1943); J. C. Ransom, "Poetry: A Note in Ontology," repr. in *Critiques and Essays in Crit.*, ed. R. W. Stallman (1949); F. M. Cornford, "The Unconscious Element in Lit. and Philos.," in *The Unwritten Philos. and Other Essays* (1950), "The Philosopher as Successor of the Seer-Poet," and "The Quarrel of Philos. and Poetry," both repr. in *Principium Sapientiae* (1952); Crane, *Critics;* S. K. Langer, *Feeling and Form* (1953; chs. 1 and 2), J. Maritain, *Creative Intuition in Art and Poetry* (1953); Wellek and Warren, 2d ed., ch. 10; K. Hoppe, "Philosophie und Dichtung," *Deutsche Philologie im Aufriss*, ed. W. Stammler, III (1957); E. W. Knight, *Lit. Considered as Philos.: The Fr. Example* (1957); R. Jordan, "Poetry and Philos.: Two Modes of Revelation," SR, 67 (1959); A. W. Levi, *Lit., Philos. and the Imagination* (1962); P. Wheelwright, *Metaphor and Reality* (1962); E. Vivas, *The Artistic Transaction and Essays on Theory of Lit.* (1963). P.W.

PHONEME. See PROSODY.

PHONETIC EQUIVALENCE. To acknowledge repetition, grouping, or modulation of sounds one must define the phonetic elements. If we can avoid eye-rhymes and get rid of the notion that even the most rational of spellings can accurately represent the sounds of a language, the problem appears superficially to be simple. A given recurrent sound is easily recognized, one might believe, by anyone who knows the language. It is clear that *ate / bait / great / straight / weight*, or that *beau / hoe / mow / so / though*, are rhymes, and that in England *bitter / bit her* are equivalent. Eng. *or/au, ar/ah* (e.g., *born / brawn, car / spa*), once stigmatized as "Cockney" rhymes, are now valid for so-called British Eng. (Received Standard of England). Elizabethan *throwes / trewand* may alliterate in *tr-*. Desperate rhymes, sometimes favored by Browning and Hopkins, such as *boon he on / communion*, are evidently not exact echoes. Certain 18th-c. German poets use *ei / eu(äu), i/ü, e/ö, -gen / -chen, (-de / -te),* as rhymes: with them these rhymes represent dialectical sound-fusions, but became conventional rhymes in later writers.

If a speaker of the language, dialect or standard, and the era in which the poem was composed, would accept certain sounds as equivalent (omitting naive errors), these may be called correct echoes. This covers the 18th-c. German rhymes, the "Cockney" rhymes, and the Elizabethan *tr* above, and in general it suffices for most formal sound repetitions such as true rhyme, Sp. assonance, and most Germanic alliteration. Gaelic rhymes are a special case, in which all voiceless stops are treated as equivalent, all voiced stops, or all "aspirates."

Normal ph. e. does not call for a rigid adherence to the "phonemes." In any case, different schools of linguists present different batteries of phonemes and rules of their combination, and some systems run counter to a mere commonsensical view of language; for example, *y*- and *w*- appear in some as *i* and *u*. Especially when we consider grouping or modulation of sounds, we must be free to cling to or to abandon the phoneme. But what criteria can we use? The problem is far from simple. In Am. Eng., does the first vocalic element in *pyre* really echo that in *tropic;* or in "butter tub drubbing" does the slackened -*tt*- of *butter* find equivalents in the *t* of *tub,* the *d* of *drubbing,* or in its *r*? Should an Englishman equate the *e*-vowel in *pet, pare* and *pay*? Should a German speaker equate the first vowel element in *Mann, Maus, mein*? Should a Frenchman equate the vowels in *est, et, répéter, même* (he does not altogether in rhymes), or those in *de, deux, deuil*? In Castilian Sp. the voiced *z* before *g* (*juzgo*) is close to the sound of medial *d,* for whereas initial *b* (*v*), *d, g* are stops, between vowels (etc.) those symbols represent fricatives: should a Spaniard regard these phonetic affinities and distinctions as overriding the phonemics, which equates *d*- with -*d*- and so on? This initial-vs.-medial difference must cause even more confusion in Danish, which besides presenting a transform like that in Sp., has medial *p, t, k* resembling initial *b, d, g* (as with Am. *t*).

Applying "phonetic syzygy" to "tone-color" (Lanier) we note that certain related variants from separate phonemes sometimes echo, while certain widely differing variants of a given phoneme may not. But analysis of phonemic features is advisable, and the whole of a poem should be considered. "Equivalence" is a misleading term: what we have to recognize are degrees and kinds of likeness and diversity. Their basis need not be linguistically, but must be aesthetically, distinctive for the particular crux. Where motor considerations predominate, the phonemes may be analyzed on a basis of articulation; where acoustic impression are paramount, we may analyze on an auditory-feature basis. No rigid rules are possible, but the more unlike two "sounds" are, the more compensation is needed: whether from (1) their similar *position* (a) in the syllable (e.g., *chat* / *jay*), (b) relative to other sounds (*river* / *rougher, spital* / *smitten*), (c) relative to rhythm and line; or from (2) their comparatively strong *phonetic contrast* with (d) their surroundings, (e) other more frequent phonemes in the language.

I. The least obtrusive difference between occidental phonemes is either a *lenis* / *fortis* or a voiced / unvoiced distinction: e.g. *z*-sounds and *s*-sounds (va*ll*eys / A*l*ice) or *j* and *ch* often suballiterate: "Ses ai*l*es de *g*éant l'emp*êch*ent de mar*ch*er" (Baudelaire). II. Nasals may ring together: "Sacred Virgil never sa*ng* / All the marvel there be*gun*, / But there's a stone upon my to*ngue*" (Yeats). III. Vocalic *i, ü, u* may respectively echo their corresponding semivowels in various languages, and British *u*-vowels with vocalic *l*: "dand*l*ed a sanda*l*led / Shadow that swa*m* or sa*nk* / On mea*d*ow and river and w*ind*-w*and*ering w*eed*-w*ind*ing bank" (Hopkins). IV. Sharp and dull versions of a liquid or nasal may chime together; e.g. It. *gl* with *l*: "avo*lt*e . . . scio*lt*e . . . / *l*e qua*l*i e*ll*a spargea sì do*l*cemente / e raccog*l*iea con sì *l*eggiadri" (Petrarch). V. Even wider linguistic distinctions may be overridden: thus *s* assibilates with *sh,* e.g. in "*ch*ast desire / . . . Cher*isht* but with fire" (S. Daniel); and the different vowels in "Shadow . . . On meadow" (Hopkins, above) subassonate. For broader sound classes see TONE-COLOR. See also ALLITERATION, ASSONANCE, CONSONANCE, ECHO, REPETITION, RHYME, SOUND IN POETRY, SYZYGY.—S. Lanier, *The Science of Eng. Verse* (1880; in centenary ed. of his works, 10 v., 1945); M. Grammont, *Traité de phonétique* (3e éd., 1946); M. Swadesh, "On the Analysis of Eng. Syllabics," *Language,* 33 (1947); U. K. Goldsmith, "Words Out of a Hat . . . ," JEGP, 49 (1950); H. Kökeritz, *Shakespeare's Pronunciation* (1953); R. Jakobson and M. Halle, *Fundamentals of Language* (1956); E. J. Dobson, *Eng. Pronunciation 1500–1700* (1957).   D.I.M.

PIE QUEBRADO. Although this Sp. metric term may occasionally mean any half-line used with its corresponding whole line (as the heptasyllable and/or the pentasyllable with the hendecasyllable, the hexasyllable with the dodecasyllable), p.q. usually denotes the tetrasyllable (or equivalent) used in combination with the octosyllable, particularly in the *copla de pie quebrado* (see COPLA). The use of the p.q. has been common in Sp. poetry since at least the early 14th c., when it appears in the *Libro de buen amor* of Juan Ruiz Archpriest of Hita.—Navarro.   D.C.C.

PINDARIC ODE. See ODE.

PITCH. Highness or lowness of tone. One of the four characteristics of a spoken sound, the others being duration (q.v.), loudness, and quality. P. is measured by the number of vibrations per second (8 to 30,000), is sometimes roughly described by the terms acute (high) and grave (low), and is often indicated by musical notation. A number of authorities hold that p. usually coincides with accent (q.v.) or that it is one of the constituents of accent. Despite controversy over the relation of p. to accent, most prosodists would agree that the management of p., in poetry, is one of the primary means of rhetorical emphasis or intensification.—Baum; K. M. Wilson, *Sound and Meaning in Eng. Poetry* (1930); D. Bolinger, "A Theory of P. Accent in Eng.," *Word*, 14 (1958). P.F.

PLANH. A funeral lament, in Old Prov. In form, it may be considered a specialized variety of *sirventes* (q.v.). Of the 40-odd *planhs* preserved, three-fourths bewail the death of some distinguished person, normally a patron or patroness of the poet; only 10 are laments for close friends and loved ones. The poem ordinarily consists of conventional and hyperbolic eulogies of the departed (he was generous, hospitable, gracious, chivalrous, well-mannered, wise, brave, all to a supreme degree), plus a prayer for his soul, and a statement of the poet's sense of loss, the sincerity of which is sometimes open to question.—H. Springer, *Das altprovenzalische Klagelied* (1895); Jeanroy, II. F.M.C.

PLATONISM AND POETRY. Pl. has been a persistent influence on Western poetry from the 4th c. B.C. until the present day. This is paradoxical since Plato was suspicious of poetry and banned most of its types from his ideal republic. To understand Plato's continuing influence it is necessary to consider four concepts which either originated with Plato or received their most persuasive expression in the dialogues.

I. POETRY AS EDUCATION. A characteristic feature of Plato's thought is his concern for the practical application of philosophy to personal, family, and social problems. Although he believed that the supreme values—the Good, the Beautiful, and the True—were ultimately One, it was the Good which concerned him most frequently. Because of this bias Plato believed that poetry, like all the other arts, should subserve individual and social morality. In the *Protagoras* (325–26) he showed how poetry could be used to create admiration (hence emulation) of the gods and noble heroes. The sanction against poets in *Republic* 10 is simply a corollary of this idea. The state must protect its citizens against the corrupting influence of meretricious poetry, as well as indoctrinate them in virtue. Plato did not ban *all* poetry. It is often forgotten that he permitted those poets

to remain who sang "praises of the gods and encomia of famous men" (*Republic* 10.607), a concession repeated in the *Laws* 8.801.

Plato's emphasis on the power of poetry to educate is merely the outstanding instance of a general Gr. tendency which has been explored in Werner Jaeger's *Paideia*. It was a powerful influence on late classical and medieval criticism, which often had to defend poetry against the attacks of moral bigots. During the Renaissance it continued to be used in this way. It also contributed to the theory of the poet as forger of the national consciousness of the newly emergent national state, an idea especially strong in Renaissance epic theory.

II. POETRY AS IMITATION. The theory of ideas led Plato to view the created world as an imperfect imitation of a divine archetype. In the *Republic* poetry is described as a "mimetic" (imitative) art using as its models the objects and actions which the poet sees in the created world. It is thus an imitation of an imitation, more false than that which it imitates. If this is so, it may be a pleasant pastime, but it leads away from the True rather than toward it. This is a more telling attack on poetry than the claim that much of it is immoral. It implies that poetry is inevitably trivial.

Aristotle's *Poetics* offered one solution to the problem by suggesting that the poetic imitation, being based upon general probabilities, was "more philosophical" and hence more true than history (cf. *Poetics* 9). The Neoplatonists went further than Aristotle. Beginning with Plotinus, Neoplatonists generally agreed that the poetic imitation is the highest of all imitations because the poet seeks to imitate the divine archetype, whereas the artisan merely copies an already-existing model. Plato's own terminology thus provided the means for elevating the artist to a position of supreme importance. This theory was widespread during the Renaissance and persisted unabated during the romantic period, largely because of its analogies to Kantian idealism.

III. POETRY AS INSPIRATION. In the *Ion* Plato satirized a rhapsodist who could not explain the source of his talent for reciting and talking about poetry. Half in jest Socrates explains that both poets and rhapsodists must be moved by a divine power speaking through them. Elsewhere, Plato seems to say that there can be no genuine poetry except by inspiration. In later ages inspiration, or *furor poeticus*, was interpreted as the suprahuman state during which the poet glimpsed the ultimate nature of things, the divine archetypes. Countless texts and traditions affirm the truth of this doctrine. The conventional invocation to the muse, the primitive tradition of the poet as *vates* or madman, etc. confirm the idea of poetry as a divine gift. Christian critics who inherited this idea could point to Pentateuch and Psalms for substantiation. See INSPIRATION.

IV. POETRY AS HERMETIC SYMBOLISM. Throughout the dialogues, but especially in *Symposium, Timaeus, Parmenides,* and *Republic,* Plato used myths, images, and symbols to express his ideas. Many of these (e.g., number-symbolism) were derived from pre-Socratic philosophy or primitive religion. However, Plato gave them philosophical coherence and permanent expression. In this sense the vast jumble of myths, symbols, emblems, and esoteric notions found in Orphic, Hermetic, and Neoplatonic literature may be called Platonic. On the other hand, many specific symbols and the general tendency toward allegory and jargon are not Platonic but a product of the decadent phase of Neoplatonism.

The theory of imitation and inspiration as developed by the Neoplatonists tended to emphasize the mystic and occult elements in poetry. Carried to an extreme it encouraged poetry which was consciously obscure; and obscurity is perhaps the most obvious feature of Hermetic writing from Hermes Trismegistus through Pico della Mirandola down to Blake and Yeats. This obscurity results from the conscious use of esoteric symbols, which are explained in two ways: First, the poet is by definition trying to convey a more than human vision (the divine archetypes). Since normal language is inadequate, he must resort to symbols. Second, the poet must conceal his knowledge from the profane, who would abuse it. His symbols and allegories create a veil which only the initiated can penetrate. The theory of symbolism as a veil protecting knowledge from the rabble is evident in Fulgentius' reading of the *Aeneid,* in Dante's *Convivio,* in Boccaccio's *Genealogy of the Gods,* and in numerous Renaissance critical works. Among common symbols which may with some justification be called Platonic, the following are typical: the idea of the One and the Many, the equation of Light and Truth (*Timaeus, Parmenides*); the equation of music with divine order, the music of the spheres, number-symbolism, the golden chain of creation (*Republic, Timaeus*); the Platonic ladder, Platonic love (*Symposium*); the soul as the body's prisoner; the soul as charioteer drawn by a dark and a light horse (*Republic, Symposium, Phaedrus*). Readers interested in Platonic and Hermetic symbols and their history are referred to Frutiger, Dunbar, and Merrill in the bibliography.

HISTORY: Although Pl. has never ceased to be an important influence on European poetry, its influence has sometimes been predominant, sometimes submerged. The four periods of predominance are Neoplatonic (3d–5th c. A.D.), Dionysian (10th–12th c.), High Renaissance (16th–17th c.), and Romantic (19th c.).

The Neoplatonic period is chiefly significant for commentaries on Plato and on various literary texts. Plotinus (d. 270) was the leader of the movement. Although he did not treat poetry specifically, his theory of beauty provided the basis for the idea of poetry as imitation (see above). Among Plotinus' followers, Porphyry (d. 304) wrote on *Homeric Questions* and *On the Cave of the Nymphs,* in which he interpreted *Odyssey* 13.102–12, as a detailed allegory of the universe. He thereby helped encourage the tendency toward allegorical reading of poetry and philosophy evident in Macrobius' commentary on *Somnium Scipionis* and Fulgentius' *De Continentia Virgiliana.* Iamblichus (d. 330), his pupil, emphasized the Hermetic element in Neoplatonism but added little to literary theory. On the other hand, Maximus Tyrius (fl. A.D. 150) wrote a series of *Dissertations* on Platonic topics, three of which (4, 17, 37) defend poetry from the ethical standpoint, asserting the moral probity of Homer. A much later writer, Proclus (d. 485), also defended poetry in an often-quoted commentary on the *Republic.* Finally, the Alexandrian Jew Philo Judaeus (d. ca. A.D. 50) wrote an immensely influential and long-winded allegorical interpretation of Genesis along cabalistic and Platonic lines.

The Christian Fathers, particularly Origen and Augustine (cf. *City of God* 8,10; *Confessions* 8) confessed a strong debt to Plato. Generally they were suspicious of all but spiritual poetry, and when they countenanced secular poetry at all they did so on the basis of its power to educate. From writers like Philo they inherited the technique of allegorical interpretation and read the Bible as an intricate fusion of literal, allegorical, and symbolic meanings. This approach was carried over to the interpretation of classical poets like Ovid, Statius, and Virgil, and often had a profound influence on poets engaged in original composition, Dante being the standard example.

By the 4th c. A.D. the Latin West had lost contact with Plato and the better Neoplatonists. Only the *Timaeus* (tr. Calcidius, ca. A.D. 350) and a few fragments were available in translation. For the rest, Western scholars had to rely on second- and third-hand sources such as Macrobius, Boethius, or Cicero's philosophical dialogues. However during the 9th c. Pl. was strongly revived by Scotus Erigena's translation of the *Mystical Theology, On the Divine Names,* and *The Heavenly Hierarchy* of Dionysius the pseudo-Areopagite. These works were saturated with debased Neoplatonism (especially that of Proclus), but the fact that their author was thought to be St. Paul's famous convert (Acts 17:34) caused them to be read and assimilated throughout the West. Their influence culminated in the writing of such men as Thierry and Bernard of Chartres and the poetry of Bernard Silvestris (*de Mundi Universitate*) and Alan of Lille (*Anticlaudianus; de Planctu Naturae*). Their most important influence however was a delayed one. The structure of Dante's *Paradise*, much of its symbolism, and innumerable details are drawn directly or indirectly from Dionysius.

The influence of Pl. during the High Renaissance is incalculable. It began with the completion (ca. 1482) of Marsilio Ficino's L. translation of Plato and the publication of his noble effort to reconcile Plato and Christianity, the *Theologia Platonica*. The history of Renaissance Pl. has been traced in detail by many scholars (see Robb, Harrison, Merrill in bibliography), and only a few generalizations will be made here. First, the Platonic concept of *paideia* furnished the basic justification for poetry throughout the period. Second, the Platonic theory of love, especially in popularized form, furnished the chief subject matter for the Renaissance lyric from Petrarch to Edmund Spenser, as well as appearing in countless courtesy books, epics, philosophical poems, hymns, and the like. Third, the theories of imitation and inspiration recur with monotonous regularity throughout the 16th c.

Generally speaking, Pl. yielded to naturalism during the latter half of the 16th c. in France and the first half of the 17th c. in England. This tendency was opposed by the Cambridge Platonists, and one of them, Henry More, wrote philosophical poetry of some merit (e.g., *The Song of the Soul*, 1647).

The romantic period witnessed a renewed interest in inspirational literature and literary symbolism as part of the reaction against 18th-c. rationalism. All of these tendencies favored the revival of Pl., but often as a fanciful or "poetic" means of expressing Kantian ideas rather than an independent philosophy. Wordsworth's "Intimations Ode" uses many Platonic theories—e.g., the pre-existence of the soul, the image of the body as prison house, the light imagery—but one hesitates to call it a Platonic poem. On the other hand, Blake and Shelley were conscious Platonists, the former a student of Plotinus, Maximus Tyrius, and Proclus in the translations of Wm. Taylor; the latter a reader of Plato in the original Gr. and a lifelong believer in the power of poetry to educate mankind. In Germany Hölderlin is the best example (among many) of a romantic poet strongly influenced by Pl. In America Emerson interpreted Plato for his fellow Transcendentalists, and Poe, with his Platonic concern for the concrete expression of the ideal through symbols, created a literary theory which influenced Baudelaire and the later symbolists.

Pl. has continued to influence modern poetry, particularly Eng. and German. The translation of Plato by Jowett (1871) had an important effect in diffusing knowledge of his philosophy. Among modern poets whose debt to Plato seems especially important are Rilke and Yeats, both of whom draw on the Hermetic tradition and the idea of poetry as inspiration; and Wallace Stevens, whose idealism and symbols both owe much to Plato. Despite his banishment of poets Plato was as much a poet as a philosopher. His philosophy has always been deeply appealing to the poetic temperament. There is every reason to believe that it will continue to be so in the future.

J. Harrison, *Pl. in Eng. Poetry of the 16th and 17th C.* (1903); L. Winstanley, *Pl. in Shelley* (1913); H. Dunbar, *Symbolism in Medieval Thought* (1929); P. Frutiger, *Les Mythes de Platon* (1930); N. Robb, *Pl. in the It. Renaissance* (1935); P. Shorey, *Pl., Ancient and Modern* (1938); R. Klibansky, *The Continuity of the Platonic Tradition during the Middle Ages* (1939); Mario dal Pra, *Scoto Eriugena ed il neoplatonismo medievale* (1941); I. Samuel, *Plato and Milton* (1949); R. McKeon, "Poetry and Philosophy in the 12th C.," Crane, *Critics*; P. Kristeller, *Il pensiero filosofico di Marsilio Ficino* (1953); E. Cassirer, *The Platonic Ren. in England* (1953); R. C. Lodge, *Plato's Theory of Art* (1953); R. V. Merrill and R. J. Clements, *Pl. in Fr. Ren. Poetry* (1957); R. Ellrodt, *Neo-Pl. in the Poetry of Spenser* (1960); G. Harper, *The Neopl. of William Blake* (1961).　　o.b.h.

PLÉIADE. The term, as it refers to the small group of poets of the Fr. Renaissance led by Pierre de Ronsard, originated in 1556 in an elegy in which the latter welcomed a new member to the group: ". . . Belleau, qui viens en la brigade / Des bons, pour accomplir la septiesme Pléiade" (Critical edition of Ronsard by P. Laumonier, VIII, 354). This was Ronsard's only use of the term in this sense. Until that time he had used the term *Brigade*, which had been hospitable to a much larger number of poets than the expression that replaced it. Probably with no rigid intention of thereby creating an exclusive circle of poets limited in membership to seven, Ronsard adopted the expression *Pléiade* from the well-known Alexandrine group of poets who in antiquity had gone by that name.

Although membership in the P. varied with the years, it did not at any one time surpass seven. In 1556, along with Remy Belleau and Ronsard himself, the group included Joachim du Bellay, Pontus de Tyard, Jean-Antoine de Baïf, Jacques Peletier, and Etienne Jodelle. According to Ronsard's first biographer, Claude Binet, the name of Peletier was eventually replaced by that of the poet's teacher, Jean Dorat, one of the great Hellenists of the Fr.

-[621]-

Renaissance. Within a few years of its first and last mention by Ronsard, the term P. had been found so convenient as a designation of the group immediately associated with the poet, that Henri Estienne is able to use it in his *Apologie pour Hérodote* (1566) in confident expectation that it would be understood to refer to the contemporary group of Fr. poets.

Three members of the P. were influential contributors to Fr. poetic theory of the Renaissance: Jacques Peletier, Joachim du Bellay, and Ronsard. As early as 1541, Peletier had published a translation of the *Ars poetica* of Horace prefaced by remarks of his own in which the fundamental principle which was later to be adopted by Ronsard and his associates was clearly enunciated: that Fr. writers should *defend* and *illustrate* (i.e., render illustrious) their own language by writing in Fr., and not in L. or Gr. In 1555 Peletier published an *Art Poétique* in which he reaffirms the position he had adopted in the preface to the *Ars Poetica* of 1541, insists upon the divine nature of poetry, discusses the relationship between technique and native endowment, the function of imitation, the varieties of poetic subjects, and genres.

Both Du Bellay and Ronsard may be called, in matters of theory, disciples of Peletier. The former published in 1549 the renowned *Deffence et illustration de la langue françoyse* which, though it followed by eight or more years Peletier's preface, became, because it arrived precisely at the right moment, and because of the intensity of its language, the manifesto of the new school. Du Bellay blames the alleged poverty of the Fr. language of his time on the unwillingness of earlier generations of Frenchmen to devote their energies to its cultivation. Intrinsically, he says, it is capable of the highest reaches of poetic and philosophic expression, and need not bow in these respects before any of the languages of antiquity or of modern times. This is the essence of his *deffence*. As for the *illustration*, Du Bellay rejects the position that translation of the great classics into Fr. can of itself suffice to raise Fr. literature to a status of equality with Gr., L., or It. What the Fr. poet needs is so intimate a knowledge of the classics and of the more important modern literatures, that their substance will become part of his own, and that ideally his imitation of them will result not so much in a conscious effort to reproduce their thought and feeling, as in their natural assimilation and transformation into a form congenial to the Fr. language and acceptable to cultivated Frenchmen.

The *Abregé de l'art poëtique françois* of Ronsard (1565) is a brief practical handbook intended for the young beginner in poetry.

Like Peletier and Du Bellay, Ronsard's fundamental premise is that the poet must write in Fr., although he, too, demands that the would-be writer possess as profound a classical instruction as possible. He demands that the poet, who for him is the inspired prophet of the Muses, should hold them "in singular veneration and never reduce them to a position of dishonorable servitude" (ed. Laumonier, XIV, 10).

The "revolution" of Malherbe (1605) was, in reality, the regularization, perhaps the excessively rigid codification, of tendencies already clearly apparent in Ronsard and his colleagues. With the end of the Malherbian dispensation, as the romantic period begins, qualities of subjective lyricism, equally present in the poets of the P., but somewhat neglected during the period of classicism, come once more to the fore. The influence of the P. has thus been durable and pervasive, and it is fair to say that the principles laid down by Peletier, Du Bellay, and Ronsard have not lost their vigor except among poets for whom harmony and sonority take precedence over communication.

A. Rosenbauer, *Die poetischen Theorien der Plejade nach Ronsard und Du Bellay* (1895); P. Laumonier, "L'Art poétique de Jacques Peletier du Mans," *Revue de la Renaissance* (June 1901) and *Ronsard, poète lyrique* (1909, 3d ed., 1931); C. Binet, *Vie de Ronsard*, ed. P. Laumonier (1910); Patterson; H. Chamard, *Histoire de la P.* (4 v., 1939–41); R. J. Clements, *The Crit. Theory and Practice of the P.* (1942); F. Simone, "I poeti della P. ed i loro predecessori, *Giornale italiano di filologia*, 2 (1949); *Crit. Prefaces of the Fr. Ren.*, ed. B. Weinberg (1950); F. Desonay, "Les manifestes littéraires du XVIe s. en France," BHR, 14 (1952); R. V. Merrill and R. J. Clements, *Platonism in Fr. Renaissance Poetry* (1957); J. Bonnot, *Humanisme et P., l'histoire, la doctrine, les oeuvres* (1959); I. Silver, *Ronsard and the Hellenic Renaissance in France* (1961–); G. Castor, *P. Poetics* (1964).   I.S.

PLOCE. See ANADIPLOSIS.

PLOT may be defined as the pattern of events in a narrative or a drama, either in prose or in verse. *Plot* is the Eng. word commonly used to translate Aristotle's *mythos*, a term used in the *Poetics* to describe one of the six elements of tragedy. Aristotle gives *p.* a precise critical definition, assigns it the place of honor, and calls it "the first principle, and, as it were, the soul of a tragedy." The definition given in the *Poetics* has been the basis of almost all other considerations of p., either friendly or hostile.

The concept of p. has shifted from time to

time in the history of criticism, as the critic's concern has been with the making of a work or with the responding to a work, with the creator or the spectator. Viewed in terms of the principles controlling the making of a work of art, p. has referred to action, to pattern, to structure or some variation of these elements; viewed in terms of the psychological and emotional response of the audience or reader, p. has referred to impression, to sense of unity, to purpose, or to some similar response. In terms of the latter view of p., any of many different elements may constitute the controlled affective quality of a work; it is essentially in terms of witness rather than creation that the critics of the contemporary Chicago school have attempted to broaden greatly the concept of p. (See paragraph below on "the Chicago school.") In the common usage of the term p., however, the sense of the making or shaping principle has been dominant in most criticism, and it is in that sense that this article treats the concept of p.

Aristotle called the p. "the imitation of the action" (see IMITATION) as well as "the arrangement of the incidents." He demanded that the action imitated be "a whole," i.e., have a beginning: "that which does not itself follow anything by causal necessity, but after which something naturally is or comes to be"; a middle: "that which follows something as some other thing follows it"; and an end: "that which itself naturally follows some other thing, either by necessity, or as a rule, but has nothing following it." He asked that a p. have unity, i.e., that it "imitate one action and that a whole, the structural union of the parts being such that, if any one of them is displaced or removed, the whole will be disjointed and disturbed." These well-knit plots he opposed to episodic plots "in which the acts succeed one another without probable or necessary sequence." He also distinguished between simple and complex plots, a simple p. being one in which a change of fortune takes place without Reversal of the Situation and without Recognition, and a complex p. being one in which the change of fortune is accompanied by a Reversal or by a Recognition or by both. The Reversal is a change by which the action veers round to its opposite, and a Recognition is a change from ignorance to knowledge. These should both arise, he says, from "the internal structure of the plot, so that what follows should be the necessary or probable result of the preceding action." Therefore, Aristotle's test for sound plotting appears to be "whether any given event is a case of *propter hoc* or *post hoc*." This emphasis on causality is central to the Aristotelian concept, yet he also argued against a mechanic art, declaring that "a single action, whole and complete, with a beginning, a middle, and an end" will "resemble a living organism in all its unity." There is much to be said for Humphry House's view that the episode or incident is for Aristotle the means by which the plot is realized. Aristotle's statement that, having found his story, the poet "should first sketch its general outline, and then fill in the episodes and amplify in detail," House would translate "should first sketch its general outline, and then *episodize*" (*Aristotle's Poetics*, 1956). Aristotle asserted that the poet "should be a maker of plot . . . since he is a maker because he imitates, and what he imitates are actions." House asserts that "episodizing"—i.e., realizing the plot in terms of incidents—"is the essential activity of the poet as the maker."

The distinction between story and p. is a difficult one to make. E. M. Forster says that ". . . a story [is] a narrative of events arranged in their time-sequence. A plot is also a narrative of events, the emphasis falling on causality" (*Aspects of the Novel*, 1927). Story, he believes, arouses only curiosity; whereas p. demands intelligence and memory. House is illuminating on this distinction; he says: "There is first a rambling and amorphous 'story,' often taken over from tradition or picked up from some other extraneous source . . . and then comes the serious business of *making* it into a play or an epic." This *making* is essentially the making of *story* into *plot*.

The superiority which Aristotle assigns p. over character has been a matter of great debate, with most critics since the early 19th c. defending active character as the dynamic aspect of narrative or drama and p. as the mechanic aspect. Edward J. O'Brien, writing on the short story, says: "The plot of a story is structural. . . . The action of a story, as contrasted with the plot, is a matter of dynamics. . . . Plot is merely a means to an end" (*The Short Story Case Book*, 1935). Probably the best and certainly the most graceful of the mediators between these positions is Henry James, who says: "I cannot imagine composition existing in a series of blocks, nor conceive, in any novel worth discussing at all, of a passage of description that is not in its intention narrative, a passage of dialogue that is not in its intention descriptive, a touch of truth of any sort that does not partake of the nature of incident, or an incident that derives its interest from any other source than the general and only source of the success of a work of art—that of being illustrative. . . . What is character but the determination of incident? What is incident but the illustration of character" ("The Art of Fiction," 1884). James's term *illustrative* appears to be his rough equivalent of *imitation*.

The critics of "the Chicago school" have

PLOT

attempted greatly to extend this organic view of p. Ronald S. Crane says: "The form of a given plot is a function of the particular correlation among . . . three variables which the completed work is calculated to establish, consistently and progressively, in our minds." The variables are: " (1) the general estimate we are induced to form . . . of the moral character and deserts of the hero . . . ; (2) the judgments we are led similarly to make about the nature of the events that actually befall the hero . . . as having either painful or pleasurable consequences for him . . . permanently or temporarily; and (3) the opinions we are made to entertain concerning the degree and kind of his responsibility for what happens to him . . ." (*Critics and Criticism,* 1952). Paul Goodman, also of the Chicago school, considers "Any system of parts that carries over, continuous and changing, from the beginning to the end" a p., and he applies the definition even to short poetry, making it refer to rhythm, diction, and imagery, as well as incidents" (*The Structure of Literature,* 1954).

The various views of p. have in common an attention to arrangement or pattern or structure. For all critics "pattern" seems a minimal definition; and for almost all of them "pattern of events" is a primary description, however much more than this they may also wish to include. Clearly an episode in itself does not make a p.; equally clearly the presence of two or more episodes does not make a p.; the concept of p. refers to a relationship—and an implied causality—among episodes. We may conclude, therefore, that p. is an intellectual formulation about the relationship existing among the incidents of a drama or a narrative, and that it is, therefore, a guiding principle for the author and an ordering control for the reader. It is something perceived by the reader as giving structure and unity to the work. And herein lies, perhaps, one of the greatest difficulties; for, as Percy Lubbock has argued, it is difficult for a reader to hold the pieces of a drama or a narrative in his mind and almost impossible to retain the total work firmly enough in mind to examine its informing and unifying principle (*The Craft of Fiction,* 1921).

This difficulty is illustrated by an examination of a special type of narrative structure, the framework story, i.e., the kind of work in which a narrative or a group of narratives is set within a larger controlling frame. The question of when the frame becomes a p. itself or even a portion of the p. is a delicate one. Boccaccio's *Decameron,* a collection of tales told by a group in special circumstances, has no narrative frame p. at all, for nothing is presented of the circumstances out of which the

tales come. Chaucer's *Canterbury Tales* clearly has a narrative in its frame—the pilgrims are realized as persons, the pattern of a journey is given, a contest within this journey is presented, and the tales themselves at least in part grow out of the events which occur in this framework. Yet the *Canterbury Tales* can hardly be said to have a framework p. in the sense in which p. has been described in this essay. In some cases the framework does become a p., as, for example, in Melville's *Moby-Dick,* where the narrator has his own problem and the action dealing with Ahab becomes in a sense an element in this problem. On the other hand, one might argue that the *Faerie Queene,* had it been completed, would have had no real p., but rather a conceptualized allegorical structure. This is a kind of structure which raises another critical question about p.

Many critics have suggested that theme or philosophical concept is or may be the basis of p. Now certainly the action being imitated in a p. should not be stripped of its rich complexity; yet it must be asserted that the raw materials of plots are conflicts and actions, not concepts and philosophical statements. Even in an allegory we do not think of the p. in terms of the conceptualized abstractions represented by the characters but rather in terms of the characters and their actions broadly independent of the conceptualizations that they represent. Thus, if we give a plot summary of *Everyman* similar to Aristotle's summary of the *Odyssey,* in which no names are attached to the actors, we are carried further away from rather than closer to the abstract statement beneath the play. P. may be a formulation by which the author of an allegory translates his concepts into dramatic or narrative terms, but it does not itself partake of the concept which is expressed through it.

Thus we are pointed back toward a view of p. as the controlling and unifying principle of action in a work. It is helpful to think of p. as a "planned series of interrelated actions progressing, because of the interplay of one force upon another, through a struggle of opposing forces to a climax and a *dénouement*" (W. F. Thrall, A. Hibbard and C. H. Holman, *A Handbook to Literature,* rev. ed.). Here the emphasis is on conflict as the unifying principle of action. Basically there are four kinds of conflict which may be made the basis of a p.: man against the forces of nature, man against his fellowman, man against himself, and man against some conceptualized or personalized aspect of the order of things, such as Fate or Destiny or Nemesis.

If viewed in terms of the basic conflict, the elements of a p. are: (1) The *Exposition,* i.e., the establishing of the situation within which the conflict develops. This exposition is frequently delayed until after the conflict has gotten underway and then given piecemeal. (2) The *Initiating Action*, i.e., the event which brings the opposing forces into conflict. (3) *The Rising Action*, i.e., the separate events which advance the conflict to its crucial point at which the protagonist in the conflict takes, consciously or unconsciously, the action which determines the future course of the conflict irrevocably. It is possible for this action of the protagonist to be a failure to act, as in the scene where Hamlet fails to kill Claudius at prayer. This decisive point is called the *crisis*, for upon it the action turns. It frequently, but by no means always, coincides with the *climax*, which is the point of highest interest. Crisis refers to structure; climax to emotional response. (4) The *Falling Action*, i.e., the incidents and episodes in which the force destined to be victorious establishes its supremacy. (5) The *Dénouement* or conclusion, i.e., the incidents or episode in which the conflict called forth by the initiating action is irremediably resolved. The unified p. may be considered to make an upward spiral, in that the resolution of the conflict returns us to a situation similar in its repose or the balance of its forces but not in their exact nature or alignment to that presented in the exposition.

S. H. Butcher, Aristotle's *Theory of Poetry and Fine Art, The Poetics* and ch. 9 (4th ed., 1911); P. Lubbock, *The Craft of Fiction* (1921); E. Muir, *The Structure of the Novel* (1928); C. H. Grabo, *The Technique of the Novel* (1928); J. W. Linn and H. W. Taylor, *A Foreword to Fiction* (1935; ch. 5); W. F. Thrall, A. Hibbard and C. H. Holman, *A Handbook to Lit.* (1936; rev. ed. 1960); H. D. F. Kitto, *Gr. Tragedy* (1939); F. Fergusson, *The Idea of a Theater* (1949); R. A. Brower, "The Heresy of P.," EIE *1951* (1952); R. S. Crane, "The Concept of P. and the P. of Tom Jones," *Critics and Crit. Ancient and Modern* (1952); P. Goodman, *The Structure of Lit.* (1954); H. House, *Aristotle's Poetics* (1956); W. C. Booth, *The Rhetoric of Fiction* (1961); E. Olson, *Tragedy and the Theory of Drama* (1961); J. Jones, *On Aristotle and Gr. Tragedy* (1962); R. Lattimore, *Story Patterns in Gr. Tragedy* (1964). C.H.H.

PLURISIGNATION. See SEMANTICS AND POETRY.

POÈME. A genre of poetry introduced into Fr. literature by Alfred de Vigny, who defined his *poèmes* in a preface of August 1837, as "compositions . . . in which a philosophic thought is staged under an Epic or Dramatic form." Among the *pensées philosophiques* staged in Vigny's *poèmes* are the following:

that the man of genius is irremediably lonely (*Moïse*); that man should live uncomplaining and die like the wolf without a cry (*La mort du loup*); that there is a kind of immortality for man in the knowledge or beauty he bequeaths to those who live after him (*La Bouteille à la mer* and *L'Esprit pur*). In 1844, in *Le journal d'un poète*, Vigny cites the line "J'aime la majesté des souffrances humaines" (from *La maison du berger*) with the comment: "This verse holds the meaning of all my Poèmes philosophiques."—A de Vigny, *Oeuvres complètes* (2 v., 1948). A.G.E.

POESIE is derived from Gr. *poiesis* and the latter in turn from *poiein* meaning "to make." Hence, *poiesis* means making (in general), but is usually narrowed to mean "the composition of poetry." The Eng. 16th c. word *makers* as in the phrase "courtly makers" is the exact equivalent of the word *poets*. P. was introduced into the Eng. language early in the 14th c. and has been an Eng. word long enough to beget another word which looks and sounds like a native Eng. word, *posy*, a motto in a rhyming couplet or quatrain. Later in the 14th c. the word *poetrie*, derived from L. *poetria* came into Eng. Poetrie and p. have frequently been used as synonyms; thus Philip Sidney's critical work appeared in 1595 in two editions; one was called *A Defense of Poesy*; the other, *An Apology for Poetry*. Ben Jonson in *Timber* (Schelling's ed., pp. 72 *seq.*), however, made an effort to distinguish between p. and poetry. He used poem, a word that became Eng. in the 16th c., to mean any single product of a poet's art; poetry to mean the total product of a poet's art; (e.g., the poetry of Milton) and poesy, recurring to the early Gr. practice, to mean the poet's means of composition. Jonson's remarks had little effect, but there were some later critics who expressed similar views. A.R.B.

POET LAUREATE. About to be seized by Apollo, Daphne turns into a laurel tree. Apollo takes the laurel for his emblem, and decrees that its branch or bay shall become the prize of honor for poets and victors. (Ovid, *Metamorphoses* 1). The line from Apollo to the Eng. poets l. follows the custom of kings and chieftains of maintaining a court poet to sing heroic and glorious achievement. The Scandinavian skald, the Welsh bard, and the Anglo-Saxon scop resembled the poets l. in being attached to a ruler's court and serving his purposes. Professional entertainers like William I's *ioculator regis* or Henry I's *mimus regis* develop into the *versificator regis* who is part of Henry III's royal household in England. The *versificator* suggests an official l. not only by his regular payment in money and wine, but in being ridiculed as were Jonson, Davenant, Eusden, Cibber, Pye, and even Tennyson later on. The actual term "l." arose in the medieval universities which crowned with laurel a student admitted to an academic degree in grammar, rhetoric, and poetry. In time the word applied to any notable poetic attainment, and was used as a standard compliment to Chaucer, and more formally, Petrarch. In a tradition of loosely bestowing the title "l." we find the names of Gower, Lydgate, Skelton, and Bernard Andreas, the Augustinian friar who, under Henry VII, anticipated Dryden's later double appointment as court poet and historiographer royal. Spenser, Drayton, and Daniel shared in various forms of court activity receiving official recognition, while Ben Jonson, a successful court entertainer and panegyrist, thought of himself as a formal l., having received two pensions and much popular acclaim. Davenant seems to have enjoyed a tacit recognition as poet l. under both Charles I and II, but held no official patent. The office was finally authorized with the appointment of John Dryden as the first "poet l." in 1668, and historiographer royal in 1670. The two offices were separated in 1692, and the emolument of l. was fixed at £100 a year where it has in effect remained ever since.

Since Dryden's removal in 1688, fourteen men have been chosen poet l. in succession as follows: Thomas Shadwell, 1689–92; Nahum Tate, 1692–1715; Nicholas Rowe, 1715–18; Laurence Eusden, 1718–30; Colley Cibber, 1730–57; William Whitehead, 1757–85; Thomas Warton, 1785–90; Henry James Pye, 1790–1813; Robert Southey, 1813–43; William Wordsworth, 1843–50; Alfred Tennyson, 1850–92; Alfred Austin, 1896–1913; Robert Bridges, 1913–30; John Masefield, 1930– . A number of poets have sought the laureateship in vain, including Johnson's friend Richard Savage the "volunteer l.," William Mason, Leigh Hunt, and Lewis Morris when, after Tennyson, a period of four years elapsed without a choice being made. The position has likewise been refused by Gray, Scott, Wordsworth once before accepting it, and Samuel Rogers on the death of Wordsworth.

Traditionally the laureate's duty was to write eulogies, elegies, and other celebrations of important events. In this sense, Tennyson's *Ode on the Death of the Duke of Wellington* (1852) emerges as the ideal performance. In practice, the laureateship from its beginning with Dryden falls into three periods. Dryden, Shadwell and Tate had no stated duties, and could make of the office what they chose. In Dryden's case this was to speak brilliantly and with entire conviction for the royal cause, making *Absalom and Achitophel* in its way the ideal laureate's poem. In the early 18th c., the l.

became a member of the royal household, charged with writing annually a New Year's Ode and a Birthday Ode, to be set to music and sung before the king. The office became something of a joke, until the annual odes were abandoned in the tenure of Southey. The modern phase has restored dignity to the position, with Wordsworth symbolically, and Tennyson actively standing for the best that poetry is capable of. Paradoxically, however, the laureateship will suffer until the poet is free of any subservience to the very court that first sustained him; likewise the notion of immediate continuity should be abandoned. If the laureateship ceases to be an office which must be filled as soon as it is vacant, it may gain dignity by waiting until a poet of high order is chosen. Then the difference between what it could be and what in fact it has been will diminish. (See especially E. K. Broadus, *The Laureateship*, 1921, pp. 216–18.)—W. S. Austin, Jr., and J. Ralph, *The Lives of the Poets L.* (1853); W. Hamilton, *The Poets L. of England* (1879); K. West, *The Laureates of England from Ben Jonson to Alfred Tennyson* (1895); W. F. Gray, *The Poets L. of England* (1914); K. Hopkins, *The Poets L.* (1955). B.N.S.

POÈTE MAUDIT. A phrase that mirrors the widening gulf in 19th-c. France between the gifted poet and the public upon which his survival might depend. It was given currency by Verlaine's *Les poètes maudits* (1884, 1888), a collection of essays on poets hardly known at the time, such as Corbière, Rimbaud, and Mallarmé. A half-century earlier Vigny's *Stello* (1832) had developed, in successive tales on Gilbert, Chatterton, and André Chénier, the idea that poets ("the race forever accursed [*maudite*] by those who have power on earth") are envied and hated for their superior qualities by society and its rulers who fear the truths they tell. Thereafter, a sick, impoverished or dissolute poet of significant but generally unrecognized talent came to be seen in these terms as doubly victimized by a hostile or insentient society. Thus Verlaine could write in *Les poètes maudits,* invoking Vigny's hero: ". . . is it not true that *now and forever* the sincere poet sees, feels, knows himself *accursed* by whatever system of self-interest is in power, O Stello?"—A. de Vigny, *Stello* (1832); P. Verlaine, *Les poètes maudits* (1884). A.G.E.

POETIC CONTESTS were of two kinds: imaginary and real. The earliest examples of the imaginary are in ancient Gr. comedy. In Aristophanes' *Frogs* the characters Aeschylus and Euripides debate the merits of their poetry; in the *Clouds* the Just and the Unjust Reasoning argue, and so on. L. eclogues and fables preserved the device, and in Carolingian times the device was used again in northwestern Europe. One of the earliest of these medieval L. *conflictūs* is that of Summer and Winter. Other themes were developed: wine against water, wine against beer. It has been said that poetic debates on love themes first appeared in the 12th c. The most famous is the *Altercatio Phyllidis et Florae* over the relative merits of the knight and the cleric as lovers. The violet and the rose, the sheep and the flax plant, mind and flesh, soul and body, Moslem and Jew and Christian—these were principal subjects. In the late 13th c. similar themes were handled in Fr.

In Prov. and Old Fr. is found the *tenso* (*tençon*) which probably originated as a dialogued *sirventes*, q.v. (political, or satirical poem). The oldest extant example is between Cercamon and Guilhemi in the mid-12th c. The first poet states a belief, and the other argues with him in alternating couplets; or the two poets merely converse in a deprecating way. The goodness and perversity of women was a favorite theme. Many of these dialogues were certainly imaginary, by one author alone; but some of them, by well-known poets, may have been genuine discussions. The 13th-c. *lauda* (q.v.) in Italy sometimes took this form. A *tenso* of a special kind, which has separate origins, is the *pastourelle* (q.v.). Elements of this can be found in L. as early as the 10th c. The *pastourelle* is a strictly imaginary dialogue in which a man of the upper class approaches a peasant girl and "propositions" her, with varying success. There are many surviving specimens in Old Fr. and a few in Prov. A celebrated It. example is the *Contrasto* of Cielo d'Alcamo in the 13th c., which is unusually long with several amusing climaxes. Another by Ciacco dell' Anguillaia has a most unexpected ending. Very similar to the *tenso* is the *partimen* (q.v.) or *jeu parti*. This type of poetic debate may have begun with the Delfin d'Auvergna around 1200. There are some 103 examples in Prov. The oldest Fr. example dates from 1246; there are 182 surviving *jeux partis* in that language.

The theme of the soul in opposition to the body is found also in Anglo-Saxon; but there it is not yet in dialogue form. It is found later in ME, dating ca. 1200. The debate of the Owl and the Nightingale by Nicholas of Guildford (Dorset) is an early 13th-c. masterpiece, expressing perhaps, on a higher level of interpretation, the dispute between didactic and love poetry. There were also dialogues of body and soul, and wine and water in Spain.

The second kind of poetic contest is a formally held competition at which a number of poets submit their entries on assigned themes to win a prize. This is a very ancient procedure. The tragedies and comedies performed at the Dionysia and Lenaea festivals in ancient Athens were competing in this way. In the Middle Ages, when wealthy patrons had become more scarce, the best poets in 13th c. France were also tradesmen who were associated together loosely. They supervised the poetic instruction of young aspirants, and they took part in prize contests. Such associations and competitions seem to have flourished first in Picardy and the Walloon territory. The Puy at Valenciennes was perhaps the first, dating back to 1229. It met at Notre-Dame-du Puy, hence the name. Arras had a minstrels' association in 1199 and was not slow in holding organized competitions. Others were formed at Douai, Tournai, Lille, and later at Rouen and Dieppe. In Germany the guilds of the Meistersinger (q.v.), burgher poets who flourished from the 14th to the 16th c., organized singing schools an essential feature of which was the singing contest. (The oldest literary example of such a singing contest is the Middle High German poem *Der Wartburgkrieg* [13th c.], in which the principal minnesingers [q.v.] took part.) Of great importance was the organization of the Academy of the *Jocs Florals* at Toulouse in 1323, by seven poets, and possibly a lady, Clemence Isaura. The first competition was on May 1, 1324, and the prize was a violet of gold. The Academy has had many vicissitudes but it continues still today. It was imitated by John I of Aragon in 1393 at Barcelona. This Catalan *Jocs Florals* held its meeting in New York City in 1951. Another annual festival and competition which has survived to this day is the National Eisteddfod of Wales which can be traced to the 15th c. and may date back to the bardic festival held by Lord Rhys in 1176 at Cardigan.

H. Knobloch, *Die Streitgedichte im Provenzalischen und Altfranzösischen* (1886); H. Walther, *Das Streitgedicht in der lateinischen Lit. des Mittelalters* (1920); E. Faral, "La pastourelle," *Rom.*, 49 (1923); *Recueil général des jeux-partis*, ed. A. Långfors and others (2 v., 1926); Jeanroy; A. Taylor, *Lit. Hist. of Meistergesang* (1937); E. Köhler, "Zur Entstehung des altprovenzalischen Streitgedichts," ZRP, 75 (1959).—See also PREGUNTA.   U.T.H.

POETIC CONTRACTIONS. In syllabic or accentual-syllabic poetry of a formal and rhetorical kind, p.c. (or elisions) are often used to keep contiguous lines equal in number of syllables. Two basic kinds of contractions can be distinguished: synaeresis (sometimes called synaloepha) and syncope. When contracting by synaeresis, the poet joins two vowels to create a single syllable:

Of Man's First Disobedience, and the Fruit
(*Paradise Lost* 1.1)

Here, the "ie" in "Disobedience" changes to what is called a "y-glide," and the word is read "Disobed-yence." Such a reading is clearly intended by a poet composing syllabically (see METER). Syncope, on the other hand, involves the dropping of an unstressed vowel flanked by two consonants:

Ill fares the land, to hastening ills a prey
(Goldsmith, *The Deserted Village*, 51)

In this line, "hastening," normally trisyllabic, is reduced by syncope to a dissyllable, and the line is thus kept predictably decasyllabic.

P.c. in Eng. poetry are found most frequently in verse composed from the Restoration to the end of the 18th c. In this kind of Augustan poetry, the contractions are sometimes indicated by the use of the apostrophe and sometimes not, but they were observed by the reader even if the word was printed in full, for the aesthetic of 18th-c. poetry assumes that each line will be syllabically regular (see ENG. PROSODY). There is evidence, in fact, that the contemporary reader of 18th-c. poetry derived much of his aesthetic delight from his deliberate and conscious "regularizing," through contraction, of normally irregular phonetic materials. Contraction will be found to be a basic structural tool in syllabic or accentual-syllabic verse with pretensions to formality, and, because the neglect or "modernizing" of these contractions distorts what the poems "say," the contractions should be heeded by the modern reader who wishes to re-create for himself the genuine tone of 18th-c. poetry. Contractions also occasionally appear in excessively rhetorical 19th- and 20th-c. Eng. verse (e.g., "o'er," "e'er"), but, unless the poem in which they appear is genuinely syllabic, they may often be regarded as pretentious quasi-"poetic" affectations inspired by ignorance of the structural rationale of formal syllabic or accentual-syllabic verse.—Saintsbury, *Prosody*; T. S. Omond, *Eng. Metrists* (1921); W. J. Bate, *The Stylistic Development of Keats* (1945); P. Fussell, Jr., *Theory of Prosody in 18th-C. England* (1954).
P.F.

POETIC DICTION. CRITICAL THEORY. The phrase "p.d." begins to assume importance in Eng. literature about the 19th c., when the Preface to Wordsworth's *Lyrical Ballads* (2d ed. 1800) raised the question whether the language of poetry was essentially different from that of prose. In that Preface Wordsworth is as much concerned to discredit the conventional use of words and phrases long associated with meter as to vindicate the genuine language of passion. "P.d." therefore generally means, in Wordsworth's criticism, false

p.d., a fact indicated by the author himself in his statement, "There is little in [*Lyrical Ballads*] of what is usually called poetic diction" (*Preface*, 1800). The ambiguity of the phrase has persisted to the present day, for to some writers p.d. means the collection of epithets, periphrases, archaisms, etc., which were common property to most poets of the 18th c., while to others p.d. means the specifically poetic words and phrases which express the imaginative and impassioned nature of poetry. Thus a book entitled *Poetic Diction*, by Thomas Quayle (1924), has the subtitle *A Study of Eighteenth Century Verse*, while in another book, also entitled *Poetic Diction*, by Owen Barfield (1928, 2d ed., 1952), the author says, in his opening passage, "When words are selected and arranged in such a way that their meaning either arouses or is obviously intended to arouse, aesthetic imagination, the result may be described as *poetic diction*." On a broad view, Barfield's use of the term must appear as the correct one: any special or limited application of it should be indicated by the use of some qualifying word or phrase.

The earliest instance of "diction," given in the OED, in the sense it bears on "p.d." occurs in Dryden's *Fables* (1700): "The first beauty of an Epic poem consists in diction, that is, in the choice of words, and harmony of numbers." "Diction" thus corresponds to the *lexis* of Gr. critics.

The history of the critical theory of p.d. as such is not extensive, for the subject does not much lend itself to discussion in general terms, most of the criticism being found in articles on individual poets. The few sentences of a general nature in Aristotle's *Poetics* are, however, extremely pregnant. The passage, translated by Ingram Bywater, is as follows:

"The perfection of Diction is for it to be at once clear and not mean. The clearest indeed is that made up of the ordinary words for things, but it is mean, as is shown by the poetry of Cleophon and Sthenelus. On the other hand, the diction becomes distinguished and non-prosaic by the use of unfamiliar terms, i.e. strange words, metaphors, lengthened forms, and everything that deviates from the ordinary modes of speech . . . A certain admixture, accordingly, of unfamiliar terms is necessary. These, the strange word, the metaphor, the ornamental equivalent, etc., will save the language from seeming mean and prosaic, while the ordinary words in it will secure the requisite clearness."

It might have been expected that Aristotle's successors among the Gr. critics, many of whom had an acute appreciation of poetic style, would have developed and applied the principles admirably stated in this passage. But instead, this branch of criticism was left to rhetoric, which claimed to offer rules for poetic as well as oratorical diction under the heading of style (*lexis, elocutio*). (*See* RHETORIC AND POETICS.) Rhetoric remained a determining influence on conventional p.d. from about the 1st c. A.D. until the end of the 18th c. The influence of rhetoric is best seen in the long and elaborate lists of figures of speech in works like the *Rhetorica ad Herennium* and Cicero's *De Inventione,* and in their medieval and Renaissance counterparts such as the *Poetria Nova* of Geoffrey of Vinsauf (ca. 1150) or the *Arcadian Rhetorike* of Abraham Fraunce (1590). Generally speaking, rhetoric emphasized the artificial and ornamental aspects of p.d.

In L. criticism there is even less discussion of p.d. than in Gr. The caution of the Roman mind, enforced no doubt by the L. disposition to consider design and general effect rather than the details of execution, led the critics to assume a somewhat aloof attitude towards the ornaments of poetic style. While few of the world's poets have had such skill in the magical use of words as Virgil, the critics, like practical gardeners, concerned themselves with the nature of the soil from which these flowers of speech might best spring. One pronouncement on the subject which might be quoted as the essence of sober classicism was the dictum of Horace: "Cui lecta potenter erit res, nec facundia deseret hunc nec lucidus ordo" (Whosoever shall choose a theme within his range, neither speech will fail him, nor clearness of order—*Ars poetica* 40–41, tr. H. Rushton Fairclough). According to this view, conception is the great thing: execution may be left to take care of itself. There is an almost puritanical austerity in the Horatian critics, who appear as disciplinarians against the inclinaton of poets to luxuriate in verbal extravagance.

The revival of poetry in the Middle Ages was marked by a close concern among poets with the technique of expression. They were interested in general questions of language as well as the art of versification. Short works on these matters by Prov. and Catalan poets survive, and this activity culminates in the L. treatise of Dante, *De Vulgari Eloquentia.* This work is of great importance in the history of both literature and language, and it is highly significant to find the poet discriminating between various Romance dialects, finally giving his preference to Tuscan on the score of euphony and "significance." Yet the very breadth of Dante's view (and its date) precludes that specialized discussion which marks the criticism of p.d. in the strict sense. Dante, like his medieval predecessors, is concerned with the "lingua d'arte," and his view embraces both poetry and rhetoric. He is concerned with the creation of a literary language rather than a specifically poetic one and pays little or no heed to the distinction between prose and poetry which is fundamental to the nature of p.d.

Critical thought during both the Middle Ages and the Renaissance was much concerned with the "lingua d'arte," but it viewed the matter rather in terms of rhetoric than of poetry. During the later Middle Ages and after, poetry came to be regarded as little more than a subdivision of rhetoric, and poets themselves were known as "rethors" or "rhétoriqueurs." This new emphasis fortunately came after the time of Chaucer, whose position as one of the creators of Eng. p.d. is not sufficiently recognized: he was as clearly conscious of the distinction between poetry and prose, as between poetry and rhetoric. The emphasis on rhetoric coincided with a barren period of Eng. poetry, when style was first marked by "aureate" extravagance, and later by the "drabness" (to borrow Professor C. S. Lewis's word) of versifiers who abandoned verbal ornament to their contemporaries in the sphere of prose. Strong traces of the assimilation of poetry to rhetoric appear in much Elizabethan criticism.

For reasons already noticed, the Horatian critics were disinclined to isolate p.d. as an important subject for discussion, though in Johnson's *Lives* there are many acute comments on the diction of particular poets. But in Gray's letter to his friend West (1742), there is a passage indicative of a new approach to the subject: the following sentences are original to an extent not easily appreciated today:

"The language of the age is never the language of poetry; except among the French, whose verse, where the thought or image does not support it, differs in nothing from prose. Our poetry, on the contrary, has a language peculiar to itself; to which almost every one, that has written, has added something by enriching it with foreign idioms and derivatives: nay, sometimes with words of their own composition or invention. Shakespeare and Milton have been great creators this way; and no one more licentious than Pope or Dryden, who perpetually borrow expressions from the former. . . ."

Not long after this a contribution to the *British Magazine* (1762) anticipated a future form of criticism by a detailed examination of verbal effects drawn from many authors. The paper, "On Poetry, as Distinguished from Other Writing," contains some discriminating comments on the "figurative" and "emphatical" qualities of p.d., with apt illustrations from Gr., L., and Eng. poetry.

A revival of interest in the treatise on the Sublime attributed to Longinus had far-reaching effects on poetry and criticism in the 18th c. The treatise was translated into Fr. in 1674 by Boileau, who defined "sublimity" as the quality "qui fait qu'un ouvrage enlève, ravit, transporte." The name of "Longinus" constantly appears in the writings of Eng. critics from Dryden onwards. Addison familiarized his readers with the notion that Milton was the poet of the Sublime, *par excellence*. "Longinus" was frequently appealed to, in the 18th c., against the neoclassical standard of "correctness," and "sublimity" was thus associated with a poetic style and diction which were daring, irregular, romantic. Passages in Thomson's *Seasons* which excited awe or terror were admired as "sublime." The odes of Gray, especially *The Bard*, were "sublime." In critical writings later than the 18th c. the term "sublime" tended to be replaced by others, e.g., the "grand style."

One of the most important documents on our subject is the *Preface* (1800) to Wordsworth's *Lyrical Ballads*, already mentioned. The views of this work are expressed in exaggerated terms and they are at variance with Wordsworth's own practice in most of his best poetry. Yet it remains the most comprehensive and impassioned utterance ever made by a great poet on this vital aspect of his art. Behind the *Preface* lies the conviction of the superiority of the natural to the artificial, and its main doctrines are contained in two theses: that *true* p.d. is natural, and that *false* p.d. is artificial. Wordsworth, who emphasizes the human character of the poet, considers the genuine language of passion to be itself poetical, meter being merely a "superadded" though desirable element. "The poet is a man speaking to men." On the other hand, all the conventional expressions associated with meter (faded classicism, "stock" epithets, verse equivalents for the living words of real emotion) which had accumulated over a century or more of "classical" writing create a barrier between the poet and his audience, and are to be discarded as artificial. Nor have they any justification in theory. "There neither is, nor can be any *essential* difference between the language of prose and metrical composition."

It was principally the implication of this last sentence that impelled Coleridge in his *Biographia Literaria* (chs. 14–22) to complement and correct the views of Wordsworth's *Preface*. Coleridge, with a vast range of reading to support him, appeals to the nature of meter as an outward token that the poet, in accepting its stimulus and discipline, intends to use a language differing in spirit and purpose from that of ordinary life. Poetic language is more nearly universal, more impassioned, more imaginative than other forms of utterance, and its purpose is to give aesthetic pleasure in itself as well as through "what" it expresses. Admitting that there is a "neutral style" common to prose and poetry, Coleridge finds it "a singular and noticeable fact . . . that a theory which would establish the *lingua communis* not only as the best, but as the only commendable style, should have proceeded from a poet, whose diction, next to that of Shakespeare and Milton, appears to me of all others the most *individualized* and characteristic" (*Biographia Literaria*, ch. 20). He makes a further important point in his criticism of some lines by Wordsworth in which the words, considered separately, are admittedly in everyday use; "but," he asks, "are those words *in those places* commonly employed in real life to express the same thought or outward thing? Are they the style used in the ordinary intercourse of spoken words? No! nor are the modes of connections; and still less the breaks and transitions" (*ibid.*). The whole tendency of Coleridge's arguments is to maintain the right of the poet to create a diction strongly marked by the character of his own mind, within the laws which determine the general nature and use of language.

Wordsworth, in his attacks on false p.d., and Coleridge, in his vindication of true p.d., laid down the principles and prepared the way for much valuable criticism in the 19th and 20th c. Many authors who have written excellent studies of the diction of individual poets, e.g., J. W. Mackail, Walter Raleigh, Oliver Elton, Alfred Noyes, E. de Selincourt, Ethel Seaton, Geoffrey Tillotson, George Rylands, while contributing much from their own studies, have not sought to modify the fundamental principles established by the two poet-critics.

An especially constructive contribution to the theory of p.d. is Owen Barfield's *Poetic Diction*. Barfield holds that there are naturally poetic periods of language before the birth of a distinction between poetry and prose. Language being then predominantly concrete, and meanings not yet split up, there are properly speaking, no "metaphors," which are the revolt against the "deadness" of rational speech: ". . . primary 'meanings' were *given*, as it were, by Nature, but the very condition of their being given was that they could not at the same time be apprehended in full consciousness; they could not be *known*, but only experienced, or lived. At this time, therefore, individuals cannot be said to have been responsible for the production of poetic values. . . . A history of language written, not from the logician's, but from the poet's point of view, would proceed somewhat in the following manner: it would see in the concrete vocabulary which has left us the mythologies the world's first 'poetic diction.' Moving forward, it would come, after a long interval, to the earliest ages of which we have any written record—the time of the *Vedas*, in India, the time of the *Iliad* and *Odyssey* in Greece. And at this stage it would find meaning still suffused with myth, and Nature all alive in the thinking of man. . . . The gods are never far below the surface of Homer's language—hence its unearthly sublimity." Barfield then describes the character of p.d. when meanings are "splitting up . . . and language beginning . . . to lose its intrinsic life." He notes the birth of hitherto unknown antitheses, such as those between truth and myth, between prose and poetry, and again between an objective and a subjective world. "Poetry has now passed from the 'fluid' to the 'architectural' type, and in many characteristic works the aesthetic effect corresponds to a sense of difficulties overcome. . . . In Horace's *Sapphics* and *Alcaics* the architectural element practically reaches its zenith. And again if we turn to the history of English, I do not think that we find this architectural element at all pronounced until the 17th c. It strikes us, for instance, in Milton and the metaphysicals, and frequently afterwards, but hardly in Chaucer or Shakespeare." The whole of Barfield's book is an important challenge to the view of Jespersen, and other philologists, to whom "progress in language . . . is synonymous with an increasing ability to think abstract thoughts."

THE DICTION OF ENG. POETRY. OE poetry possessed an elaborate p.d. which was closely linked with the alliterative meter then in use. It included kennings or periphrases (e.g., *swanrād*, "swan's-road," or "sea"), compound epithets (e.g., *fāmigheals*, "foamy-necked"), and mythological allusions. The new rhyming measures introduced from Fr. after the Norman Conquest fostered the creation of a "verse diction" abounding in clichés. Its worst features are amusingly parodied in Chaucer's *Sir Topas*. But Chaucer also developed in his more serious poetry the elements of a distinctively p.d., e.g., the use of mythological names such as *Flora, Zephirus (The Book of the Duchesse*, 402); decorative compound epithets such as *golden-tressed (Troilus and Criseyde*, 5.8), *laurer-crouned (Anelida and Arcite*, 43); and picturesque metaphorical verbs such as *unneste* ("fly out of the nest") (*Troilus and Criseyde*, 4.305). And sometimes there is a phrase modeled on one from Dante to remind us how the new It. style in poetry (*dolce stil nuovo*, q.v.) stimulated in Chaucer the ambition to draw higher and more imaginative effects from his native tongue. An example is: "Al the orient laugheth of the light" (*The Knight's Tale*, 1494) adapted from "Faceva tutto rider l'oriente" (*Purgatorio*, i.20).

In the poetry of Spenser, especially in *The Faerie Queene*, may be found all the chief elements of that nondramatic diction of poetry which has constituted one of the main tradi-

tions in Eng. literature. More than any other man Spenser established by the spell of his example the right of poets to draw upon words and phrases outside those of contemporary speech. As E. de Selincourt says: "He cherished words which though still in use were rapidly passing out of fashion, and the sustained colouring and atmosphere of his style is thus given by a constant use of words which are found in Marlowe, Shakespeare, or Sydney, perhaps once or twice. 'Eftsoons', 'ne', 'als', 'whilom', 'uncouth', 'wight', 'eke', 'sithens', 'ywis'—it is words like these continually woven into the texture of his diction which, even more than the Chaucerian or romance elements, give it the Spenserian colour" (Oxford *Spenser*, Introduction by E. de Selincourt). Few Eng. poets have been as archaistic as Spenser, but a select number of archaisms have colored the diction of most nondramatic Eng. poets, almost up to the present time. Spenser also cultivated epithets as an enrichment of style, occasionally filling a whole line with them, as in his description of Britain as a

"saluage wildernesse,
Unpeopled, unmanurd, unprou'd, unpraysd"
(*Faerie Queene* 2.10.5)

His compound epithets are more numerous and memorable than Chaucer's, and are of various kinds: the morally serious (e.g., *hart-murdring* love: *F.Q.* 2.5.16); the picturesque (e.g., *firie-footed* teeme: *ibid.* 1.12.2); the classical (e.g., *rosy-fingred* Morning: *ibid.* 1.2.7). Spenser's epithets were the model and inspiration of much brilliant work in Marlowe, Chatterton, Keats, Tennyson, and others, and are no less important than his conservatism which seemed bent on preserving all from the past that could still be made current.

The greatness of Shakespeare as a poet gives him a primary place in this survey. Dramatic dialogue must above all things appear unpremeditated: the archaic and literary qualities of Spenser's diction remove it far from "the real language of men." Shakespeare as a poet could not escape the influence of Spenser, and some of his earlier work (e.g., *Romeo and Juliet* and *A Midsummer Night's Dream*) contains passages of rich Spenserian "color." But his mature dramatic needs required that he should develop an extreme suppleness of diction answering to a vast range of characters and passions. The grammatical licences permitted by Elizabethan usage were effectively exploited by Shakespeare at an early date in his career. For instance, we find him using two variations on the word "king" in a couple of lines in *Richard II:* "Then am I king'd again: and by and by / Think that I am unking'd by Bolingbroke." These and similar licences, when put to the service of Shakespeare's power of metaphor, produce that astonishing flexibility of style which matures in *Hamlet* and reappears again and again as late as *The Tempest*. The vivid metaphor of the noun-as-verb in Horatio's phrase "It harrows me with fear and wonder" is typical of Shakespeare's maturely developed diction.

During the period about 1620–60 Eng. poetry divides into three major schools. The neoclassical school as represented by Ben Jonson revived the Horatian ideals of decorum, restraint, and neatness, or "curiosa felicitas." Donne and his followers among the metaphysicals (see METAPHYSICAL POETRY) valued a more elaborate diction marked by complex structure, allusion, and elaborate, often obscure metaphor. The most gifted Spenserian of the age was Milton, but the poems he wrote before 1660, exquisitely worded though they are, could not have given him the commanding place which is his in the history of p.d. In *Paradise Lost* he created a genuine epic diction. Its chief features are: use of Latinate vocabulary and syntax, emphasis on sound effects, use of classical and Hebraic allusions, use of epic simile, and subordination of blank verse line to verse paragraph.

Between 1660 and 1700 the prevailing tendency was toward simplicity seasoned by wit: the powerful secular forces of the age fostered a rational and combative diction, which, as Dryden said, was "fittest for discourse and nearest prose." But in his later years Dryden became more sensitive to the beauty of verbal ornament. In his translation of Virgil and in the *Fables, Ancient and Modern* his links with Spenser are evident. He revives or adapts many old words and expressions for their poetic color. His critical remarks helped to transmit his admiration of Milton and Spenser to the next century.

The complex pattern of 18th-c. poetry includes one dominant motif—the rivalry between the "way of Pope" and the "way of Dryden." Pope, who opened his career with a display of verbal ornament gathered from his reading of Milton and others, achieved his greatest success in the wise and witty *Moral Essays, Satires*, and *Epistles*, in which the diction is close to the best contemporary prose usage. The style and diction of Pope were so congenial to the neoclassical temper of the age that they established themselves, in the eyes of many, e.g., Johnson, as the last word in the art of poetry. Yet even at the height of Pope's reputation there survived a memory of the warmer, more colored, more wayward, and less rigid diction of Spenser, and this was imitated in the work of such professed Spenserians as Thomson, Shenstone, and—somewhat later—Beattie. The fuller and freer tradition of diction was maintained by Gray and by other learned poets such as T. Warton, who had read widely in Eng. poetry and knew how limited was Pope's mastery of diction (however perfect in its way) in comparison with the "pomp and prodigality" of Shakespeare and Milton (Gray, *Stanzas to Mr. Bentley*). The last quarter of the century witnessed the vindication of dialect as a medium of poetry in the work of Burns, and the development of a mixed style, between poetry and rhapsody, undisciplined by meter, in the earlier Prophetic Books of William Blake.

At no time in the history of Eng. poetry does diction play a more vital part than in the work of the romantic poets from Wordsworth to Keats, nor has there ever been more fruitful discussion of the subject. In Wordsworth, two impulses are evident: opposition to the "inane phraseology" of the more lifeless verse of the time—personifications, clichés, trite mythology, and the like; and an impassioned love of simple words and the poetic effects latent within them, as in the celebrated line in *Michael:* "And never lifted up a single stone." Wordsworth's love of plain language, however, does not preclude the frequent borrowing of apt phrases from other poets: his diction is, in fact, more literary than is commonly recognized. Coleridge's original achievement in diction was to raise the style of the ballad to a high poetic level, and in *Kubla Khan* to bring language to the verge of its frontier with music. Byron's diction, in general, is somewhat wanting in precision and the finer qualities, but in *Don Juan* he produced a diction, which has the ease of prose but often rises to brilliant satiric and lyric effects. The diction of Shelley clearly reflects the notions expressed in his *Defence of Poetry*. Two statements are particularly important: that poets are the true creators of language, and that "composition" can never do full justice to "inspiration." Shelley's ideal diction emanates from the primal creative elements of nature, from sunlight and from the ether, but in practice Shelley's writing is often vague and abstract. Keats, on the other hand, stressed concrete, visual description and appeal to sense (especially sight, sound, and smell); and his diction owes much to Spenser and Milton. Keats has no superior in the intense picturesqueness of his best descriptions, and at the same time he often employs language with a mythopoeic power, in which the spirit of Gr. poetry reappears with a subtle modernization.

The achievement in diction by these early 19th-c. writers is the highest attained in Eng. poetry since the age of Shakespeare. Their successors were in a difficult position. Though they were men of high poetic ability, the way to originality was less clear than it had been among the excitements and dangers of the previous age. Tennyson, a consummate artist in diction, had an almost unrivaled versatility. Those who are familiar with the grace, power, and picturesque elegance of his better-known poems should not overlook his equal success in dialect. What is most novel in Browning's diction is his use of a contemporary colloquial idiom in short dramatic lyrics and in the much longer dramatic monologues.

The decline in the poetic quality of "poetic" language in Browning is symptomatic of a change affecting nearly the whole of Eng. poetry for some eighty years. Within that period may be distinguished three main attitudes on the subject of diction. The first is that of the poets to whom the traditional diction of poetry was still a suitable vehicle for poetry. To this group belong such poets as Swinburne, Francis Thomson, Robert Bridges in his earlier work, A. E. Housman, Mrs. Meynell, Rupert Brooke, Walter de la Mare, and the present Laureate, John Masefield. The second attitude is that of the poets who respected the traditional diction, but felt that it must be vigorously rejuvenated in a changed and changing world. Fresh vitality might be infused by bold experiments in diction itself, or by novel effects in meter and rhythm. Thus, G. M. Hopkins handled his epithets in a manner suggesting "a passionate emotion which seems to try and utter all its words in one" (Charles Williams); he also enlivened his verse by what he called "sprung rhythm." Robert Bridges, the associate of Hopkins, increasingly felt the need for novel effects of diction and rhythm: in his late poem, *The Testament of Beauty*, he employed "loose Alexandrines" in which scientific and philosophical terms are woven into the older fabric of traditional diction. A concerted but less vigorous effort to rejuvenate the diction of the past was made by the group of writers associated under the title of "Georgian poets." Writers outside Great Britain often revived the older diction by expressions peculiar to their native custom and landscape. Thus Am. poets had long engrafted new local terms of their own on the traditional stock of Eng. p.d., a method used by a succession of writers from Longfellow to Robert Frost. The Ir. school of poets to which W. B. Yeats belonged did the same, with a more considered program. "Rejuvenation" also came to diction through the experiences of World War I, especially in the work of Wilfred Owen. The third attitude cannot be precisely distinguished from the second, but it is connected with the rise of free verse (q.v.). When metrical regularity disappears in an unlimited "freedom," the distinction between the poetic and the nonpoetic is blurred. Whitman's diction, for example, is powerful and original, but it is also crude and (often intentionally) prosaic.

The conditions which made Whitman acceptable in 19th-c. America were reproduced in an acute form in postwar England. The revolutionary spirit in diction appears in the work of Eliot and Auden, and most recently in Dylan Thomas who (says Anne Ridler, herself a poet) "treats words as though he were present at their creation." Nonetheless, there is a widespread instinct to distrust "revolutionary" writers as models, however much their individual work may be admired. The life of poetry is continuous. There is abundant ground for holding that the consensus of opinion among many good poets now writing is in favor, not of the abandonment of tradition, but of some form of "rejuvenation."

ANALOGIES IN OTHER LITERATURES. The many varieties of diction found in Eng. poetry are closely paralleled in the chief literatures of the Western world. The parallels are of two kinds: there are the fundamental resemblances between techniques of effective diction in classical, especially Gr., poetry and in Eng. poetry; there are also parallels—with some significant differences—between the history of p.d. in Eng. and its history in other important literatures, such as Fr., It., and Sp.

The metaphorical quality of language in Homer, Aeschylus, and Sophocles as well as in Shakespeare and his greatest successors is well known and scarcely needs illustration. Another parallel, little less significant, is the endeavor of poets in their most energetic moments to find or create (in Coleridge's phrase) *"one word* to express *one act* of imagination." The Homeric phrase "Pēlion einosiphullon" (Pelion with quivering leafage) and Aeschylus' "anērithmon gelasma" (multitudinous laughter, i.e., of the sea) are brilliant examples of this: each produces the effect described by Wordsworth in his poem on the daffodils: "Ten thousand saw I at a glance." This is the imaginative power which Coleridge called "esemplastic." The "embracing" or "extensive" epithet occurs frequently in both literatures. The compound epithets in Gr. beginning with *eury-*, and *tele-*, and *poly-* have their Eng. analogues beginning with *wide-*, *far-*, and *many-*. The *poly-* or "many" group is particularly large. By the side of Gr. epithets having the sense of "rich in flowers," "with many furrows," "with many trees," "with many ridges," "with many glens," "poluphloisbos" (loud-roaring, Homer's epithet for the sea), and many more of the like character, may be placed Milton's "wide-watered" (shore), Keats's "far-foamed" (sands), and Tennyson's "many-fountain'd" (Ida). Such epithets are imaginative in their reduction of multiplicity to unity, of complexity to simplicity. Descriptive diction at its best in both Gr. and Eng. poetry is frequently marked by these two characteristic features—the unifying (or "esemplastic") and the metaphorical.

Parallels between p.d. in Eng. and Fr. are especially instructive. The decline of medieval poetry, marked in England by aureate (q.v.) diction, produced its Fr. counterpart in the affectations of the rhétoriqueurs. Renaissance poetry in France and in England was exposed to similar influences, but the national genius of the two countries reacted differently. Sir Thomas Elyot in England and Joachim du Bellay in France both labored to enrich their respective languages with the wealth of classical Gr. and L. But whereas this movement, in England, led to "exornation" and culminated in the unsurpassed wealth of Shakespeare's poetic vocabulary, in France the critical and negative spirit of Malherbe diverted poetry into another channel. The characteristic triumph which Fr. poetry soon after achieved in the work of Racine was marked not by creative abundance of diction but by restraint, conscious elevation, and a certain economy. "La poésie de Racine," says Ste.-Beuve "élude les détails." It shows "une perpétuelle nécessité de noblesse et d'élégance"; it uses "un vocabulaire un peu restreint." In England, the natural reaction which followed Elizabethan exuberance of diction prepared the way for the neoclassical poetry of the 18th c. which is a close parallel to contemporary poetry in France. The p.d. denounced by Wordsworth has its systematized counterpart in the compilation called Le Gradus Français—a guide for the use of poets to epithet, allusion, and periphrasis.

The literary revolution of the early 19th c. had, in England, for its principal arenas, lyrical and narrative poetry, and philosophical criticism. In France, the contest was fought out more publicly on the stage, the classical drama being the stronghold of "noblesse" and "élégance" in diction, as it was of the Unities. The claim made in Victor Hugo's celebrated Préface to Cromwell (1827) to the whole truth as the province of poetry, instead of simply the Beautiful and the Sublime, aimed at removing restraints from language no less than from the handling of dramatic plot and the structure of scenes. Thus a new art of diction was introduced, and language was henceforth to be chosen for its intensity of emotion and descriptive effect, without regard for tradition. In due time romantic fervor cooled into aesthetic precision and the cult of the "mot juste," but the essence of the movement survives in a saying of the brothers Goncourt, valid for more than half the century, "l'épithète rare, voilà la marque du poète."

With the development of the "symboliste" movement some new and valuable thoughts on p.d. have been put forward by Fr. writers, of whom Paul Valéry is an outstanding example. The restricted outlook which haunted the Fr. mind so long after Malherbe is now exchanged for a conception of poetry as entirely free and autonomous. In Valéry the Eng.-speaking reader is reminded of Dryden, of Wordsworth, of Pater, and of Housman, but the breadth of Valéry's generalization is his own. For him literature is simply "un développement de certaines des propriétés du langage . . . les plus agissantes chez les peuples primitifs." Poetry must renew its diction from the "undefiled wells." "Plus la forme est belle, plus elle se sent des origines de la conscience et de l'expression; plus elle est savante et plus elle s'efforce de retrouver, par une sorte de synthèse, la plénitude, l'indivision de la parole encore neuve et dans son état créateur" (Jean Hytier, La Poétique de Valéry, p. 70). Valéry's theory of p.d. is an integral part of his conception of "la poésie absolute."

GENERAL: Aristotle, Poetics, tr. I. Bywater (1909); Dante, De Vulgari eloquentia, tr. A. G. Ferrers Howell (1890; a poet's critical contribution to the making of a literary language); Buffon, Discours sur le style (1753; for statement of neoclassical point of view); Thos. Gray, Letter to R. West, April 1742; "On Poetry, as Distinguished from Other Writing," British Magazine (1762); W. Wordsworth, Lyrical Ballads, Preface (2d ed., 1800); Appendix on what is usually called Poetic Diction (1802); Essay, Supplementary to the Preface (1815); S. T. Coleridge, Biographia Literaria, chs. 14–22; Ker; F. W. Bateson, Eng. Poetry and the Eng. Language (1934, 2d ed., 1961); F. A. Pottle, The Idiom of Poetry (2d ed., 1946); J. Miles, The Continuity of Poetic Language (1951); O. Barfield, P.D. (2d ed., 1952); B. Groom, The Diction of Poetry from Spenser to Bridges (1956).

SPECIAL STUDIES: Norden; M. Arnold, On Translating Homer, ed. W. H. D. Rouse (1905); W. Raleigh, "P.D.," Wordsworth (1921); T. Quayle, P.D.: a Study of 18th C. Verse (1924); J. W. Mackail, "The Poet of The Seasons," Studies of Eng. Poets (1926; a valuable study of James Thomson's diction); H. C. Wyld, "Diction and Imagery in Anglo-Saxon Poetry," E&S, 11 (1925); O. Elton, "The Poet's Dictionary," E&S, 14 (1928); G. Rylands, "Eng. Poetry and the Abstract Word," E&S, 16 (1930); S. H. Monk, The Sublime (1935); B. Groom, The Formation and Use of Compound Epithets in Eng. Poetry from 1579 (1937; SPE Tract no. 49); C. M. Bowra, The Heritage of Symbolism (1943); J. Arthos, The Language of Natural Description in 18th C. Poetry (1949); R. F. Jones, The Triumph of the Eng. Language (1951; ch. 6); D. Davie, Purity of Diction in Eng. Verse (1952); J. Hytier, La Poétique de Valéry (1953); D. L. Clark, Rhetoric in Greco-

Roman Education (1957); G. Tillotson, *Augustan Studies* (1962).　B.G.

POETIC DRAMA. See DRAMATIC POETRY.

POETIC LICENSE. A freedom allowed the poet to depart in subject matter, grammar, or diction from what would be proper in ordinary prose discourse. In a broad sense, the poet is exercising p.l. when he invents fictions ("tells lies," as Plato has it) or takes liberties with facts, as when Virgil makes Dido the contemporary of Aeneas. More frequently the term is confined to the poet's freedoms with language: departing from normal word order; using one part of speech for another ("As those move *easiest* who have learned to dance"); employing coined or archaic words; contracting or lengthening words (*'gainst, o'er; beweep, aweary*); altering their pronunciation (*wind* rhymed with *behind*), etc.

P.l. may be used to achieve some special effect or beauty otherwise unattainable, or merely to make the verse conform to the exigencies of meter or rhyme. In the former case, if successful, it generally receives critical commendation; in the latter case its acceptance depends upon the type of poem in which it appears and the standards of the age in which the poem was written. In general, the freedom allowed the poet in his language varies inversely with the freedom allowed him in his meter. In the 18th c., for instance, when metrical laws were very strict, licenses in language were commonly accepted which would not be allowed today when the poet has much greater metrical freedom. In all times, however, the best poets have kept to a minimum such licenses as are dictated merely by meter or rhyme.

Aristotle and Horace both recognize the right of the poet to coin, lengthen, alter, or import words to give distinction to his language, and Aristotle allows him to invent images or situations that improve upon nature: "For poetic effect a convincing impossibility is preferable to that which is unconvincing but possible." Quintilian (ca. A.D. 95) points out that "poets are usually the servants of their meters and are allowed such license that faults are given other names when they occur in poetry." George Gascoigne (1575) advises Eng. poets to place all words in their usual pronunciation and to frame all sentences in their natural idiomatic order, "and yet sometimes . . . the contrary may be borne, but that is rather where rime enforceth, or *per licentiam Poeticam*, than it is otherwise lawful or commendable." R. M. Alden (1909) states that "all these licenses are admitted sparingly in modern poetry, and are to be reckoned as blemishes unless . . . the change from the normal choice of words or order of words has a certain stylistic value of its own."—R. F. Brewer, *The Art of Versification and the Technicalities of Poetry* (1925).　L.P.

POETIC MADNESS. In *Phaedrus* 245 Socrates asserts that poets are susceptible to madness and, in fact, cannot succeed without it. In the *Ion* both poet and critic are described as possessed by a frenzy so that they do not consciously control their words. In Aristotle's *Problemata* 30 it is said that poets and philosophers are inclined to excessive melancholy. Roman poets are possessed by spirits or demons (Ovid: "Deus est in nobis / Agitante calescimus illo"—"A god is within us; when he urges, we are inspired"); write best when tipsy (Horace); are filled with the divine afflatus (Cicero); or are literally mad (the tradition that Lucretius was driven insane by a love potion). The concept of p.m., which can be found *passim* in European poetry and criticism, is summed up in two familiar quotations: "The lunatic, the lover, and the poet / Are of imagination all compact" (Shakespeare); and "Great wits are sure to madness near allied / And thin partitions do their bounds divide" (Dryden).

The parallel between poets and madmen is extremely primitive. It apparently goes back to the time when the poet, the prophet, and the priest were one and the same and when madmen were considered the special children of the gods, invested with prophetic and magical powers. By Plato's time we may assume that only a small residue of the primitive attitude survived. Although Plato evidently considered p.m. suspect, to Horace and many Neoplatonic writers it was the special dispensation which made poetry superior to other forms of discourse. In the form of *furor poeticus* (q.v.) it was identified, especially during the 16th c., with inspiration.

The question whether or not there is a scientific basis for the idea of p.m. is hard to answer. Being especially sensitive, poets may be more subject to neurosis than other men. Many poets (e.g., Sappho, Lucretius, Villon, Marlowe, Collins, Smart, Nerval, Nietzsche, Pound) were either insane or exhibited marked personality disturbances. The romantic theory of the artist as tormented outcast was subsumed by Freud in his essay "The Relation of the Poet to Day-Dreaming" and elsewhere. To Freud, the artist is neurotic and his work is a by-product—often a symbolic statement of—his disturbance. In various forms this idea has been restated by Thomas Mann, Kenneth Burke, and Lionel Trilling. It is explored in considerable detail by Edmund Wilson in *The Wound and the Bow*, where "wound" refers to the artist's neurosis, and "bow" to the art which is its compensation. In this theory poetry is a catharsis for the author—the pearl of art forms around the irritant of emotional disturbance. However, the theory is challenged by critics in the aesthetic tradition (e.g., Croce, I. A. Richards), who tend to claim that the creator is not less but more healthy than average. Among psychologists, Jung and his followers assert the health of the artist, since creative activity puts man in contact with the primal source of human vitality, the collective unconscious.—G. E. Woodberry, "P.M.," *The Inspiration of Poetry* (1910); F. C. Prescott, "The P.M. and Catharsis," *The Poetic Mind* (1922). See also L. Trilling, "Art and Neurosis," *The Liberal Imagination* (1950). See INSPIRATION.　A.R.B.

POETICS, CONCEPTIONS OF. P. is traditionally a systematic theory or doctrine of poetry. It defines poetry and its various branches and subdivisions, forms and technical resources, and discusses the principles that govern it and that distinguish it from other creative activities. The term is derived from the title of Aristotle's fragmentary work *perì poietikês,* or "on poetic (art)," which is the foundation and prototype of all later p. Aristotle himself defined it comprehensively as dealing with "poetry itself and its kinds and the specific power of each, the way in which the plot is to be constructed if the poem is to be beautiful, of how many and of what parts it is composed, and anything else that falls within the same inquiry" (ch. 1).

But even before him there were other conceptions of p. A hint of the hedonistic theory of poetry has been found in Homer's reference to the rhapsode who sings only to produce "delight" in his listeners, as in the *Odyssey* 8. But his song must be orderly and complete, *katà kósmon,* and his subject is "the deeds of men" (*Iliad* 2.484), as revealed by Apollo and the divine Muses to the poet, so it is truth. The more austere p. of Hesiod is unmistakably didactic and has no room for pretty lies. The p. of inspiration may be traced to the poet's invocation to the Muse, and received theoretical form in Democritus, who was the best known representative of that view in antiquity. The opposite view of poetry as an acquired skill or technique may be found in certain sayings of Pindar and other poets. Among the philosophical schools, the Pythagoreans with their concepts of harmony, proportion, and catharsis provide the rudiments of another conception of p., which may have been influential upon later views. Some of the early philosophers then started what Plato was to call "the ancient quarrel between poetry and philosophy" (*Republic* 10.607b), attacking the poets for spreading unworthy notions of God in the tales of mythology. In a different vein the Sophists built up their own ideas of poetry and of poetic effect, which they probably related to that of rhetoric, or persuasion by means of artfully calculated devices. Gorgias formulated a view of tragedy as "a deception by means of legends and emotions in which it was more righteous to deceive than not to deceive, and wiser to be deceived than not to be deceived." In the same spirit the Sophists made early investigations into the technique of language, i.e., grammar and synonyms, and studied rhetorical devices like irony.

In the work of Plato it is possible to find several different and even conflicting views of poetry, leading to contradictory p. The inspiration theory finds its most elaborate formulation in the *Phaedrus* and the *Symposium,* while the latter introduces in a short incidental discussion the startling definition of all art as being poetry and all poetry as being creation, or "the passing of something from not-being into being" (205b). On the other hand, the concept of mimesis which prevails in the *Republic* and elsewhere logically leads to the depreciation of poetry and art in general as the copy of a copy, and the consequent exclusion of the poets from the ideal state. To this exclusion support is also given by a resumption on the grand scale of the "ancient quarrel" in Book 2. Again, the concept of Beauty receives in Plato a definite metaphysical status and becomes one of the most important archetypes or Ideas, as in the *Phaedrus* and *Symposium,* but this notion is initially that of natural beauty, as of a beautiful human body, and not that of the beauty produced by art, particularly poetry. So p. remained in Plato's work an area of unresolved contradictions.

To it Aristotle seemed to bring order and system. He stated his intention to follow the method of philosophy, "beginning with first principles according to the nature of things" (*Poetics,* ch. 1), i.e., proceeding from the general to the particular: a deductive method followed by many later p., at least in their exposition. Several other procedures and formulas of Aristotle have passed on to his successors in this field, just as his uncertainties and vacillations have remained to plague later p. A constructive step is represented by Aristotle's bringing poetry under its general class, i.e., art or *téchne,* thus firmly grounding p. from its inception into aesthetics, considered as the general theory of art. But his definition of art as *mimesis* or the portrayal of an external object through the skilful manipulation of a medium brings us back to the difficulties that beset Plato. Poetry being the portrayal of "men in action" (ch. 2) through the medium of rhythmical speech (ch. 1), this dependence on the object produces a division of poetry according to the kind of men represented, ethically categorized: satire and comedy originate from the portrayal of despicable persons, while epic and tragedy from the portrayal of "noble actions" and of men who are above the common level (chs. 2 and 4). A still more restrictive dependence on the object is to be found in Aristotle's definition of the hero of tragedy. In contradiction with ch. 2, which had made the characters of tragedy "men better than in actual life," the hero is now defined (ch. 13) as a man "like ourselves," neither too good nor too bad, who is trapped by circumstances through committing an *hamartia* (whatever be the exact meaning of that disputed term). The characters of tragedy are elsewhere said to belong to the class of "a few noble families" famous for their misfortunes (ch. 13), with no hint of their purely mythical character.

This dependence on the object portrayed is of course in keeping with Aristotle's realistic theory of knowledge, which makes the object of knowledge a prerequisite to the act of knowing. In the *Poetics* it may at times represent an attempt to reach at the eidetic character of poetry, but its logic leaves no room for invention or for the function of the creative imagination which will play such a large part in later conceptions of p. Creative imagination is also excluded by Aristotle's psychological doctrine (*Rhetoric* 1.11.1370 a 28). This doctrine was accurately represented later in Hobbes's definition: "imagination is nothing but decaying sense" (*Leviathan* 1.2). Aristotle's view allows only for a certain manipulative skill in "putting together the fable," or plot construction, with which in relation to tragedy the most detailed discussion in the *Poetics* is concerned. Here the poetic talent seems to be identified with the capacity for classification: for the poet's job is made to consist in discerning what episodes and plots come under certain general definitions of desirable ingredients of tragedy, according to the elaborate system of divisions and subdivisions of "recognition" and "reversal." Here also the ultimate test appears to be an effect upon the emotions of the audience, so another external object is assumed as determining the poet's activity: viz. the arousal of certain arbitrarily restricted types of emotion in the minds of the future audience, or the much debated concept of *catharsis* (q.v.).

It will now be patent that from the beginning of the treatise Aristotle shifts from the conception of p. as a descriptive or philosophical statement to a very different conception that has divided critics into opposing camps throughout the ages, namely p. as prescriptive and regulative. The conflict is between a statement as to what poetry *is*, independently of the desires or requirements of the theorist, and a statement as to what poetry

should be to satisfy those requirements and to fit into a preconceived set of forms and subjects, of types of diction and meter and arrangement and kinds of content. Upon these two conceptions of p. are grounded the two opposing trends of criticism which finally crystallized into the classic-romantic dichotomy: judicial criticism, which assesses poetry from the requirements of a prescriptive p., and aesthetic or romantic criticism, which accepts all kinds of patterns and forms, of genres and of subjects, provided they are aesthetically unified, and attempts to see the poem from the point of view of its creator and to reproduce in the mind of the critic the creative process of the artist. While the latter conception was obviously not available to Aristotle, it might have been possible for him to conceive of art as mimetic without attempting to prescribe laws for it. But this he does from the very opening paragraph, already cited: "the way in which plots *are to be* constructed if a poem *is to be* beautiful" (ch. 1). This later develops into the enumeration of the rules that tragedy should follow: it should present a hero of a certain type and not of another, a plot of a certain kind rather than of another, an unhappy ending rather than a happy one (such as is actually found in several extant Gr. tragedies, as the *Philoctetes, Alcestis, Helen, Iphigenia in Tauris*, etc.), etc. These rules were multiplied by the followers of Aristotle in the tradition of prescriptive p., such as Horace. The latter laid down still narrower rules for the drama: there must be no more than three characters speaking on the stage, neither more nor less than five acts, etc., but he was saved from pedantry by his polished, urbane, man-of-the-world presentation. No such sophistication was achieved by the Renaissance Aristotelian critics, who fathered upon Aristotle the doctrine of the Dramatic Unities and whose pedantry has passed into proverb: "they proclaimed Aristotle always right, even when they translated him wrong" (F. L. Lucas). They thus paved the way to the most famous modern p. of the prescriptive kind, Boileau's *Art of Poetry* (1674), presenting in verse according to the Horatian tradition the code of Fr. neoclassicism. This view includes a doctrine of generality, or poetry as the expression of the most general thoughts in the most general terms—the acme of an intellectualistic p. for which Aristotle himself, with his excursion into a theory of the poetic universal in ch. 9, is not entirely without responsibility.

From the Renaissance onward theories of p. are to be found not only in treatises with that title but in all kinds of writings. Pope's *Essay on Criticism* (1711), inspired as it is by Boileau, includes a poetic of the neoclassical prescriptive type, the injunctions to poets ("Trust not thyself!") being much less liberal than the advice to critics, a paradoxical situation for which there is also precedent in Aristotle's *Poetics*, for his ch. 25 consists of advice to critics to avoid pedantic strictures and a defense of various kinds of poetic license. The rise of aesthetics as a philosophical science, formally achieved by J. B. Baumgarten in 1750, tended to strengthen the theoretical and objective treatment of p. rather than the prescriptive. The simultaneous rise of the historical method in literary criticism led to the purely historical handling of p. as the objective account of what poetry and theories of poetry had been in the past, one of the earliest instances being F. von Blankenburg's article on p. in his supplement to Sulzer's aesthetics, 1796–98. Since p. had become identified with the Rules under the neoclassical dispensation, it now shared the discredit which romanticism poured over them, and not many p. have been written since, or at least they have not been so authoritative. However, A. W. Schlegel's Berlin lectures on the theory of art in 1801–2 include a comprehensive survey of questions relating to poetry and constitute the most substantial p. by a romantic critic. They are surpassed in depth only by Hegel's lectures on aesthetics, published after his death. Both Schlegel and Hegel refute the theory that poetry is an imitation of nature and develop a creative concept of art and of poetry, conceiving the poem as a self-developing organism governed by its own principles. This is in keeping with the new metaphysics of mind, in which the object is conceived as an organic creation of the subject. Aristotle had used the organic metaphor, but his dissection of tragedy showed only too clearly his incapacity to conceive of the work of art as an inseparable unity of form and content. It remained for modern interpreters like Butcher to project the preeminently romantic concepts of ideality and organic unity into the text of Aristotle.

In the 19th c. p. therefore became either a part of philosophical aesthetics, or was dealt with historically. In the first alternative, a theory of poetry is to be found in all the systems of metaphysical aesthetics which were then built up, from those of the Hegelians such as Vischer (and before them of Schleiermacher and of Solger) and of the anti-Hegelian Herbart, to those of Schopenhauer, Hartmann, Lotze, etc. P., to these writers, is the theory of a particular art in the system of the arts, when the aesthetic is built around such a system, or it may be considered as a purely empirical and external classification of works of art for the sake of convenience, as in Croce's *Aesthetics* of 1902. Croce's later *Poesia* (1936) is a discussion of the problems arising from

this empirical classification of poetry, with a view to resolving them into a unified concept of art, and is in this sense a kind of p. On the other hand p. treated historically became in Germany what is there known as *Literaturwissenschaft,* or in its Am. version "the theory of literature": viz., a discussion of the problems of p. with an empirical rather than a philosophical method, grounded upon historical knowledge and assuming implicitly the validity of the theory of genres: e.g., H. Cysarz (1926), E. Ermatinger (1930), J. Petersen (1939), and W. Kayser (1948).

The relations of literary criticism to p., or more generally to aesthetic theory, are manifold and complex. The critic's main concern is usually with the evaluation and analysis of the work which is in front of him, but this evaluation logically implies standards of judgment which have their root in an aesthetic or poetic of some kind. This relationship, being by implication, may range anywhere from the conscious adherence to a definite system (e.g., in the case of the Chicago Aristotelians) to the professed rejection of all aesthetics or p., as in the impressionists à la Anatole France. Even more delicate and sensitive is the relationship between p. and actual creation. Does a poet start with a definite theory of what poetry should be, and then attempt to fit his own composition into the requirements of that theory? All intellectualistic conceptions of p. answer in the affirmative, all intuitionistic or eidetic theories in the negative. But even a critic who believes in the creative imagination may acknowledge that a poet may have before him a vague and fluctuating idea of what his poem is going to be, an orientation toward certain subjects and certain forms, a sketch, outline or "harmony of tones and feelings," from which his poem then develops, assuming definite shape and concrete verbalization in the process of expression. The ideal of the poetry that a poet may dream of or aim at may be called his p. In this sense it is possible to speak of the poetic of Shelley or of Hopkins, of Mallarmé or Valéry, deriving it from their prose statements and from their actual work, and then to present their poetry as the realization of this ideal. Since the eighties there is a symbolistic poetic of this kind, an ideal of poetry as symbol rather than representation, of suggestion rather than of expression, of musicality rather than of discourse. In the postsymbolists of the 20th c. there has been among other things a tendency to return to some of the doctrines of traditional p., to a rule of intellectual construction and technical virtuosity rather than to the p. of imagination and feeling. T. S. Eliot's p., as put forward in his critical writings, has stressed, one after the other, a series of devices considered to ensure poetic effect: he has resorted in turn to "myth," to "conventions," to the "objective correlative," and ultimately to "poetic drama." Pound's poetic has stressed the role of the intellect in the conscious elaboration of technical devices, sharpness of imagery, and metrical innovation. P. in this sense is the individual concern of each poet and finds its consummation in the production of his work. It thus becomes too multifarious for discussion here.

Other contemporary conceptions of p. are based on sociological or anthropological or psychological theories: e.g., the various schools of psychoanalysis, from Freud's complexes to the archetypes of Jung, all of which are supposed to be active in the unconscious (either individual or collective) and emerge unintentionally in poetic compositions. P. also discusses such matters as the difference between prose and verse, the various kinds of meter and the various kinds of composition (see GENRES), the nature of poetic genius, and the function of myth or the supernatural in poetry. It does not usually include fiction or drama in prose (which are included in the German term for poetry, *Dichtung*), an exclusion which has been followed in the present work, which deals with compositions in verse.

C. M. Gayley and F. N. Scott, *An Introd. to the Methods and Materials of Lit. Crit.: the Bases in Aesthetics and P.* (1899); Gayley and Kurtz (Gayley's books are out of date in many ways, but they still provide the fullest guide to the earlier lit. of the subject); Wellek and Warren (abundant references to more recent bibliog.); W. Kayser, *Das sprachliche Kunstwerk* (Bern, 1948; for the German "theory of literature," with up-to-date bibliog.); M. Fubini and others, *Tecnica e teoria letteraria* (2d ed., 1951).—T. B. L. Webster, "Gr. Theories of Art and Lit. down to 400 B.C.," CQ, 33 (1939); *Lit. Crit.: Plato to Dryden*, ed. A. H. Gilbert (1940; most usable Eng. tr. of Aristotle's *Poetics* with sel. from Plato and from Ren. p.); Aristotele, *Poetica*, ed. A. Rostagni (2d ed., 1945; best ed. of the Gr. text with commentary and important critical introd.); *The Art of Poetry: The Poetical Treatises of Horace, Vida and Boileau*, ed. A. S. Cook (1892); B. Croce, *The Defence of Poetry*, tr. E. E. Carritt (1933) and *La poesia* (1936; selections tr. by A. H. Gilbert in G. W. Allen and H. H. Clark, eds., *Lit. Crit.: Pope to Croce*, 1941); *L'Art poétique*, ed. C. Charpier and P. Seghers (1956; compreh. coll. of texts of p., esp. good for modern Fr.).

K. Borinski, *Die Antike in Poetik und Kunsttheorie* (2 v., 1914–24); M. W. Bundy, *The Theory of the Imagination in Cl. and Medieval Thought* (1927); G. F. Else, *Aristotle's P.: the Argument* (1957); J. Jones, *On Aristotle and Gr. Tragedy* (1962); *European Theories of the*

Drama, ed. B. H. Clark (2d ed., with suppl. on Am. drama, 1947; with an anthol. of dramatic theory and crit. from Aristotle to present); Curtius; Weinberg; R. P. Cowl, *The Theory of Poetry in England . . . from the 16th to the 19th C.* (1914); *18th C. Crit. Essays*, ed. S. Elledge (2 v., 1961); P. van Tieghem, *Petite hist. des grandes doctrines littéraires en France de la Pléiade au Surréalisme* (1946); Abrams; B. Markwardt, *Gesch. der deutschen Poetik* (in 6 v., 4 v. completed, 1937–61); L. Abercrombie, *The Theory of Poetry* (1926); E. Staiger, *Grundbegriffe der Poetik* (1946); E. Sewell, *The Structure of Poetry* (1951); F. Martini, "Poetik," *Deutsche Philologie im Aufriss*, 2. überarbeitete Auflage, herausgeben von W. Stammler, I (1957); L. D. Lerner, *The Truest Poetry* (1960); W. L. Schwartz, "Some 20th C. Arts Poétiques," PMLA, 47 (1932); "On Prose and Poetry: Prose Statements by Modern Poets," *A Little Treasury of Modern Poetry*, ed. O. Williams (1950); *Modern Fr. Poets on Poetry. An Anthol.*, ed. R. Gibson (1961); Frye.   G.N.G.O.

POETICS AND RHETORIC. See RHETORIC AND POETICS.

POETISCHER REALISMUS. See REALISM.

POETRY, THEORIES OF. There is no uniquely valid way to classify theories of poetry; that classification is best which best serves the particular purpose in hand. The division of theories presented here is one among many possibilities, adopted because it is relatively simple; because it stresses the notable extent to which later approaches to poetry were expansions—although under the influence of many new philosophical concepts and poetic examples—of Gr. and Roman prototypes; and because it defines in a provisional way certain large-scale shifts of emphasis during 2,500 years of Western speculation about the identity of poetry, its kinds and their relative status, the parts, qualities, and ordonnance of a single poem, and the criteria by which poems are to be evaluated. But like all general schemes, this one must be supplemented and qualified in numerous ways before it can do justice to the diversity of individual points of view.

All theorists recognize that poetry is a fabricated thing, not found in nature, and therefore contingent on a number of factors. A *poem* is produced by a *poet*, takes its subject matter from the *universe* of men, things, and events, and is addressed to, or made available to, an *audience* of hearers or readers. But although these four elements play some part in all inclusive accounts of poetry, they do not play an equal part. Commonly a critic takes one of these elements or relations as cardinal, and refers the poem either to the external world, or to the audience, or to the poet as preponderantly "the source, and end, and test of art"; or alternatively, he considers the poem as a self-sufficient entity, best regarded in theoretical isolation from the causal factors in the universe from which the poem derives its materials, or the tastes, convictions, and responses of the audience to which it appeals, or the character, intentions, thoughts, and feelings of the poet who brings it into being. These varied orientations give us, in a preliminary way, four broad types of poetic theory, which may be labeled mimetic, pragmatic, expressive, and objective.

MIMETIC THEORIES: In Plato's *Republic* 10, Socrates said that poetry is mimesis, or "imitation," and illustrated its relation to the universe by a mirror which, turned round and round, can produce an appearance of all sensible things. Plato thus bequeathed to later theorists a preoccupation with the relation of poetry to that which it imitates, and also the persistent analogy of the reflector as defining the nature of that relation. But in the cosmic structure underlying Plato's dialectic, the sensible universe is itself an imitation, or appearance, of the eternal Ideas which are the locus of all value, while all other human knowledge and products are also modes of imitation. A poem therefore turns out to be the rival of the work of the artisan, the statesman, the moralist, and the philosopher, but under the inescapable disadvantage of being an imitation of an imitation, "thrice removed from the truth," and composed not by art and knowledge, but by inspiration, at a time when the poet is not in his right mind (*Ion*). Plato thus forced many later critical theorists into a posture of defense, in a context of discussion in which poetry necessarily competes with all other human attempts to achieve the true, the beautiful, and the good.

In Aristotle's *Poetics* the various kinds of poetry are also defined as "modes of imitation" of human actions. Aristotle attributes the origin of poetry to our natural instinct to imitate and to take pleasure in imitations, and grounds in large part on the kinds of subjects which are imitated such essential concepts as the different species of poetry, the unity of a poem (since an imitation "must represent one action, a complete whole"), and the primacy of plot in tragedy (for "tragedy is essentially an imitation not of persons but of action and life"). But Aristotle's use of the term "imitation" sharply differentiates his theory of poetry from that of Plato. In Aristotle's scheme, the forms of things do not exist in an otherworldly realm, but are inherent in the things themselves, so that it is in no way derogatory to point out that poetry imitates models in the world of sense. On the contrary, poetry is more philosophic than history, because it imitates the form of things in the matter or medium of words, and so achieves statements in the mode of "universals, whereas those of history are singulars." Furthermore "imitation" in Aristotle is a term specific to the arts, distinguishing poems from all other activities and products as a class of objects having their own criteria of value and reason for being. And by exploiting systematically such distinctions as the kinds of objects imitated, the media and manner of imitation, and the variety of emotional effects on an audience, Aristotle implements his consideration of poetry as poetry by providing means for distinguishing among the poetic kinds—e.g., tragedy, comedy, epic—and for discriminating the particular parts, internal relations, power of giving pleasure, and standards of evaluation proper to each type of poem.

Later the eclectic Cicero (*Ad M. Brutum Orator* 2) and Plotinus (*Enneads* 5.8) demonstrated that it was possible to assume a world-scheme which includes Platonic Ideas, yet allow the artist to short-circuit the objects of sense so as to imitate, in Plotinus' phrase, "the Ideas from which Nature itself derives." In accordance with this strategy, later critics used building blocks from Plato's cosmos to construct aesthetic theories which raise poetry from Plato's inferior position to the highest among human endeavors. The claim that poetry imitates the eternal Forms was developed by It. Neoplatonists in the 16th c., occasionally echoed by neoclassic critics (including, in England, Dennis, Hurd, and Reynolds), and played a prominent part in the writings of German romantic philosophers such as Schelling and Novalis. Diverse cognitive claims for poetry as approximating verities beyond experience are also found in the Eng. romantic critics Blake, Coleridge, and Carlyle. Shelley, in his *Defence of Poetry*, demonstrates the radically reductive tendency of an uncompromising Neoplatonic theory. Since all good poems imitate the same Forms, and since these Forms, as the residence of all values, are the models for all other human activities and products as well, Shelley's essay all but annuls any essential differences between poem and poem, between poetic kind and poetic kind, between poems written in various times and in various places, and between poems written in words and the poetry of all other men who "express this indestructible order," including institutors of laws, founders of civil society, inventors of the arts of life, and teachers of religion. All strive for the same end and are subject to the same standards of judgment, which are at once judgments of aesthetic, ontological, and moral excellence. In our own day a formal parallel to this extreme critical monism is to be found among the critics who, after Jung, maintain that great poems, like myths, dreams, visions, and other products of the collective unconscious, all reproduce the same limited set of archetypal paradigms, and ultimately the whole or part of that archetype of archetypes, the cycle of the seasons and of death and rebirth. (See, e.g., Philip Wheelwright, *The Burning Fountain*, 1954; Northrop Frye, *Anatomy of Criticism*, 1957).

Among mimetic theorists, however, the concept that art reproduces aspects of the sensible world has been much more common than the Platonistic or transcendental variant. The doctrine that poetry and the arts are essentially imitations of this world, in a variety of systematic applications, flourished through the Renaissance and well into the 18th c. In *Les Beaux Arts réduits à un même principe* (1747), Charles Batteux found in the principle of imitation the "clear and distinct idea" from which he systematically deduced the nature and all the rules of the various arts. The Englishman Richard Hurd declared that "all poetry, to speak with Aristotle and the Greek critics (if for so plain a point authorities be thought wanting) is, properly, *imitation* . . . having all creation for its object" ("Discourse on Poetical Imitation," 1751). And Lessing's classic *Laokoon* (1766), although it set out to substitute an inductive method for the blatantly deductive theories of Batteux and other contemporaries, still discovered the "essence" of poetry and painting to be imitation, and derived the bounds of the subjects each art is competent to imitate from the differences in their media.

Since the 18th c. the mimetic doctrine has been more narrowly employed by proponents of artistic realism, or in theories limited to the more realistic literary genres. In the Renaissance there had been many echoes of the saying Donatus had attributed to Cicero that dramatic comedy is peculiarly "a copy of life, a mirror of custom, a reflection of truth." In the early 19th c., when prose fiction had superseded comedy as the primary vehicle of realism, Stendhal put the mimetic mirror on wheels: "a novel," he said "is a mirror riding along a highway." Since that time representational theories have been voiced mainly by exponents of naturalistic fiction and imagist poetry.

The mimetic approach to literature, accordingly, has been used to justify artistic procedures ranging from the most refined idealism to the rawest realism. What the various theories have in common is the tendency to look to the nature of the given universe as the clue to the nature of poetry, and to assign to the subject matter which is represented—or which ought to be represented—the primary role in determining the aims, kinds, constitution, and criteria of poems. The key word in mimetic definitions of poetry, if not "imitation," is another predicate which aligns the poem in the same direction: the poem is an "image," "reflection," "feigning," "counterfeiting," "copy," or "representation." The underlying parallel for a poem, which often comes to the surface as an express comparison, is Plato's mirror, or "a speaking picture," or a photographic plate. The focus of attention is thus on the relation between the imitable and the imitation, and the primary aesthetic criterion is "truth to nature." In purely representational theories, the patent discrepancies between the world as it is and the world as it is represented in poems tend to be explained, not by reference to the psychology of the poet or the reader, or to the conventions and internal requirements of a work of art, but by reference to the kinds or aspects of reality which are to be imitated. Transcendental theorists maintain that poetry represents the poet's intuitions of models existing in their own supramundane space. This-worldly theorists claim that poetry represents a composite of the beautiful and moral aspects of things, or "la belle nature," or the statistical average of a biological form, or the universal, typical, and generically human, or the quotidian, the particular, the unique, and "the characteristic." In all these instances, however opposed, the objects or qualities are conceived to be inherent in the constitution of the universe, and the genius of the poet is explained primarily by his acuity of observation, enabling him to discover aspects of reality hitherto unregarded, and by his artistic ingenuity, enabling him to select and arrange even the more familiar elements into novel combinations which, nevertheless, surprise us by their truth.

PRAGMATIC THEORIES: The pragmatic scheme sets a poem in a means-end relationship, regarding the matter and manner of imitation as instrumental toward achieving certain effects in the reader. "Poesy therefore," declared Sir Philip Sidney in a typical formulation, "is an art of imitation . . . a speaking picture: with this end, to teach and delight." Ancient rhetorical theory provided the conceptual frame and many of the terms for this approach to poetry, for it was held that the aim of rhetoric is to effect persuasion, and there was wide agreement (e.g., Cicero, *De Oratore* 2.28) that this end is best achieved by informing, winning, and moving the auditor. But the great prototype for the pragmatic view of poetry was Horace's *Ars Poetica*, with its persistent emphasis that the aim of the poet, and the measure of poetic success, is the pleasure and approval of the contemporary Roman audience and of posterity as well. Aristotle has been more often quoted, but Horace has been the most influential critical exemplar in the Western world. For the pragmatic orientation, exploiting the mode of reasoning and many of the concepts and topics presented in Horace's short epistle, dominated literary criticism through the Renaissance and most of the 18th c., and has made frequent, though more sporadic, reappearances ever since.

"Aut prodesse volunt, aut delectare poetae," Horace declared, although pleasure turns out to be the ultimate end, with instruction requisite only because the graver readers will not be pleased without moral matter. Later critics added from rhetoric a third term, "movere," to sum up under the three headings of instruction, emotion, and pleasure the effects of poetry on its audience. Most Renaissance humanists, like Sidney, made moral profit the ultimate aim of poetry; but from Dryden through the 18th c. it became increasingly common to subordinate instruction and emotion to the delight of the reader, as the defining end of a poetic composition. Dr. Johnson, however, continued to insist that "the end of poetry is to instruct by pleasing," and that "it is always a writer's duty to make the world better" *(Preface to Shakespeare)*. In the 19th c. the influential reviewer, Francis Jeffrey, deliberately justified writing in such a way as to please the least common denominator of public taste, and in this procedure he has been followed by later pedlars of formulae for achieving popular success. Neoclassic pragmatists, however, justified the sophisticated preferences of the classically trained connoisseurs of their own day by the claim that these accorded with the literary qualities of works whose long survival prove their adaptation to the aesthetic proclivities of man in general (Dr. Johnson's "common reader"), and that works written in accordance with these principles have the best chance to endure. The renowned masters, John Dennis said, wrote not to please only their countrymen; "they wrote to their fellow-citizens of the universe, to all countries, and to all ages."

We recognize pragmatic critics of poetry, whatever their many divergences, by their tendency to regard a poem as a made object, a craftsmanlike product which (after due allowance for the play of natural talent, inspired moments, and felicities beyond the reach of art) is still, for the most part, deliberately designed to achieve foreknown ends; we recognize them also by their tendency to derive the rationale, the chief determinants of elements and forms, and the norms of such artifacts from the legitimate requirements and springs of pleasure in the readers for whom it is written. Thus the *ars poetica*—in Ben Jonson's words, "the craft of making"—looms large in

this theory, and for centuries was often codified as a system of prescriptions and "rules." "Having thus shown that imitation pleases," as Dryden summarized the common line of reasoning, "it follows, that some rules of imitation are necessary to obtain the end; for without rules there can be no art" *(Parallel of Poetry and Painting)*. These rules were justified inductively as essential properties abstracted from works which have appealed to the natural preferences of mankind over the centuries; in the 18th c., especially in such systematic theorists as Beattie, Hurd, and Kames, they were also warranted by a confident appeal to the psychological laws governing the responses of the reader. Through the neoclassic period, most critics assumed that the rules were specific for each of the fixed genres, or kinds, but these poetic kinds in turn were usually discriminated and ranked, from epic and tragedy at the top down to the "lesser lyric" and other trifles at the bottom, by the special moral and pleasurable effects each kind is most competent to achieve. Poetic deviations from the truth of fact, which in strictly mimetic theories are justified by their conformity to forms and tendencies in the constitution of the universe, are warranted pragmatically by the reader's moral requirements, and even more emphatically, by his native inclination to take delight only in a selected, patterned, heightened, and "ornamented" reality. In 1651 Davenant *(Preface to Gondibert)* attacked the traditional use of pagan machinery and supernatural materials on the assumption that the poet undertakes to "represent the world's true image"; a point of view which Hobbes at once abetted by proscribing all poetic materials that go "beyond the conceived possibility of nature" *(Answer to Davenant)*. To this influential interpretation of poetic probability as correspondence to the empirical constitution and order of events, pragmatic critics responded by shifting the emphasis from the nature of the world to the nature of man, and by redefining poetic probability as anything which succeeds in evoking the pleasurable responsiveness of the reader. "The end of poetry is to please," Beattie wrote in his *Essays on Poetry and Music* (1776), and "greater pleasure is . . . to be expected from it, because we grant it superior indulgence, in regard to fiction," than if it were "according to real nature." Later Thomas Twining justified for poetry "not only impossibilities, but even absurdities, where that end [of yielding pleasure] appears to be better answered with them, than it would have been without them" (Preface to *Aristotle's Treatise on Poetry*, 1789).

EXPRESSIVE THEORIES: The mimetic poet is the agent who holds the mirror up to nature; the pragmatic poet is considered mainly in terms of the inherent powers ("nature") and acquired knowledge and skills ("art") he must possess to construct a poetic object intricately adapted, in its parts and as a whole, to its complex aims. In the expressive orientation, the poet moves into the center of the scheme and himself becomes the prime generator of the subject matter, attributes, and values of a poem. The chief historical source for this point of view was the treatise *On the Sublime* attributed to Longinus. In this treatise the stylistic quality of sublimity is defined by its effect of *ekstasis*, or transport, and is traced to five sources in the powers of the author. Of these sources, three have to do with expression, and are amenable to art; but the two primary sources are largely innate and instinctive, and are constituted by the author's greatness of conception and, most important of all, by his "vehement and inspired passion." Referring the major excellence of a work to its genesis in the author's mind, Longinus finds it a reflection of its author: "Sublimity is the echo of a great soul."

The influence of Longinus' essay, after it became generally known in the third quarter of the 17th c., was immense, and its emphasis on thought and passion, originally used to explain a single stylistic quality, was expanded and applied to poetry as a whole. The effect on poetic theory was supplemented by primitivistic concepts of the natural origins of language and poetry in emotional exclamations and effusions, as well as by the rise to high estate of "the greater lyric," or Pindaric ode, which critics (following the lead of Cowley) treated in Longinian terms. By 1725 the boldly speculative Giambattista Vico combined Longinian doctrines, the Lucretian theory of linguistic origins, and travelers' reports about the poetry of culturally primitive peoples into his major thesis that the first language after the flood was dominated by sense, passion, and imagination, and was therefore at once emotional, concrete, mythical, and poetic. In Vico is to be found the root concept of the common expressive origins and nature of poetry, myth, and religion which was later exploited by such influential theorists as Herder, Croce, and Cassirer; this mode of speculation is still recognizable in the current theories of Suzanne Langer and Philip Wheelwright, among many others.

In the course of the 18th c. there was a growing tendency to treat poetry, although still within a generally pragmatic frame, as primarily an emotional, in contrast to a rational, use of language, especially among such Longinian enthusiasts as John Dennis, Robert Lowth, and Joseph Warton (see, e.g., Warton's *Essay . . . on Pope*, 1756–82). By the latter part of the century, unqualifiedly expressive

theories of poetry as grounded in the faculties and feelings of the poet are to be found in Sir William Jones's "Essay on the Arts Called Imitative" (1772), J. G. Sulzer's *Allgemeine Theorie der schönen Künste* (1771–74), and Hugh Blair's "Nature of Poetry" (*Lectures on Rhetoric and Belles Lettres*, 1783). German romantic theorists such as the Schlegels, Schleiermacher, and Tieck, formulated the expressive view in the terminology of post-Kantian idealism; Novalis, e.g., said that "poetry is representation of the spirit, of the inner world in its totality" (*Die Fragmente*). In France Mme de Stael announced the new outlook on poetry in *De L'Allemagne* (1813), and in Italy it manifested itself, later on, in some of Leopardi's speculations on lyrical poetry.

Wordsworth's "Preface" to the *Lyrical Ballads* is the heir to a century of developments in this mode of thinking, and became the single most important pronouncement of the emotive theory of poetry. His key formulation, twice uttered, is that poetry "is the spontaneous overflow of powerful feelings." The key metaphor, "overflow," like the equivalent terms in the definitions of Wordsworth's contemporaries—"expression," "uttering forth," "projection"—faces in an opposite direction from "imitation," and indicates that the source of the poem is no longer the external world, but the poet himself; and the elements which, externalized, become the subject matter of the poem are, expressly, the poet's "feelings." The word "overflow" also exemplifies the water-language in which feelings are usually discussed, and suggests that the dynamics of the poetic process consists in the pressure of fluid feelings; later John Keble converted the water to steam, and described the poetic process as a release, a "safety valve," for pent-up feelings and desires. The poetic process, therefore, as Wordsworth says, is not calculated, but "spontaneous." Wordsworth still allows for the element of "art" by regarding the success of spontaneous composition to be attendant upon prior thought and practice, and takes the audience into account by insisting that "poets do not write for poets alone, but for men." But in the more radical followers and successors of Wordsworth, including Keble, Mill, and Carlyle, the art of affecting an audience, which had been the defining attribute of poetry in pragmatic theory, becomes precisely the quality which invalidates a poem. "Poetry," wrote John Stuart Mill, "is feeling, confessing itself to itself in moments of solitude." And when the utterance "is not itself the end, but a means to an end . . . of making an impression upon another mind, then it ceases to be poetry, and becomes eloquence" ("What is Poetry?", 1833). Sir Walter Scott was almost alone in his time in proposing a theory of poetry as the communication, as well as the expression of emotion: the poet, he said, has the motive "of exciting in the reader . . . a tone of feeling similar to that which existed in his own bosom" ("Essay on the Drama," 1819). Later writers also adapted the concept of poetry as emotive expression to a communicative, or pragmatic, frame of reference. That poetry is emotional communication is the basic principle of Tolstoy's "infection theory" of art (*What is Art?*, 1898), as well as of the earlier writings of I. A. Richards, who claimed that emotive language is "used for the sake of the effects in emotion and attitude produced by the reference it occasions," and that poetry "is the supreme form of emotive language" (*Principles of Literary Criticism*, 1924).

Feelings overflow into words, so that it is characteristic of Wordsworth and later emotive theorists, through the school of I. A. Richards, to give to the nature and standards of poetic diction, or "language," the systematic priority which earlier critics had given to plot, character, and considerations of form. In earlier discussions of poetry as an imitation of human actions, "feigning," or fiction, the chief instances of poetry had been narrative and dramatic forms, and the usual antithesis to poetry had been history, or the narration of events that have actually happened. But Wordsworth, Hazlitt, Mill, and many of their contemporaries, conceiving poetry as the language of feeling, thought of the lyrical poem, instead of epic or tragedy, as the exemplary form, and replaced history as the logical opposite of poetry by what Wordsworth called "matter of fact, or science." This romantic innovation in poetic theory has become predominant in our own time. It is the characteristic procedure of I. A. Richards, William Empson, Allen Tate, Cleanth Brooks, and most of the New Critics to establish primarily semantic principles for poetry, by setting up a bipolar distribution of all discourse, and by defining the "emotive," or "imaginative," or the "ambiguous," "ironic," and "paradoxical" language of poetry by systematic opposition to the attributes of the "referential," "cognitive," and unambiguously "rational" language of science.

Among expressive theorists of the 19th c., the old criterion of truth to objective or ideal nature was often reinterpreted as truth to a nature already suffused with the poet's feelings, or reshaped by the dynamics of desire. More commonly still, the criterion was turned around, in the demand that poetry be "sincere"; it was in this period that "sincerity" became a cardinal requirement of poetic excellence. "The excellence of Burns," as Carlyle said, clearly revealing the reversal of the standard, "is . . . his *sincerity*, his indisputable

air of truth. . . . The passion that is traced before us has glowed in a living heart." Or as J. S. Mill asserted, in a phrasing anticipating the theory of later symbolists and expressionists, poetry embodies "itself in symbols which are the nearest possible representations of the feeling in the exact shape in which it exists in the poet's mind." The mirror held up to nature becomes a mirror held up to the poet, or else it is rendered transparent: Shakespeare's works, according to Carlyle, "are so many windows, through which we see a glimpse of the world that was in him." Correspondingly, the elements constituting a poem become in large part qualities which it shares with its author: feelings, imagination, spirit, and (in Matthew Arnold, e.g.) such traits of character as largeness, freedom, benignity, and high seriousness. And as Carlyle shrewdly observed so early as 1827, the grand question asked by the best contemporary critics is "to be answered by discovering and delineating the peculiar nature of the poet from his poetry." Essays on Shakespeare, Milton, Dante, Homer became to a singular degree essays on the temperament and moral nature of the poet as embodied in his work. The most thorough exponent of poetry as self-expression was John Keble in his *Lectures on Poetry* (1832–41), whose thesis was that any good poem is a disguised form of wish-fulfillment—"the indirect expression," as he said in a review of Lockhart's *Scott*, "of some overpowering emotion, or ruling taste, or feeling, the direct indulgence whereof is somehow repressed"—and who specified and applied a complex set of techniques for reversing the process and reconstructing the temperament of the poet from its distorted projection in his poems. In both critical premises and practice, Keble has hardly been exceeded even by critics in the age of Freud who, like Edmund Wilson, hold that "the real elements, of course, of any work of fiction, are the elements of the author's personality: his imagination embodies in the images of characters, situations, and scenes the fundamental conflicts of his nature . . ." (*Axel's Castle*, 1936).

The principal alternative, in Eng. expressive theory, to the view that poetry is the expression of feelings or unrealized desires was Coleridge's view that "poetry" (the superlative passages which occur both in poems and other forms of discourse) is the product of "that synthetic and magical power, to which we have exclusively appropriated the name of imagination" (*Biographia Literaria*, 1817). The creative imagination of the poet, like God the Creator, is endowed with an inner source of motion, and its creative activity, generated by the tension of contraries seeking resolution in a new whole, parallels the dynamic principle underlying the created universe. Following the lead of post-Kantian German theorists, especially Schelling and A. W. Schlegel, Coleridge opposes the organic imaginative process to the mechanical operation of the fancy; that is, he deals with it, in terms that are literal for a growing plant and metaphoric for imagination, as a self-organizing process, assimilating disparate materials by an inherent lawfulness into an organic unity revealed "in the balance or reconciliation of opposite or discordant qualities: of sameness with difference; of the general, with the concrete; the idea, with the image. . . ." Coleridge thus inaugurated the organic theory of poetry in England, as well as the aesthetic principle of inclusiveness, or the "reconciliation of opposite or discordant qualities" which—in the mode of "irony," "tension," the "reconciliation of diverse impulses," or "a pattern of resolved stresses"—has become both the basic conception of poetic unity and the prime criterion of poetic excellence in I. A. Richards and many of the New Critics.

One other variant of the expressive theory deserves mention. Longinus had exemplified the sublime quality as inhering especially in the stunning image, or in brief passages characterized by "speed, power, and intensity," comparable in effect "to a thunder-bolt or flash of lightning," and recognizable by the transport or "spell that it throws over us." Most expressive theorists, assuming the lyric to be the paradigm of poetry, depart from the neoclassic emphasis on distinct and hierarchically ordered poetic kinds by minimizing other genres except as the occasion for the expression of various lyrical feelings, as well as by applying to all poems universal qualitative and evaluative terms which are independent of their generic differences. Joseph Warton and other 18th-c. Longinians went still farther, by isolating the transporting short poem, or the intense image or fragment in a longer poem, and identifying it as "pure poetry," "poetry as such," or the "poetry of a poem." In the 19th c., there emerged the explicit theory that the essentially poetic is to be found only in the incandescent and unsustainable short poem or passage, originating in the soul, unachievable by art and unanalyzable by critics, but characterized by the supreme aesthetic virtue of "intensity." This mode of thinking is to be found in Hazlitt's treatment of "gusto"; in Keats's concept that "the excellence of every art is its *intensity*"; in Poe's doctrine (picked up by Baudelaire) that "a poem is such, only inasmuch as it intensely excites, by elevating, the soul; and all intense excitements are, through a psychal necessity, brief" ("The Philosophy of Composition," 1846); in Arnold's use of fragmentary touchstones for detecting

"the very highest poetical quality"; in the Abbé Bremond's theory of "la poésie pure"; and more recently and explicitly still, in A. E. Housman's *The Name and Nature of Poetry* (1933).

OBJECTIVE THEORIES: Aristotle, after defining tragedy as an imitation of a certain kind of action with certain characteristic effects, showed the way to the further consideration of the tragic poem as an entity in itself, subject to internal requirements (such as unity, probability, progression from beginning through complication to catastrophe) which determine the selection, treatment, and ordering of the parts in an artistic whole. Despite their persistent appeal to Aristotle as exemplar, however, later critics in effect assimilated Aristotle to the Horatian theoretical frame, aligning the poem to its audience. A radically new approach to an objective theory of poetry was inaugurated by certain It. thinkers of the Renaissance (including Cristoforo Landino, Tasso, and Scaliger) who proposed that the poet or "maker" does not imitate God's world, but like the God of Genesis creates his own world, and, it was sometimes suggested, *ex nihilo*, "out of nothing." Against contemporary charges that the poet's fictions are lies, the main line of defense in England, as in Italy, was the claim that poets teach by example, through shaping amoral reality to fit a moral ideal. But Sir Philip Sidney further glorified poetry above all other human achievements by the claim that the poet alone among productive thinkers is not tied to nature, but "lifted up with the vigor of his own invention, doth grow in effect into another nature," when "with the force of a divine breath he bringeth things forth far surpassing her doings" (*Defense of Poesie*); to which Puttenham added that if poets be able to "make all these things of themselves, without any subject of verity," then "they be (by manner of speech) as creating gods" (*Art of Eng. Poesy*).

The concept of the poet as a creator continued to be echoed rather casually by critics for the next century or so; its revolutionary possibilities for critical theory began to be exploited only when it became necessary to justify pagan myth and other forms of the supernatural against the powerful claim of Hobbes and other writers in the age of the "new philosophy" that, since poetry is "an imitation of human life," the poet may not go "beyond the conceived possibility of nature" (Hobbes, "Answer to Davenant"). By the mid-18th c. the Swiss critics, Bodmer and Breitinger, expanding on Addison's suggestive *Spectator* 419 on "the fairy way of writing" in terms taken from Leibniz's cosmogony, substituted the metaphor of creation for the metaphor of the imitative mirror. They proposed that the supernatural poem is a heterocosm, a second creation, and therefore is not a reflection of this world, but its own world, with its own laws and reason for being, in which probability is not a matter of correspondence to reality, but of internal coherence and compossibility. Rational truth, Bodmer said, we shall seek in the metaphysicians, "but demand from the poet only poetry; in this we shall be satisfied with the probability and the reason which lies in its coherence with itself" (*Von dem Wunderbaren*, 1740). Or as Richard Hurd, who also developed Addison's suggestions, said in explicit refutation of Hobbes, poetical truth is not philosophical truth, for "the poet has a world of his own, where experience has less to do, than consistent imagination" (*Letters on Chivalry and Romance*, 1762). By 1788 Karl Philipp Moritz, writing "On the Formative Imitation of the Beautiful," had expanded the Renaissance metaphor of a second creation, according to lines of thinking suggested by Bodmer, Breitinger, and the aesthetician A. G. Baumgarten, into a comprehensive objective theory of art. To Moritz, the energy of the artist "creates for itself its own world, in which . . . everything is after its own fashion a self-sufficient whole"; so that a poem, like all works of art, is a microcosm which "needs no end, no purpose for its presence outside itself, but has its entire value, and the end of its existence, in itself." In the course of the 19th c. Fr. critics developed the explicit theory of *l'art pour l'art*, building especially on Poe's doctrine of the "poem *per se* . . . written solely for the poem's sake" ("The Poetic Principle"), and on the concepts of Kant and his followers that beauty is purposiveness without a purpose beyond itself, and that the contemplation of beauty is "disinterested," indifferent to the reality of the object, and without regard to its utility. The common ground of the various doctrines classified as "Art for Art's Sake" is the concept that its claim to truth, its principles of order, and its values are bounded by the confines of the work of art itself; and that the end of a poem is not to teach, nor even to please, but simply to exist and to be beautiful. Such views were sometimes cast in the venerable metaphor of the poem as a world of its own. Pure poems, as A. C. Bradley said in "Poetry for Poetry's Sake" (1901), strike us as "creations," and the nature of poetry "is to be not a part, nor yet a copy, of the real world . . . but to be a world by itself, independent, complete, autonomous."

An objective theory of poetry, in one or another critical idiom and mode of reasoning, is proposed by many of the leading critics in our own day. The emphasis in Fr. pedagogy on the method of *explication de texte*, and

the theory and procedures of the movement known as "Russian Formalism," have focused attention on the study of the poem as such and developed methods for analyzing the internal relations of its elements. Since 1930 the kind of statement most widely approved, especially in America, is that a work of art is "autotelic," and that we must consider poetry "primarily as poetry and not another thing" (T. S. Eliot); or that the first law of criticism "is that it shall be objective, shall cite the nature of the object" and shall recognize "the autonomy of the work itself as existing for its own sake" (J. C. Ransom); or that the basic premise of critical theory is "the poem *qua* poem," the "poem as an object"; or that the essential undertaking of the critic is the "intrinsic" rather than the "extrinsic" study of literature (Wellek and Warren, *Theory of Literature*).

Current ways of conceiving the identity and constitution of the independent poetic object, however, vary greatly. Sometimes we find restatements of the old heterocosmic analogue; thus Austin Warren, in *Rage for Order*, says that the poet's creation is "a kind of world or cosmos; a concretely languaged, synoptically felt world, an ikon or image of the 'real world.'" The acute and learned Chicago Critics, while recognizing the validity and uses of an "integral criticism" which considers poetry in a broad context as sharing essential characteristics with other things, themselves prefer to advocate and pursue a "differential criticism" which deals with the poem as such. They do so by expanding upon the Aristotelian method of taking a poem as a constructed artistic whole, having a particular "working or power," whose elements and structure are analyzable in terms of internal causes which are analytically separable from extra-artistic causes in the particular nature of an author, his audience, or the state of the language he inherits ("Introduction," *Critics and Criticism*, ed. R. S. Crane). The commonest approach, however, and the one characteristic of most of the New Critics, has been to proceed on the assumption that poetry in the large (with little or no attention to different kinds of poems) is a special mode of discourse, which is isolated and defined by positing for the language of poetry a set of attributes which are the contraries of the abstract, literal, and conceptual nature, the empirical claims, and the practical purpose of the language of "science." Poetry thus becomes a universe of discourse, rather than a represented physical universe of things, people, and events; and the integrity of poetry, so conceived, is often jealously guarded by prohibitions against the "personal heresy" and the "intentional fallacy"—reference to the temperament, state of mind, and purpose of the author—and against the "affective fallacy" —reference to the responses of the reader. This type of theory has been accompanied by the revival, after the romantic revolt against it, of an *ars poetica*, or the conception of poetry as a craft of making which involves a knowing application of techniques, conventions, and traditions toward a foreseen end; the end, however, is no longer the Horatian effect on the reader, but the poem itself as a perfected object, or a self-sufficient "structure of meanings."

The objective theory of the New Critics separates itself off in various ways from the theory of Art for Art's Sake, despite obvious similarities in provenience and formulation. For one thing, it replaces the mainly impressionistic criticism of the earlier theorists with a formidable apparatus for the explication of individual poems as a totality of "logical structure" and "local texture" (Ransom), or of multiple tensions in equilibrium (Tate), or of ambiguities, ironies, paradoxes, and image patterns (Brooks). For another thing, it undertakes to rescue the poem as poem from the claim that its sole function is a beautiful inutility, by engaging it with our ordinary moral consciousness and experience of life.

The common procedure of Cleanth Brooks, R. P. Warren, J. Wilson Knight, and many others is to posit a "theme" as the organizing principle of any poem which is better than merely trivial—a theme which is sometimes treated as a Jungian "archetype" shared with myths, dreams, and religious visions, but is often (in despite of caveats against the "heresy of paraphrase") formulated as a moral maxim or general philosophical proposition. This revived moral treatment of poetry is put, not in pragmatic terms, as the construction of exemplary characters and actions, nor in expressive terms, as the poet's projection of his criticism of life (Matthew Arnold and Yvor Winters), but in objective terms, as an isolated thesis or set of values which are embodied and dramatized in the poem's evolving meanings, imagery, and "symbolic action," and is to be judged by such tests as "seriousness," "maturity," "profundity," and the subtlety and complexity of "moral awareness." (See e.g., the writings of F. R. Leavis, and Brooks's "Irony as a Principle of Structure"). As W. K. Wimsatt warns us in *The Verbal Icon*, "neither the qualities of the author's mind nor the effects of a poem upon a reader's mind should be confused with the moral quality of the meaning expressed by the poem itself." Finally, a number of critics, including Blackmur, Ransom, Tate, and Wimsatt, oppose to the view of Art for Art's Sake, as well as to the positivist's claim that valid knowledge is the sole preserve of science, the insistence that poetry is "cognitive," and yields

us a "special, unique, and complete knowledge" (Allen Tate, "The Present Function of Criticism"). This would appear to be a revived mimetic view of poetry, and some of Ransom's statements seem also to bespeak for poetry a truth of simple correspondence to the real world; a poet's imagery, e.g., "is probably true in the commonest sense of true: verifiable; based on observation" (*The World's Body*). But Ransom also sets out to preserve "the autonomy of the work as existing for its own sake," and it eventuates that the particularity and "irrelevancies" of the poem as object are merely a salutary reminder-by-analogy that the world's body is "denser and more refractory" than the "docile and virtuous" world pictured by science (*The New Criticism*). Even more clearly in other cognitive theorists, what we get to know in reading the poem turns out to be the poem itself; as Tate says, "it is sufficient that here, in the poem, we get knowledge of a whole object" ("Literature as Knowledge"). And as in the earlier objective theory of the poem as a heterocosm, or "second nature," the mimetic truth of correspondence to the external world tends to be reinterpreted as a truth of coherence, or of internal relations coterminous with the poem. Thus W. K. Wimsatt, in *The Verbal Icon*, undertakes to defend the double thesis that literature is "a form of knowledge," and that "the verbal object and its analysis constitute the domain of literary criticism." Poetry "achieves concreteness, particularity, and something like sensuous shape" by "the interrelational density of words taken in their fullest, most inclusive and symbolic character. . . . It has an iconic solidity." A poem is therefore not a mirror of the world, but is thickened by multiple internal relationships into an object which is itself physical and dense, hence merely isomorphic with the world to which it stands in the relation of an icon, or analogue: "The dimension of coherence is . . . greatly enhanced and thus generates an extra dimension of correspondence to reality, the symbolic or analogical."

This classification of poetic theories, through the limitations imposed by its own premises, is not complete. Some theories of poetry bring into the center of the scheme what the older and major lines of critical development which have been listed here recognized, but left peripheral. For example, sociological critics from Thomas Blackwell, *Enquiry into the Life and Writings of Homer* (1735), through Taine, V. L. Parrington, and the Marxist critics, regard the materials and values of a literary work as determined in large part by the geographical, social, economic, and political conditions of its time and place, whether these enter a poem through the contemporary scene that is imitated, or by adaptation to the assumptions and prejudices of the audience that is addressed, or as a precipitation of collective and superpersonal ideas and forces for which the poet serves merely as a catalyst. Other critics, on the contrary, emphasize the degree to which any poem is the result of an evolving and self-perpetuating process of intrinsically literary forms, conventions, techniques, and artistic materials (Ferdinand Brunetière, *L'Evolution des genres*, 1898; Harry Levin, "Lit. as an Institution," *Accent*, 6 [1946]). And the unclassifiable Kenneth Burke deliberately experiments with a diversity of critical approaches to a poem. Simplified though this survey is, however, it reveals the remarkable multiplicity of seemingly conflicting theories of poetry, a phenomenon which in the last century has led to repeated attacks by adherents of critical impressionism against the validity and use of any systematic theory in the domain of art. The most recent and concerted attack of this sort has been launched by a group seemingly remote from the aesthetic impressionists: the philosophical analysts who take their departure mainly from the later lectures and writings of Ludwig Wittgenstein. A number of these philosophers deny the possibility of formulating any significant definitions of art and poetry, or any general theory in which these definitions play a part, on the grounds that such definitions are arbitrary, because there exists no procedure for deciding in favor of one or against another by empirical evidence or counter-evidence. Their conclusion is that traditional artistic theory is mainly a history of logical and linguistic mistakes and confusions, and that the only legitimate criticism is applied criticism, which is regarded as a set of verifiable statements about the properties of individual poems or works of art. (See e.g., *Aesthetics and Language*, ed. William Elton, 1954). Such "metacriticism," however, is founded on a radical misunderstanding of the function of theory in criticism. A valid poetic theory is empirical in that it begins and ends in an appeal to the facts of existing poems, but it is not a science, like a physical science; it is an enterprise of discovery, or what Coleridge called "a speculative instrument." Its statements are not to be judged by their empirical verifiability out of context, but by their function as stages in the total process of illuminating the qualities and structure of diverse poems. The definitions from which most theorists set out, for example—although some critics have thought that they were using these definitions to manifest the essence or ultimate nature of poetry—in practice have served as an indispensable heuristic device for blocking out an area of investigation and establishing a point of vantage; they have functioned also as a critical premise, or elected starting

point for reasoning about poetry and for developing a coherent set of terms and categories to be used in classifying, describing, and appraising particular poems. The diverse theories described in this article—however contradictory an excerpted statement from one may seem when confronted by an isolated statement from another—may in fact be alternative and complementary procedures for carrying out the critic's job of work, with each theory yielding its own distinctive insights into the properties and relations of poems. Criticism without a theoretical understructure (whether this is developed explicitly or brought in merely as occasion demands) is made up largely of desultory impressions and of unassorted concepts which are supposedly given by "common sense," but are in fact a heritage from earlier critics, in whose writings they may have implicated a whole theoretical system. And the history of criticism at the hands of its masters, from Aristotle through Coleridge to T. S. Eliot, testifies that the applied criticism which the impressionists and philosophical analysts applaud has been neither impressionistic nor *ad hoc*, but most telling when grounded on the general principles, concepts, and reasoning which constitute precisely what we mean by a theory of poetry.

D. Masson, "Theories of Poetry," *Essays Biographical and Crit.* (1856); J. E. Spingarn, *A Hist. of Lit. Crit. in the Renaissance* (1899); Saintsbury; Gayley and Kurtz; Bray; J. W. H. Atkins, *Lit. Crit. in Antiquity* (2 v., 1934) and *Eng. Lit. Crit.*, I, *The Medieval Phase* (1943); II, *The Renascence* (1947); III, *The 17th and 18th C.* (1951); Patterson; M. T. Herrick, *The Fusion of Horatian and Aristotelian Lit. Crit., 1531–1555* (1946); S. C. Pepper, *The Basis of Crit. in the Arts* (1946); S. E. Hyman, *The Armed Vision* (1948); Wellek and Warren; Crane, *Critics;* M. H. Abrams, *The Mirror and the Lamp: Romantic Theory and the Crit. Tradition* (1953; includes an expanded treatment of much of the material in this article); Crane; Wellek; J. P. Pritchard, *Crit. in America* (1956); Wimsatt and Brooks; B. Markwardt, *Gesch. der deutschen Poetik* (in 6 v., 4 v. completed, 1937–61); B. Weinberg, *A Hist. of Lit. Crit. in the It. Renaissance* (2 v., 1961); R. Foster, *The New Romantics, a Reappraisal of the New Crit.* (1962); B. Hathaway, *The Age of Crit., the Late Renaissance in Italy* (1962); Sutton, *Modern Am. Crit.;* R. Wellek, *Concepts of Crit.*, ed. S. G. Nichols (1963).

CONVENIENT ANTHOLOGIES OF POETIC THEORY: *Crit. Essays of the 17th C.*, ed. J. S. Spingarn (3 v., 1908-9); *Crit. Essays of the 18th C.*, ed. W. H. Durham (1915); *Eng. Crit. Essays, 19th C.*, ed. E. D. Jones (1916); *Kunstanschauung der Frühromantik*, ed. A. Müller (1931); *Elizabethan Crit. Essays*, ed. G. G. Smith (2 v.,

1937); *Lit. Crit. Plato to Dryden*, ed. A. H. Gilbert (1940); *Lit. Crit. Pope to Croce*, ed. G. W. Allen and H. H. Clark (1941); *Crit.: The Major Texts*, ed. W. J. Bate (1948); *Critiques and Essays in Crit., 1920–1948*, ed. R. W. Stallman (1949); *Crit. Prefaces of the Fr. Renaissance*, ed. B. Weinberg (1950); *Lit. Opinion in America*, ed. M. D. Zabel (1951); *The Achievement of Am. Crit.*, ed. C. A. Brown (1954); *Modern Lit. Crit.*, ed. I. Howe (1958); *The Continental Model, Selected Fr. Crit. Essays of the 17th C. in Eng. Tr.*, ed. S. Elledge and D. S. Schier (1960); *18th-C. Crit. Essays*, ed. S. Elledge (2 v., 1961); *Modern Fr. Poets on Poetry, an Anthol.*, ed. R. Gibson (1961).

See also: W. J. Bate, *From Classic to Romantic* (1946); Krieger; Frye.—*Modern Continental Lit. Crit.*, ed. O. B. Hardison, Jr. (1962); *Modern Crit. in Theory and Practice*, ed. W. Sutton and R. Foster (1963).   M.H.A.

POETRY AND FINE ARTS. See FINE ARTS AND POETRY. POETRY AND HISTORY. See HISTORY AND POETRY. POETRY AND KNOWLEDGE. See SCIENCE AND POETRY; MEANING, PROBLEM OF; POETRY, THEORIES OF (OBJECTIVE THEORIES); CRITICISM, FUNCTION OF (COGNITIVE THEORIES). POETRY AND MUSIC. See MUSIC AND POETRY. POETRY AND PHILOSOPHY. See PHILOSOPHY AND POETRY. POETRY AND RELIGION. See RELIGION AND POETRY. POETRY AND SCIENCE. See SCIENCE AND POETRY. POETRY AND SEMANTICS. See SEMANTICS AND POETRY. POETRY AND SOCIETY. See SOCIETY AND POETRY. POETRY AND TRUTH. See BELIEF, PROBLEM OF; MEANING, PROBLEM OF; CRITICISM, FUNCTION OF (COGNITIVE THEORIES).†

POLISH POETRY has its beginnings in the 12th c. with a religious hymn *Bogurodzica dziewica* (Mother of God and Virgin) which far surpasses anything else produced in Poland during the Middle Ages. It contains in its two oldest stanzas a plea to the Holy Virgin and to Christ. The style is sublime, simple, and expressive. The rhythmic structure is elaborate, the lines of varying length are two- or three-partite; rhyme is used both at the end of the line and internally. Analogies with medieval L. and Gr. hymns are discernible. During the 14th c. poetry of a religious character still prevailed. Among the works which have been preserved is *Pieśń o Męce Pańskiej* (Passion Song), the first work written in 13-syllable lines with a regular caesura after the seventh syllable. By the 15th c. we have both religious and secular lyrics but no epic poetry to speak of. In general, these poems do not yet constitute artistic wholes, but they do frequently contain sincere and moving passages. Among lyric poems should be mentioned *Żołtarz Jezusów* (Psalter of Jesus), whose structure is mostly syllabic bi-partite with the caesura after the seventh syllable, numerous Lenten and Easter songs, Christmas carols, etc. One of the few religious poems is the *Legenda o Św. Aleksym* (Legend of St. Alexis), based, however, on foreign sources. Secular love poetry is represented by several poems, but in this century it still is relatively poor. In general, Pol. poetry of the Middle Ages is thematically original only in part, shows a variety of metrical structure (between 5 and 13 syllables to a line) with a tendency to asymmetric lines and "grammatical" rhymes, often imperfect.

Humanism penetrated into Poland in the second half of the 15th c. and subsequently played a major role in Pol. intellectual life and literature. L. became the second language of the gentry both in writing and speaking, and L. antiquity absorbed them as much as their own past. By the middle of the 16th c. humanism had become a Pol. national trend. Outstanding poets and prose writers began to write exclusively or mainly in Pol. The "Golden Age" of Pol. literature came into being. The forerunner of this flourishing age was Nicholas Rey (1505–69), whose literary merit lies in prose. His poetry, imbued with didacticism, lacks creative imagination; his language is often clumsy and prosaic, although colorful and expressive. But he wrote exclusively in Pol., did original work reflecting contemporary Pol. life and considered literature his vocation. Among his poetic works are: *Krótka rozprawa* . . . (Short Discourse Between Three Persons . . . , 1543), which is a satire on the clergy and gentry, and *Wizerunek* . . . (The Portrait), a moral-didactic poem. Rey shows considerable invention in metric patterns; besides 8-, 10-, and 13-syllable lines we find such unusual structures as 14 and 15 syllables. Rhymes still have a primitive character with "grammatical" rhymes prevailing.

The glory of the 16th c. is Jan Kochanowski (1530–86), the greatest poet of the whole Slavic world at the time. An accomplished humanist, educated in Italy and France, he formed his "literary program" in accordance with the Fr. *Pléiade* and created a Pol. poetry imbued with the spirit of the ancients. Thanks to him, poetry in Poland became humanistic and national, ridding itself of medieval and early 16th-c. didacticism. Kochanowski was first of all an artist who sang "for himself and the Muses." Poetic genres cultivated by him are those known in ancient and classical literature: Anacreontic *Fraszki* (Trifles), Horatian *Pieśni* (Songs), *Satyry* (Satires), *Treny* (Threnodies), a tragedy in verse *Odprawa posłów greckich* (The Dismissal of the Greek Envoys), some epic poems, and a magnificent adaptation *Psałterz Dawidów* (The Psalter). All these genres acquire in his work a highly original character.

† In Supplement, see also POETRY AND THE OTHER ARTS; POLITICS AND POETRY; PSYCHOLOGY AND POETRY.

His "poetic world" is a world of deep universal feelings and thoughts; it reveals a balanced, humanistic mind, broad literary and artistic culture, and a noble and refined morality. His language is the tongue of the educated Pole raised to poetic dignity by new values of cadence, meaning, and suggestiveness. It is always "classical," lucid, and noble without exaggerated neologisms, but also without the commonplace and prosaic expressions still so frequent in Rey. Of fundamental importance is Kochanowski's merit in the field of versification. He established syllabic verse and the uniform full rhyme, and laid the foundation for the Pol. prosodic system. Kochanowski's lyric poetry influenced a number of poets both in the 16th c. and later. Among his contemporaries the most original and independent of his "pupils" was Mikolaj Sęp Szarzyński (1550–81), author of the collection *Rytmy albo wiersze polskie* (Pol. Rhythms or Verses). They contain love poems, reflective, historical, and religious poems, some of them in sonnet form. In the first half of the 17th c. we also have outstanding humanist poets: Mateusz Sarbiewski (1595–1640) who was known abroad as "the Christian Horace" for his L. odes and Szymon Szymonowicz (1558–1629) whose L. works also won him fame abroad. Among Szymonowicz's Pol. poems the finest are his *Sielanki* (Eclogues), some of which are indeed original and based on Pol. motifs.

The poetic production of the second half of the 17th c. is predominantly baroque in style. In this field Poland has a distinguished pupil of the It. poet Marino in Andrzej Morsztyn (1613–93), author of two collections of poems, *Kanikuła albo psia gwiazda* (Caniculum or the Dog Star), and *Lutnia* (The Lute). He excelled in brief compact forms, elaborate verbal combinations, striking comparisons and contrasts in depicting love and its nuances. There is also another, more local alloy of this baroque trend, characterized by a falling away from classical traditions in literary genres, careful structure, clear and noble style, strict versification. In the language, artificial loftiness is speckled with colloquialisms, even vulgarity, and Pol. with L.; complicated poetical figures and images, syntactic inversions, extravagant rhymes abound. One of the most popular genres was the historical epic; immense poems of 12,000 or more lines were written, attempting historical authenticity with little room for creative imagination. Such is the *Wojna chocimska* (War of Chocim), by Wacław Potocki (1625–96) and the *Wojna domowa* (Civil War) by Samuel Twardowski (1600–60). Another popular form was the collection of short poems, reflecting the life of the Pol. gentry in its various manifestations: Potocki's original *Moralia* and *Ogród* (The

Garden) and Wespazjan Kochowski's (1633–1700) *Niepróżnujące próżnowanie* (Unleisurely Leisure). Baroque-pastoral poetry is represented by Twardowski's dramatic idyll *Dafnis w drzewo bobkowe przemieniła sie* (Daphne Transformed into a Bay Tree), and also by a volume of love songs, *Roxolanki* (The Ruthenian Maidens), a work by Szymon Zimorowicz (1609–29), full of charm in depicting all the vicissitudes of love. Zimorowicz's style is close to that of Kochanowski, but his versification is quite original, having varied rhythmical patterns, lines of various length and internal rhymes. There were also some works of a satirical bent.

The first half of the 18th c. marks a decline in Pol. poetry; only a few works stand out above mediocrity. But the second half of the century witnesses a considerable renascence of intellectual life, including poetry. It is the period of Enlightenment influenced by Fr. literature and culture. Neoclassicism predominates; style again becomes pure, poetic images precise, structure careful; strict discipline in verse, rhythm, and rhyme is restored; mixing of different poetic genres is abandoned. Fables, parables, satires, epics and mock epics, epistles, descriptive poems, anacreontics, odes, eclogues, and occasional poems are the main genres cultivated. The old Horatian maxim of amusing and instructing through poetry triumphs without making poetic works artistically inferior.

The most representative poet of the period, and the greatest after Kochanowski, is Bishop Ignacy Krasicki (1735–1801). He wrote in most of the aforementioned genres and left true masterpieces in many of them. This applies especially to his fables and satires. The fables (two collections: 1779 and 1802) are, of course, in the traditional style (Phedrus, Lessing, and La Fontaine), but highly original in transforming known motifs in new forms. The compactness of their structure reaches its summit in 4-line fables presenting the essence of both characters and actions. The rhythmic pattern is either uniform (many 13-syllable lines) or varied; there are examples of syllabo-tonic structures, the caesura is strict, the rhyme full. His Satires (part I in 1799) are masterpieces of characterization, observation, subtle humor and wit. Among his mock epics the most amusing is *Monachomachia* (1778) directed by this talented bishop against the ignorance, laziness and drunkenness of monks. Of similar significance, although of much smaller output, is the work of Stanisław Trembecki (1735–1812). He also wrote fables, epistles, anacreontics (among them "obsceanas"), and descriptive poems. His fables are different from those of Krasicki in that they are generally longer and more elaborate in their treatment of known motifs. Another characteristic is that he does not shrink from using forceful and picturesque expressions drawn from everyday speech or from the peasant language. His imagination delights alike in strong and exuberant as well as subtle and refined phenomena.

Classicist sentimentalism expressed itself mostly in lyrics and eclogues. The finest love poems of the century were written by Franciszek Dionizy Kniaźnin (1750–1807), the most popular eclogues by Franciszek Karpiński (1741–1825). Neoclassicism in quite rigid form extended into the first decades of the 19th c. The main poets of this period are Kajetan Koźmian (1778–1856), Ludwik Osiński (1775–1838), Aloizy Feliński (1771–1820), and others. A variegated poetic activity, however, was developed by Julian Ursyn Niemcewicz (1757–1841). The kind of ballads he wrote linked with the incipient period of romanticism. There were other signs indicating a change in the literary atmosphere. The catastrophe of Poland's partition raised the emotional intensity of some poets, their religious and patriotic feelings and metaphysical longings (J. P. Woronicz). New trends penetrated into Poland from western Europe from the writings of Jean Jacques Rousseau, Chateaubriand, Klopstock, Lessing, Macpherson, Herder, Walter Scott and others.

The romantic period of Pol. poetry begins in 1822, the date of the publication of the first volume of poems by Adam Mickiewicz (1798–1855). He at once attained a position of leadership in the movement and subsequently made Pol. poetry of first importance among the Slavs. Between 1822 and 1830 he published a series of ballads which are on a level with those of Schiller and Goethe; two tales in verse, of which one (*Grażyna*) possesses a half-classical, and the other (*Konrad Wallenrod*) a highly Byronic character; two parts of a fantastic drama *Dziady* (Forefathers' Eve) combining folklore motifs with those of a "mad" romantic love; his masterpiece of this period, the *Sonety Krymskie* (Crimean Sonnets), marvels of descriptive lyricism; and a number of other lyrics among which religious poems occupy an important place. The importance of the majority of these works lies in the fact that they created genuinely Pol. romantic poetry in a language and verse that is in many respects unsurpassed. Mickiewicz's language has a truly classical clarity and conciseness even in his most romantic "flights." Artfully simple, it attains the highest poetic art by the infallible choice and placement of words and expressions and by endowing them with a new meaning. His versification enhances this quality; without ceasing to be traditional, it is highly original. Syllabic and syllabo-tonic meter is used, but there is immense variety in its adapta-

tion to various rhythmic patterns and in the distribution of accents. In *Konrad Wallenrod* alone the poet uses 5- to 13-syllable lines and creates the "Pol. hexameter" composed of 6 feet. Besides Mickiewicz, the first period of the Pol. "romantic school" includes several other young poets writing in a similar vein and cultivating similar genres (J. Słowacki, A. Malczewski, S. Goszczyński, B. Zaleski).

The second period begins after 1831 when the defeat of the insurrection against Czarist Russia caused the Pol. intellectual élite to emigrate, mostly to France, where they established the "headquarters" of Pol. poetry. Mickiewicz still dominates the scene. With his *Dziady* (Forefathers' Eve) part III, 1832, prized by George Sand above *Faust* and *Manfred*, he sets the tone for a new poetry imbued with patriotic and messianic elements and at the same time distinguished by an immense richness of styles, moods, and metrical forms. Mickiewicz' genius is revealed even more in an entirely different work: *Pan Tadeusz* (1834). An *epos* of the Pol. nation and the Pol. countryside presented against the background of the Napoleonic Wars (1812), it treats with Homeric care both great and small subjects, developing a multiform plot. The poetic language here reaches its summit of clarity and force; the meter is the traditional Pol. 13-syllable line with the caesura after the seventh syllable, modulated by varying main and secondary stresses:

Litwo! Ojczyzno moja! ty jesteś jak zdrowie;
Ile cię trzeba cenić, ten tylko się dowie.
Kto cię stracił. Dziś piękność twą w całej ozdobie
Widzę i opisuję, bo tęsknię po tobie.

Lithuania, my country, you are like health:
how much you should be prized only he can learn
who has lost you. Today your beauty in all its splendor
I see and describe, for I yearn for you.

Mickiewicz in exile shares the sceptre of poetry with three other poets: Juliusz Słowacki (1809–49), Zygmunt Krasiński (1812–59), and Cyprian Norwid (1821–83). Słowacki is the creator of the modern Pol. drama; his works embrace a rich variety of dramatic forms: the romantic-patriotic (Kordian), the romantic-legendary, the romantic-Greek (Lilla Weneda), the historic, the "realistic" (Horsztyński), the mystic (*Ksiądz Marek*—Father Marek) and an "antiromantic" comedy (*Fantazy*). In some of his late dramas, unfortunately unfinished (e.g., *Samuel Zborowski*), he went far beyond romanticism, realism, and even symbolism, approaching the modern antirealistic theater. He is also the author of tales in verse (*Podróż do*

POLISH POETRY

Ziemi Świętej—Journey to the Holy Land; *Beniowski*) and of over a hundred lyric poems, among them a number of masterpieces. His *tour de force* was his last (unfinished) poem, *Król Duch* (King Spirit), a unique combination of lyric and quasi-epic elements in an attempt to give a vision of the history of Poland conceived as the inner experience of a spirit incarnating the nation's soul. Słowacki's poetic art is romantic to the highest degree and at the same time outstrips romanticism and approaches symbolism and "surrealism." His language, far from Mickiewicz' simplicity, is unusual "by birth," full of ingenious and bold inventiveness, of amazing virtuosity in fusing sounds, colors and lights in images far more intense than the phenomena of reality. His metric forms range from 2-syllable to 15-syllable lines in numerous structural combinations, many of them entirely new, as, for instance, tonic lines which became common in Pol. poetry only much later. Equally rich and varied are his rhymes.

Of Zygmunt Krasiński's literary works those of the most lasting value are his visionary dramas, *Nie-Boska Komedia* (The Undivine Comedy) and *Irydion*. However, in lyric poetry as well, Krasiński occupied a position of importance and influence. His longer poem *Przedświt* (Pre-Dawn) and his *Psalmy przyszłości* (Psalms of the Future)—although there is more philosophy than lyricism in them—are a significant chapter in the development of the Messianistic trend in Pol. poetry. C. K. Norwid was one of the most original of all Pol. poets, self-inspired and independent of influences. His poetic world revolved around the most important problems of humanity, history, culture, and art. He expressed them in a wealth of forms: lyrics, epic poems, tragedies and comedies, aesthetical dialogues and tales. Lyric poems occupy the highest place among these genres. They are unique in objectivization and universalization of observations and experiences.

Norwid's devices are condensed to the utmost in grasping the essence of cultural processes and of great men (Socrates, Napoleon, Mickiewicz, Chopin, and others). They are no less successful in giving far-reaching perspectives to apparently average phenomena. Norwid's language is highly individual, elaborate, difficult, sometimes obscure in forging new expressions, but always forceful. His versification, e.g., his *Bema pamięci rapsod żałobny* (Funeral Rhapsody to the Memory of General Bem) is as rich as that of Słowacki.

Poets of this period who remained in Poland, cultivated patriotic and religious poetry (K. Ujejski) and various forms of lyrics and folk songs (T. Lenartowicz and K. Brzozowski). The reaction against romanticism in the sec-

ond half of the 19th c.—the epoch of "positivism" in Poland when prose predominated—found expression, too, in the poetry of Adam Asnyk (1838–97) and Maria Konopnicka (1842–1910).

The very end of the 19th c. and the beginning of the 20th c. brought a new trend in literature called "Young Poland." It was, in turn, a reaction against positivism and realism partly influenced by Fr. and Belgian symbolism and German "modernism." The trend begins with the poetry of Kazimierz Tetmajer (1865–1940), who is the most characteristic representative of "decadence" with its pessimism, agnosticism, cynicism, strong sensuality and hatred for bourgeois culture. Some of these attitudes appear also in the greatest poet of this period, Jan Kasprowicz (1860–1926), but through periods of Prometheanism, inner struggle, and religious crisis he develops to a serene acceptance of the world and its destinies. His verse, first oscillating between syllabo-tonic and tonic meter, finally takes the form of pure "tonism" which from this period on is the usual rhythmic pattern of Pol. poetry. Still bolder in introducing even definite irregularities, is the tonic versification of the leading dramatist of the period, Stanisław Wyspiański (1869–1907), a poet and painter of powerful imagination. The new drama he created combines elements of Gr. and Shakespearean tragedy, the romantic drama and the Pol. folk play. Gr. themes are treated in an original way, giving them a modern application, which is also the main motif of dramas dealing with the Pol. past and present. To his masterpieces belong *Noc listopadowa* (November Night), an impressive dramatic vision of the first night of the Pol. insurrection of 1830, where historical and fictitious characters mingle with mythological figures, and *Wesele* (The Wedding, 1901), a strong indictment of contemporary Pol. society attained by means of a "puppet" technique and fusing the world of men with that of ghosts.

To the younger generation belonged Leopold Staff (1878–1957), author of numerous volumes of lyrics. He broke with "decadence," shaping his manly, positive world-outlook in a rich variety of structure and versification. His work shows a classical command over his poetic material and an ability to crystallize it into concise objective images.

The twenty years of politically independent Poland (1918–1939) brought an important change in poetry. The "Skamandrites" (so-called after their organ *Skamander*), who dominated the literary scene during the first decade, felt free of any "duty" imposed by the nation or society; they wished to be "the poets of today" and to write the best verses possible. They enriched the language with urban and colloquial elements (like the It. and Rus. futurists) and with new and often startling images and metaphors. Their versification, without abandoning traditional syllabism and syllabo-tonism, held to the tonic line, becoming more complex and freer in rhythmic structure, rhymes, and assonances. To the outstanding representatives of this group characterized by the above common traits, but very divergent as individualities, belong: Julian Tuwim (1894–1954) distinguished by an unusual eruptive force of lyricism, mastery of language, and most daring, powerful, imaginative experiments in structure and versification; Antoni Słonimski (1895–) characterized by concentration, self-possession, discursive and rhetorical elements; Jan Lechoń (pseudonym of Leszek Serafinowicz, 1899–1956) the most "classical" and academic of the group in language and verse; Kazimierz Wierzyński (1894–), best known, perhaps, for his poems praising athletics and sport, but also for his serious reflective lyrics of perfect artistic balance; and Jarosław Iwaszkiewicz (1894–). More loosely affiliated with the Skamander group are: Kazimiera Iłłakowicz (1892–), highly original in imagination and "free" versification; Maria Pawlikowska (1895–1945) a master of brief, concise, epigrammatic forms; Władysław Broniewski (1889–1962) conservative but powerful in language and metric forms, revolutionary in social outlook; Józef Wittlin (1896–), author of inspiring *Hymny* (Hymns) and Stanisław Baliński (1899–), a sensitive lyric poet of deep patriotic tones. A more radical program advocated by the "avant-garde" group (Julian Przyboś, Czesław Miłosz, Adam Ważyk, Józef Czechowicz, K. I. Gałczyński, and others) was linked with futurism, expressionism, and surrealism. It was opposed to the "Skamander," and preached dismissal of traditional poetic language and versification. Since World War II some of these poets have worked in exile, others in the homeland. The younger postwar generation, including several gifted poets, tries to be lyrical and express the "new reality" of its country mostly in forms closer to the avant-garde than to the Skamandrite school. The most interesting and characteristic in this respect are the works of such authors as T. Różewicz, R. Bratny, S. Bieńkowski. The war experience of the young generation is perhaps best expressed in the works of T. Gajcy, Z. Stroiński (both killed in 1944) and K. Baczyński. Poets most freely experimenting with verse and even semantics are: M. Białoszewski, J. Harasymowicz, I. Iredyński, S. Grochowiak, W. Szymborska.

ANTHOLOGIES: *Polnische Klänge*, ed. L. Koppens (1922); *Moderne polnische Lyrik*, ed. L. Scherlag (1923); *Les Grands poètes polonais*, ed. W. Bugiel (1927); *Od Kochanowskiego do Staffa. Antologia liryki polskiej*, ed. W. Borowy (1930); *Antologia della poesia contemporanea polacca*, ed. S. Can and O. Skarbek-Tluchowski (1931); *Lirici della Polonia d'oggi*, ed. M. and M. Bersano-Begey (1933); *A Golden Treasury of Pol. Lyrics*, ed. W. Kirkconnel (1936); *Poètes polonais*, ed. P. Seghers (1949); *Anthol. of Pol. Poetry*, ed. M. Kridl (1957); *Five Centuries of Pol. Poetry, 1450–1950*, ed. and tr. J. Pieterkiewicz and B. Singer (1962).

HISTORY AND CRITICISM: I. Chrzanowski, *Historja literatury niepodległej Polski* (many ed.); K. Wójcicki, *Stylistyka i rytmika polska* (1919); J. Łoś, *Wiersze polskie w ich dziejowym rozwoju* (1920); J. Kleiner, *Juljusz Słowacki* (4 v., 1923–27); R. Pilat, *Historja literatury polskiej* (1926); J. Krzyżanowski, *Pol. Romantic Lit.* (1930); J. Langlade, *Jean Kochanowski* (Paris, 1932); B. Chlebowski, *La Litt. polonaise au XIXe s.* (1933); K. Czachowski, *Obraz współczesnej literatury polskiej* (3 v., 1934–36); "Dzieje literatury pięknej," *Encyklopedja polska* (1935–36); K. W. Zawodziński, *Zarys wersytikacji polskiej* (1936); F. Siedlecki, *Studja z metryki polskiej* (2 v., 1937); K. Wójcicki, *Rytm w liczbach* (1938); J. Krzyżanowski, *Od średniowiecza do baroku* (1938); K. Budzyk, *Stylistyka teoretyczna w Polsce* (1946); S. Furmanik, *Podstawy wersyfikacji polskiej* (1947); S. Szuman, *O Kunszcie i istocie poezii lirycznej* (1948); W. Borowy, *O poezji polskiej wieku XVIII* (1948); J. Kleiner, *Adam Mickiewicz* (2 v., 1948); M. R. Mayenowa, *Poetyka opisowa* (1949); M. Dłuska, *Studja z historji i teorji wersyfikacji polskiej* (2 v., 1948–50); S. Łempicki, *Renesans i humanizm* (1951); A. Ważyk, *Mickiewicz i wersyfikacja narodowa* (1951); *Adam Mickiewicz, A Symposium*, ed. M. Kridl (1951); J. Krzyżanowski, *Historja literatury polskiej. Od średniowiecza do XIX wieku* (1953); K. Budzyk, *Z dziejów Renesansu w Polsce* (1953); K. W. Zawodziński, *Studja z wersyfikacji polskiej* (1954); W. Weintraub, *The Poetry of Adam Mickiewicz* (1954); Z. Folejewski, *Studies in Modern Slavic Poetry* (1955); *Adam Mickiewicz in World Lit.*, ed. W. Lednicki (1956); M. Kridl, *A Survey of Pol. Lit. and Culture* (1956); *Poetyka: Zarys encyklopedyczny*, III. *Wersyfikacja*, ed. M. R. Mayenowa (1955–); K. Wyka, *Rzecz wyobraźni* (1959); W. Borowy, *O Norwidzie* (1960); M. Dłuska, *Próba teorii wiersza polskiego* (1962). M.K.; Z.F.

The death of Professor Manfred Kridl left the editors with only the first draft of the article on Pol. poetry. In his function as co-author of this article, Professor Folejewski has sought to preserve as much as possible the original plan as outlined by Professor Kridl. (Ed.)

POLISH PROSODY. See SLAVIC PROSODY.

POLYNESIAN POETRY. Poetry is integral to a Polynesian in his personal life from birth to death and in assemblies for organized entertainment or ceremonies of communal benefit. The value given to artful manipulation of language ensured that any individual, regardless of sex, age, or social position at birth, whether he lived in a large, populous, class-structured archipelago or a small, barren, informally organized atoll, could win social and material rewards through talent in memorizing and chanting old rhythmic formulas to control supernatural forces or in composing new songs or revising the ancient to fit new occasions. Cultural changes following European discovery of this originally nonliterate area have not destroyed native appreciation of creative verbalization nor imitation of established rhythmic models.

Cultural and linguistic homogeneity is sufficiently marked, despite inter-island diversity, to designate Polynesia a distinctive culture area of the Pacific, extending south of the Tropic of Cancer and except for New Zealand and Ellice Islands east of the 180th meridian. Westward in Melanesia and Micronesia are scattered Polyn. enclaves. Northernmost in Polynesia is the Hawaiian Islands, now the fiftieth state of the United States; the old native culture and language, including the style and content of narrative art, show it unquestionably related to the rest of Polynesia.

Poetry is inseparably entwined with ritual acts and dances to maintain traditional knowledge and to harmonize man with innumerable divine beings who ranged from departmentalized, creative gods to personal guardian spirits and with the latent impersonal supernatural force (*mana*) found throughout the universe and in varying degrees in human beings.

The Hawaiian *Kumulipo* (Source of Profundity) exemplifies a complex genealogical prayer chant (a genre called *ku'auhau*, pathway-lineage). It belonged to the family of Kalakaua and his sister Liliuokalani, 19th-c. rulers of the Hawaiian monarchy established after European discovery when their relative Kamehameha I conquered and politically united the archipelago. The *Kumulipo* may have been the temple prayer (*pule heiau*) recited, in some parts by one priest and in others by two priests in concert, during the ceremony for Captain James Cook, presumably to consecrate him as the god Lono returned to Hawaii.

Its more than 2,000 words, half of which are genealogical pairs, were a magical charm to vivify the *mana* in the individual, usually a first-born child, whose genealogy it was. Each name conducted power, like an electrical charge, and glorified the child's kinship to earthly ancestors and to those among demigods, gods, and parent-pairs symbolic of phenomena evolving during genesis, first in the era of primeval darkness and then in the era of light. The individual becomes one with the universe and its divine principle as priests intone strongly, clearly, with carefully controlled breathing and stylized vibrations of tones, the words, in which a single error or hesitation destroys the power. Compositional mechanics, serving mnemonic, magical, and aesthetic needs, include quick, mental word associations based on identities and antitheses running in groups, often with the last word or syllable suggesting the name heading the next group. The family's master poet (*haku mele*) with assistants incorporated allusive phrases and adjectives about ancestral deeds to shape a poetic encyclopedia of philosophy, cosmogony, and family tradition for the individual setting forth on the winding pathway of his lineage. An inner meaning (*kaona*) is that the cosmogonic beginnings are analogous to the sacred child's conception and birth.

Although Liliuokalani credited the poem to the poet Keaulumoku and dated it as A.D. 1700, more than likely it was only the last revision of an ancient composition, because, except for the more recent genealogy, much of the content as well as the style, is widely distributed in Polynesia as part of the shared traditional art of the area.

The following lines illustrate ancient poetic style although the version of the Hawaiian creation chant in which they occur was recorded in the mid-19th c., the time of the monarchy, by educated, Christianized Hawaiians who apparently reinterpreted the events in the light of their Biblical knowledge. These lines tell of the rising waters of the flood sent by the god Kane to destroy evil mankind.

> E ala, e ka ua, e ka la, e ka po,
> E kaiko'o, e ka pohu,
> E ka ohu kolo i uka,
> E ka ohu kolo i kai,
> Kai wahine, kai tane, e,
> Kai pupule, kai ulala,
> Kai pili'aiku,
> Ua puni ho'i na moku i ka wai.

> Awake, O rain, O sun, O night,
> O rough sea, O calm sea,
> O mists creeping inland,
> O mists creeping seaward,
> O feminine sea, masculine sea,
> Mad sea, delirious sea,
> Surrounding sea!
> The islands are surrounded by the sea!

(*Moolelo o Hawaii*. Ms. by S. M. Kamakau, tr. by M. W. Beckwith and M. K. Pukui.)

Anyone might compose a favorite Hawaiian form, the "name chant," to honor another person, and have it performed at the graduation ceremony of a hula troupe, trained in a school where it observed taboos to ensure concentration and dedication to gods of the art. Special schools for secular and religious knowledge, with emphasis on learning chants, existed in many archipelagoes. Young people also learned as members of informal troupes of traveling entertainers or in choruses required in religious ceremonies. Entrepreneurs, often poets themselves, men or women, were employed by families wishing to hold a festival to commemorate the dead or honor the living. Entrepreneurs with fellow poets composed and assembled chants, determined the rhythms and dances for their performance, and coordinated their preparations with the craftsmen and farmers who had their special duties for the festival. Chant specialists became a distinctive, well-paid, honored class in many islands. Marquesan tribes had master chanters, really masters of ceremonies, who alone could recite the initial parts of cosmogonic chants, essential to the completion of any important production, whether house or canoe, in order to link new creation with old. Craftsmen, whose knowledge of chants connected with their work was as important as their manual skill, knew the less sacred portions.

Insulting chants were often institutionalized. Rival bards engaged in traditional contests to exhibit their learning and skill and to mock their competitors. Audiences took sides, shouting belittling songs at each other and eulogies to their poets. In Pukapuka, three villages traditionally faced each other before the entire population for one whole day in a festival period to chant and dance insulting chants, some old, some new, until aggression was spent and competitors fell into each other's arms.

Everywhere women participated in composing and presenting poems, but fear of the magic of their sex excluded them from the most sacred ceremonies. No woman could be a master chanter in the Marquesas. Hawaiian poets, male and female, ascribed to Hiiaka, younger sister of the volcano goddess Pele, many of their own poems. Hiiaka, traveling through the archipelago on a mission for Pele, poured her lyric talent, so the tradition goes, into poems about her moods, her adventures, the people she met, the landscape, and the weather. In New Zealand, women's poems kept alive the memory of old insults in order to incite men to take revenge.

Objective analysis of Polyn. poetic style in terms of its own language and culture has scarcely begun. Finding a hundred different terms for poetic genres is easy in any archipelago. Defining with assurance the style and typical content of even one is impossible. Conscious organizational structure is apparent as in certain Mangaian poems, each with an introduction, a foundation, offshoots, and a conclusion, and each poem for a festival fitted into a set of different but complementary genres. Meaning, the poets say, is important. Many poems have inner meanings but the key to the symbolism is held by the poet and his immediate circle. Meter when evident seems entirely accidental. Rhyming of final letters or syllables in phrases or lines is sometimes accidental too because of the character of the language and sometimes deliberate, especially in western Polynesia. Poets or entrepreneurs add meaningless vocables according to their inner ear's determination of which vocables are "good" in each instance. Poets have not formulated their standards and compositional mechanics in rules, nor do they seem able to verbalize on why certain phrases or lines are "good" and worth using generation after generation. It is much easier to compose a new poem than to explain the old.

Collections of texts of chants, most of them with translations and accompanying ethnographic discussion, appear in most of the ethnographical bulletins, special publications, and memoirs of the Bernice P. Bishop Museum (Honolulu) and in the journals and memoirs of the Polyn. Society (New Zealand). Bishop Museum publications of special interest include vols. IV, V, and VI of the *Memoirs,* and nos. 8, 9, 17, 29, 34, 46, 69, 95, 109, 127, 148, 157, and 183 of the *Bulletins.* Of Polyn. Society. *Memoirs* see especially V. III and IV, and no. 1 in the Maori Texts series. A key to bibliog. on native narrative art is provided in "Survey of Research on Polyn. Prose and Poetry," by K. Luomala, JAF, 74 (1962).

See also W. W. Gill, *Myths and Songs from the South Pacific* (1876) and *Historical Sketches of Savage Life in Polynesia; with Illustrative Clan Songs* (1880); N. B. Emerson, *Unwritten Lit. of Hawaii: Sacred Songs of the Hula* (1909; Bureau of Am. Ethnology. *Bulletin* 38) and *Pele and Hiiaka* (1915); M. W. Pukui, "Songs (Meles) of Old Ka'u, Hawaii," JAF, 62 (1949); M. W. Beckwith, *The Kumulipo, a Hawaiian Creation Chant* (1951); S. H. Elbert, "Hawaiian Lit. Style and Culture," *Am. Anthropologist,* 53 (1951) and "Symbolism in Hawaiian Poetry," ETC, 18 (1962); K. Luomala, *Voices on the Wind, Polyn. Myths and Chants* (1955). K.L.

POLYPHONIC PROSE. The name given by Amy Lowell to a form she invented; from a foundation in the "long, flowing cadence" of oratorical prose, it reaches over into "cadenced verse" (her term for *vers libre*) and even metrical verse. The emphasis is on "absolute adequacy of manner to thought"; the determining factors (which distinguished this poetic art form from prose) are "taste and a rhythmic ear." Miss Lowell conceived her form upon reading the *versets* (q.v.) of Paul Fort; but whereas Fort uses the alexandrine as theme for his formal variations, she found its Eng. equivalent, blank verse, so insistent as to make easy slipping into and out of it impossible. Yet "to depart satisfactorily from a rhythm it is first necessary to have it," and this, presumably, is where taste and the rhythmic ear come in. Miss Lowell finds the typographical arrangement of prose "far from perfect," but apologetically admits to not having evolved a better one. Amy Lowell's polyphonic prose appeared first in the volume *Can Grande's Castle* (1918), from whose preface the above quotations are taken. The form had a brief vogue and a few imitators; it differs little, actually, from poetic prose as practiced through the ages: every formal element of *Can Grande's Castle* was used more effectively by Lautréamont, for example, half a century earlier.—Norden (showing the ancientness of Miss Lowell's "invention"); A. Lowell, "Paul Fort," *Six Fr. Poets* (2d ed., 1916); A. Cherel, *La Prose poétique française* (1940; showing that any number of writers wrote "polyphonic prose" without knowing it); P. F. Baum, *The Other Harmony of Prose* (1952; a more recent discussion of rhythm in prose—polyphonic or otherwise). J.S.

POLYRHYTHMIC. A poem composed of lines having different kinds of metrical or rhythmic patterns. Pindar's odes frequently are of this order, as are Cowley's *Odes* in Eng. and modern free verse. Variety is emphasized rather than balance or repetition. R.A.H.

POLYSCHEMATIST (Gr. "of many forms"). Term applied, with respect to Gr. lyric verse, to an octosyllabic dimeter in which each of the first 4 syllables may be either long (with resolution [q.v.] as a later development) or short, while the remaining 4 regularly form a choriamb ($- \cup \cup -$).—J. W. White, *The Verse of Gr. Comedy* (1912). R.J.G.

POLYSYLLABIC RHYME. See MULTIPLE RHYME.

POLYSYNDETON (Gr. "much compounded"). The repetition of conjunctions; the opposite of asyndeton (q.v.), which is the omission of conjunctions; common in all kinds of poetry. Quintilian remarks that "The source of them [both figures] is the same, as they render what we say more vivacious and energetic, exhibiting an appearance of vehemence, and of passion bursting forth as it were time after time," citing to illustrate p.: "Both house, and household gods, and arms, and Amyclaean dog, and quiver formed of Cretan make" ("Tectumque

laremque," etc.—Virgil, *Georgics* 3.344-45; Quintilian, 1st c. A.D., *Institutes of Oratory* 9.3.51-54). It should be observed that the effect of headlong momentum here illustrated is traceable to the repetitions *as such* only in cases where the last conjunction alone would be needed for a cool prose statement (the earlier ones thus calling attention to themselves) and that the recondite term p. had best be applied only to cases of this kind. By this rule it would be hard to find a true p. in Eng. involving any conjunction except "and" (e.g., in Sonnet 66 Shakespeare begins 10 of the 14 lines with "and"). Other repeated conjunctions, e.g., "or" or "nor" (as in the last of the Ten Commandments), being practically indispensable for mere clarity, convey *in themselves* no specially urgent effect. H.B.

PORSON'S LAW (or Porson's Canon). A rule of Gr. metric discovered by Richard Porson, an Eng. philologist (1759-1808), and explained in the supplement to the preface to his second edition of Euripides' *Hecuba* (1802): when a tragic trimeter (q.v.) or trochaic tetrameter catalectic (q.v.) ends in a cretic (q.v.) formed by one or more words, the syllable preceding the cretic is regularly short unless elision intervenes or unless the first syllable of the cretic is an enclitic which of course belongs metrically to the word before it (likewise a long proclitic monosyllable such as an article or preposition may stand before the final cretic word to which in fact it belongs). For example, Euripides' trimeter verse (*Hecuba* 343), which ends in *prosōpon toumpalin* ($\cup - - - \cup \stackrel{\cup}{\sim}$) must be emended to read *prosōpon empalin* ($\cup - \cup \cup \stackrel{\cup}{\sim}$), in so far as the syllable preceding a final cretic (of *one* word)—e.g., *empalin* ($- \cup \stackrel{\cup}{\sim}$)—must be short (normally it is anceps [see SYLLABA ANCEPS]) if it is part of a polysyllabic word—e.g., *prosōpon*. In other words, P.L. is not applicable to a line which does not end with a true cretic. P.L. is no longer considered absolute, since exceptions to it have been found in many cases.—*Euripidis tragoediae*, ed. R. Porson I (1807); recension by J. Scholefield (2d ed., 1829) pp. 27ff.; K. Witte, "Porsons Gesetz," *Hermes*, 49 (1914); Hardie; L. Laurand, *Manuel des études grecques et latines*, III (1946); K. Rupprecht, *Abriss der griechischen Verslehre* (1949); "Metre, Gr.," *Oxford Cl. Dict.* (1949); Koster; J. Perret, "Un équivalent latin de la loi de Porson," *Hommages à Léon Herrmann* (1961). R.A.S.

PORTUGUESE POETRY. Port. literature has its origins in the *cantigas* which arose in Galicia toward the end of the 12th c. In the earliest period Galician and Portuguese poetry cannot be satisfactorily separated (see GALICIAN POETRY). Gradually the center of gravity of this common poetry moves south with more and more identifiable Port. names among the *trovadores* (troubadours of upper classes), *segreis* (lower-born, paid composers), and *jograis* (minstrels or musicians of humble birth) represented in the three great *cancioneiros* (see CANTIGA). Although these collections contain much monotonous verse revealing poverty of ideas and highly conventional vocabulary, there are poetic gems of clearly personal inspiration and technical perfection, especially among the *cantigas de amigo* based on indigenous folk *cossantes* rather than on Prov. types. Some of the better known Port. poets are Joan Zorro, Vasco Gil, Joan Soares Coelho, Airas Perez Vuitorom, Lourenço Jogral, King Diniz (1261–1325) with nearly 140 songs, and this king's natural sons Afonso Sanches and Pedro Conde de Barcelos. After the death of the most prolific of these poets, Diniz, the Galician and Port. languages gradually separate, as Castilian reduces Galician to the category of a patois, and the troubadouresque tradition declines.

Much of the poetry written during the 15th c. is contained in the *Cancioneiro Geral* (General Songbook, 1516) published by Garcia de Resende (1470?–1536) with compositions by nearly 300 poets. This court poetry shows greater metrical variety and more sophisticated form than the Galician-Port. compilations. Sp. influence predominates—some poems are in this language. (Indeed, most Port. poets from this time until the 18th c. are bilingual.) Much space is devoted to such trivia as poetic competitions, collective poems on ladies, petty satire, and poetic glosses of more social or sociological than literary interest. There are, however, Garcia de Resende's *Trovas* on the death of Inês de Castro; João Roiz de Castelo Branco's *Cantiga, partindo-se* (Song on Parting); the satirical work of Alvaro de Brito Pestana; Duarte de Brito who reveals some It. influence; and poets who were to become famous later in the 16th c. One of these, Gil Vicente (1465?–1536?), the father of the Port. theater, included in his popular drama many a lyric passage, *cantigas de amigo*, and other songs of medieval and folk inspiration in Sp. as well as Port.

Although Resende's *Cancioneiro* already shows some Italianate influences, it was Francisco Sá de Miranda (ca. 1481–1558) who after his stay in Italy (1521–26) introduced into Portugal the sonnet, *canzone*, Dante's tercets and Ariosto's ottava rima and many Renaissance features that characterized the *Quinhentistas* (poets of the 1500's). Sá de Miranda was a painstaking craftsman but the moral tone and formal innovations of his work are more important than its artistic qualities. His friend Bernardim Ribeiro (1482–1552), author

of a highly sentimental pastoral novel *Menina e moça,* favored bucolic poetry and wrote the first eclogues in Port. (*Jano e Franco,* etc.). This form was to be greatly exploited for the next century, perhaps most successfully in the longish *Trovas de Crisfal* by Cristóvão Falcão (1518–57?). The patriotic António Ferreira (1528–69), who boycotted Castilian, wrote a famous tragedy, *A Castro,* as well as superior sonnets, odes, and epistles in the classical mold but of little originality.

The Renaissance imitation of classical genres inspired Luis de Camões (ca. 1524–80), who not only wrote the greatest Virgilian epic of the Iberian Peninsula, *Os Lusíadas,* but is also the outstanding Port. lyric poet of all times. His *canções* and sonnets show a rare mastery of form and genuine inspiration:

Alma minha gentil que te partiste
tam cedo desta vida descontente,
repousa tu no ceu eternamente,
e viva eu cá na terra sempre triste!

My sweet soul who departed so soon,
discontent with this life,
rest eternally in heaven
and let me live always sad on this earth!

The Lusiads, in 10 ottava-rima cantos, is perhaps the most typically national of all epics. Although Vasco de Gama's memorable expedition to India (1497–98) represents the principal subject, the hero of the poem is not the great captain but rather the Port. people collectively. Historical events (the founding of the Port. kingdom, battle of Aljubarrota, death of Inês de Castro, etc.) and legendary ones (the "Twelve of England"), episodes from the voyage (the fictitious Island of Love) and, through prophecy, Lusitanian accomplishments of the 16th c. are all magnificently described. The mingling of pagan mythology and Christianity, prosaic lines, and abuse of classical allusions in this poem have been criticized, but they are amply compensated for by the grandeur of conception, wonderfully quotable lines, sincere Port. inspiration and patriotism, erudition, and reflections of the personal experiences of a very eventful life.

Other contemporaries still popular with anthologists are two brothers: Diogo Bernardes (ca. 1530–1605?) and Frei Agostinho da Cruz (1540–1619). The former had been chosen to write an epic on King Sebastian's Alcazar-Kebir expedition (1578), but after its disastrous outcome and his imprisonment he wrote religious verses and bucolic poems that show a sincere love for Port. nature in their descriptions of the Lima River. Frei Agostinho destroyed his profane verse but left behind in his hermitage some profoundly religious songs inspired by divine mysteries and the contemplation of nature and mankind.

The 17th c. could not but represent an anticlimax. Literarily its chief distinction lies in the great prose that contributed to the development of the modern Port. language. The poetry, much of which was collected in the 5-vol. *A Fénix Renascida* (1716–28), suffered from excesses inspired by Sp. Gongorism and *culteranismo* (see CULTISM). Francisco Rodrigues Lobo (1580?–1622), however, continued the Ribeiro tradition with simple, gentle yet colorful eclogues. Sóror Violante do Céu (1601–93), a Dominican nun, was much admired for her ingenious conceits combined with mystic fervor, occasionally in a somewhat incongruous fashion. Francisco Manuel de Melo (1608–66), a polygraph in both Castilian and Port., is better in prose, but has left eclogues and epistles of technical excellence. Throughout the century there were many epics of varying literary merit, but all overshadowed by Camões' work. Perhaps in no other country has such a large part of national poetic effort gone into the production of epics.

The best poetry of the 18th c., particularly from the second half, is produced by Arcadians who represented a rejection of the Sp. influence of the 17th c. in favor of Fr. neoclassicism. The poetry from this period that is still remembered owes its reputation more to style and philosophical content than to its lyrical qualities. Many of the poets belonged to the "Arcádia Lusitana" (or "Acad. Ulissiponense," from 1756) or the "Nova Arcádia" (from 1790). Each poet adopted the name of a shepherd celebrated in antiquity, and often such pseudonyms became better known than the real names. Pedro António Correia Garção (1724–72), the "Portuguese Boileau," is remembered for his reforms and certain elegant poems such as *A cantata de Dido*. Nicolau Tolentino de Almeida (1740–1811) is the principal satirical poet, while the mock heroic *O hissope* by his contemporary António Dinis da Cruz e Silva (1731–99) is favorably compared with Boileau's *Le lutrin*. The most personal love lyrics of the century were written by a poet claimed by both Portugal and Brazil, Tomás António Gonzaga (1744–1810). His *Marília de Dirceu*, a lyric exception among many volumes of moralizing neoclassic verse of the age, has enjoyed exceptional popularity as demonstrated by the great number of editions (probably second only to Camões). This is due not only to its melodiousness and sincerity, but also to the poet's romantic personal tragedy: his involvement in the Minas Conspiracy in Brazil (1789) and subsequent exile to Angola, which frustrated his love for "Marília." Among the New Arcadians, José Agostinho de Macedo (1761–1831) attracted much contemporary attention by his irregular life, bitterly polemic and philosophic verse, and his immodest attempt to improve upon *Os Lusíadas*. Much more important was Manuel Maria Barbosa du Bocage (1765–1805), a bohemian whose life has given rise to many *piadas* (anecdotes) but whose production includes, among much that is trivial, contentious, satirical, and improvised, many sonnets of a perfection to be found only in Camões and Antero de Quental.

A transition to romanticism is provided by Francisco Manuel do Nascimento (1734–1819), "Filinto Elísio," who had great technical perfection and was considered the greatest poet of his time. The purity of his language was not influenced by 40 years of residence in Paris (Lamartine dedicated to him an ode *A un poète portugais exilé*), but he did turn toward romanticism in vogue there, thus stimulating Almeida Garrett's interest in the new movement. The Port. were further introduced to some of the newer Northern European writers by Coimbra mathematics professor José Anastácio da Cunha (1744–87) and by the "Portuguese Mme de Staël," Leonor de Almeida (Marquesa de Alorna, 1750–1839), whose abundant original verse and translations were, however, known only to a limited circle during her lifetime.

Romanticism in Portugal borrowed many features from France and elsewhere but represents a less spectacular break with the 18th c. than in other countries. Politically, events in Portugal tended to make its proponents patriotic and liberal. The beginning of the movement is usually dated from 1825 with the publication of *Camões*, an epic on the neglect of genius, by João Batista da Silva Leitão de Almeida Garrett (1799–1854). Almeida Garrett's neoclassic background, as a disciple of Filinto Elísio, prevented him from falling into romantic excesses frequent in other literatures. He contributed to literary nationalism with his collection of ballads, *Romanceiro* (1843). His best lyric verse, inspired by a late love affair, is contained in *Folhas caídas* (Fallen Leaves, 1853), ardent, elegant poetry among the best love songs in the language. He is more restrained, more modern than many contemporaries. His influence is similar to that of Sá de Miranda and his position in Port. literature has been compared with that of Goethe in German literature. With his interest in the national past, his politically liberal enthusiasms, his great versatility and mastery of all genres, Almeida Garrett personifies Port. romanticism, which thus comes as close to being a one-man movement as is possible. Contrasting with him in personality and works, Alexandre Herculano (1810–77) wrote his best poetry in *A harpa do crente* (The Harp of the Believer, 1838), imbued with an austere, Christian spirit reflecting the seriousness of purpose of the author. Herculano, best known for his histories and historical novels, is a master of the language but tends to produce more prosaic poetry than Garrett.

A third important Romantic, António Feliciano de Castilho (1800–1875), remained more apart from the political struggles and agitation of the time because of his blindness. He, too, began as a neoclassic and possesses formal perfection with occasional glimpses of inspiration. Usually, however, he must substitute mastery of language and patient craftsmanship for imagination and sensibility. His translations are excellent in both versification and style but are often excessively free.

Many of the "ultra-romantics" collaborated in the journal *O Trovador* (1844–48) under the direction of João de Lemos (1819–89), who tended to emphasize form over content. Others wrote for *O Novo Trovador* (1851–56) under the inspiration of António Soares de Passos (1826–60). Soares de Passos, a translator of Ossian, is characterized by an emotive melancholy and morbid imagination. Raimundo de Bulhão Pato (1829–1912) spent many years on a long poem *Paquita* (1866), which overly enthusiastic admirers have compared with Byron's *Don Juan*. Tomás António Ribeiro (1831–1901) is remembered for his patriotic *D. Jaime* (1862), which Castilho suggested might be substituted for *Os Lusíadas* in Port. schools! João de Deus (Ramos, 1830–96) combines some of the best features of the romantics with bourgeois sentiment and optimistic unselfishness. His effervescent *Campo de flores* (Field of Flowers, 1869, 1893) expresses best *o amor português*, fresh, chaste and simple love, described with the "vocabulary of a child and the syntax of a bird."

The reaction against Castilho, who had come to represent all that was trivial and traditional in romanticism, gave rise to the "Questão Coimbrã" (1865), a pamphlet war led by Antero de Quental (1842–91), Teófilo Braga (1843–1924), and other Coimbra students. Although they were interested in liberal political and philosophical ideas, they also were more fertile in genuine poetry. Antero's *Sonetos* are unique in Port. literature, presenting a diary of the poet's pessimism and his agonized struggle to attain a faith reconciling materialism and the spirit, a struggle that culminated in the poet's suicide. Teófilo Braga wrote verse illustrating his positivistic philosophy, but his principal merit lies more in his many literary studies and his compilations of *canções populares* and *romances* (folk songs and ballads). Abílio Manuel Guerra Junqueiro (1850–1923), reminiscent of Victor Hugo at times in his fiery rhetoric, attacks church and state in *A velhice do Padre Eterno* (The Old Age of the Eternal Father,

1885) and *A Pátria* (The Motherland, 1896), but shows some transition to symbolism in *Os simples* (1892) with episodes from the simple and virtuous life of country people. Also often iconoclastic and satirical, António Duarte Gomes Leal (1848–1921) has genial moments when he avoids the declamatory. José Joaquim Cesário Verde (1855–86) in the posthumous *Livro de Cesário Verde* has left a collection of increasing popularity. His chief quality is an adaptation of naturalism or realism to poetry, painting in concrete details the monotony of bourgeois life with some inclination to the unusual and grotesque.

Although literary schools, as can be observed above, tend to be less clear cut and rigid in Portugal than in other countries, António Cândido Gonçalves Crespo (1846–83), born in Brazil but Port. by education and residence, is clearly Parnassian. The clear, precise language, sculptural verses and rhythmic beauty of his *Miniaturas* (1870) and *Nocturnos* (1882) are outstanding. António Joaquim de Castro Feijó (1862?–1917), Parnassian in form, goes from irony to moving *saudade* (nostalgic longing). His *Cancioneiro chinês* (Chinese Songbook, 1890) uses Fr. translations in order to adapt gracefully into Port. old Chinese lyrics. António Nobre (1867–1900) lived and published his *Só* (Alone, 1892) in Paris and was quite familiar with current literary movements there, but is intensely Port. in his introspective subjectivity. His personal suffering is communicated with gentle sensitiveness and almost morbid *saudade*. Sebastianism, Port. folklore, a wealth of images, and metrical freedom lend to his work an enduring fascination. Fausto Guedes Teixeira (1872–1940) and Augusto Gil (1873–1929) may be compared in their tenderness and simple lyric qualities. José Duro (1873–99), however, tubercular like Cesário Verde and Nobre, gained notoriety with a work reminiscent of Baudelaire, *Fel* (Bile, 1898), full of despair and nostalgia inspired by a life that was ebbing away.

Some of the poets above display traits of Fr. symbolism, but usually Eugénio de Castro (1869–1944) is given credit for introducing this movement and Sp. Am. modernism to his fellow countrymen. Castro, who became the country's best known poet abroad, prefaced his manifesto to *Oaristos* (Intimate Dialogues, 1890). He advocated greater freedom of form, varied and often eccentric vocabulary, unusual rhymes, alliteration, and emphasis on the aesthetic and sensual rather than the social uses of poetry. Beginning as a refined and aristocratic poet for the élite, in *Horas* (1891), *Salomé e outros poemas* (1896), etc., he later became more restrained and national in such works as *Depois da ceifa* (After the Harvest, 1901) and *Constança* (1900). Camilo Pessanha

(1867–1926) wrote the delicate, Symbolistic *Clépsidra* (1920) and was enabled by his long residence in Macao to translate Chinese poetry.

Afonso Lopes Vieira (1878–1946), an admirer of João de Deus and the Port. classics, was not greatly influenced by current movements but strove for a literary nationalism in his numerous volumes, some of notable musicality. From Algarve in the extreme south of Portugal came João Lúcio (Pousão Pereira, 1880–1918) who has some admirable moments, especially when singing of his native region, but is uneven in style. Like Castro in his international repute, Joaquim Pereira Teixeira de Vasconcelos ("Teixeira de Pascoaes," 1878–1952) invented *saudosismo* to epitomize the Lusitanian genius, a melancholy and pantheistic solidarity with all things. His influence has been great on the traditionalist "Renascença Portuguesa" group that he gathered around him. António Sardinha (1888–1925) is a poet who represents both literary and political nationalism. Perhaps the most Port. of all poetesses was Florbela Espanca (1894–1930), "Sóror Saudade," whose reputation has continued to grow because of her personal tragedy, unfulfilled yearnings and despair that she expressed so well in her sonnets.

Mário Sá-Carneiro (1890–1916), despondent, eccentric, and finally a suicide, combined extraordinary inventiveness with traditional forms to furnish inspiration to the *Presença* poets. He had collaborated in the foundation of the Vanguard journal *Orpheu* (1915), but some of his most important poetry was published posthumously. The principal organ of the *modernista* movement was *Presença* (published 1927–40), of which the leaders were José Régio (pseudonym of José Maria dos Reis Pereira, b. 1901) and Fernando Pessoa (1888–1935). Pessoa was educated in South Africa and even wrote several volumes of Eng. verse. His dramatic versatility in dividing his production into four groups and adopting three additional names and personalities has raised questions as to the sincerity of his inspiration, but not as to his importance. His over-all impact on his fellow countrymen has been compared to that of Juan Ramón Jiménez in Spain. José Régio, poet, novelist, dramatist, and critic, is receptive to all forms of art and is independent in his thinking. The conflicts within him are reflected in his work, but he suggests no solution. *Poemas de Deus e do Diabo* (Poems of God and of the Devil, 1925) present dramatically and with verbal exuberance the conflict of good and evil.

Despite the increasing importance of the novel and short story in Portugal, such younger members of the *Presença* group as Casais Monteiro (b. 1908), Alberto de Serpa (b. 1906), Miguel Torga (b. 1907), and numerous other contemporaries of diverse orientation (cf. sample in Cabral do Nascimento's anthology *Líricas Portuguesas*, 2a. série) testify to the survival and continuation of the traditional predominance of (lyric) poetry over other literary manifestations. It is this poetry that made Bell say: "The claim that, with the exception of ancient Greece, no small country has produced so great a literature as Portugal may be a hard saying, but it can be justified."

ANTHOLOGIES: *Poems from the Port.*, ed. A. F. G. Bell (1913); *Portugal–An Anthol.*, ed. G. Young (1916); Antero de Quental, *Sonnets and Poems*, tr. S. Griswold Morley (1922); Eugénio de Castro, *Dona Briolanja and Other Poems*, tr. L. S. Downes (1944); Luis Vaz de Camoens, *The Lusiads*, tr. W. C. Atkinson (1952); *The Oxford Book of Port. Verse*, ed. A. F. G. Bell, 2d ed. B. Vidigal (1953); *Port. Poems with Translations*, ed. J. B. Trend (1954); *Líricas portuguesas*, 1a. série, ed. J. Régio (195-?); 2a. série, ed. J. Cabral de Nascimento (1945); 3a. série, ed. J. de Sena (1958).

HISTORY AND CRITICISM: T. Braga, *História da litteratura portugueza* (1896–, many v. in this series deal specifically with different phases of poetry); A. F. G. Bell, *Studies in Port. Lit.* (1914) and *Port. Lit.* (1922; Port. tr., 1931); *História da literatura portuguesa ilustrada*, ed. A. Forjaz de Sampaio *et al.* (4 v., 1929–42; lavishly illustrated, with bibliog.); F. de Figueiredo, *A épica portuguesa no século XVI* (1950) and *Lit. portuguésa* (3d ed., 1955; also available in Sp.); G. Le Gentil, *La littérature portugaise* (2d ed., 1951; the best brief introd.); H. V. Livermore *et al.*, *Portugal and Brazil, An Introd.* (1953; sections on lit., bibliog. of studies by E. Prestage and A. F. G. Bell and of tr. from Port. to Eng.); A. J. Saraiva and O. Lopes, *História da lit. portuguesa* (2d ed., 1957?); *Dicionário das literaturas portuguesa, galega e brasileira*, ed. J. do Prado Coelho (1960; entries on individual poets and works, versification, and movements); see also CANTIGA and GALICIAN POETRY.　　　　　　　　L.A.S.

POULTER'S MEASURE. A meter composed of rhyming couplets made up of a line of iambic hexameter followed by a line of iambic heptameter, thus: "Silence augmenteth grief, writing increaseth rage, / Staled are my thoughts, which loved and lost the wonder of our age." (Fulke Greville, Lord Brooke, *Epitaph on Sir Philip Sidney*.) Employed in the 16th c. by Wyatt, Surrey, Sidney, Grimald, and other Eng. poets, the meter derives its name from the poultryman's proverbial practice of giving 12 eggs for the first dozen and 14 for the second, noted by George Gascoigne in his *Steele Glas* (1576). Despite its temporary popularity, the meter has not proved a satisfactory one for sustained composition in Eng. It has a deadly tendency toward monotony, and the heavy stress accents native to the language lend it an effect of panting effort followed by ludicrous haste. Written out as an iambic quatrain instead of a couplet, a^3 b^3 c^4 b^3, the form persisted as the "short meter" (q.v.) of the Eng. hymns. —G. Stewart, *The Technique of Eng. Verse* (1930); C. S. Lewis, *Eng. Lit. of the 16th C.* (1954); J. Thompson, *The Founding of Eng. Metre* (1961).

PRACTICAL CRITICISM. See CRITICISM, FUNCTION OF.

PRĀKRITS POETRY. See INDIAN POETRY.

PRÉCIOSITÉ traditionally refers to several separable, though often confused, phenomena of Fr. history: polite society of the first half of the 17th c., literature of the same period, and certain traits of style associated with the period but not exclusively possessed by it. Besides, the word has, like "preciosity" in Eng., a general application, unconfined by time, to style and manners, and is taken to mean affectation and overingeniousness.

In reaction to the roughness of Court manners, the Marquise de Rambouillet retired about 1608 to her *hôtel,* or more precisely, to her *alcôve,* and for half a century gathered round her those who were concerned to purify both manners and literary style. Originally they drew their code and inspiration from the pastoral novel of Honoré d'Urfé, *L'Astrée,* which began to be published in 1607; and gradually they developed their own canons, which we know chiefly in the *Historiettes* of Tallemant des Réaux (not actually published till 1833–35), the enormous *romans à clef* by a rival, Mlle de Scudéry, and the *Dictionnaire des précieuses* (1660) of A. B. de Somaize. Though they were satirized notably by Molière in *Les Précieuses Ridicules* (1659), some frequenters of the Hôtel de Rambouillet helped to form the Académie Française (1635), which finally produced its dictionary in 1694.

Actually the only poet of consequence directly associated with *précieux* society was Vincent Voiture (1598–1648), whose works circulated but were not published until after his death. His elegant and casual sonnets and rondeaux made him one of the first and best composers of *vers de société.* Of greater achievement is a group of poets who are usually lumped together either as opponents of Malherbe or as *précieux.* Among them are Théophile de Viau (1590–1626), Saint-Amant (1594–1661), and Tristan l'Hermite (1601?–1655), whose reputations have been restored only recently in this century. In Théophile's ode *Le Matin,* for example, we note such possibly *précieux* details as the lion "herissant sa perruque affreuse," but also traits more generally baroque, such as the profusion of particularized images and a concern with the gradual passage of time.

It must be said that not only is there some confusion as to the scope of the word, but also there is the probability that it will be supplanted as a literary term by baroque. If *préciosité* is thought to be a universal phenomenon connected somehow with marinism and euphuism, its origins can be found in the Middle Ages and its extension can be traced to our own day. Its literary traits would be urbane wit, use of the conceit, artificiality, etc. If it is restricted to social history, it would apply to those works that reflect the cultivated taste of 17th-c. salons. If p. continues to be used of most early 17th-c. poetry, its scope must be widened to include the best as well as the narrowly "typical."—C. L. Livet, *Précieux et précieuses* (1856); E. Magne, *Voiture et l'Hôtel de Rambouillet* (1911, new ed., 1930); D. Mornet, "La Signification et l'évolution de l'idée de p. en France au XVIIe s.," JHI, 1 (1940); R. Bray, *Anthologie de la poésie précieuse de Thibaut de Champagne à Giraudoux* (1946) and *La P. et les précieux . . .* (1948); A. Adam, "Baroque et p.," *Revue des sciences humaines* (Lille), fasc. 55–56 (1949); O. de Mourgues, *Metaphysical, Baroque and Précieux Poetry* (1953). L.N.

PREGUNTA. The "p." or *requesta,* question, with the corresponding *respuesta,* answer, was a form of poetic debate practiced principally by the Sp. court poets of the late 14th and 15th c. One poet presented his question—often on such themes as morals, love, philosophy, or religion—in a poem, and another poet gave the answer in a poem of identical form, including the rhymes. Sometimes several answers were given in identical form and by more than one poet. Occasionally an answering poet was unable to follow the rhymes of the p. and might excuse himself for his substitutions.—P. Le Gentil, *La Poésie lyrique espagnole et portugaise à la fin du moyen âge.* 1e partie. *Les Thèmes et les genres* (1949); Navarro; J. G. Cummins, "Methods and Conventions in Poetic Debate," HR, 31 (1963). D.C.C.

PRE-RAPHAELITE BROTHERHOOD. A group of Eng. artists, organized in London in 1848 by Dante Gabriel Rossetti, William Holman Hunt, and John Millais. The P.R.B., as it came to be called, had as its aim the reform of the art of painting, away from academicism and toward the realism, sensuousness, and attention to detail which its members professed to find in It. painting before Raphael. However, since Rossetti, the leader of the group, was both a poet and a painter, as were several of its other members, the movement soon made itself felt in Eng. poetry. Indeed, Pre-Raphaelite painting was always distinguished by a strong literary flavor, both in choice of material and in technique. *The Germ*, the short-lived publication of the group, contained such poems as Rossetti's *The Blessed Damozel*, in which ardent medievalism as well as attention to pictorial detail expressed the aims of the Brotherhood.

Although the P.R.B. did not survive as an organized group beyond the early 1850's, it was effectively reborn as a literary phenomenon in 1856, when Rossetti met William Morris, whose artistic aims were roughly similar. Other poets to come under Rossetti's powerful influence included Swinburne, Coventry Patmore, and Austin Dobson. Rossetti's sister Christina ranks as one of the best poets of the Pre-Raphaelite school. Pre-Raphaelite poetry elicited strong reactions in Victorian England. Ruskin expressed admiration for the group in 1851, but Robert Buchanan delivered a violent attack on what he regarded as the eroticism of some of their work in 1871 in an article entitled "The Fleshly School of Poetry" (q.v.).

The antecedents of Pre-Raphaelitism, as a poetic style, are to be found in the It. poets of the 13th c., in Spenser, and, to a much greater extent, in some aspects of the work of the romantics—the sensuousness of Keats, for example, and the supernaturalism of Poe. Despite their professed aim of realism, the Pre-Raphaelite poets tended ultimately toward the creation of a poetic realm in which medievalism, musicality, and vague religious feeling combined to achieve a narcotically escapist effect. In some respects they anticipated the Fr. symbolists, although their movement had neither the profundity nor the importance of the later one.

In 1863, some fifteen years after the initial founding of the P.R.B., the *Society for the Advancement of Truth in Art* was organized in New York City. The members of this group, who never achieved the fame of their British counterparts, came to be called the "American Pre-Raphaelites," because of their adherence to the doctrines of Rossetti and Ruskin.

Ruskin: Rossetti: Preraphaelitism. Papers 1854 to 1862, arr. and ed. W. M. Rossetti (1899); W. H. Hunt, Pre-Raphaelitism and the P.R.B. (2 v., 1905–06); T. E. Welby, The Victorian Romantics, 1850–1870 (1929); F. L. Bickley, The Pre-Ralphaelite Comedy (1932); W. Gaunt, The Pre-Raphaelite Tragedy (1942); G. Hough, The Last Romantics (1949); D. H. Dickason, The Daring Young Men, the Story of the Am. Pre-Raphaelites (1953); H. M. Jones, "The Pre-Raphaelites," The Victorian Poets: A Guide to Research, ed. F. F. Faverty (1956); O. Doughty, A Victorian Romantic: Dante Gabriel Rossetti (2d ed., 1960); D. Hudson, "The Pre-Raphaelites," The Forgotten King and Other Essays (1960).   F.J.W.; A.P.

PREROMANTICISM. Those features of 18th-c. writing that reveal a turning away from neoclassicism are now commonly labeled "preromantic," although not all of them are important to romantic poetics or literature (e.g., middle-class drama). There are some preromantic elements in rococo poetry, but more appear in works of genres newly developed or undergoing radical modifications: the exotic or sentimental novel (Defoe, Prévost, Rousseau, Richardson, Goethe); bourgeois drama and nonmusical melodrama (Diderot, Sedaine, Mercier, *Sturm-und-Drang* [q.v.] playwrights); poetry of personal or individual observation (Brockes, Haller, authors of "Seasons") and experience (Günther, Klopstock, Goethe, Bürger, Chénier, Blake).

With its doctrines of progress and relativism and its view that experiment and individuality are desirable, the Enlightenment created an atmosphere favorable for the use of nonclassical mythology (Gray, Klopstock, and other Bardic poets); of primitive and exotic materials (the Noble Savage of Rousseau and others, the cult of the untutored poet in England and Germany); of forms and themes from popular literature (folk song and ballad, gothicism and medievalism, drama inspired by Shakespeare's histories, verse modeled after that of Hans Sachs); and for such novelties as prose idylls (Gessner), dialogue novels (Diderot), tragedies in prose or prose-and-verse (Lessing, *Sturm-und-Drang* writers), and unrhymed odes in Gr. meters and lyrics in free rhythms (Klopstock). By allotting an important place to feeling and the unconscious, and by ignoring large metaphysical issues and so perhaps abetting the spread of religious enthusiasm and crypto-mystic societies, philosophic speculation fostered sentimentality (*comédie larmoyante*, the sentimental novel and lyric) and sensationalism (gothic novel, much *Sturm-und-Drang* writing). The religion of Nature's God directly accessible to Human Reason permeated most religious and moral speculation; in the absence of special revelation it was widely held that Virtue subjectively felt could be objectively revealed only as feeling expressed, so that Deism, no less than such movements as Pietism and Methodism, favored sentimentality and irrational subjectivism.

Historical relativism led to the interpretation of Homer and the Old Testament as primitive or early national poetry (Young, Herder) and to the overvaluing of Ossian (Blair, Herder). With rural life thought to be closer to God-Nature than urban civilization, the idyll, sentimental or realistic, enjoyed wide popularity (Haller, Gessner, E. von Kleist, Thomson, Gray, Goldsmith, Cowper, Burns, Voss, Müller). Poetry of religious feeling, strongly reflective in tone, was given renewed life by Young, Klopstock and those they inspired. Anticlassicistic critical theories were expounded ever more vigorously (Bodmer, Breitinger, J. E. Schlegel, Gerstenberg, Lessing, Herder, Goethe, Young, Diderot, Rousseau, Mercier); in varying degrees these favored the "characteristic" as opposed to the "normative" or "ideal," so that novels of Lesage and Smollett, no less than Fr. and German plays consciously executed under their influence, may properly be considered preromantic. The concepts of the organic growth of national literatures (Herder) and of the organic structure of the work of art (Goethe) are also developed. Because the unique and the particular are considered valuable, literary language is enriched by neologisms (Klopstock), archaic forms (Chatterton), and dialectical or otherwise uncommon words (Burns, Goethe), especially in Germany, where Hamann and Herder demanded a revitalization of poetic speech.

An inept blending of disparate stylistic elements (e.g., realistic detail and neoclassical epithet; vulgarism and sentimental pathos; ballad form and insistent rhetoric) is evident in most preromantic writing. Not until conscious romanticism and its ironic self-awareness—Goethe's early works are important exceptions—does unity of tone or the successful harmonizing of dissimilar styles become general. Preromanticism is thus more than a breaking away from neoclassicism; it is a series of ideological and technical developments which effectively prepare for the triumph of romanticism (q.v.).

J. G. Robertson, Studies in the Genesis of Romantic Theory in the 18th C. (1923); P. van Tieghem, Le Préromantisme (3 v., 1924–47); A. Monglond, Le Préromantisme français (2 v., 1930); P. Trahard, Les Maîtres de la sensibilité française au XVIIIe s. (4 v., 1931–33); K. Wais, Das antiphilosophische Weltbild des französischen Sturm und Drang (1934); E. Bernbaum, Guide through the Romantic Movement (1938, 2d ed., 1949); E. Neff, A Revolution in European Poetry, 1660–1900 (1940); W. J. Bate, From Cl. to Romantic (1946); Wellek, I.; R. Ayrault, La Genèse du romantisme allemand (2 v., 1961). S.A.

PRIAMEL. Among the aphoristic poems composed by Germans from the 12th c. (Spervogel, Marner) to the 16th, the P. (L. praeambulum) occupies a niche of its own. A literary genre with "origins in many other ages and countries" (A. Taylor, The Proverb . . . , 1962, p. 179), it developed originally from epigram-

matic improvisation. Its special feature is that a series of seemingly unrelated and unconnected ideas or observations, taken from everyday life, are brought together, with a surprise effect, in the last line. The form is a kind of teasing and lends itself to humorous employment. It became very popular in the 14th-15th c., and the folk poet Hans Rosenplüt (15th c.) established it as a genre and composed a large number of Priameln. Several manuscripts containing such poems have been preserved, and the "Wolfenbüttel MS" was edited and published by K. Euling in 1908.— W. Uhl, Die deutsche P. (1897); K. Euling, Das P. bis Hans Rosenplüt (1905) and "P.," Reallexikon, II; C. Selmer and C. R. Goedsche, "The P. Manuscript of the Newberry Library, Chicago," PMLA, 53 (1938). B.Q.M.

PRIAPEAN. A measure consisting of a glyconic and a pherecratean (qq.v.), separated by a diaeresis. It was used by Anacreon and other amatory poets and is also found in dramatic poetry, especially the chorus of satyric plays. It was employed by the Alexandrian poet, Euphronius, to celebrate the god of fertility, Priapus, whence its name. In L. literature it is found in Catullus and the Priapea, e.g.,

$$\bar{O} \ C\bar{o}l\bar{o}n\breve{i}\bar{a} \ qu\bar{a}e \ c\bar{u}p\bar{i}s \ || \ p\bar{o}nt\breve{e} \ l\breve{u}d\breve{e}re \ l\bar{o}ng\bar{o}$$
(Catullus 17.1)

M. Coulon, La Poésie priapique dans l'antiquité et au moyen âge (1932); Dale; Koster, Crusius; V. Buchheit, Studien zum Corpus Priapeorum (1962). P.S.C.

PRIMITIVISM. A primitivist is a person who prefers a way of life which, when judged by one or more of the standards prevailing in his own society, would be considered less "advanced" or less "civilized." The primitivist finds the model for his preferred way of life in a culture that existed or is reputed to have existed at some time in the past; in the culture of the less sophisticated classes within his society or of primitive peoples that exist elsewhere in the world; in the experiences of his childhood or youth; in a psychological elemental (subrational or even subconscious) level of existence; or in some combination of these.

Primitivistic themes appear in almost all literatures: they are found in classical and medieval literature; in the late Renaissance, Montaigne, in his essay Des Cannibales, praises the happy and virtuous life of savages living close to nature; Pope envies the untutored Indian; 18th-c. interest in p. receives its fullest expression in Rousseau's pietistic doctrine of the children of nature; Wordsworth attributes superior wisdom to sheep-herders and children; Thoreau tells us that "we do not ride on the railroad; it rides upon us"; the poetry of Rimbaud is a record of defiance of Europe and dogmatic Christianity in favor of an Oriental "fatherland," which is his symbol of personal and essential reality; D. H. Lawrence makes a similar condemnation of Western civilization and advocates a return to an older mode of living based on a recognition of man's "blood nature." Primitivists have differed widely on the nature of the evils and weaknesses of civilized life, the causes of these evils, the positive values of the primitive life, and the degree to which a regression to the primitive is possible.

P. has also been used to support revolutions in taste and poetic theory. In the 18th c. Vico, Blackwell, Blair, Herder, and many other critics, in reaction to the rigidities of neoclassicism, admired the poetry of such "primitives" as Homer, the authors of the Old Testament, Shakespeare, Ossian, and the "peasant poets"; some of these critics held that the characteristics of this poetry (spontaneity, wildness, sublimity, free expression of powerful feeling) are the standards by which all poetry should be judged. Wordsworth's poetics reflects primitivistic tendencies in his recommendations concerning the proper subject matter and diction of poetry. Some contemporary theorists, influenced by modern psychology and anthropology, regard poetry (together with religion, myth, and ritual) as a reflection of primitive psychic activities. For example, some critics, following Jung, find the power and value of literature to consist in its effective presentation of archetypes, preserved in the racial memory of the collective unconscious, to which humanity must always return for spiritual renewal. Finally, the primitive is fully rehabilitated in the speculations of Coomaraswamy, Eliade, and other Perennial Philosophers: primitive art, which is the symbolic expression of metaphysical truths, is simply the "normal" or "traditional" art of all peoples everywhere; Western realistic and expressionistic theories of art, like Western civilization generally, are historical anomalies.

P. has had its disparagers, particularly among those who have committed themselves to a progressive view of history. Voltaire attacked Rousseau and other primitivists. In the 20th c. Babbitt sees p. as a form of escapism; in its "surrender to the subrational" it threatens the "overthrow of humanistic and religious standards"; it is no substitute for a disciplined intellect and will and a genuine social consciousness. Thus, the long historical debate between primitivist and nonprimitivist is part of the larger debate concerning the standards which determine the good life for man.

I. Babbitt, *Rousseau and Romanticism* (1919); C. B. Tinker, *Nature's Simple Plan* (1922); L. Whitney, "Eng. Primitivistic Theories of Epic Origins," MP, 21 (1924) and *P. and the Idea of Progress* (1934); H. N. Fairchild, *The Noble Savage* (1928); A. O. Lovejoy and others, *P. and Related Ideas in Antiquity* (1935); E. A. Runge, *P. and Related Ideas in Sturm und Drang Lit.* (1946); A. K. Coomaraswamy, *Figures of Speech and Figures of Thought* (1946); G. Boas, *Essays on P. and Related Ideas in the Middle Ages* (1948); M. Eliade, *The Myth of the Eternal Return*, tr. W. Trask (1954); J. Baird, *Ishmael* (1956).   J.B.; F.G.

PROCELEUSMATIC (Gr. "rousing to action beforehand"). A foot consisting of 4 short syllables ($\smile\smile\smile\smile$). It is derived, with respect to the iambic trimeter, from the resolution of the long in a dactyl, when it is called p. from thesis, or in the anapaest, when it is called p. from arsis (q.v.). It is seldom employed in Gr. lyric poetry or in tragedy and only occasionally in comedy, although in L. comedy it is fairly common, especially at the beginning of a senarius. In late tragedy it is used in dactylic *hyporchemata* and in dactylic monodies.—W. M. Lindsay, Early L. Verse (1922); Dale; Koster.   P.S.C.

PROEST. See ODL.

PRO-ODE. In Gr. dramatic and lyric poetry the term refers to a strophe, without a corresponding antistrophe, which precedes the first strophe and antistrophe of a choral ode. It can also mean simply a short verse before a longer one.—Kolář, Koster.   R.A.H.

PROSE AND VERSE. See VERSE AND PROSE.

PROSE POEM (poem in prose). A composition able to have any or all features of the lyric, except that it is put on the page—though not conceived of—as prose. It differs from poetic prose in that it is short and compact, from free verse in that it has no line breaks, from a short prose passage in that it has, usually, more pronounced rhythm, sonorous effects, imagery, and density of expression. It may contain even inner rhyme and metrical runs. Its length, generally, is from half a page (one or two paragraphs) to three or four pages, i.e., that of the average lyrical poem. If it is any longer, the tensions and impact are forfeited, and it becomes—more or less poetic-prose. The term "prose poem" has been applied irresponsibly to anything from the Bible to a novel by Faulkner, but should be used only to designate a highly conscious (sometimes even self-conscious) artform.

The tendency is to consider Aloysius Bertrand the creator of the p.p.; his *Gaspard de la nuit* of 1842 is the first published collection of indubitable prose poetry, though Bertrand was writing p. poems as early as 1827, and Maurice de Guérin, the other initiator, around 1835. But the actual beginnings are in that 18th-c. France where the Academy's rigid rules of versification were driving many a potential poet with a taste for individuality into prose. Thus came about works like Fénelon's poetic novel *Télémaque* (1699) and Montesquieu's prose pastoral *Le Temple de Gnide* (1725); these, and their many imitators, represent an approach, and encouragement, to prose poetry. Men like La Mothe-Houdar defiantly produced odes in prose, but this was mostly bravado and rhetoric. A greater incentive and more useful model was provided by translations of foreign verse into Fr. prose. The original might be *The Psalms*, Gr. or L. lyrics, Norse, oriental, or other "exotic" folk poems, Eng. preromantic verse, or such works as in the original already are more or less prose poetry, like Macpherson's *Ossian* or the *Idyls* of the Swiss poet Salomon Gessner (1756). In Fr., these emerge as prose poetry, soon to be followed by pseudo-translations which, naturally, take the same form. Best among the latter are the charming *Chansons madécasses* of Parny (1787), purporting to be folk poems of Madagascar. By this time the poetic novels may contain lyrics in prose, e.g., Chateaubriand's *Atala* (1799, publ. 1801), but these are still translations, real or supposed. Minor writers, like Volney and Rabbe, may be stepping-stones, but it is the colorful Bertrand and the limpid Guérin (*Le Centaure, La Bacchante*—unfortunately not publ. till 1861) that write the first fine, admittedly original, pieces which, though neither author is known to have used the term, are p. poems by any name.

The first widely known poems in prose, however, are those of Baudelaire, who also officially christens the genre (*Petits Poèmes en prose*, or *Le Spleen de Paris*, begun 1855, published in full 1869). By owning their filiation from Bertrand, Baudelaire bestowed recognition on a young man who died obscurely in a charity ward. Baudelaire's achievement is to have taken an artform which still went in heavily for exoticism and verbal genre-painting and given it the variety and scope, or almost, of the *Fleurs du mal*. But he does not always escape prosaism, and often becomes merely anecdotal. Rimbaud is the first, and probably only, poet whose greatest work is his prose poetry: *Les Illuminations* (date of composition uncertain, published 1886) and, somewhat less developed, *Une Saison en enfer* (1873). Here the p.p. is given the sweep of both a boundless consciousness and a creative subconscious, expressed with extraordinary, dizzying collocations of objects and ideas. Where private imagery does not turn to solipsism, stunning effects are achieved in a wholly flexible form sometimes becoming vers libre or even rhymed verse. From 1864 on, Stéphane Mallarmé was working on p. poems which appeared, along with other prose, as *Divagations* (1897). In these dozen or so pieces a revolutionary (but always carefully pondered) use of syntax, creating unusual relationships or isolations within the sentence, and a system of overlapping metaphors (tropes within tropes) produce almost infinite suggestiveness, now and then inscrutability. From the *Illuminations* and the *Divagations* direct paths lead to such important literary phenomena as free verse, the stream of consciousness, surrealism, James Joyce, and, indeed, modern literature's emphasis on private metaphor and *mélange des genres*. Significantly, the verse dramatist Claudel and the experimental novelists Gide and Proust wrote prose poetry in their youth.

By the end of the 19th c. the p.p. is firmly established, and even to list its major European and Am. practitioners would be impossible here. In the early period, however, we must note in Germany the amazing *ex nihilo* manifestation of the above-mentioned Gessner; Novalis and Hölderlin contributed to the genre at the beginning of the 19th c., the young Stefan George and Rilke at the end. Elsewhere in the past century, the p.p. or a reasonable facsimile, made interesting appearances in De Quincey and Beddoes (later in some poets of the Yellow Nineties), in Turgenyev, the Spaniard G. A. Bécquer, the Dane J. P. Jacobsen; two of Poe's short pieces, at least, fall into the category. But assertions and splendors notwithstanding, works like Lautréamont's *Maldoror*, Hölderlin's *Hyperion*, Nietzsche's *Zarathustra*, are not p. poems—unless prose epics, hence barely distinguishable from the poetic novel. The p.p. as such is with us still, but its accomplishments having been absorbed by other genres, it has become the occasional "aside" of writers whose essential utterance takes other forms.

C. Baudelaire. "A Arsène Houssaye," *Le Spleen de Paris* (1869); J.-K. Huysmans, *A rebours* (1884; end of ch. 14 first anthol. of p.p., with comment); F. Rauhut, *Das französische Prosagedicht* (1929); V. Clayton, *The Prose P. in Fr. Lit. of the 18th C.* (1936); M.-J. Durry [review of the preceding item], RHL, 44 (1937) and "Autour du poème en prose," *Mercure de France*, Feb. 1, 1937; A. Cherel, *La Prose poétique française* (1940); *Anthologie du poème en prose*, ed. M. Chapelan (1946); P. M. Jones, *The Background to Modern Fr. Poetry* (1951); "A Little Anthol. of the Poem in Prose," ed. C. H. Ford, *New Directions*, 14 (1953; possibilities and impossibilities of the p.p.: junk, jargon, and a few gems); S. Bernard, *Le Poème en prose de Baudelaire jusqu'à nos jours* (1959); M. Parent, *Saint-John Perse et quelques devanciers: Etudes sur le poème en prose* (1960). J.S.

PROSE RHYTHM. P.r. has been written off as a mere figure of speech and it has been treated seriously by both psychologists and students of literature. Much depends on the definition of rhythm that one starts with. If rhythm means simply, etymologically, "flow," p.r. is a pleasing flow of the sounds of language, and any prose which satisfies the ear is rhythmic. This is sometimes called the rhythm of the flowing line. If, on the other hand, the word has the stricter sense of a series of equal or approximately equal units, the first problem is to find a way of identifying the units. This can be done by grammatical analysis, that is, by observing the length of phrases and clauses: if they seem to fall into more or less equal and repeated patterns, the prose has a recognizable kind of rhythm, sometimes called the balanced style, as is all too common in Dr. Johnson. But this will occur without much regularity; otherwise the prose becomes offensively monotonous or sing-song. Take for example, "Priest falls, prophet rises," or Burke's "Kings will be tyrants from policy when subjects are rebels from principle." To recognize the subtler varieties, such as may occur in ordinary, to say nothing of studied and ornate prose, a trained ear is necessary, and also a careful analysis of the potential elements. And this means breaking down the sentences and paragraphs into phrases, words, and syllables with full regard to their constituents of *time* (duration), *stress* (relative emphasis), *pitch* (rising and falling of the voice in spoken language and an analogous effect in silent reading), and *tempo*, including pauses; for there are considerable differences in rhythm between rapid and retarded speech—the more rapid the speaking or reading, the longer the rhythmic units seem to become.

Another form of measurement is metrical. Owing to the formal arrangements of language (syntax), words and syllables have a natural tendency to come in set patterns ("the course of the river," "human nature," "inevitable development," etc.). The poet adopts these natural patterns, altering them for special effects and sometimes with, sometimes without forcing, molds the language into his metrical scheme. Often the difference between rhythmic prose and poetry is very slight; for example, in Pope's famous line "Most women have no character at all" or in Milton's "Of Man's First Disobedience, and the Fruit" the meter is so "irregular," that is, departs so far from the expected alternation of stressed and unstressed syllables, that without the context one would not recognize the meter at all. Conversely, a great deal of normal prose contains potential, and unintentional, meter which will be noticed only after close examination but which nevertheless is felt and so contributes to the p.r. If, however, the latent meter is allowed to become too obvious or is purposely developed for emotional effect, as in oratorical or pathetic passages, the sense of true prose is destroyed and the reader or hearer resents the trick played on him. The best prose requires therefore a careful balance of these two forces.

In the study of p.r., then, three facts must be taken into account. First, there is this natural tendency of language to assume metrical patterns. This is the most elementary aspect of p.r. Second, the established grammatical or syntactic arrangements of language are often repeated, in the form of parallelism or balance, for rhetorical purposes. Third, there is a psychological factor which both creates and satisfies a desire for rhythmical repetition and which leads us to find or feel, and sometimes to induce where it does not actually exist, a clear sense of rhythm in language. In its extreme form it develops or imposes a sense of rhythm in any prose which is easy to read or listen to, so that we are inclined to say that all good prose is rhythmical.

Great progress has been made recently in the scientific study of speech sounds, going beyond the simple groups of syllable, word, phrase, etc. *This structural analysis* has an elaborate code of symbols, including four degrees of stress and four or five of pitch. Besides the usual phonetic values of vowel and consonant, it embraces juncture, the phonemic, morphemic, and syntactic phenomena, and various formulas. This system may eventually enable us to record and interpret the many variations of speech and so come closer than hitherto to an understanding of rhythms, both in prose and in verse. Yet there will always remain a subjective element, and each reader, each listener will recognize and feel the rhythms according to his native receptivity.

The cadence or *cursus* (clausula) is a special form of prose rhythm. It was invented by the Gr. orators and was, originally, a kind of punctuation for oral delivery, marking the end of a clause or sentence. Cicero adopted the device and used the following clausulae and their numerous resolutions most often:

$$-\smile--\smile;---\smile;-\smile\smile-\smile$$

Zielinski divides Cicero's clausulae into the following classes: *verae* I = cretic ($-\smile-$) or molossus ($---$) + trochee ($-\smile$) or cretic or ditrochee; *verae* II, which permit substitution of $\smile\smile$ for $-$; *verae* III, which permit substitution of a choriamb ($-\smile\smile-$) or epitrite ($-\smile--$) for the cretic; *licitae:* the c. *licita* is a c. *vera* with a 5-syllable word at the end; *malae* and *pessimae,* so called in accordance with their degree of departure from the standard patterns; and *selectae,* which substitute spondees (‒‒) for the trochees of the *verae.* Of these the *verae* and *licitae* comprise 86.8 per cent of Cicero's clausulae, the others 12.7 per cent. Latin prosewriters whose clausulae reflect the Ciceronian pattern include Nepos, Seneca, Suetonius, and Quintilian; among those whose do not are Sallust and Livy. By the 3d c. A.D., the L. clausula had shifted from quantitative to accentual rhythm, and in the latter form it was used during the Middle Ages in three patterns of *cursus:*

> *planus* or plain (‒◡‒◡‒◡),
> *tardus* or slow (‒◡‒◡‒◡◡), and
> *velox* or fast (‒◡‒◡◡◡‒◡)

Later it became chiefly, with lexical accent substituted for syllabic length, a stylistic ornament; but in the diplomatic correspondence of the Roman Curia it was used, with modifications, as a secret code or signature. Something similar to the classical *cursus* has been noted in Eng., starting from the L. collects of the church service and passing on by aural tradition to the Eng. collects and thence into secular prose. But whether the *cursus* was transmitted to Eng. through the Prayer Book or whether Eng. developed independently its own satisfying cadences has never been fully established. Some patterns recur more frequently in Eng. than others, but they do not correspond closely to the classical *cursus.* See VERSE AND PROSE; PROSODY.

T. Zielinski, *Das Clauselgesetz in Ciceros Reden* (1904) and *Der constructive Rhythmus in Ciceros Reden* (1914); W. Thomson, *The Rhythm of Eng. Speech* (1907); A. C. Clark, *The Cursus in Mediaeval and Vulgar L.* (1910) and *P.R. in Eng.* (1913); P. Fijn van Draat, *Rhythm in Eng. Prose* (1910); G. Saintsbury, *A Hist. of Eng. P.R.* (1912, 1922); W. M. Patterson, *The Rhythm of Prose* (1917); H. D. Broadhead, *Latin P.R.* (1922); H. Griffith, *Time Patterns in Prose* (1929); B. Tomashevsky, "Ritm prozy," *O Stikhe. Statyi* (1929; an important Russ. contribution based on statistical methods); A. Classe, *The Rhythm of Eng. Prose* (1939); G. L. Trager and H. L. Smith, Jr., *An Outline of Eng. Structure* (1951, 1956); P. F. Baum, *The Other Harmony of Prose* (1952); Norden; W. Schmid, *Über die klassische Theorie und Praxis des antiken Prosarhythmus* (1959). P.F.B.

PROSODIC NOTATION. Notation of prosodic aspects of speech is of three kinds, (1) by *diacritical markings* imposed upon ordinary text; normal text in all languages includes some such marks, e.g., "accents," and all marks of punctuation are partially or wholly prosodic; (2) by a distinct *graphic transcription* either of the total phonetic content of a text (*phonetic* transcription conventionally set within square brackets, *phonemic* transcription between slant lines) or of abstracted prosodic features only; (3) by an abstract *schematic symbolism* (usually based upon 1 or 2) representing prosodic elements and values (e.g., use of letters for values, of numbers for position in series, of barring for divisions, etc.); the use of this last is especially to provide concise schematic formulas to represent abstracted patterns of rhythmic or metrical organization of prosodic features.

Of diacritical marks the most commonly used have been the acute accent (′) for primary stress, stress in general, or "ictus," sometimes lengthened (/, the virgule), the grave accent (`) for secondary stress, the macron (‒) to indicate a "long" syllable or element, and the breve (◡) for a "short"; relative length of sounds is frequently indicated by a dot above or after the symbol for the sound, protracted duration by two dots aligned vertically after it. Pauses are indicated by normal punctuation (especially the comma) or by the caret (∧). The caret is used also to indicate an omission. Relative duration of pauses is indicated with the caret by addition of macron or breve or dot(s); duration of pause may be indicated by conventional musical notation for rests. G. Trager and H. L. Smith (*Outline of Eng. Structure,* 1951), followed by many linguists, use diacritically over normal text or transcription, for stress-values the acute accent for primary, circumflex for secondary, grave for tertiary, and the breve for weakest; for degrees of openness of juncture, + for open juncture internal to a stress-group, | for "terminal" juncture after clauses or members with even or level pitch conclusion, || for such juncture with rising pitch, # for completive terminal juncture (with falling pitch), and they then use the names of these signs as designations of the grades of juncture ("plus-juncture," "single-bar-," "double-bar-," "cross-bar-" or "double-cross-"). This is in some ways the best of current diacritical systems for languages like Eng., and is in increasing use; but for abstractive prosodic analysis it has, besides the disadvantages of all merely diacritical procedures, the inconvenience that it cannot easily be generalized to fit all languages and prosodic systems, and that it uses for phonological description signs or symbols which in strictly rhythmic analysis are needed or useful for other values and better reserved for those (e.g., ◡ | ||).

In rhythmic analysis diacritical marking of normal text is less satisfactory for most purposes than some kind of graphic transcription which clearly abstracts the prosodic features relevant to a rhythmic design and presents them in separation from the qualitative phonemic and other nonrhythmic aspects of the speech in which they occur. There has been great variety in the history of prosody in provision of devices for such abstractive notation, and much diversity as to crudity or refinement in them. Perhaps the oldest is the use of letters of an alphabet to represent prosodic values, found in the fragmentary remains of ancient Gr. prosodic (and musical) notation and exploited systematically in the ancient Sanskrit *Chandahsutra* of Pingala (where G = long or heavy, *guru*, L = short or light, *laghu*; Pingala used single letters also to represent systematic combinations of these values, or "feet": M = GGG, N = LLL, R = GLG, etc.); in recent use for Eng., e.g., x = unstressed, a (more often ' or /) = stressed, F *(fort)* = stressed, f *(faible)* = weak (P. Verrier, *Métrique anglaise*, 1909), and very often (following G. R. Stewart, *Technique of Eng. Verse*, 1930) S = stressed, o = unstressed, l = light stress, p, P = pause short or long or replacing light or heavy. Less often, numbers (0 or 1 to 3, 4, or higher) have been used, to represent either degrees of prominence (J. B. Mayor; J. Lotz for Gr.) or position of stress or other value (so commonly for Romance verse; for stress-verse by J. Lotz; for prose sequences by M. Croll); numbers (1 to 4 or 6) are commonly used to note levels of pitch. Conventional musical notation has often been adapted for rhythmic analysis of verse. For Eng., occasional and partial use of musical notation begins with C. Gildon (*Complete Art of Poetry*, 1718), and recurs frequently in the later 18th and in the 19th c.; since S. Lanier (*Science of Eng. Verse*, 1880) full musical notation has often been used by writers whose analysis of verse is musical or exclusively temporal (and has therefore generally been avoided by nontemporalists). Systems of arbitrary graphic symbols often variously incorporating musical and other inherited conventional sgins have been sporadically used (J. Steele, *Essay . . . establishing the Melody and Measure of Speech . . . expressed and perpetuated by peculiar symbols*, 1775; W. Skeat, "Versification," § 98, pp. lxxxii-xcvii of "General Introduction" in his ed. of *Complete Works of G. Chaucer*, VI, 1894; W. Thomson, *Rhythm of Speech*, 1923; A. Heusler, *Deutsche Versgeschichte*, I, 1925; MLA Committee of 1923; etc.)

In the system of notation used in the article on *Prosody* in this Encyclopedia, o = the single element or unit, normally a syllable, of weak or unemphatic value when not otherwise marked; ó = a syllable or element of stressed or emphatic value. Where more than two values are required, ó = primary, ò = secondary, ȯ = terti-

ary, o = weakest; ŏ = value which may be either primary or secondary; ổ = prominence in excess of adjacent primary value. (Since of contiguous primary values the second must always be phonetically stronger if the two are to be perceptually equal, the sequence ó ó is always phonetically ó ŏ and ổ is therefore not often required.) The straight comma , is used to indicate the open juncture or break between stress-groups, the caret ᴧ for longer pause at more open junctures. (Protraction of pause may be indicated with this caret by a dot under or after it. In metrical sequences, the straight bar | may further be used to separate feet where this is felt to be desirable; the marking of values or stresses should normally suffice for indication of metrical pattern. Caesural breaks are often represented by this straight bar, single or double, or by a vertical dotted line; such breaks too are sufficiently indicated by marks for junctures and pauses.) These signs serve adequately to represent all the values of all the prosodic factors in all languages. Where temporal duration alone is to be noted, as for classical Gr. and L., the macron may be used for long and the breve for short, and o for indifferent or indeterminate quantity; for binary contrast of pitch values, as in Chinese, now commonly o (O) = flat or uninflected, x (X) = inflected; to distinguish levels of pitch, numbers may be used (1 = lowest), or the syllabic sign o placed on a musical staff with lines. When only one of two contrasting values is to be noted, and the place of occurrence of this value alone is to be represented in a schematic indication of a pattern, numbers corresponding to the place of the affected syllables in their series may be used, as by M. Croll for clausular cadences in prose, counting backward from the last syllable (5-2 = ó o o ó o; SP, 16 (1919) 1ff.). For such schemes, J. Lotz has proposed, counting from the beginning for verse, giving the number only of light syllables between the strong or emphatic in series, indicating absence of weak syllables at end or beginning by 0: (thus 2 1 1 0 = o o ó o ó o ó; *Lingua*, 6 (1956), 1ff.).

For rhythmic analysis, it is not necessary or desirable that a notation represent all the variation in the rhythmic aspects of a speech; what is necessary is representation of the rhythmic contrasts relevant to the pattern or meter to be described. The ideal rhythmic notation is therefore always abstractive and, for the total rhythmic variation, only approximative. It should also be remembered that "notational symbols . . . have nothing whatever to do with the problem of good, bad, or indifferent readings; they can, in fact, be used to record readings of any quality or character" (J. W. Hendren, *Time and Stress in Eng. Verse* [1959; Rićе Institute pamphlet 46]).

T. S. Omond, *Eng. Metrists* (1921); M. W. Croll, "Report of the Committee on Metrical Notation," PMLA, 39 (1924), lxxxvii-xciv; *Phonetic Transcription and Transliteration, Proposals of the Copenhagen Conference April 1925* (Oxford, 1926; mainly by O. Jespersen).

J.C.LAD.

PROSODION. A religious song used chiefly in the worship of Apollo in ancient Greece, sung to instrumental music by a chorus either approaching or standing at the altar of a god, hence its name ("processional"). Such a song frequently used the metrical unit called the *prosodiakon* or *prosodiacus* ≃−◡◡−◡◡−. This is sometimes known as the catalectic form of the *enoplius* (q.v.).

R.A.H.

PROSODY† is the most general term in current use to refer to the elements and structures involved in the rhythmic or dynamic aspect of speech, and the study of these elements and structures as they occur in speech and language generally (*linguistic prosody*) or in the compositions of the literary arts (*literary prosody*). Descriptive study of pros., linguistic or literary, may be *theoretical* ("achronic" or "panchronic," concerned with abstracting to the universal or general nature of the phenomena and the principles operating in them, rather than with recording the fact and particular circumstances of their actual occurrence) or *historical* (either "synchronic" or "diachronic," and either "comparative" or limited to a national or linguistic unit); theory and history are here as elsewhere reciprocally complementary. The evaluative *prosodic criticism* related to these descriptive studies is grammatical, rhetorical, or aesthetic, as the value it assesses is one of linguistic correctness, rhetorical effectiveness, or poetic form. A preceptive or prescriptive pros. attempts to provide practical rules for rhythmic composition and interpretation or delivery. Such precept has always some connection with contemporary descriptive pros. and the related prosodic criticism, and is often conflated with them, but it is properly a part, not of these disciplines, but of the arts of poetry and rhetoric, or of grammar and elocution and their pedagogy; as such it is a datum for their histories and the history of taste and literary education rather than a division of scientific literary study.

As a part of traditional study of classical grammar, which was both linguistic and literary but concentrated upon poetic texts, pros. was the study of "accent" (L. *accentus, adcantus,* = Gr. *prosoidia*), of phonetic properties (chiefly temporal) of syllables and words as relevant to the measure (Gr. *metron*) of rhythm especially in verse, and of meters and the forms of verse generally. In antiquity musical analysis of rhythm, developed also by some philosophers, notably Aristoxenus, was applied to verse by writers called *rhythmikoi,* whose procedures differed from those of the *metrikoi,* grammatical or literary metrists like Hephaestion; St. Augustine, *De musica,* represents late conflation of these. Ancient rhetoric (e.g., Cicero, *Orator*) included treatment of prose rhythm based on these grammatical, musical, and philosophical sources. Later medieval rhetoric elaborated some aspects of prose rhythm (*cursus,* etc.), and it is within the frame of rhetoric rather than grammar that versification generally is provided for in late medieval and early modern times: the Fr. *Seconde Rethorique* is the art of versification. Grammatical and rhetorical elements are often combined with musical in treatments of *ars rythmica* and verse in the late middle ages, when poetry was again in close practical association with music. Modern *linguistic* study of pros. is concerned primarily with the practical functioning of the phonetic elements of speech which accompany and vary but are not directly involved in discrimination of phonemes in the narrow sense, and with the conventions by which these elements (intensity, duration, variation of pitch, and phenomena of interruption and transition between sounds) operate in linguistic systems, by variation and distribution of sonority and massing or grouping of sounds, to produce meanings and discriminate among them; but linguistic pros. has also included investigation of verse and of metrical conventions, since wherever a conventional distinction between prose speech and verse exists within a linguistic community, the conventions relevant to this distinction (though not all the further formalizations of language involved in actual uses of verse) may be considered part of the linguistic system (the *langue* of De Saussure).

Literary pros. studies the rhythmic structure of prose and verse, not as exemplifying linguistic norms but as functioning (in the *parole* or actual speech) for literary effect as a component in rhetorical processes or constructions or as an aspect of poetic form. Literary pros. is not directly concerned with the use which language makes of rhythm for linguistic ends; it is in fact more properly concerned with the use which rhythmic impulse makes of language for its own ends when those are involved with the processes or forms of rhetoric and poetry. But literary pros. supposes some understanding of its phonetic materials, and of linguistic conventions along with other conventions in the cultural environment which affect the literary arts in their rhythmic aspect; it is part of the task of a literary pros.

† In Supplement, see also GENERATIVE METRICS.

to show how the forms it deals with come to be lodged in the material of a language. Prosodic structures differ from language to language, for languages differ in their selection and emphasis among universally available phonetic elements and modes of combining them, first for use in ordinary speech and then for application to the composition of verse; these are always somehow related, but the nature of their relation also varies (as a language too may vary, sometimes radically in these respects, from one period or dialect to another), so that the requisites and characteristics of verse do not always remain the same even in a single language throughout its history, and more than one system of versification, and various interpenetrations of verse and prose, can exist in a language at the same time.

Strictly phonetic phenomena are often more relevant to literary pros. than to linguistics, and some linguistic phenomena of more concern to literary prosodists than they have been to linguists. It is at times necessary for understanding of verbal rhythms to refer to a broader context of more general or other specialized rhythmic behavior, since the rhythm in a verbal structure may reflect or incorporate that of other rhythmic processes with which the verbal has been associated, or into which it has been assimilated, or which it imitates. Speech is a complex act involving concurrence of the verbal with other physical and mental action, and its rhythm is a property of the speech as a whole, not of its verbal part alone; and the act of speech may be conjoined with other action and so further complicated rhythmically, by the natural or stylized movements of ordinary or ceremonial activities or by the elaborated rhythms of music or the dance. The rhythm of song or of chant differs by such association from that of words only spoken or recited; and there are differences within these classes. It is of course only so much of an external rhythmic context as is somehow registered within the structure of a verbal text that is relevant to literary analysis of the text. It is certaintly an error in method to assume the reverse and analyze verbal rhythms only in terms of their correspondence with other rhythm, notably the musical. All species of rhythm have generic aspects in common, and there are indeed specific components in some verbal rhythms that are to be accounted for only by musical association or its residual influence; but there are also elements in all literary rhythms which will be ignored or misrepresented in a description based solely on current conventions of musical analysis. It is with the rhythmic structure of the dance that the verbal rhythms typical of verse have most direct affinity; this is not strange, since speech like the dance is an organization of

bodily movements, including those of the specialized "vocal" organs, and it is an ordering of the physical movements and pressures which produce sounds, even more than of the physical motion or vibration which constitutes the sound, that is the basis of rhythm in speech.

The structure of sound in speech is an organization, by relations of similarity and difference, of the elements provided by the physical constitution of speech, a succession of vocal sounds and interruptions of sound by silence occurring in time. The relations in this structure are not of sounds or silences simply or absolutely, but of properties or attributes of sound and of silence. Sounds are differentiated in quality (discriminable character or kind) and in quantity (measurable degree or amount of sonority or of general or specific acoustic magnitude, including that of duration in time; temporal duration is the only common property of sound and silence, and the only positive attribute of silence, which is thus essentially quantitative). The rhythm of speech is a structure of ordered variation in the quantitative aspects of the flow of sound in which contrast is balanced by a cyclic recurrence of some identity. Meter is a fixed schematization of the cyclically recurring identity in a rhythmic series. Structured elements may be involved simultaneously in different sets of relations, and so incorporated concurrently into structural units of different kinds. To some of the intrinsic properties and relations of sounds and silences conventional "'values" (purely constructional relations) are assigned by which they become susceptible of the special conventional organization that constitutes the phonological or "phonemic" system of a given language. All grammatical or strictly linguistic structure, the syntactic as well as the phonological, is conventional structure of this kind. Rhetorical and poetic structures are never wholly thus conventional, and the conventions observed in them are never exclusively linguistic or grammatical. Rhetoric and poetry use the constructs of a phonological system as they use grammar generally, but their own constructions, especially those of poetry, make freer use of intrinsic phonetic properties and relations apart from phonological conventionalization, so far as these are not masked beyond recognition in perception by phonological conditioning of attention. It is the sound as heard, the perceptual "phone" or "allophone" rather than the phoneme as such, that is relevant for literary, as distinct from linguistic, structure of sound.

Vocal sound is the result of vibration produced by constriction of the current of air projected from the lungs (by movements of the diaphragm and other muscles of abdomen and chest) through the larynx, throat, and mouth, with resonance in chest and head and modification of the current and vibrations by varying articulation of the parts of organs in these passages, especially in the mouth. Continuity and interruption or remission of sound depend upon and correspond to the muscular actions and pressures of expiration (during which normal speech-sound occurs) and inspiration of air and the pauses between them (which though considerable in breathing at rest are neither frequent nor lengthy in continuous speech, in which inspiration normally follows expiration with no interval of rest); it is therefore primarily to the mechanisms of respiratory pressure that most of the massing and grouping of sounds, and in general their quantitative acoustic effects (especially of intensity and duration, but also largely of pitch) are due. Larger and intermediate groupings are determined by action of the diaphragm supported by the muscles of the abdominal and thoracic walls; the smallest aggregatory (and rhythmic) unit, the syllable, as it occurs in polysyllabic utterance in most languages, appears to be the product of a single pressure ("chest-pulse") of the smaller intercostal muscles. (Uttered in isolation the syllable, like all whole-utterance units, is produced by pressure from the abdomen. In polysyllabic utterances it is a slighter pulsation within a larger stretch of sound produced by sustained abdominal pressure. This is the physiological foundation of the "rhythmic group," for which see below.) Obstruction of the current of air and articulatory modification of vibration and resonance produce qualitative differentiation of sounds, upon which phonemic discrimination of segments of sound is based.

Qualitative differences among sounds are usually described and classified in terms of the articulations involved in their production; but the foundation of phonemic distinctions is a generalizing discrimination of acoustic differences which corresponds at times only loosely to articulatory, or to very sensitive auditory, differentiation. (The phonemes of a language are roughly represented by the letters of an alphabet; hence the name *alliteration* for repetitive figuration of qualitative similarities in sounds.) Quality in vocal sound may be generally described as the acoustic effect of articulatory action, broadly including all varieties of constriction and obstruction (vocalic, consonantal, liquid, etc.) or of vibration and resonance (voiced, voiceless; oral, nasal, etc.) as well as distinction of organ, part, or place (glottal, palatal, dental, labial etc; dorsal, lateral, apical etc; front, back, high, low etc.) or mode (open, closed, rounded, unrounded; plosive, spirant, affricate, etc.) of articulation. Each vowel or consonant is a composite "bundle" of several such qualitative properties or (sub-phonemic) component "features" (now being systematically classified by Jakobson and others), and the relations upon which qualitative structure of sounds depends are relations among these properties or features rather than among the composite sounds or segments (phonemes) as such. Some qualitative differences, e.g. that between voiced and unvoiced sounds, involve accompanying difference in quantity. But qualitative differentiation of sounds, though its figuration (alliteration, assonance, rhyme) may be combined with and even assimilated to rhythmic structure, is never directly a factor in the production of rhythm, since rhythm is a structure of quantitative relations.

The properties of sound directly relevant to rhythmic structure are the quantitative or quantifiable properties of intensity, duration, and pitch. Intensity (loudness or volume) and duration are obviously quantitative in perceptual effect as well as physically measurable. Pitch (corresponding roughly to frequency of vibration, and thus easily quantified, though not subject to extensive or intensive measurement) has an ambiguous perceptual effect, in part quantitative, in part qualitative. As it is used in language, variation of pitch is normally associated with other variation that is quantitative and, whether independently or because pitch is easily conflated in perception with associated features, its effect is quantitative, increasing the prominence of the sound altered by its variation. The quantitative or prosodic properties of sound are used in language not for their absolute or "inherent" characters (as pitch is used in music) but, in contrasting juxtaposition with other variants of the same property in adjacent sounds within an utterance, to provide "relational" oppositions which have semantic effects or syntactic functions. The prosodic features are therefore often distinguished as "relational" from the "inherent" features by which segmental phonemes are characterized, because the phonologically functional characteristics of the individual phonemic segments are discernible in isolated utterance of single phonemes, whereas it is only in continuous successive utterance of sounds that prosodic contrasts can be observed. A similar distinction now in common use opposes prosodic features as "suprasegmental" to the (qualitative) features of the phonemic "segments" of sound upon which they are imposed; phonologically regulated occurrences of prosodic entities ("prosodic phonemes") may then be called "suprasegmental phonemes," patterns of these called "superfixes," and prosodic superfixes called "suprasegmental morphemes" when they have a fixed "morphological" function in the syntax of a language. (British linguists who follow J. R. Firth make different distinctions, otherwise grounded, among prosodic and "phonematic" entities: cf. R. H. Robins, "Aspects of Prosodic Analysis," Univ. of Durham Philosophical Society, *Proc.* 1, ser. B, no. 1, 1957.)

The various contrasts provided by the prosodic features are used in some languages for lexical distinctions, between words or functional classes of words (e.g. Eng. *contrast*, n. = ó o, vb. = o ó), but their most general linguistic use is that of ordering and grouping sounds to produce phonological units that function syntactically. The mechanisms of this ordering and aggregation of sounds are those of "accent" (of intensity, "dynamic"; or of pitch, "tonic"), of "intonation" (systematic successive arrangement of pitch-values) and of "pause" and "timing" (dilation or holding, contraction, and interruption of sound; transition with "juncture" of various degrees of "openness" between sounds); these mechanisms and their effects (fusion, reduction or promotion, elision of sounds) may involve accompanying qualitative changes. One of their effects is the production of what is usually called (rhythmic) "cadence," i.e. pattern of successive or positional relation of prominent ("strong" or "emphatic") elements to less prominent ("weak" or "unemphatic") elements. The prominence and weakness relevant for cadence may be of intensity, of duration, or of pitch; these factors may operate singly and distinctly or in combinations; and the phonological patterns of a single language (e.g. ancient Gr. and L., modern Czech, Chinese) may produce distinct "natural" cadences of more than one kind. Cadence involves the two aspects of "span" (the number of elements over which a unitary pattern extends) and "direction" (the positional or successional order of the elements). Direction is usually classified as "rising" (o ó, o o ó), "falling" (ó o, ó o o), "mixed" or "undulating" or "rocking" (o ó o, ó o ó), and "level" or "even" (ó ó, o o); these last and other cadence-units (as ó) exhibiting neither "rise" nor "fall," and often the undulating cadences which include both, are also called "neutral"; cadence is called "alternating" when "emphatic" and "unemphatic" elements of equal span succeed each other in a series (especially when the series begins and ends with the same value) and more loosely when equivalence of span is only approximated.

Hegel based the treatment of verse in his *Aesthetik* upon a sharp distinction between quantitative and qualitative structures of sound. It is important for analysis to distinguish clearly these two quite distinct kinds of structure; but the distinction is not well drawn in Hegel's often penetrating survey, and he mistakenly conceived the two structures as mutually exclusive alternatives. Though all four properties of sound—quality, pitch, intensity, and duration—are distinct in character and effect, and each produces a different kind of structure or figuration, they do not occur in isolation from each other, and their distinct designs may be combined and interrelated. Rhythmic structure is usually complex, and within it a distinction must be made between primary or constitutive elements which create or establish rhythm and secondary or adjunct elements whose figuration only supports or supplements a more basic rhythmic pattern established by the primary elements. The primary constitutive factors of rhythm in all systems of versification are relations of intensity or of duration; these provide rhythmic structures based upon counting of syllables, on counting or disposition of "stresses," and on general quantitative or specifically temporal "measure" or balance. Pitch is not the primary factor of rhythm in any known system of verse, though it may be used with intensity (as duration may) to enforce or even to supply a "stress," and may possibly function similarly with duration. But when either intensity or duration is the primary factor in creating rhythm, the other may operate along with it as an adjunct secondary element; and with either of these as primary, pitch and quality may be used as adjuncts for secondary figuration, as indeed (since verse is a patterning of properties in speech, not of abstracted sound) may the non-phonetic elements of syntactic construction or of semantic relationship. (These latter are related to rhythmic structure not only in figures of balance, "parallelism"—often syntactic parallel crossing semantic antithesis—and the like, but also in construction and internal division of "lines"—"caesura" etc.—and strophic units.)

Patterns of two elements may operate concurrently in a rhythmic structure, the one reinforcing the other in what then may be regarded as a single complex rhythm (from which nevertheless the distinct characters of the harmonizing components make possible regression to a simpler rhythmic base exploiting only one of them, alone or in new combination with other elements). Patterns of accentual cadence were thus combined with those of durational elements in some phases of L. verse and of late ancient Gr., and there was concurrence of numerical correspondence of syllables with durational patterns in "Aeolic" Gr. lyric verse; in Romance verse there is varying concurrence of accentual patterns, more or less regulated, with syllable-counting.

Secondary figuration of adjunct elements may be assimilated into the basic rhythmic structure created by the primary elements, as an integrated support or extension of the form either of all verse in a given language or of particular species of verse. So in all Old Germanic verse alliteration is combined with a primary stress rhythm; in all Arabic and in all the "classical" Persian and Turkish verse modeled upon it some regulated use of qualitative figuration accompanies rhythmic patterning of temporal durations; in Chinese and in almost all Romance verse some "rhyme" or assonance is used with syllable-counting. With syllable-counting the *lü-shih,* "regulated" or "new style" verse of China since the T'ang period, combines a fixed arrangement of pitches or "tones" (a phenomenon common in "tone languages," i.e. those in which variation of pitch is lexically distinctive); in the most elaborate types of traditional Welsh verse (doubtless the most developed example of the fondness for qualitative filigree universal in Celtic verse-systems) the complex qualitative figuration called *cynghanedd* (q.v.) complements a basic pattern of syllable-counting; in European verse-systems generally particular forms like the sonnet and in Eng. e.g. the "Limerick" are distinguished by fixed rhyme-schemes.

Secondary figuration may occur also as free supplementary embellishment or optional incidental design not thus integrated into the basic rhythmic form, as with alliteration in modern Eng. or other Germanic verse, or tone-arrangement in the Chinese *ku-shih* or "old style" verse. Since any entity selected for metrical schematization necessarily occurs in concomitance with other nonschematized entities (e.g. syllabic units are present in "nonsyllabic" verse), and these other entities may themselves be independently patterned or regulated, it is at times difficult to distinguish in a verse-system between elements essential to a metrical scheme and redundant concomitant elements whose concurrence with the more primary rhythmic structure is not adverted to in production or attended to in native perception of the rhythm as such.

Confusion of essential or primary factors in the constitution of standard verse with incidental secondary characteristics typical of such verse produces "doggerel" (q.v.), i.e. a structure which provides some secondary figuration characteristic of normal verse, but lacks an essential requisite of its primary rhythmic form. When elements not independently rhythmical are assimilated into a rhythmic structure (e.g. qualitative figuration or syntactic construction marking or creating divisions within such structure) it is often not easy to disassociate them from the rhythm or to describe the form of the rhythm without including them. Strictly rhythmic structure is always the basis of verse, and in some languages verse is identical with its rhythmic or metrical structure; so purely rhythmic considerations account for all aspects of the complex durational metrical verse of classical Gr. and L., or of

the simple syllable-counting verse of Japanese. But in most languages some additional figuration, most often qualitative, is characteristic of verse; and even where it is not incorporated into the *discrimen* by which verse is distinguished from prose (as alliteration appears to have been in Old Germanic verse) such pararhythmic adjunct figuration may be as meticulously elaborated as the primary rhythmic structure, and sometimes more strictly regulated (Arabic, Prov., Welsh, Icelandic). The scope of prosodic study has therefore in practice generally been extended to include phonetic elements not strictly rhythmical, and elements of syntax and meaning, when these are relevant to the structure of verse. But this extension has not generally modified the traditional conception of the "prosodic" (inherited from its connection with Gr. and L., in which verse and metrical rhythm coincided without discrepancy) as essentially restricted to the rhythmic.

It is by the dynamic functioning of the mechanisms of quantitative variation, in intensity, duration, and pitch, that sounds are aggregated together into the smaller clusters and groups, and then into the larger sequences, that make the (semantically ordered) phonetic structure of "natural" speech. The phonemes themselves are aggregates ("bundles"), and quantitative forces and relations are operative in the process of their combination of qualities as in all phonetic aggregation. But the smallest structural unit of speech in which quantitative aggregation, rather than qualitative differentiation, is felt as the primary factor is the syllable, which may be described acoustically as a single massing of sound between recessions of sonority, usually round a definite peak or center (the "syllabic" nucleus). The formation of syllables is a necessary product of the variation of sonority inevitable in any meaningful flow of speech-sound, and the syllable therefore occurs as the minimal aggregatory unit (and hence the fundamental rhythmic unit) in all languages; but there is much variety among languages in the nature of its composition. This diversity is partly in number and order of syllabic components, but especially in degree of sonority or phonetic mass required or permitted for distinction of individual syllabic nuclei, or degree of diminution of sonority regarded as constituting interstitial recession; in Eng., e.g., *splash* and *sponge* are single syllables, but in Japanese it would be difficult to form or hear such combinations as having fewer than four syllables.

In most languages the syllabic center is typically a vowel (V), which may or may not have consonant (C) accompaniment before and (less generally) after: CV, VC, CVC, CCVCC, etc. In such languages it is exceptional, but in most not impossible, that syllabic centers be consonantal (*Psst!*); but in some languages, like Japanese, a single consonant may be a syllable. An element of duration or "timing" may operate in syllabic construction. In some languages (Eng., Rus.) syllables vary freely in duration; in some (e.g. Sp.) all syllables are approximately equal in duration; in some ("mora" languages, including ancient Gr. and L.) syllabic duration varies, for perception or by convention, only within a ratio of roughly 2:1. (Japanese combines the last two conventions; its ratio of 2:1 in time between "long" and "normal" syllables involves a doubling or gemination imposed upon a basic scheme of uniformly equal timing of normal syllables.)

Where syllables are isochronous the distinct identity of the syllable is never reduced or lost, and equal timing of syllables thus provides for, and appears to induce, syllable-counting in verse, which is then itself a kind of timing. The simple ratio of durations in "mora" languages provides similarly in them for the use of this and a few other such ratios as the basis of internal "measure" in the "feet" of a quite different metrical schematization, as in ancient Gr. and classical L. When syllabic duration varies without regulation, as in the Germanic languages or Rus., it seems not to be related to metrical schematization; in these languages variation in time of syllables is absorbed into the contrast of strong and weak stress which is exploited for verse either simply as such or as forming units ("feet") of patterns of "cadence." In its internal contrast of degrees of sonority or intensity the typical syllable may be said to include the minimal presentation of a pattern of cadence; so e.g. rising or alternating cadence is represented at intrasyllabic level by sequences of the type CV-CV-CV etc., normal in many languages in which CV is the most frequent or the only arrangement used in composing syllables.

The grouping of syllables into larger aggregations is determined in natural speech primarily by the semantic functioning of these larger units in the syntactic structure of a language. (In normal speech the physiological and psychological necessity of variation of energy in production, and of some massing of sounds for perception, are subordinated and adapted to systematized semantic and syntactic ends; when these forces operate independently of conventional semantic and syntactic norms in creating phonetic units, the effect is one of artificial "stylized" histrionic or rhetorical "distortion" of "natural" speech.)

As in their construction of syllables, languages differ in their modes of combining syllables into syntactic unities, and especially in the degree of definiteness with which they mark individual units as distinct phonetic en-

tities either by creating discontinuities between units or by establishing continuity or cohesion within units. The largest units of utterance are marked by pause-boundaries which are true interruptions of sound by silence. The necessity of maintaining a degree of continuity in the phonetic microstructure of speech prohibits general use of actual silence to mark the limits of the smallest aggregatory units; the smaller units therefore depend for unitary integrity and distinctness upon internal "culminative" or concentrating factors rather than upon disruptive external "delimitative" effects generally; intermediate units variously combine culminative and delimitative elements. In the smaller units there is thus a condensation or greater concentration of the integrating factors—"prosodic superfixes" of accentual and intonational patterns and timing—which also appear, with little modification, in more diffused form and distributed over broader spans in the larger units; it may be added that the larger the unit, the more significant in this respect will intonation ("melody") be, the smaller the unit the more dependent upon the other prosodic factors for its identity. The smallest unit of aggregation, the syllable, is normally distinguished primarily by the relative prominence of its nuclear center or "syllabic"; its borders are often indeterminate.

The next phonetic aggregate beyond the syllable, the syllabic or rhythmic group, is also usually thus characterized primarily by internal nuclear concentration; it is a sound-cluster spoken with a single phonologically conventionalized pattern or "contour" of accentuation and intonation, the nuclear center or peak of which in the free or full form is a phonologically maximal or "primary" accent (either "dynamic" or "tonic"). In the group-unit it is the nuclear center that is most distinctive; the limits of the group may be marked by any degree of openness in juncture, and they are often, as in the syllable, obscure. (For the nuclear center of the rhythmic group the term *centroid* was much used in phonetic and psychological studies of rhythm early in this century, and became common in literary prosody; it has not been used in the more recently developed terminology of the newer linguistics. For rhythmic analysis it has the advantage of supplying for the group a term exactly correponding to "syllabic" for the syllable, and of abstracting from specification of factors involved to generalized neutral indication of a focus of relations.) The group-unit may be a single syllable (*Yes!*), or several "words" grouped by a single primary accent; it may stand alone as a sentence, or form part of a sentence in which several groups are combined either by subordinating hypotaxis or in paratactic coordination. The group-unit is the minimal free unit of utterance and as such the type of all free utterance-units, for the rest of which its phonological structure may be said to establish a basic norm preserved through various extensions in the larger units. No utterance can be made without this unit, and all utterances consist of such units and their extensions.

Syllabic groups are either simple or composite. A simple group includes no accent potentially "primary" other than that of its contour-nucleus; it may however, in a language provided with sufficient grading of stress or variation of pitch, include syllables with accent of "secondary" (or "tertiary") degree, normally incapable of optional utterance as primary. Composite groups include more than one potential primary or nuclear accent, all but one reduced to secondary level, under a single intonation-contour; a group is composite therefore when it is susceptible of optional utterance as a sequence of more than one group by imposition of additional contours of accentuation and intonation with secondary accents of the composite group as nuclear centers (*under these circumstances,* ò o ò ó o ò o, optionally e.g. ó o, ó, ó o ò o ᴧ). A composite group is thus a hypotactic inclusion of two or more potentially independent groups under the dominance of the contour and nuclear accent of one. The independent form of a simple group (exemplified in isolated utterance of a single word) is marked by full, if condensed, presentation of a complete intonation-contour; in the included form, this contour is reduced to its accentual nucleus alone, and this in turn reduced to secondary rank or suppressed. The varying distinctness of potential and actual group-units depends upon the definiteness with which subordinated nuclei affirm themselves as such; relatively slight nuclear concentration may suffice to assert a vestigial group-identity. Within the group-unit, even when it is monosyllabic, there appears a pattern of cadence; the accentual contour is a cadence-pattern. It is at the level of the syllabic group that cadence becomes conspicuous in speech. The *general cadence* of speech, as distinct from the succession of the unitary cadences of its group-units, is the continuous pattern within it of positional relation of prominent and unemphatic syllables, without reference to group division or group-boundaries, and hence without reference to group-contours as such.

In this general cadence, especially when it presents or suggests the regularity of alternation or other continuous recurrence, secondary accents rise to greater perceptual importance without any phonetic increase or modification. Regulation of general cadence by schematization of recurrence within it provides cadence-

meter in "stress" languages, notably the Germanic, including Eng. With such meters there can be interplay and tension between the continuous scheme of the metrically regulated general cadence and the varying patterns of the successive group-cadences; in languages with metrical schematization of cadence patterns other than those directly relevant to contours of aggregation, as in the durational feet of Gr. (aggregating by tonic accent) and L. (aggregating probably by stress of intensity), there can be contrast of these metrical patterns with "natural" aggregational cadence generally (in some forms of classical L. verse possibly regulated with reference to the patterns of the meter). The unit of recurrence in the minimal serial rhythm of normal prose seems always to be simply the phonological group-entity as such, without further schematization; to this unit nuclear concentration alone is essential, and cadence is as such irrelevant or redundant. (The group-entity itself however involves uniformity other than repetition of group-character in languages where the position of the nuclear accent within groups is fixed, as e.g. in Fr. at or near the end. Regular serial repetition of a scheme of cadence as such, which would make of this scheme a unit of recurrence distinct from the group-entity, would compromise the non-metrical character of rhythm in prose, since such schematization of recurrence is what constitutes meter.) But in the sporadic figuration which characterizes the further rhythmization of prose (and distinguishes prose called "rhythmical") patterns of cadence may have a conspicuous part, especially at the ends of syntactic or rhetorical units, where cadence patterns in systems involving two or more groups are common; cf. L. *clausulae, cursus.*

The larger rhythmic patterns of prose result from a massing and distribution of stronger and weaker elements in units corresponding to the larger syntactic and rhetorical entities ("phrases," intermediate members, sentences; the *comma, colon,* and *period* of ancient rhetoric); in these units cadence strictly so called is replaced or superseded by a larger movement, surge or swell and fall or undulation, which is only analogous to the minor if sharper contrasts of syllabic units within centroidal groups. Cadence strictly so called is a property of the macrostructure of speech and not, in the natural form of speech, conspicuously apparent in its microstructure. But in the configurational design of the larger units a cadence of their microstructural elements may have a part, and cadence in the strict sense may be one of the factors involved in the prominence or emphasis of the "emphatic" part of a large rhetorical unit.

The centroidal syllabic group-unit is often

identified by phonologists with the syntactic word-unit, and sometimes referred to as the "phonetic [or phonemic] word." Actually, both of the smallest phonological units of aggregation, the syllable and the group, are essentially phonetic entities whose correspondence with syntactic units is not fixed. Of rhetorical and syntactic groupings of sounds other than the syllable and the group-unit it may be said that in them phonetic boundaries always coincide with those of the same or similar syntactic units; but there is no single syntactic, or morphological, entity that invariably corresponds to or coincides with either the syllable or the centroidal syllabic group. The syllable may be either a part of a word or a word (in "monosyllabic" languages, e.g. Chinese, this latter is the norm; in other languages the proportion of monosyllabic to polysyllabic words, as of simple to compound words, in the lexicon varies). So the syllabic "group" may be a single word (possibly monosyllabic) or a combination of words (the accent of one the nuclear centroid of the group, other words "proclitic" or "enclitic" to this) or, more rarely, a part of a word-unit (e.g. in optional eccentric utterance, *impossible* = ó, ó o o). The word is not a phonetic unit but a syntactic (morphological-lexical) entity; phonetically it corresponds normally and typically with a single syllabic group, but not always. Any of the larger grammatical or rhetorical units (phrase, member, sentence) may also be phonetically a single centroidal group, and indeed monosyllabic. Usually and typically, of course, these larger units include more than one group. When this is the case, the phonological structure of such units includes some form of nuclear concentration (usually at or near the end), and especially a more or less diffused intonation-contour (with specific meaning-effect as well as terminal character), but the identity of larger units is established primarily by the occurrence of more open junctures at their boundaries; wholly terminal juncture is always a silence of indeterminate length.

Since their general intonation and delimitative junctures are sufficient to sustain their identity without reduction of accent in their component centroidal groups, these larger units of speech have the character of serial sequences of the smaller units rather than of systematic aggregation by nuclear accents; accentually they are sequence-units rather than strict aggregations. A distinction of this kind, between sequence-units created by imposing limits upon *series*, and units which are *systems* by virtue of internal aggregatory structure, is of use in all analysis. But the units relevant for rhythmic structure are not exclusively or even principally (in verse) the phonetic units that correspond to functional syntactic or rhetorical divisions. These divisions, of words, phrases, *cola*, and sentences or "periods," are indeed present everywhere in speech, and operate throughout its structure to create effects of "balance" and "measure," the ground of rhythm. All rhythm in speech is a relation among speech-units involved in establishment and conveyance of meaning, and relations among lexical and syntactic units, when these are regarded simply as unitary entities and their masses or characters in any way balanced or "measured" against each other, are not only rhythmic but examples of the most basic and elementary form of rhythm in speech; it is from this foundation that all the more complex rhythms of verse and meter develop by a more or less natural progression, and to this again that, whenever their progressive impulse is enfeebled or momentarily relaxed, they regress. Such elementary balancing occurs in simple paratactic series (lists of coordinate items in menus, scores, marshalings, litanies, etc.) or as relating systems hypotactically ordered internally. The items in such measured relation may be phonetically very disparate; but wherever we are conscious of pronounced balance or measure there is phonetic correspondence or congruence as well as semantic or syntactic, and not only of the balanced entities as total units but also of their component elements. The type of such balance is therefore one that rests primarily upon phonetic correspondence, as in parison or isocolon.

The rhythm thus created by patterns, especially of accentual grouping and phrasing, in the "natural" fúnctional units of speech from the group-unit to the "paragraph," is the fundamental and most basic rhythm in all speech whether prose or verse, metrical or unmetrical. When this rhythm appears alone, and the balance and measure of the speech is due exclusively to patterning of its "natural" functional units with no cyclic recurrence other than that of the group-entity, the rhythm is that of normal prose. Metrical rhythm is distinguished from that of prose by having as the unit of cyclic recurrence not the group-entity but an entity constituted "artificially" by abstraction and recombination of prosodic components of the group in some fixed scheme. The metrical schematization of cyclic entities may itself be *serial*—a counting of syllables (syllabics) or of "stresses"—producing units ("lines") larger than the typical group-unit but distinct both from it and from the rhetorical units into which groups are aggregated "naturally"; or it may be *systematic*, an arrangement or ratio of contrasting elements or values, providing units (typically "feet") distinct from the group-unit which may then be ordered by serial count or systematic arrangement into line-units distinct from the larger units of "natural" aggregation; line-units formed in either of these ways may then in turn be ordered together either serially ("stichically") or in some systematic ("strophic") arrangement, which may in its turn be repeated serially or, as in the Gr. choral ode, itself subjected to a further systematic ordering. The selection of elements for metrical schematization and of types of schemes is determined in part by the nature of a language, in part by historical accident; one could not have predicted of L. in its pre-classical stage that its classical verse would adopt Gr. schemes. Once the elements are selected, the multiple contrasts of values of these elements in "natural" speech are commonly reduced to a simple binary opposition for metrical construction (variety of stress-value to "stress" vs. "unstress," pitch variation to "level" vs. "inflected," durations to "long" and "short").

Though a scheme tends to be maintained continuously in recognizable form, once the unit of recurrence is established the essential recurrence is of its unit-character as such rather than of the scheme that specifies it; there is in the metrical verse of most languages, both at the level of the cyclic unit or foot and at that of the line, a good deal of variety in satisfaction of schematic norms ("substitution" etc.) Line-units have in common with the larger units of "natural" aggregation that their terminal sections are their most determinate parts; freedom of variation is more often permitted in the earlier part than at the end, and sometimes schematization is specially or exclusively fixed at or near the end of the line; strophic systematization of lines seems to enforce determinacy at line-ends (Vedic; cf. very general use of end-rhyme as enforcing supplement).

In general it may be said that where there is continuous recurrence of a fixed schematization of a unit roughly equal to or smaller than a typical aggregatory group (or word-unit), the rhythm of the speech is *metrical;* if there is continuous recurrence throughout of a schematized unit larger than the typical group or word-unit, the rhythm is that of *verse* (which may be unmetrical, or "free," if there is no continuous recurrence of a schematized cycle at or below the level of the group); where neither of these occurs, the rhythm is that of *prose.* Rhythmically *intermediate* speech, conventionally distinguished in many (especially Oriental) languages, though lacking the continuous cyclic schematization which would make it metrical, and the continuous division by lines which would make it verse, supplements the unschematized rhythm of ordinary prose by figuration of the same elements used in the schematizations of meter or of verse.

The datum of a prosodic analysis is ideally an oral performance (actual or conceived) rather than a written text. But every performance is governed by norms supplied by a text, and performance itself is to be judged by its conformity to the textual norm, determined from the graphic signs interpreted in turn by norms provided by the conventions of the given language generally and any relevant special conventions or usages (of period or author, possibly indicated by particular marketings etc.). In practice, a performance represents an abstraction of norms from a text; a prosodic analysis may therefore be a description in terms of such an abstraction of norms, representing perhaps more than one possible performance. Most metrical texts can be performed in more than one way within the limits of a single scansion; many can be read so as to present more than one possible metrical organization.

J. Caramuel (y Lobkowitz), *Primus Calamus ob oculis ponens Metametricam* (I, Rome 1653; II, 1665); M. Kawczynski, *Essai comparatif sur l'origine et l'histoire des rythmes* (1889); R. Westphal, *Allgemeine Metrik* (1892); P. Verrier, *Essai sur les principes de la métrique anglaise,* II (1909; *livre* 3, ch. v, "Origine et évolution des mètres poétiques," comparative survey); C. Jacob, *Foundations and Nature of Verse* (1918); A. Meillet, *Les origines indo-européennes des mètres grecs* (1923); E. A. Sonnenschein, *What is Rhythm?* (1925); O. Schröder, *Nomenclator Metricus* (1929); "Metrica" in *Enciclopedia Italiana,* XXIII (1934); A. Arnholtz, *Studier i poetisk og musikalsk Rytmik,* I (1938); E. Olson, *General Pros.* (1938); J. C. La Drière, "Prose Rhythm," "Pros.," in Shipley and "Comparative Method in . . . Pros.," *Comparative Literature,* ed. W. P. Friederich (Intern. Comparative Lit. Assoc. 2d Cong. *Proc.,* 1959); A. W. De Groot, *Algemene Versleer* (1946); *Sound and Poetry,* ed. N. Frye (1957; Whitehall, typology, pp. 143–44); *Manual of Phonetics,* ed. L. Kaiser (1957; esp. Jakobson, Halle, 215ff., Von Essen, 295ff., De Groot, 385ff.); J. Lotz, "Metric Typology," *Style in Language,* ed. T. Sebeok (1960); International Conference of Work-in-Progress Devoted to Problems of Poetics. 1st, Warsaw, 1960. *Poetics* . . . (1961); C. Watkins, "Indo-European Metrics and Archaic Ir. Verse," *Celtica,* 6 (1962); L. P. Wilkinson, *Golden L. Artistry* (1963); V. Nabokov, "Notes on Pros.," in his tr. of Pushkin, *Eugene Onegin* (1964).　　J.C.LAD.

PROSOPOPOEIA (fr. Gr. *prosōpon* "face," "person," and *poiein* "to make"). Term occasionally still used for personification (q.v.).

PROVENÇAL POETRY. The term "Prov.," applied to the poets who cultivated the language in the Middle Ages (the *trobadors*), co-incides with the ancient Roman "provincia" in what is now southern France. As a literary language it attained artificial uniformity throughout the territory, but where the same individual (e.g., Daude de Pradas) was at the same time poet and businessman, the non-literary documents he left behind show marked variations in dialect from the standard.

These writers produced largely, though not exclusively, lyric verse, which, from roughly the middle of the 11th c. through the 13th, was supreme in Europe. Since the discovery of the Sp. *jarchas*, the chronological priority of Prov. has been laid open to debate, but the basic importance of its impact on the literature of the continent remains unchallenged.

It is unexplained how it is that the first known name, that of William IX of Aquitaine (1071–ca. 1127), already shows, along with a sometimes primitive versification (aaab stanza) and themes fit for a baronial "stag party," the essentials of the courtly tone. This troublesome seigneur assumes an already conventional humility, it seems, before a quintessential *domna*, or lady far above him on a pedestal.

After him, practitioners of the art become numerous. To cite a few: the dour Marcabru, ever ready to belabor the world's foibles with the fervor of an Old Testament prophet, writing, at the same time, delightful *pastourelles*, dialogues between the "city slicker" and the no less astute shepherdess. There is Giraut de Borneil, a student in winter, but wandering minstrel in summer, accompanied by two performers who handled the *sonet*, or air that came perforce with each poem; contrasting in tone, Bernart de Ventadorn, truly sensitive in an essentially unromantic era. There was Peire Vidal, whose nimble wit and highly developed craftsmanship caused his works to be frequently misunderstood and even his biography miscolored in a modern novel.

Presentation soon becomes all-important, showing up in *rimas caras* (literally "costly rhymes"), sublimated language, and complex strophic form. Ideas were often so preciously conceived that a quarrel ensued between Giraut de Borneil and Raimbaut d'Aurenga as to whether a style should be easily comprehensible (*trobar leu*) or hermetic (*trobar clus*), an issue which may never be settled.

The supposedly resultant dearth of content was more apparent than real. True, some content themselves with an air of false, but fashionable, profundity; in many instances genuine, but equally heavy scholasticism is all too evident. Many an abstraction in the courtly terminology stems from the learning of the times.

Such a spirit often invades the genre least capable of admitting it, the *canso* (Fr. *chanson*). Here love is the almost exclusive concern, and nowhere is there displayed with so great and ceaseless complacency the poet's heart seared by amorous flames. Yet there is nothing tragic, not a single note of fatality about the whole business. The lover surrenders himself to the inexorable mistress upon due reflection and of his free will, since that is what a courtly person is expected to do in order to demonstrate his *valor*, or innate worth, and, through service to the lady, acquire *pretz*, or esteem. The identity of the mistress supposedly remained a secret and the love of the suitor completely disinterested. Both conditions could be theoretical.

Obviously such a poet was of the courts, even when his origin was lowly, and it was for the courts that he wrote. The day when the troops of Simon de Montfort, under royal or papal sponsorship, laid siege to their first castle in the Midi marks the first catastrophic step in the decline of all Prov. lyric. Thanks to the Inquisition, the adoration of the lady takes on a religious cast and the *canso* assumes a new character. Some genres get a new lease on life, like the *sirventes,* a satiric type, early immortalized by Bertran de Born, and flourishing again at the hands of the anticlerical Peire Cardenal; but the manifestation is brief. It is curious that the charming *pastourelle* takes on newer colors with the "last of the court poets," Guiraut Riquier, who makes of the songs true novelettes by grouping them in cycles.

If ideas became circumscribed, form was even more so. In the canso, the number of strophes was usually 5 to 7, with 1 or 2 additional half-strophes, called *tornadas,* serving as *envois,* dedicated to ladies or patrons, often addressed to the minstrel charged with their delivery. The stanzas had to be identical in form, sung as they were to identical melodies. They might all possess the same rhymes (*unissonans*) or differ in scheme (*utrissonans*). Sometimes a rhymeless verse was used (*estramp*), repeated in corresponding position in each stanza and serving as link between them. Especially in the earlier days, the term *vers* was used for this form, and it is hard to distinguish the two, at times, except for a greater tendency on the part of the *vers* toward masculine rhymes, a greater liberty in the number of strophes, and increased emphasis on satire or humor. The distinction, however, can scarcely be established in a short definition.

Steadier vogue was enjoyed by the dialogue forms, the *joc partit* and the *tenso,* both debates, largely on love casuistry, the difference being that, in the former, the opponent could choose any side, while in the latter he could not. The debate could involve no more than a *cobla,* or single stanza by way of statement and another in reply. Such a form often possessed a decided sting. The *planh,* or lament, reflects existing society. Reciting the virtues of a defunct patron, it dilates upon the departure of *Pretz* and Valor, by which, however, it is implied that a generous giver is no longer available. It is an exaggeration, on the other hand, to say that the genre is without emotion. Close to the modern romantic mood is the *alba* or dawn song, wherein a lover takes leave of his lady, while (at least in one case) a friend, acting as lookout, warns him of approaching day. The *alba* can also be strictly religious.

For decades, performers used crude manuscripts or learned their songs by heart. When the end of the bloom period was felt near, a great deal of extant material was gathered into beautiful anthologies, especially in Italy, where the Renaissance favored such activity. To this circumstance much Prov. lyric owes its survival. To the creation of anthologies we owe the earliest Prov. literary prose in the form of "biographical" sketches, called *vidas,* and comments, called *razos,* which purportedly showed the genesis of their accompanying poems. These so developed that they ultimately became a separate genre, later to become the *novella.*

So much for the lyric, which dominated the scene. There were epics, like the *Jaufre* and the *Girart de Roussillon,* the latter in mixed Fr. and Prov. Both are readable specimens, indeed much so, but southern epics are inferior to those of the north. Among the romances, where the south ranks high, the peer of them all is the *Flamenca,* in which the age-old subject of jealousy is treated with a skill that still excites admiration.

The 14th c. represents a drop in quantity and quality. Letting alone the uninspired treatises on versification or grammar (*Leys d'Amors, Razos de trobar*), we may indicate medieval encyclopedic works like the *Breviari d'Amor,* by the Franciscan friar Matfré Ermengaut, which, though it does include a "Perilous Treatise" on love, with copious citations from "authorities" like the *trobadors,* also takes in anything from astronomy to theology.

Religious literature multiplies in the later Middle Ages, but it is usually mediocre. The drama (e.g., the mystery play of St. Agnes) gives evidence of vitality. Production during the Renaissance is permeated with northern Fr. influence; the Toulouse academy, founded at the end of the bloom period, awarded prizes even to works not in any dialect of the Midi. Names could be cited, one of the few interesting ones available being the Gascon Pey de Garros, who shows the impact of the Reformation in the region. From the 18th c. one may perhaps select the earthy tales of Abbé Favre, notably the *Sermoun de Moussu Sistre,* popular enough, in 1919, to be sold on the newsstands of Montpellier. Favre and others showed their devotion to antiquity by translations, adaptations, even parodies of epics and the like.

Not until the 19th c. does a truly new movement like the Félibrige (q.v.) bring the humble patois back into the realm of world literature. Its chief, Frédéric Mistral, was awarded the Nobel Prize for outstanding lyrics, and for *Nerto* and *Miréio,* the latter set to music by Gounod. Mistral is one of several worthies.

Recently it has seemed, despite valiant efforts, that Prov. was fighting a losing battle, though, in contrast with other Fr. patois it is far from dead. Even the local verse written by the Résistants of World War II is evidence of real literary potentiality.

BIBLIOGRAPHIES: A. Jeanroy, *Bibliographie sommaire des chansonniers provençaux* (1916); A. Pillet and H. Carstens, *Bibliog. der Troubadours* (1933); C. Brunel, *Bibliog. des manuscrits littéraires en ancien prov.* (1935); P. L. Berthaud, *Bibliog. occitane* (1946); *Crit. Bibliog. of Fr. Lit.,* gen. ed. D. C. Cabeen, I (1952; enl. ed. U. T. Holmes).

ANTHOLOGIES: *Choix des poésies originales des troubadours,* ed. F.J.M. Raynouard (6 v., 1816–21); *Gedichte der Troubadours in provenzalischer Sprache,* ed. K.A.F. Mahn (4 v., 1856–73); *Chrestomathie provençale,* ed. K. Bartsch (6th ed., 1904); *Anthologie des tr.,* ed. J. Anglade (1927); *Anthol. des tr.,* ed. A. Jeanroy (1928); *Nouvelle anthol. des tr.,* ed. J. Audiau and R. Lavaud (1928); *Provenzalische Chrestomathie,* ed. C. Appel (6th ed., 1930); *Anthol. of the Prov. Tr.,* ed. R. T. Hill and T. G. Bergin (1941); *La lírica de los trovadores,* ed. M. de Riquer, I (1948); *Poètes provençaux d'aujourd'hui* (1957); *Leben und Lieder der provenzalischen Tr.,* ed. E. Lommatzsch (2 v., 1957–59); *Anthologie de la poésie occitane,* ed. and tr. A. Berry (1961).

GENERAL STUDIES: J. Anglade, *Hist. sommaire de la litt. méridionale* (1921); A. Jeanroy, *Poésie lyrique des tr.* (2 v., 1934) and *Hist. sommaire de la poésie occitane* (1945); P. Remy, *La litt. prov. au moyen-âge* (1944); M. de Riquer, *Resumen de literatura provenzal trovadoresca* (1948); A. Viscardi, *Storia delle letterature d'oc et d'oïl* (1952); V. Roche, *Prov. Regionalism* (1954); E. Hoepffner, *Les tr.* (1955); M. Valency, *In Praise of Love* (1958).

VERSIFICATION: G. Lote, *Hist. du vers fr.* (3 v., 1949–55); I. Frank, *Répertoire métrique de la poésie des tr.* (1953–57).—SPECIFIC GENRES: H. Springer, *Das altprovenzalische Klagelied* (1895); K. Lewent, *Das altprovenzalische Kreuzlied* (1905); J. Jones, *La tenson prov.* (1934); H. J. Chaytor, *The Prov. Chanson de*

Geste (1946); J. Boutière and A. H. Schutz, *Les biographies des tr.* (1950). A.H.S.

PROVERB. A saying current among the folk, often pithily or wittily expressed. Proverbial subjects favor customs, superstitions, legal maxims, "blasons populaires," weather and medical lore, conventional phrases, and prophecies. Proverbs are among the oldest poetic works in Sanskrit, Hebrew, Germanic, and Scandinavian literatures. "Learned" proverbs are those long current in literature, as distinct from "popular" tradition. The former come into Western European literature both from the Bible and the Church Fathers and from such classical sources as Aristophanes, Theophrastus, Lucian, and Plautus. Erasmus' *Adagia* (1500) was instrumental in spreading classical proverb lore among the European vernaculars. The first Eng. collection was *A Dialogue conteining . . . all the proverbs in the English tongue* (1546) by John Heywood. Proverbs had been commonly used by OE and ME writers, particularly Chaucer. The Elizabethan delight in proverbs is evident in John Lyly's *Euphues* (1578-80) and in countless plays of the period; proverbs are common in Shakespeare. The genres of literature in which they frequently occur are the didactic (e.g., Chaucer's *Tale of Melibeus*, Franklin's *The Way to Wealth*, Goethe's "Sprichwörtliches"); the satirical (Pope's writings, *passim*); works depicting folk characters (*Don Quixote*, J. R. Lowell's *The Biglow Papers*, Faulkner's *The Hamlet*); works reproducing local or national characteristics (E. A. Robinson's *New England*); and literary *tours de force* (Villon's *Ballade des proverbes*).—A. Taylor, *The Proverb* (1931); B. J. Whiting, *Chaucer's Use of Proverbs* (1934); W. G. Smith, *The Oxford Dict. of Eng. Proverbs* (2d ed. rev., P. Harvey, 1948); M. P. Tilley, *A Dict. of the Proverbs in England in the 16th and 17th Centuries . . .* (1950). D.H.

PRYDDEST. During much of the 19th c., and usually to this day, the "crown," which is the second highest award for a poem in the National Eisteddfod of Wales, is given for a "p.": a poem of considerable length in "free-meter" (q.v.) and not necessarily in *cynghanedd* (q.v.). The need for some such poetic form was seen by the 18th-c. poet and critic Goronwy Owen, who realized that the genius of the traditional Welsh poetic art was lyric and panegyric. Under Augustan influence he sought after a Welsh epic or heroic poem, and introduced into Wales a Miltonic ideal. Many attempts were made in the 19th c. to compose along these lines. The 20th-c. p. is usually shorter, more varied in style and lighter in touch. Romantic narrative and description have become popular, and great scope has been found within the p. form for metrical experiment, and for enlarging the scope of Welsh poetry. D.M.L.

PSEUDO-STATEMENT. Though I. A. Richards, when he introduced "pseudo-statement," in *Science and Poetry* (1926), used it fifteen times, he did not formally define it; he gave only two instances of p.-s. labeled as such (one from poetry—Blake's "O Rose, thou art sick!" [p. 69]), and his use of the term seemed to hover over at least three different but related senses. In each of these senses, *part* of what was meant by the term is a string of words that affects our feelings and attitudes (desirably or undesirably)—organizes (or disorganizes) our impulses—and, hence, is true or false only in some pragmatic sense of "true" and "false." What was *additionally* meant in Sense (1) is a string of words that is in the form of a statement but that—because factually meaningless (empirically unverifiable) and, hence, neither true nor false in the usual sense of "true" and "false"—is not in fact a statement; in Sense (2), a string of words that in certain contexts (scientific ones, e.g.) is a statement but that in certain other ones (poetic ones, at least) is not; and, in Sense (3), a false statement. Blake's line is certainly an instance of p.-s. in Sense (2). In the context of his poem, it is neither true nor false: it neither gives nor pretends to give information. Twenty-nine years later, in *Speculative Instruments*, Richards explicitly avowed Sense (2) and disavowed Sense (3), saying that "literary folk" had wrongly taken him to mean (3) and that "the more I pointed out that I didn't and couldn't mean that because I meant that—as they [pseudo-statements] occurred in the poetry—they are not statements at all, . . . the more glumly convinced my critics were that I was calling poetry names" (p. 148).

The term has had a curious history. For one thing, though the reviewers of *Science and Poetry* took little notice of the term, it was the subject of considerable controversy in the 1930's and the early 1940's—partly (one suspects) because "pseudo" is usually pejorative, partly because Richards' use of "p.-s." was, as Murry was first to point out, ambiguous, and partly because the theory in which the term had a rôle (that poetry is not cognitive but emotive) was unacceptable to some critics (Tate, preeminently). For another thing, between 1926 and 1955, though Richards often discussed the problem (of poetry and beliefs) that had occasioned his first uses of the term, he abandoned the term, perhaps because of its poor reception. And, finally, the term was, though often the subject of discussion, rarely a means of discussion—which is a pity, for, in Sense (2) at least, it could function usefully. Wheelwright proposes "poetic statement" as "a more suitable and less misleading term" in

Sense (2) ("On the Semantics of Poetry," p. 273).
—I. A. Richards, *Science and Poetry* (1926),
Practical Crit. (1929; esp. pp. 186–88), "Belief," *Sym.*, 1 (1930), and *Speculative Instruments* (1955); A. Tate, "The Revolt against
Lit.," *New Republic*, 49 (1927), "Three Types
of Poetry: III," *ibid.*, 78 (1934), "The Present
Function of Crit.," *Southern Review*, 6 (1940),
and "Lit. as Knowledge. . . ," *ibid.*, 6 (1941);
T. S. Eliot, "Lit., Science, and Dogma," *Dial*
[New York], 82 (1927) and "Dante" (1929),
Selected Essays 1917-1932 (1932); J. M. Murry,
"Beauty Is Truth," *Sym.*, 1 (1930). P. Wheelwright, "Poetry and Logic," *Sym.*, 1 (1930) and
"On the Semantics of Poetry," KR, 2 (1940).

M.S.

PSYCHOANALYSIS AND POETRY.† See SCIENCE AND POETRY.

PSYCHOLOGICAL CRITICISM.† See CRITICISM, TYPES OF.

PUN. A figure of speech depending upon a
similarity of sound and a disparity of meaning. For a successful p., the reader must recognize multiple meanings in a context where all
these meanings can be applied. The figure is
apparently as old as language, possessing irresistible appeal and appearing in all literatures.
It is discussed and analyzed in the classic
treatises of rhetoric by Aristotle, by Cicero, and
in the anonymous *Rhetorica ad Herennium*,
where three varieties are discriminated: *traductio, adnominatio*, and *significatio. Traductio*
refers to the use of the same word in different
connotations or a balancing of homonyms; *adnominatio* is the repetition of a word with the
addition of suffixes, prefixes, or with transposition of letters or sounds; *significatio* is closest
to the modern p., including *double entendre*.
The medieval rhetoricians, Geoffrey of Vinsauf
in his *Poetria Nova* and John of Garland in
his *Ars Versificandi* made the figure available
to such writers as Chaucer and the author of
the *Roman de la Rose*. The p. was not looked
upon by classical, medieval, or Renaissance
writers as primarily a vehicle for humor. For
example, the medieval *rime riche,* a form of
traductio, the use of homonyms in different
senses as the rhyming words (e.g., lief-leef
[lief-leaf]) was looked upon as a beauty rather
than a blemish. The p. could be used for comic
effect, but it was also a means of emphasis and
an instrument of persuasion. Shakespeare uses
it for both serious and bawdy purposes. Like
most Renaissance writers, Shakespeare followed
the divisions of p. by contemporary rhetoricians into antanaclasis, syllepsis, paronomasia,
and asteismus. In antanaclasis, a word is repeated, with a shift in meaning:

To England will I steal, and there I'll steal.
(*Henry V*, 5.1.92)

In syllepsis, a word is used once, with two
meanings:

At a word, hang no more about me. I am no
gibbet for you.
(*Merry Wives of Windsor* 2.2.17)

In paronomasia, the repeated words are close
but not exactly the same in sound:

Out sword, and to a sore purpose!
(*Cymbeline* 4.1.25)

In asteismus, a speaker replies to another, using the first man's words in a different sense:

Cloten: Would he had been one of my rank!
Lord: To have smell'd like a fool.
(*Cymbeline* 2.1.17)

At the same time the p. was esteemed as an
adornment for sermons, and Lancelot Andrews
can play on *gin* as both *snare* and *engine* or
contrivance without comic intent. By the end
of the 17th c., word games and excessive ingenuity had brought the p. into disrepute, and
by Addison's time, its use seemed a fault. In
Spectator no. 61, he indicts it as "false wit"
and explains it away in the works of "the most
ancient Polite Authors" by their being "destitute of all Rules and Arts of Criticism." From
the low critical esteem of the early 18th c., the
p. has never recovered full respectability. It is
negligible as a serious figure of rhetoric in the
romantic period, occurring most notably in a
far-fetched form as a sort of consciously outrageous comedy, as in Charles Lamb's "Lambpuns," or in Barham's *Ingoldsby Legends*,
where in one poem a witch is caught "by a
Hugh and a cry." The kind of serious wordplay of Verlaine's

Il pleure dans mon coeur
Comme il pleut sur la ville

would have been thoroughly unlikely in 19th-c.
England. Only in the present day, with a revival of interest in the metaphysical poets and
greater scholarly interest in medieval and
Renaissance rhetoric, has there been any kind
of rehabilitation of the p. as a figure of speech
and any serious interest in it found in criticism.
The allusiveness of modern verse is related to
punning, the original context of the quotation
standing for the second sense of the word, and
here frequently modern poetry makes an approach to the serious wit of the Renaissance
(e.g., Eliot's *The Waste Land*, "When lovely
woman stoops to folly and . . ." and "Good
night, sweet ladies, good night . . ."). However,
another influence, the exuberant word-play in
Joyce's *Ulysses* and the mass of interlingual

† In Supplement, see also PSYCHOLOGY AND POETRY.

puns in *Finnegans Wake* (balmheartzyheat—*Barmherzigkeit*) is working to keep the comic aspect of the p. dominant.

W. Empson, *Seven Types of Ambiguity* (1947); Sister Miriam Joseph, *Shakespeare's Use of the Arts of Language* (1947); H. Kökeritz, "Punning Names in Shakespeare," MLN, 65 (1950) and "Rhetorical Word-Play in Chaucer," PMLA, 69 (1954); W. K. Wimsatt, Jr., "Verbal Style, Logical and Counterlogical," PMLA, 65 (1950); P. F. Baum, "Chaucer's Puns," PMLA, 71 (1956); J. Brown, "Eight Types of Puns," PMLA, 71 (1956); M. M. Mahood, *Shakespeare's Wordplay* (1957).   S.F.F.

PURE POETRY is a prescriptive rather than a descriptive term in that it designates, not an actual body of verse, but a theoretical ideal to which poetry may aspire. Any theory of poetry which seeks to isolate one or more properties as essential and proceeds to exclude material considered to be nonessential may be classed as a doctrine of pure poetry. Interpreted in the widest sense, it could be applied to divergent points of view occurring within a broad historical range, such as Sidney's strictures on tragi-comedy and the 18th-c. idea of "sublimity."

Most specifically, the term refers to "La Poésie pure," a doctrine derived from Edgar Allan Poe by the Fr. symbolist poets, Baudelaire, Mallarmé, and Valéry, and widely discussed in the late 19th and early 20th c. In this context, "pure" is equivalent to absolute, on the analogy of absolute music. The analogy is significant in that both the theory and practice of the symbolists were influenced by the relations of poetry and music.

The doctrine was first enunciated in Poe's "The Poetic Principle." For Poe, the essential quality of poetry is a kind of lyricism distinguished by intensity and virtually identical with music in its effects. Since the duration of intensity is limited by psychological conditions, Poe concludes that the long poem is a contradiction in terms and that passages which fail to achieve a high level of intensity should not be included in the category of poetry. Poetry is regarded as being entirely an aesthetic phenomenon, differentiated from and independent of the intellect and the moral sense. The products of the latter, ideas and passions, are judged to be within the province of prose and their presence in a poem to be positively detrimental to the poetic effect.

In their desire to attain in poetry the condition of music, the symbolists were wholehearted disciples of Poe; in elaborating his theory, however, they were far more aware of the problem of language than Poe had been. The relevance of the doctrine of pure poetry to contemporary theory rests almost entirely upon its concern with the symbolic or iconic properties of language. The impetus toward this line of speculation was given in Baudelaire's rephrasing of Poe's idea: The goal of poetry is of the same nature as its principle and it should have nothing in view but itself. The general import appears to be nothing more than an affirmation of art for art's sake, but the technical implications are far reaching. The aim of the symbolists was to confer autonomy upon poetry by reducing to a minimum the semantic properties of language and by exploiting the phonetic properties of words and their marginal or suggestive meanings.

It would not be accurate to ascribe unity of aim to the whole symbolist movement. For Baudelaire, the autonomy of poetic language was incomplete in that meaning involved "correspondances" with an ultimate kind of reality. In his reference to the "supernal beauty" which pure poetry was capable of achieving, Poe had hinted at the possibility of a metaphysical or mystical significance in verbal music. The Abbé Bremond is explicit in claiming a mystical value for pure poetry, which for him is allied to the primordial incantatory element in verse. Mallarmé and Valéry are much more guarded concerning the meaning of poetry, limiting their inquiry to the technical problems of language. Mallarmé's speculations, which were intended for poets, must perhaps remain somewhat obscure to the layman. His conception of pure poetry was that of an absolute, a point at which poetry would attain complete linguistic autonomy, the words themselves taking over the initiative and creating the meanings, liberating themselves, so to speak, from the deliberate rhetoric of the poet. With Mallarmé, interest in subject matter in the traditional sense recedes almost to the vanishing point and is replaced by concern for the medium of poetry.

Speculation in this direction reached its limit in Valéry, who eventually found the processes of poetic composition more interesting than the poetry itself. Valéry's contribution to the doctrine of pure poetry focused on the most baffling aspect of poetic language, the relation of sound and sense. In his first exposition of the subject, preface to a volume of verse by Lucien Fabré, it is defined as poetry which is isolated from everything but its essence. Poe's strictures on the epic and on the didactic motive in general are repeated. Valéry acknowledges the debt of the symbolists to Wagner. The aim of pure poetry is to attain from language an effect comparable to that produced on the nervous system by music. This essay gave rise to considerable discussion and debate. Valéry, without abandoning the doctrine, was later to deny that he had advocated pure poetry in a literal sense. It represented for him a theoretical goal, an ideal rarely attainable in view of the nature of language, in which sound and meaning, sonority and idea form a union as intimate as that of the body and soul.

Poe's ideas, as is generally known, had little direct influence on Eng.-speaking critics and poets; the idea of pure poetry was mainly an importation from France. In the 1920's, George Moore brought out an anthology entitled *Pure Poetry*. Although Moore had absorbed the views of the symbolists, his notion of pure poetry actually goes back to an earlier tradition, that of the Parnassians. While the element of verbal music is not neglected, it is not of primary importance. The emphasis is on subject matter. Moore's chief aversions are abstract ideas and the intrusion of the poet's personality. Pure poetry is that which achieves the greatest possible degree of concreteness and objectivity.

It is possible to view imagism (q.v.) as an instance of pure poetry, although the doctrine itself does not employ the term and is quite distinct from the aims of the symbolists. The imagist manifesto was ready to dispense with rhyme and meter, if not with the element of verbal music itself. The qualities of vagueness and suggestiveness valued by Poe and the symbolists as an aid to the achievement of pure poetry were contrary to the imagist demand for the utmost precision in the rendering of the concrete image. The imagist doctrine may be included in the broad category of pure poetry insofar as it locates the essence of poetry in a single feature—the concrete image—and judges the other features of poetry to be superfluous.

As Robert Penn Warren has demonstrated in "Pure and Impure Poetry," the doctrine of pure poetry is hardly tenable in practice. Yet T. S. Eliot regards it as the most interesting and original development in the aesthetic of verse made in the last century. He finds its characteristically modern in its emphasis upon the medium of verse and its indifference to content. In his view, it terminated with Valéry and cannot serve as a guide to contemporary poets.

E. A. Poe, "The Poetic Principle," *Complete Works,* ed. J. A. Harrison, XIV (1902); *Pure Poetry: an Anthol.,* ed. G. Moore (1924); H. Bremond, *La Poésie pure* (1926); D. Porché, *Paul Valéry et la poésie pure* (1926); P. Valéry, *Variété,* 1 (1934); R. P. Warren, "Pure and Impure Poetry," KR, 5 (1943); J. Benda, *La France Byzantine, ou Le Triomphe de la littérature pure* (1945); T. S. Eliot, "From Poe to Valery," HR, 2 (1949); L. and F. E. Hyslop, Jr., *Baudelaire on Poe's Crit. Papers* (1952); C. Feidelson, Jr., *Symbolism and Am. Lit.* (1953); F. Scarfe, *The Art of Paul Valéry* (1954); J. Chiari, *Symbolisme from Poe to Mallarmé* (1956); H. W. Decker, *Pure Poetry, 1925–1930: Theory and Debate in France* (1962). S.F.

PURPLE PATCH. Horace in the *Ars Poetica* (*Epistles* 2.3.14–19, *purpureus . . . pannus*), explains the phrase as the irrelevant insertion of a richly described topic into a work about a totally different subject, e.g., a glowing description of a grove and altar of Diana in an epic poem. Thus two elements are necessary: extraneous subject matter and a colorful description of it. In modern usage, however, the term generally means a florid passage which stands out from the tone of the rest of the work. Such unrestrained diction causes the emotion thus aroused to exceed its object; e.g., "Oh Mother, I implore / Your scorched, blue thunderbreasts of love to pour / Buckets of blessings on my burning head . . ." (Robert Lowell, *In Memory of Arthur Winslow,* sect. 3). R.A.H.

PYRRHIC (Gr. "used in the *pyrrichē* or war dance) or *dibrach* (Gr. "of 2 short syllables"). This may be said to have been the shortest metrical foot in Gr. and L. verse, although it was not recognized as such by Aristoxenus and ancient metricians generally, who felt that feet must be of at least 3 morae or time elements (e.g., the tribrach ◡◡◡). In Eng. verse the p. foot (2 unstressed syllables) occurs frequently as variant or "substitution" (q.v.) in normal iambic series.—Kolář. R.J.G.

PYTHIAMBIC. A dactylic hexameter verse followed by an iambic dimeter (first p.) or trimeter (second p.). Is is used by Archilochus and by Horace (*Epodes* 14–15 and 16).—Koster. P.S.C.

PYTHIAN METER. See VERSUS PYTHIUS.

Q

QASĪDA. Name given to a formal ode in Eastern literature. The form originated in pre-Islamic Arabia during the 6th c., and was borrowed by Persian, Turkish, and Urdu poets. The theme may be panegyric, satire, warlike boasting, or elegiac; later the repertory was extended to include religious, mystical, didactic, and even political writing. The q. may extend to upward of a 100 couplets, all upon the same rhyme. The most famous examples are the *Muʿallaqat*, the 7 "suspended odes" of pagan Arabia; the greatest exponents were the Arabs Mutanabbī (d. 955) and Ibn al-Fāriḍ (d. 1235) and the Persians Anvarī (d. 1190), Khāqānī (d. 1200), Rūmī (d. 1273), and Saʿdī (d. 1291). In Western poetry, the form was imitated by Tennyson in his *Locksley Hall* and J. E. Flecker in his poetic drama *Hassan*. It was also used by the German poet Platen. See ARAB POETRY, PERSIAN POETRY.—R. A. Nicholson, *Lit. Hist. of the Arabs* (3d ed., 1923); E. G. Browne, *Lit. Hist. of Persia* (4 v., 1928); A. J. Arberry, *The Seven Odes* (1957).　A.J.A.

QUANTITY. See CLASSICAL PROSODY; METER; PROSODY.

QUATERNARIUS. See IAMB.

QUATORZAIN. A stanza or poem of 14 lines, e.g., a sonnet. The term, however, is now reserved for a 14-line poem similar to or like a sonnet but deviating from its patterns.

QUATRAIN. A stanza of 4 lines, rhymed or unrhymed. It is, with its many variations, the most common of all stanzaic forms in European poetry. Most rhyming quatrains fall into one of the following categories: abab, or its variant xbyb (in which x and y represent unrhymed lines), a category which includes the familiar ballad meter and the elegiac stanza (qq.v.) or heroic quatrain; abba, the so-called envelope stanza (q.v.), of which Tennyson's *In Memoriam* stanza (q.v.) is a type; aabb, in which an effect of internal balance or antithesis is achieved through the use of opposed couplets, as in Shelley's *The Sensitive Plant*. Less common quatrains are the Omar Khayyám stanza (q.v.), rhyming aaxa, and the monorhymed quatrain (e.g., Gottfried Keller's *Abendlied*). Quatrains interlinked by rhyme are also to be found, as are those displaying such complications as the alternation of masculine and feminine rhyme and the use of irregular line length. The q. has been used in Western poetry primarily as a unit of composition in longer poems, but the term is also applied to the two component parts of the octave (q.v.) of a sonnet. As a poem complete in itself, the q. lends itself to epigrammatic utterance; Landor and Yeats have shown mastery in the composition of such poems. (See EPIGRAM).

QUESTION, EPIC. In ancient epic poetry after the theme of the poem is announced, the muse, as patron goddess of the poet, is sometimes asked what started the action e.g., "Which of the gods brought them together in strife for fighting?" (*Iliad* 1.8.) The answer then offers a convenient way for the poet to begin his narration.　R.A.H.

QUINTET. A 5-line stanza of varying rhyme scheme and line length. The most frequent rhyme pattern is ababb as, for example, in Edmund Waller's *Go, Lovely Rose*. See also CINQUAIN and SP. QUINTILLA.

QUINTILLA. The q., a Sp. stanza form formerly considered a type of *redondilla* (q.v.) and so called (Rengifo, *Arte poética española*, 1592) was probably formed by the separation, in the 16th c., of the two parts of the 9- or 10-line *copla de arte menor*, where it was embryonic. It is a 5-line octosyllabic strophe having two rhymes in consonance and having the following restrictions: there may not be more than two rhymes or two consecutive rhymes and the strophe may not end with a couplet. The five possible rhyme combinations are therefore: ababa, abbab, abaab, aabab, aabba. The last two combinations, which begin with a couplet, are generally avoided in the independent q., but frequently appear as the second half of the *copla real*. The q. probably ranks among the three or four most commonly used octosyllabic strophes in Castilian. N. Fernández de Moratín's (1737–1780) famous *Fiesta de toros en Madrid* is written in *quintillas* employing four of the possible five rhyme schemes.—D. C. Clarke, "Sobre la q.," RFE, 20 (1933); Navarro.　D.C.C.

R

RAGUSAN POETRY. See YUGOSLAV POETRY.

RASA. See INDIAN POETICS.

REALISM. Following V. da Sola Pinto, we might define r. as that element in art "which is concerned with giving a truthful impression of actuality as it appears to the normal human consciousness." Realistic poetry, at its best, is likely to meet the following conditions: (1) it will describe normal situations and average characters in ordinary settings (often with emphasis on the lower strata of society); (2) it will renounce the use of far-fetched images and metaphors; (3) it will endeavor to reproduce actual speech and tend to approximate prose rhythms. An extreme of realistic poetry in the above sense is reached in Edgar Lee Masters' *Spoon River Anthology*, where no attempt is made to transcend the mental horizon of the individual speakers.

While fully inherent in the poetry of Villon and Swift (not to mention Chaucer's *Canterbury Tales, Piers Plowman* and the popular ballads, all of which reflect the medieval tradition of r.), poetic r., as a movement, must be regarded as an outgrowth of romanticism. In the Preface to the second edition of the *Lyrical Ballads* (1800), Wordsworth defends his choice of "incidents and situations of common life," while, at the same time, advocating "a certain colouring whereby ordinary things should be presented to the mind in an unusual aspect." This selective r., which presupposes a certain degree of idealization, is also championed by Crabbe, who (in the preface to his *Tales* of 1812) envisages a poetry that has "enough of reality to engage (our) sympathy, but possesses not interest sufficient to create painful sensations." In Germany, the aims of poetic r. (*Poetischer Realismus*) have been defined by Otto Ludwig as follows: "Die Poesie verfährt nach den Gesetzen der Erinnerung; sie ändert nicht, was geschehen, aber sie mildert es künstlerisch" (Poetry operates according to the laws of memory; it does not change the past but softens it artistically). This applies equally well to the poetry of Eduard Mörike and the prose of Gottfried Keller and Adalbert Stifter. In America, poetic r. is present in the poetry of Robert Frost, whom Louis Untermeyer quotes as having called himself a realist "satisfied with the potato brushed clean."

The ascendance of stark r. in poetry coincides with the arrival of the industrial age in the second quarter of the 19th c. In Germany, it takes a decidedly political turn in the social lyrics of Freiligrath, Herwegh, and Beck (*Das junge Deutschland*). Stripped of its revolutionary pathos, it is revived in the age of *Neue Sachlichkeit* (New Objectivity), especially in the poems of Bertolt Brecht's *Hauspostille* (1927). In France, Villon's macabre and naive humanitarianism (*Ballade des Pendus*) is sentimentalized in certain of Béranger's songs (*La Pauvre Femme*) and in François Coppée's *Les Humbles* of 1872. On the whole, however, modern French poetry—from Victor Hugo to Paul Valéry—is so markedly antirealistic that Baudelaire could make the statement: "The exclusive taste for the true . . . oppresses and stifles the taste for the beautiful" (*Salon of 1859*). The humanitarianism of Blake's *London* and Thomas Hood's *Song of the Shirt* remains somewhat isolated in Eng. poetry. More characteristic of the latter are the matter-of-factness of Browning ("all I want's the thing / settled for ever one way") and Hardy and the grim, almost satirical, r. of Synge (*Danny*), Kipling (*Barrack-Room Ballads*) and Siegfried Sassoon (*The Rear-Guard*). In America, E. A. Robinson (*The Children of the Night*) and Carl Sandburg (*Chicago Poems*) work in a tradition that harks back to Walt Whitman's ecstatic r. as it appears in the *Song of Myself*. (For a brief historical account of the realistic tradition in European literature see the epilogue to Erich Auerbach's *Mimesis*, 1953).— E. H. Coleridge, "R. in Poetry," Royal Soc. of Lit. *Trans.*, ser. 2, 31 (1914); J. A. Roy, "R. in Modern Poetry," QQ, 30 (1923), 31 (1924); S. Liptzin, "The Lyric of Nascent Modern R.," GR, 2 (1927); V. da Sola Pinto, "R. in Eng. Poetry," E&S, 25 (1939); M. Nussberger, "R., Poetischer" in *Reallexikon*, III; W. Silz, *R. and Reality* (1954; see p. 10–16 of Introd.); *Documents of Modern Lit. R.*, ed. G. J. Becker (1963).   U.W.

RECESSIVE ACCENT. A r.a. is said to occur when a word (usually a dissyllable) accented on its final syllable is succeeded by another strongly accented syllable. In such cases for the sake of greater ease in rhythm, the accent in the dissyllable is shifted to the front of the word: "He is compléte in feature and in mind." (Shakespeare, *Two Gentlemen of Verona* 2.4.73) and "Can pierce a cómplete bosom." (*Measure for Measure* 1.3.3). A specific variety of wrenched accent, this device has died out of versification, as it has in normal speech usage, from which it no doubt took its origin and justification. Early poets, among them Shakespeare, used it extensively, the romantics employed it, and Bridges speaks of it as a lingering custom in the common speech of Ireland (e.g., éxtreme unction).—A. Schmidt, *Shakespeare Lexicon* (2d ed., II, append. 1, 1886); C. F. Jacob, *The Foundation and Nature of Verse* (1918); R. Bridges, *Milton's Prosody* (1921); Deutsch.　　　　　　　　　　R.BE.

RECIPROCUS VERSUS. A verse which is in the same meter when the order of the words is reversed, e.g.

$$M\bar{u}s\breve{a}, m\breve{i}|h\bar{i} \ c\bar{a}u|s\bar{a}s \ m\breve{e}m\breve{o}|r\bar{a} \ qu\bar{o} \ | \ n\breve{u}m\breve{i}n\breve{e} \ |$$

$$l\bar{a}es\bar{o}$$

(Virgil, Aeneid 1.8)

which remains a dactylic hexameter when read backward:

$$l\bar{a}es\bar{o} \ | \ n\bar{u}m\breve{i}n\breve{e} \ | \ qu\bar{o} \ m\breve{e}m\breve{o}|r\bar{a} \ c\bar{a}u|s\bar{a}s \ m\breve{i}h\breve{i}, \ |$$

$$M\bar{u}s\breve{a}$$

Sidonius Apollinaris (5th c. A.D., *Epistulae* 9.14) mentions "recurrent verses" (*versus recurrentes*) which, when read backward, retain the same order of letters and meter, e.g.

　　Roma tibi subito motibus ibit amor.

H. Keil, *Grammatici latini*, I (1857), 516.24–517.14; VI (1923), 113.11–114.10.　　　　R.J.G.

RECOGNITION. See PLOT.

REDERIJKERS. (Fr. *rhétoriqueurs*.) Members of the *rederijkerskamers* (chambers of rhetoric) which flourished in the Netherlands in the 15th and 16th c. The chambers, which were organized as guilds, each with its patron, its name, and its distinctive motto and emblem, originated in Flanders and Brabant, almost certainly on the model of analogous Fr. associations, and spread gradually to the north, where they became particularly well established in the province of Holland.

The r. (the term included both practicing poets and students of poetry) tended, like their German counterparts, the Meistersinger (q.v.), toward a formalistic, almost mechanical concept of art, and some of the forms in which they expressed themselves have a remarkable complexity. Their major interest lay in dramatic and lyric poetry, and their principal forms were: in the drama, the *zinnespel* (allegorical morality play) and the *esbattement* (farce); in the lyric, the *refrein* (q.v.), a strophic

poem utilizing a recurrent 1-line refrain at the end of each stanza, and such Fr. forms as the ballade and the rondel (qq.v.).

The r., who were, on the whole, members of the prosperous burgher class, often organized sumptuous drama and poetry competitions, known variously as *landjuwelen, haagspelen,* and *refreinfeesten*. Among the more famous *rederijkerskamers* were *De Heilige Geest* and *De Drie Santinnen* at Bruges, *De Fonteine* at Ghent, *Trou moet Blycken* at Haarlem, and *De Egelantier* and *Het Wit Lavendel* at Amsterdam. The most noted of *rederijker* works are *Elckerlijk* (Everyman), which is probably the source of its Eng. analogue, the anonymous miracle play *Mariken van Nieumeghen,* Colijn van Rijssele's romantic play *Den Spieghel der Minnen,* the religious *refreinen* of Anna Bijns, and the *esbattements* of Cornelis Everaert.—J. J. Mak, *De R.* (1944); G. J. Steenbergen, *Het Landjuweel van de R.* (1950).　　F.J.W.

REDONDILLA. A Sp. stanza form, an octosyllabic quatrain rhyming abba in consonance and sometimes called *r. mayor, cuarteta, cuartilla.* Quatrains having the rhyme abab are occasionally called *redondillas,* but generally use the name *serventesio.* The r. written in lines of less than 8 syllables is called *r. menor.* The term formerly included the *quintilla* (q.v.) and was also applied to any octosyllabic strophe in which all verses rhymed in consonance. The r. apparently is the result of the breaking in two at the strophic caesura of the *copla de arte menor* (see ARTE MENOR). The separation was completed in the 16th c., and the r. has been one of the most commonly used octosyllabic strophes in Castilian ever since.—D. C. Clarke, "R. and copla de arte menor," HR, 9 (1941); Navarro.　　　　D.C.C.

REFRAIN. A line, or lines, or part of a line, repeated at intervals throughout a poem, usually at regular intervals, and most often at the end of a stanza; a burden, chorus, or repetend. (*Burden* usually indicates a whole stanza; a *chorus* is a refrain joined in by a group; a *repetend* need not occur *throughout* a poem.) The r. seems a universal feature of primitive poetry and tribal verse, an accompaniment of communal dance and communal labor. Probably the very beginnings of poetry are to be found in iterated words and phrases. Refrains occur in the Egyptian *Book of the Dead,* in the Hebrew Psalms, in the Gr. idyls of Theocritus and Bion, in the L. epithalamiums of Catullus, in the Anglo-Saxon *Deor's Lament;* they blossom in the medieval ballads, in Prov. fixed forms, in Renaissance lyrics, and in poetry of the romantic period.

A r. may be as short as a single word or as long as a stanza. Though usually recurring as a regular part of a metrical pattern, it may appear irregularly throughout a poem, and it may be used in free verse. In stanzaic verse it usually occurs at the end of a stanza, but may appear at the beginning or in the middle. It may be used in such a way that its meaning varies or develops from one recurrence to the next (Poe discusses this use in "The Philosophy of Composition"), or it may be used each time with a slight variation of wording appropriate to its immediate context (Rossetti's *Sister Helen*, Tennyson's *Lady of Shalott*).

The r. may be a nonsense phrase, apparently irrelevant to the rest of the poem, or relevant only in spirit ("With a hey, and a ho, and a hey nonino"), or it may very meaningfully emphasize some important aspect of the poem —theme, characters, or setting. The r. furnishes pleasure in its repetition of familiar sound; it serves to mark off rhythmical units, and at the same time to unify the poem; and it may be very skillfully used to reinforce emotion and meaning.—F. B. Gummere, *The Beginnings of Poetry* (1908); F. G. Ruhrmann, *Studien zur Gesch. und Charakteristik des R. in der englischen Lit.* (1927).　　　　L.P.

REFRÁN. The Sp. *refrán*, usually translated as proverb, is a short, pithy, popular saying expressing advice based on wisdom gained through common experience or observation. It may deal with any subject—such as medicine, hygiene, agriculture, morals, or philosophy, to name but a few. It is often composed of two short phrases that rhyme in consonance or assonance, or contain alliteration, or are of parallel structure, or have some other sound-device that makes them appeal to the ear and cling to the memory. The Sp. language is exceedingly rich in this sort of expression and collectors have been busy for at least half a millennium gathering them into *refraneros*. The first known collection is the mid-15th-c. *Refranes que dicen las viejas tras el fuego*, generally attributed to the Marqués de Santillana. Many thousands have been gathered by dozens of collectors since then. Some of the important collections are those of Hernán Núñez, Juan de Mal Lara, Gonzalo Correas, F. Rodríguez Marín, and J. Cejador y Frauca.　　　D.C.C.

REFREIN. A poetic form especially favored by the *rederijkers* (q.v.) in the Netherlands. It consists of 4 or more stanzas of identical length and rhyme scheme, each of which ends with an identical line (*stock*, q.v.); the number of syllables in the lines is not fixed. The last stanza, which may be shorter than the others, is usually directed to the "prince" of the chamber of rhetoric or some other person; its initial letters are sometimes used acrostically to form the name of the poet. In accordance with the highly mannered poetic of the *rederijkers*, great attention is bestowed on rhyme, the intricate use of which makes the *refrein* a difficult form.

A spoken, not a sung, form, the r. derives its name from the Fr. *refrain*, and it owes its origin largely to the Fr. ballade (q.v.). *Refreinen* are divided into *vroede* (serious, religious, didactic, satiric), *amoureuze*, and *sotte* (comic, jocular, obscene, or nonsensical) categories. *Refreinfeesten* were competitions between various chambers, on given questions or *stocks* and with a given number of stanzas and lines. The great age of the r. was ca. 1450–1600, and the most notorious examples of the form are those by Anna Bijns and those compiled by Jan van Styevoort, Jan van Doesborch, and Jan de Bruyne.—A. van Elslander, *Het r. in de Nederlanden tot 1600* (1953).　　R.F.L.

REIZIANUM (*colon Reizianum*). An acephalous pherecratean

$$(\breve{\smile}\breve{\smile}-\smile\smile-\breve{\smile})$$

named after Reiz (1733–90). Like the telesillean (q.v.) of which it is the catalectic form, it occurs with variations and resolutions in Pindar and Gr. drama as well as in early L. poetry. The *versus Reizianus* which is frequently found in Plautus is a *colon R.* preceded by an iambic dimeter acatalectic, e.g.:

$$\breve{e}g\bar{o} \ \bar{t}e \mid f\breve{a}ci\bar{a}m \mid m\breve{i}ser\vert r\bar{u}m\bar{u}s \parallel m\bar{o}rt\bar{a}li\breve{s} \ \bar{u}ti \ s\bar{i}s$$
$$(Aulularia \ 443)$$

The combination of other meters (in particular an anapaestic dimeter acatalectic) with a colon R. also occurs in Plautine cantica. There is now a tendency in Gr. metric to discard the term "R.": see A. M. Dale, *Lustrum*, 2 (1957), 12.— W. M. Lindsay, *Early L. Verse* (1922); L. Havet, "Le distique (dit 'vers') de Reiz," *Revue des études latines*, 19 (1941); Dale; Koster, Crusius; U. von Wilamowitz-Moellendorff, *Griechische Verskunst* (2d ed., 1958).　　R.J.G.

REJET. A term in Fr. versification. The r. occurs as the result of a conflict between syntax and metrical pattern in enjambement (q.v.), when the lesser part of a grammatical phrase-unit flows over from one line to the next: "C'est le sceau de l'état.—Oui, le grand sceau de cire / Rouge" (V. Hugo, *Marion de Lorme* 3.4.1–2). A more limited form, the r. *à l'hémistiche*, is identified when such overflow occurs from one hemistich to the next in the same line: "En attaquant Monsieur | Bonaparte, on me fâche" (V. Hugo, *Un bon bourgeois dans sa maison*). When the greater part of a grammatical phrase-unit overflows in this way, there results what is called a *contre-rejet*: "Le Sauveur a *veillé* | pour tous les yeux, *pleuré* / Pour tous les pleurs, *saigné* | pour toutes les blessures" (V. Hugo, *Dieu*).— M. Grammont, *Le vers français* (1913) and *Petit traité de versification française* (5e éd., revue, 1924). A.G.E.

RELATIVISM IN CRITICISM. See CRITICISM, TYPES OF.

RELIGION AND POETRY. The relations of rel. to poetry have been so varied and often so subtle or intricate, that any simple statement regarding them is likely to invite objections. On the one hand there is the view stated by Amos N. Wilder (*Modern Poetry and the Christian Tradition*) that poetic experience and religious experience "are profoundly and intimately related to each other if not consubstantial, and religion requires poetry in its discourse." At the opposite pole stands Samuel Johnson's pontifical denial that "contemplative piety, or the intercourse between God and the human soul" either can or should be poetical. For "the essence of poetry is invention" (so Johnson argues in his *Life of Waller*), and it delights by producing unexpected surprises; whereas the topics of devotion, being few, are already known to all believers, hence "they can receive no grace from novelty of sentiment and very little from novelty of expression."

It would seem that each of these contrary views pushes its point too far. Rel. and poetry can hardly be considered consubstantial, since either of them may occur without the other. Calvinism deliberately repudiates the poetic graces so far as possible, yet only by an arbitrary restriction of language could it be denied that Calvinism is a rel. Conversely, such poems as Shakespeare's *Venus and Adonis* and Keats's *Endymion* are not, in any accepted meaning of the word, religious. But if it is thus evident that rel. and poetry differ in essence since they possess demonstrably different meanings, it is equally evident that they should not be conceived in such a way as necessarily to exclude each other. In opposition to Johnson's pronouncement it may be observed that novelty of sentiment and novelty of expression have within reasonable limits a legitimate place in rel., for hackneyed phrases and the stale sentiments which they are likely to engender can do much to weaken the religious consciousness of a freshly inquisitive generation that inherits them. An agnostical reader, to whom prayer has become an expendable anachronism, may be startled into a new, though partial, awareness of its vitality by Auden's unconventional way of addressing God, in "Sir, no man's enemy . . ." Similarly, God's love, which is so inevitable and oft-repeated a theme in Christianity that it runs the double danger of being accepted perfunctorily and of being sentimentalized, has received new lifts at various times from such metaphoric conceits as Spenser's "Then shall thy ravish'd soul inspirèd be . . . / With sweet estrangement of celestial love," Donne's and the Spanish mystics' bold use of carnal union as a symbol of divine love, and the love-chase in Francis Thompson's *The Hound of Heaven*. Quite evidently the novelties of expression and of sentiment that are present in these poems do not disqualify them from being considered religious.

If the foregoing considerations are valid it follows that rel. and poetry should be defined independently of each other yet not in such a way as to imply mutual exclusion. One method of doing this is to consider the basic modes of apprehending reality which the two disciplines, poetry and rel., individually represent. The poetic mode of apprehension is largely synthetic. It works by fusion; for in the familiar words of T. S. Eliot, the poem *qua* poem is a particular medium "in which impressions and experiences combine in peculiar and unexpected ways," and consequently "the poet's mind is in fact a receptacle for seizing and storing up numberless feelings, phrases, images, which remain there until the particles which can unite to form a new compound are present together" ("Tradition and the Individual Talent"). In short, poetry works by a "fusion of elements," and it achieves its own kind of objectivity inasmuch as "impressions and experiences which are important for the man may take no place in the poetry, and those which become important in the poetry may play quite a negligible part in the man, the personality." The religious mode of apprehension, by contrast, must be defined in terms not of synthesis but of responsive belief; and it becomes objective—that is, it transcends the merely personal and subjective —to the extent that a vital harmony is achieved, often involving a large measure of paradox, between the belief and the totality of the believer's passive and active (that is, receptive and responsive) experience. A properly religious emotion, as Eliot declares in his essay on Lancelot Andrewes, "is wholly evoked by the object of contemplation, to which it is adequate"; it is "wholly contained in and explained by its object." The spheres of rel. and poetry coalesce, therefore, wherever an imaginative fusion of the elements of experience and a responsive faith in a reality transcending and potentially sanctifying the experience are both effectively present.

As a matter of fact religious language, even when it is not molded into an actual poem, and when its intent is to instruct or exhort rather than to please, tends quite naturally to employ some of the characteristic devices of poetic expression. Everyday language is inadequate to

RELIGION AND POETRY

describe such intense and largely unsharable experiences as the soul's yearning for and partial realization of God. Devotional writers, therefore, have generally resorted to figurative language, not always in lieu of an attempt at plain speaking but at least as a supplement to it. Repeatedly in the Bible the soul's relation to Divinity is expressed, for instance, by the metaphor of marriage. Jeremiah and Ezekiel speak of God as Israel's husband; Jesus speaks of himself as the Bridegroom; Paul speaks of the mystical marriage between Christ and his Church; and the Book of Revelation is climaxed by the marriage of the Lamb and his Bride. Or again, in the first chapter of the Gospel according to John, Christ is spoken of as the Word and the Light, and in the fifteenth chapter he speaks of himself as the true Vine. When these epithets are examined it will be seen that each of them represents a double semantic shift. There is a synecdochic shift from whole to part, whereby the writer, in order to speak about the Supreme Reality, concentrates upon one attribute at a time. And there is the metaphoric shift from abstract to concrete, whereby the attribute thus momentarily isolated is presented under the figure of a familiar image. Parable and allegory are further manifestations of this tendency toward figurative speaking; but as distinguished from metaphor they can be translated more or less adequately into literal expository terms, and to that extent they represent a secondary rather than a primary linguistic phenomenon.

As we pass from the scattered and incidental appearances of poetry in religious documents to actual religious poems such as the *Oresteia, The Divine Comedy,* and *Paradise Lost,* we find more deliberate and sustained uses of poetic artifice. The religious power of the *Oresteia* is found not so much in the exhortations and cosmic speculations of the Chorus as in the symbolic overtones of the imagery—particularly the images associated with watching, hunting, crimson blood and the crimson royal robes, ritual slaughter, the serpent in its dual rôle as death bringer and life bearer, the flight of birds, and the coming of light. *The Divine Comedy,* although it draws freely upon the philosophy and theology of Thomas Aquinas, is by no means merely a restatement of that teaching in more highly colored language. The peculiar perspective and quality of Dante's poem comes not from either the doctrinal content or the poetic embellishments taken separately, but mainly from the fresh insights produced by the poet's fusion of particular images and incidents with the theological ideas which they represent and which they suggest to an informed reader's mind. As for *Paradise Lost,* which to many readers will seem to deal with its subject matter more straightforwardly than

either of the other two poems here mentioned, David Daiches has pointed out that beneath the obvious scenario meaning, which is to say the paraphrasable surface meaning, Milton is presenting obliquely through mood and imagery and indirect allusion a more essential theodicy—namely that "the real justification of God's dealings with men lies in the implicit contrast between the ideal idleness of the Garden of Eden and the changing and challenging world of moral effort and natural beauty which resulted from the fall." For although the postlapsarian world may lack the unruffled bliss of Eden, yet the curse placed on mankind that he shall earn his bread by the sweat of his brow is transformed by Milton into descriptions of the procession of the seasons and the beauty and dignity of rustic labor, all of which "contradict or at least modify the explicit statement that work was imposed on man as a curse" (Daiches, in Hopper, *Spiritual Problems in Contemporary Literature*).

The 17th c. marks the highest development of religious poetry in England; for in no other period have there been so many poets—Donne, George Herbert, Henry Vaughan, Crashaw, and Traherne among the chief—who combined devotional sincerity with a readiness to experiment with poetry as a verbal and metrical medium. Whereas it had been more characteristic of Spenser, in the late 16th c., to employ simple and familiar metaphors when speaking of God—"that sovereign Light, / From Whose pure beams all perfect beauty springs"—the 17th-c. metaphysical poets sought by new and unexpected tricks of syntax and extensions of metaphor, by "pious wit" as it has been called, to communicate certain more elusive qualities of religious awareness. George Herbert, for instance, can employ such devices as tautology and reversed metaphor with startling effect. Regarding the love-union with God as the absolute of human existence he can declare: "Ah, my dear God, though I am clean forgot, / Let me not love Thee, if I love Thee not"—where the seeming tautology of the second line expresses more potently than a literal declaration could do, the identification of love of God with very existence. The reversed metaphor in the poem *Divinity*—"He doth bid us take his blood for wine"—surprises us by the interchange of vehicle and tenor, q.v. (since Christian liturgy normally treats the wine of the Eucharist as symbolizing Christ's blood rather than vice versa); but this shock of surprise produces a new depth of understanding by forcing the reminder that Blood, too, is a symbol. In fact, in the final couplet of *The Agony* Herbert merges the two symbols, declaring: "Love is that liquor, sweet, and most divine, / Which my God feels as Blood, but I as wine." Henry Vaughan, who acknowledged a large spiritual debt to Herbert, is especially concerned with such paradoxical relations as that of time to eternity ("bright shoots of everlastingness"), of death to life ("And where this dust falls to the urn, / In that state I came, return"), and of light to darkness ("The whole creation shakes off night, / And for thy shadow looks, the light").

Coming down to the present, it may be said with some assurance that no poet writing in Eng. today has made a more signal contribution to the art of religious poetry than Eliot. Two poems stand out as particular landmarks. *Ash Wednesday* is a devotional poem remaining within the Christian framework, employing much of the imagery and echoing a number of the responses of the Anglican liturgy. *Four Quartets* achieves a more inclusive synthesis. It develops freshly paradoxical insights by fusing traditionally Christian images with images drawn from secular aspects of the contemporary world: as in the "wounded surgeon" lyric in *East Coker,* or as when the dark dove in *Little Gidding* represents at once an attacking bomber and the third Persona of the Trinity, or as when the garden imagery in *Burnt Norton* becomes suddenly vitalized and estranged by a suggestion of Freudian symbolism. Such metaphoric revitalization of the great Christian themes demonstrates anew the real service to poetry and rel. alike which an effective alliance of the two can bring about.

G. Santayana, *Interpretations of Poetry and Rel.* (1900); P. H. Osmond, *The Mystical Poets of the Eng. Church* (1918); H. Bremond, *Prayer and Poetry* (1929); T. S. Eliot, *Dante* (1929, repr. in *Selected Essays,* 1932) and "Rel. and Lit.," in *Essays Ancient and Modern* (1936); H. C. White, *The Metaphysical Poets* (1936); D. G. James, *Scepticism and Poetry* (1937; ch. 8); H. N. Fairchild, *Religious Trends in Eng. Poetry* (5 v., 1939–62); G. W. Knight, *The Starlit Dome* (1941); *Spiritual Problems in Contemp. Lit.,* ed. S. R. Hopper (1952); A. N. Wilder, *Modern Poetry and the Christian Tradition* (1952) and *Theology and Modern Lit.* (1958); E. I. Watkin, *Poets and Mystics* (1953); L. L. Martz, *The Poetry of Meditation* (1954); Wheelwright; *Lit. and Belief,* ed. M. H. Abrams (1958); N. A. Scott, Jr., *Modern Lit. and the Religious Frontier* (1958); R. Stewart, *Am. Lit. and Christian Doctrine* (1958); C. I. Glicksberg, *Lit. and Rel.* (1960); R. P. Blackmur, "Religious Poetry in the United States," *Rel. in Am. Life,* ed. J. W. Smith and A. L. Jamison, II (1961); *The New Orpheus* and *The Climate of Faith in Modern Lit.,* both ed. N. A. Scott (1964).   P.W.

REMATE. A Sp. metric term denoting a short stanza placed at the end of a poem and serving as a conclusion to the poem. The r. generally repeats the last rhymes of the preceding full-length strophe. It is most commonly used at the end of the *canción* (q.v.). In it the poet addresses himself to the *canción,* giving it a special message to bear to a particular person, "recognizing some flaw in the *canción,* or making an excuse for it, or telling it what it must answer if it should be found wanting in some respect" (Rengifo). It has also been called *vuelta, commiato, despido, envío, ripressa, ritornelo (retornelo), contera.*—Rengifo, *Arte poética española* (1592, ch. 86); E. Segura Covarsí, *La canción petrarquista en la lírica española del siglo de oro* (1949); Navarro.

D.C.C.

RENAISSANCE POETICS. Despite comparative neglect, Ren. poetics is an important and influential body of criticism. It is thanks to the Ren. that literary criticism is recognized as an independent form of literature, and that the critic is accepted as an honorable citizen in the republic of letters. Nor is that all. All modern poetics is heavily indebted to the Ren. The neoclassical period did little more than normalize the precepts of the Ren., and the romantic period formulated its new doctrines in conscious opposition to neoclassicism. Much of the "newness" of romanticism is little more than the old rules turned upside down. Wordsworth and Hugo, for instance, defined their critical positions by affirming almost all that the neoclassical period negates and negating almost all that it affirms.

Ren. criticism was born in the struggle to defend imaginative literature against its enemies and since literature was attacked on moral and social grounds it had to be defended on those grounds. If today moralistic conceptions seem foreign to literary criticism, it is because the Ren. won its battle and left its heirs free to devote themselves to other matters. Boccaccio in his *Genealogia Deorum* (1360) and in his life of Dante laid down the main lines for the defense of poetry against its clerical and philistine detractors. He argued that poetry and religion are not opponents. On the contrary, the Bible *is* poetry and teaches, as does all poetry, by means of allegory. The pagan stories which seem offensive to theologians may be interpreted as the Bible is interpreted: "When the ancient poets feigned that Saturn had many children and devoured all but four of them, they wished to have understood from their picture nothing else than that Saturn is time, in which everything is produced, and as everything is produced in time, it likewise is the destroyer of all and reduces all to nothing." Boccaccio's defense of pagan writers, naive as it may seem, was a step toward complete freedom of subject matter for all artists. Leda and the Swan, for instance, could be considered as shadowing forth the Virgin and the Dove. By his method anything and everything could be defended against moral or theological criticism.

On the social level, Boccaccio's defense is suited to values of the age. Not only has poetry always been admired among all peoples, but its protectors have been kings and princes and great lords. Further, the poet himself has always been worthy of patronage. He is a creator, like God Almighty Himself. No higher function is possible for man.

These arguments were repeated again and again, not only in Italy but in the various "apologies for poetry" written in France and England. They gave an inspirational coloring to even the most practical treatises. The rule makers who flourished in the 16th c. always had these assumptions in mind, as did the practicing poets. Forgetting this, some literary historians have spoken of a disparity between the dry poetic treatises and the creative outburst of the period. This simply did not exist for the men of the time.

Once the subject matter of poetry was defended, the next problem that presented itself was whether poetry could be written in a modern language. This problem was extremely complex. First, some of the humanists were so proud of having restored good L. to the world that they had small sympathy for productions in the vernacular even when these were by Dante, Petrarch or Boccaccio. Secondly, those literary critics whose major interests were in the classical genres usually assumed that great literature demanded either L. or Gr., preferably L. Thirdly, in Italy, which set the pattern in this as in other critical matters, the situation was complicated by the fact that there was no national state and thus no national language. Those who were interested in defending literature in the vernacular had first to defend their choice of a particular dialect.

Blessed with the greatest writers in the so-called vulgar tongue, Florence took the lead in the language question. Dante's *De Vulgari Eloquentia* (ca. 1305) is the first and greatest plea for vernacular literature, and it has no worthy successor until Alberti's *Il Governo della famiglia* (1438), where it is argued that the vulgar tongue would become as polished as L. if patriotic writers gave their attention to it. Pietro Bembo in *Prose della Volgar Lingua* (1524) deserted his fellow humanists and came over to the side of the vernacular. Not content with claiming that Florentine was as good as Latin, he went on to assert that it was even superior as a medium for modern subjects. Since Florentine was the one dialect with a strong literary tradition, most Italians who wrote in the vernacular used it, yet some opposed it and called for a truly national language which they termed "Italian" or, sometimes, "Courtier's Tongue." Il Calmeta and Castiglione were the most prominent of these. Most of their arguments were borrowed from Dante's *De Vulgari Eloquentia*.

In England and France, the existence of national monarchies made the language problem easier of solution. Although the upholders of L. had to be combatted, the speech of the court was accepted as "English" or "French" and had little competition from outlying dialects. We still speak of the "King's English" in recognition of this standard. The growing national feeling in England and France sped the victory of the vernacular. Du Bellay's *Deffence et illustration de la langue françoyse* (1549) is frankly nationalistc. Borrowing many ideas from Sperone Speroni's *Dialogo della lingua* (1542), he argues that the Fr. are as good as the Romans, and that there is no reason why their language should not be as good. It is the patriotic duty of all Fr. scholars and poets to write in Fr. and enrich it. Translators in particular can enlarge the Fr. vocabulary by "capturing" words from other languages.

The Eng. were, if possible, even more patriotic. For hundreds of years the nobility had spoken Fr. and though this was no longer true in the 16th c., it had given rise to a strong popular tradition of hostility to any foreign domination of the mother tongue. Yet it was no easy thing to learn to write in the spoken language. In his *Toxophilus* (1545), Ascham confessed, "to have written this book either in Latin or Greek . . . had been more easier." Bacon, conscious of how Eng. had changed since Chaucer's day, had his *Essays* published in a L. edition because he feared that "these modern languages will at one time or other play bankrupt with books." But the flood of national pride was irresistible. Eng., which Mulcaster called the "joyful title of our liberty and freedom, the Latin tongue remembering us of our thraldom and bondage," won the day. The victory was accelerated in England, as it was on the continent also, by the Protestant movement in favor of the scriptures in translation.

The critics, having decided that it was allowable to write in the vernacular, were confronted with the fact that popular poetry in the vernacular was quite unlike the Gr. and L. poetry they admired. Desiring to imitate the ancients as closely as possible, they rejected the use of rhyme in modern poetry and characterized it as barbarous, an invention of the "Goths and Huns." Still they were not satisfied. The vernacular had to be adorned with the ancient meters before the classicizing process could be considered complete. Claudio Tolomei in his *Versi et regole della nuova poesia toscana* (1539) tried to show how It. could be written to sound something like L. verse. He was followed in France by Jacques de la Taille with his *La Manière de faire des vers en françois, comme en grec et en latin* (1573). In his preface he shows the yearning of the ultraclassicists to be as "good" as Virgil and Homer. Rhyme must be rejected because it is "as common to the unlearned as to the learned." He offers a harder road to Parnassus, one that only the learned can follow, and a hard road it is, he admits, since the language must be changed to fit the meters. What he advocates is really a new Fr. pronunciation with reformed spelling to make the pronunciation possible.

The Eng. critics gave enthusiastic support to this movement, which, though foreign to the nature of the language, was less obviously so than to It. with its plethora of rhymes, and to Fr. with its musical accent. First to begin the discussion was Ascham. His *Scholemaster* (1570) boldly declared that rhyme was the invention of barbarians who knew no better: "But now, when men know the difference, and have the examples, both of the best and of the worst, surely to follow rather the *Goths* in riming than the *Greeks* in true versifying were even to eat acorns with swine, when we may freely eat wheat bread amongst men."

Later treatises such as those of Webbe (1586) and Puttenham (1589) add a new argument as to why Protestant Englishmen should look with suspicion on rhyme. The past is not only "gothic," it is also papist. Webbe writes of "this tinkerly verse which we call rime" and condemns the monks for inventing this "brutish Poetry." He is echoed by Puttenham who speaks of rhyme as "the idle invention of Monastical men," and uses this fact to support the superiority of Protestant classicists. "Thus," he continues, "what in writing of rimes and registering of lies was the Clergy of that fabulous age wholly occupied." That even Edmund Spenser became part of this movement demonstrates its appeal. Spenser was, temporarily, a follower of Thomas Drant as this "verse" he sent to Harvey shows: "See yee the blindfoulded pretie god, that feathered Archer, / Of Lovers Miseries which maketh his bloodie Game? / Wote ye why his Moother with a Veale hath coovered his Face? / Trust me, least he my loove happely chaunce to beholde."

Nor was Spenser the only true poet of his time so to betray the natural genius of the language. At late as 1602, Campion in his *Observations* asserted that Eng. poets must forget "the childish titillation of riming" if they are ever to rival the ancients. Such examples as he gives from his own poetry prove that it is possible to write lovely lyrics without rhyme but certainly nothing more. Samuel Daniel finally put an end to his *Defence of Rime* (1603). His treatise not only shows how

much in accord with the nature of Eng. rhyme is, but also does its best to destroy the widespread prejudice concerning medieval culture.

The major virtue of the movement was negative. It showed what should not be done in vernacular verse. On the other hand, it did encourage metrical experimentation and may have had a slight influence in making more acceptable dramatic blank verse. Significantly, it seems to be one of the first attempts to pose a clearly conceived technical problem in prosody and deal with it experimentally.

Paralleling the discussions of language and of classical meters was the attempt to reestablish the classical genres in opposition to what the Ren. considered the formlessness of medieval literature. For the readers of the time the two movements must often have seemed in conflict since many of the literary critics were Latinists who had little interest in vernacular literature. However, it is apparent that the two groups were working toward a common end. The masterpieces of Ren. literature are written in the vernacular but the forms are classical, or what was thought to be classical.

The classical genres and the distinctions between them were worked out first by the commentators on Horace and Aristotle, and were codified by critics like Minturno, Scaliger, and Sidney, who wrote independent treatises on poetics. Believing imitation, q.v. (Aristotle's *mimesis* to mean "truth to life," the mirror held up to nature, the critics decided that the genres should be distinguished one from the other according to the kind of life imitated. Since poetry had been defended on moral and social grounds (and the Ren. interpretation of catharsis [q.v.] strengthened this), it was quite natural for critics to examine the genres from this point of view. The social divisions of the Ren. seemed to them to be reflected in the genres, and it was easy to make a hierarchy of the genres according to the rank of the people dealt with.

Among the dramatic genres tragedy is ranked highest because its characters are kings and princes, as well as because Aristotle's *Poetics* discussed this genre most fully. The plot is based upon the activities of kings—the affairs of state, fortress, and camp, says Scaliger in his famous *Poetices Libri Septem* (1561). Giraldi Cinthio says that we call the actions of tragedy *illustrious*, not because they are virtuous but because the characters who act are of the highest rank. The style of writing employed must be of the highest since any lower one would be unworthy of kings and princes. In Italy, especially, the stage scenery was considered important and it was ordered that magnificent palaces should serve as a background for the action.

Comedy deals with people of the middle

class. Obviously, the plots must be suitable to such persons and to the middle class customs with which the poets are familiar. Minturno suggests in *L'Arte Poetica* (1564) that although noble ladies appear in public, middle-class girls do not until after marriage, and that the poet will violate decorum if he has them do so on the stage. Castelvetro declares that members of the strong-willed aristocracy constitute a law unto themselves but that the middle-class persons of comedy are poor in heart, run to the magistrates with their troubles, and live under the law. Thus the plots of comedies must not contain *vendettas* or other actions unsuitable to the characters but be drawn from bourgeois and private life. The speech must be everyday speech in the middle style.

There is one dramatic form reserved for the lowest classes. It is the farce. Here the language is that of the gutter and the actions are appropriately low. The ability to keep decorum is considered the prime responsibility of the poet. The Fr. and Eng. critics follow this threefold division and give, almost word for word, the same definitions as do the Italians. For instance, in *L'Art Poëtique François* (1598), Pierre de Laudun sums up the matter for the Fr. as follows: "The characters of tragedy are grave people of great rank and those of comedy are low and of small position. . . . The words of Tragedy are grave and those of Comedy are light. . . . The characters in Tragedy are sumptuously dressed and those of Comedy garbed in an ordinary way." Many similar quotations could be given from Eng. critics. The practicing dramatists followed the rules of the critics. Most of Shakespeare's tragedies and comedies observe the main distinctions as to rank, action, and language. Ben Jonson, realizing he had not kept the unity of time, felt that it was unimportant in comparison with these. He writes about his *Sejanus:* "First, if it be objected, that what I publish is no true poem, in the strict law of time, I confess it. . . . In the meantime, if in truth of argument, dignity of person, gravity and height of elocution, fullness and frequency of sentence, I have discharged the other offices of a tragic writer, let not the absence of these forms be imputed to me." In the conventions of rank and subject matter the Ren. critics felt that they were following the ancients. Another important concept which they felt implicit in the classical sources was the concept of the unity (q.v.) of action, time, and place. This concept first appeared in its modern form in Castelvetro's translation and commentary, *La Poetica d'Aristotele Vulgarizzata* (1570), but it did not become a major critical dogma until the 17th c.

The area of agreement among the leading critics was so large that definition after definition could be transferred from the pages of one man's treatise to another's without being out of place. Yet in two areas—that of tragicomedy and that of romance—real arguments arose. Here the polemical tone of the treatises was evidence that the critics were dealing with modern literary forms for which the ancients were insufficient guides.

For the more conservative critics tragicomedy was by definition a bastard and therefore inadmissible form. Sidney's criticism of his contemporary dramatists in his *Apologie* (ca. 1583) is typical. He protests, "All their plays be neither right tragedies nor right comedies; mingling kings and clowns, not because the matter so carrieth it, but thrust in the clown by head and shoulders, to play a part in majestical matters, with neither decency nor discretion. So as neither the admiration and commiseration, nor the right sportfulness, is by this mongrel tragi-comedy obtained." Yet, the best playwrights paid little attention to such strictures. John Fletcher could write a tragicomedy and bluntly defend it with the assertion, "a God is as lawful in this as in a tragedy, and mean people as in a comedy." Fletcher knew of the bitter discussion which had taken place in Italy on this question. In his *Discorso intorno a . . . la Tragedia* (1587) De Nores had written that mixed genres were not even worthy of discussion. Guarini, the author of *Il Pasto fido*, however, sprang to the defense of his own practice. He argued that since the great and the lowly exist side by side in every country, it is perfectly correct to have both in the drama. De Nores answered (*Apologia*, 1590) that comedy instructs citizens on how to act. A mixed genre, since it cannot so instruct, is without any useful end. Then he asked a series of questions: How can the dramatist keep decorum if the characters are of different rank? What level of language should be used, the grand or humble? Should the stage settings be palaces or humble cottages? He answered his questions by saying that whatever the choice, it will be inappropriate for one class of characters. Guarini was afraid to answer merely by saying that he wrote to please, though he hinted at it. He, too, had to use the standard social arguments. He said, essentially, that a pastoral tragicomedy like his *Il Pastor fido* was an acceptable genre because some of the shepherds were noble and others were not. The first made for the tragedy, the second for the comedy. The two together made tragicomedy.

Of the nondramatic genres, the epic was most important and was considered by some critics to be the highest literary form. Not only did it deal with princes and kings, but the heroes were usually national heroes. In both France and England the demand was made for epic poets to come forward and celebrate the glories of the nation. Ronsard with his *Franciade* and Spenser with his *Faerie Queene* attempted to glorify their nations. The question of whether such modern poetic narratives could be considered epics was particularly agitated in Italy. In *Orlando furioso* and *Gerusalemme liberata*, Ariosto and Tasso had produced romantic poems that appealed to popular taste far more than such a classically "correct" epic as Trissino's *Italia Liberata dai Goti*. Minturno took the strict classical position and quite correctly contended that the romances could not be considered epics since they lacked classical unity. Not content with this, he poured scorn on the romances because they appealed to popular taste—an instance of the widespread Ren. assumption that what pleased the mob was bad *per se*. Giraldi Cinthio, though perhaps less sensitive to what constituted an epic, was more forward looking. Not only did he refuse to reject a poem merely because it was popular but, more important, he claimed in his *Discorsi* (1554) the right of the new age to develop poetic forms suitable to it and to free itself from overclose imitation of the ancients.

Of similar import was the argument over medieval forms of poetry. The strict classicists were as severe on Dante's *Commedia* as they were on the romances. They considered it to be obscure, gothic, barbarous and without form. They held that the great poet, himself, lacked all taste. The legion of critics who defended Dante suggested, by the mere fact of their defense, that the ancients and their disciples did not have a monopoly on good poetry.

Thanks to these controversies, the Ren. provided the seed from which, in opposition to classical or neoclassical literature, romantic and later literature was to spring.

The It. Ren. critics and their Fr. and Eng. successors were the founders of modern European literary criticism. The Dutch, the Germans, and the Sp. critics of the Ren. added little that was new. When Lope de Vega attempted a defense of his work, he paid homage to the Ren. authorities with the startling confession that of his 483 comedies, "all except six of them sin grievously against art." In other words, the only way Lope de Vega or anyone else prior to the collapse of the neoclassical spirit could talk about art was in the terms formulated by Ren. poetics.

BIBLIOGRAPHIES: For Fr. and Eng., see Patterson and Smith (below, *Collections*). For It., R. C. Williams, "It. Crit. Treatises of the 16th C.," MLN 35 (1920); and W. Bullock, "It. 16th C. Crit.," MLN, 41 (1926); For Sp., see Menéndez y Pelayo, *Historia de las ideas estéticas en España* (9 v., unfinished, 1883–91; v. II); Saintsbury is convenient though inadequate.

COLLECTIONS: Eng.: The major essays are collected in G. Smith, *Elizabethan Crit. Essays*

(2 v., 1904); and J. E. Spingarn, *Crit. Essays of the 17th C.* (3 v. 1907). Fr.: Although the work is a history, W. F. Patterson, *Three C. of Fr. Poetic Theory* (3 v., 1935) contains copious excerpts from Ren. essays; the important prefaces of the period are collected in B. Weinberg, *Crit. Prefaces of the Fr. Ren.* (1950). It.: There is no satisfactory modern coll. and in view of the mass of material available a coll. is probably impossible, but a generous selection in tr. is contained in A. Gilbert, *Lit. Crit.* (1940). The opinions and comments of most of the It. critics are collected in what amounts to a commonplace book of crit., *Proginnasmi Poetici*, by U. Nisieli (pseudonym for B. Fioretti), publ. in Florence (2 v., 1639). Sp.: No satisfactory coll.

PRIMARY WORKS: It.: Dante, *de Vulgari Eloquentia* (publ. 1529), and *Convivio;* Boccaccio, *de Genealogia Deorum*, Bks. XIV, XV (tr. Osgood, *Boccaccio on the Art of Poetry* [1931]); Pontanus, *Dialoghi* (esp. "Actius"), ed. Previtera (1943); Vida, *de Arte Poetica* (1527); Trissino, *Poetica* (Bks. i-iv, 1529; v-vi, publ., 1563); Robortello, *In Librum . . . de Arte Poetica Explicationes* (1548); Scaliger, *Poetices Libri Septem* (1561); Minturno, *L'Arte Poetica* (1563); Castelvetro, *Poetica d'Aristotele* (1571); Patrizi, *Della Poetica* (1586); Tasso, *Discorsi* (1594). Fr.: Sebillet, *Art Poétique Françoys* (1548); Du Bellay, *Deffence et Illustration de la Langue Françoyse* (1549); J. Peletier du Mans, *Art Poétique* (1555); Ronsard, *Abrégé de l'Art Poétique* (1565); Vauquelin de la Fresnaye, *Art Poétique Français* (ca. 1574; pub., 1605). Eng.: See the coll. by Smith (above, COLLECTIONS). For Spenser, see I. Langdon, *Materials for a Study of Spenser's Theory of Fine Art* (1911); and for "turn of the century" critics (esp. Jonson and Bacon), see Spingarn (above, COLLECTIONS). For Eng. rhetorical theory, a standard text is Wilson, *The Art of Rhetoric* (1553), available in the modern ed. of G. Mair (1909). Sp.: A. de Nebrija, *Arte de la Lengua Castellana* (1492); J. del Encina, *Arte de la Poesía Castellana* (1496); F. Herrera, *Anotaciones a las obras de Garcilaso de la Vega* (1580); J. Díaz Rengifo, *Arte Poética Española* (1592); A. Lopez el Pinciano, *Philosophia Antigua Poética* (1596); Cervantes, *Don Quixote*, I, 48 (1605); Lope de Vega Carpio, *Arte Nuevo de Hacer Comedias* (1609). Dutch and German crit. is unimportant prior to the 17th c., but three critics may be mentioned whose work reflects the spirit of Ren. crit.: D. Heinsius, *De Tragoediae Constitutione* (1611); M. Opitz, *Buch von der deutschen Poeterey* (1624); and G. Vossius, *de Artis Poeticae Natura* (1647).

SECONDARY WORKS: In addition to the general histories of crit. by Saintsbury, Wimsatt, and Brooks, the following studies are useful: C. De-job, *De L'Influence du Concile de Trente sur la Litt* . . . (1884); K. Borinski, *Die Poetik der Ren.* (1886); J. E. Spingarn, *A Hist. of Lit. Crit. in the Ren.* (1899); K. Vossler, *Poetische Theorien in der ital. Frühren.* (1900); F. Padelford, *Select Tr. from Scaliger's Poetics* (1905); H. Charlton, *Castelvetro's Theory of Poetry* (1913); G. Thompson, *Elizabethan Crit. of Poetry* (1914); C. Trabalza, *La Critica Letteraria nel Rinsaciamento* (1915); D. L. Clark, *Rhetoric and Poetic in the Ren.* (1922); Patterson, see above, COLLECTIONS; W. G. Crane, *Wit and Rhetoric in the Ren.* (1937); F. Markwardt, *Gesch. der deutschen Poetik,* I (1937); C. S. Baldwin, *Ren. Lit. Theory and Practice* (1939); R. J. Clements, *Crit. Theory and Practice of the Pléiade* (1942); V. Hall, Jr., *Ren. Lit. Crit.* (1945); M. T. Herrick, *The Fusion of Horatian and Aristotelian Lit. Crit.* (1946); J. W. H. Atkins, *Eng. Lit. Crit.: the Ren.* (1947); J. Cunningham, *Woe or Wonder* (1954); M. Doran, *Endeavors of Art* (1954); M. T. Herrick, *Tragicomedy* (1955); W. S. Howell, *Logic and Rhetoric in England, 1500–1700* (1956); B. Weinberg, *A Hist. of Lit. Crit. in the It. Ren.* (2 v., 1961); B. Hathaway, *The Age of Crit.: the Late Ren. in Italy* (1962); O. B. Hardison, *The Enduring Monument: a Study in the Relationship between Ren. Crit. and Lit. Practice* (1962).

Of the numerous articles on aspects of Ren. poetics, see especially M. W. Bundy, " 'Invention' and 'Imagination' in the Ren.," JEGP, 29 (1930); H. S. Wilson, "Some Meanings of 'Nature' in Ren. Lit. Theory," JHI, 2 (1941); B. Weinberg, "The Poetic Theories of Minturno," *Studies in Honor of Frederick W. Shipley* (1942), "Castelvetro's Theory of Poetics" and "Robortello on the Poetics," both in Crane, *Critics;* G. Giovannini, "Historical Realism and the Tragic Emotions in Ren. Crit.," PQ, 32 (1953); B. Sozzi, "La Poetica del Tasso," *Studi Tassiani,* 5 (1955); S. L. Bethell, "The Nature of Metaphysical Wit," *Discussions of John Donne,* ed. F. Kermode (1962).   v.h.

RENAISSANCE POETRY. The term "Ren." has occasioned much debate. Like other general terms, it embraces many exceptions and apparent contradictions. Moreover, it means different things in painting, architecture, literature; and its chronological limits vary from country to country. The notion of a "rebirth" is in itself suspect, for culture is not discontinuous. In general usage, however, the term is most commonly applied to the 16th c. With margins of half a century, roughly, on either side, that application may be accepted. By "Ren. poetry" is meant, then, European poetry produced between 1450 and 1650.

Within these limits some pervasive characteristics may be noticed. Among these is humanism, the enthusiastic "recovery" and imita-

tion of the classics, especially Gr.; the eventual displacement of L. by firmly established vernaculars; and the eminence attained by certain genres: heroic poem, sonnet, madrigal, pastoral, epigram. A heightened conception of the importance of the individual parallels the widened horizons in science and geography, presenting new worlds for poetic exploration. The religious renewal expressed in the Reformation and Counter-Reformation is both a stimulus to devotional poetry and, in its divisive effects, a factor in promoting nationalism. Intellectually and artistically, Italy has the dominant rôle as initiator and exemplar.

Certain other characteristics serve to differentiate the new age from the medieval period. The major literatures, for instance, achieve noteworthy successes in polishing and regularizing poetic vocabulary. Allegory and dream-vision tend to give way to realism and lyricism as the older didactic criteria are supplemented or replaced by the criteria of imitation and delight. The invention of printing, by rendering poetry more accessible, encouraged poets to write for a much wider audience than had been available to the medieval poet. Another difference appears in the emergence of historical self-consciousness. Whereas the Middle Ages had tended to fuse the past into one indiscriminate whole, the Ren. tended to treat the nonclassical centuries either with disdain or with critical condescension. Even where evocation of the past is most sympathetic—in Boiardo, in Du Bellay, in Spenser—this attitude may be detected. And as every great movement carries within itself the germs of its own decay, there emerges toward the end of the Ren. an increasing interest in *form* as opposed to content, whence derives the formalism of the neoclassic age.

In Italy, since the great precursors of the Ren.—Dante, Petrarch, Boccaccio—established a viable literary language, the question of the language should have been settled. It was not. Petrarch himself mistakenly pinned his hope of poetic fame upon his L. epic, *Africa;* and his humanist successors remained scornful of the vulgar tongue. No considerable It. vernacular poet appears between Boccaccio (1313?–1375) and Lorenzo de' Medici (1449–92). Within Italy and without, the poetry of the early Ren. is largely neo-Latin. The practice of Latinizing persisted throughout the entire Ren.; the same individuals wrote both L. and vernacular compositions. Among the most signal neo-L. poets may be named the gifted Giovanni Pontano (1426–1503), erotic poet of marital love; Mantuan (G.-B. Spagnuolo: 1448–1516), influential through his eclogues; Poliziano, or Politian (Angelo Ambrogini: 1454–94); Girolamo Vida (1485–1566), author of long didactic poems and an epic *Christiad;* George Buchanan (1506–82),

Scottish elegist; the Dutch Joannes Secundus (Jan Everaerts: 1511–1536), truest lyricist of the lot; and John Owen (?1560–1622), Welshman, whose *Epigrams* (1606ff.) diverted learned Europe. A word might be said also for Jacopo Sannazaro (1456–1530), author of the famed (vernacular) *Arcadia* (1504), as inventor of the piscatory eclogue; and for Andrea Alciati (1492–1550), whose *Emblematum liber* (1531) begot innumerable imitations. Many others wrote respectable L. and Gr. verse; and the practice aided in producing a native poetry with greater restraint and more disciplined form than might otherwise have resulted. But from first to last neo-Latin poetry was a graveyard of misdirected effort. The future lay elsewhere.

The magnificent story of the It. Ren., often told, cannot be reduced to a few words. In heroic poem, in lyric, and in pastoral, It. poets dominate the age and set the models for imitation. The medieval chivalric matter of the Carolingian cycle, rescued from popular balladeers and street singers, was raised into conscious art in epic pattern, now humorous and grotesque, as in the *Morgante Maggiore* of Luigi Pulci (1432–87); now serious and nobly romantic, as in the *Orlando Innamorato* of Matteo Boiardo (1434–94); now infused with satire and irony, as in the exquisitely polished *Orlando Furioso* of Lodovico Ariosto (1474–1533), stylistic masterpiece of the genre. These, together with the more lavishly descriptive and moralizing *Gerusalemme Liberata* of Torquato Tasso (1544–95) established for Italians the primacy of ottava rima as vehicle for heroic poetry and set for others a model rivaled only by the *Aeneid*. The pastoral strain traces its line of descent from the *Orfeo* (1494) of Poliziano through Sannazaro's *Arcadia* (1504) and Tasso's *Aminta* (1580) to the *Pastor Fido* (1590) of Giovanni Battista Guarini (1537–1612). The two last, dramatic in form, are lyric in feeling and highly influential upon subsequent pastoral poetry. Smooth writers of the detached lyric, as represented by *ballate, canzoni,* madrigals, and sonnets are legion; and everywhere the inspiration of Petrarch is evident. It. poetical *raccolte* of the period, very numerous, are virtually tributes to Petrarch; the masculine vigor and unpolished individuality of Michelangelo Buonarroti's (1475–1564) sonnets are rare exceptions. For It. poetic drama, see below, final section.

After Italy, France was the most effective agent in spreading the civilization of the Ren. to the rest of Europe. Under the influence, initially, of Francis I and his sister, Marguerite d'Angoulême, Fr. Ren. poetry remained largely artificial and courtly. Clément Marot (1495–1544) happily blended sympathies for the old and the new. Adhering to old forms, he invested them with ease and naturalness. His verse paraphrases of selected Psalms enjoyed great popularity; and his elegiac and pastoral poems found a reflection in Spenser's *Shepheardes Calender*. Marot's friend Melin de Saint-Gelais (1487–1558) imported the sonnet to France, beginning a vogue which soon became universal. After Marot, leadership in Fr. poetry passed briefly to Lyons. Of the flourishing Lyonnese school, Antoine Héroët (d. 1568) is now forgotten; Maurice Scève (1504–64), eminent and able Petrarchizer in *dizains,* is only now beginning to be restudied; and Louise Labé (ca. 1525–66), impassioned love poetess in elegy and sonnet, is rather a name than a living force. The Lyonnese, by virtue of proximity, were much influenced by It. neo-Platonism. All this, however, was but prelude to the concerted efforts of a Parisian group, the famous *Pléiade* (q.v.), whose dual purpose it was to create a distinguished Fr. language and a national poetry. Joachim du Bellay (1525–60), their leader and spokesman, issued their manifesto, *La Deffense et Illustration de la Langue françoyse,* in 1549. But the brightest star of the *Pléiade* was Pierre de Ronsard (1524–85), in whom the Fr. Ren. came of age. Ronsard's interests and inspirations were varied. An admirer of Petrarch, of Pindar, of Anacreon, of Horace, he was a master craftsman in sonnet, ode, and elegy. His work is characterized by delicacy of feeling and great finish. The inheritor of Ronsard's literary eminence, if not of his gifts, was Philippe Desportes (1545–1606), a copious sonneteer and imitator of It. models. Desportes's rival in the popular taste was Guillaume de Salluste du Bartas (1544–90), whose epic of creation, *La Sepmaine* (1578), had an astounding European vogue and left traces of influence upon Tasso and—in Joshua Sylvester's translation—upon Milton. A more fiery and compelling Huguenot voice is that of the soldier-poet-historian, Agrippa d'Aubigné (1552–1630). The seven books of D'Aubigné's *Les Tragiques* (1616), constituting a blistering arraignment of his Catholic enemies and a powerful picture of the sufferings of France during the Wars of Religion, are a fitting curtain to the spectacle of the Fr. Ren.

Spain and Portugal, outside the main current, had their own burst of poetic glory. They, too, finally succumbed to the It. Circe, though not without a struggle between the new schools and the adherents to traditional native forms. In Spain the issue was rather simple; in Portugal, it was complicated by the necessity of choosing between Spanish and Portuguese. Some poets, like Francisco de Sá de Miranda (ca. 1485–1558), were successful in both languages. It. forms were introduced into Spain by Juan Boscán (ca. 1490–1542) and much furthered by the poetry of his greatly gifted young friend, Garcilaso de la Vega (1503–36). Best representative of the older tradition is probably Cristóbal de Castillejo (ca. 1490–1550), who wittily but strenuously opposed the Italianizers. Most eminent of the Salamancan school was the Augustinian friar, Luis de León (ca. 1528–91), who wrote some of the most beautifully simple, direct, and personal lyrics in Sp. His counterpart in the Sevillian school was Fernando de Herrera (ca. 1534–94); and in religious verse, the ecstatic (San) Juan de la Cruz (1549–91). Worthy of mention also is Gutierre de Cetina (ca. 1520–57), another Italianizer. In epic, the age produced Alonso de Ercilla (1533–94), whose La Araucana (1569; complete, 1597) presents an American setting; and, more notably, the Portuguese Luís de Camões (1524–80), whose patriotic Os Lusiadas (1572) is the only modern epic worthy to stand beside Paradise Lost. Another Portuguese, Jorge de Montemayor, following Sannazaro, wrote (in Sp.) La Diana (1559), a prose pastoral romance with interspersed lyrics. Last may be named Luis de Góngora (1561–1627), a witty and gifted lyricist, the introducer of that cult of obscurity which beclouded the later poetry of the siglo de oro. The real giants of the age —Santa Teresa, Cervantes, Lope de Vega, Tirso de Molina, Calderón—although respectable versifiers, belong rather to the realms of prose or the drama (see below, final section).

Germany, whose contributions to the Reformation and to the Ren. were important in other directions, is negligible in vernacular poetry.

England's poetic Ren. came late. The delay was not altogether disadvantageous, for it enabled the Eng. to draw upon the riches of both Italy and France. Of the Tudor poets who preceded Wyatt and Surrey, John Skelton (ca. 1460–1529), author of rough and tumbling medieval satires in jigging short lines, was most notable. Innovation and experiment in the new spirit, al modo italico, begin with Sir Thomas Wyatt (ca. 1503–42) and Henry Howard (ca. 1517–47), Earl of Surrey. These two, whose poetry was first published in Tottel's miscellany Songs and Sonnets (1557), are credited with introducing into Eng. the sonnet, terza rima, blank verse, and the alexandrine. Less sturdily individual, as a metrist Surrey is considerably smoother than Wyatt; and he became the model for the sporadic Italianizing efforts of various minor courtly poets. Of poets belonging to the generation between these forerunners and Spenser, the ablest is George Gascoigne (ca. 1542–77), a conscientious craftsman whose innovating merit is not exclusively poetic. The once-famous Mirror for Magistrates (1559; enlarged, 1563), reproducing the medie-val fall-of-princes theme, is hardly salvageable, even with the "Induction" (ed. 1563) by Thomas Sackville (1536–1608).

A concerted and sustained effort to lift the Eng. language and poetry into rivalry with Fr. and It., as well as classic literature, does not appear until the last quarter of the 16th c. Once the movement was begun, however, it matured rapidly and produced an astounding poetic literature. An age that numbers Spenser, Sidney, Marlowe, Drayton, Shakespeare, Chapman, Donne, and Jonson among its poets need make no apologies anywhere. The great flowering begins with The Shepheardes Calender (1579) of Edmund Spenser (1552–99), eclogues in experimental meters drawing inspiration from the Gr. bucolic poets, from Virgil, Mantuan, Marot, and from Chaucer. Virtually the manifesto of the new movement, it provided an impulse comparable to that originated in the Pléiade's Deffense. This initial success Spenser followed up in his masterpiece, The Faerie Queene (1590; 1596), a bold attempt to "overgo" Ariosto and Tasso in the heroic kind.

Thereafter, success followed success. Poetical miscellanies, following Tottel's, now increased in number and lyric excellence, numbering, among others, The Phoenix Nest (1593), The Passionate Pilgrim (1599), containing poems by William Shakespeare (1564–1616), England's Helicon (1600), and Davison's A Poetical Rhapsody (1602). Narrative and erotic poems of Ovidian stamp, such as the Hero and Leander (1598) of Christopher Marlowe (1564–93) and George Chapman (?1559–?1634) and the Venus and Adonis (1593) of Shakespeare abounded. The characteristic Ren. addiction to the sonnet reached full tide in the 1590's, producing such remarkable sequences as the Astrophel and Stella (pr. 1591) of Sir Philip Sidney (1554–86), the Delia (1592, 1594) of Samuel Daniel (1562–1619), the Idea's Mirrour (1594, 1619) of Michael Drayton (1563–1631), and the Amoretti (1595) of Spenser. Shakespeare's sonnets, probably mostly written during this decade, were first printed in 1609. Contemporary with the sonnet cycles were the numerous collections of madrigals and the beginnings of formal verse satire. Nor were the translators inactive. But the noblest creation of this period is a vigorous national drama into which great poetic energies were poured. From Lyly and Peele to Beaumont and Fletcher the Eng. drama sparkles with fine songs and noble passages in a perfected blank verse, the Ren. legacy to Milton (see also below, final section). After the turn of the century, the poetry of Ben Jonson (1572–1637) shows tendencies toward neoclassic formalism; that of John Donne (1572–1631), a manneristic intellectualism and obscurity. With their followers, Milton aside, the Ren. gives way to baroque (q.v.). J.L.L.

-[697]-

Ren. poetic drama developed from the religious drama of the Middle Ages—the "sacre rappresentazioni" of Italy, the "mystère" of France, and the Eng. mysteries and moralities. Generally, medieval drama is in crude rhyming stanzas serving for both serious and comic dialogue. By the 16th c. medieval drama had proliferated into a series of vigorous popular forms, largely secular but preserving the strong moral bias of the earlier period, as in tragedy based on the "fall of princes" theme. With the advent of humanism, critics advocated a drama modeled on the work of Seneca, Plautus, and Terence. It is significant that where the humanists were most successful (Italy, France), Ren. drama is relatively weak; and where they were least influential (Spain, England), Ren. drama is magnificently successful.

In Italy, poetic drama begins with Mussato, whose *Eccerinis* (1315), the first regular drama in modern European literature, is an imitation of Seneca in L. verse. In the early 16th c. the circle of Cardinal Riario (1451–1521) made a concerted effort to revive the ancient theatre at the court of Leo X in Rome. It. vernacular tragedy may be dated from G. G. Trissino's *Sofonisba* (1515), a stiff Senecan tragedy in blank verse (*versi sciolti*) with lyric choruses. Trissino's followers include Alemanni (*Antigone*, 1532), Ciraldi Cinthio (*L'Orbecche*, 1541), and Tasso (*Il Re Torrismondo*, 1587). Far more significant is It. lyric drama imitating the music drama which critics believed to be the most ancient Gr. form. This drama began with Politian's *Orfeo* (1494) and was continued in the 16th c. by Tasso (*Aminta*, 1580), Guarini (*Il Pastor Fido*, 1590), and Rinuccini (*Dafne*, 1594, 99). It culminated in the first true opera, Striggio's *Orfeo* (1607), with music by Monteverdi.

Fr. poetic drama followed the It. lead. The earliest important Fr. drama is George Buchanan's influential *Johannes Baptistus* (1540), soon followed by the *Julius Caesar* of Muretus. Vernacular drama was established by Étienne Jodelle, a member of the *Pléiade*, in *Cleopatre captive* (1552) and *Didon se sacrificant* (1558), both frigidly correct imitations of Seneca. The second is important for its use of alexandrine meter, which thereafter became standard for Fr. tragedy. The classical style reached something of a climax in the tragedies of Robert Garnier (1544–90). While usually stiff, Garnier's verse is occasionally moving. *Les Juives* (1584) is probably his best work and has been produced successfully in the 20th c. There is no important lyric or pastoral drama in 16th c. France, and Fr. poetic comedy is unimportant until Molière, whose work belongs to the next century.

Sp. poetic drama is the glory of the *siglo del oro*. After experiments in both popular and classical forms, it blossomed in the work of Lope de Vega (1562–1635). Lope's work (ca. 400 plays survive from an estimated 1500) is usually divided into four categories: (1) *comedias de capa y espada*, consisting of upper-class intrigue and in a loose rhyming tetrameter; (2) *heróicas*, or plays on historical subjects (e.g., *Roma Abrasada*); (3) *comedias de santos*, saints' plays; and (4) *autos sacramentales*, allegorical dialogues in verse on religious themes. It is in the *heroicas* and *autos* that Lope was most successful. Second place in Sp. poetic drama belongs to Calderón de la Barca (1600–81), who wrote *autos*, *comedias de santos*, tragedies (*Il Principe Constante*), and the unique *La Vida es sueño* (Life is a Dream). Among numerous lesser dramatists are C. de Castro, whose play on the Cid influenced Corneille; Montalban; Alcaron; and Tirso de Molina, creator of Don Juan.

Like Sp. drama, Eng. Ren. drama is closely tied to medieval drama. In Bale's *King John* (1540) a group of allegorical morality-play characters are suddenly transformed into historical figures. *Gorboduc* (1562), a Senecan history play by Sackville and Norton, established blank verse as the standard meter for serious drama in Eng. The great period of Eng. drama began around 1580 with the work of Lyly, Peele, Greene, and Kyd, all skilled versifiers and experimenters in such forms as tragedy, revenge play, chronicle history, and lyric-pastoral. Christopher Marlowe (1564–93) is the most important of the early dramatists. His "mighty line" dazzled contemporaries and remains today one of the great achievements of Eng. blank verse. Shakespeare's achievements are so numerous and so profound that they cannot be listed in a brief article such as the present one. He adapted blank verse to every conceivable mood and purpose and is still the dominant influence on Eng. poetic drama. Shakespeare's contemporaries and followers include Ben Jonson (1572–1637), John Fletcher (1579–1625), George Chapman (1559–1634), and John Webster (1580–1625). A special type of poetic drama, in many ways similar to opera, was the court masque (q.v.), usually in lyric meters and set to music. Among the many authors of masques Ben Jonson and Thomas Campion were most successful; John Milton (*Comus*, 1634), the most significant and poetically moving.

After 1610 Eng. drama declined perceptibly. As the plays became more melodramatic, the poetry became more ornamental and showy. By the closing of the theatres in 1642, Eng. poetic drama was already a dead art. When the theatres were reopened in 1660, it was Fr. classical drama as perfected by Corneille and Racine which set the style of the age. See also LYRIC, NARRATIVE POETRY, TRAGEDY, etc. and the

-[698]-

relevant sections in the various national and regional poetry articles.   O.B.H.

A. Tilley, *The Lit. of the Fr. Ren.* (2 v., 1904); J. M. Berdan, *Early Tudor Poetry* (1920); A.F.G. Bell, *Luis de León, a Study of the Sp. Ren.* (1925); P. Champion, *Ronsard et son temps* (1925); W. L. Renwick, *Edmund Spenser: An Essay on Ren. Poetry* (1925; excellent general introd.); J. Fitzmaurice-Kelly, *A New Hist. of Sp. Lit.* (1926); H. Hauvette, *L'Arioste et la poésie chevaleresque à Ferrare au début du XVIe s.* (2d ed., 1927); *Poetry of the Eng. Ren.*, ed. J. W. Hebel and H. H. Hudson (1929; anthol. with good crit. apparatus); J. G. Scott, *Les Sonnets élisabéthains* (1929); *The Love Poems of Joannes Secundus*, ed. and tr. F. A. Wright (1930; with valuable essay on neo-Latin poetry); J. Plattard, *Agrippa d'Aubigné* (1931); H. Chamard, *Les Origines de la poésie fr. de la Ren.* (1932; emphasizes medieval heritage); R. Morçay, *La Ren.* (2 v., 1933–35); J. B. Fletcher, *Lit. of the It. Ren.* (1934); A. Meozzi, *Il petrarchismo europeo: secolo XVI* (1934); C. S. Lewis, *Allegory of Love* (1936) and *Eng. Lit. in the 16th C. Excluding Drama* (1954); A. Capasso, *Tre saggi sulla poesia ital. del rinascimento* (1939); G. Toffanin, *Il Cinquecento* (3d ed., 1945; basic); E.M.W. Tillyard, *Shakespeare's History Plays* (1946) and *The Eng. Epic and Its Background* (1954; pt. 3); E. Donadoni, *Torquato Tasso* (3d ed., 1946); M. Prior, *The Language of Tragedy* (1947); T. Spencer, *Shakespeare and the Nature of Man* (2d ed., 1949); M. I. Gerhardt, *La Pastorale* (1950); C. M. Ing, *Elizabethan Lyrics* (1951); H. D. Smith, *Elizabethan Poetry* (1952); P. Cruttwell, *The Shakespearean Moment and Its Place in the Poetry of the 17th C.* (1954); B. Weinberg, *Fr. Poetry of the Ren.* (1954); A. L. Sells, *It. Influence in Eng. Poetry from Chaucer to Southwell* (1955); J. W. Lever, *The Elizabethan Love Sonnet* (1956); M. Valency, *In Praise of Love* (1958); M. T. Herrick, *It. Comedy in the Ren.* (1960); A. W. Satterthwaite, *Spenser, Ronsard and Du Bellay: A Ren. Comparison* (1960); D. Bush, *Eng. Lit. in the Earlier 17th C., 1600–1660* (2d ed., 1962).   J.L.L.; O.B.H.

RENGA. See JAPANESE POETRY.

REPETEND. A recurring word, phrase, or line; loosely, a refrain (q.v.). As distinguished from refrain, r. usually refers to a repetition occurring irregularly rather than regularly in a poem, or to a partial rather than a complete repetition. E.g.: "For a breeze of morning moves, / And the planet of Love is on high, / Beginning *to faint in the light* that *she loves* / On a bed of daffodil sky, / *To faint in the light* of the sun *she loves,* / *To faint in his light,* and to die" (Tennyson, *Maud* 22.7). R. may be richly

studied in the medieval ballads, Poe's *Ulalume* and *The Raven,* Meredith's *Love in the Valley,* Eliot's *The Love Song of J. Alfred Prufrock.*   L.P.

REPETITION of a sound, syllable, word, phrase, line, stanza, or metrical pattern is a basic unifying device in all poetry. It may reinforce, supplement, or even substitute for meter, the other chief controlling factor in the arrangement of words into poetry. Primitive religious chants from all cultures show r. developing into cadence and song, with parallelism and r. still constituting, most frequently as anaphora (q.v.), an important part in the sophisticated and subtle rhetoric of contemporary liturgies (e.g., the *Beatitudes*). Frequently also, the exact r. of words in the same metrical pattern at regular intervals forms a refrain (q.v.), which serves to set off or divide narrative into segments, as in ballads, or, in lyric poetry, to indicate shifts or developments of emotion. Such repetitions may serve as commentary, a static point against which the rest of the poem develops, or it may be simply a pleasing sound pattern to fill out a form ("hey downe a-downe"). As a unifying device, independent of conventional metrics, r. is found extensively in free verse, where parallelism, q.v. (r. of grammatical pattern) reinforced by the recurrence of actual words and phrases governs the rhythm which helps to distinguish free verse from prose (e.g., Walt Whitman. *I Hear America Singing*; Carl Sandburg, *Chicago, The People Yes*; Edgar Lee Masters, *Spoon River Anthology, passim.*).

The r. of similar endings of words or even of identical syllables (*rime riche*, q.v.) constitutes rhyme, used generally to bind lines together into larger units or to set up relationships within the same line (internal rhyme). Such r., as a *tour de force*, may be the center of interest in a poem, as Southey's *The Cataract of Lodore* and Belloc's *Tarantella,* or may play a large part in establishing the mood of a poem, as in Byron's *Don Juan.* Front-rhyme, or alliteration (q.v.) the r. of initial sounds of accented syllables frequently supplements the use of other unifying devices, although in OE poetry it formed the basic structure of the line and is still so employed occasionally in modern poetry, as by G. M. Hopkins and in W. H. Auden's *The Age of Anxiety.* Alliteration also may be carried beyond the limits of a single line and may even operate in elaborate patterns throughout a poem (see SOUND IN POETRY) as a counterpoint to other relationships indicated by different sorts of r., such as rhyme, metrical pattern, and assonance (q.v.). The exact r. of sounds within a line serves as a variety of internal rhyme ("Come here, thou *worthy* of a *world* of praise," Chapman, *The*

Odyssey). Another repetitional device used chiefly in a decorative or supplemental function rather than in a structural one is assonance, the use of similar vowel sounds with identical consonant clusters. Such a poem as G. M. Hopkins' *The Leaden Echo and the Golden Echo* will illustrate abundantly how these "supplemental" devices of internal rhyme, alliteration, and assonance may be made into the chief features of the poetic line to support an unconventional system of metrics.

A single word may be repeated as a unifying device or, especially in dramatic poetry, for emphasis. The sections of a poem may be linked by repeating in the opening line of each new stanza the final word of the previous one, as in MacNeice's *Leaving Barra*. This linking device can be carried further into the formal rhetorical figure of climax, as in the following passage where each noun is picked up and repeated in some form:

And let the kettle to the trumpets speak,
The trumpet to the cannoneer without,
The cannons to the heavens, the heaven to
earth.

(Shakespeare, *Hamlet*)

The suggestions of a quality inherent in a single word may be exploited by the intensive r. of the word in every position within a conventional metrical pattern that the poet's ingenuity can devise, as in De la Mare's *Silver*, or a word may be repeated to underline an onomatopoetic effect as in the line, itself repeated at irregular intervals, from Catullus' 64th Ode, "*Currite ducentes subtegmina, currite, fusi.*" The immediate r. of a word for emphasis has an incremental emotional effect, as shown most daringly in *King Lear* with an entire line consisting of a single word repeated ("Never, never, never, never, never!"). One of the dangers of this method is that like all expressions of strong emotion it lends itself to parody rather readily. Almost the same patterns of r. are used by Shakespeare for both serious and comic purposes, the difference in effect lying in context and in metrical subtlety.

O Cressid! O false Cressid! false, false, false!
(*Troilus and Cressida*)

O night, O night! alack, alack, alack!
(*Midsummer Night's Dream*)

The same duality of effect may be observed in the following progression from Shakespeare through Nathaniel Lee to Henry Fielding:

O Desdemona, Desdemona dead! O!O!O!
(*Othello*)

O Sophonisba, Sophonisba O!
(*Sophonisba*)

O Huncamunca, Huncamunca O!
(*Tragedy of Tom Thumb the Great*)

Again it is notable that the effective line lacks complete symmetry, while the unintentionally and the intentionally comic lines are rigidly constructed, a situation which suggests caution in the use of immediate r. A special case of r. is the pun (q.v.), where not similarity but difference is pointed up, and the effect within the context in which it occurs is diffusive rather than unifying. In general, double meanings in poetry will be found more frequently within the "tight" or heavily patterned forms of verse, such as sonnets or heroic couplets, rather than in "loose" forms, such as nondramatic blank verse.

The r. of a phrase in poetry may have an incantatory effect as in the opening lines of T. S. Eliot's *Ash-Wednesday*:

Because I do not hope to turn again
Because I do not hope
Because I do not hope to turn

The remaining 38 lines of the opening section of the poem might well be studied as an example of the effects of phrasal r., containing as they do no less than 11 lines clearly related to the opening 3 and serving as a unifying factor in a poem otherwise very free in structure. Sometimes the effect of a repeated phrase in a poem will be to emphasize a development or change by means of the contrast in the words following the identical phrases. For example, the shift from the distant to the near, from the less personal to the more personal is emphasized in Coleridge's *Rime of the Ancient Mariner* by such a r. of phrases:

I looked upon the rotting sea,
And drew my eyes away;
I looked upon the rotting deck,
And there the dead men lay.

Allusion (q.v.) or quoting is a special case of r., since it relies on resources outside of the poem itself for its effect. Here, as with the pun, the effect of the r. is diffusive rather than unifying, seeming frequently to be an extraneous, if graceful, decoration. Hence, with the exception of a few poets who have used it as a basic technique (T. S. Eliot, *The Waste Land*; Ezra Pound, *Cantos*), its chief use has been humorous, as in Robert Frost's *A Masque of Reason* or in W. S. Gilbert's *Bab Ballads*.

The r. of a complete line within a poem may be related to the envelope (q.v.) stanza pattern, may be used regularly at the end of each stanza as a refrain, or in other ways. The multiple recurrence of a line at irregular intervals as in Catullus' 64th Ode, as cited *supra*, or the line "Cras amet qui numquam amavit, quique amavit cras amet," which occurs ten times in the 92 lines of the *Pervigilium Veneris,* illustrates the effect of a r. of a specific line apart from a set place as furnished by stanzaic structure. Rarely a line may be repeated entire and immediately as a means of bringing a poem to a close, an extension of the method of bringing a sequence of terza rima (q.v.) to a close with a couplet:

> And miles to go before I sleep,
> And miles to go before I sleep.
> (Frost, *Stopping by Woods on a Snowy Evening*)

Lines simply reintroduced once in a poem generally are meant to bear an altered and enriched significance on their second appearance, as:

> O all the instruments agree
> The day of his death was a dark cold day
> (W. H. Auden, *In Memory of W. B. Yeats*)

The r. of a complete stanza within a poem is generally related to the envelope pattern or to the refrain, already cited. In either case, the effect is to reintroduce into an altered situation a unit which has already provoked a response, which will now modify and be modified.

The r. of metrical pattern is one of the most important elements of poetry. Through such r. individual lines are paired as to structure and groups of lines are built and organized into larger units or stanzas. These may be relatively simple like the ballad stanza, result: ing from the breakdown of a pair of 14-syllable lines, or complex like the stanza used by Keats in *Ode to a Nightingale.* Undoubtedly part of the interest in a long poem lies in the skillful variation possible in the repetition of a single basic unit, whether the tail-rhyme strophes of metrical romance, the Spenserian stanzas of *The Faerie Queene,* or the heroic couplet in Pope's *Rape of the Lock.* Similarly in blank verse, much interest lies in the variety possible within limits of the regular beat.—C. A. Smith, *R. and Parallelism in Eng. Verse* (1894); B. R. Lewis, *Creative Poetry* (1931); C. P. Smith, *Pattern and Variation in Poetry* (1932); G. W. Allen, *Am. Prosody* (1935); Sister Miriam Joseph, *Shakespeare and the Arts of Language* (1947); J. Greenway, *Lit. among the Primitives* (1964). S.F.F.

RESOLUTION. Term restricted in Gr. and L. metric to the resolution of a long syllable into its metrical equivalent of two shorts, e.g., when an iambus ($\smile$ —) or trochee (— $\smile$) is replaced by a tribrach ($\smile\smile\smile$). See CLASSICAL PROSODY and MORA. R.J.G.

REST. A term adapted from music and generally definable as a pause that counts in the metrical scheme. Most writers seem to restrict this definition to situations where a pause

seems to compensate (see COMPENSATION) for the absence of an unstressed syllable or syllables in a foot. The standard example is Tennyson's

> Break, break, break,
> At the foot of thy crags, O sea!

However, others have suggested that a rest may take the place of an entire foot. According to Stewart the variety of metrical pause equivalent to a rest in music seems to be a late literary invention, "hardly begun until after 1920."—Baum; G. R. Stewart, Jr., *Modern Metrical Technique as Illustrated in Ballad Meter, 1700–1920* (1923); W. L. Schramm, *Approaches to a Science of Eng. Verse* (1935). R.BE.

RETROENCHA (*retroensa*). A Prov. lyric form (more talked about than actually produced, it would seem) whose chief distinction was that it had a refrain at the end of each stanza. Otherwise, it was indistinguishable from the *vers* or the *chanso* (qq.v.).—E. Levy, *Provenzalisches Supplement-Wörterbuch,* VII (1915). F.M.C.

REVERDIE. OF dance poem which celebrates the coming of spring, the new green of the woods and fields, the singing of the birds, and the time for love. The versification is usually that of the *chanson* (q.v.) of 5 or 6 stanzas without refrain. According to Jeanroy, the r. was a popular form which spread from the Franco-Prov. border. Others conceive of it as an artistic form of dance resulting from an aristocratic milieu.—J. Bédier, "Les fêtes de mai et les commencements de la poésie lyrique au moyenâge," *Revue des deux mondes,* 135 (1896); Jeanroy, *Origines.* U.T.H.

REVERSAL. See PLOT.

RHAPSODIST, rhapsode (Gr. "stitcher"). In ancient Greece a wandering minstrel or court poet who recited epic poetry partly extemporaneously and partly from memory. He selected and "stitched together" (hence the name) his own poetry or that of others into which he frequently interpolated his own work. With the establishment of what was regarded as the authentic Homeric text of the *Iliad* and *Odyssey* (ca. 500 B.C.) the term labeled a professional class who recited only the Homeric poems in correct sequence, not selected extracts. Though such a class survived in Greece until the time of Sulla, it came to be unfavorably regarded.—T. W. Allen, *Homer, the Origins and Transmission* (1924). R.A.H.

RHAPSODY. Originally a selection or a portion of epic literature, usually the *Iliad* or *Odyssey,* sung by a rhapsode or rhapsodist (q.v.) in ancient Greece. The term in literature subsequently meant any highly emotional utterance, a literary work informed by ecstasy and not by a rational organization. It is also applied to a literary miscellany or a disconnected series of literary works.   R.A.H.

RHETORIC AND POETICS. From ancient times to the present, *rhetoric* in the broad sense has meant the art of persuasion, in the narrow sense the studied ornament of speech, or eloquence. Since the time of Aristotle, *poetics* has meant the theory of making and judging poetry. Any attempt to describe the relationship between these two disciplines inevitably runs into many complications. In the first place, rhet., as Aristotle remarked in the first sentence of his *Rhetoric,* is a "counterpart" (antistrophe) of dialectic or logic. Poetry, in turn, is a counterpart of rhet. Both rhet. and poetry depend upon grammar, and lyric poetry has always been associated with music. Many attempts have been made to find the differences between these arts, but more often than not these differences have evaporated in the interpretation of some particular critic. Consequently rhet. and poetics from Plato to T. S. Eliot have been almost inextricably intertwined. Rhet. is still a part of poetics; the analyses of poems that appear in the so-called New Criticism of today are largely rhetorical, in both the broad Aristotelian-Ciceronian sense and in the narrow stylistic sense.

Plato suggested inspiration *versus* reason or madness *versus* demonstrable truth as a dividing line between the poet and the orator. Socrates, in the *Phaedrus,* remarked that no poet can hope to enter the doors of poetry unless he is mad. Socrates' ideal speaker, on the other hand, was a sober dialectician. Aristotle mentioned, in his *Poetics,* that the poet may have a touch of madness, but went no further. Other critics, especially the Neoplatonists, made much of inspiration, sometimes calling it divine *furor,* often insisting that inspiration was the essential factor in composing poetry. In the 16th c., the poet-critic Ronsard repeatedly declared that both the poet and musician must be inspired. Shakespeare perfectly expressed the concept in the last act of the *Midsummer Night's Dream,* where he made Theseus say, "The lunatic, the lover, and the poet / Are of imagination all compact." In the early 19th c. Shelley argued in his *Defence of Poetry* that the finest passages in poetry are not produced by study and have no necessary connection with the will. Inspiration, however, could hardly be analyzed and provided little matter for any systematic poetics; the critic who wished to draw up principles and rules was forced to turn to rhet. Moreover, some critics would not allow that inspiration was given only to poet and musician. In *On the Sublime* Longinus maintained that all of the truly elevated passages in literature are ecstatic, and made no distinction between poet and orator; both Homer and Demosthenes transport the reader, and so do Cicero and the author of Genesis. Inspiration and rhet. were always found together in the Bible. There was no questioning the inspired quality of either New or Old Testament, but were the prophetic books, the psalms, and Job oratory or poetry or both?

A more fruitful distinction between rhet. and poetry was provided by Aristotle when he called persuasion the characteristic of rhet. and imitation the characteristic of poetry. The orator is a good rhetorician when he masters all the available means of persuasion, and the poet is a poet because he imitates the actions of men. While Aristotle thought that poetry is more universal and a higher art than history, he did not call it more universal and higher than oratory or philosophy. Some of his Renaissance disciples, however, went so far. J. C. Scaliger (*Poetices* 1.1), for example, asserted that the poet excels the philosopher, historian, and orator because he alone is not tied to fact but represents a higher nature and in so doing creates as if he were "another god." Sir Philip Sidney and many others, including Wordsworth and Coleridge, echoed this concept.

Not every critic after Aristotle, however, accepted persuasion as a function peculiar to the rhetorician. Scaliger, while calling the poet a second deity, nevertheless maintained that philosophy and drama (i.e., poetry) have the same end as does oratory, namely, persuasion. Scaliger believed, as did most critics of the Renaissance, that poetry should be didactic. There was no explicit statement in Aristotle that the poet is a teacher, but Horace, whose rhetorical *Ars Poetica* was enormously influential for centuries, had said that the poet should teach as well as delight. Consequently most critics after Horace believed that poetry and rhet. had a common end, didacticism, which is usually identical with persuasion.

The only honest basis of teaching and persuading is knowledge. Plato's Socrates repeatedly quarreled with poets and with bad rhetoricians because they did not know enough. Cicero demanded a thorough knowledge of all the liberal arts and sciences in his ideal orator. Horace, who was doubtless influenced by Cicero, declared that the source and fountain of all good writing is "to know" (*sapere*). Scholars and critics of the Renaissance readily harmonized Ciceronian and Horatian *dicta*; they transferred the universal knowledge of

Cicero's ideal orator to the ideal poet and held up Virgil, sometimes Homer, as the exemplar of omniscience.

The concept that the true poet is an imitator or creator of fictions, not merely a versifier, was long accepted by most critics. Scaliger raised objections, arguing that verse and prose provided a satisfactory dividing line between poetry and oratory; but Scaliger was exceptional and most critics supported the Aristotelian theory, especially since it fitted Cicero's well-known statement in *De Oratore* (1.16), that the orator and poet are closely allied, the poet being somewhat more restricted in expression by his "numbers." For centuries, from Quintilian in the 1st c. to the Eng. romanticists of the 19th, it was a critical commonplace that Lucan was a rhetorician or historian who wrote in verse and that Plato and Xenophon were poets. Wordsworth's *Preface to the Lyrical Ballads* (1800) maintained that there is no difference between prose and verse save the poet's meter and rhyme. Wordsworth's more learned partner, Coleridge, objected to this theory, but on somewhat different grounds from those used by Scaliger. According to Coleridge, the very act of introducing meter and rhyme into a discourse fundamentally alters the form as well as the expression. Although he did not press his theory to the extent of excluding all prose from any close alliance with poetry—he acknowledged that Isaiah, Plato, and Jeremy Taylor wrote poetry of the "highest kind"—his discussion of the problem in the *Biographia Literaria* provided an important basis for later theories. Several present-day critics, following the lead of I. A. Richards, have incorporated Coleridge's ideas in their poetics.

Although persuasion as a characteristic did not separate rhet. from poetry, it suggested a significant difference. Since the orator must persuade, he must have an audience, and oratory was always regarded as a practical art. Such was the view of leading ancients like Aristotle, Cicero, and Quintilian, although Plato's Socrates aimed at self-conviction in his rhet. rather than at persuading the mob. The successful poet, especially the dramatist, usually had an audience; but poetry was not necessarily a practical art like rhet. This distinction has often been emphasized in modern times. The first Fr. art of poetry, Thomas Sebillet's *Art poétique françois* (1548), suggested that the ideal aim of the poet was his own personal glory or the glory of his country, not persuasion of a particular audience. Shelley described the poet as a "nightingale, who sits in darkness and sings to cheer its own solitude with sweet sounds." John Stuart Mill (*Poetry and its Varieties*, 1859) remarked that since poetry is the "natural fruit of solitude," it is *overheard* while eloquence is *heard*. Milton, in *Of Education*, said that poetry is "more simple, sensuous, and passionate" than rhet., and many critics have argued that the poet relies more upon emotion, inner emotion, than does the prose writer. In an early essay, "Tradition and the Individual Talent" (1919), T. S. Eliot tried to separate the poetic experience from other experiences, and called the poetic experience primarily an intensifying of a special kind of emotion, namely, "art emotion." But Eliot never actually defined emotion in poetry. I. A. Richards, using the techniques of behaviorist psychology, has tried to define it, with conspicuous success, according to some disciples, with no success whatever, according to others.

The brief, incomplete analysis above should indicate the impossibility of presenting any systematic history of rhet. and poetics within the space allotted here. A brief account of the historical terminology, however, may at least point out some prominent milestones along the way.

Aristotle was apparently the first critic to construct a terminology for poetics. His *Poetics* provided both a qualitative and quantitative analysis: tragedy was divided into Plot, Character (*ethos*), Thought (*dianoia*), Diction, Music, Spectacle, and into prologue, episodes, choruses, and epode. Epic poetry could be analyzed in the same qualitative way though it lacked music and spectacle. In his *Rhetoric*, on the other hand, Aristotle divided a speech into two essential parts, statement of the case and proof. A speech might also have an introduction and a peroration, but these parts were not essential. Aristotle's *Poetics* all but disappeared from Alexandrian times to the close of the 15th c., and meanwhile the terminology of Cicero became the standard for both rhet. and poetics. Cicero's youthful *De Inventione* and the pseudo-Ciceronian *Rhetorica ad Herennium* named both qualitative and quantitative parts: rhet. was divided into invention, arrangement (*dispositio*), style, memory, and delivery; the mechanical parts of a speech were exordium, statement of the case (*narratio*), proof and/or disproof, conclusion. There were three kinds of style, high, middle, and plain.

Although the author of the *Ad Herennium* was sparing in his use of poetry to illustrate rhetorical principles, Cicero himself was not, but drew freely, for example, upon Terence to show what good rhet. was. Moreover, Cicero's most distinguished follower, Quintilian, taught that Homer's writings display all the rules of art to be followed in oratory and that a careful study of the comic poet Menander would be sufficient to develop the whole art of rhet. In late classical times and throughout most of the Middle Ages poetry fell under the wing of either rhet. or grammar. When deliberative oratory disappeared under the rule of the emperors and forensic oratory became highly specialized, demonstrative oratory or declamation became the principal rhetorical study and *elocutio* or style received the major emphasis. Invention and arrangement were either neglected or returned to their original owner, the logician. Some medieval theorists in France associated poetics with music, but most medieval manuals of poetry were rhetorics and only the sections on versification made any significant distinction between poetry and oratory.

With the revival of classical learning came the recovery of the mature rhetorical treatises of Cicero, *De Oratore, Brutus, Orator, etc.* and the complete *Institutio Oratoria* of Quintilian, bringing with them a revival of the logical components of rhet., namely, invention and arrangement. One of the influential books of the early Renaissance was *De Inventione Dialectica* by Rodolphus Agricola (d. 1485). Logic or dialectic, said Agricola, is "to speak in a probable way on any matter"; grammar teaches correctness and clarity, rhet. style. Agricola had anticipated Peter Ramus (1515–72), who insisted that invention and arrangement belonged to logic, that style belonged to rhet. Meanwhile Ciceronians continued to maintain that rhet. included both logical and stylistic disciplines. And the study of poetry remained largely rhetorical; dramas, epic poems, odes, elegies were analyzed in terms of invention, arrangement, and style, and also in terms of exordium, *narratio*, proof, and conclusion. The Ciceronian hierarchy of styles (high, middle, plain) was also restored.

The recovery of Aristotle's *Poetics* in the 16th c. produced some modifications of this rhetorical poetics, for scholars like Robortelli and Castelvetro began to mingle Aristotle's poetic terminology with the Ciceronian terminology, and their work gradually found its way into poetics outside Italy. The *Pléiade* poets, Du Bellay, Ronsard, Peletier, spoke of invention, arrangement, and style. Sidney's *Defense of Poesy* was mainly rhetorical. In the next century, however, these logical-rhetorical terms appeared side by side with Plot (Fable), Character (Manners), Thought (Sentiments), and Diction, as, for example, in Rapin's *Réflexions sur la Poétique d'Aristote* (1674) and in Dryden's *Preface to the Fables* (1700). In the 18th c. the authors of poetics continued to mingle Ciceronian terminology with Aristotle's and to use rhet. in both the broad and narrow sense.

The 19th c. witnessed a romantic revolt by poets and critics of poetry against classical poetics and a professed revulsion toward all rhet. (The revulsion was actually toward oratory.) This dislike of rhet. was carried over into the 20th c., when influential scholars and critics called for a "new" poetics and a "new" rhet. Joel Spingarn and Benedetto Croce recommended a scrapping of all older techniques and terminologies. Spingarn, in his lecture of 1910 entitled "The New Criticism," recommended concentration on the *expression* of a poem. At about the same time, Croce, in his aesthetic essays, recommended abandonment of form-content and the genres of poetry and adoption of *intuition-expression*. In 1923, I. A. Richards, one of the leaders of the New Critics, proposed to abandon traditional procedures and fashion a new poetics based on modern psychology. A dozen years later, he had more or less given up psychology and was working on a new rhet. Richards, in fact, had never abandoned rhet.; as Laurence Lerner (*The Truest Poetry* [1960], pp. 76–78) has remarked, Richards belongs with the Elizabethan apologists for poetry, with Sidney and Puttenham, whose arts of poetry were rhetorical. Northrop Frye, author of the *Anatomy of Criticism*, has turned back to Plato and Aristotle; he has resurrected the genres of poetry (drama, epic, lyric) and applied rhetorical criticism to them. According to Frye (pp. 245–247), there are two kinds of rhet.: persuasion ("applied literature") and ornament ("the *lexis* or verbal texture of poetry"). The old traditional terminology, going back through the Renaissance to ancient Greece and Rome, has been modified, but the changes are not so radical as may appear on the surface. Instead of *res-verba, imitatio, fictio, inventio, dispositio, elocutio*, etc. we have Richards' *emotive* language of poetry *vs.* the *scientific* language of prose, John Crowe Ransom's *ontology*, Allen Tate's "strategies" of language, Cleanth Brooks's *paradox*, William Empson's *ambiguity*, and a host of other terms, such as *creative imagination, organicism, tension, irony, semantics*, and *communication*—all adding up, in the main, to rhet.

Plato, *Phaedrus, Gorgias, Ion, Symposium*; Aristotle, *Rhetoric, Poetics*; Cicero, *De Inventione, De Oratore, Brutus, Orator, De Partitione Oratoria*; [Cicero], *Rhetorica ad Herennium*; Horace, *Ars Poetica*; Quintilian, *Institutio Oratoria*; Longinus, *On the Sublime*; F. Robortellus, *In Librum Aristotelis de Arte Poetica Explicationes* (1548); T. Wilson, *The Arte of Rhetorique* (1553); Ramus and Talaeus, *Rhetorica e P. Rami Regii Professoris Praelectionibus Observata* (1572); J. C. Scaliger, *Poetices Libri Septem* (2d ed., 1581); Puttenham, *The Arte of Eng. Poesie* (1589); G. I. Vossius, *Commentariorum Rhetoricorum Sive Oratoriarum Institutionum, Libri Sex* (1643); F. Fénelon, *Dialogues Concerning Eloquence* (Eng. ed., 1722); G. Campbell, *The Philos. of Rhet.* (1776); H. Blair, *Lectures on Rhet. and Belles Lettres* (1783); R. Whately, *Rhet.* (1828); E. T. Channing, *Lectures [On Rhet. and Oratory]*

RHYME

Read to the Seniors in Harvard College (1856); A. Bain, *Eng. Composition and Rhet.* (1866); J. F. Genung, *The Practical Elements of Rhet.* (1886); I. A. Richards, *Practical Crit.* (1929), *The Philos. of Rhet.* (1936); K. Burke, *The Philos. of Lit. Form* (1941) and *A Rhet. of Motives* (1950).

SECONDARY SOURCES: C. S. Baldwin, *Ancient Rhet. and Poetic* (1924), *Medieval Rhet. and Poetic* (1928); D. L. Clark, *Rhet. and Poetry in the Renaissance* (1922); Patterson; M. T. Herrick, "The Place of Rhet. in Poetics," in *Comic Theory in the 16th C.* (1950); W. S. Howell, *Logic and Rhet. in England, 1500–1700* (1956); N. Frye, *Anatomy of Crit.* (1957); L. Lerner, *Truest Poetry* (1960); B. Weinberg, *A Hist. of Lit. Crit. in the It. Renaissance* (2 v., 1961); O. B. Hardison, Jr., *The Enduring Monument* (1962); G. Kennedy, *The Art of Persuasion* (1963); M. H. Nichols, *Rhet. and Crit.* (1963).　　　　M.T.H.

RHETORICAL ACCENT. See ACCENT.

RHETORICAL QUESTION. Either a word- or sentence-question asked for effect rather than information, one to which the speaker knows the answer in advance and either does not wait for it or answers the question himself: "ti oun aition einai hypolambano; ego hymin ero" (What then do I regard as the explanation? I will tell you—Plato, *Apology* 40b). The device, much more favored in Gr. than in Eng., is found rarely in Lysias, quite frequently in Plato and Isaeus, in a highly developed state in Demosthenes. Used frequently in persuasive discourse, r.q. commands attention from the audience, serves to express various shades of emotion, and sometimes acts as a transitional device to lead from one subject to another. The most famous Eng. example is probably the question at the end of Shelley's *Ode to the West Wind:* "O, Wind, / If Winter comes, can Spring be far behind?"　　　　R.O.E.

RHÉTORIQUEURS, *grands rhétoriqueurs.* Fr. poets of the late 15th and early 16th c., particularly active at the court of Burgundy and, later, at the Parisian court. Their work is characterized by extensive allegory, obscure diction, and intricately experimental meters and stanza forms, and in their technical innovations they performed an important, if usually unacknowledged, service for later Fr. poets. Despite their courtly activity, the r. were generally bourgeois in their antecedents and, in this respect as in their formalism, they are analogous to the German Meistersinger and the Dutch *rederijkers* (qq.v.). Their formalism, related to the late medieval confusion of rhetoric and poetics, makes the name by which they are known at least partially appropriate

to their work, but it ought to be recognized that they and their contemporaries did not, in all probability, call themselves *rhétoriqueurs.* It is a literary-historical designation dating from a much later period.

The first of the r. was Alain Chartier (fl. 1430), and other members of the tradition include Jean Lemaire de Belges, Meschinet, Molinet, Crétin, and Jean Marot (father of the more famous Clément Marot). The poetry of the r. was criticized harshly in the later 16th c. by the School of Lyons and by the *Pléiade* (q.v.), but modern opinion recognizes to an ever greater degree the value of their contributions not only to the technique of Fr. poetry but also to the development of satire and, in general, to a dissemination of humanist ideals which prefigures the high Renaissance.—H. Guy, "L'École des r.," *Hist. de la poésie française au 16e s.,* I (1910); W. L. Wiley, "Who Named Them R.?" *Medieval Studies in Honor of Jeremiah Denis Matthias Ford,* ed. U. T. Holmes, Jr. and A. J. Denomy (1948); A. M. Schmidt, "La Littérature humaniste à l'époque de la renaissance," *Hist. des littératures,* ed. R. Queneau (1958).　　　F.J.W.; A.P.

RHOPALIC VERSE (from Gr. "club-like," "thicker toward the end"). Wedge verse in which each word is a syllable longer than the one before it, as *Iliad* 3.182: "o makar Atreide, moiregenes, olbiodaimon," which begins with a monosyllable and closes with a word of 6 syllables.—Koster.　　　K.M.A.

RHUPYNT. See AWDL.

RHYME. NATURE AND FUNCTION. The spelling "rhyme" became common in the 17th c. and is now more usual than the older "rime." The main meaning of the word is: a metrical rhetorical device based on the sound-identities of words. The minor meanings can be summarily disposed of before the main one is elaborated: (1) a poem in rhymed verse (cf. Mrs. Browning's *Rhyme of the Duchess May* which has a "Pro-rhyme" before and an "Epi-rhyme" after); (2) rhymed verse in general (e.g., "Pope's Homer is in rhyme" (3) any kind of echoing between words besides the one specified by the main meaning above (e.g., assonance, consonance, alliteration, etc.); (4) unison or accord (e.g., J. R. Lowell, *Among My Books:* "of which he was as unaware as the blue river is of its rhyme with the blue sky"); (5) a word that echoes another (e.g., " 'Love' is a hackneyed rhyme for 'dove' ") or the sound common to two or more words (e.g., "The meanings of the words are just as important as their rhymes"); (6) a complement to "reason" (in such phrases as: "without rhyme or reason").

As a metrical-rhetorical device in Eng., r.

-[705]-

involves two or more r.-fellows. These may be: whole words (*dawn–fawn*); ends of words (ap/*plaud*–de/*fraud*); groups of whole words (*stayed with us–played with us*); or ends of words followed by one or more whole words (be/*seech him*–im/*peach him*). R.-fellows of one sort may of course rhyme with fellows of another sort (*poet–know it*). If a r.-fellow is phonetically analyzed, it will be found to have at least a stem, which must be vocalic (*awe, eye, owe*). It may have an initial, which if it is present must be consonantal (*saw, spy, low*); and it may have a terminal, consonantal (*all, eyes, own*) or vocalic (*ayah*) or both (*awful, eyot, owning*). Both initial and terminal may be present as well as stem (*lawfully, spying, known*). The stem carries the last metrical stress of the line, or possibly the second last

make of it–take of it.

The sound-identity for a perfect rhyme must begin in each r.-fellow with the stem and continue through the terminal if there is one. At least one of a pair of r.-fellows, two of a trio, and so on must have initials, no two initials being the same (*ill–fill–mill;* but not *ill–till–*un/*til*). When the r.-fellows are monosyllabic, the r. is male, masculine, or single (pala/*din*–harle/*quin*). In Eng. such rhymes far outnumber those involving more than one syllable. Rhymes are said to be female, feminine, or double when the r.-fellows are disyllabic (*master*–di/*saster*). Trisyllabic r.-fellows produce treble, triple, or sdrucciolo rhymes (*Thackeray–quackery*). R.-fellows with still more syllables are so rare in Eng. that no special names are in use for the resulting rhymes. No doubt rhymes of sorts can be concocted from nonce words, as in Lewis Carroll's *Jabberwock*. But notionally at least r. comes only from sound-identities between real words, given their accepted pronunciation, accentuation, articulation, and usage. R. which conforms to all the requirements is said to be complete, full, perfect, true, or whole. Departures from the norm are licenses, which may or may not be tolerable according to circumstances.

The origin of r. should not be sought locally or linguistically. R. is to be traced rather to the fact that the number of sounds available for any language is limited and its many words must be combinations and permutations of its few sounds. Every language, therefore, is bound to jingle now and then. It will depend on a variety of factors whether the jingles will come to be used deliberately as a device in poetry and how far that device will be carried. Systematic rhyming, however, has appeared in such widely separated languages (e.g., Chinese, Sanskrit, Arabic, Norse, Prov., Celtic) that its

spontaneous development in more than one of them can be reasonably assumed. In the rest it may have been introduced like any other device from the outside, and any language that had already acquired r., no matter how, may have learned new applications of it from its neighbors. Men must have been pleased by verbal jingles long before they realized that the jingles had a use in organizing or pointing their verses. R. is indeed only one instance of that animating principle of all the arts: the desire for similarity in dissimilarity and dissimilarity in similarity. Other results within the literary art are: alliteration, anaphora, antithesis and balance, assonance, meter and stanzas, parallelism, and refrains. Perhaps because man is a creature with paired limbs and organs, he takes pleasure in repetitions, not merely simple duplications, but approximations, complements, and counterpoints.

The functions of r. are metrical and rhetorical. From the metrical point of view end- or final r. is a device to mark the ends of lines and link them in couplets, stanzas, or verse paragraphs. It has an organizing effect, therefore, in respect of metrical units longer than the foot. It might be regarded as an ornamental stress falling on and confirming the metrical stresses at the ends of the lines. But middle-and-end r. is sometimes used to mark the ends of the two halves of a line. Such rhyming is sporadic in many ballads, as well as elsewhere. When it is systematic, it simply results from two short lines having been put down as one to save space.

R. in verse is not limited to the ends of lines and half-lines. One word may echo another anywhere in its immediate neighborhood and apart from the metrical scheme. The purpose of such inner, internal, or medial rhymes is then more rhetorical than metrical, as where Browning builds up a seriocomic climax with them in:—

How *sad* and *bad* and *mad* it was—
But then, how it was sweet!

or where Swinburne suggests the darting flight of the bird in:—

Sister, my sister, O *fleet sweet* swallow.

Rhetorical, too, rather than metrical is the practice of Shakespeare and his fellow-dramatists intermingling a good deal of end-r. with their blank verse, generally in couplets, but sometimes in greater complication; they were particularly partial to rhymed couplets for ending a speech or pointing a maxim.

Though r. is primarily a feature of verse, it has been resorted to in prose for occasional effects from the earliest Gr. orators downward. Cicero's discreet use of it was probably what commended it to the mannered stylists of the Renaissance (e.g., Rabelais; Guevara and the gongorists; John Lyly and the euphuists). It can be found in later writers as diverse as Hannah More, Disraeli, and George Meredith, not to mention the practitioners of polyphonic prose (q.v.).

Though end-r. in verse is primarily metrical, it has also a rhetorical side. "Poetry aims . . . at increasing, by metrical devices, the number of best places for the best words in the best order" (Sir Walter Raleigh, *Six Essays on Johnson*). Of these devices r. is not the least important, and the places which it signalizes are among the very best. It concentrates meaning in "ce mot sorcier, ce mot fée, ce mot magique" (Théodore de Banville, *Petit Traité de Poésie Française*). There is then little point in having good places for words if advantage is not taken of them; and r. is wasted unless its sound cooperates in some ways with the sense. That being so, the poet who has many insignificant words in rhyming places is losing some of his opportunities.

The beauty of r., for the Eng. reader at least, "is lessened by any likeness the words may have beyond that of sound" (G. M. Hopkins, *The Note-books and Papers*). Even when rhymes are separately unexceptionable, they may be weakened by repetition or near-repetition at no great interval. Such lapses, besides being unenterprising, are destructive of stanzaic patterns. Then again hackneyed rhymes (*breeze–trees*) can hardly yield the pleasure of a mild surprise; and inevitable yoke-fellows (*anguish–languish, length–strength*) still less. It does not follow, however, that bizarre rhymes are *per contra* good in any context, though they may be appropriate in *Hudibras* or *The Ingoldsby Legends*. A last weakness, to mention no more, is to let the r. too obviously dictate the sense. For part of the mastery of r. "consists in never writing it for its own sake, or at least never appearing to do so" (Leigh Hunt, *Imagination and Fancy*).

Languages differ widely in their rhymability, and different conventions have been established as to the acceptable and the unacceptable. Languages which rhyme easily may right the balance by restrictive rules; and those which rhyme less easily may tolerate near-rhymes, though retaining perfect r. as the ideal. Though Gr. and L. poetry normally did without rhyme, it was a recognized figure (*homoeoteleuton* [q.v.], *similiter desinens*). It is rarer in Gr. poetry than in L., though not unknown even in Homer and becoming rather commoner in the Alexandrian poets who delighted in all kinds of verbal correspondences. L. poetry seemed to hanker after r. The earliest remains, which are in accentual verse, frequently jingle. Among modern European languages Sp. and It. run the most readily to r., on account of the relatively small number of ways in which words end. Rhyming is further facilitated in It. by the eliding flexibility of the language. Hence the fluency of the *improvisatori* who can produce extemporary verses in complicated meters with scarcely any cogitation on any subjects suggested by their auditors. Fr. rhymes almost as readily as Sp. and It. But by authoritarian edict many phonetically perfect rhymes are declined on various grounds. Another restrictive influence was the limitation of poets to an exclusive poetic diction, until Victor Hugo "mit un bonnet rouge au vieux dictionnaire." German is less rhymable than any of the Romance languages, but more so than Eng. It has always been ready to accept into art-poetry some of the freedoms of folk-verse and to make a pronunciation in one dialect justify a r. in another. It has also resorted, more often and more successfully than Sp., It., or Fr., to unrhymed measures.

So has Eng., especially in its blank verse. It also has made a considerable use of stanzas which do not require every line to rhyme (e.g., ballad measure, long measure, etc.). Owing to the large number of ways in which Eng. words can terminate, the average number of words to an ending is under three. The number of words which rhyme with only one other is large (*mountain–fountain, babe*-astro/*labe*); and those which cannot be rhymed at all is as large or larger (*breadth, circle, desert, monarch, month, virtue, wisdom,* etc.). The result is that Eng. is more tolerant than any other European language of rhyming licenses. Though Eng. poets vary greatly in the number and the kinds of easements they discover from rhyming rigor, they all allow themselves more merely approximate rhymes than is generally realized, to say nothing of solecisms in usage for rhyme's sake. Several other points are worth mentioning in this connection: first, the anomalies of Eng. spelling which give a sort of sanction to eye or visual rhymes (*cough–plough*); secondly, the fact that so many of the most admired poets came early when the language was different from what it became; thirdly, the respect for ancient precedents and the revivalism in practically every period among poets who harked back to their predecessors for models; and finally, the frequent draughts of Eng. art-poetry from folk-poetry, if not indeed the virtual absence of any barrier between them. Moreover it is the way of art to make virtues of necessities; and so the poets have found reasons for rhyming relaxation which originate in the recognition of the beauty of imperfection and the pleasure of novelty and surprise. They are, by virtue of their calling, verbal experimenters who strain at and overleap the restrictions of the purists; and poetry is the growing end of language, in the matter of r. as in other respects.　A.M.C.

For bibliog. see HISTORY (below).

HISTORY. Saintsbury, famous British prosodist, once declared that r. in Eng. appeared no one quite knows how, or why, or whence. Indeed, in origins, in diffusion, and in function, r. is the most mysterious of all sound-pattern repetitions. It is not originally native to any European or Indo-European language. Among Oriental languages, it appears early in South-Semitic and Chinese, whence from either or both it may later have been adapted to the Sanskritic Indian languages and to Iranian. Fragments of Old Latin poems by Ennius certainly show structural r. as a factor in verse side by side with accent and alliteration, but here one suspects acculturation from a language originally from the northern Near East–Etruscan. Not only are the origins of r. mysterious; it is mysteriously complex in its literary suggestions. Obviously, in the ages before silent reading (see Augustine, *Confessions* 3) it was a useful mnemonic device. In addition, it contributes to verse a euphonic factor, a phrase and line segmentalizing factor, a pointing (deictic) semantic factor, and—particularly in modern verse—a factor that underlines irony, litotes, and the unexpected collocations of dissimilars we expect to find in the poetry of dissociation. To trace the history of r. in Western Atlantic literatures is a discursion into the unknown, particularly since early writers integrate it with assonance, consonance, alliteration, and the like under one head. In native North America, it occurs only in one Indian language, where it is probably borrowed from Eng. Most cultures' verse lacks r. either as organizational device or as ornament.

In European literatures, the first mention of anything approaching true r. is in the third book of Aristotle's *Rhetoric*—that remarkable book, long neglected in favor of the *Poetics*—which discusses practical rhetorical devices under the twin heads of *clarity* and *propriety*. Here we are introduced to the notion of homoeoteleuton at the ends, more rarely at the beginnings, of the members of prose periods, as contributing to sound harmony (paromoeosis). Whether or not Aristotle's account derives from Gorgian rhetoricians, or from lost books by Isocrates, or from Near Eastern sources, we do not certainly know. We do know that the later Alexandrian rhetoricians and critics, like some L. writers after them, understood the use of homoeoteleuton in prose.

Verse r., actually homocotcleuton rather than full r., first appears in hymns of the African Christian Church attributed to successors of Tertullian (A.D. 160?–220?). In these (as in *suscipe: tempore*) only the final inflectional syllable actually rhymed. Full r. seems first to appear in hymns associated with the followers of St. Hilarius of Poitiers (d. A.D. 368?), but was not generally adopted until some centuries later. In Byzantium, Romanus the Melode and Synesius were exploiting its possibilities in hymnology by the 6th c. A.D. The combined evidence of Aristotelian and Alexandrinian homoeoteleuton, the African Tertullian hymns, Hilarian full r., and Byzantinian full r. all points to a South-Semitic, possibly Arabian, source as the diffusion center for r. in the European literatures.

In Western Europe, full r., usually combining end-r. with in-r., seems first to have appeared in Ireland under the influence of early rhymed hymns and among poets writing both in Ir. and in L. Here, the controlling linguistic factor was the early disappearance of Ir. suffixal elements, the development of initial inflection, and the consequent development of end-stress in the word. In Welsh, which was and is a fore-stressed language, r. has always been secondary to alliteration. Very intricate combinations of end-r. with in-r. occur in Ir. as early as the Lorica of St. Patrick (attributed to A.D. 433), and wherever Ir. monks traveled on the Continent of Europe, they seem to have proselytized the use of full r. as ardently as they proselytized their Faith. They are probably responsible ultimately for the intricate rhyming patterns of the goliardic *Carmina Burana,* and eventually, for those of the 9th-c. Ambrosian hymns. From both sources, r. diffused to the Scandinavian countries, where from Bragi onward it alternated with carefully contrived end consonances (*skothendings*) in skaldic verse. In ON skaldic verse, as in Ir. hymns and L.-Ir. goliardic poems, full r. is used as a line-end marker to segmentalize such lovely stanzaic forms as those of the *Pervigilium Veneris* or the Provençal-Minnesänger stanza form abc / abc / dddd and its variants, first found in the *Carmina Burana.*

The introduction of end-r. into West Germanic verse is rather curious. In Old High German, the *Muspilli* shows a degeneration of the original alliterative technique to a point where it is rhythmically unintelligible. Otfried, or someone like Otfried, simply had to introduce end r. as a structural factor marking line-endings and inducing a new accentual verse structure. That Otfried had uneven success with his new technique merely reveals the relative unfamiliarity of end-r. in the German literature of his day. In OE, ornamental in-r. coupled with end-r. is much more common than one usually supposes. Friedrich Kluge found 28 examples in the *Beowulf* alone. Recent phonemicizations of OE, which construe *ea, eo,* and *io* as mere positional (nondistinctive) variants of *ae, e,* and *i,* add greatly to the frequency of actual full rhymes found in *Beowulf*, the so-called Elegiac poems, the Cynewulfian poems, *Judith*, and so forth. Here we may be concerned with direct or indirect influence from Ir. Yet, although OE full rhymes are ornamental—subsidiary to the primary structural device of alliteration—the *Rhyming Poem* and the *Death of Alfred* in the OE Chronicle (both 10th c.) are so similar to the ON *runhent* (like Egill's *Höfuðlausn*, composed at York) that we may suspect a well-developed OE tradition of structural full r. of which these two are the only surviving exemplars. Quite probably it originated in the Scandinavian colonies of Eastern and Northern England. The later evolution of the ME unrhymed alliterative romance in the Central and North West Midlands as compared with that of the rhymed metrical romance (quite similar to the later ON *rímur*) in the North East Midlands and East Anglia adds substance to this hypothesis. Further evidence may be derived from the emergence of such long rhymed poems as *Genesis and Exodus* and *Cursor Mundi* around A.D. 1300, the one from the Central East Midlands, the other from the Northern area.

In ME, the first influx of rhymed verse occurs in the late 12th c. with the *Owl and the Nightingale* and in the 13th c. with Layamon's *Brut* and the lyrics preserved in MS Harley 2254. The first is in form and subject matter a Prov. tenson and may owe its rhymes, as it owes its adapted theme, to direct Prov. influence. The second is curious: it blends the OE alliterative line with full rhymes, assonances, homoeoteleutons, and nunnations, and may very well owe a direct debt to contemporary Welsh verse. The lyrics raise a vexed question: is their use of stanzaic r. to be attributed directly to Prov.-Fr. influence, or to goliardic lyric, or to Saracen influence working through Prov., or to a combination of these possibilities? The earliest troubadour lyrics themselves undoubtedly derive from the goliardic L. verse of the wandering scholars, although later enriched by the intricate erotic rhymed verse of the Arabic Moors. In all probability, particularly when we consider the macaronic verse of the early ME manuscripts, we are to assume a combination of these influences. If *Alisoun* plainly recalls the Prov. influence, *Lenten is come with Love to Toune* recalls, and surpasses, the best of the goliardic lyrics. With Robert of Brunne and the Chaucerians, as with Chaucer himself, the primary influence is undoubted. It is Fr., and Northern Fr. at that. Yet to understand the intrusion of r. into ME verse, certain linguistic facts must also be taken into account. The breakdown of the OE inflectional system enormously multiplied the number of easily rhymed monosyllabic words; the widespread borrowing of Fr. disyllabic and polysyllabic words stressed on the last or next to the last syllable created words easily accessible to end-r. These factors, working in combination, created a verse milieu favorable to r. and relatively unfavorable to alliteration.

The later history of r. in Eng. calls for some preliminary observations. First, languages in which full r. or homoeoteleuton are automatic concomitants of inflection never use r. as a structural factor in verse. Examples are Japanese and certain Bantu languages. Second, end-stress rather than fore-stress facilitates the use of r. A typical example would be that of Italian. Third, when, in any language, rhyming is relatively easy, the poet tends to complicate it by employing *rime riche* (as in Fr.), or highly complex rhymed stanza forms (as in Prov. and Fr.), or by eschewing r. completely (as in the blank verse allegedly invented by Trissino for drama). Eng., greatly influenced in rhyming habit by Continental sources, shows or has shown all three tendencies. *Rime riche* occurs in Chaucer; although the ballade, rondeau, rondel, and triolet have never had the popularity of the sonnet, they have been frequently written and are still being written; blank verse achieved almost immediate popularity in drama; and unrhymed quantitative verse, first introduced by Thomas Watson (between 1530 and 1540), Richard Stanyhurst (1582), William Webbe (1586), and Thomas Campion (1602) was revived even in the 19th c. by Arthur Hugh Clough and the Reverend Rackham—this despite Daniel's brilliant *Defence of Rhyme* (1603). R., in fact, walks a tightrope between ease and difficulty: too easy rhyming or too difficult rhyming produce the same result—the poetic disuse of r.

On these lines, four periods of Eng. rhyming can be distinguished: (1) in the fore-stressed OE, r. was difficult; hence the persistence of structural alliteration; (2) in ME, r. became easier; hence its eventual victory over alliteration; (3) in Early Modern Eng. (roughly 1500–1750) the results of the Great Sound Shift made r. very easy; hence the popularity of such forms as the sonnet on the one hand and blank verse on the other; (4) in the Late Modern Eng. period (roughly from 1830), because of the victorious emergence of the former bourgeois pronunciation as a Received Standard, r. has again become difficult; hence the increasing use of eye-rhymes (based ultimately on the true rhymes of Pope) in the 19th c., and, more lately, the increasing popularity of end-consonance, slant rhymes, assonances, Donnesque rhymes, and, ultimately, through the influence of the Fr. symbolists and Whitman, of "free" (viz. syntactic) verse.   H.W.

A. Ehrenfeld, *Studien zur Theorie des Reims*

(2 v., 1897–1904); G. Mari, *Riassunto e Dizio-narietto di Ritmica Italiana* (1901); Kastner; Saintsbury, *Prosody;* A. Gabrielson, *R. as a Criterion of the Pronunciation of Spenser, Pope, Byron, and Swinburne* (1909); Schipper; F. Zschech, *Die Kritik des Reims in England* (1917); O. Brik, "Zvukovie povtory," *Poetika* (1919); T. S. Osmond, *Eng. Metrists* (1921); H. C. Wyld, *Studies in Eng. Rhymes from Surrey to Pope* (1923); V. Zhirmunsky, *Rifma, ee istoriia i teoriia* (1923); Norden; A. Heusler, *Deutsche Versgeschichte* (3 v., 1925–29); G. Young, *An Eng. Prosody on Inductive Lines* (1928); H. Lanz, *The Physical Basis of R.* (1931); A. M. Clark, *Studies in Lit. Modes* (1945); F.J.E. Raby, *Hist. of Christian L. Poetry* (2d ed. 1953) and *Secular L. Poetry* (2d ed. 2 v., 1957); J. Carney, *Studies in Ir. Lit. and Hist.* (1955); Parry; W. P. Lehmann, *The Development of Germanic Verse* (1956); Navarro; J. W. Draper, "The Origin of R.," RLC, 31 (1957). See also SOUND IN POETRY. A.M.C.; H.W.

RHYME-COUNTERPOINT. A term which designates that type of versification in which line length is systematically opposed to rhyme scheme, rhymed lines being of unequal length, unrhymed lines being of equal length. (See A. M. Hayes, "Counterpoint in Herbert," SP, 35 [1938]). Thus, the term "rhyme-harmony" describes such traditional stanzaic forms as ballad meter and limerick (qq.v.), whereas "r.-c." describes the unusual stanzaic forms employed by Donne, Vaughan, and, especially, Herbert.

Hayes sees the chief function of r.-c. as being to compel the reader's attention through the shock of unfulfilled expectation. One might add that this metrical tendency is also a kind of prosodic equivalent of other features of *metaphysical poetry* (q.v.), e.g. its nervous diction and surprising imagery.

> O cheer and tune my heartless breast;
> Defer no time,
> That so Thy favors granting my request,
> They and my mind may chime
> And mend my rhyme.

The example above (Herbert, *Denial*) is composed basically in r.-c., but the last line is in rhyme-harmony with the second line, thereby supporting the content of the stanza. F.J.W.

RHYME ROYAL. Sometimes called the Chaucerian (and Troilus) stanza. A stanza of 7 lines of iambic pentameter, rhyming ababbcc. In the hands of Chaucer, who used the form in *Troilus and Criseyde*, *The Parlement of Fowles*, and several of the *Canterbury Tales*, r.r. was an instrument of extraordinary flexibility and power. Ample enough for narrative purposes, the stanza is also suited to descrip-

tion, digression, and comment, and its rhyme scheme is remarkably subtle in its potentialities. The superb hymn which opens *The Prioress's Tale*, the leisurely narrative of *The Clerk's Tale*, and the incisive psychological insights of *Troilus and Criseyde*, all indicate the wide scope of Chaucer's use of the form.

R.r. dominated Eng. poetry in the century after Chaucer's death; it is said to have received its name during this period from its use by King James I of Scotland in *The Kingis Quair*, although some prosodists, e.g., E. Guest (*History of Eng. Rhythms*, 1882) and Schipper trace the name to the Fr. *chant royal*. As late as the second half of the 16th c., r.r. was mentioned by Gascoigne and by Puttenham as the chief Eng. stanza for serious verse, and in this period it was distinguished by being used in Spenser's *Fowre Hymnes* and Shakespeare's *Rape of Lucrece*. Some time before 1619, Michael Drayton revised his r.r. narrative *Mortimeriados* and recast it in ottava rima as *The Baron's Wars*. His action symbolized the end of r.r. as a great Eng. measure; its only important subsequent uses were in Morris' *Earthly Paradise* and Masefield's *Dauber*, in which, however, its traditional flexibility and strength are apparent.—See also G. H. Cowling, "A Note on Chaucer's Stanza," RES, 2 (1926); Hamer; P. F. Baum, *Chaucer's Verse* (1961; notes the Fr. [ballade] origin of the stanza).

RHYME SCHEME. The arrangement of rhyming words, usually at the ends of lines, though sometimes internally, which gives the poem its characteristic pattern. R. schemes may be fixed or variable, simple or complex. The sonnet and the Spenserian stanza, for example, have fixed patterns, but stanza forms not traditionally fixed may be shaped to the needs of the individual poem. Among the more useful r. schemes in Eng. verse are those of the couplet, which often suggests the epigrammatic package of meaning as in Pope, and the quatrain, which allows for some flexibility of arrangement (for example, alternating, abab, as in Gray's *Elegy Written in a Country Churchyard;* enclosing, abba, as in Tennyson's *In Memoriam;* and intermittent, xbyb, as in Coleridge's *The Rime of the Ancient Mariner*). Some r. schemes involve the repetition of whole lines, as in the triolet and the villanelle, and others require the repetition of "rhyming" words, as in the sestina. Because rhyming words must carry a semantic as well as a phonetic value, the r. scheme has a great deal to do with the emergence of meaning aesthetically embodied in the stanza or the poem. S.L.M.

RHYTHM. See PROSODY; METER; VERSE AND PROSE.

RHYTHMICAL PAUSE. By some writers apparently equated with the caesura (middle or internal pause), as distinguished from the metrical pause at the end of a line. By others it is distinguished from the sense pause and the metrical pause or the rest (q.v.), and is defined by them as the pause separating each breath group of a sentence.—G. Saintsbury, *A Historical Manual of Eng. Prosody* (1910); Baum; Deutsch. R.BE.

RHYTHMICI. See METRICI.

RIDDLE. Essentially a metaphor which draws attention to likenesses between unrelated objects, e.g., *Humpty Dumpty*. World-wide and one of the oldest forms of literature, riddles are still used by primitive peoples in times of crisis (harvesting, weddings, etc.) with the idea that solving them may, by sympathetic magic, solve the crisis. They may also be a teaching device, and the oldest recorded are Babylonian school texts. Most riddles, especially the older ones, are in verse, partially perhaps for mnemonic purposes but probably principally because of their original use in magic. Customarily a distinction is made between the literary riddle (*Kunsträtsel*) and the folk riddle (*Volksrätsel*).

The history of riddles is a long one. The Sanskrit *Rig Veda* (final version ca. 1000 B.C.) contains riddles. The most famous Arab riddler was Al-Hariri (1054–1122) whose *Assemblies* was very influential. Hebrew has a long history of riddles, e.g., Samson's exchange with the Philistines at his wedding. The most famous Persian riddles are those in Firdausi's epic the *Shah-Nameh* (10th c.). Gr. riddles stem from the 14th book of the Gr. *Anthology* and from Byzantine literature. The literary r. in western Europe begins its tradition with the 100 L. poetic riddles of Symphosius (5th c.), and under his influence the L. verse r. was cultivated from the *Berne Riddles* (7th c.) and those of Aldhelm (written A.D. 685–705) to the encyclopedic work of Nicolas Reusner, *Aenigmatographia* (1602). The oldest European vernacular riddles are the poetic riddles of the OE *Exeter Book* (8th c.), many of which are long, ingenious, and of high poetic merit. The earliest in Germany date from the 13th c., the *Warburgkrieg*; in Spain, Portugal, and France from the 16th c. In modern times riddles have flourished in France, particularly in the 17th and 18th c. in Germany in the 19th c., and most of all in Italy. In England they have had no vogue.—F. Tupper, *The Riddles of the Exeter Book* (1910); A. Taylor, *The Lit. R. before 1600* (1948); C. F. Potter, "Riddles," *Funk & Wagnalls Standard Dict. of Folklore, Mythology and Legend,* ed. M. Leach, II (1950). R.P.APR.

RIME. See RHYME.

RIME RICHE. Rhyming pairs pronounced in the same way without having the same meaning; classified as homographs (written and pronounced alike, as *stare,* the bird, and *stare,* to gaze curiously) and as homophones (pronounced alike but different in spelling, as *stare, stair*). Chaucer, observing Fr. practice, has *seke-seke* (seek, sick), *riche-rubriche, tiraunt-erraunt,* and many other such rhymes throughout the *Canterbury Tales.* Imperfectly naturalized into Eng. verse, r.r. is common and frequent in Fr., *éclaire-crépusculaire;* but rhymes on the suffix are considered weak (i.e., too facile) as *magnifiques-pacifiques, gladiateur-lecteur.* (See discussion of *rime très riche, rime suffisante,* and *rime pauvre* under PERFECT RHYME.)—J. Suberville, *Hist. et théorie de la versification française* (new ed., 1956). S.L.M.

RÍMUR (plur. of *rima*). A type of metrical romances peculiar to Iceland, which originated there in the 14th c. and retained their popularity until the 19th c. In subject matter they are most frequently based on heroic tales and chivalric romances. The basic meter is the alliterative 4-line stanza. The rhyme schemes, however, are so numerous that over 2,000 varieties have been recorded, eloquently bespeaking the ingenuity and the metrical skill of the authors. These narrative poems abound in kennings, on the pattern of skaldic poetry, but the poetical phraseology often becomes turgid and obscure. The r. contributed to Icelandic literature a verse form (*ferskeytt*) corresponding to the modern epigram and flourishing in a highly varied and elaborate form to this day.—*Sýnisbók íslenzkra rímna,* ed. W. A. Craigie (3 v., 1953; specimens of Icelandic *rímur*). R.B.

RISING ACTION. See PLOT.

RISING RHYTHM. See ASCENDING RHYTHM.

RISPETTO. An 8-line stanza (octave), rhyming abababcc. It is probably a form of Tuscan popular poetry, although now used throughout Italy. The content is generally amorous, hence the name "respect," honor paid the beloved woman in its hendecasyllabic verses. The form may vary in the last 4 verses (or *ripresa*) to 2 rhyming couplets of different rhymes. Politian and Lorenzo de' Medici wrote series of *rispetti,* likewise Lionardo Giustinian. In modern times G. Carducci composed many and G. Pascoli included a number of them in his *Myricae.* The Fr. *respit* is more peasantlike in feeling and gives admonitions with whip-lashes. This form is akin to the Sicilian octave or *stram-*

botto.—G. Lega, *Rispetti antichi pubblicati da un codice magliabechiano* (1905); M. Barbi, *Poesia popolare italiana* (1939).   L.H.G.

RITORNELLO. A group of 2 (sometimes 3) lines repeated like a refrain at the end or sometimes at the beginning of each stanza of a poem. The last 2 lines of the r. form a couplet; the first can combine with them to form a triplet or can rhyme with a line of the preceding stanza. The r. may have begun as a r. *intercalare*, an exclamation from the congregation in response to the priest who was reading a psalm or sequence. In most instances the r. remained an expression of emotional response to the idea or action treated in the stanza. The fully developed r. probably resulted when the last line of the primitive neolatinic strophe (aaaa) was divided and/or lengthened to form more than one verse. Thus the r. may serve as the refrain of a *ballata* or even the couplet coda of a sonnet. The fully developed r. strophe seems to have been used first by feminine dancers on May Day, at country fêtes, and on festival days. The term may also designate the *stornello* (q.v.).—F. Flamini, *Notizia storica dei versi e metri italiani dal medioevo ai tempi nostri* (1919).   L.H.G.

ROCKING RHYTHM. Term coined by Gerard Manley Hopkins to denote a trisyllabic meter in which a stressed syllable is felt to occur regularly between 2 unstressed (or "slack") ones. In Browning's "Behind shut the postern, the lights sank to rest" (*How They Brought the Good News from Ghent to Aix*, 5) the phenomenon of rocking rhythm seems apparent in the first half of the line. See FOOT, AMPHIBRACH, RUNNING RHYTHM, SPRUNG RHYTHM.   P.F.

ROCOCO. As in art history, r. has come to be used in literary history as a collective term for 18th-c. works of which graceful lightness is an outstanding characteristic. In literature r. (ca. 1720-70) includes the mock-heroic poem (Pope, Zachariä, Voltaire), *poésie fugitive* and the fable (Gay, Hagedorn, Gellert, Lessing), Horatian and anacreontic verse (E. von Kleist, Gleim, Uz, Götz, Bellamy, Bilderdijk, Bellman), the frivolous or lightly ironic or satirically philosophic tale in verse or prose (Voltaire, Cazotte, Wieland, Casti), the humorous novel (Sterne, Wieland), and satiric and pastoral comedy (Marivaux, Beaumarchais, the early Goethe). Although some r. writing may seem to be deliberately immoral, and some to expound gracefully what purports to be the golden mean (E. von Kleist), homely wisdom (Gellert) or even an enlightened philosophical system (Wieland), common to all is a tacit or explicit repudiation of earnestness as an absolute good. Monotony is avoided by brevity and conscious

formal variation (the *genre mêlé* is cultivated, the length of verse lines is deliberately kept irregular, colloquial tones are imitated), while wit is exploited in connection with serious themes and even at the expense of unity of action or plausibility of characterization. In tone r. writing is often frankly playful; writers cultivate the fiction that they stand in a direct, even personal relationship with their public, at times deliberately interposing themselves between their work and its audience; neoclassical forms remain important for many r. authors but are used as media for expressing the optimistic rationalism and individualism of 18th-c. middle-class intellectuals.—F. Ausfeld, *Die deutsche anakreontische Dichtung des 18. Jhs.* (1907); E. Ermatinger, *Barock und Rokoko in der deutschen Dichtung* (1928); P. Trahard, *Les Maîtres de la sensibilité française au XVIIIᵉ s.* (4 v., 1931-33); B. A. Sørensen, "Das deutsche R. und die Verserzählung im 18. Jh.," *Euphorion*, 48 (1954); E. Merker, "Graziendichtung," *Reallexikon*, 2d ed., I.; W. Widmer, "Die Welt des R.," *Imprimatur*, 2 (1958-60); W. Sypher, *R. to Cubism in Art and Lit.* (1960); A. Anger, *Literarisches R.* (1962) and *Deutsche R.-Dichtung* (1963).   S.A.

ROMANCE. The r.—the Sp. ballad—is the simplest and most widely used set poetic form in Sp. It usually is written in octosyllabic verse in which the even-numbered lines rhyme with the same assonance throughout the poem and the odd-numbered lines are left free. A few *romances* are in octosyllabic couplets in consonance. The r. *doble* rhymes all lines in alternating assonance. Other variations of the basic form (even some having a periodic refrain) have at times been popular. The learned and the semilearned—and probably even the illiterate—produce them wherever Sp. is spoken and scholars collect them by the hundreds. They reflect almost every phase of Sp. life. Since many of them are anonymous and have been transmitted largely in oral form, their origin and complete history cannot be traced. The earliest known written *romances* date from the early 15th c. In the early 16th c. *romanceros* (collections devoted exclusively to *romances*) began to appear, the first (1545-1550?) being the famous *Cancionero de romances*, often called the *Cancionero sin año* because it bears no date of publication, by Martín Nucio in Antwerp. The most convenient classification of *romances*—that summarized by S. G. Morley and adapted from those of Duran, Wolf and Hofmann, and Mila y Fontanals—covers the period from the 15th through the 17th c. It corresponds, with the exception of the *romances vulgares* to three periods of creation, traditional, erudite, artistic: (1) the anonymous *romances viejos*, primitive or traditional ballads, usually on historical themes and thought to be among the earliest; (2) the 15th- and early 16th-c. *romances juglarescos*, minstrel ballads, "longer and more personal, but still supported by tradition"; (3) *romances eruditos*, erudite ballads, written by known authors after 1550 and based on old chronicles; (4) *romances artísticos*, artistic ballads, usually lyric, on varied themes, and written by known authors from the late 15th c. through the 17th; (5) the crude *romances vulgares*, blind beggar ballads, from about 1600 on.

The *r. heroico*, also called *r. endecasílabo* or *r. real*, is a r. in Italianate hendecasyllables. A r. in lines of less than 8 syllables is called *romancillo* (see also ENDECHA). One variation of the r. is the *corrido* (ballad with guitar accompaniment), especially popular in Mexico. The *jácara* is a r. in which the activities of ruffians are recounted, usually in a boisterous manner.—E. Mérimée and S. G. Morley, *A Hist. of Sp. Lit.* (1930); S. G. Morley, "Chronological List of Early Sp. Ballads," HR, 13 (1945); R. Menéndez Pidal, *Romancero hispánico* (2 v., 1953); Navarro.   D.C.C.

ROMANCE, MEDIEVAL. See MEDIEVAL ROMANCE.

ROMANCE PROSODY. EARLY DEVELOPMENTS. Although the Rom. languages are directly derived from L., the evolution of their metrical systems from L. prosody does not show the same continuity. Rom. versification very likely originated from or developed along with that type of late L. poetry which neglects the rules of quantity (whereby 1 long syllable equals 2 short) and seems to be based on the number of syllables, marked accentual endings and rhyme. The origin of this new "rhythmic" verse has been explained in three different ways: (1) the change of L. pronunciation at the end of the Imperial period consisting in the loss of quantitative differences in vowels and in the replacement of pitch accent by stress accent (Fr. theory); (2) the importance of stress for the structure of L. verse at all times (a theory upheld by most Eng. and some German scholars); and (3) the creation by the early Christians of a syllabic verse with, at first, quantitative cadence in imitation of Syrian meters (the theory of Wilhelm Meyer aus Speyer, newly advocated by some scholars). Recently Michel Burger (*Recherches sur la structure et l'origine des vers romans*) has offered a more definite explanation of the origin of Rom. verse. He maintains that the transition from L. quantitative meters to accentual verse was a natural and gradual one. At a time when the sense for quantity had vanished, the uneducated when reading classical L. verse

disregarded the quantitative metrical scheme and considered only the normal word accent. Thus the Sapphic line *Christe servorum, regimen tuorum* ($\_\cup\_\_\_\_\|\cup\cup\_\cup\_\cup$) was recited

$$\overset{\prime}{1}\ 2\ 3\ \overset{\prime}{4}\ 5\ 6\ \overset{\prime}{7}\ 8\ 9\ \overset{\prime}{10}\ 11.$$

In composing new verse they kept the structure of their models leaving word accents where they had been in L., free in the interior of the verse line and fixed at the end and, to a certain degree, at the caesura. Due to the fact that the ratio 1 long-2 shorts had been lost, the number of syllables in a line necessarily became fixed while the syllables could be arranged in either ascending or descending rhythm. In this new system the last accented syllable of the verse line (originally coinciding with the thesis) marked the end of the verse the 1 or 2 following syllables being considered as supernumerary. The same happened at the caesura. This is one of the dominant characteristics of all Rom. verse. Burger believes that the important types of Rom. verse were already developed before the scission into the different idioms occurred. These types were later further adapted to each individual language and can still be traced back to their L. (quantitative) models: the decasyllable to the iambic trimeter and the Sapphic, the *verso de arte mayor* to the lesser asclepediac, the alexandrine to the double iambic dimeter etc.

GENERAL CHARACTERISTICS. Rom. verse has a definite rhythm indicated by at least one normally accented syllable at the end of the verse or of the hemistich. The odd or even number of syllables preceding this accented syllable produces a rising or falling movement and a division into rhythmical groups. Within the line, metrical beats and word accent do not coincide, and this free distribution of stresses gives to Rom. verse flexibility and variety which are lacking in Germanic verse. Verse based solely on accentuation in the sense of Germanic prosody, where, between fixed beats, unstressed syllables may be accumulated or omitted, would defy the prosodic features of the Rom. languages which distinguish less markedly the force and duration of their syllables.

Syllable count is based on the principles of phonetics and euphony which govern the individual languages. In Prov., It., Sp. and Portuguese the adjustment of the verse line to the required number of syllables is achieved by synaloepha (the blending of two consecutive vowels or diphthongs, one at the end of a word and the other at the beginning of the following word), by elision or by hiatus. Old Prov. had no strict rules about elision and hiatus; Fr. tolerated hiatus in the Middle Ages but ruled it out completely under Malherbe (17th c.);

It., Sp. and Port., while not banning it completely, usually eliminate it by contraction. In Fr., syllable count is complicated owing to the treatment of mute -e. At the end of a verse mute -e is never counted: hence the line with a masculine or oxytonic termination gives its name to the class of verse. Rules set up for the elision of mute e in the body of the verse have not kept pace with the evolution of the Fr. language and are therefore frequently violated by modern poets.

In every Rom. verse there is besides the last tonic syllable which must coincide with the metrical beat, at least 1 additional stress in the interior of the verse line. Archaic meters offer more fixed stresses than modern forms. Thus the Old Fr. octosyllable carried a second stress on the fourth syllable; the decasyllable, likewise, on the fourth, sometimes on the sixth and the dodecasyllable on the sixth. The It. *endecasillabo* varies its principal stresses which may fall either on the sixth, on the fourth and eighth or on the fourth and ninth syllables. In the Fr. classical alexandrine a stress on the sixth syllable with a following pause is obligatory, while the romantic poets introduced the *alexandrin ternaire* with accents on the fourth and eighth syllables. The Sp. and Portuguese 14-syllable verse had originally 4 obligatory stresses which were later reduced to only one on the seventh syllable. The *verso de arte mayor* has a primary and secondary beat in every hemistich. Port. displays more archaic patterns with beats following at regular intervals, usually placed on even syllables.

Long verses are divided by a fixed pause after a stressed tonic syllable. This pause is named after the *caesura* of classical poetry which, however, was produced by a word ending within a foot. In Rom. versification the caesura may be followed by 1 or more unstressed syllables. In Old Fr. the "epic" caesura was treated in the same way as the verse end; that is, it was preceded by an unelidable feminine syllable not reckoned in the measure. The second variety of feminine caesura found in Old Fr. is known as "lyric"; it is preceded by a stressed atonic syllable counted in the number of syllables composing the line. Usually the caesura is emphasized by the syntactic pattern except in It. where metrical pauses are very slightly perceptible.

As already mentioned, Fr. and Prov. prefer oxytonic verse ends; It., Sp. and Port. paroxytonic; It. admits even propar-oxytonic (*sdruccioli*). Fr., Prov. and It. show predilection for rhyme while Sp. and Port. have for a long time used assonance besides rhyme. Rhymeless verse is unusual but has been repeatedly tried (*versi sciolti, vers blancs, versos sueltos*). Rom. assonance consists in the identity of the final

tonic vowels of 2 successive lines (Sp. *aguinaldo- honrado*); rhyme in the identity of the last tonic vowel and all following sounds (Sp. *hermosura- procura*). One distinguishes 1-syllable, masculine, and 2-syllable, feminine rhyme; 3-syllable rhyme occurs in It.

Fr. and Prov., with their prevailing oxytonic accents, have resorted to various devices for more elaborate verse endings: *rimes riches, léonines, équivoques*, etc., artifices practiced especially at the end of the Middle Ages by the Fr. *rhétoriqueurs* (q.v.) and imitated elsewhere. Alternation of masculine and feminine rhyme was devised in France by the *Pléiade* (q.v.) poets Ronsard and Du Bellay (16th c.) and then codified by Malherbe in the 17th c. Originally, two rhymes were combined (*rims caudatz, rimes plates, rime accopiate, versos empareados*). Although verse ends coincide with syntactic pauses, *enjambement*, the overflow of a clause into the next verse line, is permitted throughout in Rom. versification but was avoided in the Alexandrine by the Fr. classicists.

The origin of the various Rom. metrical lines will not be discussed here since this problem has not yet advanced beyond the purely hypothetical stages. Most important among the early Rom. meters is the decasyllable as used in the Fr. epics. Next to it stands the 12-syllable line, also named alexandrine (q.v.) after the Fr. *Alexander Romance* of Lambert le Tort and Alexandre de Berney in which it was used. In Italy the *endecasillabo*, which corresponds to the Fr. 10-syllable line, became predominant with Dante in the 13th and 14th c., and was later imported into Spain and Portugal. The octosyllable was popular for a long time in the north and south of France where it furnished the meter for all narrative poetry destined to be read and not recited. Today it is used in lyrical poetry only. The dodecasyllable was reinstated in France by the poets of the *Pléiade* and subsequently imposed as the Fr. verse *par excellence*. Ranking as the standard verse for elevated poetry it was imitated outside of France especially in Italy and Spain (*verso francés*). Spain and Portugal give preference to an 8-syllable line which is used in the *romances* and in the drama. Since these octosyllables are so arranged that only the even numbered lines assonate and odd lines are left free, some scholars consider them as the two parts of an older 14-syllable meter. The latter may also have been the original pattern for epic poetry which, in the Iberian peninsula, varies its lines from 10 to 18 syllables. Other typically Sp. and Port. verse lines are the *verso de arte mayor* of 10 to 12 syllables with marked beats, the *redondilla de arte mayor* (8 syllables) the *serranilla* verse (7 syllables) and the *redondilla de arte menor* (5 syllables). Verses of other dimensions have also been practiced in the Rom. territory but do not compare in frequency to those mentioned above.

The most primitive strophic form originated in the division of a long line containing interior rhymes into 2 or 3 short ones, hence the Fr. *rimes couées* and *rimes brisées* (aab ccb aab, aab), and the cross rhyme (*rimes croisées* [*incatenate, encadenadas*]). Rom. strophes are original popular creations. The oldest epics were written in mono-assonanced *tirades* or *laisses,* the oldest Saints' lives in mono-rhymed quatrains (Sp. *cuaderna vía*). Dante's *terzinas,* subsequently used for longer narrative poems, are a three-lined chain with a 1-line clausula (aba bcb cdc . . . yzyz). Strophic division was further achieved through the use of the refrain (It. *ripresa,* Sp. *cabeza, estribillo,* Port. *tornel*), an echo-like repetition of part of the text and melody. Remnants of original refrains are the Prov. *rims estramps,* It. *chiave,* Sp. *palabras perdidas,* isolated rhymes without correspondence. Later the refrain was extended to two or several lines or repeated in a half strophe at the end of a poem (Fr. *envoi,* It., Prov. *tornada,* It. *commiato, congedo, ritornello*). Strophes of varying length have been used in Rom. poetry, some of which became popular even elsewhere, thus the It. ottava rima.

One of the oldest forms of refrain poetry is the ballad, which probably originated in Provence and in its primitive form was constructed on the theme BBaabBB. In France, it evolved into a 3-strophe poem with a refrain after each strophe and an *envoi* at the end. The It. *ballata* differs from the Fr. in that the first strophic part is divided into two sections and that the *ripresa,* which precedes, is not repeated after each strophe. Of northern Fr. origin is the *rondeau* which depends on the refrain and on the extent of its repetition. Its basic form, A1 A2 aA aa A1 A2, developed into many different types of rondeaux of which the 16th c. variant of 15 lines is now the only survivor. In Spain, the *estribillo* has been developed, partly under Arabic influence, into *cosante, zéjel, villancico, romance.* Unquestionably, the most important of all Rom. poetic forms is the sonnet which can be briefly defined as two quatrains followed by two tercets. It was developed in Italy by the Sicilian school and brought to perfection by Petrarch. Perhaps the most fitting vehicle of poetic thought ever devised, it has remained in constant favor not only in the Rom. but in all literary languages.

At the end of the 19th c. the traditional syllabic verse was discarded by the Fr. symbolists who replaced it with "vers libre" (free verse). It is a verse based on rhythmical groups corresponding to syntactic units and does not

observe any fixed rules. This innovation was adopted by some It. and Sp. poets.

E. Stengel, "Romanische Verslehre," in G. Gröber, *Grundriss der romanischen Philologie,* II (1902), 1–96; still remains fundamental; M. Burger, *Recherches sur la structure et l'origine des vers romans* (1957). Other works treating problems of Rom. versification include: W. Meyer aus Speyer, *Gesammelte Abhandlungen zur mittelalterlichen Rhythmik* (3 v., 1905–36); P. A. Becker, *Über den Ursprung der romanischen Versmasse* (1890); F. d'Ovidio, "Versificazione romanza," in *Opere complete,* IX (1932); Jeanroy, *Origines;* P. Henriquez Ureña, *La versificacion irregular en la poesia castellana* (1920); T. Gerold, *La musique au moyen âge* (1932); Navarro; L. A. Schökel, *Estética y estilística del ritmo poético* (1959). See also W. Suchier, *Französische Verslehre* . . . (1963).   T.F.

ROMANCE-SIX. See TAIL-RHYME.

ROMANSH POETRY. Modern Rom. poetry flourishes in the Alpine valleys of southeastern Switzerland (the Grisons), where 45,000 people speak the Rom. language, one of the three branches of Raeto-Romance, an independent language group, sister to other minor Romance languages, such as Prov. and Rumanian. Rom. was first written down when the needs of the religious factions of the Reformation created the two main written forms which have persisted to this day—Ladin in the Protestant Inn-Danube Valley (Engadine) and Surselvan in the Catholic Rhine Valley (Surselva). Because of commercial Swiss-German infiltration into the Grisons in the 18th and 19th c., the Rom.-speaking territory grew smaller and smaller, and there was danger of the extinction of the language. To combat this possibility, Rom. poets and other writers took the lead in a "Raetian Renaissance," beginning about 1886. They formed numerous societies in different regions and founded periodicals for the preservation of the Rom. language and culture. These groups eventually banded together in 1919 to form the *Lia Rumantscha* which fostered the development of Rom. in the schools, Rom. publications, and linguistic studies to show that Rom. was not an It. dialect (as Mussolini claimed with a view to territorial aggrandizement). The efforts of the "Raetian Renaissance" eventually brought about the recognition of Rom. as the fourth national language of Switzerland by a vote of all the Swiss people in 1938.

Rom. poetry has always been the most important part of Rom. literature. The first written work in Rom. was a poem by Gian de Travers (1483–1563), *Chianzun dalla guerra dagl chiasté da Müs* (1527) (Song of the War of Müs Castle), a rhymed chronicle of the Grisons' struggle to be free of Austrian domination. Political and historical songs, sometimes satirical, were characteristic of the early poetry. There were sometimes new versions of old Rom. folksongs. But most of these early works are interesting only historically and linguistically because of poor technique and often unpoetic vocabulary, making them of little literary value. Most Rom. writings, prose and poetry, of the 16th, 17th, and 18th c. were religious, since most of the writers were Protestant ministers in the Engadine and Catholic priests or monks in Surselva. There is occasionally real poetry, as in some of the versified paraphrases of the Psalms by Durich Chiampel (1510–82) and others, and in some of the biblical dramas in verse, including several partly original Passion plays. The last Passion play, performed at Sumvitg in 1811 where it had been given for nearly 200 years, is considered by some critics to be truly poetic in parts.

With the sweep of the romantic movement all over Europe at the beginning of the 19th c., Rom. literature in general, and its poetry in particular, began to flourish. Since all Rom. are bilingual from early childhood (Rom. in home and primary school but German in later schooling and business contacts), it is not surprising that the influence of modern German and Swiss-German poets should be greater than that of other nationalities. However, Rom. poets have also translated Eng. (Shakespeare, Burns, Byron and Tennyson, etc.) and Am. (Longfellow, Whitman, etc.) as well as It., Fr. and even Rus. poets. These foreign influences often show in the original creations of Rom. poets who are as diversified as the influences they reflect.

In Rom. poetry all kinds of meters are possible because of the flexibility of the language. Though the early epic and historical poems and religious dramas had very simple forms, mostly long poems of rhymed couplets, modern Rom. poetry consists almost entirely of short lyrics expressed in a wide variety of forms, antique and modern, and using all the technical devices for good poetry, such as varied rhyme schemes, internal rhymes, onomatopoeia and alliteration. As in other Romance languages, Rom. rhymes are not hard to find because of the numerous vowel endings in the language.

Though romanticism at first nourished numerous Rom. love lyrics, now as then, the really dominant theme in Rom. poetry is love of native land, of the Rom. language, the people, their customs and traditions. Many of these patriotic poems have been set to music. The second most important theme in Rom. poetry is nature, which is in a way another expression of love of this Alpine region filled with the beauty of bright wildflowers, dazzling snow on the mountains, glaciers in the valleys, and the terror of avalanches, storms, and wild winds. In many of these nature poems there is philosophic symbolism and sometimes deep religious feeling, especially among the Catholic poets in the Surselvan region.

An astounding number of Rom. people, in proportion to the small population, have written poems and published them in the many Rom. periodicals and calendars or in privately printed books and pamphlets. Much of this poetry is without great literary value. However, critics in and out of Switzerland agree that there are a few outstanding poets who have given real vitality and high literary standards to Rom. poetry: da Flugi, Pallioppi, Caderas, and Lansel in the Engadine, and Huonder, Muoth, Tuor, and Fontana in Surselva.

The first of these, Conradin da Flugi (1787–1874) of San Murezzan (St. Moritz), has been considered the father of Rom. lyric poetry. One of his loveliest poems, set to music several times, is an 8-stanza poem, *Inviern* (Winter) of which the first stanza is typical:

> La naivetta, la naivetta
> Vain da tschêl a flöch a flöch;
> Onduland scu las chürallas,
> S'mett'la giò a töch a töch.

> Little snowflakes, little snowflakes,
> Falling, heav'n sent, through the air,
> Like the butterflies in summer
> Flutt'ring, settle here and there.

Zaccaria Pallioppi (1820–73), Engadine linguist and lexicographer, was a poet of polished technique. He revived antique poetic forms, such as the asclepiadic meter, and introduced forms from the It.: the terza rima of Dante, the Calabrian octave, and the sonnet which was his favorite. His poems are truly classic in their perfection of form and in the intellectual clarity which controls his thought and feeling. Gian Fadri Caderas (1830–91), the most lyric Engadine poet of the 19th c., wrote very unevenly. Some of his prolific output is merely poor verse, but some of his poems are very fine and can rank with the best productions of Rom. poetry.

The foremost Surselvan poet of the mid-19th c. was Anton Huonder (1825–67) whose patriotic poem *La Ligia Grischa* (The Gray League), written in 1864, was set to music, translated into German and It., and made the anthem of the trilingual Canton of the Grisons. His much-loved lyric *Il Pur suveran* (The Sovereign Peasant) is one of the most often quoted Rom. poems. The greatest Surselvan poet at the end of the century, and the only epic poet of merit in Rom. literature, was Giachen Caspar

Muoth (1844–1906). Though he is well-known as a humorous poet, a lyric poet, and a short story writer, he is best remembered for his long epics of the thrilling history of that mountain region which he knew so well. His most famous long poem is *La dertgira nauscha de Valendau* (The Wicked Judgment of Valendau). In addition to his prolific literary work, Muoth did much to stimulate and encourage the "Raetian Renaissance" movement. The best lyric poet in Surselva at the turn of the century was Alfons Tuor (1871–1904). In spite of years of physical suffering, he wrote poems reflecting an optimistic faith in life and his ardent Catholicism. His well-polished poems show him to be a musician who puts his whole soul into his singing. In the 20th c., the outstanding Surselvan poet is Gian Fontana (1897–1935). Writer of scholarly articles and children's stories, he is best known for his lyric poetry which shows mastery of varied forms and poetic understanding of human emotion and of the meanings in nature.

But the most outstanding poet of 20th-c. Rom. poetry is the Engadine poet Peider Lansel (1863–1943) whom many competent critics consider the best poet that either branch of Rom. literature has ever produced. It is felt that Lansel has been to Rom. poetry what Frédéric Mistral (1830–1914) has been to Prov. Lansel's poems combine the polished technique of Pallioppi, the musicality of Caderas, the vitality of Muoth, and the poetic understanding of Fontana. Lansel's Rom. studies and his anthologies of Rom. poetry, as well as his own richly varied poetry have all contributed enormously to the modern movement for the preservation of Rom. culture.

When one considers the size of the Rom.-speaking population (less than 45,000), the fecundity and vitality of modern Rom. poetry is astounding. Though much published is the work of talented amateurs, certain young poets today, appearing in periodicals and in the Lansel anthology of 1950, show real promise. It seems perfectly possible that each generation may find at least one or two Rom. poets of the caliber of those cited here. Thus, contrary to the 19th-c. predictions of doom, Rom. culture will probably not die out but will continue to be creative, largely because of the efforts of its active poets and the influence of their poetry and song. Switzerland itself now encourages the preservation of the four different cultures within her borders which, with mutual respect for one another, in turn give Switzerland strong national unity.

BIBLIOGRAPHIES: *Bibliografia Retoromontscha 1552–1930*, ed. Ligia romontscha (1938); M. E. Maxfield, "Raeto-Romance Bibliog.," UNCSRLL, 2 (1941).

ANTHOLOGIES: *Raetoromanische Chresto-mathie*, ed. C. Decurtins (13 v., 1896–1919); *La musa ladina*, ed. P. Lansel (2d ed., 1918; selection of best modern Ladin poets, with introd. and biographies); *Engadiner Nelken. Eine Sammlung raeto-romanischer Lyrik*, ed. G. Bundi (1920); "Poesias retorumantschas," ed. R. Faesi in his *Antologia Helvetica* (Leipzig, 1920); *Musa romontscha. Musa rumantscha*, ed. P. Lansel (1950; Ladin and Surselvan poetry).

HISTORY AND CRITICISM: C. Decurtins, "Gesch. der rätoromanischen Lit.," in Gröber's *Grundriss der romanischen Philologie*, 2d ed., II (1901); T. Gartner, *Handbuch der rätoromanischen Sprache und Lit.* (1901); P. M. Carnot, *Im Lande der Rätoromanen* (1934); W. Kirkconnell, "Rhaeto-romanic Tradition," Royal Soc. of Canada. *Trans.* 31, sec. II (1937); M. E. Maxfield, *Studies in Modern Rom. Poetry in the Engadine* (1938); R. R. Bezzola, "Rom. Lit.," *Cassell's*, I; A. Decurtins, *La Suisse rhétoromane et la défense de sa latinité* (1959).
E.M.M.

ROMANTICISM. The interpretation of this thoroughly controversial term (F. L. Lucas, in *The Decline and Fall of the Romantic Ideal*, 1948, counted 11,396 definitions of r.) divides critics into roughly three camps, with loyalties overlapping. Two viewpoints derive from sharply bifurcating ideas on the scope and period of r. in *literary* history: (a) Croce, e.g. (for once in partial agreement with more traditional historians) differentiates between "r.," "later r.," and "decadence," where (b) Praz, M. Paribatra, and Albérès see in r. a complex of literary phenomena associated with a change occurring in European sensibility toward the end of the 18th c., and extending into the present—a concept which underlies our own definition. A third major trend in criticism, springing from *Geistesgeschichte*, *history of ideas*, and literary *psychology*, is exemplified by the attempts of Strich, Cazamian, and Sir Herbert Read to explain r. as one of the poles between which Occidental art in all places and periods oscillates: the pendulum swing between the Schlegels' distinction of "classical" and "romantic" (see CLASSICISM), and Nietzsche's "Apollonian-Dionysian" (q.v.) dichotomy.

Opinions also differ as to the homogeneity of European r. While (e.g.) Wellek argues for its unity, Lovejoy and others stress the diversity of its national manifestations. The truth seems to be that r. (a) does not occur simultaneously in all European literatures, (b) varies in its literary aspects from country to country, and (c), as a word, has not the same meaning everywhere. It started in Germany and England during the 1790's as *a new mode of imagination and vision*, which spread, with considerable modifications, throughout Europe between

1800 and 1830. Directly or by reaction it affects all modern literature. There are traits common to all of European r. Universally it proposes absolute creative freedom, spontaneity, "sincerity," and a sort of emotional *engagement* on the part of the poet. Romantic doctrines are generally directed against rationalism, and frequently against *genres*. To neoclassical dictates of objectivity, imitation, invention, clarity, separation of prose and poetry, the romanticists oppose demands for the free play of imagination and originality, functional rather than decorative imagery, the use of prose rhythms in poetry, and of lyrical prose in novel, essay, and criticism. They defend obscurity as a necessary by-product of myth, symbol, and intuitions of what today would be called the subconscious.

The terrain for romantic poetics was, at least in part, prepared by certain *philosophical influences*, such as Shaftesbury's concept of genius; discussions of the sublime (*Peri Hypsous*, Young, Wood, the Wartons, Burke); pietist and theosophical undercurrents of the Enlightenment (e.g., Hamann, Moritz); Herder's irrationalist search for a common bond of humanity, his organic concept of history and the universe, with its far-reaching consequences for all branches of criticism.

Foremost among the *literary sources* of the romantic sensibility were Young's *Conjectures on Original Composition*; views on the theatre voiced by La Chaussée, Diderot, and Mercier; the purported imitation of "ancient folkpoetry" by Percy, Bürger, Macpherson-"Ossian," Herder, the *Hainbund*; primitivism and exoticism (q.v.) as literary themes in Rousseau, Bernardin de Saint-Pierre, etc.; graveyard and nature poetry (Young, Blair, Cowper, Gray, Thomson, Gessner); sentimental, ironical, and gothic novels (Richardson, Sterne, Walpole, Radcliffe); nostalgic evocations of ruins (Volney); the topic of revolt against fate and the gods (Goethe's *Prometheus*); open and concealed eroticism (Crébillon fils, Rousseau, Restif de la Bretonne, Sade, Laclos, Nerciat, etc.). Rousseau's *Nouvelle Héloïse* (1761) already contains all the essential ingredients of European r.

FIRST PERIOD: 1798–1805. A first wave of romantic poetry and criticism, passing lightly over England, swept Germany between 1798 and 1805. In *France* r. was delayed for two decades by the neoclassical trends of Revolution and Empire. Despite the themes of memory, *ennui*, exoticism, and nostalgia (still clothed in a time-honoured "noble" style) which permeate *Atala* (1801) and *René* (1802), Chateaubriand's (1768–1848) lyrical and picturesque prose is still as decidedly neoclassical as the echo it finds in Lamartine's *Méditations poétiques* (1820), with alexandrines as conven-

tional as any of Parny's. In *England* the way was cleared for romantic poetry by two outsiders, the Scottish regionalist poet Robert Burns (1759–96), and William Blake (1757–1827) whose hermetic poems found their public posthumously. The first flare-up of Eng. r. marks an attempt at poetic reform and is encompassed by the three editions of *Lyrical Ballads* (1798, 1800, 1802). William Wordsworth (1770–1850) in his preface to the 2d edition defines his own poems as arising from private rather than general associations, and poetry as "the spontaneous overflow of powerful feelings," recollected in tranquillity, and presented in a language at once metric, musical, and close to everyday usage. S. T. Coleridge (1772–1834), defending in retrospect these early poems (which had appeared "obscure" to the readers) intimates (*Biographia Literaria*, 1817) that Wordsworth's contributions aimed at supernaturalizing the natural, and his own at naturalizing the supernatural.

Only in *Germany* there emerged about 1798 a fully grown romantic revolt with its own aesthetics, philosophy, and poetics, which placed sensibility and flashes of orphic insight above rational experience. H. W. Wackenroder (1773–98) animates his sentimental anecdotes about Dürer, Raphael, Leonardo, Michelangelo, etc., with the spirit of a childlike devotion. His romantic criticism substitutes emotonal effusions on religious art and the Christian Middle Ages for neoclassical analysis of form, composition, and structure (*Herzensergiessungen eines kunstliebenden Klosterbruders*, 1797, with a preface by Tieck, some of whose most important work deals with Christian legends). The medieval unity of Christendom is exalted by Novalis in *Die Christenheit oder Europa*, published as late as 1826 but in manuscript form known to the Schlegels and their circle since 1799. Awakening new interest in medieval Christianity, these works early planted the seeds for Z. Werner's, Friedrich and Dorothea Schlegel's conversions to Catholicism between 1808 and 1810. In *Athenaeum*, a literary review published by A. W. Schlegel (1767–1845) and his brother Friedrich (1772–1829), German romantic criticism formulated new concepts of myth, symbol, irony, wit, and imagination; it formulated demands for collective endeavours and a fusion of the rational and irrational powers of the human mind in a total artistic creation (*Sympoesie, Symphilosophie*). It derived from the metaphysics of J. G. Fichte (1762–1814), his disciple F. W. J. Schelling (1775–1854) and Friedrich Schleiermacher (1768–1834), whose systems continued Kant's transcendentalism. To Novalis, Tieck, the Schlegels, and E. T. A. Hoffmann, Fichte's principle of the individual's boundless creative freedom as the highest realization of the spirit justifies the unrestrained activity of *imagination* (q.v.) and its rational complement, *wit*. K. W. F. Solger (1780–1819) analyzes in depth the dialectical playfulness of imagination and wit which results in *romantic irony*, i.e., the poet's ever-attentive consciousness that mirrors the antinomy of *mind in its unfettered freedom* and the *material boundaries of literary form*. It is knowledge about this irremediable conflict, opposing an infinite vision to the limitations of finite poetic form, that leads the artist to mock his public and his art, and to shatter the literary illusion by thrusting himself into his work, often under the mask of grotesque self-mockery. Hence the predominance of paradox, aphorisms, and the "fragment" whose sudden illuminations are preferred to systematically expressed thought, since they appear to be more spontaneous, more truthful, and more sincere.

While Friedrich Schlegel, the foremost theoretician of the movement, admired the balance of nature and spirit in classical .Gr. art, he was aware that this perfection—the result of an harmonious reconciliation of opposites— cannot be achieved by the modern artist, whose work is marked by the unbridgeable split which not only the development of Reason but also Christian doctrine, brought about between the finite world of nature and the infinite surge of the spirit. Where classical literature aims at the *perfection of being*, the romanticist, torn between the ideal and physical reality, expresses in his work the *dialectics of becoming*, a flux which corresponds to his inner conflict. In an almost existential sense he *engages* the free subjectivity of his mind, transforming the stuff of reality into poetry, i.e., into a function of his soul and mind as fragments of the infinite. Imagination moved by nostalgia for the infinite is that creative power which can metamorphose reality into spiritual experience. The aim of romantic creation is a sort of mystic union of the mind with a transcendental reality; its perfect literary vehicle—freed from the fetters of *genres*—the novel (*Roman*) as a farrago (*Mischgedicht*), a magic mixture of literary forms, in which poetry, prose, criticism, and philosophy can mingle, transforming reality into dream, dream into reality. On the cosmic level, Schelling's organic view of the physical world (governed as all romantic thought by Platonist and Neoplatonist philosophy) supersedes post-Cartesian mechanistic theories. On this point—despite their open feud on contemporary painting, on Fr. neoclassicism vs. the "r." of Christian authors like Shakespeare, Dante, Cervantes—the opinions of the *Romantiker* strangely coincide with those of the *Klassiker*. Novalis, the Schlegels, Tieck, Schelling, and Goethe alike— just as decades later in France Hugo, Nerval,

and Baudelaire—seemed convinced of secret and ambiguous correspondences between nature and a cosmic spirit in which latter phenomenon the human mind participates.

The contrast of *Klassik* and *Romantik*, real within the framework of the German literary situation, appears artificial from the viewpoint of *European r.*; all the more so since even the last lines of Goethe's *Faust* (2d part) are permeated with myth and symbolism of the Schlegel-Novalis variety, and since, paradoxically, Schiller (unromantic to the Germans) is considered in France to be eminently romantic. Likewise Goethe's theory of colors derives from the same organic view of nature which characterizes Schelling's philosophy, just as his concept of art for art's sake approximates Schleiermacher's idea of religion as a mystical transformation of reality into spirit, and a "sense of the infinite." As to Goethe in his last years so to Novalis (F. L. von Hardenberg, 1772– 1801), author of the hermetic prose poems *Hymns to the Night* (1800) and theoretician of a "magic idealism," all finite things are mere symbols, hieroglyphs, whose archetypal meaning can be deciphered by the poet's intuition and the interpretative art of the scientist. Poetry and *Naturphilosophie* (uniting spirit and nature) are seen as separate keys to the direct knowledge of a deeper reality, where the pulsations of the external universe are analogous to the mysterious impulses of the human spirit. This concept of the *poeta-magus* as an intuitive interpreter of nature's analogies with the human spirit, developed in Berlin and Jena between 1798 and 1805, emerged more than half a century later in France with the *Fleurs du Mal*, the Hugo of *la Légende des Siècles* (1859– 83), Rimbaud, Mallarmé, and the Fr. symbolists; it is reflected in E. A. Poe's aesthetics, and since 1817 in Coleridge's *Biographia Literaria*. Early German r. provides at once a metaphysical and an aesthetic foundation for most European romantic and symbolist schools of poetry.

SECOND PERIOD: AFTER 1806. *German r.* underwent radical changes during the Napoleonic occupation. At the outset cosmopolitan, urbane, progressive, pantheistic, it now turned to chauvinism and an historical preoccupation with the German Middle Ages. Leading romantics found their way into the Roman Catholic Church. Dissatisfaction with the present had driven the early romanticists toward self-deification and the future. After 1806 the individual submerged in Church and Nation (deified as organic entities), while poetry, philology, and history attempted to transfigure the national past which was explored back to its dim beginnings in prehistory. A predilection for chapbooks, folk songs, and *Märchen* prompted Joseph Görres (1776–1848) to publish the *Teutschen Volksbücher* (1807), C. M. Brentano

(1778–1842) and A. von Arnim (1781–1832) to collect, and upon occasion to forge, German folk songs (*Des Knaben Wunderhorn*, 1806–08) and the brothers Jakob Grimm (1785–1863) and Wilhelm Grimm (1786–1859) to write down traditional fairy tales. Simultaneously the Swabian school of poetry (Uhland, Mörike, Schwab, Kerner) drew on folklore for its lyrical production. A century later, the surrealists (q.v.) went back to these same sources of magic inspiration and archetypal myths, which owe much to the romanticists' interest in the nocturnal side of nature (*magnetism, mesmerism*, etc.). Friedrich Schlegel's investigations into the history of myth and religion had led him to a revolutionary concept of the orphic aspects of Hellenism, later to be defined by Nietzsche as the Dionysian element which he opposed to Winckelmann's Apollonian ideal of classical antiquity (see "APOLLONIAN-DIONYSIAN"). Independently, Friedrich Hölderlin's (1770–1843) poetry descended into the depths of orphism. Against the rising tide of German nationalism, Heinrich Heine (1797–1856)—praised by Nietzsche as the greatest German lyricist—launched from his Paris exile the last (and possibly highest) realizations of romantic irony, his mock epics *Atta Troll* (1843) and *Germany, a Wintertale* (1844).

While German r., from its very beginnings, was a movement conscious of its aims, the *Eng. romantics* remained, on the whole, unaware of their romantic trends, and refused to apply the term romantic to their own production. The authors of the Lake school (Coleridge, Wordsworth, and de Quincey) are perhaps the closest approximation to an Eng. school of r. Wordsworth, exalting the "purity" of childhood in *Intimations of Immortality* (1802–6), in the long autobiographical poems *The Prelude* (1798–1805) and *The Excursion* (1814), drew from his pantheism the naive morality that love for nature must needs lead to love for mankind. Together with Coleridge he stressed the superiority of creative imagination over intelligence in its spontaneous intuition of truth (*Preface to Poems*, 1815). Coleridge, in his poetic period (1795–1802), differed profoundly from Wordsworth, inasmuch as exoticism, magic, dream, imagination prevail in his verse. His *Biographia Literaria* (1817) and *Lectures on Shakespeare* (1818), both reflecting the thought of Kant, the Schlegels, and Schiller, were by far the most influential works of literary criticism, together with those of Hazlitt, Arnold, and Ruskin, in 19th-c. England. Lord Byron (1788–1824) regarded himself as a neoclassical poet, continuing the tradition of Pope; to the Germans and the Fr. he became the very personification of r. His poetic travelogue *Childe Harold's Pilgrimage* (1812–18), *The Giaour* (1813), *Lara* (1814), *The Corsair* (1814), *Mazeppa* (1818), *Don Juan* (1819–24) introduce to literature the semi-autobiographical *homme fatal*, prototype of the melancholy antihero torn by unbearable guilt feelings, who haunts Fr. romantic literature between 1820 and 1860. Shelley's (1792–1822) Platonism fuses ideals of freedom and world-brotherhood with concepts of love and the perfection of beauty. Pain over the inaccessibility of the world of ideals is tempered by a Pantheism which sees in the fleeting moment revelations of divine beauty and truth. In his *Defence of Poetry* (1821), Shelley continued Sidney's theories, defining poetry as prophecy and an intuition of ultimate reality. The contribution of Eng. r. to the theatre seems negligible; Byron's *Manfred* (1817) and *Cain* (1821), and Shelley's *The Cenci* (1819) are more pregnant with ideas than excelling in dramatic quality.

Of all British romanticists, Sir Walter Scott (1771–1832) exerted by far the greatest influence on the development of the European novel (in France on Balzac and V. Hugo; in England on Marryat, Reade, and Thackeray; in Germany on Hauff, Scheffel, Alexis, Fontane). R., undergoing subtle modifications, persisted in England throughout the 19th c. Elizabeth Barrett Browning (1806–61) with her *Sonnets from the Portuguese* continued the Renaissance and romantic tradition of the sonnet; Robert Browning (1812–89) wrote his Faustian poem with *Paracelsus* (1835) and attained mature symbolism with *The Ring and the Book* (1868–9). The Pre-Raphaelites, in particular D. G. Rossetti (1828–82), with their adoration of Giotto and the It. *Trecento*, developed the highly romantic metaphysics of love and death and, in their cultivation of spiritual allegory, started a mystical "art for art's sake" movement, which found its erotic and symbolist counterpart in the lyricism of A. C. Swinburne (1837–1909). Continuing the themes of Byron's poetry, Swinburne's *Poems and Ballads* (1866, 1878, 1889) bear affinities with the lyricism of Gautier and Baudelaire.

In *France*—as in Italy, Spain, Portugal, Russia, Poland, the New World, etc.—r. is largely derivative. In 1816 (hardly more than a word in France) it is decried as an unpatriotic attempt to glorify the poetry of the victors of Waterloo, and as a blow struck at the very foundations of national (i.e., neoclassical) taste. At Milan, Stendhal (Henri Beyle, 1783–1842) joined forces in 1816 with the It. liberal romanticists Manzoni, Pellico, Visconti, Monti, and Berchet, whose literary aspirations merged with the political aims of the *risorgimento*. Fr. r. found all its models abroad; across the Channel with "Ossian," Shakespeare (in 1822 still booed in Paris), W. Scott (the "slanderer" of Bonaparte), and Byron; across the Rhine with Schiller (sic), and (to a lesser degree) Jean Paul and Goethe. The vogue of Schiller had been launched from Mme de Staël's headquarters in exile by Barante and Constant. Mme de Staël's *De l'Allemagne* (1813), creating the fateful mirage of an idyllic Germany (which persisted in England and France until 1870), had awakened an interest in the German romantics. It introduced to France the antinomy "classical-romantic" (see CLASSICISM), gleaned from the Schlegels, which was to split literary and artistic France throughout the *Restauration* (1815–30) into at least four opposing (yet in their loyalties fluid) factions of royalist classicists, liberal classicists, royalist romanticists, and liberal romanticists.

In the 1820's there developed from these confused beginnings a coherent movement, led since 1827 by Victor Hugo (in 1822 still a royalist classicist; now, as the author of *Cromwell,* a liberal romantic). R. had matured around three centers: (1) the royalist *Muse française* (1823–24), edited by Emile Deschamps, conservative and opposed to excesses but exalting Byron, W. Scott, and Shakespeare, and publishing poetry by Hugo, Vigny, and Marceline Desbordes-Valmore; (2) since 1824 the eclectic *salon* of Ch. Nodier, the librarian of the *Arsénal,* who (before defecting after 1830) received on Sundays Deschamps, Vigny, Hugo, Dumas, Mérimée, Nerval, Lamartine (when in Paris), Gautier, Balzac, Delacroix, Devéria, David d'Angers; (3) *Le Globe* (1824–32), a liberal newspaper founded by Paul Dubois, with Stendhal, Mérimée, and Sainte-Beuve (all still unknown) among its contributors, and Rémusat, Vitet, and Ampère (whose translation of E. T. A. Hoffmann appeared in 1828) formulating a doctrine of independent taste and freedom from neoclassical rules. Alessandro Manzoni (1785–1873) in his *Lettre à M. Chauvet* (1823) had postulated the liberation of genius from the fetters of literary conventions, and defined the new movement (somewhat awkwardly) as a classicism broadened by history.

By 1830, most Fr. romanticists were moving away from Byronic frenzy and bizarre ostentation; the necrophily, cult of magic clairvoyance and sadism of A. Rabbe, Pétrus Borel, and Philotée O'Neddy are extravagant but turn into vibrant lyricism when transposed and deepened in Baudelaire's poetry. The dominant figure remains Victor Hugo (1802–85) whose lyricism—traditional in the *Odes* (1822), picturesque and medieval in the *Ballades* (1826), exotic with brilliant virtuosity in *les Orientales* (1829)—became more personal between 1830 and 1840, his odes in a Bonapartist spirit foreshadowing the short epic, cultivated by Vigny and Leconte de Lisle, and flourishing in his own *Légende des Siècles* (1859–83). *Poeta-magus*

in his late verse (1856–85), Hugo becomes a Neoplatonist visionary whose charity, transcending mere social pity, extends to all creatures. His vast poetic structures—dominated by the idea of the great chain of being—prophesy the final liberation of suffering matter in its irresistible progress from heaviness and obscurity toward spirituality and light. His "Ce que dit la bouche d'ombre" approaches the hermetic rhythms of Nerval, Mallarmé, and Valéry.

Diametrically opposed to Hugo's optimism is the stoic impassivity of Alfred de Vigny (1797–1863). This disenchanted poet turns his creation into the living symbol of an idea; his terse and impersonal poetry, philosophical and often of epic quality, set a pattern later to be continued by Leconte de Lisle and the *Parnassiens,* whose ascetic cult of "art for art's sake" bears a marked affinity with that of Théophile Gautier (1811–72). The themes and stylistic aspirations of Fr. r. found their fulfillment only in Baudelaire, whose *Fleurs du Mal* transformed into ferocious and diabolical obsessions the *spleen* of the dandy and the *ennui* and remorse which, since Chateaubriand, haunted all Fr. literature. In frenzied and majestic images, Baudelaire's *Flowers of Evil* expressed the existential anguish of modern Man, while his *Spleen de Paris* may be considered the first successful attempt to introduce the prose poem into Fr. poetry.

In France, as elsewhere in Europe and the New World of Poe, Melville, and Whitman, r. and its later developments opposed to the neatly rational, universal, and orderly *solutions* of neoclassicism the untidy and *problematic* world of Man—as a *creator* freely probing the irrational and inventing new forms, and as an *individual* dispossessed of beliefs, traditions, and affiliations, torn by *ennui* and laden with guilt, a stranger among strangers, and a stranger unto himself. The 20th c., reviving "everything that reinforces our irrationalism" (Malraux), with its poetics ever widening the gap between neoclassical *genres* and free experimentation in aesthetics, and with its poetry sounding the depth of the subconscious, is producing a literature which, in its ontological quest, is now largely regarded by critics like Albert Béguin, A. Malraux, F. M. Albérès, and Marsi Paribatra, as an extension of r., and labeled "neoromantic."

I. Babbit, *Rousseau and R.* (1919); P. L. Smith, "Four Words: Romantic, Originality, Creative, Genius," *SPE Tract* 17 (1924); T. E. Hulme, *Speculations* (1924); A. O. Lovejoy, "On the Discrimination of Romanticisms," PMLA, 39 (1924); A. Castro, *Les grands romantiques espagnols* (1924); P. Kluckhohn, *Die deutsche Romantik* (1924); P. Hazard, "Romantisme italien et r. européen," RLC, 6 (1926);

J. Petersen, *Die Wesensbestimmung der deutschen R.* (1926); M. Souriau, *Histoire du r. en France* (3 v., 1927); A. Farinelli, *Il Romanticismo nel mondo latino* (3 v., 1927); A. Viatte, *Les Sources occultes du r.* (2 v., 1928); F. Strich, *Deutsche Klassik and R.* (1928); G. Calgari, *Il R. in Germania e in Italia* (1929); A. Monglond, *Le Préromantisme français* (2 v., 1930); J. v. Frakas, *Die ungarische R.* (1931); M. Praz, *The Romantic Agony* (1933; 2d ed., 1951); E. Seillière, *Sur la psychologie du r. allemand* (1933); *Krisenjahre der Frühromantik* (letters from and to the Schlegels, 2 v., ed. J. Körner, 1936–37); H. A. Korff, *Geist der Goethezeit* (5 v., 1940–1957); N. Neusser, "Barock and R.," (Diss. Zurich, 1942); G. Diaz-Plaja, *Introducción al estudio del romanticismo español* (2d ed., 1942); Ph. van Tieghem, *Le R. français* (1947); A. Béguin, *L'Âme romantique et le rêve* (1946); E. A. Peers, *A Short Hist. of the Romantic Movement in Spain* (1949); R. Wellek, "The Concept of 'R.' in Lit. Hist.," CL,.1 (1949) and *A Hist. of Modern Crit., 1750–1950* (v. 2., *The Romantic Age*, 1955); *The Eng. Romantic Poets: A Review of Research*, ed. T. M. Raysor (1950); K. Weinberg, *Henri Heine, "romantique défroqué," héraut du symbolisme fr.* (1954); M. Paribatra, *Le R. contemporain . . . 1850–1950* (1954); R.-M. Albérès, *Bilan littéraire du XXᵉ s.* (1956); R. H. Fogle, "The Romantic Movement," in *Contemp. Lit. Scholarship*, ed. L. Leary (1958); E. C. Mason, *Deutsche und englische Romantik* (1959); *Eng. Romantic Poets. Modern Essays in Crit.*, ed. M. H. Abrams (1960); R. Ayrault, *La Genèse du r. allemand* (2 v., 1961); *R.: Points of View*, ed. R. F. Gleckner and G. E. Enscoe (1962); *R. Reconsidered: Selected Papers from the Eng. Institute*, ed. N. Frye (1963). Consult also bibliog. to MODERN POETICS, 1750–1900. See PREROMANTICISM. K.W.

ROMANY POETRY. See GYPSY POETRY.

RONDEAU. One of the Fr. fixed forms, comparable in its strictness of construction to the triolet (q.v.). The most common type of r., as practiced by Clément Marot in the early 16th c., consists of 13 lines of 8 or 10 syllables each, divided into stanzas of 5, 3, and 5 lines. The whole is constructed on 2 rhymes only, and the first word, or first few words, of the first line are used as a *rentrement* (partial repetition), which occurs independently of the rhyme scheme, after the eighth and the thirteenth lines, that is, after the end of the second and third stanzas. If we allow R to stand for the *rentrement*, the following scheme describes the rondeau: (R) aabba aabR aabbaR. The popularity of the r. diminished toward the first third of the 16th c., and toward the middle of the same century the form disappeared. It was

used again at the beginning of the 17th c. by the *précieux* poets, especially Vincent Voiture. In the latter part of the 17th c. and during the entire 18th it was employed to a lesser extent. The r. had a new vogue among some of the romantics, notably Musset, who took some liberty with the arrangement of the rhymes. Théodore de Banville and Maurice Rollinat used the form subsequently.

Aside from an occasional r. in Eng. as early as the latter 18th c., the form did not flourish in England until near the end of the 19th, at which time it attracted the attention of Swinburne, Dobson, and other poets who experimented with the Fr. forms. In Eng. it has, unlike the triolet, often been used as a vehicle for serious verse. In Germany, where it has also been called the *Ringel-Gedicht*, *Ringelreim*, or *Rundreim*, the r. was cultivated by Weckherlin, Götz, and Fischart. An accomplished r. demands extraordinary skill in managing a natural return of the *rentrement*. Often the *rentrement* embodies a pun or an ambiguity of some sort.—Kastner, H. G. Atkins, *A Hist. of German Versification* (1923); Patterson; M. Françon, "La pratique et la théorie du r. et du rondel chez Théodore de Banville," MLN, 52 (1937; states that triolets, rondels, and rondeaux are a single genre with variations). L.B.P.

RONDEAU REDOUBLÉ. A strict poetic form similar to the older Fr. forms. Hardly used before the 16th c., it is rare even at the time of Clément Marot, who is known to have composed one in 1526 (publ. in 1534). In the 17th c. a few isolated examples occur in the works of Mme Deshoulières and Jean de La Fontaine. In the 19th c. Théodore de Banville used the form. Marot's r.r. may be schematized as follows: ABA'B' babA abaB babA' abaB' babaR (R here signifying a *rentrement* or partial repetition composed of the first 2 words or the first phrase of the poem's initial line). In addition, each line of stanza 1 is employed in turn as the last line of each of the following 4 stanzas. Stanzas 2, 3, 4, and 5 thus serve as developments of the content of stanza 1, and the final stanza makes a comment or summation. In Eng. light verse the form has been used by such writers as Dorothy Parker and Louis Untermeyer.—M. Grammont, *Petit traité de versification française* (7th ed., 1930). L.B.P.

RONDEL. A Fr. fixed form, which has had a long and varied history. Its simplest form: AB aA ab AB, reaching back to the 13th c., became known later as the triolet (q.v.). Another early variation was the *rondel double*, which had the following rhyme scheme: ABBA abBA abba ABBA (the capital letters indicate the repeated lines). In the 15th c. the terms "rondel" and "rondeau" (q.v.) seem to have been used interchangeably, and one finds the words *un rondel, des rondeaux*. The rondel best known today is a poem of 3 stanzas and built on 2 rhymes, the scheme being ABba abAB abbaA(B). It is composed of 13 lines in which a 2-line refrain occurs twice in the first 8 lines (lines 1–2 and 7–8) and the first line is repeated as the last line; or it may consist of 14 lines in which case a 2-line refrain appears thrice in the poem. Henley, Gosse, Dobson, R. L. Stevenson, and others have written Eng. rondels.—Kastner; M. Françon, "La pratique et la théorie du rondeau et du rondel chez Théodore de Banville," MLN, 52 (1937). L.B.P.

ROUNDEL. According to the OED, used as a synonym for rondeau and/or rondel by Chaucer (e.g., *Knight's Tale* 1529) and others. Yet the term now is usually reserved for the variant form introduced by Swinburne and published in his *A Century of Roundels* (1883). The form consists of 11 lines (3 stanzas), rhyming abaR bab abaR, *R* standing in this scheme for the refrain (more correctly the *rentrement*), which is either the first word of the poem or some part of its first line. If the *rentrement* is more than one word, it usually rhymes with the *b*-rhyme of the poem. Swinburne's *The Roundel* is at once a definition and an example of the form. L.B.P.

RUBĀ‘Ī (quatrain). See OMAR KHAYYÁM QUATRAIN; PERSIAN POETRY.

RULES. Formulations of poetic "r." have commonly been founded on the assumption that literary composition is partly at least a matter of conscious "art" (*technē*) for which one may construct a more or less systematic body of principles and precepts (*technologos; ars*). It is an assumption which, when employed with wisdom and flexibility, has been a basis of much valuable literary theory, criticism, and scholarship. Sometimes, however (as in the 16th and 17th c.), the "art" of poetry has been viewed as a system of highly detailed and inviolable specifications for the subject matter, arrangement, presentation, and style of the various poetic genres; e.g., a play must have five acts; only three actors can be placed on the stage at one time; the established subject matters of the genres cannot be mixed; the pastoral or eclogue must be written in the "simple" style, about shepherds; tragedies must be about kings, princes, and generals; comedies must be about soldiers, servants, farmers, and prostitutes; the "Aristotelian" unities of time and place (limiting the action depicted in a play to no more than two days' duration and usually to a single locale) must be faithfully

observed; the time limit of an epic story is one year; etc.

Most 16th- and 17th-c. collections of such r. were in a large degree codifications of artistic practices of classical antiquity, combined with fragmentary citations of various ancient critics; but they were also quite heavily supported by general theorizing about art, nature, the audience, and the poet—from a number of points of view—and particular regulations were frequently defended by different writers on entirely different theoretical grounds. For example, Castelvetro, viewing poetry primarily as designed for the pleasure of a common, ignorant, and unimaginative audience, defends the unity of time on the basis of the impossibility—so he reasons—of making such persons "believe that several days and nights have passed when they know through their senses that only a few hours have passed" (*Poetica d'Aristotele* [1570]); Minturno, however, viewing poetry both as the product of natural and artistic faculties and as a collection of naturally separate genres all designed for the edification of a more general kind of audience, defends the unity of time as one of the standard "intellectual" requirements of artistic achievement for a "good" (hence socially useful) dramatic poem, and does not argue that it is demanded by laws of credibility (*De poeta* [1559]). At the same time, a particular rule could be rejected by one critic on grounds very similar to those on which another had defended it; for example, Pierre de Laudun argued, in his *Art poétique françois* (1597), that strict adherence to the unity of time is unwise, precisely because it tends to force the poet to present impossible and incredible things. (Cf. F. Ogier, *Préface au lecteur* to Schelandre's *Tyr et Sidon* [1628].)

Notwithstanding the volume and earnestness of this earlier theorizing, in the 17th c. a gradual general undermining of the so-called neoclassical r. began, influenced partly by trends toward a more independent "philosophical" kind of criticism, and toward a kind of "circumstantial" criticism by which specific r. of the past were rejected as appropriate only to specific past conditions and circumstances of authorship (see R. S. Crane, in UTQ, 22 [1953], 389–90); and by the middle of the 18th c., especially in England, most of the more notorious r. had been discredited (cf. S. Johnson, *Rambler*, no. 125 [1751]; *Preface to Shakespeare* [1765]). The concentration particularly on the r. of the established genres give way first to more flexible definitions of those genres, then to more inclusive lists of legitimate ones (including, e.g., "heroic plays," comedies of manners, and domestic tragedies), and finally to a shift of interest largely away from genres to aspects and qualities of nature and art relevant to poetry in general (see NEOCLASSICAL POETICS). With this shift, however, there was not a general denial of the need for artistic r. The tendency was rather to establish new ones, and they were usually based on the ancient principle that achievement of peculiarly poetic qualities is at least partly an "art," not merely a natural process; Wordsworth, for example, in his Preface to the *Lyrical Ballads* (1800; 1802); while rejecting the "artificial" practices of most 18th-c. poets, announced the presumably innovative r. of "human" subject matter and style by which true poetry could consciously be achieved. Nor was the "neoclassical" principal of guidance by the practices of past masters ever completely abandoned. Rather, rejection of "ancient" examples was commonly accompanied by endorsement of "modern" ones, especially of those who departed from the "neo-classical" r. (see BATTLE OF THE ANCIENTS AND MODERNS). For example, writers as diverse in theory as Lessing, Herder, Voltaire, and Dr. Johnson frequently cited the example of medieval or "folk" poetry, as well as of such non-classical authors as Shakespeare and Milton.

Many of the changes which occur from time to time in "accepted" poetic r. thus seem to result as much from changes of taste and prejudice in poetry itself as from changes in theoretical conceptions of it. Even some recent anti-technical approaches to poetry (from which the concept of artistic intention and r. has been virtually eliminated and the central problem is the accomplished "meaning" of poems) tend to imply the highly restrictive modern rule that "true" or "good" poetry must be made—by conscious intention or not—of paradoxical metaphors like those (say) of the Metaphysical poets of the 17th c. It is not inevitable, however, that the r. of poetic art, whether stated or implied, should be so narrowly conceived and restrictive; much poetic theory and criticism exists, ancient and modern (for example, that of Plato, Aristotle, and Longinus, or of Dr. Johnson, Lessing, and Coleridge), whose principles and methods of reasoning, and the "r." which follow from them, may be positively useful to both the critics and the poets of any age, because they are based intelligently and flexibly on aspects of literary achievement and kinds of general theory which have survived the accidental changes of literary fashion and dogma.—Bray; B. Weinberg, *Critical Prefaces of the Fr. Renaissance* (1950) and *A Hist. of Lit. Crit. in the It. Ren.* (2 v., 1961); Abrams. R.M.

RUMANIAN POETRY. Rumania, at the crossroads between the Orient and the Occident, was bound to undergo numerous cultural influences after the year A.D. 107, when the Ro-

man Emperor Trajan conquered Dacia. This ancient realm comprising the territories of Wallachia, Moldavia, Transylvania, Bukovina, Bessarabia, and a small part of Macedonia, has been populated by a large and homogeneous people, 80 per cent peasantry, whose speech belongs to the great family of Romance languages. The beginnings of its poetry are oral, and the lyrical *doina* of the villagers expresses grief, exile, loneliness, and death, celebrates wine and carousal, revolts against oppression, contemplates and worships the creation of the Lord, and persistently intones love. Some of the erotic stanzas are ironic or satiric. And they all run the gamut of sentiment. They are sung or recited, and usually begin with the apostrophe "green leaf" followed by the name of an appropriate bough or flower. As the peasant lives in the midst of nature, under the blue or clouded sky, bent over the black earth he cultivates to nourish him, the animals, birds, and plants play an important part in his life. The smallest insect and tiniest blade of grass are known to the rustic poet. Lyricism characterizes even *Miorița* (The Lambkin), the most quoted poem, which is probably a fragment from a longer epic lost in the distant past. Vasile Alecsandri (1819–90) published it in his collection of ballads (1852–53), gathered from the lips of village minstrels, and "corrected" in order to emphasize their beauty. Lines of 5 syllables (an anapaest preceding an iamb) depict the epoch when vagrant shepherds roamed through pasture fields of aboriginal mountaineers. Its plot is naive, but the verses are concise and heartfelt:

Pe-un picior de plai,
Pe-o gură de rai.

At the foot of a high mountain,
At the entrance to paradise.

And the ancestral song proceeds to tell that there came along the road three flocks of sheep with their shepherds, a Moldavian, a Transylvanian, and a Vrancean of the small land bordering on three Carpathian territories. Two of them plot to slay the Moldavian as he is richer in herds, trained horses, and brave dogs. But Miorița, the little lamb of golden wool, proves its fairy nature. It can talk, and advises its master to change his course toward the dark willow wood where there is grass and shade, and thus outwit the murderers. The fatalist herdsman, however, is resigned to die and asks Lambkin to tell his foes that he wishes to be buried in the nearby fold to be always with his sheep, to hear his dogs bark, and, so that the mourning winds may blow through it plaintively, to have on his grave a "Little pipe of beech."

Even though we find written poetry as early as the 16th c., all texts are influenced by Slavonic, Latin, and modern Gr. cultures, the last becoming dominant. The chronicler Miron Costin (1633–91) gives in his *Life of the World* a philosophic-theologic poem to show that one can create *stihuri* (verses) in the vernacular. But lay works are totally absent. The first lyric poet, one of the foremost Wallachian boyars and a high dignitary, Ienache Văcărescu (1740–99) shows a genuine love for the lore of his people, but it is more of a presentiment than a realization. When Johan Gottfried von Herder (1774–1803) published his *Stimmen der Völker in Liedern* (1778–79), the boyar pursued his modern Gr. predilections listening to his gypsy band and exalting the faithful turtledove, amid woeful interjections. The Transylvanian Ioan Budai-Deleanu (1770–1830), who, unlike Văcărescu, was a commoner, wrote in 1800 the epic *Ţiganiada,* published posthumously in 1875–77, a satirical comic poem in 12 cantos. Budai-Deleanu read with profit the masterworks of the ancients and moderns, and his work merges the classic and the popular.

The Fr. Revolution and the Napoleonic Wars were decisive in strengthening Fr. influence in the Rum. principalities, its foundation being laid by the Latinist movement originating in Transylvania. Translations of poems are few, but some of the tragedies are in verse. Gradually, the Fr. more than any other of the major European literatures infiltrated Rum. poetry. Mihail Eminescu (1850–89) built a monument of romantic dreams. Blending his Western education with painstaking study of ancient peasant lore and vernacular, he actually molded his masterpieces in the true spirit of the soil, adding the magic of his genius. Disappointed in love, fleeing the commonplace and tedious, sinking into his inborn sadness, he became fascinated by Kant and Schopenhauer. Descending deeper into pessimism, his mind darkened in the prime of life and death followed in an insane asylum. Among his sixty completed poems, in which occidental technique and Rum. folklore fuse with unprecedented craftsmanship, one beholds in *Împărat şi Proletar* the conflict between the emperor and the proletarian in revolutionary France: "The century is ashes—Paris its sepulcher." And in *Luceafărul* (in iambic feet) Hyperion, the evening star, pleads with God to be made a man for the sake of a beautiful princess:

> Often she would gaze at him
> With childish ecstasy,
> As he rose and shone and led
> Black ships upon the sea.

When Eminescu's statue was unveiled at Galatz in 1911, Dimitrie Anghel (1872–1914) seized this opportunity to read at the official exercises his *Prinosul unui Iconoclast* (Offerings of an Iconoclast), a proclamation of independence from the master's sway which grew to the extent of absorbing generations of writers. With Anghel, a new movement of great diversity spread over Rum. poetry, and many young poets were inspired by him. Excessively sensitive, his verse is a garden of discreetly scented gossamer-like flowers. An unhappy love life, complicated by poverty and disillusionment, caused him to commit suicide. Tudor Arghezi (b. 1880) furthers the independent trend. He was too personal, too original, to let himself be carried away by the charm of European poets he read. Thus his motif is of the soil, his idioms taken from life, artistically transposed, and his stark realism verges on surrealism. All forms of contemporary poetry flourish, and we find Tristan Tzara (born in 1896) in Fr. and Rum. anthologies and histories of literature, since one of the originators of dadaism hails from Rumania, as well as Eugen Ionesco (born in 1912), author of *The Bald Soprano* and other plays.

Of the two extreme views B. Munteano in his *Contemporary Rum. Literature* states the traditional idea: "When people speak of Rumania as a Balkan country, they misuse words. It has kept its own peculiar character, bound up with the Carpathians, not the Balkans, with the Danube plains, not the Don steppes." The permanent instinct of being different from his Slav and oriental surroundings "has become in the nineteenth century a conscious and combative act of will. The Rumanian lived through a political and literary pre-renaissance which was accomplished thanks to a passionate attempt to draw near the West." And further: "In place of the metaphysical themes of yesterday, there appear political and economic themes with no spiritual echoes and no perspective. The most important consists in a base flattery, a humiliating idolatry of Soviet Russia and her heroes, the conquest of her *genius* in all fields. . . ."

The other view, according to official statements, shows that there is one single front with poets like Demostene Botez (b. 1893), Enric Furtună (b. 1881), Panait Cerna (1881–1913) and a number of the younger generation, Nina Cassian being one of the most appreciated due to her liveliness of inspiration and novelty of verse. This front is characterized by its attachment to life, actuality, reality, and the people. Its major preoccupation is with the *fond*, the idea content in artistic forms. It avoids formalism, hermeticism, and mysticism in favor of clarity and a positive optimism. Much of its poetry is narrative, tending to epic celebration of heroic deeds during the revolutions of liberation and of heroes like those in the great ballads. Reliance on popular forms and rhythms has been at times excessive, but the better poets have outgrown it. The Fr. influence is still strong. Am. (Walt Whitman, Edgar Allan Poe), Eng., German, It., and Sp. models have also had an important influence, especially on the many emigrants living outside of Rumania but writing in their native language. At present Rum. poetry is a vigorous and diversified body of literature outstanding in its love of native land and people.

ANTHOLOGIES: *Antologia Poeților de Azi*, ed. I. Pillat și Perpessicius (2 v., 1925; collection of modern poetry); *Antol. romana*, ed. S. Puscariu (Halle, 1938); *Antol. Poeziei Rominesti de la începuturi pînă astăzi* (1954); *Rum. Prose and Verse*, ed. E. D. Tappe (1956); *Antol. della poesia romena*, ed. and tr. M. de Micheli e D. Vranceanu (1961).

HISTORY AND CRITICISM: G. Adamescu, *Contribuțiune la bibliografia românească* (3 v., 1921–28); L. Feraru, *The Development of Rum. Poetry* (1929), "Rum. Lit.," *New Internat. Ency.* supp. 1930, II, "Rum. Lit.," *Columbia Diction. of Modern European Lit.* (1947); O. Densusianu, *Literatura romana moderna* (2 v., 1929); P. V. Hanes, *Hist. de la litt. roumaine* (1934); B. Munteano, *Modern Rum. Lit.*, tr. C. Sprietsma (1939) and "Contemporary Rum. Lit.," BA, 30 (1956); G. Lupi, *Storia della lett. romena* (1955); G. Nandriș, "Rum. Lit.," *Ency. Britannica* (1958); Al. Piru, *Literatura romînă veche* (1961). L.F.

RUNE. A character of the Old Germanic alphabet (or *futhark*, as it is named from the first letters of its series), probably derived partly from Gr. and partly from L. characters. From about the 4th c. A.D. runes were widely used for inscriptions on weapons, coins, memorial stones, etc., and they occur also in Anglo-Saxon, Icelandic, and Norwegian poems, where the individual letters are to be translated into the body of the verse as common nouns. Certain runes (as for example in Eng. the rune-words *wyn*, *thorn*, *ethel*, *dæg*, and *man*) were introduced into native scripts with the advent of Christianity, and served thereafter as regular characters, or, more occasionally, as a kind of shorthand. From early times runes were associated with incantation and magical practices (the word itself meant "whisper, mystery, secret counsel"). The surviving Old Germanic poems which use them as special letters are either gnomic-didactic in character or else they dimly recall more superstitious uses, as when the OE poet Cynewulf signs his works with the runes for his name woven into the verses, so that his readers may pray for him.— B. Dickins, *Runic and Heroic Poems of the Old Teutonic Peoples* (1915); O. von Friesen, "Runenschrift," J. Hoops, *Reallexikon der germanischen Altertumskunde*, IV (1918–19); H. Arntz, *Handbuch der Runenkunde* (1935); R. Dérolez, *Runica Manuscripta* (1954); R. W. V. Elliott, *Runes: An Introd.* (1959). J.B.B.

RUNNING RHYTHM (common rhythm). Term coined by Gerard Manley Hopkins to denote the standard rhythm of Eng. verse measured by feet of 2 or 3 syllables (with only occasional extra unaccented syllables). The rhythm is said to be rising if the stress occurs at the end of the foot, falling if the stress occurs at the beginning of the foot (see ASCENDING and DESCENDING RHYTHM). If the stress occurs between 2 unstressed (or "slack") syllables (as in the amphibrachic foot), the rhythm, according to Hopkins, is "rocking" (q.v.). Running rhythm, in Hopkins' conception, is opposed to sprung rhythm (q.v.).—"Author's Preface," *Poems of Gerard Manley Hopkins*, ed. R. Bridges and W. H. Gardner (3d ed., 1948). P.F.

RUN-ON LINE. See ENJAMBEMENT.

RUSSIAN FORMALISM. A school in Rus. literary scholarship which originated in the second decade of this century and was championed by unorthodox philologists and students of literature such as B. Eichenbaum, R. Jakobson, V. Shklovsky, B. Tomashevsky, Yu. Tynyanov. The main strongholds of the Rus. formalist movement were the Moscow Linguistic Circle, founded in 1915, and the Petrograd "Society for the Study of Poetic Language" (*Opoyaz*), formed in 1916. The initial statement of the formalist position is found in the symposium *Poetics. Studies in the Theory of Poetic Language* (1919) and in *Modern Rus. Poetry* by R. Jakobson.

The formalists viewed literature as a distinct field of human endeavor, as a verbal *art* rather than a reflection of society or a battleground of ideas. They were more interested in the poetry than in the poet, in the actual works of literature than in their alleged roots or effects. Intent upon delimiting literary scholarship from contiguous disciplines such as psychology, sociology, or intellectual history, the formalist theoreticians focused on "distinguishing features" of literature, on the artistic devices peculiar to imaginative writing. In Jakobson's words, "the subject of literary scholarship is not literature in its totality, but *literariness*, i.e., that which makes of a given work a work of literature."

According to the formalists, imaginative literature is a unique mode of discourse, characterized by the "emphasis on the medium" (Jakobson) or "perceptibility of the mode of expression." In literary art, especially in poetry, it was argued, language is not

RUSSIAN POETRY

simply a vehicle of communication. From a mere proxy for an object, the word becomes here an object in its own right, an autonomous source of pleasure as multiple devices at the poet's disposal—rhythm, meter, euphony, imagery—converge upon the verbal sign in order to dramatize its complex texture.

These methodological assumptions were tested in acute studies of rhythm, style, and narrative structure. Probably, the most fruitful field of formalist endeavor was the theory of versification. To the formalists, verse is not merely a matter of external embellishments, such as meter, rhyme or alliteration, superimposed upon ordinary speech. It is an integrated type of discourse, qualitatively different from prose, with a hierarchy of elements and internal laws of its own—"a speech organized throughout in its phonic texture." The notion of rhythm as a *Gestaltqualität,* a structural property operative at all levels of poetic language, helped elucidate a crucial problem of poetics—that of relationship between sound and meaning in verse.

The formalist approach to literature was a far cry from that single-minded concern with "social significance" and "message," which dominated so much 19th-c. Rus. literary criticism. Consequently, the formalist research in the masters of Rus. literature resulted in drastic reexaminations. Gogol's famous story, "The Overcoat," hailed by the contemporaries as a moving plea for the "little man," became under the pen of B. Eichenbaum primarily a piece of grotesque stylization. Pushkin, viewed this time at the level of style and genre rather than that of *Weltanschauung,* appeared as a magnificent culmination of 18th-c. Rus. poetry rather than as the father of Rus. romanticism. And the moral crisis of the young Tolstoy was reinterpreted in largely aesthetic terms as a struggle for a new style, as a challenge to romantic clichés grown stale. In dealing with the current literary production, the formalist critics favored inventiveness, aesthetic sophistication, a search for new modes of expression. In visual arts they encouraged such trends as constructivism or cubism.

At first the formalist spokesmen extravagantly overstated their case. In their early studies Jakobson and Shklovsky played down the links between literature and society and denied the relevance of any "extra-aesthetic" considerations. Eventually, in the face of a concerted attack on the part of the Soviet Marxists, they made an effort to combine aesthetic analysis with a sociological approach to literature. But this attempt at synthesis came too late. In 1929–30 the methodological debate in the Soviet Union was rudely discontinued. With Soviet criticism being whipped into orthodoxy, formalism was suppressed as a heresy. Ever since 1930 "formalism" has been in Soviet parlance a term of censure, connoting undue preoccupation with "mere" form, bourgeois "escapism" and like offenses.

If in Russia the formalist movement was stopped in its tracks, during the thirties its influence was felt in other Slavic countries, especially, in Czechoslovakia and Poland. The theorists of so-called Czech structuralism grouped around the Prague Linguistic Circle, Dimitry Cizevsky, Jan Mukařovsky, René Wellek, and last but not least, Roman Jakobson who had lived in Prague since 1920, restated the basic tenets of Rus. formalism in more judicious and rigorous terms.

Viewed in a broader perspective, Rus. formalism appears as one of the most vigorous manifestations of the recent trend toward structural analysis of literature and art, which in the last two decades has made substantial inroads into Eng. and Am. literary study. Formalist doctrine has many points of contact with "new criticisms" (q.v.), especially with its "organicist" variant, as represented by Cleanth Brooks and Robert Penn Warren. C. Brooks' emphasis on the organic unity of a poem, with the concomitant warning against the "heresy of paraphrase," his keen awareness of the "ambiguity" of poetic idiom and "the conflict-structures" resulting from this ambiguity, such as irony and paradox—all this is closely akin to their later phase of formalist theorizing. Perhaps one should add that the affinity between these two schools of thought rests on analytical procedures rather than on criteria of evaluation. While the majority of Anglo-Am. New Critics have worked toward some flexible yet absolute standards applicable to literature of various ages, the Rus. formalists frankly espoused critical relativism.

Poetika. Sborniki po teorii poeticheskogo yazyka (1919); R. Jakobson, *O cheshskom stikhe* (1923); B. Tomashevsky, *O stikhe* (1929); V. Erlich, *Rus. Formalism: History-Doctrine* (1955). V.E.

RUSSIAN POETICS. See MODERN POETICS.

RUSSIAN POETRY. Rus. literature, which had its beginnings in the 11th c., was preceded by folk poetry which has always been unusually rich on Russian soil but began to be regularly recorded only in the 19th c. Many folklore genres were not only verbal, but musical as well, and they were sung or chanted by the people or professional performers, sometimes with instrumental accompaniment. There were lyrical and ceremonial songs, divinations, charms, laments. There were religious chants (*dukhovnye stikhi*) performed by wandering religious mendicants, and "historical songs" telling about great persons or events. Finally, there were *byliny* (q.v.), epics of legendary content, which are probably the most original and famous genre in Rus. oral poetic tradition. Also, one should add proverbs and riddles with their interesting rhythmic structure and original imagery. Folk poetry often influenced, and occasionally was influenced by, Rus. literary poetry, and it continued to develop. For instance, as late as in the 19th c., a new genre, the now popular *chastushka* (q.v.) made its appearance.

Among the poetic works of early Rus. literature, which primarily consisted of ecclesiastic works and chronicles, *Slovo o pŭlku Igorevě* (Lay of Igor's Campaign), written in Old Rus. rhythmic prose, stands out as a supreme masterpiece. It tells the story of the unsuccessful campaign of a Rus. prince in the 12th c. against the nomadic tribes, his captivity, and escape. A 16th-c. copy of this 12th-c. poem was found at the end of the 18th c., but later was destroyed in a fire. The work has ties with both its contemporary literary tradition and folklore, and contains pagan elements. It is not an epic narrative, but rather a series of lyrical pictures and patriotic apostrophes. Intensity of lyricism, rich imagery, complex sound patterns, and the variety and subtlety of *Slovo*'s rhythms led some to regard it as a verse composition, and others to question its authenticity. *Slovo* has become a national classic and has been a source of inspiration for Rus. poets, artists, and composers for more than a century.

Rus. literary verse is a relatively recent development, although it existed in a rudimentary shape, in works written in prose, since the 11th c. Nor should one ignore the Byzantine tradition of Rus. liturgical poetry, written in Old Church Slavonic and having the appearance of free verse with its pronounced line beginnings, syntactical parallelisms, and occasional use of the acrostic form. Formal Rus. verse, however, made its appearance at the beginning of the 17th c. as crude, doggerel-like *virshi*. In the second half of the 17th c. the earlier form was replaced by isosyllabic *virshi* which imitated Polish verse and required a constant number of syllables in a line, a fixed caesura, and feminine rhyme. This "syllabic verse" was brought to Russia by the learned Byelorussian monk, Simeon of Polotsk (1629–80), who used it for his long and ornate court panegyrics. The language of syllabic poetry was Old Church Slavonic with admixture of Rus.

The 18th c. was of extreme importance for the development of Rus. poetry. As the result of the reforms of Peter I, a new Russia emerged, and it was eager to adopt European ways and to find expression for individual human feelings. The old syllabic verse, prosaic and amorphous, which was not based on the prosodic structure of the Rus. language, was an inconvenient vehicle for this. The most important poets of the period experimented with new forms of versification, and the 18th c. can rightfully be called the laboratory of modern Rus. poetry. Despite the fact that Rus. 18th-c. poets drew heavily on the ideas and techniques of Fr. neoclassicism, their work is distinctly Rus. The brilliant poet-diplomat Antiokh Kantemir (1708–44) stubbornly continued to use the antiquated syllabic meter (though his vocabulary was almost purely Rus.), but he championed enlightenment and criticized society in his satires which contained elements of realism. Vasily Tredyakovsky (1703–69) was the first to see the inadequacy of syllabic verse, and he looked to the folk song for the basis of the new Rus. verse, which was to be accentual. Tredyakovsky was a paradoxical figure, being both a pioneer in many important poetic fields and also the father of all subsequent archaists in Rus. poetry. An indefatigable translator and scholar, he was historically sensitive, but apt to stop at half-measures. For almost two centuries his poetry was dismissed by many as unreadable trash, but critics now usually admit that it deserves attention and contains interspersed passages of genius. In spite of Tredyakovsky's insights into the nature of Rus. verse, it was given not to him, but to his foe, the "Russian Leonardo," Mikhaylo Lomonosov (1711–65), the great scientist, scholar, and poet, to create the first poem in the new meter, based on word-stress and usually referred to as syllabo-tonic. After him, iamb became the most popular Rus. meter and remains so at present. Lomonosov wrote sonorous odes in which he praised the ideal Rus. empire, but probably his best poetry is to be found in his two "razmyshleniya" (meditations) with their grandiose vision of nature, and in his "spiritual odes" in general. Lomonosov put an end to stylistic confusion by offering his "theory of three styles," which allowed the use of rare Church Slavonisms in the "high style" genres (heroic epics, odes), limited their use in the "middle style" (most dramas, satires, lyrical poetry) to those already accepted into Rus. spoken language, and did not permit them in the "low style" works (comedies, songs). In comparison with Lomonosov, his foe, Alexander Sumarokov (1718–77) was a lesser poet, but he emphasized what Lomonosov termed the "middle style," i.e., the language of educated classes, which was to become the main instrument of Rus. poetry for more than a century. Sumarokov also introduced a great variety of genres and meters, but, in spite of his efforts to preach brevity, economy, and precision in expression and to fight against the loud sound and uncontrolled flights of fancy in the odes of his contemporaries, these latter dominated the poetry of the greatest poet of the Rus. 18th c., Gavrilo Derzhavin (1743–1816) who was a giant of poetic imagination. This man, who began his career as a simple soldier and ended as a cabinet minister, was possessed by a passion for justice, and in his magnificent odes, he continued the Lomonosov tradition. But he also daringly mixed diction and genres, combining ode with satire (*Felitsa*) and Pindaric heights with realistic description. Thus, in an ode to the Empress, he mentions his wife looking for lice in his hair. Derzhavin's odes are an encyclopedia of Rus. life in his time, but they also present examples of profound tragic art, as in his famous monodies *Na smert' knyazya Meshcherskogo* (On the Death of Prince Meshchersky) and *Vodopad* (Waterfall), and of astounding spiritual rhetoric (the ode *Bog* [God]). This barbarian classicist filled his lines with splendid sound and unsurpassed visual richness. He also could speak softly and good-naturedly, and with him the intonation of spoken Rus. appeared in Rus. poetry for the first time, as in his late poem *Zhizn' zvanskaya* (Life in Zvanka) where he described his day in the country from morning to night and which is a masterpiece of mood and color, anticipating all subsequent attempts to treat poetry in a realistic way. One of Derzhavin's most original achievements was the fact that in his poems a real man, complete with sublime ideas and belching after a good dinner, unashamedly entered Rus. poetry. Rus. poetic fable was developed by several poets during the 18th c., but yielded its finest results when Ivan Krylov (1769–1844) began to write in this genre at the beginning of the 19th c. His fables are not so much satires of the society as the best expression of the common sense of the Rus. people in verse. The racy colloquialisms of his proverb-like lines make one forget the foreign sources of many of his fables completely.

The most prominent figure of the transition from the 18th to the 19th c. is Nikolay Karamzin (1766–1826), who, although a minor poet, affected Rus. poetry greatly with his reform of the literary language, aimed at purging it of archaic Church Slavonisms, at giving it European garb and at making it flexible enough for modern sensibility. Karamzin was a leading figure of Rus. sentimentalism which did not produce great poets, but helped to refine Rus. literary manners and to shift emphasis from universal and state affairs to the themes of individual life. The beginning of the 19th c. was the period of polemics between the circles close to Karamzin (see ARZAMAS) and the literary conservatives who desired to retain archaic diction as the mark of poetry and resisted the excessive Europeanization of the language. The modern party won, but the

conservatives, for a variety of reasons, never lacked individual defenders of their cause throughout the subsequent development of Rus. poetry.

The first three decades of the 19th c. are often referred to as the "Golden Age of Rus. Poetry." The tender and self-effacing Vasily Zhukovsky (1783–1852) was the first great name in the long list of Rus. poets of the 19th c., and, quite appropriately, the human soul is in the center of his poetry. Zhukovsky's poems were both sentimentalist and romantic, and his own unhappy love colored them with melancholy and infused them with motives of resignation and yielding to one's destiny. Zhukovsky became very popular through his translations and adaptations (*Svetlana*) of German romantic ballads, and he is still considered the greatest Rus. translator (*Odyssey*); but it would be difficult to draw a line between his original and translated works as he often used the latter for his most intimate personal outpourings, frequently improving on the originals. This pious tutor of the future Rus. emperor made of the Rus. language a most refined vehicle. He was the first to be able to express shades and subtle transitions of meaning, and few Rus. poets could equal the beauty of his melody, his rhythmic variety, and the purity of his style. Zhukovsky can be credited with creating for Rus. poetry a new language, the language of the human soul. His contribution was complemented by Constantine Batyushkov (1787–1855), also a member of the "Arzamas," and an officer who participated in campaigns against Napoleon and fell victim to hereditary madness in the middle of his life. If Zhukovsky's was usually the poetry of heaven, Batyushkov remained on the earth, but this earth was an ideal one. His eroticism was purified, and he was tender rather than passionate in his love poetry. In his early idyllic and hedonistic poems, Batyushkov sang of simple love, friendship, and solitude, but melancholy crept in gradually and added tragic shades to his last poems which are full of strange beauty. In general, his neoclassic imagery went hand in hand with a romantic treatment of words. Batyushkov consciously tried to make Rus. flexible, purged of Church Slavonisms and in sound as close as possible to his favorite It., and he often succeeded: in sheer beauty, his best poems were hardly equaled even by greater poets than he was. Such is the case, for instance, with the beginning of his *Ten' druga* (The Shade of a Friend). Rus. poets of our times discovered Batyushkov after a century of neglect, probably attracted by the inimitable combination of outward harmony and inner discord in his verse.

Both Zhukovsky and Batyushkov prepared

the way for Alexander Pushkin (1799–1837), who is not only regarded as the greatest Rus. poet, but probably is one of the four or five greatest poets of postmedieval Europe. He summed up the Rus. 18th c., and his art was essentially classicistic; however, his name was closely connected with the contemporary romanticism and even with the future realism. Contrary to what is often said, he was not the creator of the Rus. literary language, but his verbal perfection, in combination with his stylistic and ideological Proteanism, made several subsequent poetic movements claim him as their predecessor. Pushkin was endowed with the unique ability to assimilate all the valuable things he met on his way and to accept life with all its conflicts, combining them in a higher harmony. Thus, he was the first (and perhaps the last) to combine folklore and the European tradition successfully in Rus. poetry. One critic called him "the poet of the empire and of freedom," and, when applied to Pushkin, this does not sound paradoxical. Pushkin's early poetry, which he wrote at school, was imitative but not immature. He became famous after publishing his *poema* (Rus. for a longer poem) *Ruslan i Lyudmila* (Ruslan and Ludmila), a delightful tale of adventure, full of irony and parody, which started a literary controversy. Having been exiled to the south for writing political verse, Pushkin began his romantic period, which has been often termed "Byronic." However, the romanticism of his "southern" narrative *poemy* is skin-deep. Only in *Bakhchisarayskiy fontan* (The Fountain of Bakhchisaray), a love story with Oriental background, did he indulge in extreme beauty of sound. In the following *Tsygany* (The Gypsies) and the later *Poltava*, the familiar Pushkin objectivity and impersonality can be observed. The former, a story about a flight from civilization and about love and jealousy, not only cuts a Byronic hero down to size, but also is a complex treatise on the nature of freedom, whereas the latter adds a national epic to the romantic love story and marks Pushkin's ever-increasing interest in history.

Still in exile, though moved to his estate in the north, he finally completed his magnum opus, *Evgeny Onegin*, which was probably his greatest work in verse. It is both a novel in verse and an "encyclopedia of Rus. life," to quote a famous critic. *Onegin*'s simple story, noble ending, and portrayal of the main characters (a "superfluous" man, an ideal Rus. girl) greatly affected Rus. literature. But this is also a lyrical poem with the author as one of the heroes. The lyrical themes accompany the narrative and are often almost undistinguishable from the informal chat with which the poet interrupts the action continually;

they are made by him to appear and disappear with a Mozartian ease and skill of modulation. The entire work gives the appearance of "a work in progress" with its natural and, on the surface, disorganized growth as well as its immediate adaptation of tone and style to the change in theme and action. Many Pushkin admirers consider, however, *Medny vsadnik* (The Bronze Horseman) his masterpiece, and this work is as tight and somber as *Evgeny Onegin* was fluent and light. The action centers here on the famous flood of 1824 in St. Petersburg, but the theme is "state vs. individual," and the poet, with tragic objectivity, recognizes the claims of either party without trying to reconcile or take sides in the conflict. Pushkin's late years were mainly devoted to writing prose, and his lyrical poetry of this period made a further step toward stripping verse of all ornament and toward a nonviolent inclusion of prosaisms in the texture. These lonely years were also characterized by growing inner despair and by the poet's moving politically to the right.

But whether in his earlier romantic elegies or in his later experiments with folklore, the essential qualities of Pushkin's poetry remained the same: individual experience became universalized, and he handled words in the classical way, aiming at simplicity, brevity, and precision of expression. Few poets had such a perfect ear and such ability to stop where necessary.

Imagery was used by him sparingly, and one would in vain look in his lines for "interesting" ideas, since Pushkin was a genius of the obvious and normal. All this makes it difficult to translate him, and in a foreign language Pushkin may sound flat and banal. Some of his most beautiful lines, like

Kak grustno mne tvoyo yavlenye,
Vesna, vesna! pora lyubvi!
Kakoe tomnoe volnenye
V moey dushe, v moey krovi!

How sad looks to me your arrival,
Spring, Spring, the season of love!
What languorous excitement
In my soul, in my blood!

rely entirely on intonation too elusive for an analysis or a reproduction. After an eclipse in reputation which lasted several decades, Pushkin, at the end of the 19th c., became the object of practically unchallenged adoration which continues to grow.

Pushkin was surrounded by a handful of poets, mostly his friends, who are known under the name of the "Pushkin Pleiad," and some of them were first-rate talents, only slightly overshadowed by his genius. Though different in their temperament and subject matter, they all were classicists in more than one respect. Two of them stand out in particular. Evgeny Boratynsky (also spelled Baratynsky) (1800–44) attained popularity as the author of melancholy elegies and Byronic narrative *poemy*, but even in these he remained essentially a "poet of thought," as he was called. Restraint, logical development, and verbal precision were his typical traits. Toward the end of his days, his philosophical pessimism grew and his poetic meditations became visions of the approaching end of poetry (*Posledniy poet* [The Last Poet]) and of human life (*Poslednyaya smert'* [The Last Death], *Osen'* [Autumn]). Their tragic grandeur was intensified by Boratynsky's use of archaic diction reminiscent of the 18th-c. odes. In many respects his opposite was Nikolay Yazykov (1803–46), whose sensual songs with their abandon and hedonism are unique in their power and the combination of lightness with audacity, and rapid movement with majesty. Yazykov's poetry is highly original, and it abounds in daring imagery. His sonorous alliterations and bold new word coinages produce the effect of an almost physical intoxication. Yazykov was extolled by his Slavophil admirers as a perfect specimen of the truly Rus. "breadth of soul," but his ideological polemics in verse failed to produce anything first-rate. Nevertheless, in his imitations of psalms he again showed verbal magnificence, and in his foreign-diary poems there is charm of everyday detail and of intimate intonation. Other names in the "Pleiad" are the dry and witty Prince P. Vyazemsky, and the indolent Baron A. Delvig who wrote imitations of folk songs, classical idylls, and impersonal sonnets. Both were Pushkin's closest friends. There were also poets who did not belong poetically to the Pleiad and went their own ways as, for instance, the religious poet Fyodor Glinka and the freedom-loving Wilhelm Kuechelbecker, a participant in the Decembrist revolt, who was exiled to Siberia. Decembrist ideas had an important influence on contemporary poets (including Pushkin), and one of the Decembrist leaders, Kondraty Ryleev, hanged for his part in the revolt, was also a poet of note.

Critics and the reading audience recognized Mikhail Lermontov (1814–41) as Pushkin's heir, although his work represents a new departure for Rus. poetry both in mood and in subject matter, particularly in its almost complete severance of ties with the 18th c. This army officer, who lived a short and unhappy life, was Russia's greatest romantic poet, and his Byronism was more than just a fashionable pose. His poetry of great passions and proud loneliness found its best expression in two *poemy*. *Demon*, set against a Caucasian background, is the story of the love of a demon, who bears a resemblance to Lucifer, for a mortal beauty. *Mtsyri*, also a Caucasian *poema*, is the confession of a dying novice at a monastery, full of unrestrained passion, rhetorical richness, and a powerful desire for freedom. For the first time in Rus. poetry, in Lermontov's works, nature appears as a hero, not merely an aesthetic fact; and the Rousseauist theme of flight from civilization is sounded more distinctly and convincingly than ever before. Lermontov's rebellious spirit cannot be interpreted merely politically, for he was a metaphysical rebel. He was also the best religious poet of Russia, and no other poet left such sincere prayers or expressed better the homesickness of the human soul while bound to this earth. There was also a strong prophetic element in his poetry. On the other hand, realism made its first distinct appearance in Lermontov's poems—in those written from another man's viewpoint (usually a man of humble origin) as well as in those resembling a page from a diary, extremely sincere and full of self-observation and self-criticism. Lermontov not only excelled in oratorical meditation, he also introduced journalism into poetry, and this connects him with such later poets as Nekrasov. But Lermontov also marked the end of the Rus. poetical Golden Age. After him, there began a gradual loss of poetic culture, deterioration of technique and the general decline of attention to poetry. It is customary to mention at the end of the Golden Age the name of the folk poet Alexey Koltsov, who left a few original songs about peasants' life, but actually he was already the beginning of the decline.

There was, however, a poet who began writing at the beginning of the century and lived through the decline, while standing apart from his contemporary literary life. He was Fyodor Tyutchev (1803–73), one of the greatest Rus. lyrical poets, who lived for many years abroad as a diplomat and later was a government official in Russia. As a poet, he was twice "discovered" during his lifetime and once posthumously. Tyutchev was first of all a philosophical poet whose poems were full of profound metaphysical vision and symbols. His pessimistic world outlook was based on the image of primordial chaos which is the foundation of our universe and its true reality. This chaos is hidden from us behind "the golden cover" of the day, but during the night hours and in the howling of the wind it reveals itself to us, and it has a strong attraction for the poet. This dualism of chaos and cosmos is complemented by that of lonely and ignorant man and the nature surrounding him. However, as presented by Tyutchev, the pantheist, this nature is far from being completely indifferent, and in his most popular poems (*Vesenn-*

yaya groza [The Thunderstorm in the Spring])
it lives and breathes like a human being. The
dualism continues in the portrayal of human
soul by Tyutchev:

O thou, my wizard soul, oh heart
That whelming agony immerses,
The threshold of two universes
In cleaving thee, tears thee apart.

The romantic vision of his poetry is presented
with the rhetorical art of a classicist, and he
adds to the melody of Zhukovsky the archaic
diction and oratorical structure of Derzhavin.
Subtle impressionism goes hand in hand with
aphoristic quality in his fragment-like poems.
Tyutchev also wrote much political verse, reacting to contemporary events and defending
the religious mission of Russia in the world;
but his most original contribution, next to
his somber metaphysical revelations, was his
love poetry which reflected his own love affair
and his suffering after his mistress' death. Love
was for Tyutchev a "fatal duel" between the
sexes, and its portrayal had much in common
with that in Dostoevsky's novels. Tyutchev
greatly influenced Rus. symbolists of the 20th
c. by his form, his vision, and the prophetic
character of his poetry.

The second half of the 19th c. was a time of
conflict between two camps. One of these insisted that poetry had the civic duty of contributing to the social struggle of the period
for the improvement of conditions under which
the majority of the Rus. people lived, and the
poetic slogan was "You do not have to be a
poet, but you must be a citizen" (Nekrasov).
The opposite party, known under the misleading label of the "poets of art for art's sake"
considered it poetry's sacred task to create
beauty. Among the civic-minded (who usually
coincided with the political left), there was
only one poet worth mention, Nekrasov, but
he was a giant, comparable in the scope of his
achievements only to Pushkin and Lermontov.
Nikolay Nekrasov (1821–78)—praised by his
contemporaries on the ground of his message
and subject matter, but only after his death
appreciated as a poet of great talent and
craftsmanship—was early in his career persuaded by the influential critic Belinsky to
draw material directly from life and to place
his poetry at the service of the social cause.
Nekrasov enjoyed enormous popular success
during his lifetime, and he was a complex
personality, an unscrupulous and shrewd, but
discerning, publisher, a gambler, a social snob,
but simultaneously a man of "wounded heart"
(Dostoevsky), a sensitive and guilt-ridden hypo-
chondriac who penitently confessed in his
poems a discrepancy between his democratic
ideals and his way of life. Among his *poemy*,

there are the social satire *Zheleznaya doroga*
(The Railroad), the peasant love and murder
story *Korobeyniki* (The Pedlars), the realistic
fantasy *Moroz krasny nos* (Frost the Red-
Nosed), and the huge epic *Komu na Rusi zhit'
khorosho* (Who is Happy in Russia), a satiric
crosscut through contemporary society, ending
with a glorification of Rus. populist intelligentsia. In spite of the fact that even now
Nekrasov's poetry is often extolled or rejected
on the ground of his humanitarian or revolutionary message, he was the greatest and the
most representative poet of his time. The "suffering of the people," which he sang all his
life, may well have been the symbol of his own
tortured soul rather than an expression of
group feelings. It is for this reason that his
uneven "muse of vengeance and sorrow," as he
himself called his poetry, so often achieved
immediacy and white-hot intensity. His originality lies not only in his masterly, broad,
and compassionate treatment of the Rus. peasant theme (and this includes some of the best
Rus. rustic idylls, not only the poems about
"suffering"), but in the combination of conversational style and folk song and in the daring use of "prosaic" diction. Variety was also
Nekrasov's mark. Next to a sobbing melody,
tortuous reflections, sad landscapes, pictures
of rural and urban poverty as well as the portrayal of pain in human love relations, one
finds healthy humor and racy vigor.

The "art-for-art's-sake" school was richer in
names, but not a single one among those
poets, with the probable exception of Fet, ever
reached Nekrasov's stature. Also, they suffered
as much as their civic-minded adversaries from
the decline in poetic technique. Most of them
were eclectics who considered themselves, or
were considered, Pushkin's heirs. Among them,
the following were the most prominent: Alexey
K. Tolstoy, who also wrote the best Rus. nonsense poetry, a Rus. "Victorian," Apollon
Maykov, and the poet with a gift of song,
Yakov Polonsky. But only Afanasy Fet (1820–
92) can be considered Nekrasov's rightful rival,
despite the fact that many of his contemporaries turned their backs at him for his "reactionary" behavior. Fet was an army officer, and
later a practical landowner, but he was also
one of the most tender and subtle Rus. poets.
His inner poetical freedom was comparable
only to Pushkin's. He was primarily the poet
of nature and love, but his late poems, published under the title *Vechernie ogni* (The
Evening Lights), showed a distinct turn to
metaphysical subjects and the influence of
Schopenhauer. Fet was close to the Zhukovsky
tradition in Rus. poetry in his ability to express nuances of feeling and catch elusive and
fleeting impressions, as well as in the suggestiveness of his verse, its high musicality and

RUSSIAN POETRY

rhythmic variety. Nature in his poems seems to dissolve in lyrical emotion, and in his love poetry Fet is both passionate and subtle. All these qualities made him particularly dear to Rus. symbolists who dominated Rus. poetry around the turn of the century.

The general poetic decline continued, and toward the end of the 19th c., the poetic level of the idols of the radicals (S. Nadson), or of their antagonists (A. Apukhtin), or even of the predecessors of the coming poetic renascence (C. Sluchevsky), was extremely low. Slightly above this level was the mystical poetry of the famous philosopher Vladimir Solovyov. But in the 1890's, there began the aesthetic and spiritual revolution which, in poetry, resulted in the complex and heterogeneous phenomenon of Rus. modernism which has often, and rather misleadingly, been called symbolism. This movement opposed the realistic tradition of Rus. literature and its social-progress orientation. It emphasized aesthetic individualism with overtones of anarchism and amoralism, and in many respects was based on the Western European art and poetry of the *fin de siècle* (however, later the Slavophil elements grew and began to predominate). There was a renewal of interest in spiritual problems and of intense quest in philosophy, religion, and mysticism. There was also an active revaluation of the past, which returned to their rightful places many important figures of Rus. literature, art, and thought. A salient feature of this modernist movement was attention to poetic form; craftsmanship, variety, and subtlety in poetry ceased to be an exception. First-rate poets began to appear in great numbers, and the period was afterward called by some the "Second Golden Age," whereas others, taking into consideration its prevalent 'decadent' features, insisted on the name "Silver Age."

The first decades brought into prominence several poets. Constantine Balmont (1867–1943) infused Rus. poetry with unusual richness of sound. His often heavily alliterated lines dazzled the ear and enchanted it with a real song quality. The scholarly Valery Bryusov (1873–1924) soon became the recognized leader of the movement, and in his poems Rus. poetry regained the previously lost cultural level. His stylized, often oratorical verse, with its heavy rhythm (*Urbi et orbi*), emphasized proud solitude and almost allegorical eroticism. Fyodor Sologub (1863–1927) presented symbols of evil and praised the beauty of death in his deceptively simple and unadorned poems with their Manichaean world outlook and the general mood of tiredness, cruelty, pain and yearning. The intellectual poetry of Zinaida Gippius (1869–1945) was also bare of ornament, but this Pushkin-like feature was counterbalanced by a Lermontovian metaphysical *Sehnsucht*.

Apart from the movement stood Innokenty Annensky (1856–1909) whose nervous poetry, perfect in form, subtle and precise in expression, continues to be the object of admiration among poets, although the general public has never been particularly aware of him.

The next generation of Rus. symbolists had more right to use this name because in their literary works and activities aesthetic considerations were definitely subordinated to a mystical atmosphere and apocalyptic expectations. Individualistic self-assertion was clearly on the wane. A leading figure of the period was Vyacheslav Ivanov (1866–1949), scholarly and antidecadent in outlook. In his heavily ornamented, static, and priestly poems (*Cor ardens*), full of classical allusions, archaic diction, and "symbol-myths," he spoke about the coming transfiguration of the world, which would bring about the triumph of "collective individualism." But the real king of the Rus. poets of the 20th c. has so far been Alexander Blok (1880–1921) whose first success was the romantic and mystical *Stikhi o Prekrasnoy Dame* (Verses About the Beautiful Lady) with its atmosphere of eschatological expectation. Despite the fact that Blok lacked the erudition and sophistication of other leaders of the movement, he felt his symbolism more profoundly and sincerely; and his poetry, in which life and creation are blended, is full of ups and downs, moving from exaltation to disillusionment. Soon he abandoned celestial heights and plunged into reality, but this reality continued to be transformed by his mysticism for years to come, resulting in a most peculiar mixture of realism and mystical vision. The expectations alternate in his poems with moments of doubt, emptiness, gloom and despair. Romantic irony, blasphemy, and self-parody appear, as well as hauntingly beautiful cycles of love poetry. Blok's poems are uneven in quality, but the best of them are unique in the force of their passion and intoxicating rhythm and melody. His late poetry (*Strashny mir* [The Frightening World], *Vozmezdie* [Retaliation]) became increasingly tragic despite a short period of relief in his poems on Russia, which appeared now as the poet's wife, i.e., another incarnation of his mystical love. Blok accepted the revolution of 1917 in his enigmatic *poema Dvenadtsat'* (The Twelve) which not only astounded with contrasting images and rhythms, but also gave birth to a host of interpreters of its puzzling end in which twelve Red soldiers (the apostles of the new world) are preceded on their march by Jesus Christ. Blok's friend, and intermittently a foe, was Andrey Bely (1880–1934), another leader of Rus. symbolism and a complex figure who mixed solemn predictions with outright foolery in his brilliant poems. He changed style drastically and often, and was apt to produce a collection of abstract meditations (*Urna* [The Urn]) after a book containing realistic pictures of Rus. life (*Pepel* [Ashes]). Bely was a tireless experimenter in both prose and verse, especially in the field of rhythm, and he was probably the only Rus. symbolist who could be genuinely humorous.

Symbolism's universal aspirations and its constant aiming at overstepping the borders of art were bound to arouse an opposition. The poet Mikhail Kuzmin (1875–1936), who was close to symbolist circles and wrote verse of great charm, ease, and variety, demanded publicly a return to "beautiful clarity." This was soon followed by the neoclassicist movement of acmeism (q.v.) whose leaders protested symbolism's neglect of this world and the vagueness and "mistiness" of its doctrine. The acmeists also put a special emphasis on poetic craftsmanship, and the movement's recognized leader, Nikolay Gumilyov (1886–1921) also headed the Guild of Poets, to which many younger poets owed their technical brilliance. In his early poetry, Gumilyov had a particular predilection for the exotic, and he devoted a whole book to "geographic" poems about his favorite continent of Africa (*Shatyor* [The Tent]). He admired virility and glorified in his poems warriors, adventurers, and discoverers of new lands. War was to him an almost mystical activity and the natural outlet for human heroism. His best collection, *Ognenny stolp* (The Pillar of Fire), a book of great promise, was published after its author was executed for his participation in an anti-Soviet conspiracy. Gumilyov's wife, Anna Akhmatova (b. 1889), was a greater artist than her husband. She early became famous with her book of short love-poems, *Chotki* (Beads). These poetic cameos are little masterpieces of compactness. They are written in a conversational style, which Akhmatova later abandoned in the solemn and austere poems on the Russian war and revolution (*Anno Domini*). Akhmatova's most recent major work, the somber and obscure *Poema bez geroya* (The Poem Without a Hero), is autobiographical. The third great acmeist, Osip Mandelshtam (1891–1939) wrote militant critical essays in which he tried to deepen the rather flat aesthetics of the movement. In his neoclassicist verse (*Kamen'* [The Stone]), a keen feeling for history, especially classical antiquity, is revealed, and words are treated with perfect balance and strange detachment, so that his Rus. sounds like Latin. In Mandelshtam's best book, *Tristia*, there is a tendency toward loosening of semantics. His later poetry has a complex texture, but its theme remains the poet's dialogue with time in general and his own time in particular. Mandelshtam's poetry written in concentration

camps (where the poet died) was recently published outside Russia. It is poignant, though elusive, and occasionally reaches the heights of tragic lyricism.

Another reaction to symbolism was that of the Rus. futurists (see EGO-FUTURISM and CUBO-FUTURISM) who began their movement with a nihilistic rebellion against the past. Their poetry often sounded like a cross of the *poètes maudits* and the dadaists, but soon revealed not only points of affinity with the Rus. 18th c., but also a very productive doctrine of the essentially verbal nature of poetry. Their theories of the "self-oriented word" (*samovitoe slovo*) and the "trans-rational language" (*zaumny yazyk*) asserted that words are not simply means of expression, but the source and essence of poetry. The greatest poet of Rus. futurism was Victor (Velimir) Khlebnikov (1885–1922), a tireless experimenter with words, the creator of interesting linguistic mythology and a supreme craftsman. This bizarre and lonely man was also a Utopian dreamer who hoped to find the mathematical foundations of history. He combined, in a paradoxical way, rationalistic dreams of the harmonious future life based on science with attraction to the old Slavic past and an almost prehistoric mentality. The enormous variety of his work and his continuous mixing of forms and genres make Khlebnikov a difficult poet to classify, but his greatest poetic achievements are to be found among his numerous *poemy* in which he lovingly described the pagan world (*Vnuchka Malushi* [Malusha's Granddaughter]), created the best specimens of Rus. primitivistic idyll (*I i E*) and later portrayed revolution with genuine tragic art (*Nochnoy obysk* [A Night Search]). Khlebnikov was anti-Western and stressed the Asiatic ties of Russia. He was one of the strongest influences on Rus. poetry during the first years after the Communist revolution.

Another great poet with a futurist background was Vladimir Mayakovsky (1894–1930) whose loud and rebellious expressionist poems (*Oblako v shtanakh* [The Cloud in Pants]) are among the most original literary events of Russia just before the revolution. He wanted to create the poetry of the streets, extrovert and devoid of any sentimentality and sweetness, but in his work social satire and oratory alternate with some of the most passionate love poems ever written (*Fleyta-pozvonochnik* [The Spine Flute], *Pro eto* [About That]). Mayakovsky also created his own highly effective verse system, based on stress only, in which a word, rather than a line, was the unit. He used elaborate rhyme and had a predilection for hyperbole. After the revolution of 1917, Mayakovsky placed his work at the service of the Communist state and wrote some of the best Rus. propaganda poetry (*Vladimir Ilyich Lenin, Khorosho!* [It's Good!]). After his suicide, he was officially proclaimed the best poet of Soviet Russia, and he is still the poetic hero of the Soviet youth. Mayakovsky's rival in popular esteem, but until recently under a semi-ban, was Sergey Esenin (1895–1925), a boy from the village who attracted the attention of prerevolutionary poetic circles with his melodious verse about the Rus. countryside. For some time, he was associated with the Peasant Poets' group, which was headed by Nikolay Klyuev (1885–1937) who wrote heavily ornamented poetry, often based on the imagery of Rus. religious sects. Later, Esenin joined the modernist group of imagists, who considered the autonomous trope the basis of poetry and abundantly used it in their rudely erotic and blasphemous poems. Esenin became particularly popular after the revolution with his melancholic love poems which often stressed the theme of the end of the Rus. peasant's old way of life, so dear to the poet. Motives of death predominate in this poetry, and they further increase in his later "tavern" poems (*Moskva kabatskaya* [The Moscow of Saloons]) with their devil-may-care tragic abandon. Esenin's late poetry, written just before his suicide, produced both realistic, mildly humorous pictures of the Soviet village (*Rus' ukhodyashchaya* [The Disappearing Russia]) which he observed with a sad smile, and morbid alcoholic visions (*Chorny chelovek* [The Black Man]).

The 1920's were the most active period in the development of Soviet Rus. poetry. From the formal point of view, it was a continuation of the traditions of the prerevolutionary "Silver Age," with futurist ideas predominating. In subject matter, it was usually the poetry of factories and cosmic revolution (see SMITHY POETS) or the romanticism of the Civil War (Bagritsky, Aseev, Tikhonov). The group of constructivists (q.v.) aimed at an alliance between poetry and technology (Selvinsky). However, at the beginning of the 1930's, the government forced poetry, together with the rest of literature, to become part of its political machinery and to accept the method of "socialist realism" which can be best defined as party line in literature and art. After this, poets did whatever was required by the party. Most of them glorified Stalin's wisdom, extolled the collective farm labor or attacked capitalism and the alleged internal enemies of communism. During World War II, spontaneous patriotism produced a few sincere poetic works (Simonov, Tvardovsky), but it failed to create great poetry or major poets. The only new name during this decade is Nikolay Zabolotsky (1903–58), who began as a master of satirical grotesque, but, after criticism, switched over to the more acceptable Soviet brand of neoclassicism. Neither was the postwar period very productive in this respect. Recently the young Evgeny Evtushenko (b. 1933) has attracted much attention both inside and outside Russia with his energetic and often courageous poetry reflecting the new Soviet generation's search for truth, and characterized by mastery of realistic detail and a mild tendency to formal innovation (mainly in rhyme). However, the most consistent representative of Soviet nonconformism remains the towering, lonely figure of Boris Pasternak (1890–1960), who began his poetic activities before the revolution as a moderate futurist, but very soon found his individual voice. In most of his poems, he remained a poet of nature and love, and he stubbornly refused to write poetic propaganda for the creation of the new society according to official prescriptions. In one of his poems he said:

The great Soviet gives to the highest passions
In these brave days each one its rightful place,
Yet vainly leaves one vacant for the poet.
When that's not empty, look for danger's face.

For decades, Pasternak was severely criticized for his apolitical attitude and was finally forced to turn exclusively to translating. His outstanding feature as a poet is his combination of culture and sophistication with intense passion and freshness. In his rushing, syntactically complex lines, colloquialisms jostle "poetic" words, and unexpected metaphors are created by free association. There is a special vision of life in his poetry. Things come alive, the commonplace becomes strange, and natural optimism reigns. Pasternak's most famous book of poems remains his early *Sestra moya zhizn'* (My Sister Life). His late poems, while remaining primarily poetry of nature, show more preoccupation with moral and religious problems, especially the poems concluding his novel *Dr. Zhivago*. The diction is more simple, and the general tone shows more restraint.

The poetry of the Rus. exiles has never had enough attention from critics, and yet its achievements were not inferior to those of the poets who remained after the revolution in their country. The émigré literature concentrated in Paris, and there numerous poets contributed to what was later named "the Parisian tone" (*parizhskaya nota*). It is the poetry of simplicity and brevity, which avoided loud tone and stressed the theme of human loneliness. However, the greatest poets of Rus. exile belonged to the older generation and had begun their careers before the revolution, although they fully developed only in emigration. Vladislav Khodasevich (1886–1939) was the virtual head and the feared critic of Rus. poets in Paris. Being a scholar of note, he

RUSSIAN PROSODY

consciously imitated the style of the Pushkin period, but in content his mystical poetry was a direct descendant of symbolism. There is a deep discord in it between the "quiet inferno" of this ugly world and the regions where the soul dwells (*Tyazholaya lira* [The Heavy Lyre]). The growing despair at the inability of poetry to change the state of things led Khodasevich to the poetic silence near the end of his life. Quite different was the loud-voiced and high-pitched poetry of Marina Tsvetaeva (1892–1941) who lived in poverty in exile and then returned to Russia only to commit suicide there. Rus. folklore, the Rus. 18th c., Goethe and Rilke are combined in her rhythmically luxurious and verbally magnificent poems, full of archaic diction and colloquialisms, high rhetoric and intimate confessions,, genuine passion and verbal virtuosity (*Remeslo* [Craft], *Posle Rossii* [After Russia]). In poetry, as in life, she yearned for true nobility and never failed to defend lost causes (*Lebediny stan* [The Camp of Swans]) or move against the stream, and, as a consequence, she was an outcast wherever she lived. Probably the greatest Rus. lyric poet in exile was Georgy Ivanov (1894–1958) who began as a minor acmeist, but developed into a major poetic force in Paris. His diary-like poetry, where he now indulged in irresponsible *jemenfoutisme*, now created poems of almost unbearable beauty, was the logical conclusion of the period of Alexander Blok. Melancholy at the loss of his native country develops in it into a cynical nihilism and the conviction that art and beauty have deceived man (*Portret bez skhodstva* [A Portrait Without Likeness]). In his poems, there is a combination of utter simplicity and brevity with elusiveness, of modern consciousness with a nostalgia for things past, and of acid beauty with a desire to tease the reader.

ANTHOLOGIES: *Specimens of the Rus. Poets*, tr. J. Bowring (2 v., 1821, 1823); *Russkaya poeziya*, ed. S. A. Vengerov (issues I-VII, 1893–97; the most complete anthol. of the 18th-c. poetry); L. Wiener, *Anthol. of Rus. Lit. from the Earliest Period to the Present Time* (2 v., 1902–3); Yu. N. Verkhovsky, *Poety pushkinskoy pory* (1919; standard anthol. of the poets of Pushkin's time); *Rus. poetry, an Anthol.*, tr. B. Deutsch and A. Yarmolinsky (1927); *Russkaya lirika, malen'kaya antologiya ot Lomonosova do Pasternaka*, ed. D. Mirsky (1924; the best little anthol.); I. S. Ezhov and E. I. Shamurin, *Russkaya poeziya XX veka* (1925;

standard); N. K. Chadwick, *Rus. Heroic Poetry* (1932); *Soviet Lit., an Anthol.*, ed. and tr. G. Reavey and M. Slonim (1934); *Modern Poems from Russia*, tr. G. Shelley (1942); *A Book of Rus. Verse*, ed. C. M. Bowra (1943); *Three Rus. Poets, Selections from Pushkin, Lermontov and Tyutchev*, tr. V. Nabokov (1944); *The Oxford Book of Rus. Verse* (2d ed., 1948; Rus. texts, Eng. preface and commentaries); *A Second Book of Rus. Verse*, ed. C. M. Bowra (1948); *Priglushonnye golosa, Poeziya za zheleznym zanavesom*, ed. V. Markov (1952; the best poetry by the best Rus. poets who lived in Soviet Russia); Yu. P. Ivask, *Na zapade* (1953; the widest selection of Rus. poets in exile); *Antologiya russkoy sovetskoy poezii, 1917–1957*, ed. V. Lugovskoy et al. (2 v., 1957; the most complete recent Soviet anthol.); *Poety XVIII veka*, ed. G. P. Makogonenko (2 v., 1958, the latest anthol. of the poets of the 18th c.); *Russkie poety XIX veka*, ed. N. Gaydenkov (1958; the widest sel. of 19th-c. poets). *Russkoe narodnoe poeticheskoe tvorchestvo*, ed. E. V. Pomerantseva and S. I. Mints (1959; the latest anthol. of Rus. folklore); *An Anthol. of Rus. Verse 1812–1960*, ed. A. Yarmolinsky (1962).

HISTORY AND CRITICISM: I. N. Rozanov, *Russkaya lirika* (1914; standard on the end of the 18th c. and the beginning of the 19th c.); L. A. Magnus, *The Heroic Ballads of Russia* (1921); D. S. Mirsky, *Pushkin* (1926); V. Khodasevich, *Nekropol'* (1939; brilliant portraits of some of the leading figures of the poetical "Silver Age"); A. S. Kaun, *Soviet Poets and Poetry* (1942); N. K. Gudzy, *Hist. of Early Rus. Lit.* (1949); D. S. Mirsky, *A Hist. of Rus. Lit.* (1949); L. Strakhovsky, *Craftsmen of the Word, Three Poets of Modern Russia* (1949); M. Slonim, *The Epic of Rus. Lit.* (1950); Y. M. Sokolov, *Rus. Folklore* (1950); G. Struve, *Soviet Rus. Lit., 1917–1950* (1951); O. A. Maslenikov, *The Frenzied Poets, Andrey Biely and the Rus. Symbolists* (1952); M. Slonim, *Modern Rus. Lit., From Chekhov to the Present* (1953); Akademiya Nauk SSR, *Istoriya russkoy literatury* (10 v., 1941–54); G. Struve, *Russkaya literatura v izgnanii* (1956; standard on Rus. lit. in exile); B. O. Unbegaun, *Rus. Versification* (1956); R. Poggioli, *The Poets of Russia, 1890–1930* (1960); D. D. Blagoy, *Istoriya russkoy literatury XVIII veka* (preferably last ed., 1960; standard).　V.M.

RUSSIAN PROSODY. See SLAVIC PROSODY.

S

S.M. Abbreviation for short measure or meter. Hymn stanza.

SANSKRIT POETRY. See INDIAN POETRY.

SAPPHIC. An important Aeolic (q.v.) verse form named after Sappho, a Gr. poetess from Lesbos of the 7th-6th c. B.C. The S. stanza consists of three Lesser S. lines

$$-\cup-\cup\breve{\cup}-\cup\cup-\cup\breve{\cup}$$

followed by one Adonic

or Adoneus, $-\cup\cup-\breve{\cup}$

Sappho's contemporary, Alcaeus, also used the stanza and may have been its inventor. Catullus (84–54 B.C.?) made an adaptation of one of Sappho's odes (Catullus 51) and composed another in the meter (Catullus 11); with these poems he probably introduced the S. into L. poetry, but it is not certain. Horace (65–8 B.C.) provided the S. model for subsequent Roman and European poets; he used the meter 27 times, second in frequency only to the alcaics (q.v.) among his poems. Horace also makes a single use of the Greater S. strophe, i.e., an Aristophanic ($-\cup\cup-\cup\breve{>}$) followed by a Greater S. line ($-\cup\cup->-\|\cup\cup-\|$ $-\cup\cup-\cup->$). Seneca (4 B.C.–A.D. 65) sometimes uses the separate elements in a different order, e.g., by arranging a continuous series of longer lines with an Adonic clausula. The S. stanza is today read in two quite different ways. We may stress the long third and fifth syllables ("integer vitae") or the fourth and sixth syllables, which in the Horatian pattern bear the word accent ("integer vitae scelerisque purus"). This second method is suggested by medieval rhyme in, e.g.,

vita sanctórum, decus angelórum.

Late medieval German Sapphics are rhymed.

The stanza was popular with poets and metricians in Italy, France (see CLASSICAL METERS IN MODERN LANGUAGES), Germany, England, and Spain during the Renaissance and, in varying extent, during later periods. Leonardo Dati used it for the first time in It. (1441, cf. HEXAMETER). He was followed by Galeotto del Carretto (1455–1530), Claudio Tolomei (1492–1555), and others. Felice Cavallotti (1842–98) experimented with the Horatian Greater S. Spain's Estéban de Villegas (1589–

1669) is the chief practitioner of this meter in his country. In the 18th c. F. G. Klopstock varied an unrhymed stanza with regular positional changes of the trisyllabic foot in the Lesser S. lines; H. von Platen and others in Germany sustained the strict Horatian form. The Victorians, Tennyson and Swinburne in particular, included Sapphics among their many reproductions of classical meter.

Recent examples of the S. ode are in abundance. Translators of Horace and Catullus are constantly attracted by the deceptively simple scheme, e.g.

... I'll adore my Lalage's pleasant laughter,
pleasant discoursing.
(J. B. Leishman)

For an example of original Sapphics today see Ezra Pound's *Apparuit*, one stanza of which reads as follows: "Half the graven shoulder, the throat aflash with / strands of light inwoven about it, loveli- / est of all things, frail alabaster, ah me! / swift in departing."—For bibliography, see CLASSICAL METERS IN MODERN LANGUAGES. Also, G. Mazzoni, "Per la storia della saffica in Italia," *Atti* dell' Acc. Scienze lett. arti, 10 (1894); C. H. Moore, *Horace . . .* (1902), 42; H. G. Atkins, *A Hist. of German Versification* (1923); G. Highet, *The Cl. Tradition* (1949); Koster; Navarro.   R.A.S.

SATANIC SCHOOL. A term applied in the early 19th c. to a group of romantic poets, it was originated by Robert Southey in his preface to *A Vision of Judgment,* an attack on Shelley, Keats, and, especially, Byron. Southey attacked the second generation of Eng. romantics on the basis of an alleged immorality in their work and lives, coupled with their rejection of the revelations of the Christian religion. The term "Satanic school" seems in particular to designate that interest in the exotic, the passionate, the violent, and the perverse which distinguishes one group of romantics. Moreover, Southey's condemnation was susceptible of extension to other Eng. poets—Leigh Hunt and Thomas Moore, for example. Some critics (M. Praz, *The Romantic Agony,* 2d ed., 1951) have associated this attitude with the Marquis de Sade. Continental poets who show such "Satanic" elements include Hugo, Musset, and Baudelaire in France, and Kleist in Germany.

SATIRE, says Dr. Johnson, is "a poem in which wickedness or folly is censured"; and more elaborate definitions are rarely more satisfactory. No strict definition can encompass the complexity of a word which signifies, on one hand, a kind of literature, and on the other, a spirit or tone which expresses itself in many literary genres. The difficulty is pointed up by a phrase of Quintilian (*Institutio Oratoria*, 10.93): "satura [as opposed to other literary forms] tota nostra est"; Quintilian seems to be claiming s. as a wholly Roman phenomenon, although he had read Aristophanes, and was familiar with a number of Gr. forms that we would call satiric. The point is that by *satura* (which meant originally something like "medley" and from which comes our "satire") he intended to specify that kind of poem "invented" by Lucilius, written in hexameters on certain appropriate themes, dominated by a Lucilian-Horatian tone. *Satura* referred, in short, to a poetic form, established and fixed by Roman practice. After Quintilian's day the signification of the term broadened to include works that were "satirical" in tone, but not in form; then, according to Hendrickson, from Gr. *satyros* and its derivatives were appropriated terms which became our *satirist, satiric, satirize*, etc. This confused etymology made for confusion: *satura* was modified orthographically into *satyra* and then, in Eng., into *satyre*. Elizabethan writers, anxious to follow classical models but misled by a false etymology, believed that "satyre" derived from the Gr. satyr-play; satyrs being notoriously rude, unmannerly creatures, "spiers out of . . . secret faults," it seemed to follow that "satyre" should be harsh, coarse, rough:

The *Satyre* should be like the *Porcupine*,
That shoots sharp quilles out in each angry
    line. . . .
                    (Hall, *Virgidemiarum*, 5.3)

Isaac Casaubon exposed the false etymology of the satire-satyr relation in 1605; but the tradition has remained strong.

The formal verse s. as composed by Horace, Persius, and Juvenal is the only satiric form to have even a remotely determinate structure, and it furnishes exceptions to every generalization ("qui dit satire latine, dit mélange," writes Lejay). Generally speaking, the formal s. is a quasi-dramatic poem, "framed" by an encounter between the Satirist (or, more reasonably, his *persona*, the "I" of the poem) and an Adversarius who impels the satirist to speech. Within this frame, as M. C. Randolph has shown, vice and folly are exposed to critical analysis by means of any number of literary and rhetorical devices: the satirist may use beast fables, Theophrastian "characters," dramatic incidents, fictional experiences, anecdotes, proverbs, homilies; he may employ invective, sarcasm, irony, mockery, raillery, exaggeration, understatement—wit in any of its forms—anything to make the object of attack abhorrent or ridiculous. Complementing this negative aspect of the poem is a positive appeal, explicit or implicit, to virtue and rational behavior—to a norm, that is, against which the vicious and the foolish are to be judged. Thus, though the materials of the s. are astonishingly varied, there is pressure toward order internally from the arraignment of vice and appeal to virtue, and externally from the (often shadowy) dramatic situation which frames the poem.

Formal satires are written in the middle style; they are discursive, colloquial, as befits a form unremittingly aware of its low estate in the hierarchy of genres. Juvenal's occasional self-conscious flights into the grand style, however, sanctioned the "tragicall" s. of later writers, and his *saeva indignatio* contrasts with the tone of urbane mockery characteristic of Horace.

In addition to attacking vice and folly on nearly all levels, the formal satirist has from the beginning felt impelled to justify his ungrateful art. His *apologiae* (Horace, 1.4; 2.1; Persius, 1; Juvenal, 1; Régnier, 12; Boileau, 9; Pope, *Epistle to Dr. Arbuthnot*) are conventional; they project an image of the satirist as a plain honest man, wishing harm to no upright person, but appalled at the evil he sees about him and forced by his conscience (*facit indignatio versum*) to write s. Readers have not always been convinced. While the influence of Roman practice on later satirists in matters of theme, point of view, tone, literary and rhetorical device, etc., has been enormous, relatively few poets have attempted to adapt precisely the Roman form. Boileau and Pope are great exceptions.

The satiric spirit as it is manifested in verse seems to appear (whether as mockery, raillery, ridicule, or formalized invective) in the literature or folklore of all peoples, early and late, preliterate and civilized. According to Aristotle (*Poetics* 4. 1448^b–1449^a), Gr. Old Comedy developed out of ritualistic invective—out of satiric utterances, that is, improvised and hurled at individuals by the Leaders of the Phallic Songs. The function of these "iambic" utterances was magical, as F. M. Cornford has shown; they were thought to drive away evil influences so that the positive fertility magic of the phallus might be operative. This early connection of primitive "s." with magic has a remarkably widespread history. Archilochus (7th c. B.C.), the "first" Gr. literary satirist, composed iambics of such potency against Lycambes that he and his daughters are said to have hung themselves. In the next century the sculptors Bupalus and Athenis "knit their necks in halters," it is said, as a result of the "bitter rimes and biting libels" of the satirical poet Hipponax. Similar tales exist in other cultures. The chief function of the ancient Arabic poet was to compose s. (*hijá*) against the tribal enemy. The satires were thought always to be fatal and the poet led his people into battle, hurling his verses as he would hurl a spear. Old Ir. literature is laced with accounts of the extraordinary power of the poets, whose satires brought disgrace and death to their victims: ". . . saith [King] Lugh to his poet, 'what power can *you* wield in battle?' 'Not hard to say,' quoth Carpre '. . . I will satirize them and shame them, so that through the spell of my art they will not resist warriors'" (*The Second Battle of Moytura*, tr. W. Stokes, *Revue Celtique*, 12 [1891], 91–92). (F. N. Robinson adduces linguistic, thematic, and other evidence to show a functional relation between primitive s., like that of Carpre, and the "real" s. of more sophisticated times.) Today, among the Eskimo, the loss of a duel in s. (the drum-match, in which two enemies alternately hurl verses of ridicule and abuse at each other) may lead to exile and even death. Primitive s. such as that described above can hardly be spoken of in literary terms; its affiliations are rather with the magical incantation and the curse.

When the satiric utterance breaks loose from its background in ritual and magic, as in ancient Greece (when it is free, that is, to develop according to literary rather than "practical" impulsions), it is found embodied in an indefinite number of literary forms which profess to convey moral instruction by means of laughter, ridicule, mockery—forms such as Aristophanic comedy, the Bionean diatribe, the mime, the beast fable, the Theophrastian character, etc., all of which contribute to the developed formal s. of Rome. But the spirit which informs them is too mercurial to be confined to exclusive literary structures; it proliferates everywhere, adapting itself to whatever mode (verse or prose) seems congenial. Its range is enormous: from an anonymous medieval invective against social injustice to the superb wit of some of Chaucer's portraits and the somber power of the Vision of Piers the Ploughman; from the burlesque of Pulci to the scurrilities of Aretino; from the flailings of Marston and the mordancies of Quevedo to the bite of La Fontaine and the great dramatic structures of Jonson and Molière.

By and large the satiric spirit seems to fuse most readily with the comic genres: when s. was prohibited by law in Elizabethan England, and it was ordered that the verses of Hall and Marston be burned, the satirists turned promptly to the comic drama ("comicall

satyre") as the form most appropriate for their purposes. But, as in all generalizations about s., the qualifications are important. Juvenal deliberately sought to rise above the prescriptive bounds of the comic; at the end of the scarifying Sixth S. he enforces a comparison in theme and tone with Sophocles. In the modern Age of S. Alexander Pope catches beautifully, when he likes, the deft Horatian tone; but his wit (like that of Dryden in *Absalom and Achitophel*) is also a serious wit, deeply probing and prophetic. The last lines of the *Dunciad* rise to a terrifying sublimity as they celebrate the restoration of chaos, the obliterating triumph of the anti-Logos. Such passages transcend easy generic distinctions.

The private motivations of the satirist we cannot know. The public function of s.—how it works in its social, psychological, cultural dimensions—we understand only obscurely. (Approaches to these problems by way of psychoanalytic theory, cultural anthropology, etc., are promising; e.g., the work of E. Kris and E. H. Gombrich on caricature in Kris, *Psychoanalytic Explorations in Art* [1952].) But the public motivation of the satirist is explicit and self-justificatory; he writes, so he claims, to reform. His audience may be small (a few "right-thinking men") but it must share with him commitment to certain intellectual and moral beliefs which validate his critique of aberration. Ridicule, which in some cultures may kill and in our own kills symbolically, depends on shared assumptions against which the aberrant stands in naked relief. The greatest s. has been written in periods when ethical and rational norms were sufficiently powerful to attract widespread assent, yet not so powerful as to compel absolute conformity—those periods when the satirist could be of his society and apart from it; could exercise the "double vision." Neoclassic poets had available to them as a kind of implicit metaphor the mighty standard of the classical past; witness the success in the period of the mock-heroic genres. These mock not primarily the ancient forms (although there may be affectionate laughter at some aspects of the epic) but present society, which in the context of past grandeur shows contemptible and mean.

The 20th c., like the 19th, lacks such available norms; but unlike the 19th (Byron's *Vision of Judgment* and *Don Juan* and Heine's *Atta Troll* are hardly characteristic of their period) it has a taste for s. Yet though this may be a satirical age, it is hardly an age of great verse s. The alienation of poet from society is notorious; and when the poet has struggled through to the adoption of beliefs and values adequate to his needs, it is a question whether they will serve as metaphors for poetry. Three exceptions (to speak only of poets writing in Eng.) may be noted: Yeats, his vision radically private, and Eliot, his values at the time of *The Waste Land* generally religious, have both written powerful s.; and Auden, his orientation at first social-political, later religious, has demonstrated that a poet writing consciously within the 18th-c. satiric tradition can speak sharply, eloquently, effectively—can speak *satirically*—even to our fragmented society.

J. Dryden, "A Discourse concerning the Original and Progress of S." (1693), *Works*, ed. W. Scott and G. Saintsbury (1882–93), XIII, 1–123; P. Lejay, "Les origines et la nature de la satire d'Horace," in his ed. of Horace, *Satires* (1911); F. N. Robinson, "Satirists and Enchanters in Early Ir. Lit.," *Studies in the Hist. of Religions. . .*, ed. D. G. Lyon and G. F. Moore (1912); H. Walker, *English S. and Satirists* (1925); G. L. Hendrickson, "Archilochus and the Victims of his Iambics," AJP, 46 (1925) and "Satura tota nostra est," CP, 22 (1927); J. W. Duff, *Roman S.* (1936); O. J. Campbell, *Comicall Satyre* (1938); V. Cian, *La satira* (2 v., 1939); D. Worcester, *The Art of S.* (1940); M. C. Randolph, "The Structural Design of the Formal Verse S.," PQ, 21 (1942); I. Jack, *Augustan S.* (1952); M. Mack, "The Muse of S.," *Studies in the Lit. of the Augustan Age*, ed. R. C. Boys (1952); J. Peter, *S. and Complaint in Early Eng. Lit.* (1956); J. Sutherland, *Eng. S.* (1958); A. Kernan, *The Cankered Muse* (1959); R. C. Elliott, *The Power of S.* (1960); G. Highet, *The Anatomy of S.* (1962).   R.C.E.

SATURA. See SATIRE.

SATURNIAN. This early L. meter, related as it was subsequently by the imagination of Roman writers to the age of Saturn, is generally thought to have been indigenous, although Caesius Bassus (1st c. A.D.) held that its ultimate source was a Gr. lyric verse of the type:

Ĕrăsmŏnīdĕ Chărílāe, || chrēmă tŏī gĕloīŏn.

Whether it was quantitative or accentual remains an unsolved problem because of the perplexing variety displayed by the 160 or so lines which survive in inscriptions and in the epic fragments of the poets Livius Andronicus and Naevius (second half of 3d c. B.C.). The lines, however, are regularly divisible into two cola, between which elision of vowels plays no part, e.g.

vǐrum mǐhi, Cāmēnă, || īnsēcĕ vērsūtum,

where the presumed metrical stresses indicate the rhythm of Macaulay's famous imitation:

The queén was ín her párlour || eating bread

, and honey

and are those of the quantitative theory whereby, at any rate in this example, the first colon has the appearance of an iambic dimeter catalectic and the second that of an ithyphallic. Accentual scansion on the other hand, according to the law of the penultimate, would give:

vírum míhi, Caména, || ínsece versútum.

Lines like this with 7 syllables in the first colon and 6 in the second or 13 in all are more common than those with a total of 12 or 14. After Naevius the Saturnian disappeared from L. literature, and the hexameter took its place as the meter of epic. Horace's description of the *horridus numerus Saturnius* as an offensive poison (*grave virus*) is an example of later taste in regard to it.—W. Beare, "*Pollicis Ictus*, the Saturnian, and *Beowulf*," CP, 50 (1955; good discussion of previous views and argument that the rival theories concerning quantity and accent are largely unreal) and *L. Verse and European Song* (1957); F. Novotný, "De versu Saturnio," *Studia Salač* (1955); G. B. Pighi, "Il Verso Saturnio," *Rivista di filologia e di istruzione classica*, 35 (1957); P. W. Harsh, *Lustrum* 3 (1958); R. G. Tanner, "The Arval Hymn and Early Latin Verse," CQ n.s., 11 (1961).   R.J.G.

SCALD. See SKALD.

SCANSION. The system of describing more or less conventional poetic rhythms by visual symbols for purposes of metrical analysis and study. Three methods of scanning Eng. verse are generally recognized: the graphic, the musical, and the acoustic. The primary symbols most commonly used in traditional graphic s. are: ˟ or ˘ representing a syllable which, in poetic context, is unstressed; and ′ or –, representing a syllable which is stressed. Secondary symbols are: |, representing a division between feet; and ||, representing a caesura (q.v.). In performing s. of a line or group of lines, the reader first marks stressed and unstressed syllables, not according to any preconceived pattern, but according to the degree of sense emphasis transmitted by the syllables. For example:

I sométimes thínk that néver blóws so réd

The Róse as whére some buríed Caésar bled;

That évery Hyácinth the Gárden wéars

Dropt ín her láp from some ónce lóvely héad.
(FitzGerald, *The Rubaiyat*)

After ascertaining whether the lines are generally in ascending or descending rhythm (q.v.), the reader next marks the feet, as follows:

Í some|times thínk | that ne|ver blóws | so réd |

The Róse | as where|some bur|ied Cae|sar bléd;|

That év|ery Hy|acinth | the Gár|den wears |

Drópt ín | her láp | from sóme | once love|ly head. |

S. does not make rhythm: it reveals it by transferring it from a temporal into a spatial dimension. By giving the reader a visual representation of the metrical situation underlying the words of the poem, s. helps to make clear the function of metrical variations (q.v.): in the fourth line of FitzGerald's stanza, for example, the s. makes visually apparent the substitution of a trochee for the expected iamb in the first position; this variation reinforces the suddenness and the rapidity of the fall of the drops of blood.

The s. of the following stanza also serves to reveal in visual symbols meaningful variations from the expected metrical pattern:

Her líps| were réd, | her lóoks | were frée, |

Her lócks |were yel|low as góld: |

Her skín | was whíte | as lep|rosy, |

The Níght|mare Life|-in-Death | was shé, |

Who thícks | men's blóod | with cóld. |
(Coleridge, *Rime of the Ancient Mariner*)

Here the s. of the last line reveals that a spondaic substitution has occurred in the second position, and that the added metrical weight performs the function of reinforcing the sense of the slow, heavy movement of chilled and thickened blood (see METRICAL VARIATIONS).

Total stanzaic structure is often recorded by indicating the rhyme scheme in letters, and the number of feet per line in numbers. For example, the FitzGerald stanza may be represented thus: $a\ a\ b\ a_5$; and the Coleridge thus: $a_4b_3aa_4b_3$.

Some prosodists reject the traditional graphic s. symbols, as illustrated above, and use instead musical symbols. In s. systems of this kind, eighth notes may represent unstressed syllables and quarter or half notes stressed syllables of varying degrees of emphasis. Caesuras are sometimes indicated by musical rests of various lengths. Musical s. has the advantage of representing more accurately than graphic s. delicate differences in degree of stress: it is obvious to anyone that an Eng. line has more than two "kinds" of syllables in it, and yet graphic s.,

preferring convenience to accuracy, gives the impression that any syllable in a line is either clearly stressed or clearly unstressed. On the other hand, the major disadvantage of musical s. is its complexity; a lesser disadvantage is that it tends to imply that poetry follows musical principles, an assumption not universally accepted.

The third method of s., the acoustic, has been developed by modern linguists working with such machines as the kymograph and the oscillograph. Like musical s., it is a system advantageous in the accuracy of its representations of the empirical phenomena of spoken verse but disadvantageous in its complexity.

Some theorists reject all three kinds of s. and prefer to mark the rhythmical movements of verse by cadences (q.v.), often indicated by wavy lines or brackets drawn above the poetic line.

E. Smith, *The Principles of Eng. Metre* (1923; on the s. of free verse); Y. Winters, *Primitivism and Decadence* (1937; free verse); "Eng. Verse and What It Sounds Like," KR, 18 (1956; articles by J. C. Ransom and others); W. K. Wimsatt, Jr. and M. C. Beardsley, "The Concept of Meter: an Exercise in Abstraction," PMLA, 74 (1959; on the s. of Eng. verse).   P.F.

SCAZON. See CHOLIAMBUS.

SCHOOL OF NIGHT. A philosophical and literary society believed by some scholars to have existed in England in the closing years of the 16th c. Among its members are supposed to have been Sir Walter Raleigh (its founder and patron), the poets Chapman and Marlowe, and the mathematician Harriot. The existence of the society as such cannot be definitely proved. Modern scholars who accept its existence (the theory was first pronounced by Arthur Acheson, *Shakespeare and the Rival Poet*, 1903) see Chapman's obscure and ambitious poems *The Shadow of Night* and *Ovid's Banquet of Sense* as expressions of the group's theologico-scientific interests and esoteric learning, particularly in his use of "night" as the symbol of divine and hidden knowledge. The writers associated with the group had an undeserved contemporary reputation for atheism, due no doubt to their relation to the modernist thought which was beginning to shake Europe at that time, but in their grandiose pretensions as in their enthusiastic classicism they were typical late-Renaissance men. The "school of night" theory relies heavily for specific evidence on an interpretation of Shakespeare's *Love's Labour's Lost* 4.3.254: "O paradox! Black is the badge of hell, / The hue of dungeons, and the school of night," which is seen as a satiric reference to the esoteric and learned claims of the group.

But the passage, undoubtedly puzzling and often emended, admits of diverse readings, and the "school of night" theory remains an unproved, if fascinating, hypothesis.—M. C. Bradbrook, *The School of Night* (1936); J. H. P. Pafford, "Schoole of Night," N&Q, 202 (1957). See also J. D. Wilson's comments in his 2d ed. (1962) of *LLL*.   F.J.W.

SCHOOL OF SPENSER. A group of Eng. poets of the earlier 17th c., strongly under the influence of Edmund Spenser (1552-99). Their work is sharply distinguished from the more radical poetic movements of the time, movements epitomized by the classicism of Jonson and by the "metaphysical" (q.v.) style of Donne. The principal poets of the Spenserian school —Browne, Wither, Giles, and Phineas Fletcher, and the Scottish poets Drummond of Hawthornden and Sir William Alexander—show the influence of Spenser in their sensuous imagery, their smooth meter, their archaic diction, and their fondness for narrative and pastoral modes of expression. They also owe to Spenser their allegorical and moral tendencies. Such ambitious narrative poems as Giles Fletcher's *Christ's Victory and Triumph* and Phineas Fletcher's *The Apollyonists* suggest Spenser's *Faerie Queene* in their pictorial quality and in their stanzaic forms (modified Spenserian); they also anticipate Milton, who, occasionally echoing the Fletchers, follows them in the use of Christian material for epic purposes and himself acknowledged his indebtedness to Spenser whom he termed *master*.

SCHÜTTELREIM. A double rhyme based on the principle of the Spoonerism, that is, on the transposition or "shaking" of the initial consonants of two words or syllables. It lends itself peculiarly well to humorous and satirical verse in German. It is found in couplets or in longer line series, some of which have become popular quotations while their authors have been forgotten, e.g., "Nicht jeder, der da freite zwo, ward über seine zweite froh," or "Als Gottes Atem leiser ging, schuf er den Grafen Keyserling" (attributed to Friedrich Gundolf). The shortest known Sch. is "Du bist Buddhist." Regine Mirsky-Tauber (*Schüttelreime*, 1904) and Anton Kippenberg (*Benno Papentrigks Schüttelreime*, 1943) have written whole cycles of light verse in this form. U.K.G.

SCIENCE AND POETRY. I. INTRODUCTORY. In a general way, the relation between sci. and poetry has had its critics since Plato's suggestion in *The Republic* that there may be a fundamental opposition between the aims of the poet and those of the philosopher. Clearly, the relation could not be considered in modern terms until sci. itself assumed its present forms.

There is general agreement that modern sci. emerged during the 17th c., when the rival claims of sci. and poetry (truth and fiction, method and imagination) were first examined in ways that would sound familiar to a reader of Matthew Arnold's "Literature and Sci." or I. A. Richards' *Sci. and Poetry*.

Comments on sci. and poetry have in every period of history ranged far beyond the limits suggested by the phrase "sci. vs. poetry." An adequate treatment of the subject must approach it from two directions—historical and analytical. But because of the philosophic nature of the problem, attitudes and positions overlap, so that they cannot always be confined within given categories and under fixed rubrics. Both approaches must recognize that comments on sci. and poetry are related to larger assumptions about the place of each in the scheme of human knowledge.

The Aristotelian approach was to lead to considerations of a rapprochement between sci. and poetry. This was to be effected through an interplay of disciplines in a widening conception of the nature of poetry on the one hand and of knowledge or sci. on the other. Neoplatonists from Plotinus to the romantic period felt that art was an avenue to absolute truth and that it was therefore one of the highest of the sciences. And where poetry was related to divine inspiration and revelation, it was free of any opposition to sci.

The "system of the sciences" derived from Aristotle was passed on to the high Middle Ages in a tripartite division of the theoretical, the rational, and the practical categories, all "scientific" in the sense that they were concerned with truth. The question of poetry vs. sci. did not arise. There was a swerving between the idea that poetry was only a secondary rhetoric and as such was deficient in knowledge, and the notion that the absorption of sci. in poetry made the latter a worthy vehicle of all knowledge. When it was considered as a "theoretical sci.," poetry became a method of discovering ultimate truth, as well as a vehicle for philosophy (as in Lucretius).

The chief concern from the 17th c. down to our present day has been the mind's tilting with a pervasive dualism which would keep poetry and sci. apart as two antithetic activities of mental operation. Entrenched in the argument for dualism is a vulgar or crude empiricism. In one form or another, it is the basis of most discussions involving the relation of poetry and sci. For Kant, the fountainhead of idealism, there was no opposition between art and sci.; though they are different modes of intellection, they are both implicated in the contemplation of phenomena. "A rose is a rose is a rose" is as valid a statement as "A rose is a plant." Sci. and poetry are distinguished in that the scientist refers the phenomenon to a law "explaining" it (the fall of an apple—the law of gravitation), whereas the poet and his reader—once the phenomenon has been expressed in significant form—appreciate it for its own sake as a unique experience. Thus, in the light of recent testimony by both scientists and poets, the neo-Kantian tendency to associate sci. with abstraction and poetry with particularity is an oversimplification.

Historically, our problem takes us, in the classical period, from Plato for whom the poet was impractical and remote from truth to Aristotle who looked upon art as a force complementary to nature and upon poetry as capable of reducing contraries to harmonious form and in this respect contributing to knowledge. From the Plotinian affinity between subject and object and the Augustinian opposition to dualism we move to a nexus between sense (poetry) and truth. For Scholasticism, poetry was a secondary rhetoric, and the true *scientia* was beyond reason. During the Renaissance, the so-called Dante quarrel turned upon the merits of his linking in his poetic work ethics, philosophy, and sci. The tension between the desire for knowledge and the urgency of the expression of feeling made itself felt in the Renaissance, one of whose chief preoccupations was sci. Elizabethan psychology and astronomy certainly are fundamental to the poetry of the period. The metaphor of the circle, inherited from the Greeks, appealed to the 17th-c. imagination largely because it symbolized a "unified sensibility" which resulted when thought and feeling were brought together. *Paradise Lost* registers the "tension between the inner and the outer life of man." The 18th c. that gave rise to the concept of man as a machine (La Mettrie) was rife with divisiveness between the claims of reason (sci.) and desire (imagination, poetry). With the romantic movement, we enter a period when, in spite of dissident voices (like that of Peacock), poetic genius was conceived of as having the power to encompass scientific insight as well as intuitive penetration. Yet it is true that much of romantic theory turned on the disparity between imaginative and scientific perception. Coleridge, whose potency is felt in present-day criticism, was for a conjunction of poetry and sci., because he held, as Hegel did, that man's highest faculty included both the emotional and rational elements. Even the 19th-c. positivist Buckle argued that there was an organic relationship between poetry and sciences "simply because the emotions are a part of the mind." In the latter part of the century, Matthew Arnold reiterated the plea for wholeness.

Analytically, we find in current viewpoints a continued tension between the claims of poetry and sci. as well as an effort to relate them in a theory of cognition. Man among his machines has still not been emptied of desire and idealism. To save himself from fragmentation, he resorts, in both sci. and poetry, to transformism and symbolism. In his effort to "musicalize" his experiences, man reasserts a "poetic monism" suggested by Kant and Schelling and entertained by Coleridge. Granted a difference in aims between the scientist and the poet, the true scientist, who is also a philosopher (like Poincaré, Heisenberg et al.), will turn from mere pointer readings to pregnant experience which also engages the poet. The scientist will join the poet on the way to a new sensibility; for already sci. itself has furnished both with new psychic experience and, at least, with intimations of a new cognition. Poetry and sci., through symbolist abstraction, become two complementary symbol systems that, with the dissolution of the old realist faith in objects, illumine and correct the perceptual world. Nonetheless, since the time of I. A. Richards' *Sci. and Poetry* (1926), critics have continued to envisage the poetry-sci. problem in a bipolar manner, saying that the language of the one is referential and that of the other emotive. The whole problem has received further critical consideration in the framework of *poetry as knowledge*. Tate adduces Richards' testimony that Coleridge's claims for a poetic order of truth were not coherent. If Coleridge is found wanting in his attempt to unify poetry and sci., Richards is far from offering a final solution, and (according to Tate) modern semiotic or logical positivism implies an ultimate assimilation of poetry and sci. in a strict instrumentalism. In Vivas' view, the poet, wrenching form from nature and creating novelty, brings a new sense of reality and thus may be said to contribute knowledge. Though it is not a knowledge "of which we may demand correspondence with the actual world," it is, by the fact that it is constitutive of culture, prior to all knowledge. L. D. Lerner, who oscillates critically between "literature is knowledge" and "literature is not knowledge," finds Richards' differentiation between referential and emotive language rigid and even false. Perhaps (he suggests) we ought to regard language as a continuum between the poles of mathematics and dream.

II. HISTORICAL ASPECTS. The history of the emergence of self-consciousness in man is still lost in obscurity. However, with the progressive development of his analytic powers, he began to differentiate between forms of thought and forms of feeling, between reason and emotion. In time, sci. came to be associated with the one and poetry with the other;

and this in spite of the fact that often no hard and fast line could be drawn between the two, since sci. could inspire certain emotions (as the sense of vastness in astronomy) and poetry could be reflective as well as lyrical.

1. Classical and medieval. In classical antiquity, this divisiveness comes to the fore explicitly in Plato. Favoring mathematical thought, his view of reality put poetry on the defensive as something that is at best an imitation of reality and, at worst, a distortion of it. There is at present no satisfactory treatment of the relationship between poetry and sci. in Plato's thought. The dominant assumption of his philosophy is that branches of human knowledge are to be ranked according to their contribution to man's ethical and political welfare. Since poetry is impractical and, at least apparently, indifferent to truth, it is trivial and even pernicious. Sci., on the other hand, though less important than ethics, is directly concerned with truth and is therefore of great value. A subdominant strain in Plato, inherited from primitive tradition and the Pythagoreans, and evident in the *Timaeus* and the *Symposium*, assumes that the highest good is the perception of absolute truth which is most perfectly manifested in the harmony of numbers. The ideal scientist is the mathematician. Since his tool is *measure*, Plato's theory of knowledge is loaded in favor of sci. This view seems to be supported by the image of God as a Geometer (see Theaetetus, 143b).

With Aristotle, Plato's pupil, the situation is considerably different. The author of the *Poetics*, it must be kept in mind, is also the author of the *Physics* as well as the *Metaphysics*. There are indications that he wished the first of these works to be interpreted in the light of the others. Thus, while he was engaged in constituting a morphology of bone structure in terms of homology and, as an empiricist, was opposed to Plato's other-worldliness, he was at the same time concerned with ideal types which "must surpass the reality," with form and essence, and with the concept of the whole which surpasses its parts. All these ideas come into play in his *Poetics,* often as echoes from the *Physics* and *Metaphysics.* In his elements of tragic structure—"matter," "medium" and "manner," which may also be taken as the elements of poetry as such—we have the essential *operanda* of his *Physics* and *Metaphysics.* Implicit in these elements are form, which inheres in anything as one of its causes; the dynamic principle of change in a given direction; and oneness or unity, which embraces a heterogeneity of interacting parts. The principle of imitation finds expression in his *Meteorology* and in the *Physics.* There art is conceived as a force which helps nature to attain its goal; or, if nature is found wanting, art finishes the job, so to speak, by imitating the parts. Thus art or poetry helps nature realize its fullest potential. In addition, poetry imitates the harmony that, in nature, arises from contraries: it does so for the soul by reducing the clashes of passion to harmonious form. Thus we find poetry and sci. converging on a common goal: the stabilization of the soul.

The affinity that Plotinus envisioned between subject and object would suggest, at least to the modern student, the common delight that poetry and sci. share when they bring objects into harmony with the senses and so engage the whole nature of man. St. Augustine, who was opposed to dualism as a form of evil, embraced the Plotinian monism and conceived of an "ascent from rhythm in sense to the immortal rhythm which is truth" which would (to our way of thinking) engage poetry and sci. in a common partnership of *beate contemplari* or delighted contemplation.

Only obliquely can the problem of poetry and sci. be approached in Albertus or in St. Thomas: in the former through the notion of the *splendor of form* and in both (as in a good many of the theologians of their period) through what has later come to be known as the aesthetic of light (*claritas, splendor, lux,* etc.) [see Wimsatt and Brooks, 128]. For Scholasticism, a true relation between poetry and sci. could be thinkable only if the two were conceived as engaged together in the common enterprise of capturing and expressing the *resplendentia formae* in nature and thus flooding man's mind with that *fulgor* which is revealed understanding. In general, however, poetry was regarded as "a secondary rhetoric" or as a propaedeutic to logic. Poetic knowledge, deficient in truth, had to resort to metaphoric evasion. As for sci., the true *scientia* was above reason.

Contrary to the views just expressed, both poetry and sci. (imagination and reason) were, for Dante, in the service of revelation. Renaissance scholars credited him with encyclopedic knowledge in the arts and the sciences as well. His treatment of natural things reflected that knowledge in its "modo poetico." Those who questioned the right of Empedocles and Lucretius to the title of poet readily assented to Dante's merit in this respect because of his use of *persona* and figurative language. There were those, however, like Ridolfo Castravilla, who denied Dante's preeminence as poet, because they held that the arts and sciences were *not* acceptable subjects of poetry. Contrariwise, Vincenzo Borghini found the *Divina Commedia* great poetry precisely because it makes use of all the sciences in the service of the poem. The so-called Dante quarrel turned on this issue and oscillated between derogation and adulation: those who held that the introduction of learned matter interfered with the rendition of a "legitimate and well-understood imitation" and those who found a most worthy "concatenation" of elements in the poet's work because in the persona of the philosopher he linked successfully ethics, philosophy, and sci. (see Weinberg, pp. 823-94, *passim*). It is in this historic light that one can understand Chaucer's artistic use of sci. in the development of his characters.

2. *Renaissance*. With the Renaissance, we enter a period in which (as Bernard Weinberg authoritatively indicates) the study of any subject of necessity entailed consideration of its place in the entire framework of the arts and sciences and particularly of its relation to philosophy. Accordingly, poetics had to justify itself in relation to truth, and poetry was considered among the discursive sciences. Some writers on poetry (e.g., Giovanni Battista Pigna and Gabriele Zinano) saw the poet as one who "participates in every science" and poetry as a universal sci. encompassing all the others; and some (e.g., Benedetto Varchi), considering poetry as the greatest of all human activities, assigned to poetics a position more exalted "than all the other faculties, arts and sciences" (Weinberg, pp. 1-9, *passim*). Scipione Ammirato held that the poet's divine furor itself constitutes a kind of knowledge—one, in the long run, superior to that obtained through sci. Among Platonists there were those who, through their own researches, came to conclusions opposed to Plato, because of the testimony of the ancients that the first contributions to civilization were made by the poets and that as a result "poetry became the first of the arts and the sciences and mother of all the rest" (Weinberg, p. 296). But the signal event in the history of literary criticism in the It. Renaissance, we are told, was the discovery of Aristotle's *Poetics*. Its interpreters were engaged with the problem of *imitation* in its various aspects. Thus Lionardo Salviati, in his *Poetica d'Aristotile parafrasta e comentata*, is concerned with the fact that (1) poetry is an imitation of verisimilar objects; (2) it is an imitation in verse; (3) its ends are to profit and please. By comparing poetry with nature, a causal relationship is seen between objects, senses, and pleasure in nature; whereas in poetry, the causal chain (Weinberg, p. 614) is objects-appearances-imitation-senses (pleasure). Since the ideal of necessary order and catenation found in nature is wanting in poetry, the poet has to resort to verisimilitude— the resemblances whereby he produces the world of reality (see Tasso, *Delle differenze poetiche*, ca. 1585: Weinberg, p. 630). For Scaliger, the poet (Virgil) *is* nature, since what is represented in it only imperfectly by objects

is given perfection in his poetry (Weinberg, p. 747).

Even the Renaissance was on the defensive with regard to the uses of the imagination. The type of orthodox humanist represented by Peletier was torn between the desire for knowledge (sci.) and the compulsion for the expression of feeling in poetry. Yet sci. was one of the chief preoccupations of 16th-c. poetic humanism. Ronsard's irrepressible pessimism is, at least in part, the expression of the tension between the claims of sci. and technology (for which he evinced great enthusiasm) and the mandate for the expression of feeling in poetry. For Maurice Scève (see his three songs of the *Microcosme*), poetry, consisting of "numbers," carries intimations of celestial numbers which rule the universe. In general, certain syntagmic structures bring into focus the sci.-poetry polarity: the Platonic-astrologic synthesis of Peletier, the astrologic-demonic synthesis of Ronsard, the microcosm synthesis of Scève. The search for order in the welter of Renaissance thought becomes, in one of its aspects, the quest for a literary form worthy of presenting the dignity of the human mind.

Closely allied to Ronsardian pessimism is Renaissance "star-crossed" melancholy born of a psychology of humors compounded with an astronomy of omens. Somehow, this weird combination was supposed to foster "intellectual and imaginative powers." The poetry-sci. tension also encouraged a certain type of solitude which was at once a response to, and an alienation from, "the infected world." In Milton's *Il Penseroso* we find an historical adumbration of the romantic poet over his "lamp at midnight hour" in "some high lonely tower." Milton looks toward William Butler Yeats; and Burton, writing his *Anatomy of Melancholy* as "an antidote out of that which was the prime cause of my disease," looks toward a galaxy of Freudian introspectivists.

3. *17th and 18th c.* The 17th c. poses an historical paradox in that it is at once committed to order on a cosmic scale and to divisiveness on the psychological plane; matter and mind, extension and thought. This situation gives rise to a new sensibility and a complex vision. The intellectual climate, it is claimed, became inimical to poetry. A legend was promulgated that Descartes had cut the throat of poetry. Yet with Henry More, a great admirer of Descartes, there was a motion to transcend the divisiveness of matter and mind by claiming extension for spirit. In such a tendency, the confrontation of poetry and sci. in a possible theory of cognition was inevitable. By mutual fructification, they form jointly a *scientia intuitiva*. The subjection of "the shows of things to the desires of the

mind" (Bacon) need not mean that the mind remains unaware of the difference between appearance and reality.

Try as he might, man could not escape the use of analogy in his attempt to articulate his experience of the world as a system. Thus (to follow Marjorie Nicolson), while we think of our universe in similes, the Elizabethans thought of theirs in metaphors; and the 17th c. inherited the metaphor of the circle (itself of ancient origin). In their desire for unity, poets and philosophers had tried for 300 years to put together the pieces of a circle; they tried to do so in the interest of preserving a "unified sensibility" of feeling and thinking. Miss Nicholson's succinct statement summarizes the situation: "The language of poetry and science was no longer one when the world was no longer one." The decisive break in the so-called Circle of Perfection came with the shift from the Gr. view that the world was permeated with mind to the Cartesian that the world is a lifeless machine. Thinking and feeling had ceased to be parts of the same process. This is expressed by Donne:

And New Philosophy calls all in doubt,
The element of fire is quite put out:
The sun is lost, and the earth, and no man's wit
Can well direct him where to look for it.

The Circle of Perfection was disturbed by the persistence of the idea of infinity. Because the "human understanding is unquiet," as Bacon tells us, the vast spaces engaged not only the reason of Pascal but his emotions as well. In him we find the clue for the study of the infinite as an aesthetic entity: a study of the mutual fructification of poetic feeling and mathematical expression. It is not that we find here the genesis of romanticism but an indication of its perpetuity. Conversely, *Paradise Lost,* the greatest poem of the 17th c., attempts to confront the sci. of its age, particularly in its cosmology, and to reiterate the traditional affirmations. It is filled with the "tension between the inner and the outer life of man" (Svendsen), but its sci. is not so much an incursion from without as it is an invitation from within. Whatever Milton's limitations, his attempt places him in the great tradition of poetry that uses sci. to find an order in which feeling and thought are harmoniously orchestrated, from Lucretius to Goethe; from Rabelais to Pascal; from Chaucer to Donne and Shelley. And it was always more than a question of versifying sci. or of making poetry "scientific."

As we turn to the 18th c., we go from an aesthetic of vastness to one of light in which (again we are instructed by Nicolson) poetry and sci. had mutual commerce. Burke's essay on the Sublime and Beautiful (ca. 1757) bears witness to this; for here the scientific facts of light and color are brought into alignment with the poetic response which in turn communicates the scientific facts in depth. But privations of light, in that they are terrible, are productive of Vacuity, Darkness, Solitude, and Silence, according to Burke. We are back in the Pascalian vastness. When we compound "A Newton's genius" with "a Milton's flame," we have plenitude indeed. One must not overlook, however, the pervasive impression that the poets of the 18th c. were divided between the claims of reason and those of desire, between the intellect and the imagination as often opposed to each other. In 18th-c. discussions of the relation of poetry to sci. and other forms of discourse, poetry (according to Abrams) was considered truth ornamented with certain devices, while the bare representation of truth was non-poetry. Newton himself thought with Barrow that poetry was "a kind of ingenious nonsense."

With the movement of the 18th c. toward the Fr. Revolution, poetry had to sustain itself against rising odds. In view of this, André Chénier (1762–94), for instance, recommended a new content for poetry, namely modern sci. His own attempt may be found in his poem *Hermès.* With Wordsworth's idea of poetry as a "science of feelings," we move in the same direction as Alexander Baumgarten's conception of aesthetics as the "science of sensuous cognition" (see Wellek).

In any consideration of the relation of poetry to sci., Blake is a seminal figure. As Miss Nicolson remarked on the basis of the poet's marginalia: ". . . [The] aesthetics which came to a climax in Burke was to Blake a corollary of the metaphysics supposedly engendered by Newton." In a lengthy passage cited by her from the Annotations, Blake declares himself against both the sci. and metaphysics of Burke. Urizen wept as he beheld the philosophy of five senses—the product of "the terrible race of Los and Enitharmon"—put "into the hands of Newton and Locke" (*The Song of Los*). Blake's rejection of sci. was but an extreme form of the general trend, from the end of the 18th c., toward a monism embracing man and nature.

4. 19th c. Pope's declaration that "all are parts of one stupendous whole" was accepted by Shelley as his "favorite theory." *Prometheus* expresses the mystical union of man and nature and identifies the energies of life and love with that of electricity (see Grabo). Significantly, Whitehead makes much of Shelley's power to visualize geometric facts and give them poetic expression. Of course, the Promethean myth itself, as used by Shelley, allegorizes man's conflict with the forces of nature and his attempt to master them.

For Keats, the "innate universality" of a Shakespeare seemed to suggest that poetic genius had the power to encompass all scientific insight. Yet in *Lamia*, he indicted sci. memorably: "Philosophy will clip an Angel's wings . . . Unweave a rainbow." For Abrams, Keats exemplifies "a romantic tendency to shift the debate about the discrepancy between science and poetry from the question of poetic myth and fable to the difference between the visible universe of concrete imaginative observation and that of scientific analysis and explanation." Thus, Peacock (*Four Ages of Poetry*) maintains that poetry arouses emotion at the expense of truth, and that as such it is a waste of time. And Macaulay, in the main, agrees with him. He can find no way of uniting "the incompatible advantage of reality" and "the exquisite enjoyment of fiction." Poe's sonnet *To Science* echoes phrases from *Lamia*. In fact, almost all the important romantic theorists comment on the disparity between imaginative and scientific perception and deplore the neglect of the former.

Working from the idea that the highest faculty includes both the emotional and rational elements, Coleridge urged the conjunction of poetry and sci. This conjunction is further suggested by Hegel's idea of thought becoming incandescent by its own acceleration and "philosophy in its last synthesis showing itself to be poetry"; and by Mill's declaration that "every great poet has been a great thinker." Another aspect of this thought is reflected in the romantic Emersonian notion that the mind itself is involved in a universal metaphor, a Universal Analogy, according to which the natural world is the reproduction of the spiritual world, and that it is the business of poetic genius to interpret this analogy (see Baym's "Baudelaire and Shakespeare," *The Shakespeare Assoc. Bull.*, 15, nos. 3 and 4 [1940]). Sci., therefore, joins poetry in a magnificent harmony of universal knowledge. Hence hymns to intellectual beauty and the equation of beauty with truth.

Between 1800 and 1850, the romantic poets in France and elsewhere had before them a rich array of scientists (see Ampère, *Essai sur la philosophie des sciences*). Though Fusil maintains that romanticism, contrary to the 18th c., had momentarily broken the chains of sci., we find Lamartine singing a lyrical obligato to the astronomy of Tycho Brahe, Kepler, Herschel, and Newton, with man's love and desire written into space (*L'Infini des cieux*). Vigny sings, though pessimistically,

La distance et le temps sont vaincus! La Science Trace autour de la terre un sentier triste et droit . . .

Hugo's *Le Satyre*, for which Shelley's *Prometheus* is suggested as a source, celebrates evolution and universal progress. In spite of many ineptitudes and exaggerations, the romantic poets prepared the way for the finer and more profitable coalescence of poetry and sci. in the literature that was to follow in the second half of the 19th c. and the first half of the 20th.

August Comte's great insight was the idea that all knowledge had a progressive historical character. But his big error consisted in his attempt to impose upon knowledge, nevertheless, a rigid pattern from which he himself, having undergone a "méditation exceptionnelle," had to recoil. It is a curious fact that, in the midst of the progress of positivism in England, Buckle pointed to an organic relationship between poetry and sci. His central idea was that in abrogating any portion of the mind's activities, one impoverished and even injured another. The operations of the imagination (and the emotions associated with it) were central to the total activity of the mind. For historical support of his idea, Buckle turned to 17th-c. England, rich in scientific discoveries as well as in poetry. Seeing in this a causal relationship, he warned the physical scientists of his own day, who were inclined "to separate philosophy from poetry, and to look upon them, not only as indifferent, but as hostile," that they might be taking too narrow a view of the functions of the human mind and of "the manner in which truth is obtained." Pretty much in the spirit of Spinoza before him and of Freud after, he maintained that the emotions, too, obeyed fixed laws and that "they [had] their logic and method of reference." Poetry, he concluded, was "a part of philosophy [or sci.], simply because the emotions are a part of the mind." Like Shelley in his *Defense*, Buckle held that vast masses of observations were useless unless they were connected with a presiding idea and that "the most effective way of turning them to account would be to give more scope to the imagination" and to incorporate the spirit of poetry with the spirit of science" (*Hist. Civil. in Engl.*, 2d ed., II [1901] 395–99).

If the influence of Erasmus Darwin is felt among the poets of the first half of the 19th c., that of Charles Darwin is powerful after the publication of the *Origin of Species*. Lionel Stevenson has studied that impact on such poets as Tennyson, Robert Browning, George Meredith, Thomas Hardy, and others. Implicit in the response of Meredith and Hardy to evolution is the unconscious desire to resolve the tension which the Ego experiences in the Chain of Being. Meredith's response took the form of poetic irony which found beneficence in the drama of development from mud to mind. Hardy's reaction assumed the form of a tragic catharsis which comes from a stark confrontation with an immanent, blind will pervading the endless variety of things in a process called nature. Both Meredith and Hardy herald a growing awareness in modern sensibility of the fragmentation of knowledge which (as Bonamy Dobrée says) "We all deplore while we all so busily further it." This situation is poignantly expressed by Anthony Woodhouse in *Song at Twilight:*

> We must go on from here
> - - - - - -
> The bridge behind is down
> - - - - - -
> The Canyon-crack of knowing
> Divides us now from Spring . . .

In a sense, the whole problem of the poetry-sci. relationship is expressed in these words: how to fill in "the canyon-crack of knowing." The shadow of Pascal is with us again.

The great plea for relating poetry and sci.—though he admitted ignorance as to the manner of bringing it about—came in Matthew Arnold's "Literature and Sci." Echoing Wolf, he maintained that "a genuine humanism is scientific." He argued that there was a general tendency in human nature to relate poetry and sci. in obedience to an emotional need for wholeness or completeness, reflected in human conduct. The effecting of such a relationship is further called for by the dire need for recapturing an antique symmetry (*symmetria prisca*) once possessed by the Greeks—"fit details strictly combined, in view of a large general result nobly conceived."

Conversely, the great spokesman for the antithesis between poetry and sci. in the 19th c. is Nietzsche. Already in *The Birth of Tragedy* (1872) Nietzsche maintained that the *malaise* of contemporary culture stems from the rise of the analytic intellect, typified by Socrates and (in poetic art) Euripides. To escape the sterility of the analytic world view, man must rediscover the Dionysian elements of life which Nietzsche felt at an early stage in his career were exemplified in Wagner. If "the canyon-crack of knowing" divides us from "Spring," the way to return is to destroy the "knowing" —an idea which recurs in D. H. Lawrence and others.

III. PRESENT VIEWPOINTS. The age-old question of "reality" inevitably and recurrently comes to plague poet and scientist alike. In retrospect, the 19th-c. division between analysis and synthesis appears an over-simplification. Today the correlativity of the two has come to be recognized. Newton did not expel God from nature; nor Darwin from life; nor Freud from the soul. The act of transcendence which produced the concept of God also impelled man to proceed into the bowels of the earth and the vastness of the heavens, as well as into the awesome domain of the mind. At each stage of his quest he experienced the shock of discovery whose correlative came to be known as the aesthetic shiver (*frisson esthétique*). In each instance, poetry and reality became one, like water and shore—a reciprocal action expressed by the Abbé Delille:

Du mobile océan tels les flots onduleux
Vont façonner leurs bords, ou sont moulés par
  eux.

1. Transformism and symbolism. It is at least debatable whether the world of the actual—the average man's "higgledy-piggledy" world —remains the same when touched by the visions of the poet and the scientist. Transformism is the order of both. Both tend to de-phlegmatize inert matter, to infuse it with energy; and, in doing so, to raise it to a higher potential, of which music is the type and mathematics the notation. Thus the aspirations of scientists and artists converge in musicality—a purity of representation which leaves the senses behind on the way to form. This is represented by symbolism, with Valéry as its later representative. But the so-called "quest for a pure representation" may be traced from Novalis to Rilke and Valéry.

With the intermittent death of idealism after Hegel, not only philosophy but poetry as well was at the mercy of sci. which now presided over reality. To redeem this atmosphere symbolism brought a new enthusiasm. Man, isolated among his machines, falls back on his desire. The orientation is an idealistic one. Paul Fort and Whitman sang of a cosmic unanimism: "La terre et le soleil en moi sont en cadence, et toute la nature est entrée dans mon coeur" (*La grande ivresse*). The elements themselves—"air, soil, water, fire—those are words. / I myself am a word with them" (*A Song of the Rolling Earth*). And "The words of true poems are the tuft and final applause of science" (*Song of the Answerer*).

2. Toward a poetic monism. Here we have the mutual salute of intelligence and sensibility with which our contemporary philosophers of art and literature are concerned. Herbert Read has struggled with the possible rapprochement of the two in the forms of sci. and poetry—the one said to be discursive, the other "more exactly, a mode of symbolic communication." For him, intelligence would unite poetry and sci. In the last analysis, Read reasserts a "poetic monism" which was first suggested by the *Critique of Judgement* and was then more firmly outlined by Schelling and held many attractions for Coleridge. This effort toward a poetic monism was made not without certain misgivings which plagued Coleridge and still agitate all thinking men (see Read's *The True Voice of Feeling*).

The appetite for unity or monism manifests itself especially in the study of origins as a clue to common tendencies. Only a conception which would still relate poetry to magic would regard it (poetry) as totally apart from sci. C. Day Lewis feels that as physical scientists have moved during the last half century toward the study of the micro-event, they have been brought nearer to the poets. That the imaginative leap is necessary to scientist and poet alike, is attested by men like Poincaré, Bronowski, and Keuklé. All languages (even mathematics as Scott Buchanan emphasizes when he says, "Almost every term [in analytic geometry] is a metaphorical expression for a proportion" [p. 118]) have recourse to metaphor. Indeed, for Lewis sci. is a kind of poetry; and so it is for many others. Sherrington (quoted by Lewis) points to the ghostliness of mind in its indivisibility and intangibility, and asks the question which he answers himself: "What then does that amount to? All that counts in life, Desire, zest, truth, love, knowledge, 'values.'"

3. Toward a new sensibility. While for the present the aims of the scientist, in Herbert Dingle's view, are different from those of the poet, there will come a time when the scientist will "pass beyond the inspid observations of pointer readings and find something to say about the pregnant experiences that have been the poet's concern from the beginning." In essence, what is implicit in Dingle's remark is that a progressive philosophy of sci., whether it succeeds in reconciling the poet to the scientist or not, will give pause to both to see experience in its *rich* variety. This is attested to by the names of Leonardo da Vinci, Pascal, Goethe, and Valéry.

One of the chief problems entailed in the sci.-poetry relationship is the total sensibility of the observer and the observed. Experimental sci. too often fails to elicit the answers we should so much like to have to this question. Heinrich Henel ("Goethe and Sci." in *Sci. and Literature*) calls our attention to the fact that Goethe's remark that nature falls silent when put on the rack by experimental sci., has recently been corroborated by Heisenberg. Of course, even his disciples held that Goethe was neither a scientist nor a philosopher. Goethe himself conceived of a sci. of ideas which would "give poetic form to reality rather than to realize the so-called poetic, the merely fanciful." This purpose, according to Henel, was common to his poetry and his studies of nature. Goethe's approach to the art-nature relationship is based on a paradox according to which the law-giving artist (*gesetzgebende Künstler*) strives for artistic truth which obeys a lawless, blind impulse; that is, the realism of nature bears the imprint of his own laws. For Goethe, then, the poet and the scientist often remain apart while they have much in common. For a German poet of a century later, Rainer Maria Rilke, sci. could be the best and the worst of things. He is almost overwhelmed by the opposition of poetry (imagination) to sci., and especially technology. For him, this constitutes an element of disharmony and disequilibrium (see "Rainer Maria Rilke et la Science Moderne" by Adrien de Clery in *Sci. and Literature*).

4. The psyche and cognition. The advance of sci. has furnished the poet with new psychic experience. We may assume with William Rose that the roots of the creative imagination reach into the unconscious. This is, of course, supported by Freud. But error lurks on both sides: the literary analyst dare not neglect the unconscious, if he is to reach the heart of the matter he deals with; the psychoanalyst who leaves out of account the conscious striving for form will come to grips with the work of art only partially. The student of literature and the anthropologist should have a common field of research. But turning to Freud's essay on "The Relation of the Poet to Day-Dreaming," we find him saying that poets themselves give no satisfactory explanation of the power their art has to move others. Clearly, the full possibility of a satisfactory rapprochement between scientist and poet waits upon the perfection of a deeper sci. of cognition than we now possess. Such a sci. would go beyond Freud in the exploration of phantasy and of the rôle of language as its vehicle. Yet the investigator of the poetry-sci. tension has much to learn from recent psychoanalytic work in metaphor, for instance, which is one of the great essentials of poetry. For Ella Freeman Sharpe, "the intellectual life of man is only possible through the development of metaphor (see Baym, "The Present State of the Study of Metaphor," BA, 35 [1961]). In metaphoric language *idea* and *affect* hurtle each other and interfuse. The metaphysical becomes a transmutation of the physical.

5. Abstraction in poetry and sci. We come now to the question of abstraction in sci. and poetry, whereby the imagination conjures up a world independent of common sense. Some recent thinkers (for instance, E. R. Briggs) find that in studying the impact of sci. upon the concept of the imagination, they must go back to Descartes. For him, imagination is the ability to form images precisely and to carry to the brain the imprint of external objects received through the senses. Though he normally uses the term pejoratively, he tends, nevertheless, to invest the 'imagination' with a vague status, higher than that of matter but lower than that of spirit, when he implicitly abandons his dream of a purely deductive method requiring only reason. Briggs finds a much keener approach in Baudelaire's suggestion that the function of the imagination is to detect relationships between things,—'correspondences.' Every image tends to suggest relationship. In pointing to the ultra-sensitive, analogical intelligence of the artist, Baudelaire (Briggs thinks) has gone beyond Descartes.

For abstract sci., theoretical concepts displace the idea of a solid world of sight and touch. We are in the world of relativity and quantum mechanics. The old realist faith in *objects with qualities* is replaced by faith in *images* and symbolisms that incorporate sensibility in the thing seen or heard. Poetry and sci. become two complementary symbol systems that illumine nature and correct the perceptual world. As Ronald Peacock puts it ("Abstraction and Reality in Modern Sci.," in *Sci. and Literature*), "the point of reference of symbolic systems, including the perceptual, must lie not in one or the other separately but in their equilibrium. Sci., art, poetry, and the study of language all attempt a constant adjustment of thought in the search for this equilibrium." Thus, symbolist abstraction in Valéry, for example, reveals itself as a vehicle for "sensibility." Frost will speak of himself as a "sensibilitist" even if he might object to the label "symbolist poet." Rilke will see in the poetic process an attempt to replace a chaotic outside ("ideal") world by an ordered inside world of symbols.

6. Poetry and knowledge. In any thorough investigation, then, of the relation of poetry and sci., there inevitably arises the general problem of *poetry as knowledge*. This problem is dealt with in varying degrees of analytic insight by Allen Tate, Eliseo Vivas, and Laurence D. Lerner, among others. The first (*Limits of Poetry*, 1948) brings into his discussion Coleridge, Matthew Arnold, I. A. Richards, and logical positivism in the person of Charles W. Morris. Arnold gave the case for poetry away to the real scientist who demands a one-to-one relevance of language to the objects and events to which it refers. The positivists have replaced "meaning" by a concept of "operational validity" which dispenses with cognition and "mind." While the word *poetry* appears frequently in Morris' two articles on aesthetics ("Esthetics and the Theory of Signs," *J. of Unified Sci.*, 8 [1939]; "Sci., Art & Technology," KR, 1 [1939]), there is no actual analysis, Tate regrets, of a passage or even a line of verse. Morris' sci. of semiotic implies an ultimate

assimilation of poetry and knowledge (sci.) in obedience to a rigorous instrumentalism. Tate goes back to Coleridge and his definition of poetry: "A poem is that species of composition, which is opposed to works of science, by proposing for its immediate object pleasure, not truth. . . ." Coleridge's failure "to get out of the dilemma of Intellect-or-Feeling," says Tate, "has been passed on to us as a fatal legacy." Tate adduces I. A. Richards' testimony (*Coleridge on the Imagination*) that Coleridge's claims for a poetic order of truth were not coherent. For logical positivism, the knowledge or truth of poetry is immature; and for modern psychology, pleasure is a response to a stimulus. Poetry has come under the general idea of "operational validity." Tate defers to Richards who will not accept the notion that language is a "mere signaling system." "It is the instrument of all our distinctively human development, of everything in which we go beyond the animals." Tate considers *Coleridge on the Imagination* the most ambitious attempt of a modern critic to force into unity the longstanding antithesis of language and subject, of pleasure and truth. In the chapter "The Wind Harp" two doctrines are expressed: (1) The poet's mind, with an insight into reality, reads nature as a symbol of something behind or within nature not ordinarily perceived. (2) The mind of the poet creates a nature into which he projects his own feelings and aspirations. At this point, Tate finds a confusion, especially in the light of positivism which would eliminate both "mind" and cognition. By following the positivist road, we lose "everything in which we go beyond the animals." By embracing the second doctrine, we have a knowing mind without anything that it can know. Tate finds that Richards' conception of the imagination (quite different from Coleridge's) closely resembles a Hegelian synthesis. Richards' two doctrines are neither consequences of *a priori* decisions, nor verifiable as the empirical statements of sci. are verifiable. He certainly does not offer a final solution of the problem of the unified imagination, but he asserts: "It is the privilege of poetry to preserve us from mistaking our notions either for things or for ourselves. *Poetry is the completest mode of utterance*" (*Coleridge on the Imagination*, 163). Here Tate adds: "[The] completeness of *Hamlet* is not of the experimental order, but of the experienced order." Correlative with all this is Richards' insight that myths are "hard realities in projection. The opposite and discordant qualities in things in them acquire a form. . . . Without his mythologies man is only a cruel animal, without a soul . . . a congeries of possibilities without order or aim." Tate comments: "Man, without his mythologies, is an interpretant." We have "the failure of the modern mind to understand poetry on the assumptions underlying the demi-religion of positivism."

According to the second critic, Eliseo Vivas, the artist or poet is one who "wrenches form from the heart of nature" (*Creation and Discovery*, 1955). Vivas differentiates his view from that of Aristotle (*catharsis*), that of Suzanne Langer (*presentational symbol*), and that of Wimsatt (*icon*), by what he (Vivas) calls the facts of *intransitivity* and *creativity*. The first is an assertion of novelty, which is the equivalent of the creation of new knowledge. The second maintains that the artist creates form and so a new sense of reality where before there was a blurred and cliché-cluttered reality (p. 120). Through his originality, the artist captivates the reader's mind by creating within him a state of "ecstasy" and thus supplies him with "something very similar to what we experience when we acquire knowledge." As a subscriber to Bergson's dictum that art reveals the reality of things, one would expect Vivas to equate poetry and sci. in their common effort toward that goal. But he adds the qualifying phrase "superior reality" and explains that the reality symbolized by a work of art is "superior not to the reality of the work of physics, but to the alleged reality of our physical world, that is, of the cliché-cluttered, hastily grasped, by-passion-blurred world in which we daily live" (p. 120). It is difficult to distinguish the cognitive from the aesthetic mode of experience. The artist refurbishes our world picture in concrete terms and by presenting the dramatic pattern of human life defines for us its sense. He gives us an aesthetically ordered picture. In a broad sense, literature (a product of the mind) does give us "knowledge" which has "undeniable similarities with the symbolic constructions of knowledge in the narrow sense." In the latter sense literature or poetry does not give us knowledge "since it does not give us a picture of which we may demand correspondence with the actual world." But, urges Vivas, it ought to be recognized that literature "is prior in the order of logic to all knowledge, since it is constitutive of culture, which is one of the conditions of knowledge" (p. 127).

The third critic, L. D. Lerner (*The Truest Poetry: An Essay on the Question What is Literature?* 1960) devotes one section of his work to the assertion that literature (for him the poet is one who is engaged in any form of imaginative writing) is knowledge and another section to the negation of this statement. Lerner goes back to Shelley's statement that poetic language "remarks the before unapprehended relations of things." This would seem to argue that the poet—at any rate, the great poet—gives us original knowledge (see

Vivas' theory of *intransitivity*). No wholly cognitive theory is by itself satisfactory for the future of poetry. Even in the realm of ideas, intellectual susceptibility is promoted by cathexis. (Lerner quotes Freud's "Introductory Lecture," 18 and 27 to this effect.) The romantic movement contributed the notable insight that no subject is as important as the growth of the poet's sensibility. Hence Lerner links *The Prelude* of Wordsworth with Proust's *A la Recherche du Temps Perdu* as "poems" that deal with two faculties that have a great deal in common, namely, *memory* and *poetic power*. The chief motive for writing poetry is *relief*: emotion pressing for expression in words. While Lerner credits Collingwood (*The Principles of Art*, Bk. 2: "The Theory of Imagination") with placing an idealist and rationalist philosophical approach in the service of the romantic view of art, he is aware that we owe the expression theory to Wordsworth's declaration that poetry is the "spontaneous overflow of powerful feelings" and that "it takes its origin from emotion recollected in tranquility" (pp. 39, 56). To this is related the *furor poeticus*, whose history stretches from Plato through the Renaissance. Lerner confronts, in all honesty, the contrary winds of opinion concerning the relative functions of poetry as knowledge. Wordsworth had thought about the cognitive status of poetry and reflected on

Those sweet counsels between head and heart
Whence grew that genuine knowledge fraught
  with peace
      (Lerner, p. 140; *The Prelude* 353)

At the same time the poet inveighed against "Our meddling intellect" which "Mis-shapes the forms of things: / We murder to dissect." Our critic finds Richards' differentiation between referential and emotive language rigid and to that extent false. It should prove surprising to Richards, on his own theory, that "almost all the illuminating criticism before this century, and a great deal since, has been written by poets" (p. 129). This raises the question as to whether, instead of classifying language into two kinds, we ought not to regard it as a continuum between the poles of mathematics and dream (*ibid.*). Lerner takes issue with Valéry's anti-intellectual intellectualism which would reserve the very existence of poetry for those who hold the correct theories of its nature: "it exists (says Lerner) for those who can appreciate it" (p. 181). In the end, our critic's position, with respect to the question *Is literature (poetry) knowledge?*, is a conservative one. He does say (p. 219) that literature cannot have the same cognitive function as sci. In conclusion, one may quote his words: "In the end, there are two types of literary theory, and two types of literature. One is constantly tugging literature in the direction of music [compare Valéry's idea of "musicalization" of experience], because music seems the type of pure creation. The other tugs literature toward ordinary human activity —and essentially toward speech. There has been the threat that if literature clings too obstinately to its cognitive function, it may die out before the advancing sciences of man" (p. 221).

CONCLUSION. In 1889 Charles Morice wrote: "One asks how science and art will effect that large understanding on which the future counts. Pascal, Balzac, Edgar Allan Poe, and Villiers de l'Isle Adam know the answer: 'Art will touch science with its foot to gain assurance of a solid foundation and will with one swoop cross over it on the wings of Intuition.'" This is, of course, a statement born of an enthusiastic wish. Poetry constantly makes the error, from a scientific point of view, of attributing to nature or the universe something of man's own nature. Once called the pathetic fallacy, it has also come to be known as metaphysical pathos. Poetry has always lived on this anthropomorphism. The so-called universal analogy stems from it. But, even granting this error, what poetry does is to declare that there is a relationship between a subject and an object, between a sensorium and that which is sensed. Without such a relationship no knowledge would be possible. The so-called error of poetry turns out to be a necessity analogous to the necessity of hypothesis in sci. In a Freudian age, we must recognize the "deep unconscious processes in the creative act" and such a recognition, as Jerome Bruner remarks, will go far "toward enriching our understanding of the kinship between the artist, the humanist, and the man of science."

It is not without significance for our problem that the world-renowned physicist Louis de Broglie was asked to write a preface to Paul Valéry's *Cahiers*. Faced with the question of what could have led the great poet to his prolonged studies in the field of sci., de Broglie answered: "What actually complemented in a unique manner Paul Valéry's qualities of imagination and poetic sensibility was a great love of general ideas, a constant tendency towards precision in images and terms, a *finesse d'esprit* at times reaching subtlety. Thus, he could find in the development of modern science all that suited his mind: the clarity of concepts and words, the suddenly discovered vast intellectual horizons, the fine subtlety of theories which, revealing lapses of logic, unforeseen properties of forms and numbers, the relativity of time and space and the uncertainties of the atomic world, have opened for human thought strange new perspectives. And Paul Valéry, poet with a penetrating insight, knew how to envision, behind the dryness of experimental facts and the coldness of logarithms and theories, this triumphant conquest of the unknown, this ascendant march toward the splendor of the True, which constitutes the value and the poetry of Science." The image of the mind reflected in its own mirror, so patent in Valéry's poetry and poetics (as Elizabeth Sewell has so brilliantly shown) indicates the poet's struggle—and the struggle of many artists and scientists—to get rid of a dualism such as the poetry-sci. division presents.

But the debate continues. In a symposium on sci. and poetry held at Yale in 1961 (see *Rev. of Metaphysics*, 15 [1961] 236–55), in which scientists and humanists participated, it was suggested that the semantic problem involved in the cultural schism between the arts and the sciences could be cleared up with a little aesthetic cultivation on the one hand and more vigorous education on the other. At the same time it was said that whereas the poet uses the self instrumentally to test his intuitions of existence, the scientist finds that instrument inadequate in probing the secrets of the cosmos. It was admitted, however, that "the arrogance of the scientist comes in thinking his the only discipline. . . ." A common ground was found in the use of metaphor by both sci. and poetry. A geologist suggested that "there is a continuous series running from pure poetic metaphor (perhaps the haiku would be an example), in which the meaning is almost entirely dependent on a *resonance* with human awareness, to the pure symbolic analogue (say a mathematical formulation of the phase rule), in which the meaning is entirely contained within the terms as formally defined" (p. 242). Ultimately (and paradoxically), the scientist's analogues "become his means of grasping experience. They become resonant with his personal response and begin to function poetically as his metaphors." We are advised by a scientist to "have no illusions that the scientist is set apart from other men by the pure, objective quality of his mind" (p. 244). The scientific jargon itself may be a defense against poetry creeping in." Matt Walton (whose words have been quoted above) sums the matter up thus: "We are inescapably concerned with two genuinely different ways of grasping reality, poetically as a function of human response, scientifically as something independent and subsuming the human response." He adds that both senses of reality, functioning in some degree in everybody, are necessary for a full awareness of the meaning of existence (p. 246). In the over-all picture, the tension between poetry and sci. translates the tensions of both poets and scientists in confrontation with an elusive reality.

A. A. Fusil, *La Poésie scientifique de 1750 à nos jours* (1918); S. Freud, "The Relation of the Poet to Day-Dreaming," *Collected Papers*, IV (1924); A. N. Whitehead, *Sci. and the Modern World* (1925); W. C. Curry, *Chaucer and the Mediaeval Sciences* (1926); I. A. Richards, *Sci. and Poetry* (1926); S. Buchanan, *Poetry and Mathematics* (1929, repr. 1962); C. H. Grabo, *A Newton Among Poets* (1930); L. Stevenson, *Darwin Among the Poets* (1932); B. Willey, *The 17th C. Background* (1934); J. W. Beach, *The Concept of Nature in 19th-C. Eng. Poetry* (1936); A. O. Lovejoy, *The Great Chain of Being* (1936); F. R. Johnson, *Astronomical Thought in Renaissance England* (1937); H. V. Routh, *Towards the 20th C.* (1937); A.-M. Schmidt, *La Poésie scientifique en France au 16ᵉ s.* (1938); D. C. Allen, *The Star-Crossed Renaissance* (1941); A. Gode-von Aesch, *Natural Science in German Romanticism* (1941); H. J. Muller, *Sci. and Crit.* (1943); F. J. Hoffman, *Freudianism and the Lit. Mind* (1945, 2d ed., 1957); M. H. Nicolson, *Newton Demands the Muse* (1946), *The Breaking of the Circle* (1950, rev. 1962), and *Sci. and Imagination* (1956); D. Bush, *Sci. and Eng. Poetry* (1950); N. H. Pearson, "The Am. Poet in Relation to Sci.," *The Am. Writer and the European Tradition* (1950); H. H. Waggoner, *The Heel of Elohim: Sci. and Values in Modern Am. Poetry* (1950); L. Babb, *The Elizabethan Malady* (1951); H. Read, *The True Voice of Feeling* (1953); Abrams; B. Dobrée, "Scientism I, II," chaps. 3, 4 in *The Broken Cistern* (1954); J. Z. Fullmer, "Contemporary Sci. and the Poets," *Science*, 119 (1954); replies and rejoinder, *Science*, 120 (1954); A. R. Hall, *The Scientific Revolution, 1500–1800* (1954); *Sci. and Lit.;* Wellek; M. I. Baym, "On the Relationship between Poetry and Sci.," *Yearbook of Comparative Lit.*, 5 (1956); J. Bronowski, *Sci. and Human Values* (1956); K. Svendsen, *Milton and Sci.* (1956); C. D. Lewis, *The Poet's Way of Knowledge* (1957); Wimsatt and Brooks; E. Sewell, *The Orphic Voice: Poetry and Natural Hist.* (1960); P. Ginestier, *Poet and the Machine*, tr. M. B. Friedman (1961); *17th C. Sci. and the Arts*, ed. H. H. Rhys (1961); A. Huxley, *Lit. and Sci.* (1963).　M.I.B.

SCOLION. An early type of Gr. lyric poetry, a sort of after-dinner or drinking song. The exact origin of the term is difficult to trace and its etymology cannot be established with certainty. Tradition ascribes its origin to Terpander who was the first to give it artistic form. Its stanzas were composed of 2 phalaecians or hendecasyllabics (q.v.), a colon of the form ◡◡—◡◡——◡◡—, and another with —◡◡—◡◡—repeated. The s. was sung by choruses accompanied by the lyre or the flute and dealt with historical events or expressed deep personal feeling and shrewd and trenchant comments on daily life. In the course of the 5th c. this type of poetry was considerably simplified. Often the scolia were pure extemporized pieces, excerpts from lyric poetry or even selections from Homer's poems.—R. Reitzenstein, *Epigramm und Skolion* (1893); Smyth; Schmid and Stählin.　P.S.C.

SCOP. An OE name, like "gleeman," with which it is interchangeably used, for the professional entertainer, a harpist and poet-singer, normally a member of a royal household, who was the shaper and conservator in England of Old Germanic poetic tradition. He was of an old and honored class, sharing with his audience a critical interest in his craft; he commanded a mastery of the complex oral-formulaic materials of Old Germanic prosody (q.v.) hardly comprehensible to lettered societies. His repertory included more than encomiastic court verse: he was also a folk historian; and his narrative celebrations of heroic boldness and sacrifice, mingled with lyrical reflection and secular or Christian morality, have been preserved in later written forms as a central part of the Anglo-Saxon poetical corpus. There are no extant full-length biographies of OE scops, as there are of some of the Icelandic court poets, for instance; but a fictional biography in verse of one Widsith, together with a quasi-autobiographical lyric by a certain Deor, afford glimpses of the bard's social status and of some of his professional techniques. It is likely, however, that the transmission of verse depended less upon the personality and talent of an individual scop than upon the formulaic materials with which he worked, the cooperative appreciation of his audience, and their common familiarity with traditional themes. It is sometimes hard to distinguish between the art of popular and courtly poetry, between the art of a court gleeman and that perhaps of a chieftain who might take up the harp and recite a lay himself; or that of a warrior-singer whose function as a singer would be incidental to his personal knowledge of a battle; or even that of an humble person like Cædmon (Cædman), described in Bede's *Historia Ecclesiastica* (A.D. 721), who had no training as a singer, but who nevertheless developed the art of narrative verse on Christian themes in what must have been, technically, a thoroughly traditional manner.—L. F. Anderson, *The Anglo-Saxon Scop* (1903); R. W. Chambers, *Widsith* (1912); K. Malone, *Deor* (1933, 1962); *Widsith* (1936); D. Whitelock, *The Audience of Beowulf* (1951); F. P. Magoun, Jr., "Bede's Story of Cædman: The Case Hist. of an Anglo-Saxon Oral Singer," *Speculum*, 30 (1955).　J.B.B

SCOTTISH CHAUCERIANS. A name applied to a group of Sc. poets of the 15th and 16th c., whose work, although the freshest and most original Eng. poetry of the period, shows a common indebtedness to the example of Chaucer. The most important Sc. Chaucerians were King James I of Scotland, Robert Henryson, William Dunbar, Gavin Douglas, and Sir David Lindsay, and of these Henryson and Dunbar were poets of major importance. Henryson is remembered for *Robene and Makyne,* a superb pastoral, and for *The Testament of Cresseid,* a profound and moving elaboration and continuation of Chaucer's *Troilus and Criseyde.* Dunbar, a poet of wider range, wrote elaborate occasional verse, biting satires, and such memorable short poems as his famous elegiac *Lament for the Makaris.* In formal terms, the Sc. Chaucerians continued the vogue of the 7-line stanza introduced into Eng. poetry by Chaucer. Indeed, it has been said by some prosodists (though denied by others) that its name of "rhyme royal" (q.v.) derives from the use of this stanza by James I in his poem *The Kingis Quair.*—G. Gregory Smith, "The Sc. Chaucerians," CHEL, II (1949); C. S. Lewis, *Eng. Lit. in the 16th C., Excluding Drama* (1954).

SCOTTISH GAELIC POETRY. The origins of Scot. Gael. poetry are naturally identical with those of Ir. This identity is preserved in classical or "bardic" poetry, which continued to be written without significant regional variation in both countries—up to the 17th c. in Ireland, the 18th in Scotland, which held the status of a cultural province vis-à-vis the mother country. This fact, as well as destruction of manuscripts, has to be considered when noting the comparative rarity of poems of Scot. provenance or authorship. Nevertheless, there are examples of poems connected with Scotland extant from as early as the 11th or 12th c. Identity is constituted by the same literary dialect; the same expression of "heroic" values; the same metrical forms (although Gael. is a stressed language, classical poetry, based on late L. verse, observes regularity of syllable grouping rather than stress); the same rigorous and almost incredibly complex rules of ornamentation. Not all poems of course conform to this austere standard. *Oglàchas* or "prentice-work," which utilizes an easier, modified technique, is fairly common whether written by members of the hereditary caste of learned men who had undergone the arduous training of the bardic schools or by members of the aristocracy who had not, but who knew the literary language and possessed a facility for composing dilettante or occasional verse. All these features of style and authorship are admirably displayed in the earliest and principal compilation of classi-cal verse to have survived in Scotland, viz. the Book of the Dean of Lismore (ca. 1512–26). It also provides a fair sample of the range and variety of the themes of bardic verse: encomia of court poets for their patrons, satire, religious poetry, "ballads" of Fionn and Oisean, etc. (formally the Gael. "ballad," in this context, belongs with the rest of bardic poetry), a sprinkling of moral and didactic verse, and a few love poems in the *amour courtois* tradition. These limited examples serve to remind us of the relative paucity of that genre in classical poetry until the notion of courtly love, introduced with the Anglo-Norman invasion of Ireland, became rooted in Gael. tradition. The excellence of bardic verse lies in the highly developed language employed, with its sophisticated and allusive style, and, above all, in the elaborate and subtly modulated music of its intricate metrical patterns. Its limitations are in fact inherent neither in subject matter nor technique but derive rather from a formality of approach inseparable from the conventions of the professional poet's office, that of public panegyrist to the great men of his society.

The classical poets were by definition literate; their counterparts, the vernacular poets, on the whole were not; and with some exceptions their work has been recovered from oral tradition by 18th-c. and later collectors. But too much can be made of this disjunction. Syllabic versification did not die out with the professional poets nor, in the stressed meters, do we at once find a poetry of totally different content or thought. Stressed poetry exists in a multiplicity of forms, the most interesting, because restricted to Scotland, being the so-called strophic meter (minimally, two lines each of two stresses, followed by a triple-stressed line —but extensions and elaborations occur). The two great early practitioners of this type of verse whose work has survived, Mairi Nighean Alasdair Ruaidh (ca. 1615–1707) and Iain Lom (ca. 1620–1710) are not innovators. Although the latter is exercised by national issues, both are clan poets, still in the panegyric tradition, and both have clearly the security of established practice behind them—stretching back perhaps to a point anterior to the introduction of Latin learning and the syllabic meters. The rhetoric of their verse at its best has a splendidly affirmative quality.

Syllabic verse persisted in Scotland both in written and orally composed vernacular poetry. The anthology known as the Fernaig MS, compiled between 1688 and 1693, contains distinctive examples of poems (religious, political, elegiac etc.) that help to point the steps in the development from classical to vernacular syllabic meters, while oral poetry displaying substantial vestiges of syllabic meter is being composed at the present day. In this connection one must note the significance of the great collections from MSS and oral recitation of vernacular Fionn and Oisean ballads. These collections were mostly made after the publication of James MacPherson's *Ossian* (1760), which was ultimately based on the ballads.

Of obscure origin but almost certainly indigenous is the corpus of oral songs sung in single lines or couplets followed by meaningless and sometimes highly elaborate refrains. Again restricted to Scotland and composed largely by women, these songs contain some of the most vivid and arresting poetry in Gael. Often it has a strong pagan tone. Possibly from the 17th c., which appears to be the heyday of the tradition, comes the *Lament for Seathan*, which concludes thus:

A Sheathain, mo ghile-gréine,
Och dha m'aindeoin ghlac an t-eug thu,
'S dh'fhàg siod mise dubhach deurach
'S iargain ghointeach orm ad dhéidh-sa;
'S masa fior na their na cléirich
Gu bheil Irinn 's gu bheil Nèamh ann,
Mo chuid-sa Nèamh, di-beath an éig e,
Air son oidhche mar ris an eudail,
Mar ri Sheathain donn mo chéile.

O Seathan, my brightness of the sun!
Alas! despite me death has seized thee,
And that has left me sad and tearful,
Lamenting bitterly that thou art gone;
And if all the clerics say is true,
That there is a Hell and a Heaven,
My share of Heaven—it is my welcome to death—
For a night with my darling,
With my spouse, brown-haired Seathan.

In the 18th c. a fresh dimension was added to the scope and expressiveness of poetry by Alexander MacDonald (1700-1770), the perfervid nationalist and poet of the "Forty-Five," and by Duncan Bàn Macintyre (1724-1812), the hunter-poet. A highly literate man—he was formally educated at Glasgow University—drawing on all the resources of Gael., MacDonald is the outstanding figure of his age. The resonant verse of John MacCodrum (1693-1779) seems more of the 17th c. by comparison, but the controlled, detailed naturalism of Macintyre's *Praise of Ben Dorain* embodies a movement away from clan poetry. These two were completely oral poets, as was Rob Donn (1714-78), the best satirist in vernacular Gael. The poetry of William Ross (1762-90) manifests a wider sensibility, which certainly owes something to his learning in Eng. and in the classical languages. Ross's tender, anguished love poems merit a special place in the history of Gael. literature.

The nadir of Gael. verse falls in the 19th c. when the breakup of Gael. society, due to Eng. intrusion and forced emigration, partially destroyed the Gael. spirit. Moreover, a good deal of published work is the product of urbanized Gaels influenced by romanticism and other alien conventions. Yet an appreciable body of vigorous oral poetry was composed, in which the verse of Mary MacPherson of Skye (1821–98) is notable.

Gael. poetry throughout its history has suffered from being largely excluded from external influences. The importance of this is underlined by pointing out that it has been almost totally unaffected by the Renaissance. Less important, but equally significant, is the fact that (with perhaps some minor exceptions) all Gael. poetry appears to have been sung or chanted. But partly because it is mainly an oral poetry, and partly too because verse and not prose has always been the prime literary medium of Gael., a strong, supple, rich language has been evolved, capable of expressing immense diversity in form and mood.

In our own time it has been triumphantly recharged by Somhairle Maclean (b. 1911) in *Dàin do Eimhir* (1943) the publication of which marks a revolution in Gael. writing. Like George Campbell Hay (b. 1915), whose verse rehabilitates the subtle movement of the older syllabic meters, Maclean writes with an intense private awareness of international problems of the 20th c. Of younger poets Derick Thomson (b. 1922) and Iain Crichton Smith (b. 1928) are the most significant. With these writers Gael. poetry, without compromising its intrinsic virtues, suddenly has become "modern."

ANTHOLOGIES: *Ortha nan Gaidheal: Carmina Gadelica*, ed. A. Carmichael (5 v., 1928–54; with parallel tr.); *Highland Songs of the Forty-Five*, ed. J. L. Campbell (1933); *Scot. Verse from the Book of the Dean of Lismore*, ed. W. J. Watson (1937); *Heroic Poetry from the Book of the Dean of Lismore*, ed. N. Ross (1939); *Bardachd Ghàidhlig: Specimens of Gael. Poetry 1550-1900*, ed. W. J. Watson (3d ed., 1959; contains useful bibliog. of printed and manuscript sources).

HISTORY AND CRITICISM: D. Maclean, *The Lit. of the Scot. Gael* (1912); M. Maclean, *The Lit. of the Highlands* (2d ed., 1925) and *The Lit. of the Celts* (2d ed., 1926); N. MacNeill, *The Lit. of the Highlanders* (2d ed., 1929); D. Young, "A Note on Scot. Gael. Poetry," *Scot. Poetry: A Critical Survey*, ed. J. Kinsley (1955); K. Wittig, "The Scot. Gael. Trad.," *The Scot. Tradition in Lit.* (1958). J.MACI.

SCOTTISH POETRY. A brief description of Scot. poetry can be most clearly indicated with-the year 1603 in mind. That year took Queen Elizabeth from the English; it also took James VI from his throne in Auld Reekie to sit as James I in Whitehall. The departure of James signified the end of Scotland's identity as a kingdom and the loss of her individual culture. It also closed the first volume of Scot. poetry.

Long before 1603 a Scot. tongue had developed slowly from Northumbrian Eng. to the point where it was regarded as literary. As early as the 13th c. poets like Rhymer and Huchowne had left their names linked with metrical romances, ballads, and songs. And out of those beginnings three figures had emerged to fix in verse-history the national pride of the Scots: John Barbour, author of *The Bruce*; Andrew of Wyntoun, author of a rhymed chronicle; and Blind Harry, author of *The Wallace*. Barbour (ca. 1357), first and foremost of these poet-chroniclers, is remembered by Scotland today chiefly because he remembered the men of the Scot. War of Independence as heroes and patriots in such lines as "and certes, thai suld weill hawe pryss / That in thair tyme war wycht and wise, / And led their lyff in gret trawaill, / And oft, in hard stour of bataill, / Wan eycht gret price off chewalry, / And was woydyt off cowardy."

In the 15th c., when Blind Harry composed his eleven books of heroic couplets on Wallace, James I of Scotland, the reputed poet of *The Kingis Quair*, was living out his 18 years of imprisonment in England. Knowledge of Chaucer and Gower gained through these years spread in Scotland upon James's return and became an important stimulus for Scotland's richest body of poetry.

This Renaissance poetry was the work of the Scot. Chaucerians or makars—Henryson, Douglas, and Dunbar—who, like James, held Chaucer and his Eng. imitators as their "maisteris dear." The makars borrowed from Chaucer as he had borrowed from the best in medieval poetry; of such, for example, was their use of the rhyme-royal stanza (q.v.). More or less on their own, they completed the development of a literary language (Middle Scots) so fully sophisticated and metropolitan that it remained adequate for expressing Scot. culture until Eng. was substituted for that purpose in 1603.

Robert Henryson (1425–1503) opened this memorable period with a retelling of the Troilus and Criseyde story, a number of moral fables after Aesop, and *Robene and Makyne,* perhaps the earliest pastoral in British poetry. Bishop Gavin Douglas of Dunkeld (1474–1522) followed with the first translation of a classic into Scots (*Eneados*) in which the prologues, notably that for Book VII, reveal an able poet with the typical Scots poet's eye for the natural scene.

William Dunbar (1463–1535) most severely tested the capabilities of Middle Scots in poems like *The Golden Targe* (for many his masterpiece), *The Flyting of Dunbar and Kennedy,* and *Ane Ballat of Our Lady.* Never long, his poems are often pessimistic, free and brilliant after Horace, forceful, coarse, and sententious. Dunbar employed a variety of metrics (he was the first to write blank verse in the Scots vernacular), a variety of tone—now religious, now violently satiric, now bawdy—and a variety of diction.

The last of the notable figures in this period was Sir David Lyndsay (1490–1557): an early defender of writing for Iok and Thome in the maternal language, the most popular Scots poet before Burns, and the tutor of James V, Lyndsay is known primarily for his *Ane Pleasant Satire of the Thrie Estaitis* striking out against the corruption of the clergy and nobles.

With the poetry of the makars and anonymous pieces like *Rauf Coilyear* and *The Bewteis of the Fute-ball*; with the lyrics of poets like Scott and Montgomerie; and with the manuscript collections of Maitland and Bannatyne, which show lyrics and ballads to be the staples of Scot. poetry, national Scotland approached the year of Elizabeth's death and the subsequent loss of its own court and independent life. This loss and the prolonged dissipation of intellectual efforts in theological speculation and controversy make it impossible to name a Scot. poet of high distinction during the entire 17th c., not excluding William Drummond, who showed with some success what a Scotsman could compose in Eng.

Scotland's great corpus of folk poetry, a major part of what is now known as "the Ballads," coexisted with and even predated the court poetry of the makars. These vivid verse narratives, whether of national history (*The Battle of Otterbourn*), of legendary local feud or farce (*Jock o' the Side; Get up and Bar the Door*), or of doomed romance and the supernatural (*Edward; Thomas of Ersseldoune*), reveal constant techniques of dramatic immediacy and economy. The language, stark and nonliterary except for a few often repeated epithets and "kennings" (q.v.), acquires a dynamic urgency from the relentless beat of the ballad rhythm: "At kirk or market where we meet, / We dare nae mair avow"; or evokes "the abomination of desolation": "Ower his white banes, when they are bare, / The wind sall blaw for evermair"; or freezes us with the shudder of mortality and the unknown: "The cock doth craw, the day doth daw, / The channerin' worm doth chide." In their dramatic intensity, their laconic understatement, and their pervasive undertone of grim humor, the ballads come nearer than almost any other literary form to expressing the elemental values of a rugged people for whom struggle was the basic condition of life.

From 1603 to the present day Scotland has produced a number of excellent poets who chose literary Eng. as their medium because they thought it was impossible to write in Scots and yet write seriously. James Thomson (1700–1748), poet of *The Seasons*, Robert Blair, Alexander Ross, James Beattie, and John Home used standard Eng. for the works by which they are remembered. Byron and Campbell were Scotsmen, but hardly Scots poets. Sir Walter Scott's long poems are in Eng., so are such later works as James Thomson's (1834–82) *The City of Dreadful Night* and Stevenson's *A Child's Garden of Verses*.

Modern Scot. poetry—to be distinguished from that of the makars and of those poets coming after them who wrote principally in Eng.—had rather inauspicious beginnings in the 17th and early 18th c. as literary jokes like Semple's *Epitaph of Habbie Simson, Piper of Kilbarchen* and Allan Ramsay's burlesque elegy on John Cooper, a kirk treasurer who could smell out a bawd. Because of the vogue of pastoral poetry, Ramsay selected Scots also for his poetic drama *The Gentle Shepherd* and by so doing increased the growing sentiment that Scots with its rural origin and popular character encouraged a homely directness of approach and was well suited to express simple ideas.

Ramsay, Robert Fergusson, and Robert Burns all were discontented with the lowly state of Scot. verse during their time; yet all three, the only Scotsmen to write significant Scot. poetry in the 18th c., were fully aware that exclusive use of Scots had become the mark of the vulgar. Ramsay's poetry became the principal source of Fergusson's, whose poetry, in turn, became the principal source of Burns's. The types which all three favored were the epistle, ode, elegy, and satire—Ramsay and Burns being interested, moreover, in the song. All three poets relied heavily upon four verse forms: the octosyllabic couplet, the standard "Habbie," the heroic couplet, and the Christ's Kirk stanza. Fergusson and Burns were successful also in the Spenserian stanza, introduced to Scot. poetry by Fergusson.

Such poetry as Fergusson's gave to Burns the example of completely free self-expression in Scots—something unknown to Ramsay. But the poetry of Burns is most easily distinguishable from that of Fergusson by its power of concentrating thought upon theme. Not only such powers as this, but also Burns's wisdom in staying away from standard Eng. or using it sparingly for a particular effect is evident in his best poems. Had *The Jolly Beggars* served as *the* anthology piece of Burns instead of *The Cotter's Saturday Night*, there would be today a truer picture of Burns's poetic genius, for it is here that his characteristic merits of description, narration, dramatic effect, metrical diversity, energy, sensitivity to the beauties inherent in Scots music and language, and keen discernment of country folk are to be appreciated. Hundreds of songs, moreover, show these merits of Burns. No poet—certainly in Great Britain—has left so many memorable ones or so much evidence of masterful skill in uniting words with music! Let a Scotsman sing *Come Boat Me O'er, The Banks o' Doon*, or *Scots Wha Hae* and the genius of Robert Burns explains itself. These songs are a contribution to world poetry made by Burns and Scotland. Many of them describe the continuation of the collecting of folk songs and ballads which Ramsay had begun and which Percy, Herd, Ritson, Burns, Scott, Child, and others carried on.

In the 19th and 20th c. there have been very few fish in the sea. Poets have been at work and have produced infrequently a piece or two like *Caller Herrin'* or *The Bush aboon Traquair* to turn up in anthologies. Sentimentality and heavy use of the diminutive, as in the popular *Cuddle Doon*, mark much of their poetry as Scot.

More recently, a group of Scots poets, led by Hugh MacDiarmid (C. M. Grieve), has determined that the practice of vernacular verse shall not involve any surrendering of the poet's cultural dignity or any loss of his intellectual personality. Refusing to accept the 18th-c. limitations of the vernacular, these poets have tackled the problem of having to create a Scots idiom of their own. One answer has been their battle cry "Back to Dunbar!"— that is, back to Dunbar's "literary" stature, his variety of expression, and his richness of vocabulary. How successful contemporary Scot. poets have been in freeing Scots from the cultural bonds of a class and dialect speech forged after 1603 and in using current Scots for the profounder utterances of the spirit may be judged by reading George Campbell Hay's volume *Wind on Loch Fyne*, William Soutar's poem *The Gowk*, or MacDiarmid's brief lyric with which we conclude:

The Bonnie Broukit Bairn

Mars is braw in crammasy,
Venus in a green silk goun,
The auld mune shaks her gowden feathers,
Their starry talk's a wheen o' blethers,
Nane for thee a thochtie sparin,
Earth, thou bonnie broukit bairn!
　　—But greet, an' in your tears ye'll droun
　　The haill clanjamfrie!

ANTHOLOGIES: *Specimens of Middle Scots,* ed. G. Smith (1902); *The Poets of Ayrshire,* ed. J. Macintosh (1910); *The Edinburgh Book of Scot. Verse: 1300–1900,* ed. W. Dixon (1910); *The Northern Muse,* ed. J. Buchan (1936); *The Golden Treasury of Scot. Poetry,* ed. H. MacDiarmid (1941); *A Scots Anthol.,* ed. J. Oliver and J. Smith (1949); *Scot. Verse: 1851–1951,* ed. D. Young (1952).

BALLADS AND SONGS: *Ancient and Modern Scots Songs,* ed. D. Herd (1769); *The Scots Musical Museum,* ed. J. Johnson (6 v., 1786–1803); *Bishop Percy's Folio Manuscript,* ed. J. Hales and F. Furnivall (3 v., 1867–68); *Eng. and Scot. Popular Ballads,* ed. F. J. Child (5 v., 1883–98); *Scott's Minstrelsy of the Scot. Border,* ed. T. Henderson (4 v., 1902); *Border Ballads,* ed. W. Beattie (1952); *The Traditional Tunes of the Child Ballads,* ed. B. Bronson (1959–   ).

HISTORY AND CRITICISM: G. Douglas, *Scot. Poetry* (1911); A. Mackenzie, *Historical Survey of Scot. Lit. to 1714* (1933); W. Craigie, "The Scot. Alliterative Poems," *Proc.* of the British Academy (1942); P. Brown, *A Short Hist. of Scotland,* ed. and rev. by H. Meikle (2d ed., 1951); *Scot. Poetry: A Crit. Survey,* ed. J. Kinsley (1955); K. Wittig, *The Scot. Trad. in Lit.* (1958); T. Crawford, *Burns: A Study of the Poems and Songs* (1960); D. Craig, *Scot. Lit. and the Scot. People* (1961); see also introd. to anthol. listed above, esp. MacDiarmid's.   R.D.T.

SEA SHANTIES (chanteys, chanties). The work songs of sailors aboard square-rigged sailing vessels, as distinct from fo'c's'le songs, the story-songs and lyrics sung by sailors for their off-duty amusement. Shanty singing goes back at least to the days of the Tudor carracks, and one song of that period, *Haul on the Bowline,* has been preserved. The heyday of the shanty was the clipper era (1830–80). Sh. were not permitted in the Am. or British navies. The purpose of the shanty was partly to keep up morale but primarily to coordinate group labor. Sh. therefore are grouped by the kind of labor they could accompany, since different jobs required different rhythms. The short-haul shanty (*Boney, Haul Away, Joe*) coordinated a job that could be done with a few hard pulls, such as "sweating up" halyards; halyard sh. accompanied heavy, prolonged jobs, such as hoisting sail. Examples are *Blow the Man Down* and *Hanging Johnny.* The capstan shanty (*The Fair Maid of Amsterdam, Shenandoah*) was for pulling in anchor cable and similar sustained work of moderate difficulty. A shantyman—Irishmen or Negroes were preferred—directed the singing, coming down heavily on the word on which the gang was to heave in concert. The narrative line in sh. is generally incoherent; the songs tended to be compounded of independent stanzas so that they could be curtailed or expanded as the job required.—COLLECTIONS: *Sea Songs and Sh.,* comp. W. B. Whall (1927); *Songs of Am. Sailormen,* comp. J. C. Colcord (1938); *Shantymen and Shantyboys,* comp. W. M. Doerflinger (1951); *Sh. from the Seven Seas,* ed. S. Hugill (1961).   A.B.F.

SEGUIDILLA. A Sp. poetic form of popular origin. It probably originated as a dance song and was popular, at least in the underworld, early in the 17th c. In the beginning it was probably a 4-line strophe of alternating long (usually of 7 or 8 syllables) and short (usually of 5 or 6 syllables) lines, the short (even-numbered) lines assonating (called *s. simple* or *s. para cantar*). Later, probably, in the 17th c., a second, semi-independent part of 3 lines—short, long, short—was added, the short lines having a new assonance. Eventually the strophe became regularized as a literary form to lines of 7,5,7,5: 5,7,5 (the colon denotes a pause in thought), lines 2 and 4 having one assonance, lines 5 and 7 another (called *s. compuesta* or *s. para bailar*) and was often used by the poets of the 18th c. Sometimes the rhythm only has been used in lines of 7-plus-5 syllables as by Rubén Darío in his *Elogio de la seguidilla.* The s. favors all paroxytonic verses except when hexasyllabic oxytones are substituted for the pentasyllabic lines. The s. is sometimes used to serve as a conclusion (*estribillo*) to another song.

The *s. gitana* (Gypsy s.), also called *flamenca* or *playera,* is usually a 5-line strophe of successively 6,6,5,6,6 syllables, lines 2 and 5 assonating. Lines 3 and 4 may be written together as one line of from 10 to 12 syllables.—F. Hanssen, "La s.," AUC, 125 (1909); F. Rodríguez Marín, *La copla* (1910); P. Henríquez Ureña, *La versificación irregular en la poesía castellana* (2d ed., 1933); D. C. Clarke, "The Early s.," HR, 12 (1944); Navarro.   D.C.C.

SEMANTICS AND POETRY. The word "semantics," derived from the Gr. *semainein,* denotes properly "the study of meaning." Although the word was brought into modern use by the publication of Bréal's *Essai de Semantique* (1897; Eng. tr. 1900), it was employed there in a more limitedly philological sense than has subsequently been the custom.

Wherever meaning is present (and where it is not present we cannot properly think or speak) there are always two terms involved: that which means, and that which is meant; or the indicator (in the broadest sense) and the meaning. When the meaning is definite enough to be pointed to or otherwise clearly identified, it is also called the referend; when it is too general or too elusive to define exactly, it may be called the reference.

Indicators may be grouped, according to their methods of functioning, into three main classes: natural signs, steno-signs, and symbols. Natural signs are those which indicate a certain referend or referential situation by reason of some actual (usually causal) connection in the real world. In this sense a rapidly clouding sky is a sign of a storm; if it suggests appropriate action, such as running for cover, it is a signal as well. Natural signs are the primitive materials out of which both steno-signs and symbols are developed by different routes.

By a steno-sign is meant an indicator whose meaning has become fixed and definite, whether by gradual habituation or by stipulative agreement, for those who understand the particular language-convention that governs it: e.g., the word "tree" (for those who speak Eng.), the sign + (for those who know arithmetic), and a red traffic light (for motorists and most pedestrians). The third of these steno-signs functions also as a signal, and the second may do so where there is a problem to be solved. Four characteristics of the steno-sign deserve notice. (1) Since the relation of steno-sign to its meaning is governed by convention, the sign and the meaning tend to be quite distinct. The word "tree" is replaceable by the word *"Baum"* or *"arbre"* without semantic loss when the linguistic context is changed to German or French; there is no more of the character of tree attached to any one of these words than to the others. Nor is there any character of plusness in the sign +. (2) The relation of steno-sign to its meaning is properly univocal. In a given context it should have only one meaning, or, if more than one, these should be so distinguishable that they could be represented by distinct symbols if the occasion should require. Moreover, this meaning should be definite, and for the course of a given argument or given science, invariant. (3) The referend of any steno-sign is characterized by either of two kinds of mental (often preconscious) integration: logical universality, established by definition based on definite similarities or analogies, and existential particularity, established by space-time continuities. These two familiar modes of meaning are what Santayana has called concretions in discourse and concretions in existence; the one is normally expressed by common names ("man"), the other by proper names or particularized common names ("John," "the man I met yesterday"). (4) Steno-signs lend themselves to the making of steno-statements, or propositions. It is characteristic of a proposition, in this logical sense, that it should be internally coherent (not self-contradictory) and that its truth be a function of the potential evidence on which it rests.

The obvious utilitarian value of steno-signs has given rise to a type of semantics which takes the operations of such signs, on whatever level of abstraction, as coextensive with semantic functioning in general; consequently treating all other modes of semantic functioning, particularly those found in religion and in poetry, as either variations or violations of these. For brevity of reference this type of theory may be described as steno-semantics. The usual way of interpreting poetry from the standpoint of steno-semantics is to deny that it functions semantically at all—that is, in its proper character as poetry—and to emphasize rather its psychic effects. This reemphasis (termed "the affective fallacy" [q.v.] by Beardsley and Wimsatt) is exemplified in Morris' statement that poetry is "an example of discourse which is appraisive-valuative" and that "its primary aim is to cause the interpreter to accord to what is signified the preferential place in his behavior signified by the appraisors." Similarly I. A. Richards, in his earlier writings, distinguishes between the "statements" of science and the "pseudo-statements" which are typical of poetry; defining a pseudo-statement as one whose validity is entirely subjective—"entirely governed by its effects upon our feelings and attitudes."

The third type of indicator, supremely important for poetry and such related disciplines as religion and mythology, is the expressive symbol, or depth symbol. The qualifying adjectives are designed to distinguish this use of the word "symbol," justified by a long popular and literary tradition, from its technical use in logic and mathematics, where, in terms of our present definitions, it is taken as a specially abstract type of steno-sign. The steno-sign and the depth symbol represent two complementary and interpenetrating uses of language, which are the outgrowth, by and large, of two complementary semantic needs—to designate clearly as a means to efficient and assured communication, and to express with maximum fullness. The role of a depth symbol is thus to evoke richness and suggestiveness of meaning, usually at some sacrifice of conventional and utilitarian exactness: e.g., the Cross to a believing Christian, the ominous contrasting connotations of the blood and darkness imagery in *Macbeth*, the mythic Father and Mother archetypes associated respectively with the powers of sky and earth. It is evident that the more interesting and important semantic problems of poetry have to do with its employment of, and shifting relations to, depth symbols. As distinguished from steno-semantics, which undertakes to interpret the meanings of poetry according to the rigid laws of steno-signs, the method of a poeto-semantics must be to examine the actual character and semantic action of depth symbols in a variety of particular poems and to construct a theory of meaning that does something like adequate justice to these. As opposed to the four characteristics of steno-signs above noted, the characteristics of the depth symbol, or poeto-symbol, in its most typical manifestations, may be set down as follows.

1. The depth symbol, although pointing to a meaning beyond itself, is to some extent *participative* in that meaning. The Cross, the holy image, and the liturgical act have received into themselves, through the associative power of long tradition, much of the religious character which properly belongs to the transcendental reality which is their meaning and justification. In poetry and the arts the participative nature of the symbols employed shows itself in the artist's and the beholder's love for the medium itself. Not only what is said but the way of saying it counts; where the double condition is lacking, art falls into mere abstractionism and experimentalism on the one hand, or into either allegory or propaganda on the other.

2. As distinguished from the univocality of the steno-sign, the depth symbol tends to be *plurisignative;* which is to say, its intended meanings are likely to be more or less multiple, yet so fused as to produce an integral meaning which radically transcends the sum of the ingredient meanings, and hence which defies any adequate analysis into monosignative components. In this latter respect real plurisignation differs from simple punning or wit-writing. The power of the Cross for a Christian resides semantically in its double meaning of sacrificial death and resurrected life, both as represented archetypally in the Christ and as constituting the ultimate vocation of each believer. Lady Macbeth's reply, "And when goes hence?" to her husband's announcement of King Duncan's forthcoming visit is more than a pun, for the innuendo carries an air of ominous foreboding that is functionally related to the movement of the drama. Empson's use of the term "ambiguity" generally refers to the plurisignative character of poetic language; his word is inappropriate, however, since ambiguity implies an "either-or" relation, plurisignation a "both-and."

3. One mode of plurisignation is of such importance as to require separate treatment—namely, the *archetypal* character which resides perhaps implicitly and somewhat darkly, in many a depth symbol. An archetypal meaning is present wherever the transient image and the particular idea are permeated and enriched by suggestions of something more universal and perduring. Such archetypes as the Divine Father, the Earth Mother, new life growing out of death, the bread of life and the wine of the spirit, angels of light and demons of darkness, have powers of emotional and cognitive association which enable a poet, by deftly evoking them, to give an added referential dimension to his discourse. (See ARCHETYPE, MYTH). The archetypal character of the true symbol should not be confused with allegory, where the particular has status merely as an instance and example of the universal. Archetypal symbolism, by contrast, is what Hegel and more recently Wimsatt have called "concrete universality" and what Goethe has called "a living-moment disclosure of the inscrutable."

4. Whereas the steno-sign is, in principle at least, strictly invariant throughout a given discourse, the depth symbol, involving as it does some fusion of multiple meanings, tends to exhibit some degree of *contextual variation*—that is, to be semantically influenced and freshened by each particular context, even though there will also be a relatively persistent core of meaning which unites or relates the various semantic occasions together.

5. Poetic expression, striving more after semantic fullness than after logical exactitude, is hospitable to meanings which do not have definite outlines and which cannot be adequately represented by terms that are strictly defined. This property may be called, by photographic analogy, *soft focus*. Logical exactitude can be attained only by the systematic neglect of all the overtones of meaning and allusion that do not fit into the stipulated definition. But these overtones are the very life of the depth symbol, and while a poet controls them as well as he can, it would be unrealistic to suppose that they can ever be exactly the same for different readers. "Poetry is implication, don't try to turn it into explication," Robert Frost warns his readers. But T. S. Eliot's counter-warning should also be heeded, that "the suggestiveness is the aura around a bright clear centre, that you cannot have the aura alone."

6. As opposed to the third characteristic of the steno-sign, depth symbols tend to represent other concretions of meaning than those two stereotyped ones, existential particularity (the individual thing) and logical universality (the class concept). The one represents our common ways of identifying things in the public world, the other represents our common ways of grouping qualities and functions under class-concepts in order to draw logical inferences about them. But the role of the poet is not simply to repeat identifications and generalizations that have already been made. "The sole excuse which a man can have for writing," said Remy de Gourmont, "is to unveil for others the sort of world which mirrors itself in his individual glass." To express that individual world will always require to some

degree what Coleridge has called the "balance or reconciliation of discordant qualities." There will be realignments of meaning, "produced by bringing into relation without explicit comparison two distant realities whose relations the mind alone has seized" (Paul Reverdy). The linguistic device by which this is achieved Allen Tate calls *"fused metaphor"* —that is to say, not metaphor in Aristotle's, Quintilian's, and the grammarians' sense of an abbreviated simile, but rather, according to Herbert Read's definition, as "the synthesis of several units of observation into one commanding image" and as "the expression of a complex idea, not by analysis, nor by direct statement, but by a sudden perception of an objective relation."

7. As distinguished from the fourth property of steno-signs, the depth symbol enters into the making not of logical propositions, but of *depth statements*. As shown by Wheelwright (*The Burning Fountain*, chap. 13), the difference between a depth statement and a pure proposition is not only a result of the six forementioned differences between depth symbols and steno-signs, but consists also in this, that whereas the meaning of a pure proposition is strictly declarative, the declarative element in a depth statement is fused with one or more of the four other modes of sentence-formation: the interrogative, exclamatory, hortatory, and acquiescent. As a consequence, *paradox* is a frequent property of depth statements. They can be paradoxical because of the softening effect of the nondeclarative elements in them, and they are likely to be para-doxical to some degree or other by reason of the tension of conflicting meanings struggling for quasi-assertion. Paradoxes in poetry may be either rhetorical or metaphysical. The former type may be an affair purely of surface, as in the conventional oxymoron of Romeo's "O heavy lightness! serious vanity!" Or it may result from an assertion made overtly and a counter-assertion implicit in the imagery or in the context. The metaphysical type of paradox is found in such a line as Eliot's "So the darkness shall be light, and the stillness the dancing"—where the paradoxical language is aimed at expressing a truth that transcends the area of ordinary experience, and where such transcendence is expressed symbolically by a flouting of the conventional laws of contradiction.

S. T. Coleridge, *Biographia Literaria* (1817; chaps. 13, 14); J. M. Murry, *The Problem of Style* (1922) and "Metaphor," in *Countries of the Mind* (2d ser., 1931); I. A. Richards, *Science and Poetry* (1926); *Coleridge on Imagination* (1934); *Philos. of Rhetoric* (1936); *Speculative Instruments* (1955; secs. 2, 3); O. Barfield, *Poetic Diction* (1928); G. Rylands, *Words and Poetry* (1928); W. Empson, *Seven Types of Ambiguity* (1930); *Some Versions of Pastoral* (1935); *The Structure of Complex Words* (1951); J. Sparrow, *Sense and Poetry* (1934); E. M. W. Tillyard, *Poetry Direct and Oblique* (1934; rev. ed. 1945); A. Tate, "Tension in Poetry" (1938; repr. in *On the Limits of Poetry*, 1948); K. Britton, *Communication* (1939); W. M. Urban, *Language and Reality* (1939); K. Burke, "Semantic and Poetic Meaning," in *The Philos. of Lit. Form* (1941); S. K. Langer, *Philos. in a New Key* (1942) and *Feeling and Form* (1953); T. C. Pollock, *The Nature of Lit.* (1942); J. Hospers, *Meaning and Truth in the Arts* (1946); C. Brooks, *The Well Wrought Urn* (1947); M. Foss, *Symbol and Metaphor in Human Experience* (1949); S. K. Coffman, *Imagism* (1951); R. McKeon, "Semantics, Science, and Poetry," MP, 49 (1952); P. Wheelwright, *The Burning Fountain* (1954) and *Metaphor and Reality* (1962); Wimsatt.　　　P.W.

SENARIUS (L. "of 6 each"). The Roman equivalent of the Gr. iambic trimeter. Whereas the latter name recognizes the division of this meter into 3 pairs of feet or dipodies, each ending in an iambus (or its equivalent tribrach in the first or second dipody), the senarius of early Roman drama ignored Gr. dipodic structure and admitted spondees in the second and fourth feet (but not in lieu of the pure iambus of the sixth foot). In the first 5 feet there are frequent resolutions of long syllables and the fifth foot is rarely an iambus. Later Roman poets, with the exception of Phaedrus, wrote trimeters rather than senarii.—W. M. Lindsay, *Early L. Verse* (1922); Crusius.　　　R.J.G.

SENHAL. A fanciful name ("My Magnet," "Tristan," "Good Hope") used in Old Prov. poems to address ladies, patrons, or friends. A few of the persons so addressed have been identified with some certainty, but for the most part they remain either completely unknown or the objects of more or less probable conjectures.　　　F.M.C.

SENRYŪ. See JAPANESE POETRY.

SENSIBILITY first became prominent as a literary term in the mid-18th c., with the meaning "susceptibility to tender feelings." It links the (possibly undesirable) quality of feeling sorry for oneself and conscious of one's own woes, with a morally praiseworthy quality—susceptibility to the sorrows of others—and an aesthetically praiseworthy quality, responsiveness to beauty. This complex of qualities is naturally popular in the age of Sterne, Goldsmith, and Cowper. The Man of Feeling (there is a novel of this title by Mackenzie) represents much of what the later 18th c. admired:

he is the opposite of the Stoic (the cult of sensibility sometimes involved a conscious rejection of Stoicism) and an obvious anticipation of the romantics.

Perhaps the first important use of "s." in this way comes in a passage from the periodical *The Prompter* in 1735: the writer is defending that Humanity which "is not satisfy'd with good-Natured Actions alone, but feels the Misery of others with inward Pain. It is then deservedly nam'd Sensibility." The term seems to become popular in the 1760's, and there are a good number of odes to s. from then on; Goldsmith's *Deserted Village* was no doubt thought of as a poem not lacking in s., and the youth at the end of Gray's *Elegy* who "gave to Mis'ry all he had, a tear," is a Man of Feeling. The famous lines from Cowper's *Task*:

I would not enter on my list of friends
(Though grac'd with polish'd manners and fine
    sense,
Yet wanting sensibility) the man,
Who needlessly sets foot upon a worm

suggest that its opposite is not only insensibility but also (he goes on to use the word) cruelty.

Several other favorite terms of the period overlap with "s.": especially "delicacy" and "sentimentality." "Delicacy" perhaps differs in stressing fineness rather than intensity of feeling, though it is often used as a synonym; while to distinguish "sentimentality" from "s." is even more difficult, perhaps impossible.

The concept of s. is probably most familiar today from the attacks made on it, by Dr. Johnson and (especially) Jane Austen. *Sense and Sensibility* is the most famous of these; less profound, but more convenient for the literary historian, is Jane Austen's portrait of Sir Edward Denham in *Sanditon,* who, talking of the sea and the sea shore, "ran with Energy through all the usual Phrases employed in praise of their Sublimity, and descriptive of the *undescribable* Emotions they excite in the Mind of Sensibility."

In the 19th c. the adjective "sensible" underwent a semantic change, attaching itself to "sense" and not to "s." It was—more or less—replaced by "sensitive," but "sensitivity" never became a technical term of literary discussion as "s." had been. The concept itself seemed to disappear: perhaps the advent of romanticism had made it unnecessary to defend the Man of Feeling. At any rate, when the term "s." returned to criticism, it was with an altogether new meaning: one which draws on the (non-literary) history of the word.

This modern meaning was anticipated by Baudelaire. In his essay on Constantin Guys he suggests that the child, the convalescent, and the artist are alike in possessing "the ability

(*la faculté*) of being vividly interested in things, even those that appear most trivial . . . . The child sees everything *afresh* (*en nouveauté*); he is always *drunk.*" The man of genius is he who adds powers of analysis and expression to the s. of the child. We can see here the linking of physical and emotional responsiveness that is the essence of the modern meaning of the word. Baudelaire's view of s. involves an emphasis on the physical strain of thought, a special awareness of flux, and a mingling of the senses. Almost all his essay could apply to Proust (he even says "le génie n'est que l'enfance retrouvée à volonté"— genius is simply the deliberate recapturing of childhood), and a great deal to the whole stream-of-consciousness tradition. Both Virginia Woolf and Joyce are peculiarly aware of the flux of the world of sensations, and of the physical strain accompanying intense emotional experience; and next to Baudelaire's assertion that "inspiration has some connexion with *congestion*" we can set the experience of Lily Briscoe, in Virginia Woolf's *To the Lighthouse,* who when she has had her vision "with a sudden intensity, as if she saw it clear for a second," then lays down her brush "in extreme fatigue." It seems just to speak of Proust and Virginia Woolf as "novelists of sensibility" (in this modern use of the term); and the attitudes and limitations of this kind of novel are discussed by William Troy, who lays stress on the fascination of instability, the withdrawal from action of the essentially solitary characters, and the vicarious nature of their experience.

The philosophical background to this literary concept is in Bergson, and in his Eng. disciple, T. E. Hulme. Reality is a flux of interpenetrated elements, unseizable by the intellect: art is a more direct communication of reality than we can normally have. Hulme stresses the freshness of the artist's vision (the perfect artist would "perceive all things in their inner purity"—a sentence that could have come from Baudelaire's essay); he remarks, following Bergson, that those characteristics of mental life which art combats are imposed on us by the necessity of action. This certainly anticipates Virginia Woolf, and the theory seems to come full circle when Troy attacks her for constantly depicting states of mind that are almost totally withdrawn from action. Hulme does not use the word "s.," but he accepts the major assumption that its modern sense indicates: that the perception of sounds and colors is closely allied to emotional awareness (perception of "the subtlest movements of the inner life"), and is quite independent of the intellect.

But of all modern critics, it is T. S. Eliot who has done most to bring the term into common use. For him, too, its physical connections are very strong: "a thought to Donne was an experience: it modified his sensibility" —this means that he perceived it with his five senses—"like the odour of a rose." But for Eliot the term does not indicate one special kind of awareness, nor is its exploitation the mark of one kind of writing: s. is simply a name for the artistic faculty, as found in every poet. As a result, he brings the term closer to intellect. It may not actually include intelligence, but it is very closely related to it, and seems to include the ability to offer resistance —intellectual resistance—to the dangers of generalization. Hence the remark that Henry James had not merely a sensibility but a "*mind* so fine that no idea could violate it." Eliot's famous doctrine of dissociation of sensibility (q.v.) refers to a dissociation between the intellect and the senses.

Since Eliot the term (now very common) has widened still more, and today a poet's s. may mean simply "the sort of man he is." This meaning is already covered by "personality" or "character," and it may be that this widening has robbed the term of much of its original interest.

So distinct are the two uses of "s." that this bibliog. is divided into two sections. I. THE 18TH-C. USAGE: *The Guardian*, no. 19 (1713); *The Prompter*, no. 63 (17 June 1735); L. Sterne, *Tristram Shandy* (1759–67; see especially such episodes as Uncle Toby's speech to the fly, v. II, chap. 12), *A Sentimental Journey* (1768); Wm. Cowper, *The Task* (1785; esp. Book VI); R. S. Crane, "Suggestions towards a Genealogy of the Man of Feeling," ELH, 1 (1934); C. S. Lewis, *Studies in Words* (1960); L. I. Bredvold, *The Natural History of S.* (1962); C. J. Rawson, "Some Remarks on 18th C. Delicacy . . . ," JEGP, 61 (1962). II. THE MODERN USAGE: C. Baudelaire, "Le Peintre de la Vie Moderne," *L'Art Romantique* (1869); H. James, "The Art of Fiction," *Partial Portraits* (1888); T. E. Hulme, *Speculations* (1924); V. Woolf, "Mr. Bennett and Mrs. Brown," *The Common Reader* (1925); T. S. Eliot, "The Metaphysical Poets," "Andrew Marvell," *Selected Essays* (1932); W. Troy, "Virginia Woolf: The Novel of S.," *Lit. Opinion in America*, ed. M. D. Zabel (3d ed. rev., 2 v., 1962).   L.D.L.

SENSIBILITY, DISSOCIATION OF. See DISSOCIATION OF SENSIBILITY.

SENTIMENTALITY in poetry. (1) Poetic indulgence in the exhibition of pathetic emotions for their own sake; (2) poetic indulgence of more emotion (often of a self-regarding kind) than seems warranted by the stimulus; (3) excessively direct poetic expression of pathos without a sufficient poetic correlative. Whether found in poet or reader, s. (a form of emo-

tional redundancy, and thus a fault of rhetoric as well as of ethics) often suggests the presence of self-pity and the absence of mature emotional self-control. The poetic sentimentalist appears to be interested in pathos as an end rather than as an artistic means or a constituent of a larger, less merely personal experience. The sentimentalist will often be found to be afflicted with an uncritically romantic sensibility: dogs, children, old women, the poor, and the unfortunate, regardless of any inherent merit, are not merely objects of interest and pity to the sentimentalist: they are frequently objects of reverence and even envy.

S. in poetry tends to express itself in the tags of popular journalism: adjectives are frequently clichés, and emotions remain vague and oversimplified; they somehow never become transmuted into something more meaningful than the bare, uncomplicated emotion itself. A good example of sentimental treatment is the journalistic habit of using invariably the redundant adjective "little" when some unfortunate child is being described. A similar technique of emotional redundancy is apparent in the following example: "When love meets love, breast urged to breast, / God interposes, / An unacknowledged guest, / And leaves a little child among our roses" (T. E. Brown, *When Love Meets Love*).

The quality of self-indulgence in the following example (a parody, by Coleridge, of the standard late 18th-c. sentimental poem) is noteworthy: the speaker characteristically tells us (and not once, but many times) that he is experiencing emotion; he does not present the emotion—he merely describes it: "Pensive at eve on the hard world I mused, / And my poor heart was sad: so at the Moon / I gazed—and sighed and sighed—for ah! how soon / Eve darkens into night" ("Nehemiah Higginbottom"). In this parody, the feeling has not found its poetic correlatives (images, symbols) but remains instead naked and untransmuted.

Poetic s. also tends to manifest an unconvincing hyperbole, and the hyperbole often fails because the imagery is trite or vapid: "If I can stop one heart from breaking, / I shall not live in vain; / If I can ease one life the aching, / Or cool one pain, / Or help one fainting robin / Unto his nest again, / I shall not live in vain" (Emily Dickinson). These last two examples will suggest that the sentimental poet generally expects to be admired for the feeling he exhibits; he reveals that, at the moment of composition, he has been more interested in the poet than the poem.

Historically, s. (at least in the modern sense of the term) seems not to have entered poetry much before the 18th c.; its appearance (for example, in Cowper, Gray, Shelley) can perhaps be ascribed in part to a strong current of philosophic optimism which transmitted itself to the public from the writings of Shaftesbury and Rousseau. Its appearance would also seem to be related to the tendency towards increasing subjectivity in 18th-c. aesthetics. It is perhaps connected with the gradual decay of medieval and Renaissance conceptions of the inherent evil of mankind. Viewed historically, s. can be seen to be a uniquely "romantic" phenomenon and thus one of the inherited constituents of the modern sensibility.

It is well to remember, finally, that the presentation of pathos (or of any strong emotion) is not in itself a poetic vice; s. (and bad verse) results only when the pathos, for whatever reason, is inadequately transformed into poetry.—Richards, *Practical;* Brooks and Warren; L. Lerner, "A Note on S.," *The Truest Poetry* (1960). P.F.

SEPTENARIUS (L. "of 7 each"). The Roman equivalent of the Gr. catalectic tetrameter. Whereas the latter was divided into 4 pairs of feet or dipodies (the last of course being incomplete), the iambic, trochaic, and anapaestic s. of early Roman drama were each regarded as composed of 7 feet and an additional syllable.—W. M. Lindsay, *Early L. Verse* (1922); L. Strzelecki, "De septenariis anapaesticis," Société des Sciences et des Lettres de Wroclaw, *Travaux,* series A, no. 54 (1954); Crusius. R.J.G.

SEPTENARY. A metrical line of 7 feet, usually in trochaic tetrameter:

mihi est propositum in taberna mori
(*Confessio Goliae* of Archpoet)

The s. is metrically the same as the heptameter (q.v.) and the fourteener, but the term is now rarely used and best restricted to medieval L. verse and to such vernacular compositions as the Middle Eng. *Orrmulum* and *Poema Morale,* which are predominantly iambic.—Schipper.

SEPTET, *septette* (It.); also *septain* (Fr.). A 7-line stanza of varying meter and rhyme scheme, usually reserved for lyric poetry. In Fr. employed as early as Guillaume de Poitiers; not infrequently heterometric (characterized by diversity of meter), as in *Cantique de Gottschalk sur la douleur du Péché.* Also, more generally, the 7-line iambic pentameter stanza of rhyme royal, q.v. (Chaucer's *Man of Law's Tale, Troilus and Criseyde*—Lydgate, Hoccleve, Dunbar, Skelton, Wyatt, Morris, etc.) is a form of septet. Term is not in general use with reference to Eng. prosody. R.O.E.

SERBO-CROATIAN POETRY. See YUGOSLAV POETRY.

SERRANILLA. A Sp. poem composed in any short meter, but especially in the *arte mayor* (q.v.) half-line, and dealing lightly with the subject of the meeting of a gentleman and a pretty country girl. Sometimes, especially if it is octosyllabic, it is called *serrana.* The *serranilla* was particularly characteristic of the late medieval period. The most famous are those of the Archpriest of Hita (1283?–1350?), and especially those of the Marqués de Santillana (1398–1458). The latter may have been influenced by the ". . . great volume of Portuguese and Galician *cantigas, serranas,* and *decires . . ."* to which he says he had access in his early youth.—P. Le Gentil, *La poésie lyrique espagnole et portugaise à la fin du moyen âge. 2e partie. Les formes* (1953); Navarro. D.C.C.

SESTET(T), *sestette, sestetto.* (a) The minor division or last 6 lines of an It. type sonnet (q.v.), preceded by an octet (see OCTAVE). Sometimes the octet states a proposition or situation and the s. a conclusion, but no fast rules for content can be formulated. The rhyme scheme of the s. varies. (b) Any separable 6-line section of a stanza, but s. is not generally used to describe an entire stanza. R.O.E.

SESTINA. The most complicated of the verse forms initiated by the troubadours. It is composed of 6 stanzas of 6 lines each, followed by an envoy of 3 lines, all of which are usually unrhymed. The function of rhyme in the s. is taken over by a recurrent pattern of end-words; the same 6 end-words occur in each stanza, but in a constantly shifting order which follows a fixed pattern.

If we let the letters A through F stand for the 6 end-words of a s., we may schematize the recurrence pattern as follows:

stanza 1: ABCDEF
2: FAEBDC
3: CFDABE
4: ECBFAD
5: DEACFB
6: BDFECA
envoy : ECA *or* ACE

Most commonly, the envoy, or *tornada,* is further complicated by the fact that the remaining 3 end-words, BDF, must occur in the course of the lines, so that the 3-line envoy will contain all 6 recurrent words.

The invention of the s. is usually attributed to Arnaut Daniel (fl. 1190), and the form was widely cultivated both by his Prov. followers and by Dante and Petrarch in Italy. It was introduced into Fr. by Pontus de Tyard (ca. 1521–1605), a member of the *Pléiade,* and was practiced in 17th-c. Germany by Opitz, Gryphius, and Weckherlin. In the 19th c. the foremost writers of sestinas were the Comte de Gramont, who wrote an astonishing number of them, and Swinburne, who sometimes varied the pattern, even using rhyme, and who composed, in his *Complaint of Lisa,* a double s. of 12 stanzas. The form has had a certain popularity in the 20th c., and Ezra Pound, T. S. Eliot and W. H. Auden have all written sestinas of distinction.—Kastner; F. J. A. Davidson, "The Origin of the S.," MLN, 25 (1910); A. Jeanroy, "La 's. doppia' de Dante et les origines de la sestine," *Romania,* 42 (1912); L. A. Fiedler, "Green Thoughts in a Green Shade: Reflections on the Stony S. of Dante Alighieri," KR, 18 (1956).

SEXAIN, sixain, sextain, sextet, sestet, hexastich. Names variously and indiscriminately applied to the great variety of 6-line stanzas found in Western poetry. The term "sestet" (q.v.), properly speaking, is restricted to the concluding 6 lines of a sonnet (q.v.), especially an It. sonnet, in distinction to the octave (q.v.), or first 8 lines. The remaining terms are applied interchangeably to such forms as the Burns stanza and tail-rhyme (qq.v.), as well as to the many 6-line stanzas which have no distinctive names. The most familiar types of sexain in Eng. poetry are the following: (1) ababcc, in iambic pentameter (the so-called *Venus and Adonis* stanza, q.v.); (2) ababcc, in iambic tetrameter (Wordsworth's *The Daffodils*; also a familiar stanzaic form in German lyric poetry); (3) tail-rhyme, aa⁴b³cc⁴b³ (Chaucer, *Tale of Sir Thopas*); (4) Burns stanza, aaa⁴b²a⁴b²; (5) xayaza (Rossetti, *The Blessed Damozel*). The sestina (q.v.) uses a 6-line stanza in which word recurrence rather than rhyme is used as a principle of organization. Six-line stanzas occur more frequently than do 5-line stanzas. Indeed, their incidence ranks only after that of the quatrain and the couplet (qq.v.).

SEXTILLA. A Sp. stanza form of 6 octosyllabic or shorter lines. In the classic period the usual rhyme schemes were abbaab, ababba, ababab, abbaba, aabbab, and abaabb; modern definitions often call for aabccb or ababcc (sometimes this last is called *sestina*) and occasionally stipulate that the *b* lines be oxytones and the others paroxytones. *Sextillas* have been pointed out in the prologue to Alfonso the Wise's (13th c.) Galician-Portuguese *Cantigas a Santa María* and in the Archpriest of Hita's (14th c.) *Libro de buen amor:*

> ¡Ventura astrosa,
> cruel, enojosa,
> captiva, mesquina!
> ¿Por qué eres sañosa,
> contra mí tan dañosa,
> e falsa vesina?

Rengifo, *Arte poética española* (1592); A. de Trueba, *Arte de hacer versos* (1905); Navarro. D.C.C.

SHANTY (less correct chanty). See SEA SHANTIES.

SHIH. See CHINESE POETRY.

SHORT (syllable). See MORA; CLASSICAL PROSODY.

SHORT METER (S.M. of the hymn books). In effect a variant of ballad meter (q.v.), for if the first tetrameter of that 4343 pattern is shortened, the 3343 arrangement of s.m. results. The form is also similar to the "Poulter's measure" (q.v.) of the 16th c. (if the "Poulter's" couplets are divided at the caesuras, but it is susceptible of greater variety than is found in the monotonous alternations of hexameters and heptameters in the latter. It is most frequently, but by no means exclusively, found in hymnals. S.m. rhymes abcb or abab, and is sometimes written in trochees, but more frequently in iambics, as in Emerson's

> To clothe the fiery thought
> In simple words succeeds,
> For still the craft of genius is
> To mask a king in weeds.
> L.J.Z.

SIAMESE POETRY. See THAI POETRY.

SICILIAN OCTAVE, or *strambotto popolare.* An 8-line It. stanza, rhyming abababab, composed of hendecasyllabic verses. The name is applied with the content in mind, not the metrical form (which may be even 6-line with the same rhyme scheme). Originally its content was satiric, akin to the Fr. *estrabot* of the Middle Ages. According to a minority of present-day scholars, this type of octave existed early in the 13th c. in Southern Italy and Sicily, and toward the end of that century in Tuscany. Recent investigations tend to place its origin in Tuscany and to consider it a derivation from the octave of the sonnet. E. H. Wilkins suggests that what we today call "ottava rima" was the popular borrowing in the 14th c. on the part of some minstrel or minstrels of the *strambotto* form for long poems (*cantari*) of less than epic length. In the last analysis, no one knows accurately the origin, the precise development, or connections, nor etymology [*strammotto, strammuoto* (Sicilian); *strambo* (squint-eyed, sidelong glancing); *motto* (dictum)]. This form remained in popular use until the 15th c., when art-poets (Politian, Lionardo Giustinian) took it up; then in the first half of the 16th c. it disappeared from the literary scene, yielding its place to the madrigal.—F. Flamini, *Notizia storica dei versi e metri italiani* . . . (1919); E. LiGotti, "Lo Strambotto," *Convivium* (1949); R. M. Ruggieri, "Protostoria dello strambotto romanzo," sfi, 11 (1953); Wilkins. L.H.G.

SICILIAN SCHOOL (also known as Frederician poets). A group of poets writing in the vernacular, who were active at the court of the Hohenstaufen monarchs in Sicily during the first three quarters of the 13th c. They flourished particularly under King Frederic II and his son Manfred. Some thirty poets are associated with the Sic. school; the majority of them were Sicilians, but a fair proportion came from the It. mainland, some from as far north as Tuscany.

The major importance of the Sic. poets is that they established It. as a literary language. The content of their work is derived from troubadour models, but, unlike their northern It. contemporaries, they abandoned Prov., the traditional language of the love lyric, and wrote in their own tongue. Of almost equal importance is the formal achievement of the Sicilians; they invented the sonnet and the *canzone* (qq.v.), the two most important lyric forms of It. poetry. The sonnet of the Sic. school, as written by Giacomo da Lentino and others, shows already the distinctive separation into octave and sestet. The octave always rhymes abababab and the sestet is either cdecde or cdcdcd.

These first It. poets (whose use of the vernacular may have been suggested by their acquaintance with the work of the *trouvères* and the Minnesinger (qq.v.) exerted a powerful effect on all subsequent It. lyric verse through their influence, both formal and thematic, on the Tuscan poets of the 13th and 14th c., on Guittone d'Arezzo, Guido Guinicelli, Dante, and Petrarch. Indeed, their influence was linguistic as well as literary, and the occurrence of typically southern locutions in the Tuscan, which became the standard literary language of Italy, may be traced to their example. The best of the Sic. poets, in addition to Giacomo da Lentino, are Giacomino Pugliese and Rinaldo d'Aquino.

La scuola poetica siciliana. Le canzoni dei rimatori nativi di Sicilia. Testo critico (1955) and *La scuola poetica siciliana. Le canzoni dei rimatori non siciliani* (2v., 1957–58), both ed. B. Panvini; *Poeti del Duecento*, ed. G. Contini

(2 v., 1960); G. A. Cesareo, *Le origini della poesia lirica e la poesia siciliana sotto gli Svevi* (2d ed., 1924); V. de Bartholomaeis, *Primordi della lirica d'arte in Italia* (1943); Wilkins; W. T. Elwert, *Per una valutazione stilistica dell' elemento provenzale nel linguaggio della scuola poetica siciliana* (1955); A. del Monte, *Le origini* (1958). F.J.W.; A.P.

SIGN. See SEMANTICS AND POETRY.

SIGNIFICATIO. See PUN.

SIJO. See KOREAN POETRY.

SILESIAN SCHOOL. A designation applied to two distinct poetic groups in 17th-c. Germany. Both groups included chiefly men from the middle classes, who had received their strongest intellectual stimuli in or from the Netherlands (e.g., from Lipsius, Heinsius, Grotius, Salmasius). The so-called First Silesian School was made up of those poets, not all from Silesia, who followed the stylistic reforms of Martin Opitz early in the century. These reforms, based largely on the theories of Ronsard and the Fr. *Pléiade* (q.v.), introduced the stricter forms and more precious diction of Renaissance classicism into German verse, but contributed to a decline in its native vigor. One of the major technical innovations of the group was the substitution of the alexandrine line for the indigenous *Knittelvers* (qq.v.). The term "Second Silesian School" has been applied to the poetry of Hofmann von Hofmannswaldau, Casper von Lohenstein and their followers in the middle and later years of the 17th c. The work of the later Silesians is distinctly baroque and shows marked affinities to that of Marino and his It. imitators (see MARINISM). Eccentric imagery and supercharged eroticism characterize the school, and in the work of Lohenstein these features degenerate into the tasteless bombast which later German critics called *Schwulst*.

The absence of a dominating poetic figure, together with the chaos brought about by the Thirty Years' War, prevented the Silesians from achieving major work or leaving a permanent mark on G. poetry. Modern scholars, recognizing the vagueness of the concept of a "First Silesian School," have preferred to restrict the term to Hofmannswaldau, Lohenstein, and the later group, together with their greater predecessor, Andreas Gryphius, whose lyrics and dramas (the latter composed under Dutch influence) stand as the most important monuments of the school.—H. Heckel, *Gesch. der deutschen Lit. in Schlesien* (1929); J. Nadler, *Literaturgesch. der deutschen Stämme und Landschaften*, II (1931); H. Schöffler, *Deutscher Osten im deutschen Geist von*

Opitz zu Wolff (1940); R. Newald, Die deutsche Lit. vom Späthumanismus zur Empfindsamkeit, 1570–1750 (3d ed., 1960).　　　　F.J.W.; A.P.

SILLOGRAPHER. A writer of silloi ("squint-eyed" pieces), satirical poems or lampoons directed not against personalities but against the doctrines of individuals or schools. Perhaps the first sillographer of antiquity was Xenophanes of Colophon, who criticized the mythology of Homer and Hesiod. However, the most famous was Timon of Phlius (fl. 250 B.C.), who in his main poem, entitled silloi and written in pseudo-heroic hexameters, ridiculed all dogmatic philosophers.—C. Wachsmuth, Sillographi Graeci (1885); Schmid and Stählin, I.　　　　P.S.C.

SILVA. A Sp. poem in Italianate hendecasyllables and heptasyllables in which the poet makes his strophic divisions at will, usually in unequal lengths, and rhymes most of the lines without set pattern, sometimes leaving a few lines unrhymed. Other meters may be used. The s., introduced in the 16th c., is sometimes considered a form of Italianate canción (q.v.) and called canción libre. Morley-Bruerton (The Chronology of Lope de Vega's Comedias, 1940, p. 12) distinguishes four types in Lope's silvas, which are also the types generally used by other poets: (1) "silva de consonantes, aAbB-cCdD, etc." which "could be called pareados [couplets] de 7 y 11"; (2) "sevens and elevens mixed irregularly, no fixed order of length or rime, some unrimed lines"; (3) "all elevens, the majority . . . rimed, not counting the final couplet, no fixed order, mostly pairs, some ABAB and ABBA. May approximate to sueltos [free-riming lines] or pareados [couplets] de 11"; (4) "sevens and elevens mixed irregularly, all rimes in pairs."—Navarro.　　　　D.C.C.

SIMILE. A comparison of one thing with another, explicitly announced by the word "like" or "as."

Aristotle granted that good similes "give an effect of brilliance," but preferred metaphor to simile because s., being longer, was less attractive, and because the s. "does not say outright that 'this' is 'that' . . . the hearer is less interested in the idea." (Rhetoric 1410a). As a figure of speech, s. merges with and to some extent overlaps the "prosaic" metaphor of comparison, substitution, or description, differing from it only by the presence of "like" or "as" (see e.g. Rhetoric 1406a, 1410a). Not every s. is a metaphor, though some similes can be compressed or converted into metaphors; and only some metaphors can be expanded into similes. At the level of comparison, substitution, or description it is useful to preserve the formal distinction between "metaphor-form" and "simile-form," and to apply the term "submerged s." to figures of metaphor-form which are in fact similes with the word "like" or "as" omitted. For example, "Thou Moon beyond the clouds! . . . Thou Star above the Storm!" is a submerged s. (Many of the more vigorous submerged similes are of the 4-term analogical type A is to X as B is to Y [e.g. "a poisonous resentment"] and are in their origins at least truly metaphorical.) On the other hand, some figures in s.-form may be converted into genuine metaphor, usually by the resonance of the context.

Dull brown a cloak enwraps, Don Juan,
Both thy lean shanks, one arm,
That old bird-cage thy breast, where like magpie
Thy heart hopped on alarm.

Whereas metaphor is a mode of condensation and compression, s. through its descriptive function readily leads to diffuseness and extension, even to the digressive development of the figurative scene, action, or object as an object of beauty in itself. Homer's brief similes (e.g. Thetis rises out of the sea like a mist, Apollo descends like the night, "And with them followed a cloud of foot-soldiers") suggest clearly their origin in metaphor; for, although comparison is explicitly indicated by the word "like" or "as," the two things are not primarily compared but identified, yet without any loss of individual character. Such a use of the metaphor in s.-form may be a natural mark of young and vital speech. (See Bowra, Tradition and Design.) Indeed Chaucer's characteristic brief similes are of this kind: "hir eyen greye as glas," "His eyen twynkled in his heed aryght, / As doon the sterres in the frosty nyght." Such similes are also found in Old Fr. romance. But W. P. Ker has pointed out that "similes are not used much in English poetry before Chaucer, or in medieval vernacular poetry before Dante"; that similes, though commonly used by medieval L. writers, are uncommon in Old Eng. and Old Icelandic (Form and Style, p. 253).

The true epic s. involves the comparison of one composite action or relation with another composite action or relation. For example, in Iliad 4.275 the Gr. host led by Ajax is compared to a storm-cloud: "As when a goatherd looks out from a watch-tower of a hill over the sea, and sees a cloud coming afar off over the sea, carrying with it much tempest, showing to him blacker than pitch, coming on driven by the west wind, and he shudders to see it, and drives his flock into a cave, so appeared the march of the Greek warriors." It is to Homer's epic s. that the whole European tradition of extended s. may be traced. In Homer too is to be found an insistently digressive tendency in s. The example cited above has a double reference (for more complex relations see e.g. *Iliad* 13.271–76, 586); but his aim is usually to provide some single common characteristic in the comparison. His favorite source of material for similes is his direct observation of the life around him; he will sometimes, from delight in the material, follow his fancy and develop the picture without much care for the initial comparison (e.g. *Iliad* 4.141–45, 12.278–86). Homer uses his similes for a variety of purposes: for relief, suspense, decoration, magnificence. The Homeric similes—striking, various, self-contained, if not always completely apposite—seldom fail to heighten the narrative and to give pleasure for their own sake.

In succession, Virgil and Dante refined the epic s. in order to develop with precision a multiplicity of comparisons within a single extensive image or action, to "make us see more definitely the scene" (T. S. Eliot, *Dante*, p. 24). This process reaches its culmination in Milton who, as Newton noticed, surpassed all his predecessors in the matter of consistency. Historically, the process may be seen as a process of degeneration from metaphor in the direction of descriptive and logical consistency; from the specifically poetic mode to a discursive mode; from the simple vivid s.-form metaphor discernible in Homer to an extended comparison through imagery, the success of which depends upon the multiplicity and precision of logical, actual, and visual correspondence. (This, in Coleridgean terms, could be described as a movement from Imagination to Fancy.) Homer's success in s. often depends upon violent heterogeneity between the elements of s.—a practice implicitly commended by Quintilian: "The more remote the simile is from the subject to which it is applied, the greater will be the impression of novelty and the unexpected which it produces" (*Institutio Oratoria* 8.3.74; cf. Johnson's dictum: "A simile may be compared to lines converging at a point, and is more excellent as the lines approach from a greater distance"). This striking heterogeneity, often found also in Virgil, may be taken as a mark of the origin of s. in metaphor, being a kind of parataxis or "confrontation" (see METAPHOR). Milton, on the other hand, avoids digressive tendencies in his choice of illustrative material, and chooses his imagery with an almost mathematical subtlety to secure a delicate and complex consistency of internal relations. The organic correspondence of many of Milton's similes with their context and with the whole poem, their exquisite finish, and relentless logical and imaginative consistency, carry them paradoxically out of the field of discursive comparison toward the field of identity and of metaphor, e.g., *Paradise Lost* 3.431–41:

As when a Vultur on *Imaus* bred,
Whose snowie ridge the roving *Tartar* bounds,
Dislodging from a Region scarce of prey
To gorge the flesh of Lambs or yeanling Kids
On Hills where Flocks are fed, flies toward the
    Springs
Of *Ganges* or *Hydaspes, Indian* streams;
But in his way lights on the barren plaines
Of *Sericana*, where *Chineses* drive
With Sails and Wind thir canie Waggons light:
So on this windie Sea of Land, the Fiend
Walk'd up and down alone bent on his
    prey, . . .

The extended s. is not confined to epic poetry. Jeremy Taylor and Sir Thomas Browne are only two of several 17th-c. prose-writers capable of using s. with perspicuous accuracy and florid invention. Shakespeare had handled extended s. with unerring point and carried it to unmatched depths of implication. But after Milton no poet uses the epic s. with his force or precision. Keats shows craftsmanlike skill in *Hyperion*, his comparison of the fallen gods to Stonehenge being justly celebrated; Byron, through carelessness, misuses the epic s. in *Childe Harold;* Matthew Arnold cultivated the heroic manner rather too sedulously in *Sohrab and Rustum* but not without a few notable successes. Shelley has a curious habit, in passages of transcendent emotion, of accumulating a shower of approximate similes (both in explicit s.-form and in metaphor-form); prime examples occur in *Epipsychidion* 26–34, 115–23 (but cf. *Adonais* 17). The art of extended s. had a vogue in later 19th-c. journalism but has now happily passed out of fashion. And now that power rather than revelation has become the central concern of the public orator, the more grotesque manifestations of extended s. (e.g. "Like a paralytic who finds his arms useless to move his wheel-chair from the murderous flame that would snuff out his life, I am powerless to strain the muscles of coincidence's arm by suggesting any connexion between the mayor's timely affluence and the loss of the Party funds") are seldom heard now even on political platforms.

The distinction drawn by C. S. Lewis (*The Allegory of Love*) between symbolic allegory and "formulated" allegory can be seen to be parallel to the distinction between metaphor and s. Symbolic allegory (e.g. *Roman de la Rose, The Faerie Queene* (in part at least), *Pilgrim's Progress,* Kafka's *Trial*) develops two or more levels of meaning simultaneously. The "formulated" allegory (e.g. Dryden's *Absalom and Achitophel,* Swift's *Tale of a Tub*), in which the "real meaning" is derived by direct substitution from the details and context of the "story," may be regarded as an extension of "submerged s."; for the comparison unfolds in the manner of an extended s., though the primary subject for comparison is withheld and the fact that a comparison is intended is (for a variety of reasons) not explicitly stated. This relation of "formulated" allegory to s. tends to be overlooked because of the habit—to be seen, for example, in Coleridge, Yeats and Fowler—of assuming that all allegory is of the type of "formulated" allegory and concluding that allegory is the contrary term to symbol.

H. Fränkel, *Die homerischen Gleichnisse* (1921); Ker, p. 250–59; C. M. Bowra, *Tradition and Design in the Iliad* (1930); J. Whaler, "Grammatical *Nexus* of the Miltonic S.," JEGP, 30 (1931), "Compounding and Distribution of Similes in *Paradise Lost*," MP, 28 (1931), "The Miltonic S.," PMLA, 46 (1931); I. F. Green, "Observations on the Epic Similes in the *Faerie Queene*," PQ, 14 (1935); L. D. Lerner, "The Miltonic S.," EIC, 4 (1954); M. Coffey, "Function of the Homeric S.," AJP, 78 (1957); J. Notopoulos, "Homeric Similes in the Light of Oral Poetry," CJ, 52 (1957); K. Widmer, "The Iconography of Renunciation: The Miltonic S.," ELH, 25 (1958).　　　　G.W.

SINCERITY. As a poetic criterion s. can be either helpful or harmful, according to the tact with which it is employed. With the Eng. romantics s. was a genuine correspondence with or expression of the poet's state of mind and feelings, from which the poem derived its vitality. The Victorians gave s. even more importance, and a more exclusively moral meaning. For them it was the chief and indispensable value, and the integrity of the poet's character became the principal question. The romantics inclined to treat s. as a guarantee of the poet's natural gift. Thus Leigh Hunt praised Keats's *Eve of St. Agnes* for its naturalness and spontaneity: "All flows out of sincerity and passion." G. H. Lewes, John Keble, Carlyle, and Matthew Arnold, however, all gave s. stronger moral implications than did the romantics. "To every poet, to every writer," exclaimed Carlyle, "we might say: Be true, if you would be believed. Let a man but speak forth with genuine earnestness the thought, the emotion, the actual condition of his own heart." To Arnold the touchstone of great poetry was "the high seriousness which comes from absolute sincerity." Henry James returned to s. its aesthetic meaning, proposing as "the one measure of the worth of a given subject . . . is it valid, in a word, is it genuine, is it sincere, the result of some direct impression or perception of life?"

In so questioning, James returned to the best romantic version of s., though doubtless his emphasis is more exclusively aesthetic. For Wordsworth in his rejection of "poetic dic-

tion" and in his claim that "I have at all times endeavoured to look steadily at my subject" was simply requiring that poetic language should be "the result of some direct impression or perception of life." Likewise Shelley is expounding the most profitable doctrine of s. when he calls the poets the creators of language: "Their language is vitally metaphorical; that is, it marks the before unapprehended relations of things and perpetuates their apprehension."—Wellek and Warren; Abrams; Wellek. For a crit. hist. of the term, see H. Peyre, *Lit. and S.* (1963); D. Perkins, *Wordsworth and the Poetry of S.* (1964).
　　　　　　　　　　　　　　　　R.H.F.

SINHALESE POETRY. The earliest extant specimens of Sinh. poetry go as far back as the 1st c. A.D. These verses, limited to about half a dozen unrhymed couplets, are found in the form of inscriptions carved on rock. One of these couplets perpetuates the memory of a royal lapidary who had died while on duty. Though there is evidence to show that this tradition of poetry continued to exist, no examples have survived, and one has to wait till the 5th or the 6th c. to get further examples of early Sinh. poetry.

The graffiti incised on the Mirror Wall at Sigiriya range from 5th c. to 13th c. These graffiti, essentially lyrical in character, embody the reactions of visitors to the Sigiriya Rock when they viewed the well-known paintings executed in some pockets there. A variety of metrical forms is used in these verses, and they range from the unrhymed couplet to the rhymed 4-line stanza, a form which became very popular in later times.

The earliest extant full length Sinh. poem, however, is assigned to the 10th c. This work, *Siyabaslakara*, based on earlier Sanskrit works, is a treatise on rhetorics, and is devoted to a discussion of the different types of poetic embellishments and figures of speech with illustrations. The verse form employed in this work is known as *gī*, i.e. an unrhymed couplet, employing a variable number of syllabic instants in the 2 lines of verse.

This is followed by three poems, the *Sasadāvata* (Birth story of the Hare), the *Muvadevdāvata* (Birth story of the Deer) and the *Kav-Silumiṇa* (Diadem of Poetry) in all of which the *gī* form of verse is employed. The first was composed in the reign of Queen Līlāvatī (A.D. 1197–1200) while the *Kav-Silumiṇa* is attributed to King Parākramabāhu II (A.D. 1234–1269). The *Muvadevdāvata*, whose author is not identified, is considered to have been written after the *Sasadāvata* but before the *Kav-Silumiṇa*.

Each of these poems is based on a *Jātaka*,

i.e. a previous life of the Buddha. The authors of these poems attempted to follow closely the rules laid down by writers on the Indian theory of poetry, and as a result these poems contain a considerable amount of irrelevant descriptions which detract from their organic unity.

Toward the middle of the 14th c. a new literary form known as *Sandeśa* was adopted by Sinh. poets. In this form, a messenger, usually a bird such as a peacock or a parrot, is supposed to take a message from the author to a god or a high religious dignitary asking the latter to give his blessings to the King or to a Minister of State. In describing the route the messenger had to take, the authors indulged in profuse descriptions of the villages, towns, rivers and shrines the messenger would see or visit on his way. The earliest Sinh. *Sandeśa* are the *Mayūra-Sandeśa* and the *Tisara-Sandeśa*, and later in the middle of the 15th c. the well known *Sälalihiṇi-Sandeśa,* the *Kokila-Sandeśa,* and the *Girā-Sandeśa* were composed by autors who were contemporaries. The *Sandeśa* as a literary form became popular with Sinh. poets and a considerable number was composed in later times. Even in the present day one hears occasionally of a new *Sandeśa* being published. Though the authors of *Sandeśa* poems generally followed the established poetic conventions, this new literary form provided Sinh. poets with an opportunity, for the first time, of giving expression to their own experience and observation. In these poems passages of considerable literary merit are occasionally found.

During the same period the *Kāvyasekharaya* and the *Guttila Kāvyaya,* two poems based on the previous lives of the Buddha, were also written. The *Budugunālankāraya,* based on an event in the life of the Buddha and the *Lōvāḍa-Sangarāva*—a popular exposition of Buddhist ethics—were also composed during this period. In all these poems *gī* verse is replaced by the rhymed stanza of 4 lines.

This period was followed by one of internal strife and strain. The Portuguese, followed by the Dutch and the Eng., invaded Ceylon. Literary activity during these troublous times appears to have suffered a setback, though mention has to be made of the poet Alagiyavanna (2d half of 16th c.) and the poets of the Matara School (2d half of the 18th c.) whose works are characterized by signs of decadence and decline.

Recent and present day Sinh. poetry is characterized by an admixture of both the old and the new in respect of form and content. An attempt at what is termed social realism can also be discerned, particularly in the works of the present day poets that have come under the influence of radical ideologies. An important feature of this recent and present phase is the appearance of free verse with neither rhyme nor meter.

M. Wickramasinghe, *Sinh. Lit.,* tr. E. R. Sarathchandra (1949); C. E. Godakumbura, *Sinh. Lit.* (1955); *Sigiri Graffiti,* ed. S. Paranavitana (1956); *Padyāvalī,* pts. I and II, ed. S. Palansuriya (1959–60). P.E.E.F.

SIRVENTES. A poem in Old Prov. which is strophic in form but which is not a love poem. The main themes are personal abuse or (occasionally) praise; literary satire of a superficial nature; moralizing on the evil state of the world; politics and current events; and the crusades (exhortations to go, songs of parting, etc.). The tone is mostly satiric, and gross vituperation is common. In form, the s. came to be regarded as a subservient genre, deserving less originality than the *chanso* (q.v.). Indeed, it became a recognized practice to write a s. to the tune of a popular *chanso,* and even in many cases to adopt the actual rhyme sounds of the *chanso* whose tune was borrowed. This custom was so general that the s. was sometimes defined in these terms, as an imitative poem; but it seems most unlikely that this imitation was ever considered by the poets themselves as an essential condition of the genre.—Jeanroy, II; J. Storost, *Ursprung und Entwicklung des altprovenzal. S.* (1931); F. M. Chambers, "Imitation of Form in the Old Prov. Lyric," *RPh,* 6 (1952–53). F.M.C.

SKALD (scald). The word *skáld* had the general meaning "poet" in ON, and still does in Icelandic. In Eng., however, it is applied specifically to the Scandinavian poets of old who were attached to the courts of kings, earls, and other chieftains in the Northern countries, England, and elsewhere. The first skalds were Norwegian. The oldest whose work we know was Bragi Boddason the Old of the first half of the 9th c.; he was the forerunner of a number of other Norwegian skalds, but from the end of the 10th c. and down to the close of the 13th, when the court poetry went out of fashion, the Icelanders dominated the field almost exclusively. Altogether, the names of about 250 skalds have come down to us. See also OLD NORSE POETRY.—W. Craigie, *The Art of Poetry in Iceland* (1937); *The Skalds,* tr. and ed. L. M. Hollander (1945). R.B.

SKELTONIC VERSE. A verse form (sometimes treated as part of a generic type called tumbling verse, q.v.) named after its originator and principal practitioner, John Skelton (ca. 1460–1529). Its characteristics are: a line that is usually quite short (from 3 to 6 or 7 syllables and of 2 or 3 stresses), though longer lines with the typical skeltonic feel are not uncommon; a rhyme scheme in which a rhyme set may be extended indefinitely, though rhymes are never crossed; the elevation of parallelism to a major rhetorical element.

> And if ye stand in doubt
> Who brought this rhyme about
> My name is Colin Clout.
> I propose to shake out
> All my conning bag,
> Like a clerkly hag.
> For though my rhyme be ragged,
> Tattered and jagged
> Rudely rain-beaten,
> Rusty and moth-eaten,
> If ye take well therewith
> It hath in it some pith.
> —Colin Clout

The effect of this highly irregular verse struck a number of generations as "rude rayling," but beginning with favorable comments by various eminent romantics, including Coleridge and Wordsworth, a revaluation has taken place, till skeltonic is much admired by many modern poets.

The traditional roots of the verse form have been variously described as Anglo-Saxon rhyming poems (Guest), as a fine form of native doggerel bent on escaping the dullness of post-Chaucerian poetics (Saintsbury), as an adaptation of rhymed accentual verse of medieval Latinists (Berdan), as a fusion of the Anglo-Saxon 4-accent alliterative line (broken into halves), and the aforementioned Latinists (de Sola Pinto). The most specific suggestion from this later group is Kinsman's, who traces a close relationship from both medieval Eng. and L. poems on the "Signs of Death" to Skelton's *Uppon a Deedmans Hed*. Nelson has advanced a persuasive theory, namely, that the principal forbear of skeltonic is the *similiter desinens* or rhymed prose of the Latins which, combined with *clausulae* (short parallel clauses), enjoyed a vogue from the 11th to the 14th c., and which Skelton himself practiced.—Saintsbury, *Prosody*, I; J. M. Berdan, *Early Tudor Poetry* (1920); R. Graves, *John Skelton. Selections* (1927); W. Nelson, *John Skelton: Laureate* (1939); *John Skelton: A Selection from his Poems*, ed. V. de Sola Pinto (1950); R. S. Kinsman, "Skelton's 'Uppon a Deedmans Hed': New Light on the Origin of the Skeltonic," SP, 50 (1953). R.BE.

SLANT RHYME. See NEAR RHYME.

SLAVIC POETICS. See MODERN POETICS (20TH CENTURY).

SLAVIC PROSODY. A comparative study of Slav. pros. has as its aim both the reconstruction of Common Slav. versification and the description of the individual Slav. prosodic systems which evolved after the breakdown of Slav. unity, around the 10th c. A.D. These systems comprise an oral (declamatory or sung) popular tradition, which to some extent is the continuation of Common Slav. pros., and a tradition of written poetry, which is genetically and structurally connected with the former, but has been subject to various foreign as well as cross-cultural Slav. influences. Whatever metrical system exerted an influence on or was adopted by a given Slav. pros., its needs must be adjusted to the prosodic possibilities of the particular Slav. language implementing it. In recognizing this fact, modern study of versification does not limit itself to an enumeration of ideal metrical schemes, but views verse as a structure within which the metrical constants correlate to rhythmic tendencies.

Attempts to reconstruct Common Slav. pros. have so far yielded the following results. Common Slav. had two types of verse: a spoken asyllabic verse, based on syntactic parallelism of the lines; and a syllabic verse, based on a fixed number of syllables in each line and syntactic pause at the end of the lines. Specimens of the first type are found in Slav. folklore in the form of wedding-speeches and sayings and in the imparisyllabic lines found in older Western (e.g. 14th-c. Czech epic poems) and Rus. (17th-c.) poetry. The syllabic type was recitative or sung. Direct descendants of the recitative type are the laments (*tužbalice*, *plači*) and epic songs (*junačke pesme, byliny*) preserved among the Balkan Slavs and in Northern Great Russia. The laments consisted of short or long lines with a trochaic cadence, which were divided into uniform cola (4 + 4 or 4 + 4 + 4). The epic songs also consisted of long or short lines and were divided into asymmetrical cola: (4 + 6) with a trochaic cadence and (5 + 3 or 3 + 5) with an iambic cadence. The epic verse also had a quantitative clausula. All four types of the recitative verse are very well preserved in the South Slav. area. In the Northern Rus. area the recitative verse changed its structure considerably after the loss of phonemic length and intonation. The asymmetrical verse of epic songs, both long and short, had lost its syllabic pattern just because of its asymmetry, and became a purely accentual verse with a two-syllable anacrusis and a dactylic clausula (which replaced the quantitative one). The symmetrical verse of the laments preserved its syllabic pattern much better. It also developed a new dactylic clausula owing to an additional syllable. Thus it now consists, as a rule, of 9-syllable or 13-syllable lines with a trochaic cadence.

The oldest learned Slav. poetry, that of the Old Church Slavonic-Moravian period, was based on isosyllabism without rhyme and owed its origin to Common Slav. syllabic verse as well as to Byzantine-Gr. forms.

The new political, religious, and linguistic developments which took place around the 10th c. A.D. created the conditions for independent Slav. poetic traditions and prosodic systems. The formation of Slav. states and their subsequent destinies, the adoption of Christianity, and the Schism affected the growth and functions of poetry in the various Slav. countries in different ways. The longest uninterrupted tradition of learned poetry existed among the Western Slavs and, to a lesser degree, in the Catholic Southern Slav world where it started among Croats and Serbs on the Dalmatian coast during the flowering of the Renaissance in this area. In the Orthodox Slav. world learned poetry developed much later: among Eastern Slavs in the 17th c. and among Balkan Slavs (Serbs and Bulgarians) in the 18th and 19th c., respectively. As a consequence of the breakdown of Common Slav., a new word-prosody developed in the various Slav. languages, which can be formulated as follows: (1) Czech and Slovak; (2) Serbo-Croatian; and (3) Slovenian preserved phonemic quantity. In Czech and Slovak, stress has the function only of delimiting word boundaries, being fixed on the initial syllable of a word. In Serbo-Croatian and Slovenian, stress is concomitant with pitch, which is distinctive but metrically irrelevant, or in the absence of the latter, it delimits the word boundary, falling on the first (Serbo-Croatian) or final syllable of a word (Slovenian). In the Eastern Slav. languages and in Bulgarian, stress has a distinctive function, whereas in Polish it is bound to the penultimate syllable of a word.

Syllabism has been up to now the basis of *Polish* versification. In the 14th-15th c., isosyllabism of the lines was merely a tendency, which was pronounced in the works influenced by medieval L. poetry. The greatest innovator of Pol. syllabic verse was J. Kochanowski. He canonized the principle of strict isosyllabism, eliminated syntactic parallelism of the lines as a constant, and stabilized the place of the caesura in longer (over 8-syllable) lines. He also introduced a full, 1½ rhyme (with a penultimate stress), which was not strictly adhered to by his 17th- and 18th-c. followers. These innovations lent Pol. verse new flexibility: they allowed the use of lines and hemistichs of various length and released syntactic phrasing for expressive effects. The consistent adherence to the syllabic principle accounts for the popularity of the longer lines, especially of 11 (5 + 6) and 13 (7 + 6) syllables, in which the best Pol. lyric and epic poetry has been written. The shorter octosyllable has generally been used in learned poetry without a caesura. In popular verse, this line is divided into hemistichs (5 + 3 or 4 + 4), which entails a breakdown of the line into word groups with an equal number of stresses or a strong trochaic tendency.

The rhythmical measures of the folk song enter at first into Pol. romantic poetry as a form of popular stylization. The impulse for syllabic-accentual pros. was, however, given mainly by the imitation of classical, quantitative meters and by foreign (Rus.) models. Syllabic-accentual meters are used by the romantics in smaller lyric poems and in sections of dramatic works. The great romantics, who introduced masculine rhyme and iambic and anapestic feet (Mickiewicz, Słowacki), used these meters with moderation. Syllabic-accentual verse became the norm with the "positivist" poets (Konopnicka, Asnyk), who practiced it with extreme rigor. Modern poets admit frequent deviations from the metrical scheme. The imitation of classical meters, especially the hexameter, actually led to the introduction of purely accentual meters, based on an equal number of stresses in each line. In our times, these meters, as well as free verse, compete successfully with the traditional syllabic verse.

In *Czech* the 8-syllable line formed the backbone of both lyric and epic Old Czech poetry, with a pronounced trochaic tendency in the former, and syntactic parallelism approaching a constant in the latter. Dramatic works, on the other hand, were based on asyllabism. Syllabic-accentual meters, with a trochaic and iambic cadence, became popular during the Hussite movement with the flourishing of religious songs. But as a consequence of the frequent discrepancy between music and meter, and the general decline of secular poetry, the 15th and 16th c. saw a return to purely syllabic meters, a development which coincided with the Pol. syllabic versification and was partly influenced by it. In this system, quantity served only as an element of variation. However, in the poems and songs of the Czech humanists who imitate classical versification (Komenský, Blahoslav), it becomes the metrical principle.

At the end of the 18th c., syllabic-accentual meters, based on the congruence of foot and word boundaries, triumph in Czech poetry. The poets of the Puchmajer school adhere strictly to the metrical scheme. Later on this rigor is considerably attenuated through the use of quantity, of polysyllabic words, and of heterosyllabic, mainly dactylo-trochaic feet. The romantics (Mácha) make very skillful use of iambic feet, which are contrary to the dactylo-trochaic cadence of the Czech language. Toward the end of the 19th c., the metrical scheme is again rigorously implemented (by the *Lumírovci*) to finally cede place to the modified syllabic-accentual meters and to the vers libre of the symbolists (Březina).

In its early, Štúr period, *Slovak* poetry drew its inspiration from the local folk poetry, which is syllabic. In the last quarter of the 19th c., the Slovak poets (Hviezdoslav, Vajansky) abandoned syllabism for the syllabic-accentual meters of Czech origin, which was strictly adhered to toward the end of that century. Subsequently the syllabic-accentual frame became more flexible, to mark the transition to free rhythms.

Serbo-Croatian popular verse shows striking similarities to that of Czech and Slovak, with the difference that quantity is sometimes endowed with a metrical function (e.g. the quantitative clausula of the epic decasyllable). Dalmatian poetry of the Renaissance owed its verse forms to popular inspiration. The influence of Western (It.) poetry has here been responsible for the introduction of rhyme (and *media rima*), which replaced syntactic parallelism as a constant. Besides the epic asymmetric $(4 + 6)$ and the lyric, symmetric $(5 + 5)$ decasyllable, the most common meters are (8 and 12) syllabic lines $(4 + 4$ and $6 + 6)$ with a pronounced trochaic cadence. Modern poetry employs, in addition, 11-syllable lines $(5 + 6)$. Syllabic-accentual meters appeared under foreign (German and Rus.) influence during the 19th c. (Radičević, Zmaj, Kostić; Vraz, Preradović, Šenoa, F. Marković). The division into feet is, as in Czech, dependent upon the arrangement of word boundaries. Quantity serves mainly as an element of variation, although in some positions it may substitute for stress (especially in rhymes).

The meters of modern *Slovenian* poetry, which developed in the 19th c., are syllabic-accentual. The role of quantity as a rhythmic factor is more restricted here than in Serbo-Croatian. In the poetry of Prešeren, the greatest romantic poet, who used primarily the iambic pentameter (with feminine rhyme), the metrical scheme is still rigorously observed. Modern versification (Aškerc, Župančič) has moved in the direction of relaxing the metrical requirements; it also adopted ternary meters and free verse.

Syllabic-accentual meters became the basis of *Rus.* prosody in the 1740's under German influence, following a period of syllabic verse which had reached Russia from Poland, via the Ukraine, in the 17th c. (Simeon of Polotsk, Istomin, Kantemir). From the time of Lomonosov, Trediakovsky, and Sumarokov, binary meters were used almost exclusively in the poetry of the 18th c., especially iambic tetrameter, iambic hexameter (alexandrine) and trochaic tetrameter. At the beginning of the 19th c. the iambic pentameter became widespread in the poetry of Zhukovsky, Pushkin, and others, replacing the alexandrine in dramatic poetry. In the 19th c. ternary meters also became more popular, especially in the second half of the century (Nekrasov, A. Tolstoy, Fet). While in Rus. ternary meters all downbeats, as a rule, are always stressed, in binary meters only the last downbeat in the line has a compulsory stress; stress on the other downbeats is merely a tendency. In ternary meters the excess of constants led in the 20th c. to the admission of a variable number of unstressed syllables (usually one or two) between the downbeats, giving rise to the *dol'niki* in the poetry of the symbolists and acmeists (Bryusov, Blok, Akhmatova, Gumilev, etc.) and, later, to purely accentual verse with a still freer number of unstressed syllables between downbeats (especially in some poems of Mayakovsky). Free verse (vers libre), based primarily on phrase intonation rather than on the number of stresses per line, was introduced into Rus. poetry by Blok and Kuzmin, but it was never widely adopted as it was in other Slavic literatures (Czech, Polish, and Serbo-Croatian). Syllabic-accentual meters, especially the iambic, constitute the bulk of Rus. verse up to the present. In addition to the stress and syllabics, in Rus. prosody the arrangement of word boundaries is also free to serve as an element of variation.

Ukrainian and *Bulgarian* learned poetry of the 19th c. (Shevchenko, Botev) is indebted for its verse forms to the popular tradition of the folk song, which shows a strong tendency toward a fixed arrangement of word groups within the short line and a division into hemistichs in the long line. Subsequently Bulgarian and Ukrainian poetry underwent the influence of Rus. syllabic-accentual versification, which became the prevailing norm, with the exception of Western Ukrainian poetry, where purely syllabic verse is still written. In this century, the *dol'niki* (Tychina, Javorov) and vers libre have competed also with the syllabotonic meters.

See especially R. Jakobson, "Studies in Comparative Slav. Metrics," OSP, 3 (1952) and "The Kernel of Comp. Slav. Lit.," HSS, I (1953). The most recent and most comprehensive attempts at a reconstruction of Common Slav. pros.—S. Furmanik, *Podstawy wersyfikacji polskiej* (1947; a clear, though somewhat mechanical survey of the principles of Polish pros.); M. R. Mayenowa (ed.), *Wiersz*, II cz. I (1963), *Sylabizm*, III (1956), *Sylabotonizm*, IV (1957), (*Wersyfikacja*, important ser. *Poetyka, Polska Akademja Nauk*). The most comprehensive v. on two types of Pol. meters.—J. Mukařovský, "Český verš. Obecné zásady a vývoj novočeského verše"; R. Jakobson, "Verš staročeský," 376–429, 429–459, *Československá Vlastivěda*, III (1934; compreh. outlines of the hist. of Czech verse); M. Bakoš, *Vývin slovenského verša od školy Štúrovej* (2d ed., 1949; a synthetic survey of Slovak versification); K. Horálek, *Zarys dziejów czeskiego wiersza* (1957; a brief historical survey of Czech and Slovak verse).— S. Matić, "Principi umetničke versifikacje srpske," *Godišnica N. Čupića* (1930–32; a thorough, though one-sided, study of Serbo-Croatian syllabic meters); R. Košutić, *O tonskoj metrici u novoj srpskoj poeziji* (1941; a compreh. study of syllabo-tonic versific., but with a normative bias); K. Taranovski, "Principi srpskohrvatske versifikacije," *Prilozi za književnost*, 20 (1954) and "The Prosodic Structure of Serbo-Croat Verse," OSP, 9 (1960; briefer treatment); A. V. Isačenko, *Slovenski verz* (1939; brief survey of Slovenian metrics, with a comparative outlook). —B. V. Tomashevsky, *Russkoe stikhoslozhenie* (1923; a balanced and compreh. work on the structure of Rus. verse); B. M. Zhirmunsky, *Vvedenie v metriku. Teoriya stikha* (1925; clear and well-documented, somewhat controversial study on the structure of Rus. verse); K. Taranovski, *Ruski dvodelni ritmovi* I–II (1953); B. O. Unbegaun, *Rus. Versification* (1956; useful introd. to the hist. and structure of Rus. verse). —V. Jakubs'kyj, *Nauka viršuvannja* (1922; a compreh. study of the principles of Ukrainian pros.)—A. Balabanov, "B' 'lgarski stix," *Iz edin život* (1934); M. Janakiev, *B' 'lgarsko stixoznamie* (1960; up-to-date survey of the hist. of Bulgarian verse).   E.ST.

ŚLOKA or *anuṣṭubh*. Verse form in which the bulk of Sanskrit metrical literature is composed. Being rather free, it is generally used for narrative, epic, mythology, and scientific treatises; and being brief it is also used effectively for epigrams and maxims. S. originally meant "praise" or "fame" or "the act of praising." Later, the word came to mean verse in general. Anuṣṭubh, a name for s. going back to the *Veda*, refers to its octosyllabic class having 4 feet of 8 syllables each. It is a completion of the Vedic *gayatri* of 3 feet of 8 syllables each.

The s. or anuṣṭubh continued to be a fluid meter when all quantitative meters had become rigidly fixed. The standard rules in a s. are that the sixth syllable shall always be long, the fifth short, and the seventh short in the even feet, giving them an iambic cadence. However, only the last rule is strictly enforced in the classical s.; and in archaic writings, ślokas with a long 7th giving a trochaic cadence to the even feet are to be found. Perhaps the most basic requirement of a s. is that it should give a true "sloka-feeling" to the ear. The following is a typical s. from the *Bhagavad Gita* 18:

5th 6th
sarvadharmān parityajya

6th 7th 8th
mām ēkam saraṇam vrajā

(Abandoning all duties, take refuge in Me alone.)

For bibliog., see INDIAN PROSODY.   V.R.

SLOVAK POETRY. Until the last century the Slovaks had virtually no literature in their own language; L. and Czech served as written languages, and only sporadic attempts were made to write in Slovak. The 17th c. saw what may be regarded as the beginnings of a national literature in two great hymnals, the Protestant *Cithara sanctorum* (1636) and the Catholic *Cantus catholici* (1655). The first collection contained mostly Czech hymns, but a few were Slov. and employed vernacular expressions. The language of *Cantus catholici* represented an attempt by the Jesuits of the University of Trnava to write in Slov., using Western Slov. dialects. Throughout the latter part of the 17th and most of the 18th c., the baroque period in Slovakia, poetry continued to be almost entirely religious or didactic.

Neoclassicism dominated Slov. literature at the end of the 18th and in the first three decades of the 19th c. A new attempt to standardize Slov. was made at this time by Anton Bernolák (1762–1813), a Catholic priest. Bernolák's Slov. was likewise based on Western Slov. dialects. His follower, Ján Hollý (1785–1849), wrote ponderous epics on patriotic historical subjects, drawing heavily for inspiration on antique poets. The failure of Bernolák's Slov. to win acceptance doomed Hollý's work to oblivion. More successful was Ján Kollár (1793–1852), who wrote in Czech. His great sonnet cycle, *Slávy dcera* (The Daughter of Sláva, 1824), laments the impotence of the Slavic peoples, but predicts their future greatness.

Not until the 1840's and the first romantic generation was a standard Slov. language which would endure created. Based on Central Slov. dialects, and hence more widely acceptable, it was largely the work of two Protestant nationalists, L'udovít Štúr (1815–56) and J. M. Hurban (1817–88). The romantic poets who surrounded Štúr were strongly influenced by the Slov. folk song; ardent patriots, they largely defined national literature by its use of popular speech and folk forms. They finally solved the question of prosody, which had vexed Slov. poets almost as much as the language problem: both quantitative and qualitative versification had been employed. On the model of the folk song, the romantics now adopted qualitative (accentual) verse.

The romantic generation included a number of significant poets. Andrej Sládkovič (pseudonym of Ondrej Braxatoris, 1820–72) created a historical epic, *Detvan* (1853), an idyllic but accurate description of the life of the peasants of the region of Detva. Janko Král' (1822–76), the greatest of the romantics, produced ballads interesting for their use of Oedipal themes. Ján Botto's (1829–81) *Smrt' Janošíka* (The Death of Janošík, 1862) eulogized the famous bandit of the Carpathians, who had become a symbol of liberty for the common people. Ján Kalinčiak (1812–71) treated national historical subjects, but with more realistic detail than the other romantics.

The hope of the romantic generation for liberty was shattered by the failure of the Revolution of 1848. As the century wore on and Hungarian rule grew more severe, a mood of helplessness set in. Svétozar Hurban Vajanský (1847–1916) and Pavol Országh (1849–1921), who wrote under the pseudonym of Hviezdoslav, were the greatest poets of the era. Hurban Vajanský, the son of J. M. Hurban, was a romantic, but with a vein of irony and satire new to Slov. literature. Hviezdoslav was a Parnassian poet. His translations from Shakespeare, Goethe, Pushkin, and others gave Slov. poetry a new stimulus. In keeping with his cosmopolitanism, he avoided the hitherto dominant tone of the folk song. Though he was a lyric, epic, and dramatic poet, his masterpiece is probably the *Krvavé sonety* (Bloody Sonnets, 1919), which mirror the horror of World War I. His last poetry became more and more disillusioned, though he lived to see Slovakia win freedom.

Symbolism, or *Moderna*, as the Slovaks called it, had its chief poet in Ivan Krasko (pseudonym of Ján Botto, 1876–), the son of the older Botto. Krasko shares Hviezdoslav's pessimism, but his poetry is more modern in its use of the lexicon and the subtler shades of introspective feeling of symbolism. Janko Jesenský (1874–1945) cultivated a cosmopolitan satire relatively unique in Slov. poetry. Among recent writers, Emil B. Lukáč (1900–) is a complex and contradictory religious poet influenced by Paul Claudel. Ján Smrek (pseudonym of Ján Cietek, 1899–) is a vitalist who delights in sensual descriptions of female beauty. He has also flirted with poetism, an indigenous Czechoslovak poetic movement which arose in the 1920's and which contained traits of futurism, dadaism, and surrealism (qq.v.). Another poetist was Laco Novomeský (1904–), a Communist journalist who has recently been in prison for nationalist "deviation" under the Communist regime. Since 1948 Communist rule has silenced most of the older poets and greatly restricted the range of themes.

The chief foreign influences on Slov. poetry have been Czech, German, and Rus. literature. Like Czech, Slov. has fixed stress on the first syllable, which facilitates the use of trochaic rhythm. Still, iambic verse—usually with considerable metrical freedom in the opening foot of the line—is very common, and more popular than trochaic in the second half of the 19th c. Pure trinary meters are virtually impossible in Slov. because the stress tends to fall on every odd syllable. Dactylic feet may alternate with trochees, however; such purely tonic rhythms were popular under the influence of antique meters and of native folk songs, both in the romantic era and again in modern times.

The severity of the national problem in Slovakia and the political role played by many Slov. writers have given poetry a strongly nationalistic coloring. Those poetic forms are popular in which national ideas can be expressed or implied: narrative poetry, occasional verse, the popular song, and the reflective lyric.

ANTHOLOGIES: *Slovenská poesie XIX. století*, ed. Fr. Frýdecký (1920); *Sborník mladej slovenskej literatúry*, ed. J. Smrek (1924; 19th and early 20th c.); *Slovenské jaro; ze slovenské poesie, 1945–1955*, ed. C. Stitnický (1955); *The Linden Tree*, ed. M. Otruba and Z. Pešat (1963).

HISTORY AND CRITICISM: P. Bujnák, *Hviezdoslav* (1919); S. Krčméry, "A Survey of Modern Slov. Lit.," SEER, 6 (1928) and "Úvod do dejín slovenskej literatúry, najmä poézie," *Sborník Matice slovenskej*, 18 (1943); M. Pišút, *K počiatkom básnickej školy Štúrovej* (On the Beginnings of Štúr's Poetic School, 1938); M. Bakoš, *Vývin slovenského verša* (The Development of Slov. Verse, 1939); A. Kostolný, *O Hviezdoslavovej tvorbe* (On Hviezdoslav's Work, 1939); A. Mráz, *Die Lit. der Slovaken* (1942) and "Dejiny slovenskej literatúry" (Hist. of Slov. Lit.), *Slovenská vlastiveda*, 5, 1 (1948); J. Brezina, *Ivan Krasko* (1946); W. E. Harkins and K. Šimončič, *Czech and Slov. Lit.* (1950; brief surveys with a bibliog.); B. Meriggi, *Storia della letteratura ceca e slovacca* (1958). W.E.H.

SMITHY POETS. A group of Soviet poets who wrote on such themes as the role of industrialization and the solidarity of the proletariat in the new Soviet society. Formed in 1920, they included Vladimir Kirillov, Vasili Kazin, Alexei Gastev, and others. Their verse, which they strove to make rhythmically free and "modern," was often crude and naive.—G. Z. Patrick, *Popular Poetry in Soviet Russia* (1929); "Kuznitsa" (Smithy), *Literaturnaya entsiklopediya*, v (1931). W.E.H.

SOCIETY AND POETRY. The most obvious truth concerning the relations of poets and poetry to soc. is diversity. Pope spat as much as he praised, Yeats cursed, Shelley fled and prophesied, and Shakespeare's and Racine's

aristocratically ordered worlds are always un-
derthreatened by the elemental and savage
power of human sin. Homer, Virgil, the Germanic *scops*, and the Hebrew prophets spoke
in and for their societies, but not with simple
acceptance, rather with heroic exaltation, or
tragic breadth, or denunciation.

The diversity is not surprising. Neither is
the lack of simple relations. No man or poet
can wholly reject his soc.; if he accepts it
genuinely, he accepts its moral standards and
finds, on observing social actualities, much
cause for lamentation, satire, and fear. Societies
do not stand still; nor do poets. Most societies
have seen themselves as incomplete against the
measure of the divine. Those that have not
are fragmented, pluralistic, and individualistic,
like modern America; or see themselves as incomplete against the immanent measure of unfolding historical process, like modern Russia;
or are tyrannically stultifying, like Nazi Germany. Therefore men seldom find their relation to soc. simple and secure; poets are men.
They are also poets; societies assign poets to
various roles, high or low; or they ignore poetry, in which case the alienation of the poet
becomes a social issue.

Men are individuals through and through:
they are born alone; they live and decide alone;
they die alone, and much of their labor is
spent in a never completely successful effort
to close down the gap of their separation from
God and their neighbors. Men are social
through and through: the conception that gives
them existence, and the childbirth that brings
them into the world (even if there is no mid-
wife or doctor, there are mother and child),
are social acts; the food that becomes their
physical substance, the language with which
they think, decide, and perhaps rebel, are
given them by their soc. The relations between
these counter-truths are mysterious. As long
as this is true, there can be no adequate theory
of the relation of the individual to soc., and
hence no adequate statement of the relation of
the poet to soc. This general truth, which applies to all men, is complicated by the historical complexity of the poet's economic relations
to his soc. and his various degrees of feeling
in or out of, for or against his soc., by the
varied way in which he uses social "tools" in
his poetry, the varied ways in which he speaks
about his soc. In selecting illustrative examples,
this article will deal with poet and poetry at
once. The divisions that follow are neither exhaustive nor exclusive, nor make any claim to
be of value to the social historian. They are
useful for showing some responses and relations
involving poets, poetry, and soc.

UNIFIED SOCIETY. A soc. is unified, in this
sense, if it achieves social solidarity, if it is
felt to be unified by enough relevant members.

Primitive societies, Gr. city-states (and Greece
in the imagination of later men), Rome, the
Jewish nation, medieval Christendom, 17th-c.
royalist France, are examples. The poet is apt
to feel himself part of such a soc., rather than
a rebel from it, a conveyor of old truth, rather
than a discoverer of new. The epics of Homer
and Virgil convey and dignify the history of
a people, the good wars, and the gods; they
presume the moral dignity of man, the value
of civilizing labor, an informed and sympathetic audience. Social wisdom is conveyed by
the choruses of Gr. plays. The sufferings of the
individual in high station are bound to the
soc. and even to the fields and harvest by
natural, social, and supernatural ties. Social
wisdom requires a sense of the mysteries beyond soc., of the limits of human expectation:
here Odysseus, Oedipus, Aeneas agree.

A soc. may achieve unity—in spite of temporal insecurities and failures—by a dominant
and continued purpose. The Jewish nation is
one major example. Church is state, the profound agony of the psalmists and the prophets
is the agony of Israel. The soc., its lore, its
acts are holy and one, even in exile and
separation. The unified soc. is apt to have firm
belief, a clear sense of hierarchy. In the Jewish
soc. of the Old Testament and the early Christian soc. of the New, the social hierarchy matters less than the reality of God. The prophets
threaten the social structure with sublime
derogation. Those who are high shall be
brought down. Christian paradox informs the
rhetoric as well as the theology of the New
Testament and, through it, of much Christian
literature. Jesus is a humble carpenter, a
titular descendant of David, the Messiah. The
homeliest things—sheep, work, bread—are
exalted, great things are brought low.

But in classical soc., hierarchy tends to prevail. The rhetoric of Cicero and Quintilian,
which exerted a major influence on Western
thought about poetry through the Renaissance,
divides styles into three: high, middle, and
plain. There are social connections, especially
between the high style and aristocratic dignity.
Theories about poetic and dramatic characterization tend toward the typical, toward a simple
propriety of class and function. Horace simplifies Aristotle in this respect, and, more than
1700 years later, Rymer attacks Shakespeare
for making a soldier kindly. The acceptance of
standards can make for variety as well as for
uniformity. For instance, Virgil, Ovid, Juvenal,
and Horace partake of one firm culture, but
Virgil tends to idealize, deepen, and heighten
links between past and present, between man,
nature, ancestors, and gods; Ovid in *The Art
of Love* accepts the standards of a sophisticated
soc. playfully and cynically, but turns to a
strong sense of the past and the lore of his

people in the *Metamorphoses;* Juvenal holds high standards of civilized behavior and lashes those who depart from them; Horace's poetry has perhaps its greatest influence in its vision of the good man in retirement taking a large and sane view of men and affairs.

Security—real or apparent—can make for frivolity, for self-conscious elegance, for setting a high value on witty expression and brilliant entertainments. The *précieux* of 17th-c. France have their highly artificial games, but also show, in their elaborate restraints and "Platonic" devotions something of the ascetic side of their Catholic tradition. In the Eng. Restoration, the complex protocol of seduction in plays is an attempt to systematize, civilize, and justify the debauched morals of a social class. One of the loveliest of courtly entertainments is the masque, especially in the hands of Jonson and Milton, where high aristocrats themselves take part and allegorical figuration of noble ideals blends into the festivity of an evening.

All patriotic poetry presumes or seeks the unity of a people. It is easy for moderns to forget how much of the world's great poetry is profoundly patriotic—Homer, Virgil, David, Dante, Chaucer, Shakespeare, Spenser, Corneille, Whitman, Wordsworth, René Char, as perhaps most important poets, have all written patriotic poetry. The power of such poetry and its social value can be great, even if all of it shares in varying degrees the tendency to idealize the nation or people and then defend the actuality by the idealization. When such poetry is war poetry, as it often is, the enemy is (more or less subtly and completely) both ennobled—that the victory may be noble—and debased—that the slaughter may be morally admirable.

Those who describe the unified soc. as a theoretical ideal have been liable (from Plato to modern communism) to give poetry its marching orders or its dishonorable discharge. Poetry must, they insist, transmit social ideals, form social virtues, praise great men, idealize the system. (We should remember that poets have often done these things without being told). Censorship may be a corollary. Plato in the *Republic* excludes poets from the ideal state because they tell lies, malign the gods, soften character, confuse the unreal and real.

DIVIDED SOCIETY. A soc. is divided when there are in it distinct sides to be chosen. A soc. locked in civil war is the clearest example, but not the only one. A poet in such a soc. may firmly choose a side, like Milton in his attack on the Anglican clergy in *Lycidas* or Dryden in his defense of Charles II in *Absalom and Achitophel.* Or he may vacillate, as Venantius Fortunatus who, in the 6th c., both wrote panegyrics of his barbarian patrons and

the powerfully liturgical *Vexilla Regis.* All Christendom has been, in such a sense, a divided soc. through much of history, since the choice between the worldly and the holy has been recurrently and variously possible, a fact that provides for the literary kind of the medieval debate between body and soul. Or the poet (or his culture) may reconcile. An extremely important example is the Christianization of the classics by allegory (so that such an unpalatable story as that of Saturn eating his children comes to mean merely Time bearing all his sons away, and the *Aeneid* becomes a pilgrim's progress) and by the continuation and re-creation of classical ideas and literary forms (as Aquinas is to Aristotelian philosophy so is—so to speak—Milton to the Virgilian epic).

THREATENED SOCIETY. The threat may come from God's wrath; plague or famine; military force; a new, potent system of thought and feeling; or internal social decay. The essential condition is that men face changes they intensely fear. All tragedy and all apocalyptic poetry envisions soc. as fearfully unstable, and such fears may be felt at the time of greatest unity and achievement. The plague underwrites Chaucer's *Pardoner's Tale* and Thomas Nashe's "Adieu farewell earth's bliss" (and even, as background and contrast for social comedy, Boccaccio's *Decameron*); the theme of the Last Judgment figures in poems as diverse as the *Dies Irae,* the close of Dryden's *Song for St. Cecilia's Day,* Michael Wigglesworth's popular *The Day of Doom,* and Dylan Thomas' "And death shall have no dominion." Shakespeare, in *King Lear* and *Hamlet* and expressly in the famous "degree" speech in *Troilus and Cressida,* sees the overturn of social hierarchy reechoed in nature, and adumbrating apocalypse. The 16th and 17th c. debate whether nature (and hence soc.) has decayed, which issues on the one hand into Baconian optimism, also provides pessimistic motifs for poetry, for example in Donne's Anniversaries. Racine's *Phèdre* images the underworld of sinful human passion as an explosive and mysterious social force. So does Baudelaire in such poems as *Les Sept Vieillards.* In both works, the image focuses in an agonized individual consciousness, but the social consequences are plainer in Racine. Phèdre is a queen, Baudelaire's *persona* an alienated poet. The close of Pope's Dunciad rises to pessimistic grandeur, telling and foretelling how men fall away from great norms of thought and conduct.

Poets have responded in many other ways to threatened, or present, or imagined social cataclysm. A poet may turn from the cataclysm to the universal in common experience, as did Hardy in *In Time of Breaking of Nations,* Herrick in most of his poems. A poet may express violent reversal of feeling and commitment like Coleridge in *France: An Ode.* He may, like Yeats, adopt dozens of variant, persuasively expressed attitudes, then attempt to unify them into a contemplative whole. He may simply call for a greater allegiance to the common cause: Donald Stauffer, writing as a Marine captain in World War II, invented a memorable phrase—"Get thee behind me, Buddha." He may call for vindication of the oppressed, like Hugo in *L'Enfant;* or he may triumphantly express, among greater things, the vindication of a nation (the final chorus of Milton's *Samson Agonistes*). He may indict deity with Voltaire in his poem on Lisbon, or call men back to God with Johnson in the peroration of *The Vanity of Human Wishes,* or achieve pessimistic universality, like Juvenal in his 10th Satire (from which Johnson adapted his poem) or de Vigny in *La Mort du Loup.*

FRAGMENTED SOCIETY. Such a soc. is ours, in many ways: individualistic, pluralistic, and uncertain of its values. There have been several major responses to it.

1. *eclecticism.* The poet imaginatively and temporarily appropriates values of this culture and that and expresses them. Karl Shapiro has stated that he writes as a Jew one day, a Christian the next. Yeats, Eliot, Auden, Stevens, Pound, Valéry, all share something of the quality that Yvor Winters castigated in Pound when he called him, in a memorably savage phrase, "a barbarian on the loose in a museum."

2. *syncretism.* No sharp line is fixed between the eclectic and the syncretic. It depends on how much is *joined.* A successful syncretism in modern poetry is yet to come. Yeats's *A Vision* is the most bold attempt (though in prose, it is a system for poetry), though it is not surprising that he spoke of it ambiguously; and his poetry—great in its power and beauty and in its deep cultural awareness—is more various than unified.

3. *mystical unity.* A long way from traditional mysticism, this is the solution of Walt Whitman, Hart Crane, and (at times) Emerson. Relativism and pluralism may themselves be praised, but a cultural unity assumed: Whitman assumes a cultural unity in American democratic brotherhood, feels (perhaps more deeply) a unity of life with death. Crane tries to achieve such unity by his powerful, many-stranded image of the bridge.

4. *Marxist futurism.* This tremendously powerful cultural force has not had much place in 20th-c. poetry, though it has had its say in literary criticism and had revolutionary forebears of the stature of Shelley. Stephen Spender's sentimental and unconvincing "Death is

another milestone on the way" is an example.

5. *alienation of the individual* (from soc., himself, the past, and God). This is surely the favorite theme of modern poetry. It is nostalgic, pathetic, yet dignified in the best of MacLeish's earlier poetry; powerfully complex and tragic in Tate's *Ode to the Confederate Dead;* multifariously and pretentiously sly in Steven's *The Comedian as the Letter C;* modest and precise in several of Donald Justice's poems; arrogantly stoic in Jeffers; ragingly bitter in the later Yeats. It flavors, or occasions, several of the other responses.

6. *imaging the disorder by disorder.* Disorder as expressive of social disorder, recommended by Henry Adams, is a major feature of Eliot's *The Waste Land* and Pound's Cantos, and of many shorter poems by such writers as E. E. Cummings, Stevens, and Dylan Thomas, reaching its extremes in Dadaism and surrealism in France and the trivial, noisy San Francisco school of the American 1950's. Outside of Eliot—perhaps not even excluding his work—the most powerful writing of this kind is that of Robert Lowell, notably in *The Quaker Graveyard in Nantucket* and *New Year's Day.*

7. *regionalism.* The most important exemplars of this 'strategy' (a word they have significantly liked) are the Southern traditionalists, particularly Ransom, Tate, and Warren. They look to the past to judge the present, the region to judge the nation, but do not accept simple nostalgia, idealization, or patriotism as adequate responses. Rather they express division, tragic inconclusiveness, and deal with their subject with irony and ambiguity.

8. *other responses.* Poets turn to the personal life (Delmore Schwartz, E. E. Cummings, E. A. Robinson among others), whether lyrically or unhappily. Others turn to the permanent and universal in human experience, and by an act of will appropriate and continue the major tradition of Western ethics. Yvor Winters is the most distinguished example. There are various, not very bold versions of Art for Art's Sake, taking such forms as the concentration on physical details in the work of Marianne Moore and William Carlos Williams, the playful variety of synaesthetic and vocal effects in Edith Sitwell, the mannered and graceful and apologetic elegance of Richard Wilbur.

No modern poet submits tamely to total inclusion in any one of these categories, and it is perhaps a measure of the stature of Robert Frost that he fits them least well.

POETRY AS SOCIAL. Language itself is social. Poetry is refined speech, hence is always (1) communicative, (2) invented. Sir Philip Sidney said that poetry asserts nothing, hence cannot be accused of lying. I. A. Richards held, at least in part of his career, a similar doctrine, and Suzanne Langer holds that poetry is never "about" soc., since it is always pure invention. Without maintaining such bold and refutable paradoxes, one can clearly see that the soc. in poetry is always, *in a sense,* invented rather than actual. Further, all poetry is about invented soc., since—even in the most abstractly didactic or personally expressive of poems—the fundamental invention of each poem is a voice, a someone speaking to someone. Still, one needs to distinguish between the soc. of voice and listener, the invented soc. within the poem, and the actual soc. imitated. And poetry does offer various invented societies that have their own attractiveness as inventions as well as their multifold moral bearings on our experience: the world of pastoral, the world of folk belief, the world of the Faerie Queene, the world of medieval dream visions. There are many degrees of re-creation of soc. Herrick's country people and scenes are less realistic than Goldsmith's, Goldsmith's less than Crabbe's. But there is always re-creation *and* imitation, however mixed. Poetry, then, is always social in its instrument, its chief purpose, its subject, and its invention. It also constitutes a unified soc. Its great themes and great continuities of form are one of the real strands of unity in our history, across nations, across bitter religious and political differences, across centuries. The ideal of literary emulation is one of the greatest Western ideals and of immeasurable social utility.

But if poetry is social, it is not only social. The individual towers above soc. in the very act of naming it; poets universalize as well as express their times; they see soc. in change, limited by history and apocalypse; they imagine men alienated from soc. in exile and fear (so all men always to some degree are). They can also see soc. in relation to permanent standards and realities that transcend civilization and make it possible. Such a view was taken by Longinus, one of the greatest of critics of poetry, in a permanently noble passage: "What is it they saw, those godlike writers who in their work aim at what is greatest and overlook precision in every detail? This, among other things: that nature judged man to be no lowly or ignoble creature when she brought us into this life and into the whole universe as into a great celebration, to be spectators of her whole performance and most ambitious actors. She implanted at once into our souls an invincible love for all that is great and more divine than ourselves. That is why the whole universe gives insufficient scope to man's power of contemplation and reflection, but his thoughts often pass beyond the boundaries of the surrounding world. Anyone

who looks at life in all its aspects will see how far the remarkable, the great, and the beautiful predominate in all things, and he will soon understand to what end we have been born." See also CRITICISM, TYPES OF for sociological criticism.

BIBLIOGRAPHIES: A. Beljame, *Men of Letters and the Eng. Public in the 18th C.* (1948); H. D. Duncan, *Language and Lit. in Soc.* (1953), pp. 143–214; Wellek and Warren, 2d ed., pp. 322–24.

GENERAL: L. Cooper, *The Poetics of Aristotle* (1923); V. F. Calverton, *The Newer Spirit: A Sociological Crit. of Lit.* (1925); H. N. Fairchild, *The Noble Savage* (1928); L. I. Bredvold, *The Intellectual Milieu of John Dryden* (1934); T. R. Henn, *Longinus and Eng. Crit.* (1934); Lewis; A. O. Lovejoy, *The Great Chain of Being* (1936); M. W. Bundy, *The Theory of Imagination in Cl. and Medieval Thought* (1927); D. Daiches, *Lit. and Soc.* (1938); Gilbert and Kuhn; G. N. Shuster, *The Eng. Ode from Milton to Keats* (1940); J. C. Ransom, *The New Crit.* (1941); T. Spencer, *Shakespeare and the Nature of Man* (1942); Wellek and Warren, 2d ed., pp. 82–98; E. M. W. Tillyard, *The Elizabethan World Picture* (1943); Auerbach; L. C. Knights, *Explorations* (1947); Y. Winters, *In Defense of Reason* (1947); J. F. Danby, *Shakespeare's Doctrine of Nature* (1949); C. Dawson, *Religion and the Rise of Western Culture* (1950); R. C. Wallerstein, *Studies in 17th-C. Poetic* (1950); H. Baker, *The Wars of Truth* (1952); Crane, *Critics;* I. Jack, *Augustan Satire* (1952); A. Tate, *The Forlorn Demon* (1953); G. Whicher, *Poetry and Civilization* (1955); D. de Rougemont, *Love in the Western World* (2d ed., 1956); Krieger; Frye; H. Levin, *Contexts of Crit.* (1957); A. Salomon, "Sociology and the Lit. Artist," *Spiritual Problems in Contemp. Lit.,* ed. S. R. Hopper (2d ed., 1957); W. J. Ong, "Voice as Summons for Belief," *Thought,* 33 (1958); R. P. Warren, *Selected Essays* (1958); R. N. Wilson, *Man Made Plain: The Poet in Contemp. Soc.* (1958); P. Ginestier, *The Poet and the Machine,* tr. from Fr. by M. B. Friedman (1961); B. Snell, *Poetry and Soc.* (1961). P.R.

SOCIETY VERSE. See LIGHT VERSE.

SOCIOLOGICAL CRITICISM. See CRITICISM, TYPES OF.

SOLILOQUY. See MONOLOGUE.

SONG. In general, any music of the human voice, most often modulating the words of speech; more specifically, a poem or other formalized utterance and its musical setting, whether composed together or separately, the text before the melody, or vice versa. One might distinguish "s." from what is thought of as "chant" with reference to the smaller melodic range and less sharply defined contours of the latter, and to the fact that one seldom speaks of an accompanied s. as a "chant." It might be observed that we tend to apply the notion of "chanting" to what we consider either primitive or else highly ritualized passages of singing, whether the indigenous singing of non-Indo-European cultures, unfamiliar to Western ears, or, on the other hand, to the prolonged intonation of narrative or scriptural texts. Another useful distinction between s. proper (in its literal, modern sense) and the word's more extended range of applicability can best be pointed out by invoking a distinction between the modern Fr. *chant* and *chanson:* the latter being generally used to refer to what are literally "songs," the former covering the extended senses of "poem," "lyric utterance," "recitation," etc. (Occurrences of such usage apparently as perverse as in *Le Chanson de Roland* and, generically, in *chanson de geste,* however, resulted from their application to long poems which were nevertheless sung to short, interminably repeated, melodic fragments.) At various times, particularly before the development of modern conceptions of literary or musical genres, we may find "s." standing for poems, narratives, and musical compositions almost indiscriminately; but at such times there is almost always a wealth of nomenclature whereby different sorts of forms and functions serve to draw any necessary distinctions. The types of troubadour lyric, for example, are organized with respect not only to verse form (*vers*) but to purpose (*planh, sirventes*) and peculiarities of genesis (*tenso*) as well. In these cases, incidentally, the melodic structure of the music is by and large entailed by the versification, and since both text and melody were generally composed by the troubadour himself, we might almost wish to employ him as the model of the "singer" (in every sense but that of actual performer) in postclassical times.

Up through the Renaissance, "s." continues to refer either to a musico-poetic entity or, at times (and particularly under the influence of antiquity), to a poetic text alone. It is only during the later 15th and the 16th c., however, that modern categories of type of s. begin to be useful. Even assuming (in the 16th c., at any rate) one basic canonical musical language, that of high-Renaissance polyphony, a category of musical types, such as songs of various numbers of parts, those with prescribed accompaniments and those without, etc. may be employed. And categories of subject (amatory, pastoral, satiric, narrative, religious, etc.), poetic form (sonnet, various ode forms, etc.) and function (dramatic lyrics,

masque songs, postprandial madrigals, etc.) become necessary, in the light of 16th-c. practice, as descriptive terms.

It is with the notion of s. as *chant* rather than as *chanson,* however, that literary history is primarily concerned. The processes by which more purely literary senses accrued to the word "s." must themselves be studied, of course, against the background of the tangled history of musico-poetic relations. The splitting into separate practices and concepts, in postclassic times, of music, poetry, and dance in no way interfered with the transmission of a literary heritage in which "singing" could now be taken metaphorically as "writing" and the Apollonian lyre as an inspiring muse. The 12th and 13th c., it is true, saw a reunification of music and lyric poetry in the art of the troubadours, trouvères and Minnesänger; even the 14th c. saw an important lyric poet as well as a truly great polyphonic composer in Guillaume de Machaut, and there are cases, like that of the German Oswald von Wolkenstein, of poet-composers as late as the 15th c. After this, however, such names as that of Thomas Campion come to represent the extremely rare exceptions.

But if the 16th c. saw the final separation of roles of poet and musician, there nevertheless occurred a temporary identification of *chant* and *chanson*. Short lyric poems of almost any kind, including those like the sonnet whose real heritage was purely literary and intellectual, were written in the conscious knowledge that they were candidates for musical setting. Secular vocal composers turned to plays, sonnet sequences, pastorals, miscellanies, etc. for their texts, and any poem, regardless of its particular literary intention, might end up in a s. book. But even amidst this burst of harmonious musical and literary activity, the notion of *chant* began to crystallize out. An early and significant case is that of the envoy of Spenser's *Epithalamion,* in the lines that seem to summarize so nicely much of the Elizabethan aesthetic (ll. 427–8):

Song, made in lieu of many ornaments
With which my love should duly have bene
    dect. . . .

Here, "song" = "literary composition," pure and simple; and it is thus that "s." comes to designate lyric poems, not necessarily composed as candidates for possible setting at all, throughout the 17th c. The metaphysical lyric, commencing perhaps with Donne's *Songs and Sonnets,* poses a special problem. If we were to contrast the Elizabethan and metaphysical lyric with respect to their musical status, we should have to remark that it is the former that models itself on the *chanson* text, and that the latter tends to approach more and more a formal argument, a quasi-scriptural or philosophical "text" for study, contemplation, exegesis, etc. The metaphysical lyric may be said to be more semantically dense than we would expect the text of a *chanson* to be: the rapidity, that is, with which its highly complex statement moves forward is even greater than the movement of the formal verse itself. The density of a *chanson* text, on the other hand, would be lessened to the degree that its thought progressed less slowly than its own (prosodic) or accompanying (actual) music. Musicians will recognize here a useful analogy to the musical concept of *harmonic rhythm*, which similarly treats of the "density" or rapidity of harmonic change with respect to rhythmic flow.

By and large, it is this rarer semantic density which characterizes the actual s. text throughout the later 17th and 18th c.; and even within the context of the over-all development of lyric poetry, the *chanson* remains a more or less trivial poetic form. In drama, with the possible sole exception of the opening, programmatic lyric in Dryden's *Marriage à la Mode,* nothing approaches the variety and intricacy of purpose to which songs are put by Shakespeare. The development of opera and the exigencies of libretto-writing gradually eclipse in importance, while perhaps never surpassing, the proto-operatic songs of Jonson's masques.

In general, it is only rarely that long or ambitious lyric poems like Smart's *A Song to David* or Blake's *Songs of Innocence* are actually so called, and it is interesting that the title of so important a manifesto as the Wordsworth-Coleridge *Lyrical Ballads* avoids the word almost pointedly. Throughout the 19th c., nevertheless, a greater tendency may be noted to unify *chant* and *chanson,* the German lyric appearing as a *Lied,* for example, and the flourishing of the art-song in general as a musical development contributing to this in no small part. In the latter half of the century, however, the notion of *chant* seems to undergo its greatest extended application; with the heritage of the *symboliste* movement and its reverberations in the poetry of many languages up through the present century, "s." comes to be used more and more in perverse and ironic ways, finally coming to name or describe any poem, in verse or prose, and of whatever length. Interestingly enough, it is during this same later 19th c. that an overextended musical sense of "s." begins to develop, in the short instrumental (usually piano) solo piece entitled *chant sans paroles,* and later, simply, "song." See LYRIC; MUSIC AND POETRY.

J. B. Beck, *La Musique des troubadours* (1910); J. R. Noble, *Shakespeare's Use of S.*

(1923); E. H. Fellowes, *The Eng. Madrigal* (1925); P. Warlock, *The Eng. Ayre* (1926); J. M. Edmonds, "An Account of Gr. Lyric Poetry," *Lyra Graeca,* ed. and tr. J. Edmonds (2d ed., III, 1928); G. Bontoux, *Le Chanson en Angleterre au temps d'Elizabeth* (1936); M. Bukofzer, *Music in the Baroque Era* (1947); *Historical Anthol. of Music,* ed. A. T. Davison and W. Apel (2v., 1949–50); A. Einstein, *Essays on Music* (1956); Beare; *A Hist. of S.,* ed. D. Stevens (1960); C. M. Bowra, *Primitive S.* (1962).   J.H.

SONNET (fr. It. *sonetto,* a little sound or song). A 14-line poem in iambic pentameter (normally iambic hexameter in France) whose rhyme scheme has, in practice, been widely varied despite the traditional assumption of limited freedom in this respect. The three most widely recognized forms of the s., with their traditional rhyme schemes, are the It. or Petrarchan (octave: *abbaabba;* sestet: *cdecde* or *cdcdcd* or a similar combination that avoids the closing couplet), the Spenserian (*abab bcbc cdcd ee*), and the Eng. or Shakespearean (*abab cdcd efef gg*). With respect to the It. pattern (by far the most widely used of the three) it will be observed that a two-part division of thought is invited, and that the octave offers an admirably unified pattern and leads to the *volta* (q.v.) or "turn" of thought in the more varied sestet. The effect of the *abbaabba* octave is truly remarkable. It is actually a blend of 3 brace-rhyme quatrains, since the middle 4 verses, whose sounds overlap the others and echo their pattern, impress the reader with a similar rhyme pattern, thus, ab*baab*ba. Normally, too, a definite pause is made in thought development at the end of the eighth verse, serving to increase the independent unity of an octave that has already progressed with the greatest economy in rhyme sounds. Certainly it would be difficult to conceive a more artistically compact and phonologically effective pattern. The sestet, in turn, leads out of the octave and, if the closing couplet is avoided, assures a commendable variety within uniformity to the poem as a whole. The Spenserian and Shakespearean patterns, on the other hand, offer some relief to the difficulty of rhyming in Eng. and invite a division of thought into 3 quatrains and a closing or summarizing couplet; and even though such arbitrary divisions are frequently ignored by the poet, the more open rhyme schemes tend to impress the fourfold structure on the reader's ear and to suggest a stepped progression toward the closing couplet. Such matters of relationship between form and content are, however, susceptible of considerable control in the hands of a skilled poet, and the ultimate effect in any given instance may override theoretical considerations in achievement of artistic integrity.

Most deviations from the foregoing patterns have resulted from liberties taken in rhyming, but there have been a few novelties in use of the s. that may be mentioned, among them the following: *caudate* (q.v.), with "tails" of added verses; *continuous or iterating*, on one or two rhyme sounds throughout; *retrograde*, reading the same backward as forward; *chained or linked*, each verse beginning with the last word of the preceding verse; *interwoven*, with medial as well as end rhyme; *crown of sonnets* (q.v.), a series joined together by rhyme or repeated verses, for panegyric; *terza rima sonnet* (q.v.), with a rhyme scheme corresponding to terza rima; *tetrameter*, in tetrameters instead of pentameters. Meredith's *Modern Love* sequence is clearly related to the s. in its themes and its *abba cddc effe ghhg* rhyme pattern, but whether these 16-line poems should be admitted to the canon is questionable.

Historically, s. beginnings centered about the It. pattern, and it is probable that the form resulted from the addition of a double refrain of 6 lines (2 tercets) to the 2-quatrain Sicilian *strambotto* (q.v.). In any event (for the origins must remain uncertain) the earliest antecedents of the "true" It. s. are credited to Giacomo da Lentino (fl. 1215-1233) whose hendecasyllables usually rhymed *abababab cdecde*. Although others of Lentino's contemporaries (the Abbot of Tivoli, Jacopo Mostacii, Pierro delle Vigne, Monaldo d'Aquino) used the form and established the octave-sestet divisions (with quatrain-tercet subdivisions), it remained for Guittone d'Arezzo (1230-1294) to establish the *abbaabba* octave, which became traditional through its preference by Dante (*Vita Nuova; Canzoniere*) and Petrarch (*Canzoniere*); and for Antonio da Tempo, in his *Summa Artis Rithimici* (1332), to enunciate the first theoretical discussion of the s. as a type. The sonnets of Dante to Beatrice, and of Petrarch to Laura ("spells which unseal the inmost enchanted fountains of the delight which is the grief of love" [Shelley]) normally opened with a strong statement which was then developed; but they were not unmarked by the artificiality of treatment that stemmed from variations on the Platonic love themes, an artificiality that was to be exported with the form in the 15th and 16th c. as the s. made its way to Spain, Portugal, France, the Netherlands, Poland, and England, and later to Germany, Scandinavia, and Russia; until its use was world-wide and the number of poets not using it negligible. Following Petrarch there was in Italy some diminution of dignity in use of the form (as in Serafino dall'Aquila [1466-1500]), but with the work of Tasso (1544-1595) and his contemporaries (Michelangelo, Bembo, Castiglioni) the

s. was reaffirmed as a structure admirably suited to the expression of emotion in lyrical mood, adaptable to a wide range of subject matter (love, politics, religion, etc.), and employed with skill by many writers in the centuries to follow (Alfieri, Foscolo, Carducci, D'Annunzio).

It was the Marquis de Santillana (1398-1458) who introduced the pattern to Spain, although it was not established there until the time of Juan Boscán (1490-1552) and, especially, Garcilaso de la Vega (1503-1536), and Lope de Vega (1562-1635) and other dramatists of the *siglo de oro*. Sá de Miranda (1485-1558) and his disciple, Antonio Ferreira, brought the s. to Portugal, where it is better known in the *Rimas* of Camões (1524-1580) and, more recently, in the exquisite work of Anthero de Quental (1842-1891). Clément Marot (1496-1544) and Mellin de Saint Gelais (1491-1558) introduced it to France, but it was Joachim du Bellay (1522-1560) who was most active, writing (in the Petrarchan pattern) the first non-Italian cycle, *L'Olive*, as well as *Regrets* and *Les Antiquités de Rome* (translated by Spenser as *The Ruins of Rome*). Ronsard (1524-1585) who experimented with the form in alexandrines, and Philippe Desportes (1546-1606) wrote many sonnets and were instrumental in stimulating interest both at home and in England; while Malherbe (1555-1628) put the weight of his authority behind the *abbaabba ccdede* or *ccdced* pattern in alexandrines, which became the accepted line length. After a period of decline (general throughout Europe) in the 18th c., Theophile Gautier (1811-1872) and Baudelaire (1821-1867) revived the form, which soon reached new heights in the work of Heredia, Lecomte de Lisle, Valéry, Mallarmé, and Rimbaud. Germany received the form relatively late, in the writings of G. R. Weckherlin (1584-1653) and, especially insofar as creative achievement is concerned, Andreas Gryphius (1616-1664). There followed a period of disuse until Gottfried Bürger (1747-1794) revived the form and anticipated its use by Schlegel, Eichendorff, Tieck, and other romantic writers. The sonnets of August Graf von Platen (1796-1835; *Sonette aus Venedig*) rank among the best in modern times, while in more recent years the mystical sequence, *Sonette an Orpheus* (1923), of Rilke and the writings of R. A. Schröder have brought the German s. to another high point.

In England the s. has had a fruitful history. Wyatt (1503-1542) brought the form from Italy but showed an immediate preference (possibly influenced by the work of minor writers while he was abroad) for a closing couplet in the sestet. Wyatt did, however, adhere to the Petrarchan octave, and it was Surrey (1517-1547) who established the accepted *abab cdcd efef gg,* a pattern more congenial to the comparatively rhyme-poor Eng. language. This pattern was used extensively in the period, but by no means exclusively for there was wide variety in rhyme schemes and line lengths. It was brought to its finest representation by Shakespeare. A rhyme scheme more attractive to Spenser (and in its first 9 lines paralleling his Spenserian stanza) was *abab bcbc cdcd ee,* in effect a compromise between the more rigid It. and the less rigid Eng. patterns. The period also saw many s. cycles, beginning with Sidney's *Astrophel and Stella* (1580) and continuing in the sequences of Daniel (*Delia*), Drayton (*Idea*), Spenser (*Amoretti*), and Shakespeare; with a shift to religious themes shortly thereafter in John Donne's *Holy Sonnets.* It remained for Milton to introduce the true It. pattern, to break from sequences to occasional sonnets, to give a greater unity to the form by frequently permitting octave to run into sestet (the "Miltonic" sonnet, but anticipated by the Elizabethans), and a greater richness to the texture by employing his principle of "apt numbers, fit quantity of syllables, and the sense variously drawn out from one verse into another," as in his blank verse. Milton's was the strongest influence when, after a century of disuse, the s. was revived in the late 18th c. by Gray, T. Warton, Cowper, and Bowles; and reestablished in the early 19th by Wordsworth (also under Milton's influence but easing rhyme demands by use of an *abbaacca* octave in nearly half of his more than 500 sonnets); and by Keats, whose frequent use of the Shakespearean pattern did much to reaffirm it as a worthy companion to the generally favored Miltonic-Italian. By this time the scope of s. themes had broadened widely, and in Leigh Hunt and Keats it even embraced an unaccustomed humor. S. theory was also developing tentatively during this period (as in Hunt's "Essay on the Sonnet") to eventuate in an unrealistic extreme of purism in T.W.H. Crosland's *The Eng. Sonnet* (1917) before it was more temperately approached by later writers. Since the impetus of the romantic revival, the form has had a continuing and at times distinguished use, as in D. G. Rossetti (*The House of Life*), Christina Rossetti, E. B. Browning (*Sonnets from the Portugese*), and the facile work of Swinburne. Few writers in the present century (W. H. Auden and Dylan Thomas might be named) have matched the consistent level of production found in the earlier work, although an occasional single s., such as Yeats's "Leda and the Swan," has rare beauty.

The s. did not appear in America until the last quarter of the 18th c., in the work of Colonel David Humphreys, but once introduced, the form spread rapidly if not distinctively until Longfellow (1807–1882), using the

It. pattern, lifted it in dignity and lyric tone (especially in the *Divina Commedia* sequence) to a level easily equal to its counterpart in England. Following him there was wide variety in form and theme, with commendable work from such writers as Lowell, George Henry Boker, and Paul Hamilton Hayne. Of the later writers E. A. Robinson, Edna St. Vincent Millay, Merrill Moore, Allen Tate, and E. E. Cummings hold a recognized place, although, space permitting, many others might be named who stand well above what Robinson called

. . . these little sonnet men
Who fashion, in a shrewd mechanic way,
Songs without souls, that flicker for a day,
To vanish in irrevocable night.

During the past century s. themes in both Europe and America have broadened to include almost any subject and mood, even though the main line of development has remained remarkably stable. Structurally, even within the traditional patterns, the type has reflected the principal influences evident in modern poetry as a whole: the sprung rhythm of Hopkins and free-verse innovations have frequently led to less metronomic movement within the iambic norm; substitutions for exact rhymes have supplied fresher sound relationships; and a more natural idiom has removed much of the artificiality that had long been a burden. This adaptability within a tradition of eight centuries' standing suggests that there will be no diminution of interest in and use of the form in the foreseeable future, and that the inherent difficulties that have kept the numbers of truly fine sonnets to an extremely small percentage of those that have been written will deter neither versifier nor genius from testing for himself the challenge of what Rossetti called

. . . a moment's monument,—
Memorial from the Soul's eternity
To one dead deathless hour.

S. Lee, *Elizabethan Sonnets* (2 v., 1904); E. H. Wilkins, "The Invention of the S.," MP, 13 (1915; rewritten and brought up to date in his collected *Studies in It. Lit.,* Rome, 1957); T.W.H. Crosland, *The Eng. S.* (1917); R. D. Havens, "Milton and the S.," *The Influence of Milton on Eng. Poetry* (1922; excellent survey of the s. in 18th- and 19th-c. England); W. L. Bullock, "The Genesis of the Eng. S. Form," PMLA, 38 (1923); G. Bertoni, *Il Duocento* (1930); L. G. Sterner, *The S. in Am. Lit.* (1930); A. Meozzi, *Il Petrarchismo Europeo: Secolo XVI* (1934); E. Hamer, *The Eng. S.* (1936); L. C. John, *The Elizabethan S. Sequences* (1938); W. Mönch, *Das Sonett* (1955; the most comprehensive study to date, with extended

SONNET CYCLE

bibliog.); J. W. Lever, *The Elizabethan Love S.* (1956); E. T. Prince, "The S. from Wyatt to Shakespeare," *Elizabethan Poetry*, ed. J. R. Brown and B. Harris (1960). L.J.Z.

SONNET CYCLE or sequence. A series of sonnets on a given theme or to a given individual. The effect is that of stanzas in a longer work, but with the difference that each sonnet retains its integrity as an independent poem. When this is not the case, as in William Ellery Leonard's moving *Two Lives* (1925), the sonnet loses much of its force as a type and becomes in fact "stanzaic." At times the sequence will be given added unity by use of repetition, either of rhymes or of lines, between the different poems, as in the "crown of sonnets" (q.v.). From the earliest times the cycle has been used to amplify the limited scope of the single sonnet and to reflect the many facets of the chosen theme. Among the most famous or noteworthy of these cycles may be named Dante's *Vita Nuova*, Petrarch's *Canzoniere*, du Bellay's *L'Olive* (the first non-It. cycle), Camões' *Rimas*, Sidney's *Astrophel and Stella* (the first cycle in England), Spenser's *Amoretti*, Shakespeare's *Sonnets*, Donne's *Holy Sonnets*, Wordsworth's *Ecclesiastical Sonnets*, Rossetti's *The House of Life*, E. B. Browning's *Sonnets from the Portuguese*, George Henry Boker's *A Sequence on Profane Love*, Longfellow's *Divina Commedia*, Arthur Davison Ficke's *Sonnets of a Portrait Painter*, Edna St. Vincent Millay's *Fatal Interview*, and Rilke's *Sonette an Orpheus*. L.J.Z.

SORITES. See CLIMAX.

SOTADEAN (fr. Sotades, an Alexandrian poet of the 3d c. B.C.). A verse form based on the major ionic (*ionicus a maiore*) and essentially an ionic tetrameter brachycatalectic (−−◡◡|−−◡◡|−−◡◡|−−). Anaclasis (q.v. and see IONIC) and resolutions and contractions of long syllables may occur. The S. was introduced to Latin in nondramatic verse by Ennius, but was never extensively used (Accius, Varro in his *Menippean Satires*, Petronius twice, and Martial once). The strictest form occurs in Petronius and Martial (3. 29):

hās cŭm gĕmī|nā cŏmpĕdĕ | dēdĭcăt că|tēnās

Sătŭrnĕ tī|bĭ Zŏīlŭs | ănŭlŏs prī|ōrēs,

with anaclasis (−◡◡− in place of −−◡◡) in the third foot or, as some prefer to say, as a system of two ionics plus three trochees. See also PALINDROME.—Koster; Crusius. K.M.A.

SOUND IN POETRY. This subject has attracted much controversy. One reason is our psycho-physiological variety. Human beings are divisible into pure verbalizers who can think only in words, pure visualizers who use only visual images, and two larger groups, *predominantly* verbal or visual; a verbalizer unconsciously says words for his thoughts over to himself, as betrayed by his breathing. (Cf. *Science News*, 24 [May 1952], 7–21.) Presumably most poets "verbalize"; poems by exclusive visualizers must depend solely on images, and their sound structure must be conventional or scarcely organized (Blake? Whitman?). Many poets "chant" their verses and, even if they recite in monotone, give full play to vowel and consonant values. Berry (1962) claims that a poet's work matches the physical characteristics of his voice. With Valéry, we may consider a poem on paper as merely an inadequate "musical score."

SOURCE. Human prelanguage may have been a set of predispositions towards fluid utterances partly expressing emotion and need. Poetry, concerned so much with expression, can embody such primitive mechanisms. Expression through sound utterance (now under its own conventions) involves pitch, stress, duration, voice quality, articulatory gesture, phonetic *timbre*, and pattern in time: all can be organized into a formally satisfying poem or chant, or used expressively and decoratively. As music and poetry differentiate, pitch and duration are drawn more into music, articulation and phonetic timbre more into poetry.

A tendency to reduplicative phonetic patterns seems innate in man. They occur in infant babbling; in certain languages; in strong feeling; in spells; in oaths; in proverbial expressions; in oratory; and in advertisements. The chants of modern "primitive" tribes reveal a repetitive structure: refrains, word repetitions, syllable echoes; but these features are already often stylized.

SOUND AS STRUCTURE. Sound effects must be felt against the whole phonology of a language (see TONE-COLOR), the fundamentals of its verse (see ALLITERATIVE METER, CLASSICAL PROSODY, RHYME, CELTIC PROSODY, CYNGHANEDD, and [for syllabic verse] METER, PROSODY); and the particular verse form. Welsh *cynghanedd* crystallized complex phonetic sequences. Legitimate changes rung on structural forms are often exploited musically or expressively. Thus in *pollá d' ánanta kátanta páranta te dókhmid t' élthon* dactyls replace spondees wherever permissible: one reason why the line is appropriate to horses cantering. If *ictus* (metrical beat) was present in classical verse, effects could be achieved by counterpoint with the prose accent, as claimed by W. F. Jackson Knight in Virgil; "reversal of foot" and "ionic foot" are expressive in accentual, and stress-clumping in nonsyllabic verse. The line-internal pause or

SOUND IN POETRY

caesura can be expressively shifted. Variation, and grouping, of rhyme-vowels (and rhyme-consonants) has been observed in, e.g., the Eng. Renaissance by Oras.

SOUND AS TEXTURE. The whole body of free sound in verse is available for exploitation. There are periods, usually those in which spoken verse existed side by side with sung verse, as in the Elizabethan or the European Renaissance, when conscious virtuosity in varieties of word repetition, in wordplay, and in sound echoes, is the rule; individuals have also used blatant alliteration etc.; but in civilized verse, alliteration at the expense of sincere expression often defeats the objects of poetry: cf. Poe, Swinburne. Duration-variation may be achieved by grouping sounds either "cloggingly" or "trippingly": contrast the two 5-beat "iambic" lines "Rocks, Caves, Lakes, Fens, Bogs, Dens, and shades of death" (Milton) and "For the ripple to run over in its mirth" (Browning). Classes of vowel or consonant, somber or bright, liquid or harsh, may be grouped (see TONE-COLOR). The tissue of most verse forms a web of sound-patterning, often related to sense and mood; the poet may not have worked for it, the reader may not be aware of it, but the words were chosen, and the reader/listener reacts, under its influence; words first chosen may "attract" others of like sound, which then seem to reinforce their aura. And "le style, c'est l'homme même" is as true (and untrue) of sound as of any other feature.

FUNCTIONS OF SOUND-MANIPULATION. These may be divided into (overlapping) types, in practice rarely isolated pure. Behind them are (a) associations of sound arrangements with certain sets of words; (b) familiarity with the grammatical function, and hence with any arbitrary use, of sounds as mere labels; (c) traditional and accepted synaesthesias (see ONO-MATOPOEIA, TONE-COLOR); (d) vocal/facial emotive expression; (e) instinctive satisfaction in sounds, articulations, and reiterations. Types A-C below are especially concerned with (aspect 1) the *formal structure* of the verse; types D-H, with (2) the *sense;* I-K (also D, H) with (3) the *scene;* L-O (G) with (4) the *feeling;* and P-R with (5) the *aesthetic flavor.* We start each of these five groups here with its crudest type. Apart from the Emphases (A, D, L) the functions in group 2 are mainly symbolic, in groups 3 and 4 mainly representational. In the face of sound effects under aspect 2 it is helpful to list the words involved in each phonetic theme; under 3 and 4 careful study of the subtleties of sensory metaphor is essential; under 5 an analysis of the patterning is needed for full understanding. Many of our examples here are necessarily too short.

A. (Under aspect 1.) *Structural Emphasis* (i.e.

of the form). A rhetorical addition to the formally required sound structure. E.g. gratuitous rich-rhymes; scene-end rhyming couplets in blank verse; alliterative support as in "Against this nearest cruelest of *Foes* / What shall *Wit* meditate, or *Force* oppose?" (Prior).

B. (Under 1.) *Underpinning:* relatively subtle reinforcement of the verse structure. E.g. unobtrusive sporadically rich rhymes; Milton's compensatory line-end assonance and consonance in his blank verse (Oras, 1953). Sometimes combined with C, as follows.

C. (1.) *Counterpoising:* arrangement of some sounds in opposition to the verse structure. Notice the imperfect rhymes, distractingly echoed by internal rhyme and submerged alliteration, in "violet,— / Solution sweet: meantime the frost-wind blows / . . . sleet /Against . . . St. Agnes' . . . set." (Keats); this compensates for the next stanza repeating this rhyme, in a different place, with "beat" and a second "sleet." Owen's *Exposure* (with a *structure* of dissonant rich-rhymes) has some complicated counterpoising.

D. (2, 3.) *Rubricating Emphasis* (i.e. of words or images). Common; in England richest in Tudor verse. In "The *turtle to* her make hath *tolde* her *tale. / Sommer* is *come,* for *euery spray* nowe *springes; / The hart hath hong his* olde *hed* on the pale; / The *buck* in *brake* his winter *cote* he flings; / The *fishes flote* with newe repaired scale; / The [ ]adder [ ]all her sloughe away she *slinges; / The swift swallow* pursueth the *flyes smale; / The busy bee her honye* now she minges; / *Winter* is *worne,* that *was* the flowers *bale*" (Surrey) striking echoes rubricate each image (besides cross-links such as *make—brake, tolde—olde, cote—flings—flote —flyes—flowers* and others).

E. (2.) *Tagging:* punctuation of syntax or thought by sounds. Common before the romantics. In "The *baiting*-place of *wit,* the *balme* of *woe*" (Sidney), the analogous nouns in the two parallel phrases are respectively labeled with *b-* and *w-;* in "The pallor of girls' brows shall be their *pall*" (Wilfred Owen) the metaphor is *primarily* underlined by *p—l / p—l.*

F. (2.) *Correlation:* indirect support of argument by related echoes. Very common. Notice the relevance of the repeated sound-groupings in "Then farewell, world; thy vttermost I see: / Eternal Loue, maintaine thy life in me" (Sidney); "Five! the finding and sake / And cypher of suffering Christ. / . . . Sacrificed" (Hopkins). Types E and F also occur as pun and near-pun (paronomasia).

G. (2, 4.) *Implication:* more involved interconnection of sound, meaning, and feeling. Almost universal. Wordplay and hidden associations sometimes take part. "With his loll'd tongue he faintly licks his Prey; / His warm breath blows her flix up as she lies; / She,

-[785]-

trembling, creeps upon the ground away, / And looks back to him with beseeching eyes" (Dryden) swarms with interlocking echoes too numerous to analyze, but including *f—liliks / bl—z / fliks / l—ks*; cf. "At length himself unsettling, he the pond / Stirr'd with his staff, and fixedly did look" (Wordsworth).

H. (2, 3.) *Diagramming:* the abstract pattern symbolizes the sense. Notice the criss-crossing sound patterns in Dryden's account of the Fire of London: "He wades the Streets, and streight he reaches cross." This has the sounds [e:dz] (*w-ades*) invading [stri:ts] (*Streets*) and transforming it into [dstre:t] (*and streight*), then in *reaches* (pronounced with [ri:tš—z] or [re:tš—z]) sending their [z] one syllable ahead to leap over in "-s cross" [zkr—s]; thus inspiredly "imitating" the mode of spread of the flames.

I. (3.) *Sound-Representation:* some similarity to the relevant sounds (see ONOMATOPOEIA). Rather rare unless adulterated; its worst excesses are baroque. "The double double double beat / Of the thund'ring DRUM" (Dryden); "Sudden successive flights of bullets streak the silence" (Owen).

J. (3.) *Illustrative Mime:* mouth-movements recall motion or shape (cf. TONE-COLOR). Rare pure. "When *Péarse súmmoned* Cuchulain to his *side,* / What *stálked* thróugh the *Post-Óffice?*" (Yeats); here a reader's half-conscious mouthing of the words may evoke a looming, slow-striding figure.

K. (3.) *Illustrative Painting:* articulations, sounds, or their patterns, correspond to appearances and nonacoustic sensations. "The horrid crags, by toppling convent crown'd, / The cork-trees hoar that clothe the shaggy steep, / The mountain-moss by scorching skies imbrown'd" (Byron) is chiefly appropriate to the ruggedness, dark tints, and dizzy heights (for analysis see TONE-COLOR).

L. (4.) *Passionate Emphasis* (as from the emotion). E.g. "Ruin seize thee, ruthless King" (Gray).

M. (4.) *Mood-Evocation:* choice of tone-colors resembling vocalizations natural to the emotion. Rare pure. Milton's sonnet of anger and grief on the massacre at Piedmont has all the octet rhymes and one of the two sestet rhymes in [o:], plus resonant octet-rhyme consonants.

N. (4.) *Expressive Mime:* mouth-movements ape the expression of emotion. Chiefly in dialogue. "Out of my sight, thou Serpent, that name best / Befits thee with him leagu'd, thy self as false / And hateful" (Milton): in the succession *s—t / s—p—t / b—st / b—f—ts / s—lf—zf—ls / tf—l* the reader's mouth is made to spit out Adam's hatred.

O. (4.) *Expressive Painting:* sounds, articulations, or their arrangement, correspond to feel-

ings or impressions. Certain repeated sounds express monotony in "And the dull wheel hums doleful through the day" (Crabbe); Shelley's revolutionary fervour is conveyed in the *s, sk,* and *sp* sounds of "Liberty . . . o'er Spain, / Scattering contagious fire into the sky, / Gleamed. My soul spurned the chains of its dismay"; for analyses see TONE-COLOR.

P. (5.) *Ebullience:* pure exuberance or pleasure in sound. Seldom alone. "The wealthy crops of whit'ning rice / 'Mongst thyine woods and groves of spice, / For ADORATION grow; / . . . Where wild carnations blow" (Smart) includes the ten interwoven motifs *w—l, th (—)i, kr—s / gr—z, ps / sp, wĭ, wĭ'n / ĭnw, r—s / r—z, w—d, grō, ation.*

Q. (5.) *Embellishment:* superficially "musical." More frequent through the Renaissance (cf. Surrey under D), possibly as compensation for verse not sung. "No clowde was seene, but christaline the ayre, / Laughing for joy vpon my louely fayre" (Drayton) includes the five motifs *n—kl/k . . . l—n, s—n/s . . . n, r . . . l/rl, l—f/l—v, l(—)if—r.*

R. (5.) *Incantation:* profoundly musical or magical. Not infrequent pure, but disappears during the neoclassical period. Adequate analyses impossible here. Enobarbus describing Cleopatra in the barge (*A. & C.* 2.2.191–94); "The *Sounds, and Seas with* all their *finny drove / Now* to the *Moon* in *wavering Morrice move*" (Milton); "Of perilous seas in faery lands forlorn" (Keats), esp. *v . . . l . . . n / f . . . l—n / f—l—n;* "Shrill music reach'd them on the middle sea" (Tennyson) with *ilm / i / them / themi—l;* "That dolphin-torn, that gong-tormented sea" (Yeats).

SURVEY (Classical, Romance, Eng. and Germanic, Slavonic). *Gr. civilization* achieved refinements of sound effect. Such writers as Homer, Sappho, Aeschylus, Pindar afford florid sound-patternings. Gr. and L. suffered from excess of like-endings, but other consonances are common, usually parceled out rather as in It. or Fr.: "*Diomēdea d' ámbroton ksanthá pote* Glaukôpis *éthēke theon;* / gaîa d' en *Thēbais* hüpédekto kerauno*theîsa Dios* bélesin / mántin Oikleídan, polémoio néphos" (Pindar); which also includes such echo-progressions as: *oto/ot/to/oth, po/po/pho, ám/má, deaddám/den/éde/eidan, éthēketh/édekt—ke.* Demetrius *On Style* writes of imitative words and the virtues of vivid cacophony in Homer; cites musicians who distinguish "smooth" words (vocalic, e.g. *Aias*), "rough" (*bébrōke*), etc.; defends juxtaposed vowels as harmonious; and commends long vowels and lengthened consonants (*Kallistratos*). In the 1st c. B.C. Dionysius of Halicarnassus writes an elaborate analysis of composition, especially sound; double letters like *x* are preferred for sonority, *sigmatism* is condemned, short vowels (especially *e*) are thought ugly; imitative words are illustrated from Homer (e.g. *rhókhthei* "crashes out"); many Homeric examples of sound echoing sense are analyzed, some mainly rhythmical like the famous lines on Sisyphus' stone, but most phonemic.

L. writers (rhetorician-inspired?) use abundant sound-patterning, too rich for a structural code which has been suggested. There is much underpinning, embellishment, painting, sound representation, and mime. Catullus, Virgil especially, Horace, Ovid, even Juvenal, are the great practitioners: "frīgora mītescunt Zephirīs, uēr prōterit aestās / interitūra, simul / pōmifer autumnus frūgēs effūderit, et mox / brūma recurrit iners" (Horace) has recurrent motifs in *fr—g* and *ī* (for cold), *fr/f—r, fu, rŭ/urr/ŭr, mu/um/ŭm, pō, cu, terit, in, erit, t—m/tm*, etc. Herescu's study concentrates much on patterns in ictus-bearing vowels (italicized in the quotation above), but without "long/short" distinction.

Early medieval L. hymns became accentual and developed rhyme. They also show texture: "Pange, lingua, gloriosi proelium certaminis, / Et super crucis tropaeo dic triumphum nobilem, / Qualiter redemptor orbis immolatus vicerit" (Venantius Fortunatus, c. 600) includes the four themes *p—eli/préli/pér/r—pé, čert/ ét/pér/r—č/čerìt, up—rkru/tr—p/ktr—úmpu/ mpt—r, ór/pr/p—r/rop/óbil/ptorórbi/ol.*

Mediterranean vernacular poets developed a host of rhymed song-forms, etc., some with intricate repetitions like the *leixa-pren.* But rich textures appear too: "Quant l'erba fresqu' e·l fuelha par / E la flors botona el verjan, / E·l rossinhols autet e clar / Leva sa votz e mou son chan, / Joy ai de luy e joy ai de la flor / E joy de me e de midons major; / Daus totas partz suy de joy claus e sens, / Mas sel es joys que totz autres joys vens" (Bernart de Ventadorn, ca. 1150, in Provençal) includes the following in succession: *ler / fre / elfwe(lh) / flors / ver /lros / olsaut / levasav / laflor / jóidemé, edem—dó'm—jó / aus / aus / esens / seles / saut;* cf., e.g., such diverse poets as Arnaut Daniel in Provençal, Chrétien de Troyes and Guy de Coucy in Fr., Giacomo Pugliese in It., all 1150–1250.

It. Dante's word-classification betters Demetrius'; his onomatopoeia, implication, harmony recall Virgil's: "Ora incomincian le dolenti note / A [f]farmisi sentire: or son venuto / Là [d]dove [m]molto pianto mi percuote" includes "ear-striking" *òt / to / ólto / to / òt* and at least 13 other motifs, some with stress-shunting in *co, om/mo, mi, ián, l—do, le, enti, ent/en—t, nt, ol, s—n, ve, m . . . p . . . t.* Later masters are Petrarch, Boiardo, Tasso, Marino, Testi; 19–20th c.: Leopardi, Carducci, D'Annunzio, Ungaretti, Montale, Quasimodo.

In Sp., the few different vowels, never "long,"

go with a tendency to simple vowel patterns which embellish or underpin a line or neighboring lines. Renaissance masters, preluded by Mena, include Garcilaso, Luis de León, Carrillo y Sotomayor, Góngora: "De *púrpura,* y de *nieve* [-εβε] / *florida* la *cabeza* [-βε-] *coronado, / a* dulces *pastos mueve, /* sin *honda,* ni *cayado /* el *buen pastor, en* ti su *hato amado"* (León); 19–20th c.: Darío, Lorca, Jiménez. *Portuguese*—Renaissance—Sá de Miranda and the great Camões; 17th c.: Rodriguez Lobo; 18th c.: Bocage; 19–20th c.: Quental, Junqueiro, Nobre, Castro, Pessanha, "Modernists" Sá-Carneiro and Pessoa, also Mourão-Ferreira and others of today.

Fr. The 15th-c. *Grands Rhétoriqueurs* use a host of conscious echoes and repetitions for embellishment. The 16th-c. *Pléiade* and their followers are rich in deliberate patterning, chiefly for implication, rubrication, painting, or incantation: "Puis tout à coup, avec sa trouppe belle / D'un saut léger en l'onde se lança, / L'eau jette un son, et en tournoyant toute" (Du Bellay) has the succession *tout / oup / troup / léjè / anl / lan / l— jè / antour / antout;* in 1587 he remarks that *a, o, u, m, b, s, r* "sont une grande sonnerie et batterie aux vers." The Pléiade were influenced by Dionysius; they restored sung verse, and regarded recital as an important test of a harmonious style. Jacques Pelletier had introduced the notion of *harmonie imitative* (chiefly sound-representation); this could be exceedingly crude, as in the punning "La gentille Alouette avec son tire-lire, / Tire l'ire à l'iré, et tire-lirant tire / Vers la voute du ciel; puis son vol vers ce lieu / Vire, et désire dire: adieu Dieu, adieu Dieu" (Du Bartas).

Reaction against excess begins with Malherbe, whose echoes are discreet and more logical: "Je crains à l'avenir la *faute* que j'ai *faite"* (tagging). In the supreme artist Racine some celebrated lines are richly patterned for correlation or, as in the *afflige* line, for dramatic mood-evocation; usually he produces for implication a quieter sound-scrambling: "Que, sévère aux méchants, et des bons le refuge, / Entre le pauvre et vous, vous prendrez Dieu pour juge" includes the 5 themes *évèr/vrév, leref/relep, chan/jan, p—vr/voupr/pour, antrelep/prandr—d.*

Romantics such as Vigny, Hugo (more bristling), Musset revived wealth of sound (including rich-rhymes), sound-representation and illustrative painting: "J'aime le son du cor, le soir, au fond des bois, / Soit qu'il chante les pleurs de la biche aux abois, / Ou l'adieu du chasseur que l'écho faible accueille, / Et que le vent du nord porte de feuille en feuille" (Vigny) includes the 8 themes: *swa/bwa/swa/ bwa, leurdeula/ladyeud/euy* (3ce); *óf/óf* and *ab/ab* with dissonances; *f . . . euy/feuy/feuy, ilch/ich/uch, pl/bl, or/or/or;* and "imitative" vowels. Baudelaire employs rather subtler patterns for mystical correlation and expressive painting. The *symbolistes* meant various things by "music," but their practice often involved elaborate incantation. Mallarmé occasionally has wordplay, perhaps from Poe: "Tristement dort une mandore"; his swan-sonnet in *i* is his best-known example of extended complex patterning, there for painting and implication; but the most intricately interbonded wholes in any language are perhaps his shipwreck and *ptyx* sonnets, partly syllable for syllable, partly in whole lines and rhymes. Verlaine's "music" often depends on short lines with well-focused consonants or vowels. The Belgian Verhaeren's clamant echoings (only onomatopoeic in "Un long appel, qui long, parmi l'écho, ricoche") often amount to word-play. Valéry's exuberant patterns, for painting or emphasis, are sustained but virile: "Harmonieuse MOI, différente d'un songe, / Femme flexible et ferme aux silences suivis / D'actes purs! . . . Front limpide, et par ondes ravis, / Si loin que le vent vague et velu les achève" (© Editions Gallimard 1917 *tous droits réservés*).

Jules Romains and others instituted ACCORD (q.v.—vowel-less rhymes classified like true Fr. rhymes). Trannoy and Grammont recognize the importance of total vowel-melody in Fr.: e.g. "Voici la verte Écosse et la brune Italie" (Musset) has *a i / a è / é o / / é a u / i a i* with satisfying grouping and contrast; Grammont's classification (see TONE-COLOR, as also for the earlier *instrumentalistes* and a modern Belgian critic of sound-suggestion, Delbouille) is more helpful than Trannoy's.

Eng. (see also section FUNCTIONS in this article). In contrast to the simpler syllabic structure of Fr., Eng. fosters strung-out and scrambled patterns, often all-consonant. Alliterative meter (q.v.) persisted to ca. 1400, but Chaucer's occasional patternings could represent ex-classical rhetoric. After a relatively dead period while the phonology underwent rapid changes, Wyatt's songs and Surrey's poems usher in the Renaissance; owing much to It. influence, including Surrey's assonances. Encouraged by Fr. and It. models and a new joy in language, writers produced a wealth of (syntactically) repetitive devices, codified by, e.g., Puttenham. Pun and wordplay mingled with often florid alliteration: Drayton writes one sonnet "Nothing but No and I, and I and No . . ." which is a *pas-de-deux* for these two syllables. Edwardes, Sackville, Greville, Nashe, Raleigh, Daniel, Drayton, employ plangent echoes; Constable, Spenser, Southwell are more subdued: "The sea of *Fortune* doth not *ever flow,* / She *draws* her *favours* to the *lowest ebb,* / Her *tides* hath *equal times to come* and go, / Her *loom* doth *weave* the *fine*

and *coarsest web,*" with *weave* assonating with *favours.* Shakespeare, sharing all the rhetorical tricks in his poems and early plays, also develops painting, implication, incantation: "Come, seeling Night, / Skarfe vp . . . pittiful . . . bloodie and inuisible Hand / Cancell and teare to pieces that great Bond / Which keepes me pale. Light thickens, and the Crow / Makes Wing to th' Rookie Wood" (including the seven themes [k—ms—l / sk—f / f—l / v—z—b—l / k—ns—l / k—psm—p—l], [bl—d / nd / bl / nd / b—nd], [pi:s / i:ps], [nd / nd], [k—sm . . . e: / me:ks], [θɪk / ð—k / ð . . . kɪ], [ks / k—sm / θɪk—z / m—kswɪ / ð—kɪw]). Writers like William Browne, Quarles, Herbert, continue repetition and harmony into the next century. Milton in maturity develops expression, correlation, implication, underpinning.

With Waller and Dryden and the heroic couplet forthright rhetoric increases and incantation dies down: "A *R*ace un*c*on*q*uer'd, by their *C*lime *m*a*d*e *b*ol*d,* / The *C*ali*d*onians." Pope is richest in correlation and implicatory harmonies: "awakens ev'ry grace, / And calls forth all the wonders of her face"; he often conducts melodiously varied repetition of stressed vowels within alliteration: "Now feels my heart its long forgotten heat"; but "The Sound must seem an echo to the Sense" *may* refer to rhythm. Thomson's rubrication and Johnson's rhetoric are heavy; Dyer, Akenside, Goldsmith, more subtly implicatory: "The spring / Distills her dews, and from the silken gem / Its lucid leaves unfolds"; Gray paints delicately; Collins and Smart are flamboyant.

The commonest rhyme-vowel was and is *ā/ai* (now pronounced [eɪ]), but Pope seems especially addicted to it (25 per cent, less *-r,* of perfect rhymes in *Windsor Forest,* especially "shades"; and assonance everywhere); however, *ee, ĭ, oh* appear to gain ground through Keats to Tennyson; later short and dark rhyme-vowels increase. Romantics gave jostling variations their head: Keats is lushly incantatory (with some false notes), Shelley passionate, often overwrought: "I stood within the city disinterred; / And heard the autumnal leaves like light footfalls / Of spirits passing through the streets; and heard / The mountain's slumberous voice at intervals / Thrill through these roofless halls; / The oracular thunder penetrating shook / The listening soul in my suspended blood" (Latinesque in its richness and onomatopoeia). Tennyson weaves rather facile spells. Poe, though hailed apostle by Baudelaire and Mallarmé, recalls baroque excess and effect-seeking. Arnold is a milder Gray. Swinburne whips his verses along with consonants. Hopkins' welter of patterns reflects his richly "inscaped" visual world and intensity of response, as well as his interest in Welsh *cynghanedd;* he reintroduced nonsyllabic verse:

"Evening strains to be tíme's vást, | womb-of-all, home-of-all, hearse-of-all night" (4+4 beats). Housman revived a starker alliterative rhetoric. Owen experimented with florid echoes, some for prophetic emphasis, and introduced vowel-less rich-rhyme (*brutes / brats*) expressing 1914–18 shock and disillusionment. Yeats developed (with arresting rhythms) oscasional richness and rarer "musical" organization of the whole (*Byzantium*); Eliot also, but with much wordplay; both often use thin sounds (abstract vocabulary). Wallace Stevens, another word-repeater, could offer a suave resonance or an untamed clangor. Dylan Thomas used Welsh extravagance eventually subordinated to traceable implications.

German. Simple alliteration survives piecemeal (Luther). The 17th c. has baroque devices. Klopstock and Claudius are subtler. G. sound-echoes, denser than Fr. or Eng., are more florid than It. or Sp. Theorists attend most to vowels. Goethe sets the tone (musical, pictorial): "Ihr seid mir hold, ihr gönnt mir diese Träume, / Sie schmeicheln mir und locken alte Reime. / Mir wieder selbst, von allen Menschen fern, / Wie bad' ich mich in euren Düften gern!" includes (for him) the succession *ihr'aitmihr / traime / / schmai'elnmihr / teraime / / mihr / lenm—nschen / m / inairen;* the *Erlkönig* is noted for painting, the *Hochzeitslied* for crude onomatopoeia.

Hölderlin is sonorously rich, then starker. Tieck experiments with blatant echoes; Eichendorff is plangently,˙sustainedly Shelleian: "Und sie sehn ihn fröhlich steigen / Nach den Waldeshöhn hinaus, / Hören ihn von fern noch geigen, / Und gehn all vergnügt nach Haus" (cf. Vigny): note motifs in *fr/fer, n—ch, al, f—n, hö-n, gn/gen, ehn.* Droste-Hülshoff has bold syllabic effects; Mörike, Storm, fine painting, incantation. C. F. Meyer has dense echoes (implication): "Wolken, meine Kinder, wandern gehen / Wollt ihr? Fahret wohl! auf Wiedersehen! / Eure wandellustigen Gestalten / Kann ich nicht in Mutterbanden halten." George is measured, tableau-depictive; Hofmannsthal is incantatory; Rilke develops from undisciplined floridity to richness organized for bizarre correlations and implications.

Dutch Renaissance masters include Hooft and Vondel; 19–20th c.: Perk, Kloos, above all Verwey (e.g. *De Terrassen van Meudon*), and Mok.

Rus. masters include: Pushkin; symbolists such as Bryusov, Bal'mont (overdone alliteration) and Blok; Svetaeva, Akhmatova, and Pasternak. The postsymbolist formalist movement, which spread to other Slav countries, had much to say on the interaction of sound (i.e. both "verbal orchestration" through phonetic repetitions, and rhythm) with meaning. *Polish* masters of sound include Mickiewicz,

Słowacki, Tuwim, and Pawlikowska; *Czech:* Kollár, Neruda, Wolker.

See also ACCORD, ALLITERATION, ASSONANCE, CONSONANCE, DISSONANCE, ECHO, EUPHONY, NEAR RHYME, ONOMATOPOEIA, PHONETIC EQUIVALENCE, REPETITION, RHYME, SYZYGY, TONE-COLOR.

H. Werner, *Die Ursprünge der Lyrik* (1924); A. I. Trannoy, *La musique des vers* (1929); Patterson; M. M. Macdermott, *Vowel Sounds in Poetry* (1940); L. P. Wilkinson, "Onomatopoeia and the Sceptics," CQ, 36 (1942) W. F. J. Knight, *Roman Vergil* (1944); S. Bonneau, *L'univers poétique d'Alexandre Blok* (1946); M. Cressot, *Le style et ses techniques* (1947); M. Grammont, *Petit traité de versification française* (13e éd., 1949); T. Pfeiffer, *Umgang mit Dichtung* (6. Aufl., 1949); A. Spire, *Plaisir poétique et plaisir musculaire* (1949); D. Alonso, *Poesía española: ensayo de métodos y límites estilísticos* (1950); D. T. Mace, "The Doctrine of Sound and Sense in Augustan Poetic Theory," RES, n.s. 2 (1951); D. I. Masson, "Patterns of Vowel and Consonant in a Rilkean Sonnet," MLR, 46 (1951); A. Oras, "Surrey's Technique of Phonetic Echoes," JEGP, 50 (1951); R. Peacock, "Probleme des Musikalischen in der Sprache," *Weltliteratur, Festg. f. F. Strich* (1952); S. S. Prawer, *German Lyric Poetry* (1952); D. I. Masson, "Vowel and Consonant Patterns in Poetry," JAAC, 12 (1953); D. I. Masson, "Word and Sound in Yeats' *Byzantium*," ELH, 20 (1953); A. Oras, "Echoing Verse Endings in *Paradise Lost*," *South Atl. Studies f. S. E. Leavitt* (1953); A. Stein, "Structures of Sound in Milton's Verse," KR, 15 (1953); Wellek and Warren; D. I. Masson, "Free Phonetic Patterns in Shakespeare's Sonnets," *Neophilologus*, 38 (1954); H. W. Belmore, *Rilke's Craftsmanship* (1954); W. Kayser, *Das sprachliche Kunstwerk* (3. Aufl., 1954); H. Kökeritz, "Rhetorical Word-Play in Chaucer," PMLA, 69 (1954); F. Scarfe, *The Art of Paul Valéry* (1954); D. Alonso, *Estudios y ensayos gongorinos* (1955); V. Erlich, *Rus. Formalism: History—Doctrine* (1955); D. I. Masson, "Wilfred Owen's Free Phonetic Patterns," JAAC, 13 (1955); A. Oras, "Intensified Rhyme Links in *The Faerie Queene*," JEGP, 54 (1955); E. R. Vincent, "Dante's Choice of Words," *It. Studies*, 10 (1955); J. Hollander, "The Music of Poetry," JAAC, 15 (1956); *Sound and Poetry*, ed. N. Frye (1957); *John Keats: a Reassessment*, ed. K. Muir (1958); N. I. Herescu, *La poésie latine: étude des structures phoniques* (1960); D. I. Masson, "Thematic Analysis of Sound in Poetry," *Proc. of the Leeds Phil. & Lit. Soc., Lit. & Hist. Sec., 9,* pt. 4 (1960); F. Berry, *Poetry and the Physical Voice* (1962); C. C. Smith, "La musicalidad del *Polifemo*" [Góngora], RFE, 44 (1962); D. I. Masson, "Sound & Sense in a Line of Poetry," *Brit. J. of Aesth.*, 3 (1963). See also I. Fónagy,

"Communication in Poetry," *Word*, 17 (1961); L. P. Wilkinson, *Golden L. Artistry* (1963).

D.I.M.

SOUTH AFRICAN POETRY. I. IN AFRIKAANS. The Afrik. language had to struggle for recognition. It developed, like Eng. and the Romance languages, by dropping the inflections and has become, as Sir Patrick Duncan said, an instrument fit for use in the universities and capable of expressing the subtle needs of poetry. In an unpublished letter Roy Campbell said some twenty-five years ago: "The Afrikaans language is today as full of adventure for the bold and daring as was ever any language in history and unique among contemporary tongues for youth and freshness." Sir Thomas Holland, the late Principal of Edinburgh University, wrote in 1936: "Could any man fail to regard with less than admiration the true portrait of the rough old Voortrekker that A. G. Visser has outlined in a few words? For English readers I will offer a translation: 'With children about my bed, / I feel my pilgrimage is done; this is the last outspan—'.".

When Afrik. first appeared in printed form (from ca. 1875), it leaned heavily on the literature of Europe. President Reitz translated Scott and humorous pieces from Burns, incidentally showing a quality that has distinguished the Afrikaner from most of his forebears in Holland, a sense of humor. This quality is seen preeminently in A. G. Visser and in some of C. M. van den Heever's work, but has become obscured in the stress and strain of modern conflicts, and has been superseded sometimes by verse that is itself obscure.

Even in the early days, Afrik. poetry diverged from the poetry of Holland with which the cultural contacts were always tenuous and uncertain. It became deeply rooted in the soil and did not look to another home overseas. The most telling descriptions of the S. Afr. scene are in Afrik., but, as in the case of Eng. verse, the later Afrik. poets developed the universal sense of poetry. The most spontaneous of the Afrik. poets, and also the most careless, is the late C. L. Leipoldt (1880–1947). He had a very intimate knowledge and experience of nature and a wide sympathy with human beings. Writing after the S. Afr. War (1899–1902), he expressed the bitter suffering of his people; but he outgrew bitterness and attained a generous humanity. Technically his work is criticized by the younger poets; but it contains more of the real substance of poetry than theirs, in spite of its apparent artlessness: He wants to hear songs of the veld and its denizens, "of clouds and of seas and of mountains, / But never, no never, of gold." The shadow side of the gold discoveries is frequently found in the earlier poets. Similar to Leipoldt is Toon van den Heever (1894–1956): "In the Highveld, in the open, where the sky is broad above, / Where the grasses skip like lambs that leave the fold," it is still possible to breathe freely and to believe in the love of Heaven, while the gold mines that draw the labor of the impoverished farmer are the negation of these values.

Politics have had a marked effect on Afrik. poetry, but the major poets have risen above party strife. C. M. van den Heever (1902–57) published in 1955 *Hundred Sonnets*, which show depth and beauty. He is one of the older poets who preferred traditional forms, a disciple of the late J. D. du Toit (Totius, 1877–1953), who, with Jan Celliers and D. F. Malherbe and Leipoldt form the pillars of the earlier Afrik. poetry. A writer of very great merit and sensitivity, who may in the future be ranked above many of the popular ones, is Eugène Marais: "A drop of gall is in the sweetest wine; / In joyous mirth there yet are tears of grief" (tr. A. E. Thorpe).

With the widening interest in technique it was inevitable a new school of poets should arise in the 1930's. They were influenced by writers like T. S. Eliot and sought new forms of expression and new themes. They turned away from the romantic idea and from what they called rhetoric. They adapted themselves to the streamlined world of modern technology and looked on language with a semantic eye. Chief of these poets is N. P. van Wyk Louw, who has become celebrated for beauty of expression in a modern form, as has D. J. Opperman, and for his search for new values. There are indications, as in the case of van Wyk Louw's brother, W. E. G. Louw, that the search for new values may lead back to ancient universal standards. In Ernst van Heerden, too, we find a modern poet with a fine feeling for language. Peter Blum has a strange attraction and is full of influences derived from continental Europe.

Sensitive poetry has been published by W. A. de Klerk and G. A. Watermeyer; by Elisabeth Eybers and the Jewess Olga Kirsch, now living in Israel; and by the colored writers S. V. Petersen (whose poetry was crowned in 1959 by the Suid-Afrikaanse Akademie), P. J. Philander, and Adam Small. A new development is poetry in the mixed (Eng.-Afrik.) language of the colored folk written vividly by the Uys Krige and Adam Small. I. W. van der Merwe (Boerneef) has recently gone in the same direction and reproduced in verse the actual patois of the nonwhites, sometimes obtaining very vivid and striking effects and penetrating into the soul of primitive people. This new interest in the feelings and habits of the underprivileged may be of great significance.

I. D. du Plessis, however, a distinguished poet of the older group, ably interpreted the life of the Cape Malays in melodious traditional meters. More than anyone else, he has identified himself with the traditions of the "Colored People." Elisabeth Eybers is outstanding among women writers of Afrik. poetry. She preserves a fine melody in her verse and a fine sense of form. But it is her deep and genuine feeling and her keen observation that specially distinguish her writing. In this poetry that springs from the soil, but is widening its horizons, perhaps the most remarkable figure is that of Uys Krige who spent years in the Mediterranean with Roy Campbell, and has expressed his deep sympathy with Sp. work. Often in his work, as in Leipoldt's, we find phrases of Afrik. so rooted in the soil that they defy translation.

Thus Afrik. poetry has developed from a pioneering stage to a position that will bear comparison with modern verse in most parts of the world.

ANTHOLOGIES: *Afrikaanse Natuurpoësie*, ed. P. J. Nienaber (1949); *Zuid-Afrikaanse Poësie*, ed. R. Antonissen (1950); *Lied van die Land* (1954) and *Groot Verseboek* (4th ed., 1955), both ed. D. J. Opperman; *Afrikaanse Verse*, ed. D. F. Malherbe (1955); *Digterstemme*, ed. J. Kromhout (1956); *Janus*, ed. L. Herrman and S. Goldblatt (1962; bilingual anthol.).

HISTORY AND CRITICISM: C. M. v. d. Heever and T. J. Haarhoff, *The Achievement of Afrik.* (1934); T. J. Haarhoff, *Afrik., Its Origin and Development* (1936) and "S. Afr. Lit. in Afrik.," *Chambers Ency.* (1950; F. E. J. Malherbe, *Aspekte van Afrikaanse Literatuur* (1940); P. J. Nienaber, *Ons Eerste Digters* (1940), *Geskiedenis van die Afrikaanse Letterkunde*, I (with G. S. Nienaber, 1941) and *Perspektief en Profiel* (1951); R. Antonissen, *Schets van den Ontwikkelingsgang der Zuid-Afrik. Letterkunde* (1946); G. Dekker, *Afrik. Literatuurgeskiedenis* (4th ed., 1947); F. E. J. Malherbe, *Afrik. Lewe en Letterkunde* (1958); N. P. van Wyk Louw, *Swaarte en Ligtepunte* (1958); D. J. Opperman, *Wiggelstok* (1959); E. van Heerden, *Rekenskap* (1963).

II. IN ENGLISH. The British settlers came to S. Africa in 1820, and like the early Romans, they had to bend to the task of colonization and opening up the country, with little time for the cultural side of life. When they did begin to write poetry it was of a nostalgic type, following closely the forms established in Britain. Yet even as early as Thomas Pringle (1789–1834), of whose poem, *The Desert*, Coleridge wrote that it was "among the most perfect lyrics in our language," we find that the spirit of the veld: ". . . I sit apart by the desert stone / Like Elijah at Horeb's cave alone."

It has been held against the earlier poets that their verse was merely descriptive. But Francis Carey Slater (1876–1958) did more than write strikingly descriptive lines like: "The wing-foot sprinkbok's leaping loveliness." In *The Trek* he made a generous effort to understand the Afrikaner and in *Dark Folk* he showed his sympathy for the Bantu. The late Arthur Shearley Cripps (1869–1952) was a Rhodesian missionary who interpreted the life of the native in terms of haunting pathos and beauty and expressed his gratitude to the veld "that gave me my lost manhood back."

It was realized more and more that genuine poetry must be based on direct personal experience and that symbols and colors cannot be the same as those of Eng. poetry in Britain in a land where nature takes a different form and May falls in mid-winter. And similarly, the experience of a multiracial society produced an outlook that was necessarily different from that of those who formed their opinions by looking on from a distance.

A poet who has not yet received due recognition is Mary Morison Webster. She represents an advance (to the universality of art), from merely descriptive poetry and poetry related to local affairs. Her verse has great beauty and reminds us of Elizabeth Barrett Browning: "Now with this love shall I walk regally, / Henceforth shall I go proudly as a queen. . . ."

Another poet whose work will be recognized is Adèle Naudé who is deeply concerned with the interpretation of nature and the spiritual sources of inspiration. Like most S. Afr. poets, she keeps a balance between the traditional and the free forms of verse. To the same group belong the younger poets, like Roy Macnab and Anthony Delius who has established himself as a sensitive poet, versed in the use of modern technique and alive to the racial problems of our time. The younger poets are feeling their way to a significant symbolism and trying to transcend the one dimensional type of verse that used to dominate the scene. Especially is this true of Guy Butler who holds the chair of Eng. at Rhodes University in Grahamstown and who has edited the Oxford *Book of South Afr. Verse*. He has been interpreting the racial problems of the country in verse; but his dramatic verse is less successful than his lyrics. Racial themes enter inevitably into the writing of the younger generation and they have established a fashion that is not always followed with balance and sanity. An Afrik. poet, G. A. Watermeyer, has essayed a long poem in Eng.: *Atlantis, or The Crying of the Waters*, which contains some remarkable descriptive poetry, though the language needs revision.

But the chief poet on the Eng. side is without doubt Roy Campbell (1902–57). He kept,

SPANISH AMERICAN POETRY

throughout, to the traditional form of poetry. There is a virility in his verse that stands out in contrast to the introverted and affected poetry that is merely self-centered. He spent many years away from his native land, yet he had a stronger and healthier S. Afr. feeling than many who have never left their country. His poem on the Zulu Girl breathes the spirit of Africa, and his verse is taut like a strung bow. His poems contain much of his experience in Spain: "Toledo, when I saw you die / And heard the roof of Carmel crash. . . ."

On the whole we see a steady progress to an Eng. S. Afr. poetry that is not merely an imitation of British tradition, but contains a spirit that springs from the soil. It is here that Afrik. poetry has an advantage: it has greater direct inspiration and is not related to Holland as the earlier Eng. verse in S. Africa was related to England. There is a corresponding danger of inbreeding and parochialism; but this is being surmounted.

ANTHOLOGIES: *The Centenary Book of S. Afr. Verse, 1800 to 1925* (1925) and *The New Centenary Book of S. Afr. Verse* (1945), both ed. F. C. Slater; *Rhodesian Verse, 1888–1928* (1938) and *A New Anthol. of Rhodesian Verse*, both ed. J. Snelling (1950); *S. Afr. Poetry*, ed. R. Macnab and C. Gulston (1948); *Poets in S. Africa*, ed. R. Macnab (1958); *A Book of S. Afr. Verse*, ed. G. Butler (1959).

HISTORY AND CRITICISM: M. Nathan, *S. Afr. Lit.* (1925); E. R. Seary, "S. Afr. Lit. in Eng.," *Chambers Ency.* (1950); G. M. Miller and H. Sergeant, *A Crit. Survey of S. Afr. Poetry in Eng.* (1957). T.J.H.

SPANISH AMERICAN POETRY† had its origins in the classical tradition of the Sp. and It. Renaissance. At first, it was written by Spaniards for Spaniards. The Am. setting appeared only as an exotic world to captivate the fancy of Europeans. As some of the soldier-poets stayed in America a strange sense of attachment and loyalty for the New World developed in their writings. Soon they began to express the saga of the Conquest with a social consciousness which was not entirely European, but rather the result of humanism tested under the forces of war and death in the dramatic adventure of the Am. Conquest. These fabulous soldier-poets, of whom Alonso de Ercilla (1533–1594) is the most eminent example, could not bring themselves to follow exactly the fashion of It. epic poetry. There was no need to make up adventures in America. The poet had hardly anything to invent. Not only was he fighting Indians, but his own allies as well, and quite often he wrote his poems to secure royal favor, or to promote the cause of a kind patron or to thwart a personal enemy. His characters were very real indeed.

Heroines were a luxury with which he could dispense. Romance was used sparingly and only to break the monotony of narrative. Touched by the self-sacrificing attitude of the Indian people and by the un-Christian exploitation of which they were victims, these poets glorified their enemies and presented them to the European reader of the 16th and 17th c. as pure and noble creatures driven to desperation by the evil ambitions of Western Civilization. The Black Legend thus was born and the foundations were laid for the idealization of the primitive man to be expounded by the Fr. philosophers of the 18th c.

Sp. Am. epic poetry of the 16th and 17th c., then, differed somewhat from the epic poetry of the European Renaissance and one could say that a poet such as Ercilla actually developed an original form of epic which might be described as follows: his poem has no individual hero, and the poet sings the birth of a nation, exalting the people, both of Spain and of America; Ercilla devotes a great deal of space to the narrative of his own adventures; the intention is more political and social than purely artistic. From the purely literary viewpoint Ercilla's epic blends the direct realism of primitive epic poetry and the artistic flair of the It. *Romanzi*. Ercilla's masterpiece *La Araucana* is divided into three parts and they appeared separately in 1569, 1578, and 1589. He had a school of imitators and among them one is still remembered by critics: Pedro de Oña (1570–1643?), a Chilean, whose poem *Arauco domado* appeared in 1596 and who is more appreciated now for the lyric quality of *El Vasauro*.

There was another kind of soldier in the Sp. conquest of America, just as fearless and determined as the heavily armored Conquistador: the missionary. Between the cross and the sword the Am. Indian found his way into the literary world of Western civilization. Since the priest-poet could not deal directly with contemporary wars, he wrote sacred verse on subjects taken from the Middle Ages and ancient history. The best examples of this type of epic produced in Sp. America are: *La Cristiada* by Fray Diego de Hojeda (1570?–1615), an Andalusian by birth, who lived and died in Lima; and *El Bernardo o la victoria de Roncesvalles* (1624) by Bernardo de Balbuena (1561–1627), who lived in Mexico. Relegated to obscurity by the popular success of Ercilla, the priest-poets withdrew more and more into the learned isolation of their monasteries and from there engaged in rhetorical contests which marked the beginning of baroque poetry in Sp. America. They opened their hearts and their minds to the intellectual pyrotechnics of the great Góngora, the Sp. master of euphuism, and vied with each other in the art of expressing deep

† In Supplement, see also PUERTO RICAN POETRY.

concepts in a syntax laden with L. and Gr. complexities. Testimony of these contests is Carlos de Sigüenza y Góngora's (1645–1700) *Triunfo parténico,* and proof of Góngora's predominance among the Sp. Am. baroque poets is the *Apologético en favor de don Luis de Góngora* (1662) by the Peruvian Juan de Espinosa Medrano (1632–1688), also known by the nickname of "El Lunarejo." It is obvious that these and other poets of the same period did have an inkling of what Góngora was attempting to accomplish in his poetry. They knew that in his rhetorical labyrinth he was creating a poetic language of his own and building with it a world of fantasy that stood defiantly against the logic of classical realism. He was the precursor of present day "Abstractionists." But, in general, his disciples failed him. One alone approached him in deepness of thought and poetic charm: Sor Juana Inés de la Cruz (1648–1695), the Mexican nun who excelled in every literary genre in which she chose to write. She produced comedies, dramas, and religious plays; she wrote an autobiographical essay, *Respuesta a Sor Filotea de la Cruz* (1691) that stands even today as a model of independent thinking and brilliant argumentation; she wrote poetry in the popular vein, and her "Villancicos" can be counted among the most charming lyric poetry in the history of Sp. letters; she emulated the great euphuistic poets of Spain, Góngora and Calderón, in *Primero Sueño,* and produced an interpretation of the subconscious world which, for its imagery and fascinating poetic structure stands today with the best creations of surrealism; she wrote of love with an insight and a profound understanding which have made the critics wonder if a real passion might not have been the reason for her religious seclusion. One example might give the reader an idea of the excellence of her love sonnets, which the critics have compared to those of Lope de Vega and Shakespeare:

Love, at the first, is fashioned of agitation,
Ardors, anxiety, and wakeful hours;
By danger, risk, and fear it spreads its powers,
And feeds on weeping and on supplication.

It learns from coolness and indifference,
Preserves its life beneath faithless veneers,
Until, with jealousy or with offense,
It extinguishes its fire in its tears.

Love's beginning, middle, and its end are these:
Then why, Alcino, does it so displease
That Celia, who once loved you, now should leave you?

Is that a cause for sorrow and remorse?
Alcino mine, no, love did not deceive you:
It merely ran its customary course.
(Translated by S. G. Morley.)

Sp. Am. baroque poetry was a hothouse flower, nursed by artifice, and killed by artifice. Far away from literary academies and the solitude of the cloisters a new poetry was slowly coming into being: a rough, impetuous song of mountains, pampas, rivers, and seas. This poetry was the Am. descendant of the Sp. *Romancero.* Old Sp. ballads were on the lips of the Conquistadors and, used as they were in the manner of proverbs, served to illustrate many a decision or to give a historical twist to local incidents. Hernán Cortés was quick to quote an old ballad, if we are to believe his historian Bernal Díaz del Castillo. Perpetuated by oral tradition, these ballads underwent colorful modifications and eventually came to express the Am. spirit that was treasuring them. From the great variety of subjects in the Sp. *Romancero* Sp. Am. people chose those that specially appealed to their imagination, and worked on them with exuberant fantasy. They made and remade the adventures of Charlemagne, El Cid, Los Infantes de Lara, Conde Alarcos and Juan de Austria. They memorized the deeds of famous bandits and invented new outlaws, romantically brave, full of vengeance against the Sp. masters and the wealthy creoles. This was the birth of the so-called Gaucho poetry (q.v.), which developed from the time of the arrival of the Conquistadors in the 15th c. through colonial times and reached its peak in the second half of the 19th c.

Heavily influenced by the liberal philosophy of the Fr. encyclopaedists and expressing themselves in the verbose manner of the Spaniard Manuel José Quintana, Sp. Am. poets rose at the beginning of the 19th c. to sing the War of Independence. Their poetry was lofty in ideas but exceedingly poor if judged from a strict artistic viewpoint. The most eminent of these poets were the Argentine Vicente López (1815–1903), the Chilean Camilo Henríquez (1769–1824?), and the Mexicans Andrés Quintana Roo (1787–1851) and Anastasio de Ochoa (1783–1833).

The young scions of wealthy Am. families, who had the fortune to study in France, Spain, and England, absorbed the political and literary effervescence created by the romantic movement. They were joined by the exiles, who plotted from Paris and London the overthrow of the Sp. rulers in America. Napoleon's invasion of Spain brought about the political independence of Sp. America and as the new republics were coming into existence the political and literary expatriates started their journey back home. Romanticism took root in Sp. America without the structure of a movement. Poets wrote romantic poems without realizing they were doing so. A Cuban, José María Heredia (1803–1839), brought up in the

SPANISH AMERICAN POETRY

best neoclassical tradition, wrote the first romantic poem in the Sp. language: *En el Teocalli de Cholula* (1820), ten years before the romantic movement was launched in Spain. His themes were an idealization of the Mexican landscape, decadence, and death. The poet searches for the expression of an ideal beauty but his words are only approximations lost among mysterious echoes in an atmosphere of melancholy and disillusionment. Another of his compositions, *Niagara,* was perhaps his best poem. His description of the waterfall, eloquent and impassioned, his masterly blending of landscape and mood—solitude, homesickness, an invocation to God—make of this poem a true example of the best Sp. Am. romanticism. Two other poets contributed also to the introduction of romanticism in Sp. America: José Joaquín Olmedo (1780–1847) born in Ecuador and author of *A la victoria de Junín: Canto a Bolívar;* and Andrés Bello (1781–1865), the eminent Venezuelan humanist whose poem *Silva a la agricultura de la zona tórrida,* although of dubious artistic merit, is truly Am. in subject matter and intent. The expression of both these poets is strictly bound to classical norms, but the love for their homeland, their deep lyrical feeling for the beauties of the Am. landscape, their glorification of Am. heroes, their use of Indian words, transcend rhetorical limitations and give their compositions an undeniable romantic meaning.

Sp. Am. romanticism bloomed in the second half of the 19th c. Its success as a school was strengthened by the presence of a number of distinguished Sp. poets who had come to America in search of wealth and honors. Among these poets two should be remembered for the influence they had on their Sp. Am. contemporaries: José Joaquín de Mora (1783–1864), who settled down as a teacher in Chile and traveled extensively in America before returning to Spain, and the famous José Zorrilla, who spent a short time in Mexico. Perhaps because of the fact that romanticism had come late to the New World many of its most important representatives wrote in the romantic fashion denying all the time that they belonged to this school. They realized that romanticism was a thing of the past in Europe and they knew that Fr. poetry was already undergoing a transformation which soon would crystallize in parnassianism and symbolism. This reluctance to accept the romantic nature of their poetry produced an odd situation: Andrés Bello and his Chilean disciples, and the Argentine Domingo Faustino Sarmiento and his own disciples, polemicized on the need to create a literary style truly American; Bello was identified as a classicist and Sarmiento as a defender of romanticism. But Bello

had been a powerful factor in the establishment of romanticism in Sp. America, not only as a poet but as a translator as well, and Sarmiento had savagely ridiculed romanticism in his newspaper articles. . . . The fact is that they both were arguing for one and the same thing, only from different viewpoints: they wanted a poetry that would reflect the genius of the New World, a new and forceful expression which would exalt its people to create their own civilization. Bello had an eclectic mind and wished to benefit from the classical heritage as well as from modern achievements; above all, he had complete faith in the genius of Spain. Sarmiento, on the other hand, took the view that Spain had run its course, that Sp. Americans should sever all ties with her and open their minds to the fresh and invigorating influence of France.

The young poets, whether following Bello or Sarmiento, emulated models which sang in a surprisingly similar key: Zorrilla or Espronceda, Chateaubriand or Lamartine or Hugo. Sp. Am. poets suddenly discovered themselves at odds with bourgeois society, they fought tyranny, they went into exile, they longed for the homeland, they felt bitter and rejected, they sang of the glories of Greece, Poland, and Mexico in the struggle for their independence, they even evoked the Middle Ages, although more often historical interest led them to a colorful Indian past; they took the ocean as a symbol, twilight as the emblem of their melancholy; they wrote legends and historical plays —in a word, they produced romanticism. They are too numerous to list; few are remembered today as first-rate poets; among these one should mention: the Cuban Gabriel de la Concepción Valdés (1809–1844) also known as Plácido el Mulato; the Argentines José Mármol (1817–1871) whose fiery diatribes against Rosas, the dictator, gained him the admiration of his people, Esteban Echeverría (1805–1851) Rafael Obligado (1851–1920), and Olegario Andrade (1839–1882); Guillermo Blest Gana, a Chilean (1829–1905), author of two or three memorable sonnets; the Peruvians Carlos Augusto Salaverry (1831–1890) and Manuel González Prada (1848–1918); the Mexicans Manuel Acuña (1849–1873) and Juan de Dios Peza (1852–1910); and the Uruguayan Juan Zorrilla de San Martín (1855–1931) whose poem *Tabaré* (1888) is one of the landmarks of Sp. Am. romanticism.

Gradually the romantic fever subsided and the poets who began to write in the last third of the 19th c. showed a growing concern for refinement and sophistication: Eloquence is toned down. The desire to escape reality becomes a search for the exotic and the decadent. No longer do the expatriates weep for a distant homeland; they enjoy the foreign places they

-[794]-

visit and write about them with elegance and a sort of wicked irresponsibility. They are still romantic, of course, and many refuse to go the way of damnation singing its praises. Instead, they pine away in touching "Nocturnos" and commit suicide. These, the suicides, are referred to by some critics as "the precursors of modernism." Two of them are good, brilliant poets in a dated sort of way: Julián del Casal (1863–1893), a Cuban, author of some of the saddest poetry written in Sp., and José Asunción Silva (1865–1896) a Colombian, perhaps the greatest Sp. Am. lyric poet of the 19th c. What makes these poets, and the others referred to as "precursors of modernism," different from their romantic predecessors? A touch of sophistication, one would say, symbolism and Parnassianism borrowed from Fr. literature, nothing else. They wrote short bits of melancholy amorousness, whereas their predecessors wrote vast cascades of passionate lamentations. They show no concern for historical events, except that they condescend sometimes to attack the United States for its budding imperialism in Sp. America. If they feel at odds with society they do not confront it, but escape from it sometimes literarily and sometimes literally by doing away with themselves. The most socially conscious of them, the Cuban José Martí (1853–1895), is the least "modernistic." The more refined and artistic they become the more they distinguish themselves from romanticism. Salvador Díaz Mirón (1853–1928), a Mexican, is a good example of this: neoclassic in his descriptions of nature, romantic in his love poems, he is at all times obsessed by the importance of novelty and uniqueness in the choice of words, so he adorns and overadorns, and because of it is praised by the master of modernism, Rubén Darío. Another Mexican poet Manuel Gutiérrez Nájera (1859–1895) can be rescued from romanticism only because of his contrived and rather naive symbolism.

Therefore the critics say a new poetic movement was born in Sp. America and they name it "modernism." They exaggerate, or, rather, they mistake the facts. What happened is that a new poet, a great poet, was born in Central America, and this poet absolutely dominated Sp. and Sp. Am. poetry for about twenty years. *He* was modernism, he and a few talented disciples, and when he died modernism died with him. His name was Rubén Darío (1867–1916) and he was born in Nicaragua. At a very young age he left his native land, lived for a while in Guatemala and El Salvador, and settled for a few years in Santiago de Chile. In Chile he came into contact with writers who introduced him to the works of Fr. symbolists. Under a strong Fr. influence he published a book of poems and short stories,

Azul . . . (1888), which immediately gained for him an international reputation. His later works further convinced the critics of his extraordinary powers. At the turn of the century, his books—*Prosas profanas*, (1896); *Cantos de vida y esperanza* (1905); *El canto errante* (1907) —were the Bible of the new poets and his name was immensely revered. Critics and historians of Sp. Am. literature have written scores of books dealing with modernism. It would not be too daring to say that in future years the word "modernism" as the denomination for a literary school will have lost its meaning, and instead the name of the great Nicaraguan will stand to mark an epoch and to give significance to the hundreds of minor poets who sang under his wing. At any rate, whether one calls it "modernism" or "rubenismo" or something similar, the poetic trend dominating Sp. America at the turn of this century and lasting to about 1920 could be described more or less as the Sp. Am. expression of Fr. *Parnasse* and *Symbolisme*. In its beginnings it represented an escape from reality —it was then that exoticism was one of its main features—later it turned its attention to America—influenced somewhat by Walt Whitman's Americanism. From Parnassianism it inherited a fastidious concern for beauty of form. From symbolism it learned to subdue emotions, replacing exclamation by suggestion, and also it inherited a liking for pure fantasy and a playful curiosity about decadence and sin. From gongorism, which Darío revived in all its splendor, modernism took a fondness for intricate and brilliant imagery. Putting all this together was the fascinating miracle wrought by Rubén Darío. He made people think that a "new civilization" was being born, but today one realizes that with Darío an old historical fact found its affirmation in the work of art: Sp. Am. "new civilization" was the blossoming of European culture, mainly Fr. and Sp., in the midst of a continent whose soul and whose natural forces were still unknown entities. Darío awakened many a dream in the minds of Sp. Am. intellectuals. His magic touch sent his disciples away with the dangerous notion that they too were demi-gods. After his disappearance modernism faded in the winds of our materialistic age like a cloud of golden dust.

A number of poets achieved true distinction following the steps of the Nicaraguan master. Here are a few names: Leopoldo Díaz (1862–1947) and Leopoldo Lugones (1874–1938), both Argentines, the first an outstanding sonnetist, the latter, Lugones, an eloquent, rather overpowering poet in whose works—*Las montañas del oro* (1897), *Los crepúsculos del jardín* (1905), *Los poemas solariegos* (1928)—one finds an amazing blend of all the major literary currents of the 19th c.; Amado Nervo (1870–1919), the refined, gently religious, amiable Mexican, a genuine romanticist, one of the greatest in the Sp. language, author of *Elevación* (1917), *Plenitud* (1918), *Serenidad* (1914) and many other books; Luis G. Urbina (1868–1934) also a Mexican, sentimental, ironic, surprisingly original in the treatment of certain subjects considered "prosaic" in his own times (*Lámparas en agonía*, 1914, *El glosario de la vida vulgar*, 1916); Rufino Blanco Fombona (1874–1944), Venezuelan, a brilliant, colorful, poet, too strongly bound by the current likings of his epoch (*Pequeña ópera lírica*, 1904 and *Cancionero del amor infeliz*, 1918); Julio Herrera y Reissig (1875–1910), Uruguayan, undoubtedly the greatest poet of modernism after Darío, a true representative of the baroque, deeply preoccupied with the creation of a poetic language that would combine the best elements of gongorism, symbolism, and Parnassianism; he is the real link between the poetry of the 19th and 20th c. in Sp. America; Ricardo Jaimes Freyre (1868–1933), Bolivian, exquisite in his already outmoded exoticism, a true master of versification (*Castalia bárbara*, 1899; *Los sueños son vida*, 1917); Guillermo Valencia (1872–1943), Colombian, a poet of profound pictorial sense, whose classical aloofness in the midst of a period when color and brilliance were used with naive profuseness is proving to be the reason for his permanent popularity (*Ritos*, 1898; enl. London, 1914); José Santos Chocano (1875–1934), Peruvian, a bombastic versifier, self-styled interpreter of the American world (*La selva virgen*, 1901; *Alma América* (1906); and the Chileans Manuel Magallanes Moure (1878–1924) and Carlos Pezoa Véliz (1879–1908).

Some poets, too young to accompany Darío as disciples, but too old to overtake the avant-garde forces, found themselves stranded with the remnants of modernism. A few of them became excellent poets and for a number of years they have held their own against newcomers, but as a group they represent a lost generation. The best known among them are: Álvaro Armando Vasseur (1878), and Sabat Ercasty (1887) from Uruguay; Angel Cruchaga Santa María (1893), Juan Guzmán Cruchaga (1896), Daniel de la Vega (1892) from Chile; R. López Velarde (1888–1921), Juan José Tablada (1871–1945), E. González Martínez (1871–1952), J. Torres-Bodet (1902), Alfonso Reyes (1889–1959) from Mexico; Porfirio Barba Jacob (1883–1942) from Colombia; Ricardo Miró (1883–1940) from Panama; R. Arévalo Martínez (1884) from Guatemala; R. Brenes Mesén (1874–1947) from Costa Rica; L. Llorens Torens (1878–1944) from Puerto Rico; and, in a place by themselves, the four poetesses of modern Spanish America: Gabriela Mistral, Juana de Irbar-bourou, Alfonsina Storni, and Delmira Agustini.

The mention of these women brings one to the threshold of contemporary Sp. Am. poetry, that is to say, the poetry that is being written today, halfway into the 20th c. In the maturing of the new schools that followed Rubén Darío, France again played an important role, for it was the spirit of *Dada* that killed the nostalgic decadentism of Darío's late disciples, and it was surrealism and creationism (qq.v.) that offered the aesthetic ideas which materialized that break with Spain's classical and neoclassical tradition promoted by Sarmiento in the mid-19th c. Contemporary poetry seems to have come into its own through the combined action of three main factors: the personal influence of Gabriela Mistral, Delmira Agustini, Alfonsina Storni, and Juana de Ibarbourou; the reaction against Darío; and the return to realism led by Pablo Neruda. The poetesses just mentioned helped to bring about a social revolution of far-reaching effect: they fought for the social and psychological emancipation of Sp. Am. women. Gabriela Mistral (1889–1957), especially, who won the Nobel Prize in 1945, became the living banner of a movement for child welfare, for women's rights, and for social laws to protect the Indian and the Negro. It has been said that the Nobel Prize may have been given to her as a reward for an entire life devoted to defending the poor and the outcast, and that her glorification of motherhood convinced the Swedish Academy of the true universality of her poetry. To the student of Sp. Am. literature her greatness reaches beyond the limits of mere philanthropy. In her three books, *Desolación* (1922), *Tala* (1938), and *Lagar* (1954), the Chilean poetess created a style that is entirely her own. Solidly realistic, direct and forceful, deeply religious in a biblical sense, and oddly rural in its vocabulary, her language offered a sharp contrast to the decadent elegance of modernism. The Uruguayan Delmira Agustini (1886–1914) began writing before she was 17 years old. Her presentiment of violent death—she was killed when she was 28 years old—her yearning for an all-satisfying love, her passionate descriptions of masculine beauty, her direct and voluptuous allusions to the sexual act, were taken by the critics as the daring but innocent poetical exercises of an extremely gifted adolescent. But when her poems appeared in book form Darío and his disciples recognized in amazement that a new major poet had arrived. Her work is thoroughly human. Not a shade of artifice mars the pathos of her sensuous pleas. Touched by the sublime emotion of a real artist, the crude reality of her naked figures assumes a classical aloofness. She had the depth that Darío never attained, not even in the mystic period of his belated religiosity. Her style is baroque but it would be difficult to find another poetry in which the twisting elaborateness of form is more genuinely motivated by a corresponding complexity of soul. In the Argentine poetess Alfonsina Storni (1892–1938) the tragic story of Delmira Agustini is repeated. After a nightmarish routine of loneliness and economic strain, she committed suicide. Sex flashes violently in her metaphors. But she lacks the natural refinement of Delmira Agustini, and her verse, after pounding on the emotions of the reader who senses the coming unhappy climax, falls to earth in a mixture of childish bewilderment and sad, prosaic, almost cynical defeat. The Uruguayan Juana de Ibarbourou (1895–), on the other hand, devotes her wholesome life to singing of motherhood and youth. With her the revolutionary period of feminine poetry in Sp. America comes to an end.

Around 1920 there came a strong reaction against Darío's *preciosité*. The Mexican *Estridentismo*, the Whitmanism of Armando Vasseur and Sabat Ercasty; the sensual pessimism of Barba Jacob; the *Creationism* of Vicente Huidobro, and the Argentine Jorge Luis Borges' *Nativism*, led the fight against a "modernist" revolution which in less than thirty years had already become reactionary. These poets, with the exception of the Whitmanists, replaced one formula by another. They abandoned the objective or "representational" approach to nature, they outlawed rhyme and, transitorily, even punctuation. They created a new form of exoticism: the escape into abstraction. The most brilliant of these poets was the Chilean Vicente Huidobro (1893–1948). In his country he was followed by a gifted group of poets: Rosamel del Valle (1900), Humberto Díaz Casanueva (1908), Juvencio Valle (1907), among others.

In the early 1930's it was another Chilean who directed a new rebellion against abstract poetry: Pablo Neruda (1904), who evolved from the melodious symbolism of *20 poemas de amor y una canción desesperada* (1924), to an astonishing glorification of the most prosaic elements of reality. Slowly and deliberately he proceeded to destroy all that modernism considered sacred. In conceiving the monumental chaos which constitutes the essence of *Residencia en la tierra* (1925–35), Pablo Neruda has expressed, as no one had done before, the metaphysical anguish of the Sp. Am. man, his terrors, his superstitions, his sense of guilt imposed on him by religious teachings and the broken tradition of his Indian forefathers, his loneliness in the midst of a strange civilization that he does not understand and cannot appreciate, his consternation before Nature that crushes him with its untamed jungles, oceans, and mountains, his decadence coming as the result of exploitation, malnutrition, alcoholism, poverty, and disease. *Residencia en la tierra* is really an expression of the psychological and social drama affecting great numbers of Sp. Am. people today. In recent years Neruda has become a political propagandist. His latest books include: *Canto General* (1950), an epic of the Am. world, *Las uvas y el viento* (1954), and *Odas elementales* (1954, 1955, 1957); also, *Estravagario* (1958), and *Navegaciones y regresos* (1959).

Surrealism has assumed a strong political undertone in the works of two leading Sp. Am. poets: César Vallejo (1892–1938), the great and mysterious Peruvian who expressed the soul of the Indian in the tormented notes of *Los heraldos negros* (1918) and *Trilce* (1922); and the Chilean Pablo de Rokha (1895) whose poetry, *Gran temperatura* (1937), *Escritura de Raimundo Contreras* (1929), *Morfología del espanto* (1942), is a fascinating combination of baroque imagery, Rabelaisian humor, and Chilean slang. Two other first-rate poets, the Ecuadorean Jorge Carrera Andrade (1902) and the Cuban Nicolás Guillén (1902), have established themselves as the great interpreters of the tropical world. They are experts in the use of a magic realism that permits them to condense the beauty of their land into few but excellently chosen metaphors.

Mexican poetry offers a strange picture of isolation. Untouched by the portentous events of the Mexican Revolution, which had deep effects on the novel, on painting, and on music, suspicious of foreign influences and extremely reluctant to allow itself to show enthusiasm for any lately arrived *ism*, Mexican poetry suffers from a case of what one might call "sorjuanismo," that is to say, a persistent attachment to the most conservative Sp. tradition. Loyal to classical form, Mexican poets experiment, however, with subjects of varied and profound significance. The love poetry of Xavier Villaurrutia (1903–1950) is the epitome of exquisite sophistication. José Gorostiza (1901), on the other hand, explores the metaphysical meanings in everyday life, and Carlos Pellicer (1899), the third in a distinguished group of poets, encompasses a world of music and color in highly stylized form. Among the young poets of Mexico, Octavio Paz (1914) seems to stand out with a poetic expression that is surrealistic in form and genuinely philosophical in content. His preoccupation with the soul and the fate of his people lends a serious, almost tragic, tone to his recent poetry.

ANTHOLOGIES: *Antología de poetas hispanoamericanos*, ed. M. Menéndez y Pelayo (4 v., 1893–95; mostly 19th c.); *Poetas jóvenas de América*, ed. A. Guillén (1930); *Antol. de poetas . . . hispanoamericanos modernos*, ed. F. Monterde (1931); *The Modernist Trend in*

Sp. Am. Poetry, ed. G. D. Craig (1934); *Antol. de la poesía española e hispanoamericana*, ed. F. de Onís (1934, 1961; excellent); *Some Sp. Am. Poets*, ed. A. S. Blackwell (2d ed., 1937); *Anthol. of Contemporary L. Am. Poetry*, ed. D. Fitts (1942; Sp. and Eng. texts); *Three Sp. Am. Poets*, ed. J. L. Grucci and others (1942); *12 Sp. Am. Poets*, ed. H. R. Hays (1943; Sp. and Eng. texts); *Antol. de la poesía hispano-americana*, ed. G. de Albareda and F. Garfias (10 v., 1957–); —*Indice de la poesía argentina contemporánea*, ed. J. González Carbalho (1937); *Argentine Anthol. of Modern Verse*, ed. P. Gannon and H. Manning (1942); —*La poesía chilena nueva*, ed. E. Anguita and V. Teitelboin (1935); —*Orbita de la poesía afrocubana*, ed. R. Guirao (1938); —*Indice de la poesía ecuatoriana contemporánea*, ed. B. Carrión (1937); *Antol. de poetas ecuatorianos*, ed. A. Arias and A. Montalvo (1944); —*A Brief Anthol. of Mexican Verse*, ed. S.L.M. Rosenberg and E. H. Templin (1928); *La décima en México*, ed. V. T. Mendoza (1947); *La poesía mexicana moderna*, ed. A. Castro Leal (1953); *Anthol. of Mexican Poetry*, comp. O. Paz, tr. S. Beckett (1958). —*Cien años de poesía en Panamá*, ed. R. Miró (1953); —*Indice de la poesía paraguaya*, ed. S. Buzó Gómez (1943); —*Las cien mejores poesías (líricas) peruanas*, ed. M. Beltroy (1921); *Indice de la poesía peruana contemporánea*, ed. L. A. Sánchez (1938); —*Indice de la poesía uruguaya contemporánea*, ed. A. Zum Felde (1935); —*Nuevos poetas venezolanos*, ed. R. Olivares Figueroa (1939).

HISTORY AND CRITICISM: A. Donoso, *La otra América* (1925); J. E. Englekirk, *Edgar Allan Poe in Hispanic Lit.* (1934); S. Rosenbaum, *Modern Women Poets of Sp. Am.* (1945; best treatment of the subject, excellent biblio.); E. Anderson Imbert, *Historia de la lit. hispano-americana* (2 v., 1961, Eng. tr. 1963); F. Alegría, *Walt Whitman en Hispanoamérica* (1954); M. Henríquez Ureña, *Breve historia del Modernismo* (1954). —A. Alonso, *Poesía y estilo de Pablo Neruda* (1940, 2d ed., 1951); A. de Undurraga, *El arte poético de Pablo de Rokha* (1945); E. Anguita, *Antología de Vicente Huidobro* (1954; the introd. is the best study available on Huidobro's poetry); F. Alegría, *La poesía chilena* (1954); —E. Neale-Silva, *Estudios sobre José Eustasio Rivera: El arte poético* (1951); —R. Fernández Retamar, *La poesía contemporánea en Cuba* (1954); M. Henríquez Ureña, *Panorama histórico de la lit. cubana* (1963); I. J. Barrera, *Historia de la lit. ecuatoriana* (4 v., 1944–55); H. R. Hays, "Jorge Carrera Andrade, Magician of Metaphors," BA, 17 (1943); —M. del Carmen Millán, *El paisaje en la poesía mexicana* (1952; 19th c. esp.); F. Dauster, *Breve historia de la poesía mexicana* (1956); —A. Torres-Ríoseco, *Rubén Darío: casticismo y americanismo* (1931); —

L. Monguió, *César Vallejo* (1952; introd., biblio., anthol.) and *La poesía post-modernista peruana* (1954); —F. Manrique Cabrera, *Historia de la lit. puertorriquena* (1956); —J. F. Toruño, *Indice de poetas de El Salvador en un siglo, 1840–1940* (1941).

See also: *Lit. hispanoamericana*, ed. E. Anderson Imbert and E. Florit (1960). —P. Henríques Ureña, *Literary Currents in Hispanic America* (1945); *Panorama das literaturas das Américas, de 1900 à actualidade*, ed. J. de Montezuma de Carvalho (1958–).   F.A.

SPANISH POETICS. See MEDIEVAL, RENAISSANCE, BAROQUE, NEOCLASSICAL, MODERN POETICS.

SPANISH POETRY. THE EARLIEST LYRICS. Sp. poetry originated, no doubt, simultaneously with the Sp. language itself, or more precisely, with those Romance dialects which developed on the Iberian peninsula during the Middle Ages. The dialects began, of course, not as written, but as spoken languages; the first Sp. poetry was, naturally, oral poetry. Only almost indecipherable fragments of this poetry have been preserved, transcribed in Arabic or Hebrew letters, as refrains (*kharjas*) appended to longer, more learned poems written as early as the 11th c. by Moorish or Jewish poets of southern Spain. The dialect of the *kharjas*, known as Mozarabic, reflects the earliest stage of a recognizably Sp. language. These *kharjas*, which antedate even the lyric poems of the Prov. troubadours, are predominantly love songs, snatches of lamentation in which girls bewail the absence of their lovers; the poetic intensity of these fragments, tremulously chaste in the Hebrew poems, more sensual in the Arabic ones, can still be felt by the Sp. reader, despite one or two archaic words of Semitic origin:

> Vayse meu corazón de míb.
> ¿Ya, Rab, si se me tornarád?
> ¡Tan mal meu dolor li-l-habib!
> Enfermo yed: ¿Cuándo sanarád?

My heart is leaving me. / Oh God, I wonder whether it will return? / My grief for my beloved is so great! / He is sick: when will he be well?

Such fragments are the only survivors of a body of oral poetry which must have been common to most communities of the Iberian peninsula. The first Sp. poetry recorded in the L. alphabet, that of the 13th-c. Galician-Portuguese *cancioneiros* or collections of songs, include *cantigas de amigo* which are quite similar to the *kharjas* in theme; and in the traditional folk poetry of Castile, as well, the *villancicos* or refrain carols, deriving from the Hispano-Arabic *zajal*, are frequently *Frauenlieder* of a similar sort.

THE MEDIEVAL EPIC. The oldest major work of Sp. literature is the anonymous *Poema del Cid* or *Cantar de Mío Cid*; written about 1140, it is the best surviving example of the Sp. medieval epic. Like the Fr. *chansons de geste*, the *Poema del Cid* reflects feudal customs of Germanic origin, which may be traced back to the Visigothic period; it also shows signs of the direct influence of Fr. literary models and, perhaps, of certain Arabic sources. The word "cid" itself is of Arabic origin and means feudal lord; it is the title of the poem's hero, Rodrigo Díaz de Vivar, a well-documented historical personage who, exiled by Alfonso VI of Castile and Leon between 1079 and 1099, took the city of Valencia from the Moors in 1089. Given a degree of historicity and of geographical precision which clearly distinguishes this poem's level of realism from the fantasy of Fr. epics such as the *Chanson de Roland*, the *Poema del Cid* is essentially the dramatic depiction of a relatively restrained and modest type of feudal hero.

Written in lines of variable length (14-syllable lines predominate) which divide into hemistichs, with assonant or vowel rhyme at the end of each line, the poem was evidently composed for dramatic oral recitation by a *jongleur* or professional court entertainer. It begins with the pathos of the hero's unjust exile. But Rodrigo Díaz is always a faithful vassal to the king, sending him booty from each of the battles that he wins in Moslem land. After taking Valencia, the king restores him to his good graces and honors him by sponsoring his daughters' marriage to two Leonese noblemen. But the sons-in-law turn out to be as decadent and cowardly as they are proud. When they beat and abandon their wives, the Cid does not take vengeance into his own hands, but appeals to the king for justice to be administered in accordance with law. His second vindication is even more glorious than his first.

The sober understatement of this epic poem's style reflects the orderly, measured character of its hero. Thus, the first major work in the history of Sp. poetry has none of the baroque exuberance or picaresque cynicism which are often considered typical of Sp. literature; it is, in fact, quite classically subtle in its balanced avoidance of all extremes.

Other Sp. medieval epics existed and can be reconstructed from later chronicles and ballads, but the original versions are, for the most part, lost. Among the surviving texts are a 13th-c. clerkly reworking of an epic on Fernán González, and the much later *Mocedades de Rodrigo*, in which the Cid is depicted, not as an austere feudal vassal, but as an arrogant, fiery youth. It is this later, more romantic Cid who was to become famous in ballads and in plays.

MONASTIC POETRY. In the 13th c., the scholarly poet of the cloister begins to compete with the *jongleur* of the feudal court. He replaces the militaristic Romanesque virtues of feudal society by the Gothic virtues of devotion to Our Lady, to the saints, and to the Mass. His sources are not recent Sp. history or oral legends, but L. manuscripts: the Bible, the lives and miracles of the saints, even legends of classical antiquity. And he uses, not a loose oral meter, but a fixed stanzaic form known as "cuaderna vía": four 14-syllable lines (*alejandrinos*) all with the same full rhyme.

Gonzalo de Berceo (ca. 1200–1265) is the best representative of this poetic school. A secular priest and confessor of La Rioja, he was closely associated with the important monasteries of San Millán de la Cogolla and Santo Domingo de Silos. His works deal exclusively with religious subjects: lives of saints, theology, the Virgin Mary. His *Milagros de Nuestra Señora* (Miracles of Our Lady), for example, consist of 25 brief stories, each telling of a miracle wrought by the Virgin's intercession. These stories are almost all adapted from standard L. sources common to most of medieval Europe. Berceo's poetic achievement was to popularize and humanize these legends by retelling them in Castilian, the local language of the people. His style is simple and clear to the point of being almost prosaic; but his attitude of childlike faith and his rustic images are often charming and occasionally quite lyrical. A spirit of Christian equalitarianism and a sense of humor further contribute to the 20th-c. revival of Berceo's popularity as a Sp. poet.

Somewhat different, though of the same metric genre and period (the first half of the 13th c.), is the *Libro de Alexandre*, doubtfully attributed to a Leonese cleric, Juan Lorenzo "Segura" de Astorga. Following L. and Fr. sources, it reveals Alexander the Great in the medieval guise of a legendary hero. It is encyclopedic in scope, combining classical reminiscences, exotic fantasies, mythology, evocations of the springtime garden of love, and moral didacticism. It is definitely more sophisticated than Berceo's works, more formally polished in style. Other poems of this school are the *Libro de Apolonio*, the *Poema de Yusuf* (the story of Joseph based on the Koran rather than on the Old Testament and written in the Arabic rather than the Latin alphabet), and the *Vida de Santa María Egipciaca*.

POETRY OF THE 14TH C. It is significant, as has been emphasized recently by Criado del Val, that Spain's greatest medieval poet lived south of the Guadarrama Mountains, that is, not in the more soberly European Old Castile of Burgos and the Cid but in the Mozarabic New Castile of Toledo. Juan Ruiz (ca. 1283–1350), probably born in Alcalá de Henares, no doubt studied at the episcopal seminary of Toledo; here the archbishop, primate of Spain, maintained a strongly clerical center of studies in the midst of a peculiarly Sp. goliardic atmosphere of taverns and Moorish dancing girls. Though ordained and made Archpriest of Hita, Juan Ruiz conveys in his poetry this Mozarabic atmosphere as he assimilates to it his readings in the medieval L. literature of Europe, ranging from the Bible and the Breviary to preachers' moral fables and aphorisms to goliardic love songs and Ovid's erotic poems.

Though his great poem, the *Libro de buen amor* (The Book of Good Love), is written chiefly in the same "cuaderna vía" stanzas that Berceo had used in the previous century, it really belongs to a different genre altogether. It is, in fact, *sui generis* so far as European literature is concerned; its peculiar autobiographical and didactic form has recently been related by María Rosa Lida to the Semitic *maqāmat*, a genre cultivated by various Hispano-Hebraic authors preceding Juan Ruiz. In a general way its picaresque tone and content might remind the Eng. reader most of the contemporary Chaucerian Wife of Bath's prologue and tale. Its essentially equivocal nature allows the author to play constantly between poles which are usually considered to be mutually exclusive: personal experiences and adaptations from L. sources, moral didacticism and irrepressible humor, ascetic fervor, and erotic fever. The author seems simultaneously to be a priest and a sidewalk *jongleur*.

When one analyzes more literally the objective content of the *Libro de buen amor*, one can distinguish from the basic plot, which is a series of erotic adventures told in the first person, several elements which are more or less loosely attached: moral fables, adaptations of Ovid's *Ars amandi* and of the 12th-c. L. comedy *Pamphilus*, burlesque allegories associated with Lent and Easter, assorted satires, and a few lyric poems, mostly devoted to the Virgin. The *Libro de buen amor* is, in sum, Spain's poetic synthesis of Gothic culture, a crudely human comedy worthy of comparison with Dante's refined divine one: full of the joy and pathos of life under the shadow of death, permeated by a deeply ironic humor and childlike sense of playfulness.

There is only one poem worthy of note in the second half of the 14th c.: The *Rimado de palacio* by the solemn Basque Chancellor Pero López de Ayala (1332–1407). This "palace rhyme" is primarily political in its emphasis; it is austerely, severely moralistic as it fiercely satirizes contemporary decadence of church and state.

THE REIGN OF JUAN II. Lyric poetry as an independent written genre developed much later in Castilian than it did in Galician-Portuguese or Catalan (qq.v.), the western and eastern dialects of the peninsula. Early Catalan poetry is, in fact, part of the history of the troubadour lyric, the linguistic difference between Prov. and Catalan being relatively slight. In the west, lyric poetry written in the Galician-Portuguese dialect included both the *cantigas de amigo*, which we have seen were related to the same aboriginal folk poetry reflected earlier in the Mozarabic *kharjas*, and more sophisticated love poems stemming from the direct influence of the Prov. troubadours. Thus, the cult of courtly love entered Sp. literature; even poets who spoke Castilian as their native dialect used Galician for writing lyric poetry during the 13th and most of the 14th c. The scholarly Alfonso X of Castile (1221–1284) wrote his 430 *Cantigas de Santa María* in Galician, illustrating a wide range of metrical virtuosity *à la provençale*. But between 1350 and 1450 the center of Sp. lyric poetry shifts from Galician to Castilian; the first collection of Castilian lyrics, the *Cancionero de Baena*, is dated 1445. In this collection the troubadour style predominates, but the allegorical and philosophical influence of It. poetry, particularly Dante, is also apparent.

The two major prehumanistic poets of Juan II's reign are Íñigo López de Mendoza, first Marquis of Santillana (1398–1458) and Juan de Mena. Santillana was a leading aristocratic figure of the northern Castilian nobility, involved militarily in the civil wars of Juan II's reign. His youthful lyrics include witty *dezires*, courtly *canciones*, and pseudo-rustic *serranillas* (*pastourelles*); the latter, based on the encounter of traveling knight with mountain lass, are delightfully sophisticated variations of a popular genre. More ambitious is his *Comedieta de Ponça* (1436), an elaborate allegorical narrative in the It. tradition. An interesting product of Santillana's final twenty years are 42 sonnets, the first to be written in any language other than It.; they reveal the influence of the "dolce stil nuovo" and of Petrarch. A final category of poetry includes mature works treating of moral, political, and religious themes; typical is *Bías contra Fortuna* (ca. 1450), in which the semi-legendary philosopher-statesman of ancient Greece engages in Stoic debate with an arbitrary and tyrannical Fortuna.

Juan de Mena (1411–1456), born in Cordova the son of a leading family of converts from Judaism, is the typically scholarly humanist of southern Spain; he studied at the University of Salamanca and at Rome and was named L. secretary at the court of Juan II. His poetry is

SPANISH POETRY

of two basic types: troubadour love poetry as it had developed in Spain, marked by scholastic "wit," psychological subtleties, and a strong tendency to use pseudo-religious hyperbole; and politico-moral poetry such as *La coronación,* a difficult allegory in which literary personages are presented as though either in Hell or in Paradise, with the Marquis of Santillana crowned as perfect knight in both arms and letters. Mena's most ambitious poem is the *Laberinto de Fortuna,* consisting of almost 300 *arte mayor* stanzas (eight 12-syllable lines each). In it the poet visits the crystal palace of Fortune under the guidance of a maiden representing Providence. Allegorical wheels and planetary circles lead up to the culminating vision of Jupiter and Saturn, representing Juan II and his minister Don Álvaro de Luna, prophesying the achievement of national unity. His rhetorical grandiloquence, Latinized vocabulary, aesthetic use of classical allusion, and emphatic nationalism make of Juan de Mena the most significant herald of the Renaissance in 15th-c. Sp. poetry.

One other poem of this period deserves special mention: the *Coplas por la muerte de su padre* of Jorge Manrique. This elegy for the death of his father is one of the most perfectly controlled poems in Sp. literature; its classical flow of simple language makes it a perennial favorite of the Sp.-speaking world. Its themes are late medieval commonplaces: the fugacity of earthly life ("Ubi sunt qui ante nos in mundo fuere?") and a compensating Christian faith in eternal life. But these themes receive at the hands of Jorge Manrique a molding of verbal expression that is inimitable:

. . . cuán presto se va el placer,
cómo después de acordado
da dolor,
cómo a nuestro parecer
cualquiera tiempo pasado
fue mejor.

. . . how swiftly pleasure leaves us; how, when we recall it, it grieves us; how, in our opinion, any time past was better than now.

THE REIGN OF FERDINAND AND ISABELLA. With the marriage of Ferdinand of Aragon and Isabella of Castile, the political unity of the peninsula (except for Portugal) was achieved; religious unity was achieved in 1492 by the expulsion of all unconverted Jews and by the capture of Granada, the sole remaining Moslem kingdom on Sp. soil. The Middle Ages were receding; in art and in education the It. Renaissance was clearly arriving. But in poetry it was still a transitional period. The Hispanized troubadour lyric continued without great change. Religious poetry took on a more personal sentimental coloration in the works of the popular Franciscan poets Íñigo de Mendoza and Ambrosio Montesino. The most important development was a new interest, on the part of literate poets, in the folk tradition; *villancicos* or refrain-carols, which go back to the Mozarabic *kharjas,* and *romances* or ballads, deriving from the fragmentation of the old epic cycles, were now being collected, elaborated upon, and published. All of the above elements may be observed in the great folio *Cancionero general* published by Hernando del Castillo in 1511 and republished, with modifications, several times during the 16th c. This late medieval corpus of poetry continued to exert an influence upon Renaissance poets of the succeeding generations, including those of the 17th c.

The ballads or *romances* are especially interesting and important in the history of Sp. literature. The semi-lyrical fragments deriving from national epics such as the *Poema del Cid* maintained an epic meter: 16-syllable lines divided into 8-syllable hemistichs with a continuous assonant rhyme at the end of each line. (In modern editions the hemistichs are usually printed as complete octosyllabic lines, and the assonance thus appears at the ends of the even-numbered lines only.) Similar ballads grew out of Carolingian, Arthurian, Moorish, and other romantic or popular stories. They were published first in small groups as single-sheet broadsides; these were gradually collected and reprinted as small volumes; finally, in 1600, a voluminous *Romancero general* was published. Famous Golden Age plays were based upon the more popular cycles; everyone seems to have been familiar with the *romances,* for they were constantly cited and alluded to. As a genre it has been familiar to every generation, from the Golden Age to the romantics and the neopopularists of Lorca's generation; even the oral tradition has lived on into the 20th c. among the more isolated communities of Spain, the Sephardic Balkans and North Africa, and Sp. America.

RENAISSANCE POETRY OF THE 16TH C. In 1526, at the court of Charles V in Granada, the Venetian ambassador Andrea Navagero suggested to the courtier-poet Juan Boscán (ca. 1490–1542) that he try his hand at writing sonnets and other It. forms in Sp. With the encouragement and collaboration of his friend Garcilaso de la Vega (1503–1536), Boscán's experiment was successful; a new type of poetry eventually took root in Spain, marking a distinct shift of poetic sensibility. The success of this revolution was due largely to the superior aesthetic gifts of Garcilaso, who not only assimilated It. metric forms (the hendecasyllabic line in sonnets, *canzoni, terza rima, ottava rima, rima al mezzo,* and blank verse), but also captured an essential part of the It. Renaissance spirit in his poetry: a sensuous, metaphoric flow of bucolic, erotic, and mythological themes expressing a new sense of beauty in grief and in idealized classical scenes and landscapes. Despite his many stylistic debts to Virgil and Sannazaro, to Petrarch and to Ovid, Garcilaso's Sp. poetry (he also wrote L. odes) strikes a new note which belongs to him alone.

> Cerca del Tajo en soledad amena
> de verdes sauces hay una espesura
> toda de hiedra revestida y llena
> que por el tronco va hasta el altura
> y así la teje arriba y encadena
> que el sol no halla paso a la verdura;
> el agua baña el prado con sonido,
> alegrando la hierba y el oído.

Near the Tagus River in sweet solitude / there is a thicket of green willows / all covered over and filled with ivy / which climbs the trunk to the top / and so weaves and enchains it up there / that the sun can not penetrate the verdure; / the water bathes the greensward with sound, making joyful the grass and the human ear.

The poetry of Boscán and Garcilaso was published posthumously, in a single volume, in 1543, and was republished many times during the 16th c. Garcilaso's poetry was published separately for the first time in 1570; it was treated as a humanistic classic by being annotated by a professor at the University of Salamanca in 1574 and by the scholar-poet Fernando de Herrera, of Seville, in 1580. Thus Garcilaso's 35 sonnets, 5 odes, 2 elegies, 1 epistle, and 3 eclogues become the foundation of a Renaissance tradition of poetry in Spain; very little poetry has been written in Sp. since the 16th c. that has not been influenced to some extent by that of Garcilaso de la Vega. We could list innumerable 16th-c. poets belonging to Garcilaso's new school: Diego Hurtado de Mendoza (1503–1575), Hernando de Acuña (1520?–1580), Baltasar del Alcázar (1530–1606), Francisco de Figueroa (1536–1617?), Francisco de Aldana (1537–1578), Gutierre de Cetina (1520–1557?), et al. There was a more or less serious movement of nationalistic resistance against the new It. meters, headed by Cristóbal de Castillejo (1490?–1550); his own poetry, however, while avoiding the new meters, frequently reflects the Renaissance spirit much more than it does the spirit of the Sp. 15th c.

Christianity and the Renaissance join forces in the poetry of the Augustinian friar Luis de León (1527–1591) and of the reformed Carmelite monk San Juan de la Cruz (or St. John of the Cross, 1542–1591). Luis de León was a biblical scholar and professor at the University of Salamanca. In his vigorously classical odes he manages to fuse the satirical rusticity of

Horace with a soaring Neoplatonic Christianity which at times approaches true mysticism. Because of its explicit philosophical content, his poetry often receives more serious attention than does that of Garcilaso; it seems to reconcile again the Greco-Roman and the Hebraic-Christian traditions and certainly reaches more than once the heights of truly great classical poetry. Much more etherially mystical is the even smaller body of lyrics by San Juan de la Cruz. His major poem, the *Cántico espiritual*, draws directly upon the Song of Solomon and indirectly upon Garcilaso's eclogues; the resultant imagery, tremulously sensual, lends itself to an extended allegory of the soul's mystic love for God. Nowhere else in Western poetry is erotic intensity so essential to the expression of an overwhelming religious experience; St. John of the Cross is without doubt one of the few great mystic poets. After a climax, he writes these lines:

> Quedéme y olvidéme,
> el rostro recliné sobre el Amado;
> cesó todo y dejéme,
> dejando mi cuidado
> entre las azucenas olvidado.

I stayed there forgetting myself, / I leaned my face over the Beloved; / everything stopped and I let myself go, / leaving my cares / forgotten among the lilies.

At the same time, on a lower plane, poets continue to use the traditional Sp. meters, especially the 8-syllable line. Scholastic wit of a 15th-c. sort is revived for religious purposes in the *Conceptos espirituales* (1600), for example, of Alonso de Ledesma (1562–1623).

The most serious attempt to continue Garcilaso's tradition was that of his annotator Fernando de Herrera (1534–1597), the central figure of a school of poets developing in Andalusia, principally in Seville. His voluminous notes to Garcilaso's works are, in fact, a poetic manifesto of a Neoplatonic sort. Herrera declares that erudition is necessary for great poetry, that the Sp. language is as richly expressive as the It., and that the poetic genius expresses divine reality. His classical learning is inexhaustible; in his notes he writes veritable histories of the poetic genres and uses a large Gr. vocabulary in making rhetorical analyses. Thus his *Anotaciones* (1580) are a major contribution to Renaissance poetics (q.v.), second in Spain only to the Aristotelian *Filosofía antigua poética* (1596) of A. López Pinciano.

Having taken minor orders, Herrera devoted his entire life to scholarship and poetry. He wrote several heroic odes or hymns on national themes; their grandiloquent echoes of the Old Testament define Herrera's organ voice. But the social center of his life was the literary *tertulia*, or salon, of the Count and Countess of Gelves; here Herrera found it natural to focus his poetry, in the manner of Petrarch, upon the lovely young countess. These sonnets, odes, and elegies, in which he exquisitely suffers and delights, reflect primarily a literary experience within an aristocratic, scholarly setting; they won for him among his contemporaries the title of "the Divine," when in 1582, a year after the countess's death, he published them with the modest title of *Algunas obras de Fernando de Herrera*. Other members of this Andalusian school of poets are Luis Barahona de Soto (1548–1595), Pedro de Espinosa (1578–1650), Francisco de Rioja (1583–1659), and Francisco de Medrano (1570–1607).

Mention should here be made of Renaissance epic poetry. Spain has nothing to compare with Portugal's *Lusiadas* (1572), but the epic of the conquest of Chile, *La Araucana* (1569–1590) by Alonso de Ercilla (1533–1596?), can still be read with interest and pleasure. Worthy of note is the literary treatment of the Indian chieftain Caupolicán as a "noble savage."

Baroque poetry of the 17th C. From among the dozens of considerable poets of 17th-c. Spain, we can select for special attention the three who are generally considered greatest: Luis de Góngora (1561–1627), Lope de Vega (1562–1635), and Francisco de Quevedo (1580–1645). Among them they represent the main trends of Sp. lyric poetry during the second half of the Golden Age. Góngora, like Juan de Mena, was born in Cordova and, like Herrera, took minor orders entitling him to an ecclesiastical benefice; in classical erudition and aristocratic intellect he was second to neither of his Andalusian predecessors, rivaling Garcilaso himself as a major creative figure of Sp. poetry. In a sense he continues and elaborates upon Garcilaso's tradition, carrying each of his stylistic traits out to its ultimate poetic consequences, achieving an aesthetic purity almost devoid of any everyday human emotion deriving directly from such common themes as love, religion, or politics.

Like Lope and Quevedo, Góngora cultivated poetry, not only of the Renaissance tradition in Italianate meters, but also of the more medieval folkloric tradition in octosyllabic and other short lines. His *romances* and *villancicos* (or *letrillas*) show a thorough familiarity with the more popular themes and meters; Góngora characteristically polishes and elaborates upon them, however, in such a way that we could never mistake his exquisite poems for those of the anonymous tradition. His burlesque and satirical poems are equally polished. And his sonnets realize a final formal perfection, whether heroic, funereal, erotic, or burlesque in theme. His most ambitious classical poems are quite difficult to read, both because of their unusual syntax and word order and because of the intellectual complexity of their metaphors, conceits, and mythological allusions. His masterpieces in this style are baroque pastorals: the *Fábula de Polifemo y Galatea*, based on Ovid's Polyphemus, and the *Soledades*, the "plot" of which is more original, though hardly a line is without classical allusions. This style of his, traditionally labeled *culteranismo* or *cultismo* (q.v.), though widely imitated in Spain and Sp. America, was never surpassed:

> No la Trinacria en sus montañas, fiera
> armó de crueldad, calzó de viento,
> que redima feroz, salve ligera,
> su piel manchada de colores ciento:
> pellico es ya la que en los bosques era
> mortal horror al que con paso lento
> los bueyes a su albergue reducía,
> pisando la dudosa luz del día.

Sicily in its mountains never armed a beast with such ferocity nor shod it with such wind that it might either fiercely or swiftly save its many-colored skin: it is already a jacket, that former mortal terror of the woods, for him who with slow step brought back the oxen to his shelter, treading the doubtful light of day [i.e., twilight].

The world of Góngora's major poems is a material world of solid substances and glittering colors in which the poet, using words, attempts to rival the artificiality of nature, of *Natura Artifex*, herself. It is no accident that a taste for this poetry has been revived in the 20th c. by Spain's most sophisticated modern poets.

Lope de Vega, the creator of Spain's lyrical Golden Age theater, was also a very productive poet; his sonnets alone number 1,600 or more! He wrote many long narrative poems, of which perhaps his Tassoesque *Jerusalén conquistada* is the most noteworthy. Between 1604 and 1637 five important collections of his lyric poems were published; they are not so polished as those of Góngora, but they are full of variety, spontaneity, and flowing grace. His odes, eclogues, elegies, and sonnets belong to Garcilaso's classical tradition, with light baroque elaborations of all sorts; he occasionally attempts to rival even Góngora. His poems actually do surpass Góngora's in subjective personal emotion, if not in erudition and technical skill. At the other pole, Lope's folkloric lyrics are unexcelled; unlike Góngora's, they are often indistinguishable from those of the anonymous tradition. And his ability to fuse these two traditions, the learned and the popular, is likewise unexcelled. No other poet could compete with Lope de Vega's facile abundance;

he was indeed a veritable phenomenon, "Nature's monster."

Finally, Francisco de Quevedo, though his poetry too is extremely various, represents chiefly a severe moralistic trend, an awareness of universal human corruption, in Spain's baroque poetry. An incisive satirical wit characterizes most of Quevedo's poetry, which at times is quite obscene; his colloquial puns and other witticisms are often very funny in a grim sort of way. His profoundest lyrical note is struck when he faces death with stoic desperation:

Ya formidable y espantoso suena
dentro del corazón el postrer día;
y la última hora, negra y fría,
se acerca, de temor y sombras llena . . .

Now fearfully within the heart resounds the final day; and the last hour, black and cold, draws near, filled with terrible shadows. . . .

It is traditional, though inaccurate, to list Spain's 17th-c. poets either as *cultista* followers of Góngora (Jáuregui, Bocángel, Espinosa, Soto de Rojas, Villamediana, Polo de Medina, et al.) or as *conceptistas* like Quevedo (the Argensola brothers, Esquilache, the anonymous author of the *Epístola moral a Fabio*). As a matter of fact, classical erudition and mythological allusions, the trademarks of *cultismo*, were almost universal in 17th-c. poetry; and few poets completely avoided indulging in puns, conceits, and other forms of baroque wit. The question is, with regard to each poet, how he developed an individual style and poetic mode as he made use of the contemporarily popular devices. The modern critic can usefully study the poetics of the period: the *Libro de erudición poética* (1611) by L. Carrillo y Sotomayor; the *Discurso poético* (1623) by J. de Jáuregui; and, above all, the *Agudeza y arte de ingenio* (1642), in which the great Jesuit *conceptista* Baltasar Gracián (1601–1658) cites Góngora far more than any other poet. Among 17th-c. epic poems, perhaps two are worthy of mention here: *La Christíada* (1611), based on Christ's Passion, by Diego de Hojeda (1571?–1615), and *El Bernardo* (1624), on a national epic hero, by Bernardo de Balbuena (1568–1627).

Neoclassical poetry of the 18th C. The second half of the 17th c. in Spain was marked by a general cultural decadence; baroque poetry continued to be turned out almost automatically, according to established formulas, but further development or self-renovation seemed impossible. Ignacio de Luzán (1702–1754) brought into Spain, from his studies in Italy and France, a neoclassical standard of "good taste" by which all baroque extremism could be cleared away to make room for a new, philosophical, international sort of poetry. Luzán's treatise, the *Poética* (1737), was based largely upon the neo-Aristotelianism of Muratori and others; it gave rise to many polemics concerning Sp. literature of the 17th c., in which the classical rules had usually been ignored. The result was a return to Garcilaso and Luis de León, the classical poets of the 16th c. The best of the Sp. neoclassical poets of the 18th c. was Juan Meléndez Valdés (1754–1817), whose elegiac and pastoral melancholy shows a classical restraint and a delicate preromantic sensibility. In the 16th c. he would have been appreciated as a minor poet; in the 18th he dominates the otherwise almost deserted scene of Sp. lyric poetry. La Fontaine and Voltaire are visible influences in the verse fables of Félix Samaniego (1745–1801) and Tomás Iriarte (1750–1791).

Romantic and post-romantic poetry of the 19th C. The romantic movement, like neoclassicism, came into Spain from outside; it was the Germans and the Eng. who helped Spaniards to rediscover and appreciate anew their own *romances* or ballads and Golden Age lyrics. This leads eventually to the publication of the *Romances históricos* (1841), new poems by the Duke of Rivas (1791–1865), in which national legends and atmospheres are nostalgically evoked in colorful pictures. More passionately romantic and lyrical was José de Espronceda (1808–1842), an active Byronic personality pregnant with political and amorous escapades. His *Poesías líricas* (1840) are filled with emotions which are violent, if not profound, and with the sound and rhythm of a renovated poetic language; his erotic and libertarian impulses are often colored with a rebellious, nihilistic Satanism. The best example of this is his Don Juanesque *Estudiante de Salamanca*, full of vitality and technical virtuosity. Greatly influenced by Rivas and Espronceda was José Zorrilla (1817–1893), whose romantic stage version of the Don Juan story is filled with similar poetry and is still played annually. With Zorrilla the romantic movement put roots deep down into Sp. history. Zorrilla wrote verse facilely and in tremendous quantities; by the time he died, he had become himself a national monument to romanticism, a 19th-c. Lope de Vega.

The only Sp. poet of the 19th c. whose works can still be read without condescension in the 20th is Gustavo Adolfo Bécquer (1836–1870). Romantic idealism of a vaguely Platonic variety and neat economy of form are, in general terms, his distinctive traits. His 76 short *Rimas* (1871) are marked externally by a direct simplicity and musicality of language reminiscent of folk song; their inner dream-world of sentiment is, however, more ethereal, sophisticated, deliberately artistic. A constant theme is the ineffability of love, despair, memories, and all profound emotional values.

¿Será verdad que cuando toca el sueño
con sus dedos de rosa nuestros ojos,
de la cárcel que habita huye el espíritu
en vuelo presuroso?

Can it be true that when sleep touches / our eyes with its rose-colored fingers, / our spirit flees the prison it inhabits / and soars away in haste?

Perhaps two non-Castilian poets, writing in dialects revived literarily by romantic regionalists, are remotely comparable in quality to Bécquer: Rosalía de Castro (1837–1885), writing in Galician, and Jacinto Verdaguer (1845–1902), writing in Catalan. More widely read than any of these, however, were two postromantic, solidly bourgeois poets, the prosaic humorist Ramón de Campoamor (1817–1901) and the rhetorical idealist Gaspar Núñez de Arce (1832–1903); with these two, Sp. lyricism reached a nadir from which it was to rise only under the impulse of Ruben Darío's modernism (q.v.).

The 20th C. Ruben Darío (1867–1916) was born in Nicaragua, but his poetic innovations reached every corner of the Sp.-speaking world. His cult of beauty, evinced in his rhythmic metrical experiments, in his Parnassian sensuousness, and even in his Verlainean religiosity, amounted to a stylistic revolution hardly less important than that of the 16th c. Yet Spain's first great poet in the 20th c. was not a modernist; in fact, Antonio Machado (1875–1939) seems to illustrate, as an Andalusian living in somber Castile, a reaction against all that was showy and external in Darío, a deliberate turning within, a searching for his own unknown God. His style is simple, apparently almost prosaic at times; yet there are always deep inner resonances. Even his landscapes have their true existence, not in the world of geography, but upon the contours of the soul. His most typical symbolic scene is that of a fountain trickling in a deserted square at sunset.

Las ascuas de un crepúsculo morado
detrás del negro cipresal humean . . .
En la glorieta en sombra está la fuente
con su alado y desnudo Amor de piedra,
que sueña mudo. En la marmórea taza
reposa el agua muerta.

The embers of a purple twilight / smoke behind the dark cypress grove . . . / In the shadowy arbor is the fountain / with its winged nude Cupid of stone / silently dreaming. In the marble basin / reposes the still water.

More directly related to Darío is the poet of transition who stands between Modernism and

Lorca's generation, Juan Ramón Jiménez (1881–1958). A perfectionist like Valéry, Jiménez spent his life working on his poetry, stripping it of all nonessentials, seeking forms of expression to reflect as precisely as possible the subtle shadings of his emotional world. In 1956 he received the Nobel Prize, both for his own work and, vicariously, for that of two Sp. poets no longer living at that time: Antonio Machado and Federico García Lorca.

Lorca (1899–1936) is the most widely known member of the major constellation of 20th-c Sp. poets, which reached maturity during the 1920's. With Alberti (1902–) he represents primarily the Andalusian, folkloric tendency: a popular intuitive genius of great lyrical power, fusing in his poetry elements drawn from many currents within the Sp. cultural heritage, ranging from childlike ingenuousness to the sophistication of a Góngora. The Civil Guard attacks the gypsy town:

En el portal de Belén
los gitanos se congregan.
San José, lleno de heridas,
amortaja a una doncella . . .

In the doorway of Bethlehem / the gypsies congregate. / Saint Joseph, full of wounds, / enshrouds a maiden . . .

More cosmopolitan and intellectual members of the same group are the Castilians Pedro Salinas (1892–1952) and Jorge Guillén (1893–). Guillen's perfectionism is reminiscent of Juan Ramón Jiménez's. He owes something, no doubt, to Rimbaud and other Fr. poets, but his poetry as contained in *Cántico* (definitive edition 1950) is very much his own creation: an attitude of boundless wonder and joy at human existence in this physical world. In recent years, however, his poetry has taken on a somewhat more anguished, less exuberantly optimistic color; we do not yet know what new worlds he will create and reveal. At least two other important members of Lorca's generation should be mentioned here, both having continued to write poetry in Spain since the Civil War: Dámaso Alonso (1898–) and Vicente Aleixandre (1900–). Aleixandre is generally categorized as Spain's greatest surrealist; he has patronized and encouraged many younger poets. Alonso, Spain's leading philologian and literary critic, initiated a distinctly existentialist movement in Sp. poetry with his *Hijos de la ira* (1944), which with its God-forsaken anguish at human suffering echoes in modern terms certain notes of the Hebrew Psalms.

During and since the Civil War many poets have made themselves known in Spain; poetry has, in fact, been less stunted by the Franco regime than either drama or fiction. One very promising poet, Miguel Hernández (1910–1942), died in prison; a country boy with very little formal education, he read Sp. baroque poetry for himself and wrote some highly original verse. A relatively conservative group of poets who had participated actively in the Civil War published in the postwar review *Escorial:* Luis Felipe Vivanco (born 1907), Leopoldo Panero (1909), Luis Rosales (1910), Dionisio Ridruejo (1912). The younger poets have tended to gravitate toward two poles. The more neoclassical, orthodox ones, following the lead of the *Escorial* poets, characteristically entitled their review *Garcilaso:* José García Nieto (1914), Rafael Morales (1919), José María Valverde (1926), and others. A more baroquely existentialist group looked rather to Quevedo and *Hijos de la ira* for guidance, centering around the review *Espadaña:* Gabriel Celaya (1911), Blas de Otero (1916), Leopoldo de Luis (1918), Vicente Gaos (1919), Carlos Bousoño (1923), Eugenio de Nora (1923). In this younger generation as a whole there is a definite reaction against the aestheticism of Juan Ramón Jiménez and the Lorca generation; their poetry is often directly concerned even with questions of social justice. But the definitive history of postwar Sp. poetry has, of course, yet to be written; the poet José Luis Cano (1912) is the author of the best interim history of this period.

ANTHOLOGIES: *Contemporary Sp. Poetry* (1945) and *Ten Centuries of Sp. Poetry* (1955), both ed. E. L. Turnbull; *The Heroic Poem of the Sp. Golden Age,* ed. F. Pierce (1947); *Antología de la poesía lírica española,* ed. E. Moreno Báez (1952); *Sp. Lyrics of the Golden Age,* ed. P. D. Tettenborn (1952); *The Penguin Book of Sp. Verse,* ed. J. M. Cohen (1956); *Floresta lírica española,* ed. J. M. Blecua (1957); *Poesía española,* ed. D. Marín (1958); *Ren. and Baroque Poetry of Spain,* ed. E. L. Rivers (1964).

HISTORY AND CRITICISM: A. Coster, *Fernando de Herrera* (1908); H. A. Rennert and A. Castro, *Vida de Lope de Vega* (1919); A. F. G. Bell, *Luis de León* (1925); J. Cano, *La poética de Luzán* (1928); K. Vossler, *Lope de Vega und seine Zeit* (1930); J. Baruzi, *St. Jean de la Croix* (1930); A. Valbuena Prat, *La poesía española contemporánea* (1930); E. Joiner Gates, *The Metaphors of Luis de Góngora* (1933); F. Lecoy, *Recherches sur le Libro de buen amor* . . . (1938); R. Menéndez Pidal, *La España del Cid* (1939); E. A. Peers, *A Hist. of the Romantic Movement in Spain* (1940); W. E. Colford, *Juan Meléndez Valdés* (1942); A. del Río, *Pedro Salinas* (1942); J. Guillén, "La poética de Bécquer," *Revista Hispanica Moderna,* 8 (1942); E. Honig, *García Lorca* (1944); M. Menéndez y Pelayo, *Antología de poetas líricos castellanos* (1945); J. Casalduero,

Jorge Guillén: Cántico (1946); R. Menéndez Pidal, *Le epopeya castellana a través de la literatura española* (1946); P. Salinas, *Jorge Manrique, o tradición y originalidad* (1947); G. Díaz-Plaja, *Historia de la poesía lírica española* (1948); R. Lapesa, *La trayectoria poética de Garcilaso* (1948); M. R. Lida de Malkiel, *Juan de Mena, poeta del prerrenacimiento español* (1950); R. Menéndez Pidal, *Los orígenes de las literaturas románicas* (1951); G. Brenan, *Lit. of the Sp. People* (1951); D. Alonso, *Poesía española* (1952); A. Castro, *La realidad histórica esp.* (1954); D. Alonso, *Estudios y ensayos gongorinos* (1955); Navarro; F. Cantera, *La canción mozárabe* (1957); E. Asensio, *Poética y realidad en el cancionero peninsular de la edad media* (1957); R. Lapesa, *La obra literaria del marqués de Santillana* (1957); D. Alonso, *De los siglos oscuros al de oro* (1958); S. Pellegrini, *Studi su trove e trovatori della prima lirica ispano-portoghese* (1959); M. Criado del Val, *Teoría de Castilla la Nueva* (1960); M. Arce, *Garcilaso* (1961); M. R. Lida de Malkiel, *Two Sp. Masterpieces: The Book of Good Love and The Celestina* (1961); C. D. Ley, *Sp. Poetry Since 1939* (1962); O. H. Green, *Spain and the Western Tradition* (1963–   ).   F.L.R.

SPANISH PROSODY. See ROMANCE PROSODY.

SPASMODIC SCHOOL. A derisive term applied first (1853) by Kingsley and more strikingly (1854) by Aytoun to a group of poets then popular. Neoromantic yearners toward the cosmic, exploiters of intensity and formlessness, they were made ridiculous by Aytoun's parody, *Firmilian: A Spasmodic Tragedy.* The hero, himself a tragedian, was represented as "Gathering by piecemeal all the noble thoughts / And fierce sensations of the mind," and hoping to "utter such tremendous cadences / That the mere babe who hears them at the breast . . . / Shall be an idiot to its dying hour!" Charter members of the school were P. J. Bailey (*Festus*), S. Dobell (*Balder*), Alexander Smith (*A Life Drama*), and perhaps J. S. Bigg. Other critics then and later applied the name to various poetasters, including G. Massey, J. W. Marston, G. Gilfillan, Ebenezer and Ernest Jones, R. H. Horne, W. B. Scott, and others. They have been called Shelleyan or Byronic; they may have been the feeble Keatsians whom Browning belittled in his poem *Popularity.* Mrs. Browning, however, is recognizably "spasmodic" in some of her work both before and after marriage, as is Tennyson in *Maud.*—[W. E. Aytoun] hoax review of *Firmilian: A Tragedy,* by "T. Percy Jones," *Blackwood,* 75 (1854); NED; G. Saintsbury, CHEL, XIII, part of ch. 6, pp. 164–249; J. H. Buckley, *The Victorian Temper* (1951);

J. Thale, "Browning's 'Popularity' and the Spasmodic Poets," JEGP, 54 (1955).　F.A.D.

SPELL. See CHARM.

SPENSERIAN STANZA. An important stanza in Eng. poetry, composed of 9 iambic lines, the first 8 being pentameter and the last hexameter (alexandrine), rhyming ababbcbcc. The form was invented by Edmund Spenser for his *The Faerie Queene*, and, despite some similarity to ottava rima and to the linked octave used by Chaucer in *The Monk's Tale*, it stands out as one of the most remarkably original metrical innovations in the history of Eng. verse. The stanza is perfectly suited to the nature of Spenser's great poem, at once dreamlike and intellectual, by turns vividly narrative and lushly descriptive, for it is short enough to contain sharply etched vignettes of action and yet ample enough to lend itself to digression, description, and comment. The subtly recurring pattern of rhyme gives the stanza a formal unity, and the final alexandrine is suited to limpidly expressive emotional effects rather than, like the closing couplet of ottava rima (q.v.), to epigrammatic and witty observations.

The Sp. stanza fell into general disuse in the 17th c., although complex variations of it occurred early in the century in the work of Giles and Phineas Fletcher, and although, later, the philosopher Henry More used it in his largely forgotten allegorical narratives. Some poets of the mid-18th c. revived the stanza with enthusiasm; Shenstone's *The Schoolmistress* (1742) and, particularly, James Thomson's *Castle of Indolence* (1748) show a real grasp of its varied possibilities. Beattie's *The Minstrel* (1771–74) provides a transition to the Eng. romantics, who made the stanza one of their principal vehicles. Wordsworth's early *Guilt and Sorrow* is written in this measure, but it remained for the younger generation of romantics to produce poems in the Sp. stanza equal in merit to *The Faerie Queene*. Byron's *Childe Harold's Pilgrimage* (1812, 1816), with its frequent changes in tone and attitude, utilizes the stanza to advantage; Keats's *Eve of St. Agnes* (1820) revives the rich sensuousness associated with Spenser's stanza as with his whole art; and Shelley's *Revolt of Islam* (1818) and *Adonais* (1821) show their author to be the greatest master of the form since its creator himself. The Sp. stanza has been seldom used since the middle of the 19th c.; an interesting example of a 20th-c. poem in this stanza is the *Dieper Levensinkijk* (Deeper Life-Vision) of the Dutch poet Willem Kloos, which is also one of the rare examples of non-Eng. Sp. stanza.—Schipper; E. Taboureux, "The Sp. Stanza," *Revue de l'enseignement des langues vivantes*, 15 (1899), 16 (1900); E. F. Pope, "The Critical Background of the Sp. Stanza," MP, 24 (1926); L. Bradner, "Forerunners of the Sp. Stanza," RES, 4 (1928); Hamer.　F.J.W.; A.P.

SPIRITUALS. These religious folk songs of the Am. Negro were known until quite recently as Jubilee Songs because of the Fisk Jubilee Singers who introduced them to the musical world in 1871. Circumstantial evidence, like the survival of *Roll, Jordan, Roll* among slaves from the U.S. isolated on a Caribbean island since 1824, would seem to place the beginnings of these songs very early in the 19th c., if not, indeed, in the 18th, allowing for the time it usually took such music to develop and become generally known. Musically, the s. often take the Africa-derived form of "call and response chants," but sustained, long-phrase melodies as well as syncopated, segmented ones are used freqently. Their lyrics have no set form, but an indication of the language as well as the subject matter of this most influential body of folk art is contained in such titles as *Swing Low Sweet Chariot, Deep River, My Lord What a Morning, Shout All Over God's Heab'n*, and *Go Down, Moses*.—J. B. Marsh, *The Story of the Jubilee Singers* (1875); *Folk Songs of the Am. Negro*, ed. J. W. and F. J. Work (1907); *Negro Folk Rhymes*, ed. T. W. Talley (1922); *The Book of Am. Negro S.* (1925) and *Second Book of Negro S.* (1926), both ed. J. R. and J. W. Johnson; *Am. Negro Songs and S.*, ed. J. W. Work (1960).　A.B.

SPONDAIC VERSE. A dactylic hexameter (q.v.) whose fifth foot contains a spondee rather than a dactyl, thus causing the verse to end in (at least) 2 spondees:

$$\bar{con}stiti|t,\ \bar{a}tque\ \breve{ocu}|l\bar{i}s\ Phr\breve{y}g\breve{i}|a\ \bar{a}gm\breve{i}n\breve{a}|$$

$$c\bar{i}rcum|sp\bar{e}x\bar{i}t$$
(Virgil, *Aeneid* 2.68)

Occasional in Homer, common in his Alexandrian imitators (especially in lines which end with quadrisyllabic words, e.g., Catullus 64.78–80 has 3 such lines in succession), rarer in succeeding L. poets (e.g., Virgil's use of spondaic endings is perhaps most frequent within words borrowed from Gr.), almost disappearing after Ovid.—Hardie; Koster.　D.S.P.

SPONDEE (Gr. "used at a libation" poured to the accompaniment of the 2 long notes). In classical metric, a unit consisting of 2 long syllables:

$$(--;\ \bar{fec}\bar{i})$$

Meters entirely composed of spondees are rare, but do occur:

$$\overline{Ze\bar{u}}\ pa\bar{n}|to\bar{n}\ a\bar{r}|cha\bar{}, pa\bar{n}|to\bar{n}\ ha|ge\hat{}to\hat{r}}$$
(Terpander, fr. 1)

In the common meters, a s. may replace dactyl, iamb, trochee, or anapaest. In Eng. stressed verse, the s. (′ ′ ; ámén) is rarer than might be expected, the instance of 2 equally stressed syllables in the same foot being almost wholly confined to compound words or 2 adjacent monosyllables:

The long|day wanes;|the slow|moon climbs
(Tennyson, *Ulysses*)

It is the basis of no Eng. verse, occurring only as a variation. Most Eng. attempts at the foot in classical imitations result in trochees.— Hamer; U. v. Wilamowitz-Moellendorff, *Griechische Verskunst* (2d ed., 1958); P. Maas, *Gr. Metre*, tr. H. Lloyd-Jones (1962).   D.S.P.

SPONTANEITY. Like sincerity, spontaneity is for the romantics the hallmark of the genuine poet. For Wordsworth, "Poetry is the spontaneous overflow of powerful feelings." Coleridge distinguishes between "promises and specific symptoms of poetic power," and "general talent determined to poetic composition by accidental motives, by an act of the will, rather than by the inspiration of a genial and productive nature." Such promises are "the sense of musical delight," the choice of subjects remote from the private interests and circumstances of the writer, the modification of imagery by a predominant passion, and depth and energy of thought. J. S. Mill follows Coleridge in distinguishing poets "by nature," and poets "by culture." Keats maintains that "if Poetry comes not as naturally as the Leaves to a tree it had better not come at all." "I appeal," says Shelley, "to the greatest poets of the present day whether it is not an error to assert that the finest passages of poetry are produced by labor and study. The toil and the delay recommended by critics can be justly interpreted to mean no more than a careful observation of the inspired moments, and an artificial connection of the spaces between their suggestions." The doctrine of spontaneity is now largely discredited as dangerous in its implications for the practice of poetry. Taken with caution and common sense, however, it will be found to contain a substantial element of truth.—Abrams.   R.H.F.

SPRUCH. Ever since the extension of the term to the short lyrical poem of the minnesingers (q.v.) one has to distinguish between the lyrical Sp. and the Sp. proper (*Sprechspruch*). Thematically, there is no sharp dividing line between the two. The former is set to music and contains subjective emotional elements,

even when dealing with matters other than *minne*. It is not restricted to one stanza. Before Walther v.d. Vogelweide, only the spurious Spervogel (some identify him as Herger) stands out as a lyrical Sp. poet. Walther developed the genre to an art which in his later years outweighed his *lied* production. He found many imitators (Bruder Werner, Reinmar von Zweter).

The *Sprechspruch*, however, is meant to be spoken and read. It is gnomic poetry, including pithy sayings of practical wisdom; religious admonitions; fables or *novellas* which point a moral (the latter type occurs under the name of *bispel*; cf. also the popular, often jocular *Priamel* [q.v.]). Its form is the 4-beat line, arranged in rhyme pairs. It is nonstrophic, but may be subdivided in line groups of varying length. Such *Sprüche* first appear in the 12th c. The bourgeois poet Freidank's collection *Bescheidenheit* (early 13th c.) enjoyed wide popularity into the 16th. The flowery, rhymed speeches (*Reimreden*) of the Austrian Heinrich der Teichner and his friend Peter Suchenwirt (14th c.) may be considered extended *Sprüche*. In the 15th c. both Sp. types can be found in the works of the same poets. Hans Sachs made a clear distinction between his *Meistergesang* and Sp. poetry. Goethe, in his old age, was fond of the Sp. form. The works of Stefan George (the most gnomic of modern German poets) abound in *Sprüche;* nearly all 100 poems of *Der Stern des Bundes* are variants of this genre (most of them being unrhymed).

H. Jantzen, *Gesch. des deutschen Streitgedichts* (1896); W. Nickel, *Sirventes und Spruchdichtung* (1907); W. Wilmanns and V. Michels, *Walther v. d. Vogelweide* (4th ed., 1916); H Schneider, "Spruchdichtung, mittelhochdeutsche," *Reallexikon*, III; W. Preisendanz, *Die Spruchform in der Lyrik des alten Goethe und ihre Vorgesch.* (1952); A. Schmidt, "Der politische Sp.," *Wolfram-Jahrbuch* (1954); H. de Boor, *Die höfische Literatur 1170–1250* (3d ed., 1957); R. Kienast, "Deutschsprachige Lyrik des Mittelalters," *Dt. Philologie im Aufriss*, II (1958).   U.K.G.

SPRUNG RHYTHM. Term coined by Gerard Manley Hopkins to describe what he thought to be his most important metrical rediscovery. As Hopkins describes it, "Sprung rhythm . . . is measured by feet of from one to four syllables, regularly, and for particular effects any number of weak or slack syllables may be used. It has one stress, which falls on the only syllable, if there is only one, or, if there are more, then scanning as above, on the first, and so gives rise to four sorts of feet, a monosyllable and the so-called accentual Trochee, Dactyl, and the First Paeon [q.v.]. . . . Sprung Rhythm cannot be counterpointed [q.v.]. . . ."

Sprung (or "abrupt") rhythm differs from running rhythm (q.v.) in that it may use rests, monosyllabic feet, and the first paeon ($\prime$ x x x); running rhythm, if scanned from the first stress in the line, will consist of accentual trochees and dactyls only, while s. rhythm can juxtapose monosyllabic feet to produce effects of slowness and weight not possible in running (or "alternating") rhythm.

Hopkins points out that s. rhythm is found in nursery rhymes, and a good illustration of the rhythm is to be found in

> One,   two,
> Buckle my shoe.

Here, line 1 is in s., line 2 in running rhythm. Another example given by Hopkins is

> March dust, April showers
> Bring forth May flowers,

where, if "showers" and "flowers" are considered monosyllables, both lines are in s. rhythm. These examples will make clear that s. rhythm is essentially a system of overstressing; the poet practicing s. rhythm composes almost as if the spondee were a normal Eng. foot. As has been said of s. rhythm, "Its external distinguishing feature is the free occurrence of juxtaposed stresses without intermediate unstressed syllables."

S. rhythm, by approximating the movements of emotion-charged natural speech, suggests a tone of frank sincerity and intimate emotional involvement. Good examples of the tone most natural to s. rhythm are Hopkins' poems *At the Wedding March* and *Spring and Fall: To a Young Child.*

H. Whitehall, "S. Rhythm," in The Kenyon Critics, *Gerard Manley Hopkins* (1945); Sister M. M. Holloway, *The Prosodic Theory of Gerard Manley Hopkins* (1947); "Author's Preface," *Poems of Gerard Manley Hopkins,* ed. R. Bridges and W. H. Gardner (3d ed; 1948); *A Hopkins Reader,* ed. John Pick (1953). See also P. F. Baum, "S. Rhythm," PMLA, 74 (1959).   P.F.

STANZA (It. "station, stopping-place"). A basic structural unit in verse composition, a sequence of lines arranged in a definite pattern of meter and rhyme scheme which is repeated throughout the work. Stanzas range from such simple patterns as the couplet or the quatrain (qq.v.) to such complex stanza forms as the Spenserian (q.v.) or those used by Keats in his odes. The term "stanza" is sometimes restricted to verse units of 4 lines or more, "couplet" and "tercet" being the preferred terms for the shorter forms. The term is also sometimes employed to designate irregular formal divisions found in nonstanzaic poetry (e.g., *Paradise Lost*), but

the term "verse paragraph" (q.v.) is here more expressive and less confusing.

Some narrative poetry, particularly of the epic type, is nonstanzaic (i.e., stichic) in structure (e.g., the *Iliad,* the *Aeneid, Paradise Lost, The Ring and the Book*) and thus achieves an effect of linear development in which the narrative line in itself provides the essential structure. Such compositions as Pope's *Rape of the Lock* (in couplets) and Dante's *Divina Commedia* (in tercets, or, more properly, in terza rima) achieve a similar effect. True stanzaic composition, as in Spenser's *Faerie Queene* (Spenserian stanza), Ariosto's *Orlando Furioso* (ottava rima), and Chaucer's *Troilus and Criseyde* (rhyme royal), lends itself to a kind of tension between narrative structure and lyric, elegiac, didactic, or satiric digression. Although the essence of stanzaic composition lies in the regular repetition of the pattern, stanzaic verse often employs variation, not only through metrical substitution but also through irregularities in s. form, as in Coleridge's *Ancient Mariner,* with its subtle rhetorical embroideries on the basic ballad measure.

The term "s." is sometimes applied to independent poems of complex metrical pattern, such as the ballade, the sestina, and the sonnet (qq.v.). Synonymous or analogous terms include the Gr. strophe (q.v.) and the early Eng. batch and stave (q.v.).   F.J.W.; A.P.

STASIMON (Gr. "stationary song"). An ode sung by the Gr. chorus after it has taken its position in the orchestra. Aristotle distinguishes the s. from the *parodos,* the song of the chorus in anapaestic meter as it marches into the orchestra, and defines it as "a song of the chorus without anapaests or trochees" (*Poetics* 1452 b. 20ff.). The *stasima* alternate with the episodes, the dialogue passages delivered by the actors, and their number in tragedy varies between three and five. Originally, and during the longer part of the 5th c. B.C., the *stasima* were intimately connected with the subject matter of the episodes. However, this connection became, gradually, very tenuous, until, finally, Agathon (ca. 447–400 B.C.) replaced them by the *embolima,* intercalary pieces, mere choral interludes which could be introduced into any play (*Poetics* 1456 a 29–30).—W. Aly, "S.," in Pauly-Wissowa, *Real-encyklopädie der classischen Altertumswissenschaft,* 2d ser., III (1926), 2156–66; W. Kranz, S. (1933); W. J. W. Koster, "De metris stasimi I et II Electrae Euripidis," *Mélanges Emile Boisacq,* II (1938).   P.S.C.

STAVE (a back formation from the plural *staves,* of *staff*). A group of lines of verse or a stanza of a poem or song, particularly a hymn or drinking song; possibly the term was once restricted to poems intended to be sung. Also, the initial alliterative sound in a verse: e.g., the s in the line, "Or snorted we in the Seven Sleepers den" (Donne). This special meaning possibly comes from analogy with German *Stab*, meaning *staff*; in German *stabreimender Vers* means alliterative verse. R.O.E.

STICHOMYTHIA. Line by line conversation between two characters in the Gr. drama. It occurs in argumentative passages and is characterized by contrasted statements, repetition of the opponent's words, and angry retort. S. is very frequent in Seneca and is often used by Elizabethan dramatists, especially in plays written in imitation of Seneca's tragedies. Shakespeare employs it in *King Richard III*, 4.4, and in *Hamlet*, 3.4, as does Molière in *Les Femmes Savantes*, 3.5. It is occasionally referred to as "cut and parry" or "cut and thrust" dialogue.—J. L. Hancock, *Studies in S.* (1917); J. L. Myres, *The Structure of S. in Gr. Tragedy* (1950). P.S.C.

STICH(OS) (Gr. "row," "line"). A line of Gr. or L. verse. More precisely a single line (or a poem 1 line long, of which *Anthologia Palatina* 11.312 cites an example) is called a monostich, a couplet a distich, and a half-line or section of a verse a hemistich. "Stichic" verse is that which was composed in recurrent and homogeneous lines, whereas in "stanzaic" verse a limited number of lines or cola (often, in the case of personal lyric, in quatrains and generally of varying length and movement) are combined in recurrent groups or stanzas. Stichic arrangement was normal for recitative poetry, whereas that which was sung was generally stanzaic.—J. W. White, *The Verse of Gr. Comedy* (1912); Dale. R.J.G.

STILFORSCHUNG. See STYLISTICS.

STILNOVISMO. See DOLCE STIL NUOVO.

STOCK (also called *sto(c)kreg(h)el, reg(h)el, sluutvers*). The identical line which concludes each stanza of the *refrein* (q.v.) practiced by the *rederijkers* (q.v.). It expresses the theme or leading thought of the poem and is borrowed from the Fr. ballade. Occasionally, the s. may consist of 2 or 1½ lines, or even of a half-line. —A. Borguet, "De 'stok' van het referein," *Tijdschrift voor Levende Talen* (1946); A. van Elslander, *Het refrein in de Nederlanden tot 1600* (1953). R.F.L.

STOCK RESPONSE. This usually pejorative term, probably coined by I. A. Richards in *Principles* . . . , has two main senses: (1) "Response evoked partly by a present stimulus— e.g., a word ('mother,' say) or a topic (mother-

hood) in a poem—but largely by past, associated stimuli—e.g., other poems with similar words or topics." If the context of the present stimulus is a poem, then such a response results in misreading, in neglecting the rest of the context. (2) "Stimulus likely to evoke a stock response in Sense (1)." "Here . . . the stock response is actually in the poem" (*Practical Criticism*, p. 244); if, however, such a response is in some sense "appropriate," then such a poem may be good (". . . [Gray's] *Elegy* is perhaps the best example in English of a good poem built upon a foundation of stock responses"—*ibid.*, p. 253). But in either sense s. responses are generally bad; for they generally stand between someone and reality—either between the reader and the reality mirrored in the poem (Sense 1) or between the poet and reality (Sense 2). They are "stereotyped reactions" (*ibid.*, p. 246)—inappropriate, unrealistic, and inefficient.

"S. reponse" is, of course, a metaphor; and the vehicle of the metaphor—something readymade, carried in stock, and sold without alteration—has inspired other terms: ". . . [a passage from Charles Reade] works on the *feelings* known already to be in *stock* with the suitable reader . . . in tapping the Great Heart of his Public he stresses 'little' and 'white-headed boys' and gives the bird human attributes, thus bringing off a *response* to his indecently false pathos" (D. Thompson, *Reading and Discrimination* [1934] p. 19; italics supplied); "The emotional appeal of stock phrases is probably very considerable . . ." (E. G. Biaggini, *Eng. in Australia* [1933] p. 21).—I. A. Richards, *Principles of Lit. Crit.* (1924) and *Practical Crit.* (1929); A. West, *Crisis and Crit.* (1937). See also N. Frye, *The Well-Tempered Critic* (1963). M.S.

STORNELLO (sometimes called *fiore, ritornello, motteto, novella*). A short It. folk verse form customarily divided so that it can be sung responsively. It took root in Tuscany in the 17th c. and from there has spread throughout central and southern Italy. Originally, it must have consisted of a rhymed distich, a type now common in Sicily, but the 2 principal types that have prevailed are (1) a composition of 3 hendecasyllables the first and third having a consonantal or assonantal rhyme, and the second an atonic rhyme (-ore, -åre, -ire); and (2) a composition of 2 hendecasyllables prefixed by a pentameter or some other short verse line which consists of an invocation to a flower or plant, or an exclamatory or vocative phrase. Often between one s. and another or between its parts a refrain (*ritornello, rifiorita*) is intercalated. The s. lends itself to easy improvisation.—V. Santoli, *I Canti popolari italiani* (1940). J.G.F.

STRAMBOTTO. A 1-stanza composition in hendecasyllables and one of the oldest of It. verse forms. Though the number of its verses varies, particularly from region to region, the two dominant patterns which it assumes are the octave with the rhyme scheme:

AB AB AB AB
AB AB CC DD
AB AB AB CC
AA BB CC DD

and the sestet with the rhyme scheme:

AB AB AB
AB AB CC
AA BB CC

Of these the octave type is characteristic of Sicily where the form is supposed to have originated. The sestet type, on the other hand, is Tuscan and is presumed by some authorities to be a modification of the Sicilian octave (q.v.). Critical opinion is now tending to oppose this monogenetic thesis by a polygenetic one.

The term derives from Fr. *estrabot,* but whereas the Fr. have used it to apply to satirical compositions, the Italians have restricted it to rhymes that are sentimental and amorous in content.—G. D'Aronco, *Guida bibliografica allo studio dello strambotto* (1951).
J.G.F.

"STRATEGY" began to appear in literary criticism in the 1930's. (1) Kenneth Burke defined literature as "symbolic action" in which a "situation" is "sized up" and a "strategy" (or "attitude") is indicated for "handling" or "encompassing" it. Thus *The Rime of the Ancient Mariner* reflects (in part) Coleridge's s. for the "redemption" of his drug habit; and the typical s. of Blake is "purification by excess." (2) For other critics (Ransom, Brooks) s. means "art," "craft," "method," or "technique." S. is an author's selection and deployment of various formal elements (whether of style or structure) for the achievement of poetic ends, however these ends may be defined. (3) Finally, the principles of the various systems of criticism have been called strategies (by R. P. Warren, Tate, Fiedler, Pollock) in the sense (a) that by different "approaches" they seek the "defeat" of the artistic work, or (b) that they are polemical devices for "attacking" established reputations and "defending" revolutions in taste, or (c) that, logically considered, they are proposals for the redefinition of normative terms and as such carry implicit recommendations whether the critic or his reader realizes this or not.—K. Burke, *The Philosophy of Literary Form* (1941); T. C. Pollock, "The Strategy of Classification," *The Nature of Lit.* (1942).
F.G.

STRESS. The vocal emphasis received by a syllable as part of a metrical pattern. S. is held by some linguists and prosodists to be equal to accent (q.v.); it is held by others to be one of the constituents of accent; the term is used by still others to mean metrical accent as distinguished from rhetorical accent. In this latter sense, the term "stress" is often used instead of "accent" to refer to the ideal or normal pattern of accents in a regular accentual or accentual-syllabic poetic line: e.g., "Swift was fond of the four-stress line." The term "stress-unit" has recently attained some popularity as a synonym for "foot," but in fact the two are distinct although they may coincide. Free s. is emphasis which may fall on any syllable of a word according to rhetorical weight; fixed s. is emphasis which falls always on the same syllable of a word regardless of the word's rhetorical context. Four degrees of s. are sometimes discriminated: strong, secondary, tertiary, weak. See ACCENT, METER, PROSODY.
P.F.

STRICT-METRE POETRY. The earliest extant attempt at a metrical analysis of Welsh poetry is attributed to Einion the Priest, and dates from the 1st half of the 14th c. His division of "metres" into the three categories of *awdl, cywydd,* and *englyn* and, subject to the modifications by Dafydd ab Edmwnd in 1450, his arrangement of the "twenty-four metres" comprised in these three classes, became the accepted forms of "strict-metre" poetry and have remained so to this day. See AWDL, CYWYDD, DYFALU, ENGLYN, ODL.
D.M.L.

STROPHE. Originally, the initial component of a choral ode, as in the classical Gr. drama. The s. derives its name from the first of the tripartite divisions of a Gr. choral interlude, which the chorus chanted while moving from one side of the stage to the other; it was followed by the antistrophe (q.v.) of identical metrical structure, chanted in accompaniment to a reverse movement, and then by the epode (q.v.), of different metrical structure, chanted as the chorus stood still.

In later periods the term was extended to apply to a structural division of any irregularly stanzaic poem of intermediate length, particularly of the ode type. It is thus partially synonymous with stanza (q.v.). In the modern period the term "s." has also been applied to the irregular rhetorical unit of free verse, possibly because the original classical s. was free from any prescribed limit of length or meter. The free-verse s. is a unit determined by rhythmic or emotional completeness rather than by metrical pattern.

STRUCTURE. The term "s." in the sense of "sum of the relationships of the parts of a literary whole to one another" has a long history. The NED cites instances as early as 1746; but there is at least one nearly a century and a half older: ". . . call it [i.e., dimeter] what you please," Campion wrote in 1602, "for I will not wrangle about names, only intending to set down the nature of it and true structure. It consists of two feet and one odde sillable" (*Observations in the Art of Eng. Poesie*, p. 16). The whole referred to in the definition is usually a literary work but may be a chapter, a scene, or a stanza; a sentence or a line; or a part of a line (as in Campion) or even a word. The parts may be *formal* subdivisions of the whole, certain significant marks on the page or certain significant sounds (the parts of a line, e.g., may be phrases or words, feet or syllables, or morphemes or phonemes), or *nonformal* subdivisions (certain topics or events, e.g.).

The relationship of one *formal* part to another is always either linear (marks on the page) or temporal (sounds). To say that the line "And smote him, thus" consists of "and," "smote," "him," and "thus" in that order; or of a conjunction, a verb, a pronoun, and an adverb in that order; or of two iambs is to describe its formal s. The relationship of one *nonformal* part to another is sometimes linear or temporal but not always. To say that *Paradise Lost* consists of certain topics or events (the revolt of the angels, the fall of the angels, the fall of Eve, etc.) presented in a certain serial or temporal order is to describe *one* of its nonformal structures. An account of the plot of an epic or a novel (such as Milton himself gives in the argument preceding each book) is, thus, a description of *a* nonformal s. of that work; and a topical outline of an essay represents *a* nonformal s. of that essay. Sometimes, however, the relationship of one nonformal part to another is quite otherwise. To say, as Aristotle would, that *Paradise Lost* consists of fable, characters, diction, and thought—or, as Tillyard does (*Milton*, Pt. 3), that, like an onion, it consists of at least two layers of meaning: the "conscious" or "professed" meaning (man's disobedience, etc.) and the "unconscious" or "real" ("the true state of Milton's mind when he wrote it") —is to describe (truly or falsely) another of its nonformal structures. And to say, as Empson does, that a single word consists of senses, implications, emotions, and moods is to describe a nonformal s. of that word (*The Structure of Complex Words*, pp. 15–39).

The concept designated by the term "s." is even older than the term. Its rôle has always, and necessarily, been prominent in any criticism (such as Aristotle's) whose focus is (a)

the work itself rather than "nature," the writer, or his audience; (b) the work as a function of one of these other things (as, e.g., an imitation of "nature"); or (c) one of these other things as a function of the work (the emotion of pity in the audience, e.g., as a function of certain properties of the fable and the characters of a tragedy). Its rôle is smaller in criticism (such as Johnson's) whose focus is "nature" (mimesis) or the audience (*dulce et utile*), or criticism (such as Coleridge's) whose focus is the writer (the imagination).

Aristotle, in defining "tragedy," considers "nature" and the audience as well as the work itself but carefully establishes a functional relationship between the work and the other two. The tragedy itself has six qualitative or formative parts: fable, characters, diction, thought, spectacle, and melody (*Poetics* 6.1450a14). The fable imitates "nature": a serious, complete action of some magnitude etc. (7.1450b23–25); and the fable and the main character are such (13.1453a7–17) as to arouse certain emotions in the audience: pity and fear (9.1452a2). A tragedy has four quantitative parts also: the prologue, the epeisodia, the exode, and the choral parts (the parode and the stasima) (12.1452b17–24). The qualitative or formative parts constitute a nonformal s.; the quantitative (insofar as they may be distinguished by formal criteria), a formal.

Disagreements about s. are only rarely factual —at least, rarely exclusively factual. Critics disagree about what s. a work *ought to* have (if it is to be rightly denominated a "true" lyric, e.g.). They rarely disagree about what s. it *has*. At the root of most disagreements lie rival persuasive definitions of "poetry"—statements of policy rather than statements of fact (about actual usage of the term); and they largely determine critics' answers to the two questions that are, as Crane shows (*The Languages of Criticism and the Structure of Poetry*, pp. 5–6), the loci of disagreements about s.: (a) whether all species of poetry (say) ought to have the same s. or each have its own and (b) what that structure or those structures ought to be. These questions have been variously answered by ancients and moderns; but—since the answers are many, and analysis of them complex—a few observations must suffice. As to (a), Aristotle and Crane himself (and the Chicago neo-Aristotelians generally) are pluralists; most modern critics (especially New Critics), monists. Some of Aristotle's answers to (b) appear above; perhaps the best-known modern answer is Brooks' in *The Well Wrought Urn: Studies in the Structure of Poetry*. A poem, Brooks holds, is essentially a s. of paradoxes (in an extended sense of "paradox" that counts as paradoxes, not only apparent contradictions, but also descriptions of surprising states of affairs—e.g., London's looking attractive in "Westminster Bridge"): ". . . the language of poetry is the language of paradox" (p. 3). Since for him poetry is by (persuasive) definition (i) a form of discourse and (ii) discourse differing from other ("scientific") discourse by its use of paradox ("It is the scientist whose truth requires a language purged of every trace of paradox; apparently the truth which the poet utters can be approached only in terms of paradox" [*ibid.*]), his answer to (b) could have been predicted.

Perhaps "s." would be more critically useful if part of its meaning were taken over by "style," so that "s." would mean "sum of the relationships of the *nonformal* parts of a literary whole to one another" and "style" ". . . *formal* parts. . . ." This distinction would reserve "style" for remarks about words and their syntax, and "s." for ones about the things designated by the words and about the relationships among these things. See FORM; STYLE.

Aristotle, *Poetics* (ca. 325 B.C.); T. Campion, *Observations in the Art of Eng. Poesie* (1602; ed. G. B. Harrison, 1925); E. M. W. Tillyard, *Milton* (1930); C. Brooks, *The Well Wrought Urn* (1947); W. Empson, *The S. of Complex Words* (1951); Crane.　　　M.S.

STURM UND DRANG (Storm and Stress). The title of a wildly bombastic play (1776) by Klinger, and a hendiadys for the impulse to give violent expression to one's individuality, S.u.D. was quickly used to describe a revolutionary literary movement that flourished in Germany from the late 1760's to the early 1780's; because most of its representatives calmed down with advancing years, the term often denotes a period of youthful exuberance and/or maladjustment.

Hostile to neoclassicism as exemplified in Fr. literature, S.u.D. was greatly influenced by preromantic developments in France and, especially, England, whose literature had been regarded as the more congenial to the German national character since the 1740's (Bodmer, Breitinger, Klopstock, Lessing). A general repudiation of normative aesthetics based itself upon (1) the new sense of historical relativism and the importance attributed to environmental forces (Montesquieu, Herder); (2) the revaluation of primitive and early national literature and art (Rousseau, Macpherson and Ossian; popular balladry, the Gothic revival, Homer as interpreted by Young and Shakespeare by Herder); and (3) the cult of original genius (Shaftesbury, Young), which Herder conceived of as dynamic. S.u.D. developed in Germany as the optimism of the Enlightenment began to appear unwarranted by its in-

tellectual and social achievements. Herder and his teacher Hamann were both centrally concerned with religious issues, and many S.-u.-D. writers subscribed to a voluntaristic pantheism in which Spinozistic and Leibnizian elements were fused with pietistic subjectivism. With nature felt to be a demonic force not entirely accessible to reason, a deliberate cult of the irrational became widespread.

For the drama Shakespeare, as formally unconventional, and Diderot and Mercier, as socially realistic, were inspirations and models (Goethe, Lenz, H. L. Wagner, F. Müller). The lyric was permanently enriched with folk song elements (new structural freedom, simpler and more direct language), although the ode in Klopstock's manner continued to be cultivated, especially by members of the Göttinger *Hainbund*, q.v. (Society of the Grove—grove as home of bards). The novel, largely concerned with emotional crises, showed the influence of Rousseau, Richardson, Goldsmith, and Sterne. Emphasis on the "characteristic" as opposed to the "ideal" marks most S.-u.-D. writing; in the drama violently individualistic heroes—extroverts, misfits, outlaws—dominate (Goethe, Schiller), while the novel of psychological development, often partly autobiographical, begins to flourish (Goethe, Jung-Stilling, F. H. Jacobi, Heinse, K. P. Moritz).

Despite novel, almost expressionistic, technical experiments in drama and lyric, the movement was abortive. Individualistic rather than social (apparent interest in contemporary social issues often reflects only a choice of unconventional naturalistic themes), it could not realize in a complex and sophisticated age its vision of a universally popular national literature such as Homer and Shakespeare were held once to have exemplified. A direct contemporary influence was exerted in Swedish and, more feebly, Eng. literature; analogous features have been discerned in some other literatures, but only in Germany was S.u.D. a self-conscious group movement. By radically undermining traditional concepts of poetry it undoubtedly hastened the first flowering of a conscious romanticism, that of Germany in the 1790's.

H. A. Korff, *Geist der Goethezeit*, I (1923); B. Markwardt, "S.u.D., Geniezeit," *Reallexikon*, III; K. Wais, *Das antiphilosophische Weltbild des französischen S. u. Drangs* (1934); E. A. Runge, *Primitivism and Related Ideas in S.u.D. Lit.* (1946); H. B. Garland, *Storm and Stress* (1952); R. Pascal, *The German S.u.D.* (1953); Wellek, I.; E. Blackall, "The Language of S.u.D.," *Stil-und Formprobleme in der Literatur*, ed. P. Böckmann (1959); E. Braemer, *Goethes Prometheus und die Grundpositionen des S.u.D.* (1959); S. Atkins, "Zeitalter der Aufklärung," *Fischer-Lexikon* (Lit. II, 1, 1965). S.A.

STYLE. How are we to distinguish between what a poem says and the language in which it says it? On the one hand, there is no such thing as a "content" which does exist quite apart from the words; on the other hand the very existence of the word "style" shows that something can be said about the words which does not refer directly to the content. The relation between the two must be described metaphorically; and looking at the metaphors that have been used, we see that they are of two kinds. The first suggest that the relation is mechanical, that s. is something added, more or less at the poet's discretion; if on the other hand we see the relation as closer and more intimate, we are likely to use an organic metaphor.

The first kind is common in Renaissance and neoclassic criticism. Puttenham compares "ornament" (the term had a very wide meaning for him, almost that of "s.") to flowers, to jewels or embroidery, even to "the crimson taint which should be laid upon a lady's lips." Even commoner is the comparison of s. to a garment: says Sir William Alexander (1634): "Language is but the apparel of Poesy, which may give beauty but not strength." The same conception survives into neoclassic criticism: for Chapelain (1668) the essentials of a poem are "l'invention, la disposition, les moeurs et les passions"; diction, s., and versification are unimportant—"de petite consideration." Rosamund Tuve has made an attempt (which has not convinced everyone) to claim that some of these apparently mechanical views are really organic: pointing out that the garment image, for example, was also applied to the body in relation to the soul.

It is possible to find the organic view in Renaissance theory (Ben Jonson uses the body / soul analogy); but it comes into its own only with the romantics. Coleridge states it as well as anybody: images, he says in the *Biographia Literaria,* "become proofs of original genius only as far as they are modified by a predominant passion; or by associated thoughts or images awakened by that passion;" or in several other ways which would give an inner unity to the s. This passage, incidentally, says almost exactly the same as the 17th section of Longinus' treatise *On the Sublime,* the one notable statement of the organic view in antiquity.

After Coleridge there are innumerable statements of the organic view: for Pater, for instance, the process of polishing one's style may seem mechanical, but the result, when successful, is organic—"the house he has built is rather a body he has informed." Two modern statements worth special mention are those of Middleton Murry and Leo Spitzer. Murry, who actually uses the word *organic* ("style is

organic—not the clothes a man wears, but the flesh and bone of his body") holds that metaphor is more than an ornament, more even than an act of comparison: in creative literature of the highest kind it becomes "almost a mode of apprehension." This is confined to imaginative writing: in the case of argument and exposition, he is prepared to allow that s. is detachable from content. Spitzer assumes the organic view of s. in his account of the "philological circle": the process of arguing from details of a linguistic structure to its postulated cause, "mental centre" or "inner significance," and then back again to other details. Spitzer regards this process as the same whether the "cause" is the artistic purpose behind a particular poem, or the hypothetical vulgar L. prototype behind the details of modern Fr. and It.: the process applies both to linguistics and to literary study. "The reader must seek to place himself in the creative centre of the artist himself and recreate the artistic organism." This assumes that stylistic details in a poem, like verbal details in a language, are not an inchoate chance aggregation, but part of a related whole: that seems a fair and even a necessary assumption, though many of Spitzer's readers will not follow him in the religious corollaries he deduces from it.

S., then, may be considered as something added, or as part of an organic whole. We need to ask next what it is added to, what it depends on or reflects. There are three main answers to this: that s. depends on subject, or an author, or on period. The first view was systematized in the Renaissance doctrine of the three styles: "to have the style decent and comely it behoveth the maker or Poet to follow the nature of his subject, that is if his matter be high and lofty that the style be so too, if mean, the style also to be mean, if base, the style humble and base accordingly" (Puttenham). The high s. suited epic and, in theory, tragedy; the middle s. verse epistles, "common poesies of love," elegies, and matters "that concern mean men, their life and business, as lawyers, gentlemen and merchants"; the base s. was for satire, and for pastoral, "the doings of the common artificer, servingman, yeoman," etc. Decorum demanded the use of "words, phrases, sentences, and figures, high, lofty, eloquent and magnific" for a poem like the *Faerie Queene:* "Dread sovereign goddess that dost highest sit / In seat of judgement in th'Almighty's stead, / And with magnific might and wondrous wit / Dost to thy people righteous doom aread. . . ." At the other extreme, here is the base s., as used by Donne in a satire: "But he is worst, who (beggarly) doth chaw / Others wits fruits, and in his ravenous maw / Rankly digested, doth those things out-spew / As his own things. . . ."

Each s. is bad if applied to the wrong subject: and Puttenham offers examples of such indecorum. Aeneas should not *trudge* out of Troy, Juno should not *tug* Aeneas, for these terms are "better to be spoken of a beggar, or of a rogue, or a lackey" than a prince and the hero of an epic. The theory of decorum has a social basis.

Naturally it is the grand s. that receives most discussion. For the supreme example of its use, we need to move forward to the next age, to the plays of Racine. It is in fact not easy to find the grand s. in Elizabethan literature, for the stylistic practice of the Elizabethans was much less doctrinaire than their theory. Donne and Marlowe mingle the styles and apply them to inappropriate subjects, with daring and successful results. No one does this more than Shakespeare: the language of Cleopatra and Lear, at their finest moments, is full of low terms. For the theory of stylistic decorum runs counter to the great strength of Elizabethan literature, and especially drama—its linguistic flexibility and boldness.

The s. of Racine's plays is discussed by Erich Auerbach as the culmination of a movement toward the grand s. that goes back for centuries. He appreciates the effect that this s. yields in the baroque plays of Racine, but is very conscious of the price paid. Auerbach considers all European literature in relation to the division of styles: this is not really found in Homer, he claims, and it is contradicted by the very spirit of both Old and New Testaments. In the world of Christianity, "sermo gravis" and "sermo humilis" are merged: the effect of Christianity has been to merge tragedy in the everyday, not to isolate it, and so to contribute to the realistic tradition that Auerbach so admires. W. H. Auden, too, rejects the grand s., though for another reason: "All words like peace and love, All sane affirmative speech" have been degraded by their use in a commercial age, "pawed at and gossiped over;" so that the writer of integrity is driven to use "the wry, the sotto voce."

Neoclassic interest in the grand s. almost drove out interest in the others: and the idea that there are three styles (or even more than three, as the Elizabethans often concede) is replaced by the idea that there is only one s., based not on the subject of a poem, but merely on the fact that it is a poem, and must therefore differ from the language of speech or prose. "The language of the age," said Gray, "is never the language of poetry . . . our poetry has a language peculiar to itself." This results in the theory of poetic diction (q.v.), aggressively rejected later by Wordsworth, who maintained, in direct opposition to Gray, that "there neither is nor can be any *essential* difference between the language of prose and metrical composition." Wordsworth's best practice often (though not always) contradicts this; and Coleridge partly reinstated the idea of a special language for poetry in his discussion of Wordsworth's theories. In Coleridge, however, this is not described in terms of choice of words, or any criterion that can be applied mechanically, but it is the result of the poet's "inward vision" and "modifying powers."

So much for subject: next there is the theory that s. reflects the individual author. "Le style est l'homme même": the famous sentence of Buffon seems to sum up this view, though when we look at it in context we see that it is not a view of personality expressed through s. or of "self-expression." For Buffon a fine s. depends on impersonal factors, the truths it presents, the arrangement of the thoughts. In this he is still in the Renaissance/neoclassic tradition (and incidentally is echoed by the demi-romantic Flaubert). It is easy to find assertions in Renaissance criticism that s. is "mentis character," a reflection of the man himself. Puttenham points out that although s. reflects subject, "men do choose their subjects according to the metal of their minds;" and since it is accepted that the personages of a play should speak in character, the extension of this to the poet speaking in his own person needs only a simple analogy. Nonetheless, no preromantic critic sees s. as the man himself in the full sense that this would now be claimed, for this depends on the new emphasis the romantics gave to the individual personality of the writer. The idea that deeper levels of a man's mind are revealed, sometimes even despite himself, in his style, is a comparatively modern one: and its most sophisticated versions (such as that of William Empson) are likely to use the insights of Freud. The traditional view of s. as "l'homme même" was a moral view (as in Longinus and Cicero); the modern version, if not actually psychoanalytic, will certainly emphasize the individual creative act. S. as personality is now a truth universally acknowledged; and the first impulse of a modern is to describe the difference between the two passages quoted earlier in terms of the difference between Spenser and Donne. Here is matter for controversy between the New Critics and the New Scholars. Is an epic by X more like a satire by X or an epic by his contemporary Y? The New Critics tend to emphasize the continuity of author; the others, of subject.

The s. of an author can be subdivided chronologically (Shakespeare, Milton, Dryden, Yeats are clear examples); and this division may overlap (it does with Dryden and Yeats, it does not with Milton) with the third way of considering s., as depending on the age. According to this view, it is possible to date a poem by the way it uses language: and there have been attempts (such as that of Bateson) to see a number of main phases of Eng. poetry, depending on the changing state of the language. As an example of period s., we may take the famous perspicuity of the Augustans. The Augustan ideals, as is well known, were clarity, perspicuity, good sense, nature, correctness, and reason: these preferences being based on the growing importance of science, the social influence of the bourgeoisie, the philosophy of Hobbes and Descartes. Obviously it is correct to say that this outlook is reflected in the prose of Addison, Defoe, and Swift, the poetry of Denham, Dryden, and Pope, and that there is therefore such a thing as an Augustan s., of the late 17th and earlier 18th c. What qualifications are needed to this simple view? First, that there is more strain among the Augustan ideals than they themselves always recognized: e.g. between reason and good sense, or between correctness and naturalness. This strain is mirrored in stylistic contrasts, e.g. between the coolness of the prose of Addison and the savage energy of Swift's (yet both are Augustan), or between the language of Pope's pastorals and that of his satires. Further, much of the energy of Augustan writing went into the characterizing of what they did not altogether approve of. "One glaring chaos and wild heap of wit," writes Pope in the *Essay on Criticism*, with a creative fire that in *The Dunciad* was to become an inspired condemning.

Relating s. to period, though prefigured in such a document as Coleridge's essay on s., is on the whole characteristic of the historical approach of the 20th c. There have been many interesting attempts to discuss the mechanism behind the formation of a period s. F. W. Bateson, for example, emphasizes that social and ethical influences can act on poetry only indirectly through their influence on the language. Promising as this sounds, it issues either in truism or in an utterly unprovable determinism, asserting that the characteristics of a group of poets are "imposed on the poets willy nilly" by the state of the language. Indeed, a theory of "period s." can hardly escape determinism, as we can see in two much subtler critics, Erich Auerbach and Patrick Cruttwell. "At any given moment," says Cruttwell, "there are not more than one or two poetic manners in which success is possible;" and his book (*The Shakespearean Moment*) analyzes those in which it was possible in the 17th c. Cruttwell has not the magnificent sweep of Auerbach's immense learning, but he has the one quality which the attentive reader of Auerbach begins to miss: he recognizes the importance of the creative act. For Auerbach, s. is often (especially in early periods) the reflection of a tension between the author's intent and the pressure of social forces: thus the s. of Ammianus Marcellinus is the resultant of a stoical "respect for the past" in Ammianus being acted upon by the sombre realism, the social violence, and the sensory prominence of gesture found in his material and, behind that, in his age: the author's control, as maker, is almost ignored. And discussing Racine, the s. and the theory behind it, Auerbach offers a "sociological" interpretation of the apparent contradiction (paying tribute to Taine), in terms of an elite with more prestige than function. The determinism of Auerbach is subtler and more specious than that of Cruttwell, but also more rigid; for although Cruttwell offers a less complex version of the social forces at work, he sees these forces not as themselves determining s., but merely as imposing a limit to the kind of creative act possible.

The problem of what determines s. (subject, author, or period: or yet further possibilities, such as the language itself, or certain philosophical positions) is in one sense a philosophical not a literary problem; and it can be shelved while we are actually analyzing styles, or suggesting ways of comparing them. It is impossible even to mention all the worthwhile analyses of styles which exist, but a word seems in place on some of the classifications that have been suggested, into kinds of s. There is the contrast between a plain and an ornate s.: the plain s. of course overlaps with the period s. of the Augustans, but at almost any time there is some sort of movement for plainness. What it attacks can vary, and a later age may not find it plain at all: thus George Herbert claimed to prefer "honest plainness" to veiled sense and baroque imagery (cf. *Jordan*), and yet is accused by the Augustans of those very qualities himself. Bagehot suggested a threefold distinction, between the pure s. of Wordsworth, the ornate s. of Tennyson (he calls this romantic, but it is really *parnassien*), and the grotesque s. of Browning. Remy de Gourmont suggested a distinction between visual and emotive styles, and regarded the first as the essentially poetic: few modern critics would follow him here. Many accounts of the classical romantic distinction have been offered, one of the best being Valéry's ("Tout classicisme suppose un romantisme antérieure. L'essence du classicisme est de venir après.")

Finally, it must be said that the discussion of s. is a part of literary criticism. The nature of literary creation is such that if it is successful, every detail of the product is of significance only as pointing to a total meaning: the better a poem, the more certain we may be that the organic view of s. is the true one for it. This means that there can be no worthwhile discussion of "figures," stylistic details, and ornament apart from their function in the poem.

–[816]–

"Longinus," *On the Sublime* (1st c. A.D.); Puttenham, *The Art of Eng. Poesy* (1589; esp. Bk. III, chaps. 5, 23); Ben Jonson, *Timber, or Discoveries* (1640; esp. sections cxv-end); Boileau, *L'Art Poétique* (1674); Addison, *The Spectator,* no. 285 (1712; on poetic diction); Pope, *Essay on Crit.* (1711), *The Dunciad* (1728–43), *To Augustus: the First Epistle of the Second Book of Horace Imitated* (1737; a survey of Eng. poetry); G. Buffon, *Discours sur le S.* (1753); Wordsworth, *Preface* to the 2d ed. of *Lyrical Ballads* (1800); Coleridge, *Biographia Literaria* (1817; esp. chaps. 15–22) and "On Style," no. 14 of *A Course of Lectures* (1818); Keats, *Letters* (esp. that to Shelley, Aug. 10, 1820); Bagehot, *Wordsworth, Tennyson and Browning* or *Pure, Ornate and Grotesque Art in Eng. Poetry* (1864); Pater, "S.," in *Appreciations* (1889); R. de Gourmont, *Le Problème du S.* (1902); M. Proust, *A L'Ombre des Jeunes Filles en Fleurs* (NRF ed., v. III, 1919, pp. 156–57; s. as the revelation of personality); J. M. Murry, *The Problem of S.* (1925); P. Valéry, 'Situation de Baudelaire,' *Variété,* II (1929), 141; F. W. Bateson, *Eng. Poetry and the Eng. Language* (1932) and *Eng. Poetry* (1950); Tuve; L. Spitzer, *Linguistics and Lit. Hist.* (1948); Wellek and Warren, esp. ch. 14, and excellent biblio.); W. H. Auden, dedicatory poem to *Nones* (1952); Auerbach; M. C. Bradbrook, "Fifty Years of Crit. of Shakespeare's S.," *ShS,* 7 (1954); P. Cruttwell, *The Shakespearean Moment* (1954); W. Nowottny, *The Language Poets Use* (1962).   L.D.L.

STYLISTICS. Deriving from grammar and rhetoric, stylistics was, prior to this century, normative and prescriptive. With modern linguistics and semantics, it has become analytical and has increased its scope to cover all the expressive aspects of language. It ranges over phonology and prosody, morphology, syntax, and lexicology, and the study of figures and tropes. Although it usually proceeds from the linguistic form to the idea or feeling embodied therein (semasiology), it may reverse the procedure and seek what means of expression are available to embody an idea or feeling (onomasiology). It may examine a single passage, an entire work or group of works, a genre, period, or national language (idiomatology). Essentially interpretative, it can reach evaluation by comparing texts or determining the degree of coherence of stylistic traits. It may also serve to fix authorship and chronology.

Internationally, stylistics is polarized between two tendencies which are most clearly formulated in Fr. *stylistique* and German *Stilforschung. Stylistique* considers itself closely linked to linguistics and merely an auxiliary of literary history and criticism, to which it supplies observations, definitions, and classifications. Its orientation is positivistic and its ultimate aim is to create a science of style, or repertory of all the stylistic elements of language. Literary language is but one of the numerous systems which together constitute a language; any one of these systems may be studied stylistically. Lack of emphasis on individual literary works gives rise to a large number of monographs on stylistic procedures either within a given period (synchronic) or across periods (diachronic). When *stylistique* turns to a specific work, it considers all style resources as present potentially in language, defines style as choice from among available means of expression, and determines the author's originality by comparison of his choice with generally accepted usage. Consequently, it utilizes a series of categories into which it sorts the work's constituent elements. Striving for completeness, it lists, for example, vowel and consonant sounds, rhythms and rhymes, parts of speech, kinds of vocabulary, types of sentences, figures, devices, and images. It establishes charts, graphs, and frequency tables. It has made great use of statistical methods and, recently, of electronic tabulations. There is usually no concern with determining relations among the style elements within the work or grouping them around a unifying principle. Its findings consequently take the form of quantitative analysis and linear description. Although *stylistique* occasionally confuses style with grammar, it remains within the language system and points up the relationship between literary language and ordinary language. Its findings are always verifiable.

Stilforschung identifies itself with literary history or criticism. It diminishes the importance of the concrete linguistic form and emphasizes the "spirit," or psychological attitude, behind the form. It follows Croce in maintaining that all language is style and individual creation and can therefore be seized only in literary works; in Saussurean terms, only in *parole* (individual), not in *langue* (general). No external categories may be applied to the work, which must be intuited as a whole. The goal is a grasp on inner form, which determines outer form and the relation of the whole to the parts. An unusual linguistic trait (outer form) reflects a similar deviation in the inner form which the investigator is thus able to penetrate. The entire work may then be recreated synthetically by the to-and-fro movement between inner and outer form. The approach is qualitative and concentrates on one or several key style elements. The concept of inner form offers difficulties, because it rarely turns out to be strictly aesthetic and is usually a psychic irregularity in the author or his metaphysical vision. Emphasis on inner form often results in leaving the original linguistic observation (and Croce) behind and in merging the author's spirit in that of his period and his nation. Since, at the period level, all cultural manifestations are felt to reflect the same time spirit, it becomes legitimate to assimilate literary to art history and to apply Wölfflin's style pairs to literary works. Thus, despite its having been originally a reaction against *Geistesgeschichte*, *Stilforschung* tends to fall back into psychological biography or history of ideas. Many of its insights are extremely valuable, but by soaring so far above linguistic phenomena, it is sometimes open to the charge of first determining the "spirit" of a work and then looking for a stylisticum which is supposed, not always convincingly, to embody it.

To *stylistique* may be likened the work of members of the first phase or generation of the New Criticism as well as certain of the more systematic aspects of Slavic formalism, e.g., phonostylistics, use of statistics, study of the relation between literary and other types of language. *Stilforschung*, by its concern with words in context, meaning structure, interrelation of form and content elements, and holism, offers analogies with other aspects of Slavic formalism and the New Criticism in its mature stage. Also, a few practitioners of *Stilforschung* concentrate on the work as an artistic object, to the exclusion of the poet's psyche or cultural history. However, Slavic formalism and the New Criticism have shown distrust of intuition, placed greater emphasis on the linguistic medium, and insisted on the *differentia* of literary language—the *how* and *what* rather than the *why*. Slavic formalism combines the objective thoroughness of *stylistique* with the integralism of *Stilforschung*. The New Criticism, with its interest in image-clusters, plurisignation, ambiguity, paradox, and irony, as observed in groups of poems spread over several literary periods, has created a modern rhetoric, or "science of tropes." Stylistics has discredited the impressionistic evaluation of style and has become an indispensable part of literary scholarship, creating techniques which may be said to constitute an intrinsic approach to literature.

H. A. Hatzfeld, *A Crit. Bibliog. of the New Stylistics Applied to the Romance Literatures* (1953); Wellek and Warren, 1956, pp. 282–96, 325–39; H. A. Hatzfeld and Y. Le Hir, *Essai de bibliographie critique de stylistique française et romane (1955–1960)* (1961).—GENERAL: D. Alonso, *Poesía española: Ensayo de métodos y límites estilicos* (1950); T. Spoerri, "Eléments d'une critique constructive," *Trivium*, 8 (1950); C. Bruneau, "La Stylistique," RPH, 5 (1951); L. Spitzer, "Les Théories de la stylistique," FM, 20 (1952) and "Stylistique et critique littéraire," *Critique*, 98 (1955); A. Schiaffini, "La stilistica letteraria," *Momenti*

di storia della lingua italiana (1953); H. Seidler, *Allgemeine Stilistik* (1953); P. Guiraud, *La Stylistique* (1954); W. K. Wimsatt, Jr., "Verbal Style," *The Verbal Icon* (1954); H. Hatzfeld, "Methods of Stylistic Investigation," *Lit. and Science* (1955), pp. 44–51; E. R. Vincent, "Mechanical Aids for the Study of Language and Literary Style," *Lit. and Science*, pp. 56–60; J. Miles, *Eras and Modes in Eng. Poetry* (1957); Wimsatt and Brooks; G. Antoine, "La Stylistique française," *Revue de l'enseignment supérieur*, 1 (1959); J.-P. Richard, "Quelques aspects nouveaux de la critique littéraire en France," *Filología moderna*, 1 (1961; relation of phenomenological critics to *Stilforschung*). A.A.E.

SUBJECTIVITY AND OBJECTIVITY. This distinction is the result of the 17th-c. Cartesian separation between thought and thing, which along with the rise of science has been baneful to poetry. In the 18th c. it limited the scope of poetry to amusement and morality, and greatly hampered the Eng. poets up to Blake. Blake asserted the power of art, poetry, and the imagination by denying objective reality to God and Nature, or by refusing to admit any distinction whatever between the internal and the external, between the subjective and the objective. The effect of his beliefs is evident in the wholly non-naturalistic imagery of his poetry. Wordsworth and Coleridge posited an ideal correlation between Nature and the human mind, and Coleridge's exposition of "the poetry of nature" (*Biographia Literaria*, chap. 14) illustrates his conception of the fusion of subject and object, or of imagination and observation, by the image of sunset or moonlight upon "a known and familiar landscape." Keats's "What the imagination seizes as beauty must be truth" is his solution of the problem, though he was not always confident of its correctness.

In such Victorians as Tennyson and Arnold the breach between subjective and objective widened. In general there is a discrepancy between the Victorian sensibility and the Victorian beliefs, as witness the exquisite nature poetry, unbased in doctrine, of Hardy and Housman. Modern poets, bolstered by depth-psychology and myth, have evolved a position akin to Blake's. The hallucinatory vividness of Yeats's "Byzantium," for example, is an assertion of the reality of imagination, a new kind of "willing suspension of disbelief." Yet it is to be remarked that most modern critics have taken subjectivity to mean solipsism and self-indulgence, as in the 20th-c. treatment of Shelley, while objectivity has been equated with honesty and insight. This is a decided shift from Blake's attitude toward free will and the power of the individual.—S. T. Coleridge,

Biographia Literaria, ed. J. Shawcross (1907), I. XII–XIII; A. Tate, *Reason in Madness* (1939); J. C. Ransom, *The New Criticism* (1941); Abrams; Wimsatt; A. Gérard, *L'Idée romantique de la poésie en Angleterre* (1955). R.H.F.

"SUBLIME," a Latin-derived word meaning literally "(on) high, lofty, elevated," owes its currency as a critical and aesthetic term to the anonymous Gr. treatise *Peri Hypsous* (*hypsos,* "height, elevation"), formerly ascribed to the rhetorician Cassius Longinus, 3rd c. A.D., but now generally agreed to belong to the 1st c., perhaps around 50 A.D. Whatever his name and origin, its author was certainly a rhetorician and a teacher of the art, but one of uncommon mold. His essay, with its intimacy of tone (it is addressed to a favorite pupil, a young Roman) and breadth of spirit, stands more or less isolated in its own time, but has had a recurrent fascination for modern minds since the 17th c.

The idea of sublimity had its roots in the rhetorical distinction, well established before "Longinus," of three styles of speech, high, middle, and low. His achievement was to draw it out of the technical sphere, where it had to do with style primarily, and associate it with the general phenomenon of greatness in literature, prose and poetry alike. "Longinus" regards sublimity above all as a thing of the spirit, a spark that leaps from the soul of the writer to the soul of his reader, and only secondarily as a matter of technique and expression. "Sublimity is the echo of greatness of spirit." Being of the soul, it may pervade a whole work (speech, history, or poem: "Longinus" pays little attention to *genre* distinctions); or it may flash out at particular moments. "Father Zeus, kill us if thou wilt, but kill us in the light." "God said, 'Let there be light,' and there was light." In such quotations as these "Longinus" shows among other things his sharp eye for the particular passage and his capacity for *Einfühlung* into the actual work: qualities that are rare in ancient criticism and presage the modern spirit.

The distinguishing mark of sublimity, for "Longinus," is a certain quality of feeling. But he will not allow it to be simply identified with emotion, for not all emotions are true or noble. Only art can guard against exaggerated or misplaced feeling. Nevertheless art plays second fiddle to genius in his thinking. There are five sources of the sublime which he enumerates: great thoughts, noble feeling, lofty figures, diction, and arrangement. The first two, the crucial ones, are the gift of nature, not art. "Longinus" even prefers the faults of a great spirit, a Homer, a Plato, or a Demosthenes, to the faultless mediocrity that is achieved by following rules.

The treatise remained unknown, or at least

exercised little influence, in later antiquity. It was first published by Robortelli in 1554, then translated into L. in 1572 and into Eng. in 1652 (by John Hall). But it made no great impression until the late 17th c. Paradoxically enough it was Boileau, the archpriest of neoclassicism, who launched the *Peri Hypsous* on its great career and thus helped to prepare the ultimate downfall of classicism. His translation (1672) had immense reverberation, especially in England. The Eng., always restive under the "French rules," instinctively welcomed "Longinus" as an ally. The Augustans duly admired him as "himself that great Sublime he draws" (Pope), but at the same time he was being invoked by John Dennis in support of the thesis that "Passion is the Principal thing in Poetry" (1701) and by Samuel Cobb as a champion of "the Liberty of Writing" (1707). As the 18th c. advanced, the sublime was absorbed into the bloodstream of Eng. thinking not only about literature but about art in general and even external nature. Under it were subsumed all the loftier feelings—"admiration," "transport," "enthusiasm," vehemence, even awe and terror—which literature, art, and nature are capable of inspiring, but for which neoclassicism had no clearly marked place. More and more frequently the sublime was distinguished from the beautiful—and ranked above it. Thus it played no small part in the drift toward subjectivism, the psychologizing of literature and literary experience, the concept of "original genius" unfettered by rules (Edward Young, the Wartons, Robert Wood, ca. 1760–70), and ultimately in the rise of romanticism in poetry and the concurrent establishment of aesthetics as a new, separate branch of philosophy (Kant, Hegel, etc.).

In this development the sublime left its beginnings in "Longinus" far behind; it became an independent concept with an intellectual history of its own. Burke's *Enquiry into the Origin of our Ideas on the Sublime and Beautiful* (1757) and Kant's *Critique of Aesthetic Judgment* (1790) make little use of the *Peri Hypsous.* But its significance is not exhausted by its historical role. Though not greatly in fashion today, it remains a perennially moving plea for greatness of spirit in literature, and it can also provide—coming as it does from a rhetorician—a timely corrective for overabsorption in poetic language and style.

PRIMARY WORKS: "Longinus on the Sublime," ed. and tr., with introd. and appendices, W. Rhys Roberts (2d ed., 1907; best and fullest ed.); *Anonimo del Sublime,* ed. and tr. A. Rostagni (1947). Tr.: W. H. Fyfe (1927; Loeb ed.); B. Einarson (1945); G.M.A. Grube (1958); D. A. Russell (1965; text and commentary, 1964).

SECONDARY WORKS: T. R. Henn, *L. and Eng. Crit.* (1934; spotty); S. H. Monk, *The S.: A*

Study of Crit. Theories in 18th-C. England (1935; definitive); E. Olson, "The · Argument of Longinus' 'On the S.'," MP, 39 (1942; repr. in Crane, Critics; subtle, overmodernizes "L."); F. Wehrli, "Der erhabene und der schlichte Stil in der poetisch-rhetorischen Theorie der Antike," Phyllobolia für P. von der Mühll (1946); W. J. Hipple, The Beautiful, The S., and the Picturesque (1957); J. Brody, Boileau and Longinus (1958); J. Arthos, Dante, Michelangelo and Milton (1963).　　　　G.F.E.

SUBSTITUTION. In most Gr. and L. verse forms one metrical foot, under certain conditions, might be substituted for another, e.g., in a Gr. iambic trimeter a spondee could replace the initial iambus of each dipody:

$$\text{≅}-\cup-|\text{≅}-\cup-|\text{≅}-\cup-$$

See also METRICAL VARIATIONS.　　　R.J.G.

SUMERIAN POETRY. The Sumerians lived in Southern Babylonia along the lower Euphrates during the 3d millennium B.C. Their language is agglutinative, but has no close relations with any other known language. Their literature, written on clay tablets in cuneiform characters derived from actual pictures, flourished chiefly from 2500 to 2000 B.C.

The poetry of the Sumerians, like that of the ancient Hebrews, Egyptians, Hittites, and Babylonians, consisted of verses having an accentuating rhythm and a variable number of syllables. The verse was divided into two equal parts and appears in Eng. translation as a distich. Often the two halves of the verse either complete one another or stand in parallelism, as in the poem on Inanna-Ishtar's descent to the Underworld:

u-da kur-še Du-na-mu-de

an du-du-dam gar-gar-ma-ni-ib

eš-gu-en-na tuku-a-ma-ni-ib

e-dingir-ri-e-ne-ke nigin-na-ma-ni-ib
(33–36)

When I shall have come to the nether world,
Fill heaven with complaints for me;
In the assembly shrine cry out for me,
In the house of the gods rush about for me.
(Tr. S. N. Kramer)

The standard verse in Sum., as in the ancient Near East, was divided into equal halves, each having 4 stress accents (8 beats for the verse). The meter is therefore identical with that of the following stanza of Coleridge (corresponding to 2 verses in Sum.):

The lovely lady, Christabel,

Whom her father loves so well,

What makes her in the wood so late,

A furlong from the castle gate?

Some scholars believe that the 4:4 verse should be regarded as two 2:2 verses, as conventionally printed above; but such a metrical structure would eliminate the parallelism. Occasionally Sum. poetry used the elegiac meter, known also in ancient Egyptian and Hebrew (Lamentations 1–4; Amos 5:2) literature, in which a silence takes the place of the last beat (4:3 + silence; some scholars scan it as 3:2 + silence).

The earliest poetry may have been that of workers songs, as in Egypt (cf. the song of the well-diggers in Numbers 21:17–18), but only a few Assyrian ones have survived. Extant Sum. poetry is religious in character, consisting of mythological epics, hymns, and prayers. All ancient Near Eastern poetry was sung, usually to the accompaniment of wind and string instruments. Such Sum. hymns and prayers have come down for the most part in Akkadian translations, or with interlinear Akkadian translation. Almost all other known Sum. poetry is mythological, except for a few lamentations and proverbs; most of the poetic texts were excavated by the University of Pennsylvania at Nippur (modern Nuffar) from 1889 to 1900.

Among the hymns to gods we may mention those to Nannar (Sin, the moon god), to Ningirsu and Gatumdug (the god and goddess of the city Lagash), to Ninkarrak (goddess of Isin). The hymns to Inanna-Ishtar and Anu were sung antiphonally. We have a lamentation for Dumuzi-Tammuz (Adonis, the dying god of vegetation) and one about the destructive anger of Enlil (god of Nippur).

The human, semi-divine or divine protagonists of the epics are: Enmerkar (who conquered Aratta for Erech), Lugalbanda (who succeeded in bringing Enmerkar's message to Inanna at Aratta), Gilgamesh (king of Erech, son of Lugalbanda), Ninurta, and Inanna (who fought against Entiki). The mythological poems deal with the creation of the world and its organization, the slaying of the dragon (the myth common to all Mediterranean peoples), the descent of Inanna-Ishtar to the nether world, the deluge, the marriage of the god Martu (the god of the Amorites), "Inanna-Ishtar prefers the farmer," and others.

The best Eng. tr. (by S. N. Kramer) are found in Ancient Near Eastern Texts Relating to the Old Testament, ed. J. B. Pritchard (1950; these tr. are repr. in an inexpensive ed. by I. Mendelsohn, Religions of the Ancient Near

East, 1955).—For general and literary histories, see: M. Jastrow, Jr., *The Civilization of Babylonia and Assyria* (1915); B. Meissner, *Babylonien und Assyrien*, II (1925) and *Die babylonisch-assyrische Literatur* (1930); S. N. Kramer, "Sum. Lit., a Preliminary Survey of the Oldest Lit. in the World," *Proc. of the Am. Philos. Soc.*, 83 (1942), *Sum. Mythology* (1944, rev. ed., 1962; standard work), "Enki and Ninhursag," *Bulletin of the Am. Schools of Oriental Research*, supp. studies, no. 1 (1945) and *From the Tablets of Sumer* (1956) as well as *The Sumerians* (1963).—See also *Sumerische und akkadische Hymnen und Gebete*, tr. A. Falkenstein and W. von Soden (1953; important introd.). R.H.P.

SURREALISM. In its beginnings s. was presented by its chief spokesman, André Breton, in his first *Manifesto* (1924) as an attempt to give expression to the "real functioning of thought" through pure psychic automatism, by means of the spoken or written word, or by any other means available. He proclaimed its main interest to be that of furthering a revolution destined to liberate the mind of man, and its superior aim to be the unification of exterior reality with interior reality. Thus, s. resolutely placed itself apart from literature. However, the talent of those who, with Breton, furthered the cause of s. made of this movement the principal poetic as well as artistic current of the first half of the 20th c.

The study of dreams, of hallucinations, the practice of automatic writing under the dictation of the subconscious are considered by the surrealists as the true means of knowledge. They ascribe a great importance to the analysis of the interpenetration of the sleeping and waking states. Hallucinations, either spontaneous or provoked, are for them revelatory of the workings of the mind when liberated from the control of reason, as well as from conscious aesthetic or moral preoccupations. Automatic writing, equally free from aesthetic or rational control, reveals the life of the subconscious and widens the range of Baudelairian correspondences.

All these methods allow the surrealist to liberate his mind from the censorship of habits, of social conventions, and of education. He is then free to participate in the world of "surreality," which alone reveals the true relationship between man and the universe.

Later Breton was to enlarge this definition in his *Second Manifeste du S.*, which first appeared in the December 1929 issue of *La Révolution Surréaliste*:

"The idea of s. tends simply to the total recuperation of our psychic forces by a means which is no other than a vertiginous descent within ourselves, the systematic illumination of hidden places and the progressive darkening of all other places, the perpetual rambling in the depth of the forbidden zone. . . . Everything leads one to believe that there exists a certain point in the mind from which life and death, the real and the imaginary, the past and the future, what is communicable and what is incommunicable, the high and the low, cease to be perceived as contradictory. Vainly would one assign to surrealist activity another ambition than the hope of determining this point."

Surrealist poetry is primarily an instrument of knowledge which brings the poet to a clearer awareness of the world perceived by the senses. In turn the poet becomes a revolutionary in that he seeks, by solving the principal problems of life, to change the human condition. There is no attempt, in this poetry, to adhere to established rules of versification, nor even to create new ones. Very often the poem is indistinguishable from prose; a certain rhythm is, however, to be found in the works of the best surrealist poets such as Breton and Eluard. By considering words as images having an autonomous life of their own and by bringing together word-images of widely removed species (e.g. "Sur le pont la rosée à tête de chatte se berçait," A. Breton), the surrealist poet creates new images of a remarkable ignascent quality. This, rather than the use of metaphors, or other figures of rhetoric, is the basis of surrealist imagery.

The main themes of surrealist poetry are love, revolt, the marvelous, freedom, the exaltation of desire, "black humor" and the universe of subconscious thought. The love of woman, of a frankly erotic character, is considered as a form of liberation. Revolt, for the surrealists, is directed principally against logic, social morality, and conventional norms. These they would replace by an unconditional pursuit of the marvelous in everyday life, especially as it manifests itself in urban civilization. "Black humor" is also an expression of revolt in that it is characterized by an explosive and liberating effect. The exaltation of desire is upheld because of a belief in the ultimate worth of all passions.

The chief surrealist writers in France have been: Louis Aragon (1897–), Antonin Artaud (1895–1948), André Breton (1896–), Aimé Césaire (1913–), René Char (1907–), René Crevel (1900–35), Robert Desnos (1900–45), Paul Eluard (1895–1952), Julien Gracq (1909–), Michel Leiris (1901–), Benjamin Péret (1899–), Francis Picabia (1878–), Raymond Queneau (1903–), Philippe Soupault (1897–), Tristan Tzara (1896–).

It is difficult to ascribe a precise date for the beginning of the s. movement. As Breton has pointed out, the movement presented itself

SURREALISM

from the start as a codification of a state of mind that has manifested itself sporadically throughout the centuries and in every country. The first to use the word s., but in its adjectival form and with a humoristic connotation, was Guillaume Apollinaire (1880–1918). His farce *Les Mamelles de Tirésias* (1917) was subtitled: *drame surréaliste*. The word acquired new meaning and a precise definition in Breton's *Manifeste du S.* (1924) and, in the same year, appeared in the title of the movement's review: *La Révolution surréaliste*, directed at first by Pierre Naville and Benjamin Péret and later (1925–30) by Breton. The first surrealist text, however, was *Les Champs Magnétiques*, written jointly, as an exercise in automatic writing, by Breton and Philippe Soupault and published in the 1919 review *Littérature*, directed by these two poets and by Louis Aragon. The first manifesto summed up the conclusions drawn by the surrealists in what Breton calls the "heroic period" of their movement.

In 1922 Breton and his friends broke away from dadaism (q.v.), and Breton took over the direction of the review *Littérature*. From then until 1924 the surrealists sought, and found, the fields for their experiments which were to be hypnotically induced sleep and the subconscious probed by automatic writing. In 1921 Breton had been received by Freud, for whom he had conceived an enthusiastic admiration and whose theories were to have an important influence on the development of surrealist methods.

Many other influences can be cited. In Fr. literature, the surrealists recognized their indebtedness to the Marquis de Sade (1740–1814), in whom they saw an example of perfect revolt, to Gérard de Nerval (1808–55), who had affirmed that there was a link to be found between the external and the internal worlds and who had first used the word *supernaturalism*, to Charles Baudelaire (1821–67), who first described the chaos of modern man, to Stéphane Mallarmé (1842–98), who considered the main function of the poet to be that of magician, to Isidore Ducasse "comte de Lautréamont" (1846–70) for the spiritual torment and the concern for the human condition that they found in his work *Les Chants de Maldoror*, to Arthur Rimbaud (1854–91), who had proclaimed the unity and innocence of life and had recommended the cultivation of hallucinations and other abnormal states of mind, to Alfred Jarry (1873–1907) for his violent and obscene humor, and to Guillaume Apollinaire.

In foreign literatures, the surrealists drew from Novalis and von Arnim, from Blake and Coleridge, Ann Radcliffe and Horace Walpole, as well as from the philosophy of Hegel and the psychology of Freud. The personality of Jacques Vaché (1896–1919), whom Breton met

in 1916 in a hospital at Nantes, and who, through his suicide in 1919, became for the surrealists a symbol of their revolt, played a major role in determining the climate of s. Lastly the surrealists were inspired by the arts of the primitives of all lands and of all times.

From 1924 to the outbreak of the Second World War, s. produced many poetic works such as Aragon's *Le mouvement perpétuel* (1925), René Crevel's *Etes-vous fous?* (1929), Robert Desnos' *Corps et Biens* (1930), Paul Eluard's *L'amour la poésie* (1929), Benjamin Péret's *Le grand jeu* (1928), and Breton's *Le revolver à cheveux blancs* (1932) which, together with numerous prose works, testified to the vitality of the movement.

S., from its beginnings, had refused to draw a dividing line between the arts. Thus, painters, sculptors, and poets worked hand in hand and borrowed freely from each other. Salvador Dali (b. 1904) gave the movement a new impetus in 1933 through his method of paranoiaccriticism, based on critical interpretation of states of delirium. From the application of this method issued the surrealist objects, i.e., objects made gratuitously or following the dictates of the subconscious or of dreams. In 1938 an international exhibit of s. was held in Paris, to which eighteen nations sent representative works of art, showing thereby that the movement had spread to all parts of the globe.

In 1930 *La Révolution Surréaliste* became *Le Surréalisme au Service de la Révolution* to indicate the importance attached by the surrealists to social revolution, especially after the Moroccan war of 1925. After the break with the Communist party in 1933 this review ceased to appear. In 1934 the review *Minotaure* became the vehicle for surrealist publications, and in 1937 Breton became one of its directors.

During the Second World War Breton came to the United States. He founded the review vvv and in 1942 gave an important lecture at Yale University, entitled *La situation du s. entre les deux guerres*, which was shortly followed by the *Prolégomènes à un troisième Manifeste du S. ou non* (published in 1946 with the two previous *Manifestes*). Most of the other members of the surrealist movement stayed in France during the war and participated in the Resistance against the Nazis. Aragon, who had been "excommunicated" by Breton some years before the war, and Eluard, who left the movement in 1942, wrote poetry inspired by fervent patriotism but still preserving much of the surrealist technique.

Since 1945 s. has attracted many young writers and its influence is still important, though it can no longer be considered as an integrated movement. In 1949 twenty-four nations participated in an International Exposition in Paris.

Breton's major recent works: *Arcane 17* (1945), *Ode à Charles Fourier* (1947), *Poèmes* (1948), *Anthologie de l'Humour Noir* (1950—first published in 1940), bear witness to his continued optimism as to man's progress towards a better condition. No review has been able to take the place of *S.A.S.D.L.R.* but Breton, after having directed the short-lived *Le S. même,* has recently, with Robert Benayoun, founded *La Brèche* (March 1962). Apart from Breton, other writers have since the Second World War produced interesting surrealist works: Pierre de Mandiargues, *Dans les années sordides* (1948), Georges Schehadé, *Poésie II* (1948), Henri Pichette, *Les Epiphanies* (1948), Aimé Césaire, *Les Armes Miraculeuses* (1946), etc.

S. has exercised an undeniable influence on poetry during the last thirty-eight years. The poem is no longer considered merely as a vehicle for aesthetic pleasure but as a springboard for metaphysical knowledge, and this transformation is, in great part, due to the surrealists. The experimentations in language have left their mark on poetic language in France and in other countries as well. The surrealist conceptions of love, of liberty, of humor, and of the marvelous have helped to fashion the modern mentality. Aside from poetry, s. has left its mark on the theatre (through Antonin Artaud principally), the novel, the cinema, and on painting and sculpture. This influence has been felt in and outside France, for s. has been a major international movement in the arts of the Twentieth Century. Japan, Egypt, Yugoslavia, Czechoslovakia, Germany, Poland, Sweden, England, Spain, Italy, Argentina, Mexico, and the United States have all had their surrealist poets and painters and their surrealist reviews. In all these countries the surrealist affirmation that the poet and the artist belong to the same species and are interdependent has been amply demonstrated.

M. Raymond, *De Baudelaire au S.* (1933); A. Breton, *Qu'est-ce le S.?* (1934), *Situation du S. entre les deux guerres* (1945), *Les Manifestes du S.* suivis de *Prolégomènes à un troisième Manifeste du S. ou non* (1946), *Entretiens avec André Parinaud* (1952); D. Gascoyne, *A Short Survey of S.* (1935); H. R. Hays, "Surrealist Influence in Contemporary Eng. and American Poetry," *Poetry,* 54 (1939); R. Mabille, *Le miroir du merveilleux* (1940); G. Lemaître, *From Cubism to S. in Fr. Lit.* (1941); N. Calas, *Confound the Wise* (1942); C. Bo, *Antologia del Surrealismo* (1944), *Bilancio del Surrealismo* (1944); J. Monnerot, *La poésie moderne et le sacré* (1945); M. Nadeau, *Histoire du S.* (1945), *Documents Surréalistes* (1946); M. Blanchot, "A propos du S.," *L'Arche,* 8 (1945), "Surréalistes étrangers," *Cahiers du Sud,* 280 (1946); A. Balakian, *Literary Origins of S.* (1947), *S.: The Road to the Absolute*

(1959); J. Gracq, *André Breton* (1948); F. Alquié, "Humanisme surréaliste et humanisme existentialiste," *Cahiers du Collège philosophique* (1948), *Philosophie du S.* (1955); M. Gilman, "From Imagination to Immediacy in Fr. Poetry," *RR,* 39 (1948); C. Mauriac, *André Breton* (1949); A.-M. Schmidt, "Constances baroques dans la littérature française," *Trivium,* 7 (1949); A. Bosquet, *Surrealismus* (1950); W. Fowlie, *Age of S.* (1950); M. Carrouges, *André Breton et les données fondamentales du S.* (1950); L. Lesage, *Jean Giraudoux, S., and the German Romantic Ideal* (1952); R. Warnier, "Trente ans après . . . le s.," *Romanische Forschungen,* 67 (1956); H. M. Block, "S. and Modern Poetry: Outline for an Approach," JAAC, 18 (1959); J. Hardré, "Present State of Studies on Literary S.," *Yearbook of Comparative and General Lit.,* 9 (1960); "S.," YFS, 31 (1964). J.HA.

SWEDISH-FINNISH MODERNISTS, THE. A group of significant poets in the Swed.-speaking part of Finland about and following the time of World War I. The chief members of the group were Edith Södergran (1892–1923), Elmer Diktonius (1896–1961), Gunnar Björling (1887–1960), and Rabbe Enckell (b. 1903). Although these poets were influenced by a great many foreign poetic programs, ranging from Rus. futurism to Am. modernism, the principal external stimulus was provided by expressionist and futurist painting and music, from Van Gogh to Schönberg. Their aims, set forth in the two periodicals *Ultra* (1922) and *Quosego* (1928–29), were not only to create a new revolutionary aesthetic and a new poetic technique, but also to establish the poet in a more active social role. By means of a freely associative imagery that startled and shocked, a verse following free rhythms, and a language unencumbered by external ornament, they endeavored to express both their own innermost feelings and the submerged humanity of the age. In their romantic emphasis on the instinctual and the spontaneous as well as in their free form, these poets were inspirational both to *Fem unga* (Five Young Poets), the surrealist Gunnar Ekelöf, and *fyrtiotalisterna,* q.v. ("The Poets of the Forties") in Sweden.—*Voices from Finland,* ed. E. Tompuri (1947); *20th-C. Scandinavian Poetry,* ed. M. Allwood (1950); B. Holmqvist, *Modern finlandssvensk litt.* (1951); *40 år finlandssvensk lyrik,* ed. S. Carlson (1955). S.L.

SWEDISH POETRY. Very little is known about the earliest Swed. poetry, none of which has been recorded. Rune (q.v.) inscriptions, however, show that *fornyrðislag* (q.v.), the Edda stanza, was known, possibly also *drótt-*

SWEDISH POETRY

kvætt (q.v.), the classical scaldic verse form.
There is evidence that an extensive oral poetry
existed, comprising pagan religious hymns and
heroic and mythological poems. Traces of
Sweden's heroic poetry may have been preserved in *Beowulf* and in the scaldic poem
Ynglingatal.

The chief monuments of medieval Swed.
poetry are the folk ballads, at their height in
the 13th and 14th c. Strongly dramatic, the
Swed. ballad in both spirit and structure approximates the Scotch ballad. Of individual
poems, the versified chronicles, from *Eriks-
krönikan* (Eric's Chronicle, 1320-21) to *Stora
rimkrönikan* (The Great Rhymed Chronicle,
ca. 1500), were significant productions in *knittelvers* (q.v.). Of the known poets the best was
Tomas af Strängnäs (d. 1443), whose patriotic
lyrics, like *Frihetsvisan* (The Song of Freedom), adumbrated a national tradition that
was to be sustained throughout the centuries.
The 16th c. (1511-1611) produced mostly the-
ological-didactic poetry, typified by the first
Swed. attempt at drama, the Bible play *Tobiae
comedia* (ca. 1550) ascribed to Olavus Petri
(1493-1552).

In the 17th c. (1611-1718) Swed. poets endeavored to create a literature in the vernacular to match the achievements of classical antiquity. The greatest of these poets was Georg
Stiernhielm (1598-1672), whose principal work
was the allegorical-didactic epic *Hercules* (1648;
pub. 1658), epoch-making in respect to both
form and content: it demonstrated the aptness
of the Swed. language for hexameter verse and
exploited a classical-mythological subject without incurring triteness and artificiality. These
faults Stiernhielm avoided by nationalizing the
Greco-Roman gods and by introducing vividly
described personified abstractions. The resultant merging of Gothicism—or generally nationalism—and classicism established a pattern
in Swed. poetry which was to remain a shaping
poetic force up to the end of the 19th c., and
to leave its imprint upon the style of such
poets as Tegnér, Rydberg, and Heidenstam. On
the whole, Stiernhielm's art was broadly realistic, a trait derived possibly from his intimate
acquaintance with Dutch poets, especially Jacob
Cats. Stiernhielm also introduced the sonnet,
according to Fr. models composed in alexandrines, a practice abandoned only in the romantic period. Samuel Columbus (1642-79),
who with Urban Hiärne (1641-1724) and a few
others made up the first Swed. literary coterie,
was the most important of Stiernhielm's followers. His lyric verse, best represented by
Odae Sveticae (1674), is more melodious than
that of Stiernhielm. Intimately personal as well
as national was the inspiration of Lars Wivallius (1605-69), first in a fairly continuous line
of unschooled singers who have contributed a

rich store of spontaneous popular lyricism to
Swed. poetry. He was followed by Lars Johans-
son, or Lucidor (1638-74), whose forte was the
convivial song, where he provides a link between Wivallius and Bellman, the 18th-c. virtuoso of the genre.

In the late 17th c. baroque poetry found a
practitioner in Gunno Eurelius Dahlstierna
(1661-1709), whose *Kungaskald* (King-Scald,
1697) was intended as an allegorical epic in the
It. style. This is proved by the use of ottava
rima (q.v.), a meter Dahlstierna was the first
to practice in Swed., characteristically in alexandrines. The poem, however, lacks all narrative unity, and the marinistic style is too uneven to sustain the mood. Somewhat later,
Samuel Triewald (1688-1743) advocated Fr.
neoclassicism, while the Finn Jacob Frese
(1691-1729) became Sweden's first significant
subjective-emotional poet. Frese's Christian epic
Passionstankar (Thoughts on the Passion, 1728)
was fraught with a profound religiousness;
after being imaginatively transformed by the
romantics, the introspective emotionalism here
introduced crystallized into an enduring tradition in Swed. poetry. Johan Runius (1679-
1713) was a virtuoso rhymer celebrating bourgeois jocundity. Together, Triewald, Frese, and
Runius sum up the tendencies that would prevail in the 18th c.: Fr. neoclassicism, sentimental romanticism, and Swed.-Carolinian poetic
realism.

The outstanding event in 18th-c. Swed. poetry was the consolidation of neoclassical principles, both in epic, with its obligatory alexandrine, and in drama. The first great advocate
of these principles, Olof von Dalin (1708-63),
gave his age both a tragedy and an epic in
the prescribed style; modern readers, however,
are attracted chiefly by his excellent ballads
and epigrammatic satires. In the 1750's Mrs.
Hedvig Charlotta Nordenflycht (1718-63) established a literary *salon,* the purpose of which
was to maintain, and further refine, the poetic
standards of Dalin; its principal habitués were
Finnish-born Gustaf Filip Creutz (1731-85) and
Gustaf Fredrik Gyllenborg (1731-1808). With
Atis och Camilla (1761) Creutz produced
Sweden's loveliest pastoral poem. Gyllenborg,
a lesser poet, was more didactic; his best work,
Människans elände (The Wretchedness of
Man, 1761), shows traces of Rousseau. Carl
Michael Bellman (1740-1809), who continued
the poetic realism of Runius, wrote poetry
which was at the same time peculiarly individual and broadly national. His work exhibits
a wide gamut of moods, ranging from genuine,
intoxicated, and burlesque rapture to profound
melancholy and sorrow; it is, however his *joie
de vivre* that has made him a universally beloved poet. Although primarily a lyrist, Bellman was also a superb narrator and portrayer

-[824]-

of types: his gallery of comic figures is unforgettable.

The Gustavian Age (1772–1802) was *par excellence* the age of Enlightenment and of Fr. taste in art and literature, enforced by such literary societies as *Utile Dulci* and *Svenska akademien* (The Swedish Academy, est. 1786). Rationalism and neoclassicism found their contrary, however, in a preromantic movement inspired by Rousseau, Eng. preromantics, Klopstock, and *Sturm und Drang* (q.v.). The best poet of the period was the satirist Johan Henrik Kellgren (1751–95), who, initially an advocate of neoclassicism, in his best poem, the magnificent *Den nya skapelsen* (The New Creation, 1789), expressed a profound idealism that foreshadowed the romantic age. But of 18th-c. poets, excepting Bellman, it is Anna Maria Lenngren (1755–1817) who has best preserved her reputation in modern times, because of her everyday subjects, simple style, and common sense. Of preromantic Gustavians one may mention Bengt Lidner (1757–93), who in *Grevinnan Spastaras död* (The Death of Countess Spastara, 1783) displayed a virtuoso mastery of stanzaic forms and metrical effects, and the Finn Frans Michael Franzén (1772–1847), who in *Människans anlete* (The Countenance of Man, 1793) employed a richly imaginative and musical style as the vehicle of an aesthetic and religious idealism.

With the 19th c., which initiated a great period in Swed. poetry, German romanticism and philosophical idealism became the chief foreign sources of poetic inspiration. Through Germany Swed. poets became acquainted with Shakespeare and with Romance Renaissance authors. Formally, therefore, the new poetry was exceedingly varied, classical and medieval measures alternating with those of Southern romance and of contemporary German verse. The first romantic group was active mainly through a literary association founded at Uppsala in 1807, *Auroraförbundet* (The Aurora League), whose chief organ, the periodical *Phosphoros* (1810–13), conferred on its members the nickname "Phosphorists." Per Daniel Amadeus Atterbom (1790–1855), who was inspired by German Jena romanticism, emerged with *Blommorna* (The Flowers, 1812–37) as the finest Phosphorist poet. His most ambitious work, *Lycksalighetens ö* (The Isle of Bliss, 1824–27), is an allegorical fairy-tale play which embodies the conflict between romantic aestheticism and an ethical-religious ideal. Closely related to Phosphorist poetry is the work of Erik Johan Stagnelius (1793–1823), one of the most gifted of Sweden's poets. Combining imaginative fervor with classical form, he is the Shelley and Keats of Swed. literature. His lyric cycle *Liljor i Saron* (Lilies of Sharon, 1821–23) contains moods ranging from world-weary mysticism to passionate eroticism. His last and greatest work, *Bacchanterna* (The Bacchae, 1822), which deals with the fate of Orpheus in the classical Gr. style, dramatizes the contrast between inspired rapture and sensual intoxication. Stagnelius first brought to full development the subjective-emotional mode in Swed. poetry. He has been vastly influential, largely because of his ability to convey intense emotion and to concretize involved abstractions.

The second group of Swed. romantics are identified by their connection with *Götiska förbundet* (The Gothic League), which called for a national revival in literature. Its head, Erik Gustaf Geijer (1783–1847), is significant as a poet mainly because of his artlessly simple style and his regionalism. It was Esaias Tegnér (1782–1846), one of the foremost of Swed. poets, who came closest to realizing the program of the Gothicists. Drawing upon German Heidelberg romanticism and the classicism of Goethe and Schiller, Tegnér achieved a new poetic synthesis on a national basis. His most important productions are *Nattvardsbarnen* (The Children of the Lord's Supper, 1820), a religious-didactic narrative in hexameter verse influenced by Goethe's *Hermann und Dorothea*, and *Frithiofs saga* (1825), which marks the high point of his achievement. The noble figure of Frithiof may lack historical verisimilitude, but his character, in its union of virility, courage, and courtliness, became the ideal of the age. The poem is a free rendering of an Old Icelandic saga in a cycle of 24 romances in various meters, a form modeled on the Danish poet Oehlenschläger's *Helge*. It owes much of its staying-power to the skill with which Tegnér conjured with stanzaic forms and metrical patterns to evoke the mood of the various episodes. Worthy of special mention is the poet's masterful handling of Homeric hexameter; here Tegnér was a worthy heir to Stiernhielm, whom he also recalls in his lofty dignity and exalted national fervor. The 1830's and 1840's produced only one original romantic, Byron-inspired Carl Johan Love Almquist (1793–1866), a bizarre and exotic writer whose poems are notable for their free-verse qualities and their emotional wizardry. His chief work, *Törnrosens bok* (The Book of the Briar Rose, 1832–51), contained lyric, narrative, and dramatic pieces—and prose. Of most enduring value are his *Songes*, whose deliberately artless form, musical suggestiveness, and intensely gripping tone ally Almquist to Stagnelius, with whom he also belongs as a forerunner of poetic modernism in Sweden.

The Finn Johan Ludvig Runeberg (1804–77), one of the greatest poets who ever wrote in Swed., attained in his work a perfect fusion of realism and romantic idealism. Though influenced by his countryman Franzén and classical Gr. poetry, Runeberg is in his tone and technique uniquely individual. Of his narratives may be mentioned *Elgskyttarne* (The Elk-hunters, 1832), written in Homeric hexameter, and *Kung Fjalar* (1844), his best work. In the latter, a somber historical epic, influences from primitive Nordic myth, Ossian, and classical antiquity interpenetrate. But the verse forms, modeled on Nordic meters, were worked out individually by the poet himself. Runeberg, however, is best known for his immortal cycle *Fänrik Ståls sägner* (The Tales of Ensign Stål, 1848–60), into which both narrative and lyric elements entered. Of his purely lyric poetry, the cycle *Idyll och epigram* (1830–33), with its laconic verses in trochaic rhythm, displays a striking originality.

After a couple of relatively barren decades, in the 1870's Carl Snoilsky and Viktor Rydberg ushered in a period of high achievement. Snoilsky (1841–1903) was a member of *Namnlösa Sällskapet* (The Nameless Society, est. 1860), a literary association with a realistic poetic program inspired by Runeberg and by contemporary Norwegian poetry. In his *Dikter* (Poems, 1369) Snoilsky showed a versatile talent; the keynote was a joyous love of life and freedom. His later lyricism was richer, combining, as in *Afrodite och Sliparen* (Aphrodite and the Knife-Grinder), an alert social awareness with the expression of personal moods. Rydberg (1828–95) harmonized in his work romantic idealism, classical form, and national inspiration; thus he appears a successor to Stiernhielm and Tegnér. But the liberal ideology of *Dikter* (1882, 1891)—whose loftiness and formal perfection are reminiscent of Matthew Arnold at his best—informed his lyricism of profound reflection with a distinctly modern note. Definitely social in tendency were the later poems, like *Den nya Grottesången* (The New Song of Grotti, 1891), with its fiery imprecations against industrial slavery.

The best poet of the 1880's was August Strindberg (1849–1912), who, primarily a prose dramatist, possessed a lyrical gift of high distinction. By its deep concern with actuality and by its free, deliberately careless rhythm, his poetry signified the final break with the ideas and the style of late romanticism. Moreover, his fresh and daring imagery became inspirational for the 1890's. Strindberg's *Dikter på vers och prosa* (Poems in Verse and Prose, 1883) and *Ordalek och småkonst* (Word-Play and Minor Art, 1902–5) contain a world of impressions, moods, and visions. Scenes from the big city coexist with family idylls, and both are effectively contrasted with chords of passion in poems like *Chrysaetos* and *Holländarn* (The Dutchman). With its loose rhythm and its mathematical-scientific imagery,

his powerful hymn to the female body in the latter poem anticipated the poetry of recent decades. Like Stagnelius and Almquist, Strindberg in his lyricism as well as in his later expressionistic plays prepared the way for the poetic modernism of the postwar period. Of other poets of the 1880's, Ola Hansson (1860–1925) renounced realism in an attempt, inspired by Poe, Nietzsche, and Mallarmé, to penetrate beneath appearances. In this endeavor he was aided effectively by a superb sense of rhythm.

In the 1890's Swed. poetry experienced a veritable renascence. Ideologically no great novelties emerged, as the *Weltanschauung* remained naturalistic; and technically the new poetry inherited the minute observation and psychological analysis of the naturalists. Yet, the renascence was decidedly neoromantic in character: sensuous beauty, the imagination, and the self were apotheosized. In the matter of the self the concern was not purely individualistic, but national as well; the decade evinced, in its choice of subjects from Swed. history as also in the deeper local patriotism expressed in the regional poetry, a desire to rediscover its roots and redefine the nation's identity. Even technically, the poets reverted to romanticism, as they desired to create a grand style and practiced a variety of forms.

Four lyrists, Heidenstam, Levertin, Fröding, and Karlfeldt, were the vehicles of this poetic renewal. Verner von Heidenstam (1859–1940), originally a painter, already with his first collection, *Vallfart och vandringsår* (Pilgrimage and Wander-Years, 1888), created an epoch in Swed. poetry. It was written in an impressionistic, richly visual style replete with baroque images and daring coinings. This romanticism schooled in realism, later called "imaginative naturalism" by Heidenstam himself, would have been impossible without the example of Strindberg, although Heidenstam, to be sure, was no disciple. In *Dikter* (1895) —supported theoretically by *Renässans* (Renascence, 1889) and *Pepitas bröllop* (Pepita's Wedding, 1890), which settled with "shoemaker realism" both in art and philosophy—the central themes of his lyricism appeared. These themes, the glories of the imagination, of his native region, and of his country, were also the basis of *Ett folk* (One People, 1920), a narrative cycle in which Heidenstam did homage to the knightly and heroic virtues that he considered distinctively Swed. Oscar Levertin (1862–1906), Heidenstam's friend, both as critic and poet contributed to the new movement, of whose exponents he was the most romantic. The main themes of his work, love and death, were treated in a richly textured style influenced by the Eng. Pre-Raphaelites.

Gustaf Fröding (1860–1911) is one of the

greatest lyric poets of Sweden. Already *Guitarr och dragharmonika* (Guitar and Concertina, 1891), which had been theoretically prepared for by his essay *Om humor* (On Humor, 1890), displayed a fully matured talent. It was precisely its brilliant, contagiously gay humor that differentiated this collection from the rest of contemporary poetry. *Nya dikter* (New Poems, 1894) contained also poems that were serious, even somber, in tone, like *Bibliska fantasier* (Biblical Fantasies), in which a dark *Weltschmerz* found expression. But it was only in *Stänk och flikar* (Splashes and Rags, 1896) that Fröding laid bare the deepest layers of his psyche, whether in the form of Nietzschean superman fantasies, in erotic poems celebrating pagan beauty, or in harrowing personal confessions like *Narkissos*. Here also, in *Sagan om Gral* (The Grail Saga), one observes his first attempt to attain a mystical catharsis of life's paradoxes by way of metaphysical humor. The last great figure in the peculiar Swed. tradition of spontaneous realistic lyricism beginning with Wivallius, Fröding is the most beloved of all native poets in his own country, excelling both Tegnér and Heidenstam despite their openly professed national programs. He is also more immediately attractive to non-Swedes. This universal appeal is due partly to his wide range of theme and emotion, but chiefly, one suspects, to his naked intensity and the innate skill with which he exploits the lyrical potentialities of the Swed. language. This language, with its undulating rhythm, rich modulation, and great variety of expressive vowel sounds, is admirably suited for lyric poetry, and it is not surprising that the strength of Swed. poetry lies precisely in this genre. Swed. is an especially eloquent medium for the expression of surging passion and grotesque humor, and both Bellman and Fröding display a prodigious virtuosity in these modes. The latter could conjure with rhythm, rhyme, and alliteration to produce the finest nuance of melody, tone, and mood. To suggest both the qualities of Swed. and the rich music of Fröding's verse, here are a few lines from his poem *En vårmorgon* (A Spring Morning), in trochaic meter:

Vårens vindar äro ljuva,
glädjens vemod milt de tala
till en själ, som sörjt sig sjuk,
livets vårfröjd kuttrar duva,
kvittrar gråsparv, visslar svala,
gungar björkens krona mjuk.

The winds of spring caress with love
A soul in pain from ceaseless sorrow.
Softly they speak of joys decaying.
Life's spring rapture stirs in the dove,
The chirping sparrow, the whistling swallow,
In the crown of the birch, gently swaying.

The last great poet of the 1890's, Erik Axel Karlfeldt (1864–1931), was the voice of his native region, Dalecarlia, whose landscape, people, and customs he presented in *Fridolins visor* (The Songs of Fridolin, 1898) and *Fridolins lustgård* (Fridolin's Pleasure Garden, 1901).

The writers who appeared after the turn of the century inherited both the realism of the 1880's and the neoromanticism of the 1890's; yet they worked out their own forms of expression. Bo Bergman (b. 1869), who with *Marionetterna* (The Puppets, 1903) initiated the pessimistic poetry of the big city, created a new style marked by clarity, everyday idiom, and simple rhythms. Vilhelm Ekelund (1880–1949), whose first poems evoked *fin de siècle* moods, developed a lyricism of deep reflection and showed a preference for unrhymed verse and free rhythms in the manner of Pindar, Hölderlin, and Strindberg. Anders Österling (b. 1884) kept within the limits of traditional verse and adopted in *Idyllernas bok* (The Book of Idylls, 1917) a moderate poetic realism inspired by the Eng. Georgian poets.

World War I affected Swed. poetry profoundly, imbuing it with pessimism and religious questing. Metaphysical unrest is evident in the work of Dan Andersson (1888–1920), who formally, however, followed the tradition of the 1890's. More significant was the early poetry of Pär Lagerkvist (b. 1891), whose manifesto *Ordkonst och bildkonst* (Verbal and Pictorial Art, 1913) announced a radical modernism, related to Ekelund's experiments and to expressionism in painting. In *Ångest* (Anguish, 1916) he expressed moods of anxiety in an unadorned, unrhythmical verse of striking novelty. Slightly anticipating the Swed.-Finnish modernists (q.v.), Lagerkvist laid the groundwork for the subsequent modernist movement in Swed. poetry. Close to him intellectually was Erik Blomberg (b. 1894), whose Faustian lyric confession *Den fångne guden* (The Captive God, 1927) inspired younger writers. Blomberg's evolutionary humanism became an important rallying-point for poets in an age of religious skepticism. In the 1920's the melancholy idyll, related to Österling's poetry, was the predominant genre. The bourgeois idyll was dissolved, however, in the work of Erik Lindorm (1889–1941), a realistic proletarian poet of everyday city life, similar in technique to Bo Bergman. With Birger Sjöberg (1885–1929), a troubadour of disillusion not unlike Bellman, a new spirit and style came to fruition. Sjöberg's *Kriser och kransar* (Crises and Laurel Wreaths, 1926) expressed postwar anxiety in an idiom characterized by violent dissonances, achieved through fearless use of slang and jargon in serious and solemn contexts.

The definite breakthrough of modernism—

the development of which constitutes a central movement in 20th-c. Swed. poetry—came with the appearance in 1929 of the anthology *Fem unga* (Five Young Poets), two of whose contributors, Harry Martinson (b. 1904) and Artur Lundkvist (b. 1906), should be noted. These writers, whose program found a nonliterary complement in a primitivism inspired by D. H. Lawrence, reinforced Lagerkvist's emphasis on immediacy of poetic expression by demanding the use of objective visual imagery—a doctrine derived, however belatedly, from the American imagists. Spiritually akin to primitivist modernism was the work of Karin Boye (1900–41), probably Sweden's most gifted poetess. With the critical 1930's a distinction became apparent between "pure" and "engaged" poets. Of the former, Gunnar Ekelöf (b. 1907), a Swed. surrealist, further elaborated the modernistic technique by employing musical principles of poetic structure, nonlogical syntax, and verbal telescoping *à la* James Joyce. The leading "engaged" poets were Hjalmar Gullberg (1898–1961), Johannes Edfelt (b. 1904), and Bertil Malmberg (1889–1958), none of whom was a programmatic modernist. But both Gullberg and Edfelt practiced Sjöberg's disturbing reversals in rhythm and idiom; and when drawing upon classical tradition, they used it in a characteristically modern manner: to reinforce their somber probings of the contemporary psyche through ironical contrast. During the 1940's the modernist movement, headed by Erik Lindegren (b. 1910) and Karl Vennberg (b. 1910), advanced on a broad front. Encompassing the programs and techniques of both the "pure" and the "engaged" poets of the 1930's, it was in scope comparable to the Phosphorist movement, from which it differed, however, by combining universalism with a relentless social and cultural awareness. Epochal was Lindegren's *Mannen utan väg* (The Man Without a Way, 1942), a cycle of irregular sonnets in which the disorder of the war years was given a deliberately chaotic expression. Of *fyrtiotalisterna*, q.v. ("The Poets of the Forties"), most of whom followed Vennberg, one may mention Werner Aspenström (b. 1918), Bernt Erikson (b. 1918), and Stig Carlson (b. 1920). Strongly influenced by T. S. Eliot, Vennberg's poetry is critical-analytical in method as well as in aim; but beneath his intellectual scepticism one discerns a quest for a viable *Weltanschauung*. In the 1950's a new aesthetic-religious romanticism appeared, in counterbalance to the largely culturally oriented poetry of the 1940's. Significant of the new intellectual climate was Bo Setterlind (b. 1923), whose objective nature poetry with symbolic overtones is pervaded with mysticism and cosmic wonder. Foremost among the numerous new poets are Folke Isaksson (b. 1927) and Tomas Tranströmer (b. 1931). Besides these may be mentioned Sandro Key-Aberg (b. 1922), Lars Forssell (b. 1928), Ingemar Gustafson (b. 1928), Paul Andersson (b. 1930), and Göran Printz-Påhlson (b. 1932). Though the 1950's were far less originative than the preceding decade, the sheer number of practicing young poets in Sweden raise high expectations of future achievement.

WORKS AND ANTHOLOGIES: *Poems by Tegnér*, tr. H. W. Longfellow and W. L. Blackley (1872); E. Tegnér, *Fritiofs saga*, ed. G. T. Flom (1909; annotated ed.); G. Fröding, *Selected Poems*, tr. C. W. Stork (1916); *Svensk diktning*, ed. J. Mauritzson (2 v., 1917; an annotated anthol.); *The Oxford Book of Scandinavian Verse*, ed. E. W. Gosse and W. A. Craigie (1925); *A Selection from Modern Swed. Poetry*, ed. C. D. Locock (1930); *Anthol. of Swed. Lyrics from 1750–1925*, ed. C. W. Stork (1930; poems in tr.); *Levande svensk dikt från fem sekel* (2 v., 1945; a compreh. anthol.); *Swed. Songs and Ballads*, ed. M. S. Allwood (1950); *20th C. Scandinavian Poetry*, ed. M. S. Allwood (1950); *Lyrikboken*, ed. Tage Nilsson (1951; an illustrated anthol.); *40-talslyrik*, ed. B. Holmqvist (1951); *50-talslyrik*, ed. B. Holmqvist and F. Isaksson (1955).

HISTORY AND CRITICISM: E. W. Gosse, *Northern Studies* (1890); A. B. Benson, *The Old Norse Element in Swed. Romanticism* (1914); H. Schück, *Hist. de la litt. suédoise* (1923); H. Boor, *Schwedische Lit.* (1924); O. Sylwan *et al.*, *Svenska litteraturens historia* (2d rev. ed., 3 v., 1929); H. G. Topsøe-Jensen, *Scandinavian Lit. from Brandes to Our Own Day*, tr. I. Anderson (1929); O. Sylwan, *Den svenska versen från 1600-talets början* (3 v., 1925–34) and *Svensk verskonst från Wivallius till Karlfeldt* (1934; studies in the formal aspects of Swed. verse); L. Maury, *Panorama de la litt. suédoise contemporaine* (1940); E. N. Tigerstedt, *Svensk litteraturh.* (1948; stimulating crit. survey); E. Bredsdorff *et al.*, *An Introd. to Scandinavian Lit.* (1951; useful short survey); C. A. D. Fehrman, *Kyrkogårdsromantik: Studier i engelsk och svensk 1700-talsdiktning* (1954; a comparative study, summarized in Eng.); I. Holm and M. von Platen, *La Litt. suédoise* (1957); E. N. Tigerstedt *et al.*, *Ny illustrerad svensk litteraturh.* (5 v., 1955–58; standard lit. hist., with annotated bibliog.); G. Brandell, *Svensk litt. 1900–1950* (1958); A. Gustafson, *A Hist. of Swed. Lit.* (1961; best crit. hist. in Eng., with bibliog.); R. B. Vowles, "Post-War Swed. Poetry . . . ," *Western Humanities Rev.*, 15 (1961); G. C. Schoolfield, "The Recent Scandinavian Lyric," BA, 36 (1962). S.L.

SWISS POETRY. It is extremely difficult to conceive a Swiss national literature because of the four languages—German, French, Italian, Romansh—spoken in Switzerland. The poetry of German Switzerland is a part of G. literature just as the poetry of Fr. and It. Switzerland is a part of Fr. and It. literature. Only the Romansh-speaking areas are linguistically independent and only there does the spoken language completely coincide with the language of literature (see ROMANSH POETRY), whereas in all other parts, especially in G. and It. Switzerland, the colloquial language (dialect) differs considerably from the written language. The common basis of the polylingual Swiss nation—the common political (democratic) ideals and institutions, the common history, tradition and culture—does not automatically weld four linguistic media into a national literature. There may be found, however, a unity in this diversity.

GERMAN-SWISS POETRY. In G. Switzerland a paucity of lyric poetry may be almost a characteristic feature. A vivid sense of reality, inimical to speculation and abstraction, is furthermore not conducive to purely dramatic creation, particularly in tragedy. The accent falls above all upon plastic presentation, upon the projection of images, upon display, upon spectacle. Pictorial actualization and descriptive imagery are essential stylistic characteristics of Alemanic-Swiss poetry. Significantly enough, the only important G.-Swiss handbook of poetics, the *Critische Dichtkunst* (1740) by J. J. Breitinger, 1701–76 (inspired by J. J. Bodmer, 1698–1783), places in the foreground the theory of "poetic painting." The imagination of the reader is compared to an empty canvas upon which the poet paints his ideas in clear, graphic depiction. The works of nature are the prototypes of all art and must be duplicated as faithfully as possible. This proximity to nature is likewise a dominating characteristic of Swiss poets and, to an extent, may be attributed to the peasant origin of their culture. The beauty and omnipotence of nature (above all of the mountain landscape), the struggle for and against nature, have left distinct traces in Swiss poetry. (Jeremias Gotthelf, 1797–1854, exclusively a prose-writer, is the greatest representative of this peasant attachment to nature.) It is astonishing how many poet-painters are to be found in G.-Swiss literature, for example, N. Manuel, S. Gessner, G. Keller. Sheer delight in observation and a naive joy in contemplation dominate. One may regard the verses from Keller's *Abendlied* as a "Leitmotif" of Swiss poetry:

Augen, meine lieben Fensterlein, . . .
Lasset freundlich Bild um Bild herein.

However, Bodmer and Breitinger also permit the poet to imitate invisible nature. The poet becomes a creator when he brings an invisible reality to a tangible realization and endows it with body, hence with poetic reality. Thus there is room in this rationalistic 18th-c. theory for irrational, fantastic elements. The epic genre is most commensurable to such a background: the great poets of Switzerland have all been significant prose story-tellers. It is indicative that Bodmer's and Breitinger's poetic conceptions have been popularized and continued by J. G. Sulzer in his encyclopedic *Allgemeine Theorie der schönen Künste* (1771–74).

Swiss poetry is far more intimately connected with the development of the state than is G. poetry. Common political ideals are the basic strength of the Swiss nation. The growth of the confederacy was accompanied by a plethora of political songs, often of meager artistic quality, such as the songs of the legendary hero William Tell; battle songs and war ballads (e.g. the *Sempacherlied*); rhymed chronicles, etc. From the foundation of the confederacy, literature concerned itself, both critically and eulogistically, with the Swiss state and with Swiss customs. Note especially Wittenweiler's *Ring;* the epigrams of J. Grob; J. C. Lavater's (1741–1801) *Schweizerlieder;* and many poems of G. Keller. With J. G. von Salis (1762–1834), one of the few lyric poets, an uninterrupted series of "Heimwehgedichte" (poems of homesickness) begins. From the outbreak of World War I, however, attention concentrates more and more upon the world outside Switzerland, particularly upon Europe and humanity, as, for example, in the poems of K. Stamm or R. Faesi (b. 1883):

Völker, wir wollen euch Leidgenossen,
Dir, Heimat, Eidgenossen sein.

As the result of a rationalistic attitude, which concentrated upon the present and upon fitness for life, a didactic tendency may be perceived throughout the whole history of Swiss poetry, from Haller's philosophical poems to the anthroposophic mission of A. Steffen 1884–1963. Bodmer and Breitinger emphasize specifically the didactic fable as the most desirable genre of poetry. (Note the original animal fables by J. L. Meyer von Knonau, 1705–85.) The artist solely as artist is basically suspect. In the presence of such an attitude, one should not expect experiments in form. Two poets, who proved to have a true talent for form, H. Leuthold (1827–79) and Dranmor (L. F. Schmid, 1823–88), significantly enough, practiced their virtuosity not upon Swiss soil but in foreign countries.

As early as 1300, the minnesingers B. Steinmar von Klingnau and J. Hadlaub showed Swiss traits. They did their best work in the vivid description of external events rather than in introspective probing into their own souls.

H. Wittenweiler's *Ring* (ca. 1420), simultaneously a mirror and satire of customs and a textbook of knowledge, reveals an unusual understanding of the people. His brilliant imagination, often unbridled, is combined with humor without which it is hard to imagine any Swiss poet. In the belligerent poems of the Reformation a similar combination of realism and humanism appears (P. Gengenbach, 1480–1525; N. Manuel, 1484–1530). The Swiss contribution to the poetry of the baroque is negligible. Only the lively epigrams of J. Grob (1643–97) deserve attention. A. von Haller (1708–77) provides the most significant realization of the poetic theories of Bodmer and Breitinger: in his poem *Die Alpen* he was the first to describe in picturesque language and with scientific accuracy the beauty and divine scheme inherent in the mountains. In rhythmic prose S. Gessner (1730–88) adds the more gentle nature of his idylls to this rugged world.

The most prominent Swiss prose writer, G. Keller (1819–90), is also the most representative lyric poet. In his poems are combined all the features which find typical Swiss representation: a most lively imagination; a joy in external realities; a love for nature, home and humor; a sense of democracy, which is cosmopolitan in its perspective but keeps an awareness of local tradition. The aristocratic C. F. Meyer (1825–98) found in art a substitute for a vigorous contact with life. Far from crass reality, he reached out into the past and into the realm of art to create poems of great perfection. Many of them anticipated in their unified imagery the later accomplishments of symbolism. C. Spitteler's (1845–1924) relationship to his time and to democracy was one of defiance. His cosmic verse-epics (e.g. the mammoth *Olympischer Frühling*, 18,000 verses) give evidence of an undeniable spaciousness of thought. A fascinating grace of expression—rare in G.-Swiss literature—distinguishes the anachronistic verse-idylls of Spitteler's friend J. V. Widmann (1842–1911).

In a predominantly urbane generation, the "awakening of the heart" at the time of World War I led to a renewed prominence of lyric poetry which has lasted until today. The upheavals of the time are reflected in the rhythmically erratic, symbolic language of K. Stamm (1890–1919) and A. Zollinger (1895–1941). Many poems of the following contemporary poets demonstrate that G.-Swiss poetry is on the point of acquiring musical dimensions which it has lacked hitherto: S. Lang (b. 1887); M. Rychner (b. 1897); W. Zemp (1906–59); A. Ehrismann (b. 1908); U. M. Strub (b. 1910); Silja Walter (b. 1919); A. X. Gwerder (1923–52); H. Boesch (b. 1926).

ANTHOLOGIES: *Die Schweizer Minnesinger*, ed.

K. Bartsch (1886); *Silhouetten*, ed. P. Kägi (I, II, 1917); *Historische Volkslieder der deutschen Schweiz*, ed. F. Waldmann, O. v. Greyerz (1922); *Schweizer Balladen*, ed. A. Fischli (1924); *Die Ernte schweizerischer Lyrik*, ed. R. Faesi (1928; G., Fr., It., Romansh, L., folk songs); *Schweizer Dichtung im Querschnitt*, ed. S. Lang (1938; G., Fr., It., Romansh); *Schweizer Lyrik*, ed. G. Zürcher (1944); *Minnesangs Frühling in der Schweiz*, ed. and tr. M. Geilinger (1945); *Zürcher Lyrik* (1955; contemporary poetry); *Lyriker der deutschen Schweiz, 1850–1950*, ed. H. Helmerking (1957).

HISTORY AND CRITICISM: J. Bächtold, *Gesch. der deutschen Lit. in der Schweiz* (1892); H. E. Jenny, *Die Alpen-Dichtung der deutschen Schweiz* (1905); O. Walzel, *Die Wirklichkeitsfreude der neueren schweizerischen Dichtung* (1908); H. E. Tièche, *Die politische Lyrik in der deutschen Schweiz, 1830/50* (1917); O. v. Greyerz, *Das Volkslied der deutschen Schweiz* (1927); S. Singer, *Die mittelalterliche Lit. der deutschen Schweiz* (1930); J. Nadler, *Literaturgeschichte der deutschen Schweiz* (1932); E. Ermatinger, *Dichtung und Geistesleben der deutschen Schweiz* (1933; best general survey); A. Bruggisser, *Heimat- und Weltgefühl in der schweizerischen Lyrik* (1945); M. Blöchliger, *La poésie lyrique contemporaine en Suisse Allemande* (1947); A. Bettex, *Die Lit. der deutschen Schweiz von heute* (1950); A. Zäch, *Die Dichtung der deutschen Schweiz* (1951; best introd.); E. S. Trümpler, "Zur Lit. der deutschen Schweiz von heute," *Monatshefte*, 47 (1955); F. Ernst, *Gibt es eine schweizerische Nationallit.?* (1955); K. Schmid, "Versuch über die schweizerische Nationalität," *Aufsätze und Reden* (1957); M. Wehrli, "Gegenwartsdichtung der deutschen Schweiz," *Deutsche Lit. in unserer Zeit* (2d ed., 1959).—The following include other Swiss literatures as well: E. Jenny and V. Rossel, *Gesch. der schweizerischen Lit.* (2 v., 1909f); G. de Reynold, *Histoire littéraire de la Suisse au XVIIIe siècle* (1912; v. II, Bodmer et l'Ecole suisse); J. Moser, Ch. Clerc, et al., *Littératures de la Suisse* (1938); H. de Ziègler, *La Suisse littéraire d'aujourd'hui* (1944); G. Calgari, *Storia delle quattro letterature della Svizzera* (1959).

DIALECT POETRY: In G. Switzerland, from the 17th c. on, a rich dialect poetry has paralleled that of the literary language. This literature possesses, to an even greater degree, the joy in reality, the nearness to the soil, the picturesque and homely elements, which appear in more elevated literature. Since this dialect poetry remains an almost closed book to the non-Swiss, mention of a few names may suffice: J. M. Usteri (1763–1827); G. J. Kuhn (1775–1849); A. Corrodi (1826–85); M. Lienert (1865–1933); Sophie Hämmerli-Marti (1868–1942); D. Müller (1871–1953); J. Reinhart (1875–

1957).—ANTHOLOGIES: *Silhouetten,* ed. P. Kägi (III, 1918); *Schwyzer Meie,* ed. A. Guggenbühl, G. Thürer (3d ed., 1938); *Bluemen us euserem Garte,* ed. A. Guggenbühl, K. Hafner (1942).— HISTORY AND CRITICISM: O. v. Greyerz, *Die Mundartdichtung der deutschen Schweiz* (1924); H. Trümpy, *Schweizerdeutsche Sprache und Lit. im 17. und 18. Jh.* (1955).   E.S.T.

FRENCH-SWISS POETRY. Although the literature of Fr. Switzerland is a part of Fr. literature, the literary works produced here offer certain common characteristics. They reflect the social life and structure of small towns and small independent republics. Most often they express the uneasiness and isolation of one who feels divided in the very sources of his culture: on one side, history—on the other, language. Whenever France becomes a danger for the independence of Switzerland, the Fr.-Swiss literature stresses its essentially Swiss qualities; whenever political centralization tends to give too much influence to G. Switzerland, the Fr.-Swiss literature turns toward France and thus reveals its indestructible ties to the language. Calvinistic Protestantism offers an explanation for the fact that the problems of conscience, psychological analysis, and introspection are of chief importance.

These generalizations hold good for poetry, too. The result of political independence was at first an almost total sterility in literary matters in the 16th and 17th c. The refusal of the Fr. materialist philosophy of the 18th c. led to the so-called "helvétisme littéraire," to the admiration of rural virtues, to the imitation of Salomon Gessner. After the Federal Constitution of 1848 which brought about a greater national unity, Fr.-Swiss poetry tended once more away from G.-Swiss influence into the sphere of influence of modern Fr. poetry. The 20th c. came to be the richest period of the "poésie romande," no doubt because the pains taken with language are the starting point of all poetry. Besides, "poésie pure" (not talking about one's feelings unless by farfetched analogies) agrees with Protestant reserve and its need for detours.

The following are the principal Fr.-Swiss poets and works from the beginnings to the present day. Middle Ages: Oton de Grandson (d. 1397) in his songs remained true to the tradition of the troubadours.—18th c.: Philippe-Sirice Bridel (1757–1845) published the *Poésies helvétiennes* (1782) in which he pictured alpine scenes in accordance with his own program for a Fr.-Swiss national poetry.—19th c.: Some spirited poets inspired by Béranger joined in the "Caveau genevois." The least forgotten of these patriotic humorists is J. Petit-Senn (1792–1870). The Genevan romantic Jacques-Imbert Galloix (1807–28) reveals in his posthumous collection of poems *Méditations lyriques* (1834) an extraordinary sensitiveness. Frédéric Monneron (1813–37) wrote beautiful love songs and metaphysical poems: *Poésies* (1852). Juste Olivier (1807–76) gives expression to the local atmosphere in his poems *Le Léman* and *Helvétie. Les chansons lointaines* (1847) are composed of political couplets à la Béranger. The most gifted of the romantics, Etienne Eggis (1830–67), was influenced by Germany. His *En causant avec la lune* (1851) has been called a "sumptuous babbling." Louis Duchosal (1862–1901), under the influence of Baudelaire, Verlaine and, later, Albert Samain, at the same time managed to maintain a personal note: *Rameau d'or* (1894). Henry Warnery (1859–1902), an idealist preoccupied with his own salvation, abandoned the traditional versification in *Sur l'Alpe* (1895); in *Aux vents de la vie* (1904) the religious feeling springs from the contemplation of nature.— 20th c.: The truly lyric Henry Spiess (1876–1940) made use of his musical talent to express the dilemma of man, torn between the desire of the flesh and the thirst of God: *Les chansons captives* (1910), *Saisons divines* (1920). The two most prominent authors of the 20th c. are C. F. Ramuz (1870–1947) and G. de Reynold (b. 1880). Ramuz, predominantly a prose writer, first tried his hand at poetry in *Le Petit Village* (1903). De Reynold, who made a name for himself as a historian and essayist, has been tempted to write verse as well; his poetry, collected in *Aux Pays des Aieux* and *Les Bannières Flammées,* is mainly concerned with the military, the heroic, and the legendary in the life and history of the Swiss.

René-Louis Piachaud (1896–1941), representative of a classic art, wrote verse of admirabe density in *L'indifférent* (1923), and in the *Poème paternel* (1932) Edmond-Henri Crisinel (1897–1948) strangely repeats the experience of Nerval. Pierre-Louis Matthey is the most powerful of the Fr.-Swiss poets; his poetic work can be said to be without a flaw: *Poésies* (1943). Gustave Roud is a man of untiring poetic quest across the country-side: *Ecrits* (1950). The rich literary production of Gilbert Trolliet has found a large reading public: *Offrande* (1944), *La Colline* (1955). Philippe Jaccottet devotes himself to the search of new rhythms: *L'Effraie* (1954).

ANTHOLOGIES: *Les chants du pays* (1883); *En pays romands,* ed. Sociétés de Belles-Lettres (1883–85); *Anthologie des poètes de la Suisse romande,* ed. E. de Boccard (1946).—HISTORY AND CRITICISM: Gonzague de Reynold, "Evolution de la litt. romande," *La Suisse une et diverse* (1923); C. Clerc, "La Suisse Romande," *L'Hist. de la litt. française,* ed. J. Bédier and P. Hazard (2 v., 1923–24); P. Kohler, "La litt. de la Suisse Romande," *L'Hist. de la litt. fr.,* III (1949); Weber-Perret, "La poésie," *Ecrivains*

Romands, 1900–1950 (1951).   w.-p. (tr. e.s.t.)

ITALIAN-SWISS. It. Switzerland is an extremely small country of limited resources and with a population of hardly 200,000. It is therefore not surprising that its literary production is equally modest in size. In the 16th c. there were several humanists; then in the 17th and 18th, poets busied themselves mostly with the translation of works by poets from other countries. Francesco Soave (1743–1806) must be mentioned here. His version of Salomon Gessner's *New Idylls* exercised a certain influence on the preromantic movement in Italy. In the 19th and 20th c. Francesco Chiesa, born in 1871, is of foremost significance. In his prose as well as in his lyrics he keeps up throughout an essentially poetic quality. In 1897 his first collection of poetry, *Preludio,* appeared; ten years later, the epic trilogy *Calliope,* the parts of which are: *La Cattedrale*—symbol of the Middle Ages where religious feeling predominates; *La Reggia*—the palace of a Renaissance prince, here symbol of the Renaissance governed by a spirit of wordliness and splendor; *La Città*—representative of the modern period, in a way the synthesis of those preceding. All in all there are 220 sonnets, many of them admirable, which remind us of the Fr. Parnassians (q.v.). A little later appeared *I viali d'oro* (1910). But the most beautiful of his poems are found in *Fuochi di primavera* (1919). Although Chiesa is recognized as the greatest It.-Swiss poet, there are others who deserve to be named. Giuseppe Zoppi (1896–1952) likewise excelled in prose and verse. *La nuvola bianca* (1923) is his best known collection of poetry. Valerio Abbondio has left several collections noted for their delicacy of feeling and language: *Betulle* (1922), *Cuore notturno* (1947).

ANTHOLOGIES: *Antologia di prose e poesie moderne,* ed. P. Tosetti (1902); *Scrittori della Svizzera italiana* (2 v., 1936); *Scrittori ticinesi da Rinascimento a oggi,* ed. G. Zoppi (1936).— HISTORY AND CRITICISM: G. Zoppi, *La poesia di F. Chiesa* (1920) and *La Svizzera nella lett. ital.* (1944); G. Locarnini, *Die literarischen Beziehungen zwischen der italienischen und der deutschen Schweiz* (1946); G. Calgari in *Storia delle quattro lett. della Svizzera* (1959).

     H.DE Z. (tr. e.s.t.)

RECENT TITLES: *Holderbluescht,* ed. G. Thürer (1962; dialect); *Schweizer Lyrik,* ed. W. Weber (1964; contemp.); W. Günther, *Dichter der neueren Schweiz,* I (1963); *Bestand und Versuch,* ed. B. Mariacher and F. Witz (1964).   E.S.T.

SYLLABA ANCEPS (L. "twofold syllable," the noun being from Gr.). A syllable which, independently of its real metrical value, can be counted as long or short, according to the requirements of the meter. This is especially true of the syllable at the end of a verse or of a few cola.—Koster; W. S. Barrett, "Dactylo-Epitrites in Bacchylides," *Hermes,* 84 (1956).   P.S.C.

SYLLABISM. See METER.

SYLLABLE. Linguistically, the domain of any degree of accent in spoken utterance. The s. is the smallest measurable unit of poetic sound, the fundamental building-block of metrical structure, and, in pure syllabic prosody (see METER), the only constituent to be regarded in the metrically normal line. See also PROSODY.   P.F.

SYLLEPSIS (Gr. "a taking together"). According to Herodian, the Gr. rhetorician of the 2d c. A.D. and two of his Gr. successors, the inclusive reference of a predicate to a compound subject where the predicate states a proposition true of only one part of the subject and untrue of the other part, e.g., "The north wind and the west wind that blow from Thrace" (true only of the north wind, *Iliad* 9.5; C. Walz, *Rhetores Graeci,* 9 v., 1832–36, v. 8, p. 604; cf. pp. 720, 753). This meaning is of little but historical interest, the quotation illustrating rather a trivial rhetorical fault than any virtue. The term was applied by the Byzantine rhetorician Gregory of Corinth (12th c.) to an expression in the *Iliad* that is not properly a figure of speech at all (*Iliad* 2.226–28), wherein the poet has subtly implied the pretentiousness of Thersites by making him include himself among the Achaean military aristocrats when he tells of spoils "we Achaeans" have taken. Here the subject of the verb, though plural, is not compound, nor would the statement convey any implicit meaning to a reader not already familiar with the worthless character of the speaker (Walz, v. 8, p. 776).

Later authorities distinguish two useful definitions of the term: (1). A kind of grammatical ellipsis, usually unobjectionable, in which, for the sake of economy, one word is used to refer to two or more other words with only one of which it agrees grammatically (so Johannes Susenbrotus, *Epitome troporum ac schematum,* 1541, ed. of 1621, pp. 25–26; contrast zeugma, q.v.), e.g., "Good Paulina, / Lead us from hence, where we may leisurely / Each one demand and answer to his part" (Shakespeare, *The Winter's Tale* 5.3.151–3); "My Ladie laughs for ioy, and I for wo" (George Puttenham, *The Arte of Eng. Poesie,* 1589, ed. of 1936, p. 165). (2). The use of any part of speech comparably related to two other words or phrases, correctly with respect to each taken separately, as to both syntax and meaning, but in different ways, so as to produce a witty effect, e.g., "Alta petens, pariterque oculos

SYMBOL

telumque tetendit" (he looked up [at the target, a captive pigeon] with gaze and arrow alike on the stretch—Virgil, *Aeneid* 5.508); "Whether the nymph shall . . . / Or stain her honor or her new brocade" (Pope, *The Rape of the Lock* 2.105-7). See *The Oxford Companion to Eng. Lit.,* 2d ed., 1937; H. L. Yelland and others, *A Handbook of Lit. Terms,* 1950.

S. should not be confused in any of the senses here defined with zeugma, q.v.   H.B.

SYMBOL. The word "symbol" derives from the Gr. verb, *symballein,* meaning "to put together," and the related noun, *symbolon,* meaning "mark," "token," or "sign," in the sense of the half-coin carried away by each of the two parties of an agreement as a pledge. Hence, it means basically a joining or combination, and, consequently, something once so joined or combined as standing for or representing in itself, when seen alone, the entire complex. This term in literary usage refers most specifically to a manner of representation in which what is shown (normally referring to something material) means, by virtue of association, something *more* or something *else* (normally referring to something immaterial). Thus a literary s. unites an image (the analogy) and an idea or conception (the subject) which that image suggests or evokes—as when, for example, the image of climbing a staircase (the difficulty involved in the effort to raise oneself) is used to suggest the idea of "raising" oneself spiritually or becoming purified (T. S. Eliot's *Ash Wednesday*).

A s. thus resembles what are known traditionally as "figures of speech" (cf. IMAGERY), which themselves comprise "tropes," or departures (turns) from the commonplace modes of signification, and "schemes," or artful elaborations of the forms of words and sentences. A s. is like a trope, in that a simile, metaphor, personification, allegory (qq.v.), and so on, each represent a manner of speaking in which what is said means something more or something else. But a s. is not a trope, and may be distinguished in terms of how it relates subject and analogy in a poem. In the other figures mentioned, what is said (analogy) is distinct from what is meant (subject), and their relationship is based upon a stated or implied resemblance within difference.

A s., on the other hand, puts the analogy in place of the subject (and may thus be thought of as an "expanded" metaphor—and, conversely, recurring metaphors in a given work are often spoken of as symbolic) so that we read what is said (climbing a staircase) as if that were what is meant, but are made to infer, by virtue of the associations provoked by what is said and the manner in which it is expressed, something more or something else as

the additional or true meaning (spiritual purification). Thus, an idea which would be difficult, flat, lengthy, or unmoving when expressed prosaically and by itself, may be made intelligible, vivid, economical, and emotionally effective by the use of symbols.

A s., then, may be called, for purely technical purposes, a "pseudo-subject." Nor need the relationship between what is said and what is to be inferred be based, as in metaphor and simile, merely upon resemblance, for many images have become potentially symbolic not through likeness only but also through one sort of association or another—as when the loss of a man's hair symbolizes the loss of strength (Samson) or the rejection of worldly desires (monastic and ascetic practice), not because of any resemblance between them but rather because a primitive and magical connection has been established between secondary sex characteristics, virility, and desire. Of course, an associative relationship may be established having resemblance as its basis when a metaphor or simile is repeated so often, either in the work of a single author or in literary tradition, that the analogue can be used alone to summon up the subject with which it was once connected. Similarly, many interpreters have pointed out that poets tend to use the metaphors and similes of their earlier work as symbols in their later work because of the associative relations thus established. Critics rightly warn, moreover, that symbolic associations of imagery should be made neither too explicit nor too fixed, for implications of this sort are best felt rather than explained, and vary from work to work depending upon the individual context.

The first question, however, which faces the reader of a poem is whether or not a given image is indeed symbolic to begin with. This question may be answered in at least three related ways: (1) the connection between s. and thing symbolized may be made explicit in the work, as with the "Sea of Faith" in Arnold's *Dover Beach;* (2) the image may be presented in such a way as to discourage a merely literal interpretation, as with Byzantium in Yeats's *Sailing to Byzantium,* since no such thing actually exists, or to encourage a more than merely literal interpretation, as with the garden in Marvell's poem of that name, since, although it does actually exist, it is made into something more by virtue of the speaker's reactions to it; or (3) the pressure of implicit association may be so great as to demand a symbolic interpretation, as with Ulysses in Tennyson's poem of that name, since that figure has received such extensive previous treatment in myth, legend, and literature (cf. Homer and Dante). Because there is today a tendency to apply symbolic interpretation rather loosely, it bears emphasizing at this point that an image in a work is not symbolic unless a literal interpretation fails to do it justice; that is to say, a negative test often helps—an image is literal until proved otherwise—and if a literal interpretation can account satisfactorily for its place and function in the work then it is probably not symbolic.

Once the presence of symbols has been established, however, the next question is how to interpret their place and function in the work. This question may be answered in terms of at least three overlapping areas of inquiry: (1) the source of their imagery in experience, whether from the natural world, the human body, man-made artifacts, and so on; (2) the status of their imagery in a given work, whether presented literally as an actual experience (so that it symbolizes something more) or nonliterally as a dream or vision (so that it symbolizes something else altogether); and (3) the way in which their imagery has acquired associative power, whether mainly by virtue of universal human experience (see ARCHETYPE), or particular historical conventions, or the internal relationships which obtain among the elements of a given work (whereby one thing becomes associated with another by virtue of structural emphasis, arrangement, position, or development—this aspect, is, of course, involved to some degree in all works containing symbols), or some private system invented by the poet, or some combination. Regarding the third area of inquiry, examples of universally understood symbols would include climbing a staircase (or mountain) as spiritual purification, crossing a body of water as some sort of spiritual transition, sunset as death and sunrise as rebirth, and so on; examples of conventional symbols would include the transmutation of lead to gold as redemption, the lily as chastity and the rose as passion, the tiger as Christ, and so on; examples of internal-relationship symbols would include the wall as the division between the primitive and the civilized or natural chaos and human order in Robert Frost, the guitar and the color blue as the aesthetic imagination in Wallace Stevens, the island as complacency and the sea as courage in W. H. Auden, and so on; and examples of private symbols would include the phases of the moon as the cycles of history combined with the psychology of individuals in W. B. Yeats, embalmment as an obstacle that cannot be overcome in the attempt to resurrect the spirit in Dylan Thomas (see Olson [bibliog.]), and so on.

In Frost's famous poem, *Birches,* for example, the speaker talks of climbing to the top of a birch tree and swinging on it back down to earth again in such a way that the reader is given to understand that this action means something more than just climbing up and swinging down. That is to say, in the context of this poem the action comes to mean for its speaker a temporary release from the difficulties and responsibilities of daily life (climbing up and away from earth toward heaven) and a subsequent return to those mundane limitations once again refreshed (swinging back down to earth). Climbing, then, stands for his desire to get away, while swinging down stands for his recognition that he must, after all, live out his life on earth where the gods have placed him. Thus this action, which at first seemed to be the speaker's subject, turns out ultimately to be an analogue of his subject (which in no way, of course, diminishes the value and interest of the imagery in itself).

According to the three areas of inquiry outlined above, this symbolic imagery may first be analyzed as coming from the natural world in combination with actions of the human body: earth, heaven, tree, climbing up and swinging down. It is presented, secondly, as literal occurrence. And thirdly, its associative power derives from universal experience—earth as limitation and heaven as release—in combination with internal relationships—the act of swinging from a birch as seen in this context.

Yeats's *Sailing to Byzantium,* on the other hand, is rather more complicated in its symbolism. Here the speaker talks of sailing the seas and coming to the holy city of Byzantium, but, because this cannot be taken literally, what he actually means (again the warning against being too specific in explaining the meaning of symbols must be recalled) is that he wants to divest himself of mortality and its limitations and dwell—probably through the forms of art—in eternity. Notice, however, in the first place, that Byzantium as a symbolic image is derived from man-made artifact (although sailing as transition is not); secondly, that it is presented as a vision and not as something which has literally happened or could literally happen; and thirdly, that, in addition to internal relationships, the associative power of this image depends for its force upon—or at least is aided greatly by—a knowledge of exactly what it meant to Yeats in his private symbology. Thus the symbolism of different writers may be distinguished, characterized, and interpreted. (Even here, however, such categories must be applied flexibly, for Yeats's Byzantium image, although it does indeed have crucial private associations, is also related to the universal image of the "holy city" [e.g., Jerusalem] as fulfillment or redemption.)

Historically, men once tended to see the physical world in terms of spiritual values, not only by way of generating universal symbols (the world as a body, for example, or man's body as a state, and so on) but also of developing—through myth, lore, legend, craft, and learning—special conventions. And it is one of the doctrines of modern criticism that, partly due to the Protestant Reformation, partly to the changes gradually effected in school curricula, partly to the growth of science, and partly to the mere passing of time, not only have many conventional symbols been rendered meaningless to poets and readers alike but also the very power of seeing the physical world in terms of spiritual values has disappeared. Thus symbolism has been called in the 20th c. the "lost" or the "forgotten" language.

Certain 20th-c. poets, following the lead of the 19th-c. Fr. "symbolists" (Baudelaire, Verlaine, Rimbaud, and Mallarmé each in his own way explored afresh the possibilities of the private symbolism of vision and dreams), and partly under the influence of a renewal of interest in Donne, Blake, and Hopkins, have attempted not only a revival of conventional religious and legendary symbolism, as has Eliot in *Ash Wednesday*, for example, but also have tried, in what they have felt to be a collapse of spiritual values, to invent their own symbolic conventions (Yeats is only the most obvious, with Ezra Pound, Hart Crane, Wallace Stevens, and Dylan Thomas working along similar if less systematic lines). Other poets, such as Frost, William Carlos Williams, and E. E. Cummings, have by and large been content to use natural, literal, universal, and contextual symbols.

The differences of opinion which exist today regarding the nature and function of symbolism in literature are due principally to the variety of ways in which the term is used in the service of different critical theories. This is true for many other terms as well, for a critic's use of any given term is governed by the assumptions he makes about literature and the kind of knowledge he is interested in obtaining. One cannot, therefore, compare and contrast the interpretations of different critics without first realizing what their assumptions and goals are, and consequently how they use their various terms.

Elder Olson, for example, as a neo-Aristotelian, is primarily concerned with literary works in their aspect as artistic wholes of certain kinds. Since he sees artistic wholeness in terms of the over-all effect which a work is designed to have upon the reader—whether doctrinal, as in the case of didactic works, or emotional, as in the case of mimetic works—and since a s. cannot produce such an effect apart from the poem of which it is a part, he regards symbolism as a device which is sometimes used by an author in the service of that effect (to aid in the expression of remote ideas, to vivify

what otherwise would be faint, to aid in determining the reader's emotional reactions, and so on).

Other critics, however, having a more general notion of artistic form, are less precise in their definitions. Because Yeats, for example, as a symbolist, is primarily interested in the suggestive powers of poetry, he extends his definition of symbolism to include not only images, metaphors, and myths, but also all the "musical relations" of a poem (rhythm, diction, rhyme, and so on). Because Krieger, Wheelwright, Langer, Cassirer, and Urban, as anti-positivists, are concerned with defending poetry as having epistemological status, they stress in their use of the term its powers of bodying forth nondiscursive meaning, truth, or vision. Because Kenneth Burke, as a student of language in terms of human motives, deduces the form of a literary work from speculation as to how it functions in relation to the poet's inner life, he emphasizes the way in which various elements of that work symbolize an enactment of the poet's psychological tensions. Because the writers in Bryson's anthologies, as social critics, are interested in the uses of symbolism in a cultural context, they focus on the term as referring to the ways in which societal phenomena in general (insigne, designs on currency, structure of public buildings, motion pictures, and so on) serve as indicators of the values of a people.

Thus, if symbolism refers generally to the use of one thing to stand for another, then its specific meanings will vary according to the framework in which this relationship is viewed. A s. is a device of the poetic art when it refes to something in the poem as standing for something else in the poem; it is a power of poetic language when it refers to the way words and rhythms can evoke mystery; it is a function of the whole poem when it refers to the kinds of meaning a literary work can stand for; it is a form of therapeutic disguise when it refers to the ways in which a poem stands for the working out of the author's inner disturbances; and it is an index of cultural values when it refers to the ways in which man's products reveal his attitudes. Since the word is thus capable of such protean meanings—some of them overlapping at certain points—it is obviously best, when using the term, to specify the exact sense intended.

W. B. Yeats, "The Symbolism of Poetry" (1900), *Ideas of Good and Evil* (2d ed., 1903); H. Bayley, *The Lost Lang. of Symbolism* (2 v., 1912, repr. 1951, 1952); D. A. Mackenzie, *The Migration of Symbols* (1926); H. Flanders Dunbar, *Symbolism in Medieval Thought* (1929); W. M. Urban, "The Principles of Symbolism," *Lang. and Reality* (1939); K. Burke, *The Philos. of Lit. Form: Studies in Symbolic Ac-*

tion (1941); Langer; C. M. Bowra, *The Herit-age of Symbolism* (1943); E. Cassirer, *An Essay on Man* (1944); M. Krieger, "Creative Crit.: A Broader View of Symbolism," sr, 58 (1950); T. Mischel, "The Meanings of 'S.' in Lit.," *Arizona Quar.*, 8 (1952); E. Olson, "A Dialogue on Symbolism," in Crane, *Critics*; Special Issue of yfs, no. 9 (1952–53); Special Issue of jaac, 12 (Sept. 1953); C. Feidelson, *Symbolism and Am. Lit.* (1953); B. Kimpel, *The Symbols of Religious Faith* (1954); E. Olson, "The Universe of the Early Poems," *The Poetry of Dylan Thomas* (1954); *Symbols and Values* (1954) and *Symbols and Society* (1955), both ed. L. Bryson *et al.*; P. Wheelwright, *The Burning Fountain* (1954) and *Metaphor and Reality* (1962); W. Y. Tindall, *The Lit. S.* (1955); H. Levin, *Symbolism and Fiction* (1956); Frye; F. Kermode, *Romantic Image* (1957); J. W. Beach, *Obsessive Images: Symbolism in the Poetry of the 1930's and 1940's* (1960); *Lit. Symbolism*, ed. M. Beebe (1960); *Metaphor and S.*, ed. L. C. Knights and B. Cottle (1960); B. Seward, *The Symbolic Rose* (1960); *Symbolism in Religion and Lit.*, ed. R. May (1960); H. Musurillo, *S. and Myth in Ancient Poetry* (1961); *Myth and S.*, ed. B. Slote (1963). N.FRIE.

SYMBOLIC ACTION is a term used by Kenneth Burke to signify, first, that poetry is different from practical action, but parallel to it and, in a sense, symptomatic of it. Poetry is a way of "acting out" tensions and symbolically resolving irresolutions in the poet. His fundamental trope in criticism is poetry as drama. The poet forms a role and then transforms it, symbolic death and rebirth being the primary pattern. At times Burke speaks of three levels of symbolic action (*Philosophy of Literary Form*, 36–37): biological, familistic, and abstract, but more typically he deals with "act, scene, agent, agency, purpose" as the best modes for understanding literature and philosophy. Polar oppositions (sublime-ridiculous) and image clusters (often elaborately interpreted) are important in and to his method, and synecdoche, or the part for the whole, is to him the *basic* literary device. The resemblance to Freudian criticism is evident, but he carefully avoids the Freudian metaphysical reduction of all levels of meaning and motive to the sexual, biological level, and attempts to interpret motive more charitably than does Freudian criticism generally.—S. Freud, *Psychopathology of Everyday Life* (1901; chap. 9); K. Burke, *Counter-Statement* (1931), *The Philos. of Lit. Form* (1941), "Symbol and Association," hr, 9 (1956); Y. Winters, *In Defense of Reason* (1947); G. Knox, *Crit. Moments: Kenneth Burke's Categories and Critiques* (1957). See also W. H. Rueckert, *Kenneth Burke and the Drama of Human Relations* (1963). P.R.

SYMBOLISM (movement). Historically, s. follows Parnassianism (see PARNASSIANS) as a continuation of the great romantic revolution in Fr. poetry of the 19th c. Its subject matter shows a return to the intimate emotional and aesthetic experience of the individual after the more objective stress of the Parnasse; but s. differs from historical Fr. romanticism in its greater subtlety and preoccupation with the inner life and in its general avoidance of sentimentality, rhetoric, narration, direct statement, description, public and political themes, and overt didacticism of any kind. It marks a fusion of the sensibility and imagination, which the romantics had restored to Fr. poetry, with the lucid craftsmanship of the Parnassians, and a turn toward music and *le rêve* for evocative expression. Symbolist poetry is a poetry of indirection, in which objects tend to be suggested rather than named, or to be used primarily for an evocation of mood. Ideas may be important, but are characteristically presented obliquely through a variety of symbols and must be apprehended largely by intuition and feeling. Symbolist poets use words for their magical suggestiveness—what Rimbaud termed *l'alchimie du verbe* and Baudelaire *une sorcellerie évocatoire*; and one of their essential aims is to arouse response beyond the level of ordinary consciousness, in what was called after Hartmann *l'inconscient*. For the symbolists the power of the Word goes far beyond ordinary denotative verbal limits through suggestive developments in syntax and interrelated images and through what may be termed the "phonetic s." of musicality and connotative sound-relationships. Profoundly evocative poetry of this sort is essentially different from that which had predominated in France since the late Renaissance; and its appearance in Fr. literature entailed a more evident renovation of lyric poetry than would have been possible in England and Germany, many of whose earlier poets had already much in common with the later Fr. symbolists.

Among the more important foreign writers and philosophers influencing or showing affinities with Fr. s. may be cited, from the British Isles: Berkeley, Coleridge, Shelley, Keats, Carlyle, Ruskin, Rossetti, Morris, Swinburne and Pater; from Germany: Schiller, Fichte, Hegel, Hölderlin, Novalis, Schelling, E.T.A. Hoffmann, Schopenhauer, and Wagner; and from the United States: Emerson, Poe, and Whitman. Wagner was especially important, not only for his music but for his insistence upon the ideal relation between music and poetry (". . . the most complete work of the poet must be that which, in its final achievement, would be a perfect music"). But the greatest single influence was exerted by Poe, who came to prefigure an ideal of the poet for several of the

SYMBOLISM

great Fr. symbolists. More important than his poems, Poe's theories proclaimed the idea of an absolute Beauty and the importance of the poem "written solely for the poem's sake"; urged in poetry "a certain taint of sadness," the need for images with indefinite sensations, and the "absolute essentiality" and vast importance of music; and represented the poet as a thoroughly conscious artist.

Among native Fr. writers, links have been seen between the symbolists and the mystical and idealistic predecessors of the *Pléiade* (q.v.) in *l'école lyonnaise* (Antoine Héroët, Gilles Corrozet, Maurice Scève, and Louise Labé). Rousseau and Chateaubriand ("the Enchanter") may be considered precursors of s. in their use of musical and affective language. The *tristesse lamartinienne* with its remarkable musicality is a prelude to the more delicate music of Verlaine. In the poetry of Vigny, the function of such symbols as the waterfall (in *Le cor*) that establishes the strange ambience for the fall of Roland and the Peers at Roncevaux, and the sound of the weathercock *en deuil* (in *La mort du loup*), with its premonitory note of mourning, anticipate symbolist techniques. Sainte-Beuve is a precursor of Fr. s.; and Victor Hugo, in his visionary power and his evocative mingling of image and music, often shows symbolist qualities. But of all the Fr. romantic poets Gérard de Nerval (1808–55) is nearest to the new poetry, and in the compressed, musical, and difficult sonnets of *Les chimères* (1854) seems to anticipate the art of both Verlaine and Mallarmé.

Charles Baudelaire (1821–67) is the first great symbolist poet of France. It has become apparent that with Baudelaire's *Les Fleurs du Mal* (1857) Fr. poetry had assimilated the lessons of Eng. and German romanticism and rejoined the great European lyric tradition from which it had been in great part separated since the Renaissance. With *Les Fleurs du Mal*, Baudelaire (in his proclaimed effort to "extraire la *beauté du Mal*") brought to Fr. poetry a renewed sense of the magical power of words and a symbolic, mythical vision of the great modern city and of modern man ("l'héroisme de la vie moderne"). His sonnet *Correspondances* describes man moving through a "forest of symbols" familiarly related to his existence, and proclaims two kinds of interrelated *correspondences*: (1) those (in the manner of Swedenborg and the great mystics generally since Plato) between the material world and spiritual realities, and (2) those between the different human sense modalities (see SYNAESTHESIA). Baudelaire's memorable depiction of the "delicate monster" Ennui and of the struggle in man between Spleen and the Ideal; his Satanism; his exploiting of the various senses, especially that of smell; his interest in

the "artificial paradises" (opium, hashish, wine), in dandyism, in decadence; his development of the *prose poem* (q.v.); his theories on *correspondences* and on art and the artist; his translations and adaptations from Poe; and his enthusiasm for Wagner combined with the general prestige of *Les Fleurs du Mal* to make Baudelaire the most significant native influence upon the rising symbolist movement in France.

Verlaine, Rimbaud, and Mallarmé, the three great symbolist poets of the later 19th c., all felt Baudelaire's influence. Paul Verlaine (1844–96), one of the most delicate Fr. lyricists, published his first volume of poetry (*Poèmes saturniens*) in 1866. Already in this collection, where Verlaine shows himself still influenced by Parnassian theory, such poems as *Chanson d'automne* and *Mon rêve familier* sound a characteristic note of musical nostalgia in which "the language is vaporized and reabsorbed into the melody" (Michaud). Among Verlaine's significant later volumes are *Fêtes galantes* (1869), *La bonne chanson* (1870), *Romances sans paroles* (1874), *Sagesse* (1881), and *Jadis et naguère* (1884). Verlaine's "Art poétique" advocates "music before everything," use of *le vers impair* (verse of an uneven number of syllables: 5,7,9,11 instead of the usual 6,8,10,12), and urges that ideal poetry should be as fugitive and intangible as the scent of mint and thyme on the morning wind—something very like the conception of *poésie pure* (see PURE POETRY) championed in the 20th c. by the Abbé Bremond. Aside from his influence on Fr. prosody, Verlaine was influential as a symbol of "decadence." His lyric gifts were personal, and his evocative poems introduced into Fr. literature an intimate impressionism hardly known before his time. Verlaine was not by nature a theorist or a poet of ideas. But he brought music and poetry into a relationship that is in itself a kind of miracle.

Arthur Rimbaud (1854–91), the precocious boy-genius among the symbolists who gave up poetry before he was nineteen, inspired a "myth" that has not yet lost its fascination and that in itself symbolizes a rebellious aspect of the modern creative mind. Rimbaud saw the poet as a *mage*, a *seer*, and wrote that "le poète se fait *voyant* par un long, immense et raisonné *dérèglement* de tous les sens." (The poet makes himself *a seer* by a long, immense and reasoned *derangement* of all the senses.) Rimbaud's *Bateau ivre* (September 1871), composed before his seventeenth birthday, is one of the most memorable poems of the century. Its strange rhythms, hallucinatory descriptions of land and sea, brilliant colors, and alternating violence and calms; its employment of symbols concerned with the beginning of the world (Tohu-Bohu, Behemoth, Leviathan); its

-[837]-

powerful mingling of fresh, adolescent sensations with apocalyptic visions; and the ultimate evocation, from what seems at first a chaos of images, of impressive form and meaning combine to make the poem a masterpiece of Fr. s. The sonnet *Voyelles* (1871) is of less importance; but its sensational proclamation that the vowels are colored ("A noir, E blanc, I rouge, U vert, O bleu, voyelles. . . ."), though not original (see AUDITION COLORÉE), aroused violent controversy and led to exteme exaggeration in such analogous attempts as René Ghil's *Traité du verbe* (1885) and P.-N. Roinard's *Cantique des cantiques* (1891). Between 1871 and 1873 Rimbaud wrote a collection of verses and prose poems (*Les illuminations*) published in 1886, and the autobiographical *Une saison en enfer* (published by Rimbaud in 1873, but never circulated; reprinted in 1892). Rimbaud's experiments with rhythm in *Les illuminations* (e.g., in *Mouvement* and *Marine*) have led to his being identified by some critics as the inventor of vers libre (q.v.). His influence has been enormous. Dame Edith Sitwell calls this marvelous boy "the originator of modern prose rhythms" and adds that "Rimbaud is, to modern English verse and to modern English and American prose poems, what Edgar Allan Poe was to Baudelaire and Mallarmé." In the words of Pierre Jean Jouve: "Avec Rimbaud nous entrons dans la langue moderne de la Poésie."

The last of the great Fr. symbolist poets of the 19th c. is Stéphane Mallarmé (1842–98), the exquisite, hermetic master whose Tuesday evenings in his apartment on the Rue de Rome were attended at one time or another by most of the famous symbolists of the day. Mallarmé's early poems show already the influence of Baudelaire, along with that of Hugo, Gautier, and Banville. Poems of the second period (e.g., *Hérodiade* and *L'après-midi d'un faune*) have more characteristic developments of complex suggestion, imagery and verbal music; and those of the third period become increasingly condensed and remote and culminate in the variously interpreted *Un coup de dés jamais n'abolira le hasard*. Mallarmé is known as one of the most difficult Fr. poets; and the bitterness of his frustration in not finding words for the ideal is seen in his symbol of the white swan with wings imprisoned in a frozen lake ("Le vierge, le vivace et le bel aujourd'hui, . . ."), and in his unhappy admission to Louis le Cardonnel: "Mon art est une impasse." But Mallarmé was by no means a sterile poet. He saw life differently from those around him, and evolved his own technique of combining symbols with verbal music, typography and patterned suggestion to *evoke* as nearly as possible his aesthetic and metaphysical ideal. According to Mallarmé, a poem is a mystery whose key must be sought by the reader, and poetry is primarily suggestion: "Nommer un objet, c'est supprimer les trois quarts de la jouissance du poème qui est faite du bonheur de deviner peu à peu: le *suggérer*, voilà le rêve" (To name an object is to suppress three-fourths of the delight of the poem which is derived from the pleasure of divining little by little: to *suggest* it, that is the dream). A passage in "Crise de vers" (from *Divagations*, 1897) indicates at once the difficulties and fascination of his method: "Abolie, la prétention, esthétiquement une erreur, quoiqu'elle régit les chefs-d'oeuvre, d'inclure au papier subtil du volume autre chose que par exemple l'horreur de la forêt, ou le tonnerre muet épars au feuillage; non le bois intrinsèque et dense des arbres" (Abolished, the claim, aesthetically an error, although it governs masterpieces, of including on the subtle paper of the volume anything more for example than the horror of the forest, or the silent thunder scattered through the leaves: not the intrinsic, dense wood of the trees). Although critics find Hegelian influence in Mallarmé (e.g., in *Igitur*), ideas in his poems are not meant to be apprehended directly by reason, but indirectly, symbolically, through poetic intuition. "Je dis: une fleur!" he writes, "et, hors de l'oubli où ma voix relègue aucun contour, en tant que quelque chose d'autre que les calices sus, musicalement se lève, idée même et suave, l'absente de tous bouquets" (I say: a flower! and, out of the oblivion into which my voice consigns every outline, apart from the known calyxes, there arises musically, the delicate idea itself, the flower absent from all bouquets).

About 1885, the year of Hugo's death, the symbolists became more widely known through such works as Verlaine's *Les poètes maudits* (1884), Huysmans' *A rebours* (1884), and the amusing parodies in Gabriel Vicaire's and Henri Beauclair's *Les déliquescences d'Adoré Floupette, poète décadent* (1885). This period saw the discovery of two "decadent" poets related to s. who introduce a new note of irony into Fr. poetry: Tristan Corbière (1845–75), the author of *Les amours jaunes* (1875), who was brought to the attention of the public as one of Verlaine's *poètes maudits* (q.v.), and Jules Laforgue (1860–87) with *Les complaintes* (1885) and *L'imitation de Notre-Dame la Lune* (1886).

Between Baudelaire, Verlaine, Rimbaud, and Mallarmé and the last great symbolist poets (Claudel and Valéry) Fr. symbolists like René Ghil, Stuart Merrill, Vielé Griffin, Jean Moréas, Henri de Régnier, and Gustave Kahn seem on the whole less important than their Belgian contemporaries (Rodenbach, Verhaeren, Maeterlinck, Van Lerberghe, Elskamp). The last years of the century teemed with theoretical discussion in print and in the symbolist cafés of the Latin Quarter (Le François Ier, Le Vachette, Le Panthéon, Le Procope, Le Soleil d'Or). On September 8, 1886, *Le Figaro* published the symbolist manifesto of Jean Moréas. Important periodicals championed the symbolist cause: *La revue wagnérienne* (1885–88), *La Wallonie* (1886–92), *La plume* (1889–1905), *Mercure de France* (1890–), *L'Ermitage* (1890–1906), *La revue blanche* (1891–1903); and s. became recognized as a movement. But the greatest symbolist poets had already done their work. In 1891, Jules Huret's famous *Enquête sur l'évolution littéraire* indicated the triumph of the symbolists and the fading prestige of naturalism in France.

In the 20th c., Guillaume Apollinaire echoes at times the music of Verlaine; Paul Claudel, turning to Catholicism under the influence of Rimbaud, brings a liturgical quality to his s.; and Paul Valéry, the follower of Mallarmé, in *La jeune Parque* and *Le cimetière marin* creates two of the most memorable of symbolist poems. The surrealists discovered Isidore Ducasse ("le comte de Lautréamont"), whose *Chants de Maldoror* (1868–69) afford another link between s. and the *poème en prose*. Fr. symbolists are important in the background of surrealism (q.v.) itself, as André Breton recognized in remarks on Nerval, Baudelaire, Rimbaud, and Mallarmé. Their influence is evident also in contemporary drama and brief fiction and in the novel since Flaubert. (D. Hayman has recently shown the significant influence of Mallarmé on *Finnegans Wake*, and Fiser identifies Marcel Proust as the greatest symbolist of all.) Thus the music, the dream, and the poetic symbol of s., like romantic lyricism and imagination in an earlier day, have invaded the most important literary genres of the present century.

Influence of the Fr. symbolists may be traced in many poets from other lands; e.g., the British Isles: in Arthur Symons, Ernest Dowson, Walter de la Mare, Lionel Johnson, Oscar Wilde, George Russell ("Æ"), and William Butler Yeats; Germany: in Stefan George and Rainer Maria Rilke; Austria: in Hugo von Hofmannsthal; Russia: in Valery Bryusov, Innokenty Annensky, Zinaida Gippius, Fyodor Sologub, Constantine Balmont, Alexander Blok, Andrey Bely, and Vyacheslav Ivanov; Spain: in Antonio Machado, Juan Ramón Jiménez, and Jorge Guillén; Portugal: in Eugenio de Castro; also, Nicaragua: in Rubén Darío; Uruguay: in Julio Herrera y Reissig; and the United States: in Amy Lowell, Hilda Doolittle ("H. D."), John Gould Fletcher, Ezra Pound, T. S. Eliot, Hart Crane, E. E. Cummings, and Wallace Stevens. (See also NATIONAL POETRY ARTICLES.)

A. Symons, *The Symbolist Movement in Lit.* (1899); W. B. Yeats, "The S. of Poetry" (1900)

in *Ideas of Good and Evil* (2d ed., 1903); A. Barre, *Le symbolisme: essai historique . . .* (1911); J. Charpentier, *Le s.* (1927); R. Taupin, *L'influence du s. français sur la poésie américaine (de 1910 à 1920)* (1929); Martino; Wilson; E. L. Duthie, *L'influence du s. fr. dans le renouveau poétique de l'Allemagne* (1933); E. Fiser, *Le symbole littéraire: essai sur la signification du symbole chez Wagner, Baudelaire, Mallarmé, Bergson et Marcel Proust* (1941); C. M. Bowra, *The Heritage of S.* (1943); S. Johansen, *Le s.: étude sur le style . . .* (1945); L. Cazamian, *S. et poésie: l'exemple anglais* (1947); G. Davies, "Stéphane Mallarmé: Fifty Years of Research," FS, 1 (1947); A. J. Mathews, *La Wallonie, 1886–1892: The Symbolist Movement in Belgium* (1947); G. Michaud, *La doctrine symboliste: Documents* (1947) and *Message poétique du s.* (3 v., 1947); T. S. Eliot, *From Poe to Valéry* (1948); Raymond; Lehmann; K. Cornell, *The Symbolist Movement* (1951) and *The Post-Symbolist Period* (1958); O. A. Maslenikov, *The Frenzied Poets: Andrey Biely and the Rus. Symbolists* (1952); G.-E. Clancier, *De Rimbaud au surréalisme* (1953); R. Z. Temple, *The Critic's Alchemy: A Study of the Introd. of Fr. S. into England* (1953); L. J. Austin, *L'univers poétique de Baudelaire: s. et symbolique* (1956); J. Chiari, *S. from Poe to Mallarmé: The Growth of a Myth* (1956); B. Gicovate, *Julio Herrera y Reissig and the Symbolists* (1957); H. Hatzfeld, *Trends and Styles in 20th C. Fr. Lit.* (1957); O. Ragusa, *Mallarmé in Italy* (1957); G. Donchin, *The Influence of Fr. S. on Russian Poetry* (1958); M. Décaudin, *La crise des valeurs symbolistes* (1960); H. M. Block, *Mallarmé and the Symbolist Drama* (1963).   A.G.E.

SYMBOLS, PROSODIC. See PROSODIC NOTATION.

SYMPATHY. See EMPATHY AND SYMPATHY.

SYMPLOCE. See ANADIPLOSIS.

SYNAERESIS (Gr. "a drawing together"), often synonymous with synizesis. In Gr. and L. poetry it occurs when two adjacent vowels of a word which are ordinarily separate syllables are combined for metrical purposes into one syllable, e.g.,

$\overline{\text{theoi}}$ for *theoi* (*Iliad* 1.18) or Theudosius for

Theodosius

In Eng. poetry it similarly occurs, e.g., "seest" for "seëst" or "zoo" for "zoö."—Hardie.   R.A.H.

SYNAESTHESIA. Term denoting the perception, or description of the perception, of one sense modality in terms of another; e.g., perceiving or describing a voice as velvety, warm, heavy, or sweet, or a trumpet-blast as scarlet. The word occurs in 1891 in *The Century Dictionary*, but in the sense concerned here seems to have been first employed by Jules Millet in his thesis on *Audition colorée* (Montpellier, 1892). S. was popularized by two sonnets (Baudelaire's *Correspondances* [1857] and Rimbaud's *Voyelles* [in MS, 1871]) and Huysmans' novel *A rebours* (1884); but it had been widely employed earlier in German and Eng. romantic poetry, and it occurs in the earliest literature of the West (e.g., in *Iliad* 3.152, where the voices of the old Trojans are likened to the *lily-like* voices of cicalas; in *Iliad* 3.222, where Odysseus' words fall like winter snowflakes; and in *Odyssey* 12.187 in the *honey-voice* of the Sirens). In Aeschylus' *Persians* (line 395), "the trumpet set all the shores ablaze with its sound." Horace writes (*Odes* 1.24.3–4) of a *liquidam vocem*. Hebrews 6.5 and Revelations 1.12 refer to *tasting* the word of God and *seeing* a voice. John Donne mentions a *loud perfume*, Crashaw a *sparkling noyse*. Shelley refers to the fragrance of the hyacinth as *music*, and Heine to words *sweet as moonlight and delicate as the scent of the rose*. Silence is *perfumed* (Rimbaud), *black* (Pindar), *dark* ("Ossian" [Macpherson]), *green* (Carducci), *silver* (Wilde), *blue* (D'Annunzio), *chill* (Edith Sitwell), *green water* (Louis Aragon). For Milosz the smell of silence is "so old"; for Sartre it is like violets. Dylan Thomas writes of the *light of sound* and *sound of light*. Kipling's dawn *comes up like thunder*. Lorca refers to *green wind* and Mary Webb to the *icy voices* of curlews. S. has been exploited for varied purposes, but attempts to establish it as in itself a sign of illness, degeneration, or decadence seem to be inspired largely by prejudice or ignorance; for s. occurs very widely in language and literature in an apparently universal role among civilized peoples as the metaphor of the senses.—V. Ségalen, "Les synesthésies et l'école symboliste," *MdF*, 42 (1902); I. Babbitt, *The New Laokoön: An Essay on the Confusion of the Arts* (1910; chap. 6); E. v. Siebold, "Synästhesien in der . . . Dichtung des 19. Jhs.," *Englische Studien*, 53 (1919–20); W. B. Stanford, *Gr. Metaphor* (1936); G. Maurevert, "Des sons, des goûts et des couleurs: Essai sur les correspondances sensorielles," *MdF*, 292 (1939); S. de Ullmann, "Laws of Language and Laws of Nature," *MLR*, 38 (1943) and "Romanticism and S.," PMLA, 60 (1945); A. G. Engstrom, "In Defense of S. in Lit.," PQ, 25 (1946); G. O'Malley, "Literary S.," JAAC, 15 (1957).   A.G.E.

SYNALOEPHA, synalepha, synalephe (Gr. "coalescing"). In Gr. and L. poetry the contraction of a long vowel or diphthong at the end of one word with a vowel or diphthong at the beginning of the next into a long syllable.—Koster; L. Brunner, "Zur Elision langer Vokale im lateinischen Vers," *Museum Helveticum*, 13 (1956).   R.J.G.

SYNCOPATION. See COUNTERPOINT.

SYNCOPE (Gr. "a cutting up"). Omission of a letter from the middle of a word (see POETIC CONTRACTIONS). In Gr. poetry the compression of a rhythmical unit such as a trochee or dactyl into one syllable which is then felt to be exceptionally long. L. poetry appears not to do this.   R.A.H.

SYNECDOCHE (Gr. "act of taking together," "understanding one thing with another"). An important figure, often quite properly regarded as a special type of metonymy (q.v.), wherein the part is substituted for the whole, or sometimes the whole for the part: *elephas* (ivory for elephant); *melissa* (honey for bee). Quintilian (*Institutes of Oratory* 8.6.19–21) illustrates from L.: *mucro* (point for sword); *tectum* (roof for house), etc., but forbids others like *puppis* (stern for ship). Besides being a common device in ordinary speech and a rhetorical ornament, s. is sometimes used to describe cases where something is assumed that has not been expressed: "Arcades ad portas ruere" (The Arcadians to the gates *began* to rush—Virgil, *Aeneid* 11.142), though Quintilian considers such omission, when it creates a blemish, to be an ellipse (q.v.), a narrower definition than usual.

Generally, any internal relation of entity or concept may be used in synecdochic expression, as species for genus, material for thing made, abstract quality for being possessing it, etc., but some rhetoricians limit s. to four types: part for whole, species for genus, whole for part, genus for species, thus separating s. from *merismus*, or *partitio*, wherein the whole is distributed into its parts (Sister Miriam Joseph, *Shakespeare's Use of the Arts of Language*, 1947, p. 315). Often s. assumes intricate forms: "Two thousand souls and twenty thousand ducats / Will not debate the question of this straw," *Hamlet* 4.4.25.

Kenneth Burke sees s. as implying a relation of convertibility between its terms. He emphasizes the philosophical implications of the figure, pointing out the synecdochic nature of the ancient metaphysical doctrines of microcosm and macrocosm, in which the individual entity is seen as recapitulating the nature and structure of the universe ("Four Master Tropes" in *A Grammar of Motives*, 1945, pp. 503f.). Lausberg investigates s. as (1) trope, (2) word-trope, (3) figure of thought (i.e., "*Gedanken-Tropus*"), and (4) ellipse.   R.O.E.

TAGELIED

SYNTHESIS. See ANALYSIS.

SYNTHETIC RHYME results from the alteration by contraction, protraction, or distortion of one or more rhyme-fellows to produce phonetic identity or at least approximation, e.g.:

> The consequence was he was lost to*tally,*
> And married a girl in the corps de *bally.*
> (W. S. Gilbert, *Patience*)

Such liberties with language are not confined to light or humorous verse, common as they are in Butler, Byron, Barham, and Ogden Nash, to raise a smile. There are many, for example, in *The Faerie Queene,* some of them very forced; and plenty of others, less licentious perhaps, can be found in quite serious poetry at any period. A.M.C.

SYNTHETIC RHYTHM is one maintained by repeating a word to fill up the line, or by padding it out with an expletive or extra syllable. It is common in balladry, e.g.: "He hadna gane a step, a step, / A step but barely ane . . ."

(*The Ballad of Sir Patrick Spens*) and in folk songs. A.M.C.

SYSTEM (Gr. *systema*). In Gr. metric a sequence of cola (see COLON) in the same meter. Hephaestion (2d c. A.D.) in his longer treatise *On Meters* used this term instead of *periodos* to describe a metrical "period" of several cola. —Kolář; Koster. R.J.G.

SYZYGY (also phonetic syzygy). A term from classical prosody used to describe the combining of two feet into a single metrical unit. Phonetic s. is a term apparently originated by Sylvester and adopted by Lanier and others to describe consonant sound patterns and repetitions not covered by the term "alliteration" (q.v.). It has been objected to by Saintsbury and other critics as unnecessary, obscure, and confusing. Such terms as "mosaic alliteration" and "colliteration," among others, have been advanced as names for the same phenomenon. See also SOUND IN POETRY.—J. J. Sylvester, *Laws of Verse* (1870); S. Lanier, *The Science of Eng. Verse* (1880); G. Saintsbury, *A Historical Manual of Eng. Prosody* (1910); K. Burke, *The Philos. of Lit. Form* (1941), pp. 369–78. R.BE.

T

TACHTIGERS ('80ers, the generation of the 1880's). A group of young Dutch poets and prose writers who, in the last two decades of the 19th c., revived their country's literature from a lethargy of almost 200 years and restored it to a respectable position in European letters. In reaction against the then dominant sentimentalism, didacticism, and domesticity of Dutch poetry, the poets Kloos, Verwey, and van Eeden organized *De Nieuwe Gids* (The New Guide), a publication in which their doctrines of individualism, aestheticism, and realism were preached by precept and example. In addition to the *Nieuwe Gids* group, which also included the poet Herman Gorter, the short-lived Jacques Perk (1859–81) deserves mention as a Tachtiger. The T. were sensitive to a variety of foreign influences, chiefly Eng. romanticism, contemporary Fr. symbolism and naturalism, and the German *Kunst für die Kunst* movement. The very diversity of Tachtiger ideals prophesied the instability of any formal school of T.; the major figures of the movement developed in different directions after 1890. But their metrical and lexical innovations and, even more important, their example of artistic dedication assured the vitality

of 20th-c. Dutch verse. See also DUTCH POETRY. —F. Coenen, *Studiën van de Tachtiger Beweging* (1924); A. Donker, *De episode van de vernieuwing onzer poëzie* (1929); G. Stuiveling, *Versbouw en ritme in de tijd van '80* (1934); G. Colmjon, *De oorsprong van de renaissance der litteratuur in Nederland in het laatste kwart der negentiende eeuw* (1947). F.J.W.

TAGELIED ("Dawn Song"). A type of medieval German love lyric, analogous to and derived from the alba (q.v.) of the troubadours. The type first appears in a poem by Dietmar von Aist (fl. 1140–70), the earliest minnesinger who seems to have an acquaintance with troubadour lyrics. But neither Dietmar's poem nor Heinrich von Morungen's so-called T. are typical of the genre; the T. is best represented by and receives its highest development at the hands of Wolfram von Eschenbach. Wolfram introduced the Prov. figure of the watchman who warns the lovers of the coming of dawn, when they must part, and he gives depth and dramatic force to his poems. Later writers of the T. include Hadlaub and Oswald von Wolkenstein. Parodies of the type also occur in the late Middle Ages, e.g., Steinmar's *Lied* 8.

According to de Boor and other scholars, the T. made its way into bourgeois-social lyrical poetry (*Gesellschaftslied*, q.v.), turned into the folk song, and—by way of conscious elevation to a spiritual level—took on the form of the religious song of admonition or reveille. However, a sort of later revival of the T., in a dramatic context, can be seen in the parting scenes in Shakespeare's *Romeo and Juliet* (3.5) and in Wagner's *Tristan und Isolde* (Act 2).— F. Nicklas, *Untersuchung über Stil und Gesch. des deutschen Tageliedes* (1929); *Texte zur Gesch. des dt. Tageliedes*, comp. E. Scheunemann and F. Ranke (1947); H. de Boor and R. Newald, *Gesch. der dt. Lit. von den Anfängen bis zur Gegenwart*, II (3d ed., 1957), III, pt.1 (1962); A. T. Hatto, "Das T. in der Weltlit.," DVLG, 36 (1962); *Eos*, ed. A. T. Hatto (1965; a monumental coll.).   A.P.

TAIL-RHYME (or tailed rhyme or, rarely, caudate rhyme) is the modern Eng. rendering of ME *rime couwee*, from Fr. *rime couée*, which in turn is from medieval L. *rhythmus caudatus* or *versus caudati* (cf. G. *Schweifreim*). The phrase designates a group of lines consisting of (a) a couplet, triplet, or stanza and (b) a following tail or additional shorter line. It could be applied to any such group; but it is generally reserved for a schematic recurrence. The tail may rhyme to a line in the couplet, triplet, or stanza, or to another shorter line after another couplet, triplet, or stanza; or it may be unrhymed to anything; or it may be a refrain, in the same formula throughout (as in Longfellow's *Excelsior* or Tennyson's *Ask me no more*) or in a varying formula (as in Burns's *Holy Fair*, "Fu' sweet that day," "Wi' fright that day," etc.). The most typical tail-rhyme is the romance-six, common in medieval romances and familiar from Chaucer's parody thereof, *The Rime of Sir Thopas*. Its scheme is 8,8,6,8,8,6 syllables, rhyming aabaab. Whittier in *Barclay of Ury* and O. W. Holmes in *The Last Leaf* keep the rhyme arrangement but reduce the syllables to 7,7,6,7,7,6 and 6,6,3,6,6,3 respectively. A similar grouping is Drayton's stanza in *The Ballad of Agincourt*, 6,6,6,5,6,6,6,5, rhyming aaabcccb. Many other arrangements of longer and shorter lines exhibit the phenomenon of tailing.—Schipper; Ker; A. McI. Trounce, "The Eng. Tail-Rhyme Romances," *Medium Aevum*, 1-3 (1932-34).   A.M.C.

TAMIL POETRY. See INDIAN POETRY.

TANKA (also called *waka* or *uta*). This Japanese lyric form of 31 syllables in lines of 5,7,5,7,7 syllables originated ca. 7th c. A.D., has continued to the present, and may be called the classic Japanese poetic form. Identified for centuries with the court, its diction has been traditional and elevated, and its subjects most often nature, love, laments, or such occasions as travel and felicitations.

The influence of tanka upon modern Western poetry has been vaguer and less extensive than that of haiku (q.v.) and is, therefore, more difficult to assess. The principal obstacles to fruitful understanding of t. have been ignorance—of its language, tradition, and techniques—and the fact that until recently the form has usually been viewed in terms of the exotic and poor translations of one anthology, the *Hyakunin Isshu* (One Poem from Each of a Hundred Poets). The exotic concept of t. merged with the impressionist view of the color print to represent Japanese poetry in terms of delicate, sensitive, coloristic, amoral, and (in theory at least) precise images. Although t. tends to treat separately its different subjects, Western conceptions and imitations of it usually merged nature, love, and the tone of the laments, in techniques borrowed from haiku.

This confusion of genres, in a haze of exoticism, often makes it difficult to distinguish the influence of one form from that of the other. This is particularly true of early Fr. interest (ca. 1905-10) and early Anglo-Am. interest (ca. 1910-15). Although none of our major poets has benefited materially from t., a few lesser figures have imitated it or translated translations (e.g., Amy Lowell, Ernest Fenollosa) or devised poetic forms on tanka lines (e.g., Adelaide Crapsey). As a model for experiment, t. was imitated by the imagists and some of their predecessors in France and England, but with less enthusiasm or profit than haiku.

Western estimation of t. probably has suffered from 19th-20th c. Japanese primitivizing of their own culture, a process which has led to a condemnation of the Court tradition of t. and to praise of the imagined greater "sincerity" of haiku. This attitude tended to keep certain of the most influential earlier translators and commentators from tanka; and although excellent Fr., Am., and German translations of this form in recent years have somewhat tempered exoticism and moderated attitudes toward these two genres, t. has not yet become as fruitful a source of poetic theory and technique as haiku and nō (q.v.). See also JAPANESE POETRY.—H. L. Seaver, "The Asian Lyric and Eng. Lit.," *Essays in Honor of Barrett Wendell* (1926); W. L. Schwartz, *The Imaginative Interpretation of the Far East in Modern Fr. Lit. 1800-1925* (1927); E. V. Gatenby, "The Influence of Japan on Eng. Lang. and Lit.," Japan Society (London), *Trans. and Proceed.*, 34 (1936-37); E. Miner, *The Japanese Tradition in British and Am.*

Lit. (1958); R. H. Brower and E. Miner, *Japanese Court Poetry* (1961). E.M.

TAPINOSIS (Gr. "lowering"). Abasement, diminution or deflation of something by means of degrading terms, calling someone bad names. It should not be confused with *meiosis* (q.v.), which means, literally, belittling and is allied with amplification. While t. is most prominent in comedy, satire, and vituperation, and in modern writing is more common in prose than in verse, it has been pointed out in a wide variety of compositions. Quintilian (8.3.48) cited the misguided tragic poet who spoke of a "stony wart on the brow of the mountain" ("saxea est verruca in summo montis vertice"). Servius called Virgil's "in gurgite vasto" (*Aeneid* 1.118) a t. because the poet referred to the great sea as a "gulf" (*gurges*). T. has been extended to include violations of *decorum:* Cicero's illustration in *Orator* 21 of discussing cases of roof-drainage in the grand style and then using beggarly language in speaking of the majesty of the Roman people; Horace's illustration in *Ars Poetica* 1 of the painter who joins a human head to the neck of a horse. The clearest examples, however, are familiar, vulgar terms used in place of polite terms. Puttenham, in the *Arte of Eng. Poesie,* used the example of the man who said to Queen Elizabeth's coachman, "Stay thy cart, good fellow, stay thy cart, that I may speak to the Queen." The exchanges of abuse between Thersites and his fellow soldiers in *Troilus and Cressida,* similar exchanges between Falstaff and his friends, and Petruchio's abuse of the tailor in *The Taming of the Shrew* 4.3.107–12 are obvious examples. Petruchio says: "Thou liest, thou thread, / Thou thimble, / Thou yard, three-quarters, half-yard, quarter, nail! / Thou flea, thou nit, thou winter-cricket, thou! / Braved in mine own house with a skein of thread! / Away! thou rag, thou quantity, thou remnant!" M.T.H.

TASTE. The term "t.," used in an aesthetic context, commonly refers (1) to a person's capacity to respond to aesthetic objects or (2) to the preferences that result from an exercise of this capacity. The capacity or the preferences may be treated factually: we have histories that describe national tastes or try to account for changes in taste from epoch to epoch; we have psychological studies of the nature of the capacity and sociological studies of the genetic, cultural, economic, and other conditioning forces that determine the aesthetic preferences of individuals or groups. However, in aesthetic theory, the term "t." frequently takes on normative overtones; it becomes synonymous with "good t." or "correct t." Thus, "He is a man of t." may mean "He is a person with the capacity for appreciating the truly excellent in art." Since theories differ as to the nature of the aesthetic experience, its value, and the kinds of reasons that justify aesthetic value judgments, the nature of the capacity to be possessed by the man of t. will inevitably differ from theory to theory. If the theory demands a precise adjustment of sound to sense, the man of t. must be one who can perceive and enjoy such an adjustment even to its finest shades. If the theory demands that a poem should have a desirable moral effect on a reader, the man of t. must be an expert judge of the quality of the message and of the power of the poem to convey this message. If the theory demands that poetry incorporate structures symbolic of archetypes in the subconscious, the man of t. must be one who is sensitive to the subconscious reverberations that such images produce.

Historically, the term "t." has been most closely associated with aesthetic theories that define their subject matter as the investigation of such qualities as beauty and sublimity, whether found in nature or the fine arts, and of the "aesthetic" responses that these qualities arouse. According to Spingarn, "t." first became an important term in European criticism in the late 17th c. Some critics, in reaction to the authority of neoclassic rules, interpreted t. as a special faculty of the mind that spontaneously and instinctively responds to aesthetic objects. Its relations, they said, are with "sentiment" or the "heart" rather than with the reason. The rules, the product of reason, hamper rather than encourage the production of certain types of valuable aesthetic effects; and the ability of an artist to create and a man of t. to perceive "the grace beyond the reach of art" (the *je ne sais quoi,* q.v.) was enthusiastically praised. It is the position of the "School of T." (Spingarn's term) that Reynolds had in mind when, in 1776, he said, "To speak of genius and t., as in any way connected with reason or common sense, would be, in the opinion of some towering talkers, to speak like a man who possessed neither; who had never felt that enthusiasm, or, to use their own inflated language, was never warmed by that Promethean fire which animates the canvas and vivifies the marble" (*Discourses on Art,* VII).

The School of T. had popularized the term "t.," and during the 18th c. a considerable amount of aesthetic discussion revolved around the term. In 1712 Addison, in his *Spectator* papers on t. and on the pleasures of the imagination (nos. 409, 411–421), formulated the main topics for this discussion. In these papers, he defines t. as "that faculty of the soul which discerns the beauties of an author with pleasure, and the imperfections with dislike." He points out that the term is a metaphor, found in most languages, based on a likeness of "mental t." to the "sensitive t. which gives us a relish of every different flavor that affects the palate." The chief signs of a well-developed state of this faculty are an ability to discriminate differences and to take pleasure in excellencies. Though t. is a natural faculty, it can be improved by reading the authors whose works have stood the test of time, by conversation with men of refined t., and by a familiarity with the views of the best ancient and modern critics. The critic whom Addison singles out for particular praise is "Longinus." "Longinus" is almost the only critic who has described a class of excellencies that are "more essential to the art" than the excellencies produced by adherence to "mechanical rules which a man of very little t. may discourse upon." The excellencies that Addison is particularly interested in are aesthetic qualities, which, in his papers on the pleasures of the imagination, he enumerates as novelty, beauty, and grandeur (sublimity).

An important line of 18th-c. critics (the chief of whom were Hutcheson, Hume, Gerard, Burke, Kames, Blair, Reynolds, and Alison) explored in detail this new approach to aesthetic problems. All of these critics were concerned, at least in part, with aesthetic qualities (to those listed by Addison a number of others were added, e.g., the picturesque, the witty, the humorous, the pathetic) and the nature of the faculty (t.) that perceives and enjoys them. Some of the questions concerning t. that these critics tried to answer were the following: Is t. a natural or acquired faculty? What is its relation to genius? Is it an independent faculty, a special internal sense, or is it derivative from man's other faculties? Is it a single faculty or a combination of simpler faculties? What is the relation of t. to reason, emotion, and morality? What is the relation of t. to the rules? To what extent can t. be changed or corrected and by what methods? Is there a standard that determines the correctness of t.? If there is such a standard, how can it be validated? How are divergencies in t. to be explained?

Eng. and Fr. 18th-c. critics, most of whom were empiricists, gave a bewildering variety of answers to these questions. The variety became even more bewildering when German transcendental philosophers and their followers in other countries began to speculate on beauty, sublimity, and other aesthetic qualities. The complex meaning of Kant's explanation of beauty ("purposiveness without a purpose") or Hegel's ("the sensuous appearance of the Idea") can be understood only in the light of each philosopher's transcendental assumptions. The transcendentalists also discovered faculties in the human mind undreamed of in empirical

philosophy, and t. achieved a dignity that it never had before. For example, Coleridge, echoing Kant, defines "t." as "the intermediate faculty which connects the active with the passive powers of our nature, the intellect with the senses; and its appointed function is to elevate the *images* of the latter, while it realizes the *ideas* of the former"; t. is "a sense, and a regulative principle, which may indeed be stifled and latent in some, and be perverted and denaturalized in others, yet is nevertheless universal in a given state of intellectual and moral culture; which is independent of local and temporary circumstances, and dependent only on the degree in which the faculties of the mind are developed" ("On the Principles of Genial Criticism," 1814).

T. remained an important concept for later beauty theorists, particularly for those who, like Poe and Pater, defended an "art for art's sake" position. Today, there are signs that this great tradition in aesthetics is coming to an end. Toward the end of the 19th c., Tolstoi severely attacked the philosophies of beauty and t. that had dominated 18th- and 19th-c. aesthetics. More recently, I. A. Richards has rejected the "phantom aesthetic state" (*Principles of Literary Criticism*, 1924, chap. II). And T. Munro describes the contemporary situation as follows: "Aesthetics was formerly regarded as 'the philosophy of beauty,' a subject devoted largely to explaining the nature of beauty and ugliness, with a few related ideas such as 'good taste' and 'the sublime.' These words occur much less often in contemporary discussion. There is no other small set of concepts to take their place, but a much wider range, to cope with the diverse phenomena of art and behavior toward art. . . . The psychology of art . . . is no longer limited to 'the sense of beauty,' 'good taste,' and the 'aesthetic attitude' in a narrow sense. . . . It studies a great variety of responses to art, of ways of experiencing and using it, all of which are in a broad sense aesthetic phenomena" (*Toward Science in Aesthetics*, 1956, p. 97; see also pp. 154–55). This new orientation, explicitly pluralistic, together with increased knowledge about the operations of the mind, has led to an abandonment or reformulation of the 18th-c. questions about t.

Throughout the history of criticism, a perennial problem has been the relation of t. (in the sense of preference or liking) to evaluation (q.v.). It is proverbial that there is no disputing about tastes ("de gustibus non est disputandum"); but the extreme position "I like this; therefore it is good" (where "I" may refer to any speaker) has seldom been defended by theoretical critics. Bentham (in *The Rationale of Reward*, 1825, Bk. III, chap. 1) argues that reading poetry may be for some people a less pleasurable and thus a less valuable activity than playing push-pin. Therefore, "it is only from custom and prejudice that, in matters of t., we speak of false and true." Indeed, critics like Addison, under the "pretense of purifying the public t.," have deprived "mankind of a larger or smaller part of the sources of their amusement." But then Bentham quickly adds that it is not only legitimate but necessary to speak of good and bad t. when the instrumental values of a preferred activity are included in the evaluation. Explicitly or implicitly, most theorists have placed evaluation above t. (whether the evaluative judgment is determined by the degree to which an artistic work conforms to theoretical principles or by the response of the cultivated mind of a man of good t.). They have not hesitated to call actual tastes good or bad when judged by the standards defended in their theories, nor have they hesitated to recommend that a person should make his tastes conform to what he *ought* to like. Thus Arnold, as part of his plea for the development of a "conscience" in intellectual and aesthetic matters, quotes Sainte-Beuve approvingly: " 'In France . . . the first consideration for us is not whether we are amused and pleased by a work of art or mind, nor is it whether we are touched by it. What we seek above all to learn is, whether *we were right* in being amused with it, and in applauding it, and in being moved by it' " ("The Literary Influence of Academies," *Essays in Criticism*, 1865). Most theorists agree with Arnold and Sainte-Beuve. But literature has many values, and different species of literature have different values. As long as each theorist insists on building a system that prescribes a class of values that literature ought to have and excludes all of its other possible values, a universally acceptable definition of "good t." cannot be formulated.

J. E. Spingarn, *Crit. Essays of the 17th C.* (1908); B. Croce, *Aesthetic*, tr. D. Ainslie (1909, best ed. 1922); I. Kant, *Critique of Aesthetic Judgment*, tr. J. C. Meredith (1911); A.F.B. Clark, *Boileau and the Fr. Classical Critics in England, 1660–1830* (1925); F. P. Chambers, *Cycles of T.* (1928) and *The History of T.* (1932); E. E. Kellett, *The Whirligig of T.* (1929) and *Fashion in Lit.* (1931); E. N. Hooker, "The Discussion of T., from 1750 to 1770, and the New Trend in Lit. Crit.," PMLA, 49 (1934); L. Venturi, *Hist. of Art Crit.*, tr. C. Marriott (1936); J. Steegmann, *The Rule of T.* (1936); J. Evans, *T. and Temperament* (1939); B. Heyl, "T.," in Shipley; H. H. Creed, "Coleridge on 'T.,' " ELH, 13 (1946); G. Boas, *Wingless Pegasus* (1950); F. L. Lucas, *Lit. and Psychology*, especially chap. XI "The Relativity of T.," (1951); H. A. Needham, *T. and Crit. in the 18th C.* (1952); A. Bosker, *Lit. Crit. in the Age*

of Johnson (2d ed. rev., 1953); W. J. Hipple, *The Beautiful, the Sublime and the Picturesque in 18th-C. British Aesthetic Theory* (1957); B. Markwardt, "Geschmack," *Reallexikon*, 2d ed., I (includes extended bibliog.); B. Jessup, "T. and Judgment in Aesthetic Experience," JAAC, 19 (1960).   F.G.

TECHNICAL CRITICISM. See CRITICISM, TYPES OF.

TELESILLEUM. An acephalous glyconic ($\simeq - \smile \smile - \smile -$), named after Telesilla, a poetess of Argos of the early 5th c. B.C. Like the Reizianum (q.v.), it occurs in Pindar and Gr. drama. A hymn to the Great Mother of the gods, written entirely in this meter and dating from the 2d c. A.D., was discovered in an inscription from Epidaurus.—J. U. Powell, *New Chapters in the Hist. of Gr. Lit.* (3d ser., 1932); P. Maas, *Epidaurische Hymnen* (1933); Dale; Koster.   P.S.C.

TELESTICH. See ACROSTIC.

TELIAMBOS. See MEIURUS.

TELUGU POETRY. See INDIAN POETRY.

TENOR AND VEHICLE. Because he was dissatisfied with the traditional account of metaphor in what he conceived of as a too exclusively grammatical and rhetorical manner, I. A. Richards coined this pair of terms to improve upon the old theory of metaphor by introducing the notion of "a borrowing between and intercourse of thoughts." Since any metaphor, at its simplest, gives us two ideas, he used "t." to mean purport or general drift of thought regarding the subject of the metaphor, and "v." to mean that which serves to carry or embody the t. as the analogy brought to the subject. Although this was by no means the first modern attempt to analyze the fundamental duality of metaphor—previous writers had already distinguished between "major term" and "minor term," or "thing meant" and "thing said," or "meaning" and "picture," and so on—Richards' distinction and the terms he introduced have gained wide currency among modern critics.

Having traced out t. and v. as the essential ingredients of metaphor, Richards (and the critics who followed him) went on to distinguish between the poetic metaphor and other kinds. In attempting to show that the truly poetic metaphor is never merely decorative or logical or explanatory or illustrative, he claimed that the "transaction" which it sets up between t. and v. "results in a meaning (to be clearly distinguished from the t.) which is not attainable without their interaction." The v., he continued, "is not normally mere embellishment of a tenor which is otherwise unchanged by it but . . . vehicle and tenor in cooperation give a meaning of more varied powers than can be ascribed to either."

These peculiar powers of the poetic metaphor he ascribed to the way in which the v. brings with it, by virtue of its being an aspect of human experience outside of or different from the experience portrayed in the poem, a host of implicit associations which, although circumscribed by the t., are never quite shut out entirely. This unsuppressible range of associations closely resembles what John Crowe Ransom has called "irrelevant texture," which he (and many other modern critics) value as the very essence of the poetic art itself. Such terms and the assumptions which give rise to them reveal an approach to poetry which looks for its lines of differentiation in the special qualities of poetic language—richness, ambiguity, irony, paradox, etc.—and which locates the cause of these qualities chiefly in the tension set up in a poetic figure between the t. and the emotional, sensory, and/or conceptual overtones brought into the poem by the v. Such an approach can frequently go beyond simply ascribing emotional and imaginative powers to metaphor and claim for it a special kind of cognitive power as well.

Thus, for example, it has become very common to interpret the well-known "stiff twin compasses" simile in Donne's "Valediction" in terms of a conflict supposedly set up between the warmth and passion binding the souls of the two lovers together (t.) and the rationality and metallic coldness implied by the mechanical compasses (v.). This analysis is seen as revealing the nobility of the speaker's conceptual powers in recognizing the subtle contradictions and complexities of the experience of love, as well as explaining the cause of our pleasure in this poem in terms of the filling in of such connections between t. and v. which our minds are stimulated to do. A less ambitious interpretation, however, would begin by pointing out that the figure is based on the notion of being separate but joined—a notion which the v. exemplifies and which the speaker is using as part of the argument he is fashioning to console his lady regarding their impending separation (t.). See IMAGERY, METAPHOR.—H. W. Wells, *Poetic Imagery* (1924); K. Burke, "Perspective as Metaphor," *Permanence and Change* (1935); W. B. Stanford, *Gr. Metaphor* (1936); I. A. Richards, *The Philos. of Rhetoric* (1936); C. Brooks, *Modern Poetry and the Tradition* (1939), pp. 1-17; J. C. Ransom, *Poems and Essays* (1955), pp. 159-85. N.FRIE.

TENSION. The concept of t. in imaginative literature, although not always the term itself,

is found at many points in modern criticism and aesthetic theory. This, for example, is a statement by John Dewey: "Without internal tension there would be a fluid rush to a straightway mark; there would be nothing that could be called development and fulfillment. The existence of resistance defines the place of intelligence in the production of an object." A further example is this comment on the poet's imagination by T. E. Hulme: "A powerful imaginative mind seizes and combines at the same instant all the important ideas of its poem or picture, and while it works with one of them, it is at the same instant working with and modifying all in their relation to it and never losing sight of their bearings on each other—as the motion of a snake's belly goes through all parts at once and its volition acts at the same instant in coils which go contrary ways." Comparable views are to be found in Coleridge's *Biographia Literaria* and in Henry James's "The Art of Fiction." The concept of t. is related to the organic theory of poetry and fiction, especially to the part of the theory that emphasizes the place of mind and intelligence in imaginative literature. It is also related to Richards' doctrine of synthesis, the reconciling of inharmonious elements, and to Brooks's doctrine of irony (q.v.). The criticism preoccupied with or aware of t. in imaginative literature tries to define the relationship between intelligence and medium, to demonstrate and to evaluate the ways in which an idea is reconciled with another idea and the appropriateness with which all of it is expressed in its medium.

Allen Tate, in "Tension in Poetry," has given a somewhat special meaning to the term, which he derives by "lopping the prefixes off the logical *ex*tension and *in*tension. . . ." He says that "the remotest figurative significance that we can derive does not invalidate the extensions of the literal statement. Or we may begin with the literal statement and by stages develop the complications of metaphor: at every stage we may pause to state the meaning so far apprehended, and at every stage the meaning will be coherent." Tate looks, for example, at *The Vine* by James Thomson:

The wine of love is music,
And the feast of love is song:
And when love sits down to the banquet,
Love sits long:

Sits long and ariseth drunken,
But not with the feast and the wine,
He reeleth with his own heart,
That great rich Vine.

"The language here appeals to an existing affective state; it has no coherent meaning either literally or in terms of ambiguity or implication; it may be wholly replaced by one of its several paraphrases, which are already latent in our mind." It is apparent, for example, that music might more appropriately be the feast of love, and song the wine of love. The imagery of the opening stanza bears little or no relationship to the self-intoxication of love, nor does there seem to be any appropriate relationship between love conceived as drunkard and one's ordinary reverence for love. In other words, the poem is one that cannot stand very much contemplation.

R. P. Warren has further complicated the concept of t. by discussing "pure" and "impure" poetry, asking whether certain things have to be left out of poetry if it is to be pure and other things put in. Warren says that if we added up the things that certain critics would leave out as unpoetic we would have "a list like this: 1. ideas, truths, generalizations, 'meaning.' 2. precise, complicated, 'intellectual' images. 3. unbeautiful, disagreeable, or neutral materials. 4. situation, narrative, logical transition. 5. realistic details, exact descriptions, realism in general. 6. shifts in tone or mood. 7. irony. 8. metrical variation, dramatic adaptations of rhythms, cacophony, etc. 9. meter itself. 10. subjective and personal elements. No one theory of pure poetry excludes all of these items, and, as a matter of fact, the items listed are not on the same level of importance." Warren's position is that nothing human should be legislated out of a poem, not even a chemical formula if the formula is made to function properly in its context. He says that, "other things being equal, the greatness of a poet depends upon the extent of the area of experience which he can master poetically." Warren also uses a memorable phrase, "coming to terms with Mercutio," by which he meants that a piece of fiction or a poem makes a proposition, and having made it should come to terms with opposing propositions. For example, the intensely romantic love of Romeo and Juliet is subjected to the ironic barbs of Mercutio and to the basic cynicism of the Nurse. If the poet's "proposition" is justifiable it can withstand the ridicule.

This theory of literature implies a preference for the dramatic play of ideas as against the pageant, the loosely strung narrative, or the simple lyric cry. It would prefer, for example, Yeats's "We had fed the heart on fantasies,/The heart's grown brutal from the fare" to Whitman's "The blab of the pave, tires of carts, sluff of boot-soles, talk of the promenaders, / The heavy omnibus, the driver with his interrogating thumb, the clank of the shod horses on the granite floor, / The snow-sleighs, clinking, shouted jokes, pelts of snow-balls, / The hurrahs for popular favorites, the fury of roused mobs, / The flab of the curtain'd litter, a sick man inside borne to the hospital." In Yeats's lines there is a suggestion of the paradoxical, of idea that promises insight and understanding. Pushed far enough, Yeats's lines imply a subtle philosophical position. Whitman's lines, on the other hand, give the texture of the world, and, by implication, ask for, without arguing toward, a simple optimism. There are, of course, degrees in such a matter, but perhaps one can say that those by whom the theory of t. is held most dearly and closely would prefer *The Tempest* to *A Midsummer Night's Dream* and *Light in August* to "The Bear." It does not follow that they would find either *A Midsummer Night's Dream* or "The Bear" to have little or no merit.—Richards, *Principles*; A. Tate, "T. in Poetry," *Reason in Madness* (1941); R. P. Warren, "Pure and Impure Poetry," KR, 5 (1943); W. Van O'Connor, "T. and Structure in Poetry," SR, 51 (1943); Wimsatt and Brooks; W. K. Wimsatt, Jr., "Poetic T.: A Summary," *New Scholasticism*, 32 (1958). w.v.o'c.

TENSO(N). Prov. (Fr. *tençon*). See TENZONE.

TENZONE (from *tenson, tençon*). An amoebean type of poetic composition which matured in Provence early in the 12th c. It consists of a verbal exchange largely in the form of invective expressed through the medium of *sirventes* or *coblas* (qq.v.). The earliest example seems to be by Cercamon and Guilhelmi. Later it developed into the *partimen* (q.v.) or *joc partit*, an exchange minus the personal element, and was applied to moral, literary or political problems. In many cases the subject matter is imaginary, and often the original argument and the exchange are by the same person. The wandering troubadours carried the device into Italy where we find Lanzia Marques and Alberto Malaspina making use of it in Prov. compositions. In Sicily the feigned *tenzone* in canzone-form called *contrasto* was quite popular. Giacomo da Lentino and Jacopo Mostacci, however, were among those who indulged in personal *tenzoni*, for which they utilized the sonnet (q.v.), thus setting the t. pattern adopted by later Italians. In Tuscany the example of Guittone d'Arezzo was extremely influential in making it common among the *guittoniani* and the poets of the *dolce stil nuovo* (q.v.), including Dante.— H. Stiefel, *Die italienische T. des XII Jhdts. und ihr Verhältnis zur provenzalischen T.* (1914); Jeanroy; D. J. Jones, *La Tenson prov.* (1934). J.G.F.

TERCET. See TRIPLET.

TERZA RIMA. A verse form composed of iambic tercets rhyming aba bcb, etc., the second line of the first tercet supplying the rhyme for the second tercet, the second line of the second tercet supplying the rhyme for the third, and so on, thus giving an effect of linkage to the entire composition. In t.r., the conclusion of a formal unit is generally signified by the occurrence of a single line which completes the rhyme structure by rhyming with the middle line of the preceding tercet, thus: xyx y.

T.r. was invented by Dante as an appropriate form for his *Divina Commedia;* the symbolic reference to the Holy Trinity is obvious. Furthermore, the intricate harmony which Dante achieves through his mastery of the form gives to the poem a structure at once massive and subtle, a structure which can only be suggested by any passage taken out of context. Most probably, Dante developed t.r. from the tercets of the *sirventes* (q.v.) but, whatever the origins of the form, it found immediate popularity with Boccaccio, who used it in his *Amorosa Visione*, and Petrarch, who used it in his *I Trionfi*. The implicit difficulty of the form, however, discouraged its widespread use after the 14th c., although Monti in the late 18th and Foscolo in the early 19th wrote noteworthy poems in t.r.

The form makes even greater demands on poets who write in a language less rich in rhymes than It. T.r. was introduced into Eng. by Chaucer in his *Complaint to his Lady* and was used by Wyatt and by Daniel. Some of the Eng. romantics experimented with the form, Byron in *The Prophecy of Dante* and Shelley in *Prince Athanase* and *The Triumph of Life*. The latter poet's *Ode to the West Wind* is composed of five sections, each rhyming aba bcb cdc ded ee. In the 20th c. the form has been used, among others, by W. H. Auden (*The Sea and the Mirror*) and, with marked variations, by MacLeish (*Conquistador*). European poets of the 19th and 20th c. who employed t.r. include the Dutch Potgieter and van Eeden and the German A. W. Schlegel, Chamisso, Liliencron, Heyse, and von Hofmannsthal.—Schipper; Hamer; Th. Spoerri, "Wie Dantes Vers entstand," *Vox romanica*, 2 (1937); V. Pernicone, "Storia e svolgimento della metrica," in *Problemi ed orientamenti critici di lingua e di letteratura italiana*, ed. A. Momigliano, II (1948); Wilkins.

TERZA RIMA SONNET. A term sometimes used to describe a quatorzain whose rhyme scheme makes use of the interweaving characteristic of terza rima (aba bcb cdc, etc.). Thus a pattern aba bcb cdc ded ee (the form of each section of Shelley's *Ode to the West Wind*, it may be noted) is not unlike the development of the Spenserian sonnet with its couplet ending; but there is an excess of interweaving

for so short a poem, and a theoretical demand for a five-part division instead of the normally expected four. Moreover, the principal charm of the t.r.—its cumulative melody—is lost in so short a passage. It is, however, of interest to note that the Sicilian sonnet has been suggested as the source of the t.r. as such.   L.J.Z.

TETRALOGY. A set of four plays, three tragedies and a satyr play (so-called because the chorus were dressed as satyrs), dealing with the same subject matter and treating of various aspects of the same legend. This custom of dramatic presentations, which is believed to have begun with Aeschylus, was discontinued by later playwrights. In modern usage, the term is applied to a group of four connected works, e.g., dramas and operas. See TRILOGY.   P.S.C.

TETRAMETER (Gr. "of 4 measures"). A line consisting of 4 measures. In classical iambic ($\smile-$), trochaic ($-\smile$), and anapaestic ($\smile\smile-$) verse the measure is a dipody (pair of feet). There are four classical types: iambic t. acatalectic and trochaic t. acatalectic (8 feet. 16 syllables each; see OCTONARIUS) and iambic t. catalectic and trochaic t. catalectic (7 feet. 15 syllables each; see SEPTENARIUS). A spondee ($--$) was allowed in the odd iambic and the even trochaic feet. Resolution of a long into 2 shorts was allowed in certain circumstances. A break (diaeresis) was compulsory after the second dipody. The catalectic types are the commoner. The iambic t. catalectic was common in L. comedy; indeed it had rather vulgar associations. The trochaic t. catalectic is one of the oldest and most popular of meters; it was used in drama for excited dialogue, and it was the rhythm of the Roman soldiers' marching-songs and of some of the most famous Christian hymns, e.g.,

pānge, līnguă, glōriŏsī prŏeliŭ: certāminĭs

Eng. t. (a line of 4 feet; strictly speaking the term is incorrectly used for the Eng. 4-stress line) is less strict than the classical varieties. Usually it is iambic or trochaic, or both, with accentual feet. It was used by Milton (*L'Allegro, Il Penseroso*) and many others, and conspicuously by Scott and Byron in long narratives.—Hardie; Beare.   W.B.

TÉTRAMÈTRE. Term applied to the 12-syllable Fr. classical alexandrine (q.v.), which has 4 divisions to the line, as distinguished from the 12-syllable *vers romantique* or *trimètre* (q.v.), which has only 3. The *tétramètre* (unlike the *vers romantique*) has a caesural pause after the sixth syllable. Racine's *Phèdre* (1.3.306) affords a famous example: "C'est Vénus | tout entière || à sa proie | attachée."

The Fr. t., whose roots go back at least to *Le pèlerinage de Charlemagne* (12th c.), was shaped in the classical age by the firm rules of Malherbe into the form championed by Boileau and brought to perfection in the tragedies of Corneille and Racine.—M. Grammont, *Le vers français* (1913) and *Petit traité de versification française* (5ᵉ éd. revue, 1924); G. Lote, *Hist. du vers fr.*, II (1951)   A.G.E.

TETRAPODY (Gr. "4 feet"). A group or line of 4 feet. The most common tetrapodies in Gr. dramatic poetry are the anapaestic, logaoedic, dactylic and the dactylic myuric.—Koster.
TETRASTICH. A group, stanza or poem of 4 lines. A quatrain (q.v.).   P.S.C.

TEXTUAL CRITICISM is the analysis of the existing forms or states of a text to determine the nature of the form or state from which they are all descended, and the emendation of the state so determined to remove as far as possible any errors it contains. It is sometimes called *lower criticism* to distinguish it from *higher criticism,* which is the analysis of the text provided by lower criticism to determine its unity or diversity of date and authorship. Textual c. may sometimes draw conclusions from information provided by explication (q.v.), but in general the relationship is reversed. It finds its chief justification as a discipline ancillary to literary history and criticism, but it has its own attractiveness as a rational exercise.

The boundary between lower and higher c. is not rigidly determined, each critic making his own decision as to how far he will carry the process of emendation. In the biblical poem of Job, for instance, many critics are convinced that the division of the speeches between Job and his three friends has been corrupted, but only a few (e.g. Moulton, Bates) have produced texts in which they set forth the speeches as they conceive the author intended. Within lower c., too, are shifting boundaries. Some critics prefer not to emend at all; others do nothing else. A text that has not been emended is an antiquarian text. One that has been produced by combining the best parts of the various states in which the text has been preserved (which is in practice nothing but emending one state on the basis of the others) is an eclectic text. A text that has been produced by the processes envisioned in the definition of textual c. given above is a critical text.

The process of producing an eclectic text of a poem is seldom employed unless the evidence as to which state is the ancestor of the others is badly confused or any connection at all between the states seems doubtful—and then the critic feels on the defensive. The work of Wolf and Leishman illustrates careful use of the method (see bibliography; the poems in question were evidently transmitted by word of mouth before finding their way into commonplace books and into print). Kane's edition of *Piers Plowman: The A Version* is a major recent example.

Experience shows that if there is more than one manuscript of a poem of moderate length, each manuscript will differ from the rest. If the poem is printed, each setting of type is almost certain to differ from the rest, even with careful proofreading, and early books preserved in only a few copies may differ in every copy because of the old practice of starting to print before the completion of proofreading, the press being stopped as necessary to make corrections. Some critics are willing to assume that an extant manuscript or typesetting is an exact transcript of an earlier lost form of the text; others hold that experience prevents such an assumption.

Faced with a poem that has come down to him in more than one state, the critic asks himself how the states came to agree and how they came to differ. He reasons that some likenesses result from the desire of the copyists to transmit the text as they received it, and some differences from the failure of the copyists to accomplish their intention. He recognizes that some likenesses may result from the correction of errors recognized as such by editors, and some differences from tendentious alterations by editors; further, that some differences may result from the author's revisions, and some likeness from the author's giving up revisions in favor of his first thoughts. And he accepts the possibility that some likenesses result from chance. Experience suggests to him that on the whole it is more likely that copying has caused both likenesses and differences, and he guides himself accordingly.

A critic who follows the method introduced by Karl Lachmann first discards all states that he is satisfied descend from any other extant state. He accepts the rest as descended from one or more nonextant states. Acting on the principle that agreements in the text imply identity of source, he groups together in families those states that commonly agree together. If, as often happens, the states do not fall into clearly defined groups, he groups them on the basis of common errors, or, failing these, of striking likenesses, or, failing even these, on what seem to him the probabilities (see for example, Grierson, Gardner, and Redpath on the grouping of manuscripts in their editions of Donne). Some critics, however, maintain that looking for common errors is the basic step. Sometimes the critic may conclude that a state has two or more distinct ancestries, in other words, that the scribe compared two or more states of the poem instead of merely copying one. Individual judgment, which will rest upon the critic's experience and theories of how men behave or ought to behave, plays a large part in his decisions, and it is not too much to call the division of the states into families an art. The rest of the analysis proceeds according to rule. The critic assigns a nonextant ancestor to each family, and to these ancestors and any states belonging to no family he assigns a further ancestor, the archetype.

Dryden's "Epilogue to *The Man of Mode*" is found in a printed version, which may be designated A, and three manuscript versions, which may be designated B, C, and D. The date of A only is known exactly, but the others are apparently contemporary with it. None can be shown to descend from any other. Where the versions disagree, we find three agreements each of two against two in the pattern AB:CD and of three against one in the pattern B:ACD; there are four examples of C:ABD, eight of D:ABC, one of A:BC:D and two of AB:C:D. A critic following Lachmann's method will ignore the division of the states shown by AB:CD because of the large preponderance of D:ABC, and will assign an ancestor x to the family ABC, and an archetype y to x and D.

Sir Walter Greg also adopts the principle that agreements in the text imply identity of source, but he assigns an ancestor for each type of agreement. Furthermore, he does not suppose that the immediate ancestor of one family may not be a remoter ancestor of another. Most of Greg's discussion proceeds on the assumption that none of the states is the ancestor of any of the others, but he points out that if any exant state fails to stand alone against agreements in the rest, it is (unless it has a double ancestry) the ancestor of one or more of the rest, and that any state which does stand alone and is consistently superior to the rest is their ancestor, with one or more nonextant descendants between it and the rest. A critic following Greg's method will see eleven possible patterns of ancestors for the "Epilogue": (1) x for A and B, y for x and C, and z for y and D; (2) x for A and B, y for x and D, and z for y and C; (3) x for A and B, and y for x, C, and D; (4) x for A and B, y for C and D, and z for x and y; (5) x for C and D, and y for x, A, and B; (6) x for C and D, y for x and B; and z for y and A; (7) x for C and D, y for x and A, and z for y and B; (8) x for A and B, y for x and C, and D for y; (9) x for A and B, y for x and D, and C for y; (10) x for C and D, y for x and A, and B for y; (11) x for C and D, y for x and B, and A for y. If some manuscripts are measurably closer than others to what the author intended, then alternate superiority of ABC (i.e. when they agree) over D, and of D over ABC points to (1); of ABD and C to (2); of AB and CD to (4); of A and BCD to (6); and of B and ACD to (7); while consistent superiority of CD over AB points to (3); and of AB over CD to (5), of D to (8), of C to (9), of B to (10), and of A to (11).

Willard Thorp argues for (1); the text in the California Dryden is based on (11); the text in the Oxford Poets Dryden is based on (3).

Archibald A. Hill sometimes understands the evidence provided by the patterns of agreement in a different fashion from Greg. Hill asserts that a reasonable balance of AB:CD and AC:BD indicates that all the states descend independently from the archetype x; Greg would say that one of the states had two distinct lines of ancestry. Hill maintains that a reasonable balance of AB:C:D and A:B:CD indicates an ancestor x for A and B and another, y, for C and D, one being also the ancestor of the other, i.e., the archetype; Greg would say that any state might be the archetype and the others descended from it in series, provided only that neither A nor B came between C and D and the reverse, and that if all were descendants, any of the first seven patterns above would fit the situation, depending upon the manuscripts' closeness to the author's intentions.

Hill points out that a set of states of a poem may not provide enough evidence to determine a pattern of ancestors exactly, and proposes to decide between the possibilities by weighing the assumptions implied in each. A first assumption, that an archetype exists, he regards as basic, and does not count. A second assumption, that the extant descendants were copied, he counts once for each. A third assumption, that any of these states has a nonexistent ancestor short of the archetype, he counts as a double assumption for each ancestor and as doubling the assumptions to be counted for its immediate descendants. In the patterns of ancestors for Dryden's "Epilogue," therefore, those numbered (1), (2), (6) and (7) above have 11 assumptions each, (3) and (5) have 8, (4) has 12, the rest 10. It will be seen that if the pattern of ancestors includes a nonextant state, Hill's system of weighing assumptions will prevent the choice of an extant state as the archetype. Hill admits the weights are arbitrary, but holds that the results will conform to the facts. But the results *are* the facts, as determined by the method, so there is no external check. In the case of Dryden's "Epilogue," Hill's method will only reduce the choice to (3) or (5), and if either of them could then be decided on, it could have been decided on without the method. Sometimes, however, the method will at once point to a single possibility.

Dom Henri Quentin's principle is that if one state of a poem agrees now with a second, now with a third, now with both, while they never or almost never agree against it, it is the descendant of one and the ancestor of the other, or it is the ancestor of both, neither being the ancestor of the other, or it is the descendant of both, neither being the descendant of the other (double ancestry); and on the other hand, if the second and third states do fairly regularly agree against the first, then the three have a common intermediary from which they radiate. Unless it is a question of the archetype, the decision as to which state is to stand at the head will depend upon which manuscript is earliest, or where this cannot be determined, upon the closeness of the states to the author's intentions. The archetype will never be an extant state if the earliest extant states radiate, but if one state is always intermediary in its triads, it is the archetype. The method is inconsistent here, and is somewhat more cumbrous than the others because the states are examined three at a time. J. Burke Severs has shown that Quentin's method of dealing with states with double ancestry is unsatisfactory.

With Dryden's "Epilogue," a critic following Quentin's method will test the four triads ABC, ABD, ACD, BCD. Because A almost never stands alone, it will be intermediary in the first three triads. The states in the last triad radiate. It follows that they radiate from A, which is then the archetype. Quentin's method will always reduce the number of nonextant ancestors to a minimum.

Vinton A. Dearing's principle is an inversion and generalization of Quentin's, namely, that if two or more states agree, no other state can come between them if they are in the same line of descent, or between them and their common ancestor if they are in different lines of descent. This way of putting the principle allows the analysis of all the states at once, and at the same time eliminates the need of a special procedure (Greg's "resolution of complex variants," not expounded here) to analyze agreements against diversity or against two or more counteragreements or both. Dearing holds that two states agree against a third not only when they differ from it in the text, but also when they are both earlier than the third, or when one has developed out of the other and the third is not an intermediate stage in the development. He chooses among the alternate patterns of ancestors on the grounds of simplicity, but estimates simplicity differently from Hill: the minimum conditions for transmission of the text are that the archetype have one descendant, itself the ancestor of a single descendant, and so on to the last descendant; and the complications of the simplest arrangement are in order of increasing weight, (1) increasing the number of immediate descendants of an ancestor, (2) introducing nonextant ancestors, and (3) giving a descendant more than one independent ancestor. Dearing weighs both the dates of the manuscripts and the closeness of the states to the author's intentions, maintaining that a good text in a late manuscript is not to be taken as a perfect copy of an earlier manuscript.

The critic who follows Dearing's method will see as the simplest possible patterns of ancestors for Dryden's "Epilogue" those numbered (8) to (11) above, and if it is possible he will chose the best state as the archetype. If, however, the best state is inferior to the others in some way, he will choose between (3) and (5), provided that one archetype is consistently superior to the other states (the readings of an archetype are those of the majority of its immediate descendants, as long as none has a double ancestry). He will choose among the others only as a last resort. If the dates of the manuscripts could be distinguished, this would also affect his choice; that is, if he were to choose from (8) to (11), the archetype would have to be the earliest of the states; if it were not, he would be limited to (1) to (7).

It will be seen that the different methods may lead to different conclusions from the same evidence; and other practicing critics have felt free to employ any amalgamation of methods. The same critic may vary his methods as his views mature. Greg has proposed a concise and clear method of expressing the patterns of difference that may occur in states of a poem, and he, Hill, and Dearing have all developed precise terminologies, but each terminology differs in some respects, and other practicing critics have never felt bound to use any standard language. As a result, close attention and considerable flexibility of mind are necessary to understand any given analysis, and mastery of one does not necessarily lead to easier understanding of another.

Manuscripts and books that are not dated may be given dates on the basis of their physical characteristics as well as by tracing the development of the text they record from one to another. Details of script or type, design, and manufacture change over the years, and once the trends are established from dated examples, undated examples may be fitted in their places. Very old manuscripts may profitably be dated by carbon-14 analysis. Occasionally details of manufacture allow identification of a specific ancestor for a given descendant. Surely the most amusing example of this is in the manuscripts of Propertius, where Laurentianus 36, 49 has for line iv. 8. 3 a blank, followed by "vetus est tutela draconis," with a marginal note, "non potuit legi in exemplari hoc quod deficit"; and Neopolitanus 268 gives the line as "non potuit legi vetus est tutela draconis."

One state may be accepted as representing the author's intentions better than another if where they differ the second state may be shown probably to have developed out of the first, but the first can be shown probably not to have developed out of the second (Dearing lists and gives examples of nonreversible types).

The critic also seeks to identify instances where only the corruption has been preserved, and to restore the original by emendation. The rules for emendation are that the change must be necessary, and that there be only one possible change. Bentley did not observe the first rule in his notorious emendations of Milton (though he thought he was observing it). The second rule is harder, for the passage may cry out for emendation when there is no way to choose among several possibilities, as for instance in the second line of Shakespeare's Sonnet CXLVI, which has lost its first two syllables. In such a case, the critic who sticks to the rule will put an ellipsis in the text, and discuss the possible emendations in his notes, but most critics woud probably put one emendation into the text, say "Thrall to," and discuss the rest in the notes. It is only by intuition that many corruptions can be identified, intuition based on a deep feeling for the author being emended and a penetrating understanding of his drift in every passage; and if the critic is to hit upon the necessary corrections, he needs the same qualities, coupled with a thorough knowledge of how and what kinds of errors may creep into a poem.

Similar problems confront the critic faced with a poem revised by the author. Not all the differences between the revised and original versions are authoritative, in all probability, because copying errors are so hard to avoid, and the critic must therefore decide which changes are authoritative, which are not. Greg suggests that here the critic ask himself whether the readings are apparently authoritative; if one is and the other is not, accept the one that is; if both are, accept the later; and if neither are, accept the earlier. The result is to deny to the author any changes that the critic feels are not characteristic of him. Another procedure is to accept the revised text as it stands (only emending any corruptions). Here the result is to deny to the copyist any changes that the critic feels are not characteristic of him. Normally there will be a set of changes that might, as far as the critic can tell, have resulted equally well from the author's revision or from errors in copying,

and as we have just said, very likely the set contains some of each kind. Even if it is possible to reach some conclusion as to how many of each kind are in the set, it is still impossible to identify any one as being of one kind or the other; the critic must accept all the doubtful changes or reject them all. Acceptance is usually called conservatism, but rejection is only conservatism in the other direction. At present practicing critics disagree in this, as in every aspect of textual c.

Although no detailed account exists in print, some advances have been made in automating textual c. There are now programs of instructions for computers for comparing texts, for determining patterns of descent, for compiling concordances (used in emending), and for restoring text lost through damage to manuscripts. Computers will also be necessary, in all probability, to make full use of probabilistic methods for determining patterns of descent, now being introduced especially by Antonin Hruby (see his "Statistical Methods in Textual C.," *General Linguistics*, 3, no. 3, suppl. [1962]). More information will be available with the publication of Dearing's *Introd. to Computer Programming for Literary Students.*

For Lachmann's method, see F. W. Hall, *A Companion to Classical Texts* (1913), K. Lake, *The Text of the New Testament* (6th ed., rev. S. Lake, 1928); J. P. Postgate, "Textual C.," in *A Companion to Latin Studies,* ed. J. E. Sandys (3d ed., 1921) and his article on the same subject in the *Ency. Britannica* (11th ed.), R. C. Jebb, "Textual C.," in *A Companion to Gr. Studies,* ed. L. Whibley (2d ed., 1906); some traces of the old method continue in P. Maas, *Textual C.,* tr. B. Flower (1958), which otherwise forms an extremely valuable supplement to Greg's method. J. Bédier, Introduction to his ed. of *Le Lai de l'Ombre* (1913), etc., largely discredited textual c. among Romance philologists; a new tack, but resembling Jebb, is E. Vinaver, "Principles of Textual Emendation," in *Studies in Fr. Language and Medieval Lit.* (1939). W. W. Greg, *The Calculus of Variants* (1927); A. A. Hill, "Postulates for Distributional Study of Texts," SB, 3 (1950–51); H. Quentin, *Mémoire sur l'Etablissement du Texte de la Vulgate* (1922) and, with additional examples, *Essais de Critique Textuelle* (1926); J. Burke Severs, "Quentin's Theory of Textual C.," *EIE, 1941;* V. A. Dearing, *A Manual of Textual Analysis* (1959), with examples; for additional references see Hill. For the principles of emendation, see Hall, A. E. Housman in his editions of Manilius (1903–20), Juvenal (1906), and Lucan (1926), R. B. McKerrow, *Prolegomena for the Oxford Shakespeare* (1939), Greg, *The Editorial Problem in Shakespeare* (2d ed., 1951) and "The Rationale of Copy-Text," SB, 3 (1950–51); F. Bowers, *Textual and Literary C.*

(1959). A. L. Clark, *The Descent of Manuscripts;* McKerrow, *An Introd. to Bibliog. for Literary Students;* and similar works (McKerrow has a brief introd. to paleography and type design). Severs, *The Literary Relations of Chaucer's Clerke's Tale* (1942); J. M. Manly and E. Rickert, *The Text of the Canterbury Tales* (1940); cf. G. Dempster, "A Chapter in the Manuscript History of the *Canterbury Tales*," PMLA, 63 (1948); J. B. Leishman, "'You Meaner Beauties of the Night,'" *The Library,* 4th ser., 26 (1945); E. Wolf, 2d, "'If Shadows be a Picture's Excellence'; An Experiment in Critical Bibliog.," PMLA, 63 (1948). For setting out a critical apparatus, an important subject not treated in this article, see Lake, McKerrow, and Greg on Shakespeare, Dearing, and International Union of Academies, *Emploi des signes critiques, disposition de l'apparat dans les editions savantes de textes grecs et latins; conseils et recommendations* (1932).   V.A.D.

TEXTURE. In modern criticism "texture" usually designates the concrete, particular details of a poem as differentiated from abstract or general ideas. The term is derived from the plastic arts, where it normally refers to the surface qualities of a work as against the larger elements of form or design.

In the context of prosody, t. denotes euphony, the actual physical effects of vowels and consonants as distinguished from meter, considered as a temporal and dynamic phenomenon. T., in this sense, is a matter of great subtlety; since the judgment of phonetic qualities is necessarily subjective to a certain degree, t. is not amenable to systematic analysis. Aside from the observation of such well-established devices as assonance and alliteration, the description of t. depends on analogy with non-aural phenomena: hardness, softness; thickness, thinness; darkness, richness, sweetness, harshness. The subject of phonetic t. is further complicated by its interaction with meter; according to Edith Sitwell, it has "incredibly subtle" effects on rhythm and variations of speed.

In the field of poetics, "t." has a much broader reference, including euphony and meter but extending also to the topic of poetic language. It has a special importance in the criticism of John Crowe Ransom as one of two key terms in a general theory of poetry. Ransom has consistently opposed the tendency in modern poetics to create a unitary theory by reducing poetry to a single essence. In his view, poetry is a composite art containing three distinct and irreducible ingredients. One of these comes under the heading of structure; the others under t. The nature or condition of poetry is defined by the relationship of structure and t.

Structure is the argument of the poem, that element which is governed by logic and reason and which, since it belongs to the order of discursive language, may be extracted from the poem in the form of a prose paraphrase. Ransom maintains that without the prose argument there can be no poem, and is therefore opposed to tendencies in modern poetry which would dispense with structure and have the poem consist entirely of what he calls texture.

T. is the valuable element of poetry, since the structure exists for its sake rather than the reverse. T. includes all the local, heterogeneous detail which differentiates the poem from a prose statement. The detail is characterized by its concreteness and particularity. Furthermore, it is essentially irrelevant to the structure. Ransom's notion of t. is grounded upon empirical knowledge of the process of poetic composition. He perceived that the t. is unpredictable, that it arises adventitiously during the poetic process; generally, it retards or even impedes the argument. In adjusting the details which arise from the logical structure to the requirements of meter and euphony, the poet discovers new facts which belong to the details but not the structure. T. includes a whole realm of meanings, therefore, which exist apart from the structure. These meanings, peculiar to poetry, constitute that aspect of poetry which has occupied the interest of the majority of linguistically oriented critics.

J. C. Ransom, *The World's Body* (1932), *The New Crit.* (1941), "Crit. as Pure Speculation," in *The Intent of the Critic,* ed. D. A. Stauffer (1941), "The Inorganic Muses," KR, 5 (1943), "Poetry: The Formal Analysis," and "Poetry: The Final Cause," KR, 9 (1947); W. Elton, *A Glossary of the New Crit.* (1948); R. W. Stallman, "The New Critics," *Critiques and Essays in Crit.* (1949); E. Sitwell, "Poetry," in *Cassell's;* Wimsatt and Brooks.   S.F.

THAI POETRY. Thai literature possesses a written history going back to the 13th c. A.D. From the earliest period of its history one finds poetic forms and throughout Thai writing poetry is the dominant literary form. The Thai or Siamese language is a tone language with five significant tones which further complicates the structure of the various verse forms. The latter are five in number and are called *chanta, kap, khlong, klon,* and *ray.* The *chanta* consists of lines of unstressed and stressed words in varying combinations. A typical example is the *totok* which is a 4-line stanza of 12 syllables, each line consisting of 4 consecutive groups of 2 shorts and a long. *Kap,* which means a "poetic production," is restricted to certain types of verse and closely resembles the *chanta* but without adhering to long and short syllables. In *kap* verse, however, rhyme is significant. *Khlong*, meaning "to rhyme," has been the most popular among poets in spite of the fact that its requirement of rhyme renders it quite difficult to manipulate. The *khlong* may be of 2, 3, or even 4 stanzas but must conform to the tonal and rhyme requirements. The fourth type of verse, called the *klon*, conforms to a rhyming scheme only. One of the more common types is the 8-syllable *klon* which permits as many interior rhymes as one desires; each verse is connected with the following by the rhyme of the last syllable, which in turns falls on one of the first in the succeeding verse. The *klon* is much used in the theater, in popular songs and recitations. *Ray*, "to recite," is blank verse and is used primarily in Buddhist religious literature.

Some of the earliest Thai poetry may well have been Thai versions of the *Rāmāyana*, called *Ramakirti* (and pronounced *Ramakien*), but the various versions now extant date from the 16th and 17th c. and later. In most instances they are court products, often with several collaborators such as king or prince and court poets, the result being a collective composition. The Thai renderings of the *Rāmāyana* have become very much Thaicized in locale and proper names of the personages. Though there is a considerable body of literature, oral and written, in poetic form in the Thai language prior to the reign of P'hra Narai (1656–88), this period is generally called the 'Golden Age of Thai Poetry.' It was during this period that the famous *P'hra Lo* was probably composed though it may be a century earlier. This long poem is in a verse form known as *lilit* whose 7-meter 4-line strophes are intermixed with *kap* verses. An example from *P'hra Lo* is the following stanza:

Satavan van chauy ron   rew pai nung ru
Bok kao pra lo klai   klin choo
Sadet yoo asai   suan raj ni na
Hai jong song tao roo   ti ron ram si

O thou wind which whirls through space, seek
  our prince,
Go to him, waft him to us!
And you, myriad stars, tell him to hasten,
Use lanterns and light his way.

A favorite poetic form, almost always a love poem, is the *nirat* meaning "separation." It sings of the charms of the loved one the poet has left behind. As he progresses on his journey he relates what he sees to memories he holds dear. In a sense, the *nirat* is a series of travel notes to one's beloved, interspersed with comments about her. One of the most widely imitated *nirats* in the 18th and 19th c. was *Khamsoun* by Si Prat who lived in the early 18th c. This *nirat* was written while the poet was on his way to exile in south Thailand. He is the

author of a number of others which have become famous in the history of Thai literature.

During the reign of Thonburi (1770–82) the king himself composed certain episodes from the *Rāmāyana* and his successor encouraged a literary renaissance in which the latter's son Phuttaleutla (Rama II) actively participated by writing down the first *sepha*, an oral genre traditionally handed down from master to disciple. Entitled *The Adventures of Khun Chang and Khun Phen*, it is actually the work of several authors and is written in a lively and amusing style in 40,000 lines. One of the most accomplished poets was Sunthorn Bhu (1786–1855) who as a boy exhibited exceptional poetical talents. Author of several well-known *nirats* and assistant to Phuttaleutla in the preparation of the latter's collaborative version of the *Ramayana*, he is best known for his *Phra Abhai Mani*, a long imaginative romance, composed in a number of cantos. The first and foremost poetess was Khun Phum (1815–80). Her home was a literary salon for the last forty years of her life, and some of her poems, especially her *nirats*, hold an important place in Thai literature. Since her period greater contact with the West has had the effect of replacing, to a very great extent, poetry with prose, and modern Thai students of literature voice the fear that poetry will become a relic of the past. In fact, poetry in the classical style has virtually disappeared in the past twenty years but there are now half a dozen poets in their late twenties and early thirties who are variously styled "idealistic," "realistic," or "imaginary" and who are quite popular. More outlets for publication and a resurgence of interest for poetry can be noted.

ANTHOLOGIES AND TRANSLATIONS: *Chrestomathie siamoise*, ed. J. Burnay (1938); *Magic Lotus, a Romantic Fantasy*, ed. and tr. Prem Chaya (1949; Eng. adaptation of *P'hra Lo*); *The Ramakirti (Ramakien), or the Thai version of the Rāmāyana*, ed. Swami Satyananda Puri and Charoen Sarahiran (1949); Sunthorn Bhu, *The Story of Phra Abhai Mani* (1952); Khun S'ra Prasot, *Siamsänge* (1955).

HISTORIES AND CRITICISM: H. H. Prince Bidyalankarana, "Sebha Recitation and the Story of Khun Chang Khun Phan," *Jour. of the Siam Society*, 33 (1941); Saiyuda Bhakdi, "Siamese Lit.," in *Encyclopedia of Lit.*, ed. J. T. Shipley, II (1946); P. Schweisguth, *Étude sur la litt. siamoise* (1951; the best study of Thai lit. in a Western lang.); Phya Anuman Rajadhon, *Thai Lit. and Swasdi Raksa* (1953); Kasem Sibunruang, "Litt. siamoise," in *Histoire des littératures*, ed. R. Quéneau, I (1955); P. Purachatra, "Thailand and Her Lit.," *Diliman Review*, 6 (1958); J. N. Mosel, *A Survey of Cl. Thai Poetry* (1959) and *Trends and Structure in Contemporary Thai Poetry* (1961). J.M.E.

THEORETICAL CRITICISM. See CRITICISM, FUNCTION OF.

THESIS. See ARSIS AND THESIS.

THRENODY (Gr. "a dirge sung over some-one or something"). The ancient Gr. word for a song of lamentation, a dirge (q.v.), or a funeral song. Although originally a choral ode, it was changed to a monody (q.v.) which was strophic in form employing various metrical systems. Such a poem was not only a lamentation but also an encomium for the dead. From the 6th c. B.C. it became common in Gr. literature whence it spread to other literatures. In modern usage the term may be applied to any lyric of lamentation or memorial, e.g., Emerson's *Threnody on His Young Son,* or even Tennyson's *In Memoriam.*
R.A.H.

TIBETAN POETRY. The extreme scarcity of available material on Tib. poetry makes it almost impossible to treat the subject satisfactorily. Terms such as "poems" and "poets" are nonexistent in the Tib. language. The closest approximation to the word "poems" is *glu bzhas* (honorific *gsungs bzhas*), which means "songs." *Glu bzhas* are mainly folk songs; they are lively, colorful, and often naive in their simplicity and frankness. These popular songs constitute one part of the main body of Tib. poetry. The other part is to be found in various religious writings such as prayers, hymns, or ceremonious songs. Generally called *dbyangs* or *mgur*, they are the compositions of learned scholars and priests and are essentially poetic as well as intensely religious in nature. The popular songs are usually without definite authorship, and are spread mainly through oral transmission. They present extensive textual variations and are characterized by colloquialism. On the other hand, the religious songs are composed in the classical language, which was stabilized in the 8th c. with the introduction of Buddhism from India.

In the development of Tib. poetry two different traditions can be distinguished: Tib. native literary creations and Indic Buddhistic translations. In general, the secular poetry always contains an even number of syllables in each line, while the religious treatises usually contain an odd number of syllables. The former have more variations, whereas the latter are more regular in form. There is no distinction of long and short syllables in Tib. versification. The significance of the distinction between accented and unaccented syllables is doubtful. Rhyming is not universal among all types of poetry. Structurally, all poetic pieces differ from one another only in the number of syllables. Parallelism has been observed by Francke in his *Ladakhi Songs.*

The following is a tentative classification of Tib. poetic pieces: (1) folk songs, (2) ritualistic songs, (3) poetic passages in plays, (4) *Gling glu* (songs for the *Kesar* festival), (5) poetic passages in the *Kesar Saga,* (6) poetic passages in historical works, (7) historical songs, (8) religious songs, prayers, and hymns, (9) Milaraspa's *Mgur 'Bum.* Within the brief space of this article, only the more important types can be considered. Of folk songs there are many varieties, including work songs for sowing, harvesting, building a house, etc. Special mention should be made of the love songs attributed to the 6th Dalai Lama. Simple, fresh, artless, and imbued with great feeling for nature, they reveal the struggle between passion and propriety, from which there is no respite:

shar phyogs ri bo'i rtse nas
dkar gsal zla ba shar byung
ma skyes a ma'i zhal ras
yid la 'khor byas byung.

From the mountain peaks in the east,
The silvery moon has peeped out.
And the face of that young maiden,
Has gradually appeared in my mind.

The best known epic is the *Kesar Saga.* The Tib. versions of this epic, which is widely circulated in Central Asia and which revolves around the heroic deeds of the mystical king Kesar, are written in verses which intermingle with prose. Of religious writings, the several poetical works in the *Kanjur* (translated word) and the *Tanjur* (translated treatises) should be singled out. Faithful translations of the Sanskrit Buddhist works of India, they are composed in verse, consisting of two or four lines, each of 7–21 syllables. Many native compositions of a religious nature are modeled on the Buddhistic translations.

Milaraspa (1040–1123), a Buddhist missionary of the *Bka rgyud pa* sect, is above all a poet. The chief work ascribed to him is the "One Hundred Thousand Songs" (*Mgur 'Bum*), which comprises a narrative of a part of his wanderings, plentifully interspersed with ditties and poetical expositions of doctrine. The songs, however, number less than 200 instead of 100,000 as stated in the metaphorical title. His poetry has a personal touch which is rarely found in Tib. literature.

Trois mystères tibétains, tr. J. Bacot (1912); *Milaraspa,* ed. B. Laufer (1922); T. C. Yu and Y. R. Chao, *Love Songs of the 6th Dalai Lama Tshang dbyangs rgya mtsho* (1930; Academia Sinica, Institute of Hist. and Phil., *Monographs,* ser. A., no. 5); *Tib. Folksongs from the District of Gyantse,* ed. and tr. G. Tucci,

(1949); P. Poucha, "Les vers tibétains," *Archiv Orientalni*, 18 (1950); J. Vekerdi, "Some Remarks on Tib. Prosody," *Academiae Scientiarum Hungaricae, Acta Orientalia*, 2 (1952); K. Chang, "On Tib. Poetry," *Central Asiatic Jour.*, 2 (1956); *L'Epopée tibétaine de Gesar dans sa version lamaique de Ling*, tr. R. A. Stein (1956); J. W. de Jong, *Mi la ras pa'i rnam thar* (1959; Tib. text of the life of Milarepa); *Message of Milarepa: New Light upon the Tib. Way*, tr. H. Clarke (1960); *The Hundred-Thousand Songs. Selections from Milarepa, Poet-Saint of Tibet*, tr. A. K. Gordon (1961); *The Hundred Thousand Songs of Milarepa*, tr. and annotated by G. C. C. Chang (2 v., 1962).   K.C.

TMESIS (Gr. "a cutting"). In Gr. syntax it means the separation of a preposition from its verb to which in postepic language it was completely joined. In Attic Gr. poetry the two elements were separated by unimportant words, e.g.,

kat' oūn ĕlaben for *oūn katélaben*

for the sake of emphasis. L. poetry does the same thing, e.g., *seque gregari* for *segregarique*. In Eng. the breaking up of any compound word, e.g., "what place soever" for "whatsoever place." Another example of t. is G. M. Hopkins' "See his wind—lilylocks—laced" (*Harry Ploughman*).   R.A.H.

TONE. Traditionally, "t." has denoted an intangible quality, frequently an affective one, which is metaphorically predicated of a literary work or of some part of it such as its style. It is said to pervade and "color" the whole, like a mood in a human being, and in various ways to contribute to the aesthetic excellence of the work. Some of the other terms naming the same concept are "Gestalt-quality," "impression," "spirit," "atmosphere," "aura," and "accent." In *Practical Criticism* (1929) I. A. Richards compared t. to social manners and defined it as the reflection in a discourse of the author's attitude towards his audience. Successful management of t., on which the rhetorical effectiveness of a discourse largely depends, consists primarily in the tactful selection of content and in the adjustment of style to suit a particular audience. Other recent critics have analogized t. in literature to a quality of speech. The t. in which something is said may add to, qualify, or even reverse the meaning of what is said, as in sarcasm. Thus the t. of a speaker's voice may reveal information about his feelings, wishes, attitudes, beliefs, etc. Presumably on the assumption that vocal tones are used only or primarily to convey attitudes, critics who have adopted this

analogy maintain that any indirect expression of attitude in a poem (by choice of words, imagery, slanting, syntax, etc.) is a problem of t. Thus attitudes determine t., and t. reflects attitudes. Since poetry is regarded as a specialization of language for the communication of attitudes, the determination of the exact shading of t. in a particular poem is one of the most important duties of the explicator. The t. of a poem is also a source of value judgments; a poem is deemed poor if the attitudes it expresses are vague, confused, unsustained, unjustified, unmotivated, inappropriate, simple, conventional, or sentimental. —I. A. Richards, *Practical Crit.* (1929); Brooks and Warren; I. C. Hungerland, *Poetic Discourse* (1958).   F.G.

TONE-COLOR. Characteristic auditory quality of a speech-sound or musical instrument (German *Tonfarbe, Klangfarbe*; Fr., Eng. *timbre*). Extended to cover the kinesthetic "feel" of articulation and utterance. The relations of both aspects of tone-color to sound-associations are here examined. (See also ONOMATOPOEIA, SOUND IN POETRY.)

The key to poetic tone-color is phonology. The reader who has, for instance, digested sound spectrograms in their linguistic significance, has a far clearer understanding of the bases of timbre. One such basis is the relation of the *formants* of a given sound to each other and to those of other sounds: *formants* may be crudely defined as pitch zones in which voice overtones are strengthened, owing to the voice-cavity configuration. But a sound may be abrupt or lingering, noise-like or music-like. Jakobson thinks each speech sound in a given language is recognized by its "reading" against a selection from some dozen "either-or" pairs of characteristics. Though their function is linguistic, such features can have aesthetic qualities and natural associations, while in poetry *all* sound qualities come in. When considering the associations of sounds, *articulation* is more important in stops and fricatives, *timbre* in vowels and final nasals or liquids; but the student should be familiar with the "vowel-polygon."

From Plato's *Cratylus* onward the power of sounds has been recognized. A. W. Schlegel connected each vowel with a hue and a feeling-tone; romantics and symbolists made much of universal *correspondances* and synaesthesias; the *instrumentalistes* equated each vowel class with a class of musical instrument; Rimbaud's vowel/color sonnet is suspect, but Ernst Jünger elaborates a nexus of ideas for each vowel. Psychological investigators record synaesthesias, some conflicting; Gestalt theorists invoke *coenesthesia*, basic feelings underlying all pairs of contrasting sensations. Grammont notes as-

-[856]-

ociations with emotive expression, percepts, and (metaphorically) abstracts; German writers discuss the general problem, lexical and poetic. Paget and others back articulatory "gesture." Macdermott relates Eng. vowel types predominant in verse passages, to the subject. Imitative and suggestive words have been adduced in all tongues. Wundt distinguishes noise imitation, other percepts suggested by sound, and "metaphors" in which speech sound and object arouse related feelings. Bühler distinguishes objective from relational fidelity (*Relationstreue*) such as that of a fever chart to the fever. The poetic vowel classifications of Grammont and Macdermott are well enough founded to be approximable with Jakobson's linguistic ones. But the most painstaking of the skeptics, P. Delbouille, in a highly critical review of theories, assigns to sound suggestion a very rare derivative rôle.

It is clear that every sound (-collocation) has multiple affinities. The whole picture is distorted by lexical associations. Thus one word (or set) may attract others *in the language* (*swing, sway, swirl, swill, swish, swash, swoop, swat, switch*) and/or *in verse*, where Trannoy speaks of the harmony-generating word: in "Se mêlaient au bruit sourd des ruisseaux sur la mousse" (Hugo), *ruisseaux* is supposed to generate *bruit sourd* since we would expect *bruit clair*: over-simply, since *sur* and *mousse* also echo.

Nevertheless, potential associations are activated in certain milieux. In "And the dull wheel hums doleful through the day" (Crabbe) the monotony is conveyed by the doubled *d-l*, lingering *l*'s and *m*, driving *d*'s, flat British *u*'s. In "Liberty . . . o'er Spain, / Scattering contagious fire into the sky, / Gleamed. My soul spurned the chains of its dismay" (Shelley) the release and ardor are expressed by the swishing *s*'s, leaping *sp*'s, flinging *sk*'s, gay *ā/ai*'s. In "The horrid crags, by toppling convent crown'd, / The cork-trees hoar that clothe the shaggy steep, / The mountain-moss by scorching skies imbrown'd" (Byron), the scene is suggested by the gasping *h*'s, dark *or*'s and *ŏ*'s, rugged *kr*'s, hard-edged *k*'s and *ag*'s, sweeping *mount/m-own'd*, abrupt *-p*'s, dizzy *sk*'s and spiring *trees/steep*. In Mallarmé's swan-sonnet the *i*'s illuminate white bird, frozen winter, spiritual intensity, sterility. Rilke uses *i*-sounds similarly in the unicorn Sonnet to Orpheus, but almost confined to certain lines, set in contrast with *a*-sounds in the first quatrain and *au* in the second, and in modulation with *ei* in the sestet. (Tone-colors can also be used for themselves alone without "program.")

To systematize is possible. Depending on the language (see below), vowels like [e, i, y] tend to be appropriate to height, intensity, sharpness, thinness, delicacy, minuteness, insignificance, pallidity, purity, rarefaction, mobility; but such as [a, ɒ, ɔ] to the opposite notions; like [u, o] to hollowness, roundness, solemnity, gloom, depth, softness, malleability, liquidity; but such as [a, æ, ɛ] to their opposites; like [y, ø, œ] to preciosity, charm, melancholy; but such as [ʌ, ɑ] to their antitheses; rounded vowels generally to interest, rich hue or form; but others to the reverse; vowels like [u, y, i] to mystery, tenderness, cool tints; but such as [a, ɑ, ɒ] to their contraries; short vowels can be brisk or trite, long vowels operatic (diphthongs plastically expressive). *Consonants:—resonants* (nasals, liquids) can suggest harmony, flow, protraction (especially as finals), malleability; *stops:* the opposites; *voiceless:* levity, agitation; *voiced:* the converse; *hissing:* scorn, tenuity; *hushing:* swarm, effusion; *both the last:* speed, harshness; *r*'s: roughness, menace, warmth; *labials:* warm emotions; *velars:* cold emotions; *stops juxtaposed:* obstacle shapes; *fricatives combined with other cons.:* movement shapes. (Cf. Hevner, Macdermott, Grammont, Lockemann, Jakobson.)

But each language differs phonologically, and hence in its aesthetic resources. Thus Gr. words (cf. Norwegian, Swedish, etc.) were probably pitch-accented, L. stress-accented; Germanic tongues have forceful expiratory stress, weak syllables being often slurred, galloped over, or even dropped (today especially in S. England); Romance languages (except European Portuguese) are more evenly stressed and precisely articulated (Fr. especially); weak Rus. syllables are also phonetically reduced. Eng. and Rus. bristle with difficult consonant groups, and in general Germanic and Slavonic contrast in this respect with the simpler syllables of Romance. Danish, and partly Sp., seriously weaken noninitial "stops" (see PHONETIC EQUIVALENCE). L., Gr., early Germanic tongues, It., Finnish, Hungarian, etc., possess double-duration consonants (It. *chi* [s]*sono, hanno*) as well as vowels. In It. and Sp. few syllables end with a consonant, and there are 7 or 5 vowel sounds to England's twenty-odd. Eng., Dutch, German, etc., possess gently "falling" diphthongs (which in Eng. replace most "long" vowels); German, Fr., Dutch, etc., possess rounded front vowels; Fr., Polish, and Portuguese have their nasal vowels. Most Rus. vowels are dull and lax, and so are the "short" vowels in Eng. and other Germanic tongues; Rus. and standard Sp. have no "long" vowels. Many Slav tongues are rich in hissing and hushing consonants, and possess a palatalized set of consonants and (in effect) vowels. Romance languages possess palatal *n* and, usually, *l*. Fr., Portuguese, Icelandic, Welsh, Finnish, etc., lack affricates.

Some Germanic phonologies have perhaps more affinity with the violent, unstable, rugged, distinctive aspects of existence; Romance ones, with the harmonious, steady, smooth, reiterative. If so, the *reverse* aspects should be expressed more easily with less means: hardness and roughness more economically in Romance than in Germanic, e.g. by *a*'s, *r*'s, stops: "un choc d'armures, / Quand la sourde mêlée étreint les escadrons" (Hugo) (helped by the hiatus); fullness, peace, richness more economically in Germanic, e.g. by long sonorous syllables (*Paradise Lost* 4.242–50). Languor is expressible by nasal vowels in Fr., by dull vowels and final resonants in Eng.; excitement or movement by acute vowels in Fr., by *sp*, *sw*, *sl*, *st*, *sh*, *nce* in Eng. (as in Shelley). Sounds too common in discourse tend to neutralize their effects: e.g. *th*-, *-s*, [ə], [ɪ] in Eng. Grammatical like-endings bind speech or verse more monotonously together in Gr., L. (German, It., Sp., Portuguese, Slavonic), Finnish, etc.; and paucity of vowel types does the same in Sp. or It.; but Eng. and Fr. starkness is partly cluttered up through analytical syntax and particles.

W. M. Wundt, *Völkerpsychologie* (v. 1–2, 1904); A. I. Trannoy, *La musique des vers* (1929); Sir R. A. S. Paget, *Human Speech* (1930); H. Werner, *Grundfragen der Sprachphysiognomik* (1932) ; K. Bühler, *Sprachtheòrie: die Darstellungsfunktion der Sprache* (1934); K. Hevner, "An Experimental Study of the Affective Value of Sounds in Poetry," *Am. J. of Psych.*, 49 (1937); H. Lützeler, "Die Lautgestaltung in der Lyrik," *Zeitschrift für Aesth.*, 29 (1935); W. Schneider, "Über die Lautbedeutsamkeit," *ZDP*, 63 (1938); M. M. Macdermott, *Vowel Sounds in Poetry* (1940); E. Jünger, "Lob der Vokale" in his *Blätter und Steine* (1942); M. Grammont, *Traité de phonétique* (3e éd., 1946, pt. 3); R. K. Potter, G. A. Kapp and H. C. Green, *Visible Speech* (1947); P. Delattre, "The Physiological Interpretation of Sound Spectrograms," *PMLA*, 66 (1951); F. Lockemann, *Das Gedicht und seine Klanggestalt* (1952); J. J. Lynch, "The Tonality of Lyric Poetry," *Word*, 9 (1953); W. Wandruschka, "Ausdruckswerte der Sprachlaute," *Germ.-Rom.Monatsschr.*, n.F., 4 (1954); R. Jakobson and M. Halle, *Fundamentals of Language* (1956); P. Delbouille, *Poésie et sonorités: la critique contemporaine devant le pouvoir suggestif des sons* (1961).　　D.I.M.

TOPOGRAPHICAL POEM. T. poetry was defined in 1799 by Dr. Johnson as "*local poetry*, of which the fundamental subject is some particular landscape . . . with the addition of . . . historical retrospection or incidental meditation." Known to the ancients in versegeographies and in accounts of voyages, the genre was established in Eng. poetry by Sir John Denham's *Cooper Hill* (1642). Through-

out the next century and a half, it flourished luxuriously in Eng. verse, where as many as nine subcategories (hills, towns, rivers, buildings, caves, etc.), each with numerous representatives, may be distinguished. Thomson, Dyer, Crabbe, and a multitude of minor poets wrote t. poetry, but its importance as a separate genre was largely outmoded by the extensive use of descriptive detail for other purposes in romantic poetry, as in Wordsworth's *Tintern Abbey* or *Ode on Intimations of Immortality*. John Betjeman has recently revived t. verse in short works with humorous effect, but no major serious works have appeared.—D. L. Durling, *Georgic Tradition in Eng. Poetry* (1935); R. A. Aubin, *T. Poetry in 18th-C. England* (1936); R. M. Thale, "Crabbe's *Village* and T. Poetry," *JEGP*, 55 (1956).　　S.F.F.

TORNADA. A final short stanza, comparable to the Fr. *envoi*, added to many Old Prov. poems as a kind of dedication to a patron or friend. In form, the t. usually reproduces the metrical structure and the rhymes of the last part of the preceding stanza. Some poems have 2 or even 3 *tornadas*, addressed to different persons.　　F.M.C.

TOUCHSTONE. A term used by Matthew Arnold in "The Study of Poetry," first published in 1880 as a general introduction to Ward's *The Eng. Poets*. Arnold's touchstones are "lines and expressions of the great masters" which are supposed to reveal "the presence or absence of high poetic quality, and also the degree of this quality" in poems placed beside them. Arnold advocates his touchstone method of criticism as the basis of a "real," as opposed to a "historic" or "personal," estimate of poetry. Passages have "high poetic quality" if they have high seriousness and the grand style. Of the touchstones Arnold applies in his survey of Eng. poets, three each are from Homer, Dante, and Milton, and two are from Shakespeare. Though Arnold's touchstones strikingly express certain moods, they are not essences of the poetry from which they are taken but rather of certain states of Arnold's mind. Eight of them reflect melancholy, two devotion, one courage. Even if Arnold's touchstones did convey the quality of their sources, they would have limitations as critical tools. No part conveys a whole, and Arnold's parts are themselves limited. Arnold thought of seriousness as solemnity and offered no touchstones for natural magic or merriment.

Arnold did not originate the use of the poetical fragment as a touchstone. Longinus conveyed the quality of the greatest poetry by quoting quintessential passages, and so did John Dennis and Joseph Warton.—M. Arnold, "The Study of Poetry," *Essays in Crit.*, 2d ser.

(1888); L. Trilling, *Matthew Arnold* (1939); Abrams, ch. 6; J. S. Eells, Jr., *The Touchstones of Matthew Arnold* (1955).   J.K.R.

TRADITION. To treat comprehensively the idea of t. as related to poetry would involve the whole history of poetry, since t. in the widest sense signifies consciousness of the past. Antitraditionalism is relatively rare in literary history; with the exception of the experimental school of contemporary poets and possibly the 19th-c. romantics, poets have normally emulated the achievement of their predecessors. Traditionalism is one of the constant ingredients of the classical outlook, which has survived beyond the neoclassic period in the work of such writers as Matthew Arnold and T. S. Eliot. To regard literary history as a continuous cyclical alternation of t. and revolt is inaccurate, since the proportion of innovation to t. has always been slight.

In contemporary criticism, the term is employed in two different but not unrelated senses. It refers, in one instance, not to literature, but to culture and society. A number of critics have been occupied with the problem of the poet's relation to society; the peculiar difficulties of modern poetry have been attributed to the disintegration of traditional society which has gradually been taking place since the Renaissance, and to the consequent loss of religious and moral authority.

The poets and critics who have been aware of the absence of traditional society in the modern world have also been those who have been most concerned with t. in poetry. In this context, t. usually signifies "the tradition," as in the title of Cleanth Brooks's *Modern Poetry and the Tradition*. The writings of T. E. Hulme and T. S. Eliot's "Tradition and the Individual Talent" (1917) were largely responsible for reestablishing traditionalism as a central concept in modern poetry. Eliot's essay, appearing at a time when experimentalism in poetry was at its height, had a tremendous impact upon subsequent speculation and taste. In retrospect it appears to be a moderate enough statement of the classical point of view, stressing the continuity of the present with the past and affirming the objectivity of the work of art, hence its essential impersonality. For Eliot, t. involves the historical sense —the perception of the presence of the past as well as its pastness. He postulates, furthermore, the simultaneous existence of the works of the past. The most important statement in the essay with respect to subsequent criticism concerns the main current of Eng. poetry which, according to Eliot, does not necessarily flow through the most distinguished reputations. The t. or main current is not specified, but later essays, among them the essay on

"The Metaphysical Poets," were devoted to it. Other influential critics and poets, notably the Nashville group consisting of Allen Tate, John Crowe Ransom, and Robert Penn Warren, were also contributing to the idea of a main t. in Eng. poetry, which has since become the contemporary equivalent of "the classical tradition" of former periods.

The lines of the t. are clearly defined. The criteria for inclusion are based on a conception of a poetic sensibility capable of assimilating and fusing experiences of a widely divergent kind. Traditional poetry, sometimes called poetry of synthesis, is recognized principally by its use of metaphor, which is functional rather than decorative, involving the union of thought and sensation. Eliot perceived the current as having risen in the 16th-c. poets, having reached its climax in the late Elizabethan dramatists and the 17th-c. metaphysical poets —Donne, Crashaw, Vaughan, Herbert, Lord Herbert, Marvell, King, Cowley—and ceasing suddenly with the "dissociation of sensibility," the bifurcation of sensation and intellect, which set in with Milton and Dryden and survived throughout the 18th and 19th c. in England.

The peculiar intellectual qualities of the 16th- and 17th-c. Eng. poetry reappeared in the work of two late 19th-c. Fr. poets, Jules Laforgue and Tristran Corbière; the symbolists are assimilated into the t. available to modern poets. Cleanth Brooks's *Modern Poetry and the Tradition* contains the fullest exposition of the continuation of the metaphysical-symbolist t. in modern poetry. It is interesting to note that within the last generation there have been gradual changes in the outlines of the t. The exclusions are not so rigid, and several neoclassic and romantic poets who had previously been excluded are now admitted.

An objection voiced against the contemporary traditionalists is that their revision of the history of Eng. poetry was undertaken in the interests of a single school of contemporary poetry. The objection is partly anticipated in "Tradition and the Individual Talent," for there Eliot points out that the relations of the present and past are reciprocal rather than static and that the appearance of a really new work alters the "order" formed by the monuments of the past. Without providing for flexibility and change, traditionalism actually becomes as stultifying as it is imagined to be by the most violent antitraditionalist.

T. S. Eliot, *The Sacred Wood: Essays on Poetry and Crit.* (1921), *After Strange Gods: a Primer of Modern Heresy* (1934) and *The Idea of a Christian Society* (1939); T. E. Hulme, *Speculations*, ed. H. Read (1924); G. Murray, *The Classical T. in Poetry* (1927); J. L. Lowes, *T. and Revolt* (1930); A. Nicoll, "Eliot and the

Revival of Classicism," *Eng. Jour.*, 23 (1934); F. R. Leavis, *Revaluation* (1936); A. Tate, *Reactionary Essays on Poetry and Ideas* (1936) and *Reason in Madness* (1941); C. Brooks, *Modern Poetry and the T.* (1939); G. Hough, *Reflections on a Literary Revolution* (1960); J. V. Cunningham, *T. and Poetic Structure* (1961); S. Lucy, *T. S. Eliot and the Idea of T.* (1961).

s.f.

TRADUCTIO. See ANADIPLOSIS.

TRAGEDY. Courage and inevitable defeat: when we confront the great literature of t. from our everyday world, it is perhaps these two qualities that strike us most forcibly, for the first in any society is rare and the second is a prospect most men find intolerable. Without courage or endurance, the exceptional action or commitment which characterizes t. would not be undertaken or sustained; without defeat, it would not be placed in the perspective of the ordinary world. For the tragic gesture or thrust is on too grand a scale to conform to the ways of the world or to find means to alter them. After comedy and most other literary forms, life goes on; but t. stops history, it is a summit or end stage, always concerned with problems of value; it is human life seen in an ultimate perspective. The tragic protagonist's courage must seem possible—not absurd, but astonishing or praiseworthy in the extreme. Without such courage, there is no compelling example. But it must also be doomed. If not, action and thought are not internalized, character is not fully developed, values are not transformed. Courage without an overpowering challenge, moreover, can be mere bravado or foolhardiness. Defeat without a great attempt can be mere pathos. T. as a literary form demands that both be brought into a unity. Great action is probably rarer in literature, even, than it is in life, but in Greece of the 5th c. B.C. (Aeschylus, Sophocles, and Euripides), and late 16th- and 17th-c. England (Marlowe, Shakespeare, Webster, and their contemporaries), Spain (Lope de Vega and Calderón), and France (Corneille and Racine), it recommends itself to the writer in the boldest forms.

The word "tragedy" will here be employed to refer to a form of the drama which can be distinguished from plays of mere violence or disaster in the close relationships which it establishes between character and fate and the fitness of its means to its ends. And it can be distinguished from the drama of sentiment in the stern logic of its events and the grandeur of its conceptions. Terror and pity, to use the conventional terms, should be caught in equipoise. Other elements, too, are usually in balance. The hero's struggle in t. does not seem

meaningless nor his universe too ordered, for either extreme would deprive his action of its full significance. And this struggle itself, which is central, suggests, especially since the Greeks, that man's will is neither wholly predetermined nor wholly free. Strangely, t. is almost wholly a phenomenon of the Western world.

Many of the characteristics posited here for t. would seem to apply equally well, of course, to an epic like *Paradise Lost,* or to novels, say, by Dostoevsky or Hardy or Faulkner. The tragic view of life is clearly not limited to dramatic form. Perhaps two or three hundred years or more before Aeschylus, Homer in the *Iliad* seems to have established, once and for all, the broad outlines of the tragic experience. In the fierce absoluteness of Achilles' withdrawal and the terror of his return, in his mysterious collaboration with forces either divine or in nature above and beyond himself, Homer seems to have created the archetypal tragic hero. Nevertheless, it seems wise to limit our use of the word to the formal drama—to suggest structure and form as well as idea, situation, character, and tone.

T. has proved to be as flexible as the other major genres, and generalizations about the nature of the form do not of course apply in detail to the tragedies of all times and places. The Greeks did not even insist, as we see in the *Philoctetes* and other plays, that tragedies must always have unhappy endings. There are, however, a surprising number of similarities in form and content between the tragedies of ancient Greece and those of the modern world. All exhibit a central character (or characters) isolated from his fellows who is caught in a difficult situation, usually ending with his death. Surrounding him are various other persons who are involved with the hero in his predicament or who respond variously to his actions, with support or with bitter criticism. Their function in part is to place the hero's struggle in perspective—to afford us norms of vision or judgment by which we can appraise it. This struggle itself may take many different forms. The hero's predicament can arise primarily through elements in his own make-up, through the plotting of another or others, through the very nature of his environment, through the will or heaven, or, more probably, through a combination of these. Essentially, this predicament is part of the plot, the "given" of the play. The protagonist may respond to a challenge with energy and defiance, or he may confront his destiny more stoically. He may go through several stages or changes in the course of this experience or may fall quite suddenly from well-being to disaster. He may arrive sooner or later at a recognition of his place in the universe, of a relationship between his character and his fate, or he may apprehend less about his experience than do other characters or members of a chorus or the audience, thus creating situations of tragic irony. These alternatives are not, of course, mutually exclusive, and they may predominate variously at different times in the same play.

The relationship between character and plot in most great t. is so intimate that we speak of the "inevitability" of a series of events in this form, and of the particular challenge confronting the hero and the end to which he comes as part of his "fate." A man's fate, like his character, is usually the shape or result of a collaboration between forces working from within and from without. In the *Iliad* and Aeschylus, these outer forces are primarily divine in origin; in Sophocles and Euripides, often less clearly so. In Shakespeare, whether divine or infernal, superhuman forces supply primary motivation for action in two plays (*Hamlet* and *Macbeth*); in the others, external forces, when not human, are difficult to define, but they seem—as is usually true with the Greeks—either hostile to the hero's actions or indifferent to them. And forces working from within the hero, initiating or echoing those without, are often contradictory or divisive and threaten to split him apart.

The predicaments in which protagonists find themselves—men who would appear to be impervious to temptation or folly in other situations—seem calculated to baffle, try, or torture them. And opportunists or villains in t. choose their mighty victims and, like the fates, appear to manipulate the machinery of the plot to destroy them with appalling ingenuity. Indeed, the actions of these lesser persons and the movements of the plot form an instrument finely adapted to the testing and laying bare of the nature of heroism. The gods or fates, or the great tragedians, rarely select weak men for heroic destinies. Since Aristotle, students of t. have debated endlessly the character of the protagonist. Frequently, the traditional theory of the "tragic flaw" (q.v.), Aristotle's *hamartia*, when applied to specific cases, simplifies and indeed prejudges this character. Were it not for the protagonist's "flaw," we are told—his folly, obsessions, or crimes—he would not find himself the target of so menacing a concert of forces, in heaven, society, other individuals, and in himself. Or at least he would be able to master or transcend them.

To be sure, the tragic protagonist is rarely thought by those around him to be without fault. Among the attitudes which he exhibits when confronted with an overwhelming challenge is a courage or an inflexible dedication which easily becomes stubbornness, arrogance, foolhardiness, or blind rage, and which others inevitably think outrageous, wicked, or blasphemous. We could scarcely expect them to respond otherwise, and we may frequently ally ourselves with their point of view. The chorus in Greek t. often speaks for traditional communal and religious values which it knows are threatened by the protagonist's attitudes or behavior, especially his *hybris* or pride. And in t. written in Christian times, choral voices chronicling the hero's progress can speak, if occasion demands, with all of the Church's or society's sanctions against the unregenerate will or against man's assuming the prerogatives of the gods. But we rarely ally ourselves wholly with the chorus or with these voices. With his emphasis upon pity and terror, Aristotle has suggested a kind of double response in ourselves to the fate of the hero. Through a process (catharsis, q.v.) which is still debated, he speaks of our "purging" ourselves of these powerful emotions by entertaining them vicariously. It may be wiser, however, to speak of t. as enabling us to experience these heightened and contradictory emotions rather than as purging us of them.

Comedy often seems to prompt in us a degree of detachment from a person or group, t. a degree of identification with a central character. We do not identify ourselves wholly and at all times with the protagonist, nor do we fail to withdraw in amazement from his willfulness or daring. And yet we do seem to be experiencing something of the fate of the hero as we hear or read, and to see the central dilemma primarily through his eyes. A negative or moralistic approach to t. undervalues the hero's strength and in effect short-circuits the tragic experience. The "sin" or weakness of the hero is often inextricably associated with the strength which enables him to struggle or endure; it is a condition of his being. Furthermore, the disparity in t. between the protagonist's folly and its consequences in suffering, between his agonizing sense of guilt or loneliness and the remoteness of the powers that might acknowledge or forgive him, does not encourage us to form simple moral judgments. It may therefore be more helpful to speak of tragic virtue than of a tragic flaw, of the hero as a man elected or selected for his fate because of his greatness, rather than spotted for it because of his folly, and of the solemn spectacle of his experience as an exalted example—not to be pursued literally, of course —rather than as a warning. The price that the hero pays for his exceptional action is suffering and death, to be sure. But the emphasis is not only on his folly and punishment, but on the way in which he responds to the challenge which confronts him, on his daring, or on his ability to bear the worst that heaven and earth can devise. The focus is thus upon his grandness rather than his goodness. T. brings sheer power and human spirit into opposition, and it is the triumph of the latter, at whatever cost, that we admire. When during a crisis most men would make the minor or major compromises that might save them from disaster, resign themselves to numb passivity or to tears, abandon their course as sheer folly, or buckle under their burdens, the tragic protagonist frequently seems with each new challenge or stroke of fate to grow bolder or more absolute.

The periods of major t. are probably nourished by many different, even conflicting, attitudes, philosophies, and religious beliefs, and rarely can be made to conform to single systems of belief, whether Christian or pagan. It is clear that theories of "poetic justice" in literature or life—careful adjustment of the punishment to fit the crime, the reward to match the virtue—are alien to the spirit of the tragic world. And ages characterized by certain dominant attitudes—implicit trust in a universe wholly rational, predictable, or divine, in which whatever is, is right—or by a disbelief in the finality of evil—have not turned to t. as a characteristic form of expression. If the hero is fairly sure from the outset that he will be forgiven, redeemed, or even rewarded for his actions, then the bewilderment, helplessness, and transformation of values we associate with the tragic experience are greatly qualified. The grimmer attitudes of other ages also have not given rise to t. Classical fatalism alone does not provide the grounds for t., and the medieval Fortune's wheel is not an adequate image for the tragic experience—indeed, the wheel turned in an age without formal t. If the relationship between a man's acts and his consequent suffering is wholly capricious, there clearly can be little of the inevitability about his experience that we associate with t. All generalizations about this subject are hazardous, however. In Euripides, for instance, Hecuba and Heracles, who are without fault, struggle and are overwhelmed in a universe of total disorder.

In Greece, t. seems to have arisen in the 6th c. B.C. out of the festivals in honor of Dionysus, the god principally associated with the death and rebirth of the year. From the outset, its basis is communal and ritualistic, its medium poetry, and its accompaniments dance, song, and spectacle. And it is associated with a sense of mystery or wonder. As with many other forms of art, it achieves a greatness very early in its development which in certain respects has never been surpassed. Three dramatists of the 5th c. B.C. are primarily responsible for bringing the Gr. theatre to preeminence. From Aeschylus' first extant play (472 B.C. or earlier) to Euripides' last (406), the movement of Gr. t. is from ritual and a concern with the gods and fate, to a concern with the passions of everyday men and women. Over this period, t. begins to give way to tragicomedy, romance, and other forms. In Aeschylus (525–456), the chorus is of the utmost importance to the meaning and structure of the play, and the two (and later three) actors usually represent persons of divine or heroic stature. A series of related plays (three tragedies and a satyr play) form a unified work of art, like the *Oresteia*, dealing with themes of justice, of sin, and punishment. In Euripides (480?–?406), the chorus is far less significant, the plays in a series are not necessarily related, and the three or more actors move in a world of greater psychological realism. Contemporary with these two dramatists, Sophocles (496?–406), in plays like those in his Theban cycle, combines something of Aeschylus' concern for the will of the gods with Euripides' concern for more detailed probings of the heart. It is Sophocles' drama which serves as the basis for Aristotle's remarks on t. in the *Poetics*. Sophocles' elegant and perfected verse lies somewhere between the richly metaphoric, heroic language of Aeschylus and the restless and subtle verse of Euripides. Though he was ridiculed by Aristophanes during his lifetime, Euripides has had the greatest influence upon later writers of t., from Hellenistic times down to the 17th c. in France and beyond.

Classical t. on the highest level dies as suddenly as it is born, and it is about twenty centuries before t. is written again by men who are at once practical men of the theatre and great poets. Many of Euripides' plays are later freely revised by Seneca (4 B.C.?–A.D. 65), the Roman who is the next important tragedian whose plays we possess, now chiefly of historical significance. Roman t., throughout imitative of Gr. example, heightens the melodramatic elements in Euripides and is thus often characterized by extravagant rhetoric and violence. The Stoicism of Seneca and the dominant characteristics of his theatre—the use of revenge motifs, of ghosts and portents, and so on— exert a great influence, across some 1600 years, over the reviving drama of the Renaissance. The fact that Seneca writes a drama probably not intended for performance on a stage may partly explain why Chaucer and others, who knew him during the long medieval period when there is practically no serious drama along classical lines, consider t. a narrative with an unhappy ending merely to be read or recited.

The body of poetic t. in the late 16th and the 17th c., inspired partly by the revered example of Seneca and later the Greeks, partly by the full use of the power inherent in native folk and religious traditions (the moralities, mysteries, and miracle plays), is the richest of all of those in the Western world of which we have fairly full record. Appearing and disappearing as suddenly as did the Greek, this drama has not been surpassed in poetic power since the 17th c. In Spain, in Lope de Vega (1562–1635) and Calderón (1600–81) and others, it rarely takes the form of "pure" t., but of intrigues of love and honor, and plays on patriotic, historical, philosophical, and religious themes. But it possesses undeniable dignity and great variety, and the breadth of its appeal to the wide public which attended its performances, and its use of interlocking plots, themes, and many poetic styles are very similar to the practice of drama in Elizabethan England.

The great period of Eng. t. is very brief—on the highest level about twenty-five years, all told about fifty. Toward the end of the 16th c., traditions of the classical theatre (especially Seneca) and native Eng. subject matter and forms are crossed very swiftly, and a wide variety of tragedies suddenly appears—of revenge, of honor, of ambition, of love, pride or blind heroism, and of many other kinds. The large casts of characters in these plays, their complicated balancing of tragic and comic elements, plot and subplot, hero and fool, their vivid and violent action and frequent passages of philosophical reflection, and their richly metaphoric blank verse, interspersed with rhymed verse and songs, render these plays in many ways unique in the history of world theatre. Though Shakespeare's tragedies—from *Romeo and Juliet* (ca. 1595) to *Coriolanus* (1608)—are the masterpieces of this period, many writers, from Marlowe through Webster, Beaumont and Fletcher, Middleton, and so on, produce tragedies of great poetic power. Like Shakespeare, they often employ a language which ranges from lyric to rhetoric, from prose to formal couplets and blank verse, from simple exposition to a highly embellished figurative style.

Fr. t., like the Gr., focuses upon a few characters, usually historical or mythological, confronting one another at a moment of crisis. It is unlike the Eng., which pursues the development of several characters through a variety of events and changes of mood. Though the first Fr. writers of t. share something of the native linguistic exuberance of earlier writers like Rabelais, the triumph of the unities in France, under the influence of Richelieu and others, prompts tragedians to turn toward matter drawn from Spain, Rome, and Greece, and toward discipline and decorum in style. The Golden Age of Fr. t. develops from *Le Cid* of Corneille (1606–84), with its emphasis upon conflicts between love and duty, to the more perfectly proportioned tragedies of Racine (1639–99), with their psychologically subtle studies of irresistible passion, conveyed in masterfully controlled alexandrines. In the 18th and 19th c., the heroic figures of 17th-c. t. become either more commonplace or more extravagant. In the *drame tragique* and the *drame bourgeois*, Fr. classical t. is replaced, as t. is in England, by various forms of melodrama and tragicomedy, and poetry is almost wholly replaced by prose. Among the few remaining writers of verse t., Voltaire combines 17th-c. forms with 18th-c. attitudes, and Hugo heralds the triumph of romanticism. In the 18th and early 19th c., several writers in other countries of Europe produce verse t., or near-t., of great power, especially the It. Alfieri (1749–1803), the Rus. Pushkin (1799–1837), and the Germans Goethe (1749–1832) and Schiller (1759–1805), followed by Kleist, Grillparzer, and others.

Since the 17th c., t. throughout the Western world has undergone several fundamental changes. The assumptions of neoclassicism, romanticism, and of related movements of the past hundred years or so, such as naturalism or realism, are in varying ways quite different from those that underlie both ancient t. and that of the 16th and 17th c. With a vanishing of a pervasive belief in and of images for the interrelatedness of all things, the dramatist's placing of man's struggle in a mysterious cosmos at once of nature, of human society, and of the divine becomes increasingly difficult. After the 17th c. and the disappearance of the partly communal or ceremonial function of the drama—a function which prompted audiences to seek edification as well as entertainment, through a heightened and compressed poetic language—there has developed an enormous new reading public for the novel, and thus new writers who wished to explore the basic problems in more relaxed and expansive forms. This new public has often sought dramatic forms that are less demanding —images of itself less aristocratic or uncompromising than those provided by earlier t., and less unsentimentally detached than those provided by much earlier comedy. This is not to say, of course, that Ibsen and Strindberg, Chekhov, Hauptmann, Shaw, Pirandello, O'Neill, and other dramatists, writing chiefly in prose during the last century or so, have not written great or at least impressive plays. But, with the possible exception of Ibsen, the work of these playwrights cannot be said to equal in scope and expressive power the work of the greatest of modern novelists, who have attempted and achieved something commensurate with earlier verse t. In a world skeptical, as it has had to become, of "heroes" or of innate superiority founded upon birth or class, and often distrustful of independent action which threatens the fabric of society, the novelists have probably managed to create the only images of human life in our time worthy to be set alongside those of Aeschylus, Racine, or Shakespeare. In another form of theatre in the 19th c., t. has come to fullest expressiveness in opera, especially in the work of Wagner and Verdi. The work of the few modern dramatists who have written something like verse t. in recent times—Yeats, Synge, Eliot, Claudel, Brecht, Lorca, and others—may, however, lead to further experimentation and achievement.

A. E. Haigh, *The Tragic Drama of the Greeks* (1896); A. C. Bradley, *Shakespearean T.* (1904); G. Norwood, *Gr. T.* (1920); M. de Unamuno, *The Tragic Sense of Life,* tr. J.E.C. Flitch (1921); F. Nietzsche, "The Birth of T.," *Complete Works,* I (1924); W. B. Yeats, "Tragic Theatre," *Essays* (1924); H. C. Lancaster, *A Hist. of Fr. Dramatic Literature in the 17th C.* (1929–42); A. A. Tilley, *Three Fr. Dramatists* (1933); H.D.F. Kitto, *Gr. T.* (1939); D. L. Savory, *Jean Racine* (1940); M. E. Prior,. *The Language of T.* (1947); M. Turnell, *The Cl. Moment* (1947); L. Spitzer, *Linguistics and Lit. Hist.* (1948); C. Leech, *Shakespeare's Tragedies and Other Studies in the 17th C. Drama* (1950); A. Sewell, *Character and Society in Shakespeare* (1951); C. Whitman, *Sophocles* (1951); *Tragic Themes in Western Lit.,* ed. C. Brooks (1955); T. R. Henn, *The Harvest of T.* (1956); H. J. Muller, *The Spirit of T.* (1956); Frye; L. Lowenthal, *Lit. and the Image of Man* (1957); R. Langbaum, *The Poetry of Experience* (1957); R. Lattimore, *The Poetry of Gr. T.* (1958); R. B. Sewall, *The Vision of T.* (1959); D. D. Raphael, *The Paradox of T.* (1960); R. Ornstein, *The Moral Vision of Jacobean T.* (1960); G. Steiner, *The Death of T.* (1961); E. Olson, *Tr. and the Theory of Drama* (1961). See also J. Jones, *On Aristotle and Gr. T.* (1962); *Le Théâtre tragique,* ed. J. Jacquot (1962); *T.: Modern Essays in Crit.,* ed. L. Michel and R. B. Sewall (1963).   R.J.D.

TRAGIC FLAW. The defect in character which brings about the ruin of the protagonist. Before tragedy had been differentiated from ritual, there was no need to "understand" the fall of the hero. He fell because the ceremony demanded his fall, much as a dancer performs a pirouette because the choreographer calls for one. The first step in the transition from ritual to problem play is the idea that characters suffer because of "fate" or "destiny." The tragedies of Aeschylus, still close to the primitive myths which inspired them, emphasize fate. When fate is identified with the will of the gods, as in *Prometheus Bound*, the gods necessarily emerge as cruel taskmasters who derive pleasure from the agonies of the hero.

Aristotle's *Poetics* contains the first—and still a basic—discussion of t.f. (Gr. *hamartia*), although critics disagree concerning the interpretation of several of his remarks and the proper definition of *hamartia*. According to Aristotle the tragic hero must have nobility (be "better than" ourselves, but he must also have a defect: ". . . the intermediate kind of personage, a man not pre-eminently virtuous and just, whose misfortune, however, is brought upon him *not by vice and depravity but by some error of judgment. . . ."* It should be noted that this is not a moral flaw. The Aristotelian definition takes us one step beyond the tragedy of fate, but it does not justify interpreting the tragic catastrophe as the just punishment of some crime committed by the protagonist. It combines two discordant elements, nobility and proneness to error, without reconciling them. It thus suggests the element of paradox which seems essential to the greatest tragedy.

Later critics tended to destroy the Aristotelian balance by eliminating the paradox. In consonance with the pervasive classical theory of *paideia* (literature as education), they emphasized the moral implications of the t.f. The t.f. became a vice—usually *hamartia* was interpreted as "pride"—and the fall of the protagonist served to illustrate the folly of succumbing to vice. To Sir Philip Sidney, for example, tragedy "openeth the greatest wounds, and showeth forth the ulcers that are covered with tissue, that maketh kings fear to be tyrants, and tyrants manifest their tyrannical humors. . . ." Something like this view of tragedy can be found in germinal form in Euripides (*Medea, Hippolytus*), and in less attractive but more consistent form in Seneca (e.g., *Thyestes, Hercules Furens*). Despite its logical soundness, it was damaging to tragedy in the Hellenistic and late Roman period. The more vice was emphasized, the less noble became the tragic hero. In Seneca, the hero's fall is generally so well deserved that it fails to move the reader any more than a newspaper report announcing the execution of a convicted criminal.

Traces of classical theory persisted during the Middle Ages in authors like Euanthius, Isidore of Seville, and Vincent of Beauvais, but tragedy itself was a dead form. Its rebirth began with medieval religious dramas (*Quem quaeritis,* the Corpus Christi plays), which were like the earliest Gr. dramas in being ritualistic. The first theory of tragedy to be found in medieval writers resembles Gr. fatalism. According to the tradition traced by Willard Farnham (*The Medieval Heritage of Elizabethan Tragedy*) from Boccaccio, Chaucer, and Lydgate through *The Mirror for Magistrates,* a tragedy was defined as the fall of a great man from high station because of fickle fortune. At first, character was unimportant. Men rose or fell as Fortune turned her wheel, not because of virtues or defects of character.

Although this view persisted in the 16th c. and even had some influence on Shakespeare (*Romeo and Juliet, Lear*), it gradually gave way to the theory of the t.f.

16th-c. theory was dominated by two forces, humanism and Christianity. These combined to emphasize the moral purpose of literature (a revived *paideia*), and the didactic theory of tragedy prevailed until the late 18th c. Aristotle's *Poetics* was read to conform to this theory by critics such as Robortello, Maggi, and Varchi; and the moral theory of t.f. appears in numerous eclectic works such as Tasso's *Discorsi*, Minturno's *De Poeta*, Corneille's prefaces, Sidney's *Defense*, and Dryden's essays. The practice of Shakespeare and his Eng. contemporaries tends to conform to critical theory in a general way (e.g., *Macbeth* and *Othello* can be read as exemplary, the one illustrating the folly of ambition, and the other, of jealousy), but the didacticism is never simple, and there are many mythic and irrational elements which were unknown to the critics. In fact, several scholars have denied that Aristotle is applicable to Shakespeare. Neoclassic drama (Garnier, Racine, Corneille, Dryden) is somewhat more explicitly didactic, and becomes still more so in the 18th c. (Voltaire, Addison). During this period tragedy degenerated into pompous moralizing seen at its dull best in a work like Addison's *Cato*, and at its worst in Lillo's *London Merchant*.

During the romantic period writers consciously rebelled against neoclassic rationalism. Shakespeare and Aeschylus were praised at the expense of Corneille and Euripides; and there was a marked effort to produce a tragedy with mythic overtones. The most successful example of this effort is Goethe's *Faust*, in which the convention of t.f. is employed with. something of an Aristotelian balance between nobility and error, and myth and morality; however, the works of Schiller (*Wallenstein*) and Kleist (*Penthesilea*) also deserve mention. Fr. and Eng. romantics (e.g. Hugo, Shelley, Browning) worked in the same direction as the Germans but were less successful. Modern dramatists from Ibsen and Strindberg through Eliot and Arthur Miller have generally followed the romantics in avoiding a simple, moral explanation of the t.f. At times (especially Yeats and Synge) they have gone behind Aristotle to the mythic roots of tragedy. Both tendencies have been healthy. They illustrate the paradox that the t.f. is both a necessary element in first-rate tragedy, and a factor which can destroy tragedy if not used with great care.   O.B.H.

For bibliography see TRAGEDY.

TRAGICOMEDY. The term "t." came from Plautus' facetious reference to the unconventional mixture of kings and gods and servants in his own *Amphitryon* as *tragicocomoedia*. The idea of t. as poetic drama that combined elements of both tragedy and comedy was at least as old as Euripides and Aristotle; Euripides wrote tragedies with a happy ending, e.g. *Alcestis* and *Iphigenia in Tauris,* and Aristotle remarked in the *Poetics* that the popular audience preferred tragedy with a double ending—"an opposite issue for the good and bad personages"—to a single unhappy issue. Moreover, Aristotle admitted that a successful tragedy could be based on a fictitious argument, like that of comedy, although most tragic poets used plots drawn from historic or legendary matter.

T. in modern times stemmed from two sources: (1) classical theory and practice, (2) the "people's choice," namely, the reward of virtue and the punishment of vice. There was some overlapping, but the two branches can be distinguished, the classical one springing from classical tragedy and the popular one from the native mysteries, miracles, moralities, and chronicle plays which freely mingled kings with clowns, tears with mirth. Neoclassical t. developed in Italy under the guidance of Giraldi Cinthio, who wrote several tragedies with a happy ending which he called mixed tragedies (*tragedie miste*). Cinthio distrusted Plautus' *tragicocomoedia*, but admitted that his own *Altile* (1543) could be called a *tragicomedia*. His mixed tragedies combined plots patterned after those of the comic poet Terence with the royal or noble characters of tragedy and attempted the lofty style of Seneca and Euripides. The author justified his violation of the classical prescription for separate tragic and comic genres by citing the authority of Aristotle and the example of Euripides. Popular t., on the other hand, developed as an extension of medieval practice, which more often than not ignored classical prescriptions, and this popular t. appeared as "tragical comedies" or "comical tragedies" or "histories," with serious main .plots and comic subplots. The L. school plays of the Christian Terence and vernacular tragicomedies flourished side by side in France, Holland, Germany, and England.

These classical and popular branches grew together before the end of the 16th c. While Cinthio catered to the popular taste for poetic justice, he never admitted comic incidents, sentiments, or diction in his mixed tragedies. One of his successors, Giovanni Battista Guarini, drawing upon still another tradition which lent itself to t., i.e. the pastoral, wrote the best known t. of the century, the *Pastor fido*, and then prescribed formulas for the "new" genre in the critical controversy that followed the appearance of his play. Like Cinthio, Guarini mingled the great personages and lofty sentiments of tragedy with the comic order of plot; unlike Cinthio, he admitted some comic incidents, characters, sentiments, and diction as well. In his *Compendio della poesia tragicomica* (1601), he carefully explained what he was trying to do. Of special interest is his insistence upon a middle style of poetry between tragic grandeur and comic plainness: "In the *Pastor fido* the verse is not turgid, not noisy, not dithyrambic. Its periods are not prolonged, not short, not intricate, not hard, not difficult to understand; they need not be reread many times. Its figures of speech are taken from significant qualities, from proper and not from remote qualities. Its diction is clear but not low, proper but not vulgar, figurative but not enigmatical, beautiful but not affected, sustained but not inflated, pliant but not languishing; and, to conclude in a word, such as is not remote from common speech and yet not close to that of the common herd."

Guarini's own style hardly realized this ideal, but both his critical prescriptions and his "Faithful Shepherd" exerted a widespread influence in France and England as well as in Italy. Jean de Mairet in France and John Fletcher in England, for example, reproduced both the theory and the practice of Guarini. Moreover, leading dramatic poets of both these countries—e.g. Garnier, Hardy, Mairet, Corneille, Du Ryer, Rotrou, Beaumont and Fletcher, Shakespeare, Marston, Thomas Heywood, Massinger, Shirley, Dryden, Davenant—wrote tragicomedies.

When poetic drama went out of fashion, as it did in the 18th c., t. in the old sense disappeared except for an occasional *tour de force* like Rostand's *Cyrano*, and was succeeded in the theatre by the prosaic *drame* and problem play. It might be said, however, that the spirit of t., with its mingling of tragic and comic genres, continues in poetry under the heritage of "metaphysical" poetry, which unites wit with seriousness and often employs in one way or another the old device of "tragic kingcomic people."—H. C. Lancaster, *The Fr. T.* (1907); F. H. Ristine, *Eng. T.* (1910); W. Empson, *Some Versions of Pastoral* (1935); E. M. Waith, *The Pattern of T. in Beaumont and Fletcher* (1952); M. T. Herrick, *T.* (1955); K. S. Guthke, *Gesch. und Poetik der deutschen Tragikomödie* (1961).   M.T.H.

TRANSLATION. That "poetry cannot be translated" is a cliché begotten by romantic poetics, nourished by bad translations, and chiefly serviceable in apostrophes to ineffable poesy. It is deducible from the *Biographia Literaria* (1817), but not from the *Lives of the Poets* (1783) or the *Essay on Criticism* (1711), to say nothing of the practice of Chaucer. It obviously applies to certain kinds of poetry,

and will seem an unshakable truism to anyone whose conception of poetry is limited to those kinds. The extent to which a poetic effect relies on the sound of words, or on their tricks of context or association, is a measure of its resistance to the translating process; on the other hand, quite complicated structures of imagery will often metaphorphose virtually intact, and the gnomic and aphoristic can come through with remarkable force. The first scientific statement about this subject was made by Ezra Pound in 1933, when he remarked of his three "components of poetry," phanopoeia, melopoeia, and logopoeia, that the first can be translated and the second cannot, while the third, though it is untranslatable, implies an attitude of mind, a "tone," which will frequently pass through paraphrase. Obviously a great deal depends on what the translator regards as the main strand of the original, and what he is willing to modify or abandon as secondary; it was because the 18th c. chiefly prized the classical poets as transmitters of moral wisdom that it failed to suppose them untranslatable, the translator's task being chiefly to supply an Eng. mode of elegance which should correspond to the concision inherent in the original tongues. The epigraphs to Johnson's essays afford a handy anthology of this genre.

On the other hand, just as "Forlorn! The very word is like a bell" achieves an effect restricted to the Eng. language, so one could hardly expect Homer's *poluphloisboio thalasses* to survive a divorce from the Gr.; and anyone preoccupied with the Homeric "surge and thunder" or the Virgilian cello sonorities will naturally find prose translations less offensive than any verse which perforce scamps these qualities. It follows that a very large class of distinguished translations serve to define the aspects of the originals which the translators found not merely reproducible but essential. Dryden's *Aeneid*, for instance, doesn't provide an impression of Virgil's effects but an analysis of them; there is, typically, a separate word for each nuance Dryden could discover in the original: he rendered "varium et mutabile semper femina" by "Woman's a various and changeful *thing*" to register the presence of neuter adjectives. Pope's *Iliad*, on the other hand, represents a highly selective understanding of Homer, in whom Pope seems to have permitted himself to perceive only what his exceptionally supple and substantial idiom could regenerate. Into yet a third species fall the fidelities obtained when some affinity of temperament, or some intuition of analogous historical situations, underlies the translator's ability and willingness to confront the theme his author confronted and write, as if for the first time, an analogous poem by pursuing analogous processes. The best parts of Marianne Moore's *Fables of La Fontaine* reproduce his stanzaic schemes not because they are part of the problem set but because analysis has disclosed their expressive appropriateness; the idiom remains sufficiently Miss Moore's to sustain an illusion that, given the theme, she would have written the poem she did if La Fontaine had never existed.

These three kinds of tr., differing in their manner of apprehending the original, all have the air of lying within the compass of the translator's normal idiom. Another kind of translator entirely—Marlowe in the *Amores* or Pound in the *Seafarer*—is concerned neither with domesticating the familiar classics nor with giving his reader some idea of the contents of the unfamiliar, but with enhancing the resources of his own language by incorporating into it poetic qualities hitherto foreign. (This motive is to be distinguished from, say, Pope's, who was less concerned with extending the Eng. language to encompass the strangeness of Homer's than with consolidating Eng. literature by incorporating an Iliad within it.) The *Seafarer* isn't a performance with an existing Eng. idiom into which the sense of the original is put; it is the continuous invention of an idiom necessary to accommodate the Anglo-Saxon, and henceforth available to other poets for other uses. Much Renaissance song-writing, with an eye on L. or It. models, constitutes invention of this order; so do Chaucer's translations and adaptations from the It. and Fr.

In a final category we have the transfusion of foreign blood into the veins of an independent creation: the passages of L. rescription in Pound's *Homage to Sextus Propertius*, the intermittently intimate paraphrases of the *Filostrato* in Chaucer's *Troilus and Criseyde*, Shakespeare condensing whole paragraphs of Plutarch (North's Eng. Plutarch, it is true) into his late plays. These examples serve to emphasize the place of tr. in the system of allusion by which, from Virgil to Eliot, literature has always grown.

The misunderstandings that make for bad tr. are worth enumerating. Inadequate acquaintance with the original will naturally lead to mistakes, but what prevents an inferior tr. from holding the reader's interest is less likely to be inaccuracy than incompetence in managing the new language, or an imperfect idea of its resources. Though he cannot know his original too well, it is easy for the scholarly translator to be too familiar with it. Familiarity blunts his sense of when it is best to be literal; though all his predecessors had registered the adjective in one way or another, Pound was the first to notice that Sophocles was calling Nessus an "old ruffian with hair on his chest." A tr., so far as the reader is concerned, is a

poem written in his own language. He cannot be expected to take an interest in the translator's sense of duty toward the original, though this commonly accounts for dead passages. The first mistake of the inept translator is unwillingness to leave anything out, though reflection will show the wisdom of not admitting into the new poem what one can't cause to function within it. The classic instance is the usual tr. of Aeschylus, rendered unreadable through a determination to reproduce Gr. syntax, though Eng. word order is thereby rendered impenetrable and a host of words incorporated whose function in the original is wholly syntactic. The second cause of failure is uncertainty about why the original is worth translating: not why it has some claim on the attention of a specialist, but why it is needed in the economy of the new language or in the *paideuma* of the new reader. The third is unsuitable choice of idiom: T. S. Eliot noted in 1920 that Gilbert Murray, having "stretched the Greek brevity to fit the loose frame of William Morris, and blurred the Greek lyric to the fluid haze of Swinburne," had "interposed between Euripides and ourselves a barrier more impenetrable than the Greek language." To this is related the not uncommon supposition that an idiom once chosen is simpler to sustain than it is. To the acres of mechanical couplets turned out in the shadow of Pope may be added the reams of "free verse" to which 20th c. translators have had recourse under the impression that it is a form so unexacting as to be no more difficult than bad prose.

While it is a fallacy to suppose that any tr. can be definitive, it is equally fallacious to suppose that a new tr. eclipses an old one solely by being "up to date." The translations in the following list are not offered as standard versions; they are either of historical or technical interest, like Browning's versions of Euripides, or else they uphold certain criteria for the writing of Eng. verse better than do other or later versions of the same works. Versions of single short poems, like Ben Jonson's *Come, my Celia*, have not been included, nor have works like Fitzgerald's *Rubaiyat* which occupy an ambiguous ground between tr. and original composition.

SOME SIGNIFICANT TRANSLATIONS INTO ENG.: A. Golding, *Ovid's Metamorphoses* (1565–67); C. Marlowe, *Ovid's Elegies* (1590); G. Chapman, *Homer's Iliad* (1598–1611); J. Dryden, *Poems of Virgil* (1697); A. Pope, *Homer's Iliad* (1715–20); R. Browning, *Balaustion's Adventure* (1871) and *Aristophanes' Apology* (1875); E. Pound, *The Translations of Ezra Pound* (1953) and *"The Women of Trachis,"* in HR, 6 (1954); M. Moore, *The Fables of La Fontaine* (1954).

HISTORICAL AND THEORETICAL: J. Dryden,

Preface to *Ovid's Epistles Translated by Several Hands* (1680); W. Dillon, Earl of Roscommon, *An Essay on Tr. Verse* (1684); J. Dryden, Dedication to *The Works of Virgil* (1697); A. Pope, Preface to *The Iliad of Homer* (1715); T. Parnell, Preface to *Homer's Battle of the Frogs and Mice* (1717); J. Spence, *An Essay on Mr. Pope's Odyssey* (1726-27); W. Benson, *Letters Concerning Poetical Translations* (1739); A. F. Tytler, Baron Woodhouselee, *Essay on the Principles of Tr.* (1791); M. Arnold, *On Translating Homer, Three Lectures* (1861); J. Conington, "Eng. Translations of Virgil," QR, 110 (1861); O. L. Hatcher, "Aims and Methods of Elizabethan Translators," *Englische Studien*, 44 (1910); C. Whibley, "Translators," *Cambridge Hist. of Eng. Lit.*, IV (1909) and "Tudor Translators," in his *Lit. Studies* (1919); F. R. Amos, *Early Theories of Tr.* (1920); J. W. Draper, "The Theory of Tr. in the 18th C.," *Neophil*, 6 (1920); D. Bush, "Eng. Translations of Homer," PMLA, 41 (1926); R. C. Whitford, "Juvenal in England, 1750-1802," PQ, 7 (1928); F. O. Matthiessen, *Tr., an Elizabethan Art* (1931); E. Pound, *ABC of Reading* (1933) and *Lit. Essays* (1954); H. J. C. Grierson, *Verse Tr.* (1949); W. Frost, *Dryden and the Art of Tr.* (1955); *On Tr.*, ed. R. A. Brower (1959); *The Craft and Context of Tr.*, ed. W. Arrowsmith and R. Shattuck (1961).—See also *The Poem Itself*, ed. S. Burnshaw (1960) for an interesting approach to the problem of tr.   H.K.

TRIAD. In Gr. lyric poetry (e.g., the odes of Pindar and Bacchylides) a combination of strophe, antistrophe, and epode (qq.v.).   K.M.A.

TRIBE OF BEN, sons of Ben. A name adopted by a group of Eng. poets of the first half of the 17th c. who wrote lyric poetry strongly influenced by the precept and example of Ben Jonson (1572-1637). Most of them imbibed Jonsonian wit and classicism in highly informal meetings at various London taverns frequented by their master. In their lyrics, the sons of Ben cultivated a tight and chiseled form, modeled on the lyrics of the *Gr. Anthology*, and employed, in general, shorter lines and crisper rhythms than their Elizabethan predecessors. Their preference for the genres of epigram and satire also indicates their classical orientation. The Jonsonian "school" represents one direction of revolt from the Italianate and moralistic aspects of the "school of Spenser" (q.v.), the other being represented by the "metaphysical poetry" (q.v.) initiated by Donne. The greatest of the tribe of Ben was Robert Herrick (1591-1674), who praised his master in *An Ode for Ben Jonson* (1637). Others include Carew, Suckling, Lovelace, Randolph, Cartwright, and Godolphin.—K. A.

McEuen, *Cl. Influence upon the Tribe of Ben* (1939).

TRIBRACH (Gr. "of 3 short syllables'"). Such a foot ($\smile\smile\smile$) in Gr. and L. verse was usually a resolved iamb or trochee. It is seldom found as an independent foot. The ictus, as a rule, falls on the second syllable if it replaces an iamb and on the first if it replaces a trochee. —Koster.   P.S.C.

TRIHEMIMERAL. See CAESURA.

TRILOGY. A group of 3 tragedies presented by each poet at the dramatic festivals in Athens. The general name for such a group was *didascalia*, "a teaching." However, if the 3 tragedies dealt with the same subject matter and were combined into a single and connected whole, they were referred to as a trilogy. This practice is said to have been introduced by Aeschylus, whose *Oresteia* is the only complete t. that has come down to us, but later dramatists, beginning with Sophocles, abandoned it in favor of single plays each dealing with a different story. In modern usage, the term is applied to a literary (or operatic) work, written in 3 parts, each of which is in itself a complete unit. Shakespeare's *Henry VI*, Schiller's *Wallenstein*, and O'Neill's *Mourning Becomes Electra* are examples in the field of drama.—A. E. Haigh, *The Attic Theatre* (1907); R. C. Flickinger, *The Gr. Theater and its Drama* (4th ed., new impression, 1960).   P.S.C.

TRIMETER (Gr. "of 3 measures"). Line composed of 3 measures, each measure being in classical verse a pair of iambic feet ($\smile-\smile-$), or else a spondee followed by an iambus ($--\smile-$). Developed (probably) by Archilochus of Paros, the t. is the usual meter for invective and for dialogue in Gr. drama. A caesura (q.v.) was obligatory in the inside of the third or fourth foot. Resolution (q.v.) of a short into 2 longs gave Gr. tragedy the possibility of an anapaest ($\smile\smile-$) in the first foot, a dactyl ($-\smile\smile$) in the first and third, and a tribrach ($\smile\smile\smile$) in any of the first 4. In comedy, resolution was more freely allowed. The L. modification of the t., the senarius (q.v.), is the characteristic dialogue meter of Old L. drama. In the senarius of the drama of the republican period and popular verse of later times the Gr. distinction between the even and odd feet was abandoned; spondees were allowed in the first 5 feet, and resolution was carried to its extreme (thus giving the proceleusmatic [$\smile\smile\smile\smile$] as another possible form). This Roman disregard of the "Dipody Law" (that the alternate feet should not exceed the value of 3 morae or shorts) is thought by some to be explicable only in terms of Roman regard for word-accent. A semiaccentual form of the t. was popular in the Middle Ages:

O tu qui sérvas || armis ista móenia
  (Carmen Mutinense)

Eng. t. (a 3-foot line; strictly speaking, the term is incorrectly used for the Eng. 3-stress line) tends to be monotonous. Variation is often secured by the use of a dimeter (as in Browning's *A Woman's Last Word*) or tetrameter in a trimeter pattern. See IAMB.—Hardie; J. Descroix, *Le trimètre iambique* (1931).
                                                W.B.

TRIMÈTRE. Term applied to the 12-syllable *vers romantique* or romantic alexandrine, which has 3 divisions to the line, as distinguished from the 12-syllable classical alexandrine or *tétramètre* (q.v.), which has 4. A memorable example of the *trimètre* occurs in Baudelaire's *Que diras-tu ce soir*: "A la très belle,| à la très bonne,| à la très chère . . ." The t. often appeared in the 16th c. in the rather free alexandrines of the *Pléiade* and survived the classical period especially in the comedy and secondary genres, where it was used by Molière and La Fontaine. It came back into more general favor with the romantic poets of the 19th c. who developed its rhythms, employed it more widely, and championed its use as part of their moderate reform of Fr. versification.—M. ·Grammont, *Le vers français* (1913) and *Petit traité de versification française* (5ᵉ éd. revue, 1924).   A.G.E.

TRIOLET. A Fr. fixed form. It is composed of 8 lines and uses only 2 rhymes, disposed in the following scheme: AB aA ab AB (a capital letter indicates a repeated line): "Easy is the triolet, / If you really learn to make it! / Once a neat refrain you get, / Easy is the triolet. / As you see!—I pay my debt / With another rhyme. Deuce take it, / Easy is the triolet, / If you really learn to make it!" (W. E. Henley). The challenge of the form lies in managing the intricate repetition so that it seems to be natural and inevitable, and in achieving in the repetitions a variety of meaning or, at least, a shift in emphasis.
    According to O. Bloch and W. von Wartburg (*Dictionnaire étymologique de la langue française*, 3d ed., 1960), the word "triolet" is not found until 1486, but the poem, as we know it, is much older and, as the simplest form of the rondel (q.v.), can be traced back to the 13th c., e.g., in the *Cléomadès* of Adenet-le-Roi. Subsequently, the form was cultivated by such medieval poets as Deschamps and Froissart. It began to be neglected toward the end of the 15th c. and fell into disuse during the 16th,

although it had a brief vogue as revived by Vincent Voiture and Jean de La Fontaine in the 17th c. It was revived again in the 19th c. by Alphonse Daudet and, particularly, by Théodore de Banville.
    With the exception of a few religious triolets composed in 1651 by the obscure devotional poet Patrick Carey, there were no triolets written in Eng. before recent times. Introduced by Robert Bridges, the form enjoyed considerable favor in the later years of the 19th c. The modern writers of triolets—Austin Dobson, H. C. Bunner, W. E. Henley and others—recognized, on the whole, the suitability of the form to light or humorous themes.—Kastner; P. Champion, *Hist. poétique du XVᵉ s.* (2 v., 1923); M. Françon, "La pratique et la théorie du rondeau et du rondel chez Théodore de Banville," MLN, 52 (1937; states that triolets, rondels, and rondeaux are a single genre with variations); L. Spitzer, "T.," RR, 39 (1948).   A.P.

TRIPLE METER. (1) Any poetic measure consisting of 3 units, such as a foot of 3 syllables. Hence anapestic, dactylic, tribrachic, cretic, bacchiac feet, etc. are a sort of t.m. (2) Also any larger unit consisting of 3 feet or measures; thus a tripody is a measure of 3 feet. Fr. 12-syllable trimètre (q.v.) is an example of t.m. Spenser's "Iambic Trimetrum" (cf. correspondence with Gabriel Harvey) also employs a variety of t.m., which is more common in quantitative than in syllabic verse, especially L. hymns.   R.O.E.

TRIPLE RHYME. See MULTIPLE OR POLYSYLLABIC RHYME.

TRIPLET, tercet. A verse unit of 3 lines, usually containing rhyme, employed as a stanzaic form, as a variation from couplet structure, or, occasionally, as a complete poem in itself. Known to It. poetry as the *terzina* (see TERZA RIMA). "Triplet" is a generic term; "tercet" generally .implies the use of rhyme. The sestet (q.v.) of a sonnet is frequently made up of two triplets. The interlinking *sestine* of Dante's *Divina Commedia* are certainly the outstanding example of triplet composition; other noteworthy users of the t. include Donne, who wrote most of his verse epistles in monorhymed iambic triplets; Herrick, whose *Whenas in Silks my Julia Goes* is written in the same stanza form; and Shelley, who employed terza rima in his *Ode to the West Wind* and *The Triumph of Life*. William Carlos Williams has used free verse arranged in irregular triplets in some of the poems of his volume *The Desert Music*. A special use of the t. is exemplified in the heroic couplet writings of the Eng. poets of the Augustan

Age. In the poems of Dryden and, to a lesser degree, in those of Pope, the heroic couplets are sometimes varied by the interposition of 3 rhyming lines: "A fiery Soul, which working out its way, / Fretted the Pigmy Body to decay: / And o'r inform'd the Tenement of Clay" (Dryden, *Absalom and Achitophel*). The t. has never been used as widely as the couplet or the quatrain (qq.v.).

TRIPODY (Gr. "3 feet"). Three metrical feet treated as one. The most common tripodies in classical poetry are the dactylic, trochaic, iambic and anapaestic. TRISTICH. A group or stanza of 3 lines. See also TRIPLET.　　P.S.C.

TRISEMIC (Gr. "of 3 time-units"). Term applied to the principle whereby musical theorists like Aristoxenus (4th c. B.C.) and Aristides Quintilianus (3d or 4th c. A.D.) postulated the existence of syllables equivalent in length to 3 morae. See CLASSICAL PROSODY, DISEMIC, and MORA.　　R.J.G.

TROBAR CLUS. The intentionally difficult or hermetic style cultivated by many Old Prov. poets, in contrast to the *trobar leu* or easy style of less sophisticated writing. It may be divided into the *trobar clus* proper and the *trobar ric*. Both are difficult, but not to the same degree or for the same reasons. Exponents of the *t.c.* (e.g., Marcabru) had, or fancied that they had, something profound to say; and they increased the profundity of their subject by cloaking it in enigmatic words, deliberately designed to keep out the uninitiated. Adepts of the *t.r.* (e.g., Arnaut Daniel) make no pretense of profundity, but perform incredible feats of virtuosity in juggling with rare rhymes and in overcoming other technical obstacles. The result is sometimes amusing, often ingenious, and usually quite superficial.—Jeanroy, II.　　F.M.C.

TROCHEE, *choree* (respectively from Gr. "running" and "belonging to the dance"). A metrical unit, in quantitative verse, of a long syllable followed by a short:

$$-\cup; \; \bar{a}n\breve{t}e$$

The rhythm of the trochaic foot was therefore the reverse of the iambic (q.v.), i.e. "falling" instead of "rising." In Gr. and L. verse, where the feet could be varied by the use of spondees or tribrachs (less often by dactyls or anapaests), trochaic measures were used from the time of Archilochus onward, particularly in lyric and drama. (In comedy especially they lent themselves to rapid movement and dancing). Most common was the trochaic tetrameter catalectic, i.e., 7½ trochees or their variations

called *septenarius* (q.v.) by the Romans. The term has been adopted into Eng. for the accentual foot of a stressed followed by an unstressed syllable:

$$\acute{}\; \times; \; \acute{silver}$$

Though common in ME verse, the trochaic base was almost wholly absent from Eng. poetry until the end of the 16th c. when it was employed both in lyric and in dramatic monologues and songs:

Honour, | riches, | marriage|-blessing
(Shakespeare, *Tempest* 4.1.106)

The 4-foot line remained predominant until Blake, whose innovations in length and variation opened up the way for subsequent developments. The 19th c. saw more frequent and broader use, chiefly, however, as substitution in predominantly iambic lines; but by itself it has never been a favorite in Eng., owing no doubt to the difficulty of finding words or phrases to begin the line with a stressed syllable (cf. the variations in Milton's *L'Allegro* and *Il Penseroso*). Used mechanically, as in *Hiawatha*, the trochee becomes monotonous; but in short passages it is often handled with success.—J. W. White, *The Verse of Gr. Comedy* (1912); Baum; Hamer; Crusius; U. v. Wilamowitz-Moellendorff, *Griechische Verskunst* (2d ed., 1958).　　D.S.P.

TROPE. Ancient rhetoric in treating elocution or style as the presentation of thought and feeling in "decent and comely order" classified the language so arranged in schemes and tropes. Schemes are figures or patterns of speech which are out of the ordinary; they include figures of thought, which in the 16th c. were called figures of sentence or amplification, and figures of words. Tropes were figures also, but different in nature to the degree that they used words or phrases in senses that were not proper to them. These classifications were easy to maintain as such, but there was much confusion concerning the placing of particular figures. Antithesis was at once a scheme and a figure of thought. Periphrasis was sometimes classified as a trope and sometimes as a scheme. Metaphor, metonymy, synecdoche, and irony were central tropes. In the 16th c. metaphor and metonymy were regarded as tropes of words, and allegory, irony and hyperbole were tropes of sentences. The basis of these distinctions are in Aristotle and Isocrates, and a summary of the ancient teaching on tropes is made by Quintilian (8.6).

Elocution and style from early times were understood to belong equally to the arts of oratory and poetry, but the difficulty of maintaining the distinction in the nature of figures used by arts of different purpose increased with the sophistication of rhetorical practice and teaching and the allegorization of poetry in later Antiquity and the early Christian period. The root of the confusion lay in the doctrine that the orator himself must be moved, for in the extreme this was taken to justify ornament and figures for their own sake, a development of the emphasis of the pseudo-Ciceronian *Ad Herennium*. In the Middle Ages the Venerable Bede's work on schemes and tropes, which became a standard medieval text, initiated a tradition of stylistic rhetoric in England. From his analysis there led such doctrines that neither the Middle nor Low styles permitted the use of tropes, but that the High Style allowed ten of them, which were called "difficult ornaments." The treatment of tropes in the Renaissance went no farther than the extreme stylistic interpretation of Ramus, where schemes and tropes were regarded as the whole of elocution from which even considerations of grammar were excluded. It was not till the 18th c. and Vico that the base of the analysis was radically changed, with the doctrine that tropes belonged to the primitive imagination and were the necessary means of communication.

A special development in the use of tropes in the Middle Ages had spectacular consequences. An elaboration of the liturgy that is associated with the Carolingian Renaissance, and particularly in the rituals of Easter and the days preceding it, has been shown to have given rise to church drama itself. These tropes have been defined as verbal amplifications of passages in the authorized liturgy made to adorn the text, to enforce its meaning, and to enlarge its emotional appeal. One of the earliest examples is in the amplification of the *Kyrie eleïson:*

> Kyrie,
> magnæ Deus potentiæ,
> liberator hominis,
> transgressoris mandati,
> eleïson.

The *Introit* of the Mass at Easter, "Quem quæritis," developed into a completely dramatized form and detached from the Mass became, first, part of the Procession, then of the Matins, and later still was made into a representation of the Visitation.—A. Sorrentino, *La Retorica e la Poetica di Vico* (1927); W. G. Crane, *Wit and Rhetoric in the Renaissance* (1937); K. Burke, "Four Master Tropes," KR, 3 (1941); D. L. Clark, *John Milton at Saint Paul's School* (1948) and *Rhetoric in Greco-Roman Education* (1957); K. Young, *The Drama of the Medieval Church* (1951); W. S. Howell,

Logic and Rhetoric in England, 1500–1700 (1956). J.A.

TROUBADOUR (from Prov. *trobar*, "invent"). A Prov. poet of the high Middle Ages. The troubadours flourished between 1100 and 1350 and were attached to various courts in the south of France. Their contributions to European poetry, which concern both subject matter and form, were of incalculable importance.

The troubadours made sexual love their almost exclusive theme, and developed the social phenomenon of courtly love (q.v.), which left its stamp on European culture for centuries. The principal features of the love extolled by the troubadours were: an attitude of subservience and fidelity to a cold and cruel mistress, exorbitant and quasi-religious praise of the lady's beauty, and a requirement that the love be extramarital. Though the love celebrated by the troubadours was sensual, their ideal of "pure" love prohibited sexual intercourse between the lovers—at least in theory. This prohibition had the effect of endowing any casual contact, gesture, or token with enormous erotic significance, and thus bequeathed to later European love poetry a whole vocabulary and grammar of amorous symbol. Most t. lyrics are, thus, amorous in the extreme, but some are satirical or political.

The major genres cultivated by the troubadours, who were at once poets and composers of music, were the *canso d'amor* (see CHANSO), a love song, the *pastorela* (see PASTOURELLE), an account of the attempted seduction of a shepherdess by a poet, the *alba* (q.v.), a lament of lovers who must separate at the coming of dawn, the *tenso, partimen,* or *joc-partit* (qq.v.), debates on the fine points of the code of love, and the *sirventes* (q.v.), a political invective or satire. These genres were expressed in a variety of metrical forms, some of them, like the *sestina* (q.v.), of extraordinary complexity.

Among the troubadours whose work has come down to us are Guillaume d'Aquitaine, Arnaut Daniel, and Bertrand de Born. Some of the troubadours, such as Sordello, were Italians, although they composed in the Prov. established by tradition.

The t. influence on Dante and Petrarch was immense, in both theme and form. Indeed, the example of the troubadours quickened and formed the lyrical impulse throughout western Europe, as expressed in the poetry of the *trouvères* and *Minnesinger* (qq.v.) as well as in that of late medieval Portuguese and Sicilian poets. F.J.W.; A.P.

For bibliog. see PROVENÇAL POETRY.

TROUVÈRE. Medieval poet of Northern France, especially Picardy. Contemporary of the troubadour (q.v.), who composed his poems in the *langue d'oc* of the South (or Prov.), the trouvère wrote in the *langue d'oïl*, which prevailed and became the Fr. language. In addition to courtly lyrical poetry, which shows the influence of the troubadour in form and sentiment, the trouvère composed *chansons de geste* (q.v.) and *romans bretons*. Notable trouvères include Jean Bodel, Blondel de Nesle, the Châtelain de Coucy, Conon de Béthune and Thibaud de Champagne.—Jeanroy, *Origines; Minnesinger et trouvères*, ed. I. Frank (I, texts, 1952) and J. M. Müller-Blattau (II, music, 1956); R. Dragonetti, *La Technique poétique des trouvères dans la chanson courtoise* (1960).

TRUNCATION (catalexis). The omission of the last (generally unstressed) syllable or syllables in a line of conventional metrical structure. A line lacking one syllable of the normal number is called catalectic; one lacking two is called brachycatalectic. (When no syllable is lacking, the line is acatalectic and when there are one or more syllables in excess of the normal number, the line is said to be hypercatalectic or hypermetrical, q.v.) Truncation is frequent in trochaic verse, where the line of complete trochaic feet tends to create an effect of monotony. The following trochaic lines exhibit t.: "Simple maiden, void of art, / Babbling out the very heart" (Ambrose Philips). T. is also frequently employed in dactylic lines to avoid an effect of excessive bounciness; Hood's second line is truncated: "Take her up tenderly, / Lift her with care." T. in the blank verse of the 17th-c. drama is frequently encountered in passages representing informal utterance: "Good morrow to this fair assembly" (*Much Ado About Nothing* 5.4). The term "initial t." is used to describe the omission of the first syllable of a (generally iambic) line. A line so truncated is also called a "headless" (acephalous) line. See also DEFECTIVE FOOT, LINE ENDINGS. P.F.

TRUTH AND POETRY. See BELIEF, PROBLEM OF; MEANING, PROBLEM OF; CRITICISM, FUNCTION OF (COGNITIVE THEORIES).

TUMBLING VERSE. A phrase first used by James I in his *Reulis and Cautelis* (1585) to apply to 4-foot trisyllabic (anapaestic or dactylic) verse in Eng. which goes back through the alliterative verse of the Middle Ages to the Old Germanic alliterative verse and probably even further to a common Indo-European meter: "I was wery forwandred and went me to rest." The meter was reinforced by the 6/8 dance tune of popular song and was much used in Elizabethan poetry (e.g., Tusser, *Five Hundred Points of Good Husbandry*, 1557). Aside

from England the only European country in which this meter was prominent was Spain where, as the *arte mayor* (q.v.), it was used for the most serious poetry. Juan de Mena (ca. 1411–56), the most famous poet to use this measure, employed it in his chief work, *El Laberinto*.—Ker. R.P.APR.

TURKISH POETRY. There is sufficient data, i.e. vestiges of epics, to indicate that poetic sensibility must have dawned in the Turk. consciousness several centuries before Christ. However, the actual beginnings of the Turks' poetic tradition lie in the period between late 9th and mid-11th c. A.D. when Turk. tribes moved into and settled parts of Anatolia. The *Oğuz* Turks brought with them a dialect already rich in expressive resources and a developed popular literature. At the time, however, Anatolia was under the influence of Islam and of Arabic and Persian cultures. By the end of the 11th c., Turks became converted to Islam and imbibed its prevalent culture, including its philosophy and literature. Out of this assimilation came the first poetic work of stature that clearly bears the imprint of the new literary tradition with which the Turks became familiar: *Kutadgu Bilig* (1069 or 1070) by Yusuf Has Hacib. Composed in *aruz* (Arabic-Persian prosody), *Kutadgu Bilig* (The Knowledge of Bliss), which consists of close to 6,500 couplets, is a vast philosophical treatise in verse on government, justice, and ethics. Kaşgârlı Mahmut's *Divan ü Lûgat-it Türk*, a dictionary and grammar of the Turk. language, written in the period 1071–77, included many specimens (some fragmentary) of pre-Islamic and early Islamic Turk. poetry particularly in the epic, lyric, and didactic genres.

From the end of the 13th c., when the Ottoman state came into being through the mid-19th c., three main traditions of Turk. poetry evolved: (1) Persian-influenced *Divan* (classical) poetry, (2) Religious or *Tekke* poetry, (3) Indigenous folk poetry. From mid-19th c. through the present day, Turk. poetry has gone through an extensive European orientation.

DIVAN (CLASSICAL) POETRY. *Divan* poetry (also referred to as Court poetry), whose course ran almost parallel to the glories and decline of the Ottoman Empire, spanned over six centuries. Composed by and for an intellectual elite mostly affiliated with the Court, its main vehicle of expression was Anatolian Turk., with the *Çağatay* and *Azerî* dialects also boasting of some distinguished output. From beginning to end, classical Turk. poetry remained under the impact of Persian and Arabic poetry: It imitated and tried to emulate the verse forms, rhyme-and-rhythm patterns, meters, and mythology used by Persian and Arab poets. It also adopted a substantial portion of their vocabulary. *Aruz,* the quantitative prosody originated by Arabs, dominated *Divan* poetry. *Aruz* afforded a definite structure of its own and to suit its metric requirements *Divan* poets often deliberately distorted Turk. vowels or employed words of Arabic and Persian origin which lent themselves better to *Aruz. Divan* poetry also used the major verse forms of Persian and Arabic literature: *gazel, kaside, mesnevi, rubâi, tuyuǧ, şarkı* (originally *murabba), musammat, tarih* (chronogram), etc.

Form reigned supreme over *Divan* poetry, with content of secondary importance. Content, most *Divan* poets felt, was the self-generating substance of a literary tradition whose concepts and values were not to be questioned, let alone renovated. At best, originality was considered fortuitous; they preferred to achieve perfection in craftsmanship and to equal, if not excel, their Turk. or Persian rivals by using the same subject matter as competently or more effectively.

Despite the tyranny of form, prominent *Divan* poets often attained a profound spirituality, a trenchant sensitivity, an overflowing eroticism. Perhaps no *Divan* poet can be said to show a broad range of poetic sensibilities. Tradition sanctioned not range, but depth. Between the given extremes of the continuum of subject matter, the masters, i.e. Fuzulî, Baki, Şeyh Galip *et al.,* achieved an impressive profundity of passion expressed with gripping power—from self-glorification to self-abnegation, from agony to ebullient joy, from fanatic continence to uninhibited hedonism. Islamic mysticism, as the human soul's passionate yearning to merge with God, formed the superstructure of most of *Divan* poetry. In the hands of the first-rate poets, the *Divan* tradition produced a corpus of exquisite lyric and mystic poetry which has retained and will retain its impressive literary significance.

Early *Divan* masters were Şeyhî (d. ca. 1431), Ahmedî (1334–1413), Ahmet Paşa (d. 1497), Ahmed-i Dâî (15th c.), and Necati (d. 1509). The greatest figures of the *Divan* tradition emerged in the period of the Ottoman Empire's grandeur. Fuzulî (1494–1556) stands as the most impressive creative artist of classical Turk. literature. He published three *Divans* (major collections of poems), one in Turk., one in Arabic, and one in Persian, in addition to several *mesnevîs* (verse narratives). His masterpiece, *Leylâ vü Mecnun* is a *mesnevi* of close to 4,000 couplets, in which Fuzulî made a philosophical and dramatic exploration into worldly and mystic love. Perhaps no other poet exerted as much influence as Fuzulî on the *Divan* poetry of the following centuries. Among his most memorable lines are: "Min cân olaydı kâş men-i dilşikestede / Tâ her biriyle bir gez

olaydım fedâ sana" (I wish I had a thousand lives in this broken heart of mine / So that I could sacrifice myself for you once with each life). Fuzulî chose to write his Turk. poems in the *Azeri* dialect in the manner of Nesimî (d. 1404). Baki (1526–99) achieved wide fame for the aesthetic perfection of his secular *gazels* and *kasides.* Baki's lines and couplets often had an epigrammatic concentration; the following line, his best-known, has become a proverb among Turks: "Baki kalan bu kubbede bir hoş sedâ imiş" (What endures in this dome is but a pleasant sound). Hayalî (d. 1557) and Taşlıcalı Yahya Bey (d. 1582) attained renown for their craftsmanship and sensitive lyricism. Rûhi-i Baǧdadi (d. 1605) composed a *Terkib-i Bend,* which still stands as a masterpiece of social and philosophical satire with a strong moral concern. The supreme satirist of the *Divan* tradition, however, was Nef'i (1582–1635) who, in his masterful *kasides,* courageously lampooned hypocrisy and affectation. Şeyhülislâm Yahya (1552–1644) produced refined *gazels,* while Nailî (d. ca. 1666) won renown for his elegant, delicate lyrics. Intellectual exploration and social commentary abounded in the poetry of Nâbi (1642–1712). Nedim (d. 1730) sang the joys of living and the beauties of nature (particularly in the city of Istanbul). He contributed to *Divan* poetry a lilting, entrancing style derived mainly from the colloquial Istanbul Turk. of his day. The last master of *Divan* poetry was Şeyh Galip (1757–99) who, in addition to a superb *Divan,* produced *Hüsn ü Aşk* (Beauty and Love), an allegorical work of passionate mysticism. Although the classical tradition continued until the early part of the 20th c., after Şeyh Galip it fostered no major figures and produced no work of literary significance.

RELIGIOUS OR TEKKE POETRY. Religious poetry flourished among the mystics, Muslim clergy, and the adherents of various doctrines and denominations. Members of the *tekkes* (theological centers) were particularly prolific in the domain of religious poetry, which drew upon and overlapped both *Divan* and folk traditions. Ahmet Yesevî (d. 1166) and Ahmet Fakih (d. ca. 1250) were early masters. Perhaps the greatest figure of religious literature was the poet-saint Mevlânâ Celâleddin-i Rumi (1207–73) who wrote a six-volume Persian *mesnevi* of nearly 26,000 couplets about the ways of mysticism. In late 13th and early 14th c., Sultan Veled (Mevlânâ's son), Âşık Paşa and Gülşehrî achieved distinction. The most renowned Turk. masterpiece to come out of the religious tradition was *Mevlid-i Şerif* (1409), composed by Süleyman Çelebi (d. 1422). *Mevlid,* an adulation of the Prophet Mahomet, is chanted as a requiem among Muslim-Turks. Two folk poets, Kaygusuz Abdal (15th c.) and

Pir Sultan Abdal (16th c.), have made substantial contributions to Turk. religious poetry. Their poetry represents the Alevî-Bektaşi movement (long considered heretical), and is a deviation from and a reaction against some of the tenets of traditional Islam.

INDIGENOUS FOLK POETRY. Parallel to *Divan* poetry, Turk. folk poetry has run its own evolutionary course. Its roots lay in the epic tradition of the pre-Islamic times of the peripatetic Turk. tribes which handed down various epics. Although most of these epic poems became lost or did not remain intact, one major epic entitled *Oğuznâme* reveals that Turks had a developed poetic faculty long before they came under the influence of Islam-oriented Persian and Arabic cultures. The *Dede Korkut Tales* of the Oğuz tribes contain poems in rather free renditions which also stand at the source of the folk tradition. Folk poetry was created and kept alive to our day by the *ozans, saz şairleri* (poet-musicians) and *âşıks*. It has voiced, in its spontaneous, sincere, and often matter-of-fact fashion, the poetic sensibilities of the uneducated classes, in contrast to classical poetry which was composed and read by the intellectual elite. In indigenous verse forms, i.e. *türkü, koşma, mani, destan, semai, varsağı*, etc., mostly extemporized and sung to music, replete with assonances and inexact rhymes, and composed in simple syllabic meters, folk poetry harped on the themes of love, heroism, beauties of nature, and, at times, Islamic mysticism. Unsophisticated and unpretentious, folk poetry evolved a serene realism, an earthy humor, and a mellifluous lyric quality. Although the poems often lose part of their euphony when taken out of their musical context, the folk tradition still remains alive in Turkey's rural areas as well as among devotees of literature. It has exerted an appreciable influence on the Turk. poetry of modern times. In fact, many verse-makers in the late 19th and 20th c. have adopted the vivid rhythms and much of the vocabulary and idiom of folk poetry, not to mention its flair and flavor. One genius emerged out of the folk tradition: Yunus Emre (1238-1320/1). Equally at home with folk and *Divan* verse, he created a voluminous body of poetry (some of it is extinct) rich in philosophical content, intensely mystical, steeped in the best folk idiom, melodious, full of vivid imagery and fresh metaphor. Later centuries, dominated by Yunus Emre's impact, witnessed the first-rate works of Karacaoğlan (ca. 1606-1679/80), a poet of love and pastoral beauty, Âşık Ömer (d. 1707), Gevherî (d. ca. 1740), Dadaloğlu (1785-1868), Dertli (1772-1845), Bayburtlu Zihni (d. 1859), Erzurumlu Emrah (d. 1860) and Seyrani (1807-1866).

EUROPEANIZATION OF TURK. POETRY. Ottoman Empire's decline reached a critical point by the middle of the 19th c. Younger Turk. intellectuals started seeking the Empire's salvation in technological development, political reform, and cultural progress fashioned after European models. The so-called *Tanzimat* (Transformations) of the 1840's aimed at realizing some of these far-reaching changes. A new orientation toward Europe (France, in particular) brought the younger poets into contact with the aesthetic theories and verse forms of French poetry. While *aruz* was not abandoned, experiments were undertaken with forms, rhythms, and styles. A reaction set in against words of Arabic and Persian origin. Poetry acquired a social awareness and a political function in the hands of some poets who endeavored to establish freedom within the country and to gain independence from external political domination. Ziya Paşa (1825-80), Şinasi (1826-71) who ushered new concepts and genres into Turk. literature, and Namık Kemal (1840-88) emerged as champions of nationalism. Recaizade Ekrem (1847-1914) and Abdülhak Hâmit Tarhan (1852-1937) echoed the French romantics. The latter, a prolific poet and author of numerous verse dramas, gained stature as a ceaseless renovator. His poetry, which covered a wide range of topics, had a philosophic bent as well as dramatic impact.

In the late 19th and early 20th c., under Sultan Abdülhamit's suppression, most Turk. poets retired into a world of innocent, picturesque beauty, where, in a mood of meek sentimentality and lackadaisical affection, they attempted to forge the aesthetics of the simple, the pure, and the delectable. Their lyric transformation of reality abounded in new rhythms and imaginative metaphors expressed by dint of a predominantly Arabic-Persian vocabulary and an appreciably relaxed *aruz*. A French-oriented group of poets, referred to as *Servet-i Fünun* after the literary magazine they published, became prominent on the literary scene. Its leader Tevfik Fikret (1867-1915) also wrote angry political poems against the Sultan's despotism and the Empire's crumbling institutions. His poetry represented a new direction for the formal and conceptual progress of Turk. poetry. Together with Cenap Şehabettin (1870-1934), Fikret furthered the Europeanization of modern verse.

In the same period, many traditions and forms of Turk. poetry were alive and active on the literary scene. *Divan* poetry was continued by a few minor poets. Folk poetry not only maintained much of its vigor but also exerted considerable influence on many younger poets who were striving to create a pervasive national consciousness and to purify the Turk. language by eliminating Arabic and Persian loan words. Ziya Gökalp (1875–1924), social philosopher and poet, wrote poems expounding the ideals and aspirations of Turk. nationalism. Mehmet Emin Yurdakul (1869–1944) and Rıza Tevfik Bölükbaşı (1869–1949) used folk meters and forms as well as an unadorned colloquial language in their poems. Mehmet Âkif Ersoy (1873–1936), a meticulous craftsman and a deft master of *aruz*, wrote mainly of Turk. glory and of Islam's *summum bonum*. Eşref (1846–1912) emerged as Turkey's best satirical poet in the past hundred years. The *Fecr-i Âti* movement contributed in some measure to the strides toward the creation of a poetry that Turks could claim as their own.

The Turk. Republic came into being in 1923 to supersede the Ottoman Empire. It consolidated national unity and moved swiftly to eliminate Islamic elements from Turk. life. Emphasis was placed on Westernization, including the introduction of the L. alphabet. In the early part of the Republican era, poetry served primarily as a vehicle for the propagation of nationalism. Younger poets branded *Divan* forms and meters as anathema. Native forms of verse and syllabic meters gained popularity. Intense efforts were undertaken toward a systematic purification of Turk. *Beş Hececiler* (Five Syllabic Poets), Faruk Nafiz Çamlıbel (1898–), who was equally adept at *aruz*, Orhan Seyfi Orhon (1890–), Enis Behiç Koryürek (1898–1949), Halit Fahri Ozansoy (1891–) and Yusuf Ziya Ortaç (1896–) produced simple, unadorned poems celebrating love, the beauties of nature, and the glories of the Turk. nation.

Some poets, however, shied away from chauvinism and evolved individualistic worldviews and styles. Symbolism attained success in the consummate poetry of Ahmet Hâşim (1884–1933), who employed *aruz* freely. Neoclassicism gained considerable popularity under the aegis of Yahya Kemal Beyatlı (1884–1958). A supreme craftsman, Beyatlı wrote of love, nostalgia for the Ottoman past, the beauties of Istanbul, and the metaphysics of life and death in poems which are memorable for their refined language and melodiousness. Necip Fazıl Kısakürek (1905–) engaged in teleological explorations into modern man's agony. Ahmet Muhip Dranas (1909–) and Ahmet Hamdi Tanpınar (1901–61) wrote some of the best lyric poems to come out of modern Turkey. Nazim Hikmet Ran (1902–63) became an exponent of the Communist ideology. It was Ran who introduced free verse as adapted from Mayakovski. However, the wide popularity of free verse was to materialize through the efforts of younger poets who imported it from France.

In the years following the end of World War II, poets furthered most of the experiments and renovations started in the preceding decades. After surrealism cast a brief spell on the literary scene, a new school emerged setting forth what may be defined as poetic realism. Introduced by Orhan Veli Kanık (1914–1950), Oktay Rifat (1914–), and Melih Cevdet Anday (1915–) and subscribed to by a cluster of others, including Bedri Rahmi Eyüboğlu (1913–) and Cahit Külebi (1917–), this doctrine placed the poet in the center of the complex system of society. It made poetry's function a utilitarian one. In the late 1940's, most Turk. poets served as standard-bearers of the social problems of their day. Their verse reflected the frustrations and aspirations of the man in the street. Poetry became a vehicle for the expression, not of subjective experience, but of objective truth. Written in free verse (occasionally in folk forms and meters), postwar poems drew on all that was alive, vivid and colorful in the Turk idiom. One critic, Nurullah Ataç (1898–1957), played a major role in setting the directions of modern poetry in the 1940's and 1950's. In the same period, Cahit Sıtkı Tarancı (1910–56) produced impeccable lyrics expressing universal human sentiments. Fazıl Hüsnü Dağlarca (1914–) emerged as a superior poet of impressive range. His is the poetry of philosophical quest, and it displays a wealth of metaphor and a sonority almost unequalled in 20th-c. Turk. verse. Asaf Halet Çelebi (1907–58) gave some early, if deficient, specimens of surrealist poetry, while Behçet Necatigil (1916–) writes poems rich in intellectual substance. Salâh Birsel (1919–) interfuses ingenious verbal patterns and sonic capers.

The latest development in Turk. poetry is the abstract movement (also referred to as "meaningless poetry") which started in the mid-1950's. It seeks to mobilize the imaginative resources of Turk. and explores abstract phenomena and formulations. İlhan Berk (1916–), Attilâ İlhan (1925–), Turgut Uyar (1926–), Edip Cansever (1928–), and Cemal Süreya (1931–) are the protagonists. By the end of the present decade, a new Turk. poetry may be expected to develop wherein the aesthetics of form and the emotive power of substance will converge into a unity. Consequently, modern Turk. poetry may soon move from national significance to a universal level.

ANTHOLOGIES: E. J. W. Gibb, *Ottoman Lit. —The Poets and Poetry of Turkey* (1901); *The Star and the Crescent*, ed. D. Patmore (1946); *Başlangıcından Bugüne Türk Şiiri Antolojisi*, ed. V. M. Kocatürk *et al.* (4 v., 1949); *Anthologie des poètes turcs contemporains*, ed. N. Arzık (1953); N. Menemencioğlu, "Modern Turk. Poetry," *Western Review*, 23 (1959); *The Literary Review*, 4 (1960–1961; Turk. issue); *Contemp. Turk. Poetry*, ed. T. S. Halman (1965).

HISTORY AND CRITICISM: E. M. Koltsova-Masalskaya, *La Poésie des Ottomans* (1871); J. W. Redhouse, *On the History, System and Varieties of Turk. Poetry* (1879); E. J. W. Gibb, *A Hist. of Ottoman Poetry* (6 v., 1900–1909); G. Jacob, *Türkische Volkliteratur* (1901); K. J. Basmadjian, *Essai sur l'histoire de la litt. Ottomane* (1910); T. Menzel, *Die türkische Lit.* (1915); O. Hachtmann, *Die türkische Lit. des 20. Jh.* (1916); I. Kunos, *De la poésie populaire turque* (1925); F. Köprülü, *Türk Edebiyatı Tarihi* (1926; hist. of Turk. lit.), "Ottoman Turk. Lit.," *Encyclopaedia of Islam*, IV (1934) and *Türk Dili ve Edebiyatı hakkında Arastır-*

malar (1934; Studies on Turk. language and lit.); J. G. Blanco Villalta, *Literatura turca contemporánea* (1940); H. A. Yücel, *Ein Gesamtüberblick über die türkische Lit.* (1941); A. S. Levend, *Divan Edebiyatı* (1943; Divan Lit.); N. S. Banarlı, *Resimli Türk Edebiyatı Tarihi* (1948; illustrated hist. of Turk. lit.); H. T. Gönensay, *Türk Edebiyatı Tarihi-Tanzimattan Zamanımıza Kadar* (1949; Hist. of Turk. lit. from Tanzimat to present); A. Bombaci, *Storia della letteratura turca* (1956).   T.S.H.

TZ'U. See CHINESE POETRY.

UBI SUNT (L. "where are . . . ?"). A motif of great vogue in medieval L. poetry. Beginning the poem and sometimes every stanza with the phrase, the poet proceeded to list, often at interminable length, the names of those who were dead or gone. Hence the name for the motif. The lists are generally of two sorts, though sometimes combined in the same poem: the names of heroes who fought and died nobly and of beautiful women who have since perished. The Bible with its genealogical lists may be the source for the former type; pagan tradition, particularly L. love elegy, for the latter. The motif emphasized the transitoriness of life, the fragility of beauty, and could also suggest the degeneracy of the current age by harking back to a glorious epoch. Villon's "Mais ou sont les neiges d'antan?" is perhaps the greatest medieval example of the motif. Although not very popular today, occasionally it recurs as in Edgar Lee Master's *Spoon River Anthology*.—J. L. Lowes, *Convention and Revolt in Poetry* (1919); E. Gilson, *Les Idées et les lettres* (1932); L. J. Friedman, "The *Ubi Sunt*, The Regrets and *Effictio*," MLN, 72 (1957).   R.A.H.

UKRAINIAN POETRY. The old Kievan state established by the 9th c. extended its rule over all the Eastern Slavs but it collapsed after the Tatar invasion and came under the control of its eastern and western neighbors, the Russians and the Poles. The struggle of the Ukr. people to escape this domination has left a deep mark upon Ukr. poetry.

Their folk songs, which reflect all the many rites of the old Ukr. agricultural cycle, seem in some cases to point back to pagan customs existing before the introduction of Christianity from Byzantium at the end of the 10th c., but

the "Christmas songs," the *Kolyady* and *Shchedrivky*, have been influenced by Christianity and so have the laments and the many songs dealing with all the events of life and death.

The old epic poetry dealing with the court of the Grand Prince Volodymyr (Vladimir), a sort of Table Round, apparently vanished from Ukr. lands by the late 16th c. and, with the rise of the Zaporozhian Kozaks to a commanding position, there developed a new type of oral poetry, the *dumy*. These are sung to a kind of recitatif. They appear to date from the 16th and later centuries and deal with the leaders of the Kozaks (e.g. Bayda Vyshonovetsky, who was captured and tortured by the Turks), their wars (the Kozak wars with Poland at the time of Hetman Bohdan Khmelnytsky in the 17th c.) and later sufferings, or with tragic situations of nameless heroes during the same period. Yet they are more than mere chronicles of historical songs and form a distinct Ukr. contribution to folk poetry and music.

Kiev accepted Christianity and learning from Constantinople but did not remain without contacts with the Scandinavian north and with western Europe in the early days. Religious works were accepted in the Church Slavic language, but soon translators and original writers began to insert purely Ukr. forms. The artificial language thus formed continued with varying stresses on the Church Slavic and native elements until the end of the 18th c., when the use of the vernacular commenced.

There was little pure poetry in the written literature of the pre-Tatar period. The outstanding poetic work is the *Slovo o Polku Igoreve'* (The Tale of the Armament of Igor), an account of an attack in 1185 by Prince Igor Svyatoslavych of Novgorod Siversky and his allies on a horde of Polovtsy, his defeat, capture, and escape. It was apparently written soon after the events and shows close contact with both the oral poetry and the Chronicles. The author is unknown, and we are perhaps not justified in treating it merely as a type of the secular court poetry of the day, although the author alludes to other poets who sang the praise of various princes such as Boyan. The poem (it is really a prose poem) is a strong plea for cooperation among the princes. Nature plays an active role, and there is a scarcely veiled paganism in many passages. With all of its virtues the work stands alone and offers many problems, for the one late manuscript, apparently from Pskov, was burned before it was adequately studied. However, there are obvious references to the poem in some works of the next centuries.

Poetry returned in the late 16th c. It was fostered by the Jesuit Uniat colleges under Polish influences and by the Orthodox Mohylanska Academy in Kiev which was developed by the great Orthodox metropolitan, educator and theologian, Peter Mohyla, into the leading Orthodox institution north of Constantinople. It produced a large number of spiritual songs of every character, a mass of secular lyrics and historical poetry, and many eulogies to the various Hetmans, some of whom like Ivan Mazepa were themselves not inconsiderable poets. The great majority of the lines are based on Polish usage and written in syllabic verse, a line with a varying number of syllables divided by a caesura and with the rhymes almost invariably feminine. Much of the poetry is in a baroque style with an abundance of classical references, but it is still in the old mixture of Church Slavic and the vernacular. A good example is the elegy on the death of Hetman Sahaydachny. The theme of death is treated from all angles (sometimes in a form reminiscent of the *dumy* by Kyrylo Trankvilion Stavrovetsky).

There were also dramas based on Polish models as the *Volodymyr* of Teofan Prokopovych (1687–1736) dedicated to Mazepa but later changed after his defeat at Poltava, and the anonymous *Love of God.* There are also many religious dramas based on the lives of the saints, the Christmas drama of St. Dmytro Tuptalo, bishop of Rostov, etc. Both Prokopovych and Tuptalo were later lost to Rus. literature as were many of the better educated Ukrainians, especially in the 18th c. Comedy was represented especially in the *intermedia,* short scenes of a comic character representing well-known and standard national types, which were inserted in more serious performances often at the will of the producers and carried around the country by wandering scholars during vacation periods. These had a great effect on the development of the popular puppet shows.

With the defeat of Ukr. hopes for liberation after the battle of Poltava (1709), Russian influence increased both on the thought and language, and even Hryhori Skovoroda (1722–94), with his shorter poems written more or less under the influence of the Enlightenment, did not oppose prevailing tendencies. A new movement began when in 1798 Ivan Kotlyarevsky (1769–1838) published his travesty on Virgil's *Aeneid,* the *Eneida,* in the colloquial language of Poltava. In this, the first book printed in the vernacular, he parodied the *Aeneid* by representing Aeneas and his fellows as Zaporozhian Kozaks wandering around the world in search of a new home after the fall of Troy. Whatever his intentions, Kotlyarevsky started the modern Ukr. movement and later contributed to it with his musical comedy *Natalka Poltavka* (1819), in the same colloquial style. He abandoned syllabic verse for iambic pentameter. His example was followed by various minor writers such as Vasyl Hohol-Yanovsky (d. 1825)—father of the more famous Nikolay Gogol—with comedies like *Roman and Parashka;* and Petro Hulak-Artemovsky (1790–1865) with his still popular operetta *Zaporozhets za Dunayem* (The Zaporozhian across the Danube) and many odes written as travesties. In general this early Ukr. literature was "incomplete," for it lacked any attempt to produce the higher forms of literature and it portrayed the peasants often in a sentimental manner.

The revival of the vernacular spread to the Western Ukr. lands under Austria in the early days of romanticism. In Western Ukraine it began among students of the Uniat theological seminaries such as Fr. Markiyan Shashkevych (1811–43) who after some preliminary work brought out in Budapest the *Rusalka Dnistrovaya* (The Rusalka of the Dniester), a collection of romantic poems with the vernacular taking predominance over Church Slavic. He was helped by the other members of the so-called Rus. Triad, Ivan Vahylevych (1811–66) and Yakiv Holovatsky (1814–88), though the two last were soon lost to Ukr. literature, one to Polish and the other to Russian. Their work was continued by Mykola Ustyyanovych (1811–85) in the same tradition.

On the other hand extensive work was done in the populist and ethnographical fields in the Eastern Ukraine by the collection and adaptation of Ukr. folk songs by such men as I. Sreznevsky (1812–80), Lev Borovykovsky (1806–89) and by the verse of Amvrosi Metlynsky (1814–70) and Mykola Kostomariv (1817–85), later a distinguished historian.

Ukr. poetry reached its maturity in the work of Taras Shevchenko (1814–61). Born a serf on

UKRAINIAN POETRY

the Right Bank of the Dnieper, he was liberated because of his artistic talents by a group in Petersburg headed by the poet Zhukovsky and the painter Karl Bryulov. Eight years later, for his participation in the idealistic Brotherhood of Sts. Cyril and Methodius in Kiev, he was arrested and confined for ten years in a Rus. disciplinary battalion in Central Asia and was only liberated as a broken man in 1857. His first collection of poems *Kobzar* (the Bard) appeared in 1840 in a marked romantic vein, stressing typical romantic motifs and the exploits of the Zaporozhian Kozaks against the Poles. His *Kateryna* is an exceptional poem on the sufferings of a Ukr. girl seduced by a Russian. In 1841 came the *Haydamaky*, an account of the Ukr. uprising against the Poles in 1768. Later, after his return to the Ukraine in 1843, he poured out the sufferings of his people at the hands of the Russians in a long series of poems in various forms—*Son* (The Dream), *Kavkaz* (The Caucasus), and *Velyky Lyokh* (The Great Grave)—while in his shorter poems he gave lyric expression to the deepest sentiments of his people and their love of freedom:

Bury me and then rise boldly,
Break in twain your fetters
And with the foul blood of foemen
Sprinkle well your freedom
(*Testament*)

To these sentiments he added appeals to his people for love and toleration of one another. On his return from Asia, his versions of the Psalms and Old Testament Prophets spoke for a humanity outraged by human cruelty. His songs now became more universal in character, but his more personal notes of devotion to country still sounded as did his desire to have a home on the Dnieper banks in the Ukraine.

Shevchenko's successors, such as his friend P. Kulish (1819–97) who was primarily a romanticist, began experimenting with realism, but they were hampered by tsarist decrees in 1863 and 1876 which practically forbade the publication of books in Ukr. The next important figure was the Western Ukr. Ivan Franko (1856–1916), who displayed an amazing energy in all fields, poetry, drama, novels, and stories. His poems, starting with a stress on the need for reform, culminated in *Ivan Vyshensky* and *Moses*, in which he spoke as the undisputed leader of his people. A newer sense of contact with Europe appeared in the work of Lesya Ukrainka (pen name of Larysa Kvitka-Kosach, 1872–1913). A hopeless invalid with a broad knowledge of foreign languages, she composed poems and verse dramas largely on world themes but applicable to the Ukraine;

and in *The Forest Song* she gave beautiful expression to Ukr. folklore and traditions.

In the 1890's modernism and symbolism appeared, especially in the works of Oles (pen name of Ol. Kandyba, 1878–1944). Oles was really the poet of the Revolution of 1905, but he also wrote important poems in 1917 and then finally emigrated and died in Prague. With him we may group Hryhori Chuprynka (1879–1921) who published several collections before World War I.

With the Revolution of 1917, the establishment of the Ukr. National Republic and the final triumph of the Soviets, the older writers died, emigrated, or became silent. Yet during the 1920's a younger group appeared to reflect the changed conditions and the newer developments in world poetry. The foremost melodically was Pavlo Tychyna (b. 1891), an adherent of symbolism; Mykhaylo Semenko (1892–193?) was the leader of futurism. The neoclassicists Mykola Zerov (1890–193?), Pavlo Fylypovych (1891–193?) Mykhaylo Dray-Khmara (1889–193?), Osvald Burghardt (Yuri Klen, 1891–1947), and Maksym Rylsky (b. 1895) appealed for high art and a return to the European sources of world culture. In addition there were proletarian poets who warmly supported the Soviet system, expressionists like Todos Osmachka (1895–1962) and Mykola Bazhan (b. 1904), as well as neoromantic authors like Dmytro Falkivsky (1898–1934) and Oleksa Vlyzko (1908–34).

In the early 1930's, in connection with the artificial famine in the Ukraine, orders were issued to force all authors into a Union of Soviet Writers. The vast majority of the Ukr. poets disappeared in the labor camps of the far north and Siberia. The only authors who survived were those who, like Tychyna, Rylsky, Bazhan, and Volodymyr Sosyura (b. 1898), put themselves at the disposal of the regime and wrote at its command without regard to the standards of art.

Meanwhile a significant literature developed in the Western Ukraine under Polish rule (1919–1939). Especially noteworthy is Bohdan Lepky (1872–1941), a delicate lyricist, and there were several groups reflecting the various political and artistic developments of the time. Among the writers we can mention Yuri Lypa (1900–1944) and Yevhen Malanyuk (b. 1897) and above all the Lemky poet Bohdan Ihor Antonych (1909–37), a poet somewhat pantheistic in his expression of himself as the brother of the universe but with a strong sense of the joy of life, which was ended for him all too soon. We must mention also from World War II two poets who died at the hands of the Germans, Oleh Olzhych Kandyba (1909–44), a vivid exponent of the cruelty of the day, and

Olena Teliha (1907–42), a truly intimate and heroic writer who was shot in Kiev while work-in the Ukr. liberation movement.

There was another flowering of poetry in the camps in Germany after the war, but most authors who wrote in Germany have found new homes in America, e.g., Vasyl Barka, Yar Slavutych, M. Orest, and many others.

The ways of the poets in Eastern Ukraine have been hard especially during the last years of the cult of Stalin as Sosyura found out when he received a Stalin Prize for a poem *Love Ukraine* and then was bitterly attacked a few years later for the same work on ideological grounds. Of the poets who became prominent we may mention L. Pervomaysky (b. 1908), a poet with a broad palette of colors for modern Soviet literature, and A. Malyshko, who follows the general classical pattern. Since the "thaw," which affected Ukr. poetry only slightly, a new group of poets has arisen. These have been born and educated under Soviet conditions, and in the last five years such writers as Lyna Kostenko, Mykola Vinhranovsky, Vitali Korotych, and above all Ivan Drach (b. 1936) have developed some originality and a proper appreciation of modernism; and despite political criticism, they have shown themselves able to strike new notes in the long history of Ukr. poetry.

It may be questioned today whether Ukr. poetry is better represented by the poets who have emigrated or those at home. It is hard to foresee the next step, but as the last years have shown, poetry has revived whenever there has been a relaxation of pressure, and we cannot doubt that it will do so again in the future.

ANTHOLOGIES: *Struny, antologiya ukrayinskoyi poeziyi,* ed. P. Lepky (1922); *Gelb und blau, moderne ukrainische Dichtung in Auswahl,* ed. and tr. W. Derzhawin (1948); *Die ukrainische Lyrik, 1840–1940,* ed. and tr. H. Koch (1955); V. Slavutych, *The Muse in Prison* (1956); *Weinstock der Wiedergeburt, moderne ukr. Lyrik,* ed. and tr. E. Kottmeier (1957); *The Ukr. Poets, 1189–1962,* ed. C. H. Andrusyshen and W. Kirkconnell (1963).

HISTORY AND CRITICISM: M. Tyszkiewicz, *La Littérature ukrainienne* (1919); M. Hrushevsky, *Istoriya ukrayinskoyi literatury* (5 v., 1923–26); S. Efremov, *Ist. ukr. lit.* (1924); V. H. Kowalski, *Ukr. Folksongs* (1925); A. P. Coleman, *Brief Survey of Ukr. Lit.* (1936); C. A. Manning, *Ukr. Lit.* (1944); Y. Slavutych, *Modern Ukr. Poetry, 1900–1950* (1950); V. D. Chyzhevsky, *Ist. ukr. lit.* (1956); G. Luckyj, *Lit. Politics in the Soviet Ukraine, 1917–1934* (1956) and "Ukr. Lit., the last 20 Years," BA, 30 (1956); G. Luznycky, *Ukr. Lit. within the Framework of World Lit.: A Short Outline of Ukr. Lit. from Renaissance to Romanticism* (1961). C.A.M.

ULTRAISM. Hispanic literary movement (1919–1923) which best reflected the postwar emotional crisis among writers in the Sp. tongue. Gerardo Diego, Juan Larrea, and, in particular, Guillermo de Torre of Spain, César Vallejo of Peru, and Jorge Luis Borges of Argentina are the best known writers of the Hispanic aspect of U. Strange new metaphors, strings of metaphors tumbling out, and strenuous avoidance of the old patterns of language are characteristic of the ultraistic style. For example, "The guitar is a well with wind in place of water," wrote Gerardo Diego. And, "No one knows that the sky is a garden."

The movement began in Spain in 1919 among the younger poets who owed dual allegiance to Juan Ramón Jiménez and to Ramón Gómez de la Serna, but who also kept their ears keenly attuned to the series of literary "isms" that rapidly arose and fell in France in an attempt to capture the agony of the times. Creationism (q.v.), a prior movement brought to Spain by Vicente Huidobro of Chile in 1918, was also blended with U. in the peninsula. By 1923 U. was dead, and all that remained was the name. The only present value of the movement lies in the individual worth of the poets who briefly espoused its cause. Federico García Lorca of Spain, least touched by the extremes of U., was the finest poet of the generation.—J. L. Borges, "Ultraísmo," *Nosotros* (Buenos Aires), 15 (1921); G. de Torre, *Las literaturas europeas de vanguardia* (1925) and *La aventura y el orden* (1948); R. Cansinos-Assens, *La nueva literatura,* III (1927); G. Videla, *El ultraísmo* (1963). J.A.C.

UNANIMISM. Term applied by Jules Romains [Louis Farigoule, 1885–   ] to his ideal of human participation in collective life, in group rhythms, and group consciousness. According to his own account, Romains' first overwhelming intuition of u. came one evening in October 1903 while he was walking with a friend, Georges Chennevière: "I am in Amsterdam Street like a cell in the flesh of a man or in the leaves of a tree. And I am at the moment the only one conscious of this. It is up to me to grasp all the life in the street, in its thick mass of carriages and passers-by. It is up to me to bring it into the light of consciousness, beyond the explosions of its motors and the movements and thoughts of each of its individuals." The unanimist conception of the group and its ambience is related to the earlier imaginative representations of collective experience in such writers as Hugo, Whitman, and Zola, and to the vision of the great industrial city in Verhaeren; but u. entails an empathic absorption of individual wills, and sees the resulting union of experience as a consolation for man's loss of belief in immortality.

Such early volumes as *La vie unanime* (1908) and *Odes et prières* (1913) exemplify the inspiration of u. in Romains' lyric verse. Notable here among his individual poems is the *Ode à la Foule*. Romains is best known, however, not for his poetry but for his long stream of novels published under the title *Les hommes de bonne volonté*. In the theatre, his unanimist verse-plays (*L'armée dans la ville* [1911] and *Cromedeyre-le-Vieil* [1920]) have an early predecessor in Lope de Vega's *Fuente Ovejuna*. *Cromedeyre-le-Vieil*, admittedly one of its author's favorites, is concerned with the unanimist hero Emanuel's shaping the collective consciousness of his village and with the surrender to its rhythms and the unity of its psychic life by the women from outside abducted into it. Romains writes of this strange play, which has caught with haunting poetry a sense of the unanimist ideal: "It offers the image of a humanity still very close to its origins . . . of a humanity reduced to the fierce unity of the tribe." Romains and Georges Chennevière experimented with new rhythms for unanimist poetry and published in 1923 their *Petit traité de versification,* among whose most notable innovations was the theory of the *accord* (q.v.).—A. Cuisinier, *Jules Romains et l'unanimisme* [I] (1935) and *L'art de Jules Romains* (1948); S. A. Rhodes, *The Contemporary Fr. Theatre* (1942); P. Jolivet, "Le théâtre poétique de Jules Romains," *Orbis Litterarum,* 9 (1954); P. J. Norrish, *Drama of the Group: a Study of U. in the Plays of Jules Romains* (1958); B. F. Stoltzfus, "U. Revisited," MLQ, 21 (1960).   A.G.E.

UNDERSTATEMENT. See LITOTES; MEIOSIS.

UNITY is the most fundamental and comprehensive aesthetic criterion, upon which all others depend. Plato first among Western thinkers proposed an artistic doctrine of u.; in the *Phaedrus* he perceived an analogy between u. of discourse and the organic u. of a living creature. In the *Symposium* he suggested in connection with the musical scale that u. is a reconciliation of opposites or discords. Organic u. is obtainable by means of conscious arrangement of parts. Aristotle's *Poetics* provides our first great statement on dramatic u. Aristotle emphasizes functionalism; tragedy is superior to epic because of its tighter internal relationships (5.23–24). U. is an ideal relationship of beginning, middle, and end. The ideal tragedy is an imitation of a unified action, large enough to be perspicuous and small enough to be comprehensible. Aristotle's conception of u. is closely related to his artistic requirements of probability and necessity, as

they constitute the criteria for the connection of parts (6–9). The famous "three unities" of action, time and place were often ascribed to the *Poetics* though he actually sponsors the u. of action only.

Aristotle is concerned with dramatic action; Horace's looser, more informal *Art of Poetry* deals indiscriminately with action, words, metaphor, and poetic or rhetorical devices. The *Art of Poetry* contains the definitive neoclassic statement: "I shall aim at a poem so deftly fashioned out of familiar matter that anybody might hope to emulate the feat, yet for all his efforts sweat and labor in vain. Such is the power of order and arrangement; such the charm that waits upon common things." Horace conceives of u. as an effect of harmony, obtained by skillful "order and arrangement," analogous either to music or more significantly to the harmonious blending of colors, light, and shadow in painting ("ut pictura poesis"). Pope's *Essay on Criticism* in the 18th c. is a classic adaptation of Horace, as Boileau had a little earlier adapted "Longinus." Longinus' *On the Sublime* is the most useful ancient document on lyric poetry. The conception of u. presented in it is relatively romantic, although in its account of arrangement and oratorical "amplification" it has affinities with both Plato and Horace. In his analysis of Sappho's Ode Longinus detects an organic u. derived from intensity of feeling and thought, which manifests itself as a reconciliation of opposing elements, and which artistically declares itself as a process of selection (10).

From antiquity to the end of the 18th c. theories of u. have been primarily theories of dramatic u., with the three unities of "the rules" the dominant issue. The It. Castelvetro has generally been credited or taxed with them in his translation and commentary on Aristotle's *Poetics* (1570). U. for Castelvetro is a quasi-legal consequence of the limitation of a dramatic action to twelve hours; by way of artistic satisfaction, it displays the skill of the poet in doing much with little (Gilbert, *Literary Criticism,* pp. 309–10, 318–19, 354). In general, the larger purposes of the three unities throughout their reign were to foster verisimilitude (q.v.) and to obtain artistic concentration, and for these purposes, as T. S. Eliot has remarked in "A Dialogue on Dramatic Poetry" (1928), there is much to be said for them. Under them grew up the great Fr. classical drama of the 17th c., despite the occasional grumblings of Corneille. For whatever reason, the three unities were never entirely naturalized in England, although the "regular" play received due critical respect. Whether because of the whole trend of native Elizabethan and Jacobean drama, or the great counterexample of Shakespeare, or, as Englishmen were wont to maintain, because of the superior independence and originality of the Eng. mind, the unities were only casually observed. Dryden's *An Essay of Dramatic Poesy* (1668, 1684), with its brilliant defense of the Eng. use of subplot (*Essays*, 1.69–71), is a full and fair discussion of the issues. Dr. Johnson was to strike a semifinal blow against the unities by denying their claims to "nature" and verisimilitude ("Preface to Shakespeare," 1765), and Coleridge completely demolished their philosophical and psychological pretensions, as had A. W. von Schlegel, in his lectures on Shakespeare (*Shakespearean Criticism*, I).

Up to the second half of the 18th c. theories of poetic u. for the most part dealt with drama, with some attention to epic (Le Bossu, *Traité du Poëme Épique*, or Addison's *Spectator* papers on *Paradise Lost*, for example) and to narrative poetry in general. Such theories were usually objective, since their subject matter was external action, and analytical, since they were concerned with the known components of recognized genres. With the rise of psychological aesthetics in the 18th c., however, came ideas better suited to lyric poetry, or capable of application to all poetry. New and enlarged conceptions of poetic imagination and a general shift from a mechanical to a vitalist worldview brought forth the romantic organic u., which had various aspects; it appeared as u. of feeling, u. as a vision of a vital, sentient nature, u. as an imitation of the poet's mind in the act of creation, and imaginative u., with the imagination the shaping, unifying, and reconciling power (Coleridge, *Biographia Literaria*, chap. 14).

20th c. theories of u., although they are often direct reactions against romanticism, are nevertheless basically romantic. The concept of u., especially of organic u., has never been more important than in the formalist, the psychological, and the mythicist criticism of the last twenty years, both as a standard of judgment and a method of exposition. Thus poetic u. has been explained by I. A. Richards in *Principles of Literary Criticism* as a reconciliation of impulses, by Cleanth Brooks and others as a reconciliation of thought and feeling manifested in the interaction of theme with language and metaphor, by the surrealists as a unifying of the total mind by freeing the unconscious, by the Freudians through dream-pattern and Freudian symbol, and by the Jungians by detection of archetypal myth-motifs (T. S. Eliot, *The Waste Land*; Maud Bodkin, *Archetypal Patterns in Poetry*). All 20th-c. versions of u., however, can be distinguished from their romantic predecessors by their common radicalism and their common effort to banish the subject-object problem of external reference.

Plato, *Dialogues*, tr. B. Jowett, I and III (4th ed., 1953); S. H. Butcher, *Aristotle's Theory of Poetry and Fine Art* (4th ed., 1911, 1932, 1951); Longinus, *On the Sublime*, tr. W. Rhys Roberts (1907); T. R. Henn, *Longinus and Eng. Crit.* (1934); L. Castelvetro, *Poetica d'Aristotele vulgarizzata et sposta* (1571); H. B. Charlton, *Castelvetro's Theory of Poetry* (1913); R. Le Bossu, *Traité du poëme épique* (1675); *Treatise of the Epick Poem*, tr. "W. J." (1695); J. Dryden, *The Essays of John Dryden*, ed. W. P. Ker (2 v., 1926); S. T. Coleridge, *Biographia Literaria*, ed. J. Shawcross (2 v., 1907); *Coleridge's Shakespearean Crit.*, ed. T. M. Raysor (2 v., 1930); I. A. Richards, *Principles*; M. Bodkin, *Archetypal Patterns in Poetry* (1934) and *Studies of Type-Images in Poetry, Religion, and Philosophy* (1951); J.W.H. Atkins, *Lit. Crit. in Antiquity* (1934); *Lit. Crit., Plato to Dryden*, ed. A. H. Gilbert (1940); C. Brooks, *The Well Wrought Urn* (1947); S. E. Hyman, *The Armed Vision* (1948); Abrams; Wellek; Wimsatt and Brooks. See also G. F. Else, *Aristotle's Poetics* (1957).   R.H.F.

UPAJATI. A mixed meter which combines varieties of the 11- and 12-syllable measures, especially the former. The 11- and 12-syllable classes called *triṣṭubh* and *jagati* were popular in the *Veda*, and from these many classical meters evolved. In the *Mahābhārata* particularly, several forms of this "11-12 syllable meter" are found. The u., one of these forms, is also called *ākhyānakī*, showing that it was used for epic and heroic narratives. The normal u. mixes an *indravajrā* and a *upendravajrā*, which, between them, differ only in the opening pair of syllables: the former starting on a trochaic unit and the latter on an iambic (cf. opening stanza of Kālidāsa's *Kumārasambhava*). For bibliog., see INDIAN PROSODY.   V.R.

URDU POETRY. See INDIAN POETRY.

URUGUAYAN POETRY. See SPANISH AMERICAN POETRY.

UT PICTURA POESIS. Few expressions of aesthetic criticism have led to more comment over a period of several centuries than *u.p.p.*, "as is painting so is poetry" (Horace, *Ars Poetica* 361). Even with partial explanation (362–65, 1–47, 343–45), the Horatian comparison of painting and poetry was as tentative as the proper Augustan wished it to be. The notion that poetry and painting are alike had had some currency even before Horace, who probably knew—even if he may not have assumed that his audience would recall—the more explicit earlier statement of Simonides of Keos (first recorded by Plutarch, *De gloria Atheniensium*, 3.347a, more than a century after *Ars*

-[881]-

Poetica): "Pocma pictura loquens, pictura poema silens" (poetry is a speaking picture, painting a silent [mute] poetry).

The views of Aristotle—especially that poetry and painting as arts of imitation should use the same principal element of composition (structure), namely, *plot* in tragedy and *design* (outline) in painting (see *Poetics*, 6.19–21)—furnished additional authority for Renaissance and later attempts to measure the degree and the nature of the kinship of the arts (the "parallel" of the arts) and to determine the order of precedence among them (the "*paragone*" of the arts). Moreover, as Rensselaer W. Lee observed in his illuminating analysis of the humanistic theory or doctrine of painting for which the Horatian dictum served as a kind of final sanction, "writers on art expected one to read [*u.p.p.*] 'as is poetry so is painting.'"

The Horatian simile, however interpreted, asserted the likeness, if not the identity, of painting and poetry; and from so small a kernel came an extensive body of aesthetic speculation and, in particular, an impressive theory of art which prevailed in the 16th, 17th, and most of the 18th c. While a few poets assented to the proposition that painting surpasses poetry in imitating human nature in action as well as in showing a Neoplatonic Ideal Beauty above nature, more of them raided the province of painting for the greater glory of poetry and announced that the preeminent painters are the poets. Lucian's praise of Homer as painter (*Eikones* 8) gave ancient authority for that view, which Petrarch and others reinforced. Among the poets described as master-painters have been Theocritus, Virgil, Tasso, Ariosto, Spenser, Shakespeare, and Milton, not to mention numerous later landscapists in descriptive poetry, the Pre-Raphaelites, and the Parnassians. Painter and critic, Reynolds instanced Michelangelo as the prime witness to "the poetical part of our art" of painting (*Discourse* 15, 1790). Thus a "poetical" or highly imaginative painter could be compared with the "painting" poets.

U.p.p. offered a formula—the success of which "one can hardly deny," René Wellek remarked—for analyzing the relationship of poetry and painting (and other arts). However successful, the Horatian formula proved useful—at least was used—on many occasions as a precept to guide artistic endeavor, as an incitement to aesthetic argument, and as a basic element in several theories of poetry and the arts. Alone and with many accretions, modifications, and transformations, *u.p.p.* inspired a number of meaningful comments about the arts and poetry and even contributed to the [actual] work and theory of several painters, most notably, "learned Poussin."

Moreover, like other commonplaces of criticism, the Horatian formula stimulated and attracted to itself a variety of views of poetry and painting that are hard to relate to the original statement.

Another part of the story of the Horatian simile concerns adverse criticism and opposition. In *Plastics* (1712) Shaftesbury warned, "Comparisons and parallel[s] . . . between painting and poetry . . . almost ever absurd and at best constrained, lame and defective." The chief counterattack came in *Laokoön* (1766), with Lessing contending that the theories of art associated with *u.p.p.* had been the principal, if not the only, begetter of the confusion of the arts which he deplored in artistic practice and theory of the time. R. G. Saisselin has lately shown that the "relations between the sister arts . . . were more complex than a reading of Lessing might lead one to believe" (JAAC, Winter 1961). Since then similar charges have been raised occasionally, as in Irving Babbitt's *The New Laokoön: An Essay on the Confusion of the Arts* (1910), a stumbling block until very recently.

On the other hand, from late in the 19th c. the kinship of poetry and painting appeared in a more favorable light in connection with the arts of the East—in generalizations about the "poetic feeling" of Oriental painting and the pictorial characteristics of Chinese and Japanese poetry and, with the ever-increasing knowledge of Eastern art, in historical and critical studies setting forth the close relationships between Oriental poetry and painting. In China poets were often painters; and critics, particularly in the 11th and 12th c., stated the parallelism of poetry and painting in language close to that of Simonides and Horace. According to Chou Sun, "Painting and writing are one and the same art." *Writing* implied calligraphy, which linked painting with poetry. Thus, a poet might "paint poetry," and a painter *wrote* "soundless poems."

These Eastern views led a number of poets in Europe and America to follow Japanese rules for poems and Chinese canons of painting and even to write-paint "Oriental" poems—"images" directly presented to the eye, "free" impressions in a few strokes of syllables and lines, evocations of mood, lyrical epigrams, and representations rather than reproductions of nature. Yet the poems reflecting the Eastern tendency to regard poetry and painting as "two sides of the same thing" were experimental and specialized works that included only a few of the resources of the two arts. Moreover, the critical analysis of "the same thing," with its "two sides" of painting and poetry, remains at least as difficult as the explanation of the Horatian observation, "as is painting so is poetry."

VERISIMILITUDE

Today, painters and poets seldom study the Horatian simile and the expanded "texts" of the It., Fr., and Eng. treatises on the humanistic theory of painting, and few artists care whether painting ever had a superior, an elder, or any sister. Oriental theories of the blending, not to say confusion, of art forms are more likely to arouse interest in the kinship and rivalry of poetry and painting. If painting now seems too varied to allow anyone to define it precisely, the same is true of poetry. Whatever painting is, poetry is the same! Since the Horatian proposition may be useful again, it had best remain unresolved: if poetry and painting *are* the same and were born at one and the same time, they may to-gether fall.—W. G. Howard, "*U.P.P.*," PMLA, 24 (1909); and (ed.) *Laokoön: Lessing, Herder, Goethe* (1910; full bibliog.); I. Babbitt, *The New Laokoön* (1910); E. Manwaring, *It. Landscape in 18th C. England* (1925); C. Davies, "*U.P.P.*," MLR, 30 (1935); R. W. Lee, "*U.P.P.*," *Art Bull.*, 22 (1940) and "*U.P.P.*" in Shipley; Wellek and Warren (2d ed., chap. 11); H. H. Frankel, "Poetry and Painting: Chinese and Western Views of their Convertibility," CL, 9 (1957); J. H. Hagstrum, *The Sister Arts* (1958); R. G. Saisselin, "*U.P.P.*: Du Bos to Diderot," JAAC, 20 (1961). S.A.L.

UTA. See TANKA; JAPANESE POETRY.

VALUE. See EVALUATION.

VEHICLE. See TENOR AND VEHICLE.

VENEZUELAN POETRY. See SPANISH AMERICAN POETRY.

VENUS AND ADONIS STANZA. So called from its use by Shakespeare in the poem *Venus and Adonis*. A 6-line stanza in 5-foot iambic lines, rhyming ababcc, it did not originate with Shakespeare, but had been used earlier, e.g., by Sidney in his *Arcadia* and by Spenser in the Januarie eclogue of his *Shepheardes Calender*. Shakespeare employed this form again in *Romeo and Juliet, Love's Labour's Lost*, and other plays. The stanza proved particularly attractive to American poets, e.g., Freneau, *To Sylvius on His Preparing to Leave the Town*, Bryant, *Lines on Revisiting the Country*, and Lowell, *April Birthday at Sea*. R.O.E.

VERISIMILITUDE. The doctrine that poetry should be "probable" or "likely" or "lifelike." Almost all critical theory has in some measure accepted the idea, though differences in strictness and laxness of interpretation are major.

The primary source is the concept of *to eikos* (the probable, the verisimilar) in Aristotle's *Poetics*. It is closely related to his fundamental notion of the imitation of nature. If a poem is not lifelike (at least in some sense), it can hardly be called an imitation. Aristotle's account is perceptive, brief, and left a good bit to the judgment of later critics. He says, in Chapter 9, that the poet describes not histori-cal actions but "the kind of thing that might happen . . . as being probable or necessary." Historical occurrences may *or may not* be probable in this sense, and in tragedy the marvelous or astonishing must be included and the supernatural may be included. He gives some scope, though not very much, in Chapter 15, to propriety of character, as he allows "consistent inconsistency," and a great deal of scope, in Chapter 25, to the impossible so long as it is "convincing," and even some allowance to the improbable, since it is probable that some improbable events will happen. And the writer may depart from representation of common reality in depicting the ideal or in following common opinion. What he insists on is universality and the *apparent* moral and psychological consequentiality of actions. Cicero, Quintilian, Plutarch, Horace accept the idea and tend to restrict it somewhat more than did Aristotle, in the direction of the ordinary and the commonly probable.

In Renaissance thought, theorists from Scaliger through the "querelle du Cid" and later, take the concept very seriously and debate its range and meaning. Propriety of character, where Aristotle himself gave little enough freedom, is interpreted so strictly that stock characters tend to become the exclusive ideal (most notoriously in Thomas Rymer's animadversions against Shakespeare), though in one notable instance Dryden defends the character of Caliban in a brilliant argument, on strict grounds of propriety and verisimilitude (*Essays of John Dryden*, ed. W. P. Ker, I, 219–20). Somewhat more freedom is allowed in the handling of the marvelous (Christian critics being hardly willing to deny supernature a

-[883]-

place in serious literature), though there is major disagreement here. Castelvetro, Maggio, Chapelain, and d'Aubignac discriminate between ordinary and extraordinary verisimilitude. Rymer, and later—rather surprisingly—Johnson, take a conservative view with respect to this point, Dryden and Rapin take moderate positions, and Chapelain (who wants a more Christian poetry) a radical one.

It was on grounds of *vraisemblance* that the Academy censured *The Cid* of Corneille. Corneille and Racine accepted the principle of *vraisemblance* or verisimilitude quite genuinely, and the struggle in each of them between the abstracted rules and the pressures of their artistic habits and desires was, for both, fruitful.

Though the term has had much less use in the last two centuries, the idea, as a perennial and inescapable demand, persists in various, often implicit, forms: Wordsworth's turning to the common realities and the language of men, Coleridge's frequent appeals to "good sense," Arnold's "criticism of life," and the New Critics' concern for paradox, irony, "toughness" as giving an adequate, which is to say verisimilar, image of our experience.—R. M. Alden, "The Doctrine of Verisimilitude," *Matzke Memorial Volume* (1911); Bray; P. van Tieghem, *Petite histoire des grandes doctrines littéraires en France* (1946); Tuve, esp. chap. 9; B. Weinberg, *A Hist. of Lit. Crit. in the It. Renaissance* (2 v., 1961).   P.R.

VERS. A kind of song in Old Prov., fundamentally indistinguishable from the *chanso* (q.v.). But v. was the older term, in use before the literature became rigidly formalized; consequently, it was used more loosely than *chanso,* sometimes designating poems on almost any subject, and not exclusively love poems. The v. is also apt to have shorter and less complicated stanzas, but more of them.—Jeanroy, II.   F.M.C.

VERS DE SOCIÉTÉ. See LIGHT VERSE.

VERS LIBRE. Rhymed, syllabic verse, mainly the product of the Middle Ages, was not to remain long unchallenged: the *versi sciolti* (q.v.) of the It. Renaissance, prosodic experiments by Antoine de Baïf, alternations of verse lengths in La Fontaine begin a loosening which is climaxed by the v.l. of 19th-c. France. Whitman's free verse may have served as model, but the form appears in the *Illuminations* (1873?) of Rimbaud, who was probably unaware of the *Leaves of Grass* (1855) which, anyhow, seem closer to the *verset* (q.v.) than to v.l. The two v.-l. poems of Rimbaud were first printed in the review *La Vogue* in 1886. Gustave Kahn, the editor, published his own

v.l. there shortly afterwards, and haughtily insisted that he was nowise influenced by Rimbaud, to whose v.l. he, moreover, denied that appellation. About this time Jules Laforgue, Kahn's friend, produced his—infinitely superior —v.l., to be followed (it would seem) by that of Jean Moréas. These men have claimed, or been credited with, inventing the form; but it is fairer to say the form invented itself through them, the tyrannical strictures of Fr. versification eliciting a strong, if gradual, reaction—first in poetic prose, then prose poem (q.v.), then *vers libéré,* and finally v.l. This last can be defined as verse in which neither syllable nor metrical rules obtain, and only rhythm matters. Though rhyme (as opposed to most Eng. free verse) *may* persist, the traditional Fr. regulations for caesura, hiatus, counting of mute *e*'s, etc., are ignored. Consecutive lines may vary greatly in length, or may not, and the only unity generally maintained is one of sense or syntax.

The key problem is rhythm: how can it be defined—or at least demonstrated—in v.l., so as to justify the form's claim to poetic status? According to Herbert Read (following Professor Sonnenschein), we have in v.l. the substitution of the "element of proportion . . . for the element of regularity." Edouard Dujardin, himself an early *verslibriste,* sees it as "a form able to rhythmify or derhythmify itself instantaneously," and so suited to changes of mood in longer, particularly dramatic, poems. Professor V. Černý views v.l. as the spontaneous expression of inner rhythm, fighting "against formalism and, implicitly, for the self-assertion of poetic content" (a characteristically leftist position). One could adduce numerous further descriptions from scholars or practitioners, but it may be safely asserted that v.l. defies precise definition. Whatever is put on paper as free verse and moves us as poetry is v.l.: the rhythm may be simply a question of emotional and intellectual response.

Among other early *verslibristes* should be mentioned Vielé-Griffin, Henri de Régnier, Maeterlinck, and Verhaeren (the first half-Am., the last two Belgians). The movement spread to other countries. It was imported into Italy both by the futurists and the post-symbolist Gabriele d'Annunzio in his plays. In Spain, the "Generation of '98" produced some admirable v.l., especially, perhaps, Juan Ramón Jiménez. The so-called *freien Rhythmen* of Germany go back to Klopstock and the 18th c., and come down through Goethe, Hölderlin, and others; but they have been especially popular in the modern period. Rilke's *Duino Elegies* and the lyrics and dramas of expressionism are the best-known examples. There is probably no occidental literature now without its variety of v.l. The theatre has proved especially receptive to the flexible but effective form. It has also been used frequently in poetry of spiritual (e.g., Francis Jammes, P.-J. Jouve) or socio-political (e.g., V. Mayakovsky, Bert Brecht) exaltation. At present v.l. is a vigorous and developing form. A recent innovation (E. E. Cummings) has been the shift of the line breaks away from the natural speech rests, creating an effect of syncopation. See also FREE VERSE.

G. Kahn, "Préface," *Premiers poèmes* (1897); C. C. Clarke, *Concerning Fr. Verse* (1922; last ch.); M. M. Dondo, *V.L., a Logical Development of Fr. Verse* (1922); J. Hytier, *Les Techniques modernes du vers français* (1923); E. Dujardin, "Les Premiers poètes du v.l.," *Mallarmé par un des siens* (1936); H. Morier, *Le Rythme du v.l. symboliste* (3 v., 1944); A. Closs, *Die freien Rhythmen in der deutschen Lyrik* (1947); P. M. Jones, *The Background to Modern Fr. Poetry* (1951; part two, best introd. to the subject); W. Ramsey, *Jules Laforgue and the Ironic Inheritance* (1953; ch. 9); V. Černý, *Verhaeren a jeho misto v dejinach volného verše* (Prague, 1955; the Communist view). J.S.

VERSE AND PROSE. Words are used (1) for ordinary speech, (2) for discursive or logical thought, and (3) for literature.

Discursive language makes statements of fact, is judged by standards of truth and falsehood, and is in the form of prose. Literature makes no real statements of fact, proceeds hypothetically, and is judged by its imaginative consistency. Literature includes a great deal which is written in some form of regular recurrence, whether meter, accent, vowel quantity, rhyme, alliteration, parallelism, or any combination of these, and which we may call verse. All verse is literary, and philosophical or historical works written in verse are almost invariably classified as literature. We can exclude them from literature only by some kind of value-judgement, not by a categorical judgement, and to introduce value-judgements before we understand what our categories are is only to invite confusion. But although verse seems to be in some central and peculiar way the typical language of literature, all literature is not verse. The question thus arises: what is the status of literary prose? The best way to distinguish literary from nonliterary prose is by what we may call, cautiously and tentatively, its intention. If it is intended to describe and represent facts and to be judged by its truth, it normally belongs in some nonliterary category; if it is to be judged primarily by its imaginative consistency, it normally belongs to literature. We say *normally*, because it is quite possible to look at some works, such as Gibbon's *Decline and Fall of the Roman Empire,* from either point of view.

A subordinate problem also arises in passing: what is the meaning of the word poetry? Aristotle remarked in the *Poetics* that meter was not the distinguishing feature of "poetry." But Aristotle also remarked that the work of literary art as such, whether poem or play or essay, is "to this day without a name," and to *this* day, 2,500 years later, the statement is still true. The word "poetry" has always meant primarily "composition in meter," so that while *Tom Jones,* for instance, is certainly a work of literature, nobody would call it a poem.

The first point to get clear about prose is that the language of ordinary speech is not prose, or at least is prose only to the extent that it is not verse. Ordinary speech, especially colloquial or vulgar speech, is a discontinuous, repetitive, heavily accented rhetoric which is as readily distinguishable from prose as it is from regular meter. Any fiction writer who is a close observer of common speech will show in his dialogue a markedly different rhythm from what he himself uses in narration or description. Prose is ordinary speech on its best behavior: it is the conventionalization of speech that is made by the educated or articulate person when he is trying to assimilate his speech to the patterns of discursive thought. Anyone listening to the asyntactic prolixity of uneducated speech, or to the chanting or whining of children, can see that regular meter is in fact a much simpler way of stylizing ordinary speech than prose is, which explains why prose is normally a late and sophisticated development in the history of a literature.

There are, then, at least two ways of conventionalizing ordinary speech: the simple and primitive way of regularly recurring meter, and the more intellectualized way of developing a consistent and logical sentence structure. When recurrent rhythm takes the lead and the sentence structure is subordinated to it, we have verse. When the sentence structure takes the lead and all patterns of repetition are subordinated to it and become irregular, we have prose. Literary prose results from the imitation for literary purposes of the language of discursive thought. Of all the differentia between prose and verse, the only essential one is this difference of rhythm. Verse is able to absorb a much higher concentration of metaphorical and figurative speech than prose, but this difference is one of degree; the difference in rhythm which makes the higher concentration possible is a difference of kind.

This division between prose and verse is however complicated by the various forms of "free verse," which are unmistakably literary and yet are not in meter or any other form of regular recurrence. The naive assumption that any poetry not in some recognizable recurrent pattern must really be prose clearly will not do, and we have to assume the existence of a third type of conventionalized utterance. This third type has a peculiar relation to ordinary speech, or at least to soliloquy and inner speech. We may call it an oracular or associational rhythm, the unit of which is neither the prose sentence nor the metrical line, but a kind of thought-breath or phrase. Associational rhythm predominates in free verse and in certain types of literary prose, such as "stream of consciousness" prose.

A historical treatment of this threefold division of verbal rhythm—discursive, metrical, and associational—would require an encyclopaedia in itself. It will be best if we proceed inductively, confining our examples to the single language of Eng., and look at some of the literary phenomena which may be explained by it. Each of the three rhythms, in literature, may exist in a relatively pure state or in combination with either of its neighbors.

VARIETIES OF PROSE RHYTHM. Prose, we have said, is typically either the language of discursive thought or an imitation of that language for literary purposes. In pure prose the logical or descriptive features are at a maximum, and the stylistic, or rhetorical, features at a minimum. The rhythm of the sentence predominates; all repetition, whether of sound or rhythm, is eliminated as far as possible, and recurring rhetorical devices, or tricks of style, are noticed only with irritation. The aim is to present a certain content or meaning in as unobtrusive and transparent a way as possible. When prose is like this it is at the furthest possible remove from metrical or associative influences. Pure prose has two chief types of rhythm: the more informal and colloquial type which represents the rhythm of educated speech transferred to the printed page, and the more formal type which is thought of from the beginning as something to be read in a book. Let us take a passage from Darwin's *Origin of Species:* "The great and inherited development of the udders in cows and goats in countries where they are habitually milked, in comparison with these organs in other countries, is probably another instance of the effects of use. Not one of our domestic animals can be named which has not in some country drooping ears; and the view which has been suggested that the drooping is due to the disuse of the muscles of the ear, from the animals being seldom much alarmed, seems probable." This passage plainly does not lack either rhythm or readability; there is certainly a literary pleasure in reading it. The pleasure however is in seeing prose expertly

used for its own descriptive purposes, and from our confidence that such alliteration as "the drooping is due to the disuse" is purely accidental. Let us compare Darwin's prose with a passage from Gibbon's *Decline and Fall of the Roman Empire:*

"The mystic sacrifices were performed, during three nights, on the banks of the Tiber; and the Campus Martius resounded with music and dances, and was illuminated with innumerable lamps and torches. . . . A chorus of twenty-seven youths, and as many virgins, of noble families, and whose parents were both alive, implored the propitious gods in favour of the present, and for the hope of the rising generation; requesting in religious hymns, that, according to the faith of their ancient oracles, they would still maintain the virtue, the felicity, and the empire of the Roman people." Here, along with the information given about the secular games of Philip, we are aware of certain tricks of style, such as antithetical balance and doubled adjectives. If we are intent only on the history, the tricks of style obstruct our path. But we notice that a specifically literary intention is visible in Gibbon beside the descriptive one. He is suggesting a *meditative* interest in the decline of Rome, and for this meditative interest a certain formal symmetry in the style is appropriate.

We notice also that the more obtrusive stylizing of Gibbon's prose makes it more oratorical, a quality of deliberate rhetoric being present. Another step would take us all the way into oratorical prose, where the formalized style is of equal importance with the subject matter. This is the normal area of all great oratory, as from Cicero down to Lincoln's Gettysburg Address and Churchill's 1940 speeches, the most memorable passages of oratory have usually been passages of formal repetition. Samuel Johnson's letter to Chesterfield provides similar examples:

"The notice which you have been pleased to take of my labours, had it been early, had been kind; but it has been delayed till I am indifferent, and cannot enjoy it; till I am solitary, and cannot impart it; till I am known, and do not want it." With the increase of the rhetorical or symmetrical element in the style, the prose is taking on an increasingly *metrical* quality, and is moving closer to verse. This metrical quality is strongly marked in Ciceronian prose, in the long formal sentences broken in two by an "and" out of which the 17th-c. character books are constructed, in the deliberately symmetrical arrangements of phrases and clauses in Sir Thomas Browne's *Urn Burial* and Jeremy Taylor's *Holy Dying.*

A slight exaggeration of this metrical element would take us into the area of euphuism, which is a deliberate attempt to give to prose the rhetorical features of verse, including rhyme and alliteration as well as metrical balance. Here is a sentence from Robert Greene's euphuistic romance *The Carde of Fancie:* "This loathsome lyfe of *Gwydonius,* was such a cutting corasive to his Fathers carefull conscience, and such a haplesse clogge to his heavie heart, that no joye could make him injoye any joye, no mirth could make him merrie, no prosperitie could make him pleasant, but abandoning all delight, and avoyding all companie, he spent his dolefull dayes in dumpes and dolours, which he uttered in these words." Here we are almost as far away as we can get from anything that we now think of as prose: the predominating rhythm is still the sentence, but the writer has done everything that a descriptive prose writer would try to avoid. Euphuism is of course an intensely rhetorical form of prose: one would expect to find it in sermons, where it has been prominent from Anglo-Saxon times; and in euphuist stories the writer strives for situations where the characters may write letters, lament, or harangue. We notice that the sentence quoted above leads up to a harangue.

Now let us return to the type of pure prose that is more informal and colloquial, designed to suggest good talk rather than good exposition, of which perhaps the greatest practitioner is Montaigne. Let us take a passage from one of Bernard Shaw's Prefaces:

"After all, what man is capable of the insane self-conceit of believing that an eternity of himself would be tolerable even to himself? Those who try to believe it postulate that they shall be made perfect first. But if you make me perfect I shall no longer be myself, nor will it be possible for me to conceive my present imperfections (and what I cannot conceive I cannot remember); so that you may just as well give me a new name and face the fact that I am a new person and that the old Bernard Shaw is as dead as mutton." As compared with the Darwin passage, there is here some influence of an associational rhythm: we can see the easy use of parenthesis, the imaginary conversation with the reader, and similar signs of the associative process of speech. But everything here is on an impersonal plane, the conscious mind and logical argument being assumed to be in charge. Continuous prose, or writing with a logical shape, assumes an equality between writer and reader. The writer buttonholes his reader, so to speak, when he talks to him continuously. If he wishes to suggest aloofness or some barrier against his reader, or if he simply wishes to suggest that there are greater reserves in his mind than he is ready to display all at once, he would naturally turn to a more discontinuous form.

We find such a form in the series of apho-

risms of which many prose works, such as books of recorded table talk, are constructed. Philosophers in particular seem to be fond of it: Pascal, Bacon, Spinoza, Wittgenstein, Nietzsche, are a few random examples. The aphorism is oracular: it suggests that one should stop and ponder on it. Like oratorical prose, it suggests meditation, but the reader is being directed into the writer's mind instead of outward to the subject. In such discontinuous and aphoristic prose the associational rhythm can be clearly heard. Donne's *Devotions Upon Emergent Occasions* provide examples, especially in those passages cast in the form of prayer, where the reader is not being directly addressed: ". . . thou callest *Gennezareth,* which was but a Lake, and not *salt,* a *Sea;* so thou callest the *Mediterranean Sea,* still the *great Sea,* because the *inhabitants* saw no other *Sea;* they that dwelt there, thought a *Lake,* a *Sea,* and the others thought a *little Sea,* the *greatest,* and wee that know not the *afflictions* of others, call our owne the heaviest."

A step further in this direction takes us toward the oracular and associational prose poem of which Ossian is the best known Eng. example, though there is so little intellectual or logical interest in Ossian that there is not much sense of prose left. Eng. does not provide as clear examples of the aphoristic prose poem as German has in Nietzsche's *Also Sprach Zarathustra* or as Fr. has in Rimbaud's *Saison en Enfer.* But it is clear that in the opening of Dylan Thomas's *Under Milk Wood* prose is being as strongly influenced by an associational rhythm as it can well be and still remain prose: "It is Spring, moonless night in the small town, starless and bible-black, the cobblestreets silent and the hunched, courters'-and-rabbits' wood limping invisible down to the sloeblack, slow, black, crowblack, fishing-boat-bobbing sea."

VARIETIES OF VERSE RHYTHM. This subject really belongs to PROSODY, but a few additional suggestions may find a place here. In Eng. such forms as the stopped heroic couplet and the octosyllabic couplet represent the rhythm of metrical verse at its purest, equidistant from prose and from the associational rhythm. The following passage from Pope is typical:

Alike in ignorance, his reason such,
Whether he thinks too little, or too much:
Chaos of Thought and Passion, all confus'd;
Still by himself abus'd, or disabus'd;
Created half to rise, and half to fall;
Great lord of all things, yet a prey to all;
Sole judge of Truth, in endless Error hurl'd:
The glory, jest, and riddle of the world!

The one recurrent sound is the rhyme; assonance and alliteration are kept to a minimum, and even the sentence structure tends to fall into the suggested metrical unit; hence the inevitable and unforced use of antithesis and the regular fall of the caesura. In Dryden and Pope, in the octosyllabics of Marvell, in the simple quatrains of Housman, where a strictly controlled meter makes the words step along in a precise and disciplined order, the predominant sense is one of conscious wit. This sense arises from the technical dexterity displayed in neutralizing prose sense with associative sound, on approximately equal terms.

In blank verse, so easy to write accurately and so hard to write well, we move much further in the direction of prose. For in blank verse there is little place for the metrical absorption of the sentence structure: a long series of blank-verse lines in which the sentence structure closely followed the iambic pentameter would produce intolerable singsong. Hence blank verse tends to develop syncopation and run-on lines, and as it does so a second prose rhythm is set up beside the metrical one. This process may continue until the pentameter approximates prose. The following passage from Browning's *Ring and the Book* has been chosen as less extreme in its approximation than many that might have been selected:

So
Did I stand question, and make answer, still
With the same result of smiling disbelief,
Polite impossibility of faith
In such affected virtue in a priest;
But a showing fair play, an indulgence, even,
To one no worse than others after all—
Who had not brought disgrace to the order,
    played
Discreetly, ruffled gown nor ripped the cloth
In a bungling game at romps . . .

In such discursive or narrative blank verse as the above the listener hardly hears a definite pentameter at all: what he hears is a rhythm that seems just on the point of becoming prose, but is prevented from achieving the distinctively semantic rhythm of prose by some other rhythmical influence. The rhythm of Jacobean blank-verse drama has its center of gravity somewhere between verse and prose, so that it can move easily from one to the other at the requirements of dramatic decorum, which are chiefly the mood and the social rank of the speaker. In *The Tempest*, especially the speeches of Caliban, and in some late plays of Webster and Tourneur, the barrier between verse and prose often comes near dissolving, and hence the third associational rhythm peeps through, as in this passage from *The Tempest*:

I will stand to, and feed,
Although my last: no matter, since I feel

The best is past. Brother, my lord the Duke,
Stand to, and do as we.

A strong bias toward a prose sentence structure combined with a more elaborate rhyming scheme often produces the kind of intentional doggerel that is a regular feature of satire, as in *Hudibras* or *Don Juan,* or in Ogden Nash today. Wordsworth, who stressed the identity of language between verse and prose, sometimes had trouble in keeping the simple flat sentences in the *Lyrical Ballads* from sounding like doggerel. One of Donne's Satire (the fourth) opens as follows:

Well; I may now receive, and die; My sinne
Indeed is great, but I have beene in
A Purgatorie, such as fear'd hell is
A recreation to, and scarse map of this.

Nobody hearing these lines read aloud would realize that they were pentameter couplets: the whole metrical scheme is parody, and as such it fits the satirical context.

In relation to prose, associational writing shows itself chiefly in a change of direction in meaning, away from the logical and toward the emotional and private. In relation to verse, it shows its influence chiefly in an increase in sound patterns. We notice this particularly in stanzaic verse, for the natural tendency of the stanza is to develop elaborate rhyming patterns, often supported by alliteration, assonance, and similar devices. Words tend to echo each other, and an evocative rhythm is superimposed on the metrical one, as in this lovely madrigal from *The Faerie Queene:*

Wrath, gealosie, griefe, loue do thus expell:
    Wrath is a fire, and gealosie a weede,
    Griefe is a flood, and loue a monster fell;
    The fire of sparkes, the weede of little seede,
    The flood of drops, the Monster filth did
        breede:
    But sparks, seed, drops, and filth do thus
        delay;
    The sparks soone quench, the springing seed
        outweed,
    The drops dry vp, and filth wipe cleane
        away:
So shall wrath, gealosie, griefe, loue dye and
    decay.

A further step in this direction would make the sound-patterns obsessive, as happens occasionally, by way of experiment, in *The Faerie Queene* itself. Edgar Allan Poe, who made the discontinuity and the evocative effect of verse his "poetic principle," shows in such experiments in sound as *The Bells* and in such lines as the famous "The viol, the violet and the vine" the permeation of meter by associative sound. In Hopkins a similar unifying of metrical and associative rhythms takes place, but in a much more intellectualized context:

'Some find me a sword; some
The flange and the rail; flame
Fang, or flood' goes Death on drum,
And storms bugle his fame.
But we dream we are rooted in earth—Dust!
Flesh falls within sight of us, we, though
our flower the same,
Wave with the meadow, forget that there
must
The sour scythe cringe, and the blear share
come.

This passage illustrates another important principle. As associational patterns increase, and as alliteration and assonance appear beside rhyme, a more vigorous rhythm than a strict meter may be required to prevent the poem from becoming a soggy mass of echolalia. The rhythm in the Hopkins passage is accentual rather than metrical: like the rhythm of music, which it closely resembles, it sets up a series of accented beats, with a good deal of variety in the number of syllables that may intervene between beats. The sixth line of the above passage begins with an accentual spondee, though the prevailing rhythm of the line is anapestic. This accentual rhythm, usually with four main beats to a line, has run through Eng. from Anglo-Saxon alliterative verse to our own day, and often syncopates against the metrical rhythm. Thus "Whan that Aprill with his shoures soote," "To be or not to be, that is the question," and "Of man's first disobedience, and the fruit" are all iambic pentameter lines with four accented beats.

VARIETIES OF ASSOCIATIONAL RHYTHM. It is only in the more experimental writing of the last century or so, with its strongly psychological bias and its interest in the processes of creation, that any serious attempts have been made to isolate the associational rhythm in literature. Owing to this late development, its earlier manifestations have fallen within the normal categories of prose and metrical verse.

The associational rhythm has always been a feature of oracular writing, as in the Koran and in many parts of the Bible, as well as a regular literary device for expressing insanity, as in some of the Tom o' Bedlam speeches in King Lear. These uses are solemn or tragic, yet associative rhythms and mental processes have also a close connection with the comic, and, in the form of puns and malapropisms, have been one of the chief sources of humor. The conscious wit that was mentioned as an effect of expertly handled meter is quite distinct from associational wit, which results rather from an involuntary release from the subconscious. The most striking examples of associational rhythm at its purest before our own day are dramatic attempts to render the speech of uneducated or confused people who make no effort to organize their language into prose, such as Mistress Quickly in Shakespeare or Jingle and Mrs. Nickleby in Dickens. This curious duality of the oracular and the comic is peculiar to associational rhythm, and has been illustrated in passages quoted above.

Rabelais is the great progenitor of associational prose, especially in passages depicting drunkenness or other oracular states of mind, as in the fifth chapter of Gargantua. But of course in Eng. the tradition of associational prose writing was established by Sterne. Almost any page of Sterne, notably the famous opening page of the Sentimental Journey, illustrates the lightning changes of mood and rhythm and the dislocation of the ordinary logic of narrative or thought that are characteristic of associative style. Modern "stream of consciousness" writing is heavily indebted to Sterne. In such passages as this from Ulysses we can see the predominance of what we have called the "thought-breath" rhythm of association as distinct from the poetic line and the prose sentence: "Confession. Everyone wants to. Then I will tell you all. Penance. Punish me, please. Great weapon in their hands. More than doctor or solicitor. Woman dying to. And I schschschschschsch. And did you chachachachacha? And why did you? Look down at her ring to find an excuse. Whispering gallery walls have ears. Husband learn to his surprise. God's little joke. Then out she comes. Repentance skindeep. Lovely shame. Pray at an altar. Hail Mary and Holy Mary." The speed of this is andante and the monologue of Molly Bloom at the end of the book presto, but the rhythmical units are the same.

Associational prose develops in two directions, which may be called the disjunctive and the conjunctive. In disjunctive writing, as illustrated most typically by Gertrude Stein, and also found in Hemingway, Faulkner, and D. H. Lawrence, there is a technique of deliberate prolixity, a hypnotic repetition of words and ideas. In dialogue this may express simple inarticulateness or fumbling for meaning: in short, the original naive speech out of which associational writing grows. In more sophisticated contexts it expresses rather a breaking down of the more customary logical prose structures preparatory to replacing them with the psychological and emotional structures of associational prose. In conjunctive writing the aim is the reverse: to pack into the words as great a concentration of association as possible, whether of allusion, of sound (as in punning or paronomasia), or of ideas. The logical culmination of this process is Finnegans Wake, where the dream language used shows the influence of Freud's demonstrations of the incredible associative complexity of states of mind below consciousness.

In verse, associational rhythm very seldom predominates over meter before Whitman's time: about the only clear examples are poems written in abnormal states of mind, such as Christopher Smart's *Jubilate Agno*. Whitman's own rhythm shows many formalizing influences, such as that of biblical parallelism, and the relation to prose is also often close. But in Whitman's oracular lines, with a strong pause at the end of each and with no regular metrical pattern connecting them, the distinctive associational rhythm has been fully emancipated. Whitman's natural tendency is disjunctive, and in some later free verse, especially in imagism (q.v.), this tendency is developed. Thus Amy Lowell:

Lilacs,
False blue,
White,
Purple,
Color of lilac,
Heart-leaves of lilac all over New England,
Roots of lilac under all the soil of New England,
Lilac in me because I am New England . . .

But the prevailing tendency in modern associational verse is conjunctive or evocative, as it is in the erudite literary allusiveness of Eliot and Pound, in the catachresis (q.v.) metaphors of Hart Crane and Dylan Thomas, or in the symbolic clusters of the later Yeats.

In pure prose, where the emphasis is on descriptive meaning, figures of speech are used sparingly, an occasional illustration or analogy being normally the only figuration employed. The more rhetorical the prose, the more naturally figurative the style becomes. In Jeremy Taylor, for instance, there appear elaborately drawn-out similes, and in euphuism similes from natural history (or what then passed as such) are a regularly recurring feature. Verse also, when it steers its middle course between prose and associational rhythm, often finds its figurative center of gravity in the illustrative simile, so prominent in the classical epic. But in verse, words are associated for sound as well as sense, rhyme being as important as reason, and the more intensified the sound patterns are, the greater the opportunities for puns and similar verbal echoes. Associational writing, when conjunctive, tends to violently juxtaposed metaphor and to a thick figurative texture.

S. Lanier, *The Science of Eng. Verse* (1880); T. S. Omond, *A Study of Metre* (1903) and *Eng. Metrists* (1921); G. Saintsbury, *A Hist. of Eng. Prosody* (3 v., 1906–10) and *A Hist. of Eng. Prose Rhythm* (1912); Schipper;

L. Abercrombie, *Poetry and Contemporary Speech* (1914; Eng. Assoc. pamphlet no. 14); Baum; D. L. Clark, *Rhetoric and Poetry in the Renaissance* (1922); C. P. Smith, *Pattern and Variation in Poetry* (1932); O. Barfield, *Poetic Diction* (2d ed., 1952); M. Boulton, *Anatomy of Poetry* (1953) and *Anatomy of Prose* (1954); J. Thompson, *The Founding of Eng. Metre* (1961). N.FR.

VERSE DRAMA. See DRAMATIC POETRY.

VERSE PARAGRAPH. Like prose, poetry tends to move forward in units which may be called, by analogy, v. paragraphs. The tendency is particularly strong in narrative and descriptive poetry, where the paragraphs are often indicated by indentation or spacing between lines. Elaborate stanzaic forms like the Spenserian stanza or ottava rima are often developed as v. paragraphs, and in inferior poetry the result is usually monotonous. If a paragraph is defined as one or more sentences unified by a dominant mood or thought, many lyrics could be described as single v. paragraphs, a point especially obvious in the case of the sonnet.

By general consent, the greatest master of the v. paragraph is John Milton. Many of the characteristic effects of *Paradise Lost*—its majesty, its epic sweep, its rich counterpoint of line and sentence rhythms—are produced or enhanced by Milton's v. paragraphs. To sustain his paragraphs Milton employed enjambment ("the sense variously drawn out from one Verse into another"), interruption, inversion, and suspension, or *Spannung*, the device of the periodic sentence whereby the completion of the thought is delayed until the end of the period.—G. Hübner, *Die stilistische Spannung in Milton's P.L.* (1913); E. Smith, *The Principles of Eng. Metre* (1923); J. H. Hanford, *Milton Handbook* (4th ed., 1946); J. Whaler, *Counterpoint and Symbol: An Inquiry into . . . Milton's . . . Style* (1956).

VERSET. A form derived from the "verses" of the Bible (especially The Song of Songs, Psalms, Prophets). Its earliest application, accordingly, is in religious or mystical works of biblical inspiration, like the 15th-c. *Imitations of Christ* (Thomas à Kempis?). More recently, the form appears in parts of Hölderlin's *Hyperion* (1797–99) and throughout two apocalyptic works: *The Books of Polish Pilgrimage* by Adam Mickiewicz and its immediate offshoot, Lamennais' *Paroles d'un croyant* (1834). The charismatic character of both books stems largely from the v.: the long line—actually perhaps several lines of print—is a powerful, rhythmic verbal surge corresponding roughly to one outpouring of breath from full lungs.

Alliteration and assonance, possibly rhyme, anaphora and other types of repetition, rhetorical figures like antithesis, parallelism etc., bolster the *verset's* aural and emotional suasion. Inasmuch as maximum freedom (this side of the prose poem, q.v.) is allowed in the number of words per unit, an exciting oscillation obtains between vers libre and poetic prose, depending on the greater or lesser symmetry in a sequence of *versets*.

The fervor of the v. is usually religious or patriotic—Péguy, Claudel; or the (not altogether different) opposite—Nietzsche's *Also sprach Zarathustra;* it can accommodate also the pure passions of Paul Fort (*Ballades françaises*) and the cloudier ones of St.-John Perse. It has found favor with the inward-echoing receptivity of impressionism (e.g. Max Dauthendey), as with the intensified expansiveness of expressionism (Werfel, Ernst Stadler). The poetic drama made excellent use of the v.: Claudel and Péguy again, and expressionists like Walter Hasenclever (*Der Sohn*). Here its rousing quality can prove most felicitous.

P. Fort, "Préface," *Le Roman de Louis XI* (1898); L. Spitzer, "Zu Charles Péguys Stil," *Stilstudien* (2 v., 1928); P. Claudel, "Réflexions et propositions sur le vers français," *Positions et propositions* (2 v., 1928); E. Dujardin, "Les premiers poètes du vers libre," *Mallarmé par un des siens* (1936); W. Weintraub, "A Gospel for the Refugees," *The Poetry of Adam Mickiewicz* (2 v., 1954); F. Martini, "Also sprach Zarathustra," *Das Wagnis der Sprache* (2d ed., 1956). J.S.

VERSI SCIOLTI. Also, *endecasillabi sciolti.* Hendecasyllabic lines with principal accent on the tenth syllable and without rhyme. They were used as early as the 13th c. (in the *Mare amoroso*) but were first cultivated during the Renaissance as the It. equivalent of classical epic hexameter. Trissino used them in his epic *Italia liberata dai goti,* and his tragedy *Sofonisba.* Despite his lack of success a controversy arose between the advocates of classical austerity and the advocates of rhyme. In the 16th c. rhyme won the day, but in the 18th c. and thereafter, v.s. were used with great success, particularly by Parini (*Il Giorno*), Foscolo (*I Sepolcri*), and Manzoni (*Urania*). Alfieri almost singlehanded made them the standard meter for tragedy. More recently the dramatist Sem Benelli used them in several dramas, and Pascoli adopted them for all but the last of his *Poemi conviviali. Endecasillabi sciolti* are equivalent to blank verse (q.v.) and may have influenced the development of that form in Eng.—F. Flamini, *Notizia Storica dei Versi e Metri Italiani* . . . (1919). L.H.G.

VERSIFICATION. See PROSODY.

VERSO PIANO. Also, *endecasillabo.* In It. prosody applied to any line that has a feminine ending with the accent on the next-to-last syllable. In particular, a line of 11 syllables with principal accent on the tenth. V.p. is the standard narrative line in It. corresponding to iambic pentameter in Eng. It was used in the earliest It. (and Sicilian) poetry in the first half of the 13th c. The opening line of the *Divine Comedy* is a famous example: "Nel mezzo del cammin di nostra vita." See also VERSI SCIOLTI; VERSO TRONCO. L.H.G.

VERSO SDRUCCIOLO. Also, *endecasillabo sdrucciolo.* In It. prosody a line with the principal accent on the tenth syllable and ending in a *parola sdrucciola,* a word accented on the antepenultimate syllable, giving the verse a dactylic ending as well as actually 12 syllables. An example from Dante's *Divine Comedy* (*Inferno* 24.64) is: "Parlando andava per non parer fievole." This line was cultivated in the 16th c. instead of the L. iambic trimeter. Ariosto used it in his Comedies to imitate the meter in the Theater of Plautus and Terence. Monti used it later in the *Canto d'Apollo,* in his *Prometeo;* and Carducci, still later, in his *Canto di Marzo,* wherein he tried to reproduce the accents and pauses of the L. iambic trimeter. This system applies to the L. *settenario* verse as well.—F. Flamini, *Notizia Storica dei Versi e Metri Italiani* . . . (1919); C. H. Grandgent, Introd. to Dante's *Divina Commedia* (1933). L.H.G.

VERSO TRONCO. Also, *endecasillabo tronco.* In It. prosody applied to any line ending with an accented syllable; in particular, a line with principal accent on the tenth syllable and with a masculine ending. Because the final unstressed syllable has been dropped (*tronco,* from *troncato,* lopped off), the *endecasyllabo* has 10 rather than the usual 11 syllables. Dante may have used v.t. (*Inferno* 4.60), but uncertainty about his pronunciation makes it impossible to decide definitely. In the generation after Dante, Antonio Pucci began a sonnet with a v.t.: "Caro Sonetto mio, con gran pietà." In another of his sonnets, *versi tronchi* are used throughout the octave. Later poets sometimes used them as a metrical stunt. See VERSO PIANO. L.H.G

VERSUS POLITICUS. A verse of 15 accentual iambic syllables, rare before the 10th c. A.D. but common from the late Byzantine period to the present day. It consists of two cola, one of 8 and one of 7 syllables, with a caesura after the eighth syllable. It has two main accents, one on the eighth or sixth and one on the fourteenth syllable. The origin of the verse is not very certain but, in all probability, it goes back to the beginning of the Eastern Roman Empire. Eustathius thought that it originated in the ancient trochaic tetrameter and Krumbacher considered it a mixture of the two most popular ancient meters, the trochaic and iambic tetrameter. The widespread use of the verse in late Byzantine and modern Gr. folk poetry argues in favor of its popular origin.—K. L. Struve, *Ueber den politischen Vers der Mittelgriechen* (1828); K. Krumbacher, *Geschichte der byzantinischen Literatur* (2d ed., 1897); P. Maas, *Gr. Metre*, tr. H. Lloyd-Jones (1962). P.S.C.

VERSUS PYTHIUS. Name given to the dactylic hexameter, e.g., by Aphthonius (3d c. A.D.), because it was the meter used in the Pythian (i.e., Delphic) oracles. Combinations of hexameters and iambic dimeters or trimeters were called *pythiambics*, examples of which are provided by Horace, *Epodes* 14, 15, and 16. R.J.G.

VERSUS SPONDAICUS. Roman grammarians differ as to whether this was a verse (notably hexameter) consisting entirely of spondees, e.g., Ennius, *Annales* 169 (Vahlen):

$$\bar{ci}ves \mid \bar{Ro}ma \mid \bar{ni} \; tu\bar{nc} \mid fac\bar{ti} \mid su\bar{nt} \; Ca\bar{m} \mid pa\bar{ni},$$

or a dactylic hexameter with a spondee in its fifth foot, i.e., a spondaic verse (q.v.). The latter meaning is generally adopted by modern metricians (e.g., Kolář) for *versus spondaicus* (cf. the Gr. [*stichos*] *spondeiazon* as attested by Cicero, *Epistulae ad Atticum* 7.2.1). R.J.G.

VIETNAMESE POETRY. The earliest forms of Viet. poetry show the influence of Chinese domination over a long period and indeed were written in the Chinese language. What might be called the classical form was subject to the rigid rules of versification found in Chinese poetics. A common verse form was the poem of 8 lines of 7 syllables each. Since Viet., like Chinese, is a tonal language, each line provided a fixed position for various tones with little variation permitted. The 8 lines consisted of 4 couplets which, as Cung-giu-Nguyên phrases it, "served successively to introduce, describe, discuss and conclude." This Chinese influence and the Sino-Viet. literature were ultimately replaced to a very large extent by a national literature in Viet. The outstanding representative of the national literature is Nguyên-Du (1765–1820) who adapted and composed in poetry a Chinese novel, called in Viet. by the names of its three chief characters *Kim-vân-Kiêu*. This the Viet. people consider the national poem of their country and the masterpiece of their literature. Besides this

work, Viet. literature possesses two other poetic masterpieces, *Cung oan Ngâm Khuc* (Lament of a Lady of the Palace), and *Chinh phu Ngâm* (Lament of a Warrior's Wife). The first was written by the well-known poet On-nhu-Hau (1741–98), the second by one of the several outstanding poetesses in Viet. literature, Đoàn-thi-Điêm (1705–46). On-nhu-Hau depicts the sad fate of a beautiful woman whom he compares with the sunflower which is born with the sun and with the sun it dies. This poem still remains one of the most popular in all Vietnam. Đoàn-thi-Điêm's masterpiece of Viet. poetry was first written in Chinese by another Viet. Her version in the vernacular of her country has made her famous and rendered the poem among the best-loved in her country. It is the plaint of a young and beautiful woman waiting for her husband, who is away at war and in the end does not return.

Some reaction to the classical poetic tradition began to appear shortly after the turn of the century and in 1930 La Fontaine's *Fables* were translated into Viet. in free verse. The new poetry of the younger writers which began to appear from 1930 on was sharply criticized by the older poets who deplored the break with the classical verse forms and the inability or unwillingness to compose according to the long-established rules of versification. A famous classical poet of a later generation was Nguyên-khac-Hiêu (1889–1939), better known by the name Tan-Da, a Bohemian by nature, whose poems reflect the unhappiness of one who is unable to make his way in the world and retreats to live frugally, detached from the mainstream of life. Another is Trân-tuan-Khai who sings in classical style of his homeland and of its great heroes. As late as 1940 Quach Tan published a collection of poems in the same style but the younger generation exhibited no enthusiasm for them.

In 1936 Thê Lu's poems in modern rhythms, new to the Viet. ear, appeared. Pessimistic in tone, they charmed the younger generation of listeners. Several of his poems are considered masterpieces of modern Viet. literature. In the same year the first collection of poems by a leper, Hàn-mặc-Tù (1913–40), appeared. Entitled *Gái-Quê* (Country Maidens), they were written in free verse and sing of the simplicity of rustic life and people. Though suffering greatly from his malady and withdrawn from society, he continued to compose until his death in September 1940. An example of his poetry is this stanza describing his imminent death:

One of these mornings, near a limpid source,
With the stars and the dew I shall die like
    the moon

Finding none of these beautiful fairies to weep
  for me,
Embrace me and heal the wounds of my heart.

Viet. poets did not limit themselves to composition in Chinese and the vernacular of their country. So strong was Fr. influence that several Viet. poets became well known in France. One of these is Pham-van-Ky (1913–) who shows the influence of Baudelaire in his collection called *Une Voix sur la Voie* (A Voice Along the Way). One of the more successful modern poets in Viet. has been Vu-hoang-Chuong who has been publishing his work since 1940. He is regarded as an example of one who has been able to bridge the ancient and the modern as well as the Eastern and the Western. Some of his poems have been translated into Eng. and Fr.

ANTHOLOGIES: *Morceaux choisis d'auteurs annamites . . .* , ed. and tr. G. Cordier (2d ed., 1935); *Poésies de l'Extrême-Orient*, tr. Tran-van-Tung (1945); Vu-hoang-Chuong, *Communion: Poems* (1960).

HISTORY AND CRITICISM: Pham-Quynh, *La poésie annamite* (1931); G. Cordier, *Étude sur la litt. annamite* (3 v., 1933–40; best general survey); Tran-cuu-Chan, *Étude critique du Kim-văn-Kiêu, Poème national du Viêt-Nam* (1948), *Essais sur la litt. vietnamienne* (1950) and *Les grandes poétesses du Viêt-Nam* (1950); Thai-van-Kiem, *Un grand poète vietnamien: Hàn-mặc-Tù* (2d ed., 1950) and *Étude littéraire, philosophique et scientifique du "Kim-văn-Kiêu"* (1951); R. Maran, "Three Indo-Chinese Poets," BA, 21 (1947); Cung-giu-Nguyen, "Contemporary Viet. Writing," BA, 29 (1955); M. Durand, "Litt. Vietnamienne," in *Histoire des littératures*, ed. R. Queneau, I (1955). J.M.E.

VILLANCICO. The v., a Sp. song form of popular origin, has come to mean simply a carol, particularly now a Christmas carol or a popular song on some other religious theme. Formerly the theme was not so restricted in subject matter. According to P. Henríquez Ureña, ". . . the line may be of any length, regular or variable, although the typical compositions are in octosyllables or hexasyllables, and have an *estribillo* (refrain) of two, three, or four lines, and stanzas of six, plus the *retornelo* (chorus) alternating with them." Rengifo describes the Golden Age form thus: "The lines [*pies*] of each strophe of the v. ordinarily are six. The first two are called the first *mudanza* [change], and the following two, second *mudanza*, because in them the *sonada* [tune] of the *cabeza* [introductory stanza presenting the theme] is varied and changed. The last two are called *vuelta* [return], because in them one returns to the

first *tono* [tune], and after them is repeated the last line or the last two lines of the *represa* [repetition]. The rhyme-scheme of the *pies* [lines] will follow that of the *cabeza*. Thus when in the *cabeza* of the v. there are four lines rhyming first with fourth and second with third, the *mudanzas* will have the same rhyme scheme and the *vuelta* will be like the last two lines of the *cabeza*." Le Gentil classifies the v. as a form developed from the cantiga.—Rengifo, *Arte poética española* (1592); P. Henríquez Ureña, *Versificación irregular en la poesía castellana* (2d ed., 1933); P. Le Gentil, *La poésie lyrique espagnole et portugaise . . . 2e partie: Les formes* (1953) and *Le virelai et le villancico* (1954); Navarro. D.C.C.

VILLANELLE. A Fr. verse form, derived from an It. folk song of the late 15th–early 17th c. and first employed for pastoral subjects. According to L. E. Kastner (*History of Fr. Versification*, 1903), Fr. 17th c. prosodists such as Richelet reserved the term "villanelle" for one of the rustic songs by Jean Passerat (1534–1602). Although the earlier forms show considerable variation, the v. has since Passerat retained the following pattern: usually 5 tercets rhyming aba, followed by a quatrain rhyming abaa, with the first line of the initial tercet serving as the last line of the second and fourth tercets and the third line of the initial tercet serving as the last line of the third and fifth tercets, these 2 refrain-lines following each other to constitute the last 2 lines of the closing quatrain. If we let a^1 and a^2 stand for the first and third lines of the first tercet, we may schematize the form thus: a^1ba^2 aba^1 aba^2 aba^1 aba^2 aba^1a^2.

Like the older Fr. forms, the v. was employed in 19th-c. Eng. poetry primarily as a light verse form by such experimental dilettantes as Andrew Lang. However, Leconte de Lisle used it in 19th-c. France as a vehicle for philosophical content, and in the 20th c. E. A. Robinson's *House on the Hill* achieved a somber effect. More recently, Dylan Thomas' *Do not go gentle into that good night* restored a majestic seriousness to the v.

VIRELAI (also called *chanson baladée*, and *vireli*). Fr. medieval lyric. Originally a variant of the common dance song with refrain of which the rondeau (q.v.) is the most prominent type. This form developed in the 13th c. and at first may have been performed by one or more leading voices and a chorus. It begins with a refrain; this is followed by a stanza of 4 lines of which the first 2 have a musical line (repeated) different from that of the refrain. The last 2 lines of this stanza use the music of the refrain. The opening refrain, words and

-[893]-

music, is then sung again. The v. usually continues with 2 more stanzas presented in this same way. A v. with only 1 stanza would be a *bergerette.* In Italy the 13th c. *laude,* and in Spain the *cantigas,* follow the same form. The syllables *vireli* and *virelai* were probably meaningless refrains which later designated the type.—F. Gennrich, *Rondeaux, Virelais und Balladen* (2 v., 1928). For additional information, see P. Le Gentil, *La Poésie lyrique espagnole et portugaise à la fin du moyen âge, 2ᵉ partie. Les Formes* (1953) and *Le V. et le villancico* (1954); M. Francon, "On the Nature of the V.," *Sym.,* 9 (1955; briefly surveys various schemes and proposes own formula).

U.T.H.

VOLTA, or volte. A turn or a repetition (used also of music, dance, etc.). In sonnet development the word was used in Italy to refer to the tercets of the sestet, either because of the repetition of the tercet or, more probably, because of the "turn of thought" which followed the close of the octave. The term would thus be applicable to any point in the thought development, regardless of the sonnet type, where such a turn might occur, as in Shakespeare's Sonnet 18, line 9: "But thy eternal summer shall not fade . . ." or in Keats's *On First Looking Into Chapman's Homer,* line 9: "Then felt I like some watcher of the skies. . . ." It is more than coincidence that both of these occur in line 9, inasmuch as the organization of thought within the limited scope of the form invites (though it does not demand) a division at that point. See SONNET.

L.J.Z.

VORTICISM. Though essentially a manifestation of certain ideas and developments in the visual arts, v. is related directly to modern poetry through Ezra Pound's interest in it and his claim for it as a movement parallel to imagism (q.v.) in poetry. Organized by Wyndham Lewis in 1914, v. was in short-lived reaction to the romantic and vitalist theories of futurism (q.v.), and stood most positively and clearly for the abstract and nonrepresenta-

tional in art. Abstraction was important, of course, as a reflection of certain qualities of a machine-age consciousness; and in the criticism of T. E. Hulme it occasionally and for different reasons assumes a status roughly equal to that of the absolutes of metaphysics. Its value for the vorticist, however, lay in its forcing the artist upon his own invention, in its inhibiting his tendency to make art an imitation of nature which would necessarily be inferior to the original. The vortex or whirlpool is energy, but it is energy that has undergone a metamorphosis into form; the two are inextricable in this analogy, but the significant point is the creation of a form that is still and yet moving, a paradox that is central to modern poetics from Hulme's "analogy" to Pound's "Image" to the formalist theories of the New Criticism (q.v.) and the speculations of *Burnt Norton.* The abstract demanded that the artist invent rather than copy and put a premium on the intellect rather than the emotions; but vorticism's relation to poetry is through its suggestion of a symbolist concept of form and structure.—*Blast* 1 (1914) and 2 (1915); E. Pound, "V.," *The Fortnightly Review,* 96 (1914), "Affirmations," *The New Age,* 16 (1915), *Gaudier-Brzeska: A Memoir* (1916), *The Letters of E. P.,* ed. D. D. Paige (1950); W. Lewis, *Time and Western Man* (1928), *Blasting and Bombardiering* (1937), *Wyndham Lewis the Artist* (1939); H. Kenner, *The Poetry of E. P.* (1951); S. K. Coffman, *Imagism* (1951); T. E. Hulme, *Further Speculations,* ed. S. Hynes (1955); G. Wagner, *Wyndham Lewis: a Portrait of the Artist as the Enemy* (1957).

S.K.C.

VOWEL RHYME. Used by some writers instead of the terms "assonance" or "assonantal rhyme," to describe that rhyme which requires phonetic identity only in the ultimate accented vowel (e.g., roof, tooth). Others use it to describe rhyme in which "any vowel is allowed to agree with any other" (Deutsch), for example, "falling, it."—E. Guest, *A Hist. of Eng. Rhythms* (1838, new ed., 1882); C. Wood, *The Art and Technique of Writing Poetry* (1945); Deutsch.

R.BE.

W

WAKA. See TANKA; JAPANESE POETRY.

WEAK ENDING. See LINE ENDINGS.

WEDGE VERSE. See RHOPALIC VERSE.

WELSH POETRY has a history of 14 centuries from the odes of Taliesin and Aneirin to the present day. We learn from Gildas' attack on the bards of Maelgwn Gwynedd's court (d. A.D. 547) that theirs was a secular tradition of panegyric, a thing apart from ecclesiastical learning and music, and having its high moments in feastings and on public occasions. Basically this remained true in succeeding ages although the influence of L. rhetoric, *ars poetica*, and other forms of medieval culture became marked.

Most of the extant poetry prior to the loss of Welsh independence in 1282 is found in the *Black Book of Carmarthen*, the *Book of Taliesin*, the *Book of Aneirin*, the *Red Book of Hergest*, and the *Hendregadredd MS*. Modern W. scholarship has led to the unraveling of several strands. The earliest is the *Hengerdd* (old-song). This includes the historic odes of Taliesin in praise of the rulers of Rheged (in S. W. Scotland) and North Wales, and also the poetry of Aneirin—a series of poignant and graphic elegies to the young men of the retinue of Mynyddog, a ruler of Edinburgh late in the 6th c., who had nearly all been destroyed by superior numbers of Northumbrians in an attempt to recover Catraeth (Catterick), a place of strategic importance. The *Hengerdd*, short poems of strong feeling, terse antitheses, and graphic description, became the chief models of W. poetry for hundreds of years, both for the outlook on life which they presented and for metrical form and ornament. The bardic tradition was molded around them.

There is no strong tradition of W. narrative poetry; prose was long considered to be the proper medium for story-telling (e.g. the *Mabinogion*). But the story-teller would break into verse at peak moments of tension. The 9th-c. poetry about Llywarch the Aged, and of Heledd and her brothers, are all that remains of tales of W. rulers who are depicted as having held sway over rich low-lying lands around Shrewsbury before being driven to the hills by the Eng. These *englynion* (see ENGLYN) of unknown authorship, with terse economy of words, and stark directness of expression, show great dramatic perception and maturity of reflection.

Y deilen honn, neus kennired gwynt.
Gwae hi o'e thynghet!
Hi hen; eleni ganet.

This leaf, driven by the wind,
Woeful her fate!
She is old; born only this year.

The taunting of brave sons by a garrulous aging father, the pathos of the old man's lonely helplessness after the death to which he had driven them, the desolation of the burnt-out hall of Cynddylan, and the tortured conscience of Heledd who feared that her lack of charity had provoked the powers that be—

these are among the permanent things of W. poetry.

The precariousness of national existence led to much vaticinatory poetry. *The Prophecy of Britain* (ca. A.D. 900) is a notable example. Goaded by the exactions of Athelstan, a Glamorgan poet who was a master of vigorous expression envisages a grand coalition of Cornish, W., Clydesmen, Gaels, and Dublin Norse who are destined to force the Eng. back on Sandwich whence they would reembark and leave the island in peace! Most of the prophetic poems up to the 13th c. however are in a more nostalgic strain, and are attributed to Myrddin (Merlin) to whose mind, deranged by the horrors of war, is attributed the gift of prophecy. These short poems have a touching tenderness as when he talks to his little pig, but also a stark directness: he sees his people crushingly defeated in a battle fought on a Wednesday, but assures them that "Thursday will come."

There is much early nature poetry, mostly in *englyn* meters: graphic and sensitive, with a rare economy of words closely knitted with alliteration and internal rhyme ("Wind keen, hill bare, ford unsafe, pool frozen, man can stand on a single straw-stump"). Most of this verse dates from the 9th to the 12th c., and some of it seems to have been composed by hermits. Often the scenes from nature are interspersed with gnomic phrases. The earliest religious poems are englynion to the Son of Mary (9th c.). *The Black Book of Carmarthen* contains a number of varied religious poems, typically medieval, including a debate between soul and body.

Norman aggression in Wales was repulsed in the 12th and 13th c. under the leadership mainly of the House of Gwynedd, following the return of Gruffudd ap Cynan from exile in Ireland. He brought in Ir. influences and reestablished the W. bardic orders. His dynasty (together with rulers of Powys and the South) were the patrons of the *Gogynfeirdd*, composers of court panegyric, modeled on the *hengerdd*, but more ornate, complex, and verbose. The *penceirddiaid* (chiefs of song) sang odes of praise to God and to the prince. Below them were the household bards, who sang in somewhat simpler style to the court ladies and the prince's chosen warriors. Nature, love, and vaunting themes lend variety. and the freshest poems are by two of the rulers themselves (1) Prince Owain Cyfeiliog who emulates Aneirin in stirring descriptions in *awdl* meters of forays (Covered with sweat were they all when they returned, and lo! valley and long hillside were full of sun) and (2) Prince Hywel ab Owain Gwynedd, of mixed W. and Ir. blood, in whose joyous love poems, Continental influences blend with a percipient delight in the W. countryside and community. The greatest of the court panegyrists were Cynddelw (12th c.), Llywarch ap Llywelyn, Dafydd Benfras, and Bleddyn Fardd (13th c.). They were men of high office in the inner circles of the princes, and they depict well the tensions and ideals on which the fate of the nation depended. This with the artistry of their *awdlau* gives to their verse dignity and reality.

Cistercian houses were established in the heart of Wales by her princes. The content of Gogynfeirdd religious poetry benefits by this contact. After the fall of the native princes (1282), several of the abbots became active patrons of the poets; the *Ars Poetica* was introduced to Wales through the influence of the church, and as a result, from the 14th to the 16th c., disquisitions in verse on matters of poetic theory—such as the sincerity of panegyric, the source of the poetic gift, etc.—were to become a marked feature. It culminated in a long verse discussion in *cywydd* meter (q.v.) between Edmwnd Prys and Wiliam Cynwal, on the respective merits of the medieval and Renaissance viewpoints on the function of poetry. Franciscan influence appears late in the 12th c. in Madog ap Gwallter, particularly in the fresh visual imagery and tenderness of his nativity poem. After 1282 patronage devolved mainly on the numerous small estate-holders. Stratification of bards into functional grades became far less rigid. Lower orders emerge with their simpler diction and meters such as the *traethodl*. Then appeared Wales's greatest poet, Dafydd ap Gwilym, who seized this meter and embellished it with the rich ornament of *cynghanedd* (q.v.), thus creating a fitting medium for expressing energetically the exciting miracle of creation which with his untiring eye for detail he saw daily renewed. Love and the exuberance of nature were his twin themes, and through the device of *dyfalu* (q.v.) he tirelessly strings together a chain of comparisons. His new *cywydd* meter became the normal form for two centuries, was ably revived in the 18th, and is still popular.

He had many imitators, and although panegyric was reestablished in the 15th c., a new sensuousness had come into W. poetry. Domestic comfort had increased, and householdership became the main theme of the bards. A more mellifluous style prevailed, and during the *grand siècle*, 1435–1535, delight in fine houses, gardens, and the arts of domesticity, tasteful appreciation of poetry and harp music in the homes of the small estate-holders, love of horses and treasured possessions of fine craftsmanship were the main themes. In *eisteddfodau*—bardic assemblies—meters and *cynghanedd* were given their final form, and

emphasis was on artistic perfection. A challenge to the prevailing outlook, however, was provided by the school of Siôn Cent in reminders of mortality and in a demand for a more chastening "reality." Not only was it a period of great masters of verse like Dafydd Nanmor, Dafydd ab Edmwnd and Tudur Aled, but the general level of literary competence had never been higher, and as the poets "perambulated" the country they were a cohesive force, maintaining a refined literary tongue and a unity of outlook.

The growth of the Renaissance was hindered by the social changes of the Tudor period. Landed families became anglicized. Dr. Gruffydd Robert, of Milan, and Edmwnd Prys, less radical than du Bellay, wished to pour new wine into the old bottles of strict meters (q.v.). Prys urged the poets to turn for their themes to the wonder of man's growing knowledge and command over nature. A new questioning spirit is felt, but with the generation of Siôn Phylip (early 17th c.) the old bardic life of perambulation, patronage and the practice of poetry as a profession comes to an end. The Tudor period, however, saw the growth of much popular verse closely akin in form and content to similar types in England. Ballads and songs of the sea and of various aspects of the life of the common people were greatly in favor, and the impulse of the Reformation is best seen in the fine W. metrical Psalter of the scholarly Edmwnd Prys. The 17th c. saw much decay but a new kind of poetic life emerged. Owen Gruffydd, of Llanystumdwy, marks the appearance of the local poet, untrained in bardic schools, but inheriting many scraps of the tradition, who sings the daily affairs of his own village in free meters (q.v.) but garnished with much alliteration and internal rhyme. Huw Morus, was foremost in borrowing the meters of popular song-tunes and decorating them in the same manner, in a loose version of *cynghanedd*. This "manner of Huw Morris" remained popular for two centuries, and poems for watchnight services at Christmastide were generally in this style.

The long decline was arrested in the second half of the 18th c. by the classical revival and by the hymn-writers. Lewis Morris, Goronwy Owen, and Ieuan Fardd studied the best W. poetry of former ages in manuscripts, and restored *awdl* and *cywydd* to their former excellence. They combined an Augustan outlook with their medievalism. The letters of Goronwy Owen were the greatest influence in W. literary criticism down to the time of Sir John Morris-Jones, and the standards of the Eisteddfod throughout the 19th c. derived from them. Another aspect of 18th-c. classicism were the pastorals of Edward Richard in "three-stroke" meter. Free-meter poetry un-trammelled by the old poetic ornament came into its own with the hymns of Pantycelyn and others, and it is from the hymn that the 19th-c. W. lyric grew. The 18th c. also saw in the interludes of Twm o'r Nant the best dra-matic verse in W. before the work of Saunders Lewis. Blank verse and very long free-meter narrative and descriptive poems first appear in W. from the pen of Pantycelyn. Many awdlau and pryddestau (qq.v.) were composed throughout the 19th c. with eisteddfod chairs and crowns in view, but a deterioration set in as the century advanced. Notable among long free-meter poems are those of Islwyn, with their reflection on life, profound and moving at best, but often turgid. Much good lyrical poetry was written in the 19th c., patterned on hymn meters and also on Eng. lyric forms. The song lyrics of Ceiriog, nostalgic and melodious, were immensely popular.

As the century drew to its somewhat dull close, there was little to show that the next half-century was destined to be one of the greatest periods of W. poetry. Verse was de-rivative, a spent force, feebly pietistic, the language without freshness and purity of idiom, horizons narrow through lack of con-tact with the great ages of the past and with Europe. The challenge was met, however, at every point. Sir John Morris-Jones, the lead-ing critic of the early 20th c. led men back to the fine qualities of medieval and 18th-c. cynghanedd, purified idiom, translated Heine and other European lyric poets, and led other poets to find inspiration in themes of Celtic romance. The new age was heralded at the Bangor Eisteddfod (1902) by the appearance of T. Gwynn Jones's Passing of Arthur, W. J. Gruffydd's Tristan and Iseult and Eifion Wyn's lyrics. T. Gwynn Jones wrote a number of long poems in cynghanedd on the romance of the Celtic past with a mastery over words and metrical forms which led him to experiment with new adaptations of the old bardic forms culminating in his application of cynghanedd to vers libre. Gruffydd expresses his deep feel-ing for the present-day community life and characters of Caernarvonshire in free-meter forms. The sonnet makes a late appearance in Wales but is powerfully used by R. Williams-Parry, T. H. Parry-Williams, and D. Gwenallt Jones. The ferment of 20th-c. W. poetry has taken many forms, old and new. The later work of Gwenallt Jones shows bold metrical experiment in an effort to capture the rhythms of impassioned speech. Of recent years new ground has been broken by Saunders Lewis in his verse-plays, where he has closely studied ways of reproducing speech rhythms within various verse patterns.

ANTHOLOGIES (in W.): The Myvyrian Ar-chaiology of Wales, ed. O. Jones and others (3 v., 1801–7); Ceinion Llenyddiaeth Gymreig (Beauties of W. Lit.), ed. O. Jones (4 v., 1876); Cywyddau Cymru, ed. A. Hughes (1908); Blodeuglwm o Englynion, ed. W. J. Gruffydd (1920); Y Gelfyddyd Gwta. Englynion a Phenil-lion, ed. T. Gwynn Jones (1929); Y Flodeu-gerdd Gymraeg (The W. Anthol.), ed. W. J. Gruffydd (1931); Cywyddau Iolo Goch ac eraill, ed. H. Lewis and others (2d ed., 1937); Blodeugerdd o'r Ddeunawfed Ganrif, ed. D. G. Jones (4th ed., 1947; 18th c. anth.); The Ox-ford Book of W. Verse, ed. T. Parry (1962).

ANTHOLOGIES (in translation): H. I. Bell, Poems from the W. (1919); K. H. Jackson, A Celtic Miscellany (1951); D. M. and E. M. Lloyd, A Book of Wales (1953); G. Williams, The Burning Tree (1956) and Presenting W. Poetry (1959).

HISTORY AND CRITICISM: · S. Lewis, Braslun o Hanes Llenyddiaeth Gymraeg hyd 1535 (1932); H. I. Bell, The Development of W. Poetry (1936); G. Williams, An Introduction to W. Poetry (1953); Parry.

PROSODY: J. Loth, La Métrique galloise (3 v., 1900–1902); Morris-Jones.   D.M.L.

WELSH PROSODY. See CELTIC PROSODY.

WHEEL. See BOB AND WHEEL.

WIT. In Aristotle's Rhetoric, w. is treated as the ability to make apt comparisons, and also (1389ᵇ) as "well-bred insolence." The L. term (ingenium) meant unique personal character-istics, or "genius" in the 18th-c. sense of the term. It was used by the rhetoricians to mean "cleverness" or "ingenuity." During the Ren-aissance it was used in a sense similar to the classical meaning, with perhaps more emphasis on ingenuity and the ability to create the bizarre, the extraordinary, and the unique. Renaissance discussions of invention (e.g. Leo-nardi, Dialoghi dell'Inventione) tended to identify w. with the ability to discover and amplify new subjects; while in discussions of style, particularly during the 17th c., it was identified with the ability to discover brilliant, paradoxical, and far-fetched figures, especially metaphor, irony, paradox, pun, antithesis, etc. (e.g., Baltasar Gracián, Agudeza y arte de ingenio, 1642; Emmanuele Tesauro, Il Can-nocchiale Aristotelico, 1654). Among the many terms used for w. are It. ingegno; Sp. ingenio, argudeza; Fr. esprit, ingenuité; G. Witz, Geist; and Eng. wit. (Cf. J. E. Spingarn, Crit. Essays of the 17th C., I, xxiv).

The high point in the career of w. came in the latter half of the 17th and the first two decades of the 18th c. in the wake of such "witty" poetic movements as It. marinism, Sp. gongorism, Fr. préciosité, and Eng. metaphysical style (qq.v.). Thomas Hobbes used the term in *Human Nature* (1650), as follows: "And both Fancie and Judgement are commonly comprehended under the name of *Wit*, which seemeth to be a Tenuity and Agilitie of Spirits, contrary to the resitness of the Spirits supposed in thou that are dull." And in *Leviathan* (1651): "*Naturall Wit*, consisteth principally in two things; *Celerity of Imagining*. (that is, swift succession of one thought to another;) and *steddy direction* to some approved end." Sir William Davenant's *Discourse upon Gondibert* (1650) associates w. with memory; and Dryden, in the preface to his opera *The State of Innocence* (1684), says, "*The* definition of Wit . . . *is only this: That it is* a Propriety of Thoughts and Words; or in other Terms, Thoughts and Words elegantly adapted to the Subject." In general, authors of the early 17th c. consider w. an essential quality of poetry. Emmanuele Tesauro, for example, believed that the process of divine creation is the defining example of w. and the more w. an author reveals, the more godlike he becomes. Later authors, particularly such rationalists as Hobbes, regarded w. as a psychological faculty.

As the 17th c. progressed, discussions of w. became numerous. Any list would have to include Cowley ("Of Wit," 1656), Dryden (numerous comments throughout the critical works), Flecknoe (*Discourse*, 1664), Boyle (*Reflections*, 1665), Sheffield (*Essay on Poetry*, 1682), Pope (*Essay on Criticism*, 1711), Addison (numerous *Spectators;* e.g., 58–61), Richard Blackmore (*Essay upon Wit*, 1716), Gay (*The Present State of Wit*, 1711), Corbyn Morris (*Essay towards Fixing the True Standards of Wit*, 1744), and others. It is impossible to reduce the mass of material on w. to any simple form. W. was sometimes contrasted to fancy or judgment; sometimes identified with one or the other faculty. At times it was contrasted to humor, raillery, satire, and ridicule; at times compared to them. "True w." was often contrasted with "false w." (generally, writing which dazzles without appealing to the understanding). As William Empson has pointed out (see bibliography), Pope uses w. no less than 46 times in the *Essay on Criticism*, and with at least six different meanings. At times w. suggests conceited style (*argudeza*); at times it is quickness at invention in the rhetorical sense of that term; at times it is "Nature to advantage dressed;" and at times it is

apt expression. As is natural, the vagueness of the term eventually led critics to suspect its validity. Dr. Johnson attacked Cowley in his *Lives* (1779) for his "heterogeneous ideas . . . yoked by violence together. . . ." Hazlitt ("Wit and Humour," 1819) contrasted w., which is artificial, with imagination, which is valid. On the other hand Schiller's concept of the *Spieltrieb* (*Über die ästhetische Erziehung des Menschen,* 1793) would seem to be a revival of the notion that w. (in the sense here of the play-impulse) is an essential ingredient of poetry.

During the 19th c. *imagination* was used to designate the capacity to see resemblances, ability to invent, etc.; and w. became associated with levity. Matthew Arnold rejected Chaucer and Pope from his list of the greatest poets because of their wittiness: they lacked "high seriousness." But T. S. Eliot, placing Donne and Marvell high in the hierarchy of Eng. poets, insisted upon the rightness of "a tough reasonableness beneath the slight lyric grace," and he said that these poets were successful by virtue of their "alliance of levity and seriousness (by which the seriousness is intensified)." Most modern critics, from I. A. Richards to Cleanth Brooks, have agreed with him. And modern poets have insisted upon allowing w. a place in their conceptions of the nature of poetry. The meaning of the term, however, seems not to have come quite full circle: it is not commonly associated with imagination or conceptual power; on the other hand, it is associated with irony, and irony *is* associated with them.

Crit. Essays of the 17th C., ed. J. E. Spingarn, I (1908; see introd.); M. A. Grant, *The Ancient Rhetorical Theories of the Laughable* (1924); T. S. Eliot, "The Metaphysical Poets," and "Andrew Marvell," *Selected Essays* (1932); W. G. Crane, *W. and Rhetoric in the Renaissance* (1937); C. Brooks, *Modern Poetry and the Tradition* (1939); W. Empson, "W. in the *Essay on Criticism,"* *The Structure of Complex Words* (1951); A. Stein, "On Elizabethan W.," *Studies in Eng. Lit.,* 1 (1961); G. Williamson, *The Proper W. of Poetry* (1961); S. L. Bethell, "The Nature of Metaphysical W.," *Discussions of John Donne,* ed. F. Kermode (1962).   w.v.o'c.

WORD ACCENT. See ACCENT.

WRENCHED ACCENT. See ACCENT.

Y

YIDDISH POETRY. 1. SHIFTING FUNCTION OF POETRY IN THE CULTURE. Modern Yidd. poetry recognizes no circumscription on its scope: it lays claim to every type of subject and technique known in the literatures of Europe and America, and derives an extra measure of cosmopolitanism from the enormous geographic base lent it by a readership distributed over all five continents. But out of its combined prehistory and history of nearly a millennium, only the past two or three generations have witnessed this unrestricted flourishing. In traditional Ashkenazic culture, it was rather study —the continuous interpretation of basic Talmudic law in the light of changing conditions of life—that absorbed the creative passions of the society. Literary expression in the "Western" sense was unimportant, and Jewish poetry (Yidd. as well as Hebrew) of the premodern period stands out, for all its diversity, by its generally ancillary character. Then, with the revolutionary upheavals in East European Jewry in the late 19th and 20th c.—urbanization, industrialization, internal migration and emigration, political organization and eventual civic emancipation, attended by widespread secularization and thorough "Europeanization" of Jewish culture—Jewish poetry in both languages was lifted to the very top of the cultural values of the group. It attracted a mass of talent which in previous centuries would have been otherwise engaged, and, in accordance with the increased receptivity of its writers and readers to outside influences, it set out on a forced march to catch up with the common European accomplishments. Yidd. poetry "in one grand leap landed in the general twentieth century" (Hrushovski). Developments came too fast, and in an age too amorphous in its tastes, to allow a normative poetic to form except in its barest outlines; yet a certain all-European poetic standard was automatically taken for granted. The call of I. L. Peretz (d. 1915) "to barter, not to beg . . . [for] the crossing of cultures is the only possibility of human development," was put into effect. Even in its treatment of specifically Jewish themes in an imagery full of traditional allusions, Yidd. poetry became avowedly and factually part and parcel of modern European-American poetic culture: ". . . Mízrakh-zere máyrevdik tseshtrómt iz undzer dor. / Shtendik iz er—tsi geyankevt, tsi gelovnt— / a gemísh fun mórgnland mit land fun ovnt" (Leyeles). (Our generation is Eastern seed aflow the

Western way. Always—whether going the ways of Jacob or of Laban—it is a blend of the Orient and the Occident.)

2. PRE-19TH C. VERSE. The beginnings of Yidd. literature have been lost, but early contemporary references to it as well as the developed poetic technique of the recently discovered oldest dated works (A.D. 1382) indicate several centuries of prehistory. Prior to the 19th c., Yidd. literature, the bulk of which is in verse, was written in an idiom based predominantly on Western Yidd. dialects, a standardized language which functioned without interruption until it fell into disuse in Western Europe about 1800 and was superseded by a rapidly evolving new standard on an East European interdialectal base. The influence of medieval German poetic traditions and a stylistic irradiation from the intentionally literal Bible translations caused literary Yidd. to be highly stylized, only an indirect reflection of contemporary colloquial speech. Much of this verse was for oral performance, by professional minstrels or by laymen; even after the introduction of printing, the tune was often specified at the beginning or end of a work. Epic poems, both of the general European repertoire (King Arthur, Gudrun, etc., with specifically Christian references deleted as offensive) and on Old Testament themes (Samuel, the Sacrifice of Isaac, etc.) are available in 14th- and 15th-c. recensions which show relatively strict meters and, generally, "long-line" stanza structure of the *xaxa xbxb* type. Beginning with two verse novels by Elye Bokher (d. 1549), composed under It. influence, the elaborate ottava rima (ababcc) was established in Yidd. well over a century before it was tried in German poetry. It also seems that Elye Bokher was the first to use accentual iambs in any European poetry.

With the decline of the minstrel tradition, the meters decreased in regularity until the number of syllables per measure of music varied widely, and occasionally grew quite high. This is in evidence not only in the collections of 16th- and 17th-c. popular songs (which reflect a convergence of traditional with current German models), but also in the religious lyrics, in the many verse chronicles and dirges describing historical (usually disastrous) events; and in the satirical or moralizing occasional pieces. Yidd. verse of early modern times thus corresponds in its free-tonic basis to most contemporary German verse. Drawing on the Hebrew liturgical tradition, Yidd. verse sometimes made use of acrostic devices and ornamental extravagances such as making all lines of a longish poem end in the same syllable.

3. THE 19TH C. Through most of the century the folk song flourished and the recitative improvisation, narrative (on biblical subjects) or moralizing (by wedding jesters), remained productive genres. Meanwhile Yidd. literature made a new beginning, centered this time in Eastern Europe and carried by the emigrations toward the end of the century to England, the United States, and the far corners of the earth. The new writers were stimulated mostly by the Haskalah (Enlightenment) movement, which encouraged familiarity with European (especially German and Rus.) literature and made the Jewish writers increasingly self-conscious about the "underdeveloped" state of their languages, Yidd. and Hebrew, for the purposes of high-level social criticism, philosophy of national history, and the spread of secular education. While Hebrew literature toyed with a biblical manner, Yidd. writers explored the culturally specific framework offered by the folk song, which was noticed at last after a "submerged" existence of hundreds of years during which it was neither recorded nor reflected in literature. The Yidd. folk song favored an *xaxa* stanza and a free-tonic meter (usually 4 stresses per line) in which, compared with German folk song, the use of unstressed syllables to fill the musical measures was increased, probably as a result of the Slavicized prosodic structure of the language. However, more "European" standards of song construction and song phrasing introduced more elaborate rhyme patterns (*abab* and *aabccb* became widespread), and strict syllabo-tonic meters became *de rigueur* in the theatre and quasi-theatre songs. The rising labor movement furnished a new public for poetry to be sung, but also for declamatory verse—an additional factor conducive to the establishment of regular syllabo-tonic meters in the literature.

In the 1890's Yidd. poetry seems to have hit its stride at last. Though it lagged noticeably behind the development of prose—particularly of the shorter forms of prose—it now became the vehicle of truly lyrical expression (S. Frug [d. 1916], I. L. Peretz, M. Rosenfeld [d. 1923]). These authors, who had all complained about the lexical and stylistic "inadequacy" of Yidd., now laid the foundations of its modern poetry by their efforts to master a lyrical viewpoint and by experimenting with a variety of imagery and constructional patterns.

4. THE 20TH C. The existence of a new intelligentsia with secular education, some of it acquired in Yidd. language schools up to the college level, cast Yidd. poetry in this period of its culmination into the mainstream of the problems of contemporary world trends. Yidd. literature now showed itself more sensitive than ever to developments in other literatures with which it was in contact through multilingual reading and diversified and intensified translation. There were the interest and the formal means to attempt modernism along Am., German, and Rus. lines. At the same time, in the poetic culture of growing firmness there appeared genuine internal responses to innovations. The *Yunge* (Young Ones) in America (Mani Leib [d. 1953], Z. Landau [d. 1937], and others) early in the century reacted to the political tendentiousness and rhetoric of the labor poets by trying to write poetry that would be "more poetic" in diction and subject matter, more individual in its sentiments. They in turn called forth the protest of *Inzikh* (Introspectivists), a group (A. Leyeles [b. 1889], J. Glatstein [b. 1896], N. B. Minkoff [d. 1958], *et al.*) which, inspired by Yehoyosh [d. 1927], denied in principle the distinction between the intellectual and the emotional and opened the door of its poetry wide to all themes, all words, all rhythms no matter how free or how regular, as long as they embodied the personal experience of the poet.

As the cumulative effect of a growing corpus of poetic writing made itself felt, requirements of originality pushed Yidd. poets into new paths. Assonance as a rhyme substitute was explored (e.g. by P. Markish [d. about 1950] and other Soviet poets). Sonnet sequences and works in the most difficult "romance forms" were successfully created (L. Naydus [d. 1918] and others). Syntactic parallelism, etymological figures, and consonance were mobilized to recreate biblical effects in a new Jewish medium. Epic poems, verse novels, and poetic plays (especially by H. Leivick [d. 1962]) were produced and acclaimed. Interest in Old Yidd. poetry was awakened and several writers attempted new works in 16th-c. language. The poems of S. Etinger, a forgotten modernist who died in 1856, were published posthumously. The folk song reappeared, but this time in subtly stylized forms (e.g. by M. L. Halpern [d. 1932], I. Manger [b. 1901]). Regional constellations like *Yung-Vilne* set themselves specialized tasks against a common literary background. The sweet awareness of a poetic tradition being formed was reflected in poetic allusions to well-known poems. A standardized literary language came into use in which dialectal rhymes and expressions grew ever rarer.

In this period, the "discovery of the mother tongue," now emancipated in its functions, was completed. Poets by the scores, following the major prose writers of the late 19th c., learned to use the language to the full extent of its inherent possibilities. Yidd. prosodic structure, Germanic but remodeled presumably along Slavic lines, was employed to create easy triple and even paeonic meters. The syntax of conversational folk Yidd. was channeled into poetry (notably by E. Shteynbarg [d. 1932]), and by its idiomatic character refreshed the more conventional styles. The pernicious etymologizing approach of the past was dead: words were used according to their precise Yidd. phonology and semantics, without reference to—and sometimes in defiance of—their form and meaning in the stock languages. Sound frequencies typical of a particular component of Yidd. were forged into a new poetic device, making it possible, for instance, to suggest "Slavicness," and hence village earthiness, by an accumulation of $\check{z}$-and $\check{c}$ sounds (thus M. Kulbak [d. about 1940]). The common European intellectual and technical vocabulary was absorbed into Yidd. At the same time, the idiom of traditional Jewish study was annexed to the modern literary language; it found employment not only when it was required by the subject (e.g. in the poetry of a M. Boraisho [d. 1949], A. Zeitlin [b. 1889] or Kh. Grade [b. 1910]), but also in thematically unspecialized writing, where it functions simply as a flexible abstract vocabulary. Above all, the many derivational patterns of Yidd. grammar were exploited for the self-enrichment of the language. New coinages abound in the works of most poets, and some, like *umkum* (violent death) or *vogl* (restless wandering), have become common elements of the language. J. Glatstein and A. Sutskever [b. 1913] have achieved particular virtuosity in novel derivation.

With the genocide of six million Jews by Germany and her collaborators, Jewish cultural life in most of Eastern Europe was destroyed; it received another deadly blow through the total ban on Yidd. culture and the physical destruction of Yidd. writers in the USSR after 1949. The catastrophe of the war years naturally became the central theme of Yidd. literature not only in the Nazi-made ghettos themselves, but everywhere else. After 1948, the rebirth of a Jewish state opened new subjects, descriptive, psychological, and ethical, to Yidd. poetry in Israel as well as in other countries. The technical brilliance of Yidd. poetry has never been greater than in the postwar period. In its rhythmic features, however, postwar writing seems to have retreated from the experimentation of the previous period. As Leyeles put it: "Ven keyn grenets iz nishtó far di yesurem, / Veytik oys a syog fun shtreng getsoymtn furem" (When there are no bounds to suffering, create, through

pain, a ritual fence [i.e. a preventive measure] of rigorously restrained patterning).

ANTHOLOGIES: *Antologye: finf hundert yor yidishe poezye*, ed. M. Bassin (2 v., 1917); *Naje jidiše dichtung*, ed. Ch. Gininger *et al.* (Cernauti, 1934; in L. transcription); *Modern Yidd. Poetry*, ed. S. J. Imber (1927; Eng. prose versions); *The Golden Peacock*, ed. J. Leftwich (1939, 2d ed., 1961; Eng. verse tr.); *Naye yidishe dikhtung*, ed. Y. Paner and E. Frenkl (Bucharest, 1946); *Dos lid iz geblibn*, ed. B. Heller (Warsaw, 1951); *Mivḥar Shirei Yidd.*, tr. into Hebrew by M. Basuk (1963).

HISTORY AND CRITICISM: L. Wiener, *A Hist. of Yidd. Lit. in the 19th C.* (1899); I. Goldberg, [Notes on the Poetic Style of the Yidd. Folk Song], *Tsaytshrift far yidisher geshikhte . . .*, I (Minsk, 1926); M. Weinreich, *Bilder fun der yidisher literatur-geshikhte* (Vilna, 1928); D. Hofshteyn and F. Shames, *Literatur-kentenish (poetik)* (2 v., Moscow, 1927, 1928); M. Erik, *Di geshikhte fun der yidisher lit. . . .* (Warsaw, 1928); Z. Reyzen, *Leksikon fun der yidisher lit. . . .* (4 v., Vilna, 1928ff.); Y. Tsinberg, *Di geshikhte fun der lit. bay yidn*, VI (Vilna, 1935); N. B. Minkoff, *Yidishe klasiker poetn* (2d ed., 1939); A. A. Roback, *The Story of Yidd. Lit.* (1940) and *Contemporary Yidd. Lit.* (1957); Y. Mark, "Yidd. Lit.," *Encyclopedia of Lit.*, ed. J. T. Shipley, II (1946) and "Yidd. Lit.," *The Jews*, ed. L. Finkelstein, II (1949); N. B. Minkoff and J. A. Joffe, "Old-Yidd. Lit.," *The Jewish People Past and Present*, III (1952); S. Niger, "Yidd. Lit. of the Past 200 Years," *ibid.*; B. Hrushovski, "On Free Rhythms in Modern Yidd. Poetry," *The Field of Yidd.: Studies in Yidd. Language, Folklore, and Lit.*, ed. U. Weinreich (1954); *Leksikon fun der nayer yidisher literatur* (1956ff.); N. B. Minkoff, *Pyonern fun yidisher poezye in Amerike* (3 v., 1956); U. Weinreich "On the Cultural Hist. of Yidd. Rime," in *Essays on Jewish Life and Thought*, ed. J. L. Blau (1959); B. Hrushovski, "The Creation of Accentual Iambs . . . ," *For Max Weinreich on his 70th Birthday: Studies in Jewish Languages, Lit., and Society* (1964); S. Liptzin, *The Flowering of Yidd. Lit.* (1964).   UR.W.

YOUNG VIENNA. A group of poets and writers in Vienna around 1900. United in their rejection of the naturalism of Northern Germany, they tended toward impressionism and symbolism in their works, with some of them writing decadent poetry. Within German letters these authors express best the European *fin de siècle* atmosphere. They excel in the sensitive recording of delicate emotional changes. The group found an enthusiastic advocate of new literary movements in Hermann Bahr, who is best known for his critical essays and light comedies. Arthur Schnitzler, the author of subtle sketches of the Viennese society, and particularly Hugo von Hofmannsthal, whose versatile genius was to surpass all other members of the group, form the center of Young Vienna. The group met at cafés, as did so many intellectual circles in Vienna. Other writers associated with Young Vienna were Peter Altenberg, Richard Beer-Hofmann, and Felix Salten.—*Deutsch-österreichische Literaturgesch.*, ed. J. W. Nagl, J. Zeidler, and E. Castle, IV (1937), 1649-1930.　　　c.f.s.

YUGOSLAV POETRY. The natural aptitude of the Yugoslav peoples for poetic invention throughout their history is demonstrated by the wealth and beauty of their traditional folk poetry. This poetry is of two kinds, "heroic" or epic, and lyric. The lyric poems, with lines of varying lengths and meters, express every emotion and every aspect of the life of the people. There are ritual and ceremonial songs, dirges, love songs, and songs sung at work or to accompany dancing or various celebrations and customs. The majority of the epic (heroic) songs relate events from the country's past. Mythological or semi-legendary themes occur in those of earlier origin: the more recent the ballad the more authentic its subject. The ballads with historical subjects deal for the most part with the struggles against the Turks. The cycle describing incidents connected with the disastrous battle of Kosovo in 1389 has the greatest aesthetic value and is the most moving. A regular example of the line of the majority of the epic ballads is decasyllabic, with a caesura after the fourth syllable, and a clearly expressed tendency to trochaic distribution of stresses and with a quantitative close: ⌣–⌣–⌣. (When stressed, the ninth syllable is usually long, and the eighth and seventh are short.) The basis of this meter is thus both stress and quantity, and is a matter for detailed study. There is little or no rhyme. The line of a small minority of epic ballads consists of 15, 16, or even more syllables, with varying meters.

As regards written verse, the earliest consisted principally of 13th- and 14th-c. translations of hymns and other poems of an ecclesiastical nature. The liturgical verse of the Orthodox Church, influenced by Byzantium, was mostly translated from Gr., and was written in Serbian recensions of Old Church Slavonic in the Cyrillic alphabet. That of the Roman Catholic church, in the Glagolitic alphabet, was similar in character, but Catholic religious verse, not purely liturgical, was also written in the vernacular. The earliest extant records of this poetry date from the 15th c.

When the cultural development of the peoples of the interior was suppressed under foreign domination, conditions were favorable for the cultivation of literature only in the free republic of Dubrovnik (Ragusa) and elsewhere in Dalmatia. Here poetry began to flourish in the 15th c. under the influence of the It. Renaissance. The Petrarchan lyric was imitated in Dubrovnik first by the "troubadour" poets Šiško Menčetić (1457-1527) and Džore Držić (1451-1501), of whom the latter was less imitative and more sincere. These poets favored a slightly modified form of the *strambotto* (q.v.) as well as the Petrarchan sonnet. The conceits employed by the It. lyricists were introduced with ingenuity into this poetry, which yet retained some indigenous elements and certain reminiscences of folk ballads. Love is the predominant motive, but other themes such as patriotism and religion occur. The meter is usually a dodecasyllabic line with internal rhyme, but an octosyllabic line was also employed by certain of the innumerable subsequent poets and versifiers who kept alive the poetic tradition thus established. Songs of a similar character, sung by shepherds, were introduced into the "pastoral novel" *Planine* (The Mountains) by Petar Zoranić (b. 1508?) of Zadar. Another aspect of It. influence is seen in imitations of Florentine carnival poetry. Of these, *Jedjupka* (The Gypsy) by Mikša Pelegrinović (d. 1563) of Hvar, has the greatest charm and originality. (This work was until recently attributed to Andrija Cubranović, of Dubrovnik, who is now proved only to have altered it slightly and contributed its final section.) The earliest epic was *Judita* (1501) by Marko Marulić of Split. Using the dodecasyllabic line, and in verse in which fashionable adornments are not absent, he relates the biblical story of Judith, suggesting an analogy between its background and his own country's perils. Other notable poetic works of the 16th c., in the same meter, were *Robinja* (The Slave-girl) by Hanibal Lucić, (1485-1553) of Hvar, the earliest secular dramatic work in Croatian literature, though a narrative poem in dialogue form rather than a drama; and *Ribanje i ribarsko prigovaranje* (Fishing and Fishermen's Talk) by Petar Hektorović, (1487-1572) also of Hvar. Although this poem, describing a fishing expedition, is to some extent reminiscent of It. piscatorial eclogues, it is one of the most original and realistic works of the period. Folk epic songs sung by fishermen in the poem represent the earliest written record of Yugoslav traditional poetry. The lyrical, contemplative, and epic poetry of Mavro Vetranović (1482-1576), often with a moralizing purpose, was relatively free from foreign influences but generally of little aesthetic value. New metrical forms, imitated or adapted from It. lyrics, were introduced to Ragusan poetry by Dinko Ranjina (1536-1607) and Dinko Zlatarić (1558-1609), whose

YUGOSLAV POETRY

work as translators of Gr. and L. verse also reflects the revival of interest in classical literature in Italy.

With the works of Ivan Gundulić (1588–1638) Ragusan literature is generally considered to have reached its "Golden Age." The influence of the Renaissance had given way to that of the Counter-Reformation; national consciousness, a moral purpose, religious feeling, and philosophical meditations—elements to be found among the works of most of his predecessors—are supreme in those of Gundulić. His *Suze sina razmetnoga* (The Tears of the Prodigal Son), in 3 cantos, is a confession of sin and a meditation on the transitoriness of earthly things. In his greatest work, the epic *Osman*, a poem inspired by his faith in the Slavs and Christianity, Gundulić weaves a complex pattern of incidents around his central theme—an event in the contemporary war between Poles and Turks. The epic is akin to those of Tasso and Ariosto, with marinistic traits of style. It is composed in stanzas of 4 octosyllabic lines rhyming abab.

The Ragusan love lyric continued to flourish, in the verse—with characteristics of marinism—of Stijepo Djurdjević (1579–1632), best known for his satirical *Derviš*, describing the emotions of an elderly dervish in love; and in the exquisite, concise, and erotic poems of Ivan Bunić (1594–1658). Both Bunić and the last great Ragusan lyricist, Ignjat Djurdjević (1675–1737), in whose work the baroque influence predominates, also treated the subject of the repentant Mary Magdalene in longer works inspired by Gundulić.

As literature slowly revived elsewhere in the Yugoslav lands, verse was at first put to practical uses. Employing the convenient decasyllabic line of the epic folk ballads A. Kačić-Miošić (1704–60), of central Dalmatia, wrote a chronicle of the South Slavs, and M. Reljković (1732–98), a Slavonian, composed his admonitory poem *Satir* (The Satyr). The Serb Jovan Rajić (1726–1801) composed, among other works, an allegorical-historical epic *Boj zmaja s orlovi* (The Battle of the Dragon with the Eagles) in the artificial *rusko-slovenski* language cultivated by Serbian writers of his period. The didactic element, characteristic of the literature of this time, is present in the pseudo-classical lyric poetry of the Serb Lukijan Mušicki (1777–1837). Meanwhile the foundations of Slovene poetry were laid by Valentin Vodnik (1758–1819), the first Slovene poet to write in the vernacular.

With the romantic movement came the revival of poetic composition as an art and the inspiration derived from the indigenous folk poetry, vast collections of which were made in the first half of the 19th c. by Vuk Karadžić (1787–1864), to whom future Serbian and

Croatian writers were also indebted for his linguistic reforms. The folk poetry element is a characteristic of the work of S. Milutinović (1791–1847), whose epic and lyric poetry, glorifying the Serbs, is a confusion of realism and fantasy. It is also a characteristic of the work of the great Serbian poet, Petar Petrović Njegoš (1813–1851), Prince-Bishop of Montenegro. Njegoš's lyric and epic poetry, composed in intellectual isolation, expresses his intense patriotic emotion and his groping for a solution to the philosophical problems which tormented him. His *Luča mikrokozma* (The Torch of the Microcosm) treats a subject similar to that of Milton's *Paradise Lost;* his greatest work, *Gorski vijenac* (The Mountain Wreath), is an epic in dramatic form, and a synthesis of aspects of Montenegrin life. The epic *Smrt Smail-Age Čengića*, by the Croat Ivan Mažuranić (1814–90), also in the style of the epic songs, graphically and powerfully depicts the sufferings of Montenegrins under Turkish oppression. The sonnet was introduced to the Croatian literature of the period by Stanko Vraz (1810–51), who wrote also in the style of the folk ballads. Both he and Petar Preradović (1818–72) composed moving love lyrics at a time when poetic output in Croatia consisted mainly of patriotic verse.

The work of Slovenia's greatest poet, France Prešeren (1800–49) showed for the first time the potentialities of Slovene as a literary language. His sonnets, sincere expressions of emotion, are examples of perfect harmony of form and theme.

New inspiration was brought to Serbian poetry by the fresh, spontaneous lyrics of Branko Radičević (1824–53). The meter is again often that of the folk ballads, but the themes are very diverse. Lyric poetry became the principal literary product of young Serbian writers after the middle of the century: J. Jovanović Zmaj (1833–1904) wrote simple and moving subjective lyrics, and later poured out verses commenting on contemporary events; Djura Jakšić (1833–78) composed patriotic verse whose stridency contrasts with the tone of his melancholy emotional poems, e.g. his poignant *Na Liparu* (In the Lime-grove). The last of the great Serbian romantic poets was Laza Kostić (1841–1910), a translator of Shakespeare and composer of "Shakespearean" dramas in verse, and of lyric poetry.

The cultivation of lyric poetry, in various forms, continued in Slovenia. That of Fran Levstik (1831–87) is sincere and expressive; Josip Stritar (1836–1923) skillfully experimented with various meters and poetic forms. This concern with form is seen also in the lyrics of Simon Gregorčič (1844–1906), expressing his love of nature and his longing to promote kindness and tolerance. The influ-

-[903]-

ence of folk poetry is evident in the lyrics of Simon Jenko (1835–69), a poet of patriotism, nature, and love; and the historical ballads which Anton Aškerc (1856–1912), nationalist and social critic, made the vehicle for the expression of his principles were sometimes composed in the decasyllabic line; but no one meter can from this period onward be considered as characteristic of Yugoslav verse.

In Croatia the symbolist Silvije Strahimir Kranjčević (1865–1908) wrote with great violence or pathos, his work reflecting his nationalistic, socialistic and anticlerical views, and his pessimism and bitterness. Meanwhile the Croatan critic A. G. Matoš (1873–1914), himself a poet, demanded complete freedom of expression in poetry, which should be untrammelled by any tendentious elements, and in which aesthetic value should be of supreme importance. To his teaching were added lessons in form and technique derived from the *Parnassiens*. Prominent among Matoš' contemporaries, the Croatian "modernists," were the poets Dragutin Domjanić (1875–1933), Vladimir Vidrić (1875–1909), and Milan Begović (1876–1948). Ljubo Wiesner (1805–1951) and Nikola Polić (1890–1960) were among those who continued the tradition of the subjective, aesthetic lyric, and an outstanding Croatian lyricist, Tin Ujević (1891–1955), with verse of great diversity of subject, emotion, expression, and form, may be counted as a disciple of Matoš. The eminent Croat Vladimir Nazor (1876–1949), optimistic and exuberant, expressed an intense love of all forms of life and nature in lyric verse or in epics with legendary or historical themes.

In Serbia Vojislav Ilić (1862–94), a pure lyricist of fertile inspiration, provided examples of poetic technique for future poets. The works of a trio of lyric poets, Aleksa Šantić (1868–1924), a writer of patriotic and emotional verse; Jovan Dučić (1871–1943), whose lyrics, exquisite in phrasing and form, show the influence of the *Parnassiens*, and Milan Rakić (1876–1938), equally a perfectionist but a poet of profounder ideas and emotions, represent some of the best and purest in Serbian poetry of the next decades. Meanwhile there appeared a great Serbian lyricist of another school, Vladislav Petković-Dis (1880–1917), a poet of dreams and despair, to whom the sincere expression of emotions was of more importance than a studied perfection of form. Characteristics of the "decadent" movement in Serbian poetry before the First World War are found also in the melancholy verse of the symbolist Sima Pandurović (1883–1960); Veljko Petrović (b. 1884)—now better known as a prose writer—wrote verse in which sympathy for the victims of social injustices is given expression, as well as vigorous patriotic verse, contrasting with the poetry of the majority of his contemporaries. Pessimism is again characteristic of the lyrics of the Serbs Velimir Živojinović-Massuka (b. 1886) and Dušan Vasiljev (1900–1924), the former a poet of melancholy, the latter of revolt. One of the most prominent 20th-c. Serbian poets, Miloš Crnjanski (b. 1893), now living in London, expresses his emotions and disillusionment in verses of great originality of both form and theme. The poetry of Rade Drainac (1899–1943) and of the poetess Desanka Maksimović (b. 1898) is also intimate, subjective, and emotional; but while that of the former may be bitter in tone, that of the latter is sensitive and delicate, and notable for its beauty and purity of expression. Branko Ćopić (b. 1915), both poet and prose writer, has described in realistic verse the exploits and sufferings of the Partisans during the Second World War. The works of two other of the more prominent of the younger generation of Serbian poets, Vasko Popa (b. 1922) and Stevan Raičković (b. 1928) present a striking contrast; Popa's verse, which includes patriotic poetry, is experimental and original; Raičković adheres to a more conventional poetic tradition.

Miroslav Krleža (b. 1893), the dominant figure in contemporary Croatian literature, has composed ballads and lyrics, many of which are indictments of social injustices, and are for the most part, like his prose works, vigorous and intense. The Croat Ivan Goran Kovačić (1913–43) will be remembered chiefly as a poet of the Second World War, with his impressive cycle *Jama* (The Pit). Gustav Krklec (b. 1899), Dobriša Cesarić (b. 1902), Nikola Šop (b. 1904), Dragutin Tadijanović (b. 1905), and—of the younger generation— Jure Kaštelan (b. 1919) and the poetess Vesna Parun (b. 1922) are prominent among those who contribute to the wealth of 20th-c. Croatian lyric poetry, remarkable for its variety, spontaneity and originality, and the directness of its appeal to the senses and intellect. The work of Krklec has been described as a "lyrical monologue," reflecting as it does the varying emotions of the poet's life; Cesarić, perhaps the greatest of contemporary Croatian poets, without striving after unconvenional forms of expression has enriched Croatian poetry with works of great aesthetic value; Šop, earlier best known for his sensitive lyrics with a religious tendency, has now turned his attention to longer philosophical works inspired by poetic visions of space; the spontaneous and sincere lyrics of Tadijanović express his dreams and emotions, his love of nature and his nostalgia for the simple life in verse which, while unpretentious, is of great beauty. The works of Kaštelan—whose style has been compared with that of Walt Whitman—and of

Vesna Parun, while still subjective, are concerned with more general human problems.

Oton Župančič (1878–1949), the greatest Slovene poet of the 20th c., turned from the early influence of the symbolists to the composition of lyrics which are striking in their individuality, beauty, and variety in form and phrasing and in their originality in the expression of emotions and ideas. His influence is seen in the work of Alojz Gradnik (b. 1882). Between the wars criticism of the social system was the concern not only of Slovene prose writers but of poets; outstanding among the latter were Anton Podbevšek (1898) and Mile Klopčič (b. 1905). Župančič, and the poet and dramatist Matej Bor (b. 1913) composed verse inspired by events of the Second World War. Other prominent Slovene poets of the present century are Srečko Kosovel (1904–26), Edvard Kocbek (b. 1904), and Miran Jarc (1900–1942), one of the foremost exponents of expressionism.

Lastly, mention must be made of the youngest branch of Yugoslav poetry, that of the Macedonian Slavs, which has only developed in the 20th c. and is the most fruitful branch of their literature. The revolutionary works of Kosta Racin (1909–43) between the wars were of significance on account not only of their tendentious nature but of their contribution to the cultivation of the Macedonian literary language. Among the most notable of those Macedonian poets whose work has come into prominence in the last decades are Venko Markovski (b. 1915), Slavko Janevski (b. 1920), and Blaže Koneski (b. 1921) with verse of a predominantly nationalistic character.

ANTHOLOGIES: *Heroic Ballads of Serbia*, tr. G. R. Noyes and L. R. Bacon (1913); *Serbian Songs and Poems*, tr. J. W. Wiles (1917); *Kossovo: Heroic Songs of the Serbs*, tr. H. Rootham (1920); *Sto let slovenske lirike od Vodnika do Moderne*, ed. C. Golar (1920); *Ballads of Marko Kraljević*, tr. D. H. Low (1922); *Antologija novije hrvatske lirike*, ed. M. Kombol (1934); *Anthologie de la poésie Yougoslave des XIXᵉ et XXᵉ s.*, tr. and ed. M. and S. Ibrovac (1935); *The Revolt of the Serbs against the Turks, 1804–1813*, tr. W. A. Morison (1942; tr. from national ballads of the period); *Antologija na makedonskata lirika* (1951); *Srpske narodne pjesme*, collected Vuk Karadžić, I–IV (1953–58); *Antologija novije srpske lirike*, ed. B. Popović (9th ed., 1953); *The Parnassus of a Small Nation, an Anthol. of Slovene Lyrics*, tr. and ed. W. K. Matthews and A. Slodnjak (1957); *Antologija dubrovačke lirike*, ed. D. Pavlović (1960); *An Anthol. of Modern Yugoslav Poetry*, ed. J. Lavrin (1962).

HISTORY AND CRITICISM: J. Torbarina, *It. Influence on the Poets of the Ragusan Republic* (1931); D. Subotić, *Yugoslav Popular Ballads* (1932); L. Salvini, *Poeti sloveni moderni* (1951); A. Cronia, *Storia della letteratura serbo-croata* (1956); A. Slodnjak, *Geschichte der slowenischen Lit.* (1958); K. Taranovski, "The Prosodic Structure of Serbo-Croat Verse," *Oxford Slavonic Papers*, 9 (1960); A. Kadić, *Contemporary Croatian Lit.* (1960); R. Jakobson, "The Slavic Response to Byzantine Poetry," Congrès International des Études Byzantines. 12th, Ohrid, 1961. *Rapport* 18 (1961).　　　　v.j.

Z

ZÉJEL. A Sp. poem consisting of an introductory strophe containing the theme to be developed in the poem and followed by strophes each patterned as follows: a monorhymed tiercet, called the *mudanza*, followed by the *vuelta* (repetition) of one line or more rhyming with the introductory stanza. The simplest form of this strophe is the 4-verse rhyming aaab, cccb, and so on, the *b* rhyme remaining constant throughout the poem. Multiple variations of this basic form are found. The octosyllable is a frequent verse measure, though other verse lengths are also used. The z. is believed to be a song form of Arabic origin. It was popular in Spain in the late medieval period.—P. Le Gentil, "A propos de la 'strophe zéjelesque,'" RLR, 70 (1949) and *Le virelai et le*

villancico. Le problème des origines arabes (1954); Navarro.　　　　D.C.C.

ZEUGMA (Gr. "means of binding"; cf. Gr. *zeugos*, "yoke"). According to a Gr. rhetorician of the 2d c. A.D., Alexander Numenius, and two of his Gr. successors of undetermined date, the use of a single verb with a compound object (C. Walz, *Rhetores Graeci*, 9 v., 1832–36, v. 8, pp. 474, 686, 709), the construction called *synezeugmenon* by Quintilian, 1st c. A.D. (*Institutes of Oratory* 9.3.62), in whose examples the subject or object or both may be compound. Later rhetoricians very properly extend the definition to the "yoking" together of any two parts of speech by means of any other, normally with no breach of syntax, though some make for confusion by including cases in which the "yoking" word agrees syntactically with only one of the "yoked," thus making z. partly synonymous with *syllepsis* 1., q.v. (e.g., John Smith, *The Mysterie of Rhetorique Unvailed*, 1657, pp. 179–81); and others, past and present, make for worse confusion by assigning to z. the meaning of *syllepsis* 2.

Three varieties of z. have been distinguished, as by Johannes Susenbrotus (*Epitome troporum ac schematum*, 1541, ed. 1621, p. 25), according to whether the "yoking" word precedes the words it "yokes," i.e., *prozeugma* ("All fools have still an itching to deride, / And fain would be upon the laughing side," Pope, *An Essay on Criticism* 32–33); or follows them, i.e., *hypozeugma* ("Not marble, nor the gilded monuments / Of princes, shall outlive this powerful rime," Shakespeare, Sonnet 55); or stands between them, i.e., *mesozeugma* ("Much he the place admired, the person more," Milton, *Paradise Lost* 9.444).—Lausberg.

H.B.

-[906]-

SUPPLEMENT

SUPPLEMENT.

A

AFRICAN POETRY, VERNACULAR: ORAL. Vernacular poetry in Africa is mostly oral, and the greater part is still unrecorded. The conventions of oral v.p. belong to the whole performance and its occasion, and are therefore not exclusively literary. Internal classifications within the society have no reference to the Western categories of prose and poetry, and Afr. definitions of "literary" do not necessarily coincide with those of Eng.-Am. culture. For instance, Afr. proverbs and riddles are major, not minor, literary forms for which the term "poetry," if it is applied, need not relate only to the forms with rhyme. The evaluation even of these identifiable genres can be made only by a complete understanding of the significance of any given member (e.g., a particular praise song) of a genre (e.g., praise poetry) within the society at the time of utterance. Convention involves not only the verbal content, but also such factors as status of the performer(s), nature of the audience, mode of performance, and character of the related arts, especially music, which act interdependently in the representation of the genre. Literary distinctions may be irrelevant in a performance which has no overt literary function. Babalola's work on Yoruba poetry, for instance, shows that the mode of performance is as significant for the Afr. critic as actual content or structure, and many other cases could be cited in support of this.

There are growing signs of a fuller appreciation of the extent and nature of Afr. v.p., but even now it is only beginning to be established as a serious field of systematic study for Afr. scholars. Where the poetic tradition is strong, oral v.p. is adapted to changing conditions, as in topical and political songs and modern praise poems. Generally speaking, however, the extensive corpus of Afr. oral v.p. which forms the basis for description and discussion today belongs to, or is derived from, traditional Afr. society. The relevant language preserves its soul, and in translation the soul is lost. The survival of Afr. v.p. in the future is dependent, among other things, upon the status of the vernacular in particular communities as the medium for both oral and written forms. At the present time evaluation of recorded texts from oral performance is heavily dependent upon nonliterary factors, but it is recognized that Afr. v.p. has its own artistic features analogous to, but not always identical with, literary forms from a literate society.

Although the question of genres has not been seriously discussed, Finnegan has drawn attention to the multiplicity of local classifications. A basic distinction must be made between ritual and nonritual forms; by far the most important are the ritual forms associated, either in origin or in present reality, with formal customary rites and activities. Modern public occasions may include traditional ritual forms suitably adapted. Nonritual forms, of course, belong to informal occasions. In either general category the creative role of the performer(s) is important, for even within customary rites the evaluation is of the contemporary performance. Ritual forms include panegyric and lyric, whereas nonritual forms include lyric and, possibly, narrative.

Panegyric is one of the most developed and elaborate poetic genres in Africa. Its specialized form is best exemplified in the court poetry of the Southern Bantu, about which there is a large literature by scholars in South Africa. These praise poems have been described as intermediary between epic and ode, a combination of exclamatory narration and laudatory apostrophizing. Similar poems occur elsewhere among the Bantu, notably among the cattle-owning peoples of East Central Africa. While praise poems can be concerned with almost anything—animals, divining bones, birds, beer, clans—the most developed forms are those in which people, living or dead, are directly praised and addressed. Praise poetry often plays an essential part in rites of passage when an individual or group moves from one status to another in society. Self-praises by boys at initiation, as among the Sotho or the Galla, are an important aspect of their claim to adulthood.

The eulogies involved in funeral dirges, as among the Akan-speaking peoples of southern Ghana, are also included in this category, as are oral poems in praise of the Prophet Mohammed by the Hausa and other Islamic societies. Finnegan has noted that one cannot always draw the line between Afr. military poetry and panegyric. Southern Bantu praise poems have war and military prowess as one of their main themes, and the same blend of praise and interest in battle heroism can be seen in the "heroic recitations" of the Ankole Hima. In Rwanda military poetry, the form called *ibyivugo* is panegyric, but the narrative element is more marked in a second form, called *ibitekerezo*, songs preserved by the court bards and taught to military recruits. Narrative poetry as a ritual form is not extensive enough, however, to be assigned a special category. In hunting songs praise and celebration are often reserved for the killing of particularly outstanding or dangerous game. A dominant theme in the Yoruba hunting poems called *ijala* is verbal salute and praise, but Ambo hunting poetry is lyrical poetry characterized by the mode of delivery. It is not always possible to make a firm distinction between ritual and nonritual forms. There are derived forms, like the nonritual praise songs of the Hausa itinerant singers, which are relatable to the ritual *kirāri*, a sung proverb, traditionally performed as court poetry.

Lyric, probably the most common genre of oral poetry in Africa, has a great variety of forms, but basically it is a short poem sung or recited either antiphonally or by an individual. As a ritual form, lyric has as its most common occasions rites of passage such as birth, child-naming, initiation, betrothal, marriage, acquiring a new title or status, and funeral ceremonies. The occasions for lyric are extended in urbanized Afr. society to informal, nonritual occasions, like the drinking and dancing town songs of the Zulu and the Sotho in South Africa. The radio provides opportunities for nonritual lyrics to be performed. It is a common pattern for a prose narrative to be marked structurally from time to time by the inclusion of a song, led by the storyteller and sung by the audience. The song is relevant to the story, but may or may not forward the narrative. The subjects of lyric are about every conceivable topic in the Afr. experience. Songs about, or attributed to, birds are very common, but the main interest is human life and conduct. Love poetry has a rich tradition among certain peoples, and is often by women, as among the Zulu of South Africa and the Luo of Kenya. Songs to accompany rhythmic work seem to occur in all Afr. societies.

Narrative in oral v.p., in the sense of a relatively long narrative poem, is of infrequent occurrence. Finnegan considers that although many of the lengthy praise poems, particularly those of South Africa, do contain some narrative elements, narrative poetry does not seem to be a typically Afr. form. The most frequent mentions come from the equatorial areas of the Congo, but even there the traditional pattern, as exemplified in the Lianja and Mwindo epics, is of a prose narrative incorporating most of the local literary forms in both poetry and prose. The narrative poetry in these long epics is important enough, however, to be considered in its own right. The *mvet* poetry of Gabon, Spanish Guinea, and the Southern Cameroons (particularly the Fang people) also includes narrative poetry sung to the accompaniment of the *mvet*, a type of lyre. It is possible that further narrative poems, nonritual in character, remain to be found, but at the present time the evidence is insufficient to establish the existence of narrative as a separate genre of Afr. oral v.p.

The Oxford Library of Afr. Literature, Oxford at the Clarendon Press, presents studies of particular Afr. traditions of oral v.p., notably in works by B. W. Andrzejewski and I. M. Lewis (Somali), S. A. Babalola (Yoruba), T. Cope (Zulu), A. Coupez and T. Kamanzi (Ruanda), D. Kunene (Southern Sotho), H. F. Morris (Ankole), and I. Schapera (Tswana).— W. R. Bascom, "Folklore and Lit." in *The Afr. World: A Survey of Social Research*, ed. R. A. Lystad (1965); *The Mwindo Epic from the Banyanga*, tr. and ed. D. Biebuyck and K. C. Mateene (1967); R. Finnegan, *Oral Lit. in Africa* (1970).   L.H.

WRITTEN. Except for the v.p. derived directly from oral poetry and written in roman script, like the v.p. of South Africa and Ethiopia, Afr. written v.p. as a direct literary activity is a feature of Islamic societies. Arabic speakers, mostly in North Africa, outnumber the speakers of any other single vernacular on the African continent. Besides written v.p. in Arabic there is the Islamic written v.p. of non-Arabic speaking peoples, particularly the Fulani, the Hausa, and the Swahili. North Afr. written v.p. in Arabic was no doubt a vehicle for the spread of Islamic poetry in West Afr. vernaculars, while in East Africa Swahili written v.p. derives from the popular Islamic poetry of the Hadramawt and the Persian Gulf. Some of the same popularizations are found wherever the v.p. is Islamic, as, for instance, vernacular adaptations of early Arabic *maġāzī* (raids) literature occurring in North Africa (Arabic) and in East Africa (Swahili), as well as *mūlūdīya*, poems composed in honor of the Prophet's birth, occurring in North Africa (Arabic and Berber) and in West and East Africa (Hausa and Swahili, respectively).

In Arabic written v.p. of North Africa the term *qaṣīda* (q.v.) has a much wider range of application than the classical form, with replacement of classical monorhyme by a stanzaic structure and multiple rhyme scheme. The two most conspicuous features are profusion of rhyme and absence of inflection. The emphasis on rhyme in non-Arabic written v.p. is derivative from Arabic poetry. Stock themes, such as the cynegetic (*taradīya*), the gnomic or didactic (*ḥikam, waṣāyā*), the bacchic (*khamarīya*), and the nostalgic (*waṭanīya*) are found in shorter v. poems. The *waṭanīya*, originally an expression of nostalgia for one's place of birth, has developed into patriotic poetry in Algeria and Tunisia. More subtle than the *waṭanīya* is the satire (*čenk*), probably derived from the lampoons of Sidi Ahmed bin Yusuf (d. 1525) and Sidi Mejdub (d. 1569). North Afr. v.p., both written and oral, is a vast field still largely uninvestigated.

In sub-Saharan Africa the best-known Islamic written v.p. is in Swahili, Hausa, and Fula. It is found in other languages, such as Wolof, Songhai, and Manding, but comparatively few texts have been published in these languages. This is the poetry of the Islamic elite, based on Arabian models, and passed on to the majority by oral transmission. (See SWAHILI POETRY and HAUSA POETRY). The script is 'ajāmi, modified Arabic script adapted for the relevant language. Today roman is more generally used, particularly in derivative poetry of a more secular nature in the popular press. The authors, when they are known, are not usually well-versed in Islamic classical poetry, and may not even be able to write Arabic. They are familiar with, and are called upon to copy, earlier translations of such Arabic models as al-Būṣīrī's Burdah or al-Fazzazi's 'Ishriniya. Even in the more secular derived poetry the poets maintain the same conservative attitudes whereby their work is justified only if it serves to edify the faithful, but there is more freedom for the poet to choose personal themes.

As a consequence of Western education, oral poetry has been written down in various Afr. languages (e.g., in Yoruba, in the Akan languages of Ghana, in Kikongo), and in many instances this has resulted in a literary form of existing oral material rather than innovative forms deriving from oral poetry. A large part of printed v.p. from Ethiopia (since 1917) and from South Africa (since 1862) has consisted of praise poetry similar in function to oral panegyric. Among the Nguni peoples of South Africa the techniques and aims of praise poetry were transferred to the writing of Christian hymns, but the more internalized forms of lyricism were hardly practiced at all.

Works in the Ge'ez language of Ethiopia were printed in Europe in the 16th c. The first pieces of imaginative writing in modern Amharic were printed in Rome. The author was Afäwärq Gäbeä iYasus, who should be regarded as the true founder of modern Amharic literature. In Ethiopia itself, the proclamation of Ras Tafäri as Regent in 1917 marked the beginning of publication in Ge'ez and Amharic, and Amharic odes in honor of the Regent and of Empress Zäwditu were among the first works to be produced at the Imprimerie Ethiopienne.

The first book to be published in Addis Ababa after the liberation of the city in 1941 was an anthology of praise poems. Ethiopia stands exceptionally high in the production in print of creative v.p., but, of course, in comparison with what is published in the Western world the Ethiopian output is still very small. The Ethiopian writer, like Afr. writers of the vernacular almost everywhere, has been valued in proportion to the edifying

character and didactic significance of his message and to his skill in handling the language. Such criteria make for conformity, but in South Africa some attempts were made to innovate. Bereng's Lithothokiso tsa Moshoeshoe (The Praises of King Moshoeshoe), published in 1931, was the first collection of original poems to appear in any South Afr. language, in this case Southern Sotho, and in 1936 Jolobe's Omyezo (The Orchard) was a landmark in the history of written Xhosa poetry for its experimentation in theme and structure. B. W. Vilakazi's collection of Zulu songs, Inkondlo kaZulu, printed in 1935, showed differences from traditional v.p. in themes, in emotional tenor, and in prosody. It was in South Africa that Africans first began to discuss, through the printed word, the relationship between Afr. oral v.p. and the written v.p. The discussion still continues, but before a much wider public both inside and outside Africa.

See: On South Afr. and Ethiopian written v.p.: A. S. Gérard, Four Afr. Literatures (1971). On Afr. v.p. in Arabic: J. Wansbrough, "Theme, Convention and Prosody in the V.P. of North Africa," Bull. of School of Oriental and Afr. Studies, 32 (1969). On Hausa v.p.: M. Hiskett, "Hausa Islamic Verse: Its Sources and Development Prior to 1920" (unpub. Ph.D. diss., Univ. of London, 1969). On Fula v.p.: Poésie peule de l'Adamawa, ed. P. F. Lacroix (2 v., 1965). On Songhai v.p.: B. Hama, "L'Esprit de la culture sonrhaie," Présence Africaine, 14/15 (1957). On Swahili v.p.: L. Harries, Swahili Poetry (1962); J. Knappert, Traditional Swahili Poetry (1967) and Swahili Islamic Poetry (1971). The Johari za Kiswahili series publ. by the East Afr. Literature Bureau consists of edited tenzi (plural of utenzi, a type of heroic or narrative or homiletic poem. See SWAHILI POETRY*). L.H.

IN ENGLISH (Recent). With the end of the colonial period, and the consequent increase of literacy and higher education came a vast efflorescence of Afr. poetry written in Eng. It displays the variety to be expected in so diverse a continent, and regional styles have arisen. Nevertheless, the most eminent poets have created an international community of values and influences.

Generally Afr. Eng. poetry eschews rhyme in favor of alliteration and assonance. Instead of metrical verse, rhythms subject to the poet's syntax, logic, emotion, or rhetoric determine the verse length. Visual poetry is rare. Ambiguity is more often syntactic than lexical. The same austerity leads to avoidance of extended fanciful conceits unless these are buttressed by hard or sardonic reason and concrete, down-to-earth imagery. Oral and other traditional poetry influences recent Eng. poems primarily in more fundamental elements such as the poet's stance as defender of communal values, his integral allusions to the history, customs, and artifacts of his culture, and the architectonic features which sometimes relate poems to traditional forms of love song, praise song, proverbial tale, epic, etc. Afr. experiments in the transmutation of traditional poetic form into Eng. are perhaps best represented by Taban lo Liyong (Uganda 1938—) and Mazisi Kunene (South Africa 1932—). In *Eating Chiefs* lo Liyong experiments with novel forms to convey in Eng. the original poetic effects of Lwo myth, poetry, and song. Kunene's *Zulu Poems* apply traditional Zulu devices and forms to original subjects and thoughts. Most other Afr. poets as well, particularly those who have resided outside of Africa, display complete mastery of the functions of form in modern Eng. and Am. poetry. One indication of their freedom from these forms is the number of dramas and novels consisting partly or entirely of poetry.

The oldest tradition of sophisticated poetry in Eng. is West Afr., particularly in Ghana and Nigeria. In recent years other regions have been profoundly influenced by West Afr. poets, particularly the Nigerians Christopher Okigbo (1932–67, *Labyrinths*), John Pepper Clark (1935— *Reed in the Tide; Casualties*) and Wole Soyinka (1934— *Idandre; Shuttle in the Crypt*). This poetry combines lyricism with audacious leaps of thought, and individualistic feeling with steadfast social commitment. The authors rely heavily upon references to metaphysical, religious, and social concepts of their own ethnic groups, and less upon allusions to European cultural history.

> Before you, mother Idoto
>   naked I stand;
> before your watery presence,
>   a prodigal
> leaning on an oilbean,
> lost in your legend . . .
>   (Okigbo, *Heavensgate*)

When social protest occurs, it is presented in a tone of intellectual and emotional complexity rather than prophetic, simplistic fervor. Two other such poets are Kofi Awoonor (Ghana, 1935— *Rediscovery; Night of My Blood*) and Lenri Peters (The Gambia, 1932— *Satellites; Katchikali*). The graceful poetry of Gabriel Okara (Nigeria, 1921—) is less obscure and idiosyncratic in its forms, allusions, and thought.

East Afr. poetry is dominated by two styles. As exemplified by Okot p'Bitek (Uganda, 1931— *Song of Lawino; Song of Ocol; Song of Prisoner; Song of Malaya*) and Okello Oculi (Uganda, 1942—*Orphan*), one style has longer, rhetorical, lucid social commentary lamenting the disruptions attending modern urbanization. The poem's speaker is usually the dispossessed, arguing with the cogent similes and vivid evocation of a more humane past. The other style, more indebted to West Afr. poetry, is a tighter nexus of subtler images and covert allusions, composing a mordant, singular vision and response to modern life. It includes a wider range of subjects and tones and is more likely to employ a narrative structure or focus on some single event. Its preeminent writers are Jared Augira (Kenya 1947— *Juices; Silent Voices; Soft Corals*), Richard C. Ntiru (Uganda 1946— *Tensions*) and Taban lo Liyong (*Meditations in Limbo; Franz Fanon's Uneven Ribs; Another Nigger Dead; 13 Offensives against Our Enemies*).

Of necessity South Afr. poetry is most concerned with social upheaval, subjugation, poverty, prisons, revolt, and the private griefs of public injustice, as in O. M. Mtshali, *Sounds of a Cowhide Drum*. Since most works available to the world are by poets in exile, subjects, allusions, and forms reflect British and Am. life frequently, as in the works of Keroapetse Kgositsile (1938—, *Spirits Unchained; For Melba; My Name is Afrika*) and the consummate poetry of Dennis Brutus (1924— *A Simple Lust*):

> Then the keening crescendo
> of faces split by pain
> the wordless, endless wail
> only the unfree know . . .

Often a setting of expansive and serene nature is evoked in lyrics as a contrast to human distress. The speaker is usually an observer with a unique combination of passionate concern and reflective distance.

Despite the infinite variety of individual genius and experience which shapes Afr. writing, one can hear a distinctive, characteristic Afr. voice in Eng. poetry. It speaks of personal involvement in the culture and history of its people, their ideals, and their behavior. It is individualistic in its perceptions but not in its ethics. It often relies on allusion and logical relationships particularly obscure to those who do not share all the poet's European or Afr. cultural resources. Its style, independent of European canons, is lyrical, imagistic, prone to philosophical musing, and wary of obtrusive technique which might mitigate a tone of sincerity. In short, there is emerging an international tradition discernibly Afr. in subjects and styles, and contributing much to the variety and vigor of poetry in Eng.

BIBLIOGRAPHIES: J. Jahn, *Bibliog. of Neo-Afr. Lit.* (1965); B. Abrash, *Black Afr. Lit. in Eng. since 1952* (1967); J. Jahn and C. P. Dressler,

Bibliog. of Creative Afr. Writing (1971); H. Zell and H. Silver, *Reader's Guide to Afr. Lit.* (1971); D. E. Herdeck, *Afr. Authors* (v. I, 1973).

ANTHOLOGIES: *Modern Poetry from Africa*, ed. G. Moore and U. Beier (1963); *Book of Afr. Verse*, ed. J. Reed and C. Wake (1964); *Poems from Black Africa*, ed. L. Hughes (1966); *West Afr. Verse*, ed. D. I. Nwoga (1967); *Drum Beat*, ed. L. Okala (1967); *Pulsations*, ed. A. Kemoli (1971); *Poems from East Africa*, ed. D. Cook and D. Rubadiri (1971); *Seven South Afr. Poets*, ed. C. Pieterse (1971); *Messages, Poems from Ghana*, ed. K. Awoonor and G. Adali-Mortty (1971); *The Word Is Here*, ed. K. Kgositsile (1973); *Poems from Africa*, ed. S. Allen (1973).

HISTORY AND CRITICISM: E. Mphahlele, *The Afr. Image* (1962) and *Voices in the Whirlwind* (1972); *Afr. Lit. and the Universities*, ed. G. Moore (1965); *Introd. to Afr. Lit.*, ed. U. Beier (1967); W. Cartey, *Whispers from a Continent: The Lit. of Contemporary Black Africa* (1969); *Protest and Conflict in Afr. Lit.*, ed. C. Pieterse and D. Munro (1969); B. King, *Introd. to Nigerian Lit.* (1971); A. Roscoe, *Mother Gold* (1971); *Standpoints on Afr. Lit.*, ed. C. L. Wanjala (1973). D.F.D.

IN FRENCH (Contemporary). Although black poetry in Fr. is a comparatively recent phenomenon, it is already possible to discern several phases in its development. Black poetry in European tongues (as opposed to traditional Afr. poetry), arose initially through the displacement of Afr. populations as a result of the ·slave trade and subsequently through colonization of Africa itself and has come to be spoken of by some literary historians as "neo-Afr." or "*néo-nègre.*" Such a term would include black American, Haitian, and much of Latin Am. literature. However, Afr. poetry in Fr., as part of a cohesive and far-flung literary movement supported by a philosophical basis can be traced back only as far as the Paris of the 1930's, when black students from various parts of the Fr. colonies in Africa and the Antilles began to examine and question the concept of exclusively Fr. models of behavior, culture, and literary expression, and turned instead for inspiration to Haitian literature and also to the Harlem Renaissance* writers Langston Hughes and Claude McKay. This awakening, commonly termed Negritude, began operating and came to fruition during the years 1932–48. The postwar years 1948–60 witnessed an increasing agitation among the growing numbers of European-educated Africans, which culminated in the independence by 1960 for all of black Africa formerly controlled by France and the former Belgian Congo. In respect to poetry, this period is sometimes referred to as the period of militant Negritude. The period 1960 to the present is considered by some to have gone beyond Negritude toward new preoccupations.

The Negritude movement was launched when, in 1932, seven Martinican students published in Paris the journal *Légitime Défense*, in which they harshly criticized the Martinican middle class for its emulation of Western bourgeois culture. In 1934 three young poets who were to become the towering figures of Negritude—Léopold Sédar Senghor (b.1906) of Senegal, Léon Gontran Damas (b.1912) of Fr. Guiana, and Aimé Césaire (b.1913) of Martinique—established the journal *L'Etudiant Noir*, attracting a group of young Afr. poets and critics. Although the journal was short-lived, the group of writers which it spawned continued to be an active and cohesive unit until about 1940, when World War II disrupted their activities. Unlike its predecessor, *L'Etudiant Noir* addressed itself to the whole of the black community within the Fr. colonial empire, and its writers believed that ultimately their reaffirmation of Afr. values would "contribute to universal life, to the humanization of Humanity." Their poetry began also to appear in Parisian publications, such as *L'Esprit*. The journal, *Présence Africaine*, founded in 1947 by Alioune Diop, has continued to be a vital force in the development and diffusion of black literature in Fr. In 1948, Senghor published his now-famous *Anthologie de la nouvelle poésie nègre et malgache de langue française*, prefaced by Jean-Paul Sartre's penetrating analysis of Negritude, "*L'Orphée noir.*" The Anthology brought together for the first time a body of poetry with aims recognizably different from those of Continental Fr. literature.

Objectively, Negritude has been defined by Senghor as the culture—that is, the sum total of the economic and political, intellectual and moral, artistic and social values—of the peoples of black Africa and of the Afr.-derived peoples of America, Asia, and Oceania. But Negritude is also a subjective state: it is the acceptance on the part of black men of their distinct culture and of themselves as perpetrators of a distinctive style and world view. In *L'Orphée noir*, Sartre spoke of a dialectical progression, in which the black man at first rejects the white world and the white race as a necessary prerequisite for reintegration with his personality and rediscovery of his heritage, but soon recognizes his recent slave past and suffering as a potential basis on which to create a new humanism in which the whole of mankind will ultimately participate, and therefore, Negritude will disappear into universalism. Sartre's views have provoked much debate. In any case, it seems clear that Negritude seeks to rehabilitate the black man through a point-for-point negation of white values. Thus, white civilization, based on technology and rationality, cannot reach the source of life and expends itself in senseless hurrying about. But the black soul, existing in intuitive harmony with nature, creates a civilization wherein sensitivity and authentic humanity prevail. Césaire's long epico-lyric work, *Cahier d'un retour au pays natal* (*Return to my native land*) provides one of the finest examples of Negritude poetry:

Eia pour ceux qui n'ont jamais rien inventé
. . . .
insoucieux de dompter, mais jouant le jeu
du monde.
Eia for those who invented nothing
. . . .
not caring to conquer, but playing the
game of the world.

David Diop (1927–60) was looked to by the first generation of Negritude poets as a promising new star on the horizon. His poetry generally continues the bitterly anti-colonialist themes of the era of militant Negritude. However, there is in a great many of his poems a consistent internal development from revolt against present oppression toward a visionary hope of future redemption. This vision of future fulfillment arises directly out of the experience of suffering on the part of the colonized Afr., and David Diop's poems thus provide perhaps the most apt illustration of Sartre's contention regarding the messianic role of the black man, and at the same time, reveal Diop's historical importance as a bridge between the militant and post-Independence eras.

With political independence, many of the social preoccupations mirrored in the poetry lost their *raison d'être*. The tone and themes of black Afr. poetry in Fr. have been affected accordingly. However, the profusion of small volumes, published by Art houses, by a growing number of younger poets, attests to a still vigorous movement. The more recent poetry tends to be less concerned with revolt, to use less direct language, to be less impersonal, more lyrical; the poet appears as visionary or repository of a renewed or self-renewing race. The two poets most worthy of note of the new generation are Tchicaya U Tam'si (b. 1931) of Congo-Kinshasa and Edouard Maunick (b. 1931) of Mauritius. U Tam'si and Maunick express themes of race, of the Afr. heritage glimpsed through scenes remembered from childhood, of pilgrimage, purification, and renewal, of humanist destiny and the bardic mission, the whole through a complex system of motif symbols. Militancy is still present, but

addresses itself to the grief of a divided, still-warring Africa, as in U Tam'si's *Epitomé* or Maunick's *Fusillez-moi*, works which treat the Lumumba-Congo and the Biafran tragedies. Militancy in the more recent poetry enlarges itself in the humanistic way envisioned by Senghor, Sartre, and the writers of *L'Etudiant Noir* to include a concern for all peoples of the world, hampered by warfare and oppression from achieving true Humanity, as in Maunick's *Fusillez-moi*:

je continuerai à réciter Hiroshima Nagasaki
. . . .
et Prague et Mozambique j'apprendrai
tout le reste . . .
I will continue to recite Hiroshima Nagasaki
. . . .
and Prague and Mozambique I shall
learn all the rest . . .

ANTHOLOGIES: *Poètes d'expression française, 1900–1945*, ed. L. Dumas (1947); *Anthologie de la nouvelle poésie nègre et malgache de langue fr.*, ed. L. Senghor (1948); *Huit poètes de Madagascar*, ed. J. Aubert (1959); *An Anthol. of Afr. and Malagasy Poetry in Fr.*, ed. C. Wake (1965); *Neuf poètes camerounais*, ed. L. Lagneau [L. Kesteloot] (1965) and *Anthol. négro-africaine*, ed. L. Kesteloot (1967); *Nouvelle somme de poésie du monde noir* (Présence Africaine, 1966); *La Poésie des noirs*, ed. R. Mercier (1967); *Negritude: Black Poetry from Africa and the Caribbean*, ed. N. Shapiro (1970); B. J. Fouda et al., *Littérature camerounaise* (Kraus reprint, 1971); *Black Poets in Fr.*, ed. M. Collins (1972).

HISTORY AND CRITICISM: J.-P. Sartre, "Orphée noir" in *Anthol. de la nouvelle poésie nègre et malgache . . .* (1948); T. Melone, *De la négritude dans la littérature négro-africaine* (1962); L. Kesteloot, *Les Ecrivains noirs de langue fr....* (1963; 3d ed., 1967; Eng. tr. by E. C. Kennedy in 1974); L. Senghor, *Liberté I: Négritude et humanisme* (1964); *Negritude: Essays and Studies*, ed. A. Berrian and R. Long (1967); J. Jahn, *Neo-Afr. Lit.: A Hist. of Black Writing* (1968); J.-M. Abanda Ndengue, *De la négritude au négrisme* (Yaoundé, 1970); J.-P. Makouta-Mboukou, *Introd. à la litt. noire* (Yaoundé, 1970); J. Nantet, *Panorama de la litt. noire d'expression fr.* (1972); D. E. Herdeck, *Afr. Authors* (v.I, 1973). C.F.G.

IN PORTUGUESE. Despite the common stamp Port. occupation gave to the culture of its different Afr. possessions—Angola, Mozambique, the islands of São Tomé and Príncipe, the Cape Verde islands and Guinea, each of these territories (with the exception of Moslem Guinea) has produced a distinctive poetry. This literature is the work of a minority of educated intellectuals cut off from their roots in Afr. culture, often educated in Portugal and with a

AFRICAN POETRY

strong sense of their mission as spokesmen and reformers. Far from rejecting the Port. language, they appreciate the common instrument it offers, though a few poets have chosen to write in Creole dialect. Curiously, some of the earliest poets came from the smallest possessions. Two were mulattoes—Caetano da Costa Alegre (1864–90) from São Tomé, whose poems, written in the last decades of the 19th c., were published in 1916; and Eugénio Tavares (1867–1930) from the Cape Verde islands, who wrote some of his poetry in Creole. However, the earliest black poet, Joaquim Cordeiro da Mata (1857–94), came from Angola. The absence of a strong Afr. culture possibly acted as an indirect stimulus on the poetry of the islands, for the verse of José Lopes da Silva (1872–1962) respects Port. tradition. "Não prostituo a língua de Camões" (I do not prostitute the language of Camões), he wrote. With the influence of Brazilian Modernism in the thirties, the problem of color began to be introduced into Cape Verdean poetry. Pedro Monteiro Cardoso (ca. 1890-1942) published some bilingual poems in Port. and Creole. With the founding of *Claridade* by Jorge Barbosa (1902–71), Manuel Lopes (b. 1907), and others in 1936, literature increasingly focused attention on the islands and their peoples. The sea was an all important element, for, as Barbosa wrote in his poem, *To the Sea*, "Nos dilata sonhos e nos sufoca desejos" (it opens up dreams and stifles desires). On the other hand, another of the founders, Pedro Corsino Azevedo (1905–42), drew on the oral traditions of the island and wrote in Creole. One of his characteristically humorous poems is a detailed description of his snuffbox: *Nha tabaquero* which he lovingly evokes as made "di djacranda/co' prata tchuquido" (of jacaranda with inlaid silver). *Claridade* continued to appear intermittently, though by the sixties the young Cape Verdean poets had gone beyond the discovery of their island toward social themes such as hunger and emigration. Among these poets are Gabriel Mariano (b. 1928), Ovídio Martins (b. 1928), and Onésimo Silveira (b. 1935), who have taken emigration as their major theme. That is why in his *Um poema diferente*, Onésimo Silveira evokes a Utopian future as against the negatives of the present, a poem "sem barcos lastrados de gente/A caminho do Sul" (without boats crammed with people and heading for the South). In the small island of São Tomé, poetry has a strong social content and there has been some influence of the Cuban poet Nicolás Guillén on António Alves Tomás Medeiros (b. 1931) and Francisco José de Vasques Tenreiro (1921–63), the latter a prolific writer on *négritude* themes. A well-known woman poet of São Tomé, Alda do Espírito Santo (b. 1926) is author of an impassioned lament on the Batepa massacre of

1953—"Onde estão os homens caçados neste vento de loucura" (Where are the men pursued by this wind of madness?). The poetry of Angola and Mozambique has also arisen for the most part in response to the *négritude* movement and out of the social situation, though one of the earliest poets, Rui de Noronha (Mozambique, 1909–43) expressed little more than sad resignation at his colonial fate. With the founding of the reviews, *Mensagem* (1950) and, after its suppression, *Cultura* (both in Angola), there began a real movement of poetic discovery of Angola and Mozambique. Of great importance, too, because it drew together poets from different parts of Africa was the Casa dos Estudantes do Império in Lisbon, a student center which published many Afr. poets before it closed down in the 1960's. During the years of its existence, the *Casa* brought together writers, intellectuals, and future leaders of the Independence movement such as Amilcar Cabral, Agostinho Neto (b. Angola, 1922), and Mário de Andrade (b. Angola, 1928). The poetry of this period begins by rediscovering the peoples of Angola and Mozambique. For instance, many of the poems of Viriato da Cruz (b. Angola, 1928) take the form of portraits of typical local characters, e.g., *Só Santo*, the local potentate who is presented in the language and from the viewpoint of the people: "Hum-hum/Mas deixa .../Quando o sô Santo morrer, /Vamos chamar um kimbanda/Para 'Nghombo nos dizer/Se a sua grande desgraça/Foi desamparo de Sandu/Ou se é já própia da Raça" (Hum, but never mind. When Mr. Saint dies, we'll bring the sorcerer so that the Truth God will tell us whether his great misfortune was due to the Spirit having forsaken him or if it is in the blood). As in other parts of Africa, there is the emergence of certain *négritude* themes—the feeling of black brotherhood, for instance, in some of the poems of Agostinho Neto; of black defiance in José Craveirinha (b. Mozambique, 1922) whose *Grito Negro* compares his blackness to coal that will someday consume the boss; of the rape of mother Africa in the poetry of the woman poet, Noémia de Sousa (b. Mozambique, 1927). With the outbreak of armed struggle between 1961–64 many of these poets were to find themselves involved in the war—Agostinho Neto, Kalungano (Marcelino dos Santos, b. Mozambique, 1929), Jorge Rebelo (b. Mozambique, 1940) have all become leaders of the liberation movement and several others, António Jacinto do Amaral Martins (b. Angola, 1924) and José Craveirinha, have suffered periods of imprisonment. Not unnaturally in these poets, the theme of social exploitation is uppermost, and there are many poems written on the theme of war itself, for instance, the *Poema quarto* of Fernando Costa Andrade (b. Angola, 1936) who writes "Há sobre a terra

50,000 mortos que ninguém chorou" (There are upon the earth 50,000 unwept dead). In contrast to the poetry of the militants is that of the mulatto Mário António Fernandes de Oliveira (b. Angola, 1934) whose poetry often expresses the mystical bond between the Afr. and nature and that of Geraldo Bessa Victor (b. Angola, 1917), whose verse looks forward to a time when racial divisions will be overcome. The social and political nature of the poetry of Angola and Mozambique has had a strong influence on language and style, for it is a poetry of unequivocal statement which depends for its effect on a strong emotional tone of lament or protest. The use of Afr. words is restrained, though there is often the evocation of the drum beat.

ANTHOLOGIES: *Modernos poetas cabo-verdianos*, ed. J. de Figueiredo (1961); *Poetas e covetistas africanos de expressão portuguesa*, ed. J. Alves das Neves (São Paulo, 1963); *Literatura africana de expressão portuguesa*, I: *Poesia*, ed. M. de Andrade (Algiers, 2d ed., 1967; tr. into Fr. as *La Poésie africaine d'expression portugaise* [Honfleur], 1969).

HISTORY AND CRITICISM: M. de Andrade, "A poesia africana de expressão portuguesa: evolucão e tendencias actuais" in his anthol. cited above; N. Araujo, *A Study of Cape Verdean Lit.* (1966); G. M. Moser, *Essays in Port.-Afr. Lit.* (1969); R. A. Preto-Rodas, *Negritude as a Theme in the Poetry of the Portuguese-Speaking World* (1970); D. E. Herdeck, *Afr. Authors* (v.i, 1973). JE.F.

AGRARIANS. See FUGITIVES, THE.

AMERICAN POETIC SCHOOLS AND TECHNIQUES (CONTEMPORARY). "Ask the fact for the form," Emerson said, but the history of Am. poetry has tended to illustrate a rival quest, which is to beg the form for the fact. Emerson urged the Am. bards to emulate his Merlin, who mounted to paradise by the stairway of surprise, but even the greatest among Emerson's immediate progeny, Whitman and Dickinson, chose to present their poetic selves through repetitive modes of continuous and overwhelming formal innovation. Am. poetry since the end of World War II is an epitome of this reverse Emersonianism: no other poets in Western history have so self-deceivingly organized themselves along the supposed lines of formal divisions. The mimic wars of "closed" against "open" formers have masqueraded as conflicts between spiritual stances and ideological commitments: closed form, governed by metric and stanza, could thus be writ large as a settled insulation from experience, whereas open form, free-style and full of vatic self-confidence, reduced all experience to a chaos. And yet if we stand back now, after a quarter-cen-

tury, we behold mostly a welter of wholly shared anxieties that unite the feuding camps.

The poets who were gathered together at their first full strength ca. 1945 would include Robert Penn Warren, Richard Eberhart, Theodore Roethke, Elizabeth Bishop, Robert Lowell, John Berryman, Delmore Schwartz, J. V. Cunningham, Randall Jarrell, Richard Wilbur, Charles Olson, and Robert Duncan. They had as predecessors the most formidable group of poets in Am. tradition, one that began with Edwin Arlington Robinson and Frost and proceeded through Pound, Eliot, Moore, Williams, Stevens, Ransom, and Jeffers down to a somewhat younger trio of E. E. Cummings, Hart Crane, and Allen Tate. Almost all of the poets born in the first two decades of the 20th c. seem diminished today when juxtaposed very closely with those born in the last two or three decades of the 19th. Great achievement by the fathers sometimes exacts a price from the children, and something of the current strength of Am. poets born during the 1920's may derive from the sorrows and sacrifice of the middle generation of Roethke, Berryman, Jarrell, Lowell, and others.

We can distinguish two formal strains in the important Am. poets born during the closing decades of the 19th c. If we examine Am. poetic practice as opposed to theory in the 19th c., we see that the main British line of Spenserian-Miltonic poetry, which emerges as the romantic tradition, was carried on through Bryant, Poe, Longfellow, Timrod, and Lanier, while native strains were invented most plainly by Whitman, and more subtly by a gnomic group that includes Emerson, Thoreau, Melville, and, most grandly, Dickinson. The two strains, those of the Eng. Romantic and the Emersonian gnomic, met and mingled in Robinson and Frost.

A third strain of Whitmanian innovation ensued in the major outburst of 1915 and afterwards. The immediate influence of Whitman here—on Edgar Lee Masters, Vachel Lindsay, Carl Sandburg—was not fructifying, though these poets continue to be popular and their simplified idiom has much to do with the recent development of a quasi-folk music. However, a Whitmanian element in Pound, Williams, and even Eliot, today seems far more central and vitalizing than the European influences so directly exalted by Eliot and Pound themselves and by their followers. An even more elusive Whitmanian influence, wholly divorced from formal considerations, was crucial for Stevens, whose major formal inheritance is as close to Wordsworth, Keats, and Tennyson as ever Bryant, Poe, and Longfellow were.

Despite its enormous range and power, Stevens's poetry has waited until the late 1960's and early 1970's to find a strong disciple in John Ashbery, whose own work took a turn away from surrealism (q.v.) and automatic writing in *The Double Dream of Spring, Three Poems*, and a number of uncollected lyrics. In Ashbery's best poems we look back through Stevens to Whitman in the employment of a long line, and in a rather oblique use of the cataloguing effect. There is a similar background for poets whose middle range of ancestry and poetic temperament appears to be occupied by Eliot. For instance, W. S. Merwin began during the mid-1960's to experiment with a celebratory kind of neo-primitivism: in *The Moving Target* and *The Lice*, broken syntax is making the dissociation Eliot saw as historically unfortunate but necessary. Yet Merwin has recovered the consolatory strain that belonged to Whitman and decisively affected *The Waste Land* and *Four Quartets*, though Eliot in his own quite ambivalent public pronouncements had tried to eliminate Whitman from the acceptable "tradition" of poetry in the Eng. language.

These cases illustrate the emergence during the past few years of a transcendentalism that has always been essential to Am. poetry but was for a time anxiously rejected by its surest descendants. The poets of the generation of Roethke-Lowell-Wilbur began with the sober admonition of Eliot and Auden; they were to return to closed forms, and forsake metrical innovation. They, together with their younger followers in the 1950's—Ashbery, Merwin, James Dickey, James Merrill, Anthony Hecht, James Wright, Louis Simpson, Richard Howard, John Hollander—discovered in their various ways that neither closed nor open forms could be anything but an evasion. Poets who came into their force somewhat later, such as Gary Snyder, A. R. Ammons, Galway Kinnell, and Mark Strand, were less troubled by constraints of form and so could start more comfortably from the fact. In short, never having labored under the illusion that there was some cross-cultural modern idiom to which they ought to aspire, they declared themselves from the first to be successors of Emerson and Whitman.

Among the closed formers it is Auden rather than Eliot who has been the steadiest influence. His idiom is still going strong in the most recent work of Merrill, Howard Moss, and Wilbur, had a determining effect on the early efforts of Hollander and Howard, and never left Jarrell. What separates the Am. disciples of Auden from many of their British counterparts is a revision of Auden's characteristic irony, which (as D. Davie has remarked in a slightly different context) begins to realize in it the attitude that nature strikes in confronting man: not merely a man's own pose in confronting himself. This shift is evident also in matters of detail. Wilbur can be representative: his early

and late poems look very nearly the same, but their technical evenness covers a progress away from the metaphysical conceits which used to lie thick on his pages. Similarly, Jarrell in his last work moved to the Wordsworthian pathos that had been his theme all along, and wrote increasingly in a loose iambic that allowed for much of the "inclusiveness" he had explicitly admired in Whitman. Howard in his most recent volumes has written dramatic monologues after the manner of Browning, while Hollander has tended to favor syllabics or else a highly enjambed accentual verse. Such a list might go on: the point is that poets who had their beginning in Auden, and whose early work can often be mistaken for Auden's, have by whatever route found a resting place in the native tradition.

Our emphasis ought to fall on a Wordsworthian-Whitmanian *subjectivity* that is just and inevitable. Against this stands the mode of confessional verse, a matrix that has produced W. D. Snodgrass, Sylvia Plath, Anne Sexton, and many other figures. Confessional poetry owes its genesis to Lowell, whose earliest writing looked like a late metaphysical pastiche for which his only precursors might be Edward Taylor and Allen Tate. In *Life Studies* Lowell opened himself to the type of free verse pioneered by Williams, while using the form, as Williams had not done, to write his own life's story by way of the strictly clinical facts. In later works Lowell has put the same subject, himself, under a still more minute examination, reverting to the format of a diary and adopting the form of a fourteen-line entry written in flat pentameter. He is certainly the poet central to this movement, or tendency, in Am. poetry, and, though he has been a less imposing as well as a less domineering presence, he seems to be the logical successor to Eliot in the poetry of belief or anxious unbelief which ranges itself against the poetry of vision. Although the issue of form is as always bogus, the larger opposition here will probably be lasting.

Critics have ordinarily associated Lowell in this phase with the later work of Berryman, which belongs more appropriately to a consideration of Pound's influence. Berryman's *Dream Songs* have much of the terseness that Pound asked to be communicated from the tone of a poem to its prosody, and their way of setting an expressionistic personal stance over against imagistic hardness was also anticipated by Pound. It is only in his last and less individually realized songs that Berryman approaches Lowell.

Iris Murdoch has observed that imagism (q.v.) itself was never more than a fantastically stripped down version of late romanticism: personality was being reduced to its smallest points of perception without ever being expunged, so that a large claim for the self was at all events implicitly maintained. There was never any "extinction of personality," in Eliot's phrase. Pound recognized this when he embarked on his own private quest poem, the enormous and deliberately uncompleted *Cantos*, and his followers have taken roughly the same path. The Black Mountain School, including primarily Olson, Duncan, and Robert Creeley, can be counted among his most faithful. Olson's own epic was composed largely in Poundian cadences, though he professed to write according to a different rationale. Thus, projective verse* is the name given to his exhortation to future bards to write by "field"— that is, using all the resources of a typewriter to complicate what the eye sees on the written page—and at the same time to plan their metric according to breath—that is, with a respect for the full and varied possibilities of exhalation helped by the human voice. Olson felt that he was licensed in principle as in practice by the metric of Shakespeare's later plays.

As all the manifestos show, there is an obscure but profound spiritual kinship that binds together Williams, Pound, Olson, and a much younger poet, Allen Ginsberg. The self-discoveries of Ginsberg, Gregory Corso, Lawrence Ferlinghetti, William Everson, and a host of lesser eminences, who were first heard from in the mid-1950's, are occasionally referred to as making a San Francisco Renaissance. The advent of the Beat Poets (q.v.), and the writing Duncan issued out of San Francisco, may be set under the rubric of this event. Since the Beat Poets were noisiest in being reborn, have stayed active through their connection with Ferlinghetti's publishing enterprise, and compose the largest subset of this group, they have a special claim on our attention. In one sense these poets are Whitman's authentic heirs: they have his expansiveness, his belief in the democracy of the spirit, his sexual frankness, and they sing of the open road. But the myth has become a mystique in their hands, which merely to invoke is apparently to justify. In much of Ginsberg's work during the late 1950's and early 1960's, the elliptical image-making faculty of Williams has also been brought to bear, and it is to be noted that Williams associated himself with this poet's Whitmanian incarnation at its most aggressive pitch. At least one current in Williams' own poetry, however, ran directly contrary to Whitman, for Williams tended to freeze any given image in order to isolate it for contemplation, rather than immersing its solitariness in some wider flow of reverie. This is where the style of a poet and the deepest facts of his personality intersect, and on this point of style a disciple

far truer to Williams than any of the "Howl"-Whitmanians has been Denise Levertov.

Williams' habit of regarding a poem as "observations," enlivened by the colloquial diction of Pound, helped to encourage Marianne Moore in one generation and Elizabeth Bishop in the next. An ingratiating element in both of these poets is that they seem to claim nothing for their role, or for their craft. The type of syllabic verse invented by Moore makes the prose of life concede very little to the poetry and sets nervousness very high among the faculties that aid perception. Similar qualities, though with a certain loosening as to form and a less jagged conception of what a poem ought to be, are notable throughout Bishop's work. The "mad exactness" that has often been remarked in her poetry is itself an exacting discipline, and may eventually be viewed as a corrective reaction against the thaumaturgical excesses of the modern tradition.

Another kind of reaction against modernism accounts for the group of New York poets in which Frank O'Hara, Kenneth Koch, James Schuyler, and Ashbery figure as significant names. The *opéra bouffe* of Am. silent films as well as a native surrealism is at work in the writing of this school: O'Hara's *Second Avenue* can be considered an exemplum of the new mode thereby brought into being, which might be described as comic phantasmagoria. Such a poetics is in the last degree an urban phenomenon, and will be found irrevocably at odds with the school of pre-Wordsworthian, or indeed—as it likes to be thought—prehistorical clarity which we connect with the names of James Wright and Robert Bly.

Sooner or later, as has been noted, the proliferation of schools and methods must be understood as an impediment, not an aid to appreciation. There are two innovations that have some importance: first, the definitive sloughing off of the Georgian diction by Pound, Frost, and a few others. That the advance took place at a certain time and place has come to seem a truism, yet it holds within it an essential truth. There is also, a bit later, Williams' reassertion in free verse of the full range of ambiguity made possible by enjambment (q.v.), when, as J. Hollander has indicated, the rhetorical flexibility of that particular feature of Eng. poetry had been allowed to lapse after Milton in the poetry of the late romantics and the Victorians. But, once we have taken these into account, the arguments within and between self-proclaiming schools are at best misleading. In the strongest and most characteristic poetry of the late 1960's and early 1970's, a transcendental synthesis of the various native strains seems to be developing, and what is emerging is clearly an expressionistic and severe version of Am. ro-

manticism. At any rate, that is our safest
generalization as we trace the continuity of
individual careers. Thus Simpson, who was
once allied with Bly and the mid-West clari-
fiers, appears in his liveliest work to have
been relatively free of their defining impulse.
Ashbery, sometimes categorized quite simply
as one of the New York poets, instead moves
together with Schuyler in an enormous ambience that includes the otherwise very diverse
Merrill, Wright, Hecht, Ammons, Merwin,
Hollander, Alvin Feinman, Kinnell, Strand,
and many others, who are visionary, as Emerson prophesied they must be. The *stance* of
all these poets makes impossible an expression
in either closed or open phrased fields, and
each has been compelled, in order to escape
the fall into the confessional, to perform a
deliberate curtailment of the revisionary impulse toward an endlessly journalistic scrutiny
of himself, while simultaneously asking the
fact for the form.

For what, finally, can poetic form mean to
an Am.? Every Am. poet who aspires to
strength knows that he starts in the evening-
land, realizes he is a latecomer, fears to be
only a secondary man.

Solitary,
Patient for the last voices of the dusk to
    die down, and the dusk
To die down,
Listeners waiting for courteous rivers
To rise and be known . . .

. . . but in the large view, no
lines or changeless shapes: the working in
and out, together
        and against, of millions of events: this,
            so that I make
                no form of
                    formlessness . . .

Suspended somewhere in summer between the
    ceremonies
Remembered from childhood and the histori-
    cal conflagrations
Imagined in sad, learned youth—somewhere
    there always hangs
The American moment.
        Burning, restless, between the deed
And the dream is the life remembered . . .

In new rocks new insects are sitting
With the lights off
And once more I remember that the begin-
    ning
Is broken

No wonder the addresses are torn . . .

Glad of the changes already and if there are
    more
        it will never be you that minds
Since it will not be you to be changed, but in
    the evening in the severe lamplight
    doubts come
From many scattered distances, and do not
    come too near.
As it falls along the house, your treasure
Cries to the other men; the darkness will have
    none of you, and your are folded into it
    like mint into the sound of haying . . .

These are five representative poets of their
generation; the excerpts have been taken at
random from a recent anthology. Every passage, whether in tone, in cognitive aim, or in
human stance, shows the same anxiety: to ask
the fact for the form, while being fearful that
the fact no longer has a form. This is what
G. Hartman has called "the anxiety of demand": that which can be used can be used
up. The generation of poets who stand together
now, mature and ready to write the major Am.
verse of the 1970's, may yet be seen as what
Stevens called "a great shadow's last embellishment," the shadow being Emerson's.

ANTHOLOGIES: *New Poets of England and
America,* ed. D. Hall, R. Pack, and L. Simpson
(1957); *The New Am. Poetry,* ed. D. M. Allen
(1960); *Contemporary Am. Poetry,* ed. D. Hall
(1962); *Poems of Our Moment,* ed. J. Hollander
(1968); *The Contemporary Am. Poets,* ed. M.
Strand (1969); *Preferences: 51 Am. Poets
Choose Poems from Their Own Work and
from the Past,* comm. and introd. by R. Howard (1974). Cf. also the Yale Series of Younger
Poets, the Pitt Poetry Series of the University
of Pittsburgh, the Contemporary Poetry Series of the University of North Carolina Press,
the Wesleyan Poetry Program.

CRITICISM: E. Pound, *A.B.C. of Reading*
(1934); Y. Winters, *Primitivism and Decadence*
(1937); W. Stevens, *The Necessary Angel*
(1951); R. Jarrell, *Poetry and the Age* (1953);
W. C. Williams, *Selected Essays* (1954); A. Tate,
The Man of Letters in the Modern World
(1955); R. J. Mills, Jr. *Contemporary Am.
Poetry* (1965); C. Olson, *Human Universe*
(1967); M. L. Rosenthal, *The New Poets*
(1967); A. Alvarez, *Beyond All This Fiddle*
(1968); D. Davie, "On Sincerity," *Encounter,*
31 (1968) and *Six Epistles to Eva Hesse* (1970);
The Survival of Poetry, ed. M. Dodsworth
(1970); R. Howard, *Alone with America*
(1970); H. Bloom, *The Ringers in the Tower*
(1971); D. Bromwich, "Some Am. Masks," *Dis-*

sent, 20 (1973); K. Malkoff, *Crowell's Handbook of Contemporary Am. Poetry* (1973); L. Simpson, *North of Jamaica* (1973); *Am. Poetry since 1960*, ed. R. B. Shaw (1974); M. Bewley, D. Donoghue, R. W. Flint, R. Mazzocco in *The Hudson Review, The New York Review of Books, Partisan Review, passim.*

HA.B.; D.B.

AMERIND (a combination of syllables for American and Indian). See AMERICAN INDIAN POETRY.

ANIMAL EPIC. See BEAST EPIC.

ANTIMASQUE. See MASQUE.

ATTITUDE. See TONE.

B

BARDIC VERSE. See CELTIC PROSODY.

BEAST FABLE. See FABLE IN VERSE; BEAST EPIC.

BIBLICAL POETRY. See HEBREW POETRY.

BLACK MOUNTAIN SCHOOL OF POETS. See PROJECTIVE VERSE.*

BLACK POETRY, Recent (U.S.). The term, and perhaps the very concept, "Black Poetry" entered popular usage in the early 1960's along with "Black Power," "Black Nationalism," and "The Black Arts Movement." In part each of these rests on the premise of Pan-Africanism, that is, the belief that all B. communities in Africa and elsewhere share a fundamental cultural heritage and certain historical experiences and current political concerns, especially vis-à-vis Western culture. B. poetry, then, can mean poetry by persons of African descent, but more specifically it designates poetry by such persons which is addressed to the B. heritage aesthetically and to the B. community politically.

Recent B. poetry in the United States therefore continues the tradition of spirituals (q.v.) and of the luminaries such as Phillis Wheatley, George Moses Horton, Paul Laurence Dunbar, Claude McKay, Langston Hughes, Melvin B. Tolson, and Gwendolyn Brooks (see NEGRO POETRY. AMERICAN [U.S.]). It is distinguished from this tradition primarily by a heightened consciousness of alienation from non-B. audiences—a consciousness emerging from the Civil Rights and B. Power movements of the 1960's, the assassinations of Malcolm X and Martin Luther King, the big-city riots, and the rekindling of interest in B. Nationalism. It is further characterized by a consciously B. aesthetic which regards critical concepts and criteria of academic traditionalism as founded on principles alien to the B. culture. Such norms are rejected as racist, stifling, and parochial, even under the shibboleth of "uni-

versality." Such new B. poets as Don L. Lee and Clarence Major speak within a developing B. aesthetic similar to the mature one existing in music, a context where the B. artist, utterly independent of "scholarly criticism," interprets the cultural experience which he shares with his B. audience.

Since emancipation from traditional Western poetic criteria is relatively new, the formal elements of the new emphasis are quite varied and eclectic, as is indicated by the haiku (q.v.) of Etheridge Knight, the South African sort of praise poems by Keorapetse Kgositsile, the paeons of Nikki Giovanni, and the combination of music with poetry (not lyrics) by "The Last Poets" and many others. Often the figures of speech and prosody borrow from current oral folk poetry, thus continuing the tradition of "dialect poetry," "jazz poetry," and the many other written styles based on verbal art endemic to the whole B. community in America, but foreign to Euro-Am. literary tradition. Frequently, choices of orthography, vocabulary, tone, etc., seem intended precisely to contradict academically enshrined canons. Thus form itself is applied to the task of "decolonizing the mind" of both reader and writer. The poets' concept of a "colonized people" follows closely the thought of such political philosophers as Frantz Fanon and Kwame Nkrumah.

But it is in content that this poetry is most strikingly directed toward the B. community's emancipation ideologically and in every other sense. Typical is the poem *B. Art* by Imamu Baraka, which focuses aesthetic principles upon content—content which teaches, inspires, and hence contributes to liberation.

The recurrent themes of recent B. poetry might be provisionally categorized as either "negative" or "positive"—even though the most bleak poem may involve a subtle affirmation of B. values, and the most affirmative poem may evoke images of intense suffering. On the negative side, there are exposures of the abuses and inconsistencies of Western religion and aesthetics (Yusef Iman's *Love Your Enemy*, Dudley Randall's *B. Poet, White Critic*); demonstrations of the loss of B. selfhood which characterizes a colonial mentality (Don L. Lee's *The Self-Hatred of Don L. Lee*); and dramatizations of various forms of modern oppression (Carolyn Rodgers' *The Last M. F.*, Etheridge Knight's *Hard Rock Returns to Prison*, Johari Amini's *Upon Being B. One Friday Night in July*).

On the positive side, there are explicit calls to revolt (Sonia Sanchez' *A Coltrane Poem*, Don L. Lee's *a poem to complement other poems*) as well as less militant, inward-looking affirmations. Nikki Giovanni illustrates a transition from one stance to the other, from the mid-1960's *Nigger, Can You Kill?* to the more recent concerns of *My House*. The reintegration of the B. "sense of self" is the implicit aim of many contemporary B. poems which celebrate oft-disparaged forms of B. beauty—physical, spiritual, and cultural (Conrad Kent Rivers' *For All Things B. and Beautiful*, Everett Hoagland's *love child—a b. aesthetic*, and many B. poets' tributes to B. musicians). Another important development is the effort to provide a B. and Pan-Africanist cosmology (Larry Neal's *Kuntu*, Sun Ra's *Of Cosmic Blue Prints*, Sarah Fabio's *Evil Is No B. Thing*).

The authors cited above probably constitute a fair list of the contemporary B. poets most celebrated by their fellow artists and the B. community. Among the most seminal are Imamu Baraka (Leroi Jones) and Don L. Lee. In addition other established poets, notably Gwendolyn Brooks, have participated in the B. poetry movement, whose centers of activity are New York and Newark, New Jersey, Chicago, Detroit, and to a lesser extent San Francisco and Los Angeles. Independence has required reliance on new publishing houses such as Jihad Productions, Broadside Press, and Third World Press, and on journals such as *The Journal of B. Poetry*, *Soulbook*, and the preexisting *B. World*. The determined aspiration to speak in the idiom of Blacks has so succeeded that B. poetry has generated in its intended audience an interest challenged by no other serious contemporary B. art except music, and, possibly, drama.

ANTHOLOGIES: *B. Expressions: An Anthol. of New B. Poets*, ed. E. Perkins (1967); *B. Fire*, ed. L. Jones and L. Neal (1968); *I Am the Darker Brother: An Anthol. of Modern Poems by B. Americans* (1968) and *The Poetry of B. America: Anthol. of the 20th C.* (1973), both ed. A. Adoff; *The New B. Poetry*, ed. C. Major (1969); *Soulscript: Afro-Am. Poetry*, ed. J. Jordan (1970); *Dices or B. Bones: B. Voices of the Seventies*, ed. A. D. Miller (1970); *19 Necromancers from Now: An Anthol. of Original Am. Writing for the 70's*, ed. I. Reed (1970); *We Speak as Liberators*, ed. O. Coombs (1970); *A Broadside Treasury*, ed. G. Brooks (1971).

HISTORY AND CRITICISM: A. Bontemps, "The New B. Renaissance," *Negro Digest*, 11 (1961) and "The Umbra Poets," *Mainstream*, 16 (1963); *Anger and Beyond: The Negro Writer in the United States*, ed. H. Hill (1966); L. Neal, "The B. Arts Movement," *Drama Rev.*, 12 (1968); R. Barksdale, "Urban Crisis and the B. Poetic Avant-Garde," *Negro Am. Lit. Forum*, 3 (1969); *B. Expression: Essays by and about B. Americans in the Creative Arts*, ed. A. Gayle (1969); M. Cook and S. Henderson, *The Militant B. Writer in Africa and the United States* (1969); C. Gerald, "The B. Writer and His Role," *Negro Digest*, 18 (1969); J. Lester, "The Arts and the B. Revolution," *Arts in Society*, 5 (1969); C. Rodgers, "B. Poetry–where It's at," *Negro Digest*, 18 (1969); A. P. Davis, "The New Poetry of B. Hate," *CLA Jour.*, 11 (1970); M. Evans, "Contemporary B. Lit.," *B. World*, 19 (1970); *The B. Aesthetic*, ed. A. Gayle (1971); *Dynamite Voices: B. Poetry of the 1960's*, ed. D. L. Lee (1971); J. H. Bryant, "The B. Rebellion in Lit. and Music," *Nation*, April 24, 1972; B. Bell, "Contemporary Afro-Am. Poetry as Folk Art," *B. World*, 22 (1973); S. Henderson, *Understanding the New B. Poetry* (1973); *Modern B. Poets: A Collection of Crit. Essays*, ed. D. B. Gibson (1973). **D.J.**

C

CALLIGRAMME. The c. takes its name from Guillaume Apollinaire's figure-poems (*idéogrammes lyriques*, as he first called them) in his volume *Calligrammes* (1918). It has been termed "both unique and non-unique, both avant-garde and historically grounded" (E. E. George). While recognizing the personal quality in Apollinaire's use of the form, one may cite in its background the subtle metaphorical elements of the Chinese written character and, among others, such historical precedents as Alexandrian figure-poems (*technopaignia*) attributed to Simias of Rhodes, Theocritus, and Dosiadas; the Latin *carmina figurata*; Rabelais' "Dive Bouteille"; George Herbert's wings; and the mouse-tail of *Alice's Adventures in Wonderland*. The c. thus falls somewhere between the pattern poem (see PATTERN POETRY) and contemporary concrete poetry.* When Apollinaire shapes his verses variously into a necktie, a watch, a crown, a flower, a mandolin, a Browning pistol, the façade of Notre-Dame, a fountain, the Eiffel Tower, or a shower of rain, there is often an integral lyric quality preserved within the form. Yet the c. remains essentially a virtuosity, a visual conceit, a sort of modern blending of verse and emblem (q.v.) in one.—F. J. Carmody, *Evolution of Apollinaire's Poetics 1901–1914* (1963); S. Themerson, *Apollinaire's Lyrical Ideograms* (1966, rev. ed., 1968); E. E. George, "Calligrams in Apollinaire and in Trakl: A Psycho-Stylistic Study," *Language and Style*, 1 (1968); P. Renaud, *Lecture d'Apollinaire* (1969); G. M. Masters, "Rabelais and Ren. Figure Poems," *Etudes Rabelaisiennes*, 8 (1969); A. H. Greet, "Wordplay in Apollinaire's *Calligrammes*," *L'Esprit Créateur*, 10 (1970). A.G.E.

CENSORSHIP. Compared to prose fiction, poetry has seldom been censored. C. consists of suppression before or after publication in the name of some political, religious, or moral principle invoked by a state, church, or public pressure group. For over 2,000 years the basic principle behind such suppression has been the idea asserted in Plato's *Republic* that susceptible minds must be protected from harm. In all this time, poetry, for various reasons, has been held relatively harmless. After Aristophanes lampooned the reigning tyrant, Athens outlawed invective from the stage (437–35 B.C.) but exempted the chorus because of its roots in religious ritual. This attitude toward poetry as a part-sacred, communal activity probably provided a measure of immunity in earlier times. Today, as censors concentrate on protecting the greatest number of people from greatest moral harm, they fear poetry only in proportion to its popularity and usually leave it alone.

Wherever c. has been public policy and poetry has been as vulnerable as any other form of expression, persecution of poets has not been as dramatic as legend would lead us to believe. The famous story of Ovid being banished for obscene poetry is fanciful. He was banished for riotous living or opposition politics, not poetry. When the infamous Restoration rake Sir Charles Sedley was jailed in 1663, it was not, as some say, for "mannerly obscene" poems, but for standing on a balcony in Covent Garden "throwing down bottles (pist in)" upon the populace below. There is

little way of knowing how effectively c. inhibited poets from writing, but the record is clear that they enjoyed relative freedom until the growth of a mass reading public brought about the need for moral c. on an unprecedented scale.

Previously c. had been invoked to support the established churches or governments. With the advent of widespread printing, the Church in 1487 imposed a formal system of licensing books before publication. Charles V in 1521 made publishing without the Church's license a civil offense, and Henry VIII countered with a wholly secular licensing system under the dreaded Star Chamber. Still, no major poet is known to have suffered for his poetry even after the Church buttressed its system with an *Index of Prohibited Books* (1559). Frequently revised, the Index was subject to the whims of presiding authorities and at one time listed 11 lines of the *Divine Comedy* (from *Inferno*, 11 and 19), later the whole of *Paradise Lost* in It. translation. In post-Napoleonic Austria under the "Metternich System," the Index was combined with secular restrictions to impose excessively harsh c. on poets or anyone else expressing liberal views. Yet within Catholic nations, like Spain, the Index gradually fell into disuse until formally abrogated in 1966.

Secular restrictions, however, remain, especially in nations subject to rigorous political c. Licensing and blacklisting are standard measures controlling poetry and other forms of literary expression. In the USSR, where the state publishes all books and controls all bookstores, "ideological administrators" decide what will be written and read and what will not be written or read, including books imported from abroad. The state, the party, and the powerful Writers' Union keep watch for books lacking literary or social merit. In 1947 a decree against westernizing influences on Russian culture quickly consigned "harmful" poets like Anna Akhmatova and Boris Pasternak to silence and their works to instant oblivion. In 1972, while young poets like Iosif Brodsky endure "government service" followed by exile, others are free to read abroad, hinting at some relaxation of complete, uncompromising control.

As other states have granted increasing degrees of individual freedom, political and religious c. have declined but moral c. has flourished as a concomitant of democracy. The most dramatic shift coincided with the romantic movement in England where Lord Chancellor Eldon, seeking to shelter the morals of millions among a new mass reading class, invoked the principle, still current, that a potentially harmful work can have no existence in the eyes of the law and thus no copyright protection. He permitted piracy of

-[922]-

any work suspected of libel, blasphemy, or immorality or one written by an author whose reputation was merely suspect.

In 1817, when a pirate printed Southey's *Wat Tyler*, an effusion of his radical youth, Lord Eldon refused even the conservative laureate an injunction. In the same year, Eldon denied Shelley custody of his child because of the blasphemy in *Queen Mab*. Byron, whose wealth and power enabled him to beat off pirates of *Don Juan* and *Cain*, was yet so stunned by this injustice that he refused to go on with *Don Juan*. And Coleridge refused to translate *Faust*, fearing he would be blamed for Goethe's blasphemy and exposed to Eldon's lash. Thus for a quarter-century Eldon ruled, ably abetted in the marketplace by the Society for the Suppression of Vice, so that by the close of his career reputable publishers, like Byron's John Murray, were simply refusing to issue any new poetry as "quite unsaleable."

The Society, like its successors in America, used boycotts, blacklists, and moral suasion along with the constant threat of criminal prosecution under obscenity laws. These laws evolved with expansion of the reading public. In the U.S., the Tariff Act of 1842 banned importation of obscene books, including "classics" (exempted only in 1930), without defining obscenity. After mid-century both U.S. and British law held any book obscene that tended to corrupt corruptible minds. In 1933, in the "*Ulysses* case," Judge John Woolsey ruled that a book must be tested by its effect on "a person with average sex instincts," and this principle was embraced by the Supreme Court's "Roth decision" (1957) which held that the test of obscenity should be "whether to the average person, applying contemporary standards, the dominant theme of the material taken as a whole appeals to prurient interest" (354 U.S. 487).

At the same time, this landmark decision extended immunity to any book with ideas having "the slightest redeeming social importance" even though otherwise "unorthodox, controversial, or hateful to the prevailing climate of opinion"—a decision that effectively deprived pressure groups of their most formidable weapon. During 1972, however, the Court said that the test was solely whether the dominant theme of the work appealed to prurient interest, and that "an attempt at serious art" was not inevitably a guarantee against a finding of obscenity.

Then in 1973, the test was narrowed: "whether the work, taken as a whole, lacks serious literary, artistic, political or scientific value." More, the Court also limited the scope of the test by relating it to community standards: "whether the work depicts or describes, in a patently offensive way, sexual conduct specifically defined by the applicable state law." This revision emphasizing state jurisdiction gives pressure groups a formidable weapon for grass-roots prosecutions.

Over the past century in the free world, pressure groups and police have been notoriously unsuccessful in convicting any major poet. In fact, a judgment of obscenity against six poems in Baudelaire's *Fleurs du Mal* levied in 1857 was finally annulled by Fr. courts in 1949. In 1929, D. H. Lawrence cunningly arranged for British postal authorities to impound the MS of *Pansies*, igniting popular furore in his favor. In 1957, after U.S. Customs impounded Ginzberg's *Howl and Other Poems*, thousands cheered as Judge Clayton Horn threw the case out of court.

In 1970 the President's Commission on Obscenity and Pornography recommended relaxing what few restrictions remain. President Nixon rejected the Commission's report, and the mere possibility of relaxation caused pressure groups to redouble their efforts. Nevertheless, on the national level, poetry continues to enjoy immunity from their concerns as they focus on widely circulating books and the mass media. On local levels, however, great poems along with literary classics of all kinds continue to feel the occasional lash of latter-day Lord Eldons. Bimonthly the American Library Association issues a *Newsletter on Intellectual Freedom*, reporting harassment of bookstores, public libraries and public schools, a continuing record of democracy's voice in the republic of letters, assuring us that Plato is alive and well and living among the grassroots.

The First Freedom, ed. R. B. Downs (1960); R. W. Haney, *Comstockery in America* (1960); A. Craig, *Banned Books of England and Other Countries* (1962); M. L. Ernst and A. U. Schwartz, *C.: The Search for the Obscene* (1964); R. E. McCoy, *Freedom of the Press* (1968); D. Thomas, *A Long Time Burning: History of Literary C.* (1969); U. S. Commission on Obscenity and Pornography. *The Report* (1970).　　　　　　　　P.M.Z.

CLOSURE, POETIC. See POETIC CLOSURE.*

COLLECTIONS, UNIFIED. Groups of poems possessing a sequential or other holistic form. Virgil's ten *Eclogues* and four *Georgics* have recently been examined in detail for their symmetrical properties, involving pairs of poems within the larger whole, passages on similar topics at similar length in similar places, etc. Such thematic forms have been shown to unify the episodes of Ovid's *Metamorphoses*; and some looser form has long been observed in Martial's *Epigrams* and Statius' *Silvae*. Occasionally a form was provided, as with some Renaissance editions of Juvenal dividing his sixteen satires into books.

In the Middle Ages and the Renaissance, narrative and lyric sequences were very common, often employing other devices to impart unity. Dante's *Vita Nuova* and Petrarch's *Canzoniere* give sequences of love poems in which an idealized profane love may lead by stages to divine love, and recent criticism has discovered in these collections certain calendrical or other structures that provide one version of numerological form. The sonnet sequences (see SONNET CYCLE) of Edmund Spenser (*Amoretti*), of Sir Philip Sidney (*Astrophel and Stella*) and, less certainly, of Shakespeare incorporate narrative features, along with other symptoms of order in unified collections. Two of the best Eng. examples of u.c. appeared in the 17th c.: George Herbert's collection of divine poems, *The Temple*, and John Dryden's collection, chiefly of narratives and translations, *Fables Ancient and Modern*. Varieties of linking by echoing of words, development of plot, and variations on themes assist Herbert and Dryden, the former in developing ideas of the vicissitudes of the soul in a eucharistic series; and the latter, versions of the good life. Emblem (q.v.) books frequently showed such a progression, and particularly in dealing with the vanity of earthly things or the vicissitudes of the soul. Francis Quarles treats the former topic in the first two books of his *Emblemes* and the latter in the last three. Because discovery of the unifying principles of such collections has come so recently, it seems most likely that further study will show that numerous other u.c. can be found in classical, Renaissance, and subsequent times.

The extraordinary features of certain Japanese collections have also become known not long ago. The first imperial collection, the *Kokinshū* (early 10th c.) contains 1,111 poems in twenty books. The most important groups of books are those on the seasons and on love, both of which are ordered temporally, the former on a natural basis and in relation to the *Ceremonies of the Year* (*Nenchū Gyōji*), the latter on the pattern of a courtly love affair. Implicit in the progressive integration of the *Kokinshū* was the possibility, partly realized in that collection, of associative linkage in terms of diction, imagery, and topic. Such possibilities were fully realized by the eighth imperial collection, the *Shinkokinshū* (early 13th c.), in which the twenty books of almost 2,000 poems are integrated editorially into a sequence of nearly 10,000 lines. The central feature of such integration is the art of the editors or compilers in bringing together poems written by different poets of different ages into a single whole, with integration rather than authorship or historical chronology determining order. On the model of such imperial collections, various shorter collections employing

associative and progressive integration came into being. Some of these involved editorial integration: e.g., *Superior Poems of Our Time* (*Kindai Shūka*), a sequence integrated by the poet Fujiwara Teika. Other such Japanese u.c. were modeled on the imperial collections and were made up of poems composed by a single poet and editorially ordered by him (or her). The most frequent version of such u.c. was the hundred-poem sequence (*hyakushuuta*), out of which developed later linked forms by poets writing stanzas in alteration. The brevity of the Japanese *tanka* (q.v.) enabled other editorial manipulation into episodes accompanied by prose. In the 19th and 20th c. somewhat similar groupings of poems will be found in various literatures. A few examples of such include Charles Pierre Baudelaire's *Fleurs du mal*, Rainer Maria Rilke's *Sonette an Orpheus*, and Edgar Lee Masters' *Spoon River Anthology*.

In numerous poetic traditions, various methods of bringing two or more poems together have existed; e.g., see COMPANION POEMS.*—On Virgil, see B. Otis, *Virgil: A Study in Civilized Poetry* (1963) and M. J. C. Putnam, *Virgil's Pastoral Art* (1970). On Ovid, see B. Otis, *Ovid as an Epic Poet* (1966). On Dante and Petrarch, see C. S. Singleton, *An Essay on the Vita Nuova* (1958); T. P. Roche, "Calendrical Structure in Petrarch's *Canzoniere*," SP, 71 (1974). On Renaissance sonnet sequences, see T. P. Roche, "Shakespeare and the Sonnet Sequence" in *Hist. of Lit. in the Eng. Language*, II (1540–1674), ed. C. Ricks (1970; ch. 5). On Herbert, see L. L. Martz, *The Poetry of Meditation* (1954) and on Dryden, E. Miner, *Dryden's Poetry* (1967). On Japanese poetry, see R. H. Brower and E. Miner, *Japanese Court Poetry* (1961).   E.M.

COMPANION POEMS. Two poems designed to be read as complements, opposites, or replies. The best known c.p. in Eng. poetry are Milton's *L'Allegro* and *Il Penseroso*, which are truly paired, in the manner of rhetorical essays preferring the rival claims of day and night, youth and age, etc., as in Milton's own academic exercises (see *Prolusions*, 1.7), which imply a paired oration on the other side. Because rhetorical amplification could work to augment or diminish, and because satire and panegyric shared numerous topics, such sets of opposites were common in many forms of writing. Truly paired poems are not numerous in Eng. literature. After Milton, there are Abraham Cowley's *Against Hope* and *For Hope*, the former of which was also paired with Richard Crashaw's *For Hope*; and John Oldham's *Satyr against Virtue*, with the *Counterpart to the Satyr against Virtue*. Such opposed poems were sometimes printed together in alternating stanzas: so Cowley and Crashaw on hope; Maria Tesselschade Visscher's (a 17th-c. Dutch poet) *Wilde en Tamme Zangster* (Wild and Tame Singer); Robert Burton's *Author's Abstract of Melancholy*; and Edmund Waller's *In Answer of Sir John Suckling's Verses*, interwoven with Suckling's *Against Fruition*. Some of the poems paired by one author against those by another are answer poems with parodic elements. Christopher Marlowe's *Come live with me and be my love* excited a number of replies with parodic features.

True answer poems, implying social intercourse in verse address, will be found in large numbers in collections of Chinese, Korean, and Japanese poetry. The classical poetic traditions of those countries assumed that the persons addressed were also poets, and in fact poetry was often exchanged on occasions that today would call for prose or telephone communication. It sometimes happened that Japanese poems not actually paired were brought together editorially with a headnote describing the (imaginary) situation, leading to a genre known as "tales of poems" (*uta-monogatari*) of which *The Tales of Ise* (*Ise Monogatari*) is the best known example. Another Japanese example that flourished in classical times was the poetry-match (*utaawase*), in which two or more people competed by writing poems on given topics, with a judgment given by one or more judges. Such matches often were great occasions of state, and they had a variant in the poetry-match with oneself (*jikaawase*), in which a single poet wrote two poems on each topic and sent them to an esteemed critic for judgment.

Poems composed over a period of time might also be paired. Recent study of Virgil's *Eclogues* and *Georgics* shows that individual poems in the former ten and latter four have symmetrical features. Other recent study has shown such symmetry to characterize larger poetic collections such as Petrarch's *Canzoniere* and Edmund Spenser's *Amoretti*. The symmetry of such collections often employs a calendrical or other numerological basis. John Donne's two *Anniversaries—The Anatomy of the World* and *The Progress of the Soul*—are c.p. more by virtue of relation and contrast in theme, tone, and occasion.

The art of c.p. is sufficiently natural for it to be continued into later times. William Blake's *Songs of Innocence* and *Songs of Experience* include a number of poems set against each other and understood only by their contrasts. Similarly, Robert Browning's *Meeting at Night* and *Parting at Morning* pair two related experiences. The pairing will also be found in the works of later poets, often in question-and-answer or "straight" and parodic versions. See also COLLECTIONS, UNIFIED;* PARTIMEN; POETIC CONTESTS; PREGUNTA; TENZONE.   F.J.W.; E.M.

COMPUTER POETRY. A c. is not only a calculator; it is also a data-processing machine, which can manipulate symbols of any kind. That is, it can be programmed to "generate" graphics (line drawings), musical compositions, and verbal strings such as sentences.

Simply described, a c. poem is one or more sentences generated by a specially designed c. program. One current poetic aesthetic would identify as poetic a sentence such as the following: "What did she put four whistles beside heated rugs for?" Although this sentence is syntactically well formed, it violates some of the semantic rules which govern the combination of words in Eng. Any sentence which is well formed but which is difficult to interpret, or any pair or sequence of sentences whose logical connection is obscure is likely to be interpreted as poetry: "The old horse staggers along the road. Newspapers are on sale in Wall Street. The sun will set again this evening." Although the average reader of prose would consider the sequence incoherent, the reader of modern poetry, conditioned to allusive symbolism, will seek or invent relationships to create coherence from three such random utterances. The reader of Shakespeare, Milton, or Pope, however, would not have responded in the same manner because the poetry of earlier eras was governed by a logic of discourse similar to prose. Evidently, c. poetry is possible only in the age of the c., which happens to be an age that demands more logic from prose than from poetry. For this reason, c. prose is extremely difficult to produce.

C. poems are basically of two kinds: formulary and derivative. Formulary poems consist of strings of generated sentences. A c.-generated sentence at the simplest level is produced by means of a formula (sentence rule) like the following:

SENTENCE = NOUN + VERB + ADVERB

Each word-class in the formula is like a bin containing a pile of cards on each of which a word is written (e.g., VERB = *scavenge, misplace, corrupt, vary, yawn*). When the program runs, it is as if someone had picked the top card from each successive bin and arranged the words so drawn into a sequence. If three bins each contained five cards, according to the rule given above the following sentences would be generated: 1. *Craters scavenge nervously*; 2. *Suits misplace wrongly*; 3. *Messiahs corrupt ably*; 4. *Sentiments vary never*; 5. *Graves yawn hungrily*. It will be noticed that the sentences produced are of quite different orders of regularity: 3 is well formed, 2 is ill formed (*misplace* requires an object), 4 is inverted (*never* normally comes before the verb), both 5 and 1 are well formed but violate semantic rules

-[925]-

(*yawn* and *scavenge* both require mammal or animate subjects) and 5 produces an acceptable metaphor, whereas 1 creates something like a nonsense metaphor. To generate more than five of the 625 possible sentences, it is necessary to return the cards to the bins after each use but without preserving the original order. Thus any word has the chance of being drawn during any pass and all combinations will eventually occur.

To create poetic objects by such a process, it is necessary only to devise a variety of sentence rules of greater complexity along with rules for combining them. In addition, it may be desirable to place such constraints on the output as length of line, meter, and rhyme—all of which are possible but difficult. Metrical constraints require the prior syllabification of each word and the location of its stress, if it is polysyllabic. To achieve rhyming, it is necessary to recode letter symbols into phonetic equivalents so that similar sounds rather than letter combinations may be matched, although the same can be achieved on a small scale by storing sets of rhyming words. This is easier in most other languages than in Eng.

The following stanzas result from a formulary generation:

The landscape of your clay mitigates me.
Coldly,
By your recognizable shape,
I am wronged.

The perspective of your frog feeds me.
Dimly,
By your wet love,
I am raked.

(M. Borroff)

These two stanzas, resulting from two sentence rules and one stanza rule (Sentence 1 = Nominal + Prepositional phrase + Verb + Personal Pronoun; Sentence 2 = Adverb + Prepositional phrase + Pronoun + Passive verb; Stanza = Sentence 1, Sentence 2) display the unexpectedness of juxtaposition characteristic of this process. At the same time, the repetitive structure may undermine the poetic effect by betraying the mechanical originator. The most sophisticated efforts provide variety of structure along with unusual juxtapositions.

Although documentation is lacking, it is probable that c. poetry was invented simultaneously at various locations during the 1950's by engineers occupied in language tasks (such as machine translation) who relished the opportunity of engaging in complex word play. The earliest examples appear in the pages of technical journals and represent purely sporadic efforts at entertainment. During the following decade, these developments came to the atten-

tion of poets, critics, and scholars interested in poetry with some access to c. techniques and vocabulary. They have been interested both in the possibilities offered by this new tool and by the disturbing implications of its use: its apparently superhuman inventiveness and the inability of the reader to distinguish with certainty between the machine and the human product. At the same time, a curiosity about the discoveries made possible by such activity led to derivative c. poetry.

The basic principle of derivative c. poetry is to take an existing poem or line and to alter it in some systematic way. Hamlet's "To be or not to be, that is the question" might become "To speak or not to speak, that is the riddle," "To know or not to know, that is the struggle," etc. . . . If the line were not so well known, the identification of the original might be uncertain. The following stanza is based on one from Dylan Thomas's *In the beginning* and is the result of marking all the nouns, verbs, and adjectives in the original, arranging them in alphabetical order, and replacing them in the poem. The result is a set of stanzas containing only Thomas's own words yet evidently not his work. Some of the collocations are as unusual as his own. Although the question of which is better need not arise, it is noteworthy that, in a number of experiments, college students have usually failed to identify the original except by chance:

In the beginning was the root, the rock
That from the solid star of the smile
Set all the substance of the sun;
And from the secret space of the signature
The smile spouted up, translating to the stamp
Three-pointed sign of spark and spark.

Dylan Thomas more than most poets strove for the exceptional collocation, even at times using mechanical means to achieve it. According to a friend, Thomas recorded likely short ordinary words in a notebook he carried with him (and called his "dictionary") and which he would consult at random when he was at a loss for a word or phrase in a poem (see bibliog.: Milic, "Possible Usefulness . . . ," p. 172). That it is difficult to distinguish between his own "rooting air," "secret oils," and "letters of the void" and the computer's "rooting imprint," "secret space," and "three-pointed sign of spark and spark" perhaps reveals less about c. poetry than about his. Because words have connections with each other in our minds, certain collocations are regularly inhibited even for poets, who are freer than the norm in this regard. The complete disregard of these inhibitions in c. poetry gives it both its fresh and its outrageous character.

Derivative c. poetry is a species of parody

when it is practiced on well-known lines. As such, it calls into question the inevitability of the original: "Spring is the nepenthean desert, scrambling . . . ," "April is the vacuous land, inverting. . . ." T. S. Eliot acknowledged that some of the word combinations in parts of *The Waste Land* were incomprehensible to him. This kind of substitution is the active principle of a program called ERATO (by L. T. Milic), which is based on a dozen opening lines by poets of the last hundred years, each of which is provided with vocabulary alternatives for key words. Cummings's "Darling! because my blood can sing" can take many forms if only the noun and verb are altered: "my mouth [life, soul, spirit, heart, hand] can [wing, play, skip, chime, leap, laugh, jump]." Each poem in the series results from the choice of a number of the original lines in random order with key words permuted, the number of lines in each poem and the degree of repetition being determined by random numbers. One example follows:

HEMS

(1) This is my news to the multitude:
(2) Turn to me in the chaos of the day.
(3) I have suspected what capricious
 maidens say,
(4) I strutted upon a loathsome place,
(5) Above the new hems of the sea.
(6) I stopped upon a loathsome station,
(7) Still here lying beneath the roof,
(8) Above the humid hems of the surf.

The lines by E. Dickinson (1), C. Rossetti (2), Yeats (3), S. Crane (4,6), Hart Crane (5,8), and MacLeish (7), altered as they have been, constitute a new whole still somehow related to the originals. The relation of line (1) to Emily Dickinson's "This is my letter to the world" is that of paraphrase, but this is not true of lines (4) and (6) to their original, Stephen Crane's "I stood upon a high place." The grammatical structure, especially that conveyed by the choice and arrangement of function words, signals the kinship between derivations and originals. But the new collocations are unique, even when they depart from the original in predictable ways, as lines (5) and (8) plainly connect with Hart Crane's "Above the fresh ruffles of the surf" in the imagery of the edge of the sea as a garment. ERATO evidently produces new poems, even if only in the legal sense that the publisher has no need to seek permission from the owners of the copyright of the originating poets. (It is noteworthy that existing copyright laws protect only sequences of words, not structures or ideas.)

Needless to say, only a fraction of the output of a c. poetry program is displayed as poetry. Editing is inevitable, especially in view of the mountains of paper produced by the machine. Normal poems, however, also undergo a weeding or pruning process, though c. poetry is not edited by a c., but by a person. Editing poetry by c. is not beyond possibility if the criteria for poetic acceptability could be explicitly stated. This would be not unlike defining "good" poetry.

The peculiar affinity of computers and poetry is based on the previously noted tendency of the modern reader to puzzle out a sense in the obscurest work that is called poetry. The achievement of c. poetry is in the direction of providing a more accurate notion of the workings of poetry, and especially of poetic language. No important c. poems have been produced and none are likely, though one poet (A. Turner) has found inspiration enough in the RETURNER poems, which were based on an original work of hers, to write further poems based on the derivations. The inevitable question on this subject concerns the identity of the author of c. poetry. It is unquestionable that the poet is not the assemblage of wires, transistors, and print trains called a c. The poet is the programmer, whose ideas of what poetry ought to be, whose choice of structures and of vocabulary determine to a considerable extent what the finished product will be. The poem is both the actual verse object and the program, the abstract structure of instructions and data, of which the actual output is only the incidental product. C. poetry is a new way of producing the poetry of our time. If it should ever develop its own aesthetic and break away from the mainstream, it will become a new kind of poetry.

J. A. Baudot, *La Machine à écrire* (Montreal, 1964); *Cybernetic Serendipity*, ed. J. Reichardt (1969); M. Krause and G. F. Schaudt, *C.-Lyrik* (1969); M. Borroff, "C. as Poet," *Yale Alumni Magazine*, 34 (1971); L. T. Milic, "The Possible Usefulness of Poetry Generation," in *The C. in Lit. and Linguistic Research* (1971), *Erato* (1971) and "The 'Returner' Poetry Program," ITL (Institute of Applied Linguistics), 11 (1971); A. Turner, " 'Returner' Re-turned," *Midwest Quarterly*, 13 (1972). L.T.M.

CONCRETE POETRY. A mode of graphic art, employing graphemes of a given language and selected typeface, used by themselves, in clusters, morphemes, words, or phrases, and so patterned that an evocative or witty reading of an otherwise minimal utterance may result. Alternatively, a mode of inscription poem—and hence vaguely linked to epigram—embodied totally and (imbedded irretrievably) in a unique typographical instance. In this aspect, c.p. is allied to its contemporary concept of *musique concrète*, in which the musical work—whether synthesized electronically, drawn directly (rather than recorded) on a cinema sound track, etc.—exists not as a text to be performed by an instrumental interpreter, but in a canonical and uninterpretable form. A self-conscious literary movement crystallized around the *Constellations* (1953) of the Swiss Eugen Gomringer. This volume contained minimal inscriptions of words in sanserif type, the words, perhaps significantly, being in various languages (an alienated *Sprachgefühl* being in some way characteristic of most c.p.). Gomringer claimed to be intensifying and authenticating linguistic experience by means of varied spatial presentations of words and other elements (a concern with reading as scanning that goes back to Mallarmé); and he and his followers have drawn elaborate and sometimes labored analogies between spatial, musical, and abstract conceptual patternings. An international movement, reminiscent in its many manifestos and group publications of futurist, surrealist and Dadaist (qq.v.) literary parties, has embraced practitioners in Brazil (the so-called Noigandres Group), France, England, the U.S., and other countries. The best known of these include Ian Hamilton Finlay (Great Britain), whose more recent inscriptions on wood or stone have fled the page entirely for the outdoors; Mary Ellen Solt (U.S.), a scholar of the movement; Augusto de Campos (Brazil), Helmut Heissenbüttel (Germany), Carlo Belloli (Italy), and Emmett Williams (U.S.).

Writers on the subject have distinguished among "type poems," "typewriter poems," "object poems," and so forth, and such sub- or related movements as *Spatialisme* or *Lettrisme*. A good rule of thumb for identifying a concrete poem might be to try and read the inscription aloud without describing the format (type style, graphic arrangement, etc.) as one might a print. A poem will yield up its heart to oral reading; if a concrete poem will not, it is because no picture will. Consider, for example, e.e. cummings' poem #1 from *95 Poems* (1958):

l(a

le
af
fa

ll

s)
one
l

iness

A *haiku*-like evaded simile is here so arranged that the vehicle is literally troped into the tenor (q.v.): "loneliness" *contains* the single leafall, its emblem (q.v.). This might have been done in a single horizontal line, but the vertical format graphically represents the dropping, enforces a slow scanning (and hence, reading), discovers hidden "ones" in the words (with graphic puns based on the identity of the 12th letter of the alphabet with the first arabic numeral in many typefaces), etc. Needless to say, this is more complex and sophisticated than many formal instances of c.p., and developed from cummings' lifelong experiments with format and its relation to poetic form.

There is some debate about how the many varieties of typographical experiment in modern European and Am. poetry constitute actual c.p. The shaped poems (arranged for the typewriter's one-em-per-character) of May Swenson's *Iconographs* (1970) and John Hollander's *Types of Shape* (1969) clearly belong to the tradition of the *technopaignia* or pattern poetry (q.v.) stretching from Hellenistic times through Apollinaire's *Calligrammes*;* in all these cases, the poems on being read aloud lose only the accompanying pictorial emblem made up by their shaping. More direct precursors of c.p. are: Mallarmé's *Un Coup de Dés*; Christian Morgenstern's *Fisches Nachtgesang* (composed of the metrical signs "∪" and "—", so arranged as to suggest a gaping fish-mouth); the experiments of Henri Barzun; the posterlike texts of the futurists and of such Dada poets as Richard Huelsenbeck; Valéry's inscriptions for the façade of the Trocadero, etc. Then, too, there was the entire typographic ambience of modernist art, including the aesthetics of the Bauhaus, and the specific work of such designers as Jan Tschichold (in his *Typographische Gestaltung*, 1935). A recent and brilliant development in the area of pictured inscription has been the great graphic artist Saul Steinberg's conceptual maps, wherein groups of related pronouns, auxiliary verbs in different tenses, etc. are diagrammed out in a painted and drawn landscape, in such a way as to depict and schematize their relationship.

ANTHOLOGIES: *Anthol. of C.P.*, ed. E. Williams (1967); *C.P.: A World View*, ed. M. E. Solt (2d ed., 1970); *Imaged Word & Worded Images*, ed. R. Kostelanetz (1970); *The Word as Image*, ed. B. Bowler (1970); *Kon-krete Poesie*, ed. E. Gomringer (1972).

HISTORY AND CRITICISM: A. Leide, *Dichtung als Spiel* (1963); M. Weaver, "C.P.," *Lugano Review*, nos. 5–6 (1966); E. Lucie-Smith, "C.P.," *Encounter*, 26 (1966); R. P. Draper, "C.P.," NLH, 2 (1971).   J.H.

CONFESSIONAL POETRY. See AMERICAN POETIC SCHOOLS AND TECHNIQUES (CONTEMPORARY).*

CONTEXTUALISM. The name now commonly used to describe certain critical doctrines of the new criticism and of later theoretical developments made in sympathy with new critical attitudes. The term c. can be a misleading description for these doctrines, inasmuch as there are ambiguities in it which permit it to be applied to various literary theories.

Critics have thought of themselves as contextualists who have maintained doctrines far from those of the new criticism. For example, it has always seemed appropriate to use this term to characterize those who see literature within its social context; that is, those who see a continuity of meaning flowing between the literary work and its surroundings. For such critics, all interpretation treats meaning as a function of a language that is an expression of its cultural moment. Thus the context which gives each word its meaning is seen as that total cultural-personal situation which defines and limits that word's function. Stephen C. Pepper himself termed such a theory "contextualist," though his model for it was Deweyan and instrumentalist, and not at all new critical. (See *Aesthetic Quality: A Contextualistic Theory of Beauty* [1938] and his later works.) Of course, the biographical critic could, similarly, see himself as a contextualist who treats each meaning within a continuity that flows among all the works of a poet as a function of his sensibility and vision, as these feed and frame those works. Or the archetypal critic could be a contextualist working from a continuity among all works of the human imagination seen as a single structure expressing a monomyth. And so the applications could go on to other methods of criticism. In each case the critic would see his interpretation controlled by, and referring to, an autonomous context made up of the continuities between the poem and the particular world of meanings of which it is a function. Indeed, we could claim that each critic's approach can be defined as we discover what constitutes the context of the work for him—which is to say, as we discover what sort of contextualist he is.

Clearly, what is today termed c. is more narrowly and exclusively defined. It refers to critics for whom the verbal structure of the properly literary work itself becomes the autonomous context that generates meanings which become self-referential. Such critics see the work as beginning with "old words" that become transformed into Mallarmé's "new word," a "total" word whose definition is provided by the internal relations of the work itself, and nowhere else. Unlike other contextualisms, which emphasize the continuity between the work and the extramural elements that determine its context, this c. begins with the need to establish the discontinuity of the work's intramural structure, its independence of all extrapoetic discourse. It assumes that the work, when it is constructed to function as a proper poem ought to, has provided such a structure.

C. has been used in this limited way since the term was taken from Murray Krieger's *The New Apologists for Poetry* (1956) and more broadly applied, as if to a school of critics (see the articles by Walter Sutton in the bibliog.). Krieger's use of the term was largely fashioned after Cleanth Brooks's sense of context in *The Well Wrought Urn* (1947). And Brooks, like Krieger's teacher, Eliseo Vivas, followed upon the work of the early I. A. Richards (from *Principles of Literary Criticism* [1924] to *The Philosophy of Rhetoric* [1936]). Richards distinguished poetry from science by employing the opposition between emotive and referential discourse. In science the verbal signs, with fixed and single meanings, were to reach out of their discourse to point to their objects; the efficacy of the discourse was tested by the accuracy of that pointing. In poetry such reference was to be blocked by the multiplication of ironic complexities which were meant to feed an emotion-seeking rather than a knowledge-seeking occasion. Brooks, shaking off what he saw as Richards' commitment to behavioral psychologism, extended his interest in complexity by conceiving of an objective poetic context, whose dramatic structure was controlled by cross-referential ironies and paradoxes: the referential-emotive dichotomy was transformed into a referential-contextual dichotomy. Poetry was defined by its capacity— through its juxtapositions of words—to generate new meanings out of old as it remade language into the unique structure composed of "the right words in the right order," as Eliot had put it.

Although Brooks had failed to do so, it had to be pointed out, by way of concession, that it was theoretically naive to claim that only poetry was contextual, that in nonpoetry signs "do not change under the pressure of context" but are "pure denotations" which "are defined in advance." Instead, all language must of course be seen as contextual; this is why there are so many possible kinds of c. But the post–new-critical contextualist still can claim that a poem is discontinuous with other forms of discourse, in that only its meaning is radically untranslatable, since that meaning is an immanent and hence inseparable feature of the poem's actual verbal configuration.

The contextualist has come a long way from Richards' subjectivism. By the time he came to *The Philosophy of Rhetoric*, Richards himself had turned toward the sort of c. which Brooks was to practice. But the earlier Richards had begun by limiting himself to one or another subjective experience of the poem, either from the poet's side or the reader's. He could not postulate a normative poetic context which was to be a transformation of the contexts active in either the poet's or the reader's experiences of the words prior to encountering them in the poem. For the contextualist, however, the reading of the poem must be more than the interaction of these two subjective contexts, the poet's and the reader's: the meanings of the poem cannot be reduced to either of them. The reader is rather seen to discover, in the interrelations among the features of the work, those transformations of recognizable elements which create a new and sovereign context—out there. He recognizes these elements from his own experiences in language prior to this poem, and from what his research leads him to discover about the poet's original range of contextual elements of meaning. But, as his habits of reading poems lead to his discovery of a context of transformed elements, the reader permits himself to be overcome by it, surrendering his own contexts to it. The poet has probably done much the same with his contexts while creating the poem as his completed object. In this manner—a manner consistent with Vivas' definition of aesthetic experience as "intransitive"—the context in the poem comes to be the controlling one, working to enclose the reader within his experience of the enrapturing aesthetic object. It must end by changing and enlarging his contexts (as they preexisted this poem) by imposing its own, thus making possible his education: it leads him out of himself by leading him into the fuller world of the poem.

As one would expect, such a critical doctrine must meet with wide opposition. Its claim

about the poem's discontinuity with other discourse, the completeness of its contextual system, rests on the postulation of an ideal object. Such an object may seem to many to lie beyond the incompleteness of our actual experiences of poems and the imperfections of poems themselves if they should seek to seal themselves off. In their more candid moments one senses in contextualists a tension between the completed object they must heuristically postulate and their doubts that they can experience it in that wholeness. They know how they must allow the language of poetic discourse to function, and they fear for the limits of their own capacities to sustain so self-sufficient a language experience. Those who deny the power of poems to function as c. requires (see Walter Sutton in the bibliog.) simply assert the continuity of our actual language experience without seeing any need to create an ideal, discontinuous object which can direct and educate that experience. On his side, the contextualist will not forfeit the poem's chance to transform language—and its capacity to transform us.

I. A. Richards, *Principles of Lit. Crit.* (1924) and *The Philosophy of Rhetoric* (1936); S. C. Pepper, *Aesthetic Quality: A Contextualistic Theory of Beauty* (1938) and "The Development of Contextualistic Aesthetics," *Antioch Rev.*, 28 (1968); E. Vivas, "A Definition of the Esthetic Experience," *Jour. of Philosophy*, 34 (1937) and "C. Reconsidered," JAAC, 18 (1959); C. Brooks, "The Heresy of Paraphrase," *The Well Wrought Urn* (1947); M. Krieger, *The New Apologists for Poetry* (1956) and *The Play and Place of Crit.* (1967); W. Sutton, "The Contextualist Dilemma—or Fallacy?" JAAC, 17 (1958) and "Contextualist Theory and Crit. as a Social Act," JAAC, 19 (1961).   M.K.

D

DIONYSIAN. See APOLLONIAN-DIONYSIAN.

E

ESEMPLASTIC. Coleridge (*Biographia Literaria*, ch. 10) coined the word ("to shape into one") "because, having to convey a new sense,

I thought that a new term would both aid the recollection of my meaning, and prevent its being confounded with the usual import of the word, imagination." *Imaginatio*, that is, connoted passive reception of image-impressions, and Coleridge wished to emphasize active creativity. Considering, as he did, the imagination to be "a repetition in the finite mind of the eternal act of creation in the infinite I AM" (ibid., ch. 13), he sought for metaphors to express this act. Among these the shaping or plastic power is perhaps most characteristic, and unity ("to shape into one") is the end that creation seeks. Thus in a famous illustration of imaginative power from Shakespeare's *Venus and Adonis* the poet achieves unity-in-variety, or "the liveliest image of succession

with the feeling of simultaneousness" (ibid., ch. 15). In his early poem *The Eolian Harp* Coleridge describes organic unity-in-variety and the plastic power that achieves it:

And what if all of animated nature
Be but organic Harps diversely fram'd,
That tremble into thought, as o'er them sweeps
Plastic and vast, one intellectual breeze,
At once the Soul of each, and God of all?

S. T. Coleridge, *Biographia Literaria*, ed. J. Shawcross (2 v., 1907); B. Willey, *Nineteenth Century Studies* (1949, pp. 13ff). R.H.F.

F

FILID (pl. *fili*). See IRISH POETRY. Early period.

FORMALISM, RUSSIAN. See RUSSIAN FORMALISM.

G

GENERATIVE METRICS is a term used to refer to several forms of metrical theory or linguistic prosody that emerged in the middle 1960's and early 1970's as a kind of off-shoot or by-product of transformational generative linguistic theory. (See LINGUISTICS AND POETICS, to which this entry may be regarded as a supplement. See also METER and PROSODY.) The common aim of these various theories was an attempt to state descriptive "rules" of meter which would "account for" what is felt to be the "metricality" (cf. "grammaticality" in linguistic theory) of the great majority of metered lines of verse in a language, and which would include and explain those phenomena which in earlier theories had to be listed as unexplained "exceptions." Thus, for example, most varieties of g.m. account automatically for the phenomenon of initial trochees in Eng. iambic verse, whereas this phenomenon remains unexplained (i.e., must be listed as an "exception") in a "foot theory" which says that a line of iambic verse is a sequence of so many iambic feet, each of which consists of two syllables, the second of which is more accented than the first. The foot theory then has to recognize that in fact there are many (intuitively metrical) iambic lines that contain trochees, but it has no explanation why these trochees occur

more often than not at the beginning of lines.

Thus it may be correct to regard g.m. as a more rigorous form of metrical theory than any that had been attempted before, just as it might be correct to say that transformational-generative linguistic theory was a more rigorous attempt to account for grammatical utterances in a language, and to distinguish between grammatical and ungrammatical ones. Both employ (and in a sense, are made possible by) the formalism of some aspects of modern mathematics. The parallelism may in some sense be extended to the set of base rules and transformations which in a generative grammar may be thought of as "generating" utterances; the metrical rules may be thought of as "generating" metrical lines of poetry. The rules of a generative grammar assign a "structural description" to a sentence; the rules of a generative metric do the same for a line of verse. The rules of the grammar are at least partially ordered; the metrical rules, being in essence rules which are "plugged in" or inserted after some contiguous bank of phonological rules in the grammar, adhere also to the ordering principle. Finally, those who have done the initial explorations in g.m. are linguists brought up in, or working in, the transformational-generative tradition.

The immediate source of g.m. was a study of Chaucer's meter by Morris Halle and Samuel Jay Keyser in 1966. Here a theory of meter was advanced (specifically, a theory of iambic pentameter) which held that a verse line should be conceived of essentially as a sequence of positions—10, in the case of iambic pentameter—where the odd positions were characterized as Weak, and the even positions as Strong. A *stress maximum* may not occur in a weak position. The *stress maximum* is defined as a linguistically assigned stress greater than that found on either adjacent syllable without intervening juncture. Conditions for occupancy of a position by more than one syllable (i.e., phenomena such as synaeresis, synaloepha, qq.v.) are also provided, as is the condition for zero occupancy (the beheaded line; see ACEPHALOUS).

The striking features of the Halle-Keyser system were the concept of the *stress maximum* and the conception of the line as a sequence of *positions* (not, that is, as a collection of feet). Such a theory would accept as metrical various configurations of stresses and syllabic disposition which one finds in well-known lines of iambic pentameter (e.g., "Sílent, upon a péak in Dárien," where there are only three linguistically assigned stresses, in positions 1, 6, and 8), while rejecting as unmetrical such a line as "How many bards gild the lápses of time," with its *stress maximum* in position 7. It is important to note that the concept of stress is not a phonetic one, but a phonological one, and the theory is therefore in no direct sense dependent upon performance. Note also that the phrase "linguistically assigned" implies a system of grammar, a set of rules, that does assign stress to certain syllables of words, and to certain syllables within phrases, and that "greater than" (that found on adjacent syllables) implies that a final utterance will exhibit various stress levels, and that it is *relativity* of stress level that counts. To illustrate the foregoing sentences, a reader might place actual (i.e., phonetic) stress on the second syllable of the line "Whenever Richard Cory went down town," but a particular phonological system may not assign stress to adverbs of the type represented by "whenever" and this syllable would therefore not constitute a stress maximum, no matter how it is read.

As the original theory underwent elaboration, chiefly at the hands of those attempting to use it for stylistic analysis, certain problems presented themselves. Central among these was the discovery of a good many intuitively metrical lines where stress maxima did occur in odd position, by virtue of certain phrasal stress rules, notably the rule that assigns greater stress to the rightmost member within a syntactic unit (called by Chomsky and Halle the "Nuclear Stress Rule"). Thus in "So let the blue lump poise between my knees," greater linguistically assigned stress is found on "lump" than on either "blue" or "poise," which would establish a stress maximum in position 5. Accordingly, it was necessary either to revise the metrical theory, or to revise the phonological component of the grammar to account for such deviant stress patterns. Halle and Keyser chose the first course, and weakened the theory so that the notion of relative stress (though introduced by the phonological component of the grammar) does not figure in the metrical rules; in short, the notion "greater than" is eliminated, and *stress maximum* is redefined as major word stress occurring between two unstressed syllables. Beaver, who first pointed out the problem, chose the second course, and proposed that forms of rhythm-adjustment rules, much as his "stress exchange rule," should be introduced directly into the phonological component of the grammar.

Applications of g.m. to other meters than iambic pentameter have not received very full investigation. It would appear that necessary adaptations of the theory would be minor technical ones, such as that Weak and Strong would be assigned to even and odd in trochaic structures, etc. But difficulties do arise, and some of Hascall's work on triple meters suggests that the matter may not be quite that simple. As for older metrical forms, Keyser advanced a theory of Old Eng. prosody in a 1969 study in CE.

Acquaintance with the theory of g.m. spread rather quickly, and interesting work was done by Jacqueline Guéron in France (on Eng. nursery rhymes), and by Walter Bernhart in Germany. Applications to stylistics was an obvious development, and such works as those by Freeman, Beaver, and others witness to the vitality of the g.m. approach.

For historical purposes, it should be noted that adumbrations of g.m. appear in earlier metricists. Otto Jesperson had in 1903 theorized that the "foot" concept was untenable, and had offered a systematic explanation of the phenomenon of reversed initial feet in iambic meters. The notion of the verse line as a sequence of *positions* (rather than a sequence of feet) appeared over two centuries ago in Edward Bysshe, *The Art of Poetry* (1737).

Another system of metrics developing about the same time as that evolved by Halle, Keyser, Beaver, and others meets the general definition given earlier of g.m., and therefore will be touched upon briefly here, even though in some respects it differs markedly from the approach already described. Karl Magnuson and Frank Ryder, working originally in German poetry, advanced a metrical system which might be called a "Distinctive Feature" theory.

-[932]-

Magnuson and Ryder theorize that a syllable may be considered as a bundle of four features which figure in the realization of more and less metrical lines: [±Strong], [±Weak], [±Word Onset], and [±Pre-Strong]. A syllable is [+Strong] if it receives lexical stress assignment, or if it is the accented syllable of a non-lexical polysyllabic. A syllable is [+Word Onset] just in case it begins a word. A syllable is [+Pre-Strong] if it occurs anywhere in a word before a [+Strong] syllable. The feature [+Weak] is made necessary by the different metrical behavior in German of suffixes based on —i— and —u— (—isch, —ung, etc.) from those based on —a— and —ei— (—sam, —heit, etc.). The former are designated [+Weak], the latter [—Weak]. This feature is carried over into English in a somewhat different manner: [+Weak] is assigned to monosyllabic nonlexical words, all unstressed syllables of polysyllabics, and, in addition, to stressed syllables of non-lexical polysyllabics (e.g., the first syllable in *many* will be both [+Strong] and [+Weak]).

Now the central assumption of the Magnuson-Ryder metric is that there exists an "Expectation Matrix," an ideal combination of features for an even (strong) metrical position and an ideal combination, or syllable type for an odd (or weak) metrical position:

	Even	Odd
WO (Word Onset)	+	—
WK (Weak)	—	+
ST (Strong)	+	—
PS (Pre-Strong)	—	+

Since the expectation matrix can never be fulfilled completely, it follows that one must assume all poetry to be unmetrical in some degree, and the task of prosody is to find the constraints upon the conditions under which a feature may occur in a nonaffirming relation to the matrix. These constraints are the Base Rules. The rules deal with relations between metrical slots: between even-odd, odd-even, even-even, and odd-odd. It is found that the even-odd relationship is "more highly governed" than any other—constraints must always be placed on occurrences in this relationship but not necessarily in the other relationships. The discovery of the rules is the goal of this metric, for within these will be found, if any, all the discriminating features of degrees of metricality that we may expect in an author, a period, or whatever provides the corpus. The prosodist tabulates all the sequences of occurring and nonoccurring syllable types in the corpus under investigation, and then deduces the rules from this data.

According to Frank Ryder, the distinctive feature metric has historical origins as far back as Philip von Zesen, a 17th-c. German poet. An especially interesting aspect of the theory, as elaborated by Magnuson and Ryder, is that the use of the feature *Word Onset* amounts to the claim—unique in current Eng. prosody, so far as this writer knows—that placement of word boundary is an essential element in Eng. versification.

M. Halle and S. J. Keyser, "Chaucer and the Study of Prosody," CE, 28 (1966), "Illustration and Defense of a Theory of the Iambic Pentameter," CE, 33 (1971), *Eng. Stress. Its Form, Its Growth, and Its Role in Verse* (1971); J. C. Beaver, "A Grammar of Prosody," CE, 29 (1968), "Contrastive Stress and Metered Verse," *Language and Style*, 2 (1969), "The Rules of Stress in Eng. Verse," *Language*, 47 (1971), "Current Metrical Issues," CE, 33 (1971), review of Halle and Keyser, *Eng. Stress*, in *Language Sciences*, 18 (1971); D. C. Freeman, "On the Primes of Metrical Style," *Language and Style*, 1 (1968), "Metrical Position Constituency and G.M.," *Language and Style*, 2 (1969); D. Hascall, "Some Contributions to the Halle-Keyser Theory of Prosody," CE, 30 (1969); K. Magnuson and F. Ryder, "The Study of Eng. Prosody: An Alternative Proposal," CE, 31 (1970), "Second Thoughts on Eng. Prosody," CE, 33 (1971); J. Maling, "Sentence Stress in Old. Eng.," *Linguistic Inquiry*, 2 (1971); J. Roubaud, "Mètre et vers: Deux applications de la métrique générative de Halle-Keyser," *Poétique, revue de théorie et d'analyse littéraires*, 7 (1971); "G.M.," special issue of *Poetics*, no. 11 (1974; articles by J. C. Beaver, A. W. Bernhart, J. Guéron, D. L. Hascall, W. Klein, K. Magnuson). J.C.B.

GENERIC RHYME. See CELTIC PROSODY.

GENEVA SCHOOL, THE. The G.S. of literary criticism brings together a group of critics with varying ties to Geneva. They are united by friendship and by a common vision of literature as a network of existential expressions combining in the work to delineate the figure of an individual artistic consciousness. Marcel Raymond and Albert Béguin, the earliest members of the school, and Jean Starobinski and Jean Rousset are all directly associated with the University of Geneva; Georges Poulet, born a Belgian, taught in Switzerland for many years and was directly influenced by Raymond; Jean-Pierre Richard, a Frenchman, and J. Hillis Miller, an American, both recognize Poulet's influence on their own work. This G.S. should not be confused with an earlier G.S. of linguistic theory associated with Ferdinand de Saussure, Charles Bally, and Albert Sechehaye. Although the second G.S. is aware of and has commented on Saussure's work, the roots of their literary criticism lie not in structural linguistics but in existential and phenomenological theory

(Husserl, Jaspers, and Bachelard), in the romantic tradition, in a certain academic historicism (A. O. Lovejoy), and in Bergson's analyses of perception of time.

While the Geneva critics develop highly individual critiques, they hold basically to the same philosophy of artistic creation. Reacting against "objective" views of a work (whether that of continental scholarship or Am. new criticism), they still rely exclusively on the written text as evidence. The poem must not be seen as an object, however; it is the structural record of an individual human consciousness. The author cannot be reached as an historical being, but the critic can analyze the tracery of interlocking terms left in the work, and deduce from there a pattern of individual consciousness which is no less human for being artistically created. There are many methods for arriving at this pattern of consciousness: words indicating perception of space and time can be extrapolated and juxtaposed; recurrent types of experience can be compared and followed through the text; these perceptions and experiences themselves can be seen from a more subjective (Cartesian) point of view or in an object-centered vision. Since the Geneva critics believe that literature expresses an author's attempt to formulate and cope with his experience, they often link these patterns of consciousness with larger metaphysical problems: with an awareness of true presence (Poulet), of divinity (Béguin) or an immanent reality (Miller), and of the precarious viability of expressive forms themselves (Starobinski, Miller, Rousset). A basic metaphor is that of an inner mental space, an initial void from which consciousness emerges to plot the characteristic architecture of its experience.

The Geneva critics see literature as a structure of consciousness, and therefore consider the proper poetic response an act of sympathetic reading. The reader tries to efface his own presuppositions, and awaits a "signal" from the work that will direct him to penetrate its structure from a given angle. Evidently, the poem as consciousness surpasses any one attempt to plot its coordinates; each reader finds his own way into the work, and uses each time a slightly different avenue of penetration. Since the properly literary act is a meeting of minds, there can be no judgment or evaluation according to exterior criteria be they aesthetic, psychological, sociological, or political. Again, since the critic aims at communicating with an embodied textual consciousness, he need not limit himself to separate works. Georges Poulet and Jean-Pierre Richard prefer to draw upon an author's complete works to establish his *cogito*, while Rousset and Miller treat individual works as well. The Geneva critics have been criticized for not keeping to the objective

structures of separate texts, and for going beyond acceptable boundaries of linguistic interpretation. It is true that their analysis of the individual creative imagination can apply also to other media, and Starobinski and Rousset have written on artistic and architectural form. Only Miller regularly equates forms of perception with structures of syntax. Miller's example shows that Geneva criticism can apply to linguistic structures, and that the real distinction lies not here but in the school's assumption of an individual consciousness available in an authentically personal expression. Those who see literature as an objective pattern of greater or lesser beauty, or as an impersonal construction of language determined by transindividual coordinates, will not agree with Geneva criticism.

There is a surprising variety of methods inside the G.S. Marcel Raymond and Albert Béguin retain a traditional historical framework for their analyses of spiritual careers in Fr. symbolist and German romantic poetry. Béguin later limited his sympathetic readings to a decreasing circle of Catholic authors. Georges Poulet, the first to propose a complete methodological approach and the main figure of the modern G.S., plots with subtlety and encyclopedic knowledge the temporal and spatial coordinates of the developing creative consciousness in an author's work. Poulet envisages histories of artistic consciousness, in which he would include the works of gifted critics. In contrast with Poulet's Cartesian orientation, and like Gaston Bachelard, Jean-Pierre Richard stresses the pattern of metamorphosed objects appearing in the text's mental universe. Jean Starobinski, trained in medicine as well as in literature, is a versatile critic who describes processes of the creative imagination in art, literature, and illness. His colleague Jean Rousset is especially interested in transformations of style, and the structures of consciousness he perceives in a work are more formal and less personal than those of the other European Geneva critics. Hillis Miller blends the objective traditions of Am. new criticism with the Geneva interest in spiritual careers; like Poulet and Starobinski, Miller in his later work embarks on the criticism of criticism. Poulet, Starobinski, Rousset, and Miller locate their individual critiques inside the framework of a changing history of consciousness.

Later developments in the G.S. point to an increasing awareness of other modes of criticism, and of the work's relationship to the society from which it springs. Unchanging, however, is the group's primary attachment to patterns of individual consciousness, and to the concept of literature as an intersubjective experience fully realized only in the act of reading.

M. Raymond, *De Baudelaire au surréalisme* (1933), *Génies de France* (1942), *Senancour, sensations et révélations* (1965); A. Béguin, *L'Ame romantique et le rêve* (1937), *Balzac visionnaire* (1946), *Pascal par lui-même* (1952); G. Poulet, *Etudes sur le temps humain I-IV* (1949–1968), *L'Espace proustien* (1963), *La Conscience critique* (1971); J. Rousset, *La Littérature de l'âge baroque en France* (1953), *Forme et signification* (1962), *L'Intérieur et l'extérieur* (1968); J.-P. Richard, *Poésie et profondeur* (1955), *L'Univers imaginaire de Mallarmé*

(1961), *Onze Etudes sur la poésie moderne* (1964), *Etudes sur le romantisme* (1970); J. Starobinski, *Jean-Jacques Rousseau, la transparence et l'obstacle* (1957, enl. ed., 1971), *L'Oeil vivant I-II* (1961, 1970), *L'Invention de la liberté* (1964); J. H. Miller, *Charles Dickens, The World of His Novels* (1958), *Poets of Reality* (1965), *The Form of Victorian Fiction* (1968), *Thomas Hardy, Distance and Desire* (1970); S. N. Lawall, *Critics of Consciousness: The Existential Structures of Lit.* (1968); J. H. Miller, "The Geneva School," *Modern Fr. Crit.*, ed. J. K. Simon (1972).   S.N.L.

H

HARLEM RENAISSANCE. Extending roughly from the end of World War I to the onset of the Depression, the literary movement known as the H.R. represented a startling burst of creativity among Am. black writers. Most of the principal figures of the movement—Claude McKay, Jean Toomer, Langston Hughes, and Countee Cullen—were poets, and it was in the verse of the H.R. that the "New Negro" most emphatically announced his arrival. The spirit of this poetry is perhaps best exemplified in Hughes's 1926 declaration that the younger black writers "now intend to express our individual dark-skinned selves without fear or shame."

As its name indicates, the movement was centered in New York's Harlem, swollen by the Great Migration of southern blacks into a "Negro capital," a cultural hub which attracted the young artists and intellectuals who made the Renaissance. A new stage in Am. black consciousness was evident. The experience of the war rendered many blacks less willing than ever to tolerate white racism, and the violence of postwar anti-black feeling only hardened this resolve. Moral leadership had passed from Booker T. Washington to W.E.B. DuBois, and the aims of black awareness were furthered by such organizations as the NAACP, the National Urban League, and the Association for the Study of Negro Life and History. The Universal Negro Improvement Association, founded by Marcus Garvey "to promote the spirit of race pride and love," was short-lived but very influential on the writings of the H.R.

One result of the new consciousness was a great increase in publishing opportunities for black writers. Some of the work of the H.R. writers appeared in recently launched black periodicals—e.g., the NAACP's *Crisis* (1910) and the Urban League's *Opportunity* (1923). Such established publishing houses as Knopf and Harper's recognized that there was a growing white audience for works about black life (especially when presented as the embodiment of the uninhibited sensibility popularized by the Jazz Age). Moreover, the new movements in Am. poetry associated with *Poetry* magazine—free verse, imagism (qq.v.), and other breaks with tradition—provided a hospitable environment for much new black writing.

The poetry of the H.R. was different in both manner and matter from the tradition of Am. black verse that had extended from Phillis Wheatley to Paul Laurence Dunbar. Most of the H.R. poets, with the major exception of Countee Cullen, made use of a markedly modernistic style: they not only took advantage of the latest formal innovations in verse, but also mined their own resources of blues and jazz, folk speech, and jive talk. The content of this poetry—stressing black pride and bold protests of racism and social injustice—also represented a new emphasis. Claude McKay's sonnet *If We Must Die*, published during the race riots of the Red Summer of 1919, crystallized the new consciousness in its final couplet: "Like men we'll face the murderous, cowardly pack,/ Pressed to the wall, dying, but fighting back!" The H.R. poets declared a kinship with blacks world-wide, sometimes expressing nostalgia for the lost African past, as in Cullen's *Heritage*. But they also presented realistic pictures of Am. black life from cane fields to Pullman porters' closets to Harlem cabarets, and they affirmed and celebrated their Am. folk tradition. For example, James Weldon Johnson, who had earlier praised the "black and unknown bards" who created the spirituals (q.v.), now turned the folk art of the black sermon into the literary art of his *God's Trombones* (1927).

Johnson—like DuBois, William Stanley Braithwaite, and, above all, Alain Leroy Locke —served as critic and mentor for many of the H.R. poets, and his 1922 anthology, *The Book of Am. Negro Poetry*, helped to introduce one of the movement's most important figures: Claude McKay (1890–1948). McKay was born in Jamaica and had already published dialect poetry there before coming to the United States. *Spring in New Hampshire* (1920) and *Harlem Shadows* (1922) present his major themes of militant protest and earthy lyricism. Another of the movement's major figures, Jean Toomer (1894–1967), published an extraordinary and influential collection of poetry and poetic prose in *Cane* (1923). But Toomer did not want to be labeled a "Negro" poet, and his subsequent (and somewhat disappointing) work stands apart from the H.R. By his own request, none of his poetry appeared in the 1931 edition of Johnson's anthology.

Langston Hughes (1902–67), who outlasted the Renaissance to become the "poet laureate" of black America, demonstrates a feeling for folk expression, folk speech, and folk music in *The Weary Blues* (1926) and *Fine Clothes to the Jew* (1927), and was especially successful in his poetic adaptations of jazz and blues. On the other hand, Countee Cullen (1903–46) wrote a much more personal and conventional kind of poetry, represented in *Color* (1925), *Copper Sun* (1927), and *The Black Christ* (1929). Cullen's devotion to Victorian models of scansion and diction won him great respect among the major Am. critics of the 1920's, but rendered his style atypical of the H.R.

Many lesser-known poets also contributed to the sense of achievement of the H.R. Arna Bontemps, whose H.R. poems were not collected in a volume, displayed a profound philosophical and historical vision in *Nocturne at Bethesda*. Waring Cuney and Frank Horne presented in their work intensely personal perceptions of the black experience. And Sterling Brown, in even purer accents than Hughes, speaks with the voice of the folk Negro in such poems as *Southern Road* and *Long Gone*.

Among the women poets of the H.R., Jessie Fauset and Georgia Douglas Johnson occupied themselves primarily with issues of love and the loss of love, and the concerns of the female sensibility. Anne Spencer presented more tough-minded, less subjectively romantic versions of these same themes. By contrast, Gwendolyn Bennett and Helene Johnson eschewed a specifically feminine point of view in poems imbued with black pride.

There can be no question that the H.R. was a poetic success. The distance marked by black poets in the 1920's may be measured by the two editions of Johnson's *The Book of Am. Negro Poetry*. Between the two editions of 1922 and 1931 there was a great burgeoning of talent: among the poets who emerged during this interval, and whose work appears in the later edition, are Cullen, Hughes, Bontemps, Horne, Cuney, and Helene Johnson. Not until the 1960's was there to be so much poetic activity and achievement by Am. black writers (see BLACK POETRY, RECENT).

Despite the charges which have been leveled at the H.R.—superficiality, lack of concern for ordinary folk and real issues, and failure to realize the potential for long-term cultural and artistic development of black people—it represents a coming of age for black Am. poetry. The H.R. liberated black expression and produced some classic figures and an enduring body of poetry. Almost all of what has come after builds on the new consciousness and literary foundations established by these poets of the H.R.

A. Gayle, Jr., "The H.R.: Toward a Black Aesthetic," *Midcontinent Am. Studies Journal*, 11 (1970); ["The H.R. Issue,"] *Black World*, 19 (1970); N. I. Huggins, The *H.R.* (1971); *The H.R. Remembered*, ed. A. Bontemps (1972); "Intro." to *Afro-Am. Writing* (part 3), ed. R. A. Long and E. Collier, II (1972); *Modern Black Poets: A Collection of Crit. Essays*, ed. D. B. Gibson (1973); J. Wagner, *Black Poets of the U.S.: From Paul Laurence Dunbar to Langston Hughes*, tr. K. Douglas (1973).

R.A.L.; G.T.H.

HAUSA POETRY. For the Hausa people of West Africa an essential feature of poetry (*wāk'a*, poem, song) is that it should have a tune. Prosodic features, such as quantitative meter, rhyme, and either couplet or 5-line stanza form, distinguish poetry from other forms of *wāk'a*, e.g., the songs of Mamman Shata, where normally they do not occur. Drumming is normal for popular song, but not for the sung or chanted poetry with religious and social themes.

Apart from folksong, the main pre-Islamic source for H.p. is praise-singing (*kirāri*), but the Islamic *jihād* (holy war) of Sheikh Usumanu dan Fodio in the early 19th c. introduced new themes and prosodic forms. To encourage the spread of his reforming message, the Sheikh experimented with the vernacular instead of Arabic. He and his children and successors first used their native Fula, and, later and increasingly, H. in order that their Islamic teaching should reach the common people. Of the sixteen classical Arabic meters, H. uses about twelve, including all of the common ones. H. poets are not usually conversant with the analytic terminology of Arabic prosody, but they have adhered fairly strictly to the patterns.

Thus, in his comic poem about a *mālam's* (scholar) experience with a bicycle, Aliyu Na Mangi, a popular modern poet, uses a *wāfir* (abundant) trimeter catalectic, e.g.,

∪ _ ∪ ∪ _|∪ _ _ ∪ _|∪ _ _
zama zamaninsu ne aka zo da faifa
∪ _ _ _|∪ _ _ _|∪ _ ∪ ∪
ku'di ba masu nauyaya aljihu ba

because in their day paper money was introduced not heavy for the pocket.

But a small number of purely H. deviations are often allowed so long as they do not obscure the fundamental rhythm.

The main themes of the poetry of Sheikh Usumanu and his immediate successors were: praise of the Prophet, correct Muslim doctrine, threats of hellfire and promises of Paradise, and Islamic law. Legitimization of the Fulani political order established by the *jihād* was also an important part of the message, but sometimes a H. poet like Muhammadu Birnin Gwari (ca. 1880) would write verse tò express the opinions of H. subjects rather than those of the Fulani rulers. After the British occupation in 1903, the resentment felt against the new rulers appeared, somewhat disguised, in poetry, as, for example, in that of Aliyu dan Sidi, Emir of Zaria, who was deposed by the British in 1920. These poems, and many by less famous poets, survive in manuscripts written in *ajami* (Arabic script). One, the *Bagauda*, which contains an account of the pre-Islamic rulers of Kano and which has been attributed to Shehu Na Salga, has been translated and edited by M. Hiskett (see bibliog.). However, with the slow spread of Western education and ideas and the emergence of a new elite, first from Katsina College and later from many new schools, themes have multiplied and developed, while poetic form has remained largely unchanged. H. poets received impetus especially from the "introduction of politics" in the years between 1945 and Independence (1960) and, more recently, from the Civil War. Since the 1930's, too, poetry, previously conveyed through the memories of men or in *ajami*, has appeared more and more in roman script and in print, either in the newspaper *Gaskiya Ta Fi Kwabo* (began 1939) or in booklets emanating from the publishing center of Zaria. It is through these media and, increasingly, the radio that modern H. poets—such as Aliyu Na Mangi, Mu'azu Ha'deja, Sa'ad Zungur, Mudi Sipikin, Ak'ilu Aliyu, Salihu Kontagora, Na'ibi Wali, and many others —are becoming better known.

Modern poets have added contemporary themes, both social and political, of a communal nature. The personal, lyric note is rare, and when it occurs it is seldom passed on.

However, in praise and satire the poet's feelings often shine through, as in Na Mangi's *Imfiraji* (Comfort), a long poem with many hundreds of verses. Where he is praising the Prophet, he sometimes sounds a note of mysticism, love, and longing.

There is little, if any, written criticism of H.p. A good H. poet has something for all his listeners: images and tune for the less sophisticated, and, for the more sophisticated, skilled use of the language and close adherence to the metrical pattern.

COLLECTIONS: *Wak'ok'in Hausa* (1956; H. poems by various poets); *Wak'ar Bagauda ta Kano* ("The Kano Poem about Bagauda," 1969); *Gangar Wa'azu* ("Drum of Homily," 1969); *Wak'ok'in* ["Poems of"] *Mu'azu Ha'deja* (1970); *Wak'ok'in* ["Poems of"] *Sa'adu Zungur* (1971); Aliyu Na Mangi, *Wak'ok'in Imfiraji* ("Songs of Comfort," 1972); Salihu Kontagora, *Kimiyya da Fasaha* ("Science and Wit," 1972).

HISTORY AND CRITICISM: J. H. Greenberg, "H. Verse Prosody," *Jour. Am. Oriental Studies*, 69 (1949); M. Hiskett, "The 'Song of Bagauda': A Hausa King List and Homily in Verse," *Bulletin of the School of Oriental and African Studies*, 27 (1964), 28 (1965) and "H. Islamic Verse: Its Sources and Development prior to 1920" (unpubl. Ph.D. diss., Univ. of London, 1969); J. N. Paden, "Kano H. Poetry," *Kano Studies*, 1 (1965); D. W. Arnott, "The Song of the Rains," *Afr. Language Studies*, 9 (1968); A. N. Skinner, "A. H. Poet in Lighter Vein," *Afr. Language Review*, 8 (1969).   A.N.S.

HERMENEUTICS. See INTERPRETATION;* HISTORICISM.*

HISTORICISM. Although the term h. (sometimes spelled "historism") has long been known to philosophers of history, it has only recently been widely employed by aestheticians in an effort to develop a theory of poetic interpretation. Its general usage by historiographers, however, is often vague and uninformative for poetry criticism. Benedetto Croce (*History as the Story of Liberty*, 1941) defines h. broadly as the philosophy or science of history. Friedrich Meinecke (*Die Entstehung des Historismus*, 1936) applies the term to the awakening historical consciousness which developed out of the 19th-c. rebellion against 18th-c. rationalism and empiricism, that is, as a description of a *Weltanschauung*. Ernst Troeltsch (*Der Historismus und seine Probleme*, 1922) sees h. as a synonym for intellectual history or *Geistesgeschichte*. Similarly, poetry critics have employed the term loosely to indicate little more than the necessity of reading any poetic text more or less as an historical document. H. is confused, therefore, with "literary history" or the various types of "historical criticism" which resemble traditional antiquarian or scholarly pursuits (see CRITICISM. TYPES). The meaning of the poem is determined by its sociohistorical milieu, and value judgments are ignored or dismissed as mere subjective responses. As a result, this approach falls into what René Wellek calls a "crippling relativism and an anarchy of values" (*The History of Modern Criticism*, III, xiii). The poem can mean only what it meant to the author and his contemporary audience and can express values which are valid only for the author's world; any other meanings and values are imposed upon it by the critic.

Partly as a result of this misuse, h. has also been the focal point of bitter condemnation by historians and critics alike, and these attacks reflect the inherent contradictions in the term. Karl Popper argues that h. leads to a general theory of society as "closed"; h., he claims, establishes a universal historical point of view through which the meaning and value of any particular event (or poetic text) is determined (Wesley Morris, *Toward a New H.*, 1972, p. 5). Conversely, J. Hillis Miller states that h. eventuates in a "subjectivist" philosophy and is characterized by the absence of "any one point of view" (*The Disappearance of God*, 1965, pp. 10, 107). The first emphasizes the influence of Hegelian Idealism on h. and the second focuses on the origins of an h. attitude in 19th-c. aestheticism. To limit h. to either of these extremes, however, is inaccurate. Moreover, it is on the basis of these contradictions that a viable "new" h. has recently emerged in poetic theory, and this new critical school traces its origins through h. theory to the very source of these conflicting impulses in romantic poetics (see ROMANTICISM). (For arguments on much earlier sources for h. see Meinecke; and George Huppert, "The Renaissance Background of H.," *History and Theory*, 5 [1966], 48–60.)

Within these general definitions one can distinguish four major types of traditional h., three of which develop various aspects of the old "historical criticism." The broadest type may be labeled "metaphysical," for it derives principally from Hegelian Idealism and focuses on the transcendental continuity of historical development which allows the critic of poetry to determine the meaning of any poem by merely locating its position in the grand historical scheme. On one level this leads to an historical relativism of the type described by Wellek, but its most damning weakness for poetic theory is that it shifts the critic's attention away from the particular details of the work toward the universal meanings and values of the transcendent scheme which are reflected in that work. The second type, "naturalistic" (sometimes "positivistic" or "scientific") h.,

stands directly opposed to the transcendental Idealism of metaphysical h. As a methodology of poetic interpretation it forces the critic to treat the poetic text as a peculiar (and often unreliable) kind of sociological document, as a transparent key to contemporary social meanings and values. In varying degrees Sainte-Beuve, Taine, and Brunetière were the leading exponents of this theory which derived much support from 19th-c. positivism. A third type of h., originated by Michelet, Comte, Goethe, and Brandes, and adopted by a substantial portion of early 20th-c. Am. critics, can best be called "nationalistic." Like metaphysical h., nationalistic h. is characterized by the effort to place the individual poem in a general sociohistorical scheme, but the boundaries of this general context are clearly drawn according to national frontiers. Poetry, therefore, is seen as either the expression of native political ideals or as the manifestation of racial folk myths.

The fourth type of h. marks a radical departure from the first three. Designated "aesthetic" h., it is the product of the philosophy of history promoted by Croce and R. G. Collingwood (*An Essay on Philosophical Method*, 1950). Aesthetic h. shifts the focus of the critic's attention from the extrinsic historical or cultural context, which determines the poem's meaning, to the creative act of the poet who in writing the poem is seen to *make* cultural meanings and values, not merely reflect them. This type of h. emphasizes the poet's imaginative or intuitive powers as he gives form to culture through the act of poetic composition (see IMAGINATION. THE ROMANTICS).

If aesthetic h., however, directs the critic's attention away from the extrinsic meanings and values of the poet's culture, it bypasses the intrinsic meanings and values of the text itself in its haste to refocus attention on the poet as an intuitive seer. As a result, aesthetic h. finally loses the distinction between the poem and external reality by collapsing both into the poet's mind. Nevertheless, it is this emphasis on aesthetics or creativity that has most directly influenced the "new" h. in poetry criticism. Harry Levin, in what appears to be an effort to join aesthetic h. with the more traditional forms of historical criticism, claims that we must see that "literature is not only the effect of social causes; it is also the cause of social effects" (*The Gates of Horn*, 1963, p. 17). The poet, then, is both the maker of history and the chronicler of his times. To this dualistic position contemporary formalist schools of criticism, particularly the Am. "new criticism" (see NEW CRITICISM), have added a third important field of interest for the critic of poetry: the text as a meaningful object in itself. Thus the "new" h. critic must affirm the unique creative powers of the poet and the unique, inviolable structure of the poem while he also maintains that both poet and poem are products of their cultural-historical milieu. The "new" h. clearly develops from the many phases of romanticism, preserving in its interpretive methodology the organicist's concern with the integrity of the poem's structure and the Idealist's interest in connecting the particular poetic expression to the transcendental or sociohistorical scheme.

The varied tradition of h. is clearly problematic. Moreover, it is the tension between the tendency to seek order and meaning in external (or extrinsic) historical continuity and the emphasis on free creative activity which generates (intrinsic) meaning within the poetic text that is central to "new" h. theory. This movement has been largely the work of literary theorists; and because the primary interest here is in the interpretation of individual texts, the greatest problem is to avoid falling into the determinism of Idealistic historians like Hegel without giving up the very sensible idea that in some degree poems are always related to external sociohistorical meanings and values. "New" h. critics are consequently wary of the term "continuity" which suggests a permanent, even transcendent, historical scheme (Morris, *Toward a New H.*; Fredric Jameson, *Marxism and Form*, 1971, particularly pp. 257–79). Yet without some external linking of events history is reduced to mere random change, and the connections between individual poetic texts are merely fortuitous. The primary goal of "new" h. critics is to join the interests of "literary history," with its methodological basis in historical scholarship and its focus on cultural generalizations, and "literary criticism," with its penchant for aesthetic (and ahistorical) values and its formalist bias, into one, complete, and adequate critical activity. The practical problem, as Wellek says, is that a poem is of its own time and of the present (hence somehow above time); the poem has a "dual mode of existence" ("Periods and Movements in Literary History," EIE, 1940; *Toward a New H.*, ch. 2).

Consciously or unconsciously, the "new" h. critic confronts in this dilemma the general problems of poetic interpretation which have been the central concern of hermeneutic philosophy. The goal is a viable interpretive methodology which allows us to understand poetic texts written in remote historical periods. Wilhelm Dilthey (*Das geschichtliche Bewusstsein und die Weltanschauungen, Gesammelte Schriften*, VIII, 1913–67), one of the most influential philosophers of art and history to devise an answer to these problems, attempted to construct a hermeneutic theory based on his hypothesis that man's individual thoughts and expressions are universally "sharable," that understanding and communication are possible at a high level of generalization. He also argued that particular manifestations of thought (man's consciousness revealed in poetry) are subject to the determining forces of the poet's *Weltanschauung* (identifiable as historically meaningful psychological types). The critic's or historian's task, therefore, is to read himself into the dynamic structure of the text which is an expression of the poet's age. But Dilthey's theory results in historical relativism, for the act of interpretation becomes for him no more than a "reperformance" of the author's original experience as he composed the text. In reading backward from present to past he has resigned the role of "active" interpreter; the historian becomes passive very much in the way that the phenomenologist Georges Poulet has defined the role of all readers as giving oneself up to the thoughts of another ("The Phenomenology of Reading," NLH, 1 [1969], 53–68). E. D. Hirsch, Jr., in his recent proposal of a hermeneutic theory, has preserved the relativism of Dilthey's theory in order to explain the difference between a text's "meaning" and its "significance" (*Validity in Interpretation*, 1967). The former is historically determined, a product of the author's conscious "will" and unconscious cultural attitudes. It is discovered by a somewhat statistically oriented interpretive methodology that measures the validity of possible "meanings" against the determining possibilities of the period. A poem's "significance" is merely a subjective evaluation made by a literary critic according to his own and his society's value system. In this approach, however, Hirsch has deepened the split between the literary historian and the literary critic.

Jean-Paul Sartre (*Critique de la raison dialectique*, 1960) offers a partial solution to this dilemma in seeing history as the continuity of man's acts of self-projection which create both himself and his world. History, therefore, has no metaphysical support, nor is it merely a collection of isolated acts of self-awareness. Consciousness is dialectical, and the historical process is the product of man's free, individual projections of his future which arise only through his opposition as a free consciousness to the determining forces of his own socioeconomic milieu.

In bare outline Sartre's theory is much like the "new" h. proposed by some literary theorists of the 1950's and 1960's. Harry Levin's interest in poetry's effect on social change resembles a similar interest in poetry as a cultural force voiced by Lionel Trilling: that poetry makes man aware of his "opposing self," aware of the conflict between the individual and his cultural context captured in the poem (*The Liberal Imagination*, 1950). So, too, the phenomenologically oriented neo-Marxism of Lucien Goldmann proposes that the creative artist is both a product of and spokesman for socio-economic change (*Pour une sociologie du roman*, 1964). Roy Harvey Pearce (*H. Once More*, 1969) argues that the artist is a man of his times, but he is such because his own unique world vision (encompassing both his own existence and his culture) arises from the opposition between individual consciousness and social structures. The tensions developed in the artist through the dialectical nature of his self-awareness are captured in the structure of his verbal expressions; the "individual style" of the poem grows out of and yet opposes the "basic style" of the culture which produced it.

Those critics whose tradition is more in line with the theories of the Am. "new criticism" have also made efforts to develop a "new" h. Eliseo Vivas claims that the unique poetic context is at once the poet's "creation" of an aesthetic order and his "discovery" of meanings and values "existent" in his culture (*Creation and Discovery*, 1955). Charles Feidelson, enlarging upon the conceptions of the symbolist tradition, develops a peculiarly Am. symbolism which in its own history—and in the individual works of Am. authors—reveals the growth of an Am. poetic imagination (*Symbolism and Am. Literature*, 1953). Murray Krieger (*The Play and Place of Criticism*, 1967) sees the metaphorical structure of the poem as both a discrete, inviolable and timeless aesthetic object and a structure of meaning constituted from the elements of the artist's culturally determined language system. Krieger assumes that language always carries with it the fundamental values and meanings of society, but these "old words" are wrought into a new "Word" (the poem) under the power of the artist's creative imagination. The tension between artist and society described by Trilling and Pearce is, for Krieger, the essential tension faced by any literary artist as he confronts the cultural limitations of his language.

The renewed interest in h. in modern literary theory inevitably must confront the problems of the origin and nature of language. Historicist literary critics have turned most frequently to the philosophy of Ernst Cassirer (*The Philosophy of Symbolic Forms*, 1953) to argue that language and cognition are so intimately related that man's perception of the world is constituted in his acts of speech, and most particularly in his creative utterances. Thus the dialectic of consciousness which establishes a dynamic relationship between the "self" of the author and the restrictive structure of his society is perhaps most immediately reflected in the similar dialectical relationship between the individual poetic expression and the language system which circumscribes all verbal utterances. This is a profound problem for both linguistic studies and poetics, but it suggests that one can read from the text into the artist's society without reducing one aspect to the other. Leo Spitzer (*Linguistics and Literary History*, 1948) and Eric Auerbach (*Mimesis*, 1953) have both approached the study of individual stylistic traits in literature with this assumption. They have attempted to link the poem to the author's perception of his world and to the cultural tradition within which he lived. Moreover, in their sympathy with h., both men have searched for a continuous pattern of such relationships, for a historical organization of the dynamic interplay between man's verbal expressions and his culture. Such an approach seems to defy the precision of a scientific methodology, but it has reopened poetry to historical interpretation without denying the other extreme of its dual mode of existence, its timeless, aesthetic value.

In addition to the works already cited, the following are useful for the study of h. For general theory see: F. Engel-Janosi, *The Growth of H.* (1944); D. Lee and R. Beck, "The Meaning of H.," *Am. Historical Review*, 59 (1954); K. Popper, *The Poverty of H.* (1957); C. Antoni, *From History to Sociology* (1959) and *L'Historisme* (1961); W. B. Gallie, *Philos. and Historical Understanding* (1964); H. White, *The Uses of History* (1968; comp. and ed.) and *Metahistory* (1973). — For works on h. and related literary problems see: V. W. Brooks, "On Constructing a Usable Past," *Dial*, 64 (1918); V. L. Parrington, *Main Currents in Am. Thought* (1927); G. Hicks, *The Great Tradition* (1935); A. O. Lovejoy, *The Great Chain of Being* (1936); E. Wilson, *To the Finland Station* (1940); K. Burke, *The Philos. of Lit. Form* (1941); F. O. Matthiessen, *Am. Renaissance* (1941); M. Bewley, *The Complex Fate* (1952); L. Goldmann, *Le Dieu caché* (1955); R.W.B. Lewis, *The Am. Adam* (1955) and *The Picaresque Saint* (1959); S. Burckhardt, "Poetry, Language and the Condition of Modern Man," *Century Review*, 4 (1960); M. Krieger, *The Tragic Vision* (1960), *A Window to Crit.* (1964), and *The Classic Vision* (1971); R. H. Pearce, *The Continuity of Am. Lit.* (1961); G. Lukács, *The Historical Novel*, tr. H. and S. Mitchell (1962) and *Aesthetik* (pt. 1, 2 v., 1963); F. Hoffman, *The Mortal No* (1964); R. B. Heilman, "Historian and Critic: Notes on Attitudes," sr, 73 (1965); H. Levin, "Toward a Sociology of the Novel," jhi, 26 (1965); G. Hartman, "Beyond Formalism" and "Toward Lit. History" in *Beyond Formalism* (1970).   w.mo.

I

ICON AND ICONOLOGY. *Eikon* appears in Aristotle's *Rhetoric* (3.4) in the sense of comparison or simile. To later classical and Renaissance theorists this term meant a verbal description of a person or thing, in which similes may be used either to evaluate or simply to present vividly the subject of the description: Quintilian speaks of a kind of comparison "which the Greeks call *eikon*, and which expresses the appearance of things and persons" (*Institutio Oratoria* 5.11.24); H. Peacham defines "icon" as a "forme of speech which painteth out the image of a person or thing, by comparing forme with forme, quality with quality, and one likenesse with another" (*The Garden of Eloquence*, 1577). With the passing of the Renaissance interest in the discovery, naming, and systematic classification of stylistic and rhetorical devices, "icon" almost disappeared from poetics.

The revival of the term in modern poetics is primarily due to the influence of several articles (1939) on the nature of art written by the philosopher and semiotician Charles Morris. In these articles he sketches an aesthetics grounded on modern sign theory. The doctrine that art is a language, he says, has a history going back to Plato, but a full exploitation of this theory had to await the development of a systematic and scientific semiotic. Art differs from other forms of discourse both in the kind of sign that the artist uses and also in the kind of referent that he wishes the sign to convey. Taking his terminology from C. S. Peirce, Morris divides all signs into iconic and noniconic signs. An icon is a sign which is similar to the referent that it denotes in one or more significant respects; thus maps, blueprints, pictures, and photographs are examples of icons. Obviously, not all icons are works of art, and so Morris completes his definition by saying that the referent of the icon used in art is a human value. The iconic sign enables the artist to "present" (rather than simply assert) the value; that is, the sign provides the audience with an actual instance of the value which it denotes. Morris later (1946) modified his claim that the iconic presentation of a value is a definition of art, but he has continued to defend the position that art is a use of language for appraisive signifying and that it typically makes a generous use of iconic signs.

Morris's position attracted widespread attention among aestheticians, art historians, and literary critics. His early articles appeared at a time of growing interest, stimulated by the semantics of I. A. Richards, in the nature of the language of poetry, and his iconic hypothesis suggested a possible criterion for distinguishing the language of poetry from that used in other modes of discourse. It also appealed to critics who wished to stress the density of poetic language, the sensuous particularity of good poetry, and the crucial importance of the medium. Morris himself had discussed some of the more important iconic elements in poetry: onomatopoeia (q.v.); the general relation of sound to sense (see TONE-COLOR); the possible iconic relation of style to subject matter; and the iconicity involved in the signification of metaphors and symbols. Later theorists have explored these and other iconic elements in poetry. However, all of the issues discussed above remain highly controversial, and the fruitfulness of the iconic hypothesis is still undetermined.

"Icon," in the sense of "image" or "picture," has also had a long history of use in the criticism of the visual arts. The study of images—their origin, distribution, transformation, classification, and, particularly, the interpretation of their meaning—has been called "iconography" or "iconology." In modern use, these two terms are sometimes synonymous, sometimes defined so as to point to different concerns of the art critic (an influential distinction between the meanings of these two terms has been made by Erwin Panofsky, 1939, 1955). In recent years, some critics of poetry have discovered a fundamental similarity between their interests in poetry and the aims and methods of iconologists. Poetry, like the visual arts, uses images, and a legitimate concern of the critic of poetry is in the origin, distribution, etc. of verbal images. Furthermore, since the same image may be used in poetry and the visual arts, these critics have found a wealth of information in the writings of art historians and critics that has been of immense help in the interpretation of medieval, Renaissance, and 17th-c. poetry, especially that which employs allegorical imagery (see FINE ARTS AND POETRY).

Rosemond Tuve is a good example of a critic whose theoretical and practical criticism shows the strong influence of iconology. Like Panofsky, she assumes that the images that appear in paintings or poems are a language whose meanings must be fathomed before the work can have any aesthetic effect. When the images in an artistic work have the same meaning for all interpreters, including the artist, no problems of interpretation arise and every interpreter is his own iconologist. However, in the interpretation of poetry, especially the poetry of the distant past, this happy state is rare. The images in such poetry may have changed their meanings or may even have lost them altogether. For example, Tuve points out that George Herbert's *The Sacrifice* is unintelligible to a reader who does not recognize that the poem is filled with conventionalized symbolic imagery provided by a long iconographical tradition. The layers of suggested meanings, not to speak of the profound thematic center of the poem, are lost to a reader who does not know, for example, that in the medieval religious tradition Noah and Moses were types of Christ; that manna prefigured the Eucharist; that the creation of Eve from the rib of sleeping Adam was paralleled with the flowing of the sacraments from the pierced side of Christ; and that the tree of Adam's sin became the cross which bore Christ as its fruit. To support such interpretations Tuve uses Panofsky's "saturation" technique. She quotes from the Bible, the liturgy, Latin and vernacular lyrics, hymns and other church music, prayer books, sermons, missals, Biblical commentary, and the drama of the guilds; she reproduces photographs of church windows, illuminated manuscripts, and woodcuts. Her primary aim is, of course, to present the evidence on which she grounds her interpretations. But she also wants to build up an apperceptive mass in the reader's mind which will help him to respond to the poem's images with the immediacy that characterized the response of Herbert's contemporary readers. Such are the revitalizing services that iconology can render.

The adoption by some critics of iconological aims and methods has resulted in a large body of practical criticism that has thrown new light on the poetry of Chaucer, Spenser, Milton, and their contemporaries. It has also led to the further exploration of the ancient analogy of poetry and painting (see UT PICTURA POESIS). And it has created an interest in such hybrid art forms as emblems (q.v.) and a reconsideration of the aesthetics of the productions of poet-painters like William Blake.

C. W. Morris, "Esthetics and the Theory of Signs," *Jour. of Unified Science*, 8 (1939), "Science, Art, and Technology," KR, 1 (1939), *Signs, Language, and Behavior* (1946), *Signification and Significance* (1964); E. Panofsky, *Studies in Iconology* (1939), *Meaning in the Visual Arts* (1955); E. H. Gombrich, "Icones Symbolicae: The Visual Image in Neo-Platonic Thought," JWCI, 11 (1948); R. Tuve, *A Reading of George Herbert* (1952), *Images and Themes in Five Poems by Milton* (1957), *Allegorical Imagery* (1966); Wheelwright; M. Rieser, "The Semiotic Theory of Art in America," JAAC, 15 (1956); P. Henle, "Metaphor" in *Language, Thought, and Culture* (1958); W. K. Wimsatt, *The Verbal Icon* (1958); D. W. Robertson, *A Preface to Chaucer* (1962); S. C. Chew, *The Pilgrimage of Life* (1962); J. Bialostocki, "Iconography and Iconology" in *Encyclopedia of World Art* (1963); J. H. Hagstrum, *William Blake: Poet and Painter* (1964); P. J. Alpers, *The Poetry of the Faerie Queene* (1967); M. B. Hester, *The Meaning of Poetic Metaphor* (1967); L. A. Sonnino, *A Handbook to 16th-C. Rhetoric* (1968); J. Aptekar, *Icons of Justice: Iconography and Thematic Imagery in Book V of the Faerie Queene* (1969); J. V. Fleming, *The "Roman de la Rose": A Study in Allegory and Iconography* (1969). F.G.

INTERPRETATION. FOURFOLD METHOD. This term, or a number of minor variations on it, is normally used to refer to the classified system of biblical interpretation dominant in the Middle Ages and Renaissance, going back to Patristic theorizing on and systematizing of biblical hermeneutics. It is by no means an exact term inasmuch as not all theories of biblical i. in either the Patristic or later periods classified in a fourfold way. The common fourfold system—the literal or historical level, the allegorical (theological), the tropological (moral) level and the anagogical (eschatological) level—was not in fact widely accepted until the 12th c.

At no time was the formula ever slavishly applied, nor does it fit all or even most biblical verses. Above all, it is more appropriate for the Old Testament than the New. A more basic and satisfactory division, which we also often find in fact, would be the literal as opposed to the spiritual or fuller ("plenior") meaning, both of which were subdivided in many ways. The basic Christian argument for Jesus' divinity and the genuineness of his claims was based in the New Testament itself on the notion of a deeper meaning in the Old Testament to be discovered in the fullness of time. Furthermore, i. of a highly regarded text was normally "allegorized" to keep it current and up to date. This last purpose is first systematically applied in the Alexandrine exegesis of Homer. Alexandria, carrying on this pagan and Rabbinic tradition especially in Philo (d. ca. A.D. 54), developed a lively school of biblical exegesis. This was christianized largely by Origen of Alexandria (d. 254). This school tended to emphasize the spiritual or allegorical meaning as opposed to the Antiochene school which emphasized the literal and textual meaning. Allegory *in* the text of the Bible is usually typological or figural, in which the actions and events of the Old Testament are seen to foreshadow true events in the New Testament and in the future, a kind of horizontal allegory. Allegory *on* the Bible is more frequently but by no means exclusively vertical in which the one, two, three, or more levels are found. However, a strict division between typological and level allegory is not always possible.

One can only briefly trace here the development of biblical exegesis. Origen had a three-fold system—somatic, psychic, and pneumatic based on Hebraic and Greek psychology. Cassian (d. 435) was the first to take Origenic and triadic allegory to the West when founding southern Gaulish monasticism. Augustine in his *De doctrina christiana* provided justification to later times for the use of allegorical methods although his own system applied to the Bible usually refers to the way Jesus Himself taught rather than to current biblical exegesis. He, however, certainly distinguished the spiritual from the literal sense and provided an aesthetic of allegory in which the beauty of figurative and obscure biblical language is praised. Gregory the Great (d. 604), especially in his *Homilies on Ezechiel* and *Moralia* (a moralized commentary on Job), proposed a threefold method and was even more influential in medieval biblical allegorizing than Augustine. Various medieval schools of exegesis flourished and carried on the tradition: the Irish Monastic School, the Benedictines, the School of Laon, the Victorine School, Scholastic exegesis, and above all a "scientific" school from the 12th c. on which was remarkably open-minded and yet respectful toward tradition, culminating in Nicholas of Lyra of the 14th c., the great unifier of exegetical traditions for subsequent Christianity. Sermons in particular were much indebted to the exegetical biblical tradition and helped to make various interpretations well known. Pictures, illuminations, statues, and stained glass were also instrumental in educating the medieval and early Renaissance masses in traditional exegetical interpretations.

In modern literary scholarship and theory, the medieval and Renaissance use of the so-called fourfold system of allegory in literature has been much debated. Was there a "four-fold" meaning in the *Romance of the Rose*, in Chaucer, in Chrétien de Troyes, and so on? It is certain that any literary work worthy of the name is polysemous. That biblical symbolism and exegesis had influence on medieval and Renaissance works there can be no doubt, but the degree and extent of that influence is difficult to establish, especially in an age like

ours which is seeking for both religion and relevance. See also ALLEGORY.

F. W. Farrar, *Hist. of I.* (1886); B. Smalley, *The Study of the Bible in the Middle Ages* (2d ed., 1952); R. W. Frank, "The Art of Reading Medieval Personification Allegory," ELH, 20 (1953); H. de Lubac, *Exégèse médiévale . . .* (4 v., 1959–64); *Crit. Approaches to Medieval Lit.*, ed. D. Bethurum (1960; papers from the Eng. Institute 1958–59, esp. articles by Donaldson, Kaske, Donahue); D. W. Robertson, Jr., *A Preface to Chaucer: Studies in Medieval Perspectives* (1962); *The Cambridge Hist. of the Bible*, ed. P. R. Ackroyd et al. (3 v., 1963–69; esp. II, 155–279); H. R. Jauss, *Entstehung und Strukturwandel der allegorischen Dichtung* (1968); J. Pépin, *Dante et la tradition de l'allégorie* (1971); M. W. Bloomfield, "Allegory as I.," NLH, 3 (1971–72). M.W.B.

INTERPRETATION. MODERN. In the most generally accepted sense, literary i. is explication and explanation of the meaning, theme, or significance of a work. Although sometimes used as if it were synonymous with "i.," the word "hermeneutics," traditionally associated with biblical exegesis, is now generally employed to designate interpretive theory. Some critics think that i. need not be encumbered with discussion of methods and principles, in that it is essentially an intuitive activity leading in as many directions as literary study itself. But the purpose of relating practical criticism to articulated theory is to secure agreement concerning the results of i., not to determine how it should proceed. If a distinction between "an acceptable i." and "my i." is desirable, some means must be found to decide what will count as evidence for or against interpretive statements. Of the many theories of literary i., five of contemporary importance have been selected for treatment in this article. Philosophical and empirical aspects of interpretive theory as a whole are discussed briefly in the concluding paragraphs.

Proponents of what will here be called "autonomous i." assert that literary meaning is intrinsic and can be discovered only through sensitive attention to the verbal structure of the work itself. The articles on *explication, criticism—practical, imagery,* and *metaphor* discuss doctrines and methods relevant to this theory. In the most explicit formulations of *new criticism* (q.v.) and *contextualism,** autonomous i. is associated with the following assumptions: (1) "literary works are self-sufficient entities, whose properties are decisive in checking interpretations" (Beardsley); (2) complexity, within the limits of overall unity, is a positive aesthetic value; and (3) when properly pursued, i. leads to statements concerning the themes, situations, and attitudes embodied in literature, rather than to statements about propositional or emotive "meaning" (didactic and propagandistic works are, in this view, sub-literary). The third assumption is often accompanied by a distinction between ordinary (referential) uses of language and the language of literature, which is autonomous because it does not entail reference in the usual sense. Cleanth Brooks, W. K. Wimsatt, M. C. Beardsley, and Murray Krieger are the most articulate spokesmen of this theory of i., though important differences in their positions are perforce blurred in a skeletal exposition.

These assumptions delimit a context of i. and provide a means of validating its results. An immense variety of information may be brought to bear in discussion of a literary work; if only that contained in the work itself is considered "decisive," the problem of i. is reduced to manageable proportions. Rules governing interpretive practice are implicit in (1) and (2): the elements of a work are presumably interrelated in such a way as to attain structural unity, and the interpreter will attempt to discover their internal coherence rather than their correspondence to something outside the work. The theory enables us to discover the law whereby a literary work is a law unto itself.

The rich and diversified body of interpretive commentary produced by autonomous i. reveals that its assumptions have unanticipated consequences. In reducing the *number* of elements relevant to an i., assumption (1) eliminates extrinsic *determinants* of how these elements are to be construed (such as those that can be inferred from biography and literary history). Reduction in the quantity and determinacy of interpretive factors leads to greater ambiguity— which in turn, by virtue of assumption (2), may become a positive aesthetic value. If complexity is a desirable characteristic of literature, how can it be increased, given a text of a certain length? The obvious answer is that its elements must acquire multiple functions or meanings; and this can be achieved through ambiguity, paradox, irony, and (in general) heterogeneity. The consequent problem is to determine how such a complexity can be subsumed in the "unity" required by assumption (2), and the answer lies in assumption (3). Unity is distinguished from univocity; complexity and indeterminacy of meaning are subsumed in "situation" and "attitude." While most proponents of autonomous i. believe that it is desirable to secure agreement regarding the i. of a work, their method can lead to uncontrolled proliferation of textual commentary.

A more serious difficulty results from the literary autonomy granted in (1). As in the Kantian tradition, the literary work is seen as an object in its own right. It is not, however, seen as embodying Kantian "purposiveness";

consequently, there is nothing in the definition of the literary object to distinguish it from natural objects. Burkhardt discerningly relates autonomous i. (his term is "*werkimmanente Deutung*") to the *interpretatio naturae* of the empirical sciences in their post-Reformation development. Both presuppose that their objects (literature and nature) contain within themselves the laws in terms of which they are to be understood. However, most advocates of autonomous i., while denying the theoretical relevance of "intentions," assume in practice that literary works entail intentionality. Their explications are controlled by their awareness that although some meanings may be elusive, others are apparent, and the whole work embodies a consciously created theme. But if their theoretical statements concerning the autonomy of the literary object are considered apart from their unstated assumptions, there is reason to interpret literature as the anthropologist interprets taboos, or the psychoanalyst dreams—as human products embodying meanings of which their creators are unconscious.

These considerations lead to a definition of "i." as "explanation of the symbolic content of a text." A symbol means something more or something other than its denotation (see the articles on SYMBOL, MYTH, ARCHETYPE, and CRITICISM—PSYCHOLOGICAL, all of which are relevant to this conception of i.). Through "explanation," a particular phenomenon is seen as exemplifying a class that can be accounted for by a reference to a general law. The domains of classification involved in symbolic i. are not exclusively literary; in this respect it is opposed to autonomous i., since the latter considers the aesthetic realm *sui generis*. Symbolic i. is usually based on the following assumptions: (1) literary works and their elements are particular examples of forms and symbols appearing elsewhere in literature and in other sociocultural domains; (2) the purpose of i. is to identify the general categories in which particular literary works are properly subsumed; and (3) symbols and forms of cultural/literary expression themselves require explication because they are inherently equivocal and embody meanings of which their users are unaware.

The context within which interpretive problems arise offers some evidence favorable to this point of view. We undertake i. on encountering something we do not understand; otherwise it is unnecessary. Literary texts entice us toward realization by appearing to conceal their meanings. It is difficult to draw a line between the "implicit meaning" of autonomous i. and the "latent meaning" of symbolic i. because any form of expression involving concealment or duplicity raises the question of why the speaker hid what he would reveal, and this question cannot be answered within the framework of the text itself. The speaker may not be aware of why he conceals, or even what he conceals. When propositional meaning and explicit intentionality are considered inappropriate as the basis of i., all forms of cultural expression are called into question.

The 19th-c. attempt to apply the empirical methods of the natural sciences to the study of man made possible the modern emergence of symbolic i. Once conscious intentions had been eliminated as the decisive criteria governing the i. of social and cultural phenomena, the stage was set for the emergence of what Ricoeur refers to as "the hermeneutics of suspicion." Marx, Nietzsche, and Freud invented interpretive methods based on the premise that generally accepted explanations of human behavior were in fact illusions. "Henceforward," says Ricoeur, "to seek meaning is no longer to spell out the consciousness of meaning, but to *decipher its expressions*." While psychology, mythology, and cultural anthropology were among the earliest and remain the most influential disciplines employing this conception of i., it has recently influenced other sciences of man. M. Foucault has combined it with structural i. to identify the conceptual categories that have controlled man's perception (and hence his i.) of reality.

The diversity of the literary criticism based on what is here generically called symbolic i. results from variations in the fundamental symbolic categories employed and the indeterminacy of its assumptions. Northrop Frye, Leslie Fiedler, Gaston Bachelard, and Georg Lukács are among its best-known practitioners, but no short list of critics can indicate its varied forms. (For a discussion of the critics who have contributed to the development of a "Marxist hermeneutic," see Fredric Jameson, *Marxism and Form*, 1971.) Archetypal, psychoanalytic, Marxist, and mythic criticism differ in the meanings they educe from literature, but their methods—which involve finding something more or something other than enthymeme in the text—are quite similar. The terms Freud used in his discussions of multiple meaning (condensation, displacement, overelaboration, sublimation) identify specific techniques of symbolic i., and it is possible to envisage a lexicon of such terms correlated with rhetorical devices on the assumption that language, rather than culture or the psyche, is the fundamental source of plurivocity (as suggested by Jacques Lacan). However, even if one accepts the assumption that literary meaning does not differ in kind from meaning in general, symbolic i. has two besetting weaknesses. It remains speculative, none of its manifestations having gained more than skeptical tolerance in the social sciences; and

the methods it employs are so indeterminate as to yield incompatible results in the hands of different practitioners.

Two reactions against symbolic i. attracted attention in the 1960's. In one of these, "i." is defined as "paraphrase; exact reproduction of a text's meaning in different words," in accordance with an accepted philosophic sense of the term. In opposition to the interpretive traditions discussed above, this one insists that a text's meaning is determined by its author's intentions, which are recoverable because the text objectifies his thought and emotions, and that literary meaning is not different in kind from nonliterary meaning. Originating in the biblical and classical hermeneutics of Schleiermacher (1768–1834) and Boeckh (1785–1867), what is here called (for convenience of reference) "exegetical i." survived in the writings of Dilthey and re-emerged in recent works by E. D. Hirsch and E. Betti.

The Cartesian premises of the 19th-c. tradition are retained in restatements of the theory. Understanding (*Verstehen*) is the mental act whereby the interpreter re-experiences or recognizes the text's original meaning; i. is the subsequent act of objectifying this understanding in language. Historical and linguistic knowledge of the milieu in which the text was produced, together with an understanding of the life and works of its author, are indispensable for accurate i. By knowledging the otherness of the text, an interpreter can understand its meaning in his own time; and through knowledge of its historical context and its author, he can understand it better than did the author himself. Exegetical i. has been associated with the attempt to state rules or "canons" of i., but Boeckh and Hirsch doubt that any can be found which would be both useful and nontrivial. Most of the theorists in this tradition distinguish "i.," a restatement of inherent meaning, from "criticism," an attribution of significance to the text; the latter term would include all that is called "i." in the autonomous and symbolic traditions.

Although they provide a rationale for the methods of traditional literary scholarship, contemporary theorists of exegetical i. have had little influence on interpretive practice. Having burdened themselves with 19th-c. conceptions of "subject," "object," and "intention," they have been unable to revitalize Dilthey's distinction between the natural and humane sciences. The concept of i. as synonymous restatement of a text, which involved significant philological issues when the Bible and classical works were first subjected to textual criticism, today seems unnecessarily narrow. It would be pointless to apply i. in this sense to narrative, and impossible to apply it to much modern poetry. However, two aspects of exegetical theory are of considerable importance. One is its distinction between "explanation" and "understanding," which will be mentioned in the concluding paragraphs. The other is its assertion that since there is no logical or empirical justification for nonliteral readings of a text, "i." in the usual sense can be justified only by reference to conventions.

Structuralism (q.v.), which protean term will here be used to refer primarily to the writings of Barthes and Todorov, carries the critique of interpretive practice even further. The structuralist definition of "i." is taken from logic, in which a primitive term or sign, inherently without meaning, is accorded one arbitrarily. Where other interpreters would distinguish form from content, or fuse the two in a statement regarding "theme," the rigorous structuralist takes any identifiable meaning in a work as a locus for further formal analysis. Meaning vanishes in the multiple elaboration of structures; every content is unfolded as a form. "I." is entirely arbitrary, and by implication irrelevant to criticism. It would seem that this view constitutes a logically final step in the analysis of i. But after the effort to discover meaning has been turned inside out, the outside remains to be interpreted.

In still another of its technical uses (in philosophy and semiology—cf. Husserl, Ogden and Richards, C. W. Morris), "i." means "the act of using or construing anything as a sign." When we apprehend certain sense impressions as stimulated by a chair, or recognize certain sounds as a word, we are performing acts of i. In this sense the structuralist's structures, and language itself, are interpretations. In order to understand how i. is constituted, according to Heidegger, we must attempt to place ourselves in the moment at which we see an object *as* a chair, or use a word *to mean* something. Through hermeneutics, we elucidate "as" and "to mean." Because all experience is conditioned and mediated by language, we are endowed with an i. of reality of which we become conscious only in moments of rupture, when caught by the unexpected. Some of the literary consequences of this view, as discussed in the writings of H.-G. Gadamer, are summarized in the following paragraphs.

Because the linguistic and cultural experience which we bring to a text have constituted our very being and understanding, it is meaningless to speak of i. apart from our historical existence. "Objective" i. is impossible; we always understand literary works separated from us in time through our own mode of vision, which is largely unconscious and apart from which we do not exist. Yet since tradition has constituted our being, we can, by opening ourselves to the past, let it speak in our present. Attempts to characterize the past are vitiated by the contemporary categories we (inescapably) use in doing so, and they spring from a desire to dominate the past which distorts its voice. Meaning is always for here-and-now; it cannot be other.

Literature is misunderstood when placed in a special category called the "aesthetic"; literary and ordinary language differ only insofar as the former embodies greater intensity. Literature speaks to us by disconfirming our expectations, and in this respect it is similar to "experience," as opposed to mere habit. Herein lies the explanation of why i. always begins from something we *don't* understand. In such circumstances, we question the text. But the text itself is an answer; and if the question which it answers is a genuine one, we must assume that other answers were possible. True i. is the act of going beyond the text to the question that called it into being. If the interpreter opens his being to that which created the text, his i. will differ from all others—not because of his subjectivity, and not because the text has an infinite number of meanings, but because an infinity of texts and interpretive moments are the being of being from which subject and object are subsequently constituted in philosophic speculation.

Anglo-Am. philosophy has viewed the foregoing accounts of literary i. with skepticism. Linguistic analysts think that there must be some reasonable explanation of what practical critics are doing, regardless of what they think they are doing and the rationalizations of theoretical critics. C. L. Stevenson sees interpretations as based upon normative recommendations regarding modes of response. M. Weitz argues that many interpretations are in fact explanations, by virtue of their appeal to relevant general hypotheses; interpretive disagreements arise because of the variety of explanatory frameworks employed and the failure to recognize that these bear a provisional rather than essential relation to literary texts. J. Casey sees interpretations as explanations of how to construe a text; guided by the skillful critic, we come to see what he has seen. J. Margolis and S. Hampshire say that the existence of disparate interpretations of a work cannot be disallowed, so long as they are plausible. Few contemporary aestheticians argue that it is in principle possible to discover the "correct i." of a text.

Some problems that persistently vex interpretive theory deserve brief mention. Nearly all critics assume that literary works are coherent and that a satisfactory i. should be complete—i.e., that every part of a work should be accounted for in relation to an inclusive unity. Why? Burkhardt admits that only the greatest literature achieves unity; but R. M. Adams argues that many great works

-[946]-

contain irreconcilable "strains of discord," and Ihab Hassan sees deliberate fragmentation as characteristic of contemporary literature. There is by no means agreement regarding where coherence is to be sought. An author's complete works, or his works and his life may be posited as the unity requiring explanation. Rather than attempting to integrate the surface of the *oeuvre*, many critics subject it to transformations in a search for deep structures. Thus it is less usual to find interpretations incompatible than to find them incommensurable.

Once a critic succeeds in showing that a work is unified, his i. may be vitiated by circularity, in that the whole has been explained by reference to the parts, and vice versa (Seebohm has analyzed this problem in detail: see bibliog.). Quite apart from this problem, there is the widespread feeling that the proliferation of incompatible interpretations can be explained only by retreating to relativism. Alternative explanations are available (in instrumentalism, Pepper's contextualism, and phenomenology). The extent to which recent philosophic speculation concerning language, the theory of meaning, and general hermeneutics are of relevance to interpretive criticism remains problematic. If philosophy can provide a theoretical foundation for the distinction between scientific explanation and humanistic understanding, its influence on the theory of literary i. may be pronounced (see bibliog.: works by Apel and von Wright).

The history of practical criticism and of the ways in which literary scholarship has influenced i. remains to be written. Theoreticians who have little to say about scholarship should recognize that it continues to transform interpretive practice. Robertson's *A Preface to Chaucer* (1962) is a case in point, and it reinforces the historicist's contention that in order to understand the literature of any age, we can profit from an acquaintance with the interpretive conventions that its authors used in reading. It is evident that interpretive methods that were originally developed because of their appropriateness to the literature of a particular age are often subsequently applied, with more dubious results, to the literature of another age. An account of what contemporary interpreters of literature in fact do, regardless of what they say they do, might answer questions that have been left unresolved by theorists.

Some contemporary critics have argued that literary i. is an otiose art of divination that forestalls aesthetic response by turning it into something else. The technical innovations of contemporary literature can be seen as in part motivated by a desire to obviate i. and confute those critical theories that consider literature similar to other forms of discourse. But critics continue to prove the justice of Valéry's remark that "there is no discourse so obscure, no tale so odd or remark so incoherent that it cannot be given a meaning."

F.D.E. Schleiermacher, *Sämmtliche Werke*, Abteil. 1, v. 7 (1838) and *Hermeneutik* (1959); A. Boeckh, *Encyclopaedie . . .* (1877; selections tr. as *On I. and Crit.*, 1968); W. Dilthey, "Die Entstehung der Hermeneutik," *Gesammelte Schriften*, v (1924; tr. in NLH, 3 [1972]); C. L. Stevenson, "I. and Evaluation in Aesthetics," *Philosophical Analysis*, ed. Max Black (1950); W. K. Wimsatt, *The Verbal Icon* (1954), *Hateful Contraries* (1965; pt. 4); E. Betti, *Teoria generale della interpretazione* (2 vols., 1955), *Die Hermeneutik als allgemeine Methodik . . .* (1962); M. C. Beardsley, *Aesthetics* (1958; chs. 3, 9), *The Possibility of Crit.* (1970); H. Lipps, *Untersuchungen zu einer hermeneutischen Logik* (1959); *The New Hermeneutic*, ed. J. B. Cobb and J. M. Robinson (1964); M. Weitz, *Hamlet and the Philosophy of Lit. Crit.* (1964; chs. 13–18); A. Child, *I.: A General Theory* (1965); H.-G. Gadamer, *Wahrheit und Methode* (2d ed., 1965); P. Ricoeur, *De l'interprétation, essai sur Freud* (1965; Eng. tr. 1970), *Le Conflit des interprétations* (1969); R. Barthes, *Critique et vérité* (1966), *S/Z* (1970); J. Casey, *The Language of Crit.* (1966); E. D. Hirsch, *Validity in I.* (1967); K.-O. Apel, *Analytic Philosophy of Language and the Geisteswissenschaften*, tr. by H. Holstelilie (1967); S. Burckhardt, "Notes on the Theory of Intrinsic Meaning," *Shakespearian Meanings* (1968); E. Coreth, *Grundfragen der Hermeneutik* (1969); R. E. Palmer, *Hermeneutics* (1969); *Hermeneutik als Weg heutiger Wissenschaft*, ed. V. Warnach (1971); G. H. von Wright, *Explanation and Understanding* (1971); T. M. Seebohm, *Zur Kritik der hermeneutischen Vernunft* (1972); NLH, 3, 4 (Winter 1972, Winter 1973). w.m.

INTUITION. Theories of poetry as a form of i. are even today somewhat alien to our ways of thinking. In his book on Benedetto Croce, G.N.G. Orsini observes that Am. literary critics are profoundly distrustful of their intuitive capacities and, one might add, of the intuitive power of poetry itself. Am. histories of aesthetics do contain clear descriptions of theories of poetry as i., but their clarity depends on their remoteness from that which they are ostensibly describing. Even when most objective, they seem to suggest that such theories are simply untenable. Of course, the theories may in truth be untenable. But because they have emerged in cultures with much richer traditions of poetry and art than our own, we should reject them only with extreme caution.

In its most fully developed form, the theory of poetry as essentially intuitive is based on the belief that lines like the following are exemplary: "the dry sound of bees/ Stretching across a lucid space" (Hart Crane, *Praise for an Urn*) and "As a calm darkens among water lights" (Wallace Stevens, *Sunday Morning*). To be sure, any line of verse, according to this theory, is poetic only if it is intuitive. But the lines quoted from Crane and Stevens seem to exhibit what is meant by poetic i. with unusual clarity and vividness. Even these lines, it is true, do not force the reader to respond to them as intuitive. The lines may be taken to be imitative of certain natural events or as illustrations of visual illusions or even as instances of rhetorical catachresis (q.v.). But if the reader takes these lines in as they really are—or so the theory goes—then he will experience them as poetic intuitions, as an immediate fusion of feeling and image. The awesome stillness and brilliance of Crane's space, strung together by the dry hum of golden immortality, is at one with the poet's anguished desire to eternalize the dead man he loves. The reader is pulled into a new place and time and becomes one with its desperate beauty. If he meditates within this intuitive moment, it will enfold his whole world, Crane's world will become his world, and he will see everything afresh, colored by a pain and lucidity as never before. In experiences such as this, life and language, the world and the word, are absolutely one. Further, the experience one has of the poetry and one's knowledge of the experience are identical. Poetry is immediate knowledge of individual experience. The poetry creates the experience—as a fusion of the world as experienced and of the person as experiencing—and gives knowledge of the experience as an identity of world and person in a single, seamless act of i.

This theory does not equate poetry with the creative act of God, for it views poetic i. not as a creation out of nothing but as the creation of man and the world, of language and being, out of a material which is its prior condition. But this condition is utterly formless; it is only a hum and buzz, or a pure flux of sensation. In effect, then, poetic i. discovers only what it creates, it knows that which it itself makes. Moreover, in this theory, poetry as we ordinarily think of it is only the highest form of that creative experience in which each of us becomes a human being living in a world. Essentially the creative-knowing act of Stevens' *Sunday Morning* is the same as the act of a mother singing to her baby, the very act in which the mother evokes in the baby directed love and focused vision and discriminating hearing.

Poetic i. differs from sensation because it is neither passive nor psychological; it is a oneness of person and world expressed in language;

and its language may be words or song or drawing or gesture. It is knowledge, but of an immediate kind, and thus it is prior to conceptual, judgmental, discursive knowledge. There is no claim in poetic i. that its world is either real or unreal or that that world and the experiencing person are distinct; because it is not a self-conscious experience, it does not even contain the claim that it is itself poetic i. Although it is possible to extract concepts and abstract ideas from a poem, in the poem experienced as a poem, these ideas are fused within the i. Vico, who may be credited as the father of this conception of poetry, argued that Homer conceived of Achilles not as a courageous individual or as an example of courage or as courage itself, but as an utter fusion of all of these. In poetic i., in other words, individuality and universality are identical. Poetic i., moreover, is radically distinct from perception, which is the basis of empirical knowledge. If one perceives "the green spot here and now," he observes it as part of a spatial and temporal and chromatic framework, a structure already composed by conceptual thought. It is, of course, possible to perceive rather than intuit poems, to consider their space and time as part of some large, conventional structure within which we live our days. But to do so is to miss the poems as poems. Space and time are abstractions by means of which we think and perceive the world. But poetic i. creates the world and with it our living sense of space and time. The crudeness or fineness of our very ideas of space and time is thus derivative from the quality of our poetic, intuitive experience. Finally, in its purest form, the concept of poetry as i. is at odds with the idea of poetry as self-expression. In a poetic i., self and world, subject and object, are immediately identical. This is the way the world begins. This is the way the self begins. On its basis alone we construct our distinctions, self and world, space and time, real and unreal, truth and error, even beauty and ugliness.

So long as it was believed that a person could intuit an object and then express that intuited object without his act of i. or his act of expression in any way affecting the nature of the object, i. was a useful idea, but not difficult, problematic, illuminating, or fruitful. In all naïvely realistic theories of knowledge, theories based on the belief that an object can be known, as it is, independent of its being known, i. as immediate knowledge, both of images and of ideas, occupied a comfortable but uninteresting place. Of course, such a claim can be argued, and, indeed, A. Grabar has argued that reverse perspective in medieval painting—where the artist, losing himself in the object represented, unfolds his vision out of the object rather than from his own standpoint

INTUITION

—has its origin in Plotinus' conception of the soul's losing itself in a simple i. of all reality ("Plotin et les origines de l'estétique médiévale," *Cahiers Archéologiques*, 1945). And E. Panofsky has related the emergence in the art of Giotto and Duccio of a perspectival interpretation of space to the Occamite notion that the quality of reality belongs exclusively to particular "things," to those things which can be apprehended by *notitia intuitiva* (*Gothic Architecture and Scholasticism*, 1951). Interesting as they are, these connections between theories of i. and certain forms of art have been made consciously only in our century.

Only with Vico and Kant, both of whom recognized that knowing involves making and that therefore i. must be considered as both an object and an act, does the idea of i. become helpful to our understanding of poetry and art. It is true that Baumgarten, who founded and named the discipline of aesthetics, established the aesthetic sphere as *cognitio sensitiva*, a clear but indistinct form of knowledge anterior to logical cognition. But he found nothing intuitive in poetry, claiming that its knowledge is simply unarticulated (clear but indistinct) logical knowledge. Even Kant, for that matter, does not make a significant connection between poetry and i. But he does explicate i. in such a way as to make it possible for others to explore that connection. According to Kant, men are incapable of intellectual intuitions and therefore cannot know noumena, or things in themselves, immediately. But men can know sensible phenomena immediately. Now it is Kant's explication of sensible, intuitive knowledge which is important for our purposes. He does, it is true, insist, in a conventionally realistic sense, that phenomena are givens, are intuitions which we simply receive. But he discovers an active element in the way we receive them. Phenomena appear to us as they do because of the way in which we receive them. We do this, he finds, according to a priori principles of space and time, principles which themselves are not concepts, but intuitions. The phenomena of a concept are outside it, beneath it, as its instances. The phenomena of space and time, as we intuit them rather than think about them, are embedded within those a priori forms. We see an object in space without reflection, immediately; space as a formative, determining principle and the given object are fused and utterly at one as we experience them intuitively. As fused with their sensible content, space and time are empirical intuitions. Taken in themselves, deprived of content, they are pure intuitions. From this innovative concept of i. as both active and passive it is no great leap to Croce's concept of poetry as pure i. or to Bergson's notion of music as pure *durée*. Kant did not make the leap himself, either in the *Critique of Pure Reason*, where he developed the concept of i., or in the *Critique of Judgment*, where he considers art and poetry.

In the history of thought, often the most popular theories are not creative discoveries like Kant's, but the regressive theories composed out of fear of the originality of the great thinker. The desire to associate i. with a divine instinct by means of which we become identical with God surely did not lapse because of Kant's critical analysis of i. Schopenhauer, for example, identified artistic genius with intellectual i.—which Kant found to be outside man's capacity—with the pure contemplation of Eternal Ideas. Along with his uncritical notion of the objects of i., Schopenhauer also regressed into old-time fancy with his claim that i. has no active element, but is purely passive and contemplative. For him the agent of i. ceases, in effect, to be an agent. As a "pure knowing subject," he sees in such a way as to leave the object seen unaffected by his seeing. His is "the completest objectivity"; he strips off his individuality, becomes free of time and space, and loses himself in the object. Such a Platonic notion of the annihilation of the viewer in the vision is still to be found in certain theories of poetry as impersonally visionary.

Contrary to the opinion of T. E. Hulme—who translated Bergson's metaphysics into an aesthetics—Bergson's notion of i. is quite different from Schopenhauer's. For Bergson the object of i. is not an Eternal Idea, but the flux of life itself. It is an "intensive manifold"; as Hulme says, it is "an absolute interpenetration," "a complex thing which yet cannot be said to have parts because the parts run into each other, forming a continuous whole" (*Speculations*, p. 181). Moreover, there is an active element in Bergson's i.: it is a sympathetic and instinctive compenetration of actor and object and is the very opposite of intellectual thinking, which is exterior and fragmentary ("Introduction à la métaphysique," 1893). Such a notion of i. may be found as a subordinate element in some recent Fr. criticism, notably in that of Poulet. Also related to Bergsonian i. is J. Maritain's conception of a poet's i. as "an obscure grasping of his own Self and of things in a knowledge through union or through connaturality which is born in the spiritual unconscious, and which fructifies only in the work" (*Creative I. in Art and Poetry*, p. 115). Maritain, however, emphasizes "things" in a way alien to Bergson; he even argues that abstract art, by "breaking away from the existential world of Nature, from things and the grasping of things," must fall short of the deepest purposes of art (p. 218). Neo-Thomism (q.v.) is evident in this twist given to i. as object. In the act of i., Maritain like Bergson finds a deep, pulsating self at work, although, unlike Bergson, he finds that the intellect, rather than being excluded from i. as analytical, is caught up in its creative surge and works in harmony with it.

Benedetto Croce brought the concept of poetry as i. to its full fruition. Like Kant, he thinks of i. as an a priori formative principle. Whereas Bergson had distinguished i. as an inner, temporal sense from the exterior, spatializing intellect, Croce conceives of i. as superior to and prior to both our sense of space and our sense of time and as creative of both. Further, he rejects Kant's notion that the a priori intuitive form receives phenomena as given. Abstractly speaking, he will call the flux of feelings the material of poetic i.; but for him the flux takes its first form only within the poetic i., and thus that i. is creative and not imitative. Even though it is creative, it is also a form of knowledge. It is the one way in which one knows (as he creates) people, things, even the world in their individuality and uniqueness. Croce emphasizes his belief that i. involves both making and knowing by means of his formula of poetry as "intuition-expression."

Throughout his career, Croce distinguishes i. sharply from anything passive, like "sensation." One has an i. only if he expresses it, only if he articulates it fully. Against all who felt that he was slighting expression, externalization, all matters of technique and media and genre, Croce insisted that an i. is itself only if fully articulated as an individual and unique expression. It could, he admits, happen in one's head; but distinctions like inner and outer, mind and body, insight and realization, are irrelevant to i. Indeed, so concerned was Croce to insist on the active, expressive element in his notion of poetic i., that from 1912 to 1917 he was advocating the idea that poetic i. is an a priori synthesis of feeling and image. This advocacy was extremely disruptive for his theory, because any such synthesis would of necessity involve mediation and resolution, whereas poetic i., just as necessarily, is nonmediate, an immediate fusion and identity. The result of Croce's effort to treat poetry as both an i. and an a priori synthesis was that the elements of the synthesis, the feeling, the image, and the i., collapsed into each other even as he sought to distinguish them, just as i. and expression were collapsed into an identity in the earliest form of his aesthetics. Croce's theory of poetry has been called an expressive theory, but because of these collapses into immediate identity, the theory is always an intuitive one, even when appearances suggest otherwise. The most significant changes in Croce's theory occurred not in the act but in the object of i. The act remains at all times an immediate awareness which is a shaping, an "intuition-expression." But the object, in 1902, is a fusion

of the real and the unreal; in 1908, it is a fusion of unrealized desire and realized action, both experienced as feeling; in 1917, it is a fusion of individuality and universality; and by 1928, it is a fusion of vitality and morality, so that poets without moral preoccupations (like D'Annunzio) are found to be nonpoetic.

In Italy, Croce's theory of poetry as i. was superseded as early as 1932, with the publication of Gentile's *Philosophy of Art*. But with their emphasis on tradition, most Italians have sought to retain as much as possible of Croce's theory even as they went beyond him. Thus, as Bergsonian intuition works within more advanced Fr. theories of poetry, so Crocian i. is still a ferment in It. theories of poetry as nonintuitive. Such efforts to sustain past achievements when progressing beyond them are distinctive of cultures with rich traditions of poetry.

Brief mention must be made of E. Cassirer's Kantian usage of i. It provides a basis for S. Langer's notion of poetry as immediate "knowledge by acquaintance," as an imitation of the forms of psychic feeling, and also for E. Vivas' theory of poetry as creation and discovery, as an object to be apprehended intuitively, by "intransitive attention." In England R. G. Collingwood developed a theory of poetry dependent on Croce's, but he vacillated indecisively between the idea of poetry as intuitively immediate and a Gentilean notion of poetry as actively mediate. Quite recently M. Oakeshott has argued for what is a Crocean theory of poetry freed of all cognitive claims. Croce no doubt would have called this a theory of poetry as play rather than i.

A. Schopenhauer, *The World as Will and Idea*, tr. R. B. Haldane and J. Kemp (3 v., 1883); B. Croce, *The Essence of Aesthetic*, tr. D. Ainslie (1921), *Aesthetic*, tr. D. Ainslie (2d ed., 1922) and *Philos., Poetry, Hist.*, tr. C. Sprigge (1966); T. E. Hulme, *Speculations* (1924); I. Kant, *Critique of Pure Reason*, tr. N. K. Smith (2d print., 1933); R. G. Collingwood, *The Principles of Art* (1938); E. Cassirer, *An Essay on Man* (1944) and *The Philos. of Symbolic Forms*, tr. R. Manheim (II, 1953); S. Langer, *Philos. in a New Key* (1948); G. de Ruggiero, *Da Vico a Kant* (4th ed., 1952); J. Maritain, *Creative I. in Art and Poetry* (1953); E. Vivas, *Creation and Discovery* (1955); M. C. Beardsley, *Aesthetics* (1958); H. Bergson, *Oeuvres* (centennial ed., 1959); M. Oakeshott, *The Voice of Poetry in the Conversation of Mankind* (1959); G.N.G. Orsini, *Benedetto Croce* (1961); J. Starobinski, *L'Oeil vivant* (1961); G. Svenaeus, *Méthodologie et spéculation estétique* (1961); G. Gentile, *The Philos. of Art*, tr. G. Gullace (1972). M.E.B.

L

M

LAUREATE. See POET LAUREATE.

METACRITICISM. The best use so far found for the prefix "meta-" is that to which it has been put by contemporary philosophers and logicians: it marks a step upward in the language level, from what is talked *about* to what is talked *in*. There is the literary work, a discourse, or linguistic entity, which itself may or may not refer to the actual world and may or may not (in some sense) say something about it. There is the discourse of the critic, which refers to the literary work and (presumably) says something about it. And there is metacriticism, which is discourse about criticism. These distinctions have turned out to be no less crucial in literary study than in those fields where they were first developed and are most firmly entrenched: e.g., mathematics vs. metamathematics, science vs. philosophy of science. Nor are they invalidated even if many poems are implicitly "metapoetic," or self-referring, as argued by Rosalie L. Colie, in *"My Ecchoing Song": Andrew Marvell's Poetry of Crit.* (1970).

The task of metacriticism is the critical examination of criticism: of its technical terms, its logical structure, its fundamental principles and premises. If the critic asserts that Keats's *Lamia* is a masterpiece because it embodies the woman-into-serpent archetype (q.v.), the metacritic will ask: How does the critic know this? What sorts of evidence could establish such an embodiment? Is the concept of *archetype* sufficiently articulated to serve as a critical tool? Why is the presence of an archetype in a literary work a reason for judging it to be great? These questions go beyond the scope of the critic's concern, which is with the work itself, and which apparently must presuppose, rather than provide, answers to them.

1. RELATIONSHIP TO OTHER DISCIPLINES. In a conveniently broad sense, literary criticism (q.v.) can be said to consist of the class of all existing statements about literary works of art, whether or not made by professional critics. And this class can be considered the subject matter of metacriticism. But a further distinc-

tion within this class has come to be widely acknowledged and employed: that between "internal" and "external" statements. Among the remarks made about literary works are two external sorts: (1) *comparative* statements, noting the likenesses and differences of literary works or of literary works and other cultural products, and (2) *causal* statements about the influence of antecedent conditions (including biographical and political conditions as well as previous literary works), about the effects of literary works on individual readers or social processes, and about the ways in which literary works and other objects and events may be symptoms of underlying conditions. These external remarks are frequently assigned to the province of *literary history*, which is thus distinguished from criticism defined, in its narrower sense, as consisting of statements about the internal properties of literary works (including their semantical properties, if any). This distinction need not commit us to any assumptions about the logical connections, or lack of logical connections, between critical statements and the statements of literary history: it is merely a preliminary way of sorting things out and arranging a reasonable distribution of tasks. The task of the critic would then be to tell us what he knows (or as much as is worth imparting) about the form and content of individual works, and that of the literary historian to trace its conditions and consequences. The question is left open (it is itself a metacritical question) whether, to what extent, or in what ways, the performance of either task depends on the completion of the other.

If we think of criticism—in the narrower sense from now on—as consisting of singular statements about particular poems, short stories, etc., then we immediately wonder whether such statements can be generalized into principles of criticism and, if so, whether these principles can be brought together into a system, in which some principles are seen as logical consequences of other, more fundamental, ones. The endeavor to discover such principles and so connect them belongs to the *theory of literature*, which is sometimes called "poetics" (q.v.). Two very different examples of this genre are Northrop Frye's *Anatomy of Crit.* (1957) and Barbara Herrnstein Smith's *Poetic Closure* (1968). In attempting such a theory, we are still on the same language-level as the critic; we have merely moved (but it is a big move) from the particular to the general, and from isolated generalizations to system. How far criticism can be, or ought to be, systematized in this way is itself an important (metacritical) question; but it is hard to think of any eminent and productive critic who has been content to utter only singular statements, without suggesting some general principles and making an effort to justify them by appeal to other general principles.

Literary theory, moving toward the highest generality of which it is capable, impinges on music theory (e.g., L. B. Meyer, *Emotion and Meaning in Music*, 1956), art theory (e.g., E. H. Gombrich, *Art and Illusion*, 2d ed., 1961), etc. It therefore makes sense, though it may be rather bold, to inquire whether the combining of these several theories could not yield generalizations (say, about form, or expression, or meaning, or truth) that would hold for works of art in all media. The search for such a general theory of art—undertaken in very different ways, e.g., by B. Croce (*Aesthetic*, 1902), T. M. Greene (*The Arts and the Art of Crit.*, 1947), and N. Goodman (*Languages of Art*, 1968)—is often assigned to *aesthetics*, as a branch of philosophy. And this is not an unreasonable way of characterizing aesthetics (see T. Munro, *The Arts and their Interrelations*, 1949).

There is, however, another way, now more generally accepted by philosophers in Eng.-speaking countries who practice philosophical analysis. On this view, the problems of (philosophical, as distinct from psychological) aesthetics are precisely the general and fundamental problems of metacriticism. No one is quite happy about adopting this usage without qualification, for, in the first place, some of the problems of aesthetics can arise in reflection on, say, our tendency to ascribe various beauties and sublimities to natural objects, as well as works of art; and, in the second place, not all of the problems of aesthetics lend themselves readily to formulation as metalinguistic problems, i.e., as problems about the language of criticism. Still, we might say that the central role and dominant character of aesthetics derives from the fact that its main problems are those philosophical problems that arise when we reflect critically on the meaning and logical justification of critical statements (including, of course, literary critical statements).

We must not expect all of these borders to be precisely marked, nor require that every question we ask be instantly and confidently pigeonholed. But the sorting out is extremely important, and clarifies the nature of each of the enterprises. And developments in philosophy and logic and theory of language in recent decades have certainly enabled us to know what we are doing better than earlier theorists could. I. A. Richards' *Principles of Literary Crit.* (1925) was, in large part, a pioneering work in metacriticism, though it also encompassed some critical theory and some criticism. In his provocative first chapter on "The Chaos of Critical Theories," he listed a number of questions:

What gives the experience of reading a certain poem its value? How is this experience better than another? Why prefer this picture to that? In which ways should we listen to music so as to receive the most valuable moments? Why is one opinion about works of art not as good as another? These are the fundamental questions which criticism is required to answer, together with such preliminary questions—What *is* a picture, a poem, a piece of music? How can experiences be compared? What is value?—as may be required in order to approach these questions (pp. 5–6).

Some of these questions are not easy to classify without more context, but others clearly belong to different logical realms, and, indeed, one of the reasons for the failure of that most remarkable book is precisely that so many diverse sorts of inquiry were lumped together as though they were of the same order. Certainly, "Why prefer Pope's *Rape of the Lock* to Tennyson's *Locksley Hall*?" is precisely a question for the critic. But "What makes one opinion about a poem better than another?" is a metacritical question, since it inquires into the logic of critical judgment. And "What is a poem (i.e., what is the word 'poem' best taken to mean)?" is also a metacritical question, though, once the class of poems has been marked out (if that can be done), then the question what other properties poems always, or generally, have in common is a question for literary theory.

2. THE CLASSIFICATION OF CRITICAL STATEMENTS. Criticism, even in the narrower sense, encompasses a variety of statements, and different kinds of statement give rise to different metacritical problems. So the first, preliminary, task of the metacritic is to find the basic categories into which all critical statements can be sorted. There appear to be at least four such categories:

(a) *Descriptions*. A critic, or anyone else talking seriously about literary works, may say that a poem contains such-and-such words in such-and-such syntactical combinations; that a poem has a certain pattern of meter or rhyme; that a novel contains certain characters involved in certain events at a certain place and time (see ANALYSIS). More complex (and problematical) descriptions are those that classify literary works into certain *genres*: this is a sonnet, a tragedy, a pastoral lyric, an epic. (See, e.g., Paul Hernadi, *Beyond Genre*, 1972.)

(b) *Interpretations*. Using the term "interpretation"* in the broadest way, to encompass any statement that purports to say what a literary work means, we can distinguish several interpretational tasks, each having its own special features and problems. (i) Unraveling an obscurity or complexity in the texture of the work: saying how a syntactical construction is to be read, or unpacking the meanings of a metaphor. This is called Explication (q.v.). (ii) Interpreting implicit motives or traits of character in the fictional world. This might be called Enucleation. (iii) Interpreting the symbols (q.v.) in a literary work or (what probably comes to the same thing) identifying its themes. This might be called Thematic Elucidation. (iv) Saying what implicit propositions, philosophical or political or other, are embodied in the work. This may be called Exegesis. It has recently been argued (by Guy Sircello, in *Mind and Art*, 1972) that there is a fifth kind of interpretation, (v) saying what "artistic acts" are performed in the work: e.g., that the author has treated certain characters or events sentimentally, coldly, compassionately, ironically, with calm detachment or with moral indignation.

(c) *Explanations*. Some of the properties found in literary works are "regional qualities," in that they are qualities of the whole work or of some complex part of it: the overall metrical character, its liveliness, melancholy, or wit (for. the term "regional quality," see M. C. Beardsley, *Aesthetics*, 1958, ch. 2). Since these qualities are dependent on the (comparatively local) properties of the subordinate parts, the critic may ask: What specific features of the poem give it its metrical character, its liveliness, melancholy, or wit? A critical explanation will have the form: "It is the presence of such-and-such details (devices) that makes (or helps to make) the poem have such-and-such a regional quality."

(d) *Evaluations*. To say that a literary work is a good or poor one, or is a better or worse literary work (or poem, or novel, etc.) than another, is to offer an evaluation (q.v.). To say, on the other hand, "I like this poem," or "I prefer this poem to that," or "The poem moves me," is not to evaluate, though such remarks, in certain contexts, may suggest that the speaker

is not merely evincing his own feelings but is making, or is prepared to make, a judgment of (literary) value. Statements attributing such regional qualities as beauty, wit, tension, paradox, integrity, power to literary works are sometimes classified as evaluations, and may indeed suggest positive judgments; but they are probably best taken to affirm the presence, not of literary goodness itself, but of *grounds* of literary goodness. This (basic metacritical) issue is in dispute.

3. SOME PROBLEMS OF METACRITICISM. The problems of metacriticism can be classified in terms of the kinds of critical statement that give rise to them, or, more fundamentally, in terms of the fields of philosophic inquiry into which they lead the pursuer. Instead of attempting a systematic survey here, it will be useful, and will help to clarify the concerns and methods of metacriticism, to list briefly a representative selection of metacritical problems.

(1) When explications conflict, as they sometimes do, the questions arise, first, which of the incompatible explications is correct; and, second, by what procedure the critic can show that an explication is correct or incorrect. The second question invites inquiry into the "logic of explication"—whether, for example, appeal to the author's intention (q.v.) is decisive. The intentional theory is one (but only one) of the nonrelativistic theories of explication; relativism denies that there is in fact any objective way of showing that one explication is better than another. These disputes lead into fundamental questions in the philosophy of language, such as the nature of meaning.

(2) When the novelist makes up a story about nonexistent characters, he uses declarative sentences, but his use of language differs in puzzling ways from the use of language in, say, historical narration. What is distinctive and essential in the fictional use of language? Are the sentences of a work of fiction simply false, like many sentences in works of nonfiction, or "true" in some Pickwickian way about imaginary worlds, or neither true nor false, but exempt from these semantic categories?

(3) When evaluations conflict, as they seem very often to do, is there an objective procedure by which the conflict can be resolved and one judgment can be shown to be more reasonable or more acceptable than the other? Again, the relativist metacritical theory is that no such procedure exists, at least in some cases —perhaps (depending on the kind of relativism) when the disputants are of different periods, or cultures, or simply personal tastes. Nonrelativists tend to stress the role of reasons, or criteria of evaluation, in critical discussion— noting, for example, that the discovery of a

high degree of unity (q.v.) in a poem is taken by most critics to be a reason for saying that the poem is good, and is never (or practically never) taken to be a reason for condemning a poem—except, of course, that a highly unified poem may be weak on other grounds, just as a rather disorganized poem may have redeeming merits. Whether critical evaluations can be supported by genuine reasons is an extremely far-reaching problem that leads (as Richards notes in the quotation above) into fundamental problems about the nature of value, especially that kind of value sought in literature.

(4) Whether or not the explicit sentences of a work of fiction may be taken to be true or false, many literary works seem to embody implicit theses of a very general sort—religious, philosophical, etc. (see PHILOSOPHY AND POETRY). The problem of truth in literature is (concisely) whether the truth or falsity of such embodied theses has any logical bearing on the literary goodness or poorness of the work. This problem is closely connected with, though not identical to, the problem of belief (q.v.), which deals (roughly) with the connection between the reader's antecedent beliefs and his understanding and evaluation of the work.

(5) Analogous to the problem of truth is the problem of art and morality: whether any facts about moral aspects of the work (its potentially undesirable political effects, its pornographic nature) have a bearing on its literary goodness. Though the issues involved here trouble the metacritic today less than at earlier periods, they have perennial features and arise in new forms—as, for example, from time to time when Ezra Pound has come up for an award, or when the constitutional problems about obscenity are publicly debated.

4. METACRITICISM AS PHILOSOPHY. Taken most broadly, as philosophy of criticism, metacriticism deals with all aspects of criticism: its language, its procedures, its presuppositions, its functions and values. It may undertake a systematic classification of critical "approaches" or methods, or even devise and propose new strategies: see, for example, the "modes" of criticism distinguished by Richard McKeon, "The Philosophic Bases of Art and Criticism," in R. S. Crane, ed., Critics and Crit. (1953), pp. 530–45, and "Imitation and Criticism," in Thought, Action, and Passion (1954). But its central concern is with the logic of criticism, whose problems (as can be seen from the sample just presented) fall into two large groups: those arising in the attempt to understand and clarify the meaning of the key terms in which criticism is conducted, and those arising in the attempt to analyze and appraise the logical soundness of the critic's arguments in support of his statements.

If there is no such thing as a logic of criti-

cism, in this sense, then metacriticism becomes fairly limited, though of course it is itself a philosophical question whether there is a logic of criticism. It has sometimes been suggested that language works in a special way in critical discourse, and that such key terms as "form" and "beauty" are cognitively meaningless; if such a view could be made plausible, it would eliminate the first group of metacritical problems—unless so-called "emotive meaning" be considered a kind of meaning. It has sometimes been suggested that critical statements work in a special way—are not to be taken as true or false—and that critical argument is not argument in the usual sense (i.e., the supporting of a statement by reasons), but only a way of calling attention to features of literary works and communicating a response to them. If this view could be sustained, then there would be no such thing as a logical justification for the critic's remarks, and no call for an appraisal of it. Certainly advertising literary merits and celebrating the importance of literature may be considered important critical services, but it is hard to see how critics could perform these services if they make no genuine statements or give no genuine reasons to back them up.

The metacritic's first enterprise—the analysis of meaning—raises a conflict within metacriticism (or a metametacritical issue) concerning the scope and limits of metacriticism. Semantic descriptivists take the technical terms of criticism as the critic uses them, and are content merely to study, and make explicit, the way these terms are used—the varied senses of "form," as it is contrasted with other terms; the concept of the "objective correlative" (q.v.) as introduced by Eliot and applied or modified by others. Semantic revisionists are uneasy about stopping there: they consider it part of the metacritic's job to point out where critical vocabulary goes astray (the ambiguities, the areas of vagueness, the inconsistencies in such concepts as that of the "objective correlative"), and where possible to recommend clearer definitions or new terminology (e.g., that the word "form" be used always for the set of relationships within a work). Prescriptivists do not necessarily hope to standardize all critical language, but they think that criticism would be improved and much less discussion wasted if critics could use their key terms in the same clear and explicit senses. Those who conceive of criticism primarily as a literary art are suspicious of such an aim.

The metacritic's second enterprise—the logical appraisal of critical reasoning—raises a second conflict within metacriticism, about the ultimate relationship between criticism and philosophy. Does criticism rest on philosophic (aesthetic) foundations, and does it require to be justified (i.e., to be shown to be a reasonable enterprise) by philosophic arguments? The *autonomist* view (the view that criticism is independent of philosophy) has been firmly stated by Robert J. Matthews (*Diacritics* [Spring 1972], p. 28): "Criticism is all right as it stands. It needs no justification." The metacritic, on this view, has enough to do in getting and making clear the actual reasoning of the critic, bringing out his tacit assumptions, and perhaps even helping him understand better what he is doing. But he does not need to justify criticism itself, or any of its practices. The *heteronomist* view is that criticism necessarily rests on philosophical foundations whose truth, or at least reasonableness, can be established only by philosophical inquiry. If explication presupposes certain propositions about the nature of meaning, if evaluation presupposes certain propositions about the nature of truth and value, then (on this view) the critic may talk nonsense, or go wildly astray in his work, unless the propositions presupposed are philosophically sound. Some of the issues in the autonomy/heteronomy dispute are articulated by W. K. Wimsatt and T. M. Greene in a symposium, "Is a General Theory of the Arts of Any Practical Value in the Study of Literature?" JAAC (June 1950).

In addition to the works already cited, see also: S. C. Pepper, *The Basis of Crit. in the Arts* (1945); Abrams (ch. 1); W. K. Wimsatt, *The Verbal Icon* (1954) and *Hateful Contraries* (1965); Wellek and Warren; M. C. Beardsley, *Aesthetics* (1958, esp. Intro.) and (ed.) *Lit. and Aesthetics* (1968); *Aesthetics and Language*, ed. W. Elton (1959); J. Stolnitz, *Aesthetics and Philos. of Art Crit.* (1960); R. E. Lane, *The Liberties of Wit: Humanism, Crit. and the Civic Mind* (1961); J. Margolis, *The Language of Art and Art Crit.* (1965); J. Casey, *The Language of Crit.* (1966); E. Olson, "The Dialectical Foundations of Crit. Pluralism," *Texas Quarterly*, 9 (1966); M. C. Beardsley, *The Possibility of Crit.* (1970); M. Peckham, "Theory of Crit.," *The Triumph of Romanticism* (1970); R. Wellek, *Discriminations* (1970); F. Jameson, "Metacommentary," PMLA, 86 (1971); *In Search of Lit. Theory*, ed. M. W. Bloomfield (1972).   M.C.B.

MYTH CRITICISM. Much poetry is mythical in the sense of being about supernatural characters and events or of drawing upon them as a frame of reference. And even when poetry is not overtly mythical—when it is, say, concerned with merely human characters in a world without gods—it often has covert connections with myth (q.v.), as when 20th-c. poets describe the destruction of the world, which is an ancient and widespread mythologem or archetype (q.v.). Myth makers are poets, and m. comes into being through mythopoesis, or poetic making; whether or not all poets make myths—some critics (such as R. Chase) regard "m." and "poetry" as largely synonymous—m. provides an essential matrix of all, or at least much, poetry. Focusing upon this mythical matrix, one may say that "literature is only a part, though a central part, of the total mythopoeic structure of concern which extends into religion, philosophy, political theory, and many aspects of history, the vision a society has of its situation, destiny, and ideals, and of reality in terms of those human factors" (N. Frye, 1967). Such a reflection takes one less far from poetry than might appear, since some of the basic elements that poetry derives from m. are recognizable in mathematics and the physical sciences (S. Buchanan, E. Schrödinger). The very development of philosophy required discrimination of *mythos* from *logos*, or thinking about m. But it is only recently that thinking about the mythical matrix of literature, and about mythical elements in it, assumed the form that has been called m. criticism. Such criticism expresses concerns felt strongly in the second half of the 20th c., but groundwork for it was laid by many writers earlier, including G. Vico, various of the German romantics, Friedrich Nietzsche, E. B. Tylor, J. G. Frazer, Sigmund Freud, and C. G. Jung. Indeed, since "m." embraces ancient and persistent human concerns, observations about its relation to literature are to be found among numerous earlier literary critics, for example, Samuel Johnson, who has much to say about the aesthetic value of myths incorporated in poetry. It may be useful to regard 20th-c. m. criticism as the outcome of a succession of overlapping cultural moments, which help to define its central concerns; a few names may roughly suggest this development. Richard Wagner saw himself, as an artist, faced by opposing claims of m. and history and consciously chose those of m.; and Friedrich Nietzsche's writings directly reflected kinds of experience that give rise to m. and prophesy, though Nietzsche's Zarathustra declared that God was dead. Writers exploring the possibilities of symbolism (q.v.) created hermetic personal poetry, which, according to some critics (including T. S. Eliot) drew upon the "primitive psyche" expressed in the collective m. of earlier times. Despite Frazer's positivistic assumptions, his massive *Golden Bough* betrayed a fascination with mythical, magical, and religious materials, which it served to retrieve from the cultural trash heap for writers reacting against positivism. James Joyce, T. S. Eliot, D. H. Lawrence, Thomas Mann, and W. B. Yeats used m. in ways that demanded explication. And the new criticism (q.v.), in demonstrating not only the strengths but also the limits of a largely formalist approach to literature, led, as one reaction, to an emphasis upon m. in literary criticism. As a result of tendencies suggested by these names, a number of critics came to feel that literature "cannot be limited to the working out of a pattern within the framework imposed by an art form, but rather must be viewed as part of the totality of human experience. Thus the simple separation of form and content, intrinsic and extrinsic values, or the like, falls away even for the purposes of analysis—indeed, especially for such purposes. From this central assumption it is but one further step to assert that literature is part of a social situation and that literary works must be approached primarily as modes of collective belief and action. Myth and ritual, then, become essential qualities of literary expression" (H. M. Block in Vickery). And since m. and ritual also reflect the workings of the human mind, m. criticism overlaps the criticism of psychology and poetry.*

As the name of Nietzsche will suggest, much m. criticism has been directly or indirectly concerned with the origin and nature of drama. The influence of the Cambridge Anthropologists on literary criticism, heralded by G. Murray's essay on Hamlet and Orestes (1914), has been pervasive. Concern with elements of m. and ritual has led F. Fergusson, in an effective study, to see *Hamlet* as a celebration of the mystery of human life achieved through ceremonious invocations of the well-being of society, these invocations being themselves the means of securing that well-being. Though *Hamlet* is in important ways modern and skeptical, "even the most cutting ironies of Hamlet do not disavow the mystery which the rituals celebrate, or reject the purposes that inform them" (Fergusson). J.I.M. Stewart has seen Falstaff as a ritual scapegoat, and J. Holloway finds the scapegoat essential to Shakespeare's tragedies. More generally, H. Weisinger has traced the conception of tragedy back to its roots in m. and ritual in the ancient Near East. C. L. Barber has analyzed ways in which Shakespearean comedy achieves "clarification" related to that brought about by folk festivals. The early studies of C. Still (1921) and G. W. Knight (1929) initiated a continuing concern with mythical elements in Shakespeare's last plays. And various critics have studied such elements in Henrik Ibsen and more recent drama (O. Holton, K. Burkman).

Though m. criticism has been largely concerned with narrative, and especially dramatic, content rather than with details of poetic form and technique, several works of nondramatic poetry have been seen as embodying mythical motifs. Critics of *Sir Gawain and the Green*

Knight, for example, have arrived at differing views of such motifs in the poem (H. Zimmer, J. Speirs, and C. Moorman). In discussing the visionary landscape of medieval allegory, P. Piehler attempts to define allegory and its relations to m. Milton's *Lycidas* has been seen as conforming to a cycle of death and rebirth, expressed in vegetation sacred to fertility gods, and in a descent into water and reemergence from it, paralleling the setting and rising of the sun (R. P. Adams in Vickery). Keats's *Endymion* has also been seen as conforming to a cyclical m., consisting of the Call to the Quest, Acceptance and Descent into the Underworld, Fulfillment of the Quest, and Return, apotheosized by a sacred marriage (R. Harrison in Vickery). Indeed, the m.-making propensities of the romantic poets—their m.-like constructions derived not so much from inherited collective belief as from the impulse to individual symbol formation (Jung)—have received much attention (Frye, 1947, H. Bloom). And indeed, Frye has pointed to Blake as one of the main inspirations behind his own critical labors.

The interests and ideas guiding the works of exegesis reviewed till now have also found expression in the critical system elaborated by Frye, principally in his *Anatomy of Crit.* This work provides an all-embracing view of literature, with special attention to modes and genres, to thematic and mythical recurrence in literature, and to the ways in which literature, like m., ultimately rests on preconscious ritual. After a "Polemical Introduction," Frye's *Anatomy* goes on to "Historical Criticism: Theory of Modes," an essay which sees the literary past as consisting of two cycles of five periods each, with each of these periods corresponding to a "mode," defined as a measure of the strength of the hero (for example, of Achilles or of Leopold Bloom) in relation to the world of the fiction in which he occurs, this fictional world, in turn, reflecting the world of the audience for which the work was written. The second essay, "Ethical Crit.: Theory of Symbols," discusses five phases of symbolism—literal, descriptive, formal, archetypal, and anagogical—paralleling the five modes of the first essay. The third essay, "Archetypal Crit.: Theory of Myths," is concerned with the ways in which myths and archetypal conventions undergo historical transformation, these elements often serving as structural principles, which may affect the audience without its awareness. The transformations of these elements parallel those of the hero and the symbol, discussed in the first essays. The fourth essay, "Rhetorical Criticism: Theory of Genres," is concerned with genre as something based on its own characteristic rhythm, which may be seen in the overall, continuous flow of the epic or in minute prosodic effects. All of the elements and processes described in the *Anatomy* arise from "displacements" of m., through which m. is modified by culture so as to be logical, plausible, acceptable in accordance with prevailing stylistic and other norms. But m. remains effective even in these "displacements," since "the structural principles of literature are as closely related to mythology and comparative literature as those of painting are to geometry."

The immense appeal of Frye's critical viewpoint lies, first, in its heuristic aspect—in the way in which it invites the reader to see parallels and interconnections among forms and devices and specific literary works usually regarded as discrete, and second, in its insistence on the derivation of literature from m., not simply as "poetry" but as a fundamental way of apprehending the world. Its appeal was so great that in 1966 M. Krieger could claim that "in what approaches a decade since the publication of his masterwork, he has had an influence—indeed an absolute hold—on a generation of developing literary critics greater and more exclusive than that of any one theorist in recent critical history." Frye's work has been criticized—for being overly schematic, for neglecting style, for remaining too far from a close reading of texts, for using common literary terms in idiosyncratic ways, for surreptitiously gaining vital rhetorical effects through such emotionally colored terms as "archetype" where such plain words as "model" would do as well—and some of the criticisms of Frye shade off into criticisms that have been raised against 20th-c. m. criticism in general. One of these is that m. critics find m. a flight from the reality of history, this flight expressing certain social and political attitudes (P. Rahv). Another is that current interest in m. grants pleasant glimpses of transcendence without the bother of religious commitment and of the threat to intellectual integrity that such commitment might entail. Another is that m. criticism tends to remain on the level of coarse structure, comparing works on the basis of broad similarities, without adequately accounting for specific poetic effects. And still another is that the basic concepts and issues of m. criticism have not been adequately formulated (Weisinger in H. Murray). In general, "m. criticism" names an area of interest, rather than a specific method or viewpoint; indeed, modern criticism attributes a wide range of meanings to "m."—R. Wellek and A. Warren distinguish several—and m. critics are most often heavily indebted to one or more anthropologists, cultural historians, and philosophers for their notably various approaches. Moreover, theoretical m. critics (e.g.,

N. Frye, R. Graves, and J. Campbell) frequently aspire to a global view—for example through the assumption of a universal Monomyth or Ur-m. that brings all m. and literature into a unity. M. criticism was especially prominent in a period which may be roughly fixed between the dates of Frye's *Anatomy*, 1957, and of an excellent anthology by Vickery, 1966, which includes essays most of which were written within twenty years of that date. But the mythical matrix of poetry is sufficiently well established and sufficiently important that valuable work in this area will surely continue to be done. This sanguine view is supported by such studies as that of J. Armstrong, who regards the tree and the snake in Sumerian and Greek mythology as a single form expressing a basic imaginative polarity, and with critical sensitivity traces this form in Botticelli's *Primavera*, in three plays of Shakespeare, in Milton's *Paradise Lost*, and in Coleridge's *The Ancient Mariner* and *Kubla Khan*. As Armstrong asserts, "Myths are the most accurate means that the human mind has devised of representing its own immeasurably complex structure and content. They are essentially poetic formations, and express areas of thought and feeling where, as Blake puts it, 'ideas can only be given in their minutely appropriate words.'"

J. L. Weston, *From Ritual to Romance* (1920); C. Still, *Shakespeare's Mystery Play* (1921), *The Timeless Theme* (1936); G. Murray, *The Classical Tradition in Poetry* (1927); S. Buchanan, *Poetry and Mathematics* (1929); G. W. Knight, *M. and Miracle* (1929); N. Frye, *Fearful Symmetry* (1947), *Anatomy of Crit.* (1957), "Lit. and M." [bibliog.], in *Relations of Lit. Study*, ed. J. Thorpe (1967); R. Graves, *The White Goddess* (1948); H. Zimmer, *The King and the Corpse* (1948); J.I.M. Stewart, *Character and Motive in Shakespeare* (1949); R. Chase, *Quest for M.* (1949); F. Fergusson, *The Idea of a Theater* (1953); H. Weisinger, *Tragedy and the Paradox of the Fortunate Fall* (1953); E. Schrödinger, *Nature and the Greeks* (1954); Wellek and Warren; H. Bloom, *Shelley's Mythmaking* (1957); J. Speirs, *Medieval Eng. Poetry* (1957); C. L. Barber, *Festive Comedy in Shakespeare* (1959); C. Moorman, *Arthurian Triptych* (1960); *M. and Mythmaking*, ed. H. A. Murray (1960); J. Holloway, *The Story of the Night* (1961); *M. and Symbol*, ed. B. Slote (1963); G. Durand, *Les Structures anthropologiques de l'imaginaire* (1963); G. Bachelard, *The Poetics of Space*, tr. M. Jolas (1964), *The Psychoanalysis of Fire*, tr. A. Ross (1964); P. Rahv, *The M. and the Powerhouse* (1965); G. Hartman, "Structuralism: The Anglo American Adventure," YFS, 36–37 (1966) and *Beyond Formalism*

(1970); *M. and Lit.*, ed. J. B. Vickery (1966); *Northrop Frye in Modern Crit.*, ed. M. Krieger (1966); D. Hoffman, *Barbarous Knowledge* (1967); J. Armstrong, *The Paradise M.* (1969); W. Willeford, *The Fool and His Scepter* (1969); O. Holton, *Mythic Patterns in Ibsen's*

Last Plays (1970); H. Slochower, *Mythopoesis* (1970); K. Burkman, *The Dramatic World of Harold Pinter* (1971); P. Piehler, *The Visionary Landscape* (1971); W. A. Strauss, *Descent and Return* (1971); L. Feder, *Ancient Myth in Modern Poetry* (1972). w.w.

N

NEGATIVE CAPABILITY. Keats himself defines his famous phrase as "capable of being in uncertainties, Mysteries, doubts, without any irritable reaching after fact & reason." He adds, "This pursued through Volumes would perhaps take us no further than this, that with a great poet the sense of Beauty overcomes every other consideration, or rather obliterates all consideration." Earlier in the same letter he had said that "the excellence of every Art is its intensity, capable of making all disagreeables evaporate, from their being in close relationship with Beauty & Truth." Later on he was to speak of the virtues of passive receptivity, "budding patiently under the eye of Apollo and taking hints from every noble insect that favors us with a visit." Again, he says of the "poetical character," "It has no

character—it enjoys light and shade; it lives in gusto, be it foul or fair, high or low, rich or poor, mean or elevated—It has as much delight in conceiving an Iago as an Imogen."

Keats's statement is an affirmation of the self-contained integrity of art. Beyond this, it is peculiarly characteristic of Keats's own honest and deliberate tentativeness of approach, and it strikingly expresses his preference for the objective and the dramatic modes of poetry.—*The Letters of John Keats*, ed. H. E. Rollins (2 v., 1958, I, 193, 387); W. J. Bate, *Negative Capability: The Intuitive Approach in Keats* (1939) and *John Keats* (1963). R.H.F.

NEW YORK POETS. See AMERICAN POETIC SCHOOLS AND TECHNIQUES (CONTEMPORARY).*

O

ORNAMENT. An embellishment or decoration. Its values are intrinsic rather than instrumental. It is praised for its grace, charm, beauty, its capability of producing an immediate pleasurable response in the spectator. (An o. may, of course, have incidental utilitarian values, and a basically practical object, like a piece of furniture, may have ornamental values added to it.) In certain ages and cultures, the fine arts, including poetry, have been regarded as ornaments. They have been associated with discriminating taste, refinement, leisure, and a high level of civilization. At other times, a stress on the ornamental values of poetry has connoted superficiality, frivolity, and the decadence of a period in which poets cultivate art for its own sake.

Within poetics, the term "o." has appeared regularly in the long tradition of pragmatic criticism, particularly in those forms of pragmatic criticism that see a close relationship

between poetry and rhetoric (see POETRY, THEORIES OF [PRAGMATIC THEORIES]). In classical rhetoric, "o." is a part of the vocabulary of discussions of style (q.v.). After the content of a speech has been invented and outlined, it is dressed in language and, if desirable, decked out in appropriate o. An ornate style is defined as an artistic deviation of considerable degree from ordinary usage in choice of words or word orders. Such deviations, because of their artistry and novelty, give pleasure to the hearer (and may also contribute to the orator's persuasive purpose). The means for the heightening and exornation of style that apply in oratory apply even more fully to poetry. Thus classical, medieval, and Renaissance theorists spent much time in identifying and classifying these "flowers," "gems," and "colors" of expression. Distinctions were made between schemes and tropes, figures of speech (q.v.) and figures of thought, and "difficult" and "easy" ornaments (as in Geoffrey of Vinsauf; also see TROPE). Also characteristic of rhetorical poetics was the attempt to determine the kind and amount of stylistic o. that should be included in a poem. Although there always have been practitioners and admirers of the florid (a style which, since classical times, has been known as "Asiatic"; see also AUREATE LANGUAGE, EUPHUISM, and MANNERISM), most theorists sought to develop a set of principles for guiding an author in the tasteful and effective use of o. These principles involved considerations of decorum and genre and, most important, appropriateness to an author's subject, purpose, or audience. Thus, as R. Tuve has pointed out, the justification in medieval and Renaissance theory for figurative language stressed the functional as well as the ornamental values of figures. Figures are good because they catch the reader's attention, keep him in a state of pleasurable anticipation, and delight his imagination. They can also have more directly functional values; they can assist the persuasive process by clarifying and vivifying the abstract, generating emotion, and moving the will. The functional justification of figures was most complete in Platonizing thinkers of the Middle Ages and the Renaissance who considered some figures—notably allegory, symbol, and metaphor—to be the indispensable means for revealing the light, beauty, and harmony of spiritual reality; thus in a successful figure ornamental and functional values coalesce.

Neoclassical critics, particularly those who stressed the intrinsic values of poetry, continued to find use for the term "o." As in earlier criticism, o. was used to refer not only to figurative language but also to other parts of a poem. For example, the musical qualities of language are pleasing accessories or added embellishments. Dryden speaks of adorning a poem with noble thoughts. Sometimes the plot of a dramatic poem is regarded as a naked structure which is ornamented with a variety of interesting characters, moving episodes (including digressions), and finely wrought

speeches. Indeed, almost any aspect of a poem which could be a separate source of pleasure could be called an o. Neoclassical critics who stressed instruction, the other of the Horatian twin aims of poetry, also continued to speak of the "beauties" or "ornaments" of poetry. Pleasure, though a secondary aim, is the necessary sugarcoating to get the audience to swallow the pill of instruction.

The theory of o. gradually disappeared during the 19th c. Romantic critics formulated theories of the interdependence or identity of form and content, thought and expression. Thus the term "o.," with its connotation of adventitiousness, was no longer applicable. Similarly, in the 20th c., theories of poetry as organism (q.v.) explicitly oppose themselves to ornamentalist views. The possible intrinsic values of any part of a poem are declared unimportant or irrelevant, and only functional values are praised. Functional values are defined in terms of the interdependence of the parts of a poem and their contribution to the organic unity of the poem. When, as in Cleanth Brooks, the organic unity is described as a structure of meanings, metaphor and other figures are said to be functional only when they contribute to this structure. Organicism refuses to praise any part of a poem as a source of independent pleasure, and the term "o." is regarded with suspicion.

G. Puttenham, *The Arte of Eng. Poesie* (1589, esp. Book III, "Of O."); B. Croce, *Aesthetic* (1901); E. Faral, *Les Arts poétiques du xiie et du xiiie siècle* (1924); E. de Bruyne, *Études d'esthétique médiévale* (3 v., 1946); A. Coomaraswamy, *Figures of Speech or Figures of Thought* (1946); R. Tuve, *Elizabethan and Metaphysical Imagery* (1947); W. S. Howell, *Logic and Rhetoric in England, 1500-1700* (1956); Weinberg; Geoffrey of Vinsauf, *Documentum de Modo et Arte Dictandi et Versificandi*, tr. R. P. Parr (1968) and *Poetria Nova*, tr. J. B. Kopp, in *Three Medieval Rhetorical Arts*, ed. J. J. Murphy (1971); W. Wetherbee, *Platonism and Poetry in the Twelfth C.* (1972). F.G.

P

PERSONA. An ancient distinction, explicit in Plato and Aristotle, is between poems or parts of poems in which a poet speaks in his own person and those in which a character that he has created is speaking. Poets themselves have written in terms of this distinction: Wordsworth obviously intended that the speaker of *The Prelude* be taken as himself; just as obviously he intended that the speaker of *The Affliction of Margaret* be taken as a dramatic character.

In "The Three Voices of Poetry," T. S.

Eliot has refined upon this distinction. When a poet is speaking in his own person, he may be either speaking to himself (his meditative voice) or addressing a real-life audience (his rhetorical voice). The rhetorical voice is heard in satire and other forms of didactic poetry. It is also heard, according to Eliot, in the dramatic monologue, whose peculiar aesthetic effect is due to the reader's recognition that the poet is not creating a true dramatic personality but is merely mimicking a character, whether historical or invented. He approves of Ezra Pound's use of the term "persona" as a name for the voice of the poet heard in the dramatic monologue. He equates "p." with "assuming a role" and "speaking through a mask."

Other modern critics have asked whether it is ever legitimate or desirable to say, as Eliot does, that a poet is speaking in his own person in a poem. For example, modern objectivist critics argue that this position is a relic of romantic expressionism (Wordsworth said that the poet is a "man speaking to men"), which sends critics off on wild-goose chases after authors' intentions. Further, whether a poem, dramatic or nondramatic, reflects its author's attitudes and beliefs is a question that belongs to biography and not to criticism; frequently, particularly with older or anonymous poems, it is a question impossible to settle. And, finally, the expressionist position inevitably raises the question of the author's sincerity (q.v.), a standard of evaluation, beloved by the romantics, whose correct application, however, seems to necessitate an act of intuitive insight. Since a poem is good only if it is an entity complete in itself, criticism of the poem should proceed without reference to its author. Hence objectivist critics have recommended that all poems be regarded as dramatic fictions and that the term "p.," rather than the name of the author, be used to refer to the speaker of the poem (if it has one). Thus the lyric, which in the 19th c. meant a poem "directly expressing the poet's own thoughts and sentiments" (*O.E.D.*), becomes assimilated to the dramatic monologue. And the term "p." is applied indiscriminately to the speakers in Browning's *My Last Duchess, Rabbi Ben Ezra,* and *By the Fireside.*

Rhetorically oriented modern critics, like Wayne C. Booth, also recommend making a sharp distinction between the real-life author and the "implied author" (the "second self" or "p.") that the real-life author, consciously or unconsciously, incorporates into his work. The implied author, who may or may not be the narrator, is a fictional personality present in every literary work, even in a purely dramatic work like a Shakespearean play. His presence may serve many functions, but the principal one is to supply the norms in terms of which the characters and their actions are judged. The degree to which the implied author reveals himself and the nature of the norms that he espouses are dictated by the effects that the author wishes his work to have. This is clearly seen in didactic works; for example, Elder Olson shows how Pope's persuasive purpose in *The Epistle to Dr. Arbuthnot* is served by his endowing the "p." of the poem with admirable intellectual and moral qualities. According to Booth, the author of an imaginative or mimetic work must exercise similar care in creating his implied author if his work is to secure the intended emotional response from his readers. As in objectivist criticism, considerations of the sincerity of the author and the degree to which the implied author does or does not represent the norms of the real-life author are relegated to biography.

The reaction of modern criticism to romantic expressionism is not the only cause for the present popularity of the term "p." The advantages that accrue to the artist from his use of a p. or mask or disguise have been widely discussed by Yeats and others. The mask permits the poet to say things that for various reasons he could not say in his own person or could say only with a loss of artistic detachment; the mask permits the poet to explore various life-styles without making an ultimate commitment; it is a means for creating, discovering, or defining the self; it prevents the artist from being hurt by self-exposure or being duped by the limitations of his own vision; it is a means for the expression of ideals that the poet may not be able to realize in his personal life; it is an indispensable condition for effective personal communication. Recent studies in psychology and sociology also have influenced literary critics in their use of the concept of p. Depth psychologists need the concept to talk about the relations between the conscious and unconscious parts of the psyche (Jung opposes the p., the self a man assumes to play his social role, to the anima, a man's true inner being). Behaviorist psychologists stress the importance of role-playing for the development of personality and for satisfactory adjustment to life. These ideas have required the formulation of new definitions of "self," "personal identity," "hypocrisy," and "sincerity," both for the purposes of psychology and literary criticism. See also VOICE.*

E. Olson, "Rhetoric and the Appreciation of Pope," MP, 37 (1939); W. K. Wimsatt and M. C. Beardsley, "The Intentional Fallacy," SR, 54 (1946); T. S. Eliot, "The Three Voices of Poetry," in *On Poetry and Poets* (1957); M. C. Beardsley, *Aesthetics* (1958); G. T. Wright, *The Poet in the Poem* (1960); W. C. Booth, *The*

Rhetoric of Fiction (1961); W. J. Ong, *The Barbarian Within* (1962); I. Ehrenpreis, "Personae," *Restoration and 18th-C. Lit.*, ed. C. Camden (1963); A. Cook, "Person" in his *Prisms: Studies in Modern Lit.* (1967); D. Geiger, *The Dramatic Impulse in Modern Poetics* (1967); L. Trilling, *Sincerity and Authenticity* (1972).   F.G.

PHENOMENOLOGY. Modern p. presents itself as an epistemologically neutral instrument for inspecting the data of consciousness. Its founder, Edmund Husserl, characterized it as a "return to experience," insofar as it tries to delineate the very textures of the lived world, the taken-for-granted orbit of immediate and concrete awareness. Husserl defined the goals of p. as twofold: (1) "a pure psychology, parallel to natural science," in which the psychical would be cleanly separated from the physical; and (2) a universal methodology for the restructuring of all the sciences, a transcendental philosophy in the sense that it would disclose the fundamental structures or permanent categories of consciousness itself.

As a starting point Husserl adapted Franz Brentano's axiom that all psychical being is "intentional": awareness exists only in terms of a relation between subject and object; mental states (even hallucinations) always have reference to a content. In Husserl's synthesis this principle means that to be conscious of something is not simply to possess that something passively, as if consciousness were merely a kind of container. While an object may have independent existence, it has no independent intelligibility; it requires a consciousness to give it genuine reality. Accordingly, Husserl's exploration of phenomena is unconcerned with a noumenal realm "behind" them: p. aims at an acausal analysis that restricts itself to exhaustive description of what is directly given in awareness.

Such analysis can begin only when we move away from the "natural attitude"—in which we remain unreflectively oriented toward the object-pole of our knowledge—and into "phenomenological meditation." Husserl proposed that p. proceed by means of a positive naiveté, a mode of scrutiny in which common-sense assumptions about reality undergo "suspension" (*epoché*). A phenomenon under consideration is "bracketed": all presuppositions, inferences, and judgments about it, including the issue of its spatio-temporal existence, are held in abeyance. This purifying phase of meditation frees the phenomenologist to examine the essential structure of the individual phenomenon. As he attends to the residual given, he may describe the object of consciousness in its multiple perspectives and attempt a series of "reductions," focusing awareness so as to intuit whatever reveals itself as essential in the phenomenon (eidetic reduction)—or even in the pure stream of consciousness itself (transcendental reduction). Thus, as Monroe Beardsley has commented, the term "reduction" is in one sense misleading, since the phenomenologist "proposes only to face, without management or manipulation, experience in all its richness."

P. AND POETRY. The aims and methods of p. have much in common with those of art, and of poetry in particular. First, insofar as p. explores through language the is-ness of experience and the textures of the lived world, its quest might be construed as essentially literary. P. here adumbrates an existential concern with the irreducibility of experience. Logical analysis, as a philosophical method, may be seen as a threat to the integrity of consciousness, as in Maurice Merleau-Ponty's observation, "The world is not what I think, but what I live." Merleau-Ponty, Martin Heidegger, and others influenced by p. have been led to express many philosophical insights in poetic and fictional terms, to suggest that literature may represent the truest form of philosophy, and to use art (especially poetry) as an important source of information about perception and various mental states. All literature ultimately engages in analyzing the data of consciousness, and even apparent records of subconscious activity are given in terms of conscious apprehension.

Some commentators have gone even further in pointing out the aesthetic orientation of p. Fritz Kaufman defines art as a reformation of consciousness, and thus as essentially phenomenological in converting "the natural attitude toward the experienced world" into a meditative attitude toward one's experiencing of the world. In the art work, as in p., the question of the existence or nonexistence of represented objects is "neutralized," and "reductions, methodically carried through in p., happen to find an automatic fulfillment in art." Neal Oxenhandler, in a seminal essay on Mallarmé, applies this insight more specifically to poetry. Every poet may be said to perform an *epoché*, suspending his belief in the spatio-temporal world "in order to consider objects anew within the field of pure consciousness." Both p. and poetry proceed from the assumption of the priority of consciousness: p. tells us that "objects can be apprehended only as correlates of intentional consciousness"; and in poetry, language "*summons* or creates the world to live within itself." Mallarmé provides the paradigm of the power of creative consciousness to constitute a world by means of language: "I say: a flower! and, from out of that oblivion to which my voice relegates any contour, insofar as it differs from the calices as known, musically arises, idea selfsame and suave, the one that is absent from all bouquets."

Oxenhandler claims that even literary "realism" is a form of p., because the relationship it posits between the imaginary world and the fact-world is always tentative, "*as if* we were directly regarding the world of contingent, factual experience." But p. would seem to have stronger affinities with literary works in which the imaginary world has no primary connection to the fact-world, but rather "a direct and immediate relationship to pure consciousness.": This would account for the popularized use of the term "phenomenological" to describe some contemporary experimental literature (e.g., the fiction of Alain Robbe-Grillet) in which the experiencing mind is rendered as directly as possible, without regard to conventional psychological interpretation or to standard expectations of point of view, character, or plot. More importantly, it would account for the attraction of many phenomenologists and phenomenological critics to lyrically subjective poets (e.g., Mallarmé, Hölderlin, Wallace Stevens) whose works set up coherent imaginative universes of their own.

P. AND POETICS. The concerns of p. have influenced most modern Continental critics, especially existentialists, and have found an extremely vital application in the work of the Geneva School.* But the clearest relations between p. and poetics have been drawn by three theorists—Gaston Bachelard, Roman Ingarden, and Mikel Dufrenne—whose conclusions, although not fully consonant with one another, converge on an *aesthetic* orientation to literature. In the comparisons between p. and poetry cited above, certain themes—such as the active nature of all knowledge, the autonomy of the aesthetic object and its invulnerability to paraphrase, and the disinterestedness of aesthetic experience—suggest analogies to the critical position first developed by Immanuel Kant. Bachelard, Ingarden, and Dufrenne provide interesting modifications of this position, and their precise applications of p. may be examined in terms of three traditional issues.

1. *Imagination.* Because its descriptions of experience leave aside standard issues of causality, p. tends to use "consciousness" as an inclusive concept and to avoid the vocabulary of faculty psychologies. The term "imagination" would seem to be an exception, but it is in fact used to designate a kind of *act* rather than a power. In this regard, p. emphasizes a radical contrast between imagination and perception. In his early work in p., Jean-Paul Sartre characterizes all functions of imagination (including daydream images) as negations of perception (making present what is absent, and absent what is present), and he offers this capacity for "unrealizing" as evidence of human freedom. Imagination-as-freedom is a major theme in phenomenological poetics: it is a means of countering

physicalist and psychoanalytical oversimplifications of experience, and of arguing that the aesthetic object can constitute a self-sufficient world of its own. Bachelard defines imagination as a fundamental *openness,* even a mode of "escape," and he sees its exercise as a means of psychic wholeness: "A being deprived of the function of the unreal is a neurotic just as much as one deprived of the function of the real." For Bachelard poetry can provide the fullest manifestation of imagination, but artistic functions are not qualitatively different from other imaginative acts. For Dufrenne, however, aesthetic experience is correlated with a specifically "transcendental" imagination which can create an autonomous spatio-temporal field having no connection to our previous experience. By means of imagination, an aesthetic object carries its own meaning completely within itself, so much so that all art could in a sense be characterized as nonrepresentational.

Insofar as these theorists define imagination almost exclusively as a mode of freedom, they undercut traditional emphases on the creative faculty as an essentially unifying and synthesizing power. The fact is that phenomenological critics are generally less concerned with *formal* imagination than *material* imagination. Bachelard best exemplifies this tendency. Although he describes his total critical endeavor as a "p. of the imagination," he proposes to say nothing about how the poetic mind labors to bring a whole work to completion; in examining a poem, he restricts himself to "the level of detached images" and tries to gauge their dynamism, suggestiveness, and richness of ambivalence. His exploration of the subjective structure of material images is presented in a series of books on earth, air, fire, and water—considered not as objective substances, but as archetypal categories of lived experience. Material imagination can also be studied through its manipulation of the categories of space and time, a method epitomized in *The Poetics of Space.* Here Bachelard treats "images of felicitous space" in literature, examining various "worlds"—such as houses, wardrobes, and nests—as lived spaces which have been seized on by the imagination and invested with psychical values (e.g., intimacy or openness). A similar approach has been used extensively by the Geneva critics, as in Georges Poulet's *Studies in Human Time* or Jean Rousset's *The Interior and the Exterior.*

2. *Poetic ontology.* One analogue in American criticism to the phenomenological analysis of imagination is John Crowe Ransom's neo-Kantian emphasis on "irrelevant texture" in poetry, by means of which the fullness and richness of phenomenal particularity ("the world's body") is returned to us. But the gen-

PHENOMENOLOGY

eral tendency among Ransom's fellow critics (see NEW CRITICISM) has been toward a theory of *formal* imagination, and thus toward the explication of whole poems in terms of unity as an aesthetic value. Oxenhandler has observed that the new-critical conception of literary being is essentially Aristotelian—the poem as a made object, having a discrete existence and a special ontology. For phenomenological critics on the other hand, "the poem does *not* have an independent existence. It is simply part of consciousness; and in the measure that it appears to us, within consciousness, it has being—it *is*."

This contrast accounts for some of the most striking features of Geneva criticism: unabashed affectivity; a "sympathy" that blurs the distinction between the creative and critical acts; a de-emphasis of the wholeness of any one text, in favor of the consistency and uniqueness of the imaginary universe projected throughout an author's total body of work. A sharp contrast with new criticism, however, does not fully illuminate the somewhat ambiguous positions of Dufrenne and Ingarden on the question of poetic ontology. Both propose to deal not with the "work of art" as such, but with the "aesthetic object"—i.e., the work as incarnated in experience. Both then proceed to discuss this object as if it were a coherent entity with a special mode of being. Dufrenne denies that a work of art has an ideal existence, but he asserts that the aesthetic object, unlike other objects in our phenomenal field, can step out of the ordinary world of space and time. It has not only an "outside" but an "inside": an autonomous spatio-temporal world of its own. Moreover, it has an "expressed" world; a unique soul that permeates and gives life to the matter of the work. Thus the object is also a quasi-subject. Dufrenne, ascribing to it "the coherence of a character," seems to grant it some measure of aesthetic integrity.

Ingarden, accused by Dufrenne of "rationalism," goes even further toward a rapprochement with the Aristotelian conception of literary being. He claims that Aristotle was "naive" in giving a pseudo-empirical account of literary objects, but that the *Poetics* is genuinely significant for its unremitting attention to general structural features of works. Aristotelian analysis is akin to p. insofar as it encourages exhaustive description of a work's inherent qualities and their organization, before attempting (if at all) to relate the work to the world external to it.

For Ingarden a poem is an "intentional object" which achieves distinctness and self-presence only as it is concretized in a direct experience by a reader or listener. But the nature of this experience is in part governed by qualities and relationships in the four "strata" of the work: word-sounds, the meanings of the words and sentences (which exist in a literary work only as quasi-meanings, because their function of affirmation has been "neutralized"), the objects represented (people, things, incidents), and schematized images of these objects (made more complete in the imagination of each reader). Ingarden explores various literary possibilities within each stratum, and he examines the progressive series of determinations—from sound to sense to representation to appearance—that gives a sense of depth to the aesthetic object. When he finally argues that the "polyphonic harmony" of all of these elements is a key aesthetic value, Ingarden establishes a standard of coherence at least vaguely analogous to that of Aristotle or the new critics.

3. *Aesthetic Experience.* Although p. does not encourage evaluation in criticism, it does provide an excellent set of concepts and terms for the celebration of aesthetic experience in general. First of all, it characterizes literary response as fundamentally active: a process of "bracketing" in which the reader leaves aside all presuppositions and attends to the aesthetic object as directly given, becoming fully absorbed in it. Poulet describes this openness as a healthy kind of surrender which gives at least the *sense* of true intersubjectivity: "When I read as I ought, i.e. without mental reservation, without any desire to preserve my independence of judgment, and with the total commitment required of any reader, my comprehension becomes intuitive and any feeling proposed to me is immediately assumed by me." In this state "I am persuaded . . . that I am freed from my usual sense of incompatibility between my consciousness and its objects."

These comments accord with Bachelard's presentation of imagination as a liberating transformation of our ordinary sense of reality. Bachelard discusses aesthetic experience as a mode of "reverie"—not a nebulous dream state, but a condition of repose (like phenomenological meditation) in which consciousness is fully engaged and finely focused. Moreover, he treats this experience as archetypal—a return to the primordial images and structures of consciousness—and thus as a special fulfillment and refreshment of our humanity.

Dufrenne points out the paradox in aesthetic experience of a psychological detachment coexisting with a profound involvement, and he sees this as an affirmative response of the whole self. Although meaning in art remains completely immanent, aesthetic experience is a valid form of knowledge—ultimately a self-epiphany. The object's aura of imaginative freedom evokes a response of imaginative freedom, and the object's depth reveals a corresponding depth within the self.

Ingarden's account of aesthetic experience is

grounded in a consideration of representational literature. He attributes "value-qualities" to each stratum of a work, but the most important are those emanating from its represented world. Ingarden identifies them as aspects of life itself (e.g., the tragic, the seductive, the charming) which suffuse a whole work with a generic character or distinctive tone. In calling these qualities "metaphysical," Ingarden suggests that meaning in literature does not remain merely immanent. One value of aesthetic experience is that certain aspects of life, including those which might cause distress if encountered in personal experience, can be contemplated in serenity and detachment, and we may thus arrive at new insights into our existence. (Again, Ingarden's position is analogous to Aristotle's.)

The critical themes which have been sketched here—imagination as a source of freedom and as an act grounded in material categories, the literary work as an autonomous intentional object, the experiencing of the work as a humanly fulfilling meditation—all suggest the fundamentally aesthetic orientation of phenomenological poetics. This same orientation is evident in other applications of p., both direct and indirect: the lively practical criticism of the Geneva School; the elaboration in modern fictional theory of such traditional concepts as the authorial self, symbolism, and character (e.g., by J. Hillis Miller, Paul Brodtkorb, and William Gass, respectively); and analyses of arts other than literature—most interestingly, the treatments of film by Ingarden, Eugene Kaelin, and some contemporary "auteur critics." The rhetoric of p. gives priority to such aesthetic qualities as intensity or élan, novelty, universality, and complexity of texture. But equally significant is the readiness of phenomenological critics to delineate all that is given in aesthetic awareness, to speak as if even the most tenuous features of a work—what Beardsley calls "human regional qualities" (e.g., warmth, elegance, plenitude)—were no less "real" than those qualities we normally think of as objective.

E. Husserl, "P.," tr. C. V. Solomon, in *Encyclopedia Britannica* (14th ed., 1927), *Ideas*, tr. W.R.B. Gibson (1931), *Cartesian Meditations*, tr. D. Cairns (1960); F. Kaufman, "Art and P.," in *Philosophical Essays in Memory of Edmund Husserl*, ed. M. Farber (1940); G. Bachelard, *L'Air et les songes* (1943), *The Poetics of Space*, tr. M. Jolas (1964), *On Poetic Imagination and Reverie*, ed. and tr. C. Gaudin (1971); J.-P. Sartre, *The Psychology of Imagination*, tr. B. Frechtman (1948); M. Heidegger, *Erläuterungen zu Hölderlins Dichtung* (2d ed., 1951), *Being and Time*, tr. J. Macquarrie and E. Robinson (1962); M. Dufrenne, *Phénoménologie de l'expérience esthétique* (2 v., 1953; Eng. tr. by E. S. Casey and others in 1973),

Le Poétique (1963), "Critique littéraire et phénoménologie," *Revue internationale de philosophie*, 69 (1964); M. C. Beardsley, *Aesthetics* (1958), *Aesthetics from Classical Greece to the Present* (1966); J. H. Miller, *Charles Dickens: The World of His Novels* (1958); H. Spiegelberg, *The Phenomenological Movement* (2 v., 1960), "On Some Human Uses of P.," in *P. in Perspective*, ed. F. J. Smith (1970); N. Oxenhandler, "Ontological Crit. in America and France," MLR, 55 (1960), "The Quest for Pure Consciousness in Husserl and Mallarmé," in *The Quest for Imagination*, ed. O. B. Hardison (1971); R. Ingarden, "A Marginal Commentary on Aristotle's *Poetics*," tr. H. R. Michejda, JAAC, 20 (1962), *Das literarische Kunstwerk* (4th ed., 1972); M. Merleau-Ponty, *Sense and Nonsense*, tr. H. L. and P. A. Dreyfus (1964), *Signs*, tr. R. C. McCleary (1964); P. Brodtkorb, *Ishmael's White World* (1965); P. Ricoeur, *Husserl*, tr. E. G. Ballard and L. E. Embree (1967); S. N. Lawall, *Critics of Consciousness* (1968); G. Poulet, "P. of Reading," NLH, 1 (1969); E. F. Kaelin, *Art and Existence* (1970); W. Gass, *Fiction and the Figures of Life* (1971); R. Magliola, "The Phenomenological Approach to Lit.: Its Theory and Methodology," *Language and Style*, 5 (1972).   K.K.

PLAINT. See COMPLAINT.

POETIC CLOSURE refers most broadly to the manner in which poems end or the qualities that characterize their conclusions. More specifically, the term is used to refer to the achievement of an effect of finality, resolution, and stability at the end of a poem. In the latter sense, p.c. appears to be a universally valued quality, the achievement of which is not confined to the poetry of any particular period or nation. Its modes and the techniques by which it is secured do, however, vary in accord with stylistic, particularly structural, variables.

Closural effects are primarily a function of the reader's perception of a poem's total structure; i.e., they depend upon his experience of the relation of the concluding portion of a poem to the entire composition. The generating principles that constitute a poem's formal and thematic structure characteristically arouse in the reader continuously changing sets of expectations, which elicit from him various "hypotheses" concerning the poem's immediate direction and ultimate design. Successful closure occurs when, at the end of a poem, the reader is left without residual expectations: his developing hypotheses have been confirmed and validated (or, in the case of "surprise" endings, the unexpected turn has been accommodated and justified retrospectively), and he is left with a sense of the poem's completeness, which is to say of the integrity of his own experience of it and the appropriateness of its cessation at that point.

Closure may be strengthened by certain specifically *terminal* features in a poem, i.e., things that happen at the end of it. These include the repetition and balance of formal elements (as in alliteration and parallelism), explicit allusions to finality and repose, and the terminal return, after a deviation, to a previously established structural "norm" (e.g., a metrical norm). Closural failures (e.g., anticlimax) usually involve factors that, for one reason or another, leave the reader with residual expectations. They may also arise from weak or incompatible structural principles or from a stylistic discrepancy between the structure of the poem and its mode of closure. Weak closure may, however, be deliberately cultivated, and it has been observed that much modern poetry shares with modern works in other genres and artforms a tendency toward apparent "anticlosure," i.e., the rejection of strong closural effects in favor of irresolution, incompleteness and, more generally, a quality of "openness."—B. H. Smith, *Poetic Closure: A Study of How Poems End* (1968).   B.H.S.

POETRY AND THE OTHER ARTS. PARALLELISM AND INTERRELATIONS. At the beginning of his *Poetics* Aristotle sees various art-forms as having in common an essential representation of life or *mimesis*; and Cicero later remarks generally in his *Pro Archia* (1.2) upon "the subtle bond of mutual relationship" among the arts. More specifically, Simonides of Ceos (ca. 556–468 B.C.) is cited in an early work of Plutarch (*De Gloria Atheniensium* 3.347a) as calling poetry "a speaking picture" and referring to painting as "silent poetry." Horace, in a famous passage (*Ars Poetica* 361), similarly likens a poem to a picture (see UT PICTURA POESIS) and further urges "the labor of the file" (*limae labor*) in the fashioning of verse.

If poetry, in the terms of Horace and Simonides, thus has certain affinities with painting and the plastic arts in general, its relationships with music are deeply rooted in the very concept of *lyric* poetry (originally conceived among the Greeks to mean poetry sung to the accompaniment of the lyre). In medieval Europe this immediate interrelationship survived in the troubadour poets of Provence and the German minnesingers; but, with continuing development of music as a discrete artform, music and poetry lost much of the immediacy of their earlier communion, while a somewhat confusing vocabulary of related terms (*music, harmony, rhythm*, etc.) survives in relation to both arts to perplex us even today. Yet music and poetry continue their mutual inspiration, and many of the parallels and interrelations between them still fascinate

critical and poetic minds and challenge and puzzle philosophers.

Persistence of numerology and number-symbolism in Western thought is important in certain aspects of interrelationship between poetry and the other arts. The chapter of Mario Praz's *Mnemosyne* entitled "Sameness of Structure in a Variety of Media" shows the significance of the domination of Greek art by Pythagorean and Platonic ideas with their mystical cosmological number-symbolism. In such terms Hans Kayser has equated the structure of a Greek temple to music, and Praz considers it equally appropriate to compare it to the structure of a Greek tragedy. He traces in similar fashion the influence of the Pythagorean tradition during the medieval period in the building of the Gothic cathedrals and cites Willi Drost and Erwin Panofsky as seeing "a perfect correspondence between the Gothic cathedral and scholastic philosophy." According to medieval theories of numerical structure, as R. A. Peck has observed, "things measured by the same numbers were thought to be in some way correspondent" and could therefore help one to comprehend something of the patterning of God's creation. Thus numerology and number-symbolism (drawing upon the famous phrase from the Wisdom of Solomon, 11:21: "sed omnia in mensura et numero et pondere disposuisti"—"But You [God] arranged all things in proportion and number and weight") permeated medieval man's theory of poetics as well as his theory of Nature and served with their attendant religious orientation to provide a powerful uniting force between poetry and all the other arts. Ernst Robert Curtius has remarkable sections in his *European Literature and the Latin Middle Ages* (1953) on "Numerical Composition" and "Numerical Apothegms" which demonstrate at least something of the superficies of the matter and show the persistent influence of a philosophic and mystical numerically controlled form in poetry.

In a less mystical and less philosophical sense, it is obvious that poetry frequently borrows from the other arts and that they in turn borrow from poetry. A few examples will serve here to suggest how rich this interchange has been. Poetry draws striking effects from painting or the plastic arts generally in such famous examples as Homer's description of the shield of Achilles (*Iliad* 18.478–608) and Vergil's of the shield of Aeneas (*Aeneid* 8.625–731) —the paintings on the garden wall in Guillaume de Lorris's first part of *Le Roman de la Rose*—Dante's "visible speech" in the lovely sculpture of the Annunciation and the sculptures of David and Trajan in the tenth canto of the *Purgatory*—Chaucer's description of the monuments to episodes from the *Aeneid* in *The House of Fame* (1.119–467)—and, in more modern times, Keats's *Ode on a Grecian Urn* and Gautier's and the Parnassians' numerous *transpositions d'art*. Examples are limitless. Jean Hagstrum has even shown how descriptive poets created romantic landscapes by turning into verse the themes of such seventeenth-century painters as Claude Lorrain and Salvator Rosa. A gallery of pictures drawn from poetry could be similarly impressive in illustrations for the writings of such poets as Homer, Vergil, Dante, Shakespeare, Milton, La Fontaine, Goethe, and Byron. Baudelaire, one of the finest of literary art critics, wrote that the best critical account of a painting may be a sonnet or an elegy and offered in his poem *Les Phares* eight notable impressionistic quatrains on the work of eight separate painters and sculptors.

Poets have written fine poems inspired by music, like Fray Luis de Leon's *Oda a Francisco Salinas* and Dryden's two *Songs for Saint Cecilia's Day* (1687, 1697); and innumerable poems have been set to music (as an extreme example one may cite *Les papillons* by Théophile Gautier for which 43 different composers are listed by Spoelberch de Lovenjoul). As for relations in poetic form, Calvin Brown has shown through a detailed analysis of Walt Whitman's *When Lilacs Last in the Dooryard Bloom'd* that, though the poem has no specific musical structure, it yet conforms to certain general structural principles which he finds "more musical than literary." Many poems (like Lamartine's *Préludes*) have inspired independent musical compositions; and Mallarmé's *L'Après-midi d'un faune* was the inspiration for illustrations by Manet, music by Debussy, and a ballet by Nijinsky which was presented in 1912 with décor, costumes and setting by Bakst, under the overall direction of the great impresario Diaghilev.

On the subject of subtle correspondences between poetry and the other arts and between the arts in general there has been long controversy, and critical and impressionistic discussion on the subject has been pursued with undiminished interest over the years. In *A Parallel of Poetry and Painting* (1695), Dryden equated "bold metaphors" in poetry with "strong and glowing colors" and saw similar effects resulting from certain tropes and figures in poetry and lights and shadows on a painter's canvas. Lessing, on the contrary, in his *Laokoon* (1766), distinguished sharply between temporal and spatial forms in art and the different effects of their internal structures, and later Irving Babbitt, in *The New Laokoon* (1910), inveighed against the confusion of the arts; but their obvious interrelationships continue to tempt literary critics into many winding paths.

René Wellek and G. Giovannini have shown some of the excesses to which this sort of comparison can lead, and Maurice Souriau has called for rigorous definition in such discussion and avoidance of metaphor, which he terms "[la] peste de l'esthétique comparée." Yet there are memorable parallels and correspondences expressed; and one can hardly allow the claim that the intuitive impressions of poets and critics are of no value here and that the only voices worth heeding are those of aesthetic philosophers or descriptive analysts.

Examples of supposed parallelism between poetry and other arts provide an odd assortment of plausible and implausible relationships. A. W. Schlegel, for example, saw classical literature as sculpturesque in nature, and modern and romantic poetry as pictorial. Pope's couplets have been elaborately compared to Palladian architecture, and relationships have been proclaimed between Gothic architecture and poems as different as Spenser's *Faerie Queene* and an Old Fr. epic. For Sir Herbert Read the meter of the Anglo-Saxons is comparable with their ornaments, and an early landscape by Gainsborough recalls Collins' *Ode to Evening*, while his later landscapes recall qualities of Wordsworth. Impressions of baroque architecture are discovered by F. W. Bateson in Thomson, Young, Gray, and Collins; and the poetry of John Keats has been compared variously with sculpture, painting, and music. The parallels between the *Ode on a Grecian Urn* and sculpture are obvious enough even in the poem's inspiration; but this is only a beginning. Keats's blue has been likened to the blue of Reynolds; his *Ode to a Nightingale* has been related to the andante movement of Brahms' First Symphony; his effects have been compared to Turner's; and Yeats once wrote to his father that Keats "makes pictures one cannot forget and sees them as full of rhythm as a Chinese painting."

In the present century Mario Praz finds remarkable parallels between painting and poetry. He sees Rimbaud and Lautréamont along with Freud in the background of Picasso and Dali, compares with surrealist painting the nine lines of Eliot's *The Waste Land* beginning "A rat crept softly through the vegetation," and discovers abstract art already in Apollinaire's *Calligrammes*.* The poems of E. E. Cummings remind him of the paintings of Mondrian, Kandinsky, and Klee; and he calls Cummings' *technopaignia* "poetry and painting at the same time, a new application of the Alexandrian principle *ut pictura poesis*. . . ."

The whole problem of the interrelationships of poetry and the other arts is still unsettled and seems likely to remain so. Paul Maury, while seeing great variety in formal aspects of the different arts, would seek an explanation of their harmony in their common socio-ideological origins; but G. Giovannini contends that the relation of the fine arts to reality is very delicate and complex and that their history seems to show that "reality is often merely a suggestion for design" and is, at all events, extremely variable. René Wellek urges that current methods of comparing the arts are of little value, that they should be studied rather in the structural relations between them and not through metaphor and analogy. But this will call for a new system of aesthetics. Wellek considers misleading the once-popular idea of a unitary time-spirit pervading all the arts of a given period and notes pertinently that the arts "do not evolve with the same speed at the same time." He would stress the importance of genuine parallels between the arts, and he remarks that norms of art are "tied to specific classes" so that revolutions bring changes in aesthetic values. Clive Bell, on the other hand, implies that if the arts are one it is primarily in their absolute detachment from life.

Etienne Souriau urges that in the imitative arts it is the design rather than the representational element that gives pleasure, so that the study of harmony among the arts should be a study of their isolable formal elements. For this, according to Souriau, one must take each art in its own idiom and carefully and patiently establish the lexicon of translations and not hesitate at need to write *intraduisible*. Thomas Munroe in the second edition of *The Arts and Their Interrelations* (1967) includes a systematic classification of "Four Hundred Arts and Types of Art," which shows something of the extent and nature of the problem. In *Feeling and Form* (1953), Susanne Langer urges the need to recognize "the deep divisions among the arts . . . that set apart their very worlds" and to examine their differences and trace their distinctions as far as this is possible. But she sees ultimately a limit to such distinctions and expresses a belief that "the symbolic function is the same in every kind of artistic expression" and that all divisions end at a final depth in unity—a point which recalls Croce's insistence in *La Poesia* (1937) that the ultimate aesthetic concepts are the same in all the arts.

It seems unlikely that 20th-c. aestheticians will be able to afford for the problem anything like the encompassing framework of a Charles Batteux in the 18th c., who (in an age governed at the highest cultural level by the general idea of "taste") could reduce all the fine arts to the single principle of the imitation of "beautiful nature"—or that of medieval numerology, whose mathematical bases for the arts bound them so firmly into religion and mystical philosophy. Yet we have recurrent examples of the urge to bring the arts once more together in Pater's statement within the last

century that they all aspire to the condition of music, and in the abbé Bremond's more recent rejoinder in *La Poésie pure* (1926) as a prelude to his *Prière et poésie* that, on the contrary, they all aspire to the condition of prayer.

See also Batteux, *Les Beaux arts réduits à un même principe* (1746); P. Maury, *Arts et littérature comparés* (1934); R. Wellek, "The Parallelism between Lit. and the Arts," EIE, *1941* (1942); E. Souriau, *La Correspondence des arts: Eléments de l'esthétique comparée* (1947); C. S. Brown, *Music and Lit.: A Comparison of the Arts* (1948); G. Giovannini, "Method in the Study of Lit. in Its Relation to the Other Fine Arts," JAAC, 8 (1950); H. Hatzfeld, *Lit. through Art: A New Approach to Fr. Lit.* (1952); J. H. Hagstrum, *The Sister Arts: The Tradition of Lit. Pictorialism and Eng. Poetry from Dryden to Gray* (1958); R. G. Saisselin, "Ut Pictura Poesis: Du Bos to Diderot," JAAC, 20 (1961); M. Praz, *Mnemosyne: The Parellel between Lit. and the Visual Arts* (1970); R. A. Peck, "Numerology and Chaucer's *Troilus and Criseyde*," Mosaic, 5 (1972). A.G.E.

POETRY READING. The formal presentation of poetry read aloud either by its author or by an actor-interpreter. Settings for a p.r. can be a literary *salon*, a poetry workshop, an invitational event like Johann Wolfgang von Goethe's (1749–1832) readings from his work before the Court of Weimar, or a quasi-theatrical performance at which a poet, poets, or interpreters of poetry address a wide public. By extension to the electronic media, p. readings can also take place via radio or television broadcasts, as well as through phonograph records and electromagnetic tapes. It is assumed, however, that work presented in a p.r. has been committed to writing and may be available in published form. Thus defined, the p.r. is differentiated from oral poetry (q.v.: "composed *in* oral performance by people who cannot read or write"), from productions of a poet's dramatic works, and from the classroom reading of poetry for teaching purposes.

Occidental p. readings from the Greeks to the 19th c. centered on invitational performances in courtly settings. This tradition appears also in read presentations of Chinese and Japanese poetry (qq.v.) and continues in 20th c. Japan. It is likely that p. readings took place at the Alexandrian court of the Ptolemies (ca. 325–ca. 30 B.C.) and in the aristocratic residence of C. Cilnius Maecenas (d. 8 B.C.), who encouraged the work of Vergil (70–19 B.C.), Horace (65–8 B.C.), and Propertius (ca. 47–15 B.C.). Trimalchio, in the fiction of Petronius' (d. A.D. 66) *Satyricon*, first writes, then recites his own "poetry" to the guests at his banquet. Written poetry was recited at the 13th-c. court of Frederick II (see SICILIAN SCHOOL), in the Florentine circle of Lorenzo de'Medici (1449–92) and, according to La Bruyère (1645–96), in the late 17th-c. *salons* of the Princes de Condé. Within Goethe's long life, the p.r. changed from a courtly to a public function. As a young poet of the late 1770's, Goethe read his work at the Weimar court of Carl August; on the occasion of a production of *Faust* to commemorate his eightieth birthday in 1829, he personally coached the actors in the elocution and delivery of lines. Public recitation of their work by poets and their admirers became commonplace in the 19th c. The format was generally quasi-theatrical. Edgar Allan Poe (1809–49) in America, Victor Hugo (1802–85) in France, and Alfred, Lord Tennyson (1809–92) in England are examples of major poets noted for the dramatic quality of their readings. The work of Robert Browning (1812–89) was recited in meetings of the Browning Society (founded 1881), an organization which produced hundreds of offshoots in the U.S. of the 1880's and 1890's. A *Goethe Gesellschaft* (founded 1885) brought readings from the poet's work to places as distant from each other as St. Petersburg, Manchester, and New York, for each of which an 1890 membership list shows a sizeable potential audience. Richard Wagner's (1813–83) opera *Die Meistersinger von Nürnberg* (musical version, 1867) brought the late medieval German tradition of p. readings by members of craft guilds to the attention of a vast international audience. Centered on the historic figure of Hans Sachs (1494–1576), Wagner's work favors "spontaneous" oral poetry in the tradition of Greek rhapsodists, Provençal troubadours, and German minnesingers (qq.v.) over a reading of poems written by others than the poets. Wagner stresses the superiority of national over foreign idiom, of aristocratic over bourgeois poetic voices (Stolzing vs. Beckmesser), and of desirability of correlation between the physical appearance of the poet and the quality of his work.

Wagner's poetics, as expressed in *Die Meistersinger*, is central to symbolist conceptions of the p.r. Stéphane Mallarmé (1842–98) read his poetry to a select audience of never more than twelve, on designated "Tuesdays" at which the poet himself played both host and reader in quasi-cultic, priestly style. While Mallarmé's poetry was anything but spontaneously written, his oral presentation as part of the dramatic monologue which characterized his "Tuesdays" both personalized and socialized the work. Stefan George's (1868–1934) mode of reading poetry was consciously influenced by Mallarmé's: the audience was restricted to the poet's circle of disciples (*Kreis*) and the occasion of the p.r. was perceived as cultic and sacral. While George read from manuscript, he followed a self-prescribed, strict mode of

rhapsodic recitation. His poetry was written to be read aloud. Disciples permitted to participate in the p.r. were obligated to follow George's style of reading both for his and for their own work. As the *Kreis* became, during World War I and after, ever more consciously German and xenophobic in outlook and as the poet's style of dress and demeanor grew increasingly reminiscent of Richard Wagner's, the p. readings approached ideals implied in *Die Meistersinger* even more closely than the practices of Mallarmé's "Tuesdays."

Some of these ideals carried over to modes of p.r. characteristic of the first half of the 20th c. William Butler Yeats (1865–1939) was much concerned with having his work sound spontaneous and natural. Though his style of reading was dramatic and incantatory, he deliberately revised some poems so that they would sound like an ordinary man talking under normal circumstances. By contrast, T. S. Eliot's (1888–1965) p. readings were aristocratic and cultic in style. The Wagnerian prescription of having the reader seem at once spontaneous in expression but, in his person, remote from an audience had its most splendid 20th c. exemplification in the p. readings of Dylan Thomas (1914–53). Thomas's regal, dramatic stance, and sacral incantations offered sharp contrast to the secular, conversational p. readings of Robert Frost (1875–1963) and W. H. Auden (1907–74), in which the poet presents himself as if in dialogue with his audience, to whom he offers commentary and asides in the course of the reading. Auden's and Frost's style of presentation became normative for many modes of p.r. developing in the second half of the 20th c.

Dadaism and surrealism (qq.v.) also helped shape the conventions of the later p.r. These vanguardistic European movements of the second and third decades of the century generated presentations in which p. readings were staged simultaneously with music, dance, or film. The at least apparently unplanned, spontaneous character of dadaist and surrealist events influenced p. readings of the 1950's and 1960's in their function as components in both multimedia presentations and random artistic "happenings." P. readings held during World War I and in the decade to follow as vehicles of social protest and as revolutionary proclamations were models for similar presentations in the second half of the century. This was true not only for dadaist and surrealist p. readings but also for those held in early post-revolutionary Soviet Russia (see RUSSIAN POETRY). Vladimir Mayakovsky (1894–1930), self-proclaimed "drummer of the October Revolution" sang its praises in lyrics written to be read aloud. Mayakovsky's dramatic p. readings attracted mass audiences not only in the U.S.S.R. but also in Western Europe and in the U.S. His use of the p.r. as a forum of political declamation has been internationally emulated into the 1970's. In the U.S.S.R. itself, the politicized p.r. has been institutionalized through the observance, since 1955, of an official, annual "Poetry Day" held in Moscow, Leningrad, and other large cities. During World War II, the B.B.C. broadcast p. readings by poets exiled from countries then occupied by the Germans for the specific purpose of sustaining national consciousness.

Since the 1950's, the p.r. on the Western side of the Iron Curtain has been overwhelmingly an Am. phenomenon. Its tone is "democratic," ranging from polite conversational idiom to street language. P. readings by one poet only have been increasingly rare; the more usual format ranges from two to six, with marathon p. readings by a multitude not uncommon. The separation of the poet from his audience has all but vanished. Conversation between stage and auditorium in the course of the p.r. is usual; "open p. readings" are events to which anyone may bring his work to read. Locales and audio-visual dimensions for p. readings are diversified: church basements, coffee houses, and public parks serve as often as theaters, college auditoriums, and private homes. In many p. readings the physical presence of either poets or live actors is unnecessary, since cassette tapes, loudspeakers, phonograph records, radios, or television sets can transmit the work presented. Moreover, language is no longer the p. reading's sole medium of communication, since jazz or rock music, electronic visual effects, and spontaneous dramatic presentations ("happenings") may accompany the event. Costumes for poets reading are arbitrary, ranging from business suits and evening dress to coveralls and, occasionally, total nudity. In spite of what may appear a partial merging of the p.r. with a variety of other social and cultural phenomena, it has not lost its sacral character. Many audiences consider the p.r. a cultic group experience, a sharing of special sentiments. Features beyond the presentation of poetry itself (e.g., reading it naked, to the accompaniment of bongo drums) are perceived as reinforcements of this sharing. Consumption of mind-altering drugs and alcohol during the p.r. is not uncommon for the same purpose.

Prominent innovators were the beat poets (q.v.), notably Allen Ginsberg (b. 1926), Gregory Corso (b. 1930), and Lawrence Ferlinghetti (b. 1919), all participants in an important 1957 San Francisco p.r. to the accompaniment of jazz. In the 1960's and 1970's, New York and San Francisco have been the two major Am. p.r. centers, with London, Amsterdam, and West Berlin constituting European counterparts, these latter marked by contacts and actual p. readings involving Ginsberg, Corso, and Fer-

linghetti. The German poet Peter Rühmkorf (b. 1929), the Austrian Ernst Jandl (b. 1925), the Dutch Simon Vinkenoog (b. 1928), and the Russian Andrei Voznesensky (b. 1933) are strongly connected to European p.r. presentations in the San Francisco style.

Whatever the style or era, the problem arises whether the actual audience reception of a work coincides with its intentions (q.v.). As the examples of Dylan Thomas and Robert Frost show, a poet's own staging of his work can make it appear more meaningful and commanding than a reader might gather from the printed page. Whether the poem is read by himself or by another, there is no guarantee that a p.r. audience will hear what was "intended" in the making of the poem. Ways of assessing refraction between poetic intentions and what is heard in a p.r. have only begun to be studied. Widely different approaches to the problem by descriptive linguists (Seymour Chatman, Samuel R. Levin), on the one hand, and by phenomenological critics (Georges Poulet, Wolfgang Iser) on the other, agree that identity between poetic intentions and what emerges from the act of reading is highly unlikely. For phenomenologists a poem achieves a true existence only as it is "animated" within the consciousness of a reader. The principle applies even if the reader is the poet himself: when he approaches his poem at any moment other than that of its inception, he is incarnating the text in a new way. Linguists see the necessary choice of one particular interpretation for reading purposes as a barrier between identity of intention and performance; also, they note that phonetic differences between written text and spoken delivery, constrained by the range and pitch limitations of the human voice often make impossible oral replication of texts in the p.r. The strong 20th-c. popularity of the p.r., which seems greater than general interest in reading poems from the printed page in private, is probably more deeply rooted in the dramatic-sacral character of the event than in the literary quality of poetry presented. M. v. Boehn, "Faust und die Kunst," in J. W. v. Goethe, Faust (Centennial Ed., 1932); H. Mondor, La Vie de Stéphane Mallarmé (1941); E. R. Boehringer, Mein Bild von Stefan George (1951); K. Wais, Mallarmé (2d ed., 1952); E. Salin, Um Stefan George (2d ed., 1954); S. Chatman, "Linguistics, Poetics, and Interpretations: The Phonemic Dimension," Quarterly Jour. of Speech, 43 (1957); Evergreen Review, 1, no. 2 (1957); A. B. Lord, The Singer of Tales (1960); The Penguin Book of Russian Verse, ed. D. Obolensky (1962); S. Levin, "Suprasegmentals and the Performance of Poetry," Quarterly Jour. of Speech, 48 (1962); K. T. Loesch, "Lit. Ambiguity and Oral Performance," ibid., 51 (1965); D. Levertov, "Approach to Public Poetry Listenings," *Virginia Quarterly Review*, 41 (1965); E. Lucie-Smith, "Wild Night," *Encounter*, 25 (1965); *The New Russian Poets 1953-1968*, ed. G. Reavey (1966); *Ein Gedicht und sein Autor*, ed. W. Höllerer (1969); G. Poulet, "Phenomenology of Reading," NLH, 1 (1969); P. Dickinson, "Spoken Words," *Encounter*, 34 (1970); *The San Francisco Poets*, ed. D. Meltzer (1971); *The East Side Scene*, ed. A. De Loach (1972); W. Iser, "The Reading Process: A Phenomenological Approach," NLH, 3 (1972); S. Massie, *The Living Mirror: Five Young Poets from Leningrad* (1972); P. Turner, "Introd." to R. Browning, *Men and Women 1855* (1972).

W.B.F.

POETRY THERAPY. See PSYCHOLOGY AND POETRY.*

POLITICS AND POETRY. Poetry deals with man's whole sentient being, with his ideas and with his response to what is happening in the world around him, and it is not surprising that for centuries poets have attempted to shape into art their understanding of political ideas or to render permanent their perception of the political process. Briefly, political poetry may be defined as poetry that deals with public themes or public figures, with events that extend beyond the concerns of the individual self.

While such poetry has been written in various historical periods and has never been confined to any particular country, it is more abundantly called forth in times and places of intense political activity. Although the Middle Ages, for example, was, as a whole, not productive of political poetry, one particular period of political ferment, the late 12th and early 13th c. in Germany and France, produced a great concentration of political lyrics. The history and politics of these times were dominated by major struggles—feudal struggles in France, imperialistic struggles in Germany, and continuing struggles between the Pope and secular rulers. Aside from numerous minor poets who wrote political songs, the events of the time led two major poets, Bertran de Born in Southern France and Walther von der Vogelweide in Germany, to write a substantial body of political lyrics. Sometimes in response to particular events but more often to particular figures worthy of attack, Bertran and Walther wrote poetry that was intensely partisan and pragmatic.

Similarly, the nationalistic struggles and revolutions of later times generated much political poetry. The Fr. Revolution provided the master theme of the epoch for poets in England and Germany. The poetry of Blake, Wordsworth, Coleridge, and Shelley in England

and of Hölderlin, Novalis, and Schiller in Germany reflects the course of events in France, moving from exalted hopes for a regained paradise to growing bitterness and disillusionment. The Gr. nationalistic movement for independence from the Turks in the late 18th and early 19th c. stirred not only the Gr. poets, Rhigas Pheraios and Dionysios Solomos, but also Bryon and Shelley in England and Hölderlin in Germany. In Russia the Revolution inspired some of the poems of Alexander Blok and Andrey Bely (in which apocalyptic notes were heard). A much stronger response was that of the futurist poets, many of whom saw the revolution as a fulfillment of their dreams about the future. A response equally intense but of a different nature was inspired by the Sp. Civil War. Bitterness, indignation, and harsh condemnation of country propels the poetry of the Sp. poets, León Felipe and Luis Cernuda.

In general, of all the kinds of attitudes and situations that stimulate the writing of political poetry, the most consistently compelling forces in all ages have been love of country and response to war. Unfortunately, patriotism has more often generated the kind of strained and vociferous national ardor one finds in the works of, for example, Gabriele D'Annunzio of Italy than the reasoned patriotism of Aristophanes or the understated, tender love of country apparent in *The Soldier* by Rupert Brooke.

Often the pressure of war causes a poet to change his direction. In response to the Sp. Civil War, Raphael Alberti, a poet of considerable power, forsook his surrealistic poetry of inner conflict for more conventional methods that would allow him to deal successfully with public events. Similarly, the fall of France and the German occupation stung the surrealistic poets Louis Aragon and Paul Eluard into poetry of protest. In Aragon's case, in particular, his political poetry is far more powerful than his poems of private experience. While the contemporary Am. poet Robert Bly has always been concerned with social and political themes, the recent war in Viet Nam has driven him to substitute for his earlier expressionistic mode a poetry of more direct and plangent protest.

The degree to which politics and art mingle in any poem depends upon the approach as well as competence of the poet. When transmuted into poetry, political attitudes may merge into the texture of a poem to produce, as in Yeats's *Easter, 1916*, a complex blending of personal and public passion. Equally pervasive in political poetry is the specificity and explicitness one finds, for example, in the war poems of Karl Shapiro or Richard Eberhart, as in his well-known *Fury of Aerial Bombardment*; in Bly's current work, particularly in such a poem as *The Teeth-Mother Naked at Last* (1970); in most of the poetry of Yevtushenko; or in some of Aragon's poems, one of which begins, for example, "Salut à toi Parti qui nias la misère/Et montras l'homme frère à ses frères armés" ("Hail to you Party which denied misery/And showed man as a brother to his brothers in arms" [*Les Yeux et la mémoire*, 1954]).

Aside from obvious distinctions to be made between good or bad poets, the question that remains is what causes or constitutes the success or failure of political poetry. One may clarify the range of the relationship between politics and poetry by reference to two poems of varying success by William Wordsworth, both inspired, in part, by political responses, *The Prelude*, which we will discuss later, and the *Ode, 1815*.

In the *Ode, 1815* Wordsworth's nationalistic fervor responded to Wellington's victory over Napoleon in an apostrophe to God:

> But Thy most dreaded instrument,
> In working out a pure intent,
> Is Man—arrayed for mutual slaughter,
> —Yea, Carnage is thy daughter!
>
> (ll. 106–109)

Although Wordsworth later deleted these lines, the vatic strain and the static, unreasoned attitude displayed in them and in much of the *Ode*, in general, is illustrative of the kind of pitfall into which a poet may fall when he writes on political subjects.

Only in Greek society, where the poet saw himself as a characteristic member of his society and where poetry acquired sufficient social status to become a determinant of social and political forces, could poetry actually derive its strength from the poet's assumption of a public manner and from his conviction that he spoke for the mass of men. In later times, and particularly after the 18th c., the poet writing upon public events has had to address an audience which may no longer share his convictions and has had to deal with a scale of action and event that exceeds the grasp of his own personal experience. Like Wordsworth in the *Ode, 1815*, the poet may attempt to overcome these barriers to communication by choosing to deal with standardized responses and beliefs, relying upon his display of emotion and on technical virtuosity to reach and overwhelm his audience. His assumption of a public manner allows him to cloak with an air of importance and validity the commonplace notions of political life, the actual validity of which he need not attempt to probe.

Such an approach to political poetry is sometimes apparent in the abundant political poetry of Victor Hugo and is characteristic of the poets who wrote in England in the second half of the 19th c. Filled with the available clichés of the time, the political poetry of, for example, Tennyson, Browning, or Swinburne relies on a public manner, on vatic utterances, and on emotional impact to achieve finally a kind of comfortable didacticism. The similar dependence on vague rhetoric and cliché in some of the poetry of the thirties in this c. and in much of the contemporary verse produced in the U.S.S.R. by such poets, for example, as Nikolai Aseyev, Andrei Voznesensky, or Alexander Mezhinov, springs from the same desire to reach and speak for large masses of people and again illustrates the debilitating effects of attempting to shape poetry to suit conventional public sentiment and to reflect accepted doctrine. All this is not to suggest that there is an unbridgeable gap between poetry and politics but to point out that poetry seldom submits with success to conformity of ideas or feelings.

To understand what successful political poetry seems to require, we may turn now for a brief look at those books of Wordsworth's *Prelude* that deal with political and social conflict. What is striking about these books is the completely personal yet wide-ranging vision against which the poet measures the political, economic, and utilitarian creeds of his time, as well as the major event of the age, the Fr. Revolution. Because Wordsworth examines doctrine and event in terms of values based on a personal vision of the potential within the human mind, the political poetry in *The Prelude* successfully avoids the static or cloudy attitudes of the *Ode, 1815* or of Victorian political poetry and exhibits rather a susceptibility to experience and a dimension of intellectual effort that Shelley had in mind when he observed that poets are "the unacknowledged legislators of the world" (*Defense of Poetry*, 1821).

What Shelley seems to have meant is that poets influence politics insofar as they carry the seminal ideas that finally determine human history. Whether or not a poet writing on politics speaks to the great issues of man and answers them finally, whether or not he has the power to inform the thoughts of men in later times, the success of his political verse will depend upon the extent to which he brings both his own personal insight to bear upon public issues and a purview that extends beyond any particular issue or event.

This approach is evident in the best political poetry of all ages, in Homer and in Aeschylus; in Dante, whose *Divine Comedy* is as political as it is theological, and in Shakespeare, particularly in the later political plays like *Richard II* and *Coriolanus*. Milton's political sonnets are sometimes flawed by dogmatism, but *Paradise Lost* successfully incorporates the political issues of liberty and tyranny into the larger questions the poem raises about human nature. The Eng. romantics as a group are perhaps the most successful in their search for poetic ways of harnessing political impulse. They generally bring to their political poetry commitment, vision, and the ability to face conflicts. Political satire, pervasive in the verse of the 18th c. as well as our own, seems to create its own limitations since its end often is to carry the reader to an acceptance of a one-sided case. The strength or maturity of political satire depends on whether the poet can convey a feeling for what is attacked or a sense that he is defending values of society and civilization rather than of a particular cause or group. In this sense, Pope's political satire is more successful than that of Dryden, Auden's than that of Aragon. Generally, contemporary political poets, particularly the "committed" poets, seem each to veer between the extremes depicted in the two poems of Wordsworth. Poets like Spender, Ginsberg, Neruda, Mayakovsky, Yevtushenko, and Zbigniew Herbert, sometimes produce static political rhetoric unredeemed by imagination and sometimes poems of remarkable strength which cut through the clouded abstractions that dominate modern political life.

To paraphrase Lionel Trilling, a poet writing on public issues must organize a union between our political ideas and our imagination (*The Liberal Imagination*, 1953), and he succeeds in doing so to the extent that he is deeply concerned with values in the realm beyond politics. Politics itself, after all, has to do with the "binding allocation of values" (D. Easton, *A Framework for Political Analysis*, 1965), and it becomes the poet's task to negotiate between particular political fact and the ultimate values that politics are intended to serve.

ANTHOLOGIES: *Political Poems and Songs Relating to Eng. Hist.*, ed. T. Wright (1859); *Poems on Affairs of State, 1660–1714*, I-VI (1963-72); *Of Poetry and Power*, ed. E. A. Gilkes and P. Schwaber (1964); *The Eloquence of Protest: Voices of the 70's*, ed. H. Salisbury (1972).

CRITICISM: C. Brinton, *The Political Ideas of the Eng. Romantics* (1926); M. Schorer, *William Blake: The Politics of Vision* (1946); A. P. d'Entrèves, *Dante as a Political Thinker* (1952); D. V. Erdman, *Blake: Prophet against Empire* (1954); F. M. Todd, *Politics and the Poet: A Study of Wordsworth* (1957); C. V. Wedgewood, *Poetry and Politics under the Stuarts* (1960); B. Snell, *Poetry and Society in Ancient Greece* (1961); C. Woodring, *Politics in the Poetry of Coleridge* (1961), *Politics in Eng. Romantic Poetry* (1971); A. W. Gomme,

More Essays on Gr. Hist. and Lit. (1962); I. Howe, *A World More Attractive: A View of Modern Lit. and Politics* (1963); M. Adler, *Poetry and Politics* (1965); A. Mazzeo, *Rennaissance and Revolution* (1965); C. M. Bowra, *Poetry and Politics 1900–1960* (1966); M. Adereth, *Commitment in Modern Fr. Lit.* (1967); M. Mack, *The Garden and the City: Retirement and Politics in the Poetry of Pope* (1969); G. McNeice, *Shelley and the Revolutionary Idea* (1969); T. R. Edwards, *Imagination and Power: A Study of Poetry on Public Themes* (1971); K. W. Klein, *The Partisan Voice: A Study of the Political Lyric in France and Germany, 1180–1230* (1971); J. Lucas, *Lit. and Politics in the 19th C.* (1971); V. J. Scattergood, *Politics and Poetry in the 15th C.* (1971); H. J. Cargas, *Daniel Berrigan and Contemporary Protest Poetry* (1972); L. C. Knights, *Public Voices* (1972).   J.Q.K.

PROJECTIVE VERSE. P.v. is a kind of free verse. It is like other free verse in that it represents "open" or "field" composition. It is not "closed" verse; that is, it does not depend on meter and stanzaic patterns for its form. It differs from other free verse in that it is said to be energized by the poet's breath (his life force) and moves without excessive modification or ornamentation by a series of content-heavy lines, many of them of a run-on sort. The word "projective" suggests the propulsive character of this kind of verse. Charles Olson, the chief theoretician of the p.v. movement, declares that a poem must be a "high energy-construct and, at all points, an energy-discharge." He also insists—in his influential essay "P.V.," first published in *Poetry New York* in 1950—that "form is never more than an extension of content," a precept he attributes to Robert Creeley, and that "one perception must immediately and directly lead to a further perception," a dictum that he credits to Edward Dahlberg.

The birth of the verse line, according to Olson, occurs as a combined operation of the head and the heart. The head, by way of the ear, creates the syllable: it is there that logopoeia, the dance of intellect among words, takes place. The heart, by way of the breath, creates the line: "And the line comes (I swear it) from the breath, from the breathing of the man who writes, at the moment that he writes, and thus is, it is here that, the daily work, the WORK, gets in, for only he, the man who writes, can declare, at every moment, the line its metric and its ending—where its breathing, shall come to, termination."

This emphasis on breathing has produced what is called the "breath line." The poet organizes his poem in terms of breath units or explosions of breath. He pauses momentarily at the end of a line, inhales, and proceeds to the next line, with its own push of content. When reading his work aloud, the p.v. poet sometimes exaggerates this pause for breath, interrupting the natural, propulsive character of the language of the poem. A sensitive reading permits only a short pause, a "semi-comma," to use Denise Levertov's word. P.v. is sometimes called "breath-line poetry."

The poets of the p.v. movement are also called "The Black Mountain School" because the three major figures—Charles Olson, Robert Creeley, and Robert Duncan—taught at Black Mountain College in North Carolina in the early 1950's and published the *Black Mountain Review* there. They drew the attention of Denise Levertov and other lively talents of the time, including Paul Blackburn, Joel Oppenheimer, and Edward Dorn. And they provided the aesthetic rationale for at least one of the beat generation poets, Allen Ginsberg.

In the history of poetic movements of the 20th c., p.v. can be seen as a reaction against the new criticism (q.v.) of John Crowe Ransom, Allen Tate, and Cleanth Brooks, which had dominated Am. poetic theory and practice from 1935 to 1950 and emphasized the virtues of irony, paradox, and meter. But p.v. was not without antecedents. One can trace a line of development from the Am. transcendentalist theories of organic form—the idea that a poem should be as natural in its shape as a tree is—to the practice of such poets as Walt Whitman, Ezra Pound, William Carlos Williams, and the Objectivists (see OBJECTIVISM) of the 1930's: Louis Zukofsky, George Oppen, and Charles Reznikoff. The idea of "open" as opposed to "closed" form Olson may have derived from *Poésie ouverte, Poésie fermé*, a critical work by the Fr. critic René Nelli.

Some aspects of projectivist theory are shaky —especially the insistence on the "breath line," since both poet and reader breathe whenever they like, without reference to the verse line— but it has served to energize a whole generation of poets and has produced a remarkable body of poems that are much closer to the idiom and speech rhythms of the Am. people than the work of the poets of the 1940's was. If, in pragmatic fashion, one judges the consequences of theory rather than the theory itself, one must say that the p.v. movement has been a success.

S. Stepanchev, *Am. Poetry since 1945: A Critical Survey* (1965); M. L. Rosenthal, *The New Poets, Am. and British Poetry since World War II* (1967); J. Dickey, *Babel to Byzantium: Poets and Poetry Now* (1968).　　　s.s.

PSALM. See HEBREW POETRY.

PSYCHIC DISTANCE. See AESTHETIC DISTANCE.

PSYCHOLOGY AND POETRY. That poetry and psych. impinge upon one another is obvious, since sensations, thoughts, feelings, and fantasies provide much of the necessary stuff of poetry, and since the psyche is necessary as an organ of response to it. Less obvious are the limits of this impingement and the extent to which they demarcate a special area of critical investigation. This is so because it is difficult to draw the boundaries either of poetry or of psychology. If one regards all mental contents and processes, up to the point at which they hypothetically become either pure instinct or pure spirit, as psychic, then all of reality that can be known is psychic; and every aspect of poetry might in principle be the subject of psychological investigation. And indeed, any piece of criticism that respects "the reality of the psyche" (C. G. Jung), to which poets have borne witness throughout the ages, may in a broad but sometimes telling sense be psychological. Moreover, the meeting between psych., even in a narrower sense, and poetry has from the outset been complex. Thus when S. Freud turned to an ancient text of dramatic poetry for the name of a concept, the Oedipus complex, he was deriving psych. from literature and myth; the story and the pattern of meaning that he perceived in it. not only preceded but colored the scientific concept. Matters are also complicated by the fact that many valuable psychological observations about poetry have been made in passing or by implication in works about literature not specifically poetic or in works even more generally about art and the artist. Thus "psychological" may be fairly thought to describe qualities derived from any of several forms of "knowledge of the psyche," rather than a distinct critical area or approach. But in what follows the focus will be on conscious attempts to cultivate such qualities by bringing criticism into conformity with psych. as a science striving to be empirical.

Every age has its psych. in the sense of a more or less systematic view of the workings of the human mind; such a view is either assumed or countered by the poet, and a knowledge of it may elucidate his work, for example, as knowledge of Elizabethan doctrines of the soul elucidates Shakespeare (Anderson) or as knowledge of W. James's *Principles of Psychology* (1890), with its treatment of "stream of consciousness," does modern poetry and fiction. And J. L. Lowes' study of S. T. Coleridge demonstrates that criticism may say much about the workings of the poetic mind without being continuously buttressed by psych. as a systematized discipline. But the bulk of criticism using psych. to illumine poetry is derived from psychoanalysis, which first came to literary attention with Freud's *The Interpretation of Dreams* (1900). Indeed, psychoanalysis reflects a historical moment that is also a moment in the life of literature. As K. Burke observes, "In great eras of drama, the audience *know* why characters act as they do," and as H. J. Muller elaborates, "Stable cultures bring stable and standard patterns of behavior; motives are as socialized as manners. Although characters may be momentarily confused and bewildered, or rebellious, they finally perceive their motives as clearly as the audience always do." In a period of cultural breakdown, in which a novelist and poet such as D. H. Lawrence could claim to be turning his attention from "the old stable ego" to "allotropic states" of the same psychic element, Freud was of enormous importance in supplying a new socialization of motives. And psychoanalysis allowed literary critics to concentrate on elements of poetic creation and response that had not received attention before.

Although Freud did upon occasion write about literary art, as in a book-length study of W. Jensen's *Gradiva*, much psychoanalytic theory about literature developed from suggestions in his treatment of religious and cultural history, of jokes, of slips of the tongue, of the uncanny, and especially of dreams. In approaching literature, along with other products of mental life, through the dream, Freud was following a path partly adumbrated by ideas of L. Tieck, A. Schopenhauer, J. Paul, F. Nietzsche, F. Vischer, W. Dilthey, and others, who had seen parallels between dreaming and artistic creation. In the psychoanalytic view, dreams provide hallucinatory satisfaction of instinctual impulses, and art occupies "an intermediate territory between wish-denying reality and the wish-fulfilling world of fantasy" (Freud). Like the dream, the work of art has not only manifest content but also latent content derived from the instinct-charged unconscious, and much early psychoanalytic criticism aimed at revealing the dynamism latent within the literary work. Thus Freud, and later E. Jones, saw *Hamlet* as being about the hero's incestuous longings for his mother and his ambivalence toward his father, and as achieving much of its dramatic and poetic effect by activating and giving expression to Oedipal feelings in the audience. Meaning, in this view, primarily serves to satisfy the mind's demand for sense and logic, thus permitting the satisfaction of forbidden wishes while allaying objections to them. Similarly, "The real pleasure in artistic form comes from illogic and nonsense, which, in turn, represent 'the economy of psychic expenditures or alleviation from the pressure of reason.' Our sense of pleasure comes from releasing or economizing on energy normally used to keep ourselves logical; we experience a sudden sense of psychic energy to spare, a sudden psychic profit from cutting down expenses" (N. Holland, 1966, summarizing Freud).

More recent criticism has reflected later developments in psychoanalytic theory, effected by Freud from the 1920's on, by A. Freud, H. Hartmann, E. Kris, M. Klein, and others. These developments have largely been concerned with the powers of the ego to maintain itself and to achieve some sort of viable balance amid the forces acting upon it from both within and without. Reflecting these interests, psychoanalytic criticism has come to see the literary work not only as a disguised expression of forbidden wishes but also as a reflection of various strategies of the ego for dealing with such wishes and with the moral feelings they awaken. Manifest content thus reflects the transformation of unconscious fantasies; and form and meaning, rather than being merely a disguise, serve the process of that transformation. Art effects the shift of psychic energy from one level to another, and this is in itself pleasurable (Kris). Moreover, these transformations and shifts resemble successful sublimations of illicit unconscious fantasy. Literary form "acts out defensive maneuvers for us: splitting, isolating, undoing, displacing from, omitting (repressing or denying) elements of the [pleasurable but anxiety-provoking] fantasy." These same principles operate more specifically in the sound structures of poetry (Holland, 1968). Among the more important psychoanalytic concepts relating to poetic form are those of condensation, when an image or character expresses more than one psychic tendency, and displacement, when one psychic tendency is given more than one embodiment, as in Freud's view (following L. Jekels) of the Macbeths as aspects of a single personality. Used with discretion, these concepts may illumine poetry, as they do in G. Hough's discussion of *The Faerie Queene*.

Much psychoanalytic criticism has really been a form of what has come to be called psychobiography, often occupied with ferreting out (and in moments of zeal, conjuring up) "facts" not clearly present in the biographical record but inferable in accordance with psychoanalytical theory. In some literary biographies, such as B. Meyer's of Joseph Conrad, pschoanalysis convincingly affords important glimpses into obscure parts both of the writer's life and of his work. Several poets have been treated extensively in this way, including Edgar Allan Poe by M. Bonaparte and Emily Dickinson by J. Cody, who bases his conclusions on psychoanalytic theory and on recent developments in clinical psychiatry. Suggestive refinements of the psychoanalytic approach to poetry may be found in P. Dettering's study of Rainer Maria Rilke, whose essential poetic motives are traceable not only to the classical Oedipus complex but also to the pre-Oedipal phases of development with which psychoanalysis has been concerned in recent decades. Rilke's "narcissism" is seen as a complex motivational pattern, expressed in a complex, variable and developing set of poetic symbols, including that of the angel. Moreover, such writers as Kris, Holland, and A. Ehrenzweig have in recent years dealt more subtly with questions of literary response than earlier critics had. Psychoanalysis has touched on areas still awaiting exploration that may turn out to be important for the criticism of poetry, for example, the area suggested by J.A.M. Meerloo's undeveloped hunch (in Leedy) that poetic rhythm expresses infantile archaic responses of the organism, the innate biological signal code. Another area is suggested by H. Kohut's description of a narcissistic self prefiguring and then underlying the development of the ego and, by implication, visible in certain forms of creativity and of its disturbance. Still another is suggested by Ehrenzweig's attention to ordering processes beyond conscious control that contribute to artistic form. Moreover, in the fullness of its elaboration as a system, psychoanalysis often has no rivals in offering at least some psychological explanation of important literary phenomena.

Aside from Freud, the psychologist who has figured most largely in psychological criticism is Jung, though in it he appears more often as a name for an attitude or set of ideas than as an active influence. Unlike Freud, Jung's main interest was in the transpersonal elements in literature; the focus of that interest was the *archetype* (q.v.). Since archetypes belong roughly to the realm of what Aristotle called formal causes, as distinct from the efficient causes studied by psychoanalytic literary criticism, the concept of the archetype may help the psychological critic to bridge lower and higher levels of poetic organization. The literary artist is for Jung vatic, and his view of art puts him in the line of Plato, Sidney, and those romantics who stress the relations between poetry and prophecy. His prospective or finalistic view of psychic processes, and his view of the unconscious as being composed of collective as well as personal elements, suggest a different relation of the poet to the unconscious than that described by psychoanalysis. It is largely the archetype, in its form-creating capacity and its numinosity, that accounts for the form of the work and its effect upon the reader (M. Bodkin). Art does not, then, gain its effects primarily through a partial lifting of repression; rather, the artist

often expresses contents that have not yet been known to consciousness but that have been fully formed in the unconscious. These contents have a compensatory character, providing not only the artist but also his age with materials necessary to correct a one-sided world view and to restore contact with the life-giving unconscious matrix of consciousness. The artist may indeed have psychopathological traits, but this fact does not explain his work, which in the psychoanalytic view serves the artist's ego by strengthening its mastery over forces that threaten it. Rather, Jung sees the artist as disturbed because his gift and his calling require the exaggerated development of certain psychological functions at the neglect of others important to normal life. T. Chouinard (1971) has used Jung's concept of the anima in an analysis of T. S. Eliot's poetry—G. Hough, incidentally, has commented more generally on "Poetry and the Anima"—and Chouinard has also (1970) tried to clarify use of the term "archetype" in literary criticism and analytical psych. The Jungian approach might seem more promising for criticism than for literary biography, but K. Wilson has used Jungian ideas in a sensitive discussion of Keats's *Ode to a Nightingale* and of its importance in Keats's life. In her view that poem was based upon an experience of the archetype of the self, the deepest center of the personality, an experience which resulted in a transformation of Keats's view of poetry and his relation to sources of inspiration within himself. The same critic also uses Jung's typology of psychological attitudes and functions to elucidate specific qualities of Keats's poetic language. And G. Bachelard follows Jung in seeking to create a partly transpersonal "phenomenology of the soul." For Bachelard the poetic image is a product of "the *dreaming consciousness*," in which "the duality of subject and object is iridescent, shimmering, unceasingly active in its inversions."

The ideas of such Gestalt psychologists as K. Koffka have occasionally been used by critics (Muller), but they have not found an abiding place in literary discussion. Continuing and extending the interest of the Gestalt psychologists in the holistic qualities of perception, M. Peckham has developed a comprehensive view of art, including poetry. In his view, man "desires above all a predictable and ordered world, . . . But because man desires such a world so passionately, he is very much inclined to ignore anything that intimates that he does not have it. And to anything that disorients him, anything that requires him to experience cognitive tension he ascribes negative value. Only in protected situations, characterized by high walls of psychic insulation, can he afford to let himself be aware of the disparity between his interests, that is, his expectancy or set or orientation, and the data his interaction with the environment actually produces." Art, in Peckham's view, offers this experience. J. O. Love has analyzed mythopoetic aspects of Virginia Woolf's fiction in accordance with ideas drawn from developmental cognitive psychology. And psycholinguistics, which has some claim to the first half of its name, has begun to be used in the criticism of poetry. Since poetry is rich with insights into the human condition, and since it evokes moods and provides models for dealing with them, poetry has been used as a means of psychotherapy (Leedy). But it is largely the consolatory, homiletic qualities that poetry shares with prose that are emphasized in these efforts, rather than the qualities of epiphany that make poetry subjunctive rather than indicative, a matter of being rather than of becoming (Lawler); the student of literature will learn very little from them.

The implicit parallels between dreaming, on the one hand, and literary creation and response, on the other, continue to be suggestive, as may be seen in the fact that both Burke and N. Frye have used "dream" as a critical term. Moreover, views of dreaming that diverge from those of Freud have been developed by Jung, A. Adler, E. S. Tauber, K. Horney, B. S. Robbins, E. Fromm, W. Bonime, and others, and these views supply a useful perspective on some psychological criticism. Thus for Jung, "The dream is an experience in self-confrontation. Its intent is to reveal rather than conceal. The symbols exist not as subterfuges and disguises but as metaphorical referents" (M. Ullman in Bonime, summarizing Jung). In Jung's view of dreams Freud's distinction between latent and manifest content is largely ignored; neither the content nor the structure is regarded as arbitrary, but both are thought to have the kind of necessity that governs the materials of drama, and the dream is thought not primarily to provide wish-fulfillment but to serve the self-regulation of the psyche, and the integration of the personality by compensating a one-sided conscious viewpoint. (Jung did not write a single, major study of dreams comparable to Freud's, but there are good systematic treatments of dreams from a Jungian viewpoint by C. A. Meier and H. Dieckmann.) For Adler and several others, "the dynamic meaning of the dream could be preserved without the concept of the unconscious as a reservoir of aggressive and libidinal impulses. . . . The peculiarities of dream thought are to be understood as a particular mode of presentation of one's experience and not as the eruption of an unconscious mode of thought" (Ullman). Such views would seem to have a bearing on the ancient analogy between dream

and poetry, and more generally, upon questions concerning the sources, nature, and functions of the fantasy essential to poetry. Some of these views have had little resonance in literary discussion; this fact may suggest something of the range of possibilities yet to be explored in psychological criticism.

Psychological critics often assume more agreement about first principles than exists; infelicities of tone in some of their writings often seem expressions of defensiveness about the conflict of scientific paradigms (T. S. Kuhn). Standing his ground, the literary reader may take heart from a remark by C. S. Lewis, "that the ease with which a scientific theory assumes the dignity and rigidity of fact varies inversely with the individual's scientific education," and from Jung's contention, in his Tavistock lectures, that every psychological viewpoint contains an important element of subjective confession and that the time has not yet come for a general psychology to be possible. Moreover, the literary reader may feel that on the whole the psychological critic does better, for example, with the primitive and infantile impulses of sex and aggression in *King Lear* than with the level of what Aristotle would call *theoria*, or knowledge as a form of ethical action, in the play. But even if such qualifications sometimes deserve attention, and even if the first exhilaration of psychoanalytic criticism is past, the interrelations between psych. and poetry have by now been well established as a fruitful and abiding area of critical concern.

R. Anderson, *Elizabethan Psych. and Shakespeare's Plays* (1927); J. L. Lowes, *The Road to Xanadu* (1927); K. Burke, *Counter-Statement* (1931); M. Bodkin, *Archetypal Patterns in Poetry* (1934); K. Muller, *Modern Fiction* (1937); M. Bonaparte, *The Life and Works of Edgar Allan Poe* (1949); E. Jones, *Hamlet and Oedipus* (1949); E. Kris, *Psychoanalytic Explorations in Art* (1952); S. Freud, Standard Ed. (1953–64), III, IV, VIII, IX; F. Hoffman, *Freudianism and the Literary Mind* (2d ed., 1957); W. Bonime, *The Clinical Use of Dreams* (1962); G. Hough, *A Preface to The Faerie Queene* (1962) and "Poetry and the Anima," *Spring* (1973); T. S. Kuhn, *The Structure of Scientific Revolutions* (1962); W. Kiell, *Psychoanalysis, Psych. and Lit.* (1963; bibliog.); G. Bachelard, *The Poetics of Space*, tr. M. Jolas (1964); M. Peckham, *Man's Rage for Chaos* (1965); K. Wilson, *The Nightingale and the Hawk* (1965); N. Holland, *Psychoanalysis and Shakespeare* (1966) and *The Dynamics of Lit. Response* (1968); C. G. Jung, *Collected Works*, XV (1966) and *Analytical Psych.: Its Theory and Practice* (1968; the Tavistock Lectures); F. C. Crews, "Lit. and Psych." [bibliog.], in *Relations of Lit. Study*, ed. J. Thorpe (1967)

and *Psychoanalysis and Lit. Process* (1970);
A. Ehrenzweig, *The Hidden Order of Art*
(1967); B. Meyer, *Joseph Conrad* (1967);
P. Dettmering, *Dichtung und Psychoanalyse*
(1969); J. Leedy, *Poetry Therapy* (1969);
T. Chouinard, in the *Jour. of Analytical Psych.*,
15 (July 1970), 16 (Jan. 1971); L. Edel, "Psych.
and Lit.," in *Encyclopedia of World Lit. in
the 20th C.*, ed. W. B. Fleischmann, III (1970);
J. O. Love, *Worlds in Consciousness* (1970);
J. Starobinski, *La Relation critique* (1970);
H. Kohut, *The Analysis of the Self* (1971);
J. G. Lawler, in *Psychiatry*, 35 (Aug. 1972);
C. A. Meier, *Die Bedeutung des Traumes*
(1972); N. Holland, *Poems in Persons* (1973).

SELECTED READINGS: *Art and Psychoanalysis*,
ed. W. Phillips (1957); Freud, *On Creativity
and the Unconscious*, ed. B. Nelson (1958);
Hidden Patterns, ed. L. and E. Manheim
(1966).

JOURNALS: *American Imago* (1939—); *Lit.
and Psych.* (1951— ; valuable annual bibliog.
beginning with v. 18, which covers 1964–65).
w.w.

PUERTO RICAN POETRY. The island of
Puerto Rico has been a fertile ground for
poetry since the early 16th c. The Sp. conquis-
tadores and the church prelates who wrote
their impressions of the land left the mark of
their emotional encounter with this Caribbean colony in verse and in poetic prose. Juan
de Castellanos (1522–1607) dedicated the sixth
of his *Elegies of Illustrious Men of the Indies*
to Juan Ponce de Leon and Borinquen (Puerto
Rico), while the first P.R. born poet, Francisco
de Ayerra y Santamaría (1630–1708), excelled
as a baroque poet in Mexico. The popular
ballads, couplets, and traditional religious
songs dedicated to the Epiphany, the ceremonies of Passion Week and other Catholic
inspired festivities, mingled with the music
and the rhythms of the black slaves and the
remnants of the choral Taino Areyto, survived
in a rich oral folklore of poetic enchantment.

By the 19th c. Puerto Rico had developed
a varied and interesting literary life in which
poetry was the most important of all the
genres. Young poets gathered their verse in
anthologies called "Aguinaldo," "Album," or
"Cancionero"; the custom of reciting poetry
and improvising verse in public and official
ceremonies became widespread; poetry contests were celebrated with all the adornments
of the gallant art of love, and the disputes and
satirical criticism provoked by social and political problems left their mark in some poems
of the period. The founding of the Atheneum
in 1873, to serve as the intellectual center to
express the creative urge of the writers, marked
a very important step in the development of
poetry. Lectures and recitals were regular ac-

tivities at the Atheneum, and all the important
writers of that time participated in these programs. Following the trends prevalent in
Spain, romantic lyricism dominated the scene,
from the most passionate nuance to the most
subtle and refined. Some of the best known
poets wrote about love, but they also excelled
in revealing their patriotism and rejoicing in
the beautiful landscape of the tropical paradise. Alejandro Tapia y Rivera (1826–82), Lola
Rodríguez de Tió (1843–1924), and José Gautier Benítez (1851–80), are the best representatives of the poetry of the romantic period.
Tapia exalted the past and wrote the most
extensive poem of the 19th c. in Puerto Rico,
La Sataniada. The thirty cantos in 8-line
stanzas of the composition are reminiscent of
Espronceda's *El Diablo Mundo*. Lola Rodríguez de Tió was the first outstanding woman
in the literature of the island. Her love poetry
is subtle and delicate, while her patriotic verses
are full of vigor and fire. She lived for some
years in Caracas and in New York as an exile,
and considered Cuba, where she died, her
second homeland. One of her contributions to
the culture of her country is the lyrics that
she wrote for the national anthem, *La Borin-
queña*. Gautier Benítez was a refined and sentimental poet whose tender and moving chants
to Borinquen are comparable to Bécquer's
Rhymes. The lyricism of his poems expressing
the melancholy of being absent from his birth-
place and the happiness of the return to the
shores of his homeland are considered masterpieces of romantic P.R. poetry:

Borinquen, nombre al pensamiento grato
como el recuerdo de un amor profundo
bello jardín, de América el ornato,
siendo el jardín América del mundo.

Borinquen, a name loving to the mind
as the memory of an intense love,
beautiful garden, flower of America,
America being the garden of the world.

At the close of the century the first impulse
toward a renovation of style and an introduction of metrical innovations was already present in the works of José de Diego (1866–1918),
an outstanding member of the generation that
experienced the transfer of Puerto Rico from
the domain of Spain to that of the United
States. De Diego is celebrated for both his
patriotic verse and love poems. The symbolism
attached to the flag, the anthem, the birds and
trees of the landscape of the island are some
of his favorite topics.

Modernismo (q.v.) in Puerto Rico, besides
following the aesthetic credo of Rubén Darío's
musical poetry, enriched with new rhythms
and beautiful imagery, served the purpose of

expanding the creative horizons of the island's poets in search of universal values. Luis Lloréns Torres (1878–1944), Virgilio Dávila (1869–1943), Luis Palés Matos (1898–1959), and Evaristo Ribera Chevremont (1896–   ) represent this period, although they surpassed the modernistic movement and opened the way toward the Vanguard modalities after the First World War (1914–18). Lloréns Torres founded a literary magazine, *Revista de las Antillas* (1913), which became the vehicle for innovations in style and the defense of the Sp. cultural traditions of the land. The ideal of Antillean unity was a profound motive of inspiration present in two of his best poems: *Song of the Antilles* and *Mare Nostrum*. Luis Palés Matos became a master of Afro-Antillean poetry in his famous book *Tun Tun de Pasa y Grifería* (1937), in which the mythology of black culture is re-created with magical cadence and artistic enchantment.

> Calabó y bambú
> bambú y calabó
> Es el sol de fuego que arde en Tumbuctú
> Es la danza negra de Fernando Poo
> El alma africana que vibrando está
> en el ritmo gordo del mariyandá.

> Calabó and bamboo
> bamboo and calabó
> It's the iron sun that burns in Timbuctoo
> It's the black dance of Fernando Poo
> The African soul that is vibrating,
> in the thick rhythm of the mariyandá.

In other poems Palés expresses the pessimism of his generation, and in his last days he wrote moving poems of love and death.

Many Vanguard movements, all short-lived but impressive in their manifestos, have succeeded one after the other during the decades following *modernismo*. Some of the theories were influenced by the European and Am. poets of the 20th c., although insistence in defending the identity of P.R. culture has never been absent from their poetry in this century. The Sp. names of some of these movements are significant: "noismo," based on the concept of the negative NO; "trascendentalismo," suggesting the impulse toward the metaphysical and the beyond; and "atalayismo," a bold and forceful attempt to emphasize the extravagant side of every possible idea. The relation with ultraism, cubism, dadaism (qq.v.), and other avant-garde groups, besides the nationalistic themes used by some of the poets, characterized these movements in Puerto Rico. Among the most important poets related to them are Francisco Manrique Cabrera (1908–   ), author of *Poemas de mi Tierra, Tierra*; Julia de Burgos (1914–53), who wrote exquisite poems inspired by her childhood memories and her passionate love for P.R. independence; Juan Antonio Corretjer (1908–   ), political leader and poet deeply involved with the essence of the Indian and Sp. roots of the culture of Puerto Rico; Francisco Matos Paoli (1915–   ), a refined voice in search of spiritual and transcendental meanings, and Luis Hernández Aquino (1907–   ), a scholar whose poetry reveals his quest for the cultural soul of his people.

Poetry magazines published for a short time (*Mester, Versiones, Lorca*) and the literary reviews *Asomante* and *Sin Nombre* have served the purpose of publishing many poems by young writers who have already been acclaimed by the critics. Some P.R. poets have done their work in New York City, and this group represents the continuity of what their peers have been doing in the island. Although some may have spent most of their lives in the United States, they continue to write in Sp. and their principal concern is to express their feelings and their attachment to the homeland. Diana Ramírez de Arellano (1919–   ), Juan Avilés (1904–   ), Graciany Miranda Archilla (1910–   ), and Clemente Soto Vélez (1905–   ), have written most of their books in the United States, where a younger generation, represented by Víctor Hernández Cruz, is exploring new areas of expression, writing in Eng. but creating new speech patterns by introducing Sp. and Am.-Sp. terms.

Perfect integration of a culture leads to stagnation. Every cultural complex is itself a microcosm, in which opposing factors are constantly meeting and clashing so that sometimes one, sometimes its opposite, prevails. This is applicable to the way in which poetry has been developing in the literature of P.R., and it is evident that the theater, the essay, and modern fiction, especially the short story, have been revitalized in the 20th c. by poetry itself, the genre par excellence in P.R. letters.

ANTHOLOGIES: *Poesía puertorriqueña*, ed. L. Hernández Aquino (1954); *Aguinaldo lírico de la poesía puertorriqueña*, ed. C. Rosa-Nieves (3 v., 1957); *Antología de jóvenes poetas*, ed. J. M. Torres Santiago (1965); *Poesía nueva puertorriqueña*, ed. L. A. Rosario Quiles (1971); *The P.R. Poets*, ed. A. Matilla and I. Silén (1973).

HISTORY AND CRITICISM: L. Hernández Aquino, *Movimientos literarios del siglo XX en P.R.* (1951), *Nuestra aventura literaria* (1966) and *El modernismo en P.R.* (1967; also an anthol.); E. Rivera, *La poesía en P.R. antes de 1843* (1965); M. T. Babín, *Jornadas literarias* (1967) and *The Puerto Ricans' Spirit* (1971); C. Rosa-Nieves, *Plumas estelares en las letras de P.R.* (v. I, 1967); J. E. González, *La poesía contemporanea de P.R., 1930–1960* (1972); M. D. Hill and H. B. Schleifer, *P.R. Authors: A Bibliographic Handbook* (1974).   M.T.B.

R

RECANTATION. See PALINODE.

ROCK LYRIC. From the middle of the 1950's to the early 1960's r.l. meant any set of words used in conjunction with r. and roll music which had as a distinguishing feature a strong, evenly accentuated beat most often in four-quarter but occasionally in three-quarter time. These lyrics rarely made any claim to poetic status. Nevertheless, taken as a whole, they projected the problems and fantasies of post-Korean war adolescence. It is in this sense that Richard Goldstein characterizes Chuck Berry as the "mythmaker" for millions of young listeners: Berry's lyrics both reflected and created a world of fast cars and sexual rivalries (*Mabellene*), mild protest against adult institutions (*School Day*), and ultimate fulfillment through the new music (*Reelin' and Rockin'*). Perhaps the main theme of early r. lyrics was in fact r. music itself, a celebrating of its sense of primal energy and the new kinds of dancing it made possible.

The other major theme of these lyrics was, of course, love. Most early r. songs maintained the romantic attitudes of the Tin Pan Alley popular lyric (the sorrow of unrequited love, the certainty of happiness through true love), adapting these to a teen-age audience in simple forms designed to fit a steady r. beat. But the blues tradition within r. allowed for more realistic portrayals of love relationships, and many r. lyrics (*Money Honey, Hound Dog*) expressed cynical, hostile, or abrasive tones previously underdeveloped in popular music. Moreover, within the blues tradition, the word "rock" (like the word "jazz") had often referred to sex (as in the traditional *Rock Me, Baby*), and some r. songs introduced a new sexual dimension in the popular lyric—either directly (*Work with Me, Annie*) or through innuendo (*Let the Good Times Roll*).

Through the 1960's r. lyrics continued to draw much of their vitality from the blues tradition. In England such groups as the Rolling Stones relied heavily on an earthy, frank sexuality, epitomized in *Satisfaction*. But in America black lyricists like Ray Charles and Otis Redding were adding new complexity to standard themes, and using the traditional blues technique of the repeated line in more intricate ways. The toughness of blues could be combined with secularized gospel lyrics to fashion a poetry of "soul"—or softened, as in the lyrics of Smokey Robinson, into romantic r. poetry. By the end of the decade black lyricists such as Marvin Gaye and Curtis Mayfield were using r. lyrics to articulate new subtleties of social awareness.

The major thematic development in the r. lyrics of the 1960's was a complete broadening of subject matter. Coexisting with the by now traditional treatments of music and love were lyrics reflecting rapid changes and dislocations in society itself, including a growing rejection of middle-class attitudes. Drug experience became a common topic in r. lyrics, as in Jimi Hendrix's *Purple Haze*. Lines such as the Beatles' "She's leaving home after living alone for so many years" described the actions as well as the wishful dreams of thousands of teenagers. After writing protest songs, which took on the status of anthems for the youth counter-culture (*Blowin' in the Wind, The Times They Are A-Changing*), Bob Dylan brought about a fusion of folk and r. Such albums as *Highway 61 Revisited* mingled elements of protest with nightmare visions of the modern industrial landscape. Such lyricists as Joni Mitchell and Paul Kantner often transformed protest into the vision of a new beginning, another Eden.

In addition to a broadening of themes, r. lyrics of the 1960's were distinguished by a more self-consciously *literary* tone. A number of traditional poems (*Dover Beach, Richard Cory*) were adapted to r. music, and original lyrics took on, often superficially, elements of modern poetry. (1) The use of archetypal narrative frameworks: Eric Clapton's *Tales of Brave Ulysses*, David Crosby's *Guinnevere*. (2) Alienation as objectified in a dissociated modern sensibility: Paul Simon's *The Dangling Conversation*, Dylan's *Desolation Row* (which refers specifically to Pound and Eliot). (3) A corresponding reliance on fragmentation, dissonance, and disjunction in verbal surface of the lyric: the Beatles' *A Day in the Life*. (4) Surrealism—used either to render a sense of social chaos (Dylan's *Memphis Blues Again*) or to reflect strange, perhaps psychedelic, visions (the Beatles' *Lucy in the Sky with Diamonds*). (5) Ambiguity and allusion, especially in dealing with drugs: the Jefferson Airplane's *White Rabbit* (which combines *double entendres* about pills and hashish with references to *Alice in Wonderland*). (6) Obscure, personal symbolism that resists paraphrase: the Beatles'

Strawberry Fields Forever. (7) Highly complex wordplay and intricate rhymes: Dylan's *Subterranean Homesick Blues.* (8) The development of an ironic mode, analogous to the dramatic monologue (Randy Newman's *Political Science*), and adaptable to use in serious drama (as in the interpolated sardonic rock commentary of Sam Shepard's play *Operation Sidewinder*). (9) A tendency toward sustained compositions, in which whole groups of songs form an aesthetic unit (the Beatles' *Sergeant Pepper*) or even a "rock opera" (the Who's *Tommy*).

At the beginning of the 1970's the r. opera *Jesus Christ Superstar* explored two themes which were incipient in many lyrics of the 1960's, and which have since become more powerful in r. The first is an overt religious affirmation, with the r.l. serving as prayer or hymn. The second is the examination of superstardom as a contemporary cultural phenomenon, the r. star's rise and fall (together with his roles of troubadour, sex symbol, and Byronic hero) serving as a mythic paradigm. Two other recent developments in the subject matter of the r.l. are deviant sexuality and science-fiction, both exemplified in the lyrics of David Bowie. At the same time many contemporary lyricists seem to be attempting to return to the roots of r., either through 1950's nostalgia or the still vital blues tradition.

Just as at an earlier time the popular song and the blues influenced modern poets as diverse as Eliot (*Fragment of an Agon*) and Auden (*Refugee Blues*), some contemporary poets have either been influenced by r. lyrics (William Matthews' *Ball and Chain*) or, like Leonard Cohen and Michael Benedikt, written r. songs of their own. At present, however, the r.l. has borrowed much more from modern poetry than vice-versa, and there remains the question of how well r. lyrics can survive on the printed page. With increasing frequency, anthologies of contemporary poetry are including lyrics by Paul Simon, Bob Dylan, and the Beatles. But Allen Ginsberg has suggested that the r.l. should be taken together with its music as a unique poetic construct: because many r. lyricists "*think* not only in words but in music simultaneously," they have created a new genre of "personal realistic imaginative rhymed verse."

The Age of R., ed. J. Eisen (1967); *The Poetry of R.*, ed. R. Goldstein (1969); R. Christgau, "R. Lyrics Are Poetry (Maybe)," *Cheetah*, 1 (1967); H. Davies, *The Beatles* (1968; ch. 30); J. Carey, "Changing Courtship Patterns in the Popular Song," *Am. Jour. of Sociology*, 74 (1969); L. Roxon, *Lillian Roxon's R. Encyclopedia* (1969); *Bob Dylan: A Retrospective*, ed. C. McGregor (1972); F. Kermode, S. Spender, "Bob Dylan: The Metaphor at the End of the Tunnel," *Esquire*, 77 (1972); R. Joffe, "Is R. 'n' Roll *Really* Here to Stay?" *Village Voice*, June 14, 1973; B. Sarlin, *Turn It Up (I Can't Hear the Words)* (1973); D. Swanger, *The Poem as Process* (1974).

S

SAN FRANCISCO RENAISSANCE. See AMERICAN POETIC SCHOOLS AND TECHNIQUES (CONTEMPORARY).*

SEMIOTICS (or semiology). The science of signs. Considering social and cultural phenomena as signs, s. studies the systems of rules and conventions which enable them to have meaning. In the field of literary criticism, s. involves the analysis of literature as a use of language which depends upon supplementary conventions and which explores the signifying properties of various modes of discourse.

Although reflection on the sign has a venerable philosophical history, s. or semiology in the modern sense dates from Ferdinand de Saussure (1857–1913), who argued that linguistics should form part of a general science of signs, which he called semiology. His contemporary C. S. Peirce (1839–1914) had independently worked out an elaborate typology of signs and a metalanguage for discussing them, but his s. was conceived as an expansion of logic, and since most work in s. has looked to linguistics rather than to logic as a model, Saussure has been the more influential figure. A behaviorist s. associated with Charles Morris has also been developed, but its stimulus-response psychology has made it less useful to the literary critic than a semiology based on linguistics.

Linguistics might serve as a model for semiology, Saussure argued, because it stresses the conventional nature of the sign and thus prevents the analyst from assuming that non-linguistic signs are in some way "natural" and require no explanation. By considering cultural phenomena as the products of various "languages" one is led to study the systems of convention which enable them to have meaning. Certain types of signs which lack this conventional basis are thus generally taken to fall outside the field of semiology. If the relationship between form (or signifier) and meaning (or signified) is causal rather than conventional (those clouds mean rain; those spots mean measles), one has an *index*, which is properly studied by the relevant science. If the relation be one of natural resemblance or representation (a photograph of a horse signifies a horse), one is dealing with an *icon**, which might be treated by a philosophical theory of representation. If the relationship be *motivated*—grounded in properties of the signifier and the signified—one has a symbol, which falls within the domain of semiology but which can be analyzed by noting the basis of the relationship between individual signifier and individual signified (given the role of the cross in Christianity, it is a motivated symbol of Christianity). Finally, if the relationship is unmotivated and purely conventional (as in the case of words in natural languages), one is dealing with signs proper, which can be explained only by reconstructing the system from which they derive. The relationship between the form and meaning of "relate" is itself arbitrary, but it can be explained with reference to the morphological rules of the language which place it within a system that includes *relate: relation, dictate: dictation, narrate: narration*, etc.

Semiological explanation takes objects or acts as the *parole* (speech acts) of an underlying *langue* (linguistic system) whose "grammar" must be analyzed. One must attempt to isolate the minimal units which the system employs, determine the contrasts between units that produce meaning (paradigmatic relations) and the rules of combination which enable units to be grouped together as constituents of larger structures (syntagmatic relations). The semiological study of literature is an attempt to analyze literature as a system of signs and thus to determine what conventions enable literary works to have meaning. By seeing what variations in internal structure or context would produce differences of meaning, the analyst isolates the functional units and operative conventions of literature.

Poetry is a second-order semiological system in that items which are already signs in the first-order system of the Eng. or Fr. language are organized according to supplementary conventions which give them meanings and effects other than those they would have in ordinary prose. If one takes a prose sentence and sets it down on a page as verse, its linguistic meaning is not altered, but it acquires considerable literary meaning; and the task of the semiologist is to explain what are the conventions which produce the new signs responsible for this supplementary meaning. When the following sentence is set down on the page as a poem

As the cat
climbed over
the top of

the jamcloset
first the right
forefoot

carefully
then the hind
stepped down

into the pit of
the empty
flowerpot

it acquires meaning it would not have as part of a description in a novel, and to account for this meaning we must try to state the conventions which enable readers or critics to give it meaning. Among those that make possible an interpretation of this poem are the following: the convention of reference—that the meaning of a lyric is not restricted by ostensible reference (e.g., to a particular cat); the convention of coherence—that all the parts should be shown to relate to the effect of the whole; the convention of mimetic form—that we may read line endings as spatial or temporal gaps (suspense, isolation, stepping down); the convention of significance—read a short, apparently banal lyric as a moment of epiphany; the convention of symbolic extrapolation—make thematic capital of the emptiness of the flowerpot and the careful stepping of the cat; the convention of self-reflexivity—one way of giving poems thematic coherence is to read them as about poetry. If the poem is given a meaning other than that of the prose sentence, it is because conventions of this sort, which constitute the institution of poetry, produce supplementary signs. A semiology of poetry attempts to analyze the signs of this particular semiotic system.

The task of a semiology of poetry would be to make explicit, as conventions of the institution of literature, the implicit assumptions which govern the production of meaning in poetry. These conventions are of various kinds: first, those which govern the ways in which formal features, such as enjambment, caesura, metrical deviation, rhyme, and repetition of sounds, may become signs and contribute to poetic effect; second, the conventions of genre, which by permitting or excluding certain subjects, tones, and linguistic modes, enable the poet to produce meaning by conforming to

SUPPLEMENT

them or deviating from them; third, the general expectations concerning the ways in which poems may cohere or the types of structures which readers are trained to look for (e.g., the irony and paradox which new critics [see NEW CRITICISM] sought in lyrics); and finally the conventions of symbolic reading (of plausible and implausible extrapolation) which enable readers to make poems into unified structures expressing complex attitudes. The conventions which constitute poetry as a semiotic system change, of course, from one period to another. *The Waste Land* and *Un Coup de dés* seem less incoherent now than they once did because conventions for reading them have been developed. Indeed, changes in ways of reading provide semiology with some of its best evidence about the conventions operative at particular periods.

Semiological studies may thus bear on the functioning of particular poetic devices, such as metaphor, synecdoche, repetition of sounds, line endings, and on the implicit poetics of various historical periods. One important result of seminological study has been the renewal of interest in rhetoric, as an earlier attempt to formalize the operations of poetic signs, and the desire to reorganize rhetoric in accordance with modern linguistics.

A semiology of literature is interested in the ways in which literary signs differ from those of other types of discourse, and consequently one specialized form of semiology has developed which considers literature as an activity which foregrounds and questions other types of signs. This *sémanalyse*, as Julia Kristeva calls it, opposes the traditional theory of the sign which takes the signifier as the expression of the signified and argues instead that the reality of the sign lies in its form, its signifier, which holds out the promise of a meaning but does not express it. The meaning does not lie "behind" the signifier, as something which the speaker originally "had in mind" and which the reader must recover; rather the signifier holds out the promise of a meaning which the reader must try to produce. Literature, and especially poetry where the priority of the text to its paraphrase has long been obvious, has always explored the ways in which the "work of the signifier" could lend to the open-ended production of meanings rather than to the recovery of "a" meaning. In this sense, literature can be studied as a form of discourse which undermines the conception of the sign that seems appropriate to ordinary discourse, where the signifier is the means of access to a communicative intention. *Sémanalyse* is a critical semiology in that it works on systems of signs while attempting to show that both the systems themselves and the analyses of semiotic systems are based on premises which are highly

questionable, though they may well be the very conditions of meaning and hence unavoidable.

F. de Saussure, *Cours de linguistique générale* (1916); W. Empson, *Seven Types of Ambiguity* (1930); C. Peirce, *Collected Papers* (1931–58); C. Morris, *Signs, Language and Behaviour* (1946), *Writings on the General Theory of Signs* (1971); R. Barthes, "Eléments de sémiologie," *Communications*, 4 (1964), *Système de la mode* (1967), *Sade, Fourier, Loyola* (1971); T. Sebeok, ed. *Approaches to S.* (1964), *S.* (forthcoming); A. J. Greimas, *Sémantique structurale* (1966), *Du Sens* (1970), ed. *Essais de sémiotique poétique* (1971), ed. *Sign, Language, Culture* (1971); L. Prieto, *Messages et signaux* (1966); J. Derrida, *De la grammatologie* (1967), *La Dissémination* (1972), *Marges de la philosophie* (1972); U. Eco, *La struttura assente* (1968), "La critica sémiologica," *I Metodi attuali della critica in Italia*, ed. M. Corte and C. Segre (1970); M. Serres, *Hermès, ou la communication* (1968); *Hermès II: L'Interférence* (1972); P. Sollers, *Logiques* (1968); E. Benveniste, "Sémiologie de la langue," *Semiotica*, 1 (1969); G. Deleuze, *Logique du sens* (1969); *Proust et les signes* (1970); N. Goodman, *Languages of Art* (1969); J. Kristeva, *Semiotike: Recherches pour une sémanalyse* (1969), ed. *Essays in S.* (1971); N. Mouloud, *Langage et structures* (1969); C. Segre, *I Segni et la critica* (1969); D'A. S. Avalle, *L'Analisi letteraria in Italia: Formalismo, strutturalismo, semiologia* (1970); J. Dubois et al. (Groupe de Liège), *Rhétorique générale* (1970); G. Mounin, *Introd. à la sémiologie* (1970); "Recherches rhétoriques," *Communications*, 16 (1970); P. Guiraud, *La Sémiologie* (1971); E. Meletinsky and D. Segal, "Structuralism and S. in the U.S.S.R.," *Diogenes*, 73 (1971); J. Pelc, *Studies in Functional Logical S. of Natural Language* (1971); G. Wienold, *Semiotik der Literatur* (1972); P. Zumthor, *Essai de poétique médiévale* (1972); *Recherches sur les systèmes signifiants*, ed. J. Rey-Débove (1973); J. Culler, *Structuralist Poetics* (1974).

JOURNALS: *Centrum; Communications; Jour. of Lit. Semantics; Poetics; Semiotica; Tezisy dokaladov letnej shkoly po vtorichnym modelirujushchim sistemam; Trudy po znakovym sistemam.* J.D.C.

SHAPED VERSE. See PATTERN POETRY.

STANCES. Fr. verse form often confused with *strophes* (which are Eng. "stanzas"), but differing therefrom by its restriction to lyrical themes and, in conformity with its etymology (It. "stopping places"), a more definite pause at the end of each division. Introduced from Italy in the second half of the 16th c. to designate a less ambitious form than the ode with its *strophes*, st. continued well into the 19th c.

(e.g., Musset, Sully Prudhomme). They reached their climax however in the early 17th-c. theater, particularly tragedy, where they were utilized as highly organized lyric monologues; their thematic density, varied meters, and complex rhyme schemes contrasted vividly with the alexandrine couplets of dialogue. About 1660 st. were banished from the theater in the name of verisimilitude: that characters should possess such poetic skill when in the throes of violent emotion was no longer considered logical.—P. Martinon, *Les Strophes* (1912, appendix II); J. Scherer, *La Dramaturgie classique en France* (1950, 2ᵉ partie, ch. 6).　　　A.E.

STRUCTURALISM. In literary criticism s. is a method of analysis and a theory of literature inspired by developments in structural linguistics and structural anthropology which reached its height in France in the 1960's. It has been assimilated and developed in various ways by practitioners in other countries, but it remains, in its most distinctive and characterizable form, a Fr. movement whose principal figures are Roland Barthes, Gérard Genette, Tzvetan Todorov, Julia Kristeva, and A. J. Greimas. The work of Roman Jakobson, Gilles Deleuze, and Jacques Derrida may also be considered structuralist, and outside the literary field the leaders of the movement are Claude Lévi-Strauss, Michel Foucault, Jacques Lacan, and Louis Althusser.

In general terms, s. can be opposed to an atomism which attempts to explain phenomena individually. Ferdinand de Saussure (1857–1913), the founder of modern linguistics, distinguished between concrete speech acts (*parole*) and the underlying system of a language (*la langue*), arguing that the latter was a formal entity whose elements had no positive or essential qualities but must be defined solely in relational terms. Language must be studied as a formal system of interrelated elements. Claude Lévi-Strauss, who is regarded by many as the central figure of s., adopted this perspective in anthropology and rejected attempts to explain social and cultural phenomena in piecemeal fashion, especially by explanations of a psychological kind, preferring to treat them as manifestations of underlying formal systems. His studies of primitive logic, totemism, and myth were attempts to reconstruct a "logic of the concrete": instead of relating particular practices or tales to the beliefs they imply, one should consider them as elements in conceptual systems which enable people to think about and organize the world. The various codes by which myths operate are sets of binary oppositions drawn from different areas of experience which can be used to express a variety of contrasts, and they thus bear striking resemblance to those operative in poetic discourse. One might say, for example, that in his sonnet *Two loves I have of comfort and despair* Shakespeare takes the opposition good/evil and explores it through a variety of codes: the religious (angel/devil, saint/fiend), the moral (purity/pride), and the physical (fair/colored ill).

Structural analysis of this subconscious logic of the concrete is related to semiology (see SEMIOTICS), the study of sign systems. Indeed, one might say that the two fundamental insights on which s. is based are (1) that social and cultural phenomena do not have essences but are defined both by their internal structures and by their place in the structures of the relevant social and cultural systems, and (2) that social and cultural phenomena are signs: not physical events only, but events with meaning. One may try to separate the structural from the semiological—the study of patterns from the study of signs—but the most successful structural analyses isolate those structures which permit phenomena to function as signs.

S. in literary criticism began as a revolt against the particular types of erudition—literary history and biographical criticism—which dominated the Fr. university orthodoxy. S. sought to return to the text, but unlike Anglo-Am. new criticism (q.v.) it assumed that one could not study a text without preconceptions, that naive empiricism was an impossible critical position, and that in order to discover structures one required a methodological model. The goal of s. was not interpretation of texts but rather the elaboration, through encounters with particular texts, of an account of the modes of literary discourse and their operation. Roland Barthes distinguished between a criticism which places the text in a particular context or situation and assigns meaning to it and a science of literature or poetics which studies the conditions of meaning: the formal structures which organize a text and make possible a range of meanings. Translation of the Russian formalists (see RUSSIAN FORMALISM) in the late 1960's gave structuralists analogues to their own work and stimulated, in particular, the study of literature as an autonomous institution with its own modes of self-transcendence, but the principal model was linguistics. Two versions of s. can be distinguished by their different uses of linguistics: as a technique applied directly to the description of the language of texts or as the model for a poetics which would stand to literature as linguistics stands to language.

The first strain involves above all study of the patterns formed by the distribution in the text of elements defined by phonological and syntactic theory. Roman Jakobson's characterization of the poetic function of language as "the projection of the principle of equivalence from the axis of selection into the axis of combination" led to study of the ways in which items which are paradigmatically equivalent (related by membership of a grammatical, lexical, or phonological class) are distributed in linguistic sequence (on the axis of combination). Jakobson's own analyses of poems focus on symmetrical and asymmetrical patterns of distribution which unify the text and throw certain elements into relief. It has been argued that many of the patterns he discovers are irrelevant to the meaning and coherence that readers experience, but the reply would be that formal patterns need not contribute to meaning in order to have a unifying effect, albeit experienced subconsciously, and that they are objectively present in relief. Others, such as Nicolas Ruwet and Jacques Geninasca, though working with Jakobson's theories and techniques, have preferred to concentrate on ways in which linguistic patterning supports semantic effects (SEE LINGUISTICS AND POETICS). This version of s., though it has revealed the intricacy of poems' formal organization, tends to separate the structural from the semiological and has been a less important mode of s. than the attempt to develop a poetics modeled on linguistics.

Structuralist poetics is founded on the belief that while literature uses language it is also itself like a language in that its meanings are made possible by systems of convention. Analyzing a literature is analogous to analyzing a language, and one must develop a series of concepts designed to account for the operation of literature as a system. The work of Kristeva, Derrida, and especially Barthes, has contributed to an elaborate metalanguage which serves both as a theory of literature and as the outline of an analytical method.

Literature is not just sentences but sentences made signs in a second-order literary system. The same sentence, for example, will have very different meanings, depending on whether it is used in a lyric poem or in a newspaper report. And thus within the literary system the sentence, itself a linguistic sign, becomes a form or *signifiant* whose *signifié* is its special meaning in literary discourse. The conventions which give the sentence additional meanings and functions are those of an *écriture*: a particular mode of writing which involves an implicit contract between author and reader. The system or institution of literature is made up of a series of *écritures* which constitute its historical or generic moments. In reading a sentence in a lyric differently from a sentence in a newspaper report one is implicitly recognizing and employing the conventions of a particular lyric *écriture*.

Cultures tend to *naturalize* their signs, to *motivate* the connection between signifier and signified so that meanings seem natural and not the result of convention; literature may therefore be described according to the ways in which it resists or complies with this process. Interpretation is itself a mode of *naturalization* or *recuperation*: the attempt to bring the text within a logical discursive order by making it the expression of a meaning. We read texts in accordance with a series of *codes* which provide, on the one hand, models of human behavior (coherence and incoherence of personality, plausible and implausible relations between action and motive, logical and illogical chains of events), and on the other hand, models of literary intelligibility (coherence and incoherence, plausible and implausible symbolic extrapolations, significance and insignificance) which enable us to make sense of texts by organizing their elements into coherent series. These codes are models of the *vraisemblable*, in the broad sense in which structuralists use the term—models of the natural and intelligible—; and a work which lends itself to this process of recuperation is *lisible* (readable), whereas one that is unintelligible in terms of our traditional models is *scriptible* (writable): it can be written but not read, except in a kind of vicarious writing. A structuralist analysis of a work aims less at interpreting and thereby recuperating it than at examining the ways in which it responds to the reader's attempts to make it unified and coherent. The critic does not discover its structure so much as observe its *structuration*, and he therefore attends to its *différance* (difference/deferment): the play of its signifiers which defer meaning by offering material which is different from and in excess of meanings that can be assigned them (in poetry, meter, rhyme, and sound patterns generally are instances of the surplus of the signifier). The play of the signifier is the *productivity* of the text because it forces the reader to become not the passive consumer of an intelligibility he need only recognize but the active producer of meaning and participant in the exploration of possible modes of order.

This series of concepts leads to a critique of the representational aesthetic (which locates values in what is represented) and to stress on the literality or *materiality* of the text as linguistic surface. The play of language is valued for the ways in which it leads to a questioning of the relationship between language and experience; and hence critics attend to effects of *intertextuality*: the interaction within a text of various modes of discourse or of languages drawn from other literary texts and from discourse about the world. Whereas the Russian formalists saw the text as a way of "making strange" ordinary objects or activities, structuralists emphasize the "making strange" of discourses which order the world and which the work puts on display. The value of literature is thus related to its recognition of the arbitrary nature of the sign: undermining culture's attempts to make meanings natural, it asserts its own status as artifice and produces in the reader a self-conscious exploration of ways of ordering experience.

Although structuralist criticism has focused primarily on the novel, there is a body of work on poetry which may be grouped under several subheadings. (1) The reconstruction of poetic codes or systems: Gérard Genette has described baroque imagery as a system of interrelated items defined less by individual connotation than by oppositions and has analyzed images of day and night as a poetic code; Paul Zumthor has reconstructed the codes of medieval poetry, from the generic types of discourse to systems of *topoi* (see TOPOS), rhythmical formulae, descriptive schema, and conventionalized knowledge. (2) The correlation of particular structures with the interpretive operations they require: Michael Riffaterre has analyzed a variety of poetic devices, from the revitalized cliché to the extended metaphor of surrealist poetry; Samuel Levin's theory of couplings shows how phonological or grammatical equivalence affects semantic interpretation; A. J. Greimas and his followers have attempted to show how a level of coherence or *isotopie* is attained in the interpretation of poetic sequences. (3) The rehabilitation of rhetoric: Genette, the Groupe de Liège, and others have redefined rhetorical figures in linguistic terms and opened the way to a theory which would treat the figures as instructions for symbolic reading, as sets of conventional operations which readers may perform on poetic texts. (4) The reinvention of poetic artifice: Julia Kristeva, Jacques Derrida, Philippe Sollers, and poets of the *Tel Quel* school (Marcelin Pleynet, Denis Roche) have undertaken readings of poets designed to show how they undermine by their formal invention the traditional operations of the sign and have emphasized the need for contemporary poets to question and write against the codes and implicit contracts of poetry; Veronica Forrest-Thomson stresses the constructive rather than destructive aspect of their project, arguing that only the invention of new conventions and explicit artifice can enable poetry to play its traditional role of investigating and criticizing our unexamined ordering of experience and our assumptions about the relationship between language and the world. Generally, the structuralist study of poetry investigates the implicit conventions which enable poetry to be read and understood and focuses on the unsettled dialectical relationship between these conventions, always threatened by naturalization, and poetic texts.

BIBLIOGRAPHIES: *S.: A Reader*, ed. M. Lane (1970); J. Harari, *Structuralists and Structuralisms* (1917); *Roman Jakobson, A Bibliog. of His Writings* (1971); *Tel Quel*, 47 (1971); J. Culler, *Structuralist Poetics* (1974).

R. Barthes, *Le Degré zéro de l'écriture* (1953), *Mythologies* (1957), *Essais critiques* (1964), *Critique et vérité* (1966), *S/Z* (1970); C. Lévi-Strauss, *La Pensée sauvage* (1962), *Le Cru et le cuit* (1964); S. Levin, *Linguistic Structures in Poetry* (1962); M. Foucault, *Raymond Roussel* (1963); "Recherches sémiologiques," *Communications*, 4 (1964); M. Pleynet, *Comme* (1965); "Analyse structurale du récit," *Communications*, 8 (1966); G. Genette, *Figures* (1966), *Figures II* (1969), *Figures III* (1972); A. J. Greimas, *Sémantique structurale* (1966); "S.," *YFS*, 36–37 (1966); J. Derrida, *L'Ecriture et la différence* (1967), *La Dissémination* (1972), *Marges de la philosophie* (1972); "Structuralismes: Idéologie et méthode," *Esprit*, 35 (1967); "Colloque de Cluny," *La Nouvelle critique*, spec. issue (1968); U. Eco, *La struttura assente* (1968); "Linguistique et littérature," *Langages*, 12 (1968); M. Lotman, *Lektsi po struktural'noi poetike; vvedenie, teoriia stikha* [Lectures in Structural Poetics: Introd., Theory of Verse] and *Struktura khudozhestvennogo teksta* [Structure of the Artistic Text] (both Providence, R.I., 1968 and 1971, Brown Univ. Slavic reprints, 5 and 9); D. Roche, *Eros énergumène* (1968), *Le Mécrit* (1972); P. Sollers, *Logiques* (1968); Tel Quel, *Théorie d'ensemble* (1968); "Le Vraisemblable," *Communications*, 11 (1968); *Qu'est-ce que le structuralisme?* ed. F. Wahl (1968); J. Kristeva, *Semiotike: Recherches pour une sémanalyse* (1969); C. Segre, *I Segni e la critica* (1969); "La Stylistique," *Langue française*, 3 (1969); G. Deleuze, *Proust et les signes* (1970); J. Dubois et al. (Groupe de Liège), *Rhétorique générale* (1970); *The Languages of Crit. and the Sciences of Man*, ed. R. Macksey and E. Donato (1970); "Linguistique et texte littéraire," *Langue française*, 7 (1970); "Recherches rhétoriques," *Communications*, 16 (1970); "S.," *Twentieth C. Studies*, 3 (1970); V. Forrest-Thomson, "Levels in Poetic Convention," *Jour. of European Studies*, 2 (1971); J. Geninasca, *Analyse structurale des Chimères de Nerval* (1971); *Essais de sémiotique poétique*, ed. A. J. Greimas (1971); M. Riffaterre, *Essais de stylistique structurale* (1971); T. Todorov, *Poétique de la prose* (1971), "Introduction à la symbolique," *Poétique*, 11 (1972); F. Jameson, *The Prison-House of Language: A Critical Account of S. and Russian Formalism* (1972); N. Ruwet, *Langage, musique, poésie* (1972); P. Zumthor, *Essai de poétique médiévale* (1972); R. Jakobson, *Questions de poétique* (1973), *Selected Writings*,

iii (forthcoming); J. Culler, *Structuralist Poetics* (1974); R. Scholes, *S. in Lit.* (1974); *S. around the World*, ed. T. Sebeok (forthcoming).
JOURNALS: *Poétique*, passim; *Tel Quel*, passim.   J.D.C.

SWAHILI POETRY. S.p. can be traced directly to Arabic models of Islamic verse from the Hadramawt and the Persian Gulf. The development of S.p. in the 19th c. shows the Africanization of a foreign medium by the coastal community of East Africa. The earliest extant S. manuscripts are from the early 18th c., namely, *al-Hamziya*, a S. version in 460 stanzas of al-Būsīrī's Arabic poem *Umm al-Qura* (Mother of Villages [Medina]), and *Tambuka* or *Herekali*, 1,150 stanzas dealing with the war between the Arabs and the Byzantines from A.D. 628 to 636. S.p. is still written in modified Arabic script, but only for private circulation by Muslims belonging to traditional Muslim-S. society. Most S.p. now appears in roman script, in books, and in the press.

The most important prosodic features in S.p. are rhyme and fixed patterns of syllabic measure. The earliest extant wedding songs, serenades, and praise songs are in indeterminate long measure of at least 15 syllables. Another early form is the *takhmis*, in which each stanza is of 5 lines rhyming *aaaab* and with no medial rest. The Hadrami Saiyids occasionally adopted this form, e.g., the version in the British Museum (No. Or. 4534) of the Liyongo legend by Sheikh Saiyid Abdallah bin Nasir (1725–1820). The Hadrami Saiyids in descent from Sheikh Abu Bakr bin Salim, who died in A.D. 1584, had considerable influence on the development of S.p. The author of *al-Hamziya* was Saiyid Aidarus, great-grandson of Sheikh Abu Bakr; Sheikh Saiyid Abdallah bin Nasir also wrote the *utendi* poem *al-Inkishafi* (Self-examination), an extremely popular work on the passing of the Arab city states on the East African coast; Sheikh Saiyid Mansab showed skill in composing acrostic and homiletic poems of varied form.

The *utendi* verse form consists of 4 short hemistichs of which the first 3 rhyme together and the fourth carries a rhyme repeated as the terminal rhyme of each stanza. This verse form was employed for writing long narrative poems embodying oral tradition, e.g., the story of the legendary hero Liyongo, as well as for circumstantial accounts of historical and contemporary events, e.g., the Maji-Maji rebellion of 1905, or the recent struggle for independence in Kenya and Tanzania. Some of the longer *tendi* derive from the Arabian narratives, mostly in rhymed prose, called Maghazi literature (Arabic *magāzī*, raids), consisting of legendary accounts based on a modicum of

historical facts dealing with the wars of the Prophet Mohammed after the Hegira. Some of the shorter *tendi* are related to Arabian Maulid literature, dealing with the birth and early life of the Prophet.

The most popular verse form in S. for topical and lyric themes is verse of 8 hemistichs, each of 8 syllables, with rhyming pattern *ababbbc*, the terminal rhyme of each stanza being repeated throughout the poem. Although in the scripts verse of this type is written either as a single line or in two lines, it is generally referred to by scholars as a quatrain. There appears to be no generally accepted name for this verse form in S., and it owes much less to Arabian sources for form and subject matter than the *utendi* or the *takhmis*. There are variations in the syllabic measure, but innovation is not encouraged. The outstanding exponent of S. quatrains is Muyaka bin Haji al-Ghassaniy of Mombasa (1776–1840), who encouraged the Mazrui governors of Fort Jesus, Mombasa, in opposing the overlordship of the Sultan Muscat. Muyaka's extension of S. poetry to the expression of attitudes arising from contemporary events was an important step toward the secularization of S. verse.

Most modern S. poetry in quatrains is secular, but conservative. The prestige of Shaaban Robert (1909–62) as a transitional writer is related to the political prestige of the S. language in Tanzania. He was the first to widen the literary uses of S. in forms borrowed from Eng. literature, e.g., the essay, the novelette, the autobiography. His poetry remains conventional and therefore acceptable. Mathias Mnyampala (1919–69) was among those Tanzanian poets invited by President Nyerere in 1968 to use their talents to familiarize the peasants with national politics. Mnyampala initiated the public performance of S. song poems (*ngonjera*) with the express intention of teaching "good conduct, indigenous culture and national politics." This attempt to put versification into national service maintained the functional aspect of much S. poetry. In contrast, poetry sung in the S. musical clubs of coastal East Africa was, and still is, topical, deeply allusive, close to oral tradition. The female singer, Siti binti Saad (1880–1950), is perhaps the best-known S. artist from that milieu.

Ahmad Nassir bin Juma Bhalo of Mombasa is a genuine contemporary S. poet whose poetry has features common to other early literatures of the world, and yet its composition and performance on the radio is contemporary. The poems are chanted by a professional singer to a pattern of melody based on one of the Arabian modal scales, a traditional manner of presentation. The verses are heavily gnomic, and the poet has the same specialized task of "orating" as the *thyle* (orator, statesman) of the Anglo-Saxon *Beowulf*. As he says:

walumbi haya lumbani
ni mimi simba marara ningurumaye chakani.

O orators, come then, orate!
it is I, the roaring lion I who roar in the bush.

Ahmad Nassir's poems are in the Mvita dialect, are full of local allusions, and so are difficult to interpret, even for Africans who speak S. well, but who do not belong to the S. coastal community.

The development of S.p. as a part of the national literatures of Kenya and Tanzania is largely dependent upon the status of S. as a national language. At the present time the cultural background within the national context has its counterpart only in national politics. This may not be enough to guarantee within the national context compositions of a value comparable to that of poems from S. traditional society.

COLLECTIONS: *Diwani ya* [Collected Works of] *Muyaka bin Haji*, ed. W. Hichens (Johannesburg, 1940); A. Nassir, *Poems from Kenya*, ed. L. Harries (1966); Mw. Shabaan et al., *Waimbaji wa Juzi* (Singers of Yesteryear, 1966), ed. A. A. Jahadhmy et al.; *Diwani ya Shaaban*, ed. J.W.T. Allen (1968); *Malenga wa Mvita* (Mombasan Poet, 1971), ed. S. Chiraghdin; *S. Islamic Poetry* (1971) and *An Anthology of S. Love Poetry* (1972), both tr. and ed. J. Knappert; *Johari za Kiswahili* (series of edited *tenzi*, publ. by the East Afr. Lit. Bureau).

HISTORY AND CRITICISM: L. Harries, *S. Poetry* (1962) and "S. Lit. in the National Context," *Review of National Literatures*, 11 (1971); J. Knappert, *Traditional S. Poetry* (1967); *Uchambuzi wa Maandishi ya Kiswahili* (Analysis of S. Writings, 1971), ed. F. Topan.   L.H.

T

TENZI. See SWAHILI POETRY.*

THEME. To speak of the t. of a poem may be only to give a brief and unsophisticated answer to the question, "What is this poem about?" But t. as subject or topic (sometimes equated with and sometimes distinguished from such concepts as motif and archetype [q.v.]) is indispensable for the folklorist, the archetypal or myth critic, the historian of culture or ideas, or any other critic whose concern is to study characters, objects, situations, images, or ideas that recur within a particular work, in the works of a single author, or in the works of various authors. In a closely related sense, t. is equivalent to a summary statement of the main course of action or line of thought and feeling that is depicted in a poem: the t. of *The Prelude* is the growth of a poet's mind; the t. of *The Rime of the Ancient Mariner* is the consequences of the killing of an albatross. Another sense of t. involves a reference not only to the subject of a poem but also to its intention: the t. of *To Althea, from Prison* is to define true liberty; the t. of *Ode on Melancholy* is to give advice to someone who finds himself in a state of depression; the t. of *Paradise Lost* is to justify the ways of God to man. Finally, t. is used to refer to a summary statement of the doctrinal (usually, moral, religious, or philosophical) content of a poem.

"T." in the last of the senses distinguished above has appeared in criticism under a variety of other names: "moral," "message," "precept," "thesis," "meaning," "interpretation," "sentence," "idea," "comment," etc. One or another of these terms has formed part of the vocabulary of most critics who assign a primary position to the instrumental values of poetry. Much medieval, Renaissance, and neoclassical criticism was didactically oriented. Medieval literary theory conceived of poetry as an adjunct to religion and philosophy. The aim of the poet, like that of a preacher, should be to present persuasively a valid moral precept; his means is the use of attractive parable, allegory, or exemplum. The moral precept is the "t.," "nucleus," "sentence," "fruit," or "grain" of the poem. Renaissance didactic criticism, of which Sidney's *Apologie for Poetrie* (1595) is a good example, was similar to the medieval position. The aim of human life, says Sidney, is virtuous action, and poetry is a discipline worthy of man's most serious attention because it is more effective than any other human learning in molding human behavior morally. Poetry is a "medicine of cherries." The center of a good poem is a moral universal, and the poem is good if it presents a correct and lively image of this universal. Neoclassical criticism, following Horace, assigned pleasure and instruction as a double aim for poetry. This position resulted in a continued stress on the instrumental values of poetry, and the terms "moral" and "t." were

-[987]-

used to point to the final cause of a poem and to its principle of unity. Thus Dryden: "The first rule which Bossu prescribes to the writer of an Heroic Poem, and which holds too by the same reason in all Dramatic Poetry, is to make the moral of the work; that is, to lay down to yourself what that precept of morality shall be, which you would insinuate into the people; as, namely, Homer's (which I have copied in my *Conquest of Granada*), was, that union preserves a commonwealth, and discord destroys it; Sophocles, in his *Oedipus*, that no man is to be accounted happy before his death. 'Tis the moral that directs the whole action of the play to one centre; and that action or fable is the example built upon the moral, which confirms the truth of it to our experience" ("The Grounds of Criticism in Tragedy" [1679]).

Many modern critics regard with suspicion expressions such as the "moral" or the "message" of a poem. But they do talk of poetry as a kind of knowledge, and, when induced to speak of the uses of poetry, they speak of its cognitive and moral values. As a consequence, like other instrumentalist critics, they have found the term "t." (or "meaning," "significance," "interpretation," "dominant attitude," "evaluation") indispensable both for pointing to the values of poetry and for indicating the principle of unity of a poem. However, they warn that the poem, or at least the good poem, is not a rhetorical device for ornamenting the t. or making it more persuasive.

The dangers of this didactic interpretation of the nature of poetry are so great that sometimes the recommendation appears to use "t." not to point to a general formulation of the meaning realized in a poem but rather to the moral problem or human situation that is dramatized in the poem. Thus the t. of *Antigone* is difficult choice; the t. of *Dr. Faustus* is the search for·knowledge; the t. of *King Lear* is self-discovery. The purpose of the good poet is to explore these problems or situations in a particularized and concrete context. The net result may be simply a detailed diagnosis of the nature and complexities of the problem. More often the poet comes up with a moral judgment or evaluation which is a possible solution to the problem. Such tentative solutions may also be called "themes"; however, the ·reader of poetry is warned to regard them only as hypotheses which the good poem clarifies, tests, qualifies, and subjects to the fires of irony. In this process of testing, the original t. may be so qualified that no general statement of it will represent it accurately. Murray Krieger uses the word "thematics" (opposing it to the older, didactic use of "t.") to stress that the meaning of a poem must be studied in this way. The good poem, then, does not assert its

t. and invite the reader's acceptance of it. Rather the poem should be regarded as a form of exploratory discourse, in which a poet explores an area of moral concern and discovers or realizes the meaning of an experience, a meaning which may or may not have universal application.

The concept of t. plays a strikingly different role in critical theories that stress the terminal rather than the instrumental values of poetry. Terminalist critics regard the poem as an end in itself, an intrinsic good, an object of beauty, a source of aesthetic experience. If they discuss t. at all, they usually consider it, along with everything else in the poem, as influencing the quality or intensity of the aesthetic experience. Edgar Allan Poe, for example, protested against the "heresy of the didactic" and insisted that poetry should be written and read "simply for the poem's sake." To read a poem for the poem's sake is to experience a pure, elevating, and intense pleasure. A t. can be a "soul-elevating" idea: "Love . . . the true, the divine Eros . . . is unquestionably the purest and truest of all poetical themes" ("The Poetic Principle" [1850]). It is so because this t., more than any other, is the means to intense aesthetic experience. More recently, M. C. Beardsley has argued in a similar fashion. Though not denying that poetry may have moral and cognitive "side effects," he recommends that poetry, like the other fine arts, should be cultivated and valued for the sake of aesthetic experience. Aesthetic value, he says, depends on unity, complexity, and the intensity of the emotive qualities of a work of art. Philosophical, religious, and moral concepts and doctrines ("themes" and "theses" in his terminology), whether explicit or implicit in the literary work, may add significantly to the unity, complexity, and intensity of the work and thus be aesthetically valuable.

Finally, the Chicago critics (q.v.) divide poems into didactic poems and presentative or mimetic poems. The critic, when faced with the task of analyzing and evaluating a didactic poem, must, of course, use the word "t." or one of its synonyms to point to the unifying principle of the work. This is the proper procedure when discussing such masterpieces of didactic art as *The Divine Comedy* or *The Faerie Queene*. Mimetic poems, however, have a principle of unity very different from didactic poems. Their final cause is aesthetic pleasure derived from the reader's contemplation of a picture of a sequence of human actions, thoughts, or feelings so structured as to give the poem moving power. In the criticism of mimetic works, "t." may be useful to point to the nature of the moral or philosophical problems which are frequently part of the depicted action of the poem. Or the term may be useful to point to the set of moral norms, implied or expressed, in terms of which the author or his narrator judges the characters and their actions. But to use "t." to point to the organizing principle of the work is, for the Chicago critics, to assimilate mimetic works to didactic works and to miss their distinctive excellence.—Crane; Frye; M. C. Beardsley, *Aesthetics* (1958); M. Krieger, *The Tragic Vision* (1960); C. Brooks, *A Shaping Joy* (1971).

F.G.

TOPOS (pl. *topoi*). A commonplace appropriate for literary treatment, an "intellectual theme suitable for development and modification" according to the imagination of the individual author (Curtius). In his *Rhetoric*, Aristotle used an adapted sense of physical place or t. to represent a rhetorical commonplace, and such *topoi* became the *loci communes* or commonplaces of the Roman rhetoricians, sometimes retaining a degree of their original physical sense by the association, in memory-systems, of specific places at the scene of an oration with specific topics in the speech. Aristotle's use of the term in his *Topics* is not essentially different; in that work *topoi* designate the commonplaces upon which dialectic reasoning bases its arguments and through which the philosopher may effectively communicate with non-philosophers. Ernst Robert Curtius adapted the rhetorical conception to literary use in *European Lit. and the Late Middle Ages*, tr. W. R. Trask (1953). Examples of *topoi* are: the inexpressibility t., in which a poet decries his inability to do his subject justice; the "world upsidedown" (*mundus inversus*) t., in which the world's disorder is shown by fish in the trees, children ruling parents, etc.; and set pieces like the standardized description of an ideal garden (*locus amoenus*). Critics following Curtius have extended the conception of a t. to include traditional metaphors such as the world as stage, the world as book, etc. Curtius distinguished between these "metaphorics" and the other "topics," although in many instances the distinction is difficult to maintain.

F.J.W.

V

VERBLESS POETRY. The function of the various parts of speech in works of literature and the fact that such categories as, e.g., the verb and the adjective have been in and out of fashion at various times and for various reasons, have been often discussed by both writers and scholars of various persuasions. The problem, however, is very elusive and no definitive study exists on the subject.

A common generalization is the assertion that there is a direct relationship between the frequency of verbs in a poem and its "dynamic" quality. Scholars invoke W. Humboldt's remarks about the verb as an energy-giving element or A. M. Peškovskij's slogan, "back to the verb" from his paper, "The Verb as a Means of Expressiveness," in which he voiced the view that the peculiar abstract aura of vagueness, "lack of outspokenness" in symbolist poetry was due to these poets avoiding verbal constructions.

Indeed, such a tendency is quite common in symbolist poetry, notably Fr. and Russian. (Verlaine's and Balmont's efforts to avoid verbs are a matter of record.) The same goes for some other earlier and later poets: "Rires oiseux, pleurs sans raisons,/ Mains indéfiniment pressées,/ Tristesses moites, pâmoisons,/ Et quel vague dans les pensées!" (P. Verlaine); "Whis-per, timid breathing/ Nightingale's trills/ Silver and rippling/ Of a sleepy stream" (A. Fet); "Cold, wet leaves/ Floating on moss-colored water/ And the croaking of frogs/ Cracked bellnotes in the twilight" (Amy Lowell); "Flowers through the window/ lavender and yellow// changed by white curtains—/ smell of cleanliness// Sunshine through the afternoon—/ On the glass tray// a glass pitcher . . ." (W. C. Williams).

However, the assertions that the above-mentioned features are due to the lack of verbs are subject to question. It is possible, as pointed out by O. Jespersen ("The Role of the Verb") to quote verbless construction "giving a very definite impression of motion." And vice versa, one should add, i.e., a poem packed full with verbs may be static. Marinetti's slogan of *les mots en liberté* and his celebrated example of a man who, on seeing a house on fire, naturally shouts nouns (Fire! Fire!) rather than constructing sentences with verbs, was a simple statement of fact. Many of the 20th-c. poets, but notably the futurists (see FUTURISM), turned against the conventional syntax and viewed the verb as the most mechanical "conductor of grammar," and they resorted to verbless construction in search of a more striking dynamic vision of the rapidly changing world. Marinetti's poem *Zang-Tumb-Tuum* is a good example of the violence and chaos of the bombardment of Adrianople given in a form of a "telegraphic" compression based mainly on the principle of free associations of nouns not connected by verbs (commands of officers clattering like brass plates, *bang* from here *bang* from there, *boom-cling-clang* fast *clinkclingclingclingclang* up down there around high up attention over the head *clang* beautiful blaze blaze blaze blaze . . .).

O. Jespersen, "The Role of the Verb," GRM, 3 (1911); A. Lombard, *Les Constructions nominales dans le français moderne* (1930); N. A. Nilsson, *The Russian Imaginists* (Stockholm, 1970; ch. 3: "Verbless Poetry"; see also bibliog.); Z. Folejewski, "Dynamic or Static? The Function of the Verb in Modern Poetry" in *Canadian Contributions to the 7th Congress of Slavists*, ed. Z. Folejewski (The Hague, 1972). Z.F.

VISION. "V." has been a favorite word in the vocabulary of poets, but it has become common in criticism only in the modern period. It is a word rich in ambiguities and overtones of meaning, which frequently generate ironies in the contexts in which it is used. There is the v. of the physical eye; there is Coleridge's "armed v.," perception guided and assisted by a higher mental faculty; and there is transfiguration, apocalypse, and the beatific v. V. suggests the vividly concrete, but also the archetypal, ideal, and spiritual. It may be a revelation granted to the semi-divine man, the poet, prophet, or saint; but it also may have connections with ghosts, witches, and madness. In dream, intuition, or trance, the visionary sees what is or what ought to be; heaven or hell; a past Golden Age, present misery, or a future brave new world. V. makes a claim to truth and invites assent, but it may also refer to that which is illusory, impractical, wild, or foolish. Its language—allegory, metaphor, symbol, and other devices for expressing depth meanings—frequently requires special skills of interpretation.

The tradition that great poets have drunk the milk of paradise or that they are gifted with mysterious and uncommon powers of perception is an ancient one (see INSPIRATION). Both poets and critics have encouraged this view. This claim has been in part an attempt to explain the wondrous creative power of the great artist and in part a rhetoric of praise to exalt the character of the poet in order to make his message more persuasive. Convention too enters here, as in the epic poet's address to his Muse.

Poetry of v. is not a recognized literary genre. However, a body of poetry exists for which the claim has been made that the content is a record of visionary experience (in one or another of the senses distinguished above) granted to the poet or to a character he has created. For example, there are the dream visions (see DREAM ALLEGORY) popular in the Middle Ages and later; in these poems the claim to visionary experience is clearly a convention—the poem is only a mimesis of a visionary experience. On the other hand, there are poets like Blake, who have analyzed carefully the conditions of visionary experience and have claimed the authority of v. for the content of what they wrote. Indeed, most of the great romantics saw themselves as chosen poet-seers; they felt themselves to belong to "the visionary company" together with great poets like Milton and the Hebrew prophets; their mission was to trumpet a prophecy of a world renewed whose forms they had seen in imaginative v. M. H. Abrams has distinguished three principal kinds of transforming perception claimed by the romantics (and earlier and later poets): to see the wonder of the old and familiar (to return to the freshness of sensation of the child); to experience an epiphany in which an ordinary object or event is seen as suddenly and transitorily charged with a mysterious significance (Wordsworth's "spots of time"); and to perceive objects as invested with values different from those that custom has accorded to them (the sublimity of the lowly and humble).

Contemporary criticism uses "v." in a variety of senses. Occasionally, "v." refers simply to a poet's visual images (see IMAGERY) as these appear in descriptive passages or figures of speech (see Zimmermann in bibliog.). On the other hand, a critic like Frye uses "v." in an extended sense as a synonym for literature itself, or at least for the thematic component of literature. According to Frye, literature is not an imitation of nature and makes no reference to reality; rather it is the dream of man, an imaginative projection of man's desires and fears. Thus all literary works, taken together, constitute a total v. ("the vision of the end of social effort, the innocent world of fulfilled desires, the free human society"), whose parts Frye sometimes classifies metaphorically as the spring v., the summer v., the fall v., and the winter v. But the sense in which "v." is most frequently used in contemporary criticism is that given to it by expressionist critics, who use the term (with or without Orphic connotations) to refer to an author's world view—his ideas, attitudes, feelings, and evaluations about God, nature, and man. It is held that a poet necessarily expresses some part of his philosophy of life in the poems that he writes and that the aesthetic experience consists in the reader's evolving insight into this v. (or "perspective" or "point of view" or "ideology") and ultimate identification with the consciousness of the author. In a poem, parts of the author's v. may be explicitly stated (as in Wordsworth's *Tintern Abbey*); but much of it exists on noncognitive levels of the mind and is revealed in the structure, style, images, and figurative language of his work. The chief function of the critic is to reconstruct and clarify the poet's v. In discharging this function, the critic may not be very much concerned about traditional genre or even about the analysis of poems as discrete artistic wholes. All the works of an author express some part of his v., and the critic's aim is to display the v. in its totality. (M. Krieger has condemned visionary critics for returning to pre-new criticism positions. Although he likes the term "v.," respect for the autonomy of the literary work makes him use "v." to refer to the thematic content—richly ambiguous and resisting any simple formulation—inhering in the work's unique totality and not to a set of abstract propositions and attitudes preexisting in the mind of the author and reflected in the work he composes.)

The visionary critic's most difficult problem is that of evaluation (unless, like Frye, he excludes evaluation from criticism). Visions have been praised for being complex, deep, comprehensive, original, or authentic. They have been blamed for being simple, shallow, narrow, standardized, or inauthentic. Such criteria do not seem to be entirely adequate. Any view of life, whether dramatized in a poem or systematized in philosophy, invites serious consideration of its truth and validity (see BELIEF, PROBLEM OF). Regardless of how intuitive or emotionally grounded a v. may be, it necessarily involves some elements that seem to make assertions with respect to the universe or the ongoing course of human life. Keats's questions then seem unavoidable: How does one distinguish v. from a waking dream? How does one know that he has achieved a "power to see as a god sees"? Santayana echoes Keats's words: "The height of poetry is to speak the language of the gods." The goal of the poet and the philosopher, he says, is *theoria*, "a steady contemplation of all things in their order and worth. Such contemplation is imaginative. . . . A philosopher who attains it is, for the moment, a poet; and a poet who turns his practised and passionate imagination on the order of all things, or on anything in the light of the whole, is for that moment a philosopher." Santayana evaluates the poetry of Lucretius, Dante, and Goethe in terms of this standard. On the other hand, Wheelwright argues that because of the nature of reality and the limitations of the human mind, no such synoptic view is possible. All v. is necessarily partial. He is sensitive to the need for distinguishing v. from illusion, and he says that the visions of the great artists are incommensurable (the world of T. S. Eliot cannot be subsumed by or

subsume the world of Blake); but he insists that the truth claims of all the great artists must be respected, as revelatory of some aspect of a complex and mysterious reality. To other critics, the multiplicity of visions expressed in literature is a sign of irremediable relativism. If men can get no ultimate answers about the nature of the universe or their destiny in it, then they are left with a variety of purely personal points of view by means of which they order their experience and structure their works of art. A poet's v. must be regarded simply as a series of hypotheses generated in a sensitive mind reacting to life's experiences. These hypotheses may have heuristic value for others, but the authority of v. cannot be called upon to support a claim to their partial or universal validity. Indeed, an artist is to be praised who fills his works with ironies and conflicting perspectives to dramatize the limitations of all visions and suggest the impossibility of any single correct view.

G. Santayana, *Three Philosophical Poets* (1910); P. Wheelwright, *The Burning Fountain* (1954) and *Metaphor and Reality* (1962); N. Frye, *The Anatomy of Criticism* (1957) and *Fables of Identity* (1963); M. Krieger, *The Tragic Vision* (1960) and *The Classic Vision* (1971); H. Bloom, *The Visionary Company* (1961); E. Zimmermann, " 'V.' in Poetry" in *The Disciplines of Criticism*, ed. P. Demetz (1968); M. H. Abrams, *Natural Supernaturalism* (1971).　　　　　　　　　　　　　　F.G.

VOICE. To stress "v." in discussions of poetry may be simply a reminder of the large extent to which the effects of poetry depend on sound. The qualities of vocal sounds enter directly into the aesthetic experience in the witnessing of dramatic productions or listening to the oral interpretation of poetry. But there is also listening with the "inner ear" that occurs in the silent reading of poetry. The cultivation of what T. S. Eliot has called the "auditory imagination" is indispensable for the full appreciation of poetry.

More often, modern critics use "v." in a metaphorical and extended sense. A poem is regarded as a human utterance or an imitation of a human utterance. "V." is used to refer to the person or persons who utter the words that constitute the poem. The analysis of v. in a poem is an attempt to identify the v. or combination of voices that are heard in the poem (with the help of such distinctions as those suggested by T. S. Eliot in his "The Three Voices of Poetry") and then to characterize the tonal qualities, attitudes, or even the entire personality of this speaker as it reveals itself directly or indirectly (through sound, choice of diction, and other stylistic devices). The concept of v. reminds the reader that the meaning of what is said is qualified by who says it and by the attitude that the speaker takes toward his subject and audience. More important, stress on v. is a recommendation to place greater critical emphasis on the extent to which the reader's consciousness of the quality of mind and personality of a speaker determines the kind and intensity of the response that is made to what he says. V. reminds us that a human being is behind the words of a poem, that he is revealing his individuality by means of the poem, and that this revelation may be the most significant part of what we receive from the poem.

Thus, like "vision,"* "v." is an important term in the vocabulary of recent critics who wish to rehabilitate some form of romantic expressionism or return to a view of poetry as personal communication. This recommendation is usually set in explicit reaction to contemporary objectivist theories of poetry. By stressing the autonomy of poetry and recommending the neglect of the author and the reader in the analysis and evaluation of poetry, objectivism

has, it is alleged, depersonalized and dehumanized poetry. Poetry, it is argued, should be brought back to human concerns out of which it has arisen and within which it has great influence. To do so, W. J. Ong, for example, using the language of modern phenomenological and personalist philosophers, suggests that all literature be regarded essentially as "a cry." The v. is the key to the "I-thou world where, through the mysterious interior resonance which sound best of all provides, persons commune with persons, reaching one another's interiors in a way in which one can never reach the interior of an 'object.' " Thus the aesthetic experience must not be regarded as the contemplation of a dramatic situation that the process of art has distanced from real life. Rather, it is a participation in the dialogue that the human race has been engaged in from the beginning of history. See also PERSONA.*—T. S. Eliot, "The Three Voices of Poetry" in On Poetry and Poets (1957); W. J. Ong, The Barbarian Within (1962); F. Berry, Poetry and the Physical V. (1962).

F.G.

Y

Z

YORUBA POETRY. See AFRICAN POETRY: VERNACULAR.*

ZULU POETRY. See AFRICAN POETRY: VERNACULAR.*